THE NEW DOUBLEDAY COOKBOOK

Also by Jean Anderson and Elaine Hanna

THE DOUBLEDAY COOKBOOK *(original edition)**

Also by Jean Anderson

THE ART OF AMERICAN INDIAN COOKING
(with Yeffe Kimball)

FOOD IS MORE THAN COOKING

HENRY THE NAVIGATOR, PRINCE OF PORTUGAL

THE HAUNTING OF AMERICA

THE FAMILY CIRCLE COOKBOOK
(with the Food Editors of *Family Circle*)

RECIPES FROM AMERICA'S RESTORED VILLAGES

THE GREEN THUMB PRESERVING GUIDE

THE GRASS ROOTS COOKBOOK

JEAN ANDERSON'S PROCESSOR COOKING

HALF A CAN OF TOMATO PASTE & OTHER CULINARY DILEMMAS**
(with Ruth Buchan)

JEAN ANDERSON COOKS

UNFORBIDDEN SWEETS

JEAN ANDERSON'S *NEW* PROCESSOR COOKING

*Winner of the R. T. French Tastemaker Award, Best Cookbook of the Year (1975)
**Winner of the R. T. French Tastemaker Award, Best Specialty Cookbook of the Year (1980)

THE NEW DOUBLEDAY COOKBOOK

Jean Anderson and Elaine Hanna

DOUBLEDAY

New York   London   Toronto   Sydney   Auckland

PUBLISHED BY DOUBLEDAY
a division of Bantam Doubleday Dell Publishing Group, Inc.
666 Fifth Avenue, New York, New York 10103

DOUBLEDAY and the portrayal of an anchor
with a dolphin are trademarks of Doubleday,
a division of Bantam Doubleday Dell
Publishing Group, Inc.

Library of Congress Cataloging-in-Publication Data

Anderson, Jean, 1929–
The new Doubleday cookbook.

Rev. ed. of: The Doubleday cookbook. 1975.
Includes index.
1. Cookery. I. Hanna, Elaine. II. Anderson,
Jean, 1929–   Doubleday cookbook. III. Title.
TX651.A57 1985   641.5   85-16844
ISBN 0-385-19577-X

DESIGNED BY LAURENCE ALEXANDER
ILLUSTRATIONS BY MEL KLAPHOLZ
INDEX PREPARED BY MARO RIOFRANCOS

Acknowledgments

We are greatly indebted to the following companies for providing equipment to use in the testing and development of recipes:

Farberware, Kidde, Inc., Bronx, New York (convection oven); *General Electric Company,* Louisville, Kentucky (electric and microwave range); *KitchenAid Division, Hobart Corporation,* Troy, Ohio (dishwashers and heavy-duty electric mixers); *Personal Computer Industries,* Chatsworth, California (diet/kitchen computer); *Regal Ware, Inc.,* Kewaskum, Wisconsin (small electric appliances, microwave cookware and bakeware).

We should also like to thank the following individuals and companies for so graciously supplying quantities of valuable information:

American Dietetic Association; American Home Economics Association; American Home Foods, Division of American Home Products Corporation; American Medical Association; Amstar Corporation; Armour and Company; Borden, Inc.; Campbell Soup Company; Carnation Company; Commercial Aluminum Company; Cookware Manufacturer's Association; Carl Sontheimer, Mayburn Koss, Cuisinarts, Inc.; Nach Waxman, Culinary Arts & Letters; Dairy Council of Metropolitan New York; Matt Lewis, Dean & Deluca; Del Monte Corporation; Anita Mizner, Dudley-Anderson-Yutzy; Richard Lord, Fishery Council; Mary Lyons, Food and Wines from France; R. T. French Company; Frieda's Finest Produce Specialties, Inc.; Loys Malmgren and Doris Koch, General Foods Corporation; General Mills, Inc.; Tony Fornarotto, Grand Union; Hamilton Beach, Scovill Inc.; Hershey Foods Corporation; Jenn-Air Corporation; Maryann Dalbey, Just Chocolate; Kraft, Inc.; Land O' Lakes, Inc., Lawry's Foods, Inc.; Margaret Beutel, Thomas J. Lipton, Inc.; Luhr Jensen and Sons; Marguerite Leahy, Nabisco Brands, Inc.; National Academy of Sciences; National Broiler Council; National Dairy Council; National Marine Fisheries; National Research Council; Nestlé Company; New York State College of Agriculture, Cornell University; New York State College of Human Ecology, Cornell University; New York State Cooperative Extension Service; North Carolina Agricultural Extension Service; Pillsbury Company; Quaker Oats Company; Ralston Purina Company; Reco International Corporation; Mary Ellen Griffin, Joseph E. Seagram/USA; Sun-Diamond Growers of California; Tea Council of the USA; Thermador/Waste King Company; Toastmaster Inc.; United Fresh Fruit and Vegetable Information Service; U.S. Department of Agriculture, Agriculture and Marketing Services; Linda Posati, U.S. Department of Agriculture, Science and Education Administration; U.S. Department of the Treasury, Bureau of Alcohol, Tobacco and Firearms.

Contents

Introduction

What has happened in the world of food since *The Doubleday Cookbook* was first published in 1975 is little short of phenomenal. The food processor, originally considered nothing more than a souped-up blender with an outrageous price tag, has become a necessity. So, for that matter, have microwave and convection ovens as more and more women enter the work force and more and more men pride themselves on their culinary prowess.

We have witnessed, moreover, a growing awareness of the importance of sound nutrition, a deep concern for both the wholesomeness and healthfulness of the food we eat. We have watched whole grains replace highly refined flours and polished rice, we have seen high-fiber fruits and vegetables assume greater prominence in the daily diet to say nothing of a decreased consumption of fats and sugars. Americans, as never before, have come to understand that they *are* what they eat.

Thanks to improved methods of shipping and handling, we find supermarket counters laden with foods unknown to most of us ten years ago: *carambolas* and *cherimoyas,* for example . . . *jicama* and *tomatillos* . . . not to mention such succulent forest mushrooms as *cèpes, pleurotes,* and *morels.* Pita bread can now be bought in the majority of supermarkets, as can frozen phyllo leaves. Tofu is no longer the mainstay of health food stores; it is routinely stocked by many supermarkets and most specialty food shops. *Crème fraîche* and *Devonshire cream* are cropping up in dairy counters everywhere, as is a whole new world of imported cheeses. There are the snowy goat cheeses known as *chèvres,* the buttery double and triple *crèmes,* the pungent monastery cheeses, a vast spectrum of blues.

We can buy fresh herbs today in little pots, mustards in dozens of textures and tastes, berry vinegars, herbal vinegars, and not least that mellow brown aged Italian grape vinegar known as *aceto balsamico.* Then there's the proliferation of pasta! Who could have predicted ten years ago that it would be available fresh as well as dried, stuffed and unstuffed, and in a positively dizzying array of shapes, flavors, and colors? Or that we could buy machines (or machine attachments) to mix, knead, and shape our own?

Suffice it to say that *The Doubleday Cookbook,* although first published a mere ten years ago, had considerable catching up to do. When friends heard that we were planning a major revision of the book, their reaction was immediate: "Whatever for? I love the book just the way it is."

But once we began to enumerate all the things that had been happening in the food world in the interim, they agreed that perhaps an update was due after all. "I guess there *are* a lot of developments," they would admit, then caution us about deleting this or that. *"Please* don't take out all the variations on basic recipes," one might say. "I use them all the time." Or, "You're not going to omit all those wonderful leftover ideas, are you?" Or, "For heaven's sakes, *don't cut all the calorie counts!"*

Not only did we not cut out the calorie counts, we added nutritional counts for the other two items most apt to be troublesome in diets: cholesterol and sodium. So now in addition to finding calorie counts per serving for each of the book's nearly 5,000 recipes, you will also find milligrams cholesterol and sodium given.

What we did prune from the original book were many of the recipes based upon the mixes and instants so popular ten years ago because we've found that as people become more additive-aware, they use packaged foods less and less frequently. We also plead "guilty" to axing a number of overly rich desserts and such fussy or outdated recipes as Beef Wellington and Shrimp Wiggle.

On balance, we have added more of substance than we have cut: chapter-by-chapter directions for using microwave and convection ovens (for roasting meats, for example, or baking pies and pastries) . . . detailed instructions for using that new miracle machine, the food processor . . . latest consumer information on all foods . . . new roasting times and temperatures for meats . . . updated drink and punch recipes incorporating the recently adopted metric-size bottles . . . a dictionary of commonly used food additives (see rear endpaper) that tells not only *what* they are, but also *why* they are used and *whether they are safe.*

What hasn't changed is *The Doubleday Cookbook*'s original purpose: To assemble between two covers the most complete, up-to-date information available about food and cooking. To be the cook's—*every* cook's—book. To answer his or her most pressing questions, no matter how rudimentary (What kind of potato boils best? What kind of apples make the best pie?), to provide solid background information on the selection, preparation, storage, and serving of food, wines, and spirits.

But this new edition isn't devoted to fundamentals alone. It is a book filled with appealing and unusual recipes: a sophisticated sampling of the *tapas* of Spain and *mezze* of the Middle East (appetizers both) in place of the dreary dips, dunks, and spreads so dear to the heart of the seventies' hostess . . . a hefty helping of tofu-, nut-, and/or grain-based vegetarian pâtés and entrées . . . a nutritious new collection of vegetable and whole grain breads (quick breads, yeast breads, breads to stir up by hand, by electric mixer, by food processor) . . . a wealth of from-scratch pastas, vegetables (including today's supermarket exotics), salads (some showy composed salads here). There's a heavier emphasis in this edition on the economical cuts of meat (breast, shoulder, shanks). Also upon poultry, especially turkey, which can be substituted for pricey veal in many recipes (thinnest slices of turkey breast make dandy scaloppine and boneless turkey roll can be simmered into a supremely succulent, cents-saving *Tonnato* that tastes for all the world like the veal original).

Those blasé about food insist that there are no new recipes. We disagree. Certainly there are new-to-print recipes, and it is these that we have concentrated upon in updating *The Doubleday Cookbook* although we have not forsaken those recipes essential to a basic cookbook. These, you'll note, are offered not as ends in themselves but as foundations of innumerable variations, points of embarkation for the beginner. There are now more recipes than ever for those who yearn for firsthand involvement with the raw materials of cooking, who long to make soup the old-fashioned way or feel a yeast dough respond to their touch. There are recipes for busy men and women who must put a good meal on the table fast. And there are culinary tours de force for the occasional showpiece dinner.

The recipes come from many sources: from our own imaginations, from friends and relatives; from centuries-old handwritten receipt files; from regional inns, restaurants, and hotels, gathered on our travels around the world. And each is as true to the original as it was possible to make it given American ingredients and implements.

Every recipe has been tested—retested whenever necessary—so that every specific might be included: number of servings (figured in average-size portions); pan, casserole, or mold size whenever that size is important to the recipe's success; exact cooking times and temperatures together with descriptions of what a particular recipe should look, taste, or feel like when "done." And, lest the cook mistake a natural cooking phenomenon for failure, he or she is alerted to any surprises that may be encountered as a particular recipe is prepared. The cook is also advised how to rescue such genuine failures as curdled hollandaise or runny jelly.

Leftovers, instead of being lumped together in a single chapter, have been placed where they will be most useful—following a robust turkey, for example, or a giant ham. And, to help the cook budget time, recipes that can be partially made in advance are so indicated along with the point at which they may be refrigerated or frozen and the final touches each requires before being served.

This book, more than ten years in the original writing and two years more in the revising and updating, has not been built upon a gimmick. Its intent, simply, is to be a contemporary guide to good cooking and eating, to teach the *whys* of cooking as well as the *hows.*

Its purpose is to coax the timid into the kitchen, to motivate the indifferent, and to challenge accomplished cooks into realizing their creative potential. In short, to share the fun of cooking as well as the fundamentals, to offer something of value to all who cook as well as to those who have not yet learned how.

How to Use This Book

All recipes in this book call for specific products by their generic (general descriptive) names, not the brand names; "quick-cooking rice," for example, is the fully precooked minute variety, "liquid hot red pepper seasoning" is the fiery bottled sauce made with tabasco peppers.

Whenever the name of a recipe is capitalized (Medium White Sauce, for example, or Flaky Pastry I), the recipe is included elsewhere in the book; consult Index for page numbers.

Whenever a method or technique is marked with an asterisk* ("if lobsters are live, clean,*" for example, or "caramelize the sugar*"), how-to information is described in full detail elsewhere in the book; see Index for page numbers.

Three symbols are used throughout the book to key recipes:

⚖ = **Low-Calorie**
¢ = **Budget**
⌛ = **Quick and Easy**

Specific sizes of pan, casserole, or mold are given whenever those sizes are essential to the success of a recipe.

Unless a recipe specifies alternate ingredients, do not make substitutions—margarine for butter, for example; oil for shortening; syrup for sugar. *And never substitute soft margarine for regular margarine or no-sift flour for sifted all-purpose flour.*

Suggestions for garnishes, seasonings, and leftovers are included within each chapter wherever appropriate.

Preheat conventional oven or broiler a full 15 minutes before using. *Tip:* Have oven checked frequently for accuracy (many utility companies provide this service free of charge).

Use middle oven rack for general baking and roasting; whenever a higher or lower rack position is essential, recipe will so direct.

"Cool" as used in recipes means to bring a hot food to room temperature; "chill" means to refrigerate or place in an ice bath until chilled throughout.

Read each recipe through carefully before beginning it, making sure that all necessary ingredients and utensils are on hand and that you understand the instructions.

Recipe yields are given in average-size servings or portions. A recipe that reads "4 Servings," for example, will feed 4 persons of *average* appetite.

An Explanation of How the Nutritional Counts Were Calculated

Calorie, cholesterol, and sodium counts for average-size servings are set down in round numbers (130 calories per serving instead of 128.5, 25 mg cholesterol instead of 23.25, and 395 mg sodium instead of 396 or 397). *Note:* To save space, the following abbreviations are used: NPS *(nutrients per serving),* NP *(nutrients per* as in *per cookie, per piece, per tablespoon, per teaspoon);* C *(calorie),* CH *(cholesterol),* and S *(sodium).* Also, g = gram, mg = milligram. If a recipe yields a variable number of servings (4–6, 6–8, etc.), nutritive counts are abbreviated thus: NPS (4–6): 200–135 C, 25–15 mg CH, 40–25 mg S (in each instance the higher number represents 4 servings; the lower, 6). *Note: Unless otherwise indicated, all nutritional counts are based solely upon recipe ingredients and do not include any suggested accompaniments (rice, for example, or potatoes).* Also, whenever recipes call for variable amounts (1–2 tablespoons, 1/4–1/2 cup), the count is figured using the first, or lower, quantity only. Finally, if a recipe suggests alternative ingredients, the calorie count is based upon the principal ingredient, not the alternative. The asterisk (*) appearing at the end of each nutrient count refers the reader to the above explanation of abbreviations.

About Ingredients

Unless recipes specify otherwise:

Flour called for is all-purpose flour, sifted before measuring.

Baking powder is double-acting baking powder.

Butter is salted butter.

Sour cream is the commercial type.

Eggs are large eggs.

Brown sugar is measured firmly packed.

Garlic cloves are of medium size (about like the first joint of the little finger).

Herbs and spices are dried.

Pepper is black pepper, preferably freshly ground.

"Celery stalk" means 1 branch of a bunch; some recipe books call the branch a "rib," the bunch a "stalk." As used here, "stalk" and "rib" are synonymous.

All measures are standard, all measurements level.

Oven Temperatures

Below 300° F. = very slow
300° F. = slow
325° F. = moderately slow
350° F. = moderate
375° F. = moderately hot
400°–425° F. = hot
450°–475° F. = very hot
500° F. or more = extremely hot

Table of Equivalents

NOTE: All measures are level.

Pinch or dash = less than 1/8 teaspoon

3 teaspoons = 1 tablespoon

2 tablespoons = 1 fluid ounce

1 jigger = 1 1/2 fluid ounces

4 tablespoons = 1/4 cup

5 tablespoons + 1 teaspoon = 1/3 cup

8 tablespoons = 1/2 cup

10 tablespoons + 2 teaspoons = 2/3 cup

12 tablespoons = 3/4 cup

16 tablespoons = 1 cup

1 cup = 8 fluid ounces

2 cups = 1 pint

2 pints = 1 quart

4/5 quart = 25.6 fluid ounces

1 quart = 32 fluid ounces

4 quarts = 1 gallon

SOME FRACTIONAL MEASURES

1/2 of 1/4 cup = 2 tablespoons

1/2 of 1/3 cup = 2 tablespoons + 2 tsp.

1/2 of 1/2 cup = 1/4 cup

1/2 of 2/3 cup = 1/3 cup

1/2 of 3/4 cup = 1/4 cup + 2 tablespoons

1/3 of 1/4 cup = 1 tablespoon + 1 tsp.

1/3 of 1/3 cup = 1 tablespoon + 2 1/3 tsp.

1/3 of 1/2 cup = 2 tablespoons + 2 tsp.

1/3 of 2/3 cup = 3 tablespoons + 1 2/3 tsp.

1/3 of 3/4 cup = 1/4 cup

SOME DRY WEIGHTS *(Avoirdupois)*

4 ounces = 1/4 pound

8 ounces = 1/2 pound

16 ounces = 1 pound

2 gallons (dry measure) = 1 peck

4 pecks = 1 bushel

Tips for Dieters

Low-Sodium Diets: Delete salt from recipes (1 t. salt = 1,955 mg sodium) or use a salt substitute (1 mg. sodium per t.); use unsalted butter (1 mg sodium per T. vs. 116 for the salted) or unsalted margarine (3–4 mg sodium per T. vs 87–96 for salted).

Low-Cholesterol Diets: Substitute polyunsatured vegetable oils or margarine (little or no cholesterol) for butter (31 mg cholesterol per T.) *except in recipes specifying no substitute.*

Low-Calorie Diets: Eliminate sugar from savory soups, stews, sauces (1 T. sugar = 46 calories); use aspartame sweetener (200 times sweeter than sugar, but 4 calories per 1-gram packet) to sweeten ice creams, sherbets, cold fruit desserts and sauces.

A Quick Dictionary of Widely Used Food Additives

NOTE: FDA = U.S. Food & Drug Administration   GRAS = Generally Recognized as Safe by the FDA

- **Acetic Acid:** The acid in vinegar (4–6%) and one of the oldest known food additives. Used to flavor fruit beverages, cheeses, pickles, ketchup, baked products. GRAS.

- **Acetone Peroxide:** A conditioner and bleacher of flour. GRAS, but further testing expected.

- **Alginates (Ammonium, Calcium, Potassium):** Gelatinous substances obtained from seaweeds, used to keep ice creams creamy, breads, cakes, cookies, and candies moist. Also used to remove mineral particles from cheeses, cheese products, and sugar-free jams and jellies. GRAS.

- **Alpha-tocopherol (Vitamin E):** Reduces risk of rancidity in fats, oils. GRAS.

- **Aluminum Sulfate (Cake Alum, Patent Alum):** Used to crispen and firm pickles. GRAS.

- **Ammoniated Glycyrrhizin:** A supersweet licorice flavoring used in candies, root beer, and items that taste of wintergreen. Though regarded as safe by the FDA, it can raise blood pressure, cause headaches, edema, and fatigue. There is now talk of label warnings for foods containing this additive.

- **Ammonium Bicarbonate:** An alkali used in leavening quick breads, cakes, cookies, confections, and cocoa products. GRAS.

- **Ammonium Chloride:** Used in baking to provide "food" for yeast and to condition doughs. Can acidify urine, act as an expectorant, and, in 0.5–1-gram doses, cause nausea. GRAS.

- **Ammonium Phosphate (Monobasic, Dibasic and Ammonium Sulfate:** Used as buffers, leaveners, and acidifiers in the baking and brewing industries. GRAS.

- **Ammonium Sulfide:** Artificial spice flavoring used in baking. Because it is used in such minute quantities, it need not be listed on package labels.

- **Ascorbic Acid (Vitamin C):** Used to keep fruits and vegetables from darkening. Safe.

- **Aspartame:** An artificial sweetener made from two amino acids—L-aspartic acid and L-phenylalanine. Still controversial after years of FDA test; unsafe for those with phenylketonuria.

- **Benzoic Acid:** See *Sodium Benzoate*.

- **Beta-carotene:** A yellow vegetable dye used widely in the food industry that is a precursor of vitamin A. GRAS.

- **BHA (Butylated Hydroxyanisole) and BHT (Butylated Hydroxytoluene):** Similar chemical compounds not only used to prolong shelf life of foods containing fat or oil but also added to breakfast cereals, enriched rice, chewing gum, and many convenience foods. Though ranked GRAS, BHA and BHT are increasingly controversial, and there is pressure for further testing.

- **Bromates (Potassium and Calcium):** Used in milling to improve the baking properties of flour. GRAS.

- **Bromated Vegetable Oil (BVO):** A possibly toxic additive made by combining bromine with cor, olive, or sesame oil. Its purpose? To disperse flavorings in a variety of carbonated and noncarbonated soft drinks. The FDA removed BVO, found hazardous by Canadian researchers, from its GRAS list. It is still being used, however, in soft drinks and snack foods.

- **Calcium Disodium:** See *EDTA.*
- **Calcium (and Sodium) Propionate:** Preservatives used to stop mold and bacterial growth in baked goods. Calcium propionate is preferred for yeast breads, sodium propionate for cakes, pies, cookies. GRAS.
- **Calcium Salts (Carbonate, Caseinate, Chloride, Citrate, Phosphates [Monobasic, Di-, and Tribasic], Sulfate):** For the most part firming or jelling agents or acid neutralizers. Most are on the FDA's GRAS list although calcium chloride can cause stomach upset and heart irregulatities.
- **Calcium Silicate:** An anticaking agent used in table salt and baking powders. GRAS, although further studies are needed to determine whether breathing the substance causes respiratory problems.
- **Carrageenan:** Emulsifier abtained from Irish moss, used in ice creams, sherberts, salad dressings, assorted chocolate products, whipped "creams" in squirt cans, sugar-free jams and jellies. GRAS.
- **Citric Acid:** One of the oldest safest, and most versatile additives. It is used, among other things, to impart fruit flavor; cure meats; firm peppers, tomatoes, potatoes; and prevent potatoes and fruits from darkening. Completely safe.
- **Dextrin (Starch Gum):** Used to keep candies from crystallizing, as a thickening agent, ans as a stabilizer of beer foam. Completely safe.
- **Disodium Guanylate (GMP) and Disoldium Inosinate (IMP):** Flavor enhancers used in dry soup mixes, sauces, canned vegetables, ham and chicken spreads. Not safe for gout sufferers or those on low-sodium diets.
- **Disodium Phosphate:** Used to emulsify cheeses, to inactivate trace metals in pasta and evaporated milk, to keep hams and processed meats juicy. GRAS.
- **EDTA (Calcium Disodium):** A versatile additive of questionable safety. It appears in beverages (to entrap metal impurities that cause clouding), in salad dressings, margarine, amyonnaise, sandwich spreads (to retard staline), in canned shellfish (to prevent discoloration). Careful testing overdue.
- **Erthorbic Acid (Isoascorbic Acic):** A color fixer added pickles, beverages, cured meats, bakery items. GRAS.

- **Ethyl Acetate:** Flavoring agent used in fruit sodas, ice creams, puddings, gelatins, chewing gum. GRAS.
- **Food Colors:** Accepted for general use today: Reds Nos. 3 and 40, Yellows 5 and 6, Blues 1 and 2, and Green No. 3. Possibly harmful Orange B is used exclusively for hot dogs, and Citrus Red No. 2 to dye orange peels.
- **Fumaric Acid:** Used to add tartness to fruit gelatins, puddings, pie fillings, beverages, baked goods. Harmless.
- **Glycerin (Glycerol):** Clear, viscous, sweet liquid used to keep foods—notably candies—moist. GRAS.
- **Gums (Arabic, Guar, Tragacanth):** These vegetable gums are used primarily as thickeners, stabilizers, and emulsifiers in candies, jellies, frostings, cheeses, frozen desserts, salad dressings. GRAS.
- **Hydrolized Vegetable Protein (HVP):** A flavor enhancer derived from soybean or other vegetable protein used in soup or sauce mixes, canned chilis and stews, hot dogs. GRAS.
- **Isopropyl Citrate and Stearyl Citrate:** Chemicals added to fats and oils to reduce risk of rancidity. GRAS, but many scientists demand further tests to assess potential liver/kidney damage.
- **Lactic Acid (Butyl Lactate, Ethyl Lactate, Calcium Lactate):** Lactic acid is used to boost or adjust acid in cheese and olives, to add tartness to beverages, ices, and ice creams. The non-acidic lactates prevent discoloration of fruits and vegetables. GRAS.
- **Lecithin:** An antioxidant used to retard spoilage in fats and oils; also an emulsifier used candies, ice creams, and bakery goods. Safe and Nutritious.
- **Malic Acid:** The acid of apples It's used to add tartness to fruit candies, drinks, ice creams, and preserves. GRAS.
- **Maltol and Ethyl Maltol:** Flavor enhancers added to such high-carbohydrate foods as ice creams, gelatin desserts, soft drinks. Testing for safety continues.
- **Mannitol:** A sweet substance extracted from the manna ash tree. Used primarily in "sugarless" chewing gum and dietetic desserts. Considered GRAS despite its diuretic and laxative effect.
- **Monoglycerides, Diglycerides:** Stabilizers and emulsifiers widely used in margarines, peanut butters, bakery cakes and breads. Safe, although their chemical derivatives—*ethoxylated mono- and diglycerides, sodium sulfoacetate mono- and diglycer-*

ides, and *diacetyl tartaric acid ester of mono- and diglycerides*—all require careful testing.

- **Monosodium Glutamate (MSG):** A popular but still controversil flavor enhancer despite its GRAS rating. Should be avoided by pregnant women and those on low-sodium diets. May cause allergic reactions in some people.
- **Polysorbate 60, 65, 80:** Emulsifiers and flavor disperser used in candies, cake mixes, frostings, beverages, gelatin desserts, salad dressings, milk and cream substitutes. Despite much discussion on their safety, the FAO/WHO Committee on Additives considers them safe.
- **Propyl Gallate:** Added to fats, oils, meat products, etc., to increase keeping qualities. GRAS, but new tests due.
- **Propylene Glycol:** Used to keep candies, baked goods, coconut products moist. GRAS.
- **Saccharin:** Artificial sweetener that continues to be controversial.
- **Silicon Dioxide:** Anticaking agent used in salt, baking powder, powdered coffee creamers. GRAS.
- **Sodium Benzoate:** A preservative used in such acid foods as pickles and fruit juices. GRAS.
- **Sodium bisulfite:** A bleaching agent used to keep potatoes white and to reduce discoloration in wines, beers, sliced fruits and vegetables. GRAS, although enough people are seriously allergic to sulfiting agents to warrant label warnings.
- **Sodium Carboxymethyl Cellulose (CMC):** Versatile stablizer, texturizer, emulsifier added to wide variety of foods. GRAS.
- **Sodium Erythorbate:** Color brightener for cired meats. GRAS.
- **Sodium Nitrate, Nitrite:** Highly controversial additives used in curing meats. Nitrite is particularly toxic. Bacons containing nitrite, if cooked at high temperatures, produce carcinogenic *nitrosamines.*
- **Sorbic Acid:** Inhibitor of molds added to cheeses, mayonnaises, jellies, canned frostings, soft drinks, dried fruits, and many other foods. GRAS.
- **Sorbitol:** A sugar subsitute. GRAS.
- **TBHQ (Tertiary Butylhydroquinone):** A potentially dangerous preservative used with fats and oils.
- **Textured Vegetable Protein (TVP):** Soy protein combined with additives to form a meat substitute. Safety and wholesomeness depend on additives used.
- **Vanillin:** Artificial vanilla. GRAS.

THE NEW DOUBLEDAY COOKBOOK

ONE

The Fundamentals of Cooking

Housewares departments offer so many glamorous lines of cookware it is difficult to choose which is best. That porcelain-lined, double-weight copper asparagus steamer with brass handles *is* stunning. But is it necessary? Not at $90, it isn't, unless you are rich and fond of steamed asparagus ($90 will buy many of the basics of the beginning kitchen). The point is to buy what utensils you will use frequently, then to add the more specialized items as you need them. Quality counts and should not be sacrificed for the sake of a pretty pot. Here are some shopping tips to guide you when buying.

SELECTING POTS AND PANS

Look for:
• Utensils durable enough to withstand daily use without wearing thin, denting, warping, chipping, pitting, cracking, or discoloring.
• Medium to heavyweight cookware, sturdily constructed with flat bottoms, straight or gently flared sides, and snug (but easy-to-remove) lids. *Note:* Decorative enamelware is sometimes too lightweight to cook food without scorching it.
• Well-balanced skillets and saucepans that will stand squarely on burners whether lids are on or off (always test for tippiness with the lids off).
• Easy-to-clean utensils with rounded corners and no ridges, protruding rivets, or crevices to catch and hold bits of food.
• Utensils with firmly mounted, heatproof handles and knobs.

• Utensils that can be hung or nested to save space.

Some Specifics About Different Kinds of Cookware

Aluminum: People still shy away from aluminum, believing the old wives' tale that it poisons food. *Not so.* Aluminum is one of the best all-around cooking materials available. It is inexpensive; a quick, even conductor of heat, sturdy enough to take daily wear and tear, yet lightweight enough to handle comfortably. It is stamped into lightweight and medium-weight saucepans, kettles, and bakeware and cast into heavy skillets, kettles, and griddles. Moreover, it is available plain or colored (anodized). Some people insist that aluminum gives tomatoes and other acid foods a metallic taste, yet just as many disagree. Aluminum, however, is not entirely fault free: It darkens and pits when exposed to alkaline or mineral-rich foods or when left to soak in sudsy water; it must be scoured frequently and, if anodized, cannot be washed in a dishwasher. Latest aluminum entries: Cleanly designed restaurant-gauge pots and pans with gunmetal-gray, hard-coat anodized finishes and tinned, cast-iron handles. Superb conductors of heat, these heavyweights are scratch-, chip-, and stain-resistant but must not be put through the dishwasher lest they spot or fade. *Cleaning Tip:* To brighten drab aluminum *(not nonstick),* boil an acid solution (2 tablespoons cream of tartar or 1 cup vinegar to each 1 quart water) in utensil 5–10 minutes, then scour with a soap pad, rinse, and dry.

Stainless Steel: Extremely sturdy and long suffering. Stainless steel's greatest shortcoming is that it is a poor conductor of heat and must be bonded to a good conductor—usually copper or aluminum—if it is to cook properly (even thus, it is better for stove-top cooking than baking). Sometimes pan bottoms only are clad with copper or aluminum, sometimes the entire utensil is two-ply (stainless steel inside and aluminum outside), sometimes it is three-ply (a copper, carbon steel, or aluminum core sandwiched between two layers of stainless steel), or even four-ply as in the case of chromium-plated steel (successive layers of copper, nickel, and chromium are electrolytically fused to steel, forming a hard, nonporous, nontarnishing, mirror-bright finish). Stainless-steel cookware costs more than aluminum but is easier to clean and slower to dent or scratch. It *will* heat-streak if permitted to boil dry, but unless it is seriously discolored it can be brightened with one of the special stainless-steel cleansers.

Cast Iron: The work horse of days past and still the favorite for frying chicken and baking popovers and corn sticks because of its ability to absorb and hold heat. But cast iron is leaden and cumbersome and unless well seasoned or enameled (as much of it now is) it is likely to rust; unenameled cast iron should never be used for liquid recipes—they will taste of rust. Most modern cast-iron cookware is preseasoned and ready to use, but the old-fashioned ware must be seasoned before using. *To Season* (or reseason): Wash and dry utensil, rub with unsalted shortening, and heat, uncovered, 2 hours in a 350° F. oven. *Cleaning Tip:* Use soap instead of synthetic detergents so that a utensil's seasoning will last through several washings, then dry over lowest burner heat; store uncovered to prevent beads of "sweat" from collecting and rusting the iron.

Copper: The choice of gourmets because of its ability to transmit the merest flicker of heat evenly, slowly, constantly. But, to do the job well, the copper must be heavy gauge (thin decorator sets look good—*but do not cook well*), and, to be safe for cooking, copper utensils must be lined with stainless steel, nonstick finish, or tin (the tin must be retinned whenever copper begins to show through). Copper, unquestionably, makes the handsomest pots and pans, but it is luxury priced, quick to scar, and pesky to clean and polish. An additional shortcoming of copper cookware: Most of it is made with metal handles and knobs, meaning that you must use potholders constantly.

Enameled Metals (also called *Agateware, Graniteware,* and *Enamelware):* Metal utensils coated inside and out with thin layers of porcelain. Available in dazzling colors and decorator patterns, enamel utensils are nonporous and inert (unreacting in the presence of acid or alkaline foods) and for that reason are well suited to pickling and preserving. They are, however, easily chipped, cracked, scratched, and stained. *Cleaning Tip:* To float charred foods magically off the bottoms of enamel pots, boil a baking soda solution in the pots several minutes (2–3 tablespoons baking soda to each quart water).

Nonstick Finishes: Originally so delicate they required special nylon implements and "soft" scouring pads, they are now hardier, less easily scratched or scraped. They permit virtually fat-free cooking (a blessing to the calorie and cholesterol conscious); they cannot, however, take intensive heat, so should not be used for broiling. Though most nonstick finishes are dishwasher-safe, they rarely require more than a quick sponging. If you must scour, use plastic mesh pads *only.*

Flameproof Glass: Good all-around stove-top and ovenware, inert like enamelware, easy to clean. Relatively sturdy although the glass will break if dropped or subjected to abrupt temperature changes.

Freezer-to-Stove Ceramic Ware: A Space Age material, inert, extremely durable that's now available in a multitude of sizes, styles, and patterns. All can be used in microwave and convection ovens as well as conventional ovens. The ideal container for freezer-to-oven-to-table casseroles.

Stoneware: Available in a broad range of designs, it is chip-resistant, oven-, microwave-, and dishwasher-safe.

Earthenware: Clay bakeware, glazed until nonporous, nonabsorbent; it may be high-fired and hard, low-fired and crumbly. Expert cooks insist that earthenware alone, because of its ability to release heat slowly, can impart to baked beans, *cassoulet,* and other long-simmering oven dishes the proper mellowness and consistency. Earthenware must be handled gingerly, however, cooled thoroughly before it is washed lest its glaze crack. *Warning:* Within the last decade or so, certain Mexican pottery glazes were found to be poisonous. Play it safe. Use Mexican pottery for decoration only.

Unglazed Terra-cotta: Used 2,500 years ago by Etruscans to cook food slowly, these porous, covered clay cookers remain popular today (they can be used in microwave, convection, and conventional ovens). Many must be soaked in cold water 15 minutes before *each* use; during baking, they will dry, misting food inside with steam. This "steam heat" prevents food from sticking *(no pan greasing needed)*. The most popular clay cooker today is the "Russian Pot" (Römertopf), but terra-cotta bread, Bundt, deep and shallow pie plates are the choice of experienced bakers because they inject "brick-oven" flavor. Much clay bakeware must be seasoned before it's used (follow manufacturer's instructions carefully). *Tip:* Because these cookers hold cooking odors, reserve one exclusively for fish.

SELECTING AND CARING FOR KNIVES

Fine knives are the cook's best friends—sturdily constructed, well balanced and designed knives that can be honed to long-lasting razor keenness. It is the dull knife that cuts the cook, rarely the sharp one, because the dull knife must be forced. Good knives are expensive, but justifiably so because they will perform well over a period of years. What distinguishes the fine knife from the inferior? Here are a few indicators:
• Choose knives that feel comfortable in the hand. Top quality knives have handles of close-grained hardwood, rubbed to satiny smoothness; they will not warp, split, or splinter. Shoddy knives may have handles of soft wood (usually painted) or molded out of some synthetic (often rough around the seams).
• Look for blades well anchored in handles. In fine knives, blades extend to the tops of the handles and are held fast by two or three broad, double-headed rivets lying flush with the handle. Cheaper blades may be sunk only halfway into the handle, held by one or two small wire rivets or simply glued in place.

• Insist upon forged carbon or no-stain high-carbon steel knives, budget permitting. They are the choice of chefs and gourmets because of their fine, hard smoothness that will take and keep a keen cutting edge. Carbon steel knives *will* stain and rust, however, unless washed and dried as soon as they are used. Conventional stainless steel, made stainproof and rustproof by the addition of chromium and nickel, is softer, quicker to dull.
• Select knives with well-shaped blades. The *forged,* tapering from both blunt edge to sharp and handle to point, are choicest. *Stamped blades,* cut out of uniformly thick metal, usually indicate poor quality; *beveled blades,* cut from metal thicker on one edge than the other, taper from blunt side to sharp but not from handle to point—popular construction for medium-priced knives.

Hollow-ground blades, also in the medium price range, have broad, concave cutting surfaces; they are adept at slicing but easily damaged. *Shopping Tip:* If a brand name is stamped on a knife blade, the knife is probably a good one; manufacturers of inferior merchandise don't bother.

Some Knife Care Tips:
• Treat knives with respect, washing and drying them as soon as they are used, gently scouring off any darkened spots with metal soap pads. Do not wash in the dishwasher, do not soak; either can loosen rivets, rot handles and rust blades.
• Always use knife on a cutting surface softer than the blade—hardwood is ideal, makes the knife last longer.
• Store knives in a knife rack or block, never jammed into a drawer where the blade may be bent or nicked (and the cook injured).
• Use knives strictly for slicing, cutting, and chopping, never for prying off lids and bottle tops; it's damaging to the knife, dangerous, too.
• Sharpen knives frequently. Because each person tends to hold a blade to the steel or stone at a slightly different angle, it's best if the same person does all the knife sharpening—the knives will last longer.

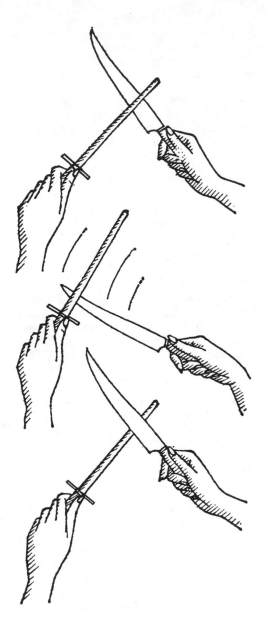

How to Sharpen a Knife

To sharpen on an electric sharpener, follow manufacturer's instructions.

MICROWAVE OVENS

Microwaves are very short, high-frequency radio waves. When absorbed by food, they cause its molecules to vibrate, producing heat, which in turn cooks the food. If proper utensils are used, microwaves pass right through them, penetrating food from the bottom, sides, and top to a depth of about 1"

(the center of a food cooks more slowly by conduction). Because microwaves cannot penetrate metal, all energy stays inside a microwave oven; if food is to cook evenly, this energy must be evenly distributed. Usually this is done with turntables, which move the food, and/or rotating antennae or stirrers which circulate the microwaves (inevitably, however, certain foods will still require manual rearranging).

Microwave Safety

Since 1971, all U.S. microwave ovens have had to meet rigid radiation safety standards that not only limit microwave leakage but also require two independent interlocks that stop microwave production whenever the oven door is opened (there must even be a separate system to monitor the interlocks).

What to Look For in a Microwave

If you only want to defrost or heat food, the simplest countertop model with one or two power levels will suffice. But if you intend to cook and bake by microwave, a more versatile, full-size unit (countertop or built-in) makes sense. Choose a size and model that not only meets your culinary needs but also fits the kitchen space available (countertop models need 1½"–2" air space on all sides *plus* their own electric circuits). Built-ins require venting. If space is limited, consider a *combination oven,* which puts two ovens into one (there are microwave-convection oven combinations—either gas or electric); most allow you to cook by either method or even to use the two in tandem. Consider wattage, too (microwaves range from 400 to 1,000 "cooking watts," the lower wattage ovens being the slower). Finally, choose microwaves with quick-to-read controls and low maintenance. *Desirable "Extras":* These include *Variable Power Controls* (ranging on some models from a low of 10 per cent to a high of 100 per cent) . . . *Memory* (for programmed, sequential cooking) . . . *Automatic Cooking* and/or *Defrosting* . . . and *Temperature Probes* (these shut oven off when food reaches desired internal temperature).

Microwave Utensils

Buying a microwave need not mean a whole new set of cookware. In general round or ring-shaped, straight-sided containers are best because they promote even heat distribution. Most suitable materials are those that transmit microwaves while remaining reasonably cool. Avoid using metal (unless utensil is labeled "suitable for microwaves"); also avoid containers with metal trim, metallic glazes, glued-on handles (these may fall off as microwave dehydrates glue). When in doubt, refer to Microwave Utensil Guide.

Some Cooking Techniques Unique to Microwaves

Arrangement: Place foods in oven to expose as many sides as possible. Center a single item on oven shelf, place two items side by side, three in a triangle, four in a square, and five or more in a circle with no item in center. Set larger or slower-to-cook foods around outer edge and smaller, quicker-cooking ones toward center.

Rearrangement: Foods must sometimes be rearranged *during cooking* if they are to cook evenly. This may be done by *stirring* (stir from *outside* to *center*) . . . *shifting or reversing positions* of items midway through cooking . . . *rotating* (by a quarter or half turn) half-cooked breads, cakes, layered casseroles, etc., that cannot be stirred or otherwise rearranged . . . *turning* (at half time) dense and/or large foods (roasts, whole birds, hamburgers, potatoes).

Shielding: Irregularly shaped foods (turkeys, for example) cook unevenly, so to keep small parts (drumsticks) from overcooking, cover with bits of foil (secure with toothpicks), which will deflect microwaves. *Note: Foil must never touch oven walls or temperature probe.*

Standing Time: Many microwaved foods must *stand* before being served because they continue to cook (or heat) after they come from the oven. For small, low-density items (bread, bacon, most vegetables, liquids) this will mean a few minutes only. But roasts, turkeys, and potatoes, etc., may require 10–15 minutes. *Standing time depends on the amount of food being microwaved, as well as its size, density, and moisture content.*

Heating Food by Microwave

Most foods heat or reheat beautifully in a microwave without losing quality. Still, there are a few tricks: *Cover* most foods (see Microwave Utensil Guide for specifics) . . . *Use a temperature probe* (if your microwave oven is equipped with one) for perfect results . . . *Allow extra time* for reheating refrigerated foods . . . *Stir, rearrange, or rotate* large amounts of food halfway through heating period . . . *Make sure food is hot throughout* (steaming or bubbling at edges is no guarantee) . . . *When heating a single plate of food,* place thick or dense pieces around edge, small ones in center. Also spread foods for a low, even profile, cover or sauce food to keep it moist, and microwave at *MEDIUM TO HIGH* 3–5 minutes. *Tip:* When food is properly heated, bottom of plate will feel *warm.*

Microwave Power Levels and Timing

The Consumer Appliance Section, International Microwave Power Institute, is working to standardize the power levels commonly used in recipes as follows: *HIGH (100 per cent power;* best for browning, boiling liquids, cooking or heating fish, ground meats, and bacon), *MEDIUM-HIGH (about 70 per cent;* for roasting meat and poultry, baking pie shells, cookies, casseroles, and convenience foods), *MEDIUM (about 50 per cent;* for defrosting and slow-cooking), *LOW (about 30 per cent;* for simmering delicate sauces, casseroles), and *WARM (about 10 per cent;* for heating breads, keeping food warm, softening butter, cheese, and chocolate). How long it takes to cook food by microwave depends upon the volume of food, its size, shape, density, and starting temperature. The increase in cooking time, however, is not necessarily proportional to the increase in volume (2 potatoes will bake more slowly than 1 but will not take twice as long). Fats and sugars heat very quickly (a cheese topping, for example, may burn before a casserole is warm; using a lower power setting or adding topping halfway through cooking will solve this problem).

Not Recommended for the Microwave

• Anything in a bottle with a narrow neck
• Eggs in the shell
• Popcorn (except in microwave poppers)
• Yeast breads or crispy filled pastries
• Huge food loads (a 25-pound turkey will cook faster in a conventional oven and so will 12 baking potatoes)
• Deep fat frying (fats will burn in a microwave and fried foods, when reheated, become soggy)
• Processing home-canned foods

Converting Conventional Recipes for Use in the Microwave

With practice, you can prepare by microwave old family favorites once cooked the conventional way. There are *do's* and *don'ts,* though.
• Avoid microwaving fat- or sugar-rich foods, sautéed or fried foods, filled crisp pastries, or yeast breads.
• Because liquids do not evaporate when microwaved, reduce by about ¼ amounts called for in soups, sauces, gravies, and casseroles. Also slightly reduce amount of seasonings, and salt food *after* cooking. *Note:* Although we've always heard that microwave ovens do not brown foods well, new models with browning elements are now available, also new utensils that promote browning. In addition, there are specific cooking techniques that you can use to brown meats and poultry more thoroughly (for details, see each of these chapters).

Defrosting, Heating, or Cooking Frozen Foods by Microwave

In addition to the tips given here, you'll find additional information in chapters where applicable (Meat, for example). Also refer to manual provided by maker of your particular microwave (especially helpful when calculating defrosting times).
• Break up frozen foods *before* defrosting or as soon as possible *during* defrosting.
• For crisper, drier textures, defrost sandwiches, coffee cakes, sweet rolls, and pizza on microwave-safe trivets.
• Follow microwave directions on frozen food packages (many now include them).
• When microwaving frozen dinners, make sure aluminum trays are no more than ¾" deep and that lids are removed. *Tip:* Avoid microwaving frozen dinners containing French fries or doughy desserts.
• Stir or rotate food halfway through defrosting or heating; flex frozen bags of food.
• Turn large or dense foods midway through microwaving.
• Let casseroles, stews, meat loaves, and other large or high-density foods *stand 15– 20 minutes between defrosting and cooking or heating;* fish fillets, meat balls, vegetables, and chicken parts should *stand 5–10 minutes.* Only whopping amounts of soups or sauces require any *standing time.*

MICROWAVE UTENSIL GUIDE

Note: When using a dual oven (microwave-convection), choose containers and lids suitable for the microwave. Whenever you question a container's microwavability, perform this *Dish Test:* Pour 1 cup water into a flameproof glass measure and set *inside* or *beside* container to be tested. Microwave 1 minute on *HIGH.* If *water heats,* container is microwave-safe; *if container heats, it is unsafe.*

Utensil/ Material	Microwave-Suitable?	Comments
Flameproof glass	Yes	Good for heating/cooking (2-quart measures are ideal for soups/sauces/gravies). Close-fitting covers seal steam in.
Freezer-to-stove ceramics	Yes	Good for cooking/heating/defrosting. Snug lids seal steam in, keep foods juicy.
China, pottery, earthenware, terra-cotta	Yes	For brief heating/cooking only.
Plastics	Thermoset types best	Neither high temperatures nor fatty foods deform stain- and odor-resistant, dishwasher-safe thermoset plastics. Most withstand conventional/convection oven heats up to 400° F. Other plastics may melt. When using plastic freezer/cooking pouches, close with floss or string *(not metal twist-ties)* and pierce with a knife to vent steam. *Plastic food wrap* is the covering to use when you want to seal steam in and keep foods moist or juicy; always turn back one corner of wrap *before microwaving* so it won't split during cooking.

Utensil/ Material	Microwave- Suitable?	Comments
Paper toweling, napkins, plates	Yes	Use plain paper products only (colors may bleed into food); never use recycled paper, that containing nylon (it may ignite), or newspaper. Use *dry paper toweling* as *cover* or *wrapper* when heating sandwiches, crisping cookies, or chips (it absorbs moisture but allows steam to escape). Use *damp toweling* for steaming fish, warming tortillas, etc.
Wax paper	Yes	Use as a *cover* or *wrapper;* wax paper holds heat, speeds cooking, and prevents spattering.
Metal	No	*Except for "Active" microwave cookware (see below),* aluminum *frozen dinner trays (if no more than ³⁄₄″ deep), and* aluminum *foil,* (use *small pieces* to shield [cover] portions of food cooking too fast). Other metal utensils (even thermometers) cause *arcing* (sparking), which pits oven walls and may start a fire. *Note: Never heat food in a can.*
"Passive" microwave cookware	Yes	Glass-filled polyester made for microwave, convection, and conventional oven use (at temperatures up to 450° F.). These can go safely from freezer or refrigerator to oven, they are stain-resistant and dishwasher-safe.
"Active" microwave cookware	Yes	A fairly new concept—plastic-coated metal cookware in which foods brown, broil, bake, steam, and fry well. Use for crisp-crusted pizzas, fried potatoes, richly browned roasts.
Straw baskets	Yes	Use only if devoid of metal trim and then for brief periods only.
Wooden spoons, whisks, skewers, toothpicks	Yes	Use *clean* implements for short-term heating only. Do not use wooden bowls in microwave ovens; they will dry, split, and crack.
Lacquer ware	No	Apt to crack and/or discolor.
Shells (natural)	Yes	For brief heating or cooking only.
Glass jars	Yes	*But only heatproof, wide-mouth jars.*
Styrofoam	No	It may melt.

CONVECTION OVENS

Convection ovens, like conventional ovens, may be gas or electric. But there is a difference. In a convection oven, a fan circulates hot air around food continuously so that it cooks more evenly and, in many instances, 20–25 per cent faster. Other advantages: cold ovens heat zip-quick, reducing or eliminating the need to preheat . . . foods rarely need to be turned or basted . . . meats may often be roasted at lower temperatures (meaning less shrinkage and more succulence). Unlike microwave ovens, convection ovens require no special equipment or major adjustment in cooking techniques. Their strong suits are roasting and baking although they may also be used as "proofing ovens" for yeast breads (for specifics, see the chapter on Breads).

What to Look For in a Convection Oven

There's a bewildering array of models available: *electric countertop* (these require plenty of space all round *and* individual electric circuits) . . . *gas and electric built-ins . . . gas and electric free-standing ranges . . .* and *micro-convection combinations* (both gas and electric). All share two features: first, *a fan* (be sure you hear a convection oven's fan *running* before you buy to see if you can stand the noise) and second, *air vents* (these must not be blocked or placed directly underneath wall cabinets). *Desirable "Extras": Variable Temperature Controls . . . Memory* (for programmed cooking) . . . *Automatic Cooking and Defrosting . . . Temperature Probes* (to switch oven off when roast, cake, or casserole, etc., is done).

Converting Conventional Recipes for Use in Convection Ovens

Cooking via convection is little different from cooking the old-fashioned gas or electric way. Basically, it's faster. Here are some tips to ease the transition:

For meats and poultry, reduce recipe temperature about 25° F. (but never lower than 300° F.). Use temperature probe or meat thermometer; check for doneness when cooking time is 75 per cent up. *Note:* Quickest way to roast meat is directly on oven rack with drip tray underneath (roasting pan blocks air circulation).

For fish, reduce temperature 25° F. and test for doneness three fourths of the way through cooking.

For eggs and cheese, lower temperature 25° F. (except for soufflés, which fare best at 350° F.); check often for doneness during last baking quarter.

For casseroles, reduce temperature 25° F. but do not shorten baking time.

For vegetables, reduce *either* cooking time *or* oven temperature about 25 per cent.

For breads, cakes, and cookies, lower oven temperature 50°–75° F., but keep baking time the same.

For frozen convenience foods: Little change needed but check for doneness 5–10 minutes earlier. *Note:* Some pies bake better at temperatures 50° F. lower than normal (follow manufacturer's directions). *Tip:* For crisp-crusted pizzas, bake directly on oven rack (with drip pan or piece of foil on rack underneath).

FOOD PROCESSORS

What ten years ago was considered a jazzy overpriced blender has revolutionized the way America cooks. "Better than a maid," one wit quipped. Perhaps. Certainly food processors chop, mince, dice, slice, shred, grind, cream, and purée quickly and without complaint. The sturdiest of them also knead bread doughs in a matter of seconds and, with the proper attachments, mix, knead, and shape pasta, juice citrus fruits, and cut French fries. Who could ask for more?

Processor Safety

Because a processor's blades are scalpel-sharp and spin at formidable speed, manufacturers have built in as many fail-safe mechanisms as possible to prevent serious injuries: feed tubes too small and tall for hands to reach inside, blades that snap firmly into place, interlocks that prevent processors from operating when lids are not securely closed, and braking systems that bring whirling blades to rest almost as soon as the motor is shut off. There are, moreover, circuit breakers to stop the motor should it stall or overheat.

What to Look For in a Food Processor

Because of their versatility, reliability, and durability, large-capacity, heavy-duty processors with powerful motors are best if you intend to use them for a wide variety of kitchen jobs. However, if your processor needs involve little more than chopping onions or making baby food, a smaller, more limited model may serve. Whatever machine you choose, make sure that it stands squarely on the counter at all times (welter-weights tend to wobble or wander under heavy chopping loads), that its motor is not unduly noisy, that it has a pulse switch or button (essential for precision chopping), and that the accessories available (both standard and optional) suit your present and future cooking needs.

Desirable "Extras": Processor-makers continue to dream up new uses for their machines, but the most useful accessories to date are: *thick and thin slicing discs . . . fine and coarse shredding discs . . . French fry cutters . . . fine julienners . . . citrus juicers . . . pasta makers.*

Some Special Processor Techniques

The single most important processor tool is the *S-shaped metal chopping blade* (you will use it for everything except slicing and shredding); the second is the *pulse switch or button,* which allows you to chop onions as fine or coarse as you like—or to reduce them to mush. Becoming processor-proficient, thus, is as easy as developing a quick "trigger finger," because the pulse button not only controls chopping, mincing, grinding, mixing, puréeing, creaming, and kneading (all of which the metal chopping blade does) but also slicing and shredding (done by the discs that ride at the top of the work bowl).

Using Slicing and Shredding Discs: Cut foods in lengths (and widths) to fit the food processor feed tube, pack snugly in feed tube (with tapered foods such as carrots, stand some large-end-up, others large-end-down); depress pulse button, and guide food down feed tube using light pressure on the pusher. *Note:* Exerting no pressure at all on the pusher will yield slightly thinner slices, applying heavy pressure, somewhat thicker ones. *Tip:* Chill or *partially* freeze any soft foods (meats, mozzarella cheese, etc.) *before* attempting to slice or shred otherwise they will be churned to paste.

Using the Metal Chopping Blade: Chopping such watery, crisp vegetables as onions and sweet peppers is probably the single most difficult processor technique to master, but other foods can present problems too. The Food Processor Metal Blade Chopping Guide that follows should solve most of the problems this versatile blade presents and also show how to adapt recipes throughout this book to preparation by processor.

FOOD PROCESSOR METAL BLADE CHOPPING GUIDE

Note: For best results, chop no more than 2 cups food at a time (large processors can chop 4 cups at once).

BREAD (soft)

Preparation for Processor: Tear into small pieces.

Processor Technique: To crumb: pulse 5–6 times for *coarse crumbs;* use 2–3 (5-second) churnings for *fine crumbs.*

Comments: 1 slice bread = ½ cup coarse or fine crumbs.

BREAD (dry), CRISP COOKIES, CRACKERS

Preparation for Processor: Break into 1″–1½″ pieces or crumble coarsely.

Processor Technique: To crumb: pulse 5–6 times for *coarse crumbs;* churn 15–20 seconds nonstop for *fine crumbs.*

Comments: 15 (2¼″-square) Graham crackers, 24 vanilla wafers = 1 cup crumbs respectively.

CABBAGE

Preparation for Processor: Quarter, core, and cut in 1½″ cubes or chunks.

Processor Technique: To grate: pulse about 5 times for a good *slaw texture,* 6–7 times for *fairly fine texture.*

Comments: Shredding discs reduce cabbage to mush.

CHEESE (Parmesan, Romano, and other hard types only)

Preparation for Processor: Cut into 1″–1½″ cubes.

Processor Technique: To grate: snap motor on, then drop cubes, one by one, down feed tube into spinning blade; buzz 15–30 seconds nonstop until as fine as you like.

Comments: Stored in tightly covered glass jar, cheese will keep "fresh" 2–3 weeks.

COCONUT

Preparation for Processor: Rap shell with hammer to loosen meat, pierce "eyes," and drain out liquid. Crack shell, pry meat from shell, peel off brown skin with swivel-bladed vegetable peeler. Cut into 1″ chunks.

Processor Technique: To grate: turn processor on, drop coconut down feed tube; churn 10 seconds for fairly *coarse texture,* 10 seconds longer for *moderately fine texture,* and 10 seconds longer still for *fine texture.*

Comments: Coconut is so hard it is difficult to grate or shred without dulling or deforming some shredding discs.

CORN (fresh or thawed, frozen whole-kernel)

Preparation for Processor: Husk corn and remove silks. Cut kernels from cob by running paring knife straight down rows.

Processor Technique: To make cream-style corn: pulse 5–6 times.

Comments: Making cream-style corn was never easier—or neater!

EGGS (hard-cooked)

Preparation for Processor: Chill well, peel, then quarter lengthwise.

Processor Technique: To chop: pulse twice for a *coarse chop,* 3 times for a *moderately coarse chop,* and 4–5 times for *fairly fine texture.*

Comments: To keep green ring from forming between yolk and white, plunge just-cooked eggs into ice water.

FRUIT (candied or dried to be used in breads, cakes, cookies, etc.)

Preparation for Processor: Cut large fruits in 1″ cubes; chill fruit in freezer 15–20 minutes, then dredge in about 1 cup flour called for by recipe.

Processor Technique: To chop: pulse 2–3 times for *coarse texture,* 4–5 times for *moderately fine texture,* and 6–7 times for *fine texture.*

Comments: You may find it quicker to chop raisins and dried currants by hand.

FRUIT, RAW (soft pulpy fruits such as apricots, peaches, berries)

Preparation for Processor: Peel and pit, if necessary, then cut in 1½″ chunks or slim wedges. Wash berries, hull, and pat very dry on paper toweling.

Processor Technique: To chop: snap processor on and off once or twice for a *coarse chop. To purée:* churn 10–15 seconds nonstop; sieve berry purées to remove seeds.

Comments: To keep apricots, nectarines, and peaches from darkening, sprinkle with lemon juice.

FRUIT, RAW (crisp, watery fruits such as apples, pears)

Preparation for Processor: Peel and core, then cut in 1″ cubes or in slim wedges.

Processor Technique: To chop: pulse 2–3 times for a *coarse chop,* 4–5 times for a *moderately fine chop. To purée:* churn 10–15 seconds.

Comments: Sprinkle apples and pears with lemon juice to prevent browning.

HERBS (parsley, chervil, basil, mint, etc.)

Preparation for Processor: Wash well, remove coarse stems, and blot herbs *very dry* between several thicknesses paper toweling. Chill until needed.

Processor Technique: To chop: pulse 3–4 times for a *coarse chop,* 5–6 times for *moderately fine chop,* and 7–8 times for a *fine chop* or *mince.*

Comments: Herbs to be used in the same recipe can be chopped together.

MEAT, RAW (beef, veal, lamb, pork)

Preparation for Processor: Trim of all sinew and excess fat, then cut in ¾″ cubes.

Processor Technique: To grind: place 1 cup meat cubes in processor and pulse 3–4 times for a *moderately coarse grind,* 5–6 times for a *moderate grind,* and churn 8–10 seconds nonstop for a *fine grind.*

Comments: After grinding *raw pork,* wash all processor parts meticulously in hot sudsy water before using again.

MEAT, COOKED (beef, veal, lamb, pork, ham, poultry)

Preparation for Processor: Trim of fat and gristle, cut in 1″ cubes, and if meat is quite rare (soft), chill about 30 minutes in the freezer before grinding.

Processor Technique: To grind: use 3–4 (1-second) pulses for a *coarse grind,* 5–6 for a *moderate grind,* and 7–8 for a *fairly fine grind.* For *very finely ground meat* (good for croquettes and spreads), churn 15–20 seconds nonstop. *Caution:* Do not attempt to grind more than 1 cup of meat at a time.

Comments: Different leftover meats may be ground together provided you do not grind more than 1 cup of meat at once.

NUTS (almonds, peanuts, pecans, pine nuts, pistachios, walnuts)

Preparation for Processor: Shell, then blanch, if desired.

Processor Technique: To chop: pulse 2–3 times for a *coarse chop,* 4–5 times for a *moderate chop,* and 6–7 times for a *moderately fine chop.* For *feathery-fine nuts* (good for pastries and tortes), grind nuts 15–20 seconds nonstop.

Comments: Raw and roasted nuts chop equally well.

VEGETABLES, RAW
Very soft (avocados, tomatoes) *Tip:* **For best results, choose firm-ripe specimens.**

Preparation for Processor: Peel, pit, if necessary, then cut in 1″ cubes or slim wedges. To keep avocado from darkening, sprinkle liberally with lemon juice the instant you cut it.

Processor Technique: To chop: pulse briskly 1–3 times for a *coarse chop. To purée:* use 2 (5-second) churnings, scraping work bowl sides down between each. Sieve tomato purée to remove seeds.

Comments: Botanically speaking, avocados and tomatoes are fruits, but since they are used more like vegetables in cooking, we include them here.

Soft (eggplant, mushrooms, yellow squash, zucchini, etc.)
Preparation for Processor: Wash, trim, peel, if necessary, and cut in 1″–1½″ chunks or rounds. Small mushrooms may be chopped whole; halve or quarter large ones.

Processor Technique: To chop: pulse 3–4 times for a *coarse chop,* 5–6 times for a *moderate chop,* and 7–8 times for a *fine texture.*

Comments: If you want to brown a chopped vegetable in a skillet, do not chop it fine; it will ooze too much liquid to brown.

Crisp (celery, cucumber, fennel, onions, sweet peppers, shallots, etc.)
Preparation for Processor: Wash or peel, if necessary. Trim; cut large vegetables in 1″–1½″ cubes or rounds or slim wedges. Peppers should also be cored and seeded.

Processor Technique: To chop: pulse briskly once or twice for a *coarse chop,* 2–3 times for a *moderate chop,* and 4–5 times for a *fairly fine chop.*

Comments: If using garlic with onions, snap processor on, drop garlic down feed tube; stop machine, add onions and chop as directed.

Firm (carrots, cauliflower, gingerroot, parsnips, etc.)
Preparation for Processor: Wash or peel, as needed. Trim, cut in 1″ chunks or rounds or slim wedges; divide cauliflower into flowerets.

Processor Technique: To chop: pulse 2–3 times for a *coarse chop,* 4–5 times for a *moderate chop,* and 6–7 times for a *fairly fine chop.*

Comments: If a recipe calls for gingerroot or carrots and garlic, chop the two together as directed.

Very hard (beets, horseradish, celery root, rutabaga, winter squash, etc.)
Preparation for Processor: Peel, seed, if necessary, then cut into ½″ cubes.

Processor Technique: To chop: use 2–3 (5-second) churnings for a *moderately coarse chop* and 2–4 (10-second) churnings for a *fairly fine chop.*

Comments: Do not attempt to chop these tough vegetables in any but the sturdiest heavy-duty processors.

VEGETABLES, COOKED

Preparation for Processor: Peel and seed, if necessary; cut large vegetables into 1″ cubes or rounds or slim wedges.

Processor Technique: To purée: churn 2 cups vegetables with 2–3 tablespoons cooking water, milk, or cream or 1½ tablespoons butter 5 seconds nonstop; repeat 2–3 times. Sieve, if needed.

Comments: Do not purée cooked Irish potatoes; the processor will churn them into a dismal, gray, gluey mass.

To grate citrus rind: If you need finely grated lemon, lime, grapefruit, or orange rind for a cake or frosting, the processor will do the job in seconds. With a vegetable peeler, strip zest (colored part) of rind from fruit, buzz 3–4 times, 10 seconds each, with 1 cup of the sugar or confectioners' sugar recipe calls for.

What the Processor *Doesn't* Do Well

• Mash or whip cooked Irish potatoes (they turn to paste).
• Chop, shred, or slice cooked Irish potatoes (they become gluey).
• Mill whole grains into flour.
• Grind whole spices.
• Grind coffee beans.
• Beat egg whites to great volume or stiff peaks (processor knocks the air out of them).
• Whip heavy cream to great volume or stiff peaks (it will overwhip).
• Mince or chop dried currants or raisins (unless soaked 10–15 minutes in fruit juice, water, wine, or spirits, they will merely rattle around the processor work bowl).
• Churn heavy cream to butter.
• Churn peanuts into a first-class peanut butter (you must add plenty of soft margarine or butter to produce an acceptable spread).

SOME COOKING TERMS DEFINED

The language of food, so clear cut and routine to experienced cooks, often bewilders the beginner. Defined here are the more common general terms; elsewhere in the book, in the sections where they most apply, are the more specific terms—*muddle,* for example, a bar technique, is defined in the beverages chapter; *soft ball,* a test used in making candy, is explained in that chapter.

adjust: To taste before serving and increase seasoning as needed.
agneau: The French word for "lamb."
ajinomoto: The Japanese word for "monosodium glutamate."
à la: A French idiom loosely translated to mean "in the style of." *À la maison,* for example, is "as prepared at this house or restaurant, the house specialty," and *à la bourguignonne* ("as prepared in Burgundy"—with Burgundy wine).
à la king: Cut up food, usually chicken or turkey, in cream sauce, often with slivered pimiento and sliced mushrooms added.
à la mode: As used in America, pie or other dessert topped with a scoop of ice cream. In French cuisine, braised meat smothered in gravy.
al dente: An Italian phrase meaning "to the tooth," used to describe pasta cooked the way Italians like it—tender but still firm.
allumette: The French word for "match," used to describe food cut in matchstick shapes; also a slim, bite-size puff pastry hors d'oeuvre.
amandine: Made or served with almonds.
à point: A French phrase used to describe food cooked just to the point of doneness.
aubergine: The French word for "eggplant."
au gratin: A dish browned in oven or broiler, usually topped with buttered bread crumbs or grated cheese or both. *Gratiné* means the same thing.
au jus: Food, usually roast beef, served in its own juices.

baba: A sweet yeast cake, studded with raisins and dried fruit, saturated with brandy, kirsch, or rum *(baba au rhum).*
baguette: A long, baton-shaped "everyday" bread popular in France. It has a crisp brown crust and chewy texture.
bain marie: French for a "steam table" or "hot water bath" (which see).
bake: To cook by dry oven heat.
ball: To cut into balls.
barbecue: To cook in a hot spicy sauce, often over a grill; also the food so cooked and the grill used for cooking it.
bard: To tie bacon, suet, or fatback around lean meats to prevent their drying out in cooking. For barding instructions, see Some Special Ways to Prepare Meat for Cooking in the meat chapter.
Bar-le-Duc: A red or white currant preserve named for Bar-le-Duc, France, where it is made.
baste: To ladle or brush drippings, liquid, butter, or sauce over food as it cooks, the purpose being to add flavor and prevent drying.
batter: An uncooked mixture, usually of eggs, flour, leavening, and liquid, that is thin enough to pour.
batterie de cuisine: A French phrase used to describe all the implements, utensils, and paraphernalia of cooking.
beard: To cut the hairy fibers off unshucked mussels.
beat: To mix briskly with a spoon, whisk, rotary or electric beater using an over-and-over or round-and-round motion.
beignet: The French word for "fritter."
beurre: The French word for "butter." *Beurre manié* is a mixture of butter and flour, kneaded until smooth, that is added as a thickener to sauces and stews. *Beurre noir* is butter heated until dark brown; *beurre noisette,* butter heated until the color of amber.
bien fatigué: A French term meaning "wilted"; it is used to describe salad greens dressed with hot dressing, then tossed until properly limp.

bind: To stir egg, sauce, or other thick ingredient into a mixture to make it hold together.

bisque: A creamed soup, usually with a shellfish base.

blanch: To immerse briefly in boiling water to loosen skins or to heighten and set color and flavor.

blaze (flame, flambé): To set a match to liquor-drenched food so that it bursts into flames.

blend: To mix two or more ingredients together until smooth.

boeuf: The French word for "beef."

boil: To heat liquid until bubbles break at the surface (212° F. for water at sea level); also to cook food in boiling liquid.

Bombay duck: Dried East Indian fish *(bummalo)* used to flavor curries.

bone: To remove bones.

braise: To brown in fat, then to cook covered on top of the stove or in the oven with some liquid.

bread: To coat with bread crumbs.

brine: To preserve in a strong salt solution; also the solution itself.

brown: To cook at high heat, usually on the topstove in fat, until brown; also to set under a broiler until touched with brown.

bruise: To partially crush—as a clove of garlic in a mortar and pestle—to release flavor.

brûlé, brûlée: The French word for "burned," used in cooking to describe foods glazed with caramelized sugar.

brunoise: A French cooking term used to describe diced or shredded vegetables, usually a mixture of them cooked in butter or just enough stock to moisten. *Brunoise* is used to flavor soups and sauces.

brush: To apply butter, liquid, or glaze with a brush.

butterfly: To split food down the center, almost but not quite all the way through, so that the two halves can be opened flat like butterfly wings.

café: The French word for "coffee."

calamari: The Italian word for "squid."

candy: To preserve in or glaze with sugar syrup.

caramelize: To heat sugar until it melts and turns golden brown; also to glaze food with caramelized sugar. *Caramel* is liquid, browned sugar used to flavor and color gravies and sauces.

chapati: A plate-shaped, unleavened East Indian bread made of whole wheat flour.

chapon: A chunk or cube of bread, rubbed with oil and garlic, that is tossed with green salads to impart a subtle garlic flavor; it is discarded before serving. For still subtler flavor, the chapon can simply be rubbed over the salad bowl before the greens are added.

chiffonade: A soup garnish composed of finely cut vegetable strips (commonly lettuce and sorrel).

chill: To let stand in the refrigerator or crushed ice until cold.

chinois: A conical, fine-meshed French sieve used for puréeing or straining.

chop: To cut into small pieces with a knife or chopper; chopped foods are more coarsely cut than the minced.

clarify: To make cloudy liquid clear, usually by heating with raw egg white, then straining through cloth. For instructions, see Some Basic Soup-Making Techniques in the soup chapter.

clove (of garlic): One small almond-sized segment of the head or bulb of garlic.

coat: To dip in crumbs, flour, or other dry ingredient; also to cover with sauce or aspic.

coat a spoon: A doneness test for custards and other cooked egg-thickened mixtures; when the egg has thickened (cooked) sufficiently, it will leave a thin, custardlike film on a metal spoon.

cocotte: The French word for "casserole"; *en cocotte* simply means "cooked in a casserole." *Cocottes* can be whopping or just large enough to serve one person.

coddle: To poach in water just below the boiling point.

combine: To mix together two or more ingredients.

confit: Meats (usually duck, goose, game birds, stewing fowl, turkey, pork, and rabbit) that are salted, cooked in the company of fat, then "put down" in earthenware crocks, sealed with a layer of fat, and stored in a cool spot. This is an ancient way of preserving meats still popular in the Southwest of France. *Confit,* in fact, comes from the French word meaning "to preserve" *(confire).*

cool: To bring hot food to room temperature.

coq: The French word for "cock" or "rooster."

core: To remove the core.

cream: To beat butter or other fat either solo or with sugar or other ingredients until smooth and creamy.

crème: The French word for "cream."

crimp: To seal the edge of a pie or pastry with a decorative edge.

croûte: The French word for "crust" or "pastry." Something prepared *en croûte* is wrapped in or topped with a crust.

crumble: To break up with the fingers.

crush: To reduce to crumbs.

cube: To cut into cubes.

cuisine minceur: The innovative low-calorie cuisine developed by French chef Michel Guérard during the 1970s. It all but eliminates butter and cream and relies upon puréed fruits and vegetables to thicken sauces instead of starches.

cure: To preserve meat, fish, or cheese by salting, drying, and/or smoking.

cut in: To mix shortening or other solid fat into dry ingredients until the texture is coarse and mealy.

dashi: A Japanese stock or sauce made with dried fish *(bonito),* sea kelp *(konbu),* and water.

deep-fat-fry: To cook by immersing in hot (usually about 360° F.) deep fat.

deglaze: To scrape the browned bits off the bottom of a skillet or roasting pan, usually by adding a small amount of liquid and heating gently; this mixture is added to the dish for flavor.

degrease: To skim or blot grease from a soup, sauce, or broth or, easier still, to chill it until the grease rises to the top and hardens; it can then be lifted off.

demi-glace: A rich brown sauce or gravy made by boiling down meat stock.

devil: To mix with hot seasonings (commonly mustard and cayenne).

dice: To cut into fine cubes, usually ⅛″–¼″.

dilute: To weaken or thin by adding liquid.

dim sum: Small Chinese snacks, most often steamed or fried dumplings, buns, and pastries, served with tea.

disjoint: To separate at the joint, most often poultry or small game.

dissolve: To pass a solid (sugar, salt, etc.) into solution; also to melt or liquefy.

dot: To distribute small bits (usually butter or other fat) over the surface of a food.

dough: A pliable raw mixture, usually containing flour, sugar, egg, milk, leavening, and seasoning, that is stiff enough to work with the hands.

dragées: Candy shot used in decorating cookies, cakes, and candies. Silver dragées are the hard BB-like shot.

drain: To pour off liquid.

draw: To remove the entrails of poultry, game, or fish; to eviscerate.

dredge: To coat lightly with flour, confectioners' sugar, or other powdery ingredient.

dress: To draw or eviscerate; also to add dressing to a salad.

drippings: The melted fat and juices that collect in the pan of meat, poultry, or other food as it cooks.

drizzle: To pour melted butter, syrup, sauce, or other liquid over the surface of food in a very fine stream.

drop: To drop from a spoon, as cookie dough onto a baking sheet.

dust: To coat very lightly with flour, confectioners' sugar, or other powdery mixture. Dusted foods are more lightly coated than the dredged.

duxelles: A thick, almost pastelike mixture of minced sautéed mushrooms, sometimes seasoned with shallots, salt, and pepper, that is mixed into sauces, stuffings, and other recipes.

en brochette: Food cooked on a skewer.

en papillote: Food cooked in oiled parchment or in a packet.

entree: The main course of a meal.

essence, extract: Concentrated flavoring.

eviscerate: To remove entrails, to draw.

filet, fillet: A boneless piece of meat or fish. *Fillet* is the English spelling, *filet* the French; *filet* is also the spelling used to identify beef tenderloin *(filet mignon).*

filter: To strain through several thicknesses of cloth.

finish: To garnish a dish before serving, to add the finishing touches.

flake: To break into small pieces with a fork.

flambé: See Blaze.

flour: To coat with flour.

fluff: To fork up until light and fluffy; also a spongy gelatin dessert.

flute: To make a decorative edge on pies or pastries; to crimp. Also to cut mushrooms or other small vegetables into fluted or scalloped shapes.

fold: To mix using a gentle over-and-over motion. Also, literally, to fold rolled-out pastry into a neat package as when making puff pastry.

fold in: To mix a light ingredient (beaten egg white, whipped cream) into a heavier one using a light over-and-over motion so that no air or volume is lost.

forcemeat (farce): Finely ground meat, poultry, or fish often combined with ground vegetables, bread crumbs, and seasonings used in making stuffings, *quenelles,* and croquettes.

fouet: The French word for the "balloon whip" or "whisk."

freeze: To chill until hard and icy.

French-fry: To cook in deep hot fat. See Deep-fat-fry.

fricassee: A way of braising cut-up chicken and small game. The pieces are dredged and browned, then cooked, covered, in liquid or sauce, often in the company of vegetables. Food can be fricasseed on top of the stove or in the oven.

frizzle: To fry thinly sliced meat at intense heat until crisp and curled.

fromage: The French word for "cheese."

frost: To spread with frosting or coat with sugar; also to chill until ice crystals form, as when frosting mint julep cups.

frothy: Light and foamy.

fry: See Panfry.

fumet: A concentrated stock used as a base for sauces.

ganâche: An exceedingly rich butter cream (usually chocolate or mocha) used to fill tortes and pastries.

garnish: To decorate a dish before serving. The *garniture* is the decoration.

gâteau: The French word for "cake."

giblets: The heart, liver, and gizzard of fowl and small game.

glace: The French word for "ice cream."

glacé: A French word used to describe candied or sugared food; *marrons glacés,* for instance, are candied chestnuts.

glace de viande: A rich brown meat glaze made by boiling meat stock down until dark and syrupy; it is added to sauces and gravies for flavor and color.

glaze: To cover food with a glossy coating, most often syrup, aspic, melted jellies or preserves. Also to brush pastry with milk or beaten egg to make it glisten.

grate: To cut food into small particles by passing through a grater.

grease: To rub with grease.

grease and flour: To rub with grease, then dust lightly with flour. *Note:* Most pans need greasing only, but those in which extrasweet or fruit-heavy batters will be baked will probably require greasing *and* flouring to keep the cake or bread from sticking.

grill: To broil on a grill, commonly over charcoal.

grind: To reduce to fine particles or paste by putting through a grinder.

grissini: Slim Italian bread sticks.

harissa sauce: A fiery Moroccan condiment redolent of garlic, caraway, cumin, and coriander. Canned *harissa paste* is available at Middle Eastern groceries and specialty food shops.

hot water bath, water jacket: A large kettle in which preserving jars are processed, also a pan of water in which a dish of custard or other apt-to-curdle dish is placed during baking. *Note:* If the water in the kettle boils, it becomes a *boiling water bath.*

husk: To remove the coarse outer covering, as when husking corn. Also, the covering itself.

ice: To spread with icing; also, to chill until hard and icy.

infusion: Hot liquid in which tea, coffee, herbs, or spices have been steeped.

jell (also gel): To congeal with gelatin. Also, to cook into jelly.

jelly-roll style: A flat piece of meat, fish, or cake rolled up around a filling.

julienne: Food cut into small matchstick-like strips.

junket: Tablets or powder made of rennet (an enzyme extracted from the lining of cows' stomachs) used to curd or coagulate milk. Junket is essential to cheese-making and is also used to thicken an old-fashioned pudding called *junket.*

kimchi: Incendiary Korean pickles made with cabbage, radishes, cucumbers, onions, garlic, and hot red peppers.

knead: To work with the hands in a rhythmic pressing-folding-turning pattern until smooth and satiny.

kosher: Food prepared or processed according to Jewish ritual law.

lait: The French word for "milk."

lard: To insert bits of lard or other fat into lean meat to keep it moist and succulent throughout cooking. Also, the rendered fat of hogs.

leaven: To lighten the texture and increase the volume of breads, cakes, and cookies by using baking powder, soda, or yeast, which send gases bubbling through the batter or dough during baking. Angel cakes and sponge cakes are leavened by the air beaten into the egg whites.

lecithin: A fatty substance obtained from egg yolks and legumes that's used to preserve, emulsify, and moisturize food. Lecithin sprays (available in every supermarket) can be used in lieu of higher-calorie butter, margarine, and oils for browning foods and greasing pans.

legumes: A protein-rich family of plants that includes beans, peas, lentils, and peanuts.

let down: To dilute by adding liquid.

liaison: A thickening agent (flour, cornstarch, arrowroot, egg, or cream) used to thicken soups and sauces or bind together stuffings and croquettes.

line: To cover the bottom and sides of a pan or mold with paper, a layer of cake or crumbs before adding the food to be cooked, chilled, or frozen.

macerate: To soak fruits in spirits.

marinate: To steep meat, fish, fowl, vegetables, or other savory food in a spicy liquid several hours until food absorbs the flavoring. Technically, *macerating* and *marinating* are the same; *macerate,* however, applies to *fruits, marinate* to savory food. The steeping medium is called a *marinade.*

marmite: A tall French stock pot, often made of earthenware.

marron: The French word for "chestnut." See Glacé.

marrow: The soft buttery substance found in the hollows of bones; gourmets consider it a delicacy. *Marrow spoons* are the long, slender-bowled spoons designed specifically for digging the marrow out of bones.

mash: To reduce to pulp, usually with a potato masher.

mask: To coat with sauce or aspic.

matzo: The flat unleavened bread traditionally eaten by Jews during Passover.

mealy: Resembling meal in texture; as used to describe baked potatoes, it means that they are light and crumbly, almost flaky.

meat glaze: See Glace de viande.

medallion: Small coin-shaped pieces of meat, commonly beef.

melt: To liquefy by heating.

mince: To cut into fine pieces. Minced foods are more finely cut than the chopped.

mirepoix: A mixture of minced sautéed vegetables—traditionally carrots, celery, and onions—used in French cooking to flavor sauces, stuffings, stews, and other savory dishes.

mirin: Sweet Japanese rice wine used in cooking.

miso: High-protein, Japanese soybean paste used to flavor soups, stews, sauces, dips, even desserts. It can be sweet or salty.

mix: To stir together using a round-and-round motion.

mocha: The combined flavors of coffee and chocolate.

moisten: To dampen with liquid.

mold: To cook, chill, or freeze in a mold so that the food takes on the shape of the mold. To *unmold* simply means to remove from the mold.

mortar and pestle: An old-fashioned implement, still basic to the gourmet kitchen. The mortar is a bowl-shaped container, usually made of porcelain or wood, the pestle a heavy blunt instrument of the same material used for pulverizing seasonings against the walls of the mortar.

mound: To stand in a mound when taken on or dropped from a spoon; the term is used to describe the consistency of gelatin-thickened mixtures.

mull: To heat fruit juice (frequently cider or grape juice), wine, ale, or other alcoholic beverage with sugar and spices.

nan: A lightly leavened East Indian bread made of white flour and baked in a clay oven.

nap: To coat with sauce.

noisette: A small round slice of meat, usually lamb.

nonpareilles: Another name for dragées or candy shot used in decorating cakes, cookies, and candies.

nouvelle cuisine: The "new French cooking" that has freed chefs from the rigid confines of classical French cooking. It is characterized by small portions of food artfully arranged on oversized plates, barely cooked vegetables, unusual combinations of tastes, textures, and colors. Unlike *cuisine minceur,* it is not necessarily low in calories. The Italian equivalent is *nuova cucina.*

oeuf: The French word for "egg."

oie: The French word for "goose."

pain: The French word for "bread."

panada (panade): A very thick sauce usually thickened with bread used to bind quenelles and forcemeats, etc. Also, in France, a bread-thickened broth.

panbroil: To cook in a skillet over direct heat with as little fat as possible; drippings are poured off as they accumulate.

panfry: To cook in a skillet *with* some fat *without* pouring off drippings. The French word for it is *sauté.*

pappadams: Crispy baked or deep-fat-fried East Indian wafers served with curry. They are made of pulse or lentil flour.

parch: To dry corn or other starchy vegetable by roasting.

pare: To cut the peeling from fruits or vegetables.

paste: A smooth blend of fat and flour or other starch thickener. Also, any food pounded to a paste. Also, a dough, specifically that of puff or *choux* pastry.

pavé: A square or oblong, many-layered sponge cake sandwiched together with a variety of fillings, then showily frosted. It is named after the French cobblestone *(pavé),* whose shape it resembles.

peel: To remove the peeling from fruits or vegetables by pulling off rather than cutting away.

pepper: To season with pepper.

pickle: To preserve in brine or vinegar.

pinch: The amount of salt, sugar, herb, or spice, etc., that can be taken up between the thumb and forefinger, less than 1/8 teaspoon.

pipe: To apply a frilly border, usually of frosting or mashed potatoes, by squirting through a pastry bag fitted with a decorative tip.

pit: To remove pits.

plank: To broil on a wooden plank.

pluck: To pull the feathers from poultry.

plump: To soak raisins or other dried fruit in liquid until they soften and plump up.

poach: To cook submerged in simmering liquid.

poisson: The French word for "fish."

pone: Flat and round or oval in shape, as a corn pone.

poulet: The French word for "chicken."

pound: To flatten with a mallet or cutlet bat.

preheat: To bring oven or broiler to required temperature before adding food.

prick: To pierce with the tines of a sharp fork. Pricking is necessary to keep pie shells from shrinking and warping during baking, also to free fat underneath the skin of ducks and geese as they roast.

proof: To set a yeast mixture in a warm, dry spot to rise.

pulses: Dried seeds of legumes (beans, peas, lentils, etc.)

purée: To grind to paste either by pressing through a food mill or whirling in an electric blender or food processor.

puri (poori, pooree): Puffy deep-fried East Indian bread.

quenelles: Soufflé-light, poached forcemeat dumplings sauced and served as is or used to garnish meat or fish platters.

ragout: A hearty brown stew.

ramekin: A small baking dish big enough for one portion, commonly made of earthenware.

rancid: A word used to describe the rank, musky aroma and taste of stale nuts, oils, butters, cheeses, and other fatty or oily foods.

réchauffé: A French cooking term meaning "reheated."

reconstitute: To restore milk or other dehydrated food to a liquid or moist state by mixing in water.

reduce: To boil down rapidly until volume is reduced and flavors are concentrated.

refresh: To plunge hot food (most often vegetables) into ice water to set the color and flavor. Just before serving the food is warmed in butter or sauce.

render: To heat lard or other animal fat so that it melts away from connective tissue and other solid particles. Rendered lard is smooth and creamy, almost pure fat and an excellent shortening for pastries. Another term for *render* is *try out.*

rennet: An enzyme extracted from the lining of cows' stomachs that is used to curd or coagulate milk.

rib: One branch (stalk) of a bunch of celery. *Note:* In some cookbooks, stalk means the entire bunch or head of celery; *as used here, however, stalk and rib are synonymous.*

rice: To put through a ricer.

rissole: A filled sweet or savory deep-fat-fried pie or turnover.

roast: To cook uncovered in the oven by dry heat.

roe: Fish eggs.

roll out: To roll into a thin flat sheet with a rolling pin.

roux: A butter and flour paste, sometimes browned, sometimes not, used as a thickener for soups and stews. It is the soul of Cajun and Creole cooking.

rusk: A crisp brown piece of bread, usually twice baked to make it extra light and dry; it may be sweet or plain.

salpicon: Mixed cubed foods served in a sauce or dressing.

salt: To season with salt.

sambal: Any of the many condiments served with curry.

sauce: To combine or cover with sauce.

sauté: See Panbroil.

scald: To heat a liquid, most frequently milk or cream, just short of the boiling point until bubbles begin to gather around the edge of the pan. Also, to plunge tomatoes or peaches, etc., into boiling water to loosen their skins; to blanch.

scale: To remove scales from fish.

scallop: To bake in cream or a cream sauce underneath a bread crumb topping.

score: To make shallow knife cuts over the surface of food, usually in a crisscross pattern.

scrape: To scrape the skin from a fruit or vegetable with a knife.

sear: To brown meat quickly, either in a very hot oven or in a skillet over high heat, to seal in the juices.

season: To add salt, pepper, herbs, spices, or other seasonings.

seasoned flour: Flour seasoned with salt and pepper.

seed: To remove seeds.

serrate: To cut a decorative zigzag border into food, pastries, for example, using a zigzag pastry wheel, or orange, lemon, or grapefruit halves or baskets.

set, set up: To congeal, as when thickened with gelatin.

shell: To remove the shells—most commonly of eggs, nuts, or shrimp.

shirr: To cook whole eggs in ramekins with cream and sometimes a topping of buttered bread crumbs.

short: An adjective used to describe pastry or cookies made crumbly or flaky by a high proportion of shortening.

---

shoyu: The Japanese word for soy sauce.

shred: To cut in small, thin strips or shreds, usually by pressing through a grater.

shuck: To remove the shells of clams, oysters, mussels, or scallops; also to remove husks from corn.

sieve: To strain liquid through a sieve; also the strainer itself.

sift: To pass flour or other dry ingredient through a fine sieve or sifter.

simmer: To heat liquid to about 185° F., just until bubbles begin to form; also to cook food in simmering liquid.

singe: To burn hairs off the skin of plucked poultry.

skewer: To thread small chunks of food on long metal or wooden pins; also the pin itself.

skim: To scoop fat, froth, or other material from the surface of a liquid with a spoon.

skin: To remove the skin of poultry, game, or fish.

sliver: To cut in fine, thin pieces, usually no more than 1/2″ long and a fraction of that wide.

snip: To cut in fine pieces or to gash with scissors.

soak: To let stand in liquid.

soft peaks: Phrase used to describe a mixture beaten until peaks will form but curl over at the top instead of standing up straight.

spit: To cook on a spit.

sponge: A frothy gelatin dessert; also the puffy yeast culture used to leaven bread.

steam: To cook, covered, *over* a small amount of boiling liquid so that the steam formed in the pan does the cooking.

steep: To let tea leaves, coffee grounds, herbs, or spices stand in hot liquid until their flavor is extracted.

sterilize: To kill microorganisms of spoilage by boiling or subjecting to steam under pressure.

stew: To cook submerged in simmering liquid; also the food so cooked.

stiff but not dry: Term used to describe egg whites beaten until they will stand in stiff but moist and glistening peaks.

stir: To mix with a spoon or whisk using a round-and-round motion.

stir-fry: Oriental method of briskly tossing or stirring foods as they fry.

stock: The broth strained from stewed or boiled meats, seafood, poultry, or vegetables.

strain: To separate liquids from solids by passing through a sieve.

stud: To insert whole cloves, slivers of garlic, or other seasoning over the surface of food.

stuff: To fill with stuffing.

swirl: To whirl liquid gently in a pan; also to ease a new ingredient—an egg, for example—into swirling liquid.

syrupy: Of the consistency of syrup; the term is applied most often to partially congealed gelatin. When syrupy, it is ready to whip or use as a glaze.

tahini: Sesame seed paste, a popular ingredient of Middle Eastern recipes.

tamari: A dark and pungent Japanese liquid soy seasoning used to baste *yakitori* (chunks of chicken or beef broiled on bamboo skewers).

tenderize: To make tender, especially meat, either by pounding or scoring to break up connective tissues or by adding a chemical tenderizer or acidic marinade to soften them.

terrine: An earthenware container used for baking pâté and other minced or ground meat mixtures. Also the dish so cooked.

thick and lemony: A not particularly apt phrase used to describe stiffly beaten egg yolks; at this consistency they are more nearly the color and texture of mayonnaise.

thicken: To thicken a liquid by adding flour or other starch thickener, by adding eggs or by boiling down.

thin: To dilute by adding liquid.

timbale: A custard-thickened mixture of meat, poultry, fish, or vegetables usually baked in a small mold or ramekin or served in a crisp timbale (rosette) case (see breads chapter for recipe).

toast: To brown bread by heating.

toast points: Small triangular pieces of toast.

tofu: Soybean curd.

toss: To mix by flipping or turning food over and over as when dressing a green salad or combining stuffing ingredients.

treacle: The English word for "molasses."

truss: To tie poultry or other food into a compact shape before roasting.

try out: See Render.

turn: To flute or scallop food, especially mushrooms or other small round vegetables. Also, literally, to turn food over as it cooks or steeps.

veau: The French word for "veal."

viande: The French word for "meat."

vin: The French word for "wine."

volaille: The French word for "poultry."

wasabi: Japanese "horseradish" used as a condiment for *sushi.*

whey: The watery liquid that separates from the solid curds when milk or cream curdles.

whip: To beat until stiff, usually with a whisk, rotary or electric beater.

whisk: A handy beating implement made of looped wires.

wok: A broad, bowl-shaped Oriental pan particularly suited to stir-frying because of its thin metal construction, round bottom and high sides. Set upon a metal ring or collar, it can be used on American burners.
work: To mix slowly with the fingers, to knead.

zest: The colored part of citrus rind used as a flavoring; also the oil pressed from it.

HOW TO MEASURE INGREDIENTS

Although "born cooks" can produce success after success without measuring a thing, most of us fail whenever we resort to such haphazard methods. We must not only measure but *measure correctly,* a special skill in itself.

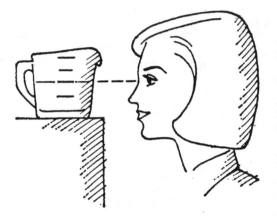

Liquids, Oils
Stand cup on level surface, fill to mark, stoop to check quantity at eye level.

Dry Ingredients, Crumbs, Minced/Grated Foods
Sift flour, confectioners' sugar *before* measuring (granulated sugar, too, if lumpy); pile food lightly in measure without tapping cup or shaking contents down; level off as shown.

Exception: Brown sugar must be packed firmly into measure; if lumpy, roll between sheets of wax paper with a rolling pin before measuring.

Melted Fats
If fat is soft, measure as directed for solid fat, then melt and use. If fat is brittle and hard, melt, estimating as nearly as possible amount you'll need, then measure as directed for oils.

Tips: Measure syrups, molasses, honey, other sticky liquids in lightly greased cups *or* dry measures (so surface can be leveled off); scrape measure out well with a rubber spatula.

Solid Fats
Pack, a little at a time, in a dry measure cup, pressing out air pockets; level off, then scrape cup out well with rubber spatula.

Note: The old water-displacement method is no longer considered accurate.

How to Use Measuring Spoons

HOW TO MEASURE PANS

All recipes in this book specify baking pan, casserole, or mold size when that size is essential to the success of a recipe. Modern containers usually have their vital statistics (length, width, depth, and volume) stamped on the bottom. If not, here is the correct way to take them.

Linear Measurements: For length, width, and diameter, measure pan across the top, inside edge to inside edge. For depth, stand ruler in pan, noting distance from rim to bottom.

Volume: Pour water into container, using a measuring cup, and record how many cups or quarts are needed to fill it.

Tip: Once measurements are taken, scratch them on the outside of the container so that they need not be retaken.

THE TECHNIQUES OF CHOPPING, MINCING, SLICING

A skilled chef wields his knife with all the grace of a swordsman, and to the novice his knife seems swordlike. Its weight and size, however, speed the cutting. Those timid about knives often choose knives too small for the job. For all round use, an 8″ blade is best; for bulkier, tougher foods, a 10″ blade and for small foods a 4″–6″ blade. Here are the basic cutting techniques, applicable with

only minor adjustments to all kinds of food. Work slowly at first; speed will come.

To Slice Food
Peel; halve lengthwise or cut a thin slice off bottom so food is steady on cutting board. Slice straight through in thickness desired.

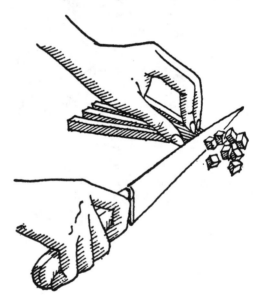

To Cube and Dice
Peel and slice—1/2″–1″ for cubes, 1/8″–1/4″ for dice. Stack slices and cut in strips of the same thickness, then gather several strips together and cut crosswise into uniform cubes.

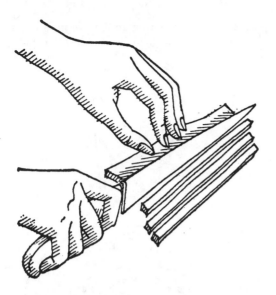

To Cut in Strips, Julienne
Peel and slice—1/4" thick for regular strips, 1/8" for julienne; stack 3–4 slices and cut in 1/8" strips. For julienne, cut strips in uniform lengths as desired.

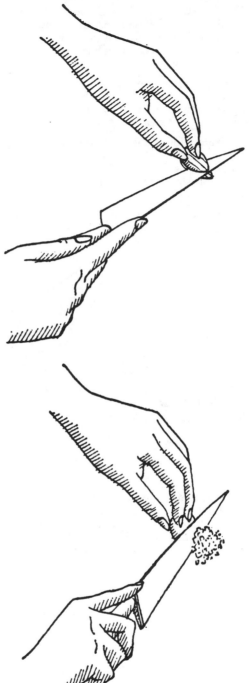

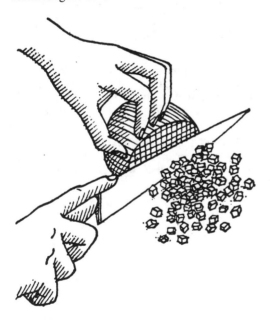

To Chop and Mince Solid Foods
Peel, halve lengthwise, place cut side down on board and, cutting almost—but not quite —through food, make evenly spaced vertical and horizontal cuts in a crisscross pattern— about 1/4" apart for chopped foods, closer together for minced, then slice straight through.

Tip: Garlic, shallots, and other small foods are less apt to slip if *lightly* salted.

To Mince or Dice Celery
Make a series of cuts the length of the stalk without cutting clear through the end, then

slice crosswise into desired widths. If stalks are thick, they should be split lengthwise first, again almost but not quite through the end. *Note:* Carrots, thinly sliced lengthwise, can be similarly minced.

To Snip Herbs with Scissors
Bunch chives, dill tops, or other wispy herbs together, then cut straight across with scissors at 1/8″ intervals—or more or less.

To Grate Rind, Onion, Hard Cheese
Rub in short quick strokes over fine side of grater onto wax paper; brush grater with a pastry brush to free clinging bits.

To Shred Cabbage
Quarter, core, then slice fine or grate on coarse side of grater.

To Chop and Mince Leafy Foods
Bundle leaves together and slice straight across, then, anchoring knife point to board with 1 hand, move knife up and down over leaves in an arc as though it were hinged to board, again and again to desired fineness.

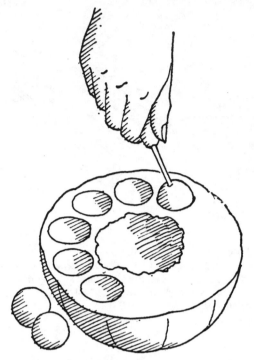

To Make Melon or Vegetable Balls
Peel vegetable; halve and seed melon. Press ball cutter firmly straight into food, rotate until embedded, then twist out and remove ball.

To Use a Chopping Bowl
Coarsely cut or break up food, place in bowl, then chop vigorously with curved chopper.

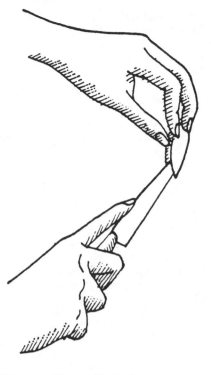

To Sliver or Shave Almonds
Blanch, peel, halve, and while still moist cut lengthwise in 1/8″ strips. To shave, cut lengthwise with a vegetable peeler.

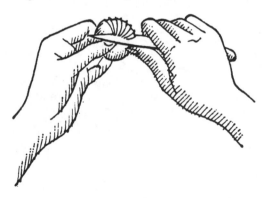

To Flute (Turn) Mushrooms
Holding mushroom cap in left hand and paring knife rigidly in right, rotate mushroom toward you and against *stationary* blade, making fluted indentations from crown to bottom.

To Make Onion Chrysanthemums
Peel, then, slicing about 3/4 way down toward root end, cut onion into 1/8″ sections. Hold under hot tap and spread "petals" gently. Tint rose or yellow, if you like, in water mixed with food coloring.

SOME OTHER COOKING TECHNIQUES

To Make Butter Balls
Scald butter paddles and chill in ice water; cut an ice cold butter stick in 1/2″ pats and roll each between paddles into a ball; drop in ice water to "set."

To Make Butter Curls
Chill butter curler in ice water; also chill butter (in refrigerator). Pulling toward you, draw curler full length of butter stick, scooping out curl; drop in ice water to "set" curl.

To Make Bacon Curls
Fry bacon until limp, spear one end with a fork, and wind around tines. Continue frying until brown and crisp, turning frequently so bacon is evenly cooked. Remove from fork.

To Line Pans with Ladyfingers
Cut ladyfingers lengthwise in long, slim wedges and arrange, rounded sides down, over bottom of pan in a sunburst pattern, fitting close together. Stand ladyfingers upright, touching one another, around sides. If mold is flared, trim ladyfingers as needed to fit close together around sides.

To Line Pans with Crumbs or Sugar
Butter pan well, spoon in fine crumbs or granulated sugar, and tilt pan back and forth, rotating and shaking lightly until evenly coated all over. Tip out excess crumbs or sugar.

To Glaze Molds and Pans with Gelatin
Chill mold; prepare any clear gelatin mixture (Basic or Quick and Easy Aspic or any other gelatin mixture according to package directions). To glaze a 1-pint mold, you'll need about 1 cup; for a 1–1 1/2-quart mold, about 1 pint. Chill gelatin until thick and syrupy, pour into chilled mold, and tilt back and forth, rolling around until bottom and sides are evenly coated. Tip out excess and keep its consistency syrupy. Quick-chill mold until gelatin is tacky. Continue pouring in gelatin, building up layers, until desired thickness is reached; 2–3 layers will glaze most mixtures, but for spiky foods add an extra layer or 2. Fill mold and chill until firm. Unmold very carefully, using only the briefest dip in hot water—glaze will quickly melt.

Note: Numerous other cooking techniques (seeding and juicing of tomatoes, for example, separating eggs, etc.) are included elsewhere in the book in the sections where they seem most appropriate. Consult Index for page numbers.

SOME PREPARATION SHORT CUTS, COOKING TIPS AND TRICKS

Preparation:
• To anchor wax paper to a counter (when rolling dough or grating food), dampen counter, then press paper to it.
• To deaden the clattery sound of a rotary beater, stand bowl on a folded, dampened dishcloth or towel.
• To strain stock or other liquid through "cloth" when there is none, substitute paper toweling (but *not* the new super-absorbent type).
• To roll bread or cracker crumbs *neatly,* seal bread or crackers inside a plastic bag, then roll with a rolling pin. Or crush in an electric blender or food processor instead.
• To melt small amounts of chocolate, place in a custard cup and stand in a small pan of simmering water.
• To fill without incident small, easily tipped-over molds, stand them in muffin pans.
• To prevent fish or meat ball mixtures from sticking to your hands as you shape the balls, rinse hands frequently in cold water.
• To avoid overcoloring foods, add liquid food coloring with an eyedropper, paste color by daubing on the end of a toothpick.
• To prevent slippery foods from slipping as you slice or chop, dip fingers in salt. It also may help to lightly salt the cutting board.
• To measure out ½ egg, beat 1 whole egg, then spoon out ½ (add remaining ½ to a sauce or scrambled eggs).
• To crush whole cardamom seeds if you have no mortar and pestle, remove puffy white outer shell, then pulverize dark inner seeds by placing in the bowl of a spoon, fitting another spoon on top and grinding the two together. *Note:* Other small seeds—cumin, coriander, etc.—can be ground the same way.
• To expedite peeling of boiled potatoes, score lightly around middle before cooking; afterward, simply spear potatoes with a fork and peel skin back from the score marks.
• To "frost" grapes, brush lightly with beaten egg white, then dip in granulated sugar and dry on a cake rack.
• To peel an onion zip-quick, cut a thin slice off top or bottom, then pull away papery outer skin.

Cooking and Baking:
• To brighten beets and red cabbage, add 1 tablespoon cider vinegar or lemon juice to the cooking water.
• To scald milk without scorching it, heat in a very heavy saucepan or top of a double boiler over just-boiling water until tiny bubbles appear at edges of milk.
• To help keep sour cream from curdling, bring to room temperature before adding to hot mixtures and never allow to boil.
• To keep butter from burning during frying or sautéing, mix 2-to-1 with cooking oil or use clarified butter.*
• To soften hard, dry brown sugar, heat, uncovered, in a 200° F. oven until dry and crumbly, then pulverize in an electric blender. *Note:* If you have a microwave oven, place sugar in a flameproof glass measure, add an apple slice, cover with plastic food wrap, and microwave on *LOW* 1–2 minutes.
• To prevent food from overbrowning as it bakes, wrap in foil with the shiny side out.
• To keep cooked, drained spaghetti from clumping when it must be held a few minutes, toss lightly with 1 tablespoon warm olive or other cooking oil.
• To prevent pancakes from sticking to the griddle, sprinkle it lightly with salt instead of greasing.
• To douse a small burner or oven fire, sprinkle with baking soda or salt.
• To soothe a superficial burn, hold under cold running water, rub with cold, heavy cream or apply a baking soda-water paste.
• To test oven temperature when gauge is broken, preheat oven 15 minutes, then place a sheet of white paper (typewriter bond is a good weight) on center rack for 5 minutes; if paper blackens, oven is 500° F. or more; if it turns deep brown, oven is 450°–500° F.; if golden brown, oven is 400°–450° F.; if light brown 350°–400° F.; and if a pale biscuit color, 300° F. or less.

Serving and Storing:
• To clean spills from serving dishes before carrying them to the table, wipe with cotton swabs or swab sticks.
• To keep plastic food wrap from sticking to itself, store in refrigerator.
• To build up a supply of ice cubes, remove from trays when frozen hard and very dry, bundle into large plastic bags and store in freezer. If dry enough when removed from trays, cubes will not stick to one another.
• To apportion vegetables evenly—and quickly—for a crowd, use an ice-cream scoop; No. 10 size = ½ cup; No. 12 = ¾ cup.

• To cover a cake frosted with a soft or fluffy icing, stick toothpicks in top and sides, then drape foil or plastic food wrap over toothpicks.
• To keep fruit pies as fresh-tasting as possible, cover with foil or plastic food wrap and store at room temperature, then warm, uncovered, 10 minutes in a 350° F. oven before serving.
• To loosen a sticking crumb crust, set piepan on a hot damp cloth and hold cloth ends against sides of pan 1–2 minutes.
• To cut extra-fresh soft bread in thin slices, dip knife in boiling water, shaking off extra drops, then slice.

Cleaning:
• To remove the smell of onions or garlic from hands, rinse hands in cold water, rub with salt or baking soda, rinse again, then wash with soap and water.
• To remove stains from fingers, rub with a cut lemon.

OVEN TEMPERATURES

Below 300° F. = very slow
300° F. = slow
325° F. = moderately slow
350° F. = moderate
375° F. = moderately hot
400°–425° F. = hot
450°–475° F. = very hot
500° F. or more = extremely hot

Conversion Formulas:
Fahrenheit to Celsius (Centigrade): Subtract 32 from Fahrenheit reading, multiply by 5, then divide by 9. For example: 212° F. − 32 = 180 × 5 = 900 ÷ 9 = 100° C.
Celsius to Fahrenheit: Multiply centigrade reading by 9, divide by 5, and add 32. For example: 100° C. × 9 = 900 ÷ 5 = 180 + 32 = 212° F.

FAHRENHEIT/CELSIUS SCALE

	Boiling Point F.		Boiling Point C.	
(of Water)	212°	– – – –	100°	(of Water)
	200°	– – – –	93.3°	
	190°	– – – –	87.8°	
	180°	– – – –	82.2°	
	170°	– – – –	76.7°	
	160°	– – – –	71.1°	
	150°	– – – –	65.6°	
	140°	– – – –	60°	
	130°	– – – –	54.4°	
	120°	– – – –	48.9°	
	110°	– – – –	43.3°	
	100°	– – – –	37.8°	
	90°	– – – –	32.2°	
	80°	– – – –	26.7°	
	70°	– – – –	21.1°	
	60°	– – – –	15.6°	
Freezing Point (of Water)	50°	– – – –	10°	Freezing Point (of Water)
	40°	– – – –	4.4°	
	32°	– – – –	0°	

WHAT IT WILL MEAN TO COOK WITH METRIC MEASURES

Will America one day adopt the metric system of measuring? Perhaps. But a full-scale changeover is not likely to happen anytime soon because the Metric Conversion Act of 1975 makes the switch *voluntary,* not mandatory. It's true that all wines and spirits are now sold in metric measures, also true that a number of large manufacturers, in order to compete in the world market, have gone metric. Still, the first generation of American *consumers* to go metric will probably be the children now studying this system of measuring in school.

What, exactly, is the metric system? A way of measuring, far simpler than our own, because it is based on the decimal system with larger measures being subdivided into units of ten.

Food researchers have always used the metric system because it is more precise than American weights and measures. European cooks use it, too, and have found nothing mystifying or complicated about it (they, in truth, would be baffled by our own system of pounds and ounces, yards and inches, which are not based on logical units of ten).

In recipes, the principal difference between our present way of measuring and the metric is that dry ingredients like flour and sugar are weighed rather than measured in a cup. It's an easier, more efficient method because the flour can be sifted directly onto a piece of wax paper on a scale, the dial indicating exactly when the proper amount of flour has been added. Meats, fruits, and vegetables, whether sliced, diced, or whole, will be called for by weight rather than by cup, and, of course, they will be sold in supermarkets by the kilogram instead of the pound.

In Europe, small measures—tablespoons, teaspoons, and fractions thereof—are usually called for by soup spoons or coffee spoons, a system less accurate than our own, so hang on to your measuring spoons.

In the metric system, liquids are measured

in measuring cups, but the calibrations are marked in liters, 1/2 liters, 1/4 liters, and milliliters instead of in cups. Again, the system is more refined because each liter is subdivided into 10 deciliters, each deciliter into 10 centiliters, each centiliter into 10 milliliters. One advantage is immediately obvious: there will be no more such cumbersome measurements as 1/2 cup plus 1 tablespoon, or 1 cup minus 3 teaspoons.

Many manufacturers of scales and measuring cups are already using dual markings, showing quantities in liters and cups for liquids, grams and ounces for weights.

To give you an idea of how the metric system works, we have included in the pages that follow a table of Metric Weights and Measures as well as conversion tables for weights, fluid and linear measures, the ones most apt to affect the cook.

METRIC WEIGHTS AND MEASURES

FLUID MEASURES

10 milliliters	= 1 centiliter
10 centiliters	= 1 deciliter
10 deciliters	= 1 liter
10 liters	= 1 decaliter
10 decaliters	= 1 hectoliter
10 hectoliters	= 1 kiloliter

WEIGHTS

10 milligrams	= 1 centigram
10 centigrams	= 1 decigram
10 decigrams	= 1 gram
10 grams	= 1 decagram
10 decagrams	= 1 hectogram
10 hectograms	= 1 kilogram

LINEAR MEASURES

10 millimeters	= 1 centimeter
10 centimeters	= 1 decimeter
10 decimeters	= 1 meter
10 meters	= 1 decameter
10 decameters	= 1 hectometer
10 hectometers	= 1 kilometer

METRIC EQUIVALENTS OF U.S. WEIGHTS AND MEASURES

WEIGHTS (AVOIRDUPOIS)

5 grams	= 1 teaspoon (approx.)
28.35 grams	= 1 ounce
50 grams	= 1 3/4 ounces
100 grams	= 3 1/2 ounces
227 grams	= 8 ounces
1 kilogram (1000 grams)	= 2 pounds 3 1/4 ounces

FLUID MEASURES

1 deciliter	= 6 tablespoons + 2 teaspoons
1/4 liter	= 1 cup + 2 1/4 teaspoons
1/2 liter	= 1 pint + 4 1/2 teaspoons
1 liter	= 1 quart + 4 scant tablespoons
4 liters	= 1 gallon + 1 scant cup
10 liters	= 2 1/2 gallons + 2 1/2 cups (approx.)

LINEAR MEASURES

2 1/2 centimeters	= 1 inch
1 meter (100 centimeters)	= 39 1/3 inches

Some Abbreviations Used in European Cookbooks: g = gram; kg = kilogram; cm = centimeter; c. = cuiller (spoon), usually qualified by type (coffee spoon, soupspoon, or tablespoon); dl = deciliter.

TABLE OF EQUIVALENTS

Note: All measures are level.

Pinch or dash = less than 1/8 teaspoon
3 teaspoons = 1 tablespoon
2 tablespoons = 1 fluid ounce
1 jigger = 1 1/2 fluid ounces
4 tablespoons = 1/4 cup
5 tablespoons + 1 teaspoon = 1/3 cup
8 tablespoons = 1/2 cup
10 tablespoons + 2 teaspoons = 2/3 cup
12 tablespoons = 3/4 cup
16 tablespoons = 1 cup
1 cup = 8 fluid ounces
2 cups = 1 pint
2 pints = 1 quart
4/5 quart = 25.6 fluid ounces
1 quart = 32 fluid ounces
4 quarts = 1 gallon
2 gallons (dry measure) = 1 peck
4 pecks = 1 bushel

SOME FRACTIONAL MEASURES

1/2 of 1/4 cup = 2 tablespoons
1/2 of 1/3 cup = 2 tablespoons + 2 teaspoons
1/2 of 1/2 cup = 1/4 cup
1/2 of 2/3 cup = 1/3 cup
1/2 of 3/4 cup = 1/4 cup + 2 tablespoons
1/3 of 1/4 cup = 1 tablespoon + 1 teaspoon
1/3 of 1/3 cup = 1 tablespoon + 2 1/3 teaspoons
1/3 of 1/2 cup = 2 tablespoons + 2 teaspoons

$\frac{1}{3}$ of $\frac{2}{3}$ cup = 3 tablespoons + $1\frac{2}{3}$ teaspoons
$\frac{1}{3}$ of $\frac{3}{4}$ cup = $\frac{1}{4}$ cup

SOME DRY WEIGHTS (AVOIRDUPOIS)

4 ounces = $\frac{1}{4}$ pound
8 ounces = $\frac{1}{2}$ pound
16 ounces = 1 pound

SOME EMERGENCY SUBSTITUTIONS

In a pinch, any of the following ingredient substitutions can be made successfully *except* in temperamental cakes, breads, cookies, or pastries.

Leavening:
• $1\frac{1}{2}$ teaspoons phosphate or tartrate baking powder = 1 teaspoon double-acting baking powder.
• $\frac{1}{4}$ teaspoon baking soda + $\frac{1}{2}$ teaspoon cream of tartar = 1 teaspoon double-acting baking powder.
• $\frac{1}{4}$ teaspoon baking soda + $\frac{1}{2}$ cup sour milk = 1 teaspoon double-acting baking powder *in liquid mixtures;* reduce recipe liquid content by $\frac{1}{2}$ cup.

Thickening:
• 1 tablespoon cornstarch = 2 tablespoons all-purpose flour.
• 1 tablespoon potato flour = 2 tablespoons all-purpose flour.
• 1 tablespoon arrowroot = $2\frac{1}{2}$ tablespoons all-purpose flour.
• 2 teaspoons quick-cooking tapioca = 1 tablespoon all-purpose flour (use in soups only).

Sweetening, Flavoring:
• $1\frac{1}{4}$ cups sugar + $\frac{1}{3}$ cup liquid = 1 cup light corn syrup or honey.
• 3 tablespoons cocoa + 1 tablespoon butter = 1 (1-ounce) square unsweetened chocolate.
• $\frac{1}{8}$ teaspoon cayenne pepper = 3–4 drops liquid hot red pepper seasoning.

Flour:
• 1 cup sifted all-purpose flour − 2 tablespoons = 1 cup sifted cake flour.
• 1 cup + 2 tablespoons sifted cake flour = 1 cup sifted all-purpose flour.
• 1 cup sifted self-rising flour = 1 cup sifted all-purpose flour + $1\frac{1}{4}$ teaspoons baking powder and a pinch of salt; when using, substitute measure for measure for all-purpose flour, then omit baking powder and salt in recipe.

Dairy:
• $\frac{1}{2}$ cup evaporated milk + $\frac{1}{2}$ cup water = 1 cup whole milk.
• 1 cup skim milk + 2 teaspoons melted butter = 1 cup whole milk.
• 1 cup milk + 1 tablespoon lemon juice or white vinegar = 1 cup sour milk (let stand 5–10 minutes before using).
• $\frac{3}{4}$ cup milk + $\frac{1}{4}$ cup melted butter = 1 cup light cream.

Eggs:
• 2 egg yolks = 1 egg (for thickening sauces, custards).
• 2 egg yolks + 1 tablespoon cold water = 1 egg (for baking).
• $1\frac{1}{2}$ tablespoons stirred egg yolks = 1 egg yolk.
• 2 tablespoons stirred egg whites = 1 egg white.
• 3 tablespoons mixed broken yolks and whites = 1 medium-size egg.

Miscellaneous:
• 1 cup boiling water + 1 bouillon cube or envelope instant broth mix = 1 cup broth.
• 1 teaspoon beef extract blended with 1 cup boiling water = 1 cup beef broth.
• 1 cup fine bread crumbs = $\frac{3}{4}$ cup fine cracker crumbs.
• $\frac{1}{2}$ cup minced, plumped, pitted prunes or dates = $\frac{1}{2}$ cup seedless raisins or dried currants.
• 6 tablespoons mayonnaise blended with 2 tablespoons minced pickles or pickle relish = $\frac{1}{2}$ cup tartar sauce.

SOME USEFUL EQUIVALENTS

Food	Weight or Amount	Approximate Equivalent Volume or Number
Fruits		
Apples	1 pound	3–4 medium (2½–3 cups sliced)
Apricots (fresh)	1 pound	5–8 medium (2–2½ cups sliced)
Apricots (dried)	1 pound	4½ cups cooked
Bananas	1 pound	3–4 medium (1¼–1½ cups mashed)
Berries (except strawberries)	1 pound	2 cups
Cherries	1 quart	2 cups pitted
Cranberries	1 pound	1 quart sauce
Dates (unpitted)	1 pound	2 cups pitted
Dates (diced, sugared)	1 pound	2⅔ cups
Figs (dried)	1 pound	3 cups chopped, 4 cups cooked
Grapes	1 pound	2½–3 cups seeded
Lemons	1 pound	5–6 medium (1 cup juice)
	1 lemon	3 T. juice, 2 t. grated rind
Limes	1 pound	6–8 medium (⅓–⅔ cup juice)
	1 lime	1–2 T. juice, 1 t. grated rind
Oranges	1 pound	3 medium (1 cup juice)
	1 orange	⅓ cup juice, 1 T. grated rind
Peaches, pears	1 pound	4 medium (2–2½ cups sliced)
Peaches (dried)	1 pound	4 cups cooked
Prunes	1 pound	4 cups cooked
Raisins (seedless)	1 pound	3 cups
Raisins (seeded)	1 pound	2½ cups
Rhubarb	1 pound, cut up	2 cups cooked
Strawberries	1 pint	1½–2 cups sliced
Vegetables		
Beans, peas (dried)	1 pound	2¼–2½ cups raw, 5–6 cups cooked
Cabbage	1 pound	4½ cups shredded
Green peas in the pod	1 pound	1½ cups shelled peas
Limas in the pod	1 pound	¾–1 cup shelled limas
Mushrooms	½ pound	3 cups sliced, 1 cup sliced sautéed
Onions (yellow)	1 medium	½ cup minced
Pepper (sweet green or red)	1 large	1 cup minced
Potatoes (Irish)	1 pound	3 medium, 1¾ cups mashed
Tomatoes	1 pound	3 large, 4 medium
Dairy, Fats		
Milk (whole, skim, buttermilk)	1 quart	4 cups
Milk (evaporated)	13-ounce can	1⅔ cups
	5¾-ounce can	¾ cup
Milk (sweetened, condensed)	14-ounce can	1⅓ cups
Cream (heavy)	½ pint	2 cups, whipped
Cream (sour cream)	½ pint	1 cup
Cheese (Cheddar, process)	½ pound	2 cups grated
Cheese (cottage)	½ pound	1 cup
Cheese (cream)	3-ounce package	6 tablespoons
Butter, margarine (not whipped)	1 pound	2 cups
	1 (¼-pound) stick	½ cup
	⅛ (¼-pound) stick	1 tablespoon

Food	Weight or Amount	Approximate Equivalent Volume or Number
Lard or vegetable shortening	1 pound	2 cups
Eggs (whole)	4–6	1 cup
Egg whites	10–12	1 cup
Egg yolks	13–14	1 cup

Cereal, Pasta

Food	Weight or Amount	Approximate Equivalent Volume or Number
Buckwheat groats	1 cup raw	4 cups cooked
Bulgur wheat	1 cup raw	4 cups cooked
Corn meal	1 pound	3 cups
	1 cup raw	4 cups cooked
Cornstarch	1 pound	3 cups
Flour (all-purpose)	1 pound	4 cups, sifted
Flour (cake)	1 pound	4 1/2–5 cups, sifted
Flour (whole-wheat)	1 pound	3 1/2 cups, unsifted
Oats (rolled)	1 pound	5 cups
	1 cup raw	1 3/4 cups cooked
Pasta:		
Macaroni	1 pound	4 cups raw, 8 cups cooked
Noodles	1 pound	6 cups raw, 7 cups cooked
Spaghetti	1 pound	4 cups raw, 7–8 cups cooked
Rice (regular)	1 pound	2 1/4 cups raw; 6 3/4 cups cooked
Rice (converted)	14 ounces	2 cups raw; 8 cups cooked
Rice (quick-cooking)	14 ounces	4 cups raw; 8 cups cooked
Rice (brown)	12 ounces	2 cups raw; 8 cups cooked
Rice (wild)	1 pound	3 cups raw; 11–12 cups cooked

Breads, Crackers, Crumbs

Food	Weight or Amount	Approximate Equivalent Volume or Number
Bread	1 slice, fresh	1/2 cup soft crumbs or cubes
	1 slice, dry	1/3 cup dry crumbs
Soda crackers	28	1 cup fine crumbs
Graham crackers	15	1 cup fine crumbs
Chocolate wafers	19	1 cup fine crumbs
Vanilla wafers	22	1 cup fine crumbs

Sugar, Salt, Coffee

Food	Weight or Amount	Approximate Equivalent Volume or Number
Coffee (ground)	1 pound	3 1/3 cups grounds
Salt	1 pound	2 cups
Sugar (granulated)	1 pound	2 cups
Sugar (superfine)	1 pound	2 1/4–2 1/2 cups
Sugar (brown)	1 pound	2 1/4–2 1/3 cups
Sugar (confectioners')	1 pound	4 1/2 cups, sifted

Nuts, Candy

Food	Weight or Amount	Approximate Equivalent Volume or Number
Candied fruit and peel	1 pound	3 cups chopped
Coconut	1 pound	5–6 cups flaked or shredded
Unshelled Nuts:		
Almonds	1 pound	1 1/4 cups nut meats
Brazil nuts	1 pound	1 1/2 cups nut meats
Peanuts	1 pound	2 cups nuts
Pecans	1 pound	2 1/4 cups nut meats
Walnuts	1 pound	1 3/4 cups nut meats

Food	Weight or Amount	Approximate Equivalent Volume or Number
Shelled almonds, pecans, peanuts, walnuts	1 pound	4–4½ cups nut meats
Shelled Brazil nuts	1 pound	3 cups nut meats
Marshmallows	¼ pound	16 regular size

T W O

The Larder

Today's larder includes the cupboard, the pantry, the refrigerator, the freezer, and the spice shelf. Storing it efficiently demands skill. Before setting out for the market, familiarize yourself with the ingredients you use and need most.

INGREDIENTS

Science continues to revolutionize cooking *and* eating; each year supermarket shelves grow longer, accommodating new products that bewilder the shopper with an infinite variety of choices. What is the best buy? The all-purpose, the presifted, or the self-rising flour? Corn, peanut, olive, safflower, or blended vegetable oil? The following list is intended to explain the differences between certain basic ingredients. Other ingredients—and some not so basic—can be found elsewhere in the book in chapters where they are most frequently used: yeast in the breads chapter, for instance, and baking powders in the section on cakes (consult the Index for page numbers).

DAIRY PRODUCTS

Milk: Nearly all milk sold today is *pasteurized. (Certified milk,* sometimes sold locally, is raw milk handled and bottled under strict sanitary conditions.)

Pasteurized milk has been heated, then quick-cooled to destroy microorganisms of spoilage, thereby improving keeping qualities. It is available in a variety of fluid forms.

Fluid Milks

Homogenized Milk: Uniformly smooth rich milk that will stay uniformly smooth and rich (no cream floating to the top) because the butter particles have been broken up and dispersed evenly throughout.

Low-fat and Nonfat Milks: In this age of growing calorie and cholesterol consciousness, there are nine different low-fat and nonfat milks available. The basic types are *2 per cent low-fat milk,* with 98 per cent of the butterfat removed; *1 per cent low-fat milk,* with 99 per cent of the butterfat removed; and *skim (nonfat) milk,* containing less than 0.5 per cent butterfat. Each of these three basic types is also available in the three following forms: 1. *With no milk solids added;* 2. *with milk solids added* (labels will claim *"less than 10 grams protein per cup";* and 3. *"Protein-Fortified Milk"* (fluid milk with enough nonfat dry milk solids added to boost the nutritive value to "10 grams or more of protein per cup"). Usually sold under trade or brand names, protein-fortified milk is not widely available. *Note: Federal law mandates that all low-fat and nonfat milks be fortified with 2,000 International Units (IU) of vitamin A per quart. And although it makes optional the additional fortification of each quart of milk with 400 IU of vitamin D, 98 per cent of America's milk producers do add it.*

Flavored Milk: Chocolate or other flavored whole, skim, or partly skim milk. Such milks often have sugar, salt, and stabilizers added. (Also available powdered as drink mixes.)

Buttermilk: Originally the residue left after churning butter, but today a simulated version, usually made with skim milk and flecked with butter.

Low-Sodium Milk: A special diet milk in which 90 per cent of the sodium has been replaced by potassium. The fluid form is available only in limited amounts.

Lactose-Reduced Low-Fat Milk: With a lactose content of only 30 per cent, this milk is a good choice for those unable to digest that complex milk sugar. The milk's butterfat content is about 1 per cent.

Soy Milk: Though not a dairy product, this milky liquid pressed from ground cooked soybeans is higher in protein than cow's milk. It's also rich in iron but low in sodium, calcium, and fat, and devoid of cholesterol. Soybean milk is a good choice for those allergic to milk, but because of its potent protein supply should not be fed to infants. It keeps 5–7 days in the refrigerator and may be frozen. *Note:* Soybean milk is quick to curdle when cooked with wine, soy sauce, Worcestershire sauce, lemon juice (or other acid), even salt.

Yogurt: Whole or low-fat milk fermented into a thick creamy curd; plain yogurt is high in protein and calcium, relatively low in calories (about 140 per cup of whole-milk yogurt, 125 per cup of low-fat yogurt). Also available in a variety of flavors.

Canned Milks

Evaporated Milk: Homogenized milk with about 60 per cent of the water removed and vitamin D added. Mixed 1/2 and 1/2 with water, it has the consistency and food value of whole milk, for which it may be substituted. Use full strength to increase the creaminess of sauces and soups, to coat chicken or chops before crumbing or breading, to top fruits and puddings.

Evaporated Skim Milk: Containing 0.5 per cent butterfat, or less, this is a good choice for calorie counters. If partially frozen and mixed with several drops lemon juice, it will even whip.

Sweetened Condensed Milk: A sticky-sweet evaporated blend of whole milk and sugar, usually used to sweeten beverages, to make candy, ice creams, and other desserts.

Powdered Milks

Nonfat Dry Milk: Whole milk from which almost all water and butterfat have been removed, processed to dissolve rapidly in liquid. To reconstitute, follow package directions. One cup milk powder will make about 3 cups fluid milk, best when covered and refrigerated overnight to develop full flavor.

Reconstituted dry milk can be substituted for the fresh; as powder, it can be added to hamburgers, meat loaves, and mashed potatoes to enrich flavor and nutritive value. *Whole Dry Milk Powder* is also available, but in limited quantities. Because of its butterfat content, it must be kept refrigerated.

Cream and Cream Substitutes

Heavy (Whipping) Cream: Rich and thick (35–40 per cent butterfat) and thicker still after a brief stretch in the refrigerator.

Crème Fraîche: Heavy cream (originally unpasteurized) allowed to mature until nutty and slightly tart, spoon-up-thick, and the color of ivory. A specialty of Normandy, *crème fraîche* is now produced in the U.S. and routinely stocked by many fancy supermarkets (at fancy prices).

To Make Crème Fraîche: Mix 1 pint heavy cream with 2 tablespoons buttermilk, cover and let stand about 24 hours at room temperature (a few hours only if kitchen is hot). Stored tightly covered in refrigerator, *crème fraîche* will keep well several days. Use as a topping for fresh fruits or pastries.

Devonshire (Clotted) Cream: Heavy cream (from scalded butterfat-rich milk) that has been heated gently several hours in a water bath until a spoon will stand in it upright. It's an English (Devonshire) favorite spread on scones (with jam) instead of butter. It's equally luscious ladled over fresh berries and pastries.

Light (Coffee) Cream: With half the butterfat (18–20 per cent) of heavy cream, light cream is a better all-purpose cream, the choice for creaming coffee and tea. It will not whip.

Half-and-Half: A 1/2 and 1/2 mixture of milk and light cream (12–15 per cent butterfat). It will not whip but can be substituted for light cream in puddings and ice creams to shave calories a bit.

Sour Cream: A thick, silky-smooth commercial product made by souring light cream (it has the same butterfat content). Also available: *Half-and-Half Sour Cream* made from a 1/2 and 1/2 mixture of milk and light cream. It has about half the calories of regular sour cream. There's even a *Non-Butterfat Sour Cream Substitute* made from vegetable oil and tapioca flour.

Powdered (Instant) Cream: A mixture of dehydrated light cream and milk solids, with stabilizer added. Use as label directs.

Pressurized Whipped Cream: Sweetened cream, emulsifiers, and stabilizer in an aerosol can that whip into snowy drifts at the touch of a button.

Cream Substitutes: Nondairy products in liquid, powder, and pressurized form, some low-calorie, are usually composed of hydrogenated vegetable oils, sugar, emulsifiers, and preservatives. Depending upon form, these may be used in beverages, in cooking, and as dessert toppings.

FATS AND OILS

Butter: Federal requirements demand that butter be 80 per cent butterfat. In addition, it is federally graded as to flavor, color, texture, and body, the finest quality being U.S. Grade AA (or U.S. Grade Score 93, the figure representing the grader's quality points). The remaining grades, in descending order, are A (U.S. Score 92), B (Score 90), and C (Score 89). The AA and A are the grades most commonly available. Butter may be (and often is) artificially colored; it may be *salted* or *unsalted,* often called *sweet butter,* though true sweet butter is any butter— salted or unsalted—churned from sweet cream instead of sour. *Whipped butter* has simply been beaten full of air to soften it into a better spreading consistency. Whipped butter is lighter in weight than standard butter—6 sticks per pound as opposed to 4— and it must not be substituted for standard butter in recipes.

Butter-Flavor Granules: A blend of butter oil and spray-dried butter that pares calories to about 6 per tablespoon (butter is 100!) and virtually eliminates cholesterol. To use, dissolve granules in water as package directs and spoon over food to add "buttery" flavor. The granules can be sprinkled dry into mashed potatoes and scrambled eggs. *Note:* Never substitute for butter in recipes in this book or use for frying, sautéing, or greasing pans.

Ghee: Clarified butter* used in Asian—and especially Indian—cooking.

Margarine: A butter substitute compounded of vegetable (primarily soybean) and animal oils. To make margarine taste more like butter, cream and milk are sometimes added; to make it look more like butter, yellow food coloring is blended in. Margarine is frequently fortified with vitamins A and D and may contain preservatives and emulsifiers as well. Also available: *butter-margarine blends*

(usually 40–60 per cent), both salted and unsalted. Some contain 50 per cent fewer calories and at least one is cholesterol-free. Specialty margarines include *diet spreads,* the polyunsaturated, the *soft,* the *squeeze-on,* and the *whipped,* even a *no-burn* variety. *Note:* Margarine has slightly greater shortening power than butter and should not be substituted for it in temperamental cake, cookie, or pastry recipes.

Vegetable Shortening: Fluffy-soft all-purpose cooking fats made by pumping hydrogen into vegetable oils; usually snow white but sometimes tinted yellow, and given artificial butter flavor. These are particularly good for deep fat frying because of their high smoking point; superior, too, for making pastries, cookies, and cakes. Do not refrigerate because the shortening may break down.

Lard: Pork fat, rendered and clarified. It is often hydrogenated and stabilized with emulsifiers and preservatives so that no refrigeration is needed (read label carefully and store as directed). Because lard has subtle meat flavor and a more brittle texture than other shortenings, it is particularly suited to making pastries.

Suet: The brittle, snowy fat encasing beef kidneys; it makes superbly crisp, short pastries and is sometimes sold grated for use in steamed puddings.

Cooking and Salad Oils: The two are the same *except* that certain oils—olive, for one —taste better in salads than others and, having relatively low smoking points, are poor choices for deep fat frying. Oils are pressed from myriad vegetables, nuts, seeds, and fruits. The best all-round cooking-salad oils are *corn, cottonseed, peanut,* and *soybean* or blends of these. Lightest of all is the nearly colorless *safflower oil,* favored by the cholesterol conscious. Among the other oils available are *coconut, palm (dendê,* a thick orange oil integral to Brazilian—and especially Bahian—cooking), *sesame* (a dark, heavy Oriental favorite), *sunflower seed, avocado, grape seed, hazelnut, walnut,* and *almond oils.* To Mediterranean Europe, however, oil is olive oil. No other will do. *Virgin olive oil,* highly esteemed by connoisseurs, is unrefined oil from the first pressing. Subsequent pressings yield coarser, stronger oils, sometimes with a greenish cast (a sure sign of strong flavor). The most delicate of all is the champagne-pale (and champagne-priced) olive oil of France, best reserved for very special salads although many cooks prefer the more full-bodied Tuscan olive oils of Italy. Spain, Greece, and California all produce good all-round olive oils—straw-colored, aromatic, but not overly strong. Whenever possible, buy olive oil by the can rather than by the bottle so that it's shielded from the light and does not go stale. If you have neither the taste nor the pocketbook for pure olive oil, mix 1/2 and 1/2 with another vegetable oil. It's best not to refrigerate olive oil—or, for that matter, other oils; they will clump and turn cloudy. However, if you buy large bottles and use oil only occasionally, you may want to refrigerate the oil to keep it from turning rancid. When using, measure out only what you need and let come to room temperature—most of the cloudiness will disappear. *Cooking Tip:* When sautéing with olive oil, keep the heat a shade lower than usual to reduce spattering.

Spray-on Vegetable Oils: Mixtures of vegetable oil, water, and preservatives used to keep food from sticking to pans.

WHEAT FLOURS

The milling industry is well into the Age of Specialization, grinding out bleached and unbleached flours in a variety of textures and types. The plain, white general-purpose flours, as required by the *Federal Enrichment Program,* have had B vitamins (thiamine, riboflavin, and niacin) and iron added so that their food value equals that of whole wheat flour. Some millers further enrich their flours by adding vitamins A and D and calcium.

All-Purpose Flour: The everything flour, equally good for baking cakes, pies, breads, and cookies, for thickening sauces and gravies, and for dredging foods to be fried. It is milled from hard and soft wheats, is *enriched,* and may be bleached or unbleached.

Bread Flour: An *enriched* hard wheat flour with a high content of the protein (gluten) needed to give bread its framework. Available bleached and unbleached.

Cake Flour: An *unenriched* superfine flour milled from soft wheat. Too delicate for general use, it produces cakes of exceedingly fine and feathery grain.

Pastry Flour: Neither as coarse as all-purpose flour nor as fine as cake flour, pastry flour has just enough body to produce flaky-tender piecrusts. It is not as widely distributed as it once was. Most people today use all-purpose flour for pastry.

Self-Rising Flour: *Enriched* all-purpose flour to which baking powder and salt have been added. It can be substituted for all-purpose flour in recipes that call for baking powder and salt; to use, measure out the quantity of flour called for and omit the baking powder and salt. *Note:* To be effective, self-rising flour must be strictly fresh.

Presifted Flour: A timesaving, *enriched,* all-purpose flour that does not require sifting before measuring *except* for tall and tender cakes or other critical (easily-thrown-off-balance) recipes.

Instant-Type Flour: The sauce and gravy specialist, a granular white flour that blends into hot or cold liquids without lumping. It needs no sifting before measuring. Use for thickening only, not for baking or dredging, *except* as label instructs. *Not enriched* as a rule.

Whole Wheat Flour (Graham Flour): Unrefined, unbleached flour containing the iron- and vitamin B-rich wheat bran and germ. Never sift. These—and especially the *"naturally grown and milled"* varieties sold in health food stores—quickly go rancid, so should be stored in tightly covered glass jars in the refrigerator.

Gluten Flour: High-protein, low-starch (and low-calorie) flour milled from hard wheat; it is used to make gluten and other "slimming" breads.

Bran, Cracked Wheat, Wheat Germ Flours: All-purpose flours to which bran, cracked wheat, or wheat germ has been added; do not sift. Because of their coarse textures, these flours are particularly suitable for breads. Buy in small quantities and store in tightly capped glass jars in the refrigerator.

Note: Other wheat products (semolina, etc.) are discussed along with other grains in the chapter on cereals and rice.

OTHER FLOURS

Cereals other than wheat—*barley, buckwheat, corn, oats, rice,* and *rye*—are also milled into rough and smooth flours. They are available at specialty food stores, primarily, and most of them bake into supremely good breads.

Tortilla flour (also called *masa harina)* is a powdery meal made from corn that has been treated with lye. It, along with the other specialty flours, is available at most specialty groceries and some supermarkets. In addition, there are *noncereal flours: potato, soy* and *lima bean, peanut, cottonseed, tapioca, chestnut, water chestnut, lotus root,* and *carob* (the St.-John's-bread of the Mediterranean). These, however, with the exception of potato flour, which makes exceptionally fine angel cake and is a splendid thickener of sauces and gravies, are seldom used solo but are blended with other flours or foods to boost flavor and nutritive value. Water chestnut flour is what the Chinese use to give deep-fried foods crunchy coatings. *Note:* As a thickener, potato flour, like cornstarch and arrowroot, will thin down if overheated.

THICKENERS

Arrowroot: Extracted from a tropical tuber once used to treat arrow wounds, this delicate, flavorless starch thickens without turning cloudy. Use it when a glistening, jewel-like glaze is needed.

Cornstarch: Fine white starch ground from the hearts of dried corn. It has about twice the thickening power of all-purpose flour, *but will thin down after thickening if over-stirred or overcooked and will refuse to thicken at all if mixture is too acid or too sweet.* Handle carefully, as label directs.

Flour: See all-purpose and instant-type flours.

Note: Additional information on starch thickeners can be found in the chapter on sauces, gravies and butters.

LEAVENINGS

Baking Powders: See the chapter on cakes.

Baking Soda: Pure bicarbonate of soda used to leaven acid batters and doughs (those containing molasses, sour milk or buttermilk, vinegar).

Cream of Tartar: A fine white powder crystallized from grape acid used in commercial baking powders. It will also whiten and "cream" candies and frostings, increase the volume and stability of beaten egg whites.

Yeasts: See the chapter on breads.

SUGARS AND SYRUPS

Granulated (White) Sugar: Highly refined, free-pouring, 99+per cent pure all-purpose sugar crystallized from sugar cane or beets.

As a convenience, it is also pressed into cubes.

Superfine (Castor) Sugar: Extra-fine-grain, quick-dissolving sugar. A boon to drink mixing, it also makes unusually good cakes and frostings.

Confectioners' (10X, Powdered) Sugar: Pulverized sugar mixed with cornstarch; particularly suited to making uncooked candies and frostings. Always sift before measuring.

Brown Sugar: Soft, molasses-flavored crystals left behind after the refining of granulated sugar. Brown sugar has a higher mineral content than granulated sugar. The *light brown* is more delicate than the *dark.* You can now buy free-pouring (nonclumping) *brown sugar granules* and *liquid brown sugar* (neither should be substituted for regular brown sugar in recipes). *Muscovado sugar,* integral to many fruit cakes and East Indian recipes, is light brown, molasses-y, and moist.

Raw Sugar: Sugary residue left in the vat after molasses is run off. It is crude, coursegrained, and brown. It contains more minerals, notably potassium, than refined sugar. Potassium, however, is not a mineral apt to be lacking in the normal diet. *Barbados sugar* is fine-grained, moist, and "rummy" and *Demerara* (from the Demerara area of Guyana) is dry and coarse, a favorite topper for puddings, porridges, and cereals.

Maple Sugar: Crystallized, concentrated maple syrup.

Two Special Sugars, Both Decorative: *Rock Candy,* several-carat-big sugar crystals on a string; *colored granulated sugars.*

Fructose (levulose): Because it is the sweetest of all natural sugars (it's the sugar of honey and certain fruits), fructose can be used in smaller amounts than regular sugar (*sucrose,* a compound of equal parts *glucose* and *fructose).* But it must be used only in recipes especially devised for fructose or for sweetening sauces, beverages, fruits, etc. Heat destroys some of its sweetening power.

Noncaloric and Low-Calorie Sweeteners: Liquid, tablet, and powdered calorie-free sugar substitute. Saccharine is the best known. *Aspartame,* the newest sugar substitute, has none of the bitter aftertaste of saccharine and is also safe for diabetics. Synthesized from two amino acids (L-aspartic acid and L-phenylalanine), the building blocks of protein, aspartame is 200 times sweeter than sugar, yet a 1-gram packet of fine granules (the best form, by the way, to use in recipes) contains just 4 calories. *Aspartame should not be heated or used in baking (it breaks down and loses sweetness),* but is superb for sweetening cold mousses and soufflés, sherbets, ices and ice creams, fresh fruits, sauces, etc. Although approved by the U.S. Food and Drug Administration for use in diet beverages and foods as well as for sale as a low-calorie sweetener, aspartame continues to be controversial on several counts. It should be used in moderation and avoided altogether by those with such metabolic disorders as phenylketonuria.

Corn Syrups: *Light* and *dark syrups* made from hydrolyzed cornstarch.

Maple Syrup: The concentrated sap of the sugar maple tree. Also available: *Maple Blended Syrup,* a mixture of maple and other syrups, and *Buttered Maple Syrup.*

Golden Syrup: A pale golden syrup made by evaporating sugar cane juice until the consistency of corn syrup. It is particularly popular in the Deep South (where it is also called *King Syrup)* and in Britain.

Molasses: Available in many grades from the smooth, sweet, dark amber syrup extracted directly from sugar cane juices to the rougher, browner, not-so-sweet by-products of sugar refining. *Blackstrap,* the darkest and coarsest and least sweet of all, amounts to the dregs; it is not, as some believe, a nutritional powerhouse because some of its minerals are not assimilable by the body. Any grade of molasses can be *sulfured* or *unsulfured* depending upon whether sulfur was used in the sugar refining. The unsulfured is preferable because of its lighter color and more full-bodied cane-sugar flavor.

Sorghum: A molasses-like syrup extracted from sorghum.

Honey: Flower nectar that has been processed and condensed by bees. Flavors vary according to the flowers bees have fed upon; among those considered especially choice are heather honey, orange blossom, sourwood, rosemary, and the famous Hymettus (from the wild thyme carpeting the slopes of Mount Hymettus near Athens). Honey may be liquid and golden, creamy and brown, or still in the comb. Do not refrigerate; the honey will turn grainy. Honey averages about 20 calories more per tablespoon than granulated sugar, but contains only the merest traces of vitamins and minerals despite faddist claims to the contrary.

CHOCOLATE AND COCOA

Unsweetened Chocolate: The bitter, all-purpose, unadulterated chocolate rendered out of ground, roasted cocoa beans.

Semisweet Chocolate: Bitter chocolate sweetened with sugar and softened somewhat with extra cocoa butter. It is ideal for dipping because it melts smoothly and rehardens without streaking. Especially highly prized are the Belgian and Swiss chocolates. Semisweet chocolate is available as *bits* and *miniature bits.* Because these are lightly glazed, they hold their shape during baking.

Milk Chocolate: A blend of chocolate, sugar, and powdered milk meant to be eaten out-of-hand. The newest form: lightly glazed *milk chocolate bits* (both miniature and standard size), similar to the semisweet but sweeter, milder, milkier.

Dark German's (Sweet Cooking) Chocolate: Sweetened pure bitter chocolate, darker and more brittle than the semisweet because it lacks the extra cocoa butter.

No-Melt Unsweetened Chocolate: A pudding-thick blend of cocoa, vegetable oil, and preservatives ready to mix into candies, frostings, and batters. Each 1-ounce packet equals 1 (1-ounce) square unsweetened chocolate.

White Chocolate: Milk and sugar boiled down until almost solid, then blended with cocoa butter. White chocolate is temperamental, difficult to melt to satin-smoothness.

Cocoa: All-purpose chocolate powder ground from roasted cocoa beans. It contains virtually no cocoa butter, therefore fewer calories and saturated fats.

Dutch-Type Cocoa: Cocoa processed with alkali to mellow the flavor and darken the color.

Instant Cocoa Mixes: Assorted blends of cocoa, sugar, flavorings, emulsifiers, and sometimes milk powder processed to dissolve instantly in beverages. Some are reduced in calories, others sugar-free.

Carob: The sweet, perfumy powder of the dried locust bean (the "locusts" eaten by John the Baptist) has chocolaty flavor but none of the caffeine-like kick. In this muscle-flexing age of fitness, it's being used as a chocolate substitute.

SALT

Table (Cooking) Salt: A fine salt manufactured from rock salt and brine. It may be *iodized* (have sodium or potassium iodide added as a goiter preventive) or *plain;* often contains desiccants to keep it free-flowing.

Sea Salt: Seawater evaporated to the point of crystallization.

Kosher Salt: Originally a coarse salt made under rabbinical supervision but more commonly today a generic term meaning any coarse natural sea salt. Alternate names are *Dairy, Cheese,* and *Flake Salt.*

Pickling Salt: Pure fine-grain salt with no additives.

Rock (Ice Cream) Salt: Coarse, crude salt used in freezing ice cream.

Flavored Salts: The repertoire is lengthy, including combinations of dehydrated vegetables and salt, charcoal and salt, assorted herbs, spices, and salt.

PEPPER

See The Herb and Spice Shelf.

COMMERCIAL CONDIMENTS, SAUCES, AND SEASONINGS

Vinegar: See the chapter on salads and salad dressings.

Worcestershire Sauce: A secret, spicy blend of soy sauce, shallots, anchovies, vinegar, garlic, molasses, and other ingredients designed to pep up meats and savory dishes.

Soy Sauce: Salty brown sauce extracted from lightly fermented soybeans.

Steak Sauce: A generic name for various thick brown bottled sauces concocted specifically to serve over broiled steaks and chops.

Liquid Hot Red Pepper Seasoning: Another generic name used to identify the incendiary sauces made of tabasco peppers, vinegar, and salt. Use drop by drop.

Liquid Gravy Browner: A blend of caramel, vegetable protein, vinegar, salt, and other flavorings used to brown gravies and sauces and impart a lusty meaty flavor.

Prepared (Wet, Bottled) Mustards: There are dozens of blends, some sunny and mild, some brown and spicy, some superhot.

Mustard *The Milds:* Prepared mild yellow mustard (the old hot-dog favorite). *Spicy But Not Fiery: Bordeaux* and some *Dijon* (spicy French wine-flavored mustards); *Dijon-type* (in the style of—but not necessarily from—Dijon), *Sweet Bavarian Mustard* (the mellow, sweet-sour blend that traditionally accompanies weisswurst), most *Düsseldorf* and other *German Mustards; Creole* (a pungent beige mixture lightly flecked with spice); and the ever-increasing array of *Flavored* and *Herbal Mustards.* *The Hots:* Certain of the *Dijon Mustards,* the French *Moutarde de Meaux,* most of the *Whole Grain Mustards, English* (or *Chinese) Mustard,* and *Bahamian Mustard.* Pretty hot stuff, too, is the *American Horseradish Mustard.*

Note: A discussion of whole and powdered mustards follows in the Herb and Spice Chart.

SOME MARKETING TIPS

• Make a shopping list, setting down first any staples in low supply, then adding those foods needed in preparing the week's meals. Consider seasonal specials—both nonperishables or "freezables"—and buy in bulk whenever storage space permits.
• Buy only what quantities your family can use without waste or what can be stored properly in cupboard, pantry, refrigerator, or freezer.
• Read package labels carefully. By law they must include: net weight, all ingredients, including such additives as vitamins, minerals, preservatives, emulsifiers, artificial sweetener, flavoring, and coloring; identification of dietetic properties (sugar-free or sugar-reduced, low sodium, etc.). The latest ruling states that, if any food contains more artificial flavoring than natural, the name of the food must indicate that fact (i.e., Maple-Flavor Syrup rather than Maple Syrup). Helpful labels may also list proportions of saturated, monounsaturated, and polyunsaturated fats and calorie counts; they may indicate number of servings, provide descriptions of the food (diced, sliced, whole, etc.), and offer a recipe. When buying, suit the style of the food to the use: Why pay more for fancy whole tomatoes if they will be made into sauce?
• When buying "instants," and preprepared foods, consider whether the extra cost is worth the time saved.
• Reject bulging or leaking cans; dented ones are all right provided they do not bulge or

leak. Also reject soft or uneven packages of frozen food, ripped or torn packages of cereals, flours, pasta, breads, and crackers.
• When you discover a food that is spoiled or less than top quality, return it to the grocer. Most markets welcome valid complaints because they are then able to trace and correct the difficulty.
• Hurry all food home, unload and store properly, using the following charts as guides.

STORING FOOD IN THE FREEZER

General Tips:
• Check commercial frozen foods before storing, overwrapping any torn or damaged packages in foil or plastic food wrap.
• If package has been badly damaged and food exposed, use food as soon as possible.
• Date packages as they go into the freezer and use the oldest ones first.
• Update freezer inventory with every new addition.

STORING FOOD IN THE REFRIGERATOR

General Tips:
• Clean refrigerator out regularly, preferably before marketing.

• Store new supplies behind the old so the old will be used first.
• Group often used foods together in accessible spots. If possible, reserve a special corner for leftovers.
• *If power fails,* keep refrigerator door shut; food will remain cool several hours.

Storing Meats, Poultry, Seafood:
• Never wash before storing.
• Always remove market wrapping from fresh uncooked meats, poultry, or seafood and *rewrap loosely* in wax paper or foil unless directed otherwise. *Exception:* Prepackaged meats to be cooked within two days and all ground meat.
• Store in coldest part of refrigerator (it varies from model to model; check manufacturer's instruction booklet).

Storing Vegetables, Fruits:
• Wash only if storage chart recommends it.
• Unless chart directs otherwise, vegetables to be stored in the hydrator should be put in perforated plastic bags, those to be stored on shelves in plain plastic bags.

Storing Leftover, Cooked Foods:
• Quick-cool hot food (in an ice or ice water bath) and package airtight.
• Remove any stuffing from meat, poultry, or seafood and wrap separately.
• Leftover canned foods can be covered and stored in the can 3–4 days.

MAXIMUM RECOMMENDED STORAGE TIME FOR FROZEN FOODS AT 0° F.

Because the type of food and packaging and the number of times a freezer is opened all affect the keeping quality of frozen foods, storage times can only be approximate. Use foods *before* maximum time is up; they are unlikely to spoil immediately afterward, but their quality will deteriorate rapidly.

Food	*Storage Time in months*
Fresh, Uncooked Meats	
Beef, veal, lamb roasts, steaks, and chops	6–12
Ground beef, veal, lamb	3–4
Beef, veal, lamb liver, heart, and kidneys	3–4
Pork roasts, chops	3–6
Ground pork, fresh sausage meat	1–3
Pork liver	1–2
Smoked and Cured Meats	
Ham, slab bacon, frankfurters	1–2
Sausages	1–2
Cooked Meats	
Beef, veal, and lamb roasts	2–4

Food	Storage Time in months
Pork roasts	2–4
Stews, meats in gravy or sauce, meat loaves and balls, meat pies, hash	2–4
Fresh, Uncooked Poultry	
Chicken	12
Turkey, duckling, goose, game birds	6
Giblets	2–3
Cooked Poultry	
Chicken	4–6
Turkey, duckling, goose	2–4
Fresh, Uncooked Seafood	
Lean, white fish	4–6
Oily, gamy fish	3–4
Shucked clams, oysters, scallops, shrimp	3–4
Cooked Seafood	
Fish (all kinds)	1–2
Crab and lobster meat	2–3
Shrimp	1–2
Shellfish in sauce (Newburg, thermidor, etc.)	1
Vegetables	12
Herbs	6
Dairy Products	
Butter	6–8
Cream (whipped)	3–4
Hard cheeses	6–8
Ice cream, sherbet, ices	1–2
Margarine	12
Eggs (Yolks, Whites)	12
Breads	
Baked yeast breads and rolls	6–8
Baked quick breads	2–4
Sandwiches (avoid mayonnaise or cream cheese based spreads, jelly or hard-cooked-egg fillings)	2–3 weeks
Cakes and Cookies	
Baked cakes and cookies (unfrosted)	6–8
Baked cakes and cookies (frosted or filled)	2–4
Cookie dough	2–4
Pastries	
Unbaked pie shells	6–8
Unbaked pies (fruit or mince)	6–8
Baked pies (fruit or mince)	2–4

Note: The storage chart includes only those homemade cakes and pastries suitable for home freezing. There are, of course, commercially frozen cheese cakes, cream and custard pies—silky-smooth ones— but food companies use stabilizers unavailable to the home cook.

MAXIMUM RECOMMENDED STORAGE TIME
FOR REFRIGERATED FOOD

Note: Use following times as a guide only, checking highly perishable foods every day or so. Refrigerator load, how often door is opened, food packaging all affect storage time.

Food	Special Storage Tips	Storage Time
Fresh, Uncooked Meats		
Roasts		4 days
Steaks, chops		3–5 days
Ground meat, stew meat		2 days
Variety meats		1–2 days
Cured and Smoked Meats		
Ham (roasts), bacon	Leave in original wrapper or wrap loosely in plastic food wrap. Store canned hams as labels direct.	1 week
Sliced ham, luncheon meats, sausages		2–3 days
Frankfurters		4–5 days
Cooked Meats, Leftovers		3–4 days
Fresh, Uncooked Poultry	Store giblets separately in a plastic bag.	2–3 days
Cooked Poultry, Leftovers	Remove stuffing and wrap airtight separately.	2 days
Fresh, Uncooked Seafood		
Fish	Clean and dress* before storing. Wrap loosely.	1–2 days
Live lobsters, crabs	Have claws pegged and animals packed in seaweed in double-thick moistureproof bag. Pop bundle into a large plastic bag and refrigerate. Do not cover animals with water; they will die.	6–8 hours
Shrimp	Store shelled or unshelled in plastic bags.	1–2 days
Clams, mussels, oysters, scallops	Store the unshucked in plastic bags, the shucked in their liquor in airtight containers.	1 day
Smoked and Pickled Fish		1–2 weeks
Cooked Seafood, Leftovers		1–2 days
Raw Vegetables		
Artichokes, beans, broccoli, Brussels sprouts, cauliflower, chayotes, eggplant, fennel, peas (in the pod), peppers	Remove any blemished leaves, stalks.	3–5 days
Asparagus	If limp, remove ½" stems; stand in cold water 1 hour.	3–4 days
Beets, carrots, parsnips	Remove all but 1" tops; rinse if dirty.	2 weeks
Cabbage, cardoons, celeriac, celery	Remove blemished leaves, stalks; wash celery if dirty.	3–7 days
Corn on the cob	Store in the husk in plastic bags.	1 day
Cucumbers, summer squash	Wipe if very dirty.	1 week
Leeks, scallions, salsify	Trim roots, unusable tops; rinse salsify.	3–7 days
Lettuces, all salad greens, spinach, dark leafy greens	Wash and dry well. Do not break up salad greens until salad-making time.	3–8 days
Mushrooms	Do not trim or wipe; cover loosely.	1 week

Food	Special Storage Tips	Storage Time
New potatoes, breadfruit	*Note:* Potatoes need not be refrigerated, but cold storage makes them stay sweet longer.	1 week
Okra	Wash if very dirty; dry.	3–4 days
Plantain (dead ripe only)	*Note:* Ripen the green at room temperature.	1–2 days
Tomatoes (dead ripe only)	Store unwrapped, uncovered.	2–3 days
	Note: Slightly underripe tomatoes can be ripened in the refrigerator; takes 8–12 days.	

Cooked Vegetables, Leftovers		2–4 days

Fresh, Ripe Fruits	(All except avocados, bananas, melons, pineapple, stored at room temperature)	
Berries	Discard bruised berries; cover loosely.	2–3 days
Soft fruits	Discard damaged fruits; cover loosely or store in perforated plastic bags.	3–7 days
Firm fruits	Same as for soft fruits.	1–2 weeks
Leftover Raw or Cooked Fruits	Store airtight.	3–5 days
Fruit Juices (fresh, canned, frozen)	Store in airtight containers.	5–7 days

Dairy Products		
Fresh milk, cream, buttermilk	Store in original or airtight nonmetal container.	3–4 days
Sour cream, yogurt	Same as for milk.	1 week
Canned milk	After opening, store covered in original container.	10 days
Cottage, cream, process cheese, spreads	Store airtight in original container.	1–3 weeks
Semi-hard and hard, mild and strong cheese	Butter cut edges to prevent drying; double wrap in foil or plastic food wrap.	3–9 months
	For long storage, wrap in vinegar-moistened cheesecloth (keep cloth moist). Cut off mold (it is harmless, merely unattractive).	
Cheese scraps	Grate and store in an airtight jar.	2–3 weeks
Butter	Store in original wrapper in "butter keeper section."	1–2 weeks

Eggs		
Whole raw	Store small end down, covered, in egg keeper or carton.	10 days
Raw whites, broken eggs	Store in airtight nonmetal container.	1 week
Raw yolks	Cover with cool water and store in airtight jar.	2–3 days
Hard cooked	Store in the shell or shelled and individually wrapped in foil or plastic food wrap. Label eggs "cooked."	10 days

Food	Special Storage Tips	Storage Time
Miscellaneous Foods		
Brown sugar	To keep moist, store box in airtight plastic bag in hydrator.	3–6 months
Coffee (ground)	Store airtight in original can.	3–4 weeks
Custards	Quick-cool, cover, and refrigerate at once.	1 day
Custard and cream cakes and pies	Quick-cool, cover loosely with plastic food wrap, and refrigerate at once.	3–5 days
Drippings	Store in tightly covered can or jar.	2 months
Gravies, sauces	Quick-cool, cover, and refrigerate at once.	2–3 days
Lard	Store in original carton or wrapped airtight. *Note:* New types need no refrigeration; read label carefully.	2 weeks– 2 months
Maple syrup (genuine without preservative)	After opening, store airtight.	2–4 months
Margarine	Store in original wrapper.	2–4 weeks
Nuts (shelled)	Store in airtight jar.	3–4 months
Leftover cooked rice, cereal, pasta, puddings, gelatins	Cool rapidly and store tightly covered.	3–4 days
Relishes, ketchup, pickles, mayonnaise	After opening, store airtight.	2–3 months

STORING FOOD IN CUPBOARD OR PANTRY

"Pantry" is a marvelously old-fashioned word, calling to mind trips to Grandmother's house with its bright shelf parade of home-preserved foods. But a pantry is not a thing of the past. It is as essential today as a refrigerator or freezer. Ideally, it should be a step away from the kitchen—big and airy, reasonably cool, dry, and dark. Cupboard shelves, too, should be well ventilated, cool, dry, and dark.

General Tips:
• Keep pantry and cupboards scrupulously clean, protecting shelves with spill-resistant, easy-to-clean coated paper or vinyl shelf liners. Reline shelves frequently and in the interim wipe regularly with a weak vinegar-water solution to keep ants, roaches, and silverfish at bay.
• Check often for food spoilage (bulging or leaky cans, frothing bottles), for mice (tattered packages are a sure sign if there are also droppings), weevils, roaches, ants, or silverfish. *When Pests Attack:* Clear the shelves, destroying any infested foods (flours, cornstarch, cereals, nuts, raisins, and meals are favorite breeding grounds). Transfer uninfested foods to large screw-top jars (the quart and half-gallon preserving jars are perfect for flours, meals, cereals, nuts, rai-

sins, etc.). Burn old shelf liners; thoroughly vacuum floors, shelves, walls; spackle all holes, cracks, and crevices, then scrub down the entire pantry with the vinegar-water solution. Use an appropriate insecticide—*following label directions carefully*—then let pantry or cupboards stand open several days before restocking with food.
• Be especially selective about the shelf to be used for storing tea, coffee, flavorings, and leavenings. It should be extra cool, dry, and dark.
• When adding supplies to pantry or cupboard, place the new behind the old so that the old will be used first.
• Seal opened packages airtight *(bug-tight)*, either by transferring contents to large preserving jars or by overwrapping in plastic bags and closing with rubber bands or "twisters."
• Get rid of market bags and cartons as soon as they're emptied. *Never* save, *never* store in cupboards. They're an open invitation to roaches, weevils, silverfish, ants. But most of all to roaches. These pests are fond of the glue used in manufacturing bags and cartons and females seek out the snug dark folds and crevices in which to lay their eggs. A market bag or carton, seemingly free of roaches, may in fact harbor hundreds of soon-to-hatch eggs.

THE HERB AND SPICE SHELF

Man has always cherished herbs and spices. Squabbled and fought over them, too. And journeyed to the ends of the earth. The discovery of America, everyone knows, was a happy accident; what Columbus was really after was a direct sea route to the spice treasures of the East.

To primitive man, herbs and spices were magic plants possessing powers of creation, regeneration, and immortality. Much later, kings counted their wealth in peppercorns, gladiators munched fennel to bolster their courage, and prophets wore crowns of laurel to sharpen their "vision." Up until the Middle Ages, mothers strung necklaces of cloves for their children to keep evil spirits away and tucked sprigs of dill in their own buttonholes. Still later, Englishmen devoured pounds of sage each spring, believing "He that would live for aye must eat sage in May."

Today we attribute no magic to herbs and spices other than their power to uplift mundane fare. What are these aromatics so indispensable to mankind? What, in fact, is an herb? A spice? Generally speaking, an herb is the leaf of tender, fragrant annuals and biennials that grow in temperate climates. Spices are the more pungent roots, barks, stems, buds, fruits, and leaves of tropical or subtropical plants, usually perennials. Crossing boundaries are the aromatic seeds, produced by both herb and spice plants.

Some General Tips on Buying, Storing, and Using Herbs and Spices:
• Buy in small amounts and store no longer than one year; flavors fade fast. Toss stale herbs onto hearth or charcoal fires to scent the air.
• Try using whole spices, grinding or grating them as needed. They are far more aromatic than the preground. Whole spices can also be used to season soups, stocks, and stews. You'll need about 1½ times more whole spices than ground, so adjust recipe accordingly. Tie spices in cheesecloth and simmer along with soup or stew or whatever, then lift out before serving.
• Store herbs and spices tightly capped away from direct sunlight in a cool, dry place.
• Use herbs and spices sparingly, discriminatingly, never combining too many in a single recipe. Be particularly cautious about hot peppers.
• Crush dried herbs between your fingers as

you add; body heat will intensify their flavor. Always taste for seasoning *after* herbs or spices have been warmed through.
• If an herb or spice is unfamiliar, taste *before* adding. The best way—though you may not want to go to the trouble—is to blend with a little softened cream cheese or butter, then to let stand at room temperature several minutes so that the seasoning's flavor will develop fully.
• When herbs or spices are being added "cold" to cold dishes—dips and spreads, for example—allow flavors to mature and ripen about ½ hour at room temperature before serving. Or warm the seasoning in a little butter over low heat before adding—especially advisable for raw-tasting chili and curry powders.
• Use fresh herbs as often as possible; they are so much more fragrant than the dry and are being stocked in greater and greater variety by big city grocers. Better still, grow your own.
• Use a light hand with garlic powders and juices; they gather strength on the shelf. Remember, too, that a crushed clove of garlic has two to three times the impact of a minced one.

If a dish is overseasoned, try one or more of the following remedies:
• Strain out bits of herb or spice.
• Simmer a raw, peeled, quartered potato in mixture 10–15 minutes, then remove; it will absorb some of the excess flavor.
• Reduce amount of salt (if it has not already been added) and stir in a little sugar or brown sugar.
• Thicken gravy or stew with a flour or cornstarch and water paste.
• If mixture is overly sweet, sharpen with about 1 teaspoon lemon juice or vinegar.
• Serve mixture well chilled; cold numbs the palate.
• Prepare a second batch—*unseasoned*—and combine with the first.

When making recipes in quantity, adjust seasonings as follows:

QUANTITY BEING MADE	HERB AND SPICE ADJUSTMENT
2 times the recipe	Use 1½ times amounts called for
3 times the recipe	Use 2 times amounts called for
4 times the recipe	Use 2½ times amounts called for

AN HERB AND SPICE CHART

| Herb or Spice | Popular Forms | Essential to Herb/Spice Shelf | | Easy to Grow |
		Basic	Gourmet	
Allspice *Spice.* Berry of a Caribbean tree with combined flavor of cinnamon, cloves, and nutmeg. Use primarily for cakes, cookies, pies, puddings, breads.	Dried whole; powdered	X	X	
Anise *Aromatic seed.* Licorice-flavored cousin to the carrot; used in candies, liqueurs, Scandinavian and German breads, pastries, cookies, beef stews.	Dried whole; powdered		X	
Basil *Herb.* Bitter, clove-flavored relative of mint. Good with any tomato dish, especially Italian.	Dried crushed or ground leaves; fresh	X	X	X
Bay leaves (Bay Laurel) *Herb.* Woodsy, faint flavor of cinnamon-sarsaparilla; bitter when overused; good with veal, fowl, fish.	Dried whole; powdered	X	X	
Capers *Herb.* Tart flower buds of Mediterranean caper bush; superb with eggs, seafood, veal, tomatoes. Choicest are tiny.	Pickled or brined whole		X	
Cardamom *Spice.* Lemony-gingery seeds, especially popular in Scandinavia for breads, cakes.	Dried whole; powdered		X	
Caraway *Aromatic seed.* Delicately licorice, nutty. Used in rye bread, German and Nordic cheeses; good with cabbage and sauerkraut.	Whole dry seeds		X	
Celery seed *Aromatic seed.* Concentrated celery flavor.	Whole dry seeds; powdered	X	X	
Chervil *Herb.* Delicate, sweet, parsley-licorice flavor; component of *fines herbes.* Excellent with seafood, green salads.	Dried whole or ground leaves; fresh		X	X
Chives *Herb.* The most delicate onion; wispy green tops; all-purpose herb for savory dishes.	Minced dried, frozen, freeze-dried; fresh	X	X	X
Cinnamon *Spice.* Sweet, slightly "hot" bark of the cassia tree. Used primarily for cookies, cakes, pies, puddings, spicy beverages.	Sticks; powdered	X	X	
Cloves *Spice.* Pungent flower buds of the clove tree. Used mainly in cakes, pies, puddings, spicy sauces and drinks.	Whole dried buds; powdered	X	X	
Coriander *Aromatic seed.* Nutty seed of a plant of the parsley family; principal seasoning of Latin American sausages, meat dishes. *Herb:* A member of the parsley family that's intensely lemony. Also called Chinese parsley or *cilantro,* coriander is a staple of both Latin American and Oriental cooking.	Whole dried seeds; powdered; fresh		X	
Cumin *Aromatic seed.* Similar to caraway but more medicinal; one of the chief ingredients of chili and curry powders. Good with cabbage, sauerkraut, in meat loaves.	Whole dry seeds; powdered		X	

Herb or Spice	Popular Forms	Essential to Herb/Spice Shelf		
		Basic	Gourmet	Easy to Grow
Dill *Herb.* Lemony-tart; enchances seafood, egg and cheese dishes, salads, cucumbers, tomatoes.	Dried whole and powdered seeds; weed (dried leaves); fresh	X	X	X
Fennel (Finocchio) *Herb.* Feathery, faintly licorice member of the parsley family. Superb with seafood; a favorite Scandinavian flavoring for sweet breads, pastries, cakes, cookies.	Dried whole and powdered seeds, leaves; fresh bulbs		X	X
Fenugreek *Aromatic seed.* Bitter red-brown seeds with a burnt sugar taste. A component of curry powder, imitation maple flavoring, chutney.	Whole dry seeds; powdered		X	
Filé powder *Herb.* Dried sassafras leaves; flavor woodsy, root beer-like. Used to flavor and thicken gumbos, other Creole dishes.	Powder		X	X
Garlic See Specialty Onions (vegetable chapter).	Fresh bulbs; powder; salt; juice	X	X	
Geranium *Herb.* Many flavors (rose, lemon, apple), all good in confections, jellies, fruit compotes. A particularly fragrant, pretty garnish.	Fresh potted plants		X	X
Ginger *Spice.* Biting but sweet root of an Asian plant. One of the most versatile spices, essential to Oriental sweet-sour dishes, pickles, cakes, cookies, pies.	Dried whole and cracked roots; crystallized; preserved; powdered; fresh	X	X	
Horseradish *Herb.* Peppery white root with a turnip-like flavor. Used primarily to add zip to sauces, dips, spreads, salad dressings. Red horseradish has beets added.	Prepared (bottled); fresh	X	X	
Juniper *Aromatic berry.* Dried, smoky-blue, resinous, bittersweet berry of the juniper bush. Used to flavor gin, game, salmon, goose, duck, pork.	Dried whole berries		X	X
Lemon verbena *Herb.* Sweet lemon-flavored leaves; best used to flavor or garnish fruit salads, desserts.	Fresh potted plants		X	X
Mace *Spice.* Fibrous husk of nutmeg; flavor similar but milder. All-purpose spice, equally at home in savory and sweet dishes.	Dried blades; powdered	X	X	
Marjoram *Herb.* Mild cousin of oregano with musky-mellow, almost nutty bouquet. Particularly good with veal, lamb, fowl, potatoes, and tomatoes.	Dried whole leaves; powdered	X	X	X
Mint *Herb.* More than thirty varieties; peppermint and spearmint (the two most popular), apple, lemon and orange, etc. Best in jellies, confections, fruit salads, and desserts, as a pretty, perky garnish.	Whole, crushed and powdered dried leaves; as extracts, oils; fresh	X	X	X

Herb or Spice	Popular Forms	Essential to Herb/Spice Shelf		Easy to Grow
		Basic	Gourmet	
Mustard *Spice.* Bitter and biting; *two main types* are relatively mild *White* and extra-strong *Brown* or *Oriental.* Used primarily in zippy sauces, pickles, salad dressings, deviled foods. Of the prepared, the Dijon-type, made with wine, is considered choicest.	Whole dried or powdered seeds; variety of prepared (bottled) blends.	X	X	X
Nasturtium *Herb.* Leaves of the popular flower, peppery and tart, not unlike watercress. Use in salads. Blossoms also good in salads, as garnishes.	Fresh		X	X
Nutmeg *Spice.* Mellow, sweet-nutty seed of the nutmeg tree. Like mace, an all-purpose spice, equally good with sweets and meats, fruits and vegetables.	Dried whole seeds; ground	X	X	
Oregano *Herb.* Wild marjoram with a bitter, marigold-like flavor. An Italian favorite for spaghetti sauces, pizza, other tomato-rich dishes.	Dried whole or crushed leaves; powdered	X	X	X
Paprika *Spice.* Ground dried pods of fleshy, mild-to-slightly-hot Capsicum peppers, native to Latin America but now the soul of Hungarian cooking. The Hungarian sweet rose paprika is the reddest, sweetest, mildest. *Note:* All paprika is extremely high in vitamin C.	Ground	X	X	
Parsley *Herb.* There are dozens of varieties, but the two most popular are the curly and the somewhat stronger Italian or plain-leaf. A multipurpose herb, a component of *fines herbes* and *bouquet garni.*	Fresh; flakes (dried leaves)	X	X	X
Pepper (true) *Spice.* "The Master Spice," once as rare and costly as gold. There are three types, all from the same tropical vine: the pungent *Black* (dried, unhusked, immature berries), the milder *White* (dried inner white cores of ripe berries), and the *Green* (unripe whole berries). The white is preferable for seasoning light soups and sauces, the green for those who want a less peppery black pepper. Sweet but pungent *Pink Peppercorns* (dried Baies rose berries imported from Madagascar via France), after much controversy, have been deemed safe by the Food and Drug Administration. *Note:* Florida pink peppercorns are altogether different and may cause allergic reactions.	Black dried peppercorns; cracked, ground, seasoned, and lemon-flavor black pepper; whole and ground white pepper; whole dried and liquid-packed green peppercorns	X	X	
Peppers (Capsicums) *Spice.* Not true peppers but a large group of New World pods called "peppers" by Columbus because they were as fiery as the Indian pepper. Capsicums are both red and green, mild and hot (the hot are collectively called *Chili Peppers).* There are dozens of Capsicums, all important to Latin American cuisine, but the following are the most available. *Popular Red Peppers: Cayenne* (ground hot red pepper); plump, sweet, scarlet *Ancho;* sharper, browner, elongated *Mulato;* long skinny, torrid *Pasilla;* and the tiny incendiary	Ground (cayenne); crushed and whole dried pods; canned and pickled whole pods; fresh whole pods; liquid hot red pepper seasoning	X	X	

Herb or Spice	Popular Forms	Essential to Herb/Spice Shelf Basic	Gourmet	Easy to Grow
Pequin. *Popular Green Peppers:* The superhot *Serrano* and *Jalapeño* and the milder, though sometimes hot *Poblano. CAUTION:* Never rub eyes when working with hot peppers—pain is excruciating. Always wash hands well when preparations are done. *(Note:* To "cool" hot peppers, rinse well, remove seeds, stems, veins, then soak 1 hour in lightly salted cold water.)				
Poppy seed *Aromatic seed.* Tiny, nutty, silver-blue seeds of the poppy (they contain no opium). Good in breads, pastries, cakes, salads, with noodles. There are also white poppy seeds, which Oriental chefs favor.	Whole seeds		X	
Rocket (Rugula) See Other Salad Greens in the salad chapter.	Fresh			
Rosemary *Herb.* Heady, lemony-resinous, needle-like leaves. Good with lamb, green peas, pork.	Dried whole or powdered leaves		X	X
Saffron *Spice.* Expensive, dried orange stigmas of the saffron crocus (it takes 225,000 hand-plucked stigmas to yield 1 pound, hence the high price). Flavor is medicinal, the key seasoning of Paella, Spanish breads, cakes. *To Use:* Soak strands in tepid water, then use this infusion to flavor and color recipes.	Dried whole stigmas; powdered		X	
Sage *Herb.* Musky, lime-scented silver-green leaves; the identifiable herb of poultry seasoning and stuffings.	Dried whole, crushed and powdered leaves	X	X	X
Savory *Herb.* There are two savories, the delicate, aromatic *Summer Savory* and the more bitter *Winter Savory.* The *Summer* is the better herb, especially delicious with eggs and cheese.	Dried whole and powdered leaves		X	X
Sesame seed (Benne) *Aromatic seed.* Small flat seeds, nutty with a tinge of bitterness. They may be red, brown, or black in addition to the familiar pearly shade. Good in breads and pastries, toasted in salads. *(Note:* These stale and go rancid quite rapidly; buy as needed.) *To Toast:* Warm uncovered in piepan 10–15 minutes at 350° F., stirring often until golden, or 1–2 minutes in a heavy skillet over moderate heat.	Whole seeds		X	
Shallots See Specialty Onions (vegetable chapter).	Fresh		X	
Tarragon *Herb.* Succulent, licorice-flavored green leaves. Superlative with seafood, eggs, crisp green salads. Component of *fines herbes.*	Dried whole and powdered leaves; fresh sprigs		X	X
Thyme *Herb.* All-round meat, fowl and fish herb with a vaguely minty, vaguely tea-like flavor. Customarily included in a *bouquet garni.* Particularly fragrant is lemon thyme.	Whole dried or powdered leaves	X	X	X

Herb or Spice	Popular Forms	Essential to Herb/Spice Shelf		Easy to Grow
		Basic	Gourmet	
Turmeric *Spice.* Deep yellow-orange root of an Asian plant related to ginger. Dried and ground, it becomes an integral part of curry powder, the "yellow" of mustard. Turmeric alone has a thin, flat, medicinal taste. Used primarily in pickles, chutneys, curries.	Powdered		X	
Vanilla bean *Aromatic seed capsule.* Long black seed pod of a wild Mexican orchid, sweet and perfume-like.	Beans; extract	X	X	
Woodruff *Herb.* Sweet-musky woodland herb, the leaves of which are used in the *Maibowle* (Rhine wine afloat with strawberries).	Fresh		X	

Some Less Used Herbs and Spices

Achiote: Small red seeds of a Latin American tree similar to and used as a substitute for saffron in Mexican cooking.

Angelica: Sweet, succulently stalked member of the parsley family, most often available candied and used as a decoration in confectionery.

Borage: Medicinal-tasting European herb used in teas and other beverages.

Burnet: A leafy cucumber-flavored herb, excellent in salads.

Costmary: Minty but bitter herb used in making ale; good used *sparingly* in salads.

Horehound: A bitter herb aromatic of tobacco, once popular for flavoring candies and cough drops.

Hyssop: An astringent variety of mint used in liqueurs; scatter a few leaves into green salads for bite.

Lavender: "The old ladies' herb," the clean and lemony perfumer of bureaus and closets. Few people cook with lavender, but a leaf or two, minced into a fruit cup or salad, injects a pleasing, elusive scent.

Lemon balm: Crisp lemony-minty leaves that double nicely for mint.

Lemon grass: Fibrous stalks (the outer layers must be peeled off) with distinct lemon flavor that figure prominently in much Oriental—and especially Thai—cooking.

Lovage: A celery-flavored herb, particularly compatible with fowl and game.

Marigold: The pungent garden variety; use sparingly to pep up salads, poultry stuffings. The flower stamens can be dried and substituted for saffron.

Parsley root: This tough root is a pet Russian and Middle European flavoring for soups and stews. It belongs to the parsley family, looks like a small, knobby parsnip, and tastes like a cross between turnip and celery root.

Rose hips: The tart, crab-apple-like fruit of the rose; delicious boiled into jelly or minced into venison or rabbit stews. Extremely high in vitamin C.

Rue: An old-fashioned acrid herb used in minute quantities to perk up fruit cups and salads.

Sweet cicely: A kind of chervil often—but erroneously—called myrrh because both have a faintly licorice-parsley flavor. True myrrh is an aromatic gum.

Sweet flag: An iris with cinnamon-and-ginger-flavored rhizomes used in seasoning confections and puddings.

The Herb Blends

Bouquet garni: A bouquet of herbs—fresh parsley and thyme plus a bay leaf—bundled together, simmered in soups, stews, stocks, or other liquid recipes, then fished out before serving. The French way to prepare the bouquet is to wrap the parsley around the two other herbs, but Americans may prefer to tie all three in a tiny cheesecloth bag (imperative, by the way, if dry spices are used so that they don't float out and overseason the dish). A *bouquet garni* may contain other seasoners—a celery stalk, perhaps, a garlic clove—but it must begin with parsley, thyme, and bay leaf. Food companies now market dried blends called *bouquet garni,* which should be used as labels direct.

Fines herbes: A French favorite—minced fresh or dried chervil, tarragon, parsley, chives, and sometimes basil, sage, marjoram, fennel, or oregano employed as a multipurpose seasoner. Particularly good in salads. Now available bottled.

Poultry seasoning: All the good poultry and poultry stuffing seasoners—sage, marjoram, powdered onion, pepper, and sometimes thyme—premixed and ready to use.

The Spice Blends

Barbecue spice: Zippy blend of chili peppers, cumin, garlic, cloves, paprika, sugar, and salt created specifically for barbecued foods but also good mixed into salad dressings, meat loaves and patties, egg, cheese, and potato dishes.

Charcoal seasoning: A smoky mix of powdered charcoal, herbs, spices, salt, and sometimes sugar and monosodium glutamate designed to impart a charcoal-broiled flavor.

Chili powder: Ground chili peppers, cumin seeds, oregano, garlic, salt, and occasionally cloves, allspice, and onion—the staples of Mexican and Tex-Mex cooking.

Cinnamon sugar: Simply that, cinnamon and sugar premixed and ready to sprinkle onto hot buttered toast, waffles, pancakes, or fresh-from-the-oven breads.

Crab boil (shrimp spice): Peppercorns, crumbled bay leaves, dried red peppers, mustard seeds, chips of dried ginger, and other whole spices suitable for seasoning boiled crab and shrimp.

Curry powder: An Occidental invention; Indian cooks would never dream of using curry powder, but grind their own spices, varying the combinations according to the food to be curried. Commercial curry powders contain as many as 16–20 spices, predominantly cinnamon, cloves, cumin, fenugreek, ginger, turmeric, red and black pepper, the quantity of pepper determining the curry's "hotness." *Tip:* When adding curry powder to a cold dish (such as a dip or spread), always warm it a few minutes first in butter over low heat to mellow the "raw" taste.

A HOMEMADE CURRY POWDER

¼ cup

2 tablespoons ground coriander
1 tablespoon ground turmeric
1 teaspoon *each* ground cumin, fenugreek, ginger, and allspice
½ teaspoon *each* ground mace and crushed dried hot red chili peppers
¼ teaspoon *each* powdered mustard and black pepper

Work all ingredients together in a mortar and pestle until well blended. Store airtight.

Curry paste: A blend of curry powder, ghee (clarified butter), and vinegar available in specialty food shops. Use in place of curry powder, allowing about 1–2 tablespoons paste to season a curry for 6 persons.

Five fragrance (five spice) powder: A mixture of powdered star anise, cloves, cinnamon, fennel, and peppercorns used extensively in Chinese cooking.

Seven spice mixture: Another staple of the Chinese kitchen, this one a blend of powdered chili and sansho peppers, mandarin orange rind, black hemp, white poppy seeds, dried seaweed, and sesame seeds.

Seto fuumi: A popular Japanese seasoning compounded of dried seaweed and tuna, sesame seeds, and monosodium glutamate.

Pickling spice: Mixture of mustard and coriander seeds, white and black peppercorns, whole cloves and allspice, whole hot red chili peppers, broken cinnamon sticks and bay leaves, chunks of gingerroot; versatile enough to use for a variety of pickles, preserves, and condiments.

Apple pie spice: Blend of cinnamon, nutmeg, and sometimes allspice.

Pumpkin pie spice: Mixture of cinnamon, ginger, nutmeg, allspice, and cloves.

Pizza spice: A garlicky, oniony blend similar to Barbecue spice compounded specifically for pizza toppings.

Quatre-épices: A French blend of four spices —cloves, ginger, nutmeg, and white pepper —used as an all-purpose seasoner for meats and vegetables, soups and sauces. *To Make:* Mix together 5 tablespoons ground cloves and 3 tablespoons *each* ground ginger, nutmeg, and white pepper. Store airtight. Particularly good on carrots, turnips, and parsnips, broiled steaks and chops.

Seasoned salt: The formula varies from processor to processor, but essentially an aromatic blend of salt, spices, and herbs that can be used as an all-purpose seasoning.

Some Herb and Spice Substitutions

Because a number of herbs and spices taste somewhat the same, the following can be interchanged in a pinch (substitute measure for measure):

Herbs
Basil and Oregano
Caraway and Anise
Celery Seeds and Minced Celery Tops
Chervil and Parsley
Chervil and Tarragon
Fennel and Anise
Fennel and Tarragon
Oregano and Marjoram
Sage and Thyme

Spices
Allspice and *equal parts* Cinnamon, Cloves, and Nutmeg
Chili Peppers and Cayenne
Commercial Curry Powder and Homemade Curry Powder
Nutmeg and Mace

ABOUT OTHER ADDITIVES

Monosodium glutamate *(MSG; the aji-nomoto* of Japanese cuisine): Neither herb nor spice, this white crystalline vegetable extract must nonetheless be included because of its popularity as a flavor enhancer. Long an Oriental standby, it is tasteless, yet has the mysterious power of freshening and developing other foods' flavors. *Note:* MSG has recently come under medical scrutiny, some researchers believing overdoses cause giddiness, fainting spells.

Meat tenderizers: These are discussed fully in the meat chapter (see The Ways of Tenderizing Meat).

Note: Those block-long scientific words cluttering package-label ingredient lists are additives. To learn what each is—and does—see *A Dictionary of Additives* on the rear endpaper.

Using Fresh Herbs

• Cut and use herbs often; snipping promotes growth. To cut, reach down near the soil and snip each stalk separately with scissors. Resist the temptation (especially strong with chives) to shear the tops right off in a crew cut. Also avoid cutting too deeply into woody stems. *(Note:* Herbs are said to be at their headiest just before blooming, also early in the day when touched with dew. *But* herbs are rarely used first thing in the morning, so it makes more sense to cut them when they are needed.)

• Wash herbs gently, swishing them up and down in cool water, then drain, shaking lightly or patting dry on paper toweling.

• Mince herbs as they are needed and in quantities needed. If herbs are tender, mince stems and all; otherwise, use the leaves only. Wispy herbs like dill, chives, and fennel are most efficiently minced by gathering a dozen or so strands or tops together, then snipping straight across with scissors. A chopping knife makes short shrift of larger, coarser herbs.

• To store unused fresh herbs, wrap stalks loosely in damp paper toweling and tuck into the hydrator or stand stalks upright in 1/4″ cold water in a wide-mouth preserving jar, cover loosely with a plastic bag, and refrigerate. *(Note:* Minced herbs store poorly; better to freeze them.)

• When substituting fresh herbs for the dry, double or triple the quantity called for, tasting as you add until the flavors seem well balanced. Fresh herbs are far more subtle than the dry.

How to Dry Fresh Herbs

• Pick prime leaves, preferably just before herbs bloom and early in the morning as soon as the dew has evaporated.

• Wash herbs gently and pat dry on paper toweling.

• Spread out on a cheesecloth-covered cookie rack and dry outdoors in a warm shady spot (bring inside at night), in a dry, airy room or in a 200° F. oven, or on dehydration racks in a convection oven (at the *dehydrate setting;* follow manufacturer's directions). Drying times will vary according to humidity and herb variety; test leaves often for crumbliness. You can also tie 2–3 herb stalks together and hang upside down in a dry, airy spot; the herbs will dry in a week or two under favorable conditions.

• When herbs are dry and crumbly, remove any twigs and stems and pack leaves whole in airtight jars. Or, if you prefer, crush with a rolling pin between sheets of wax paper, then bottle airtight.

THREE

Beverages

The French are master chefs, the Viennese master confectioners, but when it comes to mixing drinks, Americans are the masters. So many drinks—hard and soft—are American inventions: ice-cream sodas, fizzy colas and floats, not to mention cocktails (and cocktail parties). We drink, perhaps, a greater variety of beverages than any other people and are constantly concocting new ones. Moreover, we have developed a European fondness for fine wines and choice brews and an adventurous spirit in sampling exotic liqueurs.

ALCOHOLIC BEVERAGES

BEERS AND ALES

Beer and ale are closely related fermented malt beverages, brewed in different ways. The technical differences matter not so much here as the results. *Ale* tastes more strongly of hops than beer, particularly *stout* and *porter,* which are heavy, dark, and bittersweet.

The most popular *beer* is bubbly, golden *lager,* a light brew held in the cask until cleared of sediment *(lager* is from *lagern,* the German word meaning *to store).* It is carbonated (hence the bubbles), bottled or canned, and pasteurized. *Draft beer* is drawn straight from the cask and not pasteurized. American lagers average 3.2–5 per cent alcohol, European lagers slightly more. *Bock beer,* available in spring, is a dark, sweetish, heavy lager brewed from dark-roasted malt. *Pilsner* is pale lager, originally from Pilsen, Czechoslovakia, made with natural mineral water. Also now available are *light beers* that weigh in at some 30 per cent fewer calories

than regular beer (they average 8 calories per ounce as compared with 12 or 13).

Serving Beers and Ales: The ideal temperature for serving beer is said to be 40° F., cool but not as cold as Americans like it. Europeans frown upon the American practice of serving ice-cold beer, insisting that it destroys the flavor. Should beer be poured so that there is no head? Depends on personal preference. Connoisseurs insist upon a creamy head about 1″ thick because it proves the beer isn't flat and seals in the flavor. To achieve a good head, tilt glass and pour enough beer gently down the side to one-third full, then stand glass upright and pour beer straight in. To minimize head, fill tilted glass.

WINES

The subject of wine (by definition the fermented juice of freshly pressed grapes) is nearly inexhaustible, and in a basic cookbook there simply is not room to do more than capsulize. Whole volumes have been devoted to wines, indeed to single wines.

The Types of Wine

TABLE WINES

(Natural wines served with meals; they have an alcoholic content of 10–14 per cent.)

Dry Red Wines

FRENCH:

Bordeaux (called claret by the British): Many experts consider these the finest of all table wines. When good, they are rich, fragrant, full-bodied. Bordeaux include *Médoc, Pomerol, Saint-Émilion, Graves.* Outstanding chateaux are *Château Lafite-Rothschild,*

APÉRITIF WINES AND WINE-BASED DRINKS

Wine (those served before meals)	Appropriate Glass	How to Serve
Byrrh	6-ounce old-fashioned glass	on the rocks
Dry Champagne (Brut)	9-ounce tulip goblet	well chilled
Dry Sherry (Fino or Manzanilla)	6-ounce sherry glass	well chilled
Dubonnet or Dubonnet Blonde	6-ounce sherry glass	well chilled
Half-and-Half (a blend of sweet and dry vermouths)	6-ounce old-fashioned glass	on the rocks
Lillet (similar to vermouth, made of white wine, brandy, herbs)	6-ounce old-fashioned glass or sherry glass	on the rocks or well chilled
Punt e Mes (Italian vermouth-based apéritif meaning "a point of bitters and a half of sweet")	6-ounce old-fashioned glass	on the rocks with club soda
Rosso Antico (herb-infused red wine)	6-ounce old-fashioned glass	on the rocks
Vermouth (dry and sweet)	6-ounce old-fashioned glass or sherry glass	on the rocks or well chilled

Château Latour, Château Mouton-Rothschild.

Burgundy: Another superb group of French wines, heavier than Bordeaux and more robust. Some better known red Burgundies are *Beaujolais* (and *Beaujolais Nouveau,* unaged wines that usually reach the U.S. by Thanksgiving amid much fanfare), *Échézeaux, Volnay, Pommard, Beaune,* and, three of the best: *Chambertin, Romanée-Conti,* and *La Tâche.*

Loire Valley Wine: Chinon, Anjou (both light bodied and well balanced).

Rhône Valley Wine: Châteauneuf-du-Pape, Côte Rôtie (heady and rich), and *Hermitage* (generously full flavored).

ITALIAN:
Popular imports are *Barbera, Barbaresco, Bardolino* (much like Chianti but smoother), *Barolo* (which some consider Italy's greatest dry red wine), *Chianti* (the best may not come in the *fiasco,* or straw-covered bottle; look for the neckband imprinted with the black rooster), *Lambrusco* (a crackling red) and *Valpolicella* (delicate).

SPANISH AND PORTUGUESE:
Both countries produce good—if sometimes rough—red table wines. Most readily available are the Spanish *Rioja* and Portuguese *Dão.*

AMERICAN:
California vineyards produce first-rate dry red wines, notably *Cabernet Sauvignon* (a Bordeaux-type), *Pinot Noir* (similar to Burgundy), *Gamay, Zinfandel* and *Barbera.*

Dry White Wines

FRENCH:

Bordeaux: Graves (both dry and semidry).

Burgundy: Chablis (light and very dry), *Meursault* (soft, flowery, feminine), *Montrachet* (Dumas declared that Montrachet "should be drunk while kneeling"), and *Pouilly-Fuissé* (dry but fruity).

Loire Valley Wine: Muscadet (very dry), *Pouilly-Fumé* and *Sancerre* (both still and dry), and *Vouvray* (still or crackling, dry or semidry).

Alsatian Wine: Gewürztraminer (fruity, almost gingery), *Riesling* (dry and elegant), *Sylvaner* (fresh, light, and fruity), and *Traminer* (similar to *Gewürztraminer* but subtler).

ITALIAN:

Brolio Bianco (light), *Est! Est!! Est!!!* and *Orvieto* (dry or semidry), *Frascati, Soave* (very light and smooth), *Verdicchio* (dry or semidry with a touch of bitterness).

GERMAN:
The noble grape of Germany is the Riesling, hence the varietal name Riesling may appear on labels of both Rhine and Moselle wines. To tell Rhine wines from the Moselle at a glance, look at the bottle. Both come in tall slim bottles but the Rhine bottle is brown, the Moselle green.

Rhine Wine: The choicest are from the Rheingau, a 20-mile stretch on the right bank of the Rhine between Wiesbaden and Rüdesheim. Ones to seek out are *Hochheimer* (called hock by the British),

Rüdesheimer, and *Johannisberg* (Schloss Johannisberg may be Germany's most famous vineyard). The *Rheinhessen,* just across the river from the Rheingau, produces the popular *Liebfraumilch,* not a single wine but a blend. It is produced throughout the Rheinhessen, thus can be very good (look for such labels as Blue Nun, Hans Christof, Crown of Crowns), or it can be disappointing. Rhine wines, generally, are pleasantly light and dry.

Moselle Wine: The best are from the *Mittel (Middle) Moselle* and include *Piesporter, Bernkasteler* (Bernkasteler Doktor is perhaps the most renowned), *Kroever, Zeltinger,* and *Wehlener.*

Steinwein: One of the best wines from Franconia (valleys of the Main and its tributaries), this light wine comes in the squatty *Bocksbeutel* instead of the tall, graceful bottles of Rhine and Moselle wines. There are other wines from Franconia, but Steinwein is best known to Americans.

SPANISH AND PORTUGUESE:
As with the Spanish table reds, *Rioja* is the name to look for in white table wines. Probably the best known Portuguese white wine is *vinho verde,* a tart young green wine, best drunk very cold.

AMERICAN:
California vintners produce excellent dry white wines. Some to try: *Semillon* and *Sauvignon Blanc* (similar to but drier than Sauternes), *Chardonnay, Chenin Blanc,* and *Pinot Blanc* (chablis types), *Riesling, Traminer, Sylvaner,* and *Grey Riesling.* A number of Eastern vineyards also produce creditable Rieslings.

Rosé Wines

There are fewer good rosé wines than dry reds or whites. The best imports are *Tavel* and *Anjou* from France, *Mateus* from Portugal. California also has good rosés: *Grenache* and *Gamay.*

Light (Low-Calorie) Wines

Rosés, Chablis, and *Rhine-type* wines are all now available in less alcoholic, low-calorie versions, averaging 25–33 per cent fewer calories than standard table wines.

DESSERT WINES

(Sweet, still, or fortified wines that are especially compatible with dessert; fortified wines are those that have had spirits added, often brandy, to bring the alcoholic content up to about 20 per cent.)

Sauternes: People quibble as to whether these white Bordeaux are table or dessert wines. They are sweetish, however, and connoisseurs prefer them with dessert, particularly fruit. Among the greats are *Château d'Yquem* and *Château La Tour-Blanche.*

Madeira: There are many Madeira wines, all fortified, all classified according to sweetness. The driest is *Sercial,* then *Verdelho,* then *Boal* and, sweetest of all, *Malmsey. Rainwater Madeira* is a blend, which though light in color can be fairly rich or dry. Madeira, by the way, is a superb wine to use in cooking, especially in soups, sauces, and desserts. Sercial is also popularly served with turtle soup.

Port, Porto: True Porto comes from Porto, Portugal, and is a far cry from domestic imitations, which are spelled simply port. Some are exquisitely light and golden, some tawny and mellow, some thick and sweet. All are fortified. The classifications of port are: *Ruby* (fruity, sweet, young red wine), *Tawny* (aged in wood and amber in color), *Vintage* (wine of a single excellent year, carefully aged and costly), *Crusted* (aged port, not necessarily of one vintage; *crusted* refers to the sediment that accumulates in the bottle. These wines should be decanted so that the sediment doesn't land in the glass).

Sherry: The best known of the dessert wines, sherries come from Jerez, Spain, after which they are named. They are fortified but mellower, nuttier than either the ports or Madeiras. *Dry sherries* are *Fino, Manzanilla,* and *Vino de Pasto* (these are best served cold as apéritifs); the *medium dry* is *Amontillado* (very nutty and a good all-purpose sherry); and the *sweet* are *Amoroso, Oloroso,* and *Brown. Cream sherry* is a very sweet *Oloroso.*

Tokay: White or amber sweet Hungarian wine from Tokay grapes. Tokays are also made in California.

Other Dessert Wines: Málaga (from Spain), *Marsala* (from Sicily), *Mavrodaphne* (from Greece), and *Muscatel* (Greece, Spain, and Portugal produce good ones). These are generally very sweet, some quite syrupy and raisiny.

Champagne and Other Sparkling Wines

Champagne: True champagne comes from the ancient province of Champagne around Rheims, and it and only it can be sold as "Champagne" in France and most of Europe. This is the reason why domestic champagne is labeled "California Champagne" or "Ohio" or "New York State Champagne." (Some of the domestics are very good, too.) Champagne is a white wine made from the Pinot Noir and Pinot Chardonnay grapes, twice fermented—once before bottling, once afterward (which produces the bubbles). All champagnes are blends, usually made from both varieties of Pinot grapes. When the white grapes alone (Chardonnay) are used, the results are a lighter champagne called *blanc de blanc.* Depending upon the amount of sweetening added *after* the first fermentation, champagne may be dry or sweet. The terms used to denote degree of sweetness are: *brut* or, in the case of California champagne, *natur* (the driest), *extra dry* (not as dry as brut), *demi-sec* (fairly sweet), and *sec* or *doux* (quite sweet). Pink champagne is simply champagne made from pressings allowed to stay on the skins a bit longer than usual (the pigment in the *pinot noir* grape skins pinkens the juice). When should champagne be served? It is the one wine that can be served at any time of the day, any course of the meal. The sweeter champagnes, however, are more suited to dessert. *Tip on Opening Champagne Bottles:* Don't pop the cork, ease it out slowly and steadily so you don't shake up the champagne.

Other Sparkling Wines: There are many bubbling red and white wines, but sparkling Burgundy is the one Americans know best (Americans like it, the French don't). It is produced in much the same way as champagne except that the wine used is red Burgundy. France also makes a sparkling *Anjou* (rosé) and a sparkling *Vouvray* (dry or semi-dry white). Portugal makes some bubbling rosés, Germany some sparkling whites, Italy, too, including the famous *Asti Spumante.* California makes a version of nearly every sparkling French wine.

COOKING WINES

The idea of "cooking wine" is an absurd holdover from the days of prohibition. Cooking wines are "salted" so they won't be drunk. It is pointless to buy them, because the best wines to cook with are "drinking" wines (except, of course, those that cost the earth).

Some Terms and Techniques Having to Do with Wines

The Language of Wine Labels: Because so many wines are imported and their labels written in foreign languages, the beginner

has trouble decoding the message. The labels carrying the most meaningful information are those of French and German wines. Here then, are some of the common label terms and what they mean:

Appellation d'Origine Contrôlée: A French term meaning that the wine was produced where it says it was, a guarantee of place of origin, so to speak, entitling the wine to a regional name—Bordeaux, for example, or Burgundy (the more specific the regional name, by the way, the better the wine will probably be). It further means that the traditional standards of the locale were upheld in the production of the wine.

Cave: The French word for *wine cellar; cave* on a label is not a guarantee of quality.

Clos: The French word for *vineyard;* if a label contains the phrase *"clos de"* followed by the name of a vineyard, it means the wine was produced at the local vineyard, and if the vineyard (and vintage) is a good one, the wine should be good.

Crus Classés: In 1855 the vineyards of Médoc and Sauternes in Bordeaux were classified according to excellence, and 62 were rated *Grands Crus* (great growths), a designation many Bordeaux labels still carry. Within the *Grands Crus* were five subdivisions, from the first and finest *(Premiers Crus)* through second, third, and fourth to fifth growths. Some bottles still display *Premiers Crus* on their labels, meaning they were the finest of the 1855 classification. Wines marked *Crus Exceptionnels* were in the category just below the *Grands Crus,* and those marked *Crus Bourgeois* and *Crus Artisans,* etc., were lower still. Since 1855, however, vineyards have changed hands, qualities have changed, and there is much pressure for a new system of classification that will give credit where credit is due today. The new system, however, has not been determined, so the 1855 terms still hold.

Kabinet: A German label term meaning that the grower guarantees this particular wine to be the highest quality.

Mise en Bouteilles au (or *du) Château:* A French term meaning *estate-bottled.* Because most wine-producing châteaux are in Bordeaux, this particular phrase appears primarily on Bordeaux wines. With Burgundies, the equivalent phrase is *Mise en* (or *du) Domaine.* Other French phrases meaning estate-bottled are *Mise en Bouteille par le Propriétaire* or, more simply, *Mise à la Propriété.* The German equivalents: *Abfüllung, Kellerabfüllung,* and *Schlossabzug.*

V.D.Q.S. An abbreviation on French labels for *Vins Délimités de Qualité Supérieure.* It merely means that the wine has been produced according to government regulation and is not an indication of quality.

Other Wine Terms and Techniques

Claret: The British name for red Bordeaux table wines.

Decant: To pour from one container to another. Aged wines need to be decanted so that any sediment stays in the original bottle. Decanting also is important for many dry red wines because it aerates them and brings out their full flavor.

Dry: A term meaning not sweet.

Lees: Sediment in a liquor or wine.

Marc: The grape skins and seeds left in the press after the juice has been run off. It is used to make *marc,* a potent *eau de vie.*

May Wine: Light German spring wine punch flavored with woodruff. Also called *Maibowle.* Some May wine is bottled.

Must: Pressed grape juice before and during fermentation.

Room Temperature: Ideally 60° F. and the temperature at which most dry red table wines are at their best.

Solerization: A process used in making Madeira and sherry in which casks of certain vintages are stacked, one on top of the other, the oldest being at the bottom. During the blending of the wines, a little from each tier is added in carefully worked-out proportions. When the bottom casks are empty, they are refilled from those directly above. Not all Madeira and sherry are made by this process, but those that are are marked *Solera.*

Varietal Wine: A wine named for the variety of grape from which it was made. *Riesling* is a varietal wine and so are *Semillon, Pinot Noir* and *Gamay* from California.

Vin Blanc: French for *white wine.*

Vin du Pays: Local wine and the one to drink when traveling abroad. Much of it cannot be sampled out of its own locale, and much of it is very pleasant indeed.

Vin Rouge: French for *red wine.*

Vins Ordinaires: Ordinary table wines, red or white, usually served in a carafe. These are the wines served in many French *bistros* and inns.

Vintage: Considerable fuss is made about vintage, more perhaps than is justified, because in off years wine of a great vineyard is likely to be better than that of a so-so vineyard in a great year. Vintage refers to the year's crop, and grapes, like other crops, experience good years and bad. Vintage matters most with French and German wines where weather is more changeable than in warmer, sunnier climes (vintage means little with Italian, Spanish, California, and Portuguese wines—except for Porto).

Bottle Shapes and Sizes

Certain types of wines are sold in certain types of bottles, and as you come to know wines, you'll be able to recognize the wine by glancing at the bottle. Sizes vary, too. And to complicate matters, we must contend with metric measures instead of the more familiar fifths and quarts. The best bottle sizes to buy are those that you will use up in the course of an evening. The standard bottle size for most still wines is now 750 milliliters (25.4 fluid ounces and just shy of a fifth), enough for 2–3 people at dinner if one wine only is being served. Many are available in half bottles (375 milliliters or 12.7 fluid ounces), enough for 1–2 persons. A number of domestic and imported wines are also bottled by the liter (33.8 fluid ounces), magnum (1.5 liters, 50.7 fluid ounces), and 3-liter jugs (101 fluid ounces)—a money saver when a great many people are to be served. For general use, however, the standard 750-milliliter bottle size is best.

Serving Wines

When a wine is to be served and what it is to accompany determine the type that should be served. But the rules aren't as rigid as they once were, and the old business about red wines with red meats and white wines with white meats shouldn't be taken as law. A full-bodied red wine complements rare roast beef, it's true, but that same wine might not pair as happily as a dry white wine with *pot-au-feu* or other boiled beef dishes. What you choose, then, is largely a matter of personal preference and common sense. Obviously, a rich dry red wine would be inappropriate with delicate white fish. And a fragile white would do nothing for venison. It would be foolish to lavish a fine wine on meat loaf, but equally so to downgrade filet mignon with a poor one. Generally speaking, white wines are the best choices for seafood, the humbler wines accompanying the humbler fish. The wine that goes best with poultry depends upon how the poultry was cooked—that in a white sauce calls for white wine, but *coq au vin* or chicken with a robust tomato sauce will team better with red wine. With experience, one begins to know instinctively happy partnerships of food and wine. And a good way to gain that experience is by eating in fine restaurants and asking the sommelier (wine steward) what he recommends with your choice of menu.

When Two Wines Are to Be Served: The rules again are fairly simple: white wine before red, young wine before old, and dry wine before sweet. *Tip:* Avoid serving wine with salad or other vinegary food—the vinegar deadens the palate to the taste of the wine.

Wineglasses: Few people have room today to store several kinds of wineglasses, so the best idea is to have an all-purpose glass and, shelf space permitting, a special tulip goblet for champagne. The all-purpose glass should be large—anywhere from 10 to 20 ounces, stemmed, round-bowled, and of clear, thin uncut crystal or glass (the better to appreciate the color of the wine).

Wine-Serving Temperatures: Red wines should be served at room temperature provided the room isn't sweltering. To wine connoisseurs, room temperature is 60° F.—a bit cool for those used to heated houses—but a red wine served at a room temperature in the 70°'s will still be good. White and rosé wines should be chilled before serving, not so much that they lose flavor, just enough to enhance them (about 40°–45° F.). Two to three hours in the refrigerator should do it. Don't try to quick-chill wine in the freezer—too much danger of its freezing. Champagnes should be served well chilled and so should sparkling Burgundies. *Note:* When chilling wine in an ice bucket, rotate bottle frequently so the wine chills evenly.

Uncorking and Pouring Wines: First of all, get a proper corkscrew—one that gently lifts out the cork—and learn to use it before tackling a fine wine. To open a bottle, cut around the metal covering over the cork about 1″ below the top of the bottle and peel off; wipe mouth of bottle with a dry, clean napkin. Center tip of corkscrew in cork and twist into cork, using the proper technique for the particular corkscrew, then *ease* cork out. Don't pop the cork or jerk it out—doing so unsettles the wine.

Red wines should be uncorked about an hour before serving so that they have a chance to "breathe" and develop full flavor.

If the wine is an old one with sediment in the bottle, decant carefully into a clean, dry decanter and leave unstoppered. Or, if wine is very old and precious, cradle gently in a wine basket (its purpose is to keep wine as nearly as possible in its cellar position so that a minimum of sediment is stirred up).

White and rosé wines should be uncorked just before serving. Wrapping a wine bottle in a white linen napkin is unnecessary unless the wine has been chilled in an ice bucket and is dripping. If in doubt about the quality of a wine, pour a little into your own glass and sample before serving guests (this is routinely done by sommeliers in restaurants). When pouring, never fill each glass more than one third to one half (another reason for having large wineglasses; the air space in the glass allows you to swirl the wine, bringing out its full bouquet). *Tip:* As you finish pouring wine into a glass, twist bottle slightly as you lift it to prevent dripping.

Leftover Wines: Once opened, wines quickly turn to vinegar. White wines will keep refrigerated several days, red and fortified wines somewhat longer (uncork the leftover red wine and let it stand at room temperature about an hour before serving). If the wine should turn to vinegar, don't despair. Use it to dress salads.

WHISKEYS AND LIQUORS

All whiskeys are liquor but all liquors aren't whiskey, the difference being that whiskey is distilled from grain mash (rye, corn, barley, wheat) and liquor from a variety of things—grain, sugar cane (rum), cactus (tequila), potatoes (vodka—although much of today's vodka is made of grain). Another clarification: *Whiskey* is the common spelling, *whisky* the British (used for scotch and Canadian whisky). Here, then, is a quick alphabet of popular liquors:

Aquavit: Potent, colorless Scandinavian liquor distilled from grain mash or potatoes, usually flavored with caraway. It is drunk ice cold, neat, sometimes with a beer chaser.

Arrack: A strong rumlike liquor distilled from fermented coconut juice. It is popular in Indonesia, Asia, and the Middle East.

Blended Whiskey: A blend, one-fifth 100-proof straight whiskey, four-fifths other whiskeys and neutral spirits. Blended whiskeys must be at least 80 proof, but they are almost always light and smooth.

Bourbon: The American liquor—amber brown, rich, and smooth—distilled from a fermented mash of rye, corn, and malted barley. *Straight bourbon* is distilled from a mash containing at least 51 per cent corn; *blended bourbon* is a whiskey blend containing at least 51 per cent straight bourbon. *Sour mash* is a type of bourbon made by fermenting each new load of mash with "working yeast" from the previous batch. Rather like sour dough bread, for which yeast starters are kept alive and used over and over, each successive dough replenishing the starter.

Cachaça: A clear, colorless, deceptively smooth Brazilian "firewater" fermented from sugar cane juice. It's the foundation of such Brazilian drinks as *batidas* and *caipirinhas.*

Canadian Whisky: Liquor distilled from blends of rye, corn, wheat, and barley. It is similar to rye and bourbon but smoother and lighter.

Corn Whiskey: Liquor distilled from fermented corn mash. To qualify as *straight corn whiskey,* it must contain at least 51 per cent corn. Corn whiskey is, of course, the *white lightning* or *moonshine* of Southern bootleggers.

Gin: Distilled neutral grain spirits, crisp, colorless, and lightly flavored with juniper. There are two types: *London dry gin,* the type Americans know, and *Dutch* or *Holland gin (Jenever* or *Geneva),* a heavier, stronger variety, which the Dutch drink neat. Actually, there are many *Jenevers,* the dark and the light and those steeped with secret blends of herbs and spices.

Irish Whiskey: An Irish liquor distilled from grain, primarily barley. It is dry and light, has none of the smokiness of scotch.

Rum: Liquor distilled from sugar syrup or molasses. Made primarily in the Caribbean, rum can be light and soft, it can be golden, amber, or rich dark brown, and it can be full-bodied. Darkest of all is *Demerara* rum, made from sugar cane grown along the Demerara River in Guyana.

Rye: Whiskey distilled wholly or partly from rye mash. Its flavor is similar to bourbon, but many people find it smoother, more full bodied. *Rock and Rye* is rye flavored with rock candy, lemon, and orange.

Schnapps (also Snaps): A generic word meaning in Holland and Germany any strong dry colorless liquor such as gin, in Scandinavia (except Finland) aquavit, and in Finland vodka.

Scotch: A well-aged blend of grain and malt whiskies made in Scotland. The smoky flavor comes from the peat fires over which the malted barley is dried. Long a Scottish favorite, *Single-Malt Scotches* (straight malt whisky rather than the better-known blends containing 30–50 per cent malt whisky and 70–50 per cent grain whisky) have only recently become popular here. The best are aged 10–12 years and possess a deep smoky-peaty flavor.

Sour Mash: See Bourbon.

Southern Comfort: Bourbon mixed with peach liqueur and fresh, peeled, and pitted peaches, then aged several months. It is sweeter, mellower than bourbon but has a deceptive kick.

Straight Whiskey: Pure, unblended grain whiskey from 80 to 110 proof that has been aged at least two years. The term is usually used in conjunction with bourbon or rye.

Tequila: A colorless or pale yellow liquor, usually 100+ proof, distilled from the fermented juice of the agave cactus.

Vodka: Highly distilled, charcoal-filtered, colorless liquor made from fermented grain mash or potatoes. Vodka is unaged, flavorless, odorless and ranges from about 65 to 98 proof.

BRANDIES AND LIQUEURS

These are usually served after meals or used in mixing drinks.

Absinthe: A bitter licorice-flavored liqueur made with wormwood and herbs. Because of the harmful effects of wormwood, absinthe was banned in France in 1915 and subsequently by many other countries including the United States.

Advokaat: A creamy egg liqueur.

Amaretto: An extremely popular Italian cordial with a pronounced almond flavor that's extracted, oddly enough, from crushed apricot pits. There is also a *Chocolate Amaretto.*

Anesone: A smooth and dry, clear and colorless anise liqueur.

Anis: Clear anise (licorice) liqueur popular in France and Spain. It is mixed with water (which turns it milky) and drunk as an apéritif.

Anisette: Clear sweet liqueur aromatic of anise seeds; unlike anis, it is drunk neat as a cordial.

Applejack: The American version of apple brandy.

Apricot Liqueur: A liqueur made from apricots; syrupy and fragrant.

Armagnac: See Brandy.

B&B: A ½ and ½ mixture of Benedictine and brandy, available bottled.

Benedictine: A sweet, fruity, herby liqueur made originally by Benedictine monks at the abbey of Fécamp in France. Though laymen today make Benedictine, they carry on in the tradition of the monks, using their secret recipe.

Brandy: Technically, distilled wine or other fermented fruit juice, well aged, usually in wood. There are many brandies: *Cognac* (one of the choicest, made in Cognac, France), *Armagnac* (another fine dry French brandy, this one from Armagnac), *Calvados* (the fine apple brandy of Normandy), and *Marc* (or *Grappa),* distilled from the grape skins, pulp, and seeds left in the wine press after the juice has been drained off.

Chambord: A rich, intensely fruity black raspberry liqueur from the Burgundy Province of France.

Chartreuse: A brandy-based liqueur made by monks of the monastery of La Grande Chartreuse near Grenoble, France. Pale green or golden in color, it is flavored with hyssop, angelica, balm, cinnamon, and other herbs and spices.

Cherry Heering: A dark Danish cherry liqueur.

Cherry Suisse: A Swiss cherry-chocolate liqueur.

Cognac: See Brandy.

Cointreau: A choice French orange-flavored liqueur.

Cranberria: A ruby-hued American cordial made with ripe cranberries. Refreshingly tart.

Crème: Crème liqueurs have been sweetened, are thick and syrupy. The list of them is long, but among the better known are: *Crème d'Ananas* (pineapple), *Crème de Banane* (Banana), *Crème de Cacao* (chocolate), *Crème de Café* (coffee), *Crème de Cassis* (black currant), *Crème de Fraise* (strawberry), *Crème de Framboise* (raspberry), *Crème de Menthe* (mint—both a white and

green are available), *Crème de Roses* (rose), *Crème de Vanille* (vanilla) and *Crème de Violette* (violet). There is even now a *Crème de Grand Marnier* (orange). More popular than any of the French *crèmes,* however, is the family of *Irish creams,* almost cloyingly rich mixes of Irish whiskey, Irish cream, and assorted flavorings.

Cuarenta y Tres: Also called *43 Liqueur,* this orange-colored Spanish liqueur tastes strongly of vanilla.

Curaçao: An orange-flavored liqueur made on the Caribbean island of Curaçao from the dried rind of bitter (Seville) oranges.

Danziger Goldwasser: A German herb-and-orange-flavored liqueur adrift with flecks of gold leaf (they are harmless to drink).

Drambuie: Pale, amber scotch-based liqueur sweetened with heather honey and flavored with herbs.

Eau de Vie: "Water of life," a colorless, potent liqueur distilled from fermented fruit juices and/or skins and pits. If the fruit is the grape (as in Marc, see Brandy), the *eau de vie* is a brandy. If a fruit other than grape, it is technically not brandy. *Kirsch* and *framboise,* for example, are *eaux de vie* but not brandies.

Forbidden Fruit: An American brandy-based liqueur flavored with shaddock (a variety of grapefruit).

Fraise: A French *eau de vie* made from strawberries.

Framboise: A French *eau de vie* made from raspberries.

Frangelico: A hazelnut liqueur said to have been invented 300 years ago by an Italian monk.

Galliano: A spicy, golden Italian anisette liqueur.

Grand Marnier: A French cognac-based liqueur flavored with orange.

Grappa: An Italian *eau de vie* made from grape skins and seeds left in the wine press (see Brandy).

Irish Mist: A liqueur distilled from Irish whiskey and sweetened with heather honey.

Kahlúa: A syrupy Mexican liqueur made of coffee and cocoa beans.

Kirsch: A crisp, colorless cherry *eau de vie.* Also called *Kirchwasser.*

Kümmel: A colorless German liqueur aromatic of caraway seeds.

Lochan Ora: A scotch-whisky-based herbal liqueur the color of ripe grain.

Maraschino: An Italian wild cherry liqueur.

Marc: See Brandy.

Metaxa: A heavy, dark, sweet Greek brandy.

Midori: A light, green, melon liqueur from Japan that's honeydew sweet.

Mirabelle: A deliciously smooth and flowery *eau de vie* made from the golden mirabelle plums of Alsace.

Nocello: An Italian walnut liqueur (it's pronounced no-CHELL-o).

Ouzo: A clear licorice-flavored Greek brandy, mixed with water and drunk as an apéritif. Like anis, it turns cloudy when mixed with water.

Parfait Amour: A perfumy lavender liqueur.

Pernod: Yellow, licorice-flavored liqueur much like absinthe except that it contains no wormwood. Mixed with water, it is a favorite French apéritif.

Pisco: A Peruvian grape brandy.

Poire William: Clear, colorless pear *eau de vie,* the finest of which contains a ripe pear inside the bottle.

Prunelle: Brown, brandy-based French liqueur flavored with sloes (bitter plums).

Quetsch: An Alsatian *eau de vie* made of fermented purple plum juice.

Raki: A fiery anise-flavored spirit popular in Greece, Turkey, and the Middle East.

Ratafia: A fruit liqueur, often homemade.

Sabra: An orange-chocolate Israeli liqueur made from Jaffa oranges.

Sambuca Romana: An Italian anise (licorice) liqueur; not very sweet; often served with 3 crisp-roasted dark coffee beans in the bottom of the glass.

Slivovitz: A plum brandy made in Hungary and the Balkans.

Sloe Gin: A liqueur made by steeping sloes (small tart plums) in gin.

Strega: A flowery golden Italian liqueur.

Tia Maria: A heavy rum-based, coffee-flavored Jamaican liqueur.

Triple Sec: A clear, orange-flavored liqueur much like curaçao.

Vandermint: A Dutch chocolate-mint liqueur.

A MISCELLANY OF MIXERS AND ALCOHOLIC BEVERAGES

These do not fit neatly into any of the preceding categories, yet are commonly used today.

Falernum: Not really a liqueur but a colorless West Indian lime-almond-ginger syrup, about 6 per cent alcohol. It is used in mixing many "tropical" drinks.

Grenadine: Pink pomegranate syrup, sometimes containing alcohol.

Hard Cider: Fermented apple cider; it often has quite a kick.

Orgeat: A milky, sweet, nonalcoholic syrup used in such mixed drinks as mai tais.

Pimm's Cup: There are four Pimm's Cups, all cordial-like drink mixes, said to have been originated by a bartender at Pimm's Restaurant in London. Because of popular demand, the mixes were bottled. Pimm's No. 1 is a gin-based mix, No. 2 a whisky-based mix, No. 3 rum-based, and No. 4 brandy-based. All are commonly used in mixing cocktails.

Pulque: The fermented sap of the agave cactus and practically the national drink of Mexico. Pulque is thick, sweetish and looks rather like buttermilk.

Sake: People often call this Japanese fermented rice drink wine; technically, it isn't because wine is fermented grape juice. Sake is nearer beer because both are fermented grain drinks; however, sake's alcoholic content at 20 per cent is well above that of conventional beers. In Japan, sake is served warm in doll-size china cups, usually at the start of a meal. *Mirin* is another rice drink, similar to sake but sweeter. It is used more for cooking than drinking.

Vermouth: Vermouth is not so much wine as a wine-based drink, heavily infused with herbs. Dry vermouth is pale (the best comes from France), sweet vermouth is dark or light and usually Italian. Dry vermouth is integral to martinis, sweet vermouth to manhattans.

BITTERS

These are used in making cocktails, also taken as apéritifs, liqueurs, and medicine (many bitters are said to be good for digestion). Bitters are made of aromatic seeds, herbs, barks, and plants from carefully guarded recipes. Many have high alcoholic content, all are bitter or bittersweet.

Abbott's Aged Bitters: American bitters prepared for more than 100 years by the Abbott family in Baltimore.

Amer Picon: Popular French bitters.

Angostura: Probably the best known of all bitters, these were created by a German doctor in Trinidad.

Boonekamp: Famous Dutch bitters.

Campari: Italy's most popular bitters, drunk everywhere mixed with club soda (campari sodas are now bottled in Italy the way colas are here).

Fernet Branca: Another popular Italian bitters, this one heavy and dark and more often used for medicinal purposes than for mixing drinks.

Orange Bitters: Bitters made from the dried peel of Seville (bitter) oranges.

Unicum: Popular bitters made in Hungary.

MINERAL WATERS, SELTZERS, AND SODAS

Spring and spa waters are mineral-rich (usually in bicarbonates, sulfates, chlorides, calcium, magnesium, and/or iron). They may be pungent or bland, bubbly or still. Some are low in sodium or sodium-free, but check labels carefully if you are on a low-sodium diet.

Imported Mineral Waters: Among the best known are the French *Evian* (still, slightly sweet), *Perrier* (bland and bubbly), *Vichy* (effervescent), and Vittel (still, alkaline); the Italian *San Pellegrino* (bubbly but metallic, so better drunk than used as a mixer); and the German *Apollinaris* (naturally carbonated; wonderfully refreshing) and *Peters Val* (a sparkly water of good flavor from the Black Forest).

Domestic Mineral Waters: The major American mineral waters are: *Deer Park* (still, salt-free spring water from Pennsylvania), *Mountain Valley* (bracing, very low-salt mineral water from Hot Springs, Arkansas), and *Poland Spring* (a still, low-salt, neutral-tasting mineral water from Maine).

Club Sodas: Carbonic acid is what makes them fizzy. These may contain as much as 45 milligrams sodium per 6-ounce glass, but new *low-salt* or *no-salt-added* club sodas are also now widely available.

Seltzers: As bubbly as club soda but usually much lower in sodium (about 10 milligrams per 6-ounce glass). There are also *low-salt* and *no-salt-added* varieties.

How to Buy Wine and Liquor for a Party

It's usually wise to buy by the liter or magnum (you have more stock in fewer bottles and you may also be able to save a little money). If the party is small and you know your guests well, you probably also know what each drinks and can order accordingly. If a party is large, be guided by the drinking habits and fads in your area. In some communities, people prefer dry white wine to liquor; in others, people drink a great deal of scotch and gin but little else; in still others (the South, for example), people prefer bourbon. Order a good supply of the two or three popular liquors and wines, then also buy a few bottles of the next most popular—just in case. Here, then, is a guide to ordering.

Some Terms and Techniques of Drink Mixing

Bottled in Bond: This phrase is not a mark of quality in whiskey. It merely means that certain government regulations have been met, that the whiskey is at least four years old and 100 proof, that it was produced by a single distiller, and that it will be stored in a bonded warehouse until federal excise taxes have been paid by the distiller (this usually is done as the whiskey is ready to be shipped to the retailer).

Dash: A bar measure—6–8 drops.

Fifth: 4/5 of a quart or 25.6 fluid ounces. This measure is obsolete now that wines and spirits are sold in metric-size bottles. The nearest metric equivalent is the 750-milliliter bottle containing 25.4 fluid ounces.

Frost: To chill a glass until frost forms on the outside.

To Frost Rims of Glasses: Dip rims of glasses in lemon, lime, or orange juice or in lightly beaten egg white, then in sugar or salt to frost (salt for margaritas, sugar for most sweet fruit drinks), then let harden 3–4 minutes.

Jigger (or *Shot*): A bar measure—1½ ounces. A large jigger is 2 ounces.

Muddle: To mix together ingredients, lightly bruising and mashing with a pestlelike muddler.

PARTY DRINK CALCULATOR

No. of Guests	Approx. Drink Consumption	Liquor Needed
	For a Dinner Party	
4	8–12	1 (750-ml) bottle
6	12–18	1 (1-liter) bottle
8	16–24	1 (1.75-liter) bottle
12	24–36	2 (1-liter) bottles
20	40–60	3 (1-liter) bottles
40	80–120	4 (1.75-liter) bottles
	For a Cocktail Party	
4	12–16	1 (1-liter) bottle
6	18–24	2 (750-ml) bottles
8	24–32	2 (1-liter) bottles
12	36–48	2 (1.75-liter) bottles
20	60–80	3 (1.75-liter) bottles
40	120–160	5 (1.75-liter) bottles

Note: To be safe, substitute a liter wherever a (750-ml) bottle is called for. It's always good to have a little liquor on reserve.

Neat: A way of drinking liquor—in straight shots without ice.

On the Rocks: Descriptive term for a drink served with ice cubes.

Pony: A bar measure—1 ounce.

Proof: The measure of alcoholic content of liquor; in the U.S., proof is exactly twice the percentage of alcohol. Thus, something marked 100 proof is 50 per cent alcohol.

Shake: To blend by shaking vigorously in a covered shaker. Shaking produces a cloudy drink, stirring a clear one.

Standing: A term used to describe a cocktail served without ice.

Stir: To mix, using a long-handled spoon or stirring rod in a gentle circular motion. The purpose is to mingle ingredients, not to agitate them.

Twist: A twisted piece of lemon or orange rind, usually about 1½″ long and ¼″ wide. The technique is to twist the rind over the drink to extract the oil, then to drop the rind into the drink.

Up: A term used to describe a cocktail served without ice.

V.S.: An abbreviation often seen on liquor labels. It stands for *very superior*. Others are: *V.S.O. (very superior old), V.V.O. (very, very old),* and *V.V.S. (very, very superior).*

SANGRIA

8–10 servings

A Spanish wine and fruit drink, cooling on a hot summer day.

1 (750-ml) bottle dry red wine
1 orange
1 lemon or lime
½ (1-liter) bottle club soda
6–8 ice cubes
1 peeled, sliced peach or ⅓ cup stemmed ripe strawberries or ⅓ cup raspberries (optional)

Pour wine into a large pitcher. Using a vegetable peeler, peel rinds from orange and lemon in long spirals and add to wine; add juice from the orange and half the lemon. Stir in soda, add ice and the peach. Let stand 5 minutes, then serve in large wine goblets.

NPS (8–10): 90–70 C, 0 mg CH, 5–5 mg S*

ROYAL EGGNOG

36 servings

This recipe is a modern version of an old family favorite. In copper-plate script at the side was noted, "For cases of Exhaustion. If the case is not serious, half the quantity of brandy may be used. Give every *hour* in cases of extreme weakness!"

NUMBER OF 1½-OUNCE DRINKS IN:

Bottle Size	1 Bottle	2 Bottles	4 Bottles	6 Bottles	8 Bottles	10 Bottles
750 ml (25.4 fluid ounces, corresponds to the fifth)	16	33	67	101	135	169
1 liter (33.8 fluid ounces, corresponds to the quart)	22	45	90	135	180	225
1.75 liter (59.2 fluid ounces, corresponds to the half-gallon)	39	78	157	236	315	394

Note: When serving martinis or manhattans, allow 1 (750-ml) bottle of vermouth to 3 liters of liquor.

12 eggs, separated
1½ cups sugar
1 quart milk
1 (1-liter) bottle brandy or 1 (500-ml) bottle
each whiskey and brandy
1 quart light cream
¾ cup light rum (optional)
½ teaspoon nutmeg

Cover and refrigerate egg whites until needed; beat yolks until thick in a large bowl; add sugar, a little at a time, and beat until pale and fluffy. Slowly beat in milk, alternately with brandy; cover and chill 3–4 hours. About ½ hour before serving, take egg whites from refrigerator. Just before serving, beat yolk mixture well, add cream and, if you like, rum. Whip egg whites to soft peaks and fold into yolk mixture. Pour into a well-chilled punch bowl and sprinkle with nutmeg. *(Note:* So that eggnog will be fresh for late arrivals or "seconds," whip up only half of the egg whites and mix with half of the yolk mixture. Mix the remainder when needed.)

NPS: 195 C, 110 mg CH, 50 mg S*
NPS (with rum): 210 C, 110 mg CH, 50 mg S*

MICROWAVING BEVERAGES

Microwave ovens heat (and reheat) liquids zip-quick (a minute is about all it takes to make a cup of instant tea, coffee, or bouillon). Here are some points to bear in mind that apply specifically to beverages both alcoholic and nonalcoholic (also read carefully Microwave Ovens in Chapter 1).

• Use heatproof paper (not Styrofoam), glass, pottery, or china cups, mugs, pitchers, or punch bowls (not cut glass) devoid of metal trim.

• Heat water-based beverages uncovered on *HIGH.*

• Because microwaves exaggerate boiling in milk-based beverages, use *LOW* to *MEDIUM* setting and watch carefully.

• If your microwave has a *temperature probe,* use it to minimize risk of "boil-overs." Insert probe in middle of drink, and set as follows: at 125°–130° F. for "warm-to-drink," at 140° F. for milk-based beverages, and at 170°–180° F. for "steaming hot" coffees and teas.

• To keep beverages hot some minutes, use *temperature hold* setting with the *temperature probe*—130° F. for children's drinks, 165° F. for hot punches. *(Note:* Though you will use the microwave most often for nonalcoholic drinks, you may be interested to know that such spirited drinks as Glögg and Mulled Wine can be held at 165° F. without losing their punch.)

• When heating 4 or more cups of a beverage, arrange in a circle for even heating; rearrange midway, reversing the order. For large quantities, use 3- or 4-quart casseroles; stir beverage once or twice as it heats, let stand 1–2 minutes, stir again and serve.

• Never heat or defrost a liquid in a bottle or can; it may explode. To defrost frozen juice concentrates, spoon into a microwave-safe glass or pitcher, then microwave on *HIGH* about 1½ minutes until liquefied.

NONALCOHOLIC
BEVERAGES

COFFEE

When Islam spread through Arabia forbidding Moslems to drink alcoholic beverages, the faithful turned to something else with "kick." That something was coffee. The Arabs introduced coffee to the Turks, who glorified it with coffeehouses, then Turkish invaders carried coffee into Europe. Coffee came to the New World with the colonists; the first coffee plant was brought over by a Dutchman about fifty years later, and from it, the story goes, the Latin American coffee industry took root.

Today Central and South America are top coffee producers along with Indonesia (especially Java and Sumatra), Yemen, Kenya, Hawaii, and a number of Caribbean islands. Coffee varieties often take their names from the areas where they're grown—Colombian coffee, for example, Brazilian, Puerto Rican, Arabian Mocha, Blue Mountain Jamaican. Most brands are skillful blends because coffee made from a single variety is insipid; indeed, it takes many different coffees to produce rich, well-rounded flavor. It is possible, however, to buy beans of a particular variety —Mocha or Colombian—and have them ground or mixed to order. The best plan is to try a number of brands and blends until you hit upon the one you like.

About Roasts: If variety and blend determine the flavor of coffee, so, too, does the roast, which can vary from *light* and *cinnamon* through *medium, high, city,* and *French* to *Italian* (nearly black and the roast to use for demitasse and espresso). The darker the roast, incidentally, the less the caffeine.

About Grinds: Coffee can be bought in the bean, the best way to buy it if you have a coffee mill, because coffee stays fresh in the bean far longer than it does after being ground. Once ground—and exposed to the air—coffee stales fast. That's why it is best to buy only a pound at a time and to store in the refrigerator once the tin is opened. There are three grinds of coffee available today:

Regular Grind	Use for Percolators
Drip Grind	Use for Drip or Old-fashioned Coffeepots
Fine Grind	Use for Vacuum Coffee Makers (*Note:* Drip grind may also be used)

In addition, there is the powdery coffee used in making Turkish coffee, but it is available only at specialty food shops or Middle Eastern groceries and must be especially sought out.

About Decaffeinated Coffee: Caffeine is a stimulant that affects many people adversely, so it was inevitable that someone would discover a way of extracting most of the caffeine from coffee. Decaffeinated coffees are widely available in all standard grinds, also as instant coffee.

About Coffee with Chicory: Chicory—the same one used for salads—has a long brown root, which, when roasted and ground, can be brewed into a bitter dark drink. When Napoleon banned the importation of coffee, the French hit upon mixing their dwindling reserves with roasted chicory, and they do yet, though there is no shortage of coffee. Coffee with chicory is strong and bitter but popular still around New Orleans.

About Instant Coffees: In the beginning, these seemed feeble imitations of freshly brewed coffee. But research has perfected the process so that modern instant coffees are very good indeed. One of the advantages —in addition to instant cups of coffee—is that the powder or granules can be used in recipes as easily as cocoa. So popular have the instants become that there is now instant *espresso* not to mention such *flavored coffees* as *Café Française, Irish Creme, Amaretto,* and *Swiss Mocha.*

About Freeze-Dried Coffees: These are the best instant coffees because they taste remarkably like freshly brewed coffee. They are made by flash-freezing strong, fresh coffee, then drawing off the ice crystals by a special vacuum process that does not affect the flavor of the coffee as heat dehydrating does (this is the method used for conventional instants). Freeze-dried crystals can also be used in recipes if the mixture they're being added to is liquid or at least moist— the crystals dissolve on contact.

About Coffee Substitutes: These (Postum, to name one) are made of dark roasted cereals and are good for those unable to take any coffee at all. They are available as ground or instant types.

How to Make Coffee

In an Old-fashioned Pot: Measure coffee *(drip grind)* into pot, allowing 1 standard coffee measure or 2 level tablespoons for each serving, add cold water (3/4 cup for each 2 tablespoons coffee), and stir. Set over moderately high heat, cover, and when mixture bubbles up once, remove from heat and add 3–4 tablespoons cold water to settle grounds. Set pot over low heat and steep 5 minutes—do not allow to boil. To serve, pour through a very fine small strainer into cups.

In a Percolator: Measure cold water into pot, allowing 3/4 cup for each serving. Set percolator basket in place in pot, measure *regular grind* coffee into it, using 1 standard coffee measure or 2 level tablespoons for each 3/4 cup water. Cover with lid. Set pot over moderately high heat and, when coffee begins to perk (when it bubbles in glass lid dome) and turns pale amber, turn heat to moderately low and let coffee perk gently 6–8 minutes. Remove basket of grounds, stir coffee, and serve. Keep hot over low heat but do not let coffee boil.

In a Drip Pot:

Filter-Flask Type: Roll filter paper into a cone and stick into neck of flask. In a saucepan or teakettle, measure amount of cold water needed—3/4 cup for each serving—and bring to a boil over high heat. Meanwhile, measure *drip grind* coffee into filter cone, allowing 1 standard coffee measure or 2 level tablespoons for each 3/4 cup water. Set flask on a burner topped with an asbestos flame tamer, but do not turn burner on. When water boils, take from heat, let bubbling subside and pour over coffee grounds; stir once, then let drip through. Lift out paper of grounds, turn on burner heat (to low) and let coffee steep 1–2 minutes. Pour and serve.

Conventional Drip Pot: Measure amount of cold water needed—3/4 cup per serving—into a teakettle or saucepan and bring to a boil. Meanwhile, rinse coffeepot with scalding hot water. Fit basket into bottom part of pot and measure in *drip grind* coffee, allowing 1 standard coffee measure or 2 level tablespoons for each 3/4 cup water. Fit upper compartment over basket and set pot on a burner (not turned on). When water boils, take from heat, let bubbling subside, and pour into upper compartment, cover, and let water drip through. When about half of the water has dripped through, turn burner under pot to low. When all water has dripped through, lift off upper compartment and basket of grounds. Stir coffee, let mellow 1–2 minutes over low heat, then serve.

In a Vacuum-Style Coffee Maker: For each cup of coffee wanted, measure 3/4 cup cold water into lower compartment. Fit filter into upper bowl and measure in *fine or drip grind* coffee—1 standard coffee measure or 2 level tablespoons for each 3/4 cup water. Set pot over high heat and, when water comes to a full rolling boil, insert upper part of coffee maker into bottom, using a slight twist to ensure a tight seal. When water rises into top part, stir well and turn heat to low. Let brew bubble in top part 2–3 minutes, then remove coffee maker from heat (this creates a vacuum, causing coffee to plunge into lower part of coffee maker). When coffee has filtered back into lower part, lift off top part. Keep coffee hot over low heat.

In an Automatic Coffee Maker: Follow manufacturer's instructions closely, experimenting with the mild-strong control until you achieve the brew you like. *(Note:* For clearer, mellower coffee, wet the grounds basket with cold water before adding the coffee. This helps keep small bits from drifting through the basket.)

In an Espresso Pot: These aren't espresso pots (true espresso is made by passing steam under pressure over the coffee grounds) but Italian-style drip pots. But they make espresso-like coffee and are easy to use. For each serving use 6 tablespoons cold water (in a standard measuring cup, 6 tablespoons is midway between the 1/3 and 1/2 cup marks) and 1 standard coffee measure or 2 level tablespoons of *French or Italian roast drip grind* coffee. Place water in bottom part of pot, grounds in middle basket; fit all parts of pot together, cover and set over moderately high heat. When water comes to a full boil, turn pot upside down, turn heat off, and let coffee drip through. Serve in demitasse cups with a twist of lemon and, if you like, sugar. But never cream. To be really Italian, skip the lemon, too. *(Note:* Some housewares shops sell home-size steam-pressured espresso machines in 3-, 6-, and 9-cup sizes; use exactly as the manufacturer directs.)

HOW TO MAKE COFFEE FOR A CROWD

Number of Servings	Coffee Needed (Regular Grind)	Water Needed
20	1/2 pound	1 gallon
40	1 pound	2 gallons
60	1 1/2 pounds	3 gallons

Tie coffee in a muslin or cheesecloth bag large enough to hold at least twice the quantity you're using, drop into a kettle of just boiling water, reduce heat immediately so water no longer boils, and let stand 10–12 minutes. Plunge bag up and down several times, then remove. Keep coffee hot over low heat but do not allow to boil. *(Note:* If you're making coffee for more than 60, set up 2 kettles.) To clear coffee, add 1–2 eggshells to each kettle.

Quantity Instant Coffee: From 2 ounces instant coffee you can make 20 cups of coffee. Simply empty coffee powder or granules into a large kettle and for each 2 ounces add 1 gallon simmering water. Stir, let steep a few minutes, then serve. *Note:* Always add the hot water to the coffee, never the other way around.

Some Tips for Making Better Coffee

• Buy only a week's supply of coffee at a time and, once the can is opened, store tightly covered in the refrigerator.
• Do not mix any stale coffee with a freshly opened tin.
• If you buy coffee in the bean, grind it as you need it (and keep grinder spotless). Whole roasted beans will keep their flavor about one month.
• Use the proper grind of coffee for your coffee maker.
• Keep coffee maker spanking clean. This means washing after each use with soap and water, getting at spouts and crevices with a small bottle brush, rinsing well in hot water, and drying thoroughly. Occasionally pot may need to be scoured (though those with metal-plated insides should never be). If you prefer, remove stains and chemical deposits with one of the commercial preparations instead of the scouring pad.
• Store coffee maker unassembled so air can circulate.
• Measure coffee and water carefully, using 1 standard coffee measure or 2 level tablespoons for each ¾ cup water. *Note:* If you like really strong coffee, use 3 level tablespoons for each ¾ cup water; if you prefer it weak, use 2 scant tablespoons for each ¾ cup water.
• Always use cold water when making coffee; hot tap water tastes flat. Also use naturally soft (or chemically softened) water; hard water gives coffee an unpleasant metallic taste.
• Never allow coffee to boil—it becomes a bitter potion. The most desirable tempera-

ture for brewing coffee is between 185° F. and 205° F.
• Use a coffee maker of the right size for the amount of coffee you need. All coffee makers should be used to at least three fourths of their capacity, so if you often make small amounts, keep a special small pot for just that purpose.
• Remove coffee grounds from the coffee maker as soon as the coffee is brewed.
• Keep coffee hot until it is served. Reheated coffee tastes stale.
• Serve coffee as soon after making as possible; don't try to keep hot longer than one hour because coffee deteriorates rapidly on standing.

Some Variations on Coffee

Demitasse: This is simply extra-strong black coffee served in small (demi, or half-size) cups. To make, use one of the standard methods, substituting a dark *French* or *Italian* roast for the regular *or* increasing the amount of regular roast coffee to 3–4 level tablespoons per ¾ cup of water.

Iced Coffee: Brew demitasse using one of the basic methods. Fill tall glasses with ice and pour in hot demitasse. Or, if you prefer, brew regular strength coffee and cool. Serve over ice or, for stronger coffee, over coffee ice cubes (coffee frozen in ice cube trays).

Café au Lait: This is the traditional breakfast beverage throughout Europe. Brew demitasse by one of the basic methods. At the same time, heat an equal quantity of milk to scalding. Pour milk into a pitcher and fill cups by pouring the hot milk and coffee simultaneously and adding about equal amounts of each.

Viennese Coffee:

Hot: Brew strong coffee and mix with an equal quantity of hot milk or light cream. Pour into a tall glass, sweeten to taste, and top with a float of whipped cream.

Frosted: Brew strong coffee. Place a scoop of vanilla ice cream in a tall glass, slowly pour in coffee, top with whipped cream, and dust with confectioners' sugar.

Café Brûlot *(Makes 6 servings):* Here's a showy after-dinner drink. Place 6 sugar lumps, 8 cloves, a 1″ strip each of lemon and orange rind, and ⅓ cup cognac or Cointreau in a chafing dish but do not mix. Blaze cognac with a match, then stir. Add 1 quart very strong hot coffee, heat about 1 minute, ladle into cups, and serve.

CAPPUCCINO

4–6 servings ⚖

This popular Italian coffee drink is thought to have been named for Capuchin monks, who wear coffee-brown robes.

1 pint hot espresso
1 cup scalding hot milk
Cinnamon or nutmeg (optional)
4–6 sticks cinnamon (optional)

Beat espresso and milk in a heated bowl until frothy; pour into cups. *(Note:* The correct size is something between a demitasse and a regular coffee cup, but either of these will do just as well.) Sprinkle lightly with cinnamon, add cinnamon sticks for stirring, and serve. Set out the sugar bowl for those who want it.

NPS (4–6): 40–30 C, 10–5 mg CH, 30–20 mg S*

TEA

All teas can be divided into three groups: *black,* fermented teas, obtained principally from India, Sri Lanka (Ceylon), Taiwan, and Kenya; *green,* unfermented teas (most come from Japan and China); and *oolong,* semifermented teas from Taiwan.

Black Teas: Americans know these best. They produce fragrant, amber brews, the blend (most contain as many as 20 different teas) determining flavor; it may be brisk and strong, nutty, fruity, flowery, even winelike. Popular black teas include *Assam,* a robust tea from northeast India (when blended with Ceylon tea, it is called *Irish Breakfast Tea); Darjeeling,* from the Himalayas, more delicate and, some people insist, India's finest tea; *Earl Grey* (a full-bodied blend of Taiwan teas); *English Breakfast* (choice, mellow blend of India and Ceylon teas); *Lapsang Souchong* (a strong, smoky Taiwan tea); and *Sumatra* (an Indonesian tea commonly used in blends).

Black tea leaves are graded as to size. The largest are *souchong,* second largest *orange pekoe* or simply, *pekoe.* Smaller, cut or broken leaves are called *broken orange pekoe* or *broken pekoe souchong* (these make especially aromatic tea). *Fannings* are smaller still and used for tea bags.

Green Teas: These astringent yellow-green brews are beloved by Orientals. The four principal sizes are *gunpowder* (so called because, on drying, the tiny leaves roll into balls), *imperial* (slightly larger balls), *young hyson* (longer, twisted leaves), and *hyson* (the longest, most loosely twisted). Japanese green teas are *basket-fired* (dried in bamboo baskets over charcoal until deep olive brown), *pan-fired* (dried in iron pans over coals), or *natural leaf* (coarse leaves panfired for short periods of time). Basket-fired is considered choicest.

Oolong Teas: These semifermented teas combine the mellowness of black teas with the tang of the green; they make deceptively light-colored brews. *Formosa Oolong* is the mildest and most popular. *Note:* For an exceptionally good pot of tea, mix 1 teaspoon *Formosa Oolong* with your favorite black tea blend; if, for example, you need 6 teaspoons tea, use 1 teaspoon Formosa Oolong and 5 teaspoons black tea.

Scented Teas: Teas, particularly Oolong, are often mixed with dried flowers or herbs. Among the common blends are *Jasmine* and *Peppermint* teas.

Instant Teas: These are pulverized black teas mixed sometimes with malto-dextrin, which preserves their flavor. They are available plain or mixed with sugar and lemon and dissolve in both hot or cold water.

Tea-like Beverages:

Herbal Teas and Tisanes: When England taxed tea, colonial American women swore off it and began making infusions of raspberry leaves, sage, and a variety of other herbs, seeds, and flowers. Many of these tisanes remain popular today, and a number —comfrey, hyssop, peppermint, verbena, sassafras, linden, rose hips and camomile together with such modern blends as Red Zinger—can be bought as "tea bags."

Maté: Also known as Paraguay tea, these are the dried leaves of the young shoots of a variety of holly. They brew into a strangely smoky, oily drink that tastes a little like green tea.

Buying Tea

As with coffee, the best way to determine the tea you like best is to experiment, trying first one blend, then another. Most popular blends are available both by the half pound or pound as loose tea or in tea bags. Teas keep far better than coffee, but they should be stored tightly covered and far away from foods whose flavors they might absorb.

How to Make Tea

Hot Tea: Use a china, heatproof glass, or porcelain pot rather than a metal one (metal makes tea taste metallic). Scald the pot with boiling water. For each serving, use 3/4 cup water and 1 teaspoon *(not* measuring teaspoon) loose tea (or 1 tea bag). Place required quantity of water—*cold water*—in a saucepan or teakettle and bring to a full boil. Meanwhile, place tea in teapot. Pour boiling water directly over tea, let steep 3–5 minutes. Stir and serve with lemon, sugar, and, if you like, milk or cream. *Note:* Tea, like coffee, should never boil. If tea is too strong (color is less an indicator than flavor), simply weaken with additional boiling water.

VARIATIONS

Spiced Tea: Prepare as directed but add 6–8 cloves and a cinnamon stick to the teapot along with the tea.

Iced Tea: Prepare hot tea as directed but use 1 1/2 teaspoons tea to each 3/4 cup water. Pour hot tea into tall glasses filled with ice cubes. Add lemon and sugar to taste, sprig with mint, if you wish, and serve. *To Make a Pitcherful* (8–10 servings): Bring 1 quart cold water to a full boil in a large enamel or heatproof glass saucepan, remove from heat, add 1/3 cup loose tea (or 15 tea bags) and let steep 4–5 minutes. Stir well, then strain through a very fine sieve into a pitcher containing 1 quart ice water. Pour into tall glasses filled with ice. *Note:* If you refrigerate tea while it is still hot, it will cloud. To clear, stir in a little boiling water.

HOW TO MAKE HOT TEA FOR A CROWD

Number of Servings	Tea Needed	Water Needed
20	2 ounces (7 tablespoons) loose tea OR 20 tea bags	3 cups
40	1/4 pound (1 cup − 2 tablespoons) loose tea OR 40 tea bags	1 1/2 quarts
60	6 ounces (1 1/4 cups + 1 tablespoon) loose tea OR 60 tea bags	2 quarts + 1 cup

Bring water to a rolling boil in a saucepan (not aluminum). Remove from heat, add tea, stir, cover, and brew 5 minutes. Scald teapot and strain tea into pot. To serve: Pour about 2 tablespoons tea into each cup and fill with piping hot freshly boiled water, adjusting strength by varying amount of tea. *(Note:* For a quantity Tea Punch, see the Party Punch Chart.)

RUSSIAN-STYLE TEA

6 servings ⊴⊵

Russians serve tea in slim heatproof glasses instead of cups—a 6- to 8-ounce size is about right.

2 quarts boiling water (about)
8 teaspoons black tea (Indian or Ceylon)
Thinly sliced lemon
Strawberry or raspberry jam
Lump sugar

Have water boiling furiously and keep boiling throughout the tea service (use a samovar if you have one). Pour a little boiling water into a teapot to warm it, swish around, and pour out. Place tea in teapot, add 1 1/2 cups boiling water, cover, and let steep 3–5 minutes. Strain tea into a second warmed teapot and keep warm. To serve, pour about 1/4 cup tea into each glass and add boiling water to fill; adjust amount of tea according to strength desired. Pass lemon, jam, and sugar. *(Note:* Russians often stir a spoonful of jam into their tea or place a lump of sugar in their mouths and drink the tea through it.)

NPS: 30 C, 0 mg CH, 1.5 mg S*
Note: Sugar is not included.

Some Tips for Making Better Milk Drinks

• For richer flavor, use evaporated milk or a 1/2 and 1/2 mixture of evaporated and fresh milk (especially good in chocolate drinks).
• To reduce calories, use skim or reconstituted nonfat dry milk instead of whole milk—their calorie content is approximately half that of whole milk.
• To prevent "skin" from forming on hot milk or hot milk drinks, stir often with a wire whisk.
• Use a low heat for hot milk or chocolate drinks—both scorch easily.
• Never try to mix cocoa or cinnamon directly with milk or other liquid; blend first with an equal quantity of sugar.
• When combining milk and an acid fruit juice, slowly mix fruit juice into milk rather than vice versa—less chance of curdling.

Some Garnishes for Milk Drinks
(Choose garnishes compatible in flavor with the drink):
Dustings of cinnamon, cinnamon sugar, nutmeg, instant cocoa mix, or confectioners' sugar (all drinks)
Grated or shaved chocolate (for chocolate or mocha drinks)
Marshmallows (especially good for cocoa)

Whipped cream fluffs (all drinks)
Cinnamon stick stirrers (good with chocolate drinks)

SOME QUICK MILK DRINKS

Each makes 1 serving ☒

Pour 1¼ cups cold milk into a 12-ounce glass and blend in any of the following:

Chocolate Milk: 2–3 tablespoons chocolate syrup and ¼ teaspoon vanilla.

NPS: 280 C, 40 mg CH, 170 mg S*

Mocha Milk: 2 tablespoons chocolate syrup, 1 teaspoon instant coffee powder blended with 1 tablespoon tepid water and ¼ teaspoon vanilla.

NPS: 285 C, 40 mg CH, 170 mg S*

Vanilla Milk: 1 tablespoon superfine sugar and 1 teaspoon vanilla.

NPS: 250 C, 40 mg CH, 150 mg S*

Maple Milk: 3–4 tablespoons maple syrup.

NPS: 335 C, 40 mg CH, 155 mg S*

Milk and Honey: 3–4 tablespoons honey and a pinch nutmeg or mace.

NPS: 380 C, 40 mg CH, 150 mg S*

Molasses Milk: 3–4 tablespoons molasses.

NPS: 340 C, 40 mg CH, 160 mg S*

To Make Malted Milk: Prepare any of the Quick Milk Drinks as directed but add 2 tablespoons malted milk powder (plain or chocolate depending upon flavor of drink) and beat well. *(Note:* 2 tablespoons malted milk will increase total calories per serving by about 115 calories, cholesterol by 0 mg, sodium by 125 mg.)

SOME MILK SHAKES

Each makes 1 serving ☒

The electric blender whips up shakes best, but a rotary or portable electric mixer works fairly well. A milk shake becomes a "frosted" when ice cream is beaten in, a "float" when a scoopful is dropped in after beating.

Pour 1 cup cold milk into blender container and blend in any of the following:

Banana Milk Shake: 1 small very ripe peeled and well-mashed banana and ¼ teaspoon vanilla. Serve sprinkled with cinnamon or nutmeg.

NPS: 235 C, 35 mg CH, 120 mg S*

Berry Milk Shake: ⅓ cup puréed strawberries or raspberries, 3–4 tablespoons berry preserves and, if you like, 1–2 drops red food coloring.

NPS: 325 C, 35 mg CH, 125 mg S*

Chocolate Milk Shake: 2–3 tablespoons chocolate syrup.

NPS: 240 C, 35 mg CH, 140 mg S*

Coffee Milk Shake: 2 teaspoons each instant coffee powder and sugar.

NPS: 185 C, 35 mg CH, 120 mg S*

Mocha Milk Shake: 2 tablespoons chocolate syrup and 1 teaspoon each instant coffee powder and sugar.

NPS: 260 C, 35 mg CH, 140 mg S*

To Make Frosted Milk Shakes: Add 1–2 scoops of an appropriate ice cream to milk along with flavoring and blend until thick and creamy and no lumps of ice cream remain. *Note:* For each scoop of ice cream used, add 135 C, 30 mg CH, 60 mg S.*

To Make Malted Milk Shakes: Add 1–2 tablespoons malted milk powder to any milk shake recipe before blending, then blend as directed. *(Note:* Chocolate malted milk powder is especially good in the Chocolate, Coffee, and Mocha Milk Shakes.) For each tablespoon malted milk powder used, add 60 C, 0 mg CH, 65 mg S.*

BASIC ICE CREAM SODA

1 serving ☒

As good as the corner drugstore ever made.

¼ cup cold milk or light cream
2 scoops vanilla or any flavor ice cream
Chilled club soda (or ginger ale, cola, or other favorite carbonated drink)
Garnishes (optional): whipped cream, maraschino cherry

Pour milk into a 12-ounce glass, add 1 scoop ice cream, pour in a little soda, and stir briskly, mashing ice cream. Add second scoop of ice cream, fill with soda, stir again, and garnish. *Note:* For each tablespoon whipped cream used, increase the Basic Ice Cream Soda nutritional count by 20 C, 10 mg CH, 5 mg S; for each cherry add 5 C, 0 mg CH, 0 mg S.*

NPS (with milk): 305 C, 70 mg CH, 145 mg S*
NPS (with light cream): 385 C, 100 mg CH, 140 mg S*

Chocolate Ice Cream Soda: Mix milk with 2–3 tablespoons chocolate syrup, then proceed as directed, using chocolate or vanilla ice cream. *Note:* For each tablespoon chocolate syrup used, increase the Basic Ice Cream Soda nutritional count by 45 C, 0 mg CH, 10 mg S.*

Mocha Ice Cream Soda: Prepare Chocolate Ice Cream Soda but use coffee ice cream. Nutritional count is the same as for Chocolate Ice Cream Soda.

Coffee Ice Cream Soda: Mix milk and 1 teaspoon instant coffee powder, then proceed as directed, using coffee ice cream.

*NPS: 305 C, 70 mg CH, 145 mg S**

Strawberry or Raspberry Ice Cream Soda: Mix milk with 1/4 cup crushed strawberries or raspberries or 2–3 tablespoons strawberry or raspberry syrup and proceed as directed, using vanilla, strawberry, or raspberry ice cream. Garnish with a berry instead of cherry.

*NPS (with strawberries): 315 C, 70 mg CH, 145 mg S**
*NPS (with raspberries): 320 C, 70 mg CH, 145 mg S**
*NPS (with syrup): 405 C, 70 mg CH, 145 mg S**

HOT COCOA

1 serving   ¢ ▨

Inexpensive, easy, and good.

1 tablespoon cocoa
1 tablespoon sugar
Pinch salt
1/3 cup water
2/3 cup milk

Mix cocoa, sugar, and salt in a small saucepan, slowly stir in water. Heat and stir over moderately low heat until mixture boils, then boil slowly, stirring constantly, 2 minutes. Add milk and heat to scalding but do not boil.

*NPS: 160 C, 25 mg CH, 210 mg S**

Cocoa for a Crowd *(12 servings):* Mix 3/4 cup cocoa with 3/4 cup sugar and 1/2 teaspoon salt in a large saucepan. Gradually stir in 1 quart warm water, set over low heat, and heat, stirring now and then, 8–10 minutes. Add 2 quarts milk and heat to scalding. Serve in mugs, sprinkled, if you like, with cinnamon or nutmeg or topped with marshmallows.

*NPS: 160 C, 25 mg CH, 170 mg S**

Iced Cocoa: Prepare cocoa as directed, then cool, stirring occasionally. Pour over ice cubes, top with a dollop of whipped cream, and sprinkle with cinnamon.

*NPS: 160 C, 25 mg CH, 170 mg S**

OLD-FASHIONED HOT CHOCOLATE

4–6 servings

The kind Grandmother used to make—dark and rich.

2 (1-ounce) squares unsweetened chocolate
1 cup water
1/4 cup sugar
Pinch salt
3 cups milk
1/3 cup heavy cream

Heat and stir chocolate, water, sugar, and salt in the top of a double boiler over simmering water until chocolate melts. Slowly stir in milk and heat uncovered to serving temperature. Meanwhile, whip cream. Serve in mugs or cups topped with whipped cream.

*NPS (4–6): 300–200 C, 55–35 mg CH, 130–90 mg S**

Some Tips for Making Better Fruit Drinks

• Use freshly squeezed, unstrained juice whenever possible.
• Freeze some of the fruit juice or drink mixture to use as "ice cubes."
• When making punch in quantity, use a large ice block in punch bowl rather than crushed or cubed ice; it melts more slowly, waters the punch down less.
• For extra-tangy fruit drinks, add a little grated orange, lemon, or lime rind.
• When a recipe calls for both fruit juice and rind, grate the rind first.
• Try sweetening drinks with honey or light corn syrup instead of sugar—they dissolve more easily and make drinks mellower.
• For really sparkling drinks, add ginger ale or other carbonated beverage just before serving.
• Have drink ingredients well chilled before mixing together.
• Avoid putting tinted ice cubes in colorful fruit drinks that might gray the drinks as they melt.

• Avoid heavy, awkward garnishes that make beverages difficult to drink.

Some Garnishes for Fruit Drinks
(Choose those compatible in flavor with the drink):
Plain or fancily cut orange, lemon, or lime slices or wedges
Cocktail cherries, fresh cherries or berries
Pineapple chunks or melon balls
Fruit kebabs (grapes, cherries, melon balls, whole berries, or pineapple chunks threaded alternately on long wooden skewers)
Pineapple stick stirrers (simply, long, thin sticks of pineapple)
Cinnamon stick stirrers (for hot drinks)

SOME QUICK COOLERS

Each makes 1 serving ⊠

For best results, have fruit juices, ginger ale, club soda, colas, etc., well chilled.

Ginger-Grapefruit Cooler: Put 3–4 ice cubes in a 12-ounce glass, then fill, using equal quantities grapefruit juice (or pineapple, orange, tangerine, grape, or cranberry juice) and ginger ale. Sprig with mint and, if you like, add a slice of orange or lime.

NPS (with grapefruit juice): 105 C, 0 mg CH, 1 mg S*
NPS (with orange, grape, or pineapple juice): 115 C, 0 mg CH, 1 mg S*
NPS (with tangerine juice): 110 C, 0 mg CH, 1 mg S*
NPS (with cranberry juice): 135 C, 0 mg CH, 5 mg S*

Minted Apple-Lime Cooler: Bruise 2 mint leaves with 1/2 teaspoon sugar in a 12-ounce glass. Add apple juice or cider to half fill and mix well. Add 1 tablespoon lime juice and 2–3 ice cubes and mix again. Fill with ginger ale and add a wedge of lime.

NPS: 135 C, 0 mg CH, 10 mg S*

Cranberry Sparkle: Put 3–4 ice cubes in a 12-ounce glass, then fill, using equal quantities cranberry juice, lemonade, and club soda.

NPS: 95 C, 0 mg CH, 5 mg S*

⊲⊳ **Orange-Tea Cooler:** Mix 2 teaspoons instant tea powder with 1/2 cup orange juice in a 12-ounce glass. Add 2 ice cubes and fill with club soda or ginger ale. Sprig with mint.

NPS: 60 C, 0 mg CH, 5 mg S*

Wine Cooler: Half fill a 12-ounce glass with crushed ice, then fill with equal quantities sweet or dry red or white wine and ginger ale or club soda.

NPS: 100 C, 0 mg CH, 5 mg S*
NPS (with club soda): 75 C, 0 mg CH, 5 mg S*

EASY LEMONADE MIX

1 1/2 quarts, enough for 2 dozen glasses of lemonade ⊠

A handy mix to have on hand in the refrigerator (also handy to have on long car trips). Whenever anyone wants a glass of lemonade, all he or she has to do is add water and ice and stir.

1 quart lemon juice
1 cup sugar
2 cups light corn syrup

Stir all ingredients together until sugar dissolves. Pour into screw-top jar, cover, and store in refrigerator. To serve, shake well and pour 1/4 cup mix into a 12-ounce glass, add ice, fill with water or club soda, and stir well. *Note:* This mix keeps well several weeks. To make in a pitcher, allow 1/4 cup mix to 1 cup ice water.

NPS: 120 C, 0 mg CH, 30 mg S*

V A R I A T I O N S

⊠ **Easy Limeade Mix:** Substitute 1 quart lime juice for lemon juice; if you like, add a few drops green food coloring.

NPS: 120 C, 0 mg CH, 25 mg S*

⊠ **Easy Orangeade Mix** *(12 servings):* Substitute 1 quart freshly squeezed orange juice for lemon juice, omit sugar, and reduce corn syrup to 1 1/2 cups; proceed as directed but use 1/2 cup mix per serving.

NPS: 155 C, 0 mg CH, 30 mg S*

⊠ **Easy Pink Lemonade:** Prepare Easy Lemonade Mix and add 3/4 cup grenadine syrup; if you like, add a few drops red food coloring. Use 1/4 cup mix per serving. *(Note:* Cranberry juice gives a nice color, too, but makes a tarter drink: Mix 1 quart cranberry juice with the Easy Lemonade Mix and use 1/2 cup mix per serving.)

NPS: 145 C, 0 mg CH, 30 mg S*
NPS (with cranberry juice): 115 C, 0 mg CH, 25 mg S*

⊠ **Easy Grape Lemonade:** Pour 1/2 cup Easy Lemonade Mix into an ice-filled 12-ounce glass, fill with grape juice, and stir well.

NPS: 320 C, 0 mg CH, 60 mg S*

CRANBERRY SHRUB

8 servings

Shrubs are a colonial holdover. Originally spiked with rum or brandy, they are today an acid fruit juice served on the rocks or mixed with water or club soda. They make refreshing apéritifs, especially if served with scoops of tart sherbet.

1 quart cranberry juice
2 cups sugar
Rind of 1 lemon (cut in thin strips)
1/2 cup white vinegar or 2/3 cup lemon juice
1 (1-liter) bottle club soda (optional)
1 pint tart fruit ice or sherbet (optional)

Simmer cranberry juice, sugar, and rind, uncovered, in a saucepan (not aluminum) 10 minutes, stirring now and then. Off heat, mix in vinegar; cool, pour into a bottle, cover, and refrigerate. Serve as is on the rocks in punch cups or small glasses. Or half fill a tall glass with shrub, add ice, and fill with water or club soda. Or pour into punch cups and top each serving with a scoop of tart fruit ice.

NPS (without fruit ice or sherbet): 270 C, 0 mg CH, 5 mg S*
NPS (with fruit ice): 330 C, 0 mg CH, 5 mg S*
NPS (with sherbet): 335 C, 5 mg CH, 30 mg S*

VARIATIONS

Raspberry or Blackberry Shrub: Crush 2 quarts ripe berries with 2 cups sugar, cover, and let stand overnight. Press through a cheesecloth-lined sieve, extracting as much juice as possible. Omit lemon rind but mix in vinegar. Taste for sweetness and, if too tart, add a bit more sugar, stirring until dissolved. Store and serve as directed.

NPS (without fruit ice): 250 C, 0 mg CH, .5 mg S*
NPS (with fruit ice): 315 C, 0 mg CH, .5 mg S*

Spiked Shrub: Prepare any of the 3 shrubs as directed, omitting sherbet; mix in 3 cups light rum or brandy. Pour into bottles, cover, and store in a cool place at least 1 week before serving. Serve as is over crushed ice or mixed 1/2 and 1/2 with club soda in tall glasses with plenty of ice. Makes 16 servings.

NPS (cranberry): 240 C, 0 mg CH, 5 mg S*
NPS (raspberry or blackberry): 235 C, 0 mg CH, .5 mg S*

TOMATO COCKTAIL

4 servings　⚖ ☒

1 pint tomato juice
2 tablespoons lemon juice
1 tablespoon sugar

1 tablespoon minced yellow onion
1 bay leaf, crumbled
Pinch pepper

Mix all ingredients, cover, and chill 1–2 hours. Strain and serve in juice glasses.

NPS: 40 C, 0 mg CH, 245 mg S*

VARIATIONS

⚖ ☒ **Tomato-Celery Cocktail:** Prepare as directed but add 1/2 cup diced celery and substitute 1 tablespoon cider vinegar for 1 tablespoon of the lemon juice.

NPS: 40 C, 0 mg CH, 260 mg S*

⚖ ☒ **Spicy Tomato Cocktail:** Prepare as directed but add 1 teaspoon prepared horseradish, 1 crushed clove garlic, 1/2 teaspoon Worcestershire sauce and substitute minced scallions for yellow onion.

NPS: 40 C, 0 mg CH, 255 mg S*

⚖ ☒ **Tomato Bouillon** *(4–6 servings):* Prepare as directed but omit lemon juice and sugar and add 1 cup beef broth or consommé and 1/2 teaspoon Worcestershire sauce. Serve on the rocks in small old-fashioned glasses.

NPS (4–6): 30–20 C, 0 mg CH, 445–300 mg S*

⚖ ☒ **Tomato-Clam Cocktail** *(8 servings):* Prepare as directed, then mix in 2 (8-ounce) bottles clam juice and 3–4 dashes liquid hot red pepper seasoning.

NPS: 30 C, 5 mg CH, 365 mg S*

SOME EASY APPETIZER BEVERAGES

Serve in 4- to 6-ounce glasses on small plates lined with paper coasters. Suitably garnished, these can substitute for appetizer or soup courses. Pass them around before the meal or serve at the table. The following recipes all make 4 servings.

☒ ⚖ **Clam Juice on the Rocks:** Mix 2 cups chilled clam juice with 2 tablespoons lemon juice, 1 tablespoon minced chives, 1 teaspoon Worcestershire sauce, and 2–3 drops liquid hot red pepper seasoning. If you like, add 1/4 cup light cream and 1/8 teaspoon garlic salt. Serve on the rocks.

NPS: 25 C, 10 mg CH, 495 mg S*

☒ ⚖ **Clam Chickee:** Mix 1 cup each chilled clam juice and chicken broth. Season to taste with celery salt and top each serving with a dollop of sour cream; sprinkle with salt and paprika.

Substitute madrilène for chicken broth.

NPS: 20 C, 5 mg CH, 435 mg S*

⊠ ⚖ **Sauerkraut Juice Cocktail:** Mix 2 cups chilled sauerkraut juice with 2 tablespoons lemon juice, 1/2 teaspoon prepared horseradish, and 1/4 teaspoon bruised caraway seeds.

NPS: 15 C, 0 mg CH, 955 mg S*

Or use 1 cup each sauerkraut juice and tomato juice. Serve with a slice of lemon.

NPS (with tomato juice): 20 C, 0 mg CH, 600 mg S*

⊠ ⚖ **Bullseye:** Mix 1 (10½-ounce) can chilled condensed beef bouillon and 1 cup chilled tomato-vegetable juice; serve with a twist of lemon peel.

NPS: 25 C, 0 mg CH, 820 mg S*

SOME DECORATIVE ICES AND ICE RINGS FOR PUNCH BOWLS

Note: Chilled, boiled water makes clearer ice than water straight out of the tap. To unmold decorative ice blocks, dip in hot—not boiling—water. Boiling water may crack the block.

Float: Half fill a metal loaf pan, metal bowl, decorative gelatin or ring mold with cold boiled water; freeze solid. Arrange washed strawberries, pineapple chunks or rings, black and/or green grapes, melon balls, lemon, lime, or orange slices, drained maraschino cherries on ice in a decorative pattern; add 1/4″ cold boiled water and freeze. Fill mold with cold boiled water and freeze. Unmold and float in punch bowl.

Christmas Wreath: Arrange 1 dozen each red and green maraschino cherries and a few mint leaves in a decorative pattern in the bottom of a 5-cup ring mold. Carefully pour in 1″ cold boiled water and freeze solid. Fill with cold boiled water and freeze. Unmold and float in punch bowl.

Wedding Ring: Pour 1″ cold boiled water in any large ring mold and freeze solid. Arrange rinsed sweetheart roses close together on ice, add 1/2″ cold boiled water, and freeze. Fill ring with more water and freeze. Unmold and float in Champagne Punch.

Ice Bowl: Half fill a 3-quart metal bowl with cold boiled water; set a 1-quart metal bowl inside larger bowl, weighting down so it will stay in center; freeze solid. Remove weights from small bowl, fill with hot water, then lift small bowl out. Unmold ice bowl by dipping large bowl in hot water, float right-side-up in punch bowl and fill with fresh flowers or fruit. *(Note:* Ice bowl can also be set in a deep platter and used as a container for ice cream or fruit desserts. It can be made ahead of time and stored in the freezer.)

Party Ice Cubes: Half fill ice cube trays with cold boiled water; freeze solid. Into each cube, place a cherry, berry, wedge of pineapple, lemon, lime, or orange, or a mint leaf. Fill with cold boiled water and freeze. *(Note:* Water can be tinted with food coloring, a colorful fruit liqueur, maraschino or cranberry juice, but it will color the punch as it melts.)

Iced Fruits: Rinse and dry any pretty chunky fruits and freeze solid on foil-lined baking sheets. *(Note:* Frozen cherries and grapes tend to sink to the bottom of a punch bowl; berries, pineapple rings, peach halves, citrus slices, and melon balls float.) To use iced fruits, simply peel off foil and drop into punch bowl. They will keep punch cool without diluting it.

PARTY PUNCH CHART

Note: Not only are all wines and distilled spirits now sold in metric-size bottles but also many sodas and mixers. To save space in the charts below, we use the abbreviation "ml" for the metric measure milliliter. Whenever possible, buy punch ingredients in large containers: 3- or 4-liter jugs of wine, 1.5-liter bottles (magnums), or 3-liter bottles (jeroboams) of champagne, and institution-size cans of fruit juice. You may have to order ahead, but you'll save money. Unless you have use of an institutional kitchen and its giant kettles, do not try to mix punch for 100 at one time; make 2 batches for 50 or, if necessary, 4–5 batches for 2 dozen (especially important if a mixture must be heated). All servings are 4 ounces.

NONALCOHOLIC PUNCHES	*Quantities for:*			
	1 Dozen	*2 Dozen*	*50 People*	*100 People*
Autumn Apple Punch	*Calories per serving: 55*			
Apple juice	1½ quarts	3 quarts	1½ gallons	3 gallons
Cinnamon sticks	2	4	8	16
Whole cloves	8	1 dozen	1½ dozen	2 dozen
Pineapple juice	1⅓ cups	1½ pints	1½ quarts	3 quarts
Lemon juice	½ cup	1 cup	1 pint	1 quart
Orange juice	1 pint	1 quart	2 quarts	1 gallon
Ginger ale	1 (1-liter) bottle	1 (2-liter) bottle	3½ (1-liter) bottles	7 (1-liter) bottles

Place 1–2 quarts apple juice in a large kettle (not aluminum); tie spices in cheesecloth, add to kettle, and simmer uncovered 15 minutes; discard spice bag. Mix spiced juice with remaining fruit juices. To serve, place a large block of ice in a large punch bowl, add fruit juice and ginger ale. *(Note:* For large quantities, mix batches as needed, using 1 [1-liter] bottle ginger ale to each 2½ quarts fruit juice mixture.)

Hot Party Mocha	*Calories per serving: 180*			
Unsweetened chocolate	4 ounces	½ pound	1 pound	2 pounds
Sugar	1 cup	1 pound	2 pounds	4 pounds
Water	½ cup	1 cup	1 pint	1 quart
Instant coffee powder	2 teaspoons	4 teaspoons	8 teaspoons	⅓ cup
Cinnamon	¼ teaspoon	½ teaspoon	1 teaspoon	2 teaspoons
Heavy cream	½ cup	1 cup	1 pint	1 quart
Scalding hot milk	2½ quarts	5 quarts	2½ gallons	5 gallons

Heat and stir chocolate, sugar, water, coffee, and cinnamon in a heavy saucepan over low heat until chocolate melts; cover and cool. Beat cream to soft peaks and fold into chocolate mixture. To serve, pour chocolate mixture into a large silver punch bowl, add hot milk, and stir to mix. *(Note:* For large quantities, mix chocolate mixture and hot milk as needed to fill punch bowl, allowing about 1¼ cups chocolate mixture to 2½ quarts milk.)

Hot Spicy Grape Juice	*Calories per serving: 75*			
Oranges	1	2	4	8
Whole nutmegs, cracked	2	3	5	8
Whole cloves	1 dozen	1½ dozen	2 dozen	3 dozen
Cinnamon sticks	2	4	8	16
Grape juice	2 quarts	1 gallon	2 gallons	4 gallons
Boiling water	1 quart	2 quarts	1 gallon	2 gallons
Lemon juice	½ cup	1 cup	1 pint	1 quart
Sugar	1 cup	1 pound	2 pounds	4 pounds

With a vegetable peeler, cut rind from oranges in long strips; tie in cheesecloth with spices; save oranges to use another time. Place spices and remaining ingredients in a very large heavy kettle (not aluminum) and simmer, uncovered, stirring occasionally 10–15 minutes; discard spice bag. Serve hot from a large silver punch bowl.

PARTY PUNCH CHART (continued)

	1 Dozen	*2 Dozen*	*50 People*	*100 People*
		Quantities for:		

Hot Spiced Cider — *Calories per serving: 115*

	1 Dozen	*2 Dozen*	*50 People*	*100 People*
Apple cider	3 quarts	1½ gallons	3 gallons	6 gallons
Light brown sugar	1 pound	2 pounds	4 pounds	8 pounds
Cinnamon sticks	3	6	1 dozen	2 dozen
Whole cloves	1 dozen	1½ dozen	2 dozen	3 dozen

Place cider and sugar in a large kettle (not aluminum); tie spices in cheesecloth, add, and simmer uncovered 15 minutes; discard spice bag. Serve from a silver punch bowl or large coffee or teapot.

Jubilee Punch — *Calories per serving: 65*

Orange juice	1½ quarts	3 quarts	1½ gallons	3 gallons
Lemon juice	1½ cups	3 cups	1½ quarts	3 quarts
Maraschino cherries (and liquid)	⅓ cup	⅔ cup	1½ cups	3 cups
Sparkling white grape juice	2½ (750-ml) bottles	5⅓ (750-ml) bottles	10½ (750-ml) bottles	21 (750-ml) bottles

Mix orange and lemon juice with cherries. To serve, place a large block of ice in a large punch bowl, add fruit mixture, then pour in grape juice. (*Note:* For large quantities, mix batches as needed, using about equal quantities fruit mixture and grape juice.)

Lemonade or Limeade — *Calories per serving: 90*

Sugar	3 cups	3 pounds	6 pounds	12 pounds
Water	2½ quarts	5 quarts	2½ gallons	5 gallons
Lemon or lime juice	3 cups	1½ quarts	3 quarts	1½ gallons

Heat sugar and water in a large kettle (not aluminum), stirring until sugar dissolves; cool, and mix in lemon juice. To serve, place a large block of ice in a large punch bowl and pour in lemonade.

Pineapple-Raspberry Cream Punch — *Calories per serving: 95*

Pineapple juice	1 quart	2 quarts	1 gallon	2 gallons
Ginger ale	1 (2-liter) bottle	2 (2-liter) bottles	7 (1-liter) bottles	13 (1-liter) bottles
Vanilla ice cream	1 quart	2 quarts	1 gallon	2 gallons
Raspberry sherbet	1 quart	2 quarts	1 gallon	2 gallons

Pour pineapple juice and ginger ale over ice cream and sherbet and stir until melted and blended.

Tea Punch — *Calories per serving: 50*

Superfine sugar	1 cup	1 pound	2 pounds	4 pounds
Oranges, sliced	2	4	8	16
Lemons, sliced	6	9	1 dozen	1½ dozen
Hot strong tea	1 quart	2 quarts	1 gallon	2 gallons
Boiling water	1 quart	2 quarts	1 gallon	2 gallons
Ginger ale	1 (2-liter) bottle	2 (2-liter) bottles	7 (1-liter) bottles	13 (1-liter) bottles

Place all but last ingredient in a large, heavy kettle (not aluminum) and stir, bruising fruit slightly, until sugar dissolves; cover and cool 1–2 hours. To serve, place a large block of ice in a large punch bowl, then fill, adding about equal quantities tea mixture and ginger ale.

	Quantities for:			
	1 Dozen	*2 Dozen*	*50 People*	*100 People*

Three Fruit Punch   *Calories per serving: 60*

	1 Dozen	*2 Dozen*	*50 People*	*100 People*
Superfine sugar	1/3 cup	2/3 cup	11/3 cups	22/3 cups
Grapefruit juice	11/2 cups	3 cups	11/2 quarts	3 quarts
Orange juice	11/2 cups	3 cups	11/2 quarts	3 quarts
Apricot or peach nectar	2 quarts	1 gallon	2 gallons	4 gallons
Finely grated orange rind	11/2 teaspoons	1 tablespoon	2 tablespoons	1/4 cup
Club soda	1 (1-liter) bottle	1 (2-liter) bottle	31/2 (1-liter) bottles	7 (1-liter) bottles
Oranges, sliced (garnish)	1	1	2	3

Place sugar and grapefruit juice in a large kettle (not aluminum) and stir until sugar dissolves. *(Note:* For large quantities, you may need to heat slightly; do not boil; cool to room temperature.) Mix in all but last 2 ingredients. To serve, place a large block of ice in a large punch bowl, then fill, adding 1 bottle club soda for each 23/4 quarts fruit juice mixture. Float orange slices on top and replenish, as needed, with fresh slices.

ALCOHOLIC PUNCHES

Champagne Punch   *Calories per serving: 90*

	1 Dozen	*2 Dozen*	*50 People*	*100 People*
Lemon juice	2/3 cup	11/3 cups	21/2 cups	1 quart
Superfine sugar	1/3 cup	2/3 cup	11/4 cups	1 pound
Cranberry juice	3 cups	11/2 quarts	3 quarts	11/2 gallons
Champagne	3 (750-ml) bottles	3 (1.5-liter) bottles	6 (1.5-liter) bottles	12 (1.5-liter) bottles
Ginger ale	1 (1-liter) bottle	1 (2-liter) bottle	31/2 (1-liter) bottles	7 (1-liter) bottles
Brandy (optional)	1/2 cup	1 cup	1 (500-ml) bottle	1 (1-liter) bottle

Stir lemon juice and sugar together in a large kettle (not aluminum) until sugar dissolves. *(Note:* For large quantities, you may need to heat gently to dissolve sugar; do not boil; cool to room temperature.) Mix in cranberry juice. To serve, place a large block of ice or decorative ice ring* in a large punch bowl; add fruit juice mixture, champagne, ginger ale, and, if you like, brandy; mix gently. *(Note:* For large amounts, mix in batches as needed, using 2 quarts fruit juice mixture to 4 bottles champagne, 2 bottles ginger ale, and 1 cup brandy.) Calorie count does not include brandy.

Claret Cup   *Calories per serving: 60*

	1 Dozen	*2 Dozen*	*50 People*	*100 People*
Red Bordeaux wine	3 (750-ml) bottles	6 (750-ml) bottles	12 (750-ml) bottles	24 (750-ml) bottles
Superfine sugar	3/4 cup	11/2 cups	3 cups	3 pounds
Nutmeg	1/2 teaspoon	1 teaspoon	11/2 teaspoons	1 tablespoon
Maraschino liqueur	1/4 cup	1/2 cup	1 cup	2 cups
Club soda	21/2 (1-liter) bottles	5 (1-liter) bottles	5 (2-liter) bottles	10 (2-liter) bottles
Unpeeled cucumber, sliced thin	1 small	1 large	2 large	3 large
Borage sprigs (optional garnish)	3–4	5–6	8–10	12–15

Stir wine and sugar together in a large punch bowl until sugar dissolves. *(Note:* For very large quantities, heat 1–2 bottles wine with sugar, stirring constantly, in a large saucepan [not aluminum] until sugar dissolves; do not boil; cool completely.) Mix nutmeg and maraschino liqueur into wine mixture. To

	Quantities for:			
	1 Dozen	*2 Dozen*	*50 People*	*100 People*

serve, place a large block of ice in a large punch bowl and fill by pouring in equal quantities wine mixture and club soda; stir lightly. Float cucumber slices on top and, if you like, sprig with borage. Replenish cucumber and borage as needed.

Fish House Punch	*Calories per serving: 275*			
Superfine sugar	1½ cups	3 cups	3 pounds	6 pounds
Water	1 cup	1 pint	1 quart	2 quarts
Lemon juice	1 quart	2 quarts	1 gallon	2 gallons
Dark Jamaican rum	2 (1-liter) bottles	4 (1-liter) bottles	4⅓ (1.75-liter) bottles	8¾ (1.75-liter) bottles
Brandy	1 (1-liter) bottle	2 (1-liter) bottles	4 (1-liter) bottles	4⅓ (1.75-liter) bottles
Peach brandy	½ cup	1 cup	1 (500-ml) bottle	1 (1-liter) bottle

Heat and stir sugar and water in a large saucepan over moderate heat until sugar dissolves; cool to room temperature. Mix sugar syrup with remaining ingredients in a large punch bowl and let "ripen" at room temperature 2 hours. Add a large block of ice and let stand ½ hour longer. Mix gently and serve. (*Note:* For large quantities [for 50 or 100], mix in batches for 2 dozen and omit ripening time.)

Glögg	*Calories per serving: 255*			
Oranges	1	2	4	8
Whole cloves	8	16	2 dozen	3 dozen
Cardamom seeds	1 tablespoon	2 tablespoons	¼ cup	½ cup
Cinnamon sticks	2	4	8	16
Water	1 pint	1 quart	2 quarts	1 gallon
Sugar	1 cup	1 pound	2 pounds	4 pounds
Seedless raisins	1 cup	2 cups	1 pound	1½ pounds
Whole blanched almonds	1 cup	2 cups	1 pound	1½ pounds
Dry port or red Bordeaux wine	2 (750-ml) bottles	4 (750-ml) bottles	8 (750-ml) bottles	16 (750-ml) bottles
Aquavit or vodka	2 (750-ml) bottles	3 (1-liter) bottles	3¼ (1.75-liter) bottles	6½ (1.75-liter) bottles

With a vegetable peeler, cut rind from oranges in long strips; tie in cheesecloth with spices; save oranges to use another time. Place spice bag in a large kettle (not aluminum), add water and sugar, and simmer uncovered, stirring until sugar is dissolved, 5–10 minutes. Add raisins and almonds and simmer 3–5 minutes; cool slightly, mix in wine and aquavit, then cool, cover, and store overnight. To serve, remove spice bag and heat glögg to steaming, but not boiling. Pour into a large silver punch bowl and ladle into mugs or heatproof punch cups, adding a few raisins and almonds to each serving.

Mulled Wine	*Calories per serving: 100*			
Whole cloves	1 dozen	1½ dozen	2 dozen	3 dozen
Cinnamon sticks	4	8	16	2½ dozen
Water	3 cups	1½ quarts	3 quarts	1½ gallons
Sugar	1 cup	1 pound	2 pounds	4 pounds
Lemons, sliced thin	2	4	8	16
Red Bordeaux, Burgundy, or other dry red wine	3 (750-ml) bottles	6 (750-ml) bottles	3 (3-liter) bottles	6 (3-liter) bottles

Tie spices in cheesecloth, place in a large kettle (not aluminum), add water and sugar, and simmer uncovered 10 minutes, stirring now and then. Add lemons, bruise slightly, and let stand off heat 10

	Quantities for:			
	1 Dozen	*2 Dozen*	*50 People*	*100 People*

minutes. Add wine and slowly bring to a simmer; do not boil. Pour into a large silver punch bowl or ladle into heatproof mugs.

Orange Blossom Cup — *Calories per serving: 170*

Orange juice	1 quart	2 quarts	1 gallon	2 gallons
Rhine, Moselle, or Riesling wine	1 (1.5-liter) bottle	1 (3-liter) bottle	2 (3-liter) bottles	4 (3-liter) bottles
Light rum	1 (1-liter) bottle	2 (1-liter) bottles	4 (1-liter) bottles	4 1/3 (1.75-liter) bottles
Superfine sugar (optional)	1/4 cup	1/2–1/3 cup	1 cup	1 pound
Oranges, sliced thin	1	2	3	4

Mix juice, wine, and rum; taste and add sugar if needed. *(Note: If quantities are large, you may have to heat mixture slightly so sugar will dissolve. Cool well.)* To serve, place a large block of ice in a large punch bowl, pour in punch, and float orange slices on top, replenishing them as needed.

Party Daiquiris — *Calories per serving: 205*

Cracked ice	3 cups	1 1/2 quarts	3 quarts	1 1/2 gallons
Frozen limeade or lemonade concentrate or frozen daiquiri mix	1 (6-ounce) can	2 (6-ounce) cans	4 (6-ounce) cans	8 (6-ounce) cans
White or light rum	1 (750-ml) bottle	2 (750-ml) bottles	3 (1-liter) bottles	3 1/2 (1.75-liter) bottles

(Note: Make in batches for 1 dozen.*)* Place all ingredients in a 1/2-gallon jar that has a tight-fitting lid (mayonnaise jars are good) and shake vigorously about 1/2 minute until frothy. Strain into cocktail glasses and serve at once.

Party Milk Punch — *Calories per serving: 120*

Superfine sugar	1/4 cup	1/2 cup	1 cup	1 pound
Bourbon, rye or blended whiskey	1 (500-ml) bottle	1 (1-liter) bottle	2 (1-liter) bottles	4 (1-liter) bottles
Ice cold milk	3 1/2 quarts	7 quarts	3 1/2 gallons	7 gallons
Nutmeg	1/4 teaspoon	1/4 teaspoon	1/2 teaspoon	3/4 teaspoon

Mix all but last ingredient in a large kettle, ladle over an ice block in a large punch bowl, and sprinkle with nutmeg.

Quick Party Eggnog — *Calories per serving: 250*

Chilled eggnog mix	2 quarts	4 quarts	8 quarts	16 quarts
Light rum	1 (750-ml) bottle	2 (750-ml) bottles	3 (1-liter) bottles	3 (1.75-liter) bottles
Heavy cream	1 pint	1 quart	2 quarts	4 quarts
Nutmeg	1/4 teaspoon	1/4 teaspoon	1/2 teaspoon	3/4 teaspoon

Mix eggnog and rum; whip cream to soft peaks and fold in; cover and chill 1 hour. Ladle into a large punch bowl and sprinkle with nutmeg. *(Note:* For large amounts, make up in batches for 2 dozen, keep cold, and refill punch bowl as needed.*)*

DRINK CHART

(Each Recipe Makes 1 Serving)

Tips for Making Better Drinks:
• Measure all ingredients carefully.
• Use the freshest and best ingredients possible.
• *Shaking* is for cloudy drinks. Shake drinks in a cocktail shaker—*vigorously*—to blend.
• *Stirring* is for clear drinks. Use a glass pitcher and glass stirrer.
• Use clean ice that has been stored away from foods (ice absorbs odors). *To crush,* wrap cubes in a dish towel and pound with a hammer; or use an ice crusher. *To crack,* tap ice block with ice cracker. *To shave,* pull ice shaver (a gadget rather like a wood plane) across ice block.
• Use *superfine* sugar (not confectioners' or granulated); use domino-shape sugar cubes; 1 small cube equals about 1/2 domino cube.
• Add liquor last when mixing with fruit juice, milk, cream, or egg.
• Mix drinks to order and serve as soon as they're made in chilled glasses.

Drink	Approx. Calories per Serving	Type of Glass	Best Time to Serve	Kind and Amount of Wine or Liquor	Ice
Alexander (Brandy or Gin)	225	4 1/2- or 6-oz. cocktail glass	After dinner	1 1/2 oz. brandy or gin	1/2 cup cracked ice
Americano	120	8-oz. highball glass	Before or between meals	2 oz. sweet vermouth	2–3 ice cubes
B & B	100	2-oz. liqueur glass	After dinner	1/2 oz. brandy	—
Bacardi	190	4 1/2-oz. cocktail glass	Before meals	2 oz. Bacardi rum	1/2 cup cracked ice
Black Russian	245	6-oz. old-fashioned glass	Before meals	2 oz. vodka	2 ice cubes
Black Velvet	280	12-oz. tankard or beer glass	Between meals	1 (6–6 1/2-oz.) split chilled dry champagne	—
Bloody Mary	140	8-oz. highball glass	Before meals	1 1/2 oz. vodka	1/2 cup cracked ice
Bullshot	135	6-oz. old-fashioned glass	Before or between meals	1 1/2 oz. vodka	2 ice cubes
Campari Soda	40	8-oz. highball glass	Before or between meals	1 oz. Campari	2 ice cubes
Champagne Cocktail	180	6–8-oz. champagne goblet	Before meals	Chilled champagne to fill glass	—

Note: Calorie counts for all alcoholic beverages that follow were computed on the basis of 100-proof liquor. By using a lower proof, you can reduce the number of calories somewhat:

Proof (all liquors)	Measure	Number of Calories
80	1 fluid ounce	65
86	1 fluid ounce	70
90	1 fluid ounce	73
100	1 fluid ounce	84

Other Liquid or Liqueur	Seasonings	How to Mix	Garnishes
½ oz. heavy cream ¾ oz. crème de cacao	—	Shake all ingredients with ice and strain into glass.	Sprinkling of nutmeg
Club soda to fill glass	1 oz. Campari	Place ice, vermouth, and Campari in glass, fill with soda and stir to mix.	Twist of lemon peel
½ oz. Benedictine	—	Pour Benedictine in glass, then pour in brandy.	—
Juice of ½ lime	3–4 dashes grenadine ½ teaspoon sugar	Shake all ingredients with ice and strain into glass.	—
1 oz. coffee liqueur	—	Stir all ingredients with ice in glass.	—
¾ cup chilled stout	—	Pour champagne and stout simultaneously into tankard.	—
⅓ cup tomato juice 1 teaspoon lemon juice	2 dashes Worcestershire 1–2 dashes liquid hot red pepper seasoning Pinch each salt and cayenne	Shake all ingredients with ice and strain into glass.	—
Beef consommé to fill glass	Salt to taste	Place vodka and ice in glass, fill with consommé, season, and stir.	Twist of lemon peel
Club soda to fill glass	—	Place ice and Campari in glass and pour in soda.	—
—	1 lump sugar 2–3 dashes aromatic bitters	Place sugar in glass, drop bitters on sugar, and pour in champagne.	Twist of lemon peel

Drink	Approx. Calories per Serving	Type of Glass	Best Time to Serve	Kind and Amount of Wine or Liquor	Ice
Collins (basic recipe)	230	10–12-oz. collins glass	Before or between meals	2 oz. liquor (gin for Tom Collins, blended whiskey for John Collins, rum for Rum Collins, etc.)	¾–1 cup cracked ice
Crème de Menthe Frappé	100	2–2½-oz. sherry glass	After dinner	1 oz. green crème de menthe	¼ cup crushed ice
(*Note:* Any liqueur may be prepared as a frappé using this method.)					
Cuba Libre	285	12-oz. collins glass	As a midafternoon cooler	2 oz. rum	3–4 ice cubes
Daiquiri (plain)	185	4½-oz. cocktail glass	Before meals	1 oz. light rum	½ cup cracked ice
Daiquiri (frozen)	185	6–8-oz. champagne goblet	Before meals	2 oz. light rum	½ cup shaved or crushed ice
Eggnog	435	12-oz. collins glass	As a between-meals refresher	2 oz. brandy, light rum, sherry, or port	½ cup cracked ice
French 75	245	8-oz. highball glass	Before meals	2 oz. gin	½ cup cracked ice
Gibson (see Martini)					
Gimlet	210	4½-oz. cocktail glass	Before meals	2 oz. gin or vodka	½ cup cracked ice
Gin or Vodka and Tonic	170	8-oz. highball glass	Before meals or between meals	1½ oz. gin or vodka	3 ice cubes
Gin or Sloe Gin Fizz	150 with gin 110 with sloe gin	8-oz. highball glass	Before or between meals	1½ oz. gin or sloe gin	½ cup cracked ice 2 ice cubes
Gin Rickey	130	8-oz. highball glass	Before or between meals	1½ oz. gin	2–3 ice cubes
Grasshopper	250	4½-oz. cocktail glass	After dinner	1 oz. white crème de cacao	½ cup cracked ice

Other Liquid or Liqueur	Seasonings	How to Mix	Garnishes
Juice of 1 lemon Club soda to fill glass	1 teaspoon sugar	Place juice, sugar, ice, and liquor in glass, fill with soda, and stir.	Cocktail cherry Slice of lemon
—	—	Fill glass with ice and pour liqueur evenly over all. Insert straws.	—
Juice of ½ lime Chilled cola to fill glass	—	Place juice, ice and rum in glass, fill with cola, and stir to mix.	Small lime wedge
Juice of ½ lime	¾ teaspoon sugar	Shake all ingredients with ice and strain into glass.	—
Juice of ½ lime	¾ teaspoon sugar 3–4 dashes Maraschino	Buzz all ingredients with ice in an electric blender at high speed about 1 minute until fluffy; spoon into glass, insert short straws.	—
1 cup milk	1 egg 2 teaspoons sugar	Shake all ingredients with ice and strain into glass.	A sprinkling of nutmeg
Juice of 1 lemon Chilled champagne to fill glass	1 teaspoon sugar	Place lemon juice, sugar, and gin in glass and stir to mix; add ice and pour in champagne.	—
Juice of ½ lime or 1 tablespoon bottled lime juice	1½ teaspoons Triple Sec	Shake all ingredients with ice and strain into glass.	—
Quinine water to fill glass	1 lime wedge	Squeeze lime wedge over glass, then drop in; add gin, ice, quinine water; stir slightly.	—
Juice of ½ lemon Club soda to fill glass	1 teaspoon sugar	Shake all ingredients but soda with cracked ice and strain over ice cubes in glass. Fill with soda and stir.	—
Juice of ½ lime Club soda to fill glass	—	Squeeze lime over glass and drop in, add ice, gin, and soda, and stir.	—
1 oz. green crème de menthe ¾ oz. heavy cream	—	Shake all ingredients with ice and strain into glass.	—

DRINK CHART (continued)

Drink	Approx. Calories per Serving	Type of Glass	Best Time to Serve	Kind and Amount of Wine or Liquor	Ice
Grog	190	8-oz. mug	Anytime as a cold-weather bracer	2 oz. dark rum or brandy	—
Hot Buttered Rum	235	8-oz. mug	Anytime as a cold-weather bracer	2 oz. dark rum	—
Hot Toddy	170	6-oz. old-fashioned glass	Anytime as a cold-weather bracer	1½ oz. dark rum, brandy, bourbon, rye, or scotch	—
Irish Coffee	290	6–8-oz. mug or cup	Anytime as a cold-weather bracer	1½ oz. Irish whiskey	—
Kir	200	8-oz. wineglass	Before meals	6 oz. Aligoté, Muscadet, or Chablis	2 ice cubes
Manhattan (regular)	200	4½-oz. cocktail glass	Before meals	2 oz. rye	1–2 ice cubes
Manhattan (dry)	190	4½-oz. cocktail glass	Before meals	2 oz. rye	1–2 ice cubes
Margarita	175	4½-oz. cocktail glass (dip rim in lime juice, then in salt to "frost")	Before meals	2 oz. tequila	½ cup cracked ice
Martini (*Note:* Connoisseurs keep both gin and vermouth in the refrigerator.)					
Regular	142	4½-oz. cocktail glass	Before meals	1½ oz. gin or vodka	2–3 ice cubes
Dry	138	4½-oz. cocktail glass	Before meals	1½ oz. gin or vodka	2–3 ice cubes
Extra dry	135	4½-oz. cocktail glass	Before meals	1¾ oz. gin or vodka	2–3 ice cubes
Gibson	175	4½-oz. cocktail glass	Before meals	2 oz. gin or vodka	2–3 ice cubes

Other Liquid or Liqueur	Seasonings	How to Mix	Garnishes
Juice of ½ lemon Boiling water to fill mug	1 lump sugar 1 lemon slice 2 cloves ½ cinnamon stick	Place lemon juice, rum, and seasonings in mug, fill with boiling water, and stir to mix.	—
1 teaspoon brandy Boiling water to fill mug	1 teaspoon light brown sugar 4 cloves 1 strip orange peel 1 teaspoon unsalted butter 1 cinnamon stick	Place rum and brandy in mug, add sugar, cloves and orange peel; place butter on a spoon in mug and pour boiling water over butter; stir with cinnamon stick.	—
Boiling water to fill glass	1 lemon slice stuck with 3 cloves ¼ cinnamon stick 1 teaspoon sugar	Put rum and seasonings in glass, insert metal spoon, and slowly pour in water; stir to mix.	—
½–¾ cup hot strong black coffee	2 teaspoons sugar	Pour coffee into mug, add whiskey and sugar and stir; let whipped cream slide over a metal spoon to float on coffee. Do not stir.	2 tablespoons *very* lightly whipped cream
½ oz. crème de cassis	1 strip lemon peel	Place ice, wine and crème de cassis in glass, twist lemon peel over glass, and drop in. Stir gently.	—
¾ oz. sweet vermouth ¾ oz. dry vermouth	— —	Stir rye and vermouth gently with ice, strain into glass, and garnish.	Cocktail cherry Twist of lemon peel
Juice of ½ lime	2–3 dashes Triple Sec or curaçao	Shake all ingredients with ice and strain into glass.	—
½ oz. extra dry vermouth ⅓ oz. extra dry vermouth ¼ oz. extra dry vermouth ¼ oz. extra dry vermouth	— — — —	Stir gin or vodka and vermouth very gently with ice, strain into glass, and garnish.	Green olive Twist of lemon peel Twist of lemon peel 2–3 cocktail onions

Drink	Approx. Calories per Serving	Type of Glass	Best Time to Serve	Kind and Amount of Wine or Liquor	Ice
Mint Julep	185	10–12-oz. collins glass or silver julep cup	Anytime as a refresher	2 oz. bourbon	2 cups cracked ice
Mist					
Scotch	165	6-oz. old-fashioned glass	Before meals for scotch and Irish mist, after dinner for heather mist	2 oz. scotch	1/2 cup shaved ice
Heather	220	6-oz. old-fashioned glass		2 oz. Drambuie	1/2 cup shaved ice
Irish	165	6-oz. old-fashioned glass		2 oz. Irish whiskey	1/2 cup shaved ice
Moscow Mule	220	8-oz. pewter or silver mug	Before or between meals	2 oz. vodka	2–3 ice cubes
Negroni	170	10–12-oz. collins glass	Before or between meals	1 oz. gin	2–3 ice cubes
Old-fashioned	135	6-oz. old-fashioned glass	Before meals	1 1/2 oz. blended whiskey or, if you specify it, rye, scotch, bourbon, or rum	1–2 ice cubes
Orange Blossom	155	4 1/2-oz. cocktail glass	Before meals	1 1/2 oz. gin	1/2 cup cracked ice
Pimm's Cup	160	10–12-oz. collins glass	Before or between meals	2 oz. Pimm's No. 1	2–3 ice cubes
Piña Colada	226	10–12-oz. collins glass	Before or between meals	1 1/2 oz. light rum	1/3 cup crushed ice
Pink Lady	195	4 1/2- or 6-oz. cocktail glass	Before meals	2 oz. gin	1/2 cup cracked ice

Other Liquid or Liqueur	Seasonings	How to Mix	Garnishes
—	12 large tender mint leaves 1 teaspoon sugar	Place leaves and sugar in glass and muddle, pressing leaves against sides of glass to extract flavor; discard mint. Pack glass with ice and let stand 1–2 minutes to "frost" outside; slowly pour in bourbon, rotating glass; garnish and serve with straws. SIP SLOWLY!	3–4 sprigs mint
—	—	Fill glass with ice, drizzle in whiskey or liqueur, and garnish.	Twist of lemon peel
—	—		Twist of lemon peel
—	—		Twist of lemon peel
Juice of ½ lime Ginger beer to fill mug	—	Place ice in mug, add lime and vodka; stir, then fill with ginger beer.	Slice of lime
1 oz. Campari 1 oz. sweet vermouth Club soda to fill glass	—	Place ice, gin, Campari, and vermouth in glass, fill with soda and stir.	Slice of orange
1 teaspoon club soda	½ lump sugar saturated with 1–2 dashes aromatic bitters; for an extra good drink, also add 2 drops scotch and 3 drops curaçao.	Place sugar and soda in glass, add ice and whiskey, stir, and garnish.	Twist of lemon peel Slice of orange Maraschino cherry
1 oz. orange juice	1 teaspoon sugar	Shake all ingredients with ice and strain into glass.	—
Lemon soda to fill glass	—	Place ice, garnishes, and Pimm's in glass, fill with soda, and stir.	Slice of lemon Strip of cucumber peel
1 oz. cream of coconut 2 oz. unsweetened pineapple juice	—	Buzz all ingredients with ice in electric blender at high speed 1 minute until fluffy. Pour into glass; insert straw.	Pineapple stick Cocktail cherry
Juice of ½ lemon 3–4 dashes apple brandy	3–4 dashes grenadine 1 egg white	Shake all ingredients with ice and strain into glass.	—

DRINK CHART (continued)

Drink	Approx. Calories per Serving	Type of Glass	Best Time to Serve	Kind and Amount of Wine or Liquor	Ice
Pisco Sour	165	5-oz. Delmonico or juice glass	Before meals	1½ oz. Pisco brandy	½ cup cracked ice
Planter's Punch	190	10–12-oz. collins glass	Before or between meals	2 oz. dark rum	½ cup cracked ice, shaved ice to fill glass
Port Wine Cooler	130	12-oz. collins glass	Before or between meals	½ cup dry port wine	Crushed ice to ½ fill glass
Pousse-Café	95	1-oz. liqueur glass	After dinner	1 teaspoon grenadine 1 teaspoon green crème de menthe 1 teaspoon yellow Chartreuse 1 teaspoon Triple Sec 1 teaspoon brandy	—
Rob Roy	190	4½-oz. cocktail glass	Before meals	2 oz. scotch	½ cup shaved or cracked ice
Rum Swizzle	190	8-oz. highball glass	Before or between meals	2 oz. rum	½ cup crushed ice
Salty Dog	230	8-oz. highball glass	Before meals	2 oz. vodka	2 ice cubes
Screwdriver	300	12-oz. collins glass	Before meals	2 oz. vodka	½–⅔ cup crushed ice
Side Car	230	4½-oz. cocktail glass	After dinner	1½ oz. brandy	½ cup cracked ice
Singapore Sling	260	12-oz. collins glass	Before or between meals	2 oz. gin	¾ cup cracked ice

Other Liquid or Liqueur	Seasonings	How to Mix	Garnishes
Juice of ½ lemon	1 egg white 1 teaspoon sugar	Shake all ingredients with ice and strain into glass.	—
Juice of ½ lemon or lime Juice of ½ orange	½ oz. Falernum or 1 teaspoon sugar	Shake all ingredients with cracked ice and strain into glass filled with shaved ice, garnish, add straws.	½ orange slice 1 stick fresh pineapple Maraschino cherry Mint
½ cup ginger ale	—	Place ice in glass, add wine and ginger ale, and stir to mix.	—
—	—	Pour grenadine into glass and let stand a few seconds. Gently place a glass stirrer in grenadine and very slowly pour in each liqueur down along stirrer in order listed so each floats on the other.	—
¾ oz. dry vermouth	Dash aromatic bitters	Stir scotch and vermouth with ice and bitters and strain into glass. Add garnishes.	Strip of lemon peel Maraschino cherry
Juice of ½ lime Club soda to fill glass	1 teaspoon sugar 3–4 dashes aromatic bitters	Stir lime juice, rum, seasonings, and ice in a pitcher until it "frosts," strain into glass, and add soda.	—
Grapefruit juice to fill glass	Pinch salt	Place all ingredients in glass and stir.	—
Orange juice to fill glass	—	Place all ingredients in glass and stir.	—
Juice of ½ lime 1 oz. Cointreau	—	Shake all ingredients with ice and strain into glass.	—
Juice of ½ lemon or lime 1 oz. cherry brandy or liqueur Club soda to fill glass	2–3 drops Benedictine 2–3 drops brandy	Place ice, juice, gin, cherry brandy and soda in glass and stir; with a medicine dropper, add Benedictine, then brandy by inserting halfway into glass. Float orange slice on top and place cherry in center.	Thin orange slice Maraschino cherry

DRINK CHART (continued)

Drink	Approx. Calories per Serving	Type of Glass	Best Time to Serve	Kind and Amount of Wine or Liquor	Ice
Sour (basic recipe)	190	5-oz. Delmonico or juice glass or 6-oz. sour glass	Before meals	2 oz. rye, bourbon, scotch, rum, brandy, or gin	1/2 cup cracked ice
Spritzer	90	12-oz. collins glass	With or between meals	1/2 cup Rhine wine	3/4 cup cracked ice
Stinger	245	4 1/2-oz. cocktail glass	After dinner	1 3/4 oz. brandy	1/2 cup cracked ice
Vermouth Cassis	190	8-oz. wineglass	Before meals	—	2 ice cubes
Zombie	450	12-oz. collins glass	Before meals	1 1/2 oz. light rum 1 1/2 oz. dark rum 1 1/2 oz. Demerara rum	1/2 cup cracked ice 4 ice cubes

Other Liquid or Liqueur	Seasonings	How to Mix	Garnishes
Juice of ½ lemon	1 teaspoon sugar 2 dashes aromatic bitters	Shake all ingredients with ice and strain into glass. Add garnishes.	Small orange wedge Maraschino cherry
Club soda to fill glass	—	Place all ingredients in glass and stir.	—
1 oz. white crème de menthe	—	Shake all ingredients with ice and strain into glass.	—
4 oz. dry vermouth ½ oz. crème de cassis 2 oz. chilled club soda	Twist of lemon peel	Place ice in glass, pour in vermouth, twist lemon peel over glass and drop in. Add crème de cassis, club soda and stir gently.	—
Juice of ½ lime 1 tablespoon apricot liqueur 1 tablespoon pineapple juice	1½ teaspoons Falernum	Shake all ingredients with cracked ice, strain into glass, add ice cubes and garnishes. Insert straws and SIP VERY SLOWLY!	Thin orange slice Mint sprigs

Appetizers and Hors d'Oeuvre

The cocktail party may be an American invention, but the practice of nibbling while drinking dates back to the Greeks and Romans. (Nibbling is perhaps the wrong word because these early gluttons stuffed themselves.)

Appetizers today are served with more restraint, their purpose being to whet the appetite and set the tone of the meal—unless, of course, cocktails only are being served, in which case appetizers are there to serve as a sop.

The difference between hors d'oeuvre and appetizers isn't as sharply defined as it once was. Hors d'oeuvre, meaning "outside the work," is a French phrase used to describe the hot or cold savories served at the start of a meal. In France hors d'oeuvre, often a selection of tart foods, are served at the table. In America hors d'oeuvre have come to mean the finger foods passed around with cocktails. Appetizer is a more encompassing word, including not only hors d'oeuvre but also any beverage or savory food served before the meal.

Making appetizers appeals to the drama in most of us—a fine thing as long as they don't upstage the foods to follow or prove so irresistible that guests overeat. The best practice is to keep appetizers simple.

Microwaving Appetizers and Hors d'Oeuvre

Because of their small size, appetizers and hors d'oeuvre can be microwaved with ease and speed. Many, moreover—meat balls, croquettes, hot dips and spreads, stuffed clams, cocktail sausages—can be cooked (or heated) and served in the same container. Particularly helpful are microwaves with temperature probes that will turn the oven off when the proper serving temperature has been reached. (*Note:* Don't forget to allow for *standing time* when figuring over-all cooking times because microwaved foods continue to cook for some minutes after they're removed from the oven. And don't forget to stir all mixtures after the *standing time* so that the heat is evenly distributed.) *And just what does the microwave do best when it comes to preparing hors d'oeuvre?*

• Reheating precooked appetizers (both the frozen and unfrozen) in seconds. (*Note:* Pastries and batter-fried foods are best *prepared* by conventional methods, then *reheated* by microwave.)

• Refreshing stale potato chips, popcorn, pretzels, and crackers (spread out on paper toweling, then microwave on *HIGH* for a few seconds; remove from the oven and let stand, uncovered, for a few minutes to crisp).

• Popping corn (in microwave poppers) with stunning speed. *Note:* Also read carefully Microwave Ovens in Chapter 1.

Preparing Appetizers and Hors d'Oeuvre in a Convection Oven

Convection ovens that cook via circulating hot air are faster than conventional ovens but slower than microwaves. They rarely need to be preheated (a saving right there of some 10–15 minutes). They further trim baking (or reheating) time by about 25 per cent. Most manufacturers recommend that you use whatever oven temperature a recipe specifies but that you begin checking for doneness about three fourths of the way through baking. The safest policy, however, is to follow the directions set forth by the manufacturer of your particular convection oven. *Note:* Also refer to Convection Ovens in Chapter 1.

PÂTÉ

There are dozens of *pâtés,* all liver and/or meat pastes of one kind or another. Most luxurious is *pâté de foie gras,* made of the livers of force-fed geese, seasoned with spices and sometimes brandy or Madeira. It is sold canned, also fresh, by the pound (the fresh must be kept refrigerated until ready to be served; the canned need not and, in fact, actually mellows and ages on the shelf like fine wine). *Pâté de foie gras truffé* has had truffles added, sometimes minced and mixed throughout but more often in a row down the middle of the pâté. *Pâté de foie d'oie* contains about 25 per cent pork liver, 75 per cent goose liver. Some other famous pâtés:

à la Meau: Meat pâté made of game; it usually contains some liver.

à la Périgueux: A truffled meat-liver pâté made of poultry and game.

à la Rouennaise: Duckling pâté.

d'Amiens: Pâté made of duckling and other livers.

de Campagne: A term used by many of America's fancy food shops to describe a rough-textured, often highly seasoned pâté compounded primarily of ground pork and pork liver.

Foie gras en bloc: Delicately seasoned whole fresh, fat goose or duck livers pressed into a block. Such blocks are pale pink and faintly marbleized, proving they contain several fresh livers. Because of U.S. government restrictions, *foie gras en bloc* is unavailable here, but it's something to try in France.

Lorraine: Meat pâté made from a mixture of veal, pork, and game.

Pâté en Croûte: Pâté baked in a crust (the crust need not be eaten).

Pâté Maison: The specialty of the particular restaurant. These usually contain a mixture of livers (poultry, calf, pork), also some ground meat.

Terrine: A mixture of liver and game or poultry leftovers baked in and served from a terrine (small earthenware dish).

How to Serve Pâté

All pâtés should be served cold (chill cans at least 24 hours before opening). When the pâté is to be served as a spread with cocktails, unwrap or slide out of can (dip can briefly in hot water, if necessary, to loosen pâté, or open both ends of can and push pâté out). Center pâté on a small serving plate and smooth fat layer with a spatula. Serve with melba rounds or hot buttered toast triangles and a pâté knife for spreading.

To Glaze Pâté with Aspic: This adds a festive touch. Scrape fat layer from block of pâté, then smooth surface. Make about 1 pint aspic, using beef or chicken broth,* and chill until syrupy. Spoon 2–3 layers of aspic over pâté, 1 at a time, and chill until tacky before adding next layer. Decorate top of pâté with herb sprigs, pimiento and truffle cutouts, seal under a final layer of glaze, and chill until firm. Also chill any leftover aspic, then chop and wreathe around plate of pâté.

If pâté is to be served at the table as a first course, slice 1/4″–1/2″ thick (do not remove fat layer) and overlap 2–3 slices (depending on size and richness) on each plate. Add a ruff of watercress or pepper grass sprouts, if you like, provide pâté spreaders, and pass hot buttered or unbuttered toast triangles.

How Much Pâté Is Enough? Depends on the richness, but generally, 1/8–1/4 pound per person is ample.

COUNTRY-STYLE LIVER PÂTÉ

16–18 servings

**1 medium-size yellow onion, peeled and coarsely
  chopped**
**1 pound calf's liver, trimmed of membrane and
  veins and cubed**
1/2 cup light cream
2 eggs, separated
2 teaspoons salt
1/4 teaspoon pepper
1/4 teaspoon ginger
Pinch allspice
**1/4 cup melted bacon drippings, butter, or
  margarine**

Preheat oven to 300° F. Purée onion in an electric blender at high speed or in a food processor fitted with the metal chopping blade; add liver, a little at a time, puréeing until creamy; strain through a fine sieve.

Mix in cream; lightly beat yolks and add along with remaining ingredients. Beat egg whites to soft peaks and fold in. Spoon into a well-greased 9″ × 5″ × 3″ loaf pan, set in a hot water bath, and bake, uncovered, 1–1¼ hours until a knife inserted in the center comes out clean. Cool pâté upright in pan on a wire rack, cover, and chill at least 12 hours. Invert on a platter and serve.

NPS (16–18): 90–80 C, 125–110 mg CH, 310–275 mg S*

VARIATIONS

Pretty Party Pâté: Prepare, chill, and unmold pâté; trim so loaf is about ¼″ smaller all around than its pan. Make a clear aspic by dissolving 1 envelope unflavored gelatin in 3 cups hot beef consommé. Pour ⅔ cup aspic into a clean 9″ × 5″ × 3″ loaf pan and chill until tacky; keep remaining aspic warm. Arrange truffle, radish, and/or lemon rind cutouts, tarragon or parsley sprigs in desired design on aspic, spoon a little warm aspic on top, and chill until tacky. Fit pâté loaf into pan, fill to brim with aspic, and chill until firm; also chill any remaining aspic; unmold. Chop extra chilled aspic and use to garnish platter along with radish roses and watercress sprigs.

NPS (16–18): 95–85 C, 125–110 mg CH, 445–395 mg S*

EASY CHICKEN LIVER PÂTÉ

6–8 servings

1 pound chicken livers, halved at the natural separation
3 tablespoons butter or margarine
2 (3-ounce) packages cream cheese, softened to room temperature
3–4 tablespoons brandy
1 teaspoon salt (about)
⅛ teaspoon pepper
⅛ teaspoon nutmeg
2 teaspoons finely grated yellow onion

GLAZE
1 (10½-ounce) can madrilène or beef consommé
1 teaspoon unflavored gelatin
Cutouts of truffle and pimiento; parsley or tarragon sprigs (decoration)

Brown livers in butter in a skillet over moderately high heat 4–5 minutes; transfer to an electric blender cup or a food processor fitted with the metal chopping blade; add drippings and scraped-up browned bits, also all remaining ingredients except glaze, and blend 20–30 seconds until smooth. Taste for salt and adjust as needed. Spoon into a small shallow serving bowl (about 1-pint size) and chill 2–3 hours. For glaze: Heat madrilène and gelatin over low heat, stirring constantly, until gelatin dissolves. Chill until thick and syrupy; spoon a thin layer on top of pâté and chill until tacky. Decorate with truffle and pimiento cutouts and herb sprigs. Add more madrilène to seal in design and chill until firm. Serve with melba rounds.

NPS (6–8): 280–210 C, 380–285 mg CH, 830–620 mg S*

EGG, NUT, AND MUSHROOM PÂTÉ

3 cups ⊠

A good vegetarian spread.

1 large yellow onion, peeled and sliced thin
1 large clove garlic, peeled and minced
¼ pound mushrooms, wiped clean and sliced thin
½ cup butter or margarine
6 hard-cooked eggs, peeled and quartered
1 cup walnuts
½ cup unblanched almonds
1 tablespoon Worcestershire sauce
1 teaspoon salt
¼ teaspoon pepper

Stir-fry onion, garlic, and mushrooms in butter in a heavy skillet over moderate heat 5 minutes until onion is soft, not brown; remove from heat. Mince eggs, walnuts, and almonds by pulsing 6–8 times in an electric blender at high speed or 3–5 times in a food processor fitted with the metal chopping blade. Add skillet mixture and all remaining ingredients; buzz 3–5 seconds to mix. Spoon into a decorative bowl, cover, and chill 1–2 hours to blend flavors. Let stand 30 minutes at room temperature before serving.

NP Tablespoon: 55 C, 40 mg CH, 80 mg S*

SPINACH, CARROT, AND WHITE KIDNEY BEAN PÂTÉ

25 servings ⚖ ¢

2 (10-ounce) packages frozen chopped spinach
2 medium-size carrots, peeled and cut in 1″ chunks
1 small yellow onion, peeled and quartered
¼ pound mushrooms, wiped clean and halved
¾ pound zucchini, scrubbed and cut in 1″ chunks
2 stalks celery, cut in 1″ chunks
1 (1-pound 3-ounce) can white kidney beans, drained
2 eggs, lightly beaten
1 teaspoon salt

1/4 teaspoon pepper
1 hard-cooked egg, peeled and chopped (optional garnish)

Preheat oven to 350° F. Cook spinach by package directions, dump into a large sieve set over a large heatproof bowl; press with the back of a spoon to extract as much liquid as possible. Measure out and reserve 1/4 cup spinach cooking liquid. Chop spinach, carrots, onion, and mushrooms very fine by pulsing in an electric blender at high speed 10–12 times or 6–8 times in a food processor fitted with the metal chopping blade; dump into a large bowl. Now chop zucchini, celery, and beans the same way; add to bowl along with all remaining ingredients except the garnish. Mix well. Pack into a well-buttered 9″ × 5″ × 3″ baking pan lined on the bottom with buttered wax paper. Cover with buttered wax paper (buttered-side-down), set in a large shallow baking pan, pour hot water into pan to a depth of 1 1/2″, and bake, uncovered, 1 1/4 hours until set. Remove wax paper cover and cool pâté in pan, right-side-up, on a wire rack to room temperature. Unmold carefully on small oblong platter, peel off wax paper, cover, and chill 3–4 hours. Before serving, let pâté stand about 20 minutes at room temperature. Sprinkle, if you like, with chopped hard-cooked egg.

NPS: 40 C, 20 mg CH, 185 mg S*

BLACK OLIVE PÂTÉ

1 1/2 cups

1/2 medium-size bulb garlic (about 6–7 cloves), not peeled
1/2 pound ripe Brie or Fontina cheese, cut in 1″ cubes
1 cup oil-cured Mediterranean or Greek black olives, pitted
1/4 cup olive oil (no substitute)

Preheat oven to 350° F. Wrap garlic in aluminum foil and bake 30 minutes; unwrap and cool to room temperature. Squeeze each clove at root end, popping out soft garlic pulp. Heat cheese in double boiler top over just-simmering water until melted, about 15 minutes. Meanwhile, purée garlic and olives with oil by buzzing 10–15 seconds in an electric blender at high speed or in a food processor fitted with the metal chopping blade. Add melted cheese and buzz 5–10 seconds longer. Cover and chill 2–3 hours. Let pâté stand at room temperature 20–30 minutes, then serve as a spread for chunks of Italian bread or slices of raw zucchini.

NP Tablespoon: 70 C, 10 mg CH, 245 mg S*

LAYERED FISH TERRINE

18 servings

1 1/2 pounds white fish fillets (haddock, flounder, cod, halibut, hake, etc.)
1/2 cup water
1 tablespoon lemon juice
1/4 teaspoon salt
1 egg, lightly beaten
3/4 pound smoked trout or whiting, skinned and boned
1/2 cup mayonnaise
1/4 cup watercress leaves, minced
1/2 pound thinly sliced smoked salmon

Preheat oven to 325° F. Simmer fish fillets in water with lemon juice and salt in a large covered skillet 5 minutes over low heat *just* until fish flakes. Drain fish well, then purée by buzzing 10–15 seconds in an electric blender at high speed or in a food processor fitted with the metal chopping blade. Mix in egg and set aside. Flake smoked trout very fine; set aside. Combine mayonnaise and watercress and set aside also. Butter a 2-quart oval terrine well, line bottom with wax paper cut to fit, and butter paper well. Spoon half the fish fillet mixture over bottom of the terrine, spread with 2–3 tablespoons watercress mixture, layer in all slices of salmon, spread with 2–3 tablespoons watercress mixture; spoon in smoked trout, smoothing surface and spreading with 2–3 tablespoons watercress mixture. Finally, add remaining white fish fillet mixture, again smoothing surface. Top with buttered wax paper, buttered-side-down. Place terrine in a large shallow baking pan, pour in hot water to a depth of 1 1/2″, and bake, uncovered, 30 minutes. Remove wax paper cover and cool terrine upright in its dish on a wire rack to room temperature. Carefully turn out on a serving platter. *(Note:* If fish sticks to dish, loosen by dipping dish briefly in hot water.) Peel off wax paper. Cover terrine and chill overnight before serving. Garnish, if you like, with lemon twists and ruffs of watercress.

NPS: 120 C, 60 mg CH, 2055 mg S*

CAVIAR

At $300 or more a pound, fresh imported caviar is hardly the everyday appetizer, and any meal beginning with it had better be elegant. What determines the quality of caviar and rockets the price sky high is the size of the eggs (caviar is the roe of sturgeon, screened and lightly salted). Costliest is the *beluga* from sturgeon that swims in the Caspian Sea, surrounded by Russia and Iran. The eggs are giant size, sometimes as big as peas; they are soft and translucent and range in color from silvery gray to black. Next come *osetra* (medium-size caviar, usually gray or gray green) and *sevruga* (smaller gray grains; one in 2,000 sevruga sturgeon has golden roe, so rare a delicacy that any found in Iran was once reserved for the Shah). Still smaller grained are *sterlet* and *ship* caviars. *(Note: Malossol* is not a kind of caviar but the Russian way of preserving it with minimal salt—*malossol* means "little salt.")* The good news today is that America is once again producing true (sturgeon) caviar of increasingly good quality. It costs a mere fraction of the Russian or Iranian.

There are other caviars: tiny, gritty black *lumpfish caviar* (usually from the Baltic Sea), *red caviar* (salmon roe), orange carp roe, or *tarama,* and "American Golden" or whitefish roe. These are not nearly so choice or costly as sturgeon caviar.

Fresh caviar is extremely perishable and must be kept refrigerated from the instant it is taken from the fish until the moment it is served. Malossol and pasteurized caviar, packed in small jars, are less perishable but may need refrigeration (read labels carefully). Pressed caviar, also less perishable than the fresh, has been treated in an acid solution, then brined, drained, and pressed. None of these is a match for the fresh.

How to Serve Caviar

The only way to serve fresh caviar, gourmets insist, is from its own tin, imbedded in crushed ice with nothing more to accompany than buttered toast points and, perhaps, lemon wedges, each guest helping himself or herself. Anything more is lily gilding. Others, however, like to accompany caviar with small bowls of minced onion, chopped hard-cooked egg white, sieved egg yolks, and occasionally a bowl of sour cream and plate of sliced pumpernickel. It's a matter of taste. The classic "caviar" drinks are chilled fine dry champagne or icy cold vodka drunk neat from liqueur glasses.

The less princely caviars are best used for making hors d'oeuvre and canapés, dips, spreads, and salad dressings and a variety of other recipes. They also make colorful garnishes.

How much caviar per person? 1–2 ounces, depending on your bank balance.

SMOKED SALMON

Another elegant, expensive appetizer. The salmon is raw but salted and smoked so that it has a cool velvety texture, a rosy, translucent look, and a delicately balanced woodsy-sea flavor. Smoked salmon should never seem oily or show grains of salt; taste before buying, rejecting any that is overpoweringly salty or smoky. The choicest smoked salmon comes from Scotland, but that from Nova Scotia, Norway, Denmark, and the Columbia River area is very good too. Lox is Jewish smoked salmon, slightly saltier than the regular, and a breakfast favorite with cream cheese and bagels.

The best way to buy smoked salmon is from the center cut, sliced thin but not so thin the slices tear (allow about 3 ounces per person). Like most seafoods, smoked salmon is perishable and must be kept refrigerated.

There are other smoked fish; sturgeon, which is very like salmon and best served like it; whitefish, eel, and trout, which need to be skinned and boned before serving. In addition, there are many canned smoked fish and shellfish, best served as cocktail tidbits or minced and mixed into dips and spreads.

How to Serve Smoked Salmon

The more simply the better. Trim away ragged edges (save to mix into scrambled eggs or make into a spread or dip with cream cheese and mayonnaise). Overlap slices neatly (about 3 per portion) on small chilled plates. Garnish with lemon wedges and sprinkle, if you like, with capers; set out the pepper mill. Or, if you prefer, forgo the capers and pass a cruet of olive oil and small dishes of minced yellow onion and hard-cooked egg.

Another way to serve smoked salmon is on cut-to-fit, thin slices of pumpernickel spread with unsalted butter. Cut bite size, these make luxurious canapés.

SALMON NORI-ROLL SUSHI (NORI-MAKI)

2 dozen 3/4" slices

The Japanese "rice sandwich" called *sushi* comes in many forms but owes its unique flavor and texture to vinegared rice *(sushi* means *vinegared rice).* Most *sushi* requires years of practice to shape, but this recipe is easy enough for beginners. Although traditionally served with green tea, sake, or beer, *sushi* makes stunning cocktail appetizers.

VINEGARED RICE
1 cup short grain rice
2 cups water
1/4 cup rice vinegar
3 tablespoons + 1 teaspoon sugar
2 1/2 teaspoons salt

FILLING
2 eggs, lightly beaten
1/2 teaspoon sugar
1/8 teaspoon salt
1 teaspoon cooking oil
1/4 pound thinly sliced smoked salmon

WRAPPING
3 sheets Asakusa nori (sheets of dried seaweed),
  each approximately 6" × 8" (available in
  Oriental groceries)

HAND VINEGAR
1 teaspoon rice vinegar mixed with 3
  tablespoons cold water

FOR DIPPING
3/4 cup Japanese soy sauce mixed with a few
  shreds or slices pickled ginger

Wash rice in a sieve under cold running water until water runs clear. Bring rice and water to a rapid boil in a covered heavy saucepan over high heat; boil 2 minutes; reduce heat to moderate and cook 5 minutes; reduce heat to very low and simmer 15 minutes. *Note:* Do not uncover pan at any time. Meanwhile, heat vinegar, sugar, and salt in a small saucepan over low heat until sugar dissolves; cool to room temperature and reserve. For the Filling: Prepare an omelet by combining eggs, sugar, and salt; heat oil in a 9" heavy skillet over moderately low heat and swirl to film bottom. Add egg mixture, tilt pan to spread evenly, then cook without stirring until eggs are just set. Invert onto a baking sheet, cool, and cut in strips 5" long and 1/8" wide; reserve. Cut smoked salmon in strips the same size and set aside also. When rice is done, turn out on a shallow tray, sprinkle with vinegar mixture, and toss with 2 wooden spoons to mix. To assemble *sushi:* Place a sheet of *nori,* shiny-side-down, on an 8" × 10" slatted bamboo mat (or a heavy cloth napkin or piece of aluminum foil topped by wax paper; the short side should be toward you). Dip one hand in hand vinegar, spread a scant 2 cups rice about 1/4" thick evenly over *nori,* leaving 1/2" margins on three sides and 2" at the far end. Lay one third each of omelet and salmon strips across the rice, in the exact center. Now using the bamboo mat to guide and compact mixture, tightly roll *sushi* up jelly-roll style so *nori* overlaps itself at the end. Press mat firmly around *sushi* and let stand 2 minutes. Remove mat, place roll of *sushi* seam-side-down on a cutting board and with a sharp knife dipped in cold water, cut into 8 slices. *Note:* Dip knife in water before each new cut. Make and slice 2 more rolls of *sushi* just as you did the first. To serve, center a small bowl of soy dipping mixture on a round platter and wreathe with slices of *sushi.* *Note:* You may find it easier to roll the *sushi* ahead of time, to refrigerate, then to slice the rolls shortly before serving.

NP Slice: 55 C, 25 mg CH, 545 mg S*
NP Slice (dipping sauce): 5 C, 0 mg CH, 665 mg S*

VARIATION

Shrimp, Cucumber, and Scallion Sushi: Prepare and spread vinegared rice on *nori* as directed. For the salmon, substitute 1/2 pound small shrimp, parboiled 1 minute, then shelled and deveined. Omit the omelet and roll shrimp instead with long thin slivers peeled cucumber and scallion (include green tops). Shape and slice as directed. Recipe too flexible for meaningful nutritional count.

CRUDITÉS

Crudités is simply a French term for crisp, raw vegetables eaten out-of-hand as appetizers. Any colorful combination can be used; in fact, the more colorful the better. Choose tenderest young vegetables, pare only if necessary, then cut into easy-to-eat sticks or chunks. Certain vegetables—cherry tomatoes, radishes, button mushrooms, etc.—are naturally bite-size and best left whole with a sprig of stem to make dipping easier. Group vegetables spoke fashion on a bed of crushed ice and center with a bowl of kosher or seasoned salt (makes a very low-calorie appetizer), or, if you prefer something heartier, serve with a savory dressing or dip. Some good vegetable choices:

To Serve in Long (2"–3") Slim Sticks
  Carrots
  Celery and celeriac
  Cucumbers (peel only if waxed)
  Fennel
  Scallions
  Sweet green and/or red peppers
  Turnips
  Zucchini

To Serve Whole
  Asparagus tips
  Button mushrooms
  Cherry tomatoes
  Endive leaves

Radishes
Snow peas

To Serve in Bite-size Chunks
Broccoli and cauliflowerets

Some Appropriate Dips
(see Index for page numbers)
Any flavored mayonnaise
Avocado Dressing
Cold Béarnaise
Cold Ravigote Sauce
Green Goddess Dressing
Horseradish Cream Sauce
Russian Dressing
Green Sauce (Salsa Verde)
Sour Cream-Anchovy, -Chive, or
  -Curry Sauce
Tapenade
Thousand Island Dressing

BAGNA CAUDA

1 1/2 cups ▨

Italians like *crudités,* too, especially chunks of cardoon, broccoli flowerets, and sticks of zucchini, sweet red or green pepper when dipped into this famous Piemontese "hot bath." Some recipes add a little red or white wine—or even scalded heavy cream—to this basic sauce.

8 cloves garlic, peeled and coarsely chopped
2/3 cup clarified butter*
2/3 cup olive oil (top quality)
2 (2-ounce) cans anchovy fillets, drained and minced
1 small white truffle, minced (optional)

Sauté garlic in butter and oil in a small heavy saucepan over moderate heat 5 minutes; do not brown. Strain and discard garlic; return mixture to saucepan, add anchovies and, if you like, the truffle. Heat and stir over moderately low heat 4–5 minutes. Transfer to a small chafing dish or fondue pot and keep hot. Serve as a dip, scooping anchovies up from the bottom, with an assortment of bite-size raw vegetables.

*NP Tablespoon: 115 C, 15 mg CH, 40 mg S**

ANTIPASTO

Antipasto, an Italian word meaning "before the meal," is simply a combination plate of raw, cooked, or pickled vegetables, meats and fish, hard-cooked eggs, and cheese served at the table as an appetizer and eaten with a fork. Any colorful, tart combination, artfully arranged, is appropriate. One of the best ways to serve antipasto is to load a giant platter and let each guest help himself or herself. Have the foods as nearly bite size as possible, or at least easy to serve (thin slices of cheese and meat, for example, should be rolled into tubes or cornucopias, hard-cooked eggs halved or quartered). Serve with cruets of olive oil and red wine vinegar.

Some Popular Components of Antipasto

(Many are available at supermarkets, others at specialty food shops.)

Meats: Thinly sliced *prosciutto* or boiled ham, salami, pastrami, dry hot Italian sausages

Fish: Oil-packed tuna, sardines, or anchovies

Eggs: Hard-cooked, deviled, or stuffed

Cheese: Thinly sliced provolone, mozzarella, or Gorgonzola

Vegetables: Caponata; any dried bean or chick-pea salad; marinated or pickled beets or artichoke hearts; green or ripe olives; radishes; celery or carrot sticks; fennel or celery hearts; pickled hot green or red peppers; roasted sweet green or red peppers; oil-packed pimientos; cherry tomatoes

SERVING CHEESES AS APPETIZERS

The best cheeses to serve before dinner are pungent or rich ones that are not likely to be overeaten. Bland cheeses may seem a better choice, but they aren't because guests tend to keep nibbling them until their appetites fade.

Two kinds of cheese, usually, are sufficient. Place well apart on a large cheese board or, failing that, on two small ones. Let stand at room temperature at least an hour before serving, longer if cheeses are particularly hard or cold—they need plenty of time to soften and mellow.

If the cheeses are to be fully appreciated, they should be served with unsalted, unseasoned crackers, French or Italian bread, thinly sliced. Serve these on a separate plate, not ringed around the cheeses. And provide a separate knife for each cheese so the flavors do not mix.

For a full rundown on the kinds of cheese and additional tips on serving them, see the chapter on eggs, cheese, and dairy.

NUTS AS APPETIZERS

Salted and seasoned nuts may be served as cocktail nibbles, but avoid putting out so many guests overeat. Supermarkets carry dazzling varieties of ready-to-serve cocktail nuts, some of them very good. None, however, can compare with those you roast or deep-fry yourself (see chapter on candies and nuts for directions).

HOLLOWED-OUT STUFFED VEGETABLES

These make attractive and neat-to-eat cocktail tidbits. Simply hollow out cherry tomatoes, radishes, raw baby zucchini or carrots, cucumbers and fill with red or black caviar, any savory cocktail spread, or tart spreadable cheese, any savory egg, seafood, meat, or poultry salad, chopping ingredients for these a little more finely than usual. Long vegetables like cucumbers, zucchini, and carrots can be hollowed out, stuffed, chilled, then sliced 3/4"–1" thick. Others should be filled shortly before serving. A number of vegetables—mushroom caps, celery stalks, small artichoke bottoms, snow peas, split along one side—are tailor-made for stuffing, no need to hollow out. The only precautions to take when stuffing vegetables: make the vegetables bite size and the filling firm enough to stay inside them.

CANAPÉS

Canapés are decorative open-face sandwiches small enough to eat in a bite or two. Whether hot or cold, they should look neat and freshly made, never fussed over (or left over). The best are salty or savory, colorful, and appetizing.

Canapés can be nothing more than a bread cutout spread with a savory filling (any of the following spreads are suitable, also any egg, seafood, meat, or chicken salad, provided the ingredients are minced instead of chopped). Canapés can be much more elaborate, rather like mini Danish sandwiches, spread first with a savory butter or mayonnaise, then mounted with a dab of caviar, sliver of smoked salmon, or *pâté de foie gras,* round of cucumber or cherry tomato or hard-cooked egg, cluster of tiny Danish shrimp. The spread is essential—to keep the bread from drying out (or the topping from seeping in) and to hold the canapé together.

Any firm-textured bread, thinly sliced and cut in fancy shapes, makes a good base for canapés (sourdough bread, whole wheat, pumpernickel, rye, French, or Italian bread). It can be toasted or not or fried golden brown in butter. Other good canapé foundations or "couches" *(canapé* is French for "couch") are crisp bland crackers, melba toast, piecrusts cut in fancy shapes, Puff Pastry shaped into tiny patty shells, or Choux Pastry into doll-size puffs (see Carolines).

How Many Canapés Are Enough? Better figure on 3–4 per person. Put out a variety—2 or 3 different kinds, perhaps 1 hot and 2 cold.

Some Canapé Spreads

Any of the savory butters and mayonnaises given in the sandwich and sauce chapters can be used. Very moist spreads should be applied shortly before serving, otherwise the bread becomes soggy. Others, however, may be put on ahead of time. *(Tip:* It's easier to spread the bread, then cut into fancy shapes.) Slices can be divided into trim squares, rectangles, or triangles or cut with small decorative cookie cutters. For a professional touch, spread canapés with one kind of spread, then pipe on a decorative border or design using another spread of contrasting color but compatible flavor. *(Note:* Only creamy spreads should be put through pastry tubes; any containing bits of solid food will merely clog the works.)

How Much Spread Is Needed? 1 cup should do about 8 dozen canapés—if thinly applied.

Roquefort Spread *(Makes about 3/4 cup):* Cream together 4 ounces Roquefort or blue cheese, 1/4 cup each unsalted butter and softened cream cheese, and 2 tablespoons brandy. For quick flavor variations: Substitute Stilton and port, Cheddar and sherry, or Caerphilly and stout for the Roquefort and brandy.
NP Teaspoon: 30 C, 10 mg CH, 60 mg S*

Caviar Spread *(Makes about 1/3 cup):* Blend 1/4 cup unsalted butter with 3 tablespoons black caviar, 1 teaspoon lemon juice, and 1/4 teaspoon finely grated onion.
NP Teaspoon: 35 C, 20 mg CH, 70 mg S*

Sardine Spread *(Makes about 1/2 cup):* Blend together 1/4 cup each unsalted butter and mashed, skinless, boneless sardines; season to taste with lemon juice and pepper.
NP Teaspoon: 25 C, 10 mg CH, 25 mg S*

Some Canapé Suggestions

Shrimp: Spread bread or toast rounds with Caper Butter, top with tiny Danish shrimp and a rosette of Tartar Sauce or curlicue of pimiento.

Sardine: Spread a cracker (any bland kind) with Herb Butter, top with 2–3 boneless, skinless sardines and a red onion ring filled with sieved hard-cooked egg yolk.

Chicken: Spread bread or toast rectangles with Anchovy Butter, top with cut-to-fit slices of chicken, and garnish with a fluff of Green Mayonnaise and a rolled anchovy fillet.

Smoked Oyster: Spread crackers with softened cream cheese, top with smoked oysters, and garnish with a border of Caviar Mayonnaise and a twisted lemon slice.

Broiled Anchovy: Spread toast rounds with any cheese spread, broil until bubbly, and top with crossed anchovy fillets.

Aspic: Cover bread slices with cut-to-fit slices of cold meat, poultry, or fish fillets, glaze with thin layers of aspic made from meat, poultry, or fish stock,* and chill until tacky. Cut in small squares, triangles, or rectangles, decorate, if you like, with herb sprigs, pimiento slivers, or olive slices, and seal under a thin glaze of aspic. Chill well before serving.

Stuffed Rolls: Cut ends from long, skinny loaves of French or Italian bread, scoop out soft insides and fill with any savory, not-too-soupy spread or seafood, egg, meat, or chicken salad. Wrap in foil and chill 6–8 hours. Slice thin and serve.

Garnishing Canapés
Any sandwich garnish, done on a doll's scale, will work (see Sandwich Garnishes).

Party Sandwiches
These are covered fully in the chapter on sandwiches.

CRISP CUCUMBER ROUNDS TOKYO STYLE

4–6 servings   ⊲⊳ ▨

This is such a good recipe it's difficult to believe there are only two ingredients.

3/4 cup Japanese soy sauce, chilled well
2 medium-size cucumbers, chilled well, peeled, and sliced 1/2" thick

Pour soy sauce into a small, deep mixing bowl, add cucumbers, and toss lightly to mix. Cover and chill 2 hours. To serve, transfer to a serving bowl and set out a separate small container of toothpicks.

*NPS (4–6): 30–20 C, 0 mg CH, 650–430 mg S.**

VARIATION

Substitute 2 1/2 cups of almost any crisp raw vegetable for the cucumbers: short carrot sticks, bite-size cauliflowerets, whole radishes or water chestnuts, small chunks of celery, or a combination of these.

PROSCIUTTO-STUFFED MUSHROOM HORS D'OEUVRE

3 1/2–4 dozen hors d'oeuvre   ⊲⊳

1 (3-ounce) package cream cheese, softened to room temperature
1/2 (2-ounce) tube anchovy paste
1/4 pound prosciutto, finely chopped
1 tablespoon capers
1 tablespoon minced parsley
1 tablespoon minced watercress
1/2 teaspoon Worcestershire sauce
3–4 tablespoons light cream
1 pound 1" mushrooms, stemmed and peeled (save stems to use later)

Mix cheese, anchovy paste, *prosciutto,* capers, parsley, watercress, and Worcestershire, adding enough cream to give mixture the consistency of pâté. Stuff mushroom caps, heaping mixture in center, cover, and refrigerate until about 1/2 hour before serving. Let come to room temperature, then serve with cocktails.

*NP Piece: 15 C, 5 mg CH, 60 mg S**

CRAB-STUFFED SNOW PEA PODS

40 stuffed pea pods

Substitute finely minced cooked shrimp or lobster meat for the crab, if you like. Both are equally delicious.

40 small snow pea pods, washed and trimmed
1/2 pound lump crab meat, well picked over, or 1 (6-ounce) can snow crab meat, drained
1 hard-cooked egg, peeled
1/3 cup mayonnaise
1/4 cup finely chopped celery
1 tablespoon minced capers
1 teaspoon Dijon mustard
1/8 teaspoon pepper

Blanch pea pods in boiling water 10 seconds; drain, plunge into ice water, drain again, and pat dry on paper toweling. Split pea pods open along the straight edge, not quite to the ends, to form "pockets." Mince the crab very fine; mash the egg yolk to a paste and chop the white fine; mix into the crab along with all remaining ingredients. Fill each pea pod with about 3/4 teaspoon of the crab mixture and flatten slightly. Arrange the pods close together in a shallow dish, cover, and chill 1–2 hours.

NP Pod: 20 C, 10 mg CH, 65 mg S*

MELON AND HAM

4 servings ⚖

A popular European first course.

1/2 ripe honeydew, casaba, or crenshaw melon, well chilled
6 ounces paper-thin slices prosciutto, Bayonne, or Westphalian ham, well chilled
Freshly ground pepper

Cut rind from melon, remove seeds, and slice lengthwise into thin crescents. Alternate slices of ham and melon on chilled plates and pass the pepper mill.

NPS: 130 C, 25 mg CH, 655 mg S*

VARIATIONS

⚖ **Figs or Mangoes and Ham:** Prepare as directed, substituting thinly sliced, peeled ripe figs or mangoes for the melon.

NPS: 145 C, 25 mg CH, 640 mg S*

⚖ **Melon and Ham Tidbits:** Cut peeled and seeded melon in 3/4" cubes, wrap in thin strips of ham, and secure with toothpicks. Serve as cocktail food; pass a pepper mill.

NP Piece: 20 C, 5 mg CH, 110 mg S*

MARINATED MUSHROOMS

4–6 servings ⚖

1 cup water
1/2 cup olive or other cooking oil
1/2 cup lemon juice or white vinegar
1 clove garlic, peeled and bruised
1 teaspoon thyme
1 teaspoon tarragon
1 bay leaf
1 teaspoon salt
1/2 teaspoon peppercorns
1 pound button mushrooms, wiped clean

Simmer all ingredients except mushrooms, uncovered, 5 minutes. Add mushrooms, boil 1 minute, then cool, cover, and refrigerate overnight. Remove from refrigerator about 1/2 hour before serving, mix well, and serve

in marinade or drained and speared with toothpicks.

NPS (4–6): 280–185 C, 0 mg CH, 195–125 mg S*

VARIATION

Marinated Artichoke Hearts: Substitute 1 (1-pound) can drained artichoke hearts for the mushrooms (halved if large) and proceed as directed. *(Note:* Quartered artichoke bottoms are good this way, too.)

NPS (4–6): 290–195 C, 0 mg CH, 205–135 mg S*

ARMENIAN BEAN APPETIZER

4–6 servings ¢

A good addition to antipasto.

1/4 cup olive oil
2 tablespoons lemon juice
3/4 teaspoon salt (about)
1/8 teaspoon white pepper
1 clove garlic, peeled and crushed
3 tablespoons minced parsley
2 cups cooked, drained dried pea beans or navy beans, flageolets, or cannellini (white kidney beans)

Beat oil with lemon juice and salt until creamy, mix in pepper, garlic, and 2 tablespoons parsley. Pour over beans, mix lightly, cover, and marinate 3–4 hours in refrigerator, stirring now and then. Remove from refrigerator, stir well, let stand at room temperature 15–20 minutes, then serve sprinkled with remaining parsley either as a first course in lettuce cups with lemon wedges or spooned onto sesame seed wafers.

NPS (4–6): 235–155 C, 0 mg CH, 420–280 mg S*

VARIATION

¢ **Turkish Bean Appetizer:** Prepare as directed but add 1 tablespoon minced fresh dill and 1 teaspoon minced fresh mint. Serve topped with paper-thin, raw onion rings. Nutritional count same as basic recipe.

COLD MARINATED SHRIMP

6 servings

1 pound boiled, shelled, and deveined medium-size shrimp
1/3 cup tart salad dressing (French, Tarragon French, Spanish Vinaigrette)
1 clove garlic, peeled, bruised, and stuck on a toothpick
1 tablespoon snipped fresh dill or 1 teaspoon dried dill

Mix all ingredients, cover, and chill 6–8 hours, tossing shrimp in marinade now and then. Drain shrimp, discarding garlic, and serve with toothpicks (marinade can be saved and used again with other shellfish).

NPS: 150 C, 75 mg CH, 90 mg S*

VARIATIONS

Cold Marinated Scallops: Prepare as directed but substitute 1 pound poached or, if tiny, *raw* bay scallops for shrimp; chill only 4 hours.

NPS (4–6): 165–140 C, 40–25 mg CH, 230–225 mg S*

Cold Marinated Oysters: Poach 1½ pints shucked oysters in their liquor 3–4 minutes just until edges ruffle, drain (save liquor for soup) and marinate as directed for shrimp.

NPS: 160 C, 60 mg CH, 120 mg S*

Cold Marinated Mussels: Steam open 2 dozen mussels and shuck*; marinate as directed for shrimp.

NPS: 105 C, 15 mg CH, 105 mg S*

⚖ **Low-Calorie Marinated Cold Shellfish:** Prepare any of the above recipes as directed using a low-calorie French, Italian, or herb dressing. Recipe too flexible for meaningful nutritional count.

SPICED OLIVES

3 cups ⊠

1 cup large unpitted ripe olives
1 cup large unpitted green olives
2 cups French Dressing
4 thick lemon slices
1 tablespoon mixed pickling spices
2 large cloves garlic, peeled and bruised

Place all ingredients in a large wide-mouthed jar with a tight-fitting lid. Cover tightly and shake well. Store in refrigerator at least 2 days before serving; shake jar from time to time. Drain liquid from olives (save it for another batch), remove lemon slices and garlic. Serve with toothpicks.

NP Olive: 30 C, 0 mg CH, 140 mg S*

DILL AND GARLIC OLIVES

1 pint ⊠

2 cups unpitted green olives
1 clove garlic, peeled and crushed
2 tablespoons olive oil
3 large sprigs fresh dill

Empty olives and their juice into a small bowl, add remaining ingredients, and toss to mix. Cover and chill at least 24 hours before serving.

NP Olive: 10 C, 0 mg CH, 95 mg S*

SAUTÉED CHICK-PEAS (GARBANZOS)

8 servings ¢

Serve warm as a cocktail nibble instead of salted nuts.

½ pound dried chick-peas, washed, boiled until tender* and drained, or 1 (1-pound 3-ounce) can chick-peas, drained well
⅓ cup olive oil or other cooking oil
1 teaspoon salt (about)

Pat chick-peas very dry between several thicknesses of paper toweling. Heat oil in a large heavy skillet over moderate heat 30 seconds. Add one third of the chick-peas and sauté, stirring constantly, 2–3 minutes until slightly crisp (reduce heat if peas brown too fast). Remove peas with a slotted spoon to paper toweling to drain; keep warm while you sauté remaining peas the same way in two batches. Add salt and toss chick-peas lightly to mix. Taste and add more salt, if needed.

NPS: 180 C, 0 mg CH, 280 mg S*

DRY-ROASTED HERBED MUSHROOMS

4–6 servings ⚖

An unusual appetizer and oh! so low in calories.

½ teaspoon garlic salt
1 pound medium-size mushrooms, wiped clean and sliced thin
1 teaspoon seasoned salt
½ teaspoon oregano
½ teaspoon powdered rosemary

Preheat oven to 200° F. Sprinkle 2 *lightly* oiled baking sheets with garlic salt and arrange mushrooms 1 layer deep on sheets. Mix seasoned salt and herbs and sprinkle evenly over mushrooms. Bake, uncovered, about 1½ hours until dry and crisp but not brown. Cool slightly and serve as a cocktail nibble. *(Note:* Store airtight; these absorb moisture rapidly.)

NPS (4–6): 35–25 C, 0 mg CH, 550–350 mg S*

HEALTH MIX

7 cups

A nutritious high-fiber, high-protein snack.

**6 slices wheat germ or whole grain bread, cut in
  1/4″ cubes (do not trim off crusts)**
1/4 cup butter or margarine
2 cloves garlic, peeled and crushed
2 tablespoons Japanese soy sauce
2 tablespoons Worcestershire sauce
1 cup pepitas (Mexican pumpkin seeds)
1 cup shelled unblanched peanuts
1 cup dry-roasted soybean nuts
1/2 cup whole unblanched almonds
1/2 cup shelled, blanched pistachio nuts
1 cup ready-to-eat high-fiber cereal
1 teaspoon salt (optional)

Preheat oven to 400° F. Spread bread cubes
one layer deep on an ungreased baking
sheet; toast in oven 8–10 minutes, stirring
after 4–5 minutes. (*Note:* Some breads toast
faster than others, so watch carefully.)
Meanwhile, heat butter and garlic in a small
saucepan over moderate heat till bubbly but
not brown; off heat, mix in soy and Worcestershire sauce; set aside. When bread cubes
are toasted, reduce heat to 200° F. Mix
in pepitas, all nuts, and cereal. Drizzle
evenly with seasoned butter, taste, and add
salt, if needed; toss well. Spread mix out in a
large ungreased roasting pan and bake, uncovered, 1 hour, stirring now and then. Cool
to room temperature, then serve as a cocktail nibble. Store airtight.

NP Tablespoon: 35 C, 1 mg CH, 60 mg S*

VARIATION

Trail Mix (*About 7 cups*): Mix 1 cup *each*
ready-to-eat high-fiber cereal, pepitas, peanuts, dry-roasted soybean nuts, 1/2 cup *each*
whole unblanched almonds and shelled unblanched pistachios, and 2 cups mixed dried
fruits such as small apricots, apples, figs, or
raisins. Store airtight.

NP Tablespoon: 35 C, 0 mg CH, 5 mg S*

CHEESE CRACKERS

6–7 dozen   ⚖ ¢

1 1/2 cups sifted flour
1 teaspoon salt
1/8 teaspoon paprika
1/8 teaspoon cayenne pepper
1/2 cup chilled margarine (no substitute)
1/2 pound sharp Cheddar cheese, coarsely grated
2 1/2–3 tablespoons ice water

Mix flour, salt, paprika, and cayenne in a
shallow bowl and cut in margarine with a
pastry blender until mixture resembles
coarse meal. Add cheese and toss to mix.
Sprinkle water evenly over surface, 1 tablespoon at a time, mixing lightly with a fork;
dough should just hold together. Divide
dough in half and shape each on a lightly
floured board into a roll about 9″ long and
1 1/2″ in diameter; wrap in foil and chill well.
About 10 minutes before crackers are to be
baked, heat oven to 375° F. Slice rolls 1/4″
thick, space 1″ apart on ungreased baking
sheets, and bake 10 minutes until golden;
transfer at once to wire racks to cool. Store
airtight. Serve at room temperature or, if
you prefer, reheat about 5 minutes at 350° F.

NP Cracker: 35 C, 5 mg CH, 65 mg S*

SHRIMP TOAST

6–8 servings

**4 ounces cooked or canned shrimp, drained and
  minced very fine**
2 tablespoons minced water chestnuts
3 scallions, minced (white part only)
1 teaspoon minced gingerroot
1 teaspoon cornstarch
1 teaspoon dry sherry
1/4 teaspoon sugar
1/4 teaspoon salt
2 egg whites, lightly beaten
Peanut or other cooking oil for deep fat frying
**4 thin slices firm-textured, day-old white bread,
  trimmed of crusts**

Mix all but last 2 ingredients. Begin heating
oil in a deep fat fryer with a basket and deep
fat thermometer over moderately high heat.
Pile shrimp mixture on bread, dividing total
amount evenly, and spread just to edges;
press down lightly. Cut each slice into 4 triangles. When oil reaches 350° F., place 2 or
3 triangles, spread sides up, in fryer basket,
lower into oil, and fry about 1 minute until
golden and puffed. (*Note:* Triangles should
automatically flip over; if not, turn to brown
evenly.) Drain on paper toweling and keep
warm in a 250° F. oven while you fry the
rest. Serve hot.

*NPS (6–8): 85–65 C, 30–20 mg CH, 200–150
  mg S**

QUICHE LORRAINE TARTLETS

1 1/2 dozen

Serve warm as hors d'oeuvre.

1 recipe Flaky Pastry II

FILLING

3/4 cup coarsely grated Gruyère or Swiss cheese
1/4 cup crumbled crisply cooked bacon
2 eggs, lightly beaten
3/4 cup light cream
1/2 teaspoon salt
Pinch white pepper
Pinch nutmeg
Pinch cayenne pepper

Preheat oven to 425° F. Prepare pastry, divide in half, and roll out 1 piece at a time into a circle about 1/8″ thick. Cut with a 3″ biscuit cutter and line fluted or plain tart tins about 2 1/2″ in diameter. Set tins on baking sheets. Dividing total amount evenly, sprinkle cheese and bacon into pastry shells. Mix remaining ingredients and pour into shells. Bake on center oven rack 10 minutes, remove from oven, and let stand 2 minutes. Meanwhile, reduce oven to 350° F. Return tartlets to oven and bake 5 minutes until filling is puffed and pastry golden. Cool in tins 2–3 minutes, then lift from tins and cool slightly on a wire rack. Serve warm. *(Note: Tartlets may be baked ahead of time, then cooled and refrigerated until shortly before serving. Reheat on a baking sheet 5–8 minutes at 350° F.)*

NP Tartlet: 190 C, 50 mg CH, 250 mg S*

VARIATION

Any Quiche Lorraine variations (see Eggs, Cheese, and Dairy) can be prepared as tartlets instead of full-size pies.

GOUGÈRE (BURGUNDIAN CHEESE PASTRY RING)

20 servings

Usually served cold, but we like it hot.

1 cup water
1/2 cup butter or margarine
1/2 teaspoon salt
1/4 teaspoon cayenne pepper
1 cup sifted flour
6 ounces Gruyère or Swiss cheese, coarsely
  grated
4 eggs, at room temperature
2 tablespoons grated Parmesan cheese

Preheat oven to 400° F. In a heavy medium-size saucepan set over high heat, bring water, butter, salt, and cayenne to a boil; pull pan almost off burner and reduce heat to moderate. Add flour *all at once* and stir briskly with a wooden spoon until mixture forms a ball; add Gruyère, beating well to blend. Set pan on a damp cloth; add the eggs, one at a time, beating each in thor-

oughly before adding the next egg. *(Note: The mixture may look curdled at first, but as you beat, it will become smooth.)* Drop pastry by rounded tablespoonfuls, almost touching each other, to form a 10″ circle on a lightly greased baking sheet or put through a pastry bag fitted with a large plain tip. Sprinkle the pastry evenly with the Parmesan. Bake, uncovered, 20 minutes until puffed and lightly browned, then *without opening the oven door,* reduce temperature to 350° F. and bake 10 minutes longer. Make slits in the sides of the *gougère* every 4″ and let it dry out in the turned-off oven 15 minutes. Cut the *gougère* into slim wedges and serve warm or cold.

NPS: 115 C, 75 mg CH, 155 mg S*

FRIED MOZZARELLA CUBES

3 dozen

1 pound mozzarella or Fontina cheese
1/4 cup unsifted flour
1 egg, lightly beaten
1 cup fine dry bread crumbs
Shortening or cooking oil for deep fat frying

Cut the cheese into 36 small (about 2/3″) cubes. Dredge cubes in flour, dip in egg, then roll in crumbs. Press crumbs onto cubes lightly, then again dip in egg and roll in crumbs. Let breaded cubes dry on a rack at room temperature 1/2 hour. Meanwhile, heat fat in a deep fat fryer fitted with the fryer basket over moderate heat to 350° F. on a deep fat thermometer. Fry the cheese cubes, a few at a time, about 1 minute until golden brown. Do not overcook or the cheese will burst through the crumb coating. *(Note: The crumb coating should be nice and crisp, but the cheese inside meltingly soft.)* Drain the cubes on paper toweling and serve at once with spicy mustard or chutney.

NP Cube: 60 C, 20 mg CH, 70 mg S*

BEEF BOREKS

25–30 servings

Fresh phyllo pastry leaves (sheets) are sold by Middle Eastern groceries and bakeries. They are also available frozen at many specialty food shops and some supermarkets. Thaw as directed before using.

1/2 (1-pound) package phyllo pastry leaves, at
  room temperature (refrigerate or freeze
  remainder to use another time)
1/2 cup (about) melted butter (no substitute)

FILLING

½ pound ground beef chuck
1 small yellow onion, peeled and minced
1 clove garlic, peeled and crushed
2 tablespoons tomato purée
1 egg yolk, lightly beaten
1 tablespoon minced parsley
½ teaspoon salt
⅛ teaspoon pepper
⅛ teaspoon cinnamon
⅛ teaspoon allspice

Unroll pastry, arrange leaves in an even stack, then halve lengthwise *and* crosswise, making 4 stacks about 8″ × 6″. Pile stacks on top of each other and cover with cloth to prevent drying. Prepare filling: Brown beef 5 minutes over moderately high heat, add onion and garlic, and continue cooking until meat is no longer pink; drain off drippings. Off heat, mix in remaining ingredients; cool to room temperature. Preheat oven to 350° F. Lift 1 pastry leaf to a flat surface so short side faces you and brush with butter. Place a rounded ½ teaspoon filling 1″ from bottom and slightly off center and fold as shown; brush with melted butter, then fold over and over into a small, neat triangle. Fill and fold remaining boreks the same way.

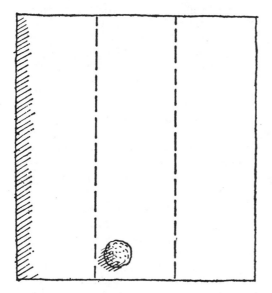

Space 1″ apart on buttered baking sheets, brush with melted butter, and bake about 25 minutes until well browned. Serve hot. *(Note:* These can be made up to the point of baking several hours ahead of time; cover and refrigerate until needed.)

NPS (25–30): 85–70 C, 25–20 mg CH, 90–75 mg S*

VARIATIONS

Spinach and Mozzarella Boreks: Prepare as directed but use the following filling instead of the beef: Thaw 1 (10-ounce) package frozen chopped spinach and drain well; mince spinach very fine, mix in ¼ pound finely minced mozzarella cheese, ¼ cup finely grated Parmesan, ½ teaspoon salt, and ⅛ teaspoon pepper.

NPS (25–30): 80–65 C, 15–10 mg CH, 120–100 mg S*

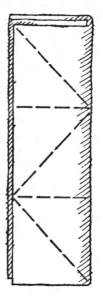

Cheese Boreks: Prepare as directed but substitute the following filling for the beef: Mix 1 (3-ounce) package softened cream cheese with 1 cup each crumbled feta and cottage cheeses, 1 lightly beaten egg yolk, ½ teaspoon salt, ⅛ teaspoon pepper, and 1 tablespoon minced fresh dill, chives, or parsley.

NPS (25–30): 100–80 C, 30–25 mg CH, 185–155 mg S*

EMPANADITAS

32 empanaditas

Cocktail-size, meat-filled Spanish turnovers, one of the many *tapas* Spaniards like with drinks.

PASTRY
1 recipe Flaky Pastry I

FILLING
3 ounces ground veal
2 tablespoons minced yellow onion
2 tablespoons olive oil
2 ounces ground lean cooked ham

2 tablespoons butter or margarine
2 tablespoons seedless raisins (optional)
2 tablespoons minced pimiento
2 tablespoons minced ripe olives
1/2 teaspoon liquid hot red pepper seasoning
1/2 teaspoon salt (about)
Shortening or cooking oil for deep fat frying

Prepare pastry as directed, wrap in wax paper, and chill while you make the filling. Sauté veal and onion in oil in a heavy skillet over moderate heat 3–4 minutes until lightly browned. Add all remaining ingredients except shortening for deep fat frying and cook, stirring, over low heat 1 minute. Taste for salt and add more, if needed; cool to room temperature. Roll pastry into a 14″ circle on a lightly floured pastry cloth and cut into 3″ rounds with a floured cookie cutter. Gather pastry scraps, reroll and cut. Brush edges of pastry rounds with cold water, place a scant teaspoon of filling on the lower half of each round, fold pastry over and crimp edges with a fork to seal. Let turnovers dry, uncovered, at room temperature while you heat the shortening over moderate heat in a deep fat fryer fitted with a fryer basket and deep fat thermometer. When temperature reaches 365° F., fry turnovers, a few at a time, 2½–3 minutes until well browned (do not undercook or pastry may be raw underneath). Drain turnovers on paper toweling while you fry the rest. Serve hot.

NPS: 65 C, 5 mg CH, 105 mg S*

VARIATION

Baked Empanaditas: Prepare as directed. Brush turnovers lightly with a glaze made by beating 1 egg with 1 tablespoon cold water, then place about 1½″ apart on an ungreased baking sheet. Bake, uncovered, in a preheated 400° F. oven about 20 minutes until golden brown. Serve hot.

NPS: 60 C, 15 mg CH, 105 mg S*

BUÑUELITOS (SPANISH HAM FRITTERS)

32 buñuelitos

Shortening or cooking oil for deep fat frying
2 cups ground lean cooked ham (about 1/2 pound)
2 tablespoons finely chopped pimiento
2 tablespoons finely grated yellow onion
1/3 cup soft white bread crumbs
1/2 teaspoon salt
1/4 teaspoon pepper
2 eggs, separated
2 tablespoons flour

1/2 teaspoon baking powder
2 tablespoons milk

Place shortening in a deep fat fryer, insert a deep fat thermometer, and begin heating over moderate heat. Meanwhile, mix ham, pimiento, onion, bread crumbs, salt, pepper, and egg yolks. Whisk flour and baking powder with milk until smooth, add to ham mixture, and blend well. Beat egg whites to soft peaks, then fold into ham mixture. When fat reaches 350° F., drop mixture by teaspoonfuls into fat. Fry *buñuelitos,* a few at a time, 1½–2 minutes until golden brown. (*Note:* You may have to flip the fritters over so they brown evenly.) Drain on paper toweling and serve hot.

NPS: 30 C, 20 mg CH, 135 mg S*

CHEESE NACHOS WITH GREEN CHILIES

2 dozen ⊠

24 round tortilla chips (about 2½″ across)
2 cups coarsely grated Monterey Jack or sharp Cheddar cheese
1 (4-ounce) can peeled green chili peppers, drained and finely chopped

Preheat broiler. Arrange tortilla chips on a large ungreased baking sheet; sprinkle each with cheese and top with about 1/2 teaspoon green chilies. Broil about 6″ from the heat 1–2 minutes until cheese melts. Serve hot.

NP Nacho: 60 C, 10 mg CH, 75 mg S*

VARIATIONS

Bean, Bacon, and Cheese Nachos: Arrange chips on baking sheet as directed; top each with a small spoonful of Refried Beans, sprinkle with a little crisply cooked bacon, then with the cheese and green chilies. Broil as directed.

NP Nacho: 65 C, 10 mg CH, 95 mg S*

Potato-Skin Nachos with Cheese and Chilies: Bake 6 Idaho potatoes,* halve lengthwise, and scoop out most of the flesh (save this for potato pancakes, for soups or for mashing). Take care not to break the potato skins. Place the skins on an ungreased baking sheet, sprinkle with salt and pepper, and bake, uncovered, in a preheated 400° F. oven for 10 minutes. Now prepare Cheese Nachos with Green Chilies as directed above but substitute the baked potato skins for the tortilla chips. After broiling the *nachos,* halve crosswise and serve hot.

NP Nacho: 50 C, 10 mg CH, 75 mg S*

HOT GLAZED COCKTAIL SAUSAGES

6–8 servings ⊠

GLAZE

1 cup tomato purée
3 tablespoons cider vinegar
1/3 cup firmly packed light brown sugar
1 1/2 teaspoons chili powder
1 clove garlic, peeled and crushed

2 (5 1/2-ounce) packages cocktail frankfurters

Mix glaze ingredients in a skillet and simmer, uncovered, 2–3 minutes, stirring now and then. Add frankfurters and simmer, uncovered, stirring occasionally, about 10 minutes until lightly glazed. Pour into a chafing dish and serve with toothpicks.

NPS (6–8): 230–175 C, 25–20 mg CH, 760–570 mg S*

VARIATIONS

⊠ **Orange and Mustard-Glazed Cocktail Sausages:** Prepare as directed but substitute the following glaze for that above: 1 cup orange juice, 1/3 cup medium-dry sherry, 3 tablespoons each sugar and molasses, and 4 teaspoons spicy brown prepared mustard.

NPS (6–8): 245–180 C, 25–20 mg CH, 620–465 mg S*

⊠ **Cocktail Sausages Glazed with Plum Sauce:** Prepare as directed but substitute 1 recipe Plum Sauce for the glaze above.

NPS (6–8): 365–275 C, 25–20 mg CH, 635–475 mg S*

⊠ **Sweet-Sour Cocktail Sausages:** Prepare as directed but substitute 1/2 recipe Sweet-Sour Sauce for the above glaze.

NPS (6–8): 210–155 C, 25–20 mg CH, 1025–770 mg S*

HOT SPICY MEAT BALLS

12 servings

MEAT BALLS

1 pound ground beef chuck
1 medium-size yellow onion, peeled and finely grated
1 clove garlic, peeled and crushed
3/4 teaspoon salt
1 tablespoon steak sauce
1/4 teaspoon pepper
1/8 teaspoon crushed dried hot red chili peppers
3/4 cup soft white bread crumbs soaked in 1/4 cup cold water
1 egg, lightly beaten
2 tablespoons cooking oil (for browning)

SAUCE (optional)

3 tablespoons flour
2 tablespoons pan drippings
1 1/2 cups beef broth
2 tablespoons tomato paste
2 tablespoons dry red wine or 1 tablespoon red wine vinegar
1/8 teaspoon pepper

Mix all meat ball ingredients except oil and shape in 1" balls. Brown well in oil, a few balls at a time, 5–7 minutes in a heavy skillet over moderately high heat; remove to paper toweling with a slotted spoon. Drain all but 1 tablespoon drippings from pan, add balls, turn heat to low, cover, and simmer 10–15 minutes, adding about 2 tablespoons water, if needed, to keep balls from sticking. Serve hot on toothpicks with or without a savory dip (Béarnaise, Chinese-Style Sweet-Sour, and Plum Sauce are particularly good). Or, if you prefer, serve in the above sauce: Brown and drain balls as directed; before returning to pan, blend flour into drippings, add remaining ingredients, and heat and stir until thickened. Add meat balls, cover, and simmer 10–15 minutes. Serve from a chafing dish with toothpicks.

NPS: 115 C, 50 mg CH, 195 mg S*
NPS (sauce): 45 C, 5 mg CH, 180 mg S*

VARIATIONS

Roman Meat Balls: For the meat balls, use 1/2 pound each ground beef chuck and hot or sweet Italian sausages removed from casings; stir-fry 10 minutes over moderately high heat until cooked through. Drain off drippings and cool meat slightly; then mince. Mix with ingredients called for but omit hot red peppers; add 3 tablespoons grated Parmesan. Shape into 1" balls, brown and cook as directed.

NPS: 175 C, 70 mg CH, 510 mg S*

Chutney-Nut Meat Balls: To the meat ball mixture add 1/3 cup minced walnuts or toasted almonds. Proceed as directed, simmering in the sauce to which 1/3 cup well-drained, minced chutney has been added.

NPS: 280 C, 75 mg CH, 495 mg S*

Chili Meat Balls: Prepare meat balls as directed, omitting hot red chili peppers and adding 1 tablespoon chili powder and 2 tablespoons chili sauce. Also prepare sauce, blending 1 teaspoon chili powder into drippings along with flour.

NPS: 225 C, 75 mg CH, 545 mg S*

Blue Cheese Meat Balls: Prepare meat balls as directed, omitting hot red chili peppers and salt and adding 3–4 tablespoons crumbled blue cheese. Serve without sauce but pass Sour Cream Dressing as a dip.

NPS: 185 C, 75 mg CH, 340 mg S*

RUMAKIS (HOT BACON AND CHICKEN LIVER HORS D'OEUVRE)

6 servings

6 chicken livers, quartered
3/4 cup Japanese soy sauce
1/4 cup sake or medium-dry sherry
1/2 clove garlic, peeled and crushed
2 (1/2″) cubes fresh gingerroot, peeled and crushed
8 water chestnuts (about), each cut in 3 thin slivers
3/4 cup light brown sugar
1/2 pound lean bacon, each strip halved crosswise

Marinate chicken livers in refrigerator in a mixture of soy sauce, sake, garlic, and ginger about 12 hours or overnight. Make a slit in the center of each piece of liver, insert a sliver of water chestnut, and roll in brown sugar; wrap each in a piece of bacon and secure with a toothpick. Place *rumakis* in a piepan, add marinade, cover, and marinate 2–3 hours longer in refrigerator, turning occasionally in marinade. Preheat oven to 400° F. Drain marinade from *rumakis* and reserve. Roast *rumakis*, uncovered, 1/2–3/4 hour, pouring off drippings as they accumulate and basting often with marinade until nicely glazed and brown.

NPS: 255 C, 150 mg CH, 2770 mg S*

SIZZLING CHICKEN LIVERS

6 servings

1/4 cup soy sauce
2 tablespoons dry sherry or sake
1 tablespoon dark brown sugar
1 clove garlic, peeled and quartered
1/2 pound chicken livers, halved at the natural separation
1 tablespoon cornstarch blended with 1/4 cup canned condensed beef broth
1–2 tablespoons flour
2 tablespoons peanut or other cooking oil

Mix soy sauce, sherry, sugar, and garlic in a bowl, add livers, cover, and marinate in refrigerator 1–2 hours. Drain marinade into a small saucepan; discard garlic. Bring to a simmer, blend in cornstarch paste, and heat, stirring constantly, until thickened and clear; transfer to a small chafing dish and keep warm. Dredge chicken livers in flour and stir-fry in oil 3–4 minutes until lightly browned. Transfer to chafing dish and heat 1–2 minutes. Serve from chafing dish with toothpicks for spearing livers.

NPS: 115 C, 165 mg CH, 950 mg S*

Dips and Spreads

There's something convivial about dips and spreads. Dips are an American invention, and a very good one, too. Spreads are not, though Americans have certainly enlarged the repertoire. The main caution to bear in mind when preparing either is to keep them the right consistency: dips should be thick enough not to dribble or splash, spreads soft enough to spread easily without tearing the bread or breaking the crackers. Another good practice: Make dips and spreads ahead of time so that their flavor will mellow.

Sauces to Use as Dips *(see Sauces Chapter for Recipes):*	*Particularly Good with:*
Béarnaise	Meat, Seafood, Vegetables
Caper and Horseradish	Seafood, Vegetables
Chinese-Style Sweet-Sour	Meat, Seafood
Cold Ravigote	Vegetables
Easy Sour Cream (and Variations)	Meat, Seafood, Vegetables
Gribiche	Seafood
Hot Chinese Mustard	Meat
Mayonnaise (and Variations)	Meat, Seafood, Vegetables
Plum Sauce	Meat
Tartar	Seafood, Vegetables
Tempura	Seafood

TAPENADE

2 cups

A traditional Provençal spread or dip. Serve with chunks of French or Italian bread, with raw sticks of zucchini, or with raw cauliflower or broccoli flowerets.

1 cup oil-cured Mediterranean or Greek black olives, pitted
6–7 anchovy fillets
1/3 cup well-drained capers
1 large clove garlic, peeled and crushed
1 (6 1/2-ounce) can tuna, drained and flaked
2 tablespoons lemon juice
1 tablespoon Dijon mustard
1/2 cup olive oil
1/8 teaspoon pepper
1/4 teaspoon minced fresh thyme or 1/8 teaspoon dried thyme

Purée all ingredients by buzzing 20–30 seconds in an electric blender at high speed or 15–20 seconds in a food processor fitted with the metal chopping blade. Cover and chill 2–3 hours. Let *tapenade* stand at room temperature 30 minutes before serving.

NP Tablespoon: 55 C, 1 mg CH, 220 mg S*

DILLED DEVILED HAM DIP

1 pint

1 cup sour cream
1 (8-ounce) package cream cheese, softened to room temperature
1 (4 1/2-ounce) can deviled ham
1 tablespoon minced onion
2 teaspoons prepared spicy brown mustard
1 tablespoon minced dill pickle

Beat all ingredients together with an electric mixer or in a food processor fitted with the metal chopping blade about 30 seconds until smooth and creamy. Cover and let stand at room temperature 1 hour before serving to blend flavors.

NP Tablespoon: 55 C, 10 mg CH, 70 mg S*

CREAM CHEESE, BACON AND HORSERADISH DIP

1 1/2 cups

1/2 cup milk or light cream
1 (8-ounce) package cream cheese, softened to room temperature
1 tablespoon prepared horseradish
1 teaspoon Worcestershire sauce
1/3 cup crisp, crumbled bacon

Blend milk and cheese until smooth, mix in remaining ingredients, cover, and let stand at room temperature 1 hour before serving.

NP Tablespoon: 45 C, 10 mg CH, 60 mg S*

CLAM AND CREAM CHEESE DIP

1 1/2 cups

1 (8-ounce) package cream cheese, softened to room temperature
1/4 cup light cream
1 tablespoon lemon juice
1 tablespoon Worcestershire sauce
1/4 teaspoon prepared horseradish
1/4 teaspoon salt
Pinch white pepper
1 (6 1/2-ounce) can minced clams, drained

Blend cream cheese and cream until smooth, mix in remaining ingredients, cover, and chill 1–2 hours to blend flavors.

NP Tablespoon: 45 C, 15 mg CH, 65 mg S*

VARIATION

Deviled Clam Dip: Prepare as directed, reducing cream to 2 tablespoons and adding 2 tablespoons spicy brown mustard, 1 tablespoon grated onion, 1/4 crushed clove garlic, and 1/8 teaspoon liquid hot red pepper seasoning.

NP Tablespoon: 40 C, 15 mg CH, 75 mg S*

SHERRIED GREEN CHEESE DIP

2 cups

A particularly good dip for small celery sticks.

8 ounces sharp Cheddar cheese spread, softened to room temperature
6 ounces Roquefort cheese, softened to room temperature
1/4–1/3 cup medium-dry sherry

With an electric mixer or in a food processor fitted with the metal chopping blade, beat cheeses and 1/4 cup sherry 15–20 seconds until smooth; if you like a softer dip, add more sherry. Cover and let stand 1 hour at room temperature to blend flavors before serving.

NP Tablespoon: 50 C, 10 mg CH, 140 mg S*

CURRY DIP

2 1/2 cups

Good as a dip for crisp sticks of celery, carrot, or finocchio.

2 (8-ounce) packages cream cheese, softened to
   room temperature
1/3 cup milk
1 tablespoon Worcestershire sauce
1/4 teaspoon liquid hot red pepper seasoning
1 tablespoon curry powder
1 tablespoon finely grated yellow onion
1/2 teaspoon salt

Beat all ingredients together with an electric
mixer or in a food processor fitted with the
metal chopping blade 20–30 seconds until
creamy. Cover and chill several hours. Let
stand 1/2 hour at room temperature before
serving. If mixture still seems a bit stiff for
dipping, thin with a little milk.

*NP Tablespoon: 40 C, 15 mg CH, 65 mg S**

GUACAMOLE

2 cups ⊠

Because they are firm and flavorful, Hass avocados from California and Mexico are the
best to use for Guacamole. They're in season
in summer and when properly ripe, their
thin, pebbly skins will be black.

Juice of 1/2 lemon
2 medium-size ripe avocados
1 tablespoon grated yellow onion
1 tablespoon olive oil
1/2–1 small pickled hot green chili pepper,
   drained, seeded, and minced
1/2 teaspoon salt

Place lemon juice in a small bowl; halve avocados lengthwise, remove pits, scoop flesh
into bowl, and mash with a fork (mixture
should be quite lumpy). Mix in all remaining
ingredients. Place a piece of plastic food
wrap directly on surface of Guacamole (to
retard browning) and let stand at room temperature 1 hour to blend flavors. Stir well
and serve as a dip with crisp corn chips.

*NP Tablespoon: 25 C, 0 mg CH, 35 mg S**

VARIATION

Guacamole with Tomato: Prepare Guacamole as directed above, then stir in 1 small
firm-ripe tomato that has been peeled, cored,
seeded, and coarsely chopped. Cover and let
stand as recipe directs. Stir well and serve as
a dip with crisp corn chips or bed on lettuce
and serve as a salad.

*NP Tablespoon: 25 C, 0 mg CH, 35 mg S**

BLACK BEAN DIP

2 cups ⊲⊳ ¢ ⊠

2 cups cooked or canned black beans, drained
   (reserve 1/2 cup liquid)
1 small yellow onion, peeled and minced
1 large clove garlic, peeled and crushed
1/4 teaspoon liquid hot red pepper seasoning
2 tablespoons dark rum or dry sherry
1 teaspoon salt
1 tablespoon lemon juice
2 tablespoons sour cream (optional)

Purée all ingredients except sour cream by
buzzing 20–30 seconds in an electric blender
at high speed or 15–20 seconds in a food
processor fitted with the metal chopping
blade. Transfer to a small serving bowl,
cover, and chill 2–3 hours. Let dip stand at
room temperature about 30 minutes before
serving. Top, if you like, with sour cream,
then serve with crisp corn chips or cubes of
rough country bread.

*NP Tablespoon: 15 C, 0 mg CH, 70 mg S**

HUMMUS (MIDDLE EASTERN CHICK-PEA SPREAD)

1 1/4 cups ⊠

1 cup cooked or canned chick-peas, drained
   (reserve 2 tablespoons liquid)
1/3 cup tahini (sesame seed paste)
1 large clove garlic, peeled and crushed
6 tablespoons lemon juice
1/2 teaspoon salt
1 tablespoon olive oil (garnish)
1 tablespoon minced parsley (garnish)

Purée chick-peas with cooking or can liquid,
tahini, garlic, lemon juice, and salt by buzzing 20–30 seconds in an electric blender at
high speed or in a food processor fitted with
the metal chopping blade. Spoon into a
small shallow bowl and make a shallow well
in the center. Spoon in olive oil and scatter
parsley on top. Serve as a dip or spread for
Armenian flat bread, pita, or sesame seed
crackers.

*NP Tablespoon: 50 C, 0 mg CH, 55 mg S**

BEER CHEESE SPREAD

1 quart

This spread is best if allowed to age about a
week in the refrigerator before using.

1 pound mild Cheddar cheese, finely grated
1 pound sharp Cheddar cheese, finely grated
1/4 cup finely grated Bermuda onion
1/2 clove garlic, peeled and crushed

1/4 cup ketchup
1 tablespoon Worcestershire sauce
1/8 teaspoon liquid hot red pepper seasoning
1 (12-ounce) can beer

Let cheeses soften at room temperature at least 1 hour. With an electric mixer or in a food processor fitted with the metal chopping blade, mix cheeses and all remaining ingredients except beer by snapping motor on and off several times. With motor running, beat in the beer, a little at a time; continue beating until light and fluffy. Chill well before serving.

NP Tablespoon: 60 C, 15 mg CH, 100 mg S*

TARAMASALATA (GREEK FISH ROE DIP)

1 cup ▨

This thick, creamy Greek appetizer is made with *tarama* (pale orange carp roe). Greek and Middle Eastern groceries sell it, but if unavailable use red or "American Golden" (whitefish) caviar.

1/4 cup tarama (carp roe)
2 tablespoons lemon juice
2 slices white bread, trimmed of crusts, soaked in cold water, and squeezed dry
1/2 cup olive oil
1/4 cup cooking oil
1/4 teaspoon onion juice

Blend *tarama,* lemon juice, bread, and olive oil in an electric blender or in a food processor fitted with the metal chopping blade about 1 minute, scrape blender cup or work bowl sides down with a rubber spatula, and blend again 1/2 minute. Add cooking oil and blend 1/2 minute. Stir in onion juice and serve at room temperature as a dip for raw vegetables or unsalted crackers. Or use as a spread for pumpernickel rounds or melba toast.

NP Tablespoon: 100 C, 10 mg CH, 15 mg S*

EGG-DILL SPREAD

1 pint ¢ ▨

5 hard-cooked eggs, peeled and minced
1/3 cup melted butter or margarine
1 teaspoon prepared Dijon-style mustard
1 tablespoon minced fresh dill
1 tablespoon white wine vinegar
1/2 teaspoon salt
1/2 teaspoon Worcestershire sauce
1/8 teaspoon pepper
2–3 dashes liquid hot red pepper seasoning

Mix all ingredients together and use as a cocktail spread. Especially good on small squares of pumpernickel.

NP Tablespoon: 30 C, 50 mg CH, 70 mg S*

LIPTAUER CHEESE SPREAD

1 cup

1/2 pound chèvre (goat cheese), trimmed of any rind, at room temperature, or 1 (8-ounce) package cream cheese, at room temperature
1/4 cup butter or margarine, at room temperature
2 anchovy fillets, minced fine
1/2 teaspoon crushed caraway seeds
1 teaspoon minced chives
1 teaspoon grated yellow onion
1/2 teaspoon paprika
1 teaspoon Dijon mustard
2 teaspoons minced drained capers (optional)

Blend all ingredients together well, pack in an 8- or 10-ounce crock, cover, and chill 3–4 hours. Let spread stand at room temperature about 30 minutes before serving so it is a good spreading consistency.

NP Tablespoon: 75 C, 25 mg CH, 95 mg S*

CAPONATA (SICILIAN EGGPLANT SPREAD)

3 cups ⚖

Refrigerated, this will keep about a week. Bring to room temperature before serving.

4 tablespoons olive oil
1 small eggplant, cut in 1″ cubes but not peeled
1 medium-size yellow onion, peeled and minced
1/3 cup minced celery
1 cup tomato purée
1/3 cup coarsely chopped, pitted green and/or ripe olives
4 anchovy fillets, minced
2 tablespoons capers
2 tablespoons red wine vinegar
1 tablespoon sugar
1/2 teaspoon salt (about)
1/4 teaspoon pepper
1 tablespoon minced parsley

Heat 3 tablespoons oil in a large, heavy saucepan 1 minute over moderately high heat, add eggplant and sauté, stirring now and then, 10 minutes until golden and nearly translucent. Add remaining oil, onion, and celery and stir-fry 5–8 minutes until pale golden. Add remaining ingredients except parsley, cover, and simmer 1 1/4–1 1/2 hours until quite thick, stirring now and then. Mix in parsley, cool to room temperature, taste for salt and adjust as needed. Serve as a spread for crackers.

NP Tablespoon: 20 C, 0 mg CH, 60 mg S*

BABA GANOUJ (MIDDLE EASTERN EGGPLANT SPREAD)

2 cups ◁▷

Baba ganouj is integral to *mezze,* that seemingly endless parade of hors d'oeuvre that begins every important Middle Eastern meal. It is mounded onto a plate, swirled around so there's a shallow crater in the center into which a tablespoon or two of olive oil is then spooned. Sometimes ruby pomegranate seeds are strewn on top, sometimes minced pistachios or black olives. But usually *baba ganouj* is sprinkled with coarsely chopped Italian (flat-leaf) parsley.

1 eggplant (about 1 pound)
1 large clove garlic, peeled and crushed
⅓ cup tahini (sesame seed paste)
5 tablespoons lemon juice
¾ teaspoon salt
1 tablespoon olive oil (top quality)
1 tablespoon coarsely chopped Italian parsley

Preheat broiler. Prick eggplant all over with a sharp fork and broil 6″ from the heat about 20 minutes, turning every 5 minutes until skin blackens and eggplant is soft. Cool until easy to handle; slip off the skin. Place eggplant, garlic, tahini, lemon juice, and salt in an electric blender cup or food processor fitted with the metal chopping blade and purée by buzzing 5–10 seconds (use highest blender speed). Ladle onto a plate, make a shallow well in the center, and spoon in the olive oil. Scatter parsley on top and serve with crisp Middle Eastern flat bread or with triangles of pita bread.

NP Tablespoon: 25 C, 0 mg CH, 50 mg S*

MUSHROOM CAVIAR

1¾ cups ◁▷

If you are a vegetarian, omit the bacon and bring the mixture to a good spreading consistency by adding 2–3 tablespoons tawny port or dry sherry.

2 slices bacon, snipped crosswise in small strips
¼ cup butter or margarine
1 pound mushrooms, wiped clean and sliced thin
1 cup minced scallions (include tops)
2 cloves garlic, peeled and crushed
½ teaspoon salt (about)
¼ teaspoon pepper

Fry bacon in a large heavy skillet about 5 minutes over moderate heat until crisp; drain bacon crumbles on paper toweling. Reserve skillet drippings, add butter, then sauté mushrooms, scallions, and garlic over moderately high heat about 10 minutes until most of the juices have evaporated. Stir often to prevent burning. Purée reserved bacon and skillet mixture with the salt and pepper by buzzing 10–15 seconds in an electric blender at high speed or 5–10 seconds in a food processor fitted with the metal chopping blade. Taste and adjust the seasoning, if needed. Cover and chill 1–2 hours. Let stand about 20 minutes at room temperature before serving. *(Note:* This spread is also delicious served slightly warm.)

NP Tablespoon: 25 C, 5 mg CH, 65 mg S*

COCKTAILS

These are not alcoholic cocktails but chilled fruits or seafoods served at the start of a meal. They are easy to prepare and can be quite glamorous, depending upon the presentation.

Fruit Cocktails

Tart fruits (grapefruit, kiwis, pineapple) are the best appetite whetters. They may be fresh, frozen, or canned (or a combination), they can be served solo, mixed together, or teamed with blander fruits such as mangoes, papayas, peaches, pears, avocados, apples, apricots, melons, or berries. Fruits, of course, should be peeled whenever the skin is hard or thick, cored or sectioned, seeded and cut in bite-size chunks, then chilled several hours. They may be spiked with champagne or dry wine, grenadine or crème de menthe or sprigged with fresh mint, rose geranium, or lemon verbena (if these leaves are tucked into the fruits before chilling, their bouquet will permeate the fruit). If fruits are not naturally tart, drizzle with lemon, lime, orange, or cranberry juice.

Fruit cocktails may be simply served in stemmed goblets, more elaborately presented by dishing into small bowls and imbedding in larger bowls of crushed ice or by mounding into grapefruit or orange shells, avocado or mango halves. Serve unadorned or crown with scoops of fruit ice or sherbet or dabs of tart fruit jelly. The main point to bear in mind when making fruit cocktails: Keep the fruit mixtures tart and light, varied and colorful.

Fruit Juice Cocktails

(These are included in the beverage chapter.)

Seafood Cocktails

Shrimp cocktail is America's favorite, especially when the shrimp are plump and tender, cooked in a fragrant court bouillon and served well chilled on beds of crushed ice with a horseradish-hot cocktail sauce. Other cold, cooked shellfish make delicious cocktails, too—lobster, crab, Alaska king crab, tiny bay scallops, especially with Green Mayonnaise. Full instructions for preparing and cooking shellfish are included in the seafood chapter, also directions for serving oysters and clams on the half shell, for pickling shrimp and oysters. Here, too, are recipes for Ceviche (Peruvian Raw Pickled Fish), Sashimi (raw fish Japanese style), and a number of other unusual cold fish dishes that can double as appetizers.

Seafood cocktails are routinely served in small stemmed glasses with ruffs of greenery and dabs of cocktail sauce. They're far more appealing arranged on beds of crushed ice or piled into avocado, papaya, or mango halves. However served, seafood cocktails should be accompanied by a tart rather than a rich dressing. And the portions should be small.

FIVE

Soups

With so many soups coming out of cans and boxes, few of us bother to make them the old-fashioned way. Too bad, because we're missing the friendliness of the soup kettle singing on the back of the stove. Such headiness it sends through the house, such promise of goodness. Making soup, time consuming as it may be (and it isn't always), *is* virtually effortless because the kettle can bubble away unattended.

The varieties of soup are nearly endless (as supermarket shelves testify), but basically there are four types: *thin clear soups, cream soups, thick vegetable and/or meat soups,* and *sweet or dessert soups.* Within these categories are the hot and the cold, the delicate and the husky, some of which are closer to stews than soups (certain of these— Bouillabaisse, Philadelphia Pepper Pot, Ukrainian-Style Borscht—are included in meat or seafood chapters; for page numbers, see the Index). There has always been some confusion about the difference between bouillons and consommés, bisques and other creamed soups, so to clarify:

A QUICK DICTIONARY OF SOUPS

Bisque: A rich creamed soup, usually of puréed crab, lobster, shrimp, or other shellfish.

Bouillon, Broth, Stock: Used interchangeably, all three terms mean the rich, savory liquid made by simmering meat, fish, or poultry with vegetables and seasonings in water. *Bouillon,* from the French verb *bouillir* (to boil) is sometimes made of a combination of meats; *broths and stocks,* however, are usually made of one meat only. *Brown stocks* are brewed from beef and beef bones and *white stocks* from veal.

Chowder: A lusty fish or shellfish soup, usually made with milk and often made with vegetables.

Consommé: A rich, clarified meat or poultry broth. *Double consommé* is simply double strength, made either by boiling down regular consommé or by using a higher proportion of meat and bones to liquid. *Jellied consommé* is just that; if rich enough, consommé will jell naturally when chilled; weaker consommés must be fortified with gelatin.

Madrilène: A sparkling, clear, ruby blend of beef or chicken consommé and tomatoes. When chilled, as it usually is before serving, madrilène jells slightly.

Potage: The French word for *soup;* as used today, it often means a creamed vegetable soup, especially a thick one.

Velouté: A soup enriched with egg yolks and cream.

SOME BASIC SOUP-MAKING TECHNIQUES

How to Clarify Broths: For each quart, allow 1 egg white and 1 crushed eggshell. Beat egg white until soft peaks form, stir into cooled broth along with shell, set over lowest heat, and heat, stirring with a whisk, until mixture foams up. Remove from heat, stir once, then let stand undisturbed 1 hour at room temperature. Line a sieve with a fine dish towel wrung out in cold water, set over a deep bowl, and ladle in broth, egg, shell and all, taking care not to stir up sediment in bottom of pan. Let drip through undisturbed. Remove any specks of fat from clarified liquid by blotting up with a paper towel. *Note:* An easier way to clarify is simply to pour the broth through the cloth-lined sieve, but for jewel-clear liquid, use the egg white and shell.

How to Color Stocks and Broths: Mix in a little commercial gravy browner or, for more delicate flavor, caramelized sugar* (it won't make the broth sweet):

Caramelized Sugar: Melt 1 cup sugar in a very heavy saucepan (not iron) over lowest heat, stirring. When dark brown, remove from heat and cool to room temperature. Add 1 cup boiling water, drop by drop, stirring all the while. Return to low heat and heat, stirring, until caramelized sugar dissolves.

How to Degrease Soups: The easiest way is to chill the soup, then lift off the hardened fat. Second best: skim off as much fat as possible, then blot up the rest by spreading paper toweling flat on the surface of the soup.

How to Dilute Soups: When held too long on the stove or chilled, soups often need thinning before serving. Thin cream soups with milk or light cream; meat, poultry, or fish soups with meat, poultry, or fish broth; vegetable soups with a meat or chicken broth or, if the soup contains tomatoes, with tomato juice. Cabbage and dried bean soups can be thinned with beer.

How to Reduce Soups: Boil uncovered until reduced to desired strength.

How to Thicken Soups

With Flour (best for cream soups): For each 1 cup soup, add any of the following:
• 1 tablespoon flour blended with 2 tablespoons cold water, milk, or broth
• 2 tablespoons rice, potato, soya, peanut, or wheat germ flour blended with ¼ cup cold water, milk, or broth
• 1 tablespoon flour blended with 1 tablespoon softened butter or margarine

Method: Blend a little hot soup into thickening agent, then quickly return to soup and heat, stirring, until thickened and smooth. For best flavor, let soup mellow 5–10 minutes after thickening.

With Raw Cereal (best for meat or vegetable soups): For each 1 cup soup, add any one of the following:
• 1 teaspoon medium pearl barley
• 1 teaspoon rice
• 1 teaspoon oatmeal

Method: About 1 hour before soup is done, mix in cereal, cover, and simmer, stirring now and then.

With Raw Potato (best for meat and vegetable soups; excellent for those with wheat and/or egg allergies): Allow 3 tablespoons grated raw potato for each cup soup; mix in 15–20 minutes before soup is done and cook, stirring now and then.

With Raw Egg (best for cream soups): For each 1 cup soup, add any one of the following:
• 2 egg yolks, lightly beaten
• 1 whole egg, lightly beaten

Method: Blend a little hot soup into egg, return to soup, set over *lowest* heat, and cook, stirring briskly, about 2 minutes until slightly thickened and no raw taste of egg remains; do not boil. *Note:* For easier blending, beat egg or yolks with about 2 tablespoons cold milk or broth or, for added zip, dry sherry.

With Hard-cooked Egg (excellent for dried bean soups): For each 2 cups soup, mix in 1 finely chopped hard-cooked egg just before serving. *Note:* If you prefer, scatter egg on top of each portion instead of mixing in.

With Pasta (best for consommés, meat and vegetable soups): Pasta doesn't thicken soup so much as give it body. Any thin spaghetti or macaroni, broken in short lengths, or tiny pasta shapes such as *stellette* (stars), *semini* (seeds), or alphabet letters will work. Depending on how hearty a soup you want, add 1–2 tablespoons uncooked pasta per cup. The pasta can be cooked in the soup (use package directions as a guide) or separately and added just before serving (this is the method to use when a clear broth is wanted).

With Bread Crumbs (good for meat or vegetable soups): Allow 1–2 tablespoons soft or dry bread crumbs per cup of soup and mix in just before serving.

Some Tips for Making Better Soups

• Most soups taste better if made 1–2 days ahead of time; reheat just before serving.
• Use vegetable cooking water in making soups, also in thinning condensed canned soups.
• Best bones to use for stocks: shin, marrow, neck, oxtail.
• Best bones to use for jellied stocks: veal knuckles.
• Whenever a soup tastes bland, add a little salt and pepper. Sometimes that's all that's needed to bring out the flavor.
• Use bouillon cubes or powders to strengthen weak soups.

• Cool soups uncovered and as quickly as possible.
• Always taste a cold soup before serving and adjust seasonings as needed; cold foods dull the taste buds and usually need more seasoning than hot foods.
• When a soup is flavored with wine or beer, reduce the salt slightly.
• Always add wine to soup shortly before serving and do not let soup boil.
• Use a light hand in adding wine to soup—1/4–1/3 cup per quart is usually enough. Too much wine will merely make the soup bitter.
• If a soup is to be reduced (boiled down), add the salt at the very end.
• If a soup seems *slightly* salty, add a peeled, halved raw potato and simmer about 15 minutes; it will absorb some of the salt. Remove the potato before serving.
• To mellow tomato soup, add 1 tablespoon sugar or light brown sugar.
• To give vegetable cream soups more character, purée the vegetables in a food mill; a blender or processor may reduce them to "mush."

Pressure-Cooking Soups

Soups suffer when cooked under pressure so use the pressure cooker only when necessary and only for making stocks. For best results, use 15 pounds pressure and process meat bones and stock 40 minutes, poultry 20 minutes, and vegetables 5. Release pressure and finish cooking over low heat. To reach their peak of flavor, meat stocks may take as much as 1 hour of slow simmering, poultry stocks about 1/2 hour, and vegetable stocks 15 minutes. This method seems to produce stocks that don't taste of the pressure cooker.

Microwaving Soups

Microwaves excel at making and heating soups because they are both fast and efficient (if you use a *temperature probe,* there is even little danger of scorching). Here are some tips that apply specifically to microwaving soups. (*Note:* Also study very carefully Microwave Ovens in Chapter 1 and Microwaving Beverages in Chapter 3—like beverages, soups are mostly liquid, so many techniques are similar.)
• Heat soup right in the soup bowl or cup provided there are no glued-on handles or metal trim. A microwave set at *HIGH* can heat a cup of soup in 2–3 minutes (chilled soups take slightly longer and should be stirred often).

• Dilute canned condensed soups with water in a 1-quart glass measuring cup or 1 1/2-quart casserole, then heat 5–7 minutes in microwave set on *HIGH;* stir frequently to distribute heat evenly.
• If your microwave has a *SIMMER* or *SLOW-COOK* setting, you can make stocks and soups from scratch without having to watch the pot. Place *temperature probe* in center of soup (not touching a meat or vegetable) with tip resting on utensil bottom. Cover with plastic food wrap, gathering it loosely around probe so steam can escape, then *SIMMER* or *SLOW-COOK* as manufacturer directs.
• Freeze leftover soup in individual serving-size containers. Come serving time, defrost, then reheat in microwave as manufacturer directs. If soup is thick, cover with plastic food wrap and pierce with a knife to allow steam egress.
• To keep soups hot, use *temperature hold* with the *temperature probe* set at 165° F.

SERVING SOUPS

How to Choose a Soup: Soups can be the prelude to an elegant meal or, in the case of a family-style lunch or supper, the meal itself. Soup served as a first course should set the tone of the meal and complement what's to follow. Thus, if the main course is rich or spicy, the soup should be light or bland (never serve a cream soup with a creamed entree). If the main course is roast meat or fowl, the soup may be richer, a bisque, perhaps, or a cream vegetable soup. Pay attention to flavors, too, never duplicating within a meal. Soup should be the counterpoint, offering a contrast of flavor, texture, color, and sometimes temperature (a steaming soup is splendid before cold salmon, a cool Vichyssoise before broiled steak). Cool soups, obviously, are welcome when the temperature's nudging 90°, warm soups in winter.

How to Figure Number of Servings: As a general rule, 1 quart soup will make 6 first-course servings, 3–4 main course.

How to Choose the Proper Soup Bowl and Spoon: The kind of soup and the formality of the meal both dictate which to use. See the list of popular soup bowls and spoons together with tips for using each.

Tureens: When a meal is informal and soup the main course, a tureen adds a note of importance; it also keeps the soup hot for "seconds."

Type of Soup Bowl	Appropriate Spoon	Appropriate Soup
Bouillon cup	Teaspoon	Bouillon, consommé, or other thin, clear soup that can be drunk
Double-eared bouillon cup	Round-bowled soup spoon	Bouillon, consommé, or other thin, clear soup that can be drunk
Oriental soup bowl	Teaspoon	Clear Oriental soups such as Won Ton or Egg Drop
Soup plate	Round- or oval-bowled soup spoons	Chowders, thick meat, poultry, or vegetable soups
Marmite	Any soup spoon	Baked or broiled soups
Multipurpose American soup bowls	Any soup spoon	Any soup
Mugs	———	Any hot or cold soup that can be drunk
Glasses	———	Any cold soup that can be drunk

Some Tips on Serving Soups

Hot Soups: Have the soup steaming hot and ladle into heated soup bowls.

Cold Soups: Have soup well chilled and serve in chilled bowls. For a festive touch, bed the soup bowls in larger bowls of crushed ice or, if the soup is a thin one, serve in glasses on the rocks.

Some Ways to Garnish Soups

Clear Soups (Hot)
Avocado slices or cubes
Chiffonade (butter-sautéed shreds of lettuce or sorrel)
Crumbled French-fried onions
Cubed, peeled, seeded tomato
Dumplings (liver, farina)
Gnocchi
Julienne strips of cooked meat or vegetables or brunoise (butter-sautéed shreds of carrot, leeks, and celery)
Lemon, lime, or orange slices
Matzo Balls
Minced fresh chives, chervil, dill, mint, parsley, or tarragon
Pasta (Nockerln, Spätzle, Viennese soup "peas," Won Tons)
Quenelles (especially for fish broth)
Royale Custard
Sliced, cooked beef marrow
Slivered pimiento or sliced green or ripe olives
Tofu cubes

Clear Soups (Cold or Jellied)
Avocado slices or cubes

Cubed, peeled, seeded tomato
Cubed, peeled, or unpeeled cucumber
Lemon, lime, or orange slices or wedges
Minced fresh chives, chervil, dill, fennel, mint, parsley, tarragon, or watercress
Minced radishes or scallions
Sour cream sprinkled with one of the minced herbs listed above

Cream Soups (Hot or Cold)
Bacon crumbles
Croutons (plain or seasoned)
Crumbled French-fried onions
Crumbled or grated cheese
Finely grated lemon or orange rind
Minced cashews, peanuts, pistachio or piñon nuts, or slivered blanched or toasted almonds, soybean nuts
Minced fresh basil, chives, chervil, dill, fennel, mint, parsley, tarragon, or watercress
Minced or thinly sliced truffles
Paprika, chili or curry powder
Poppy or caraway seeds
Sesame seeds, lightly toasted
Sliced ripe or green olives
Slivered pimiento

Thick Vegetable, Meat, or Fish Soups
Bacon crumbles
Croutons (plain or seasoned)
Grated sharp cheese
Lemon or orange slices (especially for fish soups)
Minced chives, dill, parsley, or watercress
Sliced frankfurters or sautéed pepperoni, *chorizos,* kielbasa, or other garlic sausage (especially for dried pea or bean soups)

ALL-PURPOSE STOCK

1 quart   ¢ ⚖

Before freezers and refrigerators there was the stock pot. It's still a good way to use meat and vegetable leftovers, vegetable cooking water, celery tops, mushroom stems, tomato peelings, and other vegetable parings.

2–3 cups finely chopped mixed leftover lean meat and vegetables
1 pound beef, veal, or lamb bones
2 quarts water
1 bay leaf and 1 sprig each parsley and thyme, tied in cheesecloth *(bouquet garni)*
Salt
Pepper

Simmer leftovers, bones, water, and *bouquet garni,* covered, in a large, heavy kettle 2–3 hours; add salt and pepper to taste. Strain through a fine sieve, cool, chill, and skim off fat. Store in refrigerator or freezer and use as a base for soups, stews, and sauces.

NP Cup: 20 C, 0 mg CH, 415 mg S*

CHICKEN BROTH (STOCK)

2 quarts   ⚖

The perfect base for soups and stews.

1 (5½–6-pound) stewing hen, cleaned and dressed
2 quarts water
1 medium-size yellow onion, peeled and quartered
1 stalk celery (include top)
1 medium-size carrot, peeled
2 sprigs parsley
1 bay leaf
6 peppercorns
1½ teaspoons salt

Place hen, giblets, and all remaining ingredients in a large heavy kettle, cover, and simmer 1½–2 hours until hen is tender; lift hen and giblets from broth and cool. *Note:* For more tender giblets, remove after 15–20 minutes' simmering. Strain broth, cool, then chill and skim off fat; save fat, if you like, clarify,* and keep on hand to use in cooking. Discard chicken skin, remove meat from bones, and save to use in recipes calling for cooked chicken meat.

NP Cup: 40 C, 0 mg CH, 410 mg S*

VARIATIONS

¢ ⚖   **Economy Chicken Broth:** Proceed as directed, using 4–5 pounds chicken backs and wings instead of the hen and simmering about 1 hour. Nutritional count same as basic recipe.

⚖   **Delicate Chicken Broth:** Proceed as directed, using 4 quarts water instead of 2.

NP Cup: 20 C, 0 mg CH, 205 mg S*

⚖   **Turkey Broth:** Prepare as directed, substituting 1 (6-pound) turkey for the hen. Recipe too flexible for meaningful nutritional count.

CHICKEN GIBLET STOCK

1 pint   ⚖ ¢

Use as a base for soups, sauces, and gravies.

Giblets and neck from 1 chicken, washed
2 cups cold water
½ small yellow onion, peeled and coarsely chopped
½ stalk celery
½ carrot, peeled
1 bay leaf
2 peppercorns
½ teaspoon salt (about)

Simmer giblets and remaining ingredients, covered, 15 minutes. Remove liver and reserve, also remove heart if it is tender. Recover and simmer remaining giblets until tender, 1–2 hours, replenishing water as needed. Strain stock, taste for seasoning, and adjust as needed; chill and skim off fat. Mince giblets and, if you like, meat from neck. Save to use in gravy or sauce recipes or mix into recipes calling for cooked chicken meat.

NP Cup: 35 C, 35 mg CH, 580 mg S*

VARIATIONS

Recipes too flexible for meaningful nutritional count.

⚖   **Turkey Giblet Stock** *(Makes about 1 quart):* Cook turkey giblets and neck as directed for chicken, using 1 quart water and doubling all remaining ingredients.

⚖   **Giblet Stock from Other Poultry and Game Birds:** Prepare as directed for Chicken Giblet Stock, adjusting quantity of water and seasonings to number of giblets.

⚖   **Quantity Giblet Stock:** For each additional pint of stock needed over and above what basic recipe makes, use 1 pint chicken broth, 2–3 chicken livers, ¼ yellow onion, peeled, ½ stalk celery, and ½ bay leaf. Simmer as directed, removing 1 liver after 15 minutes (so stock will not be overly strong of liver). Simmer remaining giblets 1–2 hours, replenishing liquid with chicken broth as needed. Strain and season to taste as directed. Mince giblets and add to stock or save to use in other recipes.

BEEF BROTH (STOCK)

3 quarts ¢ ⚖️

A rich brown broth to use in making soups and sauces.

**4–5 pounds beef shin and marrowbones, cracked
  (a 1/2 and 1/2 mixture is best)**
**1 large yellow onion, peeled and coarsely
  chopped**
2 leeks, washed, trimmed, and coarsely chopped
**2 medium-size carrots, peeled and coarsely
  chopped**
2 stalks celery, coarsely chopped
5 quarts water
**2–3 sprigs parsley or 1 bay leaf and 1 sprig each
  parsley and thyme, tied in cheesecloth
  (*bouquet garni*)**
6 peppercorns
1 bay leaf, crumbled
1 tablespoon salt (about)

Bring all ingredients to a boil in a large heavy kettle, turn heat to low, skim off froth, cover, and simmer 4–5 hours; check pot occasionally and add extra water if needed. Skim off fat, then strain stock through a sieve lined with a double thickness of cheesecloth; pour into a clean kettle and boil rapidly, uncovered, until reduced to about 3 quarts. Taste for salt and adjust as needed. Cool, then chill; lift off solidified fat. Stock is now ready to use in recipes. Store in refrigerator or freezer.

NP Cup: 25 C, 0 mg CH, 560 mg S*

VARIATIONS

¢ ⚖️ **Brown Beef Stock:** Roast bones uncovered in a shallow roasting pan in a 425° F. oven 3/4–1 hour until brown. Meanwhile, stir-fry onion, leeks, carrots, and celery in 2 tablespoons beef drippings or margarine in kettle 12–15 minutes over moderate heat until well browned. Add bones, 4 quarts water, and remaining ingredients. Drain fat from roasting pan, add remaining water, stirring to scrape up browned bits; pour into kettle and proceed as directed.

NP Cup: 50 C, 0 mg CH, 1120 mg S*

⚖️ **Double-Strength Beef Broth:** Brown bones as for Brown Beef Stock (above). Also brown 2 pounds boned beef chuck, shank, or neck, cut in 1″ cubes, in 2 tablespoons beef drippings or margarine in a large kettle; add vegetables, brown, then proceed as above.

Note: Boned beef may be saved after cooking and used in hash, stuffing, or sandwich spreads.

NP Cup: 60 C, 5 mg CH, 565 mg S*

⚖️ **Veal (White) Stock:** Prepare as for Beef Broth (above), using 2 veal shanks and 4–5 pounds veal bones or a 1/2 and 1/2 mixture of veal and beef bones. Recipe too flexible for meaningful nutritional count.

BEEF CONSOMMÉ

1 quart ⚖️

Richer than Beef Broth and delicious hot or cold.

**1 quart Beef Broth or Double-Strength Beef
  Broth**
1/2 pound very lean ground beef
1/2 medium-size carrot, peeled and minced
1 small yellow onion, peeled and minced
1/2 stalk celery, minced

Simmer all ingredients, covered, 1 hour; strain through a fine sieve lined with cheesecloth, cool, chill, and remove all fat. Clarify,* taste for salt, and adjust as needed. Serve hot or cold.

NP Cup: 45 C, 5 mg CH, 570 mg S*

VARIATIONS

⚖️ **Double Consommé:** Prepare as directed; after clarifying, boil rapidly, uncovered, until reduced by half. If you like, stir in 1/2 cup dry sherry or Madeira. Serve hot or cold.

NP Cup: 90 C, 10 mg CH, 1135 mg S*
*NP Cup (with sherry): 170 C, 10 mg CH, 1140
  mg S**

⚖️ **Consommé Royale:** Prepare 1 recipe Royale Custard (made with beef consommé), cut in fancy shapes, and float a few pieces in each soup bowl.

⚖️ **Jellied Consommé:** Prepare consommé as directed and chill 1 cup about 2 hours to test firmness. If firm, no extra gelatin is needed. If semifirm, mix 1 envelope unflavored gelatin into consommé; if liquid, 2 envelopes. Heat, stirring, until gelatin dissolves, then cool and chill until firm. Before serving, break up consommé with a fork. Serve in chilled bowls or bowls set in larger bowls of crushed ice. Sprinkle with minced chives, scallions, or parsley and garnish with lemon wedges.

*NP Cup (1 envelope gelatin): 50 C, 5 mg CH, 570
  mg S**
*NP Cup (2 envelopes gelatin): 55 C, 5 mg CH, 570
  mg S**

EASY FISH STOCK

2 quarts   ⚖ ¢

Bones of haddock, halibut, cod, sea bass, and/or pike produce a fragrant stock. Use for making seafood soups and sauces.

2 quarts cold water
1 pound fishbones, heads and trimmings
1 tablespoon salt

Place all ingredients in a kettle, cover, and simmer 1 hour. Strain liquid through a fine sieve and use for poaching fish, making soups or sauces. *(Note:* This stock freezes well.)

NP Cup: 5 C, 5 mg CH, 830 mg S*

VEGETABLE STOCK

3 quarts   ¢ ⚖

Use this stock as a base for vegetable soups or sauces.

2 large yellow onions, peeled and minced
2 cups coarsely chopped, scrubbed, *unpeeled* carrots
2 cups coarsely chopped celery (include some tops)
2 cups coarsely chopped, *unpeeled* tomatoes
2 cups coarsely chopped mushrooms (include stems)
2 leeks, washed, trimmed, and coarsely chopped
1 cup coarsely chopped cabbage or cauliflower heart and trimmings (optional)
4 sprigs parsley
2 bay leaves, crumbled
6 peppercorns
4 teaspoons salt (about)
1 gallon water

Simmer all ingredients in a large covered kettle 2 hours; check liquid occasionally and add water as needed to maintain level at about 3 quarts. Strain stock through a fine sieve and measure; if you have more than 3 quarts, boil rapidly, uncovered, to reduce; if less than 3 quarts, add boiling water to round out measure. Taste for salt and adjust as needed. Cool, then store in refrigerator or freezer.

NP Cup: 15 C, 0 mg CH, 745 mg S*

CONSOMMÉ MADRILÈNE

4 servings   ⚖

Madrilène should be made with sun-ripened tomatoes, but since they are scarce, this recipe substitutes canned purée.

2 cups tomato purée
1 quart beef consommé or fat-free chicken broth
1 teaspoon minced chives
1 teaspoon minced parsley
1/8 teaspoon cayenne pepper
1/4 cup dry sherry or Madeira wine (optional)
1 tablespoon slivered pimiento (optional)

Mix purée, consommé, chives, parsley, and cayenne in a saucepan, cover, and heat over lowest heat 15 minutes; mixture should barely simmer. Strain through a fine sieve lined with several thicknesses of cheesecloth. For a sparkling madrilène, let drip through undisturbed. Bring liquid to a boil and, if you like, stir in sherry and pimiento.

NPS: 80 C, 0 mg CH, 1130 mg S*
NPS (with sherry): 100 C, 0 mg CH, 1130 mg S*

VARIATION

⚖ **Jellied Consommé Madrilène:** Prepare as directed using beef consommé. Heat 1 envelope unflavored gelatin in 1/3 cup water over moderate heat, stirring until dissolved. Stir into madrilène, add sherry and, if you like, pimiento. Taste for salt and adjust as needed. Cool, then chill until firm. Break madrilène up with a fork, ladle into chilled bowls, garnish with minced chives or watercress and lemon wedges, and serve.

NPS: 85 C, 0 mg CH, 1135 mg S*

BASIC ASPIC

1 quart   ⚖

Clear aspic is sometimes used to coat or glaze party food—a whole ham, for example, poached fresh salmon, a *chaudfroid,* meat or poultry, or vegetable canapés. Any clear meat, poultry, vegetable, or fish stock can be used. *(Note:* A recipe for Court Bouillon for Aspics and directions for clarifying it are included in the fish chapter.)

1 quart clarified* Beef Broth, Brown Beef Broth, Veal (White) Stock, Chicken Broth, or Vegetable Stock
1–2 envelopes unflavored gelatin (optional)
1/4–1/2 cup cold water (optional)

First, determine broth's jelling power by chilling 1 cup. If it sets up firmly, it will need no gelatin; if soft, it will need 1 envelope gelatin, if soupy, 2 envelopes. *(Note:* Vegetable stock will always need the full amount of gelatin.) Soften required amount of gelatin in cold water—1/4 cup cold water to each envelope gelatin—then add to broth (including that chilled for jelling test) and heat and stir over low heat until dissolved. To prevent bubble formation, stir gently; do not beat. Chill until thick and syrupy. *(Note:* To quick-chill, set over ice cubes.) Aspic is now ready to use for glazing foods or as recipes direct.

NP Cup (1 envelope gelatin): 5 C, 0 mg CH, 1 mg S*

NP Cup (2 envelopes gelatin): 10 C, 0 mg CH, 5 mg S*

VARIATIONS

⊠ ⫡ **Quick and Easy Aspic:** Slowly heat 1 envelope unflavored gelatin and 3 cups beef consommé or madrilène, stirring until dissolved. If you like, mix in 2–3 tablespoons medium-dry sherry.

NP Cup: 50 C, 0 mg CH, 640 mg S*

⊠ ⫡ **Quick and Easy Light Aspic:** Soften 1 envelope unflavored gelatin in 1 cup cold water, then heat and stir until dissolved. Add 1/2 cup each chicken broth and beef consommé.

NP Cup: 30 C, 0 mg CH, 355 mg S*

CHICKEN NOODLE SOUP

4 servings ¢ ⫡ ⊠

1 quart Chicken Broth
1 cup fine noodles
1 cup diced cooked chicken meat
Salt
Pepper
2 teaspoons minced parsley

Bring broth to a boil in a large saucepan, add noodles and chicken, and simmer, uncovered, about 10 minutes until noodles are tender. Taste for salt and pepper and adjust as needed. Stir in parsley and serve.

NPS: 175 C, 50 mg CH, 810 mg S*

VARIATION

¢ ⫡ ⊠ **Chicken and Rice Soup:** Prepare as directed, substituting 1/3 cup uncooked rice for the noodles and cooking 15–20 minutes until rice is tender. Season and serve as directed.

NPS: 165 C, 30 mg CH, 810 mg S*

EGG DROP SOUP

4 servings ¢ ⫡ ⊠

1 quart Chicken Broth
1 scallion, minced (optional)
1/2 teaspoon sugar
1 teaspoon soy sauce
2 tablespoons cornstarch blended with 1/4 cup cold water

1 egg lightly beaten with 1 tablespoon cold water

Heat broth and, if you like, scallion to boiling in a heavy saucepan over moderate heat. Mix in sugar, soy sauce, and cornstarch paste and heat, stirring constantly, until slightly thickened. Bring mixture to a full boil, remove from heat and drizzle in egg mixture, stirring constantly. Ladle into hot bowls and serve.

NPS: 80 C, 70 mg CH, 905 mg S*

WON TON SOUP

8 servings

Fresh squares of noodle dough called won ton skins or wrappers can usually be bought in Chinese groceries. They should be refrigerated in foil or plastic food wrap and used within 4–5 days. If you're unable to buy them, here's how to make your own.

WON TON DOUGH
1 1/2 cups sifted flour
1 teaspoon salt
1 egg lightly beaten with 3 tablespoons cold water

FILLING
1/4 pound very lean uncooked pork, ground twice, or 1/2 cup minced cooked chicken meat or shrimp
2 water chestnuts, minced
2 scallions, minced
1 teaspoon grated fresh gingerroot or 1/8 teaspoon ginger
1 teaspoon soy sauce
1/2 teaspoon salt
Pinch pepper

BROTH
2 quarts + 1 cup chicken broth
1/2 cup julienne strips of cooked chicken meat or roast pork (optional)

For dough, sift flour with salt, add egg mixture all at once, and stir briskly with a fork until dough holds together; turn onto a lightly floured board and knead 2–3 minutes until smooth. Cover and let rest 1/2 hour. Dust board and rolling pin lightly with cornstarch and roll dough as thin as possible into a square about 16"; cut in 2 1/2" squares. Mix filling ingredients. Arrange noodle squares on counter, spoon about 1/2 teaspoon filling onto each, a little above center, then roll, as shown, sealing by moistening edges with cold water. Bring broth to a boil in a large kettle, drop in 6–8 won tons, and boil, uncovered, 5 minutes; lift out won tons and cover with a damp towel. Cook remaining

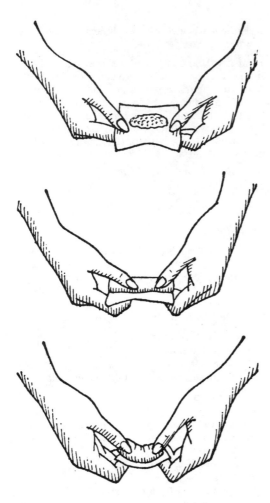

won tons the same way. When all won tons are done, return to broth and simmer, uncovered, 1 minute. Ladle broth into soup bowls, add 3 won tons to each, and serve. If you like, float a few strips chicken or pork in each bowl.

NPS (pork): 160 C, 45 mg CH, 1360 mg S*
NPS (chicken): 155 C, 40 mg CH, 1360 mg S*
NPS (shrimp): 150 C, 50 mg CH, 1365 mg S*

TOMATO VEGETABLE BOUILLON

4 servings ⚖

This Southern recipe has been handed down for generations. Rumor has it that it was Robert E. Lee's favorite soup.

6 large ripe tomatoes, peeled, seeded, and coarsely chopped
1 medium-size yellow onion, peeled and coarsely chopped
1 stalk celery, coarsely chopped
2 carrots, peeled and coarsely chopped

1/2 sweet green pepper, cored, seeded, and coarsely chopped
1 pint water
1 bay leaf
1 tablespoon sugar
1/4 cup dry sherry
1 teaspoon salt (about)
Pinch pepper

Place vegetables, water, bay leaf, and sugar in a large saucepan, cover, and simmer 1/2 hour. Strain through a fine sieve and return to pan. Add sherry, salt to taste, and pepper. Serve steaming hot.

NPS: 110 C, 0 mg CH, 590 mg S*

CLEAR MUSHROOM BROTH

6 servings ⚖

Glorious when made with morels, *chanterelles,* or other edible wild mushrooms.

1 pound mushrooms, wiped clean and minced
1 1/2 quarts beef bouillon or consommé, skimmed of any fat
1 small sprig each thyme, parsley, and marjoram, tied in cheesecloth (optional)
1/2 teaspoon finely grated onion
6 thin slices lemon

Place all ingredients except lemon in a large saucepan (not aluminum), cover, and simmer over lowest heat 1 hour, using an asbestos flame tamer, if necessary, to keep bouillon just trembling. Taste for salt and adjust as needed. Cool broth and chill overnight. Strain through a sieve lined with a double thickness of cheesecloth. Serve cold or piping hot with a lemon slice floating in each soup bowl.

NPS: 50 C, 0 mg CH, 650 mg S*

VARIATION

⚖ **Sherried Mushroom Broth:** Prepare as directed; just before serving, stir in 1/4–1/3 cup medium-dry sherry and, if you like, 2–3 very thinly sliced raw mushrooms or 1 thinly sliced truffle.

NPS: 65 C, 0 mg CH, 650 mg S*

FRENCH ONION SOUP

4 servings ⚖

If broth is pale, color a rich amber brown with liquid gravy browner or caramelized sugar.*

1/2 pound Spanish or yellow onions, peeled and sliced paper thin
2 tablespoons butter (no substitute)

1 quart beef broth, bouillon, or consommé
1/8 teaspoon pepper

Stir-fry onions in butter in a large, heavy saucepan over low heat 10–15 minutes until pale golden. Add broth and pepper, cover, and simmer 20–25 minutes, stirring occasionally, until onions are very tender. Taste for salt and add if needed. Serve steaming hot with French bread.

NPS: 90 C, 15 mg CH, 845 mg S*

V A R I A T I O N

French Onion Soup au Gratin: Prepare soup as directed and, while it simmers, preheat oven to 400° F.; also lightly toast 4 slices French bread. Ladle soup into 4 ovenproof soup bowls (individual casseroles or marmites are perfect), float a piece of toast in each, and sprinkle generously with grated Parmesan or shredded mozzarella cheese. Bake, uncovered, 5–7 minutes until cheese is lightly browned and bread puffed up. Serve at once.

NPS: 195 C, 20 mg CH, 1080 mg S*

DE LUXE CREAM OF VEGETABLE SOUP

4 servings

Thickened with cream and egg, not flour.

1 1/2 cups diced raw vegetable (asparagus, celery, peas, broccoli, spinach, carrots, onion, cauliflower, zucchini, or mushrooms)
2 tablespoons butter (no substitute)
1 pint chicken broth
1 teaspoon finely grated onion
1 cup heavy cream
2 egg yolks, lightly beaten

Stir-fry vegetable in butter in a heavy saucepan over moderately low heat about 10 minutes until wilted, not brown. Add broth and onion, cover, and simmer 10–15 minutes until vegetable is very soft. Purée by buzzing 20–30 seconds in an electric blender at low speed or 10–15 seconds in a food processor fitted with the metal chopping blade. Pour into the top of a large double boiler and set over simmering water. Mix cream and egg yolks and stir into soup; heat, stirring constantly, until slightly thickened. Taste for salt and pepper and adjust as needed. Serve piping hot.

NPS: 325 C, 235 mg CH, 490 mg S*

CREAM OF ALMOND SOUP

4 servings

Serve hot or icy cold.

1 stalk celery, minced
1 clove garlic, peeled and crushed
2 tablespoons butter or margarine
3 cups chicken broth
2/3 cup finely ground blanched almonds
1/8 teaspoon mace
1 cup heavy cream
1–2 tablespoons toasted, slivered almonds

Stir-fry celery and garlic in butter in a heavy saucepan 4–5 minutes over moderate heat until limp; add broth, ground almonds, and mace, cover, and simmer 30–40 minutes, stirring occasionally. Remove from heat and let stand at room temperature 1 hour. Purée by buzzing 20–30 seconds in two batches in an electric blender at low speed or 15–20 seconds in a single batch in a food processor fitted with the metal chopping blade. Return mixture to saucepan, smooth in cream, and heat, uncovered, stirring occasionally, 2–3 minutes; do not boil. Taste for salt and add if needed. Ladle into hot bowls, sprinkle with toasted almonds, and, if you like, dust with paprika. Or chill well and serve cold.

NPS: 430 C, 95 mg CH, 675 mg S*

CURRIED AVOCADO SOUP

6 servings　☒

2 2/3 cups rich chicken broth
1 teaspoon grated onion
1/4 garlic clove, peeled and crushed
2 teaspoons curry powder
2 ripe medium-size avocados
2 teaspoons lemon juice
1 cup milk or light cream

Simmer broth, onion, garlic, and curry powder, uncovered, in a small saucepan 8–10 minutes. Halve avocados lengthwise, remove pits, and scoop out flesh. Purée with lemon juice and 1 cup hot broth by buzzing 15–20 seconds in an electric blender at high speed or in a food processor fitted with the metal chopping blade. Add to broth in pan, stir in milk, and heat, stirring occasionally, 2–3 minutes. Serve hot or chill and serve cold.

NPS (with milk): 170 C, 5 mg CH, 725 mg S*
NPS (with cream): 225 C, 25 mg CH, 720 mg S*

BASIC PROPORTIONS FOR CREAMED VEGETABLE SOUPS

(6 servings)

Variety	Butter	Flour	Liquid	Cooked Vegetable Purée	Salt	White Pepper	Optional Seasonings
Artichoke (globe and Jerusalem) *NPS: 155 C, 25 mg CH, 755 mg S** **Asparagus** *NPS: 145 C, 25 mg CH, 725 mg S** **Celery** *NPS: 135 C, 25 mg CH, 780 mg S** **Endive** *NPS: 140 C, 25 mg CH, 730 mg S**	3 T.	3 T.	1 pint each milk and chicken or vegetable broth	2½ cups	1 t.	⅛ t.	Pinch each thyme and nutmeg and ¼ cup dry white wine
Broccoli *NPS: 135 C, 25 mg CH, 735 mg S** **Cauliflower** *NPS: 135 C, 25 mg CH, 730 mg S** **Onion** *NPS: 140 C, 25 mg CH, 730 mg S** **Leek** *NPS: 140 C, 25 mg CH, 730 mg S** **Brussels Sprouts** *NPS: 140 C, 25 mg CH, 730 mg S** **Cabbage** *NPS: 135 C, 25 mg CH, 730 mg S** **Kale** *NPS: 135 C, 25 mg CH, 740 mg S**	3 T.	3 T.	1 pint each milk and beef, chicken, or vegetable broth	2 cups	1 t.	⅛ t.	Pinch each cardamom and mace and ¼ cup grated mild Cheddar or Gruyère
Carrot *NPS: 120 C, 20 mg CH, 720 mg S** **Green Pea** *NPS: 140 C, 20 mg CH, 765 mg S**	2 T.	2 T.	1 pint each milk and chicken or vegetable broth	2 cups	1 t.	⅛ t.	1 t. grated orange rind, pinch rosemary, nutmeg, or savory or 1 T. minced fresh tarragon or chervil
Parsnip *NPS: 130 C, 20 mg CH, 710 mg S** **Turnip** *NPS: 110 C, 20 mg CH, 725 mg S** **Rutabaga** *NPS: 120 C, 20 mg CH, 710 mg S**	2 T.	2 T.	1 pint each milk and beef or chicken broth	2 cups	1 t.	⅛ t.	Pinch each cinnamon, allspice and ginger
Potato, tomato	SEE INDEX FOR RECIPES IN THIS CHAPTER						

Variety	Butter	Flour	Liquid	Cooked Vegetable Purée	Salt	White Pepper	Optional Seasonings
Spinach *NPS: 145 C, 25 mg* *CH, 760 mg S** **Watercress** *NPS: 140 C, 25 mg* *CH, 745 mg S**	3 T.	3 T.	1 pint each milk and chicken broth	2½ cups	1 t.	⅛ t.	2 T. each grated onion and lemon juice or curry powder, pinch nutmeg
Summer Squash *NPS: 180 C, 30 mg* *CH, 615 mg S**	3 T.	3 T.	3 cups milk and 1 cup beef or chicken broth	3 cups	1 t.	⅛ t.	¼ cup minced onion, ¼ t. each savory and oregano, pinch cinnamon or mace
Winter Squash *NPS: 130 C, 20 mg* *CH, 705 mg S** **Sweet Potato, Yam** *NPS: 175 C, 20 mg* *CH, 735 mg S** **Pumpkin** *NPS: 130 C, 20 mg* *CH, 900 mg S**	2 T.	1 T.	1 pint each milk and chicken broth	2 cups	1 t.	⅛ t.	¼ cup each orange juice and honey, ¼ t. each cinnamon, ginger, and cloves

METHOD: Melt butter in a large, heavy saucepan over moderate heat, blend in flour, add liquid, and heat, stirring, until mixture boils; turn heat to low, smooth in purée and seasonings, cover, and let mellow 5–10 minutes to blend flavors. Serve hot or chill and serve cold. (*Note:* For a silky-smooth soup, strain through a fine sieve, then heat to serving temperature or chill.)

VARIATIONS: In addition to the all-of-a-flavor soups above, many vegetables team well. To prepare, follow basic proportions above, using a ½ and ½ mixture of any of the following purées:

Carrot and Jerusalem artichoke	Carrot and winter squash	Onion and carrot
Carrot and celery	Carrot and pumpkin	Onion and green pea
Carrot and green pea	Carrot and sweet potato or yam	Onion and spinach
Carrot and parsnip	Celery and green pea	Onion and celery
Carrot and turnip	Celery and spinach	Onion and summer squash
Carrot and rutabaga	Celery and summer squash	Onion and pumpkin

CHESTNUT SOUP

6 servings

In the Pyrenees chestnut soup is sometimes enriched with leftover scraps of game bird; use it if you have it, or bits of turkey, goose, duck, or chicken.

1 medium-size yellow onion, peeled and minced
1 stalk celery, minced
2 tablespoons butter or margarine
1 tablespoon flour
1 pint chicken broth or water
1 pound shelled, peeled chestnuts
6 cups milk
1 cup heavy cream
½–¾ cup minced, cooked chicken, goose, turkey, duck, or game bird (optional)
1½ teaspoons salt
⅛ teaspoon white pepper
⅛ teaspoon mace
⅓ cup croutons

Stir-fry onion and celery in butter in a large, heavy saucepan over moderately low heat 5–8 minutes until pale golden. Sprinkle with flour, mix well, then slowly stir in broth. Add chestnuts, cover, and simmer about ½ hour until very soft. Put through a food mill or purée by churning 20–30 seconds in a food processor fitted with the metal chopping blade; return to pan and set over moderate heat. Add all remaining ingredients except croutons and heat, stirring, about 5 minutes; do not allow to boil. Taste for salt and adjust; ladle into soup bowls and pass croutons separately. (*Note:* This soup will be mellower if made the day before and reheated in the top of a double boiler.)

NPS: 545 C, 100 mg CH, 1110 mg S*

CUCUMBER VELOUTÉ

4–6 servings

6 tablespoons butter or margarine
2 medium-size yellow onions, peeled and
    coarsely chopped
3 medium-size cucumbers, peeled, seeded, and
    diced
1 teaspoon salt
1/8 teaspoon white pepper
Pinch mace
3 1/2 cups chicken broth
2 tablespoons flour
2 egg yolks, lightly beaten
1 cup light cream
2 tablespoons minced parsley

Melt 4 tablespoons butter in a large skillet over moderate heat, add onions and cucumbers, and sauté, stirring, 8–10 minutes until onions are golden. Stir in salt, pepper, mace, and broth, cover, and simmer 15 minutes until vegetables are soft. Put through a food mill or purée by buzzing 20–30 seconds in a food processor fitted with the metal chopping blade. In a large saucepan, melt remaining butter over moderate heat. Blend in flour, add purée, and heat, stirring constantly, until thickened and smooth. Spoon a little hot mixture into yolks, then return all to saucepan. Mix in cream, reduce heat to lowest point, and warm 1–2 minutes longer, stirring; do not boil. Serve hot or cold garnished with minced parsley.

NPS (4–6): 390–260 C, 220–150 mg CH, 1450–965 mg S*

DELUXE CREAM OF MUSHROOM SOUP

4 servings

3/4 pound mushrooms, wiped clean and minced
2 tablespoons butter (no substitute)
1 tablespoon cornstarch
1 1/2 cups chicken broth
1 1/2 cups light cream
1/2 teaspoon salt (about)
1/8 teaspoon white pepper
1 teaspoon Worcestershire sauce

Stir-fry mushrooms in butter in a heavy saucepan over low heat 5–7 minutes until limp; blend in cornstarch, add broth, and heat, stirring, 3–4 minutes. Cover and simmer over lowest heat 12–15 minutes, stirring occasionally. Purée by buzzing 20–30 seconds in a food processor fitted with the metal chopping blade or put through a food mill; return to pan. Add remaining ingredients and heat, stirring, 2–3 minutes. Taste for salt and adjust as needed.

NPS: 275 C, 75 mg CH, 685 mg S*

VARIATION

☖ **Low-Calorie Cream of Mushroom Soup:** Omit butter and cornstarch; simmer mushrooms in broth, then proceed as recipe directs, substituting skim milk for cream.

NPS: 70 C, 1 mg CH, 640 mg S*

POTAGE SAINT-GERMAIN

4 servings ☖

This soup should be made with fresh young peas, but if they're unavailable, use the frozen. Restaurants sometimes use dried split peas—very good but not authentic.

2 cups cooked green peas
2 cups White Stock or a 1/2 and 1/2 mixture of
    water and beef broth
1/2 teaspoon minced fresh chervil or 1/4 teaspoon
    dried chervil
1 tablespoon butter (no substitute)
1/4 cup croutons

Set aside 1 tablespoon peas; put the rest through a food mill or purée by buzzing with a little stock 20–30 seconds in a food processor fitted with the metal chopping blade. Mix purée and stock and strain through a fine sieve, pressing solids to extract as much liquid as possible. Pour into a saucepan, add chervil and butter, and heat, stirring now and then, about 5 minutes until a good serving temperature. Taste for seasoning and adjust as needed. Stir in reserved peas, ladle into bowls, and sprinkle with croutons.

NPS: 145 C, 10 mg CH, 445 mg S*

CREAMY PEANUT SOUP

6 servings ☒

A fragrant soup that makes a nice change of pace.

2 tablespoons butter or margarine
2 tablespoons flour

1 teaspoon salt
1/4 teaspoon cayenne pepper
Pinch nutmeg
1 pint milk
1 pint light cream
1 cup creamy peanut butter
1/4 cup tawny port or dry sherry

Melt butter in a large saucepan over moderate heat, blend in flour and seasonings, add milk and cream, and heat, stirring constantly, until thickened and smooth. Add peanut butter and continue to heat, stirring, until melted. Mix in wine and serve.

NPS: 510 C, 75 mg CH, 735 mg S*

VICHYSSOISE

6 servings

Deliciously bland and silky.

2 tablespoons butter or margarine
3 large leeks, washed, trimmed, and sliced thin
2 scallions, washed, trimmed, and sliced thin
1 small yellow onion, peeled and sliced thin
1 pound potatoes, peeled and sliced thin
2 1/2 cups chicken broth
1 1/2 teaspoons salt
Pinch white pepper
1 pint heavy cream
2 tablespoons minced fresh chives

Melt butter in a large kettle over moderate heat, add leeks, scallions, and onion, and sauté, stirring, 8–10 minutes until golden. Stir in all remaining ingredients except heavy cream and chives, cover, and simmer 45 minutes until vegetables are mushy; press all through a fine sieve. Return to kettle, add heavy cream, and heat and stir just until mixture boils. Remove from heat and put through sieve once again. Cool to room temperature, cover, and chill several hours. Serve very cold, topped with chives.

NPS: 415 C, 120 mg CH, 950 mg S*

PUMPKIN SOUP

4–6 servings

1 1/2 cups pumpkin purée
3 cups chicken broth
1 tablespoon flour
1 teaspoon salt
1/4 teaspoon ginger
1/4 teaspoon nutmeg
3/4 cup milk or light cream
1 teaspoon minced chives
2 egg yolks, lightly beaten

Heat pumpkin and broth in top of a double boiler over direct heat to a simmer. Blend flour, salt, ginger, and nutmeg with 1/4 cup milk, mix into pumpkin, and heat, stirring, 3–4 minutes. Cover, set over simmering water, and cook 20 minutes, stirring occasionally; mix in chives. Beat egg yolks lightly with remaining milk, add to soup, cook, and stir 5 minutes over simmering water, then serve. *(Note:* The flavor of this soup improves on standing. Just be sure to reheat slowly in the top of a double boiler and to stir well.)

NPS (4–6) (with milk): 125–85 C, 145–95 mg CH, 1375–910 mg S*
NPS (4–6) (with cream): 185–125 C, 165–110 mg CH, 1370–915 mg S*

POTAGE GERMINY (CREAM OF SORREL SOUP)

6 servings

1 quart chicken broth
1/2 cup finely chopped yellow onion or scallions
3 tablespoons unsalted butter (no substitute)
1 cup heavy cream
3 egg yolks, lightly beaten
1/4 teaspoon cayenne pepper
1/2 teaspoon salt (about)
1 pound tender young sorrel, washed and trimmed of stems
1–2 tablespoons lemon juice (optional)

Boil broth in a heavy uncovered saucepan over high heat 10–15 minutes until reduced to 3 cups; cover and keep warm. Stir-fry onion in butter in a small skillet over moderate heat 3–4 minutes until limp, not brown; set aside. Pour cream into a large double boiler top, set over simmering water, and heat, stirring occasionally, 5 minutes. Blend a little hot cream into egg yolks, stir back into pan, then heat, stirring constantly, 4–5 minutes until slightly thickened and no raw egg taste remains. Mix in cayenne, salt, and reserve onion mixture; cover and set aside. Toss sorrel into broth, cover, and cook over lowest heat 30 seconds; stir well, re-cover, and cook 30 seconds longer until sorrel is wilted. Purée sorrel mixture by buzzing—in two batches—20–30 seconds in an electric blender at high speed or in a single batch in a food processor fitted with the metal chopping blade. Mix sorrel purée into cream mixture, a little at a time, then bring just to serving temperature; do not allow to boil or the soup will curdle. Taste for salt, and add more, if needed. If you prefer a tarter soup, stir in the lemon juice. Serve with toasted French bread.

NPS: 270 C, 205 mg CH, 725 mg S*

VARIATION

Potage Crème d'Épinards (Cream of Spinach Soup): Prepare as directed but substitute 1 pound tender young spinach for the sorrel.

NPS: 265 C, 205 mg CH, 765 mg S*

QUICK CREAM OF TOMATO SOUP

6 servings ¢ ⚖ ☒

1/3 cup minced yellow onion
2 tablespoons butter or margarine
2 tablespoons flour
1/2 teaspoon basil
1/2 teaspoon oregano
1 1/4 teaspoons salt
1/8 teaspoon pepper
1 tablespoon tomato paste
1 tablespoon light brown sugar
1 (10 1/2-ounce) can condensed beef consommé
1 cup milk
1 (1-pound 12-ounce) can tomatoes (do not drain)

Stir-fry onion in butter in a large heavy saucepan 3–5 minutes until limp, blend in flour, herbs, salt, and pepper, then stir in tomato paste, light brown sugar, consommé, and milk and heat, stirring constantly, until thickened and smooth. Put tomatoes through a food mill or purée by churning 15–20 seconds in a food processor fitted with the metal chopping blade; add to pan and simmer, uncovered, 12–15 minutes—do not allow to boil. Ladle into soup bowls and serve piping hot.

NPS: 125 C, 15 mg CH, 970 mg S*

SHELLFISH BISQUE

6 servings

1/4 cup minced yellow onion
1/4 cup minced carrot
3 tablespoons butter or margarine
1 pound cooked lobster, shrimp, or crab meat, well picked over and minced
1/3 cup dry white wine
2 cups water, Easy Fish Stock, or Rich Court Bouillon
1 pint heavy cream
2 egg yolks, lightly beaten
1/2 teaspoon salt (about)
1/8 teaspoon white pepper
1/4 cup medium-dry sherry or brandy (optional)

Stir-fry onion and carrot in butter in a heavy saucepan over moderately low heat 5 minutes until onion is limp; add shellfish and stir-fry 2–3 minutes. Add wine and water, cover, and simmer 10 minutes. Remove from heat and let stand 1/2 hour to blend flavors. Put mixture through a food mill or purée by churning 20–30 seconds in a food processor fitted with the metal chopping blade. Pour into the top of a large double boiler, set over simmering water, add cream and heat, stirring, 5 minutes. Mix a little hot bisque into yolks, return to pan, and heat, stirring constantly, until no raw taste of egg remains. Add seasonings and, if you like, sherry; taste for salt and adjust if needed. Serve hot or chill and serve cold. *(Note:* For a pretty garnish, reserve about one fourth of the minced shellfish and scatter over each portion.)

NPS: 425 C, 280 mg CH, 435 mg S*
NPS (with sherry): 440 C, 280 mg CH, 435 mg S*
NPS (with brandy): 450 C, 280 mg CH, 435 mg S*

BILLI-BI

4 servings

A delicate mussel soup delicious hot or cold.

5 dozen mussels in the shell, prepared for cooking*
2 medium-size yellow onions, peeled and minced
2 stalks celery, minced
1/2 pound mushrooms, wiped clean and minced (include stems)
1/4 cup minced parsley
1/8 teaspoon pepper
2 1/2 cups water or 2 cups water and 1/2 cup Easy Fish Stock
1 cup dry white wine
1 cup light cream

Place mussels in a large, heavy kettle with all but last ingredient, cover, bring to a boil over moderate heat, then reduce heat and simmer 3 minutes until mussels open. With a slotted spoon lift out mussels and reserve to serve as a separate course or at another meal. Strain cooking liquid through a fine sieve lined with a triple thickness of cheesecloth, pour into a clean saucepan, and boil rapidly, uncovered, until reduced by about half. Turn heat to low, stir in cream, and heat and stir until piping hot. Taste for salt, adjust as needed and serve. Or chill well and serve cold.

NPS: 485 C, 210 mg CH, 1050 mg S*

CREAM OF CHICKEN OR TURKEY SOUP

4 servings ⊠

1 quart chicken or turkey broth
1 cup heavy cream
1/4 teaspoon salt (about)
1/8 teaspoon white pepper
1/8 teaspoon nutmeg or mace
1 tablespoon minced parsley or chives

Bring broth to a simmer and slowly mix in cream. Add salt to taste, pepper, and nutmeg. Cover and let mellow over lowest heat about 10 minutes. Serve hot or icy cold, topped with minced parsley.

NPS (chicken): 245 C, 80 mg CH, 935 mg S*

VARIATIONS

Home-Style Cream of Chicken or Turkey Soup: Melt 4 tablespoons butter in a large heavy saucepan over moderate heat and blend in 4 tablespoons flour. Add broth and 1 cup light cream or half-and-half and heat, stirring constantly, until thickened and smooth. Mix in all seasonings and 1 cup diced, cooked chicken or turkey meat and, if you like, 1/2 cup diced, cooked carrots; cover, let mellow over low heat as recipe directs, then serve hot.

NPS (chicken with light cream): 360 C, 100 mg CH, 1090 mg S*
NPS (chicken with half-and-half): 320 C, 85 mg CH, 1090 mg S*
NPS (turkey with light cream): 350 C, 100 mg CH, 1085 mg S*
NPS (turkey with half-and-half): 310 C, 80 mg CH, 1085 mg S*

⊠ **Chicken or Turkey Velouté:** Melt 4 tablespoons butter in a large, heavy saucepan and blend in 4 tablespoons flour. Add broth and cream and heat, stirring constantly, until thickened and smooth; mix in all seasonings. Blend a little hot soup into 3 lightly beaten egg yolks, return to saucepan, set over lowest heat, and warm, stirring constantly, 1–2 minutes until no raw taste of egg remains; do not allow to boil. Serve hot topped with minced parsley.

NPS: 420 C, 315 mg CH, 1055 mg S*

AVGOLEMONO SOUP (GREEK CHICKEN-LEMON SOUP)

4 servings ⚖

1 quart chicken broth
1/4 cup uncooked rice
Pince mace or nutmeg
3 egg yolks

Juice of 1 lemon
Salt
Pepper

Place broth, rice, and mace in a large saucepan, cover, and simmer 25–30 minutes until rice is very tender. Beat yolks with lemon juice; spoon a little hot broth into egg mixture, return to pan, and heat over lowest heat 1–2 minutes, stirring constantly, until no taste of raw egg remains; do not boil. Taste for salt and pepper and season as needed.

NPS: 135 C, 205 mg CH, 785 mg S*

CHEDDAR CHEESE SOUP

6 servings

2 tablespoons butter or margarine
2 tablespoons flour
6 cups milk
1 clove garlic, peeled and bruised (optional)
1 1/2 cups coarsely grated sharp Cheddar cheese
1 cup dry white wine or water
2 egg yolks, lightly beaten
1/4 cup heavy cream
1 teaspoon salt (about)
1/8 teaspoon white pepper
Pinch nutmeg
1/3 cup finely grated mild Cheddar cheese

Melt butter in the top of a double boiler set over simmering water. Blend in flour, then slowly stir in milk; add garlic if you wish. Heat, uncovered, stirring frequently, 10 minutes; mix in cheese and stir until melted; add wine. Mix egg yolks and cream, stir a little hot mixture into yolks, return to pan, and heat, stirring constantly, until no raw taste of egg remains. Remove garlic, mix in salt, pepper, and nutmeg, taste for salt, and adjust as needed. Ladle into bowls, sprinkle with the mild Cheddar, and serve.

NPS: 395 C, 185 mg CH, 750 mg S*

OXTAIL SOUP

6 servings ¢

2 pounds oxtail, cut in 1"–1 1/2" chunks and trimmed of excess fat
1/2 cup unsifted flour + 2 tablespoons
2 tablespoons beef drippings or cooking oil
2 medium-size yellow onions, peeled and minced
2 quarts water, or 6 cups water and 1 pint beef broth or bouillon
2 tablespoons tomato paste
2 teaspoons salt
1/4 teaspoon pepper
1 bay leaf

1/2 teaspoon thyme
3 cloves
2 sprigs parsley
2 medium-size carrots, peeled and diced
1 stalk celery, diced
1/3 cup dry sherry or port wine (optional)

Dredge oxtail in 1/2 cup flour, then brown in drippings in a large, heavy kettle over high heat; drain on paper toweling. Turn heat to moderate and stir-fry onions 8–10 minutes until golden; sprinkle in remaining flour, mix well, and brown lightly. Slowly add water, stir in tomato paste, salt, and pepper, also bay leaf tied in cheesecloth with thyme, cloves, and parsley. Return oxtail to kettle, cover, and simmer 3 hours until meat is fork tender; cool and skim off fat; remove cheesecloth bag. Separate meat from bones, cut in bite-size pieces, and return to kettle along with carrots and celery. Cover and simmer 10–15 minutes until carrots are tender; if you like, mix in sherry. Serve as is or strain kettle liquid, serve as a first course, and follow with oxtail and vegetables.

NPS: 375 C, 5 mg CH, 800 mg S*

VARIATION

¢ **Clear Oxtail Soup:** Prepare as directed, browning oxtail without dredging and omitting all flour and tomato paste from recipe.

NPS: 325 C, 5 mg CH, 760 mg S*

SCOTCH BROTH

6–8 servings   ¢

2 pounds lean neck of mutton or lamb (with bones), cut in 2" chunks
2 medium-size yellow onions, peeled and minced
2 cups diced, peeled carrots
1/2 medium-size rutabaga, peeled and cut in small dice
2 leeks or 4 scallions, washed, trimmed, and coarsely chopped
1/2 cup medium pearl barley
1 gallon water
1 tablespoon salt (about)
1/4 teaspoon pepper
2 tablespoons minced parsley

Place all ingredients except parsley in a large kettle, cover, and bring to a boil. Skim froth from surface, reduce heat, cover, and simmer 2–2 1/2 hours, stirring now and then, until lamb is tender. Cut meat from bones in small pieces, if you like, and return to kettle. Stir, taste for salt, and adjust as needed. Sprinkle with parsley and serve in deep bowls.

NPS (6–8): 255–190 C, 35–25 mg CH, 1150–860 mg S*

RUSSIAN BORSCHT

6–8 servings

3 1/2 quarts water
2 pounds beef shank bone with some meat attached
1/2 pound ham hock
1 pound lean pork shoulder in 1 piece
2 bay leaves, crumbled
8 peppercorns
4 sprigs parsley
2 carrots, peeled and cut in 1" chunks
2 leeks, washed, trimmed, and cut in 2" chunks
2 stalks celery, cut in 2" chunks
2 pounds beets, washed, trimmed, and peeled
1 pound yellow onions, peeled and cut in thin wedges
3 cloves garlic, peeled and crushed
1 (6-ounce) can tomato paste
1/4 cup white wine vinegar
1 tablespoon salt
1/4 teaspoon pepper
2 cups thickly sliced cabbage
1 cup sour cream
1/4 cup minced fresh dill

Place water, bones and meat, bay leaves, peppercorns, parsley, carrots, leeks, and celery in a large, heavy kettle, cover, and simmer, stirring occasionally, 3–3 1/2 hours until meats almost fall from bones. Trim meat from bones and cut in bite-size pieces; set aside. Strain broth, discarding vegetables and seasonings, then chill several hours until fat rises to top and hardens; lift off fat and discard. Thinly slice all beets but 1, grate it, mix with 1/2 cup cold water, and reserve. Return strained broth to kettle, add sliced beets, onions, garlic, tomato paste, vinegar, salt, and pepper, cover, and simmer, stirring occasionally, 2 hours. Add reserved meat, cabbage, grated beet, and beet water and simmer, covered, 15–20 minutes until cabbage is crisp tender. Ladle into large soup bowls, top each serving with a float of sour cream, and sprinkle with dill.

NPS (6–8): 400–300 C, 95–70 mg CH, 1645–1235 mg S*

QUICK BORSCHT

6 servings   ¢ ⤫ ⊠

Although no quick borscht can match the old-fashioned variety made with long and slow simmering on the back of the stove, this one comes close. It contains less than half the calories of Russian Borscht.

2 tablespoons butter or margarine
1 medium-size yellow onion, peeled and sliced thin
1½ cups finely sliced cabbage
2 (10½-ounce) cans condensed beef consommé
4 (8-ounce) cans julienne beets (do not drain)
2 tablespoons tarragon vinegar
1 tablespoon tomato paste
½ teaspoon salt
Pinch pepper
¼ cup sour cream
2 tablespoons minced fresh dill or parsley

Melt butter in a large saucepan over moderately high heat, add onion and cabbage, and sauté, stirring occasionally, 8–10 minutes until cabbage is nearly tender. Add consommé and half the beets; purée remaining beets by buzzing 15–20 seconds in an electric blender at low speed or 10–15 seconds in a food processor fitted with the metal chopping blade, and add to pan along with vinegar, tomato paste, salt, and pepper. Simmer, uncovered, 15 minutes. Ladle about ½ cup borscht liquid into a small bowl and blend in sour cream; return to pan and smooth into borscht. Ladle into large, flat soup bowls and serve hot with a sprinkling of minced fresh dill or chill well and serve cold.

*NPS: 145 C, 15 mg CH, 1130 mg S**

COCKALEEKIE

4 servings   ⊡ ⊠

This old Scottish cock and leek soup used to be rich as a stew. Today you're more apt to be served the following version—with or without prunes.

1 pound leeks, washed, trimmed, halved lengthwise, and sliced ⅛″ thick (include some green tops)
1 tablespoon butter or margarine
1 quart chicken broth
½ teaspoon salt
⅛ teaspoon pepper
½ cup diced, cooked chicken meat
4–6 whole or coarsely chopped pitted prunes (optional)
1 teaspoon minced parsley

Stir-fry leeks in butter in a saucepan over moderately low heat 2–3 minutes. Add all remaining ingredients except parsley, cover, and simmer 10 minutes. Sprinkle with parsley and serve.

*NPS: 125 C, 25 mg CH, 1095 mg S**
*NPS (with prunes): 144 C, 25 mg CH, 1095 mg S**

WATERZOOIE (BELGIAN CHICKEN SOUP)

8 servings

Extra rich!

1 (6–7-pound) hen or capon, cleaned and dressed
¼ cup unsalted butter, softened to room temperature
5 large leeks, washed, trimmed, and cut in large chunks
5 large stalks celery, cut in large chunks (include tops)
2 large carrots, peeled and cut in large chunks
2 medium-size yellow onions, each peeled and stuck with 2 cloves
6 sprigs parsley
½ teaspoon thyme
¼ teaspoon nutmeg
6 peppercorns
1 bay leaf, crumbled
2 quarts chicken broth
1 cup dry white wine (optional)
4 egg yolks lightly beaten with ¾ cup heavy cream
1 lemon, sliced thin
2 tablespoons minced parsley

Preheat broiler. Rub chicken well with butter and broil 4″–5″ from heat, turning often, about 20 minutes until lightly browned. Transfer chicken to a large, heavy kettle, add giblets and all but last 3 ingredients, cover, and simmer 1–1½ hours until chicken is tender. Lift chicken and giblets from broth, cool until easy to handle, peel off skin and discard; separate meat from bones and cut in large chunks; mince giblets. Meanwhile, continue simmering vegetables, covered, in broth. When chicken is cut up, strain broth and skim off fat. Return broth to kettle, add cut-up chicken and giblets, cover, and heat 5 minutes. Mix a little hot broth into yolk mixture, return to kettle, and warm over lowest heat 2–3 minutes; do not boil. Ladle into soup bowls, top each portion with a lemon slice and scattering of parsley and serve.

*NPS: 490 C, 335 mg CH, 935 mg S**
*NPS (with wine): 495 C, 335 mg CH, 940 mg S**

MULLIGATAWNY SOUP

6 servings

A curried chicken and tomato soup.

3 tablespoons butter or margarine
1 small yellow onion, peeled and minced
1 medium-size carrot, peeled and diced fine
1 stalk celery, diced fine
1/2 green pepper, cored, seeded, and minced
1/4 cup unsifted flour
1 tablespoon curry powder
1/4 teaspoon nutmeg
3 cloves
2 sprigs parsley
1 quart chicken broth
1 teaspoon salt
1/8 teaspoon pepper
1 cup chopped tomatoes
1 cup diced cooked chicken
1/2 cup heavy cream
1 cup boiled rice

Melt butter in a large saucepan, add onion, carrot, celery, and green pepper, and stir-fry 8–10 minutes until onion is golden. Blend in flour, curry powder, and nutmeg; add cloves, parsley, broth, salt, pepper, and tomatoes, cover, and simmer 1 hour. Strain broth; pick out and discard cloves and parsley; purée vegetables with about 1 cup soup liquid by buzzing 20–30 seconds in an electric blender at low speed or 15–20 seconds in a food processor fitted with the metal chopping blade. Smooth purée into broth, return to heat, add chicken and cream, and heat, stirring, 5–10 minutes to blend flavors. Add rice, heat and stir 2–3 minutes longer, then serve.

NPS: 270 C, 65 mg CH, 990 mg S*

NEW ENGLAND CLAM CHOWDER

6 servings

1 pint shucked clams, drained (reserve liquid)
1/3 cup diced salt pork
1 medium-size yellow onion, peeled and minced
2 cups diced, peeled potatoes
1/2 cup water
2 cups milk
1 cup light cream
1 teaspoon salt (about)
1/8 teaspoon white pepper
1/8 teaspoon paprika

Pick over clams, removing any shell fragments; leave whole or, if you prefer, mince or grind medium fine. Lightly brown salt pork in a large, heavy saucepan over moderate heat, lift out, and reserve. Stir-fry onion in drippings 5–8 minutes until pale golden,

add potatoes, water, clam liquid, and salt pork. Cover and simmer 10–12 minutes until potatoes are nearly tender, stirring occasionally. Add clams, milk, cream, salt, and pepper, cover, and simmer 5 minutes to heat through; do not boil. Ladle into hot bowls, dust with paprika, and serve.

NPS: 290 C, 80 mg CH, 615 mg S*

NEW ENGLAND FISH CHOWDER

4 servings   ¢

3 tablespoons butter (no substitute)
1 medium-size yellow onion, peeled and minced
3 medium-size Irish potatoes, peeled and cut in 1/4" cubes
1/2 cup hot water
1 pound haddock or cod fillets
2 cups milk
1 teaspoon salt
1/8 teaspoon white pepper
Paprika (garnish)

Melt 2 tablespoons butter in a large, heavy saucepan over low heat. Add onion and sauté 8–10 minutes, until golden, *not brown.* Add potatoes and water, cover, and simmer 10 minutes; add fish, cover, and simmer 10 minutes longer. *(Note:* Adjust burner so mixture *simmers;* if it boils, fish may overcook and become watery.) Off heat, flake fish with a fork, add milk, salt, and pepper; cover and let stand 1 hour at room temperature to blend flavors. Reheat slowly, stirring frequently, about 10 minutes. *Do not allow to boil.* Ladle into soup bowls, sprinkle lightly with paprika, and dot with remaining butter. Serve with oyster crackers or hot crusty bread.

NPS: 335 C, 110 mg CH, 770 mg S*

VARIATION

For extra richness, substitute 1/2 cup light or heavy cream for 1/2 cup of the milk.

NPS (light cream): 375 C, 125 mg CH, 770 mg S*
NPS (heavy cream): 420 C, 145 mg CH, 770 mg S*

MANHATTAN CLAM CHOWDER

8 servings   ⚖

Manhattan-style clam chowder may contain sweet green pepper and/or corn, but it *always* contains tomatoes. New England Clam Chowder never does.

1 medium-size yellow onion, peeled and minced
2 tablespoons butter, margarine, or bacon drippings
1½ cups diced, peeled carrots

1/2 cup diced celery
2 cups diced, peeled potatoes
1 (1-pound 12-ounce) can tomatoes (do not drain)
2 cups water or Easy Fish Stock
1 1/2 teaspoons salt
1/8 teaspoon pepper
1 pint minced fresh or canned clams, drained (reserve liquid)
Drained clam liquid + enough bottled clam juice to total 1 pint
1 tablespoon minced parsley

Stir-fry onion in butter in a large, heavy kettle over moderate heat 5–8 minutes until pale golden. Add remaining vegetables (breaking up the tomatoes), water, salt, and pepper. Cover and simmer 15 minutes. Off heat, add clams and clam liquid, cover, and let stand 1/2 hour to blend flavors. Return to heat and simmer about 5 minutes, sprinkle with parsley, and serve.

NPS: 140 C, 35 mg CH, 820 mg S*

VARIATION

Prepare as directed, reducing carrots to 1 cup and adding 1/2–3/4 cup diced, seeded, cored sweet green pepper or whole kernel corn. Recipe too flexible for meaningful nutritional count.

DRIED BEAN SOUP

12 servings ¢

This soup freezes well.

1 pound dried beans (any kind), washed and sorted
1 gallon cold water, or 1 quart cold water and 3 quarts beef, chicken, or turkey broth
2 medium-size yellow onions, peeled and coarsely chopped
3 carrots, peeled and diced
2 stalks celery, diced
2 cloves garlic, peeled and crushed (optional)
1 tablespoon bacon drippings, margarine, or cooking oil
2 teaspoons salt (about)
1/4 teaspoon pepper
2 tablespoons minced parsley

Soak beans in 1 quart water overnight or use the quick method.* Drain, measure soaking water, and add enough cold water to total 3 quarts. Place beans and water in a large, heavy kettle with all but last 3 ingredients, cover, and simmer about 1 1/2 hours until very soft. Put half of mixture through a food mill or purée by churning 20–30 seconds in a food processor fitted with the metal chopping blade. Return to kettle and heat until

bubbly. Add salt and pepper, tasting and adjusting salt as needed. Sprinkle with parsley and serve.

NPS (with water only): 150 C, 1 mg CH, 400 mg S*
NPS (with broth): 170 C, 1 mg CH, 1180 mg S*

VARIATIONS

¢ **Savory Dried Bean Soup:** Prepare as directed, adding a ham bone or pig's knuckle, chunk of salt pork or bacon, or leftover roast bone to the pot. Other good additions: leftover meat, gravy, and vegetables, medium-dry sherry or Madeira to taste. Recipe too flexible for a meaningful nutritional count.

¢ **Rosy Dried Bean Soup:** Prepare as directed, smoothing 1 1/2 cups tomato purée into soup shortly before serving.

NPS (with water only): 165 C, 1 mg CH, 525 mg S*
NPS (with broth and water): 180 C, 1 mg CH, 1305 mg S*

Creamy Dried Bean Soup: Cook beans as directed, using 2 quarts water instead of 3. After puréeing, blend in 1 quart light cream and heat to serving temperature; do not boil.

NPS: 310 C, 55 mg CH, 430 mg S*

HEARTY CHICK-PEA AND SAUSAGE SOUP

8–10 servings ¢

1 pound dried chick-peas, washed and sorted
3 quarts cold water (about)
1 small lean ham bone with some meat attached
2 sprigs parsley
1/2 pound chorizos, pepperoni, or other hot sausage, skinned and sliced 1/2" thick
2 medium-size yellow onions, peeled and coarsely chopped
2 cloves garlic, peeled and crushed
2 medium-size carrots, peeled and sliced thin
1/2 teaspoon oregano
1/4 teaspoon thyme
1/4 teaspoon coriander
1 1/2 teaspoons salt (about)
1/8 teaspoon pepper (about)

Soak chick-peas overnight in 1 quart water or use the quick method.* Drain, measure soaking water, and add cold water to total 3 quarts. Place peas, water, ham bone, and parsley in a large, heavy kettle, cover, and simmer 1 hour. Meanwhile, brown *chorizos* in a large, heavy skillet; lift out with a slotted spoon and reserve. Stir-fry onions, garlic, and carrots in drippings 10–12 minutes over moderate heat to brown lightly, stir in remaining ingredients (but not sausages), and add to chick-peas. Re-cover and simmer 1–1½ hours until peas are mushy. Lift out ham bone, cut off any meat and reserve; discard parsley. Purée kettle mixture, a little at a time, by churning 20–30 seconds in a food processor fitted with the metal chopping blade or by putting through a food mill. Return all to kettle; add ham and sausages and heat, stirring, 10–15 minutes to blend flavors. Taste for salt and pepper and adjust as needed. Serve hot.

NPS (8–10): 375–300 C, 25–20 mg CH, 1105–885 mg S*

OLD-FASHIONED BLACK BEAN SOUP

6 servings   ¢

1 pound dried black beans, washed and sorted but not soaked
3 quarts cold water
2 medium-size yellow onions, peeled and minced
2 cloves garlic, peeled and crushed
3 tablespoons bacon drippings
2 medium-size tomatoes, peeled, cored, seeded, and chopped
3/4 teaspoon oregano
1/2 teaspoon crushed dried hot red chili peppers
1/4 teaspoon thyme
2 teaspoons salt
1/8 teaspoon black pepper
1/2 cup dry sherry
2 hard-cooked eggs

Place beans and water in a very large, heavy kettle, cover, and simmer 1¼–1½ hours until almost tender. Meanwhile, stir-fry onions and garlic in drippings in a heavy skillet over moderate heat 8–10 minutes until golden, stir in tomatoes, all herbs and spices, and set aside. When beans are almost tender, stir in skillet mixture, cover, and simmer 1½–2 hours longer until beans are mushy. Put mixture through a food mill or purée by pressing through a fine sieve. Return to pan, add salt, black pepper, and sherry, and heat, stirring frequently, 5–10 minutes to blend flavors. Peel eggs, sieve the yolks, and mince the whites. Ladle soup into large bowls, sprinkle with yolks and whites, and serve.

NPS: 360 C, 95 mg CH, 815 mg S*

EASY BLACK BEAN SOUP

4 servings   ¢

1 cup minced Spanish or Bermuda onion
2 cloves garlic, peeled and crushed
2 tablespoons butter or margarine
1/2 teaspoon crushed coriander seeds

1/4 teaspoon oregano
1/8 teaspoon thyme
1/4 cup dry sherry
1 (10½-ounce) can condensed beef consommé
2 (1-pound) cans black beans (do not drain)
1 bay leaf, crumbled

Stir-fry onion and garlic in butter in a large saucepan over moderate heat 8–10 minutes until golden. Blend in herbs and sherry and heat 1–2 minutes, then add remaining ingredients and simmer, uncovered, stirring occasionally, ½–¾ hour until flavors are well blended. Ladle into soup bowls and serve.

NPS: 300 C, 15 mg CH, 1200 mg S*

LAMB, PEPPER, AND BARLEY SOUP

8–10 servings   ¢

1 lamb shank, cracked, or a meaty leg or shoulder bone from a leftover roast
1 cup medium pearl barley, washed
1 cup dried green split peas, washed and sorted
2 medium-size yellow onions, peeled and minced
1 clove garlic, peeled and crushed
1 sweet green pepper, cored, seeded, and minced
3½ quarts cold water
4 teaspoons salt (about)
1/4 teaspoon pepper

Place all ingredients in a large, heavy kettle, cover, and simmer 2 hours, stirring occasionally. Cut meat from bones and return to kettle. Taste for salt and adjust if necessary. Serve hot with crusty bread or crisp crackers. *(Note: This soup keeps well in the refrigerator about 1 week. It also freezes well.)*

NPS (8–10): 215–170 C, 15–10 mg CH, 1130–900 mg S*

GOLDEN SPLIT PEA SOUP WITH HAM

8–10 servings   ¢

A Norwegian favorite, hearty enough to serve as a main course.

2 medium-size yellow onions, peeled and coarsely chopped
2 tablespoons bacon drippings, butter, or margarine
2 cups diced, cooked ham
1 pound yellow split peas, washed and sorted
3 quarts water
1/8 teaspoon rosemary
1 tablespoon salt
1/4 teaspoon pepper

Stir-fry onions in drippings 5–8 minutes in a large saucepan over moderate heat until pale golden. Add ham and stir-fry 5 minutes. Add remaining ingredients, cover, and simmer 1 hour, stirring occasionally. Serve steaming hot with buttery chunks of garlic bread.

NPS (8–10): 295–235 C, 25–20 mg CH, 1405–1125 mg S*

VARIATION

Lentil and Ham Soup: Prepare as directed, substituting 1 pound lentils for the peas and simmering 3/4 hour until tender, not mushy.

NPS (8–10): 290–230 C, 25–20 mg CH, 1400–1120 mg S*

MINESTRONE MILANESE

10 servings   ¢

Italians like minestrone made with red kidney beans; Americans more often use navy or pea beans. Either makes a husky main-dish soup.

1/2 **pound dried red kidney, navy, or pea beans, washed and sorted**
2 **cups water**
1 **large yellow onion, peeled and minced**
1 **clove garlic, peeled and minced**
1/3 **cup diced salt pork**
2 **tablespoons olive or other cooking oil**
3 **quarts beef broth or water or a 1/2 and 1/2 mixture of water and beef bouillon**
2 **medium-size carrots, peeled and diced**
2 **medium-size potatoes, peeled and diced**
2 **cups finely shredded cabbage**
1/2 **cup minced celery**
1/3 **cup tomato paste**
2 **teaspoons minced fresh basil or 1 teaspoon dried basil**
1/4 **teaspoon thyme**
2 **teaspoons salt (about)**
1/4 **teaspoon pepper**
2 **small zucchini, diced (optional)**
1 **tablespoon minced parsley**
1 **cup ditalini or elbow macaroni**
1/3 **cup grated Parmesan cheese**

Soak beans overnight in water or use the quick method,* drain. Stir-fry onion, garlic, and salt pork in oil in a large, heavy kettle 5–8 minutes over moderate heat until onion is pale golden. Add beans and broth, cover, and simmer 1 hour. Add all remaining ingredients except zucchini, parsley, ditalini, and Parmesan, cover, and simmer 1 hour, stirring now and then. Add zucchini, parsley, and ditalini, cover, and simmer 15–20 minutes longer until ditalini is tender. Taste

for salt and adjust as needed. Stir Parmesan into soup or, if you prefer, pass separately.

NPS (with broth): 230 C, 1 mg CH, 1520 mg S*

PASTA E FAGIOLI (PASTA AND BEAN SOUP)

6–8 servings   ¢

Although this soup, like Minestrone, combines beans and pasta, its taste and texture are quite different thanks to *battuto,* a mixture of minced onion, garlic, celery, and ham, lightly sautéed in olive oil, which goes into the soup kettle at the outset.

1 **cup dried cannellini or white beans, washed and sorted**
2 **quarts cold water (about)**
1 **small meaty ham or beef bone**
1 **cup tomato purée**
1/2 **teaspoon minced fresh rosemary or 1/4 teaspoon dried rosemary**
2 **tablespoons minced parsley**
1/4 **cup olive oil (no substitute)**
1 **medium-size yellow onion, peeled and minced**
2 **cloves garlic, peeled and minced**
1/4 **cup minced celery (include some leaves)**
1/4 **cup minced cooked ham**
2 1/2 **teaspoons salt (about)**
1/2 **teaspoon pepper**
3/4 **cup ditalini or 1″ pieces broken spaghettini**
1/4 **cup each grated Parmesan and Pecorino cheeses, mixed together (garnish)**

Soak beans overnight in 1 quart water or use the quick method.* Drain, measure soaking water, and add enough cold water to total 2 quarts; pour into a large heavy kettle, add beans, ham bone, tomato purée, rosemary, and parsley, and set over low heat. Heat oil in a heavy skillet over moderate heat 1 minute, add onion, garlic, celery, and ham and stir-fry 3–4 minutes until onion is pale golden; stir all into beans. Cover kettle and simmer, stirring occasionally, about 1 1/2 hours until beans are tender; add salt and pepper, stir well, cool 1 hour, then cut meat from bone in bite-size pieces and reserve; discard bone. Purée about 2 cups beans by buzzing 20–30 seconds in an electric blender at high speed or in a food processor fitted with the metal chopping blade. Stir purée into kettle along with reserved meat; add ditalini and boil slowly, uncovered, 10–12 minutes until pasta is *al dente.* Taste for salt and add more, if needed. This soup should be quite thick, but if you like it thinner, add a little dry white wine or hot water. Ladle into large soup bowls and top with a sprinkling of the combined cheeses.

NPS (6–8): 350–260 C, 20–15 mg CH, 1540–1150 mg S*

SOUPE AU PISTOU

About 6 servings ¢

Provence, home of Bouillabaisse, is equally famous for this thick vegetable soup aromatic of garlic and basil. It gets its name from *pistou,* a French variation of *pesto,* the green and garlicky basil sauce for which Genoa, Italy, is famous. Indeed, *Soupe au Pistou* is thought to have originated in Genoa.

2 tablespoons olive oil
1/2 pound leeks, washed, trimmed, and sliced thin or 1 medium-size yellow onion, peeled and finely chopped
2 medium-size potatoes, peeled and diced
3/4 cup tomato purée
1 quart + 1 cup water (about)
1 1/4 teaspoons salt (about)
1/4 teaspoon pepper
1 cup fresh or drained, canned white beans
1/2 pound fresh Italian green beans, cut in 1/2" lengths, or 1 (10-ounce) package frozen Italian green beans (do not thaw)
1/2 cup 1" pieces broken spaghettini

PISTOU
2 cloves garlic, peeled
6–7 fresh basil leaves, coarsely chopped, or 1 teaspoon dried basil
1/2 teaspoon salt
2 tablespoons grated Parmesan cheese
1 tablespoon olive oil

Heat oil in a large heavy kettle over moderate heat and stir-fry leeks about 3 minutes until wilted, not brown. Add potatoes, tomato purée, water, salt, and pepper; cover and boil slowly 10 minutes. Add white and green beans, re-cover, and boil 10 minutes more. Now add spaghettini and boil, uncovered, 10–12 minutes until pasta is barely *al dente. (Note:* If using *fresh* pasta, boil 2–3 minutes only.) Meanwhile, make the *pistou:* Mash garlic, basil, and salt in a mortar with a pestle, bruising basil well. Add Parmesan, then drizzle in oil, blending well to form a paste. When pasta is barely cooked, slowly beat 1/2 cup soup liquid into *pistou;* stir back into kettle. Cover and let stand 10–15 minutes off heat to blend flavors. Bring slowly to serving temperature, still covered; *do not boil.* Taste for salt and add more, if needed.

NPS: 220 C, 1 mg CH, 800 mg S*

GARBURE

10 servings ¢

Early spring vegetables traditionally form the foundation of this rustic Basque or Béarn "meal-in-a-pot," but cabbage and pork or preserved goose, or a piece of *lard rance* (slightly rancid Basque salt pork) are *musts.*

2 1/2 quarts water
1 1/2 pounds lean salt pork, trimmed of rind, or lean pork shoulder or 2 pounds smoked pork hocks, scrubbed
3 cloves garlic, peeled and minced
2 stalks celery, finely chopped
1/2 teaspoon minced fresh thyme or 1/4 teaspoon dried thyme
1/2 teaspoon minced fresh marjoram or 1/4 teaspoon dried marjoram
1/2 teaspoon paprika
1 1/2 teaspoons salt (about)
1 tablespoon minced parsley
1 pound carrots, peeled and cut in 1" chunks
1 1/2 pounds potatoes, peeled and cut in 2" chunks (baking potatoes won't work)
1 pound baby lima beans, shelled, or 1 (10-ounce) package frozen baby limas (do not thaw) or 1/2 pound green beans, in 2" lengths
1 (1-pound 3-ounce) can white kidney beans, drained
1 small cabbage (about 2 pounds), trimmed and cut in 8 wedges
6 thick slices French bread, toasted until uniformly crisp, dry, and golden brown

Place water, pork, garlic, celery, thyme, marjoram, paprika, salt, and parsley in a large heavy kettle, cover and simmer 1 1/2–2 hours over moderately low heat until meat is almost tender; skim off fat. Add carrots, potatoes, and limas, cover, and simmer 30 minutes. Lift meat from broth, cut into large chunks, discard skin and bones; return meat to kettle. Purée half the kidney beans by buzzing 20–30 seconds in an electric blender at high speed or in a food processor fitted with the metal chopping blade; add to kettle along with cabbage and remaining kidney beans. Cover and simmer 15–20 minutes until cabbage is crisp tender. Taste for salt and add more, if needed. Ladle the soup liquid into large soup plates, add the toasted bread, if you like, and serve as a first course. Follow with a main course of the soup meat and vegetables.

NPS: 355 C, 45 mg CH, 830 mg S*

ARTICHOKE SOUP

4 servings ⚖

An unusually delicate soup. Good hot or cold.

2 cups globe artichoke hearts (fresh, frozen, or drained canned)
2 tablespoons butter or margarine
1 cup milk
2 cups water
1 teaspoon salt
1/8 teaspoon white pepper
1 clove garlic, peeled and speared with a toothpick
1/2 cup beef consommé
1 teaspoon minced parsley

If artichokes are fresh, parboil 20–25 minutes and drain. If frozen, thaw just enough to separate. Quarter hearts, then slice thin crosswise. Stir-fry in butter in a saucepan (not aluminum) over moderately low heat 5 minutes; do not brown. Add all but last 2 ingredients, cover, and simmer over lowest heat 20 minutes. Discard garlic, purée about half the mixture by buzzing 15–20 seconds in a food processor fitted with the metal chopping blade or by putting through a food mill; return to pan. Add consommé and heat to serving temperature, stirring now and then. Serve hot sprinkled with parsley.

NPS: 125 C, 25 mg CH, 760 mg S*

VARIATION

⚖ **Cold Artichoke Soup:** Slice artichokes but do not fry; omit butter. Simmer as directed, then purée and proceed as above.

NPS: 75 C, 10 mg CH, 700 mg S*

CABBAGE SOUP

6 servings ⊠ ¢

A simple soup that can be used as the foundation of a variety of unusual European soups. Three of the best are included here as easy variations.

2 cups finely shredded green cabbage
1 medium-size yellow onion, peeled and minced
1/4 cup butter or margarine
6 cups beef broth, bouillon, or consommé
1/2 teaspoon salt
1/4 teaspoon pepper
1/2 cup finely grated Cheddar or Parmesan cheese or 1/2 cup sour cream

Stir-fry cabbage and onion in butter in a large, heavy saucepan over moderately low heat until cabbage is wilted, not brown. Add broth, salt, and pepper, cover, and simmer 15–20 minutes until cabbage is tender. Ladle into soup bowls, sprinkle with cheese or top with sour cream, and serve.

NPS: 135 C, 30 mg CH, 1110 mg S*

VARIATIONS

¢ **German Cabbage Soup:** Prepare as directed and just before serving thicken with 2 tablespoons flour blended with 1/4 cup cold water. Also stir in 1 tablespoon caraway seeds and 2 tablespoons butter or margarine; omit cheese or sour cream topping.

NPS: 145 C, 30 mg CH, 1090 mg S*

¢ **Basque Cabbage Soup:** Prepare as directed, increasing broth to 2 quarts and adding at the same time 1 cup cooked dried limas and 1 peeled and crushed clove garlic. Top each serving with 1/4 teaspoon vinegar instead of cheese or sour cream.

NPS: 135 C, 20 mg CH, 1310 mg S*

¢ **Russian Sauerkraut Soup:** Prepare as directed, substituting 2 cups drained sauerkraut for cabbage and adding 1 (1-pound) undrained can tomatoes, breaking tomatoes up. Top each serving with sour cream.

NPS: 155 C, 30 mg CH, 1765 mg S*

CORN CHOWDER

6 servings ⊠ ¢

6 slices bacon, diced
2 medium-size yellow onions, peeled and chopped
1 medium-size sweet green pepper, cored, seeded, and chopped
2½ cups fresh whole-kernel corn or 2 (10-ounce) packages frozen whole-kernel corn
3 cups milk
2 teaspoons salt
1/8 teaspoon pepper
1/8 teaspoon nutmeg

Brown bacon in a very large skillet over moderate heat and drain on paper toweling. Stir-fry onions and green pepper in drippings 8–10 minutes until onions are golden. Add corn, cover, and simmer 10–12 minutes. Uncover, break up any frozen bits of corn, if necessary, and simmer, uncovered, 5 minutes, stirring occasionally. Add remaining ingredients and simmer 5 minutes. Ladle into soup bowls and top each serving with bacon.

NPS: 280 C, 30 mg CH, 950 mg S*

BASIC POTATO SOUP

6 servings ⊠ ¢

1 small yellow onion, peeled and minced
2 tablespoons butter or margarine
2 cups diced, peeled potatoes
2 cups chicken broth or cold water
1 teaspoon salt
1/2 teaspoon celery salt
1 cup milk
1 cup light cream
1/8 teaspoon white pepper
1 tablespoon minced parsley, chives, or dill

Stir-fry onion in butter in a heavy saucepan over moderate heat 5 minutes until limp; add potatoes, broth, salt, and celery salt; cover and simmer 10–15 minutes until potatoes are nearly tender. Add milk, cream, and pepper and simmer, uncovered, stirring occasionally, 3–5 minutes until potatoes are done. Sprinkle with parsley and serve.

NPS (with broth): 190 C, 40 mg CH, 820 mg S*
NPS (with water): 175 C, 40 mg CH, 565 mg S*

VARIATIONS

¢ **Potato Soup au Gratin:** Prepare soup as directed, ladle into flameproof bowls, top each with a little grated Cheddar or Parmesan cheese and a sprinkling of nutmeg or paprika, and broil quickly to brown.

NPS (with broth): 200 C, 45 mg CH, 855 mg S*
NPS (with water): 185 C, 45 mg CH, 595 mg S*

¢ **Mashed Potato Soup:** Prepare as directed, substituting 2 cups seasoned mashed potatoes for the diced and simmering 10 minutes altogether, beating with a whisk now and then.

NPS (with broth): 220 C, 40 mg CH, 1050 mg S*
NPS (with water): 205 C, 40 mg CH, 795 mg S*

¢ **Cream of Potato Soup:** Prepare as directed; purée by buzzing 10–15 seconds in a food processor fitted with the metal chopping blade or by putting through a food mill. Serve hot or cold. Same nutritional counts as Basic Potato Soup.

CALDO VERDE (PORTUGUESE GREEN SOUP)

6 servings ¢

The Portuguese national dish.

3 large baking potatoes, peeled and cut in 1/2" cubes
2 quarts water
1/2 pound *linguiça* (garlicky Portuguese dry sausage) or *chorizo* (garlicky Spanish sausage)
or kielbasa sausage, sliced 1/4" thick (optional)
1 1/2 teaspoons salt (about)
1/4 teaspoon pepper (about)
1 pound fresh kale
1/3 cup olive oil

Boil potatoes in water in a large, heavy, covered kettle over moderate heat about 20 minutes until soft. Meanwhile, if you plan to include the sausage, sauté slices in a heavy skillet over moderately low heat until lightly browned—about 3–4 minutes per side; turn heat down low, cover, and let cook until potatoes are done. Mash the potatoes in the cooking water in the kettle with a potato masher; add the sausage, then ladle 1/2 cup potato cooking water into skillet, stirring and scraping up browned bits; add to kettle along with salt and pepper. Cover and simmer 20 minutes. Meanwhile, cut kale leaves from stems; remove coarse midribs, then bundle 8–10 leaves together, rolling them up tight, lengthwise. With a very sharp knife, slice roll of kale crosswise into hair-thin filaments; repeat until all kale is sliced. Toss kale into kettle, cover and simmer 3–4 minutes, just until kale is crisp tender and bright green. Stir in olive oil, taste soup and adjust seasonings, if needed. Ladle into large soup bowls and serve hot as a main course. The perfect accompaniment: crusty chunks of bread.

NPS: 340 C, 25 mg CH, 940 mg S*

ITALIAN-STYLE SPINACH AND RICE SOUP

6–8 servings ¢

Accompanied by garlic bread and sliced tomatoes, this makes a refreshing, light lunch.

2 medium-size yellow onions, peeled and coarsely chopped
2 tablespoons butter or margarine
7 cups chicken broth
1/2 cup uncooked rice
2 (10-ounce) packages frozen chopped spinach, thawed
2 teaspoons salt
1/4 teaspoon nutmeg
1/8 teaspoon pepper

Stir-fry onions in butter in a large saucepan over moderate heat 8–10 minutes until golden. Add broth and bring to a boil. Stir in rice and boil, uncovered, 10 minutes until rice is about half done. Add remaining ingredients and simmer 12–15 minutes longer until rice is done. Ladle into soup bowls and serve.

NPS (6–8): 170–130 C, 10–5 mg CH, 1735–1300 mg S*

FRESH TOMATO SOUP

6 servings   ¢ ⚖️

2 medium-size yellow onions, peeled and quartered
1 stalk celery, cut in 2″ chunks
1½ cups rich beef broth or consommé
6 large ripe tomatoes, peeled, cored, and quartered
1 tablespoon butter or margarine
2 teaspoons salt
⅛ teaspoon pepper
2 tablespoons minced fresh chives or dill

Place onions, celery, and broth in a large saucepan, cover, and simmer 45 minutes until onions are mushy. Add tomatoes, cover, and simmer 15–20 minutes until tomatoes have reduced to juice; cool 10 minutes, then purée by buzzing 20–30 seconds in an electric blender at low speed or 15–20 seconds in a food processor fitted with the metal chopping blade. Return to pan, add butter, salt, and pepper, and simmer, uncovered, 5 minutes. Serve hot or cold garnished with minced chives.

NPS: 65 C, 5 mg CH, 965 mg S*

ANDALUSIAN GAZPACHO (COLD SPANISH VEGETABLE SOUP)

6 servings   ¢ ⚖️

Glorious on a hot summer day. And almost a meal in itself.

¾ cup soft white bread crumbs
3 tablespoons red wine vinegar
2 cloves garlic, peeled and crushed
¼ cup olive oil
1 large cucumber, peeled, seeded, and cut in fine dice
1 sweet green pepper, cored, seeded, and minced
8 large ripe tomatoes, peeled, cored, seeded, and chopped fine
1 cup cold water
½ teaspoon salt
⅛ teaspoon pepper

Place bread crumbs, vinegar, garlic, and oil in a small bowl and mix vigorously with a fork to form a smooth paste; set aside. Mix all remaining ingredients in a large mixing bowl, then blend in bread paste. Cover and chill at least 24 hours before serving. Serve icy cold in soup bowls as a first course or as a midafternoon refresher. For a special touch, bed the soup bowls in larger bowls of crushed ice and garnish with sprigs of fresh dill or basil or, failing that, watercress or parsley.

NPS: 150 C, 0 mg CH, 220 mg S*

BASIC FRUIT SOUP

4 servings   ⚖️

Slavs and Scandinavians sometimes serve a hot or cold fruit soup before the main course; berries, cherries, and plums are the favored "soup fruits."

1 pint berries, washed and stemmed (strawberries, raspberries, blueberries, boysenberries, blackberries, or gooseberries)
1 pint water or a ½ and ½ mixture of water and dry white wine
¼ cup sugar (about)
2 teaspoons lemon juice
1 tablespoon cornstarch blended with 2 tablespoons cold water
Heavy cream, sour cream, or buttermilk (optional topping)

Simmer berries in water in a covered saucepan 10 minutes until mushy; purée by buzzing 15–20 seconds in an electric blender at low speed or 10–15 seconds in a food processor fitted with the metal chopping blade; press through a fine sieve. Return purée to pan, add remaining ingredients, and heat to a boil, stirring. Taste for sugar and add more, if needed. Serve hot or cold, topped, if you like, with cream. *Note:* For each tablespoon heavy cream used, increase the Basic Fruit Soup nutritional count by 50 C, 20 mg CH, 5 mg S; for each tablespoon sour cream, add 30 C, 5 mg CH, 5 mg S; for each tablespoon buttermilk, add 5 C, 0 mg CH, 15 mg S.*

NPS (with water only): 80 C, 0 mg CH, 1 mg S*
NPS (with strawberries & wine): 90 C, 0 mg CH, 5 mg S*
NPS (with blueberries & wine): 105 C, 0 mg CH, 10 mg S*

VARIATIONS

▢ **Quick Berry Soup:** Substitute 2 (10-ounce) packages thawed frozen berries or 1 (1-pound) undrained can berries for the fresh. Do not cook; purée and sieve, then add enough water to make 1 quart. Heat with sugar (just enough to taste), lemon juice, and cornstarch paste as directed. Nutritional count about the same as basic recipe.

Spiced Fruit Soup: Prepare as directed, adding ½ teaspoon cinnamon and ¼ teaspoon each nutmeg and cloves along with sugar. Nutritional count about the same as basic recipe.

Sweet-Sour Fruit Soup: Prepare as directed, increasing sugar to 5 tablespoons and adding, at the same time, 3 tablespoons red or white wine vinegar.

NPS: 90 C, 0 mg CH, 5 mg S*

Plum Soup: Substitute 1 pound purple plums for berries and simmer 25–30 minutes until mushy; cool slightly, pit, then purée and proceed as for Basic Fruit Soup.

NPS: 115 C, 0 mg CH, 1 mg S*

COOL HUNGARIAN CHERRY SOUP

4–6 servings

Although Hungarians traditionally serve this cold soup *before* the entree, you may find it too sweet for an appetizer. If so, serve as a hot weather dessert.

2 (1-pound 1-ounce) cans pitted dark sweet cherries (do not drain)
1 cup sour cream
¼ cup superfine sugar
¼ cup tawny port or cream sherry (optional)

Drain cherry liquid into a mixing bowl, add sour cream, sugar, and, if you like, the wine, and stir until well blended. Add cherries, cover, and chill 3–4 hours before serving.

NPS (4–6): 330–220 C, 25–15 mg CH, 40–25 mg S*
NPS (4–6) (with sherry): 355–235 C, 25–15 mg CH, 40–25 mg S*

APPLE SOUP

4–6 servings   ¢ ⚖

Serve as a first course or light dessert.

1 pound greenings or other tart cooking apples, peeled, cored, and sliced thin
3 cups water
1 teaspoon grated lemon rind
2 teaspoons lemon juice
½ cup sugar (about)
½ teaspoon cinnamon
¼ teaspoon nutmeg
1 cup sour cream blended with ½ cup milk (optional)

Place all but last ingredient in a saucepan, cover, and simmer about 20 minutes until apples are mushy. Purée by buzzing 15–20 seconds in an electric blender at low speed or 10–15 seconds in a food processor fitted with the metal chopping blade; taste for sugar and add more if needed. Serve hot or cold with a little of the sour cream mixture drizzled on top, if you like.

NPS (4–6): 155–100 C, 0 mg CH, 1 mg S*
NPS (4–6) (with topping): 295–195 C, 30–20 mg CH, 45–30 mg S*

VARIATION

Russian Apple Soup: Prepare as directed, using 2 cups water and 1 cup red Bordeaux wine for cooking the apples. Before purée-ing, add ¼ cup red or black currant jelly and stir until melted. Purée and serve hot or cold with or without cream topping.

NPS (4–6): 215–145 C, 0 mg CH, 5 mg S*
NPS (4–6) (with topping): 355–240 C, 30–20 mg CH, 50–35 mg S*

Soup Dumplings, Garnishes, and Trimmings

Note: For additional dumpling recipes, also recipes for plain and flavored croutons, see the chapter on breads.

VIENNESE SOUP "PEAS"

About 1 cup, enough to garnish 8 soup servings   ¢

An unusual soup garnish that can be made ahead of time.

½ cup sifted flour
1 teaspoon salt
1 egg, lightly beaten
¼ cup milk
Shortening or cooking oil for deep fat frying

Mix flour, salt, egg, and milk and beat until smooth. Heat shortening in a deep fat fryer over high heat until deep fat thermometer registers 375° F. Drizzle batter from the end of a teaspoon into hot fat to form small "peas" and fry 30–40 seconds until golden. Scoop out with a slotted spoon and drain on paper toweling. Fry only a few "peas" at a time so you don't crowd pan. Serve sprinkled on top of any soup. These may be made ahead, stored airtight, then reheated. Simply spread out on a baking sheet, set uncovered in a 400° F. oven, and let warm 4–5 minutes.

NPS: 70 C, 35 mg CH, 285 mg S*

ROYALE CUSTARD

Makes enough to garnish 6 soup servings

1 egg + 2 egg yolks, lightly beaten
1/2 cup beef consommé, chicken broth, or milk
1/8 teaspoon salt
Pinch cayenne pepper

Preheat oven to 325° F. Mix all ingredients and pour into a well-buttered, shallow baking dish or pie plate 6"–7" in diameter. (*Note:* Custard should be about 1/2" deep.) Set dish on a rack in a large, shallow baking pan, pour in hot water to a depth of 1/2", and bake, uncovered, 25 minutes or until a knife inserted midway between rim and center comes out clean. Lift custard from water bath and cool upright in its baking dish on a wire rack. Cut in small cubes or diamonds or into fancy shapes with truffle cutters. Float in consommé or other clear soup as a garnish, allowing 3–4 cubes or cutouts per serving.

NPS: 35 C, 136 mg CH, 115 mg S*

V A R I A T I O N

Indian Royale Custard: Prepare custard using chicken broth; whisk in 1/2 teaspoon curry powder, then bake as directed. Nutritional count same as basic recipe.

FARINA DUMPLINGS

2 dozen ¢

Good in any clear meat or vegetable soup.

1 cup milk
1/4 cup uncooked farina or cream of wheat
1 egg, lightly beaten
1 tablespoon butter or margarine
1/2 teaspoon salt
1/8 teaspoon white pepper

Heat milk almost to boiling over moderate heat, stir in farina and heat, stirring constantly, 2–3 minutes until thick. Off heat, beat in remaining ingredients. Cool to room temperature. Drop by 1/2 teaspoonfuls into 2–3 quarts just boiling soup, cover, and simmer 4–5 minutes. Do not cook more than one layer of dumplings at a time; remove first batch with a slotted spoon and keep warm while you cook the rest. Serve 3–4 dumplings in each bowl of soup.

NPS: 20 C, 15 mg CH, 60 mg S*

LIVER DUMPLINGS

2 dozen

1/4 pound calf's, beef, or lamb liver, sliced 1/4"–1/2" thick
1/2 cup water
1 egg, lightly beaten
1 1/2 cups soft white bread crumbs
2 tablespoons light cream
3/4 teaspoon salt
1/8 teaspoon pepper
1/4 teaspoon marjoram or thyme
1 teaspoon minced parsley
1/4 cup minced yellow onion
1/2 clove garlic, peeled and crushed (optional)
1 tablespoon butter or margarine

Simmer liver, uncovered, in water 5 minutes; drain and put through finest blade of a meat grinder. Mix in egg, crumbs, cream, salt, pepper, marjoram, and parsley. Stir-fry onion and, if you like, garlic in butter 3–5 minutes over moderate heat until limp; stir into liver. Drop mixture by 1/2 teaspoonfuls and cook, uncovered, a few dumplings at a time, in 2–3 quarts just boiling clear meat or vegetable soup 3–4 minutes. Lift dumplings out with a slotted spoon and keep warm while you cook the rest. Serve a few dumplings in each bowl of soup.

NP Dumpling: 25 C, 25 mg CH, 95 mg S*

POTATO DUMPLINGS

2 dozen small soup dumplings, 1 dozen stew dumplings ¢

3 medium-size potatoes, boiled in their skins, drained, and peeled
1 egg, lightly beaten
1/3 cup sifted flour
1 1/2 teaspoons salt
1/8 teaspoon white pepper
1/4 teaspoon nutmeg (optional)
1/2 cup croutons

Return potatoes to their pan and dry, uncovered, 1–2 minutes over lowest heat; mash or rice. Beat in all remaining ingredients except croutons. Shape into 1" or 2" balls, push a crouton into center of each 1" ball, 2–3 into larger balls. Drop into just boiling soup or stew and cook, uncovered, allowing 5–7 minutes for the 1" balls and 10–12 for the 2" balls. (*Note:* Don't crowd dumplings; they should be in a single layer, so cook half at a time if necessary.) Use the 1" dumplings to garnish soup, the 2" for stew.

NPS (soup dumpling): 40 C, 10 mg CH, 185 mg S*
NPS (stew dumpling): 80 C, 25 mg CH, 365 mg S*

MATZO BALLS

1 1/2 dozen ¢

2 eggs, lightly beaten
1/2 cup matzo meal
1 teaspoon salt
1/4 teaspoon ginger, cinnamon, or nutmeg
   (optional)
3 tablespoons cold water

Mix all ingredients, cover, and refrigerate 1/2 hour. Drop by rounded teaspoonfuls on top of just boiling chicken broth or other clear soup, cover, and cook at a slow boil 15–20 minutes. Serve at once.

NP Ball: 25 C, 30 mg CH, 130 mg S*

Mary's Matzo Balls: Reduce water to 2 tablespoons and add 2 minced, sautéed chicken livers and 2 teaspoons minced parsley to ingredients called for. Butter hands, roll into 1″ balls, then cook as directed.

NP Ball: 25 C, 45 mg CH, 135 mg S*

Precooked Matzo Balls: Prepare Matzo Ball mixture, then cook as directed in boiling salted water instead of soup (for this amount you'll need about 3 quarts water and 2 tablespoons salt). Lift from salted water with a slotted spoon and add 2–3 Matzo Balls to each bowl of chicken broth or clear soup. Nutritional count same as basic recipe.

SIX

Meat

Meat always gets star billing. It's the dish around which all others are planned, the one for which wines are chosen, the one that sets the tone of a meal. It's the most expensive part of our diet, the most universally well liked, the most versatile, and certainly one of the most nutritious. Meat thus deserves a worthy role and the best possible supporting cast. It needs skillful and imaginative handling, preferential treatment sometimes, and kid glove care always.

HOW TO FIND QUALITY IN MEAT

Your guarantee of wholesomeness is the federal inspector's seal, a round purple stamp about the size of a silver dollar on beef, somewhat smaller on veal, lamb, and pork. All meat entered in interstate commerce must be federally inspected and passed before it can be sold. This means that the animals have been found free of disease and that the slaughterhouse handling them has met U.S. Department of Agriculture sanitation standards. About 80 per cent of the meat sold in this country is federally inspected; most of the remaining 20 per cent is state or city inspected.

Look next for the *grade* or *degree of excellence*. Meat may be graded federally (these grades vary from animal to animal and will be discussed separately under Beef, Veal, Lamb, and Pork), or it may be graded by a packing house. The equivalent of USDA CHOICE, for example, might be labeled Premium by one packer and Star, Puritan,

or Certified by others. Packer grading is more often done with ham than other meats.

Aging

Only beef, lamb, and mutton ribs and loins of high quality are aged, the purpose being to make them as flavorful and tender as possible. They may be *dry aged* (held 3–6 weeks at low temperature and humidity), *fast aged* (held 2 days or less at 70° F. and rather high humidity), or *vacuum packaged* (covered with a moisture-vaporproof film that stays on from packer to buyer). Most dry-aged and vacuum-packaged meat goes to hotels and restaurants; what we buy is usually fast aged or unaged—except in transit from slaughterhouse to our own homes (considerable tenderizing takes place during this period of 6–10 days). Because many people prefer more well-aged meat, especially beef, butchers often age it in their own coolers.

The Food and Calorie Value of Meat

All meat is a high-quality protein food supplying substantial amounts of B vitamins, iron, and phosphorus; most is moderate or moderately high in calories. Food and calorie values of meat vary considerably from animal to animal, also from cut to cut.

The Cuts of Meat

All cuts can be fitted into two categories: *the tender* and the *less tender*. Learning which are which isn't difficult once you remember that exercise and age are what toughen meat. The most frequently exercised parts of the animal, therefore—legs, neck, shoulder, rump, flank—will be far tougher than the seldom exercised rib and loin; old cows will be more sinewy than pampered young heifers or steers. Diagrams of the various cuts appear in the sections on Beef, Veal, Lamb, and Pork, as well as rules and recipes for preparing them.

How to Make the Most of Your Meat Dollar

• Learn the cuts of meat and cook them properly. Why buy relatively expensive round for stew when neck, shank, and chuck are not only cheaper but better?
• Buy in quantity, by the side if you have a freezer. If not, buy large cuts and divide them up as follows (below):
• Make the most of leftovers (see suggestions in each of the meat sections).
• Take advantage of supermarket specials.
• Steer clear of luxury cuts—steaks, chops, rib roasts—and concentrate upon less expensive pot roasts, Swiss steaks, shanks, and stews.

Original Cut	First Meal	Second Meal
10″ Beef rib roast	Rib roast	Deviled Short Ribs
Whole ham	Ham steak	Roast ham
Square shoulder of lamb	Blade chops	Shoulder roast

THE WAYS OF TENDERIZING MEAT

Down the centuries cooks have devised ingenious ways of softening up not-so-tender cuts both mechanically and chemically.

Mechanical tenderizing merely means breaking up tough meat fibers by *pounding, cubing, scoring, or grinding.*

Chemical tenderizing means softening tough fibers with an *enzyme, acid marinade, or moist heat cooking.* Using enzymes isn't as new as it may seem, because Latin American women have been tenderizing meat with papaya juice for ages (many modern tenderizers are simply crystalline forms of its enzyme, papain). The majority of today's tenderizers are the instant type, so read directions carefully before using. Marinating, on the other hand, isn't as effective a tenderizer as originally thought because the juices of the marinade hardly penetrate meat at all

in contrast to papain. Far more effective is the moist heat cooking that follows marination.

SOME SPECIAL WAYS TO PREPARE MEAT FOR COOKING

To Bard: To tie sheets or strips of fat around lean cuts so they won't dry out during cooking.

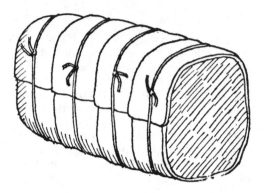

Commonly barded meats are whole beef tenderloin, filet steaks and tournedos; lean veal roasts; venison and game birds; poultry. Suet and bacon are recommended for beef and veal; bacon for pheasant and chicken; fatback or salt pork for venison and wild game birds.

Note: Many butchers will do the barding for you.

To Bone: To remove bones (have butcher do it whenever possible). *Filleting* refers to boning small pieces like steaks and chops. (*Note:* Base cooking times on *boned* weight.)

To Butterfly: To cut small boneless chops horizontally through the center, cutting almost but not quite through so that they can be opened flat like a book.

To French: To remove meat from rib ends of lamb, veal, or pork chops or crown roasts and to garnish with paper frills or small fruits.

To Lard: To insert long strips of chilled fat (lardoons) into lean meats with a larding needle. If the cut is large, strips the length of it are drawn through the center with a long-bladed larding needle.

Larding

When cuts are small, short lardoons are drawn through the surface in a technique called *piquing*. Piquing needles are fairly small, not unlike yarn needles. Piquing can also be done without a needle: make small slits at intervals over surface of meat, tuck in small cubes of fat and, if you like, garlic slivers and herbs.

Piquing

Meats often larded: beef rump and round roasts; veal leg roasts; whole beef liver and heart. Good larding fats are fatback, salt pork, fat trimmed from pork loin or fresh ham. *Note:* Always chill fat well before larding—makes the going easier. To make salt pork less salty, blanch lardoons quickly in boiling water, drain, and chill.

To Shape (also known as **To Skewer and Tie**): To make meat as compact as possible by inserting small skewers and pulling together with cord. The purpose is to make meat cook as evenly as possible.

To Slash: To cut outer fat of steaks and chops at regular intervals so they won't curl as they cook.

To Trim: To cut excess fat from outer layer of steaks and chops; most are best with fat trimmed to a thickness of 1/4".

Should Meat Come to Room Temperature Before Cooking?

Many home economists say not, but we think meat cooks more evenly, becomes more juicily tender if allowed to stand at room temperature about 1–2 hours before cooking. But there are exceptions: naturally thin cuts like flank steak, which are broiled only until rare (having them well chilled safeguards against overcooking); highly perishable meats such as hamburger, liver, kidneys, heart, and sweetbreads.

THE WAYS OF COOKING MEAT

What every cook hopes for is as succulent and tender a piece of meat as possible. Since naturally tender cuts cannot be made more tender by cooking (only less so), the object is to preserve every ounce of original tenderness. This is best done (with a few exceptions, which will be discussed as we come to them) by *dry heat cooking*. The less tender cuts, on the other hand, can be made more tender if cooked by *moist heat*. Here are the basic methods of each (with variations).

Dry Heat Cooking

Roasting: There are two schools of thought about roasting meat. Home economists and meat industry spokespersons generally recommend a continuous low heat (300°–325° F.) to reduce shrinkage and sputtering and to produce exquisitely juicy, evenly cooked roasts; classically trained chefs favor searing to brown both the roast and the pan juices. We prefer the low heat method but include both so you can take your pick. Whichever you use, place meat on a rack in a shallow roasting pan (so that it doesn't stew in its own juice); do not cover, do not baste (roast fat side up so drippings run down over meat), and do not add any liquid. Recommended for all large tender cuts of beef, veal, lamb, pork, and ham.

VARIATIONS

Spit Roasting: Meat turned on a spit in an oven or rotisserie or over a charcoal fire will generally take about 5 minutes less per pound than oven-roasted meat. To cook evenly, the meat must turn smoothly throughout cooking, which means that it must be perfectly balanced at all times. Best ways to ensure balance: choose blocky, compact cuts or, if spitting more than one piece of meat, counterbalance as needed with extra metal skewers. Despite all precautions, a roast may become unbalanced during cooking because it loses weight—unevenly—via drippings; keep an eye on the spit and rebalance roast if necessary. Many rotisseries are equipped with "compensators" that adjust the spit to a roast's changing weight and keep it turning smoothly. Rotisseries, incidentally, cook at varying speeds, so it's wise to consult the manufacturer's timetable. Also read his directions before buying a big roast—if too big, it won't stay balanced.

Smoke Roasting: This centuries-old way of cooking meat is becoming increasingly popular. Without special equipment you can still give steaks and roasts a deliciously smoky flavor by tossing packaged aromatic wood chips or mesquite on a charcoal fire or, if these are unavailable, green hardwood prunings, water-soaked shavings or sawdust (1 hour is usually long enough for the soaking). *Caution:* Never use pine or other resinous woods that will make the meat taste of turpentine.

Pit Roasting: When French explorers saw American Indians roasting whole deer and buffalo in earthen pits, they called it *barbe à queue,* meaning that the animals were cooked from "beard to tail." We now use their phrase to describe all meat cooked in pits, both open and closed. Most pit barbecuing is too complicated to try in your own back yard, so for anything grander than a clambake, hire a professional. Best bets for back-yard barbecues: beef rump or pork loin.

Broiling: Cooking in a broiler, 2"–5" from the heat (depending on thickness of cut). The meat should be placed on a rack in a broiler pan, browned on one side, turned with tongs (so savory juices aren't lost), and browned on the other side. Do not salt *until after browning*—salt draws moisture to the surface of the meat and prevents browning. Recommended for tender beef and ham steaks, lamb chops, ground beef and lamb, but not for pork or veal chops, no matter how tender. Pork must always be well cooked, and at broiling temperature it may toughen and dry. Veal, being lean and delicate, also tends to dry out. Both should be braised.

Charcoal Broiling (Grilling): Browning over glowing coals instead of under a broiler. Cooking times vary considerably, depending on amount of wind and outdoor temperature.

Gas and Electric Barbecuing with Lava Rocks: Whether done indoors or out, this is similar to, but easier than, charcoal broiling because temperatures can be easily controlled and lava rocks rarely need to be replaced.

Campfire Broiling: Essentially the same as charcoal broiling except that the fuel is wood and the fire a bit cooler.

Hibachi Broiling: This is charcoal broiling on a doll's scale (most hibachis, whether round or square, measure only 10"–16" across). But these sturdy little Japanese braziers put out a lot of heat and are perfect for grilling chops, small steaks, and such hors d'oeuvre as Teriyaki and Rumaki. Use long bamboo skewers, thoroughly water-soaked so that they won't burn.

Panbroiling: Cooking, uncovered, in a heavy skillet over moderate to moderately high heat without any fat or liquid (if meat is especially lean, lightly oil or salt skillet to prevent sticking). Cook until nicely browned on both sides and at desired doneness, turning often with tongs. Pour off drippings as they collect (this is one of the principal differences between panbroiling and frying). With the exception of extra-large steaks that are too unwieldy for skillet cooking, any cuts suitable for broiling can be panbroiled. *Browning Tips:* To brown well, meat must be dry on the surface; wipe with a damp cloth, if necessary, and do not salt until after cooking.

Frying: There are two methods:

Panfrying (Sautéing): The technique is virtually the same as for panbroiling *except* that the meat is cooked in a small amount of fat. Recommended for lean veal and lamb chops, for cube steaks and lean ground meat patties.

Deep Fat Frying: Cooking by immersing in very hot fat (usually 300°–380° F. on a deep fat thermometer). For best results, use a deep fat fryer with wire basket. Recommended for small breaded cuts or croquettes.

Moist Heat Cooking

Braising: Whether used for pot roasts, Swiss steaks, or fricassees, the technique is the same. Meat is browned in a heavy skillet or kettle in a little fat, then covered and simmered until tender over low heat or in a slow oven with a small amount of liquid (the fat is usually poured off after browning). Recommended for pork and veal chops, also for marginally tender steaks and roasts.

Cooking in Liquid (Stewing): Here's the way to tenderize the toughest cuts. Most of them (corned beef and smoked pork excepted) will taste better if browned in a little fat before being covered with liquid (water, stock, wine, or a combination) and left to simmer slowly in a covered kettle until fork tender. As with braising, the simmering can be done on top of the stove or in the oven.

Microwaving Meat

Although most meats cook and reheat beautifully in microwave ovens, power levels and cooking times vary from model to model, so it's best to follow your manufacturer's directions. These general guidelines will help you when microwaving different cuts of meat (also see Microwave Ovens in Chapter 1).

Roasts: Those with some blanketing of fat will brown more quickly than those without, yet rarely as richly as in a conventional oven. Remove roasts from the microwave oven when they are about 10° F. below the desired degree of doneness (use meat temperature charts as a guide). Allow microwaved roasts 10–15 minutes of *standing time* before you carve them so that their juices have a chance to settle. *Note:* Never salt a roast until *after* you have microwaved it (this helps keep the meat juicily tender).

Pot Roasts, Swiss Steaks, Stews: For better flavor and appearance, brown meats first on top of the stove, then pierce deeply all over with a fork so that moisture can penetrate the meat; add liquid recipe calls for, but reduce the amount by about 1/4. If you intend to add dumplings to a stew, make them small—the microwave will puff them dramatically. Do not attempt to microwave pastry- or biscuit-topped stews or casseroles; the toppings won't brown. Instead, speed-cook stew or casserole in the microwave, then add topping and brown in a conventional oven.

Steaks, Chops, and Hamburgers: For maximum browning, use a *preheated* browning tray or grill and remember to preheat it again before browning the meat's flip side. *Tip:* Try searing steaks or chops on a charcoal grill, then wrapping and freezing them. Come serving time, all you need do is pop already browned meat into the microwave.

Some Additional Do's and Don'ts:
• To microwave bacon to perfect crispness, lay between several layers paper toweling.
• Don't try to microwave breaded meats; the breading won't crispen because of the steam rising out of the meat.
• To time microwaving of meats accurately, use a *temperature probe* (make sure its tip is in center of meat, not touching fat or bone).
• To ensure even cooking, arrange such individual items as hamburgers, stuffed peppers, and meat balls in a ring in the microwave oven.
• Shape meat loaves both *round and flat* in a pie plate, then to promote browning, brush *top only* with a sweet mixture such as barbecue sauce or ketchup; also be sure to cover the meat with vented plastic food wrap before microwaving.
• To prevent hot dogs from bursting in a microwave, prick or slash them. Also try microwaving them *inside* their buns, wrapped in a napkin or paper toweling.
• To save time, double favorite meat recipes and freeze half for future enjoyment. The microwave will defrost and heat the second meal zip-quick.

Microwaving Leftovers

Microwaves reheat leftovers perfectly. Even roasts can be reheated and served *still rare* if you use a temperature probe or microwave-safe meat thermometer and time things carefully. Be sure to cover unsauced meats with wax paper or vented plastic food wrap.

Defrosting Meat in a Microwave

Being able to defrost frozen meats quickly and evenly is one of the major benefits of owning a microwave. Still, meats to be defrosted, particularly roasts, require special attention:
• Begin defrosting meat in a dish (to catch drips) in its *unopened* freezer wrapper unless that wrapper is aluminum foil; if so, remove foil and rewrap meat in plastic food wrap.
• Rotate package of meat frequently as it defrosts and unwrap when half of defrosting time has elapsed.
• Shield any warm spots with aluminum foil strips lest meat begin to cook.
• Separate steaks, chops, burgers, and stew

meat as soon as possible to hasten thawing. *Note:* Solidly frozen beef and lamb burgers can be microwaved without first being defrosted, but be forewarned, you'll never be able to have them rare, only well done. Simply allow 50–75 per cent more cooking time; to keep the burgers juicy, cover them with wax paper or vented plastic food wrap.
• To complete the defrosting of meat, allow a period of *standing time* before you begin to cook meat by microwave—20–30 minutes is usually sufficient for roasts, 5–15 minutes for burgers, chops, and steaks.
• Prepare meat and cook *immediately* after standing time or refrigerate *immediately and cook within a day.*

Cooking Meat in a Convection Oven

This oven's circulating hot air browns meats superbly, seals in their natural juices, reduces cooking times, and produces roasts done to an even turn and stews of supreme succulence. Any meat recipe can be easily adapted for use in a convection oven because it requires little more than time or temperature adjustments. Basically, a convection oven is just quicker than a conventional oven, indeed, except for broiling, it need not even be preheated. These pointers will help you cook meats perfectly in convection ovens (as will reading Convection Ovens in Chapter 1).
• To cook meats just the way you like them, use a temperature probe or meat thermometer (be sure tip rests in center of meat, touching neither bone nor fat).
• To compensate for the convection oven's speed, reduce most meat cooking temperatures by about 25° F. (but never use temperatures below 300° F.). *Note:* Such high-density foods as meat loaves and pasta-meat casseroles should be cooked at the temperatures recipes specify.
• To permit maximum air circulation, use baking pans at least 1/2″ smaller all around than the oven itself.
• For well-browned pastry or biscuit toppings, use dark or matte-finish metal pans. And to brown casseroles, cook uncovered for final 15 minutes.
• To shorten roasting times, place roasts *directly on oven rack* and a drip pan on rack underneath (roasting pans block air circulation). The best rack position for roasts is in the middle or lower half of oven. *Note:* There's no need to baste meats as they roast in a convection oven.
• To avoid spillover and flare-ups in convection ovens while large cuts roast, remove accumulated drippings from dripping pan with a bulb baster.

Defrosting Meat in a Convection Oven

For best results, use either the *automatic defrost cycle* or the *lowest temperature setting (about 100° F.).* Leave meat in its freezer wrap, place directly on middle oven rack with a drip tray on rack underneath. Separate steaks, chops, burgers, and stew meat as soon as possible to shorten overall defrosting time.

Infrared Cooking

Many of the modern, portable, plug-in broilers, roasters, and rotisseries cook by infrared heat, which produces richly browned, extra-juicy steaks, chops, and roasts a shade quicker than conventional ovens. For greatest efficiency, bring meat to room temperature before cooking and preheat unit thoroughly. Each of these units operates somewhat differently, so follow the manufacturer's directions.

Cooking Frozen Meat

To defrost or not to defrost? It really doesn't make any difference unless you intend to cook the meat in a microwave oven, in which case it must be completely defrosted (see Defrosting Meat in a Microwave). The advantage of defrosting is that the meat will cook more quickly; the advantage of not defrosting is that, if plans change and the meat cannot be cooked on schedule, all is not lost (thawed frozen meat should not be refrozen).

How to Defrost: Leave meat in its wrapper and set it in the refrigerator or on the counter top (a large roast will take 4–7 hours per pound to defrost in the refrigerator, roughly half that at room temperature; a steak 1″ thick will take 12–14 hours to thaw in the refrigerator, 3–4 hours at room temperature). Never defrost meat in warm water unless it is to be cooked in liquid. Once defrosted, meat can be cooked exactly like fresh meat.

How to Cook Solidly Frozen Meat:

Roasts: Unwrap, place on a rack in a shallow roasting pan, and begin roasting just as you would a fresh roast. When meat has partially thawed, remove from oven and insert meat thermometer in center of roast, not touching bone. Return to oven and continue roasting to desired temperature. *Note:* Solidly frozen roasts will take 1½–2 times as long to cook as the fresh in conventional ovens, a little less in convection ovens. Always defrost roasts before microwaving them.

Steaks, Chops, and Hamburgers:

To Broil: Place 1″–2″ farther away from heat than recommended for fresh meat and increase total cooking time 1½–2 times.

To Charcoal-Broil: Cook 5″–6″ above moderately hot coals, turning often, about half again as long as you would fresh meat.

To Panbroil or Panfry: Brown both sides quickly in a very hot skillet before surface has a chance to thaw (once thawing starts and juices run out, the meat will not brown). Reduce heat to moderately low and cook as you would fresh meat, but turning oftener. Cook 1½–2 times as long.

Meat Loaves: Cook exactly like fresh loaves but 1½–2 times as long. If loaf contains raw pork, insert meat thermometer when loaf is soft enough to do so and continue cooking to 185° F.

Meats to Be Breaded: Thaw just until surface is soft so that breading will stick; then proceed as for fresh meat, increasing cooking time by 1½–2.

Commercially Frozen Meat: Follow package directions.

Pressure-Cooking Meat

Meat cooked under pressure loses flavor, succulence, and attractiveness, so pressure-cook only when absolutely necessary to save time and then only for pot roasts or Swiss steaks that aren't apt to fall apart. Techniques vary from cooker to cooker, so follow the manufacturer's directions. In general, meat will suffer less if cooked at 10 pounds pressure than at 15.

Reheating Meat

Roasts, the most often leftover cuts, are also the most difficult to rehabilitate unless you have a microwave oven (see Microwaving Leftovers). Ideally, they should be transformed into entirely new dishes (see leftover recipes in beef, veal, lamb, and pork sections), but if such is not possible, any of these simple techniques will make warmed-over meat presentable:
• Slice very thin, place on heated plates, and top with hot gravy or sauce.

• Preheat oven to 300° F. Place roast on a rack in a shallow roasting pan and set, uncovered, on upper rack; place a pan of water underneath and heat 25–30 minutes.
• Preheat oven to 350° F. Slice meat thin, layer into a shallow, ungreased casserole with just enough gravy, pan juices, or sauce to cover, cover with foil, and heat 20 minutes. If you prefer, heat slices in gravy, juices, or sauce in a covered skillet about 5 minutes over moderately low heat.

Meat Stocks

Many of the world's great recipes depend upon stocks, gentle brews of bones, meat trimmings, herbs, and vegetables. Some stocks are simple, others elaborate; some delicate, others concentrated; some dark, some light. Almost all can simmer unattended on the back of the stove. For recipes, see the chapter on soups.

How to Render Fat

Clean, sweet lard (rendered pork fat) and suet (beef kidney fat) are excellent for browning meats and vegetables because they're economical and impart a mellow, meaty flavor. Lard is also such a superior pastry fat that many cooks will use no other.

Suitable Fats to Render: Beef kidney fat; pork kidney fat, clear plate, and fatback.

General Preparation: Cut fat into strips 1″ wide, remove any skin, then cut in 1″ cubes. Trim out any meat particles (these burn quickly and can give rendered fat an acrid flavor). Leave fat as cubes or put through coarse blade of meat grinder.

Stove-Top Method: Place prepared fat in a large, heavy skillet and add a little cold water to keep fat from browning before it melts (½ cup should be sufficient for 1–2 pounds fat). Heat uncovered over moderately low heat, stirring frequently, until all fat is melted, about 10 minutes. If you are rendering pork fat, the *cracklings* (cellular membranes in which the fat was held) will soon crispen and brown and rise to the surface. Skim them off and press out any remaining lard. Strain melted fat through a double thickness of cheesecloth and cool until firm. For especially fine grain, cover and chill quickly in the refrigerator. Spoon solidified fat into small crocks or glass jars, cover with lids, and store in a cool, dry, dark, well-ventilated place. Top quality lard or suet, properly stored, should keep 6–12 months.

Oven Method: Preheat oven to 250° F. Spread prepared fat over the bottom of a large, shallow pan, set uncovered in oven and let try out (melt), stirring occasionally. Skim off any cracklings, then strain, cool, and store as above.

To Clarify Rendered Fat: Place prepared fat in a large, heavy saucepan, add boiling water to cover, then boil slowly, uncovered, 10–15 minutes, stirring frequently. Cool 10 minutes, strain through several thicknesses of cheesecloth, cool, and chill without disturbing; lift off clear top layer of fat; discard liquid underneath and scrape off and discard sediment and semiliquid layer on bottom of fat. Store fat in a cool, dry, dark, airy spot.

To Clarify Meat Drippings: Let drippings solidify, then chop coarsely, place in a heavy saucepan with water to cover, and proceed as directed for clarifying rendered fat.

How to Use Meat Thermometers

Some thermometers, unfortunately, have not kept abreast of America's changing tastes. Rare roast beef, if you go by the average thermometer, has an internal temperature of 140° F. Not so. To rare beef enthusiasts, that is medium rare, perhaps even medium. Nearer the mark is 120° F. Readings for lamb are high, too. According to the thermometer, lamb should be cooked to 170° F., well done, indeed, and a disappointment to those who like it juicily pink (130°–135° F.). A few thermometers have readings as low as 130° F.; for most 140° F. is the cutoff point. If you are especially fond of very rare meat, try to obtain the new spot-check thermometer (inserted into meat only as it approaches doneness).

There are two basic types of meat thermometers: the spring-type and the mercury type, the latter preferred by some cooks because of its more detailed scale. Both are used the same way:

For Oven Roasting:
• Hold thermometer against side of meat so you can gauge location of bone, fat, and gristle.
• Insert thermometer in center of largest lean muscle, not touching bone, fat, or gristle.

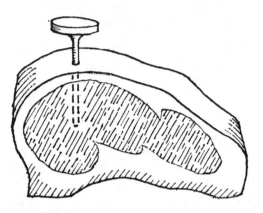

Place meat in oven with scale facing door so that you can read temperatures at a glance.

For Spit-Roasting:
• Insert thermometer into end of cut and parallel to spit so that it touches neither bone nor spit. If necessary, adjust angle slightly so thermometer will clear grill, hood, or oven walls as spit turns.
• When stopping rotisserie, see that thermometer comes to rest as far from heat as possible; otherwise it may break.

BEEF

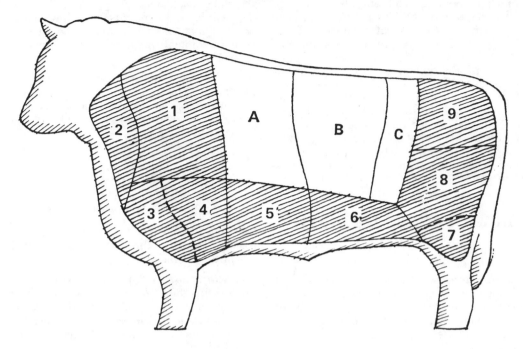

Note: Unshaded parts are the tender cuts. Shaded parts are not-so-tender.

THE TENDER CUTS:

A. RIB
   Roasts (rib, rib eye, or Delmonico)
   Steaks (rib, rib eye, or Delmonico)

B. LOIN
   Steaks (club, T-bone, porterhouse)
   Tenderloin

C. SIRLOIN
   Steaks
   Roasts

THE NOT-SO-TENDER CUTS:

1. CHUCK (shoulder)
   Pot roasts
   Swiss-style steaks (blade, arm)
   Stew beef
   Ground beef

2. NECK
   Stew beef

3. SHANK
   Stew beef
   Shank crosscuts
   Soup bones

4. BRISKET
   Corned beef
   Pot roasts

5. PLATE
   Short ribs
   Stew beef
   Ground beef

6. FLANK
   Flank steak
   London broil

7. HEEL OF ROUND
   Stew beef

8. ROUND
   Pot roasts
   Steaks (top, eye, and bottom round)
   Ground beef

9. RUMP
   Pot roasts

T-bones sizzling on a back-yard grill . . . hamburgers with all the trimmings . . . prime ribs bathed in their own natural juices —they're so American it's difficult to believe cattle are not native to America. The first arrived in Florida with the Spaniards about 400 years ago, rangy beasts of burden to the settlers, but to Indians a refreshing change from game. In a way, Indians were responsible for the birth of America's beef industry because they moved these cattle across the Mississippi into the grasslands beyond, where they thrived. Strangely, white men preferred pork and chicken to beef and may never have prized beef if Civil War shortages hadn't driven them to eat it. Suddenly long-horns were in demand, the rush was on, and with it the hell-for-leather days of cowboys and cattle barons and hundred-mile drives to market. Soon there were railroads, and beef, no longer driven to market, grew fat and lazy and succulent and tender. Ranchers quickly learned that penned steers were tenderer still and those fed corn and grain the most flavorful. Today beef production is highly scientific. And beef, itself, is our No. 1 meat.

HOW TO RECOGNIZE QUALITY IN BEEF

Look first for the *federal inspector's round purple stamp* (see discussion at beginning of this chapter), second for *grade,* which is based on *quality* (marbling or distribution of fat in lean, color and texture of lean, fat and bone) and *yield grade* (amount of usable meat). If beef has been graded by a federal agent, you will see his stamp, a series of shield-shaped purple emblems running the length of the carcass (the purple dye is harmless):

USDA Prime: The finest young beef, well marbled and blanketed with a creamy layer of fat. Little prime beef reaches the supermarket—it's the grand champion steer or heifer bought by prestige butchers, hotels, and restaurants.

USDA Choice: Finely grained, well-marbled beef just a shade under prime. It's the most readily available grade today.

USDA Good: This meat hasn't quite the well-marbled look of higher grades, but many people prefer its somewhat chewier texture.

USDA Standard: Here's an economical, all-purpose beef. Its steaks and roasts, though not the juiciest, are quite acceptable. The meat is not particularly well marbled, and the outer fat covering is apt to be skimpy.

The lowest grades—*USDA Commercial, Utility, Cutter,* and *Canner* or *Cull*—are of little concern here because they're rarely sold in retail stores. Packers use them for making sausages, frankfurters, and other process meats.

How to Tell Quality When the Grade Doesn't Show on the Cut: Tender, young beef will be bright cherry red, the fat creamy white and the chine (backbone) spongy and red. Older beef will be darker red, its fat yellowish and bones flinty. An orange cast to the fat suggests the animal was range fed and that its meat may be tough.

Note: When first cut, beef will be dark purple-brown. This doesn't mean it's spoiled, old, or tough, merely that it hasn't been exposed to the air (oxygen gives beef its vivid red color).

ROAST BEEF

The Top Tender Cuts

Standing Ribs: There are three different rib roasts, named for the part of the rib from which they come:

First-Rib Roast (5–8 pounds): Also sometimes called the *11th-and-12th-rib roast,* this cut is from the loin end of the rib. It's the most desirable and expensive rib roast because of its large, meaty center muscle, called the rib eye.

Center-Rib Roast (5–8 pounds): The mid-rib cut with a slightly smaller eye and slightly lower cost.

Sixth-and-Seventh-Rib Roast (5–8 pounds): From the chuck or shoulder end of the rib, this roast may not be so tender as the first two.

Three Styles for Standing Ribs: Each rib roast can be cut three ways:

10″ Standing Rib: The ribs are 10″ long, the backbone still intact. There's little advantage in having such long ribs because they provide almost no meat. Better to have them cut off and to cook as short ribs.

7″ Standing Rib: Probably the best style; 3″ of ribs have been sawed off and the backbone removed.

6″ Standing Rib: The newest look in rib roasts, a bit too "sawed off," perhaps, to be graceful, but a good choice for spit roasting because it is easy to balance on the spit.

Boned and Rolled Rib Roast (4–6 pounds): All rib roasts can be boned and rolled; they are easier to carve than standing ribs but take longer to cook. Some say they lack the rich, beefy flavor of standing ribs.

Rib Eye or Delmonico Roast (3–6 pounds): The boneless, meaty rib eye.

Whole Tenderloin or Filet (see Tenderloin).

Sirloin (8–12 pounds): The granddaddy of roasts adored by the English. *Boneless sirloin* has become very popular in the Northeastern U.S.

Marginally Tender Roasts

These less expensive cuts are "iffy" roasts—tender enough to roast *if* from prime or choice beef. When in doubt about them, braise.

Sirloin Tip (3–5 pounds): A chunky, lean, triangular cut.

Standing or Rolled Rump (4–7 pounds): Often underrated, this blocky, hindquarter cut has unusually good flavor.

Top Round (3–6 pounds): Though usually reserved for steaks, top round can be left whole and roasted. It's a single, large lean muscle, the tenderest one of the round.

Eye Round (2½–5 pounds): Probably the "iffiest" cut of all. Eye round looks like whole tenderloin, but there the resemblance ends; it will be tender enough to roast only if of tiptop quality.

How to Roast Beef

Suitable Cuts: Standing Rib, Boned and Rolled Rib, Rib Eye, Sirloin and, if top quality, Sirloin Tip, Standing and Rolled Rump, Top and Eye Round. Bear in mind that boneless roasts will take about 10 minutes per pound longer to cook than bone-in roasts; also that small roasts take proportionately longer to cook than large roasts.

Amount Needed: The bigger the roast, the better it will be. Standing ribs should weigh at least 5 pounds and be 2 ribs wide; boned and rolled ribs should be no less than 4 pounds. To figure number of servings, allow ⅓–½ pound boneless roast per person; ¾ pound bone-in roast.

General Preparation for Cooking: Let roast stand at room temperature 1½–2 hours if possible. Season, if you like, with salt and pepper (salt penetrates only ¼″, so it makes little difference whether a roast is salted before or after cooking). For extra savor, rub roast with a cut clove of garlic or suitable herb such as rosemary or thyme. Some cooks also like to flour a roast and start it at a high temperature to help seal in juices and give it a nice brown crust, but tests have shown it's wasted effort as far as sealing in the juices is concerned.

Continuous Low Heat Method: Preheat oven to 300° F. Place roast fat side up in a large, shallow roasting pan; all but standing ribs should be put on a rack so they're kept out of the drippings (with standing ribs, the ribs themselves act as a rack). Insert meat thermometer in lean in center of roast, not touching bone. Do not cover roast; do not add liquid to pan; do not baste roast as it cooks. Using times and temperatures in Roast Beef Chart as a guide, roast to desired degree of doneness. Transfer roast to heated platter, let "rest," if you like, then serve Au Jus or with Pan Gravy.

Searing Method: Preheat oven to 450° F. Insert meat thermometer and place in pan as for low heat method. Roast, uncovered, 25 minutes, reduce heat to 300° F. (leaving oven door open will quickly bring temperature down), and continue roasting to desired doneness. Bone-in roasts will take about 15 minutes per pound for rare (120°–125° F.), 17 for medium rare (130°–140° F.), 19–21 for medium (145°–150° F.) and 23–25 for well done (155°–165° F.); boneless roasts will require 8–10 minutes longer per pound for each degree of doneness. Transfer roast to heated platter, garnish, and serve.

How to Spit-Roast Beef

Always make sure a roast *stays* balanced and turns evenly throughout cooking. If you plan to let roast "rest" 15–20 minutes before serving, remove from spit when thermometer is 5–10° below desired doneness.

Best Cuts: A 6″ or 7″ Standing Rib or a Boned and Rolled Rib.

Amount Needed: For best results, the standing rib should weigh 5–8 pounds, the boned and rolled rib 4–6.

General Preparation for Cooking: If using the standing rib, have butcher remove backbone. Let roast stand at room temperature 1½–2 hours if possible. Season or not, as you like.

In Rotisserie, Oven, Gas or Electric Barbecue: Preheat unit. Insert spit on bias so meat is balanced; tighten holding forks. Insert meat thermometer in center of largest lean muscle, touching neither bone nor the spit. Attach spit to rotisserie and roast to desired doneness. Standing ribs will take 12–14 minutes per pound for rare (120°–125° F.), 15–17 for medium rare (130°–140° F.), 18–20 for medium (145°–150° F.) and 21–23 for well done (155°–165° F.). Boned and rolled roasts will take about 10 minutes longer per pound for each degree of doneness.

Over Charcoal: Prepare a moderately hot charcoal fire. Balance roast on spit as above and insert thermometer. Adjust fire bed height so coals are 6″ from spit, then roast to desired doneness, using approximately same times as for rotisserie. Watch thermometer closely—it's the truest indicator of doneness.

VARIATION

Spit-Barbecued Beef: Marinate roast in refrigerator 12–24 hours in 1 pint Barbecue Sauce for Beef, turning 2–3 times. Let come to room temperature in marinade, then spit-roast as above. During last ¾ hour of cooking, baste often with marinade. Serve with Barbecue Gravy for Beef.

Roast Beef Chart
(opposite)

American tastes are changing. Those who like rare roast beef like it *really* rare, about 120°–125° F. on a meat thermometer, not 140° F., as many cookbooks recommend. To rare beef buffs, 140° F. is medium rare, perhaps even medium. It depends on one's definition of rare. If you like beef juicy and red (not pink), try taking it from the oven when the thermometer reads 115°–120° F. and letting it "rest" at room temperature 15–20 minutes before carving. Letting beef rest is good practice no matter how you like it cooked—the roast will be juicier, easier to carve. Because a roast will continue cooking as it rests, it should be brought from the oven when the thermometer is 5°–10° below desired doneness.

Using the Chart
• Times can only be approximate, since shape of cut, amount of fat and bone, the way the meat was aged, and internal temperature all affect roasting time. So does size; proportionately, large roasts take less time to cook than small ones. Timetables, thus, are most useful in telling you when to put a roast in the oven so that you can gauge meal preparation time. For the truest test of doneness, use a meat thermometer.
• Times are for roasts that have stood at room temperature 1½–2 hours, then roasted at a constant low temperature (300° F.).
• To roast at 325° F. (the outer fat cover-

ing will be slightly crisper), allow about 2 minutes less per pound.
• For refrigerated roasts, allow 2–3 minutes more per pound.

How to Carve a Standing Rib Roast:
Lay roast, large side down, on platter; if wobbly, cut slice off bottom to level. Steady roast by inserting carving fork below top rib; with a short-bladed knife, cut down along ribs to loosen meat. With a carving knife, cut across face of roast to ribs, making slices ⅛″–¼″ thick and lifting each off as it is cut.

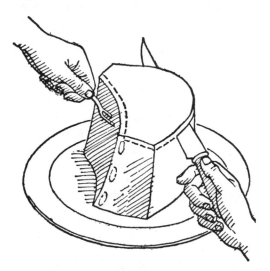

How to Carve a Boned and Rolled Rib Roast:
If roast seems firm (and carver is experienced) remove strings in kitchen. Otherwise, leave on lest roast fall apart. Lay roast on its side on platter. Steady with fork, and cut straight down through roll into ⅛″–¼″ slices, removing strings as you go. When through carving, turn roast cut side up so juices won't run out.

ROAST BEEF REVISITED

(How to Use Up Leftovers)

BEEF MIROTON

4 servings ⚖

Here's an unusually good way to use up leftover roast beef.

1 medium-size yellow onion, peeled and minced
1 tablespoon beef drippings, butter, or margarine
2 tablespoons flour

ROAST BEEF CHART

Cut	Weight in Pounds	Approximate Minutes per Pound at 300° F.	Meat Thermometer Temperature
Standing Ribs			
Rare	5–8	17–19	120°–125° F.
Medium rare	5–8	20–22	130°–140° F.
Medium	5–8	23–25	145°–150° F.
Well done	5–8	27–30	155°–165° F.
Boned and rolled	4–6	Add about 8–10 minutes per pound to each of the times given for standing ribs —and keep a close eye on the meat thermometer.	
Rib roasts			
Sirloin			
Rare	8–12	16–20	120°–125° F.
Medium rare	8–12	20–22	130°–140° F.
Medium	8–12	23–25	145°–150° F.
Well done	8–12	26–30	155°–165° F.

Note: The following cuts should be roasted only if prime or choice. Some beef connoisseurs also feel that they are better cooked to medium.

Cut	Weight in Pounds	Approximate Minutes per Pound at 300° F.	Meat Thermometer Temperature
Sirloin tip (a boneless roast)			
Rare	3–5	28–30	120°–125° F.
Medium rare	3–5	30–33	130°–140° F.
Medium	3–5	34–38	145°–150° F.
Well done	3–5	40–45	155°–165° F.
Standing rump			
Rare	5–7	20–22	120°–125° F.
Medium rare	5–7	23–25	130°–140° F.
Medium	5–7	26–28	145°–150° F.
Well done	5–7	29–32	155°–165° F.
Boned and rolled	4–6	Add 5–8 minutes per pound to each of the times given for standing rump, but use meat thermometer as the most accurate indicator.	
Rump roast			
Top round (a chunky, boneless cut)			
Rare	3–6	28–30	120°–125° F.
Medium rare	3–6	30–33	130°–140° F.
Medium	3–6	34–38	145°–150° F.
Well done	3–6	40–45	155°–165° F.

Note: Because of their long, narrow shape, rib eye (Delmonico) and eye round will cook more evenly at 350° F. than 300° F. The same is true of all small roasts (under 3 pounds).

Cut	Weight in Pounds	Approximate Minutes per Pound at 300° F.	Meat Thermometer Temperature
Rib eye and eye round			
Rare	3–6	12	120°–125° F.
Medium rare	3–6	14	130°–140° F.
Medium	3–6	16	145°–150° F.
Well done	3–6	18–20	155°–165° F.

1 cup beef broth
1 cup leftover beef gravy
2 tablespoons red wine vinegar
1/2 cup dry red or white wine (optional)
1 tablespoon tomato paste
8 slices leftover roast beef
1 tablespoon minced parsley

Sauté onion in drippings over moderate heat 8–10 minutes until golden; blend in flour, slowly add broth, and cook, stirring, until thickened. Mix in all remaining ingredients except beef and parsley, then heat, stirring, 2–3 minutes. Pour about 1/3 of the sauce into a shallow, ungreased 1 1/2-quart casserole, lay beef on top, overlapping slices, and add remaining sauce. Cover and refrigerate 1 hour. Preheat oven to 350° F. Bake, covered, 15–20 minutes until bubbly. Sprinkle with parsley and serve.

NPS: 240 C, 5 mg CH, 300 mg S*

BEEF CROQUETTES

4 servings   ¢

2 cups cubed leftover lean cooked beef
1 large yellow onion, peeled and cut in slim
  wedges
2 tablespoons butter or margarine
1/4 cup unsifted flour
1 cup strong beef broth or stock
1 1/4 teaspoons salt
1/8 teaspoon pepper
1 tablespoon steak or Worcestershire sauce
1 egg, lightly beaten
3/4 cup toasted fine bread crumbs
1/4 cup cooking oil

Grind beef with onion, using fine blade of meat grinder or finely mince the two together by churning 15–20 seconds in a food processor fitted with the metal chopping blade. Melt butter over moderately high heat, mix in flour, and brown *lightly,* stirring. Slowly add broth and heat, stirring, until thickened; add salt, pepper, and steak sauce and mix into ground meat. Spread in a shallow dish, cover, and chill until easy to work. Shape into 8 sausage-like rolls, dip in egg, then in crumbs; dry on a wire rack 10 minutes. Brown croquettes in oil in a large, heavy skillet over moderate heat 5–7 minutes, turning often; drain on paper toweling and serve. Good with gravy, Tomato or Mushroom Sauce.

NPS: 370 C, 150 mg CH, 1220 mg S*

VARIATIONS

Dressed-Up Croquettes: Add any one of the following to croquette mixture: 1 tablespoon prepared mustard or horseradish; 1/4 cup minced ripe olives; 1/2 cup chopped, sautéed mushrooms; 2 tablespoons chili sauce, minced capers, dill pickle, or sweet green pepper; 1 crushed clove garlic; 1 teaspoon oregano, marjoram, curry, or chili powder. Recipe too flexible for meaningful nutritional count.

¢ **Budget Croquettes** *(6 servings):* Add 1 1/2 cups cooked rice or mashed potatoes to croquette mixture, shape into 12 rolls, and brown as directed.

NPS: 300 C, 100 mg CH, 815 mg S*

Some Additional Ways to Use Up Leftover Roast Beef

¢ **Beef, Macaroni, and Tomato Casserole** *(6 servings):* Mix together 1/2 pound boiled, drained macaroni, 1 1/2 pints canned tomato or meatless spaghetti sauce, 2–3 cups diced cooked beef, 1/4 pound lightly sautéed sliced mushrooms, a little minced garlic, salt and pepper. Spoon into a greased 2 1/2-quart casserole, top with grated cheese, and bake, uncovered, about 30 minutes at 375° F. until bubbly.

NPS: 315 C, 50 mg CH, 650 mg S*

¢ **Beef and Potato Cakes** *(4–6 servings):* Mix together 2 cups mashed potatoes, 1 1/2 cups coarsely ground cooked beef, 1 lightly beaten egg, 1 tablespoon grated onion, and salt and pepper to taste. Shape into patties, dust lightly with flour, and brown in 2 tablespoons butter 2–3 minutes on each side over moderate heat. *(Note:* Finely crumbled leftover hamburgers can be used in place of roast.) For extra zip, mix in any of the following: 1 tablespoon minced parsley or chives, prepared mustard, horseradish, chili sauce, or ketchup.

NPS (4–6): 315–210 C, 135–90 mg CH, 460–305 mg S*

▨ **Quick Beef Paprika** *(4 servings):* Stir-fry 1/2 cup each minced yellow onion and mushrooms in 2 tablespoons butter, margarine, or drippings in a heavy skillet 8–10 minutes over moderate heat until onion is golden. Blend in 1–2 tablespoons paprika and 1/2 cup light cream and simmer, uncovered, 5 minutes. Add 2 cups cubed cooked beef, cover, and simmer over lowest heat 10–15 minutes until beef is heated through and flavors blended. Season to taste with salt and pepper, smooth in 1 cup sour cream, and serve over buttered noodles or boiled rice. *(Note:* Veal may be substituted for the beef.)

NPS: 430 C, 60 mg CH, 155 mg S*

Beef Curry *(4–6 servings):* Stir-fry 1 minced yellow onion and chopped sweet apple in 1/4 cup meat drippings or oil 8 minutes until golden; blend in 5 tablespoons flour, 3 tablespoons curry powder, 1 teaspoon salt, 1 pint beef broth (use part gravy if you have it), 1 cup water (or vegetable cooking water or tomato juice), and 1 tablespoon Worcestershire sauce and heat, stirring, until thickened. Add 3–4 cups cubed cooked beef, cover, and simmer 20 minutes. Let stand off heat 3/4–1 hour, if possible, to blend flavors, then reheat just before serving. Serve with boiled rice, chutney, a green salad, and buttery chunks of garlic bread. *(Note:* Recipe may also be made with lamb or veal.)

NPS (4–6): 480–320 C, 110–75 mg CH, 1060–705 mg S*

¢ **Beef and Vegetable Pie** *(4–6 servings):* Mix 2 cups cubed cooked beef with 2 cups mixed leftover vegetables—any compatible combination: peas and carrots, corn and green or lima beans, potatoes with almost anything. Stir in 1 1/2 cups thin leftover gravy or 1 (10 1/2-ounce) can cream of potato or celery soup thinned with 3/4 cup water and, for extra flavor, 1 minced yellow onion and 1/2 minced sweet green pepper sautéed in a little butter until limp. Spoon into a greased 6-cup casserole or deep pie dish, cover with Flaky Pastry I, Rough Puff Pastry, or Biscuit Topping for Casseroles, and bake, uncovered, 35–40 minutes at 425° F. until lightly browned. *(Note:* Lamb or veal can be used instead of beef.)

NPS (4–6): 615–410 C, 85–55 mg CH, 495–330 mg S*

¢ **Beef-Stuffed Vegetables** *(4 servings):* Prepare 4 large tomatoes, sweet green peppers, or yellow onions for stuffing.* Stir-fry 1 minced yellow onion, 2 minced stalks celery, 1/4 pound chopped mushrooms, and 1 crushed clove garlic in 1/4 cup drippings or butter 8–10 minutes over moderate heat until onion is golden. Off heat mix in 1 1/2 cups each soft white bread crumbs and coarsely ground cooked beef and 3/4 cup leftover gravy or tomato sauce. Stuff vegetables, stand upright in an ungreased 1-quart casserole, and pour in gravy, beef broth, or tomato juice to a depth of 1/2". Bake, uncovered, 30–45 minutes at 375° F. until tender. *(Note:* Veal, lamb, or ham can be used in place of beef.)

NPS: 405 C, 60 mg CH, 175 mg S*

¢ **Beef Chow Mein or Chop Suey** *(4 servings):* Stir-fry 1 minced large yellow onion or bunch scallions in 2 tablespoons oil 5 minutes over moderate heat in a large skillet; add 2 cups diced cooked beef and stir-fry 5 minutes longer. Prepare 2 (1-pound) cans chow mein or chop suey vegetables (without meat) by package directions and when hot stir in skillet mixture and 1 tablespoon soy sauce. Simmer, uncovered, 2–3 minutes and serve over chow mein noodles or boiled rice. *(Note:* Pork can be substituted for the beef.)

NPS: 310 C, 70 mg CH, 385 mg S*

¢ **Roast Beef Hash** *(4–6 servings):* Stir-fry 1 minced yellow onion in 2 tablespoons meat drippings in a large, heavy skillet over moderate heat 8–10 minutes until golden. Add 2 cups diced cooked roast beef, 2–3 cups diced boiled potatoes, 1 teaspoon salt, 1/4 teaspoon pepper, 1/2 cup evaporated milk, and 1 minced large dill pickle. Spread hash evenly in skillet, leave uncovered, and brown over moderately low heat without stirring 30–40 minutes until underside is crusty. Fold over in half as you would an omelet and slide onto a heated platter. Serve with dill pickles, chili sauce, or ketchup. *(Note:* This recipe can be halved easily. It can also be made with corned beef, canned or processed meats, tongue, leftover lamb, pork, veal, or ham.)

NPS (4–6): 345–230 C, 70–50 mg CH, 1120–745 mg S*

To Make the Most of Very Small Amounts:

• Cube beef or cut in julienne strips and toss into hearty salads (chef's salad, dried bean, egg, potato, pasta, or rice salads).
• Cube and use to stretch budget casseroles (dried bean, pasta, rice, mixed vegetables).
• Cube and substitute for raw beef in soups and broths (add bones, whenever possible, to enrich flavor). Or dice fine and add to vegetable soups—homemade or canned.
• Add lean scraps and bones to stock pot.
• Grind fine and make into sandwich spreads by mixing with softened cream cheese, mayonnaise and/or mustard, or horseradish.
• Grind fine, mix with any seasoned butter, a little minced onion or capers, mustard or other spicy condiment and use as a cocktail spread.
• Grind fine and add to any savory stuffings.
• Cut into small thin slices, trim of fat, and layer into custard cups, adding thinly sliced cooked carrots between layers, if you like. Fill to brim with Basic Aspic or Jellied Consommé Madrilène and chill until firm. Un-

mold on salad greens and serve with mayonnaise or any suitable cold sauce such as Cumberland, Rémoulade, Tartar, or Whipped Horseradish.

BEEF TENDERLOIN

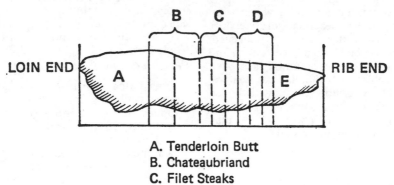

A. Tenderloin Butt
B. Chateaubriand
C. Filet Steaks
D. Tournedos
E. Filet Mignon

Butter-smooth, boneless, and so tender you scarcely need a knife to cut it, tenderloin is the Rolls-Royce of beef. It can be roasted, sliced into steaks, and broiled or sautéed, cubed for Stroganoff or Fondue Bourguignonne, even ground for Steak Tartare.

Though we tend to think of filet mignon as any small tenderloin steak, it is actually the smallest of four. Choicest is the 2″–3″ *chateaubriand,* cut from the chunky center of the tenderloin; it should weigh at least 1 pound before trimming and serve 2–3. Next in line are the individual *filet steaks,* 3″–3½″ in diameter and usually cut 1″–2″ thick.

Third are the *tournedos* or *medallions of beef,* about 1″ less in diameter but cut similarly thick. Finally come the *filets mignons* from the thin rib end. *Mignon* means *dainty* or *tiny,* and these, rarely seen in supermarkets, are often no more than 1½″ across. All tenderloin deserves special treatment, both in the cooking (always serve rare or medium rare) and in the presentation.

ROAST WHOLE BEEF TENDERLOIN

8–12 servings

Tenderloin isn't the easiest cut to roast because it tapers sharply at one end. For best results, tuck the skinny end under before barding (or buy only the plump part of the tenderloin) and roast just until rare or medium rare. Many butchers, incidentally, will do the barding for you.

Suet for barding
1 whole beef tenderloin (about 4–6 pounds), trimmed of fat and connective tissue
3–4 tablespoons softened unsalted butter or Garlic Butter
1½ teaspoons salt
¼ teaspoon pepper

SUGGESTED GARNISHES
Stuffed Mushrooms
Broiled tomato halves
Shoestring Potatoes
Watercress or parsley sprigs

SUGGESTED SAUCE
Béarnaise or Madeira

Bard tenderloin* with suet, then let stand at room temperature 1½–2 hours if convenient. Meanwhile, preheat oven to 450° F. Rub exposed tenderloin ends with 2 tablespoons butter, insert meat thermometer in center of meat, and roast, uncovered, on a rack in a shallow roasting pan 5–6 minutes per pound for rare (120°–125° F.), 7–8 minutes for medium rare (130°–140° F.). Remove suet covering during last 10–15 minutes and brush tenderloin well with remaining butter so it will brown nicely. Transfer to steak board or hot platter, cover loosely, and let "rest" 5 minutes. Sprinkle with salt and pepper and garnish with 2 or more of the suggested garnishes. Slice ½″–1″ thick and serve with Madeira or Béarnaise Sauce.

NPS (8–12): 425–285 C, 165–110 mg CH, 585–390 mg S*

To Roast a Half Tenderloin *(4–6 servings):* Choose a 2–3 pound tenderloin of as uniform thickness as possible. Bard and tie as above, insert thermometer, and roast at 450° F., using above times as a guide.

To Spit-Roast Whole Beef Tenderloin:

In Rotisserie or Oven: Preheat unit. Balance barded tenderloin on spit by skewering lengthwise; tighten holding forks, attach to rotisserie, and broil 20–25 minutes for rare, 30–35 for medium rare or according to the manufacturer's time table. Remove suet and brown quickly under broiler. Season and serve.

Over Charcoal: Prepare a hot charcoal fire. Balance barded tenderloin on spit as above, attach to rotisserie, adjust height so spit is 6″ from coals, and broil 25–30 minutes for rare, 35–40 for medium rare. Remove suet for last 10 minutes and brush often with melted unsalted butter. Season and serve.

VARIATIONS

Beef Tenderloin Rosemary: Bard and roast tenderloin as directed up to point of removing suet. When suet is removed, sprinkle tenderloin with 1/2 teaspoon crushed rosemary, 1 teaspoon salt, and 1/4 teaspoon coarsely ground pepper. Finish roasting as directed, basting often with Burgundy (you'll need about 2/3 cup in all). When serving, top each portion with some of the Burgundy pan drippings.

NPS (4–6): 435–290 C, 165–110 mg CH, 725–480 mg S*

Beef Tenderloin Madeira: Before barding, marinate tenderloin in 1 pint medium-dry Madeira 4–8 hours in the refrigerator; remove from marinade, pat dry, bard, and roast as directed. Serve with Madeira Sauce (use marinade in preparing sauce).

NPS (4–6): 440–295 C, 165–110 mg CH, 585–390 mg S*

ROAST TENDERLOIN OF BEEF SMITANE

4–6 servings

1 (2–3-pound) beef tenderloin of uniform thickness, trimmed of fat and connective tissue
1 small yellow onion, peeled and minced
1 carrot, peeled and minced
1 stalk celery, minced
2 tablespoons butter or margarine
1 tablespoon finely grated lemon rind
4–5 slices fat bacon or thin strips salt pork

1¼ cups sour cream
Paprika

SUGGESTED GARNISH
Baked Mushroom Caps Stuffed with Hazelnuts
Watercress or parsley sprigs

Let tenderloin stand at room temperature 1½–2 hours if convenient. Meanwhile, stir-fry onion, carrot, and celery in butter over low heat about 10 minutes until tender but not brown; mix in lemon rind. Preheat oven to 450° F. Spread vegetable mixture over tenderloin, lay bacon slices on top, and insert meat thermometer in center. Roast, uncovered, on a rack in a shallow roasting pan 5–6 minutes per pound for rare (120°–125° F.) and 7–8 for medium rare (130°–140° F.). Remove bacon and vegetables and discard. Transfer tenderloin to a steak board or hot platter and keep warm. Skim fat from drippings, smooth in sour cream, and warm gently, but do not boil, 1–2 minutes. Garnish beef with stuffed mushrooms and cress, top with some of the sauce, and sprinkle with paprika. Pass remaining sauce.

NPS (4–6): 560–370 C, 190–125 mg CH, 325–215 mg S*

FILET STEAKS, TOURNEDOS, AND FILETS MIGNONS

It should be reemphasized that the filet steaks here are what we commonly (and incorrectly) call filets mignons—tenderloin steaks 3–3½″ across. The filets mignons really are *mignons,* dainty chunks cut from the thin end of the filet (see Beef Tenderloin illustration). All cooking times are for steaks that have stood at room temperature 1½–2 hours. Allow 1 (1″–2″) thick filet steak per person; 1–2 (1″–2″) tournedos, and, depending on size, 2–3 filets mignons.

To Panfry (Sauté): Wrap a strip of bacon or suet around edge of each steak, if you like, and tie with string or secure with toothpicks. Warm a little butter and oil (for 4 steaks, 2 tablespoons butter and 1 of oil are about right) in a heavy skillet over moderately high heat, add steaks, and brown, uncovered, 3–4 minutes on a side for very rare, 5–6 for rare, and 7–8 for medium rare (to test for doneness, press steak in center with your finger—unlike raw filet, which is soft, it should feel slightly resilient). If you plan to leave bacon on, turn steaks on end and brown lightly. Transfer to a hot platter, remove strings or toothpicks and, if you like, bacon. Sprinkle with salt and pepper and serve with pan juices or a suitable sauce such as Béarnaise, Choron, Diable, Dijonnaise, or Poivrade. Small mushroom caps, which can be sautéed in the pan right along with the steaks, make a delicious garnish.

To Panbroil (filet steaks only): Bacon-wrap or not, as you wish. Brown filets, uncovered, in a lightly greased or salted heavy skillet over moderately high heat 3–4 minutes on a side for very rare, 5–6 for rare, and 7–8 for medium rare; pour off any drippings as they collect.

To Broil: Preheat broiler. Place bacon-wrapped steaks on lightly greased broiler rack and broil 3″ from heat 4–5 minutes on a side for very rare, 6–7 for rare, and 8–9 for medium rare. If you wish, brush both sides of steaks lightly with melted butter before broiling. *(Note:* A good way to broil very small mignons is à la shish kebab on long metal skewers with strips of bacon intertwined. They'll take slightly less time to broil than larger tenderloin steaks.)

Some Easy Ways to Dress Up Filets and Tournedos

Marinated Filets or Tournedos: Marinate steaks 8 hours in refrigerator in a good homemade French or herb dressing or in Japanese Steak Sauce. Remove from marinade, let stand at room temperature 1 hour, then bacon-wrap and broil as directed, brushing often with marinade.

Surprise Filets or Tournedos: Make small pockets in raw steaks (work from outer edge, cutting a horizontal slit deep into center of each). Place 1 teaspoon pâté in each pocket and, if you like, 1/4 teaspoon minced truffle. Or tuck a small lump Roquefort or blue cheese in each. Close with toothpicks, wrap with bacon or suet, and panfry or broil.

Savory Filets or Tournedos: Just before serving, rub steaks with a dab of Anchovy, Chive, Mustard, Shallot, or Tarragon Butter.

Filets or Tournedos in Wine: Panfry 4 steaks and transfer to a hot platter. Heat 1/4 cup dry red wine, Madeira, or port with 1/4 teaspoon tarragon, chervil, chives, or rosemary in skillet, stirring, until bubbly. Pour over steaks and serve.

Filets or Tournedos in Minute Sauce: Panfry 4 steaks and transfer to a hot platter.

Add 2 tablespoons lemon juice, 1 tablespoon Worcestershire sauce, and 1/2 teaspoon Dijon-type mustard to skillet and heat, stirring, until bubbly; pour over steaks.

Flaming Filets or Tournedos: Broil or panfry 4 steaks, then transfer to a chafing dish set over low heat. Add 1/3–1/2 cup warmed cognac, heat 1 minute, and blaze with a match. Spoon flaming cognac over steaks and season with salt and pepper. If you like, swirl in 1 tablespoon Maître d'Hôtel Butter when flames subside.

Some Classic Ways to Serve Tournedos (and Filets)

À la Béarnaise: Panfry 4–6 steaks, arrange in a circle on a hot platter, mound Château Potatoes in center, and drizzle steaks with Béarnaise; pass extra sauce.

À la Bordelaise: Top panfried steaks (any number you wish) with 1/2″ slices poached marrow (see Marrowbones) and a little minced parsley. Serve with Bordelaise Sauce.

À la Clamart: On a hot platter arrange panfried steaks, tiny buttered new potatoes, and boiled artichoke bottoms filled with buttered or Puréed Green Peas. Quickly boil and stir 1/3 cup dry white wine in steak skillet to reduce by half, pour over steaks, and serve.

Chasseur: Before cooking steaks, sauté 1/2 pound sliced mushrooms and 2 tablespoons minced shallots or scallions in 2 tablespoons butter over moderate heat 5 minutes; set aside. Panfry 6 steaks, place each on a fried crouton round, and keep warm on a hot platter. Pour fat from steak skillet, add 1/2 cup beef stock and 2 teaspoons tomato paste, and boil rapidly, stirring, until reduced by half. Mix in 1/4 cup Madeira blended with 2 teaspoons cornstarch and heat, stirring, until thickened and clear. Add mushrooms and 1 tablespoon minced parsley (or 1 teaspoon each minced parsley, tarragon, and chervil), pour over steaks, and serve.

Rossini: Serve panfried steaks on fried crouton rounds topped with 1/4″ slices *pâté de foie gras,* decorative truffle slices, and a little Madeira Sauce. *(Note:* Pâté will be more attractive if lightly dusted with flour and sautéed briefly in a little butter over low heat.) Garnish with Château Potatoes and watercress; pass extra sauce.

FONDUE BOURGUIGNONNE

6 servings

Picture a group of friends gathered round, spearing chunks of steak and cooking them in a bubbling pot of oil; picture an array of sauces and condiments, there for the dunking, and you have the idea of Fondue Bourguignonne. It's a merry Swiss dish that's perfect for a small party. Everything can be prepared well in advance and set out at the last minute.

3 pounds beef tenderloin or boneless sirloin, trimmed of fat and cut in 1″ cubes
3 cups (about) cooking oil (a ½ and ½ mixture of peanut and corn oil is especially good) or 3 cups clarified butter*

Sauces: Prepare 2 or more, choosing with an eye to variety. Any hot sauces can be reheated in the top of a double boiler or hot water bath minutes before serving. Some sauces traditionally served: Aurore, Béarnaise (a must), Cumberland, Diable, Mustard, Rémoulade Dressing, Sour Cream-Horseradish Sauce. Not traditional but good: Brown Curry, Madeira, Smitane, and Teriyaki sauces.

Condiments: Choose 3 or more, again for variety: spicy and mild mustards, chutney, tomato or mushroom ketchup, horseradish, olives, pickled onions, or mushrooms.

Special Equipment: You'll need a fondue bourguignonne pot, a deep metal or enameled-metal pot as distinguished from the heavy, shallow, ceramic cheese fondue dish (preferably the 2-quart size), either electric or with a stand and alcohol burner, fondue forks and long bamboo skewers.

How to Set the Table: Place fondue stand and burner in the center of the table. At each place provide 2 salad plates (1 for the raw chunks of beef, the other for sauces), 2–3 bamboo skewers, and a fondue fork in addition to dinner knife, fork, spoon, and napkin.

How to Serve: In the kitchen, half fill fondue pot with oil and heat slowly on the stove until a cube of bread will sizzle; set over lighted alcohol burner on dining table. Arrange a small mound of steak cubes on 1 of the salad plates at each place and garnish with watercress or parsley. Surround fondue pot with small bowls of sauces and condiments; set out salt shaker and pepper mill. *(Note:* Pour any particularly liquid sauces into small ramekins and set 1 on each sauce plate.)

How to Eat Fondue Bourguignonne: The guests first spoon an assortment of sauces and condiments onto their empty plates. Then, using a long bamboo skewer, each person spears a chunk of filet, plunges it into the fondue pot, and cooks it the way he or she likes it (allow 5–10 seconds for rare, 10–15 for medium, and 20 for well done). More than 1 chunk of meat can be cooked at a time, but it's important to regulate the burner so the oil bubbles vigorously—but does not sputter—each time a new chunk is added. To help reduce sputter, keep a small chunk of bread in the oil, replenishing whenever it threatens to burn. After cooking a piece of steak, the person transfers it to the fondue fork, dunks it in a sauce or condiment, and eats it.
Caution: Some recipes recommend using two fondue forks, one for cooking, the other for dunking and eating. But, if you forget to switch forks (and it's easy to do so), you can get a nasty mouth burn. So play it safe and use bamboo skewers.

What to Serve with Fondue Bourguignonne: Since the fondue table will be crowded, it's best to follow with a separate salad course—a cold green bean or crisp tossed salad is ideal. As for wine, uncork a good red Burgundy or Bordeaux.
*NPS: 485 C, 145 mg CH, 170 mg S**

BEEF STROGANOFF

4 servings

A true Stroganoff has very little sour cream and no mushrooms, tomato paste, or paprika. What makes it special is the spicy mustard. It's best made with beef tenderloin, but if your budget won't allow it, use sirloin.

1½ pounds beef tenderloin or boneless sirloin, trimmed of fat and cut in 2″ × ½″ strips
¼–½ teaspoon salt (depending upon saltiness of broth and mustard)
¼ teaspoon pepper
1 medium-size Bermuda onion, peeled and sliced ¼″ thick
4 tablespoons butter or margarine
2 tablespoons flour
1 cup strong beef stock or canned condensed beef broth
1 teaspoon prepared Dijon-type mustard
¼ cup sour cream, at room temperature

Spread beef strips out on heavy brown paper and sprinkle evenly with salt and pepper. Toss to mix, spread out again, top with onion slices, and let stand 2 hours at room temperature. Melt 2 tablespoons butter in a large, heavy skillet over moderately low heat and blend in flour. Mix in stock and heat, stirring, 3–5 minutes until thickened. Blend in mustard and remove sauce from heat. In a second large skillet, melt remaining butter over moderately high heat, add beef and onion, and brown quickly—this will take about 10 minutes. Add browned beef *but not the onion* to the sauce, set over moderate heat, cover, and simmer, stirring once or twice, 15 minutes (onion can be saved for hamburgers or stew). Remove from heat, stir in sour cream, and serve.

NPS: 415 C, 150 mg CH, 900 mg S*

TERIYAKI-STYLE TENDERLOIN

4 servings   ⚖

1½ pounds beef tenderloin in 1 piece

MARINADE
¾ cup Japanese soy sauce
¼ cup mirin, sake, or medium-dry sherry
1 tablespoon light brown sugar (only if sake or sherry is used)
2 teaspoons finely grated fresh gingerroot or 1 tablespoon minced preserved ginger

Place tenderloin in a large bowl. Mix marinade ingredients, pour over meat, cover, and let stand at room temperature 1½–2 hours, turning meat several times. Preheat broiler. Remove meat from marinade and broil 4″ from the heat about 15 minutes, turning every 3 minutes and basting with marinade. (*Note:* This cooking time is for a medium-rare *teriyaki.* If you like it rarer, reduce cooking time to about 10–12 minutes, if more well done, increase it to 17 minutes.) To serve, cut in thin slices and top with a little marinade.

NPS: 300 C, 110 mg CH, 1800 mg S*

VARIATION

⚖ **Teriyaki Hors d'Oeuvre** (*About 6–8 servings*): Cut tenderloin into ¾″–1″ cubes and marinate as directed; drain, reserving marinade. Broil 4″ from heat 1–2 minutes, turn, baste with marinade, and broil 1–2 minutes longer. Skewer with toothpicks or bamboo skewers. Or, if you have a hibachi, set out the raw marinated cubes, long metal skewers, or fondue forks and let everyone broil his or her own teriyaki.

NPS (6–8): 200–150 C, 75–55 mg CH, 2740–2055 mg S*

BEEF SUKIYAKI

4 servings   ⚖

Sukiyaki is a good choice for a small dinner because all ingredients can be cut up well in advance (cover and refrigerate until the last minute), because it can be cooked quickly at the table in an electric skillet, and because it needs nothing more than rice to accompany. Made the Japanese way, it contains *dashi,* a broth made of dried bonito flakes (packets are sold in Oriental groceries), *sake,* the fermented rice drink, *shirataki,* yam noodles, and soybean cake. The *shirataki* and bean cake can be omitted if necessary, the *dashi* replaced by beef broth and the sake by sherry. Some people make sukiyaki with *mirin,* a sweet sake, and omit the sugar. You can achieve the same effect by using a sweeter sherry and adding only enough sugar to "mellow" the sukiyaki. It should never taste sweet.

1 (2″) cube suet
1 cup paper-thin slices Spanish onion
6 scallions, trimmed and halved lengthwise
3 stalks celery, cut diagonally into thin slices
1 (8-ounce) can bamboo shoots, drained and sliced thin
1¼ pounds beef tenderloin or boneless sirloin, sliced paper thin
½ pound mushrooms, wiped clean and sliced thin
⅔ cup canned *shirataki* (optional)
1 soybean cake, cut in 1½″ cubes (optional)
1 quart washed, sorted spinach leaves
½ cup *dashi* or canned beef broth
½ cup sake or medium-dry sherry
½ cup Japanese soy sauce
3 tablespoons light brown sugar

Heat a large, heavy skillet over high heat 1 minute or set an electric skillet on highest heat; when good and hot, spear suet with a cooking fork and rub over bottom to grease; discard suet. Reduce heat to moderate, add onion, scallions, and celery, and stir-fry 5–8 minutes until lightly wilted; lay bamboo shoots, beef, mushrooms, *shirataki,* bean cake, and spinach on top. Mix *dashi* with sake, soy sauce, and sugar and pour over all. Cover and steam 3–4 minutes. Uncover and toss lightly as you would a salad, then simmer, uncovered, 2–3 minutes longer. Serve with rice.

NPS: 380 C, 95 mg CH, 2960 mg S*

STEAK TARTARE

4 servings ⚔

What we call steak tartare the French call steak *à l'Américaine*—a tribute to our superb beef. Strangely, our name for the dish comes from their way of serving it—with tartar sauce. But Americans prefer to use raw egg yolks and to mix in an assortment of condiments.

1½ pounds beef tenderloin or sirloin steak, trimmed of all fat and finely ground
4 raw egg yolks
1 teaspoon minced chervil (optional)
1 medium-size yellow onion, peeled and minced
2 tablespoons minced parsley

Lightly shape beef into 4 patties, place each on a chilled plate, and, using the back of a spoon, press a hollow in the center of each. Slide a raw egg yolk into each hollow and, if you like, sprinkle with chervil. Pass remaining ingredients in small bowls or arrange in separate mounds around each patty so that guests can mix in whatever—and as much of it as they like—along with the egg yolk. Set out salt and pepper. Some other optional accompaniments: cayenne pepper, Worcestershire sauce, lemon wedges, anchovy fillets, hot buttered toast—either plain or spread with anchovy paste.

NPS: 315 C, 385 mg CH, 140 mg S*

STEAKS

Sumptuous, succulent, often whopping—these are the cuts Americans do better than anyone else. The tender steaks come from the rib and loin sections, the marginally tender from the round, rump, chuck, flank, and plate. (Refer to Beef Chart.)

The Tender Steaks

Choicest of the choice are the T-bone, porterhouse, and pinbone sirloin because they contain large chunks of butter-smooth tenderloin. All tender steaks should be cut at least 1″ thick and will be juicier if closer to 2″; all are well enough marbled with fat that they can be cooked without additional fat. Broil or charcoal broil any of the following, and, except for sirloins, which are too hefty to handle easily in a skillet, panbroil.
   Rib and boneless rib steaks
   Delmonico or rib eye steak
   Club steak
   T-bone steak
   Shell steak (T-bone minus the tenderloin)
   Porterhouse steak
   Strip steak (porterhouse minus the tenderloin)
   Sirloin steaks (pinbone, flat bone, wedge bone, and boneless)
Note: Butchers sometimes remove the pinbone from the pinbone sirloin, grind the tail end and tuck it in where the bone was; this simplifies carving. Some also grind the long, lean tail of the porterhouse and tuck it underneath the tenderloin.

The Marginally Tender Steaks

If from prime or choice beef, some of these lean "budget" steaks will be tender enough to broil; others will need all the help they can get (i.e., pounding, scoring, marinating, braising). Being leaner than the tender steaks, they are also somewhat lower in calories and cholesterol; their texture is firmer, their flavor more robust.

The Broilables

(IF from top-quality beef):
   Top and eye round steaks
   Tip or sirloin tip steak
   Rump steak
   Skirt steak fillet
   Flank and flank steak fillets
   Boneless blade and blade chuck steak

   Petite steak:
   Minute steak:
   Cube steak:
Note: Though tender enough to broil, these three steaks are so thin they should be panfried as quickly as possible in butter or drippings.

The Unbroilables

Blade steak (when not first cut), arm steak, and bottom round are the cuts to braise: to use for Swiss steak, to stuff and roll, to smother with onions and mushrooms and rich brown gravy. *Note:* Any of the broilables listed above become unbroilables when cut from lower grades of beef.

How to Cook

Amount Needed: ⅓–½ pound boneless steak per person, ½–¾ pound in bone-in steak.

General Preparation for Cooking: If steaks seem unusually moist, wipe with a damp cloth so they will brown nicely. Trim off all but 1/4" outer fat and slash at 1" intervals to keep steaks from curling. Rub with pepper, if you like, also garlic, but not salt (salt draws moisture to the surface and slows browning). Let steaks stand at room temperature 1 1/2–2 hours before cooking if convenient. (*Note:* Naturally thin cuts like flank steak, also thinly cut minute, petite, or cube steaks, should be refrigerated until just before cooking so that the quick, intense heat does not carry them beyond the point of tenderness—medium rare.)

Cooking Tips

• Whenever in doubt about the tenderness of a steak, sprinkle each side with unseasoned meat tenderizer, pierce deeply all over with a sharp fork, and let stand as package directs.
• Always turn steaks with tongs to avoid piercing them and losing savory juices.
• When broiling, panbroiling, or panfrying marginally tender steaks, never cook beyond medium rare (longer cooking will merely toughen and dry them).
• When carving large, marginally tender steaks, cut across the grain in thin slices, holding the knife at a slight angle (this breaks up long, coarse fibers).

To Panfry (Sauté): Recommended for minute, petite, and cube steaks; skirt fillets, boneless blade steak, tip steak, top and eye round cut about 1" thick. Warm 1–2 tablespoons butter, margarine, drippings, or cooking oil in a large, heavy skillet over moderately high heat about 1 minute, add steaks, and brown on both sides. Minute, petite, and cube steaks will take only 1–2 minutes per side; the other steaks about 3 minutes per side for very rare, 4 for rare, and 5 for medium rare. Season and serve.

To Panbroil: Recommended for all tender steaks except large sirloins; for top and eye round, tip and boneless blade steaks. If steaks seem especially lean, grease or salt skillet *lightly;* heat over moderately high heat about 1 minute, add steaks, and cook, uncovered, turning occasionally and pouring off drippings as they accumulate, until browned on both sides and at desired doneness (use times below as a guide). Season and serve. (*Note:* Do not add water or other liquid to skillet.)

To Broil: Recommended for all tender steaks; also for top quality or tendered skirt fillets, chuck and boneless blade steak, top and eye round, tip and rump steaks. (*Note:* Flank steak requires a bit different technique

[see London Broil].) If steaks are very lean, brush lightly with melted butter. Preheat broiler. Rub rack with drippings or oil and, to save a messy clean-up, line broiler pan with foil. Place steak on rack and set in broiler so fat edge of steak is toward back of oven (this reduces spattering). Adjust height and broil to desired doneness as directed in Steak Broiling Chart (opposite), turning steak only once. Season and serve.

VARIATION

Planked Steak: A festive way to serve broiled steak is on an oak or hickory plank (most housewares departments sell them), wreathed with Duchess Potatoes, sautéed mushroom caps, and grilled tomatoes. Planks, usually rectangular or oval, should be at least 1" thick and from 15"–18" long. Most are seasoned by the manufacturer (see his directions), but, if not, here's *how to season a plank* yourself: brush top and sides with bland cooking oil, place on a sheet of foil on oven rack, and let stand in a 275° F. oven 1–1 1/2 hours. Remove from oven and wipe well with paper toweling—plank is now ready *to use* (see Planked Steak with Vegetables). *To care for plank:* wipe thoroughly with paper toweling immediately after using, then wash quickly in warm, sudsy water, rinse in cool water, pat dry, then allow to dry completely. Store, loosely wrapped, in a cool, dry place. (*Note:* If any part of plank is exposed during broiling, brush lightly with oil and cover with foil to prevent charring.)

To Charcoal-Broil: Recommended for all tender steaks; also for top-quality tip, rump, chuck, and boneless blade steaks. Prepare charcoal fire. For steaks 1"–1 3/4" thick, it should be hot (350°–375° F. on grill thermometer) or of an intensity to make you remove your hand after 2–3 seconds at grill level. For steaks 2" thick or more, it should be moderately hot (325° F.) or enough to make you withdraw your hand after 4 seconds. Spread enough glowing coals evenly over fire bed to equal area of meat and to last throughout cooking. Lightly grease grill with fat trimmed from steak, place steak on grill, adjust height, and broil as directed in Steak Broiling Chart. Turn only once during cooking. Season and serve.

To Broil on Gas or Electric Barbecues: The technique is the same as for charcoal broiling. You merely have greater control over the broiling because there are covers to divert or direct the wind, also thermostats. Broil steaks as directed in the Steak Broiling Chart, turning them one time only.

APPROXIMATE TOTAL PANBROILING TIMES

Steak Thickness	Very Rare	Rare	Medium Rare	Medium	Well Done
	Minutes	*Minutes*	*Minutes*	*Minutes*	*Minutes*
1″	6–7	8–10	11–12	13–14	15–16
1½″	8–10	11–12	13–14	15–17	18–20
2″	13–15	16–17	18–19	20–22	25–30

VARIATION

Marinated Steaks: Marginally tender steaks will be juicier if marinated 4 hours in refrigerator in Barbecue Sauce for Beef, Japanese Steak Sauce, or any good Italian, herb, or garlic dressing. Bring steak to room temperature in marinade, lift out, and pat dry. Grill as directed, brushing often with marinade.

To Braise: Here's the most sure-fire way of cooking marginally tender steaks. Braising isn't one recipe, but many—Beef Birds, Swiss Steak, and Chicken-Fried Steaks are all braised. You'll find these and other ways of braising steaks among the recipes that follow.

To Test Steaks for Doneness:

Bone-in steaks: Make a small slit near bone and check color of meat.

Boneless steaks: Make a small slit near center of steak to determine color.

Thick steaks (more than 2½″): Insert meat thermometer in center of largest lean muscle, not touching bone. A very rare steak will be 110° F., a rare one 120° F., a medium-rare one 130° F., a medium one 140° F., and a well-done one 155°–160° F.

STEAK BROILING CHART

Times (for steaks that have stood at room temperature 1½–2 hours) are approximate since shape and size of cut, amount of fat and bone, type of oven or grill all affect broiling time. In outdoor charcoal, gas or electric broiling, wind may also be a factor.

Oven Broiling	Thickness	Oven or Fire Temperature	Distance from Heat	Approximate Minutes per Side				
				Very Rare	Rare	Medium Rare	Medium	Well Done
Top and eye round, tip	1″	broil	2″	3	4	5	6	7
and rump steaks, skirt	1½″	broil	3″	6	7	8	9	10–12
fillets, chuck and	2″	broil	4″	14	15	16	17	18–19
boneless blade steak;								
all tender steaks except								
bone-in sirloins.								
Pinbone, wedge bone,	1″	broil	3″	7	8	9	10	11–13
and flat bone sirloin	1½″	broil	4″	10	11	12	13	14–15
	2″	broil	5″	18	19	20	21	22–24
Charcoal Broiling								
Tip, rump, chuck, and	1″	hot	4″	3	4–5	6	7–8	9–10
boneless blade steaks;	1½, 1¾″	hot	4″	4	5–6	7–8	9–10	12–15
all tender steaks.	2″	moderately hot	5″	6–7	8–9	10–12	14–16	18–20
	2½″	moderately hot	5″	10–12	13–15	16–18	20–22	23–25

Note: Directions and times for broiling tenderloin steaks, flank steak, and hamburgers are given in the discussion of each, since each requires a somewhat different technique.

How to Give Steak Extra Flavor
(Choose One Method Only.)

Before Cooking:
• Marinate steak 4 hours in refrigerator in Barbecue Sauce for Beef or Japanese Steak Sauce (or any good herb, Italian, or garlic dressing). Let come to room temperature, lift from marinade, pat dry, and broil, brushing often with marinade.
• Rub each side of steak with a cut clove garlic.
• Rub each side of steak with a compatible herb such as chervil, rosemary, or tarragon.
• Spread both sides of steak with 1 small grated yellow onion that has been blended with 2 tablespoons Dijon mustard and 2 teaspoons cooking oil or softened butter.
• Brush both sides of steak with 1 tablespoon soy sauce that has been mixed with 1 tablespoon each steak sauce, Worcestershire sauce, and chili sauce.

During Cooking:
• While broiling, brush or baste with Madeira, port, sherry, dry red or white wine, brandy, dark rum, or bourbon.
• While broiling, brush or baste with any barbecue sauce.
• While charcoal broiling, toss any of the following directly onto coals: 2–3 sprigs fresh sage or 1 tablespoon dried sage, a dozen bay leaves, 1 tablespoon cracked juniper berries.
• During last minutes of broiling or panbroiling, brush lightly with Herb, Chive, Garlic, Mustard, or Anchovy Butter.

Roquefort Steak: During last 1/2 minute of broiling, spread top of steak with 2–3 tablespoons Roquefort or blue cheese that have been creamed with 2 tablespoons softened butter.

After Cooking:
• Just before serving, top with 2–3 tablespoons Garlic, Herb, Marchands de Vin, Mustard, or Tarragon Butter.
• Just before serving, top with a 1/2 and 1/2 mixture of sautéed, minced yellow onions and mushrooms.
• Just before serving, top with the following: 1/2 cup each minced mushrooms and yellow onions that have been sautéed 10 minutes in butter with 1/4 cup each minced celery and sweet red or green pepper and 1 crushed clove garlic.
• Serve steak with Béarnaise, Bordelaise, Diable, Dijonnaise, Madeira, or Poivrade Sauce.

Flaming Steak: Warm 1/3 cup brandy, bourbon, rye, or dark rum, pour over hot steak, and flame, spooning flaming liquid over steak until flames subside. If you like, flame at the table.

Steak Mirabeau: Broil steak to desired doneness. Lay 9–10 anchovy fillets over steak in a crisscross pattern, dot with 2–3 tablespoons Anchovy Butter and 1/4 cup sliced pitted ripe olives. Broil 20–30 seconds to melt butter and serve.

Steak Lyonnaise: Panbroil steak, transfer to hot platter, and smother with sautéed yellow onions (about 1/2 cup is right for a 2-serving steak). To skillet add 1 tablespoon red wine vinegar, 2 tablespoons dry white wine, and 1/2 cup Rich Brown Sauce or canned beef gravy. Heat 2–3 minutes, stir in 1 tablespoon minced parsley, pour over steak, and serve.

PLANKED STEAK WITH VEGETABLES

6 servings

Unlike small or quick-cooking cuts that can be broiled altogether on a plank, sirloin steaks should be half to three-quarters done before being set on plank because plank chars easily.

1 (3–4-pound) sirloin steak, cut 1 1/2″ thick
Salt
Pepper
1 recipe Duchess Potatoes (hot)
1 egg beaten with 1 tablespoon cold water (glaze)
2 tablespoons Maître d'Hôtel, Anchovy, Bercy, Garlic, Mustard, or Tarragon Butter

G A R N I S H E S (choose 1 or 2)
1 pound mushroom caps, sautéed
3 tomatoes, halved and broiled
1 recipe French-Fried Onion Rings or 1 (8-ounce) package frozen French-fried onion rings, cooked by package directions
2 cups boiled, buttered green peas
12 boiled, buttered whole baby carrots or 12 boiled, buttered broccoli flowerets

Trim all but 1/4″ fat from steak and slash at 1″ intervals. Let steak stand at room temperature 1 1/2–2 hours if convenient. Preheat broiler. Broil steak on lightly greased rack on one side following times in Steak Broiling Chart. Meanwhile, lightly oil plank and place on rack below steak to heat. Turn steak, season lightly with salt and pepper, and broil exactly half remaining recommended time. Transfer to plank, pipe a border of potatoes around plank, and brush potatoes lightly with egg glaze. Return steak to broiler and broil to desired doneness. If potatoes brown too fast, cover loosely with foil. (*Note:* Placing foil underneath plank helps keep it clean.) Season steak with remaining salt and pepper and top with dabs of flavored butter. Arrange garnish between steak and potatoes, set plank in its holder or on a tray, and serve.

NPS: 910 C, 360 mg CH, 670 mg S*

To Plank Small Steaks (*2 servings*): Substitute 2 (1″–1½″) rib, Delmonico, club, or T-bone steaks for sirloin. Broil on one side, transfer to plank, pipe with potatoes, and broil to desired doneness. Garnish and serve.

SIRLOIN STEAK STUFFED WITH MUSHROOMS

8–10 servings

1 flat bone sirloin steak, cut 2½″–3″ thick
  (about 7 pounds)
1½ teaspoons salt
¼ teaspoon pepper
¼ cup dry port or red wine, warmed

S T U F F I N G
1 medium-size yellow onion, peeled and minced
⅓ cup butter or margarine
1 pound mushrooms, wiped clean and chopped
  fine
2 cups soft white bread crumbs
½ clove garlic, peeled and crushed
¼ teaspoon pepper
1½ teaspoons oregano
2 teaspoons minced parsley

G A R N I S H
2 recipes French-Fried Onion Rings

With a sharp knife, make a deep horizontal pocket in steak; slash fat edge at 1″ intervals and set steak aside while you prepare stuffing. Stir-fry onion in butter over moderate heat 5–8 minutes until pale golden; add mushrooms and brown over high heat 3–4 minutes. Off heat mix in remaining ingredients. Preheat broiler. Place stuffing in steak pocket and sew or skewer edges shut (to make more secure, tie steak with string, just as if wrapping a package). Broil on a lightly greased rack 5″ from heat about 20 minutes per side for rare, 22 for medium, and 24 for well done (before turning, sprinkle with half the salt and pepper). Transfer steak to steak board or heated platter, remove string and skewers, sprinkle with remaining salt and

pepper, and, to show that steak is stuffed, cut off 2–3 slices, making them ⅓″–½″ thick. Drizzle wine over steak, tipping board so it mingles with steak juices. Arrange some onion rings on top of steak and pass the rest. Top each serving with a ladling of steak juices.

NPS (8–10): 1035–830 C, 245–195 mg CH, 680–545 mg S*

To Charcoal Broil: Prepare a moderately hot charcoal fire; stuff steak as directed, and broil on lightly greased grill 5″ from coals 15 minutes per side for rare, 18 for medium rare, 20 for medium, and 25 for well done.

How to Carve Porterhouse and Sirloin Steaks:

Steady steak with carving fork, cut around bone with a small carving knife and lift out. Cut straight across steak in ¾″–1″ slices. If steak is very thick, slant knife slightly (so less juice is lost). See that each person is served some of the tenderloin.

STEAK AU POIVRE

4 servings

The quantity of pepper here is minimal for this classic steak. The best way to crush peppercorns is in a mortar and pestle or to place in a small plastic bag and roll with a rolling pin or pound with a soft drink bottle.

4 (1″-thick) club or Delmonico steaks
4 teaspoons peppercorns, crushed

Cooking oil
1 teaspoon salt
4 small pats Maître d'Hôtel Butter
2–3 tablespoons brandy

Trim fat on steaks to 1/4" and slash at 1" intervals. Sprinkle 1/2 teaspoon pepper on each side of each steak and press in well with the heel of your hand; let stand at room temperature 1/2 hour. Brush a large, heavy skillet with oil and heat over high heat 1 minute. Reduce heat to moderately high, add steaks, and panbroil, turning often, a total of 6 minutes for very rare, 8–10 for rare, 11–12 for medium rare, 13–14 for medium, and 15–16 for well done. Transfer to a hot platter, sprinkle with salt and top with butter pats. Pour brandy into skillet, stirring to scrape up brown bits, and heat 1 minute. Pour over steaks and serve.

NPS: 705 C, 150 mg CH, 745 mg S*

To Broil: Preheat broiler. Prepare steaks as directed and broil 2" from heat on lightly greased rack to desired doneness (use times in Steak Broiling Chart). Omit brandy; sprinkle with salt, top with butter, and serve.

To Charcoal Broil: Prepare a hot charcoal fire; prepare steaks as directed and broil on lightly greased grill 4" from heat to desired doneness (see Steak Broiling Chart). Omit brandy; sprinkle with salt, top with butter, and serve.

VARIATION

Steak au Poivre Flambé: Panbroil steaks as above, transfer to chafing dish, and sprinkle with salt; omit butter. Pour 1/2 cup brandy into skillet, scrape up brown bits, and pour over steaks. Heat until mixture bubbles, blaze with a match, and spoon flames over steak. Serve when flames subside.

NPS: 760 C, 130 mg CH, 655 mg S*

STEAK DIANE

2 servings   ⊠

2 (1/2-pound) Delmonico steaks, cut 1/2" thick
2 tablespoons unsalted butter
2 tablespoons minced shallots
2 tablespoons warmed cognac (optional)
1/2 teaspoon salt
1/8 teaspoon pepper
1 tablespoon minced parsley
1 tablespoon minced chives
2 teaspoons Worcestershire sauce
2 teaspoons steak sauce

Trim outer layer of fat on steaks to 1/4" and slash at 1" intervals; pound steaks between wax paper with a meat mallet until 1/4"–1/3" thick. Melt butter in a large, heavy skillet over moderate heat and sauté shallots 3–4 minutes until pale golden; push to side of skillet. Raise burner heat to moderately high, add steaks, and brown 2–3 minutes on a side. If you like, turn heat to low, pour cognac over steaks, and flame. Transfer steaks to a heated platter and sprinkle with salt and pepper. Stir remaining ingredients into skillet drippings and heat, scraping up brown bits, about 1 minute. Pour over steaks and serve.

NPS: 845 C, 160 mg CH, 800 mg S*

PANNED CHUCK STEAKS ROSEMARY

4 servings   ⊠

These steaks should only be served rare or medium rare—longer cooking makes them tough.

4 (1 1/4"–1 1/2"-thick) small boneless blade chuck steaks
3/4 teaspoon unseasoned meat tenderizer
1/2 cup butter or margarine
1/4 teaspoon powdered rosemary
1 teaspoon salt
1/4 teaspoon pepper
1 tablespoon Worcestershire sauce
1 teaspoon prepared mild yellow mustard
1 tablespoon hot water

Sprinkle both sides of each steak with tenderizer and pierce deeply with a sharp fork at 1/2" intervals. Lightly brown 1/4 cup butter in a large, heavy skillet over moderate heat and stir in rosemary. Add steaks and brown about 2 minutes on a side for very rare, 3 for rare, and 4 for medium rare. Season with salt and pepper, transfer to heated platter, and keep warm. Melt remaining butter in the skillet, add remaining ingredients, and cook and stir 1 minute; pour sauce over steaks and serve.

NPS: 1005 C, 215 mg CH, 1315 mg S*

BALINESE BEEF ON SKEWERS (SATE)

4 entree servings, enough hors d'oeuvre for 6–8

One part of the 20- or 30-dish Indonesian *rijsttafel* (rice table) is *sate*—salty-spicy beef cubes grilled over charcoal. By themselves, with their sauce or soy sauce as a dip, these make exotic cocktail fare; with rice, an original main dish.

1½ pounds boneless sirloin steak, cut in ¾″ cubes

MARINADE
1 teaspoon coriander seeds, crushed
1 teaspoon curry powder
⅛ teaspoon ginger
1 medium-size yellow onion, peeled and minced
1 clove garlic, peeled and crushed
1 tablespoon lime or lemon juice
3 tablespoons soy sauce
⅛ teaspoon pepper

SAUCE
3 tablespoons minced yellow onion
2 tablespoons cooking oil
1 teaspoon lemon juice
¼ cup peanut butter (creamy or crunchy)
1 cup hot water
Pinch hot red chili peppers (optional)

Place beef in a bowl. Mash coriander in a mortar and pestle with curry, ginger, onion, garlic, and lime juice, add to beef with soy sauce and pepper and knead well. Cover and chill 6–8 hours, turning meat one or two times in marinade. Meanwhile, prepare sauce: sauté onion in oil 5–8 minutes over moderate heat until pale golden, add remaining ingredients, and simmer, uncovered, 10 minutes; cool and reserve. For cooking sate, prepare a hot charcoal fire or preheat broiler. Skewer beef cubes on bamboo or metal skewers, not too close together, and broil 3″–4″ from heat, turning often and basting with marinade about 7 minutes for rare, 10–12 for medium, and 15 for well done. Warm sauce, uncovered, over low heat. Serve with rice, topped with some of the sauce; or as a cocktail snack.

NPS (4–6–8): 660–440–330 C, 115–75–60 mg CH, 1165–775–585 mg S*

VARIATIONS

Chicken or Pork Sate *(4 servings):* Substitute ¾″ cubes of white chicken meat or lean pork for beef and prepare as directed, broiling at least 15 minutes until well done (this is particularly important for pork; if necessary, place skewers 5″ from heat so pork cooks through without drying out).

NPS (chicken): 370 C, 100 mg CH, 1215 mg S*
NPS (pork): 450 C, 105 mg CH, 1210 mg S*

Beef Sate Padang Style *(4 servings):* Instead of using marinade above, grind 1 teaspoon caraway seeds in a mortar and pestle with ½ teaspoon each turmeric and curry powder, 1 minced yellow onion, 1 crushed clove garlic, a pinch hot red chili peppers, and 1 tablespoon lime or lemon juice; add 3 tablespoons soy sauce and ½ cup coconut liquid

or Coconut Milk. Pour marinade over beef, then marinate and broil as directed above.

NPS: 580 C, 115 mg CH, 1075 mg S*

LONDON BROIL

6 servings ⊠

The best way to make London broil tender is to serve it rare and to cut it *across the grain* in thin slices.

1 (2½–3-pound) flank steak, trimmed of excess fat
1½ teaspoons salt
¼ teaspoon pepper

Preheat broiler. Score both sides of steak in a crisscross pattern, making cuts ⅛″ deep and 1″ apart. Broil on an oiled rack 2″–3″ from heat 4 minutes, turn with tongs, and broil 4 minutes longer. Transfer to a board or platter with a well (so juices will collect) and season with salt and pepper. Carve across the grain, slanting knife slightly, into slices ⅛″–¼″ thick. Top each portion with some of the juices and, if you like, pass Madeira-Mushroom Sauce.

NPS: 245 C, 120 mg CH, 615 mg S*

To Charcoal-Broil: Prepare a hot charcoal fire; score steak as directed and broil on lightly greased grill 3″ from coals about 3–4 minutes per side. Season and serve.

VARIATION

Marinated Broiled Flank Steak: Marinate a scored flank steak in refrigerator in any meat marinade or thin barbecue sauce 4–6 hours. Remove from marinade and broil or charcoal broil, basting frequently with marinade. Slice and serve.

NPS: 280 C, 120 mg CH, 955 mg S*

BACON-WRAPPED FLANK STEAK PINWHEELS

4 servings

1 (2-pound) flank steak, trimmed of excess fat
2 tablespoons butter or margarine, softened to room temperature
1 teaspoon unseasoned meat tenderizer
¼ teaspoon salt
¼ teaspoon pepper
1 teaspoon caraway seeds
2 teaspoons oregano
6–8 slices bacon

Preheat broiler. Score one side of steak in a crisscross pattern, making cuts ⅛″ deep and 1″ apart, then spread with butter and sprinkle with tenderizer. Pierce meat deeply all over with a sharp fork, sprinkle with salt, pepper, caraway, and oregano and roll, jelly-roll style, starting from a long side: secure with skewers. Slice crosswise into rolls 1½" thick, wrap a bacon slice around each, and resecure with skewers. Broil on a lightly greased rack 3"–4" from heat 5 minutes on each side, then bake, uncovered, 5 minutes at 350° F. (no need to preheat oven). *(Note: If bacon doesn't crispen, turn pinwheels on edge and broil to brown.)* Good with broiled tomato halves topped with broiled mushroom caps.

NPS: 425 C, 165 mg CH, 805 mg S*

VARIATION

Stuffed Flank Steak Pinwheels *(6 servings):* Score steak, spread with butter, sprinkle with tenderizer, and pierce as recipe directs. Sprinkle with salt and pepper but omit caraway seeds and oregano. Spread about 2 cups any well-seasoned meat or poultry stuffing to within 1" of edges, then roll jelly-roll style, secure with skewers, slice, and wrap with bacon as directed. Broil 5 minutes on a side, 3"–4" from the heat, then bake, uncovered, 10 minutes at 350° F.

NPS: 445 C, 140 mg CH, 955 mg S*

HERB-STUFFED FLANK STEAK

6 servings

The herb-bread stuffing makes two pounds of steak do the job of three.

1 (2-pound) flank steak, trimmed of excess fat
1 medium-size yellow onion, peeled and minced
½ cup finely chopped celery
¼ cup butter or margarine
2 cups soft white bread crumbs
1½ teaspoons salt
¼ teaspoon pepper
1 tablespoon minced parsley
¼ teaspoon thyme
¼ teaspoon marjoram
¼ teaspoon sage
2 tablespoons beef drippings or cooking oil
2 cups beef broth or dry red wine
3 tablespoons flour mixed with 3 tablespoons cold water

Preheat oven to 325° F. Score one side of steak in a crisscross pattern, making cuts ⅛" deep and 1" apart. Sauté onion and celery in butter over moderately low heat 8 minutes until pale golden; off heat, mix in crumbs, 1 teaspoon salt, ⅛ teaspoon pepper, and the herbs. Sprinkle unscored side of steak with remaining salt and pepper and

spread stuffing to within 1" of edges, patting down firmly. Roll jelly-roll style, starting from a short side, and tie well with string (around the roll and end over end). Brown roll in drippings in a Dutch oven over moderate heat 7–10 minutes, add broth, cover, and bake 1½ hours until tender. Transfer meat to a platter and remove strings. Mix flour-water paste into pan liquid and heat, stirring, until thickened. Cut steak crosswise into thick slices and serve with gravy.

NPS: 390 C, 125 mg CH, 1090 mg S*

VARIATION

Argentine Stuffed Flank Steak: Score steak as directed above, then prepare the following stuffing: remove casings from ½ pound *chorizo* or other garlic-flavored sausage and sauté the meat, breaking it up, 5 minutes over moderately high heat. Add ½ cup minced celery and 4 minced scallions and sauté 5 minutes longer. Off heat mix in ½ cup soft white bread crumbs, ¼ cup minced parsley, ½ teaspoon salt, and 1 lightly beaten egg. Spread on steak as directed above, then roll, brown, and bake as directed. Serve with a peppery chili sauce.

NPS: 465 C, 175 mg CH, 905 mg S*

CHINESE BEEF AND PEPPERS

2 servings ⚔️

If you want to double this recipe, use two skillets instead of one giant one so the vegetables don't overcook and lose their crisp delicacy.

2 tablespoons peanut or other cooking oil
1 small yellow onion, peeled and minced
1 sweet green pepper, cored, seeded, and cut in 1" squares
1 teaspoon Chinese black beans, rinsed (optional)
1 clove garlic, peeled and crushed
1 thin slice gingerroot or ⅛ teaspoon ginger
1 tomato, peeled, seeded, and cut in 6 wedges
½–¾ pound flank steak, trimmed of fat and cut across the grain in slices ⅛" thick
1 teaspoon dry sherry
½ teaspoon salt
½ teaspoon sugar
1 teaspoon soy sauce

Heat oil in a large skillet or *wok* over high heat ½ minute, add onion, green pepper, black beans, garlic, and ginger, and stir-fry 2 minutes. Add tomato and stir-fry 1 minute. Reduce heat to moderately high and push vegetables to side of pan; add beef and stir-fry 1 minute, sprinkling in sherry. Mix remaining ingredients, sprinkle over beef, and stir-fry ½ minute. Serve over boiled rice or Chinese Fried Rice.

NPS: 355 C, 75 mg CH, 880 mg S*

⚖ **Chinese Beef with Snow Peas:** Substitute ¼ pound snow pea pods and, if you like, ¼ pound thinly sliced mushrooms for onion and green pepper; stir-fry as directed. Add 1 (4-ounce) can drained, thinly sliced water chestnuts in place of tomato, stir-fry 1 minute, then proceed as recipe directs.

NPS: 355 C, 75 mg CH, 880 mg S*

⚖ **Chinese Beef with Broccoli and Bean Sprouts:** Substitute ½ pound parboiled, thinly sliced broccoli for onion and green pepper and stir-fry as directed. Add ½ (1-pound) can well-drained bean sprouts along with tomato and proceed as recipe directs.

NPS: 350 C, 75 mg CH, 935 mg S*

⚖ **Chinese Beef and Cabbage:** Substitute ½ pound shredded Chinese cabbage for green pepper, proceed as recipe directs.

NPS: 330 C, 75 mg CH, 885 mg S*

BEEF BIRDS (ROULADES)

6 servings

12 (5″ × 3″ × ¼″) slices beef round pounded thin as for scaloppine
Salt
Pepper
Flour (for dredging)
¼ cup beef or bacon drippings or cooking oil
⅔ cup finely chopped celery (optional)
½ cup thinly sliced mushrooms (optional)
2 cups beef broth
3 tablespoons flour blended with 3 tablespoons cold water

STUFFING

1 large yellow onion, peeled and minced
2 tablespoons beef or bacon drippings
½ cup finely chopped mushrooms
2 cups soft white bread crumbs
½ cup water
1 egg, lightly beaten
½ teaspoon salt
⅛ teaspoon pepper
2 tablespoons minced parsley

Sprinkle beef with salt and pepper and set aside while you prepare stuffing. Sauté onion in drippings over moderate heat 5–8 minutes until pale golden, add mushrooms and stir-fry 1–2 minutes; off heat mix in remaining ingredients. Spoon about 2 tablespoons stuff-ing on each piece meat, roll, and tie well with string. Dredge rolls in flour and brown, a few at a time, in drippings in a Dutch oven 5–7 minutes over moderate heat; drain on paper toweling. If you wish, add celery and mushrooms and stir-fry 2–3 minutes. Drain all but 1 tablespoon drippings from kettle, return meat, add broth, cover, and simmer 1½ hours until tender (or bake 1½ hours at 350° F.). Transfer rolls to serving dish and remove strings. Mix flour-water paste into kettle and heat, stirring, until thickened. Serve with gravy and buttered noodles.

NPS: 464 C, 160 mg CH, 630 mg S*

⚖ **German Rouladen:** Salt and pepper beef as directed, then, instead of making stuffing, lay a thin strip dill pickle on each piece beef, also 2 teaspoons each capers and minced onion and ½ strip bacon. Roll, tie, and cook as recipe directs.

NPS: 425 C, 115 mg CH, 1180 mg S*

Italian Braciolini: Salt and pepper beef as directed, then make the following filling instead of one given above: Brown ½ cup minced onion and ½ pound ground beef chuck or sweet Italian sausage meat in 2 tablespoons olive oil 5–8 minutes over moderately high heat: drain off drippings. Off heat mix in 1 cup soft white bread crumbs, ½ teaspoon salt, ⅛ teaspoon pepper, 1 lightly beaten egg, and ½ teaspoon oregano or basil. Spoon filling onto meat, roll, tie, and proceed as recipe directs. (*Note:* If you like, cook rolls in a thin tomato sauce instead of broth, omitting chopped celery and mushrooms.) Good with Gnocchi or any buttered pasta.

NPS: 525 C, 180 mg CH, 605 mg S*

Beef Birds with Sour Cream Gravy: Prepare rolls by basic recipe above but omit flour-water paste; stir in 1 cup sour cream just before serving.

NPS: 530 C, 180 mg CH, 655 mg S*

OLD-FASHIONED SWISS STEAK

4–6 servings

¼ cup unsifted flour
1½ teaspoons salt
¼ teaspoon pepper
1 (3–4-pound) blade or arm steak, cut about 2″ thick
3 tablespoons beef or bacon drippings or cooking oil
1 large yellow onion, peeled and minced
2 stalks celery, minced

2 small carrots, peeled and minced
1 (1-pound) can tomatoes (do not drain) or 1
   (1-pound) can Spanish-style tomato sauce
1½ cups beef broth or hot water

Mix flour, salt, and pepper and sprinkle about 2 tablespoons on one side of meat; pound with a meat mallet or edge of heavy saucer. Turn meat and pound in remaining flour the same way. Melt drippings in a Dutch oven over moderately high heat 1 minute and brown meat well, about 5 minutes on each side. Remove meat and set aside. Sauté onion, celery, and carrots in remaining drippings 8 minutes until golden. Return meat to kettle, spoon vegetables on top, add tomatoes and broth. Cover and simmer 1½–2 hours until tender, basting meat once or twice. Cut into portions, top with vegetables and gravy, and serve.

NPS (4–6): 855–570 C, 215–140 mg CH, 1520–1010 mg S*

To Bake: Prepare as directed but, instead of simmering on top of stove, cover and bake 2–2½ hours in a 350° F. oven.

ESTERHAZY STEAK

2–4 servings

Steak, mushrooms, onion, celery, and carrot in a tart sour cream-caper gravy. Worth every calorie-packed forkful!

1 pound top round, cut ¼" thick and pounded
   thin as for scaloppine
⅓ cup unsifted flour
1 teaspoon salt
⅛ teaspoon pepper
3 tablespoons butter, margarine, or meat
   drippings
1 carrot, peeled and minced
2 medium-size mushrooms, wiped clean and
   minced
1 stalk celery, minced
1 small yellow onion, peeled and minced
1 tablespoon minced parsley
1 cup beef stock or broth
1 tablespoon minced capers
1 cup sour cream

Cut steak into pieces about 4" square. Mix flour, salt, and pepper and rub well into both sides of each piece of steak; reserve 1 tablespoon seasoned flour. Brown steak on both sides in butter in a large, heavy skillet over moderately high heat, push to side of skillet, add all minced vegetables and parsley, and stir-fry 5–8 minutes. Blend in reserved seasoned flour. Turn heat to low, add broth, cover, and simmer 40–45 minutes until

steak is tender. Mix in capers, then smooth in sour cream and heat (but do not boil) about 1 minute. Serve hot with boiled potatoes or buttered noodles.

NPS (2–4): 960–480 C, 250–125 mg CH, 2050–1010 mg S*

CHICKEN-FRIED STEAK

2–4 servings

Prepared much the same way as the famous Southern "batter-fried" chicken.

1 pound top or bottom round, cut ¼" thick and
   pounded thin as for scaloppine
½ cup unsifted flour
2 eggs lightly beaten with 3 tablespoons milk
1 cup fine dry bread crumbs or cracker meal
4–5 tablespoons lard, meat drippings, butter, or
   margarine
1 teaspoon salt
⅛ teaspoon pepper

Cut steak into 3" squares; dust well with flour, dip in egg, then in crumbs to coat evenly. Heat 3 tablespoons lard in a large, heavy skillet over moderately high heat and brown steak 2–3 minutes on a side, adding more lard as needed. When all pieces are browned, sprinkle with salt and pepper, turn heat to low, cover, and cook about 45 minutes until tender.

NPS (2–4): 930–465 C, 440–220 mg CH, 1660–830 mg S*

GROUND BEEF

How ground beef is to be used determines how it should be ground. For light, juicy hamburgers, it should be coarsely ground, one time only. For meat balls and meat loaves, where firmer textures are desirable, it can be finely ground two or three times. Generally speaking, the more finely—and often—meat is ground, the more compact it will be when cooked.

What kind of hamburger should you buy? Again, it depends on use. Also budget. Here are the three most popular kinds:

Regular Hamburger (ground trimmings, usually from shank, plate, and brisket): The cheapest ground beef, also the fattest (often one-quarter to one-third fat), which means it will shrink considerably during cooking as the fat melts and drippings run off.

Ground Chuck: Probably the best all-round hamburger meat. It has just enough fat (about 15 per cent) to make it juicy, an excellent flavor, and a moderate price.

Ground Round: The most expensive "hamburger," also the leanest, meaning it may dry out if cooked much beyond medium rare (when having round ground to order, make sure the butcher adds about 2 ounces suet for each pound lean). Ground round is a good choice for calorie counters—a 1/4-pound *broiled* patty averages about 220 calories.

HAMBURGERS

3–4 servings ▣

Though it's usually recommended that meat be brought to room temperature before cooking, hamburger is an exception because of its great perishability. Cooking times given here are for meat refrigerated until ready to use.

1 pound ground beef
1 teaspoon salt
1/8 teaspoon pepper

Shape beef *lightly* into 3 plump patties or 4 slim ones and cook by one of the methods below; season with salt and pepper just before serving.

To Panfry (Sauté): Especially recommended for lean meat. Brown hamburgers uncovered in 1–2 tablespoons cooking oil, butter, margarine, or drippings in a large, heavy skillet over moderately high heat; plump patties will take about 4 minutes on a side for rare, 5 for medium, and 6 for well done, thin patties about 1 minute less per side for each degree of doneness. While hamburgers cook, do not press down or "spank" with a pancake turner—you'll only force out succulent juices.

NPS (3–4): 330–250 C, 100–75 mg CH, 795–600 mg S*

▣ ⚐ **To Panbroil:** Recommended for dieters, also for meat heavily flecked with fat. Lightly brush a large, heavy skillet with oil or sprinkle with salt; heat 1 minute over moderately high heat, add hamburgers, and brown, uncovered, using the same cooking times as for panfrying. Pour off drippings as they accumulate.

NPS (3–4): 310–235 C, 100–75 mg CH, 795–600 mg S*

▣ ⚐ **To Broil:** Recommended for dieters and fatty hamburger meat. Preheat broiler; broil hamburgers 3″ from heat on a lightly greased broiler rack. Plump patties will take

5 minutes on a side for rare, 6 for medium, and 7–8 for well done, thin patties about 1 minute less per side in each instance.

NPS: 295–220 C, 100–75 mg CH, 795–600 mg S*

⚐ **To Charcoal-Broil:** Recommended for plump patties only. Prepare a moderately hot charcoal fire. Lay hamburgers on a lightly greased grill and broil 4″ from the heat about 4–5 minutes on a side for rare, 6 for medium, and 7–8 for well done.

To Braise: Brown patties quickly in a lightly greased large, heavy skillet over high heat, turn heat to low and pour in 1–1½ cups liquid (dry red wine; broth; gravy; tomato juice, soup, or sauce), cover, and simmer slowly 15–20 minutes. Recipe too flexible for meaningful nutritional count.

VARIATIONS ON HAMBURGERS

All amounts based on recipe above ▣

Cheeseburgers: Shape patties as directed, brown on one side, and season lightly; turn, season again, top with a thin slice American cheese and cook to desired doneness.

NPS (3–4): 390–310 C, 120–95 mg CH, 1000–900 mg S*

Blue Cheese Burgers: Shape meat into 6 thin patties; in the center of 3 place a scant teaspoon blue cheese spread. Top with remaining patties and pinch edges to seal. Cook as directed, season with 1/4 teaspoon salt and 1/8 teaspoon pepper and serve.

NPS: 325 C, 105 mg CH, 295 mg S*

Surprise Burgers: Shape meat into 6 thin patties; in the center of 3 place a scant teaspoon of any of the following: minced onion, dill pickle, or capers; sweet pickle relish; grated Cheddar or Swiss cheese. Top with remaining patties and pinch edges to seal. Cook and season as directed.

NPS (with onion): 310 C, 100 mg CH, 800 mg S*
NPS (with cheese): 320 C, 105 mg CH, 810 mg S*

Deviled Burgers: Mix beef with 2 tablespoons each cold water and spicy brown prepared mustard, 1 teaspoon each grated onion and Worcestershire sauce, 1/2 teaspoon salt, and 2–3 dashes liquid hot red pepper seasoning. Shape and cook as directed but do not season.

NPS (3–4): 320–240 C, 100–75 mg CH, 545–410 mg S*

Chili Burgers: Into beef mix 1 tablespoon each grated onion, chili sauce, chili powder, 1/2 crushed clove garlic, and 1/8 teaspoon cayenne pepper. Shape and cook as directed but do not season.

NPS (3–4): 325–245 C, 100–75 mg CH, 165–125 mg S*

Barbecue Burgers: Into beef mix 1 tablespoon each ketchup, Worcestershire sauce, red wine vinegar, chili powder, 1/4 teaspoon salt, and 1/8 teaspoon cayenne pepper. Shape and cook as directed but do not season.

NPS (3–4): 330–245 C, 100–75 mg CH, 385–290 mg S*

Teriyaki Burgers: Mix beef with 2 tablespoons each soy sauce, dry sherry, and minced sautéed scallions, 1/2 crushed clove garlic, 1 teaspoon grated fresh gingerroot, and 1/8 teaspoon pepper. Shape and cook as directed but do not season.

NPS (3–4): 325–245 C, 100–75 mg CH, 950–710 mg S*

Burgundy Burgers: Mix 1 minced scallion into beef, also 2 tablespoons Burgundy wine, 1/2 crushed clove garlic, 1/2 teaspoon salt, and a pinch pepper. Shape and cook as directed but do not season. About 3 minutes before serving, add 1/2 cup Burgundy to skillet and continue cooking, basting often. Serve topped with pan juices.

NPS (3–4): 415–310 C, 100–75 mg CH, 460–345 mg S*

Bacon Burgers: Mix beef with 1/4 cup each minced sautéed onion and crisp bacon bits. Shape into patties, cook and season as directed.

NPS (3–4): 350–265 C, 100–75 mg CH, 1175–880 mg S*

Burgers au Poivre: Shape into 4 patties, sprinkle each side of each with 1/4 teaspoon coarsely ground pepper and press into meat with the heel of your hand. Let stand at room temperature 20–30 minutes. Panfry hamburgers in 2 tablespoons butter 3–4 minutes on a side; remove to a hot platter, sprinkle with salt, and keep warm. To drippings add 1 tablespoon each butter, minced parsley, and cognac and heat 1–2 minutes, stirring to get up any brown bits. Spoon over burgers and serve.

NPS: 390 C, 100 mg CH, 160 mg S*

Burgers Diane: Shape into 4 patties and panfry in 2 tablespoons unsalted butter about 4 minutes on a side; remove from skillet, season with 1/2 teaspoon salt and 1/8 teaspoon pepper, and keep warm. To skillet add 3 tablespoons dry sherry, 1 tablespoon each unsalted butter, minced chives, parsley, and cognac and 1 teaspoon each Worcestershire sauce and prepared spicy brown mustard.

Heat 1–2 minutes, stirring with a wooden spoon to scrape up brown bits, pour over burgers, and serve.

NPS: 410 C, 100 mg CH, 375 mg S*

⚖ ¢ **Budget Burgers:** To extend 1 pound ground beef so it will serve 6, mix in 1 lightly beaten egg and any of the following, then shape, cook, and season as directed:
• 1 cup mashed, drained cooked beans (navy, kidney, pinto, or chick-peas).

NPS: 205 C, 95 mg CH, 410 mg S*
• 1 cup mashed potatoes, boiled rice, bulgur wheat, or pilaf and, if mixture seems a little dry, 1–2 tablespoons broth, milk, tomato juice, or water.

NPS: 205 C, 95 mg CH, 410 mg S*
• 1 cup crushed cornflakes.

NPS: 240 C, 95 mg CH, 645 mg S*
• 1 cup cracker meal or poultry stuffing mix and 1/4–1/3 cup broth, milk, or tomato juice.

NPS: 240 C, 95 mg CH, 645 mg S*
• 1 cup soft bread crumbs or crumbled corn bread and 1/4–1/3 cup broth, milk, or tomato juice.

NPS: 190 C, 95 mg CH, 480 mg S*
• 1/2 cup each minced celery and finely grated carrot and 2 tablespoons finely grated onion.

NPS: 175 C, 95 mg CH, 425 mg S*
• 1 cup finely diced boiled potatoes, 1/2 cup diced, drained cooked beets, and 2 tablespoons grated onion.

NPS: 190 C, 95 mg CH, 415 mg S*

BEEF LINDSTROM

4–6 servings ⊠ ¢

Here's a delicious way to use up leftover boiled beets and potatoes.

1 pound ground beef
2/3 cup minced boiled beets, well drained
1 cup minced boiled potatoes
1 tablespoon finely grated onion
2 teaspoons minced capers
2 egg yolks, lightly beaten
2 tablespoons light cream
1/4 teaspoon salt
Pinch pepper
2–3 tablespoons butter or margarine

Mix beef with all ingredients except butter, cover, and chill several hours until firm enough to shape. Shape into small rectangular patties about 3" long and 1" wide, then brown 5–7 minutes in butter in a large, heavy skillet over moderately high heat. To avoid crowding skillet, do about half the patties at a time, setting browned ones, uncovered, in a 250° F. oven to keep warm while you brown the rest.

NPS (4–6): 340–225 C, 225–150 mg CH, 270–180 mg S*

SALISBURY STEAK

2–4 servings

½ recipe Mushroom Gravy
1 pound ground beef
1 teaspoon salt
⅛ teaspoon pepper

Prepare gravy by recipe and keep warm. Shape beef into 2 flat oval patties and pan-broil in a large, lightly greased skillet over moderately high heat 5–6 minutes on each side for rare, 7 for medium, and 8–9 for well done. Sprinkle with salt and pepper, smother with mushroom gravy, and serve.

NPS (2–4): 825–410 C, 180–90 mg CH, 1310–655 mg S*

SLOPPY JOES

6 servings   ⊠ ¢

1 teaspoon beef drippings or cooking oil
1 pound ground beef
1 medium-size yellow onion, peeled and chopped fine
½ cup ketchup
½ cup chili sauce
1 tablespoon Worcestershire sauce
1 teaspoon salt
⅛ teaspoon pepper
⅓ cup water
6 hamburger buns, warmed

Brush a skillet with drippings and warm over moderate heat ½ minute. Add beef and onion and sauté 10 minutes, stirring frequently. Add all remaining ingredients except buns and simmer, uncovered, 10 minutes. Spoon mixture between split buns and serve.

NPS: 385 C, 55 mg CH, 1185 mg S*

VARIATIONS

⊠ ¢ **Sloppy Franks:** Add 1–2 teaspoons chili powder to meat mixture, simmer as directed, and spoon over hot dogs in hot-dog buns.

NPS: 530 C, 75 mg CH, 1670 mg S*

⊠ ¢ **Cheesy Joes:** Lightly toast bottom half of each hamburger bun, top with a slice of cheese (American, Cheddar, Swiss, etc.), and toast until cheese begins to melt. Spoon meat mixture over cheese, add bun lids, and serve.

NPS: 490 C, 80 mg CH, 1590 mg S*

ECONOMY MEAT LOAF

6 servings   ⚖ ¢

1½ pounds ground beef
1 cup rolled oats
2 teaspoons salt
¼ teaspoon pepper
1 teaspoon prepared spicy yellow mustard
1 teaspoon prepared horseradish
1 large yellow onion, peeled and chopped fine
¾ cup milk or skim milk
¼ cup cold water

Preheat oven to 350° F. Using your hands, mix all ingredients together thoroughly. Pack into an ungreased 9″ × 5″ × 3″ loaf pan. Bake, uncovered, 1 hour. Loosen loaf from pan, drain off drippings (save for gravy), invert on a heated platter, and serve.

NPS: 315 C, 80 mg CH, 810 mg S*

BEEF AND PORK LOAF

6–8 servings   ¢

¾ cup lukewarm milk
1 egg, beaten
1½ cups soft white bread crumbs
1 pound ground beef
1 pound ground lean pork
1 large yellow onion, peeled and minced
⅓ cup minced gherkins
1 tablespoon salt
¼ teaspoon pepper
1 tablespoon Worcestershire sauce

Preheat oven to 350° F. Combine milk and egg, add crumbs, and let stand 5 minutes; mix thoroughly with remaining ingredients, turn into an ungreased shallow roasting pan, and shape into a loaf. Bake, uncovered, 1½ hours, basting off excess drippings (save for gravy). Transfer loaf to a heated platter and let stand 5 minutes before cutting. Serve hot with gravy, Sweet-Sour Sauce, or Mushroom Gravy. Or chill and serve cold with Mustard Sauce.

NPS (6–8): 375–280 C, 150–115 mg CH, 1390–1045 mg S*

POT-ROASTED BEEF AND VEGETABLE ROLL

4 servings ¢

1 pound ground beef
1 teaspoon salt
1/8 teaspoon pepper
2 tablespoons bacon drippings or margarine
2 cups beef broth
2–3 tablespoons flour blended with 2 tablespoons cold water

STUFFING

1 small yellow onion, peeled and minced
1/3 cup finely chopped celery
1 small carrot, peeled and finely grated
1 tablespoon bacon drippings or margarine
3/4 cup soft white bread crumbs
1 egg, lightly beaten
2 tablespoons minced parsley
1 teaspoon salt
1/8 teaspoon pepper

Mix beef, salt, and pepper and roll with a rolling pin between 2 sheets wax paper to a rectangle about 7″ × 10″, keeping edges as straight as possible. Prepare stuffing: sauté onion, celery, carrot in drippings over moderate heat 5 minutes and mix in remaining ingredients. Spread over beef, leaving 1/2″ margins all round, then roll, jelly-roll style, pinching edges to seal. Brown roll in 2 tablespoons drippings in a heavy kettle over moderate heat 5 minutes, turning frequently and gently. Remove roll and pour off all but 1 tablespoon drippings. Place roll seam side down on a rack, return to kettle, add 1 cup broth, cover, and simmer 40 minutes. Lift roll and rack from kettle, transfer roll to a platter, and keep warm. Add remaining broth to kettle, mix in flour-water paste, and heat, stirring, until thickened. Pour a little gravy over meat roll and pass the rest.

NPS: 460 C, 155 mg CH, 1695 mg S*

VARIATION

About 1/2 hour before serving, add any of the following to kettle: peeled, halved new potatoes or turnips, carrots cut in 2″ chunks, peeled small white onions. Arrange vegetables on platter with meat and keep warm while making gravy. Recipe too flexible for meaningful nutritional count.

STUFFED GREEN PEPPERS

6–8 servings ⧖ ¢

8 medium-size sweet green peppers
1 pound ground beef
1 medium-size yellow onion, peeled and chopped fine
1 teaspoon garlic salt
1/2 teaspoon salt
1/4 teaspoon pepper
11/2 cups cooked rice (hot or cold)
21/2–3 cups canned marinara or Spanish-style tomato sauce

Prepare peppers for stuffing.* Sauté beef in a lightly greased heavy skillet over moderate heat 10 minutes until no longer pink, stirring to break up chunks; transfer to a bowl with slotted spoon. Drain all but 2 tablespoons drippings from skillet, add onion and sauté 8–10 minutes, stirring occasionally, until golden. Mix onion and all remaining ingredients except sauce into meat; stuff each pepper loosely, filling to within 1/4″ of the top. Stand peppers in a deep saucepan so they touch and support each other. Pour in sauce so it surrounds peppers but does not touch the filling. Cover and simmer slowly 1 hour until peppers are tender. Lift peppers to a heated platter, top with some of the sauce, and pass the rest.

NPS (6–8): 355–265 C, 55–40 mg CH, 970–430 mg S*

PICADILLO

4–6 servings ¢

Spicy, a little bit sweet, a little bit salty, *picadillo* is Mexican minced meat. Serve as is, use as a filling for meat pies, or for making Chiles Rellenos.

1 large yellow onion, peeled and minced
1 clove garlic, peeled and crushed
1 tablespoon olive oil
1 pound ground beef
1/2 (6-ounce) can tomato paste
1 canned jalapeño chili, seeded and minced, or
  1/4 teaspoon crushed hot red chili peppers
1/3 cup minced raisins
1/4 teaspoon oregano
1/8 teaspoon cinnamon
Pinch cloves
3/4 teaspoon salt
Pinch black pepper
1/4 cup minced blanched almonds

Sauté onion and garlic in oil in a large, heavy skillet over moderate heat 8–10 minutes until golden. Add meat and sauté 3–5 minutes, breaking up any clumps. Blend in tomato paste, add remaining ingredients, and heat, stirring, 5 minutes to blend flavors.

NPS (4–6): 455–305 C, 75–50 mg CH, 660–440 mg S*

CHILES RELLENOS (MEXICAN STUFFED PEPPERS)

6 servings

For real *chiles rellenos,* you need dark green *poblano* chilies. These aren't available fresh everywhere in this country, and even if they were, many of us would find them too hot. Sweet green peppers may be substituted and so may the canned mild green chilies (better get two cans because the chilies are very fragile and difficult to stuff).

6 *poblano* chilies, or 6 small sweet green
   peppers, roasted and peeled,* or 12 Italian
   elle peppers, or 2 (1-pound 10-ounce) cans
   peeled, roasted mild green chilies, drained
1 recipe Picadillo (recipe above)
Shortening or cooking oil for deep fat frying

COATING
4 eggs, separated
1/2 cup unsifted flour

SAUCE
1 small yellow onion, peeled and minced
1 clove garlic, peeled and crushed
2 tablespoons olive oil
1/2 (6-ounce) can tomato paste
1 (8-ounce) can tomato sauce
1 3/4 cups chicken broth
1 teaspoon sugar
1/2 teaspoon salt
Pinch pepper

If using canned chilies, rinse gently in cold water and remove seeds. Drain peppers on paper toweling. Prepare picadillo and cool to room temperature. Sauté onion and garlic for sauce in oil in a large skillet over moderate heat 8–10 minutes until golden; mix in remaining ingredients, turn heat to low, and let sauce simmer, uncovered, until you're ready for it. Begin heating shortening or oil in a deep fat fryer over moderately high heat (use a deep fat thermometer). Stuff chilies with picadillo and set aside while you prepare coating. Beat yolks and whites, separately, until thick, then fold yolks into whites. Roll stuffed chilies in flour, then dip in egg. When fat reaches 375° F., fry chilies, a few at a time, 2–3 minutes until golden. Drain on paper toweling, add to tomato sauce, and warm, uncovered, about 5 minutes. Serve chilies topped with the sauce.

NPS: 530 C, 235 mg CH, 1215 mg S*

VARIATION

Chiles Rellenos con Queso: These chilies are made just like traditional *rellenos* except that they're stuffed with cheese instead of picadillo. Use small peppers—either Italian *elle* or canned chilies—and prepare for stuffing as above. Fill with softened cream cheese, coarsely grated sharp Cheddar, or Monterey Jack (you'll need about 1/2 pound). Then proceed as recipe directs, dipping chilies in flour and beaten egg, deep frying until golden, and warming in tomato sauce.

NPS (with Monterey Jack): 360 C, 225 mg CH, 890 mg S*
NPS (with Cheddar): 380 C, 220 mg CH, 1010 mg S*

POLISH STUFFED CABBAGE ROLLS WITH LEMON SAUCE

4 servings

A friend gave us this old family recipe.

1 medium-size cabbage, trimmed of coarse outer
   leaves
1 1/2 quarts boiling water
3 1/2 teaspoons salt
1 large yellow onion, peeled and minced
1/4 cup butter or margarine
1 pound ground beef
1/2 cup uncooked rice
1/4 teaspoon black pepper
2 tablespoons lemon juice
2 tablespoons flour blended with 2 tablespoons
   cold water
1/8 teaspoon white pepper

Place cabbage, water, and 1 teaspoon salt in a large kettle and boil, uncovered, 3–4 minutes until leaves are pliable. Drain, reserving 2 1/2 cups cooking water. Cool cabbage in a colander under cold running water until easy to handle, drain well, core, and remove 12 whole outer leaves (discard any with holes). Cut base of large white vein from each leaf and discard; spread each leaf flat. (*Note:* Save rest of cabbage to use later.) Stir-fry onion in 2 tablespoons butter over moderate heat 5–8 minutes until transparent and mix with beef, rice, 2 teaspoons salt, and the black pepper. Put a spoonful of the mixture on the center of each leaf, fold sides in over filling, and roll up loosely. Secure with toothpicks. Arrange rolls 1 layer deep in a large kettle, add reserved cabbage water, lemon juice, and remaining butter. Cover and simmer 1 hour. Lift rolls to a serving dish and keep warm. Mix flour paste into kettle and cook and stir over moderate heat 3–4 minutes until liquid thickens slightly; add remaining salt and the white pepper. Pour some of the sauce over rolls and pass the rest.

NPS: 565 C, 110 mg CH, 2150 mg S*

MEAT

SWEDISH MEAT BALLS

4–6 servings

Swedish meat balls are sometimes made of one meat only, but more often with a combination of beef, pork, and/or veal. For smorgasbord, the balls are tiny (about 1/2") and served *without* sauce; for entrees they're larger and awash in pale cream gravy.

MEAT BALLS
1 medium-size yellow onion, peeled and minced
1 tablespoon butter or margarine
1 pound boned beef chuck, ground twice
1/4 pound boned lean pork shoulder, ground twice
1 1/2 teaspoons salt
1/4 teaspoon pepper
Pinch nutmeg (optional)
3/4 cup fine dry bread crumbs
1/4 cup milk
1/4 cup water
1 egg, lightly beaten
2 tablespoons butter or margarine (for browning meat balls)

GRAVY
2 tablespoons butter or margarine
2 tablespoons flour
1 1/4 cups light cream
1/2 teaspoon salt
Pinch white pepper

Sauté onion in butter 3–5 minutes over moderate heat until limp; mix well with remaining meat ball ingredients and shape into 3/4"–1" balls. Brown, 1/3 of balls at a time, in butter in a large, heavy skillet 8–10 minutes over moderate heat until well done; drain on paper toweling. *(Note:* The 1/2" smorgasbord balls will cook in 5–8 minutes.) Drain drippings from skillet and add butter for gravy. When melted, blend in flour, add cream, and heat, stirring, until thickened. Season, add meat balls, simmer uncovered 5 minutes, shaking pan occasionally, and serve.

NPS (4–6): 755–500 C, 245–165 mg CH, 1475–985 mg S*

KÖNIGSBERGER KLOPS (GERMAN MEAT BALLS IN LEMON-CAPER SAUCE)

4 servings

MEAT BALLS
1 medium-size yellow onion, peeled and chopped fine
1 tablespoon butter or margarine
2 slices white bread soaked in 1/2 cup cold water and squeezed almost dry
1/2 pound ground beef

1/2 pound ground lean pork
2 medium-size potatoes, boiled and riced
6 anchovies, chopped fine
1 egg, lightly beaten
1 teaspoon salt
1/8 teaspoon pepper
1/4 cup unsifted flour

SAUCE
1/4 cup butter or margarine
1/4 cup unsifted flour
2 cups beef broth
2 tablespoons capers
2–3 tablespoons lemon juice

Sauté onion in butter over moderate heat 8–10 minutes until golden, then mix with remaining meat ball ingredients except flour. Shape into 1" balls and roll lightly in flour. Simmer meat balls, half at a time, 5–7 minutes in salted water (about 2 teaspoons salt to 2 quarts water). Meanwhile, make the sauce: melt butter in a large saucepan over moderate heat, blend in flour, slowly add broth, and cook, stirring, until thickened. Add capers, lemon juice to taste, and meat balls, cover, and simmer 5–10 minutes. Serve with boiled potatoes.

NPS: 550 C, 190 mg CH, 1380 mg S*

SHEPHERD'S PIE

4 servings

1 large yellow onion, peeled and chopped fine
1 sweet green pepper, cored, seeded, and coarsely chopped (optional)
2 tablespoons beef or bacon drippings or cooking oil
1 1/4 pounds ground chuck
1 beef bouillon cube
1/2 cup boiling water
1 tablespoon cornstarch mixed with 2 tablespoons cold water
1 1/4 teaspoons salt
1/4 teaspoon pepper
1 tablespoon steak sauce
3 cups hot seasoned mashed potatoes

Preheat oven to 400° F. Sauté onion and green pepper in drippings in a large skillet over moderate heat 10 minutes until onion is golden. Add beef and sauté, breaking meat up with a spoon, about 10 minutes, until lightly browned; drain off fat as it accumulates. Dissolve bouillon cube in water, add to cornstarch mixture, then stir into skillet along with salt, pepper, and steak sauce. Heat, stirring, 1–2 minutes. Spoon into an ungreased 1 1/2-quart casserole, spread potatoes over surface and roughen with a fork.

(Note: Recipe may be prepared to this point ahead of time; cool, cover, and chill. Bring to room temperature before proceeding.) Bake, uncovered, 25–30 minutes, then broil 4″ from heat 2–3 minutes to brown.

NPS: 615 C, 90 mg CH, 1515 mg S*

VARIATION

Substitute 3 cups finely ground leftover cooked beef or lamb for the ground chuck; stir-fry 2–3 minutes with sautéed onion and green pepper, then proceed as recipe directs.

NPS: 685 C, 105 mg CH, 1520 mg S*

TAMALE PIE

6 servings ⊲⊳ ¢

CRUST
1 quart water
2 teaspoons salt
1 cup yellow corn meal

FILLING
1 medium-size yellow onion, peeled and coarsely chopped
1/2 sweet green pepper, cored, seeded, and coarsely chopped
1 tablespoon cooking oil or bacon drippings
1 pound lean ground beef
1 clove garlic, peeled and crushed
1 tablespoon chili powder
3/4 teaspoon salt
1/4 teaspoon oregano
Pinch pepper
1 (8-ounce) can tomato sauce

TOPPING
2 tablespoons finely grated Parmesan cheese

Preheat oven to 350° F. Bring water and salt to a boil in a large saucepan, very gradually add corn meal, beating constantly so it doesn't lump. Turn heat to low and continue cooking and stirring about 5 minutes until quite thick. Spread 2/3 of mush in the bottom of a buttered 9″ × 9″ × 2″ pan and set aside; keep rest warm. For the filling, stir-fry onion and green pepper in oil in a large skillet over moderate heat 8–10 minutes until onion is golden; mix in meat, garlic, chili powder, salt, oregano, and pepper and stir-fry 5 minutes longer, breaking up clumps of meat. Mix in tomato sauce and simmer, uncovered, about 5 minutes; spoon over mush in pan, top with remaining mush, spreading as evenly over all as possible. Sprinkle with Parmesan and bake, uncovered, 30 minutes. Let stand at room temperature 10 minutes, then cut into large squares and serve.

NPS: 340 C, 50 mg CH, 1300 mg S*

CHILI

10–12 servings ¢

4 medium-size yellow onions, peeled and coarsely chopped
3 cloves garlic, peeled and crushed
1/4 cup olive or other cooking oil
1 teaspoon oregano
2 bay leaves, crumbled
2 pounds ground beef
1/4 cup chili powder
1 (1-pound 12-ounce) can tomatoes (do not drain)
3 (1-pound 4-ounce) cans red kidney beans (do not drain)
2 teaspoons salt
3 tablespoons cider vinegar
1/8–1/4 teaspoon crushed hot red chili peppers

Sauté onions and garlic in the oil in a large, heavy kettle over moderate heat, stirring occasionally, 10 minutes until golden. Add oregano, bay leaves, and beef and sauté, breaking up meat, 10 minutes until beef is no longer pink. Add 2 tablespoons chili powder, tomatoes, 2 cans kidney beans and simmer, uncovered, over low heat, stirring occasionally, 1 1/2 hours. Add remaining chili powder and kidney beans along with salt, vinegar, and red peppers. Simmer, stirring now and then, 15 minutes longer. Serve hot, or cool and freeze for future use.

NPS (10–12): 485–405 C, 60–50 mg CH, 1195– 1000 mg S*

TEXAS RED (CHILI)

6 servings

The "bowl of red" Texans adore isn't what most of us think of as chili; it has no beans, tomatoes, or onions and is simply a torrid blend of beef, chili peppers, and herbs.

3 pounds boned beef chuck, cut in 1 1/2″ cubes and trimmed of all fat
1 tablespoon rendered suet or bacon drippings
6 dried ancho chili peppers or 6 tablespoons chili powder (anchos are the large red chilies, full-flavored but not fiery)
5 cups cold water
1 tablespoon oregano
1 tablespoon crushed cumin seeds
2 teaspoons salt
1–2 teaspoons cayenne pepper (depending on how hot you can take chili)
2 cloves garlic, peeled and crushed
2 tablespoons *masa harina* (available in Latin groceries) or 2 tablespoons corn meal

Put meat through coarse blade of meat grinder, then brown, a little at a time, in suet in a heavy skillet over moderately high heat; lift to a large, heavy kettle with a slotted spoon and set aside. Wash peppers in cold water, discard stems and seeds. Tear peppers into 2″ pieces, place in a small saucepan with 2 cups water, cover, and simmer 20 minutes; drain, reserving cooking water. Peel skin from peppers and purée with pepper water by buzzing 10–15 seconds in an electric blender at high speed or 5–10 seconds in a food processor fitted with the metal chopping blade. (Wash hands well after handling peppers and avoid touching face while working with them.) Mix pepper purée into beef, also remaining water, and bring to a boil over high heat. *(Note:* If using chili powder instead of peppers, simply place in kettle with beef and full amount of water.) Adjust heat so mixture stays at a slow simmer, cover, and cook 30 minutes. Stir in all remaining ingredients except *masa harina,* cover, and simmer 45 minutes. Mix in *masa harina,* cover, and warm over lowest heat 30 minutes longer, stirring occasionally so mixture doesn't stick. If chili seems thick, thin with 1/3–1/2 cup boiling water.

NPS: 410 C, 150 mg CH, 980 mg S*

CORNISH PASTIES

1 dozen   ¢

Cornish children take pasties to school for lunch (with their initials pricked out in the crust), and farmers munch them at apple-picking time. Although seasonings vary from town to town, the basic ingredients remain the same—beef, potatoes, and onions wrapped up in flaky pastry.

PASTRY
4 cups sifted flour
2 teaspoons salt
1 1/2 cups chilled shortening or 1 cup shortening and 1/2 cup lard
1/2 cup ice water (about)
1 egg lightly beaten with 1 tablespoon cold water (glaze)

FILLING
1 pound ground beef round
3 cups (1/4″) raw potato cubes
1/2 cup minced yellow onion
2 teaspoons salt
1/4 teaspoon pepper

Mix flour and salt in a large bowl and cut in shortening with a pastry blender until the texture of coarse meal. Sprinkle water over surface, a tablespoon at a time, mixing briskly with a fork after each addition. Pastry should *just* hold together; wrap in foil

and chill while you prepare and mix filling ingredients together. Preheat oven to 450° F. Shape pastry into 3 balls and roll, one at a time, on a lightly floured pastry cloth into a 13″ square; using a 5″–6″ saucer as a guide, cut 4 rounds from each square. Brush edges of rounds with glaze, spoon a little filling onto lower half of each round, then fold upper half over. Press edges together and crimp with a fork. Cut 2–3 small slits in top of each pastie and brush with glaze, being careful not to seal slits. Bake, uncovered, 15 minutes, reduce heat to 350° F., and bake 30 minutes longer until lightly browned. Serve warm or cold. *(Note:* To reheat pasties, set uncovered, in a 350° F. oven 10–15 minutes.)

NP Pasty: 480 C, 50 mg CH, 770 mg S*

VARIATION

¢ **Party Pasties:** Prepare as recipe directs, then cut circles with a biscuit cutter. Fill and seal as above. Bake, uncovered, 10 minutes at 450° F., then 15–20 minutes at 350° F. Makes about 2 dozen.

NP Pasty: 240 C, 25 mg CH, 385 mg S*

BEEF AND MUSHROOM PIROG (RUSSIAN MEAT PIE)

4 servings

1 recipe Sour Cream Pastry
2 teaspoons milk (glaze)

FILLING
1 medium-size yellow onion, peeled and minced
2 tablespoons butter or margarine
1/2 pound mushrooms, wiped clean and coarsely chopped
3/4 pound ground beef
1 teaspoon salt
1/8 teaspoon pepper
1/2 cup sour cream

Prepare pastry by recipe, wrap loosely in wax paper, and chill while you make the filling. Sauté onion in butter over moderate heat 5–8 minutes until pale golden. Add mushrooms and stir-fry 2 minutes, add beef, breaking up with a fork, and brown 5–7 minutes. Off heat, stir in salt, pepper, and sour cream and cool to room temperature. Preheat oven to 400° F. Divide pastry in half, shape into 2 balls, and roll, one at a time, on a lightly floured board into 9″ × 14″ rectangles. Lop 1 pastry over rolling pin and transfer to an ungreased baking sheet; brush edges with cold water. Spread filling over pastry, leaving 1/2″ margins all round. Cut 3 V-slits near center of second pastry, place on

MEAT

top of filling, press edges to seal, and crimp. Brush pastry with milk to glaze and bake, uncovered, 50–60 minutes until golden. Cut into large squares and serve.

NPS: 850 C, 160 mg CH, 1035 mg S*

POT ROASTS

In addition to the marginally tender roasts discussed earlier, these are the favorite cuts for pot roasting (see Beef Chart). Cooked slowly, with some liquid, they can be surprisingly tender.

Inside Chuck Roll
Blade Pot Roast
Arm Pot Roast
English (Boston) Cut
Rolled Shoulder Roast
Fresh Brisket
Rolled Plate
Rolled Neck
Bottom Round
Heel of Round

How to Pot-Roast Beef

Pot roast isn't one recipe but dozens. Any sizable cut that is browned, then cooked slowly in a tightly covered pot with a small amount of liquid is pot roasted. Here are some favorites.

POT ROAST

6–8 servings

Mashed potatoes are particularly good with this pot roast because of its rich brown gravy.

1 (4-pound) boned and rolled beef roast (rump, chuck, sirloin tip, bottom or eye round)
2 tablespoons beef drippings or cooking oil
1 small yellow onion, peeled and minced
2 1/2–3 teaspoons salt
1/2 teaspoon pepper (about)
1/4 cup cold water
3 cups beef stock, water, or a 1/2 and 1/2 mixture of condensed beef broth and water
6 tablespoons flour

Brown beef well on all sides in drippings in a heavy kettle over moderately high heat; remove to a bowl. Stir-fry onion in drippings 8–10 minutes until golden; return beef to kettle and sprinkle with 1 teaspoon salt and 1/4 teaspoon pepper. Add water, reduce heat to low, cover, and simmer 2–2 1/2 hours until

tender, turning meat occasionally (check pot frequently and add 1–2 tablespoons cold water if needed, but no more). When beef is tender, transfer to a heated platter, cover loosely, and keep warm. Skim all but 1–2 tablespoons fat from drippings, add 2 cups stock to kettle, and stir to scrape up browned bits. Blend remaining stock with flour and stir slowly into kettle; heat, stirring, until thickened. Reduce heat, cover, and simmer 2–3 minutes; add remaining salt and pepper to taste. Slice pot roast (not too thin) and serve with gravy.

NPS (6–8): 865–650 C, 215–160 mg CH, 1435–1075 mg S*

VARIATIONS

First 3 variations: nutritional count same as basic recipe.

Oven Pot Roast: Preheat oven to 350° F. In a large, flameproof casserole, brown beef and onion as directed; add seasonings and 1/2 cup water. Cover tight (if lid does not fit snugly, cover with foil) and bake 2–2 1/2 hours until meat is tender. Prepare gravy as directed and serve.

Electric Skillet Pot Roast: Make sure roast will fit in covered skillet before starting. Set control at 350° F., brown meat and onion as directed, add salt, pepper, and water, cover, and simmer at 200°–212° F. 2–2 1/2 hours until meat is tender. Prepare gravy as directed and serve.

Pressure Cooker Pot Roast: Brown beef and onion in open pressure cooker; add seasonings, 1/2 cup water (or amount of liquid manufacturer recommends). Seal cooker, bring to 10 pounds pressure and cook 15 minutes per pound (meat cooked at 10 pounds pressure will be more tender than that cooked at 15). Reduce pressure, open cooker, remove meat, and keep warm. Prepare gravy in open cooker, using method above.

Burgundy Pot Roast: Rub beef with 1 peeled and cut clove garlic; brown it and onion as directed. Substitute 1/2 cup Burgundy for the water, add 1 crumbled bay leaf, cover, and simmer. When making gravy, use 1/2 cup Burgundy and 2 1/2 cups stock.

NPS (6–8): 885–665 C, 215–160 mg CH, 1370–1030 mg S*

German-Style Pot Roast: Cook pot roast as directed. When making gravy, reduce flour to 3 tablespoons, add 6–8 crushed gingersnaps and 2 tablespoons dark brown sugar.

For the liquid, use 1/4 cup red wine vinegar and 2 3/4 cups stock.

NPS (6–8): 895–675 C, 215–160 mg CH, 1445–1084 mg S*

Yankee Pot Roast: About 50 minutes before roast is done, add 6 medium-size, peeled, halved potatoes, 8 peeled small carrots, 1 pound peeled small white onions, 1 small rutabaga, peeled and cut in 1" cubes, and 1/2 cup beef broth. Sprinkle vegetables with 1 teaspoon salt, cover, and simmer until meat and vegetables are both tender. Arrange vegetables around meat on platter and keep warm; make gravy as directed and serve.

NPS: 1050–785 C, 215–160 mg CH, 1905–1430 mg S*

Barbecued Pot Roast: Rub raw beef roast with a mixture of 1 teaspoon paprika and 1 teaspoon chili powder, then proceed as recipe directs. Use drippings to make Barbecue Gravy for Beef instead of basic pot roast gravy above.

NPS (6–8): 895–670 C, 215–160 mg CH, 1295–970 mg S*

Pot Roast with Sour Cream-Horseradish Gravy: Prepare beef and gravy according to recipe; just before serving, stir 1/2 pound lightly sautéed, sliced mushrooms into gravy; remove from heat, blend in 1 cup sour cream and 2 tablespoons prepared horseradish, and serve.

NPS (6–8): 960–720 C, 230–170 mg CH, 1460–1095 mg S*

BEEF À LA MODE (FRENCH POT ROAST)

8–10 servings

When preparing beef à la mode, the French lard the meat to make it more tender and flavorful. American beef, however, is so well marbled with fat it doesn't need larding. The outer covering of fat should be no more than 1/4" thick.

M A R I N A D E
2 cups dry red wine
1 medium-size yellow onion, peeled and sliced thin
1 large carrot, peeled and sliced thin
2 stalks celery, coarsely chopped (include tops)
1 clove garlic, peeled and minced
2 bay leaves, crumbled
1/2 teaspoon thyme
1/4 teaspoon pepper

1/4 teaspoon nutmeg
6 cloves
1 bay leaf and 1 sprig each parsley and thyme, tied in cheesecloth (*bouquet garni*)

P O T   R O A S T
1 (5-pound) boned and rolled beef roast (rump, chuck, sirloin tip, eye round)
1/4 cup beef or bacon drippings or lard
2 teaspoons salt
1/4 cup brandy
2 calf's feet, blanched* and split, or 1 large veal knuckle, cracked
2 cups dry red wine or a 1/2 and 1/2 mixture of wine and beef broth
2 tablespoons cornstarch or arrowroot mixed with 2 tablespoons cold water (optional)

Place marinade ingredients in a large bowl (not metal) and mix well; add beef, cover, and refrigerate 24 hours, turning beef 3–4 times. Remove beef from marinade and reserve marinade. Let meat stand on a wire rack 1/2 hour; pat dry with paper toweling. Preheat oven to 325° F. Heat drippings in a large Dutch oven over moderately high heat 1 minute, add beef and brown well on all sides, 10–15 minutes; add reserved marinade and all remaining ingredients except cornstarch mixture. Cover and bring to a boil; transfer to oven and simmer, covered, about 2 1/2–3 hours until tender, turning beef every hour. Transfer beef to a heated platter and remove strings. Strain gravy (save calf's feet if you wish—there's meat on them), skim off fat, and boil rapidly 5–10 minutes to reduce to about 3 cups. Taste for salt and pepper and adjust if needed. If you prefer a thickened gravy, stir in cornstarch paste and heat, stirring, until thickened. Pour a little gravy over beef and pass the rest. To serve, slice meat, not too thin, across the grain.

NPS (8–10): 785–630 C, 195–155 mg CH, 695–555 mg S*

V A R I A T I O N

Beef à la Mode with Vegetables: About 1 hour before beef is done, add 16 peeled whole baby carrots and 16 peeled small white onions to the pot, cover, and continue cooking until beef and vegetables are tender. Remove carrots and onions with a slotted spoon, arrange around beef on platter, and sprinkle with minced parsley. Prepare gravy as directed above and serve.

NPS (8–10): 805–645 C, 195–155 mg CH, 710–565 mg S*

SAUERBRATEN

10 servings

Begin this recipe three days before you plan to serve it.

1 (5-pound) boned and rolled beef roast (rump, chuck, bottom or eye round)
2 medium-size yellow onions, peeled and sliced thin
1 stalk celery, coarsely chopped (include top)
1 large carrot, peeled and sliced thin
3 cloves
3 peppercorns
2 bay leaves
2 cups dry red wine or red wine vinegar
3 cups cold water
1 tablespoon salt
1/2 teaspoon pepper
2 beef marrowbones (about 1 pound)
1/4 cup cooking oil
1/2 cup beef drippings, lard, or margarine
1/2 cup unsifted flour
12 gingersnaps, crumbled
1–2 tablespoons sugar

Place beef, vegetables, cloves, peppercorns, and bay leaves in a large bowl. Bring wine, water, salt, and pepper to a boil and pour over beef. Cover and refrigerate 3 days, turning beef in marinade twice a day. About 3 hours before you're ready to serve, remove beef from marinade and pat dry with paper toweling; reserve marinade. Brown beef and marrowbones well in oil in a large kettle over moderate heat, about 15 minutes. (*Note:* If bones brown before meat, remove temporarily.) Add marinade, cover, and simmer 1 1/2 hours, turn meat, re-cover, and simmer 1–1 1/2 hours longer until tender; transfer to a large platter and keep warm. Strain marinade and discard vegetables; scoop marrow from bones, sieve, and add to marinade. Heat drippings in a heavy saucepan over moderate heat, blend in flour and brown 1–2 minutes. Stir in marinade, reduce heat to low, and cook, stirring, until thickened. Mix in gingersnaps and sugar to taste. Carve meat at the table—not too thin or slices will crumble—and serve with plenty of gravy. Or carve in the kitchen, arrange slices slightly overlapping on a platter, and pour some of the gravy down the center; pass the rest. Serve with Potato Dumplings, Spätzle, or boiled potatoes.

NPS: 865 C, 160 mg CH, 855 mg S*

POT-AU-FEU

10–12 servings

Most countries have their favorite meal-in-a-pot. In France it's Pot-au-Feu, in Italy Bollito Misto. What goes into the pot depends on what the housewife has in her garden and barnyard. How the dish is served depends largely on whim—sometimes the broth is a first course; sometimes everything is eaten together like a stew.

1 (4-pound) boned and rolled beef roast with a very thin outer covering of fat (chuck, rump, or bottom round is best to use)
2 pounds beef or veal marrowbones, cracked
1 gallon cold water
5 teaspoons salt
1/4 teaspoon pepper
2 bay leaves and 2 sprigs each parsley and thyme divided between 2 cheesecloth bags (*bouquets garnis*)
2 additional bay leaves
1 medium-size yellow onion, peeled and stuck with 6 cloves
2 stalks celery, cut in 2″ lengths
1 (4-pound) stewing chicken, cut up (include giblets)
2 pounds carrots, peeled and cut in 2″ lengths
2 pounds turnips or 1 (2-pound) rutabaga, peeled and cut in 1″ cubes
2 bunches leeks, trimmed and cut in 2″ lengths, or 1 pound small white onions, peeled
1–2 tablespoons minced parsley (garnish)

Place beef on a rack in a 2 1/2-gallon kettle, add bones, water, seasonings, yellow onion, celery, and giblets, cover, and bring to a boil over moderate heat. Skim off froth, reduce heat, cover, and simmer 1 hour. Add chicken, cover, and simmer 2–2 1/2 hours until beef and chicken are nearly tender. Add carrots and turnips (also white onions if using instead of leeks) and simmer 15 minutes; add leeks, if using, and simmer 15 minutes longer until vegetables and meats are tender.

NPS (10–12): 770–640 C, 180–150 mg CH, 1285–1070 mg S*

To Serve Broth and Meats Separately: Remove strings from beef and place in the center of a large platter with chicken; wreathe with vegetables, top with a little broth, sprinkle with parsley, and keep warm in a very slow oven. Skim fat from broth, strain, taste for salt and pepper, and adjust if needed. Scoop marrow from marrowbones, spread on slices of French bread, float a slice in each bowl of broth, and serve. Traditional accompaniments are garlic croutons, freshly grated Parmesan cheese, coarsely ground black pepper, and tiny pickled white onions.

Follow broth course with the meat and vegetables, carving the beef against the grain. Pass a little extra broth for spooning over each portion.

To Serve Pot-au-Feu as a Stew: When meats are tender, cut into small slices and serve in soup bowls with vegetables, plenty of the broth, and a sprinkling of parsley. Traditional accompaniments are coarse (kosher-style) salt, gherkins, mustard, horseradish, and crusty French bread. Boiled potatoes are appropriate too.

To Make Ahead: Prepare pot-au-feu 1 day in advance—but no more—cool, cover, and refrigerate. Lift off fat, then cover and reheat very slowly. Leftover broth, incidentally, is excellent for gravies, brown sauces, and soups (especially onion).

To Halve the Recipe: Use a 2-pound beef roast and a 2½–3-pound whole frying chicken; halve all other ingredients and prepare as directed, reducing simmering time for the chicken to about 1 hour. All other simmering times will remain the same.

VARIATIONS

Polish-Style Boiled Dinner: Omit chicken, add giblets from 3 to 4 chickens along with beef and 1 (1–1½-pound) *kielbasa* sausage ring (prick skin to prevent bursting) along with the turnips and carrots. When serving, cut sausage into thick chunks.

NPS (10–12): 805–670 C, 210–175 mg CH, 1650–1375 mg S*

Bollito Misto: Add 1 (2–3-pound) fresh or smoked beef tongue to kettle along with beef, then proceed as recipe directs. When serving, remove skin and small bones from tongue, then slice. Accompany with boiled potatoes and pass two or more of the following: Green Sauce, Béarnaise, Tomato Sauce, prepared mustard or horseradish.

NPS (10–12): 955–795 C, 245–205 mg CH, 1350–1125 mg S*

BOILED BRISKET OF BEEF WITH PARSLEY DUMPLINGS

6–8 servings

1 (4-pound) lean beef brisket
3 quarts beef broth or cold water
1 large yellow onion, peeled
2 stalks celery, cut in 2″ lengths
1 tablespoon salt
¼ teaspoon pepper
2 beef bouillon cubes

1 recipe Dumplings
2 tablespoons minced parsley

Place beef on a trivet in a large kettle, add all remaining ingredients except dumplings and parsley, cover, and bring to a boil over moderately high heat. Skim froth from surface, then simmer, covered, about 3 hours until fork tender. Just before meat is done, prepare dumplings by recipe, adding parsley to dry ingredients. Lift meat to a heated platter and keep warm. Skim broth of fat and bring to a boil. Drop dumpling mixture by rounded tablespoonfuls on top of broth; simmer, uncovered, 10 minutes, cover tight, and simmer 10 minutes longer. Remove dumplings with a slotted spoon and arrange around meat. Carve meat, not too thin, across the grain. If you wish, pass a little broth in a gravy boat, or serve with Horseradish Sauce or Caper and Horseradish Sauce. Save remaining broth and use as stock.

NPS (6–8): 645–485 C, 185–140 mg CH, 2305–1730 mg S*

VARIATION

Boiled Brisket of Beef with Vegetables: Omit dumplings. Cook your choice of vegetables along with the beef—small whole carrots, cubed turnips or rutabagas, leeks, small white onions, halved or quartered parsnips, halved potatoes, cabbage wedges, timing their additions to the pot so that they—and the beef—will be done at the same time. Wreathe meat with vegetables and serve. Recipe too flexible for meaningful nutritional count.

STEWS

Stew beef comes from the sinewy, well-exercised parts of the animal (see Beef Chart) and can be cut small or left in a single large chunk. In general, the front half of the animal provides more good stew meat than the hind—these fore cuts seem to have slightly more fat, also more of the connective tissue that cooks down into gelatin, making the meat lusciously moist and tender. Ask for chuck, neck, brisket, plate, or shank.

OLD-FASHIONED BEEF STEW

4–6 servings

2 pounds boned beef chuck or bottom round, cut in 1½″ cubes
½ cup unsifted flour
2 teaspoons salt

1/4 teaspoon pepper
2–3 tablespoons beef drippings or cooking oil
1 1/2 pounds small white onions, peeled
6–8 medium-size carrots, peeled and cut in 1" chunks
1 pound small turnips, peeled and halved, or 1 pound parsnips, peeled and cut in 2" chunks (optional)
1 bay leaf
2 cups beef broth, water, dry red wine, or beer
1 tablespoon minced parsley

Dredge beef by shaking in a paper bag with flour, 1 teaspoon salt, and 1/8 teaspoon pepper; then brown, a few pieces at a time, in 2 tablespoons drippings in a large, heavy kettle over moderately high heat; transfer to a bowl. Brown onions in remaining drippings 8–10 minutes, stirring occasionally, and remove to bowl. Drain drippings from kettle, return beef and onions, and add all remaining ingredients except parsley. Cover and simmer 1 1/2–2 hours until beef is tender. (*Note:* You can prepare recipe to this point early in the day or, better still, the day before. Cool, cover, and refrigerate, or freeze for future use. Reheat slowly, stirring often.) Sprinkle with parsley and serve.

NPS (4–6): 885–590 C, 145–95 mg CH, 1670–1105 mg S*

VARIATIONS

Beef and Vegetable Stew: About 15–20 minutes before serving, stir in 2 cups fresh or frozen green peas, whole kernel corn, or diced celery (or a combination of these), cover, and simmer until tender.

NPS (4–6): 940–625 C, 145–95 mg CH, 1750–1165 mg S*

Beef Stew with Mushrooms: With the beef, onions, and carrots simmer 1/2 pound sliced mushrooms that have been lightly browned in butter.

NPS (4–6): 930–620 C, 155–100 mg CH, 1695–1130 mg S*

Beef Stew with Dumplings: About 30 minutes before serving, make Dumplings, add to stew, cover, and cook according to dumpling recipe.

NPS (4–6): 1070–710 C, 150–100 mg CH, 2105–1405 mg S*

BEEF STEW FOR A CROWD

25 servings

This recipe should be started a day before it's to be served.

12 pounds boned beef chuck or bottom round, cut in 1 1/2" cubes
2 cups sifted flour
2 tablespoons salt (about)
1/2 teaspoon pepper
3/4 cup beef drippings or cooking oil
2 quarts liquid (use liquid from canned onions, below, and round out with a 1/2 and 1/2 mixture of water and canned condensed beef broth or dry red wine)
2 beef bouillon cubes
4 tablespoons tomato paste
4 bay leaves
5 (1-pound) cans small white onions, drained (reserve liquid)
5 (1-pound) cans whole baby carrots, drained
2 tablespoons liquid gravy browner
3/4 cup sifted flour blended with 3/4 cup cold water (if needed to thicken gravy)

Dredge beef by shaking a few pieces at a time in a paper bag with flour, 1 tablespoon salt, and the pepper. For cooking the stew, use two 2-gallon kettles. Brown beef a little at a time, using 2 tablespoons drippings in each kettle; transfer to a bowl with a slotted spoon. Continue, adding more drippings as needed, until all beef is browned. This will take about 3/4 hour. Turn heat to low, return beef to kettles, then add to *each:* 1 quart liquid, 1 bouillon cube, 2 tablespoons tomato paste, and 2 bay leaves. Cover and simmer 1 1/2–2 hours until meat is tender, stirring occasionally. Cool, cover kettles, and chill overnight. Next day, skim off fat. About 1 hour before serving, set kettles on lowest heat and warm slowly. About 3/4 hour before serving, add onions and carrots, dividing them between the 2 kettles, cover and cook over moderate heat until tender. Mix in gravy browner, taste for salt, and adjust as needed. If stew seems thin, add half the flour-water to each kettle and heat, stirring, until thickened. Serve over buttered wide noodles, rice, or whole boiled potatoes.

NPS: 760 C, 140 mg CH, 1135 mg S*

BEEF AND BLACK BEAN STEW WITH PIÑON NUTS

6 servings

2 1/2 pounds boned beef chuck, cut in 1 1/2" cubes
1/4 cup olive oil
2 medium-size yellow onions, peeled and cut in thin wedges
2 cloves garlic, peeled and crushed
1 teaspoon paprika
1 bay leaf, crumbled
1/2 teaspoon thyme
1/2 teaspoon salt

1/8 teaspoon pepper
2 large ripe tomatoes, peeled, cored, and cut in
  thin wedges
2/3 cup dry white wine
1 cup boiling water
2 (1-pound) cans black beans (do not drain)
3/4 cup shelled piñon nuts

Brown meat in oil, a little at a time, in a large, heavy kettle over high heat; remove to a bowl and reserve. Add onions and garlic to kettle, reduce heat to moderate, and stir-fry 8–10 minutes until golden. Mix in paprika, herbs, salt, pepper, and tomatoes and stir-fry about 5 minutes until tomatoes have released most of their juice. Return meat to kettle, add wine and water, cover, and simmer 1 hour. Stir in 1 can beans and the nuts, cover, and simmer 1/2–1 hour longer until meat is tender. Add remaining beans, cover, and simmer 15–20 minutes to blend flavors. (*Note:* If stew seems thick, thin with 1/4–1/2 cup boiling water.) Serve over boiled rice.

*NPS: 830 C, 130 mg CH, 815 mg S**

BOEUF À LA BOURGUIGNONNE

6 servings

There are many variations of Beef Bourguignonne, each slightly different. Some call for cognac, others currant jelly, but all are basically the same—chunks of stew beef simmered in red wine (traditionally Burgundy) with herbs and onions. This version will be better if made a day ahead and reheated slowly before serving.

1 (1/4-pound) piece bacon, trimmed of rind and
  cut in 1″ × 1/4″ × 1/4″ strips
1 quart water
1 tablespoon olive oil
3 pounds boned beef chuck, cut in 1 1/2″ cubes
  and patted dry on paper toweling
1 large yellow onion, peeled and sliced thin
1 large carrot, peeled and minced
1 teaspoon salt
1/8 teaspoon pepper
2 tablespoons flour
2 cups red Burgundy or other dry red wine
1 1/3 cups strong beef stock or broth
1 tablespoon tomato paste
2 cloves garlic, peeled and crushed
2 (4″) sprigs fresh thyme or 1/2 teaspoon dried
  thyme
2 (4″) sprigs parsley
1 bay leaf, crumbled
1 recipe Pan-Braised Onions
1 pound mushrooms, wiped clean and sliced 1/4″
  thick
2 tablespoons butter or margarine

Preheat oven to 500° F. Simmer bacon, uncovered, in water 10 minutes; drain, pat dry, then brown in oil in a large, heavy skillet over moderately high heat about 5 minutes; drain on paper toweling. Brown beef in skillet in bacon drippings, a few pieces at a time, and drain on paper toweling. Reduce heat to moderate, add onion and carrot to skillet, and stir-fry 8–10 minutes until onion is golden. Place beef and bacon in an ungreased 3-quart casserole, add onion and carrot, and toss to mix. Sprinkle with salt, pepper, and flour and toss again. Set, uncovered, in oven 3–5 minutes; remove, stir well, and set in oven 3–5 minutes longer (this helps brown flour and seal in meat juices). Remove casserole from oven and reduce oven temperature to 325° F. Stir wine, stock, tomato paste, and garlic into casserole. Tie thyme, parsley, and bay leaf into cheesecloth and drop into casserole. Cover casserole, set in oven, and simmer 2 hours until beef is tender. Meanwhile, prepare onions and reserve; also stir-fry mushrooms in butter over moderate heat 8–10 minutes until tender; set aside. When beef is tender, remove it and bacon bits to a large bowl with a slotted spoon; keep warm. Discard cheesecloth bag. Put casserole liquid through a fine sieve, pressing with a wooden spoon to purée vegetables; return to casserole and boil, uncovered, about 5 minutes to reduce slightly. Return beef and bacon to casserole. Add onions and mushrooms, distributing them well, cover, and simmer slowly about 5 minutes. Serve hot with boiled new potatoes or noodles, a crisp green salad, and a red Burgundy wine.

*NPS: 945 C, 200 mg CH, 1010 mg S**

CARBONNADE FLAMANDE
(FLEMISH BEEF-BEER STEW)

6 servings

Beer gives this nut-brown stew its unusual malty flavor.

2 tablespoons butter or margarine
6 medium-size yellow onions, peeled and sliced
  thin
2 cloves garlic, peeled and crushed
1/2 cup unsifted flour
1 tablespoon salt
1/4 teaspoon pepper
3 pounds boned beef chuck, cut in 1 1/2″ cubes
  and trimmed of excess fat
1/8 teaspoon nutmeg
1/4 teaspoon thyme
2 (12-ounce) cans beer

Melt butter in a large, heavy kettle over moderate heat, add onions and garlic, and sauté, stirring occasionally, 10 minutes until golden; drain on paper toweling. Place flour, salt, and pepper in a heavy brown paper bag and dredge beef, a few cubes at a time, by shaking in the mixture. Brown beef, a little at a time, in kettle over high heat, adding more butter as needed. Reduce heat to moderate, return beef, onions, and garlic to kettle, add all remaining ingredients, cover, and simmer slowly, stirring occasionally, about 2 hours until beef is fork tender. Skim any fat from gravy. Simmer, uncovered, about 10 minutes longer, then serve with tiny boiled new potatoes and tall glasses of well-chilled beer.

*NPS: 775 C, 155 mg CH, 1215 mg S**

BEEF CATALAN

8–10 servings

Frenchwomen in the Pyrenees make a marvelous beef stew that's as much Spanish as French. Some add rice to the pot, others white kidney beans; some use a heavy hand with spices, others a light touch. This is a flexible recipe, so you can adjust the ingredients to suit your taste.

1 (1/4-pound) piece bacon, trimmed of rind and cut in 1/4" cubes
4 pounds boned beef rump or chuck, cut in 11/2" cubes and patted dry on paper toweling
1 tablespoon olive oil
3 medium-size yellow onions, peeled and sliced thin
2 cloves garlic, peeled and crushed
4 medium-size carrots, peeled and cut in 2" chunks
1/2 pound small turnips, peeled and quartered
1 (1"×3") strip orange peel (orange part only)
1 stick cinnamon
3 cloves
1 bay leaf, crumbled
2 (4") sprigs fresh thyme or 1/2 teaspoon dried thyme
3 ripe tomatoes, peeled, seeded, juiced, and coarsely chopped
2 cups dry red wine
11/3 cups strong beef stock or broth
2 (1-pound 3-ounce) cans cannellini (white kidney beans), drained
21/2 teaspoons salt
1/8 teaspoon pepper
3 tablespoons minced parsley

Preheat oven to 325° F. Brown bacon in a large, heavy kettle over high heat and drain on paper toweling. Brown beef in drippings,

a few cubes at a time, over moderately high heat; remove to a bowl and reserve. Add oil to kettle and stir-fry onions, garlic, carrots, and turnips 10–12 minutes until onions are golden. Tie orange peel, cinnamon, cloves, bay leaf, and thyme in cheesecloth and add to kettle along with bacon, beef, tomatoes, wine, and stock. Cover kettle, set in oven, and simmer 2 hours until beef is tender. Discard cheesecloth bag. *(Note:* Recipe can be made up to this point well ahead of time. Cool, cover, and refrigerate or freeze for use later. Bring to room temperature before proceeding or, if frozen, thaw gently over low heat, stirring frequently.) Add remaining ingredients except parsley and bake, uncovered, 30 minutes, stirring 1 or 2 times. Mix in parsley and serve over hot fluffy rice or Saffron Rice.

*NPS (8–10): 965–770 C, 165–130 mg CH, 1095–870 mg S**

HUNGARIAN GOULASH

4–6 servings

Though traditionally made with beef, *gulyás,* the Hungarian national dish, can be prepared with any meat or game. Here's a basic version plus three popular variations.

11/4 cups finely chopped yellow onion
1 sweet green pepper, cored, seeded, and chopped fine
1/4 cup lard, butter, or margarine
2 pounds boned beef chuck, shin, or bottom round, cut in 11/2" cubes
2 tablespoons paprika (use the Hungarian sweet rose if possible)
11/2 teaspoons salt
1/4 teaspoon pepper
1 teaspoon cider vinegar
2 cups beef stock, broth, or water

Sauté onion and green pepper in lard in a kettle over moderate heat 5–8 minutes until onion is pale golden; drain on paper toweling. Add meat to kettle and brown well over moderately high heat. Turn heat to low, add paprika, and stir 1–2 minutes. Return onion mixture to kettle, add remaining ingredients, cover, and simmer 11/2–2 hours until meat is tender. Serve with Nockerln or buttered noodles.

*NPS (4–6): 745–495 C, 165–110 mg CH, 1375–915 mg S**

VARIATIONS

Transylvanian Goulash: About 1/2 hour before goulash is done, add 1 pound drained sauerkraut, cover, and simmer until meat is tender. Mix in 1 cup sour cream and serve.

NPS (4–6): 805–535 C, 190–125 mg CH, 2250–1500 mg S*

Yugoslav Goulash: Sauté 1 clove peeled, crushed garlic with onion and green pepper, then proceed as directed, substituting 1 (1-pound 12-ounce) can undrained tomatoes for beef stock. If you prefer, use 1 cup beef stock and 1 (8-ounce) can tomato sauce.

NPS (4–6): 695–465 C, 165–110 mg CH, 1240–825 mg S*

Savory Goulash: Prepare as directed, adding 1 teaspoon caraway seeds or marjoram and/ or 1 clove peeled, crushed garlic along with other seasonings. Nutritional count same as basic recipe.

COUNTRY-STYLE UKRAINIAN BORSCHT

12–14 servings

Old country-style borscht, the national dish of the Ukraine, always has a good chunk of meat cooking along with the vegetables. A mild tartness is characteristic—beet or rye *kvas* (liquid from fermented beets or rye yeast batter) used to be traditional, but nowadays lemon, vinegar, even sorrel leaves or rhubarb juice are substituted.

1 (2-pound) boned and rolled beef roast (chuck, bottom round, or rump), trimmed of fat
1 (2-pound) smoked boneless pork shoulder butt
1 gallon cold water
2–4 teaspoons salt
1 bay leaf and 1 sprig each parsley and thyme, tied in cheesecloth with 1 peeled clove garlic and 6 peppercorns
2 medium-size yellow onions, peeled and coarsely chopped
2 carrots, peeled and cut in julienne strips
2 cups finely chopped celery
8 medium-size boiled beets, peeled and diced or cut in julienne strips
1 (1-pound 12-ounce) can tomatoes (do not drain)
4 cups finely shredded cabbage
2 cups boiled dried white beans or 1 (1-pound 3-ounce) can cannellini beans (do not drain)
3–4 tablespoons lemon juice
2 tablespoons snipped fresh dill (optional)
1 pint sour cream (optional garnish)

Place meats, water, 2 teaspoons salt, cheesecloth bag, and onions in a 3-gallon kettle, cover, and bring to a boil over moderate heat. Skim froth from surface, reduce heat, re-cover, and simmer 2–2½ hours until

meats are nearly tender. Add carrots and celery, cover, and simmer 20 minutes; add beets, tomatoes (cut them up), and cabbage, cover, and simmer 20 minutes longer. Remove cheesecloth bag and gently stir in beans and lemon juice. *(Note:* Recipe may be prepared to this point a day or so ahead; cool, cover and chill.) Heat slowly to boiling, taste for salt and pepper and adjust as needed. Stir in dill if you like. Ladle into deep soup bowls, serve with a slice or 2 of meats, and top with dollops of sour cream.

NPS (12–14): 500–430 C, 110–95 mg CH, 1250–1070 mg S*

VARIATIONS

Borscht Stew: Instead of using large chunks of beef and pork, use 2 pounds each boned chuck and pork shoulder butt, cut in 1½″ cubes. Otherwise, prepare as directed. If you prefer, use 3–4 pounds beef shank or bone-in soup meat in place of the chuck. Nutritional count same as basic recipe.

⚖ ¢ **Economy Borscht** *(12 servings):* Omit all meats; substitute strong beef stock for half the water called for, and simmer vegetables as directed.

NPS: 175 C, 15 mg CH, 1045 mg S*

Beef and Bacon Borscht for 6 Persons: Use 2 pounds boned beef chuck cut in 1½″ cubes and substitute 3–4 slices diced, lean smoked bacon for the pork shoulder butt; halve all other ingredients and prepare as recipe directs. Cooking times will be about the same.

NPS: 465 C, 120 mg CH, 715 mg S*

OLD-FASHIONED STEAK AND KIDNEY PIE

6 servings

Mashed or boiled potatoes and Brussels sprouts or carrots are traditional with steak and kidney pie.

1 pound beef kidney, free of membrane and fat
2 cups cold water mixed with 1 teaspoon salt
2½ pounds lean, boned beef chuck or bottom round, cut in 1½″ cubes
¼ cup rendered suet, beef drippings, or cooking oil
3 medium-size yellow onions, peeled and minced
3 tablespoons flour
1¼ cups beef broth
1 cup cold water
2 teaspoons salt
¼ teaspoon pepper

1 bay leaf and 1 sprig each parsley and thyme, tied in cheesecloth (optional *bouquet garni*)

PASTRY
1 recipe Flaky Pastry I
1 egg yolk mixed with 1 tablespoon cold water (glaze)

Soak kidney in salt water 1 hour, drain, and pat dry on paper toweling; remove cores and cut kidney in 1″ cubes. Brown beef, a little at a time, in suet in a large, heavy kettle over high heat; remove and reserve. Brown kidney, stirring, and add to beef. Turn heat to moderate, add onions and stir-fry 8–10 minutes until golden; mix in flour and brown 1–2 minutes. Return meat to kettle, add all but pastry ingredients, cover, and simmer 1½–2 hours until tender. Discard *bouquet garni* if used. Transfer to an ungreased 2-quart casserole that measures about 9″ across. *(Note:* If you have a pie funnel, place in center of casserole before adding meat; it will help prop up crust and keep pie from boiling over.) Preheat oven to 425° F. Roll pastry into a 10″ circle and make 3 V-slits in center. Moisten casserole rim, top with pastry, roll edges under until even with rim, press down to seal and crimp. Brush pastry with glaze, making sure not to cover slits. Bake in top third of oven (with foil under casserole to catch drips) 10–12 minutes, reduce heat to 350° F., and bake 25 minutes longer until nicely browned. To serve, cut wedge-shaped pieces of pastry and arrange on top of each helping of meat.

NPS: 705 C, 460 mg CH, 1540 mg S*

VARIATION

Just before serving, insert a small funnel in a V-slit and pour in 1–2 tablespoons dry sherry.

NPS: 705 C, 460 mg CH, 1540 mg S*

FARMHOUSE MEAT AND POTATO PIE

6 servings ¢

PASTRY
2 cups sifted flour
1 teaspoon salt
1/3 cup chilled shortening
1/3 cup chilled lard
4–5 tablespoons ice water
1 egg yolk mixed with 1 tablespoon cold water (glaze)

FILLING
1½ pounds boned beef chuck, cut in 1″ cubes
1/2 cup unsifted flour

2 teaspoons salt
3 medium-size potatoes, peeled and sliced 1/2″ thick
1 large yellow onion, peeled and sliced thin
1/4 teaspoon pepper
1 2/3 cups beef stock or 1 cup canned condensed beef broth and 2/3 cup water

Preheat oven to 425° F. Sift flour and salt for pastry into a bowl and cut in shortening and lard with a pastry blender until the texture of oatmeal. Sprinkle ice water over surface, a tablespoon at a time, mixing briskly with a fork after each addition. Pastry should *just* hold together. Wrap in foil and chill while you prepare the filling. Dredge beef by shaking in a paper bag with flour and 1 teaspoon salt. Place beef in an ungreased shallow 1½-quart casserole with a wide rim. Layer potatoes and onion on top, sprinkling pepper and remaining salt between layers. Pour stock over all. Roll pastry into a circle about 3″ larger in diameter than the casserole and cut a strip 1″ wide from around outer edge. Moisten casserole rim with cold water and lay strip on rim; moisten strip. Cut 2–3 decorative holes near center of pastry circle; place on top of filling and press edges into pastry strip. Trim pastry even with rim and crimp. Brush with glaze, avoiding decorative edge. Bake 15 minutes, reduce heat to 350° F., and bake 1¼ hours longer until meat is tender (test by poking a skewer through decorative hole). Serve hot with a crisp green salad.

NPS: 755 C, 135 mg CH, 1495 mg S*

INDONESIAN SPICED BEEF

4–6 servings

2 medium-size yellow onions, peeled and coarsely chopped
2 cloves garlic, peeled and crushed
3 tablespoons peanut oil
1 flank steak (about 2–2¼ pounds), cut crosswise into strips 1/2″ × 1½″
1 (2″) stick cinnamon
6 cloves
2 tablespoons paprika
1 tablespoon crushed coriander seeds
1–2 teaspoons cayenne pepper (depending on how hot you like things)
1 teaspoon tumeric
1 teaspoon ginger
1/4 teaspoon cumin
4 medium-size new potatoes, peeled and cut in 1/2″ cubes
2 cups Coconut Milk
1½ teaspoons salt

Stir-fry onions and garlic in oil in a heavy kettle over moderate heat 8–10 minutes until golden; remove to a bowl. Raise heat to high and brown meat, a few pieces at a time; transfer to paper toweling to drain. Reduce heat to low, return meat, onions, and garlic to kettle and mix in all remaining ingredients. Cover and simmer, stirring occasionally, about 1½ hours until meat is tender. Serve hot over fluffy boiled rice.

NPS (4–6): 875–580 C, 155–100 mg CH, 1035–690 mg S*

BRAISED OXTAIL WITH CARROTS

6–8 servings ¢

4 pounds oxtail, cut in 1½" chunks and trimmed of excess fat
2 tablespoons cooking oil
2 medium-size yellow onions, peeled and chopped fine
3 cups hot water *or* 1 (12-ounce) can beer and 1½ cups water *or* 2 cups water and 1 cup dry red wine
1 (8-ounce) can tomato sauce
½ teaspoon celery seeds
1 bay leaf, crumbled
1 tablespoon minced parsley
1 teaspoon Worcestershire sauce
1½ teaspoons salt
⅛ teaspoon pepper
6–8 medium-size carrots, peeled and sliced ½" thick
2 tablespoons flour blended with 2 tablespoons cold water

Brown oxtail in oil in a large, heavy kettle over high heat and drain on paper toweling. Reduce heat to moderate, add onions to kettle and sauté, stirring, 8–10 minutes until golden. Return meat to kettle, add remaining ingredients except carrots and flour-water paste, cover, and simmer over low heat 3 hours until meat is tender. Cool and skim off fat. (*Note:* Recipe can be prepared to this point a day or so ahead of time. Cool, cover, and refrigerate or freeze for future use. Bring to room temperature before proceeding, or if frozen thaw gently over low heat, stirring frequently.) Add carrots, cover, and simmer 20 minutes until tender. Mix in flour-water paste and heat, stirring, until thickened. Serve over buttered noodles.

NPS (6–8): 860–645 C, 0 mg CH, 790–590 mg S*

SHORT RIBS

It's curious that pork spareribs should be such a favorite and their beef counterpart, short ribs, so often slighted. These 3″ rib ends (see Beef Chart) are budget priced and, when braised and skillfully seasoned, unusually good eating.

BRAISED SHORT RIBS OF BEEF

4 servings ¢

3½–4 pounds beef short ribs, cut in 3″ pieces
2 tablespoons cooking oil or beef drippings
1 medium-size yellow onion, peeled and sliced thin
¼ pound mushrooms, wiped and sliced
1 large carrot, peeled and sliced thin
1 teaspoon salt
¼ teaspoon pepper
1 cup beef broth
2 tablespoons flour blended with 2 tablespoons cold water
¼ teaspoon liquid gravy browner

Brown ribs slowly (about 15–20 minutes) in oil in a large kettle over moderately low heat. Add onion, mushrooms, carrot, salt, pepper, and broth, cover, and simmer 1½ hours until meat is tender. Transfer ribs to a deep serving dish and keep warm. Purée vegetables and cooking liquid by buzzing 20–30 seconds in an electric blender at low speed or 15–20 seconds in a food processor fitted with the metal chopping blade; return to kettle. Mix in flour-water paste and gravy browner and cook, stirring, until thickened. Pour some gravy over short ribs and serve (remaining gravy can be passed in a gravy boat).

NPS: 795 C, 0 mg CH, 760 mg S*

DEVILED SHORT RIBS

4 servings ¢

4 pounds beef short ribs, cut in serving size pieces

M A R I N A D E
¼ cup prepared spicy brown mustard
¼ cup prepared mild yellow mustard
1 cup dry white wine
½ cup beef broth
2 tablespoons Worcestershire sauce
2 tablespoons finely grated yellow onion
1 clove garlic, peeled and crushed
½ teaspoon salt
¼ teaspoon pepper

Place ribs in a large, deep bowl; beat all marinade ingredients together until smooth and pour over ribs. Cover and refrigerate at least 12 hours, turning ribs now and then. Drain, reserving marinade. Preheat oven to 425° F. Place ribs on a rack in a roasting pan and roast, uncovered, 15–17 minutes until browned; turn and brown 15–17 minutes longer. Reduce oven temperature to 325° F. Transfer ribs to a second roasting pan (do not use rack), top with 3/4 cup marinade, cover with foil, and bake about 2 hours until tender. Just before serving, heat remaining marinade and serve as a hot sauce with the ribs.

NPS: 780 C, 0 mg CH, 805 mg S

OTHER FORMS OF BEEF

Corned Beef: Brisket (and sometimes plate or rump) cured either in brine or by having brine pumped through the arterial system. Old-fashioned corned beef is salty and gray-pink; newer, milder types, rosy red; both are available by the half or whole brisket. Newest entry is beef corned *without* sodium nitrite, which may break down in the body during metabolism and bond with other compounds to form carcinogenic nitrosamines. Allow 1/3–1/2 pound corned beef per person.

Chipped Beef (also called *Dried Beef):* Tissue-thin slices of salty dried beef; allow 1–2 ounces per person.

Beef-Bacon Slices: Rather like pastrami without the spices, these slices of cured beef are cooked just like bacon. Allow 3–4 slices per person.

Smoked Sliced Beef: Ready-to-eat sandwich meat made by pressing coarsely ground beef into rounds or squares, curing, smoking, and cooking. Allow 1–2 slices per person.

Pastrami: Cured, smoked beef plate; it's usually sliced thin and served warm in sandwiches with mustard.

Air-Dried Beef: Most famous, perhaps, is the salty, mahogany-hued Swiss *bundnerfleisch* from the Grisons although the Italian *bresaola,* salt-cured, air-dried whole beef filet from the Italian Alps, is becoming increasingly popular. Some cooks now use it in preference to fresh raw beef filet or top round when making that famous Venetian recipe *carpaccio* (named after the fifteenth-century painter and popularized by Harry's Bar) because *bresaola* can be sliced razor-thin and need not be pounded to rosy translucence. *Carpaccio,* if you don't know it, is nothing more than thinnest medallions of raw beef arrayed on a platter, ever so lightly glossed with olive oil, then decorated with anchovy fillets, roasted slivers of green pepper, and scatterings of tiny capers. In American restaurants, it is often centered with a fluff of alfalfa sprouts and served with a sharp but creamy mustard sauce. Here, as in Italy, *carpaccio* is served as an appetizer or first course.

Jerky or Jerked Beef: The original dried beef. These salty, leathery strips and chunks are still a great favorite among American Indians and Mexicans (Latin groceries are the best place to buy them).

Freeze-Dried Beef: Not much beef is being freeze-dried as yet, though the process may eventually revolutionize our lives. Freeze-dried meat requires very little storage space and no refrigeration. To date it is being used primarily in soup mixes and camp foods, also by astronauts.

NEW ENGLAND BOILED DINNER

6 servings   ¢

4 pounds corned brisket of beef, wiped with damp paper toweling
2 quarts cold water
6 peppercorns and 1 bay leaf, tied in cheesecloth
6 medium-size carrots, peeled and halved crosswise
6 medium-size potatoes, peeled and halved
1 small rutabaga, peeled and cut in 6 wedges
1 medium-size cabbage, trimmed of coarse leaves, cored, and cut in 6 wedges

If necessary, tie brisket into a neat shape; place in a very large kettle, add water and cheesecloth bag, cover, and bring to a boil over high heat. Reduce heat to low and simmer 10 minutes; uncover and skim off any scum. Re-cover and simmer about 3 hours until tender. Remove cheesecloth bag; transfer meat to a platter, cover loosely with foil and keep warm. (*Note:* Meat can be refrigerated at this point and held 1–2 days; let come to room temperature before proceeding.) Bring kettle liquid to a boil and taste; if not too salty, add carrots, potatoes, and rutabaga, cover, and boil 20 minutes; add meat and cabbage, cover, and cook 15–20 minutes longer. If liquid is too salty, cook carrots, potatoes, and rutabaga, covered, in about 2″ lightly salted water 20 minutes, add meat and cabbage, and proceed as above. Drain vegetables and make a border around a very large platter; place meat in center. Serve with horseradish, mustard, or mustard pickles. To be really traditional, add a plate of Rhode Island Jonnycake and serve apple dumplings for dessert.

NPS: 935 C, 190 mg CH, 1960 mg S*

CORNED BEEF AND CABBAGE

6–8 servings ¢

Some people say the only way to make good corned beef and cabbage is to cook the two together, but *don't* if the beef cooking water seems greasy and/or salty—boil the cabbage separately. When carving corned beef, make the slices thick or thin but always slice *against* the grain.

4 pounds corned brisket of beef, wiped with damp paper toweling
2 quarts cold water
6 peppercorns
6 whole allspice
1 bay leaf
1 medium-size yellow onion, peeled and quartered
1 medium-size cabbage, trimmed of coarse outer leaves, cored, and cut in 8 wedges

If necessary, tie brisket into a neat shape; place in a very large kettle with water, peppercorns, allspice, bay leaf, and onion, cover, and bring to a boil over high heat. Reduce heat to low and simmer 10 minutes; uncover and skim off any scum. Re-cover and simmer about 3 hours until tender. Taste cooking water and, if it seems delicate enough, add cabbage, cover, and simmer 15–20 minutes until crisp tender. Otherwise, place cabbage in a separate kettle, add about 2″ lightly salted boiling water, cover, and boil 15–20 minutes; drain. Arrange beef on a heated large platter and surround with cabbage wedges. Serve with boiled potatoes and a mustard or horseradish sauce.

NPS (6–8): 785–590 C, 190–140 mg CH, 1930–1445 mg S*

HOMEMADE CORNED BEEF HASH

4 servings ¢

1 medium-size yellow onion, peeled and chopped fine
2 tablespoons any meat drippings, butter, or margarine
2 cups diced, cooked corned beef
2 cups diced, cooked cold potatoes
2 teaspoons Worcestershire sauce
1 tablespoon minced parsley

⅛ teaspoon pepper
4 poached eggs

Stir-fry onion in drippings in a large, heavy skillet over moderate heat 5–8 minutes until transparent. Stir in corned beef and potatoes; sprinkle evenly with Worcestershire sauce, parsley, and pepper. Pat hash down with a broad spatula and cook, uncovered, without stirring, 10–12 minutes until a brown crust forms on the bottom. Turn, using 2 broad spatulas, and brown flip side 8–10 minutes. To serve, cut in 4 equal portions and top each with a poached egg.

NPS: 460 C, 345 mg CH, 845 mg S*

RED FLANNEL HASH

4–6 servings ¢ ⊲⊳

1 (12-ounce) can corned beef, minced
2 large boiled potatoes, peeled and chopped fine
1 cup minced, cooked beets
1 medium-size yellow onion, peeled and minced
Pinch pepper
3 tablespoons butter, margarine, or bacon drippings

Mix corned beef, potatoes, beets, onion, and pepper well. Melt butter in a heavy 9″ or 10″ skillet over moderately low heat, add hash, and let cook slowly about 35–40 minutes until a crisp brown crust forms on the bottom. Turn carefully and brown flip side 10–15 minutes or, if you prefer, instead of browning second side, fold as an omelet and serve. Accompany, if you like, with Sour Cream-Horseradish Sauce or top each serving with a poached egg.

NPS (4–6): 340–225 C, 105–70 mg CH, 915–610 mg S*

CREAMED CHIPPED BEEF

4 servings ¢ ▨

¼ pound chipped beef
¼ cup butter or margarine
¼ cup unsifted flour
2 cups milk
Pinch pepper

Separate beef slices and tear into medium-size shreds; taste and if too salty cover with boiling water and let stand 1 minute; drain well. Melt butter in a saucepan over moderate heat, add beef, and heat, stirring occasionally, 2–3 minutes until lightly frizzled. Off heat, blend in flour, then milk. Return to heat and cook, stirring constantly, until thickened and smooth. Add pepper, taste for salt and add if needed. Serve over slices of dry toast.

NPS: 260 C, 65 mg CH, 1395 mg S*

VARIATIONS

Parsleyed Chipped Beef: Just before serving, mix in 2 tablespoons minced parsley. Nutritional count same as basic recipe.

Creamed Chipped Beef and Mushrooms: Prepare Creamed Chipped Beef as directed, but just before serving, mix in ½ pound thinly sliced mushrooms lightly browned in

a little butter and 1 tablespoon minced parsley.

NPS: 290 C, 70 mg CH, 1415 mg S*

Chipped Beef in Cheese Sauce: Prepare as directed; add 1 cup shredded mild Cheddar, 1 tablespoon Worcestershire sauce, and 2–3 dashes liquid hot red pepper seasoning. Heat, stirring, until smooth and serve over buttered noodles or dry toast.

NPS: 380 C, 95 mg CH, 1615 mg S*

VEAL

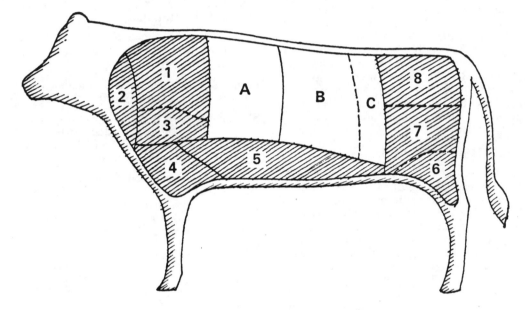

Note: Unshaded parts are the tender cuts. Shaded parts are not-so-tender.

THE TENDER CUTS:
- A. RIB
  - Roasts (rib, crown)
  - Chops (rib, boneless rib)
- B. LOIN
  - Roasts
  - Chops (loin, kidney)
- C. SIRLOIN
  - Roasts
  - Steaks

THE NOT-SO-TENDER CUTS:
- 1. SHOULDER
  - Blade roasts
  - Blade steaks
  - Stew veal
  - Ground veal
- 2. NECK
  - Stew veal
- 3. ARM
  - Arm roasts
  - Arm steaks
- 4. SHANK
  - Shank crosscuts
- 5. BREAST
  - Roasts for stuffing
  - Riblets (stew veal)
- 6. HEEL OF ROUND
  - Stew veal
- 7. ROUND (LEG)
  - Cutlets, scaloppine
  - Round steaks
  - Roasts
- 8. RUMP
  - Roasts

Compared with juicy red steaks or prime ribs, veal seems colorless, characterless. Americans tend to treat it as junior-grade beef, a mistake because veal is too lean and delicate to fling on a grill or pop in the oven. It needs coddling in butter, stock, or sauce, enhancing with herbs, rounding out with vegetables or other meats. European recipes prove how very good veal can be: *Wiener Schnitzel,* for example, tender and moist under its crispy brown crust, sagey *saltimbocca,* creamy *blanquette de veau.*

Recently better supermarkets have been selling something close to European veal (meat of suckling calves): *special-fed, nature* or *fancy-quality veal,* which is advertised as either *Plume de Veau* or *Provimi Delft Blue.* Both are fine, pale-fleshed veals from calves fed a dry skim milk formula (veal, by the way, is a by-product of the dairy industry, not the beef industry). Both of these premium veals carry fancy price tags because the animals are so young (5–16 weeks of age), also because they are penned and pampered the whole of their short lives.

How to Recognize Quality

Look for the top federal grades (USDA PRIME and CHOICE), also for federally inspected (wholesome) meat. The lean should be firm, velvety, and moist; it will have no marbling of fat and practically no outer fat covering. The color of the lean varies, depending upon the animal's age and diet. Very young milk-fed veal will be grayish-white with only the faintest blush of pink; older grass or grain-fed calves will be pink, rosy, and sometimes quite red (once an animal begins nibbling grass, its flesh begins to redden). The bones of veal should be spongy and red inside and what fat there is, creamy, sweet, and firm.

ROAST VEAL

Loin and Rib Roasts: The most luxurious veal roasts.

Rib Roast (4–6 pounds): Very lean, very expensive. There's usually more demand for rib as chops than as roasts.

Crown Roast (8 pounds up): This custom-made showpiece contains 2 or more rib sections bent into a circle. Rib ends are frenched (stripped of meat) and the trimmings ground and piled in the center of the crown (remove this ground meat before roasting the crown because it slows cooking

time; some of the ground meat can be mixed with the stuffing or all of it can be saved and used for loaves or patties). To determine the size of crown roast you need, figure 2 chops per person.

Loin Roast (4–6 pounds): The equivalent of beef short loin (steak row). With veal there's more demand for loin as chops—junior steaks containing tiny nuggets of tenderloin. In England, the favorite loin roast is that with the kidney still attached (it nestles just underneath the ribs).

Rolled Loin (3–5 pounds): Boned and rolled loin; good for stuffing.

Double Loin or Saddle (8–12 pounds): Right and left loins, still intact.

Sirloin Roast (3–4 pounds): A very tender roast from the part of the animal between the loin and rump.

Rolled Double Sirloin (5–6 pounds): Right and left sirloin roasts, boned and rolled.

Shoulder Roasts: Perfect for braising: arm roast (4–5 pounds), blade roast (4–5 pounds), and rolled shoulder (3–5 pounds; good for stuffing).

Leg Roasts: After rib and loin, these are the most tender and expensive. Good for roasting or pot roasting: Standing rump (4–6 pounds), rolled rump (3–5 pounds), center leg (3–4 pounds), and shank half of leg (5–8 pounds).

Breast: A thin, moderately priced, 3–5-pound bony cut that's best when stuffed. Also available boned and rolled (3–4 pounds).

How to Roast Veal

Because veal is so lean and delicate, it shouldn't be shoved in the oven and left to roast all by itself. It has no fat to baste it as it cooks, no marbling to make it juicy, thus will dry out if not barded, larded, and/or basted throughout cooking. Veal also suffers from searing and should only be roasted at a constant low temperature (325° F.). The best veal is that roasted with some liquid in the company of vegetables (see individual recipes that follow). Unlike beef or lamb, which are best served rare, veal does not reach its peak of flavor until it is well done (155°–160° F. on a meat thermometer) and its juices run clear. Most meat thermometers still mark 170° F. as the proper degree of doneness for veal, and some cookbooks even recommend cooking it to 175° F. or 180° F., but at that temperature it will be quite gray, dry, and tough. Try the lower temperature, then let the roast "rest" at room temperature 15–20 minutes before carving to allow its juices to settle. It will have the merest tinge of pink and be supremely tender and succulent.

Best Cuts: For simple oven roasting, leg, rib, and bone-in or rolled loin or rump are the most suitable but they must be well barded —or at least draped with bacon or slices of salt pork—if they are to be juicy.

Amount Needed: 4–5 pounds is a good all-round weight for bone-in roasts, 3–4 pounds for the boneless. To determine number of servings, allow 1/2–3/4 pound bone-in roast per person, 1/3–1/2 pound boneless roast.

General Preparation for Cooking: If the veal is very young and lean, have butcher bard* the roast well. You can do it yourself or, if roast has some fat, merely lay strips of bacon (unsmoked is best) or salt pork over it. It's a good idea to blanch the bacon or salt pork quickly in boiling water so that its flavor doesn't overpower the more delicate one of the veal. To simplify carving of rib or loin roasts, ask butcher to loosen backbone. Rub roast well with pepper and, if you like, salt. For extra savor, also rub with a cut clove of garlic and/or compatible herb such as rosemary, sage, tarragon, or thyme. Before roasting, let roast stand at room temperature 1 1/2–2 hours if possible.

Continuous Low Heat Method: Preheat oven to 325° F. Place roast fattest side up on a rack in a shallow roasting pan and insert thermometer in center, not touching bone. Roast, uncovered, 30–35 minutes per pound for bone-in roasts, about 40 for rolled roasts or until thermometer reaches 155°–160° F. For extra juiciness and flavor, baste every 15–20 minutes with melted butter or with a 1/2 and 1/2 mixture of melted butter and dry red or white wine. Remove roast from oven and let stand 15–20 minutes before serving (it will continue cooking slightly). Serve *au jus* or with Pan Gravy.

VARIATIONS

Roast Veal with Anchovies: Do not bard. Make tiny slits over roast and insert thin garlic slivers (2 cloves should be enough). Mix minced celery, minced peeled onions, and minced carrots (2 of each) in a shallow open roasting pan and lay roast on vegetables. Drape fillets from 1 (2-ounce) can anchovies over veal and pour oil from can over all. Top with 4–5 slices bacon. Insert thermometer and roast as directed; discard bacon but reserve anchovies. Strain cooking liquid into a saucepan, pressing out as much as possible. Mash anchovies and add along with 1 tablespoon anchovy paste and 1 cup Veal (White) Stock, beef or chicken broth. Heat and serve as sauce.

Cream Roasted Veal: In a shallow open roasting pan, mix together 2 peeled and sliced onions, 2 peeled and sliced carrots, 1 cup minced parsley, and 2 minced cloves garlic. Place roast on vegetables, pour 1/2 cup heavy cream over meat, and roast as directed, basting every 1/2 hour with an additional 1/4 cup lukewarm heavy cream. When roast is done, strain pan juices and pass as gravy.

About Spit-Roasting Veal: Because of its leanness veal is a poor choice for spits and rotisseries; cooked thus, it will toughen and dry out.

Some Glazes for Roast Veal

Veal is a particularly versatile meat, so experiment with some of the glazes and flavor combinations that follow to see which appeal to your family most. About 1/2 hour before roast is done, spread or drizzle any of the following over it and continue cooking as directed, basting once or twice with pan drippings:

• 1 cup sherry, port, Madeira, dry red or white wine, or apple cider.
• 1 cup beer, ale, or stout.
• 1 cup *marinara* sauce or clam juice.
• 2 peeled and chopped medium-size yellow onions simmered 1/2 hour in 2 cups milk.
• 1/2 cup soy sauce mixed with 1/2 cup honey.
• 1/2 cup honey mixed with 1/2 cup chianti or dry vermouth.

How to Carve Veal Roasts:

Rib: See How to Carve a Standing Rib Roast.

Leg or Rump: See How to Carve Leg of Lamb.

Loin: See How to Carve a Pork Loin Roast.

ROAST VEAL STUFFED WITH WALNUTS AND MUSHROOMS

8 servings

1 (4-pound) veal leg, shoulder, or rump roast, boned but not rolled (save bones for Veal Stock)
1 teaspoon salt
1/8 teaspoon pepper
6 slices bacon

2/3 cup finely chopped yellow onion
2 cloves garlic, peeled and crushed
2 tablespoons butter or margarine
2 cups finely chopped mushrooms
3/4 cup toasted bread crumbs
1 1/2 cups toasted walnuts, chopped fine
1/4 teaspoon crumbled rosemary
1 tablespoon minced parsley
1 teaspoon salt
1/4 teaspoon pepper
2 eggs, lightly beaten

Preheat oven to 325° F. Lay veal cut side up and flatten slightly with a meat mallet; sprinkle with salt and pepper. Prepare stuffing: Sauté onion and garlic in butter over moderate heat 5–8 minutes until pale golden, add mushrooms, and sauté 3–4 minutes longer. Off heat, mix in remaining stuffing ingredients. Spread stuffing on veal almost to edges and roll; tie securely in several places and set on a rack in a shallow, open roasting pan. Cover with bacon, insert meat thermometer in center of meat, making sure it doesn't rest in stuffing. Roast, uncovered, 35–40 minutes per pound until thermometer reads 155°–160° F. Lift meat from pan, discard bacon, and let roast "rest" 15–20 minutes. Remove string and slice about 1/2" thick. Serve with Pan or Au Jus Gravy.

NPS: 505 C, 195 mg CH, 790 mg S*

VARIATIONS

Omit stuffing above and use 3 cups of any of the following stuffings: Oyster; Sage and Mushroom; Sage and Onion Dressing; or prepared stuffing mix.

NPS (with Oyster): 385 C, 170 mg CH, 750 mg S*
NPS (with Sage and Mushroom): 395 C, 160 mg CH, 610 mg S*
NPS (with Sage and Onion): 345 C, 135 mg CH, 705 mg S*
NPS (with stuffing mix): 455 C, 155 mg CH, 860 mg S*

Sauerkraut-Stuffed Veal: Season veal as directed. Mix 1 (1-pound) drained can sauerkraut with 2 sautéed minced yellow onions, 1 sautéed minced sweet green pepper, 2 cups dry white bread crumbs, 1 teaspoon salt, 1/4 teaspoon pepper, and 1 lightly beaten egg. Spread stuffing on veal and proceed as recipe directs.

NPS: 395 C, 155 mg CH, 1285 mg S*

⚖ **Neapolitan Roast Stuffed Veal:** Season veal with pepper only. Mix 1/4 cup each anchovy paste and minced parsley with 3 crushed cloves garlic, 2 tablespoons each lemon juice and minced capers, 1 tablespoon grated lemon rind, 2 teaspoons prepared mild yellow mustard, and 1/4 teaspoon pepper. Spread 1/2 mixture on veal, roll, and tie; spread remainder on top of veal, cover with bacon, and roast as directed.

NPS: 315 C, 130 mg CH, 340 mg S*

Veal Roast Stuffed with Ham: Sprinkle veal with pepper only, spread with 1 cup deviled ham or 2 cups ground ham mixed with 1/3 cup heavy cream; lay 6–8 bacon slices lengthwise over filling, then roll, tie, and roast as directed, basting frequently during last 1/2 hour with chianti.

NPS: 480 C, 200 mg CH, 775 mg S*

BRAISED VEAL ROAST WITH VEGETABLE GRAVY

8 servings

1 (4–5-pound) boned and rolled veal shoulder or rump (save bones for Veal Stock)
2 tablespoons cooking oil
2 large yellow onions, peeled and coarsely chopped
1–2 cloves garlic, peeled and crushed
1 carrot, peeled and chopped fine
1 stalk celery, chopped fine
1 bay leaf and 1 sprig each parsley and thyme, tied in cheesecloth (*bouquet garni*)
2 teaspoons salt
1/4 teaspoon pepper
1/3 cup cold water
1/4 cup unsifted flour
3 cups Veal Stock or a 1/2 and 1/2 mixture of beef and chicken broths
1–2 teaspoons liquid gravy browner (optional)

Brown veal well in oil in a heavy kettle over moderate heat; add all but last 3 ingredients, cover, and simmer about 2 1/2 hours until tender, turning meat once. If pot cooks dry before veal is done, add 2–3 tablespoons cold water. Transfer veal to platter and keep warm. Discard *bouquet garni;* purée vegetables and any remaining kettle liquid by buzzing 20–30 seconds in an electric blender at low speed or 15–20 seconds in a food processor fitted with the metal chopping blade. Blend flour with 1 cup stock. Add remaining stock and purée to kettle and bring to a boil. Stir in flour paste and cook, stirring, until thickened. Cover and simmer 2–3 minutes; taste for seasoning and adjust. For a darker gravy, add browner. Slice roast about 1/4" thick and serve with plenty of gravy.

NPS: 465 C, 160 mg CH, 930 mg S*

Oven Pot Roast:

Electric Skillet Pot Roast:

Follow variations under Pot Roast in the Beef section.

Pressure Cooker Pot Roast: Brown veal and onion in oil in open pressure cooker; add all but last 3 ingredients, seal cooker, bring pressure to 10 pounds, and cook 10 minutes per pound. Reduce pressure, open cooker, remove veal and keep warm. Prepare gravy in open cooker using basic method above. All cooking methods above: nutritional count same as basic recipe.

Herbed Veal Pot Roast with Wine Gravy: Add 1 teaspoon oregano, basil, marjoram, or thyme along with other seasonings. Simmer roast in 1/3 cup dry red or white wine instead of water. For gravy, use 1 1/2 cups of the same wine and 1 1/2 cups stock.

NPS: 470 C, 160 mg CH, 825 mg S*

Veal Pot Roast with Vegetables: Prepare roast as directed; about 45 minutes before it is done, add 1/2 cup additional stock and any or a combination of the following: 16 small white onions and new potatoes, both peeled; 1 small peeled rutabaga cut in 1 1/2" cubes; 8 peeled parsnips, small whole turnips or leeks, 24 peeled whole baby carrots. Season vegetables with 1 teaspoon salt, cover, and simmer until meat and vegetables are tender. Prepare gravy as directed. Wreathe vegetables around meat and serve.

NPS: 505 C, 160 mg CH, 965 mg S*

Veal Pot Roast with Wine and Olives: Follow basic recipe but simmer roast on a trivet with 1/3 cup dry red wine instead of water. When making gravy, strain vegetables from cooking liquid; use 1 cup each dry red wine and stock and omit flour. Stir in 1/2 cup chopped pitted ripe olives, heat about 5 minutes, and serve.

NPS: 460 C, 160 mg CH, 845 mg S*

VEAL SHOULDER BRAISED WITH ROSEMARY AND VERMOUTH

6 servings

Once you've browned the meat and onions, you need only keep half an eye on the pot. This recipe literally cooks itself.

1 (3 1/2-pound) boned and rolled veal shoulder roast
1/2 teaspoon salt
1/4 teaspoon pepper

2 tablespoons flour
1/4 cup cooking oil
4 medium-size yellow onions, peeled and cut in thin wedges
1 clove garlic, peeled and crushed
1/4 teaspoon summer savory
1 (4") sprig fresh rosemary or 1/4 teaspoon crushed dried rosemary
1 (4") sprig fresh thyme or a pinch dried thyme
1 cup dry white vermouth
1 1/2 cups water

Rub veal well with salt, pepper, and flour and brown well on all sides in oil in a large, heavy kettle over moderately high heat. Reduce heat to moderate, add onions and garlic, and stir-fry 8–10 minutes until golden. Add remaining ingredients, cover, and simmer slowly about 2 hours until tender, turning veal about every hour. To serve, carve into slices about 1/4" thick and top with the juices, which will have cooked down into a rich brown gravy.

NPS: 585 C, 190 mg CH, 370 mg S*

BREAST OF VEAL STUFFED WITH SPINACH AND ZUCCHINI SOUFFLÉ

6 servings ¢

A pretty party dish that doesn't cost the earth.

4 1/2–5 pounds breast of veal, trimmed of fat but not boned
1 (10-ounce) package frozen chopped spinach
1/2 pound zucchini, scrubbed and coarsely grated
1 small yellow onion, peeled and minced
1 small clove garlic, peeled and minced
1/4 pound mushrooms, wiped clean and minced
2 tablespoons olive or cooking oil
1 tablespoon butter or margarine
1 teaspoon salt
1/4 teaspoon pepper
1 cup soft white bread crumbs
2 egg whites, beaten to soft peaks
2 cups beef broth

Preheat oven to 350° F. With a very sharp knife, cut lengthwise between bones and meat to form a long deep pocket; do not cut through meat at sides. Cook spinach by package directions until frozen block can be broken up; add zucchini, cover and cook 5 minutes; dump into a large sieve and press very dry; return to pan and set, uncovered, over lowest heat. In a skillet set over moderate heat, sauté onion, garlic, and mushrooms in 1 tablespoon oil and the butter 5–8 minutes until limp. Purée with spinach mixture by buzzing 20–30 seconds in an electric blender at high speed or in a food processor fitted with the metal chopping blade. Transfer mixture to a bowl, mix in salt, pepper, and bread crumbs; fold in egg whites. Spoon mixture into veal pocket and skewer or sew shut. Place veal on a rack in a shallow roasting pan, brush with remaining tablespoon oil, and braise, uncovered, 1 hour. Add 1/2 cup broth and braise about 30 minutes, basting often, until meat thermometer reaches 160°–165° F. *(Note:* Be sure thermometer tip is in meat, not stuffing.) Remove veal to a heated platter and keep warm. Drain fat from pan, set over 2 moderately hot burners, add remaining broth and bring to a boil, scraping up browned bits on bottom of pan. To carve the veal, simply cut down between ribs into "chops" (you'll need a large, sharp knife to sever any cartilage). Pass pan gravy separately.

NPS: 675 C, 190 mg CH, 815 mg S*

BRAISED STUFFED BREAST OF VEAL WITH RED CURRANT GRAVY

6 servings ⚖

3–4 pounds breast of veal, boned but not rolled (use bones for Veal Stock)
1 small clove garlic, peeled and crushed
1/4 teaspoon pepper
1/4 cup bacon or beef drippings
1 1/2 cups Veal Stock or 3/4 cup each beef broth and water

S T U F F I N G
1 1/2 cups soft white bread crumbs
1 medium-size yellow onion, peeled and minced
1 teaspoon summer savory
1 teaspoon sage
1 tablespoon minced parsley
1 teaspoon salt
1/4 teaspoon pepper
1 teaspoon celery seeds
1 egg, lightly beaten

G R A V Y
1/4 cup unsifted flour blended with 1/2 cup cold Veal Stock
Veal cooking liquid
1/4 cup red currant jelly

Rub veal inside and out with garlic and pepper. Mix stuffing and spread on cut side of veal almost to edges; roll and tie securely in several places. Brown veal all over in drippings in a heavy kettle over moderate heat. Place a rack under meat, add stock, cover, and simmer about 2 hours until tender. Lift meat to platter and let "rest" while you make the gravy. Blend flour paste into cooking liquid and heat, stirring, until thickened. Smooth in jelly, taste for salt and pepper and

adjust. Remove strings from veal, slice 1/4"–1/2" thick, and top with some of the gravy. Pass the rest.

NPS: 590 C, 180 mg CH, 785 mg S*

V A R I A T I O N

⚖ **Braised Stuffed Breast of Veal with Vegetable Gravy:** Stuff, roll, and tie veal as directed. Brown 2 minced, peeled carrots and 2 minced, peeled small yellow onions in drippings before browning veal; add veal and brown, then proceed as directed. When making gravy, purée vegetables and cooking liquid by buzzing 20–30 seconds in an electric blender at low speed or 15–20 seconds in a food processor fitted with the metal chopping blade; return to kettle, thicken with flour paste as directed but omit jelly.

NPS: 570 C, 180 mg CH, 790 mg S*

VITELLO TONNATO (COLD ROAST VEAL IN TUNA-MAYONNAISE SAUCE)

6–8 servings

Perfect for a summer luncheon, especially with slices of full-flavored, vine-ripened tomatoes and a well-chilled dry Italian white wine.

1 (3-pound) boned and rolled veal rump roast
2 tablespoons olive oil
2 medium-size yellow onions, peeled and sliced thin
2 stalks celery, sliced thin
1 carrot, peeled and sliced thin
2 cloves garlic, peeled and quartered
3 large sprigs parsley
1 (4") sprig fresh thyme or 1/2 teaspoon dried thyme
1 (2-ounce) can anchovy fillets, drained
1 (7-ounce) can white meat tuna, drained and flaked
3/4 cup dry vermouth
1 teaspoon salt
1/4 teaspoon pepper

T U N A - M A Y O N N A I S E   S A U C E
2 cups puréed kettle mixture
Juice of 1 lemon
1 cup mayonnaise (about)

G A R N I S H E S
2 tablespoons drained capers
2 tablespoons minced parsley
Lemon wedges

Lightly brown roast in oil in a heavy kettle over moderately high heat; add remaining ingredients (except sauce and garnishes), cover, and simmer slowly 2 hours, turning veal after 1 hour. Lift veal to a large bowl; purée kettle mixture a little at a time, by buzzing 20–30 seconds in an electric blender at low speed or 15–20 seconds in a food processor fitted with the metal chopping blade. Pour over veal, cover, and chill 24 hours, turning veal occasionally. Lift veal from purée and wipe off excess. Measure 2 cups purée and blend with lemon juice and enough mayonnaise to give it the consistency of thin cream sauce. *(Note:* Remaining purée can be used as the liquid ingredient in tuna or salmon loaves.) Slice veal about 1/4" thick, arrange, overlapping, on a large platter, spooning a little sauce over each slice; re-cover and marinate several hours in refrigerator. Just before serving, ladle a little more sauce over all, sprinkle with capers and minced parsley. Set out lemon wedges and pass remaining sauce.

NPS: (6–8): 800–600 C, 195–145 mg CH, 1025–770 mg S*

For a Milder, Less Rich Sauce: Cook veal as directed; *strain* kettle liquid, then boil, uncovered, until reduced to about 1 1/2 cups. Pour over veal, cover, and marinate as directed. Lift veal from marinade and slice; combine marinade with mayonnaise and lemon as above, spoon over veal, proceed and serve as directed.

NPS (6–8): 670–500 C, 150–115 mg CH, 920–690 mg S*

Some Ways to Use Up Leftover Roast Veal

Veal Balls in Lemon Broth *(4 servings):* Mix together 1 1/2 cups finely ground leftover veal, 1/2 cup fine soft white bread crumbs, 1 egg, 1 minced scallion, 2 tablespoons heavy cream, 1 teaspoon each anchovy paste and minced parsley, 1/4 teaspoon salt, and a pinch pepper; shape into 1/2" balls. Bring 3 1/2–4 cups chicken broth to a simmer, stir in the juice of 1/2 lemon, then add veal balls. Cover and simmer 25 minutes. Sprinkle with 1 tablespoon minced parsley and serve in soup bowls.

NPS: 230 C, 135 mg CH, 950 mg S*

Veal-Tuna Salad *(4 servings):* Mix 1 cup finely diced leftover veal with 1 (7-ounce) drained can tuna, 1 minced yellow onion, 1 tablespoon each capers, minced fresh parsley and dill, the juice of 1/2 lemon, and 1/3–1/2 cup mayonnaise (just enough for good consistency). Serve in lettuce cups or use as a sandwich spread.

NPS: 295 C, 55 mg CH, 350 mg S*

Veal-Mushroom Ramekins *(4 servings):* Stir-fry 1/2 cup minced mushrooms and 2 tablespoons minced shallots in 1 tablespoon butter 5 minutes; mix with 1 1/2 cups finely ground leftover veal, 1/2 cup heavy cream, 1/4 teaspoon dillweed, and a pinch each pepper and nutmeg. Fold in 4 egg whites beaten with 1/4 teaspoon salt until soft peaks form. Spoon into 4 buttered custard cups and top with 2 tablespoons cracker meal mixed with 1 1/2 teaspoons each melted butter and grated Parmesan. Set in a shallow baking pan, pour 1 1/2 cups hot water around cups, and bake, uncovered, 1/2 hour at 350° F. Brown quickly under broiler, if you like, and serve.

NPS: 335 C, 115 mg CH, 320 mg S*

Quick Veal Paprika:

Veal and Vegetable Pie:

Veal Stuffed Vegetables:

Roast Veal Hash:

Veal Curry:

Follow recipes given in Some Additional Ways to Use Up Leftover Roast Beef, substituting veal for beef.

Sliced Cold Veal: Slice veal about 1/4" thick and top with Anchovy Mayonnaise, Aioli Sauce, or Cumberland Sauce.

Sliced Hot Veal: Slice veal about 1/4" thick and layer into a shallow greased casserole. Add just enough Light Curry, Parsley, Portugaise, Soubise, or Tomato Sauce or gravy to cover, cover with foil, and heat 20 minutes at 350° F. Or heat veal slices in sauce about 5 minutes in a covered skillet over moderately low heat.

Hot Roast Veal Sandwiches: Heat veal slices in a suitable sauce or gravy in a skillet as for Sliced Hot Veal (above). Serve open face on toast, buns, or bread.

To Make the Most of Very Small Amounts: See suggestions given for beef.

VEAL STEAKS AND CHOPS

If you think of these simply as slices of the veal roasts described earlier, you won't have much difficulty keeping them straight. An arm steak, for example, is a slice of arm roast, a rib chop a slice of the rib, a sirloin a slice of the sirloin, and so on. The smaller cuts, logically, are the chops, the larger ones steaks. (Refer to Veal Chart.) The most popular are:
• Blade steak

- Arm steak
- Rib chops (plain and Frenched)
- Loin chops (plain, kidney, noisettes, or medallions)
- Sirloin steak
- Round steak (sometimes called cutlet)
- Cube steak
- Frozen veal steaks (plain or breaded)

How to Cook

Amount Needed: Rib and loin chops are best cut about 1″ thick; other steaks and chops range from 1/2″ to 1″. Allow 1–2 rib or loin chops per person, 1 cube or frozen veal steak. Steaks will generally serve 2 and sometimes as many as 4, depending on how thick they're cut. Allow about 1/2–3/4 pound bone-in chop or steak per person, 1/3–1/2 pound boneless.

General Preparation for Cooking: If meat seems moist, wipe with a damp cloth so it will brown well. Sprinkle with pepper but not salt (it prevents browning) and for extra savor, rub with a cut clove garlic and/or compatible herb such as sage, thyme, or marjoram. Let chops or steaks stand at room temperature 1 1/2–2 hours before cooking if convenient.

Cooking Methods Not Recommended: Broiling, panbroiling, charcoal broiling. Veal chops and steaks are too lean to cook without some fat and/or liquid; moreover, they shrivel, toughen, and dry under intense broiler heat.

To Panfry (Sauté): Best for chops and steaks cut 1/2″–3/4″ thick, also for cube and frozen veal steaks. Heat 1–2 tablespoons butter, drippings, or cooking oil in a large, heavy skillet over moderately high heat about 1/2 minute, add chops or steaks and brown well on both sides, turning frequently. Cube and frozen steaks will need only 3–5 minutes altogether; 1/2″–3/4″ steaks and chops will take 20–30 minutes and, once browned, should finish cooking over fairly low heat. Do not cover and do not add liquid.

VARIATIONS

Dredged Chops or Steaks: Dip meat in seasoned flour (about 1/3 cup unsifted flour, 1 teaspoon salt, and 1/4 teaspoon pepper), then cook as directed.

Herbed Chops or Steaks: Dip meat in 1/3 cup unsifted flour mixed with 1 teaspoon each salt and a compatible herb such as sage, marjoram, rosemary, or thyme and 1/4 teaspoon pepper. Cook as directed.

Hungarian-Style Chops or Steaks: Dip meat in 1/3 cup unsifted flour mixed with 2 tablespoons paprika, 1 teaspoon salt, and a pinch pepper. Cook as directed.

Breaded Chops or Steaks: Sprinkle both sides of meat lightly with salt and pepper, dip in 1/3 cup unsifted flour, then in 1 egg lightly beaten with 1 tablespoon cold water, finally in 1 cup fine dry bread crumbs (for extra flavor, use seasoned crumbs). To make breading stick, let breaded chops dry on a cake rack 15 minutes before browning. Cook as directed, doubling amount of butter used. Drain well on paper toweling before serving.

To Braise: Here's the very best way to cook veal chops and steaks because it allows them to cook through and at the same time remain juicily tender. Brown chops or steaks 3–4 minutes on a side over moderately high heat in 1 tablespoon butter, drippings, or cooking oil; add about 1/2 cup water to skillet, cover and simmer slowly over low heat or in a preheated 350° F. oven until cooked through. Chops will take 30–45 minutes, depending on thickness; steaks 50–60. *(Note:* Cube or frozen veal steaks will need only 10–15 minutes in all, noisettes about 20.)

For Extra Savor: Substitute any of the following for water called for above: medium-dry white or red wine, sherry, Madeira, dry vermouth, or apple cider; tomatoes (or juice or sauce); orange, apple, or mixed fruit juices; milk, buttermilk, or light cream; barbecue or meatless spaghetti sauce; chicken or beef broth.

Some Variations on Braised Veal Chops and Steaks
(All quantities based on enough chops or steaks for 4 persons)

⚖ **Flambéed with Endives:** Brown meat as directed and pour off drippings; season, add 1/4 cup cognac, and flame, spooning liquid over chops. Add 1/3 cup beef broth, 4 small whole endives, and 1/2 minced clove garlic. Cover and simmer as directed. Transfer meat and endives to a platter, add 1/4 cup heavy cream to skillet, and simmer 1–2 minutes, stirring. Pour over meat and serve.

NPS: 485 C, 150 mg CH, 750 mg S*

Budapest-Style: Brown meat as directed, season, and add 1/2 cup chicken broth. Top each chop with 1 sweet green pepper ring and 1 whole split, seeded pimiento (steaks should be completely covered with pepper and pimiento). Cover and simmer as directed. Transfer to platter and keep warm. To skillet add 2 tablespoons grated onion, 1/2 cup heavy cream, and 1/4 cup milk and simmer 2–3 minutes. Blend 1 tablespoon flour with 1/4 cup milk, add to skillet, and cook, stirring, until slightly thickened. Season to taste, pour over chops, and serve.

En Casserole: Sauté together 2 slices minced bacon, 1 minced medium-size yellow onion, and 1 diced carrot over moderate heat 5 minutes until onion is pale golden; transfer all to an ungreased 1 1/2-quart casserole. Brown meat as directed and add to casserole. Sprinkle all lightly with salt and pepper, add 1 bay leaf and 1 sprig each parsley and thyme, and 1/2 cup dry white wine. Cover and oven-simmer as directed. Uncover during last 15 minutes so juices will cook down. If you like, add 6–8 peeled small white onions or new potatoes before baking.

NPS: 575 C, 170 mg CH, 310 mg S*

⚖️ **Dijonnaise:** Brown meat as directed but do not pour off drippings. Season chops and top with 1/4 cup minced shallots or scallions and 2 tablespoons minced parsley. Add 1/2 cup beef broth, cover, and simmer as directed. Transfer meat to a platter and keep warm. To skillet add 1/4 cup beef broth and 1 tablespoon Dijon mustard. Heat and stir 1–2 minutes, pour over meat, and serve.

NPS: 315 C, 115 mg CH, 390 mg S*

Lyonnaise: Brown meat as directed, lift out, and set aside. In drippings sauté 3 thinly sliced large yellow onions 8–10 minutes until golden. Return meat to pan, season, and pile some onions on top. Add 1/3 cup chicken broth and 1 tablespoon vinegar. Cover and simmer as directed. Sprinkle with minced parsley and serve.

NPS: 350 C, 115 mg CH, 205 mg S*

À la Crème: Brown meat as directed, season, then drain off drippings. Add 1/2 cup dry white wine, Madeira, or dry sherry, cover, and simmer as directed. Transfer meat to a platter and keep warm. Quickly boil down skillet liquid to 1/4 cup, mix in 1 cup light cream and 1/2 cup Velouté or Medium White Sauce, a dash of nutmeg, and 1 teaspoon lemon juice; simmer (but do not boil) 2–3 minutes. Spoon some sauce over meat and pass the rest. If you like, scatter minced truffles, toasted slivered almonds, or minced scallions or chives over meat and add a blush of paprika.

NPS: 440 C, 160 mg CH, 310 mg S*

Chasseur (Hunter's Style): Brown meat as directed, lift out, and set aside. In pan drippings sauté 6 minced shallots or scallions and 1/2 pound sliced mushrooms 4–5 minutes until golden. Return meat to pan, season, add 1/2 cup dry white wine, cover, and simmer as directed. Transfer meat to platter and keep warm. To pan liquid, add 1 cup beef gravy, 1 tablespoon tomato paste, and 2 teaspoons each minced chervil and tarragon. Quickly bring to a boil, spoon some sauce over meat, and pass the rest.

NPS: 360 C, 115 mg CH, 205 mg S*

À la Bourguignonne: Brown meat as directed, lift out, and set aside. Drain off drippings; add 2 slices bacon to skillet, brown, remove, and crumble. In drippings sauté 1/2 pound thinly sliced mushrooms 4–5 minutes until golden; return meat and bacon to pan, season lightly, add 2/3 cup red Burgundy wine and 1 pound Pan-Braised Onions. Cover and simmer as directed. Transfer meat and vegetables to a deep dish. Thicken pan liquid with 1 tablespoon *beurre manié.** Spoon some gravy over meat and pass the rest.

NPS: 465 C, 140 mg CH, 265 mg S*

SAGE-SCENTED VEAL CHOPS STUFFED WITH PROSCIUTTO

4 servings

4 veal rib chops, cut 1 1/2" thick
4 paper-thin slices *prosciutto*
4 thin slices Gruyère cheese about 1 1/2" wide and 2" long
1 clove garlic, peeled and halved
2 tablespoons butter or margarine
2 bay leaves
4 (4") sprigs fresh sage or 1 teaspoon dried leaf sage tied in cheesecloth
1/2 cup dry white wine
1/4 teaspoon salt
Pinch pepper

Cutting from the curved outer edge, make a deep pocket in each veal chop. Flatten out each slice of *prosciutto,* top with a slice of Gruyère and wrap envelope style. Insert a *prosciutto*-Gruyère package in each veal pocket and close with toothpicks. Rub both sides of chops with garlic, then brown in butter in a large, heavy skillet over moderately high heat 2–3 minutes on each side. Add bay leaves, top each chop with a sage sprig (or drop cheesecloth bag of dried sage into skillet), pour in wine, cover, and simmer slowly 45–50 minutes until chops are just cooked through. Remove sage, bay leaves, and toothpicks, sprinkle chops with salt and pepper, and serve with some of the pan drippings spooned over each portion.

NPS: 440 C, 140 mg CH, 450 mg S*

HOTEL OASIS VEAL CHOPS

4 servings

These Roquefort-flavored chops were a specialty of the Hotel Oasis near Palma, Majorca.

4 loin veal chops, cut 3/4″ thick
1/2 cup homemade French Dressing
1 tablespoon finely grated lemon rind
1 tablespoon crumbled Roquefort cheese
1/4 cup unsifted flour
1 egg, lightly beaten with 2 tablespoons milk
3/4 cup fine toasted bread crumbs
3 tablespoons olive or other cooking oil

If chops have long, thin "tails," curl around thick portions and secure with toothpicks. Mix French dressing, lemon rind, and Roquefort, mashing cheese well; pour into a shallow enamel pan or glass baking dish, add chops and arrange in a single layer. Cover and chill 6–8 hours, turning chops in marinade one or two times. Dip chops in flour, then in egg, then in crumbs to coat evenly. Sauté in oil in a large heavy skillet 15–20 minutes on each side over moderately low heat. Drain on paper toweling and serve.

NPS: 655 C, 180 mg CH, 335 mg S*

VEAL CUTLETS (SCALLOPS)
(Refer to Veal Chart)

What the Italians call *scaloppine,* the Germans *Schnitzel,* the French *escalopes de veau,* and the English *collops* are veal cutlets or scallops to us—small, thin, boneless slices, usually from the veal leg but sometimes from the loin or rib. The choicest are those from the top round. All cutlets should be cut across the grain and slightly on the diagonal, always very thin—1/4″–3/8″—and trimmed of any filament and fat.

Usually they are pounded to between 1/8″ and 1/4″ thick (recipes here specify whether to pound or not). Most butchers will do the pounding, but, if not, you can easily do it yourself. Simply slip cutlet between two sheets of wax paper and flatten with a cutlet bat, rolling pin, or the side of a meat cleaver. Three or four resounding whacks per side per cutlet should do the job.

Though there are dozens of ways to prepare cutlets, almost all are variations on two basic cooking methods: *panfrying* (or *sautéing*) and *braising* (browning in fat, then finishing in a small amount of liquid or sauce). If you've never cooked cutlets before, don't attempt more than 4 or 6 at a time. Use as

quick and light a hand as possible and rush the cutlets to the table the instant they're done.

ESCALOPES DE VEAU À LA ZINGARA (SAUTÉED VEAL CUTLETS WITH TONGUE, HAM, AND MUSHROOMS)

4 servings

1 1/2 pounds veal round, sliced 1/4″ thick and
   pounded thin as for scaloppine
1 teaspoon salt
1/4 teaspoon pepper
1/2 cup unsifted flour
5 tablespoons butter or margarine
1/2 cup Madeira wine
3/4 cup Rich Brown Sauce (Demi-Glace)
1 tablespoon tomato paste
1/3 cup julienne strips of cooked smoked tongue
1/3 cup julienne strips of cooked ham
1/3 cup julienne strips of mushrooms
1 truffle, cut in fine julienne

Sprinkle both sides of cutlets with salt and pepper, then dredge in flour. Heat 3 tablespoons butter in a large, heavy skillet over moderately high heat until a bread cube will sizzle, and brown cutlets, a few at a time, 3–4 minutes on a side, using tongs to turn. Drain on paper toweling and keep warm at back of stove. Add Madeira to skillet and simmer, stirring to get up browned bits, until reduced by half. Blend in Rich Brown Sauce and tomato paste and simmer, stirring occasionally, until thickened and the consistency of gravy. Meanwhile, in a separate skillet, sauté tongue, ham, mushrooms, and truffle in remaining butter 2–3 minutes. Add to sauce and warm 1–2 minutes. To serve, place cutlets on a hot platter and top each with a heaping spoonful of the skillet mixture.

NPS: 640 C, 190 mg CH, 1400 mg S*

PICCATA (ITALIAN-STYLE SAUTÉED VEAL SCALLOPS)

2 servings   ☒

3/4 pound veal round, sliced 1/4″ thick and
   pounded thin as for scaloppine
3/4 teaspoon salt
1/8 teaspoon pepper
1/3 cup unsifted flour
1 tablespoon olive oil
1 tablespoon butter
2 tablespoons lemon juice
2 teaspoons minced parsley

Sprinkle both sides of veal with salt and pepper, and cut in pieces about 3″ square. Dredge veal squares in flour, shaking off excess so they're lightly dusted. Heat oil and butter in a heavy skillet over moderately high heat about 1 minute, add veal, and brown 1–2 minutes on a side; drain on paper toweling. Add lemon juice and parsley to skillet and stir quickly to get up browned bits. Return veal, warm 1–2 minutes, basting with lemon-parsley mixture, and serve.

*NPS: 470 C, 135 mg CH, 1000 mg S**

SCALOPPINE ALLA FRANCESE

4 servings ☒

1½ pounds veal round, sliced ¼″ thick and
   pounded thin as for scaloppine
1½ teaspoons salt
¼ teaspoon pepper
4 tablespoons clarified butter*
4 tablespoons olive oil
⅓ cup unsifted flour
2 eggs lightly beaten with 2 tablespoons cold
   water
2 tablespoons butter
2 tablespoons lemon juice
8 thin slices lemon (garnish)

Preheat oven to 400° F. Sprinkle both sides of cutlets with salt and pepper. Begin heating 2 tablespoons each clarified butter and oil in a large heavy skillet over moderately high heat. Dredge each cutlet well in flour, shaking off excess. When a bread cube will sizzle in skillet, begin cooking cutlets: Dip a dredged cutlet in egg to coat evenly (keep egg near skillet), then lay cutlet carefully in fat. Repeat with 3 or 4 more cutlets, allowing plenty of space between them in skillet. Brown 1–2 minutes per side; drain on paper toweling. If batter sticks to skillet, scrape up before proceeding. Dip, cook, and drain remaining cutlets the same way in remaining clarified butter and oil; arrange, not overlapping, in a shallow roasting pan and bake, uncovered, 6–7 minutes. Meanwhile, heat butter in a small skillet over moderate heat until foamy and nut brown; *do not burn.* Off heat, add lemon juice and keep warm. Arrange cutlets on heated platter, drizzle with lemon butter, garnish with lemon slices, and serve at once.

*NPS: 640 C, 305 mg CH, 1035 mg S**

WIENER SCHNITZEL (BREADED VEAL CUTLETS)

4 servings

The Viennese say a *Wiener Schnitzel* is perfect if the crust is crisp, amber brown, and puffed here and there so that you can slip a knife between it and the cutlet. Here's the trick: Bread each cutlet *just* before cooking, drop into hot (but not smoking) fat, and brown, turning one time only. *Do not* dry the breaded cutlets 15–20 minutes on a rack before cooking (the breading will stick fast and refuse to puff). Cook only as many cutlets at a time as you need and serve at once.

1½ pounds veal round, sliced ¼″ thick and
   pounded thin as for scaloppine
2 teaspoons salt (about)
¼ teaspoon pepper (about)
⅓ cup clarified butter*
⅓ cup lard
½ cup unsifted flour
2 eggs, beaten until frothy
1 cup fine dry bread crumbs
Lemon wedges (garnish)

Sprinkle both sides of cutlets with salt and pepper. If they seem too large to handle easily or to fit in your skillet, halve them (the Viennese like whopping schnitzels that hang over the edges of their plates, but if you're an inexperienced schnitzel cook, it's better to work with smaller pieces). Begin heating butter and lard in a very large, heavy skillet over moderately high heat. Dip cutlets in flour, then eggs and crumbs, each time shaking off excess (they should have a thin, even, all-over crumb coating). To test fat temperature, drop in a cube of bread; when fat bubbles vigorously about it, carefully add cutlets, allowing plenty of space between them. Brown on one side, 3–4 minutes, turn with tongs, and brown other side. Drain well on paper toweling and serve at once with lemon wedges. Bread and brown seconds as people ask for them.

*NPS: 662 C, 310 mg CH, 1400 mg S**

VARIATIONS

Schnitzel à la Holstein: Prepare Wiener Schnitzel as directed. Top each cutlet with a fried egg, drape 2 anchovy fillets over egg in an X-pattern, and sprinkle, if you like, with drained capers.

*NPS: 760 C, 560 mg CH, 1610 mg S**

Cheese Schnitzel: Season cutlets, dredge in flour, dip in egg, then in crumbs mixed with

1 tablespoon finely grated Parmesan cheese. Brown as directed and serve with lemon.

NPS: 670 C, 310 mg CH, 1420 mg S*

Sardellenschnitzel (Anchovy Schnitzel): Season cutlets with pepper but not salt, then spread each thinly with Anchovy Butter, leaving 1/4″ margins all round. Fold cutlets over, secure with toothpicks, bread and brown as for Wiener Schnitzel. Remove toothpicks and serve with lemon.

NPS: 825 C, 370 mg CH, 580 mg S*

Schnitzel Cordon Bleu: Season cutlets with pepper and a very little salt. Cut small pieces of thinly sliced Swiss cheese and Westphalian ham or *prosciutto* so they're about 1/2 the size of cutlets. Lay 1 slice ham on 1/2 of each cutlet, top with cheese, then fold cutlet over and pound one or two times between wax paper to seal. Bread and brown as for Wiener Schnitzel and serve with lemon.

NPS: 720 C, 325 mg CH, 620 mg S*

☒ **Naturschnitzel (Plain Schnitzel):** Season cutlets, dredge in flour, but do not dip in egg or crumbs. Brown as directed in 3–4 tablespoons clarified butter* and serve with lemon.

NPS: 345 C, 145 mg CH, 1180 mg S*

☒ **Rahmschnitzel (Cream Schnitzel):** Season cutlets, cut in strips 2″–3″ × 11/2″, and dredge in flour only. Brown in 3–4 tablespoons clarified butter,* remove from skillet, and drain on paper toweling. Pour off drippings; add 1 cup beef consommé to skillet and boil rapidly, stirring to scrape up browned bits, until reduced by half. Add 1 cup light cream and boil, uncovered, stirring, until reduced by half. Turn heat to low, return veal to skillet, warm 2–3 minutes, stirring, and serve.

NPS: 515 C, 175 mg CH, 1400 mg S*

☒ **Paprika Schnitzel:** Season cutlets and sprinkle both sides well with paprika. Cut into strips and proceed as for Rahmschnitzel. Just before returning veal to skillet, swirl in 2 tablespoons sour cream. Add veal, warm 2–3 minutes (but do not boil), stirring occasionally.

NPS: 535 C, 180 mg CH, 1405 mg S*

VEAL SCALOPPINE ALLA MARSALA

4–6 servings ☒

2 pounds veal round, sliced 1/4″ thick and pounded thin as for scaloppine
1/2 teaspoon salt
1/8 teaspoon pepper

3 tablespoons butter or margarine
3 tablespoons beef consommé
1/3 cup Marsala wine

Sprinkle veal with salt and pepper and let stand at room temperature 10–15 minutes. Brown a few pieces at a time, 2–3 minutes on a side, in butter in a large, heavy skillet over moderately high heat; remove to a heated platter and keep warm. Add consommé and wine to skillet and boil, uncovered, 1–2 minutes, stirring to get up browned bits. Pour over scaloppine and serve.

NPS (4–6): 455–300 C, 185–120 mg CH, 545–365 mg S*

V A R I A T I O N S

☒ **Veal Scaloppine with Parsley and Prosciutto:** Dredge in flour and brown scaloppine and set aside. In drippings, stir-fry 1/4 cup finely slivered *prosciutto;* spoon over scaloppine. Add parsley, lemon juice, consommé, and wine to skillet, boil, uncovered, pour over scaloppine and serve.

NPS (4–6): 500–335 C, 190–125 mg CH, 685–455 mg S*

☒ **Veal Scaloppine with Mushrooms:** Lightly brown 1/2 pound thinly sliced mushrooms in 2 tablespoons butter; remove from heat and set aside. Prepare Scaloppine alla Marsala as directed. Just before serving, add mushrooms to wine in skillet, warm 1–2 minutes, pour over scaloppine, and serve.

NPS (4–6): 520–345 C, 200–135 mg CH, 615–410 mg S*

VEAL PARMIGIANA

4 servings

1/2 cup fine toasted bread crumbs
1/4 cup finely grated Parmesan cheese
11/4 teaspoons salt
1/8 teaspoon pepper
1 pound veal round, sliced 1/4″ thick and pounded thin as for scaloppine
1 egg, lightly beaten
1/3 cup olive oil
2 cups Italian Tomato Sauce or 1 (151/2-ounce) jar meatless spaghetti sauce
1/2 pound mozzarella cheese, coarsely grated

Preheat oven to 375° F. Mix crumbs, Parmesan, salt, and pepper. Dip veal in egg, then in crumbs to coat evenly (pat crumbs onto veal so they stick firmly). Arrange veal on a wire rack and let dry 10–12 minutes so coating will adhere during cooking. Heat oil in a large, heavy skillet over moderately high heat about 1 minute, add half of veal, and brown 1–1½ minutes on a side; drain on paper toweling. Brown remaining veal the same way. Arrange veal in a single layer in an ungreased shallow 2-quart casserole or *au gratin* pan, top with sauce and mozzarella. Bake, uncovered, ½ hour until cheese melts and sauce is bubbly. Serve with a crisp romaine salad, chunks of hot garlic bread, and chianti.

*NPS: 465 C, 195 mg CH, 2000 mg S**

SALTIMBOCCA

4–6 servings

Prosciutto is very salty, making additional salt in the recipe unnecessary.

2 pounds veal round, sliced ¼″ thick and pounded thin as for scaloppine
¼ pound *prosciutto*, sliced paper thin
2 tablespoons minced fresh sage or 1 teaspoon dried sage
⅛ teaspoon pepper
3–4 tablespoons butter or margarine
¼ cup dry white wine

Veal slices should be about 4″ × 4″; if extra long, halve crosswise. Trim *prosciutto* slices so they're roughly the same size. Sprinkle one side of each veal slice with sage and pepper; top with *prosciutto* slice and toothpick in place. Melt butter in a large skillet over moderately high heat and brown veal quickly on both sides. Transfer to a heated platter, remove toothpicks, and keep warm. Add wine to skillet, let boil, uncovered, 1–2 minutes, scraping with a wooden spoon to get up any brown bits; pour over veal and serve.

*NPS (4–6): 500–335 C, 200–135 mg CH, 670–445 mg S**

BOCCONCINI (ITALIAN BRAISED VEAL AND CHEESE)

4 servings

1½ pounds veal round, sliced ¼″ thick and pounded thin as for scaloppine
½ pound Swiss cheese
½ teaspoon minced fresh sage or ¼ teaspoon dried sage
⅛ teaspoon pepper
2 tablespoons butter or margarine
¼ cup dry white wine
1 tablespoon lemon juice
½ teaspoon salt

Halve veal slices lengthwise; cut thin strips of cheese about ½″ smaller all round than

veal, lay 1 strip on each veal slice, roll jelly-roll style, and secure with toothpicks. Place rolls in a piepan, sprinkle with sage and pepper, cover, and chill several hours. Melt butter in a large, heavy skillet over moderate heat, add veal rolls, and brown well on all sides, about 5–10 minutes. Add remaining ingredients, cover, and simmer 18–20 minutes until veal is tender. Serve with a generous ladling of pan juices.

*NPS: 545 C, 190 mg CH, 460 mg S**

VEAL AND PEPPERS

4–6 servings

2 pounds veal round, sliced ¼″ thick and pounded thin as for scaloppine
¼ cup olive oil
2 tablespoons minced shallots
1 medium-size yellow onion, peeled and minced
1 clove garlic, peeled and crushed
¾ cup dry white wine
1½ teaspoons minced fresh sage or ¼ teaspoon dried sage
½ teaspoon minced fresh marjoram or ¼ teaspoon dried marjoram
2 medium-size sweet green peppers, cored, seeded, and cut lengthwise in strips 1″ wide
Juice of ½ lemon
1 teaspoon salt
⅛ teaspoon pepper

Cut veal crosswise into strips 1½″ wide. Heat oil in a large, heavy skillet over moderately high heat 1 minute, add veal, and brown as quickly as possible. Remove from skillet and set aside. Reduce heat to moderate, mix in shallots, onion, and garlic, and stir-fry about 8 minutes or until golden. Return veal to skillet, stir in remaining ingredients, cover, and simmer 12–15 minutes until tender. Serve with boiled rice.

*NPS (4–6): 525–350 C, 160–105 mg CH, 715–475 mg S**

VEAL BIRDS (OISEAUX SANS TÊTES)

4 servings

1½ pounds veal round, sliced ¼″ thick and pounded thin as for scaloppine
1 teaspoon salt
⅛ teaspoon pepper
2 tablespoons butter or margarine
½ cup chicken broth or dry red or white wine
½ cup beef broth
1 tablespoon flour blended with 1 tablespoon cold water

STUFFING

2 slices bacon
1 medium-size yellow onion, peeled and minced
1 clove garlic, peeled and crushed (optional)
1/4 pound mushrooms, wiped clean and chopped fine
1 cup soft white bread crumbs
1 tablespoon minced parsley
1/4 teaspoon basil

Prepare stuffing first: Brown bacon in a small skillet over moderate heat, remove, crumble, and reserve. Sauté onion and, if you like, garlic in drippings 5–8 minutes until pale golden, add mushrooms and sauté 2–3 minutes longer. Off heat mix in bacon and remaining stuffing ingredients. Cut veal into slices that measure about 3″ × 5″. Sprinkle one side of veal slices with salt and pepper, place a small dab of stuffing in center of each, roll, and secure with toothpicks. Brown rolls, 1/2 at a time, in butter in a large skillet or flameproof casserole over moderately high heat 5–10 minutes. Add chicken broth, cover, and simmer over low heat or in a preheated 350° F. oven 20–25 minutes until veal is tender. Transfer rolls to a deep dish and keep warm. Add beef broth and flour paste to skillet liquid and heat, stirring, until thickened. Pour over rolls and serve.

NPS: 455 C, 145 mg CH, 1060 mg S*

VARIATIONS

Veal Birds in Wine-Cream Sauce: Stuff, roll, and brown veal birds as directed. Add 1/2 cup dry sherry, Madeira, or apple cider, cover, and simmer until tender. Remove rolls to a deep platter and keep warm. Quickly boil down pan liquid to 1/4 cup, smooth in 1/2 cup heavy cream, and heat 1–2 minutes. Pour over veal and serve.

NPS: 555 C, 185 mg CH, 875 mg S* .

Ham- and Dill-Stuffed Veal Birds: Reduce bread crumbs in stuffing mixture to 1/2 cup and add 1/2 cup minced ham and 1/4 teaspoon thyme. *Spread* each veal slice with a little stuffing, add 1 long, slim dill pickle wedge, then roll and cook as directed.

NPS: 470 C, 155 mg CH, 1535 mg S*

Veal Birds Stuffed with Anchovies and Olives: Omit mushrooms from stuffing mixture and add 6–8 minced anchovy fillets and 1/4 cup minced pimiento-stuffed olives. Do not salt or pepper veal slices; spread each with 1 tablespoon anchovy paste, add a dab of stuffing, then roll and cook as directed. Garnish with lemon slices and capers.

NPS: 500 C, 155 mg CH, 905 mg S*

Prosciutto-Stuffed Veal Birds with Avocado: Omit stuffing and do not salt or pepper veal slices; spread each with 1 teaspoon prepared spicy brown mustard, cover with trimmed-to-size slices *prosciutto,* then roll and cook as directed. Transfer rolls to a deep dish and keep warm. Blend 1/2 cup heavy cream into pan liquid and add 1 thinly sliced, peeled, and pitted *firm* avocado. Warm gently 1–2 minutes, pour around veal, garnish with sieved hard-cooked egg yolk, and serve.

NPS: 585 C, 195 mg CH, 860 mg S*

VEAL CUTLETS OSCAR

4 servings

4 veal cutlets, cut 1/2″ thick
4 tablespoons butter or margarine
1 teaspoon salt
1/8 teaspoon pepper
1/3 cup dry white wine
1/2 pound fresh lump or backfin crab meat, carefully picked over
1/2 recipe Buttered Asparagus Tips
1 recipe Béarnaise Sauce

Brown cutlets, half at a time, in 2 tablespoons butter in a large, heavy skillet over moderately high heat 5–10 minutes. Sprinkle with salt and pepper, add wine, cover, and simmer about 20 minutes until tender. In a separate small skillet, sauté crab in remaining butter 3–4 minutes (do not brown). Arrange veal on platter and spoon crab over each cutlet. Pour veal cooking liquid into crab skillet and boil rapidly, uncovered, to reduce to 1/4 cup; pour over crab. Top each portion with a few asparagus tips and arrange rest around platter. Drizzle with Béarnaise and pass the rest. Good with Château Potatoes.

NPS: 745 C, 545 mg CH, 1540 mg S*

VARIATION

Veal Cutlets with Lobster: Prepare as directed, substituting lobster for crab.

NPS: 745 C, 535 mg CH, 1540 mg S*

GROUND VEAL

The logical cuts to grind are the sinewy, economical ones—*flank, breast, shank,* and *neck*—though some people insist upon the lean delicacy of shoulder (at half again the price). Ground veal does not make very good loaves or patties—too lean—and will be better if mixed 1/2 and 1/2 or 2 to 1 with ground pork, beef, lamb, or sausage meat or if mixed with enough vegetables or liquid to keep it moist. Once through the grinder is usually enough for veal unless you want extra-firm loaves or patties. In that case, have it ground twice.

LEMON VEAL LOAF

6–8 servings

5 slices firm-textured white bread
3/4 cup milk
2 1/2 pounds ground veal
1 medium-size yellow onion, peeled and minced
2 eggs
1 cup sour cream
1 tablespoon minced parsley
1 tablespoon minced fresh dill or 1 teaspoon dillweed
1 tablespoon minced capers
1 teaspoon finely grated lemon rind
1/4 teaspoon thyme
1/4 teaspoon salt
1/8 teaspoon pepper

Preheat oven to 350° F. Let bread soak in milk 10 minutes. Mix all ingredients together well and pat into a lightly greased 9″ × 5″ × 3″ loaf pan. Bake, uncovered, 1 hour; drain off drippings. Let loaf cool in its pan 15–20 minutes before slicing. Serve warm or chill and serve cold. Especially good with Lemon Sauce or Sour Cream-Horseradish Sauce.

NPS (6–8): 480–360 C, 240–180 mg CH, 350–260 mg S*

VIENNESE VEAL LOAF

8–10 servings

Ground veal, pork, and ham make this loaf moist and flavorful.

2 pounds veal, ground twice
1 pound lean pork, ground twice
3/4 pound lean cooked ham, ground fine
2 large yellow onions, peeled and minced
18 soda crackers, rolled to fine crumbs (about 1 1/2 cups)
2 teaspoons salt
1 teaspoon white pepper
1 1/2 teaspoons poultry seasoning
1 tablespoon Worcestershire sauce
2 eggs, lightly beaten

Preheat oven to 375° F. Using your hands, mix all ingredients together well and shape in a shallow, lightly greased roasting pan into a loaf about 9″ × 3″. Bake, uncovered, about 1 3/4 hours or until a knife inserted in center of loaf comes out clean. (*Note:* If loaf seems to brown too fast, cover with foil. Transfer loaf to a heated platter, cover loosely with foil, and let "rest" 10 minutes before slicing.) If you wish, make Pan Gravy with the drippings or Mushroom Gravy.

NPS (8–10): 380–305 C, 195–155 mg CH, 1230–985 mg S*

BUTTERMILK VEAL BALLS IN GRAVY

4–6 servings

MEAT BALLS
1 pound ground veal
1/4 pound ground pork
3/4 cup fine dry bread crumbs
1 small yellow onion, peeled and grated fine (optional)
1/4 cup buttermilk
1 small clove garlic, peeled and crushed
1 teaspoon salt
1/4 teaspoon pepper
2 tablespoons bacon drippings or cooking oil

GRAVY
3 tablespoons flour
1 cup chicken broth
1 cup beef broth

Thoroughly mix all meat ball ingredients but bacon drippings and shape into 1″ balls. Brown balls, about half at a time, 10 minutes in drippings in a large, heavy skillet over moderate heat; remove to a bowl. For gravy, blend flour into drippings, add broths, and cook and stir until thickened. Return meat balls, cover, and simmer 15 minutes.

NPS (4–6): 440–295 C, 105–70 mg CH, 1220–815 mg S*

VARIATIONS

Veal Balls with Onions and Sour Cream: Prepare and brown meat balls as recipe directs; remove to a bowl. Sauté 3 thinly sliced large yellow onions in drippings 8–10 minutes until golden. Return meat balls to skillet, add 1 cup chicken broth, cover, and simmer 15 minutes. Partially cover skillet, drain pan liquid into 1 cup sour cream, whisk together, and return to skillet. Heat (but do not boil) 1–2 minutes. Serve veal balls and sauce over noodles, rice, or mashed potatoes.

NPS (4–6): 585–390 C, 130–90 mg CH, 1070–710 mg S*

Veal and Beef Balls: In making balls use 3/4 pound each ground veal and beef; add 1 lightly beaten egg along with all other ingredients, then shape and cook as recipe directs.

NPS (4–6): 560–375 C, 190–130 mg CH, 1255–835 mg S*

Blue Cheese-Veal Balls: In making balls, increase buttermilk to ½ cup and add 2 ounces crumbled blue cheese; proceed as recipe directs.

NPS (4–6): 495–330 C, 120–80 mg CH, 1435–955 mg S*

THE LESSER CUTS OF VEAL
(See Veal Chart)

From these so-called tough cuts come some of the most famous veal dishes—blond *blanquette de veau* (a white French veal stew that the French make with *tendron,* the part of the breast containing the "false ribs" or cartilage, which cooks down to gelatinous tenderness), tomatoey brown *Marengo,* not to mention luscious Italian *Osso Buco* made with veal shanks. Hardly poor man's fare. All any of the following lesser cuts need in order to become fork tender is gentle stewing or braising in the company of liquid, vegetables, and herbs:
    Fore and hind shanks
    Breast and riblets
    Stew meat
    Neck
    Brisket rolls and pieces
    Heel of round

VEAL PAPRIKASH

4 servings

2 pounds boned veal shoulder, cut in 1″ cubes
2 tablespoons butter or margarine
2 medium-size yellow onions, peeled and minced
1 clove garlic, peeled and crushed
2 tablespoons paprika (the Hungarian sweet rose paprika is best)
½ teaspoon salt
⅛ teaspoon pepper
½ cup dry white wine
1 tomato, peeled, cored, seeded, and coarsely chopped
1 cup sour cream

Brown veal, a few pieces at a time, in butter in a large, heavy kettle over high heat; remove to a bowl. Add onions and garlic to kettle, reduce heat to moderate, and stir-fry 8–10 minutes until golden. Return veal to kettle, mix in all remaining ingredients except sour cream, cover, and simmer slowly 1½–2 hours until veal is tender. Mix in sour cream and serve over buttered wide noodles or Nockerln.

NPS: 605 C, 200 mg CH, 525 mg S*

BLANQUETTE DE VEAU (FRENCH WHITE VEAL STEW)

4–6 servings

When veal is simmered without first having been browned, it produces an ugly scum. The best preventive: Cover veal with cold water, bring to a simmer, and cook 2 minutes. Drain well, then rinse both veal *and* kettle well before beginning recipe.

2 pounds boned veal shoulder, cut in 1″ cubes and blanched to remove scum (see above)
1 large yellow onion, peeled and stuck with 4 cloves
1 carrot, peeled
1 stalk celery
1 leek, trimmed (optional)
1½ teaspoons salt (about)
⅛ teaspoon white pepper (about)
1 bay leaf and 1 sprig each parsley and thyme, tied in cheesecloth (*bouquet garni*)
1 additional bay leaf (do not crumble)
2½ cups veal stock or chicken broth
2 tablespoons butter
3 tablespoons + 2 teaspoons flour
2 egg yolks, lightly beaten
½ cup heavy cream
½ pound button mushrooms tossed with 1 tablespoon lemon juice
12 small white onions, peeled and boiled
Pinch nutmeg
2–3 tablespoons lemon juice
2 teaspoons minced parsley

Place veal, onion, carrot, celery, leek, salt, pepper, *bouquet garni,* bay leaf, and stock in a large heavy kettle; cover, and simmer slowly 1¼–1½ hours until veal is tender. Remove veal to a bowl with a slotted spoon; strain broth and discard vegetables. Boil broth in an uncovered saucepan over high heat until reduced to 2 cups. Rinse and dry kettle, add butter and melt over moderate heat; blend in flour, slowly add broth, and heat, stirring until thickened. Blend egg yolks with cream, mix in a little hot sauce, then stir back into kettle. Add mushrooms; heat and stir over moderately low heat 2–3 minutes but do not boil. Add well-drained onions and veal and heat and stir 3–4 minutes, again not allowing mixture to boil. Off heat, mix in nutmeg, and lemon juice; taste for salt and pepper and add more, if needed. Ladle into a tureen and sprinkle with parsley. Good with buttered noodles.

NPS (4–6): 675–450 C, 355–235 mg CH, 1565–1040 mg S*

BALKAN VEAL AND CHESTNUT STEW

4–6 servings

To save yourself the tedium of shelling and peeling fresh chestnuts, use the frozen, shelled, and peeled Italian chestnuts (specialty food shops stock them).

2 tablespoons butter or margarine
2 pounds boned veal shoulder, cut in 1″ cubes
1 medium-size yellow onion, peeled and coarsely chopped
1 clove garlic, peeled and crushed
1³/₄ cups chicken broth
¹/₂ cup dry white wine
1 (4″) sprig fresh thyme or ¹/₄ teaspoon dried thyme
1 teaspoon salt
¹/₈ teaspoon pepper
1 pound shelled, peeled chestnuts*

Melt butter in a large, heavy kettle over moderately high heat, add veal, and brown well on all sides, 8–10 minutes. Reduce heat to moderately low, add onion and garlic, and stir-fry 5 minutes. Add all remaining ingredients except chestnuts, cover, and simmer 1 hour; add chestnuts, cover, and simmer 30 minutes longer until chestnuts and veal are tender. Serve over rice or Bulgur Pilaf with a spicy Yugoslav traminer wine or a white Greek retsina.

NPS: 695 C, 175 mg CH, 1110 mg S*

VEAL MARENGO

6 servings

3 pounds boned veal shoulder, cut in 1¹/₂″ cubes
³/₄ cup unsifted flour
¹/₄ teaspoon pepper
1 tablespoon + ¹/₂ teaspoon salt
¹/₃ cup olive oil
2 medium-size yellow onions, peeled and coarsely chopped
1 clove garlic, peeled and crushed
1²/₃ cups dry white wine
¹/₂ cup water
1 (6-ounce) can tomato paste
¹/₂ teaspoon thyme
¹/₂ teaspoon tarragon
¹/₂ teaspoon finely grated orange rind
¹/₂ pound button mushrooms, wiped clean and trimmed of coarse stems
2 tablespoons minced parsley

Preheat oven to 325° F. Dredge veal by shaking in a paper bag with flour, pepper, and 1 tablespoon salt, then brown, a few cubes at a time, in a little of the oil in a large heavy skillet over moderately high heat; add additional oil as needed. Transfer veal to a 3-quart oven-to-table casserole. Stir-fry onions and garlic in skillet 8–10 minutes until golden, add wine, water, tomato paste, thyme, tarragon, and remaining salt, and boil, uncovered, about 2 minutes. Mix in orange rind and pour into casserole. Cover and bake 2 hours. (*Note:* Casserole can be prepared to this point 1–2 days ahead. Cool, cover, and refrigerate until about 3 hours before serving. Bring to room temperature before proceeding.) Mix in mushrooms, cover, and bake ¹/₂ hour at 325° F. Stir in parsley and serve with boiled rice or buttered wide noodles.

NPS: 610 C, 160 mg CH, 1675 mg S*

BRAISED VEAL RIBLETS

4 servings

3–3¹/₂ pounds veal riblets
¹/₄ cup unsifted flour
2 tablespoons butter or margarine
1 tablespoon cooking oil
2 tablespoons flour
1 cup beef broth
1 cup cold water
³/₄ teaspoon salt
¹/₈ teaspoon pepper
1 large yellow onion, peeled and sliced thin
1 pound carrots, peeled and cut in 2″ chunks (optional)
¹/₄ teaspoon grated lemon rind
1 teaspoon minced parsley

Dredge riblets in flour and brown, a few at a time, in butter and oil in a heavy kettle over moderately high heat; drain on paper toweling. Blend 2 tablespoons flour into drippings, slowly add broth and water, stirring until smooth. Return meat to kettle, season with salt and pepper, add onion and carrots. Cover and simmer 1 hour until veal is tender; check liquid from time to time and add a little water if necessary. Just before serving, stir in lemon and parsley. Serve with crusty bread or mashed potatoes.

NPS: 570 C, 150 mg CH, 825 mg S*

OSSO BUCO (ITALIAN-STYLE BRAISED VEAL SHANKS)

4 servings

Osso buco owes its unique flavor to *gremolata,* a mixture of lemon rind, parsley, and garlic added just before serving.

4 pounds veal shanks, cut in 3″ lengths
1/2 cup unsifted flour
1 tablespoon salt
1/4 teaspoon pepper
1/3 cup olive oil
2 cloves garlic, peeled and crushed
1 medium-size yellow onion, peeled and minced
2 large carrots, peeled and cut in small dice
1 stalk celery, chopped fine
1/2 cup dry white wine
1 3/4 cups chicken broth
1 tablespoon minced fresh basil or 1 teaspoon dried basil
1 bay leaf, crumbled
Pinch thyme

GREMOLATA
1 tablespoon minced parsley
2 teaspoons finely grated lemon rind
1 clove garlic, peeled and minced

Dredge veal by shaking in a heavy paper bag with flour, salt, and pepper, then brown in oil, a few pieces at a time; remove and reserve. Add garlic, onion, carrots, and celery to kettle and sauté 5–8 minutes until pale golden. Add wine and boil rapidly, uncovered, 4–5 minutes until reduced by half. Return veal to kettle, arranging so marrow cannot fall out, and add all remaining ingredients except gremolata. Cover and simmer 1 1/4–1 1/2 hours until veal is tender but not falling off the bones. Mix gremolata and sprinkle over shanks, cover, and simmer 5–10 minutes longer. Serve, spooning vegetables and cooking liquid over veal. Or, if you prefer, purée vegetables and cooking liquid until smooth; spoon a little over veal and pass the rest in a sauceboat. Risotto alla Milanese is the traditional accompaniment.

NPS: 670 C, 180 mg CH, 2195 mg S*

VARIATION

Braised Veal Shanks with Tomato Sauce: Prepare recipe as directed, reducing amount of chicken broth to 1/2 cup and adding, at the same time, 1 (1-pound) undrained can tomatoes.

NPS: 680 C, 180 mg CH, 2100 mg S*

VEAL SHANKS PERSILLADE

4–6 servings

Especially good with boiled noodles or rice.

4 pounds veal shanks, cut in 2″ lengths
1/2 cup unsifted flour
2 tablespoons olive oil
2 tablespoons butter
1 1/2 teaspoons salt (about)
1/4 teaspoon pepper
1 stalk celery
1 sprig fresh dill or 1/2 teaspoon dillweed
1 clove garlic, peeled
1 medium-size yellow onion, peeled
3 cups chicken broth
2 cups dry white bread crumbs
6 tablespoons minced parsley
1 tablespoon minced fresh dill or 1 teaspoon dillweed
1/4 cup finely grated Parmesan cheese
1 large clove garlic, peeled, crushed, and mixed with 1/4 cup melted butter
3 eggs, separated
3/4 cup sour cream

Dredge veal in flour. Heat oil and butter in a large heavy kettle over moderately high heat and brown veal, a few pieces at a time. Add salt, pepper, celery, dill sprig, peeled garlic clove, onion, and broth; cover and simmer 1–1 1/4 hours until veal is tender. Remove veal with slotted spoon and cool until easy to handle. Preheat oven to 425° F. Mix bread crumbs with parsley, dill, and cheese, then with garlic butter. Beat egg whites until frothy; dip each piece of veal in egg white, then in crumb mixture to coat evenly; dry on a rack at room temperature while you make the sauce. Strain veal broth into a saucepan, skim off fat, then boil rapidly, uncovered, until reduced to about 2 cups. Lower heat to simmering; beat egg yolks lightly with a little hot broth, mix into pan, and cook, stirring constantly, until slightly thickened. Smooth in sour cream, taste for salt and add more, if needed; keep warm but do not allow to boil or sauce may curdle. Arrange veal in a well-greased shallow roasting pan and bake, uncovered, 10–12 minutes until crumbs are lightly browned. To serve, arrange veal on a heated platter and drizzle with a little of the sauce. Pass the remaining sauce.

NPS (4–6): 1105–735 C, 180–120 mg CH, 2195–1465 mg S*

LAMB AND MUTTON

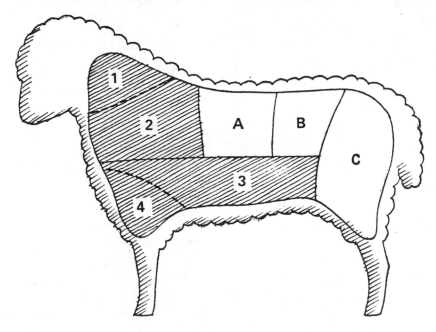

Note: Unshaded parts are the tender cuts. Shaded parts are not-so-tender.

THE TENDER CUTS:
  A. RIB
      Roasts (rib, rack, crown)
      Chops (rib, Frenched rib)
  B. LOIN
      Roasts (loin, double loin)
      Chops (loin, kidney or English)
  C. LEG
      Leg of lamb or mutton
      Leg chop or steak
      Cubes for kebabs

THE NOT-SO-TENDER CUTS:
  1. NECK
      Neck slices
  2. SHOULDER
      Roasts (rolled, cushion, square
        shoulder)
      Chops (blade, arm)
      Stew lamb or mutton
      Ground lamb or mutton
  3. BREAST
      Roasts for stuffing
      Riblets (stew lamb or mutton)
  4. SHANK
      Lamb or mutton shanks

Though adept at cooking beef and pork, we often approach lamb with uncertainty. Many of us don't like it (or think we don't), perhaps because cookbooks have for years insisted that lamb be cooked well done. Not true. Anyone who has tasted baby lamb roasted the French way—until juicily pink and not an instant longer—is quickly converted. How delicate this lamb is, and how delicious. Almost every foreign country prizes lamb as highly (or more highly) than beef, not surprising when you consider that lamb (or one of its early ancestors) was man's first meat.

Technically, lamb is a young sheep under 1 year of age, although a recent easing of USDA standards for grading lamb now permits some *yearling mutton* to be classified as *lamb. Baby or milk-fed lamb* is 6–8 weeks old, *"spring" lamb* 3–5 months old, and *lamb* 6 months to 1 year. When lamb reaches its first birthday, it becomes *yearling mutton;* at age 2, it's full-scale *mutton. Pré-salé lamb,* the French favorite, is lamb grazed on the *prés salés* (salt marshes) of Brittany and Normandy.

In the old days, lamb was available primarily in spring, hence the name "spring" lamb. Today, however, it is available the year round. Frozen New Zealand legs of lamb and lamb chops, moreover, are widely available in supermarkets; when properly stored and cooked, they're succulent and mild flavored. Choose solidly frozen lamb only, and avoid markets that sell this lamb either partially or fully thawed.

How to Recognize Quality

Buy top grades (USDA PRIME, CHOICE, or GOOD), also meat that has been federally inspected (found wholesome). It will have velvety-pink-to-red lean (the older the animal, the redder the meat), firm creamy fat, and bones that are spongy and red inside. Mutton is dark red with flinty bones and brittle fat and is generally available at retail in CHOICE and GOOD grades only.

About the Fell: The outer fat of lamb has a thin, papery covering called the *fell,* which has caused some controversy. Should it be removed before cooking? Some gourmet cooks say yes, because it gives even youngest lamb a strong flavor. Others say it should be left on legs of lamb because it helps them hold their shape during roasting, seals in juices, and speeds cooking. We've tried both ways and can't see enough difference to justify the fuss. On other cuts of lamb, especially small ones, peel the fell off *before* cooking.

About the Musk Glands: Buried in the leg of lamb (near the hock joint) and in the shoulder are large, yellowish "musk" glands (so called because people once thought they gave lamb a musky off-flavor). They don't, but they *are* conspicuous, particularly in young lamb, so most butchers routinely remove them. If your butcher hasn't, simply snip them out yourself.

A Word About the Cuts of Lamb and Mutton: They are the same in both animals, the only real difference being that in mutton they're larger, less tender (especially neck, leg, breast, and other well-exercised muscles), and more strongly flavored. The majority of recipes in this book call for lamb simply because American preferences are for it, but mutton can be substituted in any of the recipes that are braised or stewed.

ROAST LAMB

Leg: The most popular lamb roast and one of the most expensive, leg of lamb is cut the following ways:
Full (whole) leg (6–10 pounds)
Sirloin half of leg (4–5 pounds)
Shank half of leg (3–5 pounds)
Center leg (3–5 pounds)
Boned and rolled leg (3–5 pounds)

Loin and Rib Roasts: All are expensive and supremely tender:
Sirloin (2–2½ pounds)
Loin (2–2½ pounds)
Saddle or double loin (4–5 pounds)
Rolled double loin (3–4 pounds)
Rib or rack (2½–3 pounds)
Crown roast (rib roasts bent and tied into a circle; 6 pounds up)

Shoulder and Breast: More economical but less tender:
Square shoulder (4–6 pounds)
Precarved shoulder (a trimmed shoulder, cut into chops and tied back into original shape; about 5 pounds)
Cushion shoulder (the one to stuff; 3–5 pounds)
Rolled shoulder (3–5 pounds)
Breast (1½–2 pounds)
Boned and rolled breast (also good to stuff; 1½ pounds)

How to Roast Lamb

People are of many minds about the best way to roast lamb. Some prefer a constant low temperature, some a constant moderately high temperature, others a combination of high and low, which is the French way. Still others treat each cut differently: baby lamb, they say, is best roasted fast at a very high temperature, spring lamb at a lower one. Here are the three most popular methods and the preferred cuts for each.

(*Note:* Meat thermometers—many cookbooks, too—still advise cooking lamb to 170° F. or 180° F., but at those temperatures it will be depressingly gray and dry. For those who like it juicily pink, 140°–145° F. is just about perfect. Some, of course, prefer it really rare (130°–135° F.), others more well done. Try cooking a lamb roast to one of the lower temperatures; if it isn't to your liking, roast a bit longer.) Always let roast "rest"

15–20 minutes before carving so juices have a chance to settle.

Cooking times given here can only be approximate, since shape of cut, proportion of fat and bone, internal temperature at time of roasting all affect overall time. The truest test of doneness is the meat thermometer.

Amount Needed: Allow 1/3–1/2 pound boned lamb per serving, 1/2–3/4 pound bone-in lamb.

Preparation for Cooking: Legs need none (unless you elect to remove the fell); shoulders and loin should have the fell peeled off and fat trimmed to 1/8″. Let roast stand at room temperature 1 1/2–2 hours if convenient. Rub, if you like, with salt and pepper (salt only penetrates 1/4″ so it really doesn't matter whether roast is salted before cooking or not).

To Give Roast Extra Flavor:
• Rub with one of the following: 2 tablespoons curry powder or Dijon mustard; 1 teaspoon marjoram, thyme, rosemary, summer savory, or dill.
• Make tiny slits over surface of fat and insert thin garlic slivers in each, or crushed mint, sage, or basil leaves.
• Mix 1/4 cup mild yellow mustard with 2 tablespoons soy sauce, 2 crushed cloves garlic, 1 tablespoon sugar, and 1/4 teaspoon ginger; spread over roast.
• Marinate roast 24 hours in refrigerator in dry red wine, Teriyaki Sauce, All-Purpose Barbecue Sauce, or other aromatic marinade, turning occasionally. Drain and roast as directed, basting often with marinade during last 1/2 hour.

Continuous Low Heat Method (for leg of lamb, loin, saddle, and boneless roasts): Preheat oven to 325° F. Place roast fat side up on a rack in a shallow roasting pan (loin and rib roasts usually don't need racks because ribs hold them out of drippings). Insert meat thermometer in center of largest lean muscle, not touching bone. If roast is small, insert very carefully on an angle so that thermometer is secure. Do not add water, do not cover. Roast, without basting, as follows: 12–13 minutes per pound for rare (130°–135° F.), 14–16 for medium rare (140°–145° F.), 18–20 for medium (150°–160° F.), and, if you must have it well done, 20–25 minutes per pound (160°–165° F.). *(Note:* Boneless roasts, also small (3–4-pound) roasts, will take *slightly* (3–5 minutes) longer per pound for each degree of doneness.) Let roast "rest" 15–20 minutes before carving.

Continuous Moderately High Temperature (good for all but baby lamb): Preheat oven to 375° F. Place roast in pan and insert thermometer as above. Do not cover, do not add liquid. Roast, without basting, 11–13 minutes per pound for rare (130°–135° F.), 13–15 for medium rare (140°–145° F.), 16–18 for medium (150°–160° F.), 18–20 for well done (160°–165° F.), and about 3 minutes longer per pound for boneless roasts for each degree of doneness. Let roast "rest" 15–20 minutes before carving.

Searing (French) Method (good for all cuts): Preheat oven to 450° F. Place roast in pan and insert thermometer as above; do not cover or add liquid. Sear 15 minutes, reduce heat to 350° F., and roast, without basting, 10–12 minutes per pound for rare (130°–135° F.), 12–14 for medium rare (140°–145° F.), 14–16 for medium (150°–160° F.), 16–18 for well done (160°–165° F.), and slightly longer per pound for each degree of doneness for boneless roasts. Let "rest" before carving.

About Baby Lamb: Because baby lamb is so delicate and tender, it's best roasted quickly in a very hot oven, 450° F. Place fat side up on a rack, insert meat thermometer, do not add water, and do not cover. Roast 10–15 minutes per pound until medium rare (140°–145° F.). It's most succulent and flavorful at this temperature and should not be served more well done.

About Mutton: Loin, rack, and leg are the best cuts to roast, and searing is the best method. Follow directions for lamb above.

Some Glazes for Roast Lamb

Half an hour before roast is done, spread or drizzle any of the following over surface and continue cooking as directed, basting every 10 minutes.
• 1/2 cup warmed ginger, orange, or lime marmalade.
• 1/2 cup minced chutney heated with 1/2 cup apple juice, red wine, or water.
• 1/4 cup mint, apple, or red currant jelly heated with 1/4 cup honey or firmly packed light brown sugar and 1/8 teaspoon each nutmeg and cinnamon.

Some Easy Variations on Oven-Roasted Lamb

À la Bordelaise (for large roasts cooked by Continuous Low Heat Method): For each person, place 1/3 cup potato balls in pan with lamb, drizzle with 3–4 tablespoons oil or melted butter, and roast, uncovered, 40 minutes, turning balls occasionally. Add 6–8 button mushrooms for each person, toss with potatoes, and continue roasting 15–20 minutes until meat is done. Garnish meat with drained vegetables, then sprinkle with the following: 1/4 cup soft white bread crumbs that have been sautéed in 2 tablespoons butter with 1 crushed clove garlic and 1 tablespoon minced parsley.

À la Boulangère (for large roasts cooked by Continuous Low Heat Method): Begin roasting lamb as directed; meanwhile, stir-fry 2 cups coarsely chopped yellow onion in 1/4 cup butter over moderate heat until pale golden; sprinkle with 1/2 teaspoon salt and 1/8 teaspoon pepper. When roast has only 3/4 hour more to cook, take from oven and lift from pan, rack and all. Make a bed of onions in pan, place roast on top, and continue roasting to desired doneness. When serving, spoon some onions on top of roast and wreathe the rest around platter. Pass Pan Gravy.

À la Bretonne: Roast lamb by one of the methods above and serve with 1 recipe Boiled Dried White Beans, cooked as directed, but with the following changes: to the pot add 1 large yellow onion, peeled and stuck with 3 cloves, 2 peeled cloves garlic, 2 bay leaves, and 2 parsley sprigs. When beans are tender, drain, remove onion, garlic, bay leaves, and parsley and toss with 3 tablespoons melted butter, 1 crushed clove garlic, 2–3 tablespoons lamb drippings, and 1 tablespoon each tomato paste and minced parsley. Lamb can be wreathed with the beans or the two can be served separately.

À la Provençale: Buy a large, full leg of lamb, make tiny slits over surface, and tuck in anchovy fillets and thin garlic slivers; rub well with summer savory and thyme and let stand at room temperature 3 hours. Roast by one of the methods above but baste often with 1 1/2 cups lamb stock or beef broth mixed with 1/2 cup each melted butter and dry vermouth. While roast "rests," boil pan drippings and any remaining basting mixture 3–5 minutes to reduce, stir in 2 tablespoons minced parsley, and pour into a sauceboat. Accompany roast with Boiled Dried White Beans dressed with olive oil and garlic.

Arni Psito (Greek-Style Roast Lamb): Make small slits over surface of roast and tuck in thin garlic slivers (use 3 cloves garlic in all). Brush roast with 2 tablespoons olive oil or melted butter and drizzle with the juice of 2 lemons. Roast by one of the methods above and, when half done, add 2 cups boiling water to pan, 1 teaspoon salt, 1/8 teaspoon pepper. Continue roasting, uncovered, until tender. Skim pan liquid of fat and serve over lamb as sauce.

Neapolitan Roast Lamb: Make small slits over surface of roast and tuck in thin garlic slivers (use 3 cloves). Marinate lamb 24 hours in refrigerator in 2 cups dry red or white wine mixed with 1 minced small yellow onion, 2 tablespoons finely grated lemon rind, and 1 1/2 teaspoons powdered rosemary. Lift meat from marinade, brush with 2 tablespoons olive oil, and roast as directed, basting often with strained marinade. Use marinade in making Pan Gravy.

Oven-Barbecued Roast Lamb: Marinate lamb in All-Purpose Barbecue Sauce 24 hours in refrigerator, turning occasionally. Lift from marinade and roast by one of the basic methods, basting every 15 minutes with barbecue sauce.

Roast Lamb Bonne Femme: Choose a large, full leg of lamb and place in pan as directed. For each person add to pan: 1 halved, peeled medium-size potato and 3 peeled small white onions drizzled with 1/4 cup oil or melted bacon drippings. Sprinkle with 1 teaspoon salt and 1/8 teaspoon pepper and roast, uncovered, turning once or twice. These will take 1–1 1/4 hours to cook, so gauge accordingly. Drain on paper toweling and wreathe around roast on platter.

Roast Lamb with Dill-Crumb Topping: Roast lamb by one of the basic methods and about 1/2 hour before it is done, remove from oven and brush with 1 tablespoon melted butter; then pat on: 2 cups fine soft bread crumbs tossed with 2 tablespoons each minced dill, parsley, and melted butter, 1 crushed clove garlic, and 1/4 teaspoon pepper. Return to oven and roast, uncovered, to desired doneness.

Taverna-Style Roast Leg of Lamb: Choose a 5–6-pound short leg of lamb and trim off all outer covering of fat. Rub well with the juice of 1 lemon. Make tiny slits over surface and tuck in thin garlic slivers (use 2 cloves). Mix together 2 finely crumbled bay leaves, 1 teaspoon thyme, and 1/4 teaspoon each oregano and pepper and rub over lamb; pour the juice of 1 lemon over all. Let stand in a cool place 24 hours. Roast lamb by Continuous Moderately High Temperature method for exactly 1 hour (the roast will be quite rare). Remove from oven and let rest 15–20 minutes before serving.

How to Spit-Roast Lamb

Best Cuts: Leg, rolled shoulder, double loin, loin, saddle, or rack.

Amount Needed: The same as for Roast Lamb *but* avoid small roasts; 4–5 pounds is a good size (except for racks and loins that weigh only 2½–3).

Preparation for Cooking: The same as for oven roasting. When saddle, loin, or rack is to be spit-roasted over charcoal, have butcher leave flank on and roll up and tie.

In Rotisserie, Gas or Electric Barbecue, or Oven: Preheat unit. Balance roast carefully on spit: full and half legs should be skewered from butt to shank end with spit running parallel to bone; all boneless cuts are spitted lengthwise straight through the center; spit loin, rack, and saddle end to end straight through the middle so they are well balanced. Tighten holding forks. Insert meat thermometer in center of largest lean muscle, making sure it touches neither spit nor bone, also that it will not hit any part of rotisserie as it turns. The best way is to insert the thermometer on an angle or in the end of the roast. Attach spit to rotisserie and roast 5″–6″ from heat according to manufacturer's timetable or 5 minutes less per pound than recommended for lamb roasted the Continuous Low Heat Method. Keep a close eye on the thermometer and remove lamb when it registers about 5° below desired doneness. Remove roast from spit and let "rest" 15–20 minutes before carving.

Over Charcoal: Prepare a moderate charcoal fire. Balance meat on spit and insert thermometer as for rotisserie. (*Note:* Saddle, loin, and rack of lamb should be roasted only where heat can be regulated by lowering or raising spit.) Attach spit to rotisserie, place drip pan in center, and push coals to the front and back of it. Roast lamb 6″–7″ from coals, using rotisserie roasting times as a guide. Check thermometer regularly and use it as the true indicator of doneness.

VARIATIONS

For Rotisserie or Charcoal Spit Roasting:
• Marinate roast in All-Purpose Barbecue Sauce overnight, then spit-roast as directed, basting often with sauce during last ½ hour of cooking.
• Brush roast frequently with ¼ cup Garlic Butter mixed with 2 tablespoons olive or other oil.
• The day before roasting lamb, purée 2 large yellow onions, coarsely chopped, by buzzing 10–15 seconds in an electric blender at high speed or 5–10 seconds in a food processor fitted with the metal chopping blade with ⅓ cup water and 2 peeled cloves garlic. Pour over roast, cover, and refrigerate 24 hours, turning often. Lift roast from marinade, scrape off excess, and rub roast with 2 tablespoons paprika (preferably the sweet rose type). Spit and roast as directed.

How to Carve Leg of Lamb:

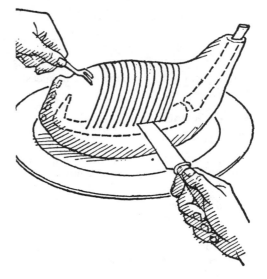

Place leg on platter so plump, meaty portion is away from carver. Cut 2–3 thin slices from near side to form a base. Stand roast on base and, beginning at shank end, cut straight down to bone. Free slices by running knife down along shank bone. Lift out and transfer to platter.

French Method

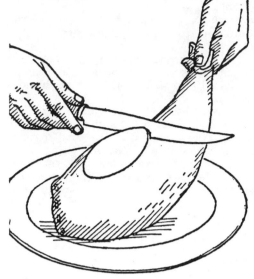

So very easy. Simply lift leg bone with hand, then with a carving knife carve the length of the leg, parallel to the bone, in thin slices.

CROWN ROAST OF LAMB

6–8 servings ⚖

This spectacular roast deserves a fine red Bordeaux, a Médoc, perhaps, Saint-Émilion, or Zinfandel.

1 (12–16-rib) crown roast of lamb
 (about 4–6 pounds) *(Note:* **Have butcher remove backbone and french ribs.)**
¼ teaspoon pepper
Chicory (pale inner leaves) and watercress sprigs (garnish)
Seedless green grapes (garnish)

If butcher has filled crown with ground trimmings, remove (save for lamb burgers). Let roast stand at room temperature 1½–2 hours if convenient. Preheat oven to 325° F. Place roast, rib ends up, in a large, shallow roasting pan (no need for a rack) and rub with pepper. Force a large foil ball into crown so it won't cook out of shape; cover rib ends with foil; insert meat thermometer between 2 ribs, not touching bone. Roast, uncovered, 12–15 minutes per pound for rare (130°–135° F. on thermometer), 15–17 for medium rare (145°–150° F.), 18–20 for medium (150°–160° F.), and 20–25 for well done (160°–170° F.). Transfer to a hot platter and let "rest" 15–20 minutes. Put paper frills on rib ends or, if you prefer, pitted green olives or preserved kumquats. Fill crown with chicory and cress and decorate base with clusters of grapes. Good with Château Potatoes and Peas à la Française.

NPS (6–8): 730–550 C, 175–130 mg CH, 90–65 mg S*

To Stuff: Before roasting, fill crown with 2 cups stuffing (Rice and Mushroom and also Pecan-Bulgur Wheat are especially good). Cover stuffing loosely with foil and roast as above, allowing about 5 minutes longer per pound; uncover stuffing for last ½ hour of cooking.

NPS (6–8) (Rice and Mushroom): 825–620 C, 185–140 mg CH, 350–260 mg S*
NPS (6–8) (Pecan and Bulgur Wheat): 900–675 C, 195–145 mg CH, 475–355 mg S*

To Carve: Separate into chops by slicing down along ribs.

VARIATION

Crown Roast of Lamb Filled with Vegetables: Omit chicory and cress and fill crown with any of the following: buttered green peas mixed with pearl onions or sliced mushrooms or Green Peas with Mint and Orange; Rice Pilaf; or Brussels Sprouts with Chestnuts; Puréed or Braised Chestnuts or Sautéed Mushrooms. Recipe too flexible for meaningful nutritional count.

ROAST LEG OF LAMB STUFFED WITH RICE, PIÑON NUTS, AND CURRANTS

6–8 servings

1 (6-pound) leg of lamb

STUFFING
2 tablespoons olive oil
½ cup uncooked rice
1 medium-size yellow onion, peeled and minced
1 clove garlic, peeled and crushed
3 tablespoons minced parsley
1 tablespoon minced mint
¼ cup dried currants
½ cup piñon nuts
1 cup chicken broth
1 teaspoon salt
¼ teaspoon pepper

Ask butcher to bone leg of lamb, leaving about 2″ of leg bone in at the narrow end (this makes the leg handsomer and easier to stuff). Preheat oven to 325° F. For stuffing, heat oil 1 minute in a saucepan over moderately high heat, add rice, onion, and garlic, and stir-fry 2–3 minutes until rice is golden. Mix in remaining ingredients, cover, and simmer 8–10 minutes until all moisture is absorbed. Cool slightly. Spoon stuffing into leg, then sew or skewer cavity shut. Place leg in a large shallow roasting pan and roast, uncovered, 3 hours. To carve, cut straight across in 1/2" slices.

NPS (6–8): 940–705 C, 260–195 mg CH, 665–495 mg S*

HERB-STUFFED ROLLED LEG OF LAMB

6–8 servings

1 (6-pound) leg of lamb, boned and opened flat but not rolled

STUFFING
1/4 cup minced parsley
3 cloves garlic, peeled and crushed
1 tablespoon minced fresh basil or 1 teaspoon dried basil
1 tablespoon olive oil
1 tablespoon softened butter
1 tablespoon lemon juice
1 teaspoon salt
1/4 teaspoon pepper

Preheat oven to 325° F. Peel fell from lamb and discard; spread lamb out fat side down on counter. Mix stuffing and spread over lamb leaving 1/2" margins; roll jelly-roll style and tie round at 2" intervals. Place on a rack and roast, uncovered, 3 hours. Serve as is with Pan Gravy (when making, use dry red wine for 1/2 the liquid) or with hot Caper Sauce.

NPS (6–8): 785–590 C, 265–200 mg CH, 550–415 mg S*

SICILIAN-STYLE BRAISED LEG OF LAMB

6 servings

1 (4-pound) half leg of lamb
2 tablespoons cooking oil
2 tablespoons flour
1 1/2 teaspoons minced fresh sage or 1/2 teaspoon dried sage
1/2 teaspoon minced fresh rosemary or 1/8 teaspoon dried rosemary
2 cloves garlic, peeled and crushed
1 teaspoon salt
1/4 teaspoon pepper
1/2 cup red wine vinegar
1/2 cup hot water
3–4 anchovy fillets, minced

Preheat oven to 325° F. Brown lamb lightly all over in oil in a Dutch oven over moderately high heat. Sprinkle flour, herbs, and garlic over lamb and continue browning 2–3 minutes, turning lamb frequently. Add all remaining ingredients except anchovies, cover, and bring to a simmer. Transfer to oven and simmer, covered, 1 1/2–2 hours until tender; baste two to three times. Lift meat to platter; stir anchovies into drippings and serve as a gravy.

NPS: 620 C, 180 mg CH, 545 mg S*

ROAST STUFFED CUSHION SHOULDER OF LAMB

6–8 servings

1 (4-pound) cushion shoulder of lamb
1 teaspoon salt
1/8 teaspoon pepper
2–3 cups stuffing (Rice Pilaf, Rice and Mushroom, Pecan-Bulgur Wheat, Rice and Kidney, and Bread and Apricot Stuffing are very good)

Preheat oven to 325° F. Skewer all but one side of roast shut, sprinkle pocket with salt and pepper, stuff loosely, and close with skewers. Place roast fat side up on a rack in a shallow roasting pan and roast, uncovered, about 2 hours until tender. Lift meat from pan and let "rest" 15–20 minutes before serving. To carve, cut across the grain in slices 1/2" thick. Serve with Au Jus or Pan Gravy. (*Note:* For an extra-special touch, glaze roast during last 1/2 hour of cooking [see Some Glazes for Roast Lamb].)

NPS (6–8): 625–470 C, 155–115 mg CH, 790–595 mg S*

EASY ATHENIAN BRAISED LAMB SHOULDER

6 servings

1 (3-pound) rolled lamb shoulder
2 tablespoons olive oil or cooking oil
1 medium-size yellow onion, peeled and coarsely chopped
1 clove garlic, peeled and crushed (optional)
2 teaspoons salt
1/4 teaspoon pepper
1 teaspoon rosemary, oregano, marjoram, or thyme (optional)
1/3 cup cold water
3 cups lamb stock or a 1/2 and 1/2 mixture of beef broth and cold water
6 tablespoons flour
1/2–1 teaspoon liquid gravy browner (optional)

Brown lamb well all over in oil in a heavy kettle over moderate heat; add onion, garlic, seasonings and water, cover, and simmer slowly about 2 1/2 hours. Keep an eye on the pot and add about 1/4 cup extra water if liquid boils away. When lamb is tender, lift to a platter and keep warm. Drain all but 1–2 tablespoons drippings from kettle, add 2 cups stock, stirring to scrape up browned bits. Blend flour and remaining stock in a shaker jar, pour into kettle, and heat, stirring, until thickened. If you like a dark gravy, add gravy browner. Slice roast about 1/4" thick and serve with plenty of gravy.

NPS: 720 C, 160 mg CH, 1080 mg S*

To Oven-Braise: Preheat oven to 350° F. Brown lamb as directed in a large, flameproof casserole, add onion, garlic, seasonings, and water, cover, and bake 2 1/2–3 hours as directed. Prepare gravy as above and serve. Nutritional count same as basic recipe.

VARIATIONS

Braised Lamb Roast with Avgolemono Sauce: Brown and simmer lamb until tender, using basic method above. When making gravy, omit flour-stock paste. Add the 3 cups stock to kettle and bring to a simmer. Beat 3 egg yolks lightly, add the juice of 1 lemon, and slowly beat in 1 cup hot stock; return all to kettle. Simmer, stirring constantly, 1–2 minutes but do not boil. Serve over lamb as you would gravy. Nutritional count same as basic recipe.

Braised Lamb Roast with Tomato Sauce: Brown lamb, add onions and seasonings, but substitute 1/3 cup tomato juice for the water; simmer as directed until tender. When making gravy, use 1 (8-ounce) can tomato sauce and 2 cups stock and reduce flour to 1/4 cup. Nutritional count same as basic recipe.

Braised Lamb Roast with Vegetables: Prepare basic recipe above and, when lamb has only 3/4 hour longer to cook, add 2 dozen peeled whole baby carrots, 12 peeled new potatoes, and 12 small peeled turnips. Sprinkle with 1 teaspoon salt, add 1/2 cup additional stock, cover, and continue simmering until meat and vegetables are tender. Lift meat to a hot platter, wreathe with vegetables, and keep warm. Prepare gravy as directed.

NPS: 965 C, 215 mg CH, 1410 mg S*

CHARCOAL SPIT-ROASTED BREAST OF LAMB

6 servings

6 pounds lean breast of lamb

MARINADE
2 cups dry red wine
2 cloves garlic, peeled and crushed
1 medium-size yellow onion, peeled and sliced thin
1 teaspoon powdered rosemary
1/4 teaspoon pepper

Place lamb in a large, shallow bowl; mix marinade, pour over lamb, cover, and marinate 24 hours in refrigerator. Prepare a moderate charcoal fire. Lift meat from marinade and weave spit in and out of ribs to balance; tighten holding forks. Attach spit to rotisserie and roast 7"–8" from coals 1 hour, basting frequently with strained marinade. Lower spit 1"–2" nearer coals and roast 20–30 minutes longer, basting, until tender and richly browned.

NPS: 600 C, 170 mg CH, 95 mg S*

VARIATION

Greek-Style Spit-Roasted Breast of Lamb: Omit marinade; instead, mix the following basting sauce: 1/4 cup melted butter or margarine, 2 tablespoons olive oil, 2 cloves garlic, crushed, and 2 tablespoons lemon juice. Spit-roast breast as above, basting every 15–20 minutes. Season with salt and pepper before serving.

NPS: 645 C, 180 mg CH, 135 mg S*

APRICOT-GLAZED STUFFED BREAST OF LAMB

4 servings

1 (1 3/4-pound) breast of lamb (have butcher crack ribs to simplify carving)

STUFFING
1/4 cup minced onion
1/2 cup diced celery
1/2 cup coarsely chopped piñon nuts
3 tablespoons butter or margarine
1/4 cup dried currants
1/2 cup diced dried apricots
1/4 cup uncooked rice
3/4 cup water
1 tablespoon minced parsley
1 tablespoon dry white wine

GLAZE
1/4 cup dried apricots
1 1/2 cups water

Preheat oven to 350° F. Carefully make a pocket in lamb breast by inserting a small sharp knife at one end and freeing meat from ribs; repeat on opposite end so pocket runs length of breast. For stuffing, stir-fry onion, celery, and nuts in butter in a large, heavy skillet 8–10 minutes over moderate heat until golden. Mix in fruits and rice and stir-fry 2–3 minutes. Add water, cover, and simmer 8–10 minutes until all moisture is absorbed. Mix in parsley and wine and cool to room temperature. Meanwhile, simmer glaze ingredients, uncovered, about 15–20 minutes; purée by buzzing 10–15 seconds in an electric blender at low speed or 5–10 seconds in a food processor fitted with the metal chopping blade; add enough water to bring measure to 2 cups. Fill lamb breast with stuffing, poking it into all corners; toothpick shut and lace with fine string to seal. Place breast in a shallow roasting pan, pour in glaze, and bake, uncovered, 2 hours, basting with glaze every 20 minutes. Remove toothpicks and lacings and serve. To carve, cut straight across between ribs.

NPS: 570 C, 100 mg CH, 150 mg S*

TURKISH LAMB SHISH KEBABS

6 servings

Developed by early travelers who would spear chunks of meat and warm them over campfires, shish kebabs are today sophisticated international fare. They can be made of beef, lamb, ham, venison, chicken, liver, even lobster, shrimp, or scallops. Broil them in the oven or, better yet, over a charcoal fire.

MARINADE
1 cup olive oil
1/2 cup lemon juice
2 cloves garlic, peeled and crushed
1/4 teaspoon pepper
1 teaspoon oregano

KEBABS
4 pounds boned leg of lamb, cut in 11/2" cubes
3 sweet green peppers, cored, seeded, and cut in 2" squares
1 pound small white onions, peeled and parboiled
1 pound medium-size mushrooms, wiped clean and stemmed
3 large, firm tomatoes, quartered (do not peel or core)
1 teaspoon salt

Mix marinade in a large bowl, add lamb, toss to mix, cover, and chill 8 hours or overnight, turning lamb two or three times. Drain off marinade and reserve. Alternate lamb, green peppers, and onions on skewers, beginning and ending with lamb; for best results, put mushrooms and tomatoes on separate skewers (so they won't overcook). Add 1/2 teaspoon salt to marinade and brush

some of it over vegetables. Arrange lamb skewers on a broiling rack or, if you have the necessary gadget, attach to rotisserie spit. Broil 3"–4" from heat 15–20 minutes for rare, 20–25 for medium, and 25–30 for well done, turning frequently so kebabs cook evenly and brushing occasionally with marinade. About 10 minutes before meat is done, lay mushroom and tomato skewers on broiler rack, brush with marinade, and broil, turning frequently, until lightly browned. Sprinkle meat with remaining salt and serve kebabs with boiled rice, bulgur wheat, or Bulgur Pilaf.

NPS: 995 C, 205 mg CH, 530 mg S*

VARIATIONS

Charcoal-Broiled Shish Kebabs: Prepare a moderately hot charcoal fire and broil kebabs 4" from coals, using times given above as a guide. Nutritional count same as basic recipe.

Beef Kebabs: Substitute sirloin or top round for the lamb and broil about 5 minutes less than times given above for rare, medium, or well done.

NPS: 1,255 C, 205 mg CH, 520 mg S*

ROAST LAMB REVISITED

(How to Use Up Leftovers)

LAMB AND EGGPLANT CASSEROLE

4 servings

A very good way to use up leftover roast lamb.

2 small yellow onions, peeled and chopped fine
1 clove garlic, peeled and crushed
2 tablespoons cooking oil
1 medium-size eggplant, peeled and cut in rounds 1/4" thick
11/2 teaspoons salt
1 (1-pound 4-ounce) can Italian plum tomatoes (do not drain)
1/4 teaspoon pepper
1/2 cup uncooked rice
8 medium-thick slices leftover roast lamb, trimmed of fat
2 tablespoons minced parsley

Stir-fry onions and garlic in oil in a deep, flameproof 21/2-quart casserole over moderate heat 8–10 minutes until golden. Layer eggplant into casserole, working onion mixture into spaces between slices. Sprinkle with 1/2 teaspoon salt. Spoon tomatoes over eggplant, sprinkle with 1/2 teaspoon salt and 1/4 teaspoon pepper. Cover and simmer slowly 30 minutes until eggplant is tender. Sprinkle in rice and top with lamb, pressing slices down slightly into mixture underneath; sprinkle with remaining salt. Cover and simmer 20 minutes; uncover and sprinkle with parsley. To serve, place 2 lamb slices on each plate and top with spoonfuls of rice-eggplant-tomato mixture.

NPS: 425 C, 115 mg CH, 1,095 mg S*

CURRIED LAMB LEFTOVERS

2 servings   ¢

2 tablespoons butter, margarine, or cooking oil
1 large yellow onion, peeled and minced
1 small tart apple, peeled, cored, and coarsely chopped
1 clove garlic, peeled and crushed
2 teaspoons curry powder
2 tablespoons dried lentils
1 cup canned tomatoes (include liquid)
1 cup hot water
1 teaspoon salt
1 1/2 cups lean leftover roast lamb, cut in 1/2" cubes

Heat butter in a saucepan over moderate heat 1 minute, add onion and sauté about 8 minutes until golden. Add apple, garlic, and curry powder and stir-fry 1 minute. Add all remaining ingredients, reduce heat to low, cover, and simmer about 45 minutes, stirring frequently. Serve hot over boiled rice and accompany, if you like, with chutney and chopped scallions.

NPS: 435 C, 135 mg CH, 1,460 mg S*

LEFTOVER LAMB PILAF

4 servings   ¢

1 cup uncooked rice
1 large yellow onion, peeled and minced
2 tablespoons butter or margarine
2 cups chicken or beef broth
1 teaspoon salt
1/8 teaspoon pepper
1/3 cup seedless raisins
2 cups coarsely chopped, lean leftover roast lamb
2 tablespoons cooking oil
1 cup leftover gravy or canned beef gravy
2 tablespoons tomato paste
1/4 teaspoon ginger
1 clove garlic, peeled and crushed
1/2 teaspoon seasoned salt

In a 2-quart saucepan stir-fry rice and onion in butter over moderate heat 3–4 minutes until rice is pale golden. Add broth, salt, pepper, and raisins, partially cover, and simmer about 20 minutes until rice is barely tender and all liquid absorbed. Meanwhile brown lamb lightly in oil over moderate heat, add all remaining ingredients, cover, and simmer until rice is tender. Toss lamb mixture into rice, using 2 forks. Serve with chutney.

NPS: 530 C, 85 mg CH, 1,300 mg S*

ARTICHOKES STUFFED WITH LAMB

6 servings

6 large globe artichokes, parboiled and drained

S T U F F I N G
2 cups ground leftover roast lamb
1 medium-size yellow onion, peeled and minced
2 tablespoons cooking oil
1 cup soft white bread crumbs
1 egg, lightly beaten
1/3 cup leftover gravy or chicken or beef broth
2 tablespoons minced parsley
1 teaspoon salt
1/8 teaspoon pepper
1 tablespoon lemon juice

T O P P I N G
1/2 cup coarse white bread crumbs tossed with 2 tablespoons melted butter or margarine

Preheat oven to 325° F. Remove chokes from artichokes,* then arrange artichokes upright and close together in an ungreased casserole. Brown lamb and onion in oil in a heavy skillet over moderate heat 10–12 minutes; off heat mix in remaining stuffing ingredients; fill artichoke centers and top each with buttered crumbs. Pour hot water around artichokes to a depth of 1"; cover and bake 45–50 minutes. Serve with Hollandaise Sauce.

NPS: 355 C, 105 mg CH, 630 mg S*

THRIFTY SCOTCH BROTH

6–8 servings   ⚖ ¢

2 medium-size yellow onions, peeled and coarsely chopped
3 medium-size carrots, peeled and cut in small dice
1/2 medium-size rutabaga, peeled and cut in small dice
1/2 cup medium pearl barley, washed
3 1/2 quarts cold water

Leftover lamb roast, leg or shoulder bone with a
  little meat attached
4 teaspoons salt
1/4 teaspoon pepper
1 tablespoon minced parsley

Place all ingredients except parsley in a large
(at least 1½-gallon) kettle, cover, and simmer 1½–2 hours. Cut meat from bones in
small pieces and return to kettle. Stir, taste
for salt, and adjust as needed. Sprinkle with
parsley and serve.

*NPS (6–8): 255–195 C, 55–40 mg CH, 1,520–1,140
  mg S**

Some Additional Ways to Use Up
Leftover Roast Lamb

Lamb and Zucchini Casserole *(4 servings):*
Stir-fry 3 cups sliced zucchini with ½ cup
chopped onion, ¼ cup minced sweet green
pepper, and 1 crushed clove garlic in 3 tablespoons olive oil in a large, heavy skillet 8–10
minutes over moderate heat until golden.
Add 2 cups canned tomatoes, 1 teaspoon
salt, and ¼ teaspoon each oregano and pepper and simmer, uncovered, 10 minutes. Stir
in 2 tablespoons flour blended with 3 tablespoons cold water and heat, stirring, until
thickened. Place 1 cup cubed cooked lamb
in a greased 1½-quart casserole, spread ½
vegetable mixture on top, and sprinkle with
½ cup grated Cheddar cheese. Add another
1 cup cubed lamb, the remaining vegetable
mixture, and ½ cup grated cheese. Top with
½ cup butter-browned bread crumbs and
bake, uncovered, 20 minutes at 350° F. until
bubbly.

NPS: 585 C, 105 mg CH, 1045 mg S*

¢ **Lamb and Black-eyed Pea Salad** *(4 servings):* Place 2 cups each diced cooked lamb
and cold, cooked, drained black-eyed peas in
a bowl. Add 2 tablespoons each minced
parsley and onion and dress with a good garlic, herb, or Italian dressing. Let stand 30
minutes, toss again, and serve.

NPS: 350 C, 70 mg CH, 50 mg S*

Shepherd's Pie: See Shepherd's Pie Variation
in the beef section.

Lamb and Vegetable Pie:
Lamb-Stuffed Vegetables:
Roast Lamb Hash:
Follow recipes given in Some Additional
Ways to Use Up Leftover Roast Beef, substi-
tuting lamb for beef.

Sliced Cold Lamb: Slice lamb about ¼"
thick, trim of fat, and top with Cumberland
Sauce or Anchovy or Herb Mayonnaise.

Sliced Hot Lamb: Slice lamb about ¼"
thick, trim off fat, and layer into an ungreased shallow casserole. Add just enough
Brown Curry, Fresh Mint, Poivrade, or
Quick Lemon-Caper Sauce to cover, cover
with foil, and heat 20 minutes at 350° F. If
you prefer, warm lamb in sauce about 5 minutes in a covered skillet over moderately low
heat.

To Make the Most of Very Small Amounts:
Follow suggestions given for beef, substituting lamb for beef.

LAMB CHOPS AND STEAKS

The choice is far broader than most of us
suspect, and so is the price range. Rib and
loin chops are the T-bones and porterhouse
of the lamb world. Far better buys are the
meatier arm and blade chops cut from the
shoulder and lamb steak, which is cut from
the leg. *(Note:* Mutton chops and steaks are
the same except that they are slightly larger
and less tender.) Here, then, are some of the
popular varieties:

Loin chops (plain or kidney—with the lamb
kidney in the center of the chop)

Rib chops (plain, double, or frenched—with
the meat stripped from the rib ends and paper frills slipped on as decoration)

Noisettes (trimmed eye of loin or rib)

Sirloin chop (the equivalent of sirloin steak)

Shoulder chops (arm, blade, boneless, Sara-
toga—boned and rolled)

Leg steak

Cube steak (knitted together from lamb
trimmings)

How to Cook

Amount Needed: Allow ⅓–½ pound boneless chops or steaks per person, ½–¾
pound of the bone-in. Loin and rib chops are
best cut 1"–1½" thick, others ¾"–1".

General Preparation for Cooking: Peel fell
from outer fat and trim fat to about ⅛";
slash at 1" intervals to prevent curling. If
meat seems moist, wipe with paper toweling
so it will brown well. Rub with pepper, if
you like, also garlic and/or rosemary, savory, tarragon, or thyme, but not salt—it
draws moisture to surface and prevents
browning. Let chops or steaks stand at room
temperature 1½–2 hours if convenient.

To Panfry (Sauté): Especially good for noisettes, cube and leg steaks, shoulder chops. Heat 1–2 tablespoons butter or cooking oil in a heavy skillet over moderately high heat about 1 minute, add chops and brown well on both sides, turning frequently with tongs. Cube steaks will take only 3 minutes altogether, noisettes 5–8, leg steaks and shoulder chops 8–12, depending upon whether you like pinkish or well-done meat. Season and serve.

VARIATION

Panfried Lamb Chops or Steaks with Minute Sauce: After cooking chops or steaks, transfer to a heated platter and keep warm. Drain all but 1 tablespoon drippings from skillet and add 2 tablespoons butter, 1 tablespoon hot water, 1 teaspoon Worcestershire sauce, and 1/2 teaspoon lemon juice. Heat 1 minute, swirling mixture round, spoon over meat, and serve.

To Panbroil: Recommended for loin, rib, arm, blade, and sirloin chops, also leg steaks. If chops seem very lean, lightly grease or salt skillet to keep meat from sticking. Heat over moderately high heat 1/2–1 minute, add chops and cook, uncovered, using times below as a guide. Turn frequently with tongs and pour off drippings as they accumulate. Season and serve.

To Broil: Recommended for the same cuts as panbroiling. Preheat broiler; line broiler pan with foil to eliminate messy clean-ups; lightly grease rack. Place chops on rack, fat edges toward back to prevent spattering. Adjust height and broil to desired doneness using times in Lamb Chop and Steak Broiling Chart as a guide. Turn chops only once during cooking, using tongs. Season and serve.

VARIATION

Planked Chops: Especially good for 1″–1 1/2″ thick rib or loin chops. Preheat broiler and prepare plank (see Planked Steak for details). Place chops close together on plank (cover any exposed areas of wood with foil to prevent charring) and broil 2″ from heat 4–5 minutes. Remove from broiler, season lightly with salt and pepper, and turn. Pipe a border of Duchess Potatoes around chops and brush lightly with Egg Glaze. Return to broiler and broil 4–5 minutes longer. Serve on plank, topping each chop with a dab of Maître d'Hôtel Butter. Garnish with broiled mushroom caps and/or tomato halves.

To Charcoal-Broil: Recommended for the same cuts as panbroiling. Prepare charcoal fire. For steaks or chops 1″–1 1/2″ thick it should be hot (350°–375° F. on grill thermometer) or of an intensity to make you remove your hand from grill level after saying, "Mississippi" three times. For 2″ chops or steaks it should be moderately hot (325° F.) or four Mississippis by the hand test. Spread glowing coals over fire bed to equal area of meat to be broiled, adjust height, and broil according to Lamb Chop and Steak Broiling Chart. Place a drip pan under meat to reduce flare-ups. Season and serve.

To Braise: Especially good for lamb and mutton arm, blade, and leg chops about 1″ thick. Brown chops 2–3 minutes on a side over moderately high heat in a large heavy skillet lightly brushed with butter, drippings, or oil; pour off all drippings. Season chops with salt and pepper, add a small amount of water (1/3 cup is about right for 4 chops), cover, and simmer slowly over low heat or cover and bake in a preheated 350° F. oven 3/4–1 hour until tender.

For Extra Savor: For the 1/3 cup water, substitute beer or dry vermouth; tomato juice, sauce or canned tomatoes; beef broth; apple cider or juice or All-Purpose Barbecue Sauce.

VARIATIONS

(All quantities based on enough chops for 4 persons)

Italian-Style: Rub chops with a cut clove garlic, then brown as directed. Season, add 1 cup meatless spaghetti sauce, cover, and simmer or bake until tender.

With Vegetables: Brown chops as directed and arrange in an ungreased roasting pan. Add 4 peeled, quartered potatoes, 4 peeled, quartered turnips, 12 peeled small white onions, and 2 stalks celery cut in 2″ lengths. Add 1 cup beef broth, sprinkle with 1 teaspoon salt and 1/4 teaspoon pepper, cover, and oven-braise as directed above 3/4–1 hour until chops and vegetables are tender. Baste one or two times during cooking. Sprinkle with 1 tablespoon minced parsley just before serving.

With Wine and Herbs: Rub chops with a cut clove garlic and 1/4 teaspoon rosemary or with 1/4 teaspoon each basil and oregano. Brown as directed, season with salt and pepper, then cover and braise in 1/2 cup dry red or white wine until tender.

To Bake: Recommended for arm, blade, or leg chops cut 1/2″–3/4″ thick. Preheat oven

APPROXIMATE TOTAL PANBROILING TIMES (IN MINUTES)

Chop Thickness	Rare	Medium Rare	Medium	Well Done
	Minutes	*Minutes*	*Minutes*	*Minutes*
1″	5–7	8–9	10–12	12–14
1½″	7–8	9–10	12–13	14–16
2″ (English chop)	8–9	10–12	13–15	16–18

to 350° F. Place steaks in a foil-lined shallow baking pan, sprinkle each with ⅛ teaspoon salt or garlic salt and a pinch pepper. Bake, uncovered, 30 minutes, turn, sprinkle again with salt and pepper, and bake, uncovered, 30 minutes longer until tender.

VARIATION

Baked Barbecued Lamb Chops: Omit seasonings, cover chops with 1 cup All-Purpose Barbecue Sauce or any favorite barbecue sauce, and bake, uncovered, as directed.

How to Test Lamb Chops and Steaks for Doneness

Bone-in Cuts: Make a small slit near bone to determine color of lean. Rare lamb will be rosy and juicy, medium faintly tinged with pink, and well done gray-brown.

Boneless Cuts: Make a small cut in center of lean and check color.

How to Give Lamb Chops and Steaks Extra Flavor

(Choose One Method Only.)

Before Panfrying, Panbroiling, Broiling, or Charcoal-Broiling:
• Marinate chops or steaks 4 hours in refrigerator in All-Purpose Barbecue Sauce or any good garlic, herb, or Italian dressing. Let come to room temperature in marinade, pat dry, and cook. If broiling or grilling, brush often with marinade.
• Brush both sides of chops or steaks with a little soy sauce or Teriyaki Sauce and let stand about 15 minutes.
• Rub both sides of chops or steaks with a little olive oil and crushed garlic and let stand 15–20 minutes.
• Rub both sides of chops or steaks with a little crushed fresh gingerroot and garlic and let stand 15–20 minutes.

During Broiling or Charcoal-Broiling:
• While broiling arm or blade chops, leg chops or steaks, brush often with the follow-ing mixture: ¼ cup melted butter, 2 tablespoons cooking oil, 1 tablespoon lemon juice, and ¼ teaspoon garlic powder.
• While charcoal broiling, toss any of the following onto the coals: 2–3 sprigs fresh sage, basil, or rosemary or 1 tablespoon of the dried; a dozen bay leaves or 1 tablespoon cracked juniper berries.
• During last minutes of broiling or grilling, brush lightly with Herb, Chive, Garlic, Lemon, or Anchovy Butter.

After Panfrying or Panbroiling:
• Serve with Tomato Sauce and garnish platter with Stuffed Tomatoes.

Lamb Chops Financière: Transfer chops to platter. Drain drippings from skillet, add ¼ cup Madeira, and cook and stir until reduced by half. Add 1 cup Rich Brown Sauce and bring to a boil. Serve chops on heart-shaped slices of butter-browned toast and top with sauce.

Lamb Chops à la Mexicaine: Transfer chops to platter. To skillet add 1 cup Rich Brown Sauce, 2 tablespoons each red wine vinegar and slivered orange rind (orange part only) and simmer 2 minutes. Spoon over chops and serve, garnished with Baked Bananas.

ENGLISH MIXED GRILL

2 servings

2 loin lamb chops, cut 1¼″ thick and trimmed of excess fat, or 2 filet mignons, cut 1¼″ thick
2 slices bacon (optional)
2 medium-size pork sausages
1 cup water
⅓ cup melted butter or margarine
½ pound calf's liver, cut in 1″ strips
4 lamb kidneys, trimmed of fat, membranes, and cores
6 medium-size mushroom caps, wiped clean
2 medium-size ripe tomatoes, halved crosswise (do not peel)
1¼ teaspoons salt (about)
¼ teaspoon pepper

2 small pats Maître d'Hôtel Butter
2 sprigs watercress (garnish)

Preheat broiler. Coil "tail" around each chop and secure with a toothpick. Or, if using filets, wrap a bacon slice around each and secure. Simmer sausages, uncovered, in the water 8 minutes; drain and pat dry on paper toweling. Arrange chops or steaks on a lightly greased broiler rack and brush with melted butter. Broil 3″ from heat for 3 minutes. Arrange sausages, liver, kidneys, mushrooms, and tomatoes around chops, brush with melted butter, and broil 5 minutes. Sprinkle all with ½ the salt and pepper, then turn. Brush again with melted butter and broil 2–3 minutes for a rare mixed grill, 3–4 minutes for medium, and 5–6 for well done; sprinkle with remaining salt and pepper. To serve, arrange chops in center of a heated platter, top each with a pat of Maître d'Hôtel Butter, and surround with sausages, liver, kidneys, mushrooms, and tomatoes. Garnish with cress and accompany with Shoestring Potatoes or French-Fried Potatoes. *(Note:* These ingredients just fit comfortably on a standard broiler rack, so if you want to double the recipe, you'll have to use 2 broilers or broil the components separately.)

NPS: 775 C, 920 mg CH, 2,375 mg S*

GROUND LAMB

Unquestionably the best cut of lamb to grind is shoulder because it has a good ratio of lean to fat, good flavor and texture. Second best are trimmings from shank and neck. Because lamb is finely grained, it needs to be ground one time only unless you want an unusually compact loaf or patty; if so, have the lamb ground twice. Like other ground meats, ground lamb is highly perishable and should be refrigerated until you're ready to use it. Ground lamb is leaner than most ground beef and more delicate in flavor.

LAMB CHOP AND STEAK BROILING CHART

Times (for chops or steaks at room temperature) are *approximate* because shape of chop, amount of fat and bone affect cooking time; outdoors, wind and temperature do too.

Cut	Thickness	Oven or Fire Temperature	Distance from Heat	Approximate Minutes per Side for		
				Rare	Medium	Well Done
Oven Broiling						
Loin, rib, and sirloin	1″	broil	2″	4–5	6	7
chops; 2″ English	1½″	broil	2″	6	7	8
chops	2″	broil	3″	8	9	10–12
Arm and blade chops;	¾″	broil	3″	not	5	6–7
leg steaks	1″	broil	3″	recommended	6	8–10
Mutton rib and loin	1″	broil	3″	not	8	9–10
chops	1½″	broil	3″	recommended	10	12–14
Charcoal Broiling						
Loin, rib, and sirloin	1″	hot	4″	5–6	7	8
chops; 2″ English	1½″	hot	4″	7	8–9	10
chops	2″	moderately hot	5″	8–10	10–12	12–14
Arm and blade chops;	¾″	moderately hot	4″	not	6	7–8
leg steaks	1″	moderately hot	4″	recommended	7	10
Mutton rib and loin	1″	moderately hot	4″	not	10	11–12
chops	1½″	moderately hot	5″	recommended	11	13–15

LAMB BURGERS

3–4 servings ☒

To be at their best, lamb burgers should be cooked until medium or well done.

1 pound ground lean lamb shoulder
1 teaspoon salt
1/8 teaspoon pepper

Lightly shape lamb into 3 plump or 4 slim patties and cook by one of the methods below; season with salt and pepper just before serving.

To Panfry (Sauté): Recommended for lean meat. Brown patties, uncovered, in 1–2 tablespoons cooking oil, butter, margarine, or drippings in a large, heavy skillet over moderately high heat. Plump patties will take about 5 minutes on a side for medium and 6 for well done, thin patties about 1 minute less per side for each degree of doneness. To keep patties juicy, avoid spanking or pressing down with a pancake turner as they cook.

NPS (3–4): 235–225 C, 105–80 mg CH, 830–625 mg S*

⚖ **To Panbroil:** Recommended for dieters, also for meat heavily flecked with fat. Lightly brush a large, heavy skillet with oil or sprinkle with salt; heat 1 minute over moderately high heat, add burgers, and brown, uncovered, using cooking times given for panfrying. Pour off drippings as they accumulate.

NPS (3–4): 225–170 C, 105–80 mg CH, 830–625 mg S*

⚖ **To Broil:** Recommended for dieters and fatty meat. Preheat broiler. Broil patties 3″ from heat on a lightly greased broiler rack. Plump patties will take about 6 minutes on a side for medium and 7–8 for well done, thin patties about 1 minute less per side in each instance.

NPS (3–4): 225–170 C, 105–80 mg CH, 830–625 mg S*

⚖ **To Charcoal-Broil:** Recommended for plump patties only. Prepare a moderately hot charcoal fire. Broil patties on a lightly greased grill 4″ from heat about 4–5 minutes on a side for medium and 6–7 for well done. Nutritional count same as basic recipe.

To Braise: Brown patties quickly in a lightly greased large, heavy skillet over high heat, turn heat to low, and pour in 1–1½ cups liquid (water; dry red or white wine; broth or gravy; tomato juice or sauce). Cover and simmer slowly 15–20 minutes. Serve patties with cooking liquid. Nutritional count same as basic recipe.

VARIATIONS

(all amounts based on recipe above)

Lamb and Sausage Burgers *(6 patties):* Mix ½ pound cooked, drained sweet or hot sausage meat with lamb; shape into 6 patties, cook until well done and season as directed.

NP Patty: 250 C, 85 mg CH, 905 mg S*

⚖ **Smothered Barbecue Burgers** *(6 patties):* Mix lamb with 1 cup soft white bread crumbs, ½ cup milk, 1 teaspoon salt, ¼ teaspoon chili powder, and 1/8 teaspoon pepper. Form into 6 patties and brown quickly in a lightly greased large, heavy skillet over high heat. Turn heat to low. Mix 2 tablespoons each Worcestershire sauce and sugar with 1 cup cider vinegar, ½ cup ketchup, and 1 tablespoon minced onion; pour over patties, cover, and simmer 10–15 minutes. Serve patties topped with plenty of sauce.

NP Patty: 195 C, 55 mg CH, 755 mg S*

Lamb Burgers in Foil *(4 servings):* Shape lamb into 4 patties; place each on a large square of heavy foil, top with thinly sliced potatoes, carrots, celery, and onion, season with salt and pepper, and wrap tight. Place on a baking sheet and bake 45–50 minutes at 350° F. until vegetables are tender; or grill 5″–6″ from a moderately hot charcoal fire 30–40 minutes, turning packages every 10 minutes.

NPS: 250 C, 80 mg CH, 680 mg S*

Note: See Variations on Hamburgers; all can be made with ground lamb instead of beef.

MOUSSAKA

8–10 servings ¢

Traditionally, *moussaka* has three layers—fried eggplant, a spicy meat mixture, and a custard-like sauce—but thrifty cooks often slip in an extra layer of leftover vegetables. The list of ingredients is long, but if you begin at the bottom and work up, you shouldn't have any trouble preparing this Greek and Turkish favorite.

BOTTOM LAYER
2 medium-size eggplants
1 teaspoon salt
2/3 cup olive oil (about)
1/4 cup fine dry bread crumbs

MIDDLE LAYER
4 medium-size yellow onions, peeled and minced
2 cloves garlic, peeled and crushed

3 tablespoons olive oil
2 pounds ground lamb shoulder or beef chuck
1/4 cup tomato paste
1/2 cup dry red wine
1/2 teaspoon oregano
1/4 teaspoon cinnamon
1 bay leaf, crumbled
2 teaspoons salt
1/8 teaspoon pepper
1/4 cup minced parsley
1/4 cup fine dry bread crumbs
2 eggs, lightly beaten
1/4 cup grated Parmesan cheese

TOP LAYER
6 tablespoons butter or margarine
6 tablespoons flour
1/8 teaspoon nutmeg
1/8 teaspoon white pepper
1 teaspoon salt
3 cups milk
1/4 cup grated Parmesan cheese
4 egg yolks, lightly beaten

Peel thin strips of skin lengthwise from eggplants every 1/2" so you have a striped effect, then cut in rounds 1/2" thick. Sprinkle rounds with salt and weight down between paper toweling 1 hour. Meanwhile, lightly oil a 14" × 10" × 2" pan and pat crumbs over bottom; set aside. Now begin middle layer: stir-fry onions and garlic in oil in a large, heavy skillet over moderate heat 8–10 minutes until golden. Add meat and brown, breaking up any chunks, 10–15 minutes. Turn heat to low, mix in all but last 4 ingredients, and simmer, uncovered, stirring occasionally, 15 minutes. Off heat, stir in parsley and crumbs; cool to room temperature and mix in eggs and Parmesan. By now, eggplants should be ready to fry. Brown rounds well on both sides, doing only 3–4 at a time and using 2 tablespoons oil—no more—for each batch; drain on paper toweling and arrange in pan in a double layer, fitting rounds as close together as possible. Spread meat sauce evenly over all. (*Note:* Recipe can be prepared to this point a day ahead and refrigerated. Bring to room temperature before proceeding.) Now begin final layer: melt butter in top of a double boiler over direct heat, blend in flour, nutmeg, pepper, and salt. Add milk and heat, stirring, until thickened; remove from heat. Mix Parmesan with yolks, then stir in a little of the hot sauce; return all to sauce, set over simmering water, and heat, stirring constantly, 2 minutes. Cool to room temperature. Preheat oven to 325° F. Spread sauce over meat and bake moussaka, uncovered, 1 1/2 hours until topping is puffy and lightly browned. Remove

from oven, let stand 10 minutes, then cut in large squares and serve.

NPS (8–10): 835–670 C, 325–260 mg CH, 1,525–1,220 mg S*

PASTÍTSIO

6–8 servings   ¢

This famous Greek lamb and macaroni casserole traditionally needs two cream sauces, one thick, one thin. But we've found a way to avoid making two separate sauces and dirtying two pans. This recipe doubles easily for a party.

1 medium-size yellow onion, peeled and minced
1 small clove garlic, peeled and crushed
1 pound ground lean lamb shoulder
2 tablespoons olive oil
1 teaspoon salt
1/4 teaspoon pepper
Pinch cinnamon
1 teaspoon oregano
1 cup Italian plum tomatoes, drained and coarsely chopped
1 cup tomato sauce
3/4 pound ziti or elbow macaroni
3/4 cup dry white bread crumbs
1/4 cup grated Romano cheese

CREAM SAUCE
4 tablespoons butter or margarine
6 tablespoons flour
2 1/4 cups milk
1 teaspoon salt
1/8 teaspoon pepper
2 egg yolks lightly beaten with 2 tablespoons milk

Stir-fry onion, garlic, and lamb in oil in a 2-quart saucepan 8–10 minutes over moderate heat, breaking lamb up with a spoon, until no longer pink. Add salt, pepper, cinnamon, oregano, tomatoes, and tomato sauce. Cover and simmer 30 minutes. Meanwhile, preheat oven to 350° F. Cook and drain ziti by package directions, rinse in cold water, and drain again. For the cream sauce: Melt butter in a saucepan over moderate heat, blend in flour, slowly add 1 3/4 cups milk and heat, stirring constantly, until very thick; blend in salt and pepper. Off heat, measure 1 1/4 cups sauce into a bowl, beat in remaining 1/2 cup milk and set aside. Mix a little of the remaining thick sauce into egg yolks, return to pan, blend all well, still off the heat, and set aside. Skim meat sauce of fat, then mix in 1/2 cup bread crumbs. Sprinkle remaining bread crumbs over bottom of a well-greased, shallow 2 1/2-quart casserole. Layer in half the ziti, spread with all the meat sauce, then half the thin cream sauce, and sprinkle with half the cheese. Top with remaining ziti and thin sauce. Using a spatula, spread thick cream sauce evenly over all, then scatter on remaining cheese. Bake, uncovered, 30 minutes, reduce temperature to 325° F., and bake 10 minutes longer until lightly browned.

NPS (6–8): 630–470 C, 180–135 mg CH, 1295–970 mg S*

BOBOTIE (CAPE MALAY CURRIED MINCED LAMB)

6–8 servings

3 slices firm-textured white bread
1 cup milk
2 large yellow onions, peeled and minced
3 cloves garlic, peeled and minced
3 tablespoons butter or margarine
2 tablespoons curry powder
3/4″ square fresh gingerroot, peeled and minced, or 1 teaspoon powdered ginger
1/4 teaspoon turmeric
1/4 teaspoon allspice
Pinch nutmeg
2 pounds ground lean lamb shoulder
1 1/4 teaspoons salt
1/4 teaspoon pepper
1/3 cup golden seedless raisins
1/4 cup lemon juice
1/4 cup beef or chicken broth
1 egg, lightly beaten
6 bay leaves

TOPPING
Milk squeezed from bread (above) + enough to total 3/4 cup
2 eggs, lightly beaten
1/4 teaspoon salt

Preheat oven to 325° F. Soak bread in milk 5–10 minutes. Meanwhile, in large heavy skillet set over moderate heat, sauté onions and garlic in butter 8–10 minutes until lightly browned. Blend in curry, gingerroot, turmeric, allspice, and nutmeg and mellow over lowest heat 5 minutes. Place lamb in large heat-proof bowl, add skillet mixture, and mix well with your hands. Squeeze bread dry, reserving all milk. Add bread to meat along with all remaining ingredients except bay leaves; mix well using hands. Pat into an ungreased 9″ × 9″ × 2″ pan or 2 1/2-quart shallow casserole. Stick bay leaves into mixture, spacing evenly. Bake *bobotie*, uncovered, 1–1 1/4 hours until *just* firm and lightly browned. Remove from oven, drain off all fat, and let stand at room temperature 5 minutes. Reduce oven heat to 300° F. Mea-

sure milk squeezed from bread and add enough additional milk to total 3/4 cup. Combine topping ingredients, pour over *bobotie*, and bake, uncovered, 20 minutes until set and touched with brown. Cut in large squares or wedges and serve.

NPS (6–8): 630–470 C, 180–135 mg CH, 1,295–970 mg S*

LEBANESE LAMB PIE (KIBBEH)

6–8 servings   ¢

TOP AND BOTTOM LAYERS
2 cups bulgur wheat
2 2/3 cups simmering water
1 medium-size yellow onion, peeled and minced
1 pound finely ground lamb shoulder
1 teaspoon salt

MIDDLE LAYER
1 medium-size yellow onion, peeled and minced
1 clove garlic, peeled and crushed
2 tablespoons olive oil
1 pound finely ground lamb shoulder
1 teaspoon salt
1/2 teaspoon cinnamon
1/8 teaspoon cardamom
Pinch pepper
1 cup coarsely chopped piñon nuts
1/2 cup dried currants or coarsely chopped raisins

TOPPING
3/4 cup melted butter or margarine
Yogurt

Preheat oven to 350° F. Soak bulgur wheat in water 20 minutes and drain well. Put onion and lamb through fine blade of meat grinder several times until reduced to paste; grind bulgur wheat until smooth and pasty and knead into lamb mixture along with salt. Pat half of mixture over the bottom of an oiled 13″ × 9″ × 2″ pan and set aside. For middle layer, stir-fry onion and garlic in oil 8–10 minutes in a large, heavy skillet over moderate heat; add lamb, salt, spices, and pepper and heat, stirring, about 10 minutes, breaking up any clumps of meat. Off heat, mix in nuts and currants; spread over wheat layer in pan. Pat remaining wheat mixture over all and press down firmly. Score top in a crisscross pattern and drizzle butter over surface. Bake, uncovered, 30–40 minutes until lightly browned. Cool slightly, cut into large squares, and serve topped with dollops of yogurt.

NPS (6–8): 975–730 C, 320–250 mg CH, 1200–950 mg S*

DOLMA (STUFFED GRAPE LEAVES)

6 servings ⚖️

Brined or preserved grape leaves can be found in specialty food shops and some supermarkets.

1 (1-pound) jar grape leaves
1 quart warm water (about)
Juice of 2 lemons

S T U F F I N G
1 pound ground lean lamb shoulder
1/2 cup uncooked rice
1/2 cup minced yellow onion
1 teaspoon salt
1/4 teaspoon allspice
1/8 teaspoon pepper
1/3 cup water
1 tablespoon minced parsley

If grape leaves seem salty, rinse well in warm water; sort leaves, selecting the most perfect to stuff; save the rest. Mix stuffing ingredients thoroughly. Place a grape leaf vein side up and stem end toward you on the counter; near the base put 1 heaping teaspoon stuffing. Fold right and left sides over stuffing and roll up—rolls should be quite tight so they won't unroll during cooking. Repeat until all stuffing is gone (you should have about 4 dozen rolls). Place a cake rack in a large, heavy kettle (it should be about 9" in diameter) and on it make a bed of the imperfect leaves. (These are merely to cushion the *dolma* and are discarded after cooking.) Arrange rolls very close together in neat rows in a single layer on top of leaves, place a dinner plate on top to weight down slightly. Pour in enough warm water to reach plate, cover, and simmer 35 minutes. Pour in lemon juice, re-cover, and simmer 15 minutes longer. When serving, pass lemon slices.

NPS: 180 C, 50 mg CH, 420 mg S*

HERBED LAMB LOAF

4–6 servings ¢

1 1/4 pounds ground lean lamb shoulder
1 medium-size yellow onion, peeled and minced
1/3 cup minced green pepper
2 eggs
2 cups packaged stuffing mix
1 tablespoon minced parsley
1/4 teaspoon thyme
1/2 teaspoon salt
1/8 teaspoon pepper
3/4 cup lamb, beef, or chicken stock

Preheat oven to 350° F. Mix all ingredients well, using your hands, and shape into a loaf in a greased shallow roasting pan. Bake, uncovered, 3/4–1 hour until loaf is firm to the touch and nicely browned. Serve as is or with Tomato Sauce.

NPS (4–6): 395–260 C, 235–160 mg CH, 1,015–675 mg S*

CURRIED LAMB AND CARROT LOAF

6 servings ¢

1 1/2 pounds ground lean lamb shoulder
1 cup very finely grated carrots
1 medium-size yellow onion, peeled and minced
1/2 cup minced celery
3 tablespoons minced chutney
2 cups crumbled corn bread
1 medium-size tart apple, peeled, cored, and minced
2 eggs
1/3 cup water
1/4 cup minced parsley
2 tablespoons curry powder
1 1/4 teaspoons salt
1/4 teaspoon cinnamon
1/8 teaspoon pepper

Preheat oven to 350° F. Mix all ingredients thoroughly with your hands and pack into a greased 9" × 5" × 3" loaf pan. Bake, uncovered, 50–60 minutes until loaf pulls from sides of pan and is firm in center. Pour off any drippings. Let loaf stand upright in pan 5 minutes before inverting and turning out.

NPS: 305 C, 190 mg CH, 760 mg S*

TURKISH LAMB BALLS BAKED IN TOMATO SAUCE

4–6 servings ¢

L A M B B A L L S
1 1/2 pounds ground lean lamb shoulder
1 medium-size yellow onion, peeled and minced
1 clove garlic, peeled and crushed
1/2 cup cracker meal
2 eggs, lightly beaten
1 1/4 teaspoons salt
1/4 teaspoon cinnamon
1/8 teaspoon anise
1/8 teaspoon pepper
3 tablespoons olive oil

S A U C E
1 cup tomato sauce
1 cup water

Preheat oven to 350° F. Mix all lamb ball ingredients except oil, using your hands, and shape into 2" balls. Brown balls well on all sides in oil in a large, heavy skillet over moderately high heat; drain on paper toweling. Transfer balls to an ungreased shallow 2-quart casserole. Mix tomato sauce and water, pour over balls, and bake, uncovered, 30–45 minutes until bubbly. Serve with rice or boiled potatoes.

NPS (4–6): 430–285 C, 255–170 mg CH, 1135–755 mg S*

CRISPY LAMB-STUFFED BULGUR BALLS

4 servings ¢

Good as an hors d'oeuvre as well as a main course.

1 cup bulgur wheat
2 cups boiling water
3/4 teaspoon salt

S T U F F I N G
1/4 pound ground lean lamb shoulder
1 small yellow onion, peeled and minced
1 tablespoon olive oil
1 tablespoon minced parsley
3/4 teaspoon salt
1/8 teaspoon pepper

C O A T I N G
2 eggs beaten with 2 tablespoons milk
2/3 cup unsifted flour

Shortening or cooking oil for deep fat frying

Stir bulgur wheat into boiling salted water, cover, and simmer about 8 minutes until all moisture is absorbed. Remove from heat and leave covered while you prepare filling. Stir-fry lamb and onion in olive oil about 10 minutes over moderate heat until lamb is no longer pink. Off heat mix in remaining stuffing ingredients; cool slightly. To roll balls, knead 1 heaping tablespoon bulgur until it holds together, shape into a small ball, then with your index finger, make a well in center; spoon in about 1/4 teaspoon stuffing and reshape into a ball to seal. Repeat until all bulgur is used up—you should have about 2 dozen balls; refrigerate them while you heat shortening. When shortening reaches 365° F. on deep fat thermometer, dip balls in egg, roll in flour, then fry 3–4 minutes until golden brown. Drain on paper toweling and serve piping hot.

NPS: 410 C, 155 mg CH, 885 mg S*

THE LESSER CUTS OF LAMB
(See Lamb and Mutton Chart)

"Lesser," in this case, means less expensive and less appreciated, but no less tender or delicious when properly prepared:

Neck slices and chunks
Shanks (fore and hind)
Riblets
Stew meat (the best comes from the shoulder)

ECONOMY LAMB STEW

4 servings ¢

A rich brown lamb and vegetable stew that costs very little to make.

2–2 1/2 pounds lean neck of lamb, cut in 1 1/2" cubes, or 2 lamb shanks, each cracked into 3 pieces
2 tablespoons cooking oil
3 medium-size yellow onions, peeled and coarsely chopped
6–8 medium-size carrots, peeled and halved crosswise
2 medium-size turnips, peeled and quartered
1/2 teaspoon minced garlic
1/2 teaspoon salt
1/4 teaspoon pepper
1 teaspoon basil
1 tablespoon minced parsley
2 cups water
1/4 cup unsifted flour blended with 1/4 cup cold water

Brown meat well, a few pieces at a time, in oil in a large, heavy kettle over moderately high heat; transfer to a bowl. In the same kettle, stir-fry onions until golden, about 8–10 minutes. Return lamb to kettle, add all remaining ingredients except flour-water paste, cover, and simmer 1 3/4 hours until lamb is tender. Mix in flour paste and heat, stirring, until thickened. Serve over boiled noodles with a crisp green salad.

NPS: 520 C, 160 mg CH, 510 mg S*

V A R I A T I O N

¢ **Economy Lamb and Potato Stew:** Prepare stew as directed and about 3/4 hour before it is done add 4–5 peeled and halved potatoes. Cover and continue cooking until potatoes and lamb are both tender.

NPS: 630 C, 160 mg CH, 515 mg S*

CASSOULET (FRENCH-STYLE BAKED BEANS WITH LAMB, PORK, AND GOOSE)

8 servings

If the following recipe seems long and involved, it is. There just isn't any short cut to a good cassoulet. There are dozens of versions, all based on dried white beans cooked with a combination of meats. Here's one of the best.

1½ pounds dried white beans (Great Northern or navy), washed and sorted
3 quarts cold water (about)
½ pound salt pork with rind left on
1 carrot, peeled
1 medium-size yellow onion, peeled and stuck with 6 cloves
1 bay leaf, 1 sprig each parsley and thyme, and 3 peeled cloves garlic, tied in cheesecloth
1 pound boned pork shoulder, cut in 1″ cubes and trimmed of excess fat
1 pound boned lamb or mutton shoulder, cut in 1″ cubes and trimmed of excess fat
2 tablespoons lard, goose, duck, or bacon drippings
2 medium-size yellow onions, peeled and minced
1 ham shank with some meat attached (leftover is fine)
1 meaty pork hock
1 clove garlic, peeled and crushed
1 cup beef broth
½ cup tomato purée
½ pound Kielbasa, Cotechino, or other garlicky pork sausage
½ pound mild pork sausage
½ preserved goose (leg and breast, obtainable in specialty food shops) or ½ roast goose or 1 small roast duckling
2 teaspoons salt (about)
¼ teaspoon pepper (about)
1 clove garlic, peeled and halved
1 cup soft white bread crumbs
2 tablespoons melted goose, duck, or bacon drippings

Soak beans in 1½ quarts water overnight or use the quick method.* Drain, measure soaking water, and add enough cold water to total 1½ quarts. Simmer beans, covered, with salt pork, carrot, onion, and cheesecloth bag 1 hour; do not drain. In another kettle brown pork and lamb, a few pieces at a time, in lard over moderately high heat; transfer to a bowl. Stir-fry onions in remaining drippings 8–10 minutes over moderate heat until golden. Return meat to kettle, add ham shank, hock, garlic, broth, and tomato purée. Cover and simmer ½ hour, add sausages, and simmer, covered, ½ hour longer. Off heat add preserved goose, scraped of ex-cess fat, and let stand 15 minutes. Preheat oven to 300° F. Cut all meats from bones in bite-sized pieces; slice sausages ½″ thick. Discard whole onion, carrot, and cheesecloth bag. Cut rind from salt pork; slice rind thin and dice the salt pork. Taste beans for salt and pepper and adjust as needed. Rub the inside of a deep 6-quart earthenware casserole or bean pot with the cut garlic, add salt pork rind, then layer in beans, salt pork, and all meats, beginning and ending with beans and sprinkling each layer with a little pepper. Pour in meat and bean broths. *(Note:* You may prepare recipe to this point early in the day or even the day before. Cover and refrigerate until about 4 hours before serving; let come to room temperature.)* Top with crumbs and drizzle with melted drippings. *(Note:* For a less rich mixture, skim fat from broths before adding.)* Bake, uncovered, 1½–2 hours until a brown crust forms on top of beans. Serve with a crisp green salad and a dry red or rosé wine.

NPS: 1,190 C, 220 mg CH, 2,085 mg S*

NAVARIN OF LAMB PRINTANIER (FRENCH LAMB STEW)

6 servings

2 pounds boned lean lamb shoulder, cut in 1½″ cubes
½ pound lean neck of lamb (with bones), cut in 1½″ cubes
2 tablespoons butter or margarine
1 tablespoon sugar
3 tablespoons flour
3 cups meat stock or a ½ and ½ mixture of chicken broth and water
¾ cup tomato purée
2 teaspoons salt
¼ teaspoon pepper
1 bay leaf and 1 sprig each parsley and thyme, tied in cheesecloth (*bouquet garni*)
1 clove garlic, peeled and crushed
12 small white onions, peeled
12 baby carrots, peeled
12 small new potatoes, peeled
4 turnips, peeled and quartered
1 pound fresh green peas, shelled, parboiled, and drained
½ pound fresh green beans, halved, parboiled, and drained

Preheat oven to 325° F. Brown lamb, a few pieces at a time, in butter in a large, heavy skillet over moderately high heat. Sprinkle last batch with sugar and let brown slightly, then transfer all to a Dutch oven. Lightly brown flour in skillet, slowly stir in stock, tomato purée, 1 teaspoon salt, and the pepper, and heat, stirring, until smooth; pour over meat. Add *bouquet garni* and garlic, cover, and bake 45 minutes. Add onions, re-cover, and bake 15 minutes. Add carrots, potatoes, and turnips, pushing them down into gravy, sprinkle with remaining salt, cover, and bake 30 minutes. Add peas and beans, cover, and bake 5–7 minutes. Ladle into a deep platter, pass the gravy separately, and serve with crusty bread.

NPS: 520 C, 130 mg CH, 1,270 mg S*

LAMB AND DHAL (DRIED PEA) CURRY

6–8 servings

3 pounds boned lamb shoulder, trimmed of excess fat and cut in 1" cubes
1 tablespoon curry powder
1 pint yogurt
1/4 cup butter or margarine
3 medium-size yellow onions, peeled and sliced thin
2 cloves garlic, peeled and crushed
1 pound yellow split peas
10 thin slices gingerroot
1 green chili pepper, sliced thin (include seeds)
2 sticks cinnamon
6 cloves
1 tablespoon powdered cumin
1 tablespoon crushed coriander seeds
2 teaspoons powdered cardamom
2 teaspoons powdered turmeric
1/2–1 teaspoon cayenne pepper (depending on how hot you like your curry)
1 (6-ounce) can tomato paste
1 quart water
1 1/2 teaspoons salt

Place lamb in a large bowl, sprinkle with curry, and toss to mix; stir in yogurt and let stand at room temperature 1 hour. Melt butter in a large, heavy kettle over moderate heat, add onions and garlic, and sauté, stirring, 12–15 minutes until golden brown. Add all but last 3 ingredients and heat, stirring, 2–3 minutes. Stir in meat-yogurt mixture, tomato paste, water, and salt, cover, and simmer slowly 1 1/2–2 hours until lamb is tender, stirring now and then. Serve over boiled rice and accompany with chutney.

NPS (6–8): 770–580 C, 190–140 mg CH, 1,070–800 mg S*

VARIATION

Lamb Curry: Prepare as directed but omit split peas and reduce water to 2 cups.

NPS (6–8): 510–380 C, 190–140 mg CH, 1,040–780 mg S*

COUSCOUS (NORTH AFRICAN LAMB STEW)

4–6 servings

Couscous is not only the name of the cooked semolina over which the stew is served but the name of the stew itself.

STEW
2 pounds boned lamb shoulder, cut in 1" cubes
2 tablespoons olive oil
2 tablespoons butter or margarine
1 (2 1/2-pound) broiler-fryer, cut up
3 medium-size yellow onions, peeled and coarsely chopped
1 clove garlic, peeled and crushed
4 ripe tomatoes, peeled, cored, seeded, and coarsely chopped
1/2 teaspoon thyme
1/4 teaspoon saffron
1 bay leaf, crumbled
6 cups chicken broth or water
2 medium-size sweet green peppers, cored, seeded, and cut in thin strips
6 medium-size carrots, peeled and cut in 1" chunks
1 tablespoon salt (about)
1/4 teaspoon pepper
1 (1-pound 4-ounce) can chick-peas, drained
2 medium-size zucchini, scrubbed and sliced 1/2" thick

COUSCOUS
1 recipe Boiled Couscous (*Note:* Use 1 cup stew liquid and 3 cups chicken broth.)

HOT SAUCE
1 cup stew liquid
2 tablespoons tomato paste
1 teaspoon paprika
1/4–1/2 teaspoon *harissa* (hot pepper sauce) or 1/2–1 teaspoon crushed dried hot red chili peppers
1/4 teaspoon coriander
1/8 teaspoon cumin

Prepare stew first: Brown lamb in oil and butter in a large, heavy kettle over moderately high heat; drain on paper toweling. Also brown and drain chicken. Add onions and garlic to kettle and brown 10–12 minutes; add tomatoes and herbs and cook and stir 2–3 minutes. Return lamb and chicken to kettle, add broth, green peppers, carrots, salt, and pepper, cover, and simmer 1/2 hour. Remove chicken, cover, and refrigerate. Continue cooking stew until lamb is nearly tender, about 1/2 hour. Remove 2 cups liquid from kettle and refrigerate (1 cup will be used for the Boiled Couscous, 1 for the Hot Sauce). Cool stew, chill, and skim off fat. (*Note:* Recipe can be prepared to this point a day or 2 in advance.) When ready to proceed, boil couscous as directed, using 1 cup of the reserved kettle liquid. Return chicken to stew and add chick-peas and zucchini. Place boiled couscous in a large colander lined with a triple thickness of dampened cheesecloth, set over kettle à la double boiler, cover with foil, and simmer stew slowly 1/2–3/4 hour until meats are very tender and flavors well blended. Meanwhile, mix remaining reserved cup kettle liquid with all hot sauce ingredients and keep warm over lowest heat. To serve: Mound boiled couscous on a large platter and top with stew. Pass hot sauce separately, letting each person take as much or little as he or she wants.

NPS (4–6): 1,915–1,275 C, 355–235 mg CH, 3,570–2,380 mg S*

RAGOUT OF MUTTON AND BEANS

6 servings ¢

1/4 pound salt pork, cut in small dice
2 pounds boned mutton shoulder, trimmed of excess fat and cut in 1" cubes
2 large yellow onions, peeled and minced
1 teaspoon sugar
1 tablespoon flour
1 cup cold water
1 clove garlic, peeled and crushed (optional)
1 pound dried white, pink, or red kidney beans, boiled 1 hour but not drained

Preheat oven to 325° F. Brown salt pork in a large, heavy skillet over moderate heat, lift out with slotted spoon and reserve. Brown mutton, a few pieces at a time, in drippings over moderately high heat, transfer to a bowl. Sauté onions in same skillet 8–10 minutes until golden; sprinkle with sugar and allow to caramelize slightly. Blend flour into skillet, add water, and heat, stirring, 1–2 minutes. Off heat return meat and salt pork to skillet. Place beans and their cooking liquid in an ungreased 1-gallon casserole or bean pot, add skillet mixture, and stir lightly. Cover and bake 1 1/2–2 hours until meat is tender.

NPS: 660 C, 120 mg CH, 340 mg S*

IRISH STEW

4 servings ¢

Prepare this stew early in the day or even a day ahead so flavors will blend and fat can be skimmed off.

5 medium-size potatoes, peeled and halved
2 1/2 pounds lean neck of lamb (with bones)

3 large yellow onions, peeled and sliced thin
4 teaspoons salt
1/4 teaspoon white pepper
1 quart cold water
2 tablespoons minced parsley (optional)

Layer potatoes, lamb, and onions into a 4-quart kettle with a tight-fitting lid, beginning and ending with potatoes. Add salt, pepper, and water, cover, and simmer about 2 hours until lamb is tender. Cool and refrigerate, covered, at least 3 hours. When ready to serve, skim fat from surface and discard. Heat stew, covered, over low heat until piping hot. Ladle into heated soup bowls, including plenty of the liquid. Sprinkle with parsley, if you wish, and serve.

NPS: 400 C, 100 mg CH, 2,310 mg S*

VARIATION

¢ **Irish Stew with Dumplings** (traditional in some parts of Ireland): Prepare and chill stew as directed. Skim off fat, then bring to a simmer over low heat. Make Dumplings by recipe, add to stew, cover, and cook as dumpling recipe directs.

NPS: 580 C, 105 mg CH, 2,760 mg S*

LAMB NECK SLICES BRAISED WITH LIMAS AND CARROTS

4 servings ¢

3 pounds lamb neck slices, cut 1" thick and trimmed of excess fat
1/3 cup unsifted flour
1 1/2 teaspoons salt
1/2 teaspoon pepper
3 tablespoons butter or margarine
1 large yellow onion, peeled and sliced thin
2/3 cup lamb or beef stock
2 tablespoons dry white wine
1 teaspoon finely grated lemon rind
1/8 teaspoon rosemary
1 (10-ounce) package frozen baby lima beans (do not thaw)
4 carrots, peeled and sliced thin
1 tablespoon minced parsley

Dredge neck slices in a mixture of flour, salt, and pepper, then brown in butter in a large, heavy skillet over moderately high heat; remove and set aside. Brown onion in drippings 10–12 minutes over moderate heat. Return lamb to skillet, pull onions on top, and add stock, wine, lemon rind, and rosemary. Cover and simmer slowly 35–40 minutes. Break up block of frozen limas by hitting package against edge of counter, scatter limas in and around neck slices, also carrots. Re-cover and simmer slowly 20–25 minutes longer until lamb and vegetables are tender. Sprinkle with parsley and serve.

NPS: 730 C, 145 mg CH, 1,285 mg S*

LANCASHIRE HOT POT

4 servings

Every town in Lancashire, England, has *its* version of Hot Pot. Here's one of the oldest.

2½ pounds lean neck of mutton or lamb (with bones), cut in 2″ chunks
1 sheep's kidney or 2–3 lamb kidneys, trimmed of fat, membranes, and cores and sliced ¼″ thick (optional)
2 large yellow onions, peeled and coarsely chopped
5–6 medium-size potatoes, peeled and sliced ¾″ thick
4 medium-size carrots, peeled and cut in 2″ chunks (optional)
1 quart cold water (about)
4 teaspoons salt
¼ teaspoon pepper

Preheat oven to 325° F. Layer lamb, kidney, onions, potatoes, and carrots in an ungreased deep 4-quart casserole; end with a layer of potatoes arranged as close together as possible. Pour in 3 cups water mixed with salt and pepper, then add enough additional water to come to bottom of potato layer. Cover with a buttered piece of foil. Bake 1 hour, uncover, and bake 1 hour longer until meat is tender and potatoes are browned on top. Serve with pickled red cabbage.

NPS: 450 C, 205 mg CH, 2,400 mg S*

YORK-STYLE LAMB RIBLETS SMOTHERED IN ONION AND CAPER SAUCE

4 servings   ¢

Economical mutton and lamb from the hilly Yorkshire Pennines made this a Victorian favorite.

3 pounds lamb riblets or spareribs, cut in serving-size pieces
1 carrot, peeled and cut in 2″ chunks
1 stalk celery, cut in half (include top)
1 cup + 1 tablespoon water
1¼ teaspoons salt
¼ teaspoon black pepper
1 Spanish onion, peeled, sliced ¼″ thick, and separated into rings
2 tablespoons butter or margarine
1 tablespoon flour
½ cup half-and-half cream or milk
2 tablespoons capers

⅛ teaspoon white pepper
⅛ teaspoon sugar
⅓ cup dry white bread crumbs

Preheat oven to 375° F. Place lamb in a large deep casserole, add carrot, celery, 1 cup water, 1 teaspoon salt, and black pepper; cover and bake 1½ hours. Meanwhile, simmer onion with butter and remaining 1 tablespoon water in a covered skillet over moderately low heat 15 minutes until limp but not brown. Blend in flour, slowly add cream, then cook and stir over moderate heat 3–5 minutes until thickened. Mix in capers, remaining ¼ teaspoon salt, white pepper, and sugar; cover and let mellow off heat. When lamb is tender, drain and save liquid; discard vegetables. Skim fat from broth, then stir ⅓ cup broth into onion mixture. Raise oven temperature to 450° F. Arrange lamb, 1 layer deep, in an ungreased roasting pan and spread evenly with onion sauce. Bake, uncovered, 10 minutes; sprinkle with crumbs and bake about 5 minutes longer or until crumbs are crisp and lightly browned. Serve each portion of lamb with some sauce and crusty topping.

NPS: 490 C, 110 mg CH, 1,015 mg S*

BARBECUED LAMB RIBLETS

4 servings   ¢

3 pounds lamb riblets or spareribs, cut in serving-size pieces
1 lemon, sliced thin
2 cups water
1 large yellow onion, peeled and sliced thin
2 tablespoons Worcestershire sauce
2 small cloves garlic, peeled
1 teaspoon salt
¼ teaspoon pepper
¼ cup chili sauce
2 cups barbecue sauce

Place all ingredients but barbecue sauce in a large, heavy kettle, cover, and simmer 1½ hours. Drain (save liquid for soups, gravies, etc.) and arrange riblets in a shallow roasting pan. Pour in barbecue sauce and let stand at room temperature 2 hours, turning ribs occasionally. Preheat oven to 325° F. Bake riblets, uncovered, 45 minutes, basting and turning often in sauce until browned, glazed, and tender.

NPS: 565 C, 85 mg CH, 2,950 mg S*

VARIATION

¢ **Charcoal-Barbecued Lamb Riblets:** Prepare riblets as directed up to point of baking. Meanwhile, prepare a moderately hot charcoal fire. Lift riblets from barbecue sauce, shaking off excess, and broil 4″–5″ from coals, turning and basting frequently, about 20 minutes until browned, glazed, and tender. Watch closely to avoid scorching. Nutritional count same as basic recipe.

BRAISED LAMB SHANKS

2 servings ¢

2 lamb shanks, each cracked into 3 pieces
2 tablespoons meat drippings or cooking oil
3/4 teaspoon salt
1/2 cup liquid (water, dry white or red wine, beer, cider, or beef consommé)
1 bay leaf and 1 sprig each parsley and thyme, tied in cheesecloth (bouquet garni)

Brown shanks well in drippings in a heavy kettle over moderate heat; pour off drippings, add remaining ingredients. Cover and simmer about 1 1/2 hours, turning shanks once or twice, until tender. Or cover and bake about 1 1/2 hours at 325° F. Skim liquid of fat and serve as gravy.

NPS: 435 C, 110 mg CH, 895 mg S*

VARIATIONS

¢ **Braised Lamb Shanks with Vegetables:** Sauté 1 coarsely chopped yellow onion along with shanks; add 4 carrots, 1 rutabaga and/or 4 turnips, all peeled and cut in large chunks, along with water, then proceed as directed. Increase salt slightly.

NPS: 625 C, 110 mg CH, 985 mg S*

Braised Lamb Shanks with Sour Cream and Capers: Cook shanks as directed and lift to a deep platter. Skim fat from broth, mix in 1/2 cup sour cream and 2 tablespoons capers. Spoon a little sauce over shanks and pass the rest.

NPS: 560 C, 135 mg CH, 1145 mg S*

¢ **Braised Lamb Shanks with Gremolata:** Sauté 1 minced yellow onion along with shanks; add 1 peeled and diced carrot with water and simmer as directed. About 10 minutes before serving, mix Gremolata, which consists of 1 tablespoon minced parsley, 1 small crushed clove garlic, and 2 teaspoons grated lemon rind; sprinkle over shanks. Thicken broth, if you like, before serving.

NPS: 470 C, 110 mg CH, 920 mg S*

Piñon- and Rice-Stuffed Lamb Shanks: Braise shanks as directed until very tender and bones are loose; cool until easy to handle, then carefully push bones out; save broth. Mix 3/4 cup cooked seasoned rice with 1 tablespoon minced parsley, 2 tablespoons coarsely chopped piñon nuts, and 1 minced scallion. Stuff shanks with mixture and arrange in an ungreased shallow baking dish. Add broth and bake, uncovered, 15–20 minutes at 350° F.

BOMBAY LAMB SHANKS

2 servings ¢ ⊲⊺⊳

2 small lamb shanks, each cracked into 3 pieces

MARINADE
1 medium-size yellow onion, peeled and coarsely chopped
1/2 cup yogurt
1/2 teaspoon curry powder
1 clove garlic, crushed
1/2 teaspoon poppy seeds, crushed in a mortar and pestle
1 teaspoon salt
1/4 teaspoon pepper
1/4 teaspoon ginger
1/4 teaspoon cinnamon
1 tablespoon lemon juice

Place lamb shanks in a large, deep bowl. Blend marinade ingredients in an electric blender at high speed 1 minute, then pour over shanks. Cover and chill 3–4 hours, turning shanks one or two times. Prepare a moderately hot charcoal fire. Place each shank on a large square of heavy foil, top with 1/4 cup marinade, and wrap tight. Reserve remaining marinade. Lay shanks on grill, not too close together, and cook 3″ from coals 1 1/4–1 1/2 hours, turning three or four times with tongs. Unwrap 1 shank and test for tenderness—meat should begin to separate from bone. If it doesn't, rewrap and cook a little longer. When tender, unwrap shanks and lay directly on grill. Broil 5–7 minutes, brushing occasionally with marinade and turning shanks so they brown evenly.

NPS: 315 C, 85 mg CH, 1200 mg S*

PORK

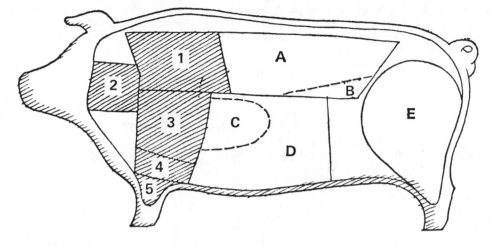

Note: Unshaded parts are the tender cuts. Shaded parts are not-so-tender.

THE TENDER CUTS:
A. LOIN
 Roasts (blade loin, center loin,
  crown, sirloin)
 Chops (rib, loin, blade, sirloin)
 Canadian bacon
 Back ribs
 Fat back
B. TENDERLOIN
C. SPARERIBS
D. BACON
 Bacon
 Salt pork
E. HAM (LEG)
 Hams (fresh and cured)
 Ham steaks

THE NOT-SO-TENDER CUTS:
1. BOSTON BUTT (SHOULDER)
 Roasts
 Steaks (blade, cube)
 Stew pork
 Ground pork
 Fat back
 Lard
2. JOWL
3. PICNIC
 Roasts (arm, fresh and smoked
  picnic)
 Steak (arm)
 Stew pork
 Ground pork
 Sausage
4. HOCK
 Fresh and smoked hock
5. FEET
 Fresh pigs' feet (trotters)
 Pickled pigs' feet

Thanks to breeders who are producing leaner, trimmer hogs, today's pork has about 1/3 fewer calories and 1/5 more protein than yesterday's. It remains one of our most nutritious meats, also one of the most economical and versatile.

How to Recognize Quality in Pork

The federal grades of pork (US 1, 2, 3, 4, Utility, Cull, etc.) are seldom used because the quality of pork varies less than that of beef, veal, or lamb, also because packers tend to use their own hallmarks of quality, e.g., *Premium* or *Star.* To be sure of good quality, look for finely grained, beige-pink lean with some marbling (very young pork will be nearly white with little marbling) and a snowy outer covering of fat. Look, too, for the federal inspector's round seal, which guarantees wholesomeness.

Cooking Pork

The cardinal rule of pork cookery: *always cook it sufficiently enough to kill the micro-*

scopic parasites that cause trichinosis, a serious, sometimes fatal illness. Not long ago cookbooks recommended cooking pork to an internal temperature of 185° F., but researchers have now proved that the trichinae (the disease causers) are killed at about 137°–140° F. As a result, some intrepid cooks are actually serving roast pork at 140° F.—risky business, it seems to us, considering the fact that the meat thermometer used to test the pork for doneness might well be a few degrees off. Other cooks, to play it safe, roast pork to an internal temperature of 150° F., but at that temperature, the pork is plenty pink. Since we don't like pink pork, we recommend roasting pork to an internal temperature of 170° F., at which stage the meat will be ivory-hued and succulent. (*Note:* Wash hands well after handling raw pork, especially ground pork, and never taste pork until after it is cooked.) *Caution:* Scientists at the Centers for Disease Control warn that *some* microwave ovens do not cook pork uniformly enough to ensure killing the trichinae. To be safe, cook pork in a microwave to at least 170° F., and test the meat in several different places with a meat thermometer to make certain that it is uniformly done throughout.

ROAST PORK

Pork is the most roastable of all meats because almost everything except the head, feet, and tail can be roasted. The choicest roasts come from the loin, the next best from the shoulder and ham.

Loin Roasts: It is possible to buy whole pork loins but not very practical; they are too cumbersome for home ovens. For extra-large parties, it is easier to cook two smaller roasts (side by side) than to tackle one giant.

Center Loin Roast (3–5 pounds): The preferred loin roast because of its sizable tenderloin.

Sirloin Roast (3–4 pounds): Second best; it may contain some tenderloin.

Blade Loin Roast (3–4 pounds): It has the shoulder blade (hence its name) but no tenderloin.

Half Loin Roast (5–7 pounds): Half the loin plus either the sirloin or blade loin.

Rolled Loin (3–5 pounds): Any of the above, boned and rolled.

Crown Roasts: Showy, super deluxe roasts made by removing the backbone from 1 or 2 half loins and shaping into a circle. Rib ends are frenched and garnished with paper frills or small fruits. Butchers sometimes grind the trimmings and pile them in the center of the crown. This ground meat should be removed because it slows roasting (mix with the dressing you're using to stuff the roasted crown, or save for meat loaf). Smallish crowns contain 10–14 ribs, large ones may have 24 or more ribs and weigh 10 pounds or more; all must be specially ordered. To determine the size you need, figure 2 ribs per person.

Tenderloin (3/4–1½ pounds): A long, lean muscle equivalent to beef filet or tenderloin. Boneless and luxury priced. Roast *or* braise.

Shoulder Roasts: Meaty, moderately priced cuts of excellent flavor.

Boston Butt (4–6 pounds): A blocky cut from the shoulder of pork. Also called *Boston Shoulder.* It is often available boned and rolled.

Fresh Picnic (5–8 pounds): Also called *Picnic Shoulder;* the lower part of the shoulder; it contains some shank.

Cushion-Style Picnic (3–5 pounds): Boned but not rolled; perfect for stuffing.

Rolled Fresh Picnic (3–5 pounds): Boned and rolled picnic.

Arm Roast (3–5 pounds): The top part of the picnic; it has no shank.

Fresh Hams: Hams are the hind legs of pork, and fresh ones are those that have not been cured and smoked. These make superlative roasts:

> Whole Ham (10–14 pounds)
> Whole Boneless Ham (7–10 pounds)
> Half Hams: Butt Portion (5–7 pounds);
> Shank Portion (5–7 pounds)

How to Roast Pork

Suitable Cuts: All fresh hams, loin and shoulder roasts. Because tenderloin and crown roasts are such luxurious cuts, there are separate recipes for each.

Amount Needed: Pork roasts should weigh at least 3 pounds and will be juicier if 4 or more. To figure number of servings, allow 1/3 pound boneless roast per person and 1/2 pound bone-in roast.

General Preparation for Cooking: To simplify carving of loin roasts, have butcher loosen backbone. With the exception of fresh hams, whose crisp roasted skin some people enjoy, roasts should have any skin removed and the outer fat layer trimmed to 1/2″. If skin is left on ham, score every 1/2″. Let roast stand at room temperature 1 1/2–2 hours if possible. Rub surface, if you like, with a little pepper and, for extra flavor, a cut clove garlic and/or compatible herb or spice such as anise, cinnamon, ginger, rosemary, sage, or thyme.

Continuous Low Heat Method: Preheat oven to 325° F. Place roast fat side up in a large, shallow roasting pan; all but bone-in loin roasts should be placed on a rack; bone-in loins can be arranged so ribs act as a rack. Insert meat thermometer in center of roast, not touching bone; if roast is stuffed, make sure thermometer is as near center as possible, but in meat, not stuffing. Roast, uncovered, until well done, without adding liquid to pan and without basting (use times in Roast Pork Chart as a guide). Transfer roast to heated platter, let "rest," if you like, 15–20 minutes to allow juices to settle and facilitate carving. Then serve.

Searing Method (recommended for loin roasts only): Preheat oven to 450° F. Insert meat thermometer and place roast in pan as for low heat method (above). Set roast in oven, reduce heat to 350° F., and roast, uncovered, 30–35 minutes per pound or until thermometer registers 170° F. Do not add water and do not baste.

Roast Pork Chart
(next page)

Times (for roasts that have stood at room temperature 1 1/2–2 hours, then roasted at a constant 325° F.) are merely approximate because size and shape of cut, proportion of fat and bone, internal temperature before roasting all affect cooking time.
• To roast at 350° F., allow 1–2 minutes less per pound and watch meat thermometer closely.
• For refrigerated roasts, allow 2–3 minutes more per pound.

How to Spit-Roast Pork

Best Cuts: Boned and rolled loin roasts. Small bone-in loins (with backbone removed) can be spit-roasted if carefully balanced and checked frequently for balance during cooking. Not recommended for spit-roasting, except over charcoal, where heat can be closely controlled by raising and lowering spit: hams and shoulder roasts (they are too chunky and/or irregularly shaped to cook evenly).

Amount Needed: Rolled roasts should weigh 4–5 pounds, bone-in roasts at least 3 if they are to be succulent and tender.

General Preparation for Cooking: Trim outer fat to 1/2″ and, if possible, let roast stand at room temperature 1 1/2–2 hours. Season or not, as you like.

In Rotisserie, Gas or Electric Barbecue, or Oven: Preheat unit. Insert spit lengthwise through center of roast so roast is balanced; tighten holding forks. Insert meat thermometer in center of largest lean muscle, touching neither bone nor the spit. Attach spit to rotisserie and roast 30 minutes per pound for bone-in roasts, 35–40 minutes per pound for rolled roasts. Thermometer should register at least 170° F. if you like no traces of pink. Remove roast from spit and let "rest" 15–20 minutes before carving.

Over Charcoal: Prepare a moderate charcoal fire toward back of grill. Balance meat on spit: Loins should be spitted lengthwise, straight through the center; bone-in hams with spit parallel to leg bone; rolled shoulder or hams on the bias. Tighten holding forks. Insert meat thermometer in center of roast, making sure it does not touch spit or bone; also make sure it will not hit anything as spit turns; attach spit to rotisserie. Because pork is rather fat, it is more likely to cause flareups than beef, veal, or lamb. To reduce flareups: Adjust height of spit so it is 7″–8″ from coals, have spit turn away from you, and place a drip pan toward front of grill, where it will catch drips (metal TV dinner trays make dandy drip pans, so does a triple-thick rectangle of heavy foil with its edges turned up). When roast is 1/2 done, lower spit 1″–2″. Roast, using the Spit-Roast Pork Chart as a guide.

VARIATION

Spit-Barbecued Pork: Marinate roast in refrigerator 8–12 hours in 2 cups All-Purpose Barbecue Sauce, turning occasionally. Lift from sauce and pat dry with paper toweling. Spit-roast as directed, brushing often with barbecue sauce during last 1/2 hour of cooking.

Some Glazes for Roast Pork

About 30 minutes before roast is done, spread or drizzle any of the following over surface and continue cooking as directed, basting once or twice:

ROAST PORK CHART

Cut	Weight in Pounds	Approximate Minutes per Pound at 325° F.	Meat Thermometer Temperature
Loin			
Center loin roast	3–5	30	170° F.
Sirloin and blade loin	3–4	40	170° F.
Half loin roast	5–7	35	170° F.
Rolled loin roast	3–5	40–45	170° F.

(Note: The following shoulder roasts and fresh hams will be more flavorful if roasted to 185° F.)

Cut	Weight in Pounds	Approximate Minutes per Pound at 325° F.	Meat Thermometer Temperature
Shoulder			
Boston butt	4–6	40	170° F.
Rolled Boston butt	3–4	45–50	170° F.
Fresh picnic	5–8	30	170° F.
Cushion-style picnic	3–5	35	170° F.
Rolled fresh picnic	3–5	40	170° F.
Arm roast	3–5	35–40	170° F.
Fresh Hams			
Whole ham	10–14	25	170° F.
Whole boneless ham	7–10	35	170° F.
Half ham (butt or shank portion)	5–7	30–35	170° F.

SPIT-ROAST PORK CHART

Cut	Weight in Pounds	Approximate Minutes per Pound over a Moderate Fire	Meat Thermometer Temperature
Bone-in loin roasts	3–7	25–35	170° F.
Rolled loin roast	3–5	30–35	170° F.
Boston butt	4–6	35–40	170° F.
Rolled Boston butt	3–4	40	170° F.
Fresh picnic	5–8	25–30	170° F.
Rolled fresh picnic	3–5	35	170° F.
Whole ham	10–14	25–30	170° F.
Whole boneless ham	7–10	30–35	170° F.
Half ham (butt or shank portion)	5–7	30–35	170° F.

- 1 cup whole or jellied cranberry sauce.
- 1 cup apricot, pineapple, peach, or cherry preserves.
- 1 cup orange, lemon, or ginger marmalade.
- 1 cup black currant, red currant, apple, or cranberry jelly.
- 1 cup maple syrup, honey, or molasses.
- 1 cup firmly packed light or dark brown sugar mixed with 1/4 cup sherry, Madeira, port, or fruit juice (cranberry, orange, apricot, apple, or pineapple).
- 1/2 cup firmly packed dark brown sugar mixed with 1 cup orange juice and 1 tablespoon each lemon juice and prepared spicy brown mustard.
- 1/2 cup soy sauce mixed with 1/4 cup maple or dark corn syrup and, if you like, 2–3 tablespoons cognac.
- 1–1 1/2 cups beer or stout.

How to Carve a Pork Arm Roast:
Separate large lean muscles from one another by making cuts at natural divisions and around the bones. Cut each large muscle across the grain into thin slices.

How to Carve Fresh Hams:
These are carved in the same way as cured hams (see carving instructions in Ham and Other Cured Pork).

How to Carve a Pork Loin Roast:

If butcher hasn't removed backbone, do so before setting roast on platter. Lay roast on platter so curved rib section will face the carver. Insert fork in top of roast and slice by cutting down along each rib.

How to Carve a Picnic Shoulder:

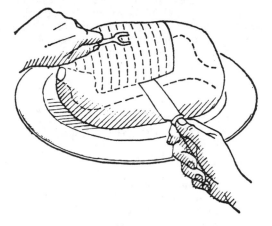

Cut a slice off side of picnic, then turn picnic so it rests on cut surface. At a point near elbow, cut straight down to armbone, then along bone; lift off this boneless piece; slice. Cut meat from both sides of armbone and cut each into thin slices.

ROAST PORK À LA BOULANGÈRE

8–10 servings

Pork roasted as an old-time French baker's wife would do it, on a buttery bed of onions and potatoes. It's a good choice for a party because it's the sort of dish everyone likes.

1 (5-pound) pork center loin roast
3 cloves garlic, peeled and crushed
3 1/2 pounds medium-size potatoes
2 cups coarsely chopped onions
1/3 cup minced parsley
1/4 cup melted butter or margarine
1 teaspoon minced fresh marjoram or 1/2 teaspoon dried marjoram (optional)
1 tablespoon salt
1/4 teaspoon pepper

Preheat oven to 350° F. Place pork fat side up in a very large, shallow roasting pan and rub well with garlic. Insert meat thermometer in center of roast, not touching bone. Roast, uncovered, 1 hour. Meanwhile, peel potatoes and slice very thin, letting slices fall into a large bowl of cold water (to prevent darkening, keep potatoes submerged until you're ready to use them). When pork has roasted 1 hour, remove from pan and set aside; pour off all drippings. Drain potatoes well and place in roasting pan, add all remaining ingredients and toss to mix. Place pork fat side up on top of potatoes. Raise oven temperature to 400° F. and roast, uncovered, 1–1½ hours longer or until thermometer registers 170° F. Stir potatoes from time to time and, if they seem dry, sprinkle with a little water or chicken broth. To serve, center pork on a large heated platter and wreathe with potatoes.

NPS (8–10): 635–505 C, 140–110 mg CH, 980–785 mg S*

CZECH-STYLE ROAST LOIN OF PORK WITH PARSNIP-SOUR CREAM SAUCE

6–8 servings

1 large parsnip, peeled, trimmed of woody central core, and coarsely grated
1 stalk celery, coarsely chopped
2 medium-size yellow onions, peeled and coarsely chopped
1 cup water
1 cup dry white wine
1 (4-pound) boned and rolled pork loin

S A U C E
Pan drippings and chopped vegetables
2 tablespoons butter or margarine
2 tablespoons flour
1 cup sour cream
2 teaspoons salt
⅛ teaspoon white pepper

Preheat oven to 325° F. Place parsnip, celery, and onions in a large, shallow roasting pan and toss lightly to mix. Pour in water and wine and lay pork fat side up on vegetables. Insert meat thermometer in center of pork. Roast, uncovered, 40–45 minutes per pound or until thermometer registers 170° F. Lift roast from pan and let "rest" while you prepare the sauce. Purée pan drippings and vegetables, a few at a time, by buzzing 20–30 seconds in an electric blender at low speed or 15–20 seconds in a food processor fitted with the metal chopping blade. Melt butter in a saucepan over moderate heat and blend in flour. Add purée and heat, stirring, until thickened and smooth. Blend in remaining ingredients and heat, stirring, 1–2 minutes until satiny. Do not boil. Carve pork into slices ¼" thick and top each serving with sauce.

NPS (6–8): 990–745 C, 240–180 mg CH, 975–735 mg S*

ROAST LOIN OF PORK STUFFED WITH APPLES AND PRUNES

4–6 servings

1 (3–3½-pound) pork loin roast (blade loin, center loin, or sirloin)
1 tart apple, peeled, cored, and sliced thin
7–8 pitted prunes, halved
1 teaspoon sugar
1 teaspoon salt
⅛ teaspoon pepper
1 recipe Pan Gravy
¼ cup currant jelly

Preheat oven to 325° F. With a sharp knife, cut down between ribs to backbone to form 8–9 chops. Force chops apart slightly and tuck a few apple slices and 2 prune halves between each. Using string, tie loin tightly together to seal in stuffing. Mix sugar, salt, and pepper and rub over roast. Place fat side up on a rack in a shallow roasting pan (loin roasts don't usually require racks, but it's a good idea to use one here because of the juiciness of the stuffing). Roast, uncovered, about 40 minutes per pound until well done (it is difficult to use a meat thermometer because of the way roast is cut, but, to be sure meat is done, insert thermometer in center of 1 chop, not touching bone; it should read 170° F.). Transfer to a heated platter, remove strings, and keep warm. Make Pan Gravy, blend in currant jelly, and serve.

NPS (4–6): 905–605 C, 195–130 mg CH, 710–475 mg S*

CROWN ROAST OF PORK

10 servings

1 (20-rib) crown roast of pork (about 7–8 pounds) (*Note:* Make sure butcher removes backbone and frenches rib ends.)
¼ teaspoon pepper
1 recipe Pecan-Bulgur Wheat Stuffing or 1½ quarts any stuffing
10 spiced crab apples or preserved kumquats (garnish)
Parsley or watercress sprigs (garnish)

If butcher has filled center of roast with ground rib trimmings, remove and save for meat loaf. Let roast stand at room temperature 1½–2 hours if possible. Preheat oven to 325° F. Arrange roast, rib ends up, in a large, shallow roasting pan (no need for a rack) and rub with pepper. Insert a meat thermometer between 2 ribs in center of meat, making sure it does not touch bone. Cover rib ends with foil to keep them from charring. Roast, uncovered, 2 hours; spoon stuffing into hollow in center of roast, cover loosely with foil, and roast 1½ hours longer. Remove all foil and roast 15–20 minutes longer or until thermometer registers 170° F. Using 2 pancake turners, transfer roast to heated platter and let "rest" 15–20 minutes. Place crab apples or kumquats on alternate rib ends and wreathe base with parsley or cress. Serve as is or with Pan Gravy.

*NPS: 760 C, 160 mg CH, 555 mg S**

For a Smaller Crown Roast *(6–8 servings):* Order a 12–16-rib crown roast (5–6 pounds) and prepare exactly like larger roast. Allow about 35 minutes per pound roasting time. Nutritional count same as basic recipe.

How to Carve a Crown Roast:
With a very sharp, rather small carving knife, slice down between each rib and remove chops one at a time. Serve 2 chops—and some stuffing—to each person.

ROAST WHOLE PORK TENDERLOIN

4 servings

1 (1½-pound) pork tenderloin
1 clove garlic, peeled and slivered
¼ teaspoon pepper
2 strips bacon (optional)
1 teaspoon salt

Preheat oven to 325° F. Make 6–8 tiny slits over surface of pork and insert a garlic sliver in each; rub well with pepper. Place tenderloin on a rack in a shallow roasting pan and insert meat thermometer in center. If meat seems lean, lay bacon strips on top. Roast, uncovered, about 1 hour until thermometer registers 170° F. Remove bacon for last 20 minutes of roasting so meat will brown. Transfer tenderloin to a hot platter, sprinkle with salt, and let "rest" 15 minutes. To serve, cut into slices ¼"–½" thick. If you like, make Pan Gravy.

*NPS: 245 C, 125 mg CH, 665 mg S**

V A R I A T I O N S

Roast Stuffed Whole Pork Tenderloin: Split tenderloin lengthwise, not quite all the way through so that one long side acts as a hinge, and spread flat like a book. Spread one cut side with 1–1½ cups Sage and Onion Dressing, close, and tie in several places to hold in stuffing. Season and roast as directed above.

*NPS: 300 C, 135 mg CH, 875 mg S**

Orange-Glazed Whole Pork Tenderloin: Prepare tenderloin and begin roasting as directed. Meanwhile prepare glaze by mixing ¼ cup orange juice with ¼ cup firmly packed light brown sugar. When tenderloin has roasted ½ hour, brush with a little glaze. Continue roasting as directed, brushing once or twice more with glaze. *(Note:* Any of the glazes recommended for pork or ham can be used in place of the orange glaze.)

*NPS: 305 C, 125 mg CH, 120 mg S**

Oven-Barbecued Pork Tenderloin: Prepare a marinade by mixing ½ cup light corn syrup with ¼ cup each soy sauce and ketchup, 2 tablespoons each Worcestershire sauce and cider vinegar, 1 teaspoon powdered mustard, and 1 crushed clove garlic. Place tenderloin in a large bowl with marinade, cover and chill 8 hours or overnight, turning occasionally. Lift meat from marinade and roast as directed above, omitting slivered garlic. Baste with marinade every 15 minutes.

*NPS: 385 C, 125 mg CH, 1,705 mg S**

Chinese-Style Pork Tenderloin: Heat and stir ½ cup each soy sauce and sugar, and 1 cup water in a small saucepan over moderate heat until sugar dissolves. Place tenderloin in a large bowl, add saucepan mixture, cover, and chill 8 hours or overnight, turning meat occasionally. Lift meat from marinade, roll in 1 cup sifted cornstarch, and roast as directed, omitting garlic slivers. Baste with marinade every 15 minutes.

*NPS: 460 C, 125 mg CH, 2,745 mg S**

BRAISED WHOLE PORK TENDERLOIN WITH MUSHROOM GRAVY

4 servings

1 (1½-pound) pork tenderloin
1⅓ cups water
3 bay leaves
1 (4") sprig fresh thyme or ¼ teaspoon dried thyme

G R A V Y
4 tablespoons butter or margarine
½ pound mushrooms, wiped clean and sliced thin
3 tablespoons flour
Drippings from pork tenderloin
1 cup water
¼ cup dry white wine
1 teaspoon salt
⅛ teaspoon pepper

Brown tenderloin well on all sides in a large, heavy skillet over moderately high heat. This will take about 10 minutes. Reduce heat to moderately low, add water, bay leaves, and thyme, cover, and simmer about

1 hour until pork is fork tender. Discard bay leaves and thyme sprig; drain liquid from skillet and reserve. Remove pork and keep warm while you make the gravy. Melt 2 tablespoons butter in the skillet and sauté mushrooms about 5 minutes over moderate heat until tender. Remove to a small plate. Melt remaining butter, blend in flour, and heat, stirring, 3–5 minutes until *roux* turns a rich amber brown. Add drippings and water and heat, stirring, until thickened and smooth. Add mushrooms, wine, salt, and pepper and continue to cook and stir 2–3 minutes. To serve, carve tenderloin crosswise into slices 1″ thick, arrange on a platter, and smother with mushroom gravy.

NPS: 335 C, 140 mg CH, 760 mg S*

BRAISED PORK TENDERLOIN FILLETS

4 servings

8 slices pork tenderloin, cut 1½″–1¾″ thick
½ cup unsifted flour
1 teaspoon salt
¼ teaspoon pepper
2 tablespoons cooking oil
¼ cup water, dry white wine, or apple juice

Dredge fillets by shaking in a paper bag with flour, salt, and pepper; brown 4 minutes on each side in oil in a heavy skillet over moderately low heat. Add water, cover and simmer 30 minutes until fork tender and no trace of pink remains. Serve with Pan Gravy, Mustard Sauce, or Poivrade Sauce.

NPS: 340 C, 125 mg CH, 640 mg S*

VARIATION

Breaded Pork Fillets: Dip fillets in flour, then in 1 egg beaten with 1 tablespoon cold water, then in seasoned bread crumbs to coat evenly; let dry on a rack at room temperature 10 minutes. Brown in ¼ cup cooking oil, drain off all but 1 tablespoon drippings, add water, cover, and simmer until tender and well done. Uncover, raise heat to moderate, and cook 1–2 minutes, turning frequently, to crispen crumb coating.

NPS: 355 C, 195 mg CH, 355 mg S*

APPLE-AND-PECAN-STUFFED ROAST SHOULDER OF PORK

8 servings

1 (4-pound) cushion-style picnic shoulder (ask butcher to give you the bones)
1 teaspoon salt

⅛ teaspoon pepper
1 quart (about) Apple and Pecan or other savory stuffing

Preheat oven to 325° F. Trim outer fat on shoulder to ½″, sprinkle cavity with salt and pepper, and loosely spoon in stuffing. Skewer edges shut every 1″–1½″ and lace with string; place fat side up on a rack in a shallow roasting pan and insert meat thermometer in center, making sure it does not rest in stuffing. Roast, uncovered, about 35 minutes per pound or until thermometer reaches 170° F. Let roast "rest" 15–20 minutes at room temperature before carving. Serve as is or with Au Jus Gravy, using stock made from bones.

NPS: 745 C, 180 mg CH, 720 mg S*

To Glaze: About ½ hour before roast is done, top with a suitable glaze (see Some Glazes for Roast Pork) and finish roasting as directed, basting once or twice. Recipe too flexible for meaningful nutritional count.

SAGE-AND-CIDER-SCENTED ROAST FRESH HAM

10–12 servings

If skin is left on a fresh ham during roasting, it will become bubbly brown and crunchy. When carving, slice into thin strips and include one or two with each portion. Eat pork skin with your fingers—it's far too crisp to catch with a fork.

1 (5–7-pound) fresh half ham (shank or butt portion)
3¾ cups apple cider
1 tablespoon powdered sage
2½ teaspoons salt (about)
5 tablespoons flour blended with ½ cup cold water
¼ teaspoon pepper

Preheat oven to 325° F. Leave skin on ham and score at ½″ intervals or, if you prefer, remove and trim fat to ½″. Place ham on a rack in a shallow roasting pan. Moisten surface with ¼ cup cider, sprinkle evenly with sage and, if you've left skin on, with 1 teaspoon salt. Insert meat thermometer in center of ham, not touching bone. Roast, uncovered, 30–35 minutes per pound or until thermometer reaches 170° F. After 1 hour's roasting, pour 1 cup cider over ham. Continue to roast, basting occasionally with pan drippings. When ham is done, transfer to hot platter and let "rest." Remove rack from roasting pan, add remaining cider, set over moderate heat, and heat, scraping browned bits from bottom. Mix in flour paste and heat, stirring, until thickened and smooth. Add remaining salt and the pepper. Strain gravy before serving.

NPS (10–12): 485–405 C, 120–100 mg CH, 660–550 mg S*

PORK "POT ROAST" WITH APPLE GRAVY

8–10 servings

This isn't the usual way of preparing pork roast, but it's a good one because it requires so little attention.

1 (5–7-pound) fresh ham or 1 (4-pound) rolled
   Boston butt or fresh picnic
1 teaspoon salt
1/4 teaspoon pepper
1/4 cup cold water

G R A V Y
6 tablespoons flour
1 1/2 cups water
1 1/2 cups apple juice
1 1/2 teaspoons salt
1/4 teaspoon pepper
1/8 teaspoon liquid gravy browner

If ham has skin on, remove; trim fat to 1/2". Render fat trimmings in a large, heavy kettle over moderately low heat; discard trimmings and pour off all but 2 tablespoons drippings. Raise heat to moderate, add pork and brown all over, about 15 minutes. Add salt, pepper, and water, cover, and simmer 3 1/2–4 hours until cooked through. Transfer to a hot platter and keep warm while making gravy. Drain off all but 1–2 tablespoons drippings; blend in flour, then remaining gravy ingredients and heat, stirring and scraping brown bits from bottom, until thickened; cover and simmer 2–3 minutes; taste and adjust seasonings if needed. Slice roast, not too thin, and serve with plenty of gravy. Potato Pancakes and red cabbage go well with this.

NPS (8–10): 405–325 C, 120–95 mg CH, 765–610 mg S*

To Cook in the Oven: Preheat oven to 325° F. Prepare pot roast as directed but simmer in oven instead of on top of stove. Check kettle occasionally to see that liquid simmers but does not boil; reduce temperature to 300° F. if needed. Nutritional count same as basic recipe.

V A R I A T I O N S

Country Inn Pork Pot Roast: About 1 hour before pork is done, add 1/2 cup water, 6–8 peeled, halved potatoes, 8 peeled small carrots, 1 pound peeled small white onions or 1 small rutabaga, peeled and cut in 1" cubes. Sprinkle vegetables with 1 teaspoon salt and 1/8 teaspoon pepper, cover, and simmer until tender. Transfer meat and vegetables to heated platter and keep warm while making gravy as directed.

NPS (8–10): 560–445 C, 120–95 mg CH, 1,080–865 mg S*

Barbecued Pork Pot Roast: Marinate pork in any zippy barbecue sauce 24–28 hours. Pat meat dry and rub with 1 tablespoon chili powder. Brown as recipe directs, add 1/4 cup barbecue sauce along with water called for, cover, and simmer as directed, turning meat once or twice. If you like, serve with additional barbecue sauce.

NPS (8–10): 395–315 C, 125–100 mg CH, 275–220 mg S*

Cranberried Pork Pot Roast: Brown pork, then add 1 cup whole or jellied cranberry sauce along with water, cover, and simmer as directed. Transfer pork to a hot platter, top with cooked-down pan juices, and keep warm; make Pan Gravy in a separate saucepan.

NPS (8–10): 585–465 C, 150–120 mg CH, 420–335 mg S*

CHOUCROUTE GARNIE (SAUERKRAUT WITH MEAT)

8 servings

Serve a well-chilled Riesling or Traminer wine with this Alsatian classic. Or beer.

1 large yellow onion, peeled and minced
2 tablespoons lard or butter
2 pounds sauerkraut, drained
1 tart apple, peeled, cored, and coarsely chopped
1 teaspoon juniper berries, tied in cheesecloth
1 (1/4-pound) piece fat bacon or salt pork
2 1/2–3 cups dry white Alsatian or other wine
1 (4-pound) center cut pork loin roast or
   (3-pound) boned and rolled loin
8 knackwurst
8 bratwurst or frankfurters

Preheat oven to 300° F. Sauté onion in lard in a heavy kettle over moderate heat 5–8 minutes until pale golden. Add kraut, apple, juniper berries, bacon, and wine; cover and bring to a simmer, then transfer to oven and bake 1 hour. Meanwhile, trim fat on loin to 1/4" and brown, fat side first, in a heavy skillet over moderate heat about 10 minutes; pour off drippings as they accumulate. When kraut has baked 1 hour, add pork, re-cover, and bake 1¾ hours longer. Check pot occasionally and add more wine if it seems dry; mixture should be moist but not soupy. Add sausages and bake 15 minutes until tender; remove cheesecloth bag. Pile sauerkraut on a large platter, top with bacon, sausages, and sliced pork. Serve with boiled potatoes sprinkled with minced parsley.

NPS: 1,025 C, 215 mg CH, 2,265 mg S*

VARIATIONS

Substitute 6–8 small meaty pork hocks for pork loin and add to sauerkraut along with wine and apple; otherwise, prepare as directed. Nutritional count same as basic recipe.

Substitute 1½ pounds kielbasa (Polish sausage) or Cotechino (Italian sausage) for either of the German sausages and add to sauerkraut along with wine and apple.

NPS: 1,050 C, 225 mg CH, 2,535 mg S*

About ½ hour before serving, stir a stout jigger of kirsch into kettle.

NPS: 1,050 C, 215 mg CH, 2,265 mg S*

ROAST PORK REVISITED

(How to Use Up Leftovers)

SLICED PORK AND BAKED BEAN CASSEROLE

4 servings   ¢

A delicious way to revive leftover roast pork.

8 slices leftover roast pork, cut ¼″ thick
2 tablespoons bacon drippings or cooking oil (about)
1 large yellow onion, peeled and minced
1 medium-size sweet green pepper, seeded, cored, and minced
¼ teaspoon powdered mustard mixed with 1 tablespoon cold water
1 (1-pound 5-ounce) can baked beans in tomato sauce
1 tablespoon Worcestershire sauce
¼ cup chili sauce
3 tablespoons dark brown sugar

Preheat oven to 350° F. Trim excess fat from pork, dice enough of it to measure 2 tablespoons, and render in a skillet over moderate heat. Measure drippings and add enough bacon drippings to total 2 tablespoons. Sauté onion and green pepper in the drippings 8–10 minutes until golden, stirring occasionally. Mix in mustard, beans, and remaining

ingredients; spoon half into an ungreased 2-quart casserole. Arrange pork slices on beans, top with remaining beans, cover, and bake ½ hour until bubbly.

NPS: 655 C, 110 mg CH, 855 mg S*

SUBGUM (10-INGREDIENT) PORK CHOW MEIN

4 servings   ⚖

¼ cup blanched, slivered almonds
2 tablespoons peanut oil
1½–2 cups diced leftover roast pork, trimmed of fat
½ pound mushrooms, wiped clean and sliced thin
1½ cups shredded celery cabbage or finely chopped celery
2 cups chicken broth
1 teaspoon salt
2 tablespoons cornstarch blended with ¼ cup cold water
1 (4-ounce) can bamboo shoots, drained and sliced thin
1 pound bean sprouts, washed

Stir-fry almonds in oil in a *wok* or heavy skillet 1–2 minutes over moderately high heat until golden; drain on paper toweling. Pour oil from skillet, add pork, mushrooms, and cabbage, and stir-fry 2 minutes. Add broth, salt, and cornstarch mixture and heat, stirring, until thickened. Add remaining ingredients and cook and stir 2–3 minutes. Serve over heated chow mein noodles topped with almonds.

NPS: 295 C, 50 mg CH, 1,045 mg S*

To Make with Raw Pork: Cut ½ pound pork tenderloin or loin across the grain into ⅛″ × ⅛″ × 2″ strips. Stir-fry almonds as directed and drain. Add pork to skillet and stir-fry 1–2 minutes; add vegetables and proceed as recipe directs.

NPS: 235 C, 35 mg CH, 1,040 mg S*

VARIATION

⚖ **Pork Lo Mein:** Boil and drain ½ pound Chinese egg noodles or spaghettini by package directions. Omit almonds. Stir-fry pork, mushrooms, and cabbage in oil 2 minutes, add ½ cup broth, salt, and cornstarch mixture, and heat, stirring, until thickened. Instead of adding bamboo shoots and bean sprouts, top with noodles, cover, and simmer 3–4 minutes. Serve with soy sauce.

NPS: 420 C, 100 mg CH, 750 mg S*

CHAR SHU DING (DICED ROAST PORK WITH CHINESE VEGETABLES)

4–6 servings ⚖

2 tablespoons cooking oil
1 cup minced yellow onion
1½ cups coarsely shredded celery cabbage
½ pound mushrooms, wiped clean and sliced thin
¼ pound snow pea pods
2 stalks celery, cut in thin diagonal slices
1 sweet green or red pepper, cored, seeded, and cut in long, thin strips
2 cups diced or sliced leftover roast pork
2 cups chicken broth
3 tablespoons soy sauce
¼ teaspoon sugar
2 tablespoons cornstarch blended with ¼ cup cold water
1 pound bean sprouts, washed
1 (3-ounce) can water chestnuts, drained and sliced thin
⅓ cup toasted, slivered almonds

Heat oil in a *wok* or large, heavy skillet over moderately high heat 1 minute; add onion, celery cabbage, mushrooms, pea pods, celery, and green pepper and stir-fry 3–4 minutes (do not brown). Add pork and stir-fry 1 minute, then broth, soy sauce, sugar, and cornstarch mixture and cook, stirring, until thickened. Toss in bean sprouts and water chestnuts and heat 1–2 minutes. Taste for salt and adjust as needed. Serve over boiled rice and top each portion with toasted, slivered almonds.

NPS (4–6): 495–330 C, 65–40 mg CH, 1,540–1,025 mg S*

CHOP SUEY

4 servings ¢ ⚖ ▯

Tag ends of peas, beans, or carrots cluttering up the refrigerator? Toss them into chop suey. This one can also be made with leftover beef or lamb.

2 tablespoons cooking oil
1 cup minced yellow onion
4 stalks celery, cut in thin diagonal slices
1 sweet green or red pepper, cored, seeded, and cut in long, thin strips
2 cups diced or sliced leftover roast pork
2 cups chicken broth
3 tablespoons soy sauce
¼ teaspoon sugar
2 tablespoons cornstarch blended with ¼ cup cold water
1 pound bean sprouts, washed

Heat oil in a *wok* or large, heavy skillet over moderately high heat 1 minute, add onion, celery, and green pepper, and stir-fry 3–4 minutes (do not brown). Add pork and stir-fry 1 minute, then all remaining ingredients except bean sprouts; cook and stir until thickened. Add sprouts and toss 1–2 minutes. Taste for salt and adjust as needed. Serve over boiled rice or chow mein noodles.

NPS: 390 C, 65 mg CH, 1,490 mg S*

To Make with Raw Pork: Slice lean tenderloin or loin across the grain into strips 2″ long and ⅛″ wide; stir-fry 1 minute in oil, then add onion, celery, and green pepper and proceed as directed.

NPS: 250 C, 45 mg CH, 1,480 mg S*

Some Additional Ways to Use Up Leftover Roast Pork

¢ ⚖ **Chinese Pork Fried Rice** *(4 servings):* Stir-fry 1½ cups minced leftover pork, 1 minced small yellow onion, and 1 crushed clove garlic in 2 tablespoons peanut oil in a large, heavy skillet over moderately high heat 5–8 minutes until lightly browned. Stir in 1 cup uncooked rice and stir-fry 3–4 minutes. Add ¼ pound lightly sautéed sliced mushrooms, 1¾ cups water, 2 tablespoons soy sauce, and a pinch pepper. Bring to a boil, cover, and simmer slowly 25 minutes until rice is tender. Top, if you like, with strips of scrambled egg.

NPS: 420 C, 50 mg CH, 705 mg S*

⚖ **Cubed Pork and Olives in Sour Cream** *(2 servings):* Melt 2 tablespoons butter in a saucepan over moderate heat and blend in 2 tablespoons flour, 1 teaspoon each paprika and salt, and 1 crushed clove garlic. Add 1 cup water and 1 tablespoon lemon juice and heat, stirring, until thickened. Add 1½ cups cubed cooked pork and ½ cup sliced, pitted ripe olives, cover, and simmer 5–10 minutes to blend flavors. Off heat, mix in ⅓ cup sour cream. Serve over boiled rice.

NPS: 625 C, 150 mg CH, 1,565 mg S*

Sliced Cold Pork: Slice pork about ¼″ thick, trim of fat, and top with mustard or Cumberland or Sour Cream-Horseradish Sauce.

Sliced Hot Pork: Slice pork about ¼″ thick, trim of fat, and layer into an ungreased shallow casserole. Add just enough gravy or Barbecue, Hot Mustard, Madeira, Plum, or Sweet-Sour Sauce to cover, cover with foil, and heat 20 minutes at 350° F. Or, if you prefer, heat pork in sauce 5 minutes in a covered skillet over moderately low heat.

Hot Roast Pork Sandwiches: Heat meat and a suitable sauce in a skillet as for Sliced Hot Pork (above) and serve, open face, on toast or bread.

To Make the Most of Very Small Amounts: See suggestions given for beef.

SUCKLING PIG

Suckling pigs call to mind medieval England, where whole pigs were spitted in open hearths, also the luaus of Hawaii, where they are pit-roasted on the beach. They are not often prepared in modern America, although they were popular at colonial feasts. Suckling pigs are 6–8 weeks old and weigh from 10 to 20 pounds. There is little meat on them, but what there is approaches pâté in richness. Some people like to munch the richly browned skin, but for most tastes it is too leathery. Suckling pigs must always be especially ordered, sometimes as much as a week or two ahead. The best size is in the 14- to 18-pound range—large enough to contain some meat, small enough to fit in most home ovens. To figure number of servings, allow about 1 1/4 pounds pig per person (most of the weight is bone). *Tip:* To keep the pig cool until roasting time (you can't get a suckling pig in the refrigerator unless you clear virtually everything else out), place in an extra-large roasting pan and set on a porch or just outside the door (suckling pig is cold-weather food, so the outdoor temperature should be just about right unless it's below freezing; in that case, you'll have to make accommodations inside). Turn a large washtub upside down over the pig and weight down with bricks or large rocks to remove temptation from neighborhood dogs. Suckling pig should be reserved for the most festive occasions. When inviting guests, tell them what you plan to serve—some people are squeamish about seeing a whole pig on a platter.

ROAST SUCKLING PIG

10–12 servings

1 (15-pound) suckling pig, dressed
1 tablespoon salt
1 teaspoon pepper
1 recipe Chestnut Mushroom Stuffing or 1

recipe Brandied Wild Rice, Corn Bread, and Chestnut Stuffing
1/4 pound butter, softened to room temperature

GARNISHES
1 small red apple or 1 lemon
1 pint fresh cranberries
12 fresh bay laurel leaves

Preheat oven to 350° F. Wipe pig inside and out with a damp cloth and dry with paper toweling. Rub inside well with salt and pepper. Lay pig on its side and stuff loosely; wrap remaining stuffing in foil and refrigerate. Close cavity with skewers and lace together to close. Place a large, sturdy rack in an extra-large shallow roasting pan; lay a triple thickness of foil diagonally on top, allowing plenty of overhang. Lift pig onto foil so it, too, is diagonal to the pan, bend hind legs forward and front legs backward into a "praying" position so pig crouches. Turn up foil edges, forming a "pan" to catch drips. Rub pig with butter; cover ears and tail with bits of foil and force a foil ball about the size of an apple into the mouth. Roast, uncovered, brushing occasionally with butter, 18 minutes per pound. Meanwhile, string cranberries and leaves into 2 garlands. Save 2 cranberries for pig's eyes. About 1 hour before serving, place foil package of stuffing in oven to heat. When pig is done, lift carefully to an extra-large platter; remove skewers, lacing, and foil. Place an apple or lemon in pig's mouth, 1 cranberry in each eye (secure with toothpicks), and lay garlands around neck. Place extra stuffing in a separate dish and skimmed drippings in a gravy boat. Recipe too flexible for meaningful nutritional count.

To Spit-Roast over Charcoal: Prepare a very large, moderate charcoal fire. Prepare and stuff pig as above, truss legs to body in kneeling position, and insert spit lengthwise through center of pig so it is balanced; use at least 4 holding forks, 2 at each end, to secure pig on spit. Arrange coals in a circle and place a drip pan in the center. Attach spit to rotisserie, adjust height so spit is 7"–8" from coals, and roast pig 15–18 minutes per pound. Arrange on platter and garnish as above.

How to Carve Suckling Pig: Set platter on table so pig's head is to left of carver. First, remove the hams or hind legs, then divide pig into chops by cutting along the backbone, then down along each rib. See that each person receives both chops and ham or leg meat.

PORK CHOPS AND STEAKS

The easiest way to learn these small cuts is to relate them to the roasts from which they come (see Pork Chart). A blade chop, for example, is simply a slice of the blade loin; a loin chop, a slice of center loin; a sirloin chop, a slice of sirloin, and so on. As with roasts, the most expensive chops and steaks are those from the loin, the most economical those from the Boston butt or picnic:

Blade Chop: A moderate sized, moderate-priced chop from the blade loin roast.

Rib Chop: A smallish, moderate-to-expensive chop from the rib end of the center loin. It is usually cut 1 rib thick.

Butterfly Chop: A double rib chop, made by removing the rib bone, cutting the meat almost in half horizontally, and opening flat like a book. It's fairly expensive and must be ordered.

Loin Chop: The choicest pork chop. It is cut from the heart of the center loin roast, usually 1 rib thick, and contains a plump nugget of tenderloin. Expensive as pork chops go.

Top Loin Chop: A loin chop with the tenderloin removed. Fairly expensive.

Sirloin Chop: A chop from the sirloin roast; any cut from the part bordering the loin may contain a tag end of tenderloin. Moderately expensive.

Tenderloin Slices: These are to pork what filet is to beef—boneless, butter-smooth, luxury-priced steaks. A whole pork tenderloin weighs only 3/4–1 1/2 pounds, so a single slice is scarcely a mouthful.

Blade Steak: A slice of Boston butt containing the shoulder blade; 1 blade steak will usually serve 2. Economical.

Arm Steak: A meaty slice of the picnic, large enough for 2. Economical.

Leg Steak: Also called pork cutlet, this is simply a slice of fresh ham, usually from the butt portion; 1 leg steak will serve 2. Moderate.

How to Cook

Amounts Needed: All pork chops and steaks should be at least 1/2″ thick and will be more attractive and succulent if cut 3/4″–1″; those to be stuffed should be 1 1/4″–1 1/2″ thick.

Tenderloin Slices: Allow 2–3 (1/4″–1/2″) slices per person.

Rib, Loin, and Top Loin Chops: Allow 1–2 per person.

Blade, Butterfly, and Sirloin Chops: Allow 1 per person.

Blade, Arm, and Leg Steaks: Allow 1 for each 2 persons.

General Preparation for Cooking: If meat seems moist, wipe with paper toweling so it will brown nicely. Trim off all but 1/4″ outer fat; rub with pepper if you like, also garlic and/or a compatible herb such as coriander, rosemary, sage, tarragon, or thyme, but not with salt (chops and steaks should not be salted until after browning). Let stand at room temperature 1 1/2–2 hours before cooking if convenient.

To Broil or Panbroil: Not recommended; by the time chops and steaks have cooked through at this intense heat, they will be dry, tough, and stringy.

To Panfry (Sauté): Recommended only for very thin pork chops or steaks (those 1/2″ or less) and then only as a change of pace from braised chops (see recipes that follow).

To Braise: Here's the preferred method for preparing all pork chops and steaks because it allows them to cook thoroughly without toughening and drying. Brown chops or steaks 3 minutes on a side over moderately high heat in a skillet brushed with oil; pour off all drippings. Sprinkle lightly with salt and pepper, add a small amount of water (1/3 cup is about right for 4 chops or 2 steaks), cover, and simmer slowly over low heat or in a preheated 350° F. oven 50–60 minutes until well done.

To Test for Doneness: Make a small slit near bone (or, if meat is boneless, in the center); flesh should show no traces of pink. Or, pierce meat with a sharp fork near center; if juices run clear with no tinges of pink, meat is well done. Serve as is or with Pan Gravy or Country Gravy.

For Extra Savor: Substitute any of the following for the water called for above: tomato juice or sauce or undrained, canned tomatoes; pineapple, orange, apple, or mixed fruit juices; milk, buttermilk, or light cream; barbecue or meatless spaghetti sauce; chicken or beef broth; beer or dry white wine.

VARIATIONS

(All quantities based on enough chops or steaks for 4 persons)

Hungarian-Style Pork Chops or Steaks: Rub chops or steaks with 1–2 teaspoons paprika, brown as directed, and remove from skillet. In drippings stir-fry 1 minced medium-size yellow onion 5–8 minutes over moderate heat until pale golden. Return chops to skillet, season with salt and pepper, add 1/2 cup beef broth and 1 bay leaf. Cover and simmer as directed. Transfer chops to a platter, blend 1 cup sour cream into pan juices, heat 1 minute but do not boil. Pour over meat and serve.

NPS: 520 C, 125 mg CH, 210 mg S*

Herbed Pork Chops or Steaks in Wine: Rub chops or steaks with a mixture of 1/4 teaspoon each powdered rosemary, sage, and 1/2 crushed clove garlic and let stand at room temperature 15 minutes. Brown as directed; pour drippings from skillet and season meat with salt and pepper. Add 1/2 cup dry white wine, cover, and simmer as directed. Transfer meat to a hot platter and keep warm. Boil down pan juices until reduced to 2–3 tablespoons; spoon over meat and serve.

NPS: 310 C, 90 mg CH, 65 mg S*

Braised Pork Chops or Steaks with Dressing: Brown chops as directed. With drippings make 1/2 recipe Pan Gravy or Mushroom Gravy. Top each chop or steak with 2–3 tablespoons poultry stuffing mix prepared by package directions, add gravy, cover, and simmer as directed. Uncover for last 5 minutes.

NPS: 460 C, 110 mg CH, 235 mg S*

Orange-Lemon Pork Chops or Steaks: Brown meat as directed and pour off drippings. Top each with a 1/4″ thick slice peeled, seeded orange and lemon. Mix 1 teaspoon salt, 1/8 teaspoon pepper, 1/4 cup firmly packed light brown sugar, and 3/4 cup orange juice; pour over meat, cover, and simmer as directed.

NPS: 390 C, 90 mg CH, 620 mg S*

Apple-Raisin Pork Chops: Brown chops as directed; pour off drippings and season meat. Top each with a 1/2″ thick slice cored tart apple (peeled or unpeeled) and fill centers with seedless raisins. Pour in 1/3 cup apple juice or cider, cover, and simmer as directed.

NPS: 325 C, 90 mg CH, 65 mg S*

Pork Chop-Corn Scallops: Brown chops as directed; pour off drippings and season meat. Arrange in a lightly greased 2-quart casserole. To skillet in which chops were browned, add 1/2 cup boiling water and heat 1–2 minutes, scraping up browned bits; pour over chops. Mix 1 (1-pound) can cream-style corn with 1 1/2 cups soft bread crumbs, 3 tablespoons each prepared mild yellow mustard and finely grated onion, 1/4 teaspoon salt, and a pinch pepper. Spoon mixture on top of each chop, mounding it up, and bake, uncovered, as directed, but without turning.

NPS: 455 C, 90 mg CH, 700 mg S*

To Bake Pork Chops: Preheat oven to 350° F. Arrange chops in a lightly greased shallow roasting pan or casserole and bake, uncovered, 1/2 hour; drain off drippings. Sprinkle with salt and a pinch pepper, turn, and bake, uncovered, 1/2 hour longer or until no trace of pink remains. Transfer to a hot platter, sprinkle with salt and pepper. Serve as is or with Pan Gravy or Country Gravy.

NPS: 405 C, 90 mg CH, 70 mg S*

For Extra Savor: About 10 minutes before chops are done, top each with any one of the following: 2 tablespoons apple jelly or whole cranberry sauce; 1/2 peach filled with red currant jelly; 1 pineapple ring or 2 tablespoons pineapple chunks sprinkled with 1 teaspoon light brown sugar. Or spread each chop with 1 tablespoon mustard (mild or spicy).

VARIATIONS

(All quantities based on enough chops for 4 persons)

Plum-Glazed Pork Chops: Arrange chops in pan as directed. Mix 1/2 cup plum jelly with 1 tablespoon red wine vinegar, 1 teaspoon salt, 1/2 teaspoon ginger, and 1/8 teaspoon pepper. Spoon over chops and bake, uncovered, without turning, 1 hour or until cooked through.

NPS: 350 C, 75 mg CH, 610 mg S*

Orange-Glazed Pork Chops: Bake chops 1/2 hour, drain off drippings, and turn. Mix 1 teaspoon salt and 1/8 teaspoon pepper with 1/2 cup orange juice, 1/4 cup firmly packed light brown sugar, and 1 teaspoon prepared mild yellow mustard; pour over chops and bake, uncovered, 1/2 hour longer until cooked through. Remove chops to a hot platter and keep warm. Mix 1 teaspoon cornstarch with 1 tablespoon cold water, stir into pan juices along with 1 tablespoon grated orange rind. Set over moderate heat and cook, stirring, until thickened and clear. Stir in 1 peeled, seeded, and sectioned orange, spoon over chops, and serve.

NPS: 335 C, 75 mg CH, 625 mg S*

Pineapple-Glazed Pork Chops: Follow Orange-Glazed Pork Chops recipe above; substitute pineapple juice for orange, omit rind, and use 1 cup pineapple tidbits instead of orange sections.

NPS: 490 C, 100 mg CH, 650 mg S*

Pork Chops 'n' Sweet Potatoes: Bake chops as basic recipe directs; 20 minutes before they are done, arrange 1 pound boiled, peeled, sliced sweet potatoes or yams around chops, brush with 2 tablespoons melted butter, and sprinkle with 3–4 tablespoons maple syrup. Continue baking as directed until done, basting potatoes once with pan juices.

NPS: 460 C, 90 mg CH, 165 mg S*

Pork Chops and Sauerkraut: Bake chops as recipe directs 30 minutes; remove from pan and drain off drippings. Spoon 1 pound undrained sauerkraut into pan and arrange over bottom; lay chops on top, season with salt and pepper, and sprinkle, if you like, with paprika. Bake, uncovered, 30 minutes longer until chops are done.

NPS: 325 C, 90 mg CH, 910 mg S*

Pork Chops and Baked Beans: Bake chops as recipe directs; 20 minutes before they are done remove from pan. Empty 1 (1-pound) can baked beans into pan, stir in 1 tablespoon each prepared mild yellow mustard, dark brown sugar, and Worcestershire sauce. Top with chops and continue baking, uncovered, 20 minutes longer or until chops are done.

NPS: 405 C, 80 mg CH, 670 mg S*

Carolina Pork Chops: Place chops in pan, top with 1¼ cups All-Purpose Barbecue Sauce, bake, basting occasionally with sauce, 1 hour until done.

NPS: 485 C, 120 mg CH, 1,495 mg S*

BRAISED PORK CHOPS AND ONIONS ROSEMARY

4 servings

4 loin pork chops, cut 1″ thick and trimmed of excess fat
¾ cup unsifted flour
1 teaspoon salt
⅛ teaspoon pepper
1 tablespoon butter or margarine
2 medium-size yellow onions, peeled and sliced thin
¾ cup dry white vermouth
¾ cup water

2 (4″) sprigs fresh rosemary or ¼ teaspoon dried rosemary

Preheat oven to 350° F. Dredge chops by shaking in a paper bag with flour, salt, and pepper. Melt butter in a heavy Dutch oven over moderately high heat and brown chops well on both sides, about 8–10 minutes. Remove from heat, lay onion slices over chops, pour in vermouth and water, and lay rosemary sprigs on top (if using dried rosemary, sprinkle evenly over all). Cover and bake 1 hour or until chops are tender. Remove herb sprigs and serve, topping each portion with onions and a generous ladling of pan juices.

NPS: 410 C, 95 mg CH, 680 mg S*

CREOLE PORK CHOPS

4 servings

4 loin or rib pork chops, cut 1″ thick and trimmed of excess fat
1 teaspoon cooking oil
1 teaspoon salt
⅛ teaspoon pepper
¼ teaspoon paprika
2 tablespoons butter or margarine
1 medium-size yellow onion, peeled and minced
1 medium-size sweet green pepper, cored, seeded, and minced
1½ cups canned tomatoes, coarsely chopped (include some liquid), or 1½ cups tomato sauce
¼ teaspoon sugar
2–3 drops liquid hot red pepper seasoning

Preheat oven to 350° F. Brown chops 5–7 minutes on each side over moderately low heat in a skillet brushed with oil. Transfer to a lightly greased 2½-quart casserole; sprinkle with salt, pepper, and paprika. Pour off all but 1 tablespoon drippings from skillet, add butter, and sauté onion and green pepper over moderate heat 8–10 minutes until onion is golden. Add remaining ingredients and simmer, uncovered, 10 minutes, stirring occasionally. Pour sauce over chops, cover, and bake 50–60 minutes until fork tender. Good with Saffron Rice.

NPS: 345 C, 105 mg CH, 825 mg S*

VARIATION

Creole Pork Steaks: Substitute 2 (¾″) blade or arm steaks for chops and proceed as directed, allowing at least 1 hour baking time.

NPS: 375 C, 90 mg CH, 785 mg S*

BARBECUED PORK CHOPS

4 servings

This dish freezes well; double or triple recipe, if you like, then let chops cool in sauce before packing in freezer containers.

4 rib or loin pork chops, cut 1″ thick and trimmed of excess fat
1 teaspoon cooking oil

CHUCK WAGON BARBECUE SAUCE
1/2 cup ketchup
1/2 cup cider vinegar
3/4 cup water
1 medium-size onion, peeled and minced
1 clove garlic, peeled and crushed
1 tablespoon chili powder
1 tablespoon Worcestershire sauce
1/4 cup firmly packed light brown sugar
1 teaspoon salt
1/4 teaspoon pepper

Preheat oven to 350° F. Brown chops well on each side 8–10 minutes over moderately high heat in a skillet brushed with oil; transfer to a small roasting pan or casserole. Meanwhile, simmer all sauce ingredients 20 minutes, stirring frequently. Pour sauce over chops and bake, uncovered, 1 hour or until tender. Turn chops once during baking.

NPS: 340 C, 90 mg CH, 1,065 mg S*

PORK CHOPS WITH GARLIC-CRUMB STUFFING

6 servings

6 rib pork chops, cut 1¼″ thick and trimmed of excess fat
1 teaspoon cooking oil
1 teaspoon salt
1/4 teaspoon pepper
1/3 cup boiling water, chicken or beef broth

STUFFING
1 small yellow onion, peeled and minced
1/4 cup minced celery
2 cloves garlic, peeled and crushed
1 tablespoon cooking oil
1 cup poultry stuffing mix
1/4 cup hot water
1 small tart apple, peeled, cored, and chopped fine
1/4 teaspoon salt
1/8 teaspoon pepper

Preheat oven to 350° F. Starting at rib bone, cut a pocket in each chop. Prepare stuffing: stir-fry onion, celery, and garlic in oil over moderate heat 5–8 minutes until pale golden. Off heat mix in remaining ingredients and spoon into chop pockets (no need to use toothpicks or skewers to seal in stuffing). Brown chops well on each side, about 8–10 minutes, over moderately high heat in a skillet brushed with oil. Transfer to an ungreased shallow roasting pan, sprinkle with salt and pepper, add boiling water, cover, and bake 1–1¼ hours or until tender.

NPS: 405 C, 115 mg CH, 700 mg S*

VARIATIONS

Oyster-Stuffed Pork Chops: Cut pockets in chops as above and fill with well-drained, coarsely chopped fresh oysters (you'll need about 1⅓ cups; save broth). Toothpick openings shut if oysters seem to slide out. Proceed as directed, substituting oyster broth for boiling water.

NPS: 365 C, 145 mg CH, 490 mg S*

Spinach-Stuffed Pork Chops: Stuff chops with about 1½ cups well-drained, cooked, minced spinach, then proceed by basic recipe above.

NPS: 340 C, 115 mg CH, 475 mg S*

Substitute 1⅓ cups Sage and Onion Dressing; Pecan-Bulgur Wheat Stuffing; Rice and Mushroom Stuffing, or any favorite for that given above. Proceed as directed. Recipes too flexible for meaningful nutritional count.

SKILLET PORK CHOPS AND RICE

4 servings

4 loin or rib pork chops, cut 1″ thick and trimmed of excess fat
1 teaspoon cooking oil
2 teaspoons salt
1/4 teaspoon pepper
1 cup uncooked rice
1¼ cups beef or chicken broth
1 cup hot water

Brown chops well on each side, about 8–10 minutes, over moderately high heat in a skillet brushed with oil. Pour off all but 1 tablespoon drippings, sprinkle chops with half the salt and pepper. Scatter rice over chops and sprinkle with remaining salt and pepper. Add broth and water, cover, and simmer 50–60 minutes until chops are tender.

NPS: 450 C, 90 mg CH, 1,435 mg S*

To Bake: Brown chops as directed, transfer to a 2-quart ungreased casserole, season, add remaining ingredients, cover and bake 1 hour at 350° F. until chops are tender.

Baked Pork Chops, Peppers, and Rice:
Brown chops as directed and transfer to an
ungreased 2-quart casserole. In drippings
stir-fry 2 diced sweet green peppers and 1
thinly sliced yellow onion 5–8 minutes over
moderate heat until onion is pale golden.
Mix in rice, spoon over chops, add seasonings, broth, and water; cover and bake 1
hour at 350° F. until chops are tender.

NPS: 440 C, 90 mg CH, 1,445 mg S*

PANFRIED PORK CHOPS

4 servings

Though it's not generally recommended that
pork chops be panfried, they can be prepared this way if cut quite thin (no more
than 1/2" thick) and cooked very gently.
Made by the following recipe, they are surprisingly tender and moist.

8 loin or rib pork chops, cut 1/2" thick and
    trimmed of excess fat
1 teaspoon cooking oil
1 teaspoon salt
1/4 teaspoon pepper

C O U N T R Y   G R A V Y (optional)
3 tablespoons flour
1 1/2 cups milk
3/4 teaspoon salt (about)
1/8 teaspoon pepper

Brown chops 2–3 minutes on each side over
moderate heat in a large, heavy skillet
brushed with oil. *(Note:* If necessary, use 2
skillets to avoid crowding pan.) Turn heat to
low and cook chops, uncovered, 10–15 minutes, turning frequently until no trace of
pink remains. Sprinkle with salt and pepper,
transfer to a hot platter, and keep warm
while making gravy. Drain all but 2 tablespoons drippings from skillet, blend in flour
and brown lightly over moderately low heat.
Add milk gradually and heat, stirring, until
thickened. Season to taste with salt and pepper. Spoon some gravy over chops before
serving, if you like, or pass separately.

NPS: 230 C, 90 mg CH, 640 mg S*
NPS (with gravy): 365 C, 105 mg CH, 1,100 mg S*

VARIATIONS

Country-Fried Pork Chops: Dredge chops,
one at a time, by shaking in a heavy paper
bag with 3/4 cup unsifted flour, the salt, and
pepper. Brown, increasing amount of oil to 1
tablespoon, then finish cooking as directed.
Serve with Country Gravy.

NPS: 445 C, 105 mg CH, 1,100 mg S*

German-Style Breaded Pork Chops: Dip
chops in 1/2 cup unsifted flour to coat
evenly, then in 1 egg beaten with 1 tablespoon cold water, then in 1 cup toasted, seasoned bread crumbs. Let dry on a rack at
room temperature 10 minutes. Panfry as directed, using 2 tablespoons cooking oil.
Serve with Country Gravy and boiled potatoes or buttered noodles.

NPS: 600 C, 175 mg CH, 1,910 mg S*

Italian-Style Breaded Pork Chops: Dip
chops in 1/2 cup unsifted flour to coat, then
in 1 egg beaten with 1 tablespoon cold water, then in 3/4 cup toasted, seasoned bread
crumbs mixed with 1/4 cup grated Parmesan
cheese. Let dry on a rack at room temperature 10 minutes. Panfry as directed in 2 tablespoons olive oil over very low heat to
avoid scorching crumb coating. Serve with
hot Tomato Sauce.

NPS: 460 C, 160 mg CH, 1,350 mg S*

SWEET-AND-SOUR PORK

2 servings

1/3 cup soy sauce mixed with 1/3 cup sugar
3/4 pound boned lean pork loin, trimmed of fat
    and cut in 3/4" cubes
Shortening or cooking oil for deep fat frying
1/4 cup sifted cornstarch
2 tablespoons cooking oil
1 clove garlic, peeled and minced
1 medium-size sweet green pepper, cored,
    seeded, and cut in 1" squares
1 medium-size carrot, peeled and cut in julienne
    strips
1 cup chicken broth
1/4 cup cider vinegar
2 tablespoons sugar
2 tablespoons soy sauce
1 1/2 teaspoons cornstarch blended with 1
    tablespoon cold water
2 pineapple rings, cut in 3/4" cubes

Heat soy sauce mixture, stirring, until sugar
dissolves; pour over pork, cover, and chill 4–
8 hours, turning meat occasionally. Begin
heating fat for deep fat frying over high heat;
insert wire basket and deep fat thermometer.
Lift meat from marinade with slotted spoon,
roll in cornstarch, and let dry 5 minutes.
When fat reaches 350° F., fry cubes 2–3 minutes until golden brown; drain in basket and
keep warm. Heat 2 tablespoons oil in *wok* or
heavy skillet over moderate heat 1 minute,
add garlic, pepper, and carrot, and stir-fry
2–3 minutes; do not brown. Mix in broth,
vinegar, sugar, and soy sauce, cover, and
simmer 2–3 minutes. Add cornstarch mix-

ture, pineapple, and pork and heat, stirring, until slightly thickened. Serve over boiled rice or Chinese Fried Rice; pass extra soy sauce.

NPS: 740 C, 105 mg CH, 3,555 mg S*

V A R I A T I O N

Sweet-and-Sour Spareribs: Substitute 1½ pounds 3″ spareribs for pork loin; cut into individual ribs, cover with water, and simmer 35–45 minutes until just tender. Drain, marinate, dredge, and fry as directed (watch ribs carefully while frying, they brown quickly). Proceed as recipe directs, adding spareribs to skillet with cornstarch mixture and pineapple.

NPS: 995 C, 160 mg CH, 3,565 mg S*

SPARERIBS, BACK RIBS, AND COUNTRY-STYLE BACKBONE

These bony cuts provide as good eating as any other part of the hog. Spareribs used to be budget fare—but no more; they've grown far too popular to remain poor man's meat. The lesser known back ribs and country-style backbone are still good buys, however, and can be substituted for spareribs in any of the following recipes.

How to Cook

Amount Needed: Allow ¾–1 pound ribs per person. Always choose ribs that are meaty between the bones and that have a thin covering of meat over the bones.

General Preparation for Cooking: If ribs are to be spit-roasted, leave in 1 piece; otherwise, cut in serving-size chunks 2-ribs wide. Marinate, if you like, in a piquant sauce—the ribs will be better.

To Roast:

Continuous Low Heat Method: Preheat oven to 325° F. Place ribs on a rack in a shallow roasting pan and roast, uncovered, about 30 minutes per pound until well done. *(Note:* Because of thinness and boniness of ribs, it is practically impossible to get an accurate meat thermometer reading. To test for doneness, make a cut near the center of a meaty section; if no pink remains, ribs are done.)

Searing Method: Preheat oven to 450° F. Place ribs on a rack in a shallow roasting pan and roast, uncovered, 30 minutes; drain off all drippings. Reduce heat to 325° F. and roast, uncovered, about 20 minutes per pound longer or until well done.

To Spit-Roast:

In Rotisserie, Gas or Electric Barbecue, or Oven: Preheat unit. Balance ribs on spit by weaving rod in and out; attach to rotisserie and roast about 20 minutes per pound until well done.

Over Charcoal: Build a moderate charcoal fire. Balance ribs on spit, attach to rotisserie, adjust height so spit is 4″–5″ from coals, and roast about 20 minutes per pound until well done (place drip pan under ribs to reduce flare-ups).

To Braise: Here is the best way to cook ribs because the meat, browned, then cooked with a little liquid, becomes extra juicy, extra flavorful, and so tender it practically falls off the bones. Technically, ribs prepared by any of the other following recipes are braised.

CHINESE-STYLE SPARERIBS

4 servings

Sweet-sour and soy-glazed.

4 pounds (3″ long) lean spareribs, cut in serving-size pieces

S A U C E
1 cup soy sauce
1 cup sugar
1 cup water
6 cloves garlic, peeled and crushed
¼ cup Hoi Sin sauce (available in Chinese groceries) or ¼ teaspoon ginger

Place ribs in a large, deep bowl. Simmer sauce ingredients 2–3 minutes, stirring, until sugar dissolves; pour over ribs, cover, and chill overnight, turning ribs occasionally. Preheat oven to 350° F. Arrange ribs in shallow roasting pan and pour in sauce. Bake, uncovered, 2 hours, turning ribs every ½ hour and basting with sauce, until fork tender and glossy brown. Serve with hot mustard and plum sauce.

NPS: 840 C, 215 mg CH, 3,085 mg S*

FAVORITE BARBECUED SPARERIBS

6 servings

Richly glazed but not too spicy.

5 pounds spareribs, cut in serving-size pieces

S A U C E
1 cup firmly packed light brown sugar
1/4 cup Worcestershire sauce
1/3 cup soy sauce
1/4 cup cider vinegar
1/4 cup chili sauce
1/2 cup ketchup
2 teaspoons prepared mild yellow mustard
2 cloves garlic, peeled and crushed
1/8 teaspoon pepper

Preheat oven to 350° F. Place ribs in a large, shallow roasting pan and bake, uncovered, 3/4 hour. Drain off all drippings. Mix sauce ingredients, pour over ribs, and bake, uncovered, 1 1/4–1 1/2 hours longer, turning and basting every 20 minutes until tender and richly browned. *(Note: For even better flavor, marinate ribs in sauce in turned-off oven 3–4 hours after first 1/4 hour of baking and drain off drippings; then bake 1 1/2 hours longer as directed.)*

NPS: 785 C, 180 mg CH, 1,840 mg S*

V A R I A T I O N

Favorite Charcoal-Barbecued Spareribs: Wrap ribs in a double thickness heavy foil and bake 1 1/2 hours at 350° F. Unwrap and drain off drippings. Marinate ribs in sauce 1–2 hours at room temperature; meanwhile, prepare a moderate charcoal fire. Remove ribs from sauce, lay on grill about 4″ from coals, taking care not to crowd them, and broil 20 minutes, basting frequently with sauce and turning often. Nutritional count same as basic recipe.

PAPRIKA SPARERIBS WITH CARAWAY SAUERKRAUT

4 servings

Spareribs the German way, oven-baked on a bed of chopped apple and sauerkraut.

3 pounds spareribs, cut in serving-size pieces
1 1/2 teaspoons salt
1 teaspoon paprika
1/8 teaspoon pepper
1 pound sauerkraut (do not drain)
1 large tart apple, peeled, cored, and coarsely chopped
1 teaspoon caraway seeds

Preheat oven to 350° F. Arrange spareribs meaty side up in a single layer in a large roasting pan; sprinkle evenly with salt, paprika, and pepper. Roast, uncovered, 1/2 hour, turn, and roast 1/2 hour longer; drain off all drippings. Mix sauerkraut, apple, and caraway seeds and place *under* spareribs. Return to oven and roast, uncovered, 1 hour, turning ribs occasionally. To serve, pile sauerkraut in the center of a large hot platter and surround with spareribs. Good with noodles and sour cream.

NPS: 570 C, 160 mg CH, 1,795 mg S*

BAKED SPARERIBS WITH APPLE-CELERY STUFFING

4 servings

Because the flavor of pork is not unlike that of chicken, you can, if you like, substitute your favorite poultry stuffing for the Apple-Celery Stuffing.

3 pounds spareribs, cut in chunks 3 or 4 ribs wide
1 teaspoon salt
1/4 teaspoon pepper

A P P L E - C E L E R Y   S T U F F I N G
1 cup soft white bread crumbs
1/2 cup finely chopped apple
1/4 cup minced celery
2 tablespoons minced yellow onion
1 tablespoon minced parsley
1/8 teaspoon cinnamon
1/2 teaspoon salt
1/8 teaspoon pepper
1 egg, lightly beaten

Preheat oven to 350° F. Toss together all stuffing ingredients. Turn half the ribs hollow side up and spread evenly with stuffing; top with remaining ribs, meaty side up, to make "sandwiches," then tie each securely with string. Place ribs in a shallow roasting pan and sprinkle with half the salt and pepper. Bake, uncovered, 1 hour and drain off drippings; turn ribs, sprinkle with remaining salt and pepper, and bake 1 hour longer or until tender and well browned. Transfer to a hot platter, remove strings and serve.

NPS: 590 C, 230 mg CH, 1,030 mg S*

GROUND PORK

Because of the danger of trichinosis, some local laws forbid butchers to grind raw pork (if the machine isn't thoroughly cleaned after grinding pork, the next batch of meat to go through may become contaminated; this is especially dangerous with beef, which is so often eaten rare). If you grind pork yourself, wash each grinding part thoroughly in hot soapy water, then rinse well in boiling water and wipe dry with a clean soft cloth.

The best cuts of pork to grind are shoulder, picnic, or lean trimmings from the side or belly. The more times and the more finely pork is ground, the more compact it will be when cooked. For a light-textured loaf, coarsely grind, once. For pork balls, where a firmer texture is preferable, grind fine, two or three times.

PORK AND VEAL RING

6 servings

1 pound ground lean pork
1 pound ground veal
4 slices white bread, trimmed of crusts
1/2 cup milk
1 medium-size yellow onion, peeled and grated fine
2 tablespoons finely grated lemon rind
1 teaspoon poultry seasoning
1 tablespoon salt
1/4 teaspoon pepper
1 egg, lightly beaten

Preheat oven to 350° F. Mix pork and veal. Cut bread into small cubes, soak in milk 5 minutes, then mix with meat and all remaining ingredients. Pack into a lightly greased 5-cup ring mold and bake, uncovered, 1 hour. Let stand 5 minutes; loosen edges and pour off drippings (save for gravy). Turn ring out on a hot platter and fill center, if you like, with mashed potatoes or yams or any creamed vegetable. Pass gravy or Mushroom Gravy.

NPS: 315 C, 150 mg CH, 1,270 mg S*

To Bake as a Loaf: Pack mixture into a lightly greased 9″ × 5″ × 3″ loaf pan or shape into a loaf in a lightly greased, shallow roasting pan. Bake as directed.

PORK BALLS IN SOUR CREAM GRAVY

4 servings

PORK BALLS
1 pound ground pork shoulder
1/4 cup sifted flour
1 medium-size yellow onion, peeled and finely grated
1/4 teaspoon sage

1/2 teaspoon finely grated lemon rind
1 teaspoon salt
1/8 teaspoon pepper
1/2 cup soft white bread crumbs
1 egg, lightly beaten
1/4 cup ice water
2 tablespoons bacon drippings or cooking oil

GRAVY
3 tablespoons flour
3/4 cup water
3/4 cup milk
1 cup beef broth or chicken broth
1/2 cup sour cream

Toss together all ingredients for meat balls except bacon drippings, then, using a rounded tablespoon as a measure, roll into small balls. Brown well in drippings in a large skillet over moderately low heat 10 minutes, remove with slotted spoon and keep warm. Drain off all but 2 tablespoons drippings, blend in flour, and brown lightly. Slowly add water, milk, and broth and heat, stirring, until thickened; simmer, uncovered, 2–3 minutes. Mix in sour cream, return pork balls to skillet, and warm 5 minutes over lowest heat; do not boil. Serve over boiled rice or buttered noodles.

NPS: 565 C, 180 mg CH, 890 mg S*

VARIATIONS

Curried Pork Balls: Omit sage from meat balls but add 1 teaspoon curry powder. When making gravy, blend 1/2 teaspoon curry powder into drippings along with flour; omit sour cream. Otherwise, prepare as directed. Serve with chutney.

NPS: 505 C, 165 mg CH, 870 mg S*

Pork and Peanut Balls: Omit sage from meat balls but add 1/4 cup finely chopped toasted peanuts. Proceed as directed.

NPS: 600 C, 180 mg CH, 890 mg S*

TOURTIÈRE

6–8 servings ¢

Tourtière is a spicy pork pie traditionally served by French Canadians at *réveillon,* the Christmas feast following midnight mass. Some tourtières contain beef, but the most authentic are made entirely of pork.

FILLING
1 1/2 pounds ground lean pork
1 teaspoon salt
1/4 teaspoon celery salt
1/4 teaspoon pepper
1/8 teaspoon cloves

½ teaspoon savory
1 small bay leaf, crumbled

PASTRY
1 recipe Flaky Pastry II

Sauté pork in a large skillet over moderate heat, breaking it up with a fork, until no pink remains. Turn heat to low, stir in all remaining filling ingredients, cover, and simmer 15 minutes. Uncover and simmer 10 minutes longer until liquid reduces to about ⅓ cup. Drain liquid into a small bowl and chill. Cool meat to room temperature. Meanwhile, prepare pastry as directed; roll and fit half into a 9″ piepan; reserve the rest for the top crust. Preheat oven to 450° F. Skim fat from reserved liquid, then mix liquid into meat and spoon into pie shell. Moisten pastry edges with cold water. Roll top crust and cut decorative steam vents near the center. Top pie with crust, seal pastry edges and crimp. Bake 10 minutes, then reduce heat to 350° F. and bake 30–35 minutes longer until pastry is lightly browned. Cut into wedges while still warm and serve with bread and butter pickles or sweet pickle relish. (*Note:* Baked tourtières can be cooled to room temperature, wrapped airtight, and frozen. To serve: Thaw, then reheat, uncovered, for ½ hour in a 350° F. oven.)

NPS (6–8): 530–405 C, 75–60 mg CH, 875–655 mg S*

THE CUTS OF PORK TO STEW

Europeans, the old saying goes, "eat everything about a pig but its squeal." We aren't so imaginative (or adventurous?) but do enjoy hocks, feet, and sinewy trimmings when well prepared.

Hocks: The fleshy, upper portion of a hog's front legs.

Pigs' Feet: Also called *trotters,* these are the feet and ankles of pigs. They are bony, full of gristle and tendons, but if stewed or pickled, the meat becomes tender and the gristle cooks down into gelatin. The forefeet are more delicate than the hind (these aren't often sold). Have your butcher clean and prepare pigs' feet for cooking.

Stew Meat: The best parts of pork to use for stew are belly (well trimmed of fat), shoulder (Boston butt), and picnic because of their well-developed flavor and firm texture.

PORK AND RED CABBAGE RAGOUT

6 servings   ¢

3 pounds boned pork shoulder, cut in 1½″ cubes and trimmed of excess fat
3 medium-size yellow onions, peeled and coarsely chopped
1 medium-size tart apple, peeled, cored, and diced
Leaves from 2 stalks celery
4 cloves
6 peppercorns
3½ cups chicken broth
1 cup dry red wine
2 teaspoons salt
½ small red cabbage, trimmed, cut in slim wedges, and parboiled
1½ cups sour cream

Brown pork, a few pieces at a time, in a large, heavy kettle over high heat (you won't need any fat) and drain on paper toweling. Reduce heat to moderate, add onions and apple, and stir-fry 8–10 minutes until golden. Return pork to kettle. Tie celery leaves, cloves, and peppercorns in cheesecloth and add to kettle along with broth, wine, and salt. Cover and simmer 1¾ hours until pork is almost tender. Add cabbage wedges, pushing them down into stew, recover, and simmer 15–20 minutes longer until pork and cabbage are tender. Discard cheesecloth bag. Remove stew from heat; using a slotted spoon, lift cabbage from kettle and wreathe around a large, deep platter; pile meat in center and keep warm. Blend sour cream into kettle liquid and heat and stir 1–2 minutes (do not boil). Ladle over cabbage and pork and serve.

NPS: 740 C, 185 mg CH, 1,350 mg S*

SPICY PORK AND TURNIP STEW

6 servings   ¢

3 pounds boned pork shoulder, cut in 1½″ cubes and trimmed of excess fat
5 large turnips, peeled and cut in ½″ cubes
2 medium-size yellow onions, peeled and coarsely chopped
1 clove garlic, peeled and crushed
4 whole allspice
6 peppercorns
4 cloves
4 sprigs parsley
1¾ cups chicken broth
½ cup dry white wine
1 cup water
1 teaspoon salt
2 tablespoons flour blended with 3 tablespoons cold water

Brown pork well on all sides in a large, heavy kettle over high heat (you won't need any fat). Reduce heat to low, add turnips, onions, and garlic, and stir-fry with pork 5 minutes. Tie spices and parsley in cheesecloth and add along with all remaining ingredients except flour-water paste, cover, and simmer 2 hours until pork is tender. Remove pork and turnips with a slotted spoon and set aside; discard cheesecloth bag. Strain cooking liquid, return to kettle, mix in flour-water paste, and heat, stirring constantly, until thickened. Remove pork and turnips to kettle and heat, uncovered, 5 minutes longer, stirring occasionally. Serve with boiled potatoes or sweet potatoes.

NPS: 620 C, 160 mg CH, 780 mg S*

PORK HOCKS WITH SAUERKRAUT

4 servings   ⚖ ¢

Pork hocks and sauerkraut can be served with or without the cooking liquid; in either case boiled potatoes and crusty bread are traditional accompaniments.

6 meaty pork hocks
1 quart cold water
1 medium-size yellow onion, peeled and sliced thin
2 bay leaves
10 peppercorns
2 sprigs parsley or 1 teaspoon dried parsley
Leaves from 2 stalks celery, coarsely chopped
1³/₄ pounds sauerkraut, drained

Scrub hocks well under cold running water; scrape skin with a sharp knife to remove any hairs. Place hocks in a 1¹/₂-gallon kettle with water and onion. Tie bay leaves, peppercorns, parsley, and celery leaves in cheesecloth and add to kettle. Cover and bring to a boil over moderate heat; uncover and skim off froth. Reduce heat to low and simmer, covered, 2–2¹/₂ hours until meat is very tender. Discard cheesecloth bag. Cool, cover, and chill several hours until fat rises to surface and hardens. When ready to serve, skim off fat (broth will be jellied), add sauerkraut, cover, and heat slowly until piping hot.

NPS: 300 C, 75 mg CH, 1,540 mg S*

STEWED PIGS' FEET (BASIC METHOD)

4 servings   ⚖ ¢

Before they can be used in recipes, pigs' feet require careful, preliminary stewing. Allow 1–2 pigs' feet per person and have butcher clean and prepare them for cooking.

S T O C K *(enough for 4–6 pigs' feet)*
1¹/₂ quarts water
³/₄ cup dry white wine
2 carrots, peeled and sliced thin
2 stalks celery, sliced thin
2 medium-size yellow onions, peeled and each stuck with 2 cloves
1 bay leaf and 1 sprig each parsley and thyme, tied in cheesecloth *(bouquet garni)*
1 tablespoon salt
4 peppercorns

Wash pigs' feet well in cool water, then tie each tightly in cheesecloth so it will keep its shape. Place in a large, heavy kettle with stock ingredients, cover, and bring to a simmer over moderate heat. Adjust heat so stock stays at a slow simmer and cook, covered, 4–5 hours until feet are very tender. Cool in liquid, drain well (save broth for soups and stews), and remove cheesecloth. Use in any of the following recipes.

NPS: 275 C, 140 mg CH, 825 mg S*

V A R I A T I O N

¢ ⚖   **Pickled Pigs' Feet:** Prepare by recipe above, but use 3 cups each cider vinegar and water for stewing instead of 1¹/₂ quarts water. When feet are tender, cool in liquid, drain, and chill well. Remove cheesecloth and serve cold with Spanish Vinaigrette Sauce.

NPS: 285 C, 140 mg CH, 825 mg S*

PIGS' FEET IN SCALLION AND JUNIPER SAUCE

4 servings   ⚖ ¢

6 pigs' feet, stewed

S A U C E
¹/₃ cup minced scallions
2 tablespoons butter or margarine
²/₃ cup white wine vinegar
6 juniper berries, crushed
Pinch nutmeg
Pinch pepper
1¹/₄ cups stock (use that from stewing pigs' feet)
2 tablespoons flour blended with 3 tablespoons cold water

After stewing pigs' feet, cool in stock just until easy to handle; drain, remove cheesecloth, and keep feet warm while preparing sauce. Sauté scallions in butter in a small saucepan 8–10 minutes, stirring occasionally, over moderate heat until golden; add vinegar, juniper berries, nutmeg, and pepper and boil, uncovered, to reduce. When almost all vinegar has evaporated, add stock. Mix in flour paste and heat, stirring, until thickened and smooth. Pour sauce over pigs' feet and serve.

NPS: 495 C, 230 mg CH, 1,165 mg S*

HAM AND OTHER CURED PORK
(See Pork Chart)

Whether served as a festive holiday ham, glistening under an amber glaze, a cool, spicy loaf, or a grilled steak, ham runs beef a close second as America's favorite meat. Although we think of any cured pork as ham, it is technically the hind leg only, and it can be fresh as well as cured. We are concerned here with all the cured and smoked cuts, the bacons and butts, picnics and jowls as well as the hams. Here's a quick dictionary to those commonly used:

Aged Hams: Heavily cured and smoked hams that have been hung from one to seven years. They are usually covered with mold (it washes off and does not mean the meat is spoiled).

Country-Cured Hams: Hams (and sometimes other cuts of pork) that have been dry-cured (preserved in a mixture of dry salt and seasonings), smoked slowly over fragrant hardwood fires, and aged at least six months. The meat is mahogany colored, salty, and firm. America's most famous country hams are the Virginia, Smithfield, Tennessee, Georgia, and Kentucky; each is salty and firm of flesh, each has a distinctive flavor, determined by breed of hog, feed, and seasonings used in the curing. Most country-cured hams are uncooked, although fully cooked ones are now available. Read labels carefully.

Cured Hams: Curing is a method of preserving, not of cooking. Large processors cure hams by soaking in brine or, more recently, by pumping brine through the meat. Cured hams may or may not be smoked and may or may not be cooked.

Cured and Smoked Hams: Hams that have been brined and smoked—but not cooked unless labels clearly say so.

Cook-Before-Eating Hams: This is the term commonly used to identify uncooked or partially cooked hams. It's a good term because the shopper knows at a glance that the meat must be cooked before serving.

Fully Cooked Hams: Hams so labeled can be eaten straight from the wrapper; they will develop richer flavor, however, if baked until meat thermometer reads 130° F.

Ready-to-Eat Hams: The same as fully cooked hams.

Smoked Ham or Pork: Meat that has been cured, then smoked, but not necessarily cooked.

Sugar-Cured Hams: Hams cured in brine or dry salt mixed with brown sugar or molasses.

Tendered or Tenderized Hams: These terms are often misinterpreted to mean "cooked hams." They are really only sales words and mean little.

Uncooked Hams: Raw hams that must be thoroughly cooked before eating. They may be cured or cured and smoked.

How to Recognize Quality in Ham and Other Cured Pork

Large cuts often—but not always—carry the round federal inspector's seal guaranteeing wholesomeness of meat. Quality is less easily determined because little pork is federally graded and because the appearance of cured pork ranges from the pale pink of processed hams to the offputting moldiness of aged country cured hams. Both may be of top quality. Your best assurance is to buy reputable brands.

Standard Processed Hams

These tender, cured packing-house hams are usually smoked (but not always). They may be fully cooked or uncooked; labels should clearly state which.

Whole Ham:

Bone-In (8–24 pounds): The full hind leg of the hog.

Semiboneless (6 pounds up): A ham from which the troublesome hip (aitch) and shank bones have been removed to simplify carving. The leg bone remains in, helping ham hold its compact oval shape, but skin and excess fat have been removed. Also sold as half hams or by the slice.

Boneless (6–14 pounds): A boned and rolled ham.

Half Ham:

Butt Portion (4–12 pounds): Also called Full Butt, this is the choice meaty, rump half of the ham, more expensive than the shank portion.

Shank Portion (4–12 pounds): Also known as Full Shank. This leg half of the ham is bonier and less expensive than the butt half.

Semiboneless (4 pounds and up): Half a semiboneless ham (see above).

Boneless (3–7 pounds): Half a boned and rolled ham (see above).

Ham End: This is what's left of a ham after the center slices or steaks have been removed. The Butt End is meaty but contains the cumbersome hipbone; the Shank End tapers sharply and may be too skimpy to roast.

Specialty Hams

Domestic:

Smithfield: So many country-cured hams claim to be the prized Smithfield hams that the Virginia General Assembly has adopted a statute: "Genuine Smithfield hams are cut from carcasses of peanut-fed hogs, raised in the peanut belt of the State of Virginia or the State of North Carolina, and cured, treated, smoked and processed in the town of Smithfield in the State of Virginia." What makes these hams so special is their firm, mahogany-hued flesh and smoky-salty flavor. Most must be cooked long and slow before eating, though some are now sold fully cooked. Available only as whole hams (12–14 pounds is a good size) through gourmet butchers or via mail order.

Virginia: Like Smithfield hams, these country-cured hams are firm of flesh and salty of flavor. They may be from hogs fattened on peanuts, or those allowed to forage for acorns, nuts, and aromatic roots. Whole hams are available uncooked or fully cooked from better butchers, also by mail order. *Note:* Some trendy food shops now advertise fine country-cured hams as "American *Prosciutto*" and claim that they can be eaten raw. *Don't you believe it!*

Canned Ham: Boned, skinned, trimmed, ready-to-eat hams. They are cured but not necessarily smoked and weigh from 1½–10 pounds (the larger the ham, the better). Though fully cooked, canned hams will have better flavor if baked or sliced and panfried.

Some come with special glazes—honey, champagne, pineapple (we've found that, to be really well glazed, most need a little longer in the oven than can directions recommend). Some require refrigeration, so read label carefully and store accordingly.

Imported:
(Note: Because trichinosis is not a problem in Europe, many European hams are eaten raw.)

Bayonne Ham: Dry-cured ham from Béarn or the Basque country of France. Many are cured in the town of Bayonne (hence the name), many simply cured with Bayonne salt. The hams are raw and the Basques like to eat them that way on buttered slabs of peasant bread. Available in specialty groceries.

Irish Ham: The best known come from Belfast. They may be bone-in or boneless, pickled or brined; what gives them their unique flavor is the smoking over peat fires. Irish hams must be soaked, scrubbed, and simmered, then baked before eating (prepare like Country-Cured Ham). Available in specialty food shops.

Prosciutto: What we call *prosciutto* is really Parma ham *(prosciutto* is simply the Italian word for *ham).* These hams come from Parma, Italy, are exquisitely seasoned, salt cured, air dried, and pressed so that their rosy brown flesh is unusually firm. *Prosciutto* is most often sliced tissue thin and eaten raw as an appetizer but can be used in recipes. Available in gourmet groceries, also in cold cut counters of many metropolitan supermarkets.

Westphalian Ham: A salty, reddish German ham similar to *prosciutto* that comes from hogs fed sugar beet mash. It, too, is sliced paper thin and eaten raw. Available in specialty food shops.

York Ham: An English ham with mild flavor and delicate pink meat. Like Irish ham, it must be cooked before eating (use recipe for Country-Cured Ham). When served hot, York ham is traditionally accompanied by Madeira Sauce.

Canned Ham: The most readily available imported canned hams are the York, Danish, Prague, and Polish, all mild-cured, all skinless and boneless. Also available in specialty food shops are canned *prosciutto* and Westphalian hams.

How to Bake Ham

Note: What we call baked ham is really roasted; it has simply been the American habit to speak of ham as baked the same way we speak of a meat loaf or potato as baked although these, too, are technically roasted.

Suitable Cuts: Any of the standard processed hams, canned hams, or country-cured hams. Each requires a somewhat different technique, however.

Amount Needed: The bigger the ham, the more succulent it will be. To figure number of servings, allow 2/3 pound per person for a bony ham (shank portion), 1/3–1/2 pound for other bone-in hams; 1/4–1/3 pound boneless ham; also 1/4–1/3 pound *net weight* canned ham per person.

General Preparation for Cooking (standard processed hams only): Remove skin, if still on, by slipping a sharp knife underneath and peeling off. Trim fat to 1/2". Let ham stand at room temperature 1 1/2–2 hours before cooking, if convenient.

Uncooked (Cook-Before-Eating) Ham: Follow manufacturer's cooking directions or prepare as follows. Preheat oven to 325° F. Place ham on a rack in a shallow roasting pan (whole hams should be fat side up, half hams cut side down). Insert meat thermometer in center, not touching bone. Bake, uncovered, until thermometer reads 160° F. Whole or boneless hams will take approximately 18–20 minutes per pound, half hams 22–24. Transfer ham to heated platter and let "rest" 15–20 minutes before carving. Serve hot or cold.

To Glaze (see Some Glazes for Baked Hams):

Liquid Glazes: Begin basting ham after 15–20 minutes in oven and continue basting at 15–20-minute intervals throughout cooking. About 1/2 hour before ham is done (no sooner or cuts will spread too much), remove from oven and score fat in a large crisscross pattern, making cuts 1/8" deep. Stud with cloves or decorate (see On Decorating Hams). Return ham to oven and finish cooking, basting frequently. For a browner glaze, finish cooking at 425° F.

Thick Glazes: Bake ham as directed but do not baste. About 1/2 hour before ham is done, remove from oven and score. Stud with cloves (avoid intricate decorations because glaze will cover them up). Pat or spread on glaze, return ham to oven, and finish cooking, basting if glaze recipe calls for it. For a richly brown glaze, finish cooking at 425° F.

Ready-to-Eat Hams: If wrapper gives cooking directions, follow them. If not, use procedure for uncooked hams above, but bake only until thermometer registers 130° F. Whole and boneless hams will require about 12–15 minutes per pound, half hams about 18–20. Glaze and decorate as above and serve hot or cold.

Canned Hams: If ham is accompanied by baking directions, use them. If not, prepare as follows. Preheat oven to 325° F. If ham has a heavy fat covering (few canned hams do), trim to 1/2". Place ham flattest side down on a rack in a shallow roasting pan. *(Note:* If using a round canned ham, cut a thin slice off bottom so ham won't roll about pan.) Insert meat thermometer in center of ham and bake, uncovered, about 20 minutes per pound or until thermometer registers 130° F. Glaze and decorate as above and serve hot or cold.

Country-Cured Hams: A day or two before you plan to serve ham, place in a very large oval kettle, sawing off hock, if necessary, to fit ham in. If ham is very salty, salt crystals will be visible. Cover with cool water and let stand 24 hours at room temperature, changing the water 3–4 times. If ham is not salty, change soaking water 1–2 times. Next day, scrub ham well under running tepid water to remove any mold and pepper. Wash well again in tepid water. Place ham on a rack in the same large kettle, add cool water to cover, cover, and bring to a boil over high heat. Skim froth from surface, re-cover, adjust heat so water stays at a slow simmer, and cook 25–30 minutes per pound or until fork tender and bone feels loose; cool ham in cooking liquid. Preheat oven to 350° F. Lift ham from liquid, peel off rind, and trim fat to 1/2". Score in a crisscross pattern and stud with cloves. Pat on a thick glaze (Brown Sugar and Bread Crumbs is the traditional glaze for Smithfield and Virginia hams). Place ham glaze side up on a rack in a shallow roasting pan and bake, uncovered, 45 minutes or until glaze is nicely browned. Transfer ham to serving platter and let cool at least 20 minutes before serving. In the South, these hams are served at room temperature (or chilled), but almost never hot. When carving, slice paper thin.

How to Spit-Roast Ham

Best Cuts: Ready-to-Eat Hams, especially skinless, boneless rolls (whole, half, or quarter); semiboneless hams can be spit-roasted if carefully balanced.

Not Recommended: Uncooked hams (heat is too intense to ensure thorough cooking) and bone-in hams (they are too irregularly shaped to cook evenly).

Amount Needed: 1/4–1/3 pound boneless or semiboneless ham per person. Do not try to spit-roast less than a quarter ham roll.

General Preparation for Cooking: Remove any casing; most ham rolls have little outer fat, so trimming is unnecessary. Tie roll as you would a parcel so it will hold its shape during cooking. Let stand at room temperature 1 1/2–2 hours if convenient.

In Rotisserie, Gas or Electric Barbecue, or Oven: Preheat unit. Insert spit lengthwise through center of ham to balance, tighten holding forks. Insert meat thermometer in center, not touching spit. Attach to rotisserie and roast, using manufacturer's or the following timetable: 10–12 minutes per pound for whole ham rolls, 15–17 for half rolls, and 20 for quarter rolls. Thermometer should read 130° F. Let ham "rest" 15–20 minutes before carving. *To Glaze:* About 1/2 hour before ham is done, baste with any liquid glaze and continue basting often (see Some Glazes for Baked Hams).

Over Charcoal: Prepare a moderate charcoal fire toward back of grill. Balance ham on spit and insert thermometer as above, attach spit to rotisserie 6"–7" from coals. Place drip pan at front of fire. Roast, using manufacturer's times or those for rotisserie roasting. Glaze, if you like, as above.

Some Glazes for Baked Hams

Basically, there are two kinds of glaze: (1) liquids that are basted on throughout cooking and (2) thick or dry mixtures that are patted or spread on about 1/2 hour before ham is done.

Liquid (Baste-On Glazes):

(Note: Hams basted with beer, champagne, wine, and fruit juice will be glossier if rubbed with a mixture of 1/4 cup light brown sugar and 1 teaspoon powdered mustard before cooking.)

Cranberry-Horseradish: 2 cups cranberry jelly, melted and mixed with 1/4 cup prepared horseradish.

Champagne or Wine (sherry, port, Madeira, sweet red or white wine).

Beer, Ale, or Stout.

Rum (dark or light).

Fruit Juices: Apple, apricot, cranberry, orange, pineapple.

Syrups: Maple, light or dark corn syrup, molasses, strained honey.

Thick Glazes:

Brown Sugar and Bread Crumbs: 1 cup firmly packed light brown sugar mixed with 1/2 cup fine soft white bread crumbs and 1 1/2 teaspoons powdered mustard. Particularly good with Smithfield or Virginia hams.

Mustard: 1 cup firmly packed light brown sugar mixed with 1/4 cup prepared mustard (any type) and 2 tablespoons cider vinegar or 3 tablespoons honey, molasses, maple syrup, or dark or light corn syrup.

Sherry or Port: Brush ham with a little warmed light corn syrup, then pat on light brown sugar to a thickness of 1/4". Slowly drizzle 1 cup sweet sherry or port over all and finish cooking, basting with additional sherry or port.

Brown Sugar: Brush a little warmed light or dark corn syrup, molasses, or honey over ham, then pat on light or dark brown sugar to a thickness of about 1/4".

Marmalade: Warm orange, lemon, or ginger marmalade slightly and spread evenly over ham.

Preserves: Use apricot, pineapple, peach, pear, or cherry preserves, sieve or purée in a blender at high speed, warm slightly, and spread evenly over ham.

Jelly: Use black or red currant, apple, or cranberry. Melt jelly, then brush over ham every 10 minutes during last 1/2 hour of baking.

On Decorating Hams

Hams glazed with syrup, fruit juice, wine, or jelly will look more festive if decorated. Use fruits and/or nuts, keeping the design simple. To make design stick to ham, brush surface with warmed corn syrup, honey, or molasses, then simply press on decoration. Larger designs, made with peaches or apricots, have a tendency to slither off, so toothpick in place (be sure to remove toothpicks before carving). It's a good idea to remove any decorations before storing leftover ham because they deteriorate rapidly.

How to Carve a Whole Bone-In Ham:

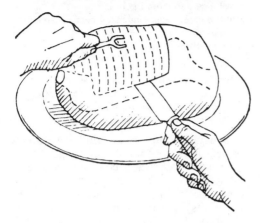

Place ham on platter, fat side up with shank to carver's right. Cut 2–3 slices parallel to leg from thin side (if ham is from left leg, thin side will face carver; if from a right leg, it will be on the far side). Cut straight down from top to bone in thin slices, then release slices by running knife along bone.

How to Carve a Shank Half Ham:

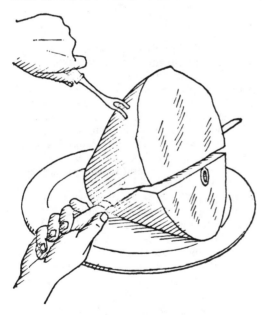

Turn platter so shank is on left; turn ham so thickest side is up, then cut along bone and lift out boneless "cushion," which is the top half of the ham. Place "cushion" cut side down and cut straight through in thin slices. Cut around leg bone and remove; turn ham so flat side is down and slice straight through as with "cushion."

How to Carve a Semiboneless Whole Ham:

Stand ham on its side and slice from right to left, cutting down to leg bone. Loosen slices by cutting along bone.

How to Carve a Butt Half Ham:

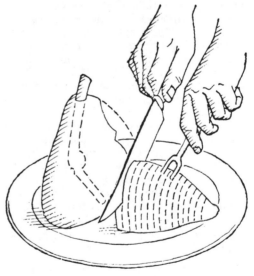

Place ham face down on platter, cut down along hip (aitch) bone, and remove large boneless chunk from side of ham. Place boneless chunk cut side down and slice straight through. Steady remaining ham with fork, slice across to bone, and loosen each slice with tip of knife.

BAKED PECAN-STUFFED HAM

18–20 servings

1 (10–12-pound) bone-in or semiboneless cook-
   before-eating ham
1 gallon cold water (about)
1/2 cup cider vinegar
1/2 cup firmly packed dark brown sugar

STUFFING
2 medium-size yellow onions, peeled and minced
1 cup minced celery
3 tablespoons bacon drippings or cooking oil
2 cups soft white bread crumbs
1/4 cup cracker crumbs
1/4 teaspoon salt
1/4 teaspoon pepper
2 tablespoons minced parsley
1 cup finely chopped pecans
2 eggs, lightly beaten

TOPPING
1 cup firmly packed light brown sugar
1/2 cup soft white bread crumbs
1 1/2 teaspoons powdered mustard

Place ham on a rack in a very large kettle, add water *just* to cover, also vinegar and sugar. Cover and simmer 1 1/2 hours. Meanwhile prepare stuffing: Stir-fry onions and celery in drippings over moderate heat 5–8 minutes until pale golden; off heat mix in remaining ingredients. When ham is tender, cool in broth until easy to handle. Begin preheating oven to 325° F. Lift ham from kettle and place lean side up on counter. With a sharp knife, cut down to and along shank bone; remove all bones (save for stock or soup). Fill cavity with stuffing, skewer shut, and, if you like, tie around with string. Place ham fat side up on a rack in a shallow roasting pan and bake, uncovered, 1 1/4 hours. Mix topping, pat over ham, and bake 15–20 minutes longer. Remove skewers and string, transfer ham to platter, and serve. Also good cold.

NPS (18–20): 535–480 C, 130–115 mg CH, 1,950–1,755 mg S*

To Halve Recipe: Use a 5–6-pound shank portion half ham. Simmer in 2 1/2 quarts water with 1/3 cup each vinegar and dark brown sugar for 1 hour. Halve stuffing recipe. Bone, stuff, and bake ham as above, reducing time to 1 hour. Cover with topping and bake 15–20 minutes longer.

HAM IN ASPIC

10–12 servings

1 (5-pound) canned ham

ASPIC
2 envelopes unflavored gelatin
3 (10 1/2-ounce) cans condensed beef consommé
   or madrilène
1/2 cup medium-dry sherry

DECORATION
2–3 truffles or pitted ripe olives, sliced thin
Small watercress, parsley, or tarragon sprigs
Thin slices cooked carrot or hard-cooked egg
   white cut in fancy shapes

Remove ham from can and chill well. Slowly heat gelatin in consommé, stirring, until dissolved; add sherry and cool over ice cubes until syrupy. Set ham on a rack over a tray, spoon on a light, even glaze of aspic. Dip decorations in aspic and arrange on ham; chill until firm. Give ham 3 more light glazes of aspic, chilling each well. (*Note:* To keep aspic syrupy, melt briefly over warm water, then return to ice bath.) Use overflow aspic on tray if reasonably clear. When final ham glaze is firm, transfer ham to platter and refrigerate. Pour remaining aspic into a shallow pan and chill until firm. To serve, cube extra aspic and arrange around base of ham.

NPS (10–12): 460–385 C, 90–75 mg CH, 3,280–2,735 mg S*

VARIATION

Pâté-Filled Ham in Aspic: Have butcher cut ham lengthwise into 1/2" slices, then tie together. For filling, mix 3 cups canned liver pâté, 1/3 cup heavy cream, 2 tablespoons prepared mild yellow mustard, 1 teaspoon Worcestershire sauce, and, if you like, 2–3 tablespoons cognac (filling should be a good spreading consistency). Untie ham carefully and thinly spread both sides of slices with filling; reshape ham and tie in several places. Wrap in foil and chill overnight; reserve remaining pâté. Next day, remove strings (ham should now hold its shape). "Frost" ham with reserved pâté and chill 2–3 hours. (*Note:* If pâté seems stiff, warm briefly over warm water.) Glaze and decorate ham as above. When serving, slice crosswise.

NPS (10–12): 780–650 C, 370–310 mg CH, 3,365–2,805 mg S*

SMOKED PICNICS AND BUTTS
(See Pork Chart)

Smoked Picnic (4–10 pounds): Also called *Picnic Ham,* this bone-in, lower shoulder portion, when cured and smoked, tastes very much like ham. It is available uncooked, fully cooked, and canned (canned picnics are boned, skinned, and trimmed).

Smoked Boneless Shoulder Butt (1–4 pounds): This long, slim boneless roll is a good choice for small families; it has a mild, smoky-sweet flavor.

How to Cook

Amount Needed: Allow 1/3–1/2 pound smoked boneless shoulder butt or canned picnic (net weight) per person, 3/4 pound smoked picnic.

Note: Fully cooked smoked picnics can be prepared by recipe for Ready-to-Eat Hams, canned picnics by that for Canned Hams. Though uncooked smoked picnics and shoulder butts can be baked like Uncooked Hams, they will be juicier if prepared by the following method.

General Preparation for Cooking: Remove skin from picnic (butt won't have any) and trim fat to 1/2".

Basic Method: Place picnic or butt on a rack in a large, heavy kettle and add just enough cold water to cover. Put lid on kettle and bring to a boil; adjust heat so water stays at a slow simmer, then cook 15 minutes per pound. Let meat cool 10 minutes in cooking water. Preheat oven to 325° F. Transfer meat to a rack in a shallow roasting pan and insert meat thermometer in center, not touching bone. Bake, uncovered, allowing 25 minutes per pound for the picnic, 30–35 for the butt or until meat thermometer reaches 170° F. *To Glaze:* Smoked picnics may be glazed like Baked Ham. Smoked butts have a very skimpy covering of fat and do not glaze well; they can, however, be drizzled with honey, maple syrup, or molasses and baked 10–15 minutes at 425° F. to make them glisten. Transfer meat to a heated platter and let "rest" 15–20 minutes before carving. Serve hot or cold.

VARIATIONS

Simmered Boneless Shoulder Butt: Place butt in kettle and add water as directed; cover and simmer 50 minutes per pound until tender. Lift from liquid, cool 10 minutes, then slice and serve with boiled vegetables and, if you like, Mustard or Horseradish Sauce.

Pickled Smoked Shoulder Butt: Place butt in kettle and add water as directed; add 1 tablespoon mixed pickling spices, 1 peeled clove garlic, and 1/2 cup cider vinegar. Simmer and bake as directed in Basic Method.

SKILLET HAM, PINEAPPLE, AND PEPPERS

6 servings ⊠

3 cups diced cooked ham
2 tablespoons butter or margarine
1 (8-ounce) can pineapple tidbits (do not drain)
2 medium-size sweet green peppers, cored, seeded, and cut in 1/4" strips
1/2 cup firmly packed light brown sugar
2 tablespoons cornstarch
1/2 cup chicken broth
1/2 cup cider vinegar
2 tablespoons soy sauce
2 pimientos, diced

In a large skillet stir-fry ham in butter 3–5 minutes over moderately high heat until lightly browned. Add pineapple and green peppers and stir-fry 3–4 minutes until peppers are crisp-tender. Mix sugar, cornstarch, broth, vinegar, and soy sauce, stir into skillet, and heat, stirring, until thickened. Add pimientos and serve over boiled rice.

NPS: 285 C, 55 mg CH, 1,640 mg S*

CREAMED HAM

4 servings ⊠

1/4 cup butter or margarine
1/4 cup unsifted flour
1/8 teaspoon pepper
1/4 teaspoon powdered mustard
1 cup milk
1/2 cup light cream
1 1/2 cups slivered or diced cooked ham
2 tablespoons minced pimiento (optional)
1/2 teaspoon salt

Melt butter in a large saucepan over moderately low heat, blend in flour, pepper, and mustard; slowly add milk and cream and heat, stirring until thickened. Add remaining ingredients, adjusting salt to taste. Serve over toast, waffles, muffins, or hot biscuits or in pastry shells or "fluffed up" baked potatoes.

NPS: 325 C, 90 mg CH, 1,245 mg S*

VARIATIONS

Creamed Ham and Eggs: Add 4 quartered hard-cooked eggs along with ham.

NPS: 400 C, 365 mg CH, 1,310 mg S*

Creamed Ham and Mushrooms: Add 1/4 pound lightly sautéed sliced mushrooms along with ham.

NPS: 330 C, 90 mg CH, 1,245 mg S*

Creamed Ham, Cheese, and Olives: Add 1/4 cup extra milk to sauce. Add 1/2 cup grated sharp Cheddar cheese and 1/4 cup sliced pimiento-stuffed green olives with ham.

NPS: 400 C, 110 mg CH, 1,540 mg S*

Creamed Ham and Vegetables: Add 1/4 cup extra milk to sauce; also 11/2–2 cups any leftover vegetable (corn, peas, cut asparagus, lima beans, broccoli, and cauliflowerets are particularly good).

NPS: 385 C, 95 mg CH, 1,250 mg S*

HAM, POTATO, AND GREEN PEPPER CASSEROLE

4 servings

1 quart thinly sliced, peeled potatoes
3 cups (1/2") cooked lean ham cubes
1/2 medium-size sweet green pepper, cored, seeded, and chopped fine
3 scallions, chopped fine (include green tops)
2 tablespoons bacon drippings, butter, or margarine
3 tablespoons flour
3/4 teaspoon powdered mustard
2 cups milk
11/2 teaspoons salt
1/8 teaspoon white pepper

Preheat oven to 375° F. Arrange half the sliced potatoes in a greased 2-quart casserole. Toss ham, green pepper, and scallions together and scatter over potatoes; top with remaining potatoes. Melt drippings in a small saucepan over moderate heat, and blend in flour and mustard. Slowly add milk and heat, stirring constantly, until smooth and thickened. Mix in salt and pepper. Pour sauce evenly over potatoes, cover, and bake 1 hour. Uncover and bake 30 minutes longer until potatoes are fork tender and golden.

NPS: 425 C, 80 mg CH, 2,155 mg S*

EASY HAM AND CORN CASSEROLE

4 servings

2 cups diced cooked ham
1 small yellow onion, peeled and grated fine
1 small sweet green pepper, cored, seeded, and minced
1 (1-pound) can cream-style corn
1 (8-ounce) can whole kernel corn, drained
1/2 cup light cream

TOPPING
11/2 cups packaged seasoned bread cubes or croutons
1/4 cup melted butter or margarine
1 tablespoon Worcestershire sauce

Preheat oven to 350° F. Mix all ingredients except topping and spoon into a buttered 11/2-quart casserole. Sprinkle with bread cubes; mix butter and Worcestershire sauce and drizzle on top. Bake, uncovered, 30 minutes until bubbly and brown.

NPS: 465 C, 95 mg CH, 1,905 mg S*

HAM AND EGG SHORTCAKE

4–6 servings ¢

3 tablespoons butter or margarine
3 tablespoons flour
2 cups milk
2 cups diced cooked ham
4 hard-cooked eggs, peeled and quartered
1/2 teaspoon salt (about)
1/4 teaspoon pepper
1 teaspoon prepared spicy brown mustard (optional)
1 tablespoon minced parsley

TOPPING
1/2 cup sifted flour
1/2 cup yellow corn meal
1/4 teaspoon salt
1–2 tablespoons sugar
2 teaspoons baking powder
1 egg, lightly beaten
2 tablespoons melted butter or margarine
1/2 cup milk

Preheat oven to 400° F. Melt butter in a saucepan over moderate heat and blend in flour; slowly add milk and heat, stirring, until thickened. Off heat add remaining ingredients except topping, taste for salt and adjust as needed. Spoon into a greased 9" × 9" × 2" pan or a 2-quart casserole. For topping, mix flour, corn meal, salt, sugar, and baking powder in a bowl. Combine egg, butter, and milk, add to dry ingredients, and beat with a rotary beater *just* until smooth. Spoon on top of ham mixture and bake, uncovered, 30 minutes until golden. Cut into squares and serve.

NPS (4–6): 600–400 C, 445–295 mg CH, 2,010–1,340 mg S*

HAM SHANK STEW WITH DUMPLINGS

4–6 servings ¢

Best made the day before with dumplings added during reheating.

1/2 pound dried whole green peas or lima beans, washed and sorted
21/2 quarts cold water (about)

1/2 pound dried split green peas, washed and sorted
1 ham shank with some meat attached (leftover is fine)
2 medium-size carrots, peeled and diced
2 medium-size yellow onions, peeled and minced
1 teaspoon salt (about)
1/4 teaspoon pepper
1 tablespoon dark brown sugar
1 tablespoon cider vinegar
1/4 teaspoon thyme (optional)
1 clove garlic, peeled and crushed
1 recipe Dumplings
1 tablespoon minced parsley

Soak whole peas or limas in 2 cups water overnight or use the quick method.* Drain, measure soaking water, and add enough cold water to make 2 1/2 quarts. Add all remaining ingredients except dumplings and parsley, adjusting salt to taste. Cover and simmer 1 1/2–2 hours until peas are tender. Remove meat from ham shank, cut into bite-size pieces, and return to kettle. Mix dumplings and drop by tablespoonfuls on top of just boiling stew; simmer, uncovered, 10 minutes, cover tightly, and simmer 10 minutes longer. Sprinkle with parsley and serve in soup bowls.

*NPS (4–6): 725–490 C, 40–25 mg CH, 1,900–1,265 mg S**

HAM LOAF

6 servings

An all-ham loaf will not slice as well as one made with part ham and part pork or veal.

1 1/2 pounds ground smoked ham
1/2 pound ground lean pork or veal shoulder
2 eggs, lightly beaten
1 1/2 cups soft white bread crumbs
1 cup milk
1 large yellow onion, peeled and minced (optional)
1/4 teaspoon pepper
1/2 teaspoon celery salt
1/2 teaspoon powdered mustard

Preheat oven to 350° F. Mix all ingredients, pack into a lightly greased 9" × 5" × 3" loaf pan, and bake, uncovered, 1 hour. Remove from oven and let "rest" 5 minutes. Drain off drippings, then turn loaf out on platter. Make Pan Gravy with some of the drippings or serve loaf with Mustard or Raisin Sauce. Or chill well and serve cold with Mustard or Sour Cream-Horseradish Sauce.

*NPS: 385 C, 190 mg CH, 1,940 mg S**

VARIATIONS

Ham Loaf Ring: Pack ham loaf mixture in a greased 5-cup ring mold instead of a loaf pan and bake as directed. When serving, fill center with mashed sweet potatoes or buttered green peas and mushrooms. Nutritional count same as basic recipe.

Spicy Ham Loaf: Add 1/4 cup minced parsley and 1/8 teaspoon each cloves, cinnamon, and nutmeg to loaf mixture and proceed as directed. Nutritional count same as basic recipe.

Caramel-Glazed Ham Loaf: Sprinkle bottom of loaf pan with 1/3 cup firmly packed light brown sugar and 1/2 teaspoon cloves before packing in meat; bake as directed.
*NPS: 430 C, 190 mg CH, 1,945 mg S**

Tomato-Glazed Ham Loaf: Substitute 1 cup tomato juice for milk when mixing loaf. Proceed as directed, basting loaf frequently with tomato juice throughout baking. About 10 minutes before loaf is done, top with 1 cup Tomato Sauce. Continue baking, and serve with additional Tomato Sauce.
*NPS: 400 C, 190 mg CH, 2,300 mg S**

Orange-Glazed Ham Loaf: Substitute 1 cup orange juice for milk when mixing loaf. Shape mixture into a loaf in a lightly greased shallow roasting pan; bake, uncovered, as directed but baste often during last 1/2 hour with Orange Glaze. *To make glaze:* mix 1/4 cup firmly packed light brown sugar with 1 tablespoon cornstarch; add 1 1/2 cups orange juice and heat, stirring, until thickened and clear. *(Note:* Any leftover glaze can be served with loaf as a sauce.) For extra tang, mix in 2 teaspoons slivered orange rind (orange part only).
*NPS: 450 C, 185 mg CH, 1,925 mg S**

TOP HAT HAM SOUFFLÉ

4 servings ⚖

1/4 cup butter or margarine
1/4 cup sifted flour
1/2 teaspoon salt
1/8 teaspoon white pepper
Pinch cayenne pepper
1 cup milk
4 eggs, separated
1 cup ground cooked ham

Preheat oven to 350° F. Melt butter in a saucepan over moderate heat, blend in flour, salt, and peppers; slowly add milk and heat, stirring, until thickened. Beat yolks lightly, mix in a little of the hot sauce, then return all to pan. Cook, stirring constantly, 1–2 minutes but do not boil. Off heat, mix in ham; cool to room temperature. Beat egg whites until fairly stiff peaks form, then fold into ham mixture. Spoon into an ungreased 1½-quart soufflé dish. To form top hat, insert a table knife in soufflé mixture about ½" deep and 1" from edge of dish and draw a circle concentric to dish. Bake, uncovered (without opening oven door), 35–45 minutes until puffed and golden. Serve at once.

NPS: 310 C, 335 mg CH, 1,030 mg S*

VARIATION

⚖ **Ham and Cheese Soufflé:** Reduce amount of butter to 3 tablespoons then proceed as recipe directs, adding ¾ cup ground ham and ⅓ cup grated sharp Cheddar cheese to hot sauce. Fold in egg whites and bake as directed.

NPS: 305 C, 330 mg CH, 925 mg S*

BAKED SWEET-AND-SOUR HAM BALLS

4 servings

MEAT BALLS
½ pound ground smoked ham
½ pound ground lean pork
1 cup soft white bread crumbs
½ cup milk
1 clove garlic, peeled and crushed
½ teaspoon salt
⅛ teaspoon pepper
1 egg, lightly beaten

SAUCE
1 cup firmly packed light brown sugar
¼ cup cider vinegar
½ cup pineapple juice
1 teaspoon powdered mustard

Preheat oven to 325° F. Mix all meat ball ingredients and shape into 16 balls about 1" in diameter. Arrange in a greased shallow baking pan. Mix sauce ingredients in a saucepan, bring to a boil, and cook, stirring constantly, 2–3 minutes. Pour sauce over meat balls and bake, uncovered, 1 hour, basting frequently.

NPS: 490 C, 145 mg CH, 1,270 mg S*

HAM THE SECOND TIME AROUND

(How to Use Up Leftovers)

HAM TIMBALES

4 servings   ⚖ ¢

1 cup milk
1 cup soft white bread crumbs
2 tablespoons butter or margarine
1 tablespoon finely grated yellow onion
½ teaspoon salt
⅛ teaspoon pepper
⅛ teaspoon cloves
2 eggs, lightly beaten
1 cup ground cooked ham

Preheat oven to 325° F. Mix all but last 2 ingredients in a saucepan and bring to a boil, stirring constantly. Off heat, stir a little hot mixture into eggs, then return to pan. Mix in ham. Spoon into 4 well-greased custard cups and set in a shallow baking pan; pour in enough water to come halfway up cups. Bake, uncovered, 35–45 minutes or until a knife inserted in center comes out clean. Loosen edges of timbales and invert gently on a hot platter. Good with hot Mushroom or Tomato Sauce.

NPS: 225 C, 185 mg CH, 995 mg S*

CRUSTY-CRUMB HAM CROQUETTES

4 servings   ¢

¼ cup butter or margarine
¼ cup sifted flour
1 cup milk
3 scallions, minced
⅛ teaspoon pepper
1 teaspoon prepared mild yellow mustard
1 teaspoon finely grated lemon rind (optional)
¼ cup minced sweet green pepper (optional)
1 egg, lightly beaten
1½ cups ground cooked ham
½ teaspoon salt (about)
1 egg lightly beaten with 1 tablespoon cold water
⅓ cup dry bread crumbs
¼ cup cooking oil

Melt butter in a large saucepan over moderate heat, blend in flour, slowly add milk, and heat, stirring, until thickened. Add scallions, pepper, mustard, and, if you like, lemon rind and green pepper. Spoon a little sauce into beaten egg, then return to saucepan. Mix in ham and salt to taste; then chill until easy to shape. Roll into 8 balls about 2″ in diameter, dip in egg-water mixture, then in crumbs to coat evenly. Let dry on a rack at room temperature 5 minutes. Heat oil in a large, heavy skillet over moderately high heat about 1 minute, then fry balls 3–4 minutes, turning frequently, until browned on all sides. Drain on paper toweling and serve. Good with Hot Mustard or Parsley Sauce.

NPS: 230 C, 215 mg CH, 990 mg S*

To Deep-Fat-Fry: Prepare balls as directed; heat fat in a deep fat fryer to 380° F., add balls a few at a time, and brown about 2 minutes; drain well and serve.

NPS: 405 C, 210 mg CH, 1,345 mg S*

CHINESE CABBAGE (PAK CHOI, BOK CHOY) AND HAM

4 servings   ¢ ⚖

1 medium-size Chinese or celery cabbage, trimmed and cored
1½ teaspoons salt
2 tablespoons cooking oil
½ cup cooked ham strips (about ⅛″ thick and 3″ long)
1 tablespoon cornstarch
1 cup chicken broth

Shred cabbage fine, cover with cold water, mix in 1 teaspoon salt, and let crispen 30 minutes; drain thoroughly. Heat oil in a large, heavy skillet or *wok* over moderately high heat 1–2 minutes. Add cabbage and ham and stir-fry 2–3 minutes until cabbage just wilts. Mix cornstarch, chicken broth, and remaining salt, add to skillet, and cook, stirring constantly, 2 minutes until mixture thickens slightly. Serve with boiled rice.

NPS: 120 C, 10 mg CH, 1,310 mg S*

Some Additional Ways to Use Up Leftover Ham

Creamed Ham and Potatoes *(4 servings):* In a large skillet mix 4 cups diced raw potatoes, 1½ cups chopped ham, ¼ cup minced yellow onion, 1 tablespoon flour, 1 teaspoon salt, and ⅛ teaspoon pepper; add 1 cup each milk and light cream, cover, and simmer, stirring occasionally, 20–30 minutes until potatoes are tender. Taste for salt and adjust as needed. Serve over toast, muffins, biscuits, or waffles.

NPS: 375 C, 80 mg CH, 1,420 mg S*

⊠ ¢ **Chinese Ham and Rice** *(4 servings):* Sauté 1½ cups slivered ham, 1 diced sweet red pepper, and 3 minced scallions in 2 tablespoons cooking oil 2–3 minutes over moderate heat. Add 1 (4-ounce) can water chestnuts, drained and sliced thin, and 3 cups cold cooked rice; stir-fry 4–5 minutes until rice is lightly browned. Stir together (do not beat) 2 eggs and 1 tablespoon soy sauce and mix into rice; heat, stirring, until eggs are just set. Serve with extra soy sauce.

NPS: 340 C, 170 mg CH, 1,190 mg S*

Ham and Egg Pie *(6 servings):* Line a 9″ piepan with pastry and sprinkle with ¾ cup minced ham. Break 5–6 eggs on top, sprinkle with ½ teaspoon salt and ⅛ teaspoon pepper, and top with ¾ cup minced ham. Cover with pastry, crimp, and cut steam vents near center. Brush with glaze if you like (1 egg beaten with 1 tablespoon cold water). Bake ½ hour at 425° F. until lightly browned. Serve hot or cold.

NPS: 430 C, 250 mg CH, 1,145 mg S*

¢ ⊠ **Ham and Baked Beans** *(2 servings):* Mix 1 (1-pound) can baked beans, 1 cup cubed or slivered ham, 2 tablespoons molasses, 1 tablespoon prepared mild yellow mustard, and 1 teaspoon prepared horseradish. Simmer, covered, 15–20 minutes until bubbly, or spoon into an ungreased 1-quart casserole, cover, and bake ½ hour at 350° F.

NPS: 460 C, 40 mg CH, 1,950 mg S*

⊠ ¢ **Ham and Potato Pie** *(4 servings):* Mix 1½ cups minced ham with 2 cups mixed cooked vegetables, succotash, or creamed corn in a buttered 1½-quart casserole. Cover with 2 cups seasoned mashed potatoes, roughen surface with fork, and bake, uncovered, ½ hour at 425° F. until touched with brown.

NPS: 260 C, 35 mg CH, 1,215 mg S*

Ham and Cheese Heroes *(Number of servings flexible):* Split thin loaves of French bread or hard rolls lengthwise, spread with Garlic Butter, prepared mild yellow mustard, and a ½ and ½ mixture of ground ham and grated cheese (Cheddar, Swiss, or Gruyère). Top with other half of loaf, wrap in foil, and bake 20 minutes at 350° F. Recipe too flexible for meaningful nutritional count.

Potted Ham *(About 1½ cups):* Mix 1 cup finely ground lean ham with 2 sieved hard-cooked egg yolks, ¼ cup soft butter, and ⅛ teaspoon powdered mustard. Beat until well blended, pack into a crock or jar, and cover with ⅛″ clarified butter.* Refrigerate and use as a canapé or sandwich spread.

NPS: 40 C, 35 mg CH, 90 mg S*

⚖ **Ham Mousse** *(4 servings):* Mix 1 envelope unflavored gelatin and ½ cup cold water and heat slowly, stirring until dissolved. Add 2 cups ground ham, 1 teaspoon prepared mild yellow mustard, 1 teaspoon prepared horseradish, and, if you like, 2 tablespoons diced pimiento. Cool to room temperature. Fold in 1 stiffly beaten egg white and ½ cup heavy cream, whipped. Spoon into an ungreased 1-quart mold and chill until firm. *(Note: Chicken or tongue may be used in place of ham.)*
NPS: 240 C, 85 mg CH, 1,125 mg S*

Ham, Olive, and Egg Salad *(4 servings):* Mix 2 cups cubed ham, 3 quartered hard-cooked eggs, 1 cup diced celery, ½ cup sliced pimiento-stuffed green olives, 2 minced gherkins, and ¾ cup mayonnaise.
NPS: 520 C, 270 mg CH, 1,875 mg S*

Ham and Chicken Salad *(4 servings):* Mix 1½ cups each cubed ham and chicken with 1 cup diced celery, 2 tablespoons each minced dill pickle, parsley, and grated yellow onion, and ¾ cup mayonnaise.
NPS: 500 C, 100 mg CH, 1,230 mg S*

Ham and Tongue Salad *(4 servings):* Mix 1½ cups each cubed ham and tongue with 1 cup diced celery, 2 tablespoons each sweet pickle relish and prepared mild yellow mustard, and ¾ cup mayonnaise.
NPS: 545 C, 105 mg CH, 1,265 mg S*

Ham Waldorf Salad *(4 servings):* Mix 2 cups each diced ham and diced unpeeled red apple, 1 cup diced celery, ½ cup coarsely chopped pecans or walnuts, 1 cup mayonnaise, and 2 tablespoons lemon juice.
NPS: 665 C, 75 mg CH, 1,430 mg S*

To Make the Most of Very Small Amounts

• Mix ½ cup ground ham with dry ingredients for Dumplings; finish mixing and cook as directed.
• Mix ½ cup ground or finely diced ham with dry ingredients for biscuits, muffins, or corn bread; finish mixing and bake as directed.
• Cube ham or cut in julienne strips and toss into hearty salads (chef's salad, dried bean, egg, potato, pasta, rice, or fruit salad).
• Dice ham and add to Hashed Brown Potatoes, Rice Pilaf, Deluxe Macaroni and Cheese, any meat sauce for spaghetti, any budget casserole.
• Grind ham fine and use in making sandwich fillings or savory stuffings (for ideas, see Some Additional Ways to Use Up Leftover Roast Beef).
• Dice ham or grind coarsely and add to omelets or scrambled eggs, waffle or pancake batter.

What to Do with Ham Bones

• Add to the pot when cooking any dried beans, peas, or lentils.
• Add to the pot when cooking fresh mustard greens, spinach, turnip greens, green or wax beans, black-eyed peas.
• Use in making dried pea, bean, or lentil soup or Corn Chowder.

HAM STEAKS AND SLICES
(See Pork Chart)

Ham Steak: Also called *Ham Center Slice,* this large oval slice from the middle of the ham is the equivalent of beef round or veal cutlet. Cut thick, it can be baked; cut thin, broiled, panbroiled, grilled, panfried, or braised. Available uncooked and ready-to-eat.

Ham Butt Slice: Cut a little higher on the ham than the center slice, this steak is not quite so large or expensive. Available uncooked or ready-to-eat.

Smoked Picnic Slice: This large oval slice resembles ham steak but is not as tender or expensive. Available uncooked or ready-to-eat.

How to Cook

Amount Needed: A ham steak or slice cut ½" thick will serve 2–4; cut 1"–2" thick, it will serve 4–6. To figure by weight: allow ⅓–½ pound per person.

General Preparation for Cooking: Remove any rind, trim off all but ¼" outer fat, then slash fat edge at 1" intervals to prevent curling.

To Panfry (Sauté): Recommended only for very lean ham steaks and slices ¼"–¾" thick. *Uncooked ham:* Brown, uncovered, in 1 tablespoon bacon drippings or cooking oil in a large, heavy skillet over moderately low heat, allowing 3 minutes per side for ¼" thick steaks, 4–5 minutes per side for ½" steaks, and 6 minutes per side for ¾" steaks. Season with pepper and, if needed, salt. *Ready-to-eat ham:* Prepare like uncooked ham but brown about half as long on each side.

Mustard Ham Steak: Before cooking, spread 1 side of ham with 1½ tablespoons mild yellow mustard and sprinkle with pepper. Place ham in skillet mustard side down and brown as directed. Before turning, spread top with 1½ tablespoons mustard and sprinkle with pepper; turn and brown as before.

To Panbroil: Recommended for steaks and slices ¼″–¾″ thick. If ham seems lean, grease or salt skillet *lightly;* heat over moderately low heat 1 minute, add ham steak, and cook, using panfrying times as a guide. Turn with tongs and drain off drippings as they collect.

VARIATION

Ham Steak in Sour Cream-Onion Gravy: Panbroil steak as directed, remove to a heated platter, and keep warm. In drippings sauté 2 thinly sliced large yellow onions 8–10 minutes over moderate heat until golden; smooth in 1 cup sour cream, ⅓ cup milk, and ¼ teaspoon paprika. Heat and stir (but do not boil) 1–2 minutes over low heat. Pour over ham and serve.

To Broil: Recommended for ham steaks or slices ½″–1½″ thick. Preheat broiler. Rub rack with drippings or oil and line pan underneath with foil. Place ham on rack, fat edge to back to reduce sputtering, then adjust height and broil using times in chart below as a guide. Use tongs for turning. For extra flavor, brush steaks often during cooking with a liquid glaze (see Some Glazes for Baked Hams).

To Charcoal-Broil: Recommended for ham steaks or slices ½″–1½″ thick. Build a moderately low charcoal fire. Lightly grease grill with drippings or oil, place ham on grill, adjust height from coals, and broil according to chart. If you like, brush often during cooking with a liquid glaze (see Some Glazes for Baked Hams).

Ham Steak Broiling Chart
(next page)

Times (for steaks refrigerated until ready to be broiled) are approximate at best because size and shape of cut, amount of fat and bone, type of oven or grill all affect broiling time. In outdoor cooking, wind and temperature must also be considered.

To Braise: Especially good for uncooked ham steaks and slices about 1″ thick. Brown both sides of steak quickly in a lightly greased large, heavy skillet over moderately high heat; pour off drippings. Add 1 cup liquid (water; orange, pineapple, apple, or apricot juice; apple cider; beer, sherry, port, Madeira, champagne, sweet or dry red or white wine), cover, turn heat to low, and simmer until done. *Uncooked hams* will take about 20 minutes (turn after 10); *ready-to-eat hams* 5–10 minutes in all.

VARIATIONS

Ham Steak Virginia: Braise steak as directed, using water for the liquid; remove ham to a heated platter and keep warm. Stir ½ cup medium-dry sherry and 2 tablespoons light brown sugar into skillet and heat, stirring, over moderate heat until sugar dissolves. Blend 2 tablespoons flour with ¼ cup cold water, mix into skillet, and heat and stir until thickened. Return steak to skillet, turn heat to low, and simmer, uncovered, 5–7 minutes, basting and turning frequently. Serve on a bed of Creamed Spinach.

Ham Steak in Port Wine Sauce: Brown steak on both sides and drain off drippings. To skillet add ¾ cup water, ⅓ cup tawny port wine, and 1 tablespoon soy sauce. Cover and simmer until done as directed above. Lift ham to a heated platter and keep warm; boil wine sauce, uncovered, 2–3 minutes until reduced to about ½ cup. Pour over ham and serve.

To Bake: Recommended for 1½″–2″ thick ham steaks and slices. Preheat oven to 325° F. Place ham on a rack in a shallow roasting pan. If you like, stud surface with cloves and top with a thin glaze (see Some Glazes for Baked Hams). Bake, uncovered, basting occasionally with glaze, if used, until tender. *Ready-to-eat hams* need only 30–35 minutes, regardless of thickness. Time *uncooked hams* as follows: 1–1¼ hours for a 1½″ steak, 1½–1¾ hours for a 2″ steak.

VARIATIONS

Marinated Ham Steak: Marinate steak in refrigerator overnight in ½ cup dry red wine or red wine vinegar mixed with ½ cup pineapple juice and ½ teaspoon ginger. Place ham and marinade in baking pan and bake as directed, basting often.

Chinese-Style Ham Steak: Marinate steak in refrigerator overnight in ⅓ cup soy sauce mixed with ¼ cup firmly packed light brown sugar, ¼ cup cider vinegar, 1 crushed clove garlic, and 1 teaspoon powdered mustard. Place ham and marinade in pan and bake as directed, basting often.

HAM STEAK BROILING CHART

Cut	Thickness	Oven or Fire Temperature	Distance from Heat	Approximate Minutes per Side
Oven Broiling				
	1/2"	broil	3"	4
Uncooked	3/4"	broil	3"	7
Ham steaks	1"	broil	4"	9
	11/2"	broil	4"	10–12
	1/2"	broil	3"	3–5 total (do not turn steak)
Ready-to-eat	3/4"	broil	3"	3
Ham steaks	1"	broil	4"	5
	11/2"	(not recommended)		
Charcoal Broiling				
	1/2"	moderately low	4"	5
Uncooked	3/4"	moderately low	4"	6–8
Ham steaks	1"	moderately low	5"	10
	11/2"	moderately low	5"	12
Ready-to-eat	1/2"	moderately low	4"	3–4
Ham steaks	3/4"	moderately low	4"	4–5
	1"	moderately low	4"	5–6

Chutney-Glazed Ham Steak: Mix 1 cup minced chutney with 1/4 cup firmly packed light brown sugar and 1/3 cup water; spread over ham and bake as directed.

BAKED HAM AND SWEET POTATOES

4–6 servings

4 medium-size sweet potatoes, parboiled, peeled, and halved
4 pineapple rings or 1 cup pineapple chunks or tidbits
1 ready-to-eat ham steak, cut 3/4" thick (about 2 pounds)
6 cloves
2 tablespoons light brown sugar
1/2 cup pineapple juice

Preheat oven to 350° F. Arrange potatoes in an ungreased 21/2-quart casserole, cover with pineapple, and top with ham. Stud ham with cloves and sprinkle with sugar. Pour pineapple juice over all and bake, uncovered, 30–40 minutes.

NPS (4–6): 720–480 C, 130–85 mg CH, 3,015–2,010 mg S*

COUNTRY-FRIED HAM WITH RED-EYE GRAVY

2–4 servings   ⊠

Country-Fried Ham with Red-Eye Gravy is one of those generations-old Southern recipes that probably seemed too simple to write down. It isn't really. To have any success, you must use country-cured ham, a heavy iron skillet, and just the right amount of heat—too much and the ham will scorch, too little and it won't brown. Some say coffee gives the gravy its red color, but most country cooks simply simmer the gravy, scraping up any browned bits, till it turns red-brown on its own.

1 teaspoon bacon drippings or lard
1 center slice country-cured ham, cut 1/4" thick
2/3 cup cold water
1 tablespoon hot strong coffee (optional)

Place a heavy iron skillet over moderately low heat and heat 1 minute; add drippings and, when melted, place ham in skillet. Fry, turning often, until ham is nicely browned on both sides; this will take about 15 minutes. Remove ham to a heated platter and keep warm. Add water to skillet and continue heating, stirring and scraping up browned bits, 3–5 minutes until gravy turns red-brown; add coffee if you like. Spoon a little gravy over ham and pass the rest. Serve with grits.

NPS (2–4): 430–215 C, 130–65 mg CH, 2,990–1,495 mg S*

BACON, SALT PORK, AND JOWL
(See Pork Chart)

"The leaner, the better" doesn't apply to bacon because fat is what gives bacon its woodsy-sweet flavor and tender crispness. Ideally, bacon should be half to two thirds fat—snowy and firm with wide, evenly distributed streakings of bright pink lean. (Because of its high fat content, bacon stores poorly, so don't buy more than a week's supply at a time.) The flavor of bacon, like that of ham, varies according to the breed of animal, feed, cut, method of curing and smoking. Your best assurance of quality is to buy brands you trust. (*Note:* In the old days, sodium nitrite was routinely used in curing bacons. But now that food researchers suspect one of its by-products, *nitrosamines,* of being carcinogenic, nitrite-free bacons are available.)

Slab Bacon: Cured and smoked side of pork. It's cheaper than presliced bacon and, according to some people, has better flavor (especially the wonderfully woodsy double-smoked bacon). Butchers will slice it for you or you can do it yourself.

Sliced Bacon: Slab bacon that has been trimmed of rind, sliced, and packaged. Available as:

Regular Sliced: The best all-round bacon, not too thick, not too thin. There are 16–20 slices per pound.

Thick Sliced: A shade thicker than regular-sliced bacon, this has an old-fashioned, hand-sliced look. About 12–16 slices per pound.

Thin Sliced: Good for sandwiches, serving with eggs or crumbling into bacon bits, but too thin and fragile to do the sort of wrapping *rumakis* need. About 35 slices per pound.

Canned Sliced: A convenience food for campers and apartment dwellers with pint-sized refrigerators, these canned precooked bacon slices need no refrigeration and can be heated in minutes. 1 can (18–20 slices) = 1 pound fresh bacon.

Ends and Pieces: These penny-saving scraps are great for soups, sandwiches, salads.

Bacon Crumbles or Bits: Crisp, cooked bits of bacon ready to toss into salads, soups, and casseroles. Usually bottled in small amounts. Also available: vegetable-based imitation bacon bits.

Country-Cured Bacon: Also called *Country-Style Bacon,* this is salty, heavily smoked bacon. Often it comes from the same hogs as Smithfield or Virginia hams. More expensive than ordinary bacon and available by the slab or slice in specialty food shops.

Irish Bacon: This Irish equivalent of country-cured bacon is a doubly long strip containing both the "streaky" we usually think of as bacon and the lean eye of loin used for Canadian bacon. For shipping, the two are cut through to the rind just below the ribs, then folded together compact-style. Whether you buy Irish bacon by the slab or have it sliced to order, you will get both parts. Like country-cured bacon, Irish bacon is heavily salted and smoked; it is more expensive than standard bacon and is available in specialty food shops.

Canadian Bacon: Sometimes called *Back Bacon,* this is the boneless, lean eye of loin, cured and smoked. In flavor and texture it resembles ham more than bacon and is best when cooked like ham. Available presliced or in rolls, also canned as *Pork Loin Roll.*

Pancetta (pronounced pan-CHET-ta): An Italian bacon roll, not smoked, but cured with spices and herbs. It's sliced like salami and used to flavor forcemeats, sauces, vegetables, and braised meats.

Smoked Loin Chops: A fairly new item closely related to Canadian bacon. These are simply cured and smoked loin chops. They're presliced and packaged with full cooking directions.

Jowl: Also called *Bacon Square,* this is the fleshy cheek of the hog trimmed into 5″–8″ squares, cured and smoked. It is boneless, fatter than bacon, and, except for that which is country-cured, budget priced. Use as you would bacon.

Salt Pork: Sometimes known as "white bacon," salt pork comes from the side of the hog. It is mostly fat (though that of top quality contains a handsome streak of lean); it is cured *but not smoked* and used primarily for seasoning. Frequently, people confuse salt pork with *fat back;* they are not at all the same. Fat back is fresh (uncured, unsmoked) fat from the back of the hog used for cooking and making lard.

How to Cook

Amounts Needed: Allow 2–4 slices bacon or Canadian bacon per person. When buying Canadian bacon by the roll, figure 1/4–1/3 pound per person.

General Preparation for Cooking: Remove any rind. Irish and country-cured bacon, because of their saltiness, will profit by 5–10 minutes simmering in water before being broiled, panbroiled, or baked. Drain well, pat dry, then follow basic methods.

To Panfry (Sauté): Especially recommended for sliced Canadian bacon. Melt about 1 teaspoon bacon drippings in a heavy skillet over moderately low heat, add bacon, and cook 4–5 minutes on a side until delicately browned.

To Panbroil: Good for all but Canadian bacon, which is too lean to cook without additional fat. Take bacon straight from refrigerator and place unseparated slices in a cold skillet. Set over moderate heat and cook, turning often with tongs and separating slices as they heat, 6–8 minutes until crisp and brown. Spoon off drippings as they collect and drain bacon well on paper toweling before serving.

To Broil: Recommended for all but Canadian bacon. Preheat broiler. Take bacon straight from refrigerator and arrange slices on broiler rack so fat edges overlap slightly. Broil 4″ from heat 2–3 minutes on a side until crisp and golden. Use tongs to turn and watch closely. Drain on paper toweling before serving.

To Bake:

Bacon: Here's the way to cook bacon for a crowd. Preheat oven to 400° F. Lay cold bacon strips, fat edges overlapping, on a large cookie rack set in a shallow roasting pan. Bake, uncovered, 12–15 minutes without turning until crisp and brown.

Canadian Bacon: Buy a roll of Canadian bacon weighing at least 2 pounds. Slip off casing and place roll fat side up on a rack in a shallow roasting pan. Insert meat thermometer in center. Preheat oven to 325° F. and bake, uncovered, about 35 minutes per pound or until meat thermometer registers 160° F. For an extra-juicy bacon, add 1 cup liquid to pan before baking (chicken stock, orange, apple, or pineapple juice, beer) and bake as directed, basting often. For more festive ways to bake Canadian bacon, see recipes that follow.

To Spit-Roast (for Canadian bacon rolls only; for best results, choose one weighing 3–4 pounds):

In Rotisserie, Gas or Electric Barbecue, or Oven: Preheat unit. Insert spit straight through roll, end to end, attach to rotisserie and insert meat thermometer in center so it does not touch spit. Roast about 25 minutes per pound or until thermometer registers 160° F. Baste every 15–20 minutes, if you like, with orange, apple, or pineapple juice or with a thin glaze (see Some Glazes for Baked Hams).

Over Charcoal: Build a moderate charcoal fire. Balance roll on spit and insert meat thermometer as above; attach to rotisserie and adjust height so spit is 4″–5″ from coals. Roast about 25 minutes per pound or until thermometer registers 160° F., basting, if you like, with orange, apple, or pineapple juice or with a thin glaze (see Some Glazes for Baked Hams).

How to Save and Use Bacon Drippings

Collect drippings in a tall coffee tin; when full, spoon drippings into a deep saucepan, add 1 cup water, and sprinkle 2–3 tablespoons flour on top (this is to make any sediment settle). Bring to a boil over moderate heat without covering or stirring. Remove from heat, cool slightly, strain through a double thickness of cheesecloth, and pour into a large jar. Cover and store in refrigerator. Use in place of butter or margarine for frying and sautéing, also for seasoning vegetables.

BAKED GINGER-GLAZED CANADIAN BACON

4–6 servings

1 (2-pound) roll ready-to-eat Canadian bacon
1½ cups ginger marmalade
¼ cup brandy

Have butcher remove casing from bacon, slice ⅛″–¼″ thick, and tie together into original shape. Preheat oven to 325° F. Place bacon fat side up on a rack in a shallow roasting pan. Mince any large pieces of ginger in marmalade, then mix all with brandy; spread half over bacon. Bake, uncovered, ½ hour; spread with remaining marmalade and bake ½ hour longer. Transfer to a hot platter, remove strings, and serve with English or Dijon-style mustard.

NPS (4–6): 890–595 C, 45–30 mg CH, 1,165–775 mg S*

VARIATION

Substitute orange or lime marmalade or chopped mango or peach chutney for ginger marmalade; proceed as directed. Nutritional count same as basic recipe.

BAKED YAMS, APPLES, AND CANADIAN BACON

4 servings

4 medium-size yams, parboiled, peeled, and sliced ½″ thick
2 tart apples, peeled, cored, and cut in ¼″ rings
½ teaspoon salt
8 slices ready-to-eat Canadian bacon, cut ¼″ thick
1 teaspoon prepared hot mustard
2 tablespoons light brown sugar
2 tablespoons butter or margarine

Preheat oven to 375° F. Layer yams and apples into a buttered 2½-quart casserole, sprinkling with salt as you go. Spread each side of bacon slices lightly with mustard and arrange on top, overlapping spoke fashion. Sprinkle with sugar and dot with butter. Bake, uncovered, 30 minutes until yams are tender and bacon lightly glazed.

NPS: 405 C, 45 mg CH, 1,165 mg S*

HOG JOWL AND BLACK-EYED PEAS

6 servings ¢

An old Southern custom, practiced yet in some communities, is to eat hog jowl and black-eyed peas on New Year's Day. Brings good luck, they say.

1 pound dried black-eyed peas, washed and sorted
2 quarts cold water
1 (½-pound) piece country-cured hog jowl
1 small dried hot red chili pepper
Salt to taste

Soak peas overnight in 1 quart water or use the quick method.* About 1 hour before peas have finished soaking, scrub jowl well under running tepid water; place in a large, heavy kettle with 1 quart water and the chili pepper. Cover and bring to a boil, adjust heat so water stays at a slow simmer, and cook 1 hour. Add peas and their soaking water to kettle, cover, and simmer about 2 hours longer until peas and jowl are both tender. Check pot occasionally and, if mixture seems thick, thin with about ½ cup hot water. Taste for salt and season as needed; discard chili pepper. Cut jowl into thin slices, return to kettle, and warm 5–10 minutes. Serve in soup bowls, making sure each person gets some of the jowl.

NPS: 510 C, 35 mg CH, 35 mg S*

SCALLOPED SALT PORK AND POTATOES

4–6 servings ¢

A good budget main dish.

½ pound salt pork, trimmed of rind and cut in small dice
Salt pork drippings and enough bacon drippings to total ¼ cup
1 quart thinly sliced, peeled potatoes (you'll need 4–5 medium-size potatoes)
1 large yellow onion, peeled and sliced thin
2 tablespoons flour
¼ cup minced parsley
⅛ teaspoon pepper
1½ cups light cream

Preheat oven to 350° F. Stir-fry salt pork 8–10 minutes in a large, heavy skillet over moderate heat until lightly browned. Pour off drippings and reserve, adding bacon drippings as needed to measure ¼ cup. In a buttered 2-quart casserole, build up alternate layers of potatoes, onion, and salt pork, beginning and ending with potatoes. Drizzle each onion layer with drippings, then sprinkle with flour, parsley, and pepper. Pour in cream, cover, and bake 1–1½ hours until potatoes are tender. Broil quickly, if you like, to brown; then serve.

NPS (4–6): 765–510 C, 100–65 mg CH, 735–490 mg S*

VARIETY MEATS

These are the other edible parts of beef, veal, lamb, and pork, the organ meats such as heart, liver, kidneys, sweetbreads, brains, tongue, and tripe. Europeans, considering them the choicest parts of the animal, lavish attention upon them, but we, alas, too often pass them up in favor of steaks, chops, and roasts. Organ meats are the most nutritious of all meats because they contain concentrated sources of certain minerals and vitamins. They are lean and thus low-calorie, but they are, for the most part, cholesterol-rich (particularly liver, kidney, and brains) and should be minimal in the diets of those with high-cholesterol blood levels.

Because there is less demand for variety meats (with the exception, perhaps, of sweetbreads and calf's liver) than for steaks, roasts, and chops, they are cheaper than the popular cuts. Correctly prepared, moreover, variety meats are surprisingly tender, delicately flavored, and good.

BRAINS

Though gourmets have long been lyrical about brains, likening their fragile texture to that of cooked mushrooms, their flavor to the most delicate white fish, they are not everyone's dish. It's the *idea* of eating brains that puts people off. If you've never tasted them, a good way to begin is by ordering *Cervelles au Beurre Noir* (Brains in Black Butter Sauce) or perhaps Brains Vinaigrette in some fine French restaurant. Delicious.

The choicest brains are those from calves or lambs; pork and beef brains have stronger flavor and less delicate texture. All brains are highly perishable (always cook within 24 hours) and for that reason are a special order item. When ordering, insist that the brains be *absolutely fresh.* Recently, frozen brains have been appearing in supermarket counters and, though they haven't quite the character of fresh brains, they are a very good substitute when the fresh aren't available. Always follow package directions when preparing.

Like sweetbreads (with which they can often be used interchangeably in recipes), brains are easily torn or broken. They require extra-gentle handling, careful cleaning and soaking, and sometimes blanching before they can be used in recipes.

Amount Needed: Allow 1/4–1/3 pound brains per serving. Lamb and pork brains usually weigh about 1/4 pound each, calf brains 1/2 pound, and beef brains 3/4 pound.

To Prepare for Cooking: Wash brains carefully in cold water, then place in a large bowl and cover with acidulated water (1 tablespoon lemon juice or white vinegar and 1 teaspoon salt to 1 quart water) and soak 1 1/2 hours. Drain, very gently peel off as much thin outer membrane as possible (it clings tightly and is almost transparent). Soak for another 1 1/2 hours in fresh acidulated water, changing the water one to two times; drain and again peel off as much membrane as possible. Also cut away opaque white bits at base of brains. *(Note:* If membrane is not peeled off before cooking, any blood trapped underneath will leave brown streaks, marring the brains' creamy color.)

To Blanch: Gourmets disagree as to whether brains should be blanched before cooking. If they are to be braised, blanching serves no real purpose and actually leaches out some of the subtle flavor. If they are to be sautéed, blanching will help make them firm, make them easier to slice and handle. To blanch, place brains in a saucepan (not aluminum), add acidulated water to cover, and simmer, uncovered, over low heat. Lamb brains will need only 15 minutes, pork and calf brains about 20, and beef brains about 30. Drain well, cover with ice water, and let stand until cold. Drain again and pat dry on paper toweling.

SAUTÉED BRAINS

4 servings ⬛

1 1/4 pounds brains
1/2 cup unsifted flour
1 teaspoon salt
1/4 teaspoon pepper
1/4 cup butter or margarine
8 small unbuttered toast triangles (optional)

SUGGESTED SAUCES
Bordelaise
Diable
Madeira

Prepare brains for cooking and blanch as directed.* Make sure they are quite dry. Slice 1/2" thick and dredge lightly in a mixture of flour, salt, and pepper. Heat butter in a large, heavy skillet over moderate heat and sauté brains 3–4 minutes on each side until nicely browned. Drain on paper toweling. Serve as is with one of the sauces suggested above or, if you like, on toast triangles.

*NPS: 335 C, 2,870 mg CH, 845 mg S**

Cervelles au Beurre Noir (Brains in Black Butter Sauce): Prepare Sautéed Brains as directed, remove from skillet and keep warm. Place 1/2 cup clarified butter* in a clean small skillet and heat, moving pan continuously, over low heat just until butter begins to brown. Mix in 2 tablespoons white vinegar or lemon juice and 1 tablespoon minced parsley. Pour over brains and serve. If you like, sprinkle brains with 2 tablespoons drained capers before adding butter.

NPS: 565 C, 2,935 mg CH, 845 mg S*

⚖ **Breaded Brains:** Prepare, slice, and dredge brains as above, then dip in 1 egg lightly beaten with 1 tablespoon cold water and finally in fine dry bread crumbs or cracker meal. Sauté in butter as directed and serve with Lemon Butter.

NPS: 405 C, 2,935 mg CH, 955 mg S*

Broiled Brains
(See Broiled Sweetbreads)

BRAINS VINAIGRETTE

4 servings

1 1/4 pounds brains
1 quart cold water
1 tablespoon white vinegar or lemon juice
1 teaspoon salt
1/4 teaspoon peppercorns and 1 bay leaf and 1 sprig each parsley and thyme, tied in cheesecloth
1/2 small yellow onion, peeled
1 small carrot, peeled

VINAIGRETTE DRESSING
1/4 cup white wine vinegar
1/4 teaspoon salt
1/8 teaspoon white pepper
3/4 cup olive oil

Prepare brains for cooking.* Place in a large enamel, stainless-steel, or Teflon-lined saucepan with all but dressing ingredients and simmer, uncovered, 20–25 minutes. Meanwhile, prepare dressing by shaking all ingredients in a shaker jar. When brains are cooked, lift out with a slotted spoon, halve, and arrange on a hot platter. Drizzle with about 1/2 cup dressing and pass the rest.

To Serve Cold: Cool brains in cooking liquid, then drain and chill well. Slice 1/2" thick, drizzle with dressing, and serve.

NPS (hot or cold): 550 C, 2,835 mg CH, 595 mg S*

COQUILLES OF BRAINS MORNAY

4 servings

1 1/4 pounds brains
2 cups hot Mornay Sauce
1/3 cup fine dry bread crumbs mixed with 2 tablespoons melted butter or margarine (optional topping)

Prepare brains for cooking and blanch as directed*; cut in small dice. Preheat oven to 350° F. Mix brains with sauce and spoon into lightly buttered scallop shells or ramekins. Top, if you like, with buttered crumbs. Set on a baking tray and bake, uncovered, 15 minutes, then brown quickly under broiler and serve.

NPS: 550 C, 2,925 mg CH, 825 mg S*

VARIATION

Coquilles of Sweetbreads Mornay: Prepare as directed, substituting sweetbreads for brains.

NPS: 640 C, 435 mg CH, 770 mg S*

HEART

The hearts of beef, veal, pork, and lamb are all good to eat. They're chewy and muscular, taste a little bit like liver, and, when stuffed and braised or stewed, make a very good meal indeed. If you are lucky enough to find very young lamb or veal hearts, you can simply slice and sauté them as you would calf's liver. All hearts are highly perishable, highly nutritious. They're also low in calories and, because there is little demand for them, budget priced. Better order ahead.

Amount Needed: Allow about 1/2 pound per serving. Beef hearts run large—from 3–5 pounds—and make a good choice for a large family; veal hearts weigh 3/4 pound and are perfect for 2 (if they don't have big appetites); pork hearts weigh about 1/2 pound, and lamb hearts between 1/4 and 1/2.

To Prepare for Cooking: Wash heart well in tepid water, remove all fat, halve lengthwise and cut out vessels and large tubes. Leave halves joined if heart is to be stuffed, otherwise, cut up as individual recipes direct. If heart seems especially muscular, soak 1–2 hours in sour milk or acidulated water (1 tablespoon vinegar or lemon juice and 1 teaspoon salt to 1 quart water) to tenderize.

To Simmer (Stew): Place heart halves in a deep pot and add broth or salted water to cover (1 teaspoon salt for each quart water).

Cover and simmer until tender, about 3–4 hours for beef heart, 2–2½ for pork and veal hearts. Serve with Pan Gravy or a suitable sauce such as Bordelaise or Madeira. *(Note: Lamb hearts should not be simmered; they're better if braised or sautéed.)* To give simmered hearts extra flavor, add an onion, carrot, celery stalk, and parsley sprigs to the pot.

To Pressure-Cook (not recommended for lamb hearts): Prepare heart for cooking; do not stuff. Brown heart in bacon drippings in open cooker, add ½ cup water or stock (or amount of liquid manufacturer recommends). Seal cooker, bring to 10 pounds pressure, and cook 15–20 minutes per pound or according to manufacturer's timetable (meat cooked at 10 pounds pressure will be more tender than that cooked at 15). Reduce pressure, open cooker, remove heart, and keep warm. Prepare Pan Gravy in open cooker.

SAUTÉED HEARTS

4 servings ¢

Only young lamb or veal hearts will be tender enough to sauté.

2 pounds lamb or veal hearts
3 tablespoons butter or margarine
¼ teaspoon salt
Pinch pepper
Pinch nutmeg (optional)
4 slices buttered toast (optional)
1 tablespoon minced parsley (optional)

Prepare hearts for cooking,* halve lengthwise, and slice ¼"–½" thick. Melt butter in a large, heavy skillet over moderately high heat, let it foam up, then subside. Add hearts, reduce heat to moderate, and stir-fry 2–3 minutes. Season and serve, if you like, on buttered toast sprinkled with parsley.

*NPS: 445 C, 365 mg CH, 420 mg S**

VARIATIONS

Sautéed Hearts and Mushrooms: Prepare and slice hearts as above. Stir-fry ½ pound thinly sliced mushrooms in butter 3–4 minutes over moderately high heat; push to side of skillet, add hearts, and sauté as directed. Season and serve.

*NPS: 460 C, 365 mg CH, 425 mg S**

Mixed Fry: Prepare and slice 1 veal heart as directed above; cut ¼ pound calf's liver into thin strips; prepare 2 lamb kidneys for cooking* and sauté halves in 2 tablespoons butter

3–4 minutes over moderate heat, turning often with tongs. Remove from skillet and slice. Raise heat to high, add heart, liver, and kidney, and stir-fry quickly 2–3 minutes. Season with salt and pepper and, if you like, 1 tablespoon each lemon juice and minced parsley. Serve as is or on buttered toast.

*NPS: 260 C, 375 mg CH, 375 mg S**

BRAISED STUFFED HEART

6 servings ¢

1 (4–5-pound) beef heart
1 teaspoon salt
¼ teaspoon pepper
2 tablespoons butter or margarine
2 cups beef broth
2 tablespoons flour blended with 2 tablespoons cold water

STUFFING
1 cup minced yellow onion
⅓ cup minced carrot
2 tablespoons minced celery
2 tablespoons butter or margarine
1½ cups cooked rice
2 tablespoons minced parsley
1 teaspoon poultry seasoning

Prepare heart for cooking* and pat dry on paper toweling. Rub inside and out with salt and pepper and let stand while you prepare stuffing. Stir-fry onion, carrot, and celery in butter in a heavy skillet over moderate heat 8–10 minutes until golden; mix with remaining stuffing ingredients. Spoon loosely into heart cavity and close opening with poultry pins and string or sew up with needle and thread. Brown heart all over in 2 tablespoons butter in a heavy kettle over moderate heat. *(Note: Use tongs for turning so you don't pierce heart and lose precious juices.)* Add broth, cover, and simmer slowly about 3 hours until tender, turning 1–2 times during cooking. Check pot occasionally and add a little water if necessary. Lift heart to a heated platter, remove pins and string or thread and keep warm. Stir flour paste into kettle liquid and heat, stirring constantly, until thickened and smooth. Taste for salt and pepper and adjust if needed. To serve: slice heart crosswise, not too thin, and pass gravy.

*NPS: 480 C, 475 mg CH, 975 mg S**

VARIATION

Substitute 2 cups Sage and Onion Dressing, Cornbread and Sausage Stuffing, or other savory stuffing for that above and proceed as directed.

NPS (Sage and Onion): 445 C, 475 mg CH, 1,205 mg S*
NPS (cornbread): 540 C, 510 mg CH, 1,445 mg S*

CASSEROLE OF VEAL HEARTS AND VEGETABLES

4 servings   ¢

2 pounds veal hearts
1/3 cup unsifted flour
1 teaspoon salt
1/4 teaspoon pepper
3 tablespoons bacon drippings or cooking oil
1 large yellow onion, peeled and minced
1 cup water
1/4 cup tomato paste
1 tablespoon Worcestershire sauce
4 carrots, peeled and cut in 2″ chunks
3 turnips, peeled and quartered
3 stalks celery, cut in 2″ chunks
1 tablespoon minced parsley

Preheat oven to 350° F. Prepare hearts for cooking* and quarter. Dredge in a mixture of flour, salt, and pepper and brown in drippings in a heavy skillet over moderate heat 3–4 minutes; transfer to an ungreased 2 1/2-quart casserole. Stir-fry onion in drippings 5–8 minutes until pale golden, stir in water, tomato paste, and Worcestershire sauce, and pour into casserole. Tuck vegetables in here and there, cover, and bake 1 1/2–2 hours until hearts are tender. Uncover, sprinkle with parsley, and serve.

NPS: 480 C, 345 mg CH, 1,075 mg S*

BALMORAL HEART PATTIES

4 servings   ¢

Good in hamburger buns.

1 pound sliced beef or veal heart, trimmed of large vessels
2 scallions
1/2 cup quick-cooking oatmeal
1/4 cup half-and-half or light cream
1 1/4 teaspoons salt
1/4 teaspoon pepper
1 tablespoon Worcestershire sauce
2 tablespoons minced parsley
3 tablespoons bacon or beef drippings, butter, or margarine
1 cup beef gravy (homemade or canned)

Put heart through finest blade of food grinder along with scallions; mix in oatmeal, milk, salt, pepper, Worcestershire sauce, and parsley, cover, and chill 1 hour. Shape into 4 plump patties and brown slowly in drippings in a heavy skillet over moderate heat; reduce heat to low and cook, uncovered, turning frequently, 10–12 minutes until cooked through but not dry. Transfer to a hot platter and keep warm. Heat gravy in skillet drippings and serve with patties.

NPS: 295 C, 185 mg CH, 860 mg S*

KIDNEYS

The kidneys of all meat animals are edible, but those of lamb and veal are the most cherished because of their delicacy and tenderness; either can be broiled or sautéed. Beef and pork kidneys are another matter; being muscular and strongly flavored, they're best when braised or stewed. All kidneys are a high-protein, low-calorie food and an excellent source of iron and B vitamins. When buying kidneys, always make sure they smell sweet and fresh.

Amount Needed: Allow 1/3–1/2 pound kidneys per person. Lamb kidneys are so tiny (only 1 1/2–3 ounces each) that you'll need 2–3 per person. Veal kidneys average 1/2–3/4 pound and will usually serve 1–2. Beef kidneys weigh about 1 pound and pork kidneys 1/4 pound.

To Prepare for Cooking: Because of their delicacy, lamb and veal kidneys should never be washed. Peel off any outer fat, the thin membrane, and then cut out the knobs of fat and tubes underneath; the job will be easier if the kidneys are first halved lengthwise. Beef and pork kidneys should be washed well in tepid water, then split and trimmed of fat and tubes.

SAUTÉED KIDNEYS

4 servings   ⊲⊳

Only lamb or veal kidneys are delicate enough to sauté. And even these are a bit tricky. If sliced, the kidneys will send a lot of juice out into the skillet so that they "stew" rather than sauté. The best method is the one that follows—sautéing the kidney halves, then slicing and returning briefly to the skillet. Kidneys, by the way, do not brown so much as turn an even gray-beige. They're best slightly rare.

1 1/2 pounds lamb or veal kidneys
3 tablespoons butter or margarine
1/4 teaspoon salt
Pinch pepper

1 tablespoon lemon juice (optional)
1 tablespoon minced parsley (optional)

Prepare kidneys for cooking.* Melt butter in a large, heavy skillet over moderately high heat, let it foam up, then subside. Add kidneys and sauté, turning often with tongs. Veal kidneys will need 8–10 minutes, lamb kidneys only 3–5. Remove from skillet and slice about 1/4″ thick (lamb kidneys may also be simply quartered). Return kidneys to skillet and warm about 2 minutes, shaking skillet. Season and, if you like, sprinkle with lemon juice and parsley. Serve as is or with suitable sauce such as Bordelaise, Diable, or Piquante.

NPS: 255 C, 660 mg CH, 565 mg S*

VARIATIONS

⚖ **Sautéed Kidneys and Mushrooms:** Prepare kidneys as above and set aside. Stir-fry 1/2 pound thinly sliced mushrooms in butter 3–5 minutes over moderately high heat, push to side of skillet, add kidneys, and proceed as directed.

NPS: 270 C, 660 mg CH, 570 mg S*

Sautéed Kidneys in Onion and Wine Sauce: Prepare and sauté whole kidneys as above; remove from skillet and keep warm. In drippings stir-fry 2 tablespoons minced scallions 3–4 minutes, add 1/2 cup dry vermouth, and boil rapidly to reduce by half. Add 1 tablespoon each lemon juice and minced parsley. Slice kidneys, return to skillet, and season. Warm, shaking skillet, 1–2 minutes and serve.

NPS: 265 C, 660 mg CH, 565 mg S*

⚖ **Low-Calorie Sautéed Kidneys:** Reduce amount of butter to 2 tablespoons and prepare as directed.

NPS: 230 C, 655 mg CH, 535 mg S*

BROILED KIDNEYS

4 servings ⚖

Lamb and veal kidneys are the most suitable for broiling, and they must be basted often with melted butter and broiled only until rare or medium if they are to remain moist and tender.

11/2 pounds lamb or veal kidneys
1/3 cup melted butter or margarine
1/2 teaspoon salt
1/8 teaspoon pepper
4 slices buttered toast, trimmed of crusts and
   halved diagonally (optional)
1 tablespoon lemon juice (optional)
1 tablespoon minced parsley (optional)

Preheat broiler. Prepare kidneys for cooking.* Place on lightly greased broiler rack and brush well with melted butter. Broil 3″ from heat, brushing often with melted butter, about 4–5 minutes on a side for rare and 5–7 for medium. Serve, if you like, on toast points sprinkled with lemon juice and parsley. Or serve with Bordelaise, Diable or Madeira Sauce.

NPS: 315 C, 680 mg CH, 770 mg S*

VARIATIONS

⚖ **Marinated Broiled Kidneys:** Prepare kidneys as above, then marinate 3–4 hours in refrigerator in French, Italian, garlic, or herb dressing. Broil as directed, brushing often with dressing instead of butter.

NPS: 260 C, 635 mg CH, 885 mg S*

⚖ **Breaded Broiled Kidneys:** Prepare kidneys as above. Dip in melted butter, then in fine dry bread crumbs. Broil as directed, basting often with melted butter.

NPS: 280 C, 660 mg CH, 610 mg S*

⚖ **Lamb Kidney en Brochette:** Prepare kidneys as above. Alternate on skewers with mushroom caps (you'll need about 12 altogether), weaving strips of bacon in and out. Broil 3″ from heat, turning often, 12–15 minutes until bacon is browned. Season and serve.

NPS: 395 C, 690 mg CH, 975 mg S*

⚖ **Low-Calorie Broiled Kidneys:** Prepare as directed, using low-calorie French, Italian, garlic, or herb dressing for basting instead of butter. Omit buttered toast slices.

NPS: 205 C, 640 mg CH, 780 mg S*

BRAISED KIDNEYS

4 servings ⚖

Beef and pork kidneys come from mature animals, thus they tend to be tough. The most successful way to tenderize them is to brown them, then to cook, covered, with a small amount of liquid.

11/2 pounds beef or pork kidneys
1/2 cup unsifted flour
1 teaspoon salt
1/4 teaspoon pepper
3 tablespoons butter, margarine, or bacon
   drippings
1/2 cup liquid (water, beef broth, dry red or
   white wine, tomato juice)

Prepare kidneys for cooking,* halve lengthwise, and slice crosswise 1/4″ thick. Dredge in a mixture of flour, salt, and pepper, then brown on both sides in butter in a large, heavy skillet over moderately high heat. Turn heat to low, add liquid, cover, and simmer slowly about 20 minutes until tender.

NPS: 355 C, 660 mg CH, 1,035 mg S*

Kidneys Lyonnaise: Prepare and dredge kidneys as above. Before browning, stir-fry 1 minced small yellow onion in butter; push to side of skillet, add kidneys and proceed as directed. Sprinkle with 1 tablespoon minced parsley before serving.

NPS: 360 C, 660 mg CH, 1,035 mg S*

⚖ **Lower-Calorie Braised Kidneys:** Prepare as directed, reducing amount of butter to 2 tablespoons and using water as the liquid.

NPS: 330 C, 655 mg CH, 910 mg S*

DEVILED KIDNEYS

4 servings

1½ pounds lamb kidneys
2 tablespoons prepared mild yellow mustard
¼ cup heavy cream
1 tablespoon steak sauce
⅛ teaspoon pepper
⅓–½ cup packaged Italian-style bread crumbs
¼ cup melted butter or margarine
4 slices hot buttered toast

Preheat oven to 325° F. Prepare kidneys for cooking.* Mix mustard, cream, steak sauce, and pepper; dip each kidney in mustard mixture, then in bread crumbs to coat evenly. Arrange in a buttered shallow baking dish and drizzle a little melted butter over each kidney. Bake, uncovered, 25 minutes until tender, basting with extra melted butter as needed to brown crumbs evenly. Serve on hot buttered toast with pan drippings ladled over kidneys.

NPS (without toast): 375 C, 690 mg CH, 890 mg S*

BRAISED VEAL KIDNEYS AND MUSHROOMS

4 servings ⚖

1½ pounds veal kidneys
¼ cup unsifted flour
3 tablespoons bacon drippings, butter, or margarine
½ pound button mushrooms, wiped clean
½ cup water, beef broth, or dry red wine
½ teaspoon salt
⅛ teaspoon pepper

Preheat oven to 350° F. Prepare kidneys for cooking* and halve lengthwise. Dredge in flour and brown lightly in 2 tablespoons drippings in a heavy skillet over moderately high heat 2–3 minutes. Transfer to an ungreased 1½-quart casserole; brown mushrooms in remaining drippings 2–3 minutes and add to kidneys. Drain off all but 1 tablespoon drippings from skillet, add water, and stir to scrape up brown bits; pour into casserole. Sprinkle with salt and pepper, cover, and bake 45 minutes until tender.

NPS: 315 C, 645 mg CH, 680 mg S*

Braised Veal Kidneys with Vegetables: Small new potatoes, 1″ chunks of carrots, turnips, or rutabagas or parboiled white onions can be cooked along with the kidneys in the same casserole; add a little extra salt and pepper. Recipe too flexible for meaningful nutritional count.

⚖ **Low-Calorie Braised Veal Kidneys:** Prepare as directed, reducing amount of drippings to 2 tablespoons and using water as the liquid.

NPS: 285 C, 643 mg CH, 580 mg S*

CLARA'S KIDNEY STEW

4 servings ¢

1½ pounds veal or beef kidneys
2 cups cold water
1 teaspoon salt
½ cup unsifted flour
⅛ teaspoon pepper
3 tablespoons beef or bacon drippings or cooking oil
1½ cups beef broth
1 bay leaf, crumbled
1 tablespoon flour blended with 1 tablespoon cold water
1 tablespoon minced parsley

If beef kidneys are used, soak in cold water mixed with 1 teaspoon salt 1 hour; drain well and pat dry on paper toweling. Prepare kidneys for cooking* and cut into ¾″–1″ cubes. Dredge lightly in mixture of flour, salt, and pepper. Sauté, half of kidneys at a time, 3–4 minutes in drippings in a heavy skillet over moderately high heat; remove with a slotted spoon to a large, heavy saucepan. Add broth to skillet, stir brown bits from bottom, and pour over kidneys. Add bay leaf, cover, and simmer until tender, about 15–20 minutes for veal kidneys, 35–40 for beef. Thicken gravy, if you like, by blending in flour paste and heating and stirring until thickened. Taste for seasoning and adjust if necessary. Sprinkle with parsley and serve. Good with boiled potatoes or hot buttered noodles.

NPS: 350 C, 645 mg CH, 1,145 mg S*

Other Kidney Recipes
Old-Fashioned Steak and Kidney Pie (see Beef)
English Mixed Grill (see Lamb)

LIVER

Liver to most people is calf's liver (or, to be more accurate, veal liver), but beef, pork, and lamb liver are good, too, especially lamb liver, which is tender enough to sauté and which can be substituted for calf's liver in the recipes that follow. Unfortunately, it is not often available. Beef and pork liver have a strong flavor but when ground into loaves or braised can be quite savory and succulent. All liver is a potent source of iron, vitamin A, and most of the B vitamins, all is low in calories.

Because of its popularity, calf's liver is rather expensive; it is now available packaged in frozen slices as well as fresh. Beef and pork livers are reasonably priced. All liver is highly perishable and should be cooked within 24 hours of purchase. Top quality calf's liver will be rosy red, moist, and quivery (so tender, someone said, you can push your thumb through it). Lamb liver will be equally delicate but redder, beef and pork liver deep red-brown and fairly firm.

Amount Needed: Allow 1/4–1/3 pound liver per serving. Beef liver weighs about 10 pounds; pork liver about 3; veal liver averages 2 1/2 pounds, and lamb liver 1.

To Prepare for Cooking: Liver needs very little preparation. Simply peel off covering membrane (so liver won't shrivel and curl during cooking), then cut out any large vessels.

Cooking Tip: Because of its quivery texture, liver is difficult to grind raw. To make the job easier, cut into strips, sauté briefly in butter or drippings to firm, then grind.

SAUTÉED CALF'S LIVER

2 servings   ⊲⊳ ▨

Liver is best on the rare side—faintly pink with rosy juices. If overcooked, it becomes tough and dry.

2 tablespoons butter or margarine
3/4 pound calf's liver, sliced 1/4″ thick
Pinch nutmeg (optional)
Pinch summer savory (optional)
1/4 teaspoon salt
1/8 teaspoon pepper

Melt butter in a large, heavy skillet over moderately high heat, let it foam up, then subside. Add liver and brown 2–3 minutes per side for rare, 3–3 1/2 for medium. Sprinkle both sides with seasonings and serve.

NPS: 340 C, 540 mg CH, 510 mg S*

VARIATIONS

⊲⊳ **Calf's Liver and Onions:** Stir-fry 1 thinly sliced small Bermuda onion in butter 5–8 minutes over moderate heat until pale golden. Push to side of pan, raise heat to moderately high, add liver, and brown as directed. Season and serve topped with onions.
NPS: 365 C, 540 mg CH, 515 mg S*

Calf's Liver and Bacon: Omit butter; brown 4 slices bacon in a large skillet over moderately high heat and drain on paper toweling. Pour off all but 1 tablespoon drippings, add liver, brown and season as directed. Serve topped with bacon.
NPS: 355 C, 525 mg CH, 630 mg S*

Calf's Liver in Mustard Sauce: Sauté liver as directed above, remove to a heated platter, and keep warm. To skillet add 1/4 cup beef broth and 1/3 cup heavy cream and boil rapidly, uncovered, to reduce by half. Off heat smooth in 2 teaspoons Dijon-style mustard and 1 teaspoon minced parsley. Pour over liver and serve.
NPS: 485 C, 595 mg CH, 775 mg S*

BROILED LIVER

4 servings   ⊲⊳ ▨

Lamb and calf's livers are the only ones suitable for broiling.

1 1/4 pounds lamb or calf's liver, sliced 1/2″ thick
1/3 cup melted butter or margarine
1/2 teaspoon salt
1/8 teaspoon pepper

Preheat broiler. Place liver on a lightly greased broiler rack and brush well with melted butter. Broil 4″ from heat 2–3 minutes per side for rare and 4 minutes per side for medium, brushing frequently with melted butter. Season and serve as is or topped with Bercy or Maître d'Hôtel Butter.
NPS (without flavored butter): 330 C, 465 mg CH, 530 mg S*

⚖️ **Low-Calorie Broiled Liver:** Broil as directed, using low-calorie Italian or French dressing for basting instead of butter.

NPS: 225 C, 425 mg CH, 545 mg S*

BRAISED LIVER

4 servings ¢

Here's the way to make beef or pork liver succulent.

1 small Bermuda onion, peeled and minced
3 tablespoons bacon drippings
1¼ pounds beef or pork liver, sliced ¼"–½" thick and cut in strips 4" long and 1" wide
½ cup unsifted flour
1 teaspoon salt
¼ teaspoon pepper
1 cup beef broth (about) or a ½ and ½ mixture of broth and dry red or white wine
1 tablespoon minced parsley

Stir-fry onion in 2 tablespoons drippings in a large, heavy skillet over moderate heat 10–12 minutes until lightly browned; lift out with a slotted spoon and set aside. Add remaining drippings to skillet. Dredge liver in a mixture of flour, salt and pepper and brown, a few pieces at a time, in drippings. Return all liver and onion to skillet, add broth, cover, and simmer over lowest heat about 45 minutes until tender. Check skillet occasionally and add a little extra broth if necessary. When liver is done, lift to a heated platter, smother with skillet gravy, and sprinkle with parsley.

NPS: 350 C, 435 mg CH, 940 mg S*

VARIATION

⚖️ **Lower-Calorie Braised Liver:** Prepare as directed, reducing amount of drippings to 2 tablespoons and using water as the liquid ingredient.

NPS: 320 C, 430 mg CH, 745 mg S*

CALF'S LIVER ALLA VENEZIANA

2 servings ⚖️ ☒

2 medium-size yellow onions, peeled and minced
2 tablespoons butter or margarine
1 tablespoon olive oil
3 tablespoons dry white wine
¼ teaspoon salt
Pinch pepper
⅔ pound calf's liver, sliced ¼"–½" thick and cut in strips about 2" long and 1" wide

1 tablespoon lemon juice
1 tablespoon minced parsley

Stir-fry onions in butter and oil in a large heavy skillet 5–8 minutes over moderate heat until pale golden; add wine, salt, and pepper and simmer 1–2 minutes to reduce. Raise heat to moderately high, add liver, and stir-fry quickly 3–5 minutes, just until redness disappears (liver will not brown). Add lemon juice and parsley and serve.

NPS: 410 C, 485 mg CH, 510 mg S*

CALF'S LIVER WITH PROSCIUTTO AND PARSLEY

4 servings

1¼ pounds calf's liver, sliced ¼"–½" thick
¾ cup unsifted flour
1½ teaspoons salt
¼ teaspoon pepper
¼ cup butter or margarine
¼ cup julienne strips of *prosciutto*
3 tablespoons minced yellow onion
½ teaspoon summer savory or sage
3 tablespoons minced parsley
1 tablespoon flour (use that from dredging liver) blended with ½ cup beef broth
½ cup dry Marsala wine
1 tablespoon lemon juice
Lemon wedges (garnish)

Dredge liver lightly in a mixture of flour, salt, and pepper and sauté in butter in a large, heavy skillet over moderately high heat, about 2–3 minutes per side for rare, 3½ for medium. Remove liver and keep warm. Turn heat to moderately low, add *prosciutto,* onion, savory, and parsley to skillet, and stir-fry 5–8 minutes until onion is pale golden. Mix in flour paste and remaining ingredients and heat, stirring, until thickened. Return liver to skillet, heat 1–2 minutes, then serve garnished with lemon wedges.

NPS: 450 C, 460 mg CH, 1,280 mg S*

LIGHTLY CURRIED CALF'S LIVER ON CRISP CAPELLINI PANCAKES

4 servings

A marvelous counterpoint of tastes and textures and our interpretation of one of the wonderful specialties at Hubert's Restaurant near New York City's Gramercy Park.

½ pound capellini or spaghettini
1¼ pounds calf's liver (about), sliced ¼" thick, then cut into 8 pieces of uniform size
⅓ cup unsifted rice flour (about)

½ teaspoon salt
⅛ teaspoon white pepper
2 tablespoons butter or margarine
6 tablespoons cooking oil

CURRIED CREAM SAUCE
2 tablespoons butter or margarine
½ teaspoon curry powder
2 tablespoons flour
1 cup light cream
¼ cup chicken broth
½ teaspoon salt
⅛ teaspoon white pepper

Cook capellini by package directions until *al dente*. Drain, rinse *briefly* under cold running water, and drain again. Divide pasta between 4 small plates (bread-and-butter size is fine) and shape into round, flat "pancakes." Cover each pancake with oiled wax paper, then stack all plates up; top with an empty plate and weight down with a large can of vegetables. Let stand at room temperature while you make the sauce: Melt butter in a saucepan over moderate heat, stir in curry powder and heat, stirring ½ minute. Blend in flour, slowly add cream and broth, and heat, stirring constantly, until thickened. Mix in salt and pepper, cover, and keep warm over lowest heat so flavors mellow. Dredge liver lightly in a mixture of rice flour, salt, and pepper, then sauté in butter and 2 tablespoons oil in a large heavy skillet about 1½–2 minutes per side for rare, 2½–3 minutes for medium. Remove liver to a heatproof plate and set, uncovered, in an oven turned to its lowest setting. Dredge pasta pancakes in rice flour mixture, then sauté in the skillet, one at a time, in 1 tablespoon oil each over moderately high heat 1½–2 minutes per side until lightly browned and crisp on both sides. To serve, top each pasta pancake with 2 slices of liver and gloss all lightly with hot curry sauce; pass the remaining sauce.

NPS: 860 C, 495 mg CH, 840 mg S*

VARIATION

If you like lacier, crisper pancakes, cook ¼ pound capellini only, then shape into pancakes and sauté as directed, using only 1–2 teaspoons oil to brown each.

NPS: 675 C, 495 mg CH, 840 mg S*

BRAISED BEEF LIVER WITH TOMATO-MUSHROOM GRAVY

8 servings   ¢ ⚖

2½ pounds young beef liver, in 1 piece
¼ cup sifted flour

2 teaspoons salt
¼ teaspoon pepper
¼ cup bacon drippings, butter, or margarine
1 medium-size yellow onion, peeled and sliced thin
¼ cup minced mushrooms
¾ cup beef broth
1 bay leaf, crumbled
1 tablespoon tomato paste

Peel any outer membrane from liver, then wipe liver with damp paper toweling; dredge in a mixture of flour, salt, and pepper and brown well on all sides in drippings in a large, heavy kettle over moderate heat about 5 minutes. Liver will swell as it browns but don't be alarmed. Turn heat to low, add all remaining ingredients except tomato paste, cover, and simmer 1½ hours until liver is tender, turning halfway through cooking. Lift liver to a platter and keep warm. Stir tomato paste into gravy; strain gravy and pour over liver. Slice thin and serve.

NPS: 270 C, 430 mg CH, 835 mg S*

FINNISH CHOPPED LIVER AND RICE CASSEROLE

4 servings   ¢

Finns serve wild mushrooms, cucumbers in sour cream, and buttered home-baked rye bread with this dish. Made with beef liver, it's a budget dish.

1¼ pounds beef or calf's liver, sliced ¼"–½" thick
3 tablespoons butter or margarine
1 large yellow onion, peeled and minced
1½ cups uncooked rice
2 cups boiling water
1 cup milk
1 cup seedless raisins
2 teaspoons salt
¼ teaspoon pepper
¼ teaspoon marjoram
2 tablespoons dark brown sugar or molasses

Preheat oven to 350° F. Sauté liver in butter in a skillet over moderately high heat 3–4 minutes until browned; cool slightly and chop fine. Brown onion in drippings 8–10 minutes and reserve. Simmer rice, water, and milk together in a saucepan with lid askew about 15 minutes until rice is barely tender; turn into a buttered 1½-quart casserole, add liver, onion, and remaining ingredients, and toss well with 2 forks. Bake, uncovered, 20–30 minutes until all liquid is absorbed.

NPS: 730 C, 455 mg CH, 1,425 mg S*

DANISH LIVER LOAF

6 servings ¢

Serve hot with bright crisp vegetables or cold on dark rye bread with pickled beets.

1/4 pound salt pork, trimmed of rind and diced
1 pound beef liver, trimmed of connective tissues and tubes and cut in strips about 2″ wide
1 medium-size yellow onion, peeled and minced
1 1/4 cups beef broth
2 dozen soda crackers, crumbled (about 1 1/2 cups)
1/2 teaspoon thyme
1 tablespoon minced parsley
1/4 teaspoon pepper
1 teaspoon dark brown sugar
1/2 teaspoon ginger
2 eggs, lightly beaten

Preheat oven to 400° F. Fry salt pork in a heavy skillet over moderately low heat 5 minutes until pale golden and rendered of all drippings; remove with a slotted spoon and reserve. Sauté liver in drippings over moderate heat 5–7 minutes, until lightly browned; remove and reserve. Sauté onion in drippings 5–8 minutes until pale golden and reserve in skillet. Pour broth over crackers and let stand. Grind liver and salt pork together, using fine blade of meat grinder, then mix thoroughly with onions and drippings, crackers and broth, and all remaining ingredients. Spoon into a lightly greased 9″ × 5″ × 3″ loaf pan and bake, uncovered, on center rack 40 minutes until firm. Cool upright in pan on rack 20 minutes; invert on serving platter and turn out. Serve hot or cold but slice fairly thick.

NPS: 345 C, 330 mg CH, 645 mg S*

SWEETBREADS

Of all the variety meats, sweetbreads are considered the most delectable. Certainly they're the most luxurious (they cost about the same as fine steak).

What are they? Technically, the thymus gland of young animals, a big double-lobed gland consisting of the large, smooth, choice *kernel* or *heart sweetbread,* located in the breast, and the smaller, more irregular *throat sweetbread.* The two, spoken of as a pair, are linked by a tube, which should be removed. Sweetbreads are ultrafragile, creamy-smooth, and faintly nutty; they resemble brains in flavor and texture and can be used interchangeably with them in many recipes. Most sweetbreads sold in this country are the milky-white, finely-grained veal sweetbreads. Lamb sweetbreads are sometimes available but are too small to be very practical; also available: yearling beef sweetbreads (rougher and redder) and pork sweetbreads (stronger flavored and a favorite with Europeans for pâtés and soufflés). No matter what animals sweetbreads come from, they will be from young ones (the thymus gland disappears with maturity).

You may also run across something called *beef breads,* not true sweetbreads but the pancreas gland of beef. Though stronger in flavor and coarser in texture, these do resemble sweetbreads and can be prepared like them.

All sweetbreads are extremely perishable; if they are not to be served on the day they're bought, they should be blanched and refrigerated and, even then, served within 24 hours. Recently, frozen sweetbreads have been available, an excellent choice because they needn't be prepared immediately (always cook by package directions). Restaurants get most of the fresh sweetbreads, so give your butcher plenty of notice. And insist that the sweetbreads be *absolutely fresh.*

Amount Needed: Because sweetbreads are so rich, 1/4–1/3 pound is about as much as a person can handle comfortably. A pair of veal sweetbreads averages 3/4–1 pound, lamb sweetbreads 1/4 pound, and yearling beef sweetbreads about 1 1/2 pounds. Pork sweetbreads run around 3/4 pound, but unless you raise your own hogs, you aren't likely to find them.

To Prepare for Cooking: Wash sweetbreads gently in cold water, then place in a large bowl and cover with cold acidulated water (1 tablespoon lemon juice or white vinegar and 1 teaspoon salt to 1 quart water) and soak 1 1/2 hours. The sweetbreads will turn white. Drain, gently peel off as much thin outer membrane as possible; it clings stubbornly and is almost transparent, so have patience. Soak for another 1 1/2 hours in fresh acidulated water, changing it one or two times; drain once more and peel away what membrane you missed the first time. Separate the 2 lobes from the tube (some people like to add it to the stock pot).

To Blanch: Connoisseurs are of two minds about blanching. Some recommend it no matter how the sweetbreads are to be cooked, others insist that it's necessary only when the sweetbreads are to be broken into smaller pieces and sautéed. Blanching does steal away some of the delicate flavor, but it also firms up the sweetbreads and makes them easier to handle. Perhaps a good rule of thumb: If sweetbreads are to be braised whole, don't blanch. Otherwise, do. Place the sweetbreads in a large enamel, stainless-steel, flameproof glass, or Teflon-lined saucepan, add acidulated water to cover, and simmer, uncovered, 15 minutes over lowest heat (young beef sweetbreads and beef breads (the pancreas) will need about 25 minutes). Drain, cover with ice water, and let stand until cold. Drain well and pat dry on paper toweling. Some cooks like to place sweetbreads between paper towels and weight with heavy plates to get out excess moisture; not a bad idea when they're to be sautéed. The sweetbreads are now ready to sauté or use in recipes. To divide into smaller pieces, gently break apart at the natural separations.

SAUTÉED SWEETBREADS

4 servings ⚖️

The following recipes are all for veal sweetbreads, but lamb or young beef sweetbreads may be substituted.

1¼ pounds sweetbreads
½ cup unsifted flour
1 teaspoon salt
¼ teaspoon pepper
¼ cup butter or margarine

S U G G E S T E D   S A U C E S
Béarnaise
Beurre Noir
Diable
Madeira

Prepare sweetbreads for cooking and blanch as directed.* Leave whole or halve at the natural separation and pat very dry on paper toweling. Dredge lightly in a mixture of flour, salt, and pepper, then sauté in butter in a large, heavy skillet over moderate to moderately high heat 3–4 minutes on a side until nicely browned. Drain on paper toweling and serve with one of the sauces suggested above.

NPS (without sauce): 450 C, 385 mg CH, 805 mg S*

V A R I A T I O N S

⚖️ **Breaded Sweetbreads:** Prepare and blanch sweetbreads as directed,* halve at the natural separation, and pat dry on paper toweling. Dredge in seasoned flour as above, dip in 1 egg lightly beaten with 1 tablespoon cold water and then in fine dry bread crumbs or cracker meal. Sauté in butter as

directed and serve with Maître d'Hôtel Butter.

NPS: 490 C, 455 mg CH, 855 mg S*

Sautéed Sweetbreads and Mushrooms: Prepare and blanch sweetbreads as directed*; divide into small pieces but do not dredge. Sauté with ½ pound wiped, sliced mushrooms in 3 tablespoons butter over moderate heat 6–8 minutes until browned. While sweetbreads are sautéing, make a thin Velouté Sauce: melt 2 tablespoons butter in a saucepan, blend in 2 tablespoons flour, add 1 cup veal or chicken stock, and heat, stirring, until thickened. Mix ⅓ cup heavy cream with 1 egg yolk, stir slowly into sauce, and heat and stir 1 minute (do not boil). Season with ½ teaspoon salt and a pinch white pepper. Spoon sweetbreads and mushrooms onto unbuttered toast triangles and smother each serving with sauce; pass any remaining sauce.

NPS: 545 C, 490 mg CH, 765 mg S*

BROILED SWEETBREADS

4 servings ⚖️

1¼ pounds sweetbreads
½ cup melted butter or margarine
½ teaspoon salt
⅛ teaspoon pepper

Prepare sweetbreads for cooking and blanch as directed,* halve at the natural separation, and pat very dry on paper toweling. Preheat broiler. Place sweetbreads on lightly greased broiler rack and brush well with melted butter. Broil 5″ from heat 2–3 minutes until lightly browned, brushing one or two times with butter; turn and broil 2–3 minutes longer, again brushing with butter. Season and serve as is or with a suitable sauce such as Béarnaise, Bordelaise, Madeira, or Périgueux.

NPS: 495 C, 415 mg CH, 645 mg S*

V A R I A T I O N S

⚖️ **Broiled Brains:** Prepare basic recipe above or the variation below as directed, substituting brains for sweetbreads.

NPS: 380 C, 2,900 mg CH, 685 mg S*

⚖️ **Broiled Breaded Sweetbreads:** Prepare sweetbreads as above, dip in melted butter, then in fine dry bread crumbs or cracker meal. Broil as directed, brushing often with melted butter. For extra flavor, use seasoned crumbs.

NPS: 540 C, 425 mg CH, 705 mg S*

BRAISED SWEETBREADS

4 servings ⚖

An elegant way to present braised sweet-breads is wreathed on a platter around buttered potato balls, baby carrots, and asparagus tips; drift with minced parsley just before serving.

1¼ pounds sweetbreads
1 carrot, peeled and sliced thin
1 large yellow onion, peeled and sliced thin
¼ cup butter or margarine
½ cup unsifted flour
1 teaspoon salt
¼ teaspoon pepper
1 cup dry white wine or chicken broth
1 bay leaf
¼ teaspoon thyme
3 sprigs parsley
2 tablespoons dry sherry

Prepare sweetbreads for cooking* but do not blanch. Preheat oven to 350° F. Pat sweetbreads dry on paper toweling; leave whole or, if very large, divide into bite-size pieces. Stir-fry carrot and onion in butter in a large, flameproof casserole 8–10 minutes over moderate heat until golden. Dredge sweetbreads lightly in flour mixed with salt and pepper. Push carrot and onion to side of casserole, add sweetbreads, and sauté 2–3 minutes on each side until golden. Add all remaining ingredients except sherry, transfer casserole to oven, cover, and bake ¾ hour (25–30 minutes if sweetbreads are in small pieces). Lift sweetbreads to a heated platter and keep warm. Purée vegetables and casserole liquid by buzzing 20–30 seconds in an electric blender at low speed or 15–20 seconds in a food processor fitted with the metal chopping blade. Bring purée to a simmer, add sherry, pour over sweetbreads, and serve.

NPS: 490 C, 385 mg CH, 820 mg S*

VARIATIONS

Braised Sweetbreads on Ham: Prepare sweetbreads as directed and serve on thin slices of broiled ham.

NPS: 540 C, 400 mg CH, 1,245 mg S*

Braised Brains: Prepare as directed, substituting brains for sweetbreads.

NPS: 375 C, 2,870 mg CH, 860 mg S*

CREAMED SWEETBREADS

4 servings

1¼ pounds sweetbreads
¼ cup butter or margarine
¼ cup unsifted flour
2 cups milk
¾–1 teaspoon salt
⅛ teaspoon white pepper
¼ cup heavy cream
4 frozen puff pastry shells, baked by package directions, or 4 slices buttered toast, trimmed of crusts and halved diagonally

Prepare sweetbreads for cooking and blanch as directed.* Melt butter in the top of a double boiler over direct heat, blend in flour, slowly add milk, and heat, stirring, until thickened. Mix in salt, pepper, and cream. Set over simmering water, break sweetbreads into small pieces, and mix gently into sauce, using a rubber spatula. Heat, uncovered, stirring occasionally, 5–10 minutes. Serve in pastry shells or on toast.

NPS: 550 C, 425 mg CH, 730 mg S*

VARIATIONS

Creamed Brains: Substitute brains for sweetbreads and prepare as directed. (*Note:* Brains may also be used in any of the variations that follow.)

NPS: 435 C, 2,905 mg CH, 770 mg S*

With Mushrooms: Add ¼ pound sautéed, thinly sliced mushrooms along with sweetbreads.

NPS: 585 C, 430 mg CH, 765 mg S*

With Ham, Tongue, or Chicken: Add an extra ¼ cup heavy cream and ½ cup diced lean boiled ham, tongue, or cooked white chicken meat along with sweetbreads; taste for salt and adjust as needed.

NPS (ham): 635 C, 455 mg CH, 1,005 mg S*
NPS (tongue): 645 C, 460 mg CH, 745 mg S*
NPS (chicken): 630 C, 460 mg CH, 750 mg S*

With Sherry or White Wine: Just before serving, stir in 2 tablespoons medium-dry sherry or white wine.

NPS: 560 C, 425 mg CH, 730 mg S*

Au Gratin: After simmering sweetbreads in sauce, turn into a buttered 1½-quart casserole, top with ¼ cup fine buttered bread crumbs, and brown quickly under broiler.

NPS: 575 C, 425 mg CH, 775 mg S*

TONGUE

Next to tripe and heart, tongue is one of the most muscular variety meats and needs special treatment to tenderize it. Beef tongue is available fresh, corned, pickled, and smoked and, in some parts of the country, ready-to-serve. Veal tongue is usually sold fresh, but lamb and pork tongues, being smaller, are almost always precooked, ready-to-eat meats.

Amount Needed: Beef tongues weigh 2½–5 pounds, veal tongues about 2 pounds, pork tongues 1 pound, and lamb tongues barely ¼ pound. Allow ⅓–½ pound per serving.

To Simmer and Prepare for Use in Recipes:

Fresh Tongue: Wash well in cool water, place in a large stainless-steel, enamel, or Teflon-lined kettle, and cover with salted water (1 teaspoon salt to 1 quart water). For extra savor, add ½ unsliced lemon, 1 peeled yellow onion stuck with 3–4 cloves, 1–2 stalks celery (include tops), 1–2 bay leaves, and a large sprig each parsley and thyme. Cover, bring to a boil, and skim off froth. Re-cover and simmer slowly until tender: veal tongue will take 2–2½ hours, beef tongue 3–4. Plunge tongue into cold water to loosen skin, lift out, and pat dry. Slit skin lengthwise on underside of tongue from root to tip and peel off; cut away root, small bones, and gristle. If tongue is to be served cold, it will be more flavorful if chilled in its own broth. Tongue is now ready to use in recipes or to serve sliced hot or cold. Good with Mustard, Madeira, or Raisin Sauce.

Smoked or Pickled Tongue: Soak 2–3 hours in cold water before simmering, then proceed as for fresh tongue.

To Parboil (use in recipes that call for cooking tongue ¾–1 hour or longer): Simmer as directed but reduce cooking time to 2 hours for beef tongue, 1½ hours for veal tongue. Proceed with preparation as directed.

PARISIAN-STYLE BRAISED SLICED BEEF TONGUE

6–8 servings

1 (3–3½-pound) fresh or smoked beef tongue

S A U C E
3 slices lean bacon, diced
1 carrot, peeled and diced
3 scallions, sliced thin
1 stalk celery, diced
4 mushrooms, wiped clean and minced

1 clove garlic, peeled and crushed
1 cup beef broth
1 cup water
⅛ teaspoon pepper
¼ cup dry sherry or cognac (optional)

Parboil tongue, remove skin, root, bone, and gristle,* and slice ⅜"–½" thick (begin at large end, slicing straight through, but as you approach small end, hold knife slightly at an angle). Prepare sauce: Stir-fry bacon and vegetables in a heavy skillet over moderate heat 8–10 minutes to brown lightly, add remaining sauce ingredients, cover, and simmer ½ hour. Cool slightly and purée by buzzing 20–30 seconds in an electric blender at low speed or 15–20 seconds in a food processor fitted with the metal chopping blade. Pour sauce into a deep, heavy skillet, add tongue slices, cover, and simmer 45 minutes until tongue is very tender. Serve with lots of sauce. *(Note:* For even richer flavor, let tongue slices marinate in sauce overnight in refrigerator before simmering.)

NPS (6–8): 510–385 C, 175–130 mg CH, 335–250 mg S*

V A R I A T I O N

Substitute veal tongue for beef and proceed as directed. Ready-to-eat lamb or pork tongues may also be used but need only be sliced and warmed 10–15 minutes in the sauce.

NPS (6–8): 365–275 C, 180–140 mg CH, 335–250 mg S*

PICKLED TONGUE

6–8 servings

1 (3–3½-pound) fresh beef tongue
2½ quarts cold water
1 cup cider vinegar
2 tablespoons pickling spice, tied in cheesecloth

Wash tongue, place in a large, heavy kettle with all ingredients, cover, and bring to a boil. Skim froth from surface, re-cover, and simmer 3–4 hours until tender. Cool tongue in broth until easy to handle, lift out, skin, cut away root, bones, and gristle. Strain and skim broth.

To Serve Hot: Place tongue in a clean kettle, add broth, cover, and reheat 8–10 minutes over moderately low heat. Lift out, drain and serve with Mustard Sauce. *To Glaze:* Instead of warming tongue in broth, place on a rack in a shallow, open roasting pan, spread with 1 cup firmly packed light brown sugar mixed with ¼ cup cider vinegar and 1 tablespoon honey or light corn syrup. Bake, uncovered, 15–20 minutes at 350° F., basting often with mixture until glazed. (*Note:* Minced chutney or chopped tart fruit jellies can be used to glaze tongue as can Plum or Sweet-Sour Sauce or any of the thin ham glazes [see Some Glazes for Baked Hams].)

To Serve Cold: Simmer tongue as directed; skin, cut away root, bones, and gristle. Return tongue to strained, skimmed broth, cover, and chill several hours. Remove from broth, slice thin, and serve with Mustard or Sour Cream-Horseradish Sauce.

NPS (6–8) (hot or cold: without sauce): 365–275 C, 120–90 mg CH, 130–100 mg S*

DEVILED TONGUE

4 servings   ⊠

2 tablespoons prepared spicy brown mustard
2 tablespoons steak sauce
8 thick slices cooked tongue
1 egg lightly beaten with 1 tablespoon cold water
1/2 cup toasted seasoned bread crumbs
3 tablespoons butter or margarine

Mix mustard and steak sauce and spread evenly on both sides of tongue slices; let stand 10 minutes. Dip tongue in egg and crumbs to coat thickly. Brown in butter, a few slices at a time, in a heavy skillet over moderate heat. Serve sprinkled with a few drops tarragon vinegar or, if you prefer, with Diable Sauce.

NPS: 580 C, 250 mg CH, 820 mg S*

TRIPE

Tripe is the lining of the stomach of meat animals, and that considered choicest is *honeycomb tripe,* the lining of the second stomach of beef. Also good are *pocket tripe,* the lower end of the second stomach, and *plain* or *smooth tripe,* which is not honeycombed and not so delicate. Tripe is available pickled, canned, and fresh. Fresh tripe is always sold partially cooked but needs still further cooking.

Amount Needed: Allow 1/4–1/2 pound tripe per person, depending upon whether it is simply prepared or served in a rich sauce.

To Prepare for Cooking: Pull or cut all fat from tripe and discard; wash well in cold water. Pickled tripe, though thoroughly

cooked, usually needs to be soaked in cold water 1–2 hours before using.

To Simmer: All fresh tripe must be simmered until tender before it can be eaten or used in many recipes (those that follow tell when it must be simmered). Cut tripe into manageable pieces so it will be easier to handle and cook more evenly. Place in a large, deep kettle (not aluminum or tripe will discolor) and cover with lightly salted water (1 teaspoon salt to each quart of water). Cover and simmer gently 1 1/2–2 hours until tender. Tripe can now be cut in 2″ squares and served hot in bowls with some of the broth; it can be cooled in its own broth, drained, chilled, and eaten with a sprinkling of vinegar. Or it can be used in recipes (cut up as individual recipes specify).

PICKLED TRIPE

4–6 servings

Pickled tripe can be kept 3–4 days in the refrigerator; if held longer, the flavor becomes unpleasantly strong.

1 1/2 pounds honeycomb tripe
2 cups cold water
1 teaspoon salt
1 small yellow onion, peeled and coarsely chopped
1 bay leaf, tied in cheesecloth with 5–6 peppercorns
1 cup white vinegar

Prepare tripe for cooking* and cut in 2″ squares. Place in a large kettle with all but last ingredient, cover, and simmer about 2 hours until very tender. Remove cheesecloth bag and add vinegar. Spoon into a large wide-mouthed jar and cover with vinegar mixture. (*Note:* if there is not enough to cover tripe, make up with a 1/2 and 1/2 mixture of water and white vinegar.) Cover tightly and store in refrigerator. Serve cold as an appetizer course or cut in smaller pieces and serve on an hors d'oeuvre tray.

NPS: 120 C, 75 mg CH, 450 mg S*

TRIPE LYONNAISE

4 servings   ⚖

2 pounds honeycomb tripe
6 tablespoons butter or margarine
2 large yellow onions, peeled and sliced thin
1 tablespoon minced parsley
1 tablespoon white vinegar
Salt
Pepper

Prepare tripe for cooking and simmer.* Drain, pat dry on paper toweling, and cut in 2″ squares. Stir-fry in 3 tablespoons butter in a large, heavy skillet over moderate heat about 2 minutes until golden; drain on paper toweling and keep warm. In a separate skillet stir-fry onions in remaining butter 8–10 minutes over moderate heat until golden. Mix tripe and onions, sprinkle with parsley and vinegar, and mix again. Taste for salt and pepper and season as needed. Toss again and serve. Good spooned over hot mashed potatoes.

NPS: 410 C, 200 mg CH, 350 mg S*

TRIPE MAÎTRE D'HÔTEL

4 servings ⚖

2 pounds honeycomb tripe
1 cup cold water
1 cup beef broth
1 cup dry white wine
1/2 teaspoon salt
1 bay leaf and 1 sprig each parsley and thyme, tied in cheesecloth with 3 thick lemon slices
2 egg yolks, lightly beaten
1/8 teaspoon nutmeg
1/8 teaspoon cayenne pepper

Prepare tripe for cooking* and cut in strips 2″ long and 3/4″ wide. Place in a large kettle (not aluminum) with water, broth, wine, salt and cheesecloth bag, cover and simmer 1 1/2– 2 hours until tender. Transfer tripe to a deep platter with a slotted spoon and keep warm. Boil broth, uncovered, over high heat until reduced to about 1 cup; discard cheesecloth bag. Mix a little hot broth into yolks, then return to broth. Set over lowest heat and cook 1–2 minutes until slightly thickened (do not boil). Mix in nutmeg and cayenne, taste for seasoning and adjust. Pour over tripe and serve.

NPS: 275 C, 290 mg CH, 640 mg S*

TRIPES À LA MODE DE CAEN

8 servings ⚖

This steaming marmite of tripe flavored with apple brandy comes from Normandy but is the favorite of all France.

4 pounds tripe
4 small yellow onions, peeled and coarsely chopped
4 carrots, peeled and cut in small dice
4 leeks, coarsely chopped
1 calf's foot, cleaned, split, and sawed in 3–4

pieces (kosher butchers will either have them or order them)
3 cloves garlic, peeled
1 bay leaf and 1 sprig each parsley and thyme, tied in cheesecloth (*bouquet garni*)
2 teaspoons salt
1/4 teaspoon white pepper
1/8 teaspoon allspice
2 quarts cold water
2–3 thin sheets barding suet (you'll need enough to cover kettle ingredients)
1/2 cup Calvados or aged cider

PASTRY
1 1/2 cups sifted flour
1/2 cup cold water

Preheat oven to 300° F. Prepare tripe for cooking,* cut in 3″ squares, and set aside. Mix vegetables in a large kettle and lay calf's foot on top. Add tripe, garlic, *bouquet garni,* seasonings, and water. Lay suet over all to cover, then place lid on kettle. Prepare pastry by mixing flour and water until sticky. Turn out on a heavily floured board, knead one or two times, then roll into a rope long enough to go around kettle. Use rope like putty to seal kettle lid to kettle. Set kettle on lowest oven rack and bake 6–7 hours. Discard pastry and suet; spoon tripe into a large tureen with a slotted spoon. Cut meat from calf's foot and add to tripe. Strain kettle liquid, discarding vegetables, garlic, and *bouquet garni.* Strain and skim off fat, then bring to a boil and stir in Calvados. Ladle over tripe and serve. Good with crusty bread or boiled potatoes.

NPS: 475 C, 170 mg CH, 730 mg S*

PHILADELPHIA PEPPER POT

8–10 servings ⚖

Begin this recipe one or even two days before you plan to serve it. Though called a soup, pepper pot is hearty enough to serve as a main dish. It was invented at Valley Forge by a chef in George Washington's army.

1 meaty veal shank
2 pounds beef marrowbones, cracked
5 quarts cold water
2 tablespoons salt (about)
1 teaspoon peppercorns
2 large yellow onions, peeled and minced
1 bay leaf and 1 sprig each parsley and thyme, tied in cheesecloth (*bouquet garni*)
2 pounds tripe
3 medium-size potatoes, peeled and cut in 1/2″ cubes
1 teaspoon marjoram

2 tablespoons minced parsley
1 recipe Dumplings

Simmer shank and marrowbones, covered, in 2 quarts water with 1 tablespoon salt, 1/2 teaspoon peppercorns, the onions, and *bouquet garni* 3–4 hours. Meanwhile, prepare tripe for cooking* and cut in 2″ squares. Place in a large kettle (not aluminum) with remaining water, salt, and peppercorns, cover, and simmer 2 hours until very tender; lift from broth and set aside; strain and save broth. When bones have simmered 3 hours, lift from broth; cut meat from shank and add to tripe; scoop out marrow, chop coarsely and also add to tripe; refrigerate. Strain broth, combine with tripe broth and refrigerate overnight. Next day place broth in a large kettle (not aluminum), add tripe and meat, potatoes and marjoram, cover, and simmer 10 minutes. Add parsley, taste for salt and adjust as needed. Prepare dumplings, bring broth to a boil and drop in dumplings from a tablespoon (make 1 for each person). Simmer, uncovered, 10 minutes, then cover and simmer 10 minutes longer. To serve, ladle out steaming bowls of soup and float a dumpling in each.

NPS (8–10): 355–285 C, 120–95 mg CH, 2,000–1,600 mg S*

SAUSAGES

How to Cook Fresh Sausages

As defined by the U.S. Department of Agriculture, *fresh sausages* contain no sodium nitrite and/or potassium nitrite, (no nitrates either). *Cured sausages,* on the other hand, have had one or more of these preservatives added. Fresh sausages may contain pork (in which case they must be cooked thoroughly before they are eaten); they may be made of beef, veal, even lamb or rabbit. Fresh sausages may be cooked or uncooked, smoked or unsmoked, dried, semidried, or simply mixtures of fresh ground meats and seasonings. Finally, fresh sausages are available as links, patties, rolls, or in bulk, by the pound. There's nothing difficult about cooking fresh sausages, although large links containing pork will require a combination of cooking methods—steaming or simmering *plus* panfrying, broiling, or grilling if they are to be done inside by the time they are brown outside.

Amount Needed: 1/4–1/3 pound sausage per person.

General Preparation for Cooking: Very little. Bulk sausage must be shaped into balls or patties, sausage rolls sliced. The biggest question concerns links. Should they be pricked before cooking? Opinions vary, but probably the best rule to follow: American sausages, no; European sausages, yes (they're moister and may burst if not pricked).

To Simmer:

Links: Place sausages in a saucepan, add just enough lightly salted boiling water—or beer or ale—to cover, cover, and simmer 10–30 minutes, depending on size, until cooked through. *To Test:* Remove 1 sausage and cut into center; it should show no traces of pink. (*Note:* If links are to be browned after simmering, they will need to be simmered only 8–10 minutes.)

Bulk Sausage: Roll into 3/4″–1″ balls, drop into lightly salted boiling water, cover, and simmer 10–15 minutes until cooked through. These are best served in a Medium White Sauce, made using 1/2 and 1/2 sausage cooking water and heavy cream. Flavor with a little dry white wine and nutmeg. Let sausages warm in sauce about 5 minutes before serving to mellow flavors.

To Steam (for links only): Place links on a rack in a saucepan, add 1–1 1/2 cups boiling water (it should not touch sausages), cover, and steam 15–20 minutes until cooked through. (*Note:* Very chunky sausages may take as long as 1/2 hour.) If sausages are to be browned later, reduce steaming time to 10–15 minutes.

To Panfry (Sauté) (for small links only): Strictly speaking, this is a combination of simmering and panfrying, but since it is all done in one skillet, it is called panfrying. Place sausages in a cold skillet, add 1/4 cup water, cover, and simmer 5–10 minutes, depending on size. Uncover and brown slowly over moderately low heat, turning often with tongs. (*Note:* Swiss and German cooks drain off the simmering water, then brown sausages slowly in 1–2 tablespoons butter or lard. Sometimes before browning, they pat sausages dry and dredge lightly in flour—gives a crisper finish. When sausages are simmered first, they need only be browned in butter.)

To Panbroil (for patties and slices): Slice a sausage roll 1/2″ thick or shape bulk sausage into patties about 1/2″ thick and 3″ across. Place patties in a cold skillet, set over moderate heat, and cook 15–20 minutes until cooked through. Turn only once during cooking; do not press down or spank with spatula.

To Braise (links and patties): Brown sausages slowly in 1–2 tablespoons butter in a large, heavy skillet over moderate heat, add 1/2 cup liquid (water, beer or ale, dry white wine, tomato juice or sauce, barbecue sauce, apple or pineapple juice, plus 1–2 tablespoons soy or teriyaki sauce), cover, and simmer 15 minutes.

To Bake:

Sausage Roll: Preheat oven to 375° F. Leave roll whole, place on a rack in a shallow roasting pan, and insert meat thermometer in center. Roast, uncovered, without basting, 45 minutes to 1 hour or until thermometer reads 185° F. Serve as is or with Pan Gravy or Tomato Sauce.

Links: Preheat oven to 400° F. Spread links out in a shallow roasting pan and roast, uncovered, 25–30 minutes, turning often with tongs so they brown evenly.

To Broil (for links that have been simmered or steamed first): Preheat broiler. Brush sausages well with melted butter or oil, place on a greased broiler pan, and broil 3″ from heat, turning often with tongs, 5–8 minutes until nicely browned.

To Charcoal-Broil (for links that have first been simmered or steamed): Prepare a moderate charcoal fire. Brush sausages with melted butter or oil, place on lightly greased grill, and broil 3″ from heat, turning often with tongs, 5–8 minutes until well browned on all sides. *Use this same method with gas or electric barbecues.*

Some Easy Ways to Dress Up Sausage Patties

All make 4 servings

Baked Sausage and Apples: Shape 1 pound bulk sausage into 4 patties and brown well on both sides over moderate heat. Transfer to an ungreased 6-cup casserole. Peel, core, and thinly slice 4 tart apples; toss with 1/4 cup firmly packed light brown sugar, 1/4 teaspoon cinnamon, a pinch nutmeg, and the juice of 1/2 lemon. Spread over patties. Top with 1/4 cup fine buttered bread crumbs and bake, uncovered, at 350° F. about 1/2 hour until lightly browned and bubbly.

NPS: 355 C, 45 mg CH, 750 mg S*

Baked Sausage and Sweet Potatoes: Shape and brown patties as above; transfer to an ungreased 6-cup casserole, top with 1 (17-ounce) can yams, drained, cover, and bake 1/2–3/4 hour at 350° F. until bubbly.

NPS: 325 C, 45 mg CH, 750 mg S*

Sausage Patties Creole: Shape and brown patties as in first variation; transfer to an ungreased 6-cup casserole. Drain all but 2 tablespoons drippings from skillet, add 1 minced medium-size yellow onion, 1 crushed clove garlic, and 1/3 cup minced sweet green pepper, and stir-fry 8–10 minutes until onion is golden. Add 1 (1-pound) can drained, chopped tomatoes, 1/2 teaspoon salt, and a pinch each marjoram and thyme. Heat, stirring, 5 minutes. Pour over sausages and bake, uncovered, 1/2–3/4 hour at 350° F. until sauce is thick and bubbly.

NPS: 290 C, 50 mg CH, 1,120 mg S*

Sauerkraut and Sausage: Shape and brown patties as in first variation; remove to an ungreased 6-cup casserole. Top with 1 pound undrained sauerkraut, sprinkle lightly with paprika, and bake uncovered 30 minutes at 350° F.

NPS: 215 C, 45 mg CH, 1,540 mg S*

Sausage "Sandwiches": Shape 1 pound bulk sausage into 8 thin patties of equal size. Top 4 with a thin layer of seasoned mashed potatoes, yams, or drained crushed pineapple. Top with remaining patties and crimp edges to seal. Brown both sides well over moderate heat. If patties are stuffed with mashed potatoes, add 1 1/2 cups Pan Gravy (or canned), cover, and simmer 1/2 hour. If stuffed with yams or pineapple, add 1/2 cup apple cider or pineapple juice, cover, and simmer 1/2 hour. Recipe too flexible for meaningful nutritional count.

Some Simple Ways to Spice Up Sausage Links

All make 4 servings

Note: Use fresh or country-style pork sausage links instead of European varieties unless otherwise specified.

Braised Sausages, Apples, and Onions: Brown 1 pound sausage links slowly in 1–2 teaspoons butter or bacon drippings in a large, heavy skillet over moderate heat; remove and drain. In drippings, stir-fry 1 thinly sliced Bermuda onion and 3 peeled, cored, and sliced tart apples 5–8 minutes until pale golden; add 1 tablespoon lemon juice, 2 tablespoons light brown sugar, 1/4 teaspoon cinnamon, and a pinch each cloves and nutmeg; toss to mix. Return sausages to skillet, pushing down into apples, cover, and simmer ½ hour.

NPS: 585 C, 80 mg CH, 930 mg S*

Country-Fried Sausage and Potatoes: Slice ½ pound country-style sausage links ½" thick and brown well in 2 tablespoons butter or oil. Add 1 chopped medium-size yellow onion, 4 raw potatoes, peeled and sliced thin, cover, and cook 8–10 minutes. Uncover and stir-fry 10–15 minutes until nicely browned. Season with ½ teaspoon salt, a pinch each pepper and thyme, and serve.

NPS: 410 C, 55 mg CH, 795 mg S*

Italian-Style Sausage and Black Beans: Begin 1 recipe Brazilian Black Beans, substituting ½ pound fresh Italian-style pork sausage for bacon. Cut sausage casings and remove meat; stir-fry in 1 tablespoon olive oil 3–5 minutes, breaking up clumps; remove to paper toweling with a slotted spoon. Brown onions and garlic in drippings as recipe directs, add sausage along with remaining ingredients, and proceed as directed.

NPS: 575 C, 55 mg CH, 1,275 mg S*

Sausage and Vegetable Gumbo: Begin 1 recipe Vegetable Gumbo but substitute ½ pound sausage links for bacon; cut in ½" slices and brown well in 1 tablespoon butter. Add onion and celery, sauté as directed, then proceed according to recipe.

NPS: 490 C, 45 mg CH, 1,195 mg S*

How to Heat and Serve Fully Cooked Sausages

Frankfurters and Other Fully Cooked Link Sausages: Franks, wieners, and knackwurst can be prepared by any of the methods below. To determine best ways of preparing the more unusual sausages, consult Quick Alphabet of Sausages, then follow directions below. *(Note:* American sausages are best *not pricked* before cooking, but the chunky, moist European sausages should be lest they burst.)

To Simmer: Cover with simmering water or, for richer flavor, with beer or a ½ and ½ mixture of water and dry white wine and *simmer* (not boil) 5–8 minutes until heated through. Or cover with simmering liquid, remove from heat, and let stand, covered, 8–10 minutes. *(Note:* If beer or wine-water mixture is used, save for making soups or stews.)

To Steam: Arrange sausages 1 layer deep on a rack in a saucepan or vegetable steamer,

add 1 cup boiling water, cover, and heat 8 minutes over moderate heat. Water should stay at a slow boil.

To Panfry (Sauté): Brown sausages in 1–2 tablespoons butter, margarine, meat drippings, or cooking oil in a heavy skillet over moderate heat 3–5 minutes, turning frequently. If you prefer, halve lengthwise and brown about 2 minutes on each side.

To Broil: Brush sausages well with oil, melted butter or margarine and broil on lightly greased broiler rack 3" from heat 4–5 minutes, turning often until evenly browned (use tongs for turning). Or split, brush with butter, and broil about 2 minutes per side.

To Charcoal-Broil: Prepare a moderately hot charcoal fire. Lay sausages in a single layer on a lightly greased grill and broil 4"–5" from heat 3–4 minutes, turning frequently with tongs, until lightly browned. *(Note:* Sausages can also be wrapped in heavy foil—not individually but in a single large package—and steamed on the grill 12–15 minutes.) *Use this same method with gas or electric barbecues.*

To Roast over a Campfire: Let fire burn down to glowing coals. Spear sausages crosswise on long-handled forks or peeled sticks (no more than 2–3 per fork or stick) and roast 3" from coals, turning frequently, 4–5 minutes until lightly browned.

Andouille: Usually this sausage is simply sliced and eaten cold, but it can be browned in butter or drippings. Slice ¼"–½" thick and brown in 2–3 tablespoons butter or bacon drippings in a large, heavy skillet over moderate heat about 2–3 minutes on each side. Or brush with melted butter or drippings and broil 4" from heat about 2 minutes on each side.

Blood Sausages: These come in different sizes and shapes, each requiring somewhat different treatment. The *small links* may simply be left whole and browned in 2–3 tablespoons bacon drippings or butter in a large, heavy skillet 3–5 minutes; turn frequently with tongs. The *large round ring* is best braised: Brown 5–7 minutes in 2–3 tablespoons bacon drippings or butter in a large, heavy skillet over moderately low heat, add 1 cup water or stock, cover, turn heat to low, and simmer about ½ hour until heated through. *Fat chunky rolls* like *Zungenwurst* can be sliced ¼"–½" thick, peeled of casings, and, if you like, dredged lightly in flour (helps reduce spattering). Brown in 2–3 tablespoons butter or bacon drippings in a large, heavy skillet over moderately low heat 3–4 minutes on each side. *Berliner Blutwurst,* another variety, should be covered with boiling water and allowed to stand 20 minutes (keep lid on pot). Remove, slice, and serve. Or, if you like, gently brown hot slices in about 2 tablespoons butter in a large, heavy skillet over moderately low heat 2–3 minutes per side.

Leberkäse: This delicate German meat pâté is nearly always served hot. Slice about 1/2″ thick and place slices on a rack over boiling water in a vegetable steamer or in the top of a double boiler. Cover and steam 25–30 minutes until heated through. Or slice 1″ thick and sauté slowly in about 3 tablespoons butter in a large, heavy skillet with 1 thinly sliced yellow onion. Keep heat low and allow about 5 minutes per side; handle with care, using a pancake turner to turn slices.

Scrapple: Slice 1/4″–1/2″ thick or cut in finger-shaped sticks; dredge lightly in flour and brown in 3–4 tablespoons butter or bacon drippings in a large, heavy skillet over moderate heat until crisply browned. Slices will take 3–5 minutes per side, fingers slightly less time but more frequent turning.

BASIC HOMEMADE SAUSAGE MEAT

6 pounds; about 2 dozen patties ¢

4 1/2 pounds lean pork (trimmings, head meat, etc.)
1 1/2 pounds fat pork (cheek, jowl, trimmings, etc.)
3 tablespoons salt
1 tablespoon pepper
1 tablespoon sage

Coarsely grind lean and fat pork together, mix with remaining ingredients, and grind two more times. Shape into patties about 3″ across and 1/2″ thick, wrap each in foil or plastic food wrap and freeze until firm. For cooking instructions, see How to Cook Fresh Sausages.

To Make Links: First of all, you need a sausage stuffing attachment for your meat grinder or electric mixer. Second you need casings (butchers can usually get them for you). Ask either for sheep casings or small artificial casings about 3/4″–1″ in diameter; they come in continuous rolls and can be bought by the pound or yard. For the quantity of sausage above, you'll need about 3 1/2 yards. Sheep and other natural casings are usually packed in salt and must be soaked about 1 hour in cold water to dissolve out the salt and soften the casings. Attach a moist casing to stuffer as electric mixer manufacturer directs, then force sausage into it. Every 3″–4″, press casing together and twist around once to form links. If you alternate direction of twisting (i.e., twisting clockwise one time and counterclockwise the next), the links will stay linked. Tying each with string in a square knot is foolproof. Work carefully, trying not to tear or break casings. Freeze sausages or store in refrigerator (don't try to keep fresh sausages in refrigerator more than a few days; they're highly perishable).

NP Patty: 325 C, 85 mg CH, 890 mg S*

VARIATIONS

Mixed Sausage: Prepare basic recipe as directed, but instead of using all pork use 3 pounds lean beef or veal, 2 pounds lean pork, and 1 pound fat pork. Recipe too flexible for meaningful nutritional count.

Hot Italian-Style Pork Sausage: Omit sage from basic recipe above and add the following: 1 medium-size chopped yellow onion, 1 minced clove garlic, 2 teaspoons paprika, 1 tablespoon crushed dried red chili peppers, 2 teaspoons fennel seeds, 1/2 teaspoon each crushed bay leaf and thyme, 1/4 teaspoon crushed coriander, and 1/2 cup dry red wine. Put through coarse blade of grinder twice to blend, then stuff into small casings as directed above, twisting into links every 6″ or so. Or do as the Italians do and make one long continuous rope of sausage, coiling it like a garden hose. Freeze or refrigerate. To use, simply cut off the amount you need (see How to Cook Fresh Sausages).

NP Link: 330 C, 85 mg CH, 890 S*

Sweet Italian-Style Pork Sausage: Follow recipe for Hot Italian-Style Pork Sausage (above) but reduce amount of crushed dried red chili peppers to 1 teaspoon. Nutritional count same as above.

Fresh Chorizos (Hot Spanish Sausages): Follow basic recipe above but omit sage and use all lean pork. Add the following: 1 tablespoon oregano, 6 minced cloves garlic, 1/3 cup chili powder, 1 teaspoon ground cumin, 1 tablespoon crushed dried red chili peppers, and 2/3 cup vinegar. Put through coarse blade of grinder twice to blend, then stuff into casings as directed for Italian-style sausages above.

NP Link: 195 C, 75 mg CH, 920 mg S*

SCRAPPLE

6 servings ⚖ ¢

At hog-butchering time the Pennsylvania Dutch cook any pork scraps with corn meal into a mush called scrapple. This version isn't the original, but it's good.

2 large meaty pork hocks
1/4 pound lean pork trimmings
1 1/2 quarts water
1 1/2 teaspoons salt
1/4 teaspoon pepper
3/4 teaspoon sage
1 1/3 cups yellow corn meal

Scrub hocks well under cold running water; scrape skin with a sharp knife to remove any hairs. Place hocks and pork trimmings in a large, heavy kettle with water and salt, cover, and simmer 2–2 1/2 hours until meat nearly falls from bones. Lift meat from kettle, discard skin and bones, and coarsely grind meat. Strain broth and skim off fat; wash and dry kettle. Measure 1 quart broth into kettle, add ground meat, pepper, and sage, and bring to a boil. Mix corn meal into remaining cold broth, then add slowly to boiling broth, stirring constantly so it doesn't lump. Continue cooking and stirring until thickened. Turn heat to lowest point, set kettle on an asbestos flame tamer, cover, and let cook about 1/2 hour. Taste for seasoning and adjust if necessary. Spoon mixture into an ungreased 9″ × 5″ × 3″ loaf pan, cover with foil, and chill until firm. To serve, unmold, slice, and panfry following directions given under How to Heat and Serve Fully Cooked Sausages.

SCOTCH EGGS

4 servings

These eggs are also good quartered and served cold as an appetizer. They are not as difficult to make as they may sound, and the only trick in making the sausage coating stick to the eggs is to make certain the shelled hard-cooked eggs are thoroughly dry.

Shortening or cooking oil for deep fat frying
1 pound sausage meat
4 hard-cooked eggs, peeled and patted dry on paper toweling
1/3 cup unsifted flour
1 egg lightly beaten with 1 tablespoon cold water
1/2 cup toasted seasoned bread crumbs

Preheat oven to 400° F. Begin heating shortening in a deep fat fryer over moderately high heat (use basket and deep fat thermometer). Meanwhile, divide sausage into 4 equal parts and mold each around an egg, making as firm and smooth as possible. Dredge lightly in flour, dip in egg, and roll in crumbs to coat evenly. When fat reaches 350° F., fry eggs, 2 at a time, 2–3 minutes until golden brown; drain on paper toweling. Place eggs in an ungreased pie tin and bake, uncovered, 10–15 minutes until sausage is cooked thoroughly. Halve each egg lengthwise and serve hot. Or cool and serve on a bed of crisp salad greens.

NPS: 445 C, 390 mg CH, 1,175 mg S*

TOAD IN THE HOLE (SAUSAGES IN YORKSHIRE PUDDING)

4–6 servings ¢

1 cup sifted flour
1 teaspoon salt
1 cup milk
1/2 cup cold water
3 eggs, lightly beaten
1 pound fresh sausage links
1/4 cup water
1/4 cup melted beef or bacon drippings or vegetable shortening
2 cups hot beef gravy (homemade or canned)

About 40 minutes before serving time, make batter: mix flour and salt in a bowl, add milk, a little at a time, beating with a rotary or electric beater until smooth. Add water and eggs and beat until bubbly. Cover loosely and set aside 1/2 hour in a cool place (do not refrigerate). Preheat oven to 450° F. Simmer sausages in water in a covered skillet 8 minutes; drain well on paper toweling. Beat batter until bubbles appear on surface. Pour drippings into a 13 1/2″ × 9″ × 2″ baking pan and heat in oven 1–2 minutes until smoking hot. Pour batter into pan and arrange sausages on top here and there. Bake, uncovered, on center oven rack 15–20 minutes until well browned, well risen, and crisp. Cut into large squares and serve piping hot with gravy.

NPS (4–6): 570–380 C, 270–180 mg CH, 1,380–920 mg S*

KIELBASA-CANNELLINI CASSEROLE

6 servings ¢

2 tablespoons olive oil
1 kielbasa sausage (about 1 1/2 pounds), cut in 1/4″ rounds
2 medium-size yellow onions, peeled and chopped fine

2 cloves garlic, peeled and crushed
⅓ cup minced parsley
½ teaspoon fennel seeds, crushed
1 teaspoon coriander seeds, crushed
1 teaspoon oregano
1 teaspoon salt
⅛ teaspoon pepper
2 (1-pound) cans zucchini in tomato sauce (do
    not drain) or 1 pound fresh zucchini, sliced
    and sautéed in butter, plus ¾ cup tomato
    sauce
2 (1-pound 3-ounce) cans cannellini (white
    kidney beans), drained
1 (6-ounce) can tomato paste

Preheat oven to 350° F. Heat oil in a large, heavy skillet over moderately high heat about 1 minute, add sausage and brown on both sides; drain on paper toweling. Add onions and garlic to skillet and sauté, stirring, 5–8 minutes until golden. Mix in parsley, herbs, salt, and pepper. Return sausage to skillet, add all remaining ingredients, and toss lightly to mix. Transfer to an ungreased shallow 3-quart casserole and bake, uncovered, 1½ hours, stirring occasionally. Serve as main dish.

NPS: 620 C, 80 mg CH, 2,255 mg S*

SOME HOT-DOG QUICKIES ⊠

Note: Luncheon meats, bologna, mild salamis, and cold cuts can be substituted in any of the recipes calling for sliced or diced frankfurters.

California Splits: Split franks lengthwise, not quite all the way through, and spread half of them with seasoned mashed potatoes or sweet potatoes; top with unspread franks, pressing together like sandwiches. Spread with mild yellow mustard, lay a slice of American or Swiss cheese over each, and bake, uncovered, 15 minutes at 400° F.

Corn Dogs: Make a batter with ½ cup yellow corn meal, 1 cup sifted flour, 1 teaspoon salt, ¼ teaspoon baking powder, 1 cup milk, and 1 egg; beat until smooth. Dip franks in batter to coat, then fry in deep fat (375° F.) until browned, 2–3 minutes. Drain on paper toweling and dip in mustard as you eat.

Texas Hounds: Serve hot dogs in buns smothered with Texas Red or other chili.

QUICK ALPHABET OF SAUSAGES

Name	How to Prepare	Good Accompaniments
FRESH SAUSAGES (uncured, unsmoked, uncooked). Cook thoroughly before eating (recipes follow).		
Bockwurst Delicate German veal sausage made in spring at bock beer time; aromatic of onion and/or chives, parsley, nutmeg.	Panfry.	Bock beer.
Bratwurst Chunky German veal and pork sausage usually seasoned with coriander or caraway, lemon, and ginger. Now being sold precooked as well as fresh.	Panfry, using beer or ale for the initial simmering; drain and brown in butter.	Hashed Brown Potatoes.
Chipolata Small Italian pork and rice sausages sometimes called "little fingers." Seasonings: chives, thyme, coriander.	Panfry. The French use chipolatas to garnish large roasts and poultry.	Potatoes, roasts, poultry.
Fresh Pork Sausage The American favorite, a mixture of ground fresh pork and pork fat, seasoned with pepper and sage. It is made under federal inspection, cannot contain more than 3 per cent added moisture or 50 per cent fat. Comes in bulk (loose for patties), links and rolls. *Country Style* is a coarser grind. *Brown 'n Serve* links and patties come plain or flavored.	*Links:* Simmer, steam, panfry, braise, bake and, if first simmered or steamed, broil or charcoal-broil. *Patties:* Panbroil, braise. *Roll:* Bake.	Eggs, grits, cooked apples, potatoes, dried beans and lentils.
Fresh Italian-Style Pork Sausage The pizza sausage, hot or sweet; usually made in continuous ropes. One type, *cotechino,* made with pork skins and white wine, is often cooked with cannellini.	Panfry or braise; use in casseroles and, removed from casings, in spaghetti sauce.	Lentils, dried beans, spaghetti.

MEAT

Name	How to Prepare	Good Accompaniments
Fresh Thuringer Finely ground pork-veal sausage aromatic of coriander, celery seed, and ginger. Now available "scalded" as well as fresh.	If not "scalded," braise or simmer and brown in butter. Good in Cassoulet.	Potatoes, dried beans.
Loukanika Greek lamb and pork sausage seasoned with orange rind. Greeks usually cut them in 1″ chunks, grill, and serve as *meze* (hors d'oeuvre).	Panfry or simmer and broil or charcoal-broil.	Fried eggs, tomatoes, rice.
Toulouse Small, coarse-textured French pork sausage; seasoned with garlic and white wine.	Braise or panfry; use in Cassoulet and other casseroles or remove from casing and use in stuffings.	Lentils, dried beans.
Weisswurst Unusually delicate, small white German sausage made of veal, cream, and eggs. Traditionally served après-midnight at Oktoberfest with rye rolls and sweet German mustard.	Bring gently to a simmer in enough water to cover; never boil or *wurst* may toughen and/or burst.	Rye rolls, sweet mustard, pretzels, beer.

FRESH SMOKED SAUSAGES. Cook thoroughly before eating.

Name	How to Prepare	Good Accompaniments
Bauernwurst (farmer sausage) A highly seasoned, super hot dog from Germany; usually coarse of texture.	Steam or simmer, then brown in butter or broil.	Sauerkraut.
Country-Style Fresh Pork Sausage A smoked version of fresh country-style sausage; it may be all pork or a combination of pork and beef. Usually sold in links.	Simmer, steam, panfry, braise, bake and, if first simmered or steamed, broil or charcoal-broil.	Eggs, grits, apples, potatoes, dried beans.
Romanian Sausage A lean pork sausage stuffed into casings and flavored with garlic and ginger.	Steam or simmer, then brown in butter or broil.	Potatoes, cabbage.

COOKED SAUSAGES. Usually these are made of fresh meats, though sometimes from cured. They are fully cooked and safe to eat as is, but most will improve if heated through before serving.

Name	How to Prepare	Good Accompaniments
Andouillette Small tripe or chitterling sausages that are a specialty of Normandy.	The French way is to make a few shallow slits in sausage and to sauté in butter or to broil or grill, brushing with melted butter.	Mashed or Lyonnaise Potatoes.
Blood Sausage A large dark sausage made of pig's blood and cubes of pork fat. Occasionally you may find uncooked ones, but most are fully cooked. Certain German varieties are smoked as well.	Uncooked ones must be simmered, then sliced and browned; cooked ones need only be sliced and browned lightly in butter.	Mashed potatoes, sauerkraut.
Boudins Blancs Very delicate, very expensive white French sausages made of pork, chicken, cream, eggs, onions, and fine bread crumbs.	Sauté gently in butter or brush with melted butter and broil just to heat.	Mashed potatoes.
Cotto A soft, cooked Italian salami, usually sold sliced as a sandwich meat.	Use for sandwiches.	Bread, mustard, dill pickles.
Leberkäse Not a sausage so much as a smooth German pork pâté eaten hot instead of cold. Germans like to joke that although *Leberkäse* means *liver-cheese,* it contains neither.	Slice and heat over boiling water in a vegetable steamer or sauté gently in butter.	Steamed: rye bread and mustard. Sautéed: fried onions.
Liver Sausages Large creamy-smooth links, some highly spiced. Usually made of pork liver mixed with pork and/or veal. American vari-	Use as sandwich filling or as a spread for crackers.	Bread (especially rye) and crackers.

eties may or may not be smoked; German types almost always are. Liver sausages can be fairly firm or soft enough to spread.

Scrapple The Pennsylvania Dutch invented this pork and corn meal mush combination as a way to use up the odds and ends of hog butchering. Scrapple comes in chunky rolls, both canned and in packages in supermarket meat coolers.	Slice and brown in butter or bacon drippings.	Eggs, grits, fried apples, cabbage, potatoes.

COOKED, SMOKED SAUSAGES: Some *(andouille, Bierwurst,* bologna, the German liver sausages) are eaten as is; others (mainly the frankfurter types) will be better if heated through. Specific directions follow.

Andouille The large French tripe or chitterling sausage is the big brother of *andouillettes*. Unlike them, it is more often sliced thin and eaten cold as an hors d'oeuvre. Occasionally it is sliced and sautéed gently in butter.	Slice and serve cold as an appetizer or heat slices by sautéing in butter.	When sautéed: mashed potatoes.
Berliner Blutwurst A smoked variation of blood sausage (see Cooked Sausages) containing bacon cubes.	Heat in boiling water, then slice; or, after heating, sauté in butter with onion and apple rings.	Cranberry sauce, sautéed onions and apples.
Berliner Bockwurst A smoky red Berlin sausage, not unlike our hot dog. It's a favorite late-night snack, served steaming from street-corner stands.	Steam or heat in boiling water, then serve.	Sauerkraut; also any of our hot-dog trappings.
Bierwurst (Beerwurst) A soft, cooked German salami, usually sold sliced as sandwich meat. Garlicky.	Use in making sandwiches.	Beer and bread.
Bologna The original Bolognese sausage is *mortadella,* a plump, creamy link studded with cubes of fat. True mortadella is air-dried briefly, putting it into the cervelat family. American mortadella is simply fat-studded American bologna—a creamy, pink pork-beef blend with lots of garlic. There are many types: *large, ring, stick* (slightly coarser), *chub* (an ultra smooth mix of beef, pork, and bacon), *Schinkenwurst* (ham bologna), *Lebanon* (a sour, briefly air-dried type from Lebanon, Pa.), all-beef bologna, and all turkey.	Use in sandwiches, salads, and soups; also see suggestions that follow.	Swiss or American cheese, lettuce, sliced tomatoes, all kinds of bread, mustard, and mayonnaise.
Frankfurters and Wieners Frankfurters came from Frankfurt, wieners from Vienna; today they're 100 per cent Americanized as hot dogs. Some are all beef (the kosher), but many are 60 per cent beef and 40 per cent pork. Casings are natural, artificial or nonexistent (as in skinless franks). *Vienna sausages* are wieners cut in short links and canned. Most popular frankfurter sizes: *regular* (9–10 franks per pound), *dinner* (5 per pound), *foot-long* (4 per pound) and *cocktail* (26–28 per pound). Also available: *smoked frankfurters* (called *Smoked Links* and sometimes just *Smokies), cheese, chicken, and turkey frankfurters.*	See recipes and suggestions that follow.	Almost anything savory.
German Liver Sausages (liverwursts) The list is long, but among those especially worth seeking out: *Braunschweiger* (mild and creamy),	All are ready-to-eat and best served cold with bread or crackers.	Bread (especially rye), crackers.

Hildesheimer Streichleberwurst (all calf's liver), *Zwiebelwurst* (with browned onion in it), *Trufflewurst* (with truffles), *Sardellenwurst* (with anchovies).

Name	How to Prepare	Good Accompaniments
Kielbasa A large garlicky Polish sausage, mostly pork but sometimes with veal or beef. Once available only fresh, *Kielbasa* is now being processed by American packers and sold "fully cooked." Check the labels.	Steam or simmer to heat; cook with sauerkraut; use in stews and casseroles.	Sauerkraut, dried peas, beans, and lentils.
Knackwurst (or knockwurst or knoblauch) Short chunky German frankfurter highly seasoned with garlic. There's also a Bavarian version called *Regensburger.*	Simmer or steam to warm or cook with sauerkraut. Can be substituted for hot dogs.	Sauerkraut, any of our hot-dog condiments.
Strasbourg Liver Sausage A French liver sausage with pistachio nuts.	Ready-to-eat; use as an appetizer.	Bread, crackers.
Strasbourg Sausage Sort of a smoked, French hot dog.	Simmer, steam or use in Choucroute Garnie.	Sauerkraut.
Tongue Sausage A large sausage made of tongue and other meats. Available sliced and in links.	Ready-to-eat; use in making sandwiches.	Cheese, bread, mustard, mayonnaise, pickles.
Zungenwurst A German blood sausage made with tongue and studded with diced fat.	Slice and brown in butter.	Sauerkraut, mashed potatoes.
SPECIALTY SAUSAGES: These two defy categorization.		
Mettwurst (Schmierwurst) A very soft, very fat German pork sausage, bright red in color and aromatic of coriander and white pepper. It is cured and smoked *but not cooked* and it is eaten raw.	Use as a spread for bread.	Bread.
Rillettes de Porc A great French favorite that is nothing more than lean and fat pork cooked, then pounded into paste; sometimes goose or rabbit is added.	Use as a spread for bread.	A good country bread.

SALAMIS AND CERVELATS (SUMMER SAUSAGES)

These are the original sausages, developed ages ago when salting, drying, and smoking were the only ways to preserve meat. The Italians came up with salamis, the Germans, cervelats. Both are mixtures of chopped pork and/or beef and secret blends of herbs and spices. With few exceptions (cooked kosher salami), both are raw and eaten that way (curing, drying, and smoking render them safe).

For all their similarities, the two are different. Salamis are laden with garlic, cervelats have none; salamis are rarely smoked, cervelats commonly are; salamis are rather coarse of texture; cervelats, generally fine. Salamis are air-dried from 1 to 6 months and thus are usually hard, dry, and shriveled. Cervelats can be dry but more often they are softer and moister—*semidry* is the trade term—having spent only 2–5 days in the drying room or smokehouse. Salamis need not be stored in the refrigerator (though they'll keep there almost forever), cervelats should be.

There are dozens of different salamis and cervelats (including an American turkey salami), most of them named after the towns where they are made, as well as other hard peppery links classified as *dry sausages.* Here are some of the more popular.

Salamis

Italian

Calabrese: A red-hot type from southern Italy.

Campagnole: Rough-textured, spicy peasant salami.

Genoa: One of the best; quite fat and studded with whole peppercorns.

Milano: Finely grained, fairly delicate, flavored with pepper and white wine.

Pepperoni: Small, dry salami-like sausage available both sweet and hot.

Soppressata: A flat oval salami—peppery, gingery, *garlicky!*

German

Hard Salami: A lean Italian type without all the garlic.

Hungarian: Called simply Hungarian salami, it is mild, often smoked.

French

Arles: Coarsely grained Provençal sausage with a crisscross cording.

Lyon: Fine, all-pork salami in large casings.

American

Alessandri, Alpino: Italian types made of pork and beef.

Frizzes: Also Italian style; sweet and peppery types are made, both scented with anise. The sweet is corded with blue string, the hot with red.

Italian: Another American-Italian salami, this one coarsely chopped pork mixed with minced beef, whole peppercorns, and red wine or grape juice.

Kosher: Soft, cooked all-beef salami made under rabbinical supervision. Available sliced and whole.

Cervelats

German

Cervelatwurst: Finely minced beef and pork, lightly smoked, mildly seasoned with mustard, red and black pepper, sugar, and salt. Semidry.

Farmer Cervelat: Rather soft, small link of coarsely chopped beef and pork in equal proportion. *Farmer Sausage* is a bigger, beefier, smokier version.

Gothaer, Göttinger: Two hard, dry cervelats, one from the town of Gotha, the other from Göttingen.

Holsteiner: Sort of a super Farmer Sausage, heavily smoked; ring-shaped.

Thuringer: Here's the favorite. Often called simply *Summer Sausage,* it's salty but mild, fairly soft. Coriander is the noticeable spice.

Italian

Mortadella: (see Bologna under Cooked, Smoked Sausages).

Swedish

Göteborg: A large cardamom-flavored, coarsely textured pork cervelat, smoked and air-dried.

Swiss

Landjäger: Very smoky, dry, wrinkled black cervelat, pressed into small sticks instead of rolls. It is made of beef and pork.

Other Dry Sausages

Chorizos: Small, hard, dry Spanish sausages, flavored with pimiento, garlic, and red pepper. Especially good with chick-peas, black beans, and other dried peas and beans.

Linguiça: Small, slim Portuguese sausages, saturated with garlic and paprika. A favorite ingredient in Portuguese and Brazilian soups, stews, and casseroles.

Some Ways to Use Salamis and Cervelats

Note about Slicing: A good general rule is "the firmer the sausage, the thinner the slice."

Thin Slices:
• In Antipasto or on hors d'oeuvre trays.
• With a savory spread as open-face sandwiches.
• In sandwiches, solo with mustard or mayonnaise, or in tandem with Swiss, American, or cream cheese.
• In making Pizza or Quick Pizzas.
• In Grilled Cheese Sandwiches.
• Wrapped around small chunks of pineapple, peach, pear, banana, mango or preserved kumquat, skewered and broiled under bastings of Sweet-Sour Sauce.
• Shaped into cornucopias, filled with a savory cheese spread, and served as cocktail snacks.

Diced or Minced (1/4–1/3 cup is enough in each instance):
• Teamed with fluffy boiled rice, mashed or Stuffed Baked Potatoes, Lyonnaise or Hashed Brown Potatoes, Macaroni and Cheese, or any meatless pasta sauce.
• Added to any boiled dried beans, spinach or other greens dressed with oil and vinegar.
• Added to stuffings for poultry or pork.
• Mixed with cheese, onion, garlic, or other savory dips and spreads.
• Added to Cheese or Mushroom Soufflé.

Julienne Strips (1/3–1/2 cup is enough):
• In crisp green salads.
• In scrambled eggs or omelets.

GAME

Cooking game is no more mysterious than roasting beef or stewing lamb. It's just that the "bag" is often brought home whole and the average cook is shocked numb at the idea of skinning and butchering. Well, cleaning game isn't as neat as peeling a potato, but fortunately the messiest job (eviscerating) will probably have been done in the field. As for the rest—skinning, aging, cutting up a carcass—there are butchers in most parts of the country who will do these jobs for you—even if you have shot the game yourself; some will even package and label cuts for the freezer. In many cities, specialty butchers sell fresh game in season and frozen game year round. More and more game (especially rabbit and buffalo) is being raised for the table.

HOW TO FIND QUALITY

Game bought from a reputable market will have been federally inspected (to ensure wholesomeness) and because of the fussiness of game fanciers, will usually be of high quality as well. But that which your husband or neighbor shoots may not be. Three factors determine quality: *age of the animal* (the younger, the better), *diet,* and *care the kill was given in the field.* As soon as an animal is shot, it should be eviscerated (especially important on warm days), and large animals must also be bled. The process is too complicated to include here; the best way to learn is firsthand from an experienced hunting guide or secondhand from a detailed hunting manual. As for the age of the animal, hunting guides can quickly judge (usu-

ally by looking at an animal's teeth). Diet, obviously, is more difficult to determine because a wild creature will eat what it must in order to survive. Still, there are clues. Certain species prefer certain kinds of food. As a general rule, vegetarians are better flavored than meat or fish eaters. Where an animal is bagged can also suggest what it's been eating. For example, a deer shot in an evergreen thicket may have nibbled evergreen berries and thus taste of them.

How do you determine quality of game in a store? Much the way you do for any other meat. Venison and other red meat should be moist (not wet) and velvety with a clean fresh smell. Small game should also be moist, its flesh springy to the touch, of good color and odor with little or no shot damage.

FOOD VALUE

Game is high-protein food; most, moreover, is lean because it is well exercised. Nutritional counts have not been supplied for game meats.

Large Animals

Choicest is venison, the meat of deer and other antlered animals. Buffalo, now being raised for the table, has a fine "beefy" flavor. There is very little wild boar around; most of that sold in this country is shipped in frozen from Europe. Cuts of large game are much like those of other meat animals (see Beef, Lamb, and Pork Charts), the tenderest coming from the little-exercised rib and loin, the toughest from the neck, leg, rump, and flank.

Small Animals

More rabbit is eaten in this country than all other furred game put together. It has light, delicate meat, much like that of chicken, and is a popular supermarket item. Squirrel is popular quarry too, though gamier and darker fleshed. Gamier still, and less often eaten, are opossum, raccoon, and muskrat.

How Much Game per Person?
When the animal or cut is unusually bony, allow 3/4–1 pound per person, otherwise 1/3–1/2 pound.

FROZEN GAME

Much of the game sold today is frozen. Thaw thoroughly before cooking, then prepare as you would fresh game. The best way to thaw game is in its original wrapper in the refrigerator; 1″ steaks will take about 12 hours, small roasts 3–4 hours per pound, and large roasts 4–6 hours per pound.

ROAST SADDLE OF VENISON

8 .ervings ⚖

Rack and loin of venison are excellent roasts, but the saddle (double loin) is choicest of all. If young and tender, it can be roasted like lamb; if of doubtful age, it should be marinated before roasting, and if mature it should be pot roasted like beef. The best way to tell an animal's age is to look at the bones. The bones of a young animal will be spongy and red inside, those of an older animal will appear flinty. Because venison is lean, it should be larded *and* barded to keep it from drying out, and it should not be roasted beyond medium rare. Though some cooks sear venison at a high temperature, then finish roasting at a low heat, it seems juiciest when roasted at 350° F. throughout.

1/2–3/4 pound fat back or salt pork
1 (5–6-pound) saddle of venison
1/2 pound suet, cut in 1/2″ cubes

Cut 1/2 the fat back into lardoons 1/4″ wide and 2″–3″ long and cut the rest into thin slices for barding.* Pique* ends of roast with lardoons, then bard outer curved side. Let roast come to room temperature; meanwhile, preheat oven to 350° F. Stand saddle fat side up in a shallow roasting pan and insert a meat thermometer in largest lean muscle, not touching bone. Scatter suet in bottom of pan. Roast, uncovered, 15–20 minutes per pound for rare (120°–125° F.) and 25 minutes per pound for medium rare (130°–140° F.), basting frequently with pan drippings and removing suet cubes as they brown. About 15 minutes before roast is done, remove barding fat. When done, lift saddle to a hot platter and let "rest" 10 minutes before carving. If you like, make Pan Gravy. Carve in long slices the length of saddle—and don't forget choice morsels of tenderloin tucked underneath the ribs. About 200 calories per serving.

VARIATION

⚖ **Marinated Roast Saddle of Venison:** Lard roast as above, cover with a marinade made by boiling 2 cups each red Burgundy and water 5 minutes with 1 peeled, bruised clove garlic, 4–6 juniper berries, 1 bay leaf, and 1 sprig each parsley and thyme, all tied in cheesecloth. Pour over venison, cover and refrigerate 1–2 days, turning meat occasionally. Lift from marinade, pat dry, bard, and roast as directed. If you like, strain marinade and use as the liquid when making Pan Gravy. About 210 calories per serving.

SMOTHERED VENISON STEAKS OR CHOPS

4 servings

Steaks and chops from very young venison can be brushed with butter or oil and broiled or panbroiled like beefsteaks. Older steaks and chops should be prepared this way.

3 pounds venison sirloin or round steak, cut 1 1/2″ thick, or 4 loin or rib chops, cut 1 1/2″ thick
1/3 cup unsifted flour
1 1/2 teaspoons salt
1/4 teaspoon pepper
3 tablespoons bacon or beef drippings or cooking oil
1 large yellow onion, peeled and minced
2 stalks celery, minced
2 small carrots, peeled and minced
2 cups hot beef broth or water
3/4 cup sour cream, at room temperature (optional)

Dredge steaks in a mixture of flour, salt, and pepper, then brown on both sides in drippings in a large, heavy skillet over moderately high heat. Remove meat and set aside. Stir-fry onion, celery, and carrots in drippings 8 minutes until golden. Return meat to pan, spoon vegetables on top, sprinkle with 1 tablespoon flour dredging mixture, and pour in broth. Turn heat to low, cover, and simmer 30–40 minutes until tender—chops will take 30–40 minutes, steaks 1–1 1/2 hours. Baste one or two times during cooking. Serve steaks topped with vegetables and pan juices, which will have thickened into gravy. If you like, smooth sour cream into gravy just before serving.

VARIATION

Oven-Braised Venison Steak: Brown venison and vegetables as directed, transfer to an ungreased 3-quart casserole, cover, and bake 1 1/2–2 hours at 300° F. until tender.
Both versions: about 400 calories per serving (without sour cream).

RAGOUT OF VENISON

4–6 servings

2 pounds boned venison shoulder, neck, or
  shank, cut in 1″–1¹/₂″ cubes
¹/₂ cup unsifted flour
1¹/₂ teaspoons salt
¹/₄ teaspoon pepper
2 tablespoons cooking oil
8 scallions, minced (include green tops)
³/₄ pound mushrooms, wiped clean and sliced
  thin
2¹/₂ cups beef broth
1 teaspoon prepared mild yellow mustard
1 tablespoon Worcestershire sauce
2 tablespoons flour blended with ¹/₄ cup cold
  water

Dredge venison by shaking in a bag with
flour, salt, and pepper. Brown in oil in a
large, heavy kettle over moderately high
heat; remove and set aside. Stir-fry scallions
and mushrooms in drippings 3–5 minutes
until mushrooms are golden, add meat to
kettle, also all but the final ingredient. Stir
well, cover, and simmer 1¹/₂–2 hours until
venison is fork tender. Mix in flour paste
and heat, stirring, until thickened and no
raw starch taste remains. Serve with wild
rice or buttered noodles. About 425 calories
for each of 4 servings (without wild rice or
noodles), 285 calories for each of 6 servings.

VENISONBURGERS

3–4 servings ⊠

Venison shank, neck, shoulder, and scraps
make excellent burgers mixed with sausage
meat or fat pork. They must be cooked well
done.

²/₃ pound venison, ground once
¹/₃ pound fat pork (cheek, jowl, trimmings),
  ground once, or ¹/₃ pound sausage meat
2 tablespoons cooking oil, butter, margarine, or
  bacon drippings
1 teaspoon salt
¹/₈ teaspoon pepper

Lightly mix venison and pork and shape into
3 plump patties or 4 slim ones. Brown in oil
in a large, heavy skillet over moderately
high heat 6–7 minutes on each side until
well done. Season with salt and pepper just
before serving. About 355 calories for each
of 3 servings, 265 calories for each of 4 servings.

About Buffalo and Beefalo
The buffalo being raised for the table is surprisingly delicate and tender, rather like lean
beef. The cuts of buffalo are similar to beef
(see Beef Chart) and similarly prepared, the
not-so-tender shoulder, rump, flank, and
shanks being best for stews and the tender
rib and loin perfect for steaks and roasts.
Where do you buy buffalo? From a specialty
meat market. *(Note:* Becoming more and
more available is *beefalo,* a cross between
the American bison and beef cattle. Its meat
is lean and dark red, and if aged for about
three weeks, it approaches prime beef in tenderness and flavor. Cook it as you would
comparable cuts of beef.)

FRIED RABBIT WITH PLANTATION GRAVY

4 servings   ¢

1 (3-pound) rabbit, cleaned, dressed, and
  disjointed
¹/₂ cup unsifted flour
1¹/₂ teaspoons salt
¹/₄ teaspoon pepper
¹/₂ cup butter or margarine

G R A V Y
3 tablespoons flour
1 cup chicken broth
1 cup milk
¹/₂ teaspoon salt
¹/₈ teaspoon pepper
¹/₈ teaspoon thyme
¹/₈ teaspoon marjoram

Dredge rabbit by shaking in a bag with
flour, salt, and pepper. Melt butter in a large
skillet over moderate heat and brown rabbit
evenly on all sides, about 5 minutes. Turn
heat to low, cover, and cook 1–1¹/₂ hours
until fork tender, turning once or twice. For
a crispy coating, cook uncovered the last 15
minutes. Transfer rabbit to a hot platter and
keep warm. For the gravy, blend flour into
pan drippings but do not brown. Add broth
and milk, then seasonings; heat, stirring, until thickened. Pass gravy separately. About
400 calories per serving.

V A R I A T I O N

Rabbit with Tarragon and White Wine:
Brown rabbit as directed, sprinkle with 2 tablespoons minced fresh tarragon or 1 teaspoon dried tarragon, cover, and cook as
above. When making gravy, substitute 1 cup
dry white wine for milk, omit the herbs, and
stir in ¹/₄ cup heavy cream just before serving. About 440 calories per serving.

HASENPFEFFER (PEPPERY RABBIT STEW)

4 servings   ¢

Germans prepare *Hasenpfeffer* many ways. In farm homes it's simply done as in the recipe below, in restaurants (and in Pennsylvania Dutch country) it's more highly spiced.

1 (3-pound) rabbit, cleaned, dressed, and
   disjointed (save liver, heart, and kidneys)
1/4 teaspoon peppercorns
1/4 teaspoon mustard seeds
4 cloves
3 bay leaves
1 cup cider vinegar
1 cup water
1 large yellow onion, peeled and sliced very thin
1/2 cup + 2 tablespoons unsifted flour
1/4 cup butter, margarine, or bacon drippings
1/2 cup dry red wine or water
1 teaspoon salt
1 teaspoon sugar

Remove all fat from rabbit; place rabbit in a deep bowl with liver, heart, and kidneys. Tie spices and bay leaves in cheesecloth and simmer, covered, with vinegar, water, and onion 5 minutes; pour over rabbit, cover, and refrigerate 1–2 days, turning rabbit occasionally. Lift rabbit from marinade (do not dry) and dredge in 1/2 cup flour; brown in butter in a large, heavy skillet over moderate heat 4–5 minutes. Transfer to a 3-quart kettle. Brown remaining flour in drippings; strain marinade, add, and heat, stirring, until thickened. Pour over rabbit, add onion and cheesecloth bag, also remaining ingredients, cover, and simmer 1–1½ hours until rabbit is tender. Shake kettle occasionally and check liquid level, adding a little extra water if mixture thickens too much. Serve with Potato Dumplings or noodles. About 370 calories per serving (without dumplings or noodles).

SQUIRREL FRICASSEE

2 servings   ¢

Gray squirrels are better eating than the red. Prepare by either of the following recipes, cook like a rabbit, or use in place of chicken in Brunswick Stew (the original Brunswick Stew was made with small furred game).

1 squirrel, cleaned, dressed, and disjointed
1/3 cup unsifted flour
1 teaspoon salt
1/4 teaspoon pepper
3 tablespoons butter or margarine
1 medium-size yellow onion, peeled and minced
1 clove garlic, peeled and crushed (optional)
1/4 cup julienne strips of lean ham
3/4 cup chicken broth
1/4 cup milk or light cream
1 tablespoon flour blended with 1/4 cup milk or
   light cream

Dredge squirrel in a mixture of flour, salt, and pepper, then brown in a heavy saucepan in butter over moderately high heat. Add all but last ingredient, cover, and simmer about 1 hour until tender. Blend in flour paste and heat, stirring, until thickened. Taste for salt and pepper and adjust as needed. Serve with hot biscuits. About 500 calories per serving (without biscuits).

SEVEN

Poultry and Game Birds

POULTRY

Of man's many meats, poultry has always been the aristocrat. The ancient Chinese domesticated a variety of exotic birds, fattened them for the table, and lavished upon them the wizardry of Oriental cuisine. From the East the birds were brought West, into Asia Minor, Greece, and Rome. It was the Romans who produced the first capon, not because they believed its flesh would be superior, but because Roman law restricted the number of hens and cocks that could be eaten. By castrating the cock, they circumvented the law and continued to feast with abandon. Thanks to today's streamlined poultry industry, there is no shortage of poultry (some 12½ *billion* [!] pounds of ready-to-cook chickens are sold each year). Birds are bred and pampered to plump succulence, most are sold dressed and ready-to-cook (sometimes even prestuffed and frozen), many are available year round, often at bargain prices. And all are unusually versatile.

The Food Value of Poultry

All poultry is a nourishing high-protein food, and much of it (ducks and geese excepted) fairly low-calorie.

THE KINDS OF POULTRY

Chicken

Squab Chicken: An infant weighing about 1 pound.

Broiler-Fryer: The all-purpose chicken, a 2–4-pounder that can be broiled, fried, roasted, braised, or poached with equal success. The term "broiler-fryer," coined by the poultry industry, is replacing the older terminology of "broiler" or "broiling chicken," "fryer," or "frying chicken."

Roaster or Roasting Chicken: A plump (4–8-pound), young (about 10 weeks) chicken perfect for roasting.

Capon: A cock castrated while young; it is full breasted, meaty, and tender, weighs 4–9½ pounds, and is superb roasted. It is also the bird to use when an especially succulent cooked chicken meat is required for a recipe.

Heavy Hen: Another of the poultry industry's coined terms, this one meaning a plump, meaty laying hen weighing 4½–6 pounds. Best when stewed.

Fowl: A stewing hen.

Stewing Hen: A tough old bird weighing 3–6½ pounds. Use for stock, soups, or recipes calling for ground or minced cooked chicken.

Turkey

(America's gift to the world of poultry):

Fryer-Roaster: A small (4–10 pound), young (usually under 16 weeks) turkey of either sex. It has tender meat, soft smooth skin, and flexible breastbone cartilage and can be broiled or oven fried as well as roasted.

Young Hen and Young Tom: Young (5–7 months) female and male with tender meat and skin. Best when roasted. Weights (see note below) vary considerably according to age and breed.

Yearling Hen and Yearling Tom: Mature female and male just over 1 year old. They have reasonably tender meat and can be roasted. Again, weights vary according to breed and age.

Mature Hen and Mature Tom: Female and male more than 15 months old; they have coarse skin, tough meat, and are rarely seen in stores today.

Note About Turkey Weights: Turkeys are also categorized by size (ready-to-cook weight): *small* (4–10 pounds), *medium* (10–19 pounds), and *large* (20 pounds or more).

Other Kinds of Poultry

Rock Cornish Hen: A breed produced by crossing a Cornish chicken and a White Rock. The baby of the chicken family, it weighs 1–2 pounds but averages 1¼. The breast is meaty and plump and the bird especially suited to roasting. It can also be braised, sautéed or prepared like medium-size game birds (see How to Cook Game Birds). Marketed frozen and ready-to-cook.

Squab: A young domesticated pigeon especially raised for the table. It weighs 1 pound or less and may be prepared like Rock Cornish hen.

Guinea Fowl: A raucous West African exotic now popular in barnyard flocks. It is a cousin to the pheasant and has rather dry, delicately gamy meat. Guinea hens are preferable to cocks; they weigh 2–4 pounds and may be prepared like chicken.

Pheasant (Farm-Raised): A plump (2–4-pound) bird with superbly flavored though somewhat dry meat. It is the wild pheasant (see Game Birds) raised in captivity for greater tenderness. Marketed frozen.

Duck: (Duckling is a better word because commercially raised ducks are marketed while still young and tender. Most famous is Long Island duckling.)

Broiler or Fryer Duckling: A very young duckling weighing about 3 pounds.

Roaster Duckling: A slightly older bird (8–16 weeks) weighing 3–5 pounds.

Goose: Geese raised for the table go to market while still *goslings;* they weigh 4–14 pounds, are fat birds, and are best when roasted.

BUYING POULTRY

All poultry moved in interstate commerce is federally inspected to ensure wholesomeness and about two thirds of it, at the packer's request, is graded for quality by the U.S. Department of Agriculture:

USDA GRADE A: The choicest bird, full fleshed and well finished.

USDA GRADE B: Second best, slightly less meaty and attractive.

USDA GRADE C: A grade used mostly for turkeys. These birds are scrawnier, may have torn skin, broken bones, and bruises. They are not handsome but, properly prepared, are good eating.

Characteristics of Quality and Freshness

Home-grown, locally marketed birds are often uninspected and ungraded, so the buyer must rely on his or her own judgment. To be sure of good poultry, look for:
• Well-fleshed breasts and short, plump legs; ducks should have broad, flat, and meaty breasts and backs well padded with fat.
• Soft, moist (but not wet), smooth, creamy, or yellow skin with a minimum of pinfeathers.
• Youthfulness—flexible breastbones in chickens and turkeys, pliable bills in ducks and geese.

Note: Reject birds with dry or purplish skin, hard scaly legs, and an "off" odor; also pass over those that have been sloppily dressed.

POPULAR MARKET FORMS OF FRESH POULTRY

Chicken

Whole, Ready-to-Cook: Such birds are cleaned and dressed inside and out, free of pinfeathers. Head, feet, and entrails were removed before weighing and pricing. The giblets have been washed, trimmed, and wrapped (they're usually tucked inside the body cavity).

Halved or Quartered: Popular supermarket forms.

Cut Up or Disjointed: Separated at the joints into breasts, backs, drumsticks, thighs, wings, etc.

Chicken Parts: It is now possible to buy just the parts of chicken you want—2 pounds of drumsticks, say, or a pound of boneless thighs, "drumettes" (the meaty part of the wing), breasts (halves or boneless, skinless halves). Chicken livers are also available by the pound.

Turkey

Whole, Ready-to-Cook: Fully cleaned and dressed birds. Some packer descriptions meaning the same thing: "Pan-Ready," "Oven-Ready," "Table-Dressed."

Quarter or Half Roast: Ready-to-cook large birds sold by the half or quarter.

Cut-Up Turkey or Turkey by the Piece: Specific parts of the bird sold separately by the pound. *Particularly popular:* Turkey rolls, boneless whole turkey breasts, "turkey tenderloin steaks" cut from the breast, and cutlets (thin slices of boneless breast meat), which savvy cooks now substitute for pricey veal scaloppine because the two are so similar in flavor and texture. These are also often called "turkey scaloppine."

Other Kinds of Poultry

Rock Cornish Hen and Squab: If you live near a hen or squab farm (most are in Pennsylvania), you may be able to buy fresh, whole, ready-to-cook birds; otherwise, you'll have to settle for the frozen.

Guinea Fowl and Farm-Raised Pheasant: Fresh, whole, ready-to-cook birds are sometimes available at specialty butchers; the frozen are far more plentiful.

Duck and Goose: These are available fresh, whole, and ready-to-cook but usually only near the source—the New York City area, Pennsylvania, and Wisconsin for duck, Wisconsin, Pennsylvania, and Minnesota for goose. Most ducks and geese come to market frozen (except during the Thanksgiving-Christmas season, when fresh birds are available). In the New York City area it is also sometimes possible to buy duck parts. *Newest Entry:* Honest-to-goodness French-style fresh *foie gras* (fat livers) from force-fed geese and ducks, which can be sliced thin and sautéed like fine calf's liver. To date, only a few gold-plated big-city markets sell fresh *foie gras* and even these do not stock it regularly.

How Much Poultry Should You Buy?

Allow 3/4–1 pound ready-to-cook bird per person; in the case of Rock Cornish hens and squabs, this will mean 1 bird per person (if appetites are hearty). *(Note:* If a turkey weighs 20 pounds or more, figure about 1/2 pound ready-to-cook bird per person.) *As for poultry parts:* Drumsticks usually weigh 4–5 ounces apiece, so allow at least 2 per person; meaty thighs average about 4 ounces each, so again allow about 2 per serving; whole breasts, the meatiest part of any bird (and the lowest in calories) weigh 12–15 ounces each, so 1/2 breast per person will be sufficient.

CLEANING AND DRESSING POULTRY

The days of chasing, catching, killing, and cleaning one's own poultry belong to history. In fact, rare is the American cook who will have to do more than unwrap (and perhaps thaw) a ready-to-cook bird. *If* you're the exception, follow the steps outlined under Game Birds for plucking, singeing, and eviscerating at the end of this chapter. Domesticated birds, of course, should not be hung.

CUTTING UP POULTRY

The best way is to have the butcher do it for you—and most will gladly. Turkey and goose are too cumbersome to tackle at home, but chicken, duck, pheasant, guinea fowl, game hen, and squab can easily be cut up:

To Halve or Quarter (for all but duck; game hen and squab should be no more than halved; they're too small to quarter): Cut closely along each side of backbone and remove (1). Cut out oil sac at base of tail. Nick breast cartilage, cut through flesh and skin; pull halves apart and remove keel bone. For quarters, cut diagonally along bottom rib (2).

To Cut Up or Disjoint Chicken: Remove wings, then legs, rolling knife along curves of ball joints. Sever legs at "knee" joints, separating into drumsticks and thighs.

Remove backbone and oil sac as directed for halving and quartering, then cut up each side of body from leg joint to wing joint, using poultry shears. Halve breast and remove keel bone as directed for halving chicken.

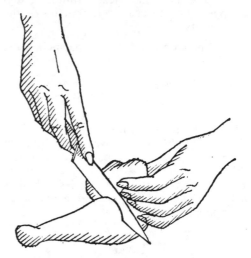

(1)

To Halve or Quarter Duck: Place breast down and with a boning knife cut from neck down each side of backbone (1). Lift backbone out. Turn breast side up, bend carcass backward so that breastbone pops up (2). Pull out breastbone. Spread duck flat and split down center to halve. To quarter, cut each half in two as shown (3).

(2)

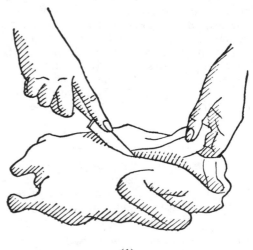

(1)

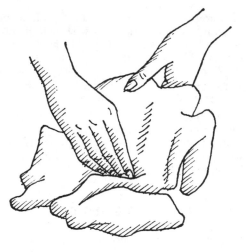

(2)

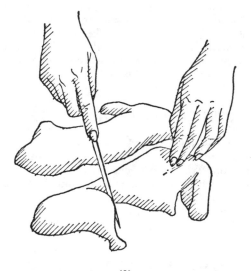

(3)

FROZEN POULTRY

All of America's popular birds come frozen and in the same market forms as fresh birds. Certain of them—Rock Cornish hens, squabs, pheasant, duck, and goose—are more readily available frozen than fresh. Among specialty items are frozen stuffed turkeys, frozen turkey rolls, and boneless roasts, frozen breaded turkey steaks (to be butter-browned like minute steaks), frozen turkey breast tenderloin (fillet), frozen whole turkey breasts, and hindquarters, frozen ground turkey, and countless precooked frozen chicken and turkey dinners.

To Be Sure of Top Quality: Buy solidly frozen birds with no discoloration or signs of freezer burn and no signs of having thawed and refrozen (a block of frozen juices at the bottom of the package).

How to Cook Frozen Poultry

You have two choices—either thaw birds thoroughly, then cook as you would fresh poultry *or* cook (whole birds or parts) from the solidly frozen state. Keep frozen poultry wrapped in foil for the first hour of cooking, then remove foil (also separate any parts); allow 1–1¼ hours *extra* cooking time. If using a *convection oven,* just increase roasting time about 50 per cent and test for doneness during the last ½ hour. *Exception:* Frozen stuffed turkeys should always be cooked from the solidly frozen state (follow package directions).

Best Ways to Thaw Frozen Poultry

Refrigerator Method: This is the safest but also the slowest. Place wrapped bird on a tray in the refrigerator. Ducks and geese will thaw in 2–3 days, chickens in 12–16 hours, chicken parts in 4–9 hours. Small birds will thaw somewhat faster.

Quick Method: Place wrapped birds in a large kettle, cover with cold water, and let stand at room temperature, changing water often. Ducks, geese, and large chickens will thaw in 2–4 hours, small chickens in about 1 hour, game hens in ½ hour.

Microwave Method: Only birds weighing 10 pounds or less should be defrosted by microwave (for larger birds, follow Special Techniques for Turkeys, next page). Leave poultry wrapped unless freezer wrapper is aluminum, in which case, unwrap, then rewrap in wax paper or plastic food wrap; remove any metal twist-ties also. Place package in a bowl (to catch drips), and defrost for half the time the microwave manufacturer recommends; unwrap for remainder of defrosting. Defrosting times will vary from microwave to microwave, also according to amount being defrosted. Two Cornish hens, for example, will take as long to defrost as one 2½–3½-pound chicken (18–22 minutes); a disjointed chicken will take 16–20 minutes with the bony pieces (wings) requiring proportionately less time than the meaty breasts and thighs (the poultry pieces should be separated as soon as possible and *rearranged* so that they will defrost evenly). Once poultry has defrosted allotted length of time, let *stand* 5–10 minutes to complete the thawing. (*Note:* After unwrapping whole birds, shield wing tips, tail, and drumstick ends with bits of foil to prevent browning or warming. The breasts of larger birds may need shielding with foil, too; check for warm or brown spots occasionally as bird defrosts.) Also, when bird is about three-fourths defrosted, remove from microwave, rinse cavity under cold running water until giblets can be removed. *Small birds* such as squabs and Rock Cornish hens should be defrosted in their wrappers for one third of the overall time, turned over and defrosted another one third of the time, still in their wrappers; unwrap for final third of time and finish defrosting as manufacturer directs.

Convection Oven Method: See Defrosting Meat in a Convection Oven; the technique is similar. Separate defrosting poultry parts (or remove giblets from body cavity) as soon as possible to speed thawing.

Special Techniques for Turkeys

Latest recommendations from the Poultry and Egg National Board are based upon how soon you want to cook the bird:

If You Want to Cook the Turkey Immediately: Unwrap frozen turkey and place on a rack in a shallow roasting pan; roast, uncovered, 1 hour at 325° F. Take turkey from oven and remove neck and giblets from body cavity and neck area; cook these immediately. Return turkey to oven *at once* and roast until done. Cook the stuffing separately.

If You Want to Cook the Turkey Later in the Day: Place wrapped turkey in a large kettle and cover with cool water; let stand at room temperature, changing water very often; or let stand in sink under a slow stream of cool water. A 5–9-pound turkey will thaw in 3–4 hours; a 12–16-pound turkey in 6–9 hours; a 16–20-pound turkey in 9–11 hours, and a 20–24-pound bird in 11–12 hours. Roast the turkey as soon as it is thawed.

If You Want to Cook the Turkey in a Day or Two: First of all, choose a bird no bigger than 12 pounds. Leave turkey in its original wrapper, set on a tray or in a baking pan and let thaw in the refrigerator.

CANNED POULTRY

Frozen and fresh poultry have all but eclipsed the canned. Most readily available are canned chicken meat (wonderful for sandwiches, salads, and casseroles), whole chicken, and an assortment of ready-to-heat dishes (fricassees, stews, à la kings, etc.). In specialty food shops you'll also find such canned delicacies as preserved goose and smoked quail or pheasant.

OTHER FORMS OF POULTRY

There is smoked turkey, some of which is ready to eat, some of which requires further cooking (read labels carefully), also, ready-to-eat barbecued turkey breast and chickens. And in Oriental groceries you'll find such exotics as dried duck feet and preserved duck.

SOME SPECIAL TERMS AND TECHNIQUES APPLYING TO POULTRY

Ballotine: A fully or partially boned bird (usually chicken or turkey), stuffed with forcemeat, reshaped, and roasted or steamed. Ballotines are usually served hot but can be served cold.

To Bard: To cover or wrap in thin sheets of fat back, salt pork, or bacon before roasting to keep a bird moist and juicy. Most poultry has enough fat of its own to ensure succulence, but guinea fowl, pheasant, and game hens may not.

To Bone: To remove all major bones; wing tips and lower leg bones are sometimes left in a bird to give it shape. Because birds are anatomically similar, all can be boned by the basic techniques below (always save bones

APPROXIMATE REFRIGERATOR THAWING TIME

Weight	Time
8 pounds	1 day
8–12 pounds	1½–2 days
12–16 pounds	2–3 days
16–20 pounds	3–4 days
20–24 pounds	3–4 days

Notes of Caution: Never thaw a bird at room temperature except by using the cool-water method (see If You Want to Cook the Turkey Later in the Day). Never let a thawed bird stand at room temperature. Refrigerate at once or, better still, roast. Never stuff a thawed bird until just before you pop it into the oven.

for making stock). Large birds are easier to bone than small ones (it's easier to see what you're doing); tiny birds like squabs or game hens are rarely boned—too tedious.

How to Bone a Whole Bird: Wipe bird with a damp cloth and pat dry; remove loose fat from body cavity. If bird is a turkey, duck, or goose, cut off wings; otherwise cut off tips at "elbow" joint. Lay bird breast side down on a board and slit center back from neck to tail (1) with a sharp knife; cut out tail and oil sac. Working down and around one side toward breast, peel flesh away from bones (2), freeing stubborn parts with the knife (it's rather like taking off a jacket). Sever ball joints at hips and shoulders (3). When you reach the ridge of the breastbone (keel bone), repeat operation on the other side, again working flesh free around back and toward breast. Lift carcass with one hand and very carefully cut against ridge, taking care not to pierce skin. Lay bird skin side down, cut and scrape all meat from leg and wing bones, turning meat and skin inside out as you go. *(Note:* If you plan to stuff and reshape the bird, leave drumstick and wing tips in; otherwise remove.) Use pliers to pull out leg tendons of turkey, goose, hen, or capon. Feel boned bird carefully for any hidden bones (the wishbone is often overlooked) and remove.

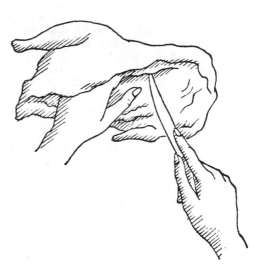

(2)

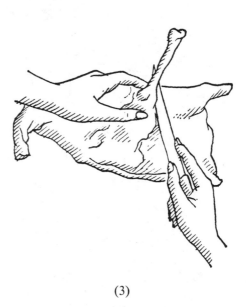

(3)

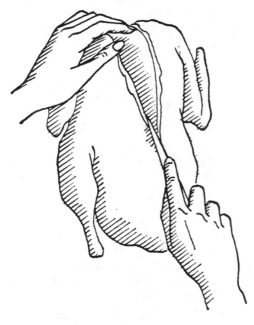

(1)

How to Bone Breasts: Whenever a recipe calls for boned breasts, buy them already boned or ask the butcher to do the boning for you. If you must do the job yourself, ask for whole breasts with left and right sides intact; they are easier to bone than split or halved breasts. Since many supermarkets sell split breasts, instructions are given here for boning whole and half breasts.

Whole Breasts: Place breast skin side down and sever white gristle at neck end of keel bone (the sharp-ridged bone in the center of the breast). Bend breast halves backward (1), then press flat, exposing keel bone. Run index finger around bone to loosen; lift out. Working with one side of breast, insert knife tip under long rib bone (2), slide knife underneath bone, cutting meat free. Work flesh free of ribs, cutting as needed around outer edge of breast up to shoulder; lift out rib cage; repeat on other side. Remove wishbone and white tendons on either side of it (3). Skin, if you like (it easily peels off).

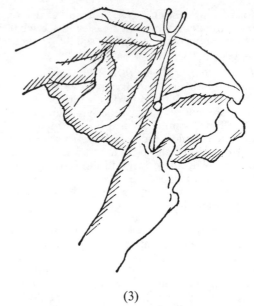

(3)

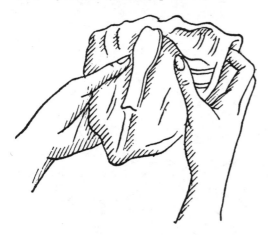

(1)

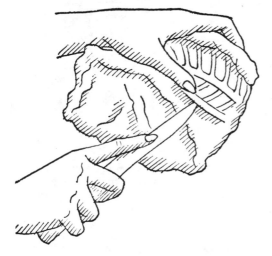

(2)

Half Breasts: Place breast skin side up, slide knife point between flesh and bottom rib, then, keeping cutting edge against rib cage, peel back flesh, using knife as needed to free stubborn bits. Lift out ribs and cut out white tendons. Skin if you like.

To Bone Drumsticks and Thighs: Cut length of drumstick or thigh on underside to bone and peel away flesh.

Deep Basted: A commercial technique of injecting butter underneath the skin of turkeys to make them buttery and juicy.

To Disjoint: To cut up a bird (usually chicken) by severing at the joints (see Cutting Up Poultry).

To Draw: To eviscerate.

Galantine: A bird, usually chicken or turkey, completely boned, then stuffed with forcemeat and shaped into a plump sausage-like roll. It is poached, then chilled and served cold, often elaborately decorated and glazed with aspic.

Giblets: The gizzard, heart, and liver of a bird (see What to Do with the Giblets).

Keel or Keel Bone: The longitudinal breastbone, sharp and ridged. In young birds it is pliable; in old birds rigid.

Oysters: The choice nuggets of dark meat found in the cavities of the hip bone.

Pinfeathers: The coarse, quill-like feathers of a bird. The easiest way to remove them is with tweezers.

To Pluck: To pick feathers from a bird.

Rack: The carcass of a bird.

To Singe: To burn off fine hairs remaining on a bird after plucking.

To Stuff: To fill the body and neck cavities of a bird with a savory dressing, with force-meat, fruit, or vegetables. Always stuff a bird loosely—so the stuffing has room to expand—and always stuff *just before cooking,* never earlier or you're flirting with food poisoning. Also, remove stuffing from leftover bird and refrigerate separately.

Suprêmes: Boned breasts of poultry (see Suprêmes of Chicken in recipe section).

To Truss: To fold a bird's wings back and under and tie its legs close to the body so it will roast more evenly (see How to Roast Poultry).

Tucked Bird: A bird (usually turkey) made more compact by having its drumsticks tucked under a flap of breast skin.

Vent: The opening at the base of the tail of a drawn bird.

Volaille: The French word for poultry.

Wishbone: The breastbone.

Should Poultry Be Brought to Room Temperature Before Cooking? Some cooks like to do so, but it is usually not practical—or even advisable—to let birds stand several hours at room temperature. Stuffed birds or those that have been thawed should never be left out on a kitchen counter—too much danger of food poisoning.

Using Meat Thermometers

Thermometers can be used when roasting large, fleshy birds, but because of the shape and boniness of poultry, the readings are not a completely reliable indicator of doneness. There are two ways to insert a thermometer in birds: in the large meaty muscle on the *inside* of the thigh so that the thermometer does not touch bone (when a chicken is done, the reading will be 185°–190° F.; for a turkey it will be 180°–185° F.); or, if a bird is stuffed, through the carcass into the center of the stuffing, again with thermometer tip not touching bone (when a bird is done, the thermometer should read 160°–165° F.).

Tests for Doneness: The old-fashioned finger tests are probably the most accurate ways to tell if a bird is done: Cover thumb and forefinger with a bit of paper towel and pinch the thickest part of the thigh; if the meat feels very soft, the bird is done. Or, grasp drumstick; if it moves easily in the hip socket, the bird is done. This last test is best for birds being stewed or steamed until very well done.

MICROWAVING POULTRY

The basic principles of cooking meat in a microwave oven apply to poultry (read Microwaving Meat in Chapter 6, also Microwave Ovens, Chapter 1). Then bear these additional guidelines in mind:

To Brown Poultry: Because of their juiciness, birds—either whole or disjointed—will not brown well in a microwave unless given extra attention. You can brown birds *before* microwaving on top of the stove or *after* microwaving in the broiler (especially good for crisping duck skin); you can use a microwave browning tray or grill; you can coat the poultry (especially appropriate for parts) with browned crumbs and/or nuts, or you can brush it at the outset with barbecue sauce, 1/4 cup melted butter brightened with about 2 teaspoons paprika, or with a 1/2 and 1/2 mix of liquid gravy browner and water.

To Cook Whole Birds: Size affects cooking time (a 3–5-pound chicken or duck will cook 30–50 per cent faster than in a conventional oven). Stuff birds or not, as you like. But if you *do* stuff, *avoid packing stuffing* into the body cavity; spoon it in *lightly.* Place bird in a microwave-safe container, breast-side down, cover with wax paper, and cook for half of allotted time; turn breast-side up, shield wings and drumstick tips with foil to prevent burning or drying, re-cover loosely with wax paper, and finish cooking. Remove from oven, cover with aluminum foil and let *stand* (5–10 minutes is usually sufficient for small birds, 15–20 for large ones), *then test for doneness* by wiggling leg in hip socket (if it moves easily, bird is done). The surest test of doneness is a microwave *temperature probe* (by all means use it, if your oven has one). *Note:* If you have stuffed the bird, insert the probe in the middle of the stuffing (or insert a spot-check thermometer at the end of the *standing time);* when the bird is done, the stuffing will be 160°–165° F. *Caution:* Do not attempt to microwave *whole* birds weighing more than 8 pounds. They will not cook evenly.

To Cook Disjointed Birds (and this includes turkey parts): Arrange meatiest pieces toward outside edge of a microwave-safe pan and cover with wax paper. Midway through cooking, rotate pan 180° or turn poultry pieces. At the end of microwaving, let *stand* about 5 minutes on the counter. This completes the cooking.

And a Few Miscellaneous Tips That Apply to Cooking All Kinds of Poultry in the Microwave:
• When stewing or braising poultry, reduce amount of liquid recipe calls for by about one fourth.
• Do not salt poultry until the final *standing time.*
• Prick poultry livers with a fork before microwaving to reduce sputtering.

COOKING POULTRY IN A CONVECTION OVEN

The principal difference between cooking poultry in a convection oven and a conventional oven is that the convection oven, thanks to its circulating hot air, is faster. Fresh and frozen birds cook in three-fourths the time. As when cooking meats, you can compensate for the convection oven's quickness by reducing oven temperatures 25° F., but never use temperatures below 300° F. (read Cooking Meat in a Convection Oven, Chapter 6, also Convection Ovens, Chapter 1). When *roasting whole birds,* place oven rack in middle or lower position, then set bird breast-side up directly on rack and slide a drip tray on the oven floor; do not cover the bird. Insert a *temperature probe* or meat thermometer in inside thigh if bird is not stuffed, otherwise insert it in the middle of the stuffing; when three fourths of roasting time has elapsed, test frequently for doneness (use internal temperatures in Poultry Roasting Chart as a guide). *(Note:* You won't need to turn or baste a bird as it roasts in a convection oven.) When *cooking casseroles in the convection oven,* use the temperatures recipes specify, but check for doneness when about 75 per cent of the cooking time is up. To brown and crispen the surface of a casserole, remove the cover for final 15 minutes of baking.

HOW TO ROAST POULTRY

Best Birds: Chickens (broiler-fryers, roasters, capons), young turkeys, Rock Cornish hens, pheasants, ducklings, and geese.

Basic Preparation for Cooking: Remove neck and giblets from body cavities (save giblets for gravy or use in stuffing; see What to Do with the Giblets). Also remove any loose fat from body cavity. Wipe bird with a damp cloth but do not wash (most birds coming to market today are beautifully cleaned and dressed; washing them merely destroys some of their flavor). Singe off any hairs and remove pinfeathers. Sprinkle neck and body cavities with salt.

To Stuff a Bird: You'll need about ½ cup stuffing per pound of bird. Choose a stuffing that complements the bird you're roasting, then spoon stuffing *loosely* into both body and neck cavities. If you pack stuffing into a bird, it will become tough and rubbery in cooking. If a particular recipe makes more stuffing than a bird will hold, simply wrap the leftover in foil and bake alongside the bird in the pan. *(Note:* Do not stuff a bird until *just* before roasting; and do not let a stuffed bird stand at room temperature. Ever.)

To Truss a Bird: After stuffing bird, skewer or sew openings shut as shown, then truss by folding the wings back and underneath body and tying drumsticks close to body so bird will have a more compact shape and roast more evenly. *Note:* "Tucked" birds (those with their drumsticks inserted under a band of skin) or turkeys with metal clamps holding their legs together need not be trussed, but *do* fold wings under against the back.

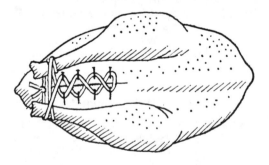

Chicken

Note: Although poultry industry spokespersons are now recommending roasting chicken at 350° F., we think it's juicier and crisper of skin when roasted at 400° F.

Whole Birds: Preheat oven to 400° F. if bird weighs 2 pounds or less, to 375° F. if between 2½ and 4 pounds, and to 325° F. if more than 4 pounds. Prepare bird for roasting as directed, place breast side up on a rack in a shallow roasting pan and brush, if you like, with melted butter or margarine or cooking oil. Insert meat thermometer in thigh or stuffing,* not touching bone. Roast, uncovered, using times given in Poultry Roasting Chart as a guide. *(Note:* For extra flavor, baste often during cooking with a seasoned butter or, if you prefer, glaze,* during last 1/2 hour of roasting—see Some Marinades and Glazes for Poultry.)

Chicken Halves or Quarters: Preheat oven to 400° F. Wipe pieces of chicken with a damp cloth and place skin side up in a lightly greased shallow roasting pan. Brush with melted butter or cooking oil and sprinkle with salt and pepper. Roast uncovered, without turning, until tender and browned, brushing, if needed to keep chicken moist, with additional butter or oil. Use times in roasting chart as a guide.

VARIATION

Oven-Barbecued Chicken: Marinate pieces of chicken in any favorite barbecue sauce 1 hour at room temperature. Preheat oven to 350° F. Place chicken skin side down in a foil-lined shallow baking pan and roast, uncovered, 1/2 hour. Turn, brush with barbecue sauce, and roast 1/2 hour longer. Brush again with sauce and roast 15 minutes longer, basting frequently with sauce.

Turkey

Breast-Up Method for a Whole Bird: This is the preferred way today; it produces an exquisitely brown bird. Preheat oven to 325° F. Prepare turkey for roasting as directed and place breast side up on a rack in a shallow roasting pan. Insert meat thermometer in thigh or stuffing,* not touching bone, and roast, uncovered, according to times given in Poultry Roasting Chart. Baste, if you like, with melted butter or margarine every 1/2–3/4 hour. If bird browns too fast, tent breast loosely with foil.

VARIATION

Beer-and-Butter-Basted Turkey: Rub turkey well with softened butter, then roast as directed, rubbing with additional softened butter every 1/2 hour and basting with about 1/2 cup beer. You'll need about 1/4 pound butter and 2–3 (12-ounce) cans of beer.

Breast-Down Method for a Whole Bird: Though this method produces juicier breast meat, it has disadvantages: The breast skin is apt to stick to the rack and tear as the turkey is being turned and the act of turning a hot, hefty turkey is both difficult and dangerous. Preheat oven to 325° F. Prepare turkey for roasting as directed and place breast side down in an oiled V rack in a shallow

roasting pan. Roast, uncovered, until half done according to roasting chart, turn breast side up, insert meat thermometer in thickest part of inside thigh,* not touching bone, and continue roasting, uncovered, until done. Baste, if you like, during cooking with drippings or melted butter.

Fast Foil Method for a Whole Bird: This is the method to use for birds, especially big ones, that must be cooked in a "hurry." Turkeys cooked this way will have more of a steamed than roasted flavor. Preheat oven to 450° F. Prepare turkey for roasting as directed and place in the center of a large sheet of heavy foil; brush well with softened butter, margarine, or shortening. Bring foil up on both sides of breast and make a simple overlapping fold at the top, smooth down around turkey, then crumple ends of foil up to hold in juices. Place turkey breast side up in a shallow roasting pan and roast as follows:

Ready-to-Cook Weight	Total Roasting Time
6–8 pounds	1 1/2–2 hours
8–12 pounds	2–2 1/2 hours
12–16 pounds	2 1/2–3 hours
16–20 pounds	3–3 1/2 hours
20–24 pounds	3 1/2–4 hours

About 30–40 minutes before turkey is done, open tent of foil and fold back and away from bird so it will brown nicely.

(Note: When roasting turkey by any of the three preceding methods, it's a good idea to cut string holding drumsticks to tail about 1 hour before bird is done so that inner legs and thighs will brown.)

Turkey Halves or Quarters: Preheat oven to 325° F. Wipe pieces of turkey with a damp cloth and pat dry; skewer skin to meat around edges to prevent it from shrinking during cooking; tie leg to tail, lay wing flat over breast meat, and tie string around to hold in place. Place pieces of turkey skin side up on a rack in a shallow roasting pan and brush well with melted butter or margarine; sprinkle with salt and pepper. Insert meat thermometer in center of inside thigh muscle. Roast, uncovered, basting occasionally with drippings or additional melted butter, using times in Poultry Roasting Chart as a guide.

Cut-Up Turkey: Preheat oven to 325° F. Wipe pieces with a damp cloth and pat dry, place skin side up on a rack in a shallow roasting pan, brush well with melted butter or margarine, and sprinkle with salt and pepper. Roast, uncovered, basting occasionally with drippings or extra melted butter, using times in Poultry Roasting Chart as a guide.

Rock Cornish Hens and Squabs

Preheat oven to 350° F. Prepare birds for roasting as directed. Rub well with softened butter or margarine or drape with strips of bacon or fat back. Place breast side up on a rack in a shallow roasting pan and roast, uncovered, basting often with drippings or melted butter, according to times given in Poultry Roasting Chart.

VARIATIONS

Napa Valley Roast Rock Cornish Hens or Squabs: Stuff each bird with 1/4 cup seedless green grapes that have been tossed with 1 teaspoon sugar. Brush generously with a hot mixture of 1/4 cup melted butter, 1 tablespoon honey, 1 teaspoon seasoned salt, and 1/8 teaspoon pepper. Place breast side up on a rack in a shallow roasting pan, add 1/2 cup each sauterne and water to pan, and roast as directed, basting often.

Mustardy Rock Cornish Hens or Squabs in Lemon Cream Sauce: Spread each hen with 1 teaspoon Dijon mustard, then roast as directed. Halve birds and set aside. For each bird, heat 1 cup heavy cream and 1 teaspoon finely grated lemon rind in a double boiler over simmering water 10 minutes; for each bird, lightly beat 1 egg yolk. Blend a little hot mixture into yolks, return to pan, and heat and stir over simmering water until slightly thickened. Pour off all but 1 tablespoon drippings from roasting pan, add cream sauce, stirring to scrape up browned bits. Add salt, pepper, and, if you like, lemon juice to taste. Return hens to pan and set in oven turned to lowest heat; let warm 10 minutes. Serve in a deep platter smothered with sauce.

Duck or Goose

Whole Birds: Preheat oven to 350° F. Prepare bird for roasting as directed. Also rub inside well with 1/2 lemon before stuffing. Prick skin well all over with a sharp fork so fat underneath will drain off during cooking. Rub skin well with salt (this helps to crispen skin). Place bird breast side up on a rack in a shallow roasting pan and roast, uncovered, draining off drippings as they accumulate and pricking as needed. Use times in Poultry Roasting Chart as a guide. (*Note:* For a particularly crisp skin, raise oven temperature to 450° F. during last 1/2 hour of roasting.) Also drain all drippings from pan and spoon 1/4–1/2 cup ice water over bird. Or, if you prefer, glaze* bird during last part of roasting—see Some Marinades and Glazes for Poultry.

Some Notes About Goose Stuffings: In Europe, very simple stuffings are popular: quartered, cored tart apples sprinkled with cinnamon or nutmeg and sometimes mixed with plumped raisins; drained sauerkraut mixed with caraway seeds; or equal parts minced apples, celery, and cranberries or pitted dried prunes or apricots.

VARIATIONS

Roast Duck or Goose with Sauerkraut and Applesauce: Roast bird as directed and 1/2 hour before it is done remove rack and drain off all drippings. Place a 1″ bed drained sauerkraut in bottom of pan, add 1/2 cup applesauce or whole cranberry sauce, and toss well to mix. Place bird breast side up on sauerkraut and finish roasting as directed. Serve wreathed with the sauerkraut.

Orange-Tea-Glazed Roast Duck or Goose: Roast bird as directed, basting every 20 minutes with the following mixture: 2 cups hot strong tea blended with 1/4 cup honey and the slivered rind of 1 orange. Sprinkle with a little extra grated rind just before serving. (*Note:* For distinctive flavor, add 1/2 teaspoon Formosa Oolong tea to the regular when brewing.)

Duckling Halves or Quarters: Preheat oven to 450° F. Wipe pieces of duckling with a damp cloth and pat dry; prick skin well all over with a sharp fork. Place skin side up on a rack in a shallow roasting pan and roast, uncovered, 1/2 hour; lower oven temperature to 350° F. and roast 1 1/2 hours longer until tender. Drain off drippings as they accumulate. Glaze,* if you like, during last 1/2 hour of cooking (see Some Marinades and Glazes for Poultry).

HOW TO SPIT-ROAST POULTRY

Best Birds: Chicken (broiler-fryers, roasters, capons), young turkeys, Rock Cornish hens, ducklings, and geese.

Basic Preparation for Cooking: The same as for roasting. *Do not stuff bird.* Tie drumsticks firmly to tail; skewer neck skin to

POULTRY ROASTING CHART

Note: Times given are for birds taken from the refrigerator and stuffed. Reduce total roasting times by about 15 minutes if small birds are unstuffed, by 30–45 minutes for unstuffed turkey or goose. Times are approximate at best, so test often for doneness toward end of cooking.

Bird	Oven Temperature	Total Cooking Time in Hours	Special Treatment Needed	Internal Temperature When Done
Chicken				
2 pounds	400° F.	1–1½	Tent bird loosely with foil if	190° F.
2½–4 pounds	375° F.	1½–2¼	it browns too fast.	190° F.
5–9 pounds	325° F.	3–5		190° F.
Halves or quarters	400° F.	¾–1		190° F.
Turkey (whole)				
4–8 pounds	325° F.	1¾–2¾	Tent bird loosely with foil	180°–185° F.
8–12 pounds	325° F.	3½–4	or cover breast with butter-	180°–185° F.
12–16 pounds	325° F.	4–4½	soaked cheesecloth if it	180°–185° F.
16–20 pounds	325° F.	4½–5	browns too fast.	180°–185° F.
20–24 pounds	325° F.	5–6		180°–185° F.
Turkey halves or quarters				
5–8 pounds	325° F.	2½–3	Tent loosely with foil if	180°–185° F.
8–10 pounds	325° F.	3–3½	browning too fast.	180°–185° F.
10–12 pounds	325° F.	3½–4		180°–185° F.
Boneless turkey rolls and roasts (unstuffed)				
3–4 pounds	325° F.	2½–3	Tent loosely with foil if	170°–175° F.
4–5 pounds	325° F.	3–3½	browning too fast.	170°–175° F.
Turkey breasts (unstuffed)				
2–4 pounds	350° F.	1–1¾	Tent loosely with foil if	180°–185° F.
4–6 pounds	350° F.	1¾–2¼	browning too fast.	180°–185° F.
6–8 pounds	350° F.	2¼–2¾		180°–185° F.
8–10 pounds	350° F.	2¾–3¼		180°–185° F.
10–12 pounds	350° F.	3¼–3¾		180°–185° F.
Rock Cornish hens and squabs				
¾–1½ pounds	350° F.	¾–1¼	Brush often with melted butter or drippings.	—
Farm-raised pheasant				
2–4 pounds	350° F.	1½–2¼	Brush or baste often with melted butter or drippings.	—
Duck (whole)				
4–5½ pounds	350° F.	2¼–2¾	Prick often with a sharp fork throughout cooking and drain off drippings as they collect.	—
Duckling halves and quarters	450° F. for ½ hour *THEN* 350° F. for 1½ hours	2		

Bird	Oven Temperature	Total Cooking Time in Hours	Special Treatment Needed	Internal Temperature When Done
Goose				
4–6 pounds	325° F.	2³/4–3	Prick goose often with a	—
6–8 pounds	325° F.	3–3¹/2	sharp fork during cooking	—
8–12 pounds	325° F.	3¹/2–4¹/2	and drain off drippings as	—
12–14 pounds	325° F.	4¹/2–5	they collect. Also allow	—
			about ¹/2 hour margin in	
			cooking times at left	
			according to breed of goose;	
			some cook faster than	
			others.	

Note: If meat thermometer is inserted in center of stuffing (not touching bone) instead of in thigh, bird should be done when thermometer reads 160°–165° F. The legs of all birds except chicken and turkeys are too skimpy to hold a meat thermometer, so if a thermometer is used, it must be inserted in the stuffing.

back, flatten wings against sides of breast, and tie string around breast to hold wings in. Insert spit lengthwise, slightly on the diagonal, through bird from vent to the top of the breastbone; tighten holding forks. Test balance of bird on spit and readjust, if necessary, so bird will turn smoothly. If bird is large enough to do so, insert meat thermometer in center of plump inside thigh muscle and make sure thermometer will clear unit as spit turns. *(Note:* If spitting several small birds, allow about ¹/2″ between birds so heat will circulate freely.)

To Spit-Roast in Oven, Gas or Electric Barbecue, or Rotisserie: Preheat unit. Prepare and spit bird as directed, attach spit to rotisserie, and roast, using times in Poultry Spit-Roasting Chart as a guide.

Note: Times are for birds taken straight from the refrigerator; they can be used as a guide only. Chicken, turkey, and boneless turkey roasts only are of a size and shape to make use of meat thermometer practical. Test birds for doneness often after minimum cooking time is up. When spit-roasting fat birds like duck or goose, watch carefully and drain off drippings as they accumulate.

To Spit-Roast over Charcoal: Build a moderately hot charcoal fire. Prepare and spit bird as directed. Attach spit to motor, adjust spit height so it is 5″ from coals, and place a drip pan where it will catch the drippings (especially important with duck and goose). Roast, increasing times given for oven spit-roasting by ¹/4–¹/2 hour, depending on size of bird and the weather (on a cool, windy day, overall cooking times may need to be increased by as much as ³/4 hour for large birds). Watch birds carefully toward end of cooking and test often for doneness.

VARIATION

Spit-Barbecued Birds: Prepare and spit-roast as directed, brushing often during last ¹/2 hour of cooking with any barbecue sauce.

HOW TO BROIL POULTRY

Basic Preparation for Cooking: Have small chickens and ducklings halved, larger ones quartered; turkeys should be cut up. Wipe the birds with a damp cloth.

To Broil in the Oven: Preheat broiler. Place bird skin side down on a lightly greased broiler rack. Brush chicken or turkey with melted butter or margarine or cooking oil, but not duckling. Duckling should be pricked well all over so that the fat underneath skin can drain off during broiling. Broil according to table above, brushing chicken or turkey well with additional melted butter after turning and throughout cooking as needed. Duckling should be pricked throughout cooking and its drippings drained off as they accumulate.

Note: Times given in the Poultry Broiling Chart can be used only as a guide; test often for doneness toward end of minimum cooking time: twist a drumstick in its socket; if it pulls loose, bird is done. Or make a tiny slit down to bone; if no pink meat remains, bird

POULTRY SPIT-ROASTING CHART

Bird	Total Spit-Roasting Time	Internal Temperature When Done
Chicken		
2–3 pounds	1–1¼ hours	190° F.
4–5 pounds	1½–2 hours	190° F.
6–8 pounds	2½–3¼ hours	190° F.
Turkey		
4–6 pounds	2–3 hours	180°–185° F.
6–8 pounds	3–3½ hours	180°–185° F.
8–10 pounds	3½–4 hours	180°–185° F.
10–12 pounds	4–5 hours	180°–185° F.
Turkey Breast (with bone)		
2–4 pounds	1½–2	170°–180° F.
4–6 pounds	2–2½	170°–180° F.
6–8 pounds	2½–3	170°–180° F.
8–10 pounds	3–3½	170°–180° F.

Boneless Turkey Roasts (If there are wrapper directions for spit-roasting, follow them; otherwise, use times below. Let roast "rest" ½ hour at room temperature before carving.)

3–4 pounds	2–3 hours	170°–175° F.
4–5 pounds	3–3½ hours	170°–175° F.
Rock Cornish Hens and Squabs		
¾–1½ pounds	40–45 minutes	—
Duck		
4–5 pounds	1½–2½ hours	—
Goose		
4–6 pounds	2–3 hours	—

is done. Livers of birds can be broiled too. Toward end of cooking, brush well with melted butter or margarine, place on broiler rack, and broil 3–5 minutes per side, depending on size.

To Charcoal-Broil: Build a moderately hot charcoal fire. Adjust height of grill so it is 6″–8″ from coals. Prepare bird as directed; brush chicken and turkey well with cooking oil, melted butter or margarine; prick duck skin all over with a sharp fork. Place bird skin side up on a lightly greased grill and broil, turning often, until tender. Chicken will need 50–60 minutes altogether, depending on size; turkey 1½–1¾ hours; and duck 1–1½ hours. Brush chicken and turkey throughout broiling with additional oil or melted butter; prick duck often (also be pre-

pared to douse flare-ups). If day is cool and gusty, you'll have to increase cooking times somewhat. (*Note:* Outdoor gas and electric barbecue grills can be used the same way; cooking times will remain the same. Remember to preheat them.)

VARIATIONS

Recipes too flexible for meaningful nutritional counts.

⚖ **Low-Calorie Broiled Chicken or Turkey:** Broil or charcoal-broil as directed, brushing with low-calorie garlic, herb, or Italian dressing instead of oil, butter, or margarine.

Marinated or Barbecued Birds: Marinate birds in any marinade or barbecue sauce 3–4 hours in refrigerator before cooking; broil or charcoal-broil as directed, brushing often

POULTRY BROILING CHART

Bird	Best Weight for Broiling	Distance from Heat	Minutes on First Side	Minutes on Second Side
Chicken	2–3 pounds	6″	20–25	15–20
Turkey	4–6 pounds	9″	40	40–50
Duckling	3 pounds or less	7″–8″	30	30–45

with marinade or sauce during last ½ hour of cooking.

Lemon-Broiled Chicken or Turkey: Mix ½ cup melted butter or margarine with the juice of 1 lemon and ½ teaspoon rosemary. *(Note:* For turkey, double quantities.) Brush liberally over bird and broil or charcoal-broil as directed, brushing often.

Portuguese-Style Charcoal-Broiled Chicken or Turkey: Mix ¼ cup olive oil with 2 peeled and crushed cloves garlic, 1 tablespoon paprika, 1 teaspoon salt, and ⅛ teaspoon pepper. *(Note:* Double amounts for turkey.) Brush bird well with mixture and let stand at room temperature ½ hour. Broil or charcoal-broil as directed, brushing often with mixture.

Chicken in a Basket over Charcoal: Place cut-up chicken in a metal rotisserie basket, balance basket in center of spit, and tighten screws. Attach spit to motor and position so center of basket is 5″–6″ from coals. Broil chicken 1½–1¾ hours or until fork tender and golden. *(Note:* Keep an eye on wings because tips sometimes catch in basket and brown unevenly. *Stop basket* before adjusting.) When chicken is done, remove from basket and sprinkle with salt and pepper. *(Note:* Chicken can be marinated 3–4 hours in any barbecue sauce in refrigerator before cooking.)

Chicken in Foil over Charcoal: Butter 4 (12″) squares heavy foil well; lay 1 chicken quarter in the center of each, sprinkle with salt and pepper, and wrap tight. Grill 3″–4″ from glowing coals 1–1¼ hours until tender, turning packages halfway through cooking. Unwrap chicken, place skin side down on grill, cover loosely with foil, and brown 4–5 minutes. *(Note:* Chicken can be marinated 3–4 hours in any barbecue sauce or marinade [see Some Marinades and Glazes for Poultry] in refrigerator before cooking. Include 1–2 tablespoons marinade in each foil package and brush with marinade during final browning.)

HOW TO FRY POULTRY

Best Birds: Chicken and very small, young turkey.

Basic Preparation for Cooking: Have birds cut up; wipe with a damp cloth but do not pat dry.

To Panfry (Sauté) Chicken

Dredge by shaking 1–2 pieces at a time in a bag in seasoned flour (⅔ cup unsifted flour, 1 teaspoon salt, ¼ teaspoon pepper, and, if you like, ¼ teaspoon paprika for 1 bird). Pour ½″ cooking oil or melted shortening in a large, heavy skillet and heat over moderately high heat until a cube of bread will sizzle. Put larger, meatier pieces of chicken skin side down in hot fat; add remaining chicken and fry, uncovered, 15–25 minutes on each side, adjusting heat as needed so chicken does not brown too fast. Turn chicken only once during cooking. Add liver and heart during last few minutes. Drain chicken on paper toweling and serve.

VARIATIONS

Chili-Fried Chicken: Prepare as directed, adding 1 tablespoon chili powder to seasoned flour.

Curry-Fried Chicken: Prepare as directed, adding 2–3 teaspoons curry powder and ¼ teaspoon ginger to seasoned flour.

Cheesy-Fried Chicken: Prepare as directed, reducing flour in seasoned flour to ½ cup and adding ½ cup finely grated Parmesan cheese and 1 teaspoon oregano or marjoram.

Crisp-Fried Chicken: Dip pieces of chicken in buttermilk, or light cream, then dredge in self-rising flour and fry as directed.

To Panfry (Sauté) Turkey

This is really a combination of frying and braising. Have a small (4–9-pound) turkey cut up. For each 5 pounds of turkey, blend together 3/4 cup unsifted flour, 2 teaspoons each salt and paprika, and 1/4 teaspoon pepper. Dredge turkey in seasoned flour by shaking in a paper bag. Pour enough cooking oil or melted shortening in a large, heavy skillet to cover bottom; heat over moderately high heat until a cube of bread will sizzle. Begin browning turkey, biggest pieces first. Slip smaller pieces in and around the large ones. Brown about 20 minutes, turning as needed with tongs so pieces brown evenly. Add 2–4 tablespoons water, cover, and cook over low heat 3/4–1 hour until turkey is tender. Turn pieces two or three times as they cook. Uncover and cook 10 minutes longer to crispen. (*Note:* The liver may be added during the last 15 minutes.)

To Pan- and Oven-Fry Chicken (Combination Method)

Preheat oven to 350° F. Dredge and brown chicken as for panfrying; transfer to an ungreased shallow baking pan, arranging pieces skin side up in a single layer. Bake, uncovered, 35–45 minutes until tender.

To Deep-Fat-Fry Chicken

Prepare a small (2–2½-pound) broiler-fryer for frying as directed above. Beat 1 egg with 1/4 cup cold milk; also mix 1 cup unsifted flour with 1 teaspoon salt and 1/4 teaspoon pepper. Dip chicken in egg, roll in flour to coat evenly, and fry, 3–4 pieces at a time, in 360° F. deep fat 15–17 minutes until richly browned all over. Drain on paper toweling.

VARIATIONS

Southern Fried Chicken: Let chicken marinate in milk to cover 1 hour at room temperature. Dip in egg mixture as directed, then dredge in 1/2 cup unsifted flour mixed with 3/4 cup cracker meal, 1 tablespoon paprika, 1½ teaspoons salt, and 1/4 teaspoon pepper. Fry in deep fat as directed.

Batter-Fried Chicken: Prepare 1 recipe Basic Batter for Fried Foods. Dip a 2–2½-pound cut-up chicken in batter, then fry, 3–4 pieces at a time, in 350°–360° F. deep fat 15–17 minutes until nut brown. Drain on paper toweling. (*Note:* Because the batter acts as an insulator and slows cooking, use only the very smallest chickens for batter-frying.)

To Oven-Fry Chicken

Preheat oven to 350° F. Place a large, shallow roasting pan in oven, add 1/4 pound butter or margarine and let melt as oven preheats. Meanwhile, dredge chicken pieces in seasoned flour as for panfrying. Roll chicken in the melted butter, then arrange skin side up 1 layer deep and bake, uncovered, 1–1¼ hours until fork tender and browned.

VARIATIONS

Chicken Italiano: Lightly beat 1 egg with the juice of 1 lemon. Dip chicken pieces in egg, then in 1 cup Italian-style seasoned bread crumbs. Place in a single layer in a greased large, shallow baking pan, drizzle with 1/2 cup melted butter or margarine, and bake as directed.

Chicken Parmesan: Dip chicken pieces in 2/3 cup melted butter or margarine into which you have crushed 1 clove garlic, then roll in 1 cup soft white bread crumbs mixed with 1/3 cup finely grated Parmesan, 2 tablespoons minced parsley, 1 teaspoon salt, and 1/8 teaspoon pepper to coat evenly. Arrange 1 layer deep in a greased large, shallow baking pan and drizzle evenly with remaining melted butter. Bake as directed.

Crispy Oven-Fried Chicken: Dredge chicken pieces in 2/3 cup unsifted flour mixed with 1 teaspoon each salt and paprika, 1/2 teaspoon savory, and 1/4 teaspoon pepper. Dip in 1 egg that has been lightly beaten with 1/4 cup cold milk, then roll in 2/3 cup cracker meal mixed with 3 tablespoons minced parsley to coat evenly. Arrange 1 layer deep in a greased large, shallow baking pan and drizzle with 1/2 cup melted butter or margarine. Bake as directed.

To Oven-Fry Turkey

Preheat oven to 400° F. Place 1 cup butter (for each 5 pounds turkey) in a large, shallow roasting pan and let melt in preheating oven. Dredge a small (4–9-pound) cut-up turkey in seasoned flour (1½ cups unsifted flour, 1 tablespoon salt, 1/2 teaspoon pepper), roll in melted butter in pan, then arrange skin side down 1 layer deep in pan. Bake, uncovered, 3/4 hour, turn skin side up, and bake 3/4 hour longer until fork tender and nicely browned.

HOW TO BRAISE POULTRY

Braising is an all-encompassing word used to describe foods that are browned in fat, then cooked, covered, with some additional liquid. Fricasseeing is a way of braising, so is cooking birds en casserole. Any bird can be braised, but it's an especially good way to deal with those that are a bit too tough to roast, broil, or fry. See the collection of recipes that follow.

HOW TO SIMMER POULTRY

Birds can be *poached* in a small amount of liquid or *stewed* in quantities of it. Disjointed young chickens or parts of them (especially the breasts) are frequently poached before being used in recipes. Stewing is usually reserved for tough, over-the-hill birds that need long and slow simmering to make them tender.

Best Birds: Any birds can be stewed, though chickens are the ones that most often end up in the kettle. The methods given below can be used for other birds as well as for chicken.

To Poach

(Also see Suprêmes of Chicken.)

Basic Preparation for Cooking: Have bird disjointed; wipe pieces with a damp cloth.

Basic Method: Place chicken pieces in a single layer in a large, heavy skillet (not iron), add water, chicken broth, or a 1/2 and 1/2 mixture of broth and dry white wine almost to cover. Also add, if you like, 1 bay leaf and 1 sprig each parsley and thyme, tied in cheesecloth. Cover and simmer 30–35 minutes until tender. Remove and use in any recipes calling for cooked or poached chicken.

To Stew

Basic Preparation for Cooking: If bird is whole, remove giblets and neck from body cavities; also pull out any loose fat and discard. Wipe bird or pieces of bird with a damp cloth.

Basic Method: Place bird or pieces in a large, heavy kettle and add water almost to cover —a large hen or capon will require about 3 quarts. Add 1 teaspoon salt and, if you like, a small onion peeled and quartered or stuck with 3–4 cloves, 2–3 stalks celery and/or parsley, 2 bay leaves, and 6 peppercorns. Or, if you prefer, add 1 bay leaf and 1 sprig each parsley and thyme, tied in cheesecloth. Cover and simmer slowly until tender. Times vary enormously according to the size and age of the bird. An old hen can take 2–3 hours to become tender, but a capon of the same or slightly larger size may be nearly falling off the bones after only 1 hour. So watch the pot closely. Plump broiler-fryers will be done in 40–55 minutes and a cut-up broiler-fryer or capon in about 25–40. Some parts (wings and backs), of course, cook more quickly than others; remove individual pieces from the kettle as they become tender. (*Note:* Neck, heart, and gizzard can be cooked along with the other parts of the chicken and will probably need the full cooking time. The liver [and sometimes heart] will cook in 10–15 minutes, so cook at the beginning, remove and reserve, or add at the end of cooking.)

HOW TO STEAM POULTRY

Best Birds: Moderately young and tender chickens or capons.

Best Preparation for Cooking: Same as for stewing.

Basic Method: Place whole or cut-up bird on a rack in a large kettle, pour in water to a depth of 1″, cover, and bring to a boil. Reduce heat so water just simmers and steam, adding additional water if kettle threatens to boil dry, until bird is tender. A cut-up bird will cook in about 3/4 hour, a whole bird in 1–1½. Use steamed chicken in recipes calling for cooked chicken.

PRESSURE-COOKING POULTRY

Only tough old birds should be pressure cooked; young tender ones will fall to pieces. Because cooker techniques differ from model to model, follow manufacturer's instructions. Place chicken, liquid and, if you like, a few chunks of celery, onion, and carrot in cooker, cover, and cook at 15 pounds pressure 25–35 minutes or as manufacturer advises. Lower pressure slowly.

WHAT TO DO WITH THE GIBLETS

You can freeze giblets separately in small plastic bags and save them until you have enough to use in a recipe (see recipes for chicken livers that follow). Or the giblets can be used immediately in stuffings or gravies or slipped into any of the recipes calling for cooked poultry. But first they must be cooked.

To Cook Giblets

Wash giblets carefully in cool water; if liver is green, discard—the gall bladder has ruptured, spilling its bitter gall and ruining the liver. Place giblets in a small saucepan and, if you like, the neck. Add *just* enough cold water to cover, cover pan, and simmer over low heat 10–15 minutes. Remove liver and reserve, also remove heart if it is tender. Recover and simmer remaining giblets until tender, 1–2 hours—time will depend on size and age of bird; add additional water during cooking as needed. Remove giblets, mince, and use in recipes calling for cooked poultry meat; also reserve cooking liquid to use in soups and gravies.

To Make Giblet Stock

Cook as directed above, but increase amount of water to 2–3 cups, depending on size of giblets, and add 1 teaspoon salt; replenish water as needed during cooking. Taste stock for seasoning and adjust; if you wish, strain through a fine sieve lined with a double thickness of cheesecloth before using in recipes. Mince giblets and use in any recipes calling for cooked poultry meat.

POULTRY STOCKS

Any liquid used for poaching or stewing a bird is stock and should be saved to use in cooking vegetables, making sauces and gravies. Specific recipes for chicken and turkey broths can be found in the chapter on soups.

HOW TO RENDER POULTRY FAT

Poultry fats are excellent for browning poultry, potatoes, and other vegetables. Carefully rendered raw chicken or goose fat can be used as the shortening in biscuits and other hot breads. Jewish cooks render chicken fat with an apple and onion into *schmaltz,* which they use as a butter substitute. Goose fat has an especially delicate flavor and is an essential ingredient of fine pâtés and *confit d'oie* (preserved goose); in the Southwest of France, the more flavorful duck fat is often used in *confits.* The best fats to render are those pulled raw from the body cavity of a bird. But pan drippings from a roasting bird can be saved, clarified* (see To Clarify Meat Drippings in the meat chapter), and used for gravies or browning meats and vegetables.

General Preparation of Fat: Pull fat from body cavity of bird, rinse in cold water, and cut in ½" cubes.

Stove-Top Method of Rendering

(Note: This method also clarifies the fat.) Place prepared fat in a large, heavy saucepan and add enough cold water to come about halfway up fat. Heat, uncovered, over moderately low heat, stirring frequently, until all fat is melted. Continue heating and stirring until nearly all water has evaporated; liquid will become clear and golden and bubbles will almost subside; strain through a double thickness of cheesecloth, cool, and chill. Carefully lift off fat and discard any liquid that has settled to the bottom; also scrape off any milky, semiliquid layer on bottom of fat. Pack fat in containers, cover, and refrigerate or freeze.

V A R I A T I O N

Seasoned Fat: Render as directed but add 1 peeled and minced onion and 1 peeled and cored tart green apple, cut in wedges, to the pan; remove apple the instant it becomes tender, but leave onion in until almost all water evaporates unless it browns too much. Strain, cool, and store as directed.

Oven Method of Rendering

Preheat oven to 250° F. Spread prepared fat in the bottom of a shallow baking pan and add about ½ cup cold water. Heat, uncovered, stirring occasionally, until fat is melted and most of the water evaporates. Strain, cool, and store as above. To clarify, follow directions for clarifying rendered fat in the meat chapter.

HOW TO CARVE POULTRY

Except for minor variations, the technique of carving is the same for all birds:

1. *Separate and Remove Leg:* Pull leg away from body and cut off, following contour of bird. Place on a separate plate.

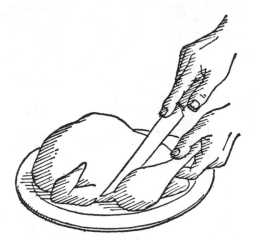

higher on the breast, keeping slices as thin and even as possible.

2. *Cut Meat from Leg:* Sever "knee" joint, separating drumstick and thigh. Hold drumstick with a napkin, tilt to a convenient angle, and slice meat parallel to bone.

3. *Cut Meat from Thigh:* Hold thigh firmly to plate with fork and slice parallel to the bone. *(Note:* If a large group is being served, remove other drumstick and thigh and slice.)

4. *Remove Wing:* Place knife parallel with and as close to breast as possible, cut through joint, and remove wing.

5. *Carve Breast:* Beginning halfway up breast, carve down, ending at cut made to remove wing. Begin each new slice a little

Slice only what meat is needed at a time. Make fresh slices for "seconds." *(Note:* Ducks are more difficult to carve than chicken or turkey, and if they are small, you may prefer to quarter them—see Cutting Up Poultry—in the kitchen before serving.)

SOME MARINADES AND GLAZES FOR POULTRY

Marinades: To enrich flavor of whole or cut-up poultry, marinate in refrigerator 3–4 hours before cooking, turning occasionally in marinade, then brush or baste often with marinade during last 20–30 minutes of cooking. Use any of the following, allowing about 1 cup marinade per chicken, 2–3 cups per large bird, and ½ cup per small bird.

Herbed or Spiced Wine or Cider (½ cup dry red, white, or rosé wine or cider mixed with ¼ cup boiling water and 1 teaspoon sage, savory, or thyme or ¼ teaspoon cinnamon, nutmeg, or mace).

Garlic Wine (½ cup dry red, white, or rosé wine mixed with ¼ cup each olive oil and boiling water and 2 crushed cloves garlic; omit oil if using for duck or goose).

Any of the following:
Beer Marinade
Buttermilk Marinade
All-Purpose Barbecue Sauce
Japanese Steak Sauce
Chinese Barbecue Sauce
South American Hot Barbecue Sauce

Glazes: For a gorgeously glistening brown bird, brush with one of the following glazes during the last 20–30 minutes of broiling or roasting. You'll need about 1/2 cup glaze for a chicken, about 1 cup for a bigger bird, and 1/4 cup for a tiny bird:
• A 1/2 and 1/2 mixture of melted apple and currant or quince jelly.
• A 1/2 and 1/2 mixture of hot apple juice and minced chutney.
• Melted orange, lime, or ginger marmalade.
• Warm wine, beer, cider, orange, or pineapple juice mixed with dark brown sugar (2 tablespoons sugar to each 1/2 cup liquid).

Butters: Instead of being marinated or glazed, chicken, turkey, and other dry-meated birds can be brushed or basted often during roasting or broiling with one of these seasoned butters: Chili, Chive, Curry, Garlic, Herb, Lemon, Maître d'Hôtel, Mustard, Paprika, or Shallot (see chapter on sauces and gravies for recipes).

CHICKEN FRICASSEE

4 servings

1 (3–3½-pound) broiler-fryer, cut up
1/4 cup butter or margarine
3 cups water
1 medium-size yellow onion, peeled and stuck with 6 cloves
1 medium-size carrot, peeled and cut in 1" chunks
1 stalk celery, cut in 1" chunks
1 bay leaf and 1 sprig each parsley and thyme, tied in cheesecloth (*bouquet garni*) with 6 peppercorns
1 teaspoon salt

S A U C E
3 tablespoons butter or margarine
1/4 cup unsifted flour
2 cups chicken broth, reserved from cooking chicken
1 egg yolk lightly beaten with 1/2 cup light or heavy cream
1 teaspoon lemon juice
1/4 teaspoon sugar
1 teaspoon salt (about)
1 tablespoon minced parsley (garnish)
4 thin lemon slices (garnish)

Brown chicken in butter in a large, heavy kettle over moderately high heat; add all but sauce ingredients, cover, and simmer 30–40 minutes until chicken is tender. Lift chicken from kettle and keep warm; strain broth, skim off fat and measure 2 cups to use in sauce. Melt butter in a large saucepan over moderate heat, blend in flour, slowly stir in broth, and heat, stirring, until thickened. Mix a little hot sauce into yolk mixture, return to pan, and heat and stir over lowest heat 1 minute; do not boil. Blend in lemon juice, sugar, and salt to taste. Add chicken to sauce and warm over lowest heat 1–2 minutes. Serve in a deep platter sprinkled with parsley and garnished with lemon. Good with boiled noodles or rice, mashed potatoes or hot biscuits.
*NPS: 675 C, 275 mg CH, 1465 mg S**

COQ AU VIN (CHICKEN IN WINE)

4 servings

2 ounces lean salt pork, cut in small dice
3–4 tablespoons butter or margarine
1 (3–3½-pound) broiler-fryer, cut up
1 pound small white onions, peeled, parboiled, and drained
1 clove garlic, peeled and crushed
1/2 pound button mushrooms, wiped clean
1/4 cup warm cognac or brandy
1 bay leaf, and 1 sprig each parsley and thyme, tied in cheesecloth (*bouquet garni*)
1/4 teaspoon pepper
1/2–1 teaspoon salt
1½ cups Burgundy or other dry red wine
3 tablespoons *Beurre Manié*

Brown salt pork in a large, heavy kettle over moderate heat; remove with a slotted spoon and reserve. Add 3 tablespoons butter to kettle and brown chicken, a few pieces at a time; remove and reserve. Add onions and brown well all over, about 10 minutes, adding more butter if necessary. Push onions to side of kettle, add garlic and mushrooms, and stir-fry 3–5 minutes until lightly browned. Return salt pork and chicken to kettle, pour cognac over chicken and blaze. When flames die, add all but final ingredient, cover, and simmer about 3/4 hour until chicken is tender. Lift chicken and vegetables to a deep casserole and keep warm. Stir small pieces of *Beurre Manié* into kettle liquid and heat, stirring, until thickened and smooth. Taste for salt and add remainder if needed. Strain gravy over chicken and serve. Good with boiled new potatoes or rice.
*NPS: 850 C, 230 mg CH, 810 mg S**

V A R I A T I O N

Coq au Vin au Casserole: Prepare as directed, but instead of cooking on top of the stove, bake in a covered casserole 30–40 minutes at 350° F. until chicken is tender. Nutritional count same as basic recipe.

POULET BASQUAIS (BASQUE-STYLE CHICKEN)

4 servings

Good with buttered noodles.

1 (3-pound) broiler-fryer, cut up
3 tablespoons olive oil
2 large ripe tomatoes, peeled, cored, seeded, and chopped
4 sweet green peppers, cored, seeded, and quartered
1/4 pound mushrooms, wiped clean and sliced thin
1/4 pound lean cooked ham, diced
1 1/2 teaspoons salt
1/4 teaspoon pepper
1/2 cup dry white wine or chicken broth
2 tablespoons tomato paste
1 tablespoon minced parsley
2 pimientos, drained and cut in thin strips

Brown chicken in oil in a heavy kettle over moderately high heat. Add tomatoes, green peppers, mushrooms, ham, salt, pepper, and wine, cover, and simmer slowly 3/4 hour until chicken is fork tender. Remove chicken to a serving platter with a slotted spoon and keep warm. Blend tomato paste into kettle liquid and boil rapidly, uncovered, 1 minute. Pour some sauce over chicken, sprinkle with parsley, and decorate with pimiento. Pass remaining sauce.

NPS: 555 C, 145 mg CH, 1380 mg S*

CHICKEN CACCIATORE

4 servings ¢

1/4 cup olive oil
1 (3–3 1/2-pound) broiler-fryer, cut up
2 medium-size yellow onions, peeled and minced
1 clove garlic, peeled and crushed
1/4 pound mushrooms, wiped clean and sliced thin
1 small sweet green pepper, cored, seeded, and coarsely chopped
1 (1-pound) can tomatoes (do not drain)
3/4 cup dry white or red wine
1/4 cup tomato paste
1/2 teaspoon rosemary
1 teaspoon salt
1/4 teaspoon pepper

Heat oil in a heavy kettle over moderately high heat 1 minute, then brown chicken well; remove and reserve. Stir-fry onions 5 minutes, add garlic, mushrooms, and green pepper, and stir-fry 3–4 minutes longer until onions are golden. Add tomatoes, breaking up clumps, blend wine and tomato paste and stir in along with rosemary. Return chicken

to kettle, sprinkle with salt and pepper, cover, and simmer, stirring now and then, about 3/4 hour until tender. Serve with spaghetti.

NPS: 550 C, 130 mg CH, 965 mg S*

CHICKEN MARENGO

4 servings ¢

Now a classic, this was originally an odds-and-ends dish made for Napoleon at the Battle of Marengo.

2 tablespoons olive oil
1 (3-pound) broiler-fryer, cut up
1/2 pound button mushrooms, wiped clean
2 cloves garlic, peeled and crushed
1 large ripe tomato, peeled, cored, seeded, and chopped or 2/3 cup coarsely chopped drained canned tomatoes
1/2 cup dry white wine
2 tablespoons tomato paste
1 teaspoon salt
1/8 teaspoon pepper
1 tablespoon minced parsley

Heat oil in a large, flameproof casserole over moderate heat. Brown chicken well on all sides, then remove and set aside. Sauté mushrooms in casserole 3–5 minutes until golden; add garlic and stir-fry 1 minute. Stir in all remaining ingredients except parsley and return chicken to casserole. Cover and simmer about 3/4 hour until tender. Sprinkle with parsley and serve.

NPS: 450 C, 130 mg CH, 750 mg S*

MAGYAR CHICKEN PAPRIKA

4 servings

2 medium-size yellow onions, peeled and sliced thin
3 tablespoons bacon drippings or 1 1/2 tablespoons each butter and cooking oil
1 (3–3 1/2-pound) broiler-fryer, cut up
1 teaspoon salt
1 tablespoon paprika (the Hungarian sweet rose paprika is best)
1/3 cup chicken broth or dry red wine
1 cup sour cream

Stir-fry onions in drippings in a large, heavy skillet over moderate heat 8–10 minutes until golden. Push to side of pan, add chicken, and fry about 10 minutes until lightly browned; turn heat to low. Arrange chicken skin side up, add salt, and sprinkle paprika evenly over all. Add broth, cover, and simmer 3/4 hour until chicken is tender. *(Note: You may prepare recipe to this point early in the day, then reheat slowly before serving.) Arrange chicken on a platter and keep warm. Mix sour cream into onions, heat 1–2 minutes but do not boil, then pour over chicken. Good with buttered noodles, kasha, or boiled potatoes.

NPS: 575 C, 165 mg CH, 820 mg S*

PAELLA

6 servings

This *paella* is geared to American rice, pans, and palates.

1/4 cup olive oil
3 (6–8-ounce) frozen rock lobster tails, cut crosswise in 1″ chunks
1/2 pound raw shrimp, shelled and deveined
1 (2 1/2–3-pound) broiler-fryer, cut up
1 large yellow onion, peeled and minced
2 cloves garlic, peeled and crushed
1 large sweet green pepper, cored, seeded, and minced
1/2 cup diced cooked ham or 1 chorizo (Spanish sausage), sliced 1/2″ thick
1 1/2 cups uncooked rice
2 3/4 cups chicken broth or water
2 teaspoons salt
1/4 teaspoon pepper
1/4–1/2 teaspoon powdered saffron
1/4 cup tomato paste
1 (10-ounce) package frozen green peas
1 1/2 dozen clams or mussels in the shell, prepared for cooking
1 pimiento, slivered (garnish)

Heat oil in a large (at least 5-quart) burner-to-table kettle over moderately high heat 1 minute, add lobster and shrimp, and stir-fry 3–4 minutes until pink; remove with a slotted spoon and reserve. Brown chicken well, remove, and reserve. Stir-fry onion in drippings 5 minutes, then add garlic, green pepper, and ham and stir-fry 3–4 minutes. Add rice, broth, 1 1/2 teaspoons salt, 1/8 teaspoon pepper, the saffron, and tomato paste. Return chicken to kettle, sprinkle with remaining salt and pepper, cover, and simmer 1/2 hour. Add lobster, shrimp, and peas (break them up when adding), cover, and simmer 10–15 minutes until chicken and peas are tender. Arrange clams on top, cover, and simmer 5 minutes until clams partially open. Sprinkle with pimiento and serve. Recipe too flexible for meaningful nutritional count.

ARROZ CON POLLO

4 servings ¢

1 (3–3 1/2-pound) broiler-fryer, cut up
1/3 cup unsifted flour
3 tablespoons olive oil
1 medium-size yellow onion, peeled and minced
1 clove garlic, peeled and crushed
1/2 cup julienne strips cooked ham
1 cup uncooked rice
1 cup chicken broth
1 (1-pound) can tomatoes (do not drain)
2 teaspoons salt
1/4 teaspoon pepper
1/4 teaspoon powdered saffron
1 bay leaf, crumbled
1 (4-ounce) can pimientos, drained and cut in 1″ pieces

Preheat oven to 350° F. Dredge chicken by shaking with flour in a bag. Heat oil in a large, heavy skillet over moderately high heat 1 minute, then brown chicken well, a few pieces at a time; drain on paper toweling. Reduce heat to moderate and stir-fry onion and garlic 5 minutes, add ham and stir-fry 3–4 minutes longer until onion is golden. Add rice, stir-fry 1 minute, then add broth, tomatoes, breaking up clumps, 1 teaspoon salt, 1/8 teaspoon pepper, the saffron, and bay leaf; mix well. Spoon into an ungreased 2 1/2-quart casserole about 2″ deep, arrange chicken on top, and sprinkle with remaining salt and pepper. Cover tightly and bake about 1 hour until chicken is fork tender. Uncover, scatter pimientos on top, and bake, uncovered, 10 minutes longer.

NPS: 745 C, 140 mg CH, 1845 mg S*

CHICKEN TERIYAKI

6 servings ⊲⊺⊳

3 large boneless chicken breasts, halved and skinned
1/2 cup soy sauce
1/4 cup *mirin* (sweet rice wine) or medium or dry sherry
1 tablespoon sugar
2 teaspoons finely grated fresh gingerroot

Place chicken breasts between wax paper and pound to flatten slightly. Marinate 1–2 hours in refrigerator in a mixture of soy sauce, *mirin,* sugar, and ginger, turning once or twice. Preheat broiler. Remove chicken from marinade and arrange on lightly oiled rack in broiler pan. Broil 5″–6″ from heat about 4 minutes on each side; brush with marinade when turning. Serve with tiny bowls of remaining marinade (sake cups are a good size) or pour a little marinade over each portion. Good with boiled rice and a spinach salad.

*NPS: 225 C, 100 mg CH, 1880 mg S**

VARIATION

⚖️ **Yakitori:** Flatten chicken breasts, then cut in 1″ cubes and marinate as directed. Thread on bamboo or thin metal skewers alternating with chunks of scallion and halved chicken livers. Broil about 8 minutes, giving skewers a quarter turn every 2 minutes; brush frequently with marinade. (*Note:* Miniatures may be served as appetizers; use 1″ chicken cubes and quartered livers.)

*NPS: 315 C, 375 mg CH, 1930 mg S**

COUNTRY CAPTAIN

6–8 servings ¢

A very mild curry popular in the South.

1 (5½–6-pound) stewing hen or capon, cleaned and dressed
2 bay leaves
2 stalks celery (include tops)
2 quarts water
2 large yellow onions, peeled and coarsely chopped
2 large sweet green peppers, cored, seeded, and coarsely chopped
2 cloves garlic, peeled and crushed
¼ cup olive or other cooking oil
⅓ cup minced parsley
1 cup dried currants or seedless raisins
1 tablespoon curry powder
1 teaspoon cayenne pepper
¼ teaspoon black pepper
½ teaspoon thyme
¼ teaspoon cloves
2 teaspoons salt
2 (1-pound 12-ounce) cans tomatoes (do not drain)
3 cups reserved chicken stock
1 cup toasted, blanched almonds (topping)

Remove fat from body cavity of bird, then place bird and giblets in a large kettle, add bay leaves, celery, and water, cover, and simmer 10–15 minutes; remove liver and reserve. Re-cover chicken and simmer about 1–1½ hours longer until tender; lift chicken from kettle and cool; strain stock and reserve. In the same kettle stir-fry onions, green peppers, and garlic in oil 8–10 minutes over moderate heat until onion is golden. Add all but last ingredient and simmer, uncovered, 45 minutes, stirring now and then. Meanwhile, skin chicken, remove meat from bones, and cut in bite-size pieces. Add chicken, reserved liver, and giblets to sauce and simmer, uncovered, 15 minutes. Serve with or over fluffy boiled rice, topped with almonds. (*Note:* Recipe can be made several days ahead and kept refrigerated until shortly before serving; it also freezes well.)

*NPS (6–8): 690–520 C, 105–80 mg CH, 1210–910 mg S**

CHICKEN JAIPUR

4–6 servings

A spicy chicken curry.

1 (4–5-pound) stewing hen, cleaned and dressed
1 quart water
1 large yellow onion, peeled and stuck with 4 cloves
1 large carrot, peeled and quartered
2½ teaspoons salt
4 peppercorns
1 large yellow onion, peeled and minced
1 clove garlic, peeled and crushed
3 tablespoons butter or margarine
⅓ cup curry powder
2 (½″) cubes fresh gingerroot, peeled and minced
¼–½ teaspoon cayenne pepper
⅛ teaspoon black pepper
1 teaspoon minced fresh mint
⅛ teaspoon cloves
½ cup coconut cream (available in specialty or Latin American groceries)
1½ cups reserved chicken stock
Juice of 1 lime
1 cup heavy cream

Remove fat from body cavity of bird, then place bird and giblets in a large kettle, add water, onion, carrot, salt, and peppercorns, cover, and simmer 15–20 minutes; remove liver and reserve. Re-cover chicken and simmer 1–1½ hours longer until tender; lift chicken and giblets from kettle and cool; strain stock and reserve. Stir-fry minced onion and garlic in butter in a very large, heavy skillet 8–10 minutes until golden; blend in curry powder, ginger, and all herbs and spices. Add coconut cream and chicken stock, cover and simmer ½ hour. Meanwhile, remove and discard chicken skin, take meat from bones, and cut in bite-size pieces. Add chicken and, if you like, liver and giblets to curry, cover, and simmer ½ hour. Mix in lime juice and cream and heat, stirring, 5–10 minutes. Serve with boiled rice. Good condiments: chutney, flaked coconut, chopped roasted peanuts, seedless raisins.

*NPS (4–6): 840–560 C, 310–210 mg CH, 1690–1125 mg S**

CHICKEN CHOW MEIN

6 servings ¢ ⊠ ⚖

1/2 pound mushrooms, wiped clean and sliced thin
6 scallions, minced (include some tops)
2 small sweet green peppers, cored, seeded, and minced
4 stalks celery, minced
2 tablespoons cooking oil
2 1/2 cups chicken broth
2 tablespoons soy sauce
1/4 cup cornstarch blended with 1/4 cup cold water
1/2 teaspoon salt
1/8 teaspoon pepper
3 cups bite-size pieces cooked chicken meat, preferably white meat
1 pound bean sprouts, washed
1 (4-ounce) can water chestnuts, drained and sliced thin

Stir-fry mushrooms, scallions, green peppers, and celery in oil in a large, heavy skillet over moderately high heat 8–10 minutes until golden brown. Add broth and soy sauce, turn heat to low, cover, and simmer 10 minutes. Mix in cornstarch paste, salt, and pepper and heat, stirring constantly, until thickened and clear. Add chicken, bean sprouts, and water chestnuts and heat and stir about 5 minutes, just to heat through. Taste for salt and adjust if needed. Serve over boiled rice.

NPS: 260 C, 60 mg CH, 1055 mg S*

MOO GOO GAI PEEN (CHICKEN WITH MUSHROOMS)

2 servings ⚖

1 large boneless chicken breast, halved and skinned
2 tablespoons peanut oil
1/2 cup thinly sliced mushrooms
1 cup finely shredded Chinese cabbage
1/3 cup thinly sliced bamboo shoots
2 (1/2") cubes fresh gingerroot, peeled and crushed
1/3 cup chicken broth
1 tablespoon dry sherry (optional)
1/4 pound snow pea pods, washed and trimmed
3 water chestnuts, sliced thin
2 teaspoons cornstarch blended with 1 tablespoon cold water
3/4 teaspoon salt (about)
1/8 teaspoon sugar

Cut chicken across the grain into strips about 2" long and 1/4" wide; set aside. Heat 1 tablespoon oil in a large, heavy skillet over

moderately high heat about 1 minute, add mushrooms, cabbage, bamboo shoots, and ginger, and stir-fry 2 minutes. Add broth, cover, and simmer 2–3 minutes. Pour all into a bowl and set aside. Wipe out skillet, heat remaining oil, and stir-fry chicken 2–3 minutes; if you like sprinkle with sherry and stir a few seconds longer. Return vegetables and broth to skillet, add snow peas and chestnuts, and heat, stirring until bubbling. Mix in cornstarch paste, salt, and sugar and heat, stirring until clear and slightly thickened; taste for salt and adjust as needed. Serve with boiled rice.

NPS: 380 C, 100 mg CH, 1080 mg S*

CHICKEN WITH SNOW PEAS AND WATER CHESTNUTS

4 servings

1 (3 1/2-pound) broiler-fryer, cut up, skinned, and boned*
1/4 cup soy sauce
1/4 cup dry sherry or port
1 clove garlic, peeled and crushed
2 (1/2") cubes fresh gingerroot, peeled and crushed
3/4 cup unsifted flour
1/3 cup peanut oil
1 (4-ounce) can water chestnuts, drained and sliced thin
1/2 pound snow pea pods washed and trimmed
1/2 cup water

Cut chicken in bite-size pieces and marinate 2–3 hours in refrigerator in a mixture of soy sauce, sherry, garlic, and ginger. Remove from marinade and dredge in flour; save marinade. Heat oil in a large, heavy skillet over moderately high heat about 1 minute, add chicken, and stir-fry 2–3 minutes to brown lightly. Add marinade and remaining ingredients and stir-fry 2–3 minutes until peas are crisp tender. Serve with or over boiled rice.

NPS: 570 C, 125 mg CH, 1460 mg S*

CHICKEN TETRAZZINI

6–8 servings

This luscious dish deserves the bravos heaped on its famous namesake, Italian coloratura Luisa Tetrazzini.

1 (5–6-pound) stewing hen, cleaned and dressed
1 quart water
1 1/2 teaspoons salt
1 small yellow onion, peeled
1 medium-size carrot, peeled

1 stalk celery
1 bay leaf
3–4 peppercorns
1 pound spaghettini or linguine
1/2 pound mushrooms, wiped clean, sliced and
    lightly sautéed in butter

S A U C E
1/4 cup butter or margarine
1/4 cup sifted flour
2 cups reserved chicken stock
1 1/2 cups milk or 3/4 cup each milk and dry
    white wine
1 cup heavy cream
2 teaspoons salt
1/8 teaspoon white pepper
1–2 tablespoons lemon juice (optional)
1/8 teaspoon nutmeg (optional)

T O P P I N G
3/4 cup soft, fine bread crumbs mixed with 3/4
    cup grated Parmesan cheese

Remove fat from body cavity of hen, then place hen, giblets, water, salt, onion, carrot, celery, bay leaf, and peppercorns in a large, heavy kettle, cover, and simmer about 2 hours until tender. (*Note:* Chicken liver should be removed after 10–15 minutes, cooled, and reserved.) Cool hen in stock, then skin and cut meat from bones in bite-size chunks; also dice all giblets; skim stock of fat, strain, and reserve. For sauce, melt butter over moderate heat, blend in flour, add stock and remaining sauce ingredients, and heat, stirring, until thickened. Preheat oven to 350° F. Cook pasta by package directions, drain and combine with sauce, mushrooms, chicken, and giblets, including liver. Place in a buttered shallow 3-quart casserole, sprinkle with topping, and bake, uncovered, 30–40 minutes until bubbly. Brown quickly under broiler and serve.
NPS (6–8): 955–715 C, 275–210 mg CH, 1750–1315 mg S*

V A R I A T I O N S

Turkey Tetrazzini: Prepare as directed, substituting a 6-pound turkey for the chicken.
NPS (6–8): 1050–790 C, 350–265 mg CH, 1830–1370 mg S*

Ham Tetrazzini: Prepare sauce as directed; also cook pasta. Toss with 3 cups diced cooked ham and the mushrooms called for, then top and bake as directed.
NPS (6–8): 750–565 C, 135–100 mg CH, 2525–1890 mg S*

CHICKEN JAMBALAYA BAKE

4–6 servings   ¢

An easy, economical chicken, rice, and tomato casserole.

1 (3–3 1/2-pound) broiler-fryer, cut up
2/3 cup unsifted flour
2 tablespoons chili powder
3 1/2 teaspoons salt
1/3 cup olive oil
1 large yellow onion, peeled and coarsely
    chopped
1 clove garlic, peeled and crushed
2/3 cup uncooked rice
1 (1-pound 12-ounce) can tomatoes (do not
    drain)
1/4 cup water
1/8–1/4 teaspoon cayenne pepper (depending on
    how hot you like things)

Preheat oven to 350° F. Dredge chicken by shaking in a bag with flour, chili powder, and 3 teaspoons salt; brown in oil in a large, heavy kettle and drain on paper toweling; pour off all but 3 tablespoons drippings. Stir-fry onion, garlic, and rice in drippings 3–5 minutes over moderate heat until rice is golden. Mix in tomatoes, water, cayenne, and remaining salt and heat, stirring, until mixture simmers. Return chicken to kettle, pushing down into liquid, cover, and bake 1 hour until chicken and rice are tender.
NPS (4–6): 750–500 C, 130–90 mg CH, 2350–1565 mg S*

CIRCASSIAN CHICKEN

6 servings

An unusual Turkish cold chicken and walnut dish that's perfect for a buffet. It's rich, needs only a green salad to accompany.

1 (6–6 1/2-pound) capon, cleaned and dressed
    (save giblets for a gravy or other recipe)
3 quarts water
1 onion, peeled and stuck with 3 cloves
2 bay leaves
1 stalk celery, cut in large chunks
1 medium-size carrot, peeled and cut in large
    chunks
6 peppercorns
1 1/2 teaspoons salt

S A U C E
1 pound shelled walnuts
3 slices white bread, trimmed of crusts and
    soaked in 1/4 cup milk
1 teaspoon salt
1/8 teaspoon pepper
2 1/3 cups reserved chicken broth (about)

2 tablespoons olive oil mixed with 1 teaspoon paprika

Place chicken, water, onion, bay leaves, celery, carrot, peppercorns, and salt in a large, heavy kettle, cover, and simmer about 1 hour until chicken is tender; lift chicken from broth and cool; strain broth and reserve. For sauce, purée walnuts, a few at a time, by buzzing 15–20 seconds in an electric blender at high speed or churn, all at once, about 10 seconds in a food processor fitted with the metal chopping blade; mix with bread, salt, pepper, and enough broth to make a sauce about the consistency of thick gravy; again purée, a little bit at a time, by buzzing 15–20 seconds in the blender at high speed or churn, all at once, about 10 seconds in the processor, still fitted with the metal chopping blade. Skin chicken, remove meat, and cut in strips about 1½" long and ¼" wide. Mound about half the chicken on a large platter and spread with half the walnut sauce; arrange remaining chicken on top and spread with remaining sauce. Cover and chill several hours. Remove from refrigerator and let stand at room temperature 1 hour. Just before serving, drizzle paprika mixture over top in a crisscross design.

NPS: 920 C, 115 mg CH, 1100 mg S*

CHICKEN MAYONNAISE

12 servings

Cool and creamy, a wise choice for a hot weather party buffet.

1 (6–6½-pound) stewing hen, cleaned and dressed (save giblets for soup or gravy)
2½ quarts water
5 teaspoons salt
1 medium-size yellow onion, peeled and stuck with 3 cloves
1 cup diced celery
1 cup finely chopped walnuts or blanched almonds
4 hard-cooked eggs, peeled and finely chopped
1 small yellow onion, peeled and finely grated
1 (10-ounce) package frozen tiny green peas, cooked by package directions and drained but not seasoned
2 envelopes unflavored gelatin
2 cups reserved chicken stock
1 cup heavy cream
1 pint thick mayonnaise
¼ teaspoon pepper

Place hen in a large, heavy kettle with water, 3 teaspoons salt, and the onion, cover, and simmer about 2 hours until tender. Lift hen from stock and cool; strain and reserve stock. Skin chicken, separate meat from bones, and mince; place in a large mixing bowl with celery, nuts, eggs, grated onion, and peas, toss well to mix, and set aside. Heat gelatin in reserved stock and cream over moderate heat, stirring until dissolved; do not boil. Off heat, blend in mayonnaise, remaining salt, and the pepper. Pour over chicken mixture and stir well to mix. Pour into a 2½-quart decorative round mold, cover with plastic food wrap, and chill several hours or overnight until firm. Unmold on a large platter, garnish as desired (stuffed eggs, marinated artichoke hearts, and sprigs of cress are especially pretty). Slice into thin wedges and serve.

NPS: 615 C, 195 mg CH, 1260 mg S*

CHICKEN KIEV

4–6 servings

Traditionally, Kiev is seasoned only with butter, salt, and pepper, though chefs nowadays often add garlic, parsley, or chives. The trick in preparing Kiev is to seal the butter inside the chicken breast so that when the meat is cut it gushes out.

3 large boneless chicken breasts, halved, skinned, and pounded flat
½ teaspoon salt
⅛ teaspoon pepper
6 finger-size slivers ice cold butter (*Note:* **The best way to make these is to halve 1 stick butter crosswise, then quarter each half lengthwise.**)
½ cup cooking oil

COATING
2 eggs, lightly beaten
2 tablespoons milk
2 tablespoons water
½ teaspoon salt
⅛ teaspoon pepper
1 cup unsifted flour
1½ cups fine dry bread crumbs

Chill chicken breasts several hours, then spread flat on a cutting board and sprinkle with salt and pepper; lay a finger of butter in the center of each, then fold top and bottom margins over butter, tightly roll jelly-roll style and secure with poultry pins; chill rolls 15 minutes. Meanwhile, for coating mix eggs with milk, water, salt, and pepper. Dip rolls in flour, then egg, then in crumbs to coat evenly; pay particular attention to the ends, making sure they're well coated; chill rolls 1 hour. Preheat oven to 350° F. Heat oil in a large, heavy skillet over moderately high heat until a cube of bread will sizzle; add rolls and fry, turning gently with a slotted spoon, until nut brown all over; drain on paper toweling. Arrange 1 layer deep in an ungreased shallow baking pan and bake, uncovered, 15 minutes. Serve at once.

NPS (4–6): 800–530 C, 335–220 mg CH, 1200–800 mg S*

VARIATIONS

Nutritional counts same as basic recipe.
Herbed Kiev: Prepare as directed, sprinkling about 1/2 teaspoon minced parsley and/or minced chives over each finger of butter and adding a dab of crushed garlic (use only 1 clove for the whole recipe). Roll breasts and proceed as directed.

Deep-Fried Kiev: Prepare as directed, then brown rolls in a deep fat fryer in 360° F. fat instead of in skillet. Drain, transfer to oven, and bake as directed.

STUFFED CHICKEN BREASTS

4 servings

Any favorite stuffing can be used for stuffing chicken breasts instead of those given below. For 4 servings, you will need 1/2 cup stuffing.

2 large boneless chicken breasts, halved, skinned, and pounded flat
1/4 teaspoon salt
1/8 teaspoon white pepper
1/3 cup liver pâté or deviled ham
1/4 cup soft white bread crumbs
2 scallions, minced
1/4 cup unsifted flour
2 tablespoons butter or margarine
1/2 cup chicken broth

Preheat oven to 350° F. Spread breasts flat and sprinkle with salt and pepper. Mix pâté, crumbs, and scallions, place 2 tablespoons on each breast, roll up, and secure with poultry pins. Dredge rolls with flour and brown in butter in a heavy skillet over moderately high heat about 5 minutes. Transfer to an ungreased shallow casserole, add broth, cover, and bake 20 minutes until tender. Remove poultry pins and serve.

NPS: 330 C, 115 mg CH, 550 mg S*

VARIATIONS

Chicken Breasts with Spicy Ham Stuffing: Prepare as directed, stuffing breasts with 1/2 cup ground boiled ham mixed with 1 lightly beaten egg yolk, 1 teaspoon prepared yellow mustard, and the bread crumbs and scallions called for. Good with Madeira Sauce.

NPS: 330 C, 190 mg CH, 700 mg S*

Ham-and-Cheese-Stuffed Chicken Breasts: Spread breasts flat, sprinkle with salt, pepper, and 2 minced scallions. Lay 1 slice cut-to-fit boiled ham and Swiss cheese on each breast, roll, and cook as directed.

NPS: 350 C, 135 mg CH, 650 mg S*

CHAUD-FROID OF CHICKEN BREASTS

4 servings

Preparing a *chaud-froid* is not difficult if the sauce is quite cold—but still liquid—and the food to be coated is well chilled. The chaud-froid sauce will then set almost immediately.

2 large boneless chicken breasts, halved
1 recipe Chaud-Froid Sauce
2 cups aspic made with chicken stock*
Cutouts of truffle and pimiento; parsley or tarragon sprigs (decoration)

Poach breasts by basic method* and cool in stock; remove from stock, skin, and chill. Strain stock and use in preparing chaud-froid sauce and aspic. When chaud-froid sauce is the proper consistency, set breasts on a rack over a tray and cover with a thin, even layer of sauce. Chill until tacky, then continue building up layers until no meat shows through. While final layer is still tacky, decorate with truffle and pimiento cutouts and herb sprigs. Seal in designs with a thin glaze of aspic and chill until firm. Also chill remaining aspic. Serve breasts on a platter wreathed with chopped aspic and sprigged with watercress.

NPS: 400 C, 125 mg CH, 500 mg S*

SUPRÊMES OF CHICKEN

Suprêmes of chicken (*suprêmes de volaille* in French) are boned, skinned *half* breasts; if the first joints of wing are attached, they become *côtelettes*. The thin strip of meat lying next to the breastbone is called the *filet*. Perfectly cooked suprêmes are springy to the touch, creamy white with juices that run clear. They may be cooked by one of the basic methods below, seasoned with salt and pepper, and served as is; they may be topped with a suitable sauce such as Mushroom, Parsley, Poulette, Soubise or Suprême, or they may be given one of the lavish classic treatments that follow.

To Poach: Arrange suprêmes in a single layer in a buttered heavy skillet or shallow, flameproof casserole. Sprinkle lightly with salt and pepper, add chicken broth almost to cover, also 1 bay leaf, and 1 sprig each parsley and thyme, tied in cheesecloth. Cover and simmer, either on top of the stove or in a 325° F. oven, about 20 minutes until tender.

To Bake: Preheat oven to 425° F. Allow 3–4 tablespoons butter for each 4 suprêmes and heat to bubbling in a shallow, flameproof casserole over moderate heat. Roll breasts in butter, cover loosely with foil, and bake 20 minutes until just tender.

To Sauté: Melt 1/4 cup butter in a large, heavy skillet; lightly dredge suprêmes in flour, then brown over moderate heat about 8 minutes, turning often, until tender.

To Broil: Preheat broiler. Flatten suprêmes slightly and arrange on oiled rack in broiler pan. Brush well with melted butter (or Herb or Lemon Butter) and broil 5″–6″ from heat 4–5 minutes on a side, brushing often with additional butter.

Some Classic Ways to Serve Suprêmes of Chicken

Suprêmes de Volaille à Blanc (in Wine and Cream Sauce): Bake 4 suprêmes as directed, transfer to a hot platter and keep warm. To pan drippings add 1/4 cup each dry white wine and chicken broth and boil, uncovered, until reduced by half. Turn heat to low and blend in 1 cup heavy cream, 3/4 teaspoon salt, 1/8 teaspoon white pepper, and 1–2 teaspoons lemon juice. Warm 1–2 minutes but do not boil; pour over suprêmes and serve sprinkled with minced parsley.

NPS: 625 C, 280 mg CH, 550 mg S*

Suprêmes de Volaille Amandine: Sauté 4 suprêmes as directed and keep warm. Stir-fry 1/4 cup blanched slivered almonds in drippings over moderate heat until golden, blend in 1 tablespoon flour and 1 cup heavy cream, and heat, stirring, until thickened. Season with salt and pepper, let mellow several minutes over low heat, add 1 teaspoon lemon juice, pour over suprêmes, and serve.

NPS: 670 C, 270 mg CH, 500 mg S*

Chicken Breasts in Champagne Sauce: Poach suprêmes as directed, using a 1/2 and 1/2 mixture of chicken broth and champagne, dry white wine, or cider. Drain off poaching liquid and measure; for each cup, lightly beat 2 egg yolks. Heat cooking liquid

in the top of a double boiler directly over moderate heat until simmering, spoon a little into yolks, return to pan, set over simmering water, and heat and stir until thickened and no raw taste of egg remains. Season to taste, pour over suprêmes and serve.

NPS: 725 C, 320 mg CH, 550 mg S*

Suprêmes Véronique: Bake 4 suprêmes as directed but add 1/2 cup dry white wine to the pan. Drain off cooking liquid, to it add 1 cup light cream, and use to make 1 1/2 cups Medium White Sauce. Pour sauce over suprêmes, garnish with peeled seedless green grapes, and serve. If you like, brown quickly under broiler before serving.

NPS: 600 C, 200 mg CH, 480 mg S*

SAUTÉED CHICKEN LIVERS

6 servings ☒ ⊲⊺⊳

1 1/2 pounds chicken livers
1/2 cup unsifted flour
1 teaspoon salt
1/4 teaspoon pepper
3–4 tablespoons bacon drippings, butter, or margarine

Halve each chicken liver at the natural separation and dredge in a mixture of flour, salt, and pepper. Stir-fry in drippings in a large, heavy skillet over moderately high heat about 5 minutes until browned all over. *(Note:* Livers will be medium rare. If you prefer them rarer, cook about 1 minute less, if more well done, turn heat to moderately low and cook 1–2 minutes longer.) Serve on buttered toast triangles for breakfast, lunch, or supper.

NPS: 230 C, 500 mg CH, 490 mg S*

BRAISED CHICKEN LIVERS WITH PARSLEY GRAVY

4–6 servings ☒ ⊲⊺⊳

1 1/2 pounds chicken livers
3 tablespoons bacon drippings, butter, or margarine
1 teaspoon salt
1/8 teaspoon pepper
4 teaspoons flour
1 cup chicken broth
2 tablespoons minced parsley
2–3 tablespoons medium-dry sherry (optional)

Halve each chicken liver at the natural separation, pat dry on paper toweling, and stir-fry in drippings in a large, heavy skillet over moderately high heat about 5 minutes until brown. Turn heat to moderately low and sprinkle livers with salt and pepper. Blend flour with ¼ cup chicken broth, add remaining broth, and pour into skillet. Cook and stir gently until slightly thickened. Add parsley and, if you like, the sherry and serve.

NPS (4–6): 305–200 C, 755–500 mg CH, 930–620 mg S*

CHICKEN LIVERS IN SOUR CREAM

4 servings   ⊠

A good chafing dish recipe.

1 pound chicken livers
2 tablespoons bacon drippings, butter, or margarine
1 cup minced scallions (include some tops)
¼ pound mushrooms, wiped clean and coarsely chopped
⅛ teaspoon rosemary
¼ teaspoon basil
1 teaspoon salt
⅛ teaspoon pepper
1 clove garlic, peeled and crushed
1 cup chicken broth
1 cup sour cream

Cut livers in two at the natural separation and pat dry on paper toweling. Stir-fry in drippings in a large, heavy skillet over moderately high heat until browned all over, about 5 minutes. Push livers to one side of skillet, add scallions, and sauté 2–3 minutes until golden. Turn heat to moderately low, mix in all remaining ingredients except sour cream, and simmer, uncovered, 7–10 minutes, stirring occasionally. If you like, transfer at this point to a chafing dish. Mix in sour cream and simmer 2–3 minutes until hot but not boiling. Serve over boiled rice, buttered noodles, or toast triangles.

NPS: 340 C, 525 mg CH, 900 mg S*

OLD-FASHIONED CREAMED CHICKEN OR TURKEY

4 servings   ⊠

¼ pound mushrooms, wiped clean and sliced thin (include stems)
¼ cup butter or margarine
¼ cup unsifted flour
1 cup chicken broth
1 cup light cream
¾ teaspoon salt (about)
⅛ teaspoon white pepper

2 cups cooked chicken or turkey meat, cut in bite-size pieces
2 tablespoons dry sherry (optional)

Sauté mushrooms in butter in the top of a double boiler directly over moderately high heat 2–3 minutes until golden. Blend in flour, slowly stir in broth and cream, and heat, stirring, until thickened. Set over just simmering water, mix in remaining ingredients, cover, and let mellow 10–15 minutes. Serve over hot buttered toast, biscuits, corn bread, toasted English muffins, pancakes, or waffles. Also good over mashed potatoes, boiled rice, or noodles or used as a filling for pancakes, crepes, or baked frozen patty shells.

NPS (Chicken): 400 C, 130 mg CH, 810 mg S*
NPS (Turkey): 385 C, 125 mg CH, 800 mg S*

VARIATIONS

Creamed Chicken or Turkey and Eggs: Prepare as directed, but just before setting mixture over water to mellow, mix in 2 peeled, hard-cooked eggs cut in wedges.

NPS (Chicken): 440 C, 270 mg CH, 845 mg S*
NPS (Turkey): 425 C, 260 mg CH, 840 mg S*

Creamed Chicken or Turkey and Ham: Prepare as directed, using a ½ and ½ mixture of chicken or turkey and ham.

NPS (Chicken): 400 C, 125 mg CH, 1320 mg S*
NPS (Turkey): 390 C, 120 mg CH, 1315 mg S*

CHICKEN OR TURKEY AND MUSHROOM CREPES

4 servings

1 recipe Crepes for Savory Fillings

FILLING
2 cups Mushroom Sauce
Pinch nutmeg
¾ teaspoon salt (about)
⅛ teaspoon pepper
2 cups minced cooked chicken or turkey meat
¼ pound mushrooms, wiped clean, sliced thin and lightly sautéed in a little butter
1 pimiento, drained and minced
Paprika

Preheat oven to 350° F. Prepare crepes as recipe directs and spread flat with most attractive sides face down. Mix sauce with all filling ingredients except paprika, taste for salt and adjust as needed. Spoon a little chicken mixture down center of each crepe, then roll up. Place crepes seam side down in a single layer in an ungreased shallow *au gratin* dish, top with remaining sauce, and bake, uncovered, 30–40 minutes until bubbly. Dust with paprika and serve.

NPS (Chicken): 410 C, 240 mg CH, 950 mg S*
NPS (Turkey): 400 C, 235 mg CH, 940 mg S*

VARIATIONS

Ham and Chicken Crepes: Prepare as directed, substituting 1 cup diced cooked ham for 1 cup chicken.

NPS: 410 C, 230 mg CH, 1460 mg S*

Chicken Crepes au Gratin: Prepare and bake crepes as directed; sprinkle ½ cup finely grated Cheddar or Parmesan cheese on top, and broil 3″–4″ from heat 2–3 minutes until flecked with brown.

NPS: 470 C, 260 mg CH, 1035 mg S*

QUICK CHICKEN OR TURKEY À LA KING

4 servings ⊠

1 (10½-ounce) can condensed cream of mushroom soup (do not dilute)
½ cup milk
1½ cups diced cooked chicken or turkey meat
2 tablespoons minced pimiento
4 English muffins, split, toasted, and lightly buttered or 4 frozen waffles, toasted

Blend soup and milk until smooth in a saucepan, cover, and heat over moderate heat 5 minutes, stirring occasionally. Add chicken, heat, and stir 3–5 minutes. Mix in pimiento, spoon over muffins, and serve.

NPS: 400 C, 180 mg CH, 500 mg S*

VARIATION

Eggs à la King: Prepare as directed, substituting 5–6 diced, hard-cooked eggs for the chicken.

NPS: 370 C, 400 mg CH, 500 mg S*

MOTHER'S CHICKEN OR TURKEY STEW

6 servings ¢

1 (5–6-pound) stewing hen or turkey, cut up
1 medium-size yellow onion, peeled and stuck with 4 cloves
5–6 medium-size carrots, peeled and cut in 2″ chunks
2 stalks celery, minced
2 sprigs parsley
2½ teaspoons salt (about)
¼ teaspoon pepper
1 quart water
1 cup milk

6 tablespoons flour blended with ⅓ cup cold milk

Place all but last ingredient in a heavy burner-to-table kettle or electric skillet set at 225° F., cover, and simmer about 2–2½ hours until chicken is tender. *(Note:* Remove chicken liver after 10–15 minutes, cool, and reserve.) Discard onion and parsley. Drain off liquid, reserving 3 cups, then skim off fat. *(Note:* If there is not enough liquid to total 3 cups, add water as needed.) Pour liquid into a saucepan, blend in flour paste, and heat, stirring, until thickened. Pour sauce over chicken, taste for salt and adjust as needed. Return chicken liver to stew, cover all, and let stand over low heat 5–10 minutes to mellow flavors. Good with boiled noodles or rice, Polenta, or mashed potatoes.

NPS (Chicken): 395 C, 140 mg CH, 1080 mg S*
NPS (Turkey): 440 C, 190 mg CH, 1130 S*

VARIATIONS

Chicken or Turkey Stew with Dumplings: Prepare stew as directed; also prepare a favorite dumpling recipe. Drop dumplings on top of stew and cook as dumpling recipe directs. Recipe too flexible for meaningful nutritional count.

Chicken or Turkey Stew with Biscuits: Prepare stew as directed and transfer to a hot, ungreased 3-quart casserole. Mix 1 recipe Baking Powder Biscuits, then cut and arrange biscuits, almost touching, on top of stew. Bake, uncovered, 15–20 minutes at 375° F. until lightly browned.

NPS (Chicken): 655 C, 145 mg CH, 1675 mg S*
NPS (Turkey): 700 C, 195 mg CH, 1725 mg S*

BRUNSWICK STEW

12–15 servings ⚖ ¢

American Indian women, who invented Brunswick Stew, used to make it with squirrel or rabbit. If you have a hunter in the family, try it their way.

1 (6-pound) stewing hen or capon, cleaned and dressed
1 gallon cold water
2 stalks celery (include tops)
1 tablespoon sugar
5 medium-size potatoes, peeled and cut in ½″ cubes
3 medium-size yellow onions, peeled and coarsely chopped
6 large ripe tomatoes, peeled, cored, seeded, and coarsely chopped
2 (10-ounce) packages frozen baby lima beans (do not thaw)

2 (10-ounce) packages frozen whole kernel corn
(do not thaw)
1 medium-size sweet green pepper, cored and cut
in short, thin slivers
2 tablespoons salt (about)
¼ teaspoon pepper

Remove fat from body cavity of bird, then
place bird and giblets in a very large kettle.
Add water and celery, cover, and simmer 1–
2 hours until *just* tender. Remove bird and
giblets from broth and cool. Strain broth
and skim off fat. Rinse kettle, pour in broth,
add sugar, all vegetables but corn and green
pepper, cover, and simmer 1 hour. Meanwhile, skin chicken, cut meat in 1″ chunks
and dice giblets. Return chicken and giblets
to kettle, add remaining ingredients, cover,
and simmer 40–45 minutes, stirring occasionally. Taste for salt, adding more if
needed. Serve piping hot in soup bowls as a
main dish. Particularly good with coleslaw
and Hushpuppies or crisp corn sticks.

*NPS (12–15): 350–280 C, 90–70 mg CH, 1250–
1000 mg S**

CHICKEN OR TURKEY HASH

4 servings   ⚖ ¢

1 medium-size yellow onion, peeled and minced
½ medium-size sweet green or red pepper,
cored, seeded, and minced (optional)
2 tablespoons bacon drippings, butter, or
margarine
2 cups diced cooked chicken or turkey meat
2 cups diced cooked cold peeled potatoes, sweet
potatoes, or yams
¼ cup applesauce
1 tablespoon minced parsley
1 teaspoon salt
⅛ teaspoon pepper
½ teaspoon poultry seasoning
4 poached or fried eggs (optional)

Stir-fry onion and, if you like, green pepper
in drippings in a large, heavy skillet over
moderate heat 5–8 minutes until onion is
pale golden. Mix in all remaining ingredients
except eggs, pat down with a broad spatula,
and cook, uncovered, without stirring about
10 minutes until a brown crust forms on the
bottom. Using 2 broad spatulas, turn hash
and brown flip side 8–10 minutes. Cut into 4
portions and serve. If you like, top each
serving with a poached or fried egg.

NPS (Chicken): 250 C, 65 mg CH, 650 mg S*
NPS (Turkey): 240 C, 60 mg CH, 640 mg S*

VARIATIONS

¢ **Chicken or Turkey 'n' Stuffing Hash:**
Prepare as directed but use 1 cup any leftover bread stuffing and 1 cup diced cooked
or mashed potatoes instead of 2 cups potatoes. Omit poultry seasoning.

NPS (Chicken): 355 C, 90 mg CH, 960 mg S*
NPS (Turkey): 340 C, 80 mg CH, 950 mg S*

Parmesan-Chicken or -Turkey Hash: Prepare as directed but substitute mashed potatoes for the diced and grated Parmesan
cheese for the applesauce; add ½ crushed
clove garlic. Fry one side as directed, turn,
sprinkle with 2–3 tablespoons grated Parmesan or Cheddar cheese, and brown under
broiler.

NPS (Chicken): 320 C, 70 mg CH, 1135 mg S*
NPS (Turkey): 310 C, 65 mg CH, 1125 mg S*

CHICKEN OR TURKEY CROQUETTES

4 servings

¼ cup butter or margarine
¼ cup sifted flour
1 cup milk
1 tablespoon minced parsley
½ teaspoon poultry seasoning
1 teaspoon finely grated lemon rind (optional)
2 tablespoons dry sherry (optional)
½ teaspoon salt (about)
⅛ teaspoon pepper
1 egg, lightly beaten
1½ cups coarsely ground cooked chicken or
turkey meat
½ cup soft white bread crumbs
Shortening or cooking oil for deep fat frying

COATING
1 egg lightly beaten with 1 tablespoon cold
water
¼ cup cracker crumbs mixed with ¼ cup
minced blanched almonds

Melt butter in a large saucepan over moderate heat and blend in flour; slowly stir in
milk, add parsley, and all seasonings, and
heat, stirring, until mixture thickens. Blend
a little hot sauce into egg, return to pan, set
over lowest heat, and heat, stirring, 1 minute; do not boil. Off heat, mix in chicken and
bread crumbs; taste for salt and adjust. Cool,
then chill until easy to shape. Shape into 8
patties or sausage-shaped rolls, dip in egg
mixture, then roll in crumbs to coat. Let dry
on a rack at room temperature while heating
fat. Place shortening in a deep fat fryer and
heat to 375° F. Fry the croquettes, half at a
time, 2–3 minutes until golden brown and

crisp; drain on paper toweling, then keep warm by setting, uncovered, in oven turned to lowest heat while you fry the rest. Good with Tomato or Parsley Sauce.

NPS (Chicken): 455 C, 225 mg CH, 575 mg S*
NPS (Turkey): 445 C, 220 mg CH, 570 mg S*

Curried Chicken or Turkey Croquettes: Prepare croquette mixture as directed but omit poultry seasoning and add 1–2 teaspoons curry powder and 1/4 cup well-drained, minced chutney. Fry as directed and serve with Chicken or Turkey Gravy or Light Curry Sauce.

NPS (Chicken): 500 C, 225 mg CH, 610 mg S*
NPS (Turkey): 485 C, 215 mg CH, 605 mg S*

Chicken and Ham, Tongue, or Shellfish Croquettes: Prepare croquette mixture as directed but use a 1/2 and 1/2 mixture of chicken and finely ground cooked ham, tongue, shrimp, lobster, or crab meat; omit poultry seasoning. Fry as directed.

NPS (Shrimp): 435 C, 240 mg CH, 590 mg S*
NPS (Lobster or crab): 430 C, 225 mg CH, 610 mg S*
NPS (Ham): 450 C, 240 mg CH, 650 mg S*
NPS (Tongue): 440 C, 240 mg CH, 640 mg S*

CHICKEN OR TURKEY DIVAN

6 servings

A luscious way to use up leftovers.

1/4 cup butter or margarine
1/4 cup sifted flour
1 cup chicken broth
1 cup milk
3/4 teaspoon salt
1/8 teaspoon white pepper
1/8 teaspoon nutmeg
1/4 cup + 2 tablespoons grated Parmesan cheese
3 tablespoons dry sherry
1 (2-pound) head broccoli or 2 pounds asparagus, trimmed and steamed just until tender
10–12 slices cooked chicken or turkey meat
1/2 cup heavy cream

Preheat oven to 350° F. Melt butter in a saucepan over moderate heat, blend in flour, slowly add broth and milk, and heat, stirring until thickened; mix in salt, pepper, nutmeg, 1/4 cup cheese, and the sherry. Arrange broccoli in a single layer in a buttered 2-quart *au gratin* dish or shallow casserole and sprinkle with remaining cheese. Top with chicken slices. Beat cream until soft peaks will form and fold into sauce; pour evenly over chicken and bake, uncovered,

about 1/2 hour until bubbly. Broil quickly to brown and serve.

NPS (Chicken): 450 C, 160 mg CH, 725 mg S*
NPS (Turkey): 425 C, 145 mg CH, 710 mg S*

Chicken Divan Hollandaise: Prepare as directed but mix 1/2 cup Hollandaise Sauce and 1 teaspoon Worcestershire sauce into cheese sauce before adding cream.

NPS: 520 C, 245 mg CH, 830 mg S*

Chicken Breasts Divan: Prepare as directed, substituting 6 poached chicken breasts for the sliced chicken and arranging them slightly overlapping on the broccoli.

NPS: 425 C, 155 mg CH, 710 mg S*

CHICKEN- OR TURKEY-NOODLE CASSEROLE

4 servings ¢

1/4 cup butter or margarine
1/4 cup sifted flour
1/2 teaspoon poultry seasoning
1 cup strong chicken broth
1 cup milk
1 teaspoon salt
1/4 teaspoon pepper
1/4 cup minced pimiento (optional)
2 cups bite-size pieces cooked chicken or turkey meat
1/2 pound thin noodles, cooked by package directions until al dente, and drained

TOPPING
1 cup soft white bread crumbs mixed with 3 tablespoons melted butter or margarine

Preheat oven to 350° F. Melt butter in a large saucepan over moderate heat and blend in flour and poultry seasoning; slowly stir in broth and milk, add salt and pepper, and heat, stirring, until mixture thickens. Off heat, mix in all remaining ingredients except topping. Spoon into a buttered 2-quart casserole, sprinkle with topping, and bake, uncovered, 1/2 hour.

NPS (Chicken): 640 C, 180 mg CH, 1100 mg S*
NPS (Turkey): 625 C, 170 mg CH, 1090 mg S*

CHICKEN OR TURKEY POT PIE

6 servings ¢

1/4 cup butter or margarine
6 tablespoons flour
1 cup milk
2 cups chicken broth or a 1/2 and 1/2 mixture of broth and apple cider or dry white wine

3 cups bite-size pieces cooked chicken or turkey
meat
1/4 teaspoon rosemary
1/4 teaspoon savory
1 tablespoon minced parsley
1 teaspoon salt
1/4 teaspoon white pepper
2 cups thinly sliced cooked carrots
2 cups cooked green peas
1 recipe Flaky Pastry I
1 egg yolk mixed with 1 tablespoon cold water
(glaze)

Preheat oven to 425° F. Melt butter in a
large saucepan over moderate heat, blend in
flour, add milk and broth, and heat, stirring,
until thickened. Add chicken and all seasonings, cover, and simmer 5–10 minutes, stirring occasionally. Cool to room temperature. Mix in carrots and peas and spoon into
an ungreased 2 1/2-quart casserole about 9"
in diameter. Prepare pastry and roll into a
circle 3" larger than casserole; make 3
V-shaped steam slits near center. Dampen
casserole rim, fit pastry on top, roll pastry
edges under even with rim, and crimp to
seal. Brush with glaze, being careful not to
cover slits. Bake 30–40 minutes until
browned and bubbly (place a sheet of foil on
rack under casserole to catch drips). To
serve, cut wedges of pastry and ladle chicken
mixture on top.

NPS (Chicken): 525 C, 135 mg CH, 1065 mg S*
NPS (Turkey): 510 C, 125 mg CH, 1055 mg S*

BASIC CHICKEN OR TURKEY SOUFFLÉ

4 servings

1/4 cup butter or margarine
1/4 cup sifted flour
1/2 teaspoon sage
1/4 teaspoon thyme
1 cup milk
1/2 teaspoon salt
1/8 teaspoon white pepper
4 eggs, separated, at room temperature
1 cup finely ground cooked chicken or turkey
meat
2 teaspoons minced chives (optional)
1/4 teaspoon cream of tartar

Melt butter in a small saucepan over moderate heat and blend in flour, sage, and thyme;
slowly stir in milk. Add salt and pepper and
heat and stir until mixture thickens. Lightly
beat yolks, blend in a little hot sauce, then
return to pan; set over lowest heat and heat,
stirring, 1–2 minutes; do not boil. Off heat,
mix in chicken and, if you like, chives. Lay a

piece of wax paper flat on top of sauce and
cool to room temperature. Preheat oven to
350° F. Beat egg whites until frothy, add
cream of tartar, and beat until stiff but not
dry. Stir about 1/4 cup egg whites into sauce,
then carefully fold in the rest, taking care
not to break down volume. Spoon into an
ungreased 1 1/2-quart soufflé dish and bake,
uncovered, 45–50 minutes until puffy and
tinged with brown. Serve at once. Good with
Tomato, Shrimp, Parsley, or Mushroom
Sauce.

NPS (Chicken): 310 C, 345 mg CH, 520 mg S*
NPS (Turkey): 305 C, 340 mg CH, 515 mg S*

VARIATIONS

**Chicken or Turkey and Ham or Tongue
Soufflé:** Prepare as directed, using 3/4 cup
ground chicken and 1/2 cup ground cooked
lean ham or tongue.

NPS (Chicken): 320 C, 345 mg CH, 720 mg S*
NPS (Turkey): 315 C, 345 mg CH, 720 mg S*
*NPS (Ham, tongue): 320 C, 350 mg CH, 740
mg S**

Curried Chicken or Turkey Soufflé: Melt
butter, blend in flour and 1 tablespoon each
curry powder and finely grated onion. Add
milk slowly and proceed as directed. About
335 calories per serving if made with
chicken, 355 calories per serving if made
with turkey. Same nutritional count as soufflé recipes above.

HOT CHICKEN OR TURKEY LOAF

8 servings   ⚖ ¢

3 cups finely chopped cooked chicken or turkey
meat
2 cups dry white bread crumbs
1/2 cup minced celery
2 pimientos, drained and coarsely chopped
1 1/2 teaspoons salt
1/4 teaspoon pepper
1 tablespoon finely grated yellow onion
1 tablespoon lemon juice
2 teaspoons Worcestershire sauce
1 tablespoon minced parsley
2 cups chicken broth
3 eggs, lightly beaten

Preheat oven to 350° F. Mix together all but
last 2 ingredients. Stir broth into eggs, then
pour over chicken mixture and mix well.
Lightly pack mixture into a greased
9" × 5" × 3" loaf pan, set in a large baking
pan, and pour in enough boiling water to
come about halfway up loaf pan. Bake, uncovered, about 1 hour until loaf begins to
pull away from sides of pan. Lift loaf pan
from water bath and cool upright 5–10 min-

utes; loosen loaf, invert on a hot platter, and ease out. Serve hot with Chicken or Mushroom Gravy. Good cold, sliced thin and accompanied by salad.

NPS (Chicken): 245 C, 150 mg CH, 890 mg S*
NPS (Turkey): 230 C, 145 mg CH, 880 mg S*

VARIATIONS

¢ ⚖ **Surprise Chicken Loaf:** Prepare chicken mixture as directed and pack half into loaf pan. Arrange 3 peeled hard-cooked eggs lengthwise down center of mixture, place rows of pimiento, stuffed green or pitted ripe olives on either side of eggs, cover with remaining chicken mixture, and bake as directed.

NPS: 275 C, 250 mg CH, 915 mg S*

¢ ⚖ **Chicken and Rice Loaf:** Prepare chicken mixture as directed but reduce bread crumbs to 1½ cups and add 1½ cups boiled rice.

NPS: 260 C, 150 mg CH, 840 mg S*

TURKEY CUTLETS IN DIJON CREAM

6 servings ⊠

This is a last-minute dish, so have at the ready every ingredient and implement you will need.

2 pounds turkey cutlets, cut ¼" thick and
   pounded thin as for scaloppine
1 teaspoon salt
¼ teaspoon white pepper
½ cup unsifted flour
8 tablespoons butter or margarine (about)
¼ cup Dijon mustard
6 tablespoons dry white wine
2 cups heavy cream
2 tablespoons minced parsley

Cut turkey into pieces about 2" × 4". Sprinkle both sides of each piece with salt and pepper, then dredge in flour. Heat 4 tablespoons butter in a large heavy skillet over moderately high heat until a bread cube will sizzle; lightly brown cutlets, a few at a time, 1–2 minutes on a side, using tongs to turn and adding more butter as needed. Drain on paper toweling and keep warm at back of stove. Combine mustard and wine, mix into skillet drippings, and simmer, uncovered, 1–2 minutes until reduced to about ¼ cup. Whisk in cream and boil slowly, stirring often, until thickened slightly—about the consistency of a thin white sauce. Return turkey to skillet and heat 1–2 minutes, stirring occasionally, over low heat. Sprinkle with parsley and serve.

NPS: 635 C, 245 mg CH, 950 mg S*

LEMONY THAI TURKEY WITH SHIITAKE MUSHROOMS AND BEAN SPROUTS

4 servings ⚖ ⊠

This recipe is "medium hot." If you like really torrid food, as many Thais do, increase amount of chili peppers to suit.

1 pound turkey cutlets, cut ¼" thick and
   pounded thin as for scaloppine
4 tablespoons peanut oil
2 cloves garlic, peeled and minced
2 (½") cubes fresh gingerroot, peeled and
   minced
⅛–¼ teaspoon crushed dried hot red chili
   peppers
1 teaspoon minced lemon grass or finely grated
   lemon rind
1 bunch scallions, washed, trimmed, and
   coarsely chopped (include some tops)
¼ pound shiitake mushrooms, rinsed, dried, and
   coarsely chopped, or ½ cup dried Chinese
   black mushrooms, prepared for cooking* and
   coarsely chopped
1 pound bean sprouts, washed
2 tablespoons dark brown sugar
¼ cup soy sauce
2 tablespoons chicken broth, water, or dried
   mushroom soaking liquid

Cut turkey cutlets across the grain into strips 2" long and ¼" wide. Stir-fry turkey in 2 tablespoons oil in a large heavy skillet or wok set over moderately high heat 2–3 minutes; remove and reserve. With a mortar and pestle, pound garlic with gingerroot, chilies, and lemon grass until well bruised; set aside. Heat remaining oil in skillet, add scallions, mushrooms, and garlic mixture and stir-fry 2 minutes. Add ¾ of bean sprouts and stir-fry 2 minutes longer. Reduce heat to moderate; combine brown sugar, soy sauce, and chicken broth and pour over vegetables; add turkey, mix well, then cook and stir 2 minutes until steaming hot. Serve at once sprinkled with remaining raw bean sprouts. Accompany with boiled rice.

NPS: 350 C, 70 mg CH, 1440 mg S*

TURKEY TONNATO

6-10 servings　¢

Like the classic Italian Vitello Tonnato, this recipe is perfect for a summer luncheon or supper. Boneless turkey roll makes it affordable—and a lot easier to prepare than the long-winded veal original.

1 (3–5-pound) frozen boneless turkey roll, thawed
1 medium-size yellow onion, peeled
1 stalk celery
2 sprigs parsley
1 bay leaf
1/4 teaspoon white pepper
2 cups dry white wine or water
1/2 (2-ounce) tin anchovy fillets (do not drain)

T U N A   S A U C E
21/4 cups turkey stock + onion reserved from cooking turkey roll (above)
1/2 cup mayonnaise
Juice of 1 lemon
1 (61/2-ounce) can white meat tuna (do not drain)
1/2 (2-ounce) tin anchovy fillets, drained
1/4 cup drained capers
2 tablespoons minced parsley
Lemon wedges (garnish)

Place turkey roll in a large heavy kettle, add onion, celery, parsley, bay leaf, pepper, wine, and anchovies together with all anchovy oil. Cover and simmer 21/2–3 hours until turkey is tender, turning it every hour to ensure even cooking. *(Note:* Liquid should just *tremble,* never boil.) Cool turkey in liquid, then lift to a platter and let drain briefly. Remove netting from turkey roll, wrap roll in aluminum foil, and chill 1 hour. For the Tuna Sauce: Strain turkey stock; pour 21/4 cups into an electric blender or food processor fitted with the metal chopping blade; add onion, mayonnaise, lemon juice, tuna (plus can liquid), and anchovies. Purée by buzzing 20–30 seconds at moderate speed in the blender or 10–15 seconds in the processor. Slice turkey roll 1/8″–1/4″ thick and arrange slices, slightly overlapping, in a large, deep platter, spooning a little sauce over each slice. Cover with aluminum foil or plastic food wrap and refrigerate at least 3 hours. Also cover and refrigerate remaining sauce. Just before serving, ladle a little more sauce over all, sprinkle with capers and minced parsley. Garnish with lemon wedges and serve. Pass remaining sauce.

NPS (6–10): 600–360 C, 155–95 mg CH, 1920–1150 mg S*

DEVILED TURKEY DRUMSTICKS

4 servings　¢

2 frozen turkey drumsticks and 2 thighs, thawed

S A U C E
1/4 cup butter or margarine
1 tablespoon powdered mustard
1 teaspoon grated yellow onion
4 teaspoons cider vinegar or lemon juice
Pinch cayenne pepper

Make 3–4 tiny lengthwise slits in each piece of turkey. Melt butter in a saucepan, stir in remaining sauce ingredients, and pour into an ungreased shallow roasting pan. Roll turkey in sauce and let stand at room temperature 1 hour. Preheat oven to 350° F. Roast turkey, uncovered, about 2 hours until tender, basting occasionally with pan drippings or a little melted butter. Turn turkey as needed to brown evenly. Tent with foil if it browns too fast.

NPS: 405 C, 175 mg CH, 270 mg S*

V A R I A T I O N S

¢　**Deviled Turkey Wings:** Substitute 6 turkey wings for the legs and proceed as directed, allowing about 11/2 hours' roasting time.

NPS: 300 C, 150 mg CH, 185 mg S*

¢　**Deviled Leftover Turkey:** Cut thick slices from cooked drumsticks and thighs, roll in sauce, and coat with dry white bread crumbs. Place in a greased baking pan and bake, uncovered, 1/2 hour at 400° F. Brown under broiler and serve. Recipe too flexible for meaningful nutritional count.

CREOLE-STYLE TURKEY DRUMSTICKS

4 servings　¢

2 frozen turkey drumsticks and 2 thighs, thawed
1/3 cup unsifted flour
3 tablespoons olive or other cooking oil
1 large yellow onion, peeled and minced
1 medium-size sweet green pepper, cored, seeded, and minced
2 stalks celery, minced
1 clove garlic, peeled and crushed
1 teaspoon salt
1/4 teaspoon pepper
1 tablespoon minced parsley
1/2 teaspoon thyme
1 bay leaf, crumbled
1 (1-pound 3-ounce) can tomatoes (do not drain)

Dredge turkey in flour and brown in oil in a very large, heavy skillet over moderate heat;

drain on paper toweling. Stir-fry onion, green pepper, celery, and garlic in drippings 8 minutes until onion is pale golden. Mix in remaining ingredients, breaking up tomatoes; return turkey to skillet, cover, and simmer 1½–2 hours until tender, basting now and then and adding a little water if pan seems dry. Or, if you prefer, transfer mixture to an ungreased 3-quart casserole, cover, and bake 1½–2 hours at 350° F. Or do the whole thing in an electric skillet, set at 350° F. Serve with boiled or Saffron Rice.

*NPS: 475 C, 145 mg CH, 910 mg S**

VARIATION

¢ **Creole-Style Turkey Parts:** Prepare as directed, substituting 6 turkey wings or a 2-pound thawed boneless turkey roll for drumsticks. Or use a 4-pound frozen whole turkey breast, thawed and split; use a larger can of tomatoes (1-pound 12-ounce size) but cook for the same length of time.

*NPS (wings): 375 C, 120 mg CH, 825 mg S**
*NPS (roll): 520 C, 125 mg CH, 2090 mg S**
*NPS (breast): 785 C, 230 mg CH, 1035 mg S**

ROCK CORNISH HENS NORMANDY STYLE

8 servings

Especially attractive when garnished with clusters of red and green grapes.

4 (1–1¼-pound) Rock Cornish hens, thawed and halved lengthwise
¼ cup cooking oil
¼ cup butter or margarine
½ pound mushrooms, wiped clean and sliced thin
2 cups apple cider or a ½ and ½ mixture of cider and dry white wine
½ clove garlic, peeled and crushed
1½ teaspoons salt
¼ teaspoon white pepper
¼ teaspoon thyme
2 tablespoons cornstarch blended with 2 tablespoons cold water
½ cup heavy cream

Preheat oven to 350° F. Pat hens dry on paper toweling and brown, 2 or 3 halves at a time, in a mixture of oil and butter in a large, heavy skillet over moderate heat. Drain hens on paper toweling, then arrange in a large, shallow roasting pan without crowding. Stir-fry mushrooms in skillet drippings 3–5 minutes over moderate heat and spoon over hens. Mix cider and garlic and pour over all; sprinkle in salt, pepper, and thyme. Cover with foil and bake ½ hour; uncover and bake 10–15 minutes longer until tender. Lift hens to a serving platter, spoon mushrooms on top, and keep warm. Pour pan liquid into a saucepan and bring to a simmer. Smooth in cornstarch paste and heat, stirring, until thickened and clear. Add cream, taste for salt and adjust as needed. Spoon some sauce over birds and pass the remainder.

*NPS: 540 C, 150 mg CH, 590 mg S**

HERBED ROCK CORNISH HENS OR SQUABS WITH MUSHROOMS AND WINE

4 servings

2 (1–1¼-pound) Rock Cornish hens or squabs, thawed
Herb Butter (see below)
3 tablespoons melted butter or margarine
1 cup dry white wine
½ cup chicken broth
1 tablespoon lemon juice
1 dozen button mushrooms, wiped clean and fluted*

HERB BUTTER

¼ cup butter or margarine, softened to room temperature
2 tablespoons minced scallions
2 tablespoons minced parsley
½ teaspoon poultry seasoning
1 teaspoon Worcestershire sauce
½ clove garlic, peeled and crushed
¼ teaspoon salt

Preheat oven to 425° F. Make a small slit in the skin on each side of the breast of each hen. Mix herb butter and, using a small, thin-bladed knife, spread evenly over breasts underneath skin. Skewer openings shut and truss* birds; place breast side up on a rack in a shallow roasting pan and roast, uncovered, 20 minutes, brushing one to two times with melted butter. Reduce oven to 350° F.; remove rack and place birds directly in pan. Pour wine, broth, and lemon juice over birds and roast, uncovered, basting frequently with drippings, about 25 minutes until just tender. Add fluted mushrooms and roast 10 minutes longer. Lift hens and mushrooms to a hot platter; if pan juices seem skimpy, stir in a little more wine or broth. Pour some pan juices over the birds and pass the rest.

*NPS: 540 C, 170 mg CH, 565 mg S**

DUCKLING WITH ORANGE SAUCE (DUCKLING À L'ORANGE, DUCKLING À LA BIGARADE)

6 servings

To be strictly authentic, this recipe should be made with bitter Seville oranges. Any clear-skinned orange will do, however, if you add lemon juice for tartness.

2 (4-pound) ducklings, cleaned, dressed, and quartered
1 tablespoon salt
1/4 teaspoon pepper
1 cup chicken broth
1 cup dry white wine
Finely slivered rind of 4 oranges (use orange part only and slice oranges to use as a garnish)
1 1/2 cups water
1/2 cup sugar
1 cup orange juice
2 tablespoons lemon juice
1/4 cup brandy
2 tablespoons butter or margarine
2 tablespoons flour
1 cup giblet stock*

Preheat oven to 450° F. Rub ducklings with 2 teaspoons salt and the pepper; place skin side up on a rack in a large shallow roasting pan and prick skin well all over. Roast, uncovered, 20–25 minutes, turning and pricking frequently; drain off fat. Pour broth and wine over ducklings, reduce oven to 350° F., and roast about 1 hour longer, basting frequently, until golden brown and leg joints move easily. Meanwhile, place rind and 1 cup water in a small saucepan and boil, uncovered, 3 minutes; drain and reserve rind. Boil remaining water and sugar, uncovered, 10–15 minutes until amber; add rind, orange and lemon juices, and brandy, cover, and keep warm over lowest heat. When ducklings are done, transfer to a heated platter and keep warm. Strain pan juices into a shallow bowl, scraping browned bits from bottom, and skim off fat. Melt butter in a saucepan, blend in flour, add pan juices, giblet stock, rind mixture, and remaining salt, and cook, stirring, until slightly thickened. Pour some sauce over the ducklings and pass the rest. Garnish platter with orange slices and sprigs of watercress or rose geranium.

*NPS: 925 C, 210 mg CH, 1500 mg S**

DUCKLING WITH BING CHERRY SAUCE (DUCKLING MORELLO)

6 servings

2 (4-pound) ducklings, cleaned, dressed, and quartered
3 teaspoons salt
1/4 teaspoon pepper
1 (1-pound 1-ounce) can pitted Bing cherries (do not drain)
1 1/2 cups giblet stock*
1 3/4 cups chicken broth
1 teaspoon lemon juice
1/4 cup cornstarch blended with 1/2 cup cold water
1/4–1/3 cup dry Madeira wine

Preheat oven to 450° F. Rub ducklings with 2 teaspoons salt and 1/8 teaspoon pepper. Place skin side up on a rack in a large, shallow roasting pan and prick skin all over with a sharp fork. Roast, uncovered, 20–25 minutes, turning and pricking frequently; drain off all drippings. Reduce oven to 350° F. and roast 1 hour longer; again drain off drippings. Drain liquid from cherries into roasting pan, baste ducklings, and roast 15–30 minutes until golden brown and leg joints move easily. Transfer to a heated platter and keep warm while you make the sauce. Pour giblet stock and broth into roasting pan and stir, scraping browned bits from bottom; transfer all to a saucepan. Add lemon juice, remaining salt and pepper, and heat, uncovered, over moderate heat 1–2 minutes. Blend in cornstarch paste and heat, stirring constantly, until thickened and clear. Add cherries and wine and heat 2–3 minutes longer. Spoon some sauce over ducklings and pass the rest.

*NPS: 875 C, 200 mg CH, 1610 mg S**

CHINESE-STYLE ROAST DUCKLING

3–4 servings

Duckling cooked this way is good at a buffet; simply slice thin and serve between small, fresh hot rolls.

1 medium-size yellow onion, peeled and minced
2 stalks celery, minced
4 dried mushrooms
1 star anise
1 clove garlic, peeled and crushed
2 teaspoons sugar
1/4 cup soy sauce
1/4 cup dry sherry
1 (5-pound) duckling, cleaned and dressed
1 teaspoon salt

BASTING SAUCE

1/4 cup honey
2 tablespoons cider vinegar
1 tablespoon soy sauce

Preheat oven to 450° F. Place onion, celery, mushrooms, anise, garlic, sugar, soy sauce, and sherry in a small saucepan and cook and stir 2–3 minutes over moderate heat. Skewer neck flap of duckling to back, then pour hot mixture into body cavity. (*Note:* If liquid tends to flow out through vent, prop lower part of duckling up with a ball of foil.) Sew up vent and tie legs together. Place duckling breast side up on a rack in a shallow roasting pan and rub well with salt. Roast, uncovered, 1/2 hour. Meanwhile, mix basting sauce and keep warm over low heat. Reduce heat to 350° F. and roast about 11/2 hours longer, basting every 20 minutes with sauce, until leg joints move easily. Transfer duckling to a heated platter and serve.

NPS (3–4): 1125–845 C, 240–180 mg CH, 3155–2365 mg S*

GERMAN-STYLE POTATO-STUFFED ROAST GOOSE

10 servings

Excellent with Sweet and Sour Red Cabbage.

1 (10–12-pound) goose, cleaned and dressed
2 large yellow onions, peeled and sliced thin
1/4 cup butter or margarine
6 large potatoes, parboiled, peeled, and cut in 1/2" cubes
2 cloves garlic, peeled and crushed
Raw goose liver, minced
1 teaspoon sage
11/2 teaspoons salt
1/4 teaspoon pepper

Preheat oven to 325° F. Remove fat from body cavity of goose and save if you like to render and use in cooking. Remove giblets, hold out liver, but save the rest for soup or giblet stock.* Prick goose well all over with a sharp fork. Sauté onions in butter in a large, heavy kettle over moderately high heat 5 minutes, add potatoes and garlic, and sauté 5 minutes. Off heat, mix in remaining ingredients. Spoon loosely into cavity of goose, skewer openings shut, and truss.* Place goose breast side up on a rack in a shallow roasting pan and roast 20–22 minutes per pound until leg joints move easily; prick every 1/2 hour and drain off drippings as they collect. If you like a crisp skin, spoon all drippings from pan, pour 1/4 cup cold water over bird, and roast 10 minutes longer.

Lift bird to a hot platter, remove skewers and strings, and let "rest" about 10 minutes. Make gravy from drippings if you like. Garnish as desired and serve.

NPS: 550 C, 225 mg CH, 515 mg S*

BRAISED GOOSE WITH CHESTNUTS AND ONIONS

10 servings

Young (4–8-pound) geese can be cooked in any of the ways suitable for duckling. The average supermarket size (about 10 pounds) is good prepared this way. *Note:* To save yourself the frustration of shelling and peeling fresh chestnuts, use the frozen shelled and peeled Italian chestnuts now available in many specialty food shops.

1 (10–12-pound) goose, cleaned, dressed, and cut up
1 tablespoon bacon drippings or rendered goose fat*
1 medium-size carrot, peeled and minced
1 medium-size yellow onion, peeled and minced
2 cloves garlic, peeled and crushed
1 teaspoon sugar
1 tablespoon flour
1 quart giblet stock* or part stock and part chicken broth
1/2 cup tomato purée
1 teaspoon salt
1/4 teaspoon pepper
1 pound small white onions, peeled
2 tablespoons rendered goose fat or clarified butter*
11/2 pounds chestnuts, shelled, peeled, and quartered

If breasts of goose are large, have butcher halve them crosswise as well as lengthwise. Early in the day, take fat from body of goose and render.* Also remove giblets and cook*; mince giblets and reserve along with stock. Preheat oven to 325° F. Prick goose well all over with a sharp fork and brown, a few pieces at a time, in a large, heavy kettle, using bacon drippings at first, about 20 minutes over moderately low heat; pour off drippings as they collect and save; also prick goose often during browning. Drain goose on paper toweling and set aside. Drain all but 2 tablespoons drippings from kettle, add carrot, onion, and garlic, and stir-fry 8–10 minutes over moderate heat until golden; sprinkle with sugar and brown 2 minutes. Blend in flour, add stock, purée, salt, and pepper and heat, stirring, until mixture boils. Return goose to kettle, cover, transfer to oven, and bake 2 hours. Meanwhile, brown whole onions in goose fat in a heavy skillet over moderate heat about 10 minutes; drain on paper toweling. When goose has cooked 2 hours, add onions, cover, and bake ½ hour; add chestnuts, cover, and bake ¼– ½ hour longer until goose is very tender. Lift goose to a hot deep platter, wreathe with onions and chestnuts, cover, and keep warm. Strain cooking liquid through a fine sieve, pressing vegetables to extract all liquid; skim off as much fat as possible. Reduce sauce to about 2 cups by boiling rapidly, uncovered, add giblets, taste for salt and pepper and adjust as needed. Ladle over goose and serve.

NPS: 570 C, 175 mg CH, 640 mg S*

SOME WAYS TO USE POULTRY LEFTOVERS

There aren't apt to be leftovers from small birds unless you've misjudged. Quarters, halves, and parts reheat well, wrapped in foil, in about ½ hour at 350° F. or in just 1– 2 minutes, loosely covered with wax paper, in a microwave. Leftover turkey, goose, duck, and chicken can be used in any recipe calling for cooked poultry meat (if recipe calls for more meat than you have, round out with canned chicken). Or they can be used as follows. *(Note:* If you prepare these by microwave, cover any sauce-rich casseroles with plastic food wrap instead of foil, and wrap sandwiches in paper toweling or napkins.)

Sliced Hot Poultry: Slice meat, not too thin, remove skin, and layer into an ungreased casserole. Add just enough hot gravy to cover, cover with foil, and heat 20 minutes at 350° F.

Hot Roast Chicken or Turkey Sandwiches: Heat slices in sauce or gravy as above and serve on toast or bread spread, if you like, with cranberry sauce, chutney, or relish. Or serve on hot leftover stuffing. To reheat stuffing, spread in a greased piepan and bake, uncovered, at 350° F., brushing occasionally with melted butter until lightly browned.

To Make the Most of Small Amounts:
• Cube, dice, or cut in julienne strips and toss into hearty salads or add to casseroles, broths, or vegetable soups.
• Add scraps and bones to stock pot.
• Grind and add to savory stuffings.
• Grind, mix with mayonnaise, a little softened cream cheese, and mustard, and use as a sandwich spread. For extra zip, add a little applesauce or minced chutney.
• Grind, mix with any seasoned butter, a little minced scallions or capers, mustard, or other spicy condiment, and use as a cocktail spread.
• Dice or slice thin, layer in custard cups, fill to the brim with Quick and Easy Aspic, chill until firm, unmold, and serve with mayonnaise.
• Stretch with an equal quantity of hot Medium White Sauce, Mornay or Parsley Sauce and serve over crepes, toast, waffles, hot biscuits, or corn bread.

GAME BIRDS

America has about a dozen different families of game birds—everything from dark-fleshed ducks and geese to delicate white-meated pheasants. With one or two exceptions, game birds can be prepared by the same basic methods. Because these methods are determined more by the size of the bird than by the kind or color of its flesh, birds are grouped here by size.

FROZEN AND CANNED GAME BIRDS

Specialty food shops and butchers sell most of the popular game birds frozen, also canned small birds. Always prepare frozen birds by wrapper directions, if any. If not, thaw in the refrigerator in the original wrapper before cooking; allow about 24 hours for small- or medium-size birds, 1½–2 days for a wild goose up to 12 pounds. Giblets are usually tucked inside the body cavity and should be removed as soon as possible; thaw separately. Once thawed, prepare frozen birds as you would the fresh; never refreeze. Canned birds are already cooked and need only be heated before serving (follow can directions). Those that have been smoked may have strong flavor; to tone it down, simmer in water to cover about 10 minutes, drain, pat dry, and then follow label instructions.

How Much Game Bird Per Serving?

Allow about 1 pound dressed bird per serving; if birds are very small, this may mean 2– 3 birds per person. Nutritional counts have not been supplied for game birds.

CLEANING AND DRESSING GAME BIRDS

The procedure is similar for all birds, though downy ducks and geese require an extra plucking. In days past, birds were bled after being shot, but newer bullets eliminate the need. When birds are eviscerated depends upon weather and whether or not they're to be hung. In cold weather, they needn't be gutted immediately, and, of course, if they are to be hung, they should not be drawn until after hanging.

To Hang: Nowadays, birds are hung only until cold or, at most, 24 hours. If you prefer a gamier flavor, however, by all means hang the bird longer. Pick a cool, dry, shady, well-ventilated spot away from insects and pets and hang undressed, undrawn birds by their feet. How long? Depends on weather (birds ripen faster in warm weather), the bird's age (old birds need to hang longer than young), and the sophistication of your palate. Usually, 2–3 days' hanging will produce a pretty "high" bird. Best tests: Pluck a feather from just above the tail; if it pulls out easily, the bird has hung long enough. Or ruffle abdomen feathers; if the skin has a blue-green tinge, the bird is ready for cooking.

To Remove Feathers: All but the smallest birds with superfragile skin should be plucked and if possible, dry-plucked (dunking a bird in hot water affects flavor). Chill bird 24 hours, then, starting at the neck, pull out feathers, a few at a time, in quick gentle jerks against the grain. Use a light touch over the breast, where skin is tender. When bird is plucked, tweeze out pinfeathers. *Tip:* The neatest way to pluck is outdoors, directly into a paper bag. Never burn feathers —the smell is horrendous. If a bird won't dry-pluck, dunk head first into a large kettle of simmering water and let stand about 15 seconds; repeat 3–4 times. Shake off excess moisture and pluck as above.

To Remove Duck and Goose Down: Pluck outer feathers. Melt paraffin in a large pot set in boiling water (for each bird you'll need 1 cake paraffin and 2 quarts water). Dip birds head first into pot to coat, remove, and cool until paraffin hardens. Peel off paraffin and the down will come away with it. Redip and peel as needed.

To Singe: After birds are plucked, burn off any hair, using long wooden matches, a candle, or spill, taking care not to scorch the flesh.

To Skin: Tiny game birds (especially woodcock, snipe, pigeon, and dove) have such tender skin they can't be plucked. To remove feathers, slit neck skin lengthwise, then carefully work skin free from breast and back, wings, and legs with fingers—it's rather like taking off coveralls.

To Eviscerate:
1. Cut off head, peel neck skin down around shoulders, then cut off neck as close to body as possible, leaving windpipe and esophagus intact. Reach under flap of breast skin and pull out crop and attached tubes.
2. Make a cut below breastbone, just big enough to admit your hand, reach in, feel around for firm, round gizzard and gently ease it out of bird (intestines, liver, and heart should come away with it).

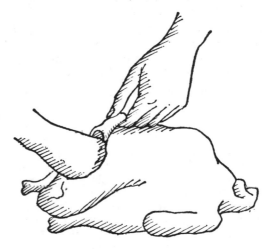

Also scoop out kidneys, lungs, and any lumps of fat. Discard all organs except gizzard, liver, and heart.

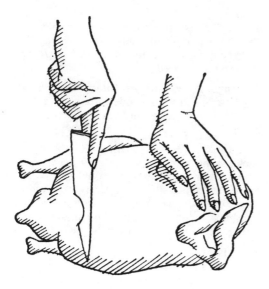

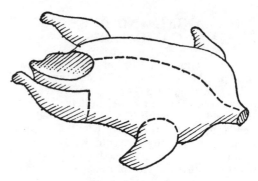

To Halve (Split)

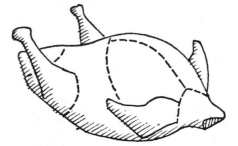

To Disjoint

3. Cut out oil sac at base of tail.

4. Wipe bird inside and out with a damp cloth, then pat dry.

To Prepare Giblets:

Liver: Separate gall bladder from liver—carefully so it doesn't rupture, spilling the bitter juices inside; trim away any greenish spots on liver.

Gizzard: Cut away fat and any bits of intestine; also scrape off outer membrane. Cut gizzard open, peel away inner membrane, bringing with it contents of gizzard.

Heart: Trim off veins and arteries, peel away membrane.

To Make Giblet Stock: *(Note:* Method may also be used for making stock from the hearts and livers of rabbits, squirrels, and other small furred game.) Wash giblets well in cool water, cover with cold salted water (1 teaspoon salt per pint water), cover, and simmer about 1 hour, replenishing water as needed. If you plan to use giblets in recipes, reduce cooking time so that they don't toughen and dry; liver, gizzard, and heart will be tender in 20 minutes, neck in 30. *(Note:* The liver of a large wild goose will need about 1/2 hour, the heart, gizzard, and neck 11/2–2 hours.) Taste stock for salt and pepper and add as needed. Use as is for making soups, sauces, and stews or, if you like, strain first through a fine sieve lined with a double thickness of cheesecloth.

To Cut Up Birds: Using poultry shears or a sharp knife, cut as follows:

The principles of cooking game birds are essentially the same as for domestic fowl—with two differences. Game birds have little or no fat and must be barded (wrapped in bacon or sheets of salt pork or other fat) and/or heavily basted to keep them from drying out. Second, dark-meated game birds like wild duck are often served rare (some people want them only passed through the oven). Otherwise, the basics are similar. Tough old birds, obviously, roast poorly and should be steamed, stewed, or braised. Young tender birds, like young tender chickens, are supremely adaptable. *(Note:* Always try to bring game birds to room temperature before cooking.)

HOW TO ROAST GAME BIRDS

Best for young small- or medium-size birds; wild goose should be roasted only if very young and small—less than 8 pounds. *Note:* This method is for well-done birds; for rare wild duck, see the separate recipe that follows:

General Preparation: Have birds cleaned and dressed; sprinkle cavities with salt and pepper.

Basic Method: Preheat oven to 350° F. Place 1/2 small peeled, cored apple and/or 1/2 small peeled yellow onion inside each bird, also 1 bay leaf, a sprig of fresh sage, thyme, parsley, or marjoram, and 1–2 tablespoons medium-dry sherry or port. Skewer or sew openings shut, then fold wings back and under and tie legs together. Arrange birds breast side up on a rack in a shallow roasting pan. Cover breast of each with a double thickness of cheesecloth saturated with melted butter, margarine, bacon drippings, or lard. Roast, uncovered, basting often with additional melted fat, until leg joints move easily and breast meat feels tender. Use the following times as a guide:

Wild Goose: 25–30 minutes per pound.

Medium-Size (1–4 pounds) Birds: 30–40 minutes per pound.

Small (under 1 pound) Birds: 50–60 minutes per pound

If birds have been skinned, leave cheesecloth cover on until last 5 minutes so they will not dry out; otherwise, remove during last 15 minutes so birds will brown. Never try to brown skinned birds. Transfer birds to a hot platter, remove strings and stuffing, and let "rest" 10 minutes before serving. Serve small birds whole, carve larger birds as you would chicken or turkey.* *For Extra Flavor:* Baste birds throughout roasting with Herb, Parsley, Tarragon, Shallot, or Garlic Butter or with a 1/2 and 1/2 mixture of melted butter and dry red or white wine, beer, or fruit juice. Stuff birds with fresh berries or cherries, brandied peaches, dates or figs, or sultana raisins sprinkled with brandy instead of apple, onion, and herbs. *To Flambé Small Birds:* Arrange roasted birds in a deep platter, pour 1/4–1/3 cup warmed brandy or rum over all, blaze with a match, and baste with flaming liquid until flames die.

VARIATIONS

Game Birds Baked in Vine Leaves: Tie fresh or brined grape leaves around each bird, cover with buttered cheesecloth, and roast as directed, removing cheesecloth and vine leaves toward end of cooking. Drain off pan drippings, pour 1/4 cup port or Madeira over each bird, and finish roasting, basting often. Remove birds to platter, add peeled seedless green grapes to pan (allow 1/4 cup grapes for each bird), and warm gently while birds "rest." Pour over birds and serve.

Game Birds with Calvados, Cream, and Truffles: Roast birds as directed through point of removing cheesecloth; drain off all but 1–2 tablespoons drippings. Pour 1/4 cup each Calvados (or brandy or champagne) and heavy cream over each bird if medium size, 2 tablespoons if small, and finish roasting as directed, basting 1–2 times. Lift birds to platter; to pan liquid add 1–2 minced truffles, warm briefly, and pour over birds.

Virginia-Style Game Birds: Roast birds as directed; if tiny, leave whole, otherwise halve or quarter according to size. Arrange on slices of sautéed, baked ham (Smithfield is best) and keep warm. Make Pan Gravy from drippings and for each cup gravy whisk in 2 tablespoons red currant jelly and 1/4 teaspoon finely grated orange rind. Pour over all and serve.

Roast Stuffed Game Birds (best for young birds weighing 3–8 pounds):

General Preparation: Same as for roasting.

Basic Method: Stuff bird loosely with any favorite stuffing, allowing 3/4–1 cup per pound of bird. Skewer openings shut, tie legs together, and fold wings back and under. Cover with butter-saturated cheesecloth and roast as for unstuffed birds, increasing cooking times about 10 minutes per pound. (*Note:* For an extra-moist bird, add a little extra liquid to stuffing.)

HOW TO BRAISE GAME BIRDS

Best for not-so-young small- and medium-size whole birds:

General Preparation: Same as for roasting.

Basic Method: Preheat oven to 350° F. Tie a 2"–3" strip of lemon or orange rind in cheesecloth with 1 bay leaf and 1 sprig each parsley and thyme, and tuck inside each bird. Tie legs together, fold wings back and under. If birds have been skinned, dredge lightly in flour. Brown birds lightly all over in 2 tablespoons butter and set aside. Make a bed of butter-sautéed, minced vegetables in an ungreased Dutch oven (for each bird allow 1/4 cup each onion, carrot, mushrooms, and celery, also 1 tablespoon minced parsley). Place birds on vegetables and pour in just enough beef or chicken broth (or a 1/2 and 1/2 mixture of chicken broth and dry red or white wine, beer, grape or orange juice) to moisten. If you like, add a peeled clove garlic. Cover and braise until leg joints move easily: Medium-size birds will take 35–45 minutes per pound, small birds 50–60. Baste 1 or 2 times with pan juices. Lift birds to a hot deep platter and keep warm. Skim fat from liquid, remove garlic clove. Purée vegetables and liquid by buzzing 20–30 seconds in an electric blender at low speed or 15–20 seconds in a food processor fitted with the metal chopping blade. Pour into a saucepan, and for each 1 cup purée add ¼ cup heavy cream or 1 tablespoon flour blended with 1 tablespoon cold water; heat, stirring, until thickened; do not boil. Pour some sauce over birds and pass the remainder. *(Note:* Birds can be halved or quartered before braising. Brown in butter as directed and arrange on vegetables. Add 1 bay leaf and 1 sprig each parsley and thyme, tied in cheesecloth, to casserole, also 1 strip lemon or orange rind. Cover and braise as directed, allowing ¾ hour for quartered medium-size birds and 30–40 minutes for small halved birds.)

VARIATIONS

Game Birds Braised with Cabbage: Prepare by basic recipe but braise on a 1½″ bed of shredded red or green cabbage instead of sautéed vegetables. Add garlic and liquid called for, also 2 fresh link sausages, sliced ½″ thick. When birds are done, remove garlic and serve on bed of cabbage.

Game Birds with Caraway, Sauerkraut, and Raisins: Brown birds as in basic method, place in a buttered casserole on a 1″ bed of drained sauerkraut sprinkled with 1 tablespoon caraway seeds and ½ cup each minced yellow onion and seedless raisins. Add 1 cup beef broth, cover, and braise until tender. Good with tall, cool glasses of beer.

Norman Game Birds: Brown birds as in basic method, place in a buttered casserole on a 1″ bed of chopped, peeled apples that have been lightly sprinkled with nutmeg and sugar and liberally dotted with butter. Add no liquid, cover, and braise as directed. When tender, lift birds to a platter, stir 2–3 tablespoons heavy cream into apples and, if you like, 2–3 tablespoons Calvados, brandy, or apple cider. Spoon mixture around birds or pass separately.

HOW TO BROIL GAME BIRDS
(in Oven or Gas or Electric Barbecue)

Best for very young tender small- or medium-size birds:

General Preparation: Have birds cleaned and dressed but not skinned. Large pheasant or duck should be halved or quartered. Tiny birds will broil more evenly if left whole, then flattened slightly with the heel of your hand.

Basic Method: Preheat broiler, setting oven temperature at 350° F. Place whole birds breast side down, pieces skin side down, on a buttered rack on a foil-lined broiler pan, sprinkle lightly with salt and pepper, and brush well with melted butter. Broil as far from heat as possible, 15–20 minutes, turn, and broil 15–20 minutes longer until evenly browned and juices run clear when thigh is pricked. *(Note:* For rare duck, broil 5″ from heat 8–10 minutes per side.) *For Extra Flavor:* Brush birds with Tarragon, Parsley, or Shallot Butter instead of plain butter.

HOW TO CHARCOAL-BROIL GAME BIRDS

Best for very young tender small- or medium-size birds:

General Preparation: Same as for oven broiling.

Basic Method: Prepare a moderately hot charcoal fire. Lay birds breast side up, pieces skin side up, on a well-oiled grill and broil 6″ from heat 30–45 minutes until fork tender, turning often and brushing frequently with melted unsalted butter or a ½ and ½ mixture of melted butter and lemon juice. Season just before serving.

VARIATIONS

Barbecued Game Birds: Marinate birds 2–3 hours in refrigerator in a favorite barbecue sauce, then broil as directed, basting often with a ½ and ½ mixture of sauce and melted butter.

Game Birds in Foil: Halve or quarter birds, brush with melted butter, and sprinkle with salt and pepper; wrap each piece in well-greased foil and cook 4″ from coals 30–40 minutes until fork tender; turn packages after 15 minutes. Unwrap, place pieces skin side down, and grill 4–5 minutes to brown.

HOW TO SPIT-ROAST GAME BIRDS

Best for young small- or medium-size birds:

General Preparation: Same as for oven broiling.

In Oven, Gas or Electric Barbecue, or Rotisserie: Preheat unit. Skewer neck skin and wings of each bird to body, tie legs together, pulling close to body. Bard* (wrap) birds with bacon or salt pork. *(Note:* Butchers will often do this for you.) Spit birds lengthwise without crowding, adjust balance as needed, and lock tines in place. Roast 5"–6" from heat, allowing 3/4–1 hour for small birds, 1–1½ hours for the medium size, basting frequently with melted unsalted butter. Remove barding fat during last 10–15 minutes so birds will brown. Take from spit, remove strings and skewers, season, and serve.

Over Charcoal: Prepare a moderately hot charcoal fire. Prepare birds as for oven spit-roasting, roast 5" from coals using above times as a guide.

HOW TO PANFRY (SAUTÉ) GAME BIRDS

Best for young small birds:

General Preparation: Have birds cleaned, dressed, and halved.

Basic Method: Lightly sprinkle birds with salt and pepper and dust with flour. Brown 2–3 minutes on a side in 1/4 cup butter, margarine, or cooking oil over moderate heat. Turn heat to low and continue cooking 10 minutes, turning frequently. Serve as is or smothered with Pan Gravy made from drippings. *For Extra Flavor:* Rub birds with garlic before dusting with flour, also, if you like, with thyme, sage, or marjoram.

VARIATIONS

Game Birds Américaine: Dip birds in flour, then beaten egg, then toasted bread crumbs, and panfry as directed. Serve on a bed of wild rice garnished with broiled, bacon-wrapped giblets and sautéed button mushrooms and cherry tomatoes.

Deviled Game Birds: Panfry birds as directed, transfer to a hot platter and keep warm; drain all but 2 tablespoons drippings from pan, add 2 tablespoons each beef broth and minced gherkins, 1 tablespoon each lemon juice and Worcestershire sauce, and 2 teaspoons Dijon mustard. Warm briefly, pour over birds, and serve.

HOW TO STEW GAME BIRDS

Best for large birds or birds of questionable age and tenderness: Follow directions for stewing a hen or capon (see Chicken).

HOW TO STEAM GAME BIRDS

Best for large birds or those of questionable tenderness: Follow directions for steaming a hen or capon (see Chicken).

PRESSURE-COOKING GAME BIRDS

Don't. It's a sacrilege to pressure-cook any succulent young bird (it will disintegrate). As for big old birds, they suffer too, becoming tougher and drier. Better to steam or stew them.

RARE ROAST WILD DUCK

2 servings

For crisp brown skin and rare meat, wild duck must be roasted fast at high heat. It should not be stuffed, so if you want stuffing, bake it separately beforehand.

1 (2–2½-pound) wild duck, cleaned and dressed
1 teaspoon salt
1/4 teaspoon pepper
1 bay leaf and 1 sprig each parsley and thyme, tied in cheesecloth *(bouquet garni)*
2 tablespoons melted butter, margarine, or bacon drippings

GRAVY
1/2 cup medium-dry red wine, chicken or beef broth, or giblet stock*
2 tablespoons minced shallots or scallions
1 bay leaf
4 peppercorns
1/8 teaspoon nutmeg (optional)

Set a shallow roasting pan and rack in oven while it preheats to 450° F. Rub duck inside and out with salt and pepper and tuck *bouquet garni* in cavity. Tie legs together, fold wings back, and brush bird with butter. Roast, uncovered, breast side up, about 15 minutes for very rare, 25 minutes for medium rare. Meanwhile, simmer gravy ingredients, uncovered, 8–10 minutes; strain and keep warm. Transfer duck to a carving board with well, remove strings, and let "rest" 5 minutes. Carve meat from duck and arrange on a hot serving platter. Drain blood and juices into gravy and warm briefly, stirring; do not boil or mixture will curdle. Taste for salt and adjust as needed. Spoon some gravy over duck and pass the rest. About 260 calories per serving.

SUPRÊMES OF WILD PHEASANT À LA CRÈME

4 servings

When pheasants have sinewy legs, use them for soup and prepare the breasts this way.

2 (2½–3-pound) pheasants, guinea fowl, grouse, or partridges, cleaned and dressed
2 cups chicken broth
1 cup water
1 small yellow onion, peeled
1 carrot, peeled
1 stalk celery, cut in 1″ lengths
4 peppercorns
3 tablespoons butter or margarine
¼ cup unsifted flour
¾ cup heavy cream
½ teaspoon salt
⅛ teaspoon nutmeg
⅛ teaspoon paprika

Place birds breast side up, side by side, on a rack in a large kettle; add broth, water, vegetables, and peppercorns. Cover and simmer ¾–1 hour until breasts are tender; cool birds in broth ½ hour, lift out, and carefully remove breasts so halves are intact. Skin breasts (save skin and remainder of birds for soup). Strain broth, then boil, uncovered, to reduce to 1½ cups. Melt butter in a large skillet over moderate heat, blend in flour, slowly add broth, cream, salt, and nutmeg, and heat, stirring, until thickened and no raw starch taste remains. Add breasts and warm slowly (do not boil), basting with sauce; lift to a hot platter, coat generously with sauce, and dust with paprika. Pass remaining sauce. About 475 calories per serving.

VARIATIONS

⚖ **Breasts of Pheasant in Aspic:** Simmer birds as directed, omitting carrot. Remove breasts, skin, and chill 3–4 hours. Save 2 cups strained cooking liquid, mix in 1 envelope unflavored gelatin, 1 egg white beaten to soft peaks, and 1 crushed eggshell. Heat, stirring with a whisk, until mixture foams up. Remove from heat, stir once, and let stand undisturbed 5 minutes. Line a sieve with a fine dish towel wrung out in cold water, set over a deep bowl, pour in hot liquid (egg, shell, and all), and let drip through to clarify. *Do not stir.* Chill clarified aspic until syrupy. Set breasts on a rack over a tray and spoon a thin, even layer of aspic over each. Chill until tacky, then decorate with truffle and pimiento cutouts and sprigs of fresh parsley or tarragon. Chill briefly to set; keep remaining aspic over warm water. Add another thin aspic layer to seal in designs; chill until firm. Also chill remaining aspic, then dice and use to garnish platter along with radish roses and watercress sprigs. About 210 calories per serving.

Breasts of Pheasant Chaud-Froid: Simmer birds as directed, omitting carrot. Remove breasts, skin, and chill. Make sauce as in Suprêmes of Pheasant (above), reducing flour to 3 tablespoons. Mix 1 envelope unflavored gelatin with ⅓ cup water and heat, stirring to dissolve; mix into sauce and chill until mixture will coat a metal spoon. Set breasts on a rack over a tray and cover with a thin, even layer of gelatin mixture. Chill until tacky, then continue building up layers until no meat shows through. While final layer is still tacky, decorate as above. If you like, seal in designs with clear aspic made using 2 cups canned chicken broth. About 475 calories per serving.

FRICASSEE OF GAME BIRDS

6 servings

A delicious way to prepare not so young and tender birds.

2 (3-pound) game birds, cleaned, dressed, and disjointed
Giblets from birds
1 yellow onion, peeled and sliced thin
1 stalk celery, cut in 1″ lengths
2½ cups chicken broth
2 tablespoons butter or margarine
½ teaspoon rosemary
1 tablespoon lemon juice
1 cup light cream (about)
⅓ cup unsifted flour blended with ⅓ cup milk
1 teaspoon salt (about)
⅛ teaspoon white pepper (about)
1 tablespoon minced parsley

Place birds, giblets, onion, celery, broth, butter, rosemary, and lemon juice in a kettle, cover, and simmer 1½–2 hours until meat is fork tender but not falling off bones; cool birds in broth ½ hour. Strain broth, measure, and add enough light cream to total 3 cups. Skin birds and, if you like, bone, keeping meat in as large pieces as possible. Pour broth mixture into a clean saucepan, blend in flour paste and heat, stirring, until thickened. Add salt and pepper, taste and adjust as needed. Add meat, mix gently, and heat, shaking pan now and then, 5 minutes. Sprinkle with parsley and serve with boiled noodles or rice. About 340 calories per serving (without noodles or rice).

EIGHT

Seafood

Few nations are more blessed with the sea's bounty than America, yet we are only beginning to learn that we can do more with fish than slosh it with batter or bread it with crumbs and plunk it into bubbling oil. There's nothing wrong with fried fish, mind you, especially if it's fresh-caught catfish served with hushpuppies. But we have too many kinds of fish and shellfish to lump into the same kettle.

From a catch less impressive than our own, the French have built an inspired repertoire of recipes. The Portuguese, it's said, know 365 ways to cook dried salt cod (bacalhau). It may be so. Certainly the Scandinavians know dozens of ways to prepare salmon and herring; the Greeks work wonders with squid and octopus; the Italians —well, it was *they* who taught the French to cook; the Chinese whisk scallops and shrimp in and out of a wok with crunches of green vegetables so that they're supremely succulent; the Japanese have made an art and ritual of *sashimi*—thinly sliced raw fish arrayed with fancily cut vegetables.

This isn't to say we haven't some classics of our own. It's hard to top a boiled Maine lobster, for example. Or Maryland crab imperial or Louisiana shrimp gumbo. But we *can* do better by our catch. If we lavished as much love on the cooking of fish as we do on the catching, we would do very well indeed.

THE KINDS OF SEAFOOD

Basically, there are two—*fish* and *shellfish.* Fish, for the sake of simplicity, have fins, backbones, and gills. Shellfish subdivide into two categories: *crustaceans* (crabs, crayfish, lobsters, shrimp, and other footed sea animals with armorlike shells) and *mollusks* (clams, mussels, oysters, scallops, and other

soft, spineless creatures living inside hard shells).

In addition to fish and shellfish, there are mavericks that defy easy classification: squid and octopus (technically mollusks that carry their shells internally); frogs and snails (amphibians). Because all require special preparation, they will be discussed individually.

The Food Value of Seafood

All seafood is high in protein; most of it is also high in minerals (notably calcium, phosphorus, copper, and iron) but low in calories. Much shellfish, alas, is also high in cholesterol. Food values vary from fish to fish, however.

SIMPLE COURT BOUILLON FOR FISH AND SHELLFISH

1 quart   ¢

The simplest court bouillon is salt water (1– 1½ teaspoons salt to 1 quart cold water). It is used to poach or steam very delicate white fish because it never masks the true flavor of the fish. The following recipe, although simple, has a touch of piquance. It is suitable for poaching any fish or shellfish.

1 large sprig parsley
1 bay leaf
1 (3"–4") sprig fresh thyme or ¼ teaspoon dried thyme
3 peppercorns
1 quart cold water
¼ cup white vinegar
1 medium-size yellow onion, peeled and stuck with 3 cloves
1 carrot, peeled and cut in small dice
1 stalk celery, chopped fine
1 teaspoon salt

Tie parsley, bay leaf, thyme, and pepper-corns in cheesecloth. Place in a saucepan, add remaining ingredients, cover, and simmer 1 hour; strain through a fine sieve.

NP Cup: 8 C, 0 mg CH, 555 mg S*

WHITE WINE COURT BOUILLON

2 quarts

Especially good for shellfish.

1/2 **pound fishbones, heads, and trimmings (from any delicate white fish)**
1 **quart water**
1 **quart dry white wine**
2 **small yellow onions, each peeled and stuck with 1 clove**
2 **bay leaves**
2 **cloves garlic, peeled**
1 **teaspoon thyme**
2 **sprigs parsley**
2 **sprigs fresh dill (optional)**
1 **teaspoon salt**
6 **bruised peppercorns**

Place fishbones and water in a large saucepan, cover, and simmer 20 minutes; strain broth through a fine sieve lined with a double thickness of cheesecloth; discard bones. Rinse out pan, add strained broth and remaining ingredients, and simmer, uncovered, 20 minutes. Again strain broth through a double thickness of cheesecloth.

NP Cup: 30 C, 2 mg CH, 285 mg S*

RICH WINE COURT BOUILLON FOR FISH AND SHELLFISH

3 quarts

An excellent base for soups, sauces, and elaborate seafood dishes.

2 **pounds fishbones, heads, and trimmings (from any delicate white fish)**
2 **quarts cold water**
1 **(1-liter) bottle dry or medium-dry red or white wine**
1/4 **cup lemon juice**
1 **medium-size yellow onion, peeled and quartered**
1 **stalk celery, coarsely chopped**
1 **bay leaf and 1 sprig each parsley and thyme, tied in cheesecloth** (*bouquet garni*)
1 **teaspoon salt**

Place all ingredients in a large kettle, cover, and simmer 1 hour. Strain through a large sieve lined with a double thickness of cheesecloth.

NP Cup: 15 C, 0 mg CH, 95 mg S*

VARIATION

Court Bouillon for Aspics: Prepare as directed, reducing water to 6 cups and wine to 2 cups; increase simmering time to 2 hours. Skim off any froth and strain liquid through a cheesecloth-lined sieve; do not press solids. Measure liquid and, if needed, add cold water to make 2 quarts. To see if liquid will jell, chill 1 cup. If it sets up as firm as commercial gelatin, you need not add gelatin. If it doesn't, mix in 1 envelope unflavored gelatin softened in 1/4 cup cold water and heat, stirring, until dissolved. *To clarify court bouillon:* Place all liquid (including chilled portion) in a large, deep saucepan. Add 2 egg whites, beaten to soft peaks, also 2 eggshells, crushed. Bring to a boil, stirring constantly with a wire whisk, and as soon as mixture foams up, remove from heat. Stir one or two times, then let stand *undisturbed* 5 minutes. Meanwhile, line a large, fine sieve with a fine linen towel or napkin wrung out in cold water and set over a deep bowl so bottom of sieve will be clear of aspic collecting in bowl. Pour aspic into sieve, egg whites, shells, and all, and let drip through undisturbed. Aspic is now ready to use as recipes direct.

NP Cup: 15 C, 2 mg CH, 285 mg S*

SOME WAYS TO USE UP LEFTOVER FISH AND SHELLFISH

It is unlikely that you'll be faced with much leftover fish unless you'd planned on eight for dinner and only four came. Here are some recipes (all can be found in the recipe section) particularly suited to leftovers, also some suggestions for using up small amounts.

Recipes Good for Leftovers:

Potato-Fish Pie
Basic Fish Soufflé (and all variations)
Fish Loaf
Fish Croquettes
Fish Cakes (or use recipe for Codfish Cakes, substituting leftover fish for salt cod)
Kedgeree
Basic Shellfish Croquettes
Basic Shellfish Soufflé

To Make the Most of Very Small Amounts:
• Combine with canned fish or shellfish, mayonnaise to bind, and seasonings to taste and use as a sandwich filling or to stuff eggs, tomatoes, or avocados.

• Stretch with an equal quantity of hot Medium White Sauce, Mornay, Parsley, or Egg Sauce and spoon over crepes, puff pastry shells, hot toast, or biscuits.

• Stretch with an equal quantity of hot Medium White Sauce, Mornay, Velouté, or Parsley Sauce, layer into buttered ramekins with hot boiled rice or thin noodles, top with grated cheese or buttered crumbs, and broil quickly to brown.

• Use in making Easy Fish Stock or any court bouillon.

FISH

All fish, whether salt- or freshwater, fall into two categories: the *lean* (delicate, low-calorie fish, whose oils are concentrated in the liver) and the *oily or fat,* whose oils are distributed throughout the flesh. Oily fish are usually darker fleshed and stronger flavored than lean fish (tuna, for example, is darker and stronger than flounder). To determine which fish are which, see the charts of America's popular salt- and freshwater fish included in this chapter.

BUYING FRESH FISH

Find a good fish market (or a supermarket with a first-rate fish section) and make friends with the owner or manager—it's the surest way of getting absolutely fresh, top-quality seafood. Also learn to recognize these *hallmarks of quality and freshness:*

• Sparkling, clear, bulging eyes.

• Rosy, sweet-smelling gills.

• Bright, shimmery, tightly clinging scales.

• Firm, springy, translucent, lifelike flesh.

• An overall fresh, clean smell.

Safety Precautions: Because of the increasing pollution of American lakes, rivers, bays, and estuaries, departments of health in many highly industrialized areas warn people *to limit their consumption of freshwater fish to ¹/2 pound a week unless they know the fish comes from clean waters. Pregnant women, nursing mothers, and children, moreover, are advised to eat no freshwater fish at all. And in no instance should anyone eat RAW freshwater fish.* Certain saltwater fish may be risky, too, if caught in waters off big metropolitan or industrial areas, particularly striped bass, bluefish, white perch,

ocean catfish, and American eel, which are showing higher and higher levels of dioxin (the federal government at present permits 50 parts per trillion). Finally, because of the danger of viral and/or bacterial pollution, never eat *raw* clams or oysters taken from inshore waters. If you are in doubt about the safety of fish or shellfish caught in your area, call your city, county, or state health department.

Federally Graded Fish

More and more supermarkets are now offering fresh fish labeled *U.S. GRADE A.* What this means is that certain grocery chains pay U.S. Department of Commerce inspectors to grade the fish they intend to sell. The characteristics that determine *GRADE A quality* are essentially the same as the *hallmarks of quality and freshness* listed above. *GRADE A,* by the way, is the only grade of fish you're likely to see.

Popular Market Forms of Fresh Fish

Whole or Round: Fish as they're taken from the water. Before cooking they must be drawn or cleaned (eviscerated) and scaled.

Drawn or Cleaned: Whole fish that have been eviscerated. Scales must be removed before cooking.

Cleaned and Dressed or Pan-Dressed: Ready-to-cook fish that have been cleaned and scaled. Usually head, tail and fins have been removed, too. *Dressed* refers to fish weighing 1 pound or more, *pan-dressed* to those weighing less.

Steaks: Cross-section cuts of large, cleaned, and dressed fish; they contain backbone.

Fillets: The boneless sides of fish or, more recently, any thin, long boneless piece of fish.

Butterfly Fillets: Both sides of the fish, boned but still attached on one side so that they can be opened flat like a book.

Chunks: Thick, cross-cut slices of large, cleaned, and dressed fish. Like steaks, they contain a cross-section of the backbone.

How Much Fish Should You Buy?

Market Form	Amount per Serving
Whole, drawn	3/4–1 pound
Whole, dressed	1/2 pound
Fillets, Steaks, Chunks	1/3 pound

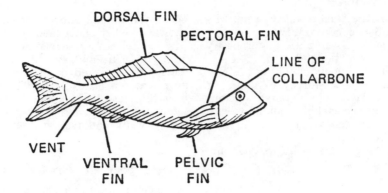

DORSAL FIN

PECTORAL FIN

LINE OF COLLARBONE

VENT

VENTRAL FIN

PELVIC FIN

HOW TO CLEAN FRESH FISH

If you buy fish, you can have the store clean and dress it. But if there are sportsmen in your family or neighborhood, you may have to cope with an uncleaned, undressed catch. The job isn't fun, but fortunately it *is* fast. Here's the procedure:

1. *Scaling:* Wash fish, place on cutting board, and with one hand hold head firmly (if you salt your hands, you'll get a better grip). With knife blade held almost vertical, scrape from tail to head, against grain of scales. Pay special attention to area around fins. A second technique is to nail fish to board through the tail with an ice pick or long, thin nail, then to scrape briskly toward head (there's less danger of slipping and cutting yourself). There are scalers to make the job easier; but many fishermen prefer a homemade gadget: a slim block of wood with bottle caps nailed upside-down on one side of it.

2. *Cleaning:* Split belly from vent to head and scoop out viscera. Cut around pelvic fins and lift them out.

3. *Removing Head and Tail:* Cut just behind collarbone so head and pectoral fins will come off in one operation. If fish is large and backbone tough, move fish to edge of cutting board so head overhangs, then snap off. Trim to even up cut; slice off tail.

4. *Finning:* Cut along each side of dorsal fin, then yank forward to remove (root bones will come away too). Remove ventral fin the same way. *(Note:* Simply snipping off fins leaves many little bones inside the fish. Rinse fish under cold running water.)

To Cut into Steaks: Slice fish crosswise, making cuts ½″–1″ or more apart, depending on how thick you like your steaks. If fish is large, rap knife with a hammer to cleave backbone neatly.

To Fillet: With an extra-sharp knife (or fillet knife), cut along back of fish from one end to the other, then with knife blade held parallel to backbone, slide it along backbone, separating meat from bones; lift off boneless piece. Turn fish over and repeat on the other side.

To Skin Fillets: Place skin side down on cutting board, hold firmly by tail end (again salt your hands for a better grip), slip knife through flesh at tail end just to skin, flatten

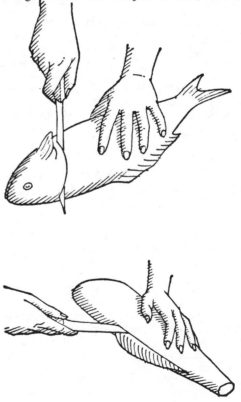

blade against skin at a 45° angle, then slide length of fillet.

To Fillet Herring (a slightly different technique): Clean and dress herring, then split entire length of stomach. Place herring cut side down, like an open book with 2 halves out to the side. Press fingertips firmly up and down backbone several times. Turn fish over, grab tail end of backbone with one hand, anchor fish to board with the other, and pull backbone up toward head. It should come away in 1 piece, bringing all the little bones with it. Now cut herring down the back into 2 fillets.

FROZEN FISH

Many of America's popular fish are available frozen in one or more of the following forms: whole, dressed, steaks, fillets, chunks, portions, and sticks.

To Be Sure of Top Quality: Buy only solidly frozen fish that shows no discoloration or freezer burn, no signs of having thawed and refrozen (a block of frozen juices at the bottom of the package); reject any fish with a strong or "off" odor. Unfortunately, much frozen fish can't be seen until the package is opened, but if you have doubts on examining the fish, return it to the market.

How to Cook Frozen Fish

Should frozen fish be thawed before cooking? It depends, on the size of the fish and how it's to be cooked. Here are some guidelines:

Fish Portions and Sticks: Cook solidly frozen.

Fillets and Steaks: Most authorities agree that it's best to thaw these 1–2 hours in the refrigerator until they're easy to separate and handle. They must be thawed (at least until soft on the outside) if they are to be breaded or the breading won't stick. If there are package directions for thawing and cooking, follow them.

Whole Fish, Dressed Fish, and Large Chunks: Whole fish must be thawed so that they can be cleaned and dressed. Dressed fish and large chunks must be thawed if they're to be stuffed. And, many experts believe, whole fish and large pieces will poach and steam more evenly if thawed before cooking. As for baking, it seems to make little difference, *except* that solidly frozen fish

will take approximately twice as long to cook as the thawed.

Best Ways to Thaw Frozen Fish

Always thaw just before cooking and, once thawed, never refreeze; thawed fish can be held in refrigerator about 1 day, but no longer. Don't unwrap fish before thawing; simply set in refrigerator and thaw, allowing about 24 hours for a 1-pound package. Don't thaw at room temperature to hasten things—the danger of spoilage is too great. Instead, thaw wrapped fish under a slow stream of *cold* running water, allowing 1–2 hours per pound. Never use warm water.

Thawing Frozen Fish and Shellfish in a Microwave

Size, shape, and weight all affect defrosting time as does microwave model (read manufacturer's directions, also Defrosting, Heating, or Cooking Frozen Foods by Microwave in Chapter 1). Be especially careful about timing small whole fish, fillets, shrimp and scallops, etc. All will thaw with awesome speed in a microwave and should be checked frequently so they neither toughen nor dry. (*Note:* A short chunky fish may take longer to defrost than a long thin one of equal weight.) Listed here are guidelines that apply to thawing both fish and shellfish in the microwave:

• Begin defrosting in a dish (to catch drips) in *unopened* original wrapper unless wrapper is foil, in which case unwrap and rewrap in plastic food wrap. (*Note:* Any fish or shellfish in metal cans should be emptied into a dish; that in nonmetal containers need not be.) Arrange lobster tails belly-up on paper toweling in dish (no need to wrap those that are bulk-packaged or unwrap those packaged singly). *Exception:* Loose-packed shrimp or other shellfish should be spread one layer deep in a shallow dish and left uncovered.

• Rotate package of fish or shellfish frequently as it defrosts and when half of defrosting time has elapsed, turn package or individual pieces (shrimp, scallops, etc.) over (also *rearrange* any individual pieces and in the case of frozen blocks of oysters, clams, and the like, break up block with a fork). *Note:* Large whole fish and lobster tails may need to have thin portions shielded with aluminum foil strips lest they begin to cook; check these areas frequently and shield at once if they feel warm.

• Continue defrosting until *barely thawed:*

whole fish, lobster tails, and king crab legs should be pliable but still somewhat icy; fillets and bulk-frozen shellfish should have begun to separate from one another; shelled shrimp and scallops should feel soft and cool but still be translucent.

• To complete defrosting, allow a period of *standing time:* 5–10 minutes for fillets, small whole fish, lobster tails, shrimp, scallops, and other small shellfish (including those that were frozen in a solid block), 15–20 minutes for whole large fish.

• After *standing time,* rinse whole fish under cold running water until cavity is no longer icy; also rinse fillets until they can be separated easily.

• Cook fish or shellfish *immediately* after standing time or refrigerate at once and cook within a day.

Caution: Never microwave frozen fish or shellfish without defrosting it first; it will be tasteless, dry, and unevenly cooked.

Thawing Frozen Fish and Shellfish in a Convection Oven

DON'T—even in one with an automatic defrost cycle. Surface of seafood will dry (or cook) before the inside thaws.

CANNED FISH

The list of canned fish is long and getting longer. Here are some of the most popular items:

Anchovies: Fillets are available either flat or rolled around capers and preserved in oil; paste comes in tubes.

Bonito: See Tuna.

Mackerel: Canned chunks are available, either plain or in sauce (tomato or wine). Mackerel roe is also canned.

Salmon: The five kinds available, from expensive to inexpensive are: red or sockeye; chinook or king; coho or silver (also sometimes called medium red); pink or humpback; and, finally, chum.

Sardines: These are packed whole in oil, also boned and skinned. The most highly prized are the Portuguese, packed in a top-grade olive oil; next best are the herbed and spiced French sardines.

Tuna: The choicest is *albacore* or *white-meat tuna. Light-meat* tuna ranges from pink to red-brown and comes from bluefin, skipjack or bonito, or yellowfin. Three packs are

available: *fancy or solid* (expensive), best used when appearance is important; *chunk* (moderate), good for salads and casseroles; and *flaked* (relatively inexpensive), good for sandwich spreads and canapés.

Some Specialty Items: Red (salmon), golden (whitefish), and black (sturgeon) caviar (see discussion in chapter on appetizers and hors d'oeuvre); eel; smoked and pickled herring; shad roe.

OTHER FORMS OF FISH

In addition to being sold fresh, frozen, and canned, many fish are also available in brine, dried, salted, and/or smoked (kippered). Consult charts of popular salt- and freshwater fish to determine which are available in which forms.

Also popular: Relatively new *seafood sticks* made of minced fish (usually pollack), egg white, starch, and crab flavoring. They resemble Alaska king crab meat in both texture and flavor. They're cheap and can be substituted for crab, shrimp, lobster, and scallops in casseroles, soups, and sauces. Not new, but becoming increasingly available in Oriental and specialty groceries are *shark's fins* (dried cartilage), which must be soaked overnight before they are used.

FRESH FISH

How to Cook Fresh Fish

Fish is as fragile as a soufflé; cooking can never make it more tender than it already is, only more attractive and flavorful. The greatest crime committed against fish is overcooking. When is fish done—and not overdone? The instant the flesh turns from translucent to opaque and flakes (falls easily into natural divisions) when probed with a fork. Flaking is the test of doneness for all fish, regardless of how it's cooked. Keep the fork handy, test often, and serve the fish the second it flakes.

To Bake

Best for whole fish, large chunks, steaks, and fillets; for names of fish that are "good bakers," consult the fish charts that follow:

To Bake Whole Fish:

General Preparation: Have fish cleaned but leave head and tail on. If you're squeamish about looking a baked fish in the eye, take the head off before transferring to platter, *but not before*—a headless fish will lose juices during cooking. Lightly sprinkle cavity of fish with salt and pepper. Do not slash skin.

Basic Method: Preheat oven to 400° F. Line a large, shallow baking pan with foil and grease well (so fish will be easier to transfer to platter and pan will be quicker to clean). Lay fish in pan (if you are baking more than 1 fish at a time, make sure they do not touch one another). If fish are lean, brush well with melted butter or margarine or drape with bacon strips. Now measure thickness of fish at the thickest point and bake, uncovered, allowing 10 minutes per inch of thickness, or, if you prefer, 10–15 minutes per pound, basting as needed with additional melted butter. It is difficult to be more specific about baking times because fish vary so in shape. Keep the testing fork handy and begin probing gently after minimum baking time is up. *(Note:* Small fish take proportionately longer to cook than large ones.) When fish is done, carefully transfer to a heated platter, top with some of the pan juices, and serve as is or with a compatible sauce such as Caper, Duxelles, Mornay, or Parsley. *For Extra Flavor:* Baste fish with a seasoned butter, a half-and-half mixture of melted butter and dry white wine, with light cream or with herb, French, or Italian dressing. *For Low-Calorie Baked Fish:* Choose a lean, low-calorie fish and baste with a low-calorie French, Italian, herb, or garlic dressing during cooking instead of butter.

Continental Method (also called *Braising):* Preheat oven to 400° F. Line pan with foil and grease, then make a 1/2″ bed of finely chopped vegetables in pan (equal parts minced onions, celery, and carrots; minced onions and mushrooms; or minced onions, tomatoes, and sweet red or green peppers); mix in 2–3 tablespoons minced fresh parsley and about 2 tablespoons melted butter or margarine. Lay fish on vegetables and proceed as in Basic Method above.

To Bake a Whole, Stuffed Fish: (Bluefish, cod, haddock, mackerel, red snapper, salmon, shad, and trout are particularly elegant when stuffed.) For other fish to stuff and bake, see charts of salt and freshwater fish.

General Preparation: Should fish be boned before stuffing? Yes, if possible. A boned fish is easier and pleasanter to eat; unfortunately, all fish are not easy to bone without filleting. Try to have your fish market bone the fish

and prepare it for stuffing. If you must prepare it yourself, here are two ways. For each it's best to have fish that has not been cleaned and dressed.

Method I. Slit fish down the back, slide a sharp, thin-bladed knife down along backbone, first on one side, then on the other, to separate meat from bone. With poultry shears, cut through backbone at both ends and lift backbone out. Remove all viscera through this opening. Scale the fish, remove fins, then rinse well in cool water and pat dry.

Method II. Slit fish down belly and eviscerate, following Method I. Deepen cut to backbone, separating meat from bones as you go. Cut through backbone at head and tail ends using poultry shears and pull backbone out through the stomach opening; vertebrae and other small bones should come away with the backbone, but examine cavity carefully for any "missed bones" and pull out. Rinse fish in cool water and pat dry.

Basic Method of Baking: Preheat oven to 400° F. Line a large, shallow baking pan with foil, then grease the foil. Loosely stuff fish with Basic Bread, Lemon Bread, or other fish stuffing such as Mushroom, Vegetable, Crab or Shrimp; you'll need about 2 cups stuffing for a 3–4-pound fish, 1 quart for a 6–7-pounder. Wrap any remaining stuffing in foil and place in baking pan. Toothpick cavity of fish shut or, if skin is tough, loosely sew up. Brush fish well with melted butter or margarine and bake, uncovered, 12–15 minutes per pound *(this is per pound of dressed weight, not stuffed weight).* While fish bakes, baste as needed with additional melted butter; remove fish from oven as soon as it will flake at the touch of a fork. *For Extra Flavor:* Use any of the suggestions given in the Basic Method above. When fish is done, carefully transfer to a hot platter and remove toothpicks or thread.

To Bake Fish Fillets, Steaks, and Chunks:

General Preparation: Pat fish dry on paper toweling. Leave fillets whole or fold envelope style, ends toward center.

Basic Method: Preheat oven to 350° F. Line a large, shallow baking pan with foil and grease well. Arrange fish pieces in a single layer, not touching. Sprinkle lightly with salt and pepper. If fish is lean, drizzle with 1/4–1/3 cup melted butter or margarine; otherwise, brush lightly with melted butter. Bake, uncovered, 20–30 minutes, basting once or twice, until fish flakes. Lift fish to a heated platter with a pancake turner, top with some of the pan juices, sprinkle with paprika and/or parsley, and serve. *For Extra Flavor:* Substitute Lemon, Parsley, or Herb Butter for the plain. *For Low-Calorie Baked Fillets, Steaks, and Chunks:* Choose a lean, low-calorie fish and baste with a low-calorie French, Italian, herb, or garlic dressing instead of butter.

To Oven-Broil

Best for steaks, fillets, and small whole or split fish:

General Preparation: If fish are whole, have cleaned or cleaned and dressed; if you like, split in half lengthwise. Pat fish, steaks, or fillets dry on paper toweling and, if you want, dredge lightly in flour.

Basic Method: Preheat broiler. Line broiler pan and rack with foil. Arrange fish on rack in a single layer, not touching each other, brush with melted butter or margarine, and sprinkle with salt and pepper. Just how long fish should be broiled can only be estimated at best because size, shape, and delicacy of fish vary greatly. The flaking test is the only true test of doneness. Use the following table as a guide:

FISH BROILING CHART

Cut	Thickness	Distance from Heat	Minutes on First Side	Minutes on Second Side
Steaks	1/2″	2″	3	3–5
Steaks	1″	2″	3–5	4–5

(Note: Lean fish like cod, halibut, and bass should be basted once during cooking with melted butter or margarine or cooking oil.)

Fillets	1/4″–1/2″	2″	4–5 minutes (do not turn)	
Fillets	3/4″–1″	2″	7–10 minutes (do not turn)	

(Note: All fillets should be basted at least once during cooking; very lean ones [cod, fluke, flounder, sole, etc.] twice. If fillets have not been skinned, broil skin side down.)

Split (halved) fish	1/2″–1″	3″	7–10 minutes (do not turn)	
Split (halved) fish	1″–11/2″	3″	10–14 minutes (do not turn)	
	Weight			
Whole fish (small)	1–2 lbs.	3″	3–5	5–6
Whole fish (medium)	3–5 lbs.	5″–6″	5–7	7–10
Whole flat fish (fluke, flounder, etc.)	—	3″	8–10 minutes (do not turn)	

(Note: Broil split fish skin side down and baste once during cooking, twice if very lean. Whole fish should be basted at least once during cooking, 2–3 times if lean.)
For Extra Flavor: Use a seasoned butter for basting or a 1/2 and 1/2 mixture of melted butter and lemon juice or dry white wine. *For Low-Calorie Broiled Fish:* Select a lean fish and baste with low-calorie herb or garlic dressing instead of butter.

To Charcoal-Broil

Best for thick (1″) fillets, small to medium whole or split fish:

General Preparation: Same as for oven broiling.

Basic Method: Prepare a moderately hot charcoal fire. Grease a long-handled, hinged wire grill well. Brush fish generously with a 1/2 and 1/2 mixture of melted butter and lemon juice, place in grill, and broil 4″ from coals 5–8 minutes on one side, basting frequently with butter mixture. Turn and grill other side 5–8 minutes, basting often, until fish flakes when touched with a fork. *(Note:* Cooking techniques (and times) are essentially the same for outdoor gas and electric grills. Be sure to preheat them.)

VARIATION

Barbecued Fish: (best for 1″ fillets and steaks): Marinate fish 1–2 hours in a favorite barbecue sauce before cooking. Charcoal broil as above but baste with barbecue sauce instead of butter.

To Panfry (Sauté)

Best for fillets, steaks, and small whole fish:

General Preparation: Have whole fish cleaned and, if you like, dressed. Pat fish very dry between several thicknesses of paper toweling.

Basic Method: Lightly sprinkle both sides of fish with salt and pepper, then dust with flour. Sauté in 3–4 tablespoons butter or magarine or cooking oil or, if you prefer, a 1/2 and 1/2 mixture of butter and cooking oil in a large, heavy skillet over moderate heat or in an electric skillet set at 350° F. Thin fillets or steaks will take 2–3 minutes per side, thicker pieces 4–5 minutes on a side, and small whole fish 3–5 minutes per side. As fish are done, drain on paper toweling, then keep warm by setting, uncovered, in oven turned to lowest heat.

VARIATIONS

Fillets or Steaks Amandine: Sauté as in Basic Method, using butter, transfer to a hot platter and keep warm. Add 2 tablespoons butter to skillet and 1/4–1/3 cup thinly sliced blanched almonds and stir-fry 2–3 minutes until bubbly and brown. Pour over fish and serve.

Fillets or Steaks à la Meunière: Dip fish in milk, then in flour lightly seasoned with salt and pepper. Sauté as above in butter, transfer to a hot platter, and sprinkle with lemon juice and a little minced parsley. Add 2 tablespoons butter to skillet and heat, stirring up any browned bits from bottom of skillet, about 2 minutes until lightly browned. Pour over fish and serve.

Breaded Fried Fish: Lightly sprinkle both sides of whole fish, fillets, or steaks with salt and pepper and dust with flour. Dip in a mixture of beaten egg and water (2 tablespoons water for each egg) and fine dry bread crumbs, cracker meal, or a 1/2 and 1/2 mixture of flour and corn meal. Sauté by Basic Method above. *For a dry, crisp crust,* let fish dry 10–15 minutes on a wire rack after breading; then sauté. *For extra flavor:* Mix 1–2 tablespoons grated Parmesan or minced parsley into crumbs, or 1/2 teaspoon sage or thyme.

To Oven-Fry

Best for steaks, fillets, and small whole fish:

General Preparation: Have whole fish cleaned and, if you like, dressed. Pat fish very dry on paper toweling.

Basic Method: Preheat oven to 500° F. Mix 1/2 cup milk with 1 teaspoon salt and 1/8 teaspoon white pepper. Dip fish in milk, then in fine dry bread crumbs, cracker meal, or crushed cornflakes. Place in a well-greased shallow baking pan and drizzle with melted butter or margarine. Bake, uncovered, without turning or basting 10–15 minutes until golden brown and fish just flakes.

To Deep-Fat-Fry

Best for fillets cut in sticks or squares or very small fish, such as smelt:

General Preparation: If using whole fish, clean but do not dress. Pat fish very dry on paper toweling.

Basic Method: Bread fish as for Breaded Fried Fish (above), arrange in a single layer in a deep fat basket, and fry 3–4 minutes in 375° F. fat until golden brown; drain on paper toweling before serving; Scoop any bits of fish or breading from fat before adding a fresh batch of fish and keep fat as nearly at 375° F. as possible. Never let the fat smoke —the whole house will reek of fish for days.

VARIATIONS

Batter-Fried Fish: See recipe for Fish and Chips.

Shallow-Fried Fish: This method is good for fillets as well as for fish sticks and small whole fish. Bread fish as for Breaded Fried Fish or dip in batter as for Fish and Chips. Pour 1"–1 1/2" cooking oil or melted shortening in a large, heavy skillet or electric skillet set at 375° F. When fat reaches 375° F. on deep fat thermometer, lower pieces of fish, one at a time, into fat using a pancake turner and arrange in a single layer; fish should not touch each other. Fry 2–3 minutes on each side until lightly browned. Drain on paper toweling before serving.

To Poach

Best for whole fish, chunks, steaks, and fillets: See charts of popular salt- and fresh-water fish for names of those that poach well. Also see special recipes for Poached Salmon and Truite au Bleu.

General Preparation: Have whole fish cleaned and, if you like, dressed.

Fillets, Steaks, Chunks, and Small Whole Fish: Arrange fish barely touching in a single layer in a large, heavy skillet (not iron); if using fragile fish, use a burner-to-table skillet to avoid excessive handling. Add Easy Fish Stock or a court bouillon to cover or, if you prefer, boiling water plus 1/4 cup lemon juice or white wine vinegar, 1 minced scallion, 1 sprig parsley, 1 teaspoon salt, 3–4 peppercorns, and 1/2 bay leaf. Cover and simmer gently until fish will flake: 5–10 minutes for steaks and fillets, 6–8 minutes per pound for small whole fish and chunks. *(Note:* It's important to keep water trembling, *not* boiling, so that fish will be moist and tender but firm.) Using a large pancake turner, transfer fish to a heated serving platter. Serve hot with a suitable sauce such as Allemande, Béchamel, Caper, Fines Herbes, or Hollandaise, or cool to room temperature, chill well, and serve with mayonnaise or a cold sauce. *(Note:* Save poaching liquid to use as a base for soups and sauces.)

Large Whole Fish and Chunks: Wrap fish in a double thickness of cheesecloth and place on a rack in a large, heavy kettle. Add Easy Fish Stock or a court bouillon to cover or, if you prefer, the water and seasonings called for in poaching fillets. *(Note:* If more than 3 cups water are needed for poaching the fish, double the amount of lemon juice and seasonings.) Cover and bring slowly to a simmer, adjust heat so water stays at a tremble, then poach 8–10 minutes per pound until fish will flake. Carefully lift fish from kettle using 2 pancake turners; remove cheesecloth and peel away fish skin. Serve hot with a compatible sauce or chill and serve cold.

To Steam

Best for whole fish, chunks, steaks, thick fillets, or rolled-up thin fillets:

General Preparation: Have whole fish cleaned or cleaned and dressed; whole fish or large chunks should be wrapped in a double thickness of cheesecloth as directed for poaching.

Basic Method: Use a fish or vegetable steamer or deep kettle fitted with a rack. Grease rack well, pour in boiling water to a depth of 1″ (or as kettle manufacturer directs), place fish on rack, sprinkle lightly with salt and white pepper, cover, and steam over boiling water as follows: 5–10 minutes for steaks and fillets; 6–8 minutes per pound for large chunks or whole fish. Lift to a heated platter and serve with an appropriate sauce or butter; or cool to room temperature, then chill well and serve cold. *For Extra Flavor:* Add 1 bay leaf and 1 sprig each parsley and thyme, tied in cheesecloth, to water in kettle or use a court bouillon, white wine, cider, or beer in place of water. *For Low-Calorie Steamed Fish:* Choose a lean fish and dress with lemon or lime juice instead of a butter or sauce.

Pressure Cooking Fish

Don't! The fish will disintegrate.

Microwaving Fish and Shellfish

If carefully timed and tended, most seafood poaches, steams, scallops, and bakes beautifully in a microwave, indeed the microwave can preserve its natural succulence. The point is to microwave seafood *just* until outer portions appear opaque because the final *standing time,* outside the oven, will finish the cooking (fish will flake at the touch of a fork; shellfish will have turned opaque at the center). Size, shape, and total quantity of seafood all affect microwave cooking times as do power levels, which vary from model to model (read your microwave's manual, also Microwave Ovens in Chapter 1). Then follow these guidelines:

To Steam Fish and Shellfish by Microwave

Fish Fillets and Steaks: Arrange one layer deep in microwave-safe dish with thickest parts of fish to the outside. Never fold or roll fillets, but *do* overlap their thin ends in center of dish. *(Note:* Such super-moist fish as flounder should be placed on a trivet.) Cover fillets with damp paper toweling, steaks with vented plastic food wrap; add no liquid. Microwave for half of recommended cooking time, then if cooking fillets, turn dish 180°; for steaks, flip each over and rearrange in dish. Re-cover and microwave until surface turns opaque and just *begins* to flake when probed with a fork. Remove from oven and let stand 2–5 minutes. *(Note:* For a prettier presentation, sprinkle fish with minced parsley or paprika.)

V A R I A T I O N

To scallop fish fillets, begin steaming as directed; at half time, add liquid recipe calls for, also crumbs, then cover with wax paper; finish microwaving and let stand as directed.

Whole Fish: Place fish in microwave-safe dish (if cooking more than one, alternate heads and tails to save space). If using a *temperature probe* (a good idea), insert it on underside of fish in meatiest area just above gill. Shield heads and tails with bits of aluminum foil. Cover dish with vented plastic food wrap, arranging loosely around probe. Microwave as manufacturer directs until fish flakes (no need to turn fish), then let *stand* 5 minutes to complete the cooking.

Whole Live Lobster: Drive point of a sharp knife into shell between body and tail (see To Split Live Lobsters), then split, removing coral and tomalley, or leave whole. If cooking whole, insert a wooden skewer lengthwise through underside of shell to hold tail straight. Lay lobster belly-up in microwave-safe dish, add 1/2 cup hot water, cover with vented plastic food wrap, and microwave half of time oven manufacturer recommends. Turn lobster, re-cover, and finish cooking as directed (cook split lobster just until flesh is opaque). Remove lobster from oven and let *stand* 5 minutes.

Lobster Tails: Place paper toweling in bottom of microwave-safe dish, arrange tails, belly-up, on top; add no water. Cover with vented plastic food wrap and microwave half of recommended time. Remove tails from oven and halve each lengthwise, cutting to *but not through* thin underside of shell. Spread shells, exposing meat, brush well with a 1/2 and 1/2 mix of melted butter and lemon juice, re-cover, and microwave until opaque. Let *stand* 3 minutes before serving.

Whole Crabs: Blanch live crabs in boiling water until they stop kicking; drain, and if dirty, scrub clean. Lay upside down in dish, add 1/2 cup hot water, cover with vented plastic food wrap, and microwave as directed for whole lobster.

King Crab Legs: Arrange legs in dish with light-colored sides up; add no water. Cover with vented plastic food wrap and microwave half the recommended time; turn legs over, re-cover, and cook till flesh at end of legs turns opaque. Let *stand* 3 minutes before serving.

Scallops: Arrange washed bay or sea scallops one layer deep in a shallow round microwave-safe container. Cover with damp paper toweling and microwave as oven manufacturer directs, rotating container 180° at half time; continue microwaving just until opaque. Allow 2–3 minutes *standing time* to complete the cooking.

Hard Shell Clams, Oysters, and Mussels: *To steam open:* arrange mollusks in a circle, their hinged edges toward the outside, in a shallow round, microwave-safe container. Microwave on *HIGH* 1 1/2 minutes, turn dish 180°, and microwave 1–2 minutes longer until shells open. (*Note:* If shellfish were icy

cold to start, meat inside will still be raw.) *To steam until done:* Arrange shellfish as directed for opening, but use a deeper dish. Add 1/2 cup water, cover with vented plastic food wrap, and microwave until shells open.

To Poach Fish and Shellfish by Microwave

Whole Fish, Fish Fillets and Steaks: Arrange fish as directed for steaming. Add just enough liquid (Easy Fish Stock, a court bouillon, water) to cover; cover with vented plastic food wrap and microwave, using steaming times as a guide.

Shrimp: If *shelled and deveined,* arrange no more than two layers deep in a circle in a glass pie plate; if *unshelled,* use a deeper dish. Cover with water, add 1 bay leaf and 1 tablespoon lemon juice. Cover with vented plastic food wrap and microwave as oven manufacturer directs or until shrimp turn pink. Remove from oven, drain off liquid, and let *stand* 2–3 minutes to complete the cooking.

To Bake Fish by Microwave

Fish Fillets and Steaks: These bake best on a buttered, preheated microwave browning tray or grill. Arrange fish as directed for steaming, brush with melted butter or sprinkle with browned crumbs, and bake as manufacturer directs, turning fish once at half time and testing often for doneness. If you have no browning tray or grill, keep fish covered with wax paper throughout microwaving. *Note:* Crumb coatings or toppings will not be as crisp or brown as when cooked in a conventional oven but preheating the browning tray a *second time* (just before you return the fish to it) helps crispen the flip side. Resist the impulse to run the fish under the broiler after microwaving; you risk overcooking (toughening and drying) it.

Whole Fish: Stuff fish or not as you like, but if you do, avoid packing stuffing into fish; simply spoon it in lightly. Arrange fish on a browning tray or grill or in a microwave-safe dish, then, if you like, brush at the outset with a favorite barbecue sauce, a 1/2 and 1/2 mix of water and liquid gravy browner or a 1/2 and 1/2 mix of lemon juice and melted butter. Insert temperature probe as directed for steaming whole fish, then if you are not using the browning tray or grill, cover with wax paper; microwave, using times for steaming whole fish as a guide. Let *stand* 5 minutes and serve.

Fish Soufflés: Use lean, dry fish when making the soufflé, then during baking, rotate soufflé dish often (a quarter turn each time) to ensure even rising. If the edges of the soufflé begin to dry before center is set, shield with strips of aluminum foil. *Note:* Although microwaved soufflés will not brown as nicely as those baked in conventional ovens, they will remain deliciously moist (read To Microwave a Soufflé in Chapter 9).

Some Additional Do's and Don'ts:
• If a seafood does not test done after the *standing time,* microwave a few *seconds* longer, but take care not to overcook.
• To ensure uniform cooking, shape any fish loaves *round* rather than oblong.
• For even heating, rotate layered casseroles that cannot be stirred.
• When microwaving gumbos, curries, soupy casseroles, scalloped seafoods, or heavily sauced dishes, reduce quantity of liquid or sauce a recipe calls for by about one quarter. Microwave *covered with wax paper* and stir or rotate dish often.
• When adding rice to stuffings or casseroles, use the quick-cooking kind only (regular rice will not cook done in the short time needed for the other ingredients).
• Puncture pouches of commercially prepared frozen seafood dishes before microwaving so they don't explode.
• Don't try to microwave recipes with pastry toppings (they won't brown), rolled stuffed fish fillets (fish will dry before stuffing cooks), frozen breaded or batter-coated fish sticks or fillets (they will not crispen properly).

Reheating Fish and Shellfish in a Microwave

As a general rule, only sauced seafoods reheat well in a microwave (curries, gumbos, jambalayas, etc.) although we have had good luck reheating such appetizers as Shrimp Rumaki, Boston-Style Stuffed Clams, and Baked Alaska King Crab Legs. Always cover seafood with wax paper or plastic food wrap when reheating it, time the reheating carefully, and stir mixtures from the edges toward the center to ensure even distribution of heat.

Cooking Fish and Shellfish in a Convection Oven

Convection cooking (via hot circulating air) is particularly suited to baking whole fish and fillets. It's quicker than conventional cooking and thus, if properly done, will yield moist and tender fish every time. Switching from conventional to convection cooking requires no major adjustment, merely lower temperatures and/or shorter cooking times. In most instances, you needn't even preheat the oven *(exceptions: broiling and oven frying)*. The following pointers will help you cook fish and shellfish perfectly in a convection oven (also read Convection Ovens in Chapter 1):
• To permit maximum air circulation in convection oven, use pans at least 1/2" smaller all around than oven itself.
• To bake stuffed or unstuffed whole fish, place oven rack in middle or lower position, set fish *directly on rack,* and place a drip tray on oven floor. Do not cover the fish. Reduce oven temperature called for in recipe 25° F. and frequently test fish for doneness after three fourths of baking time.
• To oven fry fish, preheat oven, then reduce temperature called for by about 50° F. (batter-dipped or crumbed seafood oven-fries beautifully at 400°–450° F. in about the same length of time needed to oven-fry it at 450°–500° F. in a conventional oven).
• To broil or not to broil in a convection oven? The only advantage is that you don't have to turn the fish *if* you place it *directly on lowest oven rack* (there should be a drip pan on oven floor underneath). You must preheat the convection oven for broiling, and even then, you'll find that it broils food more slowly than a conventional oven because the heating element is farther from the food.
• When adapting recipes for the convection oven, adjust as follows: *recipes calling for some liquid and a lid* should be baked at temperatures about 25° F. lower than those suggested and be checked for doneness when three fourths of cooking time has elapsed . . . *covered casseroles* should be baked as directed, but check for doneness when three fourths of cooking time is up (to brown them, simply uncover for final 15 minutes of baking) . . . *fish loaves, pasta-seafood casseroles, and other high-density foods* should be cooked at temperatures recipes specify, but test for doneness often during the final baking quarter . . . *soufflés* fare best at about 350° F. (they'll rise to stratospheric heights and brown superbly), but check frequently for doneness 5–10 minutes before allotted baking time is up.

How to Serve Whole Fish and Large Chunks

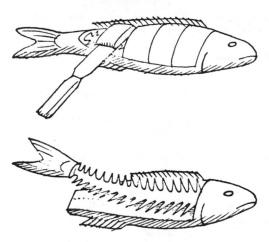

Turn platter so back of fish is away from you; beginning near head, make a cut the length of fish along backbone and loosen flesh from bone. Slice 1″–2″ wide, cutting only to bones, and lift out each slice, using a fish or pie server. Lift out backbone, pulling away vertebrae; continue slicing as before.

FISH CAKES

4 servings   ¢ ⊠

A half-and-half combination of fish and mashed potatoes that is both easy and economical.

1½ cups skinned, boned, cooked flaked fish (any kind)
1½ cups seasoned mashed potatoes
1 egg, lightly beaten
2 tablespoons minced parsley
⅛ teaspoon pepper
½ teaspoon salt (about)
1 egg lightly beaten with 1 tablespoon cold water
½ cup toasted bread crumbs
⅓ cup cooking oil

Mix fish with potatoes, egg, parsley, pepper, and salt; taste for salt and add more if needed. Shape mixture into 4 flat cakes, dip in egg mixture, then in crumbs to coat. Heat oil in a large, heavy skillet over moderate heat until a cube of bread will sizzle. Add fish cakes and brown 3–5 minutes on each side. Drain on paper toweling and serve. Pass Parsley Sauce or Tomato Sauce if you like.

NPS: 215 C, 185 mg CH, 725 mg S*

FISH CROQUETTES

4 servings

A perfect way to use up any leftover fish.

2 tablespoons butter or margarine
3 tablespoons flour
1 cup milk
½ teaspoon salt (about)
⅛ teaspoon white pepper
2 teaspoons Worcestershire sauce
1 egg yolk, lightly beaten
1½ cups soft white bread crumbs
1½ cups skinned, boned, cooked, finely ground fish (any kind)
1 tablespoon lemon juice
Shortening or cooking oil for deep fat frying

COATING
1 egg, lightly beaten
1 cup fine dry bread crumbs

Melt butter in a saucepan over moderate heat, blend in flour, slowly add milk, and heat, stirring, until thickened. Off heat, mix in seasonings, egg yolk, crumbs, fish, and lemon juice; taste for salt and adjust if needed. Cover and chill 3–4 hours. Shape mixture into 8 patties or sausage-shaped rolls, dip in egg and roll in crumbs to coat. Let stand at room temperature on a wire rack while heating fat. Place shortening in a deep fat fryer and heat to 375° F.; use a deep fat thermometer. Place 3 or 4 croquettes in fryer basket, lower into hot fat, and fry 2–3 minutes until golden brown and crisp; drain on paper toweling, then keep warm by setting, uncovered, in oven turned to lowest heat while you fry the rest. Serve hot with Tartar Sauce.

NPS: 135 C, 210 mg CH, 745 mg S*

AMERICA'S POPULAR SALTWATER FISH

Market Name and Description	Season	Where Available	Best Ways to Cook
Amberjack 10–12 lbs. Lean. Fine-fleshed, mild. *Market Forms:* whole (more often caught than bought).	Winter, spring	South Atlantic coast	Bake (stuffed or unstuffed), broil, panfry
Barracuda 10–15 lbs. Oily. Strong, dark-fleshed; Pacific barracuda is smaller, leaner. *Market Forms:* whole, occasionally fresh and frozen steaks (more often caught than bought).	Year round	Atlantic and Gulf coasts, California	Bake, broil, charcoal-broil
Bluefish 3–10 lbs. Oily. Rich, fine-grained white to silvery gray meat. *Market Forms:* whole.	Spring, summer, fall	Atlantic and Gulf coasts	Bake (stuffed or unstuffed), broil
Butterfish Average ½ lb. Oily. Also called dollarfish, pumpkinseed. Rich, tender, sweet white meat. *Market Forms:* whole.	Spring, summer, fall	Atlantic and Gulf coasts	Broil, panfry
Cobia Average 10 lbs. Oily. Firm, light flesh of good but not strong flavor. *Market Forms:* whole, steaks, chunks (more often caught than bought).	Spring	South Atlantic and Gulf coasts	Bake (stuffed or unstuffed), broil, or charcoal-broil
Cod Average 10 lbs. but can reach 100 lbs. Lean. Bland snowy meat; poorly cooked, it can be watery or woolly. Young (1½–2½-pound) cod are called scrod (so are young haddock and pollack). *Market Forms:* whole, fresh, and frozen steaks and fillets; smoked, salted, dried. Special delicacies: cod cheeks (sounds) and tongues.	Year round	North Atlantic and Pacific	*Whole or large pieces:* bake (stuffed or unstuffed), braise, poach. *Steaks:* panfry, broil, charcoal-broil. *Fillets:* panfry, poach, broil
Croaker Average 1 lb. Lean. Delicate, often underrated little fish. *Market Forms:* whole.	Year round	Middle and South Atlantic coasts	Broil, panfry
Drum (red and black) 8–10 lbs. Lean. The red drum, also called Channel bass or redfish, is choicer; black drum is bony. *Market Forms:* whole (if small), fillets, steaks; 5-pounders are called "puppy drums."	Summer, fall	New York to Texas	Bake (stuffed or unstuffed), broil or panfry steaks, fillets
Eel Average 1–4 lbs. Oily. Surprisingly mellow-flavored meat. *Market Forms:* live; also smoked, canned.	Year round	Maine to Texas	Bake, broil, panfry, deep fry, poach
Flounder Average 2–3 lbs. Lean. A family of flat fish often sold as lemon or gray sole; America has no true sole (other than that imported from Europe). Flounder is related to sole and similarly fine, white, and delicate. *Market Forms:* whole, fresh and frozen fillets.	Year round	Atlantic, Gulf, and Pacific coasts	Bake, broil, charcoal-broil, panfry, deep fry, poach
Fluke 1–5 lbs. Lean. A flounderlike fish with delicate white meat; also called plaice. *Market Forms:* whole, fresh and frozen fillets.	Spring, summer	North Atlantic	Same as for Flounder

Market Name and Description	Season	Where Available	Best Ways to Cook
Grouper Up to 700 lbs. but 5–15 pounders best. Lean. Best known: red grouper. Others are rock, speckled, Nassau, black, yellowfish, and jewfish. Remove strong-flavored skin before cooking. *Market Forms:* whole, fresh and frozen fillets, steaks.	Year round	North and South Atlantic, Gulf Coast	Bake (stuffed or unstuffed), broil, panfry, deep fry, poach
Haddock 2–5 lbs. Lean. A fine-grained codlike fish. *Market Forms:* whole, fresh and frozen fillets; smoked (finnan haddie), salted, flaked.	Year round	·Atlantic	Bake (stuffed or unstuffed), broil, panfry, deep fry, poach
Hake (see Whiting)			
Halibut 1½–50 lbs. or more. Lean. A large, moderately strong flat fish; badly cooked, it becomes dry and woolly. *Market Forms:* small (1½ pounds) fish are sold whole as "chicken halibut"; large halibut are cut into steaks and fillets and available fresh, frozen, and smoked.	Year round but best in spring	Atlantic and Pacific coasts	Bake (stuffed or unstuffed), broil, panfry, poach, steam
Herring ½–¾ lb. Oily. An enormous family that includes alewives, shad, and sardines (sardines are young herring 3″–6″ long; whitebait are young herring 2″–3″ long, sold fresh and frozen). They are so small they are cooked—and eaten—whole, heads and all. Sprats are smoked sardines; brislings are European sardines. *Matjes* herring are pickled German-style, either whole or filleted; soak in water before using. *Market Forms:* whole; brined, salted, pickled, smoked (kippered), canned.	Spring	Atlantic and Pacific coasts	Bake (stuffed or unstuffed), broil, charcoal-broil, panfry; deep fry (in the case of whitebait); brine, marinate, pickle
Jack crevalle (jack or jackfish) 2–20 lbs. Oily. This fish and its little cousin, the blue runner, are popular game fish; their meat is too gamy and bloody for most palates. *Market Forms:* whole (more often caught than bought).	Late fall, early winter	Southern Atlantic and Gulf coasts	Marinate steaks and broil or barbecue
Kingfish Average 3 lbs. Oily. Rich, firm-fleshed fish much like mackerel; a California cousin is the corbina. *Market Forms:* whole, steaks, fillets.	Late fall, winter	Southern Atlantic and Gulf coasts	Bake (stuffed or unstuffed), broil, panfry, stew
Lemon sole (see Flounder)			
Lingcod 5–20 lbs. Lean. Not a cod, despite its name, but a sleek delicate white fish. *Market Forms:* whole, steaks, fillets.	Year round	West Coast	Bake (stuffed or unstuffed), broil, panfry
Mackerel (Atlantic) 1–2 lbs. Oily. The huge mackerel family includes wahoo, chub, king, and Spanish mackerel, but the best is the small, rich, firm-fleshed Atlantic mackerel. *Market Forms:* whole, fresh and frozen fillets; smoked, salted, canned.	Spring and summer	Virginia north	Bake (stuffed or unstuffed), broil, panfry, poach
Monkfish (goosefish, anglerfish, lobsterfish, sea devil, frogfish) 5–50 lbs. Lean. Firm, white, succulent meat that resembles lobster; tail only is marketed (head is large and ugly). *Market Forms:* fresh and frozen steaks, fillets.	April–November	North Atlantic	Bake, broil, panfry, deep fry, poach

Market Name and Description	Season	Where Available	Best Ways to Cook
Mullet 2–3 lbs. Oily. Often called "poor man's meat," mullet has firm flesh and robust flavor. *Market Forms:* whole, fresh and frozen fillets; smoked, salted.	Year round	Atlantic and Gulf coasts	Bake, broil, panfry, stew
Ocean perch (silver perch, white perch) ¾–1 lb. Lean. A rather firm, coarse white fish that flakes nicely when properly cooked; flavor is delicate. *Market Forms:* frozen fillets and fish sticks.	Year round	North Atlantic	Bake, broil, panfry, deep fry, poach
Pacific mackerel 1–2 lbs. Oily. Fine, firm, dark fish of good strong flavor. *Market Forms:* whole, fillets.	All year but best in fall	California	Bake, broil, barbecue
Pacific sole ¾–7 lbs. Lean. A family of delicate, white flat fish that includes petrale and rex sole, sand dabs, flounder, and turbot. *Market Forms:* whole, fillets.	Year round	West Coast	Bake, broil, charcoal-broil, panfry, deep fry, poach
Pollock 4–12 lbs. Lean. A cousin to cod, pollock is firmer, and slightly stronger flavored. *Market Forms:* whole, steaks, fresh and frozen fillets; smoked.	Year round	North Atlantic	Bake (stuffed or unstuffed), broil, panfry, deep fry, poach
Pompano 1½–3 lbs. Oily. Often considered to be America's finest fish because of its exceptionally fine, succulent flesh and delicate flavor. *Market Forms:* whole, fresh and frozen fillets.	Year round	Southern Atlantic and Gulf coasts	Bake *en papillote*, broil, panfry
Porgies Scup: 1–2 lbs.; Sheepshead: 2–6 lbs. Lean. Scup and sheepshead both have fine flavor and white meat. *Market Forms:* whole, occasionally fillets.	Spring, early summer	Scup: North Atlantic; Sheepshead: Atlantic and Gulf coasts	Broil, panfry; Sheepshead may be stuffed and baked
Red snapper Up to 50 lbs. but 5–10-pounders are best. Lean. A beautiful fish with meaty, moist, mildly flavored flesh. *Market Forms:* whole, steaks, fresh and frozen fillets.	Year round	South Atlantic and Gulf coasts	Bake (stuffed or unstuffed), broil, panfry, poach
Rockfish 2–5 lbs. Lean. Mild fish with pinkish-white meat. *Market Forms:* whole, fillets.	Year round	West Coast	Bake (stuffed or unstuffed), broil, panfry, poach
Sablefish 4–20 lbs. Oily. Mild but buttery white fish. *Market Forms:* whole, steaks, fillets.	Year round	West Coast	Bake (stuffed or unstuffed), broil, barbecue
Salmon 6–30 lbs. Oily. Luscious, mellow meat ranging from pale to dark pink. The 5 Pacific varieties: Chinook (biggest); chum; pink or humpback; coho or silver; sockeye or red (the smallest and finest). Eastern salmon is Atlantic or Kennebec. *Market Forms:* whole, chunks, fresh and frozen steaks; smoked (lox), salted, canned, potted.	Spring and summer	Pacific Northwest, North Atlantic	*Whole Salmon or Large Chunks:* Stuff and bake, poach, steam; *Steaks:* Bake, broil, charcoal-broil, panfry, poach
Salmon trout 4–6 lbs. Oily. Larger than freshwater trout but smaller than salmon. Pale pink, delicate flesh; a choice fish for aspics. *Market Forms:* whole, chunks, fresh steaks.	Summer	North Atlantic	Same as for Salmon

Market Name and Description	Season	Where Available	Best Ways to Cook
Sardines (see Herring)			
Sea bass ½–5 lbs. Lean. A moist white fish of good flavor but many bones. *Market Forms:* whole.	Year round	Atlantic Coast	Bake (stuffed or unstuffed), broil, charcoal-broil, poach
Sea squab 4–6 ozs. Lean. This is the blowfish; when dressed, it looks like a skinless drumstick; the meat is juicy and mild. *Market Forms:* dressed.	Spring, summer, early fall	North and mid-Atlantic coast	Broil, panfry, deep fry
Sea trout (see Weakfish)			
Shad Average 3–5 lbs. Fairly oily. The king of the herring family because of its delicate, snowy meat. *Market Forms:* whole, fillets. Also available: fresh and canned shad roe.	Early spring	Atlantic and Pacific coasts	Bake (stuffed or unstuffed), broil, panfry fillets
Shark 25–40 lbs. Oily. Firm, chewy meat similar to swordfish. *Market Forms:* fresh and frozen steaks and fillets; salted, smoked.	Year round	Atlantic and Pacific coasts	Bake, broil, barbecue
Skate 10 lbs. up. Lean. This is the sting ray; only the "wings" are edible. The strangely gelatinous meat is scraped from the bones, not cut. *Market Forms:* dressed wings.	Year round	Atlantic and Pacific coasts	Poach
Smelt 2–8 ozs. Oily. Two different types of fish are called smelt: silversides (which include grunion) and true smelt (silver and surf smelt). All are small, all have firm, well-flavored meat. *Market Forms:* whole.	Year round but best in spring and summer	Atlantic and Pacific coasts, also Great Lakes, where smelt have been transplanted	Bake, broil, panfry, deep fry
Striped bass Average 1–10 lbs. Lean. These large white-meated sea bass are becoming more popular as a food fish. *Market Forms:* whole, fresh and frozen fillets.	Year round	Atlantic, Gulf, and Pacific coasts	Bake (stuffed or unstuffed), broil, charcoal-broil, poach; panfry fillets
Sturgeon 15–300 lbs. Lean. Because sturgeon swim upriver to spawn, they are mistakenly thought of as freshwater fish (they are netted in the Hudson, among other rivers, by those after their caviar). Their flesh is fine and delicate, rather like veal. *Market Forms:* boned chunks, steaks; smoked.	Year round but best in spring, summer	North Atlantic and Pacific	Bake, panfry, poach
Swordfish 200–600 lbs. Oily. Firm, salmon-colored flesh. (*Note:* Swordfish is now considered risky because of its high mercury content.)	Spring and summer	South Atlantic and Pacific	Bake, broil, charcoal-broil, barbecue
Tautog 2–5 lbs. Lean. Also called blackfish, this one is popular in New England; flesh is lean and juicy. *Market Forms:* whole (more often caught than bought).	Spring, summer, and fall	Mid- and North Atlantic coasts	Bake (stuffed or unstuffed), broil, panfry

Market Name and Description	Season	Where Available	Best Ways to Cook
Tilefish (ocean whitefish on the West Coast) 6 lbs. (average). Lean. Faintly violet fish with yellow spots. Firm, sweet, moist flesh with distinctive flavor. *Market Forms:* whole, fresh and frozen fillets and steaks.	Year round; supplies low in September and October	North Atlantic, Pacific	Chowders, soups, stews are best. Fish may also be baked, broiled, panfried
Tuna 10 to several hundred lbs. Oily. All tuna belong to the mackerel family: albacore or white-meat tuna, also the three light-meat tunas—bluefin or horse mackerel, yellowfin, and skipjack or bonito. All have firm meat with pronounced flavor. *Market Forms:* fresh and frozen steaks, large chunks and occasionally fillets; also available canned and smoked.	Spring, summer, fall	Atlantic and Pacific coasts	Bake, broil, charcoal-broil, barbecue, panfry, poach
Weakfish Sea Trout: 12 lbs.; Speckled Trout: 8 lbs. Lean. These are sea trouts, specifically the one called sea trout and the one called spotted or speckled trout. Both have lean, mild flesh. *Market Forms:* whole, fillets.	Year round	Atlantic and Gulf coasts	Bake (stuffed or unstuffed), broil, charcoal-broil, panfry
Whitebait (see Herring)			
White sea bass 12–20 lbs. Lean. This California cousin of the weakfish also has delicate white meat. *Market Forms:* whole (when small), steaks, fillets.	All year; best in summer and fall	Southern California, Mexico	Bake (stuffed or unstuffed), broil, panfry, poach
Whiting 2–5 lbs. Lean. Also called silver hake, this fine-grained, mild-fleshed white fish is extremely versatile and popular. *Market Forms:* whole, fresh and frozen fillets; also salted.	Spring, summer, fall	North Atlantic	Bake (stuffed or unstuffed), broil, charcoal-broil, panfry, deep fry, poach
Wolffish Average 10 lbs. Lean. Sometimes called ocean catfish, this fish has delicate white flesh like that of haddock. *Market Forms:* whole, steaks, fillets.	Fall, winter, spring	North Atlantic	Bake (stuffed or unstuffed), broil, panfry, deep fry, poach

AMERICA'S POPULAR FRESHWATER FISH

SEASONS: These vary from state to state and year to year, so inquire locally.

Market Name and Description	Where Available	Best Ways to Cook
Bass Average 3–5 lbs. Lean. One of the finest freshwater fish; most popular species: largemouth, smallmouth, rock, and spotted bass. *Market Forms:* whole (more often caught than bought).	One or another species found throughout most of U.S.	Bake (stuffed or unstuffed), broil, charcoal-broil, panfry
Buffalo fish 2–20 lbs. Lean. Fairly coarse-fleshed, bony family of fish. *Market Forms:* whole, steaks, fillets; also smoked.	East, Midwest	Bake, poach
Burbot 3 lbs. Lean. A freshwater cod with delicate white meat. *Market Forms:* whole.	East, Midwest, Northeast	Bake (stuffed or unstuffed), broil, panfry, poach, steam

Market Name and Description	Where Available	Best Ways to Cook
Carp 2–7 lbs. Lean. A firm, musky fish that is best eaten in winter and spring. *Market Forms:* whole, fillets, chunks.	Entire U.S.	Bake (stuffed or unstuffed), poach
Catfish 1–20 lbs. Oily. There are many kinds of catfish from the whopping blue to the medium-size Channel cat to the baby bullhead. All have cat-like chin "whiskers," tough scaleless skins (which must be removed), and firm, strong-flavored flesh.	All but the Pacific states	Panfry, deep fry, poach
Crappies Average 2 lbs. Lean. Large sunfish that are winter favorites; there are two species: black and white. *Market Forms:* whole (more often caught than bought).	Great Lakes, Mississippi Valley	Broil, panfry
Grayling and lake herring or cisco (see Whitefish)		
Perch 1–1½ lbs. Lean. Yellow, blue, and sauger perch, sometimes called pike-perch and often confused with other fish. Firm, sweet white flesh. *Market Forms:* whole, fresh and frozen fillets.	Middle Atlantic states, Great Lakes, Midwest, Mississippi River Valley	Bake, broil, panfry
Pickerel, pike, and muskellunge 1–10 lbs. or more. Lean. These three form a small but famous family, a challenge to fishermen and delight to cooks. Meat is extra delicate and tender, though bony. *Market Forms:* whole, occasionally as fillets.	Most Eastern and Central states	Bake (stuffed or unstuffed), broil, poach
Sheepshead 1–3 lbs. Lean. These are freshwater drums and have tender white meat of excellent flavor. *Market Forms:* whole, fillets.	Primarily Midwest and South	Bake (stuffed or unstuffed), broil, panfry
Salmon (landlocked) 2–8 lbs. Oily. Similar to saltwater salmon except smaller; also called Sebago salmon. *Market Forms:* whole, steaks.	New England, primarily Maine	See Saltwater Salmon
Suckers 1–5 lbs. Lean. Firm, sweet-fleshed but bony fish family; best is probably the white sucker. *Market Forms:* whole, fresh and frozen fillets; salted, smoked.	Most states but abundant in Mississippi Basin	Bake, broil, panfry, poach
Sunfish ¼–1 lb. Lean. Also called bream, this large family includes the bluegill and pumpkinseed, small fish of superior flavor. *Market Forms:* whole.	Primarily Midwest and Gulf states	Broil, panfry
Trout Best size: 1–6 lbs. Midway between lean and oily. Unquestionably the royal family of freshwater fish. Best known are Dolly Varden, brook, brown, lake, and rainbow trout. All are superb. *Market Forms:* fresh and frozen whole.	One or another species found in most of U.S. except in very warm climates	Bake (stuffed or unstuffed), broil, charcoal-broil, panfry, poach
Whitefish 1–6 lbs. Fairly oily. A distinguished group, all related to salmon. Best known: lake herring (cisco), lake whitefish, arctic and American grayling, pilotfish. Meat is firm but creamy, flavor excellent. *Market Forms:* whole, fillets; smoked. Roe is choice.	New England, Great Lakes area	Bake (stuffed or unstuffed), broil, panfry, poach, steam
Yellow perch Average 1 lb. Lean. Small fish of particularly fine flavor. *Market Forms:* whole.	New England, Great Lakes area, some parts of West and South	Bake, broil, panfry

FISH AND CHIPS

4 servings

Ideally, you should have two deep fat fryers set up so fish and chips can fry at the same time. But if you can't manage that, do the potatoes first and set in a slow oven to keep warm while you fry the fish.

BATTER
1 cup sifted flour
1 teaspoon salt
3/4 cup cold water
1/4 teaspoon baking powder

CHIPS
1 recipe French-Fried Potatoes
13/4–2 pounds haddock fillets, cut in 4″ × 3″ strips
Shortening or cooking oil for deep fat frying

Begin batter first: Mix flour, salt, and water until smooth, cover, and let stand at room temperature 20–30 minutes. Meanwhile, prepare potatoes for frying as recipe directs; also pat fish dry on paper toweling. Place shortening or oil in a deep fat fryer, insert thermometer, and begin heating over high heat. When fat reaches 375° F., fry potatoes as directed, removing to a paper-towel-lined baking sheet and setting, uncovered, in oven set at lowest temperature to keep warm while you fry fish. Stir baking powder into batter. Dip 2–3 pieces fish into batter, allowing excess to drain off. Fry 5–6 minutes in 375° F. fat, turning as needed to brown evenly. Drain on paper toweling and set, uncovered, in oven to keep warm while you fry remaining fish. Serve with salt, pepper, and cider or malt vinegar.

NPS: 615 C, 120 mg CH, 705 mg S*

EASY SCALLOPED FISH

4 servings   ¢ ⊠

11/2 pounds delicate white fish fillets (cod, haddock, fluke, flounder, halibut, etc.)
1 teaspoon salt
1/4 teaspoon pepper
1/2 cup cracker meal
2 tablespoons butter or margarine
1 cup boiling milk

Preheat oven to 400° F. Arrange fish in a single layer in a buttered shallow 2-quart casserole. Sprinkle with half the salt and pepper. Mix remaining salt and pepper with cracker meal and scatter evenly over fish. Melt butter in milk and pour over fish. Bake, uncovered, in top third of oven 20 minutes until fish just flakes when touched with a fork.

NPS: 270 C, 110 mg CH, 760 mg S*

VARIATIONS

• Prepare as directed but mix 1/4 cup grated Parmesan or 1/3 cup grated sharp Cheddar cheese into cracker meal.

NPS: 295 C, 115 mg CH, 855 mg S*

• Sprinkle fish with 1/4–1/2 teaspoon thyme, tarragon, marjoram, chervil, basil, or dill before adding meal.

NPS: 270 C, 110 mg CH, 760 mg S*

• Sprinkle fish with 1–2 tablespoons lemon juice and, if you like, 1–2 tablespoons minced parsley before adding meal.

NPS: 270 C, 110 mg CH, 760 mg S*

FISH LOAF

8 servings   ⚖ ¢

A moist, delicate fish loaf flavored with lemon and parsley.

4 cups skinned, boned, cooked, flaked fish (any kind)
3 cups soft white bread crumbs or coarse cracker crumbs
11/2 cups milk or, if you prefer, 3/4 cup milk and 3/4 cup either Easy Fish Stock or bottled clam juice
2 eggs, lightly beaten
1 medium-size yellow onion, peeled and grated
2 stalks celery, minced
1–2 teaspoons salt
1/4 teaspoon pepper
2 tablespoons lemon juice
2 tablespoons minced parsley

Preheat oven to 350° F. Mix fish and crumbs; combine milk and eggs and mix into fish along with remaining ingredients. Taste for salt and adjust as needed. Spoon into a greased 9″ × 5″ × 3″ loaf pan and bake, uncovered, 45–55 minutes until just firm. Cool upright in pan on wire cake rack 5 minutes, invert on a hot platter, and garnish with lemon wedges. If you like, pass hot Tomato Sauce or Parsley Sauce.

NPS: 235 C, 140 mg CH, 500 mg S*

VARIATIONS

⊠ ⚖ ¢ **Quick Salmon or Tuna Loaf:** Substitute 2 (1-pound) cans salmon or 4 (61/2-ounce) cans tuna for the flaked fish. Drain cans, measure liquid, and add enough milk to measure 1½ cups. Flake fish, then proceed as recipe directs.

NPS (Salmon): 250 C, 115 mg CH, 845 mg S*
NPS (Tuna): 255 C, 95 mg CH, 780 mg S*

⚖ ¢ **Herbed Fish Loaf:** Prepare as directed, adding any one of the following: 1 tablespoon minced fresh dill, tarragon, or chervil; 2 teaspoons minced fresh basil or marjoram. If fresh herbs are unavailable, substitute ½ teaspoon of the dried.

NPS: 235 C, 140 mg CH, 500 mg S*

CRISP-CRUSTED FISH AND GREEN PEPPER PIE

6 servings ¢

1 recipe Flaky Pastry II
1½ cups skinned, boned, cooked, flaked fish (any kind)
3 hard-cooked eggs, shelled and sliced thin
¼ cup butter or margarine
1 medium-size yellow onion, peeled and minced
1 small sweet green pepper, cored, seeded, and minced
1 stalk celery, minced
¼ cup unsifted flour
1½ cups milk
1 teaspoon salt
¼ teaspoon pepper

Preheat oven to 425° F. Prepare pastry and roll half into a 12″ circle; fit into a 9″ piepan but do not trim edge. Layer fish and eggs into pie shell. Roll remaining pastry into a 12″ circle, cut 3 V-shaped steam slits near center, and cover loosely with wax paper while you proceed with recipe. Melt butter in a saucepan over moderate heat, add onion, green pepper, and celery, and stir-fry 3–5 minutes until onion is very pale golden. Blend in flour, slowly add milk, and heat, stirring, until thickened; mix in salt and pepper. Pour sauce over fish, top with pastry, press edges to seal, then trim and crimp. Bake, uncovered, ½ hour until lightly browned.

NPS: 580 C, 200 mg CH, 930 mg S*

VARIATION

⚖ **Potato-Fish Pie:** Omit pastry. Layer fish into a buttered 9″ piepan and top with sauce. Spoon 3 cups hot seasoned mashed potatoes over surface and roughen with a fork. Brush lightly with beaten egg and bake 25–30 minutes as directed. Cut potato "crust" into pie-shaped wedges and top with fish mixture.

NPS: 365 C, 250 mg CH, 935 mg S*

BASIC FISH SOUFFLÉ

4 servings

¼ cup butter or margarine
¼ cup sifted flour
1 cup milk or ½ cup each milk and Easy Fish Stock
½ teaspoon salt
⅛ teaspoon white pepper
4 eggs, separated, at room temperature
1 cup skinned, boned, cooked, flaked fish (any kind)
2 teaspoons minced parsley
¼ teaspoon cream of tartar

Melt butter in a small saucepan over moderate heat, blend in flour, slowly add milk, and heat, stirring, until thickened; turn heat to low and mix in salt and pepper. Beat egg yolks lightly, blend in a little hot sauce, then return to saucepan; heat and stir 1–2 minutes but do not boil. Off heat, mix in fish and parsley. Lay a piece of wax paper directly on sauce and cool to room temperature. Preheat oven to 350° F. Beat egg whites until frothy, add cream of tartar, and continue beating until stiff but not dry. Stir about ¼ cup egg white into sauce, then carefully fold in remainder, taking care not to break down volume. Spoon into an ungreased 1½-quart soufflé dish and bake, uncovered, 45–50 minutes until puffy and tinged with brown. Serve at once. Good with Caper, Tomato, Parsley, or Shrimp Sauce.

NPS: 310 C, 345 mg CH, 535 mg S*

VARIATIONS

Curried Fish Soufflé: Prepare as directed but smooth 1 tablespoon each curry powder and finely grated onion into melted butter just after blending flour.

NPS: 320 C, 345 mg CH, 535 mg S*

Lemon Fish Soufflé: Make sauce as directed but for the liquid use the juice of ½ lemon, ½ cup Easy Fish Stock, and then enough heavy cream to total 1 cup. Proceed as directed, adding 1 teaspoon grated lemon rind to sauce along with fish.

NPS: 360 C, 370 mg CH, 615 mg S*

VELVETY FISH MOUSSE

6 servings ⚖

¾ pound delicate white fish fillets (cod, flounder, halibut, hake, turbot, etc.)
¼ cup butter or margarine
6 tablespoons flour
1 cup milk or a ½ and ½ mixture of milk and Easy Fish Stock

3 eggs, separated
1/2 cup heavy cream
1 teaspoon salt
1/8 teaspoon pepper
Pinch nutmeg
1/2 teaspoon anchovy paste
1 teaspoon lemon juice

Preheat oven to 350° F. Put fish through finest blade of meat grinder or cut into 1" chunks and grind very fine in a food processor fitted with the metal chopping blade, using 6–8 pulses or on-offs of the motor. Melt butter in a saucepan over moderate heat, blend in flour, slowly add milk, and heat, stirring, until thickened. Turn heat to low. Beat egg yolks lightly, blend in a little sauce, then return to saucepan. Heat, stirring, 1–2 minutes, but do not allow to boil. Off heat, mix in fish and all remaining ingredients except egg whites. Beat egg whites until soft peaks form, then fold into fish mixture. Spoon into a well-oiled 5-cup ring mold, set in a large baking pan, and pour in boiling water to come two thirds of the way up mold. Bake, uncovered, 45–55 minutes or until just set. Lift mold from water bath and cool 5–10 minutes, loosen mousse with a spatula, invert on hot platter, and *ease* out. Serve as is, or fill center with Shrimp in Dill Sauce, Shrimp Newburg, or Creamed Mushrooms.

NPS: 275 C, 220 mg CH, 550 mg S*

VARIATIONS

Salmon or Tuna Mousse: Substitute 1½ cups finely ground salmon or tuna for white fish and proceed as directed.

NPS (Salmon): 355 C, 210 mg CH, 555 mg S*
NPS (Tuna): 315 C, 200 mg CH, 705 mg S*

⚖ **Lobster, Shrimp, or Crab Mousse:** Substitute 1½ cups finely ground cooked lobster, shrimp, or crab meat and proceed as directed.

NPS: 265 C, 220 mg CH, 590 mg S*

⚖ **Mousse Baked in a Fish Mold** (*4 servings*): Use an easy-to-handle fish-shaped mold of about 1-quart capacity (fish will not cook evenly in larger molds). Butter mold well and make sure it will not tip in water bath (use crumpled foil as needed to prop). Prepare recipe as directed and fill mold to within 1/2" of top; spoon any remaining mixture into buttered ramekins. Bake mold as directed in water bath 1 hour; ramekins will take about 15 minutes. Cool and unmold as directed, outline "scales" with slivers of pimiento or tissue-thin cucumber slices, and

serve. Nutritional count same as basic recipe.

⚖ **Cold Fish Mousse:** Prepare and unmold mousse as directed; cool to room temperature, and chill 2–3 hours. When serving, garnish with watercress, cucumber slices, and lemon "baskets" filled with mayonnaise. Nutritional count same as basic recipe.

QUENELLES

4 servings ⚖

Quenelles are soufflé-light fish balls poached in delicate broth; they may be used to garnish fish platters or served as a light entree. The mixture may also be used as a fish stuffing.

3/4 pound delicate white fish fillets (pike, pickerel, hake, turbot, flounder, etc.)
1 egg white
2/3 cup heavy cream
1 teaspoon salt
Pinch white pepper
Pinch nutmeg
1 quart boiling water
1/2 teaspoon lemon juice

Grind fish very fine and place in a bowl over cracked ice. Add egg white and beat with a wooden spoon 2–3 minutes until mixture thickens and will cling to a spoon turned upside down. Add cream, 2 tablespoons at a time, beating 1/2 minute after each addition; mixture will be soft but should hold a shape. Stir in 1/2 teaspoon salt, pepper, and nutmeg. Pour water into a large skillet (not iron), add remaining salt and lemon juice, and adjust heat so liquid just trembles. Using 2 wet teaspoons, shape fish mixture into egg-size balls and slide into poaching liquid (liquid should just cover quenelles; if not, add a little extra water). Poach, uncovered, 6–8 quenelles at a time, 3–5 minutes until just firm. Lift out with a slotted spoon and drain on paper toweling. Loosely cover poached quenelles and keep warm in oven set at lowest heat. Shape and poach remaining mixture (you'll have to wet spoons often). Use quenelles to garnish a fish platter or top with Mushroom, Portugaise, or Normande Sauce and serve as a main course.

NPS: 275 C, 220 mg CH, 550 mg S*

VARIATIONS

Processor Quenelles: Cut fish in 1" pieces, place in food processor fitted with the metal chopping blade, along with salt, pepper, and nutmeg. Grind to paste by churning 25–30 seconds. Scrape work bowl sides down, then with machine running, drizzle cream down feed tube. Snap motor off, drop egg white down feed tube, and incorporate by pulsing or snapping motor on and off 1–2 times. Cover and chill until firm enough to hold a shape. Shape and poach quenelles as directed above. Nutritional count same as basic recipe.

Gratinéed Quenelles: Poach and drain quenelles; transfer to a buttered 1½-quart *au gratin* dish. Coat lightly with Mornay Sauce, sprinkle lightly with finely grated Parmesan or Gruyère cheese, and broil quickly to brown. Recipe too flexible for meaningful nutritional count.

Quenelles à la Florentine: Poach and drain quenelles and arrange on a bed of hot buttered, chopped spinach in a 2-quart *au gratin* dish. Gratinée as directed above. Recipe too flexible for meaningful nutritional count.

SOLE AND FLOUNDER

Unless you live in a large Eastern metropolis where English, Channel, or Dover Sole is imported, it is unlikely that you will be able to buy true sole. America has no true sole, only flounder, fluke, and other related flatfish that masquerade as sole (they're usually advertised as lemon or gray sole). These flatfish all have delicate white meat, but they lack the elegance of sole. If you can buy imported sole, by all means use it in the recipes that follow. If not use flounder, sand dabs, or any other flounder-like flatfish (see chart of America's Popular Saltwater Fish).

Some Classic Ways to Serve Fillets of Sole, Flounder, or Other Delicate White Fish

All amounts based on 1½–2 pounds fillets or enough for 4–6 servings

À la Bonne Femme: Arrange fillets 1 layer deep in a buttered, large, shallow casserole, sprinkle lightly with salt and white pepper, top with ¼ cup each minced shallots and mushroom stems. Add ½ cup each dry white wine and Easy Fish Stock, cover, and bake 20 minutes at 350° F. Draw liquid off fillets with a bulb baster and quickly reduce to 1 cup. Meanwhile, melt 3 tablespoons butter in a small saucepan and blend in 3 tablespoons flour. Add reduced liquid and heat, stirring, until thickened. Top each fillet with 4 sautéed mushroom caps, smother with sauce, and broil quickly to brown.

À la Florentine: Poach fillets by basic method and arrange flat or rolled up on a bed of hot buttered, chopped spinach. Pour enough Mornay Sauce over fish to coat evenly, sprinkle lightly with grated Parmesan cheese, and broil just until flecked with brown.

À la Niçoise: Poach fillets by basic method, arrange on a hot platter, and lay anchovy fillets on top in a crisscross pattern; top each fillet with 2 overlapping slices lemon. Wreathe platter with clusters of peeled cherry tomatoes sautéed lightly in Anchovy Butter and pitted black olives, sprinkle with capers and a little minced fresh tarragon.

À la Normande: Poach fillets by basic method and arrange on a hot platter; surround with small poached shucked oysters, steamed shucked mussels, boiled, shelled, and deveined shrimp, tiny fried smelts, and sautéed button mushrooms. Pour some Normande Sauce over fillets and dot with truffle slices. Pass extra sauce.

Amandine: Sauté fillets by basic method and arrange on a hot platter. In the same skillet, lightly brown ⅓ cup slivered blanched almonds in ¼ cup butter and pour over fish. Garnish with lemon and parsley and serve.

Aux Fines Herbes: Sauté or poach fillets by basic method. Meanwhile, melt ¼ cup butter in a small saucepan over low heat, mix in 1 tablespoon each minced fresh chives, chervil, shallots, or scallion, and parsley. Let steep until fish is done. Arrange fish on a hot platter, smother with herbed butter, and serve.

Marguery: Fold fillets envelope fashion, ends toward center, and poach by basic method in Easy Fish Stock. Arrange on a hot platter, surround with shucked, steamed mussels and boiled, shelled, and deveined shrimp. Quickly reduce poaching liquid in the top of a double boiler over direct heat to 1½ cups; beat in 3 tablespoons butter, one at a time. Add a little hot liquid to 3 lightly beaten egg yolks, set over simmering water, and heat, stirring, until thickened. Pour over fish and serve.

Mornay: Poach fillets by basic method and lift to a shallow *au gratin* dish. Cover with Mornay Sauce, sprinkle lightly with grated Parmesan cheese, and broil quickly to brown.

Véronique: Poach fillets in white wine by basic method but add 1 teaspoon lemon juice. Arrange fish on a hot platter and keep warm. Quickly reduce poaching liquid to ½ cup; smooth in 1 cup Béchamel or Thick White Sauce and 3 tablespoons whipped cream. Pour over fish and broil quickly to brown. Garnish with clusters of seedless green grapes and serve. If you prefer, simmer 1 cup peeled grapes 3 minutes in water to cover, drain, then add to sauce along with whipped cream. Pour over fish and broil to brown.

SOLE OR FLOUNDER À L'AMÉRICAINE

6 servings ⚖

2 pounds sole or flounder fillets
1 teaspoon salt
1/8 teaspoon white pepper
1 cup dry white wine
1 cup boiling water

SAUCE AMÉRICAINE
1 small yellow onion, peeled and minced
1 carrot, peeled and cut in small dice
3 tablespoons minced shallots or scallions
1 clove garlic, peeled and crushed
2 tablespoons cooking oil
1/4 cup brandy
2 large tomatoes, peeled, cored, seeded, and coarsely chopped
2 tablespoons tomato paste
1 cup Easy Fish Stock
1 cup dry white wine
1 teaspoon tarragon
1 teaspoon minced parsley
1 (6–8-ounce) frozen rock lobster tail
1 tablespoon butter or margarine
1/4 teaspoon sugar
Pinch cayenne pepper

Prepare sauce early in the day to allow flavors to blend: Sauté onion, carrot, shallots, and garlic in oil in a saucepan over moderate heat 3–5 minutes until onion is very pale golden. Add brandy, warm briefly, remove from heat, and blaze with a match. Add all but last 3 sauce ingredients, cover, and simmer 10 minutes; remove lobster, take meat from shell, slice crosswise 1/4″ thick, and refrigerate. Continue simmering sauce, *uncovered,* about 1 hour, stirring occasionally. Liquid should be reduced by half; if not, boil rapidly to reduce. Strain liquid through a fine sieve into a small saucepan, pressing vegetables lightly. Heat 1–2 minutes over low heat, whisk in butter, sugar, and cayenne, taste for salt and adjust as needed. Cover and set aside. About 10 minutes before serving, fold fillets envelope fashion, ends toward middle, and arrange in a large skillet (not iron); sprinkle with salt and pepper. Pour in wine and water, cover and

simmer slowly 7–10 minutes until fish will just flake. Meanwhile, add lobster to sauce and reheat slowly until bubbly. Using a slotted spoon, lift fish to a hot deep platter, smother with sauce, and serve.

NPS: 235 C, 95 mg CH, 730 mg S*

FILLETS OF SOLE OR FLOUNDER CARDINAL

6 servings

Genuine Sole Cardinal is sprinkled with minced lobster coral just before serving, but since that means buying a whole lobster, we've made the coral optional.

8 fillets of sole or flounder (about 2 pounds)
1 teaspoon salt
1/8 teaspoon white pepper
1 cup dry white wine
1 cup boiling water

STUFFING
1 cup cooked, minced delicate white fish (haddock, cod, fluke, halibut, etc.)
1 cup soft white bread crumbs
1 tablespoon milk
1 egg, lightly beaten
1 teaspoon minced chives
1 teaspoon minced parsley
1/2 teaspoon salt
1/8 teaspoon pepper
Pinch nutmeg

CARDINAL SAUCE
3 tablespoons butter or margarine
3 tablespoons flour
1/2 cup milk
1/2 cup Easy Fish Stock
1/2 cup heavy cream
Meat of 1 (6–8-ounce) boiled rock lobster tail or 1 (1-pound) lobster, coarsely chopped
1/2 teaspoon salt
Pinch cayenne pepper
1 tablespoon minced truffle

TOPPING (optional)
Minced coral of 1 small boiled lobster

Sprinkle fillets with salt and pepper and set aside. Pour wine and water into a large skillet (not iron) and set aside. Now prepare stuffing: Beat all ingredients together until smooth. Place about 1 tablespoon stuffing on each fillet, roll up, and secure with toothpicks. Arrange fillets seam side down in skillet, cover, and simmer slowly 7–10 minutes until fish will just flake. Meanwhile, make the sauce: Melt butter in a saucepan, blend in flour, slowly stir in milk, stock, and cream, then heat, stirring, until thickened. Mix in lobster, salt, cayenne, and truffle.

With a slotted spoon lift fish to a deep platter, top with sauce and, if you like, minced coral.

NPS: 420 C, 230 mg CH, 1150 mg S*

FILLETS OF SOLE OR FLOUNDER WITH CRAB SAUCE

4 servings

1½ pounds sole or flounder fillets
½ teaspoon salt
⅛ teaspoon white pepper

S A U C E
2 tablespoons butter or margarine
2 tablespoons flour
½ cup milk
½ cup light cream
½ teaspoon salt
⅛ teaspoon white pepper
2 teaspoons lemon juice
¼ pound fresh lump or backfin crab meat, well picked over

Preheat oven to 350° F. Fold fillets envelope fashion by lapping each end over toward center and arrange 1 layer deep in a buttered shallow 2-quart casserole or *au gratin* dish; sprinkle with salt and pepper. Bake, uncovered, 15 minutes. Meanwhile, prepare sauce: Melt butter in a saucepan over moderately low heat, blend in flour, slowly add milk and cream, and heat, stirring, until thickened. Lightly mix in salt, pepper, lemon juice, and crab, cover, and keep warm. Remove liquid from fish, using a bulb baster, then cover fish with sauce. Bake, uncovered, 10–15 minutes longer until fish flakes when touched with a fork.

NPS: 305 C, 155 mg CH, 825 mg S*

CRUMB-TOPPED BAKED FLOUNDER

4 servings

1½ pounds flounder or other delicate white fish fillets (cod, haddock, fluke, halibut, etc.)
1 teaspoon salt
⅛ teaspoon white pepper
2 cups soft white bread crumbs
1 tablespoon minced parsley
⅓ cup melted butter or margarine

Preheat oven to 350° F. Arrange fillets in a single layer in a buttered shallow 2-quart casserole; sprinkle with ½ teaspoon salt and the pepper. Toss bread crumbs with remaining salt, the parsley, and butter and scatter evenly over fish. Bake, uncovered, 25–30 minutes until fish flakes, then broil 4″ from

the heat 2–3 minutes to brown. Garnish with lemon wedges and serve.

NPS: 330 C, 125 mg CH, 950 mg S*

V A R I A T I O N S

Almond-Crumb-Topped Baked Flounder: Prepare as directed but add ½ cup coarsely chopped, blanched, toasted almonds to bread crumb mixture.

NPS: 430 C, 125 mg CH, 950 mg S*

Sesame Baked Flounder: Prepare as directed but add ¼ cup toasted sesame seeds to crumb mixture.

NPS: 380 C, 125 mg CH, 950 mg S*

LOW-CALORIE FILLETS OF FLOUNDER EN PAPILLOTE

4 servings   ⚖

4 large flounder fillets (about 1½ pounds)
1½ teaspoons salt
½ cup minced scallions
1 tablespoon butter or margarine
1 tablespoon flour
2 ripe tomatoes, peeled, cored, seeded, and chopped fine
1 teaspoon red or white wine vinegar
½ teaspoon basil or oregano
⅛ teaspoon pepper

Preheat oven to 350° F. Cut 4 large squares of cooking parchment (available at specialty food shops) or heavy duty foil (large enough to wrap fillets); lay a fillet on each and sprinkle with 1 teaspoon salt. Sauté scallions in butter in a small skillet over moderate heat 3–5 minutes until limp; sprinkle in flour, add remaining salt and all other ingredients, and heat, stirring, over low heat 3–5 minutes to blend flavors. Spoon a little sauce over each fillet and wrap tightly drugstore style.* Place packages on a baking sheet and bake 30–40 minutes; unwrap 1 package and check to see if fish flakes; if not, rewrap and bake a little longer. Serve in foil to retain all juices.

NPS: 190 C, 90 mg CH, 990 mg S*

PAUPIETTES OF SOLE OR FLOUNDER WITH ROSY SAUCE

6 servings

Paupiettes are stuffed and rolled fillets of meat or fish. They're unusually versatile because a change of stuffing or sauce creates a whole new dish.

2 pounds sole or flounder fillets
1 teaspoon salt

1/8 teaspoon white pepper
2 cups Basic Bread Stuffing for Fish
1/2 cup milk
1/2 cup water

ROSY SAUCE
2 tablespoons butter or margarine
2 tablespoons flour
Fish cooking liquid
1/4 cup heavy cream
2 tablespoons tomato paste
Pinch nutmeg

Lay fillets flat, more attractive side down, and sprinkle with salt and pepper. Place about 1/4 cup stuffing on each fillet and roll up from widest end; secure with toothpicks. (*Note:* If paupiettes are very wide, halve crosswise.) Arrange seam side down in a large skillet (not iron), add milk and water, cover, and simmer 7–10 minutes until fish will just flake. Or arrange in a buttered shallow casserole, add milk and water, cover loosely, and bake 20–30 minutes at 350° F. Lift rolls to a heated deep platter with a slotted spoon, cover, and keep warm. Strain cooking liquid and reserve. For the sauce, melt butter in a small saucepan over moderate heat, blend in flour, slowly stir in cooking liquid and remaining ingredients. Heat, stirring, until thickened. Taste for salt and pepper and adjust as needed. Pour over paupiettes and serve.

NPS: 190 C, 90 mg CH, 990 mg S*

VARIATIONS

⚖ **Mushroom-Stuffed Paupiettes:** Stuff fillets with 1 pound minced sautéed mushrooms mixed with 2 minced scallions, 1 cup soft white bread crumbs, 1/2 teaspoon salt, and 1/4 teaspoon pepper. Roll and cook as directed. Serve with Mushroom Sauce.

NPS: 285 C, 100 mg CH, 950 mg S*

Shrimp-Stuffed Paupiettes: Stuff fillets with 1 cup minced cooked shrimp mixed with 3/4 cup soft white bread crumbs, 2 tablespoons mayonnaise, and 2 teaspoons lemon juice. Roll and cook as directed; serve with Shrimp Sauce.

NPS: 280 C, 160 mg CH, 800 mg S*

Anchovy-and-Caper-Stuffed Paupiettes: Drain and mince 1 (2-ounce) can anchovy fillets, mix with 1/4 cup minced capers, spread on *unsalted* fish fillets, roll, and cook as directed. Serve with Caper Sauce.

NPS: 230 C, 100 mg CH, 660 mg S*

CREAMED SALT COD

4 servings   ¢

1 1/2 pounds filleted salt cod
2 cups hot Medium White Sauce, prepared without salt
1/8 teaspoon pepper
2 hard-cooked eggs, peeled and sliced

Soak cod overnight in cold water to cover; drain and rinse. Place in a saucepan with enough cold water to cover and simmer, covered, 10–15 minutes until fish will flake. Drain, cool slightly, and coarsely flake, removing any bones and skin. Mix fish gently into sauce, add pepper, cover, and let stand over lowest heat 10 minutes to blend flavors. Taste for salt and adjust as needed. Using eggs to garnish, serve as is or over hot boiled potatoes or buttered toast.

NPS: 465 C, 325 mg CH, 7,000 mg S*

BRANDADE DE MORUE (SALT COD WITH GARLIC, OIL, AND CREAM)

3–4 entree servings, enough cocktail spread for 12

This rich cod purée can be served hot or cold, as a luncheon entree or a cocktail spread. The best way to make it is in an electric blender or food processor.

1 pound filleted salt cod
1/2 cup heavy cream (about)
1/2 cup olive oil (about)
1 clove garlic, peeled and crushed
1/8 teaspoon pepper
4 slices French bread or 8 small triangles white bread
2–3 tablespoons olive oil or butter

Soak cod overnight in cold water to cover; drain and rinse. Place in a saucepan with just enough cold water to cover and simmer, covered, 10–15 minutes until fish will flake. Drain, cool slightly, and coarsely flake, removing any bones or skin. Purée fish with 1/4 cup each cream and oil, the garlic and pepper by buzzing 20–30 seconds in an electric blender at high speed or 15–20 seconds in a food processor fitted with the metal chopping blade. Add remaining cream and oil alternately, 1 tablespoon at a time, puréeing until the texture of mashed potatoes; if too stiff, blend in a little additional cream and oil. Heat to serving temperature in the top of a double boiler over simmering water, stirring occasionally. Meanwhile, fry bread in oil in a skillet over moderately high heat until golden. Mound fish in the center of a hot platter and surround with bread.

NPS (3): 870 C, 180 mg CH, 6,000 mg S*
NPS (4): 650 C, 135 mg CH, 4,500 mg S*
NPS (12): 220 C, 45 mg CH, 1,500 mg S*

VARIATION

To Serve Cold: Instead of warming fish, chill slightly, taste for pepper and add more if needed; also, if you like, add 1/2 teaspoon grated lemon rind and 1–2 teaspoons lemon juice. Serve with melba toast.

CODFISH CAKES

4 servings ⚖ ¢

1 (2-ounce) package dried, shredded salt cod
1½ cups cold water
1½ cups hot, unseasoned mashed potatoes
1/8 teaspoon pepper
1 tablespoon Worcestershire sauce (optional)
2 tablespoons minced fresh parsley (optional)
2 tablespoons melted butter or margarine
1 egg, lightly beaten
1/3 cup cooking oil

Soften cod in cold water 4–5 minutes; drain and squeeze dry in a strainer. Mix with all remaining ingredients except oil, shape into 4–6 flat patties, cover, and chill 1 hour. Heat oil in a large, heavy skillet over moderate heat until a cube of bread will sizzle, add fish cakes, and brown 3–5 minutes on each side. Drain on paper toweling and serve.

NPS: 205 C, 95 mg CH, 1,525 mg S*

VARIATION

⚖ **Codfish Balls:** Prepare cod mixture as directed, but instead of shaping into cakes, drop from a tablespoon into hot deep fat (375° F.) and fry 1–2 minutes until golden brown. Fry only a few balls at a time and drain well on paper toweling before serving.

NPS: 225 C, 95 mg CH, 1,525 mg S*

BAKED HADDOCK IN CREAM SAUCE

6 servings

2 pounds haddock or flounder fillets
2 tablespoons lemon juice
1 teaspoon salt
1/8 teaspoon white pepper
2 tablespoons butter or margarine

SAUCE

3 tablespoons butter or margarine
1/4 cup unsifted flour
1 cup light cream
1 teaspoon salt
1/4 teaspoon paprika

Preheat oven to 350° F. Fold fillets envelope fashion, ends toward middle, and arrange in a single layer in a buttered shallow 2-quart casserole; sprinkle with lemon juice, salt, and pepper and dot with butter. Bake, uncovered, 20–30 minutes or until fish just flakes. Meanwhile, prepare sauce: Melt butter in a saucepan over moderate heat, blend in flour, slowly add cream, and heat, stirring, until thickened; add salt, cover, and keep warm. When fish is done, drain off liquid with a bulb baster and reserve. Beat 1 cup fish liquid into sauce, pour evenly over fish, and bake, uncovered, 5–7 minutes. Dust with paprika and serve.

NPS: 300 C, 145 mg CH, 940 mg S*

VARIATIONS

Baked Haddock au Gratin: Prepare recipe as directed but, before final 5–7-minute baking, top with 1 cup soft white bread crumbs mixed with 3 tablespoons melted butter or margarine and, if you like, 2 tablespoons minced parsley. Finish baking as directed, then broil 1–2 minutes to brown.

NPS: 375 C, 160 mg CH, 1,035 mg S*

Baked Haddock in Cheese Sauce: Prepare as directed but, when making sauce, add 1 teaspoon Worcestershire sauce, 1/8 teaspoon powdered mustard, a pinch cayenne pepper, and 1 cup coarsely grated sharp Cheddar cheese. Pour sauce over fish as directed, top with 1/4 cup grated cheese, bake 5–7 minutes, then broil 1–2 minutes to brown.

NPS: 400 C, 165 mg CH, 1,095 mg S*

Baked Haddock in Shrimp Sauce: Prepare as directed, but when making sauce add 1 cup coarsely chopped cooked shrimp, 1 tablespoon tomato paste, and, if you like, 2–3 tablespoons dry sherry. Proceed as basic recipe directs, garnish with 12 cooked, shelled, and deveined small shrimp, and serve.

NPS: 340 C, 185 mg CH, 1,000 mg S*

Baked Haddock and Mushrooms: Stir-fry 1/2 pound thinly sliced mushrooms and 1/2 cup each minced onion and sweet green pepper in 2 tablespoons butter or margarine 5–8 minutes over moderate heat until onion is pale golden. Sprinkle fish with lemon juice, salt, and pepper as directed in basic recipe but omit butter; top with sautéed vegetables, then complete recipe as directed.

NPS: 270 C, 125 mg CH, 890 mg S*

FINNAN HADDIE

4–6 servings ⚖

Once upon a time, fire swept the little town of Findon, Scotland, smoking tons of haddock that had been hung to dry. Fortunately someone thought to taste the fish before it was dumped. Result: smoked haddock or finnan (Findon) haddie. Today it comes filleted or split (with backbone in). Often it is super-salty, but ½ hour of soaking in tepid water will take care of that. *Note:* The Arbroath Smokie, by most accounts the best of all smoked haddock, can now be bought here (usually by the pair) in specialty food or fish shops.

2 pounds smoked haddock fillets, rinsed and cut in serving-size pieces
1 cup milk or ½ cup milk and ½ cup water
⅛ teaspoon white pepper
2 tablespoons butter or margarine

Place haddock in a large, heavy skillet, add milk, sprinkle with pepper, and dot with butter; heat, uncovered, over moderate heat until almost boiling, turn heat to low, baste well, then cover and simmer 10 minutes until fish flakes when touched with a fork. Serve as is or, if you like, topped with plump pats of butter.

NPS (4–6): 515–345 C, 215–165 mg CH, 14,250–9,725 mg S*

VARIATIONS

Creamed Finnan Haddie: Poach haddock as directed above and drain, reserving cooking liquid. Make 2 cups Medium White Sauce, using 1 cup poaching liquid and 1 cup light cream. Add haddock, 1 tablespoon minced parsley and serve over hot buttered toast or in puff pastry shells. Nutritional count same as basic recipe.

⚖ **Scottish Nips** *(30 servings):* Poach haddock as directed above, drain, flake, and measure. To each cup haddock, add ½ cup heavy cream and a pinch cayenne pepper. Slowly bring to a simmer, spread on unbuttered small toast triangles, and serve as cocktail appetizers. Recipe too flexible for meaningful nutritional count.

⚖ **Baked Finnan Haddie:** Preheat oven to 350° F. Do not poach haddock; place instead in a single layer in a buttered shallow 2-quart casserole. Add ½ cup each milk and light cream, sprinkle with pepper and dot with butter. Cover and bake 20–25 minutes, basting occasionally, until fish flakes. Lift haddock to a hot platter, top with a little of the pan juices, then dot with 2 tablespoons butter and serve.

NPS (4–6): 380–250 C, 215–145 mg CH, 14,250–9,500 mg S*

KEDGEREE

4–6 servings ⚖

An English breakfast dish by way of India. Kedgeree doesn't have to have curry powder; in fact it's better without it if you use smoked fish in the recipe.

¼ cup butter or margarine
3 cups flaked cooked haddock or cod or 1½ cups each flaked cooked *smoked* haddock and cod
2 cups boiled rice
1 teaspoon salt (about)
⅛ teaspoon white pepper
½ teaspoon curry powder (optional)
3 hard-cooked eggs, peeled

Melt butter in the top of a double boiler over simmering water. Add fish and mix well. Add rice, salt, pepper, and curry powder if you like. Dice 2 eggs and cut the third into wedges. Mix in diced eggs, cover, and heat 10–15 minutes until heated through. Taste for salt and adjust. Mound mixture on a hot platter and garnish with egg wedges. If made with fresh haddock or cod:

NPS (4–6): 475–320 C, 330–220 mg CH, 850–565 mg S*

If made with smoked haddock and cod:

NPS (4–6): 425–285 C, 325–215 mg CH, 3,900–2,600 mg S*

HERRING IN OATMEAL

4 servings ▯

A Scottish favorite.

⅓ cup uncooked oatmeal
½ teaspoon salt
¼ teaspoon pepper
4 herring, cleaned and dressed
1 egg, lightly beaten
3 tablespoons butter or margarine

Buzz oatmeal in an electric blender at high speed a few seconds until fairly fine; mix with salt and pepper. Dip herring in egg, then in oatmeal to coat evenly. Melt butter in a large skillet over moderate heat and sauté herring about 3 minutes on each side until golden brown. (*Note:* Any small fish may be prepared this way.)

NPS: 225 C, 140 mg CH, 415 mg S*

SALT HERRING AND BEETS À LA RUSSE

4 servings

3 herring in brine
1 (1-pound) can sliced beets (do not drain)
2 tablespoons butter or margarine
2 tablespoons flour
1 tablespoon prepared horseradish
1 tablespoon lemon juice
1/8 teaspoon pepper
1 cup sour cream

Soak herring in cold water 24 hours, changing water several times. Remove heads, fillet and skin* herring, and cut in serving-size pieces. Drain beet liquid into a 1-cup measure and add enough cold water to round out measure. Melt butter in a saucepan over moderate heat, blend in flour, slowly stir in beet liquid, and heat, stirring, until thickened. Meanwhile, preheat oven to 350° F. Off heat, mix remaining ingredients into sauce, add herring, and toss to mix. Spoon into a buttered 1½-quart casserole, cover loosely, and bake 20–30 minutes. Serve with boiled potatoes.

NPS: 315 C, 75 mg CH, 2,700 mg S*

ROLLMOPS

6 servings ⚖

6 herring in brine
3 dill pickles, quartered lengthwise
2 medium-size yellow onions, peeled, sliced thin, and separated into rings
1 cup cider vinegar
1 cup water
6 peppercorns
1 bay leaf
1 clove garlic, peeled and halved
3 cloves
1/8 teaspoon crushed hot red chili peppers

Soak herring in cold water 24 hours, changing water several times. Remove heads and fillet* herring. Place a piece of dill pickle and some onion on each piece of herring, roll up, and secure with a toothpick. Arrange rolls seam side down in a heatproof glass bowl. Bring vinegar, water, and spices to a boil, cool slightly, and pour over herring. Add any remaining onion, cover tightly, and chill 3–4 days before serving.

NPS: 130 C, 45 mg CH, 3,585 mg S*

HERRING IN SOUR CREAM

4 entree servings, enough appetizers for 10–12

4 herring in brine
1 cup sour cream
3 tablespoons white wine or white wine vinegar
1 large yellow or red onion, peeled, sliced thin, and separated into rings
1/4 teaspoon powdered mustard
Pinch cayenne pepper

Soak herring in cold water 24 hours, changing water several times. Remove heads, fillet and skin* herring, and cut into bite-size pieces. Mix remaining ingredients, add herring, and pack in a 1-quart jar or glass bowl. Cover tightly and chill 1–2 days before serving.

NPS (4): 250 C, 70 mg CH, 3,150 mg S*
NPS (10): 100 C, 30 mg CH, 1,260 mg S*
NPS (12): 85 C, 25 mg CH, 1,050 mg S*

PICKLED HERRING

6 servings ⚖

6 herring in brine
2 medium-size yellow onions, peeled, sliced thin, and separated into rings
1 lemon, sliced thin
1½ cups cider vinegar
6 peppercorns
1 teaspoon mustard seeds
1 teaspoon mixed pickling spices
1 teaspoon sugar

Soak herring in cold water 24 hours, changing water several times. Remove heads, fillet* each herring, and, if you like, skin the fillets. Cut into bite-size pieces. Place half the herring in a single layer in a large shallow heatproof bowl (not metal), top with half the onions and lemon; add remaining herring, onion, and lemon. Bring vinegar, spices, and sugar to a boil and pour over herring. Cover and chill 3–5 days before serving.

NPS: 135 C, 45 mg CH, 3,120 mg S*

KIPPERED HERRING

Also called *kippers* or *bloaters,* these salted and smoked herring are usually sold whole or as fillets by the pound (allow 1 kipper per person). They also come canned. When buying, avoid any that seem leathery or dry, also any with an overpowering smell. Cook any of the following ways, and serve for breakfast (the English way), lunch, or supper.

To Bake: Preheat oven to 350° F. Line a shallow baking pan with foil and grease lightly; spread kippers flat and arrange skin side down in pan, brush lightly with melted butter or margarine, drizzle, if you like, with a very little Worcestershire sauce, and bake, uncovered, 8–10 minutes.

To Broil: Preheat broiler. Spread kippers flat and arrange skin side down on broiler pan. Spread each with 1 tablespoon butter or margarine and, if you like, sprinkle with 1 teaspoon lemon juice. Broil 3"–4" from the heat 2–3 minutes—just long enough to heat through.

To Panfry (Sauté): Spread kippers flat. Allowing about 1 tablespoon butter or margarine for each kipper, sauté gently over moderately low heat about 2 minutes on a side.

To Poach: Spread kippers flat and arrange skin side down in a single layer in a large skillet (not iron); add boiling water or milk to cover, cover skillet, and bring liquid just to a simmer over moderate heat. Lift kippers to a hot platter, dot with butter, and serve. Especially good with scrambled eggs.

To Steam: Spread kippers flat and arrange skin side down in a single layer on a steamer rack over about 1" boiling water. Cover and steam 5 minutes.

Some Ways to Use Kippered Herring
Cook by any of the methods above, then remove skin and any bones, flake, and use as follows:
• Fold into scrambled eggs or omelets, allowing about 1/2 cup flaked kippers for 4–6 eggs.
• Mix equal quantities flaked kippers and Medium White Sauce and serve on toast, split toasted muffins, in patty shells or Crepes, or over buttered noodles.
• Substitute for half the fish called for in Kedgeree.
• Spoon onto melba rounds, drizzle with lemon juice, and serve as cocktail snacks.

BAKED BLUEFISH SMOTHERED WITH HERBS AND CREAM

2–4 servings

This may seem like a long time to bake fish; it isn't, really, because the shallots, onion, herbs, and cream all insulate the fish from the heat.

1 (2–3-pound) bluefish, cleaned and dressed
1 teaspoon salt
1/8 teaspoon pepper

1/2 cup butter or margarine
5 shallots, peeled and minced
1 medium-size yellow onion, peeled and coarsely chopped
1/3 cup minced parsley
2 tablespoons minced fresh dill
1 cup light cream

Preheat oven to 375° F. Sprinkle fish inside and out with salt and pepper and place in an ungreased shallow oval casserole large enough to accommodate it. Dot fish inside and out with 1/4 cup butter. Mix shallots, onion, parsley, and dill and scatter over fish. Bake, uncovered, 15 minutes; dot with remaining butter and bake 10 minutes longer. Pour in cream and bake, uncovered, 15–20 minutes and serve.

NPS (2–4): 935–465 C, 325–165 mg CH, 1,795–900 mg S*

CHINESE SWEET-AND-SOUR CARP

4–6 servings

Carp, the lucky fish of the Chinese, is said to bring wealth and well-being to those who eat it.

1 (4–5-pound) carp, cleaned

S A U C E
2 tablespoons peanut or other cooking oil
1 clove garlic, peeled and crushed
1 medium-size sweet green pepper, cored, seeded, and cut in 1/2" squares
1 medium-size carrot, peeled and cut in julienne strips
1 cup Easy Fish Stock or 1/2 cup each water and pineapple juice
1/4 cup cider vinegar
3 tablespoons sugar
2 tablespoons soy sauce
2 teaspoons cornstarch blended with 2 tablespoons cold water
2 pineapple rings, cut in 3/4" chunks

Bend fish into an "S" shape and run 2 long skewers through from head to tail to hold in shape. Place on a rack in a fish steamer or large oval kettle over gently boiling water, cover, and steam about 25 minutes until fish will just flake. About 10 minutes before fish is done, begin sauce: Heat oil in a *wok* or heavy skillet over moderate heat 1 minute, add garlic, pepper, and carrot, and stir-fry 2–3 minutes; do not brown. Mix in stock, vinegar, sugar, and soy sauce, cover, and simmer 2–3 minutes. Add cornstarch paste and pineapple and heat, stirring, until slightly thickened and clear. Lift fish to a hot deep platter and remove skewers. Pour sauce on top and serve with boiled rice.

NPS (4–6): 300–200 C, 75–50 mg CH, 950–635 mg S*

BAKED STUFFED SHAD

6 servings   ⚖

If possible, have fish market bone and prepare fish for stuffing.

1 (4-pound) shad, prepared for stuffing*
1 teaspoon salt
¼ teaspoon pepper
2 cups Quick Mushroom or other stuffing for fish
¼ cup butter or margarine
½ cup dry white wine

Preheat oven to 400° F. Wipe shad inside and out with damp paper toweling. Sprinkle cavity with half the salt and pepper. Spoon stuffing loosely into cavity and sew up; wrap any remaining stuffing in foil. Place fish and extra stuffing in a well-buttered oven-to-table roasting pan or large casserole. Sprinkle shad with remaining salt and pepper, dot with butter, and add wine. Bake, uncovered, basting often, about 40 minutes until fish flakes easily. Remove threads and serve. (*Note:* The shad can be transferred to a hot platter, but, since it's extra fragile, the less handling the better.)

NPS: 435 C, 165 mg CH, 840 mg S*

VARIATIONS

Portuguese-Style Stuffed Shad: Prepare shad for stuffing as directed above. Make 2 cups Mushroom Stuffing for Fish, then mix in 2 thinly sliced yellow onions and ½ crushed clove garlic that have been sautéed until golden in 2 tablespoons olive oil, also ½ cup coarsely chopped, peeled, and seeded ripe tomato. Stuff fish as directed and begin baking; after 25 minutes, baste with 1 cup hot tomato sauce. Serve with pan juices.

NPS: 430 C, 145 mg CH, 965 mg S*

Empress Stuffed Shad: Prepare shad for stuffing, then stuff with the following: 1 pair blanched shad roe, broken up and mixed with ¾ cup soft white bread crumbs, 2 tablespoons each melted butter and minced chives, 1 teaspoon minced fresh tarragon or ¼ teaspoon dried tarragon, ½ teaspoon salt, and ⅛ teaspoon pepper. Bake as directed.

NPS: 405 C, 365 mg CH, 750 mg S*

POACHED SALMON

6–8 servings

2 quarts water
1½ cups dry white wine
2 bay leaves
1 sprig parsley
1 stalk celery
3 sprigs fresh dill or ¼ teaspoon dill seed
1 sprig fresh thyme or a pinch dried thyme
1 small yellow onion, peeled and quartered
10 peppercorns, bruised
1 teaspoon salt
1 (5-pound) center-cut piece fresh salmon, cleaned and dressed

Boil all ingredients except salmon, uncovered, 25 minutes and strain through a double thickness of cheesecloth. Wipe salmon with damp cloth and wrap in a double thickness of cheesecloth. Place in a large oval kettle on a rack so that loose cheesecloth ends are on top. Pour in strained liquid, cover, and simmer 40 minutes (liquid should never boil). Lift rack and salmon from kettle, remove cheesecloth, peel off skin, and carefully scrape away any darkened flesh. Serve hot with Hollandaise Sauce or cool to room temperature, chill 8–10 hours, and serve with Green Mayonnaise.

NPS (6–8): 545–410 C, 95–70 mg CH, 555–415 mg S*

VARIATIONS

Salmon in Aspic: Poach and chill salmon as directed; reserve 2 cups cooking liquid. Transfer chilled salmon to platter and keep cold. Mix 1 envelope unflavored gelatin into reserved liquid, add 1 egg white, beaten to soft peaks, and 1 eggshell, and heat, stirring with a whisk, until mixture foams up. Remove from heat, stir once, then let stand undisturbed 5 minutes. Line a sieve with a fine dish towel wrung out in cold water, set over a deep bowl, pour in hot liquid (egg, shells and all) and let drip through to clarify. Chill clarified aspic until syrupy and spoon a thin, even layer over salmon; chill until tacky, then decorate with cutouts of truffle and pimiento, sliced stuffed green olives, and sprigs of fresh tarragon or chervil; chill briefly to set but keep remaining aspic over warm water. Seal designs with another layer of aspic and chill until firm. Also chill remaining aspic, then dice and use to garnish platter along with lemon wedges and parsley fluffs. Serve with mayonnaise or other suitable cold sauce such as Chiffon, Gribiche, or Sour Cream-Dill.

NPS (6–8): 555–415 C, 95–70 mg CH, 565–425 mg S*

Whole Salmon in Aspic *(10 servings):* Substitute a whole small salmon (8 pounds) for center-cut piece and poach as directed. Peel skin from body of fish but leave it on head and tail. Glaze salmon with aspic and decorate as directed.

NPS: 330 C, 55 mg CH, 340 mg S*

Salmon in Mayonnaise Gelatin: Poach and chill salmon as directed; also make and clarify aspic as for Salmon in Aspic. In addition, prepare a mayonnaise gelatin: Heat 1 cup chicken broth, skimmed of all fat, with 1 envelope unflavored gelatin, stirring until gelatin dissolves. Smooth in 1 cup mayonnaise and chill until mixture will coat a metal spoon. Spoon a thin, even layer of mayonnaise gelatin over salmon, chill until tacky, and, if necessary, continue adding thin layers until no pink shows through. While mayonnaise gelatin is still tacky, decorate as above. Chill clear aspic until syrupy and use to seal in design.

NPS (6–8): 825–620 C, 115–90 mg CH, 900–680 mg S*

CRISPY CUCUMBER-STUFFED SALMON STEAKS

4 servings

4 salmon steaks, cut 1¼″ thick

STUFFING

3 tablespoons minced yellow onion
2 tablespoons butter or margarine
1 chicken bouillon cube, crumbled
½ cup hot water
⅓ cup diced, peeled cucumber
1 tablespoon minced parsley
1 tablespoon minced chives (fresh, frozen, or freeze-dried)
1 tablespoon minced fresh dill or ½ teaspoon dried dill
¼ teaspoon salt
⅛ teaspoon pepper
2 cups coarse soda cracker crumbs
¼ cup melted butter or margarine

Preheat oven to 375° F. Arrange salmon steaks in a greased large, shallow baking pan. Stir-fry onion in butter in a large, heavy skillet 3–5 minutes over moderate heat until limp. Mix in bouillon cube and water and heat, stirring, until dissolved. Off heat, add remaining ingredients, except melted butter, and toss lightly to mix. Mound stuffing in hollow of each steak, bring ends around to enclose and secure with toothpicks. Drizzle with melted butter and bake, uncovered, 20–

25 minutes until fish will just flake. Serve as is or with Lemon Sauce or Parsley Sauce.

NPS: 1,130 C, 195 mg CH, 1,255 mg S*

SALMON STEAKS EN CASSEROLE

4 servings ⚖

The Irish say that salmon is best baked in a sealed casserole so that none of the flavor escapes.

4 small salmon steaks, cut ¾″–1″ thick
2 tablespoons butter or margarine, softened to room temperature
¼ teaspoon salt
2–3 sprigs fresh tarragon, lemon balm, thyme, or dill
1 lemon, sliced thin
⅓ cup simmering apple cider, Easy Fish Stock, or water

Preheat oven to 325° F. Place steaks in a well-buttered large, shallow casserole that has a tight-fitting lid. Spread steaks with butter and sprinkle with salt. Lay herb on top and cover with lemon slices. Add cider, cover casserole with foil, then with lid and bake 20–30 minutes just until fish flakes when touched with a fork. Remove lemon and herb, carefully lift steaks to platter, drizzle with a little pan liquid, garnish with parsley fluffs, and serve. Tiny new potatoes, buttered green peas, and homemade mayonnaise are the perfect accompaniments.

NPS: 560 C, 105 mg CH, 365 mg S*

VARIATIONS

Liffey Salmon Steak Platter *(6 servings):* Cook salmon as directed, transfer to a large platter, and surround with clusters of the following: ½ pound hot shrimp boiled in cider, then shelled and deveined; 1–2 dozen Fried Oysters, and ½ pound button mushrooms simmered 5–7 minutes in 2 tablespoons butter and ¼ cup heavy cream. Pass Tomato Sauce.

NPS: 525 C, 155 mg CH, 370 mg S*

Tara Salmon: Prepare steaks as directed, but use milk as the cooking liquid instead of cider. Serve on a bed of Colcannon.

NPS: 560 C, 105 mg CH, 370 mg S*

TRUITE AU BLEU (BLUE TROUT)

4 servings ▨

For this classic recipe it's best if the fish are still alive or at least just out of the water.

The vinegar turns their skin silvery blue, hence the name.

4 (1-pound) fresh trout, cleaned
3 cups cold water
1 cup white vinegar
1 bay leaf and 1 sprig each parsley and thyme, tied in cheesecloth, *(bouquet garni)*
1 teaspoon salt
4 peppercorns

S A U C E
Melted butter or Hollandaise Sauce

Wipe trout with damp paper toweling. Boil remaining ingredients in a fish poacher or large kettle 2–3 minutes, add trout, cover, reduce heat, and simmer 4–5 minutes until fish just flakes when touched with a fork. Using a slotted spoon and pancake turner, carefully lift trout from water and serve at once with sauce.

NPS: 365 C, 110 mg CH, 475 mg S*

To Serve Cold: Cool trout in cooking liquid, lift out, chill well, and serve with Ravigote Sauce or Tartar Sauce.

V A R I A T I O N

⚖ **Carp au Bleu:** Substitute 1 (3–4-pound) cleaned carp for the trout; simmer as recipe directs 15–20 minutes. Nutritional count same as basic recipe.

GILLIES' SKILLET TROUT

4 servings ⊠

Gillies are Scottish hunting and fishing guides whose duties include cooking as well as directing sportsmen through the Highlands. Their simple way of preparing trout is delicious at home but unbeatable by a rippling mountain stream.

4 slices bacon
4 (1-pound) trout, cleaned
1 cup unsifted flour
1½ teaspoons salt
¼ teaspoon pepper
1 cup light cream or milk

Fry bacon in a large skillet until crisp and brown; remove, drain on paper toweling, and crumble. Set aside. Dredge trout in a mixture of flour, salt, and pepper and panfry in drippings 3–5 minutes on each side until golden brown. Add cream and simmer 2 minutes, just until bubbly. Toss in bacon and serve at once with Scottish Bannocks or thick chunks of bread.

NPS (Cream): 580 C, 165 mg CH, 1,100 mg S*
NPS (Milk): 500 C, 130 mg CH, 1,115 mg S*

BAKED MUSHROOM-SMOTHERED TROUT

4 servings

4 (1-pound) trout, cleaned
1 teaspoon salt
¼ teaspoon pepper
½ pound mushrooms, wiped clean and sliced thin
2 tablespoons butter or margarine
1 cup heavy cream
½ cup croutons* (optional)
1 tablespoon minced parsley

Preheat oven to 400° F. Rub cavity of each trout with salt and pepper, then arrange in a single layer in a buttered, large, shallow casserole. Sauté mushrooms in butter in a skillet 3–5 minutes over moderately high heat until golden; off heat stir in cream and pour over trout. Cover loosely with foil and bake 15–20 minutes, just until trout flakes when touched with a fork. Scatter croutons and parsley on top and serve. *(Note:* If you prefer, remove heads and tails before adding croutons and parsley.)

NPS: 500 C, 205 mg CH, 745 mg S*

POMPANO EN PAPILLOTE

4 servings

¼ pound button mushrooms, wiped clean
4 tablespoons butter or margarine
4 pompano fillets or 4 small pompano (about 1 pound each), cleaned and dressed
1 teaspoon salt
¼ teaspoon pepper

S A U C E
½ pound mushrooms, wiped clean and minced
3 scallions, minced
2 tablespoons butter or margarine
1 cup Thick White Sauce
1 tablespoon minced parsley

Preheat oven to 425° F. Prepare sauce first: Stir-fry mushrooms and scallions in butter over moderately high heat 3–5 minutes to brown lightly; mix with remaining sauce ingredients and set aside. Sauté button mushrooms in 2 tablespoons butter over moderately high heat 3–5 minutes until lightly browned, lift out, and reserve. Butter 4 large squares of foil and in the center of each spread 2–3 tablespoons sauce. Place a fillet on each, dot with remaining butter, and sprinkle with salt and pepper. Top each fillet with 2–3 tablespoons sauce, and a few button mushrooms, then wrap tightly, using drugstore wrap.* Place packets on a baking sheet and bake 20 minutes until fish just flakes (open 1 package to check and, if not done, bake a few minutes longer). Serve fish in packets.

NPS: 740 C, 220 mg CH, 1,110 mg S*

LEMONY BAKED STUFFED HALIBUT STEAKS

4–6 servings

2 large halibut steaks of equal size, cut ½″–¾″ thick
½ teaspoon salt
⅛ teaspoon pepper
¼ cup melted butter or margarine
Juice of 1 lemon
1 recipe Lemon Bread Stuffing for Fish

Preheat oven to 350° F. Sprinkle both sides of steaks with salt and pepper; mix butter and lemon juice and brush lightly over both sides of steaks. Place 1 steak in a well-greased shallow baking pan, cover with stuffing, and top with second steak; fasten loosely with toothpicks. Brush with butter mixture and bake, uncovered, 30–40 minutes, brushing often with remaining butter, until fish just flakes when touched with a fork. Remove toothpicks and serve hot with Parsley Sauce or Lemon Sauce or top each portion with a generous pat Maître d'Hôtel Butter.

NPS (4–6): 450–300 C, 160–105 mg CH, 830–555 mg S*

CURRIED FISH STEAKS WITH SOUR CREAM SAUCE

4 servings ⊠

⅓ cup unsifted flour
1 teaspoon salt
⅛ teaspoon white pepper
3 teaspoons curry powder
4 small halibut or salmon steaks, cut ¾″–1″ thick
⅓ cup milk
¼ cup butter or margarine
1 small yellow onion, peeled and minced
½ medium-size sweet green pepper, cored, seeded, and minced
1 cup sour cream

Mix flour, salt, pepper, and 2 teaspoons curry powder. Dip steaks in milk, then in seasoned flour. Melt butter in a large, heavy skillet over moderate heat and sauté steaks 4–5 minutes on each side until golden. Transfer to a hot platter and keep warm. Stir-fry onion and pepper in drippings 3–4 minutes until limp; smooth in remaining curry powder and sour cream, and heat, stirring, 1–2 minutes; do not boil. Pour over fish and serve.

NPS: 780 C, 145 mg CH, 880 mg S*

FISH STEAKS DUGLÉRÉ

4 servings

1 small yellow onion, peeled and minced
4 medium-size tomatoes, peeled, cored, seeded, and chopped fine
1 clove garlic, peeled and crushed
¼ cup butter or margarine
4 small delicate white fish steaks (cod, halibut, pollock, sea bass, etc.), cut ¾″–1″ thick
1 teaspoon salt
⅛ teaspoon white pepper
2 tablespoons minced parsley
⅛ teaspoon thyme
1 bay leaf
½ cup dry white wine
2 tablespoons flour blended with ¼ cup milk

In a large skillet sauté onion, tomatoes, and garlic in butter over moderate heat 4–5 minutes until onion is limp. Turn heat to moderately low, lay fish on vegetables, sprinkle with salt, pepper, 1 tablespoon parsley, and the thyme. Add bay leaf and wine, cover, and simmer 10 minutes until fish flakes when touched with a fork. Lift fish to a hot deep platter and keep warm. Remove bay leaf from sauce, mix in flour-milk paste, and heat, stirring constantly, until thickened and no raw starch taste remains. Taste for salt and adjust as needed. Pour sauce over fish, sprinkle with remaining parsley, and serve.

NPS: 345 C, 145 mg CH, 840 mg S*

DALMATIAN MARINATED FISH

4 servings

½ cup unsifted flour
1 teaspoon salt
½ teaspoon pepper
1 large tuna or halibut steak, cut 1″ thick (about 2 pounds)
¼ cup olive oil

MARINADE
2 tablespoons olive oil
1 large yellow onion, peeled, sliced thin, and separated into rings
2 carrots, peeled and sliced thin
1 large dill pickle or 2 gherkins, sliced thin
1 cup dry red or white wine
6 peppercorns
3 bay leaves
1 tablespoon capers

2 tablespoons tomato paste
1/4 cup minced pitted green olives

Mix flour with salt and pepper and set aside. Cut steaks into 1 1/2″ chunks, removing any bones and skin as you go; dredge chunks in seasoned flour. Heat oil in a large, heavy skillet over moderately high heat until a cube of bread will sizzle, and brown fish chunks well on all sides, about 5 minutes; drain on paper toweling. To the same skillet, add oil for marinade and stir-fry onion and carrots 5–8 minutes over moderate heat until golden. Mix in remaining marinade ingredients and simmer, stirring occasionally, 10 minutes. Place fish in a bowl, top with hot marinade, cool to room temperature, and serve.

NPS: 625 C, 125 mg CH, 1,460 mg S*

TAVIRA TUNA STEAK

4 servings

The men of Tavira, a small port on Portugal's Algarve coast, are tuna fishermen, and their wives are superb cooks, as this mint-flavored tuna recipe quickly proves.

1 large tuna steak, cut 1 1/2″ thick (about 2 pounds)
1/2 teaspoon salt
1/4 teaspoon pepper

MARINADE
1/4 cup olive oil
1/4 cup dry port or sherry
2 cloves garlic, peeled and crushed
2 tablespoons minced fresh mint
2 tablespoons minced parsley
Juice of 1/2 lemon

Rub both sides of steak with salt and pepper; place tuna in an ungreased large, shallow baking dish or casserole. Mix marinade and pour on top; cover and marinate in refrigerator 3–4 hours, basting several times with marinade. Preheat oven to 350° F. Bake tuna, covered, 15 minutes, uncover, and bake 15–18 minutes longer, basting often with marinade, until fish will just flake. Serve from casserole, topping each portion with some of the marinade.

NPS: 455 C, 130 mg CH, 360 mg S*

BOUILLABAISSE

6 servings

There are those who say you can't make Bouillabaisse unless you're from Marseilles

and use the local catch (especially an ugly fish called *rascasse).* But there are excellent adaptations of the classic recipe made with American fish. Here's one of them.

1 cup minced yellow onions or scallions
1/2 cup minced leeks (include green tops)
2–3 cloves garlic, peeled and crushed
1/2 cup olive oil
1 (1-pound 12-ounce) can tomatoes (do not drain)
1 1/2 quarts Easy Fish Stock or a 1/2 and 1/2 mixture of water and bottled clam juice
1 bay leaf and 1 sprig each parsley and thyme, tied in cheesecloth (*bouquet garni*)
1/2 teaspoon thyme
1/4 teaspoon fennel seeds
1/2 teaspoon saffron
1 (2″) strip orange rind (orange part only)
1 teaspoon salt
1/4 teaspoon pepper
2 (1 1/4-pound) live lobsters or 2 1/2 pounds frozen Alaska king crab legs, cut in serving-size pieces (include shells)
1 pound eel, cleaned, dressed, and cut in 1″ chunks, or 1 pound scallops, washed well
1 pound halibut, haddock, sea bass, or wolffish, cleaned, dressed, and cut in 2″ chunks
1 pound mackerel, tuna, or mullet, cleaned, dressed, and cut in 2″ chunks
1 pound flounder fillets, cut in 2″ chunks
2 dozen mussels or littleneck clams in the shell, well scrubbed (mussels should also be bearded)
1 tablespoon minced parsley

In a 3-gallon oven-to-table kettle sauté onions, leeks, and garlic in oil over moderate heat 3–5 minutes until very pale golden. Add tomatoes, breaking up clumps, stock, all herbs and seasonings, cover, and simmer 1/2 hour. Add lobsters, eel, halibut, and mackerel, cover, and simmer 5 minutes. Add flounder and mussels, cover, and simmer 7–10 minutes until mussels open. Remove *bouquet garni* and orange rind, taste for salt and pepper and adjust as needed. Ladle into hot soup plates, sprinkle with parsley, and serve with plenty of hot Garlic Bread. Set out lobster crackers and picks, also plenty of napkins. (*Note:* This recipe is best made with live lobster. If you can't get your fish market to cut the live lobsters into serving-size pieces and are squeamish about doing it yourself, parboil the lobsters 5 minutes, then cut them up.)

NPS: 620 C, 190 mg CH, 1,455 mg S*

SEAFOOD PROVENÇAL

6 servings   ⚖ ¢

2 pounds fillets or steaks of delicate white fish
   (cod, haddock, flounder, fluke, halibut, etc.)
1½ teaspoons salt
¼ teaspoon pepper
1 clove garlic, peeled and crushed
1 cup Easy Fish Stock
3 firm tomatoes, halved but not peeled
2 tablespoons olive or other cooking oil
⅛ teaspoon thyme
½ cup soft white bread crumbs
2 tablespoons melted butter or margarine

Preheat oven to 350° F. Fold fillets envelope fashion, ends toward center, and arrange in a single layer in a well-buttered shallow 2½-quart casserole. Sprinkle with 1 teaspoon salt and ⅛ teaspoon pepper. Stir garlic into stock and pour over fish. Bake, uncovered, basting two or three times, 20–30 minutes until fish will flake. Meanwhile, sauté tomatoes in oil in a skillet over moderate heat 4–5 minutes until lightly browned; keep warm. When fish is done, draw liquid off with a bulb baster. Arrange tomatoes around fish, sprinkle with thyme and remaining salt and pepper. Top with crumbs, drizzle with butter, and broil 3″–4″ from heat 1–2 minutes to brown.

NPS: 220 C, 85 mg CH, 850 mg S*

COULIBIAC

12–14 servings   ⚖

This rich Russian fish dish is usually wrapped in brioche but it's good—and good-looking—made this quick way with packaged, refrigerated dough. Much lower calorie, too.

2 (8-ounce) packages refrigerated dough for
   crescent rolls
2 cups cooked seasoned kasha or rice
2 cups skinned, boned, flaked cooked salmon
3 hard-cooked eggs, shelled and sliced thin

SAUCE
4 scallions, minced
½ pound mushrooms, wiped clean and coarsely
   chopped
2 tablespoons butter or margarine
2 tablespoons flour
1 cup Easy Fish Stock or water
2 tablespoons tomato purée
1 teaspoon salt
⅛ teaspoon pepper
1 teaspoon chervil
1 teaspoon tarragon
1 tablespoon minced parsley

GLAZE
1 egg lightly beaten with 1 tablespoon water

Preheat oven to 375° F. Make sauce first: Stir-fry scallions and mushrooms in butter in a large saucepan over moderate heat 3–5 minutes until limp; blend in flour, slowly add stock, and heat, stirring, until thickened. Off heat, mix in remaining ingredients; cool 10 minutes. Meanwhile, open 1 package of dough, spread flat, halve crosswise but do not separate into individual rolls. Fit halves together on an ungreased baking sheet so you have a rectangle about 9″ × 14″; pinch edges together to seal, also press all perforations closed so you have an unbroken sheet of dough. Spread 1½ cups *kasha* over dough, leaving ½″ margins all around, cover with fish, spread with sauce, then top with eggs and remaining kasha. Shape second roll of dough into an unbroken sheet just like the first and lay on top of filling, letting edges hang over. Brush edges of bottom dough lightly with egg glaze, bring up over top edges and pinch together to seal. Make 6 steam slits in top of coulibiac. Brush glaze over dough and bake, uncovered, on center rack ½ hour. Carefully ease onto a hot serving platter. To serve, cut straight across in thick slices.

*NPS (12–14): 270–230 C, 110–95 mg CH, 845–665
   mg S**

CEVICHE (PERUVIAN RAW PICKLED FISH)

2–3 main course servings, enough appetizers for 6

To be really authentic, serve as a main course with hot boiled sweet potatoes, peeled and sliced in thick rounds, and chunks of fresh corn on the cob.

1 pound flounder, fluke, halibut, or other firm-
   fleshed, delicate white fish fillets
3 medium-size yellow onions, peeled, sliced thin,
   and separated into rings
3 medium-size hot red chili peppers, cored,
   seeded, and cut in thin strips
3 medium-size Italian sweet peppers or 1 sweet
   green pepper, cored, seeded, and cut in thin
   strips
¾ cup lime juice
¾ cup lemon juice
1 tablespoon olive oil
½ clove garlic, peeled and crushed
½ teaspoon salt
2 tablespoons minced parsley

Cut raw fillets into strips about 3″ long and ½″ wide and place in a large glass, porcelain, or stainless-steel bowl. Add all remaining ingredients except parsley and toss well to mix. Cover and chill 24 hours, turning mixture often. When ready to serve, toss again and sprinkle with parsley. Lift out fish and top each portion with some of the vegetables and 1–2 spoonfuls of marinade.

NPS (2): 380 C, 115 mg CH, 790 mg S*
NPS (3): 255 C, 75 mg CH, 525 mg S*
NPS (6): 125 C, 35 mg CH, 265 mg S*

VARIATION

Scallops Ceviche: Prepare as directed, substituting 2 pounds whole raw bay scallops for the fish.

NPS (2): 380 C, 110 mg CH, 790 mg S*
NPS (3): 255 C, 75 mg CH, 525 mg S*
NPS (6): 125 C, 35 mg CH, 265 mg S*

SASHIMI (JAPANESE-STYLE RAW FISH AND VEGETABLES)

6 main course servings, enough appetizers for 10 ⚖

Prepare as the Japanese do, paying great attention to the artistic arrangement of fish and garnishes on small colored plates. Serve as an appetizer or main course with *sake*.

2 pounds fresh pompano, red snapper, or tuna fillets
1 cucumber, sliced paper thin (do not peel)
Watercress sprigs

CONDIMENTS
Soy sauce
1/2 cup minced white radishes
1/3 cup minced fresh gingerroot
1/4 cup prepared horseradish
Powdered mustard
Mirin or dry sherry

Insist that the fish is *ocean*-fresh; chill well, then with an extra-sharp knife, slice 1/8″ thick across the grain and slightly on the bias. Cut slices into strips about 1″ × 2″ and arrange slightly overlapping on 6 individual plates. Cover and chill until near serving time.

Setting Up the Sashimi: At each place set out a small bowl of soy sauce and, in the center of the table, group colorful bowls of minced radishes, gingerroot, horseradish, and mustard, each with its own spoon, around a bottle of *mirin* or sherry.

Serving the Sashimi: Arrange cucumber slices and watercress sprigs on plates with raw fish and set on larger plates filled with crushed ice.

Eating Sashimi: Before anyone eats anything, he or she mixes a dip by adding a little of the condiments in the center of the table to his bowl of soy sauce. The procedure is then simply to pick up slices of raw fish or cucumber, one at a time, with chopsticks or fork, dip in sauce, and eat.

NPS (6–10) (without condiments): 265–160 C, 85–50 mg CH, 85–50 mg S*

VARIATION

⚖ Scallops Sashimi: Instead of using thin slices of raw fish, substitute 2 pounds tiny whole raw bay scallops, well washed and chilled.

NPS (6–10) (without condiments): 135–80 C, 50–30 mg CH, 400–240 mg S*

SALMON LOAF WITH DILL AND LEMON

6–8 servings

2 (1-pound) cans salmon (do not drain)
2 cups coarse soda cracker crumbs
1/3 cup minced yellow onion
1/4 cup minced sweet green pepper
2 tablespoons minced fresh dill or 1 teaspoon dillweed
3 eggs
1 tablespoon lemon juice
1 teaspoon Worcestershire sauce
1/2 cup evaporated milk
1/8 teaspoon white pepper

Preheat oven to 325° F. Pick over salmon, removing any coarse bones and dark skin, then flake. Add remaining ingredients and mix well, using your hands. Pack into a well-greased 9″ × 5″ × 3″ loaf pan and bake, uncovered, about 1 hour and 20 minutes until lightly browned and firm to the touch. Let loaf stand upright in pan 5 minutes before turning out. Serve hot or cold. Particularly good with Sour Cream-Cucumber Sauce.

NPS (6–8): 390–290 C, 190–140 mg CH, 910–685 mg S*

TUNA AND CAPER SOUFFLÉ

4 servings

1/4 cup butter or margarine
2 tablespoons minced yellow onion
1/4 cup unsifted flour
1 cup milk or evaporated milk
1/2 teaspoon salt
1/8 teaspoon white pepper
4 eggs, separated, at room temperature
1 (6 1/2-ounce) can tuna, drained and flaked

1 tablespoon minced parsley
1 tablespoon minced drained capers
1/2 teaspoon dill
1/4 teaspoon cream of tartar

Melt butter in a small saucepan over moderate heat, add onion, and stir-fry 3–5 minutes until limp; blend in flour, slowly add milk, and heat, stirring, until thickened; turn heat to low and mix in salt and pepper. Beat egg yolks lightly, blend in a little hot sauce, then return to pan. Heat and stir 1–2 minutes but do not boil. Off heat, mix in tuna, parsley, capers, and dill. Place a piece of wax paper flat on the surface of the sauce to prevent a "skin" from forming, and cool to room temperature. Preheat oven to 350° F. Beat egg whites until foamy, add cream of tartar, and continue beating until stiff but not dry. Stir about 1/4 cup egg whites into sauce, then fold in remainder. Spoon into an ungreased 1 1/2-quart soufflé dish and bake, uncovered, 45–50 minutes until puffy and browned. Serve at once. Good with Caper or Parsley Sauce.

NPS: 330 C, 325 mg CH, 730 mg S*

VARIATION

Salmon Soufflé: Prepare as directed, substituting 1 cup flaked cooked or canned salmon for the tuna.

NPS: 350 C, 330 mg CH, 730 mg S*

TUNA NIÇOISE

4–6 servings

A cooling summer luncheon first course or entree made with tuna, ripe olives, and tomatoes. If made without tuna, it is the classic Salade Niçoise.

1 clove garlic, peeled and halved
1 head Boston lettuce, trimmed, broken into
  bite-size pieces, and chilled
2/3 cup French Dressing
2 (6 1/2-ounce) cans white-meat tuna, drained and
  flaked
2 cups cold diced cooked potatoes
2 cups cold cooked cut green beans
1/2 cup ripe olives
2 ripe tomatoes, cored and cut in wedges
1 (2-ounce) can anchovies, drained
1 tablespoon capers
1 teaspoon minced fresh chervil or 1/4 teaspoon
  dried chervil
1 teaspoon minced fresh tarragon or 1/2
  teaspoon dried tarragon

Rub a salad bowl with garlic, add lettuce, 2–3 tablespoons dressing, and toss. Mix 1/3 cup dressing with tuna, potatoes, and beans, then pile on lettuce. Garnish with olives, tomatoes, and anchovies, sprinkle with capers, herbs, and remaining dressing. Do not toss.

NPS (4–6): 560–370 C, 25–15 mg CH, 755–500 mg S*

VARIATION

Salade Niçoise *(4 servings):* Omit tuna; prepare salad as directed but use only 1/2 cup dressing in all; toss lettuce with 2–3 tablespoons dressing, mix 1/4 cup with potatoes and beans, then sprinkle the balance on top.

NPS: 325 C, 5 mg CH, 355 mg S*

ROE

There are two types of roe: *hard* (female eggs inside a delicate membrane) and the less familiar *soft roe* (milt or sperm, also wrapped in a tissue-thin membrane). Shad roe is the most highly prized (possibly because of its short season and scarcity), though that of herring, cod, mackerel, mullet, flounder, and whitefish are all delicious. Sizes of roe vary enormously, from the bite-size herring roe to the medium-size shad roe (5"–6" long and 3" across) to the huge cod roe (it weighs from 1 pound to 3 or more). All hard roe has a slightly gritty texture when cooked but delicate flavor; all is a high-protein food rich in B vitamins. Soft roe is paler (almost white), blander, and creamier than hard roe. The choicest comes from carp, herring, and mackerel, in that order. Like hard roe, it is highly nutritious.

Season: Spring, *early* spring for shad roe, usually March and April or, as New Englanders say, "When the shad bush blooms."

Amount Needed: Allow 1/4–1/3 pound per person. If the roe is very small, you will need several pair per person; with shad roe, 1 pair per person is ample. Larger roe will serve more than 1 person.

For Top Quality: Look for moist, firm, unbroken roe with a clean, fresh smell.

Frozen and Canned Roe

In addition to being marketed fresh, hard roe is also available frozen and canned. When salted, it becomes *caviar* (see discussion in chapter on Appetizers and Hors d'Oeuvre). Not every roe becomes caviar, however. The most delectable (black, but sometimes gray or gold) is from sturgeon, the next best (red) is from salmon. Three great pretenders are roe of lumpfish, paddlefish, and whitefish, cleverly salted and colored black.

How to Cook Frozen Roe: Thaw completely in the refrigerator, then prepare like fresh roe.

How to Prepare Canned Roe: Brown gently in butter and serve.

How to Cook Fresh Roe

Easy does it! All roe is fragile and must be given kid-glove care. Too much heat will shatter it or dry it out, too much seasoning will mask its subtle flavor. The more simply roe is cooked, the better it will be.

General Preparation:

Hard Roe: Wash *very* gently in a bowl of cool water and pat dry on paper toweling. Some cooks recommend pricking the covering membrane several places with a needle to keep it from bursting during cooking. But if the roe is cooked *gently*—as it should be— the membrane isn't likely to burst.

Soft Roe: Wash carefully in a bowl of cool water, using the lightest possible touch; pull away the blue vein running along one side of roe. Lift roe from water and pat dry on paper toweling.

To Oven-Broil (for hard roe of medium size only): This is a pretty risky way to cook roe; broiler heat is simply too intense for delicate roe and tends to shatter and shrink it. But, there are people who dote upon broiled roe, so . . . Preheat broiler. Have roe at or near room temperature to reduce chances of shattering and slather with melted butter or margarine. Place in a well-buttered piepan and broil 4″ from the heat, 4–5 minutes on a side, basting often with additional melted butter. Turn roe only once and use a pancake turner, handling lightly so membrane doesn't break. *(Note:* Some books recommend parboiling roe 10 minutes in lightly salted boiling water before broiling to reduce chances of bursting. Try it, if you like, but don't expect the roe to have much flavor.)

To Panfry (Sauté): Here's the best method for hard and soft roe. Have roe at or near room temperature. Dip in milk, then dredge in flour lightly seasoned with salt and pepper. Place in a *cold* skillet with melted butter (allow 1/4 cup butter for each 1 pound roe) and sauté slowly over moderate heat until lightly browned. Small roe will take about 2 minutes on a side, medium-size roe 31/2–4

minutes per side. Turn roe one time only and handle very carefully. *(Note:* Large roe, that of cod, for example, should be poached by the method below, patted dry on paper toweling, then just browned lightly, about 5 minutes on each side in the butter.) Serve the sautéed roe as is, topped with some of the pan juices. Or serve on lightly buttered toast, drizzled with Lemon Butter. *(Note:* Large roe is usually broken into smaller pieces, then served in the same way as smaller roe.)

VARIATIONS

Roe à la Meunière: Sauté as directed, transfer to a hot platter, and sprinkle with lemon juice and a little minced parsley. Add 1–2 tablespoons butter to skillet, heat until bubbly and the color of topaz, pour over roe and serve.

Breaded Fried Roe: Dredge roe in flour lightly seasoned with salt and pepper, dip in a mixture of beaten egg and milk (2 tablespoons milk for each egg), then roll in fine dry crumbs or cracker meal to coat. Sauté as directed.

To Poach: Arrange roe in a large, heavy skillet (not iron), add cold water barely to cover; for each 2 cups water, add 1/2 teaspoon salt and 1 tablespoon lemon juice. Cover skillet and simmer roe over moderately low heat (water should just tremble) as follows: 5 minutes for small roe, 10 minutes for medium-size roe or large roe that is to be sautéed after poaching, and 15–20 minutes for large roe that is to be poached only. When done, roe will be white and firm (but not hard). Drizzle with Parsley or Herb Butter and serve. Large roe can be broken into chunks and smothered with Béchamel, Poulette, or Shrimp Sauce or drizzled with seasoned melted butter.

SHELLFISH

BASIC SHELLFISH CROQUETTES

4 servings

If croquettes are to be light and crisp, and not the least bit greasy, the deep fat must be good and hot—in this case, 375° F.

3 tablespoons butter or margarine
3 tablespoons flour
1 cup milk or light cream
1/2 teaspoon salt

1/8 teaspoon liquid hot red pepper seasoning
1 tablespoon minced parsley
1 tablespoon minced fresh dill or 1/2 teaspoon dried dill
1 egg, lightly beaten
1 1/2 cups soft white bread crumbs
1 1/2 cups minced, cooked lobster, shrimp, crab meat, scallops, clams, mussels, or oysters
1 tablespoon lemon or lime juice
Shortening or cooking oil for deep fat frying

COATING

1 egg, lightly beaten
1 cup cracker meal or toasted, packaged, seasoned bread crumbs

Melt butter in a saucepan over moderate heat and blend in flour; slowly add milk and heat, stirring, until thickened. Off heat, mix in seasonings, egg, crumbs, shellfish, and lemon juice; cover and chill 3–4 hours. Shape into 8 patties or small balls, dip in egg, and roll in cracker meal to coat. Let stand at room temperature on a wire rack while heating fat. Place shortening in a deep fat fryer and heat to 375° F.; use a deep fat thermometer. Place 3 or 4 croquettes in fryer basket, lower into hot fat, and fry 2–3 minutes until golden brown and crisp; drain on paper toweling, then keep warm while you fry the rest by setting, uncovered, in oven turned to lowest heat. Serve hot with Tartar Sauce.

NPS (Lobster): 415 C, 215 mg CH, 635 mg S*
NPS (Scallops): 425 C, 200 mg CH, 665 mg S*

BASIC SHELLFISH SOUFFLÉ

4 servings

Delicate but not difficult to make.

1/4 cup butter or margarine
1/4 cup unsifted flour
1 cup light cream
1/2 teaspoon salt
1/8 teaspoon white pepper
1/8 teaspoon nutmeg or mace
4 eggs, separated, at room temperature
1 cup finely chopped cooked shrimp, lobster, crab meat, or well-drained minced clams
1/4 teaspoon cream of tartar

Melt butter in a small saucepan over moderate heat, blend in flour, slowly add cream, and heat, stirring, until thickened and smooth; mix in salt, pepper, and nutmeg and turn heat to low. Beat egg yolks lightly, blend in a little hot sauce, then return to saucepan. Heat and stir 1–2 minutes but do not allow to boil. Off heat, mix in shellfish; lay a piece of wax paper flat on surface of sauce to prevent a "skin" from forming, and cool to room temperature. Preheat oven to 350° F. Beat egg whites until foamy, add cream of tartar, and continue beating until stiff but not dry. Stir about 1/4 cup egg white into sauce, then carefully fold in remainder. Spoon into an ungreased 1 1/2-quart soufflé dish and bake, uncovered, about 45 minutes until puffy and tinged with brown. Rush to the table and serve. Good with Shrimp Sauce or Sauce Américaine.

NPS: 360 C, 375 mg CH, 560 mg S*

VARIATION

Herbed Shellfish Soufflé: Prepare as directed but add 1 tablespoon minced parsley and 1 tablespoon minced fresh dill, tarragon, or chervil to sauce along with shellfish.

CLAMS

Clams were probably the first New World food sampled by Pilgrims. They arrived ravenous after weeks at sea, fell upon the New England beaches in search of food, and found hard and soft clams by the bucketful. Later, they learned from the Indians how to roast clams over open fires, to simmer them into soups and stews, and to layer them into pits with corn, potatoes, and lobsters in that most convivial of picnics, the clambake.

The Kinds of Clams

The terminology is confusing because there are so many different kinds of clams, also because each has several names. Here's a quick roundup:

East Coast Clams: There are two types, the hard and soft shell.

Hard-Shell Clams: These are also called by the Indian name, *quahog,* and come in three sizes: *large or chowder* (at least 3″ in diameter and best for chowders or stuffed clams); *cherrystones* or medium (about 2″ across and good for steaming or eating on the half shell), and *littlenecks* or small (1 1/2″ across and usually reserved for eating on the half shell).

Soft Clams or Steamers: The shells are long, thin, and oval and the clams inside are long, too, and stick long black necks outside their shells (explaining their nickname, *longneck).* These are the clams harvested along beaches and mud flats, the lightning-quick burrowers.

West Coast Clams: Most famous of the 35-plus varieties are:

Butter Clams: Sweet-meated little clams from the Puget Sound area that are best eaten on the half shell. Indians used them as money, so they're also called *moneyshells.*

Geoduck (pronounced gooey-duck): These long-necked monsters are fun to dig at low tide but rarely appear in markets.

Mud Clams: Popular, large oval clams found along the Northern California and Oregon coasts; only the white flesh is eaten.

Pismo Clams: One of the choicest Pacific clams; it is big, tender, and sweet—and becoming scarce. Only clams measuring 5″ across or more may be taken. The tender adductor muscle is often served on the half shell, the body meat is usually fried, hashed, or minced into chowders. The name Pismo comes from Pismo Beach, California, where these clams were first found.

Razor Clams: These, so named because their long slender shells resemble the old-fashioned barber's razor, are so delectable many gourmets rate them higher than the Eastern soft clams.

Buying Fresh Clams

Season:

East Coast Varieties: Year round.

West Coast Varieties: Year round in the Pacific Northwest. In California the season is shorter, usually November through April. Spring and summer are the time of the dread "red tide" when microscopic organisms fill the sea, making clams and certain other shellfish unsafe to eat. At such times, many clamming beaches are closed.

Popular Market Forms: Atlantic and Pacific clams are both sold live and in the shell either by the dozen or pound; they are also sold shucked by the pint or quart. In addition, many markets, if asked, will remove the top shells and prepare clams for serving or cooking on the half shell.

Amount Needed: The quantity varies tremendously according to the size of the clams, how they are cooked and served, not to mention appetites. Here's a general guide:

Clams on the Half Shell: Allow 6–8 small- or medium-size clams per person.

Steamed or Stewed Clams: Allow 1–1½ dozen clams per serving, depending on size of clams and richness of broth.

Shucked Clams: 1 pint will serve 3–4, more if stretched with other ingredients.

For Top Quality:

Clams in the Shell: Look for tightly closed clams, or at least those that "clam up" when their shells are tapped. Any that remain open are dead and should be rejected.

Shucked Clams: Choose clams that are plump and sweet-smelling with clear liquor and no shell fragments.

Frozen and Canned Clams

Quick-frozen shucked clams are available, as are frozen, ready-to-heat-and-eat clam fritters and patties. Canned clams, both whole and minced, chowders, and clam juice are all widely marketed. *To Cook Frozen Clams:* Thaw quick-frozen shucked clams completely in refrigerator, then prepare as you would fresh clams. Once clams have thawed, cook immediately; never refreeze. Clam fritters, patties, and other frozen prepared clam dishes should be heated or cooked by package directions.

How to Use Canned Clams: These are already cooked and ideal for quick soups, salads, canapés, and casseroles.

Preparing Fresh Clams in the Shell

How to Cleanse Clams of Grit: The easiest way is to let the clams do the job themselves. Here's how: Scrub clams well to remove surface grit and mud, then place in a large, deep enamel kettle and cover with cold salted water (1 tablespoon salt to each quart water). Toss in a handful of corn meal, set kettle in a cool place, and let stand several hours or overnight. Lift clams from water and rinse well in cool water; discard any that are open or do not clamp shut when thumped.

How to Open Clams: There are two ways, one difficult, one easy. If the clams are to be served or broiled on the half shell, you'll have to use brute force. If they're to be removed from the shell and used in chowders, patties, or casseroles, they can quickly be steamed open. (*Note:* Geoducks require special attention [see method that follows].)
1. *To Pry Open:* Holding a clam in the palm of one hand, insert clam knife between upper and lower shells, then move it along rim, twisting slightly to break "seal" and force clam open (the job is much easier with soft clams than with hard). Cut clam free of shell

and remove any grit or bits of shell. Do the opening over a bowl so none of the clam juice is lost; also strain juice through a sieve lined with a double thickness of cheesecloth before using.

2. *To Steam Open:* Place clams in a large, deep kettle, pour in about ¾ cup boiling water, cover, and steam over moderate heat about 5–8 minutes until shells partially open. Drain and remove meat from shells—it will come away zip-quick if you work under a gentle stream of cool water.

How to Cook Clams

Clams can be cooked simply or glamorized in a variety of ways. Purists insist nothing surpasses a steamed clam, dunked in melted butter, but then everyone is not a purist. . . .

General Preparation: If clams are in the shell, cleanse of grit and shuck or not as recipes specify. Check extra-heavy clams carefully; they may be full of sand or mud. This is all the preparation Eastern hard and soft clams need, also the West Coast butter clam. Other Pacific varieties, however, require further attention:

Geoduck: Plunge clam into boiling water and let stand until shell opens. Drain and cut body meat from shell. Skin the clam, discard the stomach (the dark portion), and separate neck from body. Put neck through coarse blade of meat grinder and slice body into thin steaks (about ¼″ thick). The neck meat is best used in chowders, the steaks quickly panfried in butter.

Mud Clams: When clams are shucked, trim away all black portions; split the necks lengthwise and rinse away any grit. Cook as you would hard clams.

Pismo Clams: Cut hinge or adductor muscle from body meat; it is tender enough to serve raw on the half shell. Remove stomach (the dark part) from the body, rinse clam, then lightly pound any firm parts to "tenderize." These clams are particularly good fried or deep-fat-fried.

Razor Clams: Cut off tip of the neck, cut clam from shell, and split from the base of the foot (that part next to the shell) to the top of the neck. Trim off all dark parts (the gills and digestive organs). Leave clam whole and fry or deep-fry, or grind and use for chowders or patties.

To Charcoal-Broil: This is a bit of a fuss. Build a moderately hot charcoal fire. Pat shucked clams dry on paper toweling, then wrap each in a ½ slice bacon and thread on long thin skewers; or secure bacon slices with toothpicks and place clams in a well-greased hinged, long-handled wire grill. Broil 4″ from heat 3–4 minutes on a side until bacon is golden and crisp. *Note:* The techniques (and cooking times) are the same for outdoor gas and electric grills; just be sure to preheat them.

To Panfry (Sauté): Pat shucked clams dry on paper toweling. Dredge in flour lightly seasoned with salt and pepper and sauté in butter (about ⅓ cup butter for 1 pint clams) about 3 minutes over moderate heat, turning once, until clams are lightly browned. Serve with lemon wedges.

VARIATIONS

Pan-"Roasted" Clams: These aren't roasted but sautéed. Pat clams dry on paper toweling but do not dredge. Sauté in butter (about ½ cup butter for 1 pint clams) 2–3 minutes, turning once, just until clams plump up and are heated through. Serve with lemon.

Breaded Fried Clams: Pat clams dry, dredge in flour lightly seasoned with salt and pepper, dip in a mixture of beaten egg and milk (2 tablespoons milk for each egg), and roll in fine dry crumbs, cracker meal, or a half-and-half mixture of flour and corn meal. Sauté as directed until golden and drain on paper toweling before serving.

To Deep-Fat-Fry: Pat shucked clams dry on paper toweling, then bread as above. Heat cooking oil or shortening in a deep fat fryer to 375° F., place a single layer of clams in fryer basket, lower into fat, and fry 1–2 minutes until golden brown. Drain on paper toweling and serve with lemon.

VARIATION

Batter-Fried Clams (Clam Fritters): Make up batter given in Fish and Chips recipe. Pat clams dry on paper toweling, dip in batter, then fry, 6–8 at a time, in 375° F. fat about 2 minutes until golden brown. Drain on paper toweling and serve.

To Oven-Roast: Scrub clams well and cleanse of grit but do not shuck. Preheat oven to 450° F. Place clams in a shallow baking pan and roast, uncovered, 12–15 minutes until they open; reject any that do not. Serve clams in the shell with plenty of melted butter and lemon wedges.

To Roast over Charcoal: Scrub clams and cleanse but do not shuck. Build a moderately hot charcoal fire or preheat outdoor gas or electric grill. Wrap clams, about 6 to a package, in heavy foil. Place packages directly on coals and roast 4–6 minutes until clams open. Serve with lemon and melted butter.

To Steam: Steamers or soft clams are best, though small hard clams may also be steamed. Scrub clams well and cleanse of grit but do not shuck. Place clams in a large, deep kettle, add 2/3 cup boiling water, cover, and steam 5 minutes over moderate heat until clams open; discard any that don't. Serve in the shell with melted butter, a bowl of broth, and lemon wedges. When eating, peel black skin from neck and hold by the neck when dunking in broth and butter.

To Serve Clams on the Half Shell: Allow 6–8 cherrystone, littleneck, or butter clams per serving. If possible, have your fish market open clams and discard top shells. If you must do the job yourself, follow directions given earlier for cleansing and prying open clams. Fill large, shallow bowls or soup plates with crushed ice and arrange clams in ice. Garnish with lemon wedges and parsley fluffs. Set out the pepper mill (but *not* cocktail sauce unless guests insist). After eating clams on the half shell, be sure to drink the juice from each shell.

CLAMS CASINO

2 entree servings, enough appetizers for 4

Rock salt
6 slices bacon
2 dozen cherrystone clams on the half shell
1/4 cup butter or margarine, softened to room temperature
2 teaspoons anchovy paste
1/4 cup minced sweet green pepper
1/4 cup minced pimiento

Preheat oven to 450° F. Make beds of rock salt in 4 piepans (the 8″ or 9″ size is best and the jiffy foil pans work perfectly), dampen slightly with water and heat, uncovered, in oven 5 minutes. Meanwhile, cut each bacon slice into 4 equal pieces and stir-fry over moderate heat until limp; drain on paper toweling and reserve. Arrange 6 clams in each pan, pushing down into hot salt so they won't tip. Mix butter and anchovy paste until smooth and tuck about 1/2 teaspoonful under each clam. Sprinkle a little sweet green pepper and pimiento on each clam, top with a piece of bacon, and bake, uncov-

ered, 5–7 minutes until bacon is crisp. Serve clams from pans.

NPS (2–4): 545–275 C, 190–95 mg CH, 1,060–530 mg S*

VARIATION

Oysters Casino: Prepare as directed, substituting oysters on the half shell for clams.

NPS (2–4): 490–245 C, 170–85 mg CH, 750–375 mg S*

CLAMS OREGANATA

2 entree servings, enough appetizers for 4

Whenever possible, make crumbs from stale Italian bread; the recipe will have much better flavor.

Rock salt
2 dozen littleneck or cherrystone clams on the half shell
1 1/2 cups fine dry bread crumbs
2 cloves garlic, peeled and crushed
2 tablespoons minced parsley
2 teaspoons minced fresh oregano or 1 teaspoon dried oregano
3 tablespoons olive or other cooking oil
1/8 teaspoon pepper

Preheat broiler. Make beds of rock salt in 4 (8″ or 9″) piepans and dampen slightly with water; heat, uncovered, in oven 5 minutes while broiler preheats. Arrange 6 clams in each pan, pushing down into hot salt so they won't tip. Mix remaining ingredients and spoon enough on each clam to cover. Broil 5″ from the heat 3–4 minutes until lightly browned.

NPS (2–4): 615–305 C, 90–45 mg CH, 900–450 mg S*

BOSTON-STYLE STUFFED CLAMS

2–4 servings

The stuffing is a delicate blend of minced clams, onion, parsley, and soft bread crumbs.

Rock salt
1 dozen large clams on the half shell
3/4 cup soft white bread crumbs
1 tablespoon minced yellow onion
1 tablespoon minced parsley
2 teaspoons lemon juice
1/4 teaspoon pepper
1/2 cup fine dry or toasted seasoned bread crumbs mixed with 2 tablespoons melted butter or margarine

---

Preheat oven to 425° F. Make a bed of rock salt in a large, shallow baking pan and dampen slightly with water; heat, uncovered, in oven 5 minutes. Drain juice from clams, reserving 1/4 cup; mince clams and combine with juice; butter clam shells well. Mix clams and juice with all remaining ingredients except buttered crumbs and spoon into shells. Anchor shells in hot salt so they won't tip, top clams with buttered crumbs, and bake, uncovered, 10 minutes until lightly browned.

NPS (2–4): 415–205 C, 130–65 mg CH, 1,400–700 mg S*

VARIATIONS

⚔️ **Stuffed Clams au Gratin:** Prepare clam mixture as directed, adding 1/3 cup crisp crumbled bacon. Omit buttered crumb topping and top instead with 1/4 cup cracker meal mixed with 1/4 cup grated Parmesan. Bake as directed.

NPS: 285–145 C, 150–75 mg CH, 1500–750 mg S*

Creamed, Stuffed Clams: Prepare clam mixture as directed but for the liquid ingredients use 1/3 cup Thick White Sauce and 2 tablespoons medium-dry sherry instead of clam juice and lemon juice. Fill shells, top with buttered crumbs, and bake as directed.

NPS: 400–200 C, 120–60 mg CH, 1300–650 mg S*

CLAMS BULHÃO PATO

4 servings

Bulhão Pato was a Portuguese poet whose recipe for garlic- and coriander-flavored clams is better remembered than his poetry.

5–6 dozen soft clams in the shell, prepared for cooking
1 1/2 cups boiling water
1/3 cup olive oil
3 cloves garlic, peeled and crushed
1/2 cup minced parsley
1/2 cup minced fresh coriander leaves or 2 tablespoons minced carrot tops
1/8 teaspoon pepper
1/2 teaspoon salt

Place clams in a very large, deep kettle, add all remaining ingredients, cover, and steam over moderate heat 5–10 minutes just until shells open; discard any that do not open. Serve clams in shells in soup bowls topped with some of the broth. *(Note:* Tip kettle when ladling out liquid to avoid any sediment in the bottom.) Serve with hot crusty bread.

NPS: 275 C, 65 mg CH, 325 mg S*

CLAM HASH

4 servings ¢ ⊠

3 slices bacon
1 1/4 cups well-drained minced clams or 1 (10 1/2-ounce) can minced clams, drained
1/4 cup minced yellow onion
3 cups diced cooked potatoes
3 eggs, lightly beaten
1/4 cup milk or light cream
1 teaspoon salt
1/8 teaspoon pepper
Pinch nutmeg

Fry bacon in a skillet over moderate heat until crisp; drain, crumble, and reserve. Mix clams, onion, and potatoes and add to drippings in skillet, pressing down with a spatula to form a large "pancake." Fry over moderately low heat without stirring 7–10 minutes until brown on the bottom; flip mixture over, press down. Mix eggs with all remaining ingredients and pour over clams. Cook just until eggs are set, tilting pan as needed to let uncooked eggs run underneath. Sprinkle with bacon, cut in wedges, and serve.

NPS: 295 C, 255 mg CH, 815 mg S*

NEW ENGLAND CLAM PIE

6 servings

A two-crusted pie filled with clams, diced salt pork, and potatoes.

1 recipe Flaky Pastry II
1 pint shucked clams or 3 (6 1/2-ounce) cans minced clams (do not drain)
1/4 pound salt pork or bacon, cut in small dice
1 small yellow onion, peeled and minced
1 tablespoon flour
2 medium-size potatoes, boiled, drained, and cubed
1 tablespoon minced parsley
1/8 teaspoon pepper

Preheat oven to 425° F. Prepare pastry according to recipe and roll out half to form a 12" circle. Fit into a 9" piepan but do not trim edge. Roll remaining pastry into a 12" circle, cut 3 V-shaped slits near center, and cover with wax paper while preparing filling. Drain clams, reserving 1/3 cup liquor (if necessary, add milk to round out measure); mince clams. Lightly brown salt pork in a small skillet over moderately low heat; remove and reserve. Pour off all but 2 tablespoons drippings, add onion, and sauté over moderate heat 3–5 minutes until limp. Blend in flour and clam liquid and heat, stirring, until thickened. Off heat, mix in potatoes, clams, parsley, and pepper. Spoon into prepared pie shell, fit reserved pastry on top, press 2 crusts together, trim and crimp edges. Bake about 1/2 hour until pastry is lightly browned.

NPS: 585 C, 50 mg CH, 690 mg S*

INDOOR CLAMBAKE

6–8 servings

The usual order of building a clambake is clams on the bottom, then lobsters and vegetables, but the following upside-down arrangement has an advantage. The clams can be enjoyed as a first course while the slower-cooking items finish "baking." To do the indoor clambake, you'll need a giant kettle or "clambaker," obtainable in hardware and kitchen shops.

8 ears sweet corn in the husk
2 gallons cold water mixed with 1/2 cup salt
Seaweed
6 (1–1 1/4-pound) live lobsters
8 medium-size potatoes, scrubbed but not peeled
6 dozen soft clams in the shell, prepared for cooking, or 2 dozen each clams, oysters, and mussels in the shell, prepared for cooking

C O N D I M E N T S
2 cups melted butter or margarine
1 bottle liquid hot red pepper seasoning

Remove outer husks of corn but not tightly clinging inner husks; pull off tassels. Soak corn 1 hour in 6 quarts salt water. Meanwhile, pour remaining salt water in a very large deep kettle, add a rack, and cover with a thin layer of seaweed or, if unavailable, outer corn husks which have been soaked well in salt water. Drain soaked ears and arrange on rack. Add lobsters and potatoes, then top with clams and more seaweed or husks. Cover tightly and bring to a boil; reduce heat so water stays at a slow simmer and steam 3/4–1 hour. Lift out clams and serve with condiments as a first course. Meanwhile, clambake should be re-covered and allowed to steam until potatoes are tender. They will be done by the time everyone has finished with the clams. Pile lobsters, potatoes, and corn on huge platters and serve at once with the condiments. Set out bibs, lobster crackers and picks, and plenty of napkins.

NPS (6–8): 995–750 C, 325–245 mg CH, 2,100–1,575 mg S*

CONCH

Conch (pronounced *konk)* isn't everyone's dish—too tough, too strong. But those who live where it's caught—Florida, the Gulf Coast, and West Indies—consider it something special. It's available year round, live and in the shell; also frozen (cooked or uncooked) and canned.

Amount to Buy: 1 pound conch in the shell per person; 1/4–1/3 pound conch meat.

For Top Quality: Buy the conch right off the boat or from a market whose word you trust.

How to Cook Conch

Because of its rubbery texture and strong ocean flavor, conch is best stewed or ground into fritters or patties. It can also be sautéed, *if* first parboiled until tender. Frozen conch need not be thawed before using.

General Preparation (for all cooking methods): Everyone familiar with conch has a pet way to tenderize it. The most effective ways seem to be parboiling or pounding with a mallet. But first: scrub conch shell well under cold running water, place in a large heavy kettle, add boiling water to cover, 1 tablespoon salt, and 1/4 cup lemon juice. Cover and boil 3 minutes; drain in a colander under cold running water until easy to handle. Pry meat from shell with a strong, long-tined fork, cut off hard black "foot" and tightly curled tip. Wash again in cold water. Conch is now ready to simmer into soups or stews. If it is to be panfried or made into fritters, it should be parboiled.

To Parboil: Leave conch meat whole or slice thin; place in a saucepan, add water to cover, and for each pint water add 1 tablespoon lemon juice. Cover and simmer until tender, about 1 1/2–2 hours for sliced conch, 2–4 hours for the whole. Drain well.

BAHAMIAN CONCH CHOWDER

4 servings

A hearty main dish containing conch, carrots, tomatoes, and potatoes.

1 pound conch meat, prepared for cooking
3 tablespoons butter, margarine, or cooking oil
1 large yellow onion, peeled and minced
2 cloves garlic, peeled and crushed
2 carrots, peeled and cut in small dice
2 tomatoes, peeled, cored, seeded, and chopped fine

1/8 teaspoon crushed hot red chili peppers
1/8 teaspoon curry powder
1 (6-ounce) can tomato paste
1 quart water (about)
1 1/2 teaspoons salt (about)
3 small potatoes, peeled and cut in 1/2" cubes

Cut conch meat into 1/2" cubes. Melt butter in a large saucepan over moderate heat and stir-fry onion, garlic, carrots, tomatoes, peppers, and curry powder 3–5 minutes. Add conch and stir 1 minute. Add tomato paste, water, and salt, cover, and simmer 1 1/2–2 hours until conch is very tender; replenish water as needed to keep chowder from getting too thick. Add potatoes and simmer 10–15 minutes longer until tender. Serve piping hot.

NPS: 235 C, 100 mg CH, 1,115 mg S*

VARIATION

Omit potatoes and stir 1 1/2 cups boiled rice into chowder just before serving.

SCUNGILLI MARINARA

4 servings ⚖

Scungilli is the Italian word for conch, and *marinara* is a favorite Italian way of preparing it—with tomatoes, garlic, and onion.

1/2 cup minced yellow onion
1 clove garlic, peeled and crushed
2 tablespoons olive oil
1 (1-pound) can Italian plum tomatoes (do not drain)
1/4 cup tomato paste
1/2 cup dry red wine
1/2 teaspoon sugar
1 teaspoon salt
1 teaspoon oregano
1/8 teaspoon pepper
1 pound sliced parboiled conch meat
2 tablespoons finely grated Parmesan cheese

Sauté onion and garlic in oil in a large saucepan over moderate heat 8–10 minutes until golden. Turn heat to low, add all remaining ingredients except conch and cheese, cover, and simmer 1 hour, stirring occasionally. If mixture becomes too thick, thin with a little water. Cool sauce slightly and purée by buzzing 20–30 seconds in an electric blender at low speed or 15–20 seconds in a food processor fitted with the metal chopping blade. Return to pan, add conch, cover, and simmer 3–5 minutes. Mix in cheese and serve hot over spaghetti or other pasta.

NPS: 235 C, 100 mg CH, 1,115 mg S*

CONCH BURGERS

4–6 servings ⚖

2 cups finely ground parboiled conch meat
2 cups soft white bread crumbs
2 eggs, lightly beaten
1 tablespoon Worcestershire sauce
1/4 teaspoon liquid hot red pepper seasoning
1/2 teaspoon minced garlic
1 tablespoon grated yellow onion
1/4 cup unsifted flour
3 tablespoons butter, margarine, bacon drippings, or cooking oil

Mix conch with all remaining ingredients except flour and butter. Shape into 6 patties and dredge with flour. Heat butter in a large skillet over moderate heat and brown patties 3–4 minutes on each side. Serve hot with Tartar Sauce or Tomato Sauce.

NPS (4–6): 280–186 C, 220–150 mg CH, 430–285 mg S*

CRABS

After shrimp, crab rates as America's favorite shellfish. Easterners insist nothing beats blue crabs for succulence, flavor, and versatility but they get an argument from Westerners, to whom Dungeness is *the* crab. Fortunately, both coasts are blessed with an abundance of crabs. And fortunately, modern packing and shipping have brought fresh and frozen crabs to every state.

The Kinds of Crabs

There are six popular crabs in America; four are widely known, two are local specialties.

Blue Crabs: Far and away the biggest seller. Blue crabs come from Atlantic and Gulf coasts but are at their best in Chesapeake Bay. Depending upon season, they are *hard* or *soft shell.* Soft-shell crabs are nothing more than hard-shell crabs that have molted or shucked their hard shells. Choicest crab meat is that from the back—snowy, white, and sweet; claw meat has tinges of brown.

Dungeness: The king of the West Coast, two to three times the size of the blue crab. Meat is pinkish-white and delectably sweet.

Alaska King Crabs: A giant sometimes measuring 6 feet across and weighing 20 pounds. Only the scarlet-skinned white leg meat is eaten. Available frozen only.

Snow Crabs: With Alaska king crab becoming overfished, this smaller cold-water crab is taking up the slack. It's similar to Alaska king crab and like it comes from Alaska and northwestern Canada. Available frozen as legs and as meat. Prepare as you would Alaska king crab.

Rock Crabs: Taken from both New England and California coasts, these crabs are not well known elsewhere. Their meat has excellent flavor but is tan to brown in color.

Stone Crabs: This Miami-Florida Keys favorite is practically all claw. It is available frozen in fancy fish stores.

The Season for Fresh Crabs

Blue Crabs:

Hard Shell: Year round though supply is limited in cold weather.

Soft Shell: May through August.

Dungeness: Mid-November to late July in California, year round in the Pacific Northwest.

Rock Crabs: Year round with supplies limited in winter.

Stone Crabs: Mid-October to June.

Buying Fresh Crabs

Popular Market Forms:

Blue Crabs:

Hard Shell: Live in the shell; iced tins of fresh-cooked, pasteurized crab meat: choicest is *lump* or *backfin,* solid chunks from the back containing little shell or cartilage; *flake* is less expensive and contains bits and pieces of meat and considerably more shell (good for ramekins and casseroles where appearance doesn't matter so much); also sometimes available are reasonably priced *mixtures of flake and dark claw meat.*

Soft Shell: Live.

Dungeness: Live or cooked in the shell; cooked meat.

Rock Crabs: Live in the shell.

Stone Crabs: Live in the shell.

Amount Needed: Allow about 1 pound crab in the shell per person, 1/4–1/3 pound crab meat, depending upon how it is to be prepared. Hard-shell blue crabs weigh from 1/4 to 1 pound, the soft shell considerably less. Though some people can easily eat half a dozen soft-shell crabs, 3–4 make a respectable portion. Dungeness crabs weigh 13/4–

3 1/2 pounds and Alaska king crabs from 6–20. Rock crabs are small, about 1/3–1/2 pound apiece. Weight matters less with stone crabs since it's the claw that's eaten; allow about 4 claws per person.

For Top Quality: If crabs are alive, make sure they are also *lively.* When buying fresh-cooked crab meat, look for that with a sweet-clean smell.

Frozen and Canned Crabs

The best known frozen crabs are the Alaska king and snow crabs; they are precooked, then frozen in or out of the shell. Cooked Dungeness and blue crab meats are also frozen; so, too, are uncooked soft-shell crabs and stone crab claws. All of the popular American crabs are canned.

How to Use Frozen Crab: Always thaw or not as package directions or recipes direct; when crab is to be thawed, always do so in the refrigerator.

How to Use Canned Crab: This is fully cooked and particularly suited to crab cakes, deviled crab, casseroles—whenever appearance is not the first consideration.

How to Clean and Cook Crabs

With the exception of soft-shell crabs, which can be sautéed or deep-fat-fried, live crabs are best simply boiled or steamed. They may be eaten as is with a suitable sauce or butter or the meat may be taken from the shell and used in a variety of ways (see recipes that follow).

Hard-Shell Crabs:

Blue Crabs, Rock Crabs: Cook, then clean.

To Boil: Bring a large kettle of sea water or lightly salted water to a boil (allow 1 tablespoon salt to 1 quart water), grab crabs, one at a time, across center back of shell and drop into water. As soon as water returns to a boil, cover and simmer 8 minutes per pound of crabs. Drain, rinse under cool running water, and when cool enough to handle clean as directed on following pages.

To Steam: Plunge live crabs in a kettle of hot tap water—it should not be steaming hot, just a bit too hot for your hands. When crabs stop kicking, drain and, if necessary, scrub in warm water with a soft brush to remove bits of mud and sand. Old salts from crab country pooh-pooh the idea of scrubbing, but it does make the crabs more pleasant to eat. Place a rack in a large, deep kettle and pour in about 1½″ boiling water or, better yet, boiling sea water. Pile crabs up on rack so that they are well out of the water, cover and steam 25–30 minutes, just until crabs turn bright orange and their shells rise slightly. Lift crabs from kettle with tongs, drain briefly on paper toweling, and serve hot. Set out lobster or nut crackers and picks and lots of melted butter.

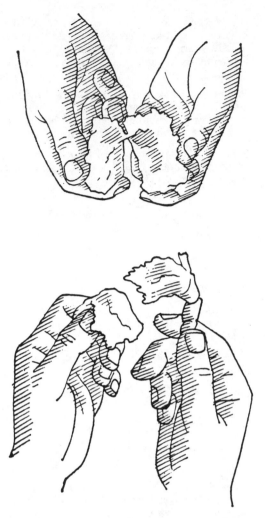

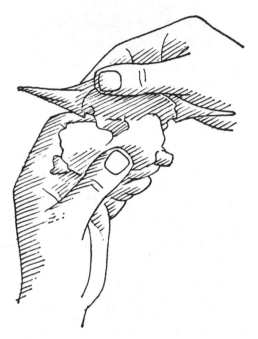

To Clean: Break off claws as close to body as possible, then cut or break off legs. Get a firm grip on top shell and pull off. Scrape all feathery, spongy material from center of body, also the soft, yellowish stomach and digestive tract. Encasing the choice lump crab meat now is a thin inner skeleton; pull or slice off either the left or right half, scrape any meat from cut-off piece and reserve, then scoop out chunks of meat in body pockets and reserve. Repeat with other half of body. Crack claws and legs and pull or pick out meat, using a lobster or nut pick for stubborn bits.

Dungeness Crabs: People disagree as to whether live Dungeness crabs should be cooked and then cleaned or vice versa. Take your choice.

To Clean: Wear rubber gloves to protect your hands from jagged pieces of shell. Grab crab from behind, getting a good grip on its body and two hind legs. Lay crab on its back on a large cutting board, place a sharp knife along midline and hit hard with a mallet to kill crab instantly. Twist off front claws, one at a time, where they join body; also twist off legs. Scrub claws and legs well and set aside. Pry off shell, using a knife if necessary, and scrape out spongy gills; save creamy "crab butter" underneath to use in sauces. Crack each segment of claws and legs and rinse well. Split crab body down midline, then cut each half into manageable (about 1½″) chunks and rinse well.

To Boil: Bring a large kettle of sea water or lightly salted water (1 tablespoon salt to each quart water) to a boil, drop in crab, and when water returns to a boil, cover and simmer 10–12 minutes for cracked crab, 15–20 for whole crab, depending on size. Drain and serve hot with melted butter. If crab has been boiled whole, clean and crack as described above before eating.

California Cold Cracked Crab: Clean and crack crab and boil as directed. Drain, cool, then chill several hours. Serve on beds of cracked ice with freshly made Mayonnaise.

Stone Crabs: Only the claw meat is eaten, so little cleaning is needed. Twist off claws, scrub well, then drop in lightly salted boiling water to cover, cover, and boil 15–20 minutes. Drain and serve hot with melted butter or cool and serve with Mayonnaise, Dill Mayonnaise, or Watercress Mayonnaise. Set out lobster crackers and picks.

Soft-Shell Blue Crabs:

To Clean: With scissors, cut off "face" portion just behind eyes. Lift up shell by the points and cut out feathery, spongy gills; also scoop or cut out yellowish digestive organs. Rinse crabs well under cool running water to remove any yellow traces and pat dry on paper toweling. Turn crab on its back and cut off apron or tail flap folded underneath body; smooth soft shell back in place. Crab is now ready to cook. Everything remaining is edible—legs, claws, soft shell, body.

To Panfry (Sauté): Clean crabs as directed. Dredge lightly in seasoned flour. Melt 1/4–1/3 cup butter or margarine in a large, heavy skillet over moderate heat and, when beginning to foam, add crabs and sauté about 3 minutes on a side until crisp and golden brown. *(Note:* Work carefully because crabs will sputter in the hot butter.) Do only 3–4 at a time, drain well on paper toweling, and set, uncovered, in an oven turned to lowest heat to keep warm while you fry the rest.

Soft-Shell Crabs à la Meunière: Dredge and sauté crabs as above. When all are done, melt 1–2 tablespoons fresh butter in skillet and squeeze in the juice of 1/2 lemon. Pour over crabs, sprinkle with minced parsley, and serve.

Breaded Soft-Shell Crabs: Clean crabs as directed. Dip in lightly beaten egg, then in fine dry bread crumbs or cracker meal to coat. Heat about 1/8" cooking oil or a 1/2 and 1/2 mixture of cooking oil and butter in a large, heavy skillet over moderate heat, add 3–4 crabs, and sauté 3 minutes on each side until crisply golden. Drain on paper toweling, sprinkle with salt and pepper, and serve with lemon wedges.

To Deep-Fat-Fry: Clean crabs as directed and bread as above. Meanwhile, heat oil or shortening in a deep fat fryer to 375° F. Place 2–3 crabs in fryer basket, lower into fat, and fry 3–4 minutes until nicely browned and crisp. Drain on paper toweling and keep warm while frying remaining crabs. Always scoop any browned crumbs from fat before adding more crabs. Serve with lemon wedges.

To Broil: Clean crabs as directed and dredge in flour or, if you prefer, bread as for panfrying. Preheat broiler. Arrange crabs on their backs on a lightly oiled broiler rack. Drizzle with melted butter or Lemon Butter and broil 4"–5" from the heat about 3 minutes until lightly browned. Turn, drizzle again with melted butter, and broil 3 minutes longer until crisp and golden brown. Watch closely toward the end.

How to Eat Crabs in the Shell

Blue Crabs, Rock Crabs:
1. Twist off claws and legs and set aside.
2. Pull off top shell, scrape out and discard feathery gray-white gills and yellowish digestive organs.
3. Peel or cut away thin inner "shell" covering body; underneath is the best part of the crab. Pull out the plump chunks of meat with a small fork or pick, dipping each morsel in accompanying sauce or butter.
4. Crack each segment of claws and twist out meat with a small fork or pick.
5. Treat legs like soda straws, sucking one end to get out any bits of meat inside.

Dungeness: Because of their size, these crabs are nearly always cleaned and cracked before they are served. If for some reason a whole crab comes to the table, attack it following directions for cleaning Dungeness crab.

Stone Crabs: Only the claws are served in the shell; crack with lobster crackers and twist out meat with a small fork or pick.

Alaska King and Snow Crab Legs: These present no problem because enough meat is exposed to make eating easy. Simply pull it out with a fork and cut as needed into bite-size chunks and eat, first dunking into any accompanying butter or sauce.

SPICED BLUE CRABS

4–6 servings ⚖ ⊠

1 quart cider vinegar
1/3 cup salt
1 celery stalk
1/4 cup powdered mustard
1/4 cup whole cloves
3 tablespoons cayenne pepper
2 tablespoons ginger
1 tablespoon mace
1 1/2 gallons boiling water
2 dozen medium-size live blue crabs

Place all ingredients except crabs in a 3-gallon enamel or stainless-steel kettle, bring to a boil, cover, and simmer 5 minutes. Add crabs, cover, and simmer 15 minutes. Drain and serve hot or cool, chill, and serve cold. Set out several sets of lobster crackers and picks.

NPS (4–6): 150–100 C, 125–85 mg CH, 835–555 mg S*

BAKED ALASKA KING CRAB LEGS

2 servings ⊠

Since Alaska king crab legs are always packaged fully cooked, they only need to be heated through before eating.

3/4 pound frozen ready split Alaska king or snow crab legs (do not thaw)
1/2 cup melted butter or margarine
1/2 clove garlic, peeled and crushed (optional)
Juice of 1/2 lemon

Preheat oven to 400° F. Place crab legs, flesh side up, in an ungreased shallow baking pan. Mix butter, garlic, and lemon juice and brush over crab legs. Bake, uncovered, 15 minutes until bubbly, brushing often with butter mixture.

NPS: 530 C, 250 mg CH, 735 mg S*

VARIATIONS

⚖ **Low-Calorie Baked King Crab Legs:** Prepare as directed, substituting low-calorie Italian, garlic, or herb dressing for the butter mixture.

NPS: 185 C, 130 mg CH, 740 mg S*

Baked Herbed King Crab Legs: Prepare as directed but omit garlic from melted butter. Add instead 2 teaspoons each minced parsley and fresh tarragon, chervil, or dill or 1 teaspoon parsley flakes and 1/4 teaspoon dried tarragon, chervil, or dill.

NPS: 530 C, 250 mg CH, 735 mg S*

Baked Italian-Style King Crab Legs: Prepare as directed, substituting olive oil for butter and adding 1/4 teaspoon oregano.

NPS: 600 C, 125 mg CH, 270 mg S*

CRAB CIOPPINO

4–6 servings

A favorite California crab stew filled with tomatoes and studded with shrimp and clams.

1 medium-size yellow onion, peeled and minced
1 stalk celery, minced
1/2 sweet green pepper, cored, seeded, and minced
1 clove garlic, peeled and crushed
1/3 cup olive oil
6 large ripe tomatoes, peeled, cored, and coarsely chopped
1/4 cup tomato paste
1 bay leaf, crumbled
1 teaspoon salt
1/2 teaspoon oregano
1/2 teaspoon basil
1/2 teaspoon pepper
1 cup dry red wine
1 1/2 cups water (about)
1 (3–3 1/2-pound) Dungeness crab, cleaned and cracked
1 pound raw shrimp in the shell
1 1/2 dozen littleneck clams in the shell, well scrubbed

Stir-fry onion, celery, green pepper, and garlic in the oil in a large, heavy kettle 8–10 minutes over moderate heat until golden; add all remaining ingredients except seafood, cover, and simmer 1 1/2–2 hours until flavors are well blended. If sauce becomes too thick (it should be about the consistency of a medium white sauce), thin with a little water or wine. Taste for salt and pepper and adjust as needed. Add all seafood to sauce, cover, and simmer 12–15 minutes longer or until shrimp and crab turn orange and clams open. Serve from a giant tureen with buttery crusts of Italian bread and a dry red wine.

NPS (4–6): 450–300 C, 250–165 mg CH, 1,080–720 mg S*

QUICK CRAB NEWBURG

6 servings ⊠

¹/₃ cup butter or margarine
1 pound crab meat (fresh, thawed frozen, or drained canned), well picked over
¹/₄ teaspoon seasoned pepper
1 pint sour cream, at room temperature
2 tablespoons tomato paste
2 tablespoons dry sherry
2 tablespoons finely grated Parmesan cheese

Melt butter in a large skillet over moderately low heat. Add crab and stir-fry 2–3 minutes. Mix in remaining ingredients and heat 2–3 minutes, stirring gently (do not boil). Serve over boiled rice or lightly buttered hot toast.

NPS: 335 C, 140 mg CH, 375 mg S*

CRAB MEAT NORFOLK

4 servings ⚖ ⊠

One of the easiest ways to prepare crab and one of the most delicately seasoned.

1 pound fresh lump or backfin crab meat, well picked over
4 teaspoons white wine vinegar
¹/₄ teaspoon salt
¹/₈ teaspoon cayenne pepper
Pinch black pepper
¹/₃ cup butter or margarine

Preheat oven to 375° F. Mix crab lightly with vinegar, salt, and pepper. Place in an ungreased 1-quart *au gratin* dish or shallow casserole and dot evenly with butter. Bake, uncovered, 15–20 minutes until bubbly.

NPS: 240 C, 155 mg CH, 530 mg S*

CRAB MORNAY

4 servings ⊠

Crab baked in a rich cheese sauce.

1 pound fresh lump or backfin crab meat, well picked over
1³/₄ cups Mornay Sauce
¹/₄ cup finely grated Gruyère or Parmesan cheese

Preheat oven to 375° F. Toss crab with Mornay Sauce to mix, spoon into an un-

greased 1-quart *au gratin* dish or shallow casserole, and scatter cheese on top. Bake, uncovered, 15–20 minutes until bubbly, then broil quickly to brown.

NPS: 365 C, 175 mg CH, 710 mg S*

VARIATION

Crab à la Florentine: Butter a 1¹/₂-quart *au gratin* dish and cover bottom with a layer of chopped, buttered cooked spinach. Mix crab and Mornay Sauce as directed and spoon over spinach. Top with ¹/₂ cup soft white bread crumbs mixed with 2 tablespoons melted butter, sprinkle lightly with paprika, and bake as directed.

NPS: 430 C, 190 mg CH, 795 mg S*

CRAB IMPERIAL NEWBURG

4–6 servings

Good with fluffy boiled rice, a crisp green salad, and a well-chilled dry white wine.

1 pound fresh lump or backfin crab meat, well picked over
3 tablespoons butter or margarine
2 tablespoons flour
1¹/₂ cups light cream
3 egg yolks, lightly beaten
1 teaspoon salt
2 teaspoons prepared horseradish
1 teaspoon powdered mustard
¹/₄ teaspoon cayenne pepper
1 tablespoon paprika
3 tablespoons dry sherry

Preheat oven to 350° F. Place crab in an ungreased 1¹/₂-quart *au gratin* dish or shallow casserole. Melt butter in a small saucepan over moderate heat and blend in flour. Add cream and heat, stirring, until thickened and smooth. Spoon a little hot sauce into yolks, then return all to saucepan; turn heat to low and warm, stirring, 1 minute—no longer. Off heat mix in remaining ingredients; pour sauce evenly over crab and bake, uncovered, ¹/₂–³/₄ hour until bubbly.

NPS (4–6): 430–285 C, 400–265 mg CH, 920–615 mg S*

DEVILED CRAB

4 servings

A delicate deviled crab.

4 hard-cooked eggs, peeled
2 tablespoons butter or margarine
2 tablespoons flour
1¹/₄ cups milk

1 tablespoon prepared spicy brown mustard
1 teaspoon paprika
1/2 teaspoon powdered mustard
1/4 teaspoon cayenne pepper
1 tablespoon Worcestershire sauce
Juice of 1/2 lemon
2 tablespoons minced parsley
1/2 teaspoon salt
1 pound fresh lump or backfin crab meat, well
  picked over

TOPPING

1/3 cup fine dry bread crumbs mixed with 2
  tablespoons melted butter or margarine

Preheat oven to 375° F. Chop egg whites
fine; sieve the yolks and set aside. Melt butter in a small saucepan over moderate heat
and blend in flour. Add milk and heat, stirring, until thickened and smooth. Off heat
mix in sieved yolks and all remaining ingredients except egg whites, crab, and topping.
Place crab and egg whites in a buttered shallow 1 1/2-quart casserole, add sauce, and stir
well to mix. Sprinkle topping over surface
and bake, uncovered, 1 hour until browned
and bubbly.

*NPS: 390 C, 430 mg CH, 875 mg S**

BAKED CRAB-STUFFED AVOCADOS

6 servings

3 tablespoons butter or margarine
2 tablespoons flour
1/2 cup light cream
1/2 cup milk
1/2 teaspoon salt
1/8 teaspoon white pepper
1 tablespoon minced chives
1 tablespoon capers
1/2 pound crab meat (fresh, thawed frozen, or
  drained canned), well picked over
3 medium-size ripe avocados
2 tablespoons lemon juice

Preheat oven to 350° F. Melt butter in a
saucepan over moderate heat. Blend in flour,
slowly add cream and milk, and cook, stirring, until thickened and smooth. Off heat
mix in salt, pepper, chives, capers, and crab.
Peel, halve, and pit avocados; brush well
with lemon juice and place in a well-buttered shallow baking pan. Fill with crab
mixture and bake, uncovered, 25–30 minutes until avocados are heated through.

*NPS: 310 C, 70 mg CH, 385 mg S**

BAKED STUFFED DUNGENESS CRAB

2 servings

1 (2-pound) Dungeness crab, boiled in the shell
  and cooled
2 tablespoons butter or margarine
2 teaspoons minced chives
1/8 teaspoon pepper
1 hard-cooked egg, peeled and chopped fine
1 tablespoon capers, drained and minced
1/4 cup fine dry bread crumbs mixed with 1
  tablespoon melted butter or margarine

Preheat oven to 450° F. Clean crab and remove meat from body, claws, and legs*;
leave large back shell intact. Pick over crab
meat, discarding bits of shell and cartilage,
and flake. Melt butter in a skillet over moderately low heat, add crab, and stir-fry 2–3
minutes; mix in chives, pepper, egg, and capers. Spoon into shell, top with buttered
crumbs, and place in a shallow baking pan.
Bake, uncovered, 10 minutes, then broil 4"
from the heat 2–3 minutes to brown lightly.
Serve in the shell.

*NPS: 340 C, 295 mg CH, 640 mg S**

VARIATION

Pilaf-Stuffed Dungeness Crab: Prepare crab
mixture as directed, but when stir-frying
crab meat in butter, add 1/2 cup cold cooked
rice. Proceed as directed.

*NPS: 495 C, 295 mg CH, 640 mg S**

MARYLAND CRAB CAKES

4 servings   ⚖ ▨

Spicily seasoned.

1 pound fresh lump or backfin crab meat, well
  picked over
2 eggs, lightly beaten
2 tablespoons mayonnaise
1 tablespoon prepared horseradish
1 tablespoon prepared spicy brown mustard
1 tablespoon minced parsley
1/4 teaspoon salt
1/4 teaspoon liquid hot red pepper seasoning
Pinch pepper
2/3 cup cracker meal
1/3 cup cooking oil

Mix crab well with all but last 2 ingredients
and shape into cakes about 3" across and
1/2" thick; dip in cracker meal to coat well.
Heat oil in a large, heavy skillet over moderately high heat until a cube of bread will
sizzle, add cakes, and brown 3–4 minutes on

a side. Drain well on paper toweling and serve with Tartar Sauce.

NPS: 310 C, 255 mg CH, 500 mg S*

CRAB LOUIS

4 servings

1 quart crisp, coarsely shredded lettuce
1 pound fresh-cooked crab meat, well picked over (Dungeness, lump, or backfin) or thawed frozen Alaska king crab
4 tomatoes, quartered
4 hard-cooked eggs, peeled and quartered

D R E S S I N G
1 cup mayonnaise
1/3 cup ketchup
1/4 cup heavy cream, whipped
2 tablespoons finely grated scallions
2 tablespoons minced parsley
2 tablespoons minced sweet green pepper
2 teaspoons lemon juice
1 teaspoon prepared horseradish
Pinch salt

On 4 luncheon-size plates, make beds of lettuce. Mound crab on top. Mix dressing and spoon over crab, then garnish each plate with tomatoes and hard-cooked eggs.

NPS: 695 C, 440 mg CH, 905 mg S*

CRAYFISH

Crawfish, crawdads, *écrevisses*—these are the sweet-tender little freshwater cousins of the lobster. To Europeans they are a delicacy unsurpassed, and in Finland, where the season begins at midnight on July 15 and lasts a short two months, the whole country rollicks with crayfish fests (by tradition, every crayfish tail must be followed by a swig of iced schnapps). The American crayfish, at 6″, is nearly twice as long as the European but no less succulent. It is found in creeks around Lake Michigan, in the Pacific Northwest, and in Gulf Coast bayous. The season varies from area to area but is usually at its peak in mid or late summer. Occasionally, crayfish are shipped live to metropolitan areas; more often they are canned.

Amount to Buy: Allow about 1 dozen crayfish in the shell per person, more if appetites are large (in Finland, 20 are considered a "decent" portion) or about 1/3 pound crayfish meat per person.

For Top Quality: Buy crayfish that are live and kicking.

How to Cook Crayfish

There is really only one way, experts will tell you—*boiling*—but the flavor of boiled crayfish varies markedly according to the seasonings used.

General Preparation: Wash crayfish carefully under cold running water; tear off the thin shell-like fin on the center-top of the tail (the dark, threadlike intestinal vein should come away with it).

To Boil: For each dozen crayfish, you will need 1 quart sea water (or 1 quart tap water mixed with 1 tablespoon salt) or 1 quart Simple Court Bouillon. Bring to a boil in a large, deep kettle, drop in live crayfish, cover, and simmer 5 minutes, just until crayfish turn scarlet. Drain and serve hot with melted butter or cool in broth and serve at room temperature.

V A R I A T I O N

Finnish-Style Crayfish: Boil crayfish as directed in sea or salt water but add 1 large bunch fresh dill, preferably that which is beginning to flower, separated into stalks. Cool crayfish in cooking liquid to room temperature before serving. If you like, marinate crayfish in liquid 1–2 days in refrigerator, then bring to room temperature before serving.

How to Eat Crayfish

This is messy work, so give every guest a large bib and plenty of paper napkins. Also set out lots of ice cold beer.

1. Twist off claws, snip off pointed tips, then separate claws at "elbow" joint. Slice off broad base of claws and suck meat out.
2. Separate body of crayfish from tail and suck any meat from body (there will not be much).
3. With the point of a knife, lift top shell from tail, take out tail meat, and remove dark vein, if any. Slosh meat in melted butter or place on lightly buttered toast and eat. This is the *pièce de résistance.*

LOBSTER

Of all America's seafoods, lobster is king. Steamed simply over sea water, or boiled in it with perhaps a sprig or two of seaweed, lobster is a thing of beauty (and a joy as long as it lasts). Underneath that scarlet armor, fat snowy chunks wait to be twisted out and sloshed in melted butter. What can top that?

The Kinds of Lobster

The best known—and best—is the giant clawed *American or Maine Lobster.* But there are others: the *rock or spiny lobster,* which swims in the Gulf of Mexico and in the warm waters off the coast of Southern California (it has no claws, but its tail is full of delectable meat) and the tiny, flat, clawless *slipper lobster* (it rarely measures more than 5″ long and its tail—the only edible part—averages 1–2 ounces). Although slipper lobsters can be found in Carolina waters, those at your supermarket have been imported from India, Indonesia, Pakistan, or Sri Lanka. Unfortunately, both rock lobsters and slipper lobsters are available to most of us only as frozen tails.

Buying Fresh Lobster

Season: Year round.

Popular Market Forms: Live in the shell; cooked in the shell; iced cooked lobster meat. It's no longer necessary to live in the East to buy live Maine lobsters; a number of firms will pack them in seaweed and airmail them to you. And more and more fine groceries are keeping tanks of live lobsters well stocked.

Amount Needed: Allow a 1–3-pound lobster per person, depending on appetites, and about 1/4–1/3 pound lobster meat. Maine lobsters are graded in 4 sizes: chickens (3/4–1 pound), quarters (1 1/4 pounds), large (1 1/2–2 1/4 pounds), jumbo (2 1/2 pounds up).

For Top Quality: Live lobsters should be thrashing about (be sure to have the claws pegged so you won't get nipped); cooked whole lobsters should have a fresh "seashore" odor and their tails, when straightened out, should spring right back. Cooked, iced lobster meat should be firm and sweetsmelling.

Frozen and Canned Lobster

Frozen uncooked rock and slipper lobster tails are widely available. Also marketed are tins of frozen, cooked lobster meat, and in the gourmet line such classics as Lobster Newburg. Canned lobster meat and tails are generally stocked by groceries, as are canned lobster bisques, Newburgs, and thermidors. *To Cook Frozen Lobsters:* The tails are usually cooked solidly frozen (but read package directions); cooked frozen meat should be thawed before using. *How to Use Canned*

Lobster: Because this meat is fully cooked, it is a good choice for salads and casseroles.

How to Cook Lobster

Lobster is marvelously adaptable, but it is at its best simply steamed, boiled, or baked. Broiling tends to dry it out (though lovers of broiled lobster will forever argue the point).

General Preparation: How lobster is prepared depends upon how it is to be cooked. For steaming or boiling it needs no preparation at all. For baking and broiling, however, it must be split live and, for certain other recipes, cut in large chunks.

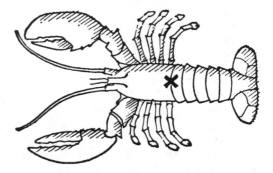

To Split Live Lobsters: Don't be squeamish about cutting into a live lobster; it has little feeling. Place lobster on its stomach with claws up over the head. Drive the point of a sharp sturdy knife into center back (X) where body meets tail (this kills lobster), and turn lobster on its back and quickly cut down through the body and head to split.

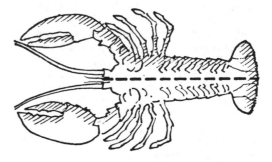

Now cut through tail (don't be alarmed if legs twitch a bit; these are simple muscular spasms and do not mean lobster is suffering). Spread halves flat, meat side up, and pull soft, beige intestinal vein from tail; discard papery stomach sac located just behind the eyes. Lift out coral (ovary and undeveloped roe) and buttery gray-green tomalley (liver)

and save if they are to be used in sauces or stuffings; otherwise leave in place in the body cavity (they're great delicacies). Once in a great while, though law forbids their being taken, you may come upon a female just ready to lay eggs. These appear as a dark caviar-like mass in the body and upper tail and are considered the choicest of delicacies. Serve separately or mix into stuffings along with coral and tomalley.

To Clean and Crack Live Lobsters: Follow all steps for splitting live lobsters; twist off claws and crack each section; cut body and tail into large or small chunks as individual recipes specify. Do not remove meat from shells unless directed otherwise. *Note to the Faint of Heart:* If you simply cannot bring yourself to cut into a live lobster, there is an alternative (although the finished lobster may not be quite so succulent). Bring a huge kettle of lightly salted water to a boil, drop in live lobsters, cover, and simmer 3–5 minutes just until they stop squirming. Drain, cool in a colander under cold running water until easy to handle, then split or clean and crack as directed.

To Boil: The best possible medium for boiling lobsters is sea water. If you haven't got it, you can fake it by adding 1 tablespoon salt to each quart water. Unless you have an absolutely colossal kettle, don't try to cook more than 2 lobsters in a pot. Bring 3–4 quarts sea or salt water to a boil, grasp lobsters, one at a time, by cupping your hand around back, and plunge head first into boiling water. Cover and, from time water returns to a boil, cook 5–6 minutes per pound (1½-pound lobsters will take 8–9 minutes, 2-pound lobsters, 10–12). If lobsters are extra large, cook 5 minutes for the first pound and 4 minutes for each additional pound. *Simple Test for Doneness:* Pull one of the antennae on the head; if it comes easily from socket, lobster is done. Color of lobsters is important, too; when cooked they will be a dazzling scarlet. Drain lobsters well (they will have absorbed plenty of cooking water), and serve hot, either whole or split and cracked, with melted butter and lemon wedges. Or cook, chill, and serve with homemade Mayonnaise or Rémoulade Dressing.

VARIATIONS

Savory Boiled Lobster: Prepare as directed, using a court bouillon instead of salt water.

Lobster Boiled in Beer: Boil as directed, using 2–2½ quarts beer or ale and 1–1½ quarts water instead of salt water. The beer gives the lobster extra-rich, slightly malty flavor.

To Steam: Pour 1″ sea or salt water into a large, heavy kettle and bring to a boil over moderately high heat. Add lobsters, cover, and steam 15 minutes. Serve hot or cold as you would boiled lobster.

To Bake: Preheat oven to 350° F. Split and clean live lobsters (the 1½–2½-pound size is best) and arrange side by side, cut side up, in a large, shallow roasting pan. Cover exposed meat with pats of butter (each lobster will take ⅓–½ stick) and squeeze the juice of ½ lemon over each lobster. Bake, uncovered, 25–30 minutes, basting often with pan juices. Sprinkle with salt and freshly ground black pepper and serve at once.

To Oven-Broil: Preheat broiler. Split and clean live lobster. Lay lobsters flesh side up as flat as possible on a foil-lined broiler pan, brush generously with melted butter or margarine, and broil 4″ from the heat 12–15 minutes, brushing often with melted butter, until lightly browned. Sprinkle with salt, pepper, and lemon juice and serve piping hot.

How to Eat Lobster

1. Twist off claws, crack each in several places with lobster or nut crackers, and twist out meat with a fork.

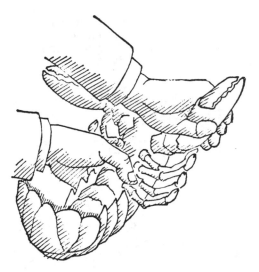

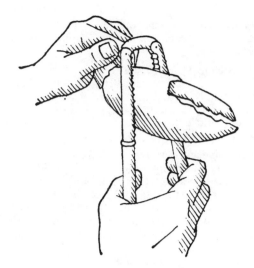

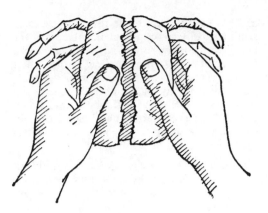

4. Pull off lobster legs and suck each as you would a straw to get out any meat or juices inside.

2. Separate tail from body by arching lobster backward until it cracks. Break off fins at base of tail and push meat from shell with a fork; remove intestinal vein. Cut meat in bite-size chunks with fork.

3. Pull body from shell and arch left and right sides backward to split in two. The green tomalley and red coral are both in this part. Avoid grayish, feathery portions.

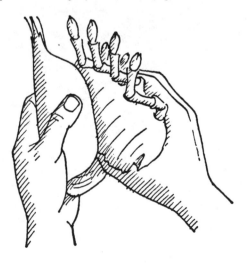

LOBSTER NEWBURG

4 servings

The simple, classic version—perfect for a chafing dish.

1 pound cooked lobster meat, cut in small chunks
1/4 cup butter or margarine
1/2 cup medium-dry sherry
1/4 teaspoon paprika
3/4 teaspoon salt
1 1/2 cups hot Velouté Sauce
1/4 cup heavy cream

Pick over lobster meat, separating out any bits of coral; sieve coral and reserve to use as a garnish. Stir-fry lobster meat in butter in a chafing dish skillet over direct, moderate heat 2–3 minutes; add sherry, paprika, and salt and simmer, uncovered, 2–3 minutes. Blend in sauce and cream, set over chafing dish warmer, and simmer, but do not boil 2–3 minutes. Sprinkle with coral, if any, or with a little paprika. Serve from chafing dish, ladling over boiled rice or into crisp pastry shells.

NPS: 470 C, 190 mg CH, 1,420 mg S*

BROILED LOBSTERS WITH HERB AND CRUMB STUFFING

4 servings

4 (1 1/4-pound) live lobsters
1/2 cup melted butter or margarine

STUFFING

1 quart soft white bread crumbs
1 clove garlic, peeled and crushed
1/2 cup butter or margarine
1/4 teaspoon salt
1/8 teaspoon pepper
2 tablespoons minced chives
2 tablespoons minced parsley

Preheat broiler. Split lobsters in half lengthwise, remove stomach and intestinal vein,* reserve any tomalley or coral. Make stuffing by sautéing crumbs and garlic in butter in a large, heavy skillet over moderate heat 2–3 minutes until pale golden; off heat mix in remaining ingredients, also any tomalley and chopped coral. Lay lobsters as flat as possible, shell side down, on a foil-lined broiler pan and brush generously with melted butter. Broil 4″ from heat 12–15 minutes until lightly browned, brushing often with butter. Remove from broiler, mound stuffing into body cavity of each lobster, return to broiler, and broil 2–3 minutes to brown lightly. Serve with melted butter and lemon wedges.

*NPS: 685 C, 260 mg CH, 1,160 mg S**

VARIATION

Broiled Stuffed Lobster Amandine: Prepare as directed, reducing bread crumbs in stuffing to 3 cups and adding 1 cup finely chopped toasted blanched almonds.

*NPS: 845 C, 260 mg CH, 1,105 mg S**

LOBSTER CARDINAL

2 servings

2 (1½-pound) lobsters, boiled, drained, split lengthwise, and cleaned
1/2 pound mushrooms, wiped clean and coarsely chopped
1 truffle, minced
3 tablespoons butter or margarine
1 tablespoon grated Parmesan cheese

SAUCE

1 cup hot Béchamel Sauce
1/2 cup boiled, minced lobster meat
1/3 cup heavy cream
1/2 teaspoon anchovy paste
Pinch cayenne pepper

Preheat broiler. Remove meat from lobsters; dice claw and body meat and slice tail 1/4″– 1/2″ thick. Mince enough tail meat to total 1/2 cup; reserve for sauce. Spread shells as flat as possible on a baking sheet and set aside. Sauté diced claw and body meat with mushrooms and truffle in butter about 5 minutes until mushrooms are limp; set aside while you prepare the sauce. Place Béchamel

Sauce in the top of a double boiler, add reserved minced lobster and remaining sauce ingredients; set over simmering water and heat, stirring, about 2–3 minutes. Mix a little sauce into mushroom mixture, just enough to bind. Make a bed of this mixture in each lobster shell, arrange tail slices on top, and spoon enough sauce over all to coat. Sprinkle with Parmesan and broil 4″–5″ from the heat 3–4 minutes until browned and bubbly.

*NPS: 745 C, 320 mg CH, 1,440 mg S**

LOBSTER À L'AMÉRICAINE

4 servings

2 (1¼–1½-pound) live lobsters or 4 (6–8-ounce) frozen rock lobster tails
1/3 cup olive oil
1/4 cup brandy

SAUCE

2 tablespoons butter or margarine
1 small yellow onion, peeled and minced
3 tablespoons minced shallots or scallions
1 clove garlic, peeled and crushed
2 large tomatoes, peeled, cored, seeded, and coarsely chopped
2 tablespoons tomato paste
2 cups dry white wine
2 tablespoons minced parsley
1 tablespoon minced fresh tarragon or 1 teaspoon dried tarragon
1 (4″) sprig fresh thyme or 1/2 teaspoon dried thyme
1/2 bay leaf
1/2 teaspoon salt
1/8 teaspoon cayenne pepper

If lobsters are live, clean*; twist off claws, crack, and reserve; cut tails crosswise into chunks at segmented divisions and cut body into 2″ chunks. Leave meat in shell and save any coral or tomalley for the sauce. If using frozen tails, simply cut crosswise into 1″ chunks while still solidly frozen. Stir-fry lobster in oil in a large, heavy skillet over moderate heat 3–5 minutes until shells turn scarlet; lift out lobster and set aside; do not drain off oil. In the same skillet, begin sauce: Melt butter and stir-fry onion, shallots, and garlic 3–5 minutes over moderate heat until limp. Mix in remaining sauce ingredients and simmer, uncovered, stirring occasionally, about 1 hour. Sauce should have reduced by half; if not, boil rapidly to reduce. Strain sauce through a fine sieve into a large saucepan and set over low heat. Pour brandy over lobster and blaze with a match; when flames die, add lobster to sauce, cover, and simmer 12–15 minutes just to blend flavors. Mix in any tomalley and chopped coral, heat 1–2 minutes longer, and serve with boiled rice or Rice Pilaf.

NPS: 340 C, 85 mg CH, 580 mg S*

LOBSTER CANTONESE

4 servings

1/2 pound ground lean pork
1 clove garlic, peeled and crushed
3 tablespoons peanut or other cooking oil
2 cups chicken broth
1/4 cup soy sauce
1 teaspoon sugar
2 (11/4–11/2-pound) live lobsters, cleaned,* cracked, and cut into 2″ chunks
2 tablespoons cornstarch blended with 1/4 cup cold water
1/4 cup scallions, minced (include green tops)
1 egg, lightly beaten

Stir-fry pork and garlic in oil in a *wok* or large, heavy skillet over moderate heat until pork is no longer pink. Mix in broth, soy sauce, and sugar; add lobsters, cover, and simmer 10 minutes. Add cornstarch mixture and heat, stirring, until thickened and clear. Stir in scallions, drizzle in egg, and cook, stirring, 2–3 minutes until egg is just set. Serve with boiled rice.

NPS: 320 C, 165 mg CH, 1,920 mg S*

COLD CURRIED LOBSTER

4 servings

11/2 pounds cooked lobster meat, well picked over and cut in bite-size chunks

D R E S S I N G
2/3 cup mayonnaise
1/3 cup sour cream
2 tablespoons minced parsley
2 tablespoons minced fresh dill
1 tablespoon minced fresh tarragon
2 tablespoons capers
1 tablespoon curry powder
2 tablespoons finely grated yellow onion
Juice of 1/2 lime
3–4 dashes liquid hot red pepper seasoning

Place lobster in a large bowl. Mix dressing ingredients until well blended, pour over lobster, and toss to mix. Cover and chill several hours. Serve as is, in lettuce cups, hollowed-out tomatoes, or avocado halves.

NPS: 475 C, 175 mg CH, 690 mg S*

LOBSTER THERMIDOR

4 servings

A showy way to prepare frozen rock lobster tails.

4 (6–8-ounce) frozen rock lobster tails, boiled by package directions and drained
3 tablespoons minced scallions (white part only)
2 tablespoons butter or margarine
1/3 cup dry white wine
1 teaspoon powdered mustard
2 cups hot Mornay Sauce
4 teaspoons grated Parmesan cheese

Preheat broiler. Remove lobster meat from shells, cut in 1/2″ chunks, and set aside; reserve shells. Stir-fry scallions in butter in a small saucepan over moderate heat 2–3 minutes until limp. Add wine and boil, uncovered, until reduced to 1/4 cup. Blend in mustard, then stir into Mornay Sauce. Mix a little hot sauce into lobster meat, just enough to bind. Place lobster shells in a shallow baking pan, fill with lobster mixture, then cover with remaining Mornay Sauce, and sprinkle each lobster with 1 teaspoon grated Parmesan. Broil 4″–5″ from heat 3–4 minutes until browned and bubbly.

NPS: 415 C, 155 mg CH, 790 mg S*

MUSSELS

Mussels are stronger flavored than clams or oysters, slightly tougher, too (or is that because we don't know how to cook them?). In Europe, especially Mediterranean Europe, people do delectable things with mussels—stuff them with rice and currants and pine nuts; simmer them, shell and all, in tomato sauces heady with garlic. We would do well to follow their lead.

The Kinds of Mussels

There is only one of importance, the *blue edible mussel,* which lives in dense colonies on wharf pilings and along rocky shores.

Buying Fresh Mussels

Season:

East Coast: Year round.

West Coast: November through April (because of the dangerous, warm weather "red tide," see Buying Fresh Clams, *West Coast Varieties*).

Popular Market Forms: Alive, in the shell; they are sold either by the dozen or the pound.

Amount Needed: Allow about 1/2–1 dozen mussels per person, depending on size of mussels and appetites.

For Top Quality: Look for mussels with tightly closed shells that will not slip or budge when pressed.

Other Forms of Mussels

To date, mussels are only available canned, not frozen. These are already cooked and best used for quick soups, fritters, patties, or casseroles.

How to Cleanse Mussels of Grit: Scrub mussels hard with a stiff brush under cold running water, pull or cut off the long beard, and scrape away any small barnacles or incrustations on the shells. Submerge mussels in a kettle of cool water and let stand 2–3 hours so they will purge themselves of sand. Discard any that float, also any with shells not tightly clamped shut.

How to Open Mussels: As with clams, there are two ways, prying and steaming. How mussels are to be prepared determines which to use.
1. *To Pry Open* (for mussels to be stuffed): Insert a paring knife into back of mussel to the right of the hinge and with blunt edge facing hinge. Move knife clockwise around crevice, twisting slightly to force shell open; take care not to cut hinge or break shell. Open mussels over a bowl so that none of their juice is lost. Once mussel is open, trim away any stray whiskers.
2. *To Steam Open and Shuck* (for mussels to be cut from shell and used in fritters, chowders, etc.): Place mussels in a large kettle, pour in about 3/4 cup boiling water, cover, and steam over moderate heat 3 minutes, just until shells open. Discard any that do not open; they are dead and full of mud. Drain mussels, remove meat from shells, and trim off any tag ends of beard. (*Note:* Before using mussel liquid, strain through a fine sieve lined with a double thickness of cheesecloth.)

How to Cook Mussels

Because of their robust flavor, mussels are better cooked in the company of vegetables, herbs, and spices than by the utterly basic methods. Even when they are steamed, they benefit from a little lily-gilding (recipes follow).

General Preparation: Cleanse as directed above and, if recipes so specify, open.

COQUILLES OF MUSSELS

6 servings   ⊲⊳

3 dozen mussels in the shell, prepared for cooking
1¼ cups hot Thick White Sauce
2 tablespoons melted butter or margarine
2 cups hot seasoned mashed potatoes
1/3 cup fine dry bread crumbs mixed with 1 tablespoon melted butter or margarine

Steam mussels open and shuck*; reserve 1/4 cup of liquid from mussels and strain, then mix with white sauce, 1 tablespoon butter, and the mussels. Spoon into 6–8 buttered large scallop shells and arrange on a baking sheet. Place potatoes in a pastry bag fitted with a small rosette tube and pipe a decorative border around edge of each shell; brush with 1 tablespoon melted butter. Scatter buttered crumbs on top of mussels and bake, uncovered, 5–7 minutes until lightly browned.
*NPS: 305 C, 65 mg CH, 675 mg S**

VARIATIONS

Creamed Mussels: Mix white sauce, mussels liquid, mussels, and butter as directed, then heat in the top of a double boiler over simmering water 4–5 minutes, stirring occasionally until piping hot. Spoon over hot buttered toast, sprinkle with parsley, and serve.
*NPS: 265 C, 60 mg CH, 505 mg S**

⊲⊳ **Creamed Mussels au Gratin:** Mix white sauce, mussels liquid, mussels, and butter as directed, stir in 2 tablespoons minced chives, spoon into an ungreased 1 1/2-quart *au gratin* dish, and top with 2/3 cup fine dry bread crumbs mixed with 2 tablespoons melted butter and 1/3 cup grated Parmesan cheese. Bake, uncovered, 10–15 minutes until bubbly and lightly browned.
*NPS: 265 C, 65 mg CH, 545 mg S**

FILEY BAY MUSSELS

4 servings   ⊲⊳

Rather like "deviled" mussels on the half shell.

Rock salt
3 dozen mussels in the shell, prepared for cooking

½ cup butter (no substitute), softened to room
  temperature
2 tablespoons minced shallots or chives
1 clove garlic, peeled and crushed
2 tablespoons minced parsley
1 tablespoon prepared mild yellow mustard
2 teaspoons steak sauce

Preheat broiler. Make a bed of rock salt in a
very large, shallow baking pan, dampen
slightly with water, and heat, uncovered, in
oven 5 minutes while broiler preheats.
Meanwhile, steam mussels open,* lift off top
shells and discard. Arrange mussels in hot
salt, pushing shells down well so they won't
tip. Cream butter with remaining ingredients and place about 1 teaspoonful on each
mussel. Broil 3"–4" from the heat 2–3 minutes until bubbly. Transfer to a hot platter or
individual plates and serve.

*NPS: 270 C, 90 mg CH, 500 mg S**

MUSSELS MARINIÈRE

4 servings

⅓ cup minced shallots or ½ cup minced yellow
  onion
½ cup butter (no substitute)
3 dozen mussels in the shell, prepared for
  cooking
4 sprigs parsley
2 (4") sprigs fresh thyme or ½ teaspoon dried
  thyme
1 bay leaf
2 cups dry white wine
2 tablespoons minced parsley

Stir-fry shallots in ¼ cup butter 5–8 minutes in a large, heavy kettle over moderate
heat until golden. Add mussels, herbs, and
wine, cover, bring to a boil, then reduce heat
and simmer 3 minutes until mussels open.
Discard any unopened mussels, also empty
half shells. Transfer mussels, still in their
shells, to a heated tureen and keep warm.
Strain cooking liquid through a double
thickness of cheesecloth, add remaining butter and minced parsley, and heat, stirring,
just until butter melts. Taste for salt and add
if needed. Pour sauce over mussels and serve
with hot French bread.

*NPS: 290 C, 90 mg CH, 415 mg S**

VARIATION

Clams Marinière: Prepare as directed, substituting steamer or cherrystone clams for
mussels. Nutritional count same as basic
recipe.

ARMENIAN MUSSELS STUFFED WITH RICE, CURRANTS, AND PIÑON NUTS

4–6 servings

⅓ cup olive oil
1 large yellow onion, peeled and minced
3 dozen mussels in the shell, prepared for
  cooking
⅓ cup dried currants
⅓ cup piñon nuts
½ teaspoon salt
¼ teaspoon cinnamon
¼ teaspoon allspice
⅛ teaspoon pepper
½ cup dry white wine
1¾ cups water
1 cup uncooked rice

Heat oil in a large, heavy kettle over moderate heat about 1 minute, add onion, and stir-
fry 3–5 minutes until limp. Add mussels,
currants, piñon nuts, salt, and spices and
heat, stirring, 2–3 minutes until mussels begin to open. Add wine and water, cover, and
simmer 3–5 minutes until mussels open
wide. Lift out all mussels; discard any that
do not open, and reserve the rest; trim off
any stray bits of beard. Bring kettle mixture
to a rapid boil, stir in rice, and boil gently,
uncovered, 12–15 minutes until rice is done
and all liquid absorbed. Stir rice well to mix
ingredients, then spoon into mussels, filling
shells full and packing ever so lightly so
mixture will not fall out. Cool to room temperature before serving.

*NPS (4–6): 510–340 C, 30–20 mg CH, 455–305
  mg S**

OYSTERS

Oysters have a long and well-documented
history. The Greeks served them at cocktail
parties as "provocatives to drinking," the
Romans imported oysters from England,
packed in snow, then parked them in
saltwater ponds until they could be fattened
up on a diet of wine and pastry. American
Indians were great oyster eaters, too, judg-
ing from the middens of shells found up and
down both coasts. Colonists were enthusiasts from the beginning, and by the early
eighteenth century, when trains began rushing fresh seafood into the Midwest, oysters
became the rage. Soon every town of conse-
quence had its own oyster parlor, and newspaper society pages devoted columns to oyster parties. The Abraham Lincolns, while
still in Illinois, gave oyster suppers at which
nothing but oysters was served. Oysters con-

tinue to be popular, so much so that, even though they are now "grown" commercially, the supply doesn't meet the demand.

The Kinds of Oysters

There are three popular American species, one taken from the Atlantic and Gulf of Mexico, two from the Pacific.

Eastern Oyster: Found along the East Coast from Massachusetts to Texas, this oyster accounts for 89 per cent of America's catch. It includes the famous *blue points,* named for Blue Point, Long Island, where they were first found (but now simply a term referring to any oyster from 2"–4" long), also the choice Virginia *Chincoteagues,* considered by many to be America's finest oyster. The subtle flavor differences among Eastern oysters depends on the oysters' diet and upon the composition of the waters in which they live.

Olympias: These sweet miniatures (it takes 300–500 to make a quart) are the pearls among oysters (and very nearly as expensive). Originally found all along the West Coast, they now come primarily from Puget Sound "farms."

Japanese or Pacific: This giant transplant from Japan is the West Coast's most popular oyster. Too large to eat on the half shell, it is usually cut up and fried, hashed, or stewed.

Buying Fresh Oysters

Season: There is some truth to the old R month theory. Though oysters are edible between May and August, they aren't very plump or tasty because this is their season to spawn. Few markets sell oysters in summer.

Popular Market Forms:

Eastern Oysters: Live and in the shell by the dozen; shucked by the pint or quart.

Olympias: Shucked and packed in small bottles.

Japanese: Shucked and packed in 10- or 12-ounce jars.

Amount Needed: It depends—on the size of the oysters (and appetites), on how the oysters are prepared and served. But here's a guide:

Oysters on the Half Shell: Allow about 1/2 dozen blue points per person, 1/2–1 dozen Chincoteagues, depending on size. If you splurge on Olympias, you'll have to order them especially and allow 3–4 dozen per person.

Oysters to Be Cooked in the Shell: Allow 1/2–1 dozen small or medium oysters per person, depending on richness of recipe.

Shucked Oysters: 1 pint will serve about 3, more if stretched with other ingredients.

For Top Quality:

Oysters in the Shell: Choose only those that are tightly shut or those that clamp shut when handled.

Shucked Oysters: Select plump, sweet-smelling oysters with clear liquor free of shell particles and grit.

Frozen and Canned Oysters

Shucked, raw Eastern oysters are now available frozen; they are also canned (either plain or smoked). Japanese or Pacific oysters are also canned. *To Cook Frozen Oysters:* Thaw in the refrigerator, then prepare as you would fresh oysters; cook immediately after thawing and never refreeze. *How to Use Canned Oysters:* Because these are fully cooked, they're best used in quick soups, stews, fritters, and casseroles. The smoked variety is usually served as cocktail snacks, though they, too, can be used in soups and stews.

How to Shuck Fresh Oysters: Wash and rinse oysters well in cool water. Place oysters on counter, flat side up, and knock off thin edge (bill) with a hammer. Insert an oyster knife into broken edge and slip it around to back of oyster; sever hinge as close to flat upper shell as possible, lift off top shell and discard. Cut muscle from lower shell; carefully feel oyster for bits of shell and grit, paying particular attention to the hinge. If oysters are to be served or cooked on the half shell, replace in deep lower shells. *Note:* Open oysters over a small bowl to catch any spilled juice and strain juice through a double thickness of cheesecloth before using.

How to Cook Oysters

There are those who say oysters should never be cooked, that the only way to savor them is on the half shell with a squirt of lemon and a grinding of black pepper. Maybe so. But just as many people insist that an oyster's true glory emerges only in the cooking. Here are the best methods.

General Preparation: Shuck oysters or not as recipes direct. Obviously, if a recipe calls for oysters to be shucked, the best plan is to buy them already out of the shell.

To Panfry (Sauté): Pat shucked oysters dry on paper toweling. Dredge in flour delicately seasoned with salt and pepper and sauté in butter or margarine (about 1/3 cup butter for 1 pint oysters) 3–4 minutes over moderate heat, turning once, just until oysters plump up and brown lightly. Serve with lemon.

VARIATIONS

Pan-"Roasted" Oysters: Pat oysters dry but do not dredge. Sauté in butter or margarine (1/2 cup per pint of oysters) 3–4 minutes over moderate heat, turning once, just until they plump up and their edges ruffle. Serve with lemon.

Spicy Pan-"Roasted" Oysters: Pan roast oysters as above but reduce amount of butter to 1/4 cup for each pint oysters. With a slotted spoon, ladle cooked oysters over slices of hot buttered toast. To pan add 2 tablespoons ketchup and 1 teaspoon Worcestershire sauce; heat and stir 1 minute, spoon over oysters and serve.

Breaded Fried Oysters: Pat shucked oysters dry and dredge in flour lightly seasoned with salt and pepper. Dip in a mixture of beaten egg and water (1 tablespoon cold water to each egg), then roll in cracker meal, fine dry crumbs, or a 1/2 and 1/2 mixture of flour and corn meal. Sauté in butter or margarine (1/2 cup for 1 pint oysters) 3–4 minutes over moderately high heat, turning once, until golden brown. Drain on paper toweling and serve with lemon.

To Deep-Fat-Fry: Pat shucked oysters dry on paper toweling and bread as above. Heat cooking oil or shortening in a deep fat fryer to 375° F., place a single layer of oysters in fryer basket, lower into fat, and fry 2–3 minutes until lightly browned. Drain on paper toweling and set, uncovered, in an oven turned to lowest heat to keep warm while you fry the rest. Serve with lemon and, if you like, Tartar Sauce or Rémoulade Sauce.

VARIATION

Batter-Fried Oysters (Oyster Fritters): Make up batter given in Fish and Chips recipe. Pat shucked oysters dry on paper toweling, dip in batter, and fry, 6–8 at a time, as directed above.

To Oven-Roast: Preheat oven to 500° F. Scrub oysters but do not shuck. Place flat side up in a large, shallow baking pan and bake, uncovered, 12–15 minutes until shells open. Serve in the shell or, if you prefer, on the half shell (simply cut hinge and lift off shallow top shell).

To Roast over Charcoal: Prepare a moderately hot charcoal fire. Scrub oysters but don't shuck. Wrap, 4–6 to a package, in heavy foil, place directly on coals, and roast, without turning, 6 minutes. Serve with lemon. *Note:* Techniques (and cooking times) are essentially the same for outdoor gas and electric grills *provided* you preheat them.

VARIATION

Do not wrap oysters; instead, place flat side up on grill 4" from coals and roast 10–15 minutes until shells open.

To Steam: Scrub oysters but do not shuck. Place in a deep kettle, add 2/3 cup boiling water, cover, and steam over moderate heat 10–12 minutes until shells open. Serve with melted butter and lemon wedges and, if you like, Worcestershire and liquid hot red pepper seasoning.

To Serve Oysters on the Half Shell: Allow 6–8 blue point oysters per person; have fish market open them and prepare for serving on the half shell. If you have to do this job yourself, see directions given earlier for opening oysters. Fill large, shallow bowls or soup plates with crushed ice and arrange oysters in ice. Garnish with lemon wedges and ruffs of parsley. Set out the pepper mill and pass thinly sliced, buttered pumpernickel or crisp thin crackers. When eating, to savor every last drop, drink the oyster liquor from each shell after eating the oyster.

VARIATION

Oysters on the Half Shell with Caviar: Prepare as directed, then top each oyster with about 1/2 teaspoon red or black caviar and a few shreds of grated fresh horseradish. Serve with lemon wedges.

GRAND CENTRAL OYSTER STEW

4 servings　⊠

The Oyster Bar in New York's Grand Central Terminal still makes oyster stew the way it did on opening day in 1912. People say the recipe can't be duplicated at home because Oyster Bar chefs never measure anything. Perhaps not, but here's a recipe that comes close. Make it fast and serve in hot, hot bowls.

1 cup milk
1 cup light cream
1 pint shucked oysters (do not drain)
2 tablespoons butter
1/4 teaspoon salt
1/4 teaspoon celery salt
Pinch pepper
Pinch paprika

Heat soup bowls. Scald milk and cream in a large, heavy saucepan over moderately high heat. Drain oyster liquor into a separate saucepan and bring to a boil. Spoon 2 tablespoons hot liquor into a third saucepan, add oysters and butter, and heat, uncovered, over moderate heat, swirling oysters around 3–4 minutes until edges just begin to curl; add oysters at once to hot milk, mix in hot oyster liquor, salt, celery salt, pepper, and paprika. Ladle into heated bowls and serve piping hot with oyster crackers.

NPS: 285 C, 125 mg CH, 425 mg S*

CREAMED OYSTERS

4 servings

1 pint shucked oysters (do not drain)
3 tablespoons butter or margarine
3 tablespoons flour
1 cup light cream
1 teaspoon lemon juice
Pinch nutmeg
1/8 teaspoon paprika
4 slices lightly buttered toast (optional)

Drain oysters and reserve 1/4 cup liquor. Melt butter in a saucepan over moderate heat, blend in flour, slowly add cream, and heat, stirring, until thickened. Add reserved liquor, lemon juice, nutmeg and paprika, reduce heat, and simmer, stirring, 1 minute. Add oysters and cook, swirling pan occasionally, 4–5 minutes just until edges begin to curl. Serve as is or spooned over buttered toast.

NPS: 295 C, 120 mg CH, 200 mg S*

VARIATIONS

Oyster Shortcake: Prepare recipe as directed and ladle over hot, split, buttered biscuits. Sprinkle with minced parsley and serve.

NPS: 385 C, 125 mg CH, 475 mg S*

Oyster Pie *(4–6 servings):* Prepare one recipe Flaky Pastry I, roll into a 12″ circle, and cut 3 steam vents in center. Prepare Creamed Oysters as directed and pour into an ungreased 9″ piepan; place a pie funnel in center of pan. Cover oysters with pastry, trim and crimp edges, and brush pastry with beaten egg. Bake 1/2 hour at 425° F. until pastry is golden.

NPS (4–6): 575–385 C, 120–80 mg CH, 475–315 mg S*

BROILED CRUMBED OYSTERS ON THE HALF SHELL

4 servings   ⚔ ▨

2 dozen oysters on the half shell
1/2 teaspoon salt
1/8 teaspoon pepper
1/2 cup soft white bread crumbs mixed with 2 tablespoons melted butter or margarine

Preheat broiler. Sprinkle oysters with salt, pepper, and buttered crumbs and arrange on foil-lined broiler pan. Broil 3″ from the heat 4–5 minutes until lightly browned.

NPS: 65 C, 15 mg CH, 360 mg S*

OYSTERS ROCKEFELLER

4 entree servings, enough appetizers for 6

There are dozens of variations of this New Orleans classic. This one may be no more original than the others, but it *is* good.

Rock salt
1/4 cup minced scallions or shallots
1/4 cup minced celery
1/2 clove garlic, peeled and crushed
1 cup butter or margarine
2 cups finely chopped watercress leaves
1/3 cup soft white bread crumbs
1/3 cup minced parsley
1/3 cup minced fresh fennel
1/4 cup Pernod or anisette
Pinch cayenne pepper
2 dozen oysters on the half shell

Preheat oven to 450° F. Make beds of rock salt in 4 piepans (the 8″ or 9″ size is best), dampen slightly with water, and heat, uncovered, in oven 5 minutes. Meanwhile, stir-fry scallions, celery, and garlic in butter over moderate heat 3–5 minutes until limp. Add watercress and stir-fry 1 minute, just until wilted. Purée skillet mixture by buzzing 10–15 seconds in an electric blender at high speed or about 5 seconds in a food processor fitted with the metal chopping blade; add remaining ingredients except oysters and buzz 5–10 seconds in the blender at high speed, about 5 seconds in the processor until smooth. Arrange 6 oysters in shells in each pan of hot salt, pushing shells down into salt so they cannot tip. Cover each oyster with 1 tablespoon purée and bake, uncovered, 5–7 minutes until bubbly. Serve at once in pans of salt.

NPS (4–6): 525–350 C, 165–110 mg CH, 575–380 mg S*

OYSTERS REMICK

4 entree servings, enough appetizers for 6

"Deviled" oysters on the half shell.

Rock salt
6 slices bacon
2 dozen oysters on the half shell
3/4 cup mayonnaise
3 tablespoons chili sauce
3/4 teaspoon prepared Dijon-style mustard
1 teaspoon lemon juice
2–3 drops liquid hot red pepper seasoning

Preheat oven to 450° F. Make beds of rock salt in 4 piepans (the 8″ or 9″ size), dampen slightly with water, and heat, uncovered, in oven 5 minutes. Meanwhile, cut each bacon strip into 4 equal-size pieces and stir-fry over moderate heat until limp. Drain on paper toweling and reserve. Arrange 6 oysters in shells in each pan, pushing shells down in hot salt so they won't tip. Blend mayonnaise with chili sauce, mustard, lemon juice, and pepper seasoning and cover each oyster with a heaping teaspoonful. Top with a piece of bacon and bake, uncovered, about 5–7 minutes until bacon is crisp. Serve from pans.

NPS (4–6): 555–370 C, 90–60 mg CH, 730–485 mg S*

OYSTERS FLORENTINE

2 entree servings, enough appetizers for 4

Oysters and spinach on the half shell topped with cheese sauce.

Rock salt
1½ dozen oysters on the half shell
1 (10-ounce) package frozen chopped spinach, cooked by package directions and drained well
2–3 scallions, trimmed and sliced thin
1 cup hot Mornay Sauce
1/3 cup grated Parmesan cheese

Preheat broiler. Make beds of rock salt in 2 (8″ or 9″) piepans, dampen slightly with water, and let heat, uncovered, in oven 5 minutes while broiler preheats. Scoop oysters and their liquor from shells into a saucepan; reserve shells. Poach oysters 3–4 minutes over moderately low heat just until edges begin to curl; drain. Purée spinach and scallions by buzzing 15–20 seconds in an electric blender at high speed or about 5 seconds in a food processor fitted with the metal chopping blade. Arrange oyster shells, 9 to a pan, in hot salt. Spoon a little spinach mixture into each shell, add an oyster, top with Mornay Sauce, then sprinkle with cheese. Broil 5″ from the heat 1–2 minutes just until flecked with brown.

NPS (2–4): 445–225 C, 140–70 mg CH, 935–465 mg S*

ANGELS ON HORSEBACK

2 servings

1 dozen shucked oysters, drained
6 slices bacon, halved, or 6 thin strips boiled ham the size of half bacon strips
2 slices hot buttered toast
1 cup Hollandaise Sauce

Preheat broiler. Pat oysters dry on paper toweling, wrap each in a piece of bacon, and secure with a toothpick. Arrange on a foil-lined broiler pan and broil 3″ from the heat, about 5 minutes, turning often so bacon browns evenly. Remove toothpicks, pile oysters on toast and smother with Hollandaise.

NPS: 670 C, 580 mg CH, 1,105 mg S*

VARIATION

Devils on Horseback: Sprinkle oysters lightly with lemon juice and liquid hot red pepper seasoning. Wrap in bacon and broil as directed. Serve on toast but omit Hollandaise.

NPS: 265 C, 70 mg CH, 535 mg S*

SCALLOPED OYSTERS

4 servings ☒

1 pint shucked oysters (do not drain)
1 cup light cream
2 cups coarse soda cracker crumbs
1/2 cup melted butter
1/2 teaspoon salt
1/4 teaspoon pepper

Preheat oven to 375° F. Drain oysters, reserving 1/4 cup liquor; mix liquor and cream and set aside. Mix crumbs with butter, salt, and pepper and sprinkle 1/3 of mixture in a buttered 1-quart casserole. Arrange half of oysters on top and pour in half of cream mixture. Cover with another 1/3 crumb mixture, add remaining oysters and cream. Top with remaining crumbs and bake, uncovered, 30–35 minutes until bubbly and lightly browned.

NPS: 555 C, 160 mg CH, 1,005 mg S*

PICKLED OYSTERS

4 first course servings ⚖

1 pint shucked oysters (do not drain)
1 medium-size yellow onion, peeled and sliced
   paper thin
1 lemon, sliced *paper* thin
1/2 cup white wine vinegar
1 teaspoon mixed pickling spices
1/8 teaspoon pepper
2 tablespoons olive or other cooking oil
2 tablespoons minced parsley

Simmer oysters in their liquor over moderately low heat 4–5 minutes just until edges begin to curl. Drain, reserve liquor, and cover oysters with ice water. Cool oysters 5 minutes in water, drain again, and arrange in a single layer in an ungreased large, shallow casserole. Cover with onion and lemon slices. Bring vinegar, reserved cooking liquor, spices, and oil to a boil, reduce heat, and simmer, uncovered, 5 minutes. Strain liquid over oysters, cool to room temperature, then cover and chill overnight. Serve sprinkled with parsley.

NPS: 155 C, 60 mg CH, 95 mg S*

SCALLOPS

Down the centuries, scallop shells have been as cherished as the tiny sea animals inside them. It is from a scallop shell that Botticelli's Venus rises; it is the scallop shell that became the emblem of St. James, patron saint of Spain; it is the scallop shell that chefs found the perfect size and shape for baking creamed seafood (hence the term "scalloped," meaning "creamed"). Scallops were so rare, in fact, that fish markets sometimes counterfeited them out of haddock and cod. They were little known in this country until vast beds of them were found off the coast of New England in the 1930s. Although Europeans eat everything inside the scallop shell and relish particularly the bean-shaped coral of the female, we tend to eat only the "eye" or firm, marshmallow-shaped muscle hinging top and bottom shells together.

The Kinds of Scallops

There are three, two harvested from deep in the Atlantic *(ocean* or *sea scallops,* also the diminutive *calico scallops)* and the third *(bay scallops)* scooped from tidewater bays and sheltered inlets up and down the East Coast. Scallops are also found on the West Coast, especially around Puget Sound.

Sea Scallops: Measuring 1"–11/2" across, these are tannish, firm, and nutty. They can be tough, however, and are best sliced across the grain or diced and used in casseroles.

Calico Scallops: These plentiful, Southern U.S. sea scallops are as tiny and tender as bay scallops. Sauté gently, or slip into soups or casseroles.

Bay Scallops: These are tiny, sometimes only 1/2" across, creamy pink, and so sweet and delicate they can (if from unpolluted waters) be eaten raw with only a drizzling of lemon or lime juice. Because of their extreme tenderness, they should be cooked as quickly and carefully as possible.

Buying Fresh Scallops

Season:

Sea Scallops: September to April.

Calico Scallops: Year round.

Bay Scallops: Autumn and winter.

Popular Market Forms: Bay and sea scallops are sold whole, out of the shell, by the pound.

Amount Needed: 1/3–1/2 pound per person.

For Top Quality: Look for sweet-smelling scallops packed in little or no liquid.

Frozen Scallops

Sea scallops are available fresh frozen, frozen breaded, and frozen precooked. Calico scallops are sometimes available frozen, but bay scallops, unfortunately, are almost never frozen. *To Cook Frozen Scallops:* Thaw uncooked scallops in refrigerator just until they can be separated or, if you prefer, thaw completely (1 pound will take 3–4 hours to thaw), then cook as you would fresh scallops. Breaded or precooked frozen scallops should be prepared by package directions.

How to Open Fresh Scallops: Occasionally you may find scallops in the shell (or perhaps dip them up yourself). If so, here are two ways to open them.
1. *To Pry Open:* Hold scallop in one hand, dark side of shell down, slip a sharp knife into hinge and slip underneath large muscle, severing it as close to shell as possible. Cut muscle just underneath top shell the same way, open, and remove scallop. Wash well in cold water to remove grit or bits of shell.
2. *To Roast Open:* Scrub scallops in cold water, place dark side down in a large, shallow roasting pan, set in a 300° F. oven, and let

stand, uncovered, about 5 minutes until shells open; discard any that don't. Remove from oven, cut out meat, and wash well in cool water.

How to Cook Scallops

Scallops are wonderfully adaptable—superb when cooked simply, sensational when dressed up. Here are the best basic ways to prepare them.

General Preparation (for all cooking methods): Wash well in cold water to remove bits of shell and grit.

To Oven-Broil: Preheat broiler. Pat scallops dry on paper toweling, dip in melted butter, margarine, or cooking oil, arrange in a single layer in a shallow baking pan, and broil 3″–4″ from the heat 5–7 minutes, without turning or basting, until lightly browned. Sprinkle with salt and pepper and serve with lemon. For extra flavor, dip scallops in Lemon, Parsley, or Herb Butter instead of plain butter.

VARIATIONS

⚖ **Low-Calorie Broiled Scallops:** Substitute low-calorie French, Italian, garlic, or herb dressing for the butter and broil as directed. Recipe too flexible for meaningful nutritional count.

Breaded Scallops: After dipping scallops in melted butter, roll in fine dry bread crumbs or cracker meal and broil as directed, turning and basting once so scallops brown evenly.

To Charcoal-Broil: Build a moderately hot charcoal fire. Wrap each scallop in a half slice bacon and thread on skewers so bacon won't unwrap; or secure bacon slices with toothpicks and arrange scallops in a well-greased, hinged, long-handled wire grill. Broil 4″ from heat 5–6 minutes on a side until bacon is brown and crisp. *Note:* The technique (and cooking times) for broiling scallops on an outdoor gas or electric grill are virtually the same *provided* you preheat the grill.

To Panfry (Sauté): Pat scallops dry on paper toweling, then sauté in butter (about 1/4 cup for 1 pound scallops) in a large, heavy skillet over moderately high heat 4–5 minutes until lightly browned. Sprinkle with salt and pepper and serve with lemon.

VARIATIONS

Scallops Amandine: Pat scallops dry, dredge in flour lightly seasoned with salt and pep-per, then sauté as above. Remove to a hot platter and keep warm. To skillet add 2–3 tablespoons butter or margarine and 1/2 cup slivered almonds and stir-fry 2–3 minutes until lightly browned. Pour over scallops and serve.

Scallops à la Meunière: Dip scallops in milk, then in flour lightly seasoned with salt and pepper. Sauté in butter as directed above, transfer to a hot platter, sprinkle with lemon juice and a little minced parsley, and keep warm. Add 1–2 tablespoons butter to skillet, heat until lightly browned and bubbly, pour over scallops, and serve.

Breaded Fried Scallops: Pat scallops dry, dip in a mixture of beaten egg and milk (2 tablespoons milk to each egg), then roll in fine dry bread crumbs or cracker meal to coat evenly. Pour 1/4″ cooking oil or a 1/2 and 1/2 mixture of cooking oil and melted butter or margarine in a large heavy skillet and heat over moderately high heat until a cube of bread will sizzle. Brown scallops, turning as necessary, 4–6 minutes until golden brown all over. Drain on paper toweling and serve with lemon wedges.

To Oven-Fry: Preheat oven to 500° F. Mix 1/4 cup milk with 1/2 teaspoon salt and a pinch white pepper; also mix 1/3 cup fine dry bread crumbs or cracker meal with 1/4 teaspoon paprika. Dip scallops in milk, then in crumbs to coat evenly. Arrange in a single layer in a buttered shallow baking pan, drizzle with melted butter, and bake, uncovered, without turning or basting, 7–9 minutes until golden.

To Deep-Fat-Fry: Pat scallops dry on paper toweling and bread as for Breaded Fried Scallops (above). Heat cooking oil or shortening in a deep fat fryer to 375° F., place a single layer of scallops in deep fat basket, lower into fat, and fry 2–3 minutes until golden brown. Drain on paper toweling and serve with lemon.

VARIATION

Batter-Fried Scallops: Make up batter given in Fish and Chips recipe. Pat scallops dry on paper toweling, dip in flour, then in batter, then fry, a few at a time, in 375° F. fat 2–3 minutes until golden brown. Drain on paper toweling and serve with lemon and Tartar Sauce.

To Poach: Place scallops in a large, heavy skillet (not iron), add lightly salted boiling water to cover, or dry white wine brought just to a simmer or, if you prefer, a boiling court bouillon. If using water or wine, add 1 bay leaf and 1 sprig each parsley and thyme, tied in cheesecloth. Cover and simmer 3–4 minutes until scallops turn milky white. Drain (cooking liquid can be used for making soups or sauces) and serve with Parsley, Caper, Mornay, or other suitable sauce.

COQUILLES ST. JACQUES À LA PARISIENNE (SCALLOPS AND MUSHROOMS IN WINE CREAM SAUCE)

6–8 servings

This is the classic *coquilles St. Jacques*. It can be served as a first course or light luncheon dish.

1½ cups dry white wine
3 tablespoons minced shallots
1 bay leaf
1 parsley sprig
½ teaspoon salt
Pinch pepper
1½ pounds bay scallops, washed
½ pound mushrooms, wiped clean and minced
1½ cups water (about)

SAUCE
4 tablespoons butter or margarine
5 tablespoons flour
¾ cup reduced scallops' cooking liquid
⅔ cup heavy cream
2 egg yolks, lightly beaten
2 teaspoons lemon juice
¼ teaspoon salt
Pinch white pepper

TOPPING
1¼ cups soft white bread crumbs
⅓ cup finely grated Gruyère cheese
¼ cup melted butter or margarine

Simmer wine, shallots, bay leaf, parsley, salt, and pepper, uncovered, 5 minutes in a large enamel or stainless-steel saucepan. Add scallops, mushrooms, and enough water to cover, and simmer, covered, 3–4 minutes until scallops turn milky white. Drain, reserving cooking liquid. Set scallops and mushrooms aside to cool, return liquid, bay leaf, and parsley to saucepan and boil rapidly, uncovered, until reduced to ¾ cup. Meanwhile, slice scallops across the grain ⅛″ thick. For the sauce, melt butter in a small saucepan and blend in flour. Strain reduced cooking liquid and add along with cream. Heat, stirring constantly, until thickened and smooth. Spoon a little hot sauce into yolks, then return to pan; set over lowest heat and cook and stir 1 minute; do not allow to boil. Mix in lemon juice, salt, and pepper. Pour over scallops and mushrooms and toss to mix. Spoon into 6–8 well-buttered very large scallop shells or into individual *au gratin* dishes; mix topping and sprinkle evenly over each. Set coquilles on a large baking sheet. *(Note: Recipe may be prepared to this point early in the day, covered and chilled until just before serving.)* Preheat broiler. If you have not made coquilles ahead and chilled them, broil 5″ from heat 4–5 minutes until bubbly and dappled with brown. If they have been chilled, set far below broiler unit (lowest oven shelf) and let warm 5–6 minutes, then move up and broil 5″ from heat 3–4 minutes until bubbly and browned.

NPS (6–8): 440–330 C, 215–160 mg CH, 810–605 mg S*

HERBED SKILLET SCALLOPS

4 servings

1½ pounds bay scallops, washed
⅓ cup butter or margarine
1 tablespoon minced parsley
1 tablespoon minced fresh dill
⅓ cup dry vermouth
Juice of ½ lemon or lime
½ teaspoon salt
4–5 dashes liquid hot red pepper seasoning

Pat scallops very dry on paper toweling. Melt butter in a large, heavy skillet over moderately high heat, add scallops and sauté, stirring often, 2–3 minutes until they turn opaque and give up most of their juices; transfer to a heatproof bowl and reserve. Add remaining ingredients to skillet and boil, uncovered, 2–3 minutes until reduced to a thick glaze on the bottom of the skillet. Return scallops to skillet together with any juices accumulated in bottom of bowl. Warm 1–2 minutes in the skillet glaze, turning often. Dish up and serve.

NPS: 280 C, 100 mg CH, 865 mg S*

SCALLOPS MARINARA

4 servings

2 medium-size yellow onions, peeled and coarsely chopped
2 cloves garlic, peeled and crushed
¼ cup olive oil
1 bay leaf, crumbled
½ teaspoon basil
½ teaspoon oregano
1 tablespoon light brown sugar
½ teaspoon salt
⅛ teaspoon pepper
½ cup dry white wine

1 (6-ounce) can tomato paste
1 (1-pound 12-ounce) can tomatoes
1½ pounds bay scallops or sea scallops, washed
   and, if large, sliced
1 tablespoon minced parsley

Stir-fry onions and garlic in olive oil in a large, heavy skillet 8–10 minutes over moderate heat until golden. Add herbs, brown sugar, salt, pepper, and wine and cook and stir 2–3 minutes. Add tomato paste and tomatoes, breaking up any large clumps, and simmer, uncovered, 40–45 minutes, stirring often, until flavors are well blended. Add scallops, cover, and simmer 3–4 minutes until milky white. Sprinkle with parsley and serve over spaghetti or boiled rice.

NPS: 370 C, 60 mg CH, 1,310 mg S*

CURRIED SCALLOPS

4 servings

1 cup dry white wine
2 cups water
1 large yellow onion, peeled and stuck with 4
   cloves
1 stick cinnamon
1 carrot, peeled and cut in large chunks
2 parsley sprigs
1 stalk celery
½ teaspoon salt
¼ teaspoon pepper
1½ pounds sea scallops, washed
1 large yellow onion, peeled and minced
1 clove garlic, peeled and crushed
3 tablespoons butter or margarine
¼ cup curry powder
¼ teaspoon cayenne pepper
1 tablespoon finely minced fresh gingerroot
⅔ cup coconut cream (available in specialty and
   Latin American groceries)
1½ cups reduced scallops' cooking liquid
Juice of 1 lime
½ cup heavy cream

Bring wine, water, onion, cinnamon stick, carrot, parsley, celery, salt, and pepper to a simmer in a large enamel or stainless-steel saucepan; add scallops and simmer, covered, 3–4 minutes until milky white. Drain scallops and cool; return cooking liquid and all of its seasonings to pan and boil, uncovered, until reduced to 1½ cups. Meanwhile, stir-fry onion and garlic in butter in a very large, heavy skillet over moderate heat 8–10 minutes until golden. Cut scallops in ½" cubes, cover, and keep cool. Blend curry powder and cayenne into onion, add ginger, coconut cream, and strained scallops' cooking liquid. Cover and simmer very slowly ½–¾ hour

until flavors are well blended. Mix in lime juice and cream, taste for salt and adjust as needed. Bring to a simmer, add scallops, and warm 2–3 minutes. Serve over boiled rice with chutney.

NPS: 530 C, 125 mg CH, 845 mg S*

CHILLED SCALLOPS IN GREEN DRESSING WITH RADICCHIO

4 servings

An unusual summer luncheon entree.

1½ pounds bay scallops, washed
⅔ cup dry white wine
2 bay leaves
1 (4") sprig fresh thyme or ¼ teaspoon dried
   thyme
1 small yellow onion, peeled and coarsely
   chopped
Crisp leaves of radicchio or bronze lettuce

GREEN DRESSING
1 tablespoon minced fresh chives
1 tablespoon minced fresh tarragon
1 tablespoon minced fresh dill
⅓ cup minced parsley
⅓ cup minced raw spinach
1 cup mayonnaise
2 teaspoons scallops' cooking liquid
¼ teaspoon salt

Pat scallops dry on paper toweling and halve any that seem extra large. Place scallops, wine, bay leaves, thyme, and onion in a small saucepan, cover, and simmer over moderate heat 3–4 minutes until scallops turn milky white. Drain, saving 2 teaspoons cooking liquid. Mix together all dressing ingredients, add scallops, and toss lightly to mix. Cover and chill several hours. Serve on leaves of radicchio, fanned out like full-blown roses.

NPS: 550 C, 90 mg CH, 890 mg S*

SHRIMP

In just 50 short years, shrimp have zoomed ahead of other shellfish to become America's favorite, all because refrigeration and quick shipping have made them as available in Nebraska as in New Orleans (also because the supply appears to be endless). Time was when the only thing most of us knew to do with shrimp was to make them into cocktails. But as Deep South shrimp reached the heartlands, so, too, did some of the great shrimp country recipes—pies, patties, puddings, not to mention gumbos and jambalayas. Then came the international specialties—from the Orient and Mediterranean, from Latin and South America—and in the process of trying them all we're putting away better than a quarter *billion* pounds of shrimp a year.

The Kinds of Shrimp

There are several kinds of shrimp—the *common gray-green;* the *brownish-pink Brazilian;* the *Gulf Coast pink;* the rare, *deep sea "royal red";* and the *cold water miniatures* from Alaska and Denmark. In addition, there are *prawns,* not just a large shrimp, as many people believe, but a bright pink European species (the French call it *langoustine* and the Italians *scampi).* Further complicating the terminology is the fact that *scampi* now means a way of cooking shrimp (broiled with lots of oil and garlic) as well as the animal itself. Actually, the varieties of shrimp matter little because all can be used interchangeably. What matters more are the sizes. As might be expected, the larger the shrimp, the more expensive.

Size	Number per Pound	Best Used for
Colossal	10 or less	Scampi, stuffed shrimp
Jumbo	12–15	Broiling, butterflying, and deep fat frying, stuffed shrimp
Medium	16–20	Casseroles, creamed dishes, cocktails
Medium-small	21–25	Casseroles, creamed dishes
Small	31–42	Casseroles, creamed dishes, salads
Miniatures (Danish or cocktail shrimp)	200 or more	Open-face sandwiches, canapés, soups, salads

Buying Fresh Shrimp

Season: Year round.

Popular Market Forms: Unless you live in a shrimping area, the shrimp you buy will be the tail part only. These are available raw and in the shell ("green shrimp," the markets call them), or shelled and deveined. In addition, you can buy fresh-cooked shrimp in the shell or shelled and deveined. A specialty item: refrigerated, ready-to-serve shrimp cocktails.

Amount Needed: Allow 1/3–1/2 pound shelled shrimp per person, about 3/4 pound unshelled shrimp, depending, of course, on appetites and richness of the dish.

For Top Quality: Raw shrimp should be firm but moist and sweet-smelling; cooked shrimp should also be firm and sweet-smelling and there should be a lot of "spring" or resilience to the tail; if the cooked shrimp have been shelled and deveined, they should look succulent, neither too moist nor too dry.

Frozen, Canned, and Dried Shrimp

You can buy frozen raw shrimp in or out of the shell, deveined or undeveined, also breaded and ready to deep-fry. Frozen cooked shrimp come shelled and deveined, also breaded and in a variety of precooked dinners. Canned shrimp have lost considerable ground since the arrival of frozen shrimp, but they are still available, deveined, or in the standard pack (not deveined). The most popular canned shrimp are probably the tiny Danish ones. Two specialty items: shrimp paste (in tubes) and dried shrimp; both should be used according to label instructions. *How to Use Frozen Shrimp:* With the exception of frozen, uncooked breaded shrimp, frozen shrimp are better if thawed before cooking (leave shrimp in their package and thaw in the refrigerator or under a gentle stream of cold running water). Once shrimp are thawed, drain well, then prepare as you would fresh shrimp; never refreeze. Most brands of frozen shrimp are accompanied by directions; follow them. *How to Use Canned Shrimp:* Because these shrimp are fully cooked, they're particularly suited for use in soups, salads, and casseroles; the tiny Danish shrimp are good for sandwich fillings, canapé spreads, and cocktail dips.

How to Cook Shrimp

Boiling is the most popular way to cook shrimp, with deep fat frying close behind. But, they may also be broiled in the oven or over charcoal and, of course, added to soups, sauces, skillet dinners, and casseroles. The greatest difficulty most people have with shrimp is overcooking them. They really only need to heat through. How can you tell if they are done and not overdone? By color. As soon as shrimp turn pink, they are done.

General Preparation: Sooner or later, all shrimp must be shelled and deveined. Sometimes it's done before cooking, sometimes afterward, and sometimes at the table, with everyone attacking his or her own portion.

To Shell and Devein Shrimp: The process is the same whether shrimp are raw or cooked. Starting at the large end, peel away the thin shell, unwinding it from around tail. If shrimp are to be deep-fat-fried, or if recipes so specify, leave tail fins on; otherwise, remove. To devein, make a shallow incision (about 1/8" deep) down center back (outer curved side) with a small, sharp knife and pull out dark vein running length of tail. Rinse away any broken bits of vein under cool running water. (*Note:* Not every shrimp will have the dark vein, but the majority will.)

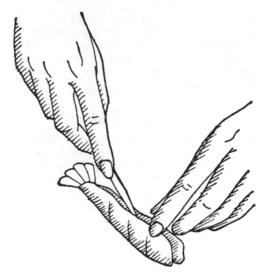

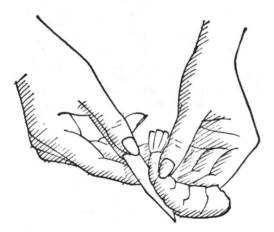

To Butterfly Shrimp: This is most often done when shrimp are to be dipped in batter and deep fat fried. Deepen incision made for deveining, cutting almost but not quite through to underside; spread shrimp as flat as possible (like an open book) and pat dry on paper toweling.

To Boil: The only real difference between boiling shrimp in the shell or out is the amount of salt needed (unshelled shrimp take twice as much). Allow 1 quart water for each pound shrimp, 2 tablespoons salt for unshelled shrimp and 1 tablespoon for the shelled. Bring salt water to a boil, add shrimp, cover, and simmer 3–5 minutes, depending on size, just until shrimp turn pink. Drain and, if in the shell, shell and devein. Serve hot with Lemon, Garlic, or Herb Butter, chill and use for shrimp cocktail; or use in any recipes calling for cooked shrimp. (*Note:* If you live near the ocean, use sea water for boiling the shrimp, adding 1 teaspoon salt if the shrimp are being cooked in the shell.)

VARIATIONS

Savory Boiled Shrimp: Boil shrimp as directed, substituting a court bouillon for salt water.

Shrimp Boiled in Beer: Boil shrimp as directed, using a 1/2 and 1/2 mixture of beer or ale and water instead of salt water.

To Oven-Broil: Select large shrimp, shell and devein. Preheat broiler. Place shrimp on a foil-lined broiler pan or in a large piepan. Brush generously with melted butter or margarine or a 1/2 and 1/2 mixture of melted butter and lemon juice, dry white wine, or sherry. Broil 3" from the heat 3–5 minutes on a side, brushing often with butter. Sprinkle with salt and pepper and serve.

VARIATION

Low-Calorie Broiled Shrimp: Broil as directed, using low-calorie Italian, herb, or garlic dressing in place of butter. Recipe too flexible for meaningful nutritional count.

To Charcoal-Broil: Select large shrimp and shell and devein. Build a moderately hot charcoal fire. Thread shrimp on large, thin skewers or place in a well-greased, hinged, long-handled wire grill. Brush shrimp generously with melted butter or margarine and broil 4″ from coals about 5 minutes on a side until pink and delicately browned. *Note:* Techniques (and cooking times) are virtually the same for broiling shrimp on an outdoor gas or electric grill; just be sure to preheat them.

To Panfry (Sauté): Shell and devein shrimp. Sauté in butter, margarine, or cooking oil (about 1/4 cup for each pound of shrimp), stirring briskly, 3–5 minutes over moderate heat, just until pink. Sprinkle with lemon juice, salt, and pepper and serve.

V A R I A T I O N

Shrimp à la Meunière: Shell and devein shrimp, dip in milk, then in flour lightly seasoned with salt and pepper. Sauté in butter as above, transfer to a hot platter, sprinkle with lemon juice and minced parsley, and keep warm. Add 1–2 tablespoons butter to skillet, heat quickly until bubbly and faintly brown, pour over shrimp and serve.

To Deep-Fat-Fry: Shell and devein shrimp and, if extra large, butterfly.* Heat shortening or cooking oil in a deep fat fryer to 375° F. Dip shrimp in flour lightly seasoned with salt and pepper, then in a mixture of beaten egg and milk (2 tablespoons milk to each egg), and then in fine dry bread crumbs, cracker meal, or a 1/2 and 1/2 mixture of flour and corn meal. Place in a single layer in fryer basket, lower into hot fat, and fry 3–5 minutes until golden. Drain on paper toweling and serve with lemon wedges and Tartar Sauce.

V A R I A T I O N

Batter-Fried Shrimp: See recipes for Hawaiian Sweet-and-Sour Shrimp and Japanese Butterfly Shrimp.

SHRIMP NEWBURG

4 servings

3 tablespoons butter or margarine
3 tablespoons flour
3/4 teaspoon salt
1/8 teaspoon cayenne pepper
1/8 teaspoon nutmeg or mace
1 pint light cream

2 egg yolks, lightly beaten
1 pound shrimp, boiled, shelled, and deveined
2 tablespoons dry sherry
4 slices hot buttered toast, halved diagonally

Melt butter in the top of a double boiler directly over moderate heat, blend in flour, salt, pepper and nutmeg, add cream and heat, stirring constantly, until thickened and smooth. Blend a little hot sauce into yolks, return to pan, and set over simmering water. Add shrimp and heat, stirring occasionally, 3–5 minutes until a good serving temperature. Stir in sherry and serve over toast.

NPS: 550 C, 390 mg CH, 840 mg S*

SHRIMP IN DILL SAUCE

6 servings

2 tablespoons butter or margarine
2 tablespoons minced shallots
1 1/4 cups dry white wine
1/2 cup water
1 bay leaf
2 pounds shelled and deveined raw shrimp
1/4 cup unsalted butter
5 tablespoons flour
1 cup heavy cream
2 tablespoons minced fresh dill
1/2 teaspoon salt
1/8 teaspoon white pepper

Melt butter in a large saucepan over moderate heat, add shallots, and sauté 5 minutes until golden. Add wine, water, bay leaf, and shrimp and simmer, uncovered, stirring occasionally, 3–5 minutes until shrimp just turn pink. Remove from heat and set aside. Melt unsalted butter in a small saucepan over moderate heat and blend in flour. Add cream and heat, stirring constantly, until thickened and smooth; mix in dill, salt, and pepper. Stir cream sauce into shrimp, return to a moderate heat, and cook, stirring constantly, 3–5 minutes until heated through (do not allow to boil); remove bay leaf. Serve over boiled rice or hot buttered toast.

NPS: 410 C, 310 mg CH, 450 mg S*

SHRIMP CURRY

6 servings

A mellow, sweet-sour curry that you can "heat up" simply by increasing the quantity of chili peppers.

3 medium-size yellow onions, peeled and coarsely chopped
3 cloves garlic, peeled and crushed
6 tablespoons butter or margarine

2/3 cup coarsely chopped celery
3 tart apples, peeled, cored, and diced
2 large tomatoes, peeled, cored, seeded, and
    coarsely chopped
3 (1/2″) cubes fresh gingerroot, peeled and
    crushed (use garlic crusher)
2 tablespoons curry powder
1/2 teaspoon turmeric
1/2 teaspoon coriander
1/4 teaspoon cumin
1/4 teaspoon cinnamon
1/4–1 teaspoon crushed hot red chili peppers
1/8 teaspoon mace
1/2 cup coconut cream (available in specialty and
    Latin American groceries)
1 cup water
1 pint yogurt
1 teaspoon salt
2 pounds shelled and deveined raw shrimp

Stir-fry onions and garlic in butter in a large,
heavy skillet over moderate heat 10–12 minutes until golden brown; mix in celery, apples, tomatoes, and all spices, cover, and
simmer 25–30 minutes. Stir in coconut
cream, water, yogurt, and salt and heat, uncovered, stirring now and then, 10 minutes.
Add shrimp and simmer, uncovered, stirring
occasionally, about 5 minutes until just pink.
Serve hot over boiled rice. (*Note:* This curry
will be even better if made a day ahead,
cooled to room temperature, then refrigerated until just before serving. Reheat
slowly.)
NPS: 430 C, 265 mg CH, 755 mg S*

SHRIMP GUMBO

4 servings

Filé powder (also called gumbo filé) is nothing more than sassafras leaves, dried and
pulverized. It is used both to flavor and to
thicken Cajun and Creole dishes.

3/4 pound small okra pods, washed, trimmed,
    and sliced 1/4″ thick, or 1 (10-ounce) package
    frozen sliced okra (do not thaw)
1/4 cup shortening or cooking oil
2/3 cup minced scallions (include some green
    tops)
2 cloves garlic, peeled and crushed
1 (1-pound 12-ounce) can tomatoes (do not
    drain)
1/2 cup boiling water
2 bay leaves
1 teaspoon salt
1/4 teaspoon liquid hot red pepper seasoning
1 pound shelled and deveined raw shrimp
1/8 teaspoon filé powder

Sauté okra 2 minutes on a side in shortening
in a large, heavy saucepan over moderate
heat until golden brown; drain on paper
toweling and reserve. Add scallions and garlic to pan and stir-fry 3–5 minutes until
limp. Add all remaining ingredients except
okra, shrimp, and filé powder and simmer,
uncovered, 20–25 minutes, stirring occasionally, until slightly thickened and flavors are
well blended. Add okra and shrimp and
cook 3–5 minutes, just until shrimp turn
pink. Remove bay leaves, stir in filé powder,
and serve over boiled rice.
NPS: 300 C, 170 mg CH, 970 mg S*

SHRIMP JAMBALAYA

4–6 servings

A Creole favorite—shrimp with ham, rice,
and tomatoes.

2 onions, peeled and coarsely chopped
1 clove garlic, peeled and crushed
1/3 cup olive oil
1 cup diced cooked ham
1 1/4 cups uncooked rice
1 (1-pound 12-ounce) can tomatoes (do not
    drain)
1 1/2 teaspoons salt
1/2 teaspoon cayenne pepper
1 tablespoon minced parsley
1 3/4 cups boiling water or chicken broth
1 pound shelled and deveined small raw shrimp

Stir-fry onions and garlic in oil in a large,
heavy kettle 5–8 minutes over moderate heat
until golden; add ham and rice and stir-fry 5
minutes until rice is very lightly browned.
Add all remaining ingredients except shrimp
and bring to a boil, stirring. Adjust heat so
mixture stays at a simmer, cover, and simmer 20 minutes until rice is very nearly
done. Add shrimp, pushing well down into
mixture, cover, and simmer 3–5 minutes just
until pink. Serve with hot buttered French
bread and a crisp green salad.
*NPS (4–6): 605–400 C, 190–125 mg CH, 1790–
1190 mg S**

SHRIMP CREOLE

4 servings

2 medium-size yellow onions, peeled and minced
2 medium-size sweet green peppers, cored,
    seeded, and minced
2 cloves garlic, peeled and crushed
2 stalks celery, minced
2 tablespoons olive or other cooking oil
2 tablespoons butter or margarine

1 (1-pound 12-ounce) can tomatoes (do not drain)
1/2 teaspoon paprika
1/8 teaspoon cayenne pepper
1 teaspoon salt
1 teaspoon filé powder (see Shrimp Gumbo)
1 1/2 pounds shelled and deveined raw shrimp

Stir-fry onions, green peppers, garlic, and celery in oil and butter in a large saucepan 5–8 minutes over moderately low heat until onions are golden. Stir in tomatoes, breaking up any large pieces, paprika, pepper, and salt; cover and simmer 35–45 minutes, stirring occasionally. If sauce seems thin, boil, uncovered, 2–3 minutes to reduce. Add filé powder and shrimp and simmer, uncovered, 3–5 minutes until shrimp are just cooked through. Serve over boiled rice.

NPS: 340 C, 270 mg CH, 1140 mg S*

SHRIMP THERMIDOR

6 servings

2 pounds shelled and deveined raw shrimp
3 tablespoons minced shallots or scallions
6 tablespoons butter or margarine
6 tablespoons flour
3/4 teaspoon salt
1/2 teaspoon powdered mustard
Pinch cayenne pepper
1 cup milk
1 cup shrimp cooking water
3 egg yolks, lightly beaten
1/3 cup grated Parmesan cheese

Preheat oven to 425° F. Boil shrimp according to basic method,* then drain, reserving 1 cup cooking water; set shrimp aside while you prepare sauce. Stir-fry shallots in butter in the top of a large double boiler directly over moderate heat 3–5 minutes until limp; blend in flour, salt, mustard and pepper, slowly add milk and shrimp cooking water, and heat, stirring, until thickened and smooth. Briskly mix 1 cup sauce into yolks, then return to pan. Set over simmering water and stir 1–2 minutes until no taste of raw egg remains. Spoon 1/2–3/4 cup sauce into an ungreased 2-quart *au gratin* dish or shallow casserole. Arrange shrimp in sauce and top with remaining sauce. Sprinkle with Parmesan. Bake, uncovered, 10–15 minutes until hot but not boiling, then broil 5"–6" from heat about 2 minutes to brown. Serve with boiled rice.

NPS: 350 C, 405 mg CH, 710 mg S*

VARIATION

Thermidor Ramekins: Prepare shrimp and sauce as directed and divide among 6 ungreased individual ramekins. Bake 10 minutes and broil 1–2 to brown.

SCAMPI

2 servings   ⚖

Broiled shrimp redolent of garlic and olive oil.

1 pound raw jumbo shrimp in the shell
1 cup olive oil
3 tablespoons dry vermouth (optional)
2 tablespoons minced parsley
1 clove garlic, peeled and crushed
1 teaspoon salt
1/4 teaspoon pepper

Shell shrimp, leaving tail ends on, then devein.* Rinse in cool water, pat dry, and place in a shallow bowl. Mix remaining ingredients and pour over shrimp; cover and chill 2–3 hours in refrigerator, turning one or two times in marinade. Preheat broiler. Place shrimp on a foil-lined broiler pan and brush generously with marinade. Broil 5"– 6" from heat 3 minutes on a side, basting often with marinade.

NPS: 410 C, 275 mg CH, 805 mg S*

VARIATION

⚖ **Scampi Italian Style:** Do not shell the shrimp; mix marinade as directed but increase garlic to 2 cloves. Cover shrimp with marinade and chill 2–3 hours, turning often. Broil 3–5 minutes on a side, basting often with marinade. Serve shrimp in the shell with plenty of paper napkins. Any remaining marinade or pan drippings can be used as a dip. Nutritional count same as basic recipe.

SHRIMP RUMAKI

4 main course servings, enough hors d'oeuvre for 8

Soy-marinated, bacon-wrapped broiled shrimp.

1 1/2 pounds shelled and deveined raw jumbo shrimp
1 cup soy sauce
1 cup medium-sweet sherry
1 tablespoon finely grated fresh gingerroot or 1/4 teaspoon dried ginger
12 slices bacon, halved crosswise

Marinate shrimp in a mixture of soy sauce, sherry, and ginger 2–3 hours in refrigerator, turning occasionally. Preheat oven to 400° F. Drain marinade from shrimp and reserve. Wrap a piece of bacon around each shrimp and secure with a toothpick. Arrange shrimp on a rack in a large, shallow roasting pan and bake, uncovered, 10 minutes, basting one or two times with marinade. Turn shrimp and bake 10 minutes longer, basting once or twice, until bacon is nicely browned. Remove toothpicks and serve as a main course, or leave toothpicks in and serve as an hors d'oeuvre.

NPS (4–8): 300–150 C, 270–135 mg CH, 900–600 mg S*

V A R I A T I O N

Scallops Rumaki: Substitute 1½ pounds bay scallops or small sea scallops for shrimp and prepare as directed.

NPS (4–8): 280–140 C, 75–35 mg CH, 900–600 mg S*

PEPPERY SZECHUAN SHRIMP

6 servings

Szechuan, a province in south central China, produces a cuisine as peppery as that of our own Southwest. By comparison, Cantonese cooking, the cuisine most familiar to Americans, seems bland. The following recipe is "hot." If you are not fond of fiery dishes, reduce the amount of hot red chili peppers. If, on the other hand, you like hot dishes truly hot, increase slightly the amount of chilies.

2 pounds shelled and deveined raw shrimp
1 cup peanut oil or ¾ cup peanut oil and ¼ cup sesame oil
½ cup thinly sliced scallions (include green tops)
2 cloves garlic, peeled and crushed
3 tablespoons finely grated fresh gingerroot
½ cup sake or dry sherry
¼ cup soy sauce
1 tablespoon sugar
1 tablespoon rice or cider vinegar
½ cup ketchup
½ cup chili sauce
¼ teaspoon crushed hot red chili peppers
¼ teaspoon salt (about)

Pat shrimp dry on paper toweling. Heat oil in a *wok* or large, heavy skillet over moderately high heat. Add shrimp, about half at a time, and stir-fry 3–4 minutes until pink.

Drain on paper toweling. Pour all but about 2 tablespoons oil from wok or skillet, add scallions and garlic, and stir-fry 3–5 minutes over moderate heat until limp. Add remaining ingredients except shrimp and heat and stir 5 minutes. Add shrimp and heat, tossing in sauce, 3–4 minutes. Taste for salt and adjust if needed. Serve with boiled rice.

NPS: 295 C, 225 mg CH, 1,730 mg S*

CANTONESE-STYLE SHRIMP WITH VEGETABLES

4–6 servings

1½ pounds shelled and deveined raw shrimp
¼ cup peanut or other cooking oil
½ pound mushrooms, wiped clean and sliced thin
1 (4-ounce) can water chestnuts, drained and sliced thin
2 cups diced celery
2 cups finely shredded Chinese cabbage
8 scallions, trimmed and minced (include tops)
1 medium-size sweet green pepper, cored, seeded, and minced
1 tablespoon minced fresh gingerroot
1 clove garlic, peeled and crushed (optional)
2 tablespoons cornstarch blended with ¼ cup cold chicken broth
1¾ cups chicken broth
2 teaspoons salt
1 teaspoon sugar

Stir-fry shrimp in 2 tablespoons oil in a large, heavy skillet or *wok* over moderately high heat 2–3 minutes until just turning pink; drain on paper toweling and reserve. Add remaining oil to skillet, also mushrooms, water chestnuts, vegetables, ginger, and, if you wish, garlic; stir-fry 2–3 minutes until crisp tender. Add shrimp and remaining ingredients and cook and stir until slightly thickened. Serve over boiled rice or thin noodles.

NPS (4–6): 370–245 C, 255–170 mg CH, 1,830–1,220 mg S*

V A R I A T I O N

Loong Ha Peen (Chicken, Shrimp, and Vegetables): Reduce amount of shrimp to 1 pound and add 1 cup coarsely chopped, cooked chicken meat. Prepare as directed, stirring chicken into sautéed vegetables along with sautéed shrimp.

NPS (4–6): 385–255 C, 200–135 mg CH, 1,780–1,185 mg S*

GINGERY CHINESE SHRIMP

2–3 main course servings, enough hors d'oeuvre for 4–6 ⚔

1 pound shelled and deveined raw shrimp
1½ teaspoons cornstarch
2 teaspoons dry vermouth or sherry
1 teaspoon salt
2 scallions, sliced ¼" thick (include some tops)
2 (¼") cubes fresh gingerroot, peeled and crushed (use garlic crusher)
¾ cup peanut or other cooking oil

If shrimp are very large, halve crosswise; place in a bowl, add cornstarch, vermouth, salt, scallions, and ginger, and toss to mix. Cover and chill 2 hours. Heat oil in a large, heavy skillet over moderately high heat until a cube of bread will sizzle, add shrimp and stir-fry 2–3 minutes or just until shrimp turn pink. Drain on paper toweling and serve with boiled rice as a main course, or spear each shrimp with a toothpick and serve hot as an hors d'oeuvre.

NPS (2–3): 460–305 C, 340–225 mg CH, 1,420–945 mg S*
NPS (4–6): 230–155 C, 170–115 mg CH, 710–475 mg S*

JAPANESE BUTTERFLY SHRIMP

6–8 entree servings, enough hors d'oeuvre for 10–12

3 pounds large raw shrimp in the shell
Shortening or cooking oil for deep fat frying
½ cup rice flour
1 recipe Tempura Batter
1 recipe Tempura Sauce

Shell shrimp, leaving tail ends on, then devein and butterfly.* Rinse shrimp in cool water, pat dry on paper toweling, cover, and chill several hours. About ½ hour before serving, begin heating shortening in a deep fat fryer; insert deep fat thermometer. Also make *tempura* batter and sauce. When fat reaches 380° F., quickly dredge shrimp in rice flour, dip in batter, and fry, 5 or 6 at a time, 3–5 minutes until golden brown. Drain on paper toweling and set, uncovered, in oven turned to lowest heat to keep warm and crisp while you fry remaining shrimp. Scoop any crumbs of batter from fat before each new batch of shrimp and keep fat temperature as near 380° F. as possible. Serve shrimp as an entree or hors d'oeuvre, using Tempura Sauce as a dip.

NPS (6–8): 365–270 C, 270–205 mg CH, 1,500–1,125 mg S*
NPS (10–12): 220–180 C, 165–135 mg CH, 895–745 mg S*

BUTTERFLY SHRIMP STUFFED WITH CRAB

4 servings

16 raw jumbo shrimp in the shell (about 1¼ pounds)
4 tablespoons butter or margarine, softened to room temperature

STUFFING
1 bunch scallions, washed, trimmed, and minced (white part only)
1 large clove garlic, peeled and minced
4 tablespoons butter or margarine
½ pound crab meat (fresh, thawed frozen, or drained canned), well picked over
1 cup soft white bread crumbs
2 tablespoons lemon juice
¼ teaspoon salt
⅛ teaspoon pepper
1 teaspoon minced fresh dill or ½ teaspoon dillweed
1 egg, lightly beaten

Preheat oven to 450° F. Shell shrimp, leaving tail ends on, then devein and butterfly*; rinse shrimp in cool water and pat dry on paper toweling. Spread softened butter on the bottom of a large shallow casserole and arrange shrimp in casserole in a single layer, cut sides up and not touching one another. Cover and refrigerate while you make the stuffing. For the Stuffing: Stir-fry scallions and garlic in butter in a small skillet 3–5 minutes over moderate heat until limp. Combine skillet mixture with all remaining stuffing ingredients and mix well. With your fingers, scoop up about 2 tablespoons stuffing and stuff into each shrimp, spreading it out evenly on top of shrimp and mounding slightly. Cover casserole and bake 15 minutes. Remove from oven and, using a bulb baster, baste each shrimp well with pan drippings. Return to oven and bake, *uncovered,* 10 minutes longer until stuffing is lightly browned. Top each portion with a little of the pan drippings.

NPS: 430 C, 360 mg CH, 725 mg S*

HAWAIIAN SWEET-AND-SOUR SHRIMP

6 servings

2 pounds large raw shrimp in the shell
Shortening or cooking oil for deep fat frying (for best flavor, use part peanut oil)

SWEET-SOUR SAUCE
1 large yellow onion, peeled and cut in thin wedges

---

1 large sweet green pepper, cored, seeded, and
   cut in 2″ × ¾″ strips
¼ cup peanut oil
⅔ cup firmly packed light brown sugar
½ cup rice vinegar or cider vinegar
¼ cup tomato paste
2 (8-ounce) cans pineapple chunks (do not drain)
⅓ cup water or dry white wine
¼ cup soy sauce
⅛ teaspoon cayenne pepper
2 tablespoons cornstarch blended with ¼ cup
   cold water

SHRIMP BATTER
1 egg
1 cup unsifted rice flour
1 tablespoon sugar
1 teaspoon salt
¾ cup ice water

Shell shrimp, leaving tail ends on, then
devein and butterfly.* Rinse shrimp in cool
water and pat dry on paper toweling. Begin
heating shortening in a deep fat fryer; insert
deep fat thermometer. Also make sweet-sour
sauce: Stir-fry onion and green pepper in
peanut oil 5–8 minutes until onion is golden;
add all remaining sauce ingredients except
cornstarch paste and simmer, uncovered,
stirring occasionally, 10 minutes. Mix in
cornstarch paste and heat, stirring constantly, until thickened and clear. Turn heat
to lowest point and let sauce cook slowly
while you prepare shrimp. For the batter,
beat egg until foamy, mix in remaining ingredients, and beat well until the consistency
of heavy cream. When fat reaches 375° F.,
dip shrimp in batter, then fry, about 5 or 6
at a time, 3–5 minutes until golden. Drain
on paper toweling. When all shrimp are
done, mound on a heated large platter,
smother with sweet-sour sauce, and serve.

NPS: 490 C, 230 mg CH, 1,535 mg S*

CHARLESTON SHRIMP PIE

6 servings

A delicate, Deep South favorite that's easy
to make.

2 pounds shrimp, boiled, shelled, and deveined
8 slices firm-textured white bread
1 pint light cream
1 pint milk
1 tablespoon melted butter or margarine
½ cup dry sherry
2 teaspoons salt
¼ teaspoon mace or nutmeg
¼ teaspoon cayenne pepper

Preheat oven to 375° F. Place shrimp in a
buttered 2½-quart casserole or soufflé dish.
Soak bread in cream and milk 15 minutes in
a large bowl, add remaining ingredients, and
beat until smooth with a wooden spoon.
Pour over shrimp and toss well to mix.
Bake, uncovered, 1 hour and 15 minutes or
until lightly browned and bubbly.

NPS: 425 C, 255 mg CH, 1,160 mg S*

BAKED SHRIMP AND RED RICE

4 servings ⊠

This Louisiana classic couldn't be easier.

¼ cup olive or other cooking oil
1 medium-size yellow onion, peeled and minced
1 clove garlic, peeled and crushed
½ cup minced green pepper
½ cup uncooked rice
1 (1-pound) can tomatoes (do not drain)
½ cup water
1½ teaspoons salt
¼ teaspoon pepper
¼ teaspoon oregano
1 bay leaf, crumbled
1½ pounds shelled and deveined raw shrimp

Preheat oven to 350° F. In a buttered 2-quart
casserole, mix all ingredients except shrimp.
Cover and bake 1 hour, stirring two or three
times. Add shrimp, pushing well down into
mixture, re-cover, and bake ½ hour longer
or until rice is done.

NPS: 400 C, 255 mg CH, 1,215 mg S*

VARIATION

Baked Scallops and Red Rice: Prepare as directed, substituting 1½ pounds bay scallops
for the shrimp.

NPS: 385 C, 60 mg CH, 1,410 mg S*

PICKLED SHRIMP À LA LORNA

*8 main course servings, enough hors d'oeuvre
for 12* ⚖

Serve as a summer luncheon entree or as
hors d'oeuvre on crisp crackers with bits of
sliced onion.

3 pounds shrimp, boiled, shelled, deveined, and
   cooled
3 medium-size yellow onions, peeled and sliced
   very thin
1 (3/16-ounce) box bay leaves
1½ cups olive or other cooking oil
1½ cups French dressing
1½ cloves garlic, peeled and halved

Place a layer of shrimp in a deep enamel kettle, top with a layer of sliced onions and a layer of bay leaves. Continue building up layers as long as shrimp last. Mix oil and French dressing and pour over all. Drop in garlic, cover, and marinate in refrigerator at least 4 hours. Drain before serving. (*Note:* These pickled shrimp will keep in the refrigerator about 1 week.)

NPS (8–12): 680–455 C, 205–135 mg CH, 810–540 mg S*

SHRIMP DE JONGHE

8 servings ⊠

Easy but impressive.

1 cup unsalted butter (no substitute), softened to room temperature
2 cloves garlic, peeled and crushed
2 shallots, peeled and minced, or 1 scallion, minced
1 tablespoon minced parsley
1 tablespoon minced chives
¼ teaspoon tarragon
¼ teaspoon marjoram
¼ teaspoon chervil
⅛ teaspoon nutmeg
3 cups soft white bread crumbs
2 tablespoons lemon juice
⅓ cup dry sherry
3 pounds shelled and deveined boiled small shrimp

Preheat oven to 375° F. Cream butter with garlic, shallots, herbs, and nutmeg until well blended; mix in crumbs, lemon juice, and sherry. Layer shrimp and crumbs into 8 well-buttered individual ramekins, ending with a layer of crumbs. Bake, uncovered, 20 minutes until topping is lightly browned and mixture heated through.

NPS: 455 C, 320 mg CH, 325 mg S*

FROGS' LEGS

Though people do still go frogging, most of the frogs' legs served today are from especially raised and pampered frogs. Only the hind legs are eaten. They are plump and tender and taste much like young chicken. Full nutritional counts on frogs' legs are unavailable.

Buying Fresh Frogs' Legs

Season: Year round.

Popular Market Forms: Dressed and ready to cook.

Amount Needed: About ½ pound or 2–4 pairs of frogs' legs per serving, depending on size; the smaller the legs, the more tender they'll be.

For Top Quality: Look for resilient, pale pink frogs' legs with a good fresh odor.

Frozen Frogs' Legs

Frozen frogs' legs are more readily available in most parts of the country than the fresh; they are dressed and ready to cook but should be thawed first in the refrigerator. Use immediately after thawing, never refreeze, and prepare as you would fresh frogs' legs.

How to Dress Fresh Frogs' Legs: It's doubtful that you'll have to do this yourself, but just in case, here's the technique: Cut off hind legs as close to the body as possible; wash well under running cold water. Cut off feet, then, starting at the top of the legs, peel off skin just as though you were removing a glove.

How to Cook Frogs' Legs

Because of their delicacy, frogs' legs should be treated simply: poached, sautéed, or deep-fat-fried. Like fish, they do not become more tender in cooking, only more appetizing.

General Preparation: Separate pairs of legs by severing at the crotch; wipe well with damp paper toweling, then pat dry. Some people like to soak frogs' legs 1–2 hours in milk before cooking, but it seems to make little difference in their tenderness or flavor.

To Panfry (Sauté): Make sure legs are very dry. Dip in milk, then in flour lightly seasoned with salt and pepper and sauté in a ½ and ½ mixture of butter and olive or other cooking oil (for 6–8 pairs of legs, you'll need about 2 tablespoons butter, 2 tablespoons oil.) Cook 5–6 minutes over moderate heat, turning often so legs brown evenly. Serve topped with some of the pan juices and with lemon.

VARIATION

Breaded Fried Frogs' Legs: Dip legs in seasoned flour, then in lightly beaten egg, and finally in fine dry bread crumbs (seasoned or plain) or cracker meal. Sauté as above.

To Deep-Fat-Fry: Select very young, tender frogs' legs, pat very dry, dip in seasoned flour, then in beaten egg, then in fine dry bread crumbs or cracker meal to coat evenly. Fry 2–3 minutes in 375° F. deep fat until golden brown. Drain on paper toweling and serve with lemon wedges and Tartar Sauce. *(Note:* If you prefer a crisp crumb coating, let breaded legs dry 10–15 minutes on a rack at room temperature before frying.)

To Poach: Place prepared legs in a large, heavy skillet (not iron), add liquid just to cover (a ½ and ½ mixture of milk and water or dry white wine); for each pint liquid, add 1 teaspoon salt and a pinch pepper. Cover and simmer 10–15 minutes, depending on size, just to cook through. Lift out legs, sprinkle with minced parsley or *fines herbes,** and drizzle with melted butter or Béchamel Sauce.

Some Classic Ways to Serve Frogs' Legs

(All amounts based on 6 pairs medium-size frogs' legs, enough for 4 servings)

À la Meunière: Sauté frogs' legs by basic method, transfer to a hot platter, and keep warm. Drain all but 2 tablespoons drippings from skillet, add ¼ cup lemon juice, and heat 1–2 minutes, stirring up browned bits. Pour over frogs' legs, sprinkle with parsley, and serve.

À la Provençale: Sauté frogs' legs by basic method. At the same time, stir-fry 2 peeled and minced medium-size yellow onions and 2 peeled and crushed cloves garlic in 2 tablespoons olive oil 5–8 minutes until pale golden. Add 3 peeled, cored, seeded, and finely chopped tomatoes, ¼ cup dry red wine, and ¼ teaspoon each salt and sugar and heat, stirring, 2–3 minutes. Pour over frogs' legs, toss very gently, sprinkle with minced parsley and serve.

Mornay: Sauté frogs' legs by basic method and transfer to a buttered 1½-quart *au gratin* dish. Smother with 2 cups hot Mornay Sauce, sprinkle with ¼ cup grated Parmesan cheese, and broil 3″–4″ from heat 2–3 minutes to brown.

Poulette: Poach frogs' legs by basic method, using part white wine, also 1 bay leaf and 1 sprig each parsley and thyme. Drain legs, transfer to a hot deep platter, and keep warm. Mix 1½ cups heavy cream with 3 lightly beaten egg yolks in the top of a double boiler; set over simmering water and heat, stirring, until slightly thickened. Off heat mix in 1 tablespoon each butter and lemon juice and 2 tablespoons minced parsley. Pour over legs, garnish, if you like, with ½ pound sautéed button mushrooms, and serve.

Vinaigrette: Poach frogs' legs by basic method, using part white wine, also 1 bay leaf and 1 sprig each parsley and thyme. Drain, cool, and chill several hours. Serve on lettuce, topped with Vinaigrette Dressing. If you prefer, cut meat from frogs' legs, toss with just enough vinaigrette to coat lightly, and marinate several hours in refrigerator.

SNAILS (ESCARGOTS)

Snails have long been a European favorite (the Romans were so fond of them they kept whole vineyards for them to feed upon), but until recently, we've been squeamish about trying them. American snails are smaller than the European (it takes about 50 of ours to make a pound). Fortunately, the fresh are relatively inexpensive and, equally fortunately, they are raised under strict supervision and do not need the "purifying" starvation period required for European snails. Canned snails are sold in gourmet shops along with bags of polished shells, but their flavor cannot compare with that of the fresh. Full nutritional counts on snails are unavailable.

Amount Needed: Allow about 1 dozen snails per person.

For Top Quality: Just make sure the snails are still alive.

How to Prepare Fresh Snails for Cooking

Place snails in a large, shallow pan, cover with lukewarm water, and let stand 10 minutes; snails should partially emerge from shells, discard any that don't. Cover "selects" with cold water, add about 1 teaspoon salt, then dampen edge of bowl and coat with salt so snails can't crawl out. Let stand at room temperature 1 hour, rinse well in cold water, then scrub shells well and rinse again. Place snails in a saucepan, cover with boiling water, cover, and simmer 5 minutes; drain and cool under cold running water, washing off the white material that looks like partially cooked egg white (it's edible, just not very attractive). Remove snails from shells by twisting out with a small skewer or snail fork; reserve shells. Remove bits of green gall from snails, also snip off heads and tiny curled black tails.

To Poach (necessary before fresh snails can be used in recipes): Place prepared snails in a saucepan, cover with water (you'll need about 1½ cups for 1 pound snails), or a ½ and ½ mixture of white wine and water or beef broth; add a peeled and quartered carrot, a celery stalk cut in chunks, a minced scallion or shallot, a bay leaf and 1 sprig each parsley and thyme, tied in cheesecloth, and a few bruised peppercorns. Cover and simmer 1½–2 hours until tender. Cool snails in broth to room temperature.

To Clean Shells: It's best to do this while snails are poaching so that both will be ready at the same time. Place scrubbed shells in a saucepan, add 1 quart boiling water mixed with 2 tablespoons baking soda and 2 teaspoons salt, cover, and simmer ½ hour. Drain, rinse in cold water, and let dry thoroughly before using. (*Note:* If carefully washed after using, the shells may be kept and used over and over again.)

How to Eat Snails: Whenever snails are served in the shell, eating them requires special implements: *escargotières* (snail plates), snail pincers, and snail forks.

To eat snails gracefully, pick them up, one at a time, with snail pincer and twist out snail as shown with the special fork. Dip in sauce, then eat.

ESCARGOTS À LA BOURGUIGNONNE

4 servings

If you've never eaten snails, this is a good way to begin, because the seasonings are superb. This particular dish is often served as a first course, but it can also be the entree.

1 pound fresh snails or 4 dozen canned snails with shells
½ cup butter, softened to room temperature
1 clove garlic, peeled and crushed
2 tablespoons minced shallots or scallions
1½ teaspoons minced parsley
¼ teaspoon salt
Pinch pepper
⅓ cup fine soft white bread crumbs

Prepare fresh snails for cooking and poach,* also clean shells.* If using canned snails, drain well and pat dry on paper toweling. Preheat oven to 350° F. Mix butter with garlic, shallots, parsley, salt, and pepper. Replace each snail in a shell and close openings with generous dabs of butter; dip buttered ends into crumbs. Arrange snails in snail plates and bake, uncovered, 10–12 minutes until piping hot. About 320 calories per serving.

VARIATION

Escargots in Chablis: Poach snails and clean shells as directed. Meanwhile, boil 1½ cups chablis with 2 teaspoons minced shallots until reduced to ¾ cup; strain through a double thickness of cheesecloth, then mix in ½ teaspoon beef extract. Before returning snails to shells, pour a little wine mixture into each shell. Replace snail and close with dabs of butter as above but omit crumbs. Arrange snails in snail plates and bake as directed. About 315 calories per serving.

BAKED ESCARGOTS CORSICAN STYLE

4 servings   ⚖

Especially good as a first course. Anchovy fillets, spinach, and lemon add piquancy.

1 pound fresh snails or 4 dozen canned snails
6–8 anchovy fillets, minced
1 cup finely shredded raw spinach
1 teaspoon lemon juice
2 tablespoons fine dry bread crumbs
¼ cup butter

Prepare fresh snails for cooking and poach.* If using canned snails, drain well. Preheat oven to 450° F. Coarsely chop snails and mix with anchovies, spinach, and lemon juice. Butter 4 large scallop shells or individual ramekins and fill with snail mixture. Sprinkle with crumbs and dot with butter. Place shells or ramekins on a baking sheet and bake, uncovered, 5–7 minutes until crumbs are lightly browned. About 240 calories per serving.

ESCARGOTS À LA PROVENÇALE

4 servings ⚖️

Unlike many Provençal recipes, this one contains no tomatoes. But the other traditional flavorings are there—garlic, onion, olive oil, and parsley.

1 pound fresh snails or 4 dozen canned snails
1 medium-size yellow onion, peeled and minced
2 cloves garlic, peeled and crushed
2 tablespoons olive oil
¼ pound mushrooms, wiped clean and minced
¼ cup dry red wine
4 slices hot buttered toast, trimmed of crusts
2 tablespoons minced parsley

Prepare fresh snails for cooking and poach.* If using canned snails, drain well and pat dry on paper toweling. Stir-fry onion and garlic in oil in a skillet 8–10 minutes over moderate heat until golden; add mushrooms and stir-fry 1–2 minutes longer. Add wine and simmer, uncovered, stirring occasionally, 5 minutes. Add snails and heat, uncovered, 5 minutes. Spoon over toast, sprinkle with parsley, and serve. About 290 calories per serving.

SQUID AND OCTOPUS

If young, tender, and properly prepared, these two can be exquisite; abused they are rubbery and tough. Squid and octopus are both inkfish, both are tentacled, and both are prepared more or less the same way. Of the two, squid is the more delicate. Most come from the North Atlantic, and the smaller they are the better. Octopus are fished from the Atlantic, too, but farther south. They may reach awesome size (about seven feet with tentacles extended), but again, the smaller the better. Canned and dried squid are sometimes available in specialty or ethnic groceries; some squid is also being frozen, but most of it goes to restau-

rants. Full nutritional counts for squid and octopus are unavailable.

Season: Year round.

Amount Needed: About ⅓–½ pound per person. The choicest squid weigh only a few ounces apiece. Octopus run larger, and even the smallest may weigh about 1 pound.

For Top Quality: Choose squid or octopus that are firm-tender and sweet-smelling with little or no liquid.

How to Prepare Squid and Octopus for Cooking

If possible, have your fish market clean squid or octopus for you. If you must do it yourself:
1. Lay squid or octopus, back side up on a counter with tentacles fully extended (the back is the side on which the eyes are most visible).
2. With a sharp knife, cut down center back, exposing cuttlebone (this is the cuttlebone used as canary food); lift it out and discard.
3. Grasp head and tentacles and pull toward you, turning octopus or squid inside out; take care not to rupture ink sac. Save sac, if you like, and use ink in broths or stews. Discard all other internal organs. The only parts you want are the meaty body covering and the tentacles.
4. Remove heads from squid; remove eyes, mouth, and parrot-like beak from octopus.
5. Cut off tentacles close to head, push out and discard bead of flesh at root of each tentacle.
6. Wash body and tentacles several times in cool water. Squid are now ready to use as recipes direct, *but octopus, unless very small and tender, must be beaten until tender.*
7. Place octopus flat on a cutting board and pound rhythmically with the blunt edge of a meat cleaver or edge of a heavy plate until meat is soft and velvety.
8. If you object to the octopus' purple skin, here's how to remove. Place octopus in a large kettle, cover with salted boiling water (about 1 teaspoon salt to 1 quart water), cover, and boil 20 minutes. Drain, plunge in ice water, and, using a stiff brush, scrub away purple skin.

About Using the Ink: Europeans often use squid or octopus ink to color and enrich soups and stews. But taste first, to see if you like the flavor. To collect the ink, hold sac over a small bowl, puncture with the point of a knife, and squeeze ink out. If used in soups or stews, it should be added along with other liquid ingredients.

FRIED SQUID

4 servings ⚖️

2 pounds small squid, prepared for cooking
1/3 cup unsifted flour
1 egg lightly beaten with 1 tablespoon cold water
3/4 cup toasted seasoned bread crumbs (about)
1/3 cup cooking oil

Cut squid in 2″ pieces (if tentacles are very small, leave whole); pat very dry on paper toweling. Dip in flour, then egg, and then in crumbs to coat evenly. Let dry on a rack at room temperature 10–15 minutes. Heat oil in a large, heavy skillet over moderate heat 1 minute. Sauté body pieces first, a few at a time, 4–5 minutes until browned on both sides; drain on paper toweling and keep warm. Sauté tentacles about 2 minutes (stand back from the pan because they sputter the way chicken livers do). Serve with lemon wedges. If you like, pass Tartar Sauce or any well-seasoned seafood sauce. About 290 calories per serving.

SQUID À LA MARSEILLAISE

4–6 servings

Squid stuffed with onion, tomatoes, and crumbs, then simmered in dry white wine.

2 pounds squid, prepared for cooking
1 large yellow onion, peeled and minced
4 tablespoons olive oil
2 cloves garlic, peeled and crushed
2 ripe tomatoes, peeled, cored, seeded, and chopped fine
1 1/2 cups soft white bread crumbs
1 tablespoon minced parsley
1/4 teaspoon salt
1/8 teaspoon pepper
1 cup dry white wine
1 cup water
1 bay leaf

Mince squid tentacles and set aside. Stir-fry onion in 2 tablespoons oil in a skillet over moderate heat 5–8 minutes until pale golden; add tentacles, garlic, and tomatoes and stir-fry 2–3 minutes. Off heat, mix in crumbs, parsley, salt, and pepper; loosely stuff into body cavities of squid and close with toothpicks. Brown squid lightly on both sides in remaining oil in a flameproof casserole over moderately high heat, add wine, water, and bay leaf; stir in any remain-

ing stuffing. Cover and simmer 20–30 minutes until squid is tender. Check consistency of liquid occasionally and, if too thick, thin with a little water or wine. Remove bay leaf and toothpicks and serve in shallow bowls with French bread or over hot boiled rice. About 405 calories for each of 4 servings (without bread or rice), about 270 calories for each of 6 servings.

GREEK-STYLE SQUID STUFFED WITH SAVORY RICE

4 servings

2 pounds squid, prepared for cooking
2 medium-size yellow onions, peeled and minced
2 tablespoons olive oil
2 cloves garlic, peeled and crushed
2 teaspoons minced parsley
1/2 teaspoon dillweed
2 cups hot cooked seasoned rice
1/3 cup dried currants (optional)
1 (1-pound) can Spanish-style tomato sauce

Preheat oven to 350° F. Chop tentacles fine and set aside. Stir-fry onions in oil in a large, heavy skillet over moderate heat 8–10 minutes until golden; add garlic and tentacles and stir-fry 1 minute. Off heat, mix in parsley, dill, rice, and, if you like, currants; stuff into body cavities of squid and close with toothpicks. Arrange squid in a single layer in a greased large casserole, pile any leftover stuffing on top, and pour in tomato sauce. Cover and bake 25 minutes until squid is tender. Remove toothpicks and serve with some sauce spooned over each portion. About 360 calories per serving.

MEDITERRANEAN-STYLE SQUID OR OCTOPUS

4–6 servings

Squid in a rich tomato-wine sauce.

2 pounds squid or octopus, prepared for cooking
2 medium-size yellow onions, peeled and minced
1/4 cup olive or other cooking oil
2–3 cloves garlic, peeled and crushed
1 (6-ounce) can tomato paste
1 cup dry white wine or dry vermouth
1 cup water
1/8 teaspoon crushed hot red chili peppers
1 tablespoon minced parsley
1/4–1/2 teaspoon salt

Cut squid or octopus in 2″ chunks and set aside. Sauté onions in oil 8–10 minutes until golden, add garlic, and stir-fry 1 minute. Add squid or octopus and all remaining ingredients except salt, mix well, cover, and simmer 3/4–1 hour, stirring occasionally, until tender (the best way to tell if squid or octopus is tender is to eat a piece). Taste for salt and add as needed. Serve over hot boiled rice. If made with squid: About 385 calories for each of 4 servings, 260 calories for each of 6 servings. If made with octopus: About 365 calories for each of 4 servings, 245 calories for each of 6 servings (without rice).

NINE

Eggs, Cheese, and Dairy

"They know, in France, 685 different ways of dressing eggs, without counting those which our savants invent every day." *De la Reynière*

Add to those 685 the dozens of ways other countries know to prepare eggs and the total staggers. No food is more versatile. Eggs can be cooked in the shell or out, simply or lavishly, solo or with something sweet or savory. They leaven angel-food cakes and soufflés, color and thicken sauces, bind croquettes, emulsify mayonnaise, clarify aspics, give batter-fried food crisp fragile crusts, glaze baked goods, smooth ice creams and candies, and enrich the flavor and food value of everything. Eggs have been called nature's "nutritional bombshells" because of their near-perfect protein and high vitamin and mineral content. Yet they are low in calories, about 80 per large egg.

EGGS

Buying Eggs

Quality: There are three federal grades for eggs, marked on the carton or tape sealing it: USDA AA (the very top quality), USDA A (second best), and USDA B. All are widely available. Choose top grades when appearance counts (as in poached or hard-cooked eggs); these eggs have excellent shape, firm whites, and high-standing yolks. Grade B eggs have thinner whites, flatter yolks, cost

less, and are good "cooking eggs" to use in making cakes and cookies, pies and puddings.

Size: Size has nothing to do with grade; weight determines. The five most common sizes, usually included in the grade stamp are:

Egg Size	Weight per Dozen
Jumbo	30 ounces
Extra-Large	27 ounces
Large	24 ounces
Medium	21 ounces
Small	18 ounces

Note: Recipes in this book are based on large eggs.

Color: The breed of hen determines shell color and personal preference the particular color you buy; white and brown eggs are equally flavorful and nutritious. Yolk color is affected by the hen's diet. Cloudy whites mean extra-fresh eggs.

Freshness: The fresher the better—*except* if eggs are to be hard-cooked. Shells cling to fresh eggs, making them difficult to peel, so use eggs several days or a week old. To determine if an egg is fresh, cover with cold water; if it floats, it's old. Beware of cracked eggs—they spoil rapidly. If you should accidentally crack an egg, use as soon as possible.

Blood Specks: Bloody eggs are removed during grading, but occasionally flecks of blood show in the yolk. They're harmless, do not mean an egg is fertile or bad. Remove with a piece of shell or paper toweling.

Fertile Eggs: These contain no magical properties, as some health faddists insist, and are no more nutritious than infertile eggs. They are overpriced and quick to spoil.

Other Kinds of Eggs

Because "eggs" so automatically mean hen eggs, we tend to overlook those of other fowl. Duck eggs are delicious (especially if ducks have swum in unbrackish ponds) and can be used interchangeably with large hen eggs (try them in custard). Eggs of geese and other domestic fowl may also be used. Simply multiply the number of hen's eggs in a recipe by 2 ounces, then substitute an equivalent weight of other fowl eggs. Small, speckled quail eggs, frequently found in specialty groceries, are most often poached or hard-cooked and served as is or in aspic. They're considered a great delicacy as are 100- or 1,000-year-old Chinese eggs. Available in many Oriental groceries, these are raw duck eggs preserved in lime, pine ash, and salt for 50–100 days. They are dark blue-green and firm enough to slice (but wash and peel them first). Serve as an appetizer (they have an "aged-cheese" or slightly "fishy" flavor).

Other Forms of Eggs

Commercially frozen egg products (whole mixed eggs, egg whites, and yolks), are available, but almost altogether on the wholesale level. Dried egg solids (whole eggs, whites, and yolks) are sometimes available in 5- or 8-ounce cartons. They are prey to bacteria, however, and should be used only for baking or in other thoroughly cooked dishes. To simplify measuring and using:

1 ounce dried whole egg = 2 large eggs
1 ounce dried egg yolk = 3½ fresh yolks
1 ounce dried egg white = 6¼ fresh whites

Good news for those on low-cholesterol diets: *frozen cholesterol-free egg product* (99 per cent real eggs from which the cholesterol has been removed). Thaw before using, also keep leftovers refrigerated. Use according to package directions, substituting ¼ cup cholesterol-free egg product for each whole egg in recipes (you can use in *any recipe calling for lightly beaten whole eggs). Tip:* When making "scrambled eggs," heat margarine until *bubbly* before adding egg mixture—keeps it from sticking to the pan.

SOME SPECIAL TERMS AND TECHNIQUES OF EGG COOKERY

To Break an Egg: Rap center of egg sharply against the edge of a counter or bowl, pull halves apart, letting egg fall into bowl. If using many eggs, break each separately into a small dish so that 1 bad egg won't destroy the lot. Here's a quick table of equivalents:

4–6 whole raw eggs = 1 cup
10–12 raw whites = 1 cup
13–14 raw yolks = 1 cup

To Separate an Egg: Break egg, catch yolk in half shell, and let white fall into a small bowl; transfer yolk to empty shell, again letting white drain into bowl. Place yolk in a separate bowl.

To Remove a Speck of Yolk from White: The merest dot of yolk will keep whites from whipping. To remove, scoop up with a piece of shell or paper toweling.

To Remove Shell Fragments: Scoop out with a piece of shell.

To Beat Whole Eggs: The point is to blend whites and yolks so that eggs will mix more quickly with other ingredients or to make the eggs fluffy and of uniform color.

EGGS, CHEESE, AND DAIRY

To Beat Whites: For best results, bring whites to room temperature and beat just before using; beaten egg whites quickly break down on standing. French chefs use unlined copper bowls and balloon whisks for greatest volume. Next best, a whisk and conventional bowl. Rotary beaters work well, electric mixers less so because they tend to break down the beaten whites.

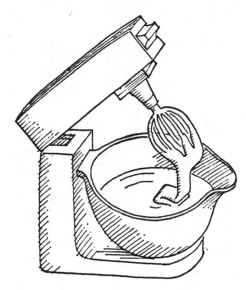

Under no circumstances attempt to beat egg whites in a food processor. You will deflate them as fast as you whip them. The greatest danger in beating whites is *overbeating.* For most recipes, whites are beaten either to *soft* peaks (as shown on previous page), or to *stiff peaks* (also described as *stiff but not dry).* Peaks can be very soft; firm but too soft to "peak"; or stiff enough to stand straight up when beater is withdrawn. But the beaten whites should never look dry. If so, they've been overbeaten and their volume is lost forever. Volume is the point of beating egg whites, because the air incorporated into them is what leavens a soufflé or omelet or angel-food cake (overbeating causes more flops than underbeating). *(Note:* Whites beaten with a pinch of salt, sugar, or cream of tartar or a drop of lemon juice or vinegar will have greater volume and stability than those beaten without.)

To Beat Yolks: These need not be at room temperature. When used to thicken sauces or custards, yolks should be beaten *lightly,* just to blend; further beating weakens their thickening power. Cake recipes often call for beating yolks until *thick and lemon-colored* (not the best description because yolks are

more nearly the color of mayonnaise) or if beaten with sugar, until mixture *makes a ribbon* (drops from beater in a thin flat ribbon that doubles back on itself in bowl).

Folding In Beaten Egg Whites: Easy does it! Once whites are beaten, they must be combined with a base mixture so that very little volume is lost. The gentle, over-and-over folding motion shown

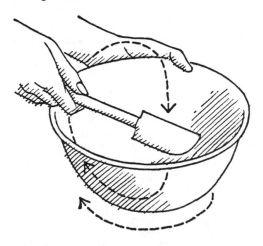

is the technique and a rubber spatula or flat whisk the best implement. If base mixture is thick, *stir in* 1/4–1/2 cup of whites to lighten it, then *fold in* the rest.

Adding Eggs to Hot Mixtures: Eggs or yolks are often blended into soups, sauces, or cream dishes shortly before serving—to thicken them, add flavor and color. Not a difficult technique, except that eggs curdle easily.

To Prevent Curdling: Beat eggs lightly, quickly blend in a little hot mixture (about 1/2 cup), then return to pan, stirring briskly. Burner should be at lowest point or, better still, topped with a "flame tamer." Cook, stirring constantly, about 2 minutes, *just until* mixture coats a metal spoon (leaves a thin, even, custard-like film).

Cooking Egg-Thickened Mixtures: The old theory was that all egg mixtures had to be cooked in the top of a double boiler over simmering, not boiling, water. And there are times when they still should be—if the cooking is prolonged, for example, as with Stirred Custard or Zabaglione, if the cook is a beginner. But most cooks can deal with simple egg-thickened mixtures over direct low heat if they stir constantly, watch closely, and take the mixture from the heat the instant it thickens. *An important point to remember: Egg mixtures continue cooking* *off heat and, unless taken from it at the critical moment, may curdle on the counter top.*

To Rescue Curdled Egg Mixtures: Strain through a fine sieve or double thickness of cheesecloth. If mixture is thin, rethicken with additional egg, taking every precaution.

What to Do with Leftover Yolks and Whites

Yolks:
• Make custard or any creamy pudding or pie filling, using 2 yolks for each egg.
• Make Mayonnaise, Hollandaise, Zabaglione, or other egg yolk sauce.
• Add yolks to creamed soups, seafood, meats, or vegetables (about 1 yolk per cup).
• Add an extra yolk or 2 to scrambled eggs.
• Hard-cook yolks,* sieve, and use in making cocktail spreads or as a garnish.

Whites:
• Make a soufflé, adding 3–4 extra whites.
• Make an angel-food cake.
• Make meringues or a meringue-topped pie.
• Make divinity or seafoam candy.
• Make a chiffon pie.
• Add an extra egg white or 2 to scrambled eggs or omelets.

HOW TO COOK EGGS

Like other high-protein foods, eggs toughen and shrivel if cooked too long, too fast or furiously. With a couple of exceptions: French omelets, which go from pan to plate in about a minute, and French-fried eggs, which bubble in deep fat. Both remain moist and tender. For egg cookery in general, however, the basic rule stands: low to moderate heat and gentle handling. *Dishwashing tip:* Soak "eggy" dishes in cold water before washing; hot water will cook egg on the dishes, making them twice as hard to wash.

To Cook in the Shell: To keep shells from cracking (especially important in Boiling Water Method), bring eggs to room temperature before cooking or warm quickly under hot tap. Use 3–4-day-old eggs for hard-cooking so eggs will peel easily. *(Note:* Eggshells badly discolor aluminum, so use pans made of other materials.)

Cold Water Method: Place eggs in pan, add enough cold water to come 1″ above eggs, bring to a boil, turn off heat, cover, and cook to desired doneness, using following table as a guide. Begin timing *after* heat is turned off. Drain eggs and plunge in cold water to stop

cooking, prevent formation of dark green around yolk, and facilitate peeling.

Boiling Water Method (Coddling): Gently lower eggs into about 6 cups boiling water (it should come 1″ above eggs). Adjust heat so water is *just below* simmering and cook according to table. Drain and chill eggs as in Cold Water Method. *Tip:* Hard-cooked eggs will be easier still to peel if you crack the large ends *before* plunging them into cold water.

To Peel: Soft-cooked eggs are usually sliced in half and scooped into small dishes or served large end up in egg cups; to eat, slice off top, sprinkle in seasonings, and eat from shell. *Oeufs mollets* and hard-cooked eggs are peeled: Crack gently on a flat surface, roll egg over surface or between hands to craze and loosen shell. Starting at the large end where there is an air space, peel off shell and membrane, dipping as needed in cold water to make the going easier. Take care not to tear white.

To Keep Peeled Eggs Warm: Immerse in hot water, *not* on the stove.

To Hard-Cook Egg Yolks: Place yolks in individual ramekins, set in 1–1½″ simmering water, cover, and cook 5–7 minutes until firm. Use in salads or spreads or as a garnish.

To Tell if an Egg Is Hard-Cooked or Raw: Spin egg on counter. If it wobbles, it's cooked; if it spins neatly, it's raw.

To Poach: Pour about 2″ water into a shallow saucepan or skillet (not iron) and bring to a boil; adjust heat so water simmers, break eggs, one at a time, into a small dish. Stir water into a whirlpool, slip egg in, stirring. Repeat with other eggs and cook 3–5 minutes to desired firmness. Lift out with a slotted spoon and serve. *(Note:* It's not necessary, as once thought, to add salt or vinegar to the water.)

V A R I A T I O N

Poach as directed, but use milk or broth instead of water.

To Steam-Poach: Break eggs into buttered cups of an egg poacher, set over simmering water, cover, and steam 3–4 minutes.

To Fry:

Method I: Heat 1–2 tablespoons butter, margarine, or bacon drippings for each egg in a large, heavy skillet over moderate heat about 1 minute, break eggs into skillet, spacing so they don't run together, reduce heat slightly,

BOILED EGG CHART

Degree of Doneness	Description	Approximate Cooking Time (in Minutes)	
		Cold Water Method	Boiling Water Method
Very soft-cooked	Jelly-like white, runny yolk	1	3
Soft-cooked	Just-set white, runny yolk	2	4
Medium-soft	Firm-tender white, soft yolk	3	5
Oeufs Mollets (a French favorite)	Firm-tender white, yolk beginning to set around the edges	—	6
Hard-cooked	Firm-tender white *and* yolk	15	10–12

and cook, basting with fat or turning, to desired firmness. Soft-fried eggs "sunny side up" will take 2–3 minutes; "over easy" eggs about 2 minutes on the first side and 1–2 minutes on the second.

Method II: Lightly grease a large, heavy skillet (not iron) and heat over moderate heat just until a drop of water will dance. Break eggs into skillet, turn heat to low, and cook just until edges turn milky, about 1 minute. Add ½ teaspoon water for each egg, cover, and steam to desired firmness.

To French-Fry: Pour about 3″ cooking oil into a small deep saucepan and heat over moderately high heat until almost smoking. Break egg into a small dish, slide into fat, roll over with 2 wooden spoons until nearly round. Fry until puffed and golden, 2–2½ minutes; drain on paper toweling and serve. *(Note:* These eggs should be cooked one at a time.)

To Scramble *(Note:* Never try to scramble just 1 egg; allow 2 per person or, if scrambling many eggs, 1½ per person):

Method I: Beat eggs just enough to blend whites and yolks, season lightly with salt and pepper. Pour into a heavy skillet (not iron) lightly coated with melted butter, margarine, or bacon drippings and cook and stir over low heat 2–3 minutes until creamy-firm.

Method II: Break eggs into a bowl, for each egg add 1 tablespoon cream, milk, or water; season lightly with salt and pepper. Beat until frothy, pour into a heavy skillet (not iron) lightly coated with melted butter, margarine, or bacon drippings, and cook and stir over low heat 2–3 minutes until creamy-firm.

Method III: Prepare eggs as for Method II. Melt 2–3 tablespoons butter in the top of a double boiler, pour in eggs, and cook and stir over simmering water 3–4 minutes to desired firmness. These eggs are super-creamy.

VARIATIONS

Prepare 6–8 eggs by any of the above methods and, about 1 minute before they're done, mix in any of the following:
• ⅓ cup minced sautéed chicken livers or pâté
• ⅓ cup minced cooked sausages or frankfurters
• ⅓ cup minced cooked ham, tongue, salami, or crisp, crumbled bacon
• ⅓ cup minced cooked fish, shellfish, chicken, or turkey
• ⅓ cup minced sautéed mushrooms, yellow onions, sweet red or green peppers
• ⅓ cup coarsely grated sharp Cheddar, Swiss, or Gruyère cheese
• ⅓ cup cooked asparagus tips, minced cooked cauliflower or broccoli
• ⅓ cup sour cream and 2 tablespoons minced chives
• ⅓ cup sour cream and 2 tablespoons red or black caviar
• ⅓ cup peeled, seeded, minced tomato
• 1 tablespoon fresh minced parsley, chives, dill, tarragon, chervil, or marjoram

To Bake or Shirr (Oeufs en Cocottes): These two techniques are similar, the only difference being that shirred eggs are started on the top of the stove and finished in the oven and baked eggs are cooked altogether in the oven. Break eggs into buttered ramekins or custard cups and top each, if you like, with 1 tablespoon light cream. Set cups in a shallow baking pan, pour in enough warm water to come halfway up cups. *To Shirr:* Cook over low heat just until whites begin to set, then transfer to a 325° F. oven and bake, uncovered, about 5 minutes until whites are milky and yolks soft but not runny. *To Bake:* Place eggs in ramekins, set in water bath, and bake, uncovered, 15–20 minutes at 325° F.

(Note: Do not sprinkle eggs with salt and pepper until after they are done, otherwise, the yolks will be spotted.)

VARIATIONS

• Place about 2 tablespoons minced cooked ham, chicken, chicken livers, fish, or shellfish into the bottom of each ramekin before adding eggs.
• Place 1 cooked artichoke bottom into each ramekin before adding eggs or, if you prefer, 2–3 tablespoons minced sautéed mushrooms, onions, or sweet peppers.
• Before baking eggs, top with a little crumbled bacon or grated cheese.
• Before baking eggs, sprinkle with a little minced parsley, fresh dill, tarragon, chervil, or chives.

COOKING EGGS AND CHEESE IN A MICROWAVE OVEN

Because they are high-protein foods, cheese and eggs can quickly toughen and dry in a microwave. Cheeses, moreover, being rich in fat, also tend to "string" easily. Still, if timed and tended with care, both can be microwaved with success, especially puffy omelets and soufflés. Needless to say, the quantity of food put into a microwave affects overall cooking times as do power levels, which vary from model to model (read your oven's instruction manual, also Microwave Ovens in Chapter 1). Then follow these general guidelines:

To Boil Eggs: Don't try it unless you have a special egg cooker made of "active" microwave cookware (see Microwave Utensil Guide in Chapter 1). *Note: Eggs boiled in water in a microwave will explode.*

To Poach Eggs: Do not attempt to poach more than 4 eggs at a time because they won't cook evenly. In a microwave-safe casserole, bring to a boil enough water to cover eggs and to help whites coagulate faster, add 1 teaspoon vinegar for each pint water; break eggs, one at a time, into a small dish, puncture yolk membrane with a toothpick (to prevent yolk's bursting during microwaving), then swirl boiling water into a whirlpool and slide egg into it; repeat with remaining eggs. Cover with vented plastic food wrap and microwave just until whites are *opaque*. Let eggs *stand* on counter 1–2 minutes to complete the poaching. *Note:* If you like soft yolks, time the poaching very carefully because yolks cook faster in a microwave than egg whites.

To Fry Eggs: For each egg to be fried, melt 2 teaspoons butter on a preheated microwave browning tray or grill; break eggs onto tray, puncture each yolk membrane with a toothpick, cover with buttered wax paper, and microwave as directed until whites are just set. Do not turn eggs because yolks will toughen.

To Scramble Eggs: In a microwave-safe container, melt 1 tablespoon butter for each egg to be cooked. *Tip:* Glass pint measures make dandy containers for scrambling 2 eggs, quart measures for 4 eggs. Break eggs into container, add 1 tablespoon water, milk, or cream for each, season lightly, and beat just enough to blend yolks and whites. Microwave *uncovered* for half the cooking time manufacturer recommends. Stir eggs from edges toward center, and continue microwaving until *just creamy-firm.* Let *stand* on counter 1–2 minutes to finish cooking to desired degree of doneness.

To Microwave Omelets: Make omelets to order, one at a time. For each, melt 2 tablespoons butter in a microwave-safe piepan in the microwave; swirl butter to coat pan. Pour in egg mixture and microwave *uncovered* as manufacturer directs but for half of recommended time only; rotate pan 180° and microwave until *just set but still creamy-moist on top.* If you like, add a filling at this time (see Some Fillings for Savory Omelets in this chapter). Run a spatula quickly around and under omelet to loosen, fold in half, and slide onto a warm plate. *Note:* If you prefer, make omelet on a peheated, buttered microwave browning tray or grill as manufacturer directs. *Note:* Since omelets do not brown well in a microwave oven, they will be prettier if topped with sauce—try Mornay, Mushroom, or Tomato.

To Microwave a Soufflé: Don't expect a microwaved soufflé to be as crusty and brown as one baked in a conventional or convection oven. It won't be. For best results, use light cream, half-and-half, or evaporated milk in the soufflé base instead of regular milk and add ¼ teaspoon cream of tartar for each egg white (both help stabilize the soufflé). Use a soufflé dish at least twice the volume of the soufflé mixture (a 6-cup dish for a 3-egg soufflé, for example), then microwave as manufacturer directs or *uncovered on a MEDIUM-LOW power setting until puffy and just set.* Serve at once—*no standing time needed.*

To Microwave a Quiche: Fit rolled-out pastry into a 9″ microwave-safe piepan and bake as directed in the microwave (see Baking Pies and Pastries in a Microwave Oven, Chapter 17) or bake in a conventional oven; cool slightly. For quiche filling, heat milk and/or cream to boiling by setting uncovered in microwave (having milk at a boil helps quiche filling cook evenly). Gradually stir hot liquid into beaten eggs as recipe directs, add remaining ingredients and pour into pie shell. Microwave *uncovered* as manufacturer directs, rotating piepan 90° after each baking quarter, until a knife inserted midway between center and edge comes out almost clean. Let quiche *stand* on counter 5 minutes to complete the cooking.

To Microwave Cheese-Rich Recipes: As a general rule, soft cheeses produce better results, so use them for toppings, casseroles, and sandwiches (they have higher moisture content and melt more smoothly). Read your microwave's instruction manual for recommended power level settings and cooking times. Also follow these pointers: Rotate and stir cheese casseroles frequently . . . stir cheese sauces every minute until cheese melts . . . add cheese toppings *after* cooking, letting heat of food melt them or microwave a *few seconds only* until melted . . . for cheese sandwiches, toast bread in a toaster first, then make sandwiches, buttering outsides of bread, too; microwave on a browning tray or grill just until cheese melts.

Reheating Eggs and Cheese in a Microwave Oven

You'll have good luck if you confine your reheating to sauce-rich casseroles. Always cover with wax paper, time reheating carefully, and stir mixtures from edges toward center. Layered casseroles should simply be rotated frequently as they reheat, a quarter turn each time.

COOKING EGGS AND CHEESE IN A CONVECTION OVEN

The only adjustments needed will be in cooking times and temperatures to compensate for the fact that convection ovens cook slightly faster than conventional ones. Their circulating hot air, however, means beautifully brown and fluffy soufflés, lighter, creamier quiches. When adapting recipes for the convection oven, read the instruction booklet accompanying your particular model. Also follow these guidelines:
• Place oven rack in middle or lower position.

• Preheat oven for soufflés (no need to for casseroles or quiches).
• Reduce oven temperatures by about 25° F. (but never lower than 300° F.). *Note:* Soufflés bake best at 350° F., quiches best at conventional oven temperatures, but reduce their baking time by about 10 minutes.
• Test dishes often for doneness after three fourths of the baking time has elapsed. *Note:* In the case of soufflés, check for doneness 5–10 minutes before baking time is up.

A Note About Serving Eggs: Have plates or platter warm, *not hot,* or eggs may cook beyond the point of desired doneness—especially important for omelets, scrambled eggs, and other simple egg dishes that quickly overcook.

Some Garnishes for Eggs

Almost anything savory and colorful is appropriate: crisp bacon strips, frizzled ham or Canadian bacon slices, glistening sausage links or patties, kippered herring, anchovy strips or rolls, sautéed chicken livers, tomato wedges or cherry tomatoes, clusters of green or black olives. And, of course, the old standbys—parsley, paprika, and watercress.

SCOTCH WOODCOCK

6 entree servings, 2 dozen appetizers

There are two ways to make Scotch Woodcock; the easiest is simply to spread hot buttered toast with anchovy paste and top with softly scrambled eggs. This is a more elaborate version.

6 slices hot buttered toast, trimmed of crusts
2 (2-ounce) cans anchovy fillets, drained and mashed
Freshly ground pepper
1 tablespoon minced parsley

SAUCE
1 cup heavy or light cream
4 egg yolks, lightly beaten
2 tablespoons butter (no substitute)

Make sauce first: Heat cream in the top of a double boiler over simmering water, mix a little into yolks, return to pan, and heat, stirring constantly, 7–10 minutes until smooth and thickened. (*Note:* Do not let water underneath boil or mixture will be scrambled eggs, not sauce.) Drop in butter and beat well; remove top of double boiler from bottom. Spread toast with anchovies, and halve diagonally, or, if to be served as appetizers, cut in "fingers." Arrange on hot plates, spoon or spread sauce over each piece, and top with a hearty grinding of pepper and sprinkling of parsley.

NPS (6–24) (with heavy cream): 330–82 C, 265–65 mg CH, 350–90 mg S*

EGGS BENEDICT

4 servings

4 thin slices boiled ham or Canadian bacon
1 tablespoon butter or margarine
2 hot, split, toasted, and buttered English muffins
4 poached eggs
1 cup hot Hollandaise Sauce

Lightly brown ham in butter over moderate heat; arrange on muffins, trimming to fit. Top with eggs, cover with sauce, and serve.

NPS: 385 C, 515 mg CH, 895 mg S*

EGGS FLORENTINE

6 servings ⚖

2 (10½-ounce) packages frozen chopped spinach, cooked by package directions and drained
6 poached eggs
1½ cups hot Mornay Sauce
¼ cup finely grated Parmesan cheese

Preheat oven to 350° F. Spoon spinach into a buttered 1-quart *au gratin* dish or shallow casserole or into 6 buttered custard cups set on a baking sheet. Make 6 depressions in spinach and slip a poached egg into each. Spoon sauce evenly over eggs, covering completely, and sprinkle with cheese. Bake, uncovered, 15 minutes, then broil 5″ from heat until speckled with brown.

NPS: 250 C, 305 mg CH, 520 mg S*

HUEVOS RANCHEROS

2–4 servings

Fried eggs on tortillas smothered with a chili-flavored tomato sauce. A Mexican classic.

4 tortillas
3 tablespoons lard or cooking oil
4 eggs
1 small yellow onion, peeled and minced
¼ cup minced sweet green pepper or 2 tablespoons minced hot green chili pepper
½ clove garlic, peeled and crushed
¾ cup tomato sauce
1½ teaspoons chili powder

¼ teaspoon salt
⅛ teaspoon sage
Pinch crushed dried hot red chili peppers (optional)

Preheat oven to 200° F. Fry tortillas on one side in 2 tablespoons lard in a large, heavy skillet over moderately low heat about 1 minute until pliable; drain on paper toweling, arrange on heatproof plates and set in oven. Fry eggs in drippings *just* until whites are set, then arrange on tortillas and keep warm in oven. Stir-fry onion and pepper in remaining lard 3–4 minutes, add remaining ingredients, and heat and stir until bubbling; turn heat to low and simmer, uncovered, 1–2 minutes. Spoon sauce over eggs and serve.

NPS (2–4): 465–230 C, 565–285 mg CH, 925–460 mg S*

EGGS FOO YUNG

4 servings

Eggs Foo Yung are a good way to use leftovers, which explains the many variations served in Chinese restaurants.

6 eggs, lightly beaten
1 cup fresh bean sprouts, washed and drained well
¼ cup minced scallions (include some tops)
¼ cup minced bamboo shoots, celery, or shredded Chinese cabbage
4 water chestnuts, minced
⅓–½ cup slivered cooked ham, chicken, or lean roast pork or minced cooked shrimp
1 teaspoon soy sauce
2–3 tablespoons peanut or other cooking oil

SAUCE
1 cup chicken broth
1 teaspoon soy sauce
½ teaspoon sugar
2 teaspoons cornstarch blended with 1 tablespoon cold water

Prepare sauce first: Heat and stir all ingredients in a small saucepan over moderate heat until slightly thickened; keep warm until needed. Mix eggs with all vegetables, meat, and soy sauce. Heat 2 teaspoons oil in a heavy 4″–6″ skillet over moderate heat ½ minute, add ⅓ cup egg mixture and fry as you would a pancake until lightly browned on bottom; turn and brown flip side. Keep warm (but do not stack) while you fry remaining "pancakes," adding more oil as needed and stirring egg mixture before each new "pancake." Serve hot topped with sauce.

NPS: 235 C, 420 mg CH, 700 mg S*

OMELETS

Omelets aren't as temperamental as they're rumored to be. Still, people approach them with trembling. By heeding the tips below, you should be able to make an acceptable omelet (the perfect one will take practice).

There are two kinds of omelets: *the plain or French,* made on top of the stove, and *the soufflé or puffed,* begun on the stove top but finished in the oven. For plain omelets, yolks and whites are beaten together just to mix; for soufflé omelets, the whites are whipped separately and folded in at the last.

Tips for Making Better Omelets

• Assemble all ingredients and implements beforehand. If omelet is to be filled, have filling ready.
• Use the freshest eggs possible and have them at room temperature (you'll get better volume). For an extra-tender omelet, add 1 teaspoon cold water per egg—*not* milk or cream, which will toughen it.
• Do not overbeat eggs. For a plain omelet, 20–30 seconds with a fork or whisk will do it. For a soufflé omelet, yolks should be briskly beaten with a fork and the whites beaten with a whisk until soft but firm peaks form.
• Use unsalted butter for cooking omelets.
• *Use a proper omelet pan* (without it, even an expert would have trouble). If the pan is too heavy, it cannot be manipulated easily as the omelet cooks; if too light, eggs may scorch. It should be round bottomed with sides that flare at the top, no more than 6″– 8″ in diameter, of medium weight, and made of cast aluminum, tin-lined copper, thick stainless steel, enameled cast iron, or Teflon-lined aluminum. It should be well seasoned and used exclusively for making omelets. *To season an omelet pan:* Half fill with cooking oil, set over lowest heat, and warm, uncovered, 1 hour. Turn off heat and let oil cool in pan to room temperature; pour out (save for cooking, if you like) and wipe pan with paper toweling. *To care for an omelet pan:* Wipe after each use with paper toweling but do not wash. If something burns on the bottom, scour with salt and fine steel wool (not soap-filled). Rinse, dry, and reseason if necessary.
• Make only 1 small omelet at a time; large ones are difficult to handle and cook unevenly.
• Once eggs are in the pan, raise burner heat to moderately high—or as high as your proficiency allows without scorching eggs. Om-

elets are an exception to the low-heat rule of egg cookery. If they are to be lightly browned on the bottom, creamy inside and moist on top, the heat must be high and the handling deft.
• Serve an omelet the second it comes from the pan on a *warm*—not hot—plate.

Filled Omelets

Plain omelets are easier to fill than the puffy, which are too bulky to fold well; these should be filled either by mixing filling with uncooked eggs or, better still, by ladling it over finished omelets before they are turned out. Plain omelets can be filled with almost any meat, fish, poultry, cheese, vegetable, fruit, preserve, or nut. Meat and vegetable fillings are usually warmed in butter in the omelet pan, then topped with the eggs (by the time the omelet is cooked, the filling will be in the center). Cheese, fruit, nuts, and other delicate fillings can be scattered over the omelet just before it's folded. Most fillings (cheese and nuts excepted) should be warm so that they do not cool the omelet.

Some Fillings for Savory Omelets

Cheese: Hard cheeses (Parmesan, romano, sapsago) can be mixed with the uncooked eggs; grate fine and allow 2–3 tablespoons cheese per 3-egg omelet. Softer cheeses (Cheddars, Gruyère, feta, mascarpone, Roquefort, mozzarella, cottage, or cream cheese) should be added in small dabs just before omelet is folded; again allow 2–3 tablespoons cheese per 3-egg omelet.

Meat: Any cooked, minced meat can be used. Allow 1/4–1/3 cup per 3-egg omelet and warm in butter in omelet pan before adding eggs.

Seafood: Any drained canned, thawed frozen, or cooked fish or shellfish can be used. Bone and flake, allow 1/4–1/3 cup per 3-egg omelet, and warm in butter in omelet pan before adding eggs.

Vegetable: Raw and cooked vegetables both make good fillings. In either case, they should be minced or diced; allow 1/4–1/3 cup per 3-egg omelet. *Best vegetables to use raw:* tomato, avocado, finocchio, spinach, sweet red or green pepper. *Best cooked vegetables:* asparagus, broccoli, cauliflower, zucchini, yellow squash, carrots, green peas, potatoes, mushrooms, spinach, onions, artichokes.

Combination Fillings: Leftover meats, seafoods, and vegetables can be minced, mixed,

---

and used to fill omelets. Allow 1/4–1/3 cup per 3-egg omelet and warm in butter in omelet pan before adding eggs. *Some good combinations:* ham and asparagus or spinach; corned beef and potatoes; franks and baked beans; beef and potatoes or onion; pork and apples or sweet potatoes; chicken and rice; rice and minced ripe or green olives; chicken liver and crumbled bacon; sautéed sausages and onions, potatoes or apples.

Dessert Omelet Fillings

Fruit: Most fruits are suitable. Small berries can be added whole, but larger fruits should be sliced thin, minced, or puréed. Allow about 1/3–1/2 cup fruit per 3-egg omelet and add just before folding. If fruits are cold, warm slightly before adding.

Jelly, Jam, or Preserves: Use 1/3 cup warmed jelly, jam, or preserves per 3-egg omelet; pour over omelet just before folding.

Nut: Use 1/3 cup minced, ground, or thinly sliced nuts per 3-egg omelet (thinly sliced *marrons glacés* are especially good). Scatter over omelet just before folding.

Liquor or Liqueur: Drizzle 1–2 tablespoons warmed liquor or liqueur (rum, cognac, kirsch, Calvados, Grand Marnier, etc.) over omelet just before folding. Fold, drizzle with 2–3 tablespoons more liquor or liqueur. Blaze with a match, if you like, and serve flaming.

PLAIN OR FRENCH OMELET

1 serving

Omelets should be made to order, one at a time.

1 tablespoon unsalted butter or margarine
3 eggs, at room temperature
1 tablespoon cold water
1/2 teaspoon salt
1/8 teaspoon white pepper

Warm butter in an 6"–8" omelet pan over low heat while you mix eggs. Beat eggs, water, salt, and pepper vigorously with a fork or whisk 20–30 seconds until blended and frothy. When butter is bubbly but not brown, tip to coat sides of pan and pour in eggs. Turn heat to moderately high and, using a fork, draw edges of eggs as they cook in toward center, at the same time tilting and gently shaking pan so uncooked portions flow underneath. Continue until omelet is just set and top creamy and moist. Take pan from heat at once, loosen omelet

edges with fork, shaking gently. If omelet should stick, slide a dab of butter underneath and tilt pan so it runs over bottom. Fold omelet in half or, if you prefer, let fold over as shown as you turn onto a warmed plate. Serve as is or topped with Tomato, Mornay, Mushroom, or other savory sauce.

NPS: 340 C, 855 mg CH, 1300 mg S*

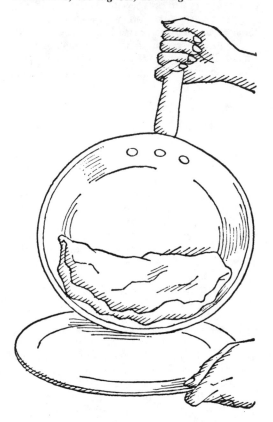

To Glaze: Fold omelet in pan, brush with melted butter, and brown quickly under broiler.

To Fill: There are two techniques (for filling ideas, see Some Fillings for Savory Omelets):
• Lightly sauté filling in pan, add eggs, and cook as directed; when omelet is done, filling will be in center.
• Sprinkle filling over omelet just before folding.

VARIATIONS

Fines Herbes Omelet: Gently warm 1 teaspoon minced chives, 1/2 teaspoon minced fresh chervil, and 1/4 teaspoon minced fresh tarragon (or 1/2 teaspoon dried *fines herbes)* in melting butter. Add eggs and cook as directed.

NPS: 340 C, 855 mg CH, 1300 mg S*

Lorraine Omelet: Prepare omelet as directed and, just before folding, top with 2 tablespoons coarsely grated Gruyère cheese, 1 tablespoon minced parsley, and 2 crisp brown slices of bacon. Fold and serve.

NPS: 530 C, 895 mg CH, 1600 mg S*

Lyonnaise Omelet: Prepare omelet as directed and, just before folding, top with 1 thinly sliced, sautéed yellow onion. Fold and serve. For extra zip, top with a drizzling of vinegar and browned butter.

NPS: 370 C, 855 mg CH, 1310 mg S*

Caviar Omelet: Prepare omelet as directed and, just before folding, top with 1/4 cup caviar (red or black) and 2 tablespoons each sour cream and minced Spanish or Bermuda onion. Fold and serve.

NPS: 625 C, 1125 mg CH, 2815 mg S*

Spanish Omelet: Stir-fry 1 slivered pimiento, 1 small peeled, cored, seeded, and coarsely chopped tomato, 1 crushed clove garlic, and 1 tablespoon minced parsley in 1 tablespoon butter 5–7 minutes over moderate heat. Cook omelet as directed, top with tomato mixture, fold, and serve.

NPS: 480 C, 885 mg CH, 1435 mg S*

Ham, Mushroom, and Tomato Omelet: Sauté 1/2 cup thinly sliced mushrooms in 1 tablespoon butter over moderate heat 3–5 minutes until golden; add 1/4 cup julienne strips cooked ham, and 1 small peeled, cored, seeded, and coarsely chopped tomato; cook and stir 5–7 minutes. Cook omelet as directed, top with ham mixture, fold, and serve.

NPS: 535 C, 905 mg CH, 1970 mg S*

Dessert Omelet: Beat eggs with water called for and 2 tablespoons sugar instead of salt and pepper. Cook as directed, sprinkle with sugar, and serve. If you like, fill with a sweet filling (see Dessert Omelet Fillings) or top with a favorite dessert sauce.

NPS: 435 C, 855 mg CH, 325 mg S*

PUFFED OR SOUFFLÉ OMELET

2 servings ⚖️

4 eggs, separated, at room temperature
1/4 cup cold water
1/2 teaspoon salt
1/8 teaspoon white pepper
1 tablespoon butter or margarine

Preheat oven to 350° F. Beat yolks briskly with a fork. In a separate bowl beat whites until frothy; add water, salt, and pepper and beat until soft peaks form; fold gently into yolks. Heat butter in an 8″ omelet pan with a heatproof handle over moderate heat until bubbly but not brown; tip pan so butter coats bottom and sides. Pour in eggs and cook, uncovered, without stirring 5 minutes until underside is pale golden. Transfer to oven and bake, uncovered, 12–15 minutes until puffy and delicately browned. Loosen omelet with a spatula, divide in half, using 2 forks, invert on a heated platter, and turn out. Or crease center with a spatula and fold omelet in half as you tip out of pan.

NPS: 210 C, 565 mg CH, 745 mg S*

VARIATIONS

Recipes too flexible for meaningful nutritional count.

Filled Soufflé Omelet: When omelet comes from oven, sprinkle filling over surface (the half nearest pan handle) and fold as above. Or fold filling into eggs *just before* cooking. (See Some Fillings for Savory Omelets.)

Sweet Soufflé Omelet: Prepare as directed but omit salt and pepper, and beat 1/4 cup sugar into egg whites. Cook as directed, sprinkle with sugar, and top with a favorite dessert sauce.

ONION FRITTATA

2–4 servings ▨

An Italian omelet that is browned on both sides.

1 medium-size Bermuda onion, peeled and sliced paper thin
3 tablespoons olive or other cooking oil
1 clove garlic, peeled and crushed
4 eggs, lightly beaten
3/4 teaspoon salt
1/8 teaspoon pepper
1 teaspoon basil
2 tablespoons grated Parmesan cheese

Sauté onion in half the oil over moderately low heat 5–8 minutes until limp, not brown; add garlic and stir-fry 1 minute. Mix onion and garlic with eggs, seasonings, and cheese. Heat remaining oil in a heavy 9″ or 10″ skillet over moderate heat 1/2 minute, add egg mixture, and cook without stirring 3–4 minutes until browned underneath and just set on top. Cut in quarters, turn, and brown flip side 2–3 minutes.

NPS (2–4): 395–200 C, 550–275 mg CH, 1065–530 mg S*

Ham and Tomato Frittata: Omit onion; sauté 1/2 cup slivered prosciutto or cooked ham and 1 coarsely chopped, peeled, and seeded tomato in oil 5 minutes, then proceed as directed.

NPS (2–4): 445–220 C, 575–285 mg CH, 1595–800 mg S*

Artichoke Frittata: Omit onion; sauté 1/2 cup thinly sliced parboiled or drained canned artichoke hearts in oil 3–4 minutes, add garlic, and proceed as directed.

NPS (2–4): 370–185 C, 550–275 mg CH, 1030–515 mg S*

PIPERADE

4–6 servings

This Basque "omelet" is closer to scrambled eggs, cooked until soft and creamy and topped with onions, tomatoes, sweet peppers, and ham.

3 medium-size yellow onions, peeled and sliced thin
2 sweet green peppers, cored, seeded, and cut in strips 1/4" wide
1 sweet red pepper, cored, seeded, and cut in strips 1/4" wide
2 tablespoons lard, olive, or other cooking oil
3 tablespoons butter or margarine
1 clove garlic, peeled and crushed
4 medium-size ripe tomatoes, peeled, cored, seeded, and coarsely chopped
1 1/2 teaspoons salt
1/8 teaspoon pepper
1/2 cup cooked ham strips cut 1/4" wide and 2" long
8 eggs, lightly beaten

Stir-fry onions and pepper in lard and 1 tablespoon butter in a large, heavy skillet over moderately low heat about 10 minutes until limp, not brown. Add garlic and tomatoes and stir-fry 5–8 minutes until almost all liquid has evaporated. Add seasonings and ham and keep warm. Melt remaining butter in a heavy 10" skillet over moderately low heat, add eggs, and scramble *just* until set. Remove from heat, spread with ham mixture, and stir lightly into *surface* of eggs. Cut in wedges and serve. Good with crusty French bread and a crisp green salad.

NPS (4–6): 400 C, 590 mg CH, 1340 mg S*

Prepare as directed but just before spreading with ham mixture sprinkle with 1/4–1/3 cup coarsely grated Gruyère cheese.

NPS (4–6): 425–285 C, 595–395 mg CH, 1365–910 mg S*

SOUFFLÉS

Like omelets, soufflés have a reputation for being difficult. They aren't, once the basic technique is learned. Soufflés are nothing more than sauces into which beaten egg whites are folded. It is the air, whipped into the whites, that leavens soufflés, so the point is to achieve the greatest possible volume of whites and to maintain it. This is done by using a balloon whip or wire whisk (and, if you have one, an unlined copper bowl), also by lightening the base sauce a bit by *stirring in* 1/4–1/2 cup beaten whites before *folding in* the balance (see To Beat Whites and Folding In Beaten Egg Whites at the beginning of this chapter).

To Grease or Not to Grease the Soufflé Dish: Opinions are sharply divided. Some insist that soufflés climb to greater heights in greased and crumbed dishes; others say not, that it's like making a monkey climb a greased pole. Recipes in this book call for ungreased dishes and have produced cloud-high soufflés. But by all means, try both methods.

To Make a Top Hat Soufflé: Just before baking soufflé, insert a table knife into soufflé mixture about 1"–1 1/2" from rim of dish and draw a circle concentric with dish. When baked, soufflé center will puff way up, forming the top hat.

Note: Other soufflé recipes are included in the meat, poultry, seafood, vegetable, and dessert chapters.

BASIC CHEESE SOUFFLÉ

4 servings ⚖️

3 tablespoons butter or margarine
3 tablespoons flour
1 cup milk
1 1/4 cups coarsely grated Cheddar cheese or 3/4 cup coarsely grated Swiss or Gruyère cheese
3 eggs, separated
1 teaspoon salt
1/8 teaspoon pepper

Melt butter in a saucepan over moderate heat, blend in flour, slowly stir in milk, and heat, stirring, until thickened. Add cheese and stir until melted. Beat yolks lightly, blend in a little hot sauce, and return to pan; heat and stir 1–2 minutes over lowest heat. Off heat, mix in salt and pepper; lay a piece of wax paper flat on surface of sauce and cool to room temperature. Meanwhile, preheat oven to 350° F. Beat egg whites until stiff but not dry, stir about 1/4 cup into sauce, then fold in remaining whites. Spoon into an ungreased 5-cup soufflé dish and bake, uncovered, 35–40 minutes until puffy and browned. Serve at once, accompanied, if you like, with Mushroom Sauce or Tomato Sauce.

NPS: 335 C, 275 mg CH, 940 mg S*

VARIATIONS

⟊ **Herbed Cheese Soufflé:** Prepare as directed, but add any of the following to cheese sauce: 1 tablespoon minced fresh dill or parsley; 1 teaspoon oregano, basil, sage, thyme, tarragon, or marjoram. Same nutritional count as for Basic Cheese Soufflé.

Deviled Cheese Soufflé: Prepare as directed but to cheese sauce add: 1 teaspoon each Worcestershire sauce and prepared spicy brown mustard, 1 tablespoon ketchup, and 1/8 teaspoon cayenne pepper.

NPS: 345 C, 275 mg CH, 1010 mg S*

⟊ **Wine and Cheese Soufflé:** Prepare as directed but substitute 1/2 cup dry white wine for 1/2 cup of the milk. Serve, if you like, with hot Mornay Sauce (lightly laced with white wine).

NPS: 325 C, 270 mg CH, 925 mg S*

Cheese and Onion Soufflé: Prepare sauce as directed but before cooling mix in 1/2 cup thinly sliced Bermuda onion rings sautéed until limp, not brown. Cool sauce, fold in whites, and bake as directed.

NPS: 345 C, 275 mg CH, 940 mg S*

Some Additional Ways to Vary Cheese Soufflé: Prepare basic recipe as directed but before cooling cheese sauce mix in any of the following:
• 1/4–1/3 cup minced cooked ham, crisp crumbled bacon, or minced sautéed chicken livers
• 1/4 cup deviled ham or pâté
• 1/4 cup minced sautéed mushrooms and 2 tablespoons minced pimiento
• 1/3 cup minced cooked vegetable (asparagus, spinach, broccoli, zucchini, carrots, cauliflower, cabbage, or Brussels sprouts)
• 1/4 cup each sautéed minced yellow onion and sweet green or red peppers
• 1/4 cup minced ripe or green olives
• 1/4 cup minced cooked fish or shellfish
Recipes too flexible for meaningful nutritional count.

BAKED EGGS IN TOMATOES

4 servings ⟊ ☒

Nutritious diet fare.

2 large firm ripe tomatoes, halved crosswise
4 eggs
1/4 cup soft white bread crumbs
1/4 cup coarsely grated sharp Cheddar
1 tablespoon minced parsley
1/4 teaspoon salt
1/8 teaspoon pepper
2 tablespoons melted butter or margarine

Preheat oven to 425° F. Scoop pulp from tomatoes, then stand cut sides up in a greased 9″ piepan and bake, uncovered, 5–7 minutes. Break eggs, one at a time, into a custard cup and slide into a tomato. Mix crumbs, cheese, parsley, salt, and pepper, sprinkle over eggs, and drizzle with butter. Bake, uncovered, about 15 minutes until eggs are just set and topping golden.

NPS: 185 C, 295 mg CH, 325 mg S*

VARIATIONS

⟊ **Low-Calorie Baked Eggs in Tomatoes:** Prepare as directed but omit drizzling of butter.

NPS: 130 C, 280 mg CH, 265 mg S*

⟊ **Baked Eggs in Toast Cups:** Prepare 4 toast cups.* Slide an egg into each cup, sprinkle with topping, drizzle with butter, and bake 15–20 minutes at 350° F. until eggs are set. Good with hot Cheese or Mushroom Sauce.

NPS: 260 C, 310 mg CH, 470 mg S*

STUFFED EGGS BAKED IN CHEESE SAUCE

4 servings

1 recipe Basic Stuffed Eggs or Deviled Eggs
2 tablespoons butter or margarine
2 tablespoons flour
1 cup milk
1/2 teaspoon salt
1/8 teaspoon pepper
1 teaspoon Worcestershire sauce
1/2 teaspoon prepared mild yellow mustard
1 cup coarsely grated sharp Cheddar cheese

Preheat oven to 350° F. Arrange eggs 1 layer deep in buttered 9″ piepan or *au gratin* dish. Melt butter over moderate heat in a small saucepan; blend in flour, slowly add milk and seasonings, and heat and stir until thickened; add cheese, stirring until melted. Pour over eggs and bake, uncovered, 20–30 minutes until bubbly; if you like, brown lightly under broiler.

NPS: 345 C, 465 mg CH, 805 mg S*

VARIATIONS

Stuffed Eggs in Mushroom Sauce: Prepare as directed but substitute 1½ cups Mushroom Sauce for the cheese sauce; if you like, sprinkle with ¼ cup grated Cheddar just before baking.

NPS: 390 C, 450 mg CH, 585 mg S*
NPS (with cheddar): 315 C, 455 mg CH, 630 mg S*

Baked Stuffed Eggs the French Way: Prepare as directed, but substitute 1½ cups Béchamel, Velouté, Suprême, or Mornay Sauce for the cheese sauce.

NPS (with Béchamel): 275 C, 450 mg CH, 1000 mg S*
NPS (with Velouté): 335 C, 455 mg CH, 890 mg S*
NPS (with Suprême): 350 C, 475 mg CH, 755 mg S*
NPS (with Mornay): 325 C, 460 mg CH, 630 mg S*

EGGS AND BROCCOLI AU GRATIN

4 servings

1 (2-pound) bunch broccoli, parboiled
4 hard-cooked eggs, peeled and quartered
3 tablespoons butter or margarine
3 tablespoons flour
¼ teaspoon powdered mustard
¼ teaspoon salt
⅛ teaspoon white pepper
1½ cups milk
1½ teaspoons Worcestershire sauce
2 cups coarsely grated sharp Cheddar cheese

Preheat oven to 350° F. Drain broccoli well and arrange in an ungreased shallow 2-quart casserole; distribute eggs evenly over broccoli. Melt butter in a saucepan over moderately low heat, blend in flour, mustard, salt, and pepper; slowly stir in milk and cook and stir until thickened and smooth. Mix in Worcestershire sauce and 1½ cups cheese. Pour sauce evenly over broccoli and eggs, top with remaining cheese, and bake, uncovered, 20–30 minutes until lightly browned and bubbly. Serve hot as a main dish.

NPS: 535 C, 370 mg CH, 745 mg S*

BACON AND EGG PIE

6–8 servings

1 recipe Flaky Pastry II
1 egg, lightly beaten (glaze)

FILLING
12 slices crisply cooked bacon
6 eggs
¼ teaspoon salt
⅛ teaspoon pepper

Preheat oven to 425° F. Prepare pastry as directed, roll out into 2 (12″) circles, and fit one in a 9″ piepan. Lay 6 slices bacon over bottom crust. Break eggs, one at a time, into a cup and gently slide on top of bacon, spacing evenly. Top with remaining bacon. Dampen rim of bottom crust; cut steam slits in top crust and fit over filling. Press edges of pastry together, trim, and crimp to seal. Brush with glaze, being careful not to cover steam slits, and bake 25–30 minutes until golden. Serve hot or cold.

NPS (6–8): 505–390 C, 330–245 mg CH, 740–555 mg S*

RANCH-STYLE EGG AND POTATO "PIE"

4 servings

4 medium-size potatoes, peeled
¼ cup cooking oil
1 teaspoon salt
⅛ teaspoon pepper
2 tablespoons minced chives
1 cup coarsely grated Cheddar cheese
8 eggs

Slice potatoes paper thin into a bowl of cold water; drain and pat dry on paper toweling. Heat oil 1–2 minutes over moderately low heat in a large, heavy skillet or flameproof casserole, spread potato slices over bottom, and press down with a pancake turner. Sauté about 30 minutes, without stirring, until a crisp brown crust forms on bottom and potatoes are tender. Meanwhile, preheat oven to 350° F. Sprinkle salt, pepper, chives, and cheese over potatoes. Break eggs, one at a time, into a cup and gently slide on top of cheese, spacing evenly. Bake, uncovered, 5–8 minutes until eggs are cooked to your liking. Cut into portions, including an egg with each, and serve.

NPS: 505 C, 575 mg CH, 870 mg S*

BASIC CREAMED EGGS

4 servings ☒

2 cups hot Medium White Sauce
1 teaspoon Worcestershire sauce (optional)
1 tablespoon minced parsley
6 hard-cooked eggs, peeled and quartered or
  sliced thin
Salt to taste

Mix all ingredients and serve over hot buttered toast or English muffins, boiled rice or frizzled ham, cooked asparagus or broccoli, or in puff pastry shells.

NPS: 325 C, 460 mg CH, 555 mg S*

VARIATIONS

Eggs in Cheese Sauce: Mix 1 cup coarsely grated sharp Cheddar cheese and 1 teaspoon prepared mild yellow mustard into sauce along with above seasonings, heat and stir until cheese melts, fold in eggs, and serve.

NPS: 440 C, 490 mg CH, 745 mg S*

Scalloped Eggs: Prepare as directed, then layer into a buttered 1½-quart casserole with 1½ cups soft buttered bread crumbs, beginning and ending with eggs. Top with ⅓ cup fine buttered crumbs and bake, uncovered, ½ hour at 350° F. until browned and bubbly.

NPS: 570 C, 520 mg CH, 870 mg S*

Curried Eggs: Prepare as directed but omit parsley; add 2 teaspoons curry powder warmed 3–5 minutes in 2 tablespoons butter over low heat, and, if you like, ¼ cup toasted slivered almonds. Serve over rice.

NPS: 375 C, 475 mg CH, 615 mg S*

Creamed Eggs, Bacon, and Onion: Prepare as directed but omit parsley and add ½ cup each minced sautéed onion and crisp crumbled bacon.

NPS: 415 C, 470 mg CH, 780 mg S*

Some Additional Ways to Vary Basic Creamed Eggs: Prepare recipe as directed, then just before serving mix in any of the following:
• ¾–1 cup diced cooked ham, tongue, luncheon meat, or sliced cooked sausages
• ¾–1 cup chipped beef
• 6–8 coarsely chopped sautéed chicken livers or 3–4 sautéed lamb kidneys
• ¾–1 cup tiny whole shelled and deveined boiled shrimp, or minced cooked crab meat or lobster
• ¾–1 cup flaked tuna or salmon
• 1 peeled and diced ripe avocado
• ¾–1 cup leftover cooked vegetables (peas, diced carrots, corn, lima beans, asparagus tips, cauliflower or broccoli flowerets)
• 1–1½ cups diced boiled potatoes
Recipes too flexible for meaningful nutritional count.

DEVILED EGGS

4 servings ⚖

6 hard-cooked eggs, peeled and halved
  lengthwise
¼ cup mayonnaise
2 teaspoons lemon juice
¼ teaspoon powdered mustard or 1 teaspoon
  prepared spicy brown mustard
1 teaspoon grated yellow onion (optional)
1 teaspoon Worcestershire sauce
¼ teaspoon salt
Pinch white pepper

SOME SUGGESTED GARNISHES
Parsley, watercress, tarragon, dill, or chervil
  sprigs
Minced chives, dill, or parsley
Pimiento strips
Sliced pitted ripe or green olives
Capers
Rolled anchovy fillets
Paprika

Mash yolks well, mix in remaining ingredients, mound into whites, and chill ½ hour. Garnish as desired and serve.

NPS: 220 C, 420 mg CH, 330 mg S*

VARIATIONS

Deviled Eggs with Cheese: Prepare yolk mixture as directed, then beat in ⅓ cup finely grated sharp Cheddar, Parmesan, or Gruyère cheese or crumbled blue cheese.

NPS: 255 C, 430 mg CH, 390 mg S*

⚖ **Anchovy Eggs:** Prepare yolk mixture as directed but omit mustard; mix in instead 2 tablespoons anchovy paste.

NPS: 235 C, 425 mg CH, 405 mg S*

⚖ **Curried Deviled Eggs:** Prepare yolk mixture as directed but increase grated onion to 2 teaspoons and add 2 teaspoons curry powder.

NPS: 225 C, 420 mg CH, 330 mg S*

BASIC STUFFED EGGS

4 servings ⚖

6 hard-cooked eggs, peeled and halved
  lengthwise
¼–⅓ cup milk, heavy, light, or sour cream

¼ teaspoon salt
Pinch white pepper

Mash yolks well, blend in remaining ingredients, and mound into whites, using a pastry bag fitted with a large decorative tip if you like. Chill ½ hour, garnish as desired, and serve.

NPS (with milk): 125 C, 415 mg CH, 245 mg S*
NPS (with heavy cream): 170 C, 430 mg CH, 245 mg S*
NPS (with light cream): 145 C, 420 mg CH, 245 mg S*
NPS (with sour cream): 150 C, 415 mg CH, 245 mg S*

Some Quick Stuffing Variations: Blend any of the following into yolk mixture, adjusting liquid as needed to make a creamy consistency:
• ¼ cup ground cooked ham, tongue, luncheon meat, chicken, or chicken livers
• ¼ cup crisp crumbled bacon
• ¼ cup minced cooked fish or shellfish
• ¼ cup red caviar and 2 teaspoons lemon juice
• 2 tablespoons anchovy paste and 1 tablespoon minced capers
• ¼ cup grated sharp cheese (any kind) and 2 tablespoons minced chutney or nuts
• ¼ cup puréed cooked spinach, asparagus, beets, peas, or carrots
Recipes too flexible for meaningful nutritional count.

EGG CROQUETTES

4 servings

4 hard-cooked eggs, peeled and minced
⅔ cup cold Thick White Sauce
½ cup soft white bread crumbs
½ teaspoon salt
⅛ teaspoon pepper
1 egg, lightly beaten
½ cup toasted fine bread crumbs
Shortening or cooking oil for deep fat frying

Mix hard-cooked eggs, sauce, soft crumbs, salt, and pepper. Using about ¼ cup for each, shape into 6 logs about 3″ long and 1″ across. Dip in beaten egg, then crumbs to coat well. Cover and chill ½ hour. Meanwhile, heat fat in a deep fat fryer with basket and deep fat thermometer over moderate heat to 375° F. Fry rolls, a few at a time, about 1½ minutes until golden. Drain on paper toweling and serve. Good with Tomato Sauce.

NPS: 280 C, 365 mg CH, 650 mg S*

Cheese Croquettes: Omit hard-cooked eggs; while sauce is still hot, stir in 1 cup coarsely grated sharp Cheddar cheese. Cool, add crumbs and seasonings, and proceed as directed.

NPS: 315 C, 120 mg CH, 755 mg S*

EGGS IN ASPIC

4 servings ⚖

2 cups aspic* made with beef or chicken broth
2–3 tablespoons Madeira or cognac
Truffle or pimiento cutouts
4 firm poached eggs, chilled

Mix aspic and Madeira, chill until syrupy, then spoon 2–3 tablespoons into each of 4 ungreased custard cups or ramekins, swirling round to coat sides and bottom; chill until firm. Keep remaining aspic syrupy. Decorate chilled aspic with cutouts, trim poached eggs to fit cups, and arrange on aspic, attractive side down. Fill cups with aspic and chill until firm. Unmold and sprig with watercress. Serve with mayonnaise as a light main course or salad.

NPS: 105 C, 270 mg CH, 540 mg S*

⚖ **Stuffed or Deviled Eggs in Aspic:** Prepare as directed but substitute 2 stuffed or deviled eggs (4 halves) for the poached, arranging stuffed sides down on aspic.

NPS: 65 C, 135 mg CH, 475 mg S*

⚖ **Tarragon Eggs in Aspic:** Begin as directed, chilling a layer of aspic in ramekins; decorate with fresh tarragon leaves and truffle diamonds, add 2 paper-thin slices boiled ham cut to fit, top with a little aspic, and chill until tacky. Add a poached or hard-cooked egg (with end sliced off so yolk shows), fill with aspic, and chill until firm.

NPS: 130 C, 280 mg CH, 750 mg S*

⚖ **Hard-Cooked Eggs in Aspic:** Prepare as directed, substituting medium-size hard-cooked eggs for the poached. Cut off about ⅓ of ends and place cut sides down in cups so yolks show when eggs are unmolded.

NPS: 75 C, 185 mg CH, 440 mg S*

PICKLED EGGS

4–6 servings ⚖ ¢

Good picnic fare.

1½ cups white vinegar
1 teaspoon mixed pickling spices
1 clove garlic, peeled and bruised
1 bay leaf
6 hard-cooked eggs, peeled

Simmer vinegar and spices, uncovered, 10 minutes; cool slightly, add garlic and bay leaf. Pack eggs into a screw-top jar, add vinegar mixture, cover, and cool to room temperature. Refrigerate 7–10 days before serving—longer for stronger flavor. Serve as an appetizer or with cold cuts and salad.

NPS (4–6): 130–85 C, 410–275 mg CH, 105–70 mg S*

VARIATION

⚖ **Pennsylvania Dutch "Red Beet" Eggs:** Prepare as directed but add 6–8 small whole boiled and peeled beets to eggs before adding vinegar. Marinate 2–3 days before serving.

NPS (4–6): 140–95 C, 410–275 mg CH, 120–80 mg S*

CHEESE AND DAIRY

No one knows who first made cheese, though legend credits an early wayfarer whose milk ration, carried in a skin pouch, turned to curds and whey. That ancient cheese would have been much like our cottage cheese. Pungent ripened cheeses arrived later, again by accident. A shepherd boy, the story goes, found that a cheese he'd left in a cave was covered with mold. He tried it, liked it, and blue cheese came into being.

Cheese is made from the milk or cream of many animals; some is unripened (cottage and cream cheese), some is mold-ripened (the whole family of blues), some bacteria-ripened (Limburger, Liederkranz). Cheeses range from hard to soft, bland to overpowering, white to dark brown. All are excellent meat substitutes because of their high-quality protein, vitamin, and mineral content. Depending upon whether cheese is made from skim or whole milk or cream, it can be low in calories or loaded.

The kinds of cheese available today are bewildering. France alone produces hundreds, including most of the great classics. Italy, Holland, England, Switzerland, Scandinavia, America, and Canada are also major producers. America's appetite for cheese has become so insatiable that cheese shops are proliferating and supermarket dairy counters are offering obscure imported varieties as well as the familiar domestics.

Confronted with dozens of cheeses, the buyer wonders which to try. Which to use in cooking, which to serve with cocktails, which to offer as dessert. The best way to bring order to the confusion is to group cheeses by type and use. But first, some oft-used terms defined:

Pasteurized Cheese

America's cheese, like its other dairy products, is pasteurized. This means, of course, that the cheese is wholesome; but it also means that the organisms responsible for the cheese's character have been destroyed and that the color, texture, and flavor won't change much as the cheese ages.

Unpasteurized (Raw-Milk) Cheese

The U.S. Food and Drug Administration restricts the sale of cheeses made from raw milk. By law, no unpasteurized cheese may be imported unless it has been aged for at least 60 days (the aging kills harmful bacteria) and most scrupulous cheese-makers and exporters comply with the law, air-shipping their cheeses to America on the 61st day (if you see *lait cru* on a French cheese label, you will know that that particular cheese was made from raw milk). Many of France's finest cheeses (Brie, Camembert, etc.) are made from unpasteurized milk and aged for less than 60 days, so to taste them at their best, you must go to France.

Process Cheese

Watered-down pasteurized cheese; preservatives, emulsifiers, artificial coloring, and flavoring are often added.

Process Cheese Food

Further watered-down and adulterated pasteurized cheese, which in some instances isn't cheese at all.

SOME POPULAR CHEESES GROUPED BY TYPE AND USE

Soft, Unripened Cheeses

(Highly perishable): Serve slightly chilled; curd cheeses can be served anytime or used in cooking. The cream cheeses, teamed with fresh berries or tart preserves, make elegant desserts, especially if accompanied by chilled champagne or moderately sweet white wine. Grouped here by country of origin, are some of the most popular soft, unripened cheeses:

FRANCE: *Fromage Blanc* (bland and creamy-crumbly) . . . *Gervais* (sour, doubly rich cream cheese) . . . *Petit-Suisse* (mild, doubly rich cream cheese) . . . *Neufchâtel* (soft cream cheese, pungent if ripe).

ITALY: *Ricotta* (fine-curded cousin of cottage cheese; now available in whole- and skim-milk American versions).

U.S.A.: *Cottage, Pot, and Farmer Cheese* (bland, sour curd cheeses; *cottage cheese* is moistest, especially cream-style; *pot cheese* is next, and *farmer cheese* the driest; all are now available in large and small curd types, low-salt and/or low-fat varieties, also fruit- and vegetable-flavored) . . . *Cream Cheese* (bland and buttery).

Soft, Ripened Cheeses

Serve at room temperature. Excellent with fruit, wine, and French bread between the main course and dessert; also good before dinner with cocktails. (*Note:* Cheese crusts are not cut away but eaten unless they are unusually moldy or soiled.) Included in this group are France's heavenly *double creams* (containing 60–74 per cent butterfat) and *triple creams* (containing 75 per cent butterfat or more!). *Compatible Fruits:* Apples, pears, peaches, grapes. *Compatible Wines:* Dry reds, *except* for Liederkranz and Limburger, which are better with beer. Listed here, according to country of origin, are some of the more popular soft, ripened cheeses:

BELGIUM: *Limburger* (creamy-firm and strong enough "to blow a safe"; not for the meek).

DENMARK: *Crema Dania* (also called *Crema Danica;* rich, creamy, and zippy when ripe; tastes faintly like blue cheese).

FRANCE: *Boursin* (a triple-cream cheese flavored with garlic and/or herbs and black peppercorns) . . . *Brie* (golden, creamy,

and if perfectly ripened, neither bland nor pungent) . . . *Brillat Savarin* (an extra-buttery triple cream) . . . *Camembert* (an ivory-hued, butter-soft Norman cheese that may be mild or strong, depending upon aging) . . . *Chèvres* (an entire family of soft, creamy cheeses made of goat's milk that includes the large logs known as *Bûcheron,* the tiny dry *Crottin de Chavignol,* the rolls wrapped in grape leaves or rolled in ashes known as *Montrachet,* and various other cones, pyramids, and logs, some steeped in *marc* [brandy], herbs, or olive oil. It's estimated that there are as many as 75 different *chèvres*) . . . *Explorateur* (a buttery triple cream) . . . *Livarot* (a round, orange-rinded cheese bound with five strands of wild grass, which accounts for its nickname, "the colonel"; one of Normandy's oldest cheeses, Livarot, when properly ripe, is creamy and ammoniac in flavor) . . . *Reblochon* (a flat, soft disc made from the rich second milking of cows that graze Alpine meadows) . . . *Tomme* (a large family of Brie-like cheeses from the Haute-Savoie made of goat's, sheep's, or cow's milk) . . . *Vacherin* (a generic name for several soft, creamy cheeses that may be plain or seasoned; they come from the French and Swiss Alps).

ITALY: *Caprini di Capra* (a smooth, soft, snowy goat cheese shaped like a little log) . . . *Mascarpone* or *Mascherpone* (a mild, nutty triple cream cheese that's good with fresh berries; some fancy cheese shops now layer it into cocktail loaves with Gorgonzola).

U.S.A.: *Liederkranz* (very strong, very creamy).

Semisoft Cheeses

Serve at room temperature. Excellent between the main course and dessert, accompanied by fruit and wine. Also good as anytime snacks and as cocktail party fare. (*Note:* Serve cheeses in the rind [unless it is unsightly] but remove rind before eating.) Fontina, mozzarella, and Monterey Jack are excellent cooking cheeses because they melt smoothly; feta is superb in salads or omelets. *Compatible Fruits:* Tart apples, crisp pears, grapes; feta is especially good with dried figs or apricots and pistachio nuts. *Compatible Wines:* Dry, full-bodied reds except for feta, which is better with a white retsina. Listed below, country by country, are some of the great semisoft cheeses:

CANADA: *Oka* (smooth, mellow, mild).

DENMARK: *Danbo* (a mild, nutty, Gruyère-like cheese with tiny holes).

FRANCE: *Morbier* (a two-layer, moderately pungent cheese with the morning milk forming one layer and the richer evening milk the second; the two are separated by a fine layer of ash, which shows in the middle of the cheese as a horizontal gray-blue line) . . . *Muenster* (sharp golden round of cheese, sometimes with caraway seeds) . . . *Pont l'Evêque* (France's most important cheese after Brie, Camembert, and Roquefort; it is square, pale, and piquant) . . . *Port du Salut* (light yellow and buttery but robust).

GERMANY: *Tilsit* (the color of cream, full of small "eyes," and fairly sharp).

GREECE: *Feta* (snowy, crumbly goat's or sheep's milk cheese preserved in brine).

ITALY: *Bel Paese* (mellow, pale yellow) . . . *Fontina* (full, firmish, faintly smoky, ivory-hued ewe's milk cheese) . . . *Mozzarella* (the delicate white pizza cheese, made with a mix of whole and skim milk).

NORWAY: *Jarlsberg* (mild, white to pale yellow cheese akin to Emmentaler; also available in low-fat versions).

SPAIN: *Manchego* (strong, salty mountain cheese).

SWITZERLAND: *Appenzeller* (buttery, slightly sharp cheese with tiny holes; scented with herbs or spices and soaked in cider or wine) . . . *Raclette* (mild, exquisitely melting cheese that's in with the *après-ski* crowd; it's melted via small braziers, then scraped onto boiled new potatoes and accompanied by pickles).

U.S.A.: *Monterey Jack* (a pale Cheddar-type made with skim or partially skim milk that comes from Monterey County, California) . . . *Muenster* (paler and blander than its French counterpart).

Firm Cheeses

Serve at room temperature. Good anytime as snacks, also between the main course and dessert with fruit and wine. These are cooking favorites because of their robust flavor and smooth-melting quality. *Compatible Fruits:* Apples, pears, grapes, plums. *Compatible Wines:* Full-bodied dry reds except for the Cheddars, which are better with beer, ale, or stout. Particularly popular firm cheeses are listed here according to country of origin:

BULGARIA: *Kashkaval* (salty, crumbly white sheep's milk cheese).

CANADA: *Cheddar* (a big family ranging from pale to dark, and mild to strong).

ENGLAND: *Cheddar* (again a huge variety) . . . *Cheshire* (rich, zesty red or white cheese of the Cheddar type; popular for Welsh Rabbit) . . . *Gloucester* (there are two—single and double, mild and sharp; both are velvety) . . . *Lancashire* (white with lots of bite; when young, it is mellow and butter-smooth) . . . *Leicester* (bright orange-rose, crumbly, sharp, and lemony) . . . *Wensleydale* (sharp pale yellow cheese that tastes of butter).

ITALY: *Provolone* (smoky-mellow, pale yellow giant trussed with rope and swung from the rafters).

NORWAY: *Gjetost* (a curious, sweet-salty, fudge-textured brown cheese made of caramelized goat's milk; it's a breakfast favorite).

NETHERLANDS: *Edam* (mild, golden "cannonball" cheese coated with red wax) . . . *Gouda* (bland, creamy cheese much like Edam; well aged, it is crumbly and piquant).

SWITZERLAND: *Gruyère* (rich, nutty-sweet, cream-colored cheese shot with small "eyes"; superb for cooking. *Note:* Wonderful *Gruyères* are also made in France) . . . *Swiss* or *Emmentaler* (pale ivory to tan cheese with big holes; it is nutty-sharp but has a sweet aftertaste; the "fondue" cheese).

U.S.A.: *Cheddar* (America makes a wonderful variety of Cheddars; among the best are Colby, Coon, Herkimer, Vermont, and Wisconsin).

WALES: *Caerphilly* (smooth, white, and salty).

The "Blues"

Serve at room temperature. Good with cocktails before dinner; delicious with fruit, rough bread, and wine between the entree and dessert; excellent crumbled into salads, salad dressings, casseroles, and omelets. *Compatible Fruits:* Apples and pears. *Compatible Wines:* Robust dry reds except for Stilton, which is committed to vintage port. Listed here, country by country, are the best-known "blues":

DENMARK: *Danish Blue* (salty, sharp, white cheese with generous blue-green marbling) . . . *Saga Blue* (mild, creamy, and soft with limited blue veining).

ENGLAND: *Blue Wensleydale* (mellow but sharp; blue-green veins) . . . *Stilton* (oyster-white, blue-green-veined cheese that's milder than other blues; it has a brown crust and a vaguely Cheddarish flavor).

FRANCE: *Bleu d'Auvergne* (smooth, full-bodied, and mellow to sharp) . . . *Bleu de Bresse* (mellow, buttery, blue-veined cheese with a white crust) . . . *Roquefort* ("the Queen of the Blues"; made of ewe's milk, it is crumbly, creamy-white with blue-green mottling; extra-strong).

ITALY: *Gorgonzola* (wonderfully biting, buttery cheese with green veins).

U.S.A.: *Maytag Blue* (a superb white cheese with limited blue marbling; available in specialty cheese shops and via mail directly from the plant in Iowa).

Hard ("Grating") Cheeses

Except for Parmesan (good eaten out of hand), these are used almost altogether as toppings (soup and pasta) or to heighten the flavor of sauces, salads, and casseroles. Use sparingly. The favorites are:

ITALY: *Asiago* (a zesty cheese reminiscent of Pecorino) . . . *Parmesan* (grainy, golden, and the foundation of Italian cuisine) . . . *Pecorino* (sharp sheep's milk cheese not unlike Parmesan) . . . *Romano* (a sheep's milk cheese similar to but more pungent than Parmesan).

SWITZERLAND: *Sapsago* (a hard, conical green cheese, sour and pungent with the flavor of dried Alpine clover).

Some Tips on Cooking with Cheese

• Use low to moderate heat. Cheese becomes rubbery, tough, and indigestible when cooked too long or at too high a heat.
• Use well-aged cheeses for cooking—especially for sauces and fondues, where smoothness counts. Badly aged cheeses will clump and separate and nothing can be done to bring them back together. Should this happen, it's best to discard the rubbery clumps and thicken the sauce with a flour paste.
• When cheeses are to be melted into a sauce, coarsely grate or dice.
• Use strong cheeses sparingly so their flavors don't dominate.

Some Tips on Serving Cheese

In General:
• Serve soft, unripened cheeses cold, *but all others at room temperature.* Bringing cheese to room temperature can take from 1/2 to 3 hours, depending on the cheese and the weather. Soft cheeses warm faster than hard, small cheeses faster than large. All, of course, come to room temperature faster in hot weather than in cold.
• Serve cheeses in their rinds or crusts unless unsightly. Crusts are usually edible; rinds are not.
• Present cheese on a simple board, wooden tray, or marble slab, not on crystal, china, or silver, which are incompatible with its earthiness.
• Put out only what cheese you expect to be eaten.
• Allow plenty of space between cheeses on a board and don't group the strongs with the milds. Provide a separate knife for each cheese.
• Don't clutter a cheese board with garnishes, which will only wilt and get smeared with cheese. The best garnish is no garnish.
• Choose simple rough breads (French or Italian) and unseasoned, unsalted crackers for cheese. Highly seasoned ones overpower the cheese.
• Serve breads and crackers separately, not on the cheese board.

Before Dinner:
• Serve 1 or, at most, 2 cheeses—rich or sharp ones (blue or Brie, perhaps) that guests aren't apt to overeat. It's easy to nibble away at bland cheeses until the appetite's gone.

At Cocktail Parties:
• Vary the cheeses, striking a balance between hard and soft, sharp and bland.
• Avoid the superstrong Limburger and Liederkranz. In a hot crowded room, they'll soon smell to high heaven.
• Put out plenty of cheese (1/4–1/2 pound per guest is a good estimate) and in whole wheels or 2–3- pound slabs so there will be enough to go around.

At the End of a Meal:
• Suit the cheese to the meal. If dinner has been rich, cheese is out of order. It is also inappropriate following an Oriental or Indian meal. But after a French, Italian, Viennese, or Scandinavian meal, it is perfect. Elegant menus deserve queenly cheeses, rougher fare, coarser cheeses. As a general rule, French cheeses are best with French wines, Italian cheeses with Italian wines,

and English or Nordic cheeses with beer or ale.
• Set out a single tray of cheese and bowl of fruit from which guests can help themselves.

WELSH RABBIT

4 servings

1 tablespoon butter or margarine
1/2 cup milk, ale, or beer
1/2 teaspoon powdered mustard
Pinch cayenne pepper
1 tablespoon Worcestershire sauce
3/4 pound sharp Cheddar cheese, coarsely grated

Heat butter, milk, mustard, cayenne, and Worcestershire sauce in the top of a double boiler or chafing dish over *just* simmering water 7–10 minutes. Add cheese, a little at a time, stirring constantly until smooth and quite thick. Remove from heat immediately and serve over hot buttered toast.

NPS (with milk): 390 C, 100 mg CH, 615 mg S*

TOMATO-CHEESE RABBIT

6 servings   ⚖

2 tablespoons butter or margarine
1/4 cup unsifted flour
1/4 teaspoon oregano
1/4 teaspoon basil
1/2 teaspoon salt
1/4 teaspoon cayenne pepper
1 cup light cream
1 tablespoon onion juice
1/2 cup coarsely grated sharp Cheddar cheese
1 cup tomato juice
1/8 teaspoon baking soda

Melt butter in a small saucepan over moderate heat and blend in flour, herbs, salt, and pepper. Mix in cream and heat, stirring, until thickened and smooth. Turn heat to low, add onion juice and Cheddar, and heat, stirring, until cheese is melted. Meanwhile, in a separate small saucepan, bring tomato juice to a boil over high heat; off heat, stir in soda. Add tomato juice slowly to cheese sauce, stirring constantly. Serve over hot buttered toast.

NPS: 180 C, 45 mg CH, 395 mg S*

CHEESE FONDUE

4 servings

Sometimes, despite all precautions, a fondue will "lump." The cheese, not the cook, is usually to blame. If the cheese is poorly aged or not *Swiss* Gruyère or Emmentaler, it may never melt smoothly. Another possible culprit is too intense a heat, which will cause the cheese to "string." Whether you use an electric fondue pot or one fueled with a denatured alcohol burner, control the heat carefully. The Swiss like to drink kirsch with fondue (usually a pony halfway through the proceedings) and to follow with broiled sausage and crisp apples or pears.

2/3 pound well-aged imported Gruyère cheese, cut in 1/4" cubes
1/3 pound well-aged imported Emmentaler cheese, cut in 1/4" cubes
3 tablespoons flour
1/2 teaspoon paprika
1/4 teaspoon nutmeg or mace
1/8 teaspoon white pepper
1 clove garlic, peeled and halved
13/4 cups Neuchâtel, Chablis, or Riesling wine
1 tablespoon lemon juice
2 tablespoons kirsch
1/4 teaspoon baking soda (optional)
11/2 loaves day-old French bread, cut in 11/2" cubes (each should have crust on one side)

Toss cheeses in a bowl with flour, paprika, nutmeg, and pepper. Rub a 2-quart fondue *caquelon* or heavy round flameproof earthenware pot well with garlic. Add wine and heat, uncovered, over low heat until bubbles dot bottom of pot. Begin adding dredged cheeses (and any loose bits of flour and spices) by the handful, stirring with a wooden spoon in a figure 8 motion. Raise heat to moderate, continue stirring and adding cheese, flour, and spices a little at a time until all are in. Mix in lemon juice. At first, cheese will clump, but keep stirring. After 15–20 minutes, fondue should begin to "cream up." When fondue is smooth and bubbling gently, stir in kirsch and, for a lighter fondue, the soda. Set caquelon over its warmer and adjust heat so fondue bubbles *gently*—too much heat will make it rubbery. Serve with bread cubes and long-handled fondue forks. (*Note:* If fondue should separate and lump, return to moderately low stove heat and beat gently with a whisk; blend 1/2 teaspoon cornstarch with 1/4 cup wine [same kind as in recipe] and blend into fondue. If fondue becomes too thick, thin with a little warmed wine.)

NPS: 1010 C, 125 mg CH, 1345 mg S*

CHEDDAR-BEER FONDUE

4 appetizer servings; 2 entree servings

Much easier and almost as good as Swiss fondue. Somewhat lower in calories, too.

1 clove garlic, peeled and halved
1 tablespoon butter or margarine
2 cups coarsely grated sharp Cheddar cheese or ½ pound American cheese, finely diced
1 tablespoon flour
⅓ cup beer
1–2 tablespoons aquavit (optional)
1 small loaf day-old French or Italian bread, cut in 1″ cubes (each should have crust on one side)

Rub inside of the top of a double boiler with garlic. Add butter and melt over simmering water. Toss cheese and flour together, add to butter along with beer and, if you like, aquavit. Heat, stirring rapidly, until smooth. Transfer to a chafing dish, set over simmering water, and serve with crusts of bread, long-handled fondue forks, and plenty of napkins.

NPS (2–4): 860–430 C, 140–70 mg CH, 140–70 mg S*

HOMEMADE COTTAGE CHEESE

1 quart ⚖

Rennet tablets, necessary for making cottage cheese, have disappeared from grocery shelves but are still available at health food stores.

1 gallon skim milk
½ cup sour cream
¼ penny-size rennet tablet crushed in 2 tablespoons cold water
1–1½ teaspoons salt
⅓ cup heavy cream (optional)

Warm milk over lowest heat in a large stainless-steel or enamel kettle to 70° F. (a household thermometer can be used to test temperature) or let stand, covered, at room temperature 2–3 hours. Blend ½ cup of this milk with sour cream, return to kettle, and mix well. Stir in rennet, cover with a dry towel, and let stand undisturbed at room temperature (about 70° F.) 12–18 hours until a firm curd forms (mixture will look set with whey visible around edges). With a long stainless-steel knife, cut curd in kettle into ½″ cubes; set kettle on a large, heavy rack *over* simmering water in a larger kettle and heat, uncovered, to 110°–115° F. (use a candy thermometer), stirring every 2–3 minutes. Maintain 110°–115° F. temperature for ½ hour, stirring every 5 minutes. Ladle into a colander lined with a double thickness of cheesecloth and let whey drain 2–3 minutes, lifting corners of cheesecloth occasionally, to move curd. Lift cheesecloth and curd, twisting top to form a bag, and plunge into cold water; move cloth gently to rinse curd. Drain and plunge into ice water; let stand 1–2 minutes. Lay bag of curd in a colander and drain well. Remove curd from cloth, season to taste with salt, and, if you like, mix in cream. Cover and chill before serving. Use within 2–3 days.

NP Cup: 405 C, 30 mg CH, 1260 mg S*

SWISS CHEESE PUFF

4 servings ¢

8 slices firm-textured white bread, trimmed of crusts
3 cups coarsely grated Swiss cheese, or sharp or mild Cheddar
3 eggs, lightly beaten
2 cups milk
1 teaspoon salt
⅛ teaspoon white pepper
2 tablespoons minced scallions
⅛ teaspoon paprika

Preheat oven to 300° F. Alternate layers of bread and cheese in a buttered shallow 1½-quart casserole, beginning with bread and ending with cheese. Mix all remaining ingredients except paprika and pour into casserole. Sprinkle with paprika and bake, uncovered, 35–40 minutes until puffed, golden, and *just* set (a silver knife inserted midway between center and rim should come out clean). Serve immediately.

NPS: 570 C, 300 mg CH, 1100 mg S*

QUICHE LORRAINE

10 appetizer servings; 6 entree servings

PASTRY
1 recipe Flaky Pastry I

FILLING
½ pound crisply cooked bacon, crumbled
½ pound Gruyère or Swiss cheese, coarsely grated
4 eggs, lightly beaten
1 teaspoon salt
⅛ teaspoon white pepper
Pinch cayenne pepper
⅛ teaspoon nutmeg (optional)
1½ cups light cream
1 tablespoon melted butter

Preheat oven to 425° F. Prepare pastry, roll into a 12″ circle, and fit into a 9″ piepan, making a high, fluted edge. Prick bottom and sides of pastry well with a fork; cover with wax paper and fill with uncooked rice or dried beans. Bake 5–7 minutes until firm but not brown, then cool slightly on a wire rack. Remove paper and rice. Sprinkle bacon and cheese evenly over pie shell. Mix together remaining ingredients and strain through a fine sieve. Place pie shell on partly pulled-out oven rack, then pour in egg mixture. Bake, uncovered, 15 minutes at 425° F., reduce heat to 350° F., and bake 10–15 minutes longer or until a knife inserted halfway between center and rim comes out clean. Cool on a wire rack 8–10 minutes before cutting into wedges. Serve as an appetizer or luncheon entree.

NPS (6–10): 755–450 C, 300–180 mg CH, 1370–820 mg S*

VARIATIONS

Roquefort Quiche: Prepare as directed, using 2 ounces Roquefort and 6 ounces Gruyère.

NPS (6–10): 745–445 C, 300–180 mg CH, 1510–905 mg S*

Spinach Quiche: Prepare as directed but omit bacon and reduce cheese to 1/4 pound; spread 1 pound finely chopped, *well-drained* cooked spinach over cheese before pouring in egg mixture.

NPS (6–10): 475–280 C, 250–150 mg CH, 740–445 mg S*

Quiche Niçoise: Prepare as directed but omit bacon; arrange thinly sliced tomatoes over crust, overlapping slices slightly; scatter with 1/3 cup thinly sliced ripe olives and sprinkle with 1/4 teaspoon garlic powder. Reduce amount of cheese to 1/4 pound and cream to 1 1/2 cups.

NPS (6–10): 470–280 C, 250–150 mg CH, 760–455 mg S*

Shellfish Quiche: Prepare as directed but substitute 1 cup well-drained minced shrimp, lobster, crab meat, or clams for the bacon. Make egg mixture using 1 cup heavy cream and 1/2 cup clam liquid instead of 1 3/4 cups cream.

NPS (6–10): 580–345 C, 300–180 mg CH, 870–520 mg S*

Swabian Onion and Caraway Tart: Prepare and bake pastry as directed; stir-fry 1 large peeled and thinly sliced Spanish onion and 2 teaspoons caraway seeds in 3 tablespoons butter 15 minutes over low heat until limp. Arrange half of onion over crust, add 1/4

pound crisply cooked, crumbled bacon, then top with remaining onion; pour in egg mixture and bake as directed.

NPS (6–10): 545–330 C, 260–155 mg CH, 1000–600 mg S*

CROQUE-MONSIEUR

2 servings

An egg-dipped, fried cheese and ham "sandwich" to be eaten with knife and fork.

4 thin slices firm-textured white bread, trimmed of crusts and buttered on one side
3 (1-ounce) packages Gruyère or Swiss cheese, coarsely grated
2 thin slices boiled ham, cut to fit bread
2 eggs lightly beaten with 2 tablespoons cold water
2–3 tablespoons butter or margarine
1/2 cup hot Medium White Sauce blended with 2 tablespoons finely grated Parmesan cheese

Sandwich cheese and ham between slices of bread pressing lightly, dip in egg, making sure edges are well coated, and brown on both sides in butter over moderate heat. Lift to warm plates and top with sauce.

NPS: 685 C, 410 mg CH, 1150 mg S*

VARIATION

Croque-Madame: Prepare as directed but substitute very thinly sliced white meat of chicken or turkey for the ham.

NPS: 680 C, 410 mg CH, 950 mg S*

CALZONE

4–8 servings

These Neapolitan filled pastries have relatives all over the world—Cornish pasties and empanadas, to name two. The ways to fill *calzone* are endless, but mozzarella cheese is a must for the classic versions.

1 recipe Pizza Dough
1/2 pound mozzarella cheese, coarsely grated
1/2 pound ricotta cheese
1/2 cup grated Parmesan cheese
1 egg, lightly beaten
3/4 teaspoon salt
1/4 teaspoon pepper
2 tablespoons minced parsley
2 tablespoons minced chives
1/2 teaspoon thyme
1 tablespoon olive oil (about)

Prepare pizza dough as directed and let rise. Meanwhile, combine all remaining ingredients except olive oil; cover and refrigerate.

When dough has doubled in bulk, preheat oven to 450° F. Punch dough down, divide into 4 equal parts, then roll, one at a time, into a circle 9″ across. Spoon ¼ of filling onto lower half of each circle, leaving a bottom margin of 1″: brush margin with cold water, fold upper half of pastry circle over filling, pressing edges together, then twist or crimp firmly to seal. (*Note:* It's important to seal the edges tightly, otherwise the cheese may bubble out during baking.) With a pancake turner, transfer *calzone* to oiled baking sheets, placing 2 on each sheet. Bake about 25 minutes until crisp and brown. Remove from oven, brush top of each with a little oil, and serve at once.

NPS (4–8): 850–425 C, 140–70 mg CH, 1450–725 mg S*

VARIATIONS

Calzone with Ham: Prepare as directed but reduce ricotta to ¼ pound and omit Parmesan cheese. After spooning filling onto lower halves of pastry circles, top each with 2 tablespoons julienned ham or *prosciutto.* Bake as directed.

NPS (4–8): 790–405 C, 130–70 mg CH, 1440–825 mg S*

Calzone with Chèvre: Prepare as directed but substitute any chèvre (goat cheese), crumbled, for the ricotta; omit egg and Parmesan.

NPS (4–8): 850–430 C, 95–45 mg CH, 1810–905 mg S*

CHEESE BLINTZES

1 dozen

½ cup sifted flour
¼ teaspoon salt
2 eggs, lightly beaten
¾ cup milk or a ½ and ½ mixture of milk and cold water
1 tablespoon melted butter or margarine
1–2 tablespoons butter or margarine

FILLING
1 pound cottage or pot cheese
2 egg yolks, lightly beaten
3–4 tablespoons sugar
⅛ teaspoon salt
⅛ teaspoon cinnamon
1–2 tablespoons milk (optional)

TOPPING
1 cup sour cream

Sift flour and salt into a bowl; mix eggs, milk, and melted butter, slowly add to flour, and beat until smooth. Butter bottom and sides of a heavy 6″ skillet and heat over moderately high heat until a drop of water will dance. Using about 2 tablespoons batter for each blintze, add to skillet and tip back and forth until bottom is evenly coated. Brown lightly on one side, about ½ minute, turn out, browned side up, on a kitchen towel or paper toweling. Cook remaining blintzes the same way. Mix filling ingredients, adding milk to moisten if needed. Place about 1½ tablespoons filling in center of each blintze, fold bottom up and sides in over filling, then roll up. Brown in remaining butter over moderate heat and serve with sour cream.

NP Blintz (with cottage cheese): 160 C, 110 mg CH, 270 mg S*
NP Blintz (with pot cheese): 145 C, 105 mg CH, 270 mg S*

VARIATION

Fruit Blintzes: Season filling to taste with finely grated lemon or orange rind and top with stewed fruit instead of sour cream. Recipe too flexible for meaningful nutritional count.

YOGURT

Legend has it that an angel told Abraham the secret of making yogurt. It may be so. Certainly this creamy cultured milk has been known since biblical times. Today, two bacteria (usually *Lactobacillus bulgaricus* and *Streptococcus thermophilus)* are used in yogurt-making to produce lactic acid in milk, which sours and thickens it into a soft curd. In India, the Middle East, and Eastern Europe, yogurt is made of cow, sheep, goat, buffalo, mare, even reindeer milk. But in America and Western Europe, cow's milk is preferred. In all instances, yogurt is more digestible than the fresh milk from which it was made.

HOMEMADE YOGURT

1 quart

For best results use commercial *unflavored* (plain) yogurt as a starter, not the gelatin-thickened variety. You can, of course, use homemade yogurt as a starter, but if you do, be sure it's good and fresh (no more than 3–4 days old). And every month or so, begin again with a fresh commercial starter. It's important to keep all implements and containers used for yogurt-making scrupulously clean.

1 quart whole, low-sodium or skim (nonfat) milk
⅓ cup nonfat dry milk powder
2 tablespoons plain yogurt

Sterilize a 1-quart wide-mouth preserving jar or prepare container of electric yogurt-maker as manufacturer directs; keep jar or container warm (about 110° F.). Combine ⅓ cup milk with milk powder; place in a large heavy saucepan, mix remaining milk in well. Set a candy thermometer in pan and heat slowly over moderately low heat until temperature reaches 190° F. Leave thermometer in pan, partly cover, and cool to 110° F. Blend yogurt with 2 tablespoons warm milk, then mix into milk in pan. If using an electric yogurt-maker, following manufacturer's directions at this point. If not, pour milk mixture into warm jar, cover tight with plastic food wrap or aluminum foil, and set in a warm, draft-free spot. You must keep the jar *undisturbed* for about 6–8 hours at a constant temperature of 105°–110° F. The best way to do so is to set jar in an insulated picnic chest along with 2 large jars of warm water (105°–110° F.); replenish warm water occasionally. When mixture is creamy-thick, refrigerate (it will keep for a week). About 185 calories per cup if made with whole or low-sodium milk, 145 calories per cup if made with skim milk.

V A R I A T I O N S

Recipes too flexible for meaningful nutritional count.

Fruit Yogurt: Mix 1 cup yogurt with 2–4 tablespoons fruit jam, jelly, or preserves or well-drained, sliced, chopped, or puréed fruit (small berries may be left whole).

Nut Yogurt: Mix 1 cup yogurt with 2–4 tablespoons finely chopped or sliced nuts (*marrons glacés* are particularly good).

Yogurt Cheese (Makes about 3 cups): Line a large sieve with a double thickness of cheesecloth and set over a large bowl. Ladle 1 quart yogurt into cloth, fold corners in toward middle, and twist tightly. Cover with aluminum foil and weight down with several heavy cans. Refrigerate overnight or at least 8 hours (the longer you let the yogurt drain, the thicker the cheese). Scrape cheese from cloth and store, tightly covered, in refrigerator (it will keep about 2 weeks). Use interchangeably with cottage or ricotta cheese.

DAIRY-LIKE SOYBEAN PRODUCTS

Inexpensive, protein-packed, low fat, and cholesterol-free, soy foods are assuming a major role in the American diet (some 52 million pounds of tofu were consumed in a single year recently). Soy foods are now being made into everything from burgers to ice cream and quiche to cheesecake. Among the more popular of them:

Tofu

(Also called *bean curd, soybean curd,* and *soy cheese):* This naturally pure, creamy white curd made from coagulated soy milk is a good substitute for eggs, cheese, and other dairy products, even meat. Most supermarkets now stock both the *firm* and the *soft* (look for them in the produce or dairy sections). Soy dairies and Oriental markets also sell *medium-firm* and *silken (kinugoshi) tofu,* this last unusually delicate and fine. There is also a *broiled tofu* (lightly mottled brown curd known as *yakidofu).* Most tofu is sold either water- or vacuum-packed (usually date-stamped) or as fresh cakes. Although most tofu will keep well 5–7 days if refrigerated, the fresher the better (once a package of tofu is opened, change the water in it daily and keep well covered). You can, if necessary, freeze tofu, although it will become chewy. Simply drain well, then wrap snugly in plastic food wrap (use within 6 months). *Note:* Thaw frozen tofu in a loosely covered sieve so water can drain off (cube or slice to speed thawing); also press it well in a dish towel to squeeze out additional water. Because of its chewy consistency, thawed frozen tofu makes an excellent meat substitute.

How to Cook with Tofu: Some recipes specify *firm tofu,* but in most instances, the *firm* and *soft* can be used interchangeably. As a general rule, *firm tofu* is best in recipes where you want cubes or slices to show (soups, omelets, salads, etc.), *soft tofu* where it is to be blended with other ingredients. (*Note:* Before using tofu, drain it very dry by standing 15 minutes on paper toweling; also pat it dry.) Tofu is wonderfully accommodating. It can be crumbled or mashed with your hands or a fork, beaten with an electric mixer, or puréed in an electric blender or food processor. *Tip:* It's best to work with a small amount (about ½ cup) at a time if you're crumbling or mashing the tofu; if using the firm variety, add ¼ cup liquid (that called for in a recipe, water, or soy milk) to speed things along.

Some Tofu Equivalent Measures

8 ounces cubed tofu = 1⅓ cups

8 ounces mashed tofu = 1 cup

---

8 ounces puréed tofu = 3/4 cup

8 ounces pressed and squeezed tofu = 2/3 cup

Tempeh

This light, springy, moist cake of fermented soy food is an Indonesian favorite; it's high in fiber, protein, and B vitamins, and its flavor ranges from *mild* (similar to mushrooms), to *medium* (closer to yeast bread), to *sharp* (like nippy cheese). Cottony threads run throughout the cake as do spots of mold. The best place to buy *tempeh?* A health food store; like tofu, *tempeh* should be tightly wrapped and refrigerated. Properly stored, it will keep 7–10 days. A particular specialty is *Dry-Roasted Tempeh.* To prepare, chop *tempeh* very fine, spread evenly on a jelly roll pan, and bake about 30 minutes at 250° F., stirring every 10 minutes, until evenly browned. Store in a tightly covered container in the refrigerator and add to salads, soufflés, quiches, bread or pastry doughs for crunch and an intense toasty flavor.

Soy Milk

(See Ingredients, Chapter 2): This creamy liquid contains no butterfat and is thus slightly thinner than milk. It can nonetheless be substituted for milk in many soups, sauces, and desserts. Soured soy milk can be used in place of buttermilk. *Note:* When heated, soy milk scorches and curdles more quickly than regular milk, so watch the pot carefully or heat it in a double boiler top set over simmering water.

TOFU AND BEAN SPROUTS IN SZECHUAN HOT SAUCE

4–6 servings ¢

Hot sauce (or *chili paste*), the traditional seasoning for many Szechuan and Hunan dishes, can be found in Oriental markets and specialty groceries.

1 pound firm tofu, drained
3 tablespoons rice flour or cornstarch
2 eggs, lightly beaten
1/2 cup peanut oil (about)
1 bunch scallions, trimmed; mince white parts, coarsely chop green tops, and keep the two separate
1 (1") cube fresh gingerroot, peeled and minced
1 large clove garlic, peeled and minced

1 medium-size sweet red or green pepper, cored, seeded, and cut in 1" squares
2 cups salt-free Vegetable Stock or chicken broth
2 teaspoons sugar
1 teaspoon hot sauce (chili paste) or 1/2–1 teaspoon crushed dried hot red chili peppers
2 tablespoons cornstarch
1/4 cup soy sauce
1 pound fresh bean sprouts, washed

Wrap tofu in a clean dish towel, place in a bowl, and weight down with several soup cans to press out liquid; set in refrigerator for 2 hours. Drain tofu well, pat dry with paper toweling, and cut into pieces 3" long, 2" wide, and 1/2" thick. Dredge tofu slices with rice flour, dip into egg, then fry, a few slices at a time, in 1/4 cup oil in a large heavy skillet over moderately high heat about 2 minutes on a side until lightly browned; drain on paper toweling, transfer to a deep serving platter, and keep warm. Add enough additional oil to skillet to total about 1/4 cup, then stir-fry white part of scallions, gingerroot, garlic, and sweet pepper 3–4 minutes over moderate heat. Add scallion tops, stock, sugar, *hot sauce,* and cornstarch blended with soy sauce. Cook and stir until thickened. Add bean sprouts, cover and cook 2–3 minutes, tossing occasionally. Pour over tofu and serve.

NPS (4–6): 490–325 C, 135–90 mg CH, 1410–940 mg S*

TOFU AND BUCKWHEAT KASHA

4–6 servings ¢

Tofu has the ability to absorb flavors, so the longer it stands in this dressing, the richer it will be. But, make a note, it will also begin to turn brown.

2 tablespoons soy sauce
1 clove garlic, peeled and minced
2 tablespoons minced parsley
1 teaspoon chervil
1 tablespoon minced chives
1 tablespoon dark brown sugar
1/4 teaspoon black pepper
1/4 cup peanut or vegetable oil
1/4 cup cider vinegar
1/3 cup finely chopped pimiento or sweet red pepper
1/3 cup finely chopped celery
1 pound firm tofu, drained well and cut in 3/4" cubes
1 recipe Basic Buckwheat Kasha
Crisp romaine, radicchio, or endive leaves
1/4 cup dry-roasted soybean nuts (optional)

Prepare dressing by combining soy, garlic, herbs, sugar, pepper, oil, and vinegar in a large bowl. Add pimiento, celery, and tofu and mix gently. Cover and refrigerate 1–2 hours, stirring now and then. Meanwhile, prepare kasha as recipe directs and cool to lukewarm. Toss kasha with tofu and dressing, pile onto lettuce leaves, and sprinkle with soybean nuts, if you like.

NPS (4–6): 450–300 C, 100–65 mg CH, 1765–1175 mg S*

TOFU AND TOASTED FILBERT LOAF

6 servings   ¢

1 large yellow onion, peeled and minced
1 clove garlic, peeled and minced
2 tablespoons cooking oil
1½ pounds firm tofu, drained well
2 cups soft whole grain or wheat germ bread crumbs
2 tablespoons minced parsley
½ teaspoon powdered mustard
2 eggs, lightly beaten
1¼ teaspoons salt
¼ teaspoon pepper
¼ cup tomato paste
½ cup soy milk or water
⅓ cup finely chopped, toasted, blanched filberts or almonds
⅓ cup nonfat dry milk powder

Preheat oven to 350° F. Stir-fry onion and garlic in oil in a medium-size heavy skillet 3–5 minutes until limp; set aside. Cut ¼ pound of the tofu into ¼″ cubes and set aside also. Mash remaining tofu with a fork, combine with skillet mixture and all remaining ingredients except cubed tofu, mixing well with your hands. Add cubed tofu and mix in gently. Spoon into a well-oiled 9″ × 5″ × 3″ loaf pan and bake, uncovered, about 1¼ hours until firm and lightly browned. Cool loaf in upright pan on a wire rack 10 minutes, then turn out on a serving platter. Slice about ½″ thick and serve with Cheese, Mushroom, or Tomato Sauce.

NPS: 260 C, 90 mg CH, 675 mg S*

TOFU AND BROCCOLI QUICHE IN BROWN RICE SHELL

6 servings

BROWN RICE SHELL
2 cups hot seasoned, cooked brown rice

FILLING
2 eggs
¾ cup soft tofu, well drained
¾ cup half-and-half or light cream
¼ cup plain yogurt
½ teaspoon salt
⅛ teaspoon white pepper
½ (10-ounce) package frozen broccoli, cooked by package directions and well drained or ½ cup cooked fresh broccoli flowerets
1½ cups coarsely grated Gruyère or Swiss cheese

Preheat oven to 350° F. Spoon rice into a well-buttered 9″ piepan and using the back of a spoon, press evenly over bottom and up sides to form a shell. Bake, uncovered, 10 minutes. Meanwhile, buzz eggs, tofu, cream, yogurt, salt, and pepper 10 seconds at high speed in an electric blender or 5 seconds in a food processor fitted with the metal chopping blade until smooth. Spread flowerets evenly over rice shell and sprinkle with cheese. Place piepan on partly pulled-out oven rack, then pour in tofu mixture. Bake, uncovered, 35–40 minutes until *just* firm. Cool slightly, cut into wedges, and serve.

NPS: 290 C, 135 mg CH, 325 mg S*

TEN

Cereals, Rice, and Pasta

CEREALS

When man discovered that seeds of certain grasses were edible, that they could be planted to provide food for himself and his family, he emerged from savagery. It was no longer necessary to kill in order to survive. Such life-giving foods, inevitably, were held sacred and became the basis of much mythology. Our word *cereal,* in fact, derives from Ceres, Roman goddess of grain and harvest.

The family of cereals is vast. All, to greater or lesser degrees, are high-energy foods with B vitamins in abundance. The more refined or polished the cereal, the less nutritious because most of the nutrients are contained in the husk. Enrichment programs, however, are replacing vitamins and minerals lost in the milling. A cereal marked *"restored"* has had the nutritive content restored to the level of whole grain. *"Enriched cereal"* has been given the added boost of nutrients not present in the whole grain (usually vitamins A or D).

THE KINDS AND FORMS OF CEREALS

The vast array of cereals available today can be divided into three basic categories: the *regular cooking,* the *quick cooking,* and the *ready to eat.* Briefly, here are the kinds of grains and forms in which they're sold:

Barley: One of man's first foods but not commonly used today except for making beer. The polished grain, or *pearl,* comes in three sizes—coarse, medium, and fine—and is a good extender of soups and stews. *Scotch barley,* sold primarily in health food stores, is husked and coarsely ground. It must be soaked overnight before using.

Bran: Not a single grain but the husk of any grain separated out in the milling.

Buckwheat: No relation to wheat but another species altogether; it is Siberian and the foundation of many Russian dishes, notably *kasha,* a pilaf-like dish of braised buckwheat groats. Kasha has become something of a generic term today, meaning any braised or baked cracked cereal. True kasha, however, is a particular recipe made of buckwheat.

Bulgur: (see Wheat).

Corn: America's gift to the world and the grain upon which much of Latin America lives yet. Both yellow and white meal are available, enriched and old-fashioned unbolted (unsifted) stone or water ground (ground on millstones), which Southerners prefer to all others.

Hominy (also called *posole):* White flint corn, the kernels of which have been skinned either mechanically or in a lye bath. It is available dry (cracked or whole) or canned (whole). *Hominy grits* are simply dried hominy ground to meal; they can be prepared like corn meal.

Couscous: The Arabic word for semolina (see Wheat).

Farina: Broadly speaking, any ground grain. Today, however, farina usually means ground wheat, either the whole grain *(dark farina)* or the refined *(light farina* or *cream of wheat).*

Grits: Finely ground grain, now almost always meaning *hominy grits* (see Corn).

Groats: Coarsely ground grain, usually buckwheat.

Kasha: (see Buckwheat).

Masa Harina: A special corn flour popular throughout Mexico and Latin America; it is what gives tortillas their characteristic nutty-sweet flavor.

Millet: An Asian grain little used in this country. Health food stores sell millet flour, also millet seeds, which can be cooked like other whole grains.

Oats: One of the most nutritious and important grains. Most are rolled into oatmeal, ground into flour, or puffed into breakfast cereal although the simpler, huskier Scottish-style *stone-cut oats* (actually stone ground) are becoming increasingly popular.

Rice: The "bread" of the Orient and a grain once so revered only emperors were permitted to plant it. There are thousands of varieties of rice (1,107 in India alone), but to simplify, there are two principal types: the *long-grain* (the fine Indian *Basmati* is of this type) and the *short-grain* (Italy's pearly *Arborio,* now readily available in specialty food shops, is a particularly good short-grain rice, perfect for making creamy risottos). The shortest of the short-grain rices is the Oriental *glutinous rice* (the Japanese use it for *sushi,* the Chinese for *dim sum,* and the Thais for a rich coconut dessert). What characterizes glutinous rice is its sweetness and stickiness (not for nothing is it also known as *sweet* or *sticky rice).* Long-grain rices are best for serving solo or using in casseroles because their grains remain separate during cooking. Short-grain rices, on the other hand, cook down into a softness more suitable for puddings. *Brown rice* is simply unpolished rice (only the husks have been removed). It is more nutritious than polished rice, cheaper, and, many people think, of better flavor. *Wild rice* is not rice (see description that follows). Polished rice is available in three popular forms: *regular, converted* (also known as processed or parboiled), and *quick cooking* (fully cooked, dehydrated rice that needs only to stand in boiling water a few minutes). Brown rice is also now available as both *regular* and *con-*

verted rice. (Note: All recipes in this book, unless otherwise noted, were tested using converted rice. This rice has been steam-treated so that its grains become tender without gumming up or losing their identity.)

Rye: The bulk of rye grown goes either into whiskey or flour. Rye groats are sometimes available, however, and should be cooked like buckwheat or other groats.

Semolina: (see Wheat).

Wheat: The staff of life for much of the world, source of flours, myriad breakfast cereals, also such ethnic exotics as *cracked wheat;* that Middle Eastern favorite called *bulgur* (parched, cracked wheat from which some of the bran has been removed); and *semolina* (the hard heart of durum wheat, ground either into the flour from which pasta is made or into granules, cooked much like farina and known to Arabs as *couscous).* Other wheat products include *wheat germ,* the tender, perishable embryo; it can be scattered over cereals, mixed into meat loaves and croquettes, slipped into casseroles and salads, or used as a topping. *Wheat berries* are whole, unpolished kernels of wheat; they've a richy wheaty flavor and chewy texture and are delicious baked into breads.

Wild Rice: A luxurious, nut-flavored, long grain marsh grass of the northern Lake States, so expensive still that Indians of the area (by law the only persons allowed to harvest it) carry small pouches of it in place of money. The longer the grain, the greater the price.

HOW TO COOK CEREALS

Except for rice and wild rice, which will be discussed separately, all cereals are cooked more or less the same way. The only variable is the proportion of liquid to cereal, determined by size of grain (whether whole, cracked, or ground) rather than by species. It's always best to cook cereal by package directions because each manufacturer knows his product best. As a general rule, however, the following methods work for all cereals (except for the quick cooking, which should be prepared strictly as the label directs).

Direct Heat Method: Bring water and salt to a full rolling boil in a heavy saucepan. Gradually sprinkle in cereal, stirring all the while. Turn heat to low and cook, uncovered, stirring often, 15–20 minutes until tender and no raw taste of starch remains. Toward end

Cereal	Quantity	Water	Salt
Rolled oats or wheat	1 cup	2 cups	1/2 teaspoon
Buckwheat or other groats, bulgur and cracked wheat, other cracked or coarsely ground cereals	1 cup	2 cups	1 teaspoon
Farina, corn meal, grits, and other granular cereals	1 cup	5 cups	1 teaspoon

of cooking, use a flame-tamer, if possible, to keep cereal from scorching.

Double Boiler Method (slower but surer): Place water and salt in top part of a double boiler and bring quickly to a boil over direct heat. Sprinkle cereal in gradually, stirring constantly. When cereal begins to thicken, set over simmering water and cook, uncovered, stirring occasionally, 20–30 minutes until done.

Microwave Method: Using proportions cereal manufacturer recommends, mix cereal (either regular or quick-cooking oatmeal, cream of wheat or rice, hominy grits, etc.) and hot tap water in a microwave-safe container large enough to prevent boil-over. Microwave, uncovered, as oven manufacturer directs, stirring once midway through cooking time. Remove from oven and let *stand* on counter 1–2 minutes to complete the cooking. *Note:* Since microwaving exaggerates boiling of milk-based foods, cereals cooked with some milk or cream require special attention to keep them from bubbling over. Use *LOW power setting* and watch carefully or use a temperature probe if your microwave oven is equipped with one.

Some Ways to Dress Up Cooked Cereals

• Cook in milk or a 1/2 and 1/2 mixture of cream and water instead of in water.
• To the cooking water, add 1 tablespoon sugar mixed with 1 teaspoon cinnamon and, if you like, a pinch nutmeg, allspice, or cloves.
• About 5 minutes before cereal is done, stir in 1/2–1 cup seedless raisins, dried currants, diced dates, dried apricots, figs, or prunes.
• About 5 minutes before cereal is done, stir in 3/4 cup coarsely chopped pecans, walnuts, roasted almonds, or peanuts.
• When serving, mound into a Baked Apple or on top of baked or fried bananas.
• When serving, make a well in the center of each portion and fill with Melba Sauce or any fruit jam, jelly, or preserves.

RICE

HOW TO COOK RICE

Note: Chicken or beef broth can be used for cooking rice instead of water, but salt should be reduced accordingly.

Basic Method (for fluffy, tender rice): Bring water and salt to a rapid boil over high heat in a heavy saucepan, add rice, cover, reduce heat so rice bubbles gently, and cook until rice is tender and all water absorbed. Regular and converted rice will take 20–25 minutes, brown rice 40–45. If you like, uncover and let dry out 3–5 minutes before serving. Fluff with a fork.

Open Pan Method (for firm, tender white rice; especially good to use if rice is to be added to casseroles or stuffings): Bring water and salt to a rapid boil over high heat in an extra-heavy saucepan, stir in rice, reduce heat slightly, and cook, uncovered, *without stirring* until water is barely visible, about 10 minutes. Turn heat to low and continue cooking, uncovered, until all moisture is absorbed, about 8–10 minutes. Fluff with a fork.

Oven Method (for mellow, nutty flavor): Preheat oven to 400° F. In a heavy flameproof casserole, melt 2 tablespoons butter or margarine over direct moderate heat. Add rice and stir-fry about 1/2 minute. Add water and salt, cover tightly, and bake until rice is tender and all liquid absorbed. White rice will take about 20 minutes, brown about 45. Fluff with a fork and serve.

VARIATION

Stir-fry 2 tablespoons minced yellow onion in butter 2–3 minutes, then add rice and proceed as directed. For added zip, add a pars-

HOW TO COOK RICE

Kind of Rice	Quantity of Uncooked Rice	Water	Salt	Yield of Cooked Rice	Number of Servings
White (regular)	1 cup	2 cups	1 teaspoon	3 cups	4
White (converted)	1 cup	2–2½ cups	1 teaspoon	4 cups	4–6
White (quick cooking)	1 cup	(cook by package directions)		2 cups	2–3
Brown (regular)	1 cup	2½ cups	1 teaspoon	4 cups	4–6
Brown (converted)	1 cup	2⅔ cups	1 teaspoon	3⅓ cups	4–5

ley sprig or celery top and 2–3 dashes liquid hot red pepper seasoning. Remove parsley or celery before serving.

Microwave Method: Because all rice (regular, converted, and quick cooking) takes about the same time to cook in a microwave as it does by the basic stove-top method, we see no advantages to cooking rice via microwave and therefore don't recommend it. *(Note:* When converting rice, meat, and/or vegetable casseroles for microwave cooking, use *quick-cooking rice* instead of the regular or converted, which may not cook as fast as the other casserole ingredients.) Remember to rotate layered casseroles that cannot be stirred often.

Tips for Making Better Rice

• Be sure to use a large enough pan; rice will quadruple or triple in bulk during cooking. Also make sure pan is heavy so there is little danger of scorching.
• Once rice comes to a boil, stir as little as possible, and use a fork if you must stir—less chance of mashing or breaking the rice.
• To help keep rice grains beautifully distinct, add 1 or 2 drops cooking oil or a dab of butter or margarine to the cooking water. Also gives rice a lovely glisten.
• If rice must be held before serving, transfer to a colander and set over simmering water; keep covered. Rice will keep hot without overcooking. Or transfer rice to a heavy casserole and set in oven turned to lowest heat. Keep tightly covered.

What to Do with Leftover Rice

To Reheat: Place rice in a large, fine sieve and with moistened hands break up any clumps. Set sieve over simmering water, cover, and steam about 10 minutes. Rice will be almost as good as it was the first time around. Or place rice in a buttered casserole and break up clumps with moistened hands.

Dot well with butter, cover, and bake ½ hour at 325° F. *Note:* In a *convection oven,* use the same temperature but check after 20 minutes.

To Reheat by Microwave: The microwave may not excel at cooking rice, but it *is* a whiz when it comes to reheating it to fluffy perfection. Simply break up rice clumps in a microwave-safe container, cover with vented plastic food wrap, and microwave about 1 minute per serving at *HIGH power level* until steaming hot. That's all there is to it. *Note:* When reheating frozen cooked rice, there's no need to thaw it first; just increase microwaving time by about 50 per cent, then break up clumps once rice defrosts.

To Use Up Small Amounts:
• Mix into meat loaves, croquettes, or stuffings.
• Combine with leftover meat and vegetables in a casserole or soup.
• Add to any creamed meat or vegetable mixture.
• Marinate in Garlic or Herb Dressing and serve in hollowed-out tomatoes.
• Add to pancake batter.
• Scramble with eggs.
• Team with custard sauce and/or fresh fruit as a dessert.

Some Quick Ways to Dress Up Rice

During Cooking (amounts based on 1 cup uncooked rice and basic method of cooking):

Saffron Rice: Add ⅛ teaspoon powdered saffron to cooking liquid or soak ¼ teaspoon saffron in ¼ cup cooking liquid about 10 minutes, then cook as directed. Season to taste with salt and pepper.
NPS: 175 C, 0 mg CH, 550 mg S*

Arroz Amarillo (Yellow Mexican Rice): Stir-fry rice in 3 tablespoons olive oil with 1 small minced yellow onion and 1 crushed clove garlic about 5 minutes over moderate heat until pale golden; mix in 2/3 cup tomato sauce and 2 cups chicken broth and cook by basic method. Season to taste with salt and freshly ground pepper.

NPS: 350 C, 0 mg CH, 1140 mg S*

Orange Rice: Cook rice in a 1/2 and 1/2 mixture of orange juice and chicken broth with 2 teaspoons grated orange rind and 1/8 teaspoon nutmeg. Just before serving, mix in 1/2 cup diced, seeded orange sections. Add a pinch of salt but omit pepper.

NPS: 225 C, 0 mg CH, 230 mg S*

Raisin, Currant, Date, Apricot, or Fig Rice: Cook as directed but add 1/4 cup seedless raisins or dried currants, diced dates, dried apricots, or figs to the pot. Season to taste with salt and pepper. Especially good with curry.

NPS (raisin, currant, date): 205 C, 0 mg CH, 555 mg S*
NPS (apricot): 195 C, 0 mg CH, 555 mg S*
NPS (fig): 210 C, 0 mg CH, 555 mg S*

Onion Rice: Stir-fry 1 minced Bermuda onion and the rice in 3 tablespoons butter about 5 minutes over moderate heat until pale golden; then cook as directed and season to taste.

NPS: 265 C, 25 mg CH, 645 mg S*

Garlic Rice: Stir-fry 1 minced clove garlic in 2 tablespoons butter 2 minutes over moderate heat; add rice and stir-fry 3 minutes longer, then cook as directed. Season to taste.

NPS: 230 C, 15 mg CH, 610 mg S*

Green Rice: Stir-fry 1/2 cup minced scallions (include tops) in 2 tablespoons butter 3–4 minutes over moderate heat until limp; add rice and cook as directed, using chicken broth. Season to taste and mix in 1 cup minced parsley.

NPS: 260 C, 15 mg CH, 1005 mg S*

Confetti Rice: Stir-fry 1/3 cup each minced yellow onion, sweet red and green pepper in 3 tablespoons butter or olive oil; add rice and cook as directed, using chicken broth. Season to taste with salt and liquid hot red pepper seasoning.

NPS: 285 C, 25 mg CH, 1035 mg S*

Curried Rice: Warm 2 teaspoons curry powder in 1 tablespoon butter 1–2 minutes over moderate heat; add rice and cook as directed, using chicken broth. Season to taste.

NPS: 225 C, 5 mg CH, 970 mg S*

Herbed Rice: Warm 2 tablespoons minced fresh dill, basil, chives, or parsley or 1 tablespoon minced fresh sage or thyme in 2 tablespoons butter 2 minutes over moderate heat; add rice and cook as directed, using chicken broth. Season to taste. *Note:* 1 teaspoon of the dried herb may be substituted for the fresh, but the flavor will not be as good.

NPS: 250 C, 15 mg CH, 1000 mg S*

Mushroom Rice: Stir-fry 1/2 pound thinly sliced or coarsely chopped mushrooms in 3 tablespoons butter over moderately high heat 2–3 minutes until golden; add rice and cook as directed, using beef or chicken broth. Season to taste.

NPS (with beef broth): 275 C, 25 mg CH, 1040 mg S*
NPS (with chicken broth): 290 C, 25 mg CH, 1035 mg S*

Just Before Serving: Cook 1 cup rice by basic method, season with salt and pepper, then mix in any of the following:

Poppy or Caraway Seed Rice: 2 tablespoons each poppy or caraway seeds and melted butter.

Rice Amandine: 1/3 cup butter-browned slivered blanched almonds.

Nut Rice: 2 tablespoons melted butter and 1/3 cup coarsely chopped pecans, walnuts, macadamia, piñon, or pistachio nuts or toasted peanuts, cashews, or soybean nuts.

Avocado-Tomato Rice: 1 coarsely chopped small firm-ripe avocado and 1/2 cup coarsely chopped, peeled, seeded tomato.

Minted Rice (delicious with lamb): 1/4 cup minced fresh mint warmed 2–3 minutes in 2 tablespoons butter.

Soy Rice: 1/4 cup minced scallions sautéed in 2 tablespoons peanut oil 2–3 minutes over moderate heat, 2 tablespoons each soy sauce and minced pimiento and 1/2 teaspoon sugar; reduce salt as needed. Cover and let stand off heat 2–3 minutes; toss and serve.

Sour Cream Rice: 3/4–1 cup warmed sour cream; cover rice and let stand off heat 5 minutes. Sprinkle with 1–2 tablespoons minced chives, toss lightly and serve.

Cheese Rice: 1/3–1/2 cup grated sharp Cheddar, Parmesan, Swiss, or mozzarella cheese; cover rice and let stand off heat 4–5 minutes to melt cheese; toss lightly and serve.

TOASTED RICE

4 servings ⟐ ⊠ ¢

If you like the nutty flavor of toasted rice, toast a pound, store airtight, and use as needed.

1 cup uncooked rice

Preheat oven to 350° F. Spread rice out in a shallow baking pan and toast, stirring now and then, 8–10 minutes until golden. Cook as you would regular rice.

NPS: 175 C, 0 mg CH, 5 mg S*

RICE RING

8 servings ⟐ ¢ ⊠

White, brown, and wild rice can all be molded by the following method. So can cracked or bulgur wheat, buckwheat groats, and all of the flavored rices (Curried, Herbed, etc.) except for very soft ones containing sauce. For variety, mold in individual ramekins or 1½-quart fluted or decorative molds instead of a ring mold.

6 cups hot seasoned cooked rice
¼ cup melted butter or margarine

Mix rice and butter with a fork and pack lightly into a *well-buttered* or oiled 1½-quart ring mold. Let stand 1 minute, then invert on a hot platter. Fill center with any creamed mixture, stew, or curry. (*Note:* If dinner must be held, don't mold rice until the very last minute; it will keep hot in the pan far better than in the mold.)

NPS: 220 C, 15 mg CH, 610 mg S*

RICE PILAF

4 servings

¼ cup butter or margarine
1 cup uncooked rice or brown rice
2 cups hot chicken or beef broth or water
½ teaspoon salt (about)
⅛ teaspoon pepper

Melt butter in a heavy saucepan over moderately low heat, add rice, and stir-fry about 5 minutes until straw-colored. Add broth, salt, and pepper, cover, and cook over lowest heat without stirring 18–20 minutes until all liquid is absorbed. Uncover and cook 3–5 minutes longer to dry out. Fluff with a fork, taste for salt, and adjust as needed.

NPS (with chicken broth): 300 C, 30 mg CH, 780 mg S*

VARIATIONS

Baked Pilaf (a good way to make pilaf in quantity): Stir-fry rice as directed in a flameproof casserole or Dutch oven-type kettle, add broth and seasonings, cover, and bake about ½ hour at 350° F. until all liquid is absorbed. For drier rice, uncover and bake 5 minutes longer. Nutritional count same as basic recipe.

Middle East Pilaf: Stir-fry 1 small minced yellow onion in butter along with rice, add broth and seasonings, also ¼ cup seedless raisins or dried currants, ¼ teaspoon each cinnamon and allspice, ⅛ teaspoon each turmeric and cardamom. Cover and cook as directed.

NPS: 330 C, 30 mg CH, 785 mg S*

Indian Pilaf: Stir-fry 1 medium-size minced yellow onion in butter along with rice, add 2 teaspoons curry powder, and stir-fry ½ minute. Add broth and seasonings, also ¼ cup seedless raisins. Cover and cook as directed. Add ¼ cup coarsely chopped toasted blanched almonds, then fluff with a fork.

NPS: 385 C, 30 mg CH, 785 mg S*

Bulgur Pilaf: Prepare any of the preceding pilafs as directed, but substitute 1 cup uncooked bulgur or cracked wheat for rice.

NPS: 280 C, 30 mg CH, 780 mg S*

Main Dish Pilaf: Prepare Rice or Bulgur Pilaf as directed; just before serving, add 1½ cups diced cooked meat, chicken, fish, or shellfish and toss lightly to mix. Recipe too flexible for meaningful nutritional count.

ARMENIAN RICE

6 servings

Delicious with roast lamb or shish kebabs.

6 tablespoons butter or margarine
⅔ cup fine egg noodles
1½ cups uncooked rice
3 cups boiling water
1 tablespoon salt

Melt butter in a large, heavy kettle over moderately high heat, toss in noodles, and stir-fry 3–5 minutes until pale brown. Add rice and stir-fry 5 minutes until tweedy and golden. Add water and salt, stir well, cover, and boil gently over moderate heat about 20 minutes until rice is tender and all water absorbed.

NPS: 310 C, 40 mg CH, 1220 mg S*

RISOTTO ALLA MILANESE

4 servings

There are dozens of *risotti* (soft rice mixtures that are to the north of Italy what pasta is to the south). This one is a classic. Delicious with veal or chicken.

2 tablespoons each butter and beef marrow or
   1/4 cup butter or margarine
1 small yellow onion, peeled and minced
1 cup uncooked short grain rice
2 cups hot chicken or beef broth or water
Pinch powdered saffron or 1/8 teaspoon saffron,
   soaked in 1/4 cup of the hot broth (strain and
   reserve broth)
1/2 teaspoon salt (about)
1/8 teaspoon pepper
1/4 cup grated Parmesan cheese

Melt butter and marrow in a heavy saucepan over moderately high heat, add onion and stir-fry 2–3 minutes until pale golden. Add rice and stir-fry 1 minute to coat with butter. Reduce heat to moderate, add 1/2 cup broth, saffron, salt, and pepper and cook, *stirring constantly,* until almost all liquid is absorbed. Continue to cook and stir, adding remaining broth by the 1/2 cup and letting rice absorb it each time before adding more broth. *Note:* This will take 30–40 minutes. When risotto is properly cooked, it will be creamy with just the slightest bit of texture. Lightly fork in the cheese, taste for salt and add as needed.

NPS: 325 C, 35 mg CH, 875 mg S*

VARIATIONS

Brown Rice Risotto: Substitute short grain brown rice for the white, omit saffron, and cook as recipe directs for 50–55 minutes.

NPS: 315 C, 35 mg CH, 875 mg S*

Mushroom Risotto: Stir-fry 1/2 pound minced mushrooms along with onion and rice; proceed as directed and toss in 1/4 cup piñon nuts along with the cheese.

NPS: 390 C, 35 mg CH, 885 mg S*

Risi e Bisi *(6 servings):* Prepare as directed, omitting saffron if you like. Mix in 1 1/4 cups drained, cooked green peas along with the cheese.

NPS: 360 C, 35 mg CH, 930 mg S*

CHICKEN LIVER RISOTTO

4 servings

1 pound chicken livers
6 tablespoons butter or margarine
1 large yellow onion, peeled and minced
1/2 cup thinly sliced mushrooms
1 cup uncooked rice
2 1/2 cups hot chicken broth
1/2 teaspoon salt
1/8 teaspoon pepper
2 tablespoons minced parsley
1/4 cup grated Parmesan cheese

Halve livers at the natural separation and pat dry on paper toweling. Melt 1/4 cup butter in a large skillet or flameproof casserole that has a tight-fitting lid over moderately high heat. Add livers and sauté 3–4 minutes, stirring, until lightly browned; remove with a slotted spoon to a heated plate, cover, and keep warm. Melt remaining butter in the same skillet, add onion, and stir-fry 4–5 minutes. Add mushrooms and stir-fry 5 minutes longer until onion and mushrooms are brown. Add rice, broth, salt, and pepper, mix well, and heat, uncovered, until just boiling. Turn heat to low, cover, and simmer 15–20 minutes until rice is tender. Add livers, parsley, and Parmesan, toss lightly with 2 forks, and serve.

NPS: 540 C, 550 mg CH, 1125 mg S*

SPANISH RICE

4 servings   ¢ ⚖

1 large yellow onion, peeled and minced
2 tablespoons cooking oil
1 small sweet green pepper, cored, seeded, and
   minced
1/2 cup uncooked rice
1/4 teaspoon chili powder
1 (1-pound) can tomatoes (do not drain)
1/2 cup water
1 bay leaf, crumbled
3/4 teaspoon salt
1/8 teaspoon pepper
1/4 teaspoon sugar

Sauté onion in oil in a heavy saucepan over moderate heat 5–8 minutes until limp. Add green pepper and stir-fry 5 minutes. Stir in rice and chili powder and brown rice lightly. Add remaining ingredients, chopping up tomatoes, cover, and simmer 20 minutes. Uncover and cook 5 minutes longer.

NPS: 195 C, 0 mg CH, 570 mg S*

VARIATION

¢ ⚖ **Baked Spanish Rice with Cheese:** Brown vegetables and rice in a flameproof casserole, add remaining ingredients and 1/2 cup grated sharp Cheddar cheese. Mix lightly, cover, and bake 1/2 hour at 350° F.;

uncover and bake 5 minutes longer. Serve as a main dish.

NPS: 250 C, 15 mg CH, 655 mg S*

JAMBALAYA

6 servings ¢

Jambalaya is a Creole rice classic. Originally made with ham (its name comes from *jamón,* the Spanish word for ham), it is as likely to be made today with sausage, shrimp, or chicken. But the method remains the same, which means making a *roux,* browned flour and fat mixture. A roux is such an integral part of Creole cooking that many recipes begin simply, "First, you make a roux." It's assumed everyone knows how. Old-time Creole cooks will "work a roux" ten times as long as the recipe below calls for to obtain a rich caramel flavor. But it really isn't necessary.

1¼ pounds pork sausage meat or diced cooked ham
¼ cup bacon drippings (optional)
3 tablespoons flour
2 medium-size yellow onions, peeled and coarsely chopped
12 scallions, sliced ½" thick (include tops)
2 cloves garlic, peeled and crushed
¼ cup minced parsley
2 teaspoons salt (slightly less if ham is used)
1 teaspoon cayenne pepper
2 cups uncooked rice
2⅔ cups chicken broth or water

Stir-fry sausage in a large, heavy kettle over moderately high heat 5 minutes, remove to a bowl with a slotted spoon. *(Note:* If using ham, stir-fry in bacon drippings. Measure drippings and add additional bacon drippings as needed to make ¼ cup.) Blend in flour and heat and stir 2–3 minutes to make a rich brown roux. Add onions, scallions, and garlic and stir-fry 10–12 minutes over moderate heat until golden brown and well worked into roux. Return sausage to kettle, add all remaining ingredients except broth and stir-fry 1–2 minutes. Add broth, bring to a boil, then turn heat to lowest point, cover, and simmer 45 minutes. Uncover, stir well, and heat 10 minutes, stirring occasionally, until rice dries out a bit. Serve hot as a budget main dish or potato substitute.

NPS (with sausage): 690 C, 65 mg CH, 1850 mg S*
NPS (with ham): 465 C, 55 mg CH, 2505 mg S*

LOUISIANA RED BEANS AND RICE

4 servings ¢

1 cup dried red kidney beans, washed and sorted
1 quart cold water
1 (2-ounce) chunk salt pork
1 medium-size yellow onion, peeled and coarsely chopped
1 clove garlic, peeled and crushed
1 stalk celery, coarsely chopped
1 bay leaf, crumbled
¼ teaspoon cumin
⅛ teaspoon pepper
1 tablespoon light brown sugar
½ teaspoon salt (about)
4 cups hot boiled rice
2 tablespoons minced parsley

Soak beans overnight in 2 cups water or use the quick method.* Drain, measure soaking water, and add enough cold water to make 2 cups. Place beans, water, and salt pork in a large, heavy saucepan, cover, and simmer ¾ hour. Add all but last 3 ingredients, cover, and simmer ½–¾ hour longer until tender. Discard salt pork; season to taste with salt. Ladle over rice, sprinkle with parsley, and serve.

NPS: 515 C, 10 mg CH, 455 mg S*

CHINESE FRIED RICE

4 servings ☒

3 cups cold cooked rice
3 tablespoons peanut or other cooking oil
½ cup julienne strips of lean cooked roast pork or ham
4 scallions, minced (white part only)
¼ cup chicken broth
1 tablespoon soy sauce
¼ teaspoon sugar
⅛ teaspoon pepper

Stir-fry rice in oil in a large, heavy skillet over moderate heat, pressing out any lumps, until pale golden. Add pork and scallions and stir-fry 1 minute. Add remaining ingredients, cover, and heat 1 minute. Serve very hot.

NPS: 265 C, 15 mg CH, 395 mg S*

VARIATION

Chinese Fried Eggs and Rice: Stir-fry rice, pork, and scallions as directed, then push to side of skillet; omit broth but add 1 or 2 lightly beaten eggs; scramble lightly, then mix into rice along with soy sauce, sugar, and pepper.

NPS: 285 C, 85 mg CH, 360 mg S*

KHICHIRI (EAST INDIAN RICE AND LENTILS)

4–6 servings ¢

Good topped with yogurt or chutney and especially good with curry.

½ cup dried lentils, washed and sorted
1 medium-size yellow onion, peeled and minced
2½ cups chicken broth or water
½ cup uncooked rice
¾ teaspoon salt (about)
Pinch crushed dried hot red chili peppers
2 tablespoons margarine
2 teaspoons cumin seeds

Simmer lentils and onion in broth in a covered heavy saucepan 25 minutes, stirring occasionally. Add rice, salt, and chili peppers, cover, and simmer 20 minutes until rice is tender and all liquid absorbed. Uncover and cook 2–3 minutes to dry out. Meanwhile, melt margarine in a small skillet over moderately low heat, add cumin seeds, and stir-fry ½ minute until they begin to pop. Pour over rice and toss with a fork. Taste for salt and adjust as needed.

NPS (4–6) (with chicken broth): 255–170 C, 0 mg CH, 975–650 mg S*

RICE CROQUETTES

6–8 servings

2 tablespoons butter or margarine
2 tablespoons flour
½ cup milk
1 egg, lightly beaten
3 cups cooked rice (leftover is fine)
¼ teaspoon salt (about)
⅛ teaspoon pepper
Shortening or cooking oil for deep fat frying
¼ cup unsifted flour
1 egg lightly beaten with 1 tablespoon cold water
½ cup toasted fine bread crumbs

Melt butter in a small saucepan over moderate heat, blend in flour, slowly stir in milk, and heat, stirring until thickened. Off heat, beat in egg; mix in rice, salt, and pepper, taste for seasoning and adjust. Cool to room temperature; shape into logs about 3″ long and 1″ wide and chill 1 hour. Begin heating shortening in a deep fat fryer with basket and deep fat thermometer over moderately high heat. Dredge logs in flour, dip in egg mixture, and roll in crumbs to coat well. When fat reaches 375° F., fry croquettes, a few at a time, 2–3 minutes until golden.

Drain on paper toweling and keep warm while frying the rest. Serve hot as a potato substitute.

NPS (6–8): 285–215 C, 105–80 mg CH, 225–165 mg S*

VARIATIONS

Savory Rice Croquettes: Prepare as directed but substitute Curried, Herbed, Mushroom or Amandine Rice for the plain.

NPS (6–8) (Curried): 325–240 C, 110–80 mg CH, 870–650 mg S*
NPS (6–8) (Herbed): 340–255 C, 115–85 mg CH, 890–665 mg S*
NPS (6–8) (Mushroom): 265–270 C, 110–90 mg CH, 915–690 mg S*

Main Dish Rice Croquettes: Prepare as directed but use 2 cups rice and 1 cup any minced leftover meat, poultry, or seafood. Good topped with Mushroom or Tomato Sauce. Recipe too flexible for meaningful nutritional count.

Cheese-Rice Croquettes: Prepare sauce as directed and stir in ½ cup grated Parmesan, Gruyère, or mozzarella cheese, then proceed as recipe directs.

NPS (6–8): 315–235 C, 110–85 mg CH, 345–260 mg S*

Bulgur or Kasha Croquettes: Prepare as directed but substitute cooked bulgur wheat or buckwheat groats for rice. Nutritional count about the same as basic recipe.

RICE PANCAKES

4 servings ¢ ⚖

Good for breakfast with ham or bacon. And a good way to use up leftover rice.

1 cup cooked rice
1 tablespoon finely grated yellow onion
⅓ cup + 2 tablespoons milk
1 egg, lightly beaten

Simmer rice, onion, and ⅓ cup milk in a covered saucepan over lowest possible heat (a flame-tamer is good) 15–20 minutes until all milk is absorbed and rice very soft. Off heat, mix in remaining milk and the egg. Heat an oiled griddle over moderate heat until a drop of water will dance (or to 350° F. if using an electric griddle). Drop mixture by rounded tablespoonfuls, spread to about 3″ in diameter, and brown lightly on both sides. Keep warm while browning the rest. Pass syrup or warm honey.

NPS: 95 C, 70 mg CH, 30 mg S*

¢ ⚖ **Dessert Rice Pancakes:** Prepare as directed but omit onion and add 2 tablespoons each sugar and seedless raisins.

NPS: 130 C, 70 mg CH, 30 mg S*

¢ **Savory Rice Pancakes:** Prepare as directed but use Curried, Herbed, Mushroom, or other flavored rice instead of plain. Recipe too flexible for meaningful nutritional count.

BASIC BOILED WILD RICE

4–6 servings

Wild rice is expensive, but it's richer than regular rice and goes further—1 cup uncooked rice equals 3⅓ cups cooked rice, enough for 4–6 servings. To extend, mix ½ and ½ with cooked brown rice or bulgur wheat.

1 cup wild rice
3 cups water
1 teaspoon salt
2–3 tablespoons melted butter or margarine

Wash rice well in a strainer under cold running water. Place in a heavy saucepan with water and salt, cover, and bring to a boil over moderate heat. Uncover and boil gently, without stirring, about 35 minutes until *just* tender. Drain, set, uncovered, over lowest possible heat (flame-tamer is handy), and dry 5 minutes, shaking pan occasionally. Mix in butter with a fork and serve. *(Note:* To keep hot, transfer to the top of a double boiler, cover, and set over simmering water. Don't try to keep warm more than 20 minutes or lovely crisp texture will be lost.)

NPS (4–6): 190–130 C, 15–10 mg CH, 610–405 mg S*

Wild Rice for Game and Poultry: Sauté 1 minced yellow onion in 2 tablespoons butter 5–8 minutes until limp, add rice, 3 cups giblet stock or chicken broth, the salt, and ¼ teaspoon each sage, thyme, and marjoram. Cook as directed but do not add butter at the end.

NPS (4–6): 230–155 C, 15–10 mg CH, 1195–795 mg S*

Wild Rice with Ham: Stir-fry ¼ pound finely diced cooked ham in 2 tablespoons bacon drippings over moderate heat 3–5 minutes until golden, add rice, water, and salt and proceed as directed but omit butter at the end.

NPS (4–6): 235–160 C, 20–15 mg CH, 980–650 mg S*

Wild Rice with Mushrooms and Bacon: Brown 6 slices bacon until crisp, remove to paper toweling, and crumble. In drippings, sauté ½ pound coarsely chopped mushrooms 3–5 minutes until golden. Add rice, 3 cups chicken broth, and ½ teaspoon salt and cook as directed. Add crumbled bacon (but not butter) and toss lightly to mix.

NPS (4–6): 375–250 C, 20–15 mg CH, 1100–735 mg S*

Herbed Wild Rice: Cook rice in 3 cups chicken broth with 2 tablespoons minced chives or scallions, 1 tablespoon minced parsley, 1 teaspoon basil or savory, and ½ teaspoon salt. Mix in butter and serve.

NPS (4–6): 225–150 C, 15–10 mg CH, 915–610 mg S*

Wild Rice with Sour Cream and Chives: Cook rice as directed but omit butter. Transfer to the top of a double boiler, set over simmering water, and fork in ¾ cup sour cream, 3 tablespoons minced chives, and, if you like, ¼ cup cooked crumbled bacon. Cover and heat 10 minutes, fluff with a fork, and serve.

NPS (4–6): 235–155 C, 20–10 mg CH, 575–385 mg S*

CASSEROLE OF WILD RICE, CHICKEN LIVERS, AND SAUSAGE

12 servings

A festive accompaniment for poultry or game birds.

1 pound pork sausage meat
¾ pound chicken livers, halved at the natural separation
2 large yellow onions, peeled and minced
1 pound mushrooms, wiped clean and sliced thin
2 cups wild rice, washed in cold water
1 quart chicken broth
1½ teaspoons salt
¼ teaspoon pepper
1 teaspoon poultry seasoning
1 cup light cream

Break up sausage meat in a large, heavy kettle and brown lightly over moderate heat, stirring now and then. Lift out with slotted spoon and reserve; drain off all but ¼ cup drippings and reserve. Sauté chicken livers in drippings over moderately high heat 3–4 minutes until lightly browned, remove, coarsely chop, and add to sausage. Add 2 tablespoons reserved drippings to kettle and sauté onions over moderate heat 5–8 minutes until pale golden; add mushrooms and sauté 2–3 minutes longer. Stir in rice, broth, and all seasonings and boil gently, uncovered, 20 minutes. Meanwhile, preheat oven to 325° F. With a fork mix in sausage, chicken livers, and cream. Spoon into a greased 3-quart casserole and bake, uncovered, 20–30 minutes until all liquid is absorbed. Fluff with a fork before serving.

NPS: 360 C, 165 mg CH, 880 mg S*

BASIC BUCKWHEAT KASHA

4–6 servings

To be strictly accurate, *kasha* is braised buckwheat groats. Serve in place of potatoes.

1 cup buckwheat groats
1 egg, lightly beaten
¼ cup butter or margarine
2 cups chicken or beef broth or water
1 teaspoon salt (about)
¼ teaspoon pepper

Mix groats and egg in a large, heavy skillet or saucepan set over moderate heat and cook and stir until dry, not brown. Add remaining ingredients, cover, and simmer 15 minutes until liquid is absorbed and groats are tender. Fluff with a fork, taste for salt, and adjust if needed.

NPS (4–6): 220–150 C, 100–65 mg CH, 1070–715 mg S*

VARIATIONS

Old World Buckwheat Kasha: Sauté 1 large minced yellow onion in the butter 8–10 minutes until golden, add groats mixed with egg and ⅓ cup minced celery, and stir-fry 1–2 minutes. Add chicken broth, salt, pepper, 1 teaspoon poultry seasoning, and ⅛ teaspoon curry powder. Cover and cook as directed.

NPS (4–6): 240–160 C, 100–65 mg CH, 1090–725 mg S*

Buckwheat-Mushroom Kasha: Sauté 1 cup coarsely chopped mushrooms in the butter 3–4 minutes until golden, add groats mixed with egg, and stir-fry 1–2 minutes. Cook as directed. Just before serving, mix in ⅓ cup minced toasted almonds, pecans, walnuts, or piñon nuts.

NPS (4–6): 290–195 C, 100–65 mg CH, 1075–715 mg S*

Kasha Varnishkas *(Makes 6 servings):* Cook the groats as directed and while they cook

boil ½ pound broad noodles by package directions; also stir-fry 1 large peeled and minced yellow onion in the ¼ cup butter 8–10 minutes until golden. Mix groats with drained noodles, onion, and 1 tablespoon poppy seeds. Place in a buttered 2½-quart casserole and bake, uncovered, 15 minutes at 350° F.

NPS: 315 C, 100 mg CH, 720 mg S*

BRAISED BULGUR WHEAT WITH ONION

4–6 servings

1 large yellow onion, peeled and minced
¼ cup butter or margarine
1 cup bulgur wheat
2 cups chicken or beef broth
1 teaspoon salt
¼ teaspoon pepper

Preheat oven to 350° F. Sauté onion in butter in a flameproof casserole over moderate heat 5–8 minutes until pale golden. Add bulgur wheat and stir-fry 2–3 minutes until golden. Add remaining ingredients, cover, and bake ½ hour until liquid is absorbed and bulgur tender. Fluff with a fork and serve as a potato substitute.

NPS (4–6): 295–195 C, 30–20 mg CH, 1060–705 mg S*

VARIATIONS

Braised Bulgur with Apples and Almonds: Prepare as directed but stir-fry 1½ cups peeled, minced tart apples along with bulgur wheat. Also add ¼ teaspoon each thyme, sage, and celery seeds and 1 tablespoon minced parsley. Cover and bake as directed; just before serving top with ½ cup slivered blanched almonds sautéed in ¼ cup butter.

NPS (4–6): 520–345 C, 60–40 mg CH, 1180–785 mg S*

Braised Bulgur with Mushrooms: Prepare as directed but stir-fry 1 cup thinly sliced mushrooms along with bulgur wheat; add 1 teaspoon poultry seasoning along with salt, and just before serving mix in ⅓ cup warmed heavy cream or sour cream.

NPS (4–6) (with heavy cream): 370–245 C, 55–40 mg CH, 1070–715 mg S*
NPS (4–6) (with sour cream): 340–225 C, 40–25 mg CH, 1075–715 mg S*

BAKED KASHA WITH WALNUTS

4 servings

Especially good with roast lamb.

1 medium-size yellow onion, peeled and minced
3 tablespoons bacon drippings, butter, or
    margarine
2 cups cooked buckwheat groats, bulgur, or
    cracked wheat
1/2 teaspoon salt
1/8 teaspoon pepper
1/2 cup coarsely chopped walnuts

Preheat oven to 350° F. Brown onion in 2 tablespoons drippings in a small skillet over moderate heat 10–12 minutes; mix into *kasha* along with salt, pepper, and walnuts and toss well. Spoon into a greased 1 1/2-quart casserole, sprinkle with remaining drippings, cover, and bake 1/2 hour. Serve in place of potatoes.

NPS: 265 C, 5 mg CH, 325 mg S*

BAKED BARLEY AND MUSHROOM CASSEROLE

4–6 servings

1 cup medium pearl barley
4 tablespoons butter or margarine
1 large yellow onion, peeled and minced
1 cup coarsely chopped mushrooms
3 cups chicken or beef broth
2 teaspoons salt
1/4 teaspoon pepper

Preheat oven to 350° F. Stir-fry barley in 2 tablespoons butter in a skillet over moderate heat about 2 minutes until lightly browned; transfer to an ungreased 1 1/2-quart casserole. Sauté onion in remaining butter 5–8 minutes until pale golden, add mushrooms, and sauté 3–5 minutes longer; add to casserole. Mix in all remaining ingredients, cover, and bake about 1 1/4 hours until barley is tender, stirring now and then. Fluff with a fork and serve as a potato substitute.

*NPS (4–6): 325–215 C, 30–20 mg CH, 1805–1205
    mg S**

CHEESE GNOCCHI

4 servings

Serve hot as a luncheon entree or as a potato substitute with veal or chicken.

GNOCCHI
1/2 pound ricotta cheese
1/2 cup sifted flour
6 tablespoons grated Parmesan cheese

2 talespoons melted butter or margarine
1/2 teaspoon salt
Pinch nutmeg
2 eggs, lightly beaten

TOPPING
1/3 cup melted butter or margarine
1/3 cup grated Parmesan cheese

Preheat oven to 350° F. Mix *gnocchi* ingredients and spoon about half into a pastry bag fitted with a large plain tube (opening should be about 1/2″ across). Heat about 5 quarts salted water to boiling in a large kettle; adjust heat so water bubbles *very gently.* Squeeze out gnocchi over water, cutting with a knife at 1″ intervals and letting drop into water. Simmer, uncovered, 2–3 minutes until gnocchi float, then remove with a slotted spoon and drain in a colander. Arrange gnocchi 1 layer deep in a buttered 1 1/2-quart *au gratin* dish or shallow casserole, drizzle with melted butter, and sprinkle with cheese. Bake, uncovered, 10 minutes, then broil about 2 minutes to brown lightly.

NPS: 420 C, 220 mg CH, 855 mg S*

VARIATION

Gnocchi with Sage-Cream Sauce: Prepare, cook, and drain gnocchi as recipe directs, then arrange, slightly overlapping, on a heated large platter and keep warm. In a large heavy skillet set over moderate heat, simmer 1 1/2 cups heavy cream, uncovered, with 3 tablespoons minced shallots, 1/3 cup finely chopped sweet red pepper, 1/4 teaspoon salt, and 1 tablespoon coarsely chopped fresh sage (or 1 1/4 teaspoons dried sage) until slightly thickened, 5–7 minutes. Pour 1/2 cup sauce over the gnocchi and pass the rest.

NPS: 575 C, 300 mg CH, 745 mg S*

POTATO GNOCCHI

4 servings

Serve as an accompaniment to veal or chicken.

GNOCCHI
2 cups hot mashed potatoes (without milk or
    seasoning)
1 cup sifted flour
2 eggs, lightly beaten
1 1/2 teaspoons salt
1/8 teaspoon white pepper
Pinch nutmeg

TOPPING
1 1/2 cups hot Italian Tomato Sauce
1/4 cup grated Parmesan cheese

Mix all *gnocchi* ingredients and spoon about half into a pastry bag fitted with a large, plain tube (opening should be about 1/2″ in diameter). Bring about 5 quarts salted water to a boil in a large kettle, then adjust heat so water bubbles *very gently*. Squeeze out gnocchi over water, cutting with a knife at 1″ intervals and letting drop into water. Simmer, uncovered, until gnocchi float, then simmer 1 minute longer. Lift out with slotted spoon, drain in a colander, and keep hot in a shallow serving dish. When all gnocchi are done, cover with sauce and sprinkle with cheese. If you like, pass extra Parmesan.

NPS: 335 C, 140 mg CH, 1590 mg S*

V A R I A T I O N

Cool uncooked gnocchi mixture to room temperature, then roll on a lightly floured board into a rope about 1/2″ thick. Cut in 1″ lengths and imprint lightly with the back of a fork. Cook and serve as directed.

FARINA GNOCCHI PARMIGIANA

6 servings

3 cups milk
2 teaspoons salt
Pinch nutmeg
1 cup quick-cooking farina
2 tablespoons melted butter or margarine
3 egg yolks, lightly beaten
1/2 cup butter
1/2 cup finely grated Parmesan cheese

Heat milk, salt, and nutmeg, covered, in the top of a double boiler over just boiling water until steaming. Add farina slowly, stirring with a wooden spoon; cook and stir until smooth and very thick, about 10 minutes. Set double boiler top on a damp cloth, mix in melted butter and yolks. Brush a large, shallow pan or casserole with cold water. Add farina mixture, spreading to a thickness of 1/2″, cover, and chill 1–2 hours. Cut into strips 3/4″ wide, turn out on a board, and roll under your palms into ropes; cut in 1″ lengths. (*Note:* Dip knife in cold water to prevent sticking.) Preheat oven to 400° F. Arrange half of *gnocchi,* slightly overlapping, over bottom of a buttered 1½-quart *au gratin* dish or shallow casserole. Dot with 1/4 cup butter and 1/4 cup Parmesan; repeat to make a second layer. Bake, uncovered, 10–15 minutes, then broil 4″–5″ from heat 2–3 minutes until lightly browned. Serve hot as a potato substitute with veal scaloppine, veal chops, or chicken, or as a luncheon entree with soup and salad.

NPS: 415 C, 210 mg CH, 1190 mg S*

BOILED COUSCOUS (SEMOLINA)

6 servings

Couscous is the Arabic word for finely ground semolina. It is also the name of the North African lamb stew served over it (see the chapter on lamb). Boiled couscous can be served in place of rice or potatoes.

1 quart beef or chicken broth or water
2 cups uncooked couscous
1/4 cup butter or margarine
1 teaspoon salt (about)

Bring broth to a rapid boil in a large, heavy saucepan, gradually add couscous, stirring briskly to prevent lumping. Cook and stir 2–3 minutes, add butter and salt, and mix lightly. Remove from heat, cover, and let stand 10–15 minutes until all moisture is absorbed and no raw taste remains. Fluff with a fork and serve smothered with gravy. (*Note:* If using to make the lamb stew called Couscous, place cooked couscous in a large colander lined with a triple thickness of dampened cheesecloth, set over kettle of stew, cover, and let steam while stew cooks. Prepared this way, the couscous will be light and moist and delicately lamb-flavored.)

NPS: 315 C, 20 mg CH, 965 mg S*

POLENTA

6 servings ⚖

Polenta, or corn meal mush Italian style, often takes the place of bread in Northern Italy. The mush is cooked until very thick, turned out, cut in chunks, and eaten with chicken, rabbit, or fish stew. Sometimes polenta is topped with the stew, sometimes with Italian sausages and Tomato Sauce. Leftovers are good fried or baked with cheese and sauce. If you have the time and patience, cook polenta the Italian way in a very heavy kettle, *stirring constantly.* Otherwise, use the more foolproof double boiler.

1 cup yellow corn meal
1 cup cold water
1½ pints boiling water
1 teaspoon salt

Mix meal and cold water in the top of a double boiler set over simmering water or in a heavy 4-quart kettle over moderately low heat (if you have one, use the unlined copper polenta pot). Stir in boiling water and salt and cook about 45 minutes until very thick; to avoid lumping stir every 5 minutes if using double boiler, constantly if using the kettle. Mixture is ready to serve when a crust forms on sides of pan. Scrape polenta onto a hot buttered platter, cool 2–3 minutes, then slice as you would bread or cut in squares and serve. (*Note:* To cut more cleanly, use string and a sawing motion.)

NPS: 85 C, 0 mg CH, 365 mg S*

VARIATIONS

⚖ **Fried Polenta:** Cut cold leftover polenta in 2″ squares 1/2″–3/4″ thick, brown lightly, 2–3 minutes on each side, in 2 tablespoons olive oil or bacon drippings over moderately low heat.

NPS: 125 C, 0 mg CH, 365 mg S*

⚖ **Polenta Parmigiana:** Prepare polenta as directed and, while hot, spoon into a buttered 8″ or 9″ square pan; smooth top and cool. Cut in 2″ or 3″ squares, arrange in a single layer in a buttered *au gratin* dish or shallow casserole. Drizzle with 1/3 cup each melted butter and grated Parmesan cheese. Bake, uncovered, 1/2 hour at 400° F., then brown lightly under broiler. Serve as potato substitute.

NPS: 195 C, 30 mg CH, 550 mg S*

BAKED HOMINY CASSEROLE

6 servings   ⚖ ¢

1 (1-pound 12-ounce) can hominy
Liquid drained from hominy + enough milk to measure 1 1/3 cups
3 eggs, lightly beaten
1 cup soft white bread crumbs
1 1/2 teaspoons salt
1/8 teaspoon white pepper
2 tablespoons minced parsley

Preheat oven to 350° F. Mix all ingredients and spoon into a buttered 2-quart casserole. Set casserole in a larger pan half full of hot water and bake, uncovered, about 1 hour until just firm. Serve hot as a potato substitute.

NPS: 150 C, 135 mg CH, 935 mg S*

VARIATIONS

Baked Hominy and Cheese Casserole: Prepare as directed but reduce eggs to 2 and add 1/2 pound grated sharp Cheddar cheese. Serve as a luncheon entree.

NPS: 285 C, 130 mg CH, 1155 mg S*

Baked Hominy Casserole with Sausages or Franks: Prepare casserole as directed and bake 1/2 hour; arrange 6 browned link sausages or frankfurters spoke fashion on top and bake 1/2 hour longer.

NPS (with sausage): 265 C, 155 mg CH, 1160 mg S*
NPS (with franks): 295 C, 160 mg CH, 1440 mg S*

HOMINY, BACON, AND EGG SCRAMBLE

4 servings   ⚖ ▨

A simple dish that is suitable for breakfast, lunch, or supper.

8 slices bacon
1 (1-pound) can hominy, drained
2 eggs lightly beaten with 1/4 cup milk
2 tablespoons grated Parmesan cheese
1/8 teaspoon pepper

Brown bacon in a large, heavy skillet, lift to paper toweling, crumble, and reserve. Drain off all but 1/4 cup drippings, add hominy, and stir-fry over moderate heat 2–3 minutes. Add eggs and scramble until soft; mix in cheese and pepper. Spoon onto warm plates and top with bacon.

NPS: 290 C, 160 mg CH, 450 mg S*

GRITS AND SMITHFIELD HAM PATTIES

6 servings

2 cups cooked hominy grits, chilled
1 cup minced Smithfield ham
1/4 teaspoon black pepper
1/8 teaspoon cayenne pepper
1 egg lightly beaten with 1 tablespoon cold water
3/4 cup fine dry bread crumbs
1/3 cup peanut or other cooking oil
2 cups hot Mushroom or Cheese Sauce

Mash grits with a fork, mix in ham and peppers. Shape into patties about the size of small hamburgers. Dip in egg, then in crumbs to coat evenly. Heat oil in a large, heavy skillet over moderately high heat until very hot but not smoking. Add patties and brown about 2 minutes on a side. Drain on paper toweling and serve topped with sauce.

NPS: 400 C, 90 mg CH, 765 mg S*

PASTA

There are dozens of stories about how pasta came to Italy from China, probably none of them true. It's now thought noodles may have originated in both places, quite independently of the other. The Chinese noodles would have been first, and they would have been made in those ancient days as they are today, of rice or soy flour. First mention of spaghetti in Italy occurred early in the Middle Ages, well before Marco Polo is said to have brought it back from the Orient. But this was pasta made of wheat flour, particularly semolina, ground from the hard golden heart of durum flour. Pasta rapidly became an Italian staple. It was cheap, satisfying, quick to prepare, and so versatile it combined equally well with harvests of land and sea. Why so many shapes and sizes? No one knows, though perhaps it was a way of adding variety to what might have become a boring routine.

Basically, there are two types of Italian pasta: *macaroni and spaghetti,* made of semolina, milled from hard durum wheat (and sometimes part whole wheat or buckwheat flour), water, and just enough egg to bind them, and *egg pasta or noodles,* containing a high proportion of egg. Green noodles have simply had spinach added, red noodles tomato paste. *Note:* Also now available is pasta made of Jerusalem artichoke flour, which is safe for diabetics to eat. There is other European pasta, notably the German *Spätzle* and Middle European *Nockerln,* both soft noodle-like dumplings used to extend the main dish and catch the gravy or sauce.

SOME POPULAR KINDS OF PASTA

Spaghettis (String Shapes):
Fedeline
Capellini
Spaghettini
Vermicelli
Spaghetti
Fideo Enrollado (long curly strands)
Spirale (long spirals)
Fusilli Bucati (tiny "springs")
Fusilli

Flat and Ribbon Shapes:
Linguine (egg pasta)
Tagliarini (egg pasta)
Fettuccine (egg pasta)
Pizzoccheri (buckwheat noodles)
Lasagne
Mafalde

Noodles:
Tagliatelle
Fine Noodles
Medium Noodles
Wide or Broad Noodles

Stuffed Pasta:
Ravioli
Cappelletti
Tortellini

Macaronis (Tubular or Hollow Shapes):
Bucatini
Penne or Mostaccioli (quills or "little mustaches")
Tubetti
Tufoli
Rigatoni
Ziti
Ditalini
Ditali
Cannelloni
Manicotti
Elbow Macaroni

Fancy Shapes:
Farfalle (bows), Farfalline (little bows) and Tripolini (tiny bows)
Conchiglie (seashell macaroni)
Ruoti, Ruotini (big and little cartwheels)
Rotelle, Rotini (little corkscrews)

Soup Pasta:
Stellette (little stars)
Semini (little seeds)
Alphabet
Anelli Campanelline (small rings)
Quadruccini (little squares)
Conchigliette (little seashells)
Acini di Pepe (little peppercorns)
Orzo (barley-shaped pasta)
Pastina (assorted tiny shaped pasta)

Oriental Noodles:
Chow Mein Noodles (crisp-fried and ready to use)
Celophane Noodles (also called bean thread and Chinese vermicelli)
Harusame (Japanese noodles made of soy flour)
Wheat Noodles (ribbons and strings)
Udon (Japanese wheat noodles)
Soba (Japanese buckwheat noodles)
Rice Stick (fine rice flour noodles)

HOW TO USE PASTA

Generally speaking, long, thin pasta and small tubes are boiled and sauced. Broad flat pasta, also the larger fancy shapes, are boiled, then baked *en casserole* with cheese, meat, seafood, or vegetable and sauce. Large tubes are boiled, stuffed, sauced, and baked. Soup pasta is added to soups or thin stews minutes before serving so that the rawness cooks out but not the firm-tenderness.

Italians intensely dislike soft or mushy pasta and eat it *al dente* (to the tooth, meaning there's still a bit of resilience). They are also likely to eat it before the main course or as an accompaniment to meat, which is why Italian cookbooks often state that a pound of pasta will serve 8–10. It won't the way we eat it.

How Much Pasta per Person: Figure 4 servings per pound if the pasta is to be eaten as the main dish, 6–8 if it is an accompaniment.

HOW TO COOK PASTA

Spaghetti and Macaroni: For each 1 pound pasta, bring 6–7 quarts water and 2 tablespoons salt to a full rolling boil in a large, heavy kettle over high heat. To keep pasta from clumping, add about a teaspoon olive or other cooking oil. Do not break strands of pasta, even if very long, but ease into the kettle, pushing farther in as ends soften, until completely submerged. Water should be boiling rapidly all the while, so if necessary add pasta a little at a time. As soon as all pasta is in the pot, begin timing it; do not cover but *do* move pasta occasionally with a long-handled fork. Depending on size and shape, dry (commercial) pasta will take 5–10 minutes to become *al dente;* very large pasta may take 15–20 minutes. Begin testing after 4 minutes, and test regularly thereafter, pulling out a strand and biting it. There should be no raw starch taste but pasta should be firm-tender. *Note:* Freshly made pasta will cook *much faster* than dry pasta—in less than 1 minute for the extra-thin, about 1–3 minutes for linquine or spaghetti, and 5–10 minutes for large pasta. Whole wheat pasta will take slightly longer, but test all freshly made pasta often to make sure that it doesn't overcook. The second the pasta is done, pull off the fire. If you've cooked a small amount, fork out or lift with tongs to serving platter, letting excess moisture run back into kettle. This method won't work, however, for more than a pound of pasta, because you can only lift out a bit at a time and that left in the pot goes mushy. So drain in a colander—fast—and return to kettle. *Do not rinse.* Set kettle over low heat and shake about 1/2 minute, then serve pasta immediately. Mound on a hot platter or individual serving plates (wide-rimmed soup plates are best), top, if you like, with a hearty lump of softened butter, then with sauce. If sauce is mixed into pasta before serving, do so with a lifting and turning motion, as though tossing salad; never stir.

If Pasta Must Wait: As soon as pasta is drained, return to kettle and dot well with butter. Cover and set in oven turned to lowest heat. Pasta will hold about 1/2 hour this way. If dinner is delayed longer than that, cook a new batch (the old can be used in stuffings, meat loaves, or casseroles).

Microwaving Pasta: Don't bother. It will take as long to cook pasta in a microwave oven as it does on top of the stove. *Casseroles containing cooked pasta,* however (macaroni and cheese, baked shells, lasagne, cannelloni, and manicotti, etc.), microwave perfectly if you use times and power levels oven manufacturer recommends. When adapting casserole recipes for the microwave, follow these guidelines:
• Reduce quantity of sauce or liquid recipe calls for by about one quarter and microwave covered with vented plastic food wrap.
• Rotate and/or stir casseroles often from edges toward center for even cooking.
• Do not add cheese toppings until after casserole comes from microwave oven; the cheese will melt quickly from residual heat and can be browned in a conventional broiler for a prettier look.
• Let all microwaved pasta casseroles stand on the counter 5–10 minutes before serving to complete the cooking.

To Reheat Leftover Pasta: Sauced pasta is no problem; simply heat slowly in a covered saucepan to serving temperature. Unsauced pasta should be covered with boiling water and allowed to stand about 2 minutes, then drained well.

To Reheat Leftover Pasta in a Microwave: If pasta is unsauced, place in a microwave-safe container, add no liquid, cover with vented plastic food wrap, and microwave about 1 minute per serving at *HIGH power level* until steaming. *If pasta is sauced,* follow guidelines given for microwaving casseroles containing cooked pasta above. *Note:* Frozen pasta, if unsauced, should be microwaved about 50 per cent longer than that taken straight from the refrigerator; sauced pasta should first be defrosted in the microwave, then reheated (see Defrosting, Heating, or Cooking Frozen Foods by Microwave in Chapter 1).

Noodles and Egg Pasta: These are softer than spaghetti and cook faster. They're also slightly saltier. Follow procedure for spaghetti but use half the amount of salt. Add noodles by handfuls to rapidly boiling water and cook uncovered. Fine noodles will be done in about 3 minutes, larger ones in 5–7. (*Note:* Homemade noodles will cook faster than the commercial, so watch carefully and taste often.) When noodles taste done, they are done. Drain quickly in a colander, again do not rinse, mound in serving dish, mix in a few dabs of butter, then sauce. Noodles do not wait well, so serve as soon as they're done.

Oriental Noodles: All of these hair-fine, translucent noodles are prepared more or less the same way. Soak in warm water about 10 minutes to soften, then drain well and use as recipes direct. They may also be deep-fat-fried without being soaked. Heat oil (preferably peanut oil) to 380° F., crumble noodles into fat a little at a time, and fry, stirring gently with a slotted spoon, 1/2–1 minute until frizzled and pale golden. Drain on paper toweling and use as a crunchy topping for Chinese dishes.

SAUCES FOR PASTA

In addition to the recipes that follow, there are a number of sauces suitable for pasta in the chapter on sauces and gravies.

HOMEMADE PASTA DOUGH

1 1/2 pounds

Semolina flour, milled from hard durum wheat, makes the best pasta because of its high gluten content, but it is very difficult to knead by hand. Bread flour, also made of hard wheat, is second best. As for all-purpose flours, the unbleached produces a firm-tender pasta, but that made from bleached flour is unpleasantly soft. Whole wheat flour, if mixed 3 to 1 with gluten flour (available in health food stores), and rye and buckwheat flours, if mixed 1/2 and 1/2 with bread flour, can all be kneaded into excellent pasta. Cook homemade pasta by the basic method,* but remember that it will boil faster than the commercial.

4 cups unsifted semolina flour or sifted bread flour or 2 cups each semolina and bread flour

1 1/2 teaspoons salt
4 eggs
1/4 cup lukewarm water
2 tablespoons olive or other cooking oil

Mix semolina flour and salt together thoroughly (or sift bread flour with salt); make a well in center and pour in eggs, water, and oil. Gradually draw dry ingredients from edges of bowl into liquids to form a fairly stiff dough (you may need to use your hands at the end). Or mix with a dough hook in an electric mixer (hold a dry towel over bowl so flour doesn't fly). Knead dough on lightly floured board about 10 minutes until smooth and elastic. Cover with dry cloth and let rest 1/2 hour. Quarter dough and roll paper thin, one piece at a time, into a 13″–14″ square on a lightly floured board, using as little additional flour as possible and keeping edges straight. Let rolled-out dough rest 5–10 minutes before cutting, turning once to dry both sides evenly. Check dough frequently; it should feel soft and supple, not dry or brittle. Cut into desired shapes (see How to Cut Pasta).

NPS (1/4 pound with semolina or bread flour): 370 C, 180 mg CH, 595 mg S*

VARIATIONS

Whole Wheat Pasta Dough: Substitute 3 cups unsifted whole wheat flour and 1 cup unsifted gluten flour for the semolina flour; increase water to 5–6 tablespoons, then proceed as recipe directs.

NPS (1/4 pound): 375 C, 180 mg CH, 595 mg S*

Pasta Verde (Green Pasta): Combine flour with 1 teaspoon salt; blend 2 eggs with 2 tablespoons water, 1 tablespoon oil, and 1/2 cup well-drained, puréed, cooked spinach. Dump spinach mixture into well in dry ingredients and proceed as directed.

NPS (1/4 pound): 330 C, 90 mg CH, 400 mg S*

Tomato Pasta (Red Pasta): Use bread flour, omit salt and eggs from basic recipe above; combine 1/2 cup tomato paste, 2/3 cup lukewarm water, and 2 tablespoons oil, pour into well in dry ingredients, and proceed as directed.

NPS (1/4 pound): 335 C, 0 mg CH, 175 mg S*

Processor Pasta: The processor is a whiz at mixing any of the above pasta doughs, but you must reverse the order of mixing as follows: Break eggs into the work bowl of a food processor fitted with the metal chopping blade, add oil and water (or other wet ingredients) and mix by snapping the motor on and off 2–3 times. Combine salt and flour and add to machine, 1 cup at a time, letting motor run nonstop about 5 seconds after each addition. When all flour has been incorporated, let processor run nonstop 8–10 seconds until dough forms a ball and rides up on the central spindle. Remove dough from processor, divide in half, shape each half into a ball, cover each with a turned-upside-down mixing bowl, and let stand on the counter about 45 minutes to "season." Roll as directed, then cut or shape as desired. (Note: Do not use this dough in the food processor's pasta-extruding attachment; it is too wet and may gum up the works.) For best results, use the recipe your processor manufacturer recommends.

To Use a Pasta Rolling Machine: Prepare dough as directed up to point of rolling. Flatten each piece of dough into a rectangle, flour it *lightly,* and feed into machine following manufacturer's instructions. For the first rolling, set dial at widest opening (No. 10), roll several times at this setting until dough is elastic, then decrease for each successive rolling until desired thickness is reached. No. 3 or 4 is good for noodles, No. 2 for cannelloni, manicotti, and ravioli. If strips become unwieldy in the rolling, halve crosswise. *(Note:* Keep remaining dough covered while rolling each piece.)

How to Cut Pasta:

For Noodles (including lasagne noodles): Roll dough up loosely, jelly-roll fashion, cut crosswise in strips of desired width, and unroll. Cover with dry cloth and let dry at room temperature 1 hour. *(Note:* Noodles may be frozen [up to 2 months] or dried overnight [turn now and then] and stored airtight; use within 1 week.)

For Cannelloni, Manicotti, or Ravioli: Cut rolled dough into squares of desired size.

To Use a Pasta-Cutting Machine: After rolled-out strips have dried 5–10 minutes, feed through appropriate blades as manufacturer directs. To keep strands of cut pasta separate, dust lightly with flour, or toss with semolina or cornmeal, or gather strands as they fall from the machine and arrange in neat rows on a flour-dusted towel, paper toweling, or wax paper.

BASIC DOUGH FOR AUTOMATIC PASTA MAKERS

1½ pounds

The easiest way to make pasta is in a machine that mixes, kneads, *and* shapes the dough (most can handle up to 2 pounds of dough at a time). Make sure the machine you buy has an automatic shut-off to prevent overheating should the machine jam, and to keep it operating smoothly, keep all parts spotless. Needless to say, you should study the instruction manual before attempting to make pasta. When making pasta dough, measure ingredients meticulously. Too much liquid will make the pasta sticky, too little, crumbly. And too much salt will make the dough extrude unevenly. It's best to *underestimate* the amount of liquid—additional water can be easily worked into the dough (flour is more difficult to incorporate). *Tip:* Keep extruding disc in hot water until ready for it—the pasta will extrude more evenly.

4 cups unsifted semolina flour
1 teaspoon salt
4 eggs, at room temperature, lightly beaten
2 tablespoons lukewarm water
2 teaspoons olive or other cooking oil

Combine flour and salt; also combine eggs, water, and oil, then mix and knead dough as machine manufacturer directs. Take up a bit of dough in your fingers and press it together; it should *just* stick together. If it is crumbly, add additional water, 1 teaspoon at a time, mixing thoroughly after each addition. If, on the other hand, the dough forms a wet ball, break it into walnut-size pieces and add more flour, 1 tablespoon at a time; mix well after each addition. When pasta is the perfect consistency, equip pasta machine with the extruding disc and extrude pasta as directed. Cut strands into uniform lengths, then lay on a dry cloth or wax paper lightly dusted with semolina, all-purpose flour, or cornmeal. Also lightly dust the pasta itself with flour or cornmeal. Let pasta dry at least 10 minutes before cooking.

NPS (¼ pound): 400 C, 180 mg CH, 415 mg S*

VARIATIONS

Bread Flour Pasta: Use 4 cups sifted bread flour and resift with 1 teaspoon salt; combine 3 lightly beaten eggs with 2 tablespoons lukewarm water and 4 teaspoons olive or other cooking oil. Mix and test consistency, then correct as needed and shape according to manufacturer's directions.

NPS (¼ pound): 345 C, 135 mg CH, 400 mg S*

Whole Wheat Pasta: Mix 3 cups unsifted whole wheat flour, 1 cup unsifted gluten flour, and 1 teaspoon salt; also combine 4 lightly beaten eggs with 2 tablespoons lukewarm water and ¼ cup olive or other cooking oil. Mix and test consistency, then correct as needed and shape as manufacturer directs.

NPS (1/4 pound): 415 C, 180 mg CH, 415 mg S*

Tomato Pasta: Combine 1/2 cup tomato paste, 1/2 cup lukewarm water, and 2 tablespoons olive or other cooking oil, then mix into a dough as manufacturer directs, using 4 cups sifted bread flour. Test dough consistency, correct as needed, then shape pasta according to manufacturer's directions.

NPS (1/4 pound): 390 C, 180 mg CH, 585 mg S*

Pasta Verde (Green Pasta): Combine 2 lightly beaten eggs, 1/2 cup well-drained, puréed cooked spinach, and 1 tablespoon lukewarm water. Following manufacturer's directions, mix into a dough using 4 cups sifted bread flour. Test the dough for consistency and correct as needed, then shape as manufacturer directs.

NPS (1/4 pound): 360 C, 275 mg CH, 445 mg S*

NOODLE RING

4 servings ¢

A festive way to serve plain buttered noodles.

1/2 pound noodles, cooked and drained by
   package directions
1/4 cup melted butter
1 teaspoon salt
1/8 teaspoon white pepper

Preheat oven to 375° F. Toss noodles with butter, salt, and pepper then *pack* into a *well-buttered* 1 1/2-quart ring mold. Place mold in a larger pan half filled with water and bake, uncovered, 20–30 minutes. Lift mold from water bath, loosen edges, and invert on a hot platter. Ring is now ready to fill with any creamed meat, fish, or vegetable.

NPS: 320 C, 85 mg CH, 670 mg S*

VARIATIONS

Egg-Noodle Ring: Prepare noodle mixture as directed but add 2 lightly beaten eggs and 1/2 cup heavy cream. Bake as directed, allowing 35–40 minutes until ring is firm. Unmold and fill with something delicate—Creamed Sweetbreads, perhaps, or asparagus tips.

NPS: 465 C, 260 mg CH, 715 mg S*

Cheese-Noodle Ring: Prepare noodle mixture as directed but add 2 lightly beaten eggs, 1/2 cup milk, and 1 cup coarsely grated sharp Cheddar cheese. Butter ring mold and coat with fine dry bread crumbs; pack in

noodle mixture and bake as directed about 40 minutes. Fill with creamed spinach, broccoli, cauliflower, chicken, or turkey.

NPS: 545 C, 265 mg CH, 970 mg S*

Some Quick Ways to Dress Up Noodles

The following amounts are for 1 pound noodles, cooked and drained by package directions. Depending upon richness of sauce, each will serve 6–8 if noodles are used as a potato substitute, 4–6 if a main course.

Savory Noodles: Dress noodles with 1/3–1/2 cup seasoned butter: Browned, Garlic, Dill, Herb, or Parsley-Lemon.

NPS (4–6–8): 575–385–290 C, 145–100–75 mg CH, 195–130–100 mg S*

Noodles Noisette: Toss noodles with 1/3 cup minced, blanched, toasted almonds or peanuts, pecans, cashews, walnuts, piñon, or pistachio nuts and 1/3–1/2 cup melted butter.

NPS (4–6–8): 640–425–320 C, 145–100–75 mg CH, 160–105–80 mg S*

Noodles Amandine: Sauté 1/2 cup slivered, blanched almonds in 1/2 cup butter until golden; off heat mix in 2 teaspoons lemon juice, pour over noodles, and toss to mix.

NPS (4–6–8): 740–495–370 C, 170–110–85 mg CH, 240–160–120 mg S*

Fried Noodles: Slowly brown cooked noodles in 1/2 cup melted butter (you'll probably have to do 2 batches), stirring occasionally, about 15 minutes.

NPS (4–6–8): 645–430–320 C, 170–110–85 mg CH, 240–160–120 mg S*

Herbed Noodles: Toss noodles with 1/2 cup melted butter and 1/4 cup minced chives or parsley, or 1–2 tablespoons minced fresh or 1 teaspoon dried basil, oregano, savory, marjoram, dill, or chervil.

NPS (4–6–8): 645–430–320 C, 170–110–85 mg CH, 240–160–120 mg S*

Poppy Seed Noodles: Toss noodles with 1/2 cup melted butter and 2 tablespoons poppy seeds. (*Note:* Toasted sesame seeds and caraway seeds are equally good.)

NPS (4–6–8): 665–445–335 C, 170–110–85 mg CH, 240–160–120 mg S*

Garlic Noodles: Toss noodles with 1 cup coarse dry bread crumbs browned in 1/2 cup Garlic Butter.

NPS (4–6–8): 740–495–370 C, 170–115–85 mg CH, 560–370–280 mg S*

Sauced Noodles: Toss noodles with 1/2 cup hot milk and 1 cup hot Parsley, Mushroom-Cheese, Velouté, Curry, Mornay, Thin White Sauce, or Egg Sauce. Or toss with 1 1/2 cups hot Tomato Sauce, or any gravy. Recipe too flexible for meaningful nutritional count.

Noodles Florentine: Toss noodles with 1 cup minced, well-drained, cooked spinach and 1/3 cup melted butter.

NPS (4–6–8): 585–390–290 C, 145–100–75 mg CH, 180–120–90 mg S*

Noodles Smetana: Toss noodles with 1/2 cup melted butter, 1 pint sour cream, 1/4 cup minced chives, 1 peeled and finely minced garlic clove, 1 teaspoon salt, and 1/8 teaspoon pepper.

NPS (4–6–8): 890–595–445 C, 220–145–110 mg CH, 300–200–150 mg S*

Noodles Hungarian: Return drained noodles to pan, add 1 pound cottage cheese, 1/2 cup melted butter or bacon drippings, and pepper to taste. Toss gently over lowest heat to warm cheese. Serve topped with crisp, crumbled bacon or crisply browned, diced salt pork.

NPS (4–6–8): 575–385–290 C, 135–90–70 mg CH, 795–530–400 mg S*

Noodles Lyonnaise: Stir-fry 1 thinly sliced large Bermuda onion in 1/2 cup butter over moderate heat until pale golden, 5–8 minutes. Serve on top of buttered noodles.

NPS (4–6–8): 540–360–270 C, 145–95–70 mg CH, 360–240–180 mg S*

Noodles Polonaise: Lightly brown 1 cup coarse white bread crumbs in 1/3 cup butter. Off heat, mix in the sieved yolks of 4 hard-cooked eggs and 2 tablespoons minced parsley. Serve on top of buttered noodles.

NPS (4–6–8): 735–490–365 C, 420–280–210 mg CH, 355–235–175 mg S*

SPÄTZLE

4 servings ¢

These tiny teardrop-shaped German noodles are served as a potato substitute (though in Germany often *in addition* to potatoes). They're good with all kinds of meats, also as a soup garnish.

1 cup sifted flour
1/2 teaspoon salt
Pinch nutmeg (optional)
Pinch paprika (optional)
1 egg, lightly beaten

1/3 cup cold water
2 tablespoons melted butter or margarine

Sift flour with salt and, if you like, spices. Mix egg and water and add slowly to dry mixture; beat hard until smooth (batter will be quite thick). Bring about 2 quarts well-salted water (or chicken or beef broth) to a slow boil in a large, heavy saucepan. Balance a colander on rim of saucepan so that it is well *above* water. Spoon about 1/3 of batter into colander, then carefully press through holes, letting *Spätzle* fall into water. Cook 3–4 minutes, lift out with a slotted spoon, and keep warm while cooking remaining spätzle. Toss spätzle with melted butter and serve hot.

NPS: 175 C, 85 mg CH, 350 mg S*

NOCKERLN

6 servings ¢

These delicate little Middle European dumplings are made to be smothered with the sauces and gravies of goulash and *paprikash*.

1/4 cup butter or margarine
1 egg, lightly beaten
6 tablespoons milk
1/2 teaspoon salt
1 cup sifted flour

Cream butter until light; mix egg with milk and salt. Add flour alternately to butter with egg mixture, beginning and ending with flour, then beat until smooth. Bring 4 quarts well-salted water to a slow boil. Drop in *Nockerln* by the 1/2 teaspoon and cook, uncovered, a few at a time, 4–5 minutes. *(Note:* Cook no more than 1 layer of nockerln at a time and wet spoon each time you dip it in the batter.) Lift cooked dumplings from kettle with a slotted spoon and keep warm while you cook the rest.

NPS: 160 C, 70 mg CH, 280 mg S*

VARIATION

Swirl cooked nockerln in 1/4 cup melted butter in a large, heavy kettle over moderately low heat, just to coat, then serve.

NPS: 225 C, 90 mg CH, 355 mg S*

DELUXE MACARONI AND CHEESE

6 servings ¢

1/4 cup butter or margarine
1/4 cup unsifted flour
1 teaspoon powdered mustard
2 1/2 cups milk

3 cups coarsely grated sharp Cheddar cheese
1/4 teaspoon salt (about)
1/8 teaspoon white pepper
1 tablespoon Worcestershire sauce
1 tablespoon finely grated yellow onion
  (optional)
1/2 pound elbow macaroni, cooked and drained
  by package directions

Preheat oven to 350° F. Melt butter in a saucepan over moderate heat, blend in flour and mustard, slowly stir in milk, and cook, stirring until thickened. Mix in 2 cups grated cheese and all remaining ingredients except macaroni. Taste for salt and add a little more if needed. Cook and stir until cheese melts. Off heat, mix in macaroni; turn into a buttered 2-quart casserole, sprinkle with remaining cheese, and bake, uncovered, about 1/2 hour until bubbly and lightly browned.

NPS: 520 C, 95 mg CH, 600 mg S*

ITALIAN MACARONI, PIMIENTO, AND CHEESE LOAF

6–8 servings   ¢

1/2 pound elbow macaroni, cooked and drained
  by package directions
2 cups milk, scalded
3 eggs, lightly beaten
2 cups soft white bread crumbs
1 cup coarsely grated mozzarella cheese
1 cup finely grated Parmesan cheese
1 cup coarsely grated provolone cheese
1/4 cup minced scallions (include some tops)
2 tablespoons minced parsley
1/4 cup minced pimiento
1 teaspoon salt (about)
1/4 teaspoon white pepper
2–3 cups hot Tomato or Mushroom Sauce
  (optional)

Preheat oven to 350° F. Mix all ingredients but sauce, taste for salt and adjust. Spoon into a well-buttered 9″ × 5″ × 3″ loaf pan and bake, uncovered, about 1 hour until firm in the center. Let stand upright 5 minutes; loosen and invert on a hot platter. Slice, not too thin, as you would a meat loaf. If you like, spoon some sauce over each serving and pass the rest.

NPS (6–8): 455–340 C, 185–140 mg CH, 1005–750 mg S*

VARIATION

Macaroni and Cheddar Loaf: Prepare as directed but substitute 3/4 pound coarsely grated sharp Cheddar for the 3 Italian cheeses.

NPS (6–8): 505–375 C, 210–155 mg CH, 870–655 mg S*

FISHERMAN'S BAKED SHELLS

6 servings   ¢

You can vary this next recipe by varying the fish. Use mussels, for example, instead of clams (but don't mince—they're nicer left whole). Or use tiny squid instead of shrimp, salmon instead of tuna.

1 medium-size yellow onion, peeled and minced
1 clove garlic, peeled and crushed
1 medium-size carrot, peeled and cut in fine dice
1 stalk celery, cut in fine dice
2 tablespoons butter or margarine
2 tablespoons flour
1 (6 1/2-ounce) can minced clams, drained
  (reserve liquid)
Liquid drained from clams + enough bottled
  clam juice to make 2 cups
1 cup dry white wine or water
1/4 teaspoon basil
1/4 teaspoon savory
3/4 pound raw shrimp, shelled and deveined
2 tablespoons cooking oil
1 (6 1/2-ounce) can tuna, drained and flaked
1/2 pound seashell macaroni, cooked and drained
  by package directions
2 tablespoons minced parsley

Stir-fry onion, garlic, carrot, and celery in butter in a 2-quart saucepan over moderate heat 3–5 minutes until limp. Mix in flour, add clam juice, wine, and herbs, cover, and simmer 30 minutes, stirring now and then. Meanwhile, stir-fry shrimp in oil over moderate heat 3–5 minutes until pink; remove and reserve. Preheat oven to 350° F. When sauce is ready, mix in clams, shrimp, and tuna. Layer macaroni and sauce in a buttered 3-quart casserole, cover, and bake 30 minutes. Sprinkle with parsley and serve.

NPS: 370 C, 105 mg CH, 585 mg S*

SPAGHETTI AND MEAT BALLS IN TOMATO SAUCE

4 servings   ¢

SAUCE
1 (1-pound) can tomatoes (do not drain)
1 (6-ounce) can tomato paste
1 cup water
1 teaspoon salt
1/4 teaspoon pepper
2 teaspoons sugar

2 teaspoons basil
1 tablespoon minced onion
1/2 teaspoon garlic juice

MEAT BALLS
1 pound ground beef
1 cup soft white bread crumbs
1/4 cup water
1/4 cup milk
1 small yellow onion, peeled and minced
1 tablespoon Worcestershire sauce
1 teaspoon salt
1/4 teaspoon pepper
2 tablespoons cooking oil (for browning)

PASTA
1 pound spaghetti

Place all sauce ingredients in a large saucepan, cover, and simmer 1 hour, stirring occasionally and breaking up tomatoes. Meanwhile, mix meat ball ingredients except oil and shape into 1″ balls. Brown 4–5 minutes in the oil in a large, heavy skillet over moderate heat, doing only 1/3 of balls at a time and draining on paper toweling. Pour all but 2 tablespoons drippings from skillet, mix in a little sauce, scraping up browned bits, and return to saucepan. Add meat balls, cover, and simmer 15 minutes. Cook spaghetti by package directions, drain, and arrange on a large, deep platter. Place meat balls on top, spoon a little sauce over all, and pass the rest.

NPS: 860 C, 85 mg CH, 1740 mg S*

HOT PASTA WITH FRESH COLD TOMATO AND BASIL SAUCE

4 servings ¢

This recipe demands red, vine-ripened tomatoes. Nothing else will do.

SAUCE
2 cloves garlic, peeled and crushed
1/4 cup olive or other cooking oil
2 pounds dead-ripe tomatoes, peeled, cored, seeded, and coarsely chopped
1/2 teaspoon sugar
1 teaspoon salt
1/4 teaspoon pepper (preferably freshly ground)
3 tablespoons minced fresh basil

PASTA
1 pound spaghetti, linguine, fettuccine, or small, fancy, shaped pasta

Sauté garlic in oil in a large heavy skillet over moderately high heat 1 minute until golden. Reduce heat to moderately low, add tomatoes and all remaining sauce ingredients except basil and stir-fry 2 minutes just to blend; *do not allow tomatoes to cook.* Off heat, mix in basil, cover and let stand at room temperature 2 hours, stirring now and then. When ready to serve, cook and drain pasta by package directions, then divide among 4 dinner plates, making a nest of the pasta on each. Top with tomato sauce, dividing total amount evenly.

NPS: 595 C, 0 mg CH, 560 mg S*

SPAGHETTI AL PESTO (GENOESE-STYLE SPAGHETTI WITH FRESH BASIL SAUCE)

4 servings

In Italy, women laboriously pound garlic, piñon nuts, basil, and spinach into *pesto* sauce using a mortar and pestle. The electric blender and food processor do a faster, better job.

SAUCE
2 cloves garlic, peeled and crushed
1/3 cup piñon nuts
2 3/4 cups fresh basil leaves, minced
1 cup olive oil
1/2 cup finely grated Parmesan cheese

PASTA
1 pound thin spaghetti
1/4 cup olive oil

Purée garlic, nuts, and basil, with 1/2 cup oil in an electric blender at low speed. (*Note:* Because mixture is thick, you'll have to stop blender often and stir.) Pour purée into a small bowl and add remaining oil, a little at a time, beating well with a fork after each addition; mix in cheese and let sauce "mellow" at room temperature at least 1 hour. Cook spaghetti by package directions, adding 1 tablespoon olive oil to the cooking water; meanwhile, warm remaining oil over low heat. When spaghetti is *al dente (just* tender), drain quickly and return to kettle; add hot oil and toss well. To serve, divide spaghetti among 4 plates and top each portion with a generous ladling of pesto sauce. Set out more freshly grated Parmesan.

NPS: 1135 C, 5 mg CH, 190 mg S*

VARIATION

Processor Pesto: Place 3 cups tightly packed whole basil leaves in the work bowl of a food processor fitted with the metal chopping blade along with garlic, nuts, olive oil, and Parmesan cheese. Churn about 1 minute nonstop until sauce is uniformly velvety. Let stand at room temperature 1 hour as directed, then cook, sauce, and serve spaghetti as recipe directs.

NPS: 1160 C, 5 mg CH, 195 mg S*

SPAGHETTI WITH WHITE CLAM SAUCE

2–4 servings ¢

SAUCE

2 cloves garlic, peeled and minced
¼ cup olive or other cooking oil
2 tablespoons flour
2 cups clam juice (use liquid drained from clams, rounding out measure as needed with bottled clam juice)
1½ cups finely chopped fresh clams or 3 (6½-ounce) cans minced clams, drained (save liquid)
1 tablespoon minced parsley
⅛ teaspoon pepper

PASTA

½ pound thin spaghetti, cooked by package directions and drained
¼ cup coarsely chopped parsley (garnish)

Stir-fry garlic in oil in a saucepan about 1 minute over low heat; do not brown. Blend in flour, add clam juice, and heat, stirring constantly, until mixture thickens slightly; cover and simmer 10–15 minutes. Add clams, minced parsley, and pepper, cover, and simmer 3–5 minutes. Pour sauce over hot spaghetti and toss with 2 forks to mix well. Sprinkle with coarsely chopped parsley and serve.

NPS (2–4): 870–435 C, 105–55 mg CH, 1170–585 mg S*

SPAGHETTI CARBONARA

4 servings

Spaghetti dressed with cream, cheese, bacon, and eggs.

1 pound thin spaghetti
¼ cup bacon drippings
6 eggs, lightly beaten
½ teaspoon salt
⅛ teaspoon white pepper
¾ cup light cream
½ pound crisply cooked bacon, crumbled
½ cup finely grated Parmesan cheese

Cook spaghetti by package directions, timing carefully so it is done just as you begin cooking the eggs. The spaghetti must be *very hot* when the eggs are poured over it so they will cling and continue to cook a bit. Heat drippings in a large, heavy skillet over moderate heat 1–2 minutes. Mix eggs, salt, pepper, and cream, pour into drippings, cook and stir 2–3 minutes until eggs just *begin* to thicken—they should be creamy but *not set;* remove from heat. Quickly drain spaghetti and arrange on a heated platter, pour eggs on top, and toss to mix. Sprinkle with bacon and Parmesan and toss again. Serve at once.

NPS: 1090 C, 505 mg CH, 1490 mg S*

VARIATION

Prepare as directed, substituting linguine, macaroni, or fusilli for the spaghetti. Nutritional count same as basic recipe.

FETTUCCINE ALFREDO

4 servings ⊠

If you prepare this recipe with homemade fettuccine, so much the better.

1 pound hot fettuccine, cooked by package directions
1 pound unsalted butter, sliced ¼″ thick and softened to room temperature
1 pound Parmesan cheese, grated fine
Freshly ground black pepper

Quickly drain fettuccine and return to kettle. Add butter and cheese and toss lightly but rapidly until fettuccine is evenly coated. Serve on heated plates and top with grindings of black pepper.

NPS: 1750 C, 390 mg CH, 2130 mg S*

VARIATION

Creamed Noodles Alfredo (not as authentic but almost as good, and certainly less caloric): Toss hot drained thin or medium-wide noodles with 1 cup melted butter, 2 cups finely grated Parmesan cheese, and 1 cup warm heavy cream. Top with freshly ground pepper.

NPS: 1235 C, 345 mg CH, 1240 mg S*

FETTUCCINE AND FISH

4 servings ¢

SAUCE

1 medium-size yellow onion, peeled, sliced thin, and separated into rings
1 medium-size sweet green or red pepper, cored, seeded, and minced
2 tablespoons olive or other cooking oil
1 (1-pound) can Italian plum tomatoes (do not drain)
2 tablespoons tomato paste
½ cup water

3/4–1 pound haddock or any lean fish fillets, cut in 1″ cubes

1 (2-ounce) can anchovy fillets, drained and minced (optional)

PASTA

1 pound fettuccine, cooked and drained by package directions

TOPPING

1 tablespoon minced fresh basil or parsley

Stir-fry onion and pepper in oil in a large skillet over moderate heat 3–5 minutes until limp. Add tomatoes, chopping as you add, tomato paste, and water; simmer, uncovered, 15 minutes. Scatter fish on top, cover, and simmer 10 minutes. Place pasta in a hot deep serving dish, top with sauce, and toss lightly. Sprinkle with basil and serve. *(Note:* If not using anchovies, taste for salt and adjust.)

NPS: 615 C, 60 mg CH, 390 mg S*

VARIATION

¢ **Fettuccine and Dried Salt Cod (Fettuccine con Baccalà):** Use 3/4 pound filleted salt cod instead of haddock; soak in cold water to cover for 4 hours, drain, pat dry, and cube. Make sauce as directed, omitting anchovies. If you like, add 1/4 cup each piñon nuts and golden seedless raisins just before pouring over pasta.

NPS: 615 C, 60 mg CH, 7000 mg S*

BUCKWHEAT PASTA WITH SESAME AND SNOW PEAS

4–6 servings

1 pound thin buckwheat spaghetti (preferably the Japanese *soba,* available in specialty food shops), cooked and drained by package directions

TOPPING

1/2 pound snow pea pods, washed and trimmed

2 teaspoons dark brown sugar

1/4 cup soy sauce

2 bunches scallions, trimmed and coarsely chopped (include green tops)

1 (10-ounce) package frozen tiny peas, cooked and drained by package directions

2 cloves garlic, peeled and minced

1/4 pound fresh water chestnuts, peeled and sliced thin, or 1 (4-ounce) can water chestnuts, drained and sliced thin

2 teaspoons hot sesame oil

1/4 cup peanut or other cooking oil

1/4 cup red rice vinegar

1/2 cup dry-roasted soybean nuts

Rinse spaghetti briefly under cold running water and drain well. Slice each snow pea pod diagonally into 3 pieces and blanch in boiling salted water 1 minute; drain well and pat very dry on paper toweling. Warm sugar with soy sauce over low heat, stirring until dissolved. Mix with snow pea pods and all remaining topping ingredients, spoon over spaghetti, toss gently, cover, and chill 2–3 hours, tossing now and then. Let stand at room temperature about 20 minutes, toss once again, and serve.

NPS (4–6): 690–460 C, 0 mg CH, 1435–955 mg S*

BEEF AND SAUSAGE STUFFED RIGATONI OR TUFOLI

6 servings   ¢

1/2 pound rigatoni or tufoli, cooked by package directions until barely *al dente,* then drained and rinsed in cool water

FILLING

1/2 pound ground beef chuck

1/2 pound sweet or hot Italian sausages, removed from casings and minced

1/4 pound mushrooms, wiped clean and minced

3/4 cup hot Italian Tomato Sauce

1/3 cup diced mozzarella cheese

TOPPING

2 1/2 cups hot Italian Tomato Sauce

1/4 cup grated Parmesan cheese

Preheat oven to 350° F. While rigatoni cool, prepare filling: Stir-fry beef and sausages in a large, heavy skillet over moderate heat 4–5 minutes until no longer pink; add mushrooms and stir-fry 2–3 minutes. Mix in sauce and simmer, uncovered, 5 minutes; cool slightly and stir in cheese. Using a small teaspoon, stuff into rigatoni; layer in an oiled 2 1/2-quart casserole or *au gratin* dish, topping with some of the 2 1/2 cups sauce as you go. Add remaining sauce, sprinkle with cheese, and bake, uncovered, 30 minutes until bubbly.

NPS: 535 C, 60 mg CH, 1280 mg S*

VARIATIONS

Prepare as directed but substitute one of the following fillings for that above: Chicken and Prosciutto, Spinach and Ricotta, or Cheese Stuffing for Ravioli.

NPS (Chicken and Prosciutto): 390 C, 140 mg CH, 1200 mg S*

NPS (Spinach and Ricotta): 330 C, 70 mg CH, 800 mg S*

NPS (Cheese Stuffing): 415 C, 90 mg CH, 1220 mg S*

MEAT-FILLED RAVIOLI

6 servings ¢

Ravioli, plump little pasta pillows stuffed with meat, eggs, vegetables, or cheese, can be made ahead, then baked in sauce just before serving. If you like, make a quantity and freeze *uncooked* (simply place 1 layer deep on foil-lined trays, cover with foil, and freeze until needed).

½ recipe Homemade Pasta Dough

F I L L I N G
1 pound beef chuck, ground twice
1 small yellow onion, peeled and minced
1 clove garlic, peeled and crushed
1 tablespoon olive or other cooking oil
2 tablespoons flour
¾ cup beef broth
¼ cup tomato paste
1 teaspoon salt
⅛ teaspoon pepper

T O P P I N G
1 cup grated Parmesan cheese
3 cups hot Italian Tomato or Marinara Sauce

Prepare dough as directed and let rest while making filling. Stir-fry beef, onion, and garlic in oil in a saucepan over moderate heat 4–5 minutes until no longer pink; put through finest blade of meat grinder, or chop very fine in a food processor fitted with the metal chopping blade by snapping motor on and off 6–8 times. Return to pan, set over moderate heat, sprinkle in flour, and slowly mix in remaining filling ingredients. Cook and stir until thickened, reduce heat, and simmer, uncovered, 5 minutes; cool to room temperature. Meanwhile, roll half of the dough on a lightly floured board into a paper-thin 14″ square. Drop rounded teaspoonfuls of filling over dough, spacing 2″ apart in neat rows. Roll remaining dough into a square of the same size and lay over the first. Press lightly around mounds of filling, then cut in 2″ squares with a ravioli cutter or pastry wheel forming "pillows." *(Note:* If you have ravioli pans [trays with 12 depressions and sharp raised edges], lay 1 sheet of rolled dough on pan, drop filling into depressions, cover with second dough sheet, and roll with a rolling pin to separate squares. Make sure edges are sealed so filling won't ooze out.) Place ravioli 1 layer deep on a lightly floured tray, dust with flour, and let stand, uncovered, ½ hour; turn and let stand ½ hour longer. Bring about 5 quarts salted water to a boil in a large kettle (to keep ravioli from sticking, add 1 teaspoon cooking oil). Drop in about a dozen ravioli and cook 7–10 minutes, moving them around so they don't stick. Lift to a hot, buttered large platter with a slotted spoon, top with 2 tablespoons cheese and 3–4 tablespoons sauce, and keep warm. Continue cooking ravioli, adding to dish and topping with cheese and sauce. Serve very hot with remaining cheese and sauce.

NPS: 610 C, 150 mg CH, 1940 mg S*

V A R I A T I O N S

¢ **Mushroom-Eggplant or Cheese Ravioli:** Prepare as directed but use Italian Mushroom-Eggplant or Italian Cheese Sauce instead of tomato sauce.

NPS (Mushroom-Eggplant): 595 C, 150 mg CH, 1715 mg S*
NPS (Cheese): 780 C, 220 mg CH, 1480 mg S*

¢ **Sausage-Stuffed Ravioli:** Prepare as directed but substitute ¾ pound sweet Italian sausages and ¼ pound salami, removed from casings and minced, for the beef.

NPS: 605 C, 150 mg CH, 2655 mg S*

Chicken-and-Prosciutto-Stuffed Ravioli: Prepare as directed but use the following filling: 1 cup each ground cooked chicken and *prosciutto* mixed with 2 lightly beaten egg yolks, ⅛ teaspoon each nutmeg and pepper, and 2 tablespoons each melted butter and grated Parmesan cheese.

NPS: 490 C, 235 mg CH, 1740 mg S*

¢ **Spinach-and-Ricotta-Stuffed Ravioli:** Prepare as directed but for the meat filling substitute: 1 cup each ricotta cheese and well-drained, puréed, cooked spinach mixed with 1 lightly beaten egg yolk and a pinch nutmeg.

NPS: 440 C, 170 mg CH, 1420 mg S*

¢ **Cheese-Stuffed Ravioli:** Prepare as directed but fill with the following mixture: 1 pound ricotta cheese mixed with ½ cup grated Parmesan or mozzarella cheese, 1 lightly beaten egg, 1 teaspoon each minced parsley and basil, and ¾ teaspoon salt. Omit sauce and sprinkle layers with 2–3 tablespoons each melted butter and grated Parmesan.

NPS: 405 C, 190 mg CH, 840 mg S*

CHEESE-FILLED TORTELLINI WITH TOMATO SAUCE

6 servings

Delicious made with plain pasta, whole wheat, Pasta Verde, or Tomato Pasta.

½ recipe Homemade Pasta Dough (or one of its variations)

FILLING
¼ pound ricotta cheese
¼ pound mozzarella cheese, coarsely grated
2 tablespoons grated Parmesan cheese
2 tablespoons heavy cream
¼ teaspoon salt
⅛ teaspoon pepper
2 tablespoons minced chives

TOPPING
3 cups hot Italian Tomato or Marinara Sauce

Prepare dough as directed and let rest while you prepare the filling. Mix all filling ingredients, cover and chill. Roll half of dough on a lightly floured board into a 12″–13″ circle; cut into 2″ circles using a floured cookie cutter. Roll and cut remaining dough the same way; also reroll and cut scraps. Drop a scant ½ teaspoon of filling in the center of each circle, brush rims with cold water, fold in half, and press edges firmly to seal so filling won't ooze out. Wrap filled half-circles around your index finger, overlapping points, and press to seal. Arrange tortellini one layer deep on a lightly floured tray, dust with flour, and let stand, uncovered, 20–30 minutes; turn and let stand 20 minutes longer. Bring about 5 quarts salted water to a boil in a large kettle and add 1 tablespoon cooking oil to keep tortellini from sticking together during cooking. Drop about 16 tortellini into kettle and cook 7–10 minutes, moving them around so they don't clump. Using a slotted spoon, lift to a large hot buttered platter, top with 3–4 tablespoons sauce, and keep hot. Continue cooking tortellini, adding to platter, and topping with sauce. Serve hot with remaining sauce; pass grated Parmesan cheese, if you wish.

NPS: 410 C, 125 mg CH, 1330 mg S*

VARIATIONS

Prepare as directed but substitute one of the following fillings for that above: Meat, Sausage, Chicken and Prosciutto, Spinach and Ricotta Stuffing for Ravioli.

NPS (Meat): 550 C, 140 mg CH, 1690 mg S*
NPS (Sausage): 545 C, 140 mg CH, 2405 mg S*
NPS (Chicken and Prosciutto): 440 C, 230 mg CH, 1575 mg S*
NPS (Spinach and Ricotta): 380 C, 155 mg CH, 1170 mg S*

BAKED STUFFED SHELLS (CONCHIGLIE)

6 servings

This recipe works equally well with any giant pasta tubes.

¾ pound large pasta shells

FILLING
1½ pounds ricotta cheese
¾ pound mozzarella cheese, coarsely grated
¼ pound grated Parmesan cheese
1 egg, lightly beaten
2 tablespoons minced parsley
2 tablespoons minced chives
1 teaspoon salt
¼ teaspoon pepper
⅛ teaspoon nutmeg

TOPPING
3 cups Italian Tomato, Marinara, or Savory American Beef and Tomato Sauce for Pasta

Preheat oven to 350° F. Cook pasta 9–10 minutes (no longer or shells may break as you stuff them) by package directions. Drain, rinse with cold water, then drain well again. Meanwhile, blend all filling ingredients and, when shells are cool enough to handle, stuff each with about 1 rounded tablespoon of filling (use a coffee or teaspoon to do the stuffing). Spoon a thin layer of sauce over the bottom of a very large shallow casserole (or use two smaller ones), then arrange shells, rounded sides down, in a single layer in the sauce. Top with remaining sauce and bake, uncovered, 30 minutes. Pass extra Parmesan cheese, if you wish.

NPS: 780 C, 160 mg CH, 1860 mg S*

VARIATION

Stuffed Shells with Meat Filling: Substitute Meat Filling for Cannelloni for that above and proceed as recipe directs.

NPS: 575 C, 45 mg CH, 1395 mg S*

LASAGNE

8–10 servings ¢

1 pound sweet Italian sausages
2 quarts (about) hot Savory American Beef and Tomato Sauce for Pasta or Marinara Sauce
1 pound lasagne, cooked and drained by package directions
1 pound ricotta cheese
⅔ cup finely grated Parmesan cheese
¾ pound mozzarella cheese, coarsely grated

Preheat oven to 350° F. Sauté sausages 15–20 minutes over moderate heat or until cooked through, drain on paper toweling, and slice 1/2" thick. Spoon a thin layer of sauce into an ungreased 13" × 9" × 2" baking pan and arrange a single layer of lasagne (about 1/4 of the total) on top, slightly overlapping. Add another thin layer of sauce, top with 1/3 of the sausage and ricotta, and sprinkle with 1/4 of the Parmesan and mozzarella. Continue building up layers until all ingredients are in the pan, ending with Parmesan and mozzarella. (*Note:* Recipe can be prepared to this point early in the day or days ahead. Cool, cover, and refrigerate or freeze until needed. Bring to room temperature before proceeding.) Bake, uncovered, 35–45 minutes until lightly browned and bubbling. Cut into squares and serve.

NPS (8–10) (with Savory Beef and Tomato Sauce): 1065–850 C, 175–140 mg CH, 2210–1765 mg S*
NPS (8–10) (with Marinara Sauce): 750–600 C, 100–80 mg CH, 1890–1515 mg S*

VARIATION

Meat Ball Lasagne: Prepare 1 recipe Savory Meat Balls as directed but omit the gravy. Simmer the meat balls 10–15 minutes in 2 quarts Marinara Sauce, then prepare the lasagne as above, substituting the meat balls, sliced 1/4" thick, for the Italian sausages.

CANNELLONI OR MANICOTTI SQUARES

1 1/2 dozen 4" squares ¢

Cannelloni and manicotti are large pasta squares (or, if bought, tubes). In this country the larger tube or square (usually 5") is manicotti, the smaller (4") one, cannelloni. Tufoli may be substituted for either.

1/2 recipe Homemade Pasta Dough
5 quarts water
2 tablespoons salt
1 teaspoon cooking oil

Prepare and roll dough as directed; cut in 4" squares, cover with cloth, and let dry 1 hour at room temperature. Bring water, salt, and oil to a boil in a large kettle and cook, uncovered, about 6 squares at a time, in rapidly boiling water 7–10 minutes until tender. Lift with a slotted spoon to a dampened dish towel. Squares are now ready to fill.

NPS: 65 C, 30 mg CH, 465 mg S*

CANNELLONI WITH MEAT FILLING

6 servings ¢

1 recipe Cannelloni Squares

FILLING
1 teaspoon cooking oil
1 pound ground beef chuck
2 tablespoons minced yellow onion
2 teaspoons salt
1/4 teaspoon pepper
1 teaspoon savory
2 tablespoons flour
3/4 cup beef broth

SAUCE
3 cups Italian Tomato Sauce or Marinara Sauce

TOPPING
1/2 pound mozzarella cheese, coarsely grated

Prepare and cook cannelloni squares as recipe directs, then reserve. Preheat oven to 375° F. Brush a large skillet with oil and heat 1–2 minutes over moderately high heat. Add beef and brown well 4–5 minutes, stirring constantly. Add onion, salt, pepper, and savory. Sprinkle flour over beef, then slowly stir in broth. Cook and stir until thickened; reduce heat to low, cover, and simmer 15–20 minutes, stirring now and then. Remove from heat and cool 10 minutes. Drop 1 1/2 tablespoons filling in center of each cannelloni square, fold bottom edge up over filling, then roll up jelly-roll style and arrange seam side down in a single layer in a buttered shallow 3-quart casserole. Cover with sauce, sprinkle with mozzarella, and bake, uncovered, 25–30 minutes until bubbling and lightly browned. (*Note:* If not brown enough, broil 4" from heat 1–2 minutes.)

NPS (with Italian Tomato Sauce): 615 C, 170 mg CH, 3240 mg S*
NPS (with Marinara Sauce): 485 C, 140 mg CH, 2865 mg S*

CANNELLONI GARIBALDI

6 servings ¢

Cannelloni filled with sweet Italian sausages, chopped spinach, and grated Parmesan cheese.

1 recipe Cannelloni Squares

FILLING
1 pound sweet Italian sausages
1 (10-ounce) package frozen chopped spinach, cooked by package directions but not seasoned
1/4 cup finely grated Parmesan cheese
1 egg, lightly beaten

SAUCE
3 cups Mushroom Marinara Sauce

TOPPING
1/4 cup finely grated Parmesan cheese

Prepare and cook cannelloni squares as recipe directs, then reserve. Preheat oven to 375° F. Remove sausage meat from casings and brown in a large, heavy skillet over moderately low heat 10–15 minutes, stirring occasionally and breaking up large clumps with a spoon; transfer with a slotted spoon to a bowl. Drain spinach in a sieve, pressing out as much water as possible with a spoon. Add spinach, cheese, and egg to sausage and toss well to mix. Divide filling evenly among cannelloni squares, roll up, and arrange seam side down in a single layer in a buttered shallow 3-quart casserole. Spoon sauce evenly over all and top with cheese. Bake, uncovered, about 30 minutes until bubbling.

NPS: 510 C, 185 mg CH, 2660 mg S*

BAKED MEATLESS "MANICOTTI"

6 servings ¢

A cheese-rich meat substitute.

MANICOTTI PANCAKES
2 eggs, lightly beaten
3/4 cup milk
1/2 teaspoon salt
1 cup sifted flour

FILLING
1 pound ricotta cheese
3 tablespoons grated Parmesan cheese
2 tablespoons minced parsley
1 teaspoon salt
1 egg, lightly beaten

TOPPING
1 1/2 pints hot Marinara or Italian Tomato Sauce

Preheat oven to 350° F. For the pancakes, mix eggs, milk, and salt; slowly add flour and beat until smooth. Using 1 tablespoon batter for each pancake, drop onto a greased griddle set over moderate heat and spread into 4″ circles. Brown lightly, turn, and brown flip side. Lay most attractive side *down* on paper toweling while you cook the rest. Mix filling ingredients, spoon about 1 1/2 tablespoons on center of each pancake, then fold top and bottom toward center, envelope fashion. Arrange seam side down in a buttered 13″ × 9 1/2″ × 2″ baking pan and top with sauce. Bake, uncovered, 1/2 hour until bubbling. Serve hot with extra grated Parmesan.

NPS (with Marinara Sauce): 350 C, 180 mg CH, 1295 mg S*
NPS (with Italian Tomato Sauce): 385 C, 180 mg CH, 1530 mg S*

VARIATION

⊄⊅ **Meatless Cannelloni:** Substitute 1 recipe Cannelloni Squares or 3/4 pound packaged cannelloni or tufoli for Manicotti Pancakes. Cook, drain, and fill; top with sauce and bake as directed.

NPS (Italian Tomato Sauce and Cannelloni Squares): 450 C, 175 mg CH, 2705 mg S*
NPS (Marinara Sauce and Cannelloni Squares): 425 C, 160 mg CH, 2740 mg S*

CHICKEN-AND-MUSHROOM STUFFED MANICOTTI

6 servings

1 recipe Manicotti Pancakes (see preceding recipe) or Manicotti Squares

FILLING
1/2 pound mushrooms, wiped clean and minced (include stems)
2 tablespoons butter or margarine
2 cups cooked minced chicken (preferably white meat)
1 teaspoon grated lemon rind
1/2 teaspoon salt
1/8 teaspoon pepper

SAUCE
2 cups Thick White Sauce
1 cup heavy cream
1/3 cup grated Parmesan cheese

Prepare manicotti as directed. Preheat oven to 375° F. For the filling: Sauté mushrooms in butter over moderate heat 3–4 minutes until golden; off heat, mix in remaining filling ingredients. Mix sauce and cream and blend 1/3 cup into chicken mixture. Spoon about 1 1/2 tablespoons filling on each manicotti, roll up, and arrange seam side down in a buttered 3-quart casserole. Sprinkle with cheese and top with remaining sauce. Bake, uncovered, 1/2 hour, then brown lightly under broiler.

NPS: 585 C, 245 mg CH, 920 mg S*

ELEVEN

Sauces, Gravies, and Butters

Sauce cookery is neither mysterious nor complicated if you consider that there are five, perhaps six, "mother" sauces from which most of the others descend: *White Sauce* (and its richer cousin Béchamel), *Velouté* (similar to White Sauce except that the liquid is light stock instead of milk), *Espagnole* (rich brown stock-based sauce), *Hollandaise* (cooked, egg-thickened sauce), *Mayonnaise* (an uncooked oil and egg emulsion), and *Vinaigrette* (oil and vinegar—it and mayonnaise are included in the salad chapter). No sauce is difficult to make (though some are tedious) and none requires more than learning a few basic techniques. The time required to prepare certain sauces may seem overlong. In some cases, slow simmering is needed to boil down liquids and concentrate flavors. In others, it is needed to give the sauce a particular finish or finesse.

In addition to the classic sauce families, there are a few orphan sauces that defy categorization: flavored butters, purées, barbecue sauces, sweet-sour sauces, not to mention the myriad sauce mixes crowding supermarket shelves. All sauces, however, the thick and the thin, the hot, the cold, the quick, and the classic, serve the same purpose: to enhance the food they accompany. They should never dominate, never inundate the food with which they are served.

SOME TERMS AND TECHNIQUES OF SAUCE MAKING

Beurre Manié: Butter-flour mixture, pinched off, a bit at a time, or rolled into small balls and beaten into hot sauces to thicken them. A wire whisk is the best tool to use when adding *beurre manié.*

Beurre Noir: Literally "black butter"; but actually, butter heated to an even nut brown.

Beurres Composés: The French term for flavored butters.

Brunoise: Diced or shredded mixed vegetables, poached in stock and used in making sauces to impart flavor. The most often used are leeks, onions, and carrots. Usually they are discarded after their flavor has been extracted.

Caramel: Liquid melted sugar, used to color and flavor sauces. See soup chapter for instructions for caramelized sugar.*

Clarified Butter: Melted butter, skimmed of milk solids; it is clear and golden and much less likely to burn than unclarified butter. *To Make:* Melt butter over low heat, watching that it does not brown. Remove from heat and let stand 2–3 minutes until solids settle. Skim off clear liquid butter and discard sediment. (*Note:* 1/2 cup butter = about 1/3 cup clarified butter.)

Cream: To mix a white or light sauce with coarsely chopped or diced meat, fish, fowl, or vegetables. A good ratio: 1 cup sauce to 2 cups solids.

Deglaze: To scrape up browned bits in a pan in which meat, fowl, or fish has browned, usually by adding a small amount of liquid and bringing to a boil. These pan scrapings enrich the color and flavor of brown sauces and gravies.

Degrease: To remove grease. The easiest—but slowest—way is to chill a mixture until fat rises to the top and hardens so that it can be lifted off. Liquid fat may be skimmed off hot sauces, or, if quantity is small, blotted up with paper toweling.

Drawn Butter: The same as clarified butter.

Emulsify: To bind oil, melted butter, or egg yolks with a nonoily liquid (vinegar, lemon juice, etc.), creating a satiny, thickened sauce. The trick is to add the oil drop by drop, beating furiously. Sometimes, as when making Hollandaise, heat is also used.

Fond: The French word for stock used as a base for soups and sauces. *Fond blanc* is white stock, *fond brun,* brown stock.

Fumet: A concentrated stock used to give body to sauces.

Ghee: The East Indian version of clarified butter.

Glace de Viande: A meat glaze made by greatly reducing brown beef stock. It is used to color and flavor sauces and gravies. Commercial beef extract makes an acceptable substitute.

Liaison: The French term for "thickener." The ways of thickening sauces are many, each requiring a different technique:

Starch Thickeners: Starches such as flour, cornstarch, or arrowroot, when heated in liquid, swell and coagulate, thickening the liquid. Whether the liquid thickens smoothly depends upon whether the starch particles were kept separate during cooking. And that depends on the cook. Raw flour, cornstarch, or other powdery thickener tossed into a bubbling liquid will lump, but if blended first with fat or a small amount of cold liquid, then blended into the hot liquid and stirred until after thickening, each will produce a silky-smooth sauce. *(Note:* The easiest way to blend starch and cold liquid is with the fingers or, if there is slightly more liquid than starch, in a shaker jar. Not all starches have the same thickening power, not all produce the same results, i.e., some will make a sauce opaque, some translucent, and others sparklingly clear. Here's a quick table (following page).

A Note About Flours: The nonlumping "sauce" flours ensure satiny sauces, even for the haphazard cook who forgets to stir; but they cost more than conventional all-purpose flours.

Eggs as Thickeners: Egg yolks are more commonly used than whole eggs; they not only thicken a sauce but enrich its color and flavor as well. Generally speaking, it will take 2 egg yolks to make 1 cup liquid about the consistency of Medium White Sauce. The egg yolks should be beaten briskly with a fork, just until uniformly liquid, then blended with a little cold liquid or beaten hard with a small amount of a hot sauce before being added to that sauce. Otherwise, the eggs will curdle. For best results, cook and stir egg-thickened sauces over lowest heat (insulated by a flame-tamer) or in the top of a double boiler over *simmering,* not boiling, water. Cook and stir only until sauce is thickened (about the consistency of stirred custard) and no raw taste of egg remains. If, despite all care, a sauce should curdle, strain through a fine sieve or double thickness of cheesecloth. If mixture is thin, rethicken with egg, taking every precaution. If sauce is Hollandaise or one of its descendants, you can salvage by following directions in the Hollandaise recipe.

Blood as a Thickener: Game sauces and gravies are sometimes thickened with blood. It should be absolutely fresh (mixing with a little vinegar helps keep it liquid), strained, then added to the sauce shortly before serving. Swirl it in slowly, as you would an egg yolk mixture, and cook and stir over low heat just until sauce thickens. Never boil a blood-thickened sauce or it will curdle.

Marinade: A spicy or piquant mixture in which food is soaked so that it absorbs some of the flavors.

Marinate: To soak in a marinade.

Mirepoix: A mixture of diced, sautéed vegetables (usually carrots, onions, shallots, celery) used as a base for sauces.

Paste: A blend of starch and cold liquid, usually 1 part starch to 2 parts liquid, used to thicken sauces.

Reduce: To boil a liquid uncovered so that it reduces in volume. The purpose is to thicken a sauce and concentrate the flavors. This is a technique used to prepare many of the sauces of *cuisine minceur* and *nouvelle cui-*

THICKENERS FOR SAUCES

Thickener	Thickening Power	Use to Thicken	Special Techniques	Sauce Appearance
Flour	1 T. will slightly thicken 1 cup liquid (see White Sauce chart)	Gravies, sweet and savory sauces	Blend with an equal quantity fat or cold liquid before adding. Cook several minutes *after thickening* to remove raw taste.	Opaque
Brown Flour	½ that of flour	Gravies, brown sauces	Same as flour	Opaque

(Note: To Make Brown Flour: Heat and stir flour in a dry heavy skillet over low heat until a pale amber color.)

Thickener	Thickening Power	Use to Thicken	Special Techniques	Sauce Appearance
Cornstarch	Twice that of flour	Sweet-sour or sweet sauces	Same as flour. Do not cook more than 3 minutes or sauce may thin.	Almost transparent
Rice Flour (available in Oriental groceries)	1–1½ times that of flour	Sweet-sour or sweet sauces; also gravies	Same as flour	Translucent
Potato Flour or Starch (available in specialty shops)	2–2½ times that of flour	Gravies, savory sauces	Same as flour but do not boil or cook after thickening—the sauce will thin out.	Translucent
Arrowroot (available in specialty shops)	2–2½ times that of flour	Sweet sauces and glazes	Mix with equal amount of sugar or about twice as much cold liquid; do not boil or reheat— sauce will thin.	Sparkling, clear

sine. A *reduction* is the reduced liquid or mixture, the end product.

Roux: A smooth blend of melted butter and flour used in thickening sauces. When the butter and flour are not browned, the roux is a *roux blanc* (white roux); when the roux is worked over low heat until pale tan it is a *roux blond,* and when it is browned still further, it becomes a *roux brun.*

Salpicon: Diced ingredients (vegetables, meats, fish, or a mixture) served in a sauce.

Skim: To scoop fat from the top of a sauce with a skimmer or large, flat spoon.

Thickener: See Liaison.

SOME TIPS FOR MAKING BETTER SAUCES

• Use heavy, flat-bottom pans of enamel, tin-lined copper, stainless steel, porcelain, or flameproof glass. Aluminum, unless anod-ized, is apt to turn white sauces gray and discolor those made with egg or vinegar.
• Use a comfortable wooden spoon for stirring or, if you prefer, a wire whisk.
• When making a thick or moderately thick sauce, keep burner heat low and stir often to prevent sauce from scorching (especially important if starch is the thickener).
• If doubling or tripling a sauce recipe, allow more cooking time so that sauce can thicken and mellow properly.
• To enrich color of gravies and brown sauces, add caramelized sugar* or liquid gravy browner.
• To enrich flavor of gravies and brown sauces, add bouillon cubes, Glace de Viande, or beef extract.
• Taste sauces often as they cook, adjusting seasonings as needed. Remember that cold sauces can take more seasoning than hot ones—cold numbs the palate.
• To prevent a skin from forming on a sauce as it cools, place a circle of wax paper *flat on sauce.*
• To smooth out a lumpy sauce, strain.

Whirling in an electric blender or food processor can turn a starch-thickened sauce gluey.

Microwaving Sauces, Gravies, and Butters

Because most sauces and gravies cook quickly on top of the stove, we find no reason to prepare them by microwave. Indeed, sauces whose consistency depends upon extended periods of reduction (evaporation) should not be microwaved because very little evaporation occurs in the microwave oven. Nor should egg-thickened sauces be microwaved because they are apt to curdle. Flavored butters, however, can be softened or melted in the microwave with little risk of their browning.

Keeping and Holding Sauces

Egg- or starch-thickened sauces, as a rule, keep poorly. About 4–5 days in the refrigerator is a maximum. Place wax paper flat on surface of sauce, then add a cover so that sauce will not absorb refrigerator odors. *Health Tip:* Never try to hold these sauces at room (or more than room) temperature for more than 20–30 minutes. You invite food poisoning. And when making creamed dishes, do not mix the sauce and the minced foods until shortly before serving unless each is cooled separately, refrigerated, and reheated. At buffets, creamed foods should be kept bubbly-hot in chafing dishes, again to reduce the risk of food poisoning.

Acid sauces are less perishable, especially tomato or other puréed vegetable sauces. Properly refrigerated, they should keep well about 2 weeks.

Freezing Sauces

Egg- and starch-thickened sauces do not freeze successfully. Most of the pasta sauces do, however.

Reheating Sauces and Gravies in a Microwave

Most sauces (except egg-thickened ones) reheat beautifully in microwave ovens. Simply cover with wax paper and microwave until steaming hot, stirring now and then from the edges toward the center. *Note:* Frozen sauces and gravies should be defrosted as oven manufacturer recommends, then reheated.

WHITE SAUCES

BASIC WHITE SAUCE

1 cup

Use the proportions given in the White Sauce Chart (next page) for the particular sauce you want. Melt fat in a small saucepan over low heat and blend in flour to form a smooth paste. Gradually stir in milk and heat, stirring constantly, until thickened and smooth. *(Note:* Don't be alarmed if sauce seems to "curdle" as milk is added—it's merely the fat hardening on contact with the cold milk; sauce will soon smooth out.) Add seasonings, then let mellow about 5 minutes, stirring occasionally over lowest heat. *(Note:* If sauce must be held a short while—up to 20–25 minutes—transfer to the top of a double boiler, set over simmering water, and cover. To hold longer, remove from heat, place a circle of wax paper flat on sauce [to prevent a skin from forming], and cool to room temperature; refrigerate until needed. Reheat in the top of a double boiler.)

VARIATIONS

Parsley Sauce: To each cup Medium White Sauce, add 2 tablespoons minced parsley and let mellow, stirring, about 5 minutes. Good with fish, carrots, or beets.
NP Tablespoon: 25 C, 5 mg CH, 55 mg S*

Mint Sauce: To each cup Medium White Sauce, add 1 tablespoon minced mint and let mellow, stirring, about 5 minutes. Good with boiled onions.
NP Tablespoon: 25 C, 5 mg CH, 55 mg S*

Cheese Sauce: To each cup Medium White Sauce, add 3/4–1 cup coarsely grated Cheddar, American, or Gruyère cheese, 1 teaspoon Worcestershire sauce, and a pinch each powdered mustard and cayenne. For a peppier sauce, increase mustard and cayenne slightly and add 1 teaspoon grated onion and 1/4 minced clove garlic. Heat and stir sauce until cheese is melted and flavors blended. Thin, if needed, with a little milk.
NP Tablespoon: 45 C, 10 mg CH, 90 mg S*

Mushroom Sauce: Begin 1 recipe Medium White Sauce as directed, but before blending in flour stir-fry 1 cup minced mushrooms in the butter 3–5 minutes. Blend in flour and proceed as directed. If you like, spike sauce with a little dry sherry or vermouth.
NP Tablespoon: 25 C, 5 mg CH, 55 mg S*

WHITE SAUCE CHART

Type	Fat (Butter, Margarine, or Drippings)		Flour	Milk	Seasonings	Use
Very thin *NP Cup: 265 C, 65 mg CH, 775 mg S**	1 tablespoon	½ tablespoon	1 cup	¼ teaspoon salt, pinch pepper	For thickening thin cream soups
Thin *NP Cup: 280 C, 65 mg CH, 775 mg S**	1 tablespoon	1 tablespoon	1 cup	¼ teaspoon salt, pinch pepper	For thickening standard cream soups
Medium *NP Cup: 410 C, 95 mg CH, 895 mg S**	2 tablespoons	2 tablespoons	1 cup	¼ teaspoon salt, pinch pepper	As a base for sauces and creamed dishes
Thick *NP Cup: 540 C, 125 mg CH, 1010 mg S**	3 tablespoons	3 tablespoons	1 cup	¼ teaspoon salt, pinch pepper	For binding casserole ingredients
Very thick *NP Cup: 670 C, 160 mg CH, 1130 mg S**	¼ cup	¼ cup	1 cup	¼ teaspoon salt, pinch pepper	For binding croquettes

Mushroom and Cheese Sauce: Begin 1 recipe Medium White Sauce as directed, but before blending in flour stir-fry 2 tablespoons minced yellow onion 3–5 minutes until limp; add ½ pound button mushrooms, cover, and simmer 7–8 minutes, stirring once or twice. Blend in flour, add 1 cup light cream or milk, ¾ cup coarsely grated sharp Cheddar cheese, and the seasonings called for. Heat and stir until thickened and smooth, then let mellow about 5 minutes longer over lowest heat, stirring occasionally. Good over boiled potatoes or summer squash.
NP Tablespoon (with cream): 40 C, 10 mg CH, 50 mg S*
NP Tablespoon (with milk): 30 C, 5 mg CH, 50 mg S*

Mustard Sauce: Into each cup Medium White Sauce blend ¼ cup prepared mild yellow or spicy brown mustard and 1–2 teaspoons cider vinegar; let mellow over lowest heat 3–5 minutes before serving. Good with ham.
NP Tablespoon: 30 C, 5 mg CH, 105 mg S*

Hot Mustard Sauce: Begin 1 recipe Medium White Sauce as directed but blend ½ teaspoon powdered mustard into butter along with flour. Proceed as for Mustard Sauce (above), adding 1 teaspoon Worcestershire sauce and 2 or 3 drops liquid hot red pepper seasoning. Good with ham.
NP Tablespoon: 25 C, 5 mg CH, 60 mg S*

Chiffon Sauce: Prepare 1 recipe Medium White Sauce in the top of a double boiler, omitting pepper and reducing salt to ⅛ teaspoon; blend a little hot sauce into 1 lightly beaten egg yolk, return to pan, set over simmering water, and cook and stir 2–3 minutes. Place a circle of wax paper flat on sauce and cool 20–30 minutes. Beat 2 tablespoons tarragon vinegar into sauce in a slow steady stream. Whip 1 egg white to soft peaks and fold into sauce; cover and chill 1–2 hours. Good with cold shellfish.
NP Tablespoon: 30 C, 25 mg CH, 45 mg S*

BEURRE MANIÉ

3 tablespoons, enough to thicken slightly 1½ cups liquid ☒

3 tablespoons butter, softened slightly
2 tablespoons flour

Blend butter and flour until smooth. Pinch off small pieces and add, one at a time, stirring constantly, to hot liquids, gravies, and sauces to thicken.
NP Tablespoon: 120 C, 30 mg CH, 115 mg S*

BÉCHAMEL SAUCE

1⅔ cups

A French white sauce from which many other sauces descend. Depending upon the food to be sauced, make with part milk, part broth (chicken broth for meat or poultry, fish stock for seafood, vegetable cooking water for eggs, cheese, or vegetables).

4 tablespoons butter (no substitute)
1/4 cup unsifted flour
2 cups milk or 1 cup each milk and chicken broth, Easy Fish Stock, or vegetable cooking water
1/2 teaspoon salt (about)
1/8 teaspoon white pepper
2 tablespoons minced yellow onion
2 ounces ground veal (use only if sauce is for meat or poultry)
1 small sprig fresh thyme or a pinch dried thyme
1/4 bay leaf
Pinch nutmeg

Melt 3 tablespoons butter in a double boiler top over direct moderate heat; blend in flour, slowly add milk, and heat, stirring, until thickened. Mix in salt and pepper. Set over simmering water. Stir-fry onion in remaining butter 3–5 minutes over moderate heat until limp, add veal if sauce is for meat or poultry, and stir-fry until no longer pink; add to sauce along with remaining ingredients, cover and cook 1 hour over simmering water, beating now and then with a whisk and scraping bottom and sides of pan with a rubber spatula. *(Note:* Be careful when removing lid not to let water condensed there drop in sauce.) Strain sauce, taste for salt and adjust. Serve hot or use as a base for other sauces. Recipe too flexible for meaningful nutritional count.

VARIATIONS

Anchovy Sauce *(12/3 cups):* Prepare Béchamel using milk and fish stock and omitting salt; before setting to simmer, blend in 4 teaspoons anchovy paste and a pinch cayenne. Proceed as above. Good with fish.

NP Tablespoon: 25 C, 5 mg CH, 60 mg S*

Caper Sauce *(2 cups):* Prepare Béchamel using milk and fish stock and omitting salt; just before serving, mix in 1/3 cup coarsely chopped capers and 1 tablespoon lemon juice. Serve with fish.

NP Tablespoon: 20 C, 5 mg CH, 80 mg S*

Caper and Horseradish Sauce *(2 cups):* Prepare Caper Sauce and mix in 2 tablespoons prepared horseradish. Good with boiled beef brisket.

NP Tablespoon: 20 C, 5 mg CH, 80 mg S*

Hot Horseradish Sauce *(2 cups):* Prepare Béchamel, mix in 1/4–1/3 cup drained prepared horseradish, 1/8 teaspoon powdered mustard blended with 2 tablespoons light cream, and heat 2–3 minutes. Good with corned or boiled beef.

NP Tablespoon: 30 C, 5 mg CH, 60 mg S*

Mornay Sauce *(21/2 cups): (Note:* This delicate cheese sauce can be used with seafood, poultry, eggs, or vegetables; let recipe decide which stock you use in making it.) Prepare Béchamel, add 1/2 cup of the same stock used in the Béchamel, and heat, uncovered, in the top of a double boiler until sauce reduces to 2 cups. Add 1/4 cup each grated Parmesan and Gruyère and heat and stir until melted. Off heat, beat in 2 tablespoons butter, 1 teaspoon at a time. *(Note:* If Mornay is to be used for a gratiné, use half as much cheese and butter.)

NP Tablespoon: 30 C, 5 mg CH, 65 mg S*

Nantua Sauce *(About 3 cups):* Prepare Béchamel using milk and fish stock, mix in 1/3 cup heavy cream, and keep warm. Boil 1/4–1/3 pound crayfish or shrimp in 11/2 cups water with 1/2 teaspoon salt 3–5 minutes; shell, devein, and mince. Boil cooking liquid, uncovered, until reduced to 1/4 cup; mix into sauce along with crayfish; add a pinch cayenne and, if you like, 1 tablespoon brandy. Off heat, beat in 2 tablespoons Shrimp Butter, 1 teaspoon at a time. Good with seafood or eggs.

NP Tablespoon: 45 C, 15 mg CH, 115 mg S*

Soubise Sauce *(About 1 quart):* Prepare Béchamel and keep warm. Meanwhile, simmer 4 coarsely chopped yellow onions, covered, with 11/2 cups water (or a 1/2 and 1/2 mixture of water and chicken or beef broth) and 3 tablespoons butter about 3/4 hour until mushy. Uncover and boil until liquid reduces to 1 cup. Purée onions and liquid by buzzing 20–30 seconds at low speed in an electric blender or 15–20 seconds in a food processor fitted with the metal chopping blade. Mix into sauce, season to taste with salt, pepper, and nutmeg. Good with poultry, fish, brains, and sweetbreads.

NP Tablespoon: 20 C, 5 mg CH, 35 mg S*

VELOUTÉ SAUCE

12/3 cups

If a velouté is used to sauce poultry, egg, or vegetable dishes, make with chicken broth; if to sauce meat, use veal stock; if seafood, fish stock.

6 tablespoons butter (no substitute)
6 tablespoons flour

---

2 cups chicken broth, Veal (White) Stock, or
  Easy Fish Stock
1/4 teaspoon salt (about)
Pinch white pepper
2–3 tablespoons coarsely chopped mushrooms
  (optional)

Melt butter in a heavy saucepan over moderate heat. Blend in flour, gradually stir in
broth, and heat, stirring constantly, until
thickened and smooth. Add seasonings,
mushrooms, if you like, reduce heat, and
simmer, uncovered, 1/2 hour, stirring often
and skimming light scum from sides of pan
as it collects. Turn heat to lowest point,
cover, and simmer 1/2 hour, stirring now and
then. (*Note:* When uncovering sauce, don't
let moisture on lid drop into sauce.) Strain
sauce through a fine sieve and serve hot.

*NP Tablespoon (with chicken broth): 35 C, 5 mg
  CH, 105 mg S**
*NP Tablespoon (with veal stock): 30 C, 5 mg CH,
  90 mg S**
*NP Tablespoon (with fish stock): 30 C, 5 mg CH,
  110 mg S**

VARIATIONS

⚖ **Allemande Sauce** *(1 quart):* Prepare Velouté with chicken broth and keep warm.
Heat 2 cups chicken broth in the top of a
double boiler and blend 1/2 cup into 4 lightly
beaten egg yolks; return to pan, set over simmering water, and cook and stir 3–4 minutes
until thickened and no raw egg taste remains. Blend in Velouté and, if you like, 3–4
teaspoons lemon juice. Strain and serve with
chicken, fish, brains, or sweetbreads.

NP Tablespoon: 20 C, 20 mg CH, 70 mg S*

⚖ **Poulette Sauce** *(1 quart):* Prepare Allemande Sauce, using lemon juice, and keep
warm in double boiler. Meanwhile, boil 1 1/2
cups chicken broth and 1/4 pound minced
mushrooms, uncovered, 20 minutes, stirring
occasionally, until liquid is reduced to 1/2
cup. Strain liquid into Allemande Sauce and
heat and stir 2–3 minutes. Mix in 2–3 tablespoons minced parsley and serve with vegetables, sweetbreads, or brains.

NP Tablespoon: 20 C, 20 mg CH, 85 mg S*

Aurore Sauce *(2 cups):* Make Velouté with
chicken broth or fish stock, blend in 1/2 cup
tomato purée, cover, and simmer 5–7 minutes. Beat in 2 tablespoons butter, 1 teaspoon at a time. Taste and, if tart, add 1/4
teaspoon sugar. Good over eggs, poultry, or
sweetbreads.

NP Tablespoon: 35 C, 5 mg CH, 110 mg S*

Bercy Sauce *(2 cups):* Make Velouté with
fish stock and keep warm. Stir-fry 2 tablespoons minced shallots or scallions (white
part) in 2 tablespoons butter over moderate
heat 3–4 minutes until limp. Add 1/2 cup
each dry white wine and fish stock and boil
slowly, uncovered, until liquid reduces to 1/2
cup; mix into sauce along with 1 tablespoon
minced parsley. Good with fish.

NP Tablespoon: 40 C, 10 mg CH, 135 mg S*

Marinière Sauce *(2 1/2 cups):* Begin Bercy
Sauce as directed, using strained liquid from
Steamed Mussels in the Velouté and in the
wine-shallot mixture instead of fish stock.
When wine-shallot mixture is reduced, blend
into 2 lightly beaten egg yolks, mix into
sauce, set over simmering water, and cook
and stir 3–4 minutes until no raw egg taste
remains. Beat in 2 tablespoons butter, 1 teaspoon at a time; add salt and pepper to taste,
strain, mix in the parsley, and serve with
seafood.

NP Tablespoon: 35 C, 20 mg CH, 95 mg S*

Egg Sauce *(2 cups):* Prepare Velouté with
fish stock, mix in 2 minced hard-cooked eggs
and, if you like, 1 teaspoon minced parsley.
Serve with white fish.

NP Tablespoon: 30 C, 25 mg CH, 95 mg S*

Indienne (Indian) Sauce *(2 cups):* Before beginning Velouté, stir-fry 1 minced large yellow onion, 1 minced stalk celery, and 2 tablespoons minced celery root in butter called
for 5–8 minutes over moderate heat until
limp. Blend in 2 teaspoons curry powder,
the flour called for, and proceed with Velouté as directed, adding 1/4 teaspoon thyme,
1/8 teaspoon mace, and 1/2 bay leaf along
with other seasonings. Strain sauce, mix in
1/2 cup heavy cream and 1 tablespoon lemon
juice. Good with cold roast lamb.

NP Tablespoon: 45 C, 10 mg CH, 100 mg S*

Lobster Sauce *(2 cups):* Prepare Velouté
with fish stock, add 1 cup dry white wine,
and simmer, uncovered, until sauce reduces
to 2 cups; beat in, 1 teaspoon at a time, 1/4
cup Lobster Butter or 1 tablespoon anchovy
paste and 2 tablespoons butter. Mix in 1/3
cup minced cooked lobster and a pinch
cayenne. Serve with seafood.

NP Tablespoon: 35 C, 10 mg CH, 100 mg S*

Normande (Normandy) Sauce *(2 cups):* Prepare Velouté with fish stock and keep warm.
Boil 1 1/2 cups chicken broth, uncovered,
with 1/4 pound minced mushrooms until reduced to 1/2 cup, stirring occasionally; strain
liquid into sauce, add 1/2 cup fish stock, and
simmer, uncovered, about 1/2 hour until reduced to 2 cups. Lightly beat 2 egg yolks
with 1/4 cup heavy cream, blend in 1/3 cup

hot sauce, return to pan, and cook and stir about 3 minutes over lowest heat until no raw egg taste remains; do not boil. Mix in a pinch cayenne. Good with fish, especially sole.

NP Tablespoon: 35 C, 25 mg CH, 140 mg S*

Diplomate Sauce *(2¹/₂ cups):* Prepare Normande Sauce and pour into a double boiler top set over simmering water. Beat in ¹/₄ cup Lobster Butter, 1 tablespoon at a time. Mix in ¹/₄ cup minced cooked lobster, 2 tablespoons brandy, and, if you like, 2 tablespoons minced truffles. Good over white fish.

NP Tablespoon: 40 C, 25 mg CH, 110 mg S*

Ravigote Sauce *(2 cups):* Prepare Velouté (use mushrooms) and keep warm. Boil ¹/₄ cup each dry white wine and white wine vinegar, uncovered, with 1 teaspoon each minced fresh (or ¹/₄ teaspoon each dried) tarragon and chervil, 1 tablespoon each minced chives and shallots or scallions, and 1 parsley sprig until reduced to ¹/₃ cup; strain liquid into sauce. Blend in ¹/₄ cup heavy cream and a pinch cayenne pepper. Good with seafood.

NP Tablespoon: 35 C, 10 mg CH, 90 mg S*

Suprême Sauce *(3 cups):* Prepare Velouté, using chicken broth, and keep warm. Boil 1¹/₂ cups chicken broth and ¹/₄ pound minced mushrooms, uncovered, about 20 minutes until liquid reduces to ¹/₂ cup; strain liquid into sauce and simmer, uncovered, ¹/₂ hour, skimming scum from pan's sides as it collects. Slowly blend in 1 cup heavy cream, then serve with poultry, sweetbreads, or brains.

NP Tablespoon: 35 C, 10 mg CH, 85 mg S*

Talleyrand Sauce *(3¹/₂ cups):* Prepare Velouté with chicken broth, mix in 2 cups chicken broth, and simmer, uncovered, until sauce reduces to 2 cups. Turn heat to low, mix in ¹/₂ cup each heavy cream and dry Madeira; beat in 2 tablespoons butter, one at a time, then strain sauce. Mix in 2 tablespoons each minced truffles, cooked tongue, and 1 tablespoon each butter-sautéed minced onion, celery, and carrot seasoned with a pinch of thyme.

NP Tablespoon: 30 C, 5 mg CH, 85 mg S*

ITALIAN CHEESE SAUCE

2¹/₂ cups, enough for 4 servings ▨

In Italy, cheese sauce is made with any available cheese and sometimes with a mixture of them. Try ¹/₂ cup Parmesan mixed with ¹/₄ cup finely grated, aged provolone, Romano, or Pecorino. Serve over pasta, accompanied, if you like, by separate bowls of grated Parmesan and minced Italian parsley.

¹/₄ **cup butter or margarine**
2 tablespoons flour
1 cup milk
1 cup light cream
1 clove garlic, peeled, bruised, and stuck on a toothpick
³/₄ **cup finely grated Parmesan cheese**
Freshly ground black pepper

Melt butter in a saucepan over moderate heat, blend in flour, slowly stir in milk and cream, add garlic, and heat, stirring constantly, until thickened. Turn heat to low, add cheese, a little at a time, and heat, stirring, until melted. Partially cover and simmer 2–3 minutes. Remove garlic, add a grating of pepper, and serve hot over pasta. *(Note:* If well-aged cheese is used, no salt is needed in this sauce.)

NPS: 340 C, 90 mg CH, 450 mg S*

LIGHT CURRY SAUCE

2 cups

2 medium-size yellow onions, peeled and minced
1 stalk celery, minced
1 clove garlic, peeled and crushed (optional)
¹/₄ **cup butter or margarine**
1 tablespoon curry powder
¹/₄ **cup unsifted flour**
2 cups chicken broth, Veal (White) Stock, or water
1 teaspoon salt
¹/₈ **teaspoon black pepper**
Pinch cayenne pepper

Stir-fry onions, celery, and, if you like, garlic in butter in a saucepan over moderate heat 5–8 minutes until limp, not brown. Add curry powder and stir-fry 1 minute. Blend in flour, slowly add broth, salt, pepper, and cayenne pepper, and heat, stirring, until thickened. Cover and simmer ¹/₂ hour, stirring now and then.

NP Tablespoon: 20 C, 5 mg CH, 135 mg S*

VARIATION

Brown Curry Sauce: Prepare as directed but brown flour in the fat. Substitute beef broth for chicken broth, also stir in 1 tablespoon each tomato paste and lemon juice and $1/8$ teaspoon crushed dried hot red chili peppers.

NP Tablespoon: 20 C, 5 mg CH, 140 mg S*

LEMON SAUCE

2 cups ⚖

Serve with veal loaf or fish.

2 cups Veal (White) Stock, chicken broth, or Easy Fish Stock (depending upon dish to be sauced)
2 tablespoons cornstarch mixed with 2 tablespoons cold water
1/4 cup butter
1 egg yolk lightly beaten with 1 tablespoon cold water
3 tablespoons lemon juice
Salt
White pepper
1 teaspoon minced parsley (optional)

Heat stock, mix in cornstarch, and cook, stirring constantly, until thickened. Add butter and beat to blend. Reduce heat, cover, and simmer 2–3 minutes. Blend a little hot sauce into egg yolk, return to pan, and heat and stir 1–2 minutes; do not boil. Off heat, mix in remaining ingredients, adding salt and pepper to taste.

NP Tablespoon (with chicken or beef broth or veal stock): 20 C, 10 mg CH, 65 mg S*
NP Tablespoon (with fish stock): 15 C, 10 mg CH, 65 mg S*

SHRIMP SAUCE

2 cups ☒

2 tablespoons butter or margarine
2 tablespoons flour
1 cup milk or light cream
2 teaspoons tomato paste
1/2 teaspoon salt
1/8 teaspoon paprika
1 cup coarsely chopped cooked shrimp
2 tablespoons dry sherry (optional)

Melt butter in a saucepan over low heat, blend in flour, gradually stir in milk and heat, stirring constantly, until thickened and smooth. Mix in remaining ingredients and cook and stir about 5 minutes to blend flavors. Serve hot as a sauce for poached, baked, or broiled white fish, for seafood soufflés or mousses.

NP Tablespoon (with milk, no sherry): 15 C, 10 mg CH, 55 mg S*
NP Tablespoon (with light cream, no sherry): 30 C, 15 mg CH, 55 mg S*

CHAUD-FROID SAUCE

2 cups

Chaud-froid sauce is used to glaze cooked foods that are served cold, usually whole chickens, small game birds, or chicken breasts.

3 tablespoons butter or margarine
3 tablespoons flour
2 cups clear chicken broth
1 envelope unflavored gelatin
1 egg yolk lightly beaten with 1/4 cup heavy cream
Salt
White pepper

Melt butter over moderate heat, blend in flour, gradually stir in $1^{1}/2$ cups chicken broth, and heat, stirring constantly, until thickened. Mix gelatin and remaining broth, add to sauce, and stir until dissolved. Reduce heat, cover, and simmer 3–4 minutes. Blend a little hot sauce into egg yolk, return to pan, and cook and stir 1–2 minutes; do not boil. Season to taste with salt and pepper, bearing in mind that cold sauces need slightly more seasoning. Place a circle of wax paper flat on sauce and cool to room temperature. Uncover, stir well, and chill until sauce coats the back of a metal spoon thickly but is still of pouring consistency. Use as recipes direct. *(Note:* If sauce becomes too thick, set over a bowl of hot water and stir until sauce thins.)

NP Tablespoon: 25 C, 15 mg CH, 60 mg S*

VARIATION

Omit butter, flour, and broth; use instead 1 recipe hot Velouté Sauce and proceed as directed, adding gelatin, egg yolk mixture, and salt and pepper to season.

NP Tablespoon: 35 C, 15 mg CH, 90 mg S*

BROWN SAUCES AND GRAVIES

PAN GRAVY

2 cups ⚖ ☒

While a roast "rests," make gravy of your choice.

2 cups hot water, vegetable cooking water, or beef broth or any combination of the 3
1/4 cup roasting pan drippings (round out amount as needed with bacon drippings or butter)
1/4 cup unsifted flour

Liquid gravy browner (optional)
Salt
Pepper

Pour water into drained roasting pan and stir, scraping up browned bits (heat, if necessary, to loosen bits). Pour drippings into a large skillet, blend in flour, and cook and stir over moderate heat until light brown. Add water mixture and heat, stirring, until thickened; reduce heat and simmer 3–5 minutes. Add gravy browner to color, if you like, salt and pepper to taste. For a silken gravy, strain through a fine sieve.

NP Tablespoon (with water or vegetable cooking water): 15 C, 1 mg CH, 0 mg S*

For Thin Gravy: Reduce flour to 2 tablespoons.

NP Tablespoon (with water or vegetable cooking water): 15 C, 1 mg CH, 0 mg S*

For Thick Gravy: Increase flour to 5–6 tablespoons.

NP Tablespoon (with water or vegetable cooking water): 20 C, 1 mg CH, 0 mg S*

For Stronger Flavor: Dissolve 1 or 2 beef bouillon cubes in the hot water.

NP Tablespoon (with water or vegetable cooking water): 15 C, 1 mg CH, 30 mg S*

For Extra-Large Roasts: Double the recipe.

NP Tablespoon (with water or vegetable cooking water): 15 C, 1 mg CH, 0 mg S*

VARIATIONS

⚖ ⚖ **Au Jus Gravy:** Drain all but 1 tablespoon clear drippings from roasting pan, add water, and heat and stir, scraping up browned bits, 2–3 minutes until slightly reduced. If you like, add a touch of gravy browner and/or dry red wine. Season to taste and ladle over each portion.

NP Tablespoon: 5 C, 0 mg CH, 0 mg S*

⚖ ⚖ **Chicken (or Turkey) Gravy:** Prepare as directed using Chicken or Turkey Broth. (*Note:* If turkey is a big one, double the recipe.) Nutritional count same as basic recipe.

⚖ **Chicken (or Turkey) Cream Gravy:** Prepare as directed using 1½ cups Chicken or Turkey Broth and ½ cup light cream.

NP Tablespoon: 15 C, 5 mg CH, 30 mg S*

⚖ ⚖ **Giblet Gravy:** Prepare as directed using Giblet Stock. Mix in minced cooked giblets and neck meat just before serving. Nutritional count same as basic recipe.

⚖ ⚖ **Herb Gravy:** Prepare as directed, warming any of the following herbs in drippings before blending in flour: ½ teaspoon savory, thyme, or marjoram (good with beef), 1 teaspoon tarragon or mint, or ¼ teaspoon rosemary (lamb or veal), ½ teaspoon sage and/or thyme (pork or poultry).

NP Tablespoon: 15 C, 0 mg CH, 0 mg S*

⚖ **Jus Lié:** Drain all drippings from roasting pan; pour 2 cups hot Veal (White) Stock or chicken broth into pan and heat, stirring, to scrape up browned bits. Stir in 2 tablespoons cornstarch blended with 2 tablespoons cold water and heat and stir until thickened and clear. Season to taste. Good with veal and chicken.

NP Tablespoon (with chicken broth or veal stock): 5 C, 0 mg CH, 50 mg S*

⚖ **Milk Gravy:** Prepare Pan Gravy as directed but use 1 cup each milk and broth. Add no gravy browner. Especially good with poultry.

NP Tablespoon: 20 C, 5 mg CH, 30 mg S*

Mushroom Gravy: Prepare Pan Gravy and mix in ½ pound thinly sliced mushrooms and 1 minced yellow onion that have been sautéed 3–5 minutes in 2 tablespoons butter. Cover and simmer 4–5 minutes; taste for seasoning and adjust as needed.

NP Tablespoon (with water or vegetable cooking water): 25 C, 5 mg CH, 10 mg S*

⚖ **Onion Gravy:** Stir-fry 2 thinly sliced medium-size yellow onions in pan drippings 8–10 minutes over moderate heat until golden, blend in flour, and proceed as Pan Gravy recipe directs.

NP Tablespoon (with water or vegetable cooking water): 20 C, 1 mg CH, 1 mg S*

⚖ **Sour Cream Gravy** *(2½ cups):* Prepare Pan Gravy as directed, smooth in 1 cup sour cream, and adjust seasonings as needed. Heat briefly but do not allow to boil.

NP Tablespoon (with water or vegetable cooking water): 25 C, 5 mg CH, 5 mg S*

⚖ ⚖ **Wine Gravy:** Make Pan Gravy using 1 cup each dry red wine and beef broth (for beef), 1 cup each rosé and water (for lamb or veal), or 1 cup each dry white wine and chicken broth (for poultry).

NP Tablespoon (red wine/beef): 20 C, 1 mg CH, 25 mg S*

NP Tablespoon (rosé/water): 20 C, 1 mg CH, 1 mg S*

NP Tablespoon (white wine/chicken): 5 C, 1 mg CH, 25 mg S*

MADEIRA-MUSHROOM SAUCE

1³/4 cups ⚖ ▨

2 tablespoons butter or margarine
¹/2 pound button mushrooms, wiped clean and halved
4 teaspoons flour
1 cup beef broth
1 teaspoon Worcestershire sauce
1 tablespoon minced chives
3 tablespoons sweet Madeira wine

Melt butter in a heavy skillet over moderately high heat, add mushrooms, and sauté 3–4 minutes until golden. Push to side of pan, blend in flour, slowly stir in broth, and cook and stir until thickened. Add remaining ingredients and cook and stir 3–5 minutes. Serve with steaks, London Broil, or sautéed kidneys.

NP Tablespoon: 10 C, 2 mg CH, 40 mg S*

ESPAGNOLE SAUCE

2²/3 cups

Serve with broiled meats, poultry, or fish or use as a base for the variations that follow.

4 slices bacon, minced
1 medium-size yellow onion, peeled and minced
1 medium-size carrot, peeled and minced
1 stalk celery, minced
6 tablespoons butter (no substitute)
6 tablespoons flour
5 cups beef broth or Easy Fish Stock (depending upon whether sauce is for meat or seafood)
Pinch minced fresh or dried thyme
¹/2 bay leaf
¹/4 cup tomato purée

Stir-fry bacon over moderate heat 3–4 minutes until crisp; drain on paper toweling. Sauté onion, carrot, and celery in drippings 8–10 minutes until golden; drain on paper toweling. Melt butter in a saucepan over moderate heat, blend in flour, then cook and stir 1–2 minutes until lightly browned. Gradually mix in broth and cook, stirring constantly, until slightly thickened. Add bacon, sautéed vegetables, and herbs. Reduce heat and boil, uncovered, very slowly ¹/2 hour, skimming light scum from pan sides as it collects. Strain sauce through a fine sieve into a clean saucepan, pressing vegetables lightly to extract juices. Mix in tomato purée, set lid on askew, and simmer 20–30 minutes until sauce coats a metal spoon. Skim or blot off any fat, then serve hot.

NP Tablespoon (with beef broth): 35 C, 5 mg CH, 135 mg S*

NP Tablespoon (with fish stock): 35 C, 6 mg CH, 140 mg S*

VARIATIONS

Bigarade (Orange) Sauce *(1 quart):* Prepare Espagnole with beef broth and keep warm. Add 1 cup dry white wine to pan drippings from roast duck or goose, heat, and stir, scraping up brown bits, then boil, uncovered, until reduced to ¹/2 cup. Strain, skim off fat, and mix into sauce along with 1 cup orange juice and 1 tablespoon lemon juice. Boil ¹/2 cup sugar and ¹/2 cup water 15 minutes until amber colored and blend into sauce. Also boil finely slivered rind (orange part only) of 4 oranges in 1 cup water 3–4 minutes; drain rind, then add rind to sauce. If you like, add 2 tablespoons curaçao. Serve with roast duck or goose.

NP Tablespoon (without curaçao): 35 C, 5 mg CH, 85 mg S*

Diable Sauce *(3¹/2 cups):* Prepare Espagnole with beef broth and keep warm. Boil 1 cup red or white wine vinegar, uncovered, with 2 tablespoons minced shallots or scallions until reduced to ¹/2 cup. Mix into sauce along with 2 tablespoons each Worcestershire and tomato purée and ¹/4 teaspoon cayenne. Good with broiled poultry, also sweetbreads, brains, and tongue.

NP Tablespoon: 30 C, 5 mg CH, 110 mg S*

Piquante Sauce: *(1 quart):* Prepare Diable and mix in ¹/4 cup minced gherkins and 2 tablespoons minced parsley. Good with liver, tongue, and tripe.

NP Tablespoon: 25 C, 5 mg CH, 100 mg S*

Poivrade (Pepper) Sauce *(3¹/2 cups):* Prepare Espagnole with beef broth and keep warm. Boil ³/4 cup dry white wine with ³/4 cup white wine vinegar until reduced by half; mix into sauce along with 6–8 crushed peppercorns, ¹/2 bay leaf, and a pinch fresh or dried thyme. Cover and simmer 5 minutes, strain through a cheesecloth-lined sieve, and serve with broiled steaks or chops.

NP Tablespoon: 25 C, 5 mg CH, 100 mg S*

Victoria Sauce *(1 quart):* Prepare Espagnole with beef broth, add 1¹/2 cups tawny port wine, ¹/3 cup red currant jelly, 3 cloves, ¹/4 teaspoon pepper, and 2 tablespoons finely grated orange rind. Boil slowly, uncovered, stirring now and then, until reduced to about 3¹/2 cups. Remove cloves, mix in ¹/3 cup orange juice and ¹/8 teaspoon cayenne. Serve with roast poultry, game, or game birds.

NP Tablespoon: 30 C, 5 mg CH, 90 mg S*

RICH BROWN SAUCE (DEMI-GLACE, OR HALF GLAZE)

3¼ cups

1 recipe Espagnole Sauce
1 cup beef broth or Easy Fish Stock (depending upon whether sauce is to be used with meat or fish)
¼ cup dry Madeira or sherry

Mix Espagnole and broth and boil slowly, uncovered, until reduced to 3 cups (sauce should coat a metal spoon). Mix in wine and serve or use as a base for other sauces.

NP Tablespoon (with beef broth): 30 C, 5 mg CH, 120 mg S*
NP Tablespoon (with fish stock): 30 C, 5 mg CH, 130 mg S*

VARIATIONS

Bordelaise Sauce *(1 quart):* Prepare Rich Brown Sauce and keep warm. Boil 2 cups dry red wine, uncovered, with 2 tablespoons minced shallots or scallions, a small sprig fresh thyme (or ¼ teaspoon dried thyme), and 1 small bay leaf until reduced to 1⅓ cups. Strain wine into sauce and simmer, uncovered, until reduced to 1 quart. Mix in ½ cup minced cooked marrow and 1 tablespoon minced parsley. Adjust salt, if needed, and serve with broiled or roasted meat, poultry, or game.

NP Tablespoon (marrow not included): 25 C, 5 mg CH, 100 mg S*

Bourguignonne (Burgundy) Sauce *(1 quart):* Prepare Rich Brown Sauce and keep warm. Stir-fry ¼ cup minced yellow onion in 2 tablespoons butter 3–5 minutes over moderate heat until limp, add 3 cups red Burgundy, 1 bay leaf and 1 sprig each parsley and thyme, tied in cheesecloth *(bouquet garni),* and boil, uncovered, until reduced by half. Stir into sauce, reduce to about 1 quart, strain, season to taste with salt and pepper, and serve with roasts, steaks, chops, or fish. *(Note:* For extra flavor, reduce wine in pan meat was cooked in.)

NP Tablespoon: 30 C, 5 mg CH, 105 mg S*

Brown Sauce Fines Herbes *(1 cup):* Mix 1 cup Rich Brown Sauce with ¼ teaspoon lemon juice and 1 tablespoon each minced fresh (or 1 teaspoon each dried) parsley, tarragon, and chervil; let stand about a minute to blend flavors. Serve with broiled meats or poultry, baked or poached fish.

NP Tablespoon: 30 C, 5 mg CH, 125 mg S*

Charcutière Sauce *(About 1 quart):* Prepare Rich Brown Sauce with beef broth and keep warm. Stir-fry ⅓ cup minced yellow onion in 2 tablespoons butter 5–8 minutes over moderate heat until pale golden; mix into sauce along with ⅓ cup minced gherkins and serve with pork.

NP Tablespoon: 30 C, 5 mg CH, 110 mg S*

Chasseur Sauce *(3 cups):* Prepare ½ recipe Rich Brown Sauce with beef broth and keep warm. Sauté ½ pound minced mushrooms in 2 tablespoons each olive oil and butter over moderate heat 2–3 minutes until pale golden; add 2 tablespoons minced shallots and sauté 2 minutes. Add 1 cup dry white wine and boil until reduced by half. Mix into sauce along with 1 cup hot Tomato Sauce and 1 tablespoon each minced fresh (or 1 teaspoon each dried) parsley, tarragon, and chervil. Adjust salt as needed and serve with roasts, steaks or chops, poultry or game.

NP Tablespoon: 30 C, 5 mg CH, 95 mg S*

Chateaubriand Sauce *(1 quart):* Prepare Rich Brown Sauce with beef broth and keep warm. Boil 2 cups dry white wine with 2 tablespoons minced shallots or scallions, a small sprig fresh thyme (or ¼ teaspoon dried thyme), and ½ bay leaf until reduced to 1⅓ cups; strain into sauce and boil until reduced to 1 quart. Stir in 2 tablespoons minced fresh (or 1½ teaspoons dried) tarragon, 1 tablespoon lemon juice, ¼ teaspoon salt, and ⅛ teaspoon cayenne. Serve with chateaubriand or other broiled steak.

NP Tablespoon: 25 C, 5 mg CH, 110 mg S*

Duxelles Sauce *(About 5 cups):* Prepare Rich Brown Sauce and keep warm. Sauté ½ pound minced mushrooms, 1 minced small yellow onion, and 2 minced shallots or scallions in 3 tablespoons butter 5 minutes over moderate heat until limp; add 1 cup dry white wine, ½ teaspoon salt, and ⅛ teaspoon each pepper and nutmeg and boil, uncovered, until liquid is reduced to ½ cup. Stir into sauce along with 1 cup tomato purée and 2 tablespoons minced parsley and simmer 5 minutes. Good with meat or game fish.

NP Tablespoon: 25 C, 5 mg CH, 110 mg S*

Lyonnaise Sauce *(3½ cups):* Prepare Rich Brown Sauce with beef broth and keep warm. Stir-fry 2 minced large yellow onions in 2 tablespoons butter 8–10 minutes over moderate heat until golden. Stir into sauce along with ⅓ cup dry white wine, 3 tablespoons white or red wine vinegar, and, if you like, 2 tablespoons tomato paste. Simmer, uncovered, ½ hour. Serve with steaks and chops.

NP Tablespoon (with tomato paste): 35 C, 5 mg CH, 125 mg S*

Madeira Sauce *(1¼ cups):* Simmer 1 cup Rich Brown Sauce with ¼ cup dry Madeira wine 2–3 minutes. Good with broiled poultry or steaks, ham, sweetbreads, brains, heart, or kidneys.

NP Tablespoon: 25 C, 5 mg CH, 100 mg S*

Financière Sauce *(1¼ cups):* Prepare Madeira Sauce and mix in 2 tablespoons minced truffles. Serve with sweetbreads or brains.

NP Tablespoon: 25 C, 5 mg CH, 95 mg S*

Raisin Sauce *(1½ cups):* Prepare Madeira Sauce as directed and mix in ¼–⅓ cup seedless raisins; simmer slowly about 10 minutes to plump raisins. Good with ham and tongue.

NP Tablespoon: 25 C, 5 mg CH, 80 mg S*

Marchands de Vin Sauce *(1 quart):* Prepare Rich Brown Sauce with beef broth and keep warm. Stir-fry 2 minced bunches scallions (white part) and ½ pound minced mushrooms in ⅓ cup butter 3–4 minutes over moderate heat; add 1½ cups dry red wine and boil, uncovered, until reduced by half. Stir into sauce along with 1 tablespoon lemon juice. Good with steaks.

NP Tablespoon: 35 C, 5 mg CH, 110 mg S*

Périgueux Sauce *(1 cup):* Mix 2 tablespoons minced truffles into 1 cup Rich Brown Sauce. Good with steak, game, and game birds.

NP Tablespoon: 30 C, 5 mg CH, 120 mg S*

Périgourdine Sauce *(1 cup):* Mix 2 thinly sliced truffles into 1 cup Rich Brown Sauce. Good with steak, game, and game birds. Same nutritional count as above recipe.

Tarragon Sauce *(3½ cups):* Prepare Rich Brown Sauce with beef broth and keep warm. Boil 1 cup dry white wine, uncovered, with 3 tablespoons minced fresh (or 2 teaspoons dried) tarragon until reduced to ¼ cup. Mix into sauce, simmer, uncovered, 5 minutes, then strain and mix in 1–2 tablespoons minced fresh tarragon. Good with roast veal.

NP Tablespoon: 30 C, 5 mg CH, 115 mg S*

Zingara Sauce *(1 quart):* Prepare Rich Brown Sauce with beef broth, mix in ½ cup tomato purée, 2 tablespoons each julienne strips cooked ham and boiled tongue, minced mushrooms and truffles, and 1 teaspoon paprika. Good with roast veal.

NP Tablespoon: 25 C, 5 mg CH, 110 mg S*

GLACE DE VIANDE

⅓ cup ⚖ ▣

Never salt a sauce until after *glace de viande* is added; then taste and salt as needed. Use sparingly to add flavor to sauces, soups, and gravies.

1 cup Brown Beef Stock or beef broth

Boil stock, uncovered, over high heat until reduced to ⅓ cup. *(Note:* A similar flavor can be obtained by dissolving 1 tablespoon beef extract in ¼ cup cold water.)

NP Tablespoon: 10 C, 0 mg CH, 210 mg S*

COLBERT SAUCE

1 cup

¼ cup Glace de Viande or 1 tablespoon beef extract dissolved in ¼ cup cold water
1 tablespoon hot water
½ cup butter, softened to room temperature (no substitute)
2 tablespoons lemon juice
1 tablespoon minced parsley
Pinch nutmeg
Pinch cayenne pepper
2 tablespoons dry Madeira wine

Heat *glace de viande* with hot water in a small saucepan. Slowly beat in butter, 1 tablespoon at a time, then mix in remaining ingredients. Drizzle sparingly over broiled meat or fish.

NP Tablespoon: 55 C, 15 mg CH, 110 mg S*

SHALLOT SAUCE

¾ cup ⚖ ▣

3 tablespoons minced shallots
2 tablespoons butter or drippings from broiled or panfried steak
½ cup beef broth
2 tablespoons dry red wine or red wine vinegar
1 teaspoon minced parsley (optional)

Sauté shallots in butter (preferably in pan steak was cooked in) over moderate heat 3–5 minutes until limp. Add remaining ingredients, heat, stirring, to boiling, then pour over steaks.

NP Tablespoon (with red wine): 20 C, 5 mg CH, 55 mg S*

GARLIC SAUCE

2 cups ⚖

1 cup beef broth
1 cup water
1 clove garlic, peeled and bruised
1 medium-size yellow onion, peeled and minced
1 bay leaf
2 tablespoons minced celery leaves
1/4 teaspoon salt (about)
1/8 teaspoon pepper
1/4 cup heavy cream
3 thin slices lemon

Simmer all but last 2 ingredients, covered, 20 minutes, then strain into a clean saucepan. Add cream and heat over lowest heat 3–5 minutes; taste for salt and pepper and adjust. Serve hot with lemon slices floating on top. Good with roast lamb or veal.

NP Tablespoon: 10 C, 5 mg CH, 40 mg S*

HERB SAUCE

2 cups

Delicious with steaks and chops.

2 cups beef broth
4 scallions, peeled and minced
1 tablespoon minced chives
1/4 teaspoon each marjoram, thyme, savory, sage, and basil
1/8 teaspoon nutmeg
1/8 teaspoon pepper
1/4 cup butter or margarine
1/4 cup unsifted flour
1/4 teaspoon salt (about)
1 tablespoon lemon juice
1 teaspoon minced fresh tarragon or 1/4 teaspoon dried tarragon
1 teaspoon minced fresh chervil or 1/4 teaspoon dried chervil

Simmer broth, scallions, chives, herbs, nutmeg, and pepper, covered, 15 minutes; strain broth through a cheesecloth-lined sieve and reserve. Melt butter in a saucepan over moderate heat, blend in flour, and cook and stir 1–2 minutes until light brown. Slowly mix in reserved broth and heat, stirring, until thickened. Lower heat and simmer 5 minutes. Mix in salt, lemon juice, tarragon, and chervil and serve.

NP Tablespoon: 20 C, 5 mg CH, 80 mg S*

HOLLANDAISE AND OTHER EGG-THICKENED SAUCES

HOLLANDAISE SAUCE

1 1/3 cups

If you remember one basic rule—that too much heat will curdle an egg-thickened sauce—you should have little difficulty making Hollandaise. Cook over *simmering,* not boiling, water, take from the heat the minute sauce thickens, and remember that all is not lost if the sauce does curdle. It can be rescued. Hollandaise should be served warm, not hot, not cold.

4 egg yolks
1 tablespoon cold water
1/2 cup butter, softened to room temperature (no substitute)
1/4 teaspoon salt
Pinch white pepper
1–2 tablespoons lemon juice

Beat yolks until thick and lemon colored, mix in water and transfer to the top of a double boiler set over barely simmering water. Heat and stir 2–3 minutes until warm, not hot. Add butter, 2 tablespoons at a time, stirring continuously and not adding more butter until previous addition is well blended in. When all butter is in, cook and stir 2–3 minutes until sauce thickens enough to coat the back of a metal spoon. Set double boiler top on counter, mix in salt, pepper, and lemon juice and stir 1–2 minutes. Serve with vegetables or seafood.

NP Tablespoon: 50 C, 65 mg CH, 70 mg S*

To Salvage Curdled Hollandaise: Add 2 tablespoons boiling water and beat vigorously until smooth. Or set pan in an ice bath, beat hard until smooth, then warm very gently over just simmering water, stirring constantly.

To Make Hollandaise Ahead of Time: Prepare as directed, then transfer to a small bowl; place a circle of wax paper flat on sauce to prevent a skin from forming. About 15 minutes before serving, set bowl of sauce in very hot—not boiling—water and stir now and then as sauce warms; replenish hot water as needed. If sauce seems thick, beat in 1–2 tablespoons hot water.

VARIATIONS

Béarnaise Sauce *(About 1 1/3 cups):* Before beginning sauce, boil 1/4 cup dry white wine, uncovered, with 1/4 cup white wine vinegar, 1 tablespoon each minced fresh (or 1 teaspoon each dried) tarragon and chervil, 1 tablespoon minced shallots or scallions (white part), 1/8 teaspoon salt, and a pinch white pepper until liquid reduces to 2 tablespoons; strain liquid and cool to room temperature. Prepare Hollandaise as directed, substituting reduced liquid for lemon juice. Just before serving, mix in 1/2 teaspoon each minced fresh tarragon and chervil and a pinch cayenne. Good with broiled meats.

NP Tablespoon: 50 C, 65 mg CH, 85 mg S*

Choron Sauce *(About 1 1/3 cups):* Prepare Béarnaise and blend in 2 tablespoons tomato paste. Good with steak.

NP Tablespoon: 55 C, 65 mg CH, 100 mg S*

Mousseline (Chantilly) Sauce *(2 cups):* Prepare Hollandaise, then fold in 1/2 cup heavy cream beaten to soft peaks. Add extra salt and pepper if needed. Good with seafood and vegetables.

NP Tablespoon: 50 C, 45 mg CH, 50 mg S*

Figaro Sauce *(1 2/3 cups):* Prepare Hollandaise, blend in 1/3 cup tomato purée and 1 tablespoon minced parsley, and heat and stir over barely simmering water 2–3 minutes. Good with seafood.

NP Tablespoon: 40 C, 50 mg CH, 70 mg S*

Maltaise (Maltese) Sauce *(1 2/3 cups):* Prepare Hollandaise, then blend in the juice of 1 orange, heated to lukewarm, and 1/4 teaspoon finely grated orange rind. Good with boiled vegetables, especially asparagus, green beans, and broccoli.

NP Tablespoon: 40 C, 50 mg CH, 55 mg S*

Mustard Hollandaise *(About 1 1/3 cups):* Prepare Hollandaise as directed but blend 1/2 teaspoon powdered mustard with lemon juice before adding to sauce. Good with boiled vegetables and fish.

NP Tablespoon: 50 C, 65 mg CH, 70 mg S*

BLENDER OR PROCESSOR HOLLANDAISE

1 1/3 cups

Quicker and easier than old-fashioned Hollandaise.

4 egg yolks
2 tablespoons lemon juice
1/4 teaspoon salt

Pinch white pepper
1/2 cup hot melted butter

Blend yolks, lemon juice, salt, and pepper by buzzing 25–30 seconds in an electric blender at high speed or 10–15 seconds in a food processor fitted with the metal chopping blade. Now, with the motor running (use highest blender speed), add melted butter drop by drop. As mixture thickens, add butter in a thin slow stream. When about half the butter is in, you can pour a little faster. Continue blending until thick and satiny, then serve.

NP Tablespoon: 50 C, 65 mg CH, 70 mg S*

VARIATION

Blender or Processor Béarnaise: Prepare reduced vinegar-herb mixture as for regular Béarnaise, then prepare recipe above, substituting vinegar mixture for lemon juice. Just before serving, mix in 1/2 teaspoon each minced fresh terragon and chervil.

NP Tablespoon: 50 C, 65 mg CH, 85 mg S*

Note: Any of the variations on standard Hollandaise can be made with the blender or processor variety.

AVGOLEMONO SAUCE

1 1/2 cups

A favorite Greek sauce, thickened with egg and lightly flavored with lemon. Serve with asparagus, broccoli, or globe artichokes. Also good with roast veal.

1 1/4 cups chicken broth
Pinch nutmeg
3 egg yolks, lightly beaten
3–4 tablespoons lemon juice
Salt
Pepper

Heat broth and nutmeg in the top of a double boiler over simmering water. Blend about 1/2 cup broth into egg yolks, return to pan, and cook, stirring constantly, until thickened. Off heat, mix in lemon juice, 1 tablespoon at a time; season to taste with salt and pepper.

NP Tablespoon: 10 C, 35 mg CH, 40 mg S*

BÂTARDE SAUCE

1 2/3 cups

An imitation Hollandaise, less caloric than the real thing.

2 tablespoons butter (no substitute)
2 tablespoons flour
1¼ cups water, vegetable cooking water, or
  Easy Fish Stock (depending upon dish to be
  sauced)
1 egg yolk lightly beaten with 1 tablespoon cold
  water
⅓ cup butter, softened to room temperature
½ teaspoon salt
⅛ teaspoon white pepper
1–2 tablespoons lemon juice

Melt butter over moderate heat, blend in flour, gradually mix in water, and cook, stirring, until thickened. Blend ¼ cup hot sauce into egg yolk, return to pan, and cook and stir over lowest heat 2 minutes until no raw taste of egg remains; do not boil. Off heat, beat in softened butter, 1 tablespoon at a time. Season with salt, pepper, and lemon juice. Serve warm—not hot—with fish or vegetables.

NP Tablespoon (with water or vegetable cooking water): 35 C, 20 mg CH, 75 mg S*

MAYONNAISE SAUCES

Note: Other mayonnaise sauces can be found in the chapter on salads and salad dressings.

SOME EASY MAYONNAISE SAUCES

To make any of the following sauces of pouring consistency, use ½ cup milk or cream and ½ cup mayonnaise instead of 1 cup mayonnaise. The cold mayonnaises will be more flavorful if allowed to stand 15–20 minutes at room temperature before serving. ☒

Aioli Sauce *(1 cup):* Blend 1 cup mayonnaise with 4 crushed garlic cloves and a pinch each sugar and cayenne. Serve slightly chilled or at room temperature with hot or cold seafood or meat, cold poultry or vegetables. Also good floated on Gazpacho.

NP Tablespoon: 100 C, 10 mg CH, 80 mg S*
NP Tablespoon (half milk): 55 C, 5 mg CH, 45 mg S*

Anchovy Mayonnaise *(1 cup):* Blend 1 cup mayonnaise with 7–8 minced anchovies (or 2 tablespoons anchovy paste) and ½ crushed clove garlic. Let mellow 1 hour before serving. *(Note:* If preparing homemade mayonnaise, omit salt.) Serve with cold seafood.

NP Tablespoon: 100 C, 10 mg CH, 95 mg S*
NP Tablespoon (half milk): 55 C, 5 mg CH, 55 mg S*

Andalouse Mayonnaise *(1½ cups):* Blend 1 cup mayonnaise with ⅓ cup tomato purée, 2 diced pimientos, and ½ crushed clove garlic. Good with cold meat or fish.

NP Tablespoon: 70 C, 5 mg CH, 65 mg S*

Avocado Mayonnaise *(1½ cups):* Blend 1 cup mayonnaise with 1 puréed ripe avocado, 1 minced pimiento, 1 tablespoon lemon juice, and salt to taste. Good with cold shellfish.

NP Tablespoon: 80 C, 5 mg CH, 55 mg S*
NP Tablespoon (half milk): 50 C, 5 mg CH, 30 mg S*

Buttermilk Mayonnaise *(1½ cups):* Blend 1 cup mayonnaise, ½ cup buttermilk, 2 tablespoons minced chives, and a few drops liquid hot red pepper seasoning. Serve over cold vegetables.

NP Tablespoon: 70 C, 5 mg CH, 60 mg S*
NP Tablespoon (half milk): 40 C, 5 mg CH, 35 mg S*

Caviar Mayonnaise *(1 cup):* Mix ¼ cup red or black caviar into 1 cup mayonnaise. *(Note:* Reduce salt if preparing homemade mayonnaise.) Serve with seafood.

NP Tablespoon: 110 C, 25 mg CH, 170 mg S*
NP Tablespoon (half milk): 65 C, 20 mg CH, 135 mg S*

Chutney Mayonnaise *(1¼ cups):* Mix 1 cup mayonnaise with ¼ cup minced chutney. Serve with cold meat or poultry.

NP Tablespoon: 85 C, 5 mg CH, 70 mg S*
NP Tablespoon (half milk): 50 C, 5 mg CH, 40 mg S*

Dill Mayonnaise *(1 cup):* Blend 1 cup mayonnaise with 1–2 tablespoons minced fresh dill. Serve with seafood.

NP Tablespoon: 100 C, 10 mg CH, 80 mg S*
NP Tablespoon (half milk): 55 C, 5 mg CH, 40 mg S*

French Mayonnaise *(1⅓ cups):* Blend 1 cup mayonnaise with ⅓ cup French dressing, 1 teaspoon finely grated onion, and ½ crushed clove garlic. Heat and stir over lowest heat 2–3 minutes; do not boil. Serve over broccoli, asparagus, or green beans.

NP Tablespoon: 90 C, 6 mg CH, 110 mg S*
NP Tablespoon (half milk): 55 C, 5 mg CH, 85 mg S*

Herb Mayonnaise *(1 cup):* Blend 1 cup mayonnaise with 1 teaspoon each minced fresh tarragon, chervil, chives, and parsley. Serve with seafood or cold meat or poultry.

NP Tablespoon: 100 C, 10 mg CH, 80 mg S*
NP Tablespoon (half milk): 55 C, 5 mg CH, 45 mg S*

Pimiento and Olive Mayonnaise *(1½ cups):* Mix 1 cup mayonnaise with ½ cup minced pimiento-stuffed green olives or ¼ cup each minced pimiento and pitted ripe olives. Serve with cold meat or seafood.

NP Tablespoon (with green olives): 70 C, 5 mg CH, 120 mg S*
NP Tablespoon (with green olives, half milk): 40 C, 5 mg CH, 95 mg S*

Quick Lemon-Caper Sauce *(1½ cups):* Mix 1 cup mayonnaise with 3 tablespoons lemon juice and 2 tablespoons each minced capers and parsley. Serve with seafood.

NP Tablespoon: 65 C, 5 mg CH, 70 mg S*
NP Tablespoon (half milk): 35 C, 5 mg CH, 45 mg S*

Mustard Mayonnaise Sauce *(1¼ cups):* Blend 1 cup mayonnaise with ¼ cup milk, 3 tablespoons prepared spicy brown mustard, and 1 tablespoon cider vinegar. Warm 2–3 minutes, stirring, over lowest heat; do not boil. Serve with ham, pork, tongue, boiled beef, or poached chicken. Also good with hot green vegetables.

NP Tablespoon: 85 C, 5 mg CH, 85 mg S*
NP Tablespoon (half milk): 45 C, 5 mg CH, 60 mg S*

Shellfish Cocktail Mayonnaise *(1¼ cups):* Mix 1 cup mayonnaise with ¼ cup each chili sauce and minced mustard pickles and 1 tablespoon each cider vinegar and Worcestershire sauce. Serve with shellfish.

NP Tablespoon: 90 C, 5 mg CH, 140 mg S*
NP Tablespoon (half milk): 50 C, 5 mg CH, 115 mg S*

Watercress Mayonnaise *(1¼ cups):* Mix 1 cup mayonnaise with ¼ cup minced watercress leaves and 2 tablespoons minced scallions. Serve with cold poultry or seafood.

NP Tablespoon: 80 C, 5 mg CH, 65 mg S*
NP Tablespoon (half milk): 45 C, 5 mg CH, 35 mg S*

MOCK HOLLANDAISE SAUCE

1½ cups

A good quick substitute for real Hollandaise.

¼ cup butter or margarine
Juice of ½ lemon
1¼ cups mayonnaise

Melt butter in a small saucepan over low heat. Beat in lemon juice and mayonnaise, then heat and beat about 2 minutes. Serve as a sauce for broccoli, cauliflower, asparagus, or globe artichokes.

NP Tablespoon: 100 C, 10 mg CH, 85 mg S*

TARTAR SAUCE I

1¼ cups

Nice and tart.

1 cup mayonnaise
3 shallots, peeled and minced, or 3 scallions, minced
1 tablespoon minced parsley
1 tablespoon minced fresh tarragon
¼ cup minced gherkins or dill pickle
2 tablespoons capers
1 teaspoon prepared Dijon-style mustard
½ teaspoon sugar
2 tablespoons red wine vinegar

Mix all ingredients, cover, and chill 2–3 hours. Serve with any seafood. *(Note:* If sauce seems thick, thin with red wine vinegar.)

NP Tablespoon: 85 C, 5 mg CH, 115 mg S*

TARTAR SAUCE II

1 cup

Olives give this version special character.

1 cup mayonnaise
1 tablespoon drained sweet pickle relish
1 tablespoon minced green olives
1 tablespoon minced parsley
1 tablespoon minced scallion
2 teaspoons drained, minced capers
1 teaspoon prepared Dijon-style mustard

Mix all ingredients and let stand at room temperature 10–15 minutes. Serve with any seafood.

NP Tablespoon: 100 C, 5 mg CH, 115 mg S*

HORSERADISH CREAM SAUCE

1 cup

½ cup heavy cream
½ cup mayonnaise or mayonnaise-type salad dressing
2 tablespoons prepared horseradish
1–2 tablespoons lemon juice
1 tablespoon finely grated lemon rind
Pinch cayenne pepper

Gradually beat cream into mayonnaise and, when smooth, stir in remaining ingredients. Chill 1/2 hour and serve with cold roast beef, ham, tongue, or poultry.

NP Tablespoon: 75 C, 15 mg CH, 45 mg S*

VARIATION

Whipped Horseradish Sauce: Beat cream to soft peaks, omit mayonnaise, and fold in remaining ingredients; season to taste with salt and pepper.

NP Tablespoon: 25 C, 10 mg CH, 5 mg S*

OIL AND VINEGAR SAUCES

Note: Other oil and vinegar sauces can be found in the chapter on salads and salad dressings.

DIJONNAISE SAUCE

3/4 cup

2 hard-cooked eggs, peeled
1/2 cup olive or other cooking oil
2 tablespoons white or red wine vinegar
1–2 tablespoons Dijon mustard
1/4 teaspoon salt
1/8 teaspoon white pepper

Press egg yolks through a fine sieve (save whites for sandwiches or salads). Beat in 1/4 cup oil, drop by drop; beat in 1 tablespoon vinegar. Add remaining oil in a fine steady stream, beating vigorously all the while. *(Note:* If mixture curdles, beat in 1–2 tablespoons boiling water.) Mix in remaining vinegar, mustard, salt, and pepper. Serve with steak or ham.

NP Tablespoon: 95 C, 45 mg CH, 95 mg S*

GRIBICHE SAUCE

1 cup

A rich tartar-like sauce that is superb with cold fish or shellfish.

2 hard-cooked eggs, peeled
1/2 cup olive or other cooking oil
2 tablespoons white vinegar
2 tablespoons minced gherkins
2 tablespoons minced capers
1 tablespoon minced parsley
1 teaspoon minced fresh chervil or 1/4 teaspoon dried chervil

1 teaspoon minced fresh tarragon or 1/4 teaspoon dried tarragon
1/4 teaspoon salt

Press egg yolks through a fine sieve and beat in 1/4 cup oil, drop by drop. Beat in 1 tablespoon vinegar, then add remaining oil in a fine, steady stream, beating vigorously all the while. *(Note:* If mixture curdles, beat in 1–2 tablespoons boiling water.) Add remaining vinegar along with other ingredients and finely chopped egg whites. Chill slightly before serving.

NP Tablespoon: 75 C, 35 mg CH, 85 mg S*

COLD RAVIGOTE SAUCE

1 1/3 cups

3/4 cup olive or other cooking oil
1/4 cup white or red wine vinegar
1/4 teaspoon salt
1/8 teaspoon pepper
2 tablespoons minced capers
2 tablespoons minced yellow onion
2 tablespoons minced chives
1 tablespoon minced parsley
1 teaspoon minced fresh tarragon or 1/4 teaspoon dried tarragon
1 teaspoon minced fresh chervil or 1/4 teaspoon dried chervil

Beat oil, vinegar, salt, and pepper until slightly thickened. Mix in remaining ingredients and let stand at room temperature 1/2 hour. Beat lightly with a fork and use to dress seafood or chicken salad.

NP Tablespoon: 70 C, 0 mg CH, 45 mg S*

GREEN SAUCE (SALSA VERDE)

1 cup

1/4 cup red or white wine vinegar
1/4 teaspoon salt
1/8 teaspoon white pepper
1/4 teaspoon powdered mustard
1 tablespoon minced parsley
1 tablespoon minced chives
1 tablespoon minced watercress or spinach
2 shallots, peeled and minced, or 2 scallions, minced (include tops)
3/4 cup olive oil

Mix vinegar, salt, pepper, and mustard in a bowl with a fork. Mix in parsley, chives, watercress, and shallots. Add oil and beat vigorously until blended and slightly thickened. Chill slightly and beat again before serving.

Good with Bollito Misto, boiled beef, or boiled tongue.

NP Tablespoon: 90 C, 0 mg CH, 35 mg S*

SOME EASY SOUR CREAM SAUCES

For best results, bring sour cream to room temperature before mixing sauce. As a general rule, serve hot with hot food, cold with cold food. Heat gently, preferably in the top of a double boiler so sour cream doesn't curdle. ⊠

Sour Cream-Almond Sauce *(1 1/4 cups):* Mix 1/4 cup minced toasted almonds (or piñon, pistachio, or peanuts) with 1 cup sour cream; salt to taste. Good with baked potatoes and broiled fish.

NP Tablespoon: 35 C, 5 mg CH, 5 mg S*

Sour Cream-Anchovy Sauce *(1 1/4 cups):* Blend 1 cup sour cream with 3 tablespoons each milk and anchovy paste and 1 tablespoon lemon juice. Serve with fish.

NP Tablespoon: 30 C, 5 mg CH, 30 mg S*

Sour Cream-Bacon Sauce *(1 1/4 cups):* Mix 1 cup sour cream with 1/4 cup crisp crumbled bacon and 2 tablespoons melted bacon drippings. Good with baked potatoes, seafood, and green vegetables.

NP Tablespoon: 45 C, 5 mg CH, 30 mg S*

Sour Cream-Blue Cheese Sauce *(2 cups):* Blend 1 cup sour cream with 1 (3-ounce) package softened cream cheese, 1/3 cup crumbled blue cheese, and 3 tablespoons evaporated milk. Good with green vegetables.

NP Tablespoon: 30 C, 5 mg CH, 35 mg S*

Sour Cream-Caper Sauce *(1 1/3 cups):* Mix 1 cup sour cream with 3 tablespoons each lemon juice (or white vinegar) and minced capers and 2 tablespoons minced chives. Serve with seafood.

NP Tablespoon: 25 C, 5 mg CH, 40 mg S*

Sour Cream-Chive Sauce *(1 1/4 cups):* Mix 1 cup sour cream with 3–4 tablespoons minced chives and salt and pepper to taste. If you like, add 1/2 crushed clove garlic. Good with baked potatoes, carrots, and seafood.

NP Tablespoon: 25 C, 5 mg CH, 5 mg S*

Sour Cream-Chutney Sauce *(1 1/4 cups):* Mix 1 cup sour cream with 1/4 cup minced chutney and 2 tablespoons Worcestershire sauce. Good with cold meat or poultry.

NP Tablespoon: 35 C, 5 mg CH, 30 mg S*

⊲⊳ **Sour Cream-Cucumber Sauce** *(2 cups):* Mix 1 cup each sour cream and peeled, diced, seeded cucumber with 2 tablespoons white wine vinegar, 1 tablespoon minced fresh dill, and salt and pepper to taste. Good with fish or ham.

NP Tablespoon: 15 C, 5 mg CH, 5 mg S*

Sour Cream-Curry Sauce *(1 cup):* Blend 1 cup sour cream with 1 teaspoon curry powder warmed 2–3 minutes with 1 tablespoon each butter and finely grated onion; add salt and pepper to taste. Good with meat or fish.

NP Tablespoon: 35 C, 10 mg CH, 15 mg S*

Sour Cream-Dill Sauce *(1 1/4 cups):* Mix 2 tablespoons each minced fresh dill and mayonnaise with 1 cup sour cream; add salt and pepper to taste. Good with seafood.

NP Tablespoon: 35 C, 5 mg CH, 15 mg S*

Sour Cream-Horseradish Sauce *(1 1/4 cups):* Blend 2 tablespoons each cider vinegar and prepared horseradish with 1 cup sour cream. Good with beef, ham, or pork.

NP Tablespoon: 25 C, 5 mg CH, 10 mg S*

Sour Cream-Mustard Sauce *(1 cup):* Blend 2–3 tablespoons any prepared mustard and 1 tablespoon cider vinegar with 1 cup sour cream. Good with beef, ham, or pork.

NP Tablespoon: 30 C, 5 mg CH, 30 mg S*

LOW-CALORIE VARIATIONS ⊲⊳

The following "sour cream" sauces will be low-calorie if made with yogurt instead of sour cream:

Sour Cream-Caper

NP Tablespoon: 10 C, 1 mg CH, 40 mg S*

Sour Cream-Chive

NP Tablespoon: 5 C, 1 mg CH, 10 mg S*

Sour Cream-Chutney

NP Tablespoon: 15 C, 0 mg CH, 30 mg S*

Sour Cream-Cucumber

NP Tablespoon: 5 C, 1 mg CH, 5 mg S*

Sour Cream-Curry

NP Tablespoon: 15 C, 0 mg CH, 15 mg S*

Sour Cream-Dill

NP Tablespoon: 15 C, 1 mg CH, 15 mg S*

Sour Cream-Horseradish

NP Tablespoon: 10 C, 1 mg CH, 10 mg S*

Sour Cream-Mustard

NP Tablespoon: 10 C, 1 mg CH, 35 mg S*

SMITANE SAUCE

1 cup

Serve with steaks and chops. Also good as a topping for baked potatoes and green vegetables.

1 large yellow onion, peeled and minced
2 tablespoons butter or margarine
1/2 cup dry white wine
1 cup sour cream
1/4 teaspoon salt
Paprika

Stir-fry onion in butter over moderate heat 3–5 minutes until limp, not brown. Add wine and simmer, uncovered, until liquid reduces to about 2 tablespoons. Turn heat to low, gradually stir in sour cream and salt, and heat gently; do not boil. Dust with paprika and serve warm.

*NP Tablespoon (with butter): 55 C, 10 mg CH, 55 mg S**

BUTTER SAUCES

DRAWN BUTTER SAUCE

1 cup ☒

1/4 cup clarified butter*
2 tablespoons flour
1 cup any warm fish or vegetable stock or water
1/2 teaspoon salt
1/8 teaspoon paprika
1/2–1 teaspoon lemon juice

Warm butter in a small saucepan over low heat and blend in flour. Add stock and heat, stirring constantly, until thickened and smooth. Mix in salt, paprika, and lemon juice to taste. Good with broiled fish or steamed green vegetables. *(Note:* Traditionalists strain this sauce before serving, but doing so is unnecessary if the sauce is correctly made and satin-smooth.)

*NP Tablespoon (with water): 30 C, 10 mg CH, 70 mg S**

BEURRE BLANC (WHITE BUTTER SAUCE)

1 cup

Beurre blanc, an emulsion of butter, wine, vinegar, and shallots, is tricky to make. Too much heat makes it oily, and once cooled, the sauce cannot be reheated. Properly prepared, however, this creamy lukewarm butter sauce is the perfect complement for poached or broiled fish and shellfish, asparagus and other green vegetables. It is superb, too, tossed with hot cooked thin noodles.

1/4 cup minced shallots
1/3 cup dry white wine
1/3 cup white wine vinegar
1 cup (2 sticks) chilled butter, each stick cut into 10 pats
Pinch white pepper

Simmer shallots, wine, and vinegar in a small covered saucepan about 15 minutes until shallots are mushy. Press mixture through a fine sieve, return to pan, and boil, uncovered, until reduced to 2 tablespoons; remove from heat and cool 2 minutes. Reduce burner to heat to its lowest point (you may even want to use a flame-tamer). Return pan to heat and add butter, 1 pat at a time, whisking constantly and adding the next butter pat only after the previous one has combined smoothly with the sauce. Whisk in pepper, taste for salt, and adjust as needed. Serve in a *slightly* warm sauceboat or use to dress food at once. *If sauce must wait:* Transfer to a double boiler top set over lukewarm water. If sauce cools too much, *do not try to reheat it;* instead, beat in 2–3 tablespoons hot water, stock, or vegetable cooking liquid. *To salvage "oily" beurre blanc:* Chill a bowl well with ice cubes, dump cubes out, then dry bowl well. Ladle 2–3 tablespoons sauce into chilled bowl and whisk hard until creamy; gradually whisk in remaining sauce, a tablespoon at a time. *Note:* Leftover *beurre blanc* can be used in place of butter when making Lemon, Caper, or Chaud-Froid Sauce. It can also be used to top any green vegetable or corn on the cob.

*NP Tablespoon: 110 C, 30 mg CH, 120 mg S**

VARIATION

Beurre Blanc aux Fines Herbes: Prepare *beurre blanc* as directed, then beat in 2 tablespoons heavy cream and mix in 1 tablespoon each minced fresh parsley, chives, chervil, and tarragon, or 1/4 teaspoon each of the dried herbs.

*NP Tablespoon: 115 C, 35 mg CH, 120 mg S**

SOME FLAVORED BUTTERS

Each makes enough to dress 6 servings of meat, fish, or vegetables ☒

Anchovy Butter: Cream 1/2 cup butter until light; mix in 4 teaspoons anchovy paste (or 4–5 minced anchovy fillets), 1/2 teaspoon lemon juice, and 2–3 drops liquid hot red pepper seasoning. Let stand 15 minutes be-

---

fore using. Spread on fish before or after broiling, on broiled steaks, or use as a sandwich spread with seafood fillings.

NPS: 145 C, 45 mg CH, 190 mg S*

Bercy Butter: Boil 1/2 cup dry white wine with 1 tablespoon minced shallots until reduced to 3 tablespoons; cool. Mix in 1/2 cup melted butter, 1/4 diced poached marrow from Marrowbones (optional), 1 tablespoon lemon juice, 2 teaspoons minced parsley, 1/4 teaspoon salt, and a pinch pepper. Serve warm with broiled meat or fish.

NPS: 40 C, 10 mg CH, 135 mg S*

Beurre Noir ("Black" Butter): Melt 1/2 cup butter over moderate heat and cook until nut brown. Off heat, mix in 1 tablespoon each minced parsley, capers, and cider vinegar. Serve with fish, vegetables, sweetbreads, or brains.

NPS: 135 C, 40 mg CH, 195 mg S*

Browned Butter: Mix 1/2 cup lightly browned butter and 4 teaspoons Worcestershire sauce; use to dress steaks, chops, fish, or vegetables (especially good with cauliflower).

NPS: 140 C, 40 mg CH, 195 mg S*

Caper Butter: Mix 1/2 cup melted butter, 1/4 cup small capers, 1 tablespoon lemon juice, and a pinch cayenne pepper; serve with fish, brains, sweetbreads, or vegetables.

NPS: 135 C, 40 mg CH, 305 mg S*

Chili Butter: Mix 1/2 cup melted butter and 1 teaspoon chili powder; warm gently 5 minutes and use to baste broiled tomatoes, meat, fish, or poultry.

NPS: 135 C, 40 mg CH, 160 mg S*

Chive Butter: Mix 1/2 cup melted butter, 2 tablespoons minced chives, 1/4 teaspoon salt, and a pinch pepper. Or cream butter until light, blend in remaining ingredients, spoon into a small crock, and chill until firm. Serve poured or dotted over steak, chops, fish, or vegetables.

NPS: 135 C, 40 mg CH, 245 mg S*

Curry Butter: Warm 1/2 cup melted butter and 1 teaspoon curry powder gently 5 minutes; serve with broiled meat, poultry, fish, or tomatoes. Also good with boiled broccoli or cauliflower.

NPS: 135 C, 40 mg CH, 155 mg S*

Dill Butter: Let 1/2 cup melted butter, 3–4 tablespoons minced fresh dill, and 1/8 teaspoon nutmeg stand in warm place 1 hour; use to dress fish or vegetables.

NPS: 135 C, 40 mg CH, 155 mg S*

Garlic Butter: Mix 1/2 cup melted butter, 1 or 2 crushed cloves garlic, 1/4 teaspoon salt, and a pinch pepper; warm 5 minutes and strain if you like. Or cream butter until light and blend in remaining ingredients. Serve on broiled meat or fish, with steamed lobster, or use to make Garlic Bread.

NPS: 135 C, 40 mg CH, 245 mg S*

Green Butter: Simmer 1/4 cup minced fresh spinach leaves with 2 tablespoons each minced parsley, chives, and water 2–3 minutes; press through a fine sieve, drain, and mix into 1/2 cup creamed butter along with a pinch each of salt and pepper. Chill and serve with fish or vegetables.

NPS: 135 C, 40 mg CH, 180 mg S*

Herb Butter: Mix 1/2 cup creamed unsalted butter with 1/2 teaspoon each minced fresh sweet marjoram and thyme (or substitute 1/2 teaspoon minced fresh rosemary). Cover and chill until firm. Serve with fish or vegetables. (*Note:* With rosemary it's delicious with lamb chops and green peas.)

NPS: 135 C, 40 mg CH, 5 mg S*

Horseradish Butter: Mix 1/2 cup creamed butter and 1 tablespoon prepared horseradish; cover and chill 1 hour. Serve with steaks and chops.

NPS: 135 C, 40 mg CH, 160 mg S*

Lemon Butter: Warm 1/2 cup melted butter, 2 tablespoons lemon juice, and a pinch pepper 2–3 minutes. Serve with fish or vegetables. *Parsley-Lemon Butter:* Add 2–3 tablespoons minced parsley to Lemon Butter.

NPS (both versions): 135 C, 40 mg CH, 155 mg S*

Lobster Butter: Finely grind 1 cup mixed cooked lobster meat, coral, and some shell. Mix with 1/2 cup melted butter and blend at high speed in an electric blender. Heat until butter melts, then blend again at high speed. Rub through a fine sieve, cool, beat with a fork, season to taste with salt and pepper, and chill until firm. Serve with fish.

NPS: 160 C, 60 mg CH, 205 mg S*

Maître d'Hôtel Butter (Parsley Butter): Mix 1/2 cup creamed butter with 2 tablespoons each minced parsley and lemon juice, 1/4 teaspoon salt, and 1/8 teaspoon white pepper. On foil shape into a roll about 1 1/4" in diameter, wrap, and chill until firm. Or roll into balls about 1/2" in diameter, place in a piepan, cover, and chill until firm. Use to season broiled steaks, chops, chicken, or fish by topping each serving with 2 or 3 balls or 1/4" thick pats.

NPS: 135 C, 40 mg CH, 250 mg S*

Marchands de Vin Butter: Boil 1/2 cup dry red wine with 2 tablespoons minced shallots until reduced to 1/4 cup. Beat in 1/2 cup soft butter, 2 tablespoons at a time, add 1 tablespoon Glace de Viande or 1 teaspoon beef extract, 1 tablespoon each minced parsley and lemon juice, and a pinch pepper. Serve on steaks and chops.

NPS: 145 C, 40 mg CH, 195 mg S*

Mushroom Butter: Sauté 1/4 pound minced mushrooms in 2 tablespoons butter 3–5 minutes until browned and tender; press through a fine sieve and cool slightly. Mix in 6 tablespoons creamed butter, 1 tablespoon sherry, 1/4 teaspoon salt, and a pinch pepper. Cover and chill; spread on steaks and chops.

NPS: 145 C, 40 mg CH, 250 mg S*

Mustard Butter: Cream 1/2 cup softened butter with 1/2 teaspoon powdered mustard and 1–2 tablespoons any prepared mustard. Use to dress broiled meats and fish or boiled vegetables (especially good with broccoli and asparagus).

NPS: 140 C, 40 mg CH, 190 mg S*

Noisette Butter: Lightly brown 1/2 cup butter over moderate heat; stir in 3 tablespoons lemon juice and pour sizzling hot over vegetables or fish.

NPS: 135 C, 40 mg CH, 160 mg S*

Orange Butter: Let 1/2 cup melted butter and 1 tablespoon finely slivered orange rind (orange part only) steep in a warm place 1/2 hour. Warm gently and serve with boiled beets, carrots, parsnips, peas, winter squash, turnips, or rutabagas.

NPS: 135 C, 40 mg CH, 155 mg S*

Paprika Butter: Blend 1/2 cup creamed butter with 1–2 teaspoons paprika (Hungarian rose, preferably), cover, and chill. Use to dress fish and vegetables.

NPS: 135 C, 40 mg CH, 155 mg S*

Pimiento Butter: Pound 2 seeded canned pimientos to a smooth paste in a mortar and pestle. Blend into 1/2 cup creamed butter along with 1/4 teaspoon salt. Cover, chill, and serve with meat, fish, or vegetables.

NPS: 140 C, 40 mg CH, 250 mg S*

Seasoned Butter: Mix 1/2 cup melted butter, 1 teaspoon salt, and 1/4 teaspoon freshly ground black pepper. Use to dress seafood or vegetables.

NPS: 135 C, 40 mg CH, 525 mg S*

Shallot Butter: Crush 6–8 peeled shallots in a garlic press, mix into 1/2 cup creamed butter along with 1/4 teaspoon salt and a pinch pepper. Cover and chill 1 hour; serve with steaks, chops, and seafood.

NPS: 145 C, 40 mg CH, 250 mg S*

Shrimp Butter: Mince 1/4 pound cooked, shelled, and deveined shrimp, add 1 tablespoon lemon juice, then pound to a paste in a mortar and pestle. Blend into 1/2 cup creamed butter, add a pinch each salt and paprika, cover, and chill 2 hours. Or mix 1–2 tablespoons shrimp paste into 1/2 cup melted butter, season, and let stand in a warm place 1 hour. Serve with seafood.

NPS: 160 C, 70 mg CH, 205 mg S*

Tarragon Butter: Let 1/2 cup melted butter steep with 1 tablespoon each minced fresh tarragon and tarragon vinegar 1 hour in a warm place. Or mix tarragon and vinegar into creamed butter and chill. Serve with meat, fish, poultry, and vegetables.

NPS: 135 C, 40 mg CH, 155 mg S*

Tomato Butter: Blend 1/2 cup creamed butter with 1/4 cup tomato paste, 1/4 teaspoon salt, and a pinch pepper; cover and chill until firm. Serve with fish.

NPS: 145 C, 40 mg CH, 330 mg S*

Watercress Butter: Mix 1/4 cup minced watercress leaves and 1/4 cup soft butter to a paste using a mortar and pestle. Blend in 1/4 cup creamed butter and add 1/4 teaspoon salt and a pinch pepper. Serve with meat, seafood, poultry, or vegetables. Good as a sandwich spread, especially with egg salad or cheese.

NPS: 135 C, 40 mg CH, 245 mg S*

TOMATO AND PASTA SAUCES

Note: Other pasta sauces can be found in the chapter on cereals, rice, and pasta.

TOMATO SAUCE

1 quart ⚒

2 tablespoons diced salt pork or bacon
1 tablespoon butter or cooking oil
2 medium-size yellow onions, peeled and minced
1 medium-size carrot, peeled and minced
1 tablespoon flour
1 (1-pound 13-ounce) can tomato purée
1 cup Veal (White) Stock or water
1 bay leaf and 1 sprig each parsley and thyme, tied in cheesecloth (*bouquet garni*)
1 clove garlic, peeled and stuck on a toothpick

1½ teaspoons salt (about)
¼ teaspoon pepper
1 teaspoon sugar

Stir-fry pork in a large, heavy saucepan over moderate heat 3–4 minutes until pale golden. Add butter, onions, and carrot and sauté 5–8 minutes until limp, not brown. Blend in flour, mix in purée and stock, then add remaining ingredients. Cover and simmer, stirring occasionally, 1 hour; remove *bouquet garni* and garlic. Purée, a little at a time, by buzzing 20–30 seconds in an electric blender at low speed, or by churning all at once 15–20 seconds in a food processor fitted with the metal chopping blade. Reheat, taste for salt and adjust as needed.

NP Cup (with water): 160 C, 15 mg CH, 1,760 mg S*

V A R I A T I O N S

⚖ **Creole Sauce:** Prepare as directed, using oil instead of butter; also sauté 2 minced and seeded sweet green peppers and 2 stalks minced celery along with onions and carrot; use 2 cloves garlic and add 1 teaspoon paprika and ⅛ teaspoon cayenne pepper along with other seasonings. Simmer, purée, then stir in 1 teaspoon filé powder, reheat briefly, and serve. Good with seafood.

NP Cup (with water): 240 C, 15 mg CH, 1,760 mg S*

⚖ **Portugaise (Portuguese) Sauce** *(1½ quarts):* Prepare as directed but omit salt pork and use 3 tablespoons olive oil for sautéing vegetables. Simmer and purée as directed; mix in 2 cups Rich Brown Sauce (or rich brown gravy), cover, and simmer 10 minutes. Stir in 3 tablespoons minced parsley and serve. Good with poultry and seafood.

NP Cup: 320 C, 15 mg CH, 1,760 mg S*

Provençal Sauce: Prepare as directed, using ¾ cup each dry white wine and veal stock instead of 1 cup stock. Just before serving, stir in 1 tablespoon minced parsley. Good with seafood.

NP Cup: 240 C, 15 mg CH, 1,760 mg S*

ITALIAN TOMATO SAUCE

1 quart, enough for 4 servings

Good with any pasta. This sauce freezes well.

2 cloves garlic, peeled and crushed
¼ cup olive or other cooking oil
1 (1-pound 13-ounce) can tomato purée
½ cup water

1½ teaspoons salt
1 teaspoon sugar
1 teaspoon basil
1 bay leaf, crumbled
⅛ teaspoon crushed dried hot red chili peppers

Sauté garlic in oil in a saucepan over moderate heat 1–2 minutes until golden. Add remaining ingredients, cover, and simmer 30–40 minutes, stirring now and then. *(Note:* If doubling recipe, use 3 cloves garlic; if tripling, 4 cloves.)

NP Cup: 205 C, 0 mg CH, 1,645 mg S*

V A R I A T I O N S

Bolognese Tomato Sauce *(5 cups):* Stir-fry ½ pound ground beef chuck with garlic, breaking beef up with a spoon, 8–10 minutes until browned. Proceed as directed, adding 1 teaspoon oregano along with other herbs.

NP Cup: 290 C, 30 mg CH, 1,345 mg S*

Italian Mushroom-Eggplant Sauce *(5 cups):* Stir-fry ½ pound thinly sliced mushrooms and 1 peeled and diced medium-size eggplant with garlic 4–5 minutes until lightly browned. Proceed as directed but simmer sauce 1 hour.

NP Cup: 200 C, 0 mg CH, 1,325 mg S*

Red Clam Sauce *(6 cups):* Prepare as directed but substitute liquid drained from 2 (6½-ounce) cans minced clams for the water. About 5 minutes before serving, mix in clams.

NP Cup: 170 C, 20 mg CH, 1,445 mg S*

MARINARA SAUCE

1½ quarts

1 cup minced yellow onion
2 cloves garlic, peeled and crushed
¼ cup olive or other cooking oil
1 (2-pound 3-ounce) can Italian plum tomatoes (do not drain)
1 (6-ounce) can tomato paste
½ cup dry red wine
½ cup water
2 teaspoons salt
1½ teaspoons sugar
¼ teaspoon pepper
1 tablespoon minced fresh oregano or 1 teaspoon dried oregano
¼ cup finely grated Romano cheese (optional)

Sauté onion and garlic in oil in a large, heavy saucepan over moderate heat 8–10 minutes until golden. Add remaining ingredients except cheese, cover, and simmer 1 hour, stirring occasionally. Press sauce through a sieve or purée by buzzing, a little at a time, 20–30 seconds in an electric blender at high speed or by churning, all at once, 15–20 seconds in a food processor fitted with the metal chopping blade. Reheat to simmering, add cheese if you wish, and serve hot with any pasta.

NP Cup: 160 C, 0 mg CH, 1,175 mg S*

VARIATIONS

Mushroom-Marinara Sauce: Prepare as directed but mix in 3/4–1 pound sautéed sliced mushrooms just before serving.

NP Cup: 175 C, 0 mg CH, 1,185 mg S*

Anchovy-Marinara Sauce: Prepare as directed but omit salt; just before serving, mix in 2 (2-ounce) cans anchovy fillets, drained and minced.

NP Cup: 160 C, 1 mg CH, 465 mg S*

MOLE SAUCE

2 cups

3 ripe tomatoes, peeled, cored, seeded, and coarsely chopped
1/2 cup ground blanched almonds or unsalted peanuts
1 (4-ounce) can peeled green chilies, drained, or 1 tablespoon chili powder
2 cloves garlic, peeled and crushed
2 tablespoons grated yellow onion
1 tablespoon sesame seeds
1/4 teaspoon coriander
1/4 teaspoon salt
1/8 teaspoon cinnamon
1 cup chicken broth
1 (1-ounce) square unsweetened chocolate, coarsely grated

Purée all ingredients by buzzing about 1 minute in an electric blender at high speed or 25–30 seconds in a food processor fitted with the metal chopping blade. Transfer to a saucepan and simmer, uncovered, stirring now and then, 1/2 hour. Sauce is now ready to add to braised chicken or turkey.

NP Cup: 375 C, 15 mg CH, 685 mg S*
NP Tablespoon: 25 C, 0 mg CH, 40 mg S*

SALSA FRÍA

2 cups   ⚖

Mexican green tomatoes *(tomatillos)*, available both fresh and canned in Latin-American groceries and many supermarkets, make a good addition to *salsa fría*. Chop 2 or 3 fine and add along with the other tomatoes.

4 ripe tomatoes, peeled, cored, seeded, and coarsely chopped
1 large red onion, peeled and minced
1 medium-size sweet green pepper, cored, seeded, and minced
1/2 small hot red chili pepper, cored and seeded, or 1 (4-ounce) can peeled green chilies, drained and minced very fine
1 clove garlic, peeled and crushed
1 tablespoon red wine vinegar
1 tablespoon olive oil
1 teaspoon salt (about)
1/4 teaspoon coriander or 1 teaspoon minced fresh coriander leaves
Pinch cloves

Mix all ingredients and chill well; taste for salt and adjust as needed. Serve cold with steaks or fish either on the side of the plate or in individual bowls.

NP Cup: 160 C, 0 mg CH, 1,120 mg S*

VARIATION

⚖ Prepare as directed but substitute 1 (1-pound) can tomatoes, drained and coarsely chopped, for fresh tomatoes, and 1/8–1/4 teaspoon crushed dried hot red chili peppers for the fresh or canned.

NP Cup: 160 C, 0 mg CH, 1,440 mg S*

BEEF, SAUSAGE, AND MUSHROOM SAUCE FOR PASTA

1 gallon, enough for 16–18 servings

Here's a versatile sauce that freezes beautifully and can be used for making lasagne or ladled over steaming spaghetti, linguine, or macaroni.

1 pound sweet Italian sausages
1 1/2 pounds ground beef chuck
3/4 pound mushrooms, wiped clean and sliced thin
3 large yellow onions, peeled and minced
4 cloves garlic, peeled and crushed
4 teaspoons salt
2 tablespoons oregano
1 tablespoon basil
1 teaspoon chili powder
1/8 teaspoon crushed dried hot red chili peppers
1 (1-quart 14-ounce) can tomato juice
4 (6-ounce) cans tomato paste
1 cup water

Slit sausage casings and remove meat; sauté over moderate heat in a large, heavy skillet, breaking meat up with a fork, about 10 minutes until golden brown. Transfer to a large kettle with a slotted spoon. Drain all but 3 tablespoons drippings from skillet, add beef and brown over moderate heat; transfer to kettle, using a slotted spoon. Drain all but 4 tablespoons drippings from skillet; add mushrooms, onions, and garlic and sauté, stirring occasionally, 8–10 minutes until golden. Transfer to kettle. Mix remaining ingredients into kettle, cover, and simmer 2 hours over moderate heat, stirring occasionally. Serve hot over pasta, or cool to room temperature and freeze for use later.

NP Cup: 270 C, 45 mg CH, 1,285 mg S*

SAVORY AMERICAN BEEF AND TOMATO SAUCE FOR PASTA

1 quart, enough for 4 servings

2 medium-size yellow onions, peeled and coarsely chopped
1 clove garlic, peeled and crushed
2 tablespoons olive oil
1 pound ground beef chuck
1 large bay leaf, crumbled
1/2 teaspoon oregano
1/4 teaspoon summer savory
1/4 teaspoon nutmeg
11/2 teaspoons salt
1/8 teaspoon pepper
2 tablespoons bourbon (optional)
1 tablespoon light brown sugar
1 (1-pound 12-ounce) can tomatoes (do not drain)
1 (6-ounce) can tomato paste
2/3 cup water

Sauté onions and garlic in oil in a large, heavy skillet over moderate heat, stirring occasionally, 10 minutes, until golden. Add beef, breaking it up with a spoon, and sauté 8–10 minutes until just pink. Stir in bay leaf, oregano, savory, nutmeg, salt, pepper, bourbon, if you like, and brown sugar and heat, stirring, 5 minutes. Reduce heat to low, stir in remaining ingredients, and simmer, uncovered, stirring occasionally, 11/2 hours. Serve hot over pasta.

NP Cup: 475 C, 75 mg CH, 1,495 mg S*

TUNA SAUCE FOR PASTA

1 cup, enough for 2 servings ⊠

1 clove garlic, peeled and crushed
2 tablespoons olive oil
2 tablespoons butter or margarine
1 (61/2-ounce) can tuna in olive oil (do not drain)
2 anchovy fillets, minced
1 teaspoon minced parsley
1/8 teaspoon freshly ground black pepper

Sauté garlic in oil and butter in a saucepan 1–2 minutes over moderate heat until

golden. Mix in tuna and anchovies, turn heat to low, and warm, breaking up tuna chunks. Cover and simmer 5 minutes. Ladle into a sauceboat, sprinkle with parsley and pepper, and serve with spaghetti or linguine.

NPS: 495 C, 85 mg CH, 890 mg S*

V A R I A T I O N

⊠ **Anchovy-Olive Sauce for Pasta:** Sauté garlic in 1/4 cup each olive oil and butter. Add 2 (2-ounce) cans anchovy fillets, drained and minced, instead of tuna and anchovies called for and cook and stir until anchovies disintegrate. Mix in 1/4 cup coarsely chopped pitted ripe olives, the parsley, and pepper and serve.

NPS: 490 C, 65 mg CH, 425 mg S*

BARBECUE SAUCES AND MARINADES

Note: Other barbecue sauces and marinades can be found in the individual meat, poultry, and seafood sections.

ALL-PURPOSE BARBECUE SAUCE

11/4 cups ¢

1/4 cup cider vinegar
1/2 cup water
2 tablespoons sugar
1 tablespoon prepared mild yellow mustard
1/2 teaspoon pepper
11/2 teaspoons salt
1/4 teaspoon paprika
1 thick slice lemon
1/2 medium-size yellow onion, peeled and sliced thin
1/4 cup butter or margarine
1/2 cup ketchup
2 tablespoons Worcestershire sauce

Simmer all but last 2 ingredients, uncovered, 20 minutes, stirring occasionally; off heat, mix in ketchup and Worcestershire sauce. Use in making any barbecued dish.

NP Cup (with butter): 575 C, 100 mg CH, 4,575 mg S*
NP Tablespoon (with butter): 35 C, 5 mg CH, 285 mg S*

BARBECUE SAUCE FOR BEEF

2 cups ⊠

1/2 cup cooking oil
1/2 cup dry red wine or red wine vinegar

2 tablespoons Worcestershire sauce
1 clove garlic, peeled and crushed
1/4 teaspoon seasoned pepper
1 cup tomato juice

Shake all ingredients in a shaker jar to blend; use as a marinade for beef or as a brush-on basting.

NP Cup (with wine): 525 C, 0 mg CH, 410 mg S*
NP Tablespoon (with wine): 35 C, 0 mg CH, 25 mg S*

BARBECUE GRAVY FOR BEEF

2 1/2 cups ⚖ ⊠

1/2 cup Barbecue Sauce for Beef
1 cup tomato juice
1 cup beef broth
2 tablespoons cornstarch blended with 2 tablespoons cold water

Heat and stir all ingredients over moderate heat until thickened and clear. Reduce heat and let mellow 3–5 minutes. Serve with any barbecued beef.

NP Tablespoon: 10 C, 0 mg CH, 35 mg S*

SOUTH AMERICAN HOT BARBECUE SAUCE

3 cups

Hot and spicy. Especially good for basting charcoal-broiled meats.

1/2 cup minced yellow onion
1/2 cup minced sweet green pepper
2 cloves garlic, peeled and crushed
1/4 cup olive oil
2 teaspoons chili powder
2 cups tomato purée
1/2 cup red wine vinegar
1/3 cup firmly packed dark brown sugar
1/4 teaspoon crushed dried hot red chili peppers
1 1/2 teaspoons salt

Stir-fry onion, green pepper, and garlic in oil in a saucepan over moderate heat 5–8 minutes until onion is pale golden. Add chili powder and stir-fry 1–2 minutes. Add remaining ingredients, cover, and simmer 1/2 hour. Use as a basting sauce for spareribs, beef, or poultry.

NP Cup: 345 C, 0 mg CH, 1,795 mg S*
NP Tablespoon: 20 C, 0 mg CH, 110 mg S*

CHINESE BARBECUE SAUCE

1/2 cup ⊠

2/3 cup firmly packed dark brown sugar
2 tablespoons cider vinegar
2 tablespoons soy sauce
1/8 teaspoon curry powder
1/2 clove garlic, peeled and crushed

Mix together all ingredients until sugar dissolves. Use for brushing barbecued spareribs, loin of pork, leg of lamb, or lamb shanks.

NP Tablespoon: 75 C, 0 mg CH, 335 mg S*

TERIYAKI SAUCE

3/4 cup ⊠ ⚖

A strong sauce best added with a light hand.

1/2 cup soy sauce
1/4 cup mirin (sweet rice wine), sake, or medium-dry sherry
1 tablespoon sugar (if sake or sherry is used)
2 teaspoons finely grated fresh gingerroot or 1 tablespoon minced preserved ginger
1/4 clove garlic, peeled and crushed (optional)

Mix all ingredients and use as a marinade or basting sauce for broiled beef or chicken or roast pork.

NP Tablespoon (with sherry and sugar): 20 C, 0 mg CH, 885 mg S*

POULTRY MARINADE

2 cups ⊠

Suit the wine or vinegar in the marinade to the bird—white for chicken, Rock Cornish hens, or turkey; red for duckling, goose, or game birds.

1 cup medium-dry white or red wine, sweet or dry Vermouth, or 1/2 cup each wine vinegar and water
1 cup olive or other cooking oil
1 clove garlic, peeled and crushed (optional)
Few crushed sprigs fresh rosemary, tarragon, or thyme
1/4 teaspoon crushed juniper berries

Place all ingredients in a large jar, cover, and shake vigorously. Use to marinate and/or baste poultry.

NP Cup (with wine): 1,055 C, 0 mg CH, 5 mg S*
NP Tablespoon (with wine): 65 C, 0 mg CH, 1 mg S*
NP Cup (with vinegar and water): 965 C, 0 mg CH, 10 mg S*
NP Tablespoon (with vinegar and water): 60 C, 0 mg CH, 1 mg S*

BUTTERMILK MARINADE

1 quart ⚖ ☒

1 quart buttermilk
2 tablespoons white vinegar
1 large yellow onion, peeled and sliced thin
2 teaspoons prepared horseradish
1/2 teaspoon sage
1 teaspoon salt
1/8 teaspoon pepper

Mix all ingredients and use to marinate poultry, game, or lamb.

NP Cup: 115 C, 10 mg CH, 815 mg S*
NP Tablespoon: 5 C, 1 mg CH, 50 mg S*

BEER MARINADE

2 cups ☒

1 (12-ounce) can beer
1/2 cup French dressing
1 clove garlic, peeled and crushed
1 teaspoon powdered mustard
1/2 teaspoon salt
1/4 teaspoon pepper

Mix all ingredients and use to marinate poultry, beef, game, or shrimp.

NP Cup: 330 C, 0 mg CH, 380 mg S*
NP Tablespoon: 20 C, 0 mg CH, 85 mg S*

OTHER SAUCES

QUICK AND EASY CHILI SAUCE

5 1/2 cups ⚖ ☒

1 (1-pound) can tomatoes (do not drain)
1 (1-pound 13-ounce) can tomato purée
1 large yellow onion, peeled and grated fine
2 cloves garlic, peeled and crushed
1/4 cup cider vinegar
1 tablespoon chili powder
1 1/2 teaspoons salt
1 teaspoon sugar
1/8 teaspoon crushed dried hot red chili peppers
1/8 teaspoon allspice
2 tablespoons cornstarch mixed with 2
    tablespoons cider vinegar

Purée tomatoes by buzzing 15–20 seconds in an electric blender at low speed or 10–15 seconds in a food processor fitted with the metal chopping blade. Mix with all but last ingredient and heat in a large saucepan until bubbling. Stir in cornstarch paste and heat, stirring constantly, 2–3 minutes. Reduce heat and simmer, uncovered, 10 minutes. Cool, ladle into sterilized jars, and seal.

Sauce will keep in a cool place without refrigeration 2–3 weeks, longer in refrigerator.

NP Cup: 80 C, 0 mg CH, 1,280 mg S*
NP Tablespoon: 5 C, 0 mg CH, 80 mg S*

COCKTAIL SAUCE

1 cup ☒

1 cup ketchup or chili sauce
1–2 tablespoons prepared horseradish
1 tablespoon lemon juice
2–3 dashes liquid hot red pepper seasoning

Mix all ingredients and let stand 1/2 hour for flavors to blend. Serve with seafood.

NP Tablespoon: 20 C, 0 mg CH, 180 mg S*

VARIATION

☒ **Fin and Claw Cocktail Sauce:** Prepare as directed but use 1/2 cup mayonnaise and 1/2 cup chili sauce instead of all ketchup.

NP Tablespoon: 60 C, 5 mg CH, 155 mg S*

BREAD SAUCE

2 cups

Traditional with game birds but good, too, with any poultry.

1 large yellow onion, peeled and stuck with 6
    cloves
2 cups milk
2 tablespoons butter
1 teaspoon salt (about)
1/4 teaspoon white pepper
Pinch mace (optional)
Pinch cayenne pepper
1 cup fine dry bread crumbs
2 tablespoons light or heavy cream

Simmer onion, covered, in milk with butter and seasonings 3/4 hour until mushy; remove onion, pick out cloves and discard. If you like, mince onion and return to milk. Mix in crumbs and heat, stirring constantly, over low heat until the consistency of oatmeal. Taste for salt and adjust, blend in cream, and serve.

NP Tablespoon: 30 C, 5 mg CH, 105 mg S*

CUMBERLAND SAUCE

2 cups

Serve with venison.

2 tablespoons finely slivered orange rind (orange
    part only)
1 tablespoon finely slivered lemon rind (yellow
    part only)

1 shallot, peeled and minced, or 1 scallion, minced (white part only)
⅓ cup water
1 cup red currant jelly
1 cup tawny port wine
½ teaspoon powdered mustard mixed with 1 teaspoon water
¼ cup orange juice
2 tablespoons lemon juice
½ teaspoon salt
⅛ teaspoon ginger
Pinch cayenne pepper

Boil orange and lemon rind and shallot in water 3–4 minutes; drain off water. Simmer remaining ingredients, covered, stirring now and then, 10 minutes. Add rinds and shallots, cover, and simmer 5 minutes.

NP Tablespoon: 30 C, 0 mg CH, 35 mg S*

SWEET-SOUR SAUCE

1⅔ cups ⊠ ⚖

1 cup pineapple juice or water or a ½ and ½ mixture of water and beef or chicken broth
¼ cup cider vinegar
¼ cup soy sauce
⅓ cup firmly packed light brown sugar
1 teaspoon finely grated fresh gingerroot or ⅛ teaspoon powdered ginger
½ clove garlic, peeled and crushed
2 tablespoons cornstarch blended with 2 tablespoons cold water

Heat together all but last ingredient; when steaming, mix in cornstarch paste and cook and stir until thickened and clear. Lower heat, cover, and simmer 5 minutes. Serve with roast pork, spareribs, broiled shrimp, or Chinese-style vegetables.

NP Tablespoon (with pineapple juice): 20 C, 0 mg CH, 205 mg S*

VARIATIONS

Pineapple-Pepper Sweet-Sour Sauce: Drain liquid from 1 (8-ounce) can pineapple chunks and add enough pineapple juice to total 1 cup. Prepare sauce as directed, using the pineapple juice and adding ½ cup minced sweet green pepper before simmering. Just before serving, stir in pineapple chunks.

NP Tablespoon: 25 C, 0 mg CH, 205 mg S*

Chinese-Style Sweet-Sour Sauce: Stir-fry 1 medium-size sweet green pepper, cored, seeded, and cut in ½″ squares, with 1 carrot, peeled and cut in julienne strips, in 2 tablespoons peanut or other cooking oil 2–3 minutes over moderate heat; do not brown. Mix in liquid and proceed as recipe directs, reducing soy sauce to 2 tablespoons. Before serving, mix in 1 tablespoon dry sherry and, if you like, ½ cup pineapple chunks.

NP Tablespoon (without pineapple chunks): 30 C, 0 mg CH, 205 mg S*

JAPANESE STEAK SAUCE

1 cup ⊠

¼ cup minced yellow onion
2 tablespoons butter or margarine
½ cup Japanese soy or teriyaki sauce
1 tablespoon chili sauce or ketchup
2 tablespoons dry sherry or sake
2 teaspoons powdered mustard
½ teaspoon pepper

Stir-fry onion in butter in a small saucepan over moderate heat 8–10 minutes until golden. Mix in remaining ingredients and simmer, uncovered, 5 minutes. Serve hot over any broiled steak. Good, too, with lamb and pork chops.

NP Tablespoon (with butter): 25 C, 5 mg CH, 695 mg S*

TEMPURA SAUCE

1½ cups ⚖ ⊠

Daikon (Japanese radish) is traditional in this sauce, but a white or red radish may be substituted.

¼ cup Japanese soy sauce
1 cup hot beef broth
1 teaspoon light brown sugar
2 tablespoons dry sherry or sake
1 tablespoon finely grated daikon or 1 medium-size radish, grated fine
¼ teaspoon finely grated fresh gingerroot

Mix all ingredients and let stand at room temperature 10 minutes. Mix well again and serve with Japanese Butterfly Shrimp or tempura.

NP Tablespoon (with sherry): 5 C, 0 mg CH, 255 mg S*

HOT CHINESE MUSTARD SAUCE

1/4 cup   ⚖ ¢ ⊠

Very hot. Use sparingly.

2 tablespoons powdered mustard
1 tablespoon cold water
1 tablespoon white vinegar
1/4 teaspoon salt
1/4 teaspoon sugar
2 or 3 drops liquid hot red pepper seasoning
Pinch turmeric
Pinch ginger

Blend mustard with water and vinegar until smooth, mix in remaining ingredients, and let stand 10 minutes to develop and blend flavors. Serve as a dip for spareribs or Chinese egg rolls.

NP Tablespoon: 15 C, 0 mg CH, 135 mg S*

HARISSA (MOROCCAN HOT SAUCE)

1/2 cup

Ever since camel caravans first brought spices to Morocco, meats, poultry, and vegetables have been heavily seasoned. A local staple, both in the kitchen and dining room, is the fiery *harissa,* which is used to flavor everything from *couscous* to *kofta.* When making *harissa,* you can substitute crushed or ground spices for the whole and omit roasting them, but the flavor of the *harissa* won't be as intense.

2 teaspoons cumin seeds
2 teaspoons coriander seeds
1/2 teaspoon cardamom seeds (dark inner seeds only)
4 teaspoons chili pequins (whole dried pods)
10 whole cloves
1/2 teaspoon black peppercorns
1/2 teaspoon cayenne pepper
1 teaspoon salt
2 large cloves garlic, peeled
1/4 cup olive oil

Place cumin, coriander, cardamom, chili pequins, cloves, and peppercorns in a small heavy saucepan, set over moderately high heat, and toast spices 3–4 minutes, shaking pan frequently. *Note:* Cumin seeds will turn bitter if browned. Cool spices 2–3 minutes, transfer to a mortar, and crush thoroughly with a pestle. Add cayenne, salt, and garlic and crush all to paste. Transfer to a small jar, add oil, cover tight, and store at room temperature. Sauce will keep several weeks. Use sparingly to flavor Hot Sauce for Couscous, meat balls, and meat loaves. Replenish oil each time you use the *harissa,* so that the spice mixture is covered at all times by about 1/4 inch of oil.

NP Tablespoon: 65 C, 0 mg CH, 275 mg S*

FRESH MINT SAUCE

1 quart   ⊠

1 1/2 cups cider or white vinegar
1 1/2 cups sugar
1 cup minced fresh mint leaves (measure loosely packed)

Wash and sterilize enough preserving jars and closures to hold 1 quart (baby food jars are ideal). Stir vinegar and sugar together in a large bowl until sugar dissolves. Add mint and mix well; ladle into jars, distributing mint evenly. Screw lids on and store in a dark, cool place (sauce will keep 2–3 months). Serve with hot or cold roast lamb, lamb chops, or tiny boiled new potatoes.

NP Tablespoon: 20 C, 0 mg CH, 1 mg S*

EASY RAISIN SAUCE

2 1/2 cups   ⊠

3 tablespoons cornstarch
2 cups apple cider
1 tablespoon orange juice
1 teaspoon finely grated orange rind
2 tablespoons butter or margarine
1 cup seedless raisins

In a closed shaker jar, blend cornstarch with 1/2 cup apple cider until smooth. Pour into a small saucepan, add all remaining ingredients, and heat, stirring constantly over moderate heat, until thickened and clear and no raw starch taste remains. Turn heat to low and let sauce mellow 2–3 minutes, stirring occasionally. Serve warm with ham or tongue.

NP Tablespoon (with butter): 25 C, 1 mg CH, 5 mg S*

PLUM SAUCE

1 1/2 cups

1/2 cup mango chutney
1 cup red plum jelly
2 teaspoons light brown sugar
2 teaspoons red wine vinegar

Drain and reserve liquid from chutney; chop solids fine. Mix chutney liquid and chopped chutney with remaining ingredients, cover, and let stand at room temperature 1 hour.

Serve with Barbecued or Chinese-Style Spareribs.

NP Tablespoon: 50 C, 0 mg CH, 15 mg S*

WHOLE CRANBERRY SAUCE

1 quart ⊠

1½ cups water
1½ cups sugar
1 pound fresh or frozen cranberries, washed and stemmed

Bring water and sugar to a boil in a large, heavy saucepan over moderate heat, stirring constantly; boil, uncovered, 5 minutes without stirring. Add cranberries, cover, and simmer 5–7 minutes until skins pop open. Serve warm or chilled with poultry or pork.

NP Tablespoon: 20 C, 0 mg CH, 0 mg S*

VARIATIONS

⊠ **Spicy Whole Cranberry Sauce:** Prepare as directed but add 1 stick cinnamon and 18 whole cloves tied in cheesecloth along with cranberries; remove before serving.

NP Tablespoon: 20 C, 0 mg CH, 0 mg S*

⊠ **Orange-Cranberry Sauce:** Prepare as directed but substitute light brown sugar for the granulated and the juice of 3 oranges and ¼ cup water for the 1½ cups water. If you like, add a cinnamon stick.

NP Tablespoon: 25 C, 0 mg CH, 1 mg S*

Stuffings and Forcemeats

Many a routine dish has been transformed into something unique by the addition of a stuffing or forcemeat *(farce,* the French call these savory mixtures of finely minced meat and vegetables). Most are easy to make (if not quick), most are economical and a good way to stretch the number of servings. The varieties of stuffings are as broad as the imagination. They can be made wholly or partly from scratch or they can be stirred up in minutes, using any of the package mixes available. Stuffings and forcemeats, by the way, are an excellent way to use up odds and ends of meats, vegetables, and breads.

SOME TIPS ON MAKING AND USING STUFFINGS AND FORCEMEATS

• Mix stuffings and forcemeats just before using—there is danger of food poisoning if they are made far ahead of time.
• To save last-minute frenzy, have all ingredients chopped or minced beforehand, but do not mix. Keep ingredients in separate containers in the refrigerator and put together just before using.
• Never put stuffing into a bird, roast, or fish until just before cooking.
• Never stuff anything that is to be frozen, either before or after cooking. It is true that prestuffed frozen turkeys are available, but commercial packers have access to preservatives the home cook doesn't.
• Always remove stuffing from leftover bird,

roast, or fish, wrap and refrigerate separately —again to reduce risk of food poisoning.
• Team rich stuffings with not so rich poultry, meat, or fish, light stuffings with heavier poultry, meat, or fish.
• Never use raw pork or pork sausage in a stuffing or forcemeat; always sauté first in a skillet until no pink color remains.
• To mellow flavor of minced onions, garlic, celery, and mushrooms, sauté lightly before mixing into stuffing.
• When using soft white commerical bread in stuffings, reduce amount of moisture in recipe slightly. These breads are already oversoft and if mixed with additional liquid may produce a soggy stuffing. *(Note:* At holiday time, many supermarkets sell special "stuffing" breads.)
• Always mix stuffings with a light hand. Never pack them into a bird, fish, or roast— just drop or spoon in lightly. Stuffings expand on heating and, if too tightly packed, may become leaden. Moreover, they may rupture the bird, fish, or roast.
• Mix forcemeats with a deft hand from start to finish. Properly made, they should be moist, velvety, and airy.

How Much Stuffing Is Enough?

For stuffing lovers, there is never enough. For practical purposes, however, figure 1/2–3/4 cup stuffing per pound of food to be stuffed. It is unlikely that you will be able to get the full amount into the bird, fish, or roast—don't try. Wrap any extra stuffing in heavy foil, then place alongside roasting pan about 1 hour before bird, fish, or roast is done. Or, if there is as much as 4 cups, spoon into a lightly greased casserole and bake, uncovered, during the last 3/4–1 hour of cooking, just until touched with brown. Use the following chart as a guide in determining quantity of stuffing needed.

Quantity of Stuffing	Size Bird It Will Stuff	Number of Servings
1 pint	3–4 pounds	2–3
1½ pints	5–6 pounds	4–5
1 quart	6–8 pounds	6
1½ quarts	8–10 pounds	8
2 quarts	10–12 pounds	10
3 quarts	12–15 pounds	12–14
4 quarts (1 gallon)	15–20 pounds	18–20

What to Do with Stuffing Leftovers

• Slice and serve cold with roast poultry or meat.
• Fluff with a fork, place on a heavy piece of foil, dot with softened butter, wrap, and heat 15–20 minutes at 350° F.
• Fluff with a fork, place in a well-greased small casserole or shallow baking pan, drizzle with melted butter or smother with sliced sautéed mushrooms, and bake about 20 minutes at 375° F. until heated through.
• Fluff with a fork and spoon into hollowed-out tomatoes or parboiled onions or parboiled, scooped-out halves of summer squash. Dot well with butter and bake 20–30 minutes at 375° F. until vegetables are tender and stuffing lightly browned.
Note: Surplus or leftover stuffing will bake or reheat a little faster in a convection oven than in a conventional one, so check stuffing often to avoid overbrowning or drying.

Microwaving Stuffings and Forcemeats

In our opinion, surplus stuffings (those which won't fit into the bird or fish) are more flavorful and attractive if baked in a conventional or convection oven. For information on how to microwave stuffed poultry and fish, read Microwaving Poultry (Chapter 7) and To Bake Fish By Microwave (Chapter 8). Also remember to use quick-cooking rices in any stuffing recipe calling for uncooked rice (converted or long-grain rice will not cook done in the short time needed for the other ingredients).

Reheating Stuffings and Forcemeats in a Microwave Oven

The microwave is ideal for reheating leftover stuffings because they remain moist and fresh. *For small amounts,* wrap in plastic food wrap and microwave as manufacturer directs, turning and rotating package often. *For large amounts,* place stuffing in a microwave-safe casserole, cover with wax paper, and microwave using times oven instruction manual recommends. Remember to rotate the casserole and stir the stuffing now and then from the outside edge toward the center to distribute heat evenly. Allow extra time to reheat frozen stuffings, also read Defrosting, Heating, or Cooking Frozen Foods by Microwave in Chapter 1.

BASIC BREAD STUFFING

2 quarts, enough to stuff a 10–12-pound turkey ¢ ☒

1 cup minced yellow onion
3/4 cup minced celery (include some leaves)
1/2 cup butter or margarine or bacon drippings
2 quarts (1/2″) stale bread cubes or 2 quarts soft white or whole wheat bread crumbs
2 teaspoons poultry seasoning or 3/4 teaspoon each sage, thyme, and marjoram
1½ teaspoons salt
1/2 teaspoon pepper
1/4 cup minced parsley
1–2 eggs, lightly beaten (optional)

Sauté onion and celery in butter in a skillet over moderate heat 5 minutes until pale golden. Mix with remaining ingredients, tossing with 2 forks. *(Note: For moister stuffing, mix in 1/3 cup chicken broth.)* Use to stuff poultry or pork. Or, if you prefer, bake, uncovered, in a well-greased 2½-quart casserole at 325° F. about 1 hour until lightly browned.

NP Cup (with butter, no eggs): 235 C, 35 mg CH, 770 mg S*
NP Cup (with butter, 2 eggs): 255 C, 100 mg CH, 785 mg S*

VARIATIONS

Stuffing Balls *(1 dozen):* Prepare as directed using 2 lightly beaten eggs or 1 egg and 1/3 cup chicken broth. Shape into 1 dozen balls and arrange 1″ apart on a well-greased baking sheet. Bake, uncovered, 35–40 minutes at 325° F. until golden brown.

NP Ball (with butter, 2 eggs): 170 C, 70 mg CH, 525 mg S*
NP Ball (with butter, egg, and broth): 165 C, 45 mg CH, 540 mg S*

Chestnut Stuffing: Prepare as directed but reduce bread cubes to 1½ quarts and poultry seasoning to 1½ teaspoons. Mix in 1 pound coarsely chopped Boiled, Sautéed, or peeled Roasted Chestnuts.

NP Cup (with butter, no eggs): 315 C, 32 mg CH, 715 mg S*
NP Cup (with butter, 2 eggs): 335 C, 100 mg CH, 735 mg S*

Pecan Stuffing: Prepare as directed but reduce bread cubes to 1½ quarts and add 1½ cups coarsely chopped pecans (or walnuts, filberts, almonds, or Brazil nuts); toast nuts first if you like.

NP Cup (with butter, no eggs): 360 C, 30 mg CH, 715 mg S*
NP Cup (with butter, 2 eggs): 370 C, 100 mg CH, 730 mg S*

Water Chestnut Stuffing (nice for Rock Cornish hens or fish): Reduce bread cubes to 1½ quarts, omit poultry seasoning but add 1 teaspoon thyme; also mix in 2 cups coarsely chopped or thinly sliced water chestnuts and 2 minced pimientos.

NP Cup (with butter, no eggs): 230 C, 30 mg CH, 720 mg S*
NP Cup (with butter, 2 eggs): 250 C, 100 mg CH, 740 mg S*

Sage and Mushroom Stuffing: Sauté 1½ pounds thinly sliced mushrooms (include stems) along with onion and celery in ⅔ cup butter. Add 1½ quarts bread cubes, 1 teaspoon sage, ½ teaspoon marjoram, and the salt and pepper called for; omit poultry seasoning and parsley. Excellent with veal.

NP Cup (no eggs): 265 C, 45 mg CH, 490 mg S*
NP Cup (2 eggs): 285 C, 110 mg CH, 780 mg S*

Oyster Stuffing: Prepare recipe using 3 cups bread cubes and 3 cups coarsely crushed crackers; reduce poultry seasoning to 1½ teaspoons and add 1 pint oysters, drained and minced.

NP Cup (with butter, no eggs): 300 C, 60 mg CH, 935 mg S*
NP Cup (with butter, 2 eggs): 320 C, 130 mg CH, 950 mg S*

Apple-Raisin Stuffing: Reduce minced onion to ½ cup, bread cubes to 1½ quarts, and poultry seasoning to 1 teaspoon. Add 3 cups coarsely chopped, peeled, tart apple and ¾ cup seedless raisins. Good with pork.

NP Cup (with butter, no eggs): 235 C, 30 mg CH, 660 mg S*
NP Cup (with butter, 2 eggs): 255 C, 100 mg CH, 675 mg S*

Corn Bread Stuffing: Prepare as directed but sauté vegetables in bacon drippings and use 3 cups bread cubes and 5 cups corn bread crumbs (preferably from corn bread made without sugar).

NP Cup (no eggs): 275 C, 60 mg CH, 875 mg S*
NP Cup (2 eggs): 295 C, 125 mg CH, 895 mg S*

Amish Potato Stuffing: Prepare as directed, using 1 quart bread cubes and 3 cups unseasoned mashed potatoes (or sweet potatoes); reduce poultry seasoning to 1½ teaspoons and add ¼ teaspoon nutmeg.

NP Cup (with butter, no eggs): 230 C, 30 mg CH, 880 mg S*
NP Cup (with butter, 2 eggs): 250 C, 100 mg CH, 890 mg S*

Savory Sausage Stuffing: Sauté 1 pound sausage meat slowly in a heavy skillet, breaking up with a fork, until lightly browned and cooked through, about 20 minutes; transfer to a bowl with slotted spoon. Proceed as directed, using ½ cup drippings for sautéing vegetables and reducing bread cubes to 7 cups.

NP Cup (no eggs): 320 C, 40 mg CH, 1,015 mg S*
NP Cup (2 eggs): 340 C, 110 mg CH, 1,035 mg S*

Bread and Apricot Stuffing: Cover 1½ cups dried apricots with boiling water and soak 10 minutes; drain and coarsely chop. Reduce onion to ½ cup, bread cubes to 1½ quarts, and poultry seasoning to ½ teaspoon. Prepare as directed, adding apricots along with bread and mixing in ½ teaspoon cinnamon and ¼ teaspoon nutmeg.

NP Cup (with butter, no eggs): 230 C, 30 mg CH, 660 mg S*
NP Cup (with butter, 2 eggs): 250 C, 100 mg CH, 675 mg S*

BASIC RICE STUFFING

About 1 quart, enough to stuff a 6–8-pound bird

1 medium-size yellow onion, peeled and minced
¼ cup minced celery
¼ cup butter or margarine
1 cup uncooked white or brown rice
2 cups chicken broth
¾ teaspoon salt (about)
¼ teaspoon pepper
¼ teaspoon each sage, thyme, and marjoram

Sauté onion and celery in butter in a heavy saucepan over moderate heat 5 minutes until pale golden. Add rice and stir-fry 1–2 minutes; add remaining ingredients, cover, reduce heat so rice bubbles gently, and cook 20–25 minutes (about 40–45 minutes for brown rice) until all liquid is absorbed. Uncover and fluff with a fork. Taste for salt and adjust as needed. Cool and use as a stuffing.

NP Cup (with butter): 310 C, 30 mg CH, 930 mg S*

VARIATIONS

Rice and Kidney Stuffing *(5 cups):* Sauté 3/4 pound lamb kidneys in the butter called for 3–5 minutes over moderately high heat; remove and mince. Stir-fry vegetables in drippings and proceed as directed, adding kidneys along with seasonings.

NP Cup (with butter); 320 C, 280 mg CH, 880 mg S*

Rice and Chicken Liver Stuffing *(5 cups):* Prepare like Rice and Kidney Stuffing, but substitute 1/2 pound chicken livers for kidneys.

NP Cup (with butter): 305 C, 225 mg CH, 780 mg S*

Sherried Rice with Raisins and Almonds *(5 cups):* Prepare Basic Rice Stuffing as directed but omit celery and herbs, use 1 1/2 cups beef broth and 1/2 cup dry sherry instead of chicken broth, and add 1/2 cup each seedless raisins and toasted slivered almonds and 1/4 teaspoon each nutmeg and allspice along with broth.

NP Cup (with butter): 365 C, 25 mg CH, 665 mg S*

Rice and Mushroom Stuffing *(5 cups):* Sauté 1/2 pound minced mushrooms (include stems) along with onion and celery in 1/3 cup butter; proceed as directed for Basic Rice Stuffing.

NP Cup: 285 C, 35 mg CH, 780 mg S*

BASIC WILD RICE STUFFING

1 quart, enough to stuff a 6–8-pound bird

Expensive as wild rice is, putting it in a stuffing is not a waste of money, because only it can provide a certain crunch and nuttiness. Use for elegant birds—game birds or a plump young turkey. If 1 cup wild rice seems an extravagance, use 1/2 cup wild rice and 1/2 cup rice, brown rice, or bulgur wheat.

1 medium-size yellow onion, peeled and minced
1/3 cup celery
1/4 cup bacon drippings
1/4 cup minced cooked ham
1 cup wild rice, washed well
1/2 teaspoon rosemary
3 cups chicken broth or water
1 teaspoon salt (about)
1/8 teaspoon pepper

Sauté onion and celery in drippings in a large, heavy saucepan over moderate heat 5–8 minutes until pale golden; add ham and stir-fry 1 minute; add rice and rosemary and stir-fry 1/2 minute. Add broth, salt, and pepper, cover, and bring to a boil; uncover and boil gently, without stirring, about 30 minutes until barely tender. Drain and set, uncovered, over lowest heat to dry 2–3 minutes, shaking pan now and then. Taste for salt and adjust as needed.

NP Cup: 310 C, 30 mg CH, 930 mg S*

VARIATIONS

Wild Rice and Cranberry Stuffing: Let 1 (8-ounce) can whole cranberry sauce drain in a fine sieve while preparing stuffing as directed; then mix in cranberries and 1 teaspoon finely grated lemon rind.

NP Cup: 375 C, 15 mg CH, 365 mg S*

Wild Rice and Mushroom Stuffing: Sauté 1/2 pound minced mushrooms along with onion and celery, then proceed as directed.

NP Cup: 305 C, 15 mg CH, 1,360 mg S*

BRANDIED WILD RICE, CORN BREAD, AND CHESTNUT STUFFING

1 gallon or enough to stuff a 15–20-pound turkey or suckling pig

1 (1/2-pound) piece lean bacon, cut in 1/4″ cubes
4 medium-size yellow onions, peeled and coarsely chopped
3 cloves garlic, peeled and crushed
1 1/2 cups finely diced celery
1 1/2 pounds mushrooms, wiped clean and sliced thin
1/2 cup minced parsley
1/4 cup minced fresh sage or 1 1/2 tablespoons dried sage
1 (8-ounce) box wild rice, cooked by package directions
8 cups crumbled dry corn bread or 2 (8-ounce) packages corn bread stuffing mix
1 1/2 pounds chestnuts, shelled, peeled, and quartered
1 1/4 cups melted butter or margarine
1 cup chicken broth or water
1/2 cup brandy
1/4 teaspoon pepper

Brown bacon in a large, heavy skillet over moderately high heat and drain on paper toweling. Stir-fry onions, garlic, and celery in drippings 8–10 minutes until golden. Add mushrooms, parsley, and sage and sauté, stirring occasionally, 8–10 minutes. Mix with all remaining ingredients (you'll have to use a very large kettle for this job) and use for stuffing a large turkey or suckling pig. Wrap any leftover stuffing in heavy foil and chill until about 1 hour before serving; place foil package alongside roasting pan and let heat as turkey or pig finishes roasting.

NP Cup (with butter): 365 C, 70 mg CH, 505 mg S*

CORN BREAD AND SAUSAGE STUFFING

About 2 1/2 quarts, enough to stuff a 12–13-pound turkey

1 1/2 pounds sausage meat
1 cup minced yellow onions
1 cup minced celery
8 cups crumbled dry corn bread or 2 (8-ounce) packages corn bread stuffing mix
1/2 teaspoon sage
1/2 teaspoon thyme
1 teaspoon poultry seasoning
2 teaspoons salt
1/2 teaspoon pepper
1 cup melted butter or margarine

Sauté sausage slowly in a heavy skillet, breaking up with a fork, until lightly browned and thoroughly cooked, about 20 minutes; transfer to a large bowl with a slotted spoon. Drain all but 1/4 cup drippings from skillet; add onions and celery and stir-fry over moderate heat 8–10 minutes until golden. Add to sausage along with remaining ingredients and toss lightly to blend. Use to stuff turkey, any poultry or game bird.

NP Cup (with butter): 495 C, 140 mg CH, 1,560 mg S*

VARIATIONS

Corn Bread and Oyster Stuffing: Omit sausage and sauté onion and celery in 1/4 cup bacon drippings as directed. Toss with corn bread, seasonings, and butter, then mix in 1 pint minced, well-drained oysters.

NP Cup (with butter): 455 C, 155 mg CH, 1,315 mg S*

Corn Bread and Cranberry Stuffing: Omit sage and sauté onion and celery in 1/4 cup butter in a large saucepan as directed; add 1 pint washed and stemmed cranberries and 1/2 cup water, cover, and simmer until berries pop. Cool slightly and toss with corn bread, seasonings, and 1/4 cup melted butter.

NP Cup: 790 C, 195 mg CH, 2,000 mg S*

SAGE AND ONION DRESSING

About 2 quarts, enough to stuff a 10–12-pound bird ¢

4 medium-size yellow onions, peeled and minced
1 cup water
6 cups soft white bread cubes
2 teaspoons sage
1/2 cup melted butter or margarine
2 teaspoons salt
1/4 teaspoon pepper

Simmer onions and water, covered, 20 minutes. Off heat, mix in remaining ingredients. Use to stuff poultry or spoon lightly into a well-greased 2 1/2-quart casserole. Bake, uncovered, 1 hour at 325° F. and serve with roast pork, ham, chicken, turkey, duckling, or goose.

NP Cup (with butter): 210 C, 30 mg CH, 840 mg S*

PECAN-BULGUR WHEAT STUFFING

About 1 quart, enough to stuff a crown roast or 6–8-pound bird

1 medium-size yellow onion, peeled and minced
1/2 cup minced celery
1/2 pound mushrooms, wiped clean and minced
1/2 cup butter or margarine
1 cup bulgur wheat
1 3/4 cups chicken broth
1 teaspoon salt (about)
1 teaspoon sage
1 teaspoon thyme
1/4 teaspoon pepper
1/2 cup minced pecans

Sauté onion, celery, and mushrooms in butter in a saucepan over moderate heat 5–8 minutes until pale golden. Add bulgur wheat and stir-fry 2–3 minutes. Add remaining ingredients except pecans, cover, and simmer 1/2 hour until liquid is absorbed and bulgur wheat tender. Mix in pecans, taste for salt and adjust as needed. (*Note:* If you wish to bake stuffing separately, spoon into a well-greased 5-cup casserole and bake 20 minutes at 350° F.)

NP Cup (with butter): 505 C, 60 mg CH, 1,155 mg S*

CHESTNUT MUSHROOM STUFFING

3 quarts or enough to stuff a 12–15-pound turkey or suckling pig

To save yourself the tedium of shelling and peeling chestnuts, use the frozen Italian chestnuts available in many specialty food shops. They have already been shelled and peeled.

4 medium-size yellow onions, peeled and coarsely chopped
2 cloves garlic, peeled and crushed
4 large stalks celery, coarsely chopped (do not include tops)
1/4 cup butter or margarine
1 pound fresh mushrooms, wiped clean and sliced thin
1/4 cup minced parsley
1/2 teaspoon sage
1/2 teaspoon thyme
1 tablespoon salt
1/4 teaspoon pepper
3/4 cup melted butter or margarine
8 cups soft bread crumbs or 2 (8-ounce) packages poultry stuffing mix
1 pound chestnuts, shelled, peeled, and quartered
1/4 cup dry sherry

Stir-fry onions, garlic, and celery in butter in a large, heavy skillet over moderate heat 8–10 minutes until golden; add mushrooms, parsley, sage, thyme, salt, and pepper and heat, stirring occasionally, 8–10 minutes. Mix with all remaining ingredients (use a 6-quart kettle) and use to stuff turkey or suckling pig. Wrap any leftover stuffing in heavy foil and chill until about an hour before serving; place foil package alongside roasting pan and let heat while turkey or pig finishes roasting.

NP Cup (with butter): 315 C, 45 mg CH, 885 mg S*

ORANGE-SWEET POTATO STUFFING

1 1/2 quarts, enough to stuff an 8–10-pound bird

1/2 cup minced yellow onion
1 medium-size carrot, peeled and cut in small dice
1/4 cup butter or margarine
2 cups hot mashed sweet potatoes
2 eggs, lightly beaten
2 cups stale bread crumbs
1/4 cup minced celery leaves
3 oranges, peeled, seeded, sectioned, and coarsely cut up
1 teaspoon finely grated orange rind
1/2 teaspoon salt (about)
1/4 teaspoon rosemary
1/4 teaspoon pepper

Sauté onion and carrot in butter in a skillet over moderate heat 5 minutes until onion is pale golden, reduce heat, and stir-fry 2–3 minutes longer until carrot is crisp tender. Beat sweet potatoes and eggs together until

light and fluffy, mix in onion and carrot and all remaining ingredients. Taste for salt and adjust as needed.

NP Cup (with butter): 365 C, 115 mg CH, 580 mg S*

SAUERKRAUT STUFFING

1 1/2 quarts, enough to stuff a 10-pound goose

1 large Spanish onion, peeled and minced
1 clove garlic, peeled and minced
1/3 cup butter, margarine, or bacon drippings
2 tart cooking apples, peeled, cored, and coarsely chopped
1/4 cup firmly packed light brown sugar
2 1/2 pounds sauerkraut, drained and chopped moderately fine
1/2 teaspoon thyme or celery seed

Sauté onion and garlic in butter in a large skillet over moderately low heat about 5 minutes until onion is limp not brown. Add apples and sugar and stir until sugar is dissolved, then mix in sauerkraut and thyme.

NP Cup (with butter): 195 C, 25 mg CH, 1,520 mg S*

SOME EASY WAYS TO SPICE UP STUFFINGS MADE FROM PACKAGE MIXES

Each variation makes about 1 1/2 quarts, enough to stuff an 8–10-pound bird

Prepare 1 (8-ounce) package poultry stuffing mix by package directions, then vary any of the following ways. To bake separately, spoon into a well-greased 1 1/2-quart casserole and bake, uncovered, about 35 minutes at 325° F. until lightly browned.

NP Cup (with butter): 275 C, 40 mg CH, 660 mg S*

Apple and Pecan Stuffing: Mix in 3/4 cup moderately finely chopped pecans and 2 peeled, cored, and coarsely chopped tart cooking apples.

NP Cup (with butter): 400 C, 45 mg CH, 660 mg S*

Herbed Bread Stuffing: Mix in 1/2 cup minced yellow onion sautéed in 1/4 cup butter over moderate heat 5 minutes until pale golden; also mix in 1/2 teaspoon each sage, thyme, chervil, and savory and 2 tablespoons minced parsley.

NP Cup (with butter): 350 C, 65 mg CH, 740 mg S*

Sausage and Mushroom Stuffing: Prepare Herbed Bread Stuffing as directed. Also sauté 1/2 pound sausage meat or thinly sliced link sausages in a skillet over moderately low heat about 15 minutes until cooked through. Remove with a slotted spoon to paper toweling, pour off all but 1/3 cup drippings, then stir-fry 1/2 cup minced yellow onion and 1/2 pound thinly sliced mushrooms (include stems) 5 minutes until pale golden. Toss into stuffing along with sausage and 1 tablespoon Worcestershire sauce.

NP Cup (with butter): 415 C, 25 mg CH, 2,980 mg S*

Herbed Fruit Stuffing: Prepare Herbed Bread Stuffing as directed, then mix in 1/2 cup each seedless raisins and halved seedless green or seeded red grapes, 2 peeled, seeded, and sectioned oranges, 1/4 cup minced celery, and, if you like, 1/4 cup minced walnuts.

NP Cup (without walnuts): 490 C, 85 mg CH, 825 mg S*

Giblet Stuffing: To the prepared stuffing mix, add the cooked and minced giblets from the bird to be stuffed; if you like, use Giblet Stock in stuffing instead of liquid called for and add an extra 2–3 sautéed minced chicken livers.

NP Cup (with butter and chicken livers): 480 C, 235 mg CH, 850 mg S*

Oyster and Almond Stuffing: Add 1/2 cup minced yellow onion sautéed in 1/4 cup butter until pale golden, also 1 cup minced, drained oysters, 1/4 cup oyster liquor, and 1 cup coarsely chopped toasted almonds.

NP Cup (with butter): 505 C, 85 mg CH, 770 mg S*

Chicken Liver and Mushroom Stuffing: Dredge 1/2 pound chicken livers in flour and sauté in 1/4 cup butter or bacon drippings over moderately high heat about 5 minutes until browned. Remove with slotted spoon and mince. Sauté 1/4 pound sliced mushrooms in drippings 2–3 minutes until golden. Mix livers, mushrooms, and 1 tablespoon minced parsley into stuffing.

NP Cup (with butter): 400 C, 230 mg CH, 770 mg S*

Corn and Pepper Stuffing: Sauté 1/2 cup minced yellow onion and 6 minced yellow-green sweet Italian peppers in 1/4 cup cooking oil over moderate heat 5 minutes until pale golden; reduce heat and simmer 2–3 minutes until peppers are tender. Mix into stuffing along with 1 cup drained canned whole kernel corn. (*Note:* This recipe is also good made with corn bread stuffing mix.)

NP Cup (with butter and corn oil): 385 C, 45 mg CH, 725 mg S*

Prune, Apple, and Cranberry Stuffing: Simmer 1 cup fresh cranberries with 1/4 cup sugar and 1/2 cup water until berries pop. Off heat, mix in 1 cup diced, pitted prunes and let stand 10 minutes. Drain off liquid and use as part of liquid called for in stuffing. Prepare stuffing mix, toss in prepared fruit, also 1 diced, peeled, and cored tart cooking apple, and 1/4 teaspoon allspice.

NP Cup (with butter): 395 C, 45 mg CH, 660 mg S*

VEAL AND PORK FORCEMEAT

About 1 1/2 pints, enough to stuff a 5-pound bird

The food processor has revolutionized the making of forcemeats (no need to pound the meat to make it velvety). If you don't have a processor, you'll have to beat the mixture vigorously with an electric mixer or wooden spoon. Any meat can be used for forcemeat, but this combination is unusually good for stuffing chicken or game birds. For a 10-pound turkey, double recipe. Forcemeat balls can be used to garnish soup, a poultry or pork platter, leftovers can be cooked like hamburgers. Small panfried patties or balls make excellent hors d'oeuvre.

1/2 cup finely minced yellow onion
2 tablespoons butter or margarine
1/3 cup scalded milk
1 cup dry bread crumbs
1/2 pound veal, ground twice
1/2 pound lean pork, ground twice
1/4 pound ground pork fat
1 turkey liver, 2–3 chicken livers, or livers from bird to be stuffed, ground fine (optional)
1 egg, lightly beaten
1/4 cup brandy
1 teaspoon finely grated lemon rind
3/4 teaspoon salt
1/2 teaspoon thyme
Pinch mace
1/8 teaspoon white pepper

Sauté onion in butter in a skillet 5 minutes over moderate heat until pale golden; set aside. Pour milk over crumbs, mix until smooth, and cool. Place onion, all meats, and fat in the work bowl of a food processor fitted with the metal chopping blade and grind very fine using 2–3 five-second churnings of the motor. Mix in remaining ingredients, including crumb paste, by snapping motor on and off 6–8 times. Use as a stuffing.

NP Cup (with butter, without livers): 850 C, 260 mg CH, 1,015 mg S*
NP Cup (with butter, with chicken livers): 865 C, 315 mg CH, 1,025 mg S*

VARIATIONS

Veal and Ham Forcemeat: Prepare as directed but substitute 1/2 pound twice-ground lean cooked ham for the pork.

NP Cup (with butter, without livers): 860 C, 250 mg CH, 2,100 mg S*
NP Cup (with butter, with chicken livers): 875 C, 310 mg CH, 2,100 mg S*

Veal and Pork Forcemeat Balls *(About 4 dozen):* Prepare as directed but omit onion and liver, also substitute 1/4 cup light cream for the brandy. Shape into marble-size balls. *To Use as a Soup Garnish:* Poach balls, a few at a time, in salted simmering water, chicken or beef broth 4–5 minutes until just cooked through. Remove with a slotted spoon and add to hot soup just before serving. *(Note: Recipe can be halved for small amounts of soup; use all veal and serve in a delicately flavored soup.) To Use as a Platter or Roast Garnish:* Brown balls, a few at a time, in about 1/2" hot lard or vegetable shortening over moderate heat 3–4 minutes, turning often. Drain on paper toweling and mound at one end of a poultry platter or use to fill center of a pork crown roast.

NP Ball (baked): 55 C, 15 mg CH, 65 mg S*

BASIC BREAD STUFFING FOR FISH

2 cups, enough to stuff a 3–4-pound fish ¢

1 medium-size yellow onion, peeled and minced
1/2 cup minced celery
1/4 cup butter or margarine
2 cups soft white bread crumbs or 2 cups (1/2")
   stale bread cubes
1/2 teaspoon salt
1/8 teaspon pepper
1 tablespoon minced parsley
1/4 teaspoon each thyme and sage or 1/2
   teaspoon poultry seasoning
1 egg, lightly beaten

Sauté onion and celery in butter in a large, heavy skillet over moderate heat 5 minutes until pale golden. Add all remaining ingredients and toss well to mix.

NP Cup (with butter): 390 C, 200 mg CH, 1,080 mg S*

LEMON BREAD STUFFING FOR FISH

1 1/2 cups, enough to stuff a 3-pound fish

1/4 cup minced yellow onion
1/4 cup minced celery
2 tablespoons butter or margarine
1 1/4 cups toasted 1/2" bread cubes
1 1/2 teaspoons finely grated lemon rind
1 tablespoon lemon juice
1 tablespoon minced parsley
1/4 teaspoon salt
1/4 teaspoon sage
1/8 teaspoon pepper
2 tablespoons milk

Stir-fry onion and celery in butter in a large, heavy skillet over moderate heat 5–8 minutes until golden. Pour over bread cubes, add remaining ingredients, and toss lightly to mix.

NP Cup (with butter): 320 C, 50 mg CH, 850 mg S*

VEGETABLE STUFFING FOR FISH

2 cups, enough to stuff a 3–4-pound fish

1/3 cup minced scallions
1/2 cup minced celery
1 small sweet green pepper, cored, seeded, and
   minced
1 medium-size carrot, peeled and cut in small
   dice
1/2 pound mushrooms, wiped clean and minced
   (include stems)
1/2 clove garlic, peeled and crushed (optional)
2 tablespoons olive or other cooking oil
2 tomatoes, peeled, seeded, and coarsely
   chopped
1 pimiento, seeded and minced
1/4 cup minced ripe olives
3/4 teaspoon salt
1/8 teaspoon pepper

Stir-fry scallions, celery, green pepper, carrot, mushrooms, and, if you like, the garlic in oil in a large, heavy skillet over moderate heat 5–8 minutes until pepper and carrot are crisp tender. Off heat, mix in remaining ingredients.

NP Cup (with butter): 255 C, 0 mg CH, 1,040 mg S*

MUSHROOM STUFFING FOR FISH

2 cups, enough to stuff a 3–4-pound fish ⊠

Especially good for stuffed, baked shad.

1/2 pound mushrooms, wiped clean and sliced
  thin
3 tablespoons melted butter or margarine
1 1/2 cups soft white bread crumbs
2 tablespoons minced chives
2 tablespoons minced parsley
1/2 teaspoon dried tarragon or marjoram
1/2 teaspoon salt
1/8 teaspoon white pepper
1 egg, lightly beaten

Sauté mushrooms in butter in a skillet 5–8 minutes over moderate heat until golden. Place all remaining ingredients in a bowl, add mushrooms and toss lightly to mix.

NP Cup (with butter): 320 C, 185 mg CH, 945 mg S*

CRAB OR SHRIMP STUFFING FOR FISH

3 cups, enough to stuff a 5–6-pound fish

1/4 cup minced scallions (include some tops)
1/4 cup minced celery
1/3 cup butter or margarine
2 cups (1/2″) soft bread cubes
1 cup flaked cooked or canned crab meat or
  minced cooked, shelled, and deveined shrimp
1 tablespoon lemon juice
Pinch nutmeg
Pinch cayenne pepper

Stir-fry scallions and celery in butter in a skillet over moderate heat 2–3 minutes. Add bread cubes and stir-fry until lightly browned. Off heat, add remaining ingredients and toss lightly to mix.

NP Cup (with butter and crab): 290 C, 105 mg CH, 430 mg S*

VARIATION

Clam Stuffing for Fish: Prepare as directed but substitute 1 (6 1/2-ounce) can drained minced clams for crab meat.

NP Cup (with butter): 275 C, 75 mg CH, 670 mg S*

EASY ALMOND STUFFING FOR FISH

2 cups, enough to stuff a 3–4-pound fish ⊠

Especially good for trout.

1 cup poultry stuffing mix
3 tablespoons melted butter
1/4 cup minced celery
2 tablespoons minced parsley
3/4 cup finely chopped, toasted, blanched
  almonds

Toss all ingredients together to mix.

NP Cup: 580 C, 50 mg CH, 665 mg S*

THIRTEEN

Vegetables

Of all the world's foods, none has greater color or variety than vegetables. None can lift a meal more quickly from the humdrum to the dramatic. And few offer cooks greater challenge.

It takes experience to whip potatoes into snowy drifts without cooling them down, to lift asparagus from the pot the second it's turning from crisp to tender, to build a soufflé out of spinach. Few people understand the art of vegetable cookery better than the Chinese and Japanese, to whom every leaf, stalk, and root is a living thing to be cooked as quickly and kindly as possible. They use practically no water, preferring to cut vegetables into delicate shapes and stir-fry them in a smidgen of oil (there are few better ways, incidentally, of preserving vitamins).

The French, too, have a talent with vegetables, particularly green vegetables, which they blanch in boiling salted water, then "refresh" in ice water. This sets the color, crunch, and flavor, meaning that a vegetable can be held several hours if necessary. It then needs only a warming in butter, broth, or sauce. Americans, strangely, have been cool toward vegetables until recently. Something—travel, perhaps, or the proliferation of ethnic restaurants—has at last glamorized vegetables and given them an importance long overdue.

HOW TO BRING OUT THE BEST IN VEGETABLES

• The quicker vegetables go from plot to pot, the better. If you grow your own, you're lucky. If not, shop on days fresh shipments arrive.
• Buy only what perishable vegetables you can use within a day or two.
• Wash vegetables before cooking, *not* before refrigerating.

• Slice, dice, chop, or mince vegetables as you're ready to cook them; never soak in water (except for potatoes and artichokes, which will darken if not soaked). *Note:* For specifics on how to chop and mince vegetables in a food processor, see the Food Processor Metal Blade Chopping Guide, Chapter 1.
• Boil vegetables whole and unpeeled whenever possible. The smaller the pieces, the greater the nutrient loss.
• Boil vegetables quickly in a minimum of water (potatoes and artichokes excepted) and use any "pot likker" in soups and sauces. The French method may seem to contradict this rule but doesn't because the final heating is the cooking.
• Cook only as much of a vegetable as you need (leftovers fade fast). The best way to reheat vegetables is in the top of a double boiler with enough broth, water, milk, or sauce to moisten and revitalize them, or in a microwave oven (see Microwaving Vegetables).

BASIC WAYS OF COOKING VEGETABLES

Boiling: Cooking *in* boiling or simmering liquid. Start vegetables in boiling liquid, then time after liquid returns to a boil. Adjust heat so liquid boils gently throughout cooking. Cover pot or not as individual recipes recommend.

Parboiling: Partial cooking; often called for when vegetables are to be added to stews, casseroles, or other recipes.

Poaching: A variation of boiling in which asparagus or broccoli is simmered flat in a skillet in an inch or so of water.

Steaming: Cooking in a covered pot on a rack over boiling water. Though standing in some water, artichokes and stalked vegetables are technically steamed; only those parts *in* water are boiled.

Frying (Sautéing): Cooking, uncovered, in a small amount of fat and/or oil until tender and/or brown. Use a skillet or French sauté pan and moderately high heat.

Stir-Frying: The Oriental technique of tossing finely cut foods as they fry.

French or Deep Fat Frying: Cooking immersed in hot fat, 360°–400° F. You'll need 3 pounds shortening or 2 quarts oil to do a proper job, also a deep fat fryer and thermometer. Vegetables to be deep-fat-fried should be cut in small pieces if they're to cook through by the time they brown.

Braising (Panning): A combination of sautéing and boiling or simmering. A popular method is to brown a vegetable lightly in butter, then add broth or wine and simmer, covered, until tender—either on top of the stove or in a 325°–350° F. oven.

Pressure Cooking: High-speed steaming in a pressure cooker.

Baking: Cooking, uncovered, without liquid or fat in the oven (this refers to baking potatoes and other vegetables solo, not *en casserole).*

Roasting: Oven cooking, usually uncovered in some fat, often in tandem with a roast.

Broiling: Quick cooking under or over intense heat. Only a few vegetables—tomatoes, eggplant—broil well; they must be sliced thick and brushed with oil or marinade.

Charcoal Broiling or Cooking in a Gas or Electric Barbecue: Cooking over hot coals; again tomatoes and eggplant are best.

Microwaving Vegetables

Vegetables steamed or baked in a microwave oven retain their natural color, taste, texture, and, best of all, most of their nutritive value (very little vitamin C is lost). Of course size, shape, and quantity affect overall vegetable cooking times as do power levels, which vary from microwave to microwave (read your model's manual, also Microwave Ovens in Chapter 1). Then follow these guidelines:

To Steam Fresh Vegetables: Prepare vegetables for cooking as directed for each individual vegetable in the pages that follow. Also cut such stalked vegetables as broccoli and

carrots in 1″ pieces and cube hard or starchy ones (potatoes, yams, turnips, winter squash, rutabaga) so that they will cook more evenly (1″ cubes are a good size). Arrange prepared vegetables in a *round* microwave-safe casserole, placing thicker pieces toward the edge, tender tops or tips in the center. Add 1/4–1/2 cup water for each 4 servings of vegetable *(add no water to washed leafy vegetables such as spinach, beet or turnip greens).* Do not salt vegetables until *after* they are cooked (salt may spot or cake on them). Cover dish of vegetables with vented plastic food wrap, then time cooking as your microwave manual directs. Halfway through cooking, turn or rearrange whole or chunky vegetables to ensure even cooking; stir small pieces. Check often for doneness; when vegetables are *barely crisp-tender,* remove from oven and let stand on counter 3–4 minutes to complete the cooking. Drain, then season to taste.

VARIATIONS

To Steam Corn on the Cob: No husking needed! Simply pull husks back, remove silks, then smooth husks back into place. Lay ears in a shallow casserole, add no water, cover with vented plastic food wrap, and microwave 2–3 minutes *per ear;* remove from oven and let stand 2–3 minutes before testing for doneness or husking.

To Steam Frozen Vegetables: Follow package directions, if any. Otherwise, microwave as directed for fresh vegetables above, but use 2–4 tablespoons water only. *Tip:* When microwaving frozen pouched vegetables, flex and turn pouch midway through cooking.

To Parboil Fresh Vegetables: Steam as directed for fresh vegetables above, but reduce cooking time by 50 per cent.

To Bake Fresh Vegetables:

Potatoes (Irish, Sweet, Yams) and Other Vegetables to Be Cooked Whole, in the Skin: Prick deeply in several places so steam can escape. Arrange vegetables on paper toweling on floor of microwave, *in a circle,* spacing about 1″ apart. Bake as microwave manual directs, turning vegetables over at half time; let stand on counter 4–5 minutes to complete the cooking. Vegetables will feel firm when taken from oven, but will soften on standing. *Note:* It is impractical to microwave more than 8 potatoes at one time— they will take as long to bake as potatoes in a conventional oven. *Tip:* If you like mealy, crisp-skinned baked potatoes, omit the standing time; instead, transfer microwaved potatoes to a conventional oven preheated to 425° F. and bake 10 minutes.

Acorn, Butternut, and Other Small Winter Squash: Halve lengthwise, seed, and arrange, cut-sides-down, in a large casserole. Add no water or salt, cover with wax paper, and microwave as your manual directs, turning squash cut-side-up and rearranging pieces midway through cooking, moving those in the center toward the outside and vice versa.

Tomatoes: Arrange washed, halved, *firm-ripe* tomatoes, cut-sides-up, in a circle in a shallow casserole. Brush with seasoned melted butter or bacon drippings, cover with wax paper, and microwave as manufacturer directs until barely soft, rotating dish 180° at half time. Let stand 1–2 minutes to complete the cooking. *Tip:* Sprinkle any grated cheese topping on tomatoes just before the standing period; the residual heat will melt the cheese. For crisp toppings, microwave as directed, then broil quickly in a conventional oven to brown.

Stuffed Vegetables: Arrange in a circle in a shallow casserole; do not cover, and microwave as manufacturer directs. *Note:* If using rice to stuff the vegetables, use the quick-cooking variety only (see How to Cook Rice —Microwave Method in Chapter 10).

Vegetable Casseroles: If using mixed vegetables, make sure the pieces are of similar size to ensure even cooking. Use a *temperature probe,* if you have one (it's the surest way to time casseroles in a microwave). Cover casserole with vented plastic food wrap and, to ensure even cooking, stir casserole often from edges toward center or, if it is layered and cannot be stirred, rotate often. Always allow *5–10 minutes standing time* to complete the cooking of a vegetable casserole. *Note:* For a crisp, brown topping, broil quickly in a conventional oven after the standing time.

Vegetables and Vegetable Recipes That Do Not Microwave Well

Dried Beans and Peas: They take as long to bake in a microwave as in a conventional oven and do not brown properly.

Breaded or Batter-Dipped Vegetables, Frozen French-Fried Potatoes: None of these will crispen or brown nicely in a microwave oven.

Vegetable Soufflés: In our experience, these are better if baked in conventional ovens. Microwaved vegetable soufflés remain runny in the center and do not brown. Conventional vegetable soufflé recipes, moreover, need adjustments if they are to be baked in a microwave (see To Microwave a Soufflé in Chapter 9).

Reheating Cooked Vegetables by Microwave: If properly timed and tended, vegetables reheated in a microwave taste as fresh as the just-picked ones. Here's the trick: Place vegetables in a shallow casserole, cover with vented plastic food wrap, and rotate or stir vegetables as they heat through. *The second they are warm enough to serve,* take vegetables from the microwave. No standing time needed. *Note:* Use a *temperature probe,* if you have one, to determine the precise internal temperature (150°–160° F. in the *center of the dish* is just right for reheated precooked vegetables). Remember, when timing the microwaving, that refrigerator-cold vegetables will take longer to reheat than room-temperature ones.

Cooking Vegetables in a Convection Oven

Most vegetables cook a little faster in convection ovens than in conventional ones, so recipe temperatures should be reduced by 25° F. (but never use oven temperatures lower than 300° F.). Because a convection oven's hot circulating air brings it to the desired temperature quickly, there's no need to preheat it before baking vegetables. It's best to read what your particular oven's manual says about cooking vegetables. Also read Convection Ovens in Chapter 1, then follow these general guidelines:

• Bake Irish potatoes, sweet potatoes, yams, and whole or halved winter squash directly on oven rack, not touching one another or oven walls.

• To avoid overbrowning of scalloped vegetables, soufflés, oven-roasted potatoes, onions, and carrots, check them frequently and turn as needed.

• When baking vegetable casseroles, cook, covered, until the final 15–20 minutes, then uncover so tops will brown nicely. Also begin testing for doneness when about 75 per cent of the recommended baking time has elapsed.

STORING VEGETABLES
(See chapter on the larder)

BABY (MINI) VEGETABLES

Miniature acorn squash no bigger than walnuts, bantam-sized beets, carrots (both finger-shaped and round), tiny leeks, turnips, corn, cauliflower, eggplant, okra, green beans, and "teardrop" tomatoes are all now showing up in supermarket vegetable bins from time to time. All are picture-perfect and fully ripe. The best way to prepare and cook them? Exactly as you would their full-size counterparts. Merely reduce the cooking time by about half and test often for doneness. *Tip:* Baby carrots, acorn squash, and turnips need no peeling, just scrub clean.

BASIC VEGETABLE SOUFFLÉ CHART

4 servings each

Use fresh, frozen, canned, or leftover vegetables in soufflés, but drain them *very well* before puréeing or chopping and measuring so that they will not thin the sauce too much. The chart below indicates which liquid ingredients and seasonings are most compatible with which vegetable, and notes any modifications that should be made in the Basic Vegetable Soufflé recipe. Choose the type of soufflé you want to make from the chart, then prepare according to the Basic Vegetable Soufflé recipe that follows. *Note:* T. = tablespoon, t. = teaspoon.

Vegetable	*Liquid*	*Seasonings*	*Special Instructions*
Artichoke (globe)	½ cup milk or light cream + ½ cup chicken broth	1 t. grated onion, ¼ cup minced mushrooms, and 1 T. grated Parmesan	Use artichoke hearts or bottoms. Stir-fry onion and mushrooms in butter called for, then blend in flour. Mix in cheese along with egg yolks.
Asparagus	½ cup milk or light cream + ½ cup chicken broth	1 T. grated Parmesan and 2 T. minced pimiento	—
Broccoli	½ cup milk + ½ cup chicken broth	1 t. finely grated lemon rind or 2 T. minced capers	Purée stems and flowerets together or use flowerets only.
Carrot	½ cup milk or light cream + ½ cup chicken broth	1 T. grated onion, 1 T. minced parsley, and a pinch of thyme OR 1 t. each finely grated orange rind and chopped mint and a pinch nutmeg or mace	Purée carrots for a full-flavored soufflé.
Cauliflower	½ cup milk or light cream + ½ cup cooking water or chicken broth	1 T. grated Parmesan, ¼ t. minced chives, chervil, or dill, and ⅛ t. nutmeg	Purée stems and flowerets together or use flowerets only.
Celery	½ cup milk or light cream + ½ cup cooking water or chicken broth	1 minced small yellow onion, 3 T. grated Parmesan, and a pinch of thyme	Cook onion with celery. Add cheese and thyme to hot sauce.

See nutrient counts at end of Basic Vegetable Soufflé recipe.

Vegetable	Liquid	Seasonings	Special Instructions
Corn (whole kernel)	½ cup milk or light cream + ½ cup cooking water or chicken broth	2 T. minced onion and 2 T. each minced green pepper and pimiento	Stir-fry onion in butter called for, mix remaining seasonings into hot sauce.
Green pea	½ cup light cream + ½ cup cooking water or chicken broth	1 T. grated onion, 1 t. finely grated orange rind, 1 T. chopped mint, and a pinch each of rosemary and nutmeg	Stir-fry onion and orange rind in butter called for, then blend in flour. Mix remaining seasonings into hot sauce.
Mushroom	½ cup light cream + ½ cup beef broth	2 T. minced onion and a pinch each of thyme and mace	Stir-fry 1⅓ cups minced raw mushrooms with onion, thyme, and mace in butter called for, then blend in flour.
Onion	½ cup light cream + ½ cup beef broth	½ small minced clove of garlic, ½ t. thyme, pinch of nutmeg, and 3 T. grated Parmesan	Use 2 cups chopped raw onion instead of 1⅓ cups cooked vegetable called for in Basic Vegetable Soufflé. Stir-fry in butter with garlic, thyme, and nutmeg. Blend in flour; add cheese to hot sauce.
Potato	½ cup milk or light cream + ½ cup beef or chicken broth	¼ cup minced onion, 2 T. minced parsley, ¼ t. each sage and thyme, and a pinch of mace	Use hot, unseasoned mashed potatoes. Stir-fry all seasonings in butter called for; blend in flour.
Pumpkin, yam, sweet potato, winter squash	½ cup milk + ½ cup chicken broth	2 T. minced onion, 1 T. light brown sugar, 1 t. each apple-pie spice and finely grated orange rind	Use hot, unseasoned mashed pumpkin, yams, sweet potatoes, or winter squash. Stir-fry all seasonings in butter called for, then blend in flour.
Spinach	½ cup light cream + ½ cup beef broth	1 minced small yellow onion and ¼ t. nutmeg	Brown butter called for, add onion and stir-fry until limp; blend in flour and nutmeg.
Summer squash	½ cup milk or light cream + ½ cup chicken broth	1 minced small yellow onion and ¼ t. each rosemary and nutmeg	Stir-fry all seasonings in butter called for, then blend in flour.

See nutrient counts at end of Basic Vegetable Soufflé recipe.

BASIC VEGETABLE SOUFFLÉ

4 servings

Because the basic proportions and methods of preparing any vegetable soufflé are very much the same, you can, by using the master recipe below, make a variety of different vegetable soufflés. If, for example, you choose to make a Mushroom Soufflé, turn first to the Basic Vegetable Soufflé Chart that precedes to determine what liquid ingredient you should use, what seasonings, what special instructions you should note, then prepare the Mushroom Soufflé following the recipe below.

3 tablespoons butter or margarine
3 tablespoons flour

1 cup liquid (see Basic Vegetable Soufflé Chart)
4 eggs, separated
1 teaspoon salt
Pinch white pepper
Seasonings (see Basic Vegetable Soufflé Chart)
1⅓ cups puréed, mashed, or finely chopped cooked vegetable (see Basic Vegetable Soufflé Chart)
Pinch cream of tartar

Melt butter in a saucepan over moderate heat, blend in flour, slowly stir in liquid, and heat, stirring, until thickened and no raw taste of flour remains. Beat egg yolks lightly, blend in a little hot sauce, then stir back into pan; heat and stir 1–2 minutes over lowest heat. Off heat, mix in salt, pepper, seasonings, and vegetable. Lay a piece of wax paper flat on sauce and cool to room temperature. *(Note:* You can make recipe up to this point ahead of time, then cover and chill until about 2 hours before serving. Let mixture come to room temperature before proceeding.) Preheat oven to 350° F. Beat egg whites until frothy, add cream of tartar, and continue beating until stiff but not dry. Fold whites into vegetable mixture, spoon into an ungreased 5-cup soufflé dish. Bake, uncovered, on center rack of oven 35–45 minutes until puffy and browned. Serve at once.

NPS (Artichoke + milk): 230 C, 300 mg CH, 870 mg S*

NPS (Artichoke + cream): 270 C, 320 mg CH, 865 mg S*

NPS (Asparagus + milk): 220 C, 300 mg CH, 845 mg S*

NPS (Asparagus + cream): 260 C, 320 mg CH, 845 mg S*

NPS (Broccoli + milk): 215 C, 300 mg CH, 835 mg S*

NPS (Broccoli + milk + capers): 220 C, 300 mg CH, 945 mg S*

NPS (Carrot + milk): 225 C, 300 mg CH, 855 mg S*

NPS (Carrot + cream): 265 C, 315 mg CH, 850 mg S*

NPS (Cauliflower + milk): 215 C, 300 mg CH, 845 mg S*

NPS (Cauliflower + cream): 255 C, 320 mg CH, 845 mg S*

NPS (Celery + milk): 230 C, 305 mg CH, 935 mg S*

NPS (Celery + cream): 270 C, 320 mg CH, 930 mg S*

NPS (Corn + milk): 250 C, 300 mg CH, 820 mg S*

NPS (Corn + cream): 290 C, 320 mg CH, 820 mg S*

NPS (Peas + cream): 280 C, 315 mg CH, 875 mg S*

NPS (Mushroom + cream): 255 C, 315 mg CH, 820 mg S*

NPS (Onion + cream): 275 C, 320 mg CH, 890 mg S*

NPS (Potato + milk): 235 C, 300 mg CH, 820 mg S*

NPS (Potato + cream): 275 C, 315 mg CH, 820 mg S*

NPS (Pumpkin): 235 C, 300 mg CH, 820 mg S*

NPS (Sweet Potato or Yam): 290 C, 300 mg CH, 850 mg S*

NPS (Winter Squash): 245 C, 300 mg CH, 820 mg S*

NPS (Spinach + cream): 255 C, 320 mg CH, 845 mg S*

NPS (Summer Squash + milk): 215 C, 300 mg CH, 820 mg S*

NPS (Summer Squash + cream): 255 C, 315 mg CH, 815 mg S*

VEGETABLE FRITTERS

4 servings

A variety of vegetables lend themselves to batter frying. Some should be parboiled first; others need not be. But all should be cut in small—about bite-size—pieces and all should be thoroughly dry before being dipped in batter and deep-fried.

SUITABLE VEGETABLES

Artichoke Hearts *(2 [9-ounce] packages frozen artichoke hearts, parboiled, drained, and patted dry on paper toweling)*

Broccoli or Cauliflower *(flowerets from 1 large head, parboiled, drained, and patted dry on paper toweling)*

Carrots *(1 pound carrots, peeled, sliced 1/2" thick, parboiled, drained, and patted dry on paper toweling)*

Parsley Fluffs *(3 cups, washed and patted dry on paper toweling)*

Parsnips *(1 pound parsnips, peeled, sliced 1/2" thick, parboiled, drained, and patted dry on paper toweling)*

Sweet Potatoes *(4 medium-size potatoes, parboiled, peeled, sliced 1/4" thick, and patted dry on paper toweling)*

Turnips or Rutabaga *(2 cups 1" cubes, parboiled, drained, and patted dry on paper toweling)*

Zucchini or Yellow Squash *(4 medium-size squash, scrubbed and sliced 1/2" thick)*

Shortening or cooking oil for deep fat frying
1 recipe Basic Batter for Fried Foods

Prepare vegetable as directed and set aside. Heat shortening or oil in a deep fat fryer over moderately high heat to 380° F. on a deep fat thermometer. Dip vegetable, a few pieces at a time, into batter, allowing excess to drain off. Drop into fat and fry 2–5 minutes until golden brown (time will vary according to vegetable). Drain on paper toweling, then keep warm in a 250° F. oven while you fry the rest (don't cover or fritters will become soggy). Serve piping hot with lemon wedges or, if you prefer, with soy sauce. Recipe too flexible for meaningful nutritional count.

VEGETABLES À LA GRECQUE

4 servings

Certain vegetables—summer squash, mushrooms, leeks, to name three—are delicious served cold in a fragrant lemon and oil dressing. Here's how to prepare them.

SUITABLE VEGETABLES

Artichoke Hearts *(8 globe artichoke hearts, parboiled and drained or 2 [9-ounce] packages* frozen artichoke hearts boiled 10 minutes and drained)

Asparagus (*2 pounds asparagus, washed, trimmed, parboiled, and drained*)

Celery Hearts (*6 medium-size celery hearts, parboiled and drained*)

Cucumbers (*8 small cucumbers, peeled, quartered, seeded, parboiled, and drained*)

Endives (*6 medium-size endives, parboiled, drained, and halved*)

Fennel (*4 bulbs of fennel, parboiled and drained*)

Green or Wax Beans (*1 pound green or wax beans, tipped, parboiled, and drained*)

Hearts of Palm (*one [14-ounce] can hearts of palm, drained and sliced ½" thick*)

Leeks (*2 bunches leeks, trimmed, parboiled, and drained*)

Mushrooms (*1 pound medium-size mushrooms, stemmed and peeled*)

Zucchini or Yellow Squash (*2 pounds zucchini or yellow squash, scrubbed, sliced ½" thick, parboiled, and drained*)

1 recipe À la Grecque Marinade

Prepare vegetable as directed above, cover with marinade, and chill 2–3 hours, turning occasionally. Serve cold as a vegetable, salad, or first course, spooning a little marinade over each portion. All versions: recipes too flexible for meaningful nutritional counts.

VARIATION

Vegetables à la Dijonnaise: Prepare vegetable as directed. Blend 1 tablespoon Dijon mustard into À la Grecque Marinade, pour over vegetable, and marinate as directed.

FRESH VEGETABLE CHART

Season	For Top Quality	Amount to Buy	Nutritive Value	Calories (unseasoned)
Globe Artichokes October–June; peak months: April, May	Pick tight, plump green buds heavy for their size.	1 (⅓–¾-pound) artichoke per person	Poor	Moderate—70–150 per steamed artichoke; 80 per cup of hearts
Jerusalem Artichokes October–March	Pick firm, un-scarred arti-chokes with tender skins.	3–4 artichokes (about ¼ pound) per person	Fairly rich in iron, phosphorus, vitamin B₁, and niacin	Low—about 30 per average serv-ing
Asparagus Late February–July; peak months: April, May	Choose straight, bright green (or pale ivory) stalks of uniform size with tight tips and moist bases.	Allow 8–10 stalks (about ½ pound) per per-son; bundles av-erage 2–2½ pounds, contain 3–4 dozen stalks.	Green has some Vitamin C and A, the white far less.	Low—35–40 per average serving
Fresh Beans Summer for Ital-ian green beans, wing beans, black-eyed peas, and fava beans. Year round for all others.	Choose firm, well-filled pods with lots of snap; wax, green, and wing beans should also be of uniform size and fairly straight.	1 pound green, wax, or wing beans will serve 4; 1 pound un-shelled limas, favas, cranberry beans, or black-eyed peas 1–2 persons.	All but wax beans are fairly high in vitamin A and contain some C.	Low for green and wax beans, 30–40 per serv-ing; high for shelled types: li-mas and favas 180 per serving. Not known for wing beans.
Dried Beans Year round	Most dried beans are boxed, so buy brands you know and trust; if buying from a	1 pound dried beans will serve 4–6 persons.	All dried beans are high in iron, most B vitamins and protein (*in-complete* protein,	High—from 230 per cup (white beans, black-eyed peas, red or pinto beans) to

Season	For Top Quality	Amount to Buy	Nutritive Value	Calories (unseasoned)
	bin, choose clean, un-withered, un-buggy beans.		but valuable in rounding out meals).	260 (limas). Fig-ures not available for favas.
Bean Sprouts Year round	Choose crisp, short sprouts with moist tips.	1/4 pound per person	Poor, although high in vitamin C and potassium	Low, about 35 per serving
Beets Year round; peak months for greens and beets: June–October	Pick crisp-tender greens; firm, un-scarred beets of equal size, 1 1/2″– 2″ in diameter.	1/2 pound beets or greens per person	Greens are rich in vitamins A and C, beets are considerably less nutritious.	Low for greens about 25 per serving; Moder-ate for beets— about 70 a serv-ing
Breadfruit July–August	Choose plump, firm but not too hard breadfruit with fairly clean skins.	1 breadfruit serves 2–4.	Some vitamin C	Moderate—about 85 per average serving
Broccoli Year round with supplies at their best in spring and again in fall; spring for broc-coli di rapa	Look for crisp, moist stalks and dark green or purplish heads. Reject any that are yellowed or flowering.	1/2 pound per person	High in vitamins A and C, fairly high in calcium	Low—about 40 per average serv-ing for broccoli; not available for broccoli di rapa but probably lower still
Brussels Sprouts September–May; peak months: October and No-vember	Choose firm, clean compact heads of a crisp green color.	A 1-pint carton will serve 2–3 persons.	Very high in vi-tamin C, fairly high in vitamin A	Low—about 40 per average serv-ing
Cabbage Year round for all cabbages ex-cept Chinese (May–November)	Buy firm, heavy heads with crisp, unblemished leaves. Green cabbages fade, so a white head may be old.	A medium-size head (3–3 1/2 pounds) will serve 4–6; 1 pound Chinese cabbage serves 2 persons.	All raw cabbage is fairly high in vitamin C, the cooked some-what less so.	Low—16–60 per cup, Chinese cabbage being lowest, red cab-bage highest
Sauerkraut Year round	Buy brands you like. Precooked kraut is sold in cans, jars, and in refrigerated plastic bags. Fresh kraut is sold by delicates-sens, specialty groceries.	1/4–1/3 pound per person	Fairly high in vi-tamin C	Low—about 45 per cup

Season	For Top Quality	Amount to Buy	Nutritive Value	Calories (unseasoned)
Cardoons Winter	Look for crisp, unblemished stalks.	1 pound cardoons serves 2–4.	Not determined	Not determined
Carrots Year round	Look for firm, bright orange carrots of equal size without cracks or splits. If buying by the bunch, make sure tops are not wilted.	1 pound carrots serves 3–4. There are 6–8 medium-size carrots per pound, 12–14 slim ones, 2–3 dozen babies.	High in vitamin A	Low—about 25 per raw, medium-size carrot
Cauliflower Year round; peak months: September–December	Choose snowy, compact heads with crisp green leaves and few or no dark spots. Reject any open, spongy heads.	1 large (3–3½-pound) cauliflower will serve 4.	High in vitamin C	Low—35–40 per average serving
Celeriac August–May	Look for firm, crisp knobs 2″–4″ in diameter with few scars or blemishes.	A 2″–4″ knob serves 1–2.	Low	Low—about 45 per average serving
Celery Year round	Whether buying white or green (Pascal) celery, choose crunchy stalks, uncracked, unbruised, with crisp green leaves.	1 large head (1½ pounds), cooked, will serve 4.	Some minerals; rather low in vitamins	Very low—about 5 per stalk
Chard June–November	Look for crisp leaves and fleshy stalks free of insect injury.	A 1-pound bunch serves 2 amply.	Very high in vitamin A	Low—about 45 per ½-pound serving
Chestnuts Fall and winter	Choose plump, unshriveled nuts with unscarred, uncracked shells.	1½ pounds unshelled nuts will yield 1 pound shelled nuts and serve about 4.	Some incomplete protein, iron, and B vitamins	Very high—about 20 per fresh nut, 40 per dried nut
Collards Year round; supply short only in April, May	Choose crisp, clean frosty blue-green leaves free of insect injury.	1 pound serves 2.	Very high in vitamins A and C, also calcium	Moderately low —55 per cup of cooked collards
Corn May–October; in big cities corn is	Buy ears in the husk from iced	2 ears per person	Fair source of vitamin A and cer-	High—70 for quite a small ear;

Season	For Top Quality	Amount to Buy	Nutritive Value	Calories (unseasoned)
available year round, but best only in summer.	bins; husks should be bright green and snug-fitting; kernels bright, plump, and milky.		tain of the B complex	170 per cup of whole kernel corn
Cucumbers Year round	Choose uniformly firm green cucumbers with no dark, soft spots.	1 medium-size cucumber will serve 1–2.	Poor	Low—about 30 per medium-size cucumber
Dandelions Spring	Choose clean, tender leaves with stems and roots attached.	1 pound serves 2.	High in vitamin A and iron	Low—about 50 per average serving
Dasheens Year round	Choose clean, unscarred tubers of uniform size.	1 average dasheen serves 2–4.	Some minerals but generally poor	Moderate to high —110 per serving
Eggplant Year round	Choose firm, evenly purple or white eggplants, without cuts or scars, that weigh heavy for their size.	1 medium-size eggplant will serve 4; allow 1–2 "frying" eggplants per person.	Poor	Low—about 40 per average serving
Endive (Belgian) October–May	Choose crisp, clean stalks with tightly clinging leaves.	1 stalk per person	Poor	Very low—about 15 per stalk
Fennel October–April	Choose crisp, plump, unscarred bulbs with fresh, feathery tops.	1 bulb will serve 1–2.	Some vitamin A and C	Low—about 25 per average serving
Ferns May	Pick young, silvery green shoots no more than 2″ above the ground and tightly curled like the scroll at the top of a fiddle.	Allow ½ cup per person.	Not determined	Not determined but probably low
Hearts of Palm Spring	Choose firm, moist, fairly clean hearts with few cuts, scars, or blemishes.	1 heart, trimmed, will weigh 1½–2½ pounds and serve 2–3. Canned hearts are smaller and will serve 1.	Not determined	Not determined

Season	For Top Quality	Amount to Buy	Nutritive Value	Calories (unseasoned)
Jicama Fall, winter, spring	Choose well-formed jicama, free of cuts and bruises.	1 pound serves 3–4 persons.	Poor	Moderately low, about 45 per 1/2 cup
Kale Fall, winter	Choose clean, crisp green leaves whether kale is sold loose or prewashed, pretrimmed, and bagged in plastic.	1 pound serves 2.	Very high in vitamin A; high in vitamin C and calcium	Moderate—about 75 per average serving
Kohlrabi May–December; peak months: June, July	Choose firm, crisp bulbs about 3″ in diameter with fresh green leaves.	Allow 1–2 bulbs per person.	High in vitamin C	Low—about 35 per average serving
Leeks Year round; two peak seasons: September–December and April–July	Look for fresh green tops and crisp, white clean stalks.	A bunch weighs about 1 pound and serves 2.	Some minerals and vitamin C, otherwise poor	Low—about 35 per leek
Lentils Year round	Buy brands you know or, if buying in bulk, choose lentils that are clean, firm, and unshriveled.	1 pound dried lentils will serve 4 persons.	High-protein food rich in vitamin A, most of the B complex, and minerals	Very high—about 350 per cup of cooked lentils
Mushrooms Year round though supplies may be short in summer.	Choose clean, snowy, plump mushrooms of equal size; the veil that joins cap to stem should be intact, hiding brown gills.	1 pound will serve 2–4.	Poor except for being fairly high in niacin	Low—about 40 per cup
Mustard Greens Year round; peak season: June–October	Choose crisp, tender leaves without holes or blemishes.	1 pound greens will serve 2.	High in vitamins A and C, also in calcium	Low—about 40 per average serving
Okra Year round; peak months: July–October	Choose young, tender clean pods 2″–4″ long; reject any with bruises or punctures.	1 pound will serve 2–4.	Some vitamin C and A	Low—about 35 per average serving
Dry Onions Year round for red, white, and	Choose firm, well-shaped on-	1 pound will serve 2–4.	Poor	Low—about 30 per 1/4 pound of

Season	For Top Quality	Amount to Buy	Nutritive Value	Calories (unseasoned)
yellow onions; March–June for Bermudas; and August–May for Spanish onions	ions with dry, clean, bright skins. Reject any that are sprouting.			cooked onions; 40 per 1/4 pound raw onions
Fresh Onions Year round for all fresh onions	Choose spring onions and scallions with succulent white stems 2″–3″ long and crisp green tops. If potted chives are unavailable, choose newly cut ones.	1 bunch scallions or spring onions contains 5–6 stalks and will serve 1–2.	Poor	Very low—about 4 per spring onion or scallion
Parsley Root Fall, winter, spring	Choose firm, clean, unblemished roots. Avoid overly large ones.	1 pound serves 3–4.	Poor	Not determined
Parsnips Year round; peak seasons: fall, winter	Look for clean, firm, well-shaped roots of medium size (large parsnips may be woody).	A 1-pound bunch will serve 2–4.	Poor	Moderate—about 74 per 1/4-pound serving
Peas Year round for snow and green peas (peak season April–August); spring and early summer for sugar snap peas	Choose bright green, tender, slightly velvety pods. Green pea pods should be well filled, snow and sugar snap pea pods slender and crisp. Cook as soon after buying as possible.	1 pound green peas in the pod serves 1–2; 1 pound snow or sugar snap peas 4–6; 1 pound dried peas 4–6.	Green, snow and sugar snap peas have fair amounts of vitamins A, C, and niacin; dried peas are high in protein and iron.	High—about 115 per cup of green peas; 290 per cup of dried peas. Not known for snow or sugar snap peas.
Peppers Year round for all; peak season: June–October	Choose bright, firm fleshy pods. Pimientos are available only canned.	1 sweet pepper per person; 2–3 Italian peppers	The red are high in vitamins A and C, the green in vitamin C.	Very low—15–20 per pepper, the red being the higher
Plantains Year round	Choose ripe black-skinned plantains unless they are to be deep-fat-fried.	1 plantain will serve 1–3 depending on size.	Some vitamin A, also some of the B group	Very high—about 125 per 1/4-pound serving

Season	For Top Quality	Amount to Buy	Nutritive Value	Calories (unseasoned)
Potatoes				

Round Whites, also marketed as Maine, Eastern, or All-purpose potatoes (for boiling, frying, and, if a mealy type, baking)

Season	For Top Quality	Amount to Buy	Nutritive Value	Calories (unseasoned)
Year round but supplies may be short in late summer and early fall.	Regardless of type, choose firm, well shaped, clean, blemish-free potatoes. Reject any with large green "sunburn spots" and those that are sprouting.	1 potato per person; there are 3–4 per pound.	Some vitamin C and a good source of potassium	Moderate—90–100 per medium potato

Round Reds, which include the luscious little New Potatoes (for boiling)

Year round but best in the spring	*(see above)*	2–4 potatoes per person, depending on size; there are 4–8 per pound, depending on size.	*(see above)*	*(see above)*

California Long Whites or White Rose; also marketed as California News (for boiling)

Mid-May to Mid-September; Mid-December to Mid-March	*(see above)*	1 potato per person; there are 3–5 per pound.	*(see above)*	*(see above)*

Russet Burbank, more often sold as Idaho Potatoes or Bakers (for baking, frying; if closely watched, can be boiled)

Year round but supplies may be short in summer.	*(see above)*	1 potato per person; there are 2–3 per pound.	*(see above)*	*(see above)*

Pumpkin Autumn	Choose small, firm, bright orange pumpkins, 6"–7" in diameter, that seem heavy for their size.	1 pound raw pumpkin yields 1 cup cooked pumpkin or 1 serving.	High in vitamin A	Moderate—about 75 per cup
Rutabaga Year round; peak months: October and November	Choose firm, fairly smooth, 2- or 3-pound rutabagas with few leaf scars around the crown.	Figure ½ pound rutabaga per serving.	High in vitamin C, fairly high in vitamin A and iron	Moderate—about 75 per ½-pound serving
Salsify Summer, fall, and winter	Choose firm roots the size and shape of small carrots.	Allow 3 roots (⅓–½ pound) per person.	Some minerals	Moderate—90–130 per average serving
Sorrel Year round	Choose young, tender, crisp leaves about 2"–3" long.	¼–½ pound per person, depending on whether sorrel is to be served alone or mixed with other greens.	High in vitamins A and C	Low—about 40 per cup

VEGETABLES

Season	For Top Quality	Amount to Buy	Nutritive Value	Calories (unseasoned)
Spinach Year round for spinach; peak months: March–July; spring and early summer for New Zealand spinach	Buy loose or bulk spinach if possible and choose crisp, dark green moist leaves with roots attached. If buying prewashed, bagged spinach, make sure it's not wilted, slimy, or dry.	½ pound bulk spinach per person; 1 (10-ounce) bag will serve 2.	Very high in vitamin A; high in iron and vitamin C	Low—about 40 per cup
Summer Squash Year round for all types	Choose firm, tender skinned, blemish-free squash that are heavy for their size.	½ pound per person	Some vitamins A and C	Low—about 50 per cup
Sweet Potatoes, Yams Year round	Choose firm, clean scar-free potatoes of uniform size.	1 potato per person; there are 2–3 per pound.	Very high in vitamin A, some vitamin C	Very high—about 145 per medium-size potato
Tomatoes Year round but the best are summer tomatoes.	Choose firm, well-formed tomatoes of good strong color (whether red, green, or yellow) with smooth, unblemished skins.	1 medium-size tomato per person; 1 pound will serve 4.	Fairly high in vitamins A and C	Very low—about 45 per medium-size tomato
Turnips, Turnip Greens Year round for turnips; peak season: fall. January–April for greens.	Choose firm, smooth turnips 2″–3″ across with few leaf scars or roots; clean, tender, crisp greens.	¼ pound turnips per person; ½ pound greens	Greens are very high in vitamins A and C; turnips contain some vitamin C.	Very low—about 30 per cup of greens; 35 per cup of turnips
Winter Squash Year round for acorn, butternut, and spaghetti squash; fall and winter for the others	Choose heavy squash with hard, clean unblemished skins.	½ pound per person	Very high in vitamin A, some vitamin C and iron	Very high—about 130 per cup

GLOBE ARTICHOKES

(Also known as French or Italian Artichokes)
These large, green flowerlike buds are possibly the most beautiful of the world's vegetables; certainly they are one of the most delicate and elegant. Native to Mediterranean Europe, artichokes were brought first to America by the French who settled in Louisiana in the eighteenth century. But it was

the Spaniards, settling in California, who first grew them with success. The mild California climate proved ideal for artichokes, and the fertile Salinas Valley below San Francisco particularly favorable (the Salinas Valley is today the "artichoke capital of the world"). With millions of artichokes now being harvested each year, we can all enjoy a luxury once reserved for the rich and the royal.

To Prepare for Cooking: Snap off stems, pulling any tough fibers from bottom of artichokes. Cut off ragged stem edges, remove blemished outer petals, then snip off prickly petal tips. Wash under cold running water and rub cut edges with lemon to prevent darkening.

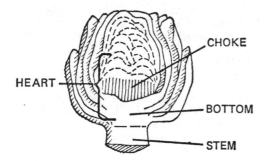

To Remove Choke (this can be done before or after cooking), spread petals and reach down into the center, pulling out thistly pieces. With a teaspoon, scoop out any remaining prickly bits. *(Note:* Dechoked artichokes will cook twice as fast as those with chokes in.) If artichokes are not to be cooked immediately, keep covered with cold acidulated water (1 tablespoon lemon juice or white vinegar to 1 quart water).

To Prepare Artichoke Hearts: Break off stems and trim away ragged edges. Remove all but inner cone of petals, lay each heart on its side and slice off prickly tips. Rub cut edges with lemon and drop into acidulated water. To keep creamy-white, don't dechoke until after cooking.

To Prepare Artichoke Bottoms: These can be made before or after cooking. In either case, begin with the hearts, remove all petals and chokes. If raw, rub with lemon and soak in acidulated water; boil as you would artichoke hearts.

To Slice an Artichoke: Cut off stem and top third of artichoke and discard; remove choke. Lay artichoke on its side and cut horizontally straight across the bud in ¼"

slices, letting them fall in acidulated water. Pat dry before sautéing or frying.

Cooking Tip: Cook artichokes in an enamel, stainless-steel, anodized aluminum, or Teflon-lined pan so they won't discolor or taste of metal.

Serving Tip: Don't serve artichokes with wine or tea—for some reason, the flavors cancel one another out.

How to Eat an Artichoke: Eating an artichoke is like playing "he-loves-me, he-loves-me-not" with a daisy. Pluck off one petal at a time, dip base in accompanying sauce, then nibble off flesh. If the choke hasn't been removed, lift out or loosen with knife and fork. Cut bottom into bite-sized chunks and eat with a fork, first dunking each into sauce.

BASIC STEAMED GLOBE ARTICHOKES

4 servings

Steaming is the preferred method for cooking artichokes because there is less chance of their overcooking. Steamed artichokes, moreover, are easier to drain than boiled artichokes because they have not been submerged in cooking water.

4 large globe artichokes, prepared for cooking
Boiling water (about 3 cups)
¼ cup cider vinegar
1 teaspoon salt
1 clove garlic, peeled and quartered (optional)

Stand artichokes stem down in a deep enamel, stainless-steel, anodized aluminum, or Teflon-lined kettle just big enough to hold them snugly. (You can stand them on a trivet, if you like, but it's not necessary.) Pour in boiling water to a depth of 1", add remaining ingredients, cover, and steam 45 minutes over moderate heat or until you can pull a leaf off easily (remember that dechoked artichokes will cook twice as fast). Lift artichokes from kettle with tongs and drain upside down in a colander. Serve hot as a first course or vegetable with melted butter or Hollandaise Sauce. Or chill and serve as a first course or salad.
NPS (plain): 85 C, 0 mg CH, 265 mg S*
NPS (butter): 185 C, 30 mg CH, 380 mg S*

To Boil Artichokes: Follow above recipe but add enough boiling water to cover.

To Boil Artichoke Hearts: For 4 servings you will need 8 artichokes. Prepare hearts* as directed. Bring 1 quart water, 2 tablespoons lemon juice, and 1½ teaspoons salt to a boil in a large, deep saucepan, add hearts, cover, and simmer 30–40 minutes until tender (liquid should cover hearts at all times, so add additional water if necessary). Drain upside down in a colander, remove chokes,* season with melted butter or margarine, and serve.

*NPS: 135 C, 30 mg CH, 365 mg S**

To Parboil Artichokes or Artichoke Hearts for Use in Other Recipes: Boil as directed above, but reduce cooking time to 25 minutes. Omit butter. (*Note:* Dechoked artichokes will parboil in 15 minutes.)

VARIATIONS

To Serve Cold: Cool artichokes or artichoke hearts in cooking liquid, then cover and chill until ready to use. Drain, pat dry on paper toweling, and remove chokes. Serve cold as a first course or salad with Italian or French Dressing.

*NPS (Italian): 150 C, 0 mg CH, 380 mg S**
*NPS (French): 145 C, 0 mg CH, 470 mg S**

⚖ **Low-Calorie Artichokes or Artichoke Hearts:** Instead of serving with butter or sauce, sprinkle artichokes with seasoned salt or drizzle with low-calorie herb or Italian dressing.

*NPS: 85 C, 0 mg CH, 415 mg S**

Artichoke Hearts DuBarry: Boil and drain artichoke hearts as directed. Return to pan, add 2 tablespoons butter, 8 small sautéed button mushrooms, 8 boiled baby carrots, and/or 8 braised small white onions.

*NPS: 105 C, 20 mg CH, 125 mg S**

ARTICHOKE BOTTOMS STUFFED WITH VEGETABLES

4 servings

8 globe artichoke hearts, boiled and drained
¼ cup butter or margarine
1½ cups hot seasoned vegetables (asparagus tips or cauliflowerets; chopped spinach; peas and diced carrots; or sautéed chopped mushrooms)
2 tablespoons minced parsley

Strip all leaves from the hearts and remove chokes.* Melt butter in a large skillet over moderately low heat and sauté bottoms 3–4 minutes, basting all the while. Fill with vegetables and sprinkle with parsley. For extra glamour, top with Lemon Butter.

*NPS (asparagus): 150 C, 30 mg CH, 160 mg S**
*NPS (spinach): 150 C, 30 mg CH, 190 mg S**
*NPS (peas and carrots): 165 C, 30 mg CH, 210 mg S**
*NPS (mushrooms): 200 C, 45 mg CH, 215 mg S**

VARIATIONS

All variations too flexible for meaningful nutritional counts.

To Serve Cold: Instead of sautéing bottoms in butter, marinate 2–3 hours in the refrigerator in French Dressing. Fill with cold, seasoned, cooked vegetables.

Florentine Style: Fill with chopped cooked, buttered spinach, top with Mornay Sauce and grated Parmesan, and brown quickly under the broiler.

Lyonnaise Style: Fill with a mixture of sautéed sausage and minced onion.

Artichoke Bottoms Princesse: Fill with puréed, cooked, seasoned green peas.

STUFFED ARTICHOKE BOTTOMS À LA PARISIENNE

4 servings

Here's an excellent dish for a ladies' lunch.

8 globe artichoke hearts, boiled and drained
1½ cups creamed chicken, ham, or shellfish
¼ cup soft white bread crumbs
¼ cup grated Parmesan cheese

Preheat oven to 375° F. Strip all leaves from hearts and remove chokes.* Arrange in a buttered shallow casserole and fill with one of the creamed mixtures. Mix crumbs with Parmesan and sprinkle over filling. Bake, uncovered, in top half of the oven 20–25 minutes until browned and bubbly. Serve as a light entree.

*NPS (chicken): 260 C, 70 mg CH, 550 mg S**
*NPS (ham): 225 C, 50 mg CH, 780 mg S**

ROMAN ARTICHOKES STUFFED WITH ANCHOVIES

4 servings

Stuffed artichokes are eaten like the steamed: pluck off petals, one at a time, then finish by eating the heart and stuffing with knife and fork.

4 large globe artichokes, prepared for cooking
½ cup soft white bread crumbs
4 anchovy fillets, chopped fine
2 tablespoons minced parsley
¼ teaspoon pepper
½ cup olive oil
2 cups boiling water

Remove chokes from artichokes.* Mix crumbs, anchovies, parsley, pepper, and 2 tablespoons olive oil and spoon into centers of artichokes. Place remaining oil and the water in a large kettle and stand artichokes in the liquid stem end down. (The liquid should only half cover artichokes, so ladle from—or add to—the pot as needed.) Cover and simmer 35–45 minutes until a leaf will pull off easily. Serve hot as a first course or vegetable with Drawn Butter Sauce or Lemon Butter.

NPS: 345 C, 2 mg CH, 190 mg S*

BRAISED ARTICHOKES PROVENÇAL

6 servings

6 large globe artichokes, parboiled and drained
1 medium-size yellow onion, peeled and sliced thin
1 carrot, peeled and sliced thin
1 clove garlic, peeled and crushed
2 tablespoons butter or margarine
2 tablespoons olive oil
1/2 teaspoon salt
1/8 teaspoon white pepper
1 sprig parsley
1/2 bay leaf
1 cup dry white wine
1 cup chicken broth
2 tablespoons lemon juice
1 tablespoon minced parsley (garnish)

Preheat oven to 325° F. Cut off top third of each artichoke and discard, then quarter remaining two thirds lengthwise and remove chokes.* In a large flameproof casserole over moderately low heat, stir-fry onion, carrot, and garlic in butter and oil 5 minutes (don't allow to brown). Lay artichokes over onion mixture and sprinkle with salt and pepper. Add all remaining ingredients except garnish and cover. When casserole begins to boil, set in oven and bake, covered, 1 1/4–1 1/2 hours until most of the liquid has bubbled away and artichokes are tender. To serve, strain cooking liquid, spoon over artichokes, and sprinkle with minced parsley. Provide a fork and spoon for scraping flesh from artichoke petals—they are too messy to eat with your fingers.

NPS: 185 C, 10 mg CH, 485 mg S*

JERUSALEM ARTICHOKES
(Sunchokes)

There's no reason why Jerusalem artichokes should be called Jerusalem artichokes. They aren't from Jerusalem and they aren't artichokes. Nut-brown and potato-flavored, they're actually tubers of a sunflower that grows wild in the Eastern United States. Eat them out of hand like a radish, or, better still, boil, bake, mash, hash, or pickle.

To Prepare for Cooking: Scrub well in cool water with a vegetable brush, cut away eyes, small knobs, or blemishes but do not peel unless recipe directs otherwise or unless the skins seem tough and inedible (because of their knobbiness, Jerusalem artichokes are the very dickens to peel).

BOILED JERUSALEM ARTICHOKES

4 servings

1 pound Jerusalem artichokes, prepared for cooking
2 cups boiling water
1/2 teaspoon salt
Butter or margarine
Salt
Pepper

Place artichokes in a large saucepan, add water and the 1/2 teaspoon salt, and simmer, covered, 8–10 minutes until just tender (artichokes will seem quite crisp and raw throughout most of the cooking, then quite suddenly become soft). Drain well and serve with plenty of butter, salt, and pepper.

NPS (with butter): 135 C, 30 mg CH, 185 mg S*

VARIATIONS

⚖ **Low-Calorie Jerusalem Artichokes:** Instead of serving with butter, sprinkle with seasoned salt or drizzle with a little low-calorie Italian salad dressing.

NPS: 30 C, 0 mg CH, 90 mg S*

Jerusalem Artichoke Purée: Follow above recipe, increasing cooking time to 10–12 minutes so artichokes are very soft. Press flesh from skins and mash or whip until creamy with an electric mixer. Beat in 2 tablespoons each butter and heavy cream (just enough to give artichokes a good consistency), then season to taste with salt, pepper and nutmeg. Warm 1–2 minutes, stirring over lowest heat, and serve.

NPS: 110 C, 25 mg CH, 130 mg S*

BAKED JERUSALEM ARTICHOKES

4 servings

1 pound uniformly large Jerusalem artichokes (they should be about 2″ long and 1 1/2″ across), prepared for cooking
Butter or margarine

Salt
Pepper

Preheat oven to 400° F. Place artichokes in a shallow roasting pan and bake, uncovered, 15–20 minutes until tender. (As with boiled artichokes, they'll seem quite crisp until 1–2 minutes before they're done, so watch carefully.) Serve oven-hot with lots of butter, salt, and freshly ground pepper.

NPS (with butter): 135 C, 30 mg CH, 185 mg S*

HASHED BROWN JERUSALEM ARTICHOKES

4 servings

1 pound Jerusalem artichokes, prepared for cooking
2 tablespoons butter or margarine
1/4 teaspoon salt
Pepper

Slice artichokes thin. Melt butter in a large skillet over moderate heat, add artichokes, and fry 5–7 minutes, stirring now and then, until tender and lightly tinged with brown. Season with salt and pepper and serve.

NPS: 80 C, 15 mg CH, 195 mg S*

CREAMED JERUSALEM ARTICHOKES

4–6 servings

It's best to make the cream sauce while the artichokes cook so the two are done at the same time.

1 1/2 pounds Jerusalem artichokes, prepared for cooking
2 cups boiling water
1 tablespoon lemon juice
2 tablespoons butter or margarine
2 tablespoons flour
1/2 teaspoon salt
Pinch white pepper
Pinch mace
1 cup light cream
1 egg yolk
1 tablespoon minced parsley or chives

Peel artichokes and cut in 1/2″ cubes. Place in a large saucepan, add water and lemon juice, cover, and simmer 5–7 minutes until just tender; drain. Meanwhile, melt butter over moderate heat in a small saucepan and blend in flour, salt, pepper, and mace. Add cream, then cook, stirring constantly, until thickened. Beat egg yolk with a fork, mix in a little of the hot sauce, then stir back into sauce in pan. Mix parsley or chives into

sauce, pour over artichokes, toss lightly, and serve.

NPS (4–6): 245–165 C, 125–80 mg CH, 360–240 mg S*

ASPARAGUS

Spring's first asparagus begins coming to market about the end of February with slim young stalks the color of budding leaves and snug, pointed tips faintly tinged with lavender. This is the asparagus Americans know best, but Europeans prefer the chunky, butter-smooth white varieties, particularly the French Argenteuil asparagus and the German *Stangenspargel.* Try them, if you should find them in your market, and prepare them as you would green asparagus—their flavor is slightly more delicate, their texture somewhat softer. Both the green and the white asparagus are fragile vegetables, best when cooked gently and *quickly* (the greatest crime perpetrated against asparagus is overcooking—when properly cooked, the stalks will be bright green, tender but *crisp,* never soft, never mushy).

To Prepare for Cooking: Snap off tough stem ends, wash asparagus well in tepid water, remove scales (they harbor grit), and, if skins seem coarse, peel with a vegetable peeler.

Serving Tip: Serve steamed asparagus, drizzled with melted butter or sauced with Hollandaise, as a separate course before or after the entree.

How to Eat: Use a fork whenever stalks are tender, limp, or drippy. It's proper, however, to eat crisp spears with your fingers (except at formal dinners).

STEAMED ASPARAGUS

4 servings

2 pounds asparagus, prepared for cooking
1/2 cup boiling water
1/4 cup melted butter or margarine
1 teaspoon salt
1/8 teaspoon pepper

Tie stalks in serving-size bunches, keeping strings loose so asparagus does not bruise. Stand stems down in a deep saucepan, add water, cover, and simmer 10–15 minutes until stems are tender. Drain, remove strings, and season with butter, salt, and pepper. Or omit butter and top with Hollandaise or Mousseline Sauce.

NPS (with butter): 135 C, 30 mg CH, 670 mg S*

To Poach: Lay individual asparagus stalks flat in a large, heavy skillet (not cast-iron), preferably in 1 layer but never more than 2. Add 1 teaspoon salt, enough boiling water to cover (about 2 cups), then cover skillet and simmer 6–8 minutes until crisp-tender (time will vary with thickness of spears). Drain well and season with butter and pepper.

To Parboil for Use in Other Recipes: Prepare as directed but reduce cooking time to 5 minutes; omit seasonings.

VARIATIONS

To Serve Cold: Lay steamed asparagus flat in a large bowl and cover with ice water. When cold, drain well, cover, and chill until ready to use. Serve with French Dressing, Hollandaise or Chiffon Sauce. Recipe too flexible for meaningful nutritional count.

⚖️ **Low-Calorie Asparagus:** Omit butter; dress with 2 tablespoons lemon juice or 1/4 cup low-calorie Italian dressing.
NPS: 35 C, 0 mg CH, 555 mg S*

Asparagus with Dill: Add 1 tablespoon minced fresh dill to the melted butter.
NPS: 135 C, 30 mg CH, 670 mg S*

Asparagus with Capers: Reduce salt to 1/2 teaspoon and mix 1 tablespoon minced capers with the melted butter.
NPS: 135 C, 30 mg CH, 445 mg S*

Buttered Asparagus Tips: Use the top 2″ of each stalk only, prepare as for Steamed Asparagus, but cook just 5–8 minutes. Season as directed.
NPS: 110 C, 30 mg CH, 670 mg S*

Creamed Asparagus Tips: Prepare Buttered Asparagus Tips but omit *all* seasonings. To each cup asparagus, add 1/2 cup hot Medium White Sauce, mix lightly, heat through, and serve. (*Note:* The Cheese, Mushroom, and Mustard variations of Basic White Sauce are equally good with asparagus tips.)
NPS: 130 C, 25 mg CH, 225 mg S*

ASPARAGUS POLONAISE

4 servings

2 pounds hot steamed or poached asparagus or 2 (10-ounce) packages frozen asparagus, boiled
3 hard-cooked egg yolks
1 tablespoon minced parsley
1/3 cup soft white bread crumbs
3 tablespoons Browned Butter

Preheat broiler. Drain asparagus well and arrange in rows in a shallow buttered casserole. Press egg yolks through a fine sieve, mix with parsley, and sprinkle over asparagus. Toss crumbs in butter and sprinkle on top. Broil 4″–5″ from the heat 2–3 minutes until lightly browned.
NPS: 195 C, 230 mg CH, 125 mg S*

CHEESE AND ASPARAGUS CASSEROLE

4 servings ⊠

2 pounds hot steamed or poached asparagus or 2 (10-ounce) packages frozen asparagus, boiled (do not drain either one)
1 pint light cream (about)
6 tablespoons butter or margarine
6 tablespoons flour
3/4 teaspoon salt
1/8 teaspoon white pepper
2 cups coarsely grated sharp Cheddar cheese
1 cup soft white bread crumbs

Preheat oven to 400° F. Drain asparagus cooking water into a quart measure and add enough light cream to measure 3 cups. Melt 4 tablespoons butter over moderate heat and blend in flour. Add the 3 cups liquid and heat, stirring constantly, until thickened. Add salt, pepper, and 1 cup cheese; cook and stir until cheese is melted. Arrange asparagus in a buttered shallow 2-quart casserole and top with cheese sauce. Toss remaining cheese with bread crumbs, sprinkle over sauce, and dot with remaining butter. Bake, uncovered, 10–12 minutes until bubbly and touched with brown.
NPS: 735 C, 185 mg CH, 1,045 mg S*

ASPARAGUS DIVAN

6 servings

2 pounds cooked Buttered Asparagus Tips
6 slices hot buttered white toast
2 tablespoons sweet Madeira or sherry
2 cups hot Cheese Sauce
1/4 cup grated Parmesan cheese

Preheat broiler. Arrange hot asparagus tips on toast in an ungreased shallow roasting pan. Stir wine into sauce, pour evenly over asparagus, and sprinkle with Parmesan. Broil 4″ from the heat 3–4 minutes until sauce is speckled with brown and bubbly.
NPS: 460 C, 95 mg CH, 1,165 mg S*

Asparagus Divan on Ham: Substitute a thick slice of cooked ham for each piece of toast. Serve as an entree.

NPS: 410 C, 100 mg CH, 1,425 mg S*

Asparagus and Egg Divan: Top asparagus with 6 very soft poached eggs before adding sauce and Parmesan. Serve as an entree.

NPS: 535 C, 370 mg CH, 1,310 mg S*

CHINESE ASPARAGUS

4–6 servings

2 pounds asparagus, prepared for cooking
1 tablespoon cornstarch
2 tablespoons cold water
1 cup chicken broth
2 teaspoons soy sauce
1 tablespoon dry sherry
¼ teaspoon sugar
3 tablespoons peanut or other vegetable oil
¼ cup thinly sliced water chestnuts or bamboo shoots

Cut each asparagus stalk diagonally into slices ¼″ thick. Blend cornstarch with water in a small saucepan, add broth, soy sauce, sherry, and sugar, and heat, stirring, over moderate heat until slightly thickened. Remove from burner but keep warm. Heat oil in a large, heavy skillet or *wok* over moderate heat 1 minute. Add asparagus and stir-fry 3 minutes until crisp-tender. Slowly stir in sauce and heat 2 minutes longer, stirring constantly. Add water chestnuts or bamboo shoots and serve.

NPS (4–6): 115–75 C, 0 mg CH, 415–280 mg S*

SPANISH-STYLE ASPARAGUS BAKE

4 servings

2 pounds hot steamed or poached asparagus or 2 (10-ounce) packages frozen asparagus, boiled
2 hard-cooked eggs, peeled and halved
2 pimientos, cut in small dice
2 tablespoons lemon juice
2 tablespoons cooking oil
2 tablespoons light cream
1 tablespoon minced chives
¼ teaspoon salt
⅛ teaspoon white pepper

Preheat oven to 350° F. Drain asparagus well; halve crosswise. Arrange in an ungreased shallow 1-quart casserole. Scoop egg yolks from whites and set aside. Mince egg whites, mix with pimientos, and scatter over asparagus. Press yolks through a fine sieve, then beat in the lemon juice, oil, and cream, one at a time. Mix in remaining ingredients, pour over asparagus, and bake, uncovered, ½ hour. Serve at once.

NPS: 165 C, 140 mg CH, 180 mg S*

BEANS

Of all vegetable families, none is quite so big or bountiful as the bean family. There are big beans and little beans, delicate and hearty beans, black beans and white (and every color in between). There are foreign exotics (the wing bean is the latest of them to reach us) and American favorites: limas, green beans, and kidney beans. These three, nutritionists maintain, are America's most valuable contribution to the world table, more so than potatoes or tomatoes because, as a protein-rich food, beans, down the ages, have nourished people unable to afford meat. The easiest way to learn the many kinds of beans is to subdivide them by type: the *fresh* and the *dried.*

The Varieties of Beans Cooked Fresh

Green Beans (also known as *snap, string,* and *haricot beans):* A kidney bean tender enough to eat pod and all.

Wax Beans: Yellow "green" beans.

Italian Green Beans: Broader, flatter than green beans, brighter, too. Most often available frozen.

Wing Beans: Long, four-sided, green, purple, or red beans (in cross-section they are square or rectangular) with four distinct "wings" or ridges running the length of each bean. The wing bean plant is completely edible—leaves, flowers, tuberous root, beans—which is why it has become a staple throughout much of the Third World.

Lima Beans (the *"butter beans"* of the South): There are large limas (Fordhooks) and baby limas, better all-round beans because they are less starchy and do not cook down to mush.

Fava Beans (called *Broad Beans* in Britain): Large, inedible, fleshy, bright green pods with a silky lining cradling pale green beans that are similar to but bigger and flatter than Fordhook limas. Favas are especially popular throughout the Mediterranean countries and Middle East.

Cranberry Beans (also called *shellouts* and *shell beans):* These pods look like outsize, splotchy red wax beans. The pods are tough but the inner cream-colored beans are nutty and tender.

Black-Eyed Peas: A Deep South favorite, small, pale green beans with black eyes. The pods are misshapen, russeted green, and inedible.

To Prepare for Cooking:

Green, Wax, or Italian Green Beans: There are few "strings" today because science has bred them out. Wash in cool water and snap off ends. If beans are tender, leave whole; if not, snap in 2″ lengths. Green and wax beans may be frenched for variety (slivered the long way); most vegetable peelers have frenchers at one end. Frenched beans will cook faster than the snapped.

Wing Beans: Snip off ends, wash in cool water, then cut in 2″ lengths.

Limas, Cranberry Beans, Black-Eyed Peas: Shell. To hasten the job, peel a strip from outer curved edge with a vegetable peeler or snip seam open with scissors.

Fava Beans: Shell, but wear rubber gloves as you work because the tannin in the pods may blacken your fingers.

Cooking Tip: Never add soda to the cooking water to brighten green beans—makes them soapy and destroys vitamin C.

An Alphabet of Dried Beans

Black Beans (also called *turtle beans*): Black skinned, creamy fleshed; the staple of South American soups and stews.

Black-Eyed and **Yellow-Eyed Peas:** Southern favorites called "peas" because their flavor resembles that of field peas. They differ only in the color of their "eyes." Black-eyed peas are available fresh in summer. Yellow-eyed peas are also known as yellow-eyed beans in some parts of the country.

Cannellini: White Italian kidney beans, available dry in Italian groceries, canned in supermarkets. Good *en casserole* with tomatoes and sausages.

Chick-Peas (also called *garbanzo beans* and *ceci*): Chick-peas resemble withered filberts and are, in fact, the most nutlike of beans. They work equally well in soups, salads, and casseroles.

Cowpeas: A sort of baby black-eyed pea used in much the same way.

Cranberry Beans: (See Fresh Beans.)

Fava Beans: Wrinkled, beige-skinned, strong-flavored giants as big as your thumb.

Flageolets: In France green beans are grown just for the tender, pale green inner beans known as *flageolets*. Though they're available fresh abroad, we must be content with the dried or canned.

Kidney Beans: Old friends, these, the red-brown beans of chili and the basis of many a Mexican recipe. They are also a popular "baking" bean in New England.

Lima Beans: Baby limas are more often dried than Fordhooks because they hold their shape better.

Pink Beans: A kissing cousin of the kidney bean, this is the bean of refried beans and other Southwestern favorites.

Pinto Beans: Another kidney bean, this one pink with brown freckles.

Red Beans: Yet another kidney bean, a smaller, redder variety that's Mexico's favorite.

White Beans: This isn't a single bean but a family of four: the big *marrowfat,* the medium-sized *Great Northern,* and the smaller *navy* (or *Yankee)* and *pea beans.*

To Prepare for Cooking: Place beans in a colander or large sieve and rinse well in cool water. Sort carefully, removing withered or broken beans and any bits of stone. Soak, using one of the following methods:

Basic Method: Allowing 1 quart cold water for 1 pound dried beans, soak overnight or for 6–8 hours (discard any beans that float). If your kitchen is very warm, soak beans, covered, in the refrigerator so they don't sour.

Quick Method: Allow 1 quart cold water for 1 pound of beans. Place beans and water in a large kettle, cover, and bring to a boil over high heat. Reduce heat to moderate and let beans boil gently 2 minutes. Remove from heat and let stand 1 hour with the lid on.

Cooking Tips:
• Always use some soaking water for cooking beans (it contains vitamins).
• Don't salt beans (or add tomatoes or other acid foods) until toward the end of cooking because they toughen the beans.
• To keep the pot from boiling over, add 1 tablespoon margarine, drippings, or cooking oil. A chunk of bacon or salt pork will do the trick too. So will a ham bone.

Some Special Beans and Bean Products

Mung Beans: We don't often see these dark, BB-sized Oriental beans, though we're thoroughly familiar with their sprouts. Many Americans today, in fact, are growing their own bean sprouts (see Bean Sprouts at the end of the section on Beans).

Soybeans: "Superbeans" might have been a better name because these beans provide oil for our margarines, a high-protein flour, soy sauce, bean pastes *(miso),* curds *(tofu),* and milk not to mention soy nuts, *tempeh* (fermented bean cakes), and *TVP* (textured vegetable protein) used both to extend meats and make artificial "meat" products.

BOILED FRESH GREEN, WAX, OR WING BEANS

4 servings

Because beans can so easily boil dry and burn it's best to cook them covered.

1 pound green, wax, or wing beans, prepared for cooking
1 teaspoon salt
2 cups boiling water (about)
2 tablespoons butter or margarine
1/8 teaspoon pepper

Place beans in a large heavy skillet, add salt and enough water to cover (about 2 cups). Cover and simmer until crisp-tender: 6–8 minutes for frenched green or wax beans, 10–12 minutes for the snapped or whole, and about 15 minutes for wing beans. Drain, season with butter and pepper, and serve.

NPS: 85 C, 0 mg CH, 350 mg S*

To Parboil for Use in Other Recipes: Follow method above, reducing cooking time to about 5 minutes for frenched beans, 8 minutes for the snapped or whole, and 10 minutes for wing beans. Omit seasonings.

VARIATIONS

To Serve Cold: Omit seasonings. Chill beans in ice water, drain, pat dry on paper toweling, wrap in plastic food wrap, and refrigerate until ready to use. Dress with a tart oil and vinegar dressing and serve as a salad.

⊲⊳ **Low-Calorie Beans:** Dress with 1/4 cup low-calorie Italian dressing instead of butter.

NPS: 35 C, 0 mg CH, 360 mg S*

Green Beans Amandine: Increase butter to 1/3 cup, melt in a small skillet, add 1/3 cup slivered blanched almonds, and stir-fry 3–5 minutes until golden. Toss with beans and serve.

NPS: 230 C, 40 mg CH, 295 mg S*

Green Beans with Mushrooms: Stir 1/2 cup sautéed sliced mushrooms into beans along with butter.

NPS: 110 C, 20 mg CH, 295 mg S*

Beans with Bacon and Dill: Just before serving, stir in 1/3 cup crisp cooked bacon and 1 tablespoon minced fresh dill.

NPS: 135 C, 25 mg CH, 350 mg S*

Beans with Oil and Vinegar: Omit butter and dress beans with 3 tablespoons olive oil and 2 tablespoons tarragon-flavored white wine vinegar.

NPS: 120 C, 0 mg CH, 140 mg S*

⊲⊳ **Sweet-Sour Beans:** Omit butter and toss beans with 1/4 cup cider vinegar and 1–1 1/2 tablespoons sugar. Serve hot or chill and serve cold.

NPS: 45 C, 0 mg CH, 140 mg S*

GREEN BEANS IN MUSTARD SAUCE

4 servings   ¢ ⊲⊳

1 pound green beans, boiled and drained (reserve cooking water)
1 tablespoon butter or margarine
1 tablespoon flour
Green bean cooking water + enough milk to total 3/4 cup
3 tablespoons prepared mild yellow mustard
1 tablespoon Worcestershire sauce
1/2 teaspoon salt
1/4 teaspoon cayenne pepper

Keep beans warm. Melt butter over moderate heat and blend in flour. Add the 3/4 cup liquid and heat, stirring constantly, until thickened. Mix in remaining ingredients and heat, stirring, 2–3 minutes to blend flavors. Pour sauce over beans, toss lightly to mix, and serve.

NPS: 75 C, 10 mg CH, 495 mg S*

GREEN OR WAX BEANS AU GRATIN

4 servings

1 pound green or wax beans or 2 (10-ounce) packages frozen green, wax, or Italian beans, boiled and drained
1 1/2 cups hot Cheese Sauce or Mornay Sauce
1/3 cup coarsely grated sharp Cheddar cheese
1 tablespoon melted butter or margarine

Preheat broiler. Arrange beans in an un-greased 2-quart *au gratin* dish or shallow casserole, cover with sauce, sprinkle with cheese, and dot with butter. Broil 5″ from heat 3–4 minutes until cheese melts and is nicely browned.

NPS (Cheese): 370 C, 85 mg CH, 645 mg S*
NPS (Mornay): 285 C, 65 mg CH, 475 mg S*

VARIATION

Lima Beans au Gratin: Substitute boiled baby lima beans (you'll need 3 pounds in the pod) or 2 (10-ounce) packages frozen limas for the green beans. Nutritional count about the same as basic recipe.

BEANS LYONNAISE

4 servings ¢

1 pound green or wax beans, frenched and parboiled
3 tablespoons butter or margarine
1 large yellow onion, peeled and sliced thin
1 teaspoon salt
1/8 teaspoon white pepper
1 teaspoon minced parsley
1 teaspoon white wine vinegar

Drain beans well and pat dry between paper toweling. Melt butter in a large, heavy skillet over moderate heat 1 minute. Add onion and sauté 5–8 minutes until pale golden. Add beans and stir-fry 3–4 minutes until *just* tender. Add remaining ingredients, toss lightly to mix, and serve.

NPS: 125 C, 25 mg CH, 650 mg S*

GREEN BEANS PROVENÇAL

4 servings ¢

Don't try to stir-fry more than this amount of beans in one skillet; if you double the rec-ipe, use two.

1 pound green beans, parboiled
2 tablespoons olive oil
1 small clove garlic, peeled and crushed
2 teaspoons minced parsley
3/4 teaspoon salt
1/8 teaspoon pepper

Drain beans well and pat dry between paper toweling. Heat oil in a large, heavy skillet over moderate heat 1 minute. Add beans and stir-fry 3–4 minutes, until crisp-tender and *very lightly* browned. Add garlic and stir-fry 1 minute. Off heat, mix in parsley, salt, and pepper and serve.

NPS: 90 C, 0 mg CH, 420 mg S*

SOFRITO WAX OR WING BEANS

6 servings

SOFRITO SAUCE
3 slices bacon, diced
2 tablespoons lard or bacon drippings
1 medium-size yellow onion, peeled and chopped fine
1 clove garlic, peeled and crushed
1 small sweet green pepper, cored, seeded, and chopped fine
1 sweet red pepper, cored, seeded, and chopped fine
1 large ripe tomato, peeled, seeded, and coarsely chopped
Pinch coriander or 2 leaves fresh coriander
4 pitted green olives, chopped fine
1/4 teaspoon capers, chopped fine (optional)
1 teaspoon oregano
1/3 cup water
1/2 teaspoon salt

1 1/2 pounds hot wax or wing beans, boiled and drained

Fry bacon 2–3 minutes over moderate heat in a large, heavy skillet, add lard or bacon drippings, onion, garlic, green and red pep-pers, and sauté 7–8 minutes until onion is pale golden. Add remaining sauce ingredi-ents, cover, and simmer slowly 7–10 min-utes, stirring once or twice. Pour sauce over beans, toss lightly to mix, and serve.

NPS: 150 C, 10 mg CH, 325 mg S*

ORIENTAL-STYLE BEANS WITH WATER CHESTNUTS

4 servings

1 pound green beans
3 tablespoons peanut or other cooking oil
12 small scallions, trimmed of green tops
1 teaspoon minced fresh gingerroot
1/4 cup chicken broth
1 teaspoon salt
1/8 teaspoon pepper
1 (4-ounce) can water chestnuts, drained and sliced paper thin

Cut beans diagonally, into 1/4″ slices or sliver lengthwise into matchstick strips. Heat oil in a large, heavy skillet or *wok* over moderate heat, add beans, scallions, and gingerroot, and stir-fry 5–7 minutes. Add chicken broth, cover tightly, reduce heat to low, and simmer 4–5 minutes until beans are tender. Off heat, mix in salt, pepper, and wa-ter chestnuts and serve.

NPS: 145 C, 0 mg CH, 615 mg S*

BOILED FRESH BABY LIMA BEANS

4 servings

The basic way to cook lima beans and a handy beginning for a number of flavor variations.

3 pounds baby lima beans, shelled
1 teaspoon salt
2 cups boiling water
2 tablespoons butter or margarine
1/8 teaspoon pepper

Place limas in a large saucepan, add salt and water, cover, and simmer 20–30 minutes until tender. Drain, season with butter and pepper, and serve.

NPS: 225 C, 15 mg CH, 420 mg S*

To Parboil for Use in Other Recipes: Use above method but reduce cooking time to 10–15 minutes; omit seasonings.

VARIATIONS

To Serve Cold: Omit seasonings; chill beans in ice water, drain, pat dry between paper toweling, wrap in plastic food wrap, and refrigerate until ready to use. Serve with Aioli Sauce, French Dressing, or Spanish Vinaigrette. Recipe too flexible for meaningful nutritional count.

Lima Beans with Bacon and Sour Cream: Reduce butter to 1 tablespoon and stir in 1/2 cup sour cream and 1/4 cup crisp, crumbled bacon just before serving.

NPS: 300 C, 25 mg CH, 520 mg S*

Lima Beans with Parsley and Paprika: Toss in 2 tablespoons minced parsley and 1 teaspoon paprika just before serving.

NPS: 225 C, 15 mg CH, 420 mg S*

Lima Beans with Dill: Reduce butter to 1 tablespoon and stir in 1/2 cup sour cream and 1 tablespoon minced fresh dill just before serving.

NPS: 260 C, 20 mg CH, 405 mg S*

Baby Limas with Pecans: Stir in 1/4 cup sour cream and 1 cup coarsely chopped pecans just before serving.

NPS: 460 C, 20 mg CH, 430 mg S*

Boiled Fresh Fava Beans: Prepare and cook favas as directed for baby lima beans, increasing cooking time slightly, if needed—the beans should not taste starchy. Fresh fava beans may be substituted for lima beans in any recipe. *Note:* Although some cooks slip the skins off cooked favas before serving them, it's not necessary if the beans you've chosen are young and tender. Nutritional count about the same as basic recipe.

LIMA BEANS WITH CARROTS AND BACON

4–6 servings

1 (1/4-pound) piece bacon, diced
2 medium-size carrots, peeled and sliced thin
1 medium-size yellow onion, peeled and sliced thin
3 pounds baby lima beans, shelled
3/4 cup boiling water
1 teaspoon salt
1 teaspoon paprika
Pinch pepper
1/4 cup dry white wine
3/4 cup sour cream
3 tablespoons minced fresh dill

Brown the bacon in a large, heavy skillet over moderately high heat, then drain on paper toweling. Sauté carrots and onion in the drippings over moderate heat about 8 minutes until onion is golden. Add beans to skillet along with water, salt, paprika, and pepper. Cover, reduce heat to moderately low, and simmer 20–25 minutes until beans are tender. Mix in bacon, wine, sour cream, and dill, heat, stirring, 1–2 minutes longer, and serve.

NPS (4–6): 455–305 C, 35–25 mg CH, 1,015–675 mg S*

BOILED FRESH CRANBERRY BEANS

4 servings   ¢

These beans can be used in place of limas in recipes.

3 pounds cranberry beans in the pod
1 teaspoon salt
2 cups boiling water
2 tablespoons butter or margarine
1/8 teaspoon pepper

Shell beans just before you're ready to use them and place in a saucepan. Add salt and water, cover, and boil slowly 10–12 minutes until tender. Drain, season with butter and pepper, and serve.

NPS: 225 C, 15 mg CH, 420 mg S*

BOILED FRESH BLACK-EYED PEAS

4 servings   ¢

3 pounds black-eyed peas in the pod
1 teaspoon salt
1 1/2 quarts boiling water

1 (¼-pound) piece lean bacon, cut in large
  chunks
⅛ teaspoon pepper

Shell peas, place in a saucepan, add salt, water, and bacon, cover, and boil slowly 1–1½ hours or until of desired tenderness. Check pot occasionally and add more water if necessary. Season with pepper, taste for salt and adjust as needed. Serve peas and "pot likker" in small bowls.

NPS: 395 C, 20 mg CH, 755 mg S*

VARIATION

¢ **Carolina-Style Black-Eyed Peas:** Prepare as directed but increase water to 2 quarts, omit salt, and substitute 1 (¼-pound) chunk salt pork or fat back for the bacon. Simmer slowly 2½–3 hours until soft-tender, adding water as needed to keep mixture soupy. Taste for salt and adjust as needed. Season with pepper. Serve peas in cooking liquid with freshly baked corn bread to accompany.

NPS: 460 C, 20 mg CH, 425 mg S*

HOPPING JOHN

6 servings   ¢

2 (10-ounce) packages frozen black-eyed peas
  (do not thaw)
3 cups boiling water
1 (¼-pound) piece lean bacon
1 yellow onion, peeled and coarscly chopped
3 cups hot fluffy cooked rice
2 tablespoons bacon drippings, butter, or
  margarine
2 teaspoons salt
⅛–¼ teaspoon crushed hot red chili peppers
⅛ teaspoon black pepper

Place peas, water, bacon, and onion in a large saucepan, cover, and simmer 30–35 minutes until peas are tender. Remove bacon, lightly mix in remaining ingredients, and serve in place of potatoes.

NPS: 355 C, 10 mg CH, 855 mg S*

BOILED DRIED BEANS

6 servings   ¢

This method works for the whole family of dried beans—only the cooking time varies.

1 pound dried beans, washed and sorted
2 quarts cold water (about)
1 tablespoon margarine, roast drippings, or
  cooking oil

Soak beans in 1 quart water overnight or use the quick method.* Drain, measure soaking water, and add enough cold water to make 1 quart. Simmer beans, covered, in the water with margarine, drippings, or oil, stirring now and then, as follows:

30–40 minutes	for black-eyed peas, cowpeas
50 minutes–1 hour	for lima beans
1–1½ hours	for chick-peas (garbanzos), flageolets, cannellini, pink or red kidney beans
1½–2 hours	for pea, navy, Great Northern, marrowfat, black, or pinto beans

Use the beans in other recipes or add salt and pepper to taste and serve. To dress them up, season with a fat chunk of Herb Butter or top with Parsley Sauce or Cheese Sauce. Recipe too flexible for meaningful nutritional count.

VARIATIONS

¢ **To Serve Cold** (for all but black beans): Cool beans in their cooking water, drain, then rinse under cold running water. Cover and chill until ready to use. Serve cold as a vegetable, dressed with oil, vinegar, and garlic, or toss into salads. Recipe too flexible for meaningful nutritional count.

¢ **Savory Beans** (for white or light beans): Simmer a ham bone or pig's knuckle with the beans, a chunk of bacon or salt pork, leftover beef bones. Other good additions to the pot: parsley sprigs, young carrots, a clove of garlic, a yellow onion stuck with a clove or two, almost any leftover vegetable. Recipe too flexible for meaningful nutritional count.

Black Beans and Sour Cream: Simmer beans with a ham bone, a medium-size onion, chopped fine, and a crushed clove of garlic. Top each serving with a dollop of sour cream.

NPS: 465 C, 15 mg CH, 230 mg S*

CREAMED PURÉE OF DRIED BEANS

4 servings

½ pound dried white or lima beans, boiled and
  drained
¼ cup milk
¼ cup light cream
2–4 tablespoons melted butter or margarine
½ clove garlic, peeled and crushed

Pinch white pepper
2 tablespoons grated Parmesan cheese (optional)

Preheat oven to 350° F. Mash beans with a potato masher, or churn with the milk and light cream 20–30 seconds in a food processor fitted with the metal chopping blade. (If you want to remove bean skins, do not drain; press beans *and* their liquid through a coarse sieve.) Beat in remaining ingredients, spoon into a buttered shallow 1½-quart casserole, roughen surface with a fork, and bake, uncovered, 25–30 minutes. To brown, broil 5″ from the heat about 4 minutes.

NPS (white beans): 300 C, 30 mg CH, 120 mg S*
NPS (limas): 300 C, 30 mg CH, 120 mg S*

V A R I A T I O N S

Purée of Beans au Gratin: Omit Parmesan. Just before broiling, sprinkle purée with ⅓ cup grated sharp Cheddar cheese and 2 tablespoons melted butter.

NPS: 370 C, 65 mg CH, 685 mg S*

Purée of Vegetables au Gratin: Combine equal quantities of puréed cooked beans and carrots or rutabaga, then proceed as for Purée of Beans au Gratin. Recipe too flexible for meaningful nutritional count.

BOSTON BAKED BEANS

4–6 servings ¢

A good meat substitute, although in New England, Boston Baked Beans are traditionally accompanied by ham, hot dogs, sausages, or meat loaf.

2 cups dried pea beans, washed and sorted
2 quarts cold water (about)
2 teaspoons salt
½ teaspoon powdered mustard
3 tablespoons dark brown sugar
3 tablespoons molasses
1 medium-size yellow onion, peeled and coarsely chopped (optional)
1 (¼-pound) piece salt pork

Soak beans overnight in 1 quart water or use the quick method.* Drain, measure soaking water, and add cold water to make 1 quart. Place beans in a large kettle, add the water, cover, and simmer, stirring occasionally, 1 hour. Drain, reserving 2 cups cooking water. Meanwhile, preheat oven to 400° F. Place beans in an ungreased 2-quart bean pot. Mix reserved cooking water with salt, mustard, sugar, and molasses and stir into beans; add onion if you like. Score rind of salt pork at ½″ intervals, then push into beans so only the rind shows. Cover and bake 1 hour; re-

duce temperature to 250° F. and bake 4 hours; uncover pot and bake 1 hour longer. Stir about every hour. Serve bubbling hot from the pot.

NPS (4–6): 655–440 C, 20–15 mg CH, 1,470–980 mg S*

ESTOUFFAT (WHITE BEAN STEW)

6 servings ¢

In France, *estouffade* means "stew," and this hearty white bean dish *is* a stew. Its name probably comes from the way people in the southern province of Languedoc pronounce *estouffade*.

1 pound dried white beans, flageolets, or limas, boiled just 1 hour but not drained
½ pound salt pork, cut into slices ¼″ thick
1 large yellow onion, peeled and chopped fine
3 large ripe tomatoes, peeled, seeded, and coarsely chopped
2 cloves garlic, peeled and crushed
1 bay leaf and 1 sprig each parsley and thyme, tied in cheesecloth *(bouquet garni)*
Salt to taste

Keep beans warm in their cooking water. Brown salt pork in a large, heavy skillet over moderate heat and drain on paper toweling. Sauté onion in the drippings 6–8 minutes until pale golden; add tomatoes and garlic and sauté 1–2 minutes longer. Add sautéed mixture to beans, also salt pork and *bouquet garni.* Cover and simmer 1 hour, stirring occasionally. Add salt to taste and serve.

NPS: 580 C, 25 mg CH, 480 mg S*

BEANS IN ONION SAUCE

4 servings ¢

A husky French country dish that is both easy and economical to make.

4 large yellow onions, peeled and quartered
¾ cup water
3 tablespoons butter or margarine
¾ cup hot Medium White Sauce
½ teaspoon salt (about)
⅛ teaspoon white pepper
3 cups hot boiled dried white or lima beans

Place onions, water, and butter in a saucepan, cover, and simmer 45 minutes or until onions are mushy. Uncover, boil slowly until liquid reduces to about ½ cup, then purée by buzzing 10–15 seconds in an electric blender at low speed or 5–10 seconds in a food processor fitted with the metal chopping blade. Mix in white sauce, salt, and pepper. Taste for salt and add a little more if needed. Pour onion sauce over hot, drained beans, mix gently, and serve.

NPS: 580 C, 25 mg CH, 480 mg S*

TURKISH "FRIED" WHITE BEANS AND CARROTS

6–8 servings

1 pound dried white beans, boiled just 1 hour but not drained
3 large yellow onions, peeled and chopped fine
2 cloves garlic, peeled and minced
1 cup olive oil
4 medium-size carrots, peeled and cut into rounds ¼″ thick
1 tablespoon salt (about)
¼ teaspoon pepper

Keep beans warm in their cooking liquid. Meanwhile, sauté onions and garlic in the oil in a large skillet over moderately low heat 5– 8 minutes until pale golden; stir into beans (include all olive oil). Add carrots, salt, and pepper, cover, and simmer 45 minutes, stirring occasionally, until vegetables are tender.

NPS (6–8): 635–475 C, 0 mg CH, 1,140–855 mg S*

SAVORY LIMA BEANS WITH WINE

6–8 servings   ¢

If the pork hock is meaty enough, this can double as a main dish.

1 pound dried large lima beans, washed and soaked
Soaking water + enough cold water to measure 3 cups
1 pork hock or pig's foot
1 medium-size yellow onion, peeled and stuck with 6 cloves
1 bay leaf, crumbled
1 tablespoon salt
⅛ teaspoon pepper
1 cup dry white wine

Place beans, water, pork hock, onion, and bay leaf in a large kettle, cover, and simmer 1 hour. Add remaining ingredients, cover, and simmer 45 minutes longer. Remove onion and pork hock. Cut meat from bones, add to beans, and serve.

NPS (6–8): 320–240 C, 15–10 mg CH, 1,115–835 mg S*

MEXICAN FRIED BEANS (FRIJOLES FRITOS)

4 servings   ¢

¼ cup lard
1 recipe Mexican Beans (following)

Melt lard in a large, heavy skillet over moderate heat. Ladle in a few of the beans and mash, adding a tablespoon or so of the bean liquid. Continue to add beans, mashing with bean liquid, until all are used up (you'll need about ½ cup liquid to give the beans the right consistency). *(Note:* You can mash all the beans, or leave about half of them whole.) Heat, stirring, until piping hot. To be really Mexican, serve with ham and Huevos Rancheros.

NPS: 310 C, 15 mg CH, 830 mg S*

VARIATIONS

¢   **Fried Beans with Cheese:** Just before serving add ½ cup coarsely grated Monterey Jack or sharp Cheddar cheese to beans and heat, stirring, about ½ minute until cheese melts.

NPS: 365 C, 25 mg CH, 905 mg S*

¢   **Fried Beans with Tomato:** After mashing beans, mix in ½ cup tomato paste, ¼–½ teaspoon chili powder, and, if you like, a touch of garlic. Heat and serve.

NPS: 335 C, 15 mg CH, 1,090 mg S*

¢   **Refried Beans (Frijoles Refritos):** As the title suggests, simply refry leftover fried beans in more lard until heated through and crisp here and there. Recipe too flexible for meaningful nutritional count.

MEXICAN BEANS (FRIJOLES MEXICANOS)

4 servings   ¢

1 cup dried pinto or red kidney beans, washed and soaked
Soaking water + enough cold water to measure 3 cups
1 tablespoon lard
1 large yellow onion, peeled and coarsely chopped (optional)
4 slices bacon, diced (optional)
1½ teaspoons salt

Place all ingredients except salt in a large saucepan, cover, and simmer until tender: 1– 1½ hours for red kidney beans, 1½–2 hours for pinto beans. Mix in salt and serve. The cooking liquid should be quite thick; if not, simmer, uncovered, until the consistency of gravy (don't boil, however, or beans may break up).

NPS: 195 C, 5 mg CH, 830 mg S*
NPS (with onion and bacon): 335 C, 20 mg CH, 990 mg S*

BARBECUED BEANS

6–8 servings ¢

This casserole improves on standing, so bake the day before and refrigerate until needed. About 1/2 hour before serving, pop, covered, into a 350° F. oven.

1 pound dried red kidney beans, washed and soaked
2 large yellow onions, peeled and chopped fine
2 cloves garlic, peeled and crushed
2 tablespoons bacon drippings
1/2 cup ketchup
1/2 cup chili sauce
1/2 cup cider vinegar
1/2 cup firmly packed dark brown sugar
1/2 teaspoon powdered mustard
1/2 teaspoon chili powder
2 teaspoons salt (about)
1/2 teaspoon pepper
5 cups water (about)

Preheat oven to 350° F. Drain beans, place in an ungreased 3-quart bean pot or casserole, and mix in all remaining ingredients. Cover tightly (use a double thickness of foil if casserole has no lid) and bake 5–6 hours, stirring occasionally, until beans are tender and sauce thick. If mixture gets too dry before beans are done, stir in a little warm water.

NPS (6–8): 435–325 C, 3–2 mg CH, 1,315–990 S*

SWEDISH BROWN BEANS

6–8 servings ¢

Somewhat like Boston Baked Beans, but more spicily flavored. These beans are popular at smorgasbords.

1 pound dried red kidney, cranberry, or pinto beans, boiled but not drained
1 medium-size yellow onion, peeled and chopped fine
1 clove garlic, peeled and crushed
1/2 cup tomato sauce
1 tablespoon Worcestershire sauce
2/3 cup firmly packed light brown sugar
2 tablespoons molasses
1/4 cup cider vinegar
1/4 teaspoon powdered mustard

1 1/2 teaspoons cornstarch
2 tablespoons cold water
6 slices bacon

Preheat oven to 325° F. Transfer beans and their cooking liquid to an ungreased 3-quart casserole and mix in onion and garlic. Blend tomato sauce, Worcestershire sauce, sugar, molasses, vinegar, and mustard and stir into beans. Blend cornstarch and water until smooth and mix in well. Lay bacon on top of beans, cover, and bake 1 1/2 hours. Raise oven temperature to 400° F., uncover, and bake 10 minutes to crisp bacon.

NPS (6–8): 515–385 C, 15–10 mg CH, 300–225 mg S*

SOUTHERN-STYLE BLACK-EYED PEAS

4–6 servings ¢

1 pound dried black-eyed peas, washed
1 (1/4-pound) piece bacon or salt pork, cut in 1″ cubes
1 1/2 quarts water
1 tablespoon salt
1/4 teaspoon cayenne pepper

Place peas, bacon, and water in a large, heavy kettle, cover, and simmer *very slowly* 2–2 1/2 hours until tender. Season with salt and pepper and serve.

NPS (4–6): 545–365 C, 20–15 mg CH, 1,880–1,255 mg S*

BAKED CHICK-PEA PILAF

6 servings ¢

1/2 medium-size Spanish onion, peeled and chopped fine
3 tablespoons olive or other cooking oil
1 (1-pound 3-ounce) can chick-peas (do not drain)
1/2 cup uncooked rice
1/4 cup boiling beef or chicken broth
1 pimiento, seeded and coarsely chopped
1 teaspoon salt

Preheat oven to 325° F. Sauté onion in oil over moderate heat 5–8 minutes until pale golden. Place chick-peas and rice in an ungreased 1 1/2-quart casserole and mix lightly. Add onion and remaining ingredients, and stir to mix. Cover and bake 1–1 1/4 hours, stirring occasionally, until rice is tender.

NPS: 200 C, 0 mg CH, 400 mg S*

CHICK-PEAS AND KASHA

4–6 servings

To be really authentic, each serving of this Syrian dish should be topped with a dollop of yogurt.

2 cups boiled dried or canned chick-peas
2 cups cooked buckwheat groats
½ cup beef bouillon
2 tablespoons butter or margarine

Preheat oven to 350° F. Drain peas, then remove skins by rubbing each pea between your thumb and forefinger. Coarsely chop peas, add buckwheat, and toss to mix. Spoon into a buttered 1½-quart casserole, pour bouillon over all, and dot with butter. Cover and bake 30 minutes.

NPS (4–6): 265–175 C, 15–10 mg CH, 165–110 mg S*

GREEK-STYLE CHICK-PEAS AND TOMATOES

6 servings   ¢

This dish has the consistency of a good, rich "spoon soup" and is easiest to eat out of soup bowls. It can also be served over spaghetti as a pasta sauce.

¼ cup olive or other cooking oil
1 medium-size Spanish onion, peeled and sliced thin
2 cloves garlic, peeled and crushed
1 pound dried chick-peas, boiled and drained, or 2 (1-pound 3-ounce) cans chick-peas, drained
2 cups tomato or marinara sauce
1 tablespoon minced parsley
¼ teaspoon finely chopped mint

Heat oil in a large saucepan over moderate heat 1 minute. Add onion and garlic and stir-fry 5 minutes, then mix in chick-peas and tomato sauce. Reduce heat to low, cover, and simmer 30 minutes. Mix in parsley and mint and serve.

NPS: 385 C, 0 mg CH, 420 mg S*

FALAFEL

1 dozen falafel

Falafel are spicy chick-pea croquettes so popular throughout the Middle East that they are sold at roadside stands like hot dogs and hamburgers. They're tucked piping hot inside freshly baked pita bread and eaten out-of-hand.

½ pound dried chick-peas, washed, boiled until tender, and drained, or 1 (1-pound, 3-ounce) can chick-peas, drained well
¼ cup soft white bread crumbs
1 teaspoon salt
⅛ teaspoon black pepper
¼ teaspoon paprika
⅛ teaspoon cayenne pepper
1 tablespoon minced parsley
¼ teaspoon marjoram
¼ teaspoon thyme
⅛ teaspoon ground cumin
¼ teaspoon ground coriander
1 small yellow onion, peeled and minced
1 small clove garlic, peeled and minced
1 egg, lightly beaten
1 tablespoon tahini (sesame seed paste)
1 cup fine dry bread crumbs (optional)
Cooking oil or vegetable shortening for deep fat frying

Pat chick-peas dry between several thicknesses paper toweling, then purée by buzzing 20–30 seconds in an electric blender at high speed or 15–20 seconds in a food processor fitted with the metal chopping blade. Add all remaining ingredients except dry bread crumbs and cooking oil, and mix well. Cover and refrigerate 30 minutes. Shape into 12 little links about 2″ long and 1″ wide or roll into balls and flatten slightly. Dredge, if you like, in dry crumbs; let stand on wax paper. Heat oil in a deep fat fryer *without basket* to 365° F. on a deep fat thermometer. Place 3 or 4 croquettes in oil and fry 2–3 minutes, turning as needed so they brown and crispen evenly. Remove with a slotted spoon to paper toweling, then keep warm while you fry the balance. Serve hot in pita bread.

NP Falafel: 140 C, 25 mg CH, 260 mg S*

VARIATION

Falafel Appetizers *(30 balls):* Using a rounded teaspoon as a measure, shape mixture into small balls, then fry about 1 minute until crisp and brown. Good with Sour Cream-Cucumber Sauce or a bowl of yogurt for dipping.

FLORIDA BLACK BEANS AND PEPPERS

6 servings   ¢

If you like black bean soup, you will also like black beans prepared this way with minced green and red peppers.

1 pound dried black beans, boiled but not drained
½ cup olive or other cooking oil
1 large Spanish onion, peeled and sliced thin
2 large sweet green peppers, cored, seeded, and chopped fine
1 large sweet red pepper, cored, seeded, and chopped fine
1 clove garlic, peeled and crushed
1 teaspoon salt (about)
⅛ teaspoon pepper
½ cup cider vinegar
2 tablespoons sugar

Keep beans warm in their cooking liquid. Heat oil in a large skillet over moderate heat 1 minute. Add onion, peppers, and garlic, sauté 5–8 minutes until onion is pale golden, then stir into beans. Add salt and pepper, cover, and simmer 45 minutes. Mix in vinegar and sugar, re-cover, and simmer 5–10 minutes longer.

NPS: 460 C, 0 mg CH, 395 mg S*

BRAZILIAN BLACK BEANS

4 servings   ⊠

6 slices bacon, cut crosswise in julienne strips
1 medium-size yellow onion, peeled and coarsely chopped
1 clove garlic, peeled and crushed
2 bay leaves
2 (1-pound) cans black beans (drain 1 can)
1 tablespoon white corn meal
1 tablespoon cider vinegar
⅛ teaspoon crushed hot red chili peppers

Brown bacon in a large, heavy skillet over moderate heat and drain on paper toweling. Pour off all but 2 tablespoons drippings, add onion and garlic to skillet, and stir-fry 8 minutes until golden. Add remaining ingredients, turn heat to low, and simmer, uncovered, stirring occasionally, about 15 minutes. Serve, topping each portion with bacon.

NPS: 540 C, 10 mg CH, 855 mg S*

BEAN SPROUTS

Integral to Oriental cooking for nearly 3,000 years, the white, cream, and yellow sprouts of *mung, azuki,* and *soybeans* add crisp succulence and nutlike flavor to salads, stir-fried meats and vegetables. Sprouted in water, they are clean and require little preparation.

To Prepare for Cooking: Rinse sprouts in a sieve under cold running water; drain well and dry between paper toweling. *Storage Tip:* Store in the refrigerator in a plastic bag or in a jar with a tight-fitting lid.

To Cook: Add to stir-fried recipes 2–3 minutes before cooking is completed and toss mixture constantly so sprouts remain crisp.

BEETS

To the ancient Greeks, the beet was a food fit for the gods (it was, in fact, the one vegetable considered worthy enough to offer the god Apollo). The first beet recipes come to us from Apicius, the first-century Roman epicure whose cookbook is still sold today. These ancients, however, ate the greens and threw away the beet (it remained for the Russians and Germans to discover how delicious the roots were). Today we have learned to enjoy both the sweet crimson beet root and the crinkly-tart green tops.

To Prepare for Cooking:

Beets: Cut off all but 1″ of the tops and leave root ends on so beets won't fade. Scrub in cold water, taking care not to break skins. Do not peel.

Greens: Sort, discarding coarse stems and blemished leaves, then wash by plunging up and down in cool water. To perk up limp leaves, soak briefly in ice water.

BOILED BEETS

4 servings   ¢

2 pounds beets, prepared for cooking
1½ teaspoons salt
1 quart boiling water
2 tablespoons butter or margarine
Pinch pepper

Place beets, salt, and boiling water in a large saucepan, cover, and boil 35–45 minutes until tender. Drain, plunge in cold water 1–2 minutes, then peel and remove any stem or root ends. If beets are small, leave whole; if not, slice thin. Return to pan, add butter and pepper, and warm, uncovered, shaking pan gently, until butter melts and gilds beets.

NPS: 115 C, 15 mg CH, 375 mg S*

To Parboil for Use in Other Recipes: Boil as directed but reduce cooking time to 20–25 minutes.

VARIATIONS

¢ **To Serve Cold:** Cook, drain, and plunge in cold water as directed. When cool, peel, remove root and stem ends, and, if you like, slice. Toss with about 1 cup good tart dressing and chill 2–3 hours. Recipe too flexible for meaningful nutritional count.

¢ **Orange-Glazed Beets:** Boil, drain, and peel as directed; stir ¼ cup orange marmalade into beets with butter and warm, uncovered, shaking pan gently, about 5 minutes until beets are glazed.

NPS: 170 C, 15 mg CH, 375 mg S*

¢ **Beets with Sour Cream and Dill:** Boil, drain, and peel; reduce butter to 1 tablespoon and stir in ⅓ cup sour cream and 1 tablespoon minced dill. Warm 2–3 minutes (but do not boil) and serve.

NPS: 130 C, 15 mg CH, 355 mg S*

¢ **Beets with Horseradish:** Cook, drain, and peel; mix 2 tablespoons each prepared horseradish and white wine vinegar into beets along with butter. Warm and serve.

NPS: 120 C, 15 mg CH, 385 mg S*

BAKED BEETS

4 servings ¢

Baked beets are mellower, sweeter, nuttier than the boiled.

2 pounds beets, prepared for cooking
1 teaspoon salt
Pinch pepper
2 tablespoons butter or margarine

Preheat oven to 350° F. Place beets in a roasting pan, cover with foil, and bake 2–2½ hours until tender. Cool until easy to handle (if you're in a hurry, plunge in ice water), then peel. If the beets are small, leave whole; otherwise slice, dice, or cut in julienne strips. Place in a saucepan with salt, pepper, and butter and warm, uncovered, over low heat, shaking pan gently, 2–3 minutes.

NPS: 115 C, 15 mg CH, 715 mg S*

HARVARD BEETS

4–6 servings ¢

½ cup sugar
2 tablespoons cornstarch

1 teaspoon salt
¼ teaspoon pepper
1 cup cider vinegar
¼ cup water
¼ cup butter or margarine
2 pounds boiled fresh beets, peeled and diced or cut in julienne strips, or 2 (1-pound) cans julienne beets, drained

Mix sugar, cornstarch, salt, and pepper in a large saucepan and slowly stir in vinegar. Add water and butter and cook, stirring, over moderate heat until thickened and clear. Reduce heat to low, add beets, cover, and simmer 15 minutes.

NPS (4–6): 285–190 C, 30–20 mg CH, 775–515 mg S*

HOT SPICY SHREDDED BEETS

4 servings

Particularly good with pork, poultry, or ham.

2 pounds beets, trimmed, peeled, and coarsely grated
½ cup coarsely grated onion
3 tablespoons butter or margarine
½ cup water
¼ cup dry red wine
Juice of ½ lemon
¼ teaspoon cinnamon
¼ teaspoon nutmeg
½ teaspoon salt
⅛ teaspoon pepper

Simmer all ingredients, covered, 25–30 minutes until beets are tender and flavors well blended. Stir once or twice during cooking.

NPS: 155 C, 25 mg CH, 475 mg S*

BEETS BAKED WITH SOUR CREAM AND CARAWAY SEEDS

4–6 servings

2 pounds fresh beets, boiled, peeled, and diced, or 2 (1-pound) cans julienne beets, drained
1½ cups sour cream
1 teaspoon caraway seeds
Pinch nutmeg or mace

Preheat oven to 350° F. Mix beets with remaining ingredients and spoon into an ungreased small casserole. Bake, uncovered, 20–25 minutes to heat through.

NPS (4–6): 255–170 C, 35–25 mg CH, 155–100 mg S*

BEETS IN BURGUNDY

3 servings   ☒

Spicy, finely cut beets in dry red wine.

1 (1-pound) can julienne beets (do not drain)
1 tablespoon cornstarch
1/3 cup sugar
1/8 teaspoon cloves
Pinch salt
1/4 cup red wine vinegar
1/2 cup red burgundy wine
2 tablespoons butter or margarine

Drain beets, saving 1/4 cup liquid. Mix cornstarch, sugar, cloves, and salt in a saucepan, slowly add beet liquid, vinegar, and wine, and cook, stirring, over moderate heat until thickened and clear. Add beets and butter, turn heat to low, cover, and simmer 15 minutes to blend flavors.

NPS: 210 C, 20 mg CH, 405 mg S*

STEAMED BEET GREENS

(See recipe for Steamed Spinach.)

BREADFRUIT

In Florida, California, and large metropolitan areas, these big pebbly green-brown fruits are not unfamiliar. Their flesh is the color and texture of bread, tastes something like globe artichokes, and is best when boiled, mashed, creamed, or baked and stuffed.

To Prepare for Cooking: Scrub well, halve, and peel deep enough that no green shows. Cut around hard, stringy core and pull out. Leave as halves or cut in 1–1½" chunks.

To Boil: Cover with lightly salted boiling water and boil, covered, until tender: about 2–2½ hours for halves, 1½–1¾ hours for chunks. Drain, season with butter, salt, and pepper, and serve.

To Parboil for Use in Other Recipes: Boil as directed, reducing cooking time to 1¼ hours for halves, 1 hour for chunks.

To Mash: Boil chunks as directed, increasing time to 2 hours so they are very soft. Drain, mash with a potato masher, and mix with a little cream, butter, salt, and pepper.

To Cream: Boil chunks as directed, drain, and mix with 1½ cups hot Medium White Sauce.

To Bake and Stuff: Parboil halves and drain; fill with any mixture you would use for stuffing yellow squash, wrap halves in foil, and bake 30–40 minutes at 350° F. Unwrap and serve, allowing a half for each person.

BROCCOLI

First cousin to cauliflower, second cousin to cabbage, broccoli was almost unknown in this country until the late 1920s, when an enterprising Italian farmer in California began advertising his broccoli crop over the radio. Most widely available is the *"heading" green variety* with thick stalks; sometimes available, the *purple "hearting" broccoli,* which looks more like cauliflower. It is blander than green broccoli and has an almost buttery texture. *Broccoli di rapa* is a pungent, somewhat bitter, nonheading Italian spring green, a leafy broccoli that can be prepared and cooked like spinach.

To Prepare for Cooking: Discard coarse stem ends and leaves. Wash broccoli in cold water; separate into stalks of about the same size and make deep X-cuts in the base of each so they'll cook as quickly as the tender heads.

STEAMED BROCCOLI

4 servings

1 (2-pound) head broccoli, prepared for cooking
1¼ cups boiling water
½ teaspoon salt
⅛ teaspoon pepper
3 tablespoons butter or margarine

Arrange broccoli, alternating heads and stems, 1 layer deep in a large, heavy skillet. Add water and salt, cover, and simmer 12–15 minutes until crisp-tender. Drain, return to pan, season with pepper and butter, and warm over low heat just until butter is melted. Taste for salt and add more if needed.

NPS: 115 C, 25 mg CH, 195 mg S*

To Parboil for Use in Other Recipes: Steam as directed, reducing cooking time to 8–10 minutes. Omit seasonings.

VARIATIONS

To Serve Cold: Steam as directed, then chill in ice water. Drain, pat dry on paper toweling, cover, and refrigerate until ready to use. Serve as an appetizer, vegetable, or salad. Sauce with Aioli, Chiffon, Ravigote, or

Spanish Vinaigrette. Recipe too flexible for meaningful nutritional count.

⚖️ **Low-Calorie Steamed Broccoli:** Dress with seasoned salt or low-calorie Italian dressing instead of butter.
NPS: 40 C, 0 mg CH, 180 mg S*

Broccoli Amandine: Increase butter to 1/3 cup, melt over moderate heat, and in it sauté 1/3 cup slivered blanched almonds, stirring, 3–5 minutes until golden brown. Add 1 tablespoon lemon juice, the pepper, and pour over drained broccoli.
NPS: 240 C, 40 mg CH, 260 mg S*

STEAMED BROCCOLI DI RAPA

4 servings

2 pounds broccoli di rapa, washed
1 cup boiling water
1/4 teaspoon salt
1/8 teaspoon pepper
3 tablespoons butter or margarine

Remove tough stems and coarse leaf veins; coarsely chop leaves. Simmer with water and salt in a covered saucepan 5–8 minutes until crisp-tender. Drain well, return to pan, season with pepper and butter, and warm over low heat until butter melts. Taste for salt and add more, if needed. Nutritional count for broccoli di rapa not available, but probably as low as spinach.

VARIATION

Italian-Style Broccoli di Rapa: Trim leaves as directed, then chop fine. Sauté 2 cloves peeled and minced garlic and 1/2 cup minced yellow onion in 1/4 cup rich, fruity olive oil over moderately high heat 3–4 minutes until limp. Add broccoli di rapa, reduce heat to moderate, and stir-fry 2–3 minutes. Cover skillet and steam 4–5 minutes until tender. Season to taste with salt and pepper, then add 2 tablespoons butter and toss lightly until butter melts. Nutritional count not available for broccoli di rapa.

BROCCOLI PARMIGIANA

4 servings

1 (2-pound) head broccoli, steamed, or 2 (10-ounce) packages frozen broccoli spears, boiled and drained

SAUCE
3 tablespoons butter or margarine
3 tablespoons flour

1 1/2 cups milk
1 egg yolk, lightly beaten
3/4 teaspoon salt
1/8 teaspoon white pepper
3/4 cup grated Parmesan cheese

TOPPING
3/4 cup soft white bread crumbs mixed with 2 tablespoons grated Parmesan cheese

While broccoli cooks, melt butter for sauce over moderate heat and blend in flour. Add milk and heat, stirring, until thickened. Mix a little sauce into yolk, stir back into sauce in pan, and mix in remaining sauce ingredients. Cook and stir 1 minute but do not boil. Preheat broiler. Spoon a little sauce into an unbuttered shallow 1 1/2-quart casserole, add broccoli, pour in remaining sauce, and sprinkle with topping. Broil 4" from the heat 2–3 minutes until flecked with brown.
NPS: 310 C, 120 mg CH, 950 mg S*

VARIATION

Eggs and Broccoli Parmigiana: For a light entree, arrange 4 soft poached eggs on broccoli before adding sauce and topping.
NPS: 390 C, 390 mg CH, 1,100 mg S*

CASTILIAN SAUTÉED BROCCOLI WITH RIPE OLIVES

4 servings

1 (2-pound) head broccoli, parboiled and drained
1 small clove garlic, peeled and crushed
2 tablespoons olive oil
1 tablespoon butter or margarine
3/4 cup thinly sliced, pitted ripe olives
1/4 teaspoon salt (about)

Cut broccoli in 2" lengths. Sauté garlic in oil and butter in a large skillet over moderate heat 1 minute, add broccoli, and stir-fry 5–7 minutes. Add olives, stir gently, cover, and let steam 3–4 minutes. Add salt to taste and serve.
NPS: 170 C, 8 mg CH, 390 mg S*

VARIATION

Sautéed Broccoli with Parmesan: Cook broccoli by the recipe above, leaving out olives. Just before serving, squeeze a lemon wedge over broccoli and sprinkle with about 1/3 cup grated Parmesan cheese.
NPS: 155 C, 15 mg CH, 325 mg S*

BROCCOLI WITH PEANUT BUTTER SAUCE

4 servings ⊠

Peanut butter may sound an odd seasoning for broccoli, but when smoothed into a golden brown sauce, it brings out the best in the broccoli.

1 (2-pound) head broccoli, steamed, or 2 (10-ounce) packages frozen broccoli spears, boiled
1/3 cup butter or margarine
2 tablespoons chopped, toasted, blanched peanuts
2 tablespoons cream-style peanut butter

Drain broccoli, place in a heated serving dish, and keep warm. Melt butter over moderately low heat, add peanuts, and sauté 2–3 minutes. Blend in peanut butter, reduce heat to low, and heat, stirring, about 2 minutes. Pour over broccoli and serve.

NPS: 235 C, 40 mg CH, 240 mg S*

OSAKA SKILLET BROCCOLI

2–4 servings ⊠

Chilled, this makes an unusually good hors d'oeuvre.

1 (2-pound) head broccoli, prepared for cooking
1/4 cup peanut oil
1 clove garlic, peeled and crushed
2 (1/2") cubes fresh gingerroot, peeled and crushed
1/4 cup water
2 tablespoons Japanese soy or teriyaki sauce

Divide broccoli into small flowerets (save stalks for soup). Heat oil in a large heavy skillet over moderate heat 1 minute, add garlic and ginger, and stir-fry 1 minute. Add broccoli and remaining ingredients, cover, and simmer 8–10 minutes until crisp-tender. Serve, topping each portion with a little pan liquid.

NPS (2–4): 335–170 C, 0 mg CH, 675–335 mg S*

BROCCOLI BAKED IN MUSTARD SAUCE

8 servings

2 (2-pound) heads broccoli, parboiled and drained (reserve cooking liquid)

S A U C E
1/4 cup butter or margarine
1/4 cup unsifted flour
Broccoli cooking liquid + enough milk to measure 2 1/4 cups
1/4 cup dry vermouth

1 cup coarsely grated Gruyère cheese
2 tablespoons prepared mild yellow mustard
2 tablespoons prepared spicy brown mustard
1/4 teaspoon salt
1/8 teaspoon cayenne pepper

T O P P I N G
1/4 cup fine dry bread crumbs mixed with 1 tablespoon melted butter or margarine

Preheat oven to 375° F. Cut broccoli in 2" lengths and place in a buttered shallow 2 1/2-quart casserole. Melt butter over moderate heat and blend in flour. Add broccoli cooking liquid-milk mixture and heat, stirring, until thickened. Mix in remaining sauce ingredients and pour over broccoli. Sprinkle with topping and bake, uncovered, 35–40 minutes until browned and bubbling.

NPS: 195 C, 35 mg CH, 335 mg S*

BROCCOLI, EGG, AND SOUR CREAM CASSEROLE

4 servings

1 (2-pound) head broccoli, steamed, drained, and coarsely chopped, or 2 (10-ounce) packages frozen chopped broccoli, boiled and drained
2 hard-cooked eggs, peeled and sliced
1 cup sour cream
1/2 cup mayonnaise
2 tablespoons tarragon vinegar
1/8 teaspoon paprika

Preheat oven to 350° F. Arrange broccoli in an ungreased shallow 1 1/2-quart casserole, top with egg slices, and set aside. Over lowest heat warm sour cream with mayonnaise and vinegar, stirring, 4–5 minutes (do not boil); pour over broccoli. Bake, uncovered, 10 minutes, sprinkle with paprika, and serve.

NPS: 400 C, 180 mg CH, 260 mg S*

BROCCOLI CREPES AU GRATIN

4 servings

For a small luncheon an elegant entree that's not difficult to make.

1/2 (2-pound) head broccoli, steamed and coarsely chopped, or 1 (10-ounce) package frozen chopped broccoli, boiled and drained
1 recipe Crepes for Savory Fillings, or 8 (6") thin pancakes made from any pancake mix
1 teaspoon salt
1/8 teaspoon pepper
1 hard-cooked egg, peeled and sliced thin
1 1/4 cups Mushroom Sauce

1/4 cup light cream
1/2 cup coarsely grated sharp Cheddar cheese

Preheat oven to 350° F. Spoon a little broccoli in the center of each pancake, sprinkle with salt and pepper, and top with a slice of egg. Roll pancakes up and place, seam side down, in a buttered 1 1/2-quart *au gratin* dish or shallow casserole. Blend sauce with cream, spoon over crepes, and sprinkle with cheese. Bake, uncovered, 20–25 minutes until bubbly, then broil 3" from the heat 2–3 minutes to brown.

NPS: 395 C, 270 mg CH, 1,175 mg S*

VARIATION

Asparagus Crepes au Gratin: Prepare as directed, substituting 2 pounds poached asparagus, or 2 (10-ounce) packages frozen asparagus spears for broccoli. Lay 2 or 3 stalks across center of each crepe, then season, top with egg, roll, and proceed as directed.

NPS: 410 C, 270 mg CH, 1,160 mg S*

BRUSSELS SPROUTS

Little more than a curiosity in this country until frozen foods made them widely available, these baby cabbages have long been popular abroad. French royalty used to reject any larger than a pea, Belgians insist yet that they be the size of a grape.

To Prepare for Cooking: Since most sprouts are washed and trimmed before they're packed, about all that's needed is a quick sorting to remove withered leaves. Trim off stems (but not too close or sprouts will fall apart). To ensure even cooking, make an X-cut in the base of each sprout with the point of a knife. Rinse sprouts in cold, lightly salted water, then drain well.

BOILED BRUSSELS SPROUTS

4–6 servings

1 quart Brussels sprouts, prepared for cooking
1 1/2 cups boiling water
1 teaspoon salt
1/4 teaspoon pepper
2 tablespoons butter or margarine

Place sprouts in a saucepan with water and salt, cover, and boil gently 15–20 minutes until crisp-tender. Drain, season with pepper and butter, and serve.

NPS (4–6): 90–60 C, 15–10 mg CH, 215–145 mg S*

To Parboil for Use in Other Recipes: Follow recipe above but cut cooking time in half. Omit seasonings.

VARIATIONS

⚗ **Low-Calorie Brussels Sprouts:** Season with 1–2 tablespoons lemon juice or tarragon vinegar and a pinch of nutmeg instead of butter.

NPS (4–6): 40–25 C, 0 mg CH, 155–105 mg S*

Brussels Sprouts Parmigiana: Boil and drain as directed but do not season. Place sprouts in a buttered 2-quart casserole, top with 1/2 cup melted butter and 1/3 cup grated Parmesan. Bake, uncovered, 15 minutes at 350° F.

NPS (4–6): 270–180 C, 55–35 mg CH, 510–340 mg S*

Dilled Sprouts in Sour Cream: Boil and drain as directed but do not season. Quarter each sprout or, if small, halve. Return to pan and stir in 1 1/2 cups sour cream, 4 minced scallions, 2 teaspoons minced fresh dill (or 1/2 teaspoon of the dried), 1/2 teaspoon salt, and a pinch white pepper. Set over lowest heat, cover, and warm 5–7 minutes, taking care cream doesn't boil.

NPS (4–6): 230–155 C, 35–25 mg CH, 475–320 mg S*

BRUSSELS SPROUTS AU GRATIN

6 servings

1 quart fresh Brussels sprouts or 2 (10-ounce) packages frozen sprouts, boiled and drained
1 1/2 cups hot Cheese Sauce or Mornay Sauce
1/3 cup coarsely grated sharp Cheddar cheese
1 tablespoon melted butter or margarine

Preheat broiler. Arrange sprouts in an ungreased 1 1/2-quart *au gratin* dish or shallow casserole. Cover with sauce, sprinkle with cheese, and drizzle with butter. Broil 4"–5" from the heat 3–4 minutes until lightly browned.

NPS (cheese): 255 C, 60 mg CH, 440 mg S*
NPS (Mornay): 200 C, 45 mg CH, 330 mg S*

BRUSSELS SPROUTS WITH CHESTNUTS

6 servings

1 quart fresh Brussels sprouts or 2 (10-ounce) packages frozen sprouts, boiled and drained
2 tablespoons butter or margarine
1 tablespoon flour
1/2 cup chicken broth
Pinch salt
Pinch pepper

1 teaspoon lemon juice
1 cup coarsely chopped cooked fresh or frozen
    Italian chestnuts or canned chestnuts

Return sprouts to pan and keep warm. Melt butter over moderate heat and blend in flour. Add chicken broth slowly and cook, stirring until slightly thickened. Mix in remaining ingredients, pour over sprouts, toss lightly, and serve.

NPS: 105 C, 10 mg CH, 140 mg S*

BRUSSELS SPROUTS IN ONION SAUCE (SOUBISE)

6 servings

3 large yellow onions, peeled and quartered
1/2 cup boiling water
2 tablespoons butter or margarine
1/2 cup hot Béchamel Sauce or Medium White
    Sauce
1/4 teaspoon salt (about)
Pinch white pepper
1 quart Brussels sprouts, boiled and drained

Simmer onions, covered, in water and butter 45 minutes until mushy. Uncover, boil slowly to reduce liquid to 1/4 cup, then purée all by buzzing 10–15 seconds in an electric blender at low speed or 5–10 seconds in a food processor fitted with the metal chopping blade. Mix Béchamel or White Sauce, salt, and pepper into onion purée; taste for salt and add more if needed. Place sprouts in an ungreased shallow 1 1/2-quart casserole, top with onion purée mixture, cover, and bake 15–20 minutes, stirring once or twice.

NPS: 125 C, 20 mg CH, 225 mg S*

VARIATION

Just before serving, sprinkle casserole with 1/2 cup finely grated sharp Cheddar cheese and broil 4"–5" from the heat 2–3 minutes to brown.

NPS: 165 C, 30 mg CH, 285 mg S*

CABBAGE

Few vegetables are surrounded by more legends than cabbage. According to Greek myth, the first cabbage sprang from the tears of a prince whom Dionysus, god of wine, punished for trampling grapes. From this legend arose another—that cabbage could prevent drunkenness. Aristotle, it's said, dined well upon cabbage before setting out for a night on the town. And the Romans preceded their orgies by consuming quantities of cabbage. The cabbages of myth, how-ever, were sprawling varieties, not the firm round heads we know today. These were brought to America by English colonists and thrived so well in the New World they soon rivaled potatoes as "the most popular vege-table." Available to us today are not only the smooth green cabbage but also the crinkly green Savoy, the red and the long slim Chinese, or celery, cabbages. These are occasionally marketed as Napa cabbage, or by their Chinese *(Pe-Tsai)* or Japanese *(Hakusai)* names. *Pak Choi (Bok Choy),* sometimes called Chinese cabbage, is actually Chinese Chard.

To Prepare for Cooking: Strip away coarse or soiled outer leaves, halve head, and core. Slice, shred, or cut in thin wedges as individual recipes specify. For *Chinese cabbage,* cut off root end, separate stalks, cut or shred leaves, then slice stalks diagonally into 1" pieces.

Serving Tip: Instead of discarding cabbage cores, trim off woody bits, parboil 10–15 minutes in lightly salted water, cool, and slice into salads.

STEAMED GREEN OR RED CABBAGE

4–6 servings   ¢

Though many recipes recommend steaming cabbage 7 to 11 minutes, we've found it's really quite raw unless cooked for 25. If you like yours crisp and pungent, by all means use the shorter time. To make red cabbage really red, add a little lemon juice, vinegar (any flavor), or dry red wine to the cooking water.

1 medium-size cabbage, cored and cut in thin
    wedges or 1" slices
1 cup boiling water
3 tablespoons butter or margarine
1 teaspoon salt
Pinch pepper

Place cabbage in a large pot, add water, cover, and steam over moderate heat 20–25 minutes, stirring occasionally. Drain, add butter, salt, and pepper, return to heat, and warm, uncovered, tossing cabbage occasionally, 2–3 minutes.

NPS (Green, 4–6): 115–80 C, 25–15 mg CH, 670–445 mg S*
NPS (Red, 4–6): 120–85 C, 25–15 mg CH, 655–435 mg S*

To Parboil for Use in Other Recipes: Use method above but steam only 15 minutes; omit seasonings.

¢ ⚖ **Low-Calorie Cabbage:** *For the green,* reduce butter to 1 tablespoon. *For the red,* omit butter and dress with 2 tablespoons vinegar.

NPS (Green, 4–6): 65–45 C, 10–5 mg CH, 610–405 mg S*
NPS (Red, 4–6): 45–30 C, 0 mg CH, 570–380 mg S*

Austrian Cabbage: Steam and season green cabbage as directed above, then chop coarsely and mix in 1 cup sour cream and 2 teaspoons poppy seeds. Spoon into a buttered 3-quart casserole, cover, and bake 15–20 minutes at 350° F.

NPS (4–6): 250–165 C, 50–30 mg CH, 700–465 mg S*

Creamy Cabbage: Steam green cabbage by recipe above, adding butter to cooking water. Do not drain. Stir in salt, pepper, 1 cup light cream, and 1/4 teaspoon nutmeg. Heat, stirring, 5 minutes (do not boil). Serve in soup bowls with lots of the cooking liquid.

NPS (4–6): 235–155 C, 60–40 mg CH, 690–460 mg S*

CREOLE CABBAGE

4 servings

1 large yellow onion, peeled and minced
1 small sweet green pepper, cored, seeded, and minced
1 small sweet red pepper, cored, seeded, and minced
1 stalk celery, minced (do not include top)
1 clove garlic, peeled and crushed
2 tablespoons cooking oil
3–4 ripe tomatoes, peeled, seeded, and coarsely chopped
1 small cabbage, shredded medium fine
1 1/2 teaspoons salt
1/8 teaspoon pepper

Stir-fry onion, sweet peppers, celery, and garlic in the oil in a large kettle 5–8 minutes until onion is pale golden. Add tomatoes and stir-fry 2 minutes; add cabbage, salt, and pepper, cover, turn heat to low, and simmer 15–20 minutes until cabbage is tender.

NPS: 140 C, 0 mg CH, 870 mg S*

PENNSYLVANIA DUTCH CABBAGE KNABRUS

4 servings　　¢

1/4 cup bacon drippings, butter, or margarine
1 small cabbage, shredded medium fine
3 medium-size yellow onions, peeled and sliced thin
1 teaspoon salt
1/4 teaspoon pepper

Melt fat in a large kettle over moderate heat, layer cabbage and onions into kettle, sprinkling each with salt. Cover and simmer 15–20 minutes, stirring once or twice, until cabbage is tender. Season with pepper, taste for salt, and add more if needed.

NPS: 145 C, 10 mg CH, 640 mg S*

COLCANNON

4 servings　　¢

Originally, Colcannon was a leftover dish, the mashed potatoes and cabbage or kale being stirred up and set in the oven to warm while the supper cooked.

1 small cabbage, steamed and chopped fine
2 cups hot seasoned mashed potatoes
2 tablespoons bacon drippings, butter, or margarine
1/4 teaspoon salt
Pinch white pepper

Preheat oven to 400° F. Mix cabbage with remaining ingredients, spoon into a well-buttered 1 1/2-quart casserole, and roughen surface with a fork. Bake, uncovered, 35–45 minutes until lightly browned.

NPS: 170 C, 5 mg CH, 535 mg S*

VARIATIONS

• Follow recipe above, substituting 1 1/2 pounds kale, steamed and finely chopped, for the cabbage.

NPS: 235 C, 5 mg CH, 640 mg S*

• Follow recipe above, stirring 1–2 tablespoons minced parsley into Colcannon before baking. Nutritional count same as basic recipe.
• Follow recipe above, adding 1–2 finely chopped, steamed leeks (they can be steamed in the same pot with the cabbage).

NPS: 175 C, 5 mg CH, 535 mg S*

SCALLOPED CABBAGE

6 servings ¢

The perfect companion for roast pork or ham.

1 medium-size cabbage, cut in 1/2″ slices, parboiled, and drained (save cooking water)

S A U C E
1/4 cup butter or margarine
1/4 cup unsifted flour
1 teaspoon salt
1/8 teaspoon mace
Pinch cayenne pepper
Pinch black pepper
Cabbage cooking water + enough milk to total 2 cups

T O P P I N G
1 cup toasted fine bread crumbs mixed with 3 tablespoons melted butter or margarine

Preheat oven to 350° F. Place cabbage in an ungreased 2-quart *au gratin* dish or shallow casserole and set aside. Melt butter and blend in flour, salt, mace, and peppers. Add the 2 cups liquid and heat, stirring, over moderate heat until thickened. Pour over cabbage, sprinkle with topping, and bake, uncovered, 30 minutes until bubbly.

NPS: 230 C, 35 mg CH, 645 mg S*

SPICY EAST INDIAN BAKED CABBAGE

4 servings

Here's an unusual vegetable to serve with curry.

4 cups finely chopped cabbage
1 medium-size yellow onion, peeled and minced
1 teaspoon salt
1/4 cup flaked coconut
1/2 teaspoon chili powder
1/4 teaspoon turmeric
Very small pinch crushed hot red chili peppers
2 eggs, lightly beaten
1/4 cup cold water

Preheat oven to 350° F. Mix all ingredients and spoon into a buttered 1 1/2-quart casserole. Cover and bake about 50 minutes until cabbage is tender; uncover and bake 10 minutes longer to crispen surface slightly.

NPS: 85 C, 135 mg CH, 605 mg S*

SWEET AND SOUR RED CABBAGE

4–6 servings ¢

1 medium-size red cabbage, sliced very thin
2/3 cup boiling water
3 tablespoons butter or margarine
1/4 cup red wine vinegar
1/2 teaspoon caraway seeds
1/8 teaspoon salt
1/8 teaspoon pepper
2 teaspoons light brown sugar
1/8 teaspoon nutmeg

Place all ingredients in a large pot, toss to mix, cover, and simmer, stirring once or twice, 15–20 minutes until cabbage is crisp-tender. Serve hot in soup bowls with plenty of the cooking liquid.

NPS (4–6): 135–90 C, 25–15 mg CH, 180–120 mg S*

RED CABBAGE AND CHESTNUTS

6 servings

This combination of cabbage and chestnuts goes particularly well with game. *Note:* If you use the shelled and peeled frozen Italian chestnuts (available in many specialty food shops), you'll spare yourself a nasty peeling job. These chestnuts only need be boiled 10 minutes.

1 medium-size red cabbage, shredded medium fine
3/4 cup beef broth
2 teaspoons cider vinegar
1/2 teaspoon salt
1/4 teaspoon pepper
18–20 chestnuts, boiled, peeled, and coarsely chopped
2 tablespoons bacon drippings

Place cabbage, broth, vinegar, salt, and pepper in a large pot, cover, and simmer 20–25 minutes until cabbage is barely tender. Mix in chestnuts and drippings and boil, uncovered, 5–7 minutes until most of the liquid has evaporated.

NPS: 70 C, 5 mg CH, 315 mg S*

V A R I A T I O N

Savoy Cabbage and Chestnuts: Follow recipe above, substituting Savoy cabbage for the red and reducing simmering time to 15 minutes.

NPS: 65 C, 5 mg CH, 325 mg S*

FLEMISH RED CABBAGE AND APPLES

4–6 servings

If you make this recipe a day or so ahead, then reheat slowly in a covered kettle, it will taste even better.

1 small red cabbage, shredded medium fine
1/2 large Spanish onion, peeled and sliced thin
4 apples (Baldwin, McIntosh, or Jonathan), peeled, cored, and sliced thin
1/4 cup firmly packed dark brown sugar
1 1/2–2 teaspoons salt
1/2 cup dry red wine or red wine vinegar
2 tablespoons butter or margarine
Pinch pepper

Place cabbage, onion, apples, sugar, 1 1/2 teaspoons salt, and wine in a large, heavy kettle, toss to mix, cover, and boil slowly, stirring once or twice, 20–25 minutes until cabbage is just tender. Mix in butter and pepper; taste for salt and add more if needed.

NPS (4–6): 225–150 C, 15–10 mg CH, 900–600 mg S*

STEAMED CHINESE CABBAGE

4 servings

2–3 heads Chinese cabbage, cut crosswise into fine shreds
1/2 cup boiling water
3/4 teaspoon salt
Pinch pepper
2 tablespoons butter or margarine

Place cabbage, water, and salt in a large saucepan, cover, and steam slowly 7–9 minutes until crisp-tender. Drain, add pepper and butter, and shake pan, uncovered, over low heat 1–2 minutes until butter melts and gilds cabbage.

NPS: 75 C, 15 mg CH, 230 mg S*

To Parboil for Use in Other Recipes: Steam as directed above, reducing cooking time to 5 minutes; omit seasonings.

V A R I A T I O N

⚖ **Low-Calorie Chinese Cabbage:** Omit salt and butter and dress with a sprinkling of seasoned salt or drizzling of low-calorie Italian or herb dressing.

NPS: 25 C, 0 mg CH, 60 mg S*

SAUTÉED CHINESE CABBAGE WITH SESAME SEEDS

4 servings

3 tablespoons peanut or other cooking oil
2–3 heads Chinese cabbage, shredded fine
1 teaspoon sesame seeds
2 teaspoons Japanese soy sauce

Heat oil in a large, heavy skillet or *wok* over moderately low heat 1 minute, add cabbage, and stir-fry 4 minutes. Add sesame seeds and stir-fry 1 minute. Mix in soy sauce. Cabbage should be crisp-tender; if not, stir-fry 1–2 minutes longer.

NPS: 120 C, 0 mg CH, 260 mg S*

V A R I A T I O N

Follow recipe above, stir-frying 6–8 minced scallions (include green tops) along with the cabbage.

NPS: 130 C, 0 mg CH, 260 mg S*

SAUERKRAUT

Sauerkraut isn't, as most of us think, a German invention. The Chinese stumbled upon the recipe centuries ago while the Great Wall was being built. Among the laborers' rations was a mixture of shredded cabbage and rice wine which, over the weeks, softened and soured into the world's first kraut.

To Prepare for Cooking: Always taste sauerkraut before cooking or heating. If it seems too salty (the fresh often is), soak 15 minutes in cold water, rinse, and drain.

To Cook Fresh Sauerkraut: Drain kraut, place in large saucepan, add just enough water, beef or chicken broth, or dry white wine to cover, and simmer, covered, 30–40 minutes until tender. Drain and serve (sauerkraut needs no additional seasoning).

To Heat Precooked Sauerkraut: Heat sauerkraut, covered, in its own liquid or, if salty, in 3/4–1 cup water or dry white wine 5–10 minutes. Drain and serve.

BRAISED SAUERKRAUT WITH JUNIPER BERRIES

4 servings

1¼ pounds sauerkraut, drained
¼ pound salt pork, cut in small dice
3 small white onions, each peeled and stuck with
  2 cloves
1 carrot, peeled and quartered
1 bay leaf, 1 sprig each parsley and thyme, and
  1 tablespoon juniper berries, tied in
  cheesecloth
½ cup beef broth
½ cup water

Preheat oven to 350° F. Squeeze sauerkraut as dry as possible. Brown salt pork in a heavy kettle over moderate heat; add sauerkraut and all remaining ingredients, cover, and bring to a boil. Transfer kettle to oven and bake, covered, 45–50 minutes, until onions are very tender. *(Note:* Check kettle occasionally and add a little hot water, if necessary, to keep it from boiling dry.) Discard carrot, cheesecloth bag, and cloves. Chop onions coarsely into sauerkraut and serve.

NPS: 255 C, 20 mg CH, 1,505 mg S*

CARDOONS

Few of us know these giant prickly green stalks, although in France and Italy they're as common as cauliflower. Cardoons are related to artichokes and, according to some botanists, they're the *original* artichoke. They are available, occasionally, in big-city specialty food shops and are a delicacy worth trying. Nutritional counts unavailable.

To Prepare for Cooking: Discard tough stalks and all leaves. Wash each stalk well, cut in 3″ lengths, remove stringy parts, and rub cut edges with lemon. Like celery stalks, cardoons have a heart; trim and quarter it.

To Cook Cardoons: Whether they're to be served in a salad or as a vegetable, cardoons must be cooked. Cover with lightly salted boiling water or chicken broth and simmer, covered, about 2 hours until tender. Drain. Chill and slice into salads, marinate in Vinaigrette or Italian Dressing, or use hot to prepare:

Herbed Cardoons: Toss cardoons with a little melted butter, minced chives, tarragon, or chervil, and salt and pepper to taste.

Sautéed Cardoons: Pat cardoons dry on paper toweling, then sauté 8–10 minutes in butter or olive oil until golden. Season with salt, pepper, and mace.

Breaded Cardoons: Dry cardoons on paper toweling, dip in beaten egg, roll in fine dry crumbs, and fry in deep fat (380° F.) 3–4 minutes until golden.

Sauced Cardoons: Warm cardoons in hot Béchamel or Mornay Sauce (1 cup sauce to 2 cups cardoons) 3–5 minutes, stirring.

CARROTS

When carrots first appeared in England some 350 years ago, ladies were so enchanted by the lacy tops they wore garlands of them in their hair. It was the English who brought carrots to America, the Indians who carried them cross country. Southwestern tribes grow much of today's crop, and to visit these areas at harvest time is to see miles of flatlands herringboned with the orange and green of freshly pulled carrots.

To Prepare for Cooking: Mature carrots should be peeled and trimmed of stem and root ends; young tender carrots need only be trimmed and scrubbed. Always try to cook carrots whole; if they seem too large, halve or quarter; if tough, slice, dice, or cut into julienne strips.

BOILED CARROTS

3–4 servings   ¢

6–8 medium-size carrots, prepared for cooking
1½ cups boiling water or beef or chicken broth
½ teaspoon salt
Pinch pepper
2 tablespoons butter or margarine

Boil carrots, covered, in lightly salted boiling water (or one of the alternate cooking liquids) as follows: 35–45 minutes for whole carrots; 20–25 for the halved or quartered; 10–15 for the thickly sliced; 5–10 for the thinly sliced, diced, or julienne. Drain, add seasonings, and warm, uncovered, over low heat 1–2 minutes until butter melts. *(Note:* When boiling cut carrots, reduce cooking liquid to 1 cup.)

NPS (3–4): 135–105 C, 20–15 mg CH, 225–170 mg S*

Boiled Baby Carrots: Follow method above and boil 8–10 minutes.

To Parboil for Use in Other Recipes: Use recipe above but boil whole carrots only 20–25 minutes; the halved or quartered 10; thickly sliced 7; thinly sliced, diced, julienne, or whole baby carrots 3–4. Omit seasonings.

¢ **To Serve Cold:** Boil and drain as directed, then chill in ice water. Drain, cover, and refrigerate. Dress with oil and lemon or lime juice.

⚖ ¢ **Low-Calorie Carrots:** Omit butter; dress with lemon or orange juice and/or 1 tablespoon minced chives.

NPS (3–4): 70–55 C, 0 mg CH, 150–110 mg S*

¢ **Lemon-Glazed Carrots:** Boil and drain carrots by above recipe and keep warm. Melt butter, mix in pepper, 1/4 cup light brown sugar, and 1/2 teaspoon grated lemon rind, and warm, stirring, 3–5 minutes until sugar dissolves. Pour over carrots and serve.

NPS (3–4): 205–155 C, 20–15 mg CH, 230–175 mg S*

¢ **Carrots Rosemary:** Boil and drain carrots as directed above. Return to heat, add pepper and butter, 1/2 teaspoon each minced fresh rosemary and summer savory (or 1/4 teaspoon of the dried), 1 tablespoon each lemon juice and light brown sugar. Warm over lowest heat, turning carrots now and then, about 5 minutes to glaze.

NPS (3–4): 155–115 C, 20–15 mg CH, 230–170 mg S*

MASHED CARROTS

4 servings

6–8 medium-size hot boiled carrots
1/4 teaspoon salt
2 tablespoons butter or margarine, softened to room temperature
2 tablespoons heavy cream
Pinch nutmeg or mace (optional)

Mash carrots with a potato masher, or purée by buzzing 15–20 seconds in an electric blender at high speed or 10–15 seconds in a food processor fitted with the metal chopping blade. Add all remaining ingredients and beat well with a fork.

NPS: 110 C, 25 mg CH, 245 mg S*

Mashed Carrots and Potatoes: Add 1 1/2 cups hot mashed potatoes to mashed carrots, mix in all seasonings, and beat until light.

NPS: 185 C, 25 mg CH, 505 mg S*

Mashed Carrots and Yams: Add 1 1/2 cups hot mashed yams or sweet potatoes, 2 tablespoons honey or maple syrup, and a pinch cinnamon to mashed carrots. Mix in the salt, butter, cream, and nutmeg and beat until light.

NPS: 225 C, 25 mg CH, 280 mg S*

Mashed Carrots and Rutabagas, Turnips, or Parsnips: Mix 1 1/2 cups hot mashed rutabagas, turnips, or parsnips into carrots, add all seasonings, and beat until light.

NPS: 140 C, 25 mg CH, 250 mg S*

CARROTS VICHY

4 servings

If you have a bottle of Vichy water, try cooking young carrots in it for particularly rich flavor. If not, use the following recipe, which substitutes tap water and a pinch of soda.

12–14 small young carrots, peeled
2 tablespoons sugar
1/2 teaspoon salt
1/2 cup boiling water
2 tablespoons butter or margarine
Pinch baking soda
Pinch white pepper
1 tablespoon minced parsley

Place carrots, sugar, salt, water, butter, and soda in a saucepan. Cover and boil gently 10–15 minutes until carrots are fork tender. Uncover and boil until almost all liquid is gone, shaking pan frequently so carrots become lightly glazed. Sprinkle with pepper and parsley and serve.

NPS: 125 C, 15 mg CH, 385 mg S*

HOT MACÉDOINE OF VEGETABLES

4–6 servings

A macédoine of vegetables is a mixture of cooked vegetables of similar size and shape. Usually they're diced, sometimes cut in diamonds or small balls. Almost any mixture can be used if the colors and flavors go well together (avoid using beets because their color runs).

1 cup diced cooked carrots
1 cup diced cooked turnips
1 cup diced cooked celery
1 cup cooked green peas
1 cup cooked baby limas
1 cup cooked green or wax beans, cut in 1/2" lengths
3–4 tablespoons butter or margarine
Salt
Pepper

Drain all vegetables well and place in a saucepan with butter and salt and pepper to taste. Warm over low heat 2–3 minutes, shaking pan, until butter melts and serve.

NPS (4–6): 200–135 C, 25–15 mg CH, 280–185 mg S*

VARIATION

Cold Macédoine of Vegetables: Chill cooked vegetables in ice water, drain, pat dry on paper toweling, and refrigerate until ready to use. Instead of seasoning with butter, salt, and pepper, dress with Spanish Vinaigrette Dressing or thin mayonnaise. Serve as a salad, cold vegetable, or hors d'oeuvre.

NPS (4–6): 220–145 C, 20–10 mg CH, 250–165 mg S*

FLEMISH-STYLE CARROTS

4 servings

Belgians have a particular talent with vegetables. Flemish-style carrots are sautéed in butter until faintly caramel, then seasoned with lemon so that they aren't too sweet.

1/4 cup butter or margarine
6–8 medium-size carrots, peeled and cut in matchstick strips
1/3 cup boiling water
1 tablespoon light brown sugar
1 teaspoon salt
1/8 teaspoon mace
2 egg yolks
1/2 cup light cream
1 tablespoon lemon juice

Melt butter in a large, heavy skillet over moderate heat, add carrots, and sauté, stirring, 12–15 minutes until lightly glazed. Add water, brown sugar, salt, and mace, cover, and simmer 8–10 minutes until carrots are crisp-tender. Uncover and cook 2 minutes longer. Beat egg yolks with cream, mix into carrots, season with lemon juice, and serve.

NPS: 255 C, 185 mg CH, 725 mg S*

CARROTS PROVENÇAL

4 servings

An unusual combination of carrots, onion, garlic, and tomatoes.

2 tablespoons olive or other cooking oil
1 medium-size yellow onion, peeled and chopped fine
1 clove garlic, peeled and crushed
2 ripe tomatoes, peeled, seeded, and coarsely chopped

6–8 medium-size carrots, cut in julienne strips and parboiled
1/2 teaspoon salt
1/8 teaspoon pepper

Heat oil in a large, heavy skillet over moderate heat 1 minute. Add onion and garlic and sauté 5–8 minutes until onion is pale golden. Add tomatoes, sauté 1–2 minutes, then add drained carrots, cover, reduce heat to low, and simmer 5 minutes until carrots are tender. Uncover and simmer 2–3 minutes longer, stirring. Season with salt and pepper and serve.

NPS: 135 C, 0 mg CH, 320 mg S*

CARROT AND ONION "PIE"

4 servings

6–8 medium-size carrots, peeled and halved or quartered
1 large yellow onion, peeled and coarsely chopped
1 1/2 cups boiling water
2 tablespoons melted butter or margarine
1 teaspoon salt (about)
1/8 teaspoon pepper
2 tablespoons butter or margarine
1 teaspoon minced parsley
1 teaspoon minced chervil (optional)

Preheat oven to 350° F. Boil carrots and onion in the water, covered, about 20 minutes until tender. Drain and purée by buzzing 20–25 seconds in an electric blender at high speed or 15–20 seconds in a food processor fitted with the metal chopping blade. Beat melted butter, salt, and pepper into carrot purée, taste for salt and add more if needed. Spoon into a well-buttered 9″ or 10″ piepan and dot with remaining butter. Bake, uncovered, 15–20 minutes. Sprinkle with parsley and, if you like, the chervil and serve.

NPS: 170 C, 30 mg CH, 715 mg S*

BAKED CARROTS AND RICE

6 servings

A mellow, crunchy combination of shredded carrots and rice that makes an unusual potato substitute.

1/4 cup butter or margarine
3 cups coarsely grated raw carrots
1/2 cup minced onion
1 teaspoon minced parsley
1 1/2 teaspoons salt
1/4 teaspoon summer savory
1/4 teaspoon mace
Pinch rosemary

Pinch pepper
3 tablespoons dry sherry
3 cups cooked rice
1 cup milk
2 eggs, lightly beaten

Preheat oven to 325° F. Melt butter in a large, heavy skillet over moderate heat, add carrots and onion, and sauté, stirring occasionally, about 15 minutes until carrots are crisp-tender. Mix in parsley, salt, savory, mace, rosemary, pepper, and sherry and heat, stirring, 1–2 minutes. Off heat, mix in rice. Beat milk with eggs, add to carrots, and stir until well blended. Spoon into a buttered 9″ × 9″ × 2″ baking dish, cover with foil, and set in a shallow pan; pour ½″ water into pan. Bake 45 minutes, remove foil, and bake 30 minutes longer.

NPS: 260 C, 115 mg CH, 690 mg S*

CAULIFLOWER

Snowy . . . succulent . . . a little bit sweet, a little bit nutty . . . that's cauliflower. "Cabbage with a college education," Mark Twain called it. Certainly it's the most elegant cabbage, a vegetable grown only for emperors and kings until twentieth-century farming made it available to all.

To Prepare for Cooking: Remove green leaves, cut off heavy stem close to base, and wash head well in cool water, holding it upside down. Leave head whole, making a deep X-cut in the base of the heavy stem to hasten cooking; or divide into bite-size flowerets, trimming each stem to a length of 1″.

Serving Tip: Try serving raw cauliflowerets with seasoned salt or Curry Dip as a cocktail hors d'oeuvre.

BOILED CAULIFLOWER

4 servings

Some say cauliflower should be cooked uncovered, some say it should be uncovered the first 5 minutes only, some say it should be covered at all times. We've tried all three ways and prefer the third because it minimizes the "cabbage-y" cooking odor. The same technique works for all members of the cabbage family.

1 large cauliflower, prepared for cooking
1½ cups boiling water
1 slice lemon (to keep cauliflower snowy)
½ teaspoon salt
⅛ teaspoon white pepper

Place cauliflower stem down in a large saucepan, add all but last ingredient, cover, and boil until crisp-tender: 20–30 minutes for a head, 5–7 for flowerets. Drain well. To keep head intact while transferring to serving dish, tilt pan and ease it out. Sprinkle with pepper, dress with Browned Butter, Béchamel, Cheese, or Hollandaise Sauce.

NPS (without butter or sauce): 40 C, 0 mg CH, 100 mg S*

To Steam Cauliflower: Place cauliflower on a rack in a steamer, pour in boiling water to a depth of 1″, cover, and steam head 30–40 minutes, flowerets 10–15.

To Parboil for Use in Other Recipes: Use either method above, reducing cooking times thus: boil heads 10 minutes, flowerets 3–5; steam heads 20 minutes, flowerets 7–10. Omit seasonings.

VARIATIONS

To Serve Cold: Chill boiled or steamed cauliflower in ice water, drain, and pat dry on paper toweling; refrigerate until ready to use. Serve as a salad or cold vegetable dressed with Aioli, Chiffon, Ravigote, or Spanish Vinaigrette Sauce. Recipe too flexible for meaningful nutritional count.

⚖ **Low-Calorie Cauliflower:** Boil or steam as directed, drain and dress with low-calorie herb or Italian dressing instead of butter or sauce. If you like, add a sprinkling of minced chives, parsley, or dill.

NPS (with dressing): 75 C, 0 mg CH, 215 mg S*

CAULIFLOWER POLONAISE

4–6 servings

1 large cauliflower, steamed and drained
2 tablespoons butter or margarine
1 cup soft white bread crumbs
2 hard-cooked eggs, peeled and chopped fine
1 tablespoon minced parsley

Transfer cauliflower to a vegetable dish and keep warm. Melt butter in a small skillet over moderate heat, add crumbs, and stir-fry 4–5 minutes until lightly browned. (*Note:* Crumbs brown slowly at first, quickly toward the end, so watch carefully.) Off heat, mix in eggs and parsley. Sprinkle crumb mixture over cauliflower and serve.

NPS (4–6): 180–120 C, 150–100 mg CH, 180–120 mg S*

CAULIFLOWER IN CIDER AND CREAM

4–6 servings

2 tablespoons butter or margarine
2 tablespoons flour
1 cup heavy cream
1/2 cup apple cider
1/2 teaspoon salt
Pinch white pepper
1 large cauliflower, divided into flowerets,
　parboiled, and drained

Melt butter in the top of a double boiler over simmering water and blend in flour; slowly mix in cream and cider. Heat, stirring, until thickened. Season with salt and pepper, add cauliflowerets, and toss gently to mix. Cover and warm, still over simmering water, 10–15 minutes to blend flavors.

NPS (4–6): 345–240 C, 95–65 mg CH, 385–255 mg S*

CAULIFLOWER CARUSO

4–6 servings

A piquant dish that goes well with veal cutlets, scaloppine, or broiled chicken.

1 large cauliflower, divided into flowerets, boiled
　and drained
1 small yellow onion, peeled and chopped fine
2 tablespoons olive or other cooking oil
1 tablespoon minced anchovies
1/4 cup dry white wine or chicken broth
1 tablespoon lemon juice
1 teaspoon minced parsley
1 teaspoon minced fresh chervil or 1/2 teaspoon
　dried chervil
1/2 teaspoon minced fresh basil or 1/4 teaspoon
　dried basil
Pinch pepper

Keep cauliflower warm. Sauté onion in oil in a large skillet over moderate heat 5–8 minutes until pale golden. Add anchovies and sauté 1 minute. Stir in wine or broth and lemon juice, reduce heat to low, cover, and simmer 10 minutes. Add cauliflower, mix gently, sprinkle with parsley, herbs, and pepper. Cover and simmer 5–7 minutes until heated through, basting cauliflower once or twice with sauce.

NPS (4–6): 135–90 C, 2–1 mg CH, 70–50 mg S*

PURÉED CAULIFLOWER À LA DUBARRY

4 servings

1 large cauliflower, boiled until very tender and
　drained
1 cup hot, seasoned mashed potatoes
1/4 cup heavy cream
2 tablespoons melted butter or margarine
1 teaspoon salt
1/8 teaspoon white pepper
Pinch mace
2 tablespoons butter or margarine

Preheat oven to 350° F. Purée cauliflower by buzzing 15–20 seconds in an electric blender at high speed or 10–15 seconds in a food processor fitted with the metal chopping blade. With a wooden spoon or wire whisk, beat purée with potatoes and cream until fluffy. Mix in melted butter, salt, pepper, and mace. Spoon into a buttered shallow 1 1/2-quart casserole and dot with butter. Bake, uncovered, 1 hour until golden brown.

NPS: 265 C, 50 mg CH, 875 mg S*

CAULIFLOWER AU GRATIN

4–6 servings

Such an easy, elegant recipe.

1 large cauliflower, divided into flowerets,
　boiled, and drained
1/2 teaspoon salt
1/8 teaspoon white pepper
1 1/2 cups hot Cheese Sauce or Mornay Sauce
1/3 cup coarsely grated sharp Cheddar cheese
1 tablespoon melted butter or margarine

Preheat broiler. Arrange flowerets in an ungreased *au gratin* dish or shallow casserole. Season with salt and pepper and cover evenly with sauce. Sprinkle with cheese and drizzle with butter. Broil 5″ from heat 3–4 minutes until cheese melts and is dappled with brown.

NPS (4–6 cheese): 410–270 C, 85–60 mg CH, 945–630 mg S*
NPS (4–6 Mornay): 320–215 C, 65–45 mg CH, 775–515 mg S*

VARIATION

After browning, top with 1/2 cup toasted, slivered almonds.

NPS (4–6 cheese): 505–325 C, 85–60 mg CH, 945–630 mg S*
NPS (4–6 Mornay): 420–280 C, 65–45 mg CH, 775–515 mg S*

CAULIFLOWER BAKED IN WINE AND CREAM SAUCE

4–6 servings

1½ cups chicken broth
1 large cauliflower, divided into flowerets
⅔ cup heavy cream (about)
¼ cup butter or margarine
¼ cup unsifted flour
Pinch mace
2 tablespoons dry white wine
½ cup finely grated Parmesan cheese
⅛ teaspoon salt
Pinch pepper

T O P P I N G
⅔ cup cracker meal
3 tablespoons melted butter or margarine
1 tablespoon finely grated Parmesan cheese

Bring broth to a boil in a large saucepan, add cauliflower, cover, and simmer 20–25 minutes until crisp-tender. Drain, reserving broth. Measure broth and add cream to make 2 cups. Melt butter over moderate heat and blend in flour and mace. Add broth mixture and heat, stirring, until thickened. Off heat, mix in wine, Parmesan, salt, and pepper. Arrange flowerets in an ungreased 2-quart *au gratin* dish and top with sauce. Mix topping and sprinkle over surface. Preheat broiler, then broil 5″ from heat 3–4 minutes until browned and bubbly.

NPS (4–6): 540–360 C, 115–75 mg CH, 825–550 mg S*

CELERIAC

(Also called Knob Celery, Turnip Celery, and German Celery)

Long treasured in Europe, this plump root celery is only now becoming popular in this country. It tastes like strong celery, has the texture of a turnip, and is best when creamed, puréed, prepared *au gratin,* or julienned raw and tossed in a Rémoulade Sauce (see salad chapter).

To Prepare for Cooking: Cut off all stalks and root ends and discard; scrub knob well in cool water, then peel (the skin is very tough and stringy). Slice, cube, or cut into julienne strips.

Cooking Tip: Substitute celeriac for celery in soups and stews.

Serving Tip: Marinate raw julienne strips of celeriac 2–3 hours in the refrigerator in a good tart dressing and serve in—or as—a salad.

BOILED CELERIAC

4 servings

If you've never tasted celeriac, try it one of these easy ways. You may discover that you like it very much.

3 knobs celeriac, prepared for cooking
1½ cups boiling water or chicken broth
1 teaspoon salt (about)
⅛ teaspoon white pepper
2 tablespoons melted butter or margarine

Place celeriac, water or broth, and salt (reduce to taste if you use broth) in a saucepan, cover, and boil until crisp-tender: 15 minutes for julienne strips, 20–30 for cubes and slices. Drain, add pepper and butter, and toss to mix.

NPS: 95 C, 15 mg CH, 445 mg S*

To Parboil for Use in Other Recipes: Use method above but reduce cooking time to 10 minutes for julienne strips, to 15 for cubes and slices. Omit seasonings.

V A R I A T I O N S

To Serve Cold: Cook and drain as recipe directs; chill in ice water. Drain, pat dry on paper toweling, and refrigerate until needed. Serve as a cold vegetable or salad, sauced with Aioli, French, or Russian Dressing. Recipe too flexible for meaningful nutritional count.

⚖ **Low-Calorie Celeriac:** Season with lemon juice instead of butter, and sprinkle with 2 tablespoons minced chives.

NPS: 45 C, 0 mg CH, 390 mg S*

Creamed Celeriac: Omit butter and mix boiled, drained celeriac with 1½ cups hot Medium White Sauce.

NPS: 200 C, 35 mg CH, 720 mg S*

Puréed Celeriac: Cook 1 small peeled cubed Irish potato with celeriac until both are very tender. Purée vegetables with ¼ cup cooking liquid by buzzing 20–25 seconds in an electric blender at low speed or 15–20 seconds in a food processor fitted with the metal chopping blade. Mix in ⅛ teaspoon white pepper, 2 tablespoons heavy cream, a pinch of nutmeg, and, for a rich purée, 2 tablespoons melted butter. If mixture has cooled, warm over low heat, stirring.

NPS: 95 C, 10 mg CH, 390 mg S*
NPS (with additional butter): 145 C, 40 mg CH, 505 mg S*

CELERIAC AU GRATIN

4 servings

An especially good casserole. Easy, too.

**3 knobs celeriac, cut in julienne strips, boiled
and drained
1½ cups hot Cheese Sauce
½ cup soft white bread crumbs
¼ cup finely grated Parmesan cheese
1 tablespoon minced parsley
2 tablespoons melted butter or margarine**

Preheat oven to 400° F. Arrange celeriac in
an ungreased 1½-quart *au gratin* dish or
shallow casserole and top with sauce. Toss
remaining ingredients together and sprinkle
over sauce. Bake, uncovered, 20 minutes until crumbs are lightly browned.

NPS: 420 C, 90 mg CH, 845 mg S*

CELERY

Celery is a Mediterranean vegetable, which
ancients looked upon as medicine rather
than food (it was said to purify the blood).
When the French began to cultivate wild celery, it was the seed they prized (and used as
an herb), not the stalk. No one knows who
first thought to eat the crisp, succulent stalks
—odd considering how much we rely on
them today to give crunch to salads and
stuffings, delicate savor to soups and stews.

To Prepare for Cooking: Cut root end and
green leafy tops from celery (save for stock
pot); separate head into individual stalks.
Wash well in cool water, slice or chop as
individual recipes specify.

To Prepare Celery Hearts: Peel away all but
inner 4 or 5 stalks (save for salads, soups, or
stews), halve lengthwise, then trim off root
ends and leafy tops so each heart is about 5"
long. Soak hearts ½ hour in ice water; rinse.

Serving Tip: To make raw stalks supercrisp,
pull threads from outer side of each; soak
stalks 20–30 minutes in 1 gallon ice water
mixed with ¼ cup sugar.

BOILED CELERY

4 servings ¢ ⚖

Cooked celery makes a delicious, low-calorie
vegetable.

**1 large bunch celery, prepared for cooking
1½ cups boiling water
½ teaspoon salt**

**Pinch pepper
2 tablespoons melted butter or margarine**

Cut stalks in 1½" lengths or dice. Boil, covered, in lightly salted water 20–30 minutes if
cut in lengths, 10–15 if diced. Drain, add
pepper and butter, and serve.

NPS: 90 C, 15 mg CH, 415 mg S*

To Parboil for Use in Other Recipes: Use recipe above but reduce cooking time to 10
minutes for celery cut in lengths, to 5 minutes for the diced. Omit seasonings.

VARIATIONS

¢ **To Serve Cold:** Boil and drain as directed; chill in ice water, drain, pat dry on
paper toweling, and refrigerate until needed.
Serve as a salad or cold vegetable with Aioli,
Mayonnaise, French, or Russian Dressing.
Recipe too flexible for meaningful nutritional count.

⚖ ¢ **Low-Calorie Celery:** Instead of seasoning with butter, dress with 2 tablespoons
low-calorie herb or Italian dressing, 2 tablespoons minced chives, and a dash of Worcestershire sauce.

NPS: 45 C, 0 mg CH, 415 mg S*

Celery au Gratin: Cut celery in 1½"
lengths, boil and drain as directed. Sprinkle
with pepper but omit butter. Mix with 1½
cups hot Mornay Sauce, spoon into an ungreased 1-quart *au gratin* dish, sprinkle with
⅓ cup grated sharp Cheddar cheese, and
broil 5" from the heat 3–4 minutes until
lightly browned.

NPS: 275 C, 55 mg CH, 795 mg S*

BRAISED CELERY HEARTS

4 servings

**4 celery hearts, parboiled and drained
2 tablespoons butter or margarine
1 cup water, chicken or beef broth or ¾ cup
water or broth and ¼ cup dry vermouth
⅛ teaspoon pepper
½ teaspoon salt (optional)**

Pat celery dry between several layers of paper toweling. Heat butter until bubbly in a
heavy skillet over moderately low heat, add
celery and cook gently, turning frequently
until pale golden. Add water, sprinkle with
pepper and salt (omit salt if using broth),
cover, and simmer about ½ hour until fork
tender. When serving, top each portion with
a little cooking liquid.

NPS (water): 70 C, 15 mg CH, 475 mg S*
NPS (broth): 80 C, 15 mg CH, 395 mg S*

CELERY AND CARROT CURRY

4–6 servings

Good with ham, pork, lamb, or chicken.

6–8 medium-size carrots, peeled and cut in
    matchstick strips
3/4 cup boiling beef broth
4 large stalks celery, cut in matchstick strips
1 1/4 cups milk (about)
2 tablespoons butter or margarine
1 small yellow onion, peeled and minced
2 tablespoons flour
1 tablespoon curry powder
1/4 teaspoon ginger
Pinch nutmeg

Place carrots in a large saucepan, add broth,
cover, and simmer 8–10 minutes. Add celery, re-cover, and simmer 10 minutes longer
until vegetables are crisp-tender. Drain
cooking liquid into a measuring cup and add
enough milk to total 1 1/2 cups. In a separate
saucepan, melt butter over moderate heat
and sauté onion, stirring, 5–8 minutes until
pale golden. Blend in flour and spices, add
milk mixture, and heat, stirring, until thickened. Pour sauce over vegetables, toss to
mix, and let "season," uncovered, over lowest heat 5–10 minutes, stirring occasionally.

*NPS (4–6): 190–125 C, 25–20 mg CH, 265–175
    mg S**

SCALLOPED CELERY WITH ALMONDS

4–6 servings

1 large bunch celery, prepared for cooking
1 1/2 cups boiling water
1–1 1/4 teaspoons salt
3 tablespoons butter or margarine
3 tablespoons flour
1/2 cup light cream
1/8 teaspoon white pepper
1/2 cup finely chopped blanched almonds
1/2 cup fine dry bread crumbs

Preheat oven to 350° F. Cut celery stalks in
3″ lengths; arrange in an ungreased shallow
2-quart flameproof casserole, add water and
1 teaspoon salt. Cover and simmer 20–25
minutes over moderate heat until crisp-tender. Drain off cooking water, reserving 1
cup. Melt butter over moderate heat and
blend in flour. Mix in cooking water and
cream and cook and stir about 5 minutes
until thickened. Season with pepper, taste
for salt, and add remaining 1/4 teaspoon if
needed. Pour sauce over celery. Mix almonds with crumbs and sprinkle on top.

Bake, uncovered, 30 minutes until browned
and bubbly.

*NPS (4–6): 340–225 C, 45–30 mg CH, 1,030–685
    mg S**

CHINESE STIR-FRIED CELERY

4 servings   ⊠ ¢

1 large bunch celery, prepared for cooking
1/4 cup peanut or other cooking oil

Cut each stalk diagonally into slices 1/8″
thick, discarding any strings. Heat oil in a
wok or large, heavy skillet over moderate
heat, add celery, and stir-fry 5–7 minutes
until crisp-tender but not brown.

NPS: 155 C, 0 mg CH, 285 mg S*

V A R I A T I O N S

⊠ ¢ **Chinese Celery with Soy and Sesame
Seeds:** Stir-fry as directed; just before serving toss in 1 tablespoon each soy sauce and
sesame seeds.

NPS: 170 C, 0 mg CH, 620 mg S*

¢ **Stir-Fried Celery, Pepper, and Scallions:**
Stir-fry 1/2 thinly slivered sweet red pepper
and 3–4 minced scallions along with the celery.

NPS: 165 C, 0 mg CH, 290 mg S*

Stir-Fried Celery and Mushrooms: Stir-fry
2/3 cup thinly sliced mushrooms along with
the celery.

NPS: 160 C, 0 mg CH, 285 mg S*

CHARD

(Also called Swiss Chard)

Chard is a bonus vegetable: the crinkly
green leaves can be steamed much like spinach, the silvery stalks can be simmered like
asparagus, or the two can be chopped and
cooked together.

To Prepare for Cooking: Discard root ends
and separate stalks from leaves. Wash leaves
2 or 3 times in cool water to remove all grit;
trim stalks of tough or woody ribs and wash
well in cool water. Keep stalks and leaves
separate.

BOILED CHARD

4 servings

2 pounds chard, prepared for cooking
1/2 cup boiling water
1/2 teaspoon salt

Pinch pepper
2 tablespoons melted butter or margarine

Coarsely chop stalks and leaves but keep the two separate. Place stalks in a large pot, add water and salt, cover, and boil 5 minutes. Add leaves, cover, and boil 5–10 minutes longer until tender. Drain, toss with pepper and butter, and serve.

NPS: 105 C, 15 mg CH, 435 mg S*

To Boil Stalks Alone: Prepare stalks for cooking, leave whole or cut in 2″–3″ lengths. Place in a pot with 1 cup boiling water and ½ teaspoon salt and boil, covered, 10–15 minutes until tender. Drain, season with pepper and butter, and serve. Nutritional count same as basic recipe.

To Boil Chard Leaves Alone: Prepare leaves for cooking, place in a large pot with ½ cup boiling water and ½ teaspoon salt, cover, and boil 5–10 minutes until tender. Drain and season with butter and pepper or oil and vinegar. Nutritional count same as basic recipe.

To Parboil for Use in Other Recipes: Boil stalks by method above but reduce cooking time to 5–7 minutes; omit seasonings. The leaves don't need parboiling.

VARIATIONS

To Serve Cold: Boil or steam as directed and drain; chill stalks and/or leaves in ice water. Drain, toss with a good tart dressing, and refrigerate several hours. Recipe too flexible for meaningful nutritional count.

⚖ **Low-Calorie Chard:** Season with red or white wine vinegar instead of butter.

NPS: 55 C, 0 mg CH, 375 mg S*

Puréed Chard: Boil and drain as directed; purée by buzzing 10–15 seconds in an electric blender at high speed or 5–10 seconds in a food processor fitted with the metal chopping blade. Mix in 2 tablespoons each butter and heavy cream, a pinch pepper and warm 1–2 minutes, stirring, over low heat.

NPS: 180 C, 40 mg CH, 495 mg S*

CHAYOTES

(Also called Christophene, Cho-Cho, Mango Squash, Mirliton, and Vegetable Pear)

These Caribbean squashes, fairly common in the Gulf States, are beginning to appear in supermarkets. The size and shape of an avocado, they have deeply furrowed, waxy, pale greenish yellow skins. They taste like sum-

mer squash and can be substituted for it in recipes. Mexican cooks team chayotes with spicy sauces or cheeses, and Indian cooks curry them. Nutritional counts unavailable.

To Prepare for Cooking: Scrub well in cool water, then peel (just as you would an apple) unless chayotes are to be stuffed and baked (you'll notice a sticky substance on your hands—it's harmless and washes right off). Halve chayotes and with a table knife pry out long, slender seed. Leave as halves, cut each in two lengthwise, or slice crosswise ¾″ thick.

To Boil: Cover with lightly salted boiling water and simmer, covered, until firm but tender: about 45 minutes for halves, 30 for quarters, 20 for slices. Drain, season with butter, salt, and pepper or top with Mornay, Basic Cheese, or Medium White Sauce.

To Parboil for Use in Other Recipes: Use method above but reduce cooking time to 30 minutes for halves, 20 for quarters, and 10–15 for slices.

To Bake and Stuff: Fill parboiled, *unpeeled,* scooped-out halves with any mixture you would use for stuffing summer squash. Bake, uncovered, at 350° F. about 30–40 minutes.

To Serve as Salad: Cool and chill boiled chayote halves or slices. Fill halves with any meat or fish salad; marinate slices in a tart dressing and toss into green salad.

CHESTNUTS

(Also called Marrons)

To us chestnuts are a luxury, something to savor before the fire with a glass of fine sherry, something to save for that special Thanksgiving stuffing. To Europeans, however, they're commonplace, a popular potato substitute. Try them their way in place of potatoes.

To Shell and Peel Fresh Chestnuts: This is a tedious job, so have patience. Make an X-cut into shell on flat side of each nut. Cover nuts with cold water, bring to a boil, cover, and boil 1–2 minutes. Remove from heat but do not drain. Using a slotted spoon, scoop 2–3 nuts from the pan at a time and peel off both the hard outer shell and the inner brown skin (use a small knife to loosen skins if necessary). Keep chestnuts in hot water until you're ready to peel them. If any seem unduly stubborn, simply reheat briefly in boiling water and try again to peel. *Note:* Now available in many specialty food shops are shelled and peeled frozen Italian chestnuts, which will save you considerable hard labor.

BOILED FRESH CHESTNUTS

4 servings

Serve in place of potatoes with poultry, pork, game, or game birds.

1 pound shelled, peeled chestnuts
2 cups boiling water or chicken broth
3 tablespoons butter or margarine
Salt
Pepper

Simmer chestnuts, covered, in water or broth 15–20 minutes until tender but not mushy. Drain, add butter, salt, and pepper to taste, and warm, uncovered, over low heat, shaking pan gently, until butter melts and gilds nuts.
NPS (water): 295 C, 25 mg CH, 95 mg S*
NPS (broth): 300 C, 25 mg CH, 190 mg S*

To Boil Dried Chestnuts: Wash and sort, carefully removing any that are withered, discolored, or buggy. Cover with cold water, remove any that float, then soak overnight. Drain, rinse several times, and scrape off bits of brown skin remaining. Cover with fresh cold water and simmer, covered, 1–1½ hours until plump and tender. Drain and use cup-for-cup in place of fresh boiled chestnuts. Nutritional count about the same as basic recipe.

VARIATIONS

Sautéed Chestnuts: Boil and drain chestnuts by recipe above, add salt and pepper but omit butter. Sauté instead in ¼ cup butter 4–5 minutes until lightly browned.
NPS (water): 320 C, 30 mg CH, 125 mg S*
NPS (broth): 325 C, 30 mg CH, 220 mg S*

Creamed Chestnuts: Boil and drain chestnuts as recipe directs, then halve. Add butter, salt, and pepper called for, also ½ cup heavy cream. Warm, uncovered, over lowest heat until just simmering. Stir occasionally.
NPS (water): 400 C, 65 mg CH, 105 mg S*
NPS (broth): 405 C, 65 mg CH, 200 mg S*

Riced Chestnut Pyramid: Boil and drain chestnuts as directed, season with salt and pepper but omit butter. Put chestnuts through a potato ricer, letting them mound into a pyramid on a heated plate. Serve with melted butter.
NPS (water): 220 C, 0 mg CH, 7 mg S*
NPS (broth): 225 C, 0 mg CH, 105 mg S*

Puréed Chestnuts: Boil as directed in chicken broth; drain and purée by buzzing 20–25 seconds in an electric blender at high speed or 15–20 seconds in a food processor fitted with the metal chopping blade. Beat in 2 tablespoons each butter and light cream; add salt and pepper to taste.
NPS: 290 C, 20 mg CH, 165 mg S*

ROASTED CHESTNUTS

4 servings

1½ pounds chestnuts in the shell
¼ cup cooking oil

Preheat oven to 400° F. With a sharp knife, make an X-shaped cut on the flat side of each shell. Arrange nuts in a roasting pan, sprinkle with oil, and toss lightly. Roast, uncovered, 10–15 minutes. Cool just until easy to handle, then shell and remove inner brown skins. The chestnuts are now ready to use in recipes or to eat out-of-hand.
NPS: 300 C, 0 mg CH, 10 mg S*

VARIATION

Hearth-Roasted Chestnuts: Do not make X-cuts on chestnuts, do not use oil. Lay chestnuts at edge of fire near glowing coals (you don't need a pan) and roast about 10 minutes, turning frequently, until nuts "pop." Shell and eat.
NPS: 270 C, 0 mg CH, 10 mg S*

BRAISED CHESTNUTS

4 servings

These chestnuts can be served as a vegetable, alone, or mixed with creamed onions, boiled cabbage, Brussels sprouts, or broccoli. They can also be used to garnish roast chicken, turkey, or game platters.

¼ cup melted butter or margarine
1 small yellow onion, peeled and minced
1 stalk celery, minced (include green tops)
1 pound shelled, peeled chestnuts, whole or
**   halved**
⅛ teaspoon white pepper
1½ cups beef or chicken broth
1 star anise (optional)

Preheat oven to 350° F. Pour butter into a 1½-quart casserole, add onion and celery, and top with chestnuts. Sprinkle with pepper, pour in broth, and, if you like, add anise. Cover and bake 35–45 minutes until chestnuts are very tender. When serving, top each portion with some of the pan juices.
NPS: 335 C, 30 mg CH, 430 mg S*

COLLARDS

Nearly every Southern farm has its collard patch, every kitchen its "mess o' greens" simmering on the back of the stove with a chunk of streaky bacon or salt pork. There's always lots of "pot likker" and oven-fresh corn bread for sopping it up.

To Prepare for Cooking: Wash well in cool water to remove grit and sand. Discard tough stems and leaf midribs; cut large leaves into bite-size pieces.

Cooking Tip: Try stir-frying finely shredded young collard leaves in bacon drippings 8–10 minutes over moderately high heat until crisp-tender.

BOILED COLLARDS, TURNIP GREENS, OR MUSTARD GREENS

4 servings   ¢

2 pounds collards, turnip greens, or mustard greens, prepared for cooking
½ cup boiling water
¾ teaspoon salt
Pinch pepper
2 tablespoons bacon drippings, melted butter or margarine

Break leaves into bite-size pieces or chop fine. Place in a large pot, add water and salt, cover, and simmer until tender: 10–15 minutes for turnip or mustard greens, 15–20 for collards. (*Note:* Very young leaves may cook in 5–7 minutes.) Drain, add pepper and drippings, and toss to mix.

NPS: 105 C, 5 mg CH, 225 mg S*

VARIATION

⚖ ¢ **Low-Calorie Boiled Greens:** Omit drippings and dress with a sprinkling of white wine vinegar.

NPS: 60 C, 0 mg CH, 190 mg S*

CORN

(Also called Maize)

One of the joys of summer is feasting upon sugary ears of sweet corn, dripping with butter and so hot you can hardly hold them. A gift from the American Indian, corn provides not only kernels to nibble off the cob but also corn meal, cornstarch, corn syrup, hominy, hominy grits, and bourbon. There are hundreds of varieties of corn, but those we like best are sweet—truly sweet, unfortunately, only when rushed from stalk to pot. If you live in a corn-growing area, try to befriend a farmer who will let you pick your own. Yellow varieties tend to have larger kernels and more mature flavor, white varieties smaller, sweeter kernels as do such variegated yellow-and-white ears as "butter and sugar corn."

To Prepare for Cooking: Just before cooking —*no earlier*—peel away husks, remove tassels and silks. Break off tip and stem end. Do not wash.

To Cut Corn off the Cob: For *cream-style,* cut down the center of each row of kernels, then, using the back of the knife, scrape corn into a bowl. *Note:* Cream-style corn is a cinch to make with a food processor (see the Food Processor Metal Blade Chopping Guide in Chapter 1). For *whole kernel corn,* simply cut kernels from cob, doing 3 or 4 rows at a time.

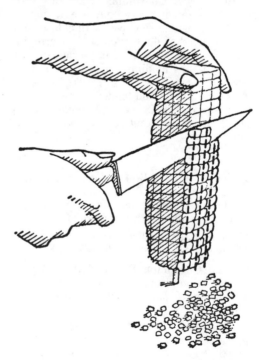

Cooking Tip: To give not so fresh corn a just-picked flavor, add 1–2 tablespoons sugar to the cooking water. Never cook corn in salted water.

BOILED FRESH CORN ON THE COB

2 ears per person ☒

4–5 quarts boiling water
Fresh ears sweet corn, prepared for cooking
Salt
Pepper
Butter or margarine

Place water in a 1½-gallon kettle over high heat and, when boiling vigorously, drop in corn. Cover and boil 5–8 minutes, depending on the size of the ears. Lift ears from water with tongs and serve with salt, pepper, and plenty of butter.

NP Ear (without butter and seasonings): 140 C, 0 mg CH, 0 mg S*

VARIATION

Substitute 1 quart milk for 1 quart water and boil as directed.

NP Ear (without butter): 150 C, 0 mg CH, 10 mg S*

CHARCOAL-ROASTED FRESH EARS OF CORN

2 ears per person

Prepare a moderately hot charcoal fire. Pull back husks to expose kernels but do not tear off. Remove silks, then smooth husks back over ears and tie at tips. Lay ears on a grill 3″–4″ from coals and roast 12–15 minutes, turning frequently. Husk while piping hot (wear gloves) and serve at once with salt, pepper, and butter.

NP Ear (without butter): 150 C, 2 mg CH, 10 mg S*

VARIATIONS

• After removing silks and tying husks at the tips as directed above, soak ears 10–15 minutes in ice water. Drain, shake off excess water, and roast as directed. If you want to roast directly in coals, soak 30 minutes. Bury in coals and roast 10 minutes.
• Husk ears, wrap in buttered squares of aluminum foil, and roast 3″ from coals 20–30 minutes, turning frequently.

OVEN ROASTING EARS

2–4 servings

An unusually good way to prepare frozen corn on the cob is to roast in the oven—it's firm yet tender and has a delightful nutty flavor.

2 (2-ear) packages frozen corn on the cob (do not thaw)
Butter or margarine
Salt
Pepper

Preheat oven to 400° F. Wrap each solidly frozen ear in several thicknesses heavy foil, twisting ends to seal. Place on lowest oven rack and roast 1 hour. Unwrap and serve with butter, salt, and pepper.

NP Ear (without butter): 245 C, 0 mg CH, 15 mg S*

VARIATION

Charcoal-Roasted Frozen Ears: Prepare a moderate charcoal fire. Wrap frozen ears as directed above and roast 3″–4″ from coals 1 hour, giving them a quarter turn every 15 minutes. Unwrap and serve with butter, salt, and pepper.

NP Ear (without butter): 245 C, 0 mg CH, 15 mg S*

BOILED FRESH WHOLE KERNEL CORN

4–6 servings

6–8 ears sweet corn, prepared for cooking
1 cup boiling water or skim milk
½ teaspoon sugar
½ teaspoon salt
Pinch white pepper
2 tablespoons butter or margarine

Cut corn from cob.* Place in a saucepan with water or milk and sugar, cover, and simmer 5–8 minutes until tender. Drain and season with salt, pepper, and butter.

NPS: 15 C, 15 mg CH, 190 mg S*

VARIATION

Boiled Corn and Vegetables: Just before serving corn, mix in 1½ cups boiled green peas, asparagus tips, or diced carrots; or ½ cup sautéed minced red or green pepper or Spanish onion. Recipe too flexible for meaningful nutritional count.

HERBED CORN IN CREAM

4–6 servings ☒

4 cups fresh whole kernel corn or 3 (10-ounce) packages frozen whole kernel corn (do not thaw)
¾ cup heavy cream
2 tablespoons butter or margarine
2 tablespoons minced chives

1 teaspoon minced fresh basil or 1/8 teaspoon
   dried basil
1/4 teaspoon minced fresh chervil or 1/8 teaspoon
   dried chervil
Salt
Pepper
Pinch paprika

Place all but last 3 ingredients in the top of a double boiler over simmering water, cover, and cook 10 minutes until corn is tender (if using frozen corn, break up clumps as corn cooks). Add salt and pepper to taste, ladle into soup bowls, and sprinkle with paprika.

NPS (4–6): 365–240 C, 75–50 mg CH, 75–50 mg S*

OLD-FASHIONED SUCCOTASH

4–6 servings

2 cups fresh whole kernel corn
2 cups fresh baby lima or cranberry beans,
   parboiled
1 cup light cream
2 tablespoons butter, margarine, or bacon
   drippings
2 teaspoons sugar
Pinch white pepper
1 teaspoon salt

Place all ingredients but salt in a saucepan and simmer, uncovered, stirring occasionally, 10–12 minutes until beans are tender. Mix in salt; ladle into soup bowls.

NPS (4–6): 365–240 C, 55–35 mg CH, 775–520 mg S*

VARIATIONS

Green Bean Succotash: Substitute 1/2 pound parboiled cut green beans for the lima beans and prepare as recipe directs.

NPS (4–6): 270–180 C, 55–35 mg CH, 635–425 mg S*

Hominy-Green Bean Succotash: Instead of using recipe above, place 2 cups each of boiled, drained hominy and boiled, drained cut green beans in a large saucepan, add 1/2 cup heavy cream, 3 tablespoons bacon drippings, and salt and pepper to taste. Warm, stirring, 3–4 minutes just to blend flavors. Serve in soup bowls, topped, if you like, with crisp bacon bits.

NPS (4–6): 260–175 C, 45–30 mg CH, 60–40 mg S*

CONFETTI CORN

4 servings ▢

1 large sweet green pepper, cored, seeded, and
   chopped fine
1 (4-ounce) can pimiento, drained and chopped
   fine
1 small yellow onion, peeled and chopped fine
1/4 cup butter or margarine
2 cups fresh whole kernel corn or 2 (10-ounce)
   packages frozen whole kernel corn, cooked
   and drained well
1/4 teaspoon salt
Pinch pepper

Stir-fry green pepper, pimiento, and onion in butter 8–10 minutes until onion is golden. Add corn, salt, and pepper, cover, and simmer 3–4 minutes, just long enough to heat through.

NPS: 200 C, 30 mg CH, 265 mg S*

SCALLOPED CORN

4 servings

A marvelously mellow corn casserole.

2 tablespoons butter or margarine
2 tablespoons flour
1 1/4 cups milk
1 teaspoon salt
1/8 teaspoon pepper
1 egg, lightly beaten
1/4 teaspoon prepared mild yellow mustard
2 cups whole kernel corn (fresh; drained frozen
   cooked or canned)
1 cup coarse soda cracker crumbs
2 tablespoons melted butter or margarine

Preheat oven to 350° F. Melt butter over moderate heat, blend in flour, then add milk and heat, stirring, until thickened and smooth. Off heat mix in salt, pepper, egg, mustard, and corn. Pour into a lightly buttered 1 1/2-quart casserole, sprinkle with crumbs, and drizzle with melted butter. Bake, uncovered, 30 minutes until lightly browned.

NPS: 340 C, 110 mg CH, 920 mg S*

CORN GUMBO

4–6 servings

1 medium-size yellow onion, peeled and minced
1/2 medium-size sweet green pepper, cored,
   seeded, and chopped fine
1 stalk celery, chopped fine
2 tablespoons bacon drippings
1 1/2 cups coarsely chopped, seeded, peeled
   tomatoes

2 cups fresh, thawed frozen, or canned whole kernel corn (drain the frozen or canned)
4–6 baby okra pods, sliced 1/2" thick
1 teaspoon salt
1/4 teaspoon gumbo filé
1/8 teaspoon pepper

Sauté onion, green pepper, and celery in drippings in a large saucepan 8–10 minutes over moderate heat until onion is golden. Add all remaining ingredients except salt, gumbo filé, and pepper, cover, and simmer slowly 10–15 minutes, stirring occasionally. Mix in salt, gumbo filé, and pepper. Ladle into soup bowls and serve.

NPS (4–6): 160–105 C, 5–3 mg CH, 600–400 mg S*

CORN PUDDING

6 servings

Everyone's favorite.

3 tablespoons butter or margarine
2 (10-ounce) packages frozen whole kernel corn (do not thaw)
1/4 teaspoon nutmeg
4 eggs
1/4 cup unsifted flour
1/2 teaspoon baking powder
1 tablespoon sugar
1 teaspoon salt
1/8 teaspoon white pepper
2 1/4 cups light cream

Preheat oven to 325° F. Melt butter in a large saucepan over moderate heat, add corn, and simmer, uncovered, stirring occasionally, 8–10 minutes until heated through. Do not drain; stir in nutmeg. Beat eggs until foamy in a large mixing bowl. Mix flour with baking powder, sugar, salt, and pepper, add to eggs, and beat until smooth. Mix in corn and cream. Pour into a buttered, shallow 1 1/2-quart casserole, set in a shallow roasting pan, and pour in enough cold water to come about halfway up casserole. Bake, uncovered, about 1 hour and 20 minutes or until a knife inserted in center of pudding comes out clean.

NPS: 385 C, 255 mg CH, 545 mg S*

CORN PIE

6 servings

PASTRY
1 recipe Flaky Pastry I

FILLING
4 eggs, lightly beaten
1 1/4 cups milk or light cream
1 1/4 teaspoons salt
Pinch white pepper
1 tablespoon grated yellow onion
1 1/2 cups cooked whole kernel corn, drained well
1/2–3/4 cup crumbled cooked bacon (optional)

Preheat oven to 425° F. Prepare pastry and fit into a 9" piepan, making a high, fluted edge. Prick bottom and sides of pastry with a fork, cover with wax paper, and fill with uncooked rice or dried beans. Bake 5–7 minutes until firm but not brown, remove rice or beans. Stir together all filling ingredients and pour into pie shell. Bake 10 minutes at 425° F., reduce heat to 350° F., and bake 30 minutes longer or until center is almost firm. Cool about 10 minutes before cutting.

NPS (milk): 365 C, 195 mg CH, 860 mg S*
NPS (cream): 430 C, 225 mg CH, 855 mg S*

CORN FRITTERS

6 servings

Lard, shortening, or cooking oil for deep fat frying

FRITTERS
1 1/2 cups sifted flour
1 1/2 teaspoons salt
2 teaspoons baking powder
2 eggs, lightly beaten
1/2 cup milk
2 cups cooked whole kernel corn, drained well

Begin heating fat in a deep fat fryer over moderately high heat; insert deep fat thermometer. Meanwhile, sift flour, salt, and baking powder together into a bowl. Add eggs, a little of the milk, and beat until smooth. Add remaining milk and beat again. Stir in corn. When fat reaches 375° F., drop in batter from a measuring tablespoon. Do only 5 or 6 fritters at a time, frying each until crisply golden and turning as needed to brown evenly. Drain on paper toweling and set, uncovered, in a 250° F. oven to keep warm while you fry the rest.

NPS: 230 C, 100 mg CH, 725 mg S*

VARIATION

Corn-Cheese Fritters: Add 1 cup coarsely grated sharp Cheddar cheese to batter. (If mixture seems thick, stir in 1–2 tablespoons cold water.) Fry as directed.

NPS: 305 C, 120 mg CH, 840 mg S*

CUCUMBERS

It was cucumbers the Israelites craved in the Wilderness, cucumbers the Emperor Tiberius ate daily, and cucumbers Charlemagne ordered grown lest he run out of pickles. Two principal types of cucumbers are available today: small "pickling" cucumbers and large "eating" or "slicing" cucumbers. The most readily available of these: the long, green-skinned "Marketer" (its skins are now routinely waxed to retard spoilage), and the more expensive, cellophane-wrapped, seedless, light-green-skinned "English" or "hothouse" cucumber. Delicious raw, cucumbers are equally so baked in butter, stir-fried in peanut oil, or smothered in cream sauce. The French and Chinese are the masters of cucumber cooking, and we include some of their favorite recipes here.

To Prepare for Cooking: Because most dark-green-skinned cucumbers are dipped in wax to keep them crisp and fresh, it's a good idea to peel before using. Cut up and seed as individual recipes specify. The easiest way to seed cucumbers is simply to scoop them out with a teaspoon.

BOILED CUCUMBERS

4 servings

3 medium-size cucumbers, peeled, halved, and seeded
1/2 cup boiling water
1/4 teaspoon salt
Pinch white pepper
2 tablespoons butter or margarine

Leave cucumbers as halves or cut in 1″ cubes. Place in a saucepan with water and salt, cover, and simmer until crisp-tender: 8–10 minutes for cubes, 10–12 for halves. Drain, add pepper and butter, set over low heat, and warm, uncovered, until butter melts.

NPS: 75 C, 15 mg CH, 140 mg S*

To Steam Cucumbers: Place halves or cubes in a steamer over rapidly boiling water, cover, and steam 8–10 minutes for cubes, 10–12 for halves. Season as above and serve.

NPS: 70 C, 15 mg CH, 70 mg S*

To Parboil for Use in Other Recipes: Boil or steam as directed above, reducing cooking times as follows: to 5 minutes for cubes, to 8 for halves. Omit seasonings.

⚖ **Low-Calorie Cucumbers:** Omit butter and dress with 1–2 tablespoons lemon juice and/or a sprinkling minced chives, parsley, or dill.

NPS: 25 C, 0 mg CH, 80 mg S*

Cucumbers au Gratin: Boil by recipe above, drain, season with pepper, and place in a buttered 1 1/2-quart *au gratin* dish. Top with 1/2 cup grated Parmesan mixed with 1/2 cup soft white bread crumbs and drizzle with 2 tablespoons melted butter. Broil 5″ from heat 2 minutes until browned (watch closely so cucumbers don't burn).

NPS: 135 C, 25 mg CH, 135 mg S*

CHINESE-STYLE CUCUMBERS IN SOY SAUCE

4 servings ⚖

3 medium-size cucumbers, peeled, quartered lengthwise, and seeded
2 tablespoons peanut oil
1 tablespoon Japanese soy sauce
1 tablespoon minced chives

Cut each cucumber quarter into slices 1/4″ thick and pat dry on paper toweling. Heat oil in a large, heavy skillet or *wok* over moderate heat 1 minute. Add cucumbers and stir-fry 3–4 minutes, until crisp-tender. Add soy sauce and toss to mix; sprinkle with chives and serve.

NPS: 85 C, 0 mg CH, 340 mg S*

CUCUMBERS PROVENÇAL

4 servings

3 medium-size cucumbers, peeled, seeded, cut in 1″ cubes, parboiled, and drained
2 tablespoons butter or margarine
2 tablespoons olive or other cooking oil
1 clove garlic, peeled and crushed
2 medium-size ripe tomatoes, peeled, seeded, and coarsely chopped
1 tablespoon minced parsley
1/2 teaspoon salt
1/8 teaspoon pepper

Pat cucumbers dry on paper toweling. Melt butter in a large, heavy skillet over moderate heat, add oil and heat 1/2 minute. Sauté garlic 1/2 minute until pale golden, add cucumbers and tomatoes, and sauté 4–5 minutes until tender, stirring constantly. Off heat, add remaining ingredients, toss lightly to mix, and serve.

NPS: 150 C, 15 mg CH, 345 mg S*

BAKED STUFFED CUCUMBERS

4 servings

2 medium-size cucumbers, peeled and halved
5–6 tablespoons melted butter or margarine
2 cups soft white bread crumbs
1/4 teaspoon salt
1/8 teaspoon pepper
1 teaspoon dried chervil
1/2 cup coarsely chopped, peeled, seeded tomatoes
3 tablespoons sliced blanched almonds

Preheat oven to 350° F. Scoop seeds and center pulp from cucumbers so they are boat-shaped. Coarsely chop pulp and reserve 1/4 cup. Parboil cucumbers 5 minutes, then drain and arrange in a well-buttered shallow baking pan. (*Note:* Use a pancake turner for handling cucumbers because they're delicate and break easily.) Brush cucumbers lightly all over with a little melted butter. Toss crumbs with reserved cucumber pulp, 1/4 cup melted butter, and all remaining ingredients except almonds and stuff cucumbers. Top with almonds and drizzle with melted butter. Bake, uncovered, 35 minutes until cucumbers are fork tender and almonds lightly browned.

NPS: 245 C, 40 mg CH, 400 mg S*

DANDELIONS

Ever wonder how dandelions got their name? It's a corruption of *dent de lion* ("tooth of the lion"), which is the way the French described the dandelion's jagged leaves. It is these leaves that are good to eat, particularly if cooked gently like spinach in a small amount of water, then tossed with butter or dressed with oil and lemon. These are the same dandelions that blight our lawns, though those sold in groceries have been especially grown for the table.

To Prepare for Cooking: Trim away roots and sort, removing yellowed or wilted leaves. Wash well in cool water and tear into bite-size pieces.

Serving Tip: Add crisped dandelion greens to tossed salads for special bite and zest.

WILTED DANDELIONS OR NETTLES

4 servings

4 slices bacon
2 pounds (3–4 quarts) dandelion or nettle leaves, prepared for cooking

1/4 cup red wine vinegar
1–2 tablespoons sugar
1/2 teaspoon salt
Pinch pepper

Brown bacon in a large, heavy kettle over moderate heat and drain on paper toweling. Add leaves to kettle along with all remaining ingredients, cover, and simmer 10–15 minutes until tender. Remove leaves from kettle and chop fine. Serve topped with any cooking liquid and crumbled bacon.

NPS: 240 C, 15 mg CH, 605 mg S*

DASHEENS

(Also known as Taro and Callaloo)

Cooked, mashed, and fermented, dasheens are the *poi* of Hawaii; boiled or baked, they are the "potatoes" of Jamaica. The plant's leaves, called *callaloo,* are integral to a lusty Caribbean soup of the same name. Like potatoes, dasheens are mealy and nutty; unlike them, they are gray-lavender inside. Some are no bigger than pullet eggs, but coconut-size dasheens are more common. Nutritional counts unavailable.

To Prepare for Cooking: Scrub in cool water with a vegetable brush. Peel and cut in 1 1/2" chunks if dasheens are to be boiled; leave whole and do not peel if they are to be baked.

To Boil: Cover dasheens with lightly salted boiling water, cover, and simmer about 1 hour until tender. Drain and mash as you would potatoes, seasoning with butter, salt, and pepper; or instead of mashing, mix chunks with hot Medium White Sauce (about 1 cup sauce to 2 cups dasheens).

To Bake: Parboil whole, unpeeled dasheens 30 minutes. Drain and bake, uncovered, in a shallow roasting pan 1–1 1/2 hours at 375° F. until a fork pierces them easily. Halve or quarter dasheens, also peel, if you like, and season as you would baked potatoes.

EGGPLANT

(Sometimes called by the French name aubergine)

For centuries eggplant stood high on Europe's list of "dangerous and immoral foods," the rumor being it drove men mad. Fortunately, Arabs and Orientals knew better; they ate eggplant with relish and created many of the recipes we consider classics. Today we appreciate eggplant for what it is—one of the most versatile of vegetables. Although the most popular variety is the glossy, deep purple "Black Beauty," there are others: babies no bigger than goose eggs, and firm, slim, dry "frying varieties" that may be either purple-skinned or white.

To Prepare for Cooking: Wash well in tepid water; peel or not as individual recipes specify (the skin is often left on to give dishes color, flavor, and texture).

Serving Tip: Salt thin strips of raw peeled eggplant, pat dry on paper toweling, toss with Vinaigrette Dressing and minced tarragon or chervil, and serve as a salad.

FRIED EGGPLANT

4–6 servings

Eggplant cooks so quickly that, when fried, it need only be browned on both sides. Use, if possible, the slim, drier "frying" variety that doesn't have to be salted and blotted on paper toweling.

1 medium-size eggplant or 6 slim "frying" eggplants cut in 1/2" rounds (do not peel)
2 teaspoons salt (about)
1 egg, lightly beaten
1/8 teaspoon mace
1/8 teaspoon pepper
1/3 cup olive or other cooking oil
1/2 cup cracker meal

If using the large eggplant, sprinkle about 1 teaspoon salt over rounds and weight down between paper toweling 1 hour. Mix egg with 1 teaspoon salt, the mace, and pepper. Heat 3–4 tablespoons oil 1–2 minutes in a large, heavy skillet over moderately high heat. Dip rounds in egg, a few at a time, then in crumbs and brown on both sides, adding more oil to skillet as needed. Drain browned rounds on paper toweling and set, uncovered, in a 250° F. oven to keep warm while you fry the rest.

NPS (4–6): 260–170 C, 70–45 mg CH, 1,125–750 mg S*

BROILED EGGPLANT

4 servings ☒

1 medium-size eggplant, cut in rounds 1/2" thick (do not peel)
1/3 cup olive or other cooking oil (about)
1 teaspoon salt
1/8 teaspoon pepper

Preheat broiler. Brush eggplant rounds generously with oil and broil 4"–5" from heat about 5 minutes until speckled with brown. Turn, brush again with oil, and broil 5 minutes longer. Sprinkle with salt and pepper and serve. For extra dash, top with chopped parsley, grated Parmesan cheese, or Tomato Sauce.

NPS: 190 C, 0 mg CH, 550 mg S*

VARIATION

⚖ **Low-Calorie Broiled Eggplant:** Brush rounds with lemon juice or low-calorie Italian dressing instead of oil and broil as directed.

NPS: 35 C, 0 mg CH, 555 mg S*

BASQUE-STYLE EGGPLANT, PEPPERS, AND TOMATOES

6–8 servings

1 medium-size eggplant, peeled and cut in 3/4" cubes
2 tablespoons flour
1/4 cup olive or other cooking oil
3 large sweet green peppers, cored, seeded, and cut in 1/2" squares
3 cups coarsely chopped, seeded, peeled ripe tomatoes
1 teaspoon salt
1 tablespoon minced parsley

Dredge eggplant in flour and stir-fry in oil in a large, heavy skillet over moderately high heat 7–8 minutes until browned. Add peppers and sauté 3–4 minutes, then add tomatoes and cook 2–3 minutes longer, stirring. Cover, reduce heat to low, and simmer 15 minutes. Mix in salt and parsley and, if mixture seems too liquid, turn up heat and boil, uncovered, stirring, until the consistency of stew. Serve with garlic bread.

NPS (6–8): 300–225 C, 0 mg CH, 380–285 mg S*

RATATOUILLE (EGGPLANT, ZUCCHINI, AND TOMATO STEW À LA PROVENÇALE)

4–6 servings

Ratatouille takes some doing, but once the pot's on, perfuming the air, the effort seems worthwhile. This dish keeps well, is even better the second time around.

1 medium-size eggplant, peeled and sliced in 1/4" rounds
3 medium-size zucchini, cut in 1/4" rounds
1 tablespoon salt (about)
3/4 cup olive oil (about)

2 medium-size yellow onions, peeled and sliced
thin
2 medium-size sweet green peppers, cored,
seeded, and sliced thin
2 cloves garlic, peeled and crushed
4 medium-size tomatoes, peeled, juiced, seeded,
and coarsely chopped
1/8 teaspoon pepper
3 tablespoons minced parsley

Sprinkle eggplant and zucchini with 1 teaspoon salt and weight down between paper toweling 1 hour. Cut eggplant in 1/4" strips and stir-fry, about one fourth at a time, 3–5 minutes in 2–3 tablespoons oil over moderately high heat. Drain on paper toweling. (Eggplant soaks up oil, but don't use more than 2–3 tablespoons for each batch or the ratatouille will be greasy). Brown all zucchini in 2 tablespoons oil and drain. Stir-fry onions with peppers and garlic in remaining oil 10 minutes over moderate heat until golden, lay tomatoes on top, add 1 1/2 teaspoons salt and the pepper, cover, and simmer 8–10 minutes. Uncover and simmer 10 minutes longer. In an ungreased shallow 2 1/2-quart flameproof casserole, build up alternate layers as follows: onion mixture (sprinkle with parsley), eggplant-zucchini (sprinkle with salt), onions (parsley), eggplant-zucchini (salt), onions (parsley). (Note: At this point ratatouille can be cooled, covered, and held in the refrigerator 1–2 days. Bring to room temperature before proceeding.) Simmer, covered, over low heat 35–40 minutes until vegetables are tender—don't stir. Uncover and simmer 40 minutes longer, also without stirring, until almost all juices are gone. Serve hot or cold as a vegetable or use for filling Crepes.

NPS (4–6): 460–310 C, 0 mg CH, 1,665–1,110 mg S*

PISTO (SPANISH VEGETABLE STEW)

16 vegetable servings, appetizers for 50   ¢

Pisto, Spanish cousin to *ratatouille,* can be eaten hot or cold, as an appetizer, vegetable, or main dish, depending on how much meat goes into it.

1 cup diced lean cooked ham
1/2 cup olive oil
4 large yellow onions, peeled and sliced thin
2 medium-size sweet red peppers, cored, seeded,
and coarsely chopped
1 (7-ounce) can pimientos, drained and cut in
1/4" strips
4 cloves garlic, peeled and crushed

1 medium-size eggplant, washed and cut in 1/2"
cubes (do not peel)
1/2 pound mushrooms, wiped clean and sliced
thin
2–3 teaspoons salt
2 (9-ounce) packages frozen artichoke hearts (do
not thaw)
2 (1-pound) cans tomatoes (do not drain)

Brown ham in the oil in a large kettle over moderate heat. Add onions, peppers, pimientos, garlic, eggplant, and mushrooms, cover, and simmer slowly, stirring occasionally, 15 minutes until onions are golden. Add remaining ingredients and simmer, covered, 30–40 minutes until artichokes are tender. Cool, cover, and chill 4–5 hours.

NPS (16–50): 130–40 C, 5–1 mg CH, 480–155 mg S*

VARIATIONS

Main Dish Ham Pisto *(12–14 servings):* Make as directed, increasing ham to 4 cups. Serve hot with fluffy cooked rice.

NPS: 245–210 C, 30–25 mg CH, 1,220–1,045 mg S*

Main Dish Beef Pisto *(12–14 servings):* Substitute 2 pounds ground beef chuck for the ham, brown lightly in the oil, then proceed as recipe directs and serve hot with rice.

NPS: 355–305 C, 50–45 mg CH, 550–470 mg S*

SULTAN'S EGGPLANT

4 servings

1 large eggplant
1/2 teaspoon lemon juice
1/4 cup light cream
1/4 cup soft white bread crumbs
1/2 teaspoon salt (about)
2 teaspoons grated Parmesan cheese
1/8 teaspoon white pepper
2 tablespoons butter or margarine
1 tablespoon minced parsley

Preheat oven to 400° F. Prick eggplant all over with a sharp fork and bake, uncovered, about 1 hour until soft. Cool until easy to handle and slip off skin. Beat eggplant briskly with a fork or rotary beater, mix in lemon juice, and heat slowly, stirring, just until warm. Add all remaining ingredients except parsley and heat, stirring, 3–5 minutes. Sprinkle with parsley and serve.

NPS: 135 C, 25 mg CH, 370 mg S*

VARIATION

Roasting the eggplant over charcoal will give the dish a woodsy flavor. Simply place well-pricked eggplant on a grill over a moderate charcoal fire and roast 5″ from the coals, turning frequently, about 45 minutes. Peel, mix with remaining ingredients, heat, and serve as directed.

NPS: 135 C, 25 mg CH, 370 mg S

EGGPLANT PARMIGIANA

6–8 servings

When making a *parmigiana,* do as the Italians do—use a light hand with the garlic and a heavy one with Parmesan.

2 small eggplants, cut in ¼″ rounds (do not peel)
2 eggs, lightly beaten
1½ cups dry bread crumbs mixed with ½ teaspoon salt and ⅛ teaspoon pepper
1 clove garlic, peeled and halved
¾ cup olive oil (about)
1 (1-pound 4-ounce) can Italian plum tomatoes (do not drain)
⅓ cup tomato paste
2 tablespoons minced fresh basil or 2 teaspoons dried basil
1 teaspoon salt
⅛ teaspoon pepper
1 cup grated Parmesan cheese
½ pound mozzarella cheese, sliced very thin

Dip eggplant rounds in eggs, then in seasoned crumbs. Cover loosely and chill 20 minutes. Sauté garlic in 2 tablespoons olive oil 1–2 minutes in a large saucepan over moderate heat, then remove. Add tomatoes, tomato paste, basil, salt, and pepper, cover, and simmer, stirring occasionally, 30 minutes. Preheat oven to 350° F. Pour oil in a large, heavy skillet to a depth of ¼″ and brown eggplant over moderately high heat, doing a few rounds at a time and adding more oil as needed. Drain on paper toweling. Spoon a thin layer of tomato sauce into an ungreased, shallow 2½-quart casserole, then build up alternate layers of eggplant, tomato sauce, Parmesan, and mozzarella, dividing ingredients equally and ending with mozzarella. Bake, uncovered, 30 minutes until bubbly. Serve as a vegetable or, for an Italian dinner, as a main dish following a hearty soup or pasta.

NPS (6–8): 590–445 C, 130–100 mg CH, 1,385–1,040 mg S

EGGPLANT STUFFED WITH PILAF AND RAISINS

4 servings

1 medium-size eggplant
1–1½ teaspoons salt
1 medium-size yellow onion, peeled and chopped fine
2 tablespoons olive oil
2 tablespoons water
1¼ cups Rice Pilaf
¼ cup seedless raisins
⅛ teaspoon pepper
1 teaspoon minced fresh dill or ½ teaspoon dried dill
1 teaspoon minced parsley

Slice 1″ off stem end of eggplant to make a lid, then, using a sharp knife, hollow out eggplant, leaving a shell ½″ thick; sprinkle inside lightly with salt. Chop flesh medium fine. Sauté onion in the oil 8–10 minutes over moderately high heat until golden, add chopped eggplant, and stir-fry 2–3 minutes. Add water, cover, and simmer over lowest heat 10–15 minutes until eggplant is tender. Mix with pilaf and remaining ingredients, fill eggplant shell, and cover with stem lid. Stand eggplant upright in a deep kettle, pour in water to a depth of 3″, cover, and simmer about 45 minutes until fork tender. Check pot occasionally to see that eggplant isn't slipping from its upright position. Lift eggplant from water, cut into wedges, and serve.

NPS: 220 C, 10 mg CH, 800 mg S

TURKISH STUFFED EGGPLANT (IMAM BAYILDI)

4 servings

A Turkish imam's wife once served her husband an eggplant dish so delicious he swooned. Here's the recipe, appropriately named Imam Bayildi, meaning "the parson fainted." Serve it hot as a vegetable, cold as an appetizer.

1 medium-size eggplant, halved lengthwise (do not peel)
2 teaspoons salt
½ cup olive oil
1 large yellow onion, peeled and minced
2 cloves garlic, peeled and crushed
3 medium-size tomatoes, peeled, seeded, and coarsely chopped
⅛ teaspoon pepper

Score cut surfaces of eggplant halves in a crisscross pattern, sprinkle each with ½ teaspoon salt, and let stand 1 hour. Press out as much liquid as possible, rinse in cold water and pat dry on paper toweling. Scoop out centers, leaving shells 1/2" thick, and brush rims with a little oil. Cut centers in 1/2" cubes. Preheat oven to 350° F. Sauté onion and garlic in 1/4 cup oil over moderate heat 8–10 minutes until golden; drain on paper toweling and reserve. Sauté tomatoes in 2 tablespoons oil 5 minutes and mix with onion; brown eggplant cubes in remaining oil, add to onion, and season with pepper and remaining salt. Taste and, if too tart, mix in a little sugar. Place eggplant shells in a lightly greased shallow casserole, cutting a slice off the bottoms, if necessary, to make them stand. Fill and bake, uncovered, 45–50 minutes until tender.

NPS: 310 C, 0 mg CH, 285 mg S*

BELGIAN ENDIVE

(Also known as French Endive, Witloof, and Chicory)

Endive was one of the "bitter herbs" God commanded the Israelites to eat with lamb at the Feast of Passover. Earlier, it was a favorite of the Egyptians, who tossed the leaves into salads and brewed the roots into a bitter drink. The recipes we prize today, however, come from the Belgians and French.

To Prepare for Cooking: Pull off any wilted or discolored outer leaves and cut a thin slice from the root end of each stalk; wash well in cool water.

Serving Tip: Crispen individual endive leaves in ice water and serve with seasoned salt as a low-caloric cocktail snack.

BOILED BELGIAN ENDIVES

4 servings

4 medium-size Belgian endives, prepared for cooking
1 cup boiling water or chicken broth
1 tablespoon lemon juice
1/4 teaspoon salt
Pinch white pepper
2 tablespoons melted butter or margarine

Leave endives whole, halve lengthwise, or cut in rounds 1/8" thick. Boil, covered, in water or broth with lemon juice and salt until tender: 5 minutes for rounds, 14 for halves, 20 for stalks. Drain, add pepper and butter, and toss gently to mix.

NPS (water): 60 C, 15 mg CH, 95 mg S*
NPS (broth): 65 C, 15 mg CH, 145 mg S*

To Parboil for Use in Other Recipes: Use method above but reduce cooking time to 2–3 minutes for rounds, 5–8 for halves, and 10 for whole stalks. Omit seasonings.

VARIATIONS

To Serve Cold: Boil and drain as directed but do not season. Chill stalks in ice water, drain, and marinate in the refrigerator several hours in a good tart dressing. Serve as a salad or cold vegetable. Recipe too flexible for meaningful nutritional count.

⚖ **Low-Calorie Endives:** Boil and drain as directed; omit butter and dress with low-calorie herb, Italian, or French dressing.

NPS: 15 C, 0 mg CH, 40 mg S*

Belgian Endives au Gratin: Boil, drain, and season endives by recipe above; place in an ungreased 1-quart *au gratin* dish, top with 1 1/2 cups hot Cheese Sauce and 1/4 cup grated Cheddar cheese. Broil 5" from heat 3–4 minutes to brown.

NPS: 375 C, 90 mg CH, 695 mg S*

Endives and Ham au Gratin: For additional elegance, roll each endive in 2 thin slices boiled ham before arranging in *au gratin* dish. Cover with sauce and cheese and broil as directed.

NPS: 395 C, 100 mg CH, 1,075 mg S*

Swiss-Style Endives: Boil, drain, and season endives by recipe above; place in a buttered 1-quart *au gratin* dish, sprinkle with about 1 teaspoon sugar and 1/3 cup grated Gruyère or Swiss cheese; broil 5" from heat 2–3 minutes until browned.

NPS: 105 C, 25 mg CH, 130 mg S*

BRAISED BELGIAN ENDIVES

4 servings

This recipe brings out the delicate flavor of endives.

4 medium-size Belgian endives, prepared for cooking
2 tablespoons butter
1/4 cup chicken broth
1/4 teaspoon salt
1 teaspoon lemon juice
Minced parsley or chives (optional garnish)

Sauté endives in butter in a heavy skillet over moderately low heat 7–12 minutes, turning frequently so they become an even nut-brown. Add all remaining ingredients except garnish, cover, and simmer 10–12 minutes until tender. Serve topped with cooking liquid and, if you like, a little minced parsley or chives.

NPS: 65 C, 15 mg CH, 245 mg S*

FENNEL

(Also called Finocchio)

This aromatic Mediterranean vegetable deserves more recognition. It looks like bulbous celery, tastes faintly of licorice, and is delicious raw in salads or cooked in a variety of ways.

To Prepare for Cooking: Discard coarse or blemished outer stalks, trim off feathery tops (save to use as a seasoning) and tough base. Wash well in cool water, using a vegetable brush if necessary to remove stubborn grit. Leave whole or cut up as individual recipes specify.

To Prepare Fennel Hearts: Peel away all heavy outer stalks (save for soups). Quarter bulbs lengthwise and wash in cool water.

Cooking Tip: Mince feathery fennel tops and use as an herb to season salads, boiled carrots, beets, parsnips, or cabbage. Fennel also adds delicate fragrance to broiled chicken and white fish.

BOILED FENNEL

4 servings

4 bulbs fennel, prepared for cooking
1½ cups boiling water or chicken broth
1 teaspoon salt (about)
Pinch white pepper
2 tablespoons butter or margarine

Prepare hearts* or cut stalks in 1″ slices. Bring water or broth to a boil, add salt (reducing amount if broth is salty) and fennel, cover, and boil until crisp-tender: 7–10 minutes for slices, 12–15 for hearts. Drain, add pepper and butter, and toss.

NPS (water): 65 C, 15 mg CH, 305 mg S*
NPS (broth): 70 C, 15 mg CH, 380 mg S*

To Parboil for Use in Other Recipes: Use recipe above but reduce cooking time to 5 minutes for slices, 10 for hearts. Omit seasonings.

VARIATIONS

To Serve Cold: Boil and drain hearts as directed but do not season. Chill in ice water, drain, toss with Vinaigrette, Spanish Vinai-

grette, Rémoulade, or Russian Dressing, and chill several hours. Serve as an appetizer, a salad, or cold vegetable. Recipe too flexible for meaningful nutritional count.

⚖ **Low-Calorie Fennel:** Boil and drain as directed. Omit butter and dress with low-calorie French or Italian dressing.

NPS: 25 C, 0 mg CH, 395 mg S*

Butter-Braised Fennel: Parboil and drain hearts but do not season. Sauté in 3 tablespoons butter 3–4 minutes, turning constantly. Add 2 tablespoons water, cover, and simmer 5–7 minutes until hearts are glazed and golden brown. Add pepper and serve.

NPS (water): 90 C, 25 mg CH, 335 mg S*
NPS (broth): 95 C, 25 mg CH, 410 mg S*

Fennel Parmigiana: Parboil hearts, drain and place in an ungreased 1-quart *au gratin* dish. Drizzle with ¼ cup melted butter, sprinkle with ¼ cup grated Parmesan, and broil 4″ from heat 3–4 minutes until lightly browned.

NPS (water): 140 C, 35 mg CH, 460 mg S*
NPS (broth): 145 C, 35 mg CH, 530 mg S*

FERNS

(Also called Fiddleheads)

The tender shoots of ferns that grow along mossy creek banks are one of spring's rare treats. Most highly prized is the cinnamon fern, which tastes of both asparagus and artichoke. Bracken and ostrich ferns are good too, though tougher and saltier. Ferns are available in specialty shops, but the best are those you pick fresh yourself.

To Prepare for Cooking: Sort, discarding any ferns that are discolored. Cut off stems—you want only the tightly curled "heads." Wash carefully in cool water to remove all traces of sand.

BUTTERED FIDDLEHEADS

4 servings

2 cups ferns, prepared for cooking
½ teaspoon salt
⅛ teaspoon white pepper
½ cup boiling water
¼ cup melted butter or margarine

Place ferns in a saucepan along with salt, pepper, and boiling water. Cover and simmer 20–30 minutes until tender. Drain well, add butter, and toss lightly to mix. Nutritional count for ferns unavailable.

HEARTS OF PALM

(Also called Swamp Cabbage, Cabbage Palm, and Palmetto Cabbage)

These smooth ivory palmetto shoots are rarely seen fresh, though once in a great while they appear in specialty food markets. Canned hearts of palm, cooked and ready to eat, are widely available.

To Prepare for Cooking: Fresh hearts are bitter and must be soaked and sometimes blanched before cooking. Peel away coarse outer layers, cut off fibrous tops, then wash well in tepid water. Leave whole or slice into rounds 1/2″ thick; soak 1 hour in cool water. Drain and taste for bitterness. If still bitter, boil 5 minutes in acidulated water to cover (1 tablespoon lemon juice to 1 quart water) and drain.

To Boil: Place prepared hearts in a saucepan, add lightly salted boiling water to cover, and simmer, covered, until tender: about 45 minutes for slices, 1 1/2–2 hours for whole hearts (when cooking whole hearts, change water at least three times to extract as much bitterness as possible). Drain well, drizzle with melted butter, or serve as you would asparagus with Hollandaise Sauce. Or chill in ice water, drain, and use in salads.

HEARTS OF PALM BRAISED IN WHITE WINE

3–4 servings

1 (14-ounce) can hearts of palm, drained
2 tablespoons butter or margarine
1/4 cup sauterne
1 tablespoon finely chopped pimiento (garnish)
1 hard-cooked egg yolk, sieved (garnish)

Slice hearts crosswise into 1/2″ rounds and sauté in butter 5 minutes over low heat, stirring once or twice. Add wine, cover, and simmer 10 minutes, basting now and then. Transfer hearts to a heated vegetable dish and keep warm; reduce cooking liquid to about 2 tablespoons by boiling rapidly, uncovered. Spoon over hearts, sprinkle with pimiento and egg, and serve.

NPS (3–4): 115–90 C, 110–85 mg CH, 80–60 mg S*

SAUTÉED HEARTS OF PALM MEDALLIONS

4 servings

1 (14-ounce) can hearts of palm, drained
1 egg lightly beaten with 1 tablespoon cold water
2/3 cup toasted seasoned bread crumbs
3 tablespoons butter or margarine

Slice hearts crosswise into rounds 1/2″ thick and pat very dry on paper toweling. Dip rounds in egg, then in crumbs to coat evenly; place on a wire rack and let dry 15 minutes. Melt butter in a large skillet over moderate heat, add rounds, a few at a time, and brown lightly about 1 minute on a side. Drain on paper toweling and set, uncovered, in a 250° F. oven to keep warm while you brown the rest.

NPS: 185 C, 90 mg CH, 635 mg S*

JICAMA
(Yambean, Sicama, Mexican Potato)

Pronounced *HIC-cah-ma,* this brown, turnip-shaped tuber has slightly sweet, crisp white flesh and tastes very much like water chestnut. It can be eaten raw with dips, tossed into salads for added crunch, simmered, sautéed, or stir-fried (strangely, it remains crisp when cooked). Nutritional count unavailable.

Storage Tip: Do not wash or trim, simply wrap in plastic food wrap and refrigerate.

To Prepare for Cooking: Trim off root and stem ends, wash, then peel. Cut in 1/2″ slices or cubes or 1/4″ strips.

To Simmer: Place sliced or cubed jicama in a saucepan, add enough lightly salted boiling water to cover, clap on the lid, and simmer 3–4 minutes over moderate heat. Drain, season with butter or a little heavy cream, salt, and pepper, and serve.

To Sauté or Stir-Fry: Brown jicama in 2–3 tablespoons cooking oil 4–5 minutes. For *sautéing,* use moderate heat and stir occasionally; for *stir-frying,* use slightly higher heat and stir constantly. Remove with a slotted spoon to paper toweling to drain, and season to taste with salt and pepper.

To Serve Cold: Cut in slices or strips, then serve with small bowls of lemon juice and chili powder to be used as dips. Or grate raw and toss into green salads, or sprinkle over Mexican or Oriental dishes as a crunchy, last-minute topping.

KALE

(Also known as Borecole and Colewort)

This sprawling, crinkly cousin of cabbage is so ancient no one knows where it originated. It is from "keal," the Scottish word for the vegetable, that we get "kale." It was also from the Scots that we obtained our first kale plants.

To Prepare for Cooking: Discard woody stems and coarse leaf midribs, then wash thoroughly in cool water. Tear large leaves into bite-size pieces.

Serving Tip: Toss tender young kale leaves into green salads for refreshing crunch.

BOILED KALE

4 servings

To minimize the strong cooking odor of kale, keep the pot tightly covered.

2 pounds kale, prepared for cooking
3 cups boiling water
1 teaspoon salt
1/8 teaspoon pepper
2 tablespoons butter, margarine, or bacon drippings

Coarsely chop kale and place in a large saucepan along with water and salt. Cover and boil slowly 15–20 minutes until tender (to keep kale as green as possible, lift lid once or twice during cooking). Drain well and, if you like, chop kale more finely. Season with pepper and butter or drippings and serve.

NPS: 125 C, 15 mg CH, 295 mg S*

VARIATIONS

⚖ **Low-Calorie Kale:** Boil and drain as directed; omit salt and butter or drippings, and dress with seasoned salt and lemon juice.

NPS: 75 C, 0 mg CH, 410 mg S*

Kale 'n' Cabbage: Combine equal amounts Boiled Kale and hot Steamed Green Cabbage, dress with Lemon Butter, and toss to mix.

NPS: 105 C, 15 mg CH, 20 mg S*

KOHLRABI

(Also known as Cabbage Turnip)

Kohlrabi is the most unusual member of the cabbage family. It looks more like a large pale green turnip than a cabbage and has a delicate, nutlike flavor all its own. Purple kohlrabi is also now coming to market, albeit in limited supply. Cook it just as you would green kohlrabi. It is delicious simply boiled and buttered, mashed, creamed, or baked in a casserole with a grated cheese topping.

To Prepare for Cooking: Remove leaves and stems and discard (if they're very young and tender, they can be cooked with other greens or tossed into salads). Wash bulbs, peel, and cut up as individual recipes specify.

Serving Tip: If you should find really young delicate kohlrabi, peel and slice raw into a green salad.

BOILED KOHLRABI

4–6 servings

8 bulbs kohlrabi, prepared for cooking
1 1/2 cups boiling water
1 teaspoon salt
1/8 teaspoon pepper
2 tablespoons butter or margarine

Cut kohlrabi in 1/2″ cubes, place in a saucepan with water and salt, cover, and boil gently 20–25 minutes until fork tender. Drain, add pepper and butter, and shake pan, uncovered, over low heat until butter melts.

NPS (4–6): 90–60 C, 15–10 mg CH, 205–135 mg S*

To Parboil for Use in Other Recipes: Use recipe above but reduce cooking time to 15 minutes; omit seasonings.

VARIATIONS

⚖ **Low-Calorie Kohlrabi:** Boil and drain as directed; omit butter and sprinkle with minced chives and lemon juice.

NPS (4–6): 40–25 C, 0 mg CH, 145–100 mg S*

Mashed Kohlrabi: Boil and drain as directed, then mash with a potato masher before seasoning. Sprinkle with pepper, add 2 tablespoons butter and 1 tablespoon heavy cream, and mix well.

NPS (4–6): 105–70 C, 20–15 mg CH, 205–135 mg S*

Kohlrabi au Gratin: Boil, drain, and season kohlrabi by recipe above. Place in an unbuttered 1½-quart *au gratin* dish, top with 1½ cups hot Cheese Sauce and ¼ cup grated Cheddar cheese, and broil 5″ from heat 3–4 minutes to brown.

NPS (4–6): 405–270 C, 90–60 mg CH, 800–535 mg S*

Creamed Kohlrabi: Boil and drain as directed but do not season; mix with 1½ cups hot Medium White Sauce or Béchamel Sauce, add a pinch of mace, and serve.

NPS (4–6) (Medium White Sauce): 195–130 C, 35– 25 mg CH, 480–320 mg S*
NPS (4–6) (Béchamel Sauce): 230–155 C, 45–30 mg CH, 560–375 mg S*

LEEKS

Leeks, of course, are onions, but they are so special and so elegant they deserve a section to themselves. Strangely, though peasant food abroad, they've never been widely grown in this country and have thus remained a luxury.

To Prepare for Cooking: Cut off roots and tough green tops, peel away coarse outer layers of stalk, and wash thoroughly in tepid water to remove all sand and grit.

BOILED LEEKS

4 servings

2 bunches leeks, prepared for cooking
1 cup boiling water, chicken or beef broth
2 tablespoons butter or margarine
½ teaspoon salt (about)
Pinch pepper

Lay leeks in a large skillet, add water or broth, cover, and simmer 12–15 minutes until crisp-tender. Drain, add butter, salt, and pepper to taste, and warm, uncovered, shaking skillet gently, 1–2 minutes until butter is melted.

NPS (water): 165 C, 15 mg CH, 345 mg S*
NPS (broth): 170 C, 15 mg CH, 390 mg S*

To Parboil for Use in Other Recipes: Use method above but reduce cooking time to 8– 10 minutes; omit seasonings.

VARIATIONS

To Serve Cold: Boil and drain as directed; chill in ice water, and drain. Cover with a fragrant dressing, and refrigerate several hours. Recipe too flexible for meaningful nutritional count.

⊲⊳ **Low-Calorie Leeks:** Boil and drain leeks; omit butter and dress with 2 tablespoons lemon juice or tarragon vinegar or 3 tablespoons low-calorie Italian or garlic dressing.

NPS: 120 C, 0 mg CH, 335 mg S*

Leeks au Gratin: Parboil and drain leeks; place in an ungreased 1½-quart *au gratin* dish and add 1 cup beef broth. Cover and bake 20 minutes at 350° F.; uncover and bake 10 minutes longer. Mix 1½ cups soft white bread crumbs with ¼ cup each grated Parmesan and melted butter. Sprinkle over leeks and broil 4″ from heat 2–3 minutes until lightly browned.

NPS: 295 C, 35 mg CH, 500 mg S*

LEEK PIE

6–8 servings

Delicious as a first course or light luncheon or supper entree.

1 recipe Flaky Pastry I
6 medium-size leeks, washed, trimmed, and sliced thin
1 cup boiling water
1¼ teaspoons salt
1½ cups light cream
¼ cup milk
2 (3-ounce) packages cream cheese, softened to room temperature
3 egg yolks, lightly beaten
⅛ teaspoon white pepper
Pinch mace

Preheat oven to 425° F. Prepare pastry as recipe directs and fit into a 9″ piepan, making a high fluted edge. Prick bottom and sides of pastry well with a fork; cover with wax paper and fill with uncooked rice or dried beans. Bake 5–7 minutes until firm but not brown, then cool slightly on a wire rack. Remove paper and rice. Lower oven temperature to 325° F. Place leeks, boiling water, and ½ teaspoon salt in a saucepan, cover, and simmer 10–12 minutes; drain leeks well, squeezing out as much liquid as possible, and reserve. In a separate saucepan, heat cream, milk, cream cheese, and remaining salt over moderate heat about 10 minutes, beating with a whisk until cheese is melted and mixture smooth. Mix a little hot sauce into yolks, then stir back into pan; mix in leeks, pepper, and mace. Pour into crust and bake, uncovered, about 45 minutes until filling is set and crust lightly browned. Cool

15–20 minutes on a wire rack, then cut into wedges and serve warm.

NPS (6–8): 505–380 C, 210–155 mg CH, 445–335 mg S*

LENTILS

The pottage Esau sold his birthright for was made of lentils, probably the red lentils of Egypt. Those we know better are the khaki-colored French lentils, although the smaller Egyptian red lentils are sometimes available in big-city Armenian or Turkish groceries. Both the red lentils and the green are only available dried.

To Prepare for Cooking: Place lentils in a colander and rinse under cool water, sorting to remove any bits of gravel or shriveled lentils.

BOILED LENTILS

4 servings   ¢

A good topping for lentils is crisply browned croutons or salt pork cubes.

1 pound dried lentils, washed and sorted
3 cups cold water, chicken or beef broth
1/2 teaspoon salt (about)
1/8 teaspoon pepper

Place all ingredients except pepper in a heavy saucepan, cover, and bring to a boil over high heat. Reduce heat to low and simmer about 45 minutes, stirring occasionally, until lentils are tender but not mushy. *(Note: Most of the water will be absorbed during cooking, so keep a close eye on the pot to make sure lentils don't stick.)* Mix in pepper, taste for salt and add more if needed.

NPS (water): 385 C, 0 mg CH, 305 mg S*
NPS (broth): 415 C, 0 mg CH, 890 mg S*

V A R I A T I O N S

Lentils and Ham: Add a ham bone or pork hock and boil as directed in water. Cut meat from bone and mix into lentils before serving.

NPS: 465 C, 15 mg CH, 1260 mg S*

Savory Lentils: Cook lentils in chicken or beef broth with 1 peeled and chopped large yellow onion, 1 bay leaf, and 1/4 teaspoon dried thyme or rosemary.

NPS: 430 C, 0 mg CH, 620 mg S*

DHAL

4–6 servings

Dhal is the Indian word for lentils, the "meat" of vegetarian sects. This dhal *can* double as meat, although you may prefer it as a potato substitute, a side dish for curry, or even a spaghetti sauce.

1 cup dried lentils, washed and sorted
1 quart cold water
3/4 teaspoon salt
1/2 teaspoon chili powder
1/4 teaspoon turmeric
2 large yellow onions, peeled and chopped fine
2 tablespoons clarified butter*
3 medium-size ripe tomatoes, peeled, cored, seeded, and coarsely chopped

Place lentils, water, salt, chili powder, and turmeric in a heavy saucepan, cover, and bring to a boil over high heat. Reduce heat to low and simmer 45 minutes, stirring occasionally, until lentils are tender, not mushy. Meanwhile, sauté onions in butter over moderate heat 8–10 minutes until golden. Add tomatoes and stir-fry 4–5 minutes. Set aside. When lentils are tender, stir in onions and tomatoes, cover, and simmer 5 minutes. If you plan to serve the dhal over rice or pasta, thin with about 1 cup boiling water until the consistency of a spaghetti sauce.

NPS (4–6): 275–180 C, 15–10 mg CH, 440–295 mg S*

RED LENTILS AND RICE

6 servings

Red lentils and rice are popular throughout the Middle East. Sometimes they're curried, sometimes reinforced with bits of meat, fish, hard-cooked eggs, or cheese (a good way to stretch the meat budget). Lebanese women top lentils and rice with salad greens—it's unusual but good.

1 cup red lentils, washed and sorted
1 quart cold water, beef or chicken broth (about)
2 teaspoons salt (about)
2 medium-size yellow onions, peeled and sliced thin
1/4 cup olive or other cooking oil
1/4 teaspoon pepper
1/2 cup uncooked rice
1 teaspoon curry powder (optional)
1 tablespoon minced parsley

Place lentils, water, and salt (reduce amount to taste if using broth) in a large, heavy saucepan, cover, and bring to a boil; adjust heat so mixture simmers gently and cook 20 minutes. Meanwhile, sauté onions in oil 5–8 minutes until pale golden. Set aside. When lentils have cooked 20 minutes, stir in onions and all remaining ingredients except parsley. Simmer, covered, 20–25 minutes until rice is tender. (*Note:* Watch pot carefully so mixture doesn't stick; add a little water if necessary to give it the consistency of thick applesauce.) Sprinkle with parsley and serve.

NPS (water): 255 C, 0 mg CH, 745 mg S*
NPS (broth): 265 C, 0 mg CH, 1270 mg S*

MUSHROOMS

To ancient Egyptians, mushrooms were "sons of gods" sent to earth on thunderbolts; to the medieval Irish they were leprechaun umbrellas, and to the English they were food, edible only if gathered under a full moon. During Louis XIV's reign, the French began growing mushrooms in caves near Paris. They're grown that way yet. Because gathering wild mushrooms is risky, we concentrate here on the commercially grown white mushrooms, also on those edible wild or imported species becoming increasingly available in both supermarkets and specialty food shops. For the most part (and unless otherwise noted), these may be prepared and cooked like cultivated mushrooms. Here, then, are the mushrooms you are most apt to encounter at the greengrocer or supermarket produce section:

Cèpes (called *Porcini* in Italian, *Steinpilze* in German). These fleshy members of the *boletus* family, gathered from dense forest floors, are dark ocher to light brown and taste of both nuts and wine.

Chanterelles (Girolles in French, *Pfifferlinge* in German). Frilly trumpet- or vase-shaped mushrooms. The egg-yolk-yellow ones taste faintly of apricots, the rarer black chanterelles of both musky earth and hot peppers. Most chanterelles, despite their delicate appearance, are firm and take somewhat longer to cook than other mushrooms.

Enoki (Enoke, Enokidake): Thumb-tack-size Japanese mushrooms with tiny white caps and elongated stems (these should be trimmed by about 1/2"). Sometimes called "Snow Puffs," enokis are moist, slightly acidic, and delicious when tossed raw into salads or stir-fried *briefly* with other vegetables.

Morels (Morilles in French): Prized by gourmands for their pungent earthy taste and meaty texture, these conical, honeycombed brown, beige, or ocher mushrooms come to market in April and May. They are superb when sautéed, creamed, or added to brown sauces and complement, in particular, roast poultry and veal, poached sweetbreads, and boiled pasta. *Note:* The American Mycological Society warns against eating morels raw because they can sometimes upset your stomach.

Pleurotes: These mushrooms average 2"–5" in diameter, they're fleshy, creamy white with tinges of reddish or brownish yellow, and grow on tree stumps and fallen branches, which accounts for their delicate woodsy flavor. The *Oyster Mushroom* (called *Abalone Mushroom* in Oriental groceries) is a shell-shaped cream, gray, or light brown and white pleurote, rather bland and chewy.

Shiitake Mushrooms (Chinese Black Mushrooms): These large, fleshy fungi, which grow on oak logs and *shii* trees, are rich in both flavor and price.

Straw Mushrooms: Planted in beds of straw or rice husks, these shaggy, conically capped beige-brown mushrooms taste mildly of woodsmoke.

Tree Ears (Wood Ears): For centuries the Chinese have gathered these creamy-gilled, brown-capped mushrooms from tree trunks, believing that to eat them regularly is to be assured of a long and happy life. It may be so. Certainly tree ears impart delicate woodsy flavor and smooth buttery texture to dozens of classic Chinese dishes.

Note: A number of these mushrooms are now available canned and dried as well as fresh, among them *morels, shiitake, straw mushrooms,* and *tree ears.*

To Prepare for Cooking: Discard woody stem ends and wipe mushrooms clean with a damp cloth; never wash or soak—you'll send the delicate flavor down the drain.

To Peel: With a paring knife, catch a bit of loose skin on underside of cap and pull up toward top of cap. Repeat until all skin is removed. It isn't necessary to peel mushrooms unless they're to be served raw (try them in salads or stuffed with a salty spread as an hors d'oeuvre).

To Prepare Dried Mushrooms for Cooking: Rinse mushrooms well under cold running water, then soak either in cold water to cover for about 2 hours until soft or in warm water to cover for about 30 minues (maximum flavor is obtained from the cold-water soak). Trim off tough stem ends. *Note: Straw mushrooms* should also be peeled before they're used. And *morels,* because of their honeycombed caps, may need several rinsings to rid them of all grit.

Storage Tip: Store dried mushrooms in glass jars with tops tightly screwed on. Also make sure your hands are dry before reaching into the jar to remove any mushrooms, otherwise you may introduce just enough moisture to mold or spoil them.

SAUTÉED MUSHROOMS

2 servings

So simple and yet so elegant.

1/2 **pound small- to medium-size mushrooms, wiped clean**
3 **tablespoons butter or margarine**
1/4 **teaspoon salt**
1/8 **teaspoon pepper**

If mushrooms are small and tender, trim stems to within 1/2" of the caps. Otherwise, pull stems out of caps and save for soups, stuffings, or meat loaves. Sauté mushrooms rapidly in butter over moderately high heat, stirring or shaking skillet, until lightly browned, about 3 minutes. Drain on paper toweling, season with salt and pepper, and serve.

NPS: 110 C, 25 mg CH, 375 mg S*

VARIATION

Sautéed Sliced Mushrooms: Thinly slice mushrooms and sauté by method above but reduce cooking time to 2 minutes. Nutritional count same as basic recipe.

BROILED MUSHROOMS

4 servings

1 **pound medium-size mushrooms, wiped clean and stemmed**
3/4 **cup melted butter or margarine or cooking oil**
1 **teaspoon salt**
1/8 **teaspoon pepper**

Using your hands, toss mushrooms in butter or oil until well coated. Cover loosely and let stand at room temperature 30 minutes, tossing once or twice. Preheat broiler. Arrange caps, cup side down, on a broiler rack and brush lightly with butter or oil. Broil 5" from heat 5 minutes until lightly browned; turn caps, brush again with butter or oil,

and broil 3 minutes longer until fork tender. Sprinkle with salt and pepper.

NPS: 335 C, 95 mg CH, 920 mg S*

SKILLET MUSHROOMS

4 servings

1 **teaspoon salt**
1 **pound mushrooms, wiped clean and sliced 1/4" thick (include stems)**
2 **tablespoons water**
Pinch pepper
4 **pats Maître d'Hôtel Butter (optional)**

Heat a large, heavy skillet over high heat 1 minute. Sprinkle in salt, add mushrooms, and stir-fry 2–3 minutes, until golden. Keep mushrooms moving constantly to avoid burning. Add water and pepper, turn heat to low, and cook 1 minute. Serve topped, if you like, with pats of Maître d'Hôtel Butter.

NPS (without butter): 30 C, 0 mg CH, 565 mg S*
NPS (with butter): 55 C, 8 mg CH, 595 mg S*

VARIATION

Low-Calorie Skillet Mushrooms: Omit butter pats and dress with a few drops onion, garlic, or lemon juice.

NPS: 30 C, 0 mg CH, 565 mg S*

CREAMED MUSHROOMS

4 servings

Ladled over hot buttered toast or used to fill puff pastry shells, Carolines, or hollowed-out rolls, these mushrooms can be served as a luncheon entree.

1 **pound medium-size mushrooms, wiped clean and sliced 1/4" thick (include stems)**
1/4 **cup butter or margarine**
2 **tablespoons flour**
11/4 **cups milk or 1/2 light cream and 1/2 chicken broth**
3/4 **teaspoon salt**
Pinch white pepper
1/2 **teaspoon Worcestershire sauce**

Stir-fry mushrooms in butter in a large skillet over moderately high heat 2–3 minutes until golden. Blend flour with milk (or cream and broth) until smooth, then slowly stir into mushrooms. Reduce heat to low and cook and stir until thickened. Mix in salt, pepper, and Worcestershire sauce and serve.

NPS (milk): 195 C, 40 mg CH, 590 mg S*
NPS (cream and broth): 230 C, 55 mg CH, 690 mg S*

Mushrooms in Madeira Sauce: Prepare recipe above and just before serving stir in 2 tablespoons sweet Madeira wine.

NPS (milk): 200 C, 40 mg CH, 590 mg S*
NPS (cream and broth): 235 C, 55 mg CH, 690 mg S*

MUSHROOMS, ONIONS, AND GREEN PEPPERS

6 servings

Delicious over broiled steak.

1 medium-size Spanish onion, peeled and chopped fine
3 tablespoons cooking oil
1 pound mushrooms, wiped clean and sliced thin (include stems)
1 large sweet green pepper, cored, seeded, and thinly slivered
1 teaspoon salt
1/8 teaspoon pepper
Pinch mace

Sauté onion in oil in a large, heavy skillet over moderately high heat 8 minutes until golden. Add mushrooms and green pepper and sauté 4–5 minutes until lightly browned. Reduce heat to low and stir-fry 2–3 minutes until pepper is tender. Season with salt, pepper, and mace and serve.

NPS: 90 C, 0 mg CH, 380 mg S*

BAKED MUSHROOM CAPS STUFFED WITH HAZELNUTS

4–6 servings

A luscious garnish for a roast platter.

24 perfect small- to medium-size mushrooms, wiped clean
1/2 cup unsalted butter, softened to room temperature
2/3 cup finely chopped unblanched hazelnuts or pecans
2 tablespoons minced chives
2 tablespoons minced parsley
1 teaspoon salt
1/8 teaspoon pepper
2 tablespoons cognac
1/4 cup cracker meal
1 1/2 cups milk (about)

Preheat oven to 300° F. Carefully remove mushroom stems from caps; set caps aside and chop stems fine. Mix chopped stems with all remaining ingredients except milk and stuff each mushroom cap, mounding mixture in the center. Place stuffed caps in an ungreased 9″ × 9″ × 2″ baking pan and pour in milk to a depth of 3/4″. Bake, uncovered, basting every 15 minutes with milk, 1 hour or until tender. Lift mushrooms from milk and use to garnish a roast or steak platter or serve hot as a vegetable with a little of the milk spooned over each serving.

NPS (4–6): 435–290 C, 75–50 mg CH, 610–405 mg S*

MUSTARD GREENS

(Also called Chinese Mustard and Mustard Spinach)

It's said that Asclepius, god of medicine, gave mustard to man. He intended that the plant be used medicinally, but man soon learned how delicious the greens were if gathered young and cooked like spinach. Nutritional count not available.

To Prepare for Cooking: Pick over greens carefully, removing any roots, woody stems or blemished leaves. Wash two to three times in cool water to remove all grit and sand.

To Boil: See recipe for Boiled Collards, Turnip Greens, or Mustard Greens under Collards.

OKRA

(Also sometimes called Gumbo)

People are generally of two minds about okra—they either adore it or abhor it. It's not the flavor they dislike (that is delicate, rather like eggplant) but the texture (too often slimy). The best preventive: don't overcook.

To Prepare for Cooking: Cut off stems (but not stem ends of pods); scrub okra well in cool water. Leave whole or slice as individual recipes specify.

Cooking Tip: Never cook okra in iron or tin pans because it will turn black (it's edible, just unattractive).

BOILED OKRA

4 servings   ☒

1 pound okra, prepared for cooking
3/4 cup boiling water
1 teaspoon salt
1/8 teaspoon pepper
2 tablespoons butter or margarine

Leave pods whole if small; if large, slice 1″ thick. Place okra in a saucepan with water and salt, cover, and boil gently until just tender: 6–10 minutes for whole pods, 3–4 minutes for slices. Drain, add pepper and butter, and set, uncovered, over low heat, shaking pan gently, until butter melts.

NPS: 85 C, 15 mg CH, 195 mg S*

To Steam Okra: Place okra in a steamer over boiling water, cover, and steam until tender: 3–5 minutes for slices, 8–10 minutes for whole pods.

NPS: 35 C, 0 mg CH, 3 mg S*

To Parboil for Use in Other Recipes: Boil or steam as directed but reduce cooking time to 2 minutes for slices, 5 minutes for pods.

VARIATION

⚖ **Low-Calorie Boiled Okra:** Omit butter and dress with low-calorie herb dressing.

NPS: 35 C, 0 mg CH, 135 mg S*

SOUTHERN FRIED OKRA

4 servings

One of the very best ways to cook okra because little of the original crispness is lost.

1 pound small okra pods, prepared for cooking
1/4 cup unsifted flour
1 egg lightly beaten with 1 tablespoon cold water
1 cup white or yellow corn meal, fine dry bread crumbs, or cracker meal
3 tablespoons butter or margarine, lard, or bacon drippings
3/4 teaspoon salt
Pinch pepper

Cut off okra stem ends and tips and slice pods crosswise into rounds 1/4″ thick. Pat dry on paper toweling. Dip rounds in flour, then in egg, then roll in meal or crumbs to coat evenly. Set on paper toweling. Heat butter, lard, or drippings in a large, heavy skillet 1 minute over moderate heat. Add okra and sauté about 2 minutes on a side until golden brown. Drain on paper toweling, sprinkle with salt and pepper.

NPS: 285 C, 90 mg CH, 520 mg S*

BATTER-FRIED OKRA

4 servings

1 pound small okra pods, parboiled and drained
Lard, shortening, or cooking oil for deep fat frying

BATTER
1 cup sifted flour
1 teaspoon salt
1 cup milk
1 egg, lightly beaten

Pat okra dry on paper toweling. Begin heating fat in a deep fat fryer over moderately high heat; insert deep fat thermometer. Sift flour and salt together into a bowl, slowly add milk and beat until smooth. Beat in egg. When fat reaches 375° F., dip okra, a few pieces at a time, into batter, allowing excess to drain off, then drop into fat. Fry 1–2 minutes until golden brown. Using a slotted spoon, remove to paper toweling to drain. Set, uncovered, in a 250° F. oven to keep warm while you fry the rest.

NPS: 255 C, 85 mg CH, 600 mg S*

VEGETABLE GUMBO

4 servings ▨

A Creole vegetable stew.

3 slices bacon, diced
1/4 cup finely chopped yellow onion
1/4 cup finely chopped celery
1 (1-pound) can tomatoes (do not drain)
1 (10-ounce) package frozen whole baby okra (thaw only to separate pods, then slice in 1″ rounds)
1 (10-ounce) package frozen whole kernel corn (do not thaw)
1 teaspoon salt
1/8 teaspoon pepper
Pinch powdered saffron
Pinch filé powder
2 cups hot cooked rice

Fry bacon in a large skillet over moderate heat 2–3 minutes; add onion and celery and sauté 8–10 minutes until golden. Add tomatoes and okra, cover, and boil gently 3–4 minutes. Add corn, salt, pepper, and saffron, re-cover, and boil 3–4 minutes longer until okra is tender. Stir in filé powder, ladle over rice, and serve.

NPS: 320 C, 10 mg CH, 825 mg S*

ONIONS

During the Civil War, General Grant notified the War Department, "I will not move my army without onions." He got them; moreover, no one thought the request odd, because armies had always traveled with onions. Originally, they were said to make men valiant, later they were used to enliven dull army food. There are many kinds of onions, each a specialist. The best way to distinguish them is to categorize as follows: *dry onions, green or fresh onions, specialty onions.*

Dry Onions

These are dry-skinned, not very perishable onions that keep well unrefrigerated.

Bermuda Onions: These large flat onions can be white, tan, even red skinned; all are mild and sweet, perfect for slicing into salads or onto hamburgers. About 2–3 per pound.

Spanish Onions: Often mistakenly called Bermudas, these fawn-colored jumbos average 1/2 pound apiece. They're mild, sweet, and juicy, good raw, French-fried, or stuffed and baked.

Pearl Onions: Once found only in Europe, these mild, sweet, white-, red-, or gold-skinned miniatures (about 60 in a 10-ounce box) are now widely available. Prepare as you would small white onions but boil 10–12 minutes only.

White Onions: Mild, shimmery little silver-skins about the size of a walnut (there are 18–24 per pound) that are best creamed or simmered in stews. Those less than 1″ in diameter are *pickling onions;* those smaller still, *cocktail onions.*

Yellow Onions: The strongest of the dry onions, these are the round, golden-skinned "cooking" onions we chop or slice and stir into everything from chili to chop suey. About 3–5 per pound.

Red or Italian Onions: Strong, purple-red onions that are best eaten raw in antipasti or salads. About 3–4 per pound.

To Prepare for Cooking: Peel. A quick and tearless way to do small white onions is to let stand 1 minute in boiling water until skins begin to shrivel, then to drain and plunge in ice water. The skins will slip off neatly as peach skins.

Green or Fresh Onions

These are perishable, freshly pulled onions that should be kept in the refrigerator.

Spring or Green Onions: Long, strong, slim onions with green tops and slightly bulbous stems.

Scallions: A sister to the spring onion but slimmer and sweeter.

Leeks: (see the special section on leeks).

Chives: These fragrant wispy green "tops" are the most delicate of all onions. Buy by the pot if possible, set on a sunny window sill, and use as an herb.

To Prepare for Cooking: Scallions and spring onions must be trimmed of roots, wilted tops, and any coarse outer stem coverings. Leave whole or cut up as individual recipes specify. Chives should be washed in cool water, patted dry on paper toweling, gathered into a bunch, and minced or snipped with scissors.

Specialty Onions

There are only two, both available year round, both used sparingly as seasonings.

Garlic: An average bulb, composed of cloves that fit together rather like sections of a tangerine, is about the size of a tangerine. Individual cloves can be small as a lima bean or big as a walnut. When a recipe calls for a clove of garlic, use one about the size of the end of your little finger (or the equivalent). Buy only one bulb of garlic at a time (they quickly dry out) and choose one that is plump and firm. Always peel garlic before using; leave whole, mince, or crush as individual recipes specify, but bear in mind that crushed garlic has about three times the impact of the minced. *Note:* The garlic that has everyone talking (and rushing to mail-order it from California) is the new sweet and mild *elephant garlic.* It's big but bland.

Shallots: Copper skinned and about the size of hazelnuts, shallots are milder than garlic but stronger than most onions. Buy about 1/4 pound at a time (shallots quickly dry up) and select ones that are plump and firm. Peel before using and cut as individual recipes specify.

In addition to the onions described above, there is an ever-widening array of *convenience onions*—powders, juices, flakes, salts, and dry soup mixes that save much in time and tears but cannot compare with fresh onions for flavor.

BOILED ONIONS

4 servings

1½ pounds small white onions, peeled
1½ cups boiling water, chicken or beef broth
1½ teaspoons salt (about)
3 tablespoons butter or margarine
¼ teaspoon paprika

Pinch mace
Pinch pepper

Place onions in a saucepan with water or
broth and 1 teaspoon salt, cover, and boil 20
minutes until tender. Drain, add remaining
salt if onions were boiled in water, the butter, paprika, mace, and pepper and warm,
shaking pan gently, 1–2 minutes until butter
melts.

NPS (water): 135 C, 25 mg CH, 375 mg S*
NPS (broth): 150 C, 25 mg CH, 665 mg S*

To Parboil for Use in Other Recipes: Use recipe above but reduce cooking time to 15
minutes; omit all seasonings.

VARIATIONS

⚔ **Low-Calorie Boiled Onions:** Cook onions as directed in water. Omit butter and
spices and dress with low-calorie Italian or
herb dressing. Recipe too flexible for meaningful nutritional count.

Glazed Onions: Boil and drain onions as directed (reserve 1 tablespoon cooking liquid).
Do not season. Melt 1/4 cup butter in a large
skillet, add reserved cooking liquid, 1/3 cup
light brown sugar, a pinch each mace and
pepper, and simmer, stirring, 3–4 minutes
until syrupy. Add onions and heat 5–8 minutes, turning frequently, until evenly glazed.
Serve hot as a vegetable or use to garnish a
roast platter.

NPS (water): 225 C, 30 mg CH, 410 mg S*
NPS (broth): 230 C, 30 mg CH, 510 mg S*

Creamed Onions: Boil and drain onions in
water as directed but do not season; combine
with 1 1/2 cups hot Medium White Sauce, 1
tablespoon light brown sugar, and a pinch
nutmeg and cayenne pepper. Warm, stirring,
2–3 minutes to blend flavors.

NPS: 230 C, 30 mg CH, 815 mg S*

Onions in Cheddar Sauce: Prepare Creamed
Onions as recipe directs but omit brown
sugar; stir in 1 1/4 cups coarsely grated sharp
Cheddar cheese, 1 teaspoon prepared spicy
brown mustard, 1/2 teaspoon Worcestershire
sauce, and, if you like, 1 tablespoon cream
sherry. Heat and stir until smooth.

NPS: 355 C, 75 mg CH, 865 mg S*

PAN-BRAISED ONIONS

4–6 servings

2 pounds small white onions, peeled
1/4 cup unsalted butter
1/2 cup dry vermouth
1/4 teaspoon salt
Pinch pepper

Sauté onions in butter in a large, heavy skillet over moderately high heat, turning frequently, 10 minutes until golden. Add vermouth, reduce heat to moderately low,
cover, and simmer 15 minutes until crisp-
tender. Sprinkle with salt and pepper and
turn onions in pan juices to glaze evenly.
Serve hot as a vegetable or use in making
such stews as Boeuf à la Bourguignonne.

*NPS (4–6): 190–125 C, 30–20 mg CH, 155–105
mg S**

SAUTÉED ONIONS

4 servings

6 medium-size yellow onions, peeled
2–3 tablespoons flour (optional)
1/4 cup butter, margarine, or cooking oil
Salt
Pepper

Thinly slice onions and separate into rings
or chop medium fine. Dredge, if you like, in
flour (onions will be a bit browner). Heat
butter or oil in a large, heavy skillet over
moderate heat 1 minute (or use an electric
skillet with temperature control set at
350° F.). Sauté onions, turning frequently,
8–10 minutes for golden, 10–12 minutes for
well browned. If you like them slightly crisp,
raise heat to moderately high at the end of
cooking and stir-fry 1 minute. Drain quickly
on paper toweling, sprinkle with salt and
pepper, and serve.

NPS: 165 C, 30 mg CH, 130 mg S*

FRENCH-FRIED ONION RINGS

4 servings

Crisp and sweet.

Lard, shortening, or cooking oil for deep fat
frying
1 large Spanish onion, peeled and sliced 1/4″
thick

BATTER
2/3 cup sifted flour
3/4 teaspoon salt
1/4 teaspoon baking powder
2/3 cup milk

Begin heating fat in a deep fat fryer over
moderately high heat; insert deep fat thermometer. Separate onion slices into rings.
Sift flour, salt, and baking powder together
into a bowl. Slowly add milk and beat until
bubbles appear on surface of batter. When
fat reaches 375° F., dip onion rings, 4 or 5 at
a time, into batter, allowing excess to drain

off, then drop into fat. Fry 1 minute until golden brown; turn rings to brown evenly if they don't flip on their own. Remove to a paper-towel-lined baking sheet and set, uncovered, in a 250° F. oven while you fry the rest. (*Note:* Skim bits of batter from fat between fryings before they burn.)

NPS: 240 C, 15 mg CH, 465 mg S*

VARIATION

Shallow-Fried Onion Rings: Pour 1½″ cooking oil into an electric skillet (temperature control set at 375° F.) or large, heavy skillet set over moderately high heat. When hot, not smoking, dip onion rings into batter and fry as recipe directs.

NPS: 240 C, 15 mg CH, 465 mg S*

BAKED ONIONS

4 servings

Baked onions are mellower and sweeter than boiled onions. They are delicious with roast meats or fowl.

4 medium-size Spanish onions (do not peel)
⅓ cup water
1 teaspoon salt
⅛ teaspoon pepper
¼ cup melted butter or margarine

Preheat oven to 400° F. Trim root end from onions and arrange in a buttered shallow casserole. Pour in water. Bake, uncovered, 1½ hours until fork tender. Using a small piece of paper toweling as a pot holder, grasp skin of onion at the top and pull off. Sprinkle onions with salt and pepper, drizzle with butter, and serve.

NPS: 160 C, 30 mg CH, 680 mg S*

ROASTED ONIONS

4 servings

Oven-roasted onions glazed with drippings.

8 medium-size yellow or Bermuda onions or 4 medium-size Spanish onions, peeled
½ cup bacon drippings, shortening, or lard
Salt
Pepper

Preheat oven to 400° F. Place onions in a roasting pan or casserole, add drippings, shortening, or lard. Roast, uncovered, until fork tender: 45–50 minutes for yellow or Bermuda onions; 1¼–1½ hours for Spanish onions. Turn onions halfway through cooking so they'll brown evenly. Drain on paper toweling, sprinkle with salt and pepper, and serve.

NPS: 215 C, 15 mg CH, 125 mg S*

CREAMED SCALLIONS

4 servings

Scallions are a good substitute for the more expensive, less available leeks, especially when creamed.

4 bunches scallions, washed and trimmed of roots and tops
1 cup boiling water
1 teaspoon salt
½ cup heavy cream
2 tablespoons butter or margarine
2 tablespoons flour blended with 2 tablespoons cold water
⅛ teaspoon white pepper

Place scallions, water, and salt in a saucepan, cover, and boil gently 5–7 minutes until just tender. Lift scallions from liquid and keep warm. Add cream and butter to scallion liquid, then stir in flour-water paste. Heat, stirring, until thickened and smooth. Add pepper, taste for salt, and add more if needed. Pour sauce over scallions, mix lightly, and serve.

NPS: 220 C, 55 mg CH, 625 mg S*

CHAMP

4 servings

Champ is a traditional dish from Northern Ireland made with scallions and mashed potatoes.

3 bunches scallions, prepared for cooking and coarsely chopped (include tops)
½ cup boiling water
½ teaspoon salt
3 cups hot seasoned mashed potatoes
2 tablespoons butter or margarine

Place scallions, water, and salt in a small saucepan, cover, and boil 4–5 minutes until scallions are very tender. Drain well and briskly beat scallions into potatoes with a fork. Spoon into a heated vegetable dish, dot with butter, and serve.

NPS: 240 C, 15 mg CH, 655 mg S*

VARIATION

Baked Champ: Spoon mixture into a buttered 1½-quart casserole, roughen surface with a fork, and drizzle with melted butter.

Bake, uncovered, 20 minutes at 400° F., then broil 4″ from the heat 1–2 minutes to brown.

NPS: 240 C, 15 mg CH, 655 mg S*

STUFFED ONIONS

4 servings

Boiled Spanish or yellow onions, hollowed out, can be filled with many vegetables: buttered peas and mushrooms; creamed diced carrots and peas; puréed spinach; mashed sweet potatoes; Harvard Beets.

4 medium-size Spanish onions, peeled
2 1/3 cups water
1 teaspoon salt
1 tablespoon cooking oil

S T U F F I N G
2 tablespoons butter or margarine
3/4 cup soft white bread crumbs
1 teaspoon salt
1/8 teaspoon pepper
1/4 cup finely grated sharp Cheddar cheese
Minced parsley (garnish)

Preheat oven to 400° F. Cut a 1/2″ slice from the top of each onion (save for other recipes). Place onions, 2 cups water, and salt in a large saucepan, cover, and simmer 20–25 minutes. Drain well. With a spoon, scoop out center of each onion and reserve, leaving a shell 1/2″ thick; place shells in a buttered shallow 1-quart casserole, and brush with oil. Pour remaining water into casserole. Chop onion centers fine and sauté 5 minutes in butter over moderate heat. Mix in all remaining stuffing ingredients except parsley, spoon into onion shells, and bake, uncovered, 30–40 minutes until lightly browned. Sprinkle with parsley and serve.

NPS: 195 C, 25 mg CH, 845 mg S*

Some Additional Stuffings for Onions

To the chopped sautéed onion centers, add any of the following:
• 3/4 cup hot cooked rice, 1/4 cup chopped peeled tomatoes, and a pinch each garlic salt and powdered saffron.
• 1/2 cup each hot cooked rice and slivered boiled ham and 2 tablespoons grated Parmesan cheese.
• 1 cup seasoned mashed potatoes and 2 tablespoons melted butter. Fill onion shells and bake as directed in basic recipe above.

FINNISH ONION FRY IN SOUR CREAM

4 servings

1/4 cup butter or margarine
1 pound Spanish onions, peeled and chopped fine
1/2 pound mushrooms, wiped clean and sliced thin
2 pimientos, seeded and slivered
1 cup sour cream
1/2 teaspoon salt
1/8 teaspoon paprika

Melt butter in a very large, heavy skillet over moderately low heat, add onions, and cook, stirring occasionally, 10–12 minutes until tender but not browned; lift from skillet and reserve. Raise heat to moderately high and sauté mushrooms 2–3 minutes until golden. Return onions to skillet, add pimientos, and mix well. Reduce heat to low, mix in sour cream and salt, and heat, stirring, 1–2 minutes (do not boil). Sprinkle with paprika and serve.

NPS: 285 C, 55 mg CH, 445 mg S*

PISSALADIÈRE (ONION TART À LA NIÇOISE)

6 servings

Nearly every French town has an onion tart, but only in Nice, where the cooking is as much Italian as French, does it resemble pizza (it's called *pissaladière*).

1 recipe Pizza Dough (see Pizza in the bread chapter)
6 medium-size yellow onions, peeled and sliced thin
1 clove garlic, peeled and crushed
1 bay leaf
1/4 cup olive oil
1 teaspoon salt
1/8 teaspoon pepper
1 (2-ounce) can anchovy fillets, drained
1 cup brined, pitted ripe Italian olives

Make pastry according to recipe and fit into a 12″ pizza pan. Preheat oven to 450° F. Sauté onions, garlic, and bay leaf in oil in a large, heavy skillet over moderate heat 8–10 minutes until onions are golden. Stir in salt; remove bay leaf. Spread onions evenly over pastry and sprinkle with pepper. Arrange anchovies, spoke fashion, over onions and dot olives here and there. Bake, uncovered, 15 minutes until pastry is browned. Cut into wedges and serve as a light entree or cut into smaller wedges and serve as an appetizer.

NPS: 515 C, 5 mg CH, 1,175 mg S*

PARSLEY ROOT (HAMBURG PARSLEY)

This subspecies of parsley produces a root that looks like a small parsnip but tastes like a cross between turnip and celeriac. Use it as European country cooks do to flavor soups and stews, or prepare and cook it as you would carrots.

To Prepare for Cooking: Remove root end and tops; scrub well in cool water and, unless skin is tough or discolored, do not peel. Slice or cube parsley root, then dip immediately in acidulated water (1 tablespoon vinegar or lemon juice to 2 quarts water) to prevent darkening.

How to Cook: Boil, mash, or sauce just as you would carrots. *Tip:* Always use an enameled, stainless-steel, or anodized aluminum pan when cooking parsley root so that it does not discolor.

PARSNIPS

The Roman Emperor Tiberius was so fond of parsnips he sent to the Rhine country each year for his supply because in that climate they grew to plump and sugary perfection. His cooks were ordered to treat the parsnips with reverence, to boil them gently and sauce them with honey wine. Parsnips later fell from favor and they have never regained their popularity. In Tudor England they were used primarily for making bread, in Ireland for brewing beer. Even today, few people relish parsnips, possibly because they have been eclipsed by their cousin, the carrot, whose sweeter, nuttier flavor most of us prefer. Parsnips are worth trying, however, because they are economical and make a welcome change of pace.

To Prepare for Cooking: Remove root ends and tops; scrub well in cool water and peel. If parsnips seem large, halve and remove woody central cores. Otherwise leave whole or cut as individual recipes specify.

Cooking Tip: To improve the flavor of parsnips, add a little brown sugar to the cooking water and, if you like, a peeled 1″ cube fresh gingerroot or blade of mace.

BOILED PARSNIPS

2–4 servings   ¢

1 pound parsnips, prepared for cooking
1½ cups boiling water
2 tablespoons butter or margarine
1 teaspoon salt
⅛ teaspoon pepper

Place parsnips in a large saucepan, add water, cover, and boil 30–35 minutes until tender; drain. Cut into thin slices or small cubes and return to pan. Add remaining ingredients and warm, uncovered, over low heat, shaking pan gently, 2–3 minutes until butter is melted and parsnips lightly glazed.

NPS (2–4): 250–125 C, 30–15 mg CH, 1,240–620 mg S*

To Parboil for Use in Other Recipes: Boil as directed above but reduce cooking time to 10 minutes; omit seasonings.

VARIATIONS

¢ **Mashed Parsnips:** Quarter and core parsnips, boil as directed, but reduce cooking time to 15–20 minutes. Drain and mash with a potato masher. Beat in butter, salt, and pepper called for, also, if you like, 1–2 tablespoons heavy cream.

NPS (2–4) (with cream): 275–135 C, 40–20 mg CH, 1,245–620 mg S*

¢ **Currant-Glazed Parsnips:** Add 2 tablespoons currant jelly to parsnips along with butter, salt, and pepper and warm as directed to glaze.

NPS (2–4): 300–150 C, 30–15 mg CH, 1,245–620 mg S*

¢ **Orange-Glazed Parsnips:** Add 2 tablespoons orange marmalade to parsnips along with butter and seasonings and warm as directed to glaze.

NPS (2–4): 300–150 C, 15 mg CH, 1,245–620 mg S*

ROASTED PARSNIPS

4 servings   ¢

½ cup melted bacon or beef drippings or shortening
1½ pounds medium-size parsnips, prepared for cooking and halved
½ teaspoon salt

Preheat oven to 400° F. Pour drippings or shortening into a 10″ flameproof glass pie-pan, add parsnips, turning in drippings to coat. Roast, uncovered, 40–45 minutes until lightly browned and fork tender, turning once or twice so they brown evenly. Drain on paper toweling, sprinkle with salt, and serve.

NPS: 265 C, 15 mg CH, 400 mg S*

PARSNIP CAKES

4–6 servings   ¢

1 egg, lightly beaten
Pinch nutmeg
Salt
Pepper
2 pounds parsnips, boiled and mashed
1 egg lightly beaten with 1 tablespoon cold
  water
¾ cup toasted seasoned bread crumbs
¼ cup butter or margarine

Mix egg, nutmeg, salt, and pepper to taste into parsnips. Cool to room temperature, cover, and chill 1 hour. Using ⅓ cup as a measure, shape mixture into 8 cakes and flatten; dip in egg, then in crumbs to coat evenly, cover, and chill ½ hour. Melt butter in a large skillet over moderate heat, add half the cakes, and brown well on both sides, about 3–4 minutes. Drain on paper toweling and set, uncovered, in a 250° F. oven to keep warm while you brown the rest.

*NPS (4–6): 370–245 C, 170–110 mg CH, 770–515
  mg S**

FRENCH-FRIED PARSNIPS

4 servings

1½ pounds parsnips, parboiled and cut in ⅜″
  strips as for French fries
Lard, shortening, or cooking oil for deep fat
  frying
Salt

Pat parsnip strips dry on paper toweling. Meanwhile, begin heating fat in a deep fat fryer over moderately high heat; insert wire basket and deep fat thermometer. When fat reaches 375° F., drop in about half the parsnips and fry 1–2 minutes until golden brown and crisp. Transfer to a paper-towel-lined baking sheet and set, uncovered, in a 250° F. oven to keep warm while you fry the rest. Sprinkle with salt and serve.

NPS: 170 C, 5 mg CH, 15 mg S*

PEAS

"This subject of peas continues to absorb all others," wrote Madame de Maintenon of the new fad at Louis XIV's court. "Some ladies, after having supped at the Royal Table and well supped, too, returning to their own homes, at the risk of suffering from indigestion, will again eat peas before going to bed. It is both a fashion and a madness." These were *petits pois,* a tiny variety of today's green peas and a far cry from the mealy, unsweet field peas of old (these are now almost unavailable except as dried whole or split yellow peas). The newest members of the pea family (at least the newest to Americans) are the tender snow peas of Chinese cooking and the sugar snap peas *(mangetout),* a shorter, somewhat plumper version of the snow pea with larger peas inside the pod.

To Prepare for Cooking:

Green Peas: Shell *just* before cooking, no sooner.

Snow or Sugar Snap Peas: Trim off stem ends and pull to remove strings; wash pods (but don't soak) in cool water.

Dried Whole Peas: Wash, sort, and soak overnight in 1 quart cold water. Or use the quick method* recommended for soaking dried beans.

Dried Split Peas: Wash and sort.

Cooking Tip: Add a pea pod to the pot when cooking green peas—gives them a just-picked flavor.

BOILED FRESH GREEN PEAS

4 servings

3 pounds green peas in the pod
½ cup boiling water
1 teaspoon sugar
1 teaspoon salt
Pinch pepper
2 tablespoons butter or margarine

Shell peas, place in a saucepan with water and sugar, cover, and boil 8–10 minutes until tender. Drain, add salt, pepper, and butter, and toss lightly to mix.

NPS: 160 C, 15 mg CH, 610 mg S*

To Parboil for Use in Other Recipes: Boil as directed but reduce cooking time to 5 minutes; omit seasonings.

VARIATIONS

To Serve Cold: Boil and drain as directed, then chill in ice water. Drain and refrigerate until needed. Use in salads or other recipes calling for cold peas.

Minted Green Peas: Boil as directed, adding a mint sprig to the pot.

NPS: 160 C, 15 mg CH, 610 mg S*

Green Peas with Rosemary: Tuck a sprig fresh rosemary into the pot, letting it perfume the peas as they boil, or add a pinch dried rosemary to peas before serving.

NPS: 160 C, 15 mg CH, 610 mg S*

Green Peas in Cream: Boil and drain peas by method above, stir in 1/4 cup heavy cream and a pinch mace or nutmeg along with seasonings called for; serve in soup bowls.

NPS: 215 C, 35 mg CH, 615 mg S*

Green Peas with Mint and Orange: Boil and drain peas as directed; keep warm. Warm 2 tablespoons finely slivered orange rind (orange part only) in 1/4 cup butter 2–3 minutes over low heat, add to peas along with 2 tablespoons chopped fresh mint, and toss lightly to mix.

NPS: 265 C, 45 mg CH, 725 mg S*

Puréed Green Peas *(2–3 servings):* Purée boiled, drained peas by buzzing 15–20 seconds in an electric blender at high speed or 10–15 seconds in a food processor fitted with the metal chopping blade. Mix in 2 tablespoons heavy cream along with seasonings called for and beat until light.

NPS (2–3): 270–180 C, 20–15 mg CH, 1,110–740 mg S*

Some Vegetables to Team with Green Peas: Diced, cooked carrots or celery; boiled tiny new potatoes; sautéed, sliced mushrooms; cooked whole kernel or cream-style corn; boiled cauliflowerets; sautéed, sliced scallions.

GREEN PEAS AND DUMPLINGS

4 servings

3 pounds green peas, shelled
1¼ cups boiling water
1 cup light cream
2 tablespoons butter or margarine
1 tablespoon sugar
1 mint sprig
1 teaspoon salt
Pinch pepper

DUMPLINGS
1 cup sifted flour
1 tablespoon sugar
1½ teaspoons baking powder
1/2 teaspoon salt
1 tablespoon butter or margarine
1/2 cup milk

Place peas, boiling water, cream, butter, sugar, mint, salt, and pepper in a large saucepan, cover, set over moderate heat, and let come to a full boil. Meanwhile, quickly sift flour with sugar, baking powder, and salt into a small bowl and cut in butter with a pastry blender until mixture is the texture of coarse meal. Pour in milk and stir briskly with a fork *just* to mix, no longer. Drop dumplings from a tablespoon on top of *boiling* pea liquid, covering surface. Cover and simmer exactly 15 minutes (don't peek or dumplings won't be light). Remove mint and serve in soup bowls, spooning lots of cooking liquid over each portion.

NPS: 450 C, 65 mg CH, 1,110 mg S*

PEAS À LA FRANÇAISE

4 servings

3 pounds green peas, shelled
1 cup finely shredded romaine or iceberg lettuce
12 scallions, trimmed and cut in rounds 1/4″ thick
1 bay leaf and 1 sprig each parsley and thyme, tied in cheesecloth *(bouquet garni)*
1/4 teaspoon sugar
1/4 cup boiling water
1/4 cup butter or margarine
1 teaspoon salt
Pinch pepper

Place all ingredients except butter, salt, and pepper in a saucepan, cover, and boil 8–10 minutes, stirring once or twice, until peas are tender. Drain and remove *bouquet garni.* Add butter, salt, and pepper, cover, and shake pan gently over low heat until butter melts. Toss lightly and serve.

NPS: 235 C, 30 mg CH, 675 mg S*

VARIATION

Substitute 2 (10-ounce) packages frozen green peas for the fresh, reducing amount of boiling water to 2 tablespoons. Add butter to saucepan before cooking, then boil peas, covered, 5–7 minutes, breaking up any large chunks after 2 minutes of cooking. Season and serve.

NPS: 230 C, 30 mg CH, 855 mg S*

BOILED FRESH SNOW PEA PODS

4–6 servings ⊠

1 pound small snow pea pods, prepared for cooking
2 cups boiling water
1/2 teaspoon salt
Pinch pepper
2–4 tablespoons melted butter or margarine

Place pea pods in a large saucepan, pour in boiling water, and set over high heat. The instant water returns to a full rolling boil, time peas and boil, uncovered, exactly 2 minutes. Drain in a colander, transfer to a heated vegetable dish, sprinkle with salt and pepper, and drizzle with butter. Toss very gently and serve.

NPS (4–6): 110–75 C, 15–10 mg CH, 335–220 mg S*

Snow Peas and Water Chestnuts: Add 3–4 thinly sliced water chestnuts to peas just before serving.

NPS (4–6): 115–75 C, 15–10 mg CH, 335–225 mg S*

Snow Peas and Scallions: Add 8 finely chopped scallions (white part only) to peas just before serving.

NPS (4–6): 125–85 C, 15–10 mg CH, 335–225 mg S*

Boiled Fresh Sugar Snap Peas: Substitute 1 pound sugar snap peas, prepared for cooking, for the snow pea pods. Cook as recipe directs, increasing boiling time to 3–4 minutes; pods should be *just* crisp-tender. Drain and season to taste. Nutritional count not available.

CHINESE-STYLE SNOW PEAS

4–6 servings

1 pound small snow pea pods, prepared for cooking
1 small yellow onion, peeled and minced
1 clove garlic, peeled and minced
1 (1″) cube fresh gingerroot, peeled and minced
2 tablespoons peanut or sesame oil
2 tablespoons hot water
1–2 tablespoons soy sauce

Pat snow peas dry on paper toweling. Stir-fry onion, garlic, and gingerroot in oil in a large heavy skillet or *wok* over moderately high heat 1–2 minutes until limp. Add snow peas and water, reduce heat to moderate, cover and cook *1 minute.* Remove lid and cook, stirring constantly, until water evaporates. Mix in soy sauce and serve.

NPS (4–6): 130–85 C, 0 mg CH, 335–225 mg S*

Chinese-Style Broccoli Flowerets: For the snow peas, substitute 1 (2-pound) head broccoli, divided into small flowerets. Proceed as recipe directs, allowing broccoli to cook 3–4 minutes.

NPS (4–6): 105–70 C, 0 mg CH, 370–245 mg S*

Chinese-Style Asparagus Tips: For the snow peas, substitute 2 pounds asparagus, prepared for cooking (use tips only, save stalks for soup). Proceed as recipe directs, allowing asparagus to cook 2 minutes.

NPS (4–6): 75–50 C, 0 mg CH, 335–220 mg S*

BOILED DRIED WHOLE PEAS

4–6 servings ¢

For special piquancy, drizzle a little vinegar over these peas before serving.

1 pound dried whole green or yellow peas, washed and sorted
2½ quarts cold water (about)
2 tablespoons butter, margarine, bacon or roast drippings
2–3 teaspoons salt
⅛ teaspoon pepper

Soak peas in 1 quart water overnight or use the quick method.* Drain, measure soaking water, and add enough cold water to total 1½ quarts. Simmer peas, covered, in the water 1¾–2 hours, stirring occasionally, until tender and almost all water has evaporated. If mixture seems soupy, simmer, uncovered, a few minutes. Stir in butter or drippings, salt to taste, add pepper, and serve.

NPS (4–6): 445–295 C, 15–10 mg CH, 1,205–800 mg S*

SAVORY SPLIT PEA PURÉE

4 servings ¢

1 cup dried split green or yellow peas, washed and sorted
2 cups chicken or beef broth, or cold water
¾ teaspoon salt
1 small yellow onion, peeled and chopped fine
1 carrot, peeled and finely chopped
2 stalks celery, minced
1 clove garlic, peeled and crushed
1 bay leaf
2 tablespoons butter or margarine

Place all ingredients in a heavy saucepan, cover, and bring to a boil over high heat. Reduce heat to moderately low and simmer 35–40 minutes, stirring occasionally, until peas are mushy. (*Note:* If lid does not fit tightly, you may have to add an extra ¼ cup boiling water toward the end of cooking so peas don't stick.) Remove from heat, discard bay leaf, and beat peas with a wooden spoon or, if you prefer, purée by buzzing 15–20 seconds in an electric blender at high speed or 10–15 seconds in a food processor fitted with the metal chopping blade. Reheat, if necessary, and serve hot, topped, if you like, by butter-browned croutons or crisp, crumbled bacon.

NPS: 260 C, 15 mg CH, 910 mg S*

PEPPERS

When Columbus discovered the West Indies, he found island natives eating scarlet and emerald pods that contained all the fire of costly East Indian black pepper. He called these pods "peppers" and "peppers" they have remained, although botanically they are not peppers but members of a large family that also includes tomatoes and potatoes. Old World cooks applauded the New World peppers, found them "more pungent than the peppers of the Caucasus," and devised delightful new ways of using them. The peppers we know today can be lumped into two large categories—the sweet and the hot. Either may be green or red because peppers, like tomatoes, turn red (or in some instances, sunny yellow, even dark purple) as they ripen.

Until recently, it was rare to find any fresh hot peppers at a supermarket, but today they are becoming fairly commonplace. As a general rule, the smaller and more pointed the pepper, the hotter it will be. Among the more available varieties:

Anaheim (Poblano) Chilies: Large, mild, plum-shaped green peppers suitable for stuffing (use them for Chiles Rellenos).

Cayenne Chilies: Slim, twisted green pods 5″–6″ long, sharply pointed at one end. They're fiery, so use with restraint to "heat up" guacamole and assorted South-of-the-Border recipes.

Fresno Chilies: Small, incendiary green or greenish red peppers. Use sparingly to flavor Tex-Mex or Szechuan dishes.

Jalapeño Chilies: Plump but pointed green peppers measuring about 2″–3″ long and 1″ across the top. They're good and hot, the choice of Southwestern cooks.

Pasilla Chilies: Big, fleshy green peppers that are sweet and only a few degrees hotter than bell peppers.

Serrano Chilies: These might be described as pint-size *jalapeños* (they average 1″–1½″). They're hot as all get-out and their seeds are pure dynamite. Mexican cooks routinely boil or roast these chilies before using them to cool their fire. Like *jalapeños,* with which they may be used interchangeably, they are

integral to a vast repertoire of Mexican and Tex-Mex sauces, stews, and stir-fried dishes.

Yellow Chilies: These medium-size, mild, bright yellow peppers are perfect for stuffing.

Note: The seeds and veins are the hottest parts of all fresh chilies, so to minimize the burn, remove them.

To Prepare for Cooking: Wash peppers in cool water; cut up as individual recipes specify. *Note:* All peppers will be mellower if first roasted and peeled.

To Roast and Peel: Spread peppers out on a baking sheet, set as close to the broiler unit as possible, then broil the peppers about 10 minutes, turning often, until their skins blacken evenly. Remove the peppers from the broiler, then wrap in a damp towel and let stand about 10 minutes until the skins loosen. Beginning at the top of each pepper, peel the skin away in strips. *Caution:* Be sure to wear plastic or rubber gloves when working with chilies and avoid rubbing your face or eyes. If you have no gloves, wash your hands thoroughly after handling chilies. They contain an oil *(capsaicin)* that can raise welts on tender skin.

To Prepare for Stuffing: Using a small sharp knife, cut a wide circle around stem of pepper and lift off (save if stem-lids are to be used to cover stuffing during baking). Scoop out core and seeds and discard.

To Parboil Before Stuffing: Because peppers will not always cook as fast as their stuffing, they must sometimes be parboiled. To do so, prepare for stuffing by method above, then lay peppers on their sides in a large kettle and add lightly salted boiling water to cover. If tops are to be used, add to kettle. Cover and boil 6–8 minutes until crisp-tender (remove tops after 4 minutes). Pour off water and drain peppers upside-down on paper toweling.

Dried Whole Chili Peppers

The most widely available of these are the *ancho* (nothing more than the dried *Anaheim* or *Poblano* chili) and the *pasilla.* Both are mild and both can be prepared the same way.

To Prepare: Soften peppers by soaking about 1 hour in just enough warm water to cover. Drain, remove stem end, slit pepper lengthwise and, if you prefer a mild flavor, scrape out all seeds. Substitute measure for measure for fresh Anaheim or pasilla peppers in recipes.

Caution: Use the same precautions when handling dried chilies as you do for the fresh.

PEPPERS STUFFED WITH SPANISH RICE

4 servings

4 large sweet green or red peppers, washed
4 cups Spanish Rice
1/4 cup coarsely grated Monterey Jack or sharp Cheddar cheese
1 cup water (about)

Preheat oven to 375° F. Prepare peppers for stuffing and parboil.* Stand close together in an ungreased shallow 1-quart casserole, fill with Spanish rice, and sprinkle with cheese. Pour water around peppers. Bake, uncovered, 45 minutes until peppers are tender, checking occasionally to make sure water hasn't boiled away—there should be a little in the bottom of the casserole at all times. Using 2 large spoons, lift peppers to a heated dish and serve.

NPS: 250 C, 5 mg CH, 625 mg S*

VARIATIONS

Peppers Stuffed with Spanish Rice and Meat: Reduce amount of Spanish Rice to 2½ cups and mix with 1½ cups chopped, cooked meat, poultry, or seafood (this is a splendid way to use up leftovers). Stuff and bake peppers as directed. Serve hot, topped if you like, with Tomato Sauce.

NPS: 315 C, 55 mg CH, 445 mg S*

Peppers Stuffed with Macaroni Marinara: Instead of stuffing peppers with Spanish Rice, stuff with 3 cups boiled macaroni shells mixed with 2 cups Marinara Sauce. Sprinkle peppers with cheese. Pour 1½ cups Marinara Sauce into kettle with peppers and bake as directed above. Serve from casserole, spooning some of the sauce over each portion.

NPS: 230 C, 5 mg CH, 495 mg S*

Some Other Stuffings for Peppers (allow 1 cup per pepper and bake as directed above): Macaroni and cheese, chili con carne, corned beef hash, Rice Pilaf, Saffron Rice, Ratatouille, Pisto, Jambalaya, any *risotto.*

SAUTÉED SWEET GREEN OR RED PEPPERS

2–4 servings

Serve these peppers as a vegetable or use to garnish meat or egg platters. They're also good mixed with sautéed sliced mushrooms, hashed brown potatoes, boiled whole kernel corn, or buttered baby limas.

2 tablespoons olive or cooking oil
2 large sweet green or red peppers, washed, cored, seeded, and cut in long, thin strips
1/4 teaspoon salt
Pepper

Heat oil in a heavy skillet over moderate heat 1 minute. Add peppers and sauté, stirring frequently, 4–6 minutes until lightly browned. Turn heat to low, cover, and simmer 2–3 minutes until crisp-tender. Using a slotted spoon, transfer to a heated vegetable dish, sprinkle with salt, a grinding or two of the pepper mill, and serve.

NPS (2–4): 115–60 C, 0 mg CH, 285–145 mg S*

ITALIAN PEPPERS AND ONIONS

4 servings

3 tablespoons olive oil
3 large sweet red or green peppers or 8 Italian sweet green peppers, washed, cored, seeded, and cut in long, thin strips
1 medium-size Spanish onion, peeled and sliced thin
1 clove garlic, peeled and crushed
1/2 teaspoon salt
Pinch pepper

Heat oil in a large, heavy skillet over moderate heat. Add peppers, onion, and garlic and stir-fry 8 minutes until onion is golden. Cover, turn heat to low, and simmer 5 minutes, shaking pan occasionally. Uncover, cook, stirring, 1–2 minutes to drive off excess moisture; add salt and pepper and serve. Especially good with veal or chicken or in a hero sandwich with hot Italian sausages.

NPS: 105 C, 0 mg CH, 275 mg S*

MARINATED ROASTED PEPPERS

2–4 servings   ⚖

An elegant cold appetizer or salad.

4 medium-size sweet red and/or green peppers, washed, roasted, and peeled*
1 tablespoon olive oil
1 tablespoon red wine vinegar
1 clove garlic, peeled and quartered

4 bay leaves
1/4 teaspoon salt
Pinch pepper

Core peppers, seed, and cut into 1" × 2" strips. Place in a small bowl, add remaining ingredients and toss gently to mix. Cover and marinate at room temperature several hours, turning occasionally. Remove garlic and bay leaves and serve.

NPS (2–4): 130–65 C, 0 mg CH, 300–150 mg S*

PEPPERS IN SWISS CHEESE SAUCE

4 servings

5 large sweet green peppers, washed, roasted, and peeled*

S A U C E
2 tablespoons butter or margarine
2 tablespoons flour
1 1/4 cups milk
1/4 pound Swiss cheese, coarsely grated
1/2 teaspoon salt
Pinch white pepper

Preheat oven to 375° F. Core peppers, seed, and cut into 2" squares. Place peppers in an ungreased 1-quart casserole and set aside while you make the sauce. Melt butter in a saucepan over moderate heat, blend in flour, then slowly stir in milk. Heat, stirring constantly, until thickened. Add cheese, salt, and pepper, cook, and stir 1–2 minutes longer until cheese melts and sauce is smooth. Pour over peppers and mix lightly. Cover and bake 20–25 minutes until peppers are very tender.

NPS: 250 C, 50 mg CH, 465 mg S*

PLANTAINS

Wherever explorers sailed in warm waters, they found plantains, starchy banana-shaped fruits, which natives knew as many ways to cook as we do potatoes. Plantains taste rather like yams and, like them, are best when baked, sautéed, or candied.

To Prepare for Cooking: Peel (just as you would a banana) unless plantains are to be baked in their skins.

To Bake: Choose ripe plantains; do not peel but slit skins lengthwise down one side. Place on a baking sheet and bake, uncovered, 20 minutes at 350° F. Turn and bake 25–30 minutes longer until tender. Serve hot with lots of butter, salt, and pepper.

To Sauté: Use ripe plantains; peel and quarter lengthwise. Sauté in 1/4 cup butter over moderate heat, turning often, 15–20 minutes until tender. Roll in sugar and serve.

To Deep-Fry: Peel hard green plantains and slice very thin on the bias so slices are oval. Soak 1 hour in lightly salted water, drain, and pat dry on paper toweling. Fry, a few chips at a time, in 2" cooking oil over high heat 2–3 minutes until golden. Drain on paper toweling, sprinkle with salt, and serve at room temperature.

To Candy: Peel ripe plantains, quarter lengthwise, and soak 1/2 hour in lightly salted water. Drain, place in a buttered 9" × 9" × 2" baking dish, dot well with butter, and sprinkle heavily with light brown sugar. Bake, uncovered, 20–25 minutes at 350° F., turn, dot again with butter, and sprinkle with sugar. Bake 25–30 minutes longer until tender.

IRISH POTATOES

The Irish potato isn't Irish. It's South American, one of the New World foods brought to Europe by the conquistadors. Europe wasn't impressed and potatoes might never have been accepted if they hadn't had boosters like Sir Francis Drake, Sir Walter Raleigh, Frederick the Great, even Marie Antoinette, who wore potato flowers in her hair. The real credit for establishing potatoes, however, belongs to the poor of Ireland and Germany, who proved that they were *enjoyable* as well as edible. There are so many kinds of potatoes even experts can't keep them straight. Grocers usually classify them simply as *all-purpose, baking,* or *boiling potatoes.* New potatoes, often hilled separately, are boiling potatoes *(new* refers both to immature potatoes and to those that haven't been in storage; they are in best supply between mid-May and mid-September). For *America's Top Potatoes* see Fresh Vegetable Chart.

And Two New Varieties: You may now find in your supermarket *Finnish Potatoes (Yellow Finn)* and *Yellow Rose Potatoes.* Both have russet to brown skins, pale yellow, choice buttery flesh, and are best when boiled. They are usually available from October to February. By all means try them and cook as you would an all-purpose potato.

To Prepare for Cooking: Scrub and remove eyes. To preserve nutrients, do not peel.

BOILED POTATOES

4–6 servings   ¢

6 medium-size potatoes, scrubbed
2 cups boiling water, chicken or beef broth
1 teaspoon salt

Peel potatoes only if they're to be boiled in broth or a stew, at the same time cutting out eyes and green "sunburned" spots; drop in cold water to prevent darkening. Place potatoes, water or broth, and salt (reduce amount if broth is salty) in a large saucepan, cover, and boil slowly about 30 minutes until tender. Drain and peel (if not already done). Return to pan, set, uncovered, over lowest heat, and shake briskly 1–2 minutes to drive off steam. Serve piping hot with butter, salt, and pepper.

NPS (4–6): 170–115 C, 0 mg CH, 280–185 mg S*

To Parboil for Use in Other Recipes: Peel potatoes and leave whole or halve. Boil halves 10 minutes in lightly salted water, whole potatoes 15–20 minutes. Do not season.

VARIATIONS

¢   **Parsleyed Potatoes:** Roll boiled, peeled potatoes in 1/4 cup each melted butter and minced parsley (or for special fragrance, 1/2 and 1/2 minced parsley and mint or basil).

NPS (4–6): 275–180 C, 30–20 mg CH, 400–265 mg S*

¢   **Potato Balls:** With a melon baller, cut raw, peeled potatoes into 1" balls. *(Note:* Because of waste, you'll need 9–12 potatoes for 4–6 servings; scraps can be cooked separately and used for mashed potatoes.) Boil potato balls 15–20 minutes until just tender; drain and serve with salt, pepper, and butter or, if you like, sprinkled with minced parsley. Recipe too flexible for meaningful nutritional count.

¢   **Riced Potatoes:** Force boiled, peeled potatoes through a ricer or fine sieve, letting them mound in a serving dish. Drizzle with 1/4 cup melted butter and sprinkle with 1 tablespoon minced parsley, basil, or chives.

NPS (4–6): 275–180 C, 30–20 mg CH, 395–265 mg S*

¢   **Mashed Potatoes:** Boil potatoes in skins as directed, drain, peel, and dry out over low heat but do not season. Mash or beat with an electric mixer. Add 1/3 cup softened butter, salt and pepper to taste, and, depending on how creamy you like your potatoes, 1/4– 1/3 cup hot milk, evaporated milk, or cream. Beat briskly with whisk or mixer *just* until

light. If potatoes grow cold, or if dinner is delayed, spoon into a buttered casserole, cover, and warm 8–10 minutes in a 250° F. oven.

NPS (4–6) (with cream): 335–220 C, 50–35 mg CH, 440–295 mg S*

BAKED POTATOES

Allow 1 large Idaho or other mealy type potato per person (always choose those of uniform size with few eyes and no green spots)   ¢

Preheat oven to 425° F. (Potatoes *can* be baked at any temperature between 300° F. and 450° F., but they'll be flakiest done at 425° F. They can also be baked along with other foods, but again, won't be so nice and dry.) Scrub potatoes well, then pierce almost to the center with a sharp fork so steam can escape. Bake directly on oven racks about 1 hour until tender (those baked at lower temperatures will take longer, of course, sometimes as much as 1/2 hour). Make an X-shaped cut in the top of each potato, press sides gently to open, then push a fat chunk of butter down inside each and sprinkle with salt and pepper.

To Oil (or Not to Oil) the Skins: If you like a soft-skinned potato, oil.

To Wrap (or Not to Wrap) in Foil: Again it's a matter of choice. Foil-wrapped potatoes will be soft skinned and moist inside.

To Speed Baking: Insert aluminum potato nails and potatoes will cook twice as fast.

To Charcoal Bake: Wrap each potato in foil and bake at edge of a moderate charcoal fire 3/4–1 hour, turning two or three times. If you like crisp, charred skins, bake without wrapping (test for doneness after 1/2 hour). *Note:* Potatoes may be baked the same way on outdoor gas and electric barbecue grills; cooking times will be about the same, too.

NPS: 220 C, 0 mg CH, 15 mg S*

To Give Baked Potatoes Special Flair, top with any of the following:
• Sour cream (or, for fewer calories, cottage cheese) and minced chives
• Melted butter and minced chives, dill, basil, parsley, or marjoram
• Melted butter, minced dill pickle, and crisp bacon bits
• Melted butter and minced onion or scallions

FRANCONIA POTATOES (OVEN-ROASTED POTATOES)

4 servings   ¢

1/2 cup melted beef or bacon drippings or
  cooking oil
6 medium-size potatoes, peeled, halved,
  parboiled, and drained
Salt

Preheat oven to 400° F. Pour drippings in a shallow roasting pan, add potatoes, turning in fat to coat. Roast, uncovered, turning occasionally, about 40 minutes until tender and nut brown. Drain on paper toweling, sprinkle with salt, and serve.

NPS: 340 C, 15 mg CH, 5 mg S*

V A R I A T I O N S

¢ **Potatoes Roasted with Meat:** When roast has about 1 hour longer to cook, add peeled, halved, parboiled potatoes to pan and roast, uncovered, turning occasionally, until meat is done. If there are few pan drippings, add 2–3 tablespoons cooking oil.

NPS: 400 C, 15 mg CH, 5 mg S*

¢ **Château Potatoes:** Peel 6 *raw* potatoes, quarter, and then trim each quarter until it is the size and shape of a jumbo olive. Roast as directed above, reducing cooking time to 30 minutes. Drain, season, and, if you like, sprinkle with minced parsley.

NPS: 310 C, 15 mg CH, 5 mg S*

¢ **Parisienne Potatoes:** With a melon baller, cut raw, peeled potatoes into 1″ balls. Roast and season as for Château Potatoes.

NPS: 280 C, 15 mg CH, 5 mg S*

¢ **Sautéed Château or Parisienne Potatoes:** Cut potatoes as directed but, instead of roasting, sauté in 1/4 cup clarified butter* 15–20 minutes over moderately low heat, turning frequently.

NPS: 255 C, 35 mg CH, 5 mg S*

SOME WAYS TO USE LEFTOVER POTATOES

2–4 servings

M A S H E D

Potato Casserole: Mix 2 cups mashed potatoes with 1/4 cup heavy cream and 2 tablespoons minced onion. Spoon into a buttered 1-quart casserole, top with 1/4 cup grated sharp Cheddar or Swiss cheese, and bake, uncovered, 30 minutes at 350° F.

NPS (2–4): 360–180 C, 55–25 mg CH, 795–395 mg S*

Potato Patties or Croquettes: Shape into patties, roll in flour, dip in lightly beaten egg, then in toasted bread crumbs. Brown 1–2 minutes on a side in 2 tablespoons butter. *For additional flavor,* mix in any of the following before shaping (1 tablespoon to 1 cup mashed potatoes): grated or fried chopped onion; minced parsley, dill, or chives; cooked crumbled bacon; finely chopped toasted peanuts, almonds, pecans, or piñon nuts. Recipe too flexible for meaningful nutritional count.

Substitute for freshly mashed potatoes when making Farmhouse Potato Topping or Cottage Potato Casserole.

B O I L E D   O R   B A K E D   *(Peel before using)*

Creamed Potatoes: Slice or dice potatoes. Measure, place in a saucepan, add 1/4 cup heavy cream for each 1 cup potatoes, and simmer, uncovered, over low heat, stirring now and then, until cream has reduced by half. Season with salt and white pepper to taste, sprinkle with minced chives, parsley, or dill, and serve. Recipe too flexible for meaningful nutritional count.

Potatoes au Gratin: Mix 2 cups sliced, diced, or coarsely grated potatoes with 1 cup Medium White Sauce or Parsley Sauce. Spoon into a buttered 1-quart *au gratin* dish, top with cracker meal or grated Cheddar cheese, and bake, uncovered, 20 minutes at 350° F. Brown under the broiler and serve. *Variation:* If you like, mix in any leftover peas, beans, corn, chopped asparagus, broccoli, or cauliflower and bake as directed. Recipe too flexible for meaningful nutritional count.

Potato-Onion Pie: Mix 2 cups thinly sliced potatoes with 1 thinly sliced sautéed yellow onion. Place in a buttered 9″ piepan, spread with 1/2 cup sour cream, and bake, uncovered, 20 minutes at 350° F. Sprinkle with paprika and serve.

NPS (2–4): 255–125 C, 25–10 mg CH, 40–20 mg S*

Substitute for freshly cooked potatoes when making any potato salad (if potatoes are firm), Hashed Brown Potatoes, O'Brien Potatoes, or Lyonnaise Potatoes.

STUFFED BAKED POTATOES

4 servings

4 large, hot baked potatoes
1/2 cup hot milk

1/4 cup butter or margarine, softened to room
   temperature
1 teaspoon salt
1/8 teaspoon white pepper
Melted butter or margarine

Preheat broiler. Cut a 1/4" lengthwise slice
from top of each potato, then scoop flesh
into a bowl, taking care not to break skins.
Mash potatoes and beat in milk, butter, salt,
and pepper. Spoon into skins, roughen surface with a fork, and brush with melted butter. Place on a lightly greased baking sheet
and broil 3"–4" from heat 2–3 minutes until
lightly browned.

NPS: 300 C, 70 mg CH, 835 mg S*

VARIATION

Add any of the following to the mashed potato mixture: 1 cup grated sharp Cheddar
cheese; 1/2 cup crumbled blue cheese; 1/4 cup
minced onion, scallions, or chives; 1 (61/2-
ounce) can drained, flaked tuna or salmon; 1
cup cooked sausage meat. Recipe too flexible
for meaningful nutritional count.

HASHED BROWN POTATOES

4 servings ¢

6 large potatoes, boiled, peeled, and cut in 1/2"
   cubes
1 medium-size yellow onion, peeled and minced
3 tablespoons bacon drippings, butter,
   margarine, or cooking oil
1 teaspoon salt
1/8 teaspoon pepper

Brown potatoes and onion 5–7 minutes in
fat in a heavy skillet over moderate heat,
pressing into a pancake. Shake pan often so
mixture doesn't stick. Sprinkle with salt and
pepper, cut in 4 wedges, turn, brown other
sides, and serve.

NPS: 305 C, 7 mg CH, 610 mg S*

VARIATIONS

¢ **O'Brien Potatoes:** Follow recipe above,
frying 1/2 minced sweet green pepper and 2
tablespoons coarsely chopped pimiento with
onion and potatoes. Fry 10–15 minutes,
turning often, until potatoes are lightly
crisp. Add salt and pepper.

NPS: 310 C, 7 mg CH, 610 mg S*

¢ **Lyonnaise Potatoes:** Slice potatoes 1/4"
thick instead of cubing; omit onion. Fry potatoes in fat 10–12 minutes until golden. In a
separate skillet, sauté 2 thinly sliced, peeled
yellow onions in 2 tablespoons butter 8–10
minutes until golden; add to potatoes, fry 1–

2 minutes longer, sprinkle with salt, pepper,
and minced parsley.

NPS: 365 C, 20 mg CH, 670 mg S*

¢ **Country-Fried Raw Potatoes:** Cut *raw*,
peeled potatoes in 1/2" slices; omit onion.
Place potatoes in a skillet with drippings
called for, cover, and cook 10 minutes. Uncover and fry 10–12 minutes, stirring, until
browned. Add salt and pepper and serve.

NPS: 295 C, 7 mg CH, 605 mg S*

¢ **Oven-Fried Potatoes for a Crowd:** Peel 9
pounds potatoes and cut in 1/2" cubes. Place
in 2 large roasting pans and drizzle each
with 1/2 cup melted drippings or oil. Cover
with foil and bake 15 minutes at 400° F.; uncover, stir, and bake 30 minutes. Raise heat
to 500° F., stir, and bake 10–15 minutes until brown. Sprinkle well with salt and pepper
and serve, using a slotted spoon. Makes
about 20 servings.

NPS: 200 C, 7 mg CH, 605 mg S*

FRENCH-FRIED POTATOES

4–6 servings

3 pounds Idaho or all-purpose potatoes
Shortening or oil for deep fat frying
Salt
Pepper

Peel potatoes, one at a time, cut into strips
the length of the potato and 3/8" wide, letting each fall into cold water. When all
strips are cut, soak 10 minutes in cold water.
Drain and pat dry on paper toweling. Meanwhile, heat shortening or oil in a deep fat
fryer over high heat (use a deep fat thermometer). When fat reaches 375° F., place
1/3 of the potatoes in frying basket and fry 8–
10 minutes until golden brown. Drain on paper toweling and keep warm in a 250° F.
oven while you fry the rest. Sprinkle with
salt and pepper and serve very hot.

NPS (4–6): 290–195 C, 0 mg CH, 10–5 mg S*

VARIATIONS

Twice-Fried French Fries: Prepare potatoes
as directed. Heat shortening or oil to 330° F.,
add potatoes, about 1 cup at a time, and fry
2 minutes until lightly golden and all sputtering stops. Drain on paper toweling. Potatoes can now be held until just before serving. For the second frying, heat fat to 375° F.
and fry, one third of the potatoes at a time, 5
minutes until crisply golden.

NPS (4–6): 290–195 C, 0 mg CH, 10–5 mg S*

Shoestring Potatoes: Cut potatoes into matchstick strips about 2″ long and ⅛″ thick. Soak in cold water as for French fries, drain, and pat dry. Fry about one third of the potatoes at a time in deep fat (375° F.) 3–5 minutes until crisp and golden. Drain on paper toweling and serve.

NPS (4–6): 290–195 C, 0 mg CH, 10–5 mg S*

SOUFFLÉ POTATOES

4 servings

For this tricky recipe, you *must* have mature storage potatoes with plenty of starch. If you can't find them, don't even try to make Soufflé Potatoes. Even when the potatoes are perfect, a few slices may refuse to "puff."

6 large mature Idaho potatoes
Cooking oil, shortening, or lard for deep fat
  frying
Salt

Peel potatoes, trimming so they're uniformly oval. Cut *lengthwise* into slices ⅛″ thick (they must be of uniform thickness) and soak 20 minutes in ice water. Meanwhile, heat fat in a deep fat fryer over moderately high heat; insert wire basket and deep fat thermometer. Drain potatoes and pat dry on paper toweling. When fat reaches 300° F., lift pan from heat and drop in enough slices to form a single layer. As they rise to surface, agitate basket to keep them covered with fat. When fat temperature drops to 200° F. (after about 4 minutes), remove slices to paper toweling to drain. Repeat with remaining slices. (*Note:* You can prepare recipe to this point early in the day; cool potatoes and cover until shortly before serving. No need to refrigerate.) Reheat fat to 400° F. Drop in slices one at a time. They should bob to the surface at once and puff. Cook 1–2 minutes, turning as needed to brown puffs evenly. Drain on paper toweling, sprinkle with salt, and serve. Puffs will deflate on standing but may be repuffed by dropping in 400° F. fat (*Note:* If you have 2 deep fat fryers, use one for the partial cooking, the other for the puffing.)

NPS: 315 C, 0 mg CH, 10 mg S*

SCALLOPED POTATOES

4–6 servings

1 quart very thinly sliced, peeled potatoes
  (you'll need 4–5 medium-size potatoes)
2 small yellow onions, peeled and sliced paper
  thin

¼ cup butter or margarine
2 tablespoons flour
1 tablespoon minced fresh dill or ¼ teaspoon
  dried dill
¼ teaspoon summer savory (optional)
1 teaspoon salt
⅛ teaspoon pepper
1½ cups milk

Preheat oven to 325° F. In a buttered 2-quart casserole build up alternate layers of potatoes and onions, beginning and ending with potatoes. Dot each onion layer with butter and sprinkle with flour, herbs, salt, and pepper. Pour in milk, cover, and bake 45 minutes. Uncover and bake 30–40 minutes until potatoes are tender and almost all liquid is absorbed. Broil, if you like, to brown, and serve.

NPS (4–6): 295–195 C, 45–30 mg CH, 720–480 mg S*

VARIATIONS

Cream-Scalloped Potatoes: Follow recipe above, substituting light or heavy cream for milk and omitting flour. Bake as directed.

NPS (4–6) (with light cream): 400–265 C, 90–60 mg CH, 710–475 mg S*
NPS (4–6) (with heavy cream): 530–355 C, 155–100 mg CH, 705–470 mg S*

¢ **Budget Scalloped Potatoes:** Follow recipe above, substituting bacon drippings for butter and water for milk. Bake as directed.

NPS (4–6): 230–150 C, 10–5 mg CH, 620–415 mg S*

Scalloped Potatoes with Ham: Use a 2½-quart casserole. Layer 2 cups diced cooked ham and ½ cup thinly sliced, butter-sautéed mushrooms in with other ingredients. Pour in milk, and bake as directed.

NPS (4–6): 425–285 C, 85–50 mg CH, 1,800–1,200 mg S*

Scalloped Potatoes with Cheese: Use a 2½-quart casserole. Layer 1½ cups grated Gruyère or sharp Cheddar cheese in with other ingredients, omitting flour. Pour 2 cups milk over all and bake as directed.

NPS (4–6): 530–355 C, 105–70 mg CH, 920–615 mg S*

FARMHOUSE POTATO TOPPING

4 servings

3 cups hot unseasoned mashed potatoes
1 egg, lightly beaten
2 tablespoons softened butter or margarine
¾ cup sour cream
⅛ teaspoon white pepper

1 teaspoon salt
1/4 teaspoon nutmeg

Mix together all ingredients and use as a topping for oven-baked stews. Or spoon into a buttered shallow 1-quart casserole and broil 4" from heat 3–4 minutes.

NPS: 310 C, 100 mg CH, 1,170 mg S*

COTTAGE POTATO CASSEROLE

6 servings

3 cups cream-style cottage cheese
4 cups hot unseasoned mashed potatoes
3/4 cup sour cream
2 tablespoons finely chopped scallions (include tops)
2 teaspoons salt
1/8 teaspoon white pepper
1–2 tablespoons melted butter or margarine

Preheat oven to 350° F. Sieve cottage cheese or purée in an electric blender at medium speed. Mix with potatoes and all remaining ingredients except butter. Spoon into a buttered 2-quart casserole, roughen surface with a fork, and brush with melted butter. Bake, uncovered, 30 minutes until lightly browned.

NPS: 320 C, 35 mg CH, 1,655 mg S*

DUCHESS POTATOES

6 servings

6 medium-size potatoes, boiled and drained
1/4 cup butter or margarine
Pinch nutmeg
1/8 teaspoon white pepper
1 teaspoon salt
2 tablespoons milk
1 egg, lightly beaten
1 egg yolk, lightly beaten
1 egg beaten with 1 tablespoon cold water (glaze)

Peel potatoes, mash, and measure 4 cups. Beat butter, nutmeg, pepper, salt, milk, egg, and egg yolk into potatoes. Meanwhile, preheat broiler. Fill a pastry bag fitted with a large rosette tip with potatoes and press out onto a lightly greased baking sheet, forming 12 spiral cones about 2 1/2" in diameter. Or simply spoon potatoes into 12 mounds. Brush lightly with egg glaze. Broil 5" from heat 3–5 minutes until lightly browned and serve.

NPS: 220 C, 160 mg CH, 475 mg S*

VARIATIONS

• Bake 10 minutes at 450° F. instead of broiling.
• Beat any one of the following into the potatoes: 1/4 teaspoon minced garlic, 1 tablespoon minced parsley or chives, 1 teaspoon minced basil, dill, or chervil. Broil or bake as directed.

NPS: 220 C, 160 mg CH, 475 mg S*

Planked Potatoes: These usually accompany planked steak, chops, or fish. When meat has browned on one side, turn and transfer to oiled plank. Pipe a ruffled border of potatoes around edge of plank, brush with egg glaze, and broil until meat is done. If potatoes brown too fast, cover loosely with foil.

NPS: 220 C, 160 mg CH, 475 mg S*

POTATO PANCAKES

4 servings   ¢

2 large Idaho potatoes, peeled
1 egg, lightly beaten
2 tablespoons flour
1 small yellow onion, peeled and finely grated
1/4 teaspoon baking powder
1 teaspoon salt
2 tablespoons cooking oil

Coarsely grate potatoes into a bowl of cold water and let stand 15–20 minutes. Meanwhile mix egg and flour until smooth and stir in all remaining ingredients except oil. Drain potatoes, squeeze as dry as possible, and stir into batter. Heat oil in a large, heavy skillet over high heat 1–2 minutes. Drop potato mixture by spoonfuls into oil, shaping into 4 or 5 large cakes and flattening slightly with a spatula. Brown 1–2 minutes on each side, turn heat down low, and cook pancakes 20–25 minutes, turning frequently, so they're cooked through. Drain on paper toweling and serve piping hot. Good with sour cream or applesauce.

NPS: 175 C, 70 mg CH, 595 mg S*

RÖSTI

4 servings

In German Switzerland this pie-sized potato pancake is served almost every day.

3 large Idaho potatoes
1/4 cup lard, butter, or margarine
1 1/2 teaspoons salt
1/8 teaspoon pepper

Peel potatoes, one at a time, and grate moderately coarsely, letting shreds fall into cold water. When all are grated, drain well and pat dry on paper toweling. Heat fat in a heavy 9″ skillet over moderate heat 1 minute, add potatoes, salt, and pepper, toss lightly in the fat, then press down gently with a pancake turner to level the surface. Turn heat to moderately low and fry slowly about 15 minutes, without stirring, until a golden brown crust forms on the bottom. Loosen "pancake" with a spatula and turn by easing out onto a plate. Invert onto a second plate, then slide back into skillet and brown the other side. To serve, slide onto platter and cut in wedges.

NPS: 230 C, 10 mg CH, 830 mg S*

VARIATION

Mix a little finely grated yellow onion into potatoes before frying.

NPS: 235 C, 10 mg CH, 830 mg S*

POTATOES ANNA

6 servings

One of the great classic potato recipes, this one is said to have been created by a lovesick French chef in honor of a beautiful lady named Anna.

1/3 cup clarified butter*
5 large potatoes (the baking varieties won't work)
1½ teaspoons salt mixed with 1/4 teaspoon pepper

Preheat oven to 450° F. Brush a 9″ ovenproof glass pie dish or shallow 1½-quart casserole with butter. (Glass is better because you can check on the final browning.) Peel potatoes and slice very thin, letting slices drop into cold water. Drain and measure potatoes (you should have 6 cups); pat dry on paper toweling. Arrange the most perfect slices in slightly overlapping concentric circles over the bottom of the pie dish, then add a row around the sides. Brush generously with butter and sprinkle with salt and pepper. Layer remaining slices the same way, brushing with butter and sprinkling with salt and pepper. You needn't be so artistic about the middle layers, but do make sure potatoes are well packed. Cover dish with foil, weight down with a heavy lid, and bake on center rack 50–55 minutes until potatoes are *just* tender. Uncover, reduce heat to 425° F., move dish to lowest rack, and bake 15–20 minutes until bottom slices turn amber-brown. Take from oven, let stand 4–5 minutes, then loosen sides and bottom with a spatula, trying not to disturb the design. Invert on a heated platter and ease out potatoes. (If any should stick to the dish, simply lift out and replace in design.) Cut in wedges and serve.

NPS: 225 C, 30 mg CH, 555 mg S*

VARIATIONS

• Sprinkle a little finely grated Parmesan cheese between potato layers.

NPS: 240 C, 30 mg CH, 615 mg S*

• Sprinkle a little minced fresh basil or chives between potato layers.

NPS: 225 C, 30 mg CH, 555 mg S*

• Spread sautéed chopped onion between potatoes, using 1/2 cup in all.

NPS: 225 C, 30 mg CH, 560 mg S*

BOILED NEW POTATOES

4 servings   ¢

Really fresh new potatoes, those dug in the spring or early summer, will cook faster than those that have been in storage.

12 medium-size new potatoes, scrubbed
3 cups boiling water
1 or 2 sprigs mint (optional)

Place all ingredients in a large saucepan, cover, and boil gently 30–45 minutes until fork tender. Drain, discarding mint, if used, and serve potatoes in or out of their skins with butter, salt, and freshly ground pepper.

NPS: 115 C, 0 mg CH, 5 mg S*

VARIATIONS

¢ **Parsleyed New Potatoes:** Just before serving, peel potatoes, roll in 1/4 cup melted butter, then in 1/4 cup minced parsley.

NPS: 215 C, 30 mg CH, 125 mg S*

¢ **Herbed New Potatoes:** Certain fresh herbs—chives, dill, basil, marjoram, coriander—go beautifully with new potatoes. Simply roll the boiled, peeled potatoes in 1/4 cup melted butter, then in 2 tablespoons minced herbs.

NPS: 215 C, 30 mg CH, 120 mg S*

NEW POTATOES IN DILL SAUCE

4 servings

16 small new potatoes, boiled in their skins

S A U C E :
3 tablespoons unsalted butter
2 tablespoons minced fresh dill
2 tablespoons flour
1 cup light cream
3/4 teaspoon salt
1/8 teaspoon white pepper

Drain potatoes, peel, return to pan, and keep warm. Melt butter in a small saucepan over moderate heat, add dill, and heat, stirring, 1–2 minutes. Blend in flour, then add cream, salt, and pepper and heat, stirring constantly, about 5 minutes until thickened and smooth. Pour sauce over potatoes, set over lowest heat, and warm, uncovered, stirring occasionally, 10–12 minutes.

NPS: 360 C, 60 mg CH, 445 mg S*

DANISH-STYLE NEW POTATOES

6–8 servings

Delectable! Young new potatoes in a buttery, brown sugar glaze.

18 medium-size new potatoes, boiled in their skins

G L A Z E
1/2 cup firmly packed light brown sugar
1/4 cup water
2 tablespoons butter or margarine
1 teaspoon salt
2 tablespoons minced fresh dill

Drain potatoes and let cool 10 minutes. Meanwhile, heat all glaze ingredients except dill in a large, heavy skillet over moderate heat, stirring, 5–8 minutes until slightly thickened and bubbly. Reduce heat to low and stir in dill. Peel potatoes, add to skillet, and warm 10–15 minutes, rolling in glaze, until they glisten and are the color of topaz.

NPS (6–8): 215–160 C, 10–7 mg CH, 415–310 mg S*

SWEET POTATOES AND YAMS

It was Columbus who introduced America's sunny, honey-sweet yams to Europe. Europeans apparently liked them from the start, because they were well established by the time Irish potatoes became acceptable. *Note:* Paler red skinned *Boniatos,* sometimes available in supermarkets, are white-fleshed South American yams. Use in any recipes calling for sweet potatoes.

To Prepare for Cooking: Scrub well; to preserve vitamins, cook in the skins.

BOILED SWEET POTATOES OR YAMS

4 servings ¢

4 medium-size sweet potatoes or yams
2 cups boiling water
1 teaspoon salt

Scrub potatoes well in cold water, cut off root end, and remove any bruised spots. Place in a large saucepan with water and salt, cover, and boil 35–40 minutes until *just* tender (sweet potatoes tend to be mushy, so watch closely during the last 5–10 minutes). Drain and serve in or out of the skins with plenty of butter, salt, and pepper.

NPS: 145 C, 0 mg CH, 285 mg S*

To Parboil for Use in Other Recipes: Boil as directed but reduce cooking time to 20 minutes.

V A R I A T I O N S

¢ **Mashed Sweet Potatoes:** Boil and drain by method above and peel. Mash with a potato masher or whip in an electric mixer. Beat in 1/4 cup softened butter, 3 tablespoons honey, 1/4 teaspoon each salt and mace, and a pinch pepper.

NPS: 295 C, 30 mg CH, 540 mg S*

¢ **Orange-Flavored Mashed Sweet Potatoes:** Prepare mashed potatoes as directed above and beat in 2 tablespoons orange juice and 1 teaspoon grated orange rind along with other seasonings.

NPS: 300 C, 30 mg CH, 540 mg S*

¢ **Maple-Flavored Mashed Sweet Potatoes:** Prepare and season mashed potatoes by basic method above, substituting maple syrup for honey and adding 1/4 teaspoon vanilla.

NPS: 285 C, 30 mg CH, 540 mg S*

BAKED SWEET POTATOES OR YAMS

4 servings ¢

4 medium-size sweet potatoes or yams

Preheat oven to 400° F. Scrub potatoes well in cold water but do not peel. Bake directly on oven rack or in a shallow baking pan 45 minutes to 1 hour or until tender. Serve piping hot with lots of butter, salt, and pepper.

NPS (no butter): 145 C, 0 mg CH, 10 mg S*

VARIATION

To Charcoal Bake: Wrap in foil and bake as directed for Irish potatoes.

ORANGE-CANDIED SWEET POTATOES OR YAMS

4 servings

2 tablespoons butter or margarine
1/2 cup firmly packed dark brown sugar
1/4 cup orange juice
1 teaspoon finely grated orange rind
4 medium-size sweet potatoes or yams, parboiled, peeled, and halved
1 navel orange, peeled and sectioned (garnish)

Heat butter, sugar, orange juice and rind, uncovered, in a very large, heavy skillet over moderately low heat, stirring occasionally, until sugar dissolves. Add potatoes and simmer, uncovered, 10–15 minutes, basting and turning to glaze evenly. Transfer to serving dish and keep warm. Warm orange sections in skillet 2–3 minutes, garnish potatoes, and serve.

NPS: 325 C, 15 mg CH, 80 mg S*

SWEET POTATO CAKES

6 servings

Nice and spicy. Delicious with baked ham.

3 medium-size sweet potatoes, boiled and peeled
1/4 cup milk
1/4 cup melted butter or margarine
3 eggs
1 teaspoon baking powder
1/2 teaspoon ginger
1/4 teaspoon cinnamon
1/8 teaspoon mace
1/2 teaspoon salt
Pinch pepper
1/4 cup cooking oil

Mash potatoes, mix in all remaining ingredients except oil, and beat until fluffy. Heat 2 tablespoons oil in a large, heavy skillet 1–2 minutes over moderately high heat, then drop in potato mixture by the tablespoon and brown 2–3 minutes (don't try to do more than 4 or 5 cakes at a time). Using a pancake turner, turn cakes gently, flatten slightly, and brown the flip side 2–3 minutes. Keep warm in a 250° F. oven while you do the rest. Fry remaining cakes in the same

way, adding more oil to the skillet as needed. Serve piping hot.

NPS: 270 C, 160 mg CH, 375 mg S*

SWEET POTATO PUFF

6–8 servings

4 medium-size sweet potatoes, boiled and peeled
1/2 cup melted butter or margarine
1/3 cup milk
3 tablespoons honey or maple syrup
4 eggs
Juice and grated rind of 1 orange
1 teaspoon baking powder
1/2 teaspoon cinnamon
1/2 teaspoon cardamom
1/4 teaspoon mace
1/4 teaspoon salt

Preheat oven to 350° F. Mash potatoes well, mix in all remaining ingredients, and beat until fluffy. Spoon into a lightly buttered 2-quart casserole and bake, uncovered, about 45 minutes until puffy and lightly browned.

NPS (6–8): 335–250 C, 225–170 mg CH, 380–285 mg S*

YAM, APPLE, AND RAISIN CASSEROLE

4–6 servings

4 medium-size yams, peeled and sliced 1/2" thick
2 apples (McIntosh, Baldwin, or Jonathan), peeled, cored, and cut in 1/4" rings
1/2 cup seedless raisins
1/2 teaspoon salt
1/2 cup firmly packed light or dark brown sugar
1/4 cup butter or margarine
1 cup soft white bread crumbs
2 tablespoons melted butter or margarine

Preheat oven to 375° F. Layer yams, apples, and raisins into a buttered 2-quart casserole, sprinkling with salt as you go. Top with sugar and dot with butter. Cover and bake 50 minutes until yams are tender, basting once or twice. Mix crumbs and melted butter and scatter over yams. Bake, uncovered, 10 minutes to brown lightly.

NPS (4–6): 525–350 C, 45–30 mg CH, 530–350 mg S*

PUMPKIN

When baked or boiled and served with butter or smoky-flavored bacon drippings, pumpkin fills that need for a different vegetable.

To Prepare for Cooking: How you plan to cook the pumpkin determines what should be done with it. Small pumpkins, for example, can be baked whole, in which case you need only cut a circle around the stem, making a "lid," and scoop out seeds and pulp. Pumpkins to be boiled should be cut into 2"–3" chunks or strips and peeled.

BOILED PUMPKIN

4 servings

1 (3–4-pound) ripe pumpkin, cut in 2"–3" chunks or strips and peeled
1 quart boiling water
1½ teaspoons salt
Pinch pepper
2–3 tablespoons butter or margarine

Place pumpkin, water, and salt in a saucepan, cover, and boil gently 25–30 minutes until fork tender. Drain, add pepper and butter, and serve.

NPS: 110 C, 15 mg CH, 470 mg S*

To Parboil for Use in Other Recipes: Boil as directed but reduce cooking time to 15 minutes; omit seasonings.

To Steam: Place pumpkin chunks or strips in a steamer over rapidly boiling water, cover, and steam 30–35 minutes until fork tender. Season and serve.

VARIATIONS

Mashed Pumpkin: Boil and drain as directed, then mash. Heat, uncovered, over low heat, shaking pan now and then, 3–5 minutes to drive off excess moisture. Add pepper and butter and, if you like, 2–3 tablespoons heavy cream; mix well or beat until fluffy with an electric mixer. Also good with a little brown sugar or honey added.

NPS: 140 C, 25 mg CH, 475 mg S*

Pumpkin au Gratin: Prepare Mashed Pumpkin as directed, spoon into a buttered 1½-quart casserole, and top with ½ cup grated Parmesan cheese mixed with ½ cup dry white bread crumbs; drizzle with 2–3 tablespoons melted butter. Bake, uncovered, 25–30 minutes at 400° F. until golden.

NPS: 260 C, 40 mg CH, 810 mg S*

Pumpkin and Potatoes: Mix equal parts seasoned Mashed Pumpkin and seasoned Mashed Potatoes, spoon into a buttered casserole, roughen top with a fork, and broil 5" from heat 2 minutes until browned. Recipe too flexible for meaningful nutritional count.

PUMPKIN PURÉE

1 quart

Use in Pumpkin Pie or any recipe calling for pumpkin purée.

1 (6–7-pound) ripe pumpkin
¼ teaspoon salt

Preheat oven to 375° F. Halve pumpkin crosswise and scoop out seeds and strings. Place halves in a large baking pan, hollow side down, and bake, uncovered, 1½–2 hours until fork tender. Remove from oven and cool. Scrape pulp from shells and purée, a little at a time, by buzzing 15–20 seconds in an electric blender at high speed or 10–15 seconds in a food processor fitted with the metal chopping blade. Mix in salt.

NP Cup: 125 C, 0 mg CH, 140 mg S*

PUMPKIN AND ONION CASSEROLE

4–6 servings

3 medium-size yellow onions, peeled, sliced thin, and separated into rings
3 tablespoons bacon drippings
1 (3–4-pound) ripe pumpkin, cut in 1" cubes, peeled, parboiled, and drained
½ teaspoon salt
⅛ teaspoon pepper
2 teaspoons minced parsley

Preheat oven to 375° F. Stir-fry onions in drippings over moderate heat 3–5 minutes until limp, not brown. Layer pumpkin and onions (include drippings) in an ungreased 1½-quart casserole, seasoning with salt and pepper as you go. Cover and bake 1 hour. Uncover, sprinkle with parsley, and serve.

NPS (4–6): 155–105 C, 7–5 mg CH, 330–220 mg S*

RUTABAGA

Rutabagas aren't just big yellow turnips but a distinct species altogether. Botanists believe they're a hybrid of turnips and cabbage and that they originated in Russia only about 250 years ago.

To Prepare for Cooking: Peel (rutabagas are dipped in melted paraffin before shipping so they'll stay fresh longer), then cut in 1" cubes or strips for easier handling. Rutabagas are often extremely hard, so use your sharpest knife and cut carefully.

BOILED RUTABAGA

4 servings   ¢

1 medium-size rutabaga, prepared for cooking
1½ cups boiling water
1½ teaspoons salt
⅛ teaspoon pepper
3–4 tablespoons butter or margarine

Place rutabaga in a large saucepan with water and salt, cover, and boil 20–30 minutes until tender. Drain well, add pepper and butter, set over low heat, and warm, shaking pan, until butter melts. Toss to mix and serve.

NPS: 155 C, 25 mg CH, 510 mg S*

To Parboil for Use in Other Recipes: Boil by method above but reduce cooking time to 12–15 minutes; omit seasonings.

V A R I A T I O N S

⚖ ¢ **Low-Calorie Rutabaga:** Boil and drain as directed but substitute seasoned salt for salt. Omit butter and sprinkle with mace.

NPS: 80 C, 0 mg CH, 235 mg S*

¢ **Mashed Rutabaga:** Boil, drain, and season as directed, then mash with a potato masher. Heat, stirring, 2–3 minutes to dry off excess moisture and serve.

NPS: 155 C, 25 mg CH, 510 mg S*

¢ **Cottage-Style Rutabaga:** Boil 1 peeled, cubed potato and 1 peeled, sliced carrot with rutabaga. Drain, season as directed, and mash.

NPS: 190 C, 25 mg CH, 515 mg S*

Rutabaga au Gratin: Boil and drain but do not season. Mix with 1½ cups hot Cheese Sauce and spoon into an ungreased 2-quart *au gratin* dish. Top with ⅓ cup grated sharp Cheddar cheese and broil 5″ from heat 3–4 minutes until bubbly.

NPS: 400 C, 80 mg CH, 1,030 mg S*

Rutabaga with Bacon and Sour Cream: Boil, drain, and season as directed. Stir in ½ cup sour cream and 4 slices cooked, crumbled bacon and serve.

NPS: 250 C, 40 mg CH, 625 mg S*

HASHED BROWN RUTABAGA

6–8 servings   ¢

3 tablespoons butter or margarine
1 medium-size rutabaga, boiled and mashed
2 cups hot seasoned mashed potatoes
2 tablespoons grated yellow onion

Melt butter in a large, heavy skillet over moderate heat. Mix rutabaga, potatoes, and onion, spoon into skillet, and pat down with a pancake turner. Brown bottom slowly about 5–7 minutes. Stir to distribute brown bits throughout, pat down again, and brown as before. Using a pancake turner, scoop into a heated vegetable dish, turning so that browned parts are on top.

NPS (6–8): 170–125 C, 15–10 mg CH, 295–220 mg S*

SCALLOPED RUTABAGA AND APPLES

6 servings

1 medium-size rutabaga, quartered and peeled
3 apples (Baldwin, McIntosh, or Jonathan), peeled, cored, and sliced thin
¼ cup butter or margarine
1½ teaspoons salt
⅛ teaspoon pepper
¼ cup firmly packed light brown sugar
1½ cups water

Preheat oven to 400° F. Halve rutabaga quarters lengthwise, then cut crosswise into slices ⅛″ thick. Arrange half the slices in a buttered 2-quart flameproof casserole and top with apples. Dot with half the butter and sprinkle with half the salt, pepper, and sugar. Top with remaining rutabaga, butter, salt, pepper, and sugar. Pour water over all, cover, set over high heat until mixture boils, then transfer to oven and bake 1 hour. Stir gently and bake, uncovered, 20–30 minutes longer until almost all liquid is gone.

NPS: 190 C, 20 mg CH, 635 mg S*

SALSIFY

(Also called Oyster Plant)

Once fairly popular, salsify now falls into the category of "forgotten vegetables." Too bad, because it has a pleasing, delicate flavor. Some people think it tastes like oysters (hence its nickname), others insist it's more like artichokes. Actually, there are two kinds of salsify, the common, or white skinned, and the rarer, more delicate black salsify. Both are prepared exactly the same way.

To Prepare for Cooking: Remove tops and upper part of roots that look to have been wound with cord. Scrub roots with a vegetable brush in cold water. Peel roots, one at a time, and cut into 2″ chunks, letting them fall into acidulated water (1 quart cold water mixed with the juice of 1 lemon) to keep them from turning brown. When all roots are prepared, soak 10 minutes longer in acidulated water.

BOILED SALSIFY

4 servings

2 bunches salsify, prepared for cooking
1½ cups boiling water
2 tablespoons butter or margarine
½ teaspoon salt
Pinch pepper

Place salsify in a saucepan with water, cover, and boil 20–25 minutes until tender. Drain, add butter, salt, and pepper, set over low heat, and warm, uncovered, shaking pan gently, 2–3 minutes until butter melts.

NPS: 185 C, 15 mg CH, 345 mg S*

To Parboil for Use in Other Recipes: Boil as directed but reduce cooking time to 15 minutes; omit seasonings.

VARIATIONS

Herbed Salsify: Prepare as directed, adding 1 tablespoon each minced parsley and chives along with butter, salt, and pepper. Nutritional count same as basic recipe.

Salsify with Dill and Sour Cream: Prepare as directed, adding ¼ cup sour cream and 2 tablespoons minced dill along with butter, salt, and pepper.

NPS: 215 C, 20 mg CH, 355 mg S*

Creamed Salsify: Boil and drain as directed but do not season; mix with 1½ cups hot Medium White Sauce, season to taste with salt and white pepper, and warm, uncovered, over low heat, stirring occasionally, 5 minutes to blend flavors.

NPS: 285 C, 35 mg CH, 625 mg S*

SORREL

(Also called Sour Dock and Patience)

Most of us find these crisp leaves too bitter to eat alone (except when puréed into sorrel soup), so we toss the youngest leaves into salads to add refreshing bite and steam the older with spinach—just a handful—to add character.

To Prepare: Wash by plunging up and down in a sinkful of tepid water; drain.

To Steam: Place sorrel in an enamel, stainless-steel, anodized aluminum, or Teflon-lined pot, add no water, cover, and steam over moderate heat 10–15 minutes until tender. Toss with melted butter or bacon drippings, season to taste with salt and pepper.

To Steam with Spinach: Use 1 part sorrel to 3 parts spinach and steam following the recipe for Steamed Spinach.

SPINACH

"Many English people that have learned it of the Dutch," wrote a seventeenth-century British herbalist, "doe stew the herbe in a pot without any other moisture than its owne and after the moisture is a little pressed from it, they put butter and a little spice unto it, and make therewith a dish that many delight to eate of." The "herbe" was spinach and we haven't found a better way to cook it today, whether it's crinkly or plain leafed or New Zealand spinach. It, by the way, isn't spinach at all; we include it here because it's best when cooked like spinach.

To Prepare for Cooking:

Bulk Spinach: Sort, removing any blemished leaves; trim off roots and coarse stems. Wash leaves by plunging up and down in a sinkful of tepid water (this helps float out sand) and rinse several times in cool water. Lift from rinse water, shake lightly, and place directly in cooking pot.

Bagged Spinach: Remove coarse stems and deteriorating leaves; rinse well.

Cooking Tip: Always cook spinach in an enamel, stainless-steel, anodized aluminum, or Teflon-lined pot so it will not darken or taste of metal.

STEAMED SPINACH

4 servings

2 pounds bulk spinach or 2 (10-ounce) bags
prewashed spinach, prepared for cooking
3 tablespoons melted butter or margarine
1 teaspoon salt
⅛ teaspoon pepper

Place spinach in a large pot, add no water, cover, and steam 3–5 minutes over moderate heat until slightly wilted but still bright green. Drain, add seasonings, and toss to mix.

NPS: 120 C, 25 mg CH, 755 mg S*

To Serve Cold: Steam as directed but do not drain or season; cool, then cover and chill. Drain well and toss with a tart dressing such as Vinaigrette. Recipe too flexible for meaningful nutritional count.

⚖️ **Low-Calorie Spinach:** Steam and drain as directed but omit butter. Dress with 3 tablespoons lemon juice or Garlic Vinegar.

NPS: 45 C, 0 mg CH, 670 mg S*

Chopped Spinach: Chop steamed, drained spinach and toss with butter, salt, and pepper.

NPS: 120 C, 25 mg CH, 755 mg S*

Puréed Spinach: Purée steamed, *undrained* spinach by buzzing 10–15 seconds in an electric blender at high speed or 5–10 seconds in a food processor fitted with the metal chopping blade. Return to pan, add seasonings, cover, and warm, stirring occasionally, 3–4 minutes.

NPS: 120 C, 25 mg CH, 755 mg S*

Italian-Style Spinach: Steam and drain as directed; omit butter and dress with 3 tablespoons olive oil; if you like, toss in 1/4 crushed clove garlic.

NPS: 130 C, 0 mg CH, 665 mg S*

Spinach with Bacon: Steam and drain as directed; omit butter and toss with 2 tablespoons bacon drippings and 1/4 cup crisp crumbled bacon.

NPS: 130 C, 10 mg CH, 810 mg S*

Creamed Spinach: Steam as directed; drain in a fine sieve, pressing as dry as possible, chop fine, and return to pan. Add 1 cup hot Medium White Sauce and warm, uncovered, over low heat, stirring occasionally, 3–5 minutes.

NPS: 145 C, 25 mg CH, 340 mg S*

Spinach au Gratin: Steam as directed; drain in a fine sieve, pressing as dry as possible, chop fine, and return to pan. Mix with 1 cup hot Cheese Sauce, place in an ungreased 1-quart casserole, top with 1/2 cup grated Cheddar cheese mixed with 1/2 cup coarse dry bread crumbs, and broil 4–5″ from heat 2–3 minutes to brown.

NPS: 340 C, 60 mg CH, 665 mg S*

SPINACH RING

8 servings

A showy way to shape spinach for a special dinner.

6 pounds fresh spinach, steamed and chopped fine, or 7 (10-ounce) packages frozen chopped spinach, cooked by package directions
3 tablespoons butter or margarine
1 teaspoon salt
1/8 teaspoon pepper
1/8 teaspoon nutmeg

Drain spinach in a strainer, pressing as dry as possible. Mix with remaining ingredients. Pack *tightly* in a lightly buttered 1-quart ring mold, then invert at once on a hot platter. If you like, fill center with hot Creamed Mushrooms or a small bowl of sauce.

NPS: 95 C, 10 mg CH, 460 mg S*

VARIATION

Baked Spinach Ring: Drain spinach as directed, mix in 2 lightly beaten eggs and all seasonings called for. Pack into mold and bake, uncovered, in a water bath at 350° F. 30–40 minutes until firm. Loosen edges, invert, and serve.

NPS: 115 C, 80 mg CH, 475 mg S*

SPINACH DRESSED WITH OIL AND VINEGAR

4 servings ▢

The Italian way to season spinach. And very good, too.

1/4 cup olive oil
2 pounds fresh spinach, prepared for cooking, or 2 (10-ounce) packages frozen leaf spinach (do not thaw)
1 clove garlic, peeled and crushed
3 tablespoons cider, white wine, or balsamic vinegar
1/2 teaspoon salt
Pinch pepper

Place olive oil, spinach, and garlic in a saucepan and simmer, uncovered, 3–5 minutes until spinach is slightly wilted (if using frozen spinach, cook about 15 minutes, breaking up any frozen clumps). Remove from heat, add remaining ingredients, and toss well to mix. Serve hot or at room temperature.

NPS: 155 C, 0 mg CH, 355 mg S*

SPINACH BAKED WITH MUSHROOMS

4–6 servings

2 pounds fresh spinach, steamed, or 2 (10-ounce) packages frozen chopped spinach, cooked by package directions

2/3 cup light cream or sour cream
1/2 teaspoon salt
Pinch pepper
3 tablespoons butter or margarine
1/2 pound mushrooms, wiped clean and sliced
thin

TOPPING
2 tablespoons butter or margarine
1 cup coarse dry white bread crumbs
1/4 cup coarsely chopped toasted, blanched
almonds

Preheat oven to 375° F. Drain spinach in a sieve, pressing as dry as possible. If using fresh spinach, chop fine. Mix spinach with cream, salt, and pepper. Melt butter in a skillet over moderately high heat, add mushrooms, and sauté 2–3 minutes until golden. Mix mushrooms and spinach, then spoon into a buttered 1-quart casserole. For the topping, melt butter in a small saucepan over moderate heat, stir in crumbs, and brown lightly 1–2 minutes. Add almonds, toss to mix, and sprinkle over spinach. Bake, uncovered, 20–30 minutes until lightly browned.

NPS (4–6): 400–265 C, 65–45 mg CH, 710–470 mg S*

SPINACH CUSTARDS

2 servings

These custards are especially good with cold baked ham.

1 pound fresh spinach, steamed, or 1 (10-ounce)
package frozen chopped spinach, cooked by
package directions
1/4 teaspoon cornstarch
1/2 cup milk
1/2 teaspoon salt
2 eggs, lightly beaten
1 tablespoon finely grated yellow onion
1 tablespoon finely chopped pimiento (optional)

Preheat oven to 375° F. Drain spinach in a fine sieve, pressing as dry as possible. Chop very fine, then return to saucepan and set over low heat to dry, 1–2 minutes. Remove from heat and set aside. Blend cornstarch with 1 tablespoon milk and mix into spinach along with all remaining ingredients including remaining milk. Ladle into 2 well-buttered custard cups, set in a shallow baking pan, and pour hot water into pan to a depth of about 1″. Bake, uncovered, on center oven rack 30–35 minutes until a knife inserted near the center of a custard comes out clean. Remove cups from water bath and cool 3–5 minutes. Serve in cups or, if you prefer, loosen edges with a spatula and invert to unmold.

NPS: 155 C, 280 mg CH, 730 mg S*

SQUASH

No American Indian food seems to have impressed Europeans more than squash, perhaps because there are so many varieties of it. Fortunately they can be classified as either *summer* (soft-skinned) or *winter* (hard-skinned) *squash.* Our word "squash," incidentally, comes from the Indian *"askutasquash,"* meaning "green thing eaten green."

The Three Kinds of Summer Squash

These tender-skinned, delicately flavored squash take equally well to saucepan, skillet, or oven. Most can be used interchangeably with one another.

Yellow Squash: There are two types, the *crookneck* and the slightly plumper *straightneck.* Both are sunny yellow outside, pale and succulent inside. About 2–4 per pound.

Pattypan (also called *cymling):* Flat, round, pale green squash with scalloped edges. They can be small as a biscuit or big as a pie. The large may weigh 1–2 pounds; the small a fraction of that.

Zucchini (also called *courgette): This* isn't one squash but four, all green skinned and white fleshed. The one called *zucchini* is cucumber-sized with dark lacy stripes. The other three are the slimmer yellow and green-striped *cocozelle,* the more rounded *caserta* with two-tone green stripes, and the dark-green-skinned *scallopini,* a cross between pattypan squash and zucchini. About 2–4 per pound.

To Prepare for Cooking:

Yellow Squash and Zucchini: Cut off ends and scrub well; peel only if skins are old. If young and tender leave whole; otherwise cut in 1/2″ slices, or halve and seed.

Pattypan: Wash in cool water, peel, seed, and cut in 1/2″ cubes.

Six Favorite Winter Squash

These hard-skinned varieties are best when boiled and mashed or baked in the skins.

Acorn Squash (also called *Table Queen):* Not much bigger than a large avocado, these are small enough to handle easily. Usually green, but sometimes orange, they're moist and tender. About 1–2 pounds each.

Butternut: A large pear-shaped squash with thin, fawn-colored skin and fine, bright orange flesh. About 2–3 pounds each.

Buttercup: Smallish, turban-shaped, green- and gray-striped squash with faintly sweet orange flesh. About 2 pounds each.

Golden Nugget: A mini, orange, pumpkin-shaped squash that also tastes of pumpkin. About 1/2 pound each.

Hubbard: A rough, tough, green or orange skinned giant often sold by the chunk. It is drier and stringier than smaller squash.

Spaghetti Squash: A big, yellow-skinned, melon-shaped squash that is unlike any other winter squash. Its pale yellow flesh, when cooked, can be forked into long spaghetti-like strands and topped with pasta or cheese sauces. About 2 pounds each and up, but the smaller the better.

To Prepare for Boiling: Halve, scoop out seeds and pulp; peel and cut in 1–2″ chunks. Work slowly and carefully because squash are hard and their skins slippery. *Note:* 1 pound squash, prepared for cooking, equals about 2 cups cooked squash.

To Prepare for Baking: If very small, leave whole; otherwise halve lengthwise and remove seeds and pulp. If extra large, quarter or cut in sixths or eighths. Do not peel. When squash are baked whole, halve and seed before serving. *Note: Spaghetti squash* is best left whole, whether boiled or baked.

Some Lesser Lights: In addition to the winter squash above, there are others, many of them used as decoration because they're not very moist or tender. Still, if cooked like Hubbard squash, they can be palatable. These varieties are:

Warren Turban, Kabocha (a newly available, jade-green Japanese turban squash), *Opu* (a green-skinned, white-fleshed, butternut-shaped Oriental squash), *Mediterranean* (a 5–7-pounder with pulpy flesh that looks like a ridged butternut squash), *Banana* (it resembles a giant banana), *Marblehead* (a variety of Hubbard), *Boston Marrow* (an orange giant thought to be America's oldest squash species), *Cushaw* (a big, ridged butternut type), and *Calabaza* (a whopping, creamy-fleshed, West Indian pumpkin). *Note:* Prepare and cook all of these hard-skinned squashes as you would butternut or acorn squash.

BOILED SUMMER SQUASH

4 servings

2 pounds summer squash (yellow, pattypan, or zucchini), prepared for cooking
1 teaspoon salt
1/2 cup boiling water
1/8 teaspoon pepper
3 tablespoons butter or margarine

Place squash in a large saucepan, add salt and water, cover, and boil until crisp tender —7–10 minutes for slices or cubes, 15–20 for halves, 25–30 for whole squash. Drain well, return to pan, and warm, uncovered, shaking pan occasionally, 2–3 minutes to drive off moisture. Season with pepper and butter and serve.

NPS: 115 C, 25 mg CH, 365 mg S*

To Steam: Place prepared squash in a steamer over boiling water, cover, and steam, using times above as a guide. Remove from steamer and season with salt, pepper, and butter.

To Parboil for Use in Other Recipes: Boil or steam as directed, reducing cooking time to 4 minutes for slices or cubes, 10 for halves, 15–20 for whole squash. Omit seasonings.

VARIATIONS

To Serve Cold: Slice or cube; boil and drain as directed. Chill in ice water, drain, mix with Vinaigrette, and chill until ready to serve. Recipe too flexible for meaningful nutritional count.

⚖ **Low-Calorie Squash:** Boil and drain as directed but omit butter. Dress with low-calorie herb, garlic, or Italian dressing.

NPS: 55 C, 0 mg CH, 365 mg S*

Squash and Carrots: Combine equal amounts sliced boiled carrots and squash, season as directed, then stir in 1 teaspoon minced fresh mint or basil.

NPS: 140 C, 25 mg CH, 395 mg S*

Squash and Scallions: Cook 4–6 minced scallions with squash and season as directed.

NPS: 125 C, 25 mg CH, 365 mg S*

Italian-Style Zucchini: Cook 1 clove peeled, halved garlic with zucchini and dress with 2 tablespoons olive oil and 1 tablespoon red wine vinegar instead of butter.

NPS: 100 C, 0 mg CH, 275 mg S*

SCALLOPED SUMMER SQUASH

4 servings

2 pounds summer squash, boiled
3 tablespoons butter or margarine
3 tablespoons grated yellow onion
3/4 teaspoon salt
1/8 teaspoon pepper

TOPPING
1/2 cup fine cracker crumbs mixed with 1
   tablespoon melted butter or margarine

Preheat oven to 350° F. Drain squash well
and mash with a potato masher. Mix in all
remaining ingredients except topping. Spoon
into a buttered shallow 1 1/2-quart casserole
and top with buttered crumbs. Bake, uncovered, 25–30 minutes until lightly browned.

NPS: 145 C, 30 mg CH, 530 mg S*

PARMESAN STUFFED SQUASH

4–6 servings

Good for a party because the squash can be
prepared well ahead of time.

6 medium-size zucchini or yellow squash, halved
   and parboiled
1 1/2 teaspoons salt
1/4 teaspoon pepper
1/4 cup butter or margarine
1/2 cup finely chopped yellow onion
3 cups soft bread crumbs
1/8 teaspoon paprika
1/2 cup grated Parmesan cheese
1 tablespoon minced parsley

Scoop out squash halves, leaving shells 1/4"
thick; discard seedy centers. Sprinkle with 1
teaspoon salt and the pepper; arrange in a
lightly buttered 13" × 9" × 2" pan. Preheat oven to 425° F. Melt butter in a skillet
over moderate heat, add onion, and sauté 8
minutes until golden. Remove from heat and
mix in all remaining ingredients including
remaining 1/2 teaspoon salt. Stuff shells with
crumb mixture. (*Note:* You may prepare recipe to this point early in the day; cool, cover,
and chill. Bring to room temperature before
proceeding.) Bake, uncovered, 20–30 minutes until crumbs are lightly browned and
squash tender.

*NPS (4–6): 280–185 C, 40–25 mg CH, 1,295–865
   mg S**

BAKED YELLOW SQUASH PUDDING

6–8 servings

A long-baking, old-fashioned Southern favorite.

4 pounds yellow squash, scrubbed and sliced 1/4"
   thick
3 medium-size yellow onions, peeled and cut in
   thin wedges
1/4 cup boiling water
1/4 cup butter or margarine
1/4 teaspoon thyme
1/8 teaspoon rosemary
1/8 teaspoon nutmeg
1 teaspoon salt
1/8 teaspoon pepper
1 tablespoon light brown sugar
1/4 cup minced parsley

Preheat oven to 350° F. Place squash, onions, water, and butter in a large kettle,
cover, and simmer 25–30 minutes until
squash is mushy. Uncover and simmer 10
minutes longer, mashing large pieces with a
fork. Stir in all remaining ingredients. Transfer to a buttered 3-quart *au gratin* dish and
bake, uncovered, 2 1/2 hours until light caramel in color.

*NPS (6–8): 150–115 C, 20–15 mg CH, 455–340
   mg S**

BAKED ZUCCHINI WITH ROSEMARY

4–6 servings

2 pounds zucchini, scrubbed
2 cups boiling water
1 medium-size yellow onion, peeled and chopped
   fine
1 clove garlic, peeled and crushed
1/4 cup olive oil
Juice of 1/2 lemon
3 tablespoons flour mixed with 1/4 cup cold
   water
1/8 teaspoon rosemary
1/8 teaspoon summer savory
1/8 teaspoon nutmeg
1 teaspoon salt
1/8 teaspoon pepper
1/4 cup grated Parmesan cheese
1/4 cup minced parsley

TOPPING
1 1/2 cups soft white bread crumbs
2 tablespoons grated Parmesan cheese
1/3 cup melted butter or margarine

Preheat oven to 325° F. Quarter each zucchini by cutting in half lengthwise, then in
half crosswise. Place in a large saucepan

with boiling water, cover, and boil 15–20 minutes until crisp-tender. Drain, reserving 1 cup cooking water. Sauté onion and garlic in oil in a heavy skillet over moderate heat 8 minutes until onion is golden. Stir in cooking water and all remaining ingredients except cheese, parsley, and topping. Heat, stirring constantly, until thickened and smooth. Off heat, mix in cheese and parsley. Arrange half the zucchini in a buttered 8" × 8" × 2" baking dish. Cover with half the sauce. Add remaining zucchini and sauce. Mix topping and sprinkle over surface. Bake, uncovered, about 1 hour until browned and bubbly.

NPS (4–6): 405–270 C, 45–30 mg CH, 935–620 mg S*

ZUCCHINI CUSTARD

4–6 servings

2 pounds zucchini, scrubbed and coarsely grated
1 medium-size yellow onion, peeled and minced
1 clove garlic, peeled and crushed
3 tablespoons olive oil
1/3 cup minced parsley
1/8 teaspoon thyme
1/8 teaspoon rosemary
1 teaspoon salt
1/8 teaspoon pepper
5 eggs
1/2 cup sifted flour
3/4 cup grated Parmesan cheese

Preheat oven to 300° F. Stir-fry zucchini, onion, and garlic in oil in a large, heavy skillet over moderate heat 10–12 minutes until zucchini is tender. Mix in parsley, thyme, rosemary, salt, and pepper. Beat eggs until frothy, then mix in flour and Parmesan. Stir zucchini mixture into eggs, spoon into a buttered 1½-quart casserole, and bake, uncovered, 1–1¼ hours until a silver knife inserted in the center comes out clean.

NPS (4–6): 355–240 C, 355–235 mg CH, 920–615 mg S*

BOILED WINTER SQUASH

4 servings

2 pounds winter squash (butternut, acorn, buttercup, or Hubbard), prepared for boiling
1½ cups boiling water
1 teaspoon salt
Pinch pepper
2 tablespoons butter or margarine

Place squash, water, and salt in a saucepan, cover, and boil gently 15–20 minutes until fork tender. Drain, add pepper and butter, and serve.

NPS: 155 C, 15 mg CH, 335 mg S*

To Parboil for Use in Other Recipes: Boil as directed, reducing cooking time to 10 minutes; omit seasonings.

VARIATIONS

Mashed Winter Squash: Boil and drain as directed and mash with a potato masher. Add pepper and butter and, if you like, 2 tablespoons cream. Mix or beat with an electric mixer until fluffly.

NPS (cream): 170 C, 25 mg CH, 335 mg S*

Spicy Mashed Squash in Orange Cups: Fill 4–6 large orange cups* with hot mashed squash, sprinkle each with cinnamon sugar, and top with a marshmallow. Broil 4"–5" from heat 2 minutes until marshmallow is lightly browned.

NPS (4–6): 190–135 C, 15–10 mg CH, 335–225 mg S*

Boiled Spaghetti Squash: Unless very large, leave squash whole; place in a large heavy kettle and pour in enough lightly salted boiling water to cover; cover kettle and cook 20–25 minutes until a fork will pierce the skin easily. Drain well. If squash is whole, halve, remove seeds, then scrape flesh with a fork (it will form long "strings"). If it's necessary to halve the squash before cooking, remove all seeds; when squash is done, scrape with a fork to form spaghetti-like strands. Toss with melted butter or, if you prefer, top with a favorite pasta or cheese sauce.

NPS (without butter): 20 C, 0 mg CH, 15 mg S*

BAKED BUTTERNUT OR ACORN SQUASH

4 servings

1 (2-pound) butternut or acorn squash, halved lengthwise and seeded
1 teaspoon salt
1/4 teaspoon pepper
2 tablespoons butter or margarine

Preheat oven to 375° F. Place each piece of squash hollow side up on a square of foil large enough to wrap it; sprinkle with salt and pepper and dot with butter. Wrap tightly. Place squash on a baking sheet and bake 45 minutes until fork tender. Unwrap and serve with extra butter if you like.

NPS: 155 C, 15 mg CH, 610 mg S*

To Charcoal Bake: Season and wrap each piece of squash as directed. Bake on a grill set 3″–4″ above a moderately hot charcoal fire 3/4–1 hour, turning two or three times. *Note:* You can cook the squash the same way on an outdoor gas or electric grill; the cooking times will be about the same.

NPS: 155 C, 15 mg CH, 610 mg S*

VARIATIONS

Before wrapping add a little honey or maple syrup, brown, maple, or cinnamon sugar, or orange marmalade to squash along with butter, salt, and pepper (about 2 tablespoons in all will be enough). Wrap and bake as directed. Recipe too flexible for meaningful nutritional count.

NPS: 185 C, 15 mg CH, 610 mg S*

Baked Spaghetti Squash: Leave squash whole; place on a lightly greased baking sheet, then bake at 375° F. about 45 minutes until you can pierce the squash easily with a fork. Remove squash from oven, halve, remove seeds, then with a fork, scrape flesh into strands. Toss with melted butter or top, if you prefer, with Tomato or Cheese Sauce.

NPS (without butter or sauce): 20 C, 0 mg CH, 15 mg S*

BAKED HUBBARD SQUASH

8 servings

Because this is such a giant squash, it requires special baking instructions.

4–5 pounds Hubbard squash (try to get a whole small squash rather than a chunk of a giant one), prepared for baking*
1 1/2 teaspoons salt
1/4 teaspoon pepper
1/4 cup butter or margarine

Preheat oven to 400° F. Place each piece of squash hollow side up on a piece of foil large enough to wrap it, sprinkle evenly with salt and pepper, and dot with butter; wrap tightly and place in a roasting pan. Bake about 1 hour until fork tender. Unwrap and serve with extra butter if you like.

NPS: 110 C, 15 mg CH, 480 mg S*

VARIATIONS

Mashed Hubbard Squash: Bake as directed, then scoop flesh from skin and mash with a potato masher; taste for salt and pepper and adjust. Add 2 tablespoons melted butter and beat until fluffy.

NPS: 135 C, 25 mg CH, 510 mg S*

"Candied" Hubbard Squash: Just before wrapping squash pieces, sprinkle with 1/4 cup light brown sugar, or drizzle with 1/4 cup maple syrup or honey. Wrap and bake as directed.

NPS: 135 C, 15 mg CH, 480 mg S*

FRUIT-GLAZED BUTTERNUT OR ACORN SQUASH

4 servings

1 (2-pound) butternut or acorn squash, halved, seeded, peeled, and sliced 1/2″ thick
1 1/2 cups pineapple or orange juice
1/4 cup firmly packed light brown sugar
1/2 teaspoon salt
3 tablespoons melted butter or margarine

Preheat oven to 350° F. Arrange squash in an ungreased 1 1/2-quart casserole. Mix remaining ingredients and pour over squash. Cover and bake about 45 minutes, basting two or three times, until fork tender. Uncover, baste, and bake 10 minutes longer to glaze lightly.

NPS: 280 C, 25 mg CH, 370 mg S*

VARIATION

Substitute Hubbard squash for the butternut or acorn and increase baking time to about 1 hour.

NPS: 235 C, 25 mg CH, 375 mg S*

BUTTERNUT SQUASH PARMIGIANA

4 servings

An unusual way to prepare butternut squash, but the butter, cheese, and bread crumbs enhance its mellow flavor.

1 (2-pound) butternut or acorn squash, halved, seeded, peeled, cut in 1″ chunks, and parboiled
1 teaspoon salt
Pinch pepper
2 tablespoons butter or margarine
1/4 cup toasted fine bread crumbs
1/4 cup grated Parmesan cheese

Preheat oven to 350° F. Arrange squash in an ungreased shallow 1 1/2-quart casserole, sprinkle evenly with salt and pepper, and dot with butter. Mix crumbs and cheese and sprinkle on top. Cover and bake 25–30 minutes until fork tender. Raise oven temperature to 400° F., uncover, and bake 10 minutes longer to brown.

NPS: 200 C, 20 mg CH, 750 mg S*

Substitute Hubbard squash for the butternut or acorn and prepare as directed.

NPS: 155 C, 20 mg CH, 755 mg S*

TOMATOES

The astonishing truth about tomatoes is that for centuries people considered them poisonous. They weren't eaten in this country until about 150 years ago, when a New Jersey farmer stood on the Salem County Courthouse lawn and ate one publicly to prove he would neither sicken nor die. He made his point and soon the most doubting Thomases were eating tomatoes. Today, of course, it's difficult to imagine life without them. Here are the most popular types plus two new exotics *(tomatillos* and *tamarillos)* and how to use them:

Red Globe Tomatoes: These are the juicy, everyday tomatoes, good either raw or cooked. There are 3–4 per pound.

Beefsteak Tomatoes: These large, firm tomatoes are perfect for broiling or slicing into sandwiches. About 1–2 per pound.

Cherry Tomatoes: Juicy, bite-size tomatoes ideal for picnics or cocktail snacks. About 30 in a 1-pint carton.

Plum Tomatoes: Sometimes red, sometimes golden, these plump, mellow Italian tomatoes cook superbly. About 5–6 per pound. *Note:* These are now available sun-dried in many supermarkets. Devoid of preservatives, sugar, or honey, they are nonetheless sweet enough to eat out of hand. They impart rich tomato flavor and color to soups, stews, and sauces, and are especially delicious when soaked several hours (or days) in fine, fruity olive oil and eaten with slices of mozzarella cheese and chunks of rough country bread.

Cranberry Tomatoes: These are the tiny, tart "wild" tomatoes occasionally carried by specialty groceries. Toss into salads or serve as a cocktail snack to be eaten like nuts. About 100 per pint.

Green Tomatoes: There are two types: the small *immature green* that are used in pickles and relishes and the larger *mature green* that are excellent for frying or broiling. From 3–8 per pound.

Tomatillos: Plum-shaped Mexican ground tomatoes enveloped in papery brown husks. Their flesh is bright green, yellow, or even deep purple, their flavor tart, rather like a green apple. They're firm of flesh, filled with tiny seeds, and available primarily in the summer months. They're best sliced raw into salads or tacos, but can be steamed into sauce in a small amount of boiling salted water (5 minutes will do the job), then seasoned with salt, pepper, minced onion, and chili powder. This sauce can be used as a dip, or condiment, or used to heighten the flavor of Mexican dishes. *Storage Tip:* Store tomatillos in a cool, well-ventilated, dry place *(not* the refrigerator).

Tamarillos: Very tart, egg-shaped New Zealand tree tomatoes that may be red, amber, or gold. Available from May to November, they're good made into sauces, chutneys, and preserves.

To Ripen Tomatoes: Do not (repeat DO NOT) stand green tomatoes on a sunny window sill, because they'll ripen unevenly and become pithy. Instead, place in a perforated bag or box with a ripe apple and set in a cool (65°–75° F.) spot.

To Peel: Do not core. Spear stem end with a long-handled fork and twirl slowly over an open flame just until skin splits. Or, if you prefer, twirl slowly in boiling water about 1/2 minute. Plunge into ice water, core, and slip off skin.

To Seed and Juice: Halve tomatoes crosswise and squeeze gently in your hand—seeds and juices will spurt out. To save juice, squeeze over a strainer set in a bowl. The strainer catches the seeds, which can be tossed out.

Serving Tip: If tomatoes are to go into a sandwich, slice from top to bottom instead of crosswise. There'll be much less juice to make the bread soggy.

FRIED TOMATOES

4 servings ☒

3 tablespoons butter, margarine, bacon drippings, or cooking oil
4 large, firm, ripe beefsteak tomatoes, washed and sliced 3/4″ thick (do not peel)
1/2 teaspoon salt
1/8 teaspoon pepper

Heat butter 1 minute in a large, heavy skillet over moderate heat. Add tomatoes and fry 3–4 minutes on a side until golden brown. Sprinkle with salt and pepper and serve.

NPS: 125 C, 25 mg CH, 370 mg S*

⊠ **Fried Tomatoes with Sour Cream:** Transfer Fried Tomatoes to platter and keep warm. Blend 2 teaspoons flour into skillet drippings, mix in ½ cup milk, and heat, stirring 1–2 minutes until thickened. Off heat, mix in ½ cup sour cream, ⅛ teaspoon paprika, and ¼ teaspoon salt. Pour over tomatoes and serve.

NPS: 210 C, 40 mg CH, 535 mg S*

⊠ **Fried Green Tomatoes:** Use green tomatoes instead of ripe, fry as directed, but sprinkle slices with sugar halfway through cooking. Nutritional count unavailable.

BROILED TOMATOES

4 servings ⊠

For an Italian touch, brush the tomatoes lightly with olive oil before sprinkling in the seasonings. And omit the butter.

**4 large firm, ripe tomatoes, washed and halved
  crosswise (do not peel)**
½ teaspoon salt
⅛ teaspoon pepper
**1 tablespoon minced fresh chervil or 1 teaspoon
  dried chervil (optional)**
**1 tablespoon minced fresh basil or 1 teaspoon
  dried basil (optional)**
¼ cup butter or margarine

Preheat broiler. Arrange tomatoes cut side up in a lightly greased shallow pan. Mix salt, pepper, and, if you like, the herbs and sprinkle over tomatoes; dot with butter. Broil 5″–6″ from heat 10–12 minutes until lightly browned.

NPS: 135 C, 30 mg CH, 395 mg S*

Deviled Tomatoes: Mix ¼ cup cracker meal, 2 tablespoons melted butter, 1 tablespoon each grated Parmesan and minced chives, 1 teaspoon prepared mild yellow mustard, and a pinch pepper. Pat on tomato halves instead of seasonings called for above and broil 5″ from heat about 3 minutes until browned.

NPS: 115 C, 15 mg CH, 105 mg S*

BAKED TOMATOES

4 servings ⊠

Serve at breakfast or brunch accompanied by ham, bacon, or sausage, and eggs.

**4 large firm, ripe beefsteak tomatoes, washed
  and halved crosswise (do not peel)**
1 teaspoon salt
⅛ teaspoon pepper
¼ cup butter or margarine

Preheat oven to 375° F. Place tomatoes cut side up in a buttered roasting pan or shallow casserole. Sprinkle with salt and pepper and dot with butter. Bake, uncovered, 15–20 minutes until fork tender. *(Note:* Winter tomatoes, being drier, will take longer to bake than summer tomatoes.)

NPS: 150 C, 30 mg CH, 675 mg S*

STUFFED TOMATOES

4 servings

A good basic recipe to vary as you wish.

4 large firm, ripe tomatoes, washed
½ teaspoon salt
⅛ teaspoon pepper

STUFFING
1 tablespoon butter or margarine
¼ cup finely chopped yellow onion
2 cups soft white bread crumbs
¾ teaspoon salt
⅛ teaspoon pepper
**1 cup chopped tomato pulp (saved from tomato
  centers)**
¼ cup grated Parmesan cheese

Preheat oven to 375° F. Cut a thin slice from top of each tomato and reserve. Using a teaspoon, scoop out pulp and seeds. Coarsely chop pulp and reserve 1 cup (use the rest in soups or stews). Sprinkle inside of tomatoes with salt and pepper. Melt butter in a small skillet over moderate heat, add onion, and sauté 8–10 minutes until golden. Mix onion with all remaining stuffing ingredients except Parmesan. Stuff tomatoes, sprinkle with Parmesan, and, if you like, replace reserved tops. Stand tomatoes in a buttered shallow casserole and bake, uncovered, ½ hour until tender.

NPS: 150 C, 10 mg CH, 925 mg S*

STEWED TOMATOES

4 servings ⊲⊳ ⊠ ¢

Another basic recipe that invites improvisation.

**4 large ripe tomatoes, peeled, cored, and
  quartered, or 1½ pounds Italian plum
  tomatoes, peeled**
1 tablespoon water (optional)
¾ teaspoon salt

1/4 teaspoon sugar
Pinch pepper

Place tomatoes in a heavy saucepan, add water (if they seem dry) and remaining ingredients. Cover and simmer 5–7 minutes until *just* soft; uncover and simmer 1/2 minute longer. Serve in small bowls as a vegetable.

NPS: 35 C, 0 mg CH, 415 mg S*

VARIATIONS

⟂ ⊠ ¢ **Savory Stewed Tomatoes:** Cook any of the following with the tomatoes: 2 tablespoons minced yellow onion or scallions and 1/2 crushed clove garlic; 1/4 cup minced celery or sweet green pepper; 1 bay leaf; 1 teaspoon minced fresh basil, oregano, or marjoram, or 1/2 teaspoon of the dried.

NPS: 35 C, 0 mg CH, 5 mg S*

⊠ ¢ **Dressed-Up Stewed Tomatoes:** Just before serving add any one of the following: 2 tablespoons butter or grated Parmesan; 1 tablespoon minced parsley; 1/3 cup soft white bread crumbs or croutons. Recipe too flexible for a meaningful nutritional count.

⊠ ¢ **Stewed Vegetables:** Just before serving, stir in any of the following: 1 cup hot cooked whole kernel corn or cream-style corn; 1 cup sautéed sliced mushrooms; 1 1/2 cups hot cooked green beans; 2 cups hot cooked baby okra pods. Recipe too flexible for a meaningful nutritional count.

TOMATO-CHEESE-CORN PIE

6 servings

A vegetable dish hearty enough to serve as an entree.

PASTRY
1 recipe Flaky Pastry I

FILLING
2 tablespoons butter or margarine
1 large yellow onion, peeled and sliced thin
2 cups coarsely grated sharp Cheddar cheese
2 medium-size, firm ripe tomatoes, peeled and sliced 1/2" thick
1/2 teaspoon salt
1/8 teaspoon pepper
1 (1-pound) can cream-style corn

Preheat oven to 425° F. Make pastry and roll to a diameter of 9 1/2". Cut 3 V-shaped slits or decorative holes near the center. Cover with cloth while you make the filling. Melt butter in a small skillet over moderate heat, add onion, and stir-fry 5–8 minutes until pale golden; set aside. Sprinkle 1/2 cup cheese over bottom of an ungreased 9" pie-pan and top with tomato slices. Sprinkle with salt, pepper, and onion. Spread corn evenly over tomatoes and top with remaining cheese. Brush rim of pan lightly with cold water. Cover pie with pastry, roll overhang under even with rim, and crimp. Bake 25 minutes until lightly browned. (*Note:* Put a piece of foil on the rack below pie to catch any drips.)

NPS: 455 C, 50 mg CH, 820 mg S*

TRUFFLES

Truffles grow only at the roots of certain trees and only in a few areas of the world; they're dug once a year by especially trained pigs or dogs and bring about $200 a pound. Oddly, though gourmets rave about truffles, they cannot agree on the flavor. Some say that truffles taste like oysters, others like mild garlic, still others like well-ripened Brie. It is flavor for which truffles are cherished, not nutritive value or beauty. Truffles are wrinkled, warty, black, brown, or beige fungi usually about the size of chestnuts or golf balls. The choicest are the black Périgord truffles of Southern France; second best are the white (actually beige) truffles from Northern Italy. Though fresh truffles make rare appearances in specialty markets, most of us must be content with the canned. And even these are a great luxury.

How to Heighten the Flavor of Canned Truffles: Open can but do not drain; add 1–2 tablespoons Madeira and let truffles stand 30–45 minutes before using.

How to Use Canned Truffles (1 truffle is usually enough for any recipe):
• Mince and stir into meat stuffing, an omelet, or potato salad (use a light hand with herbs or omit them altogether so you don't overpower the truffle).
• Slice tissue thin, cut into fancy shapes with truffle cutters, and use to decorate pâté, ham or fowl in aspic, or canapés.
• Save can liquid and use to season sauces and meat stuffings.

How to Save Leftover Canned Truffles: Wrap in foil and freeze. Or leave in the can, cover with melted bacon drippings, and refrigerate (they'll keep several weeks).

TURNIPS AND TURNIP GREENS

(The greens are often called Turnip Salad)

Most vegetables as ancient as turnips (more than 4,000 years old) have been in and out of favor half a dozen times. Not so turnips. They've never been particularly popular and only today are we beginning to appreciate their gingery piquancy.

To Prepare for Cooking:

Turnips: Trim off any stems and root ends and discard. Very tiny tender turnips can be scrubbed and cooked whole in their skins; larger turnips should be peeled and quartered or cut in 1/2" cubes.

Turnip Greens: Discard coarse stems and leaf midribs; sort greens, rejecting any that are wilted, blemished, or yellow. Wash by plunging up and down in tepid water, rinse several times, then lift from water, shake lightly, and place directly in pot.

To Boil Turnip Greens: See recipe for Boiled Collards, Turnip Greens, or Mustard Greens.

Cooking Tips:
• Always cook turnip greens in enamel, stainless-steel, anodized aluminum, or Teflon-lined pots so they don't darken or taste of metal.
• Toss young greens or thin strips of raw turnip into salads for refreshing zing.

Serving Tip: Don't serve turnips with seafood because they overpower it. They're best with pork, ham, or pot roasts.

BOILED TURNIPS

4 servings   ¢

To give turnips richer flavor, boil in beef or chicken broth instead of water.

1¼ pounds turnips, prepared for cooking
1½ cups boiling water, beef or chicken broth
1 teaspoon salt (about)
2 tablespoons butter or margarine
1/8 teaspoon pepper

Place turnips, water or broth, and salt (reduce amount if broth is salty) in a saucepan, cover, and boil until tender: 35–40 minutes for whole small turnips, 25–30 for quarters, and 15–20 for cubes. Drain, then shake pan, uncovered, over low heat to drive off steam. Add butter and continue to shake over low heat until butter melts. Add pepper and serve.

NPS (water): 85 C, 15 mg CH, 390 mg S*
NPS (broth): 95 C, 15 mg CH, 535 mg S*

To Parboil for Use in Other Recipes: Boil as directed, reducing cooking time to 25 minutes for small whole turnips, 15–20 for quarters, and 10 for cubes. Omit seasonings.

VARIATIONS

⟐ ¢ **Low-Calorie Turnips:** Boil in water and drain as directed; omit butter and sprinkle with 2 tablespoons minced chives, dill, or fennel.

NPS: 35 C, 0 mg CH, 330 mg S*

¢ **Parsleyed Turnips:** Boil in broth and season as directed; just before serving stir in 1 tablespoon lemon juice and 1 tablespoon minced parsley.

NPS: 95 C, 15 mg CH, 535 S*

¢ **Mashed Turnips:** Boil and drain as directed; mash with a potato masher or, if stringy, press through a fine sieve. Beat in butter and pepper and warm 2–3 minutes over low heat, stirring. Sprinkle with minced parsley and serve.

NPS (water): 85 C, 15 mg CH, 390 mg S*
NPS (broth): 90 C, 15 mg CH, 535 mg S*

¢ **Glazed Turnips:** Parboil quartered turnips in beef broth as directed; drain, reserving broth, but do not season. Brown turnips in a heavy skillet 3–5 minutes in 3 tablespoons oil over moderately high heat. Add broth, 2 tablespoons each sugar and butter, cover, and simmer 15–20 minutes until tender. If cooking liquid hasn't become syrupy, boil, uncovered, to reduce, turning turnips until well glazed. Sprinkle with pepper and minced parsley and serve.

NPS: 205 C, 15 mg CH, 680 mg S*

TURNIPS AU GRATIN

4 servings

Those who don't like turnips will probably eat them prepared this way.

1¼ pounds turnips, peeled, cubed, boiled, and drained
2 tablespoons butter or margarine
2 tablespoons flour
1 cup milk
1/2 teaspoon salt
1/8 teaspoon pepper
Pinch powdered mustard
3/4 cup coarsely grated sharp Cheddar cheese

Preheat oven to 400° F. Arrange turnips in an ungreased 1½-quart *au gratin* dish or shallow casserole. Melt butter over moderate heat, blend in flour, and slowly stir in milk. Heat, stirring constantly, until thickened; mix in salt, pepper, mustard, and 1/2 cup cheese. Pour sauce over turnips and mix lightly; sprinkle remaining cheese on top. Bake, uncovered, 20 minutes until bubbly.

NPS: 220 C, 45 mg CH, 550 mg S*

ROASTED TURNIPS

4 servings   ¢

Sweeter than boiled turnips, less watery, too.

1¼ pounds medium-size turnips, peeled
1/2 cup lard, bacon drippings, or cooking oil
1 teaspoon salt

Preheat oven to 375° F. Place turnips in an ungreased shallow casserole and add lard, drippings, or oil. Bake, uncovered, 50 minutes, turning turnips after 1/2 hour. Raise oven temperature to 400° F. and bake 10–15 minutes longer until lightly browned and tender. Drain on paper toweling, sprinkle with salt, and serve.

NPS: 265 C, 25 mg CH, 605 mg S*

SKILLET TURNIPS AND RED ONIONS

4 servings   ¢

1¼ pounds medium-size turnips, peeled and cubed
1 large red onion, peeled and sliced thin
1/3 cup water
3 tablespoons butter or margarine
3/4 teaspoon salt

Place all ingredients in a large, heavy skillet, cover, and simmer 15–20 minutes, shaking skillet frequently. Uncover toward end of cooking and stir gently so turnips become nicely glazed. If mixture seems dry, add 1 tablespoon water.

NPS: 125 C, 25 mg CH, 560 mg S*

TURNIPS STUFFED WITH MUSHROOM RISOTTO

4 servings

8 medium-size turnips, parboiled and drained
1½ cups Mushroom Risotto
1/4 cup grated Parmesan cheese
1½ cups chicken broth

Preheat oven to 350° F. Hollow out turnips to form "cups" (save centers for soup or stew). Stuff with risotto, sprinkle with cheese, and arrange in an ungreased shallow casserole. Pour broth around turnips, cover, and bake 20 minutes. Uncover, bake 15 minutes longer, basting two or three times.

NPS: 240 C, 15 mg CH, 805 mg S*

WATER CHESTNUTS

Fresh water chestnuts, grown like rice in flooded fields, are now available in some supermarkets and many specialty food shops. If you've tasted only the canned, you're in for a treat because fresh water chestnuts are exquisitely crisp, faintly sweet, and nutlike in flavor. They're low in calories (only 23 per ounce), and if refrigerated, will remain fresh three to four weeks. *Shopping Tip:* Choose firm, plump water chestnuts (their skins will be brown or black).

To Prepare: Wash well in cool water, cut a thin slice from root and stem ends, then peel to remove skin. Slice, chop, or mince as individual recipes direct.

Cooking Tip: Before adding to salads or prepared dishes, boil water chestnuts 2–3 minutes in lightly salted water, drain, cool, and slice. Their delicate flavor will be more pronounced, and the cooking does not destroy their crispness.

FOURTEEN

Salads and Salad Dressings

The Romans, who liked most things twice-gilded, took their salads straight—lettuce sprinkled with salt. It is, in fact, from their word for salt *(sal)* that our word salad derives. Our salads are a good deal more complex than the Roman and may appear at almost any point in a meal. Californians begin dinner with crisp green salads, simply dressed, and Southerners often end it with frozen fruit salads. The French prefer salad either before or after the main course (so that the dressing doesn't overpower the wine) and Swedes construct whole smorgasbords out of cold marinated fish and vegetables.

Salads can be nothing more than greens tossed with oil and vinegar, or they can be elaborate concoctions of meat, seafood, poultry, vegetables, pasta, or fruit. They may be bland or tart, savory or sweet, light or lavish, and they may be served hot or cold, jellied or frozen.

THE SALAD GREENS

Most salads are built around—or upon—greens. Time was when green salad was a wedge of iceberg lettuce drenched with French or Thousand Island dressing. No more, thanks to the variety of greens now available year round. Nutritionally, salad greens are low in calories and relatively high in vitamins C and A (the darker the green, the greater the vitamin content), iron, and calcium. Here, then, are the varieties of greens available:

Lettuces

Crisphead or Iceberg: The old standby, tightly packed, crunchy, pale green heads. Sweet, succulent, and bland.

Leaf or Simpson: Loose-leafed, medium to bronzy green, depending on variety (Salad Bowl, Garden, crinkly Green Leaf, frilly Red Leaf, Bronze, Ivy, and Oak are popular leaf lettuces). Coarser textured and stronger flavored than iceberg.

Boston or Butterhead: Smallish, loose, medium green heads with buttery, easily bruised leaves. Exceptionally good flavor.

Bibb or Limestone: Loveliest of lettuces. Tulip-shaped, tiny, crinkly-crisp heads of medium to pale yellow-green. Not widely available but worth hunting up. These need extra-careful washing to float out hidden caches of soil. Delicate, mellow flavor.

Romaine or Cos: Supercrisp, green, elongated heads that originated on the Aegean island of Cos. Essential to tossed green salads for crunch and a certain amount of tang.

Other Salad Greens

Chicory or Curly Endive: Frilly, sprawling heads, bright green around the edges, pale in the center. Bitter, somewhat coarse, and best when teamed with more delicate greens.

Escarole: A coarse cousin of chicory with fairly broad, bitter, flat green leaves.

Field Salad (also known as *Mâche, Corn Salad, Lamb's Lettuce,* and *Lamb's Quarter):* Small, dark, spoon-shaped leaves, loosely clustered into rosettes. A rarity in most markets and available only in fall and winter. Flavor is faintly sweet.

Garden Cress or Peppergrass: Small, spicy-hot plants of the mustard family gathered when barely out of the ground. Not often marketed in this country but worth growing from seed. A handful of leaves will revitalize a listless salad.

Nasturtium: Leaves of this sunny flower have lots of dash and bite. They're good alone or tossed with other greens. The blossoms are edible, too, and contribute color and pungency.

Radicchio (Italian Red Chicory): Tangerine-sized heads of ruby-leafed lettuce with cream-colored veins and a slightly bitter flavor. Expensive, but a few leaves only are needed to add zip and color to tossed salads (1/4 pound radicchio is sufficient for a salad for 4–6 persons).

Rugula (Arugula) or Rocket: Rugula is the Italian name and the one most often used, since these dark, bitter-sharp greens are an Italian favorite. The leaves, usually sold with the roots on, are highly perishable and very gritty, so must be washed carefully. Use sparingly in green salads.

Sorrel or Dock: Crisp, sour, tongue-shaped leaves with a fresh, spring green color. Add with a light hand.

Sprouts (Bean, Alfalfa, and Clover Radish): Relatively new additions to the salad bowl, these tiny living green and cream shoots add not only crunch and taste but also plenty of vitamins (A and C) and minerals (iron and calcium). Because they are hydroponically grown, sprouts are clean and need only the quickest trimming or sorting before they're used. Sprouts are delicious tossed into or sprinkled onto salads or layered into sandwiches instead of lettuce. For detailed descriptions of *Soy, Mung, and Azuki Bean Sprouts,* see the vegetable chapter. *Alfalfa Sprouts* are filament-thin, nutty, and mild, *Clover Radish Sprouts* (also called *2-Mamina)* are somewhat larger and delicately peppery. They should be trimmed by about 1" at the root end, but, like other sprouts, need not be washed.

Watercress: Deep green, succulent, tart, and burning. The leaves and tender young stems provide welcome crunch and piquancy.

Belgian Endive, Cabbage, Chinese Cabbages, Dandelions, and Spinach, all popular additions to the salad bowl, are described in detail in the vegetable chapter. So are *Beet, Mustard,* and *Turnip Greens,* which, if young, fresh, and tender, team well with other greens. *Pak Choi (Bok Choy),* another Chinese cabbage, is actually a leafy chard much like spinach and can be used interchangeably with it in salads.

Buying Salad Greens

Choose crisp greens free of blemishes, bruises or soft spots, nicks or cuts. Also avoid those with "rust spots" (these may go clear through the head), wilted or yellow leaves. If you are buying a head of lettuce, be sure the head is firm and compact. Whenever possible, buy unpackaged greens that you can inspect closely.

How to Wash and Crisp Salad Greens

There are two schools of thought. One insists that greens will keep longer if they are not washed until shortly before using. The second (to which we belong) maintains just the opposite, that greens should be attended to as soon as they come home from garden or grocery. Peel off and discard any wilted or damaged outer leaves, then *wash* carefully (never allow to soak).

Headed Lettuces: With point of paring knife, cut out stem end, then hold head under a stream of cold water; it will force leaves apart and cleanse them. Drain well and wrap head in paper or cloth toweling, then pop into a plastic bag and place in hydrator compartment of refrigerator. If salad is to be made fairly soon, separate leaves, blot on toweling, and roll up; refrigerate until needed. *To Make Lettuce Cups:* Carefully pull off outer leaves (they will be nicely cup-shaped) and place on a towel-lined tray. Top with another towel and crisp in refrigerator until needed.

Loose-Leafed Lettuces: Cut out stem end, pull off leaves, and slosh up and down several times in a sinkful of cool water. Repeat, changing water as needed, to float out grit and soil. Blot leaves dry on paper toweling, roll loosely in cloth or paper toweling, then store in hydrator until needed. If greens are not to be used within a day or so, slip into a plastic bag, towel and all.

Watercress, Field Salad, and Other Stemmed Greens: Open bunch and discard roots and coarse stems. Swish leaves and tender young stems up and down in several changes of cool water until free of dirt. Rinse in cold water, blot on several thicknesses of paper toweling, then roll up in dry cloth and store in hydrator. *(Note:* If watercress is not to be used right away, open bunch but do not trim; stand in a glass of cold water, cover with a plastic bag, and store in refrigerator.)

A Word About Salad Baskets and Spin-Driers: Many cooks wash greens in wire baskets, then whirl them dry by swinging the baskets through the air. An all-right method for sturdy greens, but not for fragile ones because the wire mesh will bruise them. The plastic spin-driers, which remove water from lettuce leaves via centrifugal force, are far kinder to tender greens.

Making Tossed Green Salads

The Bowl: Wooden salad bowls have become absurdly sacrosanct, hallowed things never to be rinsed, let alone washed. So they go on and on, gathering oils, essence of garlic, and rancidity. "Wash" does not mean "soak"—which would indeed ruin a wooden bowl—but a quick sudsing, rinsing, and drying after each use is good practice. Better still, choose a nonporous, washable ceramic, glass, or metal bowl, a *big* one (it's impossible to toss salad in a small bowl).

Choosing the Greens: The best green salads provide contrasts—of color (greens range from near-white through red to near-black), of texture, shape, and flavor. But the contrasts must be subtle lest one flavor or texture overshadow the others. Salad artists devote years to their art, experimenting with combinations of greens, dressings, and herbs until they achieve a delectable balance. Consider the whole meal when constructing the salad, and select greens that will complement it—strong entrees demand delicate salads, light ones something substantial.

Good Salad Herbs: Because a handful of herbs have become known as "salad herbs," we tend to slight a number of others that work very well with tossed greens. The best herbs to use are fresh herbs (if you have a sunny window and a halfway green thumb, try growing your own; it isn't difficult). Don't load a salad with herbs, but settle upon one or two (and no more than three) that are compatible with one another and your choice of greens (tasting is the best way to tell). As a rule, two tablespoons of minced fresh herbs are sufficient for one quart prepared greens. Sprinkle the herbs into the greens, or mix into the oil. If you use dried herbs, crush between your fingers, add to the oil, and let stand 20–30 minutes at room temperature so they will gain fragrance. Dried herbs are stronger than the fresh, so use only one third to one fourth as much.

Favorite Salad Herbs:

Basil	Tarragon
Chervil	Fines Herbes (a mix of
Chives	chervil, chives, parsley,
Dill	and tarragon)
Parsley	

Others to Try:

Borage
Burnet   Both are cool, cucumber-flavored
Coriander Leaves (flavor is a cross between carrots and parsley)
Fennel
Marjoram
Mint
Oregano
Rosemary
Summer Savory
Thyme

Good Vegetable Additions to Green Salads: Raw cucumbers, carrots, and radishes are naturals for tossed salads, but so are a lot of other raw vegetables. As for cooked vegetables, nearly any vegetable that can be served cold can be tossed into a green salad. Here are some suggestions (all vegetables should be cut in bite-size or at least easy-to-eat pieces):

Raw Vegetables: Broccoli flowerets, carrots, cauliflowerets, celeriac, celery, cucumbers (especially the wax-free, seedless, more easily digested English or hothouse cucumbers); fennel, jicama, kale, and kohlrabi (if young and tender), mushrooms, onions (the whole huge family), peppers, sweet and hot, radishes (the red, black, white, and big sweet Japanese daikon), turnips, and zucchini. *(Note:* Tomatoes are not particularly suitable because of their juiciness. To keep them from watering down the salad: Slice tomatoes vertically instead of horizontally; marinate tomato wedges in dressing and add at the very last minute as a garnish, or best of all, use whole cherry tomatoes.)

Cooked Vegetables: Artichoke hearts and bottoms, asparagus, beans (the whole family of fresh and dried), beets, broccoli, carrots, celeriac, celery, cucumbers, eggplant, hearts of palm, leeks, lentils, green peas and snow or sugar snap pea pods, sweet green or red peppers (especially Marinated Roasted Peppers), and Irish potatoes.

Good Fruit Additions to Green Salads: Grapefruit, orange, mandarin orange, and tangerine sections (make sure all seeds and white pith are removed): diced or sliced avocados, apples, or pears (dip in lemon juice to prevent darkening); peeled seeded grapes, blackberries, and blueberries.

Other Flavorful Additions to Green Salads:

• Cheese: cubes of Cheddar, Monterey Jack, Swiss, or Gruyère cheese, crumbles of chèvre, feta, Roquefort or blue Wensleydale cheese, or sprinkles of Parmesan or Pecorino
• Croutons (plain or seasoned)
• Capers, sweet or sour pickles, ripe or green olives, slivered pimiento
• Bacon crumbles, slivered *prosciutto* or boiled ham
• Truffles—especially good with delicate greens and French dressing
• Nuts: toasted slivered almonds, piñon nuts, peanuts, walnuts, macadamias, soybean nuts, and fresh water chestnuts
• Seeds: celery, caraway, and toasted sesame seeds
• Tofu: cubes marinated in French dressing
• Flower petals: chrysanthemums, marigolds, roses, nasturtiums, violets, pumpkin or squash blossoms

Adding Garlic: Someone once said there was no such thing as "a touch of garlic." Perhaps not, but that doesn't mean you have to add enough to blow a safe. For fairly subtle garlic flavor, use one of the following techniques:
• Rub salad bowl with a cut clove of garlic before adding greens; or for slightly stronger flavor, sprinkle a little salt in bowl, then rub with garlic.
• Toss a *chapon* with salad, then remove before serving. A *chapon* is a stale chunk of French bread rubbed well with a cut or crushed clove of garlic.
• Slice garlic into salad oil, then warm briefly over lowest heat. Cool oil to room temperature and remove garlic before dressing salad.

Choosing the Dressing: Salad greens team happily with a huge variety of dressings—any oil and vinegar type (except very sweet ones), any tart creamy dressing, any savory cheese dressing. Consider the make-up of the salad—and the entire meal—then pick a dressing compatible with both. If there are dieters, also consider the calories (there is a good selection of low-calorie dressings in the recipe section that follows).

Putting Tossed Green Salads Together

Prepare the Dressing—at least 1/2 hour ahead of time so that flavors will mellow. If you are going to make an oil and vinegar dressing, combine herbs and other seasonings with oil and let stand 1/2 hour at room temperature. (*Note:* It's best to make dressings in small quantities; few keep well. If adding cooked or raw vegetables to salad, let marinate in a little of the dressing for about 1/2 hour at room temperature.)

Prepare the Greens—just before making the salad. Use only those that have been well washed and crisped in the refrigerator. If greens still show drops of water, blot gently on paper toweling. Break, tear, or cut greens into bite-size or easy-to-eat pieces and drop into salad bowl. (*Note:* Until recently, people thought cutting greens bruised them, destroyed the food value. But that theory is being questioned. The best way today seems to be whichever is easiest, most efficient. Endive, for example, is simpler to cut than tear; iceberg lettuce just the opposite.) *How many greens for a salad?* Allow 1–2 cups prepared greens per person (depending on appetites).

Dress and Toss the Salad: Place all salad ingredients in a large bowl and drizzle with a small amount of dressing; toss lightly, lifting greens from the bottom to the top, until leaves glisten. Taste, add more dressing if needed, also salt and pepper. (*Note:* If you are dressing salad with oil and vinegar, drizzle oil in first and toss until leaves are lightly coated. Then sprinkle vinegar on top and toss again, tasting as you go and adding extra vinegar as needed.) Vinegar and salt should always be added to tossed greens at the very last minute because they will quickly wilt a salad. The best way to avoid overdressing a salad is to underdress, then to add more dressing if necessary. As a rule, 3–4 tablespoons dressing per quart of prepared greens is sufficient.

OTHER KINDS OF SALADS

There are dozens of different salads in addition to the tossed, which may be grouped roughly as follows: *Vegetable* (both cooked and raw), *Fruit* (both raw and cooked), *Main Dish* (meat, poultry, seafood, egg, and pasta salads), *Molded,* and *Frozen.* Main dish, molded, and frozen salads are treated fully in the accompanying recipe section (and there are additional recipes in the meat, poultry, seafood, and egg chapters). Vegetable and fruit salads, however, are less a matter of specific recipes than of improvisation, as, indeed, are the increasingly popular *composed salads,* which often combine meat, poultry, or seafood, fruits, and vegetables all on a single, showy plate. Here is the place to let your imagination run wild, mixing and matching flavors, combining tints and textures, contrasting the hot with the cold, always tasting as you go.

Salads to Go

Most salads are poor travelers. Best choices —*if* they can be kept well chilled in transit— are cooked vegetable, meat, or seafood salads. Salad greens are apt to wilt or crush, but if wrapped in several thicknesses of *damp* paper toweling, then tied in a plastic bag and kept cool, they should arrive on location crisp and fresh. The dressing should travel separately and be added at the very last minute.

CAESAR SALAD

6 servings

1 clove garlic, peeled
2/3 cup olive oil (about)
2 cups 1/2″ bread cubes made from stale French or Italian bread
l large head romaine, washed and crisped
1/2 teaspoon salt
1/4 teaspoon pepper
1 egg (either raw or boiled in the shell 1 minute)
3–4 tablespoons lemon juice
6 anchovy fillets, drained and minced
1/3 cup grated Parmesan cheese

Crush garlic into oil, cover, and let stand overnight at room temperature. Next day, drain oil from garlic; discard garlic. Heat 1/3 cup of the oil in a heavy skillet over moderately high heat 1–2 minutes. When hot but not smoking, add bread cubes and brown on all sides, tossing constantly. Drain on paper toweling and reserve. *(Note:* You can do these well ahead of time to avoid a last-minute rush.) Break romaine in bite-size pieces into a salad bowl. Sprinkle with remaining oil, the salt and pepper, and toss; add a few extra drops oil if needed to coat all leaves lightly. Break egg into a cup and slide onto salad, pour lemon juice directly on egg, and toss lightly. Add anchovies, Parmesan, and bread cubes, toss again, and serve.

NPS: 305 C, 50 mg CH, 380 mg S*

WINTER HEALTH SALAD

4–6 servings ⚖

A brilliant combination of vegetables.

2 cups finely shredded cabbage
1 sweet green pepper, cored, seeded, and cut in julienne strips
1 pimiento, seeded and cut in julienne strips
1 medium-size carrot, coarsely grated (scrub but do not peel)
1 small red onion, peeled and minced, or 1/4 cup minced scallions (include tops)
1/2 cup minced celery (include tops)
1/2 cup minced cucumber (do not peel unless cucumbers are waxed)
1/2 small white turnip, peeled and finely grated
1/3 cup tiny cauliflowerets or broccoli flowerets (optional)
4 radishes, thinly sliced
1/4–1/3 cup French Dressing

Chill all vegetables well; add just enough dressing to coat all lightly, toss, and serve. For lunch, top with a scoop of cottage cheese or cubed sharp Cheddar.

NPS (4–6) (with cauliflower): 130–90 C, 0 mg CH, 85–55 mg S*

VARIATION

⚖ **Extra-Low-Calorie Winter Health Salad:** Prepare as directed but dress with Tangy Low-Calorie Salad Dressing.

NPS (4–6) (with cauliflower): 65–40 C, 0 mg CH, 165–110 mg S*

NASTURTIUM SALAD

4–6 servings

Nasturtium leaves make a sharp and pungent salad.

1 pint young nasturtium leaves, washed and patted dry on paper toweling
1 quart prepared mixed salad greens

DRESSING

1/3 cup olive oil
1/2 clove garlic, peeled and crushed
1 tablespoon minced parsley
1/2 teaspoon minced fresh marjoram or 1/4 teaspoon dried marjoram
1/4 teaspoon salt
1/8 teaspoon pepper
1/4 cup sour cream
2 tablespoons tarragon vinegar

Place nasturtium leaves and greens in a salad bowl. Beat dressing ingredients until creamy, pour over greens, toss lightly to mix, and serve.

NPS (4–6): 205–135 C, 5 mg CH, 170–110 mg S*

WILTED SPINACH SALAD WITH HOT BACON DRESSING

4–6 servings

1 (10-ounce) bag fresh spinach

DRESSING
6 slices bacon, cut crosswise in julienne strips
2 scallions, washed and sliced thin (include some tops)
1/2 cup red wine vinegar
2 tablespoons ketchup
1/2 teaspoon salt
1/8 teaspoon pepper

Sort spinach carefully, removing blemished leaves and coarse stems; wash in a colander under cold running water. Pat dry on paper toweling, then place in a large salad bowl. Brown bacon in a skillet and drain on paper toweling. Stir-fry scallions in drippings 5–8 minutes until tender, mix in remaining dressing ingredients, and heat, stirring, about 5 minutes. Pour hot dressing over spinach and toss well. Sprinkle in bacon crumbles, toss again, and serve.

NPS (4–6): 225–150 C, 25–15 mg CH, 650–435 mg S*

WILTED LETTUCE

4 servings

An old Southern salad, slightly sweet-sour.

4 slices bacon
2 tablespoons cider vinegar
1 teaspoon sugar
1/4 teaspoon salt
1/8 teaspoon pepper
1 quart prepared mixed salad greens
1/4 cup minced scallions (optional)

Fry bacon until crisp, drain on paper toweling, crumble, and reserve. Drain all but 3 tablespoons drippings from skillet; mix in vinegar, sugar, salt, and pepper and heat and stir just until simmering. Pour over greens and, if you like, scallions, add bacon, toss, and serve.

NPS: 130 C, 15 mg CH, 255 mg S*

VARIATION

Carolina-Style Wilted Lettuce: Heat 1/4 cup bacon or ham drippings in a small skillet; mix in 1/2 cup boiling water, the vinegar, sugar, salt, and pepper and bring to a boil. Pour over 1 quart prepared iceberg lettuce, toss, and garnish with sliced hard-cooked eggs and scallions. Delicious with fried country ham.

NPS: 115 C, 10 mg CH, 140 mg S*

JAPANESE VEGETABLE SALAD WITH TOASTED SESAME SEED DRESSING

4 servings

Toasted sesame seeds provide a rich nutty flavor.

2 cups prepared mixed salad greens
1 cup finely shredded or sliced red cabbage
1 cup fine julienne strips of peeled, seeded cucumber
1/2 cup finely shredded radishes
1/2 cup finely shredded carrot or raw broccoli stalks
1/2 cup minced cooked shrimp, scallops, or delicate white fish (optional)

DRESSING
3 tablespoons peanut or other salad oil
2 tablespoons sesame seeds
1/4 cup rice vinegar or 2 tablespoons cider vinegar
2 tablespoons mirin or cream sherry
1 tablespoon lemon juice
1 tablespoon soy sauce

Place greens, vegetables, and, if you like, shrimp in a large salad bowl. Heat and stir oil and sesame seeds in a small, heavy skillet over moderately high heat about 1 minute until pale caramel colored; remove from heat and stir 1 minute longer. *(Note: Be careful not to overbrown seeds—they'll be bitter.)* Mix in remaining dressing ingredients, pour over salad mixture, toss lightly, and serve.

NPS (with shrimp, cider vinegar, sherry): 160 C, 25 mg CH, 375 mg S*

CARAWAY COLESLAW WITH CREAMY OIL AND VINEGAR DRESSING

6–8 servings

A fragrant sweet-sour slaw. Olive oil makes the difference.

2 quarts moderately finely grated cabbage
1 medium-size yellow onion, peeled and grated fine

DRESSING
1/3 cup olive oil
1/3 cup tarragon vinegar
2 tablespoons superfine sugar
1 tablespoon caraway seeds
1 teaspoon salt
1/8 teaspoon pepper
1 cup sour cream

Place cabbage and onion in a large bowl. Mix all dressing ingredients except sour cream and stir until sugar dissolves; blend in sour cream. Pour dressing over cabbage and toss well to mix. Cover and chill several hours before serving.

NPS (4–6): 245–185 C, 15–10 mg CH, 415–310 mg S*

VARIATION

Red and Green Slaw: Prepare as directed, using a 1/2 and 1/2 mixture of moderately finely grated red and green cabbage. Nutritional count about the same as basic recipe.

OLD-FASHIONED CAROLINA COLESLAW WITH CELERY SEED DRESSING

6 servings

The mustardy dressing has plenty of bite.

1 medium-size cabbage, trimmed, cored, and quartered

DRESSING
2 eggs
1½ teaspoons powdered mustard
3 tablespoons sugar
½ teaspoon salt
¾ cup heavy cream
⅓ cup boiling cider vinegar
1 tablespoon butter or margarine
1½ teaspoons celery seeds

Slice cabbage quarters paper thin and place in a large mixing bowl. Lightly beat eggs in the top of a double boiler and mix in mustard, sugar, and salt. Beat in cream, then add vinegar in a slow stream, stirring constantly. Heat and stir over simmering water 3–5 minutes until the consistency of stirred custard. Off heat, mix in butter and celery seeds; pour dressing over cabbage and toss well to mix. Cover and chill 2–3 hours. Just before serving, toss well again.

NPS: 205 C, 135 mg CH, 260 mg S*

RAW ZUCCHINI SALAD

4–6 servings

Use only the tenderest young zucchini for making this salad. Otherwise it may be too bitter.

2 cups thinly sliced unpeeled baby zucchini, chilled
2 medium-size firm-ripe tomatoes, cored and thinly sliced

1 medium-size red onion, peeled, sliced paper thin, and separated into rings
¾ cup thinly sliced mushrooms (optional)
⅓ cup French Dressing
2 cups prepared mixed salad greens

Mix all ingredients except greens, cover, and chill 1 hour, turning now and then. Line a salad bowl with the greens, mound zucchini mixture on top, and toss at the table (there should be enough dressing for the greens, too; if not add a little more).

NPS (4–6) (with mushrooms): 165–110 C, 0 mg CH, 60–40 mg S*

VARIATION

Okra Salad: Prepare as directed but substitute baby okra for zucchini.

NPS (4–6) (with mushrooms): 170–115 C, 0 mg CH, 60–40 mg S*

RADISH SALAD

4 servings   ¢

¾ cup very thinly sliced red radishes
¾ cup very thinly sliced white radishes
1 small sweet green pepper, cored, seeded, and cut in julienne strips
¼ cup minced celery root
¼ cup French Dressing
1 teaspoon sugar

Toss all ingredients together, chill ½ hour, and serve on crisp greens.

NPS: 110 C, 0 mg CH, 40 mg S*

RAW MUSHROOM SALAD

4 servings

A perfectly elegant salad aromatic of tarragon. Plan it for a special dinner. Delicious with poultry or seafood.

1 pound medium-size mushrooms, wiped clean and sliced thin
2 tablespoons minced fresh tarragon or 1 teaspoon dried tarragon
1 tablespoon minced chives
⅔ cup olive oil
2 tablespoons tarragon vinegar
Juice of ½ lemon
¼ teaspoon salt
⅛ teaspoon pepper

Place all ingredients in a mixing bowl and toss well to mix. Cover and marinate 1–3 hours at room temperature. Drain and serve as is or on crisp lettuce leaves.

NPS: 355 C, 0 mg CH, 155 mg S*

RAW CAULIFLOWER SALAD WITH SOUR CREAM-PARMESAN DRESSING

4–6 servings

1 medium-size cauliflower, trimmed, divided into flowerets, and sliced paper thin
1 cup thinly sliced radishes
1/2 cup minced watercress leaves
2 tablespoons minced scallions

DRESSING
1 cup sour cream
1/2 clove garlic, peeled and crushed
Juice of 1/2 lemon
2 tablespoons olive or other salad oil
1 tablespoon finely grated Parmesan cheese
1/2 teaspoon salt
1/8 teaspoon black pepper
Pinch cayenne pepper

Toss cauliflower with radishes, watercress, and scallions and chill about 1/2 hour. Meanwhile, blend together dressing ingredients. Pour dressing over salad mixture, toss well, and serve.

NPS (4–6): 245–160 C, 25–15 mg CH, 355–240 mg S*

WILTED CUCUMBERS

4 servings   ¢ ⚖

2 medium-size cucumbers, peeled or not (as you like) and sliced paper thin
1 1/2 teaspoons salt
2 tablespoons boiling water
2 tablespoons sugar
1/3 cup white, tarragon, or cider vinegar
Grinding of pepper

Layer cucumbers in a bowl, salting as you go, weight down, cover, and let stand at room temperature 1–2 hours. Drain, wash in a colander under cold running water, then drain and press out as much liquid as possible; pat dry on paper toweling. Mix water and sugar until sugar dissolves, add vinegar, pour over cucumbers, and toss well. Cover and chill 1–2 hours, mixing now and then. Top with a grinding of pepper and serve as is or in lettuce cups.

NPS: 45 C, 0 mg CH, 830 mg S*

CUCUMBERS IN SOUR CREAM

4 servings

The mild, seedless English or hothouse cucumbers are particularly suited to this recipe. Serve with fish, shellfish, or ham.

3/4 cup sour cream
1 tablespoon tarragon vinegar
1 tablespoon lemon juice
1 tablespoon minced fresh dill
1/4 teaspoon salt
1/8 teaspoon pepper
2 medium-size cucumbers, peeled and sliced 1/4" thick

Blend all ingredients but cucumbers, add cucumbers, and toss to mix. Cover and chill 1–2 hours. Toss again and serve.

NPS: 110 C, 20 mg CH, 165 mg S*

TURKISH CUCUMBER SALAD (CACIK)

6–8 servings   ⚖

A cooling salad dressed with yogurt and seasoned with fresh mint and dill.

4 medium-size cucumbers, peeled and quartered lengthwise

DRESSING
1 pint yogurt
1 clove garlic, peeled and crushed
2 tablespoons olive oil
Juice of 1/2 lemon
1 tablespoon minced fresh mint
2 tablespoons minced fresh dill
1/2 teaspoon salt
1/8 teaspoon white pepper

Slice cucumber quarters 1/8" thick and drain on paper toweling. Beat dressing ingredients until creamy, add cucumbers, and toss well to mix. Cover and chill several hours. Toss again, serve in small bowls or, if you prefer, crisp lettuce cups.

NPS (6–8): 110–85 C, 10–5 mg CH, 225–170 mg S*

ORIENTAL CUCUMBER SALAD

6 servings   ⚖ ¢

Sliced cucumbers in an unusual soy-red wine vinegar dressing.

3 large cucumbers, scrubbed well and sliced thin
3 tablespoons soy sauce
3 tablespoons red wine vinegar
3 tablespoons peanut oil
1/8 teaspoon pepper

Place cucumber slices in a large, shallow bowl. Mix remaining ingredients and pour over cucumbers. Toss well, cover, and chill several hours, tossing occasionally so all cucumber slices are marinated.

NPS: 90 C, 0 mg CH, 675 mg S*

RUSSIAN SALAD

6 servings

1 cup cold diced cooked potatoes
1 cup cold cooked cut green beans
1 cup cold diced cooked carrots
1 cup cold cooked green peas
1/3 cup French Dressing
1/3 cup mayonnaise
1 cup cold diced cooked beets
1 head Boston or romaine lettuce, trimmed and chilled
1 tablespoon capers

Mix all vegetables except beets with French Dressing, cover, and chill 2–3 hours. Drain and save dressing; mix 1 tablespoon with mayonnaise, add to vegetables along with beets, and toss well. Mound on lettuce and top with capers.

NPS: 230 C, 5 mg CH, 190 mg S*

OLD-FASHIONED POTATO SALAD

6 servings

Nothing fancy but unusually good.

6 medium-size boiled potatoes, chilled, peeled, and cubed
4 hard-cooked eggs, chilled, peeled, and diced
1/2 medium-size sweet green pepper, cored, seeded, and minced
1 medium-size yellow onion, peeled and minced
2 stalks celery, diced
1 cup mayonnaise
1/4 cup sweet pickle relish
1 1/2 teaspoons salt
1/8 teaspoon pepper

Stir all ingredients together to mix, cover, and chill several hours before serving. Serve as is or in crisp lettuce cups.

NPS: 435 C, 205 mg CH, 900 mg S*

VARIATION

Herbed Potato Salad: Prepare as directed but add 2 tablespoons minced fresh dill or 1/2 teaspoon dillweed and 1/2 teaspoon minced fresh marjoram or 1/4 teaspoon dried marjoram. Nutritional count same as basic recipe.

GERMAN POTATO SALAD

6 servings

Nice and tart.

1 tablespoon flour
3/4 cup cold water
1/4 cup cider vinegar
2 tablespoons sugar
1/4 teaspoon white pepper
2–3 teaspoons salt
6 medium-size warm boiled potatoes, peeled and cubed
1/2 cup minced yellow onion
1/2 cup minced sweet green pepper
1 cup coarsely chopped celery
3–4 slices crisp cooked bacon, crumbled
6 hard-cooked eggs, peeled and diced

Blend flour and 2 tablespoons water in a small saucepan, add remaining water, vinegar, sugar, pepper, and 2 teaspoons salt, and cook, stirring, until mixture boils. Place potatoes, onion, green pepper and celery in a large bowl and toss lightly. Pour in hot dressing and mix well. Cool to room temperature, add bacon and eggs, and toss again. Taste for salt and add more if needed. Serve at room temperature.

NPS (with 3 slices bacon): 230 C, 275 mg CH, 885 mg S*

VARIATION

Hot German Potato Salad: Cut 4 strips bacon crosswise in julienne strips, brown in a large skillet, and drain on paper toweling. In drippings stir-fry 2/3 cup minced onion until golden, 5–8 minutes. Blend in 1 tablespoon flour, add 3/4 cup water or beef broth and the vinegar, sugar, salt, and pepper called for above. Heat and stir until mixture boils; keep warm. While potatoes are still hot, slice thin into a large bowl; scatter with bacon, omit green pepper, celery, and eggs. Pour hot dressing over potatoes, toss gently to mix, sprinkle with 1 tablespoon minced parsley, and serve.

NPS: 210 C, 10 mg CH, 840 mg S*

SPANISH POTATO SALAD

6 servings

What makes it Spanish are the green olives and olive oil dressing.

6 medium-size boiled potatoes, chilled, peeled, and sliced thin
3/4 cup minced pimiento-stuffed green olives
2 tablespoons finely grated Spanish or Bermuda onion
1/3 cup olive oil
2 teaspoons white wine vinegar
1/8 teaspoon pepper

Mix all ingredients in a large bowl, cover, and chill several hours before serving.

NPS: 225 C, 0 mg CH, 410 mg S*

CELERY VICTOR

4 servings

This cool American classic was created by Victor Hirtzler, for years chef at San Francisco's stately old St. Francis Hotel.

1 large bunch celery, prepared for cooking
1½ cups boiling beef broth
1 cup French Dressing
1 small bunch watercress or 1½ cups finely shredded iceberg lettuce
¼ teaspoon salt
⅛ teaspoon pepper
1 tablespoon minced parsley
8 anchovy fillets
1 large ripe tomato, cut in 8 wedges
8–12 ripe olives

Cut celery in 3″ lengths and simmer, covered, in broth 30 minutes until tender. Drain celery, toss with dressing, cover, and marinate in the refrigerator 4–6 hours or overnight. To serve, arrange watercress or lettuce on individual salad plates. Lift celery from dressing and arrange on top. Sprinkle each portion with salt, pepper, and parsley and decorate with anchovies, tomato wedges, and olives. Serve as an appetizer or salad.

NPS (with watercress): 450 C, 5 mg CH, 995 mg S*

CELERY RÉMOULADE

4 servings

With a food processor or electric blender, you can prepare the mustardy mayonnaise dressing in minutes.

1½ pounds celery root, trimmed, peeled, and cut in matchstick strips
2 tablespoons lemon juice
½ teaspoon salt

DRESSING
2 egg yolks
⅓ cup Dijon mustard
¼ cup boiling water
2 tablespoons hot red wine vinegar
⅔ cup rich, fruity olive oil
2 tablespoons minced parsley
1 tablespoon minced fresh tarragon or 1 teaspoon dried tarragon
1 tablespoon minced fresh chervil or 1 teaspoon dried chervil
2 tablespoons minced cornichons or gherkins
⅛ teaspoon pepper (preferably freshly ground)

Toss celery root with lemon juice and salt, cover, and marinate in refrigerator 3–4 hours. For dressing, place egg yolks and mustard in electric blender cup or in work bowl of a food processor fitted with the metal chopping blade. Snap motor on and off twice to mix. With motor running (use highest blender speed), drizzle in first the water, then the hot vinegar; next add ⅓ cup oil, drop by drop, until mixture thickens, then add remaining oil in a fine steady stream. Beat 30 seconds nonstop after all oil is incorporated. Fold in remaining dressing ingredients. Toss celery root once again with marinade, then drain off all liquid. Add several heaping tablespoons of dressing and toss well; add more dressing as needed to coat celery root generously. Cover and refrigerate 6–8 hours or overnight. Also cover and refrigerate any remaining dressing. When ready to serve, let celery root stand at room temperature 15 minutes. Toss again and add a little more dressing if needed to make celery root moist. Serve as is or on rosettes of radicchio.

NPS: 460 C, 135 mg CH, 1,095 mg S*

ASPARAGUS VINAIGRETTE

4 servings

2 pounds asparagus, steamed or poached, or 2 (10-ounce) packages frozen asparagus spears, cooked by package directions
⅔ cup French Dressing or Spanish Vinaigrette

Drain asparagus well. Arrange in a large, shallow bowl, pour in dressing, cover, and marinate in refrigerator several hours, turning now and then. Serve on a bed of lettuce as a salad or first course.

NPS (with French Dressing): 305 C, 0 mg CH, 100 mg S*

VARIATION

Other Vegetables to Serve Vinaigrette: Artichoke hearts and bottoms, beans (green, wax, wing, fava, and lima), broccoli, carrots, cauliflower, celeriac, celery (especially the hearts), cucumbers, endive, fennel, hearts of palm, leeks, green peas, zucchini. Simply cook by basic method, drain well, add enough French Dressing to coat lightly, and marinate several hours in the refrigerator. Recipe too flexible for meaningful nutritional count.

CURRIED ASPARAGUS SALAD

3–4 servings

1 pound hot steamed asparagus or 1 (10-ounce) package frozen asparagus, cooked and drained
½ cup French Dressing

6–8 lettuce leaves, washed and crisped
1 pimiento, drained and cut in 1/4" strips

CURRY DRESSING
1/2 cup mayonnaise
1 tablespoon sour cream
1/2 teaspoon curry powder
1/2 teaspoon lemon juice

Marinate asparagus in French Dressing 3–4 hours in refrigerator, turning occasionally. Shortly before serving, mix Curry Dressing. Drain asparagus (reserve French Dressing for other salads later) and arrange on lettuce. Top with Curry Dressing, garnish with pimiento, and serve.

NPS (3–4): 550–420 C, 25–20 mg CH, 310–235 mg S*

GREEN BEAN SALAD

6 servings

Cooked green beans in a spicy dressing. Especially good with pork, ham, or lamb.

1 1/2 pounds green beans, boiled and drained, or
  2 (8-ounce) packages frozen cut green beans,
  cooked and drained by package directions
1 medium-size red onion, peeled and sliced thin

DRESSING
2 tablespoons minced fresh tarragon or 1/2
  teaspoon dried tarragon
1 clove garlic, peeled and crushed
2 teaspoons prepared spicy brown mustard
1/2 teaspoon salt
Pinch pepper
1/2 cup olive oil
3 tablespoons red or white wine vinegar

Place beans and onion in a large bowl. Blend together dressing ingredients, pour over beans and onion, and toss to mix. Cover and let stand at room temperature about 1 hour. Toss again and serve.

NPS: 205 C, 0 mg CH, 210 mg S*

THREE BEAN SALAD

6 servings

Green, wax, and kidney beans marinated in a sweet-sour dressing.

1 (1-pound) can cut green beans, drained
1 (1-pound) can wax beans, drained
1 (1-pound) can red kidney beans, drained
1 cup minced celery
1 cup minced sweet green pepper
1 cup minced yellow onion
1/2 cup minced sweet or dill pickle (optional)
1/2 cup olive oil

6 tablespoons cider vinegar
3 tablespoons sugar
1 teaspoon salt
1/8 teaspoon pepper

Mix all ingredients, cover, and chill several hours before serving.

NPS (with pickle): 325 C, 0 mg CH, 1,005 mg S*

HOT SWEET-SOUR BEAN SPROUT SALAD

4 servings

Delicious with roast pork, ham, chicken, or turkey.

1 pound fresh bean sprouts

DRESSING
6 slices bacon, cut crosswise in julienne strips
1 small yellow onion, peeled and coarsely
  chopped
1/2 small sweet green pepper, cored, seeded, and
  coarsely chopped
1 tablespoon ketchup
1/4 cup tarragon vinegar
1/4 teaspoon salt
Pinch pepper

Wash sprouts several times in cool water, discard any that are dark or blemished, and drain the rest in a colander. Brown bacon in a small skillet and drain on paper toweling. Stir-fry onion and green pepper in drippings over moderate heat 8–10 minutes until onion is golden. Mix in remaining dressing ingredients and simmer, uncovered, 5 minutes. Just before serving, set colander of sprouts in sink and turn on hot water full blast. Move colander about so all sprouts are heated—this will take 3–4 minutes. Quickly drain sprouts and place in a salad bowl. Pour in hot dressing, add bacon, toss to mix, and serve.

NPS: 240 C, 25 mg CH, 420 mg S*

DRIED BEAN SALAD

4 servings

2 cups any cold, well-drained, boiled dried beans
1/3 cup minced celery
1/3 cup minced sweet green pepper
1/3 cup minced yellow onion
3 tablespoons olive or other salad oil
2 tablespoons cider vinegar
1/2 teaspoon salt (about)
1/8 teaspoon pepper
2 tablespoons minced parsley

Mix all ingredients, cover, and chill several hours or overnight, tossing now and then. Taste for salt and adjust.

NPS: 215 C, 0 mg CH, 295 mg S*

V A R I A T I O N S

Creamy Dried Bean Salad: Prepare as directd but omit oil and add 1/3 cup mayonnaise and 2–3 tablespoons chili sauce.

NPS (with 2 T. chili sauce): 265 C, 10 mg CH, 515 mg S*

Parmesan Bean Salad: Prepare and chill salad as directed. Just before serving toss in 1/4 cup finely grated Parmesan cheese.

NPS: 235 C, 5 mg CH, 390 mg S*

Bean and Beet Salad *(Makes 6 servings):* Prepare as directed but add 1 (1-pound) can pickled beets, drained and diced, and 2 extra tablespoons olive oil.

NPS: 230 C, 0 mg CH, 415 mg S*

CHICK-PEA AND TOMATO SALAD

6–8 servings

Keeps well in the refrigerator and is actually better after one or two days.

2 medium-size ripe tomatoes, peeled, cored, seeded, and cubed
1/2 cup minced sweet green pepper
1/2 cup minced Bermuda or Spanish onion
1 clove garlic, peeled and crushed
3 (1-pound 3-ounce) cans chick-peas, drained well
1/4 cup minced parsley
1 tablespoon minced chives
1 teaspoon minced fresh marjoram or 1/2 teaspoon dried marjoram or oregano
1/2 teaspoon salt
1/8 teaspoon pepper
1/4 cup olive oil
3 tablespoons red wine vinegar

Place all ingredients in a large bowl and toss well to mix. Cover and marinate at room temperature at least 1 hour. Toss well again and serve.

NPS (6–8): 295–220 C, 0 mg CH, 190–140 mg S*

RICE AND BLACK-EYED PEA SALAD

6 servings

1 quart hot boiled rice
1 1/2 cups drained cooked fresh black-eyed peas, or 1 (10-ounce) package frozen black-eyed peas, cooked and drained by package directions

1 medium-size yellow onion, peeled and minced
1 clove garlic, peeled and crushed
1 large carrot, peeled and coarsely grated
1/4 cup minced parsley
1 1/2 teaspoons salt
1/8 teaspoon black or cayenne pepper
3–4 tablespoons olive oil

Mix all ingredients together, adding just enough oil to coat all lightly. Serve warm or at room temperature as a main dish salad. Good mounded in hollowed-out tomatoes.

NPS: 270 C, 0 mg CH, 565 mg S*

BASIC MACARONI SALAD

6 servings

1/2 pound elbow macaroni, cooked and drained by package directions and chilled
1 cup diced celery
1/2 cup minced scallions or 1 small yellow onion, peeled and minced
1/3 cup minced sweet green and/or red pepper
1 cup mayonnaise
2 tablespoons white vinegar or lemon juice
2 teaspoons prepared mild yellow mustard
1 1/2 teaspoons salt (about)
1/8 teaspoon pepper

Mix all ingredients, cover, and chill several hours; taste for salt and adjust. Serve garnished with tomato wedges and quartered hard-cooked egg.

NPS (with scallions, without garnish): 415 C, 20 mg CH, 805 mg S*

V A R I A T I O N S

Cheese-Macaroni Salad: Prepare as directed but add 1 cup diced sharp Cheddar, Swiss, or Gruyère cheese and use 1/2 cup each mayonnaise and Roquefort or blue cheese dressing.

NPS: 725 C, 55 mg CH, 1,250 mg S*

Macaroni and Meat, Chicken or Shellfish Salad: Prepare as directed but add 3 cups cubed cooked ham, tongue, chicken, turkey, or shellfish and an extra 1/3 cup mayonnaise or 1/4 cup French dressing. Serve as an entree.

NPS (with ham): 630 C, 70 mg CH, 1,955 mg S*
NPS (with chicken): 635 C, 90 mg CH, 935 mg S*
NPS (with shellfish): 570 C, 90 mg CH, 1,025 mg S*

"Deli" Salad: Mix 2 cups Basic Macaroni Salad with 2–2 1/2 cups mixed cubed salami, bologna, corned beef, ham, tongue, luncheon meat, or chicken roll—whatever combination pleases you; chill well and serve as an entree.

*NPS (with bologna): 425 C, 40 mg CH, 1,020 mg S**
*NPS (with chicken roll): 350 C, 40 mg CH, 815 mg S**

PASTA SHELL SALAD WITH TUNA, DILL, AND CAPERS

4 servings

To serve as an entree, double the amount of tuna in this recipe, and garnish with two chopped hard-cooked eggs.

1/2 pound small shell pasta, cooked and drained by package directions
1 (6 1/2-ounce) can tuna, drained and flaked
1/3 cup minced celery
1/3 cup minced dill pickle
1 small red onion, peeled, sliced thin, and separated into rings
2 tablespoons tarragon vinegar
1 teaspoon salt (about)
2 tablespoons snipped fresh dill or 2 teaspoons dillweed
6 tablespoons olive oil
Freshly ground black pepper to taste
3 tablespoons drained small capers
1 dozen cherry tomatoes (garnish)

Rinse pasta briefly under cold running water, drain well, and mix with tuna, celery, pickle, and onion. In a small bowl, combine vinegar with salt and dill; add oil and beat vigorously until well blended and slightly thickened. Pour dressing over pasta and toss gently to mix. Add several grindings of pepper and toss again. Taste for salt and pepper and adjust as needed. Transfer to a serving platter, scatter capers on top, and garnish with cherry tomatoes. Salad should be still slightly warm; if you prefer, cover and chill 2–3 hours, tossing now and then, then let stand at room temperature 30 minutes, toss once more, and serve.

*NPS (with tomato garnish): 485 C, 10 mg CH, 1,100 mg S**

ROTELLE, BROCCOLI, RED PEPPER, AND PIGNOLI SALAD WITH SESAME DRESSING

4–6 servings

Pignoli (the Italian word for pine nuts) are popular additions to Italian salads such as this.

1/2 pound rotelle or fusilli, cooked by package directions and drained

1 (1-pound) head broccoli, divided into flowerets, and steamed until *just* crisp-tender (save stalks for soup)
2 roasted and peeled sweet red peppers,* cored, seeded, and cut in julienne strips
1/2 pound mozzarella cheese, cut in 1/2" cubes
1/2 cup pignoli (pine nuts)
2 tablespoons white wine vinegar or 2 tablespoons red rice vinegar mixed with 1 tablespoon white wine vinegar
1/2 teaspoon salt (about)
1 large clove garlic, peeled and minced
6 tablespoons sesame oil
Freshly ground black pepper to taste

Rinse pasta quickly under cold running water, drain well, and place in a large bowl with broccoli, red peppers, cheese, and pignoli. In a small bowl, combine vinegar, salt, and garlic; add oil, and beat until well blended and slightly thickened. Pour dressing over pasta mixture, toss gently, add several grindings of pepper, and toss again. Taste for salt and pepper and adjust as needed. Serve at once, or cover and chill 2–3 hours, tossing now and then. Let stand at room temperature 30 minutes, toss once more, and serve.

*NPS (4–6): 675–450 C, 45–30 mg CH, 505–335 mg S**

VARIATION

Rotelle and Artichoke Salad: Prepare as recipe directs, substituting 10–12 globe artichoke hearts, boiled, drained, and quartered, for the broccoli, a rich, fruity olive oil for the sesame oil, and balsamic vinegar for the white wine vinegar.

*NPS (4–6): 685–450 C, 45–30 mg CH, 525–350 mg S**

RICE-STUFFED TOMATOES AL PESTO

8 servings

8 large ripe beefsteak tomatoes

STUFFING
2 cups water
1/4 cup olive oil
1 cup uncooked rice
1 medium-size yellow onion, peeled and minced
1 clove garlic, peeled and crushed
2 tablespoons minced parsley
2 tablespoons minced fresh basil
1/2 cup piñon nuts
2 tablespoons finely grated Parmesan cheese
3/4 teaspoon salt
Pinch pepper

Core tomatoes, scoop out seeds and pulp, leaving only firm outer walls; drain upside down on several thicknesses paper toweling. Bring water and 1 tablespoon olive oil to a boil in a small saucepan, stir in rice, and boil rapidly, uncovered, stirring occasionally, 10–12 minutes until almost all water is absorbed; turn heat to low and let rice dry out. Meanwhile, stir-fry onion and garlic in remaining oil in a large, heavy skillet over moderate heat 8–10 minutes until golden. Mix in rice and remaining stuffing ingredients, turn heat to low, and heat, stirring occasionally, 5 minutes; cool to room temperature. Stuff tomatoes with mixture and serve as an entree.

NPS: 260 C, 1 mg CH, 240 mg S*

TABBOULEH

4–6 servings

A Middle Eastern salad that can also be served as a first course.

1 cup uncooked bulgur wheat
2 cups boiling chicken broth or water
1 cup minced parsley
1/4 cup minced fresh mint or 2 tablespoons dried mint
1 medium-size yellow onion, peeled and minced
2 ripe tomatoes, peeled, cored, and coarsely chopped
1/4 cup olive oil
1/4 cup lemon juice
1/2 teaspoon salt (about)
1/8 teaspoon pepper
1/2 head romaine lettuce, trimmed and chilled

Mix bulgur wheat and broth, cover, and let stand at room temperature 2 hours. Fluff with a fork, add parsley, mint, onion, and tomatoes, and toss to mix. Beat oil, lemon juice, salt, and pepper until well blended, add to salad, and toss again. Cover and chill well. Taste for salt and adjust if needed. Arrange romaine leaves spoke fashion on a platter or in a shallow bowl and mound salad in center. Diners can serve themselves by scooping up salad with romaine leaves, or individual portions can be served on leaves.

NPS (4–6): 340–230 C, 0 mg CH, 685–455 mg S*

CHEF'S SALAD

4 servings

3 cups prepared mixed salad greens (include watercress if possible)
1/2 medium-size cucumber, peeled and cut in 1/4" cubes
1/2 medium-size Spanish onion, peeled and sliced thin
1 cup julienne strips boiled ham, chilled
1/2 cup julienne strips cooked tongue, chilled
1 cup julienne strips cooked white meat of chicken or turkey, chilled
1/2 cup julienne strips Swiss cheese, chilled
4 radishes, washed and sliced thin
1/2–3/4 cup French Dressing

Toss greens lightly with cucumber and onion in a large salad bowl. Group ham, tongue, chicken, and cheese on greens in a spoke fashion; fill center with radishes. Cover and chill until serving time. Dress at the table by adding about 1/2 cup dressing and tossing gently.

NPS: 420 C, 80 mg CH, 700 mg S*

VARIATIONS

Recipe variations too flexible for meaningful nutritional counts.
• Use any combination of meat and cheese instead of those listed—luncheon meat, salami, headcheese, Cheddar cheese, etc.
• Substitute boneless sardines, flaked tuna, or cooked, smoked, flaked haddock for the ham and/or tongue.
• Use washed, crisped spinach leaves as part of the greens.
• Use any favorite salad dressing instead of French—Russian, Thousand Island, Italian, Green Goddess, etc.

COMPOSED SALAD OF CHÈVRE, SPINACH, AND RADICCHIO WITH WALNUT DRESSING

6 servings

1 (10-ounce) bag fresh spinach, washed, stemmed, and chilled
1 small head radicchio, separated into leaves, washed, and chilled
1 (2½-ounce) package clover radish sprouts, trimmed of 1" of root ends, and chilled
18 pitted ripe olives
4 teaspoons red wine vinegar
4 teaspoons lemon juice
1/4 teaspoon salt
1 clove garlic, peeled and minced
3/4 cup walnut oil (about)
2 tablespoons finely chopped walnuts
3/4 pound chèvre (any firm type), cut into 6 pieces, each about 3" × 2" × 1/2"
Freshly ground black pepper

Preheat broiler. Divide spinach among 6 large plates and tuck radicchio leaves in here and there. Arrange a small cluster of radish sprouts and 3 olives on the spinach at one side of each plate. Combine vinegar, lemon juice, salt, and garlic in a small bowl, then beat in 1/2 cup oil until smooth and slightly thickened; stir in walnuts. Brush a baking sheet with walnut oil and arrange chèvre pieces there 2″ apart; brush tops with walnut oil, then broil 4″ from the heat 2–3 minutes until cheese softens. Using a pancake turner, slide a piece of cheese into center of spinach on each plate. Top with several grindings of black pepper. Whisk dressing lightly and drizzle evenly over cheese and greens.

NPS: 570 C, 0 mg CH, 560 mg S*

CHICKEN OR TURKEY SALAD

6 servings

A good basic salad to vary according to whim.

3 cups diced cold cooked chicken or turkey meat
1 cup diced celery
1/4 cup minced yellow onion or scallions
1/4 cup minced sweet green pepper
2 tablespoons minced pimiento
3/4 cup mayonnaise
2 tablespoons French Dressing, lemon juice, or milk
1/4 teaspoon salt (about)
1/8 teaspoon pepper
1 tablespoon minced parsley (garnish)

Mix all ingredients except parsley, cover, and chill 2–3 hours. Taste for salt and adjust. Sprinkle with parsley and serve. For a party, mound in avocado halves or hollowed-out tomatoes.

NPS (with chicken and French Dressing): 370 C, 80 mg CH, 345 mg S*
NPS (with chicken and lemon juice): 340 C, 80 mg CH, 335 mg S*

To Use for Sandwiches: Mince chicken instead of dicing, then proceed as directed.

VARIATIONS

Chicken, Egg, and Caper Salad: Prepare as directed using French Dressing, but mix in 3 diced, peeled, hard-cooked eggs and 2 tablespoons each capers and minced sweet or dill pickle.

NPS: 415 C, 215 mg CH, 490 mg S*

Chicken and Vegetable Salad: Reduce celery to 1/2 cup and mix in 1–1 1/2 cups any of the following combinations: mixed cooked peas and diced carrots; diced avocado and cucumber; diced cooked potatoes and cooked cut green beans; cooked asparagus tips and diced radishes; diced unpeeled raw baby zucchini and diced, peeled, cored, and seeded tomatoes; fresh bean sprouts, shredded Chinese cabbage, and slivered water chestnuts. Recipe too flexible for meaningful nutritional count.

Chicken, Olive, and Walnut Salad: Reduce celery to 1/2 cup and add 1/2 cup each sliced pitted ripe or green olives and 1/2 cup coarsely chopped walnuts.

NPS (with French Dressing, ripe olives): 455 C, 80 mg CH, 420 mg S*
NPS (with lemon juice, ripe olives): 425 C, 80 mg CH, 405 mg S*

Chicken and Ham Salad: Prepare as directed, using 1 1/2 cups each diced, cooked ham (or tongue, luncheon meat, corned beef, cooked veal or lamb) and chicken. Recipe too flexible for meaningful nutritional count.

Chicken and Seafood Salad: Prepare as directed, using 1 1/2 cups each diced, cooked fish or shellfish and chicken.

NPS (with crabmeat and French Dressing): 330 C, 80 mg CH, 380 mg S*
NPS (with crabmeat and lemon juice): 300 C, 80 mg CH, 370 mg S*

WARM COMPOSED SALAD OF ROCK CORNISH HENS, ENDIVES, AND WATERCRESS WITH DIJON DRESSING

4 servings

2 (1–1 1/4 pound) Rock Cornish hens, roasted* (reserve pan drippings)
1/4 pound mushrooms, wiped clean and sliced thin
1 bunch scallions, trimmed and sliced thin (reserve green tops for garnishing)
1 tablespoon hazelnut, walnut, or peanut oil
2 bunches watercress, washed, stalks trimmed to 1″, and chilled
2 medium-size Belgian endives, separated into individual leaves, washed, and chilled

DRESSING
1/4 cup hot pan drippings
1/4 cup hot water
1/4 cup red wine vinegar or raspberry vinegar
Pinch sugar
8 teaspoons Dijon mustard

Cool birds until easy to handle, then remove skin and cut it into thin strips. Cut meat from bones in bite-size pieces and reserve. Stir-fry mushrooms and scallions in oil in a small skillet over high heat about 2 minutes until mushrooms wilt and give up their juices. Remove mushroom mixture with a slotted spoon and reserve; drain off and reserve pan liquid. Wipe skillet with paper toweling, add skin from birds, and stir-fry over moderately high heat 2–3 minutes until crisp; remove and reserve. Pour off and discard all but 1/4 cup drippings from roasting pan (if there are less than 1/4 cup drippings, round out the measure with bacon drippings); add water, set roasting pan over moderate heat, and stir and scrape up browned bits on bottom of pan. Transfer all to a small saucepan, add remaining dressing ingredients, also reserved mushroom liquid, and whisk to blend. Set over low heat, and warm, stirring constantly, 1–2 minutes. Divide watercress among 4 large plates, arrange endive spears on top spoke fashion, then mound Cornish hen meat in the center, dividing it equally. Spoon a little mushroom mixture over each portion of meat; whisk dressing briskly and drizzle over meat and greens, dividing total amount equally. Sprinkle crispened Cornish hen skin and some of the minced scallion tops artfully over each portion. Serve at once.

NPS: 250 C, 75 mg CH, 420 mg S*

EGG SALAD

3 cups, enough for 4 salads, 6–8 sandwiches

12 hard-cooked eggs, chilled, peeled, and
  coarsely chopped
1 tablespoon minced yellow onion
1/4 cup minced celery (optional)
1 tablespoon minced parsley (optional)
1 teaspoon salt
1/8 teaspoon pepper
1/4–1/3 cup mayonnaise
3–4 tablespoons milk

Mix all ingredients together, adding just enough mayonnaise and milk to give salad a good consistency. Cover and chill several hours. Stir well and use as a main course salad—in lettuce cups or hollowed-out tomatoes—or as a sandwich spread.

NP Cup (with celery): 460 C, 1,110 mg CH, 1,135 mg S*
NP Tablespoon (with celery): 30 C, 70 mg CH, 70 mg S*

VARIATIONS

Pickle-Egg Salad: Prepare as directed but add 2 tablespoons minced dill or sweet pickle and substitute 1–2 tablespoons pickle juice for 1–2 tablespoons milk.

NP Cup (with celery): 465 C, 1,105 mg CH, 1,290 mg S*
NP Tablespoon (with celery): 30 C, 70 mg CH, 80 mg S*

Dilled Egg Salad: Prepare as directed, adding 1 tablespoon each minced fresh dill and capers. Nutritional count same as basic recipe.

Herbed Egg Salad: Prepare as directed, adding 1 tablespoon each minced parsley and chives and 1 teaspoon minced fresh or 1/4 teaspoon dried tarragon, chervil, marjoram, or rosemary.

NP Cup: 460 C, 1,110 mg CH, 1,135 mg S*
NP Tablespoon: 30 C, 70 mg CH, 70 mg S*

Anchovy-Egg Salad: Prepare as directed, adding 2 tablespoons anchovy paste and omitting salt.

NP Cup (with celery): 480 C, 1,115 mg CH, 500 mg S*
NP Tablespoon (with celery): 30 C, 70 mg CH, 30 mg S*

Curried Egg Salad: Prepare as directed, adding 2–3 teaspoons curry powder and 1–2 tablespoons minced chutney.

NP Cup (with celery): 480 C, 1,110 mg CH, 1,145 mg S*
NP Tablespoon (with celery): 30 C, 70 mg CH, 70 mg S*

BASIC HAM OR TONGUE SALAD

4–6 servings

2 cups cubed, cooked ham or tongue or 1 cup of
  each
3 hard-cooked eggs, peeled and coarsely chopped
1/2 medium-size sweet green pepper, cored,
  seeded, and cut in julienne strips
2 tablespoons minced yellow onion (optional)
1 large dill pickle, minced
1/2 cup mayonnaise
1 tablespoon lemon juice
1 tablespoon light cream
1 teaspoon Worcestershire sauce
1/2 teaspoon prepared mild yellow mustard

Mix all ingredients, cover, and chill 2–3 hours. Serve mounded in lettuce cups or in the center hollow of a tomato aspic or jellied vegetable salad ring.

NPS (4–6) (with ham, onion): 400–270 C, 265–180 mg CH, 1,795–1,200 mg S*

VARIATION

Ham and Cheese Salad: Prepare as directed, using 1 1/2 cups cubed ham and 1 cup cubed sharp Cheddar, Swiss, or Gruyère cheese.

NPS (4–6) (with Cheddar): 485–325 C, 285–190 mg CH, 1,700–1,135 mg S*

EASY TUNA SALAD

About 3 cups, enough for 4 salads or 6–8 sandwiches

2 (6½-ounce) cans tuna, drained and flaked
½ cup minced Bermuda onion
Juice of ½ lemon
¾–1 cup mayonnaise (depending on how creamy a mixture you want)
2 tablespoons minced parsley
Pinch salt
⅛ teaspoon pepper

Mix all ingredients and chill several hours before serving. Serve as a salad in hollowed-out tomatoes or on crisp lettuce leaves or as a sandwich spread.

NP Cup: 625 C, 60 mg CH, 860 mg S*
NP Tablespoon: 40 C, 5 mg CH, 55 mg S*

VARIATIONS

Tart Tuna Salad: Prepare as directed but add 2 tablespoons minced capers and 1 tablespoon minced fresh dill or ½ teaspoon dried dill.

NP Cup: 625 C, 60 mg CH, 1,005 mg S*
NP Tablespoon: 40 C, 5 mg CH, 65 mg S*

Herbed Tuna Salad: Prepare as directed but increase parsley to 3 tablespoons and add 1 tablespoon minced fresh marjoram or ½ teaspoon dried marjoram. Nutritional count same as basic recipe.

Tuna-Cucumber Salad: Prepare as directed but add ⅓ cup minced cucumber or, if you prefer, diced celery.

NP Cup: 630 C, 60 mg CH, 860 mg S*
NP Tablespoon: 40 C, 5 mg CH, 55 mg S*

Tuna-Anchovy Salad: Prepare as directed but omit salt and add 3–4 minced, drained anchovy fillets.

NP Cup: 635 C, 60 mg CH, 850 mg S*
NP Tablespoon: 40 C, 5 mg CH, 55 mg S*

SCANDINAVIAN HERRING SALAD (SILDESALAT)

4 entree servings, enough appetizers for 6–8

Serve as an appetizer or entree.

3 herring in brine
2 cups cold, diced, boiled potatoes
2 cups cold, diced, boiled beets
1 small yellow onion, peeled and minced
½ teaspoon powdered mustard blended with 1 tablespoon cider vinegar
1 teaspoon sugar
¾ cup heavy cream, whipped to soft peaks
⅛ teaspoon pepper

Soak herring in cold water 24 hours, changing water several times. Remove heads, fillet and skin* herring, and cut in 1″ cubes. Mix herring with vegetables; add remaining ingredients, and mix again. Chill well before serving.

NPS (4–6–8): 325–215–160 C, 100–65–50 mg CH, 2,395–1,595–1,195 mg S*

BASIC SHELLFISH SALAD

4 servings

The flavor will be best if shellfish is freshly cooked and still slightly warm when mixed into salad.

1 pound cooked, shelled, and deveined shrimp, diced, cooked lobster, crab meat, or scallops
½ cup mayonnaise
2 tablespoons lemon juice or French Dressing
Pinch cayenne pepper
½ teaspoon anchovy paste (optional)
1 tablespoon minced chives
½ cup diced celery, chilled
½ cup diced cucumber, chilled

Mix all but last 2 ingredients, cover, and chill 2–3 hours. Add celery and cucumber, mix well, and taste for salt if anchovy paste is not used. Serve mounded in lettuce cups, hollowed-out tomatoes, halved avocados, or in the center of a tomato aspic or jellied vegetable salad ring.

NPS (with shrimp, anchovy paste, lemon juice): 335 C, 185 mg CH, 345 mg S*
NPS (with shrimp, anchovy paste, French Dressing): 380 C, 185 mg CH, 360 mg S*

VARIATIONS

Shellfish, Egg, and Avocado Salad: Prepare as directed but add 3 coarsely chopped hard-cooked eggs and 1 diced, peeled avocado along with celery and cucumber; toss very gently.

NPS (with shrimp, anchovy paste, lemon juice): 475 C, 395 mg CH, 400 mg S*
NPS (with shrimp, anchovy paste, French Dressing): 520 C, 395 mg CH, 415 mg S*

Shellfish Salad Louisiana: Prepare as directed, using 2 cups mixed, cooked shrimp, lobster, and crab meat and adding ¼ cup chili sauce and ¼ teaspoon prepared horseradish.

NPS (with anchovy paste, lemon juice): 295 C, 100 mg CH, 530 mg S*
NPS (with anchovy paste, French Dressing): 335 C, 100 mg CH, 550 mg S*

Spanish Shellfish Salad: Prepare as directed but blend ⅛ teaspoon powdered saffron into lemon juice before mixing into salad; omit celery and cucumber and add 1 cup cubed, cooked potatoes, 1/2 cup cooked green peas, 1/3 cup coarsely chopped, pitted ripe olives, and 1 cup shredded Boston lettuce or romaine. Add a little extra mayonnaise if needed.

NPS (with shrimp, anchovy paste, without extra mayonnaise): 395 C, 185 mg CH, 430 mg S*

Shellfish and Saffron Rice Salad: Prepare as directed, adding 1 1/2 cups cold Saffron Rice, 1/4 cup minced sweet green pepper, and 1 tablespoon each olive oil and cider vinegar along with celery and cucumber.

NPS (with shrimp, anchovy paste, lemon juice): 435 C, 185 mg CH, 550 mg S*
NPS (with shrimp, anchovy paste, French Dressing): 480 C, 185 mg CH, 565 mg S*

QUICK CURRIED SHRIMP SALAD

4 servings ☒

1/3 cup mayonnaise
3 tablespoons sour cream
1 teaspoon curry powder
1 teaspoon lemon juice
1 teaspoon minced chives
1/8 teaspoon pepper
1 pound cooked, shelled, and deveined shrimp, chilled

Mix all ingredients except shrimp; add shrimp and toss to mix well. Cover and chill 30 minutes or longer. Serve in lettuce cups.

NPS: 290 C, 185 mg CH, 270 mg S*

VARIATION

Quick Curried Chicken or Turkey: Prepare as directed, substituting 3 cups 1/2″ cubes cooked chicken or turkey meat for shrimp and adding, if you like, 1/2 cup diced celery and/or apple.

NPS (with chicken, celery, apple): 370 C, 110 mg CH, 220 mg S*

CRAB RAVIGOTE

6 servings

1 1/2 pounds fresh lump or backfin crab meat, well picked over, or 4 (6-ounce) packages frozen Alaska king or snow crab meat, thawed and drained
1/4 cup tarragon vinegar
3/4 cup mayonnaise
1/2 medium-size yellow onion, peeled and minced
2 tablespoons capers, minced
1 tablespoon minced chives
1 teaspoon minced parsley
1 teaspoon minced fresh chervil

1 teaspoon minced fresh tarragon
1 tablespoon slivered pimiento

Mix crab meat and vinegar, cover, and marinate in refrigerator 2 hours, turning now and then. Drain off vinegar and mix it with all but last ingredient, pour over crab, toss well, and arrange on lettuce or in avocado halves. Garnish with pimiento and serve.

NPS: 310 C, 130 mg CH, 470 mg S*

GRAPEFRUIT AND AVOCADO SALAD

6 servings

2 grapefruit, peeled and sectioned
2 medium-size ripe avocados
Juice of 1 lemon
1/2 cup French, Roquefort French, or Sweet French Dressing

Make sure all white pith is removed from grapefruit sections. Halve, pit, and peel avocados; slice into thin crescents and dip in lemon juice to prevent darkening. Place in a large bowl with grapefruit, add dressing, and toss to mix. Serve as is or on a bed of crisp mixed greens.

NPS (with French Dressing): 255 C, 0 mg CH, 55 mg S*
NPS (with Roquefort French): 265 C, 1 mg CH, 90 mg S*

VARIATIONS

Orange and Avocado Salad: Prepare as directed but substitute 4 naval oranges for the grapefruit. Nutritional count same as basic recipe.

Papaya and Avocado Salad: Prepare as directed but substitute 1 large, ripe papaya, pitted, peeled, and thinly sliced, for the grapefruit.

NPS: 205 C, 0 mg CH, 30 mg S*

Tomato and Avocado Salad: Prepare as directed but use 3 large, ripe beefsteak tomatoes, peeled, cored, and cut in slim wedges, instead of grapefruit. Use French or Roquefort French Dressing.

NPS (with French Dressing): 255 C, 0 mg CH, 55 mg S*
NPS (with Roquefort French Dressing): 200 C, 1 mg CH, 50 mg S*

WALDORF SALAD

4 servings

4 medium-size tart red apples, cored and diced (do not peel)
3/4 cup finely chopped celery

1/3 cup coarsely chopped walnuts
2/3–1 cup mayonnaise

Stir all ingredients together, adding just enough mayonnaise for good consistency. Cover and chill 2–3 hours. Stir well and serve on lettuce leaves.

NPS: 415 C, 20 mg CH, 240 mg S*

V A R I A T I O N S

Chicken (or Turkey) Waldorf Salad: Prepare as directed but add 3 cups 1/2″ cubes cold cooked chicken or turkey meat; increase mayonnaise to 1 1/2 cups, and add about 1 teaspoon salt and 1/8 teaspoon white pepper. Stir before serving and add more salt, if needed. Serve in avocado or papaya halves, in hollowed-out tomatoes, or lettuce cups.

NPS (with chicken meat, salad only): 940 C, 140 mg CH, 1,140 mg S*

Red Grape Waldorf Salad: Prepare as directed but add 1 cup halved, seeded red grapes.

NPS: 430 C, 20 mg CH, 240 mg S*

Pear Waldorf Salad: Prepare as directed but substitute 4 ripe pears for apples.

NPS: 430 C, 20 mg CH, 240 mg S*

GELATINS AND MOLDED SALADS

Cool, shimmering, jewel-bright, these are the glamour salads. They're good party choices because they're showy, also because they can be made hours, even days, ahead of time. The vital ingredient, of course, is gelatin, either unflavored or fruit-flavored. Unflavored gelatin is 85 per cent protein and low in calories. Flavored gelatins are sweetened either with sugar or one of the noncaloric artificial sweeteners. Depending upon the calorie value of the foods being molded, gelatin salads are excellent choices for dieters.

How Much Gelatin? The perfect molded salad is tender yet strong enough to stand on its own. Too much gelatin makes the salad rubbery, too little makes it collapse. Here is the standard ratio:

To Mold 2 Cups of Liquid, Use: 1 envelope (1 tablespoon) unflavored gelatin or 1 (3-ounce) package fruit-flavored gelatin.

Note: Very sweet mixtures will "set up" softer than tart or savory ones. *Do not attempt to mold fresh or frozen pineapple or pineapple juice; they contain an enzyme that breaks down the gelatin and keeps it from setting.* Canned pineapple, however, can be used.

To Dissolve Gelatin:

Unflavored Gelatin: There are four techniques; which you use is determined by the individual recipe.

Over Direct Heat: Sprinkle gelatin over cold liquid, then heat and stir constantly over low heat until dissolved. *Note:* If cream or milk is used, gelatin will take about twice as long to dissolve.

By Adding Hot Liquid: Soften gelatin in a small amount of cold liquid, then pour in simmering-hot liquid and stir until dissolved.

By Mixing with Sugar: Mix sugar with dry gelatin, add cold liquid, and heat and stir over low heat until dissolved, or pour boiling liquid over sugar-gelatin mixture and stir until dissolved.

Over Boiling Water: Soften gelatin in a small amount of cold liquid, set over boiling water (or place in a ramekin and stand in a small amount of boiling water), and heat and stir until dissolved. Combine with remaining liquid.

Flavored Gelatins: One simple method: Pour boiling or simmering-hot liquid over gelatin and stir until dissolved.

Combining Solid Foods with Gelatin: If minced fruits, meats, or vegetables are added to gelatin while it is still liquid, they will sink or float, depending upon whether they're lighter or heavier than the gelatin. Celery, apples, pears, bananas, avocados, and peaches are all floaters. Grapes, most citrus and canned fruits, most cooked meats and vegetables are sinkers. To distribute foods evenly throughout gelatin, chill gelatin mixture until thick and syrupy (it should be about the consistency of raw egg white), then fold in foods and chill until firm.

(Note: Always drain all foods well before adding so that they do not water down gelatin. For 2 cups of gelatin mixture, allow 1–2 cups solids, either minced, cubed, or cut in small pieces.)

Gelatin Setting Times: These will vary somewhat even in standard gelatin mixtures, depending upon sweetness or tartness of mixture, shape and size of mold (large molds take proportionately longer to set up than small ones), temperature and humidity of refrigerator. The following times, however, are average *minimums:*

Clear Gelatin (with no foods mixed in): about 2 hours

Gelatins with Foods Mixed In: about 4 hours

Layered Gelatins: about 12 hours *(Note: A detailed discussion of layered gelatins and ribbon loaves follows.)*

To Hasten Jelling: Dissolve 1 envelope gelatin in 1 cup boiling liquid, then add 7–10 ice cubes and stir until mixture is syrupy; remove any unmelted ice cubes. Or prepare gelatin mixture as recipe directs, then set in an ice water bath or in a large bowl of crushed ice and stir until syrupy. *Note:* It's generally bad practice to quick-jell a mixture in the freezer—except for mousses and chiffon-type molds—because the gelatin may freeze and break down.

Molds: Clear gelatins can be molded in deeply sculptured molds (and come out as sparkling and faceted as jewels), but mixtures containing solids should be molded in something simpler; if not, they will be difficult to unmold and the intricacy of the design will be lost. Recipes occasionally call for oiled or greased molds (to facilitate unmolding), but oil leaves an unpleasant film on the gelatin. A better method is simply to rinse mold quickly in cold water, then to add gelatin mixture to the wet mold.

How to Unmold Gelatin Salads: Keep mold refrigerated and do not unmold until ready to serve.
• Dip mold in *warm* (not hot) water to depth of gelatin mixture.
• Remove from water, loosen edges with tip of a paring knife.
• Place a serving plate, quickly rinsed in cold water but not dried, flat on top of mold, then invert so plate is on the bottom and shake gently. Gelatin should ease right out. By having serving plate moist, you can easily center mold.
• Wipe up any drops of liquid, garnish as desired, and serve.

TOMATO ASPIC

4–6 servings ⚖️

Plenty of variations here to try, some simple, some sophisticated.

1 quart tomato juice
2 sprigs parsley
1 stalk celery, coarsely chopped (include tops)
2 tablespoons minced onion
1 bay leaf, crushed
1½ teaspoons salt
1½ teaspoons sugar

¼ teaspoon basil
1–2 drops liquid hot red pepper seasoning
2 envelopes unflavored gelatin
2 tablespoons lemon juice
1 pint prepared mixed salad greens

Simmer 2 cups tomato juice, covered, 20 minutes with parsley, celery, onion, bay leaf, salt, sugar, basil, and pepper seasoning, stirring occasionally; strain tomato juice, discarding the solids, mix in gelatin, and stir to dissolve. Mix in remaining tomato juice and lemon juice. Pour into an ungreased 1-quart ring mold and chill until firm, at least 4 hours. To serve, unmold on a flat round platter, fill center, and decorate base with greens. Pass French Dressing or mayonnaise.

NPS (4–6): 75–50 C, 0 mg CH, 1,335–890 mg S*

VARIATIONS

Tomato, Cream Cheese, and Olive Aspic: Begin aspic as directed and smooth 2 (3-ounce) packages softened cream cheese into hot tomato juice-gelatin mixture. Stir in remaining tomato juice and lemon juice and chill until syrupy. Mix in ¼ cup thinly sliced pimiento-stuffed green olives, pour into a 5-cup mold, and chill until firm.

NPS (4–6): 235–155 C, 45–30 mg CH, 1,665–1,110 mg S*

Vegetable Aspic *(6 servings):* Prepare aspic as directed and chill until syrupy; fold in 1½–2 cups mixed, diced raw or cooked vegetables (any combination you fancy). Spoon into a 1½-quart mold and chill until firm. Recipe too flexible for meaningful nutritional count.

Tomato-Cheese Aspic *(6 servings):* Prepare aspic and chill until syrupy; fold in 1 cup cottage cheese and ¼ cup each minced sweet green pepper and celery. Mold as directed in a 1½-quart mold. *For a 2-Layer Aspic:* Pour half of syrupy aspic into mold and chill until tacky. Mix remaining aspic with the cheese and vegetables, spoon on top, and chill until firm.

NPS: 90 C, 5 mg CH, 1,040 mg S*

⚖️ **Seafood Aspic** *(6 servings):* Prepare aspic and chill until syrupy; fold in 1 teaspoon anchovy paste and 1½ cups coarsely chopped cooked fish or shellfish; mold as directed in a 1½-quart mold.

NPS: 120 C, 35 mg CH, 945 mg S*

Ham or Tongue Aspic *(6 servings):* Prepare aspic and chill until syrupy; fold in 1½ cups diced, cooked ham or tongue and ¼ cup minced mustard pickle; mold as directed in a 1½-quart mold.

NPS (with ham): 125 C, 20 mg CH, 1,615 mg S*

Chicken or Turkey Aspic *(6 servings):* Prepare aspic and chill until syrupy; fold in 1½ cups diced cooked chicken or turkey and ¼ cup applesauce. Mold as directed in a 1½-quart mold.

NPS (with chicken): 125 C, 30 mg CH, 920 mg S*

CUCUMBER ASPIC

6–8 servings   ⚖

4 small cucumbers, peeled
2 cups water
1 teaspoon salt
2 envelopes unflavored gelatin
1 tablespoon finely grated yellow onion
4 teaspoons lemon juice
½ teaspoon Worcestershire sauce
Pinch cayenne pepper
2 or 3 drops green food coloring (optional)

Coarsely chop 2 cucumbers and simmer, covered, with water and salt about 20 minutes until mushy; drain liquid into gelatin, set over low heat, and heat and stir until dissolved. Press cooked cucumbers through a fine sieve, then mix into gelatin along with onion, lemon juice, Worcestershire, cayenne, and coloring, if you like. Cover and chill until syrupy. Meanwhile, halve and seed remaining cucumbers and coarsely grate. Mix into gelatin, spoon into an ungreased 5-cup mold, and chill until firm. Unmold and serve on crisp greens. Pass mayonnaise, if you like, or Old-Fashioned Cooked Dressing.

NPS (6–8): 25–20 C, 0 mg CH, 380–285 mg S*

AVOCADO MOUSSE

6 servings

1 envelope unflavored gelatin
1 cup cold water
1 tablespoon minced yellow onion
½ teaspoon salt
Pinch cayenne pepper
1 cup puréed ripe avocado (about 2 small ones)
¼ cup mayonnaise or sour cream

Sprinkle gelatin over water, then heat and stir until dissolved. Mix in remaining ingredients, spoon into an ungreased 3-cup mold, cover tightly, and chill until firm. Unmold (especially pretty on a bed of watercress or clover radish sprouts), and serve at once (the mousse discolors rapidly on standing); wrap any leftovers airtight.

NPS (with mayonnaise): 130 C, 5 mg CH, 240 mg S*
NPS (with sour cream): 85 C, 5 mg CH, 190 mg S*

JELLIED GARDEN VEGETABLE SALAD

8 servings

3 envelopes unflavored gelatin
½ cup sugar
3½ cups water
½ cup white vinegar
1 teaspoon salt
1 tablespoon minced parsley
1 tablespoon minced chives
½ cup cooked green peas
½ cup diced, cooked carrots or finely grated raw carrots
1 cup finely shredded cabbage
¼ cup thinly sliced radishes
½ cup diced celery
½ cup diced cucumber
¼ cup minced sweet green or red pepper
1 small red onion, peeled and minced
2 medium-size firm-ripe tomatoes, peeled, cored, seeded, and coarsely chopped

Heat and stir gelatin, sugar, and 1 cup water until dissolved. Add remaining water, vinegar, salt, parsley, and chives and chill until syrupy. Mix in remaining ingredients and spoon into an ungreased 2-quart ring mold or 9″ × 5″ × 3″ loaf pan; cover and chill until firm. Unmold and top, if you like, with a thin mayonnaise-type dressing.

NPS: 85 C, 0 mg CH, 310 mg S*

To Use Other Vegetables: Substitute any compatible combination of cooked and raw vegetables for those listed above. You'll need 1 quart minced vegetables, total.

VARIATION

Vegetable Ribbon Salad: Prepare gelatin mixture as directed and divide into 4 equal parts. Chill 1 part until syrupy, mix in peas and carrots, spoon into an ungreased decorative 2-quart mold, cover and chill until tacky. Meanwhile, chill second part of gelatin until syrupy, mix in cabbage and radishes, spoon into mold, cover, and chill until tacky. Chill third part of gelatin until syrupy, mix in celery, cucumber, and green pepper, add to mold, cover, and chill until tacky. Chill remaining gelatin until syrupy *but do not add onion and tomatoes;* pour into mold, cover, and chill until firm. Unmold and serve as directed.

NPS: 75 C, 0 mg CH, 310 mg S*

PERFECTION SALAD

6 servings ⚖

1 envelope unflavored gelatin
1/4 cup sugar
1 1/4 cups water
2 tablespoons lemon juice
1 tablespoon cider vinegar
3/4 teaspoon salt
1 1/2 cups finely shredded green, red, or Chinese cabbage or 1/2 cup of each
1/2 cup diced celery
1/4 cup coarsely chopped pimiento-stuffed green olives
1/4 cup minced sweet red or green pepper
2 tablespoons finely grated carrot

Sprinkle gelatin and sugar over water and heat, stirring, over moderately low heat until dissolved. Off heat, stir in lemon juice, vinegar, and salt; chill until syrupy. Fold in remaining ingredients, spoon into an ungreased 1-quart mold, and chill until firm. Unmold on lettuce leaves and serve with mayonnaise.

NPS: 55 C, 0 mg CH, 430 mg S*

VARIATION

⚖ **Perfection Salad for a Crowd** *(12 servings):* Double recipe and spoon into an ungreased 13″ × 9″ × 2″ baking pan. Chill until firm and cut in large squares.

NPS: 55 C, 0 mg CH, 430 mg S*

JELLIED CHICKEN OR TURKEY SALAD

8 servings

For small families, this recipe may be halved and molded in a 1-quart mold or 4 custard cups.

2 envelopes unflavored gelatin
1/2 cup cold water
3 cups chicken broth
2 tablespoons lemon juice
1/2 teaspoon salt
3 cups minced cold cooked chicken or turkey meat (preferably white meat)
1/4 cup minced celery
1/4 cup minced sweet green pepper
1/4 cup minced scallions
2 tablespoons minced pimiento

Heat and stir gelatin with water and broth until dissolved; mix in lemon juice and salt. Chill until thick and syrupy, mix in remaining ingredients, spoon into an ungreased 9″ × 5″ × 3″ loaf pan, cover, and chill un-

til firm. Loosen edges and unmold. If you like, pass a thin mayonnaise-type dressing.

NPS (with chicken): 125 C, 45 mg CH, 480 mg S*

VARIATIONS

Jellied Meat Salad: Prepare as directed, substituting 1 1/2 cups each water and beef broth for chicken broth and 3 cups minced cooked lean beef, lamb, or veal for chicken. If you like, reduce lemon juice to 1 tablespoon and add 1 teaspoon Worcestershire sauce.

NPS (with beef, no Worcestershire sauce): 115 C, 50 mg CH, 385 mg S*

Jellied Ham or Tongue Salad: Prepare as directed, using 1 1/2 cups each beef and chicken broth and 3 cups minced, cooked ham or tongue instead of chicken.

NPS (with ham): 115 C, 30 mg CH, 1,250 mg S*

Jellied Shellfish Salad: Prepare as directed, using 1 1/2 cups each chicken broth and water or tomato juice and 3 cups minced, cooked shellfish instead of chicken.

NPS (with chicken broth and water, and lobster): 70 C, 45 mg CH, 405 mg S*

MOLDED SPICY CRANBERRY SALAD

8 servings

1 pound fresh or frozen cranberries, washed
2 cups water
2 sticks cinnamon and 24 cloves, tied in cheesecloth
1 cup sugar
1/2 teaspoon salt
2 envelopes unflavored gelatin
2/3 cup minced celery
1 cup canned crushed pineapple, drained
1 cup minced walnuts

Simmer cranberries, water, and spices covered until cranberry skins pop, 5–7 minutes; discard spice bag. Purée cranberries and cooking liquid by buzzing 20–25 seconds in an electric blender at low speed or 10–15 seconds in a food processor fitted with the metal chopping blade. Return to pan, stir in sugar, salt, and gelatin, and simmer, stirring, until gelatin dissolves. Cool, then chill, stirring occasionally, until thick and syrupy. Mix in remaining ingredients, ladle into an ungreased 5-cup mold or 8 individual molds, and chill until firm. To serve, unmold and garnish with chicory or other crisp greens.

NPS: 250 C, 0 mg CH, 150 mg S*

Making Gelatin Ribbon Loaves

Any compatible gelatin mixtures can be layered—jellied meat and vegetables, jellied poultry and tart fruit or vegetables, aspic with almost anything savory. Bear in mind *combined yield* of gelatin mixtures and use a mold large enough to accommodate both. For best results:

• Keep thickness of layers in proportion to each other.

• Do not try to mold more than 3 or 4 layers in a 1- or 2-quart mold or 9″ × 5″ × 3″ loaf pan (it holds 2 quarts).

• Always chill 1 layer until *tacky-firm* before adding another. If gelatin is too firm, layers will not stick together; if too liquid, they will run together.

• Have gelatin mixtures at room temperature or, better still, chilled *just* until syrupy before adding to mold.

• Add heaviest layers last (those containing minced foods) so that when loaf is unmolded, they will be on the bottom; otherwise they may topple or slide off.

• Give a ribbon loaf plenty of time to set up before unmolding—at least 12 hours.

TOMATO AND CHEESE RIBBON LOAF

8–10 servings

1 recipe Tomato Aspic
2 envelopes unflavored gelatin
3/4 cup water
3 cups sieved cottage cheese
2/3 cup sour cream
2 tablespoons minced parsley
2 tablespoons minced scallions (include some tops)
1 teaspoon salt
1/8 teaspoon white pepper

Prepare aspic as directed and pour half into an ungreased 9″ × 5″ × 3″ loaf pan; chill until tacky-firm; keep remaining aspic syrupy over tepid water. Meanwhile, sprinkle gelatin over water and heat and stir over moderately low heat until dissolved. Mix with remaining ingredients and chill quickly until syrupy by setting in a bowl of cracked ice. Pour half of cheese gelatin on molded tomato aspic and chill until tacky; keep remaining cheese mixture syrupy over tepid water. Add remaining tomato aspic to mold, chill until tacky, then top with remaining cheese gelatin. Chill overnight until firm. Slice about 1/2″ thick and serve on crisp greens. Good with a thin mayonnaise-type dressing.

NPS (8–10): 165–135 C, 20–15 mg CH, 1,275–1,020 mg S*

VARIATION

Tomato-Chicken Ribbon Loaf: Prepare 1 recipe Tomato Aspic and 1/2 recipe Jellied Chicken Salad. Starting with Tomato Aspic, layer into loaf pan.

NPS (8–10): 100–80 C, 25–20 mg CH, 910–725 mg S*

FROZEN FRUIT SALAD

6–8 servings

More dessert than salad. It's rich but not too sweet.

1 tablespoon water mixed with 1 tablespoon lemon juice
1 teaspoon unflavored gelatin
1 tablespoon confectioners' sugar
1 (3-ounce) package cream cheese, softened to room temperature
1/3 cup mayonnaise
1/2 cup heavy cream
1 1/2 cups mixed diced fresh fruit

Place water mixture in a custard cup, sprinkle in gelatin and sugar, and set in a small pan of simmering water; heat and stir until gelatin dissolves. Beat cream cheese and mayonnaise until blended and stir in gelatin mixture; whip cream to soft peaks and fold in along with fruit. Spoon into a 9″ square pan and freeze just until firm. Cut in squares and serve on lettuce.

NPS (6–8) (1/2 cup each apple, peach, banana): 295–220 C, 50–35 mg CH, 120–90 mg S*

FROZEN CRANBERRY RIBBON SALAD

6–8 servings ▯

1 (1-pound) can whole or jellied cranberry sauce
1/4 cup lemon juice
1/2 cup mayonnaise
1/3 cup sugar
1 cup heavy cream
1/4 cup minced pecans, walnuts, or toasted almonds (optional)

If using jellied cranberry sauce, soften by standing unopened can in very hot water; mix lemon juice into sauce, spoon into a refrigerator tray, and freeze until firm. Mix mayonnaise and sugar; beat cream to soft peaks and fold in. Spread on top of cranberry layer, sprinkle, if you like, with nuts, and freeze until firm. Cut in squares and serve on lettuce.

NPS (6–8) (with nuts): 460–345 C, 65–50 mg CH, 145–110 mg S*
NPS (6–8) (without nuts): 425–320 C, 65–50 mg CH, 145–110 mg S*

SALAD DRESSINGS

The parade of bottled dressings along supermarket shelves is so long it may seem foolish to make a dressing from scratch. It isn't. Good as some commercial dressings are, they can never match the delicacy and bouquet of those made at home from first-quality oils, vinegars, and seasonings.

The Salad Oils: Keep a selection of oils on hand—on a cool, dark shelf, never in the refrigerator (cold turns oils cloudy). Unless you use oils frequently, buy in small amounts so that you can use up a bottle before it becomes rancid. Oils give salads a special mellowness and are the medium in which all flavors mingle. They can also impart a unique, subtle flavor to the well-dressed salad whether they are pressed from *olives* (the best is "extra virgin," meaning oil from the first cold pressing of choice olives; connoisseurs favor the fruity Tuscan oils of Italy), from *nuts (walnut* and *hazelnut oils* are two particularly fragrant choices), from *grape, sunflower, safflower,* or *sesame seeds* (cold-pressed sesame seed oil is mild, the Oriental variety much more intense, so use sparingly). There are now even *herbed* and *spiced oils,* scented with fresh herbs, chili peppers, garlic, or star anise. Sadly, oils are what add calories to salads (1 tablespoon salad oil averages about 125). So if you are dieting, use one of the low-calorie or cholesterol-free salad dressings now available in many supermarkets. A more detailed discussion of oils is included in the chapter The Larder.

The Vinegars: Nearly every supermarket stocks a good variety of plain and flavored vinegars. Keep an assortment on hand on a cool, dark shelf. It's best to buy in fairly small bottles because vinegars do mold and produce sediment. The sediment can be strained out, but a moldy vinegar should be discarded.

Cider Vinegar: The all-purpose, golden brown vinegar made from apples. It is good for cooked or highly seasoned dressings but too rough and coarse to use solo with oil.

Distilled Vinegar: White vinegar, acid and sour and better for pickles than salads.

Malt Vinegar: An English favorite, tart but mellow; use interchangeably with cider vinegar.

Wine Vinegars: These are simply wines that have gone a step too far, which explains why there are white, red, and rosé wine vinegars. *Note:* Save any tag ends of the wine bottle; when the wine sours into vinegar, use to dress salads.

Flavored Vinegars: These, usually made from cider or white wine vinegar, include all the herb vinegars, also garlic, pepper, honey, onion, and shallot vinegars. You can buy them at any grocery or, if you have an herb garden, make your own (recipes follow).

Fruit Vinegars: Vinegars in which ripe raspberries, blueberries, cranberries, pears, or other fruits have steeped. They're aromatic, almost perfumy, and should be used sparingly with delicate oils.

Sherry Vinegar: A dark, rich, and delicious Spanish vinegar that's a by-product of the sherry wine industry. If you want an outstanding vinaigrette, this is the vinegar to use.

Balsamic Vinegar (Aceto Balsamico di Modena): A mellow brown Italian vinegar made from white Trebbiano grape juice *(must)* that's sweet-sour and assertive without being astringent. By law, all balsamic vinegar must be aged 10 years before it can be sold. It is especially good used to dress pungent green salads, roasted peppers, cheeses, and cooked vegetables.

Rice Vinegars: These range in color from *white* (Japanese) to *red* (containing malt) to *black* (containing soy sauce). Because of their pungency, the red and black rice vinegars are usually used as condiments (Oriental restaurants commonly set them out on the table together with soy sauce). If you use them, do so with restraint. The white rice vinegars, on the other hand, are mild, less acidic, in fact, than cider or wine vinegars, so if you plan to dress a salad with them, you'll have to use nearly twice as much to achieve the proper degree of tartness.

Tips on Making Salad Dressings

• Most dressings do not keep well, so make in small quantities.
• For best flavor, dressings should be made at least a half hour ahead of time, sometimes even longer. Oil and vinegar types should

stand at room temperature so flavors marry, but cream or mayonnaise dressings should be kept refrigerated.

• Do not use garlic or onion powders and salts; they rapidly become stale and can ruin an otherwise excellent salad. It's far better to mince fresh garlic and onion; more effort, true. But worth it.

• Use fresh herbs in preference to the dry. And when using the dry, make sure they haven't been sitting on the shelf for months. An old herb adds about as much character to salad as dried grass.

• Use the finest quality oils, vinegars, and seasonings.

• Use coarse salt or kosher salt if possible and, of course, freshly ground black pepper.

• When dressing salads with oil and vinegar, use a heavy hand with the oil and a light one with the vinegar. *The classic proportion is three or four parts oil to one part vinegar.* For variety, try substituting lemon or lime juice (or part lemon or lime juice) for the vinegar.

HERB OIL

1 pint

Use the best mild extra-virgin olive oil available, also whole stalks of herbs so that they can be easily removed from the bottle.

4–6 whole stalks fresh herbs (tarragon, rosemary, chervil, sage, or thyme), washed gently in cool water and patted dry on paper toweling
1 pint top-quality olive oil

Crush herbs gently in your hands, then place in a wide-mouth 1-quart preserving jar. Pour in oil, cover tight, and let stand in a cool, dark spot 4–6 weeks (shake jar gently two to three times a week). Taste oil after 4 weeks and if flavorful enough, remove herb stalks; if too weak, let stand an additional week or 2. Use to dress salads.

NP Tablespoon: 125 C, 0 mg CH, 0 mg S*

GARLIC VINEGAR

1 pint   ⚖

1 pint boiling cider vinegar
6 cloves garlic, peeled and halved

Pour vinegar into a jar, drop in garlic, cover, and let stand 24 hours at room temperature. Discard garlic, strain vinegar through a double thickness of cheesecloth into a fresh pint jar. Use for making salad dressings and sauces.

NP Tablespoon: 3 C, 0 mg CH, 25 mg S*

HERB VINEGAR

1 pint   ⚖

Herbs will be at their peak of flavor if picked just before they bloom.

2 cups tender fresh herb leaves or sprigs (tarragon, chervil, dill, basil, or thyme) washed gently in cool water and patted dry on paper toweling
1 pint boiling vinegar (cider or white wine)

Place herbs in a wide-mouthed heatproof jar and crush lightly with the handle of a wooden spoon. Pour in vinegar and cool to room temperature. Screw on lid and let stand in a cool spot (not refrigerator) 10 days to 2 weeks; once every day, turn jar upside down, then right-side-up again. Taste vinegar after 10 days and, if strong enough, strain through several thicknesses of cheesecloth into a fresh pint jar. If too weak, let stand the full 2 weeks. If still too weak, strain off vinegar and bring to a boil; fill a fresh jar with freshly picked herbs, cover with boiling vinegar, and let stand a week to 10 days, turning once a day. Strain vinegar and use for making salad dressings and sauces.

NP Tablespoon: 3 C, 0 mg CH, 1 mg S*

À LA GRECQUE MARINADE

3 cups

Leeks, zucchini, and certain other cooked vegetables are delicious when marinated in this delicate lemon and oil dressing. They may be served as a first course, a salad, or a vegetable.

⅓ cup lemon juice
½ cup olive oil
1 pint hot water
½ teaspoon salt
⅛ teaspoon each fennel and coriander seeds tied in cheesecloth
1 bay leaf
1 (4″) sprig fresh thyme or ⅛ teaspoon dried thyme
Pinch white pepper

Mix all ingredients together and use in preparing vegetables that are to be served *à la grecque*.

NP Tablespoon: 20 C, 0 mg CH, 25 mg S*

FRENCH DRESSING (VINAIGRETTE)

1 cup ⊠

Called *vinaigrette* in France, French dressing is simply three to four parts olive oil to one part vinegar, seasoned with salt and pepper.

¼ cup red or white wine vinegar
¼ teaspoon salt
⅛ teaspoon white pepper
¾ cup olive oil

In a bowl mix vinegar, salt, and pepper with a wire whisk. Add oil and mix vigorously until well blended and slightly thickened. *(Note:* For a creamier dressing, beat over ice 1–2 minutes.) Use to dress green or vegetable salads. *(Note:* If you prefer, substitute any good salad oil for the olive oil and cider, malt, or other flavored vinegar for the wine vinegar.)

NP Tablespoon: 90 C, 0 mg CH, 35 mg S*

VARIATIONS

Garlic French Dressing: Drop 1 peeled, bruised clove garlic into dressing and let stand 1–2 hours at room temperature; remove garlic before using dressing.

NP Tablespoon: 90 C, 0 mg CH, 35 mg S*

Tarragon French Dressing: Make dressing with tarragon vinegar and add 1 tablespoon minced fresh or ½ teaspoon dried tarragon.

NP Tablespoon: 90 C, 0 mg CH, 35 mg S*

Roquefort French Dressing: Prepare dressing as directed and crumble in 3 tablespoons Roquefort cheese. Cover and let stand several hours at room temperature before using.

NP Tablespoon: 95 C, 1 mg CH, 65 mg S*

Spanish Vinaigrette: Prepare dressing as directed and place in a shaker jar with 1 tablespoon minced green olives and 1 teaspoon each minced chives, capers, parsley, and gherkin, and 1 sieved hard-cooked egg yolk. Shake, let stand at room temperature ½ hour; shake again before using.

NP Tablespoon: 95 C, 15 mg CH, 55 mg S*

Chiffonade Dressing: Prepare dressing as directed, then mix in 2 tablespoons each minced ripe olives, chives, and sweet green pepper and 1 minced hard-cooked egg.

NP Tablespoon: 95 C, 15 mg CH, 45 mg S*

Sweet French Dressing: Prepare dressing as directed, then mix in ¼ cup each orange juice and honey or superfine sugar. Use to dress fruit salads.

NP Tablespoon (with honey): 105 C, 0 mg CH, 35 mg S*

NP Tablespoon (with sugar): 105 C, 0 mg CH, 35 mg S*

FRESH HERB DRESSING

¾ cup

½ cup olive oil
1 tablespoon minced fresh dill, tarragon, chervil, or fennel
1 tablespoon minced chives
¼ teaspoon minced fresh marjoram (optional)
½ teaspoon salt
⅛ teaspoon pepper
1 clove garlic, peeled and crushed (optional)
¼ cup tarragon vinegar

Place oil, herbs, salt, pepper, and, if you like, the garlic in a shaker bottle or large glass measuring cup and let stand at room temperature 3–4 hours. Add vinegar and shake or stir well to blend. Use to dress any crisp green salad, using only enough to coat each leaf lightly. Save leftover dressing to use for other salads later (dressing will keep about 1 week).

NP Tablespoon: 80 C, 0 mg CH, 90 mg S*

SHALLOT DRESSING

½ cup

1 tablespoon minced shallots
½ teaspoon paprika
½ teaspoon powdered mustard
¼ teaspoon tarragon or chervil
½ teaspoon salt
Pinch pepper
⅓ cup olive oil
3 tablespoons tarragon vinegar

Place all ingredients except vinegar in a small bowl, stir well to mix, cover, and let stand at room temperature about 1 hour. Stir again, mix in vinegar, and use to dress crisp green salads.

NP Tablespoon: 80 C, 0 mg CH, 135 mg S*

BUTTERMILK DRESSING

1½ cups ⚖ ⊠

Dieters, note just *how* low the calories are.

½ cup cider vinegar
1 tablespoon salad oil
1 teaspoon salt
⅛ teaspoon white pepper
1 cup buttermilk

Shake all ingredients in a jar with a tight-fitting lid and use to dress cabbage or crisp green salads. (*Note:* Dressing will keep about a week in the refrigerator.)

NP Tablespoon: 10 C, 1 mg CH, 100 mg S*

LEMON-LIME DRESSING

1 cup ⊠

Juice of 1 lemon
Juice of 1/2 lime
2 tablespoons honey
2/3 cup olive oil
1 tablespoon minced chives
1 tablespoon minced fresh basil or dill
Pinch salt
Pinch pepper

Shake all ingredients in a jar and use to dress sliced tomatoes or crisp green salads.

NP Tablespoon: 90 C, 0 mg CH, 10 mg S*

WINE DRESSING

1 1/4 cups

A good way to use up any tag ends of wine.

1/3 cup dry red or white wine
1/4 cup red or white wine vinegar
1 clove garlic, peeled, bruised, and stuck on a
   toothpick
1/4 teaspoon salt
1/4 teaspoon powdered mustard
1/8 teaspoon white pepper
2/3 cup olive or other salad oil

Mix wine, vinegar, and garlic, cover, and let stand at room temperature 2 hours; remove garlic. Beat in salt, mustard, and pepper, then drizzle in oil, beating constantly. Shake well and use to dress green salads.

NP Tablespoon: 70 C, 0 mg CH, 30 mg S*

SOUR CREAM DRESSING

1 1/4 cups ⊠

1 cup sour cream
3 tablespoons white or cider vinegar
2 tablespoons sugar
1/2 teaspooon salt
Pinch cayenne pepper

Mix all ingredients, cover, and chill well. Use to dress fruit or green salads. For a thinner dressing, blend in a little milk or French dressing.

NP Tablespoon: 30 C, 5 mg CH, 60 mg S*

VARIATIONS

⟁ **Low-Calorie Yogurt Dressing:** Prepare as directed but substitute yogurt for sour

cream, reduce vinegar to 2 tablespoons and sugar to 1/2 teaspoon; also add 1/4 cup skim milk and 2 tablespoons minced chives or 1 tablespoon finely grated yellow onion.

NP Tablespoon: 10 C, 1 mg CH, 65 mg S*

California Sour Cream Dressing: Prepare as directed but use 2 tablespoons lemon juice instead of the vinegar; add 2 sieved hard-cooked egg yolks and, if you like, 1 tablespoon minced fresh dill.

NP Tablespoon: 35 C, 30 mg CH, 60 mg S*

Fruity Sour Cream Dressing: Prepare as directed but use 2 tablespoons lemon juice instead of the vinegar; increase sugar to 3 tablespoons and add 2 tablespoons orange juice and 1 teaspoon finely grated orange rind. Thin, if needed, with a little extra orange juice.

NP Tablespoon: 35 C, 5 mg CH, 60 mg S*

CREAMY ROQUEFORT DRESSING

2 1/2 cups

1 cup mayonnaise
1 tablespoon sugar
1 teaspoon prepared mild yellow mustard
1/2 teaspoon prepared horseradish
1/2 teaspoon Worcestershire sauce
1/2 teaspoon minced garlic
1 tablespoon grated onion
1/2 pound Roquefort cheese
3–4 tablespoons cider vinegar

Blend mayonnaise with sugar, mustard, horseradish, Worcestershire sauce, garlic, and onion. Crumble in Roquefort and stir well. Mix in 3–4 tablespoons vinegar, depending upon how thick a dressing you want, and use to dress green salads. (*Note:* Dressing keeps well in refrigerator several days.)

NP Tablespoon: 60 C, 10 mg CH, 135 mg S*

AVOCADO DRESSING

1 cup

It's best to make this dressing just before using, because it darkens on standing. If it must be made in advance, spread with a thin film of mayonnaise, then cover and refrigerate until needed (this will minimize discoloration). Stir mayonnaise in before serving.

2 fully ripe medium-size avocados, halved and
   pitted
3 tablespoons lemon juice
1 tablespoon finely grated yellow onion
1/2 teaspoon salt

1/4 teaspoon sugar
Few drops liquid hot red pepper seasoning

Scoop flesh from avocados and press through a fine sieve; beat in remaining ingredients. Serve over wedges of lettuce, halved endive spears, or in hollowed-out tomatoes. Or use to dress any seafood salad instead of mayonnaise.

NP Tablespoon: 40 C, 0 mg CH, 70 mg S*

LOW-CALORIE FRUIT DRESSING

1 1/3 cups ⚖

1 clove garlic, peeled, bruised, and stuck on a
  toothpick
5 tablespoons lemon juice
1 cup pineapple, orange, or tangerine juice
1 tablespoon light corn syrup or honey
1/2 teaspoon salt
1/4 teaspoon paprika

Let garlic stand in lemon juice at room temperature 2 hours, then remove. Beat in remaining ingredients, cover, and chill. Shake well and use to dress fruit salads.

NP Tablespoon: 10 C, 0 mg CH, 55 mg S*

Making Mayonnaise

Mayonnaise isn't tricky to make—*if* you follow these basic rules:
• Have all ingredients at room temperature before beginning.
• Measure oil accurately into a wide-mouthed container so you can dip it out by spoonfuls during early stages of mixing.
• If mixing by hand, place a damp cloth under bowl to keep it from sliding around as you mix. Use a fork or wire whisk for beating.
• Add oil in the beginning *by the drop* so that it will emulsify with the egg yolks.
• If you substitute vinegar for lemon juice, use the very finest quality so mayonnaise will have a delicate flavor.
• *If mayonnaise separates, use one of the following remedies:*
• Beat in 1–2 teaspoons hot water.
• Beat 1 egg yolk with 2 or 3 drops oil until very thick, then beat in curdled mayonnaise *drop by drop.*
• Buzz about 10 seconds in an electric blender at high speed or 5 seconds in a food processor fitted with the metal chopping blade.

HOMEMADE MAYONNAISE

1 1/2 cups

2 egg yolks
3/4 teaspoon salt
1/2 teaspoon powdered mustard
1/8 teaspoon sugar
Pinch cayenne pepper
4–5 teaspoons lemon juice or white vinegar
1 1/2 cups olive or other salad oil
4 teaspoons hot water

Beat yolks, salt, mustard, sugar, pepper, and 1 teaspoon lemon juice in a small bowl until very thick and pale yellow. (*Note:* If using electric mixer, beat at medium speed.) Add about 1/4 cup oil, *drop by drop,* beating vigorously all the while. Beat in 1 teaspoon each lemon juice and hot water. Add another 1/4 cup oil, a few drops at a time, beating vigorously all the while. Beat in another teaspoon each lemon juice and water. Add 1/2 cup oil in a very fine steady stream, beating constantly, then mix in remaining lemon juice and water; slowly beat in remaining oil. If you like, thin mayonnaise with a little additional hot water. Cover and refrigerate until needed. (*Note:* Store in warmest part of refrigerator—less chance of the mayonnaise's separating—and do not keep longer than 1 week.)

NP Tablespoon (with olive oil): 125 C, 25 mg CH, 70 mg S*

VARIATIONS

Blender or Processor Mayonnaise: Place yolks, salt, mustard, sugar, pepper, and 3 teaspoons lemon juice in blender cup or work bowl of a food processor fitted with the metal chopping blade, and buzz 15 seconds (use low blender speed). Now, with motor running, slowly drizzle in 1/4 cup oil (use moderately high blender speed). As mixture begins to thicken, continue adding oil in a fine steady stream, alternating with hot water and remaining lemon juice. Stop motor and scrape mixture down from sides of blender cup or work bowl as needed.

NP Tablespoon (with olive oil): 125 C, 25 mg CH, 70 mg S*

Rémoulade Dressing: Prepare mayonnaise as directed, then mix in 1 tablespoon each minced capers and gherkins, 2 teaspoons each anchovy paste and Dijon mustard, and 1 teaspoon each minced parsley and fresh chervil. Serve with seafood or use to dress cold vegetable salads or sliced tomatoes.

NP Tablespoon: 125 C, 25 mg CH, 100 mg S*

Sauce Niçoise: Prepare mayonnaise as directed and set aside. Mix 2 tablespoons tomato purée with 2 minced pimientos and 1/2 crushed clove garlic; press through a fine sieve and blend into mayonnaise.

NP Tablespoon: 125 C, 25 mg CH, 75 mg S*

Russian Mayonnaise: Prepare mayonnaise, then mix in 1/4 cup black or red caviar, 1/2 cup sour cream, and 1 tablespoon minced fresh dill.

NP Tablespoon: 145 C, 35 mg CH, 135 mg S*

Mustard Mayonnaise: Prepare mayonnaise, then mix in 4 teaspoons Dijon mustard.

NP Tablespoon: 125 C, 25 mg CH, 95 mg S*

Curry Mayonnaise: Prepare mayonnaise, then blend in 1–2 teaspoons curry powder.

NP Tablespoon: 125 C, 25 mg CH, 95 mg S*

Chantilly Mayonnaise: Prepare mayonnaise, then fold in 1/2 cup heavy cream, beaten to soft peaks.

NP Tablespoon: 140 C, 30 mg CH, 70 mg S*

Fruit Mayonnaise: Prepare mayonnaise, then beat in 3 tablespoons each orange juice and superfine sugar, 1 teaspoon finely grated orange rind, and a pinch nutmeg. For added zip, mix in 1 tablespoon Grand Marnier or other fruit liqueur. Serve with fruit salads.

NP Tablespoon (with liqueur): 135 C, 25 mg CH, 70 mg S*

Thin Mayonnaise: Prepare mayonnaise, then thin to desired consistency by beating in hot water, a tablespoon at a time. Recipe too flexible for meaningful nutrional count.

COOKED SALAD DRESSING

1 1/4 cups

Note to cholesterol counters: this dressing contains only a third as many egg yolks as old-fashioned cooked dressing.

2 tablespoons flour
2 tablespoons sugar
1 teaspoon powdered mustard
3/4 teaspoon salt
Pinch cayenne pepper
3/4 cup cold water or 1/2 cup milk and 1/4 cup water
2 egg yolks, lightly beaten
1/4 cup lemon juice or white wine vinegar
2 tablespoons salad oil

Mix flour, sugar, mustard, salt, cayenne, and water in the top of a double boiler over simmering water; beat egg yolks and lemon juice just to blend, then mix in. Heat, stirring constantly, until thickened. Beat in oil,

1 tablespoon at a time. Place a piece of wax paper flat on dressing and cool to room temperature; chill before serving. If you like, thin with a little water or milk.

NP Tablespoon (with water): 25 C, 25 mg CH, 85 mg S*
NP Tablespoon (with milk and water): 30 C, 30 mg CH, 85 mg S*

VARIATIONS

Piquant Cooked Dressing: Prepare dressing, cool, and mix in 1/2 cup sour cream, 1 teaspoon each prepared horseradish, grated yellow onion, and Worcestershire sauce. Bruise a peeled clove garlic, stick on a toothpick, and chill in dressing; remove before serving.

NP Tablespoon (with water): 40 C, 30 mg CH, 90 mg S*
NP Tablespoon (with milk and water): 45 C, 30 mg CH, 95 mg S*

Cooked Fruit Salad Dressing: Prepare dressing as directed but substitute 1 tablespoon cornstarch for the flour and use 1/2 cup orange juce and 1/4 cup pineapple juice for the water; reduce lemon juice to 2 tablespoons. If you like, fold in 1/4 teaspoon bruised celery, dill, or caraway seeds, also 1/2 cup heavy cream, whipped to soft peaks.

NP Tablespoon (without whipped cream): 30 C, 25 mg CH, 85 mg S*
NP Tablespoon (with whipped cream): 50 C, 35 mg CH, 85 mg S*

OLD-FASHIONED COOKED DRESSING

1 pint

This is such a versatile dressing. Make without seeds and serve over cold poached salmon. Or use in any of the ways that you would use mayonnaise.

6 egg yolks, lightly beaten
1/2 teaspoon powdered mustard
1/2 cup sugar
1/2 cup heavy cream
1 teaspoon salt
1/2 cup melted butter or margarine
1 cup warm cider vinegar
1 1/2 teaspoons celery or poppy seeds (optional)

Mix yolks, mustard, sugar, cream, salt, and butter in the top of a double boiler; slowly beat in vinegar, set over simmering water, and heat and stir until the consistency of custard sauce. Remove from heat and stir 1 minute; mix in seeds if you like. Place a piece of wax paper flat on dressing and cool to room temperature. Cover and chill well. Stir before using.

NP Tablespoon (with butter and celery seeds): 65 C, 65 mg CH, 100 mg S*

TANGY LOW-CALORIE SALAD DRESSING

1 1/2 cups ⚖

Good with any green salad.

1 tablespoon cornstarch
1 cup cold water
3 tablespoons salad oil
1/4 cup cider vinegar
1 teaspoon salt
1 teaspoon sugar
2 tablespoons ketchup
1 teaspoon prepared mild yellow mustard
1/2 teaspoon paprika
1/2 teaspoon prepared horseradish
1/2 teaspoon Worcestershire sauce
1/2 teaspoon oregano

Blend cornstarch and water and heat and stir over moderate heat until thickened and clear. Off heat, beat in remaining ingredients with a rotary beater or electric mixer. Cover and chill well. Shake before using.

NP Tablespoon: 20 C, 0 mg CH, 110 mg S*

MUSTARD SALAD DRESSING

1 1/2 cups ⚖

2 tablespoons butter or margarine
2 tablespoons flour
1 cup milk
1 teaspoon salt
1 1/2 teaspoons sugar
2 teaspoons powdered mustard blended with 2 tablespoons cold water
1/3 cup cider vinegar

Melt butter in a small saucepan over moderately low heat, blend in flour, add milk slowly, and cook and stir until thickened and smooth. Mix in salt, sugar, and mustard paste. Add vinegar, 1 tablespoon at a time, beating well after each addition. Cool dressing, then cover and chill 2–3 hours. Beat well before using. Use to dress any cooked vegetable or seafood salad. (*Note:* Dressing keeps well about a week in refrigerator.)

NP Tablespoon (with butter): 20 C, 5 mg CH, 105 mg S*

VARIATION

⚖ **Extra-Low-Calorie Mustard Dressing:** Prepare as directed but use skim milk instead of regular.

NP Tablespoon (with butter): 15 C, 5 mg CH, 105 mg S*

THOUSAND ISLAND DRESSING

1 1/2 cups

1 cup mayonnaise
1 hard-cooked egg, peeled and chopped fine
1 tablespoon minced onion, scallion, or chives
1/4 cup chili sauce
1/4 cup minced pimiento-stuffed green olives
1 tablespoon minced sweet green pepper
2–3 drops liquid hot red pepper seasoning

Mix all ingredients well, cover, and chill about 2 hours. Use to dress crisp wedges of lettuce. (*Note:* This dressing keeps well in the refrigerator for several days.)

NP Tablespoon: 75 C, 15 mg CH, 125 mg S*

VARIATIONS

⚖ **Low-Calorie Thousand Island Dressing** (*Makes about 1 cup*): Substitute yogurt for mayonnaise and 2 tablespoons minced parsley for the olives; use minced egg white only and reduce chili sauce to 1 tablespoon.

NP Tablespoon: 10 C, 1 mg CH, 25 mg S*

Extra-Creamy Thousand Island Dressing (*About 2 1/2 cups*): Prepare as directed but substitute minced parsley for the green pepper; mix in 1/4 cup minced dill pickle, 1 tablespoon Worcestershire sauce, and 1/4 teaspoon paprika; finally, fold in 1/2 cup heavy cream beaten until glossy but not stiff.

NP Tablespoon: 55 C, 15 mg CH, 95 mg S*

RUSSIAN DRESSING (AMERICAN STYLE)

1 3/4 cups

1 cup mayonnaise
1/4 cup French Dressing
1/4 cup chili sauce
2 tablespoons minced sweet green pepper
2 tablespoons minced pimiento
1 tablespoon minced yellow onion
1 teaspoon prepared horseradish

Blend all ingredients together and use to dress green salads.

NP Tablespoon: 75 C, 5 mg CH, 85 mg S*

Russian Dressing (Russian Style): Prepare dressing as directed and mix in 2–3 tablespoons black caviar.

NP Tablespoon: 75 C, 10 mg CH, 110 mg S*

GREEN GODDESS DRESSING I

1 quart

Years ago when George Arliss was opening in San Francisco in *The Green Goddess,* the Palace Hotel chef created a salad dressing in his honor. Of the two versions below, the first is the most like the original, the second a popular, easy variation.

1 clove garlic, peeled and halved
1/3 cup minced parsley
1/3 cup minced chives
1 tablespoon minced scallions
1/4 cup minced fresh tarragon
8 anchovy fillets, rinsed, drained, and minced
3 cups mayonnaise
1/3 cup tarragon vinegar

Rub a small bowl well with cut sides of garlic; discard garlic. Add remaining ingredients and mix well; cover and chill 1–2 hours. Use to dress crisp green salads. *(Note:* Dressing keeps well in refrigerator about 1 week.)

NP Tablespoon: 75 C, 5 mg CH, 65 mg S*

VARIATION

Green Goddess Dressing II: Prepare as directed but substitute 1/2 (2-ounce) tube anchovy paste for the minced anchovies and 1 cup sour cream for 1 cup of the mayonnaise.

NP Tablespoon: 60 C, 5 mg CH, 45 mg S*

GREEN MAYONNAISE I

1 1/2 cups

Green Mayonnaise I is nippier than Green Mayonnaise II, which substitutes spinach for watercress.

1/2 cup minced parsley
1/3 cup minced watercress
2 tablespoons minced chives
1 tablespoon minced fresh dill
1 1/4 cups mayonnaise
1 teaspoon lemon juice
1/4 teaspoon salt
2–3 drops liquid hot red pepper seasoning

Mix all ingredients well, cover, and chill several hours. Serve with cold boiled shellfish (especially lobster) or use to dress fish or vegetable salads.

NP Tablespoon: 85 C, 5 mg CH, 90 mg S*

VARIATION

Green Mayonnaise II: Prepare as directed, substituting minced raw spinach for the watercress and minced fresh tarragon or chervil for the dill. Omit chives if you like.

NP Tablespoon: 85 C, 5 mg CH, 90 mg S*

FIFTEEN

Breads and Sandwiches

Nowhere, perhaps, has our dedication to fitness affected our eating habits more profoundly than it has with bread. We want plenty of crunch and chew in our loaves today, we want them filled with healthful whole grain, high-gluten, and unbleached flours. We like them strewn, moreover, with wheat berries, oats, and such vegetables as zucchini and carrots. We are baking breads today as never before because we don't like them adulterated with preservatives. And we are all the richer for it because we are rediscovering one of cooking's true joys. Everyone should make bread once, at least, if only to feel the warm dough responding to his or her touch, if only to fill the house with the promise of fresh loaves and the memories of children with happiness.

Basically, there are two kinds of bread: *quick breads* (biscuits, muffins, pancakes, etc.), which can be cooked as soon as they're mixed, and *yeast breads,* which require more time and attention.

THE WAYS OF MIXING BREADS

Different breads require different techniques in handling; all are basic, most are easy:

Muffin Method (for muffins, popovers, waffles, pancakes, most corn breads): Dry ingredients are sifted together into a mixing bowl, liquid ingredients are combined, added all at once, and mixed in *just* enough to dampen the dry ingredients. There is great temptation to overbeat these batters, but if the bread—especially the muffin—is to be light

and meltingly tender, the batter must be lumpy. If flecks of flour show, no harm done. Too much mixing makes the muffin tough.

Biscuit or Pastry Method (for biscuits and dumplings): Dry ingredients are sifted together into a bowl, the fat is cut in with a pastry blender or 2 knives until the texture of coarse meal, then the liquid is sprinkled over the mixture and stirred briskly. Kneading follows, usually about 20 seconds on a lightly floured board. It is the distribution of small fat particles throughout the dough that produces a flaky biscuit.

Cake Method (for most quick fruit and/or nut loaves): The shortening is creamed with the sugar and eggs, then the sifted dry ingredients added alternately with the liquid; nuts and fruit are folded in at the end.

Yeast Bread: Not one method but several; see Yeast Breads.

TIPS FOR MAKING BETTER BREADS

Note: Special tips for baking breads in microwave or convection ovens can be found further on in this chapter.

Pans and Preparing Pans:

• Always use pan sizes recipes specify.
• Use baking sheets for biscuits and individually shaped rolls; if you have none, use a turned-upside-down large baking pan.
• For richly browned loaves (especially yeast

loaves), use heatproof glass or dull finish, dark metal pans.

• For greasing pans, use cooking oil, shortening, clarified* unsalted butter, or one of the low-fat, no-cholesterol, spray-on vegetable compounds. Brush over bottom and sides of pans, applying in a thin, even film with a crumple of paper toweling or a pastry brush, or spray on.

• If bread contains sticky fruit or filling, grease *and* flour pans (sprinkle a little flour into greased pans, tilt from one side to the other to coat with a thin film, then tap out excess flour).

• When using muffin tins, grease only those cups that will be used; if you've greased more cups than you need, wipe grease from those not to be used.

Mixing Breads

• Read recipe carefully before beginning.

• Assemble all utensils and measure ingredients before beginning.

• Use as light a hand as possible in mixing breads. Muffins, especially, need a delicate touch.

• Unless recipes indicate otherwise, mix breads by hand, using a comfortable long-handled wooden spoon.

• To avoid last-minute confusion, measure all ingredients for quick breads well ahead of time, then mix shortly before time to serve.

Rolling Doughs

• Use a lightly floured surface and rolling pin (experienced cooks prefer a pastry cloth and stockinette-covered pin), adding only what flour is needed to keep dough from sticking to board. Too much flour will toughen the dough.

• Roll doughs with quick, firm strokes from the center outward, keeping in mind the ultimate shape you want—circle, rectangle, square—and adjusting position of dough as needed to achieve that shape with a minimum of handling.

• Use floured cutters when cutting dough, floured scissors or knives for snipping or slicing it.

Placing Breads and Rolls in Pans

• Never fill muffin pan cups more than two thirds full when making muffins or popovers; to make popover batter go further, half fill cups.

• For soft-sided biscuits or rolls, place close together; for crusty sides, space about 1″ apart.

• Always brush any loose topping or wipe any spilled glaze from baking sheets before baking breads.

Baking Breads

(Also see Baking Yeast Breads for special techniques applying to yeast breads only):

• Let conventional oven preheat a full 15 minutes before baking.

• Bake breads as near center of oven as possible unless recipes direct otherwise.

• When baking several pans of bread at once, stagger carefully so heat will circulate as evenly as possible; never let pans touch each other or oven walls.

• Check bread after minimum cooking time, then bake full time if needed.

To Tell if Breads Are Done

Biscuits, Muffins, Rolls, and Other Small Breads: They should be dappled with brown, firm and springy to the touch, and, if baked in muffin tins, slightly pulled from sides.

Quick Loaves: They should have pulled slightly from sides of pans, be golden brown and springy to the touch.

Yeast Loaves: They should have pulled slightly from sides of pans, be richly browned and sound hollow when tapped.

Cooling Breads

• Unless recipes direct to the contrary, always remove breads from pans as soon as they come from the oven.

• Cool breads on wire racks and allow plenty of space around loaves for air to circulate. This keeps moisture from condensing on breads and spoiling them.

Serving Breads

• Serve muffins, biscuits, corn breads, popovers, and yeast rolls oven-hot; cool yeast breads and fruit or nut loaves to room temperature before serving.

• Nestle hot breads in napkin-lined baskets so they will stay hot.

• If muffins or rolls should be done before the rest of the meal, tip each slightly in its muffin cup, turn off heat, and let stand in oven until ready to serve.

• To slice fresh loaves more easily, use a hot serrated bread knife (run quickly under hot water, then dry). Or use a fine strong thread in a sawing motion.

Reheating Breads

(Also read Defrosting and Reheating Bread in a Microwave Oven):

Biscuits: Wrap in foil, not individually but en masse, and heat 15–20 minutes at 375° F. Or set unwrapped on a trivet in a large skillet, add 2–3 tablespoons water, cover and let steam over moderate heat 5–8 minutes.

Rolls, Muffins, Corn Breads: Bundle in foil and heat 8–10 minutes at 350° F. Or use the steaming method described for biscuits.

Keeping Breads: Breads do not keep well; in damp weather they mold, in fair weather they harden and dry. Wrap tightly in foil, plastic bags, or wax paper and store in a breadbox in a cool, dry place. Or, if weather is unusually damp or muggy, in the refrigerator. The refrigerator, contrary to what many people believe, is not a good place to store bread because it *hastens* staling. Breads do freeze beautifully, however. Wrap airtight in foil or plastic food wrap, label, date, and set directly on freezing surface of a 0° freezer. *Note:* Rolls can be baked until just beginning to brown, cooled, then frozen; they will finish baking as they reheat.

Baking Bread in a Microwave Oven

Because most *yeast breads and rolls* remain unappealingly moist after microwaving and fail to develop nice brown crusts, we recommend baking them in conventional or convection ovens. Microwaves *are* marvelous, however, for reheating yeast breads because they magically restore "just-baked" flavor (see Defrosting and Reheating Breads in a Microwave Oven).

Most microwave-baked *quick breads* have greater volume and more uniform texture than those baked in conventional or convection ovens. But because they do not brown, we prefer to microwave only those breads with "built-in" color—bran breads, for example, corn breads, or those containing plenty of spices, or special toppings. If you follow package directions, many quick breads made from mixes will bake satisfactorily by microwave, but most conventional quick bread recipes are iffy. Some work, some don't (popovers and Yorkshire pudding, for example). For best results, use only those recipes that have been especially formulated for microwave ovens and bake at power level your oven manufacturer recommends. *(Note:* Most manufacturers include foolproof quick bread recipes in their manuals, so read these carefully; also see Microwave Ovens in Chapter 1.) Then, when microwaving *quick breads,* follow these guidelines:
• *Biscuits:* Arrange close together in a ring in a shallow microwave-safe baking dish, brush with melted butter, and, for more color, sprinkle with caraway, poppy, or sesame seeds, minced herbs, grated Parmesan, or other suitable topping (see Some Quick Bread Toppings, which follows). Microwave, uncovered, as oven manufacturer directs, rotating dish 90° every minute. Transfer to wire rack and serve at once (no standing time needed).
• *Coffee Cakes and Sweet Breads:* Bake in a microwave baking ring or a clear, flameproof round glass dish lined on the bottom with wax paper or lightly oiled all over (do not flour dish; flour produces an ugly coating). No more than half fill baking ring or mold with batter; top, if you like, with a suitable topping (see Some Quick Bread Toppings). Microwave, uncovered, rotating bread 90° every 2–3 minutes. Check for doneness frequently by looking at *bottom* of glass dish; no raw batter should be visible in the center. Remove bread from oven and let stand on counter 10 minutes to complete baking before serving. *Tip:* You can improvise a baking ring by standing a greased water glass right-side-up in the center of the baking dish.
• *Muffins:* Line custard cups or microwave-safe muffin pans with 2 crinkly paper liners (simply set 1 liner inside another; this double thickness gives muffins needed support and makes them rise and bake more evenly). Spoon batter into liners, no more than half filling each. Sprinkle on a suitable topping, if you like (see topping suggestions below). If using custard cups, arrange them in a ring in the microwave. Microwave, uncovered, rearranging custard cups at half time or rotating muffin pans 180°. To test for doneness, insert a toothpick or cake tester in center of muffins; it should come out clean. *(Note:* Muffins may have moist spots on the surface, but these will dry out on standing.) Transfer muffins (still in liners) to wire racks and let stand 2–3 minutes before serving.

Note: If adding chopped nuts or fruits to coffee cakes, sweet breads, or muffins, chop them very fine. Batters will thin so much during the first stages of baking in a microwave that all but the most finely chopped fruits and nuts will sink to the bottom.

Some Quick Bread Toppings: Brown or cinnamon sugar; cheese, graham cracker, cookie, or toasted bread crumbs; wheat germ or crushed dry cereal; chopped nuts; toasted coconut; crisp crumbled bacon.

Defrosting and Reheating Bread in a Microwave Oven

One of the handiest features of a microwave is its ability to defrost and reheat breads in mere minutes. The size of the bread, its shape and over-all quantity all affect microwaving time, as do power levels, which vary from model to model. Read your oven's manual before defrosting or reheating any bread (some ovens have separate defrost cycles that can be used for breads, others don't). The following guidelines should be observed whether you are defrosting or reheating commercial or homemade breads:

• Remove any aluminum foil or metal twist-ties (cardboard "plates" under coffee cakes may be left in place).

• Wrap breads, biscuits, rolls, and unfilled, unglazed doughnuts in paper toweling or napkins before reheating in the microwave. All small items (rolls, doughnuts, biscuits, etc.) should be arranged in a circle in the microwave.

• Loosely cover muffins and coffee cakes with paper toweling (also arrange muffins in a circle) before reheating in the microwave. Moist breads (date-nut, banana, etc.) and glazed doughnuts should be loosely covered with wax paper.

• Use a microwave-safe trivet for warming filled rolls and doughnuts (the fillings heat faster than the bread).

• Always follow package directions (if given) when defrosting or reheating commercial or convenience breads.

Baking Bread in a Convection Oven

The circulating hot air of convection ovens browns breads superbly. Some manufacturers claim that it's not necessary to preheat their ovens before baking, and most recommend reducing baking temperatures 50°–75° F. below those recommended for all leavened breads (those containing yeast, baking powder or soda, even eggs). (Note: Never use oven temperatures lower than 300° F.) It's wise to read your oven manual carefully before you begin baking; also read Convection Ovens in Chapter 1, then follow these tips:

• Use dull metal pans for yeast breads, shiny ones for pale and tender quick breads.

• Use center oven rack for bread baking, and avoid using more than one rack at a time because you'll block air flow.

• Allow at least 1″ between pans and oven walls; baking pans should never touch oven walls or one another.

• For better air circulation, bake biscuits on baking sheets with no raised edges.

• Check breads for doneness 5–10 minutes before end of suggested baking time because some breads will bake a little faster in convection ovens than in conventional ones.

QUICK BREADS AND BATTERS

Note: Unless recipes specify otherwise, use all-purpose flour in the recipes that follow and double-acting baking powder.

BASIC MUFFINS

1¹/4 dozen   ¢ ☒

2 cups + 2 tablespoons sifted flour
1 tablespoon baking powder
2 tablespoons sugar
1 teaspoon salt
1 egg, beaten until frothy
1 cup milk
3 tablespoons cooking oil, melted butter or margarine

Preheat oven to 425° F. Sift all dry ingredients together into a mixing bowl. Mix egg, milk, and oil. Make a well in center of dry ingredients and pour in egg mixture all at once; stir lightly and quickly just to mix; *batter should be lumpy.* Spoon into muffin pans—bottoms of cups should be greased but *not* sides—filling each cup two thirds. Bake about 20 minutes until lightly browned. Serve oven-hot with plenty of butter.

NP Muffin: 105 C, 20 mg CH, 244 mg S*

V A R I A T I O N S

Bacon Muffins: Sift dry ingredients as directed but reduce salt to ¹/2 teaspoon; add ¹/4 cup minced crisp bacon and toss to dredge. Lightly beat egg and milk with 2 tablespoons each cooking oil and melted bacon drippings; mix into dry ingredients by basic method and bake as directed.

NP Muffin: 120 C, 24 mg CH, 200 mg S*

Date, Raisin, or Currant Muffins: Sift 2¹/4 cups flour, 3 tablespoons sugar, 1 tablespoon baking powder, and ¹/2 teaspoon salt into mixing bowl; add 1 teaspoon finely grated lemon rind and 1 cup diced, pitted dates, seedless raisins, or dried currants; toss to dredge. Lightly beat egg and milk with ¹/4 cup cooking oil, mix into dry ingredients by basic method, and bake as directed.

NP Muffin: 155 C, 20 mg CH, 170 mg S*

Nut Muffins: Sift 2¹/4 cups flour, ¹/4 cup light brown sugar, 1 tablespoon baking powder, and ¹/2 teaspoon salt into bowl; add ³/4 cup minced nuts (any kind) and toss to dredge. Lightly beat egg and milk with ¹/4 cup oil or melted butter; mix into dry ingredients by basic method and bake as directed.

NP Muffin: 165 C, 20 mg CH, 170 mg S*

Blueberry Muffins: Sift 2¼ cups flour, ¼ cup sugar, 1 tablespoon baking powder, and ¼ teaspoon salt into mixing bowl. Add 1 cup washed and dried blueberries and toss to mix. Beat egg and milk with ¼ cup melted butter; mix into dry ingredients by basic method and bake as directed.

NP Muffin: 130 C, 165 mg CH, 165 mg S*

Orange Muffins: Sift 2¼ cups flour, ¼ cup sugar, 2½ teaspoons baking powder, ½ teaspoon baking soda, and ¼ teaspoon salt into mixing bowl. Add finely grated rind of 1 orange and toss to dredge. Lightly beat egg with ½ cup each milk and orange juice and ¼ cup melted butter (no substitute). Mix egg mixture into dry ingredients by basic method and bake as directed.

NP Muffin: 125 C, 25 mg CH, 175 mg S*

WHOLE WHEAT MUFFINS

1 dozen   ¢

¾ cup unsifted whole wheat flour
1 cup sifted all-purpose flour
3 tablespoons sugar
1 tablespoon baking powder
1 teaspoon salt
1 egg
1 cup milk
¼ cup cooking oil
1 tablespoon molasses

Preheat oven to 425° F. Place whole wheat flour in a large mixing bowl, then sift all-purpose flour with sugar, baking powder, and salt directly into bowl; toss well to mix. Beat egg with milk, oil, and molasses until foamy. Make a well in the center of the dry ingredients, pour in liquid all at once, and stir lightly and quickly just to mix; batter should be quite lumpy. Spoon into greased muffin pans, three fourths filling each cup. (*Note:* For best results, only bottoms of cups should be greased, not sides.) Bake 20–22 minutes until lightly browned. Serve hot with plenty of butter.

NP Muffin: 135 C, 25 mg CH, 305 mg S*

BRAN MUFFINS

1 dozen   ¢

1¼ cups ready-to-eat bran cereal
1 cup milk
1¼ cups sifted flour

1 tablespoon baking powder
½ teaspoon salt
¼ cup sugar
1 egg
¼ cup cooking oil, melted butter or margarine

Preheat oven to 425° F. Soak bran in milk 2–3 minutes. Sift dry ingredients together into a mixing bowl. Beat egg and oil until blended, then stir into bran and milk. Make a well in center of dry ingredients and pour in bran mixture all at once. Stir lightly and quickly just to mix (batter should be lumpy). Spoon into muffin pans—bottoms of cups should be greased but not sides—filling each cup two thirds. Bake about 25 minutes until lightly browned and springy to the touch. Serve hot with lots of butter.

NP Muffin: 140 C, 25 mg CH, 315 mg S*

VARIATIONS

Raisin-Bran Muffins: Prepare as directed, adding ¾ cup seedless raisins to the sifted dry ingredients; toss well to dredge before combining with liquid ingredients.

NP Muffin: 170 C, 25 mg CH, 315 mg S*

Nut-Bran Muffins: Prepare as directed, adding ¾ cup minced pecans, walnuts, or soybean nuts to the sifted dry ingredients; toss well to dredge before mixing with liquid ingredients.

NP Muffin: 190 C, 25 mg CH, 315 mg S*

RYE MUFFINS

1 dozen   ¢

Not unlike pumpernickel.

1 tablespoon caraway seeds
2 tablespoons boiling water
¾ cup unsifted rye flour
3 tablespoons light brown sugar
1 cup sifted all-purpose flour
1 tablespoon baking powder
1 teaspoon salt
1 egg
1 tablespoon molasses
¾ cup milk
¼ cup cooking oil

Preheat oven to 425° F. Soak caraway seeds in boiling water 15–20 minutes. Place rye flour and sugar in a bowl and rub well between your fingers, breaking up any lumps of sugar. Sift all-purpose flour, baking powder, and salt directly into bowl and toss well to mix. Beat egg with molasses, milk, and oil until foamy, then stir in caraway seeds and water. Make a well in center of dry ingredients and pour in milk mixture all at once.

Stir quickly and lightly just enough to mix; batter should be lumpy. Spoon into muffin pans—bottoms of cups should be greased but not sides—filling each cup two thirds. Bake about 20 minutes until lightly browned. Serve hot with lots of butter.

NP Muffin: 130 C, 25 mg CH, 305 mg S*

BAKING POWDER BISCUITS

1½ dozen ¢

These will be light and feathery if you follow the directions exactly.

2 cups sifted flour
1 teaspoon salt
1 tablespoon baking powder
⅓ cup chilled vegetable shortening
¾ cup milk
Milk, melted butter or margarine (optional glaze)

Preheat oven to 450° F. Sift flour with salt and baking powder into a bowl and cut in shortening with a pastry blender until the texture of very coarse meal; make a well in center, pour in milk, and stir briskly with a fork just until dough holds together. Knead gently on a lightly floured board seven or eight times. Roll ½″ thick and cut in rounds with a floured biscuit cutter; reroll and cut scraps. Place on ungreased baking sheets— 1″ apart for crusty-sided biscuits, almost touching for soft. For glistening brown tops, brush with glaze. Bake 12–15 minutes until lightly browned. Serve oven-hot with lots of butter. *(Note:* For hot-hot-hot biscuits, bake in piepans that can come to the table. To reheat leftover biscuits, wrap together in a large foil package and warm 15–20 minutes at 350° F.)

NP Biscuit: 85 C, 1 mg CH, 200 mg S*

VARIATIONS

¢ **Drop Biscuits:** Prepare basic recipe but increase milk to 1 cup. Do not knead or roll but drop by tablespoonfuls 1″ apart on greased baking sheets. Bake as directed.

NP Biscuit: 85 C, 2 mg CH, 200 mg S*

¢ **Biscuit Topping for Casseroles:** Prepare 1 recipe Drop Biscuits (above) and drop by rounded tablespoonfuls, almost touching, on top of hot casserole mixture. *(Note:* Bake any leftover dough as basic recipe directs.) Bake casserole, uncovered, as recipe directs or 15– 20 minutes at 425° F. until lightly browned. *To serve:* Cut through biscuit topping as you would piecrust.

NP Wedge (6–8): 265–200 C, 6–4 mg CH, 600–450 mg S*

¢ **Quick Biscuit Topping for Casseroles:** For Drop Biscuits (above), substitute packaged biscuit mix prepared by label directions or canned refrigerated biscuits; drop onto casserole and bake as directed. Mixes too variable for meaningful nutritional count.

¢ **Stir-and-Roll Biscuits:** Sift dry ingredients into bowl as directed. Pour ⅓ cup cooking oil into a measuring cup, and add ⅔ cup milk; *do not stir* but pour all at once into well in dry ingredients. Mix briskly with a fork until dough holds together. Knead in bowl ten times without adding more flour. Turn onto an *unfloured* board, top with a sheet of wax paper, and roll ½″ thick. Cut and bake on ungreased baking sheets 12–14 minutes at 475° F.

NP Biscuit: 85 C, 1 mg CH, 197 mg S*

▨ **Extra-Quick Biscuits:** Prepare basic dough as directed, pat into a rectangle ½″ thick, and cut in 1½″ squares or 2″ triangles. Bake as directed. Nutritional count about the same as basic recipe.

Extra-Rich Biscuits: Prepare basic dough as directed but add 2 tablespoons sugar to dry ingredients and increase shortening to ½ cup.

NP Biscuit: 110 C, 1 mg CH, 200 mg S*

¢ **Buttermilk Biscuits:** Prepare basic or stir-and-roll dough as directed but reduce baking powder to 2 teaspoons, add ¼ teaspoon baking soda, and substitute cold buttermilk for milk.

NP Biscuit: 85 C, .40 mg CH, 190 mg S*

Sweet Pinwheel Biscuits: Prepare basic dough and roll into a rectangle about 12″ long, 6″–7″ wide, and ¼″ thick. Spread with softened butter, sprinkle with ¼ cup light brown sugar, 1 teaspoon cinnamon, ⅛ teaspoon nutmeg, and ¼–⅓ cup seedless raisins, dried currants, or coarsely chopped pecans or walnuts. Or, if you prefer, top butter with marmalade, jam, or a drizzling of honey. Roll the short way, jelly-roll style, pinch seam to seal, then slice 1″ thick. Lay pinwheels flat in greased muffin pans, brush lightly with milk, and bake 12–15 minutes at 425° F. Recipe too flexible for meaningful nutritional count.

Savory Pinwheel Biscuits: Prepare like Sweet Pinwheel Biscuits (above) but spread with deviled ham or any cheese or meat spread instead of sugar and spices. Recipe too flexible for meaningful nutritional count.

Party Biscuits: Prepare and roll basic dough as directed; cut with a 1½″ cutter and bake 10–12 minutes at 450° F. Split biscuits, fill with slices of Smithfield ham, roast chicken, or turkey, and serve as buffet food. Recipe too flexible for meaningful nutritional count.

¢ **Herb Biscuits:** Prepare basic recipe as directed, but before adding milk lightly toss in any of the following: ½ teaspoon each sage and thyme (nice with pork), ½ teaspoon each basil and oregano (good with veal), ¼ cup minced chives or parsley (delicious with chicken), 2 teaspoons dill or 1½ teaspoons caraway seeds.

NP Biscuit: 85 C, 1 mg CH, 200 mg S*

¢ **Cheese Biscuits:** Prepare basic recipe as directed, but before adding milk toss in ½ cup coarsely grated sharp Cheddar cheese.

NP Biscuit: 100 C, 5 mg CH, 220 mg S*

¢ **Make-Ahead Biscuits:** Prepare any biscuit recipe as directed, then bake 7–8 minutes at 450° F. until risen but not browned. Cool, wrap, and freeze. To serve, arrange solidly frozen biscuits on ungreased baking sheets and bake in top third of a 450° F. oven 8–10 minutes until browned.

Some Quick Toppings to Jazz Up Biscuits: Before baking, brush tops of biscuits with a little milk, melted butter or margarine, then sprinkle with any of the following:
• Poppy, caraway, or sesame seeds
• Finely ground pecans, walnuts, almonds, or peanuts
• Grated Parmesan cheese
• Corn meal

CHEESE-CORN MEAL BISCUITS

1½ dozen   ¢

½ cup corn meal
¾ cup milk, scalded
1 cup sifted flour
1 tablespoon baking powder
¾ teaspoon salt
3 tablespoons butter, margarine, or lard
¾ cup coarsely grated mild Cheddar cheese
1 egg yolk, lightly beaten (glaze)

Preheat oven to 450° F. Briskly mix corn meal into hot milk, cover, and set aside. Sift flour with baking powder and salt into a bowl. Using a pastry blender, cut in butter until mixture resembles coarse meal. Add corn meal mixture and cheese and stir lightly to blend. Turn onto a lightly floured board, knead gently about ½ minute. Roll ½″ thick and cut into rounds with a biscuit cutter. Arrange 1½″ apart on an ungreased

baking sheet and brush tops with glaze. Bake 12–15 minutes or until well risen and golden.

NP Biscuit: 85 C, 25 mg CH, 215 mg S*

BANNOCKS

2 dozen   ¢ ▣

A husky Scottish griddlecake made with oatmeal.

4¼ cups uncooked oatmeal (not quick cooking)
2 teaspoons salt
1 teaspoon baking soda
¼ cup melted bacon drippings or lard
1 cup very hot water

Preheat griddle over moderately high heat while you mix bannocks, or, if using an electric griddle, preheat to 400° F. Place 4 cups oatmeal in a mixing bowl; buzz the rest in an electric blender at high speed until moderately fine, then reserve to use in rolling out dough. Add remaining ingredients to bowl and mix well. Knead on a board lightly dusted with the fine oatmeal 1 minute, roll ¼″ thick, and cut into rounds with a 3″ cutter. Cook on an *ungreased* griddle 5–6 minutes per side until lightly browned and cooked through. Serve hot with plenty of butter.

NP Bannock: 70 C, 2 mg CH, 220 mg S*

IRISH SODA BREAD

6″ round loaf (20 slices)   ¢

In Ireland this bread is made as often with whole wheat flour as with white, and usually without shortening. It's a close-textured loaf. When serving, cut straight across the loaf into thin slices instead of dividing into wedges.

1 cup sifted all-purpose flour
2 teaspoons baking soda
1½ teaspoons salt
¼ cup vegetable shortening or margarine
3 cups unsifted whole wheat flour
1⅔ cups buttermilk or sour milk

Preheat oven to 400° F. Sift all-purpose flour, soda, and salt together into a large bowl. With a pastry blender cut in shortening until the texture of coarse meal. Mix in whole wheat flour. Pour in buttermilk all at once and mix well to blend (you may have to use your hands). Turn out on a lightly floured board and knead until fairly smooth, about 5 minutes. Shape into a round loaf about 6″ across, with a sharp knife cut a cross 1/4″ deep in top, and sprinkle with a very little flour. Place cross-side-up in a well-greased, round 2-quart casserole about 2 1/2″ deep. Bake, uncovered, about 40 minutes until crusty brown and hollow sounding when tapped. Turn loaf out on wire rack and cool before cutting.

NP Slice: 110 C, 1 mg CH, 270 mg S*

VARIATION

¢ **White Irish Soda Bread:** Sift 4 cups all-purpose flour with soda and salt and cut in shortening; omit whole wheat flour and reduce buttermilk to 1 1/2 cups; otherwise proceed as directed.

NP Slice: 120 C, 1 mg CH, 265 mg S*

HILDA'S YORKSHIRE SCONES

10 scones ¢

1 1/2 cups sifted flour
1/4 cup sugar
1/4 teaspoon salt
1 1/2 teaspoons baking powder
1/4 cup butter or margarine
1/3 cup seedless raisins
1 egg, lightly beaten
2 tablespoons milk

Preheat oven to 425° F. Sift flour, sugar, salt, and baking powder into a bowl. Using a pastry blender or 2 knives, cut in butter until the texture of coarse meal. Add raisins and toss to mix. Add egg and milk and mix with a fork until mixture forms a soft dough. Roll on a floured board or pat into a circle about 1/2″ thick, adding only enough flour to keep dough from sticking. Cut into rounds with a floured 2″ cutter; reroll and cut scraps. Bake 2″ apart on a greased baking sheet 12–15 minutes until golden. Let cool 1–2 minutes on a wire rack. Scones are best eaten warm, not hot—split in half and slathered with butter. They're also delicious spread with Devonshire cream or *crème fraîche* and berry preserves.

NP Scone: 145 C, 40 mg CH, 175 mg S*

POPOVERS

6 popovers ¢

1 cup sifted flour
1/2 teaspoon salt
3/4 cup milk
1/4 cup cold water
2 eggs

Preheat oven to 450° F. Beat all ingredients in a small bowl with a rotary beater until just smooth. Scrape bottom of bowl with rubber spatula once or twice during beating. Spoon into a well-greased muffin tin, filling each cup two thirds. Bake 40 minutes until well browned, puffed, and firm. *(Note: For dry, crisp popovers, bake 35 minutes, quickly cut a small slit in the side of each popover so steam can escape, and bake 5–10 minutes longer.)* Serve immediately with plenty of butter.

NP Popover: 115 C, 95 mg CH, 220 mg S*

YORKSHIRE PUDDING

6 servings ¢

A 100-year-old Yorkshire recipe adapted for today's silken flours. Like a soufflé, Yorkshire pudding will not wait, so serve straight from the oven.

1/2 cup sifted flour
1/2 teaspoon salt
1/2 cup milk
1/4 cup cold water
2 eggs, lightly beaten
1 tablespoon melted roast beef drippings

Mix flour and salt in a small bowl, add milk, a little at a time, beating with a rotary beater or electric mixer until smooth. Add water and eggs and beat until bubbly. Cover loosely and let stand in a cool place (not refrigerator) about 1/2 hour. Meanwhile, preheat oven to 500° F. *(Note: If you've been doing a roast, shove temperature up after roast comes from oven.)* Beat batter 1–2 minutes until bubbles appear on surface. Pour 1/2 teaspoon drippings into each of 6 muffin pan cups and heat in the oven 1–2 minutes until almost smoking hot. Spoon 3 tablespoons batter into each cup and bake 8 minutes *without opening oven door.* Reduce temperature to 400° F. and bake 8–10 minutes longer until well browned, risen, and crisp. *(Note: Do not pierce with a fork or puddings will collapse.)* Arrange puddings around roast and serve at once, allowing 1 pudding with each portion of meat and topping with plenty of hot gravy.

NPS: 90 C, 95 mg CH, 215 mg S*

VARIATION

¢ **Old-Fashioned Yorkshire Pudding:** Prepare batter and preheat oven to 500° F. Pour 3 tablespoons melted roast beef drippings into a 13″ × 9″ × 2″ baking pan (or similar-size pan in which beef was roasted) and heat in oven 2 minutes. Meanwhile beat batter until bubbles appear. Pour batter into pan and bake 10 minutes, reduce temperature to 450° F., and bake 12–15 minutes longer until well browned and crisp. Cut in large squares and serve.

NPS: 130 C, 100 mg CH, 215 mg S*

PURI (POORI, POOREE)

10 puri

Until the arrival of the British, yeast breads were virtually unknown in India. Unleavened or steam-leavened loaves such as *puri, chapati,* and *paratha* were—and still are—the breads of choice.

½ cup unsifted whole wheat flour
½ cup unsifted unbleached all-purpose flour
¼ teaspoon salt
4 teaspoons cooking oil
5 tablespoons lukewarm water
Cooking oil or vegetable shortening for deep fat frying

Combine flours and salt in a small bowl, and make a well in the center. Pour oil into well, then, with your fingers, rub oil into flour until mixture is uniformly fine and crumbly. Sprinkle 3 tablespoons lukewarm water over mixture, forking all the while, then add remaining water, 1 tablespoon at a time, again forking vigorously to form a workable dough. Lightly oil your fingers, and knead dough on a lightly floured board until satiny and elastic, about 5 minutes. Shape into a ball, place in a greased bowl, turning to grease all over. Cover with cloth and let stand at room temperature 30 minutes. Divide dough into 10 pieces of equal size, shape each into a ball, then roll, one at a time, into a 5″ circle, using a lightly floured rolling pin on a lightly floured board. Pour enough oil or melt enough vegetable shortening in a deep fat fryer or heavy kettle to measure 3″ deep; insert deep fat thermometer and heat oil to 375° F. Using tongs, drop 1 puri into oil. It will sink to the bottom; as soon as it bobs to the top—after 6–7 seconds—turn gently and cook the flip side 6–7 seconds. The point is not to brown or crispen the puri, merely to puff it softly. Drain puri on paper toweling. Fry remaining puri the same way and serve at once. Wonderful with curry.

NP Puri: 80 C, 0 mg CH, 55 mg S*

BASIC CORN BREAD

8″ × 8″ × 2″ loaf   ¢

1 cup sifted flour
1 cup sifted corn meal
1 tablespoon baking powder
¾ teaspoon salt
1 tablespoon sugar (optional)
1 egg
1 cup milk
¼ cup cooking oil, melted vegetable shortening, or bacon drippings

Preheat oven to 400° F. Sift flour, corn meal, baking powder, salt, and, if you like, sugar into a bowl; beat egg with milk and oil just to blend. Make a well in dry ingredients, pour in egg mixture, and stir until well blended. Pour into a well-greased 8″ × 8″ × 2″ baking pan and bake 20–25 minutes until bread pulls slightly from edges of pan, is lightly browned and springy to the touch. Cut in large squares and serve oven-hot with lots of butter.

NPS (12–16): 130–110 C, 20–10 mg CH, 215–195 mg S*

VARIATIONS

Jalapeño Corn Bread: Mix batter as directed increasing baking powder to 3½ teaspoons and adding 1 cup grated Monterey Jack or sharp white Cheddar cheese, 1–2 (4-ounce) cans *very well drained,* chopped Jalapeño peppers or green chilies, ¼ cup minced yellow onion, and, if you like, ¼ cup crumbled crisply cooked bacon. Bake as recipe directs 25–30 minutes.

NPS (12–16): 130–115 C, 10–5 mg CH, 215–160 mg S*

¢ **Corn Sticks** *(14 sticks):* Preheat oven to 425° F. Grease corn stick pans, set in oven, and let heat while oven preheats. Mix batter as directed, spoon into hot pans, and bake 15–20 minutes until nicely browned and springy to the touch. Serve at once.

NP Stick: 105 C, 20 mg CH, 195 mg S*

¢ **Corn Muffins** *(1 dozen):* Preheat oven to 425° F. Mix batter as directed, spoon into greased muffin pans, filling each cup two thirds. Bake 15–20 minutes until lightly browned and springy to the touch. Serve hot.

NP Muffin: 140 C, 25 mg CH, 260 mg S*

RHODE ISLAND JONNYCAKES

4 servings   ⊠ ¢

There are Rhode Island jonnycakes and Rhode Island jonnycakes (*not* spelled johnnycake, by the way). If you come from "South County," Rhode Island, you like your jonnycakes thick—the batter should be about the consistency of a soft drop-cookie dough so that it mounds on a spoon and stands up on the griddle. And the cakes themselves will be thick, 1/2"–3/4", and cooked at least 10 minutes on each side until crispy-brown. "You can't hurry jonny-cakes," they say in "South County." But if, on the other hand, you're from northern Rhode Island, you like your jonnycakes thin —almost as thin as a crepe. The recipe below is a basic one, and you can experiment with batter thickness until you determine just the consistency you like. It's best to cook jonnycakes on an old-fashioned iron griddle, but you can use an electric skillet or griddle set at a low temperature.

1 cup fine water-ground white corn meal
1/2 teaspoon salt
1 tablespoon sugar
1 cup boiling water (about)
Milk (to thin batter)
3–4 tablespoons bacon drippings or vegetable shortening

Mix together corn meal, salt, and sugar. Pour in boiling water and toss with a fork just to mix. There should be enough water just to dampen the ingredients so that no dry particles show. Next, add enough milk to thin batter to the consistency you like. Heat 2 tablespoons bacon drippings or shortening on a heavy griddle over moderate heat until a drop of water will dance about. Then drop batter by rounded tablespoonfuls onto griddle, reduce heat, and brown slowly, a few at a time, 5–10 minutes on a side, depending on thickness, until crispy and brown. Jonny-cakes should be about 2 1/2" in diameter. Lift to paper toweling and keep warm while frying the remainder (add more bacon drippings or shortening as needed). Serve hot with butter or, if you prefer, with butter and maple syrup. If the cakes are thick, try splitting and tucking in a slice of sharp Cheddar cheese—delicious!

NPS: 215 C, 5 mg CH, 275 mg S*

OLD-FASHIONED DEEP SOUTH SPOON BREAD

4–6 servings

This custard-like corn meal pudding makes a good potato substitute.

1 pint light cream
1/3 cup milk
1/4 cup unsalted butter
2 tablespoons sugar
1 teaspoon salt
1 cup sifted stone- or water-ground white corn meal

4 eggs, separated
1 teaspoon baking powder

Preheat oven to 375° F. Heat cream, milk, butter, sugar, and salt, uncovered, stirring occasionally, until scalding; off heat, mix in corn meal, beating until smooth and thick. Lightly beat yolks and stir in baking powder. Stir a little of the hot mixture into yolks, then return to pan and blend well. Beat whites until soft peaks form and fold in. Bake, uncovered, in a lightly buttered 2-quart casserole or soufflé dish 30–35 minutes until puffy and lightly browned. Serve oven-hot with lots of butter, salt, and freshly ground black pepper.

NPS (4–6): 576–385 C, 385–260 mg CH, 900–600 mg S*

CORN MEAL MUSH

4 servings ¢

A Southern breakfast favorite.

1/2 cup corn meal, preferably enriched yellow meal
2 1/2 cups boiling water
3/4 teaspoon salt

Sprinkle meal into rapidly boiling water, add salt, and heat, stirring, over very low heat about 1/2 hour until quite thick. Ladle into bowls, top with pats of butter, and serve hot for breakfast.

NPS: 60 C, 0 mg CH, 410 mg S*

VARIATION

Fried Mush: Prepare mush as directed and pour into heatproof water glasses or small tin cans (the soup size is perfect) that have been rinsed out in cold water. Cool until firm. Unmold, slice mush 1/2"–3/4" thick, and brown in hot bacon drippings, butter, or margarine. Serve with hot syrup in place of pancakes or waffles.

NPS: 110 C, 5 mg CH, 410 mg S*

HUSHPUPPIES

2 dozen

For this recipe you *must* use old-fashioned, stone- or water-ground white corn meal— enriched yellow meal flies to pieces in the hot fat. Hushpuppies, it's said, were originally tag ends of corn bread dough, deep-fat-fried and tossed to dogs at mealtime to "hush them up." Serve hushpuppies with seafood, especially breaded or batter-fried fish.

Shortening or cooking oil for deep-fat-frying
2 cups sifted fine stone- or water-ground white
   corn meal
1 tablespoon sugar
3/4 teaspoon baking soda
2 teaspoons salt
1 tablespoon minced yellow onion
1 egg
1 cup buttermilk
4–5 tablespoons cold water

Begin heating fat in a deep fat fryer; use a deep fat thermometer. Stir corn meal, sugar, soda, and salt together to mix. Place onion in a small bowl, add egg and buttermilk, and beat until frothy; pour all at once into meal and stir lightly to mix. Add just enough water to make dough a good dropping consistency—it should be about the same as drop biscuit dough. When fat reaches 375° F., scoop up rounded 1/2 tablespoons of dough, shape lightly on end of spoon to smooth out rough edges, drop into fat, and fry about 2 minutes until evenly browned. Drain quickly on paper toweling and serve—hushpuppies should be sizzling hot.

NP Hushpuppy: 60 C, 10 mg CH, 220 mg S*

TORTILLAS

15 tortillas   ¢

Masa harina is a special corn flour used to make tortillas and other Mexican breads. It's available in specialty food shops, Latin American and Spanish groceries. Tortillas are used to make tacos, enchiladas, tostadas, and a variety of other Tex-Mex favorites.

2 cups masa harina
1 teaspoon salt
11/4 cups very hot water

Mix masa and salt, stir in water, and blend well. Pinch off a piece of dough and roll into a ball about 11/2″ in diameter; flatten in a tortilla press or, if you have none, between 2 dampened 6″ double thickness squares of cheesecloth, pressing as hard as possible with a cutting board. Remove board and roll with a rolling pin until about 5″ across. Lift off top cheesecloth, very gently invert tortilla on palm of hand, and peel off bottom cheesecloth. Cook in an ungreased, heavy skillet over moderately high heat or on an electric griddle set at 400° F. 1/2–1 minute on each side, just until tortilla begins to color. It should not brown. Keep warm in a napkin or linen towel while you shape and cook remaining tortillas. Serve hot.

NP Tortilla: 65 C, 0 mg CH, 145 mg S*

CHEESE TACOS

6 servings

1/4 cup lard or vegetable shortening
6 Tortillas (homemade or packaged)

FILLING
6 slices American, Cheddar, or Monterey Jack
   cheese, coarsely cut up
1/4 cup minced yellow onion
1 teaspoon chili powder

Heat lard in a large, heavy skillet over moderate heat and dip in each tortilla 1 or 2 seconds just to soften; spread flat on a baking sheet. Top with cheese and onion and sprinkle with chili powder. Fold in half and fasten with toothpicks. Fry in lard over moderately high heat about 1 minute per side until dappled with brown; drain on paper toweling, and serve. Or, if you prefer, instead of frying, bake, uncovered, 15 minutes at 400° F. until brown and crisp.

NPS: 315 C, 30 mg CH, 775 mg S*

VARIATIONS

Recipes too flexible for meaningful nutritional count.

Chicken Tacos: Omit filling above; fill Tortillas with minced, cooked chicken (or pork or beef) moistened with canned enchilada or taco sauce; fold and fry as directed. Serve with sliced radishes, avocado, and shredded lettuce.

Sausage Tacos: Omit filling above; fill Tortillas with minced sautéed *chorizo* sausage mixed with a little minced onion; fold and fry as directed.

Bean Tacos: Omit filling above; fill Tortillas with Fried or Refried Beans, fold and fry as directed.

Chili Tacos: Prepare and cook Tortillas as directed, then fry, a few at a time, in 1/2″ lard or cooking oil over moderate heat until lightly browned. Drain on paper toweling, spread with hot chili con carne, top with shredded lettuce, a drizzling of French dressing, and a sprinkling of grated Parmesan or Cheddar cheese. Fold tortilla over filling and serve.

EASY DATE-NUT BREAD

2 (9" × 5" × 3") loaves (20 slices each)

Start this recipe the day before you bake it.

2 cups coarsely cut-up pitted dates
2 cups boiling water
2 teaspoons baking soda
1 cup sugar
1 tablespoon melted butter or margarine
1 egg, lightly beaten
2¾ cups sifted flour
1 cup coarsely chopped pecans or walnuts
1 teaspoon vanilla

Mix dates, water, and soda; cool, cover, and let stand at room temperature overnight. Next day preheat oven to 325° F. Add sugar, butter, and egg to date mixture and stir until sugar dissolves. Add flour, a few spoonfuls at a time, mixing after each addition until smooth. Stir in nuts and vanilla. Spoon into 2 greased and floured 9" × 5" × 3" loaf pans and bake about 1 hour, until loaves shrink slightly from sides of pan and are springy to the touch. Cool upright in pans on wire rack 10 minutes, turn out, and cool completely. Wrap airtight and store overnight before cutting. (*Note:* These loaves freeze well.)

NP Slice: 95 C, 5 mg CH, 45 mg S*

PRUNE AND WALNUT BREAD

9" × 5" × 3" loaf (20 slices)

This loaf tastes better and cuts more easily if wrapped airtight and "seasoned" about a day.

2 cups sifted flour
1 teaspoon baking powder
½ teaspoon salt
1 cup boiling water
1 teaspoon baking soda
1 cup coarsely chopped pitted prunes
⅔ cup sugar
1 egg
2 tablespoons melted butter or margarine
½ teaspoon vanilla
⅔ cup coarsely chopped walnuts

Preheat oven to 300° F. Sift flour with baking powder and salt and set aside. Mix boiling water, soda, and prunes and cool to lukewarm; drain off liquid and reserve. Beat sugar, egg, butter, and vanilla until well blended. Add flour mixture, about one third at a time, alternately with reserved prune liquid, beginning and ending with flour; beat just until smooth. Mix in prunes and walnuts. Spoon into a greased 9" × 5" × 3"

loaf pan and bake 1 hour until loaf shrinks slightly from sides of pan and is springy to the touch. Cool upright in pan on a wire rack 20 minutes before turning out. Cool thoroughly, slice, and serve.

NP Slice: 125 C, 15 mg CH, 130 mg S*

VARIATIONS

Apricot-Pecan Bread: Prepare as directed, substituting dried apricots for the prunes and pecans or blanched almonds for the walnuts.

NP Slice: 125 C, 15 mg CH, 135 mg S*

Raisin or Currant and Nut Bread: Prepare as directed, substituting seedless raisins or dried currants for the prunes. For the nuts use walnuts, pecans, filberts, or blanched almonds.

NP Slice: 130 C, 15 mg CH, 135 mg S*

ORANGE NUT BREAD

9" × 5" × 3" loaf (20 slices)

Delicious spread with cream cheese.

2¾ cups sifted flour
2½ teaspoons baking powder
½ teaspoon baking soda
½ teaspoon salt
2 tablespoons butter or margarine, softened to room temperature
1 cup strained honey
1 egg, lightly beaten
1½ teaspoons finely grated orange rind
¾ cup orange juice
¾ cup coarsely chopped pecans, walnuts, or blanched almonds

Preheat oven to 325° F. Sift flour with baking powder, soda, and salt and set aside. Blend butter with honey until creamy; add egg and orange rind and mix well. Add sifted ingredients alternately with orange juice, beginning and ending with the sifted. Fold in nuts. Spoon into a greased 9" × 5" × 3" loaf pan and bake 1–1¼ hours until loaf pulls slightly from sides of pan and is springy to the touch. Let cool upright in pan 10 minutes, then turn out and cool on a wire rack.

NP Slice: 160 C, 15 mg CH, 145 mg S*

CRANBERRY NUT BREAD

9" × 5" × 3" loaf (20 slices)

1 cup cranberries (fresh or frozen)
1 cup sugar
3 cups sifted flour

4 teaspoons baking powder
1/2 teaspoon salt
1/2 cup coarsely chopped walnuts or pecans
Grated rind of 1 orange
1 egg, lightly beaten
1 cup milk
2 teaspoons melted butter or margarine

Preheat oven to 350° F. Put cranberries through coarse blade of meat grinder and mix with 1/4 cup sugar. Sift remaining sugar with flour, baking powder, and salt; mix in nuts and orange rind. Lightly beat egg with milk and melted butter and stir into flour mixture. Fold in cranberries. Spoon into a buttered 9″ × 5″ × 3″ loaf pan and bake about 1 hour until loaf pulls slightly from sides of pan and is springy to the touch. Cool upright in pan 10 minutes, then turn out on a wire rack and cool before slicing.

NP Slice: 140 C, 15 mg CH, 155 mg S*

BANANA TEA BREAD

9″ × 5″ × 3″ loaf (20 slices)

1¾ cups sifted flour
2 teaspoons baking powder
1/4 teaspoon baking soda
1/2 teaspoon salt
1/3 cup vegetable shortening
2/3 cup sugar
2 eggs, well beaten
1 cup mashed ripe bananas

Preheat oven to 350° F. Sift flour with baking powder, soda, and salt and set aside. Cream shortening until light, add sugar gradually, continuing to cream until fluffy. Beat in eggs. Add flour mixture alternately with bananas, beginning and ending with flour. Spoon into a well-greased 9″ × 5″ × 3″ loaf pan and bake about 1 hour and 10 minutes until loaf pulls slightly from sides of pan and is springy to the touch. Cool upright in pan 10 minutes, then turn out on a wire rack and cool before slicing.

NP Slice: 110 C, 25 mg CH, 115 mg S*

CARROT AND RAISIN BREAD

9″ × 5″ × 3″ loaf (20 slices)

This loaf will cut more easily if you wrap it airtight and store overnight.

2½ cups sifted unbleached flour
1 tablespoon baking powder
1/2 teaspoon salt
1 cup firmly packed light brown sugar
2 eggs, lightly beaten

1/2 cup melted butter or margarine or cooking oil
1/2 cup milk
1 tablespoon finely grated orange rind (optional)
1/2 cup seedless raisins
2 cups finely grated peeled carrots

Preheat oven to 350° F. Sift flour, baking powder, and salt into a mixing bowl. Add sugar and rub well between your fingers, breaking up any lumps of sugar. Add all remaining ingredients and mix well. Spoon into a well-greased 9″ × 5″ × 3″ loaf pan and bake about 50 minutes until loaf shrinks slightly from sides of pan and is springy to the touch. (*Note:* Do not underbake; test by inserting a toothpick or cake tester in center of loaf; it should come out clean.) Cool bread upright in pan on wire rack 20 minutes, then turn out. Cool completely before cutting.

NP Slice: 160 C, 40 mg CH, 185 mg S*

VARIATION

Zucchini-Walnut Bread: Prepare as directed but reduce flour to 2 cups and add 1/2 cup unsifted whole wheat flour. Substitute 3/4 cup sugar for the brown sugar, 1/2 cup coarsely chopped walnuts for the raisins, and 2 cups finely grated zucchini (leave skin on) for the carrots.

NP Slice: 155 C, 40 mg CH, 175 mg S*

CINNAMON COFFEE CAKE

2 (9″ × 5″ × 3″) loaves (20 slices each)

2½ cups sifted flour
2½ teaspoons baking powder
1 cup butter or margarine
1 cup sugar
3 eggs
1 teaspoon vanilla
1 cup sour cream
1/2 cup coarsely chopped pitted dates
1/2 cup finely chopped pecans or walnuts
1/2 cup firmly packed light brown sugar mixed with 2 teaspoons cinnamon

Preheat oven to 350° F. Sift flour with baking powder and set aside. Cream butter and sugar until light, then beat in eggs, one at a time; mix in vanilla. Add flour, a few spoonfuls at a time, alternately with sour cream, beginning and ending with flour. Stir in dates and nuts. Spoon about half the batter into 2 greased and floured 9″ × 5″ × 3″ loaf pans and sprinkle with half the brown sugar mixture. Add remaining batter and sprinkle with remaining sugar mixture. Bake about 1 hour until loaves pull slightly from sides of pan and are springy to the touch. Cool upright in pans on a wire rack 10 minutes, then turn out and cool completely. Slice and serve with butter. (*Note:* These loaves freeze well.)

NP Slice: 130 C, 35 mg CH, 80 mg S*

BOSTON BROWN BREAD

3 small round loaves (27 slices)   ¢

A rich, dark steamed bread, which New Englanders eat with baked beans.

1 cup sifted all-purpose flour
1 teaspoon salt
1 teaspoon baking powder
1 teaspoon baking soda
1½ cups unsifted whole wheat flour
½ cup corn meal
¾ cup molasses
2 cups sour milk or buttermilk
1 cup seedless raisins

Grease 3 clean small shortening tins (the 14-ounce size) and line bottoms with greased circles of wax paper. Sift all-purpose flour with salt, baking powder, and soda into a large bowl, stir in whole wheat flour and corn meal, then mix in molasses and sour milk. Stir in raisins. Spoon into cans, filling no more than two thirds, cover with a *greased* double thickness of foil and tie or tape securely. Place on a rack in a large kettle, pour in enough boiling water to come halfway up cans, cover, and steam about 1 hour until well risen and a metal skewer inserted in center of bread comes out clean. Lift cans from water, cool upright 1–2 minutes on a wire rack, then invert and ease loaves out. Cool slightly on racks before cutting or cool to room temperature. Slice ¼" thick. (*Note:* The best way to cut this bread is with fine strong thread, using a sawing motion.) The bread can be steamed in any well-greased molds instead of shortening tins. Just make sure to fill no more than two thirds and to cover with greased foil. 1–1½-pint molds will take 1–1½ hours, 1-quart molds 2–2½ hours, and 1½-quart molds about 3 hours.

NP Slice: 85 C, .50 mg CH, 135 mg S*

SPICY BAKING POWDER DOUGHNUTS

2 dozen

Children love these.

3½ cups sifted flour
½ teaspoon salt
2 teaspoons baking powder
1 teaspoon baking soda
½ teaspoon cinnamon
½ teaspoon nutmeg
2 eggs
1 cup sugar
2 tablespoons cooking oil or vegetable shortening
¾ cup buttermilk or sour milk
Shortening or cooking oil for deep fat frying

TOPPING
½ cup superfine sugar mixed with 1 teaspoon cinnamon

Sift flour with salt, baking powder, soda, and spices and set aside. In a large mixer bowl, beat eggs, sugar, and oil at medium speed; add buttermilk. Add dry ingredients all at once and beat just until smooth. Cover and chill 1 hour. Meanwhile, begin heating fat in a deep fat fryer; insert deep fat thermometer. Roll dough ½" thick on a lightly floured surface and cut with a doughnut cutter; re-roll and cut scraps. When fat reaches 375° F., slide 4 doughnuts into fat. (*Note:* To transfer doughnuts without pushing them out of shape, use a slotted pancake turner dipped in the hot fat.) Fry doughnuts 2–3 minutes until brown all over, using tongs to turn. Drain on paper toweling; roll in topping while still warm.

NP Doughnut: 150 C, 25 mg CH, 130 mg S*

BASIC PANCAKES

1 dozen   ¢ ▣

Electric griddles or skillets are ideal for cooking pancakes because they maintain a constant heat. Follow manufacturer's directions for greasing and preheating. Batters containing fat or oil can usually be cooked in an ungreased skillet.

1 cup sifted flour
½ teaspoon salt
2 tablespoons sugar
2 teaspoons baking powder
1 egg, lightly beaten
¾ cup milk
2 tablespoons cooking oil, melted butter or margarine

Preheat griddle over moderate heat while you mix batter or, if using an electric griddle, preheat as manufacturer directs. Sift flour, salt, sugar, and baking powder into a bowl or wide-mouthed pitcher. Combine egg, milk, and oil, slowly stir into dry ingredients, and mix only until dampened—batter should be lumpy. When a drop of cold water will dance on the griddle, begin cooking pancakes, using about 3 tablespoons batter for each, allowing plenty of space between them and spreading each until about 4″ across. Cook until bubbles form over surface, turn gently, and brown flip side. *(Note: For extra-light and tender pancakes, turn before bubbles break and turn one time only.)* Stack 3–4 deep on heated plates and keep warm while cooking the rest. Serve as soon as possible with butter, maple syrup, or other topping such as sliced fruit, creamed meat, seafood or vegetables, even ice cream or any dessert sauce.

NP Pancake: 80 C, 25 mg CH, 175 mg S*

For Thinner Pancakes: Add 2–3 extra tablespoons milk.

If Batter Has Stood Awhile: Mix in about 1/4 teaspoon additional baking powder before cooking.

VARIATIONS

Nut Pancakes: Prepare batter as directed and just before cooking fold in 1/2 cup coarsely chopped pecans, walnuts, almonds, or roasted peanuts.

NP Pancake: 110 C, 25 mg CH, 175 mg S*

Berry Pancakes: Prepare batter as directed and just before cooking fold in 1/2 cup berries (any kind as long as they're small and well drained).

NP Pancake: 80 C, 25 mg CH, 175 mg S*

¢ **Apple Pancakes:** Prepare as directed, sifting 1/4 teaspoon each cinnamon and nutmeg along with dry ingredients; just before cooking, fold in 1/2–3/4 cup minced, peeled tart apple.

NP Pancake: 80 C, 25 mg CH, 175 mg S*

¢ **Rice Pancakes:** Prepare as directed but increase eggs to 2 and milk to 1 cup; just before cooking, fold in 1/2 cup cooked rice or wild rice.

NP Pancake: 100 C, 50 mg CH, 185 mg S*

¢ **Buttermilk Pancakes:** Prepare as directed but reduce baking powder to 1 teaspoon, add 3/4 teaspoon baking soda, and use 1 cup buttermilk or sour milk instead of sweet milk.

NP Pancake: 75 C, 25 mg CH, 205 mg S*

¢ **Whole Wheat Pancakes:** Prepare as directed, using 1/2 cup each unsifted whole wheat flour and sifted all-purpose flour; increase milk to 1 cup.

NP Pancake: 80 C, 25 mg CH, 180 mg S*

¢ **Buckwheat Pancakes:** Prepare as directed, using 1/2 cup each unsifted buckwheat flour and sifted all-purpose flour, increase milk to 1 cup.

NP Pancake: 80 C, 25 mg CH, 180 mg S*

Onion Pancakes: Prepare as directed but reduce sugar to 1 teaspoon. Just before cooking, mix in 1/2 cup sautéed minced onion and a pinch each sage and thyme. Cook as directed and serve for lunch or supper, topped with Welsh Rabbit or any creamed or curried meat or vegetable.

NP Pancake: 75 C, 25 mg CH, 175 mg S*

Corn and Pepper Pancakes: Prepare as directed but reduce sugar to 1 teaspoon. Just before cooking, mix in 1/2 cup well-drained cooked whole kernel corn and 1/4 cup minced sweet red or green pepper. Cook as directed and serve as is in place of potatoes or topped with chili as a main course.

NP Pancake: 80 C, 25 mg CH, 190 mg S*

YEAST-RAISED PANCAKES

1 1/2 dozen   ¢

1 3/4 cups scalded milk
2 tablespoons sugar
1/2 teaspoon salt
1/4 cup warm water (105°–115° F.)
1 packet active dry yeast
1 egg, lightly beaten
2 tablespoons cooking oil, melted butter or margarine
2 cups sifted flour

Mix milk, sugar, and salt and cool to lukewarm. Pour water into a warm mixing bowl, sprinkle in yeast and stir to dissolve; mix in cooled mixture, also egg and oil. Slowly add flour and beat until smooth. Cover and let rise in a warm draft-free place until doubled in bulk, about 35 minutes. Toward end of rising, preheat griddle over moderate heat, or, if using an electric one, by manufacturer's instructions. When batter is fully risen, stir down and pour about 1/4 cup onto griddle for each pancake; allow plenty of space between pancakes, then spread each until about 4″ across. Cook until bubbles form on surface and underside is brown, turn, and brown flip side. Keep warm while cooking the rest. Serve hot with butter and syrup or other suitable topping.

NP Pancake: 85 C, 20 mg CH, 75 mg S*

VARIATIONS

Blini: Prepare and cook pancakes as directed; fill each with 1 tablespoon red or black caviar, fold in half, and serve with sour cream.

NP Blini: 140 C, 85 mg CH, 450 mg S*

¢ **English Crumpets** *(14-crumpets):* Prepare batter as directed but reduce flour to 1⅓ cups. Cook as directed, but until bubbles on pancakes *break;* brown flip side very lightly only. Cool pancakes. When ready to serve, toast, smother "holey" sides with butter, quarter crumpets, and serve hot as a teatime snack.

NP Crumpet: 90 C, 25 mg CH, 100 mg S*

¢ **Yeast-Raised Waffles** *(8 waffles):* Prepare as directed but reduce flour to 1½ cups. Bake in a preheated waffle iron.

NP Waffle: 165 C, 40 mg CH, 170 mg S*

Using Waffle Irons

Automatic waffle irons take the frustrations out of waffle baking. But old irons, properly used, produce exquisitely crisp, nut-brown waffles. Here are a few tips for using them:
• Heat iron until a drop of water will dance over the grids.
• Pour batter in center of iron until one half to two thirds full, then close and bake until all steaming stops. Open iron gently. If top sticks, waffle probably needs to bake longer. The first waffle often sticks to an old iron, so bake it a little browner than you like and discard. Doing so will temper the iron nicely for the waffles to follow.
• Never wash or grease an iron once it has been seasoned.

BASIC WAFFLES

8 waffles ¢

And there are also a half-dozen variations here to try.

2 cups sifted flour
2 tablespoons sugar
1 tablespoon baking powder
1 teaspoon salt
2 eggs, separated
1¾ cups milk
6 tablespoons cooking oil, melted butter, margarine, or bacon drippings

Preheat waffle iron according to manufacturer's directions. Sift flour, sugar, baking powder, and salt into a bowl. Combine egg yolks, milk, and oil, pour into flour mixture, and beat with a rotary beater or electric mixer just until smooth. Beat egg whites until soft peaks form and fold into batter. Pour batter into waffle iron as manufacturer di-

rects and bake at medium heat until steaming stops and waffle is golden. Serve with plenty of butter and warm syrup or other topping.

NP Waffle: 260 C, 75 mg CH, 480 mg S*

¢ **Buttermilk Waffles:** Prepare as directed, substituting buttermilk or sour milk for sweet; reduce baking powder to 2 teaspoons and add 1 teaspoon baking soda.

NP Waffle: 250 C, 70 mg CH, 555 mg S*

Ham Waffles: Prepare as directed but omit sugar; add 1 cup finely diced lean boiled ham to batter before folding in egg whites.

NP Waffle: 270 C, 85 mg CH, 690 mg S*

Nut Waffles: Prepare as directed and add ⅓–½ cup coarsely chopped walnuts, pecans, almonds, hazelnuts, peanuts, or piñon nuts to batter before folding in egg whites.

NP Waffle: 290 C, 75 mg CH, 480 mg S*

Blueberry Waffles: Prepare as directed; scatter a few (about 2 tablespoons) washed and dried blueberries over batter in iron before baking.

NP Waffle: 270 C, 75 mg CH, 480 mg S*

Savory Waffles: Prepare as directed but omit sugar; serve topped with creamed chicken or turkey, tuna or chipped beef, Welsh Rabbit or Shrimp Newburg.

NP Waffle: 245 C, 75 mg CH, 48 mg S*

Dessert Waffles: Prepare extra-rich waffles and top with ice cream or sweetened sliced peaches or berries and whipped cream.

NP Waffle: 325 C, 90 mg CH, 505 mg S*

CREPES FOR SAVORY FILLINGS

10 crepes ¢

½ cup sifted flour
¼ teaspoon salt
2 eggs, lightly beaten
½ cup milk
1 tablespoon cold water
1 tablespoon melted butter or margarine

Sift flour and salt together into a bowl; mix all remaining ingredients and add slowly to dry ingredients, beating until smooth. Let stand at room temperature 15 minutes. Brush bottom and sides of a heavy 6″ skillet with cooking oil and set over moderate heat ½ minute. Stir batter, then add 2 tablespoonfuls to skillet, tipping it back and forth so batter *just* coats bottom (crepe should be *very thin*). Brown lightly on one side, about

30 seconds, turn and brown other side. Place on a paper-towel-lined baking sheet, most attractive side down so that when crepe is rolled it will be on the outside. Cook remaining crepes the same way; they are now ready to be filled.

NP Crepe: 65 C, 60 mg CH, 85 mg S*

VARIATION

¢ **Simple Dessert Crepes:** Add 1 tablespoon sugar to dry ingredients, then mix and cook crepes as directed; keep warm in a 250° F. oven until all are done. To serve, spread with jam, honey, or marmalade, fill with crushed berries, or simply drizzle with melted butter and sprinkle with sugar. Roll and top with dollops of sour cream. Recipe too flexible for meaningful nutritional count.

DUMPLINGS (BASIC RECIPE)

7–8 dumplings ¢

The best way to cook dumplings is uncovered for 10 minutes, then tightly covered for another 10 so that the steam will fluff up the dumplings.

1 cup sifted flour
1½ teaspoons baking powder
½ teaspoon salt
2 tablespoons chilled vegetable shortening
½ cup milk

Sift flour, baking powder, and salt together into a bowl; cut in shortening with a pastry blender until mixture resembles coarse meal. Add milk all at once and mix lightly *just* until dough holds together. Drop by rounded tablespoonfuls on top of gently bubbling soup or stew. Adjust burner so liquid just simmers, then simmer, *uncovered,* 10 minutes; cover and simmer 10 minutes longer. (*Note:* If soup or stew needs thickening, do so *after* removing dumplings.)

NP Dumpling (7–8): 105–90 C, 2.5–2 mg CH, 255–225 mg S*

VARIATIONS

Recipes for first four variations too flexible for meaningful nutritional count.

¢ **Parsley or Chive Dumplings:** Prepare as directed, mixing 2 tablespoons minced parsley or chives into dry ingredients.

¢ **Sage, Thyme, and Onion Dumplings:** Prepare as directed, mixing ¼ teaspoon each sage and thyme and 1 tablespoon grated onion into dry ingredients.

¢ **Caraway Dumplings** (especially good with goulash): Prepare as directed, mixing 1½ teaspoons caraway seeds into dry ingredients.

Saffron Dumplings: Prepare as directed, mixing ⅛ teaspoon each powdered saffron and sage or thyme into dry ingredients.

¢ **Cheese Dumplings:** Prepare as directed, mixing 2–3 tablespoons coarsely grated sharp Cheddar cheese into dry ingredients.

NP Dumpling (7–8): 110–95 C, 4–3 mg CH, 270–235 mg S*

BREAD DUMPLINGS

14–16 dumplings ¢

A delicious way to use up stale bread. These dumplings are good in soups or stews.

3 cups ½″ cubes stale bread, trimmed of crusts
¼ cup unsifted flour
1 teaspoon salt
⅛ teaspoon pepper
¼ teaspoon baking powder
⅛ teaspoon nutmeg (optional)
1 tablespoon minced parsley
2 tablespoons minced yellow onion
¼ cup milk
1 egg, lightly beaten
1 tablespoon melted butter or margarine

Mix all ingredients together, let stand 5 minutes, and mix again. Drop by rounded teaspoonfuls into a little flour, then roll into balls. Drop into *just*-boiling soup or stew, simmer, uncovered, 5 minutes, cover, and simmer 2–3 minutes longer. Do not cook more than 1 layer deep at a time. Serve in soup or stew, allowing 3–4 per serving. (*Note:* For stew, the dumplings can be made twice as large; simmer, uncovered, 7–10 minutes, cover, and simmer 5–7 minutes longer.)

NP Dumpling (14–16): 40–35 C, 25–20 mg CH, 215–185 mg S*

BASIC BATTER FOR FRIED FOODS

1½ cups

An all-purpose batter that can be used for almost any foods to be fried: chicken, fish fillets, shellfish, vegetables, fruit.

1 cup sifted flour
1 teaspoon baking powder
½ teaspoon salt
1 egg, lightly beaten
1 cup milk
2 tablespoons cooking oil

Sift flour with baking powder and salt. Mix egg, milk, and oil, slowly add to dry ingredients, and beat until smooth. Pat food to be fried very dry and, if you like, dredge lightly in flour. Dip pieces, one at a time, in batter, then fry in deep fat as individual recipes direct. (It takes about 1 tablespoon to coat a shrimp or small piece of fruit or vegetable.)

NP Tablespoon: 40 C, 15 mg CH, 70 mg S*

TEMPURA BATTER

1 pint

Low-gluten flour, teamed with egg whites, is what gives this batter its singular crispness. We've taken the liberty of substituting the more readily available cake flour and find the results excellent.

1¼ cups sifted cake flour
1 teaspoon salt
2 egg whites, lightly beaten to froth
1 cup ice water

Sift flour with salt; add egg whites and water all at once and whisk lightly and quickly just to mix. Batter should be slightly lumpy and small flecks of flour visible. Use at once for Japanese Butterfly Shrimp or for coating parsley fluffs or bite-size chunks of cucumber, carrot, cauliflower, broccoli, or zucchini before deep fat frying.

NP Tablespoon: 15 C, 0 mg CH, 70 mg S*

VEGETABLE FRITTER BATTER

1½ cups

¾ cup sifted flour
1 teaspoon baking powder
1 teaspoon salt
¾ cup milk
1 egg, lightly beaten

Sift flour, baking powder, and salt together into a bowl. Slowly add milk and beat until smooth. Add egg and beat well. Use for dipping vegetables that are to be deep-fat-fried.

NP Tablespoon: 20 C, 15 mg CH, 115 mg S*

GARLIC FRENCH BREAD

6 servings ☒

Everyone's favorite. And so easy to prepare.

1 clove garlic, peeled and crushed
¼ pound butter or margarine, softened to room
  temperature
1 loaf French bread about 18″ long

Blend garlic with butter and let stand at room temperature about 1 hour. About ½ hour before serving, preheat oven to 375° F. Meanwhile, slice bread 1″ thick, cutting *to* but not *through* the bottom and holding knife at a slight angle. Spread both sides of each slice with garlic butter and wrap loaf snugly in heavy foil. Place on a baking sheet and warm 20–25 minutes. Unwrap and serve in a long napkin-lined bread basket or break into chunks and serve in a round napkin-lined basket.

NPS: 355 C, 45 mg CH, 595 mg S*

VARIATIONS

Herbed Garlic Bread: Mix 1 teaspoon minced parsley and ¼ teaspoon each thyme and oregano or marjoram into garlic butter; proceed as directed.

NPS: 355 C, 45 mg CH, 595 mg S*

Cheese-Garlic Bread: Mix 1 tablespoon grated Parmesan, ¼ teaspoon salt, ⅛ teaspoon pepper, and ¼ teaspoon each savory and oregano or thyme into garlic butter; proceed as directed.

NPS: 360 C, 45 mg CH, 700 mg S*

How to Make Melba Toast

Slice white or any other bread ⅛″ thick, trim off crusts, and halve slices diagonally or cut in small rounds; bake, uncovered, on ungreased baking sheets 10–12 minutes at 300° F. until crisp and lightly browned. Cool and store airtight.

How to Make Rusks

Trim crusts from an unsliced loaf of firm-textured white bread, then slice ½″ thick; cut in "fingers" 3″ long and 1″–1½″ wide and bake, uncovered, on ungreased baking sheets 30–40 minutes at 300° F. until nicely browned.

How to Make Toast Cups

Trim crusts from thinly sliced, firm-textured white bread and brush one side of each slice with melted butter or margarine; press slices, buttered sides down, into muffin cups and brush insides with melted butter. Bake, uncovered, 10–12 minutes at 350° F. until golden brown. Remove from pans and use as patty shells for creamed meats or vegetables.

How to Make Croustades

Trim crusts from an unsliced loaf of firm-textured white bread, then slice 2½″ thick; cut each slice into a large cube, rectangle, or round and hollow out centers, leaving walls and bottoms ½″ thick (use centers for making bread crumbs). Brush inside and out with melted butter or margarine and bake, uncovered, on ungreased baking sheets 12–15 minutes at 350° F. until golden. Use as patty shells for creamed meats or vegetables.

How to Make Bread Cubes and Crumbs

Bread cubes and crumbs have dozens of uses. Mix into stuffings, toss into salads or casseroles, use as crunchy toppings or coatings.

For Soft Bread Cubes: Stack 2–3 slices bread on a board and cut into strips of desired width, then cut crosswise to form cubes of even size.

For Toasted Bread Cubes: Arrange soft bread cubes on an ungreased baking sheet 1 layer deep and toast in a 300° F. oven, turning occasionally, until evenly golden brown. Or broil 5″–6″ from heat, turning often and watching closely.

For Soft Bread Crumbs: Tear fresh slices of bread into small pieces, or buzz 5–10 seconds in an electric blender at high speed, or place in a food processor equipped with the metal chopping blade and pulse or snap motor on and off 5–6 times for fairly coarse crumbs; for fine crumbs, use 2–3 (5-second) churnings of the processor.

For Dry Bread Crumbs: Put slices of dry bread through fine blade of meat grinder. A neat trick is to tie or rubber-band a paper or plastic bag to end of grinder so crumbs drop directly into it. Or buzz 15–30 seconds in an electric blender at high speed until the degree of fineness you like, or place in a food processor equipped with the metal chopping blade; for coarse crumbs, pulse 5–6 times; for fine crumbs, churn 15–20 seconds nonstop. For extra-fine crumbs, sift, then store fine and coarse crumbs separately.

For Buttered Crumbs:

Soft: Toss 1 cup soft bread crumbs with ¼–⅓ cup melted butter or margarine.

Dry: Melt 3–4 tablespoons butter or margarine in a skillet over moderate heat, add 1–1½ cups dry crumbs, and heat, stirring, until golden brown.

For Seasoned Crumbs:

Garlic: Mix ¼ crushed clove garlic with ¼–⅓ cup melted butter or margarine, then toss with 1 cup soft or dry bread crumbs.

Cheese: Toss ¼ cup grated Parmesan cheese with 1 cup dry bread crumbs and 3–4 tablespoons melted butter or margarine.

Herb: Toss 1 cup dry bread crumbs with ¼ cup melted butter, margarine, or olive oil and ¼ teaspoon oregano, marjoram, or thyme.

Yields:

1 standard slice fresh bread	about ¾ cup soft bread cubes
	about ½ cup toasted bread cubes
	about ½ cup soft bread crumbs
1 standard slice dry bread	about ½ cup dry bread cubes
	about ¼ cup dry bread crumbs

CROUTONS

1 pint

Croutons add flavor and crunch to soups, salads, and casseroles. The ½″ size are best for soups and salads, the ¼″ for casserole toppings. Croutons needn't be cubes, however; cut in triangles, diamonds, or discs or into fancy shapes with truffle cutters. Make up a quantity, store airtight, or freeze, then reheat, uncovered, a few minutes at 425° F. to crispen. Packaged croutons, both plain and seasoned, are also available.

Vegetable shortening or cooking oil for deep fat frying
8 slices day-old or stale bread, trimmed of crusts and cut in ¼″ or ½″ cubes

Heat shortening in a deep fat fryer until deep fat thermometer reaches 350° F. Place about ½ cup cubes in fryer basket, lower into fat, and fry 10–15 seconds, turning, as needed, until evenly golden brown. Lift out, drain on paper toweling, and fry remaining cubes the same way. *Note:* Skim crumbs from fat before adding each fresh batch.

To Skillet-Fry: Heat 1″ cooking oil or a ½ and ½ mixture of melted butter or margarine and cooking oil in a large, heavy skillet over moderately high heat until a cube of bread will sizzle. Fry cubes about ½ cup at a time, 15–20 seconds, turning, as needed, until evenly golden brown. Drain on paper toweling.

To Oven-Fry: Preheat oven to 300° F. Butter both sides of bread or brush with melted butter and cut into cubes. Spread out on an ungreased baking sheet and bake, uncovered, 15 minutes; turn croutons and bake about 10 minutes longer until evenly browned.

VARIATIONS

Recipes too flexible for meaningful nutritional counts.

Garlic Croutons: Spread bread with Garlic Butter, cut in cubes, and oven fry as above.

Italian Croutons: Mix 1/2 cup each softened butter and grated Parmesan, 1/2 teaspoon each crushed garlic, basil, and oregano. Spread on bread, cut in cubes, and oven fry.

Herbed Croutons: Mix 2/3 cup softened butter with 2 teaspoons minced chives and 1/2 teaspoon each minced parsley, basil, and chervil. Spread on bread, cut in cubes, and oven fry.

FRENCH TOAST

4 servings   ⊠ ¢

If you have stale bread on hand, by all means use it for making French Toast.

2 eggs, lightly beaten
2/3 cup milk
1/4 teaspoon salt
1/4 cup butter, margarine, vegetable shortening, or cooking oil
8 slices firm-textured white bread

Beat egg with milk and salt just to blend and place in a piepan. Melt about 1/4 the butter in a large, heavy skillet. Quickly dip bread in egg mixture, turning to coat both sides well, then brown on each side in butter (add more butter to skillet as needed). Serve hot with honey, syrup, preserves, or tart jelly and a sprinkling of confectioners' sugar.

NPS: 295 C, 175 mg CH, 550 mg S*

VARIATION

Prepare as directed, using raisin or whole wheat bread instead of white.

NPS: 300 C, 175 mg CH, 490 mg S*

YEAST BREADS

Yeast is a delicate living thing that needs food, warmth, moisture, and air if it is to grow and leaven dough. The ingredients mixed with yeast all help provide the proper environment.

Essential Ingredients of Yeast Breads

Wheat Flour: Flour provides the framework of bread; its skeins of protein (gluten), developed in kneading, stretched as the yeast grows, and set during baking, give bread its characteristic texture. *All-purpose flour* (called for in all the following recipes unless otherwise specified) makes excellent yeast bread (we like the unbleached best); so does *bread flour,* which contains an even higher percentage of protein. *Cake or pastry flour* is too soft to make good bread. Wheat flour alone may be used in making bread, or it may be mixed with rye flour, oatmeal, corn meal, cracked wheat, buckwheat, bulgur, soy flour, or other grains. *Gluten flour,* a light brown flour made by washing the starch from wheat flour, is high in protein, low in starch, and thus good for those on starch-restricted diets. Substituted for about 1 cup all-purpose flour in bread recipes, it imparts wonderfully chewy texture.

Sugar: This is the food yeast needs; sugar also helps breads brown.

Salt: Salt isn't just for flavor. It controls the action of the yeast and keeps dough from rising too fast. Too much salt slows rising.

Fat: Lard, shortening, butter, margarine, or cooking oil can be used in making bread. Their functions: to make bread tender, give it fine texture, improve the keeping quality, and aid in browning.

Liquid: Either milk or water can be used to make bread. Milk increases the food value and keeping quality; water gives bread nuttier flavor, chewier texture, and crisper crust.

Yeast: The "life" and leavening of yeast breads. In the old days, women saved bits of yeast sponge from one baking, often mixing in leftover potato cooking water, to use as starters for the next batch. Popular, too, was sour dough—raw dough left to ferment in stone crocks, which could be used in place of yeast. And when there was no yeast, women made "salt" or "self-rising" bread by using soured corn meal batter as the leavening. Modern yeasts have made the old-fashioned ways unnecessary, though some people still make these rough breads for the joy of it. *Note:* Brewer's yeast is *not* a leavening agent; it is used mainly for brewing beer.

Active Dry Yeast: The most widely available form of yeast; it comes in 1/4-ounce packets or 4-ounce jars. Kept in a cool, dry spot, it keeps fresh several months. When dissolved in warm water, it does the work of 1 ($3/5$-ounce) cake compressed yeast. All of the following recipes call for active dry yeast; if unavailable, substitute 1 cake compressed yeast for each ¼-ounce package.

Fast-Rising Active Dry Yeast: This new "super yeast," available in ¼-ounce packets, is smaller grained than conventional active dry yeast and so viable and vigorous that it can not only speed rising times as much as 50 per cent but also, in some instances, eliminate the second rising altogether (see our recipe for Fast Single-Rising White Bread). Fast-rising yeast may be used interchangeably, measure for measure, with conventional active dry yeast; if substituted for compressed yeast, a ¼-ounce packet fast-rising active dry yeast will equal the leavening power of 1 ($3/5$-ounce) cake compressed yeast. The best way to use this new "super yeast" is to mix it directly with the dry ingredients, the method we use for Rapid-Mix White Bread (also see our recipes for Fast-Rising White Bread and Fast-Rising Cracked Wheat Bread).

Compressed Yeast: Not often seen today, this was the standard before World War II (dry yeast was developed during the war). It must be refrigerated and used within 1–2 weeks, or frozen and used within 6 months. Thaw at room temperature, then use at once. To determine if compressed yeast is still viable, crumble; if it crumbles easily, it's good.

The Care and Handling of Yeast: For most recipes (refrigerator doughs and the new cool-rise method excepted), yeast doughs must be kept warm from start to finish. And that means beginning with a warm bowl (simply rinse a bowl with warm water and dry). As you work with yeast dough, you'll learn what temperature is just right. If you are *aware* that the dough feels cool or warm, then it *is.* At the proper temperature, the dough should be so near your own body temperature that you scarcely feel it.

To Dissolve Yeast: Water (or potato cooking water) is best. It should be warm, between 105° F. and 115° F. Test using a candy thermometer or, if you have none, by the old baby's formula way of letting a drop fall on your forearm. It should feel warm, *not* hot.

Combining Dissolved Yeast with Other Liquids: A critical step, for a too hot liquid can kill the yeast, a too cold one slows its growth. The perfect temperature is lukewarm, 90°–95° F.

Nonessential (but Popular) Ingredients of Yeast Breads: Eggs, fruit, nuts, herbs, and spices are added purely for variety. Also popular: Wheat germ, wheat and rye berries (natural whole grains), and sprouted seeds and grains such as alfalfa, beans, chick-peas, flax, lentils, sesame and sunflower seeds, and wheat. These all add extra vitamins to breads (the B group, C, and E primarily). *Note:* Cracked wheat (coarsely ground whole grains) and wheat germ, because of their high fat content and tendency to turn rancid at room temperatures, should be stored, tightly covered, in the refrigerator.

Ways to Mix Yeast Breads

Standard Method: Dissolve yeast in warm (105°–115° F.) water. Scald milk, mix in sugar, salt, and shortening, and cool to lukewarm; combine with yeast, work in flour, and knead until satiny and elastic. Place in a greased, large warm bowl, turn dough to grease all over, cover with cloth (some people prefer a damp cloth, others a dry one), and set in a warm (80°–85° F.) place to rise.

Batter Method: The same as the standard method except that the mixture is much thinner and beaten to blend rather than kneaded.

Rapid-Mix: A modern refinement in which dry yeast is mixed directly with the dry ingredients (see recipe for Rapid-Mix White Bread).

Sponge Method: The old-fashioned way. Dissolve yeast in water and mix in enough flour to make a soft batter. Set in a warm, dry spot overnight or until mixture becomes "spongy." Next day prepare bread following standard method, mixing sponge into lukewarm milk mixture, then proceeding as directed.

Food Processor Method: The best part about using a food processor to mix yeast doughs is that the machine's formidable power and fast-spinning blade actually knead the dough as they mix it. Any yeast dough can be made by processor provided your machine is a heavy-duty one (lightweight models are apt to stall or burn out as they struggle to cope with heavy or sticky yeast doughs). The best blade to use for both mixing and kneading is the stubby plastic dough blade, now standard equipment with many processors. This blade, which looks like a propeller with the ends sawed off, is a whiz at kneading doughs because it has no pointed ends to become entangled in the dough. It does require a few adjustments in mixing methods, however. The sequence, essentially, is the *pastry method of mixing,* i.e. all dry ingredients are combined; half of them are placed in the work bowl of a processor fitted with the plastic dough blade; the fat (butter, margarine, vegetable shortening, etc.) is cut into small pieces and scattered over the surface of the dry ingredients; then the balance of the dry ingredients is dumped on top. A 20-second churning of the motor cuts the fat into the dry ingredients fairly coarsely. At this point the motor should be stopped, the work bowl sides scraped down, then the churning repeated three to four more times until mixture is the texture of coarse meal. Now, with the motor running, the yeast mixture, then other liquid (water, milk, etc.) should be drizzled down the feed tube and buzzed 45–60 seconds nonstop until the dough rolls into a ball and rides up on the central spindle. Churning the dough any longer may overheat it and kill the yeast. Simply remove dough from machine, shape into a ball, and let rise.

If your processor does not have the plastic dough blade, you can use the metal chopping blade both to mix and knead the dough. The method used is much more conventional (see our recipe for Processor Bread). *Note:* Before attempting to make any yeast bread by processor, read the instruction manual accompanying your machine carefully; it more than likely includes bread recipes worked out for your very model.

Kneading

This is the fun part of making bread. The technique isn't difficult, though at first it may seem so. Once you get the rhythm, however, you won't want to stop. Most doughs are kneaded on a lightly floured surface (board or pastry cloth), though extrasoft doughs should be done right in the mixing bowl. *Note:* If you're lucky enough to have one of the heavy-duty electric mixers with a dough hook, you can knead any dough in the bowl—follow manufacturer's directions.

To Knead Average Doughs: Shape dough into a large, round ball on a lightly floured bread board and fold over toward you; push down with heels of hands, give dough a quarter turn, and repeat the folding, pushing, and turning until dough is satiny, smooth, and elastic, usually 8–10 minutes. Use very little flour on your hands or board, only enough to keep dough from sticking.

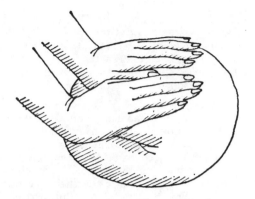

To Knead Very Soft Doughs: Use one hand only; these doughs are supersticky, and if you get both hands involved, you'll be sorry. The technique isn't so much kneading as stretching the dough right in the bowl, pulling it up again and again from the sides of the bowl. Use a large, heavy, shallow bowl, held firmly in place with your free hand. In the beginning, the dough will seem utterly unmanageable, but before long (8–10 minutes) it will begin to blister and to cling to itself, leaving your hand and the bowl relatively clean. It is now ready to rise.

The Rising Period

This is when the yeast goes to work, leavening the bread. Most breads and rolls get two risings, one before shaping, one after. Some may require three risings, others one only. For the first rising, dough should be allowed to double in bulk; for the second, to double or not as individual recipes direct. Successive risings usually take somewhat less time than the first, so watch carefully. *Note:* Braids and other intricately shaped breads should be allowed to rise fully after shaping, otherwise they may split during baking. No shaped bread, however, should more than double; if it overrises, it will be coarse and dry and have poor volume.

Optimum Rising Conditions: A warm (80°–85° F.), dry, and draftless spot. Sometimes a turned-off oven can be used (unless pilot light makes oven too hot); sometimes dough can be set over a bowl of warm water. Never, however, use the top of a refrigerator —too much uneven heat.

If Kitchen Is Cool: Use an extra package of yeast in making the dough; it will not make the bread taste too yeasty.

To Hasten Rising: Use an extra package of yeast in making dough and/or set bowl of dough over a large bowl of warm water, changing water as it cools.

Approximate Rising Time (first rising):

Soft Doughs: 3/4–1 hour to double in bulk

Average Doughs: 1–1½ hours to double in bulk

Heavy Doughs: 1½–2 hours to double in bulk

(Note: Times can be approximate at best, since warmth of kitchen and vitality of yeast both affect speed of rising.)

Letting Yeast Breads Rise (Proof) in a Convection Oven

Some convection ovens are equipped with *defrost/proof temperature settings,* which maintain a constant temperature of about 95° F. If you use this setting for proofing yeast bread doughs, follow your oven manual's instructions to the letter. Always cover the dough with a clean dry cloth, and check it frequently to prevent its overrising.

Letting Yeast Breads Rise (Proof) in a Microwave Oven

It can be done only in microwave ovens with variable power levels and then usually at the lowest setting only (read your instruction manual carefully to determine whether the manufacturer of your particular microwave recommends it as a "proofing oven"; if he does, follow his directions to the letter).

When Is Dough Doubled in Bulk?

Soft Doughs and Batter Breads: Dough or batter should look spongy, puffed, and moist. Press lightly near edge; if imprint remains, dough is doubled in bulk.

Average or Heavy Doughs: Stick two fingers into dough about ½″; if depressions remain, dough is doubled in bulk. If they disappear, give dough another 15–20 minutes to rise, then test again.

Refrigerator Doughs: The cold of a refrigerator does not kill yeast, merely retards or stops its growth. Once out of the refrigera-

tor, the yeast will begin to work again. Refrigerator doughs usually contain more yeast than standard doughs, also slightly more sugar. Any dough, thus, can be refrigerated if you up the amount of yeast by half or, better still, double it and add an extra tablespoon or so of sugar. How long dough will keep in the refrigerator depends both upon the dough and the temperature inside the refrigerator. Most doughs keep well under refrigeration 3–4 days.

Doughs can be refrigerated as soon as they're mixed or after the first rising; they must be well greased and well covered so that they remain moist and pliable.

When you're ready to bake, take dough from refrigerator. If it has not risen at all, let stand at room temperature 2–3 hours until doubled in bulk; then punch down, shape, and proceed as for unrefrigerated doughs. If the dough has had one rising before going into cold storage, shape as soon as you take it from the refrigerator, let rise until light, about 1 hour, then bake.

Punching Dough Down

There's a reason for this. Collapsing raised dough evens the texture by breaking up any large bubbles of gas.

Batters: Stir down with a spoon until batter is its original size.

Doughs: Shove a fist deep into the center of the dough so it collapses like a balloon, then fold edges of dough into center.

Shaping Breads and Rolls

(See diagrams on following pages)

Like sculptor's clay, yeast dough can be fashioned into dozens of shapes, and in European countries it is, especially for holidays and festivals. Some sculpted loaves are museum pieces.

How to Shape Loaves:

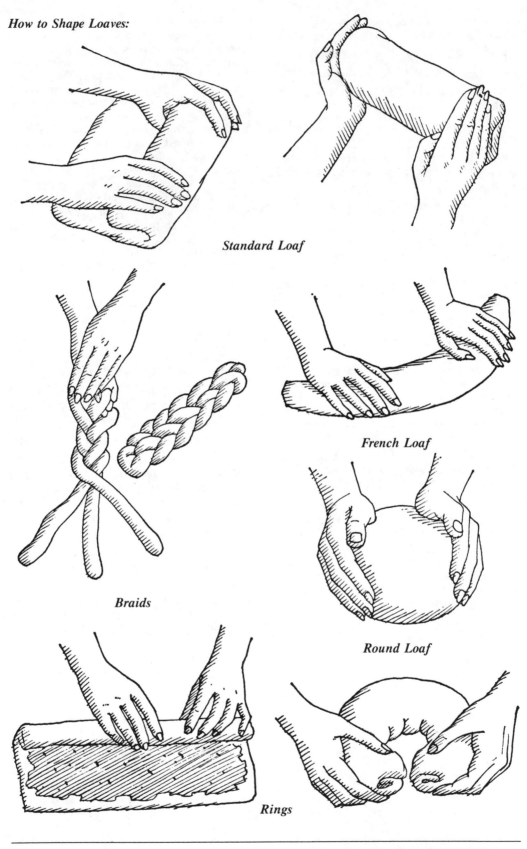

Standard Loaf

French Loaf

Braids

Round Loaf

Rings

BREADS AND SANDWICHES

How to Shape Rolls: For rolls of uniform size, divide dough into equal parts before shaping.

Pan Rolls

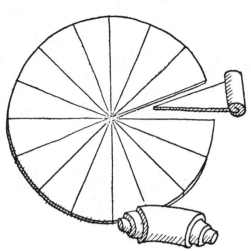

Croissants

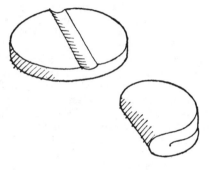

Parker House Rolls

Cloverleaf Rolls
Quick Cloverleaf Rolls

Fan Tans

Danish Pastry

Baking Yeast Breads

(Note: For information on baking breads in convection ovens, see Baking Bread in a Convection Oven earlier in this chapter.) Best temperatures are from 350° F. to 450° F., the lower heats being better for richer, sweeter breads because there's less danger of overbrowning. The first 10–15 minutes of baking—called "oven spring"—is critical; it is the time when the top of the loaf rises quickly, "breaking" or "shredding" around the edges of the pan, giving bread its characteristic shape and light texture. A perfect loaf has an evenly shredded break. If bread hasn't risen sufficiently before baking, or if the oven temperature is too low, there will be poor volume and little break. If the dough has overrisen, the strands of protein will be stretched to breaking during "oven spring" and the loaf will collapse.

To Give Crusts a Professional Finish

For Soft Brown Crusts: Brush bread or rolls before or after baking with melted butter or margarine, milk, or cream.

For Hard Crusts: Brush bread or rolls before baking with lightly beaten egg white or salty water and bake with a shallow pan of water set on rack underneath.

For Shiny Light Brown Crusts: Brush bread or rolls before baking with 1 egg white lightly beaten with 1 tablespoon cold water; or, if you prefer, brush with mixture during last 10–15 minutes of baking.

For Shiny Dark Brown Crusts: Brush bread or rolls before baking with 1 egg or 1 egg yolk lightly beaten with 1 tablespoon water, milk, or cream (the egg yolk will produce the brownest crust).

For Seed Crusts: Brush bread or rolls before baking with 1 egg or egg white lightly beaten with 1 tablespoon water and sprinkle with poppy, caraway, or sesame seeds.

For Sweet Glazes: See individual recipes for sweet breads that follow.

Why Things Sometimes Go Wrong with Yeast Breads

Small Doughy Loaves: Too much or too little heat during rising or too long or too short rising.

Sour or Too Yeasty Bread: Too much heat during rising.

Lopsided Loaves: An unlevel oven or pans touching one another and/or oven walls.

Crumbly Bread: Too long in the rising, especially after shaping.

Coarse or "Holey" Bread: Insufficient kneading; also too long in the rising.

Heavy, Dry Bread: Too much flour.

BASIC WHITE BREAD

2 (9″ × 5″ × 3″) loaves (40 slices)   ¢

If you've never made yeast bread, this is a good recipe to begin with. The recipe isn't difficult and the results are delicious.

½ cup scalded milk
3 tablespoons sugar
2 teaspoons salt
3 tablespoons butter, margarine, or lard
1½ cups warm water (105°–115° F.)
1 packet active dry yeast
6 cups sifted flour (about)
1–2 tablespoons melted butter or margarine
  (optional)

Mix milk, sugar, salt, and butter in a small bowl, stirring until sugar dissolves; cool to lukewarm. Pour warm water into a large warm bowl, sprinkle in yeast, and stir until dissolved. Stir in milk mixture, add 3 cups flour, and beat with a wooden spoon until smooth. Mix in enough additional flour, a little at a time, to make a soft dough (you will have to use your hands toward the end). Mixture will be sticky but should leave sides of bowl reasonably clean. Knead on a lightly floured board until satiny and elastic, 8–10 minutes, adding as little extra flour as possible. Shape into a smooth ball, place in a greased large bowl, turning dough to grease all over. Cover with cloth and let rise in a warm draft-free spot until doubled in bulk, about 1 hour. Punch down, turn onto lightly floured board and let rest 5 minutes; knead lightly 2 minutes. Halve piece of dough and shape* each into a loaf about 7″ long and 4″ wide; place in greased 9″ × 5″ × 3″ loaf pans, cover, and let rise about 1 hour in a warm spot until doubled in bulk. About 15 minutes before baking, preheat oven to 400° F. When loaves have risen, brush tops with melted butter if you like a soft crust. Bake 35–40 minutes until golden brown and loaves sound hollow when tapped. Turn out immediately and cool on wire racks.

NP Slice: 80 C, 4 mg CH, 125 mg S*

VARIATIONS

¢ **Cornell Bread** (a supernutritious bread): Prepare as directed, substituting 6 tablespoons *each* nonfat dry milk powder and soy flour and 2 tablespoons wheat germ for 1 cup of the flour. Mix in at the beginning with the first addition of flour.

NP Slice: 75 C, 4 mg CH, 125 mg S*

¢ **Raisin Bread:** Prepare as directed, increasing butter and sugar each to ¼ cup and mixing 1¼ cups seedless raisins in after first 3 cups of flour.

NP Slice: 95 C, 4 mg CH, 125 mg S*

¢ **Bran Bread:** Prepare as directed, substituting ¼ cup molasses for the sugar and 1 cup bran for 1 cup of the flour.

NP Slice: 75 C, 4 mg CH, 125 mg S*

Herb Bread: Prepare as recipe directs, adding 3 tablespoons minced chives, 2 teaspoons minced parsley, and 2 teaspoons dried oregano to the yeast mixture.

NP Slice: 80 C, 4 mg CH, 125 mg S*

Dill Bread: Prepare as recipe directs, adding 3 tablespoons minced fresh dill or 4 teaspoons dillweed to the yeast mixture.

NP Slice: 80 C, 4 mg CH, 125 mg S*

PROCESSOR BREAD

2 (8″) round loaves

Do not attempt this recipe unless you have a large, heavy-duty food processor.

SPONGE
2 (¼-ounce) packets active dry yeast
2 tablespoons sugar
1 cup sifted unbleached all-purpose flour
¾ cup warm milk (105°–115° F.)

BREAD
1¼ cups warm milk (105°–115° F.)
4 tablespoons unsalted butter
2 tablespoons sugar
1½ teaspoons salt
Sponge (above)
1 cup unsifted gluten flour
4½–5 cups sifted unbleached all-purpose flour
  (about)

For Sponge: Combine yeast, sugar, and flour in medium-size bowl, beat milk in, cover bowl with cloth, set in warm draft-free spot, and let rise until spongy-light, about 25 minutes. For Bread: In processor fitted with the metal chopping blade, combine milk, butter, sugar, and salt by snapping motor on and off six to eight times. As soon as sponge is properly bubbly, stir down and mix in by snapping motor on and off several times. Add gluten flour and mix in by snapping motor on and off six to eight times. Now add all-purpose flour, 1 cup at a time, mixing in by pulsing motor just as you did for gluten flour. *Note:* If you have the plastic dough blade, you can remove metal chopping blade and insert it when you've mixed in about 2 cups all-purpose flour. Add only enough flour to make a soft but *not sticky* dough. Dough will roll into a ball, then ride up on the central spindle. Now run motor 45–60 seconds nonstop—this is the kneading process. *Caution:* Do not knead longer than 60 seconds because you risk overheating the dough and killing the yeast. Remove dough from processor, shape into a ball, place in a greased large bowl, turning dough to grease all over. Cover with cloth and let rise in a warm draft-free spot about 1 hour. Punch dough down, divide in half, and knead each half about 3 minutes on lightly floured board. Shape each half into a ball, place in greased 8″ round layer cake pans, cover and let rise in a warm spot until doubled in bulk, ¾–1 hour. About 15 minutes before loaves have finished rising, preheat oven to 500° F. When loaves are properly risen, bake 15 minutes; reduce heat to 400° F. and bake 15–20 minutes longer until deeply browned and loaves sound hollow when thumped. Remove at once to wire racks to cool. Cut loaves into chunky wedges (each about ⅛ of a loaf) and serve with plenty of butter.

NP Wedge: 235 C, 12 mg CH, 220 mg S*

RAPID-MIX WHITE BREAD

2 (9″ × 5″ × 3″) loaves (40 slices) ¢ ☒

Here is the streamlined way to make yeast bread.

5½–6½ cups unsifted flour
3 tablespoons sugar
2 teaspoons salt
1 packet active dry yeast
1½ cups water
½ cup milk
3 tablespoons butter, margarine, or vegetable
  shortening, at room temperature

Mix 2 cups flour, sugar, salt, and undissolved yeast in large electric mixer bowl. Heat water, milk, and butter over low heat just until warm, not hot. Gradually add to dry ingredients and beat 2 minutes at medium mixer speed. Add about ¾ cup more flour or enough to make a thick batter and beat 2 minutes at high speed, scraping sides of bowl frequently. Stir in enough additional flour to make a soft dough. Knead dough on a lightly floured board until satiny and elastic, 8–10 minutes; place in a greased large bowl, turning to grease all over, cover, and let rise in a warm, draft-free place until doubled in bulk, about 1 hour. Punch dough down, turn onto board, cover, and let rest 15 minutes. Divide in half and shape* into 2 loaves. Place in greased 9″ × 5″ × 3″ pans, cover, and let rise until doubled in bulk. Toward end of rising, preheat oven to 400° F. Bake loaves 25–30 minutes until nicely browned and hollow sounding when tapped. Remove from pans and cool on racks.

NP Slice: 75 C, 3 mg CH, 120 mg S*

VARIATION

¢ **Cool-Rise Loaves:** Mix dough and knead as directed; leave on board, cover, and let rest 20 minutes. Divide in half, shape* into 2 loaves, and place in greased pans. Brush tops with oil, cover with oiled wax paper, then plastic food wrap. Refrigerate 2–24 hours. When ready to bake, preheat oven to 400° F. Uncover loaves and let stand at room temperature 10 minutes; prick any surface bubbles with a greased toothpick. Bake 30–40 minutes until nicely browned and hollow sounding when tapped. Cool as above. Nutritional count same as basic recipe.

FAST-RISING WHITE BREAD

2 (9″ × 5″ × 3″) loaves (40 slices)

The newest way to make bread is with fast-rising yeast, which trims dough rising time by 40–50 per cent. For a superfast bread (less than 1½ hours, start to finish), try the Fast Single-Rising White Bread variation below. Fast-rising yeast produces a denser, chewier bread than conventional active dry yeast.

6 cups sifted unbleached all-purpose flour
  (about)
3 tablespoons sugar
2 teaspoons salt
1 packet fast-rising active dry yeast
3 tablespoons butter, margarine, or lard
1½ cups water
½ cup milk
1–2 tablespoons melted butter or margarine
  (optional)

Combine 5 cups flour, the sugar, salt, and yeast in a large bowl. Heat butter, water, and milk in a saucepan to 125°–130° F. (use a candy or deep fat thermometer to check temperature). Stir hot milk mixture into dry ingredients and blend well. Mix in enough additional flour, a little at a time, to make a soft dough (you'll have to use your hands toward the end). Mixture will be sticky but should leave sides of bowl clean. Knead on a lightly floured board until satiny and elastic, 8–10 minutes. Shape into a ball, place in a greased large bowl, turning dough to grease all over. Cover with cloth and let rise in a warm draft-free spot until doubled in bulk, 30–40 minutes. Punch down, turn onto lightly floured board, and let rest 5 minutes; knead lightly 2 minutes. Halve dough and shape* each piece into a loaf about 7″ long and 4″ wide; place in greased 9″ × 5″ × 3″ loaf pans, cover, and let rise 30–40 minutes in a warm spot until doubled in bulk. About 15 minutes before baking, preheat oven to 400° F. When loaves have risen, brush tops with melted butter if you like a soft crust.

Bake 30–35 minutes until golden brown and loaves sound hollow when tapped. Turn out at once and cool on wire racks.

NP Slice: 80 C, 4 mg CH, 125 mg S*

VARIATIONS

Rapid-Mix, Fast-Rising White Bread: Prepare as recipe directs for Rapid-Mix White Bread, but heat water, milk, and butter to 125°–130° F.

NP Slice: 80 C, 4 mg CH, 125 mg S*

Fast Single-Rising White Bread: Prepare and knead Fast-Rising White Bread dough as directed, then let dough rest, covered with cloth, on counter 10 minutes. Shape* into 2 loaves, place in loaf pans, cover and let rise 30–40 minutes in a warm draft-free spot until doubled in bulk. Preheat oven and bake loaves as recipe directs.

NP Slice: 80 C, 4 mg CH, 125 mg S*

FAST-RISING CRACKED WHEAT BREAD

2 (9″ × 5″ × 3″) loaves (40 slices)

This wholesome bread needs very little kneading. We like the chewiness of *unsoaked, uncooked* cracked wheat, but if you prefer softer texture, reduce amount of cracked wheat to 1 cup, then soak or cook it according to package directions (it will double in volume).

4 cups unsifted whole wheat flour
2 cups cracked wheat
1 cup wheat germ
2 cups sifted all-purpose flour
2 teaspoons salt
2 tablespoons light brown sugar
2 packets fast-rising active dry yeast
1 cup milk
2 cups water
1 tablespoon butter, margarine, or vegetable shortening
¼ cup molasses

Mix whole wheat flour, cracked wheat, wheat germ, 1 cup of the all-purpose flour, salt, brown sugar, and yeast in a large bowl. Heat remaining ingredients (except for flour) in a saucepan to 125°–130° F., using a candy or deep fat thermometer to check the temperature. Blend hot milk mixture into dry ingredients. Turn dough onto a lightly floured board (dough will be sticky), and knead in remaining all-purpose flour, then continue kneading 2–3 minutes. Place dough in a greased large bowl, turning dough to grease all over. Cover with cloth and let rise in a warm draft-free spot until doubled in bulk, 30–40 minutes. Punch dough down and knead 1–2 minutes on a lightly floured board. Divide dough in half and shape* each into a loaf about 7″ × 4″; place in greased 9″ × 5″ × 3″ loaf pans, cover, and let rise 30–40 minutes in a warm spot until doubled in bulk. About 15 minutes before you're ready to bake, preheat oven to 400° F. When loaves have risen, bake 20 minutes; reduce oven to 375° F. and bake 20–25 minutes longer or until well browned and hollow sounding when tapped. Turn loaves out immediately and cool on wire racks.

NP Slice: 120 C, 2 mg CH, 120 mg S*

Some Tips for Making Other Breads with Fast-Rising Yeast

• If a recipe calls for water alone (as opposed to a water-milk combination), and no thermometer is available, you can safely use your hottest tap water (it will be about 130° F.).
• Whenever a recipe calls for chocolate, honey, or molasses, heat it along with the liquids.
• Whenever a recipe uses eggs, beat them lightly, then add *after* combining the hot liquid and dry ingredients.
• Whenever recipes call for herbs, spices, nuts, dried or candied fruits, even mashed potatoes, combine them with the dry ingredients.
• When mixing fast-rising yeast breads by processor, combine the yeast with the dry ingredients in the work bowl; with motor running, add first *warm (105°–115° F.) water,* then any remaining liquids *(these should be at room temperature, not at 125°–130° F.).* Hot liquids will merely cook the starch in the flour and gum up the works in a food processor.

POTATO BREAD

2 (9" × 5" × 3") loaves (40 slices) ¢

Potato gives the bread extra flavor and softer texture.

1/2 cup scalded milk
1/4 cup vegetable shortening, butter, or
  margarine
2 tablespoons sugar
2 teaspoons salt
1/3 cup warm water (105°–115° F.)
2 packets active dry yeast
1 1/2 cups lukewarm, riced, cooked, unseasoned
  potatoes
1/2 cup lukewarm potato cooking water
5 1/4–5 1/2 cups sifted flour

Mix milk, shortening, sugar, and salt; cool to lukewarm. Pour water into a warm large bowl, sprinkle in yeast, and stir to dissolve. Add cooled mixture, potatoes, potato cooking water, and about 2 cups flour; beat until smooth. Mix in enough remaining flour to make a firm dough that leaves the sides of bowl clean. Knead on a lightly floured board until elastic, about 10 minutes. Shape into a ball, place in a greased bowl, turning to grease all over. Cover with cloth and let rise in a warm, draft-free place until double in bulk, about 1 hour. Punch down, cover, and let rise again. Punch down once more and knead lightly 1–2 minutes. Divide dough in half, shape* into 2 loaves, and place in greased 9" × 5" × 3" loaf pans. Cover and let rise until almost doubled in bulk. Toward end of rising, preheat oven to 400° F. Bake loaves 10 minutes, reduce heat to 350° F., and bake 30–35 minutes longer until well browned and hollow sounding when tapped. Turn out and cool upright on a wire rack before cutting.

NP Slice: 75 C, 1 mg CH, 115 mg S*

GLUTEN BREAD

9" × 5" × 3" loaf (20 slices)

Because of its chewiness and nutty flavor, gluten bread makes superlative toast. Double this recipe, if you like, but freeze the extra loaf. Gluten bread stales rapidly at room temperature.

1/2 cup scalded milk
1 teaspoon salt
1 1/2 teaspoons sugar
1 tablespoon butter, margarine, or vegetable
  shortening
1 1/2 teaspoons active dry yeast (1/2 packet)
1 cup warm water (105°–115° F.)
3 1/4 cups sifted gluten flour (about)

1 tablespoon melted butter, margarine, or
  vegetable shortening (optional)

Combine milk, salt, sugar, and butter in a small bowl, stirring until sugar dissolves; cool to lukewarm. Sprinkle yeast over warm water in a large bowl, and mix well. Stir cooled mixture into yeast, then add 2 cups flour, and beat well. Mix in enough remaining flour to form a moderately firm dough. Knead until elastic on a board lightly floured with gluten flour—about 8–10 minutes. Place dough in a greased large bowl, turning to grease all over. Cover with cloth and let rise until doubled in bulk, about 1 hour. Punch dough down, knead lightly 1–2 minutes, shape* into a loaf about 7" long and 4" wide, place in a greased 9" × 5" × 3" loaf pan, cover, and let rise about 1 hour in a warm spot until doubled in bulk. About 15 minutes before baking, preheat oven to 350° F. When loaf has risen, brush top with melted butter if you like a soft crust. Bake about 45 minutes until golden brown and loaf sounds hollow when tapped. Turn out immediately and cool on a wire rack.

NP Slice: 100 C, 4 mg CH, 125 mg S*

SALLY LUNN

6–8 servings

A high-rising Southern bread that is almost as rich as sponge cake.

2 packets active dry yeast
1/3 cup warm water (105°–115° F.)
2/3 cup milk, scalded and cooled to lukewarm
1/2 cup butter (no substitute), softened to room
  temperature
1/3 cup sugar
4 eggs
1 teaspoon salt
4 cups sifted flour

Sprinkle yeast over warm water and stir lightly to mix; let stand 5 minutes, then mix in milk and set aside. Cream butter until light, add sugar, and continue creaming until fluffy. Add eggs, one at a time, beating well after each addition; mix in salt. Add flour alternately with yeast mixture, beginning and ending with flour. Beat vigorously with a wooden spoon or in a heavy-duty electric mixer equipped with the dough hook until smooth and elastic. Place in a well-buttered bowl, cover with cloth, and let rise in a warm, draft-free place until doubled in bulk, about 1 hour. Beat dough hard with a wooden spoon 100 strokes. Transfer to a buttered and floured 3-quart crown mold or

Bundt pan, cover, and let rise in a warm place 25–30 minutes until doubled in bulk. Meanwhile, preheat oven to 350° F. When dough has risen, bake about ½ hour until well browned and hollow sounding when tapped. Unmold, cut into thick wedges, and serve steaming hot with lots of butter.

NPS (6–8): 515–400 C, 225–170 mg CH, 570–435 mg S*

SOUR DOUGH BREAD

2 round or long, narrow loaves (40 slices) ¢

For those who *truly* want to make bread "from scratch."

SOUR DOUGH STARTER
1 cup sifted flour
1 cup cold water
1 tablespoon sugar

BREAD
5 cups sifted flour
1 tablespoon salt
1 tablespoon sugar
1 cup warm water (105°–115° F.)
1 packet active dry yeast
1 cup sour dough starter

Prepare starter at least 2 days before you plan to use it. Mix flour and water until smooth in a 1-quart bowl or glass jar; add sugar and stir until dissolved. Cover loosely and let stand in a warm (about 80° F.), draft-free place until fermented (mixture will be bubbly and smell sour); stir from time to time during fermentation. For the bread, sift flour with salt and sugar and set aside. Pour warm water into a warm large bowl, sprinkle in yeast, and stir to dissolve. Mix in starter, then flour, a little at a time, working last bit in with your hands. Knead on a lightly floured board until elastic, 8–10 minutes. Shape into a ball, place in a greased bowl, and turn to grease all over. Cover with cloth and let rise in a warm, draft-free place until doubled in bulk, about 1 hour. Punch down, knead lightly 1–2 minutes, and divide in half. Shape* into 2 round or long, tapering loaves and arrange 3″ apart on a lightly floured baking sheet. Cover and let rise until nearly doubled in bulk. Toward end of rising, preheat oven to 400° F. Brush tops of loaves with cold water and, if you like, make a diagonal ¼″ deep slash the length of loaf

with a sharp knife. Bake with a shallow pan half full of hot water on shelf below loaves 35–40 minutes until well browned and hollow sounding when tapped. Cool on wire racks before cutting.

NP Slice: 65 C, 0 mg CH, 165 mg S*

PAIN ORDINAIRE (CRUSTY FRENCH BREAD)

2 (12″) loaves (40 slices) ¢

1 packet active dry yeast
1¾ cups warm water (105°–115° F.)
2 teaspoons salt
5¼–5½ cups sifted flour
1 egg white mixed with 1 tablespoon cold water (glaze)

Sprinkle yeast over warm water and stir to dissolve. Mix salt with flour, then add to yeast mixture, a little at a time, working in enough at the end to form a fairly stiff dough. Knead on a lightly floured board until elastic, about 8 minutes. Shape into a ball, place in a greased bowl, turning to grease all over. Cover with cloth and let rise in a warm, draft-free place until doubled in bulk, about 1 hour. Punch dough down, knead lightly 1–2 minutes, and divide in half. Shape* into 2 loaves about 12″ long and 4″ wide, tapering ends; arrange 3″ apart on a baking sheet sprinkled with corn meal. Cover and let rise until doubled in bulk. Toward end of rising, preheat oven to 425° F. Brush loaves with glaze and make 3 diagonal slashes about ¼″ deep across each with a sharp knife. Bake ½ hour with a shallow baking pan half full of water on rack underneath bread, reduce heat to 350° F., and bake 20–25 minutes longer until golden brown and hollow sounding when tapped. Cool on racks before cutting.

NP Slice: 55 C, 0 mg CH, 110 mg S*

VARIATION

Hard Rolls *(2 dozen):* Prepare dough and let rise as directed; punch down, knead 1 minute, and shape into 1½″ balls. Place 2″ apart on baking sheets sprinkled with corn meal. Cover and let rise until doubled in bulk, about ½ hour. Brush with glaze and slash each roll across the top; bake 15–20 minutes at 425° F. Cool before serving.

NP Roll: 95 C, 0 mg CH, 185 mg S*

WHOLE WHEAT BREAD

2 (9" × 5" × 3") loaves (40 slices)   ¢

This hearty, wholesome bread needs no kneading and toasts beautifully.

1 cup milk
1½ cups cold water
¼ cup molasses
2 tablespoons light brown sugar
1 tablespoon butter or margarine
1 tablespoon salt
½ cup warm water (105°–115° F.)
2 packets active dry yeast
4 cups sifted all-purpose flour
5 cups unsifted whole wheat flour
2 tablespoons milk (glaze)

Bring milk and cold water to a boil in a small saucepan. Off heat, mix in molasses, sugar, butter, and salt; cool to lukewarm. Place warm water in a warm large mixing bowl and sprinkle in yeast. Stir cooled mixture into yeast, then beat in all-purpose flour, 1 cup at a time. Finally, mix in whole wheat flour, 1 cup at a time. Place dough in a greased large bowl, cover with cloth, and let rise about 1 hour in a warm draft-free place until doubled in bulk. Punch dough down and stir briefly (it will be stiff). Divide dough in half and pat firmly into 2 well-greased 9" × 5" × 3" loaf pans, rounding tops a little; brush tops with milk to glaze. Cover and let rise 30–40 minutes until almost doubled in bulk. About 15 minutes before you're ready to bake, preheat oven to 400° F. When loaves are risen, bake 20 minutes, reduce oven to 375° F., and bake 45–50 minutes longer or until richly browned and hollow sounding when tapped. Turn loaves out immediately and cool on wire racks.

NP Slice: 105 C, 2 mg CH, 170 mg S*

VARIATIONS

Nutritional counts about the same as basic recipe.

Wheat Berry and Honey Bread: Before beginning recipe, soak ½ cup wheat berries (obtainable in most health food stores) in 1 cup warm water 4 hours. Drain berries, save and measure soaking water, and add enough cold water to equal the 1½ cups called for in the recipe above. Now prepare dough as recipe directs, using 6 tablespoons honey in place of the molasses and brown sugar; reduce all-purpose flour to 2 cups, add 1 cup wheat germ, the drained wheat berries, and the whole wheat flour called for. Bake loaves at 400° F. as directed, then reduce oven to 375° F. and bake 25–30 minutes longer.

Sprouted Whole Wheat Bread: The first step is to sprout the wheat berries, which will take several days (see below). Once berries are sprouted, prepare the Wheat Berry and Honey Bread variation above but substitute 1 cup sprouted wheat berries for the soaked wheat berries.

How to Sprout Wheat Berries *(About 1 cup sprouted wheat berries):* Place ⅓ cup washed wheat berries in a 1-quart jar, cover with warm water, and soak 4 hours (no need to cover the jar). Drain (save soaking liquid for soups or stews), then cover jar with cheesecloth, securing it tightly with string or a rubber band. Tip jar from side to side so seeds stick to the sides; set jar in a warm dark place (80° F. is ideal). The next day and twice a day thereafter, add ½ cup warm water to the jar, swirling it around, then pour off the excess through the cheesecloth. The idea is to keep the berries moist, not wet. Sprouts should develop in 2–4 days, depending upon atmospheric conditions. When the sprouts are about the same length as the berries *and before rootlets appear,* the sprouted berries are ready to use. Wash them in a sieve, drain well, then store tightly covered in the refrigerator. Use within 4–5 days in yeast breads and stuffings. *Note:* You can put the sprouted berries through the fine blade of a meat grinder before using if you like more finely textured breads.

RYE BREAD

2 (7") round loaves (40 slices)   ¢

Dark, light, and medium rye flours are all available; use the medium (it's the most widely available) unless you want a particularly dark or light bread.

2 tablespoons dark brown sugar
2 tablespoons shortening
1 tablespoon salt
1 cup boiling water
½ cup cold water
½ cup warm water (105°–115° F.)
1 packet active dry yeast
2½ cups unsifted rye flour
3¼–3½ cups sifted all-purpose flour

Mix sugar, shortening, salt, and boiling water in a small bowl, add cold water, and cool to lukewarm. Pour warm water into a warm large bowl, sprinkle in yeast, and stir to dissolve. Add cooled mixture and rye flour and beat well. Mix in 3 cups all-purpose flour, a little at a time, then work in enough additional flour to make a fairly stiff dough that leaves sides of bowl reasonably clean. Knead until fairly smooth and elastic, 8–10 minutes, on a lightly floured board, adding as little extra flour as possible. Shape into a ball, place in a well-greased 3-quart bowl, and turn dough to grease all over. Cover with cloth and let rise in a warm, draft-free place until doubled in bulk, 1½–2 hours. Punch down, knead lightly 1–2 minutes, and divide dough in half. Shape* each into a round loaf about 5½" across and place 3" apart on a baking sheet sprinkled with corn meal. Cover and let rise until doubled in bulk, about 1½ hours. Toward end of rising, preheat oven to 400° F. Bake loaves 30–35 minutes until brown and hollow sounding when tapped. Cool on a wire rack before cutting.

NP Slice: 60 C, 0 mg CH, 165 mg S*

VARIATIONS

¢ **Pumpernickel Bread:** Prepare as directed, substituting ⅓ cup dark molasses for the sugar, increasing shortening to ⅓ cup, and omitting cold water. Increase rye flour to 3 cups, reduce white flour to 1⅔ cups, and add 1 cup whole wheat flour. Proceed as directed, allowing extra rising time because the dough is heavier.

NP Slice: 70 C, 0 mg CH, 170 mg S*

¢ **Swedish Limpa Bread:** Prepare as directed, increasing brown sugar to ⅓ cup and adding ⅓ cup dark molasses, 2 teaspoons each anise seeds and finely grated lemon or orange rind to shortening, salt, and boiling water; omit cold water. Otherwise, proceed as directed. For a soft crust, brush loaves with milk or melted butter before baking.

NP Slice: 70 C, 0 mg CH, 170 mg S*

OATMEAL BREAD

2 (9" × 5" × 3") loaves (40 slices) ¢

If you want a lighter, sweeter bread, use a ½ and ½ mixture of molasses and honey or molasses and maple syrup instead of molasses alone.

1 cup scalded milk
2 tablespoons vegetable shortening or margarine
2 teaspoons salt
1 cup molasses or a ½ and ½ mixture of molasses and honey or molasses and maple syrup
1 cup cold water
¼ cup warm water (105°–115° F.)
1 packet active dry yeast
1½ cups uncooked oatmeal
6 cups sifted flour

Mix milk, shortening, salt, and molasses, stir in cold water, and cool to lukewarm. Pour warm water into a warm very large bowl, sprinkle in yeast, and stir to dissolve. Add cooled mixture, oatmeal, and 4 cups flour and mix well. Mix in remaining flour and knead on a lightly floured board until elastic, 5–8 minutes. Shape into a ball, place in a greased bowl, turning to grease all over. Cover with cloth and let rise in a warm, draft-free place until doubled in bulk, about 1½ hours. Punch down and knead lightly 1–2 minutes. Divide dough in half, shape* into 2 loaves, and place in greased 9" × 5" × 3" loaf pans. Cover and let rise until almost doubled in bulk. Toward end of rising, preheat oven to 375° F. Bake loaves 40 minutes until browned and hollow sounding when tapped. Turn out and cool upright on a wire rack before cutting.

NP Slice: 105 C, 1 mg CH, 115 mg S*

ANADAMA BREAD

9" × 5" × 3" loaf (20 slices) ¢

Anadama ("Anna, damn her") was a fisherman's attempt to make something "different" out of his lazy wife Anna's same old dinner (corn meal and molasses).

½ cup corn meal
3 tablespoons vegetable shortening
¼ cup molasses
2 teaspoons salt
¾ cup boiling water
¼ cup warm water (105°–115° F.)
1 packet active dry yeast
1 egg, lightly beaten
3 cups sifted flour

Stir corn meal, shortening, molasses, salt, and boiling water in a small bowl until shortening melts; cool to lukewarm. Pour warm water into a warm large bowl, sprinkle in yeast, and stir to dissolve. Add egg, corn meal mixture, and about half the flour. Beat 300 strokes by hand or 2 minutes at medium electric mixer speed. Stir in remaining flour, using hands at the end to mix well. Spoon into a well-greased 9" × 5" × 3" loaf pan; flour hands and smooth surface. Cover and let rise in a warm, draft-free place until dough is within 1" of top of pan. Toward end of rising, preheat oven to 375° F. If you like, sprinkle top of loaf with a little corn meal; bake 30–35 minutes until well browned and hollow sounding when tapped. Turn loaf out on a wire rack and cool before cutting.

NP Slice: 105 C, 14 mg CH, 225 mg S*

¢ **Easy Oatmeal Bread:** Substitute 1/2 cup uncooked oatmeal for corn meal, reduce flour to 2 3/4 cups, and proceed as recipe directs.

NP Slice: 100 C, 14 mg CH, 225 mg S*

CHEESE BREAD

2 (9" × 5" × 3") loaves (40 slices)

Especially good toasted.

1 1/2 cups milk
2 cups finely grated sharp Cheddar cheese
2 tablespoons vegetable shortening
2 tablespoons sugar
2 teaspoons salt
1/3 cup warm water (105°–115° F.)
2 packets active dry yeast
1 egg, lightly beaten
6 1/2 cups sifted flour (about)
1 egg yolk lightly beaten with 1 tablespoon cold water (glaze)
1–2 teaspoons caraway, poppy, or toasted sesame seeds (optional)

Heat milk, cheese, shortening, sugar, and salt over moderate heat, stirring, until cheese is melted; cool to lukewarm. Pour warm water into a warm large bowl, sprinkle in yeast, and stir to dissolve. Add cooled mixture, egg, and about 3 cups flour; beat until smooth. Mix in enough remaining flour to make a firm dough. Knead on a lightly floured board until elastic, 5–8 minutes. Shape into a ball, turn in a greased bowl to grease all over, cover with cloth, and let rise in a warm, draft-free place until doubled in bulk, about 1 hour. Punch down and knead 1–2 minutes; divide dough in half, shape* into 2 loaves, and place in greased 9" × 5" × 3" loaf pans. Cover and let rise until nearly doubled in bulk, about 1 hour. Toward end of rising, preheat oven to 375° F. Brush loaves with glaze and, if you like, sprinkle with seeds. Bake 30–40 minutes until well browned and hollow sounding when tapped. Turn out and cool upright on wire rack before cutting.

NP Slice: 110 C, 20 mg CH, 150 mg S*

VARIATIONS

Cheese-Herb Bread: Prepare as directed, adding 3/4 teaspoon each marjoram and thyme or 1 1/2 teaspoons oregano to yeast mixture.

NP Slice: 110 C, 20 mg CH, 150 mg S*

Cheese-Onion Bread: Prepare as directed, adding 1/4 cup minced onion to scalded milk.

NP Slice: 110 C, 20 mg CH, 150 mg S*

Pimiento-Cheese Bread: Prepare as directed but, when shaping loaves, roll into rectangles about 14" × 9", sprinkle evenly with 1/4–1/3 cup minced pimiento, and roll up from the short side. Bake as directed.

NP Slice: 110 C, 20 mg CH, 150 mg S*

PIZZA

2 (14") pies

PIZZA DOUGH
1/4 cup warm water (105°–115° F.)
1 packet active dry yeast
4 1/4 cups sifted flour
1 teaspoon salt
1 teaspoon sugar
1 1/4 cups lukewarm water
2 tablespoons olive or other cooking oil

PIZZA SAUCE
1 cup tomato sauce
1 (6-ounce) can tomato paste
1 tablespoon olive or other cooking oil
2 tablespoons water
1 clove garlic, peeled and crushed
1 teaspoon oregano
1/2 teaspoon salt
1/2 teaspoon sugar
1/8 teaspoon crushed dried hot red chili peppers

TOPPING
3/4 pound mozzarella cheese, thinly sliced or coarsely grated
1/3–1/2 cup grated Parmesan cheese
1 teaspoon oregano

Pour warm water into a warm large bowl, sprinkle in yeast, and stir to dissolve. Mix in 2 cups flour, the salt and sugar. Add lukewarm water and oil and beat until smooth. Mix in remaining flour and knead on a lightly floured board until elastic. Shape into a ball, turn in greased bowl to grease all over, cover, and let rise in a warm, draft-free place until doubled in bulk, about 1 hour. Meanwhile, warm all sauce ingredients together in a covered saucepan over lowest heat, stirring now and then, 20 minutes; keep warm until ready to use. Preheat oven to 450° F. Punch dough down, divide in half, refrigerate 1 piece, and roll the other into a circle about 15" across. Place on a greased 14" pizza pan, roll edges under even with rim, and brush with a little oil. Spread half the sauce evenly over dough, sprinkle with half the mozzarella, Parmesan, and oregano.

Prepare remaining dough the same way. (*Note:* Dough may be rolled to fit a 15½″ × 12″ baking sheet if a pizza pan is unavailable.) Bake, uncovered, 20–25 minutes until edges are well browned and cheese bubbly. Cut each pie in 6 wedges and serve hot. Pass extra Parmesan, oregano, and chili peppers if you like.

NP Wedge: 290 C, 25 mg CH, 635 mg S*

V A R I A T I O N S

The ways to vary pizza topping are as endless as your imagination. Some favorites (to be added between the mozzarella and Parmesan): sliced *fully cooked* sweet or hot Italian sausages; sliced sautéed mushrooms; lightly sautéed strips of green and/or red peppers; lightly sautéed onion rings; drained anchovies; sliced green or ripe olives or any combination of these.

▨ **Quick Pizza** *(One 14″ pie):* Prepare 1 (13¼-ounce) package hot-roll mix by package directions but increase water to 1 cup and omit egg. *Do not let rise.* Roll out to fit a 14″ pizza pan and brush with oil. Halve sauce recipe above and mix, substituting ½ teaspoon garlic powder for the garlic; do not heat. Spread on dough and top with half the cheeses and oregano called for. Bake as directed.

NP Wedge: 375 C, 25 mg CH, 640 mg S*

▨ **Individual Muffin Pizzas** *(6 pizzas):* Split and toast 3 English muffins; arrange on an ungreased baking sheet. Spread with 1 cup meatless spaghetti sauce. Top with thin slices of mozzarella, sprinkle with Parmesan and oregano. Broil 4″–5″ from the heat about 3 minutes until bubbly.

NP Pizza: 175 C, 25 mg CH, 440 mg S*

RICH DINNER ROLLS

2½ dozen rolls ¢

1 cup scalded milk
¼ cup sugar
1 teaspoon salt
¼ cup butter or margarine
½ cup warm water (105°–115° F.)
2 packets active dry yeast
2 eggs, lightly beaten
5½ cups sifted flour (about)
1–2 tablespoons melted butter or margarine

Mix milk, sugar, salt, and butter in a small bowl, stirring until sugar dissolves; cool to lukewarm. Pour warm water into a warm large bowl, sprinkle in yeast, and stir until dissolved. Stir in milk mixture, eggs, and 2 cups flour, beating with a wooden spoon until smooth. Mix in enough additional flour, a little at a time, to make a soft dough (it will be sticky but should leave sides of bowl clean). Knead on a lightly floured board 8–10 minutes until smooth and elastic; shape into a ball, place in a greased large bowl, turning to grease all over. Cover with cloth and let rise in a warm, draft-free spot until doubled in bulk, 30–40 minutes. Punch dough down. Shape* as desired, place rolls in greased pans, cover, and let rise about ½ hour until doubled in bulk. About 15 minutes before baking, preheat oven to 375° F. Brush tops of rolls with melted butter and bake 15–20 minutes until lightly browned and hollow sounding when tapped. Serve hot.

NP Roll: 110 C, 25 mg CH, 100 mg S*

BUTTERMILK ROLLS

2 dozen rolls ¢

These are unusually light and feathery.

3 cups sifted flour
1 tablespoon sugar
1 teaspoon salt
¼ teaspoon baking soda
¼ cup chilled lard, vegetable shortening, butter, or margarine
1 packet active dry yeast
¼ cup warm water (105°–115° F.)
⅔ cup lukewarm buttermilk
1–2 tablespoons melted butter or margarine

Sift dry ingredients into a bowl and cut in lard until the texture of coarse meal. Sprinkle yeast over warm water and stir to dissolve; add buttermilk, pour into a well in flour mixture, and stir until dough comes together. Knead on a lightly floured board until elastic, about 5 minutes. Let rise in a buttered bowl, covered with cloth, in a warm, draft-free spot about ¾ hour until doubled in bulk. Punch dough down, turn onto board, and knead 1 minute. Shape into 1½″ balls, place 2″ apart on greased baking sheets, cover, and let rise until doubled, about ½ hour. Meanwhile, preheat oven to 425° F. Brush rolls with melted butter and bake 15–20 minutes until browned.

NP Roll: 80 C, 4 mg CH, 110 mg S*

V A R I A T I O N

¢ **Crusty Buttermilk Rolls:** After brushing rolls with butter, sprinkle with corn meal; bake as directed.

NP Roll: 80 C, 4 mg CH, 110 mg S*

POTATO PUFF ROLLS

3 dozen rolls

People rave about these.

3/4 cup scalded milk
3 tablespoons vegetable shortening
2 tablespoons sugar
2 teaspoons salt
1/4 cup warm water (105°–115° F.)
1 packet active dry yeast
1 egg, lightly beaten
1 cup lukewarm, unseasoned mashed potatoes
4 cups sifted flour
2 tablespoons melted butter or margarine

Mix milk, shortening, sugar, and salt and cool to lukewarm. Pour warm water into a warm mixing bowl, sprinkle in yeast and stir to dissolve. Add cooled mixture, egg, potatoes, and 2 cups flour and beat well. Mix in remaining flour and knead on a lightly floured board until satiny and elastic. Shape into a ball, place in a greased bowl, turning to grease all over. Cover and chill in refrigerator at least 3 hours or overnight. Knead dough lightly 1 minute, then divide in half. Roll 1 portion on lightly floured board to a thickness of 1/2″ and cut in rounds with a 2″ cutter. Brush tops lightly with butter and fold in half, pressing edges together lightly. Arrange rolls 1″ apart on greased baking sheets. Repeat with remaining dough. Cover rolls and let rise in a warm, draft-free place until almost doubled in bulk, about 1/2 hour. Meanwhile preheat oven to 400° F. Bake rolls 15–17 minutes until golden brown. Serve hot.

NP Roll: 75 C, 10 mg CH, 150 mg S*

CROISSANTS

2–2 1/2 dozen rolls

3/4 cup scalded milk
2 teaspoons sugar
1 teaspoon salt
1/4 cup warm water (105°–115° F.)
1 packet active dry yeast
2 1/4–2 1/2 cups sifted flour
1/2 cup cold butter (no substitute)
1 egg yolk lightly beaten with 1 tablespoon cold water (glaze)

Mix milk, sugar, and salt and cool to lukewarm. Pour warm water into a warm mixing bowl, sprinkle in yeast, and stir to dissolve. Add cooled mixture, then mix in flour, a little at a time, to make a soft dough. Knead on a lightly floured board until satiny and elastic, about 5 minutes. Shape into a ball, place in a greased bowl, turning to grease all

over. Cover with cloth and let rise in a warm, draft-free place until doubled in bulk, about 1 hour. Punch down, wrap in wax paper, and chill 20 minutes. Meanwhile work butter with your hands until pliable but still cold. Roll dough on a lightly floured board into a rectangle about 12″ × 16″. Dot half the butter over two thirds of dough and fold letter style,

bringing unbuttered third in first. Pinch all edges to seal. Give dough a quarter turn and roll quickly with short, even strokes into a 12″ × 16″ rectangle. Butter the same way, fold, and roll again using remaining butter. Roll and fold twice more (without adding any more butter), then wrap and chill 2–3 hours or overnight. (*Note:* If kitchen is warm, chill dough as needed between rollings.) Halve dough, and keep 1 piece cold while shaping the other: Roll into a 15″ circle and cut into 12 or 16 equal-size wedges.

Croissants

Roll up loosely from the wide side and place, triangle points down, 2″ apart on ungreased baking sheets. Cover and let rise until almost doubled in size, about 1 hour. Toward end of rising, preheat oven to 375° F. Brush rolls with glaze and bake 15–20 minutes until well browned. Cool slightly before serving or serve at room temperature.

NP Croissant (24–30): 80–65 C, 25–20 mg CH, 135–110 mg S*

NO-KNEAD REFRIGERATOR ROLLS

About 4 dozen rolls ¢

1 cup boiling water
1/4 cup butter or margarine
1/2 cup sugar
2 teaspoons salt
1 cup warm water (105°–115° F.)
2 packets active dry yeast
1 egg, lightly beaten
7 cups sifted flour (about)
1 egg yolk lightly beaten with 1 tablespoon cold water (glaze)

Mix boiling water, butter, sugar, and salt in a small bowl, stirring until sugar dissolves; cool to lukewarm. Pour warm water into a warm large bowl, sprinkle in yeast, and stir until dissolved. Stir in cooled mixture, egg, and about 4 cups flour; beat well with a wooden spoon until smooth. Mix in enough of the remaining flour to make a fairly soft dough, using your hands toward the end. Place dough in a greased large bowl, turn to grease all over, cover with wax paper, then a damp cloth. Refrigerate until doubled in bulk or until 2 hours before needed. *(Note:* Dough will keep 4–5 days in refrigerator and should be punched down occasionally as it rises; keep covering cloth damp.) To use, punch dough down and cut off amount needed. Shape* as desired, place rolls in greased pans, spacing 2″ apart, cover with a dry cloth, and let rise in a warm, draft-free spot 1 1/2–2 hours (size of rolls and coldness of dough will determine). About 15 minutes before baking, preheat oven to 400° F. Brush tops of rolls with glaze and bake about 15 minutes until lightly browned and hollow sounding when tapped. Serve warm.

NP Roll: 80 C, 15 mg CH, 105 mg S*

PITA (POCKET) BREAD

1 dozen pockets

Popular throughout the Middle East, this bread is round and hollow like an empty pocket. It's soft outside, chewy inside, the perfect receptacle for everything from shish kebabs to salads. Cut into triangles, pita can be used to dip up those other two Middle Eastern favorites—Baba Ganouj and Hummus.

1 packet active dry yeast
1 1/4 cups warm water (105°–115° F.)
4 cups sifted flour
1 teaspoon sugar
1/2 teaspoon salt

Sprinkle yeast over warm water and stir to dissolve. Mix flour, sugar, and salt, then add yeast mixture, mixing well to form a fairly stiff dough. Knead on a lightly floured board until elastic, about 10 minutes. Shape into a ball, place in a greased bowl, turning to grease all over. Cover with cloth and let rise in a warm draft-free place until doubled in bulk, about 1 hour. Punch dough down, knead lightly 1 minute, and divide into 12 pieces of equal size. Shape each piece into a ball, then roll, one at a time, into a 5″ circle with a lightly floured rolling pin on a lightly floured board. Transfer to a lightly floured cloth or trays, dust with flour, cover with cloth, and let rise while you preheat the oven and baking sheet. Preheat oven to 450° F., then slide a *heavy* baking sheet onto middle oven rack and heat a full 10 minutes. When ready to bake, remove baking sheet from oven, rub lightly with oiled paper toweling, and arrange 2 pita rounds 2″ apart on sheet. Bake on middle oven rack 1 1/2–2 minutes until puffed, turn with pancake turner, and bake about 1 1/2 minutes on the flip side. *Note:* Each side of pita bread should be barely touched with brown, indeed, in the Middle East, bakers sprinkle the pita dough with cold water before baking so that the bread does not brown at all. If you brown the pita bread, it will crispen on cooling instead of remaining soft and pliable. Cool first batch of pita on a wire rack while you bake the balance. Preheat baking sheet 2 full minutes before baking each new batch of pita (no need to reoil it). When all pita are baked, serve as is or tear in half and serve stuffed with a crispy green salad or shish kebab. To reheat before stuffing: Wrap pita in aluminum foil and warm 3–4 minutes in a 350° F. oven.

NP Pita: 140 C, 0 mg CH, 90 mg S*

VARIATION

Whole Wheat Pita Bread: Prepare as directed, but substitute 4 cups unsifted whole wheat flour for the all-purpose flour and increase warm water to 1 1/2 cups.

NP Pita: 135 C, 0 mg CH, 90 mg S*

BASIC SWEET DOUGH

2 (10") rings or 2 (9" × 5" × 3") loaves or 4 dozen rolls   ¢

A good all-round dough to use in making fancy yeast breads.

1 cup scalded milk
¼ cup butter or margarine
½ cup sugar
1 teaspoon salt
¼ cup warm water (105°–115° F.)
2 packets active dry yeast
2 eggs, lightly beaten
5 cups sifted flour

Mix milk, butter, sugar, and salt and cool to lukewarm. Pour warm water into a warm large bowl, sprinkle in yeast, and stir to dissolve. Add cooled mixture, eggs, and 3 cups flour and beat well. Mix in remaining flour and knead lightly on a lightly floured board until elastic. Shape into a ball, turn in a greased bowl to grease all over, cover with cloth, and let rise in a warm, draft-free place until doubled in bulk, about 1 hour. Dough is now ready to shape and use as individual recipes direct.

NP Slice (1"): 65 C, 15 mg CH, 60 mg S*
NP Roll: 200 C, 45 mg CH, 185 mg S*

HOT CROSS BUNS

4 dozen buns

1 recipe Basic Sweet Dough
1 cup seedless raisins or dried currants
1 teaspoon allspice
½ cup minced candied citron (optional)
2 egg yolks lightly beaten with 2 tablespoons cold water (glaze)
2 recipes for Easy White Icing

Prepare dough as directed, but add raisins, allspice, and, if you like, citron to yeast along with cooled mixture; proceed as directed and let rise. Divide dough in half and shape into 1½" balls. Arrange 2" apart on greased baking sheets and flatten slightly with palm of hand. Cover and let rise in a warm, draft-free place until doubled in bulk, about ¾ hour. Meanwhile, preheat oven to 400° F. Brush buns with glaze and bake 12–15 minutes until golden brown. Lift to wire racks and, while still warm, draw a cross on top of each with icing.

NP Bun: 105 C, 25 mg CH, 70 mg S*

BASIC TEA RING

10" ring (20 slices)

½ recipe Basic Sweet Dough

FILLING
2 tablespoons melted butter or margarine
¾ cup minced pecans, walnuts, or blanched almonds
½ cup sugar
1½ teaspoons cinnamon

TOPPING
1 recipe Easy White Icing

Prepare dough and let rise as directed; punch down and roll on a lightly floured board into a rectangle about 12" × 17". Brush with melted butter. Mix nuts, sugar, and cinnamon and sprinkle evenly over dough; roll up from longest side

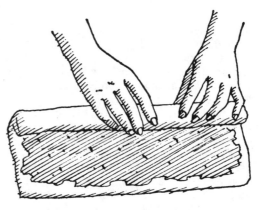

jelly-roll fashion and place seam-side-down on a greased baking sheet. Bring ends around to form a ring and pinch edges to seal.

With scissors, snip into ring every 1" and twist slices so cut sides are up. Cover and let rise in a warm, draft-free place until doubled in bulk, about 1 hour. Toward end of rising, preheat oven to 350° F. Bake 35–40 minutes until golden brown. Lift ring to a wire rack set over wax paper, and drizzle with icing while still warm.

NP Slice: 160 C, 20 mg CH, 85 mg S*

VARIATIONS

Substitute any favorite filling for the one above (see Some Fillings for Coffee Cakes).

Chelsea Buns *(1½ dozen):* Prepare and roll dough as directed. For the filling, substitute dried currants for the nuts. Roll up as directed but do not shape into a ring; instead, slice 1″ thick and arrange cut sides up 1½″ apart on greased baking sheets. Let rise, then bake 15–20 minutes until golden. Lift to racks and drizzle with icing while still warm.

NP Bun: 160 C, 25 mg CH, 45 mg S*

Caramel Sticky Buns *(1½ dozen):* Prepare Basic Tea Ring (above) as directed, but do not shape into a ring; instead, slice 1″ thick. Mix 1 cup firmly packed light or dark brown sugar with ½ cup melted butter and 2 tablespoons light corn syrup and spread over the bottom of a greased 13″ × 9″ × 2″ baking pan. Arrange rolls cut-sides-up and ½″ apart on top, cover, and let rise. Bake 25–30 minutes at 375° F. Let stand in pan 5 minutes, then invert on a wire rack set over wax paper. Serve while still warm.

NP Bun: 255 C, 35 mg CH, 150 mg S*

KUGELHUPF

10″ tube loaf (20 slices)

A fruit-filled, sweet yeast bread good with afternoon tea or coffee or as dessert.

1 recipe Basic Sweet Dough (reduce amount of flour to 4 cups)
2 egg yolks
½ cup seedless raisins
½ cup dried currants
½ cup minced mixed candied fruits (optional)
20 blanched almonds, halved
Confectioners' sugar

Prepare dough as directed, adding extra egg yolks and fruits to yeast along with cooled mixture and 3 cups flour; beat well and add remaining 1 cup flour to make a very soft dough. Do not knead. Grease and flour a 10″ tube pan or 3½-quart Bundt pan and arrange almonds in bottom. Spoon in dough, cover, and let rise in a warm, draft-free place until doubled in bulk, about 1 hour. Toward end of rising, preheat oven to 400° F. Bake 10 minutes, reduce oven to 350° F., and bake 50–60 minutes longer until lightly browned and springy to the touch. Turn out at once on a wire rack set over wax paper and dust with sifted confectioners' sugar. Slice and serve.

NP Slice: 205 C, 60 mg CH, 165 mg S*

VARIATION

Instead of using halved almonds, sprinkle prepared mold with ⅓–½ cup minced almonds; spoon in dough and proceed as directed. Nutritional count about the same as basic recipe.

DANISH PASTRY

3½ dozen pastries

1 recipe Basic Sweet Dough
1 teaspoon cardamom
1 cup butter (no substitute)
2 egg yolks lightly beaten with 2 tablespoons cold water (glaze)

FILLING
1 cup (about) jelly, jam, almond paste, applesauce, Cottage Cheese, Nut, or Prune Filling

Prepare basic dough as directed, mixing cardamom into scalded milk mixture. When dough is fully risen, punch down, cover, and chill 20 minutes. Meanwhile, knead butter until pliable but still cold. Roll dough on a lightly floured board into a rectangle about 12″ × 10″. Dot half the butter over two thirds of dough, leaving ½″ margins all round. Fold unbuttered third in toward center, then far third on top as though folding a letter; pinch edges to seal.

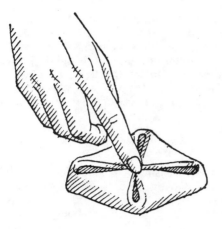

Give package a quarter turn and roll with short, even strokes into a rectangle about 12″ × 16″. Dot with remaining butter, fold, and roll as before. Turn, roll, and fold twice more, lightly flouring board and pin as needed to keep dough from sticking. Wrap and chill 1 hour. (*Note:* If kitchen is warm, you may need to chill dough between rollings.) Divide dough in half, chill 1 piece while shaping the other. Roll out 1/3″ thick and cut in 3″ or 4″ squares; place 1–2 teaspoons filling in center of each square, moisten edges and fold 2 opposite corners in toward center; press edges to seal. Arrange 2″ apart on greased baking sheets, chill 2 hours, or let rise in a warm place until about half doubled in bulk. Preheat oven to 425° F. Brush with glaze, set in oven, and reduce heat at once to 375° F. Bake 15 minutes until browned. Cool on wire racks before serving.

NP Pastry: 140 C, 40 mg CH, 115 mg S*

VARIATIONS

Danish Twists: Prepare dough as directed, let rise, then punch down and roll the butter in as above. Divide in half, chill 1 piece while shaping the other. Roll into a rectangle about 12″ × 16″, brush well with melted butter, and sprinkle with 1/4 cup sugar mixed with 1 teaspoon cinnamon. Fold dough in half the long way so you have a strip 6″ × 16″. Cut crosswise into strips 3/4″ wide. Twist ends of each in opposite directions, arrange on greased baking sheets, let rise, and bake as directed. Shape and bake remaining dough the same way.

NP Twist: 150 C, 45 mg CH, 140 mg S*

Danish Ring (*About 40 slices*): Prepare dough as directed, let rise, then punch down and roll butter into dough as above. Divide in half and chill 1 piece while shaping the other. Roll into a rectangle about 12″ × 16″, brush with melted butter, then sprinkle or spread with any of the fillings above. Roll up from the longest side jelly-roll fashion, place seam side down on a greased baking sheet, and bring ends around to form a ring, pressing edges to seal. Or, if you prefer, coil snail fashion. Let rise in a warm place until about half doubled in bulk, glaze, and sprinkle with sliced blanched almonds and granulated sugar. Bake 25–30 minutes at 375° F. until golden brown and hollow sounding when tapped. Shape and bake remaining pastry the same way. Nutritional count about the same as basic recipe.

PANETTONE (ITALIAN CHRISTMAS BREAD)

Tall 9″ loaf (16 wedges)

1 recipe Basic Sweet Dough (reduce amount of scalded milk to 3/4 cup)
1/4 cup butter or margarine
3 egg yolks, lightly beaten
1 cup golden seedless raisins
1 cup minced candied citron or mixed candied fruits
1/2 cup piñon nuts (optional)
2 tablespoons melted butter or margarine
Confectioners' sugar

Prepare basic recipe as directed, adding the 1/4 cup butter above to the scalded milk along with the butter, sugar, and salt called for in basic recipe; cool to lukewarm and stir into yeast mixture along with all but last ingredient above. Proceed as basic recipe directs. While dough is rising, prepare pan: Tear off a 30″ piece of heavy duty foil and fold over and over again until you have a strip 30″ long and 4″ wide. Grease one side of strip and stand greased side around the inside edge of a greased 9″ layer cake pan; secure with a paper clip to form a collar. Punch dough down, knead lightly 1–2 minutes, and shape into a smooth round loaf about 9″ across. Place in pan, cover, and let rise in a warm, draft-free place until doubled in bulk, about 1 hour. Toward end of rising, preheat oven to 400° F. Bake 10 minutes, reduce oven to 350° F., and bake 40–50 minutes longer until golden brown and hollow sounding when tapped. Turn out on a wire rack, dust with confectioners' sugar, and cool. To serve, cut in thin wedges.

NP Wedge: 355 C, 105 mg CH, 275 mg S*

STOLLEN

2 large loaves (40 slices)

1 recipe Basic Sweet Dough
1 cup seedless raisins
1 cup minced blanched almonds
3/4 cup minced candied fruits or a 1/2 and 1/2
  mixture of citron and candied cherries
1 tablespoon finely grated lemon rind
3 tablespoons melted butter or margarine
1 recipe Easy White Icing

Prepare dough as directed, adding raisins, almonds, candied fruit, and lemon rind to yeast along with lukewarm mixture. Add remaining flour, knead, and let rise as directed. Divide dough in half and roll or pat out half on a lightly floured board to form an oval about 12″ × 8″. Brush with melted butter, fold in half the long way, and bend ends in slightly to form a crescent; press edges firmly to seal. Transfer to a greased baking sheet and brush with melted butter. Shape remaining dough the same way and place on a baking sheet. Cover loaves and let rise in a warm, draft-free place until doubled in bulk, about 3/4 hour. Toward end of rising, preheat oven to 375° F. Bake 35–40 minutes until golden brown. Lift to wire racks set over wax paper and, while still warm, drizzle with icing. For a festive touch, decorate with "flowers" made with blanched almond halves, candied cherries, and slivered angelica.

NP Slice: 145 C, 20 mg CH, 100 mg S*

CINNAMON-RAISIN PINWHEELS

20 rolls

1/2 cup sugar
3 tablespoons butter or margarine
1 teaspoon salt
3/4 cup boiling water
1 packet active dry yeast
1/4 cup warm water (105°–115° F.)
1 egg, lightly beaten
4 1/2 cups sifted flour

FILLING
1/4 cup light corn syrup
1/4 cup melted butter or margarine
1/3 cup sugar or firmly packed light brown sugar
1 1/2 teaspoons cinnamon
1 1/2 cups seedless raisins

Stir sugar, butter, and salt into boiling water and cool to lukewarm. Dissolve yeast in the warm water in a warm large bowl; add cooled mixture, egg, and 3 cups flour and beat until smooth. Mix in remaining flour, a little at a time. Knead dough on a lightly floured board until elastic, about 5 minutes; place in a greased bowl, and let rise in a warm, draft-free spot 1 hour or until doubled in bulk. Punch dough down, turn onto board, and divide in half. Roll each into a rectangle about 15″ × 9″, brush with corn syrup and melted butter, sprinkle with sugar, cinnamon, and raisins. Roll each jelly-roll style the short way and cut into 10 slices. Lay slices flat, almost touching, in greased layer cake pans, cover, and let rise about 1/2 hour until doubled in bulk. Meanwhile, preheat oven to 350° F. Brush with melted butter and bake 30–35 minutes until lightly browned.

NP Roll: 210 C, 25 mg CH, 160 mg S*

SWEDISH CINNAMON RINGS

3 (12″) or 4 (10″) rings

This is a rich coffee cake, so cut each ring in small wedges. You should be able to get about 20 wedge-shaped slices out of each ring.

DOUGH
2 packets active dry yeast
1/2 cup warm water (105°–115° F.)
1 cup butter or margarine
3/4 cup sugar
1 tablespoon crushed cardamom seeds (it's easy
  to crush them in an electric blender)
1 teaspoon salt
1 1/2 cups light cream, scalded
2 eggs
8 cups sifted flour

FILLING
1/2 cup butter or margarine, softened to room
  temperature
1 cup firmly packed light brown sugar
2 teaspoons cinnamon

DECORATIONS (optional)
2 recipes Lemon Sugar Glaze
Diced candied red or green cherries

Sprinkle yeast over warm water in a warm large bowl and stir to dissolve. Mix butter, sugar, cardamom, and salt with cream and cool to lukewarm. Stir into yeast, then beat in eggs, one at a time. Add flour, 1 cup at a time, beating well after each addition. You will probably have to turn dough onto a board and knead in the final cup. Knead dough about 5 minutes until smooth and elastic. Place in a greased large bowl, turn so dough is greased all over, cover with cloth, and let rise in a warm, draft-free place 1 1/2–1 3/4 hours until doubled in bulk. Punch dough down, turn onto a lightly floured board, and knead 1–2 minutes. Divide dough into 3 or 4 equal parts, depending upon whether you want large- or medium-size rings. Roll each piece of dough into a rectangle (about 14″ × 18″ for medium-size rings, 18″ × 22″ for large). Spread lightly with butter; mix brown sugar and cinnamon and sprinkle over butter, then roll up jelly-roll style and shape into a ring. Using sharp scissors, make diagonal snips deep into each ring every 2″ and turn cut-side up. Place rings on lightly greased baking sheets, cover with cloth, and let rise in a warm place until doubled in bulk, 30–40 minutes. Meanwhile, preheat oven to 375° F. When rings have risen, bake 20–30 minutes until nicely browned and hollow sounding when tapped. Transfer to wire racks to cool and, if you like, glaze and decorate. Serve warm or at room temperature. To reheat, wrap in foil and heat 10 minutes at 350° F.

NP Wedge: 135 C, 25 mg CH, 90 mg S*

PUMPKIN COFFEE CAKE

8 servings

DOUGH
1/4 cup milk, scalded
1/4 cup sugar
1/2 teaspoon salt
3 tablespoons butter or margarine
1 packet active dry yeast
1/4 cup warm water (105°–115° F.)
1 egg, lightly beaten
2 1/4 cups unsifted flour (about)
1 egg yolk beaten with 1 tablespoon cold water (glaze)

FILLING
3/4 cup cooked, mashed pumpkin
1/2 cup sugar
1 teaspoon cinnamon
1/2 teaspoon ginger
1/2 teaspoon salt
1 cup chopped walnuts or pecans
1/4 cup seedless raisins

FROSTING
1/2 cup sifted confectioners' sugar
1 teaspoon milk or light cream
1/8 teaspoon vanilla

Mix milk with sugar, salt, and butter, stirring until sugar dissolves; cool to lukewarm. Sprinkle yeast over warm water and stir until dissolved. Combine milk and yeast mixtures, add egg and half the flour, and beat until smooth. Stir in remaining flour (dough will be fairly soft). Turn onto a lightly floured board and knead 7–8 minutes until smooth and elastic, adding only enough extra flour to keep dough from sticking. Place dough in a greased bowl, turn to grease all sides, cover with cloth, set in a warm, draft-free place, and let rise about 1 hour until doubled in bulk. Punch dough down, turn onto a lightly floured board, and roll into a rectangle about 22″ × 10″. Mix pumpkin with sugar, spices, and salt and spread evenly over dough, not quite to edges. Sprinkle with 1/2 cup walnuts and the raisins. Roll up jelly-roll fashion from the wide side, lift to a greased baking sheet, and coil into a ring. Cover and let rise in a warm place about 1 hour until doubled in bulk. Meanwhile, preheat oven to 350° F. Brush ring with egg glaze and bake 30–35 minutes until well browned and hollow sounding when tapped. Mix frosting ingredients together until smooth and frost ring while still warm; sprinkle with remaining nuts. Serve warm or at room temperature.

NPS: 405 C, 80 mg CH, 390 mg S*

Some Fillings for Coffee Cakes and Sweet Breads

Substitute any of the following for fillings called for in Basic Tea Ring, Danish Pastry, Pumpkin Coffee Cake, or other filled yeast bread.

Almond Paste: Cream together until light 1/3 cup each butter and sugar; add 1 egg, 1/4 teaspoon almond extract, and 1/2 cup almond paste and beat until smooth.

Nut: Cream together until light 1/4 cup butter and 1/3 cup sugar; mix in 1 tablespoon grated orange or lemon rind. Spread on dough, then sprinkle with 1 cup minced blanched almonds, pecans, or walnuts.

Prune: Heat together over low heat, stirring constantly until thickened, 1 cup coarsely chopped pitted prunes (or dates, dried apricots, or figs), 1/4 cup sugar, 2 tablespoons lemon juice, 1 teaspoon grated lemon rind, and 1 tablespoon butter.

Spiced Apple: Mix 2 tablespoons melted butter with 1/2 cup firmly packed light brown sugar, 1 teaspoon cinnamon, 1/4 teaspoon nutmeg, and 1–1 1/2 cups well-drained canned sliced apples. If you like, also mix in 1/2 cup seedless raisins.

Cottage Cheese: Mix together 1 cup cottage cheese, 1 lightly beaten egg yolk, 1/3 cup superfine sugar, 1/2 teaspoon vanilla, and 1 teaspoon finely grated lemon or orange rind.

Custard: Mix 1 cup Custard Sauce and 1/2 cup poppy seeds.

⊠ *Some Quickies:*
• 1 cup any jelly, jam, preserves, or marmalade
• 1 cup mincemeat
• 1 cup whipped cream cheese mixed with ¼ cup poppy seeds and 1 teaspoon finely grated lemon or orange rind

BRIOCHE I (TRADITIONAL METHOD)

2 dozen brioches

A difficult recipe, not for beginners.

1 packet active dry yeast
2¼ cups warm water (105°–115° F.)
4½ cups sifted flour
1 teaspoon salt
3 tablespoons sugar
6 eggs
1½ cups butter (no substitute), softened to room temperature
1 egg yolk lightly beaten with 1 tablespoon cold water (glaze)

Beat yeast with ¼ cup warm water and ½ cup flour until smooth and sticky. Pour remaining water into a warm bowl; with a rubber spatula, scrape yeast mixture into water, trying to keep in 1 piece, and let sink to the bottom. Let rise in a warm, draft-free spot until yeast mixture floats and is doubled in bulk, 7–10 minutes. Meanwhile, mix remaining flour with salt and sugar on a pastry board and make a large well in the center. Break 3 eggs into a bowl and set aside. Break remaining eggs into well in flour and, using one hand, gradually work flour from edges of well into eggs. Add remaining eggs and continue mixing until dough holds together (it will be very sticky). Keeping a metal spatula in one hand to help scrape dough from board, scoop up as much dough as possible with other hand and throw or slap hard against board. You won't be able to get all the dough at once and it will stick like glue to your fingers. But keep throwing as much as possible against board, scraping up a little more each time with the spatula. Continue throwing dough against board until it is smooth, shiny, and leaves board and your fingers almost clean, about 100 times. Squeeze one third of butter into dough with your fingers; repeat until all butter is incorporated and dough smooth. Also squeeze in yeast sponge, but not water it was floating in (dough will be soft). Scoop into a lightly buttered 3-quart bowl, cover with cloth, and let rise in a warm, draft-free place until doubled in bulk, about 2 hours. Stir dough down, cover with foil, and refrigerate 6–8 hours or overnight. Open refrigerator as little as possible during this period. Dough will rise slightly and become quite firm. Scrape dough onto a lightly floured board, knead lightly with floured hands, and shape quickly into a ball. Cut ball in 4 equal pieces with a floured knife and cut 3 of the quarters into 8 pieces, totaling 24. Roll into smooth balls and place in greased brioche or muffin pans, 1 ball per cup. With dampened index finger, make a deep depression in center of each ball. Roll remaining dough into 24 small balls and place 1 in each depression to form the "topknot." Cover brioches, set in a warm spot, and let rise until doubled in bulk, about 1 hour. About 15 minutes before you're ready to bake, preheat oven to 425° F.; set rack in lower third of oven. Gently brush brioches with glaze, taking care not to let it run into cracks around topknots (an artist's brush is best). Set pans on baking sheets and bake 12–15 minutes until well browned. *(Note:* You probably won't be able to bake all the brioches at once, so refrigerate 1 batch while baking the other.) Remove from pans at once after baking and serve hot or, if you prefer, cool on wire racks to room temperature. *(Note:* To reheat leftover brioches, bundle loosely in foil and warm 10 minutes at 350° F. These brioches freeze well; thaw before reheating.)
NP Brioche: 210 C, 110 mg CH, 225 mg S*

BRIOCHE II (EASY METHOD)

2 dozen brioches

So much less complicated than Brioche I and almost as good.

1 packet active dry yeast
¼ cup warm water (105°–115° F.)
4 cups sifted flour
3 tablespoons sugar
1 teaspoon salt
1½ cups butter or margarine, softened to room temperature
6 eggs, lightly beaten
1 egg yolk lightly beaten with 1 tablespoon cold water (glaze)

Mix yeast, warm water, and ¼ cup flour until smooth in a small bowl; set in a pan of lukewarm water (water should come one third of way up bowl) and let stand in a warm spot until bubbles form on yeast mixture, 5–10 minutes. Meanwhile, sift 3 cups flour with the sugar and salt and set aside. Cream butter in a large bowl with an electric mixer until fluffy. Add flour mixture, a little at a time, alternately with eggs. Beat 2 minutes at medium speed. Add yeast mixture, beat 1/2 minute at low speed, then 2 minutes at medium speed. Add remaining 3/4 cup flour by hand, a little at a time, beating with a wooden spoon after each addition. Cover dough with cloth, set in a warm, draft-free spot, and let rise until doubled in bulk, 2 1/2–3 hours. Stir dough down, cover with foil, and refrigerate 6–8 hours or overnight. Now divide dough, shape into 24 brioches, allow to rise, glaze, and bake as directed in Brioche I.

NP Brioche: 200 C, 110 mg CH, 225 mg S*

BRIOCHE FRUIT LOAVES

2 (9" × 5" × 3") loaves (40 slices)

Delicious toasted and buttered!

1 recipe Brioche I or II
2 cups mixed dried or candied fruits (seedless raisins, currants, coarsely chopped candied red cherries or citron)
1/3–1/2 cup slivered or sliced blanched almonds (optional)
1 egg yolk lightly beaten with 1 tablespoon cold water (glaze)

Prepare brioche up to point of shaping dough; instead of making individual brioches, halve dough. Roll each piece on a lightly floured board into a rectangle 9" × 12". Sprinkle with fruit and press in lightly. Roll up the short way, jelly-roll style, and pinch seams together. Place each loaf seam-side down in a greased 9" × 5" × 3" loaf pan. Slash tops lengthwise down center with a sharp knife and, if you like, sprinkle almonds into slits. Cover with cloth and let rise in a warm, draft-free spot until doubled in bulk, 1–1 1/2 hours. About 15 minutes before you're ready to bake, preheat oven to 350° F. Brush loaves with glaze and bake 35–40 minutes until well browned and hollow sounding when tapped. If tops or almonds brown too fast, cover loosely with foil. Turn loaves out immediately and cool upright on a wire rack. Slice and serve with plenty of butter. (*Note:* These loaves freeze well.)

NP Slice: 175 C, 75 mg CH, 175 mg S*

OLD-FASHIONED YEAST-RAISED DOUGHNUTS

3 dozen doughnuts

Stored airtight, these doughnuts keep fairly well. They're best, of course, eaten straight from the deep fat fryer.

1/4 cup butter or margarine
2/3 cup scalded milk
2/3 cup warm water (105°–115° F.)
2 packets active dry yeast
3/4 cup sugar
5 cups sifted flour (about)
2 eggs, lightly beaten
1 teaspoon salt
1 teaspoon cardamom
1/2 teaspoon cinnamon
1/2 teaspoon mace
Vegetable shortening or cooking oil for deep fat frying

TOPPING
1/2 cup superfine sugar mixed with 1 teaspoon cinnamon

Melt butter in milk and cool to lukewarm. Place water in a warm large mixing bowl, sprinkle in yeast, and stir until dissolved; add milk mixture and sugar. By hand, beat 2 1/2 cups flour in until smooth; mix in eggs, salt, and spices. Mix in remaining flour, adding a little extra, if needed, to form a soft but manageable dough. Knead lightly 1 minute on a floured pastry cloth; shape into a ball, place in a greased large bowl, cover, and let rise in a warm, draft-free spot until doubled in bulk, about 1 hour. Punch dough down, roll 1/2" thick on pastry cloth, using a floured, stockinette-covered rolling pin. Cut with a floured doughnut cutter and place 1 1/2" apart on ungreased baking sheets. Re-roll and cut scraps. Cover with cloth and let rise in a warm spot about 25 minutes until doubled in bulk. Meanwhile, begin heating fat in a deep fat fryer. When doughnuts have risen and fat reached 375° F., ease 4 doughnuts into fat, 1 at a time. Fry about 2 minutes until golden brown all over, using tongs to turn. Drain on paper toweling. (*Note:* Never fry more than 4 doughnuts at a time and keep fat as near 375° F. as possible; if too hot, doughnuts will brown before they cook inside.) While doughnuts are warm, roll in topping.

NP Doughnut: 140 C, 20 mg CH, 80 mg S*

VARIATIONS

Jelly Doughnuts: Prepare as directed, but roll dough 1/4" thick instead of 1/2". Cut in 2 1/2" rounds and put 1 teaspoonful tart jelly in the center of 1/2 the rounds. Top with remaining rounds, moisten touching edges slightly, and pinch to seal. Let rise, then fry as directed. Roll in confectioners' sugar while still warm.

NP Doughnut: 155 C, 20 mg CH, 80 mg S*

Crullers: Prepare as directed, but instead of cutting into doughnuts, cut in strips 8" long and 1/2"–3/4" wide; let rise, then twist strips several times and pinch ends. Fry at once and roll in topping while still warm.

NP Cruller: 140 C, 20 mg CH, 80 mg S*

SANDWICHES

Sandwiches are named for the Earl of Sandwich, an eighteenth-century Englishman who was so fond of gambling he had meat or other savory served between slices of bread so that he needn't interrupt his game. Open-face sandwiches are even older, dating to medieval Scandinavia when slices of bread served as plates. Open *or* shut, sandwiches have become universal favorites. And who in those early days could have predicted it?

Tips for Making Better Sandwiches

Sandwiches in General:

• Leave crusts on all but dainty tea sandwiches; they help keep sandwiches fresh.
• Assemble components, then put sandwiches together (or fill pita bread) just before serving, particularly important if fillings are drippy.
• Soften butter to room temperature so it spreads more easily.
• If filling is creamy, butter 1 slice of bread only.
• Be generous—but not lavish—with butter or mayonnaise; 1 teaspoon per slice is ample.
• Spread butter or mayonnaise *and* filling to edges of bread.
• Use several thin slices of meat or cheese rather than a single thick one.
• Make sure salad-type fillings are creamy, *not soupy.*
• Make toasted sandwiches at the very last minute and do not stack toast—it will become soggy.

Sandwiches to Go:

• Choose sandwich fillings that won't soak into bread.
• Spread bread with butter, then chill before adding filling so that butter will harden and help keep filling from seeping into bread.
• Pack lettuce leaves, pickles, tomatoes, etc., separately and slip into sandwiches just before serving.
• Keep all salad-type fillings well chilled (especially in transit) and make sandwiches on location.
• Choose less perishable fillings for lunch box sandwiches—cold cuts, sliced cheese, peanut butter, jelly, etc.—instead of quick-to-spoil creamy salad types.
• Keep lunch box sandwiches refrigerated until ready to go and eat within 4 hours.
• Halve sandwiches before wrapping—makes for easier eating.
• Wrap sandwiches individually in wax paper or plastic sandwich bags.

Sandwiches in Quantity:

To Help Compute Quantities:

• 1 (1-pound) loaf averages 20 slices; 1 pullman or sandwich loaf 33–34.
• Allowing a rounded teaspoon per slice, 1 pound butter will spread 50–60 slices or 2 1/2–3 (1-pound) loaves.
• Allowing a rounded teaspoon per slice, 1 pint mayonnaise will spread 50–60 slices or 2 1/2–3 (1-pound) loaves.
• Allowing 1/4 cup per sandwich, 1 quart filling will make 16 sandwiches.

To Stretch Butter: Add 1/2 cup milk to each 1 pound butter and cream until fluffy.

For Quickest Assembly:

• Choose the simplest sandwiches possible.
• Line bread up in rows, pairing slices so they'll match.
• Whip butter or cheese spreads until fluffy so they'll spread zip-quick.
• Place dabs of butter or mayonnaise on alternate rows of slices, then mounds of filling on remaining rows. Spread well to edges, put slices together, and press lightly.
• Use a No. 24 ice cream scoop or 1/4 cup measure for apportioning fillings.

Party Sandwiches:

• Use a firm, fine-textured bread to avoid ragged edges; if unavailable, use day-old bread and chill well before cutting.
• For attractiveness, slice bread thin and trim off crusts.
• Be sparing about fillings so they don't seep through the bread or ooze out the edges.
• When making sandwiches ahead, cover with wax paper or plastic food wrap, never a damp towel. Refrigerate until ready to serve.
• Add garnishes and decorations at the last minute.

How to Cut and Shape Party Sandwiches

(Note: Spreads included in the hors d'oeuvre chapter are perfect for party sandwiches.)

Fancy Cutouts: Trim crusts from an unsliced loaf, slice thin lengthwise, spread with filling, then cut, using a sharp bread knife or cookie cutters.

Double Deckers: Make cutouts and mix or match breads and shapes.

Ribbon Loaf: Trim crusts from an unsliced loaf, slice lengthwise about 1/2" thick, spread, and reassemble. Frost with softened cream cheese, then chill well before slicing. For variety, alternate slices of dark and light breads and 2 or more compatible fillings of contrasting color.

Ribbon Sandwiches: Prepare ribbon loaf, chill well, then slice thin. Cut slices into small squares or rectangles.

Round Ribbon Loaf: Trim crusts from unsliced bread, slice and cut slices in circles of the same size. Spread and assemble as for Ribbon Loaf (above). Frost if you like. To serve, cut in thin wedges.

Checkerboards: Prepare 2 ribbon loaves, beginning one with dark bread and the other with light.

Chill well, slice, spread, and restack slices as shown into checkerboards. Chill and slice.

Roll-Ups: Slice extra-fresh bread, spread with a soft filling, roll, and use toothpick to secure. For interest, roll around a sprig of watercress or dill, a small bunch of alfalfa or clover radish sprouts, a carrot or celery stick, cooked asparagus spear, or finger of ham, tongue, or cheese.

Pinwheels: Trim crusts from an unsliced loaf and slice thin lengthwise. Spread each slice with a colorful filling and roll up, jelly-roll style, from the short side. Wrap in dry toweling, chill several hours, then slice thin. (*Note:* If you use extra-fresh, soft bread, it should roll without cracking. Some cooks recommend flattening the bread with a rolling pin, but it shouldn't be necessary if the bread itself is soft. Besides, flattened bread tastes like damp cardboard.)

Decorated Open-Face Sandwiches: Trimmings can be as simple or lavish as time and talent permit: a sprig of dill or a tarragon leaf laid across the filling, an olive slice or fancy truffle cutout, or a showy piped-on design of cream cheese.

Sandwich Garnishes

Party sandwiches demand garnishes, dainty doll-like ones; Danish sandwiches require something flashier than everyday lunch or supper sandwiches. They don't need trimmings, but how much handsomer they are when garnished. Some trimmings to try (these same garnishes can also be used to decorate meat, fish, and fowl platters):

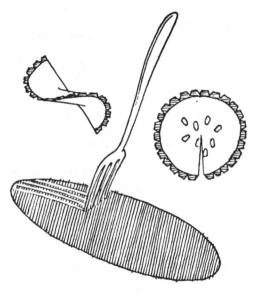

Twists or Butterflies
Thin slices of tomato, cucumber, beet, lemon, lime, and orange can all be shaped this way.

BREADS AND SANDWICHES

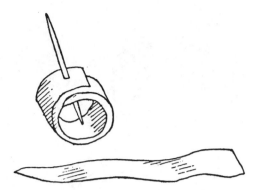

Cartwheels
Best for slices of cucumber, lemon, lime, or orange.

Carrot Curls
Bacon curls are rolled the same way. After cutting and rolling carrots, crisp in ice water.

Radish Roses

Radish Pompons
Cut, then crisp in ice water.

Celery Frills
Cut as shown above, then crisp in ice water.

Hard-Cooked Egg (Slices, Wedges, and Strips)

Anchovy Rolls and Strips

Onion Rings (Raw and French-Fried)

Herb Sprigs (Chervil, Chives, Dill, Fennel, Cress, Parsley, Tarragon)

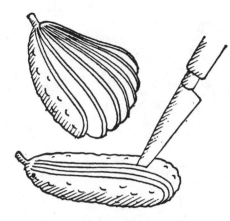

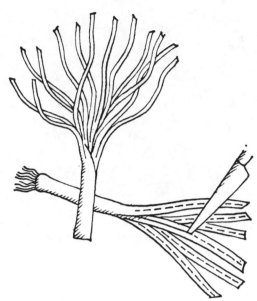

Pickle Fans

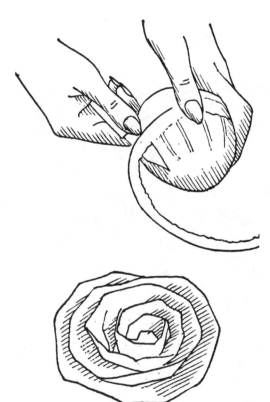

Rind or Tomato Roses
With knife or vegetable peeler, peel a long, continuous strip of rind or skin from a lemon, orange, or tomato, then roll into a rose.

Cutouts
Truffle, Pimiento, Aspic, Cooked Beet or Carrot, Hard-Cooked Egg White work best. Cut out with decorative truffle cutters.

Scallion Ruffles
Cut, then crisp in ice water.

Toasted Sandwiches

Any filling can be served on toasted bread, but favorites are bacon, lettuce, and tomato, cheese, and creamy salad types—tuna salad, egg salad, chicken salad. Toast bread just before making sandwiches and don't stack, lest toast become soggy.

Grilled Sandwiches

Best sandwiches to grill are those with fairly thick meat or cheese fillings that won't ooze out in the grilling.

How to Grill: Prepare sandwich as directed, then brown lightly 2–3 minutes on a side in 2–3 teaspoons butter or margarine over moderate heat. (*Note:* If you like, sandwich can be dipped in egg—1 egg lightly beaten with ¼ cup milk and a pinch each salt and pepper—then browned as directed. Increase amount of butter slightly if needed.)

SOME SANDWICHES TO TRY

What goes into a sandwich can be as exotic or basic as you like because there aren't any hard and fast rules. There are old favorites, of course—and the following list includes them as well as some less familiar combinations. Unless directions specify to the contrary, use any buttered bread or rolls, season fillings to taste with salt and pepper, and serve with a suitable garnish (see Sandwich Garnishes).

Meat

(Note: Hot Steak Sandwiches, Hamburgers, Sloppy Joes, and Frankfurters are all included elsewhere; see Index for page numbers.)

Basic Meat Salad: Mix any minced cooked meat with enough mayonnaise or salad dressing to make a good spreading consistency. For additional flavor, add any or a combination of the following (tasting as you mix): minced onion, celery, sweet or dill pickles, chives, or parsley; prepared mustard or horseradish; ketchup or chili sauce.

Meat Loaf: Slice any cold meat loaf, not too thin; spread with cold gravy or any of the following: prepared mustard or horseradish, mustard pickle or sweet pickle relish, chili sauce or ketchup. *Optionals:* Lettuce and sliced tomato. *Variations:* Team meat loaf with any of the following: sautéed sliced onions, pickled red cabbage, fried apple or pineapple rings, applesauce, minced chutney.

Hot Corned Beef or Pastrami: Slice thin and serve on rye bread spread with mustard.

Cold Corned Beef: Slice thin and serve on rye spread with mustard, topped with lettuce, sliced tomato, and mayonnaise. *Variations:* For the lettuce and tomato, substitute any of the following: egg salad, coleslaw, minced Harvard Beets, any sliced cheese or cheese spread.

Ham and Cheese: Sandwich thin slices boiled or baked ham and Swiss, American, or Cheddar cheese between bread spread with mustard and/or mayonnaise. Lettuce optional.

Cold Ham and Egg: Mix equal parts ground cooked ham and minced hard-cooked egg with enough mayonnaise and mustard to bind. Use as a spread. Or layer sliced ham and hard-cooked egg between bread spread with mayonnaise and mustard.

Hot Ham and Egg: Sandwich slices of fried ham and a fried egg (cooked until firm) between slices of buttered toast spread with mustard.

B.L.T.: Layer crisp bacon strips, sliced tomato, and lettuce between slices of toast spread with mayonnaise.

Bacon and Beans: Sandwich drained, mashed baked beans between slices of buttered toast with crisp bacon strips and, if you like, thin slices of Bermuda onion.

Liverwurst and Onion: Sandwich sliced liverwurst, sautéed onion rings, and crumbled crisply cooked bacon between slices of bread spread with Mustard Butter.

Poultry

(Note: Hot roast chicken or turkey sandwiches are included in the poultry chapter; see Index for page numbers.)

Basic Chicken or Turkey Salad: Follow directions for Basic Meat Salad; also see chapter on salads for specific recipes.

Curried Chicken or Turkey and Nuts: Mix minced or ground cooked chicken or turkey with minced toasted almonds, peanuts, or cashews, curry powder, and grated onion to taste, and mayonnaise to bind. Use as a spread.

Chicken or Turkey and Apple: Mix minced or ground cooked chicken or turkey with minced apple, celery, and walnuts and enough mayonnaise to bind; use as a spread.

Chicken or Turkey and Cheese: Mix minced or ground cooked chicken or turkey with grated Swiss or Cheddar cheese, sweet pickle relish to taste, and mayonnaise to bind. Use as a spread.

Chicken or Turkey and Ham: Mix equal parts minced or ground cooked chicken or turkey with minced cooked ham (or tongue, bologna, or other cold cuts), minced scallions or onion to taste, and mayonnaise to bind. Use as a spread.

Sliced Cold Chicken or Turkey: Layer between slices of buttered bread or toast with sliced tomato, lettuce, and mayonnaise. *Optionals:* Any cold cuts or sliced cheese.

Chicken and Avocado: Sandwich slices of cold chicken between slices of bread lavishly spread with Guacamole.

Chopped Chicken Liver: Mince sautéed chicken livers, mix with enough melted butter or mayonnaise to bind, and season, if you like, with a little minced onion. Use as a spread. *Optional:* Mix in a little crisp, crumbled bacon.

Seafood

(Note: Angels on Horseback and other specific seafood sandwiches are included in the seafood chapter; see Index for page numbers.)

Basic Seafood Salad: Mix any flaked cooked fish (tuna, salmon, haddock, or other delicate white fish), smoked fish, or minced cooked shellfish (shrimp, lobster, crab, etc.) with enough mayonnaise, Tartar Sauce, or Rémoulade Sauce to bind. *Some Good Additions:* Minced hard-cooked egg; minced onion and celery; minced parsley, tarragon, chervil, or dill; lemon juice; capers; curry powder. (Also see Salads for specific recipes.)

Hot Seafood Sandwiches: Sandwich any fish sticks or cakes, any breaded or batter-fried fish or shellfish between slices of bread or into buns spread with Tartar Sauce or Rémoulade Sauce.

Egg

Basic Egg Salad: Mix minced hard-cooked eggs with enough mayonnaise or relish-type sandwich spread to bind. *Some Good Additions:* Minced onion and celery; minced dill or sweet pickle; minced parsley, tarragon, chervil, dill, or marjoram; grated Cheddar or Swiss cheese; crisp crumbled bacon; minced ripe or pimiento-stuffed olives; prepared mustard or horseradish. Taste as you mix until flavors seem "just right." (Also see salad chapter for specific recipes.)

Fried Egg: Sandwich a fried egg (cooked until firm) between slices of buttered toast. *Optionals:* Sliced tomato, lettuce, minced scallions, grated Parmesan cheese.

Scrambled Egg or Omelet: Sandwich firmly cooked scrambled eggs or any small omelet between buttered toast or buns. *Optionals:* Hollandaise Sauce and/or minced, buttered spinach.

Cheese

Plain Cheese: Sandwich any thinly sliced cheese between slices of bread spread with butter or mayonnaise and, if you like, mustard. *Optionals:* Lettuce and sliced tomato; any cold cuts.

Grilled Cheese Sandwich: Make a Plain Cheese Sandwich and grill (see Grilled Sandwiches).

Some Spreads to Make with Grated Cheese: Mix coarsely grated Cheddar, American, or Swiss cheese with enough mayonnaise or salad dressing to bind, then add any of the following for flavor: minced pickles, grated onion, crumbled bacon, minced, cooked ham or cold cuts, minced chutney and ground almonds or peanuts. For piquancy, add prepared mustard or horseradish, ketchup or Worcestershire, tasting as you mix.

Cream Cheese and Jelly: Spread any bread with cream cheese, then any jam, jelly, preserves, or marmalade. *Optionals:* Any minced nuts; raisins or minced, pitted dates, prunes, dried figs or apricots.

Cream Cheese and Bacon: Sandwich toast together with cream cheese and crisp crumbled bacon. *Optionals:* Minced ripe or pimiento-stuffed olives; minced, sautéed chicken livers; deviled ham; shrimp or anchovy paste; sliced tomatoes or cucumbers.

Note: Most mild soft and semisoft cheeses can be blended with chutney; minced nuts, scallions, pickles, or olives; crumbled crisply cooked bacon, even clover radish sprouts, to make appealing spreads.

Peanut Butter

Peanut Butter and Jelly: Sandwich buttered bread together with creamy or crunchy peanut butter and any tart jelly, jam, or preserves.

Peanut Butter and Bacon: Sandwich buttered toast together with creamy or crunchy peanut butter and crisp, crumbled bacon. *Optionals:* Lettuce and sliced tomato.

Vegetables

Lettuce: Sandwich any crisp lettuce leaves between slices of bread spread with mayonnaise or other salad dressing.

Lettuce and Tomato: Layer sliced tomatoes and crisp lettuce leaves between slices of bread spread with mayonnaise or other salad dressing.

Cucumber: Layer thinly sliced cucumbers (sprinkled lightly with vinegar if you like) between buttered slices of bread.

Tomato and Onion: Layer thinly sliced tomatoes and Bermuda onion between slices of bread or toast spread with butter or mayonnaise.

Potato and Pepper: Layer thinly sliced, boiled new potatoes, Bermuda onion, and sweet green or red pepper between slices of bread spread with mayonnaise or relish-type sandwich spread. *Variation:* Substitute Roquefort or Thousand Island Dressing or sour cream for the mayonnaise.

Baked Bean: Spread slices of Boston Brown Bread with cream cheese, mound with cold baked beans, top with a bacon slice, and serve open face.

Mushroom: Sandwich sautéed, sliced mushrooms between slices of bread or toast spread with chive cheese.

Carrot and Raisin: Combine grated carrots and seedless raisins with enough mayonnaise to bind and use as a spread. *Optionals:* A little minced, cooked chicken, turkey, or ham; minced apple.

CLUB SANDWICHES

Whole meals sandwiched between 2 or 3 slices of bread or toast. Junior clubs have similar, though abbreviated, fillings and 2 slices of bread only. Here are some popular combinations with ingredients listed *in order from the bottom up.* Simply build up layers, salting and peppering as you go. When sandwiches are assembled, toothpick layers together at all 4 corners, then halve or quarter diagonally. Cover toothpick ends with olives, cocktail onions, or chunks of pickle.

SIMPLE CLUB

Buttered slice of white or whole grain toast
Slice of roast chicken or turkey
Slice of white or whole grain toast spread with mayonnaise (both sides)
Lettuce leaves
Sliced tomato
Crisp bacon strips
Buttered slice of white or whole grain toast

COUNTRY CLUB

Slice of cracked wheat toast spread with relish-type sandwich spread
Slice of Swiss cheese
Slice of boiled ham spread with mustard
Buttered slice of white toast (both sides)
Slice of roast chicken or turkey
Thin slice of cranberry jelly
Crisp romaine leaves
Crisp bacon strips
Buttered slice of cracked wheat toast

KING CLUB

Slice of buttered rye bread
Sour cream mixed with horseradish
Slice of roast beef
Crumbled French-fried onion rings
Buttered slice of rye bread (both sides)
Slice of Roquefort or blue cheese
Potato salad
Slice of rye bread

ITALIAN DOUBLE DECKER

Buttered slice of Italian bread
Anchovy fillets
Sliced hard-cooked egg
Sliced pimiento-stuffed olives drizzled with Italian dressing
Buttered slice of Italian bread (both sides)
Slice of mozzarella or provolone cheese
Slice of salami or *prosciutto*
Minced hot red pepper
Slice of Italian bread spread with mayonnaise

DELI DOUBLE DECKER

Slice of pumpernickel spread with pâté, chopped liver, or liverwurst
Slice of Bermuda onion
Sliced dill pickles
Slice of pumpernickel buttered (both sides)
Slice of roast turkey spread with Russian dressing
Slice of pumpernickel

BARNEY'S TRIPLE DECKER

Buttered slice of rye bread
Slice of corned beef spread with mustard
Drained sauerkraut
Slice of pumpernickel spread with mayonnaise (both sides)
Sliced hard-cooked egg
Minced scallions
Sliced cucumber
Slice of buttered rye bread (both sides)
Slice of pastrami
Shredded lettuce
Slice of pumpernickel spread with mayonnaise

HEROES OR SUBMARINES

Sandwiches Italian-style, whoppers filled to overflowing with sausages, cheeses, peppers —and any of a dozen other things. Begin with split and buttered small Italian loaves or hard rolls, then build up layers, adding

anything you fancy. Here are some good combinations, some Italian, some American:
• Slices of *prosciutto,* provolone cheese, and fried eggplant spread with mustard and chili sauce.
• Slices of Cheddar cheese, dill pickles, Spanish or Italian onion, boiled ham, salami, or liverwurst and tomato, green pepper rings, and shredded lettuce spread with mayonnaise or drizzled with Italian dressing.
• Slices of chicken roll or roast chicken spread with deviled ham; slices of Muenster cheese, cucumbers, and bologna spread with mayonnaise and sprinkled with minced scallions.
• Egg salad, slices of tomato and corned beef.
• Instead of buttering bread or rolls, brush with olive oil and sprinkle with garlic salt; add slices of mozzarella cheese, tomato, and salami, then anchovy fillets and Caponata or hot, sautéed, sliced sweet red peppers. Serve as is or, if you like, wrap in foil and bake 20 minutes at 400° F.
• Instead of buttering a small Italian loaf, hollow out bottom half, leaving a 1″ shell. Fill with 3–4 sliced cooked meatballs or sautéed sliced Italian sweet sausage, 1/4 cup grated mozzarella cheese, and 1/3 cup hot tomato or marinara sauce. Add top half of bread, wrap in foil, and bake 10–15 minutes at 400° F.

DANISH SANDWICHES

Lovely to look at and fun to construct. Nearly any combination of bread, meat, filling, and garnish can be used in making these open-face works of art. Here are half a dozen popular combinations, all to be eaten with knife and fork.

• Butter a slice of rye bread and top with a slice of pâté. Mound a few sautéed, sliced mushrooms in the center and lay a crisp bacon strip diagonally across. Place a gherkin fan to one side, tuck a small lettuce leaf underneath, and garnish with a twisted slice of tomato.
• Butter a slice of white bread and top with 2–3 paper-thin slices rare roast beef, crumpling slightly instead of laying flat. Add a small lettuce leaf, top with a dollop of Béarnaise, lay a twisted slice of tomato in the center, and add a few shreds of grated horseradish and crumbles of French-fried onions. Garnish with a pickle fan.

• Spread a slice of white or brown bread with unsalted butter or mayonnaise, mound with tiny Danish shrimp, top with cucumber and lemon slices.
• Spread a slice of rye or pumpernickel with butter, mound tissue-thin slices of corned beef on top. Add a twisted slice of tomato, a dill pickle fan, and a few shreds of grated horseradish.
• Spread the bottom half of a soft round bun with butter, top with thin circles of boiled ham, then mound with shrimp or other seafood salad. Garnish with twisted slices of tomato and cucumber, a frill of crinkly lettuce, and slices of hard-cooked egg.
• Spread a slice of pumpernickel with unsalted butter, top with pickled herring, small crisp onion rings, and slices of cherry tomato. Tuck a lettuce leaf to one side and add a sprig of watercress.

PIMIENTO CHEESE SPREAD

1 3/4 cups, enough for 6–8 sandwiches

3 cups coarsely grated sharp Cheddar cheese
2 tablespoons finely grated onion
1/3 cup minced pimiento
1/2 cup mayonnaise
1 teaspoon prepared spicy brown mustard
1 tablespoon milk or light cream

Mix all ingredients, then beat with a fork until creamy. Cover and let "ripen" in the refrigerator several hours or, better still, overnight. Use as a spread for any bread.

NPS (6–8): 495–405 C, 70–55 mg CH, 710–600 mg S*

CREAM CHEESE AND WATERCRESS SPREAD

1 1/2 cups, enough for 4–6 sandwiches   ☒

8 ounces cream cheese, softened to room temperature
1/2 cup minced watercress leaves
1 tablespoon grated onion
1/8 teaspoon white pepper

Cream all ingredients together until light and use as a sandwich spread. Especially good for dainty afternoon tea sandwiches. This recipe makes enough filling for 2–2 1/2 dozen tea sandwiches.

NPS (4–6): 330–265 C, 65–45 mg CH, 410–350 mg S*

EGG AND PARMESAN SANDWICH SPREAD

1½ cups, enough for 4–6 sandwiches ☒

4 hard-cooked eggs, peeled and coarsely chopped
¼ cup mayonnaise
¼ cup grated Parmesan cheese
½ teaspoon salt
⅛ teaspoon pepper

Blend all ingredients together and use as a spread for any type of bread.

NPS (4-6): 330–265 C, 290–190 mg CH, 755–585 mg S*

SALMON-CAPER SPREAD

1½ cups, enough for 6 sandwiches ☒

1 (15½-ounce) can salmon, drained
3 tablespoons mayonnaise
2 teaspoons tarragon vinegar
2 teaspoons minced capers
2 tablespoons minced chives

Pick over salmon, discarding any coarse bones and dark skin; mash well. Blend in remaining ingredients and use as a spread for white or brown bread.

NPS: 285 C, 30 mg CH, 590 mg S*

WHITSTABLE SANDWICH SPREAD

2 cups, enough for 6–8 sandwiches

Whitstable is a little fishing village east of London famous for its tiny shrimp. Women here make lovely tea sandwiches filled with Whitstable shrimp, minced watercress, scallions, and hard-cooked eggs.

1 cup cooked, shelled, and deveined shrimp, coarsely chopped
½ cup minced watercress
¼ cup minced scallions (include some tops)
2 hard-cooked eggs, peeled and coarsely chopped
2 tablespoons French dressing

Toss all ingredients together lightly and use as a sandwich spread for white or brown bread.

NPS (6–8): 205–185 C, 130–95 mg CH, 370–335 mg S*

WESTERN SANDWICHES

2 sandwiches

¼ cup minced cooked ham
¼ cup minced yellow onion
¼ cup minced sweet green pepper
1 tablespoon butter or margarine

2 eggs, lightly beaten
2 tablespoons cold water
⅛ teaspoon salt
Pinch pepper
4 slices hot buttered toast, buttered bread, or 2 hard rolls, split in half

Stir-fry ham, onion, and green pepper in butter in a heavy 9″ skillet over moderate heat 2–3 minutes until onion is limp. Mix eggs, water, salt, and pepper, pour into skillet and fry like a pancake until firm and lightly browned underneath; turn and brown flip side. Halve and sandwich between toast, folding as needed to fit.

NPS: 370 C, 320 mg CH, 860 mg S*

POTTED SALMON SANDWICHES

1¼ cups filling, enough for 4–6 sandwiches

1 (7¾-ounce) can salmon, drained
1 tablespoon anchovy paste
1 tablespoon lemon juice
Pinch cayenne pepper
⅛ teaspoon cloves
¼ cup butter or margarine, softened to room temperature
8–12 slices firm-textured white or brown bread
½ medium-size cucumber, peeled and sliced paper thin

Pick over salmon, discarding any coarse bones and dark skin; mash with a fork. Add all remaining ingredients except bread and cucumber, mix well to form a smooth paste. Spread *each* slice of bread with salmon, cover half the slices with cucumber, and top with remaining bread. *(Note:* Make these sandwiches shortly before serving—they become soggy on standing.)

NPS (4-6): 320–255 C, 55–35 mg CH, 610–490 mg S*

MONTE CRISTO SANDWICHES

1 sandwich

Crisply grilled chicken (or turkey) and cheese sandwiches.

4 tablespoons butter or margarine (about), softened to room temperature
3 slices firm-textured white bread
2 slices cold roast chicken or turkey
2 slices Monterey Jack, Swiss, or Cheddar cheese
1 egg, lightly beaten
¼ cup milk
⅛ teaspoon salt

Butter bread, 2 slices on one side only, 1 slice on both sides. Lay chicken on a buttered slice, top with doubly buttered slice, cheese, and last slice, buttered side down. Press together lightly; if you like, trim off crusts. Mix egg, milk, and salt, dip in sandwich, coating edges as well as sides. Heat 2 tablespoons butter in a skillet or griddle and brown sandwich over moderately low heat about 2 minutes on each side.

NPS: 1035 C, 510 mg CH, 1560 mg S*

VARIATIONS

Monte Carlo: Prepare as directed but substitute boiled tongue or ham for the chicken.

NPS: 1030 C, 490 mg CH, 2365 mg S*

Cocktail Monte Cristos: Prepare sandwich as directed, cut in 1″ cubes, dip in egg, and fry. Serve with toothpicks as a cocktail snack.

NP Piece: 65 C, 30 mg CH, 95 mg S*

MOZZARELLA IN CARROZZA (MOZZARELLA IN A CARRIAGE)

6 servings

Hearty enough for lunch or supper.

SAUCE
½ cup butter or margarine
¼ cup lemon juice
2 tablespoons minced, drained capers
2 tablespoons minced parsley
6 anchovy fillets, finely chopped

SANDWICHES
6 (¼-inch) slices mozzarella cheese
12 slices Italian-style or firm-textured, day-old white bread, trimmed of crusts
⅓ cup milk or evaporated milk
⅓ cup toasted bread crumbs
¾ cup olive or other cooking oil (about)
¼ cup butter or margarine
3 eggs, lightly beaten

Heat all sauce ingredients, uncovered, over low heat 15 minutes. Cover and keep warm at the back of the stove. Sandwich each slice of mozzarella between 2 slices of bread, then trim so edges of bread are even with cheese. Or, using a large round cookie cutter, cut bread and cheese so they are the same size. Dip edges of each sandwich in milk, then in crumbs to coat evenly. Heat oil and butter in a large, heavy skillet over moderately high heat about 1 minute. (*Note:* Oil should be about 1″ deep in skillet, so add more if necessary.) Dip sandwiches in beaten eggs to coat well, then fry, a few at a time, in oil about 1 minute on each side until golden brown. Drain on paper toweling. Serve hot, topped with some of the sauce.

NPS: 580 C, 225 mg CH, 860 mg S*

VARIATION

Prepare as directed, adding a cut-to-fit slice cooked ham to each sandwich.

NPS: 630 C, 240 mg CH, 1290 mg S*

SIXTEEN

Desserts and Dessert Sauces

The category of desserts includes everything from lavish architectural confections to humble bread puddings. There are fruit desserts, puddings hot and cold, ice creams and sherbets, sweet omelets and crepes.

When choosing a dessert, consider the balance of the menu. The richer the main course, the simpler the dessert should be. Cold weather calls for something hot and hearty, summer something cool and light. If the entree contains little protein, add a dessert made with milk, cream, eggs, or cheese. Remember, too, that all desserts don't zoom off the upper limits of the calorie scale. A number included here are well below 100 calories per serving.

Some Ways to Garnish Desserts

Desserts do not demand garnishes, but for a dinner party you may want to glamorize them a bit by sprigging with mint, rose geranium, or lemon verbena, by adding lemon or orange twists or wedges, clusters of grapes or berries (best for compotes, fruit cups, mousses, and sherbets); or by sprinkling with minced crystallized ginger or glacéed fruits, toasted flaked coconut, minced nuts, or chocolate curls (best for custards, ice creams, puddings).

Baking Desserts in a Microwave Oven

With three notable exceptions—fresh fruits, custards, and *pots de crème*—desserts microwave poorly, so stick to a conventional or convection oven. It goes without saying that you should scrutinize your microwave's in-struction manual before attempting to microwave any dessert. Also read Microwave Ovens in Chapter 1, then follow these guidelines:

Fresh Fruits: These retain their just-picked flavor, color, and shape when microwaved. But because power levels vary from oven to oven and because over-all cooking times depend upon both the quantity and juiciness of the fruit, follow oven manufacturer's directions. Always cook the fruit covered, use the minimum recommended microwaving time, rotate dishes 180° at half time, check frequently for doneness, and allow 2–3 minutes *standing time* on counter to complete the cooking. *Note:* Don't microwave fruit crisps, cobblers, puddings, or shortcakes; they will be soggy and pale.

Custards and Pots de Crème: Cover with wax paper, set directly on oven rack (no need for a water bath), and microwave at *LOW* power setting; rotate casserole 180° or rearrange custard cups halfway through baking. Check individual custards and *pots de crème* often for doneness (some may cook faster than others, so remove each when done). Let stand on counter 1–2 minutes to complete cooking; cool to room temperature, then chill.

How to Caramelize Sugar in a Microwave Oven: It's *so* easy! Simply mix equal amounts sugar and water in a glass measuring cup, then microwave, uncovered, at *HIGH* power setting about 8–10 minutes or until *light* brown (no need to stir). Remove from oven, and let stand on counter a few seconds; mixture will turn a rich dark brown.

Defrosting Frozen Fruit in a Microwave Oven

Remove any metal ties or aluminum foil; open tall containers of frozen fruit, then defrost at power setting recommended by oven manufacturer until fruit is *barely thawed* (it should be cold, firm, and still slightly icy). Rotate or rearrange packages or containers at half time; also flex plastic pouches at half time to speed thawing. (Also see Defrosting, Heating, or Cooking Frozen Foods by Microwave in Chapter 1.)

Baking Desserts in a Convection Oven

Fruits: Avoid crowding fresh fruits in casserole or dish, use the same temperature recommended for baking fruit in a conventional oven, but check for doneness when three fourths of baking time has elapsed. *Note:* Fruit crisps brown superbly in a convection oven.

Leavened Desserts (containing baking powder, soda, and/or eggs): Do not preheat oven (unless recipe specifies to the contrary), but do reduce temperature recommended for conventional oven 50°–75° F. *(never,* however, use temperatures below 300° F.). Place pan or pans in oven so that they touch neither oven walls nor one another. Begin checking desserts for doneness 5–10 minutes before end of suggested baking time. *Note:* For more information, read Convection Ovens in Chapter 1.

FRUIT DESSERTS

Once highly seasonal and available primarily where grown, fresh fruits are abundant today around most of the country and much of the calendar. Moreover, such tropical exotics as mangoes, papayas, and passion fruits are beginning to appear in supermarket fruit bins alongside apples and oranges.

Fruits are unusually adaptable; they team well with one another, many can be poached, baked, broiled, or sautéed as well as served *au naturel.* A fruit dessert may be as unpretentious as a pear, crisp and tart, served with a chunk of Cheddar, or as theatrical as Cherries Jubilee, carried flaming into a darkened room. It may be low-calorie (sliced oranges sprinkled with freshly minced mint) or high (strawberry shortcake drifted with whipped cream). Whatever the dessert, the fruit should look luscious, fresh, and plump, never fussed over—or left over.

The following directory describes favorite fruits (and a few not so well known), recommends which to cook (and how to cook them), which to serve raw, offers calorie counts and shopping tips.

SOME SIMPLE, BASIC WAYS OF PREPARING AND SERVING FRUIT

Peeling, Coring, and Seeding Fruit: Use a stainless-steel knife to prevent fruit from darkening and prepare fruit as you need it, not ahead of time.

Apples, Pears, Figs, and Other Thin, Hard-Skinned Fruits: Use a vegetable peeler or paring knife, paring as thinly as possible. If apples are to be left whole, core with an apple corer, then peel. Otherwise, halve or quarter and cut out core with a paring knife. Pears should be treated the same way; be sure to trim away all gritty flesh surrounding core.

Peaches, Apricots, Nectarines: Plunge fruit in boiling water, let stand about 1 minute, then plunge in cold water and slip off skins. If fruits are to be used whole, do not pit; otherwise, halve and lift pit out.

Citrus Fruits: Cut a thin slice off stem end, then with a paring knife or grapefruit knife cut away rind in an unbroken spiral, taking as much bitter white pith with it as possible.

Grapes: Slit skins lengthwise and "pop" grapes out. To seed, halve and scoop seeds out.

Avocados: If really ripe, skin can be pulled off with the hands. If firm, halve avocado lengthwise, twist out seed, halve each half lengthwise, and pull or cut skin from each quarter.

Pineapple: Slice off top and bottom; stand pineapple on counter, and peel straight down from top to bottom.

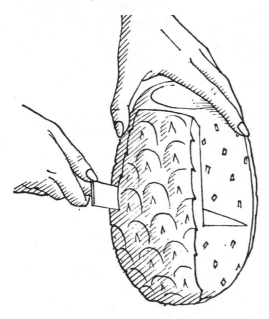

To get the "eyes" out, either (1) make spiral, grooved cuts as shown,

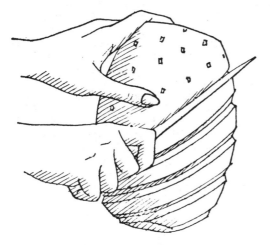

following line of eyes, or (2) peel fruit and dig eyes out with the point of a vegetable peeler or knife. *To core:* If pineapple is to be cut in rings, peel and slice, then cut core from each. Otherwise, quarter pineapple lengthwise, then slice off cores—they will be at the point of each quarter.

Others: Bananas are no problem. Cherries, berries, plums, etc., are usually eaten unpeeled.

About Fruits That Darken: Apples, apricots, avocados, bananas, peaches, nectarines, and some varieties of pear and plum darken after being cut. To keep them bright, dip in lemon or other citrus juice or in an ascorbic acid solution made by mixing ½ teaspoon powdered ascorbic acid (available at drugstores) with ½ cup cold water.

Fruit Cups

These are mixtures of fruit, sometimes fresh, sometimes fresh and frozen or canned, cut in pieces small enough to eat in one bite. For especially pretty fruit cups, team 3–4 fruits of contrasting color, size, shape, and texture: oranges, pineapple, strawberries, and kiwi fruit, for example; bananas, tangerines, peaches, and cherries, grapes, or melon balls; avocado, grapefruit, pears, and plums. For added flavor, mix in a little orange, apple, or pineapple juice, slivered crystallized ginger, grated coconut, minced mint, rose geranium, or lemon verbena. Or, if you prefer, spike with sweet sherry, port or Madeira, or with a fruit liqueur.

Macédoine of Fruit

Named after ancient Macedonia, where fruit desserts were popular, macédoines are mixtures of prettily cut fruits marinated in wine or liqueur. Choose any fresh plump ripe fruits, pare, core, and slice or cube. Layer into a large bowl, sprinkling as you go with superfine sugar, then drizzle with kirsch, Cointreau, Grand Marnier, curaçao, maraschino, other fruit liqueur, or, if you prefer, a fine cognac or brandy. Cover and chill 2–3 hours before serving. Some appealing mixtures:

• Thinly sliced strawberries, pineapple, seedless green grapes with Cointreau.
• Thinly sliced pineapple, pears, kumquats, and peaches with Grand Marnier or white crème de menthe.
• Sliced oranges with cognac, Grand Marnier, or curaçao.
• Thinly sliced apricots, bananas, and strawberries with kirsch or Cointreau.

Serve macédoines cold, set in a large bowl of crushed ice, or flame.

To Flame: First of all, arrange fruits in a flameproof bowl. After chilling, bring macédoine to room temperature. Warm about ¼ cup brandy, rum, or cognac over low heat about 1 minute, pour over fruit and blaze

---

with a match—stand back, mixture will burst into flames. Serve at once.

Fruit Fools

Wonderfully easy old-fashioned desserts, the kind Grandma served when she had sun-ripened fruits and lots of thick country cream. They are equal parts sweetened fruits and heavy cream, sometimes whipped, sometimes not. Sweet berries make glorious fruit fools; so do soft-ripe peaches and apricots, stewed apples and rhubarb. Fruit purées, if really thick, can be mixed ½ and ½ with whipped cream. A mock but very good fool can be made by combining equal parts fruit and mushy vanilla ice cream. Serve fruit fools unadorned or, for a company touch, scattered with minced pistachios or toasted almonds, slivered preserved ginger, crumbled sugar cookies, gingersnaps, or macaroons.

Fruit Purées

Any soft fruit, raw or stewed, purées well. Force through a fine sieve, a food mill, or buzz 15–20 seconds in an electric blender at high speed or 10–15 seconds in a food processor fitted with the metal chopping blade (berry purées should be sieved to remove seeds). Serve as is or as a sauce over ice creams or puddings.

Broiled and Sautéed (Fried) Fruits

(See separate recipes that follow.)

FRUIT FRITTERS (BEIGNETS)

4 servings

Many fruits are superb when batter-fried and sprinkled with sugar or cinnamon, topped with a fruit sauce or Zabaglione, or —for a show-stopper—flamed with brandy or rum. The fruits you fry should be fresh, firm-ripe, then cut in circles, rings, or medium-size wedges or chunks. The fruits may be macerated in wine, liqueur, rum, or fruit juice for 1–2 hours before they're fried. But whether macerated or not, all fruits should be patted *thoroughly dry* on paper toweling before being dipped in batter and fried.

For 4 servings, you'll need 1 recipe Basic Batter for Fried Foods sweetened with 1 tablespoon sugar and any one of the following fruits:
- *Apples* (2–3 medium-size eating variety such as Golden Delicious, Granny Smith, Jonathan, or McIntosh): Peel, core, and cut in ¼″ wedges or rings.
- *Apricots* (8 medium-size): Peel, halve, and pit.
- *Bananas* (4 small to medium-size): Peel and split lengthwise.
- *Nectarines* (8 small): Peel, halve, and pit.
- *Peaches* (4–6 small freestone type): Peel, halve, and pit.
- *Pears* (2–3 medium-size, all-purpose type): Peel, core, and slice ¼″ thick.
- *Pineapple* (1 small): Peel, core, and cut in ¼″ rings.

Sprinkle those fruits apt to darken with lemon juice. Heat cooking oil or vegetable shortening in a deep fat fryer over moderately high heat to 370° F. on a deep fat thermometer. Dip fruit, a few pieces at a time, into batter, letting excess drain off. Drop into hot fat and fry 2–3 minutes until golden brown. Drain on paper toweling, then keep warm by setting, uncovered, in a 250° F. oven while you fry the balance. Sprinkle generously with sugar (use cinnamon sugar for apples or pears). Delicious with honey, also with Currant or Honey Sauce.

FRESH FRUITS—WHEN AND HOW TO USE THEM

Description and Season	Buying Tips	Nutritive Value	Best Uses Preparation Tips
Apples (all-purpose varieties): *The following pie apples: Jonathan, McIntosh, Northern Spy, Stayman, Winesap, Yellow Transparent, York Imperial* (see Pie Apples, chapter on pies and pastries, for descriptions). *Baldwin:* Round, mottled red; juicy,	Regardless of type, select firm, fragrant, bruise- and blemish-free apples. Suit variety to use.	All apples contain some vitamin A, calcium, and phosphorus, large amounts	Eating out-of-hand; raw in salads, desserts; general cooking. *Tip:* Unless dipped in lemon or other tart fruit juice,

Description and Season	Buying Tips	Nutritive Value	Best Uses Preparation Tips

Description and Season	Buying Tips	Nutritive Value	Preparation Tips
tart-sweet. SEASON: November–April. *Cortland:* Round, red, carmine-striped; tart, snowy flesh that doesn't brown after cutting. SEASON: October–December. *Gravenstein:* Round, red-flecked yellow-green; tart, juicy. SEASON: July–September. *Grimes Golden:* Round, gold with brown flecks; juicy, sweet, crisp-tender. SEASON: October–February. *Wealthy:* Round, bright red; sweet, juicy. SEASON: August–December. **Apples (cooking varieties):** *All pie apples* (see Pies and Pastries). *Rome Beauty:* Plump, round, red, tart; hold shape in cooking. SEASON: November–May. **Apples (eating varieties):** *Delicious (Golden* and *Red):* Big, long, yellow or red; juicy-sweet. SEASON: September–April.	As a rule, tart crisp apples are best for cooking, sweet juicy ones are best for eating raw. "Windfalls," often offered as bargains, are perfect for applesauce, apple butter, jams, and jellies. Allow 1 apple per person.	of potassium. About 70 calories per medium-size apple.	apples will turn brown after being cut open. Baked apples *Tips:* Vegetable peelers speed apple peeling; corers and corer-wedgers handy.
Apricots: Smallish, oval, orange-yellow; flesh smooth, fragrant, sweet. Varietal names unimportant. SEASON: May–September.	Choose plump, firm, evenly golden fruit. Allow 1–2 per serving.	High in vitamin A, some C. About 20 calories per apricot.	Eating out-of-hand; raw in desserts, salads; simmered; in pies, puddings. *Tip:* To speed peeling, dip in boiling water.
Avocados: Pear-shaped, smooth green or pebbly black skinned; flesh bland, buttery, nutty. For flavor and texture, thin-skinned, small green *Fuerte* and black *Hass* (a summer variety) are tops. Weigh ½–3 pounds each. SEASON: Year round. *Tip:* In spring and summer look for seedless cocktail-size (1–2-ounce) avocados.	Choose heavy, medium-size fruit, firm but resilient. Allow ¼–½ avocado per person. 3–4 cocktail size.	High in B vitamins. Calories vary with maturity, variety; average about 185 per 3½-ounce serving.	Raw in fruit salads, desserts; in ice creams; as container for meat or fish salads. *Tip:* Dip flesh in lemon or other tart juice to prevent darkening. When halving, cut lengthwise.
Bananas: "Seedless," butter-smooth, fragrant tropical fruits. Varietal names unimportant to shopper. *Now available:* Short, chunky, extra-sweet *red bananas* (they are better keepers than yellow bananas). SEASON: Year round.	Buy firm bananas by the bunch; use as they soften, fleck with brown. Allow 1 banana per person.	Some vitamin A and C; low sodium, low fat; about 85 calories per medium fruit.	Eating out-of-hand; raw in salads, desserts; general cooking. *Tip:* Dip flesh in lemon juice to stop browning.
Berries: *Blackberries, Dewberries:* Plump, glossy, sweet-tart, purple-black; many seeds. *Boysenberries* are large, long Dewberries, *Loganberries* dark red ones. SEASON: Summer.	Choose full, lustrous, mold- and bruise-free berries. Allow about ¼ pound per person.	Some iron, vitamin C. About 60 calories per ¼-pound portion.	Raw with cream, sugar; in pies, puddings, ice cream, jams, preserves, cordials.
Blueberries: Small, round, dusty blue; tart; tiny seeds. SEASON: Summer.	Choose plump, unbroken berries of even size. Allow ¼ pound per person.	Some iron, vitamin C. About 65 calories per ¼ pound.	Raw with cream, sugar; in pies, puddings, pancakes, muffins.

Description and Season	Buying Tips	Nutritive Value	Best Uses Preparation Tips
Cranberries: Hard, acid, ruby hued. SEASON: September–February.	Choose bright, plump berries. Allow 1/4 pound per person.	High in vitamin C. 50 calories per 1/4 pound (unsweetened).	In sauces, relishes, pies, puddings. *Tip:* Be sure to remove wiry stems.
Currants: Small tart red, white or black cousin of gooseberries. SEASON: Summer.	Select bright, plump berries with stems attached. Allow 1/4 pound per person.	Some vitamin A, C. About 60 calories per 1/4 pound (unsweetened).	In pies, puddings, jellies, jams, preserves.
Gooseberries: Silver-green berries the size of small grapes; tart. SEASON: Summer.	Choose full, evenly sized and colored berries. Allow 1/4 pound per person.	Some vitamin A, C. 45 calories per 1/4 pound (unsweetened).	In pies, puddings, jams. *Tip:* Remove both stem and blossom ends before using.
Lingonberries: Tart red cranberry-like Northern berry. SEASON: Summer.	Same as for cranberries. Allow 1/4 pound per person.	Undetermined.	In pancakes, omelets, fruit sauces.
Raspberries: Fragile, cup-shaped, red, black, or golden; juicy-sweet. SEASON: May–December.	Choose bright, plump, uncrushed, unmoldy fruit. Allow 1 cup per serving.	Some vitamin C. 70 calories per cup.	Raw with sugar, cream; in pies, puddings, ice cream.
Strawberries: Plump, sweet, juicy, heart-shaped, bright red; gritty external seeds. SEASON: Year round, most plentiful from May–August.	Choose clean, solid, well-shaped and -colored berries with caps attached; reject leaky boxes. Allow 1 cup per person.	High in vitamin C. 55 calories per cup.	Raw with sugar, cream; in fruit cups, desserts, pies, puddings, ice cream. *Tip:* Remove stems and caps.
Carambolas (Star Fruit, Star Apple): Bright yellow, deeply furrowed, orange-sized, oval fruits with waxy skin (slices resemble stars). Carambolas are crisp, juicy, sweet-sour and taste of both apple and pineapple. SEASON: Summer and fall.	Choose bright, unblemished, firm-ripe fruit beginning to soften. Allow 1–2 per person.	High in vitamin A and C; some potassium; less than 40 calories per 1/2 cup.	Eating out-of-hand; raw in fruit salads; cooked in jellies and jams, also in Asian sauces teamed with lemon grass and chilies. *Tip:* Peel as thinly as possible.
Cherimoyas (Atemoya, Custard Apple): Heart-shaped, warty green fruits marked with "petals"; sweet, creamy-white custard inside tastes of strawberries and stewed apples. SEASON: November–May.	Choose unshriveled, plump fruit beginning to soften and brown. *Tip:* When fruit yields to gentle pressure or stem end splits, it is ready to eat. Allow 1 fruit per person.	High in niacin, thiamine, and phosphorus. About 95 calories per 1/3 cup.	Eating out-of-hand (with a spoon); in fruit salads, blender drinks, sherbets, ice creams. *To serve:* Halve and discard seeds.

Description and Season	Buying Tips	Nutritive Value	Best Uses Preparation Tips

Description and Season	Buying Tips	Nutritive Value	Preparation Tips
Cherries (sweet): Popular varieties: *Bing* (maroon, heart-shaped), *Chapman* (big, round, purple), *Lambert* (big, round, red-brown), *Royal Ann* (big, heart-shaped, salmon colored), *Tartarian* (heart-shaped, deep purple). SEASON: May–September. **Cherries (sour):** Popular types: *Early Richmond* (dark red, plump, round), *Montmorency* (round, red, juicy), *Morello* (round, black, juicy). SEASON: June–mid-August.	Choose plump, bright cherries; firm, if a sweet variety, less so if sour. Allow 1 cup per serving.	Some vitamin A. Calories: about 80 per cup sweet cherries, 60 per cup sour cherries (unsweetened).	In pies, puddings, ice cream, gelatin salads. Sweet cherries also good mixed into fruit desserts. *Tip:* Stem, then scoop out pits using a cherry pitter or point of a vegetable peeler.
Coconuts: Hard-shelled, snowy, nutty-fleshed fruits of a tropical palm. SEASON: Year round.	Buy heavy fruit in which milk sloshes. "Eyes" should not be wet or moldy.	Poor. About 400 calories per ¼ pound.	In pies, cakes, puddings, fruit desserts, candies (see candy chapter for preparation tips).
Crab Apples: Small, hard, wild apples. SEASON: Fall.	Choose those as unblemished as possible.	Poor. About 75 calories per ¼ pound.	For pickling, spicing; in jellies, jams; as garnishes.
Figs: Popular varieties: *Black Mission* (purple, rich, honey-sweet), *Calimyrna* (green, juicy), *Kadota* (green, sweet, fragrant). SEASON: June–October.	Choose soft-ripe, plump, unbruised figs; overripe ones smell sour. Allow 3–4 figs per person.	Some vitamin A, minerals. About 30 calories per small fig.	Eating out-of-hand, raw with cream; stewed, in puddings, preserves.
Grapefruit: Type (i.e., pink, seedless, Florida, which has many seeds but is luscious) more important than botanical variety. SEASON: Year round.	Choose heavy, firm fruit, not puffy or coarse skinned. Allow ½ per person.	High in vitamin C. 55 calories per medium-size ½ grapefruit.	Raw as halves, in fruit desserts, salads. *To peel:* Slice off top, cut rind away in spiral. *To section:* Cut down both sides of divider membranes.
Grapes (table varieties): *Red Grapes:* *Cardinal:* Dark red California hybrid of Tokay and Ribier. Few seeds. SEASON: June–August. *Catawba:* Oval, maroon, sweet Eastern grape. SEASON: September–November. *Delaware:* Small, sweet red Eastern grape. One of the best. SEASON: September–November. *Emperor:* Rosy, egg-shaped California grape; bland, some seeds. SEASON: November–May. *Red Malaga:* Tender-skinned, firm maroon California grape; delicate. SEASON: July–October. *Tokay:* Thick-skinned, red California grape; bland; seeds. SEASON: August–October. *Black Grapes:* *Concord:* Tart, blue-black Eastern grape; some seeds. SEASON: September–October.	Regardless of type, select plump, clean, unshriveled grapes firmly attached to stems. Bright color, especially with red or black grapes, indicates ripeness. Fully ripe green grapes have an amber cast. Allow ¼–⅓ pound per person.	All grapes contain some vitamin A and C, calcium and phosphorus. About 75 calories per ¼ pound, sour grapes somewhat less.	Eating out-of-hand; in table arrangements. Sweet varieties with few seeds (Thompson Seedless) are best for fruit salads, fruit cups, and desserts. Tart strong varieties (Concord) are best for jams and jellies. All grapes make beautiful garnishes.

Description and Season	Buying Tips	Nutritive Value	Best Uses Preparation Tips

Grapes (continued)
Ribier: Large, oblong, jet-black, tough-skinned California grape; tart, some seeds. SEASON: July–February.
Green/White Grapes:
Almeria: Tough-skinned California grape; not tart, not sweet. SEASON: October–April.
Muscadine: Large family of Southern grapes, green, russet, or black; includes Scuppernong. Juicy and sweet. SEASON: September–October.
Niagara: Strong, foxy Eastern grape. SEASON: September–November.
Thompson Seedless: Luscious, sweet, seedless green California grape. SEASON: June–January.
White Malaga: Bland California grape being replaced by Thompson Seedless. SEASON: September–November.

Buying Tips: Regardless of type, select plump, clean, unshriveled grapes firmly attached to stems. Bright color, especially with red or black grapes, indicates ripeness. Fully ripe green grapes have an amber cast. Allow 1/4–1/3 pound per person.

Nutritive Value: All grapes contain some vitamin A and C, calcium and phosphorus. About 75 calories per 1/4 pound, sour grapes somewhat less.

Preparation Tips: Eating out-of-hand; in table arrangements. Sweet varieties with few seeds (Thompson Seedless) are best for fruit salads, fruit cups, and desserts. Tart strong varieties (Concord) are best for jams and jellies. All grapes make beautiful garnishes.

Guavas: Small, oval, thick-fleshed, perfumy tropical fruit. Flesh red or golden; many seeds. Newly available *feijoas* are guavas from New Zealand and South America. SEASON: Year round in deep South, Florida, California.

Buying Tips: Choose firm-ripe fruit beginning to soften. Allow 1/4 pound per person.

Nutritive Value: High in vitamin C, A. About 70 calories per 1/4 pound.

Preparation Tips: Eating out-of-hand, raw in fruit salads; in jellies and pastes. *Tip:* Peel as thinly as possible.

Kiwi Fruits: Egg-sized and -shaped, fuzzy, brown-skinned fruits from New Zealand. Flesh is pulpy, green, and flecked with tiny, edible, black seeds. Flavor suggests plums and strawberries. SEASON: Year round.

Buying Tips: Choose firm-ripe, unblemished fruit; ripen at room temperature until soft.

Nutritive Value: Not determined, but thought to be high in vitamin C.

Preparation Tips: Eating out-of-hand; raw in fruit salads and desserts, on breakfast cereals; a favorite garnish for *nouvelle cuisine* plates and composed salads.

Kumquats: Tiny, tart, orange citrus fruits eaten skin and all. SEASON: November–February.

Buying Tips: Buy heavy, unshriveled fruit, 2–3 per person.

Nutritive Value: High in vitamin A. 70 calories per 1/4 pound.

Preparation Tips: Eating out-of-hand, raw in desserts; in preserves. *To seed:* Halve lengthwise and scrape out seeds.

Lemons: Sunny, sour citrus fruits. SEASON: Year round.

Buying Tips: Buy heavy, soft-skinned fruit; green tinges indicate super-sourness.

Nutritive Value: High in vitamin C, low in calories.

Preparation Tips: As a flavoring and garnish.

Lichees: Scarlet, cherry-size, leathery-shelled Chinese fruits; snowy, juicy, perfumy flesh. Dried lichees, eaten like raisins, are called lichee nuts. SEASON: Summer.

Buying Tips: Buy unshriveled fruit, 1/3 pound per person.

Nutritive Value: Some vitamin C. 75 calories per 1/3 pound.

Preparation Tips: Eating out-of-hand, peeled, raw in fruit desserts. *Tip:* Pit as you would cherries.

Limes: Sour, green citrus fruit. SEASON: Year round.

Buying Tips: Same as for lemons.

Nutritive Value: Same as for lemons.

Preparation Tips: Same as for lemons.

Description and Season	Buying Tips	Nutritive Value	Best Uses Preparation Tips
Loquats: Yellow-orange, tart-sweet, downy Chinese plums; many seeds. SEASON: Summer.	Buy firm-ripe, bright fruit, 2–3 per person.	Some vitamin A. 25 calories per loquat.	Eating out-of-hand, peeled, raw in fruit salads, dessert. *Tip:* Rub down skin to remove fuzz before eating.
Mangoes: Large, kidney-shaped, tropical fruits, red-orange and green skinned; flesh orange, peachlike flavor with a hint of pine; one huge seed. SEASON: May–September.	Choose fresh, firm fruit. Allow about ½ mango per person.	High in vitamins A and C. About 85 calories per ½ mango.	Raw in fruit desserts, salads; in pickles, chutney. *To seed:* Halve lengthwise, pry out seed. *Tip:* Peel as thinly as possible.
Melons: *Cantaloupe:* Plump round melon, buff rind with green netting; sweet, juicy, orange flesh. SEASON: March–December. *Casaba:* Large yellow melon, pointed at stem end, ridged rind; sweet, ivory-hued flesh. SEASON: August–November; a Christmas variety available in December. *Charentais:* Small, round, French melons with pale green skin and supremely sweet orange flesh. SEASON: Year round. *Crenshaw:* Large oval melon with pointed ends, green and yellow rind, sweet salmon flesh. SEASON: July–October. *Honeyball:* Round melon, lightly webbed, buff-pink rind; pink, sweet flesh. SEASON: June–November. *Honeydew:* Large, round pale green melon with honey-sweet green flesh. SEASON: June–October. *Persian Melon:* Like cantaloupe but bigger. SEASON: July–October. *Spanish Melon:* Large oblong melon with pointed ends, ridged green skin, pale green, sweet flesh. SEASON: June–October. *Watermelon:* Dozens of varieties, some round, some long, some light, some dark green. Newest are midgets with few seeds. SEASON: June–September.	Regardless of type, select clean, firm, plump melons with clean scars at the stem ends. Ripe cantaloupes will soften slightly at blossom end, honeydews will yield slightly when pressed. Sniffing the stem or blossom end for fragrance is a test for ripeness. Good ripe watermelons will sound hollow when thumped. Allow ½ small melon per person, slices or wedges of larger melons.	Orange-fleshed melons are high in vitamin A, all contain some vitamin C. Calories vary according to type; ½ small cantaloupe runs about 60 calories, ¼ pound watermelon about 40.	All melons can be served more or less the same way—raw, in slices, halves, cubes, or balls; mixed into fruit salads and desserts; puréed into sherbet and ice cream; as garnishes.
Nectarines: Small, smooth-skinned peaches; richer, sweeter than other types. SEASON: June–September.	Buy plump, firm, unblemished, unbruised fruit, 1–2 per person.	High in vitamin A. About 75 calories per nectarine.	Same as for peaches. *Tip:* Dip in citrus juice after cutting to prevent browning.
Oranges (juice types): *Hamlin:* Early Florida-Texas orange, smooth rind; tart, few seeds. SEASON: October–January. *Parson Brown:* Heavily seeded Florida orange; coarse flesh; tart. SEASON: October–December.	Regardless of type, oranges should weigh heavy for their size, be plump and firm. Rind	High in vitamin C; about 60 calories per medium-size orange, 100–	Squeezed into juice. Sweeter, less seedy types can be sectioned and mixed into fruit cups, salads, desserts. *To*

FRESH FRUITS—WHEN AND HOW TO USE THEM (continued)

Description and Season	Buying Tips	Nutritive Value	Best Uses — Preparation Tips
Oranges *(continued)* *Pineapple:* Midseason Florida orange; tart-sweet, many seeds. SEASON: January–March. *Valencia:* Popular variety grown in Florida, Texas, Arizona, and California; deep golden rind, sweet, juicy, few seeds. SEASON: January–November. **Oranges (eating types):** *Navel:* Large, thick-skinned, seedless Florida-California orange with navel on blossom end. Sweet, easily peeled and sectioned. SEASON: November–mid-June. *Temple:* Popular, large oval Florida orange, thought to be a hybrid of tangerine and orange. Deep orange rind, sweet, rich, and juicy. Many seeds. SEASON: December–April. **Oranges (exotic types):** *Blood:* Ruby-fleshed, honey-sweet oranges popular in Mediterranean and Middle Eastern countries. Increasingly available here. *Clementine:* Small, sweet, richly flavored, tangerine-like orange; available in specialty food markets. *Mandarin:* A variety of tangerine. *Seville or Bigarade:* Sour, bitter Mediterranean oranges, occasionally available in specialty food markets.	color has little to do with quality —many oranges are dyed; those with greenish casts may be fully ripe. Allow 1 orange per person. It takes 2–3 to make 1 cup juice.	110 calories per cup of juice, depending on sweetness.	section: Same as for grapefruit. Eating oranges are best eaten out-of-hand, sectioned or sliced raw into desserts, salads. Temples also juice well. In marmalade; for making candied orange rind.
Papayas: Tropical melon-like fruit; sweet-musky orange flesh; large cluster of dark seeds in the center; its juice contains an enzyme used in meat tenderizers. SEASON: Year round.	Choose yellow fruit, soft but not mushy. Green fruit won't ripen. Sizes: 1–20 pounds. 2–3-pound size best. Allow ¼ pound per person.	High in vitamin A and C. About 50 calories per ¼ pound.	Raw in fruit salads, desserts. Also in wedges like melon with lemon or lime. Use seeds as garnishes. *Tip:* Juice can cause skin rash, so wear gloves while peeling and preparing papayas.
Passion Fruits (granadillas): Subtropical, purple-black egg-shaped, sweet-tart fruits about 3″ long; skin is wrinkled, flesh golden-orange; many edible gray-green seeds. SEASON: Autumn.	Select plump, firm-soft, blemish-free fruits, 1–2 per person. Don't be put off by withered skin.	Undetermined. About 50 calories per ¼ pound.	Eating out-of-hand, with a spoon; in pies, puddings; also raw in fruit desserts. Juice delicious in punch. *Tip:* Halve and eat, seeds and all.
Peaches: Varieties matter less than types: *clingstone* (most are canned commercially) and *freestone* (Elberta is a favorite), best for eating, cooking because pits remove easily. Peach flesh may be white, yellow, orange. SEASON: mid-May–October.	Choose firm-tender, fragrant, blemish-free fruit showing little green. Allow 1 peach per person.	High in vitamin A, some C. About 35 calories per medium-size peach.	Eating out-of-hand; raw in fruit salads, desserts; in pies, puddings, upside-down cakes, shortcakes. *Tips:* Dip peaches in boiling water and skins will slip off. Dip cut peaches in citrus juice to prevent browning.

Description and Season	Buying Tips	Nutritive Value	Best Uses / Preparation Tips

Pears (all-purpose varieties):
Anjou: Big, yellow-russet; crisp, vinous flavor. SEASON: October–May.
Bosc: Large, thin-necked, cinnamon pear; tart. SEASON: October–April.
Clapp Favorite: Almost round, red-yellow, sweet, smooth, juicy. SEASON: August–November.
Seckel: Small russet pear; flesh gritty at core; spicy flavor. SEASON: August–December.
Winter Nelis: Large, roundish, russeted dark green pear; buttery, spicy. SEASON: October–May.
Pears (eating varieties):
Asian: Golden-skinned, apple-shaped pear with juicily crisp, cream-colored flesh. SEASON: August–February.
Bartlett: Big, bell-shaped, yellow-green pear; smooth, sweet-musky. SEASON: July–mid-October.
Comice: Large, roundish, chartreuse; fine, juicy-sweet flesh. SEASON: October–March.

Buying Tips: Regardless of type, buy firm-ripe—not hard—pears of good color and shape. Reject unclean, bruised, blemished ones. Allow 1 pear per person.

Nutritive Value: Poor for all varieties. About 100 calories per medium-size pear. Not determined for Asian pear but probably comparable.

Preparation Tips: Eating out-of-hand; poaching; canning; preserving; in upside-down cakes; sliced raw into fruit salads, cups, and desserts. *Tip:* Some types darken after cutting, so dip in citrus juice to be safe. Also trim away any gritty areas surrounding core.

Eating out-of-hand; raw in fruit cups, desserts, salads. Bartletts also good for canning.

Persimmons: Two principal types: *wild American* (small, puckery, good only after first frost) and *Oriental* (plump, vermilion fruits big as apples; flesh soft and sweet). SEASON: October–February.

Buying Tips: Choose plump, glossy, firm-tender fruit with stems and caps attached. Allow 1 per person.

Nutritive Value: High in vitamin A, some C. About 80 calories per medium-size Oriental persimmon.

Preparation Tips: Eating out-of-hand (wild varieties only if squishy-ripe); raw in fruit cups, desserts; in puddings, pies. *Tip:* Peel as thinly as possible.

Pineapples: Large prickly tropical fruits, pale to deep yellow; flesh tart and juicy. SEASON: Year round.

Buying Tips: Buy fresh, clean fruit, heavy for its size, with flat "eyes" and strong bouquet. Allow about 1/4 pound per serving.

Nutritive Value: Some vitamin C; about 60 calories per 1/4 pound serving.

Preparation Tips: Raw in fruit salads, desserts; in pies, puddings, ice creams, upside-down cake. *Tip:* Do not use with gelatin (an enzyme in pineapple keeps it from thickening).

Plums (European types): These are fairly small, tart, blue, green, or black skinned. Popular varieties: *Damson* (small, acid, black), *Greengage* (green, mild, and sweet), *Prune-Plum* (dark purple, firm, tart). SEASON: Early summer.
Plums (Japanese types): These are large, lush, scarlet, yellow, or magenta. Popular ones: *Burbank* (vermilion, sweet), *Duarte* (maroon-skinned, scarlet-fleshed, sweet), *Santa Rosa* (red-purple, tart-sweet, juicy). SEASON: August–October.

Buying Tips: Regardless of type, buy clean, plump, fresh plums, soft enough to yield when pressed. Reject bruised, sunburned (browned) ones. Allow 1–2 plums per person.

Nutritive Value: All plums are high in vitamin A and contain some C. Calories vary with sweetness: a medium-size, not too sweet plum averages about 25 calories.

Preparation Tips: Eating out-of-hand; poaching; in fruit cups, compotes, salads, desserts; in puddings, preserves.

Eating out-of-hand; raw in fruit desserts.

Description and Season	Buying Tips	Nutritive Value	Best Uses Preparation Tips
Pomegranates: Curious red Persian fruits, about the size of oranges with fleshy, ruby clusters of kernels, each encasing a dark seed. These are eaten much like grapes, the flesh being sucked from the seeds. SEASON: September–January.	Choose medium to large fruits, bright pink or red. Allow about ½ fruit per person.	Undetermined. About 40 calories per ¼ pound.	Eating out-of-hand; pulp good in sherbet, ice cream. *To eat:* Halve lengthwise, remove rind and membrane. Eat ruby kernels, discarding seeds. *To juice:* Halve crosswise and ream as you would an orange. Juice good in punch.
Prickly Pears: Fruits of *Opuntia* cactus of the Southwest; flesh may be yellow, red, purple; sweet and watery with little flavor. SEASON: Early autumn.	Choose plump, red-ripe, unshriveled fruits about the size of pears with few barbs. Allow 1 per person.	Poor. About 30 calories per medium-size fruit.	Eating out-of-hand; raw in fruit cups and desserts; in jellies. *Tip:* Barbs must be singed off before fruit is peeled.
Pumpkins (See vegetable chapter.)			
Quinces: Hard golden fruits; not edible raw. SEASON: October–December.	Buy fruits as unblemished as possible.	High in vitamin C. About 50 calories per medium-size fruit.	In jellies, jams, preserves.
Rhubarb: Succulent scarlet stalks; not eaten raw. SEASON: February–August.	Choose crisp, straight, bright red stalks. A 1-pound bunch serves 2–4.	Poor. Calories vary according to cooking method.	Stewed; in pies, jams. *Tip:* Roots are poisonous, so trim stalks carefully.
Tangelos: Grapefruit-tangerine hybrids that taste like tart oranges. SEASON: November–March.	Buy plump fruit, heavy for its size. Allow 1 per person.	High in vitamin C. About 50 calories per medium-size fruit.	Use as you would oranges or tangerines.
Tangerines: Small, flat, loose-skinned oranges of the mandarin type, easily peeled and sectioned. SEASON: November–May.	Choose plump, heavy fruits. Puffiness, flabby skins indicate poor quality. Allow 1 tangerine per person.	High in vitamin C. About 40 calories per medium-size fruit.	Eating out-of-hand; sectioned in fruit desserts and salads.
Ugli Fruits: Pale green, misshapen fruits as big as grapefruits with coarse, thick rinds. SEASON: November–May.	Choose heavy, plump fruit; when ripe, rind turns orange.	Undetermined.	Squeezed into juice; eaten out-of-hand; peeled and sectioned like an orange and added to salads, desserts.

POACHED (STEWED) FRUITS

Note: For best results, fruits should be firm, not mushy. Quantities are enough for 4 ample servings.

Fruit	Quantity and Preparation	Poaching Syrup	Method	Optional Flavorings (Choose One)
Apples (Rome Beauties are best)	1 quart peeled, cored quarters or eighths OR 4 whole peeled and cored apples	3 cups Thin	Simmer apples, uncovered, in syrup 8–10 minutes until firm-tender. Serve in some syrup.	1 stick cinnamon 3–4 cloves Piece crystallized ginger Strip lemon or orange rind Mint, rose geranium sprigs
Apricots, Pears, Oranges	4 peeled whole or halved apricots or pears, 4 peeled whole oranges	2 cups Medium	Simmer, uncovered, in syrup until heated through, about 5 minutes for apricots, 10–15 for pears and oranges. Serve in some syrup.	1 stick cinnamon 1 teaspoon curry powder Strip lemon or orange rind Piece crystallized ginger 1″ vanilla bean
Cherries	1 quart whole, pitted or unpitted	2 cups Medium	Simmer, uncovered, in syrup 3–5 minutes. Serve in some syrup.	1 stick cinnamon 2–3 cloves Strip lemon or orange rind
Berries, Peaches, Plums	1 quart whole berries, 4 whole peeled or halved peaches, 8 whole unpeeled plums	1 cup Heavy	Simmer, uncovered, in syrup until heated through—2–3 minutes for berries, 5 for plums, peaches about 10. Serve in syrup.	1 stick cinnamon and 1 teaspoon curry powder (for peaches only) 1″ vanilla bean 2 lemon or orange slices
Rhubarb	1 quart 1″ chunks	1 cup Heavy	Simmer, uncovered, in syrup about 15 minutes until crisp-tender. Serve in syrup.	1 teaspoon finely grated orange or lemon rind

VARIATION: Prepare as directed but substitute 1/4–1/3 cup fruit liqueur, rum, brandy, sherry, Porto, or Madeira for 1/4–1/3 cup syrup. (*Note:* Also see separate recipes that follow.)

POACHING SYRUPS

Type	Sugar	Water	Method	Yield
Thin	1 cup	3 cups	Boil sugar and water, uncovered, 3–5 minutes	3 cups
Medium	1 cup	2 cups	until sugar is dissolved.	2 cups
Heavy	1 cup	1 cup		1 cup

BAKED FRUITS

Fruit	Preparation and Method	Cooking Time and Temperature
Apples (see separate recipes that follow)		
Apricots, pears, peaches	Peel, core, or pit and halve; drizzle with lemon juice, sprinkle with sugar and, if you like, nutmeg and cinnamon. Dot with butter and cover.	15–20 minutes at 425° F. (canned fruit bakes in 10 minutes).
Bananas (see separate recipes that follow)		
Grapefruit, oranges (use Temple or Navel)	Halve grapefruit; peel oranges but leave whole. Sprinkle with sugar or honey and dot with butter. Do not cover.	30–40 minutes at 350° F. Baste occasionally with pan drippings.
Pineapple	Quarter lengthwise, prickly crown and all; do not peel. Cut out core, then score flesh in cubes and loosen. Sprinkle with sugar or honey, dot with butter. Do not cover	30–40 minutes at 350° F. Baste now and then with pan drippings.
Rhubarb	Cut 2 pounds rhubarb in 1″ lengths. Place in a shallow baking dish, sprinkle with 3 tablespoons water and 1½ cups superfine sugar. Also sprinkle lightly with nutmeg and cinnamon, if you like, or drizzle with lemon or orange juice. Cover.	½–¾ hour at 350° F.

Fruit Kebabs

Choose fairly firm but fleshy raw or canned fruits—1″ cubes of apricot, peach, pear, or pineapple, thick banana slices, seedless grapes, sweet cherries—and alternate colorful combinations on short metal skewers. Drizzle with honey or light corn syrup (or Heavy Poaching Syrup) and melted butter. Broil about 4″ from the heat 3–5 minutes, turning and brushing often with additional honey and melted butter. Serve sizzling hot.

Serving Fruit with Cheese

(See chapter on eggs, cheese, and dairy.)

Canned and Frozen Fruits

Nearly all popular fruits—and a number of unusual ones like lichees and papayas—are canned and/or frozen. Some are packed in syrup, others in water for the diet conscious. These are most suitable for compotes and fruit cups, for serving over or under ice creams and puddings. Canned peach, apricot, and pear halves bake and broil well (follow directions for fresh fruits, reducing times slightly).

Dried Fruits

In the dim days of history, man learned that fruits dried under the sun kept well many months. Today the drying is done mechanically, producing plump, moist, ready-to-use fruits: prunes (dried plums), dates, apricots, raisins (dried grapes). Other commonly dried fruits are apples, currants, peaches, pears, nectarines, and figs.

Dates, raisins, and currants are not cooked except as they are used in breads, cakes, puddings, and pies. Prunes, figs, apricots, and peaches (especially the extra-soft "tenderized" ones) can be used straight from the package or they may be stewed. Dried apples and pears, being a good deal drier, must be cooked.

Soaking Dried Fruits: Modern techniques have very nearly made soaking a thing of the past. Read and follow label directions carefully. Soaking too long or in too much water makes fruits mushy and flavorless.

Stewing Dried Fruits:

Apples and Pears: Soak or not as package label directs. Place in a large saucepan, add cold water to cover, set over moderate heat, cover, and simmer about 40 minutes until tender. Sweeten, if you like, adding ¼–⅓ cup sugar per cup of fruit. *For Extra Flavor:* Tuck a couple of lemon slices down into fruit, or a cinnamon stick, or several mint or rose geranium sprigs.

Apricots, Peaches, and Nectarines: Soak or not as directed. Place in a large saucepan, cover with cold water, cover pan, and simmer 40–45 minutes until tender. Sweeten, if you like, using 3–4 tablespoons sugar per cup of fruit. *For Extra Flavor:* Simmer a few slices lemon, orange, or preserved ginger or a small piece of vanilla bean along with fruit.

Figs: Soak or not as directed. Place in a large saucepan, add cold water to cover, and simmer, covered, 20–30 minutes until tender. Sweeten, if you like, using about 1 tablespoon sugar or honey per cup of fruit. *For Extra Flavor:* Simmer with a few slices lemon or crystallized ginger.

Prunes: Soak or not as label directs. Pit if you like. *(Note:* Pitted prunes are available.) Place in a large pan, add cold water just to cover, and simmer, covered, about 3/4 hour until tender. Or cover prunes with boiling water and let stand overnight. *(Note:* "Tenderized" prunes—and most of those produced in the U.S. today *are*—will take only 20 minutes. No need to add sugar.) *For Extra Flavor:* Simmer 2–3 slices lemon studded with cloves along with prunes.

(Note: Stewed dried fruits will be plumper, mellower, richer if allowed to stand overnight at room temperature in their cooking liquid before being served.)

To "Plump" Raisins and Dried Currants: If hard and dry, raisins (both the seedless and golden seedless, also called *sultanas*) and currants will sink to the bottom of breads and puddings. To prevent this, cover with boiling water and let stand about 5 minutes until they grow plump and soft. Drain well before using. Or, if you like, soak 5–10 minutes in rum or brandy.

Cutting and Mincing Dried Fruits: These are sticky and difficult to cut with a knife. Snip with scissors dipped in very hot water.

AMBROSIA

6 servings   ⚖ ⌧

A vitamin-C rich dessert that everyone likes.

4 large navel oranges, peeled
1/3 cup sifted confectioners' sugar
1 cup finely grated fresh coconut or 1 (3½-ounce) can flaked coconut
1/4 cup orange juice

Remove all outer white membrane from oranges and slice thin crosswise. Layer oranges into a serving bowl, sprinkling with sugar, coconut, and orange juice as you go. Cover and chill 2–3 hours. Mix lightly and serve.

NPS: 135 C, 0 mg CH, 5 mg S*

VARIATION

⚖ Reduce oranges to 2 or 3 and add 2–3 peeled, thinly sliced bananas or 1 small fresh pineapple, peeled, cored, and cut in thin wedges.

NPS: 145 C, 0 mg CH, 5 mg S*

HOT FRUIT COMPOTE

6–8 servings

A good basic recipe that can be varied a number of ways.

1 pound small ripe peaches or apricots, peeled, pitted, and halved
1 pound small ripe pears, peeled, cored, and halved
1 pound small ripe plums, peeled, pitted, and halved
1 cup firmly packed light brown sugar
1/2 cup orange juice mixed with 1/2 cup water
1/4 cup lemon juice
1 tablespoon finely slivered orange rind
2 tablespoons butter or margarine

Preheat oven to 350° F. Arrange fruits in a large casserole. Combine sugar, orange juice mixture, lemon juice, and orange rind; pour over fruits, then dot with butter. Bake, uncovered, 1/2 hour; serve hot with cream or cool and ladle over ice cream or pound cake.

NPS (6–8): 290–215 C, 10–5 mg CH, 50–40 mg S*

VARIATIONS

Spiced Hot Fruit Compote: Add 1/2 teaspoon cinnamon and 1/4 teaspoon each ginger, nutmeg, and allspice to sugar mixture and proceed as directed.

NPS (6–8): 290–215 C, 10–5 mg CH, 50–40 mg S*

Brandied Hot Fruit Compote: Prepare fruit compote as directed, using 1/2 cup each brandy and orange juice; also reduce lemon juice to 2 tablespoons.

NPS (6–8): 295–220 C, 10–5 mg CH, 50–40 mg S*

Curried Hot Fruit Compote: First, heat and stir 1½ teaspoons curry powder in the butter called for in a flameproof casserole 1–2 minutes over moderate heat. Add fruits, substituting 2 cups pineapple chunks for the plums, pour in sugar mixture, mix well, and bake as directed. Serve hot with meat or poultry.

NPS (6–8): 290–215 C, 10–5 mg CH, 55–40 mg S*

GINGERED HONEYDEW MELON

4–6 servings   ⚖

1 medium-size ripe honeydew melon (about 3¹/₂–
   4 pounds)
1¹/₂ cups water
¹/₂ cup sugar
6 (1-inch) squares candied ginger
¹/₂ lemon, quartered

Halve melon lengthwise and scoop out seeds; remove rind and cut melon in bite-size cubes; place in a large mixing bowl. Simmer water, uncovered, with sugar and ginger about 30 minutes, stirring occasionally. Off heat, add lemon and cool to lukewarm. Pour syrup and lemon over melon, toss to mix, cover, and chill 3–4 hours. Remove lemon, spoon melon into stemmed goblets, and top with a little of the syrup.

NPS (4–6): 210–140 C, 0 mg CH, 30–20 mg S*

STRAWBERRIES ROMANOFF

4–6 servings

A glamorized version of strawberries and cream.

1 quart fresh strawberries, washed, stemmed,
   and, if large, halved lengthwise
2–3 tablespoons superfine sugar (optional)
¹/₃ cup orange juice
¹/₄ cup curaçao
³/₄ cup heavy cream
2 tablespoons confectioners' sugar
¹/₄ teaspoon vanilla

Taste berries and, if tart, sprinkle with sugar. Let stand 10 minutes at room temperature, then toss lightly to mix. Add orange juice and curaçao and toss again; cover and chill several hours, turning berries occasionally. Spoon into a shallow serving dish. Whip cream with sugar and vanilla until soft peaks form, spoon into a pastry bag fitted with a large, fluted tube, and pipe cream over berries, covering completely.

*NPS (4–6): 290–190 C, 60–40 mg CH, 20–10
  mg S**

LICHEES IN PORT WINE

4–6 servings   ⚖

A refreshing and unique summer dessert.

2 pounds fresh lichees, peeled, seeded, and
   halved, or 3 cups halved, drained, canned
   lichees (both are available in Chinese
   groceries)
¹/₂ cup ruby port wine

Place lichees and port in a small bowl and toss well to mix; cover and chill several hours. Serve in stemmed goblets.

NPS (4–6): 130–85 C, 0 mg CH, 2–1 mg S*

OLD-FASHIONED APPLESAUCE

4–6 servings   ¢

The kind Grandmother used to make.

3 pounds greenings or other tart cooking apples,
   peeled, cored, and quartered
1 cup sugar
²/₃ cup water

Simmer all ingredients, uncovered, in a large saucepan, stirring frequently, 20–25 minutes until mushy. Serve hot or cold.

NPS (4–6): 355–240 C, 0 mg CH, ¹/₂–¹/₃ mg S*

VARIATION

¢ **Spicy Applesauce:** Prepare as directed, using light brown sugar instead of granulated, reducing water to ¹/₂ cup, and adding the juice of ¹/₂ lemon, ¹/₄ teaspoon cinnamon, ¹/₈ teaspoon nutmeg, and 1 tablespoon butter or margarine.

NPS (4–6): 395–265 C, 8–5 mg CH, 45–30 mg S*

GOLDEN SAFFRON APPLES

4 servings

¹/₈ teaspoon saffron
¹/₂ cup + 1 tablespoon water
³/₄ cup sugar
4 large tart cooking apples, peeled, cored, and
   cut in thick wedges
1 teaspoon lemon juice
1 teaspoon grated orange rind
2 tablespoons toasted, blanched, slivered
   almonds

Crush saffron and soak in 1 tablespoon water 10 minutes; boil sugar with remaining water, uncovered, stirring occasionally, 4–5 minutes to make a thin syrup. Turn heat to low, strain saffron water into syrup, add apples, lemon juice, and orange rind, cover, and simmer 7–10 minutes until apples are tender but not mushy. Cool apples in their syrup, then chill well. Serve topped with almonds.

*NPS: 280 C, 0 mg CH, .8 mg S**

BAKED APPLES

4 servings   ¢

4 large cooking apples (Rome Beauties are best)
2/3 cup sugar
2/3 cup water
1 tablespoon butter or margarine
Pinch cinnamon and/or nutmeg
2–3 drops red food coloring

Preheat oven to 350° F. Core apples, then peel about one third of the way down from the stem end, or, if you prefer, peel entirely. Arrange in an ungreased shallow baking pan. Boil remaining ingredients about 5 minutes to form a clear syrup, pour over apples, and bake, uncovered, 3/4–1 hour, basting often with syrup, until crisp-tender. Serve hot or cold, topped if you like with Custard Sauce or whipped cream.

*NPS: 265 C, 8 mg CH, 30 mg S**

VARIATIONS

¢ **Brown Sugar Glazed Apples:** Bake apples as directed, remove from oven, baste with syrup, then sprinkle each with 1 tablespoon dark brown sugar mixed with a pinch of cinnamon. Broil 4″ from the heat 1–2 minutes until sugar melts.

*NPS: 315 C, 8 mg CH, 35 mg S**

¢ **Baked Stuffed Apples:** Core and peel apples as directed, place in pan and half fill hollows with chopped pitted dates, prunes, or other dried fruit; sprinkle 2 tablespoons sugar into each hollow, finish filling with chopped fruit, and dot with butter or margarine. Omit syrup; instead, pour 1/2 cup water around apples and bake as directed, but without basting.

*NPS: 285 C, 10 mg CH, 40 mg S**

FRIED APPLE RINGS

6 servings   ⚖ ¢ ⊠

Good as dessert or as a garnish for a roast pork platter.

1/3 cup butter or margarine
4 medium-size cooking apples, cored but not
   peeled and sliced 1/2″ thick
Unsifted flour

Heat butter in a large, heavy skillet over moderate heat 1 minute. Dredge apples in flour, shake off excess, and sauté, a few at a time, in butter about 10 minutes, turning often until lightly browned. Drain on paper toweling and serve hot.

*NPS: 140 C, 20 mg CH, 80 mg S**

VARIATIONS

⚖ ¢ **Curried Apple Rings:** Prepare as directed but sprinkle with 1–1 1/2 teaspoons curry powder halfway through sautéing. (*Note:* Any of the following sautéed fruits may be curried the same way.)

*NPS: 140 C, 20 mg CH, 80 mg S**

⚖ **Sautéed Peaches or Apricots:** Pat 6 peach or apricot halves dry on paper toweling, then dredge and sauté 5–6 minutes as directed.

*NPS: 130 C, 20 mg CH, 80 mg S**

Sautéed Halved Bananas: Peel 6 underripe bananas and halve lengthwise. Dredge and sauté in butter about 5 minutes. Sprinkle lightly with salt and serve with meat or poultry.

*NPS: 190 C, 20 mg CH, 80 mg S**

BAKED BANANAS

4 servings   ⊠

4 slightly underripe bananas
1/4 cup melted butter or margarine
Sugar, dark brown sugar, or salt

Preheat oven to 350° F. Peel bananas and arrange whole or split lengthwise in a buttered 1-quart *au gratin* dish or shallow casserole; brush well with butter. Bake, uncovered, 15–20 minutes until soft and pale golden. Sprinkle with sugar and serve as dessert or sprinkle with salt and serve as an accompaniment to roast loin of pork or chicken.

*NPS: 225 C, 30 mg CH, 120 mg S**

BANANAS FLAMBÉ

4 servings   ⊠

A showy but *easy* dessert you can prepare at the table.

1/2 cup butter (no substitute)
3/4 cup firmly packed light brown sugar
2 tablespoons lemon juice
4 slightly underripe bananas, peeled and halved
   lengthwise
1/3 cup brandy or light rum

Melt butter in a chafing dish or flameproof casserole (burner-to-table type) over moderately low heat, mix in sugar and lemon juice and heat, stirring until sugar dissolves. Add bananas and simmer, uncovered, about 10 minutes, turning gently with a slotted spatula now and then, to glaze evenly. Warm brandy in a small saucepan, pour over bananas, blaze, and spoon over bananas until flames die. Serve at once.

NPS: 465 C, 60 mg CH, 250 mg S*

Peaches, Pears, or Nectarines Flambé: Substitute 4 large firm peaches, pears, or nectarines for bananas. Peel fruit and leave whole (but core the pears). Proceed as directed.

NPS: 425 C, 60 mg CH, 250 mg S*

Baked Glazed Fruit: Bake any of the above fruits, uncovered, in sugar mixture about 1/2 hour at 350° F., turning now and then in syrup to glaze. Omit brandy. Nutritional count about the same as basic recipe.

CHERRIES JUBILEE

4–6 servings ⊠

More culinary pyrotechnics. Bound to impress dinner guests if you bring flaming into a darkened room.

1 (1-pound 13-ounce) can pitted Bing cherries
1/4 cup sugar
1 tablespoon cornstarch
1 tablespoon lemon juice
1 tablespoon butter (no substitute)
1/3 cup kirsch or brandy

Drain and reserve liquid from cherries. Mix sugar and cornstarch in a saucepan, gradually mix in cherry liquid, and heat, stirring constantly, over moderate heat until boiling. Reduce heat and simmer, uncovered, 3 minutes, stirring now and then. Add lemon juice, butter, and cherries and simmer, uncovered, 2–3 minutes. Meanwhile, warm kirsch in a small saucepan. Transfer cherry mixture to a chafing dish or flameproof serving dish, pour in kirsch, blaze with a match, and carry flaming to the table. Serve as is or spooned over vanilla ice cream.

NPS (4–6): 220–145 C, 8–5 mg CH, 35–25 mg S*

STEWED FRESH FIGS

6 servings

1 quart firm-ripe figs, peeled
2 cups water
1 1/2 cups sugar
2 tablespoons lemon juice

Place all ingredients in a saucepan and simmer, uncovered, 15–30 minutes until figs are clear and tender; cover and cool in liquid. Serve at room temperature with a little liquid poured over each serving. If you like, pass heavy or light cream.

NPS: 265 C, 0 mg CH, 2 mg S*

Stewed Dried Figs: Substitute 1 pound dried figs for the fresh and simmer as directed until figs are plump and soft.

NPS: 385 C, 0 mg CH, 10 mg S*

Gingered Figs: Simmer 1 (2-inch) piece bruised, peeled fresh gingerroot along with figs; remove before serving. Or use 2 tablespoons minced crystallized ginger and serve along with figs.

NPS (fresh): 280 C, 0 mg CH, 5 mg S*

Spiced Figs: Tie 1 stick cinnamon and 4 cloves in cheesecloth and simmer along with figs; remove just before serving.

NPS (fresh): 280 C, 0 mg CH, 5 mg S*

Honeyed Figs: Quarter fresh figs and simmer with 1 cup each water and honey and the lemon juice called for. Serve as is or as a sauce over ice cream.

NPS (fresh): 240 C, 0 mg CH, 5 mg S*

BROILED GRAPEFRUIT

4 servings ⊠ ⊲⊳

Good for breakfast or dessert.

2 medium-size grapefruits, halved
4 teaspoons light brown sugar
1 tablespoon melted butter or margarine

Preheat broiler. Cut around grapefruit sections to loosen, then sprinkle each 1/2 grapefruit with 1 teaspoon brown sugar and drizzle with 3/4 teaspoon melted butter. Broil 5" from heat 5–7 minutes until golden, and serve hot.

NPS: 80 C, 8 mg CH, 30 mg S*

⊠ **Honey-Broiled Grapefruit:** Substitute 1 tablespoon honey or maple syrup for each teaspoon of brown sugar and proceed as directed.

NPS: 130 C, 8 mg CH, 30 mg S*

⊠ **Broiled Oranges, Peaches, Apricots, Pears, or Pineapples:** Halved oranges, peaches, and apricots and pineapple rings can all be broiled. Sprinkle cut sides slightly with sugar and butter and broil 3–5 minutes until delicately browned. Recipe too flexible for meaningful nutritional count.

RED-WINE-POACHED PEARS WITH CRÈME ANGLAISE

6 servings

Anjou . . . Bosc . . . Bartlett . . . Seckel. All are splendid choices for this recipe. And what about the leftover wine poaching liquid? Use it to macerate fruits.

2 cups red Burgundy (use an inexpensive jug wine)
Juice of 1/2 lemon
2/3 cup sugar
1 quart water
2 sticks cinnamon, broken
6 large firm-ripe pears
1 recipe Custard Sauce (Crème Anglaise)

Combine wine, lemon juice, sugar, and water in a large enameled or stainless-steel kettle; drop in cinnamon sticks and set over low heat. Meanwhile, core pears from bottom using a swivel-bladed vegetable peeler and working carefully so you don't bruise pears or loosen stems. Stand pears in kettle and poach, uncovered, basting often, 15–20 minutes until tender and rosy-brown. Lift pears from the poaching liquid and cool to room temperature. Cover with plastic food wrap and refrigerate until ready to serve. Meanwhile, prepare and chill Crème Anglaise. To serve, stand pears stems-up in goblets, then drizzle each with about 1/4 cup Crème Anglaise. Pass remaining sauce so guests can help themselves to more.

NPS: 280 C, 190 mg CH, 70 mg S*

BAKED PEARS AU GRATIN

4 servings

Juice of 1/2 lemon
3 large firm ripe pears, peeled, cored, and sliced 1/4" thick
1/4 cup firmly packed light brown sugar
1/4 cup light rum
2 tablespoons unsalted butter

TOPPING
1/3 cup fine dry bread crumbs
1/4 cup sugar
1 tablespoon finely grated Parmesan cheese
3 tablespoons melted unsalted butter

Preheat oven to 400° F. Place lemon juice in a 9" piepan, add pears, and toss lightly to mix; sprinkle with sugar, drizzle with rum, and dot with butter. Mix topping ingredients and sprinkle evenly over pears. Bake, uncovered, 20–25 minutes until lightly browned and bubbly. Serve hot or warm, topped, if you like, with a hearty scoop of vanilla ice cream.

NPS: 355 C, 40 mg CH, 90 mg S*

PEACH MELBA (PÊCHE MELBA)

6 servings

Also delicious this way are nectarines and pears.

1 cup water
1 cup sugar
3 large firm-ripe peaches, peeled, halved, and pitted
2 tablespoons lemon juice
1 1/2 pints vanilla ice cream
1 recipe Melba Sauce

Mix water and sugar in a large skillet (not iron) over moderate heat and heat and stir until sugar dissolves; boil, uncovered, 2 minutes. Add peaches and simmer, uncovered, 10–15 minutes, turning once, until tender but not mushy. Mix in lemon juice and cool peaches in syrup. Place scoops of ice cream in individual dessert dishes, top each with a peach half, hollow side down, and add 2–3 tablespoons Melba Sauce.

NPS: 410 C, 30 mg CH, 60 mg S*

BERRY COBBLER

6 servings

Try this when plump sweet berries are in season.

FILLING
2 quarts fresh berries (any kind), washed and stemmed
6 tablespoons cornstarch
2 cups sugar (about)
2 tablespoons butter or margarine

TOPPING
1 1/2 cups sifted flour
2 teaspoons baking powder
1/4 cup sugar
1/2 teaspoon salt
1/4 cup butter or margarine
1/2 cup milk

Preheat oven to 400° F. Place berries in an ungreased 3-quart casserole; mix cornstarch and sugar and stir into berries. Taste and, if too tart, add more sugar. Dot with butter and let stand 20 minutes; stir well. Meanwhile, prepare topping: Sift flour, baking powder, sugar, and salt into a bowl, then cut in butter with a pastry blender until mixture resembles coarse meal. Mix in milk with a fork to form a stiff dough. Drop from a tablespoon on top of berries, spacing evenly. Bake, uncovered, 30 minutes until lightly browned and bubbly. Cool to room temperature before serving. Good topped with whipped cream or vanilla ice cream.

NPS: 615 C, 35 mg CH, 450 mg S*

VARIATION

Peach Cobbler: Prepare as directed, substituting 6–8 peeled, pitted, thinly sliced ripe peaches for the berries—enough to fill casserole two thirds—and reducing sugar if peaches are very sweet.

NPS: 600 C, 35 mg CH, 450 mg S*

APPLE BROWN BETTY

4–6 servings ¢

Always popular. But try the variations, too.

1 quart (1/2-inch) bread cubes or 3 cups soft bread crumbs (made from day-old bread trimmed of crusts)
1/3 cup melted butter or margarine
1 quart thinly sliced, peeled, and cored tart cooking apples
1 cup firmly packed light brown sugar
1 teaspoon cinnamon or 1/2 teaspoon nutmeg
1 teaspoon finely grated lemon rind
2 tablespoons lemon juice
1/4 cup water

Preheat oven to 400° F. Toss bread cubes with butter; set aside. Toss apples with remaining ingredients except water. Beginning and ending with bread cubes, layer bread and apples into a buttered 2-quart casserole. Sprinkle with water, cover, and bake 1/2 hour. Uncover and bake 1/2 hour longer until lightly browned. Serve warm with cream, whipped cream, ice cream, or any suitable sauce.

NPS (4–6): 500–330 C, 40–30 mg CH, 340–225 mg S*

VARIATIONS

Peach or Apricot Brown Betty: Prepare as directed but substitute 2 (1-pound) cans drained sliced peaches or pitted quartered apricots or 3 cups thinly sliced peeled and pitted fresh peaches or apricots for the apples. If you like, substitute 1/4 cup syrup drained from canned fruit for the water.

NPS (4–6): 560–370 C, 40–30 mg CH, 350–275 mg S*

Berry-Apple Brown Betty: Prepare as directed, using 2 cups each sliced apples and stemmed blueberries or blackberries.

NPS (4–6): 505–340 C, 40–30 mg CH, 345–230 mg S*

SWISS APPLE CHARLOTTE

6 servings

6 cups thinly sliced, peeled, and cored tart cooking apples
11/2 cups sugar
1 tablespoon lemon juice
1/8–1/4 teaspoon nutmeg
1/4 cup butter or margarine
13/4–2 cups fine dry bread crumbs
Heavy cream or sweetened whipped cream (topping)

Preheat oven to 350° F. Mix apples with sugar, lemon juice, and nutmeg to taste and arrange in a buttered 2-quart casserole about 2″ deep, scattering small pieces of butter through the apples as you fill the dish. Top with crumbs, cover, and bake 35–45 minutes until apples are tender; uncover and bake 10 minutes longer to brown crumbs lightly. Cool about 5 minutes, then serve with cream.

NPS: 440 C, 20 mg CH, 295 mg S*

FRESH PEACH CRISP

4–6 servings

The spicy topping makes this Peach Crisp special.

4 large peaches, peeled, pitted, and sliced thin
Juice of 1/2 lemon
1/4 cup sugar

TOPPING
2/3 cup unsifted flour
1 cup firmly packed light brown sugar
1 teaspoon cinnamon
1/2 teaspoon ginger
1/8 teaspoon mace
1/4 teaspoon salt
1/2 cup butter or margarine, softened to room temperature

Preheat oven to 350° F. Arrange peaches in an ungreased 9″ piepan; sprinkle with lemon juice and sugar. Mix topping ingredients and pat on top of peaches. Bake, uncovered, about 45 minutes until lightly browned and bubbly. (*Note:* It's a good idea to place a piece of aluminum foil under the piepan to catch any drips.) Cool to room temperature and serve as is or topped with whipped cream or vanilla ice cream.

NPS (4–6): 655–440 C, 60–40 mg CH, 385–255 mg S*

VARIATION

Fresh Apple Crisp: Prepare as directed, substituting 5–6 peeled, cored, and thinly sliced greenings or other tart cooking apples for the peaches.

NPS (4–6): 625–420 C, 60–40 mg CH, 385–255 mg S*

SPICY PERSIMMON PUDDING

12 servings

1⅓ cups sifted flour
1 cup sugar
½ teaspoon baking soda
Pinch salt
½ teaspoon ginger
½ teaspoon cinnamon
½ teaspoon nutmeg
1 cup puréed ripe persimmons
3 eggs, lightly beaten
1 quart milk
½ cup melted butter or margarine

Preheat oven to 300° F. Sift flour with sugar, soda, salt, and spices into a large bowl. Mix persimmons with eggs, milk, and butter and add to dry ingredients, a little at a time, mixing well after each addition. Pour into a greased 13″ × 9″ × 2″ pan and bake, uncovered, about 1 hour until a knife inserted near center comes out clean. Serve warm, topped, if you like, with whipped cream.

NPS: 270 C, 100 mg CH, 180 mg S*

OLD-FASHIONED STRAWBERRY SHORTCAKE

6–8 servings

3 pints strawberries, washed and stemmed
½ cup superfine sugar
1 recipe Extra-Rich Biscuits
Butter
Sweetened whipped cream (optional)

Mash strawberries lightly with a potato masher or fork, mix with sugar, and let stand at room temperature while you make the biscuits. Prepare biscuits as directed and, while still hot, split and butter. Smother with strawberries and, if you like, top with whipped cream. For particularly pretty shortcake, save out 8–10 large perfect berries and use to garnish.

NPS (6–8): 540–405 C, 35–25 mg CH, 715–535 mg S*

VARIATIONS

Recipes too flexible for meaningful nutritional count.

Other Fruit Shortcakes: Prepare as directed but substitute 4–5 cups any prepared sweetened berries or other fruit for the strawberries.

Southern-Style Shortcake: Serve berries or other fruit on rounds or squares of sponge cake instead of on buttered biscuits. Top with whipped cream.

PUDDINGS

"Pudding," says Webster, "is a dessert of a soft, spongy or thick creamy consistency." Custard is pudding. So are mousses and Bavarians and creams, dessert soufflés, both hot and cold, gelatin fluffs and sponges. To bring order to the category, puddings are arranged here by type of thickener: custards and other egg-thickened mixtures, starch puddings, gelatin desserts, etc.

Custards

When they are good—silky-smooth and tender—they are very, very good, but when they are bad . . . well, the less said the better. What makes custards curdle and weep? Too much heat, invariably, or overcooking (which amounts to the same thing). Custards cannot be hurried. Like all egg dishes, they must be cooked gently and slowly (read about the techniques of egg cookery in the chapter on eggs, cheese, and dairy).

Stirred custards should always be cooked in the top of a double boiler *over simmering* water and stirred throughout cooking. Baked custards should bake slowly in moderate or moderately slow ovens and, as an added safeguard against curdling, in a hot water bath.

Should the milk used in custards be scalded? It isn't necessary if the milk is pasteurized; scalding dates to the days of raw milk, which needed heating to destroy microorganisms. Scalding does, however, seem to mellow the flavor of custards, particularly stirred custards, and to shorten cooking time somewhat.

To Test Custards for Doneness:

Stirred Custard: The standard test is to cook until mixture will "coat the back of a metal spoon," not as easy to determine as it sounds because uncooked custard will also leave a film on a spoon. The difference is that cooked custard should leave a thick, translucent, almost jellylike coat about the consistency of gravy. If you suspect that custard is on the verge of curdling, plunge pan into ice water to stop cooking.

Baked Custard: Insert a table knife into custard midway between rim and center *(not in the middle as cookbooks once instructed)*. If knife comes out clean, custard is done. Remove at once from water bath and cool. To chill quickly, set custard in ice water—but only if baking dish is one that can take abrupt changes of temperature without breaking.

What to Do About Curdled Custard: If it's baked custard, the best idea is to turn it into a Trifle by mixing with small hunks of cake; if stirred custard, strain out the lumps and serve as a sauce over cake, fruit, or gelatin dessert.

Caution: Keep custards refrigerated; they spoil easily, often without giving a clue.

BAKED CUSTARD

10 servings   ¢ ⚖

5 eggs (6 if you plan to bake custard in a single large dish)
2/3 cup sugar
1/4 teaspoon salt
1 teaspoon vanilla
1 quart whole or skim milk, scalded
Nutmeg or mace

Preheat oven to 325° F. Beat eggs lightly with sugar, salt, and vanilla; gradually stir in hot milk. Pour into 10 custard cups (buttered if you want to unmold custards) or a 2-quart baking dish. Sprinkle with nutmeg, set in a large shallow pan, and pour in warm water to a depth of 1″. Bake, uncovered, about 1 hour until a knife inserted midway between center and rim comes out clean. Remove custards from water bath and cool to room temperature. Chill slightly before serving.

NPS (whole milk): 150 C, 150 mg CH, 135 mg S*
NPS (skim milk): 125 C, 140 mg CH, 135 mg S*

VARIATIONS

Egg Yolk Custard: Prepare as directed, using 2 egg yolks for each whole egg.

NPS (whole milk): 175 C, 285 mg CH, 110 mg S*

⚖ **Vanilla Bean Custard:** Prepare as directed, substituting a 2″ piece vanilla bean for the extract; heat bean in milk as it scalds; remove before mixing milk into eggs. Nutritional count same as basic recipe.

¢ **Butterscotch Custard:** Prepare as directed, using light brown sugar and half-and-half cream.

NPS: 215 C, 170 mg CH, 130 mg S*

¢ **Chocolate Custard:** Prepare as directed, omitting nutmeg, melting 2 (1-ounce) grated squares unsweetened chocolate in scalding milk.

NPS: 180 C, 150 mg CH, 135 mg S*

For a richer custard, use half-and-half cream.

NPS: 245 C, 170 mg CH, 130 mg S*

¢ **Crème Caramel:** Mix custard as directed. Spoon about 1 tablespoon caramelized sugar* into each custard cup, add custard, and bake as directed. Chill, then unmold by dipping custards quickly in warm water and inverting.

NPS: 200 C, 150 mg CH, 135 mg S*

STIRRED CUSTARD OR CUSTARD SAUCE (CRÈME ANGLAISE)

6 servings, about 2 cups sauce

A good basic recipe with nearly a dozen flavor variations.

2 cups milk, scalded
5 tablespoons sugar
Pinch salt
4 egg yolks, lightly beaten
1 teaspoon vanilla

Heat milk, sugar, and salt in the top of a double boiler over direct, moderate heat, stirring until sugar dissolves. Spoon a little hot mixture into yolks, return to pan, set over *simmering* water, and cook and stir 2–3 minutes until thickened and no raw egg taste remains. Mix in vanilla and serve hot or cool quickly by setting pan in ice water and stirring briskly. Serve as is or over cake, fruit, or pudding.

NPS: 135 C, 190 mg CH, 65 mg S*

¢ ⊿⊾ **Low-Calorie Stirred Custard:** Prepare as directed but use skim milk instead of whole, reduce sugar to 1/4 cup, and use 2 lightly beaten eggs instead of all yolks.

NPS: 90 C, 90 mg CH, 90 mg S*

¢ **Thin Custard Sauce:** Prepare as directed but increase milk to 2 1/2 cups.

NP Tablespoon: 20 C, 30 mg CH, 10 mg S*

¢ **Thick Custard Sauce:** Scald 1 1/2 cups milk; blend remaining 1/2 cup milk with 1/4 cup cornstarch. Mix sugar and salt with hot milk, blend in cornstarch paste, and heat and stir over direct, moderate heat until thickened. Mix a little hot sauce into 3 lightly beaten eggs, return to pan, set over simmering water, and heat, stirring constantly, 2–3 minutes until no raw taste of egg remains. Mix in vanilla or, if you prefer, 1/8 teaspoon almond extract. Serve hot, or cool as directed and use in making Trifle or other dessert where a thick custard sauce is called for.

NP Tablespoon: 30 C, 30 mg CH, 20 mg S*

¢ **Lemon Custard Sauce:** Prepare as directed, substituting 1/4 teaspoon lemon extract and 2 teaspoons finely grated lemon rind for vanilla.

NP Tablespoon: 25 C, 35 mg CH, 13 mg S*

Orange Custard Sauce: Prepare as directed, using 1 cup each orange juice and milk and 1 tablespoon finely grated orange rind instead of vanilla.

NP Tablespoon: 25 C, 35 mg CH, 10 mg S*

¢ **Chocolate Custard Sauce:** Prepare as directed, blending 1 (1-ounce) coarsely grated square unsweetened chocolate into the scalding milk.

NP Tablespoon: 30 C, 35 mg CH, 15 mg S*

¢ **Caramel Custard Sauce:** Increase sugar to 1/3 cup, caramelize,* then add scalded milk and proceed as directed.

NP Tablespoon: 25 C, 35 mg CH, 15 mg S*

Coconut Custard Sauce: Prepare as directed but flavor with 1/4 teaspoon each vanilla and almond extract; mix in 1/3 cup flaked or toasted coconut.

NP Tablespoon: 30 C, 35 mg CH, 15 mg S*

Sour Cream Custard Sauce (*About 3 cups*): Prepare and cool as directed, then blend in, a little at a time, 1 cup sour cream.

NP Tablespoon: 25 C, 25 mg CH, 10 mg S*

CRÈME BRÛLÉE

6 servings

This extra-rich custard with a crackly, broiled-on sugar topping is showy, yet simple to make.

3 cups heavy cream
1/3 cup superfine sugar
1/2 teaspoon vanilla
6 egg yolks, lightly beaten
3/4–1 cup light brown sugar (*not* firmly packed)

Cook and stir cream, sugar, vanilla, and yolks in the top of a double boiler over simmering water 7–10 minutes until mixture coats a *wooden* spoon. Pour into an ungreased shallow 1 1/2-quart casserole and stir 1–2 minutes. Place wax paper directly on surface of *crème,* cool to room temperature, then chill 1–2 hours. Preheat broiler. Sprinkle a 1/4" layer of brown sugar evenly over *crème,* set casserole in a shallow bed of crushed ice, and broil 6"–8" from heat about 3 minutes until sugar melts and bubbles (watch so it doesn't burn). Remove from ice, chill 10–15 minutes, then serve, including some of the crackly topping with each portion.

NPS: 620 C, 435 mg CH, 60 mg S*

FLAN

6–8 servings

A popular Spanish custard dessert, unusually smooth because it is made with egg yolks only.

1/3 cup caramelized sugar*
8 egg yolks
1/2 cup sugar
1/4 teaspoon salt
1/2 teaspoon vanilla
3 cups milk, scalded

Preheat oven to 325° F. Pour caramelized sugar into a well-buttered 9" layer cake pan. Beat egg yolks lightly with sugar, salt, and vanilla; gradually mix in hot milk. Pour into pan, set in a large, shallow pan, and pour in hot water to a depth of 1/2". Bake, uncovered, about 1 hour until a knife inserted in the *center* comes out clean. Remove custard from water bath and cool to room temperature. Chill 2–3 hours. Dip pan quickly in very hot water, then invert on serving dish. Cut in wedges and serve.

NPS (6–8): 265–200 C, 380–285 mg CH, 160–120 mg S*

Rum Flan: Prepare as directed, using 1/2 cup light rum and 2 1/2 cups milk.

NPS (6–8): 255–190 C, 375–285 mg CH, 150–115 mg S*

Pineapple Flan: Prepare as directed, using 2 cups pineapple juice and 1 cup milk; reduce vanilla to 1/4 teaspoon and add 1/4 teaspoon almond extract.

NPS (6–8): 260–195 C, 370–275 mg CH, 120–90 mg S*

FLOATING ISLAND

6 servings

1 recipe Stirred Custard

MERINGUE
3 egg whites
1/8 teaspoon salt
1/3 cup sugar

Preheat broiler. Pour custard into 6 custard cups. Beat egg whites with salt until frothy, gradually beat in sugar, a little at a time, and continue to beat until stiff peaks form. Using a serving spoon dipped in cold water, float a large spoonful of meringue on each custard. Set custard cups in a large pan of ice water and broil 4″ from heat until tinged with brown. Serve at once.

NPS: 255 C, 290 mg CH, 195 mg S*

VARIATION

Oeufs à la Neige: Before making custard, prepare meringue as directed. Heat 2 cups milk to simmering in a large skillet (not iron), drop meringue by spoonfuls on milk, and poach 2–3 minutes, turning once with a spoon dipped in hot water. Using a slotted spoon, transfer meringues to a wet plate and cool. Prepare Stirred Custard as directed, using poaching milk. Cool custard. Float poached meringues on custard and chill 2–3 hours before serving. Nutritional count same as basic recipe.

TRIFLE OR TIPSY CAKE

8 servings

1 recipe Easy Sponge Loaf or 1 small sponge or yellow cake
3/4 cup strawberry jam
1 (1-pound 14-ounce) can pitted apricots, drained and puréed
1 (11-ounce) can mandarin oranges, drained (optional)
1/2 cup Marsala wine or cream sherry

1 recipe Thick Custard Sauce
1 cup heavy cream
1/4 cup superfine sugar
1/4 teaspoon vanilla
Candied cherries or fruit (garnish)

Split cake into thin layers, spread with jam and about half of the apricot purée, and sandwich back together. Cut in bars about 1″ × 2″ and pack into a 2-quart serving dish; arrange oranges in and around cake if you like. Prick cake well all over and pour Marsala on top; spread with remaining purée and smother with custard sauce. Cover and chill 2 hours. Shortly before serving, whip cream with sugar until stiff; fold in vanilla. Frost on top of Trifle and decorate with candied cherries.

NPS (with oranges, without garnish): 565 C, 290 mg CH, 135 mg S*

ZABAGLIONE (SABAYON)

6 servings

Serve this fluffy wine custard hot or cold as a dessert or dessert sauce. Especially good over fresh sliced peaches, strawberries, or homemade Angel Food Cake (a luscious way to use up the yolks).

6 egg yolks
2/3 cup superfine sugar
Pinch salt
2/3 cup Marsala wine

Beat egg yolks in top of a double boiler (set on a counter) with a rotary or electric beater until cream colored. Add sugar, a little at a time, beating hard after each addition. Beat in salt and Marsala. Set *over* simmering water (should not touch bottom of pan) and heat and beat constantly with a wire whisk until thick and foamy, about 5–7 minutes. Set double boiler top on damp cloth on counter and continue beating 2–3 minutes. Serve warm or cool further, continuing to beat so mixture does not separate.

NPS: 170 C, 270 mg CH, 30 mg S*

CLASSIC POTS DE CRÈME AU CHOCOLAT

4 servings

A dark chocolate French custard. Very rich!

1 pint heavy cream
1 (1-ounce) square unsweetened chocolate, coarsely grated
6 tablespoons sugar

4 egg yolks, lightly beaten
1/4 teaspoon vanilla

Mix cream, chocolate, and sugar in the top of a double boiler, set over simmering water, and heat, beating with a wire whisk, until sugar dissolves and chocolate is blended in. Stir a little hot mixture into egg yolks, then return to pan and cook and stir 2–3 minutes until thickened. Pour mixture into a bowl at once, stir in vanilla, and cool slightly, stirring now and then. Pour into 4 *pots de crème* or custard cups. Cool to room temperature, then chill 2 hours. Serve cold, topped, if you like, with swirls of whipped cream or a few toasted, slivered almonds.

NPS (without whipped cream or nuts): 580 C, 435 mg CH, 55 mg S*

OLD-FASHIONED BREAD AND BUTTER PUDDING

6–8 servings ¢

A perfectly delicious way to use up stale bread.

4 slices day-old or stale bread
2 tablespoons butter or margarine
1/2 cup seedless or golden seedless raisins
1/4 teaspoon each cinnamon and nutmeg, mixed
   together
3 eggs, lightly beaten
1/3 cup sugar
2 1/4 cups milk

If you like, trim crusts from bread, then butter each slice and quarter. Arrange 2 quartered slices in the bottom of a buttered 1 1/2-quart casserole, sprinkle with half the raisins and half the spice mixture. Top with remaining bread, raisins, and spice mixture. Beat eggs with sugar until cream colored, add milk, and pour over bread. Let stand at room temperature 1 hour. Preheat oven to 350° F. Set casserole in a large, shallow pan and pour in hot water to a depth of 1″. Bake, uncovered, about 1 hour until a knife inserted midway between center and rim comes out clean. Cool slightly and serve. If you like, pass cinnamon sugar to sprinkle on top.

NPS (6–8) (with butter): 250–190 C, 160–120 mg CH, 200–150 mg S*

QUEEN OF PUDDINGS

6 servings ¢

This lemon-flavored bread pudding is spread with jam, then topped with meringue.

2 cups day-old bread crumbs
1 quart milk, scalded
2 eggs + 2 egg yolks, lightly beaten
1/3 cup sugar
1/4 teaspoon salt
1/4 cup melted butter or margarine
Finely grated rind of 1 lemon
1/2 cup raspberry or strawberry jam or red
   currant jelly

MERINGUE
2 egg whites
1/4 cup superfine sugar

Preheat oven to 350° F. Place bread crumbs in a buttered 1 1/2-quart casserole. Slowly mix milk into eggs, then stir in sugar, salt, butter, and lemon rind; pour over bread and let stand 1/2 hour at room temperature. Mix lightly, set casserole in a shallow pan, pour warm water into pan to a depth of 1″, and bake, uncovered, about 1 hour or until a knife inserted midway between center and rim comes out clean. Remove from oven but leave in water bath; spread jam over pudding. Beat egg whites until frothy, slowly beat in sugar, and continue to beat until soft peaks form. Cover jam with meringue; return pudding to oven (same temperature) and bake about 15 minutes until meringue is lightly browned. Cool slightly and serve.

NPS (with butter): 410 C, 225 mg CH, 370 mg S*

CHOCOLATE MOUSSE

8 servings

6 (1-ounce) squares semisweet chocolate
2 tablespoons hot water or strong black coffee
5 eggs, separated
1 1/2 teaspoons vanilla
1 1/2 cups heavy cream
Chocolate curls* (optional decoration)

Place chocolate and hot water in the top of a double boiler, set over simmering water, and heat and stir until chocolate is melted. Lightly beat yolks, add a little hot mixture, then stir back into pan and heat and stir over simmering water 1–2 minutes until no raw taste of egg remains. Off heat, mix in vanilla. Beat cream until very thick and glossy (it should almost form soft peaks) and fold into chocolate mixture. Beat egg whites until soft peaks form and fold in, a little at a time, until no flecks of white show. Spoon into a serving dish, cover, and chill at least 12 hours. Scatter with chocolate curls, if you like, just before serving.

NPS (ungarnished): 315 C, 230 mg CH, 60 mg S*

FRUIT WHIP

6 servings ⚖

Fruit whip will have richer flavor if the dried fruit is stewed the day before and soaked overnight in its stewing liquid. Drain before puréeing.

3 egg whites
1/4 teaspoon salt
Pinch cream of tartar
1/2 cup sugar
1 cup cold puréed stewed prunes, dried apricots, peaches, or figs*
1/8 teaspoon cinnamon or nutmeg
1 tablespoon lemon juice

Beat egg whites, salt, and cream of tartar until frothy, gradually beat in sugar, then continue beating until stiff peaks form. Fold remaining ingredients into egg whites, spoon into goblets, and chill well. Serve with Custard Sauce or sweetened whipped cream.

NPS (with peaches, without Custard Sauce or whipped cream): 90 C, 0 mg CH, 120 mg S*

VARIATIONS

⚖ **Fruit and Nut Whip:** Prepare as directed, but fold in 1/4 cup minced pecans, walnuts, or toasted almonds along with egg whites.

NPS (with pecans): 125 C, 0 mg CH, 120 mg S*

⚖ **Baked Fruit Whip:** Prepare as directed but do not chill. Spoon into an ungreased 5-cup soufflé dish or casserole, set in a large, shallow baking pan, pour in hot water to a depth of 1″, and bake uncovered, 30–35 minutes at 350° F. until puffy and just firm. Serve warm with cream.

NPS (without cream): 90 C, 0 mg CH, 120 mg S*

Dessert Soufflés

Dessert soufflés are neither as fragile nor as temperamental as reputation would have them. Their biggest shortcoming is that they must be baked at the last minute. They may, however, be partially made ahead of time to avoid last-minute scurrying around. They are prepared exactly like savory soufflés (see Soufflés in the chapter on eggs, cheese, and dairy). They can be baked in unbuttered soufflé dishes or straight-sided casseroles or, for glistening brown crusts, in *well-buttered and sugared* ones (butter dish well, spoon in a little granulated sugar, then tilt from one side to the other until evenly coated with sugar; tap out excess).

BASIC HOT DESSERT SOUFFLÉ

4 servings

From this one basic recipe, you can make seven different soufflés.

2 tablespoons cornstarch
1/2 cup sugar
1 cup milk
4 egg yolks
2 teaspoons vanilla or the finely grated rind of 1 lemon
4 egg whites
1/4 teaspoon cream of tartar

Preheat oven to 350° F. Mix cornstarch and sugar in a heavy saucepan, gradually mix in milk, and heat, stirring constantly over moderate heat, until boiling. Boil and stir 1 minute; mixture will be quite thick. Off heat, beat in egg yolks, one at a time; mix in vanilla. Lay a piece of wax paper flat on sauce and cool to room temperature. *(Note:* Soufflé can be made up to this point well ahead of time to avoid last-minute rush.) Beat egg whites with cream of tartar until stiff but not dry, stir about 1/4 cup into sauce, then fold in remaining whites. Spoon into a buttered and sugared 6-cup soufflé dish and bake, uncovered, 35–45 minutes until puffy and browned. Serve at once, accompanied, if you like, with Custard Sauce or sweetened whipped cream.

NPS (without Custard Sauce or whipped cream): 235 C, 280 mg CH, 90 mg S*

VARIATIONS

Hot Coffee Soufflé: Prepare as directed, substituting 1 cup cold, very strong black coffee for the milk.

NPS: 200 C, 270 mg CH, 60 mg S*

Hot Orange Soufflé: Prepare as directed but use 3 tablespoons cornstarch and substitute 1 1/4 cups orange juice for the milk; substitute 2 teaspoons finely grated orange rind and 1 teaspoon finely grated lemon rind for the vanilla.

NPS: 235 C, 270 mg CH, 60 mg S*

Hot Chocolate Soufflé: Prepare as directed, increasing sugar to 3/4 cup. Before adding yolks, blend in 2 (1-ounce) squares grated unsweetened chocolate or 2 (1-ounce) envelopes no-melt unsweetened chocolate. Proceed as directed, reducing vanilla to 1 teaspoon.

NPS: 350 C, 280 mg CH, 90 mg S*

Hot Nut Soufflé: Prepare as directed but flavor with 1/2 teaspoon each vanilla and almond extract. Before folding in egg whites, mix in 1/2 cup minced, toasted, blanched almonds (or minced pecans, walnuts, Brazil nuts, or hazelnuts). Proceed as directed.

NPS: 330 C, 280 mg CH, 90 mg S*

Hot Fruit Soufflé: Prepare as directed but use 3 tablespoons cornstarch, 2/3 cup sugar, 1/2 cup milk, and 1 cup sieved fruit purée (peach or berry is particularly good). Proceed as directed but bake in a 7-cup soufflé dish.

NPS (with peaches): 285 C, 275 mg CH, 85 mg S*

Hot Grand Marnier Soufflé: Prepare as directed, using 3/4 cup milk and flavoring with the grated rinds of 1 orange and 1 lemon. After adding yolks, beat in 1/4–1/3 cup Grand Marnier (or curaçao, Cointreau, or rum). Proceed as directed.

NPS: 270 C, 280 mg CH, 80 mg S*

Starch-Thickened Puddings

These are really thick sweet sauces, and the techniques of preparing them are the same as for savory starch-thickened sauces (see Starch Thickeners and Some Tips for Making Better Sauces in the chapter on sauces, gravies, and butters).

The most important points to remember when making starch-thickened pudding are to use a pan heavy enough and a heat low enough to prevent scorching, also to stir constantly as mixture thickens to prevent lumping. Once thickened, starch puddings should mellow several minutes over low heat to remove all raw starch flavor. Like custards, they spoil easily and must be kept refrigerated.

BASIC STIRRED VANILLA PUDDING

4 servings ¢

2 tablespoons cornstarch
1/2 cup sugar
2 cups milk
1 egg, lightly beaten
1 teaspoon vanilla
1 tablespoon butter or margarine

Mix cornstarch and sugar in a heavy saucepan. Gradually mix in milk and heat, stirring constantly over moderate heat, until mixture boils. Boil and stir 1 minute. Turn heat to very low, mix a little hot sauce into egg, return to pan, and cook and stir 2–3 minutes until no raw taste of egg remains. Do not boil. Off heat, mix in vanilla and butter; cool slightly, pour into serving dishes and serve warm. Or place a circle of wax

paper directly on surface of pudding and cool completely; chill and serve cold. If you like decorate with swirls of whipped cream.

NPS (with butter, without whipped cream): 235 C, 95 mg CH, 105 mg S*

VARIATIONS

¢ **Caramel Pudding:** Prepare as directed but substitute 3/4 cup firmly packed dark brown sugar for the granulated. If you like, flavor with maple extract instead of vanilla.

NPS: 290 C, 95 mg CH, 120 mg S*

¢ **Chocolate Pudding:** Prepare as directed but increase sugar to 3/4 cup and add 1 square coarsely grated unsweetened chocolate along with egg. Reduce vanilla to 1/2 teaspoon, omit butter, and beat pudding briefly with a rotary beater after removing from heat.

NPS: 290 C, 85 mg CH, 75 mg S*

¢ **Mocha Pudding:** Prepare Chocolate Pudding (above) and add 1 teaspoon instant coffee powder along with chocolate. If you like, serve cold sprinkled with slivered, blanched almonds.

NPS (without almonds): 290 C, 85 mg CH, 80 mg S*

Surprise Fruit Pudding *(6 servings):* Slice stale white or yellow cake thin, spread with any jam, cut in small cubes, and place about 1/4 cup into each of 6 custard cups. Top with thinly sliced bananas, oranges, or peaches and fill with Vanilla Pudding. Cool and serve. Recipe too flexible for meaningful nutritional count.

VANILLA BLANCMANGE (CORNSTARCH PUDDING)

8 servings ¢ ⚖

Slightly thicker than Basic Stirred Vanilla Pudding and not quite so sweet. *Note:* Because this recipe contains no eggs, it is a good choice for those with egg allergies.

2/3 cup sugar
6 tablespoons cornstarch
1/4 teaspoon salt
1 quart milk
2 teaspoons vanilla

Mix sugar, cornstarch, and salt in the top of a double boiler, then gradually blend in milk. Set over just boiling water and heat, stirring constantly, until thickened. Cook 5–7 minutes, stirring now and then. Remove from heat, add vanilla, and cool 10 minutes, stirring now and then. Pour into a 5-cup mold that has been rinsed in cold water, or into 8 individual molds. Chill until firm, 3–4 hours for large mold, 1–2 hours for small ones. Unmold and serve with any dessert sauce, fresh or stewed fruit.

NPS (without sauce or fruit): 165 C, 15 mg CH, 125 mg S*

VARIATIONS

Chocolate Blancmange: Prepare as directed, using 1⅓ cups sugar and 7 tablespoons cornstarch; when thickened, add 3 (1-ounce) squares coarsely grated unsweetened chocolate, stirring until melted, then cook 5 minutes longer. Off heat, beat in 1 teaspoon vanilla. Beat occasionally with a wire whip as mixture cools. Pour into molds and chill as directed. Good with whipped cream.

NPS (without whipped cream): 285 C, 15 mg CH, 130 mg S*

Fruit Blancmange: Prepare as directed, using 2 cups each milk and sieved fruit purée (berries, peaches, pineapple, and banana are good) instead of all milk. Adjust sugar according to sweetness of fruit and tint, if you like, an appropriate color.

NPS (with peach purée): 155 C, 10 mg CH, 105 mg S*

◁▷ **Lemon Blancmange:** Prepare as directed, using 7 tablespoons cornstarch, ½ cup lemon juice, 3½ cups milk, and the finely grated rind of 1 lemon.

NPS: 160 C, 15 mg CH, 125 mg S*

◁▷ **Orange Blancmange:** Prepare as directed, using 7 tablespoons cornstarch, 2 cups each milk and orange juice, and the finely grated rind of 1 orange.

NPS: 160 C, 10 mg CH, 100 mg S*

TAPIOCA PUDDING

4 servings   ¢

Tapioca, starch from cassava roots, can be used to thicken soups, sauces, and puddings. It is made into flakes and flour, but more popular are the *granulated quick-cooking tapioca* and *quick-cooking small pearl* (this cooks in 5–8 minutes; follow package directions). Also available: *large pearl ("fisheye") tapioca,* which must be soaked before it's cooked.

⅓ cup large pearl tapioca
1 cup cold water
2 cups milk
⅓ cup sugar
⅛ teaspoon salt
¼ teaspoon vanilla

Soak tapioca in cold water at least 4 hours or overnight if you prefer; do not drain. Transfer to a large, heavy saucepan, add remaining ingredients except vanilla, and simmer over lowest heat, stirring now and then, 1 hour. Off heat, mix in vanilla; serve warm or chilled. If you like, top with cream or stewed fruit.

NPS (without cream or fruit): 185 C, 15 mg CH, 130 mg S*

VARIATIONS

Baked Tapioca Pudding: Prepare pudding as directed, but simmer only ½ hour. Mix in vanilla, pour into a buttered 1-quart casserole, dot with 1 tablespoon butter, and bake, uncovered, 1 hour at 325° F. until lightly browned.

NPS: 210 C, 25 mg CH, 160 mg S*

Chocolate Tapioca Pudding: Prepare as directed but increase sugar to ½ cup and add 1 (1-ounce) square unsweetened chocolate during last ½ hour of simmering; stir frequently until chocolate melts.

NPS: 250 C, 15 mg CH, 130 mg S*

Butterscotch Tapioca Pudding: Soak tapioca as directed. Warm ¾ cup firmly packed dark brown sugar in 2 tablespoons butter in a large saucepan over moderate heat, stirring frequently, until melted. Mix in tapioca, milk, and salt and proceed as directed.

NPS: 390 C, 30 mg CH, 200 mg S*

BAKED RICE PUDDING

4–6 servings   ¢

Short grain rice, *not* converted, makes the best pudding.

⅓ cup uncooked short grain rice
1 quart milk
½ cup sugar
⅛ teaspoon nutmeg or 1 teaspoon vanilla
2–3 tablespoons butter or margarine

Preheat oven to 300° F. Sprinkle rice evenly over the bottom of a buttered 1½-quart casserole. Mix milk and sugar, pour over rice, sprinkle with nutmeg, and dot with butter. Bake, uncovered, 2½ hours, stirring every 15 minutes for the first 1½ hours, until lightly browned. Serve warm, topped, if you like, with cream.

NPS (4–6) (with butter, without cream): 355–235 C, 50–35 mg CH, 180–120 mg S*

VARIATIONS

¢ **Raisin Rice Pudding:** Prepare as directed and bake 1½ hours; stir in ⅔–1 cup seedless or golden seedless raisins and bake 1 hour longer.

NPS (4–6): 430–285 C, 50–35 mg CH, 180–120 mg S*

Creamy Rice Pudding: Prepare pudding as directed and bake 2 hours; mix in 1/2 cup heavy cream and bake 1/2 hour longer.

NPS (4–6): 455–305 C, 90–60 mg CH, 190–125 mg S*

¢ **Cold Rice Pudding:** Reduce rice to 1/4 cup and proceed as directed. Chill pudding and serve with fresh fruit or whipped cream.

NPS (4–6) (without fruit or whipped cream): 340–225 C, 50–35 mg CH, 180–120 mg S*

⊠ ¢ **"Quick" Baked Rice Pudding:** Heat milk, sugar, nutmeg, and butter in the top of a double boiler over direct heat until just boiling. Mix in rice, set over boiling water, and cook, stirring now and then, 40 minutes. Transfer to a buttered 1-quart casserole and bake 20 minutes at 350° F. until lightly browned.

NPS (4–6): 355–235 C, 50–35 mg CH, 180–120 mg S*

¢ **Lemon or Orange Rice Pudding:** Prepare as directed but omit nutmeg; mix in 1 tablespoon finely grated lemon rind or 2 tablespoons finely grated orange rind and 1/2 teaspoon lemon or orange extract.

NPS (4–6): 360–240 C, 50–35 mg CH, 180–120 mg S*

RICE À L'IMPÉRATRICE

8 servings

An impressive cold rice pudding studded with candied fruit and molded in a decorative mold.

1 1/3 **cups milk**
1/2 **cup uncooked long grain rice**
1/3 **cup minced mixed candied fruit soaked in 1 tablespoon kirsch**
1 **cup heavy cream**
1/2 **cup sweetened whipped cream (garnish)**
Quartered candied cherries and angelica strips (garnish)

CUSTARD
1 **envelope unflavored gelatin**
1 **cup milk**
1/2 **cup sugar**
4 **egg yolks, lightly beaten**
1 **teaspoon vanilla**

Heat milk to boiling in a small, heavy saucepan, stir in rice, cover, and simmer over lowest heat, stirring now and then, 20–30 min-utes until rice is just tender. Fluff rice with a fork and cool. Meanwhile, make the custard: Sprinkle gelatin over milk, let stand 2–3 minutes, mix, and pour into the top of a double boiler. Add sugar, set over simmering water, and heat and stir until steaming. Mix a little milk into egg yolks, return to pan, and cook and stir 2–3 minutes until custard will coat the back of a metal spoon. Remove from heat, mix in vanilla, cool slightly, then stir into rice along with candied fruit; cool to room temperature. Beat cream until soft peaks form, fold into rice, spoon into an unbuttered 1 1/2-quart decorative mold, cover, and chill several hours or overnight. Unmold and decorate with fluffs of whipped cream, cherries, and angelica.

NPS (with cherries or angelica): 335 C, 195 mg CH, 85 mg S*

VARIATION

Pears or Peaches à l'Impératrice: Unmold Rice à l'Impératrice in the center of a large, shallow crystal bowl; surround with cold poached pear or peach halves, hollows filled with red currant jelly. Sprig with mint. Recipe too flexible for meaningful nutritional count.

INDIAN PUDDING

6 servings   ¢

This New England corn meal pudding is traditionally very soft and may even "weep" (separate) slightly when served. No matter, it's spicy and good.

1/4 **cup corn meal**
1 **quart milk**
3/4 **cup molasses**
1/3 **cup firmly packed light brown sugar**
1/4 **cup butter or margarine**
1/4 **teaspoon salt**
1/2 **teaspoon cinnamon**
1/2 **teaspoon ginger**
1/2 **cup seedless raisins (optional)**

Preheat oven to 325° F. Mix corn meal and 1 cup milk. Heat 2 cups milk in the top of a double boiler over simmering water until steaming. Mix in corn meal mixture and cook 15–20 minutes, stirring now and then. Stir in molasses and sugar and cook 2–3 minutes longer. Off heat, mix in butter, salt, spices, and, if you like, raisins. Spoon into a buttered 1 1/2-quart casserole and pour remaining milk evenly over top. Bake, uncovered, about 1 1/2 hours until a table knife inserted midway between center and rim comes out clean. Serve warm with whipped cream or ice cream dusted with nutmeg.

NPS (with butter and raisins, without whipped cream or ice cream): 375 C, 45 mg CH, 260 mg S*

For a Firmer Pudding: Prepare corn meal mixture as directed; instead of pouring final cup milk over pudding, mix with 2 lightly beaten eggs and blend into pudding. Bake 2 hours at 300° F. just until firm.

NPS: 375 C, 130 mg CH, 260 mg S*

VARIATION

Apple Indian Pudding: When preparing corn meal mixture, increase meal to 1/3 cup. Toss 1 1/2–2 cups thinly sliced, peeled, and cored tart cooking apples with 1/3 cup sugar, scatter over the bottom of a buttered 2-quart casserole, top with pudding mixture, and bake as directed.

NPS: 440 C, 45 mg CH, 260 mg S*

Steamed Puddings

These rich, moist puddings aren't often made today. Too troublesome, perhaps. There's no denying they require time and effort. But served on a frosty day, they add such a warm, nostalgic touch, making the bother seem supremely worthwhile.

Pudding Molds: Unless you make steamed puddings often, you probably won't want to buy proper pudding molds. You can get by using metal mixing bowls, coffee tins, ice-cream bombe molds (if you have them), even custard cups.

Preparing and Filling Pudding Molds: Butter molds well, then pour in enough pudding batter to fill mold two thirds—no more; steamed puddings must have plenty of room to expand. Cover mold snugly, either with a lid or a well-greased double thickness of aluminum foil tied securely in place.

Steaming Puddings: Any deep, heavy kettle fitted with a rack can be used for steaming puddings (if the kettle has no rack of its own, use a cake rack). Stand molds upright on rack, pour in enough boiling water to reach halfway up the sides of the molds. Tightly cover kettle and adjust burner so water simmers or boils gently. Check kettle occasionally, adding boiling water as needed to keep molds half submerged throughout steaming. *Note:* Puddings may be steamed in pressure cookers; follow manufacturer's instructions carefully.

Unmolding Steamed Puddings: Remove puddings from steamer and uncover. Let stand a few minutes, then loosen, if necessary, with a thin spatula and invert on serving plate. Or, if you prefer, before uncovering mold, dip it quickly in cold water to loosen pudding. Uncover and turn out. If you like a slightly drier pudding, warm 3–5 minutes in a 350° F. oven after unmolding.

To Serve Steamed Puddings: Cut in wedges as you would cake and top with Hard Sauce, Stirred Custard, or other sauce of compatible flavor.

BASIC STEAMED LEMON PUDDING

8 servings

To avoid a cracked pudding, uncover and let stand 2–3 minutes so that steam can escape, then unmold. There are, by the way, more than a half-dozen different ways to vary the flavor of this basic recipe.

1 1/2 cups sifted flour
2 teaspoons baking powder
1/4 teaspoon salt
1/2 cup butter, margarine, or vegetable shortening
1/2 cup sugar
2 eggs
Finely grated rind of 1 lemon
2 tablespoons lemon juice
1/2 cup milk

Sift flour with baking powder and salt and set aside. Cream butter and sugar until light, add eggs, one at a time, beating well after each addition. Beat in lemon rind and juice. Add flour alternately with milk, beginning and ending with flour; beat well after each addition. Spoon into a well-greased 1 1/2-quart mold or metal bowl, cover with a greased double thickness of foil, and tie around with string. Set on a rack in a large kettle and pour in enough boiling water to come halfway up mold. Cover and steam 1–1 1/2 hours or until metal skewer inserted in center of pudding comes out clean. Keep water simmering throughout, replenishing as needed with boiling water. Uncover mold and let stand 2–3 minutes, then invert on serving dish. Cut in wedges and serve warm with hot Lemon-Raisin Sauce or Custard Sauce. Leftover pudding may be wrapped in foil and reheated in a 350° F. oven for 20–30 minutes.

NPS (with butter, without sauce): 260 C, 100 mg CH, 315 mg S*

Steamed Orange Pudding: Substitute the grated rind of 1 large orange for the lemon; omit lemon juice and use 1/4 cup each orange juice and milk instead of all milk. Otherwise, prepare as directed.

NPS: 260 C, 100 mg CH, 315 mg S*

Steamed Chocolate Pudding: Increase sugar to 3/4 cup, beat in 3 (1-ounce) envelopes no-melt unsweetened chocolate after eggs, and substitute 1 teaspoon vanilla for lemon rind and juice.

NPS: 340 C, 100 mg CH, 315 mg S*

Steamed Ginger Pudding: Substitute 1/2 cup firmly packed light brown sugar for the granulated; omit lemon rind and juice, and add 1 1/2 teaspoons ginger.

NPS: 260 C, 100 mg CH, 320 mg S*

Steamed College Pudding: Prepare batter and mix in 1/3 cup each golden seedless raisins and dried currants and 1/4 cup minced mixed candied fruit and 1 teaspoon allspice.

NPS: 320 C, 100 mg CH, 340 mg S*

Jam- or Marmalade-Topped Steamed Pudding: Spoon 1/4 cup strawberry, raspberry, or black currant jam or orange marmalade into bottom of pudding mold, then add batter and steam as directed. Unmold and top with an additional 1/3 cup hot jam or marmalade. Serve with hot Custard Sauce.

NPS: 330 C, 100 mg CH, 320 mg S*

Steamed Date Pudding: Prepare batter as directed and mix in 1/2 pound finely cut-up pitted dates.

NPS: 335 C, 100 mg CH, 320 mg S*

Individual Steamed Puddings: Prepare any batter as directed and fill 8 greased custard cups two thirds full, cover with foil, and tie as directed; steam 1/2 hour.

NPS: 260 C, 100 mg CH, 315 mg S*

PLUM PUDDING

12 servings

The English plum pudding served at Christmas doesn't contain plums; it resembles steamed fruit cake, is made weeks ahead and mellowed in a cool, dry place. If you have no cool spot (about 50° F.), freeze the pudding or make only one week ahead and refrigerate. The English hide silver charms or coins in the pudding batter—and lucky the child who finds one.

1 1/2 cups seedless raisins
1/2 cup dried currants
1/2 cup finely chopped mixed candied fruit
1 tart apple, peeled, cored, and grated fine
Finely grated rind of 1 lemon
Finely grated rind of 1 orange
3/4 cup ale or orange juice *or* 1/2 cup ale and 1/4 cup brandy or rum
1 cup sifted flour
1 teaspoon baking powder
1/2 teaspoon salt
1 teaspoon cinnamon
1/2 teaspoon allspice
1/4 teaspoon nutmeg
1 cup fine dry bread crumbs
1 cup firmly packed dark brown sugar
1/3 cup molasses
1 cup finely ground suet
3 eggs, lightly beaten
1/2 cup minced, toasted, blanched almonds

Mix fruits, rinds, and ale and let stand 1/2 hour. Sift flour with baking powder, salt, and spices, stir in remaining ingredients, add fruit mixture, and mix well. Spoon into 2 well-buttered 1-quart molds or metal bowls, cover with double thicknesses of foil, and tie firmly in place. Set on a rack in a large kettle, add boiling water to come halfway up puddings, cover, and steam 4 hours; keep water simmering slowly and add more boiling water as needed to maintain level. Cool puddings on racks with foil still intact, then store in a cool place, freeze, or refrigerate. To reheat, steam 1 hour exactly the same way you cooked them. Unmold puddings on a hot platter and decorate with holly. If you like, pour 1/4 cup warm brandy over each pudding and blaze. Cut in wedges and serve with Hard Sauce. Also good with Brandy or Rum Sauce or Stirred Custard.

NPS (without Hard Sauce): 495 C, 90 mg CH, 245 mg S*

GELATIN DESSERTS

The beauty of gelatins is that they are both versatile *and* reliable—easy enough for the most inexperienced beginner. A gelatin dessert may be nothing fancier than fruit gelatin, prepared by package directions, chopped or diced, perhaps, then topped with sliced fruit or whipped cream. Or it may be a sparkling mold, jeweled with berries or chunks of fruit, a cool custard-smooth cream, a fluffy sponge, or silky mousse.

Some Basic Ways to Use Gelatins in Dessert

(Also see Gelatins in the chapter on salads.)

To Whip Gelatin: Dissolve fruit-flavored gelatin as label directs, then cool and chill until just beginning to thicken. Beat hard with a rotary or electric beater until light and fluffy and the consistency of whipped cream. Use in preparing gelatin sponges and mousses. *Note:* Any gelatin mixture of normal consistency *not* containing solid bits of food may be whipped.

To Mold Fruits *(4–6 servings):* The standard (3-ounce) package of fruit-flavored gelatin will set 2 cups liquid and 2 cups prepared, cut-up, drained fruits. For variety and extra flavor, dissolve gelatin in hot fruit juice instead of water, or a ½ and ½ mixture. Cool, then chill until syrupy before adding fruits so that they won't sink to the bottom or rise to the top. Mix or match fruits and gelatin flavors, putting together any combination that appeals. *Caution: Do not try to congeal fresh or frozen pineapple or pineapple juice. They destroy gelatin's jelling power.*

To Make Your Own Fruit Gelatin *(4 servings):* Mix 1 envelope unflavored gelatin and ⅓–½ cup sugar in a heavy saucepan; gradually mix in ½ cup fruit juice and heat and stir over moderately low heat until gelatin and sugar dissolve. Off heat, mix in 1 cup additional fruit juice, cool, chill until syrupy, then fold in 1½ cups prepared berries or cut-up fruit. Spoon into mold and chill until firm.

To Mold Fruit Purée *(4 servings):* Mix 1 envelope unflavored gelatin and ⅓ cup cold fruit juice in a small saucepan and heat and stir over moderately low heat until dissolved. Cool slightly, mix in 2 cups fruit purée sweetened to taste, and tint an appropriate color if you like. Pour into mold and chill until firm. Good topped with fruit sauce or whipped cream.

To Make Fruit Velvet *(4 servings):* Prepare 1 (3-ounce) package fruit-flavored gelatin as label instructs, then cool and chill until syrupy. Beat hard with a rotary or electric beater until foamy, then fold in 1 cup well-drained, prepared, cut-up fruit and 1 cup heavy cream, whipped to soft peaks. Pour into mold and chill until firm.

To Jell Ice Cream *(4–6 servings):* Dissolve 1 (3-ounce) package fruit gelatin in boiling water as label directs, cool to room temperature, then beat in 1 pint mushy ice cream of a compatible flavor. Pour into mold and chill until firm. Serve from the bowl—do not unmold.

PORT WINE JELLY

4–6 servings ⊲⊺⊳

Both simple and sophisticated.

1⅓ cups water
2 envelopes unflavored gelatin (3 envelopes if you want to mold the jelly in a decorative mold)
⅔ cup sugar
Juice of 1 lemon, strained through a fine sieve
Juice of 1 orange, strained through a fine sieve
2 cups dark ruby port wine

Place water, gelatin, and sugar in a small saucepan, stir well to mix, then heat, stirring, over moderate heat about 5 minutes until sugar and gelatin are dissolved. Remove from heat and cool slightly. Mix in fruit juices and port. Pour into an ungreased 1-quart bowl or decorative mold, cover, and chill several hours until firm. To serve, spoon jelly into dessert glasses and top, if you like, with sweetened whipped cream. Or, if you have used the decorative mold, unmold on a platter and garnish with fluffs of sweetened whipped cream.

NPS (4–6) (without whipped cream): 315–210 C, 0 mg CH, 10–5 mg S*

LEMON FLUFF

5–6 servings ⊲⊺⊳

Tart and lemony, light and billowy.

4 eggs, separated
⅔ cup superfine sugar
1½ teaspoons unflavored gelatin
¼ cup cold water
½ teaspoon grated lemon rind
¼ cup lemon juice

Beat egg yolks until very thick and light; add sugar, a little at a time, beating well after each addition, then continue beating until thick and the color of cream. Heat gelatin and water, uncovered, in a small saucepan, stirring occasionally, over low heat until gelatin dissolves; mix in lemon rind and juice and stir into egg mixture. Chill until mixture mounds when dropped from a spoon. Beat egg whites until they form stiff peaks and fold into yolk mixture. Spoon into 5 or 6 parfait glasses or into a 1-quart serving bowl. Cover and chill until serving time. Serve as is or topped with sugared fresh or thawed frozen fruit. (*Note:* Do not spoon from serving bowl into individual dishes until a few minutes before serving or mixture may liquefy.)

NPS (without topping): 170 C, 220 mg CH, 60 mg S*

BASIC COLD SOUFFLÉ (VANILLA)

4 servings

1 envelope unflavored gelatin
1/2 cup sugar
1 cup milk
2 eggs, separated
1 1/2 teaspoons vanilla
3/4 cup heavy cream

Mix gelatin and sugar in the top of a double boiler, gradually stir in milk, set over simmering water, and heat and stir until sugar dissolves; mix a little hot mixture into lightly beaten egg yolks, return to pan, and cook and stir 2–3 minutes until slightly thickened. Pour into a large bowl and mix in vanilla; cool to room temperature, stirring occasionally, then chill until mixture mounds when dropped from a spoon. Whip cream to soft peaks and fold in. With a separate beater (or the same one well washed), beat egg whites to stiff peaks and fold in. Spoon into a 1-quart soufflé dish and chill until firm. Top, if you like, with whipped cream fluffs, toasted slivered almonds, and/or fresh berries before serving.

NPS (without topping): 340 C, 205 mg CH, 85 mg S*

For a Top Hat Soufflé *(8 servings):* Extend height of a 1-quart soufflé dish by wrapping a 4"-wide, double-thickness foil strip around outside so it stands 2" above rim; fasten with cellophane tape. Double any of the cold soufflé recipes, pour into dish, and chill until firm. Remove collar carefully before serving. Nutritional count same as basic recipe.

VARIATIONS

Cold Lemon Soufflé: Prepare as directed, substituting 1/2 cup each lemon juice and water for the milk, and 1/2 teaspoon finely grated lemon rind for the vanilla.

NPS: 300 C, 200 mg CH, 60 mg S*

Cold Orange Soufflé: Prepare as directed, substituting 1 cup orange juice for milk and 1 teaspoon finely grated orange rind for vanilla.

NPS: 325 C, 200 mg CH, 55 mg S*

Cold Fruit Soufflé: Prepare as directed but substitute 1 1/4 cups any fruit purée for the milk and use 1 egg *yolk* only. Flavor with 1/4

teaspoon almond extract instead of vanilla. Otherwise, proceed as directed, folding in whipped cream and beaten egg whites.

NPS (with peach purée): 305 C, 130 mg CH, 35 mg S*

Cold Chocolate Soufflé: Prepare as directed and, while gelatin mixture is still hot, mix in 2 1/2 (1-ounce) coarsely grated squares unsweetened chocolate, stirring until melted. Garnish with chocolate curls* and fluffs of whipped cream.

NPS (without garnish): 430 C, 205 mg CH, 35 mg S*

Cold Coffee Soufflé: Prepare as directed, and while gelatin mixture is still hot, mix in 1 tablespoon instant coffee powder, stirring until dissolved. Decorate, if you like, with chocolate curls.*

NPS (without decoration): 340 C, 205 mg CH, 85 mg S*

BASIC BAVARIAN CREAM (VANILLA)

6–8 servings

1/2 cup sugar
1 envelope unflavored gelatin
1 1/2 cups milk
3 egg yolks, lightly beaten
1 1/2 teaspoons vanilla
3/4 cup heavy cream
2 tablespoons confectioners' sugar
3 egg whites (optional)

Mix sugar, gelatin, and milk in the top of a double boiler and heat over simmering water until steaming hot. Mix a little hot mixture into yolks, return to double boiler top, and cook and stir 3–5 minutes until mixture coats the back of a metal spoon. Off heat, mix in vanilla; cool, then chill, stirring occasionally, until mixture mounds when dropped from a spoon. Whip cream with confectioners' sugar until stiff peaks form, then fold into custard mixture. If you like, also beat egg whites to soft peaks and fold in. Spoon into a 1 1/2-quart mold or 6–8 custard cups or parfait glasses and chill 3–4 hours until firm. If molded, unmold on a dessert platter and wreathe, if you like, with crushed sweetened berries, sliced fresh peaches, or any stewed fruit.

NPS (6–8) (with egg whites, without garnish): 205–195 C, 185–140 mg CH, 70–55 mg S*

VARIATIONS

Rum Bavarian Cream: Prepare as directed but use 1/2 cup light rum and 1 cup milk in the custard mixture instead of all milk and reduce vanilla to 1/2 teaspoon. *(Note:*

Brandy, crème de menthe, or any fruit liqueur may be used in place of rum; tint an appropriate color.)

NPS (6–8): 295–220 C, 185–135 mg CH, 60–45 mg S*

Chocolate Bavarian Cream: Prepare as directed but add 1 (6-ounce) package semisweet chocolate bits to the hot custard mixture, stirring until melted.

NPS (6–8): 405–305 C, 185–140 mg CH, 70–55 mg S*

Mocha Bavarian Cream: Prepare Chocolate Bavarian Cream (above) as directed, using 1 cup milk and ½ cup very strong hot black coffee in the custard mixture.

NPS (6–8): 395–295 C, 185–135 mg CH, 60–45 mg S*

Fruit Bavarian Cream: Prepare as directed, using ½ cup milk and 1 cup puréed berries, peaches, apricots, bananas, or other fruit in the custard mixture; flavor with 1 tablespoon lemon juice instead of vanilla and tint, if you like, an appropriate pastel color.

NPS (6–8) (with peach purée): 250–190 C, 180–135 mg CH, 60–45 mg S*

Charlotte Russe *(12–15 servings):* Line the bottom and sides of a 9″ spring form pan with split ladyfingers (you'll need about 20), then sprinkle with ¼ cup light rum. Chill while you prepare 2 recipes Basic Bavarian Cream (omit egg whites); spoon into pan and chill 4–6 hours or overnight. Unmold by removing spring form sides and inverting on chilled platter. Garnish with fluffs of whipped cream and maraschino cherries. To serve, cut in wedges as you would a layer cake.

NPS (12–15) (without garnish): 325–260 C, 250–200 mg CH, 60–45 mg S*

SWEDISH CREAM

4 servings

So rich and smooth it never fails to impress.

1 pint light cream
1 envelope unflavored gelatin
⅔ cup sugar
1 pint sour cream
1 teaspoon vanilla
2 cups sliced fresh or frozen thawed peaches or berries

Heat cream, gelatin, and sugar in a small saucepan over lowest heat, stirring constantly, 15–20 minutes until all sugar and gelatin are dissolved; do not allow to boil. Remove from heat and cool 5 minutes; beat in sour cream with a wire whisk or rotary beater. Stir in vanilla, cover, and chill 2–3 hours until firm. To serve, spoon into individual dessert dishes and top with fruit.

NPS (with fresh peaches): 655 C, 130 mg CH, 110 mg S*

FROZEN DESSERTS

Ices and ice creams are thought to have originated in ancient China, then traveled the trade routes west to the Mediterranean. Romans served them, but it was sixteenth-century Florentine chefs who glorified them. For the wedding feasts of Catherine de Médicis and Henry II of France, they prepared a new flavor every day. Soon Italian ices and "iced creams" were fashionable throughout Western Europe and their popularity never waned. While abroad, Thomas Jefferson sampled ice cream, copied down a recipe, and on returning to America introduced it at a state dinner at the White House. Today there are many kinds of frozen desserts. Here's a quick lexicon.

The Kinds of Frozen Desserts

Bombe: Ice cream and/or sherbet or ice, frozen in a decorative mold, often in layers of contrasting color and flavor.

Coupe: Ice cream or sherbet served in a broad-bowled goblet topped with fruit and/or whipped cream and *marrons glacés* (glazed chestnuts).

Frappé: Sherbet or ice frozen to the mushy stage.

Frozen Custard: Ice cream with added eggs or egg yolks; sometimes it is whipped to incorporate more air.

Granité: A granular Italian ice frozen without stirring. When served, it is scraped into fluffy, snow-like crystals instead of being spooned.

Ice: A watery frozen dessert made of sugar, water, and flavoring (usually fruit juice).

Ice Cream: Originally, frozen sweetened and flavored cream but today almost any creamy frozen dessert. *French ice cream* has an egg custard base.

Ice Milk: Less creamy than ice cream, this frozen dessert also contains less butterfat and milk solids. It may not be as low-calorie as you think because of a high sugar content.

Mousse: An extra-rich ice cream frozen without being stirred. It often contains whipped cream.

Parfait: Ice cream or whipped cream layered into a tall footed glass with a topping—fruit, chocolate, nut—then frozen.

Sherbet: Fine-textured frozen fruit dessert, originally water-based but today more often made with milk. Gelatin and/or egg white is frequently added to make sherbets smoother.

Sorbet: The French word for *sherbet;* it has come to mean a mushy frozen fruit ice or sherbet, a frappé. It may be served between courses or as dessert.

Tofutti: A creamy frozen mixture in a variety of flavors made with dried soybean curd solids. It contains zero butterfat, zero cholesterol.

Freezing Ice Creams, Sherbets, and Ices

To Freeze in a Crank-Type Freezer (Hand or Electric): Prepare mix according to recipe, cover, and chill 1–2 hours. Meanwhile, wash and scald all freezer parts, then rinse in cold water and dry thoroughly. Set freezer can into freezer, fit dasher into place, and pour in chilled ice-cream mix. (*Note:* Mixture will expand as it freezes so never fill freezer can more than two thirds.) Put lid on can, attach crank top, and lock into place. Add enough crushed ice to fill freezer one third, distributing evenly around can. Then, using 1 part rock or kosher salt to 8 parts ice (1 to 6 if you want mixture to freeze faster), layer salt and ice into freezer until filled. Let stand 3–5 minutes, then begin turning. If freezer is the hand-crank variety, turn smoothly and slowly, always in the same direction. Stop turning only when mixture is too stiff to crank (electric freezers will shut off or begin to labor heavily). Drain water from freezer and, if necessary, scoop out enough ice to expose top third of can. Wipe away any salt, paying particular attention to seam around lid. Uncover can, lift out dasher, and scrape all frozen mixture back into can; pack down with a large spoon. Plug hole in can top with a cork (some freezers have an additional solid cover), cover can, then repack freezer, using 1 part salt to 4 parts crushed ice. Cover with heavy paper, cloth, or newspapers and let season ½ hour. Or, if you prefer, pack ice cream into plastic freezer containers and let stand ½ hour in freezer.

To Freeze in an Automatic Ice-Cream Machine: These expensive countertop appliances with built-in freezing agents make superlative ice cream because they churn as they freeze. They're a snap to use, too. Prepare ice-cream mix as recipe directs, pour into machine's drum, then freeze following manufacturer's instructions.

To Freeze in Refrigerator-Freezer: Turn temperature setting to coldest point. (*Note:* If you make ice cream often, it's a good idea to have a special set of ice cube trays for just this purpose. Frequently washed ice cube trays lose their finish, causing ice cubes to stick.) Any small excess amounts of ice-cream mix can be frozen in custard cups.

Bombes: Chill a melon or brick bombe mold well in freezer. (*Note:* If you have no mold, use a metal mixing bowl.) Meanwhile soften commercial ice cream or sherbet until workable or, if making your own, freeze only until mushy. Pack into mold, smoothing with a large spoon so that you have an even layer about 1″ thick over bottom and sides; freeze until firm. Add a second layer of contrasting color and flavor, packing tightly against the first layer, and freeze until firm. Fill center with soft ice or ice cream of yet another flavor and freeze until firm. *To Unmold:* Wipe mold with a cloth wrung out in hot water, then invert on a serving platter. (*Note:* Bombes can be frozen by packing them in a mixture of crushed ice and rock or kosher salt—1 part salt to 4 parts ice—but it seems an unnecessary lot of work unless you have no freezer.)

Ice Creams: Prepare base mix as recipe directs and freeze until mushy. Remove from tray and beat at high speed until fluffy. Also whip cream until soft peaks form, fold into base, and freeze until firm. *Note:* For extra creaminess, beat once again before freezing until firm.

Mousses: Prepare mix, spoon into shallow trays or mold, cover with foil or wax paper (because of their high cream content, mousses are more apt to pick up refrigerator odors), and freeze until firm without beating or stirring.

Parfaits: Layer ice cream or sherbet into parfait glasses with a topping of your choice, then freeze until firm. Some combinations to try:
• Vanilla ice cream with Melba Sauce or Chocolate Sauce or any puréed fruit
• Vanilla ice cream and orange sherbet with Melba Sauce or any puréed berries or peaches

---

• Chocolate ice cream and whipped cream
• Pistachio ice cream, chocolate ice cream, and Chocolate Sauce or Fudge Sauce

Sherbets and Ices: Prepare as recipe directs, spoon into refrigerator trays, and freeze until mushy. Remove from trays, beat until light, then freeze until firm. *Note:* An extra beating before freezing until firm will make the mixture more velvety.

BASIC FRUIT ICE

1¹/2 quarts (12 servings)   ⚖

An easy recipe you can experiment with. Mix two or more fruit juice flavors, if you like, or use one flavor only.

1 envelope unflavored gelatin
¹/2–1 cup sugar (depending upon sweetness of fruit juice)
1 quart sweet fruit juice (any berry, peach or apricot nectar, pineapple or orange juice) *or* **1 pint each crushed fruit and water**
2 tablespoons lemon juice
2 egg whites

Mix gelatin and ¹/2 cup sugar in a saucepan, add juice, and heat and stir over low heat until gelatin and sugar dissolve. *(Note:* If using crushed fruit, heat gelatin and sugar with the water and, when dissolved, mix in fruit.) Taste for sugar and adjust as needed. Mix in lemon juice, and pour into 2 refrigerator trays, and freeze until mushy. Spoon into a large bowl and beat hard until fluffy. Beat egg whites to very soft peaks, fold into fruit mixture, spoon into 3 refrigerator trays, cover, and freeze until firm.

NPS (with peach nectar): 80 C, 0 mg CH, 15 mg S*

VARIATIONS

⚖ **Lemon or Lime Ice:** Prepare as directed, using 1¹/2 cups sugar, 3 cups water, and 1 cup lemon or lime juice.

NPS (with lemon juice): 105 C, 0 mg CH, 15 mg S*

⚖ **Wine Ice:** Mix gelatin with ¹/2 cup sugar and 1 cup each orange juice and water and heat and stir until gelatin and sugar dissolve. Mix in 2 cups dry or sweet white, red, or rosé wine or champagne and proceed as directed. When serving, drizzle a little wine over each portion.

NPS: 80 C, 0 mg CH, 10 mg S*

⚖ **Spiked Ice:** Prepare Basic Fruit Ice as directed but add ¹/4–¹/2 cup any compatible fruit liqueur along with the beaten egg whites (orange juice and curaçao, for example, pineapple and crème de menthe, berry juice and crème de cassis, fraise, or framboise).

NPS (with curaçao): 95 C, 0 mg CH, 15 mg S*

LEMON OR LIME GRANITÉ

1¹/2 quarts (12 servings)   ▨ ⚖

Granité is a granular ice frozen without being stirred. It can be served at the mush stage or frozen hard, then scraped up in fine, feathery shavings. Particularly good topped with a little fruit liqueur or rum.

1 quart water
2 cups sugar
1 cup lemon or lime juice
1 tablespoon finely grated lemon or lime rind
Few drops yellow and/or green food coloring

Bring water and sugar to a boil in a saucepan, stirring, then reduce heat and simmer, uncovered, 5 minutes. Cool, mix in juice and rind, and tint pale yellow or green. Pour into 3 refrigerator trays, cover, and freeze to a mush without stirring. Spoon into goblets and serve or freeze hard, scrape up with a spoon, and pile into goblets.

NPS (lemon): 135 C, 0 mg CH, 5 mg S*

VARIATIONS

⚖ **Orange Granité:** Prepare as directed, substituting 1 quart orange juice for the water, reducing sugar to ³/4 cup and lemon juice to 2 tablespoons; also use orange rind instead of lemon.

NPS: 85 C, 0 mg CH, 1 mg S*

⚖ **Fruit Granité:** Boil 3 cups water and 1¹/2 cups sugar into syrup as directed. Cool, add 2 tablespoons lemon juice and 2 cups puréed fruit (any berries, peaches, pineapple, sweet cherries); omit rind. Freeze and serve as directed.

NPS (with peach purée): 115 C, 0 mg CH, 5 mg S*

⚖ **Coffee or Tea Granité:** Boil 1 cup each water and sugar into syrup as directed; cool, add 3 cups strong black coffee or tea and to tea mixture, add ¹/4 cup lemon juice. Freeze and serve as directed.

NPS (with coffee): 65 C, 0 mg CH, 1 mg S*

⚖ **Melon Granité:** Mix 1 quart puréed ripe melon (any kind) with ¹/2–1 cup sugar (depending on sweetness of melon) and 2 tablespoons lemon juice; let stand 1 hour at room temperature, stirring now and then, until sugar is dissolved. Freeze as directed.

NPS (¹/2–1 cup sugar): 35–70 C, 0 mg CH, 1 mg S*

LEMON OR LIME MILK SHERBET

1½ quarts (12 servings) ⚖

1 envelope unflavored gelatin
1⅓ cups sugar
1 quart milk
¾ cup lemon or lime juice
2 teaspoons finely grated lemon or lime rind
Few drops yellow or green food coloring
  (optional)
2 egg whites

Mix gelatin and sugar in a saucepan, gradually add milk, and heat and stir over low heat until sugar and gelatin dissolve. Cool, add juice and rind, and, if you like, tint pale yellow or green. Pour into 2 refrigerator trays and freeze until mushy. Remove from trays and beat until fluffy. Beat egg whites to very soft peaks and fold into fruit mixture. Spoon into 3 refrigerator trays and freeze until firm.

NPS: 145 C, 10 mg CH, 50 mg S*

V A R I A T I O N S

⚖ **Orange Milk Sherbet:** Heat and stir gelatin with ¾ cup sugar and 2 cups milk until dissolved; cool, add 2 tablespoons lemon juice, 2 cups orange juice, and 1 tablespoon finely grated orange rind. Proceed as directed.

NPS: 95 C, 5 mg CH, 30 mg S*

⚖ **Fruit Milk Sherbet:** Heat and stir gelatin with ¾ cup sugar and 2 cups milk until dissolved; cool, add 2 tablespoons lemon juice, ½ cup water, and 1½ cups puréed fruit (berries, sweet cherries, peaches, apricots, pineapple, etc.). Taste for sugar, adding a bit more if needed, then proceed as directed.

NPS (with peach purée): 90 C, 5 mg CH, 35 mg S*

⚖ **Extra-Low-Calorie Sherbets:** Prepare any of the above sherbets as directed but use skim milk instead of whole, reduce sugar to ½ cup, and use 1 egg white only.

NPS: 65 C, 1 mg CH, 50 mg S*

BASIC REFRIGERATOR ICE CREAM

1½ quarts (12 servings)

Turn freezer to coldest setting before beginning this recipe. From this one basic recipe, you can make 14 different flavors of ice cream.

1 cup sugar
2 teaspoons cornstarch
1 quart milk
3 eggs, separated

2 teaspoons vanilla
1 cup heavy cream, whipped

Mix sugar and cornstarch in top of a double boiler and gradually stir in milk. Add egg yolks and beat until frothy. Set over simmering water and heat 15 minutes, stirring now and then at first, constantly toward the end. Cool and stir in vanilla. Beat egg whites to soft peaks and fold in. Pour into 2 refrigerator trays and freeze until mushy. Spoon into a large bowl, beat hard until fluffy, then beat in cream. Spoon into 3 trays and freeze until firm. *(Note: For extra smoothness, beat once more before freezing until firm.)*

NPS: 205 C, 105 mg CH, 65 mg S*

V A R I A T I O N S

Berry Ice Cream: Prepare as directed but reduce vanilla to 1 teaspoon and add 2 cups any crushed, sweetened-to-taste berries (fresh, frozen, or canned) along with beaten egg whites.

NPS (with frozen raspberries): 245 C, 110 mg CH, 65 mg S*

Banana Ice Cream: Prepare as directed but reduce vanilla to 1 teaspoon and add 2 cups puréed ripe bananas (about 6 medium-size bananas) along with egg whites.

NPS: 255 C, 105 mg CH, 65 mg S*

Pineapple Ice Cream: Prepare as directed but reduce vanilla to 1 teaspoon and add 3 (8-ounce) cans crushed pineapple (undrained) along with egg whites.

NPS: 240 C, 105 mg CH, 65 mg S*

Peach or Apricot Ice Cream: Prepare as directed but reduce vanilla to ½ teaspoon and add ½ teaspoon almond extract; mix in 2 cups peach or apricot purée along with beaten egg whites.

NPS (with peach purée): 225 C, 105 mg CH, 70 mg S*

Orange Ice Cream: Prepare custard mixture as directed, using ¾ cup sugar and 3 cups milk. Add 1 (6-ounce) can thawed frozen orange juice concentrate and 1 cup freshly squeezed orange juice; omit vanilla. Proceed as directed.

NPS: 215 C, 105 mg CH, 55 mg S*

Chocolate Ice Cream: Add 2 (1-ounce) squares coarsely grated unsweetened chocolate to hot custard mixture and stir until melted. Reduce vanilla to 1 teaspoon and proceed as directed.

NPS: 230 C, 105 mg CH, 65 mg S*

Coffee Ice Cream: Sprinkle ⅓ cup instant coffee powder over hot custard mixture and stir until blended. Reduce vanilla to 1/2 teaspoon and proceed as directed.

NPS: 205 C, 105 mg CH, 65 mg S*

Burnt Almond Ice Cream: Prepare custard mixture as directed, using 1/2 cup sugar; caramelize* 1/2 cup sugar and mix in along with vanilla called for. Proceed as directed, mixing 1 cup coarsely chopped toasted, blanched almonds into beaten frozen mixture along with whipped cream.

NPS: 270 C, 105 mg CH, 65 mg S*

Butter Pecan Ice Cream: Prepare as directed, mixing 1 cup coarsely chopped, butter-browned pecans into beaten frozen mixture along with whipped cream.

NPS: 275 C, 105 mg CH, 65 mg S*

Pistachio Ice Cream: Prepare as directed but reduce vanilla to 1 teaspoon and add 1/2 teaspoon almond extract. Tint mixture pale green before freezing. Mix 3/4 cup coarsely chopped pistachio nuts into beaten frozen mixture along with whipped cream.

NPS: 260 C, 105 mg CH, 65 mg S*

Peppermint Ice Cream: Prepare as directed but omit vanilla and add 1/4 teaspoon peppermint extract; also mix 11/2 cups finely crushed peppermint candy into beaten frozen mixture along with whipped cream.

NPS: 260 C, 105 mg CH, 70 mg S*

Rum-Raisin Ice Cream: Soak 2/3 cup minced seedless raisins in 1/3 cup dark rum while preparing recipe; fold into beaten frozen mixture along with whipped cream.

NPS: 245 C, 105 mg CH, 65 mg S*

Eggnog Ice Cream: Prepare basic recipe as directed and mix 1/4 cup rum or brandy into beaten frozen mixture along with whipped cream.

NPS: 245 C, 105 mg CH, 65 mg S*

BASIC FREEZER ICE CREAM (VANILLA)

2 quarts (16 servings)

The principal difference between freezer-cranked or automatic-ice-cream-machine and refrigerator ice cream is that, with the former, the cream goes into the freezer mix in the beginning. Avoid using extra-thick or clotted cream—the freezer's churning action may turn it to butter. *(Note:* Any of the refrigerator ice creams can be frozen in a crank freezer. Simply mix in heavy cream—do not whip—at the start.)

1 quart light cream
11/2 cups superfine sugar
2 tablespoons vanilla or 1 (3-inch) piece vanilla bean, split lengthwise
1 pint heavy cream

Heat and stir light cream and sugar over moderate heat until sugar dissolves thoroughly. If using vanilla bean, heat along with mixture; remove vanilla bean (but not tiny seeds). Cool mixture, mix in vanilla extract (if bean wasn't used) and the heavy cream. Chill 1–2 hours, then freeze in a crank-type freezer* (hand or electric) or automatic ice-cream machine following manufacturer's directions.

NPS: 300 C, 80 mg CH, 35 mg S*

VARIATIONS

Chocolate Freezer Ice Cream: Prepare as directed but heat 3 squares unsweetened chocolate along with the light cream and 2 cups superfine sugar, stirring until melted.

NPS: 350 C, 80 mg CH, 35 mg S*

Coffee Freezer Ice Cream: Prepare as directed but heat 1/3 cup instant coffee powder along with light cream and sugar. If you like, stir in 1/4 cup coffee liqueur along with vanilla.

NPS (with liqueur): 310 C, 80 mg CH, 35 mg S*

Mocha Freezer Ice Cream: Prepare as directed but heat 1 square unsweetened chocolate and 1/4 cup instant coffee powder along with light cream and sugar.

NPS: 305 C, 80 mg CH, 35 mg S*

Fruit Freezer Ice Cream: Heat 1 pint cream and the sugar as directed. Cool, omit vanilla, but mix in 2 cups any fruit purée (sieved berry, fresh peach, mango, papaya, pineapple, banana, apricot, kiwi, cherimoya) and the heavy cream. Add 1/4 cup lemon or orange juice, and, if flavor is peach, apricot, or pineapple, 1 teaspoon almond extract. Proceed as directed.

NPS (with banana): 260 C, 60 mg CH, 25 mg S*

Ginger Freezer Ice Cream: Prepare vanilla mix as directed but reduce vanilla to 1 tablespoon. Add 11/2 cups minced preserved ginger, 1 cup syrup drained from bottles of ginger, and 2 tablespoons lemon juice. Freeze as directed.

NPS: 365 C, 80 mg CH, 40 mg S*

FRENCH VANILLA ICE CREAM

1 1/2 quarts (12 servings)

An extra-smooth ice cream made with egg yolks.

2 cups milk
1 cup sugar
6 egg yolks, lightly beaten
1 tablespoon vanilla
1 pint heavy cream

Beat milk, sugar, and egg yolks in the top of a double boiler until frothy. Set over simmering water and heat 15 minutes, stirring now and then at first, constantly toward the end. Cool, add vanilla and cream. Freeze in a crank-type freezer* (hand or electric) or automatic ice-cream machine, following manufacturer's directions.

NPS: 260 C, 195 mg CH, 40 mg S*

To Freeze in Refrigerator-Freezer: Prepare custard mixture as directed, cool, and mix in vanilla; pour into 2 refrigerator trays and freeze until mushy. Spoon into a large bowl and beat hard until fluffy. Whip cream until thick and satiny and fold in. Spoon into 3 refrigerator trays, cover, and freeze until firm, stirring twice during the first hour.

VARIATION

French Chocolate Ice Cream: Prepare custard mixture as directed and, while still hot, mix in 3 (1-ounce) coarsely grated squares semisweet chocolate, stirring until well blended. Cool, add 2 teaspoons vanilla, and proceed as directed, freezing either in automatic ice-cream machine or crank-type freezer* or refrigerator-freezer.

NPS: 295 C, 195 mg CH, 40 mg S*

(Note: Any of the variations given for Basic Refrigerator Ice Cream can be used for French Vanilla Ice Cream. Simply follow basic recipe above, adding amounts of fruits, flavorings, or nuts called for in the variations.)

BISCUIT TORTONI

6 servings ☒

You can buy the little paper cups used for *tortoni* in Italian delicatessens, also in some party shops. If unavailable, substitute cupcake papers but set in muffin tins to give them extra support. Once tortoni are frozen, lift from tins.

1 cup heavy cream
1/3 cup confectioners' sugar

1/2 teaspoon vanilla
1 egg white
2 tablespoons light rum
1/3 cup crushed dry macaroons
1/4 cup minced, toasted, blanched almonds

Whip cream with sugar and vanilla until soft peaks form. Beat egg white to soft peaks and fold into cream along with rum and macaroons. Spoon into paper cups, sprinkle with almonds, cover with foil circles, and freeze until firm.

NPS: 235 C, 60 mg CH, 25 mg S*

SPUMONI

1 1/2 quarts (12 servings)

This Italian ice-cream bombe comes in many flavors, textures, and colors. To vary recipe below, substitute raspberry or chocolate ice cream for the Vanilla-Almond and leave the filling white.

VANILLA-ALMOND ICE CREAM
2 cups milk
4 egg yolks, lightly beaten
3/4 cup sugar
1 1/2 teaspoons vanilla
1/3 cup minced, toasted, blanched almonds

CREAM-FRUIT FILLING
1 cup heavy cream, tinted pale pink if you like
1/2 cup sifted confectioners' sugar
1 egg white
1/4 cup minced maraschino cherries
2 tablespoons each candied citron, lemon peel, orange peel, and angelica
2 tablespoons light rum or brandy

Set a 2-quart melon mold to chill in freezer. Beat milk, egg yolks, and sugar in the top of a double boiler until frothy. Set over simmering water and heat and stir until mixture will coat a metal spoon and no raw egg taste remains; cool, mix in vanilla and almonds. Pour into a refrigerator tray and freeze until mushy; spoon into a bowl and beat hard until fluffy; return to tray, cover, and freeze until creamy-firm but not hard. Pack firmly into melon mold, smoothing with the back of a spoon to form a thick, even lining. Cover and freeze 1/2 hour. Meanwhile, prepare filling: Whip cream with sugar until soft peaks form; beat egg white to soft peaks and fold into cream along with remaining ingredients. Spoon into center of melon mold, cover, and freeze overnight. Unmold on a serving platter, loosening, if necessary, by rubbing a cloth wrung out in hot water over bottom of mold. Decorate, if you like, with candied cherries and angelica strips. To serve, cut in wedges.

NPS (without decoration): 235 C, 125 mg CH, 40 mg S*

BAKED ALASKA

8 servings

A spectacular dessert easy enough for beginners.

1 (9″) square firm white or yellow cake, homemade or bought
1 half-gallon brick ice cream (any flavor)

MERINGUE
3 egg whites
1/8 teaspoon salt
1/4 teaspoon cream of tartar
1/3 cup superfine sugar

Preheat oven to 500° F. Cut cake into a rectangle 5″ × 7″ and place on a foil-lined baking sheet (save scraps for snacks). Halve ice cream horizontally, place half on cake, and set in freezer while you prepare meringue (also returning remaining ice cream to freezer to serve another time). Beat egg whites with salt and cream of tartar until foamy, gradually beat in sugar, then continue beating until very stiff peaks form. Remove cake from freezer and quickly frost with meringue, making sure it covers cake and ice cream *entirely* and touches baking sheet all around; swirl meringue into peaks. Bake, uncovered, on center oven rack about 3 minutes until tan all over. Serve immediately, slicing with a large sharp knife.

NPS: 515 C, 80 mg CH, 415 mg S*

DESSERT OMELETS

A favorite with the French, the dessert omelet has never become very popular in this country except among gourmet cooks. Like savory omelets, dessert omelets must be made to order, one at a time. For small dinners, however, they are both practical and impressive *if* the hostess is skilled in the art of omelet making. Before trying the sweet omelet recipe included here, read Omelets in the chapter on eggs, cheese, and dairy.

APPLE AND BRANDY OMELET

2 servings

1 sweet crisp apple, peeled, cored, and sliced thin
2 tablespoons butter
3–4 tablespoons warm Calvados or brandy, warmed slightly
1 Sweet Soufflé Omelet
1 tablespoon sugar

Sauté apple in butter in a small skillet over moderately low heat 8–10 minutes until tender, lightly glazed, and golden. Add 1 tablespoon Calvados and keep warm. Prepare omelet as directed and cover with apples just before folding and turning out. Crease omelet lightly through center, fold, and ease onto a hot platter. Sprinkle with sugar, pour remaining Calvados over surface, and, if you wish, flame before serving.

NPS: 370 C, 315 mg CH, 215 mg S*

SOME SPECIALTY DESSERTS

CREPES SUZETTE

6 servings

Not as complicated to make as you might think.

1 recipe Simple Dessert Crepes with 1 tablespoon orange juice added to batter
6 sugar lumps
1 orange
1 lemon
1/2 cup orange juice
1/2 cup butter (no substitute)
2 tablespoons superfine sugar
1/4 cup Cointreau or curaçao
2 tablespoons light rum or Benedictine
1/4 cup brandy or Grand Marnier

Mix and cook crepes as recipe directs, then fold each in half and then in half again; keep warm in a 250° F. oven until all are done. Rub sugar lumps on rind of orange and lemon, drop into orange juice, and crush to dissolve. Melt butter in a chafing dish over moderately low heat, add superfine sugar and orange juice, and heat, stirring constantly, until mixture reduces slightly. Doing 1 crepe at a time, lift to chafing dish, unfold in sauce, coating well, then fold as before and push to side of chafing dish. Pour remaining ingredients over crepes—do not stir—and heat, moving pan gently over flame so crepes don't burn. Tilt pan until liqueurs ignite and spoon flaming over crepes. Serve on hot dessert plates topped with some of the sauce.

NPS: 320 C, 140 mg CH, 300 mg S*

POACHED MERINGUE RING

6 servings ⚖

A beautiful base for sliced fresh berries or any dessert sauce.

6 egg whites
1/8 teaspoon cream of tartar
1/4 teaspoon salt
3/4 cup superfine sugar
1 teaspoon vanilla
1 teaspoon lemon juice
1/4 teaspoon almond extract

Preheat oven to 325° F. Beat egg whites, cream of tartar, and salt with a rotary beater until foamy. Add sugar, a little at a time, beating well after each addition. Continue to beat until whites stand in stiff peaks. Fold in vanilla, lemon juice, and almond extract. Pack mixture in an ungreased 6-cup ring mold. Set mold in a shallow pan of cold water and bake, uncovered, 1 hour until meringue is lightly browned and pulls from the sides of mold. Remove meringue from oven and water bath and let cool upright in mold to room temperature. Loosen edges carefully with a spatula and unmold by inverting on a dessert platter. Cut into wedges and serve as is or with a generous ladling of dessert sauce (Algarve Apricot Sauce is especially good) or with sliced fresh berries.

NPS (without sauce or fruit): 115 C, 0 mg CH, 140 mg S*

COEUR À LA CRÈME

8 servings

For this dessert you will need a heart-shaped basket or perforated metal mold so that the cheese mixture can drain properly. They are stocked by housewares sections of many department stores, also by specialty food shops.

1 pound cottage cheese
1 pound cream cheese, softened to room temperature
1/8 teaspoon salt
1 pint heavy cream
1 quart fresh strawberries, washed and stemmed, or 2 (10-ounce) packages frozen strawberries, thawed
Sugar (optional)

Press cottage cheese through a fine sieve. Mix with cream cheese and salt and beat until smooth with a rotary beater. Using a wooden spoon, beat in cream, a little at a time. Line a 1½-quart heart-shaped basket or perforated mold with a double thickness of cheesecloth that has been wrung out in cold water; let ends overlap mold, and smooth out as many wrinkles as possible. Spoon cheese mixture into mold, cover with overlapping ends of cloth, and set on a tray deep enough to contain draining whey. Cover loosely with foil and refrigerate overnight; check occasionally to see that whey is not overflowing. To serve: Turn ends of cheesecloth back and invert mold on a large, shallow dish. Garnish with 10–12 large perfect berries; sweeten the rest to taste, crush slightly, and pass as a sauce.

NPS (without sugar): 485 C, 150 mg CH, 455 mg S*

MONT BLANC AUX MARRONS

8 servings

An Alp of riced chestnuts snowcapped with sweetened whipped cream. *Not* for calorie counters. *Note:* The frozen shelled and peeled Italian chestnuts available in many specialty food shops will spare you an hour or more of sheer drudgery.

1 pound shelled, peeled chestnuts (you'll need about 1½ pounds unshelled chestnuts)
3 cups milk
2/3 cup sugar
2 teaspoons vanilla
1 pint heavy cream
1/4 cup sifted confectioners' sugar

Simmer chestnuts, milk, sugar, and 1 teaspoon vanilla in the top of a double boiler over just boiling water 30–40 minutes until very tender. Drain (save milk for pudding or custard). Force chestnuts through a potato ricer or coarse sieve, mounding into a high, fluffy pyramid on a large platter. Chill 2–3 hours. Whip cream with confectioners' sugar and remaining vanilla until very soft peaks form, and gently frost pyramid, letting a bit of the base show. Serve at once.

NPS: 450 C, 95 mg CH, 70 mg S*

CLAFOUTI

6 servings

This traditional "cherry season" dessert from the Limousin district of France uses just-picked cherries. You may substitute canned cherries if you first dry them out as directed below. Apple Clafouti, although not authentically French, is a delicious variation nonetheless.

1¾ cups (about 1 pound) pitted fresh dark sweet cherries or 1 (1-pound) can dark sweet cherries, drained and pitted
4 eggs
¼ cup superfine sugar
¼ cup unsifted flour
⅛ teaspoon salt
1⅔ cups milk
1 teaspoon vanilla
1 teaspoon cornstarch
2 tablespoons confectioners' sugar

Preheat oven to 350° F. If using canned cherries, place in a single layer in a skillet, and dry over moderate heat, shaking pan now and then, 5–10 minutes until cherries give up some of their juices. Drain well, and set aside to cool briefly. Beat eggs and sugar with a balloon whip until mixture doubles in volume and is thick and lemon colored. (*Note:* You can use an electric mixer, but baked pancake will not be as light.) Gradually sift in the flour, 1 tablespoon at a time, beating lightly after each addition. Combine salt, milk, and vanilla and add all at once; stir lightly to mix. Arrange cherries in a lightly greased and floured 1½-quart shallow baking dish (an *au gratin* dish is ideal); sift cornstarch evenly over cherries, then pour in the batter. (*Note:* Batter will almost reach top of dish, but will not overflow as the clafouti bakes.) Bake, uncovered, 45–50 minutes until puffy and brown and a table knife inserted in the center comes out clean. (*Note:* Do not underbake; the batter will puff during last 15 minutes of baking only.) Cool 10 minutes on a wire rack, sift confectioners' sugar on top, and serve warm with or without whipped cream. (*Note:* The clafouti will sink slightly as it cools, but this is entirely normal.)

NPS (without whipped cream): 190 C, 190 mg CH, 125 mg S*

VARIATION

Apple Clafouti: Prepare batter as directed and pour over 1¾ cups very thinly sliced, peeled, and cored tart apples that have been tossed with the 1 teaspoon cornstarch and ¼ cup sugar. Bake as directed, cool 10 minutes on wire rack, then dust with confectioners' sugar.

NPS: 215 C, 190 mg CH, 125 mg S*

COTTAGE PUDDING

8 servings ¢

As much cake as pudding and buttery-rich.

2 cups sifted flour
1 tablespoon baking powder
¼ teaspoon salt
½ cup butter or margarine
½ cup sugar
1 egg, lightly beaten
1 teaspoon vanilla or the finely grated rind of 1 lemon
¾ cup milk

Preheat oven to 350° F. Sift flour with baking powder and salt; set aside. Cream butter and sugar until light, add egg, and beat well. Mix vanilla and milk. Add flour and milk alternately to egg mixture, beginning and ending with flour and beating after each addition. Spoon into a buttered 8″ × 8″ × 2″ baking pan and bake, uncovered, about 50 minutes until top springs back when touched. Cut in squares and serve warm with hot Custard Sauce or whipped cream.

NPS (with butter, without Custard Sauce or whipped cream): 280 C, 70 mg CH, 365 mg S*

VARIATIONS

Apple or Cherry Cottage Pudding: Prepare batter as directed and mix in 2 cups very thinly sliced, peeled, and cored tart apples or well-drained, canned pitted red cherries. Bake as directed in a buttered 9″ × 9″ × 2″ pan.

NPS (with apples): 295 C, 70 mg CH, 365 mg S*

Eve's Pudding: Spread 1½ cups applesauce in the bottom of a greased 9″ × 9″ × 2″ pan, cover with batter, and bake as directed.

NPS: 315 C, 70 mg CH, 365 mg S*

¢ **Raisin Cottage Pudding:** Prepare as directed, using grated lemon rind and adding 2 tablespoons lemon juice and ¾ cup seedless or golden seedless raisins.

NPS: 325 C, 70 mg CH, 365 mg S*

Castle Pudding: Put 2 tablespoons maple syrup, jam, or jelly into each of 8 buttered custard cups then fill two thirds with Cottage Pudding batter. Bake 25 minutes at 350° F., then invert on serving plates.

NPS (with maple syrup): 380 C, 70 mg CH, 370 mg S*

EASY DATE AND WALNUT PUDDING

20 servings

Use scissors dipped in hot water to snip dates quickly.

2 cups boiling water
2 teaspoons baking soda
1 pound pitted dates, coarsely cut up
1/4 cup butter or margarine
2 cups sugar
2 cups sifted flour
1 teaspoon vanilla
1 cup coarsely chopped walnuts

Preheat oven to 325° F. Pour water over soda, mix well, and pour over dates. Add butter and stir until melted; cool slightly. Mix sugar and flour in a large bowl, add about half the date mixture and beat well. Add remaining date mixture and vanilla and beat again. Stir in nuts. Spoon into a well-greased 13″ × 9″ × 2″ baking pan and bake 50 minutes until springy to the touch. Cut into squares and serve warm or cold with whipped cream or vanilla ice cream.

NPS (with butter, without whipped cream or ice cream): 240 C, 5 mg CH, 105 mg S*

DESSERT SAUCES

Cooking Dessert Sauces in a Microwave Oven

Because most dessert sauces cook on top of the stove in a matter of minutes, it makes little sense (and saves little time) to microwave them. So use the microwave as a handy helper to melt chocolate in a custard cup on *MEDIUM* power setting (1 square takes 2 minutes; 2 squares, 3–4 minutes), also to warm prepared sauces, toppings, and syrups. Place these in a large measuring cup, cover with wax paper or vented plastic food wrap to prevent splattering, then microwave on *MEDIUM* power setting, stirring every minute from outside toward center, until bubbly. The time needed to heat a sauce will vary from seconds to minutes depending upon the type, sweetness, and quantity of sauce. Check often.

VANILLA SAUCE

About 2 1/2 cups

A good basic sauce suited to a variety of desserts.

2 tablespoons cornstarch
1/2 cup sugar
2 cups water or milk
1/4 cup butter or margarine
1 1/2 teaspoons vanilla
Pinch nutmeg

Mix cornstarch and sugar in a heavy saucepan, gradually add water, and heat, stirring constantly, until mixture boils. Reduce heat and simmer, uncovered, 2–3 minutes, stirring now and then. Add butter, vanilla, and nutmeg and stir until butter melts and is blended. Serve hot.

NP Tablespoon (with butter and water): 20 C, 5 mg CH, 10 mg S*
NP Tablespoon (with butter and milk): 30 C, 5 mg CH, 15 mg S*

VARIATIONS

Vanilla Bean Sauce: Scald 2 cups milk, add 1/2 vanilla bean, split lengthwise, cover, and let steep 20 minutes; discard bean (but not the tiny black seeds). Combine cornstarch and sugar as directed, gradually add milk, and heat and stir until mixture boils. Proceed as directed, omitting vanilla extract and nutmeg.

NP Tablespoon: 30 C, 5 mg CH, 15 mg S*

French Vanilla Sauce: Prepare Vanilla Bean Sauce (above) as directed, spoon a little hot sauce into 2 lightly beaten egg yolks, return to pan, and heat and stir 1 minute over lowest heat; do not boil.

NP Tablespoon: 35 C, 20 mg CH, 20 mg S*

Vanilla Sauce Mousseline: Prepare any of the above vanilla sauces as directed; place a circle of wax paper flat on sauce and cool to room temperature. Whip 1/2 cup heavy cream to soft peaks, fold into sauce, and serve.

NP Tablespoon (with water): 30 C, 5 mg CH, 15 mg S*
NP Tablespoon (with milk): 40 C, 10 mg CH, 20 mg S*

EGGNOG SAUCE

About 2 cups ⊠

2 egg yolks
1/2 cup sifted confectioners' sugar
1 teaspoon vanilla
1 cup heavy cream

Beat egg yolks, sugar, and vanilla until thick and creamy. Whip cream to soft peaks, then fold in yolk mixture. Serve with fruit.

NP Tablespoon: 35 C, 25 mg CH, 5 mg S*

Orange or Lemon Eggnog Sauce: Just before serving fold in 1 tablespoon finely grated orange or lemon rind and/or 1–2 tablespoons brandy, light rum, or Marsala wine.

NP Tablespoon (without liquor): 35 C, 25 mg CH, 5 mg S*

NESSELRODE SAUCE

About 1 quart

Serve cold over pudding, fruit, or ice cream.

1 recipe Stirred Custard
1/4 cup Málaga or Marsala wine
1/4 cup golden seedless raisins
1/4 cup dried currants
2 tablespoons minced candied red cherries
2 tablespoons minced candied orange peel
2 tablespoons minced candied citron
1/2 cup shelled, peeled chestnuts, boiled and drained
1/2 cup heavy cream

Prepare and cool custard as directed. Meanwhile, pour wine over fruits and let stand 1 hour; also purée chestnuts. Mix fruits and chestnuts into custard. Whip cream to soft peaks and fold in. Cover and chill 1/2 hour before serving.

NP Tablespoon: 30 C, 20 mg CH, 10 mg S*

BASIC CHOCOLATE SAUCE

About 1 cup

Four sauces from one easy recipe.

2 (1-ounce) squares unsweetened chocolate
1/2 cup water
1/2 cup sugar
1/2 cup light corn syrup
2 tablespoons butter or margarine
1/2 teaspoon vanilla

Place chocolate, water, sugar, and syrup in a small, heavy saucepan, set over low heat, and heat, stirring now and then, until chocolate melts. Beat in butter and vanilla. Serve hot or at room temperature.

NP Tablespoon (with butter): 85 C, 5 mg CH, 20 mg S*

Creamy Chocolate Sauce: Substitute 1/2 cup light cream or evaporated milk for the water.

NP Tablespoon (with light cream): 100 C, 10 mg CH, 25 mg S*

Chocolate-Peppermint Sauce: Substitute 1/2 teaspoon peppermint extract for the vanilla.

NP Tablespoon: 85 C, 5 mg CH, 20 mg S*

Chocolate-Nut Sauce: Prepare sauce as directed and mix in 1/3 cup chopped pecans, walnuts, toasted, blanched almonds, or peanuts.

NP Tablespoon (with almonds): 100 C, 5 mg CH, 20 mg S*

HOT FUDGE SAUCE

1 1/4 cups

1 1/2 cups sugar
2 tablespoons flour
3/4 cup cold water
3 (1-ounce) squares unsweetened chocolate or 3 (1-ounce) envelopes unsweetened no-melt chocolate
3 tablespoons butter or margarine
1 teaspoon vanilla

Mix sugar and flour in a heavy saucepan, blend in water, and heat, stirring constantly over moderate heat, until boiling and thickened. Reduce heat to low, add chocolate, and heat and stir until chocolate melts. Beat in butter and vanilla. Cool slightly, beating now and then. Serve warm.

NP Tablespoon (with butter): 100 C, 5 mg CH, 15 mg S*

BUTTERSCOTCH SAUCE

About 2 cups

1 cup firmly packed dark brown sugar
1 cup maple syrup
1/4 cup butter or margarine
1 teaspoon salt
2 teaspoons vanilla
3/4 cup light cream

Heat sugar and syrup in a heavy saucepan over moderately low heat, stirring constantly until sugar dissolves. Raise heat to moderately high and boil, uncovered, 5 minutes. Off heat, add butter, salt, and vanilla. *Do not stir.* Let stand, uncovered, 5 minutes. Add cream, then beat about 1 minute until creamy, blond, and well blended. Serve warm.

NP Tablespoon (with butter): 75 C, 10 mg CH, 90 mg S*

Butterscotch Syrup *(About 3 cups):* Prepare as directed but increase light cream to 1 1/2 cups. Serve over waffles, pancakes, or ice cream.

NP Tablespoon: 60 C, 10 mg CH, 60 mg S*

CARAMEL SYRUP

2 cups ☒

1 (1-pound) box dark brown sugar
1½ cups water
2 teaspoons vanilla
¼ teaspoon salt

Heat and stir sugar in a heavy saucepan over low heat until liquid. Off heat, gradually stir in water. Return to low heat and heat and stir until smooth. Cool 5 minutes, mix in vanilla and salt. Pour into a jar, cool, cover, and refrigerate. Use as an ice-cream topping or milk flavoring.

NP Tablespoon: 55 C, 0 mg CH, 20 mg S*

BASIC NUT SYRUP

2 cups

2 cups sugar
1 cup water
¼ cup dark corn syrup
½ teaspoon vanilla
1 cup coarsely chopped walnuts, pecans, toasted almonds, hazelnuts, or blanched, roasted, unsalted peanuts

Mix sugar, water, and syrup in a 1-quart heavy saucepan, set over moderately low heat, and heat and stir until sugar dissolves. Raise heat and boil gently, uncovered, *without stirring* 3 minutes; stir once and, if the consistency of maple syrup, remove from heat; if not, boil 1 minute longer. Cool slightly and add vanilla and nuts. Stir just to mix and serve warm or cool over ice cream.

NP Tablespoon (with walnuts): 80 C, 0 mg CH, 1 mg S*

VARIATIONS

Orange-Nut Syrup: Prepare as directed, substituting orange juice for water and the grated rind of 1 orange for vanilla.

NP Tablespoon: 85 C, 0 mg CH, 1 mg S*

Pistachio Syrup: Prepare as directed, substituting light corn syrup for the dark. Add ⅛ teaspoon almond extract, tint pale green, if you like, and stir in ½ cup shelled and peeled pistachio nuts.

NP Tablespoon: 70 C, 0 mg CH, 1 mg S*

LEMON OR LIME SAUCE

2½ cups ☒

Spoon over ice cream or yellow cake.

2 tablespoons cornstarch
1 cup sugar
1½ cups water
½ cup lemon or lime juice
¼ cup butter or margarine
2 teaspoons finely grated lemon or lime rind

Mix cornstarch and sugar in a heavy saucepan, gradually add water and fruit juice, and heat, stirring constantly, until mixture boils. Reduce heat and simmer, uncovered, 2–3 minutes, stirring now and then. Add butter and rind and stir until butter is melted and well blended. Serve hot.

NP Tablespoon (with butter): 30 C, 5 mg CH, 10 mg S*

VARIATION

Orange Sauce: Prepare as directed, using 2 cups orange juice instead of water and lemon juice, and grated orange rind instead of lemon. For tartness, add 1–2 tablespoons lemon juice.

NP Tablespoon: 30 C, 5 mg CH, 10 mg S*

BRANDY OR RUM SAUCE

2½ cups ☒

Delicious over steamed puddings or ice cream.

2 tablespoons cornstarch
½ cup sugar
1¾ cups milk
¼–⅓ cup brandy or light rum
¼ cup butter or margarine
½ teaspoon vanilla
Pinch nutmeg

Mix cornstarch and sugar in a heavy saucepan, gradually add milk and brandy, and heat, stirring constantly, until mixture boils. Reduce heat and simmer, uncovered, 2–3 minutes, stirring now and then. Add butter, vanilla, and nutmeg and stir until butter melts and is well blended. Serve hot.

NP Tablespoon (with butter): 30 C, 5 mg CH, 15 mg S*

LEMON-RAISIN SAUCE

2⅔ cups

Good over gingerbread.

1 cup sugar
2 tablespoons cornstarch

1½ cups cold water
½ cup lemon juice
2 teaspoons finely grated lemon rind
1 egg yolk
2 tablespoons butter or margarine
¼ cup golden seedless raisins

Mix sugar and cornstarch in a heavy saucepan, blend in water and lemon juice, and heat, stirring constantly over moderate heat, until mixture boils. Reduce heat and simmer 2–3 minutes, stirring now and then. Mix lemon rind and egg yolk, blend a little hot sauce into egg, return to pan, and beat and stir 1–2 minutes; do not boil. Off heat, add butter and raisins and let stand 2 minutes. Serve warm.

*NP Tablespoon (with butter): 30 C, 10 mg CH, 5 mg S**

JAM OR JELLY SAUCE

1½ cups ▨

1 cup jam or jelly (any kind)
2 teaspoons cornstarch
⅔ cup cold water
2 teaspoons lemon juice

Heat jam or jelly in a small, heavy saucepan over moderately low heat. Mix cornstarch and water, blend into jam, and heat and stir until mixture boils. Reduce heat and simmer, stirring now and then, 2–3 minutes. Off heat, mix in lemon juice. Serve warm over pudding.

*NP Tablespoon: 35 C, 0 mg CH, 1 mg S**

VARIATION

Marmalade Sauce: Substitute orange, lemon, or grapefruit marmalade for jam and prepare as directed; omit lemon juice.

*NP Tablespoon: 35 C, 0 mg CH, 1 mg S**

MELBA SAUCE

1½ cups ▨

Serve as a sauce for Peach Melba, ice cream, or fruit or use to flavor milk shakes and sodas.

1 pint fresh raspberries, washed, or 2 (10-ounce) packages frozen raspberries, thawed
⅓ cup red currant jelly
⅓–½ cup sugar
1 tablespoon cornstarch blended with 2 tablespoons water

Purée raspberries by buzzing 10–15 seconds in an electric blender at high speed or 5–10 seconds in a food processor fitted with the metal chopping blade; strain through a fine sieve. Pour into a saucepan, mix in jelly, sugar, and cornstarch paste, and cook and stir over moderate heat until thickened and clear. Cool, taste for sweetness, and add more sugar if needed.

*NP Tablespoon: 30 C, 0 mg CH, 1 mg S**

VARIATIONS

Strawberry Sauce: Prepare as directed, substituting 1 pint fresh strawberries or 2 (10-ounce) packages thawed frozen strawberries for the raspberries.

*NP Tablespoon: 25 C, 0 mg CH, 1 mg S**

Currant Sauce: Substitute 1 pint very ripe red or black currants for the raspberries and omit the currant jelly. If you like, mix the cornstarch with port wine or blackberry liqueur instead of water. Proceed as directed. Recipe too flexible for meaningful nutritional count.

ALGARVE APRICOT SAUCE

2¼ cups

In the south of Portugal lies the Algarve, where figs, peaches, and apricots grow. Women make them into a variety of sweets, among them this tart apricot sauce, luscious over a poached meringue.

1 (1-pound 14-ounce) can peeled whole apricots (do not drain)
Juice and grated rind of 1 lemon
1 cup firmly packed light brown sugar
¼ cup butter

Pit apricots and purée in an electric blender at high speed or put through a food mill. Place in a small saucepan, add lemon juice, rind, and sugar, and simmer uncovered, stirring occasionally, 1 hour until thick and caramel colored. Remove from heat, stir in butter, and cool to room temperature. Serve over Poached Meringue Ring or as a dessert sauce for ice cream, sliced oranges or peaches.

*NP Tablespoon: 50 C, 5 mg CH, 15 mg S**

HONEY SAUCE

1½ cups ▨

Serve warm or cool over pudding, fruit, or ice cream.

1 cup honey
1 tablespoon cornstarch blended with 1 tablespoon cold water

1/4 cup butter or margarine
2 teaspoons lemon juice

Heat honey in a small, heavy saucepan over moderate heat. Stir in cornstarch mixture and heat and stir until boiling; reduce heat and simmer 2–3 minutes. Beat in butter and lemon juice.

NP Tablespoon (with butter): 60 C, 5 mg CH, 20 mg S*

VARIATION

Honey-Nut Sauce: Prepare sauce as directed, cool, and mix in 1/2 cup coarsely chopped pecans, walnuts, or toasted almonds.

NP Tablespoon (with pecans): 80 C, 5 mg CH, 20 mg S*

HARD SAUCE

1 cup ☒

The perfect sauce for steamed puddings.

1/2 cup butter (no substitute), softened to room temperature
2 cups sifted confectioners' sugar
1/8 teaspoon salt
1 tablespoon hot water
1 teaspoon vanilla

Beat butter until creamy; gradually beat in sugar, a little at a time. Beat in remaining ingredients and continue to beat until fluffy. Serve chilled or at room temperature.

NP Tablespoon: 100 C, 15 mg CH, 80 mg S*

VARIATIONS

Brandy or Rum Hard Sauce: Omit hot water and vanilla; add 2 tablespoons brandy or rum or 2 teaspoons brandy or rum extract.

NP Tablespoon (with brandy): 105 C, 15 mg CH, 75 mg S*

Lemon or Orange Hard Sauce: Omit water and vanilla; instead, beat in 2 tablespoons lemon or orange juice and 1 tablespoon finely grated lemon rind or 2 tablespoons finely grated orange rind.

NP Tablespoon: 100 C, 15 mg CH, 75 mg S*

SWEETENED WHIPPED CREAM

2 cups ☒

For best results, whip cream by hand just before needed, using a chilled bowl and beater.

1 cup very cold heavy cream
2 tablespoons sugar or 1/4 cup sifted confectioners' sugar
1/2 teaspoon vanilla or 1/4 teaspoon almond, maple, or peppermint extract

Beat cream in a chilled bowl until frothy; slowly beat in sugar and flavoring and continue beating until soft, glossy peaks form, scraping bowl often. *(Note:* If you should slightly overbeat cream, stir in 1–2 tablespoons cold milk.) If you must delay using it, refrigerate, then beat lightly with a wire whisk just before using.

NP Tablespoon: 30 C, 10 mg CH, 1 mg S*

VARIATIONS

Plain Whipped Cream: Whip cream as directed but omit sugar and flavoring.

NP Tablespoon: 25 C, 10 mg CH, 1 mg S*

Decorative Whipped Cream: Whip cream with 1/3 cup sifted confectioners' sugar, flavor, then tint, if you like, a pastel color. Pipe through a pastry tube fitted with a decorative tip. *To Freeze:* Do not color whipped cream; pipe onto wax-paper-lined baking sheets and freeze until hard; wrap frozen fluffs individually, then group in plastic freezer bags. Use within 2 months. Nice on warm pies.

NP Tablespoon: 30 C, 10 mg CH, 5 mg S*

Chocolate Whipped Cream: Whip as directed, beating in 3 tablespoons sugar blended with 3 tablespoons cocoa; reduce vanilla to 1/4 teaspoon.

NP Tablespoon: 30 C, 10 mg CH, 5mg S*

Spiked Whipped Cream: Whip as directed, but flavor with 2–3 tablespoons brandy, rum, bourbon, crème de menthe, or fruit liqueur instead of vanilla.

NP Tablespoon (with brandy): 30 C, 10 mg CH, 5 mg S*

Party Whipped Cream *(About 2 quarts):* Warm 2 teaspoons unflavored gelatin and 1/4 cup cold water until gelatin dissolves; cool slightly and gradually mix in 1 quart heavy cream; chill 1/2 hour. Whip cream, beating in 1 cup sifted confectioners' sugar and 2 teaspoons vanilla. *(Note:* If you use an electric mixer, hold out 1/3 cup cream and stir in after the rest is whipped.) This cream will hold well in the refrigerator about 1 hour.

NP Tablespoon: 30 C, 10 mg CH, 5 mg S*

LOW-CALORIE DESSERT TOPPING

4 servings ⊠ ⚖

3 tablespoons ice water
3 tablespoons nonfat dry milk powder
2 teaspoons lemon juice
Few drops liquid noncaloric sweetener, 2 teaspoons low-calorie granulated sugar substitute, or 2 (1-gram) packets aspartame sweetener
¼ teaspoon vanilla or almond extract

Pour ice water into a chilled bowl, sprinkle powdered milk on surface, and beat with a rotary or electric beater until soft peaks form. Add lemon juice, sweeten to taste, add vanilla, and beat until stiff peaks form. Use at once.

NP Tablespoon: 15 C, 1 mg CH, 20 mg S*

HOMEMADE SOUR CREAM

1 cup

1 cup heavy cream, at room temperature
¼ cup sour cream or buttermilk

Mix creams in a screw-top jar, cover, and let stand at room temperature about 24 hours until very thick. Chill well before using and keep refrigerated.

NP Tablespoon (with sour cream): 60 C, 20 mg CH, 10 mg S*
NP Tablespoon (with buttermilk): 55 C, 20 mg CH, 10 mg S*

SEVENTEEN

Pies and Pastries

More than any other dessert, pies are typically American. Our speech ("as easy as pie"), our songs ("I'm as normal as blueberry pie . . ."), our literature (to eat "humble pie") are strewn with references. Apple pies, traditionally, usher in autumn, pumpkin pies belong to Thanksgiving, mince pies to Christmas, and cherry pies to George Washington's birthday. Foreign countries have specialties too—if not pies, flaky pastries, honey-drenched or filled with silken creams: the éclairs, cream puffs, and Napoleons of France, the tortes of Germany and Austria, the cheese cakes of Italy, the wispy honey-laden pastries of the Middle East. Many can be made at home, some with less effort than seems possible.

THE KINDS OF PASTRY AND HOW TO MIX THEM

Conventional Pastry: The piecrust pastry, tender and flaky when properly made. The secret is to cut the fat into the flour until it is the texture of coarse meal so that, in baking, these flecks of fat melt, leaving the pastry flaky. There are a number of variations on the standard method (see recipes that follow).

Puff Pastry (Pâte Feuilletée): The feathery, many-layered French pastry used for Napoleons, Cream Horns, and dozens of lavish pastries. It is made by rolling and folding chilled butter (or sometimes lard if the pastry is a savory one) into a simple dough so that it separates into tissue-thin "leaves" when baked. A less tedious variation is *Rough Puff Pastry.*

Short French Pastry (Pâte Brisée): A versatile, butter-rich pastry (wonderfully crumbly when baked) that is used for all manner of French classics including quiches, savory single and double crust tarts.

Sweet Short Pastry (also called *Tart* or *Sweet Torte Pastry* and in French, *Pâte Sucrée;* the German *Mürbteig* is of this type): Rather like a cookie dough, this egg-rich, sweet pastry is most often used for fruit flans and tarts.

Choux Pastry (Pâte à Choux): A paste containing a high proportion of eggs that is beaten until smooth and elastic enough to "puff" during baking. This is the pastry of cream puffs and éclairs.

Phyllo Pastry (pronounced FEE-lo): The tissue-thin, crisp pastry used for Greek and Middle Eastern pastries. It requires a special hard flour, a special technique, and years of practice. Phyllo leaves, ready to fill and bake, are available in many specialty food shops and Greek groceries. Frozen phyllo pastry is now routinely stocked by many supermarkets (always follow package directions to the letter).

Strudel Pastry: An elastic dough that is kneaded, rolled, and stretched until big as a table and "thin enough to read a newspaper through." It is filled with fruit, cheese, or poppy seeds, rolled up jelly-roll style, and baked until golden brown and crisp. Strudel dough sheets—both fresh and frozen—can be bought at specialty food shops and even some supermarkets.

Crumb "Pastries": These aren't pastries but crumbs, crushed dried cereals, nuts, coconut, etc., mixed with sugar or syrup and melted butter and pressed into piepans.

ESSENTIAL INGREDIENTS OF PASTRIES

Flour: Experts use *pastry flour* for piecrusts because it makes them unusually tender. Available at specialty food shops (and occasionally through local bakeries), it is softer than all-purpose flour but not so delicate as cake flour. It is not suitable for pastries where elasticity is needed (choux and strudel).

IMPORTANT NOTE:
Use all-purpose flour for pastries in this book unless recipes specify otherwise.

Fat: For most piecrusts, a solid fat is used. It may be vegetable shortening or lard, which many cooks prefer because of its mellow flavor and brittle texture. Mixtures of shortening and butter or margarine may be used, but the proportion of butter *(do not use the whipped variety)* should be kept low (about 1 to 3) if the pastry is to be flaky. For best results, chill the fat before using. Some pastries are made with cooking oil; it produces a tender (though not very flaky) crust. *(Note:* Use cooking oil only if recipes call for it; do not use interchangeably with shortening or lard.)

Liquid: Water (but occasionally fruit juice, milk, or cream) is used to bind the fat and flour, making pastry workable. For flaky pastry, use cold water; for a denser, mealier texture, warm or hot water.

Salt: Added strictly for flavor; without it, pastries would taste flat.

Extra Ingredients of Pastries

Sugar: Added to tart or torte pastries for sweetness, tenderness, and better browning.

Eggs: Added for richness of flavor and color. Usually egg yolks, rather than whole eggs, are used.

Leavening: Used in cookie dough-type pastries when a certain lightness and sponginess are wanted.

Flavorings: These are merely embellishments—grated cheese or nuts, spices, seeds, grated orange or lemon rind, sometimes vanilla or other extracts—added for variety and interest.

SOME PASTRY-MAKING TERMS AND TECHNIQUES

To Blind-Bake (or *Bake Blind):* To bake an empty pie shell; to keep the shell from shrinking, a large square of wax paper is placed in pie shell, then filled with uncooked rice, dried beans, or metal pie weights.

To Brush: To apply a thin coating of liquid, usually glaze or melted butter, with a pastry brush to give pastry a satiny or glistening finish. Bottom crusts are sometimes brushed with beaten egg white to "waterproof" them and keep juices from soaking in.

To Crimp: To pinch or crease edges of pastry in a zigzag or fluted pattern. Crimped edges seal top and bottom crusts together and also act like dams, holding fillings in.

Croûte: The French word for *crust; en croûte* refers to something baked in a pastry.

To Cut In: To work fat into flour with a pastry blender, 2 knives, or the fingertips. The motion is literally a cutting one (except when fingers are used), the fat particles being broken up and coated with flour.

To Dot: To dab bits of butter or other solid over the surface of something, usually before baking. In pies, fruit fillings are often dotted with butter.

To Dust: To cover with a thin film of flour.

To Fill: To put filling in a pie shell or other pastry.

To Fit: To press pastry against the contours of a pan.

Flan: The French word for a flat, open-face pie usually filled with fruit or cream filling or a combination of the two; it may be larger than American-style pies or smaller. For baking flan, a *flan ring* (bottomless round metal ring with straight sides) is placed on a baking sheet and the pastry pressed into it.

To Glaze: To coat with glaze. In pastry making, both crusts and fillings may be glazed, crusts with beaten egg or milk and sugar, fillings with syrup, thin gelatin, or clear sweet sauce.

To Line: To cover a pan with a thin layer of pastry, crumb crust, or other material.

Meringue: A stiffly beaten mixture of egg whites and sugar used as a pie topping or dropped from a spoon and baked like cookies.

"Mixture Forms a Ball": The term used to describe pastry when just the right amount of liquid has been added to the flour-shortening mixture. The pastry will just hang together in a ball but be neither sticky (too much liquid) nor crumbly (too little).

Pastry Blender: A gadget indispensable to every pastry cook, 6–8 arched blades or wires, mounted on a wooden handle, that cut fat into flour in record time. If you have none, use 2 table knives instead, cutting back and forth through the fat and flour or, if you prefer, rub fat and flour together with your fingertips. The difficulty of the finger method is that the heat of the hands may melt the shortening and make the pastry tough.

Pastry Cloth: A heavy square of canvas that makes rolling pastry easier because the fabric gives up only a small amount of flour to the pastry yet keeps it from sticking.

Pastry Wheel: A handy cutting wheel with either a plain or zigzag blade mounted on a wooden handle.

To Patch: To fill in cracks, holes, uneven edges of pastry by pressing in small scraps. Sometimes it is necessary to dampen the pastry scraps so they will stick.

Pie Funnel: A heatproof ceramic funnel about 3″ high, often with a decorative top, used in deep-dish pies to help prop up the crust and keep the pie from boiling over. It stands in the center of the pie, its top poking through the pastry.

Pie Shell: Crust fitted into a piepan; it may be baked or unbaked.

To Prick: To pierce pastry, usually a bottom crust, at intervals with a fork so it will lie flat during baking.

To Roll Out: To roll pastry with a rolling pin.

To Roll Up: To roll a pastry over and over, jelly-roll style. The technique is used for making Palmiers and Strudel.

To Seal: To pinch pastry edges together, sealing in filling.

Short: Containing a high proportion of shortening; a short crust is tender and crumbly.

Spring Form Pan: A fairly deep, straight-sided round pan with removable bottom and a side seam that locks and unlocks to facilitate removing pastry. It is most often used for cheese cakes.

Steam Slits or Vents: Decorative slits or holes cut in a top crust to allow steam to escape during baking; these also help keep pies from boiling over.

Stockinette: A knitted cotton "stocking" fitted over a rolling pin to make rolling pastry easier. It works like a pastry cloth, giving up very little flour to the pastry but at the same time keeping it from sticking. Stockinettes

are inexpensive and available in nearly every dime store. Wash and dry after each use.

Tart: A small pastry, usually open-face, often with a short sweet crust. It may be bite-size or big enough for one ample dessert portion. Tart shells may be baked in muffin tins or fluted tart tins (see Making Tarts).

"Texture of Coarse Meal": The term used to describe the consistency of fat when properly cut into flour. In making pastry, the fat should be cut in only until pebbly and coarse. Some cooks prefer the particles even coarser, about the size of small beans, because these solid flecks of fat, scattered throughout the flour, are what make the pastry flaky and crisp.

To Toss: To mix quickly and lightly with a fork, using a tossing motion. This is the technique used in mixing liquid into pastries, the object being to handle as gently as possible so that the fat particles aren't mashed. When the pastry holds together, the mixing's done.

HOW TO MAKE BETTER PIES AND PASTRIES

Pans:

• For richly browned bottom crusts, use heatproof glass, dark metal, or heavy Teflon-lined pans. Bright shiny pans deflect the heat, producing pale crusts.
• For best results, use types and sizes of pans recipes call for.
• When making a juicy fruit pie, use a pan with a trough around the rim to catch "boil-ups."
• Do not grease or flour piepan; do, however, make sure it is spotless and dry.

Mixing Pastries:

• Read recipe before beginning and make sure you have all ingredients and implements on hand.
• For mixing, use a large, heavy, round-bottomed bowl.
• Measure all ingredients before beginning.
• For extra-flaky pastry, chill shortening and water 15–20 minutes before using.
• Use the lightest possible touch in mixing pastries. Cut fat into flour until "the texture of coarse meal" or for a superflaky crust, until "the size of small beans." Scatter liquid over mixture, 1 tablespoon at a time, tossing with a fork until it just "forms a ball."
• Do not knead pastry unless recipe calls for

it (strudel dough, for example, must be kneaded). But piecrusts, never.

Rolling Pastries:

• Lightly gather pastry together with hands and shape loosely into a ball.
• Chill pastry, if you like, about ½ hour before rolling. Some cooks insist that the chilling step is vital if the pastry is to be flaky and tender. But many tests have proved that, if the pastry is properly handled throughout mixing and rolling, the chilling makes little difference.
• Place pastry on a lightly floured pastry cloth, board, or plastic or marble slab, flatten lightly into a small circle (or rectangle or square, depending on shape needed), then with lightly floured, stockinette-covered rolling pin, flatten until about ½″ thick. Even up any ragged edges.
• Roll pastry from the center outward, using short, firm strokes and changing direction as needed to keep pastry as nearly circular (or rectangular or square) as possible. Always bear in mind the ultimate size and shape you want when rolling and roll toward that end. For most piecrusts, ⅛″ is a good thickness. As for diameter, pastry should be about 3″ larger in diameter than the pan you plan to use.
• Use as little flour in rolling as possible; it's the extra flour that toughens the pastry.
• If edges crack or pastry is rolled too thin in spots, patch with scraps. Dampen, then press in place and roll. The patchwork should be invisible.
• To transfer pastry easily to pan, place rolling pin across center of pastry, lop half of pastry over rolling pin, and lift gently into pan.

Fitting Pastries into Pans:

• Center pastry circle in pan so that overhang is equal all around.
• Press gently, fitting against contours of pan.
• *If a single crust pie:* Trim overhang all around with scissors so it is about 1″ larger than pan. Roll under, even with rim, and crimp as desired.
• *If a double crust pie:* Do not trim overhang. Brush bottom and sides well with beaten egg white if filling is extra juicy and let air-dry 15–20 minutes. Roll top crust as you did the bottom, making it slightly thinner if you like. Cut decorative steam slits in the center. Add filling to pie shell, mounding it up in the center. Fit top crust over filling, trim both crusts evenly all around so they overhang about ½″–1″. Roll up and over even with rim, then seal and crimp.

Fitting Pastries into Flan Rings:
The straight-sided pastry shells used for a variety of open-face tarts can be baked in bottomless flan rings set on baking sheets, or failing that, in slip-bottom layer cake pans. For professional results, we recommend the flan ring, also Torte Pastry, Pâte Brisée, or Pâte Sucrée. Roll pastry as recipe directs, then:
• Ease pastry onto a greased flan ring set on a greased baking sheet, making sure pastry is centered on ring.
• *Very gently* work pastry down against baking sheet. Using your fingers, lift edges of dough and mold against sides of flan ring, making walls of crust slightly thicker and sturdier than bottom.
• Trim off excess dough by rolling rolling pin firmly over top of flan ring; with your thumbs, gently push pastry walls up so they extend about ⅛″ above rim all around.
• Roll pastry edges under until even with rim, then crimp or flute decoratively. (*Note:* Do not let pastry overhang rim or you won't be able to remove baked shell from flan ring.) If you cannot bake flan ring immediately, refrigerate it.

Baking Pies:

• Let oven preheat a full 15 minutes before baking.
• Unless recipes direct to the contrary, bake pies as near the center of the oven as possible so they will brown evenly.
• When baking more than one pie at a time, stagger pans on rack or racks, leaving plenty of room between them for heat to circulate. Do not let pans touch oven walls.
• If crust should brown too fast, cover with a piece of foil or dampened piece of cloth. *Note:* Crimped edges, in particular, brown faster than the rest of the crust.

Baking a Flan or French Tart:
Preheat oven to 425° F. Prick bottom and sides of pastry well with a fork, line with wax paper, and fill with uncooked rice, dried beans, or metal pie weights. *For a partially baked pastry:* Bake 6–7 minutes until pastry is set; lift out paper of rice, return pastry to oven, and bake 2–4 minutes until pastry starts to brown and shrink slightly from sides of ring. *For a fully baked pastry:* Bake 4–6 minutes after removing paper of rice, just until tan. In either case, remove pastry from flan ring at once (release spring closure if ring has one) by lifting flan ring *straight up.* Using a pancake turner, ease baked flan shell onto a wire rack to cool. (*Note:* If using a slip-bottom cake pan, first loosen sides of flan shell from pan with metal spatula, then balance bottom of pan on a wide-mouth jar; push

pan sides down, freeing flan shell. Ease flan shell from pan bottom onto wire rack to cool.) *Tip:* If partially baked flan shell seems fragile, cool 10–15 minutes on wire rack, then return to flan ring or slip-bottom pan, which will provide needed support. Fill and bake tart as recipe directs, unmolding once again before serving.

To Tell When Pies Are Done:

Double Crust Pies: The crust should be tan and crisp, the filling bubbly.

Single Crust Pies: The crimped edges should be nicely browned and crisp. The filling, if a custard type, should be set (a table knife inserted midway between center and rim should come out clean).

Meringue Pies: Meringue should look "set," be very faint tan with peaks of darker brown.

Baking Pies and Pastries in a Convection Oven

Most pies and pastries bake and brown more quickly and evenly in convection ovens than in conventional ones, thanks to the hot circulating air. Time and/or temperature adjustments may be necessary, so scrutinize your oven's manual. Also read Convection Ovens in Chapter 1, then follow these guidelines:
• Reduce baking temperatures 50°–75° F. (but never lower than 300° F.), then to play it safe, check for doneness when three fourths of recommended baking time has elapsed. *Cooking Tip:* Tops of pies brown fast in convection ovens, so make certain fillings test done (especially important with egg-thickened fillings) before removing pies from oven. This surface browning usually slows as filling and/or bottom crust finish cooking. *Caution:* Meringue toppings brown zip-quick, so watch carefully.
• Use dark-finish piepans and baking sheets in convection ovens (they absorb heat faster than shiny pans). If you use flameproof glass piepans, place them on metal baking sheets for better heat distribution.
• Do not crowd pans in a convection oven. Allow at least 1″ between pans, also between pans and oven walls so air circulation isn't blocked. *Note:* Items on bottom rack may need to bake 2–3 minutes longer than those placed higher up.

Cooling Pies: Follow individual recipes carefully. Most pies should cool a few minutes on a wire rack before being cut; some should be brought to room temperature and others well chilled.

Storing and Keeping Pies: Pies with custard or cream fillings, also those with whipped cream toppings, should be kept refrigerated (let stand at room temperature about 20 minutes before serving). Other kinds of pie may simply be kept in a cool corner of the kitchen.

Reheating Pies: Fruit and mince pies are about the only ones that benefit from reheating. They will taste freshly baked if heated about 15 minutes at 325° F. and served hot.

Baking Pies and Pastries in a Microwave Oven

Because pastries and fillings bake unevenly, double crust pies should not be baked in a microwave oven, nor should open-face pies *unless* the bottom crusts were microwaved *before* the pies were filled. Power levels vary, of course, from model to model, so read instruction manual carefully to determine precise power settings and baking times. Also read Microwave Ovens in Chapter 1, and follow these general guidelines:
• *To Bake a Pie Shell:* Fit rolled pastry into a flameproof glass piepan; prick bottom and sides well with a fork, paying particular attention to the curve where sides meet bottom. For fruit pies, make a high fluted edge to minimize boil-over. Microwave, uncovered, on *HIGH* power setting 5–6 minutes or as oven manufacturer directs, rotating piepan 180° at half time. If crust seems to be baking unevenly, rotate pan 90° every 1–2 minutes. If crust bubbles up, gently push back into shape. Check frequently for doneness (thickness of crust and amount of water used in pastry both affect over-all baking time). When done, bottom of crust (clearly visible through glass piepan) will appear dry and opaque, top crust dry and blistered. (*Note:* A microwave trivet helps pie shell bake evenly.) Cool pie shell slightly before filling.
• *To Bake Fruit Pies:* Bake pie shell as directed, and keep quantity of filling skimpy (fruit fillings bubble furiously during microwaving); 1 quart of fruit is about right for a 9″ piepan. Do not cover fruit with pastry; leave open-face or scatter with streusel (crumb) topping. Place pie in oven on sheet of wax paper (to catch drips) and microwave, uncovered, on *HIGH* until fruit is tender: 7–8 minutes for berries, soft or canned fruits, and about 15 minutes for apples, pears, and firm-ripe peaches (or use

times manufacturer suggests). If fruit filling begins to bubble hard, reduce power setting to *MEDIUM-HIGH* or *MEDIUM,* and compensate by baking pie 1–2 minutes longer. Rotate piepan 90° every 4 minutes, and check fruit often for doneness. Let pie *stand* on wire rack 1–2 minutes before serving.

• *To Bake Custard Pies:* First brush baked pie shell with lightly beaten egg yolk and microwave, uncovered, on *HIGH* power setting 30 seconds to seal crust and keep filling from seeping in. Pour milk filling recipe calls for into a large glass measuring cup, set, uncovered, in microwave, and bring to a boil (about 3 minutes at *MEDIUM* power setting; having milk hot makes custard bake more evenly). Gradually stir milk into beaten eggs, add remaining ingredients, and pour into partially baked pie shell. Microwave, uncovered, on a trivet as manufacturer directs (but never at a power setting higher than *MEDIUM),* rotating piepan 90° every 3–4 minutes. Check custard frequently for doneness; it should be set around edges, and a knife inserted midway between center and edge should come out almost clean. Let custard *stand* 5 minutes on rack on counter to complete the cooking.

• *To Bake Meringue Toppings:* We don't recommend microwaving these because they fail to brown. Nor do we advocate microwaving meringues or meringue pie shells because they will not crispen.

• *To Bake Choux or Puff Pastries:* Best not.

These will never brown or crispen properly in a microwave oven.

• *To Reheat Pies in a Microwave Oven:* Whole pies (either at room temperature or refrigerator-cold) will reheat in 2–3 minutes at *MEDIUM-HIGH* power setting (do not cover them); slices will take 30–60 seconds only. *Tip:* If your microwave has a temperature probe, by all means use it, setting the temperature at 110°–120° F. (the ideal serving temperature for pie). Allow 2–3 minutes *standing time* for whole reheated pies before serving them (not necessary for slices). As for frozen pies, best follow package or manufacturer's directions because so many variables (pie's size, thickness, sweetness, etc.) all affect reheating time in a microwave oven.

Cutting Pies:

In General: Mentally divide pie into the needed number of pieces before making the first cut, then cut, using a pie server to transfer pieces to plates.

Double Crust Pies: Use a very sharp knife with a thin blade.

Single Crust Pies: Cut as you would a double crust pie, but dip knife often in hot water if filling is sticky.

Meringue Pies: Use a sharp knife, dipping into warm water after every cut to keep meringue from sticking.

How to Make Lattice-Top Crusts

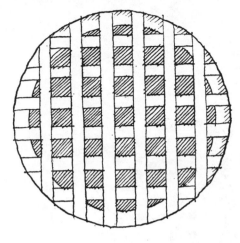

Plain Lattice

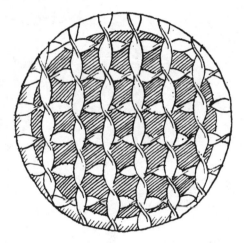

Twisted Lattice

Woven Lattice

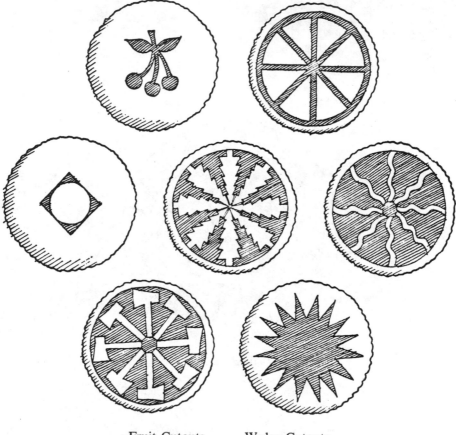

Fruit Cutouts   Wedge Cutouts

Circle in the Square   Christmas Tree Cutouts   Sunburst

Hatchet Cutouts   Star Burst

How to Crimp a Piecrust

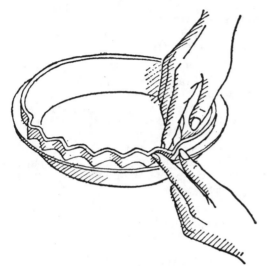

Zigzag Design

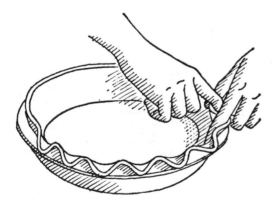

Fluted Design

Some Decorative Tricks with Pastry

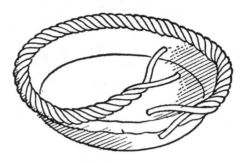

Spiral or Twist
Cut long strips of pastry about ½″ wide and twist together, tightly for a spiral, loosely for a twist. Dampen pastry rim and attach by pressing lightly.

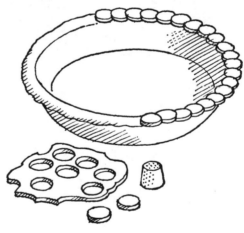

Coin
Cut out tiny pastry circles with a thimble and arrange, overlapping, on dampened rim. To make a button trim, simply perforate centers of circles with a needle so they resemble buttons.

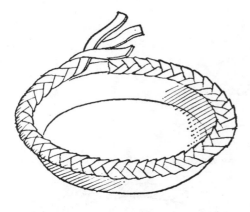

Braid
A variation on the twist made by braiding 3 long thin strips of pastry and attaching to dampened rim.

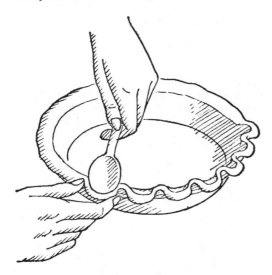

Ruffle
Simply scallop pastry edge using a measuring teaspoon.

FLAKY PASTRY I

1 single crust 8", 9", or 10" pie ¢

1¼ cups sifted flour
½ teaspoon salt
⅓ cup vegetable shortening or lard, chilled
¼ cup ice water

Place flour and salt in a shallow mixing bowl and cut in shortening with a pastry blender until mixture resembles coarse meal. Sprinkle water over surface, 1 tablespoon at a time, and mix in lightly and quickly with a fork, just until pastry holds together. Shape gently into a ball on a lightly floured pastry cloth, then flatten into a circle about 1" thick, evening up rough edges. Using a lightly floured, stockinette-covered rolling pin and short, firm strokes, roll into a circle about 3" larger than the pan you plan to use. To transfer pastry to pan, lay rolling pin across center of pastry circle, fold half of pastry over pin and ease into pan; press lightly. Seal any cracks or holes by pressing dampened scraps of pastry on top. Trim pastry so it hangs evenly 1" over rim, roll overhang under even with rim and crimp or flute as shown.

NPS (6–8) (with vegetable shortening): 185–140 C, 0 mg CH, 180–135 mg S*

To Bake an Unfilled Pie Shell: Preheat oven to 425° F. Prick bottom and sides of pastry well with a fork. To minimize shrinkage, lay a large square of wax paper over crust and fill with uncooked rice or dried beans (experienced cooks keep a jar on hand, using beans or rice over and over). Bake pastry 10–12 minutes, just until tan. Lift out paper of rice. Cool before filling unless recipes direct otherwise.

To Bake a Filled Pie Shell: Follow directions given in individual recipes.

VARIATIONS

Processor Pastry: Place flour and salt in work bowl of a food processor fitted with the metal chopping blade and snap motor on and off once or twice to blend. Cut 3 tablespoons very cold butter and 2 tablespoons very cold vegetable shortening into small pieces and scatter over surface of flour mixture; cut in using 4–5 one-second churnings of the motor (mixture should be the texture of coarse meal). Sprinkle 1½ tablespoons water over surface of fat-flour mixture and mix in by snapping motor on and off twice; repeat with another 1½ tablespoons water, then repeat a third time, working in remaining 1 tablespoon water. Mixture will be crumbly, but do not mix further because you will toughen the pastry. Transfer pastry to a piece of plastic food wrap, shape into a pone about 5" across, patting stray crumbs firmly into place. Wrap and chill 30–40 minutes before rolling. *Note:* Do not double this recipe for a two-crust pie (it's impossible to make tender pastry in quantity). Instead, make two batches of this recipe. Nutritional count same as basic recipe.

Cheese Pastry I: Prepare as directed but toss ½ cup finely grated Cheddar cheese into flour-shortening mixture before adding water. Especially good with apple pie.

NPS (6–8) (with vegetable shortening): 225–170 C, 10–7 mg CH, 240–180 mg S*

Orange Pastry I: Prepare as directed but substitute ¼ cup cold orange juice for the water and add 1–2 teaspoons finely grated lemon or orange rind to the flour-shortening mixture. Especially good with fruit or fruit-flavored chiffon pies.

NPS (6–8) (with vegetable shortening): 190–145 C, 0 mg CH, 180–135 mg S*

Nut Pastry I: Prepare as directed but toss ¼ cup finely ground nuts (pecans, walnuts, black walnuts, hazelnuts) into flour-shortening mixture before adding water. Especially good with chocolate or other cream or chiffon-type pies.

NPS (6–8) (with vegetable shortening): 220–165 C, 0 mg CH, 180–135 mg S*

¢ **Spicy Pastry I:** Mix ¼ teaspoon each cinnamon, cloves, and allspice and a pinch nutmeg, mace, or ginger with flour; proceed as directed. Good with pumpkin, apple, peach, or other spicy fruit pies.

NPS (6–8) (with vegetable shortening): 195–140 C, 0 mg CH, 185–135 mg S*

¢ **Seed Pastry I:** Prepare as directed but toss 1–2 tablespoons poppy, caraway, or toasted sesame seeds with flour-shortening mixture before adding water. The poppy seed crust is good with custard or vanilla cream pies, the caraway with apple, pear, or peach, and the toasted sesame with chocolate or butterscotch cream pies.

NPS (6–8) (with vegetable shortening): 195–145 C, 0 mg CH, 185–135 mg S*

FLAKY PASTRY II

1 double crust 8" or 9" pie   ¢

2 cups sifted flour
1 teaspoon salt
⅔ cup vegetable shortening or lard, chilled
4–6 tablespoons ice water

Mix exactly like Flaky Pastry I. Roll half the pastry as directed and fit into pan. Cover loosely and chill while you prepare filling; also wrap and chill unrolled portion. *(Note:* If filling is intricate, make it *before* the pastry.) Just before filling pie shell, roll remaining pastry as you did the first and cut 3 V-shaped slits or decorative holes near center for steam to escape. Fill pie shell and brush rim with cold water. Cover with top crust. For a high fluted edge (best for juicy

pies), roll crusts over and even with rim, then crimp. For a flat edge, trim crusts even with rim and press with tines of a fork to seal. Bake according to times given in individual recipes that follow.

NPS (6–8) (with vegetable shortening): 340–255 C, 0 mg CH, 365–275 mg S*

VARIATIONS

Cheese Pastry II: Prepare as directed but toss 1 cup finely grated Cheddar cheese into flour-shortening mixture before adding water. If necessary, add an extra tablespoon ice water.

NPS (6–8) (with vegetable shortening): 420–315 C, 0 mg CH, 485–365 mg S*

Orange Pastry II: Prepare as directed but substitute ¼–⅓ cup cold orange juice for the water and add 1 tablespoon finely grated orange or lemon rind. Good with berry or other fruit pies.

NPS (6–8) (with vegetable shortening): 345–260 C, 0 mg CH, 365–270 mg S*

¢ **Spicy Pastry II:** Mix ½ teaspoon each cinnamon and allspice and a pinch each ginger, cloves, and nutmeg with flour; then proceed as directed. Good with apple, peach, or other spicy fruit pies.

NPS (6–8) (with vegetable shortening): 355–255 C, 0 mg CH, 365–275 mg S*

¢ **Seed Pastry II:** Prepare as directed but toss 2–3 tablespoons poppy, caraway, or toasted sesame seeds with flour-shortening mixture before adding water. The poppy seed crust is good with apple or peach pies, the caraway with apple or pear, and the sesame with apple, peach, or pear.

NPS (6–8) (with vegetable shortening): 370–275 C, 0 mg CH, 370–275 mg S*

NO-CHOLESTEROL PASTRY

1 double crust 8" or 9" pie

Can be used interchangeably with the more conventional Flaky Pastry II.

2 cups sifted flour
1 teaspoon salt
½ cup polyunsaturated cooking oil
¼ cup ice water

Sift flour and salt into a bowl; beat oil and water with a fork until slightly thickened and creamy, pour all at once over flour and toss with fork to blend. Gather pastry together (it should just hold together) and, if too dry, add a few additional drops oil and toss again. Shape gently into a ball. Place half of pastry on a 12″ square of wax paper and flatten until about 1″ thick; even up rough edges. Top with a second square of wax paper and roll from center outward into a circle about 3″ larger in diameter than pan you plan to use. (*Note:* If you wipe counter with a damp cloth before rolling, wax paper won't slide around.) Peel off top paper and invert pastry on pan; peel off remaining paper and fit pastry in pan; do not trim overhang. Roll remaining pastry the same way, peel off top paper, and cut 3 V-shaped slits or decorative holes near center for steam to escape. Fill pie shell with desired filling, brush rim with cold water, and invert pastry on filling. Peel off paper and, if pie is juicy, press edges even to seal, and make a high fluted edge. If not, trim crusts even with rim and seal with tines of a fork. Bake according to times given in individual recipes.

NPS (6–8): 310–235 C, 0 mg CH, 365–275 mg S*

For a Single Crust 8″ or 9″ Pie: Prepare and roll as directed, using the following quantities: 1¼ cups flour, ½ teaspoon salt, ⅓ cup polyunsaturated cooking oil, and 2–3 tablespoons ice water. Fit into pan, crimp, and bake as directed for Flaky Pastry I.

NPS (6–8): 200–150 C, 0 mg CH, 235–180 mg S*

SOUR CREAM PASTRY

1 double crust 8″ or 9″ pie

Rich and tender and more flavorful than Flaky Pastry. Best for pies that are not too juicy.

2 cups sifted flour
½ teaspoon salt
½ teaspoon baking powder
½ cup vegetable shortening, chilled
¼ cup sour cream
1 egg, lightly beaten

Sift flour with salt and baking powder, then cut in shortening until mixture resembles coarse meal. Blend sour cream and egg, pour all at once into flour, and mix briskly with a fork until pastry *just* holds together. Wrap in wax paper and chill while you prepare filling. Divide pastry in half, shape into 2 balls, then roll, 1 at a time, on a lightly floured board into a circle 3″ larger in diameter than the piepan you're using. Fit 1 circle into pan, pressing gently to smooth out any air bubbles underneath. Fill pie, brush rim of pastry lightly with cold water, top with second pastry circle (it should have steam vents cut in center), and press edges to seal. Roll overhang over until even with rim, and crimp.

Bake according to directions given in filling recipe.

NPS (6–8): 335–250 C, 50–35 mg CH, 235–175 mg S*

SHORT FRENCH PASTRY (PÂTE BRISÉE)

1 single crust 8″ or 9″ pie

This short pastry puts the finishing touch on very special pies, whether sweet or savory. It's also perfect for tarts and turnovers, sausage rolls, or meat- or fish-filled appetizers.

1½ cups sifted flour
½ teaspoon salt
¼ cup butter or margarine, chilled
¼ cup lard or vegetable shortening, chilled
2 teaspoons lemon juice
3 tablespoons ice water (about)

Mix flour and salt in a shallow bowl and, using a pastry blender, cut in butter and lard until the texture of very coarse meal. Sprinkle lemon juice evenly over surface, then water, 1 tablespoon at a time, mixing lightly with a fork after each addition. Pastry should *just* hold together. Shape into a round about 5″ across and 1″ thick on a piece of wax paper, wrap, and chill ½ hour. Roll pastry into a circle 3″ larger in diameter than the piepan you plan to use if for a pie shell; ½″ larger if for a top crust. *For a pie shell,* fit, trim, and bake as directed in Flaky Pastry I. *For a top crust,* roll as directed for Flaky Pastry II, but do not cut steam vents until pastry is in place on pie.

NPS (6–8) (with butter and lard): 250–185, 30–20 mg CH, 260–195 mg S*

VARIATION

Processor Pâte Brisée: Place flour, salt, and ½ teaspoon baking powder in work bowl of a food processor fitted with the metal chopping blade and mix by snapping motor on and off two to three times. Cut butter and shortening into small pieces and scatter evenly over surface of dry ingredients; cut in with 2–3 one-second churnings of the motor until mixture is pebbly (it should be about the texture of uncooked oatmeal). Combine lemon juice and water and pour evenly over fat-flour mixture; churn 3–4 seconds until mixture forms a ball that rides up on chopping blade spindle. Shape pastry into a round as directed above, wrap, and chill 2–3 hours before rolling.

NPS (6–8): 250–185 C, 30–20 mg CH, 295–220 mg S*

TORTE PASTRY

1 single crust 8", 9", or 10" pie or flan

A tender, golden, egg-rich pastry.

1/2 cup unsalted butter, softened to room temperature
12/3 cups sifted flour
11/2 teaspoons baking powder
1 tablespoon sugar
3/4 teaspoon salt
2 egg yolks

Knead all ingredients in a bowl until thoroughly blended. Pat into piepan, pushing dough up sides and crimping edges.
NPS (6–8): 280–210 C, 130–100 mg CH, 385–290 mg S*

To Bake an Unfilled Pie Shell or Flan: Preheat oven to 375° F. Prick crust well all over with the tines of a fork, and bake 20–25 minutes until lightly browned. Cool before filling.

To Bake a Filled Pie Shell or Flan: Follow directions given in individual recipes that follow.

VARIATION

Sweet Torte Pastry (Pâte Sucrée): Increase flour to 13/4 cups and sugar to 1/4 cup; omit salt. Proceed as directed.
NPS (6–8): 320–240 C, 130–100 mg CH, 265–200 mg S*

CHOUX PASTRY (PÂTE À CHOUX)

1 dozen Cream Puffs or Chocolate Éclairs; 41/2–5 dozen Profiteroles

1 cup water
1/2 cup butter or margarine
1/4 teaspoon salt
1 cup sifted flour
4 eggs, at room temperature

Preheat oven to 400° F. Quickly bring water, butter, and salt to boiling. Pull pan almost off burner and turn heat to moderate. Add flour *all at once* and stir quickly with a wooden spoon until mixture forms a ball. Set pan on a damp cloth. Break an egg into a cup and slide into flour mixture. Beat hard with a wooden spoon to blend. Add remaining eggs, one at a time, beating well. Each egg *must* be blended in before the next is added; mixture will look odd at first, almost curdled, but as you beat, it will become smooth. Pastry is now ready to use in making Cream Puffs, Chocolate Éclairs, Profiteroles, Carolines, and Croquembouche.

NPS (12–60): 130–25 C, 110–20 mg CH, 145–30 mg S*

MÜRBTEIG PASTRY

1 single crust 8", 9", or 10" pie

This German pastry is perfect for fruit flans because it doesn't get soggy. It's delicate and short, so make it on a cool day.

2 cups sifted flour
1/2 cup superfine sugar
Finely grated rind of 1 lemon
3/4 cup butter or margarine, chilled
3 egg yolks, lightly beaten

Sift flour with sugar and mix in lemon rind. Cut in butter with a pastry blender until mixture resembles fine bread crumbs. Add yolks and mix with a fork until pastry forms a ball. (You may have to use your hands at the end, but handle as lightly as possible). Wrap pastry and chill 1 hour. Using short, light strokes, roll on a *lightly* floured board into a circle 3" larger than the pan you're using; fit into pan, trimming edges to hang evenly 1" all round. Roll overhang under until even with rim and crimp. (*Note:* If making a flan, see Fitting Pastries into Flan Rings at beginning of this chapter.) Chill pie or flan shell 2 hours. Preheat oven to 450° F. Prick bottom and sides of pastry with a fork, line with wax paper, and fill with rice or dried beans to weight down. Bake 5 minutes, lift out paper of rice, reduce oven to 350° F., and bake 12 minutes longer until golden. Cool pie shell before filling.
NPS (6–8): 440–330 C, 200–150 mg CH, 240–180 mg S*

VARIATION

Spicy Mürbteig (not authentic but nice with fruit pies): Prepare as directed but sift 1/4 teaspoon cinnamon and a pinch nutmeg with flour.
NPS (6–8): 440–330 C, 200–150 mg CH, 240–180 mg S*

ROUGH PUFF PASTRY

1 single crust 8" or 9" pie

Because this pastry is so rich and flaky, it makes a better top than bottom crust. It's usually reserved for pies, casseroles, or cobblers that have no bottom crusts. It can also be used to make Patty Shells and Napoleons.

11/2 cups sifted flour
1/2 teaspoon salt
1/2 cup butter or margarine, chilled

2 teaspoons lemon juice
5–6 tablespoons ice water

Mix flour and salt in a shallow bowl and cut in 1/4 cup butter with a pastry blender until the texture of coarse meal. Sprinkle in lemon juice, then water, 1 tablespoon at a time, mixing lightly and quickly with a fork until pastry *just* holds together. Shape into a "brick" on a lightly floured pastry cloth and flatten until about 1″ thick. Turn so short side faces you, and even up edges. Using a lightly floured, stockinette-covered rolling pin and short, firm strokes, roll into a rectangle 5″ × 15″. Beginning at far edge, dot one fourth of remaining butter evenly over two thirds of pastry, leaving 1/4″ margins all round. Fold near third of pastry in toward center, then far third until even with fold. Press edges lightly with rolling pin to seal. Give pastry a quarter turn and roll again into a 5″ × 15″ rectangle. Dot with butter, fold and seal as before; wrap and chill 1/2 hour. Roll, fold, and seal twice more, using as little flour as possible; wrap and chill 1/2 hour.

NP Crust: 1445 C, 250 mg CH, 2035 mg S*

To Use as a Top Crust: Roll into a circle 1/2″ larger than pan or casserole you plan to use, then trim off excess 1/2″ in a single long circular strip and reserve. Cut 3 V-shaped slits or decorative holes in center of circle. Lay strip around dampened edge of pan or casserole, center pastry circle over filling, press edges firmly to strip and crimp. Bake according to pie or casserole directions.

To Make Patty Shells (12 shells): Follow directions for making Small Patty Shells but use Rough Puff Pastry instead of regular Puff Pastry.

NP Shell: 120 C, 20 mg CH, 170 mg S*

PUFF PASTRY

1 dozen Small Patty Shells

Do not attempt this recipe on a hot day—dough will be unmanageable. Make, if possible, with some *pastry* (not cake) flour (obtainable at specialty food shops), reducing water slightly as needed.

4 cups sifted flour, preferably a 1/2 and 1/2
   mixture of pastry and all-purpose flour
1½ teaspoons salt
1 cup + 2 tablespoons ice water
1 tablespoon lemon juice
1 pound unsalted butter, chilled

Mix flour and salt in a bowl. Combine water and lemon juice, sprinkle evenly over flour,

about 1/4 cup at a time, mixing lightly and quickly with a fork after each addition (pastry should hold together, be firm yet pliable). Add a few drops more ice water if mixture seems dry. Knead on a lightly floured board about 10 minutes until smooth and elastic; cover and let stand at room temperature 1/2 hour. Meanwhile, knead and squeeze butter until malleable (about consistency of dough), free of lumps, but still cold. Shape into a 5″ square and dust with flour. Shape dough into a "brick" on a lightly floured pastry cloth and, with a lightly floured stockinette-covered rolling pin, flatten to a thickness of 1″; even up ragged edges. Place pastry so short side faces you, and roll with short, firm strokes into a rectangle 6″ × 18″. Place butter in center, fold near third of pastry in toward center, then far third. Press edges lightly with rolling pin to seal. Give pastry a quarter turn and roll again into a rectangle; fold and seal as before. Wrap and chill 3/4 hour. Roll, fold, and seal five more times, chilling dough 30 minutes between rollings and for 1 hour after the final rolling. Use as little flour as possible when rolling and handle pastry with fingertips. Lift dough with your hands or a pastry scraper occasionally, and dust underneath with flour. If butter should break through pastry as you roll, dust immediately with flour and roll it in. Pastry is now ready to use as recipes direct. To store, wrap and chill overnight or wrap airtight and freeze (thaw in refrigerator before using).

NP Shell: 410 C, 85 mg CH, 280 mg S*

SMALL PATTY SHELLS (BOUCHÉES)

1 dozen

Small puff pastry shells to be filled with sweet or savory mixtures.

1 recipe Puff Pastry
1 egg lightly beaten with 1 tablespoon cold
   water (glaze)

Make pastry as directed and roll half to a thickness of 1/4″ on a lightly floured board. Cut into rounds with an unfloured 2½″ cookie cutter (wipe cutter with a dry cloth before each cut and, to make shells rise evenly in baking, press cutter straight down through pastry). Arrange one third of the rounds on a baking sheet brushed with cold water, spacing 1″ apart. Cut centers from one third of remaining rounds with a 1¾″ round cutter. Brush tops of rings with cold water and place, tops down, on rounds. Pinch seams lightly to seal and brush rings with cold water. Press the 1¾" cutter into remaining rounds, just enough to mark with a circle, not to cut clear through. Top each shell with a marked round, marked side up, and pinch seams as before. Brush tops with glaze but do not let glaze run down sides of shells or they will not rise evenly. Roll and cut remaining pastry the same way (also any scraps). Chill shells ½ hour. Meanwhile, preheat oven to 450° F. Bake shells on center oven rack 10 minutes, reduce heat to 350° F., and bake 15–20 minutes longer until golden brown and crisp. With a sharp, pointed knife, lift off marked circle tops from patties and save to use as "lids." With a fork, scoop out and discard soft insides of shells. Return shells to oven for 3–5 minutes to dry out. Patty shells are now ready to be filled with hot creamed mixtures. Cool on wire racks before filling with cold fillings. (*Note:* Stored airtight, these will keep well several days. Reheat, uncovered, 10 minutes at 350° F.)

NP Shell: 450 C, 105 mg CH, 325 mg S*

GRAHAM CRACKER CRUST

1 single crust 9" pie   ☒

Crumb crusts can be substituted for baked pie shells in most recipes. They are especially good with chiffon and cream fillings. If a recipe calls for an unbaked crumb crust, prepare up to point of baking, then chill well, fill, and proceed as individual recipe directs.

1½ cups graham cracker crumbs (about 20 cracker squares)
⅓ cup butter or margarine, softened to room temperature
¼ cup sugar

Preheat oven to 350° F. Blend crumbs, butter, and sugar in a bowl. Spoon into a 9" piepan and, using the back of a spoon, press firmly against bottom and sides (but not over rim). Bake 8–10 minutes. Cool before filling.

NPS (6–8): 210–135 C, 25–20 mg CH, 260–200 mg S*

VARIATIONS

Vanilla Wafer Crust: Substitute vanilla wafer crumbs for the graham cracker, reduce butter to ¼ cup and sugar to 1–2 tablespoons.

NPS (6–8): 150–145 C, 25–20 mg CH, 105–80 mg S*

Chocolate Crumb Crust: Substitute crushed chocolate wafers for cracker crumbs, reduce butter to ¼ cup and sugar to 1–2 tablespoons.

NPS (6–8): 190–145 C, 25–20 mg CH, 270–205 mg S*

Gingersnap Crumb Crust: Prepare as directed but substitute crushed gingersnaps for the cracker crumbs and omit sugar.

NPS (6–8): 195–145 C, 35–25 mg CH, 245–185 mg S*

Cereal Crust: Prepare as directed but substitute 1½ cups crushed cornflakes, rice cereal, or wheat cereal for the cracker crumbs.

NPS (6–8): 230–175 C, 25–20 mg CH, 450–340 mg S*

Nut-Crumb Crust: Reduce crumbs to 1 cup and add ½ cup minced nuts (walnuts, pecans, hazelnuts, toasted blanched almonds, or Brazil nuts).

NPS (6–8): 250–190 C, 25–20 mg CH, 215–160 mg S*

Marble Crumb Crust: Prepare as directed but toss 2 (1-ounce) squares finely grated semisweet chocolate with the crumbs.

NPS (6–8): 260–195 C, 25–20 mg CH, 260–195 mg S*

TOASTED COCONUT CRUST

1 single crust 9" pie

Good with cream or chiffon fillings.

2 cups flaked coconut
¼ cup melted butter or margarine

Preheat oven to 300° F. Mix coconut and butter. Press firmly against the bottom and sides of a 9" piepan. Bake about 20 minutes until golden. Cool before filling.

NPS (6–8): 185–140 C, 20–15 mg CH, 80–60 mg S*

VARIATION

Chocolate-Coconut Crust: Prepare as directed but reduce butter to 2 tablespoons and add 2 (1-ounce) squares melted unsweetened chocolate, 2 tablespoons warm milk, and ⅓ cup sifted confectioners' sugar; mix well. Press into pan and chill 1–2 hours before filling.

NPS (6–8): 220–165 C, 12–8 mg CH, 45–35 mg S*

TOASTED NUT CRUST

1 single crust 9" pie ☒

A crunchy, rich, sweet crust, ideal for chiffon fillings.

1½ cups ground nuts (walnuts, pecans, Brazil nuts, blanched almonds, or hazelnuts)
¼ cup sugar
2 tablespoons butter or margarine, softened to room temperature

Preheat oven to 400° F. Mix nuts, sugar, and butter with your hands, press firmly against bottom and sides of a buttered 9" piepan. Bake 6–8 minutes. Cool before filling.

NPS (6–8): 260–195 C, 10–5 mg CH, 40–30 mg S*

VARIATION

Substitute 1 egg white, beaten to soft peaks, for the butter; mix with a spoon, press into buttered pan, and bake about 10 minutes until tan. Cool before filling.

NPS (6–8): 230–175 C, 0 mg CH, 10–7 mg S*

COOKIE CRUST

1 single crust 9" pie ☒

Couldn't be easier!

1 tablespoon butter or margarine, softened to room temperature
1 tablespoon sugar
1 roll refrigerated slice-and-bake cookie dough (sugar cookie, chocolate, or coconut)

Preheat oven to 375° F. Butter bottom, sides, and rim of a 9" piepan, then coat with sugar. Slice cookie dough ⅛" thick and line sides of pan, overlapping slices slightly and allowing cookies to form a scalloped edge around rim. Line bottom with slices, pressing lightly to fill spaces. Bake 8–10 minutes until tan. Cool before filling. Good with cream fillings. Recipe too flexible for meaningful nutritional count.

ICE CREAM PIE SHELL

1 single crust 9" pie ☒

1 quart vanilla or other flavor ice cream (about), slightly softened

Chill a 9" piepan in the freezer 15–20 minutes. Spoon ice cream into pan, smoothing bottom and sides with the back of a spoon to make a shell. Freeze until firm. Good filled with ice cream of contrasting flavor and color and topped with a cold fruit sauce.

Also good filled with fresh fruit and topped with whipped cream.

NPS (6–8): 180–135 C, 40–30 mg CH, 75–55 mg S*

Ground Rules for Making Meringues

• Bring egg whites to room temperature before beating.
• Make sure there are no flecks of yolk in the whites; if so, scoop out with a piece of shell.
• Make sure mixing bowl and beater are spotless.
• Follow recipe to the letter.
• Add sugar very slowly, beating well after each addition so it dissolves fully. If it does not, "beads" of syrup or sugar grains will form on baked meringue.
• Be careful not to overbeat egg whites (especially if using electric mixer). *(Note:* Unless you have a food processor with the special "whip" attachment, do not attempt to beat egg whites in a food processor. The machine's speed and power will knock the air out of them.) Properly beaten, a meringue will be *glossy and very stiff but not dry*. If meringue clumps as it's spread, it is overbeaten. To rescue, return to mixing bowl, add 1–2 tablespoons cold water and beat briefly and briskly.
• To keep meringue from shrinking during baking, spread evenly over filling, making sure it touches pie shell all around.

(Note: For additional tips, read To Beat Whites in the chapter on eggs, cheese, and dairy.)

BASIC MERINGUE TOPPING FOR PIES

TO TOP AN 8" PIE, USE
2 egg whites, at room temperature
⅛ teaspoon cream of tartar
Pinch salt
¼ cup sugar
½ teaspoon vanilla

TO TOP A 9" PIE, USE
3 egg whites, at room temperature
¼ teaspoon cream of tartar
⅛ teaspoon salt
6 tablespoons sugar
½ teaspoon vanilla

TO TOP 10" PIE, USE
4 egg whites, at room temperature
¼ teaspoon cream of tartar
⅛ teaspoon salt
½ cup sugar
1 teaspoon vanilla

Preheat oven to 350° F. Beat egg whites until frothy, using a rotary beater or electric mixer at moderate speed; add cream of tartar and salt and continue beating, adding sugar, 1 tablespoon at a time. When all sugar is incorporated, add vanilla and beat hard (highest mixer speed) until glossy and peaks stand straight up when beaters are withdrawn. Spoon about half the meringue around edge of *warm* filling, spreading so it touches pastry all around. Pile remaining meringue in center, then spread to cover all filling, pulling into peaks with the back of a spoon or swirling round. If you prefer, pipe meringue over filling, using a pastry bag fitted with a decorative tip. Bake on center oven rack 12–15 minutes until lightly browned. Cool at least 2 hours before serving. To simplify the serving of a meringue pie, dip knife in warm water before cutting each slice.

Meringue for an 8″ pie:

NPS: 40 C, 0 mg CH, 40 mg S*

Meringue for a 9″ pie:

NPS: 45 C, 0 mg CH, 55 mg S*

Meringue for a 10″ pie:

NPS: 60 C, 0 mg CH, 60 mg S*

MERINGUE PIE SHELL

1 single crust 9″ pie ⚖

3 egg whites, at room temperature
⅛ teaspoon cream of tartar
⅛ teaspoon salt
½ cup sugar
1 teaspoon vanilla or ½ teaspoon almond extract

Preheat oven to 250° F. Beat egg whites until foamy; mix in cream of tartar and salt. Add sugar, 1 tablespoon at a time, beating constantly, then continue to beat at highest speed until glossy and stiff enough to stand straight up when beaters are withdrawn. Fold in vanilla. Spoon meringue into lightly greased 9″ piepan, then spread with the back of a spoon to cover bottom and sides but not the rim; make sides a little thicker than the bottom and ½″–¾″ higher than rim of pan. Bake 1 hour until creamy white and firm, turn oven off and let meringue dry in oven without opening door until oven cools. Shell is now ready to fill as desired.

NPS (6–8) 75–55 C, 0 mg CH, 70–55 mg S*

Nut Meringue Pie Shell: Prepare meringue as directed, fold in 1 cup ground blanched almonds or hazelnuts, a little at a time, then spoon into pan and bake as directed.

NPS (6–8): 140–105 C, 0 mg CH, 70–55 mg S*

MERINGUES

2 dozen ⚖

6 egg whites, at room temperature
¼ teaspoon cream of tartar
¼ teaspoon salt
¾ cup sugar
¾ cup superfine sugar
1 teaspoon vanilla or ½ teaspoon almond extract
1 or 2 drops any food coloring (optional)

Preheat oven to 250° F. Beat egg whites until foamy; mix in cream of tartar and salt. Mix sugars and add, 1 tablespoon at a time, beating all the while. This will take some time, perhaps 10–12 minutes. Add flavoring and if you like, tint a pastel hue; beat at highest mixer speed until glossy and stiff enough to stand straight up when beaters are withdrawn. Drop by heaping spoonfuls 2″ apart on foil-lined baking sheets; smooth into mounds or, if you prefer, pipe meringue onto sheets through a pastry bag fitted with a large plain or star tip. Don't make meringues more than 2½″ across or they won't bake properly. Bake 1 hour until creamy white and firm, turn oven off, and let meringues dry several hours or overnight in oven without opening door. Lift off foil and serve as is or with ice cream or fruit. Wrapped airtight, these keep well.

NP Meringue: 50 C, 0 mg CH, 35 mg S*

⚖ **Meringue Star Shells** *(1 dozen):* Beat meringue as directed. Draw 6 (3″) circles on 2 foil-lined baking sheets, not too close together, and spread ⅓″–½″ deep with meringue. Spoon remaining meringue into a pastry bag fitted with a small star tip. Edge meringue circles with borders of small stars, one just touching another, then build up layers to form shells about 1½″ deep. Bake and dry out as directed. To serve, fill with any ice cream or fruit.

NP Shell: 105 C, 0 mg CH, 70 mg S*

⚖ **Meringues Glacées:** Make and bake meringues as directed, halve, and fill with ice cream. Or sandwich 2 meringues together with ice cream. Top with any dessert sauce or fruit.

NP Meringue (with ice cream in 1/2 meringue): 120 C, 15 mg CH, 65 mg S*
NP Meringue (with ice cream and 2 meringues): 175 C, 15 mg CH, 100 mg S*

Meringues Chantilly (12 servings): Sandwich baked meringues together with sweetened whipped cream, tinted, if you like, for a party touch. Or if you prefer, tint meringues and leave cream plain.

NPS: 220 C, 40 mg CH, 80 mg S*

COUNTRY-STYLE APPLE PIE

8 servings ¢

Aromatic of lemon, cinnamon, and nutmeg.

1 recipe Flaky Pastry II

F I L L I N G
6 medium-size tart cooking apples
3/4–1 cup sugar
2 teaspoons lemon juice
1/4 teaspoon cinnamon
1/8 teaspoon nutmeg
1/4 teaspoon salt
2 tablespoons butter or margarine

G L A Z E (optional)
1 tablespoon milk
1 tablespoon sugar

Preheat oven to 425° F. Prepare pastry as directed and fit half into a 9″ piepan; do not trim edge. Roll top crust, cut steam slits in center, and cover with cloth while you prepare filling. Peel, core, and thinly slice apples, taste, and sweeten as needed with sugar; add lemon juice, spices, and salt and toss gently. Pile apple mixture in pie shell and dot with butter. Brush pastry rim lightly with cold water, fit top crust over apples, trim, seal, and crimp edges. For a shiny crust, brush with milk and sprinkle with sugar. Bake 15–20 minutes with a piece of foil on rack below to catch drips, reduce heat to 350° F., and bake 25–30 minutes longer until crust is lightly browned. Cool 5–10 minutes before serving. Serve hot or cold with heavy cream, vanilla ice cream, or chunks of good sharp Cheddar.

NPS: 410 C, 10 mg CH, 370 mg S*

TARTE TATIN

6 servings

This caramel-glazed open-face apple tart was named after two French women from the Loire Valley who earned their living by baking their father's favorite dessert.

1 recipe Flaky Pastry I

F I L L I N G
1 1/2 pounds (4–5 large) Golden Delicious or Rome Beauty apples
1/4 cup butter
1/4 cup sugar
Finely grated rind of 1 lemon
Juice of 1/2 lemon
1/3 cup caramelized sugar*

G L A Z E
1 egg lightly beaten with 1 tablespoon milk
1 teaspoon sugar

Prepare pastry as directed, roll into a 10″ circle, prick well all over with a fork, transfer to a lightly floured baking sheet, and chill while you prepare the apples. Preheat over to 425° F. Peel, core, and cut each apple into 8 wedges. Melt butter in a large skillet over moderate heat, add sugar, and stir to dissolve. Add apples, lemon rind, and juice, mix gently, cover, and simmer apples 10 minutes, stirring now and then. Uncover, raise heat, and boil slowly, basting apples with cooking liquid, about 5 minutes until lightly glazed. *(Note: Apples should retain their shape, not become mushy.)* Pour caramelized sugar into an 11″ cast-iron or heavy cast-aluminum skillet. Using a slotted spoon, neatly arrange apples in caramelized sugar in concentric circles so that they cover entire bottom of skillet. Tuck any broken bits of apple on top. Meanwhile, boil apple cooking liquid, uncovered, until honey colored and reduced to about 2 tablespoons; spoon over apples. Gently slide pastry circle on top of apples, brush with egg mixture, then sprinkle evenly with sugar. Bake, uncovered, in lower third of oven 30 minutes until pastry browns lightly. Cool 10 minutes on a wire rack, place a 12″ serving platter over skillet, and carefully invert tart. *(Note: If a few apple wedges should stick to skillet, simply lift out with a metal spatula and replace in design; scrape any glaze remaining in skillet over apples.) (Note: If tart cools too much to unmold easily, warm 5 minutes in a 425° F. oven to soften the carmel and loosen the tart.)* Serve warm or cold, topped, if you like, with whipped cream or *crème fraîche.*

NPS: 400 C, 65 mg CH, 275 mg S*

APPLE TURNOVERS

6 servings ¢

1 recipe Flaky Pastry II

FILLING
2 cups peeled and diced tart cooking apples
⅓ cup sugar
¼ teaspoon cinnamon
¼ teaspoon nutmeg
2 tablespoons lemon juice

GLAZE
1 tablespoon milk
1 tablespoon sugar

Preheat oven to 400° F. Make pastry as directed and roll total amount into a rectangle 12″ × 18″, keeping edges as straight as possible. Cut into 6 (6″) squares; brush edges with cold water. Mix filling ingredients and place about ⅓ cup in the center of each square; fold diagonally to form triangles. Press edges together with a floured fork and snip steam slits in tops with kitchen shears.

Brush with milk and sprinkle with sugar. Arrange 2″ apart on an ungreased baking sheet and bake 25–30 minutes until golden brown. Cool a few minutes on a wire rack. Serve warm or cold with or without cream or ice cream. Or if you like, cool and drizzle with Quick Glacé Icing or Easy White Icing. *NPS: 410 C, 0 mg CH, 370 mg S**

VARIATIONS

Fruit Turnovers: Prepare as directed, substituting 2 cups any suitable fresh, frozen, or canned, drained fruit for the apples and adding sugar as needed to sweeten. Recipe too flexible for meaningful nutritional count.

Jam Turnovers *(1 dozen):* Roll out pastry into a rectangle 12″ × 16″, and cut into 12 (4″) squares. Place 2 tablespoons jam, preserves, marmalade, or mincemeat in the cen-

PIE APPLES

There are hundreds of different kinds of apples, most coming into season during the fall and remaining plentiful throughout winter and early spring. All apples, however, do not cook well—the crisp, juicy-sweet apples we love to eat out-of-hand, for example, lack the tartness and texture needed for successful pies. For best results, use one of these excellent "pie" apples:

Kind of Apple	Description	Season
Jonathan	Small to medium size, deep red with creamy-colored, tart, crisp flesh. Juicy.	October–February
McIntosh	Medium size, bright red with green around stem. White, crisp-tender, juicy flesh.	October–March
Newtown Pippin	Medium size, yellow skin, tart, hard-to-crisp juicy yellowish flesh.	February–June
Northern Spy	Large, bright red with firm, tart, juicy, yellowish flesh.	October–March
Rhode Island Greening	Medium to large, green or yellow-green skin; cream-colored, tart, crisp, juicy flesh.	October–February
Stayman	Striped, dull red apple, medium to large, with tart-crisp, juicy, ivory-hued flesh.	November–April
Winesap	Deep red, small to medium, with some green around stem; firm, crisp, tart, cream-colored flesh.	January–May
Yellow Transparent	Medium, yellow-green with white, juicy, tart flesh.	July–August
York Imperial	Medium to large, light or purple-red over yellow; ivory-colored, hard, tart flesh.	October–April

Note: Such all-purpose cooking apples as *Golden Delicious, Granny Smith, Gravenstein, Wealthy, Rome Beauty,* and *Baldwin* may also be used in pies, but the nine varieties above give especially fine flavor and texture.

ter of each, fold, seal, and glaze. Bake 15 minutes at 425° F.

NPS: 280 C, 0 mg CH, 190 mg S*

Fried Apple Pies *(8 servings):* Roll pastry 1/8″ thick and cut into 8 (4″) circles. Place 1/4 cup thick applesauce in the center of each, fold over and seal edges *well.* Do not glaze. Fry in 365° F. deep fat 2–3 minutes, turning as needed, until evenly golden brown. Drain on paper toweling, roll in sugar, and serve warm.

NPS: 350 C, 0 mg CH, 275 mg S*

FRESH FRUIT PIE

8 servings

This basic recipe can be used for making peach, apricot, plum, pear, cherry, grape, or currant pies.

1 recipe Flaky Pastry II

FILLING
1 quart sliced, pitted, and peeled fresh firm-ripe peaches, apricots, or nectarines; pitted purple or greengage plums; peeled, cored, and sliced pears; stemmed and pitted tart cherries; seeded, halved Tokay or whole seedless green grapes or stemmed currants
3/4–1 1/2 cups sugar
1/4–1/3 cup sifted flour
1/8 teaspoon salt
1 teaspoon lemon juice (optional)
1/4 teaspoon almond extract or nutmeg, cinnamon, or ginger (optional)
2 tablespoons butter or margarine

GLAZE (optional)
1 tablespoon milk
1 tablespoon sugar

Preheat oven to 425° F. Make pastry as directed and fit half into a 9″ piepan; do not trim edge. Roll out top crust, cut steam slits in center, and cover with a cloth while you prepare the filling. Place fruit in a bowl, add sugar to sweeten, and sprinkle with flour and salt; toss lightly. *(Note:* Cherries will need maximum amount of flour, firmer fruits less.) If you like, sprinkle with lemon juice and almond extract (especially good with peaches, apricots, and cherries). Spoon into pie shell and dot with butter. Brush pastry rim with cold water, fit top crust over fruit, trim, seal, and crimp edges. For a glistening crust, brush with milk and sprinkle with sugar. Bake 35–45 minutes (with a piece of foil on rack below to catch drips) until lightly browned and bubbling. Cool 5–

10 minutes before cutting. Serve warm or cold with or without cream or ice cream.

NPS: 405 C, 10 mg CH, 340 mg S*

VARIATIONS

Frozen Fruit Pie: Prepare as directed, using 1 quart solidly frozen fruit.

NPS: 405 C, 10 mg CH, 340 mg S*

Canned Fruit Pie: Prepare as directed using 2 (1-pound) cans fruit. Drain fruit well, reserving 1/2 cup liquid. Mix fruit with enough sugar to sweeten, flour, and seasonings and spoon into pie shell. Pour in reserved liquid (mixed with a few drops red food coloring if it is a cherry pie), dot with butter, and proceed as directed. Recipe too flexible for meaningful nutritional count.

Tapioca Fruit Pie: Substitute 3 tablespoons granulated quick-cooking tapioca for the flour and proceed as recipe directs.

NPS: 405 C, 10 mg CH, 340 mg S*

BASIC BERRY PIE

8 servings

1 recipe Flaky Pastry II

FILLING
1 quart ripe berries (any kind), hulled, stemmed, and drained
1–1 1/2 cups sugar
1/4 cup unsifted flour
1/8 teaspoon salt
1 teaspoon finely grated orange or lemon rind (optional)
2 tablespoons butter or margarine

GLAZE (optional)
1 tablespoon milk
1 tablespoon sugar

Preheat oven to 425° F. Make pastry as directed and fit half into a 9″ piepan; do not trim edge. Roll top crust, cut steam slits in center, and cover with cloth while you prepare filling. Dry berries on paper toweling, place in a bowl, and sprinkle with 1 cup sugar, the flour, salt, and, if you like, rind; toss *lightly.* Taste berries and if too tart add more sugar. Spoon into pie shell, and dot with butter. Brush pastry rim with cold water. Fit top crust over berries, trim, seal, and crimp edges. For a glistening crust, brush with milk and sprinkle with sugar. Bake 35–45 minutes (with a piece of foil on rack below to catch drips) until lightly browned and bubbling. Cool 5–10 minutes before cutting.

Serve hot or cold with or without cream or ice cream.

NPS: 430 C, 10 mg CH, 340 mg S*

V A R I A T I O N S

Dutch Berry Pie: Prepare and bake pie as directed. After removing from oven, funnel 1/3 cup heavy cream in through steam slits. Cool and serve.

NPS: 465 C, 20 mg CH, 345 mg S*

Frozen Berry Pie: Prepare as directed, using 1 quart solidly frozen berries for the fresh and increasing flour to 1/3 cup.

NPS: 425 C, 10 mg CH, 340 mg S*

FRESH RHUBARB PIE

8 servings

1 recipe Flaky Pastry II

F I L L I N G
2 pounds rhubarb, trimmed and cut in 1/2″ chunks
11/3–13/4 cups sugar
1/3 cup unsifted flour
1/8 teaspoon salt
2 or 3 drops red food coloring (optional)
2 tablespoons butter or margarine

G L A Z E (optional)
1 tablespoon milk
1 tablespoon sugar

Preheat oven to 425° F. Make pastry as directed and fit half into a 9″ piepan; do not trim edge. Roll remaining pastry into a 12″ circle and cut steam slits in center; cover with cloth while you prepare filling. Toss rhubarb with enough sugar to sweeten, then mix in flour, salt, and food coloring if rhubarb is pale. Pile in pie shell and dot with butter. Brush pastry rim with cold water, fit top crust over rhubarb, trim, seal, and crimp edges. For a glistening crust, brush with milk and sprinkle with sugar. Bake 40–50 minutes (with foil on rack below to catch drips) until browned and bubbling. Cool 5–10 minutes before cutting. Good with cream, whipped cream, or vanilla ice cream.

NPS: 445 C, 10 mg CH, 345 mg S*

V A R I A T I O N

Rhubarb-Strawberry Pie: Prepare as directed, using 1 pound rhubarb and 1 pint stemmed, halved strawberries; omit food coloring. For a special occasion, top with a lattice crust.*

NPS: 450 C, 10 mg CH, 340 mg S*

SOUR CREAM PEACH PIE

6–8 servings

Peaches and cream baked in a flaky crust and topped with a buttery brown sugar mixture.

1 recipe Flaky Pastry I

F I L L I N G
5 ripe peaches
1 cup sour cream
3/4 cup sugar
3 tablespoons flour
1 egg
1/8 teaspoon mace
1 tablespoon light rum
1/4 teaspoon vanilla

T O P P I N G
1/4 cup melted butter or margarine
1/3 cup unsifted flour
1/2 cup firmly packed light brown sugar

Preheat oven to 400° F. Prepare pastry as directed and fit into a 9″ piepan, making a high fluted edge; do not bake. Peel peaches, halve, pit, and slice thin directly into pie shell. Mix remaining filling ingredients and pour over peaches. Bake 25 minutes and remove from oven. Mix topping and crumble evenly over peaches. Return to oven and bake 20 minutes longer. Cool 10–20 minutes before serving.

NPS (6–8): 610–455 C, 85–60 mg CH, 300–225 mg S*

STREUSEL PEACH PIE

6–8 servings

1 recipe Flaky Pastry I

F I L L I N G
1 quart sliced, pitted, and peeled firm-ripe peaches
1/2 cup sugar
Finely grated rind and juice of 1 orange

T O P P I N G
1/2 cup firmly packed light brown sugar
1/2 cup sifted flour
1/3 cup butter or margarine

Preheat oven to 425° F. Make pastry as directed and fit into a 9″ piepan, making a high fluted edge; do not bake. Gently mix peaches, sugar, orange rind and juice and spoon into pie shell. Mix brown sugar and flour, then, using a pastry blender, cut in butter until mixture is crumbly. Sprinkle over peaches, pressing down lightly. Bake (with a piece of foil on rack below to catch drips) about 40 minutes until lightly browned. Serve warm with or without whipped cream or sour cream.

NPS (6–8): 500–375 C, 30–20 mg CH, 290–220 mg S*

V A R I A T I O N S

Streusel Pecan-Peach Pie: Make pastry and fill as directed. For the topping: Mix the sugar, 1/4 cup flour, and 1/2 teaspoon cinnamon; cut in butter and toss with 1/2 cup minced pecans. Spread over peaches and bake as directed.

NPS (6–8): 550–415 C, 30–20 mg CH, 290–220 mg S*

Streusel Apple, Pear, or Plum Pie: Substitute 1 quart peeled, cored, and sliced tart apples or pears or halved pitted plums for the peaches; adjust sugar in filling as needed to sweeten the fruit, then proceed as directed. Recipe too flexible for meaningful nutritional count.

OLD-FASHIONED PUMPKIN PIE

6–8 servings

If you like your pumpkin pie spicy, use the larger amounts of cinnamon and ginger.

1 recipe Flaky Pastry I
1 egg white, lightly beaten

F I L L I N G
1 1/2 cups pumpkin purée
2/3 cup firmly packed dark brown sugar
3/4–1 1/4 teaspoons cinnamon
1/4–1/2 teaspoon ginger
Pinch nutmeg
1/4 teaspoon maple flavoring (optional)
1/4 teaspoon salt
1 cup milk
1 cup light cream
3 eggs, lightly beaten

Make pastry as directed and fit into a 9″ piepan, making a high fluted edge; brush with egg white and chill 1 hour. Preheat oven to 450° F. For the filling, mix pumpkin and sugar until sugar dissolves. Add remaining ingredients, stirring well to blend. Set pie shell on pulled-out center oven shelf, then pour in filling. Bake 10 minutes, reduce heat to 350° F., and bake 30–35 minutes longer until a knife inserted midway between center and rim comes out clean. Serve warm or at room temperature. Good topped with sweetened whipped cream.

NPS (6–8): 445–335 C, 170–125 mg CH, 505–375 mg S*

BRANDIED MINCEMEAT IN CHEESE PASTRY

8 servings

1 recipe Cheese Pastry II

F I L L I N G
1 (1–pound 12-ounce) jar mincemeat
3–4 tablespoons brandy

Preheat oven to 450° F. Empty mincemeat into a strainer set over a bowl and drain 10 minutes; pour off at least 3–4 tablespoons liquid and discard; save the rest. Meanwhile, make pastry as directed and fit half in a 9″ or 10″ piepan. Roll top crust and make steam slits in center. Mix drained mincemeat with brandy to taste and the reserved liquid and spoon into pie shell. Moisten pastry edges lightly with cold water. Fit top crust over filling, trim edges, seal, and crimp. Bake 10 minutes (with foil on rack underneath to catch drips), reduce heat to 350° F., and bake 20–25 minutes longer until lightly browned. Serve warm or cold with Hard Sauce or wedges of sharp Cheddar.

NPS: 495 C, 15 mg CH, 445 mg S*

LEMON MERINGUE PIE

6–8 servings

1 recipe Flaky Pastry I

F I L L I N G
1/2 cup cornstarch
1 1/2 cups sugar
1/4 teaspoon salt
1 3/4 cups cold water
1 teaspoon finely grated lemon rind
4 egg yolks, lightly beaten
1/3–1/2 cup lemon juice
2 tablespoons butter or margarine

M E R I N G U E
1 recipe Basic Meringue Topping for a 9″ Pie

Make pastry, fit into a 9″ piepan, and bake as directed; reduce oven to 350° F. Mix cornstarch, sugar, and salt in a heavy saucepan, slowly blend in water, and heat, stirring constantly, until thickened and smooth. Mix in lemon rind and cook, stirring, 2–3 minutes. Blend a little hot mixture into yolks, return to pan and cook and stir over lowest heat 2–3 minutes; do not boil. Off heat, stir in 1/3 cup lemon juice (1/2 cup for really tart flavor) and the butter. Spoon filling into pie shell. Prepare meringue as directed, spread over filling, and bake 12–15 minutes until touched with brown. Cool pie at least 2 hours before serving. (*Note:* Pie will cut more easily if knife is dipped in warm water before each cut is made.)

NPS (6–8): 555–415 C, 190–145 mg CH, 390–295 mg S*

VARIATIONS

Lime Meringue Pie: Prepare as directed, substituting lime juice and rind for the lemon.

NPS (6–8): 555–415 C, 190–145 mg CH, 390–295 mg S*

Orange Meringue Pie: Prepare as directed, using 1/4 cup each orange and lemon juice and grated orange rind instead of lemon.

NPS (6–8): 560–420 C, 190–145 mg CH, 390–295 mg S*

KEY LIME PIE

6–8 servings

There are dozens of variations of this Florida Keys classic, some made with a graham cracker crust, some topped with meringue. But this particular version is most like the original: a crisp piecrust filled with a creamy, tart lime filling, then crowned with whipped cream.

1 recipe Flaky Pastry I

FILLING
4 egg yolks, lightly beaten
1 (14-ounce) can sweetened condensed milk
2/3 cup fresh lime juice
Few drops green food coloring

TOPPING
1 cup heavy cream, whipped with 3 tablespoons superfine sugar

Make pastry as directed, fit into a 9″ piepan, and bake as directed; cool while you make the filling. Beat yolks with condensed milk just to blend, add lime juice, and beat until smooth (the filling will be soft). Tint pale green and pour into baked pie shell. Chill well, then spread whipped cream topping over filling, making sure it touches pastry all around. Return to refrigerator and chill several hours before serving, or better still, overnight, so that filling will firm up somewhat (it will never really be firm).

NPS (6–8): 610–455 C, 260–195 mg CH, 285–215 mg S*

VANILLA CREAM PIE

6–8 servings

1 recipe Flaky Pastry I

FILLING
1/4 cup cornstarch
2/3 cup sugar
1/4 teaspoon salt
21/2 cups milk
3 egg yolks, lightly beaten
2 teaspoons vanilla
1 tablespoon butter or margarine

TOPPING (optional)
11/2 cups sweetened whipped cream or 1 recipe Basic Meringue Topping for a 9″ Pie

Make pastry, fit into a 9″ piepan, and bake as directed. Mix cornstarch, sugar, and salt in a saucepan, slowly blend in milk, and heat, stirring, until thickened. Turn heat to lowest point and heat and stir 1–2 minutes. Blend a little hot mixture into egg yolks, return to pan, and cook and stir 1–2 minutes over lowest heat until quite thick; do not boil. Off heat, mix in vanilla and butter. Place a circle of wax paper flat on filling and cool to lukewarm. Fill shell, then chill 2 hours at least. Serve as is or topped with whipped cream. To top with meringue: Cool filling slightly, then fill pie shell. Prepare meringue as directed, spread over filling, and back 12–15 minutes at 350° F. until touched with brown. Cool 2 hours before serving.

NPS (6–8) (without topping): 410–305 C, 155–115 mg CH, 345–260 mg S*

VARIATIONS

Coconut Cream Pie: Prepare filling as directed, then mix in 1 cup flaked or finely grated coconut. Reduce vanilla to 1 teaspoon and, if desired, serve topped with whipped cream.

NPS (6–8): 465–435 C, 155–115 mg CH, 350–260 mg S*

Butterscotch Cream Pie: Prepare filling as directed, substituting 1 cup firmly packed dark brown sugar for the sugar, increasing milk to 22/3 cups, butter to 1/4 cup, and reducing vanilla to 1 teaspoon. (*Note:* Mixture scorches easily, so watch carefully.) Pour into baked pie shell and chill as directed. Serve as is or top with Basic Meringue Topping or whipped cream.

NPS (6–8): 510–385 C, 170–130 mg CH, 420–315 mg S*

Chocolate Cream Pie: Prepare filling as directed, using 2 tablespoons flour and 3 tablespoons cornstarch and increasing sugar to 1 cup. Before adding egg yolks, blend in 3 melted (1–ounce) squares unsweetened chocolate or 3 (1–ounce) envelopes no-melt unsweetened chocolate; also reduce vanilla to 1 teaspoon. Pour into baked pie shell and chill as directed. Top with whipped cream and, if you like, chocolate curls* or chopped pistachio nuts.

NPS (6–8): 525–390 C, 155–115 mg CH, 345–260 mg S

BLACK BOTTOM PIE

6–8 servings

This two-toned pie is chocolate on the bottom, rum chiffon on top.

1 (9″) crumb crust pie shell (Graham Cracker, Gingersnap, or Chocolate), baked and cooled

FILLING
2/3 cup sugar
2 tablespoons cornstarch
1 envelope unflavored gelatin
2 1/2 cups milk
3 eggs, separated
2 (1-ounce) squares unsweetened chocolate
2 tablespoons light rum
1/4 cup superfine sugar
3/4 cup heavy cream
Chocolate curls* (garnish)

Mix sugar, cornstarch, and gelatin in the top of a double boiler, gradually mix in milk, and heat, stirring constantly, over simmering water until steaming. Beat egg yolks lightly, stir in a little hot mixture, then return to pan and cook and stir 3–5 minutes until quite thick and smooth. Place a circle of wax paper flat on sauce and cool to lukewarm. Meanwhile, melt chocolate over simmering water and cool. Measure 1 1/2 cups custard sauce into a bowl, blend in chocolate, pour into crust, and chill 1/2 hour. Cool remaining mixture until it mounds when dropped from a spoon; stir in rum. Beat egg whites until foamy, gradually beat in superfine sugar, and continue to beat until soft peaks form. Fold into rum-custard mixture. Spoon lightly on top of chocolate layer and chill until firm. Whip cream to soft peaks, spread on pie, and decorate with chocolate curls.

NPS (6–8) (with Graham Cracker crust): 605–455 C, 220–165 mg CH, 360–270 mg S

BANANA CREAM PIE

6–8 servings

1 recipe Flaky Pastry I

FILLING
2 tablespoons flour
2 tablespoons cornstarch
1/2 cup sugar

1/4 teaspoon salt
1 3/4 cups milk
3 egg yolks, lightly beaten
1 teaspoon vanilla
1 tablespoon butter or margarine
3 ripe bananas

TOPPING
3/4 cup heavy cream, whipped

Make pastry, fit into a 9″ piepan, and bake as directed. Mix flour, cornstarch, sugar, and salt in a saucepan. Slowly blend in milk and heat and stir until thickened and smooth; turn heat to lowest point and heat and stir 1–2 minutes. Blend a little hot mixture into egg yolks, return to pan, and cook and stir 1–2 minutes over lowest heat until quite thick; do not boil or mixture will curdle. Off heat, mix in vanilla and butter. Place a circle of wax paper directly on mixture and cool to room temperature. Stir filling and spoon half into pie shell. Peel bananas, slice 1/4″ thick, and arrange evenly over filling. Top with remaining filling. "Frost" with whipped cream, chill 20–30 minutes, and serve. *(Note:* If you know you won't eat all the pie at one sitting, top individual servings with whipped cream instead of frosting the whole pie—whipped cream breaks down in the refrigerator.)

NPS (6–8): 520–390 C, 190–145 mg CH, 345–255 mg S

SHOOFLY PIE

6–8 servings ¢

In Pennsylvania Dutch country you may find this pie served for breakfast. Its original function was to distract flies from other foods.

1 recipe Flaky Pastry I

FILLING
2/3 cup boiling water
1/2 teaspoon baking soda
1/2 cup molasses

CRUMB TOPPING
1 1/2 cups sifted flour
1/4 teaspoon salt
3/4 cup firmly packed light brown sugar
1/3 cup butter, margarine, or vegetable shortening

Preheat oven to 350° F. Prepare pastry as directed and fit into a 9″ piepan, making a high fluted edge; do not bake. Mix filling. Also mix flour, salt, and sugar and cut in butter with a pastry blender until the texture of coarse meal. Sprinkle about 1/3 cup topping into pie shell, pour in filling, and sprinkle evenly with remaining topping. Bake on center oven rack 35–40 minutes until well browned. Cool on a wire rack and serve slightly warm or cold. Good with whipped cream or vanilla ice cream.

NPS (6–8): 550–415 C, 25–20 mg CH, 455–340 mg S*

CUSTARD PIE

6–8 servings

For a crisp bottom crust, use the Slipped Custard Pie recipe (see Variations below).

1 recipe Flaky Pastry I

FILLING
4 eggs
2/3 cup sugar
1/2 teaspoon salt
2½ cups milk
1 teaspoon vanilla
1/4 teaspoon nutmeg

Make pastry as directed and fit into a 9″ piepan, making a high fluted edge; do not bake. Preheat oven to 425° F. With a rotary beater, beat eggs lightly, add sugar and salt, and beat until thick and cream colored. Gradually beat in milk and vanilla, then strain through a fine sieve and pour into pastry shell. Sprinkle with nutmeg and bake 15 minutes; reduce temperature to 350° F. and bake 12–15 minutes longer or until a table knife inserted midway between center and rim comes out clean. (*Note:* Center will still be soft but will set on standing.) Do not overbake or custard will curdle. Cool on a wire rack to room temperature before serving, or serve well chilled.

NPS (6–8): 400–290 C, 195–145 mg CH, 460–345 mg S*

VARIATIONS

Rich Custard Pie: Prepare as directed, substituting 1 cup heavy cream for 1 cup of the milk.

NPS (6–8): 500–375 C, 245–185 mg CH, 455–340 mg S*

Coconut Custard Pie: Prepare as directed but, just before pouring custard into pie shell, fold in 3/4 cup flaked coconut. Pour into shell, sprinkle with 1/4 cup flaked coconut (omit nutmeg), and bake as directed.

NPS (6–8): 450–335 C, 195–145 mg CH, 465–345 mg S*

Egg Yolk Custard Pie: Prepare as directed, using 8 egg yolks for custard instead of 4 whole eggs.

NPS (6–8): 420–315 C, 375–285 mg CH, 425–320 mg S*

Slipped Custard Pie: Make and bake a 9″ pie shell as directed in Flaky Pastry I. Prepare and strain custard mixture, pour into a well-buttered 9″ piepan, and sprinkle with nutmeg. Set piepan in a larger pan, add enough hot water to come halfway up piepan. Bake at 350° F. 30–35 minutes or until custard tests done; cool on a wire rack to room temperature. Gently loosen custard from sides of piepan with a spatula, hold level, and shake to loosen bottom. Now tilt and carefully slide into pie shell; hold pans close together and coax custard along. Let custard settle a few minutes before serving.

NPS (6–8): 400–290 C, 195–145 mg CH, 460–345 mg S*

RICH COCONUT PIE

6–8 servings

For a truly exquisite pie, use freshly grated coconut.

1 recipe Flaky Pastry I

FILLING
1/4 cup butter or margarine, softened to room temperature
1 cup superfine sugar
2 eggs
2 tablespoons flour
1/2 cup milk
1/4 teaspoon almond extract
2 cups finely grated coconut

Preheat oven to 350° F. Make pastry as directed and fit into a 9″ piepan, making a high fluted edge; do not bake. Cream butter and sugar until light, beat in eggs, one at a time. Sprinkle in flour and blend until smooth. Mix in remaining ingredients and spoon into pastry shell. Bake 45 minutes until browned and springy to the touch. Cool on a wire rack and serve at room temperature.

NPS (6–8): 550–410 C, 115–85 mg CH, 300–225 mg S*

VANILLA CHIFFON PIE

6–8 servings

Plenty of flavor variations here to try.

1 (9″) pie shell, baked and cooled (Flaky Pastry I or a crumb crust)

FILLING
3/4 cup sugar
1 envelope unflavored gelatin
1 cup milk
4 eggs, separated
2 teaspoons vanilla
1/3 cup heavy cream (optional)
1/4 teaspoon nutmeg

Mix 1/2 cup sugar and the gelatin in the top of a double boiler, gradually mix in milk, and heat and stir over simmering water until steaming hot. Beat egg yolks lightly, blend in a little hot milk mixture, and return to pan. Cook and stir 3–5 minutes until thickened and no raw taste of egg remains. Mix in vanilla, set pan over cold water, and place a circle of wax paper flat on sauce. Cool, stirring now and then, until mixture mounds slightly on a spoon. Whip cream, if you like, and fold into sauce. Beat egg whites until foamy, gradually beat in remaining sugar, and beat to soft peaks; fold into sauce. Spoon into pie shell and chill until firm, at least 3–4 hours. Sprinkle with nutmeg and serve. *(Note:* If you prefer, use cream to garnish pie instead of mixing into filling.)

NPS (6–8): 370–275 C, 190–140 mg CH, 250–185 mg S*

VARIATIONS

Chocolate Chiffon Pie: Prepare as directed but use only 3 egg yolks and add 2 (1-ounce) squares unsweetened chocolate. Beat 1/2 cup sugar with 3 egg whites and fold into sauce; reduce vanilla to 1 teaspoon and omit nutmeg. Decorate with chocolate curls.*

NPS (6–8): 400–300 C, 140–105 mg CH, 240–180 mg S*

Coffee Chiffon Pie: Prepare as directed but add 2 tablespoons instant coffee powder or freeze-dried coffee along with egg yolks; reduce vanilla to 1 teaspoon.

NPS (6–8): 370–275 C, 190–140 mg CH, 250–190 mg S*

Coconut Chiffon Pie: Prepare as directed but reduce vanilla to 1/2 teaspoon and add 1/2 teaspoon almond extract. Fold in 3/4 cup finely grated or flaked coconut along with beaten egg whites. Chill, then serve topped with toasted, flaked coconut.

NPS (6–8): 420–310 C, 190–140 mg CH, 250–190 mg S*

Lemon, Lime, or Orange Chiffon Pie: Prepare as directed but use 1/3 cup lemon or lime juice or 1/3 cup thawed frozen orange juice concentrate and 2/3 cup water instead of milk; also use 2 tablespoons finely grated lemon, lime, or orange rind instead of vanilla. Tint filling an appropriate color, if you like, before spooning into pie shell. Omit nutmeg.

NPS (6–8) (lemon, lime): 345–255 C, 180–135 mg CH, 230–175 mg S*
NPS (6–8) (orange): 365–275 C, 180–135 mg CH, 230–170 mg S*

Berry Chiffon Pie: Prepare as directed but substitute 1 cup crushed, sieved ripe berries for the milk, omit egg yolks, and flavor with 1 tablespoon finely grated lemon rind instead of vanilla. *(Note:* If you use frozen berries, reduce sugar to 1/2 cup—1/4 cup in the sauce, 1/4 cup in the beaten egg whites.) Fold in the whipped cream, then the beaten egg whites. Cover pie shell, if you like, with 1/2 cup sliced berries before pouring in filling. Chill until firm; omit nutmeg.

NPS (6–8): 310–235 C, 0 mg CH, 220–165 mg S*

Peach or Apricot Chiffon Pie: Prepare like Berry Chiffon Pie (above) but use 1 cup peach or apricot purée instead of berries. If you like, cover bottom of pie shell with a layer of sliced peaches or apricots before pouring in filling.

NPS (6–8): 315–235 C, 0 mg CH, 225–165 mg S*

Pumpkin Chiffon Pie: Mix 1 1/4 cups pumpkin purée with 3/4 cup firmly packed light brown sugar and the gelatin called for; proceed as recipe directs but use only 2 egg yolks. Omit vanilla and add 1/2 teaspoon each cinnamon and nutmeg. Cool, fold in 2 egg whites beaten with 1/4 cup sugar, fill pie shell, chill well, then serve topped with fluffs of whipped cream.

NPS (6–8): 395–295 C, 95–70 mg CH, 355–265 mg S*

GRASSHOPPER PIE

6–8 servings

This tastes very much like the Grasshopper cocktail—a mixture of crème de menthe and crème de cacao.

1 (9″) pie shell (Graham Cracker Crust, Flaky Pastry I, or Mürbteig), baked and cooled

FILLING
3/4 cup sugar
1 envelope unflavored gelatin
1/2 cup cold water
3 eggs, separated

⅓ cup green crème de menthe
¼ cup crème de cacao
½ cup heavy cream
Few drops green food coloring (optional)

T O P P I N G
½ cup heavy cream, whipped to soft peaks
Chocolate curls*

Heat and stir ½ cup sugar, gelatin, and water in the top of a double boiler over simmering water until gelatin dissolves. Lightly beat egg yolks, blend in a little hot mixture, then return to pan. Cook and stir 3–5 minutes until thickened and no raw taste of egg remains. Off heat, mix in liqueurs; place a circle of wax paper flat on sauce and cool until mixture mounds when dropped from a spoon. Whip cream to soft peaks, fold into sauce, and, if you like, tint pale green. Beat egg whites until foamy, gradually beat in remaining sugar, and continue to beat until soft peaks form; fold into sauce. Spoon into pie shell and chill until firm, at least 3–4 hours. Top with swirls of whipped cream and sprinkle with chocolate curls.

NPS (6–8): 565–425 C, 220–165 mg CH, 310–235 mg S*

V A R I A T I O N

Brandy Alexander Pie: Prepare as directed but substitute ⅓ cup brandy for the crème de menthe.

NPS (6–8): 550–410 C, 220–165 mg CH, 310–235 mg S*

OLD-FASHIONED SOUTHERN PECAN PIE

6–8 servings

Almost too good to be true.

1 recipe Flaky Pastry I

F I L L I N G
1 cup pecan halves
1 (1-pound) box light brown sugar
¼ cup unsifted flour
½ teaspoon salt
½ cup milk
1½ teaspoons vanilla
3 eggs
½ cup melted butter or margarine

Preheat oven to 325° F. Make pastry as directed and fit into a 9″ piepan; do not bake. Arrange pecans in concentric rings over bottom of pastry. Blend sugar, flour, and salt, then mix in milk and vanilla. Beat in eggs, one at a time, using a wire whisk or rotary beater; mix in butter, a little at a time. Pour filling over pecans. Bake pie 1 hour and 15

minutes or until filling is puffy and crust golden. Serve at room temperature. And cut the pieces small—the pie is *rich.*

NPS (6–8): 815–610 C, 180–135 mg CH, 590–440 mg S*

LEMON CHESS PIE

6–8 servings

The South's favorite pie is "chess" (probably a corruption of "cheese" from the English "lemon cheese"). Lemon is a popular chess flavor, but there are others—so many no one knows which is the original. Here are two especially good ones.

1 recipe Flaky Pastry I

F I L L I N G
1½ cups sugar
2 tablespoons flour
Finely grated rind of 2 lemons
5 eggs
Juice of 2 lemons
⅓ cup melted butter or margarine

Preheat oven to 325° F. Make pastry as directed and fit into a 9″ piepan; do not bake. Mix sugar, flour, and rind, then, beat in eggs, one at a time. Stir in lemon juice and finally the melted butter, adding a bit at a time and beating well after each addition. Pour filling into pie shell and bake about 1 hour until puffy and golden (filling will seem unset). Cool pie to room temperature (filling will settle and thicken). Serve at room temperature.

NPS (6–8): 550–410 C, 255–190 mg CH, 345–260 mg S*

BROWN SUGAR CHESS PIE

6–8 servings

Rich, rich, *rich!*

1 recipe Flaky Pastry I

F I L L I N G
1 (1-pound) box light brown sugar
4 eggs
¼ cup milk
1½ teaspoons vanilla
½ teaspoon salt
½ cup melted butter or margarine

Preheat oven to 325° F. Make pastry as directed and fit into a 9″ piepan; do not bake. Blend together all filling ingredients except butter, then mix in butter, a little at a time; pour into pie shell and bake about 1 hour until puffy and golden. Cool pie to room temperature before serving (filling will settle and thicken). Cut the pieces small.

NPS (6–8): 665–500 C, 225–170 mg CH, 595–445 mg S*

THE VERY BEST CHEESE CAKE

10 servings

Unbelievably smooth.

CRUST

18 graham crackers rolled to crumbs (there should be 1½ cups)
¼ cup sugar
5 tablespoons melted butter or margarine

FILLING

2 (8-ounce) packages cream cheese, softened to room temperature
2 eggs
½ cup sugar
1 teaspoon vanilla

TOPPING

1 cup sour cream
¼ cup sugar
1 teaspoon vanilla

Preheat oven to 375° F. Mix crust ingredients and pat firmly into the bottom and one third of the way up the sides of a 9″ spring form pan. Beat filling ingredients with a rotary beater or electric mixer until satiny and pour into crust. Bake 20 minutes, remove from oven, and cool 15 minutes. Meanwhile, raise oven to 475° F. Blend topping ingredients and spread gently over cheese filling. Return pie to oven and bake 10 minutes longer. Cool in pan to room temperature, then cover with foil and chill 10–12 hours before serving. Cut in *slim* wedges.

NPS: 370 C, 120 mg CH, 270 mg S*

CHERRY TOPPING FOR CHEESE CAKE

Enough to top a 9″ cheese cake

½ cup sugar
2 tablespoons cornstarch
1 (1-pound) can sour red cherries, drained (reserve liquid)
Cherry liquid + enough water to total ¾ cup
1 teaspoon lemon juice
Few drops red food coloring

Mix sugar and cornstarch in a saucepan, gradually blend in cherry liquid, and heat, stirring, until boiling. Reduce heat and simmer 5 minutes, stirring occasionally. Off heat, mix in lemon juice, cherries, and food coloring. Cool 5 minutes, spread on top of cooled cheese cake, and chill several hours.

NPS (topping only): 80 C, 0 mg CH, 4 mg S*

STRAWBERRY TOPPING FOR CHEESE CAKE

Enough to top a 9″ cheese cake

1 quart strawberries, washed and stemmed
⅓ cup sugar
1 tablespoon cornstarch
¼ cup water

Crush enough small berries to make 1 cup and press through a fine sieve. Mix sugar and cornstarch in a saucepan, blend in sieved berries and water, and heat and stir over moderate heat until boiling; lower heat and simmer 2–3 minutes, stirring until thickened and clear; cool slightly. Arrange whole berries, points up, on a baked, cooled cheese cake, spoon sauce over all, and chill 2 hours.

NPS (topping only): 45 C, 0 mg CH, 60 mg S*

LEMON ANGEL PIE

6–8 servings

A shattery meringue crust billowing with a creamy lemon filling.

1 (9″) Meringue Pie Shell, baked and cooled

FILLING

4 egg yolks
½ cup sugar
¼ cup lemon juice
2 tablespoons finely grated lemon rind
1 cup heavy cream

Beat egg yolks in the top of a double boiler until thick and cream colored. Gradually beat in sugar, then lemon juice and rind. Set over simmering water and cook, stirring constantly, about 5–8 minutes until thick. Remove from heat, place a circle of wax paper flat on mixture, and cool to room temperature. Whip cream until soft peaks form, and spread half in bottom of pie shell. Cover with filling and top with remaining whipped cream. Or fold lemon mixture into whipped cream, then fill pie shell. Chill overnight.

NPS (6–8): 320–240 C, 235–170 mg CH, 95–70 mg S*

VARIATIONS

Lime Angel Pie: Prepare as directed but substitute ¼ cup lime juice and 1 tablespoon grated lime rind for the lemon juice and rind.

*NPS (6–8): 320–240 C, 235–175 mg CH, 95–70 mg S**

Orange Angel Pie: Prepare as directed but substitute 1/4 cup thawed, frozen orange juice concentrate and 2 tablespoons finely grated orange rind for the lemon juice and rind.

*NPS (6–8): 340–255 C, 235–175 mg CH, 90–70 mg S**

CHOCOLATE ANGEL PIE

6–8 servings

If chocolate is your choice, you'll prefer this angel pie to the lemon.

1 (9″) Meringue Pie Shell, baked and cooled

FILLING
1/4 cup hot water
1 (12-ounce) package semisweet chocolate bits, melted
1 cup heavy cream
1/2 cup sifted confectioners' sugar
1 teaspoon vanilla

Blend water and chocolate bits until smooth and cool to room temperature. Beat cream and sugar to stiff peaks, fold into chocolate mixture, flavor with vanilla, and spoon into meringue shell. Chill well before serving.

*NPS (6–8): 535–400 C, 55–40 mg CH, 85–65 mg S**

VARIATION

Mocha Angel Pie: Prepare as directed but use 1/4 cup strong hot black coffee instead of water.

*NPS (6–8): 535–400 C, 55–40 mg CH, 85–65 mg S**

MAKING TARTS

Tarts, in classical cuisine, are short cookie-like pastry shells filled with raw or cooked fruit, often accompanied with custard or cream filling. They are usually open face (at least they are never sealed under a top crust) and may be small, medium, or large. The most beautiful are arrangements of fruit jeweled under a clear sweet glaze.

In America, tarts are simply little pies, single or double crusted, sometimes enough for one serving, sometimes no more than a mouthful. Almost any pie recipe can be used for tarts. *Note:* You will probably need 1 1/2–

2 times the amount of pastry because it takes more to line several little pans than a single large one.

Some Ways to Shape Tart Shells: Prepare pastry, roll out 1/8″ thick, then cut in circles about 1″ larger all around than tin you plan to use. Fluted tart tins, available in many housewares departments, make especially dainty tarts, but tarts can also be fitted into muffin pans or over upside-down custard cups or gelatin molds.

Baking Tarts: Follow individual pie recipes, making the following adjustments in baking times and temperatures:

Unfilled Tart Shells: Preheat oven to 450° F. Roll and fit pastry into tins, prick well all over, and bake 10–15 minutes until crisp and tan. Cool in pans on wire racks a few minutes, then ease out, using a metal skewer to free stubborn spots. Cool thoroughly before filling. *Note:* Preserves or jams may be used to fill small tarts instead of pie fillings.

Filled Tarts: Preheat oven to 425° F. Roll and fit pastry into tins; do not prick. Add filling, enough to fill each tart one half to two thirds, no more. Add top crust, if any, crimp edges or seal by pressing with the tines of a fork. Bake 15–20 minutes until pastry is crisp and tan and filling bubbly. Cool or not as individual recipes direct. *Note:* To minimize breakage, keep tarts in tins until just before serving.

Some Ways to Decorate Tarts: Keep decorations simple, in proportion to the tart and appropriate to the occasion. Here a few suggestions:

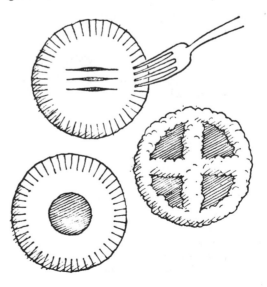

SWISS STRAWBERRY TART

6–8 servings

1 recipe Flaky Pastry I

FILLING
3 tablespoons flour
1/4 cup sugar
1/8 teaspoon salt
1 cup milk
1/2 teaspoon vanilla
2 egg yolks, lightly beaten
1/3 cup heavy cream
3 cups ripe strawberries, washed, stemmed, and dried

GLAZE
3/4 cup red currant jelly

Make pastry, fit into a 9″ piepan, and bake as directed; cool. Mix flour, sugar, and salt in the top of a double boiler, add milk slowly, stirring until smooth, then cook and stir over direct moderate heat until thickened and smooth; stir in vanilla. Blend a little hot mixture into yolks, return to top of double boiler, set over simmering water, and cook and stir 3–4 minutes until thick and no taste of raw egg remains. Remove from heat, place a circle of wax paper flat on sauce and cool to room temperature. Whip cream and fold into sauce. Spread over bottom of pie shell and arrange strawberries, points up, on top. To glaze, melt jelly over low heat, cool to barely lukewarm, then spoon evenly over berries. Cover and chill until serving time (but no longer than 1–2 hours or pastry will become soggy).

NPS (6–8): 450–335 C, 115–85 mg CH, 265–195 mg S*

VIENNESE FRUIT FLAN

8–10 servings

Cut the pieces small—this one's rich!

1 (9″) Sweet Torte or Mürbteig pie or flan shell, baked and cooled

FILLING
1 cup heavy cream
1/4 cup superfine sugar
1 teaspoon vanilla
1 quart stemmed strawberries or a mixture of sliced peaches, seedless green or seeded black grapes, and any stemmed berries

GLAZE
1 cup water
2 tablespoons sugar
4 teaspoons arrowroot or cornstarch blended with 2 tablespoons cold water

1 teaspoon lemon juice
Few drops red food coloring

Beat cream with sugar and vanilla until soft peaks form; spread over bottom of pie shell and arrange fruit artistically on top. Mix glaze (omitting coloring) and heat, stirring, over low heat until thickened and *clear.* Tint pale pink, cool to lukewarm, then spoon evenly over fruit. Keep in a cool place (not the refrigerator) and serve within 2–3 hours.

NPS (8–10): 400–320 C, 140–110 mg CH, 210–170 mg S*

TRUDY'S VIENNESE LINZERTORTE

8″ torte (12 servings)

PASTRY
1 1/2 cups sifted flour
1/4 cup sugar
1/2 teaspoon baking powder
1/2 teaspoon salt
1 teaspoon cinnamon
1/2 cup firmly packed dark brown sugar
1/2 cup butter, chilled (no substitute)
1 egg, lightly beaten
1/2 cup finely ground unblanched almonds

CREAM FILLING
1 egg
1/3 cup sugar
1/4 cup sifted flour
1/4 teaspoon salt
1 1/2 cups scalding hot milk
1 teaspoon vanilla

RASPBERRY TOPPING
1 (10-ounce) package thawed frozen raspberries (do not drain)
2 tablespoons sugar
2 tablespoons cornstarch
1 tablespoon lemon juice

Sift flour with sugar, baking powder, salt, and cinnamon, then, using a pastry blender, cut in brown sugar and butter until mixture resembles coarse meal. Add egg and almonds and blend with a fork until mixture forms a ball. Wrap half the pastry and chill. Press remaining pastry into the bottom and up the sides of an 8″ piepan, cover, and chill. To prepare filling, beat egg until frothy, add sugar gradually, and beat 2–3 minutes until thick. Add flour and salt slowly and blend until smooth. Gradually add milk, stirring constantly. Transfer to the top of a double boiler, set over simmering water, and cook, stirring, 2–3 minutes until thickened and smooth. Reduce heat, cover, and cook 5 minutes, stirring frequently. Off heat, mix in vanilla; place a piece of wax paper directly on surface and cool to room temperature. Meanwhile, prepare topping: Mix all ingredients in a saucepan and bring to a boil, stirring; reduce heat and simmer, uncovered, 5–7 minutes, stirring occasionally, until thick; cool to room temperature. Preheat oven to 375° F. Spoon filling into pastry shell and carefully spread with topping. Roll remaining pastry into an 8″ circle and cut in strips 1/2″ wide; arrange lattice fashion over filling. Lay 1–2 long strips around rim to cover lattice ends and press gently to seal. Bake 30–35 minutes until lightly browned. Cool several minutes before serving.

NPS: 305 C, 70 mg CH, 260 mg S*

APPLE STRUDEL

12 servings

You can make strudel with all-purpose flour, but bread flour will produce a thinner, flakier pastry. Remove your rings before pulling and stretching strudel pastry; also make sure fingernails are clipped so you don't tear it. *Note:* You can buy ready-to-fill strudel pastry at many specialty food shops if you don't feel up to making it from scratch.

PASTRY
1 1/2 cups sifted flour (preferably bread flour)
1/4 teaspoon salt
1 egg, lightly beaten
1 tablespoon cooking oil
1/3 cup lukewarm water
Cooking oil (for brushing pastry)

FILLING
3/4 cup (about) melted butter (no substitute)
1 cup toasted fine bread crumbs
5 medium-size tart cooking apples, peeled, cored, and minced
2/3 cup sugar mixed with 1 teaspoon cinnamon
3/4 cup seedless raisins
1/2 cup minced, blanched almonds
2 teaspoons finely grated lemon rind

TOPPING
Sifted confectioners' sugar

Mix flour and salt and make a well in the center. Combine egg, oil, and water, pour into well, and, using a fork, pull dry ingredients into liquid; mix to form a soft dough. Knead on a lightly floured board 3–4 minutes until smooth and elastic. Place dough in an oiled bowl, turn to grease all over, cover, and let stand in a warm place 1/2 hour. Meanwhile, cover a table about 3 feet square with an old tablecloth or sheet, smooth out, pull taut, and fasten underneath with tape. Sprinkle all over with flour, adding a little

extra in the center. With a lightly floured rolling pin, roll dough into an 18″ circle. Brush all over with oil. Slip floured hands, backs up, underneath pastry, then gently and evenly stretch dough, working from the center toward edges and moving hands around circle to stretch all areas as evenly and thinly as possible. The fully stretched dough should be semitransparent and cover the table. Work carefully to avoid tearing holes, but if small ones appear, ignore or pinch together (don't try to patch). Let pastry hang over edge of table and let stand, uncovered, 10 minutes (no longer or it may

How to Roll and Stretch Strudel

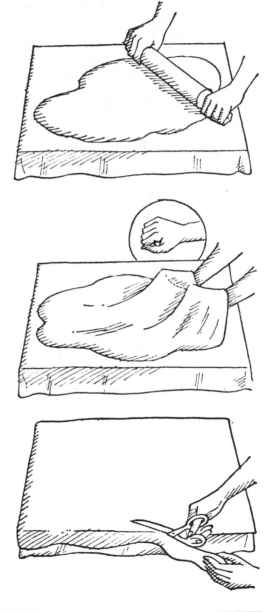

become brittle). Preheat oven to 400° F. Brush pastry generously with butter and with kitchen shears cut off thick edges and square up sides. Sprinkle crumbs over top half of pastry, leaving 2″ margins at the top and both sides. Cover crumbs with apples, sprinkle with sugar, raisins, almonds, and lemon rind; drizzle with 2–3 tablespoons melted butter. Fold top margin down and side margins in over filling. Grasping cloth at the top, tilting and holding taut with both hands, let strudel roll itself up, jelly-roll fashion. Ease strudel onto a buttered baking sheet and curve into a horseshoe. Brush with butter and bake on center rack 20 minutes; reduce oven to 350° F., brush again with butter, and bake 20–25 minutes longer, brushing once more with butter after 10 minutes or so. When strudel is richly browned, transfer to a wire rack and cool. Dust with confectioners' sugar and slice 2″ thick. Serve slightly warm or cool, with or without whipped cream.

NPS: 345 C, 55 mg CH, 230 mg S*

VARIATIONS

Cherry Strudel: Prepare as directed, using Cherry Strudel Filling instead of apple.

NPS: 265 C, 55 mg CH, 215 mg S*

Cheese Strudel: Use Cheese Strudel Filling instead of apple and place on stretched pastry in a row at the top, leaving 2″ margins at top and sides. Fold the margins in over filling, roll, and bake strudel as directed.

NPS: 265 C, 60 mg CH, 215 mg S*

Poppy Seed Strudel: Prepare and stretch pastry as directed; brush with melted butter and 1/2 cup warm honey, then sprinkle top half with crumbs. Across the top end in a single row place 2 cups ground poppy seeds, 1/2 cup sugar, 1 cup seedless raisins, the finely grated rind of 1 lemon, leaving a 2″ margin at the top and each side. Drizzle with 1/2 cup heavy cream. Fold margins in over filling, roll, and bake strudel as directed.

NPS: 480 C, 65 mg CH, 240 mg S*

Jam Strudel: Prepare and stretch pastry as directed; brush with melted butter, scatter crumbs over top half of pastry, leaving 2″ margins as above. Spread 1 1/2–2 cups warmed strawberry, raspberry, or apricot jam over crumbs, top with 3/4 cup golden seedless raisins and 1/2 cup minced blanched almonds. Fold margins in over filling, roll, and bake as directed.

NPS: 380 C, 55 mg CH, 235 mg S*

CHERRY STRUDEL FILLING

Enough to fill 1 strudel

2 (1-pound) cans pitted tart red or sweet dark cherries, drained
1/2–1 cup sugar
1/4 teaspoon almond extract
1 cup minced, blanched almonds

Quarter the cherries, toss with the minimum amount of sugar, and let stand 10 minutes; taste for sweetness and add more sugar if needed. Mix in extract and almonds and use as strudel filling.

NPS: 185 C, 0 mg CH, 70 mg S*

VARIATION

Fresh Cherry Strudel Filling: Simmer 1 quart stemmed, pitted, ripe tart red or dark sweet cherries with 1/2–1 cup sugar and 1/4 cup water 5 minutes until softened. Cool in liquid and drain; taste for sugar and adjust, then mix with extract and almonds.

NPS: 165 C, 0 mg CH, 10 mg S*

CHEESE STRUDEL FILLING

Enough to fill 1 strudel

1 pound cottage cheese
1/3 cup sugar
1 egg + 1 egg white, lightly beaten
1/4 cup heavy cream
1 cup seedless raisins
1 cup minced walnuts
Finely grated rind and juice of 1 lemon

Purée cottage cheese until smooth by buzzing 1–2 minutes in an electric blender at high speed or about 30 seconds in a food processor fitted with the metal chopping blade; or press through a fine sieve. Mix with remaining ingredients and use as strudel filling.

NPS: 190 C, 0 mg CH, 10 mg S*

PALMIERS

5 dozen

1 recipe Puff Pastry
1/2 cup sugar (about)

Make pastry as directed, divide in 3 equal parts, and roll, one at a time, into a 12 1/2″ square about 1/8″ thick. With a sharp knife, cut 1/4″ off all margins, making edges ruler straight. Brush square with cold water, sprinkle evenly with about 2 tablespoons sugar. Make a light mark down center of square and fold each side in toward center as shown so folds meet exactly; fold again through center of each half, then fold 1 roll over on top of the other. Wrap and chill 1 hour. Preheat oven to 450° F. With a very sharp knife, slice rolls crosswise every 1/2", dip both cut sides of slices in sugar, arrange 1 1/2" apart on ungreased baking sheets, and bake 5–7 minutes until browned on the bottom; turn, using a pancake turner, reduce heat to 375° F. and bake 5 minutes longer until browned underneath. Cool on wire racks. Serve as is or, if you like, sandwiched together with sweetened stiffly whipped cream.

NP Palmier: 90 C, 15 mg CH, 55 mg S*

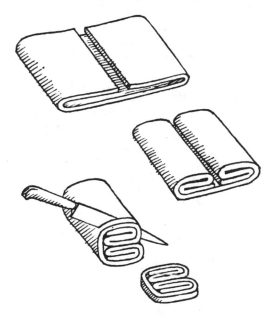

How to Fold and Cut Palmiers

NAPOLEONS

1 dozen

Napoleons are best eaten the day they're made. If you must prepare them ahead of time, spread pastry thinly with hot sieved apricot preserves before filling to keep Napoleons crisp. Also refrigerate until about 20 minutes before serving.

1 recipe Puff Pastry
2 recipes Pastry Cream or 1 quart sweetened stiffly whipped cream
Sifted confectioners' sugar

Prepare pastry as directed, divide in 3 equal parts, and roll out 1 piece on a lightly floured board into a rectangle 12 1/2" × 14 1/2" and 1/8" thick, keeping edges as straight as possible. With a sharp knife, trim 1/8" off all margins. Roll pastry over a lightly floured rolling pin and unroll on a baking sheet brushed with cold water; prick well all over, cover, and chill 1/2 hour. Meanwhile, preheat oven to 450° F. Roll remaining 2 pieces the same way, transfer to baking sheets and chill. *(Note: If you do not have 3 baking sheets, keep pastry chilled and roll when a sheet is free—make sure it is cool.)* Bake pastry, 1 sheet at a time, on center oven rack 10 minutes until golden brown and crisp. Ease onto an extra-large wire rack (or 2 racks tied together) and cool thoroughly. Place pastry sheets on a large, flat surface and even up margins (all 3 pieces should be about the same size). Cut each the long way into strips 4" wide and, as though making triple decker sandwiches, sandwich strips together, 3 deep, with filling (do not spread filling on top layer). Chill 1 hour. Using a sharp knife held vertically and a sawing motion, cut strips crosswise at 2" intervals. Dust with confectioners' sugar and serve as soon as possible.

NP Napoleon: 615 C, 275 mg CH, 390 mg S*

VARIATION

Prepare and bake 3 pastry sheets as directed. Cut 2 into strips as above; spread the third uncut sheet with 2 recipes Quick Glacé Icing. Melt 4 (1-ounce) squares semisweet chocolate and drizzle in parallel lines over icing; before it hardens, draw a toothpick across lines every 1/2" or so to make a crisscross design; when icing hardens, cut sheet into strips as you did the other two. Assemble Napoleons as above, using glazed strips as the top ones.

NP Napoleon: 885 C, 275 mg CH, 400 mg S*

PITHIVIERS (GÂTEAU D'AMANDES)

10 servings

The French town of Pithiviers is justly famous for this puff pastry tart filled with almond paste (which, you'll be pleased to know, is available in cans or links at some supermarkets and most specialty food shops).

1/2 recipe Puff Pastry

FILLING
1 egg, lightly beaten
1 tablespoon sugar
4 ounces almond paste, crumbled
2 tablespoons finely chopped toasted blanched almonds
1 tablespoon brandy (optional)

1 egg lightly beaten with 1 tablespoon milk

Make pastry as directed. Also cut a 9″ cardboard circle, then scallop the edge using a 2″–3″ biscuit cutter as a template. You'll use this as a pattern. Roll half of pastry on a lightly floured board into a circle 10″ across and ¼″ thick (if thicker, pastry won't cook properly). Using cardboard pattern as a guide, cut a scalloped circle from pastry with a sharp knife; transfer to ungreased baking sheet. Roll and cut a second circle the same way, then with tip of a sharp knife, score top lightly in a pinwheel design (curved lines radiating from center toward outer edge; make about 10 lines in all, spacing them equidistantly). For Filling: Beat egg and sugar together until light, add almond paste, and blend well. Mix in almonds and brandy, if you like. Spread filling on pastry on baking sheet, leaving a ½″ border all around. Brush border with some of the glaze and cover with second circle of dough, pressing edges *lightly* together to seal. Now make a vertical ridged pattern around sides of pastry by pressing at ¼″ intervals with the back of a knife and taking care not to damage the scalloped edge. Chill pastry 1 hour. Preheat oven to 425° F. Also remove upper rack so that pastry can puff unobstructed (it will triple in height). Brush top of pastry with remaining glaze, but do not let it run down sides or pastry will not puff evenly. Bake on center oven rack 20 minutes, reduce oven temperature to 350° F., and bake 35–40 minutes longer until well browned and crisp. (*Note:* Do not underbake or pastry will be doughy inside.) Using a pancake turner, ease pastry onto a wire rack and cool about 20 minutes. Serve slightly warm or cold. Cut the pieces small, the pastry's superrich.

NPS: 330 C, 105 mg CH, 180 mg S*

CREAM PUFFS

1 dozen puffs

1 recipe Choux Pastry
1 egg yolk mixed with 1 tablespoon cold water (glaze)
2 recipes Pastry Cream or 1 quart ice cream or any suitable cream filling
¼ cup sifted confectioners' sugar

Preheat oven to 400° F. Make pastry as directed and drop by rounded tablespoonfuls 3″ apart on ungreased baking sheet to form 12 puffs, or put through a pastry bag fitted with a large, plain tip. Brush tops with glaze and bake 45–50 minutes until puffed, golden brown, and hollow sounding when tapped. (*Note:* Do not open oven door during first quarter hour.) Cool puffs on wire racks away from drafts. To fill, cut a ¾″ slice off the top of each puff and pull out any soft dough inside. Fill, replace tops, cover, and chill until serving time. Dust with confectioners' sugar and serve.

NP Puff: 340 C, 330 mg CH, 260 mg S*

VARIATIONS

All variations too flexible for meaningful nutritional counts.
• Frost tops of filled puffs with any favorite icing.
• Top with hot or cold chocolate or butterscotch sauce.
• Fill with fresh, canned, or frozen fruit mixed with whipped cream instead of pastry cream.
• Fill with softened ice cream (any flavor); wrap airtight and freeze. Thaw 5–10 minutes before serving. These will keep about 1 month in the freezer.

CHOCOLATE ÉCLAIRS

1 dozen éclairs

1 recipe Choux Pastry
1 egg yolk mixed with 1 tablespoon cold water (glaze)
2 recipes Pastry Cream
1 recipe Chocolate Glacé Icing

Preheat oven to 400° F. Make pastry as directed and drop by rounded tablespoonfuls 2″ apart in rows that are 6″ apart on an ungreased baking sheet to form 12 equalsized mounds. Using a spoon and a spatula, shape each mound into an oval about 4″ long, 1½″ wide, and 1″ high. Or put mixture through a pastry bag fitted with a large, plain tip. Brush tops with glaze and bake 40–45 minutes until puffed, golden brown, and hollow sounding when tapped. Cool away from drafts on wire racks. Halve éclairs lengthwise and gently pull out any soft dough inside. Fill with Pastry Cream and replace tops. Arrange on a wire rack with a piece of wax paper underneath. Spoon icing evenly over each and allow to harden. Serve within 1–2 hours. Do not refrigerate.

NP Éclair: 460 C, 330 mg CH, 260 mg S*

PROFITEROLES

4¹/2 dozen

Bite-size Cream Puffs. Perfect for a tea if served plain without sauce.

1 recipe Choux Pastry
1 egg yolk mixed with 1 tablespoon cold water
  (glaze)
3 recipes Pastry Cream or 7 cups sweetened
  whipped cream (about)
¹/3 cup sifted confectioners' sugar

Preheat oven to 400° F. Prepare pastry as directed and drop by rounded teaspoonfuls 2″ apart on ungreased baking sheets or put through a pastry bag fitted with a medium-size plain tip. Smooth into little round "pillows" about 1″ high and brush tops lightly with glaze. Bake 20–25 minutes until puffed, golden brown, and crisp. Cool on wire racks away from drafts. Just before serving make a small slit in the side of each Profiterole and squirt in filling with a pastry bag fitted with a small, plain tip. Dust with confectioners' sugar and serve. Good with chocolate sauce.

NP Puff: 100 C, 95 mg CH, 70 mg S*

VARIATIONS

Profiteroles au Chocolat: Fill with Chocolate Cream Filling, arrange in a large bowl, or pile in a small pyramid and pour Basic Chocolate Sauce over all. *(Note:* Pyramid will be easier to shape if you use chocolate sauce as a "glue" to stick Profiteroles together.)

NP Puff: 110 C, 35 mg CH, 60 mg S*

Ice Cream Profiteroles: Fill with any softened ice cream; wrap airtight and freeze. Thaw 10 minutes before serving. Top with Butterscotch or Hot Fudge Sauce. These keep about 1 month in the freezer.

NP Puff: 60 C, 35 mg CH, 45 mg S*

Carolines: Make Profiteroles as directed but fill with a cold savory mixture instead of a sweet one (creamed meat, seafood, or eggs are all suitable). To serve Carolines hot, reheat pastries *before filling*—5–7 minutes at 325° F. Split, fill with hot savory mixture, and serve. Hot or cold, these make good cocktail or buffet food. Recipe too flexible for meaningful nutritional count.

CROQUEMBOUCHE

15–18 servings

This pastry pyramid must be made on a dry day so that the glaze will harden properly. It can be made with Meringue Kisses as well as Profiteroles and, for a really showy dessert, wreathed in spun sugar.*

1 recipe Profiteroles

GLAZE
1 cup water
1¹/2 cups sugar

BASE
1 (9″) cardboard circle covered with foil

TOPPING
¹/4 cup sifted confectioners' sugar

Prepare Profiteroles as directed. Heat and stir glaze ingredients until sugar dissolves, then boil, uncovered, stirring occasionally, 10–15 minutes until the color of amber; keep warm over lowest heat. Place base on a large round platter and set near range. Using glaze as a "glue," stick a ring of Profiteroles, browned sides up, around edge of base. Form a second, slightly smaller ring on top by sticking Profiteroles in spaces of first row and slanting slightly toward center. Fill middle with unglazed Profiteroles to support "walls." Continue building pyramid and top

with a single Profiterole. *(Note:* If syrup should harden, add 1–2 tablespoons boiling water and heat until again syrupy.) Dust confectioners' sugar over Croquembouche. To serve, start at the top and pull off Profiteroles with 2 forks; allow 3–4 per person.

NPS (15–18): 435–365 C, 340–285 mg CH, 250–
  210 mg S*

PARIS-BREST

8 servings

A Parisian classic made with Choux Pastry and almond-flavored Pastry Cream.

1 recipe Choux Pastry
1 egg lightly beaten with 1 tablespoon milk (glaze)
1/3 cup coarsely chopped or slivered blanched almonds

F I L L I N G
1 recipe Pastry Cream
1 cup crushed Almond Brittle
OR
2 1/2 cups Sweetened Whipped Cream

T O P P I N G
2–3 tablespoons sifted confectioners' sugar

Preheat oven to 400° F. Make pastry as directed. Lightly grease and flour a baking sheet and trace an 8" circle in the flour; now trace a 5" circle concentric to and 3" inside the 8" circle so that you have a doughnut-shaped ring about 3" wide drawn in the flour. Drop pastry by rounded tablespoonfuls, one touching the next, to fill in the ring and build it up to a thickness of 2 1/2" (if you prefer, pipe pastry through a pastry bag fitted with a large plain tip). Brush top of pastry with glaze and sprinkle with almonds. Bake 1 hour, then reduce oven temperature to 350° F. and bake 30 minutes longer until puffed, crisp, brown, and hollow sounding when tapped. *(Note:* If nuts brown too soon before pastry is done, lay a piece of aluminum foil loosely on top.) *(Caution:* Do not *underbake* pastry or it will collapse and be soggy inside.) Cool pastry ring away from drafts on a wire rack. Halve ring horizontally and gently pull out any soft dough inside. Mix Pastry Cream and Almond Brittle, then fill bottom half of ring; replace top. Dust confectioners' sugar over all and serve at once. *(Note:* If you cannot serve the ring at once, chill, uncovered, in the refrigerator —but no longer than 2 hours because the pastry will become soggy.)
NPS: 390 C, 255 mg CH, 245 mg S*

BAKLAVA

30 servings

A terrific (and calorific) Greek-Middle Eastern pastry, dripping with honey syrup. Packages of phyllo pastry leaves (sheets) are available fresh in Middle Eastern groceries and bakeries, and frozen in many supermarkets and specialty food shops.

1 (1-pound) package phyllo pastry leaves, at room temperature
1 1/2 cups (about) melted unsalted butter (no substitute)

F I L L I N G
1 pound walnuts or toasted, blanched almonds, chopped fine
1/2 cup sugar
1 teaspoon cinnamon

S Y R U P
1 cup honey
1 cup sugar
1 cup water
2 tablespoons lemon juice
2 (1") strips lemon rind

Preheat oven to 350° F. Unroll pastry leaves and separate into 3 stacks of equal height and cover loosely with wax paper, then with damp cloth to keep pastry from drying out; place 1 stack in a buttered 17" × 12" × 2" baking pan and brush every second sheet with melted butter. Mix filling and scatter one third of it over pastry stack in pan; top with half of the leaves from the second stack, brushing every other one with butter. Sprinkle with another third of the filling, top with remaining leaves from second stack, again brushing every second sheet with butter. Sprinkle with remaining filling and top with third stack of pastry leaves, again brushing every second leaf with butter. With a sharp knife, cut Baklava into 30 squares. Measure remaining butter and add a little extra, if needed, to total 1/2 cup; brown lightly over low heat, then pour evenly over pastry. Bake on center rack 1/2 hour, reduce oven to 300° F., and bake 1/2 hour longer. Meanwhile, prepare syrup: Heat and stir all ingredients in a heavy saucepan over moderate heat until sugar dissolves, then boil slowly 20 minutes. Strain syrup and pour over Baklava as soon as it comes from the oven. Serve warm or cold.
NPS: 300 C, 25 mg CH, 2 mg S*

PAVLOVA

8 servings

A meringue basket filled with whipped cream and fresh fruit, this Australian classic is named in honor of the famous ballerina Anna Pavlova.

1 recipe Meringues

F I L L I N G
2 cups Sweetened Whipped Cream
2 cups chilled fresh fruit (apricots, peaches, bananas, tangerines, pineapple, kiwi fruit cut

in bite-size pieces, and/or small whole berries or seedless green grapes)
2 tablespoons silver dragées (optional)

Preheat oven to 250° F. Trace a 9″ circle on a foil-lined baking sheet and spread ½″ deep with meringue. Spoon remaining meringue into a pastry bag fitted with a No. 6 star tip. Edge meringue circle with a border of large stars (about 1″ in diameter), each one just touching the next, then add successive borders of stars, each atop the preceding one, to form a meringue shell about 2½″ deep. Bake meringue shell 1 hour and 15 minutes until firm; turn oven off and let meringue dry in oven overnight *(do not open oven door at any time while meringue is drying)*. Next day, spread ½ cup whipped cream in bottom of meringue shell, add fruit, then top with remaining cream and decorate with *dragées,* if you like.

NPS: 320 C, 40 mg CH, 115 mg S*

DACQUOISE

8 servings

A showy, rich-as-sin pastry dessert made with layers of nut-filled meringue and butter cream frosting.

6 egg whites, at room temperature
¼ teaspoon cream of tartar
¼ teaspoon salt
¾ cup granulated sugar
¾ cup superfine sugar
1 teaspoon almond extract
1 cup finely ground blanched almonds or hazelnuts

FILLING
1 recipe Chocolate Butter Cream Frosting, or Mocha, Nut, or Basic Butter Cream Frosting

TOPPING
¼ cup sifted confectioners' sugar

Preheat oven to 250° F. Beat egg whites until foamy; mix in cream of tartar and salt. Combine granulated and superfine sugars and add, 1 tablespoon at a time, beating all the while. This will take 10–12 minutes. Add almond extract and beat at highest mixer speed until glossy and stiff enough to stand straight up when beaters are withdrawn. Gently fold in ground nuts. Draw a 9″ circle on each of 2 foil-lined baking sheets. Dividing mixture equally, spread meringue evenly over each circle, keeping edges as neat as possible. Bake 1 hour until creamy-white and firm; turn oven off, and let meringues dry several hours or overnight *(avoid opening oven door while meringues dry)*. Carefully peel foil from meringues. Arrange 1 circle on a serving platter, spread with desired butter cream filling, using three fourths of the total amount. Top with second meringue, and dust top heavily with confectioners' sugar. Spoon remaining butter cream filling into a pastry bag fitted with a star tip and pipe a decorative border around edge of filling layer. Chill Dacquoise 3–4 hours (but no longer or meringue may become soggy). To serve, cut in wedges (use the *tip only* of a very sharp knife lest you crush the fragile Dacquoise).

NPS: 630 C, 25 mg CH, 255 mg S*

EIGHTEEN

Cakes, Fillings, and Frostings

The old-fashioned art of cake making is being threatened by the dozens of mixes on the market, also by a growing calorie consciousness. Consequently, this chapter is somewhat slimmer than cake chapters of other basic cookbooks. Still, there are plenty of recipes—some easy, some involved—for those who love to make cakes from "scratch" and those who want to learn how.

THE KINDS OF CAKES AND HOW TO MIX THEM

There are dozens of different kinds of cakes, descended from three basic types: *the butter or creamed cakes* (those containing butter or some fat, also baking powder or soda to leaven), *the sponge cakes* (air-leavened cakes made with a great many eggs or egg whites) and *the chiffon* (a combination of the butter and sponge, containing some fat—usually cooking oil—and a high proportion of eggs). The type of cake determines the method of mixing:

Butter Cakes:

Conventional Method of Mixing (this can be done either by hand or electric mixer): Have butter, margarine, or shortening at room temperature (except in sultry summer weather, when butter or margarine is best used straight from the refrigerator); cream (moderate mixer speed) until light, gradually add sugar, and cream until fluffy. Add eggs (or egg yolks), one at a time, beating

well after each addition. Add sifted dry ingredients (lowest mixer speed) alternately with the liquid, beginning and ending with the dry and adding one fourth to one third at a time. Finally, if eggs have been separated, beat whites to soft peaks and fold in by hand. *(Note:* If cake contains minced fruits and/or nuts, gently fold in at the end. To keep them from sinking to the bottom of the cake during baking, hold out a bit [about one fourth to one third] of the dry ingredients, toss with the minced fruits or nuts, and fold in along with them.)

Quick or One-Bowl Method: This streamlined way of mixing cakes more or less arrived with electric mixers and should not be used for old-fashioned butter cakes. It is closer to the muffin method of mixing than the conventional cake method in that the sifted dry ingredients go into the bowl first, the combined liquids are added all at once, and the two beaten just enough to blend (use low, then moderate mixer speed and scrape down beaters and sides of bowl as needed). Sometimes the eggs are separated, the yolks being added along with the other liquid ingredients and the whites folded in at the last.

Sponge Cakes (these include Angel Food as well as the different types of sponge):

True Sponge: Have egg yolks at room temperature and beat until frothy; add sugar gradually and beat until very thick and the color of cream (use moderate to high mixer speed or lots of elbow grease if beating by hand). Add sifted dry ingredients a little at a time and mix well after each addition (low mixer speed). Beat egg whites (also at room temperature) to soft peaks and fold in by hand.

Angel Food: These cakes can be made by electric mixer, but you'll get better volume if you do the beating by hand, preferably with a balloon whip in an unlined copper bowl. The trouble with mixers is that they overbeat and break down the egg whites. Even with hand beating there is great temptation to whip the whites into tall stiff peaks. Properly beaten, however, the peaks should be soft and the whites flow, not run, when the bowl is tipped. For greatest stability, they should be beaten with a little of the sugar; the remainder is sifted and added with the flour, a little at a time.

Chiffon Cakes: These are best made with an electric mixer. Flour, sugar, and other dry ingredients go into the bowl first; oil, egg yolks, liquids, and flavorings are added to a well in the dry ingredients and the mixture beaten at slow, then moderate speed, until batter is smooth and satiny. Egg whites, beaten to very stiff peaks, are then folded in just enough to blend.

ESSENTIAL INGREDIENTS FOR CAKES

A cake will be no better than what goes into it. Choose ingredients of top quality; do not improvise, substituting one ingredient for another, but use the types of sugars, flours, shortenings, and leavenings recipes specify.

Fat: Essential to butter cakes for texture, tenderness, and flavor. Butter adds the best flavor, but vegetable shortening, some cooks believe, produces a higher, more tender cake. By combining the two, you can produce a cake of exceptionally fine flavor and volume. Do not use margarine interchangeably for butter unless recipe gives it as an alternate; margarine has somewhat greater shortening power than butter, and in a cake of delicate balance it may make the cake fall or split. Do not use hard fats like lard for making cakes and do not use cooking oil unless recipes call for it.

Sugar: This, of course, means granulated sugar unless recipe specifies light or dark brown sugar. When using brown sugar, make sure it is fresh and soft and moist (it is virtually impossible to remove or beat out hard lumps from old, dried sugar). And when measuring brown sugar, *pack* the sugar into the measuring cup.

Eggs: Egg sizes vary enormously (see chapter on eggs, cheese, and dairy); those used in developing these recipes were large. For greater cake volume, have eggs at room temperature.

Flour: Cake and all-purpose flour can both be used in making cakes but should not be used interchangeably for one another, at least, not measure for measure. To use one in place of the other, make the following adjustments:

1 cup sifted cake flour = 7/8 cup sifted all-purpose flour
1 cup sifted all-purpose flour = 1 cup + 2 tablespoons sifted cake flour

Cake flour produces an exceptionally fine-textured, tender cake, and experts prefer it, especially for butter cakes. All-purpose flour, with slightly more body, is more reliable and a better choice for beginners. Self-rising flour, which contains both baking powder and salt, can be used in recipes calling for both baking powder and salt. To use, simply sift and measure the amount of flour called for and omit baking powder and salt. A word of caution: Self-rising flour should be absolutely fresh, otherwise it may not do a proper job of leavening. No matter what kind of flour you're using, always sift before measuring, spoon into the measure lightly, and level off top with the edge, not the flat side, of a knife or spatula. *A note about the presifted flours:* Though excellent for sauces and gravies, they do not produce as fine-grained cakes as the old-fashioned sift-yourself flours.

IMPORTANT NOTE: *All cake recipes in this book should be made with all-purpose flour unless recipe specifies cake flour.*

Leavenings: Air can leaven a cake and so can steam, but when we speak of leavenings, we usually mean baking soda (if cake contains sour milk or other acid ingredient) or baking powder. There are three basic kinds of baking powders: *double-acting,* which releases leavening gases on contact with moisture and again during baking; *tartrate,* a single-acting powder that releases a volume of gas the instant it's dampened, and *phosphate,* a slightly slower-to-react single-acting powder. (*Note:* These last two baking powders are becoming more and more difficult to find in American groceries. Veteran cake bakers partial to tartrate powders now routinely stock up when traveling abroad.) Read can labels carefully to determine which type of baking powder you're dealing with. Do not substitute one type for another unless you bear in mind that 1 teaspoon double-acting powder has the leavening power of 1½ teaspoons phosphate powder and 2 teaspoons tartrate powder. Tartrate powder is particularly tricky and should not be used unless the cake is mixed zip-quick and popped straight into the oven; it does, however, produce cakes of unusually fine grain. All baking powders lose potency on standing, so it's best to buy in small quantities and store tightly covered. *To test a baking powder's effectiveness:* Mix 1 teaspoon baking powder with ⅓ cup warm water; if it fizzes, the baking powder's good; if it doesn't, better buy a new supply. If you're in the middle of a cake and discover that your can of baking powder is inactive or empty, you can get by using this *emergency homemade baking powder:*

2 teaspoons cream of tartar ⎫ to leaven
1 teaspoon baking soda ⎬ each 1 cup
½ teaspoon salt ⎭ flour

IMPORTANT NOTE: *Baking powder in the cake recipes that follow is double-acting baking powder.*

Milk: Milk, in a cake recipe, means sweet whole milk.

Flavorings: Always use finest-quality true extracts or flavorings, not perfumy imitations that can spoil an otherwise fine cake. Also make sure nuts are strictly fresh.

SOME CAKE-MAKING TERMS AND TECHNIQUES

To Beat: This refers to vigorous mixing with a spoon (use a comfortable, long-handled wooden spoon for best results) in a round-and-round motion, also to beating with a rotary or electric mixer.

To Blend: To combine one ingredient with another until absolutely homogeneous, as in blending chocolate into a batter.

To Cream: To work one or more ingredients, usually fat or fat and sugar, by beating with an electric mixer or by pressing over and over against the side of a bowl with the back of a spoon until soft and creamy. Properly creamed for a cake, butter (or butter and sugar) will be very pale yellow, fluffy, and neither greasy nor sugary. This will take 3–4 minutes in an electric mixer. Sometimes, when eggs are added, mixture will seem to curdle; this will not affect the cake.

To Dredge: To toss chopped nuts, dried or candied fruits with flour, sugar, or other dry ingredients to prevent their sinking to the bottom of a cake during baking.

Dry Ingredients: Flour, baking powder or other leavening, salt (and sometimes cocoa or other dry ingredients) sifted together.

To Fill: To put layers of a cake together with filling (usually a softer mixture than frosting).

To Fold In: To incorporate one mixture into another, usually a light one such as beaten egg whites, into a batter using a very gentle over-and-over motion with minimum loss of lightness and air.

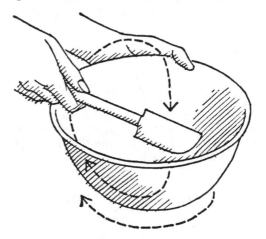

A rubber spatula is the best implement to use, though spoons, even portable electric mixers set at lowest speed and drawn through the mixture with a folding motion, work well.

To Frost: To spread with frosting.

To Glaze: To cover thinly with hard icing, fruit purée, or other shiny mixture.

To Ice: To frost.

To Mix: To blend a number of ingredients together by stirring or beating.

To Sift: To separate fine from coarse particles or to blend dry ingredients by passing them through a fine sieve or flour sifter.

To Stir: To mix in a circular motion, gently without beating.

To Whip: To beat rapidly with a whisk or rotary or electric beater to incorporate as much air as possible as in whipping cream or beating egg whites to stiff peaks.

To Work: To soften or blend by kneading or creaming.

HOW TO MAKE BETTER CAKES

Pans and Preparing Pans:

• For lightly, evenly browned cakes, use shiny baking pans rather than dark or discolored ones, which will overbrown—even burn—the cake. Do not use glass baking dishes unless you compensate for their slow heat conduction by raising oven temperature 25° F. They bake cakes too slowly, may dry them out, or form a thick hard crust all round. When using nonstick pans, follow manufacturer's directions closely, also watch baking cakes carefully until you learn how fast or slow pans conduct heat.

• Grease or grease and flour pans or not as recipes direct. As a general rule, any batter containing butter or other fat must be baked in a greased pan and, if extra rich, in a greased and floured pan. Grease bottoms of pans only unless recipes direct to the contrary. Cakes will rise more evenly all round if they can cling to ungreased pan sides.

• For greasing, use melted clarified butter* (unsalted) if you aren't on a budget, and shortening or cooking oil if you are. Apply thinly and evenly with a pastry brush or wad of paper toweling. (Note: The low-fat, no-cholesterol, spray-on vegetable compounds may also be used to grease cake pans. Use as package label directs.) (Note: If batter is extra rich or contains sticky fruit, you may even need to grease the nonstick pans.) To grease and flour, simply shake a small amount of flour into a greased pan, tilt back and forth until there is a thin, even layer of flour over bottom, then tap out excess.

• To simplify dishwashing, line pan bottoms with wax paper cut to fit or with packaged cake pan liners, available in most large department stores, then grease or not, as directed.

• For best results, always use pan sizes recipes specify. There are occasions, however, when a different shape is needed, and there are a number of batters that will bake successfully in pan shapes or sizes other than those recommended: all of the simple butter cakes, Real Sponge Cake, Devil's Food Cake, Nut Cake, Spice Cake, White Wedding Cake, Burnt Sugar Cake, Basic White Cake. Avoid changing pans for Pound Cake, any of the chiffons, other sponges and loaf cakes. Use the following table as a guide and, unless recipe specifies to the contrary, fill pans no more than half full. Bake any leftover batter as cupcakes.

Recommended Pan Size
2 (8") layers
  Alternate Pan Size
  1½–2 dozen cupcakes
3 (8") layers
  2 (9"×9"×2") pans

---

1 (9") layer
  1 (8"×8"×2") pan
2 (9") layers
  1 (13"×9"×2") pan
  1 (15½"×10½"×1") jelly-roll pan
  2 (8"×8"×2") pans
  1 (9") tube pan
  2½ dozen cupcakes

---

1 (13"×9"×2") pan
  2 (8"×8"×2") pans
  1 (10") tube pan
  2 (9") layers
  2 (15½"×10½"×1") jelly-roll pans
  2 (9"×5"×3") loaves

---

1 (9"×5"×3") pan
  1 (9"×9"×2") pan
  2 dozen cupcakes

Mixing Cakes:

• Read recipe through before beginning it and make sure you have all ingredients on hand.

• Have all utensils out, pans prepared, and ingredients measured and sifted before beginning.

• Have all ingredients at room temperature (except in very hot weather) before beginning. In summer, simply take straight from refrigerator.

• When using an electric mixer, use a medium speed for the creaming but a low speed for working in dry and liquid ingredients unless recipes direct to the contrary.

• When mixing by hand, use a comfortable, long-handled wooden spoon.

• Always cream fat and sugar thoroughly—it's virtually impossible to overbeat at this point. But mix in dry ingredients with a light touch, just enough to blend. Overbeating at this point will make the cake tough.

• Fold in beaten egg whites last, very gently, so you don't break down the volume.

Placing Batter in Pans:

• Always put batter in cool pans and never fill more than one half to two thirds full.

CAKES, FILLINGS, AND FROSTINGS

• Spread batter well to edges of pan.
• When making a layer cake, apportion batter evenly between pans so layers will be of equal size. Using an ice-cream ball scoop and filling pans by adding a scoopful of batter first to one pan and then the other is a trick experts use.
• Once pans are filled, tap gently to break any large air bubbles.

Baking:

• Have oven checked and regulated often by a local serviceman so it is as accurate as possible. Also make sure it stands level on the floor, otherwise cakes may be lopsided.
• Let oven preheat a full 15 minutes before baking.
• Unless recipes direct otherwise, bake cakes as near the center of the oven as possible. Those placed too low may burn on the bottom; those placed too high, on top.
• When baking several cakes or layers at once, stagger on shelves, leaving plenty of room around them so heat can circulate evenly. Never let pans touch each other or oven walls.
• Cake baking time breaks down into four quarters, the first two being the most critical (don't open oven door during this time or jar oven in any way).

First Quarter of Baking	. . .	cake begins to rise
Second Quarter of Baking	. . .	cake continues to rise and browns slightly
Third Quarter of Baking	. . .	cake continues browning
Fourth Quarter of Baking	. . .	cake finishes browning and shrinks from sides of pan

Baking Cakes in a Convection Oven

Baking via convection (hot circulating air) produces beautifully, *evenly* browned cakes whether those cakes are made from scratch or a commercial mix. Some convection ovens need not be preheated before they're used; most, however, should be used at temperatures 50°–75° F. below those recommended for conventional ovens, especially for baking cakes. (*Note:* Never use temperatures lower than 300° F.) Before so much as baking a cupcake, study your convection oven's instruction manual; also read Convection Ovens in Chapter 1, then observe these tips:
• Use shiny metal pans for light and tender-crusted cakes.

• Use center oven rack only for cake baking (using more than one rack blocks air circulation).
• Allow at least 1″ space between pans, also between pans and oven walls.
• Test cakes for doneness 5–10 minutes before end of suggested baking time; some cakes bake faster in convection ovens—even at reduced temperatures.

To Tell When Cakes Are Done, Use the Following Tests:
• Insert cake tester or toothpick in center of cake; if it comes out clean with no crumbs adhering, cake is done.
• Gently press top of cake; if it is springy to the touch and finger leaves no imprint, cake is done.
• Examine edges of pan; if cake has pulled away from pan, it is done.

Baking Cakes in a Microwave Oven

Microwaved cakes are uncommonly moist and feathery, and because no crust forms during baking to impede rising, they rise to great heights. Most, moreover, cook in one third the time (a single cupcake takes just 25–30 seconds!). The bad news is that cakes do not brown and often appear sticky and uneven on top (obviously, the best cakes to microwave are those that will be frosted). Recipe ingredients and quantity of batter both affect microwave baking times as do power levels, which vary from oven to oven. So study your oven manual before microwaving any cake; also read Microwave Ovens in Chapter 1, then follow these guidelines:
• Do not microwave any cake made without butter and egg yolks—angel or chiffon cake, for example. Each needs a conventional oven's dry heat to bake properly.
• For best results, use cake recipes developed specifically for the microwave (begin with those in your oven's instruction manual, or try a commercial mix, following package directions).
• Use *round, square,* or *tube* or *fluted ring molds* or *pans (not rectangular shapes)* made of flameproof glass or plastic-coated "active" microwave cookware (see Microwave Utensil Guide, Chapter 1). Glass containers allow you to check the progress of baking easily; microwave cookware makes cakes bake more evenly.
• Grease *round* or *square pans,* then line with ungreased wax paper or paper toweling (this absorbs moisture in batter and reduces cake wetness). *Tube* or *fluted ring pans or molds* should simply be greased or coated

with one of the low-fat, no-cholesterol, spray-on vegetable compounds. *(Note:* Never flour a pan; the flour covers the cake with ugly scum.) *Tip:* You can coat a greased tube pan with finely chopped nuts, graham cracker crumbs, or this *Nut-Streusel Mix* (1/3 cup finely chopped toasted blanched almonds mixed with 1/4 cup firmly packed light brown sugar and 1 teaspoon cinnamon).

• No more than half fill cake pans (bake excess batter as cupcakes; see Special Baking Tips for Cupcakes at end of this section). Cut through batter with a spatula to remove air bubbles.

• Microwave cakes on a trivet, uncovered, as manufacturer directs, rotating pans 90° every 3 minutes.

• Test often for doneness toward end of microwaving time. When done, a microwaved cake will be springy to the touch and just barely shrunk from pan sides. The top should be mostly dry, although a few damp spots are normal (these will disappear as cake *stands*). If you've used a glass container, examine cake bottom; only a small area (about 2″) in the center should be moist (this will also disappear during *standing*). If you've used a tube pan, do not remove cake from oven until top seems completely dry (these pans are so deep that moist spots will not have time to finish cooking during *standing time*).

• After removing cake from the microwave oven, let it *stand* 5 minutes on a heat-resistant counter or wooden board, then insert a toothpick in center of cake; it should come out clean. If it does not, or if moist spots have not evaporated on top and bottom of cake, or if center of cake starts to sink, microwave cake 30–60 seconds longer; let stand and test as before.

• Cool cake upright on a wire rack 10–15 minutes, then loosen edges carefully with a metal spatula, and invert cake on rack. Remove paper, if any, turn cake right-side-up, and cool thoroughly before frosting. *Note:* Do not let microwaved cakes stand uncovered for long; with no crust to retard staling, they dry out fast. *Note:* If a cooled cake seems too soft to frost, refrigerate, uncovered, 15–20 minutes. Or dust with confectioners' sugar, or sprinkle with Nut-Streusel Mix instead of frosting.

Special Baking Tips for Cupcakes: These bake so fast in a microwave that they require special handling. *Note:* Most cupcake batters can be stored in the refrigerator 3–4 days; just pour out what you need and bake cupcakes to order.

• Do not use standard muffin pans for baking cupcakes. Instead, use *custard cups* or a *round microwave cupcaker.* Line each cup with 2 paper cupcake liners, which will support the cupcakes as they rise (meaning evenly shaped cupcakes) and absorb moisture (less sticky cupcakes).

• When pouring batter into liners, no more than half fill each (cupcakes rise impressively during microwaving).

• When microwaving several cupcakes in custard cups, cluster them as nearly in a circle as possible instead of arranging in a straight line (they'll cook more evenly).

• Microwave cupcakes, uncovered, as oven manufacturer suggests, rearranging individual cups or rotating cupcaker 180° at half time.

• To test cupcakes for doneness, insert a toothpick in center; it should come out clean. *Note:* There may be small moist spots on tops of cupcakes, but worry not; these will dry as cupcakes cool.

• Remove baked cupcakes from custard cups or cupcaker, but not from paper liners. Cool on a wire rack, then frost or dust with confectioners' sugar. *Note:* If cupcakes have holes inside, try this with the next batch: cut through unbaked batter in cupcake liners several times with a toothpick. This should eliminate air bubbles and prevent holes from forming as cupcakes bake.

Cooling Cakes and Removing from Pans:

Butter Cakes:
• Cool upright in pans on a wire rack about 10 minutes before turning out.
• Loosen edges of cake with a spatula, invert cake on rack, then turn right-side-up and cool thoroughly before frosting.

Sponge and Chiffon Cakes:
• Cool cake thoroughly upside down in pan. If pan does not have "feet" so that it will stand upside down, simply "hang" on a 1-liter soft drink bottle by inserting bottle neck into pan tube.
• Loosen cake edges (and around center tube) and invert on cake plate. Do not turn right-side-up.

Storing and Keeping Cakes: Any cake with a custard or whipped cream filling or frosting should be kept refrigerated. Others last longest kept in a cake keeper in a cool spot. Fruit cakes should be wrapped in rum- or fruit-juice-soaked cheesecloth, then in foil and stored airtight in a cool, dark place. *Note:* Most unfrosted cakes freeze well; wrap snugly in foil or plastic food wrap, label, date, then store at 0° F. They will keep well several months.

How to Cut Tiered Wedding Cakes:

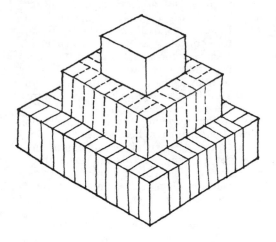

The cutting procedure for tiered cakes, whether round or square, is essentially the same. Cut bottom tier all around, then cut middle tier, again cut bottom tier, lift off top tier and present to bride, finally, cut remaining middle tier.

WHY THINGS SOMETIMES GO WRONG WITH CAKES

Occasionally, despite all care and precaution, a cake will fail. Here are some common causes of cake failures, and how to recognize and remedy them.

Description	*Cause*
Collapsed Center	Too much sugar or shortening; too little baking powder; underbaking
Fallen Cake	Same as collapsed center; also too little flour
Lopsided Cake	Unlevel oven shelves; also, sometimes, cake pans touching one another or oven walls
Cake Overflowing Pan	Using too small a pan
Heavy Cake	Too much sugar or too little baking powder
Dry Cake	Too much flour or too little shortening; also overbaking
Coarse Texture	Too much shortening or baking powder; undermixing; too low an oven heat
Uneven Texture	Undermixing
Cracked or Uneven Top	Too much flour or too hot an oven
Sticky Top or Crust	Too much sugar
Uneven Browning	Crowding oven rack; using dark pans; baking at too high a temperature

BASIC TWO-EGG BUTTER CAKE

2 (8″) layers (12 servings)   ¢

An economical all-purpose cake.

1¾ cups sifted cake flour
2 teaspoons baking powder
¼ teaspoon salt
½ cup milk
1 teaspoon vanilla
½ cup butter or margarine, softened to room
   temperature
1 cup sugar
2 eggs

Preheat oven to 375° F. Sift flour with baking powder and salt and set aside; combine milk and vanilla. Cream butter until light, add sugar gradually, continuing to cream until fluffy. Add eggs, one at a time, beating well after each addition. Add dry ingredients alternately with milk, beginning and ending with the dry and adding about one third of total at a time. Beat *just* until smooth. Spoon into 2 greased and floured 8″ layer cake pans and bake 25–30 minutes until cakes shrink slightly from sides of pans and are springy to the touch; cool upright in pans on wire racks 5–7 minutes, then invert on racks. Turn layers right-side-up and cool completely. Fill and frost as desired.

NPS (with butter, unfrosted): 205 C, 65 mg CH, 210 mg S*

BASIC THREE-EGG BUTTER CAKE

2 (9″) layers (16 servings)

Slightly richer than the Two-Egg Butter Cake (preceding recipe).

2 cups sifted cake flour
2 teaspoons baking powder
1/4 teaspoon salt
1/2 cup milk
1 teaspoon vanilla
1/2 cup butter or margarine, softened to room temperature
1 cup sugar
3 eggs, separated

Preheat oven to 375° F. Sift flour with baking powder and salt and set aside; combine milk and vanilla. Cream butter until light, add sugar gradually, continuing to cream until fluffy. Add egg yolks, one at a time, beating well after each addition. Add dry ingredients alternately with milk, beginning and ending with the dry and adding about one third of total at a time; beat *just* until smooth. Beat egg whites until soft peaks form, and gently fold into batter. Spoon into 2 greased and floured 9″ layer cake pans and bake 25–30 minutes until cakes shrink slightly from sides of pans and are springy to the touch; cool upright in pans on wire racks 5–7 minutes; then invert on racks. Turn right-side-up and cool completely. Fill and frost as desired.

NPS (with butter, unfrosted): 165 C, 70 mg CH, 165 mg S*

VARIATIONS

Basic Chocolate Butter Cake: Cream butter well with 1 1/4 cups sugar as directed, add 3 *whole* eggs, beating well after each addition; blend in 3 (1-ounce) squares unsweetened chocolate, melted, or 3 (1-ounce) envelopes no-melt unsweetened chocolate. Add dry ingredients alternately with 2/3 cup milk mixed with 1 teaspoon vanilla, then proceed as recipe directs. Fill and frost as desired.

NPS (with butter, unfrosted): 190 C, 70 mg CH, 165 mg S*

Mocha Butter Cake: Prepare Basic Chocolate Butter Cake as directed but blend 1 ta-blespoon instant coffee powder with milk and vanilla. Fill and frost with Mocha Butter Cream Frosting.

NPS (with butter, unfrosted): 190 C, 70 mg CH, 165 mg S*

Poppy Seed Cake: Pour milk called for over 1/3 cup poppy seeds and let stand at room temperature 3–4 hours, then proceed as recipe directs. Fill with Poppy Seed Cream Filling and frost with a butter cream frosting.

NPS (with butter, unfrosted): 180 C, 70 mg CH, 165 mg S*

SWEET LEMON LOAF

1 (9″ × 5″ × 3″) loaf (8 servings)

This cake is very tender, so slice it thick.

1 1/2 cups sifted flour
1 1/2 teaspoons baking powder
1/4 teaspoon salt
1/2 cup butter or margarine, softened to room temperature
1 cup sugar
2 eggs
1/2 cup milk
Finely grated rind and juice of 1 lemon
1/2 cup coarsely chopped pecans or walnuts (optional)

GLAZE
Juice of 1 lemon
1/4 cup sugar

Preheat oven to 350° F. Sift flour with baking powder and salt and set aside. Cream butter until light, slowly add sugar and beat until fluffy. Add eggs, one at a time, beating well after each addition. Add dry ingredients alternately with milk, beginning and ending with the dry and adding about one third of the total at a time. Add lemon rind and juice and beat *just* until smooth. Stir in nuts, if you like, and spoon into a greased and floured 9″ × 5″ × 3″ loaf pan. Bake about 1 hour until cake pulls from sides of pan and is springy to the touch. Let cool upright in pan on a wire rack while you make the glaze. Heat lemon juice and sugar over low heat, stirring until sugar dissolves. Pour evenly over top of cake and let cake cool thoroughly in pan before turning out. Wrap tightly and store overnight before cutting.

NPS (with butter, without nuts): 335 C, 100 mg CH, 290 mg S*

BASIC WHITE OR SILVER CAKE

2 (9") layers (16 servings)

For a really silvery cake, use vegetable shortening.

2½ cups sifted cake flour
1 tablespoon baking powder
½ teaspoon salt
⅔ cup butter, margarine, or vegetable shortening
1½ cups sugar
1 teaspoon vanilla
½ teaspoon almond extract
¾ cup milk
4 egg whites, at room temperature

Preheat oven to 375° F. Sift flour with baking powder and salt and set aside. Cream butter until light, gradually add 1¼ cups sugar, continuing to cream until fluffy. Add vanilla and almond extract and at low speed, mix in dry ingredients alternately with the milk, beginning and ending with the dry and adding about one third of the total at a time. In a separate bowl beat egg whites until frothy, slowly add remaining sugar, and beat to very soft peaks. Fold into batter just until blended. Spoon into 2 greased and floured 9" layer cake pans and bake 20–25 minutes until cakes shrink slightly from sides of pans and are springy to the touch. Cool upright in pans on wire racks 5 minutes, then invert on racks, turn right-side-up, and cool completely. Fill and frost as desired.

NPS (with butter, unfrosted): 210 C, 20 mg CH, 245 mg S*

VARIATIONS

Marble Cake: Prepare batter as directed and divide in half. Blend 3 tablespoons cocoa with 3 tablespoons hot water and mix into half the batter. Drop alternate spoonfuls of white and chocolate batter into pans, dividing amounts equally; zigzag a knife through batter to marbleize and bake as directed.

NPS (with butter, unfrosted): 210 C, 20 mg CH, 245 mg S*

Rainbow Cake: Prepare batter as directed and divide in 3 equal parts. Tint one pink, one yellow, and one green (or, if you prefer, leave one plain). Layer equal amounts of each color in each pan and bake as directed. When cool, put layers together with any white or pastel frosting (7-Minute is particularly good). Divide remaining frosting in 3 parts and tint as you did cake batter. Put alternate spoonfuls of each color on top and sides of cake, then swirl with a broad spatula to marbleize. If you like, scatter crushed peppermint candy on top.

NPS (with butter, unfrosted, without candy): 210 C, 20 mg CH, 245 mg S*

Lady Baltimore Cake: Prepare cake as directed; also prepare 1 recipe 7-Minute Frosting. To about one third of the frosting, add ¾ cup coarsely chopped pecans or walnuts, ½ cup seedless raisins, ⅓ cup diced dried figs, and ¼ teaspoon almond extract; put cake layers together with the fruit frosting, then ice with remaining 7-Minute Frosting.

NPS (with butter and pecans): 345 C, 20 mg CH, 255 mg S*

Coconut Cream Cake: Prepare cake as directed; also prepare a double recipe of Basic Vanilla Cream Filling; divide in half and mix ½ cup flaked coconut into 1 part. Put cake layers together with coconut filling. Spread remaining filling over top and sides of cake, then coat thickly with flaked coconut (about 1½ cups).

NPS (with butter): 320 C, 60 mg CH, 265 mg S*

BOSTON CREAM PIE

A 2-layer (9") cake (16 servings)

2 (9") layers Basic Three-Egg Butter Cake, Real Sponge Cake, or layers made from a yellow cake mix
1 recipe Basic Vanilla Cream Filling, Double Cream Filling, or 1½ cups sweetened whipped cream
1 recipe Chocolate Glaze

Sandwich cake layers together with filling, spread glaze on top, and let stand until glaze hardens. Store in refrigerator.

NPS (with Basic Three-Egg Butter Cake and Basic Vanilla Cream Filling): 290 C, 85 mg CH, 170 mg S*

WHITE WEDDING CAKE

1 (3-tier) cake (about 100 servings)

Begin recipe about 3–4 days before the wedding. For a 3-tier cake, each 2 cake layers thick, you will need to triple the batter recipe given below. Make 3 separate lots rather than a giant unmanageable one. You will need: 1 (13") round cake pan about 2½" deep, 2 (10"), and 2 (7") round cake pans of similar depth (these special wedding cake pans can be bought at specialty shops and confectionery supply houses); a heavy 16" circle of plywood neatly covered with heavy foil; 1 (10") and 1 (7") white cardboard cake divider; a large lazy Susan to simplify decorating; and a pastry bag and decorative star tip.

BATTER *(Make Up 3 Separate Batches)*
6 cups sifted flour
2 tablespoons baking powder
2 teaspoons salt
2 cups milk, at room temperature
2 teaspoons vanilla
1 pound butter or margarine or 1⅓ cups
margarine and ⅔ cup vegetable shortening
4 cups sugar
8 eggs, at room temperature
2 teaspoons lemon extract
2 tablespoons finely grated lemon rind

FILLING
1 recipe Pineapple-Coconut Filling

FROSTING
4 times the recipe Basic Lemon or Orange
Butter Cream Frosting, tinted pale pink or
yellow if you like

DECORATIONS
About 4 yards narrow white satin ribbon
Small sprays of artificial or real flowers
matching bride's bouquet *(Note:* **Do not use**
lilies of the valley, which are poisonous)

Preheat oven to 325° F. Sift flour with baking powder and salt and set aside. Combine milk and vanilla. Cream butter until light, add sugar gradually, continue to cream until fluffy. Add eggs, one at a time, beating well after each addition. Mix in lemon extract and rind. Add dry ingredients alternately with milk, beginning and ending with the dry and adding about one sixth of the total at a time. Beat just until smooth. Spoon into 1 ungreased 13″ and 1 ungreased 7″ round cake pan lined on the bottom with wax paper, *filling no more than half full* (this is a high-rising batter). Cover small pan with wax paper and refrigerate; bake large layer 60–65 minutes until it pulls from sides of pan and is springy to the touch. Cool upright in pan on wire rack 10 minutes, then loosen and invert on rack; peel off paper, turn right-side-up, and cool thoroughly. Meanwhile, mix a second batch of batter, cover bowl, and refrigerate until needed. Wash, dry, and reline 13″ pan with wax paper, half fill with batter; also half fill second 7″ pan, cover, and refrigerate. Bake 13″ layer as before, turn out and cool. Mix a third batch of batter, spoon into the 2 (10″) pans, ungreased but lined on the bottom with wax paper, filling no more than half full; cover with wax paper and refrigerate. When both large layers are baked, raise oven to 350° F. and bake the 2 small- and 2 medium-size layers, staggering on oven shelves and allowing plenty of space between pans. Small layers will bake in 40–45 minutes, the medium in about 50. Cool and turn out as you did the large layers. When all cakes are thoroughly cool, wrap airtight in foil and store in a cool place, not refrigerator. *(Note:* Any leftover batter can be baked as cupcakes—do not more than half fill muffin cups.)

To Assemble and Frost Cake: Center foil-covered plywood circle on lazy Susan and cover outer rim with wax paper triangles, letting points hang over (these are to catch frosting drips). Center 1 (13″) layer on board, spread with filling and top with second (13″) layer, bottom-side-up. Spread lightly with frosting, just to seal in crumbs. Place a 10″ layer on a 10″ divider, spread with filling, and center on 13″ tier; top with second (10″) layer, bottom-side-up, and frost top lightly. Set 7″ layer on 7″ divider, spread with filling, and center on 10″ tier; top with final 7″ layer. Beginning at the top, lightly frost sides of each tier to seal in crumbs and let dry at room temperature 1–2 hours. Starting again at the top, frost entire cake. *(Note:* If you plan to decorate with frosting, make surface as smooth as possible.)* For a simple finish, swirl frosting into waves with a wide metal spatula. Let dry 2 hours before decorating further.

To Decorate: Beginning at the top, pipe decorative borders around base of top and middle tiers, then add rosettes, scrolls, any designs you fancy (see Tips on Decorating Cakes). Pull out wax paper triangles around base of cake and pipe a decorative border around base of cake. Keep in a cool, dust-free place or invert a very large cardboard carton over cake, making sure top and sides do not touch.

Final Trimmings: On the day of the wedding, make rosettes from the ribbon and arrange with tiny flower sprays between the tiers, "gluing" to cake with a little frosting. Decorate top with small posies wreathed in ribbon or any suitable commercial decorations. Keep cool until serving time.

To Serve: See How to Cut Tiered Wedding Cakes.

NPS (with butter): 420 C, 105 mg CH, 395 mg S*

POUND CAKE

1 (9″ × 5″ × 3″) loaf (10 servings)

Here is a truly old-fashioned pound cake made without baking powder so the texture will be firm, fine, and moist. Top of cake will crack slightly during baking, but this is normal. *Note:* The ingredients in this cake are

---

delicately balanced, so make no substitutions.

2¼ cups sifted cake flour
¼ teaspoon salt
⅛ teaspoon nutmeg or mace
1 cup butter (no substitute), softened to room
  temperature
1 cup sugar
5 eggs, separated
1 teaspoon vanilla or orange extract or 1
  tablespoon finely grated lemon rind

Preheat oven to 350° F. Line bottom of a 9″ × 5″ × 3″ loaf pan with wax paper; grease paper well, also sides of pan. Sift flour, salt, and nutmeg together and set aside. Cream butter until light, then add sugar slowly, creaming until fluffy. Beat egg yolks until thick and light, add to butter mixture, a little at a time, beating well after each addition. Blend flour in gradually, then mix in vanilla and beat *just* until smooth. Beat egg whites until soft peaks form and fold gently into batter. Spoon into pan and bake 65–70 minutes until cake pulls slightly from sides of pan. Cool upright in pan on a wire cake rack 30 minutes; carefully turn out, peel off wax paper, turn cake right-side-up, then cool thoroughly before slicing.

NPS: 360 C, 185 mg CH, 275 mg S*

THELMA'S 1, 2, 3, 4 CAKE

1 (9″) tube cake (16 servings)

This cake keeps well if wrapped airtight; it also freezes well.

3 cups sifted flour
2 teaspoons baking powder
¼ teaspoon salt
1 cup milk
1 teaspoon vanilla, almond, lemon, or orange
  extract
1 cup butter or margarine, softened to room
  temperature, or vegetable shortening
2 cups sugar
4 eggs, separated

Preheat oven to 350° F. Sift flour with baking powder and salt and set aside; combine milk and vanilla. Cream butter until light; add sugar gradually, continuing to cream until fluffy. Beat egg yolks until thick and pale yellow; mix into creamed mixture. Add dry ingredients alternately with milk, beginning and ending with the dry and adding about one third of the total at a time. Beat *just* until smooth. Beat egg whites until soft peaks form and gently fold into batter. Spoon into a greased and floured 9″ tube

pan and bake about 1 hour until cake shrinks slightly from sides of pan and is springy to the touch. Cool cake upright in its pan on a wire rack 25–30 minutes; loosen edges, invert on rack, and cool thoroughly. Serve plain or frost with a butter cream frosting.

NPS (with butter, unfrosted): 305 C, 100 mg CH, 230 mg S*

CRAZY CHOCOLATE CAKE

2 (9″) layers (16 servings)   ⊠

"Crazy" in that the method of mixing is wholly unconventional. The cake, however, is unusually fine-grained.

G R O U P I
2 cups sugar
1 cup sour milk
1 cup butter, softened to room temperature (no
  substitute)
1½ teaspoons vanilla
3 cups sifted cake flour

G R O U P I I
2 eggs
¾ cup unsifted cocoa
2 teaspoons baking soda
¼ teaspoon salt
1 cup boiling strong coffee

Preheat oven to 325° F. Add ingredients to a large mixing bowl by alternating between Groups I and II. For example, first into bowl would be sugar, second eggs, third sour milk, fourth cocoa, and so on. Do not mix. When all ingredients are in the bowl, beat 1 minute with an electric mixer at moderate speed or 3 minutes by hand. Pour into 2 well-greased 9″ layer cake pans and bake 45–50 minutes until cakes shrink slightly from sides of pans and are springy to the touch. Cool upright in pans on wire racks 5–7 minutes, then invert to remove. Turn cakes right-side-up and cool thoroughly. Fill and frost as desired (good with 7-Minute Frosting).

NPS (unfrosted): 295 C, 65 mg CH, 270 mg S*

DEVIL'S FOOD CAKE

2 (9″) layers (16 servings)   ¢

Dark and rich.

2 cups sifted cake flour
2 cups sugar
½ cup cocoa
1 teaspoon baking soda
½ teaspoon salt

1/2 cup vegetable shortening
1¼ cups milk
1 teaspoon vanilla
3 eggs
1 teaspoon baking powder

Preheat oven to 350° F. Sift flour, sugar, co-coa, baking soda, and salt into large electric mixer bowl. Drop in shortening and add ¾ cup milk and the vanilla. Mix at lowest speed 15 seconds just to blend. (*Note:* Hold a towel over bowl to catch splatters.) Beat 2 minutes at medium speed, scraping bowl and beaters once or twice. Add remaining ingredients and beat 2 minutes longer. Spoon into 2 ungreased (9″) layer cake pans lined with wax paper and bake 40–45 minutes until cakes shrink slightly from sides of pan and are springy to the touch. Cool upright in pans on wire racks 5 minutes, then invert on racks, peel off paper, turn right-side-up, and cool completely. Fill and frost as desired.

NPS (unfrosted): 230 C, 55 mg CH, 170 mg S*

VARIATIONS

¢ **Devil's Food Loaf** (*24 servings*): Prepare as directed and bake in an ungreased 13″ × 9″ × 2″ pan lined with wax paper. Same time, same temperature.

NPS (unfrosted): 155 C, 35 mg CH, 115 mg S*

Mocha Fudge Cake (*16 servings*): Prepare as directed but substitute 3 melted (1-ounce) squares unsweetened chocolate or 3 (1-ounce) envelopes no-melt unsweetened chocolate for the cocoa, add 1 tablespoon instant coffee powder and mix in with the shortening.

NPS (unfrosted): 250 C, 55 mg CH, 170 mg S*

SACHERTORTE

1 (9″) cake (16 servings)

Sachertorte, Vienna's famous chocolate cake, is densely dark and rich. It was invented 150 years or so ago by Franz Sacher for Prince Metternich when calories meant nothing.

1 cup sifted cake flour
¼ teaspoon salt
6 (1-ounce) squares unsweetened or semisweet chocolate
¾ cup butter, softened to room temperature (no substitute)
1 cup sugar
6 egg yolks
8 egg whites
1 cup apricot preserves

1 recipe Chocolate Glaze
1 cup heavy cream, whipped to soft peaks (optional topping)

Preheat oven to 350° F. Sift flour with salt and set aside. Melt chocolate over simmering water, then cool. Cream butter until light, gradually add ¾ cup sugar and cream until fluffy. Add egg yolks, one at a time, beating well after each addition. Beat in chocolate, scraping bowl often until thoroughly blended. In a separate bowl, beat egg whites until frothy; gradually add remaining sugar and beat until soft peaks form. Stir about ½ cup egg whites into creamed mixture. Sift and fold in flour alternately with remaining egg whites, beginning and ending with flour and adding about one fourth at a time. Spoon into a 9″ spring form pan lined on the bottom with wax paper, then greased and floured on bottom *and* sides. Tap pan lightly on counter to break any large bubbles. Bake on center oven rack 45–55 minutes, until top is springy to the touch. Cool upright in pan on a wire rack 10 minutes, loosen cake, and remove spring form; invert cake on rack, remove pan bottom, and carefully peel off paper. Turn right-side-up and cool completely on rack. Halve cake horizontally, spread with preserves, put layers together and spread top thinly with preserves. Spoon Chocolate Glaze on top and let stand until set. Cut in small pieces and serve topped with whipped cream.

NPS (without cream): 385 C, 125 mg CH, 155 mg S*
NPS (with cream): 435 C, 145 mg CH, 160 mg S*

BÛCHE DE NOËL (CHRISTMAS LOG)

1 roll (12 servings)

A rich chocolate log traditionally served on Christmas Eve in France.

½ cup sifted cake flour
¾ teaspoon baking powder
¼ teaspoon salt
4 eggs, at room temperature
¾ cup sugar
1 teaspoon vanilla
3 (1-ounce) squares unsweetened chocolate, melted, or 3 (1-ounce) envelopes no-melt unsweetened chocolate
2 tablespoons very strong warm black coffee
Sifted cocoa
2 recipes Mocha or Chocolate Butter Cream Frosting

Preheat oven to 400° F. Line the bottom of a 15½″ × 10½″ × 1″ jelly-roll pan with wax paper. Sift flour with baking powder and salt and set aside. With electric or rotary beater, beat eggs at high speed until foamy; slowly add sugar, a little at a time, and beat until very thick and cream colored. Mix in vanilla, blend chocolate with coffee and mix into batter. Fold in dry ingredients just until blended. Spoon into pan, spreading batter evenly. Bake 12–14 minutes until springy to the touch. Loosen edges of cake and invert on a clean dish towel heavily sprinkled with sifted cocoa. Peel off paper and cut off crisp edges with a sharp knife. Beginning at the short side, roll cake and towel up; cool completely on a wire rack. Unroll, remove towel, spread about 1 cup mocha frosting to within 1/2″ of edges and carefully reroll. Wrap loosely in foil and chill 1 hour. With a sharp knife, cut a small piece from each end on the diagonal and reserve to make "branches." Place roll seam-side-down on serving plate and tuck a strip of wax paper under each side. Spread with remaining frosting, then draw fork tines in a wavy pattern the length of log to resemble bark or use a serrated ribbon tip and a pastry bag to force frosting out in a ridged bark effect. Lay trimmed-off ends on roll cut-side-down at an angle, off center. Press into frosting lightly, then frost edges. If you wish, sprinkle log with minced pistachio nuts and write "Noel" in white decorative icing.

NPS (with Mocha Butter Cream Frosting, no decorations): 590 C, 125 mg CH, 295 mg S*

BURNT SUGAR CAKE

A 2-layer (9″) cake (16 servings)

BURNT SUGAR SYRUP
3/4 cup sugar
3/4 cup boiling water

CAKE
3 cups sifted cake flour
1 tablespoon baking powder
1/2 teaspoon salt
1/2 cup milk
1 teaspoon vanilla
1 teaspoon maple flavoring (optional)
1/2 cup Burnt Sugar Syrup
3/4 cup butter or margarine
1 1/3 cups sugar
3 eggs

FROSTING
1/3 cup butter or margarine
1 (1-pound) box confectioners' sugar, sifted
1/4 cup Burnt Sugar Syrup
1 teaspoon vanilla
1/4 teaspoon salt

For syrup: Melt sugar in a heavy skillet or saucepan over low heat, stirring now and then. Heat, stirring constantly, until amber colored. Off heat, gradually stir in boiling water (it will foam up), return to low heat, and stir until sugar dissolves. Cool to room temperature. Preheat oven to 350° F. Sift flour with baking powder and salt and set aside. Mix milk with flavorings and 1/2 cup Burnt Sugar Syrup. Cream butter until light, add sugar gradually, creaming until fluffy. Add eggs, one at a time, beating well after each addition. Add dry ingredients alternately with milk mixture, beginning and ending with the dry and adding about one third of the total at a time. Beat just until smooth. Spoon into 2 ungreased 9″ layer pans lined with wax paper. Bake about 1/2 hour until cakes pull from sides of pan and are springy to the touch. Cool upright in pans on wire racks 5 minutes, loosen, and invert on racks; peel off paper, turn right-side-up, and cool. For the frosting: Cream butter until fluffy, beat in sugar, a little at a time, adding alternately with the syrup. Mix in vanilla and salt and beat until satiny and of good spreading consistency. If mixture seems stiff, thin with a little additional syrup. Put cake layers together with some frosting, then frost with the remainder.

NPS (with butter): 405 C, 85 mg CH, 325 mg S*

NUT CAKE

1 (13″ × 9″ × 2″) cake (24 servings)

Use the nuts you like best for making this cake.

2 cups sifted cake flour
1 1/2 teaspoons baking powder
1/2 teaspoon salt
1/3 cup milk, at room temperature
1 teaspoon vanilla
1/2 teaspoon almond extract
1 cup butter or margarine
1 cup sugar
3 eggs
1 1/4 cups finely chopped toasted nuts (pecans, walnuts or black walnuts, filberts, or almonds)
Few untoasted nut halves (garnish)

Preheat oven to 350° F. Sift flour with baking powder and salt and set aside. Mix milk, vanilla, and almond extract. Cream butter until light, add sugar gradually, continuing to cream until fluffy. Add eggs, one at a time, beating well after each addition. Add flour alternately with milk, beginning and ending with flour. Stir in chopped nuts. Spoon into an ungreased 13″ × 9″ × 2″

pan lined on the bottom with wax paper and scatter nut halves on top. Bake about 1/2 hour until cake pulls from sides of pan and is springy to the touch. Cool upright in pan on a wire rack 10 minutes, loosen edges of cake, invert on rack, peel off paper, turn right-side-up, and cool thoroughly. *(Note:* If you prefer, omit garnish and, when cake is cool, frost as desired.)

NPS (with butter and walnuts, unfrosted, no garnish): 185 C, 55 mg CH, 160 mg S*

VARIATIONS

Nut Layer Cake *(16 servings):* Prepare batter as directed, spoon into 2 ungreased 9" layer cake pans lined on the bottom with wax paper and bake 25–30 minutes at 350° F. until cakes test done. Cool as directed; fill and frost as desired.

NPS (with butter and walnuts, unfrosted, no garnish): 275 C, 85 mg CH, 240 mg S*

Nut-Seed Cake *(24 servings):* Add 2 tablespoons caraway or poppy seeds to cake batter along with flour.

NPS (with butter and walnuts, unfrosted, no garnish): 185 C, 55 mg CH, 160 mg S*

Nut-Candied Fruit Cake *(24 servings):* Add 1/2 cup minced mixed candied fruit to cake batter along with flour.

NPS (with butter and walnuts, unfrosted, no garnish): 200 C, 55 mg CH, 175 mg S*

Orange-Nut Cake *(24 servings):* Prepare as directed but add the finely grated rind of 2 oranges to creamed mixture before adding eggs.

NPS (with butter and walnuts, unfrosted, no garnish): 185 C, 55 mg CH, 160 mg S*

Chocolate-Nut Cake *(24 servings):* Prepare as directed but add 4 melted 1-ounce squares semisweet chocolate to creamed mixture before adding eggs.

NPS (with butter and walnuts, unfrosted, no garnish): 205 C, 55 mg CH, 160 mg S*

WALNUT TORTE

2 (9") layers (16 servings)

No flour needed in this *torte;* the nuts and bread crumbs give it body.

1 cup lightly packed, finely ground walnuts or black walnuts
1/2 cup fine dry bread crumbs
6 eggs, separated
1 cup sugar
1/4 teaspoon almond extract
2 teaspoons finely grated orange or lemon rind

Preheat oven to 350° F. Mix nuts and crumbs and set aside. Beat egg yolks until thick and pale yellow, slowly add 3/4 cup sugar, and beat until very thick and the color of cream. In a separate bowl, beat egg whites until frothy, gradually add remaining sugar, and beat until soft peaks form. Fold egg whites into yolk mixture alternately with nut mixture, beginning and ending with whites. Stir in almond extract and grated orange or lemon rind. Spoon into 2 ungreased 9" round pans lined on the bottom with wax paper. Bake about 20 minutes or until a faint imprint remains when top is touched. Cool upright in pans on wire racks 5–7 minutes, carefully loosen cakes with a spatula, invert on racks, peel off paper, turn right-side-up, and cool thoroughly. Fill and frost as desired—especially good with Mocha or Nut Butter Cream Frosting.

NPS (unfrosted): 140 C, 105 mg CH, 50 mg S*

VARIATION

Hazelnut Torte: Prepare as directed, using finely ground, blanched hazelnuts or filberts instead of walnuts.

NPS (with filberts): 135 C, 105 mg CH, 50 mg S*

APPLESAUCE CAKE

1 (9") cake (16 servings)

A moist old-fashioned cake. It contains no eggs, so it is suitable for those allergic to them.

2 cups sifted flour
1/2 teaspoon baking soda
1 teaspoon baking powder
1/2 teaspoon salt
3/4 teaspoon cinnamon
1/2 teaspoon nutmeg
1/4 teaspoon cloves
2 tablespoons milk
1 teaspoon vanilla
1 cup applesauce
1/2 cup butter or margarine
1 cup firmly packed light brown sugar
3/4 cup seedless raisins
3/4 cup minced pecans or walnuts

Preheat oven to 350° F. Sift flour with baking soda, baking powder, salt, and spices and set aside. Mix milk, vanilla, and applesauce. Cream butter until light, add sugar gradually, continuing to cream until fluffy. Add dry ingredients alternately with applesauce mixture, beginning and ending with the dry and adding about one third of the total at a time. Beat just until smooth. Mix in raisins and nuts. Spoon into an ungreased 9" pan lined with wax paper and bake 35 minutes until cake shrinks slightly from sides of pan and is springy to the touch. Cool upright in pan on a wire rack 5 minutes, then invert on rack, peel off paper, turn right-side-up, and cool completely. Frost or not as desired or serve slightly warm with Lemon-Raisin Sauce.

NPS (with butter and walnuts, unfrosted): 220 C, 15 mg CH, 185 mg S*

SPICE CAKE

1 (8" × 8" × 2") cake (12 servings) ¢

1½ cups sifted flour
1½ teaspoons baking powder
¼ teaspoon salt
1 teaspoon cinnamon
¾ teaspoon nutmeg
¼ teaspoon allspice
¼ teaspoon cloves
¼ teaspoon ginger
½ cup + 2 tablespoons milk
1 teaspoon vanilla
½ cup butter or margarine
1 cup sugar
1 egg

Preheat oven to 350° F. Sift flour with baking powder, salt, and spices and set aside. Mix milk and vanilla. Cream butter until light, add sugar gradually, continuing to cream until fluffy. Add egg and beat well. Add dry ingredients alternately with milk, beginning and ending with the dry and adding about one third of the total at a time. Spoon into an ungreased 8" × 8" × 2" pan lined on the bottom with wax paper. Bake about 45 minutes until cake pulls from sides of pan and is springy to the touch. Cool upright in pan on a wire rack 10 minutes, loosen edges, and invert on a rack. Peel off paper, turn right-side-up and cool. Frost or not as desired.

NPS (with butter, unfrosted): 200 C, 45 mg CH, 190 mg S*

VARIATIONS

¢ **Spice Layer Cake** *(20 servings):* Double the ingredients, prepare batter as directed, and bake in 2 ungreased 9" layer cake pans lined on the bottom with wax paper about 45 minutes at 350° F.

NPS (with butter, unfrosted): 240 C, 55 mg CH, 225 mg S*

¢ **Lemon-Spice Cake** *(12 servings):* Prepare as directed but add 1 teaspoon lemon extract and the finely grated rind of 1 lemon along with the egg.

NPS (with butter, unfrosted): 200 C, 45 mg CH, 190 mg S*

¢ **Raisin-Spice Cake** *(12 servings):* Add ¼ cup seedless raisins to batter with final addition of flour.

NPS (with butter, unfrosted): 210 C, 45 mg CH, 190 mg S*

GINGERBREAD

1 (9" × 9" × 2") cake (16 servings) ¢

2½ cups sifted flour
1½ teaspoons baking soda
½ teaspoon salt
1¼ teaspoons ginger
1 teaspoon cinnamon
½ teaspoon cloves
½ teaspoon allspice
½ cup vegetable shortening
½ cup sugar
1 egg
1 cup molasses
1 cup boiling water

Preheat oven to 350° F. Sift flour with soda, salt, and spices and set aside. Cream shortening until fluffy, then add sugar, a little at a time, beating well after each addition. Beat in egg. Combine molasses and boiling water and add alternately with the sifted dry ingredients, beginning and ending with the dry and beating after each addition just enough to mix. Pour into a greased, wax-paper-lined 9" × 9" × 2" pan and bake 50–60 minutes until gingerbread pulls from sides of pan and is springy to the touch. Cool gingerbread upright in its pan on a wire rack. Cut in large squares and serve.

NPS: 205 C, 15 mg CH, 155 mg S*

GRANDMOTHER'S SOFT GINGER CAKE

1 (9" × 9" × 2") cake (16 servings) ¢

This thin batter bakes into an unusually soft-crumbed cake.

2½ cups sifted cake flour
1½ teaspoons baking soda
¼ teaspoon salt
1 teaspoon cinnamon
1 teaspoon cloves
1 teaspoon ginger
¼ teaspoon nutmeg
½ cup vegetable shortening
⅔ cup sugar
1 egg
⅔ cup molasses
1¼ cups boiling water

Preheat oven to 375° F. Sift flour with soda, salt, and spices and set aside. Cream shortening until fluffy, add sugar, a little at a time, creaming well after each addition. Beat in egg. Combine molasses and boiling water and add alternately with sifted dry ingredients, beginning and ending with the dry. Beat after each addition to mix. Pour into a lightly greased 9" × 9" × 2" pan and bake 40–45 minutes until cake pulls from sides of pan and is springy to the touch. Cool cake upright in its pan on a wire rack. To serve, cut in large squares and top, if you like, with whipped cream or vanilla ice cream.

NPS (without topping): 185 C, 15 mg CH, 120 mg S*

PINEAPPLE UPSIDE-DOWN CAKE

1 (10" round or 9" square) cake (16 servings)

⅓ cup butter or margarine
½ cup firmly packed light or dark brown sugar
1 (1-pound 4-ounce) can sliced pineapple, drained
8 maraschino cherry halves, well drained
14–16 pecan halves

CAKE
1⅓ cups sifted flour
1 cup sugar
2 teaspoons baking powder
½ teaspoon salt
⅓ cup vegetable shortening
⅔ cup milk
1 teaspoon vanilla
½ teaspoon lemon extract
1 teaspoon finely grated lemon rind
1 egg

Preheat oven to 350° F. Melt butter in a heavy 10" skillet (with ovenproof handle) or in a 9" × 9" × 2" pan over low heat. Off heat, sprinkle brown sugar evenly over butter. Arrange pineapple in a pattern on sugar and fill spaces with cherries and pecans. Set aside while mixing cake. Sift flour, sugar, baking powder, and salt into large mixer bowl, drop in shortening and milk, and beat at lowest speed just to blend. (*Note:* It's a good idea to hold a towel over bowl to prevent spills at first.) Beat 2 minutes at medium speed, scraping bowl and beaters once or twice. Add remaining ingredients and beat 2 minutes longer, scraping bowl now and then. Pour batter evenly over fruit. Bake 40–50 minutes until cake is golden brown and pulls from sides of pan. Cool upright in pan on wire rack 3–4 minutes, loosen edges of cake, invert on heatproof serving plate, and leave pan over cake 1–2 minutes. Re-

move pan and serve warm or cold with sweetened whipped cream.

NPS (without whipped cream): 215 C, 30 mg CH, 170 mg S*

VARIATIONS

Apricot or Peach Upside-Down Cake: Substitute 2 cups drained, canned apricot or cling peach halves for pineapple rings; arrange hollow-side-up on sugar. Or use well-drained sliced cling peaches. Proceed as directed.

NPS (without whipped cream): 170 C, 20 mg CH, 135 mg S*

Apple Upside-Down Cake: Peel, core, and thinly slice 2 large tart apples and arrange in an attractive pattern on top of sugar. If you like, dot here and there with pitted cooked prunes, seedless or golden seedless raisins. Proceed as directed.

NPS (without prunes, raisins, or whipped cream): 210 C, 30 mg CH, 175 mg S*

Gingerbread Upside-Down Cake: Prepare fruit layer as directed. Prepare cake batter substituting ⅓ cup each dark molasses and boiling water for the milk; mix and cool before adding. Also add 1 teaspoon each ginger and nutmeg along with egg and other flavorings. Bake as directed.

NPS (without whipped cream): 225 C, 25 mg CH, 175 mg S*

REAL SPONGE CAKE

2 (9") layers (16 servings) ⚖

Note all the variations you can make from this one basic recipe.

6 eggs, separated, at room temperature
1 cup sifted sugar
½ teaspoon salt
2 teaspoons vanilla
1 cup sifted cake flour

Preheat oven to 350° F. Beat egg yolks until thick, slowly add sugar, salt, and vanilla, beating constantly; continue beating until very thick and the color of cream. Slowly mix in flour (lowest mixer speed). Beat egg whites to soft peaks (they should *just* flow when bowl is tipped) and fold lightly into batter, about one fourth at a time. Spoon into 2 wax-paper-lined 9" layer cake pans and bake 25 minutes until golden and springy. Cool upright in pans on a wire rack 5 minutes, then loosen carefully with a spatula and turn out. Peel off paper, turn right-side-up, and cool completely. Fill and frost as desired.

NPS (unfilled and unfrosted): 100 C, 105 mg CH, 95 mg S*

To Bake in Other Pans:

⚖ **Tube Pan** *(12 servings):* Spoon batter into an ungreased 10″ tube pan and bake 45 minutes at 350° F. Invert at once and cool completely in pan.

NPS (unfilled and unfrosted): 135 C, 135 mg CH, 125 mg S*

⚖ **Loaf Pan** *(24 servings):* Spoon batter into a wax-paper-lined 13″ × 9″ × 2″ loaf pan and bake ½ hour at 350° F. Cool upright in pan 5 minutes, invert, peel off paper, turn right-side-up, and cool.

NPS (unfilled and unfrosted): 65 C, 70 mg CH, 65 mg S*

⚖ **Muffin Pans** *(2 dozen cupcakes):* Spoon batter into muffin tins lined with cupcake papers, filling each three fourths full; bake 12–15 minutes at 350° F. Remove from pans and cool upright on wire racks.

NP Cupcake: 65 C, 70 mg CH, 65 mg S*

VARIATIONS

⚖ **Lemon Sponge Cake:** Prepare as directed but flavor with 1 teaspoon lemon extract and 1 tablespoon each lemon juice and finely grated rind instead of vanilla.

NPS (unfilled and unfrosted): 100 C, 105 mg CH, 95 mg S*

⚖ **Orange Sponge Cake:** Prepare as directed but flavor with 1 teaspoon orange extract, 1 tablespoon lemon juice, and 2 tablespoons finely grated orange rind instead of vanilla.

NPS (unfilled and unfrosted): 100 C, 105 mg CH, 95 mg S*

Nut Sponge Cake: Prepare as directed but just before folding in whites mix in ¾–1 cup minced pecans, walnuts, or toasted, blanched almonds.

NPS (with walnuts): 140 C, 105 mg CH, 95 mg S*

⚖ **Chocolate Sponge Cake:** Sift ¼ cup cocoa with flour and add to egg-sugar mixture alternately with vanilla combined with 2 tablespoons cold water, beginning and ending with flour. Proceed as directed.

NPS (unfilled and unfrosted): 105 C, 105 mg CH, 95 mg S*

⚖ **Coffee Sponge Cake:** Beat egg yolks, sugar, salt, and vanilla as directed; add flour alternately with 1 tablespoon instant coffee powder dissolved in 2 tablespoons cold water; proceed as directed.

NPS (unfilled and unfrosted): 100 C, 105 mg CH, 95 mg S*

⚖ **Mocha Sponge Cake:** Prepare Chocolate Sponge Cake as directed but dissolve 1 tablespoon instant coffee powder in the 2 tablespoons cold water. Mix in alternately with flour as directed.

NPS (unfilled and unfrosted): 105 C, 105 mg CH, 95 mg S*

Coconut Cream Sponge Cake: Prepare Real Sponge Cake as directed and put layers together with sweetened whipped cream mixed with ½ cup flaked coconut. Frost with sweetened whipped cream and sprinkle with flaked coconut (about 1 cup).

NPS: 190 C, 125 mg CH, 100 mg S*

¢ ⚖ **Economy Sponge Cake:** Sift the flour with 1½ teaspoons baking powder. Beat 3 egg yolks with the sugar as directed, then add flour alternately with ¼ cup cold water mixed with 2 teaspoons vanilla, beginning and ending with dry ingredients. Beat 3 egg whites with ¼ teaspoon cream of tartar and proceed as directed. Bake 20–25 minutes at 350° F. in the 9″ layer cake pans. Do not put layers together but serve unfrosted, each layer cut in 12 wedges.

NPS: 60 C, 35 mg CH, 35 mg S*

¢ ⚖ **Economy Chocolate Sponge Cake:** Prepare Economy Sponge Cake as directed but sift ¼ cup cocoa along with the flour.

NPS: 60 C, 35 mg CH, 35 mg S*

EASY SPONGE LOAF

1 (8″ × 8″ × 2″) cake (16 servings) ▨ ⚖

3 eggs
¾ cup sugar
⅛ teaspoon salt
1 teaspoon vanilla
¾ cup sifted flour

Preheat oven to 350° F. Beat eggs until frothy, slowly add sugar and salt, beating constantly; continue beating until thick and the color of cream. Mix in vanilla, then flour, a little at a time. Spoon into an 8″ × 8″ × 2″ pan lined with greased wax paper and bake 35 minutes until golden and springy to the touch. Cool cake upright in its pan on a wire rack 5 minutes, then loosen carefully with a spatula and turn out. Peel off wax paper and cool before cutting or using in Trifle or other recipes.

NPS: 70 C, 50 mg CH, 30 mg S*

GÉNOISE

1 (9") cake (12 servings) ⚖

Génoise, the classic European sponge cake, is the foundation of showy *Gâteaux* and *Petits Fours.* It can be made entirely by mixer instead of the more traditional way given here. But eggs should be slightly warmed before beating, then beaten until very thick and creamy in a warm bowl about 15 minutes (beware of overheating mixer).

4 eggs, at room temperature
¾ cup superfine sugar
1 teaspoon vanilla
1 teaspoon finely grated lemon or orange rind
¾ cup sifted cake flour
3 tablespoons melted clarified butter,* cooled to lukewarm (no substitute)

Preheat oven to 350° F. Butter a 9" spring form pan, line bottom with wax paper, butter paper, and dust bottom and sides of pan with flour. Place eggs, sugar, vanilla, and rind in a large stainless-steel or copper mixing bowl and set *over,* not in, a large pan one third filled with barely simmering water. With a large wire whisk, beat until mixture foams and is almost doubled in volume, about 5–6 minutes. Transfer to large mixer bowl and beat at moderately high speed until very thick (when beaters are raised, mixture should drop in a slowly dissolving ribbon). Set bowl on damp cloth, sift in ¼ cup flour, fold in gently, then fold in 1 tablespoon butter. Continue adding flour and butter the same way, the same amounts each time, until all are incorporated. Pour batter into pan, tap lightly on counter to break any large bubbles, and bake on center oven rack 30–35 minutes until cake shrinks slightly from sides of pan and is springy to the touch. Cool upright in pan on a wire rack 10 minutes (cake will sink a little in the middle), then loosen edges carefully with a spatula and remove spring form sides. Invert on rack, lift off pan bottom, peel off paper, turn cake right-side-up, and cool thoroughly. Slice into 2 or 3 layers and fill and frost as desired.

NPS (unfrosted): 125 C, 100 mg CH, 25 mg S*

VARIATIONS

Favorite Génoise: Sprinkle cut surfaces of Génoise with 2–3 tablespoons kirsch or other fruit liqueur and sandwich layers together with apricot purée and sweetened whipped cream. Frost with Basic or Coffee Butter Cream Frosting and scatter thickly with minced filberts or pistachio nuts. Rec-ipe too flexible for meaningful nutritional analysis.

⚖ **Génoise for Petits Fours** (*48 petits fours*)*:* Prepare batter as directed and pour into an ungreased 13" × 9" × 2" pan lined on the bottom with wax paper. Bake 25 minutes at 350° F. Cool as directed. Cake is now ready to cut and make into Petits Fours.

NP Petit Four: 30 C, 25 mg CH, 5 mg S*

⚖ **Génoise for a Four-Layer Cake** (*16 servings*)*:* Use 6 eggs, 1 cup superfine sugar, 1½ teaspoons each vanilla and grated rind, 1 cup sifted cake flour, and ¼ cup clarified butter.* Prepare batter as directed and divide between 4 wax-paper-lined, greased, and floured 9" layer cake pans. Bake 15 minutes at 350° F., then cool as directed.

NPS: 130 C, 110 mg CH, 25 mg S*

PETITS FOURS

4 dozen

The tricky part of Petits Fours is frosting them evenly. A base coat of Apricot Glaze seals in loose crumbs, makes the icing go on more smoothly, and keeps the little cakes moist. A help, too, is frosting with Quick Glacé Icing instead of dipping—the more traditional and tedious way—in melted fondant.

1 (1–2-day-old) Génoise for Petits Fours or any firm-textured white or yellow cake baked in a 13" × 9" × 2" pan
1 recipe Apricot Glaze
3 recipes Quick Glacé or Chocolate Glacé Icing (or some of each)
1 recipe Decorative Butter Cream Frosting or Royal Icing
Silver dragées, candied violets, chocolate shot (optional)

Cut all hard edges from cake, then even up loaf by trimming off browned top so it is uniformly 1½" thick. Cut in 1½" squares or rounds, small rectangles or triangles and brush off loose crumbs. Spear cakes, one at a time, on a fork and dip in Apricot Glaze to coat top and sides. Place uncoated side down about 2" apart on wire racks set over baking sheets. Let stand, uncovered, 1 hour. Prepare icing as directed, then, using a large spoon, ladle over cakes, one at a time, so top and sides are evenly coated. (*Note:* Enough must be poured over all at once to create a smooth finish.) Scrape up run-over on baking sheets and remelt. Let cakes dry thoroughly before decorating. Tint decorative icing as desired and pipe on tiny flowers, leaves, stars, scrolls, any design you like. Or decorate with silver *dragées,* candied violets, chocolate shot (see Tips on Decorating Cakes). Store in a cool, dry place until serving time. *(Note:* Petits Fours can be frozen but their frosting won't be quite so glossy.)

NP Petit Four (without decorations): 200 C, 30 mg CH, 35 mg S*

V A R I A T I O N

⚖️ **Simple Petits Fours:** Frost top of a trimmed sheet of cake with Basic Butter Cream Frosting or any flavored butter cream frosting, then cut in desired shapes with a sharp knife, wiping blade after each cut. Decorate with bits of candied cherries, slivered almonds, strips of angelica, colored sugar, or toasted coconut. Nutritional count about the same as basic recipe.

JELLY ROLL

1 roll (12 servings)

The filling *needn't* be jelly, as these variations prove.

³⁄₄ cup sifted cake flour
³⁄₄ teaspoon baking powder
¹⁄₄ teaspoon salt
4 eggs, at room temperature
³⁄₄ cup sugar
1 teaspoon vanilla
Confectioners' sugar
1 cup any fruit jelly or jam or 1¹⁄₂ cups
  sweetened whipped cream

Preheat oven to 400° F. Line the bottom of a 15¹⁄₂″ × 10¹⁄₂″ × 1″ jelly-roll pan with wax paper. Sift flour with baking powder and salt and set aside. With electric or rotary beater, beat eggs at high speed until foamy; slowly add sugar, a little at a time, and continue beating until very thick and the color of mayonnaise. Mix in vanilla. Fold in flour mixture just until blended. Spoon into pan, spreading batter evenly. Bake 12–14 minutes until golden and springy to the touch. Loosen edges of cake, invert on a clean dish towel lightly dusted with sifted confectioners' sugar. Peel off paper carefully and trim off crisp edges with a very sharp knife. Starting from short side, roll cake and towel up together and cool on a wire rack. Unroll, remove towel, spread jelly to within ¹⁄₂″ of edges and reroll. Place seam-side-down and sift confectioners' sugar on top. *(Note:* If jelly or jam is stiff, warm slightly before spreading.)* When serving, make slices about 1″ thick.

NPS (with jelly): 175 C, 90 mg CH, 100 mg S*

V A R I A T I O N S

Lemon Jelly Roll: Prepare cake as directed but omit vanilla; add ¹⁄₂ teaspoon lemon extract and 1 tablespoon each lemon juice and finely grated lemon rind. Fill with Lemon Cheese or Lemon Filling instead of jelly.

NPS (with Lemon Filling): 195 C, 95 mg CH, 115 mg S*

Orange Jelly Roll: Prepare as directed but omit vanilla and flavor with ¹⁄₂ teaspoon orange extract and 1 tablespoon finely grated orange rind. Fill with Orange Filling.

NPS: 205 C, 95 mg CH, 115 mg S*

Strawberry Jelly Roll: Prepare batter as directed and mix in 2 or 3 drops red food coloring; bake as directed. Spread with 1 cup heavy cream, sweetened and whipped to soft peaks, and 1¹⁄₂–2 cups thinly sliced strawberries and roll; or fill with Strawberry Filling. Wrap in foil and chill 1 hour. Sprinkle with confectioners' sugar before serving.

NPS (with strawberries and cream): 185 C, 120 mg CH, 105 mg S*
NPS (with Strawberry Filling): 215 C, 105 mg CH, 145 mg S*

Chocolate Jelly Roll: When making cake, reduce flour to ²⁄₃ cup, add ¹⁄₄ cup cocoa and sift with flour, baking powder, and salt. Add 1 tablespoon cold water along with vanilla; bake as directed. Fill with Chocolate Cream Filling or Chocolate, Mocha, or Coffee Butter Cream Frosting. Dust with confectioners' sugar before serving.

NPS (with Chocolate, Mocha, or Coffee Butter Cream Frosting): 335 C, 110 mg CH, 195 mg S*

ANGEL FOOD CAKE

1 (10″) tube cake (12 servings)   ⚖️

If you follow the directions exactly, you'll bake a tall and tender cake.

1¹⁄₂ cups sifted sugar
1 cup sifted cake flour
1 teaspoon cream of tartar
¹⁄₄ teaspoon salt
12 egg whites, at room temperature
1 teaspoon vanilla
¹⁄₂ teaspoon almond extract
1 teaspoon lemon juice

Preheat oven to 325° F. Sift ³⁄₄ cup sugar with the flour and set aside. Sprinkle cream of tartar and salt over egg whites; beat with a wire whisk or rotary beater until *very* soft peaks form (whites should *flow, not run,* when bowl is tipped). Sift a little of the remaining sugar over whites and gently fold in, using a whisk; repeat until all sugar is mixed in. Now sift a little sugar-flour mixture over whites, and fold in with the whisk; repeat until all is incorporated (it may take as many as 10 additions). Fold in vanilla, almond extract, and lemon juice. Pour batter into an *ungreased* 10″ tube pan and bake 1–1¼ hours until cake is lightly browned and has pulled from the sides of pan. Invert pan and cool cake thoroughly in pan; then loosen edges with a spatula and turn out. Leave plain or frost as desired.

NPS: 150 C, 0 mg CH, 95 mg S*

BASIC CHIFFON CAKE

1 (10″) tube cake (12 servings)

For maximum volume use 1–2 more egg whites than yolks.

2¼ cups sifted cake flour
1½ cups sugar
1 teaspoon salt
1 tablespoon baking powder
½ cup cooking oil
6 egg yolks, at room temperature
¾ cup cold water
2 teaspoons vanilla
1 teaspoon lemon juice
7–8 egg whites, at room temperature
½ teaspoon cream of tartar

Preheat oven to 325° F. Sift flour, sugar, salt, and baking powder into a bowl. Make a well in the center and add, in the order listed, the oil, egg yolks, water, vanilla, and lemon juice. Beat until smooth. Using largest bowl and electric mixer or rotary beater, beat egg whites and cream of tartar until they will form *very stiff peaks* (whites should be stiffer than for Angel Food Cake. With a rubber spatula, gently fold into batter, one fourth at a time, just until blended. Pour into an *ungreased* 10″ tube pan and bake 55 minutes; raise oven to 350° F. and bake 10 minutes longer until cake is lightly browned and has pulled from sides of pan. Invert and cool cake thoroughly in pan; loosen edges with a spatula and turn out. Leave plain or frost as desired.

NPS (unfrosted): 285 C, 135 mg CH, 325 mg S*

VARIATIONS

Lemon Chiffon Cake: Prepare as directed but reduce vanilla to 1 teaspoon and add ½ teaspoon lemon extract and 2 tablespoons finely grated lemon rind.

NPS (unfrosted): 285 C, 135 mg CH, 325 mg S*

Orange Chiffon Cake: Prepare as directed but reduce vanilla to 1 teaspoon, substitute ¾ cup orange juice for the cold water, and add 2 tablespoons finely grated orange rind.

NPS (unfrosted): 290 C, 135 mg CH, 325 mg S*

Spiced Chiffon Cake: Prepare as directed but reduce vanilla to 1 teaspoon and add 1 teaspoon cinnamon and ½ teaspoon each nutmeg, cloves, and allspice.

NPS (unfrosted): 285 C, 135 mg CH, 325 mg S*

Butterscotch-Maple Chiffon Cake: Prepare as directed but substitute 2 cups firmly packed light brown sugar for the granulated, reduce vanilla to 1 teaspoon, omit lemon juice, and add 1–2 teaspoons maple flavoring. If you like, fold in ¾ cup finely chopped pecans or walnuts just before folding in egg whites.

NPS (without nuts, unfrosted): 325 C, 135 mg CH, 335 mg S*

Chocolate Chiffon Cake: Blend ⅓ cup cocoa with ¾ cup boiling water, then cool to room temperature. Reduce flour to 1¾ cups, sift with dry ingredients as directed, then add oil, egg yolks, cocoa mixture, and 1 teaspoon vanilla (omit lemon juice) and beat until smooth. Proceed as recipe directs.

NPS (unfrosted): 275 C, 135 mg CH, 325 mg S*

Mocha Chiffon Cake: Prepare Chocolate Chiffon Cake (above) as directed but blend cocoa with ¾ cup very strong hot black coffee instead of boiling water.

NPS (unfrosted): 275 C, 135 mg CH, 325 mg S*

LIGHT FRUIT CAKE

1 (9″ × 5″ × 3″) loaf (20 servings)

1¼ cups sifted flour
½ teaspoon baking powder
½ teaspoon salt
½ teaspoon nutmeg
¼ teaspoon ginger
½ cup butter or margarine
½ cup sugar
3 eggs
1 teaspoon vanilla
½ teaspoon almond extract
1 cup golden seedless raisins
1 pound mixed candied fruits (pineapple, orange and lemon peel, citron), chopped fine
¼ pound candied red cherries, coarsely chopped
1 cup toasted, slivered almonds or coarsely chopped pecans or walnuts
Blanched almond halves (garnish)
Candied cherry halves (garnish)

Preheat oven to 300° F. Grease, then line the bottom and sides of a 9″ × 5″ × 3″ loaf pan with foil; grease foil lightly. Sift flour with baking powder, salt, and spices and set aside. Cream butter until light, gradually add sugar, continuing to cream until fluffy. Add eggs, one at a time, beating well after each addition. Mix in vanilla and almond extract. Add dry ingredients, about 1/3 cup at a time, beating just to blend. Toss raisins with candied fruits, cherries, and nuts, and stir into batter. Spoon into pan and decorate with almond and cherry halves. Bake 1 1/2–1 3/4 hours until cake shrinks slightly from sides of pan, is lightly browned, and a metal skewer inserted in center comes out clean. Cool cake upright in pan on a wire rack 1/2 hour. Invert on rack, peel off foil, turn right-side-up, and cool thoroughly. Wrap in brandy-, rum-, or fruit-juice-soaked cheese-cloth, then in foil, and store airtight 2–3 weeks before serving.

NPS (with butter, without garnish): 250 C, 55 mg CH, 205 mg S*

DARK CHRISTMAS FRUIT CAKE

1 (10″) tube cake (40 servings)

This recipe is more than 100 years old and rich enough to make 40 servings. It takes two days to make and at least three weeks to ripen. If properly stored, the cake can be made as much as two months before Christmas.

FRUIT MIXTURE

1/2 pound candied citron, chopped fine
1/4 pound candied orange peel, chopped fine
1/4 pound candied lemon peel, chopped fine
OR
1 pound mixed candied fruit, chopped (use in place of the above 3 ingredients)
2 ounces candied ginger, chopped fine
1/2 pound seedless raisins
1/2 pound golden seedless raisins
1/2 pound dried currants
1/4 pound candied cherries, coarsely chopped (save 4 whole cherries for decoration, if you like)
1/4 pound shelled walnuts or pecans, finely chopped (save 8 nut halves for decoration, if you like)
Finely grated rind of 2 lemons
1/2 cup orange marmalade
1/4 cup lemon juice
1/4 cup brandy or orange juice
1 teaspoon vanilla
1/4 teaspoon almond extract

CAKE MIXTURE
2 cups sifted flour
1 teaspoon cinnamon
1/2 teaspoon nutmeg
1/4 teaspoon mace
1/4 teaspoon cloves
1/4 teaspoon allspice
1 teaspoon baking powder
1/2 teaspoon salt
1/2 pound butter or margarine
1 cup sugar
6 eggs

Place all fruit mixture ingredients in a large bowl, toss well, cover, and let stand overnight at room temperature. Grease, then line bottom of a 10″ tube pan with wax paper. Preheat oven to 250° F. Sift together twice the flour, spices, baking powder, and salt, and set aside. Cream butter until light, add sugar gradually, and continue creaming until fluffy. Add eggs, one at a time, beating well after each addition. Add dry ingredients, about 1 cup at a time, beating just to blend. *(Note:* Unless you have an extra-large mixing bowl, you will have to transfer batter to a large kettle at this point.) Mix in the fruit mixture. Spoon batter into pan and, if you wish, decorate top with halved candied cherries and walnuts. Place on center oven rack; half fill a roasting pan with water and place on rack below. Bake, uncovered, 4 1/4 hours until cake shrinks slightly from sides of pan and a metal skewer inserted midway between edge and central tube comes out clean. Cool cake upright in pan on wire rack 1 hour. Carefully turn out, peel off wax paper, turn right-side-up, and cool thoroughly. Wrap in brandy- or rum-soaked cheesecloth, then in foil, and store in an airtight container about 3 weeks to ripen. If you wish to store the cake longer, sprinkle cheesecloth wrapping with 2–3 tablespoons brandy or rum at 3-week intervals.

NPS (with butter, citron, orange peel, and lemon peel, orange juice, and walnuts): 225 C, 55 mg CH, 115 mg S*
NPS (with butter, mixed candied fruit, orange juice, and walnuts): 210 C, 55 mg CH, 155 mg S*

CUPCAKES

Cupcakes can be made from almost any cake batter if you use the following guide for filling pans: fill each muffin pan cup two thirds full for conventional butter cake batters, fill half full for quick-method batters like that used for Easy Yellow Cupcakes, fill three fourths full for true sponge batters, and fill seven eighths full for chiffon cake batters. Use cupcake papers to save greasing and washing pans and to give cupcakes better shape. Or, if you prefer, grease and flour unlined muffin pan cups. Bake cupcakes at 375° F., 12–25 minutes, depending on batter, until springy to the touch.

EASY YELLOW CUPCAKES

1¹/2 dozen   ⊲⊳ ¢ ⊠

1¹/3 cups sifted flour
3/4 cup sugar
2 teaspoons baking powder
1/4 teaspoon salt
1/4 cup vegetable shortening
2/3 cup milk
1 egg
1 teaspoon vanilla

Preheat oven to 375° F. Sift flour, sugar, baking powder, and salt together into a large mixing bowl. Add shortening and milk, stir to blend, then beat slowly about 1¹/2 minutes with an electric mixer. Add egg and vanilla and beat slowly 1¹/2 minutes. Spoon batter into muffin tins lined with cupcake papers, filling each half full. Bake 20–25 minutes until cakes are golden brown and springy to the touch. Remove cakes from pans and cool upright on wire racks. Frost as desired.

NP Cupcake (unfrosted): 100 C, 15 mg CH, 85 mg S*

VARIATIONS

⊲⊳ ¢ ⊠ **Easy Chocolate Cupcakes:** Prepare as directed but add 2 (1-ounce) melted squares unsweetened chocolate or 2 (1-ounce) envelopes no-melt unsweetened chocolate along with egg and vanilla.

NP Cupcake (unfrosted): 115 C, 15 mg CH, 85 mg S*

⊲⊳ ¢ ⊠ **Easy Butterscotch-Spice Cupcakes:** Substitute 3/4 cup firmly packed dark brown sugar for the granulated and 1 teaspoon maple flavoring for vanilla. Also sift 1/2 teaspoon each cinnamon and nutmeg along with dry ingredients, then proceed as directed.

NP Cupcake (unfrosted): 105 C, 15 mg CH, 120 mg S*

⊠ **Easy Raisin-Nut Cupcakes:** Prepare as directed and mix in 1/2 cup each seedless raisins (or dried currants, minced pitted prunes, or dates) and minced walnuts or pecans.

NP Cupcake (unfrosted): 135 C, 15 mg CH, 85 mg S*

¢ ⊲⊳ ⊠ **Easy Orange Cupcakes:** Prepare as directed but use 1/3 cup each orange juice and milk instead of all milk; omit vanilla and add 2 teaspoons finely grated orange rind.

NP Cupcake (unfrosted): 100 C, 15 mg CH, 85 mg S*

¢ ⊲⊳ ⊠ **Easy Lemon Cupcakes:** Prepare as directed but substitute 1/4 teaspoon lemon extract for vanilla and add the finely grated rind of 1 lemon.

NP Cupcake (unfrosted): 100 C, 15 mg CH, 85 mg S*

⊠ **Chocolate Chip Cupcakes:** Prepare as directed and fold in 1 (6-ounce) package semisweet chocolate bits.

NP Cupcake (unfrosted): 145 C, 15 mg CH, 85 mg S*

FILLINGS AND FROSTINGS

"The icing on the cake" . . . the finishing touch. Not every cake needs an icing; some, in fact—pound cake, angel cake, fruit cake —are better without it. But most cakes are bare without frosting of some sort. Generally speaking, superrich cakes call for less-than-superrich icings, plain cakes for something a little showy. The same holds true for layer cakes that are filled (between the layers) as well as frosted.

SOME TIPS ON FROSTING CAKES

Preparing the Cake:
• Cool cake thoroughly before frosting unless recipe directs otherwise.
• Trim cake so that it is symmetrical.
• Brush or rub off loose crumbs and trim away ragged edges with scissors; also trim or, using a fine grater, remove any over-brown top or bottom crust.
• Choose a flat plate 2″ larger in diameter than the cake and cover plate rim, petal fashion, with triangles of wax paper, letting points hang over edge (these are to catch drips and keep plate clean). When cake is frosted, simply pull out wax paper.
• Center cake on plate, bottom-side-up if a tube cake, right-side-up if a layer or loaf cake.
• To make the frosting easier, set cake plate on a lazy Susan or turned-upside-down bowl

so that you can rotate it as you spread on frosting.

Filling the Cake:
• Place one layer bottom-side-up on plate as directed above.
• Prepare and cool filling before using unless recipe calls for a warm filling (warm fillings usually seep into cakes too much, making them soggy).
• Spread filling, not too thick, to within 1/4" of edge and, if extra soft, to within 1" of edge. Add next layer, bottom-side-up *(unless it is the top layer)* and press lightly into filling.
• Repeat until all layers are in place, remembering that the final layer should be placed right-side-up.
• Wipe off any filling that has squished out from between layers onto sides of cake.

Frosting the Cake:

If Frosting Is Thick:
• Using a metal spatula, spread a thin layer over top and sides of cake to seal in crumbs. Let dry at room temperature 10 minutes.
• Refrost sides of cake, working from bottom up, to form a slight "rim" around top of cake; this helps keep sides straight and top level.
• Pile remaining frosting on top and spread out to meet edges.
• If frosting is soft, swirl into waves with spatula or draw fork tines lightly over surface.

If Frosting Is Thin:
• Avoid using glazes or hard-drying thin frostings like Quick Glacé Icing in humid weather; they may never harden.
• Spoon frosting or glaze over top of cake and let run down sides. This is a good way to ice chiffon, angel, or sponge cakes.

Frosting Cupcakes:
• Cool cupcakes thoroughly; meanwhile, prepare frosting.
• Holding cupcakes by the bottom, dip one at a time into frosting, then lift out with a slight twirling motion so there is a curlicue on top.
• Set on wire racks and let dry thoroughly. Or, if you like, while frosting is still soft, stud with walnut or pecan halves, chocolate bits, candied cherries, raisins, or chunks of dried fruit. Or scatter lightly with flaked coconut or minced nuts, fine cookie crumbs, or grated semisweet chocolate.

What to Do with Leftover Frosting:
• Cover and refrigerate until needed.
• Bring to room temperature and use to frost cupcakes or cookies.

• Use as a dessert topping (particularly good with steamed puddings).

TIPS ON DECORATING CAKES

The Simplest Decorations: These require no icing and are usually nothing more than confectioners' sugar, sifted through a lace doily onto a cake; a poured-on glaze of melted semisweet chocolate or warmed preserves; a dusting of colored sugar, cocoa, or cinnamon sugar. Quick, easy, and inviting.

Easy Ways to Dress Up Frosted Cakes: Ready-made colored frostings in squirt-on cans or tubes make decorating a snap. They need no refrigeration, are quick and easy to use. Also available in some supermarkets and most specialty food shops: decorating jellies in assorted colors; colored sugars and decorettes; silver *dragées;* chocolate and butterscotch bits; hard candies and gumdrops; birthday candles and holders. Take whatever is available, add imagination, and create an original special-occasion cake.

Flower Cakes: Dot frosted cakes with real flowers (daisies, chrysanthemums, rosebuds, violets), crystallized violets or roses (available in specialty food shops), or fashion flowers out of blanched almonds, slivers of candied fruits, or well-drained mandarin-orange sections.

Marble Cakes: Frost top of cake with Snow Glaze (double recipe but add only 3 tablespoons milk to make frosting stiffer). Prepare 1/2 recipe Chocolate Glaze and drizzle in parallel lines over Snow Glaze. Before chocolate hardens, draw a toothpick across lines, creating a zigzag effect.

Simple Anytime Decorations:
• Frost a chocolate or mocha cake with Basic or Coffee Butter Cream Frosting and sprinkle top with chocolate curls.*
• Frost any yellow or white butter cake with Whipped Cream Frosting, arrange a ring of miniature meringues on top, and fill center with fresh strawberries.
• Frost sides of a chocolate cake with Basic Butter Cream Frosting, cover top with Chocolate Glaze, and coat sides with chocolate shot or minced nuts.

More Intricate Decorations:

Cake-Decorating Sets: These are widely available in metal or plastic and include a slim selection of decorating tips. Good for beginners.

CAKES, FILLINGS, AND FROSTINGS

Pastry (or Decorating) Bags: The best are plastic-lined cotton bags and come in a variety of sizes; they are waterproof, washable, and if properly cared for will last almost indefinitely. Also available: transparent plastic bags, also washable and reusable.

To Make Your Own Decorating Bag:
• Cut an 8″ square of parchment, wax paper, or heavy typewriter bond, then halve diagonally into 2 triangles.
• Roll into a sharp-pointed cone and fold points down.

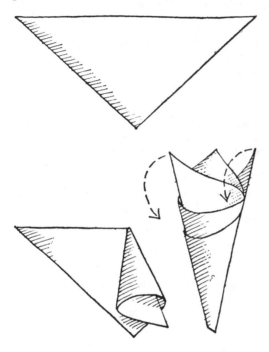

• To make fine lines (flower stems, dots, writing), snip point off to make a tiny hole.
• For broader lines, snip a little more off point.
• For making stars, scrolls, and leaves, snip still more off point and cut with a single or double notch.
• To use with decorative tips, cut ½″–¾″ off point and drop in desired tip.
• To fill: Spoon enough frosting into cone to half fill, then fold corners in and top down.
Note: If bag should go limp before decorating is done, cut off directly above decorating tip, drop tip into a fresh cone, and squeeze frosting from old bag into the new.

Decorating Tips (also called Decorating Tubes): These may be bought singly or in partial or complete sets (more than a hundred tips) from specialty food shops and confectionery supply houses. Decorating guides come with the sets.

A beginner's set might include:
Tips #2 and 5 (for writing, making flower buds, scrolls)
Tips #14, 18, 22 (for stars, swags, large scrolls)
Tip #30 (for large stars and shells)
Tip #6 (for fancy borders)
Tips #66 and 90 (for small and large leaves)

To Use Pastry Bags and Decorative Tips:
• Never more than half fill bag.
• Roll or fold top down and push frosting out, using steady, gentle pressure so decorations will have crisp outlines. Practice, if you like, on a piece of wax paper or turned-upside-down cake pan until you get the hang of it.
• If you set bag aside for a while, push out a bit of frosting before resuming decoration; some of it may have hardened.
• For really intricate designs, sketch out patterns on paper and use as a guide.

Flower Nails: These look like oversized thumbtacks, are made of metal or plastic, and are useful for shaping flowers. Top nail head with a tiny square of wax paper, form flower, then lift off paper and let flower dry. Peel off paper and place flower on cake. For a makeshift flower nail, use a small jar with a lid.

Decorating Stencils: Cardboard and plastic stencils in a variety of patterns and letters are available in specialty food shops and confectionery supply houses. You can also make your own (Manila folders work especially well). To use, hold stencil over frosting and fill cut-out spaces with colored sugar, decorettes, thin colored frosting, or melted semisweet chocolate.

Decorating Combs: Available in plastic and aluminum. To use, simply draw comb through soft frosting in straight or wavy lines.

Decorative Frostings: Use Royal Icing for intricate designs and Decorative Butter Cream Frosting for softer, simpler ones.

To Color Frostings: Use liquid or paste food colors (available in a wide range of colors at specialty food shops). Always add colors *gradually,* drop by drop for liquid colors, and dabbed on the end of a toothpick for the paste. Mix in thoroughly before adding more color. It's far better to undercolor than overcolor (many colored frostings will darken on drying). Prepare more of each color than you think you will need so that

---

CAKES, FILLINGS, AND FROSTINGS

you will not have to mix up another batch (it will be virtually impossible to match the colors exactly). *Note:* Always keep frostings covered with damp cloth or paper toweling as you work to prevent their drying out.

How to Mix Colors

Orange = red + yellow (more yellow than red)

Strawberry = red + yellow (more red than yellow)

Lime Green = yellow + green (more green than yellow)

Chartreuse = yellow + green (more yellow than green)

Violet = blue + red (more blue than red)

Maroon = blue + red (more red than blue)

Brown = yellow + red and a smidgen of green

Decorating with Chocolate: Always use type of chocolate called for in a recipe and do not substitute cocoa for chocolate.

To Grate Chocolate: Chill chocolate well, then grate into a deep bowl (it tends to fly all over).

To Melt Chocolate: Break into small pieces and melt over hot, not boiling water (chocolate scorches easily, so melt very slowly). Or place chocolate in a custard cup and set in a pan of hot water. Cool melted chocolate slightly before adding to any frosting. *(Note:* To melt chocolate in a *microwave oven,* place unwrapped pieces in a bowl, and microwave, uncovered, on *MEDIUM* power setting 2–4 minutes just until soft—no longer or chocolate will scorch.) *To Smooth Out Lumps:* If a drop of water falls into melted chocolate, the chocolate will lump. To make it smooth again, stir in 1/2–1 teaspoon vegetable shortening for each ounce of chocolate. It won't affect the flavor.

To Make Chocolate Curls: Warm chocolate (semisweet or German sweet) in wrapper in your hands, just enough to soften outside slightly. Unwrap and shave into thin curls over a piece of wax paper, using a vegetable peeler. Scatter onto cakes as decoration.

To Make Chocolate Cutouts: Melt 6 (1-ounce) packages semisweet chocolate over hot water and blend in 1 teaspoon vegetable shortening. Spread evenly and thinly on a baking sheet lined with wax paper and quick-chill in freezer or refrigerator until chocolate begins to harden. Cut out in desired shapes with cookie cutters (or, for very small decorations, with truffle cutters). Return to refrigerator or freezer and let harden

thoroughly. Lift off decorations and use to decorate cakes. To store: Layer into a cakebox, separating layers with wax paper, cover, and keep in refrigerator or freezer.

To Write with Chocolate: Melt semisweet chocolate and blend with a few drops light corn syrup; cool until slightly thickened, then drizzle off the end of a spoon in a thin even stream or, if thick enough, push through a pastry bag fitted with a fine, plain tip.

To Glaze with Chocolate: Melt unsweetened or semisweet chocolate, cool slightly, then spoon or drizzle over a frosted cake. *Note:* Let frosting harden several hours before adding chocolate. This works especially well with 7-Minute Frosting.

Some General Decorating Hints:

• Choose a firm-textured cake that will support weight of decorations rather than a delicate sponge or angel food.

• Allow plenty of time for decorating; it is often necessary to let part of the decorations harden before adding more.

• Choose a cool, dry day for the decorating, not a hot, humid one, when icings will not harden.

• If your hands are warm, put only a small amount of frosting in pastry bag at a time, lest body heat soften it too much to be workable.

• Keep designs simple, in proportion to size of cake.

• Suit the designs to the occasion.

BASIC BUTTER CREAM FROSTING

Enough to fill and frost a 9" (2-layer) cake (16 servings) or 24 cupcakes ☒

Try the flavor variations that follow or experiment with ideas of your own. This frosting is superbly adaptable.

1/3 cup butter or margarine, softened to room temperature
1 (1-pound) box confectioners' sugar, sifted
5–6 tablespoons light cream
2 teaspoons vanilla
1/4 teaspoon salt

Cream butter until fluffy; beat in sugar, a little at a time, adding alternately with cream. Mix in vanilla and salt and beat until satiny and of good spreading consistency. If mixture seems too stiff, thin with a little additional cream.

NPS (16–24) (with butter): 155–100 C, 15–10 mg CH, 75–50 mg S*

Coffee Butter Cream Frosting: Prepare by basic method above, beating 2 teaspoons instant coffee powder into butter along with sugar.

NPS (16–24) (with butter): 155–100 C, 15–10 mg CH, 75–50 mg S*

Mocha Butter Cream Frosting: Prepare by basic method above, beating 2 teaspoons instant coffee powder and 2 (1-ounce) squares melted unsweetened chocolate into creamed butter before adding sugar.

NPS (16–24) (with butter): 170–115 C, 15–10 mg CH, 75–50 mg S*

Chocolate Butter Cream Frosting: Prepare by basic method but blend 3 (1-ounce) squares melted unsweetened chocolate or 1/2 cup sifted cocoa into creamed butter before adding sugar. Proceed as directed.

NPS (16–24) (with butter): 180–120 C, 15–10 mg CH, 75–50 mg S*

Maple Butter Cream Frosting: Prepare by basic method, substituting 1/2 cup maple syrup for the light cream and reducing vanilla to 1/2 teaspoon.

NPS (16–24) (with butter): 170–110 C, 10–5 mg CH, 75–50 mg S*

Nut Butter Cream Frosting: Prepare as directed and, when of good spreading consistency, mix in 1/3–1/2 cup minced walnuts, pecans, blanched filberts, or almonds.

NPS (16–24) (with butter): 170–115 C, 15–10 mg CH, 75–50 mg S*

Orange or Lemon Butter Cream Frosting: Prepare by basic method, substituting 4–5 tablespoons orange or lemon juice for the cream; omit vanilla and add 3–4 teaspoons finely grated orange or lemon rind and 1/4 teaspoon almond extract.

NPS (16–24) (with butter): 145–95 C, 10–5 mg CH, 75–50 mg S*

Decorative Butter Cream Frosting: Prepare Basic Butter Cream Frosting as directed but reduce cream to 1–2 tablespoons; if you want a really snowy frosting, substitute vegetable shortening for butter and add a drop blue food coloring. *(Note:* Use only on firm frostings or decorations may sink in. On warm or humid days, add a little extra confectioners' sugar so decorations will hold their shape.)

NPS (16–24) (with butter): 145–100 C, 10–5 mg CH, 75–50 mg S*

CREAM CHEESE FROSTING

Enough to fill and frost a 9″ (2-layer) cake (16 servings) ☒

Slightly firmer than butter frosting, this one also invites improvisation.

2 (3-ounce) packages cream cheese, softened to room temperature
1 (1-pound) box confectioners' sugar, sifted
1 teaspoon vanilla
1–2 tablespoons milk, light cream, or evaporated milk

Beat cream cheese until very soft, then gradually beat in confectioners' sugar. Mix in vanilla and enough milk to make a good spreading consistency.

NPS (with milk): 150 C, 10 mg CH, 30 mg S*

Sour Cream-Cream Cheese Frosting: Prepare as directed but substitute 1/4 cup sour cream for the milk.

NPS: 155 C, 15 mg CH, 35 mg S*

Chocolate Cream Cheese Frosting: Beat cream cheese until soft, mix in 2 (1-ounce) squares melted unsweetened chocolate and proceed as directed, increasing milk to 3 tablespoons.

NPS (with milk): 165 C, 10 mg CH, 35 mg S*

Coffee Cream Cheese Frosting: Prepare as directed, adding 1 tablespoon instant coffee powder along with sugar.

NPS (with milk): 150 C, 10 mg CH, 30 mg S*

Orange or Lemon Cream Cheese Frosting: Prepare as directed but omit vanilla and use orange or lemon juice instead of milk. Flavor with the finely grated rind of 1 lemon or orange.

NPS: 145 C, 10 mg CH, 30 mg S*

WHIPPED CREAM FROSTING

Enough to fill and frost a 9″ tube or 2-layer cake (16 servings) ☒

Spread on cakes shortly before they're cut and eaten.

1 pint heavy cream, well chilled
1 cup sifted confectioners' sugar
1 teaspoon vanilla

In a chilled bowl with chilled beaters, beat cream until frothy. Gradually add confectioners' sugar, then vanilla. Continue beating until thick enough to spread. Use at once.

NPS: 130 C, 40 mg CH, 10 mg S*

Chocolate Whipped Cream Frosting: Sift 1/2 cup cocoa with confectioners' sugar and beat into cream as directed.

NPS: 135 C, 40 mg CH, 10 mg S*

Coffee Whipped Cream Frosting: Mix 1 tablespoon instant coffee powder with the cream and proceed as directed.

NPS: 130 C, 40 mg CH, 10 mg S*

Fruit Whipped Cream Frosting: Prepare as directed but flavor with 1/2 teaspoon orange or lemon extract, instead of vanilla, and the finely grated rind of 1 lemon or orange.

NPS: 130 C, 40 mg CH, 10 mg S*

Nut Whipped Cream Frosting: Prepare as directed but flavor with maple flavoring or almond extract instead of vanilla and fold in 3/4 cup minced pecans, filberts, shelled and peeled boiled chestnuts, or toasted almonds.

NPS (with pecans): 165 C, 40 mg CH, 10 mg S*

Tipsy Whipped Cream Frosting: Prepare as directed but flavor with brandy or rum extract instead of vanilla or 1–2 tablespoons brandy, rum, or bourbon. *(Note:* For a really Tipsy Cake, pierce unfrosted cake layers all over with a metal skewer and drizzle with a little liquor; cover loosely and let stand 1 hour before filling and frosting.)

NPS (with brandy extract): 130 C, 40 mg CH, 10 mg S*

Coconut Whipped Cream Frosting: Prepare as directed and fold in 1 cup flaked or toasted flaked coconut.

NPS: 150 C, 40 mg CH, 10 mg S*

Neapolitan Fruit Cream Filling: Use this only as a filling, it's too soft for frosting. Make half the recipe and fold in 1/2 cup minced, well-drained peaches, pears, apricots, pineapple, or fruit salad or 1/2 cup thinly sliced bananas or berries.

NPS: 70 C, 20 mg CH, 5 mg S*

Warm-Weather Whipped Cream Frosting: Blend 1 teaspoon unflavored gelatin and 2 tablespoons cold water in a custard cup. Set in a small pan of simmering water and stir until gelatin dissolves; cool. Gradually beat into cream, then proceed as recipe directs.

NPS: 130 C, 40 mg CH, 10 mg S*

7-MINUTE FROSTING

Enough to fill and frost a 9" (2-layer) cake (16 servings) or 24 cupcakes

Some electric mixers will whip up 7-Minute Frosting in *less* than 7 minutes.

2 egg whites
1 1/2 cups sugar
1/4 teaspoon cream of tartar or 1 tablespoon light corn syrup
1/3 cup cold water
1 teaspoon vanilla

Mix all ingredients except vanilla in the top of a double boiler and set over just boiling water. Beat constantly with rotary or electric beater until stiff peaks form, 4–7 minutes. Off heat, add vanilla and beat until of good spreading consistency.

NPS (16–24): 75–50 C, 0 mg CH, 5 mg S*

Orange or Lemon 7-Minute Frosting: Prepare as directed but use orange or lemon juice instead of water and 1/2 teaspoon orange or lemon extract instead of vanilla. If you like, fold in the finely grated rind of 1 orange or lemon just before using and tint pale orange or yellow.

NPS (16–24): 80–50 C, 0 mg CH, 5 mg S*

Peppermint 7-Minute Frosting: Prepare as directed but flavor with 1/2 teaspoon peppermint extract or 1/4 teaspoon oil of peppermint instead of vanilla. Tint pale pink and fold in 1/3 cup crushed peppermint candy.

NPS (16–24): 85–55 C, 0 mg CH, 5 mg S*

Coffee 7-Minute Frosting: Prepare as directed but use 1/2 cup firmly packed dark brown sugar and 1 cup granulated; also dissolve 1 tablespoon instant coffee powder in the water before adding.

NPS (16–24): 75–50 C, 0 mg CH, 10–5 mg S*

Caramel 7-Minute Frosting: Prepare as directed but use 1 cup firmly packed dark brown sugar and 1/2 cup granulated; flavor with maple flavoring instead of vanilla.

NPS (16–24): 75–50 C, 0 mg CH, 10–5 mg S*

Fruit or Nut 7-Minute Frosting: Prepare as directed, then fold in 1/2– 3/4 cup prunes or raisins or 1/2– 3/4 cup coarsely chopped nuts.

NPS (16–24) (with raisins): 90–60 C, 0 mg CH, 5 mg S*
NPS (16–24) (with walnuts): 110–75 C, 0 mg CH, 5 mg S*

Chocolate 7-Minute Frosting: Prepare as directed, then fold in 2 melted and cooled

(1-ounce) squares unsweetened chocolate. Do not beat, just stir to mix.

NPS (16–24): 95–60 C, 0 mg CH, 5 mg S*

Coconut 7–Minute Frosting: Prepare as directed, tint pastel, if you like, then fold in 1/2 cup flaked coconut. After frosting cake, sprinkle with additional flaked coconut.

NPS (16–24): 85–60 C, 0 mg CH, 5 mg S*

WHITE MOUNTAIN FROSTING

Enough to fill and frost a 9″ (2-layer) cake (16 servings)

A fluffy white frosting that you don't have to beat *on* the stove.

3/4 cup sugar
1/4 cup light corn syrup
1/4 cup water
3 egg whites, at room temperature
1 teaspoon vanilla or 1/2 teaspoon almond
   extract

Mix sugar, corn syrup, and water in a small, heavy saucepan, insert candy thermometer, partially cover pan, and bring to a boil over moderate heat. Remove cover and boil *without stirring* until thermometer registers 240°–242° F. or until a drop on the tip of a spoon will spin a 6″–8″ thread. Just before syrup reaches proper temperature, begin beating egg whites with an electric mixer until soft peaks form. When syrup reaches correct temperature, set mixer at high speed and pour syrup into whites in a slow thin stream. Continue beating until glossy and firm enough to hold a shape. Beat in vanilla.

NPS: 55 C, 0 mg CH, 15 mg S*

VARIATIONS

Lemon or Orange Mountain Frosting: Prepare as directed but substitute lemon or orange juice for water and flavor with 1/2 teaspoon lemon or orange extract and the finely grated rind of 1 lemon or orange.

NPS: 55 C, 0 mg CH, 15 mg S*

Marble Mountain Frosting: Prepare as directed and just before spreading swirl in 1 (1-ounce) square coarsely grated unsweetened chocolate or 1 (1-ounce) envelope no-melt unsweetened chocolate to create a marbleized effect.

NPS: 65 C, 0 mg CH, 15 mg S*

Maple Mountain Frosting: Use 3/4 cup firmly packed light brown sugar instead of granulated and substitute 1 teaspoon maple flavoring for vanilla.

NPS: 55 C, 0 mg CH, 15 mg S*

SEAFOAM FROSTING

Enough to fill and frost a 9″ (2-layer) cake (16 servings)

Almost as good as seafoam candy. Delicious on chocolate or burnt sugar cakes.

2/3 cup firmly packed light brown sugar
1/4 cup light corn syrup
1 egg white
1/8 teaspoon cream of tartar
1/8 teaspoon salt
2 tablespoons water
1 teaspoon vanilla

Combine all ingredients except vanilla in the top of a double boiler, set over boiling water, and beat with a rotary beater or portable electric mixer until mixture stands in peaks. Off heat, add vanilla and continue beating until mixture will hold deep swirls. Use at once.

NPS: 50 C, 0 mg CH, 25 mg S*

FUDGE FROSTING

Enough to frost a 9″ round or square cake (16 servings)

Really fudgy.

1 1/2 cups sugar
1/2 cup water or milk
1 tablespoon light corn syrup
1 tablespoon butter or margarine
2 (1-ounce) squares unsweetened chocolate,
   coarsely grated, or 2 (1-ounce) envelopes no-
   melt unsweetened chocolate
1 teaspoon vanilla

Place all ingredients except vanilla in a heavy saucepan with a candy thermometer, set over moderate heat, and stir once or twice as chocolate melts. Boil *without stirring* until thermometer reaches 234° F. or until a little mixture dropped into cold water forms a very soft ball. Remove from heat at once and cool without stirring to 120° F. (lukewarm); mix in vanilla and beat until thick and of good spreading consistency. *(Note:* If frosting seems thick, add a little milk or light cream; if too thin, beat in a little sifted confectioners' sugar.)

NPS (with water and butter): 100 C, 1 mg CH, 10
  mg S*
NPS (with milk and butter): 105 C, 5 mg CH, 10
  mg S*

Vanilla Fudge Frosting: Prepare as directed but use milk, light or sour cream instead of water and omit chocolate.

NPS (with milk and butter): 85 C, 5 mg CH, 10 mg S*

NPS (with light cream and butter): 95 C, 5 mg CH, 10 mg S*

Caramel Fudge Frosting: Prepare as directed, using 1 cup firmly packed light or dark brown sugar and 1/2 cup granulated sugar; also use milk, dark corn syrup and, if you like, add 1 teaspoon maple flavoring in addition to vanilla. Omit chocolate.

NPS (with butter): 90 C, 5 mg CH, 15 mg S*

BROILED PENUCHE ICING

Enough to top a 9" square cake (16 servings) ▢

A fast frosting for simple cakes.

2/3 cup firmly packed light or dark brown sugar
1/4 cup butter or margarine, softened to room temperature
1/4 cup heavy cream
1/2 cup finely chopped nuts

Preheat broiler. Mix all ingredients and spread evenly on warm cake. Set on wire cake rack over baking pan and broil 5" from the heat 3–4 minutes until mixture bubbles and browns lightly. Cool slightly before cutting.

NPS (with butter): 95 C, 15 mg CH, 35 mg S*

For a 13" × 9" × 2" Cake (24 servings): Use 1 cup sugar, 1/3 cup each butter and cream, and 3/4 cup nuts.

NPS (with butter): 90 C, 10 mg CH, 30 mg S*

Broiled Coconut Icing: Prepare as directed but substitute 1/2 cup flaked coconut for nuts.

NPS (with butter): 85 C, 15 mg CH, 35 mg S*

Broiled Peanut Butter Icing: Prepare as directed but substitute 1/4 cup peanut butter for butter and use 1/2 cup minced *unsalted* toasted, blanched peanuts.

NPS: 95 C, 5 mg CH, 30 mg S*

ROYAL ICING (ORNAMENTAL FROSTING)

Enough to decorate a 9" or 10" cake (16 servings) ▢

This frosting holds its shape well, dries hard, and is ideal for making durable decorations. It also helps keep cakes moist.

3 egg whites, at room temperature
1/4 teaspoon cream of tartar
1 (1-pound) box confectioners' sugar, sifted

Beat egg whites and cream of tartar until foamy. Gradually beat in sugar, then beat at high speed until very thick and glossy (beaters when withdrawn should leave sharp, firm peaks). Use to frost and decorate cakes. Keep bowl of frosting covered with damp cloth as you work to prevent "crusting." If frosting should lose stiffness, beat at high speed until firm again, or if necessary (sometimes true in humid weather) beat in a little additional confectioners' sugar.

NPS: 110 C, 0 mg CH, 10 mg S*

QUICK GLACÉ ICING

Enough to glaze about 1 1/3 dozen Petits Fours ▢

This icing dries hard with a lovely glossy finish.

3 cups sifted confectioners' sugar
3 tablespoons light corn syrup
3 tablespoons water
Few drops any food coloring (optional)

Place all ingredients except food coloring in the top of a double boiler over *simmering* water and heat, stirring, until sugar dissolves and mixture is smooth. Do not allow water underneath to boil or icing will not be glossy. Tint with food coloring as desired. Spoon over Petits Fours or any small cakes set on wire racks over baking sheets. Scrape up run-over from baking sheet, return to double boiler, and warm again until of pouring consistency. If thick, add a few drops of warm water.

NP Petit Four: 85 C, 0 mg CH, 5 mg S*

Chocolate Glacé Icing: Prepare as directed and, when sugar is dissolved, add 1 1/2 ounces semisweet chocolate broken into bits and heat, stirring until blended. Add 1–2 tablespoons warm water to thin to pouring consistency; do not overheat or icing will not be glossy.

NP Petit Four: 95 C, 0 mg CH, 5 mg S*

SNOW GLAZE

Enough to glaze a large loaf or tube cake (16 servings) or 24 cupcakes ⊠

A quick and easy topping for any simple cake.

1 cup sifted confectioners' sugar
2 tablespoons warm milk
1/4 teaspoon almond extract

Sprinkle confectioners' sugar slowly into milk and blend smooth. Mix in almond extract, spread on cake, and let stand until glaze hardens.

NPS (16–24): 25–15 C, 0 mg CH, 1 mg S*

V A R I A T I O N S

Sugar Glaze: Prepare as directed but substitute warm water for milk.

NPS (16-24): 25–15 C, 0 mg CH, 0 mg S*

Lemon or Orange Sugar Glaze: Prepare as directed but substitute warm lemon or orange juice for milk and flavor with 1 teaspoon finely grated lemon or orange rind.

NPS (16–24): 25–15 C, 0 mg CH, 1 mg S*

Tutti-Frutti Glaze: Prepare as directed but substitute 1 lightly beaten egg white for milk. Spread glaze on cake and decorate with slivered mixed candied fruit peel, candied red cherries, angelica, and thinly sliced blanched almonds. Recipe too flexible for meaningful nutritional analysis.

Easy White Icing (perfect for icing hot sweet breads): Prepare as directed but use cold milk and reduce quantity to about 1 tablespoon. Flavor with 1/4 teaspoon vanilla instead of almond extract.

NPS (16–24): 25–15 C, 0 mg CH, 1 mg S*

CHOCOLATE GLAZE

Enough to glaze a 9" cake (16 servings) or 6–8 Chocolate Éclairs ⊠

2 (1-ounce) squares unsweetened chocolate
1 teaspoon butter or margarine
1 cup sifted confectioners' sugar
3 tablespoons warm water

Melt chocolate and butter in the top of a double boiler over simmering water; stir to blend well. Set top of double boiler on a damp cloth, add 1/2 cup confectioners' sugar and 1 tablespoon water; beat until smooth. Add remaining sugar and water and beat until glossy. Use to glaze éclairs, other pastries, or the tops of cakes.

NPS (16) (with butter): 45 C, 1 mg CH, 5 mg S*

NPS (6–8) (with butter, for éclairs): 115–90 C, 1 mg CH, 5 mg S*

APRICOT GLAZE

Enough to glaze 4 dozen Petits Fours

An excellent base coat for Petits Fours and other small cakes to be covered with thin, hard, smooth icings.

2 cups apricot preserves
1/2 cup water

Heat preserves and water in a saucepan over low heat, stirring constantly, until mixture bubbles; heat and stir 2–3 minutes longer, press through a fine sieve, and cool slightly before using.

NP Petit Four: 35 C, 0 mg CH, 1 mg S*

BASIC VANILLA CREAM FILLING

About 1 cup, enough to fill a 9" (2-layer) cake (16 servings)

2 tablespoons cornstarch
1/3 cup sugar
3/4 cup milk
1 egg yolk lightly beaten with 1/4 cup milk
1 teaspoon vanilla

Blend cornstarch, sugar, and milk in a small saucepan and heat, stirring constantly, over moderate heat until mixture boils and is thick; boil and stir 1/2 minute longer. Off heat, beat a little hot mixture into egg yolk, return all to pan *gradually,* beating constantly. Mix in vanilla and cool to room temperature, beating now and then.

NPS: 35 C, 20 mg CH, 10 mg S*

V A R I A T I O N S

Poppy Seed Cream Filling: Prepare as directed and mix in 2 tablespoons poppy seeds.

NPS: 40 C, 20 mg CH, 10 mg S*

Double Cream Filling: Prepare as directed and fold in 1/3 cup heavy cream whipped to soft peaks. *(Note:* Also good with any of the flavor variations.)

NPS: 45 C, 25 mg CH, 5 mg S*

Chocolate Cream Filling: Prepare as directed but increase sugar to 1/2 cup and add 2 (1-ounce) squares melted semisweet chocolate or 2 (1-ounce) envelopes no-melt unsweetened chocolate along with vanilla; blend well. If mixture seems thick, thin with a little milk.

NPS: 55 C, 25 mg CH, 5 mg S*

Butterscotch Cream Filling: Substitute 1/2 cup firmly packed dark brown sugar for the granulated and, if you like, use maple flavoring instead of vanilla.

*NPS: 45 C, 20 mg CH, 10 mg S**

Coffee Cream Filling: Add 1 1/2 teaspoons instant coffee powder along with the sugar.

*NPS: 35 C, 20 mg CH, 10 mg S**

Fruit Cream Filling: Prepare as directed but omit vanilla and add 1/4 teaspoon lemon or orange extract and 2 teaspoons finely grated lemon or orange rind.

*NPS: 35 C, 20 mg CH, 10 mg S**

Coconut Cream Filling: Prepare as directed and mix in 1/2–2/3 cup flaked coconut.

*NPS: 45 C, 20 mg CH, 10 mg S**

PASTRY CREAM

Enough to fill a 3-layer cake (16 servings) or 1 dozen Cream Puffs or Chocolate Éclairs

What to put inside feathery French pastries.

1/2 cup sifted flour
1/2 cup sugar
1/8 teaspoon salt
2 cups milk
2 eggs + 2 egg yolks, lightly beaten
1 teaspoon vanilla

Mix flour, sugar, and salt in the top of a double boiler. Add milk slowly, blending until smooth. Heat and stir over direct moderate heat until thickened and smooth. Mix about 1/2 cup hot mixture into eggs, then return to pan. Set over simmering water and cook and stir 2–3 minutes until thick. Off heat, stir in vanilla. Place a piece of wax paper flat on sauce to prevent a skin from forming and cool. Stir well, cover, and chill until ready to use as a pastry filling.

*NPS: (12–16): 100–75 C, 95–75 mg CH, 55–40 mg S**

LEMON FILLING

Enough to fill an 8" or 9" (2-layer) cake (16 servings)

3 tablespoons cornstarch
1 cup sugar
1/2 cup lemon juice
1 cup hot water
2 tablespoons butter or margarine
2 tablespoons finely grated lemon rind
Few drops yellow food coloring

Mix cornstarch and sugar in a saucepan, stir in lemon juice and water, and bring to a full boil, stirring constantly. Reduce heat slightly and heat and stir until thickened and clear. Off heat, beat in butter and lemon rind, then tint pale yellow. Place wax paper flat on sauce and cool to room temperature. Beat with a whisk or rotary beater before using.

*NPS (with butter): 70 C, 5 mg CH, 15 mg S**

VARIATIONS

Lime Filling: Prepare as directed but substitute lime juice and rind for the lemon. Tint pale green.

*NPS (with butter): 70 C, 5 mg CH, 15 mg S**

Orange Filling: Prepare as directed, using 1 cup orange juice and 1/2 cup hot water; substitute orange rind for the lemon. Tint pale orange with a red and yellow food coloring.

*NPS (with butter): 75 C, 5 mg CH, 15 mg S**

Pineapple Filling: Mix cornstarch with sugar, add 1 cup pineapple juice, 1/4 cup hot water, and 1/2 cup well-drained crushed pineapple. Heat and stir until thickened; off heat, beat in the butter and 1/4 teaspoon lemon rind. Do not tint.

*NPS (with butter): 80 C, 5 mg CH, 15 mg S**

Rich Fruit Filling: Prepare any of the preceding recipes in the top of a double boiler over direct heat. When cornstarch mixture is thickened and clear, mix a little into 2 lightly beaten egg yolks, return to pan, set over simmering water, and heat and stir 1–2 minutes. Proceed as directed but do not tint. Recipe too flexible for meaningful nutritional analysis.

Fruit Cream Filling: Prepare Lemon, Lime, Orange, or Pineapple Filling as directed and, just before using, mix in 1 cup softly whipped cream. Recipe too flexible for meaningful nutritional count.

STRAWBERRY FILLING

Enough to fill a 9" or 10" (3-layer) cake (16 servings)

Soft and fluffy. Use to fill angel, white, or yellow cakes or jelly rolls.

1 (6-ounce) package strawberry-flavored gelatin
1 cup very hot water
1 pint fresh strawberries, hulled and sliced thin, or 1 (10-ounce) package thawed frozen, sliced strawberries
1 teaspoon almond extract
1/2 cup heavy cream

Mix gelatin and water, stirring until gelatin

dissolves. Add strawberries and almond extract and mix well. Cover and chill until thick and syrupy, but not firm. Whip cream to soft peaks, then fold into strawberry mixture. Chill 20–30 minutes until thick but not set. Use to fill Angel Food Cake, cut in 3 layers, any 3-layer white or yellow cake, or roll up inside jelly roll.

NPS: 85 C, 10 mg CH, 35 mg S*

PINEAPPLE-COCONUT FILLING

Enough to fill a 3-tier wedding cake (100 servings)

2 (1-pound 4-ounce) cans crushed pineapple (do not drain)
1½ cups sugar
¼ cup lemon juice
¼ cup cornstarch blended with ½ cup cold water or pineapple juice
2 (3½-ounce) cans flaked coconut

Mix all but last ingredient in a saucepan, set over moderate heat, and heat and stir until thickened and clear and no taste of cornstarch remains. Cool 10 minutes, stir in coconut, and cool to room temperature, stirring now and then.

NPS: 30 C, 0 mg CH, 1 mg S*

NINETEEN

Cookies

Take a wintry afternoon, add an oven full of cookies scenting the air with their warm, sugary promise and you have one of the memories dear to most of us. Cookies are where most of us begin our cooking lessons because they're fast, fun, and practically disaster-proof—a little too much liquid or flour won't destroy them *or* the cook's enthusiasm.

Basically, there are six different types of cookies: *Drop, Rolled, Molded or Pressed, Refrigerator, Bar,* and *No-Bake.* We'll discuss them one by one, but first, some tips that apply to them all.

HOW TO MAKE BETTER COOKIES

Pans and Preparing Pans:

• For delicately browned cookies, choose shiny baking sheets rather than dark ones. Dark surfaces absorb heat more quickly and cookies tend to overbrown on the bottom. When using nonstick pans, keep a close eye out until you learn how fast they bake.
• For uniform baking, make sure baking sheets are 1″–2″ smaller all round than the oven (heat must circulate freely). Also make certain pans do not touch oven walls at any point.
• Grease pans only when recipes specify doing so.
• For greasing, use melted clarified butter* (unsalted) if you can afford it and shortening or cooking oil if you can't. Apply evenly and thinly with a pastry brush or small crumple of paper toweling, coating *bottoms of pans only.* Or use one of the low-fat, no-cholesterol, spray-on vegetable compounds as label directs. To simplify dishwashing, grease only those areas cookies will actually touch. *Note:* Even nonstick pans need greasing if the cookies contain much sugar or fruit.

• When baking cookies in quantity, line baking sheets with foil. Have several sheets of foil cut to size, then as each batch of cookies comes from the oven, lift them off, foil and all, and slide a fresh sheet into place.
• If you have no baking sheets, use a turned-upside-down roasting pan—turned upside down because cookies bake poorly in high-sided pans.

Mixing Cookies:

• Read recipe through carefully before beginning it.
• Have all utensils out, pans prepared, and ingredients measured before beginning.
• When using an electric mixer, use a medium speed for creaming shortening, sugar, and eggs and low speed for working in dry ingredients unless recipes specify otherwise.
• When using a food processor: first of all, choose simple recipes only and those containing shortening of some sort, whole eggs or egg yolks. Equip machine with metal chopping blade. Cream shortening until light by churning 10–15 seconds nonstop; add sugar and churn 10–15 seconds longer. Scrape work bowl sides down, add eggs and vanilla or other flavoring, and mix in by snapping motor on and off four to six times. Now add combined dry ingredients in two installments, snapping motor on and off five to six times after each addition and scraping work bowl sides down. The instant dough is blended, remove from processor work bowl and stir in any nuts, fruits, or chocolate chips by hand (the processor will churn them to paste). *Caution:* Avoid overmixing, especially after eggs and dry ingredients have been added. You will toughen the cookies.
• When mixing by hand, use a spoon with a long, comfortable handle—wooden spoons are especially good.
• Always mix in dry ingredients with a light hand and only enough to blend. Overbeating

at this point tends to make the cookies tough.

Placing Cookies on Pans:

• Always put cookies on *cool* baking sheets; if sheets are warm, cookies will spread unnecessarily. When baking in quantity, use two or three sheets so that there is time to cool each before adding a fresh batch of cookies.
• Allow plenty of spreading room when spacing cookies on sheets (recipes specify just how much). As a rule, the thinner the dough or the higher the butter or shortening content, the more cookies will spread.
• Whenever you have less than a full sheet of cookies to bake, use a turned-upside-down pie tin or small baking pan. An unfilled sheet of cookies will bake unevenly.
• Avoid placing cookies too near edges of baking sheets; they will brown much more quickly than those in the center.
• Always scrape crumbs from a used sheet and wipe it thoroughly with paper toweling before reusing.

Baking:

• Let oven preheat a full 15 minutes before baking cookies.
• Unless recipe states otherwise, bake cookies as near the center of oven as possible. Those placed too low tend to burn on the bottom, those placed too high will be brown on top but raw in the middle.
• Unless your oven is very large, do not attempt to bake more than one sheet, certainly no more than two sheets of cookies at a time. Whenever you bake two sheets at once, stagger them, one slightly above the other, so heat can circulate freely and reverse positions of pans halfway through baking.
• Because there is some heat build-up in even the best of ovens, you can expect second, third, and fourth sheets of cookies to bake slightly faster than the first.
• Turn baking sheets as needed during baking so that cookies will brown as evenly as possible.
• Always use a timer when baking cookies.
• Check cookies after minimum baking time and, if not done, bake maximum time.
• If, despite all precautions, some cookies are done ahead of others, simply remove from baking sheet.

Baking Cookies in a Convection Oven

All kinds of cookies bake and brown beautifully via convection (hot circulating air). Most manufacturers claim that their convec-

tion ovens need no preheating, but they do recommend reducing baking temperatures 50°–75° F. below those used in conventional ovens (never, however, use temperatures lower than 300° F.). Before baking any cookies, read your convection oven's manual. Also see Convection Ovens in Chapter 1, then follow these guidelines:
• Use shiny metal baking sheets and pans for light, tender, chewy, or crisp cookies. *Note:* Baking sheets without a lip allow air to circulate more freely.
• Allow at least 1″ space between pans, also between oven walls and pans.
• Check cookies often for doneness (they may cook 5–10 minutes faster than in conventional ovens—even at reduced temperatures).
• If you should bake two sheets of cookies at a time, bake those on the bottom rack an additional 2–4 minutes to compensate for the blocked air flow.

To Tell When Cookies Are Done, Use the Following Tests:

Crisp, Thin Cookies: Check color; cookies should be firm to the touch, delicately browned or lightly ringed with brown.

Fairly Thick Dropped or Shaped Cookies: Press lightly in the center; if no imprint remains, cookies are done.

Meringue Kisses: Tap lightly; if kisses sound hollow, they are done.

Bars: Press lightly in center; mixture should feel firm yet springy. Bars should also have pulled from sides of pan.
• To rescue cookies that have burned on the bottom, grate off blackened parts with a fine lemon rind grater.

Removing Cookies from Baking Sheets:

• Use wide spatulas or pancake turners.
• Unless recipe states otherwise, lift cookies at once to wire racks to cool. Exceptions are very soft cookies, which must be firm before a spatula can be slipped underneath them.

Baking Cookies in a Microwave Oven

The only cookies that microwave well are soft and chewy bars—brownies, for example. But before attempting these, study the manual accompanying your microwave (the manufacturer probably includes recipes worked out for your particular model). Also see Microwave Ovens in Chapter 1, then observe these guidelines when microwaving bar cookies:
• For best results, use square pans of clear

flameproof glass or plastic-coated "active" microwave cookware (see Microwave Utensil Guide, Chapter 1).

• If cookie mixture is very moist, line bottom of pan with paper toweling (it will absorb excess moisture and make bars easier to remove from pan). No need to grease or flour pans. Microwave, uncovered, on a trivet or inverted saucer as manufacturer directs, rotating pan 90° every 2 minutes. If corners of mixture cook more quickly than center, shield them with triangles of foil wrapped over pan corners.

• To test for doneness, feel top of bar cookies; it should be springy (test several places). Surface should also be mostly dry although a few damp spots are normal (these will dry as cookies *stand)*. If using a clear glass pan, check bottom; center of cookie mixture should appear almost dry.

• When cookies come from microwave oven, allow 5–10 minutes *standing time* in pan directly on heat-resistant surface or wooden board to complete the cooking. *Note:* Fudge-type brownies may need as much as 20 minutes *standing time* to firm up.

• Cool bars thoroughly, then frost, if desired (this is particularly important with light-colored bars, which will appear pallid after microwaving). *Note:* If using a paper-towel-lined pan, invert cooled, uncut bars onto a wooden board, peel off paper, return bars to pan, then frost and cut.

Cooling Cookies:

• Never overlap cookies on racks and never arrange more than one layer deep; cookies will stick to one another.

• Remove to canisters as soon as cool.

Storing Cookies:

Soft Cookies: Store in canisters with tight-fitting covers and, if necessary, with a chunk of apple or bread to keep them moist (replace apple or bread often). Brownies and other bars can be stored in their baking pans, tightly wrapped in foil or plastic food wrap.

Crisp Cookies: Blanket statements can't be made because much depends on weather. Crisp cookies, for example, will soon go limp if stored in a loosely covered container in a muggy climate; in such areas they *must* be stored airtight. But in dry areas, the treatment is just the opposite: Store in loosely covered containers. If cookies should soften, crispen by heating 3–5 minutes at 350° F.

DECORATING COOKIES

Cookies can be decorated either before or after baking. Simple, sprinkled, or pressed-on designs can be applied before cookies go into the oven, but intricate designs, whether painted or piped on, are best done after baking.

To Decorate Before Baking:

Most Suitable Cookies: Simple, relatively flat cookies: dropped or rolled cookies, molded or cookie press cookies, refrigerator or commercial slice-and-bake cookies.

Sprinkle-On Decorations: Brush unbaked cookies with milk, cream, or lightly beaten egg white and sprinkle with colored sugar or coconut, silver *dragées,* chocolate jimmies, decorettes, finely chopped nuts or candied fruit, cinnamon sugar (supermarket shelves are loaded with jiffy decorator items). Brush any spilled sugar or decoration from baking sheet, then bake as directed. For an extra-special touch, cut paper stencils out of heavy paper—bells, stars, initials—and color cut-out areas only.

Press-On Decorations: Brush unbaked cookies with milk or cream and press on raisins, dried currants, candied cherries, nuts, chocolate or butterscotch bits, mini-marshmallows, gumdrops, cinnamon "red hots" in desired designs.

Paint-On Decorations: These are best for light-colored rolled cookies. Make an egg paint by mixing 1 egg yolk with 1/4 teaspoon cold water and 2 or 3 drops food coloring (this amount will be enough for 1 or 2 colors). Using fresh new paintbrushes, paint simple designs on unbaked cookies, then bake as directed until firm but not brown. If paint thickens on standing, thin with a few drops cold water.

To Decorate After Baking:

Most Suitable Cookies: Large, simple, flat cookies, especially rolled cookies.

Paint-On Decorations: Cool cookies and frost with a smooth, thin layer of Royal Icing. Keep bowl of icing covered with a damp cloth or paper toweling to keep it from hardening while you work. For an absolutely smooth surface, keep dipping knife or spatula in hot water and use long sweeping strokes. Let icing harden thoroughly. Paint on designs, using clean, fresh paintbrushes and paste food colors (liquid colors will soften icing too much).

Pipe-On Decorations: Cool cookies and, if you like, frost with Royal Icing as directed for Paint-On Decorations. Tint small amounts of icing desired colors and put through pastry tubes fitted with plain or decorative tips, tracing outlines of cookies or adding any decorative touches you like. Be sure to keep each container of icing covered with a damp cloth so it won't dry out.

To Make Hanging Cookies (wonderful as Christmas tree decorations):

Most Suitable Cookies: Large decorated rolled cookies, particularly fancy cutouts.

To Attach Hangers to Unbaked Cookies: "Stick" large loops of thin ribbon or thread to backs of unbaked cookies with tiny dabs of dough. Bake as directed, then decorate.

To Attach Hangers to Baked Cookies (good only for those that are not shattery-crisp): While cookies are still warm and pliable, quickly draw lengths of coarse thread through top, using a sturdy needle. Don't insert too close to edge or cookies may break. Allow 6"–8" thread for each cookie so it can easily be hung. Decorate as desired.

BASIC COOKIE MIX

9 cups ☒ ¢

A good mix to have on hand because there are ten different quick cookies you can make from it.

4 cups sifted flour
4 cups sugar
1½ cups skim (nonfat) dry milk powder
1½ tablespoons baking powder
1½ teaspoons salt

Place all ingredients in a large bowl and mix well with a spoon; sift mixture twice. Store in a tightly covered container. Keeps several weeks at room temperature.

NP Cup: 570 C, 5 mg CH, 645 mg S*

10 Quick Cookies to Make from the Basic Mix

Sugar Cookies *(3 dozen):* With a spoon, mix 2 cups Basic Cookie Mix, ½ cup melted butter or margarine, 1 lightly beaten egg, and 1 teaspoon vanilla. Lightly flour hands and shape in 1" balls; arrange 2" apart on well-greased baking sheets. Bake 12–15 minutes at 350° F. until golden. Cool 1–2 minutes on sheets, then transfer to wire racks to cool.

NP Cookie (with butter): 55 C, 15 mg CH, 65 mg S*

Raisin Cookies *(3 dozen):* Prepare Sugar Cookie dough as directed, mix in ½ cup seedless or golden seedless raisins, shape and bake as directed.

NP Cookie (with butter): 65 C, 15 mg CH, 65 mg S*

Coconut Cookies *(3 dozen):* Prepare Sugar Cookie dough as directed, mix in ½ cup flaked coconut, shape and bake as directed.

NP Cookie (with butter): 60 C, 15 mg CH, 65 mg S*

Easiest Ever Chocolate Chip Cookies *(3 dozen):* Prepare Sugar Cookie dough as directed, mix in ½ cup semisweet chocolate bits, shape and bake as directed.

NP Cookie (with butter): 70 C, 15 mg CH, 65 mg S*

Nut Cookies *(3 dozen):* Prepare Sugar Cookie dough as directed, mix in ½ cup chopped walnuts, pecans, or blanched almonds, shape and bake as directed.

NP Cookie (with butter): 70 C, 15 mg CH, 65 mg S*

Spice Drops *(3 dozen):* Mix 2 cups Basic Cookie Mix with 1 teaspoon cinnamon, ¼ teaspoon each ginger and allspice, and ⅛ teaspoon nutmeg. Stir in 1 lightly beaten egg, ½ cup melted butter or margarine, and 1–2 tablespoons water, just enough to make mixture a good consistency for dropping from a spoon. Drop from a teaspoon onto well-greased baking sheets, spacing cookies 2" apart, and bake 12–15 minutes at 350° F. until golden. Cool 1–2 minutes on sheets, then transfer to wire racks to cool.

NP Cookie (with butter): 55 C, 15 mg CH, 65 mg S*

Chocolate Drops *(3 dozen):* Mix 2 cups Basic Cookie Mix with ¼ cup sifted cocoa. Stir in 1 lightly beaten egg, ½ cup melted butter, ¼ cup water, and 1 teaspoon vanilla. Drop from a teaspoon onto well-greased baking sheets, spacing cookies 2" apart, and bake 12–15 minutes at 350° F. until lightly browned around edges. Let cool 1–2 minutes on sheets, then lift to wire racks to cool.

NP Cookie: 60 C, 15 mg CH, 65 mg S*

Peanut Butter Balls *(3 dozen):* Mix 2 cups Basic Cookie Mix with 1 lightly beaten egg, ¼ cup melted butter or margarine, ½ cup crunchy or creamy peanut butter, and 1 teaspoon vanilla. With lightly floured hands, shape into 1" balls and space 2" apart on lightly greased baking sheets. Bake 12 minutes at 350° F. or until the color of sand. Transfer to wire racks to cool.

NP Cookie (with butter): 65 C, 10 mg CH, 70 mg S*

Brownies *(16):* With a spoon mix 2 cups Basic Cookie Mix, 1 lightly beaten egg, 1/3 cup each cold water and melted butter or margarine, 1 teaspoon vanilla, and 2 (1-ounce) envelopes no-melt unsweetened chocolate or 1/4 cup sifted cocoa. Fold in 1/2–3/4 cup chopped pecans or walnuts. Beat by hand 1 minute, spoon into a greased 9″ × 9″ × 2″ baking pan, and bake 25 minutes at 375° F. or until top springs back when touched. Cool upright in pan on rack, then cut into large squares.

NP Brownie (with butter): 150 C, 30 mg CH, 125 mg S*

Oatmeal Bars *(32):* With a spoon mix 2 cups Basic Cookie Mix, 1 1/2 cups uncooked quick-cooking oatmeal, 1 lightly beaten egg, 3/4 cup melted butter or margarine, 1/4 cup cold water, 1 teaspoon vanilla, and 1/2 teaspoon almond extract. Spoon into a greased 13″ × 9″ × 2″ baking pan and bake 30–35 minutes at 350° F. until top is golden and sides shrink slightly from sides of pan. Cool upright in pan 10 minutes, then cut into small bars.

NP Bar (with butter): 90 C, 20 mg CH, 85 mg S*

DROP COOKIES

These are old favorites because they're so quick to mix and bake. They can be plain or studded with nuts, chocolate, or fruit; they can be crisp or chewy, thick or thin, rich or slimming (well, at least fairly low in calories). Best of all, they do not have to be rolled or shaped or pushed through a cookie press—simply dropped from a spoon and popped in the oven.

Some Tips:
• To minimize spreading during baking, chill dough slightly, then mound in center when dropping onto cookie sheets.
• Space cookies on sheets carefully, remembering that the thinner the dough, the more the cookies will spread (recipes specify just how much room to leave between cookies).
• For more interesting or uniform-size cookies, put dough through a pastry bag fitted with a large, plain round tube, piping directly onto baking sheets. Cookies without nuts, fruit, or other obstructive bits can be pressed through a large open star tip. *Note:*

Don't fill pastry bag more than two thirds full because the heat of your hands will soften the dough and make cookies spread more than usual.

LEMON WAFERS

About 4 1/2 dozen ☒

Nice and tart.

1/2 **cup butter or margarine, softened to room temperature**
1 1/3 **cups sugar**
3 **eggs**
3 **tablespoons lemon juice**
Grated rind of 1 lemon
2 **cups unsifted flour**
1/4 **teaspoon mace**
1/4 **teaspoon salt**

Preheat oven to 375° F. Cream butter until light and fluffy, then beat in sugar. Mix in eggs, one at a time, beating well after each addition. Stir in lemon juice and rind; mix in flour, mace, and salt. Drop from a teaspoon onto lightly greased baking sheets, spacing cookies 2″ apart. Bake about 15 minutes until cookies are lightly ringed with brown. While still warm, transfer to wire racks to cool.

NP Cookie (with butter): 55 C, 20 mg CH, 30 mg S*

BROWN SUGAR DROPS

6 dozen ☒ ¢

3 1/2 **cups sifted flour**
1 **teaspoon baking soda**
1 **teaspoon salt**
1 **cup butter or margarine or** 1/2 **cup each vegetable shortening and butter, softened to room temperature**
2 **cups firmly packed light or dark brown sugar**
2 **eggs**
1/2 **cup sour milk or buttermilk**
2 **teaspoons maple flavoring (optional)**

Preheat oven to 400° F. Sift flour with soda and salt and set aside. With a rotary beater or electric mixer cream butter, sugar, and eggs until well blended. Mix in sour milk and maple flavoring. Slowly mix in dry ingredients. Drop by rounded teaspoonfuls 2″ apart on greased baking sheets and bake 8–10 minutes until nearly firm (cookie should barely retain fingerprint when lightly touched). Transfer cookies to wire racks to cool.

NP Cookie (with butter): 70 C, 15 mg CH, 75 mg S*

Hermits *(About 8 dozen):* Prepare as directed but substitute 1/2 cup cold coffee for the sour milk. Mix 1 1/2 teaspoons cinnamon and 1/2 teaspoon nutmeg into dough, then 1 1/2 cups minced walnuts or pecans and 2 cups chopped seedless raisins. Bake as directed.

NP Cookie (with butter and walnuts): 70 C, 10 mg CH, 55 mg S*

Rocks *(8 dozen):* Prepare as directed, then stir in 2 cups seedless or golden seedless raisins, 1 1/2 teaspoons nutmeg, and 1/2 cup finely chopped candied citron. Bake as directed.

NP Cookie (with butter): 115 C, 20 mg CH, 115 mg S*

CHOCOLATE CHIP COOKIES

4 dozen ⊠

1 cup + 2 tablespoons sifted flour
1/2 teaspoon baking soda
1/2 teaspoon salt
1/2 cup butter or vegetable shortening, softened to room temperature
1/3 cup + 1 tablespoon sugar
1/3 cup + 1 tablespoon firmly packed light brown sugar
1 teaspoon vanilla
1 egg
1 (6-ounce) package semisweet chocolate bits
1/2 cup coarsely chopped pecans

Preheat oven to 375° F. Sift flour with baking soda and salt and set aside. Cream butter, sugars, and vanilla until light and fluffy. Beat in egg. Mix in dry ingredients; stir in chocolate bits and pecans. Drop by well-rounded 1/2 teaspoonfuls on lightly greased baking sheets, spacing cookies 2″ apart. Bake 10–12 minutes until lightly edged with brown. Transfer immediately to wire racks to cool.

NP Cookie (with butter): 70 C, 10 mg CH, 55 mg S*

PECAN CRISPS

5 dozen ⊠

Rather like a praline cookie.

1 cup butter (no substitute)
1 (1-pound) box light brown sugar
2 eggs
2 1/2 cups unsifted flour
1/2 teaspoon baking soda
1/2 teaspoon salt

1 teaspoon vanilla
1 1/2 cups coarsely chopped pecans

Preheat oven to 350° F. Cream butter until light, add sugar, and continue creaming until fluffy. Beat in eggs, one at a time. Mix in flour, soda, and salt, then remaining ingredients. Drop from a teaspoon onto lightly greased baking sheets, spacing cookies about 2″ apart, and bake 12–15 minutes until lightly browned. Remove at once to wire racks to cool.

NP Cookie: 100 C, 15 mg CH, 60 mg S*

MAUDE'S COOKIES

3 1/2–4 dozen small cookies ⚖ ⊠

A centuries-old Quaker recipe. The cookies are buttery and bland but the crystallized ginger decoration adds bite. Moreover, they are fairly low-calorie.

1/2 cup butter (no substitute), softened to room temperature
1/3 cup sugar
1 egg, well beaten
3/4 cup sifted flour
1/2 teaspoon vanilla
3 1/2–4 dozen pieces crystallized ginger about the size of raisins

Preheat oven to 350° F. Cream butter until fluffy, add sugar, and continue creaming until light. Beat in egg, then mix in flour and vanilla. Drop from a 1/2 teaspoon onto *lightly* greased baking sheets, spacing cookies 2″ apart—they spread quite a bit. Press a piece of candied ginger into the center of each cookie and bake 8–10 minutes until ringed with tan. Transfer at once to wire racks to cool.

NP Cookie: 40 C, 10 mg CH, 25 mg S*

CHOCOLATE PECAN WAFERS

4 dozen

Dark and chewy.

1/2 cup butter or margarine
1 cup sugar
1/4 teaspoon salt
1 teaspoon vanilla
2 eggs
3/4 cup sifted flour
4 (1-ounce) squares semisweet chocolate, melted
3/4 cup finely chopped pecans

Cream butter, sugar, and salt until light and fluffy, add vanilla and eggs, and beat well. Slowly mix in flour and remaining ingredients. Chill mixture in bowl 1/2 hour. Meanwhile, preheat oven to 350° F. Drop by rounded teaspoonfuls 2″ apart on greased baking sheets and flatten with bottom of a glass dipped in sugar (resugar glass for each cookie). Bake 15 minutes until tops retain almost no impression when touched. Transfer immediately to wire racks to cool.

NP Wafer: 70 C, 15 mg CH, 35 mg S*

BENNE WAFERS

4 dozen

In the South, sesame seeds are called "benne." This recipe is a Charleston favorite.

1 cup sifted flour
1/4 teaspoon salt
1/2 teaspoon baking powder
2 cups firmly packed dark brown sugar
1/2 cup butter or margarine
2 eggs, lightly beaten
1 teaspoon vanilla
2/3 cup toasted sesame seeds

Preheat oven to 325° F. Sift flour with salt and baking powder and set aside. Cream sugar and butter until thoroughly mixed; beat in eggs and vanilla. Slowly mix in flour, then sesame seeds, mixing just to blend. Drop mixture by level teaspoonfuls 5″ apart on well-greased baking sheets. Bake 10 minutes until lightly browned; cool on sheets about 1/2 minute, then lift to wire racks with a pancake turner. Store airtight when cool.

NP Wafer (with butter): 75 C, 15 mg CH, 40 mg S*

CARROT COOKIES

5 dozen ⚖ ¢

A cookie somewhat more nutritious than most.

1/2 cup butter or margarine
1 cup sugar
1 cup cooled, mashed, cooked carrots
  (unseasoned)
1 egg
1/2 teaspoon vanilla
1/2 teaspoon cinnamon
1/4 teaspoon ginger
1/4 teaspoon allspice
1 tablespoon finely grated orange rind
2 cups sifted flour
2 teaspoons baking powder
1/4 teaspoon salt

Preheat oven to 350° F. Cream butter until fluffy; add sugar gradually, beating well after each addition. Mix in carrots, egg, vanilla,

spices, and orange rind. Sift flour with baking powder and salt and beat in gradually. Drop from a teaspoon 1 1/2″ apart onto lightly greased baking sheets and bake 12–15 minutes until firm but not brown. Let cool about 1 minute on baking sheets, then transfer to wire racks to cool.

NP Cookie (with butter): 45 C, 10 mg CH, 40 mg S*

PUMPKIN COOKIES

4 dozen

Because the cookies are made with pumpkin, raisins, and nuts, they provide a little more than just "empty calories."

2 cups sifted flour
1 teaspoon baking soda
1/4 teaspoon salt
1 teaspoon cinnamon
1/4 teaspoon nutmeg
1/2 cup butter or margarine
1 cup sugar
1 teaspoon vanilla
1 cup canned pumpkin
1 cup seedless raisins
1 cup chopped pecans or walnuts

Preheat oven to 375° F. Sift flour with soda, salt, and spices and set aside. Cream butter with sugar until light, add vanilla and pumpkin, and mix well. Slowly add dry ingredients, then stir in raisins and nuts. Drop by rounded teaspoonfuls 2″ apart on greased baking sheets and bake 15 minutes until lightly browned. Transfer to wire racks to cool.

NP Cookie (with butter and pecans): 80 C, 5 mg CH, 50 mg S*

APPLESAUCE COOKIES

2 1/2 dozen ⊠

If you like caraway seeds, by all means stir them into the cookie dough. They give the cookies quite a different flavor.

2 tablespoons butter or margarine, softened to
  room temperature
1/2 cup sugar
1 egg, lightly beaten
1 cup packaged biscuit mix
1/2 cup applesauce
1 teaspoon finely grated lemon rind
1 1/2 teaspoons caraway seeds (optional)

Preheat oven to 375° F. Cream butter well with sugar and egg; mix in remaining ingredients until smooth. Drop from a teaspoon

2″ apart on well-greased baking sheets and bake 8 minutes until golden around the edges. Transfer at once to wire racks to cool. *(Note:* Since these cookies brown nicely on the underside but not on top, they're more attractive served bottom-side-up.)

NP Cookie (with butter): 45 C, 10 mg CH, 65 mg S*

OLD-FASHIONED GINGER BISCUITS

4½ dozen

For crisp cookies, store airtight; for softer ones, store loosely covered. To crispen again in humid weather, heat 3–5 minutes at 350° F., then cool.

2 cups sifted flour
½ teaspoon salt
2 teaspoons ginger
½ teaspoon cloves
2 teaspoons baking soda
¾ cup butter or margarine
1¼ cups sugar
1 egg, lightly beaten
¼ cup molasses

Preheat oven to 350° F. Sift flour with salt, spices, and baking soda and set aside. Cream butter and sugar until light and fluffy. Add egg and molasses, beating well after each addition. Mix in dry ingredients just until blended. Drop by rounded teaspoonfuls 3″ apart on greased baking sheets and bake 15 minutes until golden brown. *(Note:* Keep unused dough chilled until ready to bake.) Cool cookies on sheets 1–2 minutes, then transfer to wire racks to cool.

NP Cookie (with butter): 60 C, 10 mg CH, 80 mg S*

DROPPED OATMEAL CHIPPIES

3½ dozen ☒

1 cup sifted flour
2 teaspoons baking powder
½ teaspoon salt
½ cup butter or margarine, softened to room temperature
1 cup firmly packed light brown sugar
1½ cups uncooked quick-cooking oatmeal
2 eggs, lightly beaten
1 teaspoon vanilla
1 cup chopped pitted dates or seedless raisins

Preheat oven to 350° F. Sift flour with baking powder and salt. Stir butter and sugar together until just mixed; blend in flour, oatmeal, eggs, and vanilla. Stir in dates. Drop by rounded teaspoonfuls 2″ apart on greased baking sheets and bake 15–18 minutes until lightly browned and tops spring back when touched. Transfer at once to wire racks to cool.

NP Cookie (with butter): 75 C, 20 mg CH, 75 mg S*

MACAROONS

4½ dozen ⚖

These cookies are milk- and wheat-free, good for anyone with those specific allergies.

1 (½-pound) can almond paste
3 egg whites
1 cup sugar
½ cup sifted confectioners' sugar

Preheat oven to 300° F. Using a sharp knife, slice almond paste ¼″ thick, then chop until the consistency of coarse meal. Place in a large mixing bowl, add egg whites, and mix, using your hands. Knead in the sugar, a little bit at a time, then work in the confectioners' sugar until smooth. Line 2 baking sheets with heavy brown paper, then drop macaroons onto paper from a teaspoon, making each about 1″ in diameter and spacing about 2″ apart. Bake on lowest oven shelf 25–30 minutes until crazed and faintly tan. Remove from oven and let cool on paper to room temperature. Dampen paper by setting on top of moist towels, then peel off macaroons. Let cookies dry on wire racks at room temperature 1 hour, then store airtight.

NP Cookie: 40 C, 0 mg CH, 5 mg S*

CHOCOLATE "MACAROONS"

4 dozen ⚖

4 egg whites
2 cups sifted confectioners' sugar
2 cups fine vanilla wafer crumbs
2 (1-ounce) squares semisweet chocolate, grated
1½ teaspoons cinnamon

Preheat oven to 325° F. Beat egg whites until foamy, slowly add confectioners' sugar, and continue beating until firm peaks form. Stir in crumbs, chocolate, and cinnamon. Drop by level teaspoonfuls 2″ apart on well-greased baking sheets and bake 20 minutes. Transfer at once to wire racks to cool.

NP Cookie: 40 C, 1 mg CH, 15 mg S*

COCONUT MACAROONS

3 dozen

4 egg whites
¼ teaspoon salt
¾ teaspoon vanilla
¼ teaspoon almond extract
1⅓ cups sugar
2 (3½-ounce) cans flaked coconut

Preheat oven to 325° F. Beat egg whites with salt, vanilla, and almond extract until soft peaks form. Add sugar gradually, about 2 tablespoons at a time, and continue beating until stiff peaks form. Fold in coconut. Drop by rounded teaspoonfuls onto greased baking sheets, spacing cookies about 2″ apart. Bake 18–20 minutes until very delicately browned and firm to the touch. Cool briefly on sheets (just until macaroons can be lifted without losing their shape), then transfer to wire racks to cool.

NP Macaroon: 60 C, 0 mg CH, 20 mg S*

MERINGUE KISSES

3½ dozen ⚖

It's said that Marie Antoinette loved meringue kisses so much she often made them herself. If you've never made them, see Ground Rules for Making Meringues in the chapter on pies and pastries before beginning this recipe.

4 egg whites, at room temperature
¼ teaspoon salt
¼ teaspoon cream of tartar
1 cup sugar
¾ teaspoon vanilla or ¼ teaspoon almond extract
1 or 2 drops red or green food coloring (optional)

Preheat oven to 250° F. Line baking sheets with foil. Beat egg whites with a rotary beater or electric mixer at moderate speed until foamy; stir in salt and cream of tartar. Add sugar, 1 tablespoon at a time, beating well after each addition. Add vanilla and food coloring, if you wish, to tint meringue a pastel color. Beat hard at highest mixer speed until meringue is glossy and forms peaks that stand straight up when beater is withdrawn. Drop by rounded teaspoonfuls 2″ apart on prepared baking sheets; leave surface peaked or smooth into rounded caps. If you prefer, pipe meringue through a pastry bag fitted with a medium-size plain or star tip making each kiss about 1½″ in diameter. Bake 35–45 minutes until creamy-white and firm. For crisp kisses: Turn off

oven and let kisses cool in oven 2–3 hours without opening door. For chewier kisses, lift foil and kisses to wire rack and cool. Peel kisses from foil, using a spatula to help loosen them if necessary. Store airtight.

NP Kiss: 20 C, 0 mg CH, 20 mg S*

VARIATIONS

Filled Kisses: Sandwich 2 kisses together with a favorite filling or frosting. Recipe too flexible for meaningful nutritional count.

⚖ **Candied Kisses:** Prepare meringue mixture as directed, then fold in ⅔ cup very finely chopped candied fruits or mixed candied red and green cherries; shape and bake as directed.

NP Kiss: 35 C, 0 mg CH, 30 mg S*

⚖ **Nut Kisses:** Prepare meringue mixture as directed, then fold in 1 cup finely chopped nuts: pecans, walnuts, blanched almonds or pistachios, or unblanched hazelnuts. Shape, sprinkle tops with a few additional nuts, and bake as directed.

NP Kiss (with pecans): 40 C, 0 mg CH, 20 mg S*

⚖ **Chocolate Kisses:** Prepare meringue mixture as directed, then fold in 2 melted and cooled 1-ounce squares unsweetened or semisweet chocolate, leaving a marbled effect if you like.

NP Kiss (with unsweetened chocolate): 25 C, 0 mg CH, 20 mg S*

⚖ **Coconut Kisses:** Prepare meringue mixture as directed, fold in 1½ cups flaked coconut, shape and bake as directed.

NP Kiss: 35 C, 0 mg CH, 20 mg S*

⚖ **Brown Sugar Kisses:** When making meringue, substitute 1 cup light brown sugar for the granulated and proceed as recipe directs. (*Note:* For especially good flavor, use 1 teaspoon maple flavoring instead of vanilla, or ½ teaspoon each vanilla and maple flavoring.)

NP Kiss: 20 C, 0 mg CH, 20 mg S*

ORANGE-ALMOND LACE COOKIES

4 dozen ⚖

½ cup butter (no substitute)
½ cup sugar
½ teaspoon finely grated orange rind
½ cup ground blanched almonds
2 tablespoons flour
2 tablespoons milk

Preheat oven to 350° F. Mix all ingredients in a saucepan and heat and stir over moderate heat just until mixture bubbles; remove from heat at once. Drop by half teaspoonfuls 4" apart on ungreased baking sheets (you will only get 4 or 5 cookies on each sheet). Bake 6–7 minutes until golden brown and bubbly. Let stand 1 minute, just until cookies are firm enough to lift off sheet with a pancake turner. Cool on wire racks, then store airtight.

NP Cookie: 35 C, 5 mg CH, 20 mg S*

To Curl Cookies: As you lift each cookie from baking sheet, curl around handle of wooden spoon to form a cornucopia or "cigarette"; cool seam side down. If cookies cool too quickly to curl, return to oven briefly to soften.

FLORENTINES

2 dozen

¼ cup butter or margarine
⅓ cup firmly packed light brown sugar
¼ cup sifted flour
¼ cup + 1 tablespoon heavy cream
¾ cup finely chopped or slivered blanched almonds
⅓ cup minced candied orange peel or mixed candied peel and candied cherries
4 (1-ounce) squares semisweet chocolate
3 tablespoons butter or margarine

Preheat oven to 350° F. Cream butter and sugar until light and fluffy. Stir in flour alternately with cream; then stir in almonds and peel. Drop mixture by level teaspoonfuls 3" apart on greased and floured baking sheets; with a knife dipped in cold water, spread into 2" rounds. Bake about 12 minutes until lacy and golden brown, watching carefully toward the end. Cool 1–2 minutes on sheets, then, using a pancake turner, carefully transfer to wire racks to cool. If cookies cool too much to remove easily, return to oven 1–2 minutes to soften. Melt chocolate and butter together in a double boiler over simmering water, stirring frequently; cool slightly. Arrange cookies flat side up on wax paper and spread with chocolate. When chocolate hardens, store cookies airtight.

NP Cookie (with butter): 100 C, 15 mg CH, 35 mg S*

LADYFINGERS

1½ dozen ⚖

If you've never tasted homemade ladyfingers, you don't know what you're missing.

3 eggs, separated
⅔ cup sifted confectioners' sugar
½ teaspoon vanilla
Pinch salt
½ cup sifted cake flour

Preheat oven to 325° F. Beat egg yolks until pale lemon colored, slowly add ⅓ cup confectioners' sugar and continue beating until thick and the color of mayonnaise. Beat in vanilla. Beat egg whites until soft peaks form, add salt and 2 tablespoons confectioners' sugar, and continue beating until stiff. Mix flour with remaining confectioners' sugar. Fold egg whites into yolk mixture, about one fourth at a time and alternately with flour, beginning and ending with whites. *(Note:* Sift flour onto yolk mixture for more even distribution and don't try to fold in every speck of egg white each time before adding more.) Spoon mixture into a pastry bag (no tube necessary because the bag opening is the perfect size) and press out evenly but lightly into strips 4" long, spacing them 2" apart on buttered and floured baking sheets. *(Note:* You can shape Ladyfingers with 2 tablespoons or simply drop mixture by rounded teaspoonfuls without shaping.) Bake in center or upper third of oven 12–15 minutes until pale golden. Cool on sheets 1 minute, then, using a wide spatula, transfer to wire racks to cool. Serve as is, sprinkled with confectioners' sugar or sandwiched together with jam, chocolate frosting, or sweetened whipped cream.

NP Ladyfinger: 40 C, 45 mg CH, 20 mg S*

For a Crisper Crust (nice for Charlotte Russe): Sprinkle Ladyfingers with confectioners' sugar just before baking.

MADELEINES

2 dozen ¢ ⚖

Madeleines are spongy little cakes baked in small individual molds. The molds come in sets of a dozen and are available in kitchen departments of large department stores, also at specialty food shops. You'll need two dozen molds for this recipe because the batter is unusually light and must be baked the minute it's mixed.

2 tablespoons clarified butter*
½ cup sifted cake flour
⅛ teaspoon salt
2 eggs
⅓ cup sugar
½ teaspoon finely grated lemon rind
¼ cup butter (no substitute), melted
Confectioners' sugar

Preheat oven to 350° F. Brush madeleine molds with clarified butter and refrigerate until needed. Sift together flour and salt. Beat eggs until frothy, add sugar, 2 tablespoons at a time, beating well after each addition, then continue beating at high mixer speed until very thick and lemon colored. Fold in flour, one third at a time. Mix lemon rind and butter; fold into batter, 1 tablespoon at a time, working quickly with a rubber spatula. *(Note:* Make very sure spatula reaches bottom of bowl when folding in butter.) Fill molds two thirds full, place on baking sheets, and bake 15–17 minutes until golden and tops spring back when touched. Cool in molds 1–2 minutes, then lift out with a spatula. Cool fluted side up on wire rack. Dust generously with confectioners' sugar before serving.

NP Madeleine: 55 C, 30 mg CH, 35 mg S*

ROLLED COOKIES

Children adore these cookies—as much to make as to eat. They love the feel of the dough, they love rolling it out, cutting it into plain and fancy shapes. But most of all, they delight in decorating the cookies—strewing them with colored sugar, frosting them, and "squirting" or painting on designs (the aerosol cans of decorator frostings are perfect for children, as are the spillproof paste colors available in specialty food shops; they're as easy to use as poster paints).

All rolled cookie doughs, of course, aren't suitable for children. Many are so tender and rich even skillful cooks find them a challenge.

Temperature is all-important when it comes to rolling dough—temperature of the day, of the kitchen, of the dough, and of your hands. All should be cool if you're to succeed.

Some Tips:

• Chill dough until firm but not hard; if dough is too cold and hard, especially a butter-rich dough, it will crack and split and be difficult to roll. The perfect temperature for rolling is when dough yields slightly when pressed but does not stick to your fingers.
• If dough is unusually soft or sticky, chill board and rolling pin as well as the dough.
• If your hands are warm, keep a bowl of ice water handy and cool them from time to time by dipping into the water. Rolling dough is especially difficult for people with warm hands because the heat of their hands

oversoftens the dough, making it stick to everything.
• Roll only a small amount of dough at a time (about 1 cup) and keep the rest in the refrigerator until needed.
• Before rolling, shape dough roughly into the form you want—circle, rectangle, or square—and when rolling, shift position of dough on board and direct rolling pin strokes as needed to achieve that shape.
• When rolling, bear down on pin *lightly,* only enough to stretch and move dough in the direction you want.
• Resist the temptation of adding flour whenever the dough threatens to stick. Flour does make the dough easier to work, but it also makes the cookies tough and dry. The secret of crisp-tender rolled cookies is using little or no flour in the rolling. Here are two ways:

1. Use a pastry cloth and stockinette-covered rolling pin. Both need only the lightest flouring because the porousness of the cloth holds the flour and releases very little into the dough.

2. Roll dough between two sheets of wax paper. This method is particularly good for soft, butter-rich doughs and for cookies that must be rolled tissue-thin. The process is a bit tricky, but it does work. Place a small amount of dough between two sheets of wax paper (no flour needed) and roll quickly and lightly until dough is 1/4"–1/2" thick; peel off top sheet of paper and invert it on board so used side is down. Flop dough over onto sheet, peel off top sheet, and reverse it also so that fresh side touches dough. Continue rolling to desired thickness, reversing or replenishing wax paper as needed. If dough threatens to stick despite frequent changes of paper, simply pop into refrigerator in its semirolled state, paper and all. A few minutes' chilling will firm up the dough and make the paper peel off like magic. When dough is desired thickness, remove top sheet and cut cookies (bottom sheet should still be in place). Chill cookies briefly on wax paper so they can be lifted with ease to baking sheets. With this method, you should be able to roll dough without using any additional flour. But if at the end dough tends to stick despite all precautions, dust *very* lightly with flour (with an exceedingly soft dough, this may be necessary to keep top sheet of wax paper from sticking after final rolling).

• Flour cutters *only* if dough is soft and sticky and then only *lightly.* A quick way to do it is to sift a little flour into a shallow bowl, then simply dip cutter into it, shaking off any excess.

• When cutting cookies, cut as close together as possible so there will be few scraps to reroll. Unless you've used very little flour in rolling, the rerolls will be tough.

• If dough is unusually soft, cut into the simplest shapes—circles, diamonds, squares—to reduce breakage.

• Use a wide spatula or pancake turner for transferring cookies to baking sheets. The spatula need not be floured unless dough is supersoft.

• Space cookies 3/4"–1" apart on baking sheets unless recipes specify otherwise; most rolled cookies spread very little during baking.

COOKIE CUTTERS

Lucky the cook who owns a set of old-fashioned tin cookie cutters. They do really cut (unlike the plastic and aluminum cutters made today) and their designs are enchanting. It is still possible to find these old cutters, but it requires a bit of sleuthing in antique shops both at home and abroad. The best of the contemporary cutters are European, best in design, best in cutting ability. They're available at most specialty food shops as single cutters, cutter blocks, and cutter wheels.

You can, of course, design your own cutters. All you have to do is make a pattern, take it to a tinsmith and let him worry about the rest. Failing a handy tinsmith, you can still make cookies from your own designs. Simply sketch your designs on heavy paper (Manila file folders are the perfect weight and grease resistant to boot), cut them out, lay on rolled-out dough, and "trace" around them with a very sharp knife.

SUGAR COOKIES

7 dozen   ¢

A good basic cookie with plenty of flavor variations to try.

3¾ cups sifted flour
1½ teaspoons baking powder
1 teaspoon salt
1 cup butter or margarine
1½ cups sugar
2 teaspoons vanilla
2 eggs

Preheat oven to 375° F. Sift flour with baking powder and salt and set aside. Cream butter, sugar, and vanilla until light and fluffy. Add eggs, one at a time, beating well after each addition. Slowly mix in dry ingredients until just blended (lowest speed if you use mixer). If your kitchen is very hot, wrap dough in wax paper and chill about 1 hour so it will roll more easily. Roll one fourth of dough at a time on a lightly floured board to 1/16"–1/8" thickness and cut with plain or fluted cutters (a 2" or 3" size is good). Transfer to lightly greased baking sheets with a pancake turner, spacing cookies 2" apart. If you like, brush with milk and sprinkle lightly with sugar. Bake in top third of oven 8–9 minutes until pale tan. Transfer to wire racks to cool. Reroll and cut trimmings.

NP Cookie (with butter): 55 C, 10 mg CH, 60 mg S*

For Softer Cookies: Roll dough 1/8"–1/4" thick and cut with a 3" cutter; bake as directed 10–12 minutes until edges are just golden.

For Slice-and-Bake Cookies: Shape dough into a log about 2" in diameter, then chill several hours until firm or freeze. Slice 1/4" thick and bake about 10 minutes until firm but not brown.

VARIATIONS

Chocolate Sugar Cookies: Add 4 (1-ounce) squares melted and cooled semisweet chocolate or 4 (1-ounce) envelopes no-melt semisweet chocolate to creamed mixture after adding eggs. Proceed as recipe directs.

NP Cookie (with butter): 60 C, 10 mg CH, 60 mg S*

Pinwheels: Prepare dough as directed; mix half of it with 2 (1-ounce) envelopes no-melt semisweet chocolate. Roll one third of the plain dough into a rectangle 6" × 8" and 1/4" thick. Roll one third of chocolate dough into a rectangle the same size, and, using a pancake turner, carefully place on top of plain dough. Roll the 2 together to a thickness of 1/8", keeping shape as nearly rectangular as possible, then roll up jelly-roll style, from the short side. Repeat with remaining dough. Wrap and chill rolls 1/2 hour, then slice 1/4" thick and bake 10–12 minutes until cookies barely show a print when lightly pressed. Cool as directed.

Sugar Marbles: Reduce amount of flour to 3 cups and prepare dough as directed. Into half mix 2 (1-ounce) envelopes no-melt semisweet chocolate. Pinch off about 1/2 teaspoon each plain and chocolate dough, then roll the 2 together into a small ball, squeezing slightly, to achieve a marbled effect. Repeat until dough is used up. Space marbles 2″ apart on greased cookie sheets and bake about 10 minutes.

NP Cookie (with butter): 55 C, 10 mg CH, 60 mg S*

Butterscotch Sugar Cookies: Substitute 2 cups firmly packed light or dark brown sugar for the 1½ cups sugar and proceed as directed.

NP Cookie (with butter): 60 C, 10 mg CH, 60 mg S*

Lemon or Orange Sugar Cookies: Substitute 1 teaspoon lemon or orange extract for vanilla and add 2–3 tablespoons finely grated lemon or orange rind along with eggs. Roll and bake as directed.

NP Cookie (with butter): 55 C, 10 mg CH, 60 mg S*

Decorative Cookies: If fancy cutouts are to be made, increase amount of flour in basic recipe by about ½ cup (there'll be less breakage while you decorate cookies). Roll and cut cookies. For ideas on decorating, see Decorating Cookies.

NP Cookie (with butter): 55 C, 10 mg CH, 60 mg S*

SAND TARTS

4 dozen

This dough lends itself to all kinds of quick variations that will delight children.

²/₃ **cup butter or margarine**
1 cup sugar
¼ **teaspoon salt**
1 egg
1 teaspoon vanilla
2¾ **cups sifted flour**

GLAZE
1 egg white, lightly beaten
¼ **cup sugar**
Blanched, halved almonds (optional decoration)

Cream butter, sugar, and salt until light and fluffy; beat in egg, then vanilla. Mix in flour, one third at a time, beating just to blend. Wrap dough and chill 1 hour. Preheat oven to 375° F. Roll, a small amount of dough at a time, ⅛″ thick and cut with a 2″ round cutter. Arrange 1″ apart on greased baking sheets, brush with egg white and sprinkle with sugar. If you like, top each with an almond half. Bake 8–10 minutes until pale golden. Cool on wire racks.

NP Cookie (with butter, without almonds): 70 C, 15 mg CH, 40 mg S*

Slice-and-Bake Sandies: Prepare dough as directed and chill 1 hour; shape into a 2″ roll, wrap in foil, and chill overnight. Slice ⅛″ thick, glaze and bake as directed.

NP Cookie (with butter, without almonds): 70 C, 15 mg CH, 40 mg S*

Jumbles: Prepare and roll cookies as directed; cut with a 2½″ fluted round cutter, and in the center of half the cookies put ½ teaspoon tart jam or jelly, marmalade or mincemeat, semisweet chocolate bits or chopped mixed candied fruits. Top with remaining cookies, press edges together and snip tiny steam vents in centers with scissors. Do not glaze. Bake about 12 minutes until pale golden and cool on wire racks.

NP Cookie (with butter and jam): 145 C, 25 mg CH, 80 mg S*

Jelly Cutouts: Prepare, roll, and cut cookies as directed in basic recipe, then cut out centers of half the cookies, using a 1″ round cutter or decorative truffle cutters. Glaze cut-out cookies only. Bake all as directed, then sandwich together with jelly, using cutout cookies as the top layer. *(Note: Centers can be rerolled and cut, or baked—2–3 minutes will do it.)*

NP Cookie (with butter): 145 C, 25 mg CH, 80 mg S*

Turnovers: Prepare and roll cookies as directed but cut with a 3″ round cutter. Drop ½ teaspoon any jam or preserves on half of each cookie, fold over, and seal edges. Glaze and bake 12 minutes. Cool on wire racks.

NP Turnover (with butter and jam): 145 C, 25 mg CH, 80 mg S*

ROSE TREE COOKIES

5 dozen

A buttery-crisp old Quaker cookie that's tricky to make (don't attempt it in warm weather or in a warm kitchen). The secret is to cream the butter and sugar until fluffy and white and to roll the dough paper thin, using as little flour as possible.

1 cup butter (no substitute)
1½ **cups sugar**
1 egg
1¼ **teaspoons baking soda, dissolved in 2 teaspoons hot water**
2 teaspoons vanilla
2½ **cups sifted flour**

Cream butter and sugar until fluffy and white (about 10 minutes with an electric mixer at low speed). Beat in egg, then soda mixture and vanilla. Work in flour slowly. Divide dough in half and spoon each onto a large sheet of wax paper; flatten into large circles or rectangles about 1″ thick, wrap, and chill 1–2 hours until firm enough to roll but not brittle. When you're ready to roll dough, preheat oven to 375° F. Roll about one fourth of each package at a time between 2 sheets of wax paper. (*Note:* You should be able to roll the dough paper thin with very little additional flour if you change sheets of paper when dough begins to stick —the wax paper will peel off zip-quick if you chill all briefly.) Cut with a 2½″–3″ round cutter, chill 5–10 minutes more so circles can be lifted off paper easily, then space 1½″ apart on an ungreased baking sheet. Bake cookies 5–7 minutes until pale tan, cool on sheet about 1 minute, then lift to wire rack to cool. Store airtight.

NP Cookie: 65 C, 15 mg CH, 50 mg S*

GINGERBREAD BOYS

2 dozen

Let the children help make and decorate these.

2½ cups sifted flour
½ teaspoon salt
2 teaspoons ginger
½ cup butter or margarine
½ cup sugar
½ cup molasses
½ teaspoon baking soda
¼ cup hot water

DECORATIONS
Cinnamon candies ("red-hots")
Seedless raisins

EASY ICING
1 cup sifted confectioners' sugar
¼ teaspoon salt
½ teaspoon vanilla
1 tablespoon heavy cream (about)

Sift flour with salt and ginger and set aside. Melt butter in a large saucepan over low heat, remove from heat and mix in sugar, then molasses. Dissolve soda in hot water. Add dry ingredients to molasses mixture alternately with soda-water, beginning and ending with dry ingredients. Chill dough 2–3 hours. Preheat oven to 350° F. Roll out dough, a small portion at a time, ⅛″ thick. Cut with gingerbread boy cutter, handling dough carefully, and transfer cookies to ungreased baking sheets (they should be spaced about 2″ apart). Press on cinnamon candies

for buttons and raisins for eyes and bake 10–12 minutes until lightly browned. Cool 2–3 minutes on sheets, then lift to wire racks. While cookies cool, prepare icing: Mix sugar, salt, and vanilla; add cream, a few drops at a time, mixing well after each addition until icing is smooth and will hold a shape. Using a decorating tube, pipe outlines for collars, boots, cuffs, and belts. If you like, make a little extra icing, tint yellow, and use to pipe in hair. When frosting has hardened, store airtight. (*Note:* Gingerbread boys can be made several days ahead and piped with icing shortly before serving. If they soften in storage, warm 3–5 minutes at 350° F. to crispen, then cool on racks.)

NP Cookie (with butter, without decorations): 130 C, 10 mg CH, 125 mg S*

GOLDEN CHEDDAR RINGS

7½ dozen   ⚖

Serve as a cookie or as an appetizer with cocktails.

¾ cup butter (no substitute), softened to room temperature
2 cups sifted flour
1 teaspoon paprika
½ teaspoon salt
¼ teaspoon cayenne pepper
1 pound sharp Cheddar cheese, coarsely grated
2 tablespoons superfine sugar

Preheat oven to 400° F. Rub butter, flour, paprika, salt, and cayenne together, using your hands, until smooth and creamy. Add cheese and knead on a piece of foil 3–4 minutes until smooth and thoroughly blended. Roll dough thin, half at a time, on a lightly floured pastry cloth (it should be about as thin as piecrust). Cut into rings with doughnut cutter and bake on ungreased baking sheets 4–6 minutes until *faintly* browned. Remove at once to wire racks to cool and, while still hot, sprinkle lightly with sugar. Scraps and "holes" can be rerolled and cut.

NP Ring: 45 C, 10 mg CH, 60 mg S*

MORAVIAN CHRISTMAS COOKIES

4½ dozen   ¢

These dark ginger-molasses cookies store beautifully, so you can make them well ahead of the Christmas rush. The Moravian women of Old Salem, North Carolina, roll them paper thin and cut in fancy shapes.

4 cups sifted flour
1 teaspoon ginger

1 teaspoon cinnamon
1 teaspoon mace
1/2 teaspoon cloves
1/4 cup butter or margarine
1/4 cup lard
1/2 cup firmly packed dark brown sugar
1 cup molasses
1 1/2 teaspoons baking soda
1 tablespoon very hot water

Sift flour with spices. Cream butter, lard, and sugar until light and fluffy; add molasses and beat well. Dissolve soda in water. Mix one fourth of dry ingredients into creamed mixture, then stir in soda-water. Work in remaining dry ingredients, one third at a time. Wrap dough and chill 4–6 hours. Preheat oven to 350° F. Roll dough, a little at a time, as thin as possible (1/8″ is maximum thickness, 1/16″ far better). Cut with Christmas cutters, space cookies 1 1/2″ apart on lightly greased baking sheets, and bake about 8 minutes until lightly browned. Cool 1–2 minutes on sheets, then transfer to wire racks. When completely cool, store airtight.

NP Cookie (with butter): 70 C, 5 mg CH, 35 mg S*

MARGUERITES

4 dozen

The rose water flavoring is what makes these cookies distinctive. It is available at many drugstores, also at specialty food shops.

3 1/4 cups sifted flour
1/2 teaspoon salt
1/2 teaspoon cinnamon
1/2 teaspoon nutmeg
1/4 teaspoon mace
1 cup butter or margarine
1 cup sugar
3 egg yolks
1/4 cup rose water

T O P P I N G
3 egg whites
4 cups sifted confectioners' sugar
2 tablespoons lemon juice
1/2 (1-pound) jar peach or apricot preserves or
   marmalade

Sift flour with salt and spices. Cream butter and sugar until light and fluffy; beat in yolks, one at a time. Mix in dry ingredients alternately with rose water, beginning and ending with dry ingredients and beating only enough to blend. Chill dough 1–2 hours. Preheat oven to 350° F. Roll dough, a small amount at a time, 1/4″ thick and cut in rounds with a 2 1/2″ cutter. Space cookies 2″ apart on greased baking sheets and bake 10–12 minutes until light tan. Cool cookies on sheets 2–3 minutes, then transfer to wire racks. When all cookies are done, reduce oven temperature to 325° F. and prepare topping: Beat egg whites until frothy, add confectioners' sugar, 1/4 cup at a time, beating well after each addition. Add lemon juice and beat until stiff peaks form. Spread each cookie, not quite to edge, with 1 teaspoon preserves, top with a rounded teaspoon meringue and spread to cover. Arrange 1″ apart on ungreased baking sheets and bake 15 minutes until topping is creamy white and firm. Cool on wire racks.

NP Cookie (with butter): 130 C, 25 mg CH, 65 mg S*

CREAM-FILLED MOLASSES COOKIES

5 dozen

3/4 cup vegetable shortening
1 teaspoon salt
1 cup molasses
3/4 cup sugar
1 egg
4 1/2 cups sifted flour
2 teaspoons ginger
1 teaspoon baking soda

C R E A M   F I L L I N G
1 tablespoon butter
1 cup sifted confectioners' sugar
1/8 teaspoon salt
1/4 teaspoon ginger
1/8 teaspoon cinnamon
1 tablespoon boiling water

Preheat oven to 350° F. Cream shortening with salt, molasses, sugar, and egg until light; sift flour with ginger and soda and add, 1 cup at a time, to creamed mixture, beating smooth after each addition. If dough seems very soft, chill until firm enough to roll. Roll, about one fourth of dough at a time, on a lightly floured board to a thickness of 1/8″–1/4″. Cut half of dough with a doughnut cutter, other half with round cookie cutter of the same diameter. Repeat until all dough is rolled and cut. Bake on greased baking sheets 10–12 minutes, remove to wire racks to cool. Meanwhile, prepare filling: Cream butter, sugar, salt, ginger, and cinnamon until light, then beat in boiling water. To assemble cookies, spread rounds with filling, top with doughnut-shaped cookies, and press lightly into place.

NP Cookie: 85 C, 5 mg CH, 60 mg S*

PFEFFERNÜSSE (GERMAN PEPPERNUTS)

3 1/2 dozen

The secret of good "peppernuts" is to ripen the dough two to three days before baking and to store the cookies one to two weeks with a piece of apple before eating.

3 cups sifted flour
1 teaspoon cinnamon
1/8 teaspoon cloves
1/4 teaspoon white pepper
3 eggs
1 cup sugar
1/3 cup very finely chopped blanched almonds
1/3 cup very finely chopped mixed candied orange peel and citron
Vanilla sugar* or confectioners' sugar (for dredging, optional)

Sift flour with spices and set aside. Beat eggs until frothy, slowly add sugar, and continue beating until thick and lemon colored. Slowly mix in flour, then almonds and fruit peel. Wrap in foil and refrigerate 2–3 days. When ready to bake, preheat oven to 350° F. Roll, about one third of dough at a time, 1/4"–1/2" thick and cut with a 1 3/4" round cutter. Space cookies 1" apart on greased baking sheets and bake 15–18 minutes until light brown. Cool on wire racks and store with half an apple in a covered container 1–2 weeks before eating. If you like, dredge in vanilla sugar or dust with confectioners' sugar before serving.

*NP Cookie (dredged in sugar): 70 C, 20 mg CH, 10 mg S**
*NP Cookie (not dredged in sugar): 65 C, 20 mg CH, 10 mg S**

PEPPARKAKOR (CHRISTMAS GINGER SNAPS)

5 dozen

These gingery brown cookies are Sweden's favorite at Christmas time. They are rolled very thin, cut into stars, bells, angels, and Santa Clauses, and hung upon either the Christmas tree or the small wooden *pepparkakor* tree.

3 1/2 cups sifted flour
1 teaspoon baking soda
1/2 teaspoon salt
1 1/2 teaspoons ginger
1 1/2 teaspoons cinnamon
1 1/2 teaspoons cloves
1 cup butter or margarine
1 cup firmly packed dark brown sugar
2 egg whites

ICING
4 cups sifted confectioners' sugar
2 egg whites

Sift flour with soda, salt, and spices. Cream butter and sugar until very fluffy; beat in egg whites. Slowly work in dry ingredients. Wrap and chill 12 hours. Preheat oven to 350° F. Roll out dough, a small portion at a time, 1/8" thick on a lightly floured board and cut in decorative shapes; space cookies about 1" apart on ungreased baking sheets and bake 10–12 minutes until lightly browned around the edges. Transfer to wire racks to cool. While cookies cool, prepare icing: Slowly blend confectioners' sugar into egg whites and beat until smooth. Fit pastry bag with a fine, plain tip and pipe icing onto cookies, tracing outlines, filling in details, or adding any decorative touches you wish. (*Note:* To make hanging cookies, see directions given in Decorating Cookies.)

*NP Cookie (with butter): 90 C, 10 mg CH, 65 mg S**

LEBKUCHEN

4 1/2 dozen

A spicy German cookie studded with candied fruits.

3 cups sifted flour
1/2 teaspoon baking soda
1 teaspoon cinnamon
1/2 teaspoon nutmeg
1/2 teaspoon cloves
1 cup firmly packed dark brown sugar
1 cup honey, at room temperature
1 egg
1 teaspoon finely grated lemon rind
1 tablespoon lemon juice
1/2 cup finely chopped blanched almonds
1/2 cup finely chopped mixed candied orange peel and citron

FROSTING
1 cup sifted confectioners' sugar
4–5 teaspoons milk

DECORATION
Blanched halved almonds
Slivered or halved candied cherries

Sift flour with baking soda and spices. Beat sugar, honey, and egg until well blended; add lemon rind and juice. Slowly mix in dry ingredients just until blended; stir in almonds and fruit peel. Wrap and chill 12 hours. Preheat oven to 400° F. Roll out one third of dough at a time 1/4" thick and cut with a 2" round cookie cutter *or* cut in rectangles 2 1/2" × 1 1/2". Arrange 2" apart on lightly greased baking sheets and bake 8 minutes until edges are lightly browned and tops spring back when touched. Cool on wire racks. For the frosting: Mix sugar and milk until smooth; spread a little on top of each cookie or dip cookie tops in frosting. Decorate with almonds and cherries. Let frosting harden before storing cookies.

NP Cookie (without decorations): 80 C, 5 mg CH, 20 mg S*

For Drop Cookies: Reduce flour to 2½ cups; drop by rounded teaspoonfuls and bake as directed.

NP Cookie (without decorations): 75 C, 5 mg CH, 20 mg S*

MOLDED OR PRESSED COOKIES

These three-dimensional cookies are great favorites everywhere, but especially in Europe, where women are artists at shaping dough (Scandinavian museums exhibit cookie masterpieces alongside other folk art). Almost as soon as a little girl can toddle into the kitchen, she is given a dab of dough to shape. By the time she reaches her teens, she knows how to fashion wreaths and rings, rosettes and ribbons, pinwheels and pretzels and checkerboards. She has learned to use the cookie press with speed and skill and has built up a delectable cookie repertoire.

The dough for molded and pressed cookies is quite short (rich in butter or shortening) and has the look and feel of shortbread. There are three basic ways to handle it:
1. Roll into chunky logs (à la refrigerator cookies), chill until firm, slice thin, and bake.
2. Hand-shape into little balls, pillows, crescents, or logs.
3. Push through a pastry bag or cookie press. *Note:* Only the softer doughs are suitable for pressing.

There are a number of kinds of cookie presses. Before buying, shop around, talk with friends, and if possible borrow a press to try.

Some Tips:
• Choose a cool day for making molded or pressed cookies. Heat makes the dough too soft to hold a shape.
• When using cookie press, always follow manufacturer's instructions.
• Never fill cookie press or pastry bag more than half to two thirds full; the heat of your hands will soften dough faster than you can press it. Invariably the last of the dough must be removed from the press, chilled, and then *re*-pressed.
• Never try to press a dough containing bits of fruit or nuts that may clog the works.
• Always press cookies onto cool or cold baking sheets.
• If dough seems too soft to press or mold, chill slightly.
• When shaping cookies, flour hands only when absolutely necessary and then *very* lightly. Most doughs can be shaped with unfloured hands.

SPRINGERLE

5 dozen

The original 3-D cookies, *Springerle* date to pagan Germany when the poor, having no animals to sacrifice at the Winter Festival, made effigies of them out of cookie dough. Today, Springerle are square or rectangular cookies with pressed-in designs, made either by rolling dough on a springerle board or with a springerle rolling pin (available in specialty food shops). Sometimes used, too, are individual wooden cookie blocks called *Spekulatius* blocks.

4 cups sifted flour
1 teaspoon baking powder
½ teaspoon salt
4 eggs
2 cups sugar
2 teaspoons finely grated lemon rind (optional)
Anise seeds

Sift flour with baking powder and salt. Beat eggs until lemon colored, slowly add sugar, ½ cup at a time, beating well after each addition; continue beating until very thick and pale, about 10 minutes with a mixer. Slowly mix in lemon rind and dry ingredients, beating just to blend. Wrap and chill dough 3–4 hours. Roll, one third at a time, slightly less than 1/2" thick, keeping shape as nearly rectangular as possible and about the width of the rolling pin. Roll a lightly floured springerle rolling pin over dough one time, pressing firmly so dough is about 1/4" thick and evenly so imprint is clear. If using springerle board, roll dough 1/4" thick on lightly floured board, using regular rolling pin, then invert on lightly floured surface. If using spekulatius block, roll dough 1/4" thick, then press firmly and evenly, using block like a stamp. (*Note:* In warm weather, chill springerle pin or board along with dough to make rolling easier.) Cut on imprint lines to separate individual cookies, transfer to a lightly floured surface, and let stand, uncovered, overnight. Preheat oven to 325° F. Sprinkle greased baking sheets generously with anise seeds, lift cookies to sheets, and bake 15 minutes until golden but not brown. Cool 1 minute on sheets before transferring to racks to cool. (*Note:* Some people like to mellow Springerle about a week in an airtight canister before serving.)

NP Cookie: 60 C, 20 mg CH, 30 mg S*

BUTTERBALLS

4 dozen

They will melt in your mouth.

2 cups sifted flour
1/2 teaspoon salt
1 cup butter (no substitute)
1/2 cup superfine sugar
2 teaspoons vanilla or 1 1/2 teaspoons vanilla and
1/2 teaspoon almond extract
1/2 cup sifted confectioners' sugar or Vanilla
sugar* (for dredging, optional)

Sift together flour and salt and set aside. Cream butter and sugar until light and fluffy; add flavoring. Slowly mix in flour, 1/2 cup at a time, until just blended. Chill dough 1–2 hours. Preheat oven to 325° F. Shape dough into 1" balls, handling quickly and lightly, space 2" apart on ungreased baking sheets, and bake about 15 minutes until the color of pale sand. Transfer to wire racks to cool. If you like, roll in confectioners' sugar before serving.

NP Cookie (without sugar coating): 60 C, 10 mg CH, 60 mg S*

VARIATIONS

Almond Butterballs: Prepare as directed, using vanilla-almond extract combination and mixing in 1/2 cup finely chopped toasted blanched almonds after flour. Chill, shape into balls, roll in finely chopped toasted blanched almonds (you'll need about 3/4 cup altogether), then bake as directed. (*Note:* Other nuts may be used instead of almonds; particularly good are pecans, walnuts, hazelnuts, piñons, pistachio nuts, or unsalted peanuts.)

NP Cookie: 70 C, 10 mg CH, 60 mg S*

Thumbprint Cookies: Mix, chill, and shape cookies as directed. Make a deep thumbprint in center of each, fill with tart jam or jelly, and bake as directed.

NP Cookie: 70 C, 10 mg CH, 60 mg S*

PEANUT BUTTER COOKIES

6 dozen

2 1/2 cups sifted flour
1 teaspoon baking powder
1/2 teaspoon salt
1 cup butter or margarine or 1/2 cup each
vegetable shortening and butter
1 cup sugar
1 cup firmly packed light brown sugar
2 eggs
1 cup crunchy peanut butter

Sift flour with baking powder and salt and set aside. Cream butter and sugars until light and fluffy; add eggs, one at a time, beating well after each addition. Beat in peanut butter. Slowly mix in dry ingredients, about one third at a time, until just blended. Chill dough 2 hours. Preheat oven to 375° F. Shape dough into 1" balls, arrange 3" apart on greased baking sheets, and flatten by pressing lightly with a floured fork in a crisscross fashion. Bake 10–12 minutes until golden. Transfer to wire rack to cool. (*Note:* Dough freezes well.)

NP Cookie (with butter): 80 C, 15 mg CH, 70 mg S*

MEXICAN WEDDING CAKES

5 dozen

Meltingly tender filbert cookies.

1 cup butter or margarine, softened to room
temperature
2/3 cup + 3 tablespoons unsifted confectioners'
sugar
1 tablespoon vanilla
1/4 teaspoon salt
2 1/3 cups sifted flour

1½ cups finely ground, toasted, unblanched
filberts

Cream butter until light and fluffy. Add ⅔
cup confectioners' sugar and continue
creaming until smooth; beat in vanilla and
salt. Mix in flour, then the filberts. Wrap
dough in foil and chill several hours until
firm. Preheat oven to 350° F. Pinch off bits
of dough and roll into 1" balls. Place 2"
apart on ungreased baking sheets and flatten
each ball with the palm of your hand until
¼" thick; even up any ragged edges. Bake
12–15 minutes until edged with brown.
Transfer to wire racks to cool, then sift remaining 3 tablespoons confectioners' sugar
over cookies to dust lightly.

*NP Cookie (with butter): 65 C, 10 mg CH, 40
mg S**

KOURABIEDES

3½ dozen

These butter-rich Greek cookies are traditionally served on saints' days and at Christmas.

1 cup unsalted butter (no substitute)
⅓ cup sifted confectioners' sugar
1 egg yolk
2¼ cups sifted flour
2 tablespoons brandy
**½ cup very finely chopped walnuts or blanched
almonds (optional)**
Confectioners' sugar (for dredging)

Cream butter until light, slowly add confectioners' sugar, and continue creaming until
light and fluffy; beat in egg yolk. Slowly mix
in flour, adding alternately with brandy. If
you like, mix in nuts. Wrap dough in wax
paper and chill 1 hour. Preheat oven to
350° F. Using a rounded teaspoon as a measure, scoop up bits of dough and with lightly
floured hands roll into strips 3" long. Bend
into crescents and arrange 2" apart on ungreased baking sheets. Bake 15 minutes or
until the color of sand. Cool 2–3 minutes on
sheets, then carefully transfer to wire racks.
Cool and roll in confectioners' sugar.

*NP Cookie (with walnuts): 80 C, 20 mg CH, 1
mg S**

VARIATION

Instead of shaping into crescents, roll dough
into 1¼" balls and, if you like, stud each
with a clove. Bake 17–18 minutes.

*NP Cookie (with walnuts): 80 C, 20 mg CH, 1
mg S**

ALMOND TARTS (SWEDISH SANDBAKELSEN)

2½ dozen

**½ cup butter (no substitute), softened to room
temperature**
⅓ cup sugar
1 egg yolk, lightly beaten
½ teaspoon almond extract
1 cup + 2 tablespoons sifted flour
½ cup finely ground blanched almonds

With a wooden spoon, mix butter, sugar, egg
yolk, and almond extract until well blended.
Mix in flour and almonds; wrap and chill 1
hour. Preheat oven to 325° F. Press ¼" layers of dough into buttered and floured 1½"–
2" tartlet tins. Stand tins on a baking sheet
and bake 18–20 minutes until tarts are pale
golden (watch closely toward the end).
Transfer tins to a wire rack and cool until
easy to handle. To remove tarts from tins,
tap bottoms of tins lightly and ease tarts out.
You may need to squeeze tins lightly to
loosen tarts or use a large, sturdy needle to
help pry them out. Cool tarts thoroughly,
then store airtight. Just before serving, fill
with sweetened whipped cream or invert and
dot with crystallized fruit or dabs of red currant jelly.

NP Tart: 65 C, 15 mg CH, 30 mg S*

SPRITZ

5 dozen

From the German word meaning "to
squirt," *Spritz* are cookies "squirted"
through a cookie press into delicate designs.

**1 cup butter or margarine, softened to room
temperature**
⅔ cup sugar
2 egg yolks, lightly beaten
1 teaspoon vanilla
2½ cups sifted flour

OPTIONAL DECORATIVE
FROSTINGS

Plain: Blend 1 cup sifted confectioners'
sugar until smooth with 2 tablespoons each
softened butter and heavy cream.

Chocolate: In a double boiler over hot,
not boiling, water, heat and stir 1 cup semisweet chocolate bits with 2 tablespoons each
light corn syrup and hot water until smooth.
Keep over hot water but remove from stove
while frosting cookies.

Preheat oven to 375° F. With a wooden
spoon, beat butter, sugar, egg yolks, and vanilla until well mixed. Add flour, ½ cup at a

time, mixing well after each addition. Press dough in desired designs through a cookie press onto ungreased baking sheets, spacing cookies 1″ apart. Bake 7–9 minutes or until cookies are almost firm but not brown. Cool on sheets 2–3 minutes, then carefully transfer to wire racks. Store airtight.

NP Cookie (with butter): 55 C, 15 mg CH, 30 mg S*

To Decorate: Dip baked, cooled cookies in either of the frostings above, then sprinkle with colored sugar or decorettes, silver *dragées,* chocolate sprinkles, flaked coconut, shaved Brazil nuts, chopped, toasted almonds, pistachio nuts, walnuts or pecans, minced candied cherries or crystallized fruit.

NP Cookie (with butter, Plain Frosting, no decorations): 65 C, 20 mg CH, 35 mg S*
NP Cookie (with butter, Chocolate Frosting, no decorations): 70 C, 15 mg CH, 30 mg S*

VARIATIONS

Chocolate Spritz: Follow basic recipe above but before adding flour mix 2 (1-ounce) envelopes no-melt semisweet or unsweetened chocolate into batter. Proceed as directed. Frost and decorate if you wish.

NP Cookie (with butter, no frosting): 60 C, 15 mg CH, 30 mg S*
NP Cookie (with Plain Frosting, no decorations): 70 C, 20 mg CH, 35 mg S*
NP Cookie (with Chocolate Frosting, no decorations): 75 C, 15 mg CH, 30 mg S*

Almond Pretzels *(2½ dozen):* Prepare dough as directed, substituting almond extract for vanilla and blending in ½ cup very finely chopped toasted, blanched almonds after the flour. Spoon mixture into a pastry bag fitted with a rosette tip and pipe pretzel-shaped cookies about 3″ in diameter onto ungreased baking sheets, spacing about 2″ apart. Bake at 375° F. about 10 minutes. Transfer at once to wire racks to cool.

NP Cookie (with butter): 125 C, 35 mg CH, 65 mg S*

Sugar Pretzels *(2½ dozen):* Prepare dough as directed, but reduce flour to 2 cups + 2 tablespoons. Spoon mixture into a pastry bag fitted with a rosette tip and pipe pretzel-shaped cookies about 2½″ in diameter onto greased and floured baking sheets, spacing about 2″ apart. Brush lightly with an egg white, beaten until frothy, then sprinkle with colored or plain sugar, using about ¼ cup in all. Bake at 375° F. 10–12 minutes until *just firm,* not brown. Cool 1–2 minutes, then lift to a rack with a spatula.

NP Cookie (with butter): 115 C, 35 mg CH, 65 mg S*

Berliner Kränze (Wreaths) *(2½ dozen):* Prepare dough as directed for Sugar Pretzels and pipe into rings 1½″–2″ across on greased and floured baking sheets, spacing about 2″ apart; brush as directed with beaten egg white, then decorate with green sugar and slivers of candied red cherries. Bake and cool as directed for Sugar Pretzels.

NP Cookie (with butter): 115 C, 35 mg CH, 65 mg S*

Nut Rings *(2½ dozen):* Prepare dough and pipe into rings as directed for Berliner Kränze; brush with beaten egg white, then sprinkle with ground pecans, walnuts, filberts, or flaked coconut instead of colored sugar. Bake and cool as directed for Sugar Pretzels.

NP Cookie (with butter and walnuts): 115 C, 35 mg CH, 65 mg S*

PRESSED MOLASSES SPICE COOKIES

4 dozen   ⚖ ¢

2 cups sifted flour
½ teaspoon cinnamon
½ teaspoon nutmeg
¼ teaspoon ginger
¼ teaspoon salt
¼ teaspoon baking soda
½ cup butter or margarine
½ cup sugar
¼ cup molasses
1 egg

Preheat oven to 375° F. Sift flour with spices, salt, and soda. Cream butter and sugar until light and fluffy; beat in molasses and egg. Slowly add dry ingredients, mixing just to blend. *(Note:* If weather is cool, you may need to soften dough with 2–3 teaspoons milk to make it a good consistency for the cookie press.) Press dough through cookie press in desired designs onto ungreased baking sheets, spacing cookies 1″ apart. Bake 10 minutes until firm. Cool 2 minutes on baking sheets, then transfer to wire racks.

NP Cookie (with butter): 50 C, 10 mg CH, 35 mg S*

REFRIGERATOR COOKIES

In this day of extra-large freezers and refrigerators, refrigerator cookies are a host or hostess's best friend; a roll of cookie dough "on ice" is excellent insurance against drop-in guests. It's there whenever you need it, ready to slice and bake.

Most refrigerator cookie doughs are soft and butter-rich, much like molded or pressed cookie doughs *(these,* too, can be shaped into rolls, chilled, sliced, and baked). Extra-soft refrigerator cookie doughs need not be chilled if you're in a rush; simply drop from a spoon and bake as you would drop cookies.

Some Tips:
• If dough is extra soft, chill briefly in bowl until firm enough to shape.
• For "square" cookies, line an empty carton in which wax paper or plastic food wrap came with foil and pack dough in firmly. Chill until firm.
• For cookies with colored or flavored borders, roll chilled dough in colored or cinnamon sugar, ground nuts, or flaked coconut before slicing and baking.
• Always use your sharpest knife for slicing refrigerator cookies.
• When slicing dough, give roll a quarter turn every now and then so that it doesn't lose its round shape.
• Remember that refrigerator cookie dough freezes especially well and can be sliced and baked while still solidly frozen.

BASIC REFRIGERATOR COOKIES

6 dozen   ⚖ ¢

2 cups sifted flour
1/2 teaspoon salt
1/2 teaspoon baking soda
1/2 cup butter or margarine
1 cup granulated, light or dark brown sugar
1 egg
2 teaspoons vanilla

Sift flour with salt and baking soda and set aside. With rotary beater or electric mixer cream butter, sugar, egg, and vanilla until light and fluffy. Slowly mix in dry ingredients; shape dough into a roll about 2″ in diameter; wrap in foil or plastic food wrap and chill several hours or overnight. Preheat oven to 400° F. Slice roll 1/8″ thick and arrange slices 1/2″ apart on ungreased baking sheets. Bake 8–10 minutes until pale tan. Cool cookies on wire racks.

NP Cookie (with butter): 35 C, 5 mg CH, 35 mg S*

VARIATIONS

⚖   **Nut Refrigerator Cookies:** Prepare as directed, mixing in 1 1/2 cups minced nuts (pecans, walnuts, filberts, Brazil, pistachio, or blanched, toasted almonds) along with dry ingredients. Proceed as directed.

NP Cookie (with butter and walnuts): 50 C, 5 mg CH, 35 mg S*

⚖ ¢   **Chocolate Refrigerator Cookies:** Add 2 (1-ounce) envelopes no-melt semisweet chocolate to creamed mixture, add dry ingredients, and proceed as directed.

NP Cookie (with butter): 40 C, 5 mg CH, 35 mg S*

Filled Refrigerator Cookies: Prepare and slice cookies as directed. Make "sandwiches" by putting 2 slices together with 1 teaspoon jam, jelly, or preserves; snip a cross in center of each top cookie to expose filling. Bake about 10 minutes.

NP Cookie (with butter and jam): 45 C, 5 mg CH, 35 mg S*

⚖ ¢   **Chocolate Checkerboards:** Prepare dough as directed; into half mix 1 (1-ounce) envelope no-melt semisweet chocolate. Divide plain and chocolate doughs in half and roll each into a rope about 1/2″–3/4″ in diameter. Lay 1 chocolate and 1 plain rope side by side and touching each other on counter and top with remaining 2 ropes, reversing colors as shown to form checkerboard. Press together lightly, then wrap and chill overnight. Slice and bake as directed.

NP Cookie (with butter): 35 C, 5 mg CH, 35 mg S*

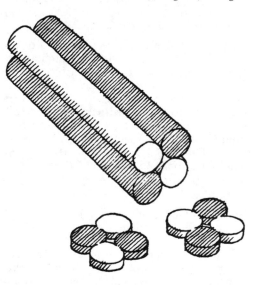

⚖ ¢   **Chocolate Pinwheels:** Prepare dough as directed; into half mix 1 (1-ounce) envelope no-melt semisweet chocolate. Flatten chocolate dough on a large piece of wax paper into a rectangle roughly 12″ × 9″ × 1/4″. On another piece of wax paper, flatten vanilla dough into a rectangle the same size. Carefully invert vanilla dough on the chocolate, aligning edges as well as possible; peel off wax paper, roll up like a jelly roll, wrap, and chill overnight. Slice and bake as directed. (*Note:* To reverse colors in pinwheels, simply invert chocolate dough on vanilla instead of vice versa.)

NP Cookie (with butter): 35 C, 5 mg CH, 35 mg S*

BUTTERSCOTCH ICEBOX COOKIES

8 dozen   ⚖

3½ cups sifted flour
2 teaspoons baking powder
½ teaspoon salt
1 cup butter, margarine, or vegetable shortening
2 cups firmly packed light brown sugar
1 egg
1½ teaspoons vanilla
3 tablespoons heavy cream

Sift flour with baking powder and salt and set aside. Cream butter and sugar until light; add egg and vanilla and beat well. Slowly add dry ingredients and cream. Shape dough into rolls about 2″ in diameter; wrap and chill several hours until firm. Preheat oven to 400° F. Slice rolls ⅛″–¼″ thick and arrange 1″ apart on ungreased baking sheets. Bake 6–10 minutes until lightly browned. Transfer to wire racks to cool.

NP Cookie (with butter): 50 C, 10 mg CH, 40 mg S*

MOLASSES ICEBOX COOKIES

6 dozen

3¼ cups sifted flour
½ teaspoon baking soda
¼ teaspoon salt
1 tablespoon ginger
½ teaspoon cinnamon
¼ teaspoon allspice
1 cup butter, margarine, or vegetable shortening
1 cup firmly packed light brown sugar
½ cup molasses

Sift flour with soda, salt, and spices and set aside. Cream butter and sugar until very light and fluffy. Work dry ingredients in alternately with molasses, beginning and ending with dry ingredients. Divide dough in half and shape into 2 rolls about 2″ in diameter. Wrap and chill several hours until firm. Preheat oven to 350° F. Slice rolls ⅛″ thick, space cookies about 1½″ apart on ungreased baking sheets and bake 8–10 minutes until just firm to the touch. Let cool

about 1 minute on baking sheets before transferring to wire racks to cool.

NP Cookie (with butter): 60 C, 5 mg CH, 40 mg S*

ALMOND-ORANGE ICEBOX COOKIES

8 dozen   ⚖

2¾ cups sifted flour
¼ teaspoon salt
¼ teaspoon baking soda
1 cup butter or vegetable shortening
½ cup sugar
½ cup firmly packed light brown sugar
2 tablespoons orange juice
1 tablespoon finely grated orange rind
1 egg
½ cup blanched, slivered almonds

Sift flour, salt, and soda together and set aside. Cream butter until fluffy and beat in sugars. Mix in orange juice, rind, and egg and beat well. Gradually stir in dry ingredients, then almonds. Shape into rolls about 1½″ in diameter, wrap and chill several hours until firm. Preheat oven to 375° F. Using a very sharp knife (because of almonds in dough), slice ⅛″ thick and place 1½″ apart on greased baking sheets. Bake 10–12 minutes until lightly ringed with brown. Transfer to wire racks to cool.

NP Cookie (with butter): 40 C, 10 mg CH, 30 mg S*

VARIATION

⚖ **Orange-Chocolate Jewels:** Prepare as directed but omit almonds; instead, stir in 2 (1-ounce) squares finely grated semisweet chocolate. Shape, chill, slice, and bake as directed.

NP Cookie (with butter): 40 C, 10 mg CH, 30 mg S*

OATMEAL ICEBOX COOKIES

6 dozen

¾ cup sifted flour
½ teaspoon salt
½ teaspoon baking soda
½ cup butter or margarine
½ cup firmly packed light brown sugar
½ cup sugar
1 egg, lightly beaten
1 teaspoon vanilla
1½ cups uncooked quick-cooking oatmeal
½ cup finely chopped pecans, walnuts, or
    blanched, toasted almonds

Sift together flour, salt, and baking soda and set aside. Cream butter and sugars until light and fluffy. Beat in egg and vanilla; mix in dry ingredients, oatmeal, and nuts. Divide dough in half, turn out on lightly floured board, and shape into 2 rolls about 10″ long and 1½″ in diameter. Wrap in foil or plastic food wrap and chill well or freeze. About 10 minutes before cookies are to be baked, preheat oven to 375° F. Slice rolls ¼″ thick and arrange cookies 2″ apart on lightly greased baking sheets. Bake about 10 minutes until tan. Cool 5 minutes on baking sheet, then transfer to wire rack and cool completely.

NP Cookie (with butter and pecans): 40 C, 5 mg CH, 35 mg S*

PEANUT BUTTER REFRIGERATOR COOKIES

5 dozen

Children especially like these.

2 cups sifted flour
¾ teaspoon baking powder
½ teaspoon cinnamon
⅓ cup butter, margarine, or vegetable shortening
¼ cup creamy or crunchy peanut butter
¾ cup sugar
1 egg
½ cup finely chopped, roasted, blanched peanuts

Sift flour with baking powder and cinnamon and set aside. Cream butter, peanut butter, and sugar until light; add egg and beat well. Slowly add dry ingredients; stir in nuts. Shape dough into a roll 2″–2½″ in diameter; wrap and chill several hours until firm. Preheat oven to 400° F. Slice roll ⅛″ thick, arrange 1″ apart on ungreased baking sheets, and bake 6–8 minutes until pale tan. Cool 1 minute on sheets before transferring to wire racks.

NP Cookie (with butter): 45 C, 5 mg CH, 25 mg S*

BAR COOKIES

Here's the fastest way to fill the cookie jar. Simply stir up a batter, bake in one pan, then cool and cut in bars or squares. Most bars are as much cake as cookie, though some, the superrich, are half cookie, half candy. The advantages of bar cookies, in addition to how fast they can be made, are that they store well and are adored by nearly everyone.

Some Tips:
• If batter is very rich or contains much fruit, grease *and* flour pan.
• Always use the pan sizes given in recipes; an incorrect size can give bars an altogether different (and often unpleasant) texture.
• When placing batter in pan, spread well to corners.
• Always let bars cool upright in their pan on a wire rack several minutes before cutting (recipes specify how long).
• Use a very sharp knife for cutting bars, and if mixture is hard or sticky, dip knife in hot water.
• If your hand is unsteady, use a metal-edged ruler to guide you when cutting bars.

BASIC BROWNIES

16 brownies

Chewy chocolate brownies. But try the variations, too.

⅓ cup butter or margarine
2 (1-ounce) squares unsweetened chocolate
¾ cup sifted flour
½ teaspoon baking powder
¼ teaspoon salt
1 cup sugar
2 eggs
1 teaspoon vanilla
¾ cup coarsely chopped pecans or walnuts

Preheat oven to 350° F. Melt butter and chocolate in a small, heavy saucepan over lowest heat; cool to room temperature. Sift flour with baking powder and salt and set aside. Beat sugar, eggs, and vanilla until light and fluffy; slowly mix in chocolate mixture, then dry ingredients. Stir in nuts. Spoon into a greased 8″ × 8″ × 2″ pan and bake 30–35 minutes until brownies just begin to pull from sides of pan. Cool to room temperature upright in pan on a wire rack. Cut into 16 squares and serve.

NP Brownie (with butter and pecans): 170 C, 45 mg CH, 95 mg S*

To Make with Cocoa: Omit chocolate. Increase amount of butter to ½ cup and, instead of melting, cream with sugar until fluffy. Beat in eggs and vanilla. Sift ⅓ cup sifted cocoa with flour, baking powder, and salt and work into creamed mixture. Stir in nuts and bake as directed. Nutritional count same as basic recipe.

To Make with No-Melt Chocolate: Instead of melting butter, soften to room temperature and mix with 2 (1-ounce) envelopes no-melt unsweetened chocolate. Beat into creamed mixture and proceed as directed. Nutritional count same as basic recipe.

Mocha Brownies: Stir 2 tablespoons instant coffee powder into melted butter and chocolate and proceed as directed.

NP Brownie (with butter and pecans): 170 C, 45 mg CH, 95 mg S*

Brown Sugar Brownies: Prepare as directed, substituting 1 cup firmly packed light brown sugar for the sugar.

NP Brownie (with butter and pecans): 170 C, 45 mg CH, 100 mg S*

Two-Tone Brownies: Prepare recipe as directed but omit chocolate. Spoon half the batter into a greased 8″ × 8″ × 2″ pan; mix 1 (1-ounce) envelope no-melt unsweetened chocolate into remaining batter and carefully spread on top. Bake as directed.

NP Brownie (with butter and pecans): 160 C, 45 mg CH, 95 mg S*

FUDGY SAUCEPAN BROWNIES

16 large brownies ⊠

Truly dark and chewy. "The best," brownie lovers say.

3/4 cup butter or margarine
4 (1-ounce) squares unsweetened chocolate
2 cups sugar
4 eggs
1 1/2 cups unsifted flour
1/2 teaspoon salt
1 1/2 teaspoons vanilla
1 3/4 cups coarsely chopped pecans

Preheat oven to 375° F. Melt butter and chocolate in a large, heavy saucepan over lowest heat. Off heat, mix in remaining ingredients in order listed, beating well after each addition. Pour batter into a greased 9″ × 9″ × 2″ pan and bake 40 minutes until brownies just begin to pull from sides of pan. Cool pan of brownies upright on a wire rack to room temperature, then cut in 16 squares.

NP Brownie (with butter): 360 C, 90 mg CH, 175 mg S*

WHEAT- AND MILK-FREE BROWNIES

2 dozen ⊠

Most children adore brownies. For those with wheat and/or milk allergies, here's a special recipe.

1/3 cup margarine, softened to room temperature
1 cup firmly packed light brown sugar
2 eggs, lightly beaten
2 (1-ounce) envelopes no-melt semisweet chocolate or 2 (1-ounce) squares semisweet chocolate, melted
1 teaspoon vanilla
2/3 cup unsifted rice flour
1/2 teaspoon baking powder
1/4 teaspoon salt
1/2 cup coarsely chopped pecans or walnuts

Preheat oven to 350° F. With a spoon, mix margarine and sugar well; add all remaining ingredients except nuts and blend until smooth. Stir in nuts and pour into a greased 8″ × 8″ × 2″ or 9″ × 9″ × 2″ pan. Bake 30 minutes or until sides shrink slightly from pan and top springs back when touched. Cool upright in pan on a wire rack, then cut into squares.

NP Brownie (with pecans): 110 C, 25 mg CH, 70 mg S*

BUTTERSCOTCH BROWNIES

16 brownies

2/3 cup sifted flour
1 teaspoon baking powder
1/4 teaspoon salt
1/4 cup butter or margarine
1 cup firmly packed light or dark brown sugar
1 egg
1 teaspoon vanilla
3/4 cup coarsely chopped walnuts or pecans

Preheat oven to 350° F. Sift flour with baking powder and salt and set aside. Melt butter in a saucepan over low heat, add sugar, and stir until dissolved; cool 5 minutes. Beat in egg and vanilla, mix in dry ingredients and nuts. Spoon into a greased 8″ × 8″ × 2″ baking pan and bake 30–35 minutes until brownies just begin to pull from sides of pan. Cool upright in pan on a wire rack to room temperature, then cut in 16 squares.

NP Brownie (with butter and walnuts): 135 C, 25 mg CH, 100 mg S*

Chocolate Chip Brownies: Prepare as directed but reduce amount of nuts to 1/2 cup; stir 1/2 cup semisweet chocolate bits into batter along with nuts and bake as directed.

NP Brownie (with butter and walnuts): 150 C, 25 mg CH, 100 mg S*

SCOTTISH SHORTBREAD

2 dozen slim, pie-shaped pieces

The secret of good shortbread lies in the kneading. The dough *must* feel satin-smooth, and getting it that way may take as long as 15 minutes.

3¼ cups sifted flour
¼ cup sifted rice flour
¼ teaspoon salt
1 cup butter (no substitute), softened to room temperature
½ cup sugar

Preheat oven to 350° F. Sift flour with rice flour and salt. Using your hand or a wooden spoon, work butter and sugar together until light in color; blend in dry ingredients. Keeping dough in bowl, knead vigorously until satin-smooth and no sugar grains remain. Divide dough in half, place each on an ungreased baking sheet, and press flat into 9″ circles, using palms of hands. Dust rolling pin with rice flour and roll surface of dough *lightly* to remove fingerprints. Crimp edges as you would piecrust and cut each circle into 12 wedges (but don't separate). Prick dough all over with a fork. Bake 20 minutes until pale golden, not brown. Cool in pans on wire rack 5 minutes, then carefully recut to separate wedges; cool thoroughly. If you like, sprinkle shortbread lightly with sugar as soon as it comes from oven.

NP Piece (with sugar topping): 145 C, 20 mg CH, 100 mg S*

VARIATION

Shortbread for Those with Milk Allergies: Make as directed, substituting ¾ cup margarine or vegetable shortening for the butter.

NP Piece (with margarine, without sugar topping): 130 C, 0 mg CH, 90 mg S*

LEMON SPONGE SQUARES

2½ dozen

CAKE
1½ cups sifted flour
½ teaspoon salt
¼ teaspoon baking powder
½ cup butter or margarine
1 cup sugar
3 eggs, separated
⅓ cup lemon juice
1 tablespoon finely grated lemon rind
1 cup sifted confectioners' sugar

FROSTING
1 cup sifted confectioners' sugar
1 tablespoon heavy cream or evaporated milk
2 tablespoons butter or margarine, softened to room temperature

Preheat oven to 350° F. Sift flour with salt and baking powder and set aside. Cream butter and sugar until light and fluffy; add egg yolks, one at a time, beating well after each addition. Mix in dry ingredients alternately with lemon juice, beginning and ending with dry ingredients. Mix in lemon rind. In a separate bowl beat egg whites until soft peaks form. Add confectioners' sugar, ¼ cup at a time, beating well after each addition, then continue to beat until stiff peaks will form. Fold egg white mixture into batter and pour into a well-greased and floured 13″ × 9″ × 2″ baking pan. Bake 35–40 minutes on center oven rack until top springs back when lightly touched. Cool upright in pan on a rack 3–5 minutes. Meanwhile, mix frosting ingredients together until smooth. While cake is still warm, spread top evenly with frosting. Cool in pan, then cut into squares.

NP Square (with butter): 115 C, 40 mg CH, 85 mg S*

CHINESE CHEWS

4 dozen

The easiest way to "chop" dates is to snip them into small pieces with kitchen shears. To simplify the job, chill dates slightly before cutting.

¾ cup sifted flour
1 cup sugar
1 teaspoon baking powder
Pinch salt
1 cup coarsely chopped dates
1 cup coarsely chopped walnuts
3 eggs, beaten until fluffy
½ teaspoon vanilla (optional)
⅔ cup sifted confectioners' sugar

Preheat oven to 350° F. Sift dry ingredients together and mix in dates and walnuts. Fold in eggs and, if you like, add vanilla. Spread evenly in a greased and floured 15½″ × 10½″ × 1″ jelly-roll pan (it will seem at first as though there isn't enough batter, but keep spreading it toward the corners; layer will be *very* thin). Bake 20 minutes until lightly browned and top springs back when touched. Cool upright in pan on a wire rack 10–12 minutes, then cut in 1¼″–1½″ squares. Using a metal spatula dipped in hot water, transfer warm squares to wax paper spread with half the confectioners' sugar; sift remaining sugar on top, then cool before serving.

NP Square: 60 C, 15 mg CH, 15 mg S*

MERINGUE NUT BARS

4 dozen

These cookies are wheat- and milk-free, good for those with either or both of these allergies.

2 egg whites
1¹/₃ cups sugar
1 tablespoon lemon juice
4 cups very finely chopped nuts (pecans, walnuts, or filberts)
1 teaspoon vanilla

Preheat oven to 325° F. Beat egg whites until frothy. Add sugar, 1 tablespoon at a time, beating well after each addition. Add lemon juice, then beat hard (highest mixer speed) 2–3 minutes. (*Note:* All sugar won't dissolve as it does in regular meringues, but mixture should be stiff and glossy.) Measure out 1 cup of the meringue mixture and set aside. Mix nuts and vanilla into remaining mixture; roll half of it out on a well-floured board into a rectangle about 6″ wide and ¹/₄″ thick (the length doesn't matter, but the width should be 6″ so that bars of uniform size can be cut easily). Spread ¹/₂ cup reserved plain meringue on top. With a floured knife, cut into bars 3″ long and 1¹/₂″ wide and arrange 2″ apart on a greased and floured baking sheet. Roll, spread, and cut remaining nut meringue mixture the same way. Bake 25 minutes or until topping is creamy white and firm. Cool on wire racks.

NP Bar (with walnuts): 85 C, 0 mg CH, 5 mg S*

GREEK WHEAT AND WALNUT BARS (KARYDATA)

16 bars

³/₄ cup butter or margarine
³/₄ cup sugar
3 eggs, separated
1 cup uncooked farina or Wheatena
1 teaspoon cinnamon
1¹/₂ cups finely chopped walnuts
¹/₄ teaspoon salt

SYRUP
¹/₄ cup sugar
2 tablespoons warm water

TOPPING
Sifted confectioners' sugar

Preheat oven to 375° F. Cream butter until fluffy and add sugar, a little at a time, beating well after each addition. Beat egg yolks in, one at a time. Stir in farina, cinnamon, and nuts. Beat egg whites with salt until soft peaks form and fold into batter. Spread in a greased and floured 9″ × 9″ × 2″ baking pan and bake 20–25 minutes until just firm to the touch. Meanwhile, prepare syrup: Boil sugar and water in a very small, heavy saucepan until clear and slightly thickened, about 3–5 minutes. Remove pan from oven, spoon syrup over top, distributing it as evenly as possible; return to oven and bake 5–10 minutes longer until mixture pulls from sides of pan. Cool upright in pan 5 minutes on a wire rack, then loosen and turn out. When cold, dust *lightly* with confectioners' sugar and cut into 16 bars.

NP Bar (with butter, without sugar topping): 255 C, 75 mg CH, 135 mg S*

HONEY-NUT GRANOLA BARS

3 dozen

You can buy unsweetened flaked coconut in many health food stores.

¹/₂ cup sifted flour
¹/₄ teaspoon salt
1¹/₂ cups uncooked quick-cooking oatmeal
¹/₂ cup wheat germ
¹/₂ cup butter or margarine, softened to room temperature
1 cup flaked or shredded coconut (preferably unsweetened)
1 cup finely chopped unsalted dry-roasted peanuts
1 cup coarsely chopped seedless raisins, dates, figs, prunes, apricots, or mixed dried fruits (optional)
¹/₃ cup honey
¹/₃ cup liquid brown sugar
1 tablespoon molasses
1 teaspoon vanilla

Preheat oven to 325° F. Sift flour with salt, add oatmeal and wheat germ. Using tips of fingers, rub butter into dry ingredients until well blended. Mix in all remaining ingredients. Wet hands thoroughly with cold water and spread mixture into a well-greased 13″ × 9″ × 2″ baking pan, patting it down firmly. Bake 30 minutes until pale tan. Cool upright in pan on wire rack 20 minutes, score surface to mark off 36 bars. Cool completely in pan, then cut to separate into bars.

NP Bar (with butter and raisins): 110 C, 5 mg CH, 45 mg S*

GERMAN DATE SQUARES

3 dozen

1/2 cup butter
1 cup sugar
3 eggs
1/2 cup sifted flour
2 teaspoons baking powder
1/4 teaspoon salt
1 cup finely chopped walnuts
1 cup finely chopped, pitted dates
1 teaspoon vanilla

Preheat oven to 250° F. Cream butter until light, add sugar and continue creaming until fluffy. Add eggs, one at a time, beating well after each addition. Sift flour with baking powder and salt and mix into batter. Stir in walnuts, dates, and vanilla. Spoon into a lightly greased 9" × 9" × 2" baking pan and bake, uncovered, 3 hours (mixture should be quite firm and tan and crackly on top). Cool upright in pan on a wire rack several hours, then cut into 1 1/2" squares (no larger because these cookies are rich).

NP Square: 90 C, 30 mg CH, 70 mg S*

LAYERED APRICOT BARS

2 dozen

2/3 cup dried apricots
1 cup water
1/2 cup butter or margarine, softened to room temperature
1/4 cup sugar
1 1/3 cups sifted flour
1/2 teaspoon baking powder
1/4 teaspoon salt
1 cup firmly packed light brown sugar
2 eggs, lightly beaten
1 1/2 teaspoons brandy flavoring or 1 teaspoon vanilla
1/2 cup finely chopped walnuts

Preheat oven to 350° F. Place apricots and water in a small saucepan, cover, and simmer 10 minutes; drain, cool, and chop fine; set aside. Stir butter and sugar together until well mixed; blend in 1 cup flour. Spread mixture in a greased 9" × 9" × 2" pan and bake 25 minutes. Meanwhile, sift remaining flour with baking powder and salt. Beat

brown sugar and eggs until thick; add flavoring. Slowly mix in dry ingredients, apricots, and walnuts. Spread lightly and evenly over baked layer and bake 1/2 hour longer. Cool upright in pan on a wire rack, then cut into bars, using a knife dipped in warm water.

NP Bar (with butter): 130 C, 35 mg CH, 80 mg S*

APPLE-OATMEAL BARS

2 dozen   ¢

1 cup sifted flour
1/2 teaspoon salt
1/2 cup firmly packed light brown sugar
1/3 cup + 2 tablespoons butter or margarine
1 cup uncooked quick-cooking oatmeal

FILLING
2 1/2 cups finely chopped or thinly sliced, peeled apples
1/4 cup sugar
1/4 teaspoon nutmeg

Preheat oven to 400° F. Sift flour with salt and add brown sugar. Using a pastry blender, cut in 1/3 cup butter until the size of small peas; mix in oatmeal. Pack half the mixture into a well-greased 9" × 9" × 2" pan; top with apples and sprinkle with sugar and nutmeg. Dot with remaining butter and cover with remaining oatmeal mixture, pressing down lightly. Bake 45–50 minutes until tan on top. Cool upright in pan on a wire rack and cut into bars.

NP Bar (with butter): 95 C, 10 mg CH, 85 mg S*

VARIATIONS

Date-Oatmeal Bars: Prepare oatmeal mixture as directed but, instead of preparing filling, simmer 2 cups chopped, pitted dates, uncovered, with 1 cup water and 2 tablespoons sugar 7–10 minutes until thick; cool to room temperature. Spread evenly over bottom oatmeal layer; do not dot with butter as above. Top with remaining oatmeal mixture and bake as directed.

NP Bar (with butter): 115 C, 5 mg CH, 75 mg S*

Fig-Oatmeal Bars: Prepare like Date-Oatmeal Bars, substituting 1 cup chopped dried figs for 1 cup of the dates.

NP Bar (with butter): 115 C, 5 mg CH, 75 mg S*

Prune-Oatmeal Bars: Prepare like Date-Oatmeal Bars, substituting 1 cup chopped, pitted prunes for 1 cup of the dates.

NP Bar (with butter): 110 C, 5 mg CH, 75 mg S*

NO-BAKE COOKIES

These are an American invention and a good one, too. They require very little time, effort, or expertise to make and, when properly stored, will keep longer than any other type of cookie. Many, especially those rich in fruit or flavored with liquor, will actually improve on standing.

NO-BAKE RUM BALLS

2¹/₂ dozen ☒

1¾ cups fine vanilla wafer crumbs
1 cup finely ground pecans
1 cup unsifted confectioners' sugar
¼ cup cocoa
3 tablespoons light corn syrup
¼ cup light rum or bourbon
⅓ cup sifted confectioners' sugar (for dredging)

Place all but last ingredient in a bowl and mix well, using your hands. Roll into 1″ balls and dredge in confectioners' sugar. (*Note:* These cookies keep well up to 10 days when stored in airtight canisters.)

NP Ball: 85 C, 5 mg CH, 15 mg S*

FOUR-FRUIT BALLS

5 dozen

These cookies are milk-, egg-, and wheat-free, good for those with any or all of these allergies.

½ pound pitted dates
1 (12-ounce) package dried figs
1½ cups seedless raisins
12 pitted prunes
2 ounces candied ginger
1½ cups walnuts or pecans
Juice of ½ lemon
2 tablespoons pineapple or other fruit juice or rum or brandy
½ teaspoon cinnamon
Confectioners' sugar (for dredging)

Put dates, figs, raisins, prunes, ginger, and nuts through fine blade of meat grinder. Mix well, using your hands, sprinkle in fruit juices and cinnamon and mix again. Shape into 1″ balls and roll in confectioners' sugar to coat. Let stand at room temperature 3–4 hours, then store airtight.

NP Ball (with walnuts and pineapple juice): 65 C, 0 mg CH, 1 mg S*

PORCUPINES

3 dozen ☒

2 eggs, lightly beaten
1 cup finely chopped, pitted dates
¾ cup sugar
1 cup finely chopped pecans or walnuts
2 cups toasted rice cereal
2 cups flaked coconut (about)

In a saucepan over moderate heat, heat eggs, dates, and sugar, stirring constantly about 10 minutes until mixture thickens. Cool 5 minutes and stir in nuts and cereal. Cool 10 minutes longer, then drop by rounded teaspoonfuls into flaked coconut; roll in coconut and shape into balls.

NP Ball (with pecans): 80 C, 15 mg CH, 25 mg S*

NO-BAKE CHOCOLATE BONBONS

2 dozen

¼ pound sweet chocolate
1 cup sifted confectioners' sugar
1 cup finely crushed vanilla wafer crumbs
¼ cup light corn syrup
2 tablespoons honey
½ cup finely chopped walnuts or pecans
Sifted confectioners' sugar (for dredging)

Melt chocolate in top of double boiler over simmering water. Off heat stir in remaining ingredients except dredging sugar in order listed; as mixture stiffens, use hands to blend well. Shape into 1″ balls and roll in confectioners' sugar. Let ripen 1–2 days before serving.

NP Bonbon (with walnuts): 95 C, 1 mg CH, 15 mg S*

FUDGE NUGGETS

3 dozen

Not as high-calorie as you might think.

2 cups sugar
1 cup milk
2 (1-ounce) squares semisweet chocolate
½ teaspoon instant coffee powder
2 tablespoons butter or margarine
1 teaspoon vanilla
1¾ cups graham cracker crumbs

Mix sugar and milk in a large, heavy saucepan; insert candy thermometer. Boil over moderate heat without stirring until thermometer registers 230° F.; mixture will foam up, so adjust heat as needed to prevent its boiling over. Off heat, stir in chocolate, coffee, butter, and vanilla; mix until chocolate

---

melts. Stir in crumbs and, working quickly, drop by rounded teaspoonfuls on wax paper. Cool thoroughly and serve.

NP Nugget (with butter): 80 C, 5 mg CH, 45 mg S*

MRS. BOULDIN'S DATE-NUT FINGERS

4 dozen

½ cup margarine
1 cup sugar
1 egg, lightly beaten
1 (8-ounce) package pitted dates, chopped fine
1¼ cups toasted rice cereal
1 cup finely chopped pecans or walnuts
1 cup finely shredded coconut (about)

Melt margarine in the top of a double boiler over simmering water. Stir in sugar and egg. Heat, stirring every 5 minutes, for 20–30 minutes over simmering—not boiling—water until mixture is thick and will coat the back of a wooden spoon. Pour over dates, add cereal and nuts, and mix well. Cool to room temperature, then shape into "fingers" about 2″ long and 1″ wide and roll in coconut to coat evenly. Store airtight.

NP Finger (with pecans): 75 C, 5 mg CH, 35 mg S*

PEANUT BUTTER BARS

4 dozen ⊠

Crunchy and sweet.

1 cup sugar
1 cup light corn syrup
1 (12-ounce) jar crunchy peanut butter
4 cups toasted rice cereal
1 cup coarsely chopped unsalted peanuts
  (optional)

Heat and stir sugar, syrup, and peanut butter in a very large saucepan over moderate heat until mixture boils. Off heat mix in remaining ingredients. Pack into a well-greased 13″ × 9″ × 2″ baking pan and cool. Cut into bars.

NP Bar (without peanuts): 85 C, 0 mg CH, 75 mg S*
NP Bar (with peanuts): 105 C, 0 mg CH, 75 mg S*

TWENTY

Candies and Nuts

How many good cooks' love of food began with a batch of fudge? Dozens, probably, because nothing draws children to the kitchen faster than candy making. And nothing *involves* them more quickly in cooking. It's fun to beat divinity, pull taffy or mints, shape fondant. Fun, too, to lick the spoon. As long as everyone's had a good time, it doesn't matter if the candy isn't perfect. The next batch will be better and the next batch better still.

TIPS FOR MAKING BETTER CANDIES

• First, the weather. It does make a difference, with cooked candies especially. So choose a dry, cool, clear day. If you must make candy on a damp day, cook 2° higher on the candy thermometer than recipe specifies so that candy will harden.
• Measure ingredients precisely.
• Do not double or halve recipes for cooked candies and do not make substitutions in ingredients.
• Follow recipes to the letter; candies are critical (apt to fail) and do not take to improvisation.
• Use a heavy, deep, straight-sided pan about four times the volume of combined recipe ingredients so that candy has plenty of room to boil up without boiling over. Also choose pan with an insulated handle so you won't burn yourself.
• Use a wooden spoon for stirring—less chance of the candy's turning to sugar and less chance of burning yourself. And make sure spoon is clean and dry each time it is put into the candy.
• *Use a candy thermometer.* Clip to side of pan, making sure bulb is immersed but does not touch bottom. Some cooks recommend inserting thermometer after candy boils (to reduce risk of crystallization), but the wait isn't necessary except for fondant. Moreover, a cold thermometer may break if shoved into boiling syrup. Keep an eye on the mercury; it will climb to 220° F. at a snail's pace, but race on thereafter and, unless watched, overshoot its mark. Read thermometer at eye level and, if in doubt about its accuracy, also use one of the tests described below. *To test accuracy of thermometer:* Insert in a pan of cold water and bring gradually to a boil; boil 10 minutes. Temperature should be 212° F. If not, note difference and adjust recipe temperatures accordingly. For example, if thermometer reads 210° F. at the boiling point, cook candy 2° lower than recipes suggest; if it registers 214° F., cook 2° higher.
• Use a marble slab for working candy or, failing that, a large ironstone platter or heavy metal tray.
• To simplify beating at the end, use a portable electric mixer.
• *To help keep creamy candies from turning to sugar:* There's no guarantee, but the following precautions should all help:
• If candy contains butter, cook in a buttered pan; also butter end of thermometer.
• Brush down crystals that collect on sides of pan and thermometer with a damp pastry brush (just one crystal can turn a whole batch of candy gritty).
• When making fondant or other simple water-sugar candies, cover and boil about three minutes after sugar is dissolved; steam will wash away crystals that have gathered on sides of pan.
• Do not stir candy after sugar has dissolved.
• Do not hurry the cooking or the cooling; let syrup cool to 110° F. before beating. If speed is important, cool in a larger pan of cold water.

CANDY-MAKING TEMPERATURES AND TESTS

Thermometer Reading	Candy Stage	Test (use fresh water for each test)
230°–234° F.	Thread	Syrup dropped from a spoon will form a 2″ thread.
234°–240° F.	Soft Ball	A drop of syrup forms a soft ball in cold water that flattens on removal.
244°–248° F.	Firm Ball	A drop of syrup forms a firm, pliable ball in cold water that holds its shape on removal.
250°–265° F.	Hard Ball	A drop of syrup forms a hard but still pliable ball in cold water.
270°–290° F.	Soft Crack	Syrup dropped in cold water forms pliable strands.
300°–310° F.	Hard Crack	Syrup dropped in cold water forms brittle strands.

Note: These thermometer readings are slightly higher than those marked on standard candy thermometers, but they have proved more reliable.

• Do not scrape pan when turning candy out.
• Knead cooled, cooked candy to reduce size of sugar crystals and work in any nuts afterward.
• Do not overcook candy; use a clean, dry spoon each time you make a test.
• Do not overbeat candy before turning out; it should be about the consistency of a butter frosting and just losing its gloss. Once candies begin turning, they turn fast, so you must work quickly. If candy becomes too hard, pick up and knead until soft again, then pat into a pan with your hands or shape into a roll and slice.

Making Candy in a Microwave Oven

It's impractical because syrups boil furiously and spatter badly in microwave ovens, also because you must use a special nonmetallic microwave candy thermometer and monitor the temperature frequently. The old stovetop method is better—and a lot more fun!

SOME SPECIAL CANDY-MAKING TECHNIQUES

To Color Sugar: Put about 1/2 cup sugar (granulated) in a small bowl and add food color, 1 drop at a time; rub sugar quickly between fingers after each addition to distribute color evenly. Be careful not to overcolor.

To Make Vanilla Sugar: Place 1 pound sugar in a canister with an airtight lid and push 2 vanilla beans deep down in. Cover and let stand at least 1 week before using. If you want a supply of vanilla sugar on hand, replenish sugar as needed and add a fresh vanilla bean every 6 months. Use vanilla sugar wherever vanilla extract is called for—in making candies, cookies, custards, dessert soufflés, and sauces. Allow 1 tablespoon vanilla sugar for each 1/4 teaspoon vanilla and decrease recipe's total quantity of sugar accordingly. Thus, in a recipe calling for 2 cups sugar and 1 teaspoon vanilla, you would use 4 tablespoons vanilla sugar and 1 3/4 cups sugar.

To Spin Sugar: Pastry cooks love to frame their masterpieces with clouds of spun sugar, and frankly, the spinning's a sticky business best left to the pros. Attempted at home without the proper technique or utensils, it can quickly wreck both cook and kitchen. However, for those who want to try their luck, here is a method that has worked fairly well at home. Pick a dry, crisp day. Place 1 cup sugar, 1/2 cup hot water, and 1/8 teaspoon cream of tartar in a small, heavy pan; insert candy thermometer. Heat, stirring until sugar dissolves, then boil slowly, uncovered, without stirring until thermometer reaches 310° F. While syrup cooks, cover counter near stove (and floor beneath it) with newspapers. Stand 2 clean quart-size soda bottles on counter about 2 feet apart. When syrup reaches 310° F., turn heat off; let cool a few minutes, then dip in a wooden spoon and pull out. If syrup spins a long, fine hair, temperature is right for spinning. Dip in a wire whisk, then spin by drawing threads from one bottle to the other, using a quick whipping motion. Continue dipping and spinning until you have an inch-wide skein of threads, then carefully lift off and set on wax paper. Continue spinning, reheating syrup if it should harden too much. *How to Use Spun Sugar:* Use as soon as possible—to wreathe a compote of fruits, a showy pastry or cake or shape into a nest on a circle of cardboard, fill with delicate candies, and use as a *bonbonnière*-centerpiece.

To Toast Grated Coconut: Spread coconut out in an ungreased shallow baking pan and toast, uncovered, stirring often, 30–40 minutes at 300° F. until golden. *Microwave Method:* Spread 1 cup flaked coconut in a flameproof glass piepan or paper plate; microwave, uncovered, at *HIGH* power 2 minutes; stir and microwave 3–4 minutes longer, stirring every minute, until evenly golden.

To Color Grated Coconut: Dip a toothpick in food color, stir through coconut, then rub with your fingers to distribute. Repeat until color is the intensity you want.

Chocolate

Real chocolate, as defined by the U.S. Food and Drug Administration (FDA), is a mixture containing a dark thick paste called *chocolate liquor* and a percentage of *cocoa butter* (at least 50 per cent but not more than 58 per cent for *bitter chocolate,* 35 per cent for *bittersweet,* 15 per cent for *sweet chocolate,* and 10 per cent for *milk chocolate).* The choicest chocolates, connoisseurs agree, come from Belgium, France, Germany, Italy, and Switzerland because chocolatiers there roast their own special blends of cocoa beans, hand-roll the chocolate liquor into paper-thin sheets *(broyage),* refine it time and again until smooth and mellow by *conching* (alternately heating, melting, and rocking the chocolate), then age it in solid blocks at strictly controlled temperatures. Mass producers short-cut the process by machine-mixing the chocolate, skipping the conching, and adding such emulsifiers as lecithin.

White Chocolate: This is not chocolate by FDA standards because it contains no chocolate liquor, only cocoa butter, sugar, milk, and flavoring.

Compound Chocolate (also known as *Confectioners' Chocolate* and *Summer Coating):* The FDA calls this *"chocolate-flavored"* because it contains less chocolate liquor or cocoa butter than required. Indeed, compound chocolate may contain cocoa instead of chocolate liquor and palm oil instead of cocoa butter. Top-quality compound chocolate does not contain paraffin or artificial ingredients, however. It can be eaten out-of-hand, but its primary function is for dipping or molding candy. Since it need not be tempered before it's used, it is less brittle than real chocolate. Other pluses: It does not discolor, it sets up (hardens) fast, and it is relatively easy for beginners to use. Compound chocolate is available as *semisweet, milk,* or *white chocolate,* also as *colored wafers.*

Coating Chocolate (Dipping Chocolate, Couverture): This choice of the pros must be alternately melted and hardened several times before it can be used. It contains a high proportion of cocoa butter (which gives it its sheen), but is tricky to use.

Dietetic Chocolate: Available as *bittersweet, sweet,* or *milk chocolate* and sweetened with *sorbitol* or *mannitol,* this is a good choice for those on sugar-restricted diets. But, make a note, this chocolate *is not lower in calories* than conventional chocolate because it has had extra vegetable oil added as a stabilizer.

Note: For information on *semisweet chocolate bits* and *no-melt unsweetened chocolate,* see Chapter 2, The Larder.

To Store Chocolate: Wrap airtight and store in a cool (68°–78° F.) dark place. Do not refrigerate because the chocolate will "sweat" and become tacky when warmed to room temperature. If stored at too high a temperature, chocolate will develop a "bloom" (white film) of cocoa butter on the surface. (*Note:* Chocolate begins to melt at temperatures above 90° F.) *How long will chocolate keep under ideal conditions?* Dark chocolates will remain fresh about 6 months, milk chocolates will stale more rapidly. *Note: Compound chocolate* may be frozen if wrapped absolutely airtight, first in plastic food wrap, then in foil. Before using, thaw the compound chocolate in its wrappings at room temperature for 24 hours.

To Melt Chocolate: All chocolate burns easily and must be melted slowly over low heat. Always use a *dry* container and spoon for stirring—a single drop of moisture can stiffen or lump the chocolate. (*Note:* Strangely, more liquid—about 1 tablespoon water, milk, fruit juice, or almost any other liquid, for that matter, to each 1 ounce chocolate—will blend into and thin the chocolate nicely.) *Cooking Tip:* Whenever adding melted chocolate to milk, blend in by beating vigorously with a wire whisk. Unsweetened chocolate will liquefy as it melts, other types will hold their shape and must be stirred. To speed the melting of chocolate, break into small pieces or grate. Here, then, are the best ways of melting the different kinds of chocolate:

• *Real (Regular) Chocolate:* Place in a double boiler top set over simmering—*not* boiling—water; stir now and then. Or place in a custard cup or flameproof glass measuring cup and set in a skillet or shallow saucepan of simmering water. *(Note:* Keep burner heat *very low* and stir the chocolate frequently.) *Microwave Method:* Place unwrapped pieces of chocolate in a microwave-safe bowl, then microwave, uncovered, on *MEDIUM* power setting 2–3 minutes just until squares soften (no longer or chocolate may scorch).

• *Compound Chocolate (Either Dark or White):* Place chocolate in a flameproof glass measuring cup and stand on an electric "hot tray" turned to its lowest temperature setting; stir occasionally. Or use the measuring-cup-and-skillet technique recommended for real chocolate above (to maintain a truly low temperature, use an electric skillet turned to its lowest setting). In a pinch, you can also melt compound chocolate in a double boiler top over simmering water, but, be forewarned, if the chocolate should overheat, it will thicken and clump (old compound chocolate is apt to lump, too).

Note: To smooth out lumpy chocolate, blend in a little vegetable shortening (about 1/2 teaspoon per pound of chocolate); compound chocolate may require slightly more shortening; it will not affect the flavor or hardening capacity of the chocolate.

Coloring White Compound Chocolate: Use artificial *powdered food coloring* only (paste or liquid food colorings will keep the chocolate from hardening). Begin by sprinkling a very small amount of the colored powder over the melted chocolate; mix well, then continue adding powder and stirring until you have just the shade you want. If the color becomes too intense, lighten it by adding a bit more melted white chocolate.

To Dip Candies in Chocolate: This isn't just a matter of melting chocolate and sloshing candy through it. It's a tricky technique requiring years to master, so don't be discouraged if your chocolates are streaked or ragged around the edges. For best results:

• Choose a cool, crisp day and have kitchen cool.

• Choose dippable candies—fondant balls, firm caramels, candied cherries.

• Have both chocolate and candies to be dipped at room temperature.

• Use semisweet chocolate (once called dot chocolate) or compound chocolate, and work with no more than 2 pounds at a time and no less than 1.

• Melt very slowly over hot—*not boiling*—water as directed.* Do not add any water to chocolate.

• Using a dipping fork or two-pronged kitchen fork, dip candies one at a time into chocolate to coat evenly; set on wax-paper-covered wire racks, twirling tail end of chocolate into curlicues on top of candies.

• Let chocolates harden about 1 hour before removing from paper. *(Note:* Those dipped in compound chocolate may be refrigerated; they will harden in 5–10 minutes.) Trim off any ragged edges and store airtight (not in the refrigerator, which will cause chocolate to whiten and streak). *Note:* You must work quickly with chocolate. If it hardens before candies are dipped, remelt and cool as before. Semisweet chocolate bits can be used for dipping but are stiffer and lack the finish of semisweet chocolate.

Special Candy Flavorings

Essences and oils are used to flavor candies as well as the familiar extracts available at supermarkets. Specialty food shops usually carry a full line of essences (butterscotch, peppermint, spearmint, not to mention such exotics as rose, violet, and orange flower water), also oils (peppermint, wintergreen, clove, lemon, and other fruit flavors). Use *oils only* to flavor melted chocolate (water- or alcohol-based extracts will make it lumpy). These are potent and must be added drop by drop.

Decorating Candies

Candies need little decoration and, in fact, are extremely difficult to decorate because of their small size. Bar candies are best left alone, but won't be overdecorated if topped by nut halves or candied cherries. Fondant and uncooked fruit balls can be rolled in finely ground nuts, grated coconut (plain, colored, or toasted), in sugar (plain or colored), in chocolate shot or decorettes. Fondant-dipped candies can be adorned with piped-on icing designs (the same decorative icings used for cakes). But keep designs simple—a tiny star or flower or leaf. When tinting icings, use a light touch, remembering that colors often darken as icing dries. Liquid food colors work well, but the number of colors is limited. For a broader palette, investigate paste and powdered colors sold in specialty food shops.

Wrapping and Keeping Candies

When it comes to wrapping and storing, candies fall into two groups: those that dry on standing and those that absorb moisture from the air. Fudges, fondants, and other creamy candies are the drying kind; caramels and hard candies just the opposite. Always store the two kinds separately so that one doesn't give up moisture to the other. Caramels and hard candies should be individually wrapped as soon as they've cooled in wax paper, cellophane, plastic food wrap, or foil, then placed in airtight canisters. The drying kind needn't be wrapped unless you hope to keep it some time, but it *should* be stored airtight.

COOKED CANDIES

FONDANT

1 pound   ¢ ⚖

Fondant is more a base for other confections than a candy to be eaten by itself.

2 cups sugar
1½ cups hot water
⅛ teaspoon cream of tartar or ¼ teaspoon lemon juice

Heat and stir all ingredients in a large, heavy saucepan over moderate heat until sugar dissolves; cover and boil 3 minutes. Uncover, insert candy thermometer that has been heated under hot water tap, and cook *without stirring* to 238° F. or until a drop of fondant forms a soft ball in cold water. (*Note:* Wipe crystals from sides of pan with a damp pastry brush as they collect—fondant will be less apt to turn grainy.) Remove fondant from heat and let stand 1–2 minutes until bubbles subside; pour—*without scraping pan*—onto a marble slab or large, heavy platter rubbed lightly with a damp cloth; cool undisturbed until barely warm. (*Note:* If you have an extra candy thermometer, insert as soon as fondant is poured.) When fondant has cooled to 110° F., scrape from edges with a broad spatula in toward center again and again until it thickens and whitens; pick up and knead until velvety. Wrap fondant in cloth wrung out in cold water and "season" ½ hour before using. (*Note:* Covered with damp cloth and stored in an airtight jar, fondant will keep 3–4 days.)

*NP Ball (1"): 25 C, 0 mg CH, 1 mg S**

To Flavor Fondant: Knead in about ½ teaspoon extract (vanilla, almond, rum, spearmint, rose or orange water) or a few drops oil of peppermint or wintergreen. Add these *by the drop,* tasting as you go so you don't *overflavor.*

To Color Fondant: Dip a toothpick in desired food color, then pierce fondant in several places. Knead to distribute color; if too pale, repeat—but keep colors pastel.

To Use Fondant for Dipping: Melt fondant (either plain or flavored) in the top of a double boiler over simmering water, stirring until smooth. Drop in candy center, nut, or fruit to be dipped, turn with a long-handled, 2-tined fork to coat evenly, lift to wax paper, and for a professional touch twirl tag end of fondant into a curlicue on top of each piece when removing fork. Let harden, then lift from paper.

VARIATIONS

⚖ **Coffee Fondant:** Prepare as directed, sustituting 1½ cups strong black coffee for the water and 2 tablespoons light corn syrup for the cream of tartar.

*NP Ball (1"): 25 C, 0 mg CH, 1 mg S**

⚖ **Butter Fondant:** Prepare as directed, using the following ingredients: 2 cups sugar, 1 cup milk, 1 tablespoon light corn syrup, and 1 tablespoon butter.

*NP Ball (1"): 30 C, 1 mg CH, 5 mg S**

⚖ **Opera Creams:** Prepare as directed, using the following ingredients: 2 cups sugar, 1 cup heavy cream, and ⅛ teaspoon cream of tartar. Do not boil covered; instead, after sugar dissolves, cook without stirring to 238° F. (*Note:* This fondant takes longer to cream up on the marble slab than regular fondant.)

*NP Ball (1"): 40 C, 5 mg CH, 1 mg S**

Confections to Make with Fondant

Stuffed Fruits: Shape fondant into small balls and stuff into pitted dates, prunes, or dried apricots. Roll in granulated sugar. Recipe too flexible for meaningful nutritional count.

Nut Bonbons: Sandwich large walnut or pecan halves together with small fondant balls. Recipe too flexible for meaningful nutritional count.

Frosted Nuts or Fruits: Dip large walnut or pecan halves, whole blanched almonds, candied cherries, pitted dates, or dried apricots into melted fondant. Recipe too flexible for meaningful nutritional count.

Pinwheels: Take equal parts fondant and fudge (without nuts) or two flavors and colors of fondant and knead separately until smooth. Flatten 1 piece into a rectangle about 6" × 8" and 1/8" thick. Pat remaining candy on top to fit, then roll jelly-roll fashion and slice 1/4" thick. Recipe too flexible for meaningful nutritional count.

⚖ **Thin Mints:** Flavor fondant with peppermint, tint pale green and flavor with spearmint, or tint pale pink and flavor with wintergreen. Melt in the top of a double boiler over simmering water, stirring until smooth; drop from a teaspoon onto wax paper and let harden. Same nutritional count as basic recipe.

Sugarplums: Roll fondant around small pieces of fruit—candied cherries, small pitted dates, cubes of preserved ginger, pieces of dried apricots. Recipe too flexible for meaningful nutritional count.

⚖ **Snowballs:** Shape fondant into small balls and roll in flaked coconut. Recipe too flexible for meaningful nutritional count.

DIVINITY

1 1/2 pounds

2 1/2 cups sugar
1/2 cup light corn syrup
1/2 cup water
2 egg whites
1 teaspoon vanilla
1 1/2 cups coarsely chopped walnuts or pecans

Place sugar, syrup, and water in a large, heavy saucepan; insert candy thermometer. Heat and stir over moderate heat until sugar dissolves, lower heat slightly and cook, uncovered, *without stirring* to 260° F. Toward end of cooking, beat egg whites until soft peaks form. When syrup reaches 260° F., add to egg whites in a very slow, fine stream, beating hard all the while. Continue adding, more quickly toward the end, until all syrup is incorporated. Add vanilla and beat until stiff peaks form; fold in nuts. Drop from rounded teaspoons onto wax-paper-lined baking sheets and cool thoroughly.

NP Ounce: 150 C, 0 mg CH, 10 mg S*

V A R I A T I O N S

Seafoam: Prepare as directed but use firmly packed light brown sugar instead of granulated.

NP Ounce: 155 C, 0 mg CH, 15 mg S*

⚖ **Confetti Divinity:** Prepare as directed but omit nuts; instead; stir in 1 cup minced mixed candied fruit.

NP Ounce: 135 C, 0 mg CH, 40 mg S*

⚖ **Fruit Divinity:** Prepare as directed but omit nuts; instead, stir in 1 cup minced pitted dates, prunes, or dried apricots.

NP Ounce: 120 C, 0 mg CH, 10 mg S*

Christmas Divinity: Prepare as directed but reduce nuts to 3/4 cup; also stir in 3/4 cup minced mixed red and green candied cherries.

NP Ounce: 140 C, 0 mg CH, 10 mg S*

⚖ **Pistachio Divinity:** Prepare as directed but reduce vanilla to 1/2 teaspoon and add 1/4 teaspoon almond extract. Tint pale green if you like, beat until stiff, and fold in 1 1/2 cups minced pistachio nuts.

NP Ounce: 145 C, 0 mg CH, 10 mg S*

BEST CHOCOLATE FUDGE

2 pounds

4 cups sugar
1 cup milk
3 (1-ounce) squares unsweetened chocolate
1/4 teaspoon salt
1/4 cup light corn syrup
1/4 cup butter or margarine
1 teaspoon vanilla
1–1 1/2 cups coarsely chopped pecans or walnuts (optional)

Heat sugar, milk, chocolate, salt, and corn syrup, uncovered, in a large, heavy saucepan with a candy thermometer over moderate heat, stirring constantly, until sugar dissolves. Continue cooking, uncovered, *without stirring* but occasionally moving a wooden spoon back and forth over bottom of pan until thermometer reaches 236°–238° F. or mixture forms a soft ball in cold water. Remove from heat, drop in butter, and cool, without stirring, to 110° F. Add vanilla and beat until fudge is quite thick and begins to lose its gloss. Quickly mix in nuts, if you like, and spread in a well-buttered 8" × 8" × 2" baking pan. Cool until firm and cut into 1" squares. For better flavor, store airtight and ripen 24 hours.

NP Ounce (without nuts): 135 C, 5 mg CH, 40 mg S*
NP Ounce (with nuts): 160 C, 5 mg CH, 40 mg S*

BLOND FUDGE

1 pound

A good choice for those allergic to chocolate.

2 cups sugar
1/4 cup light corn syrup
1 1/3 cups milk
1/3 cup light cream
1 teaspoon vanilla
1 tablespoon butter
1 1/4 cups coarsely chopped pecans or walnuts (optional)

Place sugar, syrup, milk, and cream in a large, heavy saucepan (mixture tends to boil up, so pan should be at least four times combined volume of ingredients); insert candy thermometer. Heat and stir over moderate heat until sugar dissolves, reduce heat slightly and cook, uncovered, stirring only if mixture threatens to boil over, until thermometer reaches 238° F. or a drop of candy forms a soft ball in cold water. Toward end of cooking, mixture will be very thick, so watch closely and move spoon gently across bottom of pan occasionally to keep it from scorching. Remove from heat, add vanilla and butter *without stirring,* and cool to 110° F. Beat until thick and no longer glossy, quickly mix in nuts, if you like, and turn into a buttered 8″ × 8″ × 2″ pan, spreading to edges. Cool until firm and cut in 1″ squares.

NP Ounce (without nuts): 140 C, 10 mg CH, 25 mg S*
NP Ounce (with nuts): 205 C, 10 mg CH, 25 mg S*

VARIATIONS

Coconut Fudge: Prepare as directed but omit nuts; instead, stir in 1 1/4 cups flaked coconut. Turn out, cool, and cut as directed.

NP Ounce: 170 C, 10 mg CH, 25 mg S*

Chocolate Chip Fudge: Prepare as directed but reduce nuts to 3/4 cup; at the same time, mix in 1 cup semisweet chocolate bits. Turn out, cool, and cut as directed.

NP Ounce: 230 C, 10 mg CH, 25 mg S*

PENUCHE

1 pound

1 (1-pound) box light brown sugar
3/4 cup milk
2 tablespoons butter or margarine
1 teaspoon vanilla

Heat sugar, milk, and butter in a large, heavy saucepan with a candy thermometer over moderate heat, stirring until sugar dissolves. Lower heat slightly and cook, uncovered, *without stirring* to 240° F. or until mixture forms a soft ball in cold water. Off heat, add vanilla—do not stir—and cool to 110° F. Beat until thick and no longer shiny, pour into a buttered 8″ × 8″ × 2″ pan, spreading to edges. Score in 1″ squares and cool to room temperature. Cut into 1″ squares and serve.

NP Ounce (with butter): 125 C, 5 mg CH, 30 mg S*

VARIATIONS

Nut Penuche: Prepare as directed but mix in 2/3 cup coarsely chopped pecans or walnuts just before pouring into pan.

NP Ounce: 160 C, 5 mg CH, 30 mg S*

Coconut Penuche: Prepare as directed but mix in 2/3 cup flaked coconut just before pouring into pan.

NP Ounce: 140 C, 5 mg CH, 30 mg S*

Maple Penuche: Prepare as directed but use maple flavoring instead of vanilla. For a more delicate flavor, use 1 cup granulated sugar and 1 1/4 cups firmly packed light brown sugar instead of all brown sugar.

NP Ounce (with granulated sugar and brown sugar): 130 C, 5 mg CH, 25 mg S*

PRALINES

2 dozen

A friend said of these, "Best I ever ate!"

2 cups sugar
1/2 cup firmly packed light brown sugar
1 teaspoon baking soda
1/4 teaspoon salt
1/8 teaspoon cinnamon
1 cup buttermilk
1/4 cup butter or margarine
2 cups pecan halves

Mix sugars, soda, salt, cinnamon, and buttermilk in a large, heavy saucepan; drop in butter. Insert candy thermometer. Heat, uncovered, and without stirring over moderately high heat until candy thermometer registers 238° F. or mixture forms a soft ball in cold water. Remove from heat at once and stir in pecans. Beat briskly with a wooden spoon about 1 minute, then drop onto wax-paper-lined baking sheets, making each praline 2″–2 1/2″ in diameter. Let harden thoroughly before serving.

NP Ounce (with butter): 170 C, 5 mg CH, 90 mg S*

CARAMELS

1 pound

Cook very slowly in your heaviest saucepan. This mixture is sweet and thick—apt to scorch.

1 cup sugar
2/3 cup light corn syrup
1 1/2 cups light cream
1/8 teaspoon salt
1 teaspoon vanilla

Place sugar, syrup, and 1/2 cup cream in a large, heavy saucepan; insert candy thermometer. Heat and stir over moderate heat until sugar dissolves. Turn heat to low and cook, uncovered, stirring occasionally, to 238° F. Mix in 1/2 cup cream and cook, stirring as needed to keep from sticking, to about 236° F. or until mixture forms a soft ball in cold water. Mix in remaining 1/2 cup cream and heat, stirring constantly, until very thick and a drop firms up quickly in cold water. Thermometer may register only 230° F., but if mixture firms up, take from heat. Mix in salt and vanilla and pour into a buttered 8″ × 8″ × 2″ pan. Cool until just warm and score in 1″ squares. Cool thoroughly, cut in squares, and wrap individually in wax paper or cellophane.

NP Ounce: 35 C, 5 mg CH, 10 mg S*

VARIATIONS

Nut Caramels: Prepare as directed but just before pouring into pan stir in 2/3 cup minced walnuts or pecans.

NP Ounce: 40 C, 5 mg CH, 10 mg S*

Chocolate Caramels: Prepare as directed but add 1 1/2 (1-ounce) squares melted unsweetened chocolate along with final 1/2 cup cream. Watch closely to see that mixture doesn't scorch during final cooking.

NP Ounce: 35 C, 5 mg CH, 10 mg S*

OLD ENGLISH TOFFEE

1 pound

1 cup butter (no substitute)
1/4 cup light cream or evaporated milk
2 cups firmly packed light brown sugar
1 teaspoon vanilla

Melt butter in a large, heavy saucepan over moderate heat; mix in cream and sugar, insert candy thermometer, and heat, uncovered, stirring occasionally, until sugar dissolves. Continue cooking, uncovered, moving a wooden spoon across bottom of pan *occasionally* (but not actually stirring)

until thermometer reaches 280° F. or a little mixture dropped in ice water separates into firm but not brittle strands. Remove from heat, let bubbling subside, add vanilla, and stir only to blend. Pour into a well-buttered 8″ × 8″ × 2″ pan and cool 10 minutes— candy should be hardening but still plastic. Turn onto a foil-lined board and score in 1″ squares. Cool to room temperature, break into squares, and wrap each in foil, cellophane, or wax paper. Store airtight.

NP Ounce: 210 C, 35 mg CH, 125 mg S*

PEANUT BRITTLE

1 3/4 pounds

Any nut brittle, when finely ground or minced, is delicious scattered over ice cream or custard.

2 cups roasted, blanched peanuts
2 cups sugar
1/2 cup water
1/2 cup light corn syrup
1/4 cup butter or margarine
1/4 teaspoon baking soda
1/2 teaspoon vanilla

Warm peanuts in a large, heavy skillet over low heat 5–7 minutes, shaking skillet occasionally; keep warm while making brittle. Mix sugar, water, and corn syrup in a large, heavy saucepan; insert candy thermometer. Set over high heat and heat, stirring, until sugar dissolves, then heat, uncovered, *without stirring* but moving a wooden spoon back and forth across bottom of pan occasionally to prevent scorching. When thermometer reaches 310° F. or a little hot syrup dropped in ice water turns brittle, remove from heat, add butter, peanuts, soda, and vanilla, and mix just to blend. Let bubbles subside, pour out as thin as possible on buttered baking sheets, spreading mixture with a buttered spatula. *For extra-thin brittle:* Cool until easy to handle, then pull out and stretch with buttered fingers. When brittle is cold, crack into bite-sized pieces. (*Note:* Flavor will be best if brittle ripens 24 hours in an airtight canister.)

NP Ounce (with butter): 125 C, 5 mg CH, 30 mg S*

VARIATIONS

Lacy Brittle: Prepare as directed, heating 1/4 teaspoon cream of tartar with sugar mixture and increasing soda to 1/2 teaspoon.

NP Ounce (with butter): 125 C, 5 mg CH, 35 mg S*

Pecan or Walnut Brittle: Prepare as directed, substituting roasted pecan or walnut halves, toasted, blanched whole almonds or hazelnuts for peanuts.

NP Ounce (with pecans and butter): 145 C, 5 mg CH, 30 mg S*

Almond Brittle: Prepare as directed, substituting toasted, blanched whole almonds for peanuts.

NP Ounce (with butter): 140 C, 5 mg CH, 30 mg S*

Some Pointers on Pulled Candies

• Don't attempt to make pulled candies in a cool kitchen; candies will harden too fast.
• Rally the troops; pulling candy calls for teamwork and young strong arms.
• Remove rings—candy can pull the settings out.
• Make sure counter underneath platter or tray of hot candy is heat resistant; if not, it may get scorched.
• While candy is still too hot to handle, begin the pulling with a buttered metal spatula by lifting and stretching.
• Use buttered bare hands for the pulling (gloves are hopeless) and keep rebuttering them as needed to keep candy from sticking.

VANILLA TAFFY

1 pound ¢

2 cups sugar
2/3 cup light corn syrup
1/3 cup water
3 tablespoons butter or margarine
1/2 teaspoon vanilla

Mix sugar, syrup, and water in a heavy saucepan, drop in butter, and insert candy thermometer. Heat, stirring constantly, over moderately high heat until sugar dissolves, then cook, uncovered, *without stirring* to 270° F. or until a drop of candy forms firm, pliable strands in cold water. Pour at once onto a buttered marble slab, large ironstone platter, or heavy metal tray; do not scrape pan. Cool 1–2 minutes, then sprinkle with vanilla and, using a buttered metal spatula, fold edges in toward center to distribute heat evenly. When candy is cool enough to handle, pull and stretch with buttered hands until light and no longer shiny. When too stiff to pull further, stretch into a rope about 1/2" in diameter, and with buttered kitchen shears cut across the grain every 1". Separate pieces, dry thoroughly, then wrap and store airtight.

NP Ounce (with butter): 155 C, 5 mg CH, 30 mg S*

VARIATION

¢ **Peppermint Taffy:** Prepare as directed but omit vanilla; sprinkle taffy instead with 8 drops oil of peppermint and, if you like, a few drops green coloring. Proceed as above.

NP Ounce (with butter): 155 C, 5 mg CH, 30 mg S*

MOLASSES TAFFY

1 1/4 pounds ¢

2 cups sugar
1 cup molasses
1 cup water
1/4 cup butter or margarine

Mix sugar, molasses, and water in a heavy saucepan, drop in butter, and insert candy thermometer. Heat, stirring constantly, over moderately high heat until sugar dissolves, then cook, uncovered, *without stirring* to 270° F. or until a drop of the mixture forms firm, pliable strands in cold water. Pour onto a buttered marble slab at once, or large ironstone platter or heavy metal tray. Cool 1–2 minutes, then fold edges toward center to distribute heat. When cool enough to handle, pull and stretch with buttered hands until light and no longer shiny. When too stiff to pull further, stretch into a rope about 1/2" in diameter and with buttered kitchen shears cut across the grain every 1". Separate pieces as you cut, cool thoroughly, then wrap individually and store airtight.

NP Ounce (with butter): 140 C, 5 mg CH, 25 mg S*

MRS. B's PULLED MINTS

1 1/2 pounds

A difficult recipe, not for beginners. At first these mints are chewy and taffy-like, but after several days of "ripening," they soften magically and will melt in your mouth.

4 cups sugar
2 cups boiling water
1/2 cup unsalted butter (no substitute)
6–8 drops oil of peppermint
4–5 drops green food coloring (optional)

Mix sugar and water in a heavy saucepan, drop in butter, and insert candy thermometer. Heat, stirring constantly, over moderately high heat until sugar dissolves, then cook, uncovered, *without stirring* to 258° F. or until a drop of mixture forms a hard ball in cold water. Immediately pour onto a buttered marble slab, large ironstone platter, or heavy metal tray; do not scrape out pan. Sprinkle with oil of peppermint and, if you like, coloring. Cool slightly but as soon as possible begin pulling and stretching with buttered hands. When candy pales and begins to lose its gloss, pull and twist into a rope 3/4"–1" in diameter and cut across the grain with buttered kitchen shears every 1/2"–3/4". Spread pieces out on wax paper and, when thoroughly cool, store airtight. Let "ripen" 2–3 days—mints will cream up.

NP Ounce: 160 C, 10 mg CH, 1 mg S*

APRICOT-ALMOND BALLS

4 dozen

An old-fashioned sweetmeat.

1 pound dried apricots
1½ cups sugar
¼ cup orange juice
Finely grated rind of 1 orange
1 cup minced, blanched almonds
Sifted confectioners' sugar (for dredging)

Put apricots through fine blade of meat grinder. Place in the top of a double boiler, set over just-boiling water, and mix in sugar, orange juice, and rind. Cook, stirring now and then, 1/2 hour; mix in nuts and cook 5 minutes longer. Cool in pan until just slightly warm, then drop from a teaspoon into confectioners' sugar and shape into 1" balls. When all balls have been shaped, roll again in confectioners' sugar. Store airtight.

NP Ball: 65 C, 0 mg CH, 1 mg S*

CANDIED APPLES

6 candied apples

Prepare a batch for Halloween.

6 wooden skewers or lollipop sticks
6 medium-size red apples, washed, dried, and
stemmed
2 cups sugar
2 cups light corn syrup
1 cup water
¼ cup red cinnamon candies
½ teaspoon red food coloring

Insert skewers in stem ends of apples. Place all remaining ingredients except food coloring in a heavy saucepan; insert candy thermometer and heat over moderate heat, stirring constantly, until sugar and candies dissolve; do not boil. Mix in coloring, then boil *without stirring* until thermometer reaches 300° F. or a drop of syrup turns brittle in cold water. Remove from heat. Working quickly, dip apples, one at a time, in syrup to coat evenly, twirling so excess drains off. Cool on wax-paper-lined baking sheet.

NP Apple: 675 C, 0 mg CH, 75 mg S*

VARIATION

Caramel Apples: Instead of preparing syrup above, melt 1½ pounds vanilla caramels with 3 tablespoons water in the top of a double boiler, stirring until smooth. Dip apples as directed, scraping excess caramel off on rim of pan. Cool until caramel hardens.

NP Apple: 535 C, 5 mg CH, 255 mg S*

CANDIED CITRUS PEEL

1 pound ¢

Some grapefruits have excessively bitter peel. To overcome it, soak peel overnight in heavily salted water (weight peel so it stays submerged). Rinse the peel well before beginning recipe.

Peel from 2 grapefruits, 3 large thick-skinned
oranges (navel are good), or 4 large lemons or
limes
5 quarts cold water
3 cups sugar
½ cup hot water
1 teaspoon gelatin mixed with 1 tablespoon cold
water

Cover peel with 1 quart cold water, bring to a boil, then drain. Repeat process four times until peel is tender. If peel has thick pith, scoop out excess. Cut peel in thin strips or petal shapes. Heat 2 cups sugar and hot water in a heavy saucepan over moderately low heat, stirring constantly until sugar dissolves. Add peel and boil slowly until clear and candy-like, about 25 minutes, moving a wooden spoon occasionally over bottom of pan to keep peel from sticking. Add gelatin, cook and stir 5 minutes longer. Remove from heat and let stand 3–5 minutes; remove peel, a few pieces at a time, allowing excess syrup to drain off, then roll in remaining sugar to coat thickly. (*Note:* Toothpicks are handy for doing this messy job. Dry peel on wire racks and store airtight.)

NP Ounce: 90 C, 0 mg CH, 0 mg S*

For Brightly Colored Peel: Tint syrup color of fruit used or roll candied peel in colored sugar.

NP Ounce: 90 C, 0 mg CH, 0 mg S*

UNCOOKED CANDIES

UNCOOKED FONDANT

1 pound ☒

1/4 cup butter (no substitute), softened to room
   temperature
2 tablespoons light corn syrup
3 tablespoons heavy cream
1 (1-pound) box confectioners' sugar, sifted
1/2 teaspoon vanilla

Cream butter with corn syrup and heavy
cream until smooth; slowly add sugar, a little at a time, beating well after each addition
and kneading in the last bit if necessary.
Work in vanilla. Roll into 1″ balls or use to
stuff pitted dates, prunes, or dried apricots
or to sandwich together large pecan or walnut halves.

NP Ounce: 150 C, 10 mg CH, 30 mg S*

VARIATION

Citrus-Rum Fondant: Prepare as directed,
subtituting 3 tablespoons dark rum for the
cream and 1 teaspoon grated fresh orange or
tangerine rind and 1/8 teaspoon orange extract for the vanilla.

NP Ounce: 150 C, 10 mg CH, 30 mg S*

KENTUCKY COLONELS

3 1/2 dozen

Bourbon-filled, chocolate-covered, butter
cream balls.

1/2 cup butter (no substitute)
1 (1-pound) box confectioners' sugar, sifted
1 tablespoon heavy cream or evaporated milk
2 tablespoons bourbon (about)
1 (6-ounce) package semisweet chocolate bits
1/4 cup hot water
42 pecan halves

Cream butter until light and fluffy, slowly
blend in sugar and cream, and beat until
smooth. Scoop up by rounded measuring
teaspoonfuls, shape into balls, and arrange
1 1/2″ apart on ungreased baking sheets.
With little finger, make deep dents in tops of
balls and, using an eyedropper, add a few
drops bourbon; pinch tops to seal. Chill 1/2
hour. Melt chocolate bits in the top of a
double boiler over simmering water, add water a little at a time, and beat until smooth.
Keeping chocolate warm over hot water so
it doesn't harden, spoon over balls, coating
evenly. Top each ball with a pecan. Chill 2–3

hours before serving. Store airtight in refrigerator or other cool place.

NP Ball: 90 C, 5 mg CH, 20 mg S*

UNCOOKED FUDGE

1 1/2 pounds ☒

As velvety and chocolaty as old-fashioned
cooked fudge.

2 (3-ounce) packages cream cheese, softened to
   room temperature
4 cups sifted confectioners' sugar
2 tablespoons heavy cream or evaporated milk
1 (6-ounce) package semisweet chocolate bits
1/2 teaspoon vanilla
1/8 teaspoon salt
1 cup coarsely chopped pecans

Beat cream cheese until smooth, slowly
blend in sugar and cream, and beat until
creamy. Melt chocolate bits in the top of a
double boiler over simmering water, add to
cheese mixture along with vanilla and salt,
and beat until smooth. Stir in pecans, press
into a well-buttered 9″ × 9″ × 2″ pan,
cover, and chill overnight. Cut in 1″ squares
and store in refrigerator or other cool place.

*NP Ounce (with heavy cream): 165 C, 10 mg CH,
   35 mg S**

VARIATIONS

Uncooked Almond Fudge: Prepare as directed but substitute 1/2 teaspoon almond
extract for vanilla and 1 cup coarsely
chopped blanched almonds for pecans.

*NP Ounce (with heavy cream): 160 C, 10 mg CH,
   35 mg S**

Uncooked Cocoa Fudge: Prepare as directed
but use 1/2 cup cocoa instead of chocolate
bits and add 2 extra teaspoons milk.

*NP Ounce (with heavy cream): 130 C, 10 mg CH,
   35 mg S**

Uncooked Coconut Fudge: Prepare as directed but stir in 1 cup shredded or flaked
coconut instead of pecans.

*NP Ounce (with heavy cream): 145 C, 10 mg CH,
   35 mg S**

Uncooked Peanut Butter Fudge: Prepare as
directed but omit chocolate; mix in 1 cup
creamy peanut butter and 1 cup coarsely
chopped unsalted roasted peanuts instead of
pecans.

*NP Ounce (with heavy cream): 180 C, 10 mg CH,
   100 mg S**

SPICY UNCOOKED FRUIT-NUT BARS

1½ pounds

1 cup pitted prunes
½ cup dried figs
1 cup seedless raisins
1 cup pitted dates
½ cup coarsely chopped pecans, walnuts, or
    blanched almonds
¼ teaspoon cloves
¼ teaspoon cinnamon
¼ teaspoon salt
Few drops orange juice (just to moisten)
Sifted confectioners' sugar (for dredging)

Put fruits and nuts through fine blade of meat grinder, mix in seasonings and just enough orange juice to make mixture hold together. Roll or pat out ¼" thick, cut in squares or small circles, and dredge in confectioners' sugar. If you prefer, roll into small balls and dredge.

NP Ounce (with pecans): 85 C, 0 mg CH, 25 mg S*

NUTS

Any nuts can be used in making candies, most can be toasted and eaten out-of-hand, but the favorites are almonds, walnuts, pecans, peanuts, and pistachios. For variety, try some of the less familiar: Brazil nuts, cashews, chestnuts, hazelnuts and their European cousin, filberts, macadamias, piñons (pine nuts), or if you're lucky enough to live where you can gather your own, hickory, beech, and butternuts. Nuts *do* run to calories, but fortunately not "empty calories" because they are a high-protein food with impressive vitamin and mineral content.

Buying Nuts

Supermarkets carry all the popular nuts in a variety of forms. Which you buy depends on your budget and time schedule. You'll save money by buying nuts in the shell or unblanched, but you'll spend considerable time preparing them. Obviously, the more nearly ready to use nuts are (toasted, chopped, ground, etc.), the more expensive they will be.

Nuts in the Shell (1 pound unshelled nuts = ½ pound shelled nuts): This is the way to buy nuts if they must be kept some time (some unshelled nuts will keep as long as a year). Choose nuts without splits, scars, holes, or mold. Nuts commonly available in the shell: almonds, Brazil nuts, chestnuts, filberts or hazelnuts, pecans, peanuts, pistachios, and walnuts.

Shelled, Unblanched Nuts: Recipes sometimes call for unblanched nuts (skins add color, flavor, and texture). Those often available this way: almonds, filberts and hazelnuts, peanuts, pistachios. *(Note:* Pecans and walnuts are never blanched.)

Shelled, Blanched Nuts: Almonds, Brazil nuts, filberts, hazelnuts, peanuts, piñons, and pistachio nuts are frequently sold this way.

Shelled, Blanched, Roasted, or Toasted Nuts: Almonds, pecans, peanuts, cashews, hazelnuts, filberts, and macadamias are stocked by many supermarkets and specialty food shops, as are mixed roasted nuts. Also available are dry-roasted nuts—lower in calories than the regular roasted nuts. For candies, it's best to use unsalted nuts unless recipes specify to the contrary.

Nut Halves and Meats: A handy form of almonds, pecans, and walnuts. If packaged in plastic bags, sniff for signs of rancidity (these nuts don't stay fresh long). If you are particular about your cooking, you'd do well to prepare your own nuts.

Preparing Nuts

To Crack:

Thin- or Soft-Shelled Nuts (peanuts and almonds): Crack with your hands and pull out kernels. *(Note:* Chestnuts are soft-shelled but need special techniques—see Vegetables.)

Thick- or Hard-Shelled Nuts: Crack with a nutcracker, pull off shells, and with a nut pick extract kernels. *(Note:* Pecans have a bitter red-brown inner partition that must also be removed.)

To Blanch:

Almonds, Peanuts, Pistachios: Shell, cover with boiling water, and let stand 2 minutes; drain, cool slightly, and slip off skins.

Chestnuts: See vegetable chapter.

Filberts, Hazelnuts: These nuts are so tedious to blanch you'll probably want to pay a little more and buy them already blanched. But if you're counting pennies: Shell nuts, cover with boiling water, and boil 6 minutes; drain and cover with hot tap water. Lift nuts from water, one at a time, and slip and scrape off skins, using a paring knife. The skins are stubborn, will cling to the nuts and your fingers. An easier although not a 100-

per-cent-successful method is to drain the blanched nuts, bundle in a turkish towel, and rub together briskly.

To Chop Nuts: Do only about 1/2 cup at a time, using a chopping board and heavy chopping knife. Or, if a quantity must be done, use a chopping bowl and curved chopper. *(Note:* For directions on chopping nuts in a food processor, see Food Processor Metal Blade Chopping Guide in Chapter 1.)

To Shave Nuts (almonds and Brazil nuts, either blanched or unblanched, are the most suitable): Peel off thin slivers using a vegetable peeler.

To Grate Nuts: The quickest way is to use a rotary grater.

To Grind Nuts: Buzz a few nuts at a time in an electric blender at high speed, stopping and stirring as needed to keep nuts from clumping. Do not use a meat grinder. *(Note:* For directions on grinding nuts in a food processor, see Food Processor Metal Blade Chopping Guide in Chapter 1.)

To Toast or Roast Nuts: Blanch or not, as you like. Spread out in an ungreased shallow baking pan and roast, uncovered, stirring often, 1/2–1 1/2 hours at 300° F. until lightly browned (size and kind of nut will determine, so watch closely). If you like (and if nuts are blanched), drizzle with melted butter and sprinkle with salt. Toss well to mix and store airtight. *Microwave Method:* Spread 1/2 pound nuts in a flameproof glass piepan or paper plate, and microwave, uncovered, 3–5 minutes on *HIGH* power setting, stirring once or twice.

To Deep-Fry (best for almonds and peanuts): Blanch nuts. Pour about 2″ corn or peanut oil in a large, heavy skillet and heat to 360° F. Fry nuts, about 1 cup at a time, stirring often, until pale golden. Lift to paper-towel-lined baking sheets with a slotted spoon and cool. *(Note:* Nuts will continue cooking slightly as they cool, so don't fry more than *pale* golden.) Sprinkle with salt and toss to mix. Store airtight.

FRESH COCONUT

Coconuts have double, hard shells, but most sold today wear the inner monkey-faced shell only. Choose those that are heavy for their size and full of liquid (you can tell by shaking them).

To Open: Pierce "eyes" with a screwdriver and drain liquid into a bowl (it can be used in recipes). Break coconut open with a hammer and chisel or place coconut on a baking sheet and heat 20 minutes at 400° F. Tap all over to loosen meat, then crack with a hammer or mallet. Pry chunks of white meat from shell and peel off brown skin with a knife or vegetable peeler.

To Grate: Grate coarse or fine with a flat or rotary grater, or cut in small cubes and buzz, a few at a time, in an electric blender at high speed. *(Note:* For directions on grating coconut in a food processor, see Food Processor Metal Blade Chopping Guide in Chapter 1.) From 1 medium-size coconut, you'll get 3–4 cups grated coconut and 1 cup liquid. *(Note:* When measuring grated coconut, do not pack the measure.)

How to Color or Toast Coconut: See Some Special Candy-Making Techniques.

COCONUT MILK OR CREAM

1 quart

1 medium-size coconut
Liquid from coconut + enough water, milk, or
   light cream to total 1 quart

Open coconut,* reserving liquid; grate meat moderately fine and place in a large, heavy saucepan with liquid mixture. Heat slowly, stirring constantly, just until mixture boils. Remove from heat, cover, and cool to room temperature. Press through a double thickness of cheesecloth or a fine sieve, forcing out as much liquid as possible. Discard coconut pulp. Use milk in making curries, confections, desserts, and beverages. Store in refrigerator.

*NP Cup: 85 C, 0 mg CH, 35 mg S**

To Make with Canned Coconut: Prepare as directed, substituting 3 (4-ounce) cans flaked or shredded coconut for the fresh and using 1 quart milk or light cream. *(Note:* If your Scottish nature rebels at discarding the coconut, spread out in a large, shallow baking pan, drizzle lightly with melted butter, and toast, stirring often, 3/4–1 hour until crisp and golden. Flavor will be bland, but coconut can be used to garnish candies and fruit desserts or as a condiment for curry.) Recipe too variable for meaningful nutritional count.

CHINESE COCONUT CANDY

1 pound

Sugared strips of fresh coconut.

1 medium-size coconut
Coconut liquid + enough cold water to total 1 cup
2 cups sugar

Open coconut,* reserving liquid. Remove coconut meat in as large pieces as possible and trim off brown skin with a vegetable peeler. Cut in strips about 2″ long and 3/8″ wide. Mix sugar and coconut liquid in a large, heavy saucepan, insert candy thermometer, and heat, stirring constantly, over moderate heat until sugar dissolves. Add coconut and boil, uncovered, to 240° F. or until a drop of candy forms a soft ball in cold water; stir once or twice just to keep coconut from sticking. Remove from heat and stir gently until mixture sugars and coats coconut. Using 2 forks, lift strips to wax-paper-lined baking sheets, separate into individual pieces, and cool. Store airtight.

NP Ounce: 180 C, 0 mg CH, 15 mg S*

SUGARED NUTS

1 pound

Such a dainty sweetmeat. Easy to make, too.

1¼ cups sugar
2/3 cup water
2 tablespoons light corn syrup
Pinch salt
2 cups pecan or walnut halves, whole blanched pistachio nuts, or toasted, blanched almonds or filberts

Place sugar, water, syrup, and salt in a heavy saucepan; insert candy thermometer. Heat and stir over moderate heat until sugar dissolves, reduce heat slightly, and cook, uncovered, *without stirring* to 240° F. Remove from heat, stir in nuts, and pour onto a wax-paper-lined baking sheet. Spread out as thin as possible and let cool until hard. Break apart, separating into individual nuts.

NP Ounce (with pecans): 170 C, 0 mg CH, 10 mg S*

VARIATIONS

Sugared and Spiced Nuts: Prepare as directed but mix 1 teaspoon vanilla, 1/2 teaspoon cinnamon, and a pinch nutmeg into syrup just before adding nuts. Pour out, cool, and separate as directed.

NP Ounce (with pecans): 170 C, 0 mg CH, 10 mg S*

Orange-Sugared Nuts: Prepare as directed but substitute strained orange juice for the water and add the finely grated rind of 1 orange. Proceed as above.

NP Ounce (with pecans): 175 C, 0 mg CH, 10 mg S*

GLAZED NUTS

1 pound

These must be made on a cool, dry day if they're to harden properly.

2 cups sugar
1 cup hot water
1/8 teaspoon cream of tartar
1 pound whole blanched almonds or filberts, pecan or walnut halves

Mix sugar, water, and cream of tartar in a heavy saucepan; insert candy thermometer. Heat and stir over moderate heat until sugar dissolves, reduce heat slightly, and cook, uncovered, *without stirring* until syrup is 310° F. and the color of straw. Remove from heat and set very gently in a large pan of boiling water (be careful because water will sputter). Using tongs, dip nuts into syrup, one at a time; dry on wax-paper-lined baking sheets. When thoroughly cool, store airtight. (*Note:* These candies quickly pick up moisture from the air and become sticky, so serve as soon after making as possible. If syrup should harden before all nuts are dipped reheat slowly to soften.)

NP Ounce (with almonds): 265 C, 0 mg CH, 1 mg S*

VARIATION

⚖ **Glazed Fruits:** Prepare syrup as directed and use for dipping dried apricot halves, pitted dates, firm, fresh, well-dried strawberries or grapes, well-dried orange or tangerine sections, candied cherries. Handle fruit carefully so you don't puncture it.

NP Ounce (apricots): 165 C, 0 mg CH, 5 mg S*
NP Ounce (strawberries): 105 C, 0 mg CH, 1 mg S*
NP Ounce (green grapes): 115 C, 0 mg CH, 1 mg S*
NP Ounce (orange sections): 110 C, 0 mg CH, 1 mg S*

GARLICKY COCKTAIL ALMONDS

1 pound

1 pound whole blanched almonds
2 tablespoons melted butter or margarine
1 clove garlic, peeled and crushed
3/4 teaspoon salt

Preheat oven to 275° F. Spread almonds out in a large, shallow roasting pan. Mix butter with garlic and drizzle over nuts; stir well. Roast, uncovered, stirring occasionally, about 2 hours until golden brown. Drain on paper toweling. When cool, sprinkle with salt and toss to mix.

*NP Ounce (with butter): 185 C, 5 mg CH, 120 mg S**

TOASTED CURRIED ALMONDS

1 pound

1 pound whole blanched almonds
3 tablespoons melted butter or margarine
1 tablespoon curry powder
1/2 teaspoon Worcestershire sauce
1/4 teaspoon liquid hot red pepper seasoning
1 teaspoon salt mixed with 1 teaspoon curry powder

Preheat oven to 275° F. Spread almonds out in a large, shallow roasting pan. Mix butter with curry powder, Worcestershire sauce, and liquid hot red pepper seasoning, drizzle over nuts and stir well. Roast, uncovered, stirring every 20 minutes, about 2 hours until golden brown. Drain on paper toweling. When cool, sprinkle with salt-curry powder mixture and toss well to mix. Drain on fresh paper toweling before serving.

*NP Ounce (with butter): 190 C, 5 mg CH, 165 mg S**

POPCORN BALLS

9 (3") balls or 1 1/2 dozen (1 1/2") balls

1 cup sugar
1 cup light corn syrup

1 teaspoon cider vinegar
3 tablespoons butter or margarine
1 teaspoon vanilla
2 quarts popped, unseasoned popcorn

Place sugar, corn syrup, and vinegar in a heavy saucepan; insert candy thermometer and heat and stir over moderately high heat until sugar dissolves. Cook, uncovered, *without stirring* to 260° F. or until a drop of syrup forms a hard ball in cold water. Off heat, mix in butter and vanilla. Pour over popcorn in a large bowl and stir quickly so all pieces are coated. With buttered hands, scoop up and shape into large or small balls. Cool on wax paper. Wrap individually in wax paper or plastic food wrap.

*NP Ball (9–18) (with butter): 250–125 C, 10–5 mg CH, 65–30 mg S**

VARIATIONS

Molasses Popcorn Balls: Prepare as directed but substitute 1 cup molasses for the sugar.

*NP Ball (9–18) (with butter): 240–120 C, 10–5 mg CH, 100–50 mg S**

Popcorn and Peanut Balls: Prepare as directed, but substitute 1/4 cup creamy peanut butter for the butter and add 1 cup roasted peanuts to the popcorn.

*NP Ball (9–18) (with butter): 315–160 C, 0 mg CH, 70–35 mg S**

TWENTY-ONE

Pickles, Preserves, Jams, and Jellies

Pickling and preserving are two of the oldest forms of food conservation because man learned early that overly acid, sweet, or salty foods did not spoil readily. Cleopatra adored pickles, gave them credit for her beauty, and Caesar, something of a health faddist, insisted that his legions eat pickles to stave off scurvy. In the more recent past, women pickled and preserved foods so that their families would eat well throughout the winter. Today, with the winter's food supply at the supermarket, pickling and preserving have become labors of love, especially among home gardeners who look forward each summer to the "preserving season." They enjoy the satisfaction of putting up a dozen or so jars of pickles and another of fruit preserves. Needless to add, family and friends welcome the fruits of their labor— reason enough for getting down the big kettles and cartons of jars.

Note: Because there is not space here to do more than cover the basics, we recommend the excellent and detailed booklets prepared by the U.S. Department of Agriculture, state agricultural extension services, manufacturers of preserving jars, and processors of liquid and powdered pectins.

THE WAYS OF PICKLING AND PRESERVING

Brining: This is the old-fashioned slow cure in which vegetables are submerged for weeks in heavy brine ("heavy enough to float an egg," recipes used to read). Not often used today, except for making Sauerkraut (see recipe), because there are shorter, surer methods.

Fresh-Pack or Quick Process: This is the modern way of pickling—easy, efficient, and reliable. Foods—usually vegetables or fruits —are heated in vinegar, brine, or a mixture of vinegar and salt, often with sugar and spices, then packed hot into hot sterilized jars and sealed; or they may be packed cold into jars, covered with boiling hot pickling liquid and processed in a hot water bath to prevent spoilage. *Note:* For pickles, the water bath should be hot (180°–185° F.), not boiling. Hot-pack pickles and relishes, if sufficiently acid or salty, usually need no processing.

Open-Kettle Preserving: The method recommended for preserves, jams, jellies, fruit butters, chutneys, ketchups, and conserves, which involves nothing more complicated than cooking all ingredients in a large, open kettle until of desired consistency. Very tart or sweet mixtures, ladled boiling hot into hot sterilized jars, do not need to be processed in a hot water bath; cooler or less concentrated mixtures may (as for pickles, the water bath should be 180°–185° F., not boiling).

Microwaving Pickles, Preserves, Jams, and Jellies

These *can* be cooked in a microwave oven, but there are so many drawbacks it makes little sense to do so. We don't recommend it.

THE EQUIPMENT OF PICKLING AND PRESERVING

1¹/₂–2-Gallon Kettles (or even larger): These must be large enough to provide plenty of room for boiling (especially important with jams, jellies, and preserves, which often quadruple in volume as they boil). They should also be made of an inert material that will affect neither the color nor the flavor of the foods being pickled or preserved (enameled metal, stainless steel, hard-coat anodized aluminum are all good choices). Under no circumstances use copper, tin, zinc, or galvanized metals that can react with the acid in the pickles or preserves, producing poisonous salts. As for unanodized aluminum kettles, there are those who believe that they dull the sparkling finish of pickles and preserves and inject a metallic taste. We tend to agree.

Water Bath Canner: Any big kettle fitted with a wire or wooden rack and tight lid will work.

Preserving Jars and Closures: There are a number of types, each available in half-pint, pint, quart, and half-gallon sizes, but those most suitable for home use are the half pint, pint, and quart. Most popular today are the *Standard* and *Wide-Mouth Jars with Screw Bands and Dome Caps* (use dome caps one time only but reuse screw bands if in good condition). Also available are *Jars with Porcelain-Lined Zinc Caps and Rubber Sealing Rings* (the jars and caps are reusable, but the rubber rings should be used one time only if you are to be assured of a tight vacuum seal); and finally, *Old-Fashioned Jars with Glass Lids, Clamp-Down Springs, and Rubber Sealing Rings* (again the jars and lids are reusable if in perfect condition—no chips or cracks—but the rubber rings should be used only once).

Jelly Glasses: These are available in various shapes (squat, fluted jars; tall, slim jars that resemble juice glasses, and the new wide-mouth, quilted, 8-ounce [half-pint] jelly jars fitted with dome lids). Old-fashioned jelly glasses usually hold 6 fluid ounces and must be sealed with melted paraffin. The new dome-lidded jars may be used without paraffin, provided you leave only 1/8″ head space at the top and seal immediately.

Paraffin: Pouring melted paraffin on top of hot jams, jellies, and preserves the instant they have been ladled into jelly glasses is the old-fashioned way to seal in goodness and seal out microbes. The new dome-lidded half-pint jelly jars, as has already been stated, need not be sealed with paraffin. It's a good idea, however, to process jams 5 minutes in a hot water bath since they contain whole fruits (skins and seeds may harbor microbes).

Other Useful Implements:
Scales
Cup, Pint, and Quart Measuring Cups; Measuring Spoons
Colanders and Large Strainers for washing and preparing foods to be pickled or preserved
Large and Small Knives; Long-Handled Forks, Ladles, Spoons, and Slotted Spoons
Potato Masher for crushing berries
Tongs or Bottle Holder
Food Processor, Meat Grinder, or Food Mill for chopping, mincing and slicing (*Note:* For details on mincing, chopping, and grinding foods in a food processor, see the Food Processor Metal Blade Chopping Guide in Chapter 1).
Jelly Bag and Stand or Cheesecloth for extracting fruit juices for jellies. Old-fashioned jelly bags are made of white flannel and sewn with French seams. Today's jelly bags, equipped with their own stands, are apt to be made of nylon mesh—easier to wash and quicker to dry. Jelly bags are stocked by most specialty food shops.
Jelmeter: This calibrated glass tube determines the jelling power of extracted juices, which in turn tells you how much sugar to use. These are available in better specialty food shops.
Candy Thermometer for testing temperatures (i.e., jelling stage) of jams and jellies
Wide-Mouth Funnel for easier jar filling
Clock or Timer

THE CARE OF PRESERVING JARS AND CLOSURES

• Carefully examine jars before using, rejecting any with nicks or cracks. Also discard warped, dented, or rusty lids or screw bands or caps with loose linings.
• Do not reuse rubber rings or dome caps; they may not seal properly.
• Wash jars and closures in hot soapy water after each use and then again *before* using. Rinse well in hot water.

• *To Sterilize Jars and Closures* (essential for foods *not* processed in a boiling water bath). Stand jars on a rack in a large kettle, add water to cover, bring to a full rolling boil, cover kettle, and boil 10 minutes. Closures usually need only to be scalded, but treatment varies according to type, so follow manufacturer's instructions.

• Whether sterilized or not, jars and closures should be immersed in hot water until they are needed; for pickles, preserves, jams, and jellies, they may be kept hot in a 250° F. oven.

Note: If in doubt about a jar or closure, test for leakage. Half fill with water, screw on cap, and stand jar upside down. If water oozes out, try lid on a jar you know to be good, also a good lid on the questionable jar. Discard all faulty jars and lids.

THE TERMS AND TECHNIQUES OF PICKLING AND PRESERVING

Acid and Low-Acid Foods: Any food with a high acid content—either natural, as in fruit, or artificial, as in pickles—is an acid food and may be processed in a water bath. Jellies, because of their unusually high sugar content, need not be processed. Low-acid foods (not our concerns here) are meats and vegetables; these must be processed under pressure.

To Blanch: To dip raw food in boiling water or to steam briefly to set juices, reduce bulk, intensify color, or facilitate peeling.

To Brine: To preserve foods (usually pickles or sauerkraut) by immersing for days or weeks in a heavy salt solution. Because of the growing awareness of the harmful affects of too much sodium in the diet, we do not include recipes here for brining.

Closure: A cap, lid, or its component parts used to seal preserving jars airtight.

Head Space: The distance between the food and the top of a jar. Pickles that are not to be processed in a hot water bath, and also jams and jellies, should have 1/8″ head space *only* because they will not expand in the jar. With few exceptions, foods to be processed in a water bath should have 1/4″–1/2″ head space.

Microorganisms: The microscopic yeasts, molds, and bacteria that can cause food to spoil. The purpose of processing is to destroy them.

To Pack: To fill a jar with food. When the food is hot—as it is for the majority of pickling and preserving—the method is called *hot pack.* When cold or raw foods are put into jars, the method is known as *cold pack.* Hot-packed foods may or may not need to be processed in a water bath. Cold-packed foods must be processed in either a water bath (for fruits and other high-acid foods) or a pressure canner (for low-acid foods).

Pectin: A substance found naturally in many fruits, which when in perfect balance with acid and sugar causes mixtures to jell.

To Process: To destroy microorganisms in food by heating in a water bath for prescribed lengths of time. Pickles and preserves should be processed in a *hot water bath* (water temperature 180°–185° F.). A *boiling water bath* (water temperature 212° F.) is more often used in canning.

To Seal: To make jar closures airtight.

To Sterilize: To kill microorganisms on preserving jars and lids by scalding in boiling water.

Processing in a Hot Water Bath (180°–185° F.) or a Boiling Water Bath (212° F.)

• If food has been packed into jars *cold,* have water hot but not boiling lest abrupt temperature change crack jars. If food is packed into jars *hot,* water may be very hot, even boiling, depending upon whether food is to be processed in a hot or a boiling water bath.

• Using tongs or jar holder, lower jars, one at a time, into water bath, adjusting so each stands steady on rack, does not touch its neighbor or kettle sides, and is not apt to tilt or tumble during processing.

• When all jars are in the water bath, make sure water level is 1″–2″ above jar tops. Add hot water, if needed, taking care not to pour directly on jars.

• Cover water bath and, when water comes to the correct temperature (180°–185° F. for the hot water bath, 212° F. for the boiling water bath), begin timing the processing.

• Keep water at the recommended temperature throughout processing, adding hot or boiling water to kettle as needed to keep level well above jars.

• Remove jars from water bath to a wire rack as soon as processing time is up.

Important Note: All processing times given in recipes in this chapter are for altitudes near sea level. If you live at 1,000 feet above sea level or higher, adjust processing times as the following chart directs:

WATER BATH PROCESSING TIME ADJUSTMENTS
FOR HIGH ALTITUDES

Feet Above Sea Level	IF TOTAL PROCESSING TIME Is 20 Minutes or Less, Increase by:	IF TOTAL PROCESSING TIME Is More Than 20 Minutes, Increase by:
1,000	1 minute	2 minutes
2,000	2 minutes	4 minutes
3,000	3 minutes	6 minutes
4,000	4 minutes	8 minutes
5,000	5 minutes	10 minutes
6,000	6 minutes	12 minutes
7,000	7 minutes	14 minutes
8,000	8 minutes	16 minutes
9,000	9 minutes	18 minutes
10,000	10 minutes	20 minutes

Note: For more detailed instructions, contact local agricultural extension office or home economics departments of local universities or utility companies.

PICKLES AND RELISHES

Any food almost can be pickled—preserved in brine or vinegar. But certain vegetables and fruits pickle better than other foods—cucumbers, sweet peppers, green tomatoes, cauliflower, corn, and green beans, to name a few. The difference between a pickle and a relish? It's merely a matter of size. When foods are left whole or in large chunks or slices, they are pickles. When minced or chopped, they become relishes. *(Dieter's Note:* Most tart pickles and relishes are low-calorie.)

ESSENTIAL INGREDIENTS OF PICKLING

Salt: Pickling salt (fine-grained pure salt) is best, dairy or kosher salts (coarse, flaked pure salts) next best; table salt contains adulterants that will cloud the brine. *(Note:* Because of their coarseness, dairy and kosher salts, measure for measure, are not equal to pickling salt. When substituting either one for pickling salt, use 1½ times the amount of pickling salt called for.) The recipes that follow specify which salt to use.

Vinegar: Vinegars should be plain, unflavored, of top grade and 4–6 per cent acid strength (this information is included on the label). They may be cider (brown) or distilled (white) but must be clear and free of sediment. White vinegars are best for white or delicately colored vegetables; brown vinegars will darken them. Never use a vinegar of unknown acid strength; a too weak vinegar can cause pickles to soften and spoil.

Sugar: Granulated sugar is the standard, though occasionally, when a mellower, darker product is wanted, light or dark brown sugar will be called for.

Spices: Whole dried spices, freshly bought, are preferable because they can be neatly tied in cheesecloth, simmered along with the pickles, then quickly fished out of the kettle. Powdered spices darken pickles and so will whole spices if left in too long.

Water: It should be soft—either naturally or artificially so. Hard water can produce ugly white scum on pickles or, if high in iron, turn them black. To soften water: Boil hard 15 minutes, let stand 24 hours, then skim scum from top. Carefully ladle water into a clean container, leaving any sediment behind.

Fruit and Vegetables: These should be garden fresh (never picked more than a day ahead of time), a shade underripe, free of blemishes and soft or decayed spots, and for especially pretty pickles, of small-to-medium, uniform size.

Slaked Lime (Calcium Hydroxide) and Alum: These aren't essential to pickling except when supercrisp pickles are wanted. They're used with unfermented pickles only, most often watermelon rind or green tomato. Both can be bought in drugstores and hardwares specializing in canning equipment.

TIPS FOR MAKING BETTER PICKLES AND RELISHES

• Read recipe through carefully before beginning and follow directions to the letter.
• Have all ingredients and equipment assembled before beginning. Make sure preserving jars are the proper type (those made specifically for preserving) and in perfect condition (no cracks or chips), spotless and sterilized. Lids should be perfect too—not warped, dented, or bent. If using closures requiring rubber rings, buy new ones of the proper size.
• Do not attempt to pickle vast quantities at a time; work instead with amounts you can handle comfortably in your kitchen.
• Use highest-quality fruits and vegetables, picked, if possible, just before pickling.
• Use freshly bought vinegars, spices, salts, and sugars, never those that have been sitting around on the shelf.
• Never add chemicals to pickles or relishes to heighten their color—copper sulfate, for example, or vitriol. And do not, as Grandmother did, pickle green vegetables in copper kettles to brighten the green—vinegar, coming in contact with copper, produces a poison.
• Measure or weigh ingredients carefully.
• Pack jars, one at a time, as recipes direct, allowing amount of head space (room at the top of the jar) recommended. Jars to be processed in a hot water bath should have about 1/4″ of head space so that there is room for expansion of food as it sterilizes; jars requiring no processing should be filled to within 1/8″ of tops.
• As you pack jars, run a small spatula around inside of jar to remove air bubbles.
• Make sure pickling liquid covers solids; if there is not enough, pour in a little additional vinegar or brine (same strength as that in the recipe).
• Before sealing jars, wipe tops and threading with a clean, damp cloth.
• When packing hot pickles, make sure that they *and* the pickling liquid are *boiling hot.*
• If pickles have been packed cold, do not remove metal screw bands after sealing and processing. Leave intact until jars are opened.
• When cooling sealed jars, stand several inches apart and away from drafts so that air will circulate evenly.

• Test seals after jars have cooled 12 hours. If a jar has not sealed airtight, refrigerate and serve within the week. Or empty contents into a saucepan, bring slowly to a boil, and pack into a hot sterilized jar. Reseal and cool.
• Store pickles and relishes in a dark, cool, dry place and let stand some weeks before serving so that flavors will mellow and mingle.
• To keep pickles from fading, wrap jars in newspaper before storing.

WHY THINGS SOMETIMES GO WRONG WITH PICKLES

Soft or Slippery Pickles: Vinegar too weak or pickles not kept submerged in brine or pickling liquid.

Hollow Pickles ("Floaters"): Cucumbers picked too long before pickling.

Dark Pickles: Iron in the water used.

Shriveled Pickles: Pickling solution too acid, too salty, or too sweet.

Faded Pickles: Pickles kept too long on the shelf or stored in too bright a spot.

DILL PICKLES

8 pints   ¢ ⚖

Because cucumbers brined in barrels need controlled conditions not always attainable at home, these recipes use the newer, easier fresh-pack method.

3–3 1/2 dozen small- to medium-size cucumbers (about 4″ long), washed and left whole or halved lengthwise (do not peel)
1 gallon cold water mixed with 3/4 cup pickling salt (brine)
16 sprigs fresh dill or pickling dill or 8 tablespoons dill seeds
8 teaspoons mustard seeds
1 quart white vinegar
1 quart water
1/2 cup pickling salt
1/2 cup sugar
3 tablespoons mixed pickling spices, tied in cheesecloth

Let cucumbers stand in brine overnight. Wash and sterilize 8 (1-pint) jars and closures. Drain cucumbers and pack into hot jars, leaving 1/4″ head space. To each jar add 2 sprigs dill (or 1 tablespoon dill seeds) and 1 teaspoon mustard seeds, poking halfway down in jar. Set uncovered jars on a baking sheet and keep hot in a 250° F. oven. Simmer vinegar, water, salt, sugar, and pickling spices, uncovered, 15 minutes in an enamel or stainless-steel saucepan, stirring now and then. Pour boiling hot into jars, filling to within 1/4" of tops. Wipe rims, seal, and process in a hot water bath* 10 minutes. Take from water bath and secure seals if necessary. Cool, check seals, label, and store in a cool, dark, dry place. Let pickles stand 3 weeks before using.

*NP Pickle: 30 C, 0 mg CH, 2,205 mg S**

VARIATIONS

⚖ **"Kosher" Dill Pickles:** When packing cucumbers, add to each jar 1 peeled and bruised clove garlic, 1 bay leaf, and 1 (3" × 1/2") strip hot red chili pepper in addition to seasonings above. Proceed as directed.

*NP Pickle: 30 C, 0 mg CH, 2,205 mg S**

¢ **Sweet Dill Pickles:** Prepare as directed but, instead of vinegar mixture called for, simmer 5 cups vinegar and 5 cups sugar with the 3 tablespoons spices. Proceed as directed.

*NP Pickle: 140 C, 0 mg CH, 2,200 mg S**

AUNT FLORRIE'S BREAD AND BUTTER PICKLES

6 quarts (96 servings)

4 quarts paper-thin unpeeled cucumber slices
8 medium-size white onions, peeled and sliced paper thin
2 medium-size sweet green peppers (or 1 green and 1 red), washed, cored, seeded, and coarsely chopped
1/2 cup pickling salt
1 quart cracked ice
5 cups sugar
1 1/2 teaspoons turmeric
1/2 teaspoon cloves
2 tablespoons mustard seeds
1 teaspoon celery seeds
5 cups cider or white vinegar

Mix all vegetables, salt, and ice in a very large colander, weight down, pressing out liquid, set over a large kettle, and let stand 3 hours (in refrigerator if possible). (*Note:* If kitchen is warm and you haven't refrigerator space, add more cracked ice after 1 1/2 hours.) Meanwhile, wash and sterilize 6 (1-quart) jars and closures, stand on a bak-

ing sheet, and keep hot in a 250° F. oven until needed. Mix sugar, spices, and vinegar in a very large enamel or stainless-steel kettle. Drain vegetables well and add to kettle. Heat, uncovered, over moderate heat *just* to the boiling point, moving a wooden spoon through mixture occasionally but not actually stirring. Ladle boiling hot into jars, filling to within 1/8" of tops, wipe rims, and seal. Cool, check seals, label, and store in a cool, dark, dry place. Let stand 4–6 weeks before serving.

*NPS: 50 C, 0 mg CH, 550 mg S**

MUSTARD PICKLES

4 pints (32 servings)

1 medium-size cauliflower, washed, trimmed, and divided into small flowerets
2 medium-size cucumbers, peeled, seeded, and cut in 1/4" cubes
3 medium-size sweet green peppers, washed, cored, seeded, and coarsely chopped
1 medium-size sweet red pepper, washed, cored, seeded, and coarsely chopped
1 pint tiny white onions or shallots, peeled
1 quart cold water mixed with 1/3 cup pickling salt
1/2 cup sifted flour
1 cup sugar
3 tablespoons powdered mustard
1 1/2 teaspoons turmeric
1 quart white vinegar

Place all vegetables and salt water in a large bowl, cover, and refrigerate overnight. Wash and sterilize 4 (1-pint) jars and their closures; stand on a baking sheet and keep hot in a 250° F. oven until needed. Transfer vegetables and brine to a large enamel or stainless-steel kettle, cover, bring to a boil over high heat, then boil 1 minute; drain in a colander and set aside. In the same kettle, mix flour, sugar, and spices; slowly blend in vinegar and heat, stirring constantly, over moderate heat until thickened. Add vegetables, cover, and heat, stirring occasionally, 8–10 minutes, just until boiling. Ladle into jars, filling to within 1/4" of tops, wipe rims, and seal. Process 10 minutes in a hot water bath.* Cool, check seals, label, and store in a cool, dark, dry place. Let stand 4–6 weeks before serving.

*NPS: 50 C, 0 mg CH, 1,095 mg S**

EASY ICE WATER CUCUMBER PICKLES

6 quarts ¢ ⚖

Gherkins may be substituted for cucumbers in this next recipe.

6–6½ dozen small cucumbers (do not peel)
Ice water
6 tablespoons pickling salt
6 tablespoons mixed pickling spices
12 tablespoons sugar
2–3 white onions, peeled and sliced thin
3 quarts boiling white vinegar

Cover cucumbers with ice water and let stand 3–4 hours, replenishing ice as needed. Wash and sterilize 6 (1-quart) jars and closures, stand on a baking sheet, and keep warm in a 250° F. oven until needed. Drain cucumbers and pack into hot jars, filling to within ¼″ of the top. Add 1 tablespoon salt, 1 tablespoon pickling spice, and 2 tablespoons sugar to each jar, top with 1–2 slices onion, and fill to within ¼″ of the top with vinegar. Wipe rims and seal. Process in a hot water bath* 10 minutes. Remove jars and secure seals if needed. Cool, check seals, label, and store in a cool, dark, dry place 4–6 weeks before serving.

NP Pickle: 25 C, 0 mg CH, 555 mg S*

GREEN TOMATO PICKLES

5 pints (40 servings) ⚖

2 quarts sliced, unpeeled green tomatoes (slices should be about ½″ thick)
2 tablespoons pickling salt
1 cup granulated sugar
1 cup firmly packed dark brown sugar
1 pint cider vinegar
2 tablespoons mustard seeds
1 teaspoon celery seeds
2 bay leaves, crumbled
2 large yellow onions, peeled and sliced thin
2 large sweet green peppers, cored, seeded, and minced
1 large sweet red pepper or 1 small hot chili pepper, cored, seeded, and minced

Mix tomatoes and salt, cover, and refrigerate overnight; drain well. Wash and sterilize 5 (1-pint) jars and closures, stand on a baking sheet, and keep hot in a 250° F. oven until needed. Mix sugars, vinegar, spices, and onions in a very large enamel or stainless-steel kettle, cover, and boil slowly 10 minutes. Add tomatoes and peppers and simmer, uncovered, stirring now and then, 5 minutes. Ladle boiling hot into jars filling to within ⅛″ of tops and making sure liquid

covers vegetables. Wipe rims and seal; cool, check seals, label, and store in a cool, dark, dry place 4–6 weeks before using.

NPS: 60 C, 0 mg CH, 170 mg S*

DILLED GREEN BEANS

6 pints (40 servings) ⚖

Choose the straightest beans for this recipe —makes packing jars easier.

3 pounds green beans
6 cloves garlic, peeled and halved
3 teaspoons mustard seeds
1½ teaspoons peppercorns
12 large sprigs fresh dill or 3 teaspoons dill seeds
3 cups cider vinegar
3 cups water
¼ cup pickling salt

Wash and sterilize 6 (1-pint) jars and closures. Snap ends off beans, cut in 4½″ lengths, and pack vertically in jars, filling centers with odd lengths. Add 2 halves garlic, ½ teaspoon mustard seeds, ¼ teaspoon peppercorns, and 2 sprigs fresh dill (or ½ teaspoon dill seeds) to each jar. Heat vinegar, water, and salt to boiling, then pour in jars, filling to within ¼″ of the top. Wipe rims and seal. Process in a hot water bath* 5 minutes. Tighten seals if necessary, cool, check seals, label, and store in a cool, dark, dry place 4–6 weeks before serving.

NPS: 15 C, 0 mg CH, 660 mg S*

VARIATIONS

⚖ **Dilled Carrots:** Prepare as directed but substitute 3 quarts parboiled (4″) carrot sticks or peeled whole baby carrots for beans.

NPS: 30 C, 0 mg CH, 690 mg S*

⚖ **Dilled Zucchini:** Prepare as directed but substitute 3 quarts unpeeled (4″) zucchini strips for beans. (*Note:* Baby zucchini are best.)

NPS: 10 C, 0 mg CH, 660 mg S*

PICKLED ONIONS

8 pints (64 servings) ⚖

7 pounds pearl or small white onions, peeled and parboiled 1–2 minutes
1 cup pickling salt
2 quarts cider or white vinegar
½ cup sugar
4 teaspoons mustard seeds, lightly crushed
8 bay leaves

Place onions in a large bowl, cover with cold water, add salt and stir to dissolve; cover and let stand at room temperature 24 hours. Next day, wash and sterilize 8 (1-pint) jars and closures; stand on a baking sheet and keep hot in a 250° F. oven until needed. Rinse onions under cold running water and drain well. Bring vinegar, sugar, and spices to a boil in an enamel or stainless-steel saucepan, stirring occasionally. Meanwhile, pack onions into jars; pour in boiling vinegar, filling jars to within 1/8″ of tops and distributing mustard seeds and bay leaves evenly. Wipe rims and seal. Cool, check seals, label jars, and store in a cool, dark, dry place. Let stand 1 week before using.

NPS: 30 C, 0 mg CH, 90 mg S*

PICKLED MUSHROOMS

4 pints (32 servings)   ⚖

3 pounds mushrooms (button to medium size),
   wiped clean
1 quart water mixed with 3 tablespoons pickling
   salt (brine)
4 cloves garlic, peeled and bruised
4 bay leaves
1 teaspoon whole cloves
1 teaspoon peppercorns
4 chili pequins (tiny hot dried red peppers)
1 quart white vinegar
1/4 cup olive oil

Wash and sterilize 4 (1-pint) jars and closures, stand on a baking sheet, and keep hot in a 250° F. oven until needed. Simmer mushrooms in brine, covered, 5 minutes, then drain. Into each hot jar place 1 clove garlic, 1 bay leaf, 1/4 teaspoon each cloves and peppercorns, and 1 chili pequin. Heat vinegar and oil to boiling in an enamel or stainless-steel saucepan, add mushrooms and simmer, uncovered, 5 minutes. Remove mushrooms with a slotted spoon and pack into jars, then pour in boiling vinegar mixture, filling to within 1/8″ of tops. Wipe rims and seal. Cool, check seals, label, and store in a cool, dark, dry place 2–3 weeks before serving.

NPS: 30 C, 0 mg CH, 625 mg S*

WATERMELON RIND PICKLES

4 pints (24 servings)   ¢

1 (15–16-pound) slightly underripe watermelon
   with thick, firm rind
2 quarts cold water mixed with 1/2 cup pickling
   salt (brine)

SYRUP
4 pounds sugar
1 quart cider vinegar
1 quart water
2 lemons, sliced thin
2 teaspoons whole cloves
2 teaspoons whole allspice
4 sticks cinnamon, broken up

Quarter melon, remove green skin and pink flesh, and cut rind in 1″ cubes; measure 4 quarts cubed rind, cover with brine, and soak overnight. Drain rind, rinse with cold water, place in a very large kettle, cover with water, and simmer, covered, about 1/2 hour until barely tender and translucent. Meanwhile, prepare syrup: Mix sugar, vinegar, and water in a very large enamel or stainless-steel kettle, add lemon and spices, tied in cheesecloth, and slowly boil, uncovered, 20 minutes. Also wash and sterilize 4 (1-pint) jars and closures, stand on a baking sheet in a 250° F. oven until needed. Drain rind, add to syrup, and simmer, uncovered, until rind is clear, about 1/2 hour. Remove spice bag. Using a slotted spoon, pack rind into jars, then pour in boiling syrup, filling to within 1/8″ of tops. Wipe rims and seal. Cool, check seals, label, and store in a cool, dark, dry place several weeks before serving.

NPS: 305 C, 0 mg CH, 575 mg S*

PICKLED PEACHES

10 pints (64 servings)

Dipping peaches and apricots in boiling water makes skins slip right off.

8 pounds small, firm-ripe peaches (clingstone
   varieties are best)
1 gallon cold water mixed with 2 tablespoons
   each pickling salt and white vinegar
2 tablespoons whole cloves (about)

BASIC PICKLING SYRUP
1 quart white vinegar
1 quart water
3 pounds sugar
4 sticks cinnamon, broken and tied in
   cheesecloth

Peel peaches, then dip in water-salt-vinegar mixture to prevent discoloration; leave whole or halve but do not remove pits. Stud each peach with 2 cloves. Place syrup ingredients in a large enamel or stainless-steel kettle and bring to a boil. Add peaches, a few at a time, and simmer, uncovered, 5–7 minutes until barely tender. Remove peaches with a slotted spoon and set aside while cooking the rest. When all are cooked, bring syrup to a boil and pour over peaches; cover and let stand overnight (this plumps peaches and gives them better flavor). Next day, wash and sterilize 10 (1-pint) jars and their closures. At the same time, drain syrup from peaches and bring to a boil; discard spice bag. Pack peaches into hot jars, then pour in boiling syrup, filling to within 1/4" of the top. Wipe rims and seal. Process in a hot water bath* 10 minutes. Remove jars from bath and secure seals if necessary. Cool, check seals, label, and store in a cool, dark, dry place 4–6 weeks before serving.

VARIATIONS

Pickled Apricots (64 servings): Substitute 8 pounds apricots for peaches; peel, leave whole, or halve and pit. Proceed as directed.

NPS: 100 C, 0 mg CH, 205 mg S*

Pickled Pears (20 servings): Substitute 8 pounds small, firm-ripe pears for peaches. Leave stems on but peel and remove blossom ends. Proceed as directed.

NPS: 370 C, 0 mg CH, 660 mg S*

Pickled Apples (30 servings): Substitute 10 pounds peeled, quartered, and cored small tart apples for peaches. Add cloves to pickling syrup instead of studding fruit, then proceed as directed.

NPS: 255 C, 0 mg CH, 440 mg S*

Pickled Crab Apples (64 servings): Substitute 8 pounds unpeeled crab apples for peaches. Remove blossom ends but not stems, then prick in several places to prevent bursting. Add cloves to pickling syrup and simmer crab apples 7–10 minutes, depending on size. Proceed as recipe directs.

NPS: 125 C, 0 mg CH, 205 mg S*

Pickled Quinces: Substitute 8 pounds firm-ripe quinces for peaches. Peel, quarter, core, and slice thin. For pickling syrup use 1 pint each vinegar and water and 4 pounds sugar; add cloves and cinnamon. Simmer quinces 30–40 minutes in syrup until translucent. Proceed as directed. Nutritional count not available.

Spiced Fruits: Prepare any of the preceding pickled fruits as directed, but tie cinnamon and cloves in cheesecloth along with 2 tablespoons whole allspice and 2 (2") pieces bruised, peeled fresh gingerroot. If you like, add 1 or 2 slices lemon to each jar. Nutritional count same as individual pickled fruits.

California Fruit Pickles: Prepare any of the preceding pickled fruits as directed but use a 1/2 and 1/2 mixture of granulated and light or dark brown sugar in the pickling syrup. Nutritional count same as individual pickled fruits.

BRANDIED PEACHES

4 pints (16 servings)

4 pounds small firm-ripe peaches (clingstone varieties are best)
2 quarts cold water mixed with 1 tablespoon each pickling salt and lemon juice
1 quart water
4 cups sugar
1 pint brandy (about)

Wash and sterilize 4 (1-pint) jars and closures, stand them on a baking sheet, and keep hot in a 250° F. oven until needed. Peel peaches, then dip in water-salt-lemon juice mixture to prevent darkening. Bring water and sugar to a boil in an enamel or stainless-steel saucepan; reduce heat, add peaches, a few at a time, and simmer 5–7 minutes until barely tender. Remove peaches with a slotted spoon and pack in hot jars, filling to within 1/2" of tops. When all peaches are cooked, return filled but uncovered jars to 250° F. oven. Insert candy thermometer in syrup and boil, uncovered, until thermometer registers 222° F. Cool syrup 5 minutes, measure out 1 pint, and stir in 1 pint brandy; pour into jars, filling to within 1/4" of the top. (*Note:* If you need more liquid, mix equal quantities of syrup and brandy.) Wipe jar rims and seal. Process in a hot water bath* 10 minutes. Remove jars and secure seals, if necessary. Cool, check seals, label, and store in a cool, dark, dry place. Let stand 4–6 weeks before serving.

NPS: 340 C, 0 mg CH, 410 mg S*

VARIATION

Brandied Pears (10 servings): Substitute 4 pounds small firm-ripe pears for peaches. Peel and remove blossom ends but leave stems on if you wish. Proceed as recipe directs.

NPS: 525 C, 0 mg CH, 660 mg S*

GINGERED PEARS

4 pints (32 servings)

Serve with any meat.

5 pounds firm-ripe pears, peeled, quartered, and cored
1/2 cup lemon juice
5 cups sugar
1 tablespoon finely grated lemon rind

⅓ cup minced fresh gingerroot or ½ cup
  minced preserved ginger

Wash and sterilize 4 (1-pint) jars and closures, stand them on baking sheet, and keep
warm in a 250° F. oven until needed. Simmer all ingredients, uncovered, in a heavy
enamel or stainless-steel kettle until pears
are tender and translucent, about 30–40
minutes. Ladle into hot jars, filling to within
⅛" of tops. Wipe rims and seal. Cool, check
seals, label, and store in a cool, dark, dry
place 2–3 weeks before using.

NPS: 160 C, 0 mg CH, 1 mg S*

TOMATO KETCHUP

2 pints

Ketchup can be made from mushrooms,
grapes, cranberries, green tomatoes, in fact
from many fruits and vegetables. But the favorite is bright red tomato ketchup.

**8 pounds unpeeled ripe tomatoes, coarsely
  chopped**
1 cup minced yellow onions
1 teaspoon celery seeds
1 teaspoon mustard seeds
1 teaspoon whole allspice
1 stick cinnamon
½ teaspoon peppercorns
2 bay leaves
1 tablespoon salt
1 cup white vinegar
1 cup sugar

Mix tomatoes and onions in a large (at least
1 gallon) enamel or stainless-steel kettle,
cover, and simmer 20–30 minutes, stirring
now and then, until mushy. Purée, a little at
a time, by buzzing 20–30 seconds in an electric blender at low speed or 15–20 seconds in
a food processor fitted with the metal chopping blade, or put through a food mill; press
through a fine sieve. Place in a clean large
kettle and cook, uncovered, at a slow boil
until volume reduces by half. *(Note: It's important that kettle be large to keep ketchup
from spattering kitchen.)* Meanwhile, wash
and sterilize 2 (1-pint) jars and their closures, stand them on a baking sheet, and
keep warm in a 250° F. oven until needed.
Tie all spices and bay leaves in cheesecloth
and add to kettle along with salt, set lid on
askew, and simmer ½ hour. Remove spice
bag, add vinegar and sugar, and cook, uncovered, at a slow boil, stirring frequently,
until very thick. *(Note: Toward the end, you
will have to stir constantly to prevent
scorching.)* Ladle ketchup into jars, filling to
within ⅛" of tops, wipe rims, and seal.

Cool, check seals, and store in a cool, dark,
dry place. Let stand 2 weeks before using.
(Note: To keep ketchup bright red over a
long period of time, wrap jars in foil.)

NP Tablespoon: 25 C, 0 mg CH, 105 mg S*

VARIATIONS

Easy Ketchup: Substitute 2 (1-pound 12-
ounce) cans tomato purée for fresh tomatoes, omit onion, and cook down as recipe
directs to about one third of original volume. Add spices called for but only 1½ teaspoons salt; proceed as directed.

NP Tablespoon: 25 C, 0 mg CH, 150 mg S*

Cranberry Ketchup: Substitute 2 pounds
cranberries for tomatoes and simmer with 1
cup water until mushy. Proceed as recipe directs but increase sugar to 2 cups.

NP Tablespoon: 35 C, 0 mg CH, 105 mg S*

Hot Chili Sauce: Peel and core tomatoes before chopping; simmer as directed with 2
cups each minced onions and minced, cored,
and seeded sweet red peppers and 1–2
minced, cored, and seeded hot red peppers
(or ¼–½ teaspoon crushed dried hot red
chili peppers). Purée mixture but do not
strain. Proceed as for Tomato Ketchup
(above), adding 1 tablespoon mixed pickling
spices to the spices called for and increasing
vinegar to 1½ cups.

NP Tablespoon: 30 C, 0 mg CH, 105 mg S*

APPLE CHUTNEY

4 pints

2 quarts coarsely chopped, peeled tart apples
1 cup minced, seeded sweet red peppers
1 cup minced yellow onions
1 clove garlic, peeled and minced
1 pound seedless raisins
1 (1-pound) box dark brown sugar
1 pint cider vinegar
1 tablespoon ginger
1 tablespoon cinnamon
2 teaspoons powdered mustard
2 teaspoons salt
¼ teaspoon crushed dried hot red chili peppers

Wash and sterilize 4 (1-pint) jars and their
closures and stand them on a baking sheet in
a 250° F. oven until needed. Mix all ingredients in a very large enamel or stainless-steel
kettle, cover, and bring slowly to a boil. Uncover and simmer, stirring occasionally, 1–
1½ hours until thick. *(Note: Stir more frequently toward the end to prevent scorching.)* Ladle boiling hot into jars, filling to
within ⅛" of tops. Wipe rims and seal.

When cool, check seals and label. Store in a cool, dark, dry place. Let stand 1 month before serving.

NP Tablespoon: 30 C, 0 mg CH, 35 mg S*

Pear or Peach Chutney: Prepare as directed but substitute 2 quarts coarsely chopped, peeled firm-ripe pears or peaches for apples and omit red peppers.

NP Tablespoon (with pears): 30 C, 0 mg CH, 35 mg S*

Mango Chutney: Substitute 4 pounds peeled, pitted, and thinly sliced green mangoes for apples, increase sugar to 2 pounds and vinegar to 1 quart. Add 1 pound dried currants and 3 tablespoons minced fresh gingerroot. Mix all ingredients in kettle, cover, and let stand overnight. Next day, proceed as directed.

NP Tablespoon: 60 C, 0 mg CH, 40 mg S*

CHOW CHOW RELISH

4 pints ⚖

A great way to use up garden tag ends.

4 medium-size green tomatoes, cored and minced but not peeled
4 medium-size sweet green peppers, cored, seeded, and minced
2 medium-size sweet red peppers, cored, seeded, and minced
2 large yellow onions, peeled and minced
1 small cabbage, shredded fine
1 medium-size cauliflower, separated into flowerets, or 3 cups cut green beans
2 quarts cold water mixed with 1/2 cup pickling salt (brine)
3 cups white vinegar
2 cups sugar
1 tablespoon celery seeds
1 tablespoon mustard seeds
1 teaspoon powdered mustard
1 teaspoon turmeric
1 teaspoon allspice

Mix all vegetables with brine, cover, and let stand 1 hour. Meanwhile, wash and sterilize 4 (1-pint) jars and closures, stand them on a baking sheet, and keep hot in a 250° F. oven until needed. Drain vegetables well and set aside. Mix vinegar with remaining ingredients in a very large enamel or stainless-steel kettle and simmer, uncovered, 15 minutes. Add vegetables and simmer, uncovered, 10 minutes. Ladle boiling hot into jars, filling to within 1/8″ of tops. Wipe rims and seal.

Cool, check seals, label, and store in a cool, dark, dry place 1 month before serving.

NP Tablespoon: 20 C, 0 mg CH, 415 mg S*

PEPPER RELISH

6 pints ⚖

The perfect hamburger relish.

1 dozen sweet green peppers, cored, seeded, and minced
1 dozen sweet red peppers, cored, seeded, and minced
2 cups minced yellow onions
1 cup minced celery
3 cups white vinegar
1½ cups sugar
1 tablespoon pickling salt
1 tablespoon mustard seeds
1 teaspoon celery seeds

Sterilize 6 (1-pint) jars and closures, stand them on a baking sheet, and keep warm in a 250° F. oven until needed. Mix all ingredients in a large, heavy enamel or stainless-steel kettle, cover, and simmer 15 minutes. Ladle into jars, filling to within 1/8″ of tops and making sure liquid covers vegetables. Wipe rims and seal. Or, if you prefer, leave 1/2″ head space, seal jars, and process in a hot water bath* 15 minutes. Remove jars, secure seals if necessary. Cool, check seals, label, and store in a cool, dark, dry place 3–4 weeks before using.

NP Tablespoon: 10 C, 0 mg CH, 35 mg S*

⚖ **Hot Pepper Relish:** Prepare as directed but substitute 1 dozen hot red chili peppers for the sweet red peppers.

NP Tablespoon: 10 C, 0 mg CH, 35 mg S*

⚖ **Pepper Slaw** *(About 14 pints):* Finely shred 2 large heads green cabbage, mix with 1/4 cup pickling salt, cover, and refrigerate overnight. Next day, drain thoroughly, mix with Pepper Relish ingredients, increasing sugar and vinegar each to 6 cups and mustard and celery seeds each to 2 tablespoons. Simmer 20–30 minutes, then ladle into jars and seal as directed.

NP Tablespoon: 15 C, 0 mg CH, 30 mg S*

CORN RELISH

6 pints ⚖

To simplify cutting corn from cobs, boil corn 3 minutes and plunge into cold water.

2 quarts whole kernel corn (corn cut from about
   1½ dozen ears)
1 cup minced yellow onions
1 cup minced sweet green pepper
1 cup minced sweet red pepper
1 cup minced celery
3 cups cider vinegar
1½ cups sugar
1 tablespoon pickling salt
1 tablespoon mustard seeds
2 teaspoons turmeric
1 teaspoon celery seeds

Sterilize 6 (1-pint) jars and closures, stand them on a baking sheet, and keep warm in a 250° F. oven until needed. Mix all ingredients in a large, heavy enamel or stainless-steel kettle, cover, and simmer 20 minutes. Ladle into jars, filling to within ⅛″ of tops and making sure liquid covers vegetables. Wipe rims and seal. Or leave ½″ head space, seal, and process in a hot water bath* 15 minutes. Remove jars and secure seals if needed. Cool, check seals, label, and store in a cool, dark, dry place 3–4 weeks before using.

*NP Tablespoon: 15 C, 0 mg CH, 35 mg S**

VARIATION

⚖ **Corn-Cranberry Relish** *(7½ pints):* Prepare as directed but add 1 pound moderately finely chopped washed and stemmed cranberries and increase sugar to 3 cups.

*NP Tablespoon: 15 C, 0 mg CH, 30 mg S**

JERUSALEM ARTICHOKE PICKLE RELISH

6 pints   ⚖

Note how very low in calories this relish is.

5 pounds Jerusalem artichokes
2 medium-size yellow onions, peeled and
   coarsely chopped
1 cup sugar
3 cups cider vinegar
1 tablespoon turmeric
1 tablespoon mustard seeds
1 tablespoon celery seeds
2 tablespoons pickling salt
1 stick cinnamon
½ teaspoon crushed dried hot red chili peppers

Wash and sterilize 6 (1-pint) jars and closures, stand them on a baking sheet, and keep hot in a 250° F. oven until needed. Using a stiff vegetable brush, scrub artichokes carefully under cold running water; scrape away any blemishes but do not peel, then put through the coarsest blade of a meat grinder, or coarsely chop by pulsing 3–4

times in a food processor fitted with the metal chopping blade. Place artichokes and remaining ingredients in a large, heavy enamel or stainless-steel kettle and simmer, uncovered, ½ hour, stirring occasionally; remove cinnamon. Ladle into jars, filling to within ¼″ of tops; wipe rims and seal. Process 10 minutes in a hot water bath.* Cool, check seals, label, and store in a cool, dark, dry place. Let stand 4–6 weeks before serving.

*NP Tablespoon: 10 C, 0 mg CH, 70 mg S**

BERRY RELISH

6 half pints

Tart-sweet berry relishes go well with most meats and poultry.

2 quarts firm-ripe berries (blueberries,
   huckleberries, cranberries, red or black
   currants, elderberries, or gooseberries),
   washed and stemmed
4 cups sugar
¾–1 cup cider vinegar
1½ teaspoons cinnamon
½ teaspoon allspice
¼ teaspoon ginger

Wash and sterilize 6 (half-pint) jars and closures, stand them on a baking sheet, and keep hot in a 250° F. oven until needed. Place berries in a large enamel or stainless-steel saucepan and crush a few with a potato masher. Cover and simmer, stirring now and then, until berries are soft. Mix in remaining ingredients, insert a candy thermometer, and boil slowly, stirring now and then, until thermometer registers 218° F. Ladle into jars, filling to within ⅛″ of tops. Wipe rims and seal. Cool, check seals, label, and store in a cool, dark, dry place 3–4 weeks before serving.

*NP Tablespoon: 40 C, 0 mg CH, 1 mg S**

CRANBERRY-ORANGE RELISH

1 pint   ▨

1 pound cranberries, stemmed, washed, and
   drained
2 large oranges
1¾ cups sugar
⅛ teaspoon salt

Pick cranberries over, discarding any underripe ones. Finely grate orange rinds; remove white pith and seeds from oranges, then coarsely chop. Put cranberries and oranges through the medium blade of a meat grinder. Mix with sugar and salt, cover, and

---

let stand at room temperature 1 hour; mix again. Serve as is or slightly chilled. Stored airtight in the refrigerator, relish will keep several weeks.

NP Tablespoon: 55 C, 0 mg CH, 10 mg S*

VARIATIONS

Cranberry-Pear Relish: Prepare as directed but substitute 4 peeled and cored pears (firm) for oranges and add 1/4 cup minced crystallized ginger.

NP Tablespoon: 65 C, 0 mg CH, 10 mg S*

Preserved Cranberry-Orange Relish *(4 half pints):* Leave cranberries whole, add grated rind and coarsely chopped oranges, then simmer, uncovered, with the sugar, salt, and 1 cup orange juice about 3/4 hour, stirring now and then. Ladle boiling hot into 4 sterilized half-pint jars, filling to within 1/8" of tops, wipe rims, and seal; cool, check seals, label, and store.

NP Tablespoon: 30 C, 0 mg CH, 5 mg S*

Fruit-Nut Conserve *(5 half pints):* Prepare Preserved Cranberry-Orange Relish (above) as directed but add 3/4 cup seedless raisins along with sugar and juice. After simmering, add 3/4 cup toasted, slivered almonds or coarsely chopped, blanched filberts; pack into jars as directed.

NP Tablespoon (with almonds): 35 C, 0 mg CH, 5 mg S*

SOME QUICK AND EASY RELISHES

These are jiffy relishes to mix up and serve, not ones to can. Store in the refrigerator.
⊠

⊲⊺⊳ ⊠ **Ranch Relish** *(About 3 cups):* Mix 3 peeled, seeded, and cubed medium-size ripe tomatoes, 2/3 cup each minced yellow onion and sweet green pepper, 2 teaspoons salt, and 1/2 cup chili sauce; chill well, then serve with barbecued beef, chops, and steaks.

NP Tablespoon: 5 C, 0 mg CH, 130 mg S*

Cranberry-Walnut Relish *(About 3 cups):* Mix 1 (1-pound) can undrained whole cranberry sauce with 1/3 cup each minced walnuts and celery.

NP Tablespoon: 20 C, 0 mg CH, 5 mg S*

⊲⊺⊳ **Onion Relish** *(About 1 cup):* Mix 1 large peeled and minced yellow, Bermuda, or Spanish onion with 2 tablespoons each cider vinegar and sugar and 1/4 teaspoon salt. If you like add 1 minced pimiento. Let

stand at room temperature 1/2 hour before serving.

NP Tablespoon: 10 C, 0 mg CH, 35 mg S*

⊲⊺⊳ **Pineapple Relish** *(About 3 cups):* Mix 2 cups minced fresh pineapple with 1/2 cup each minced sweet green or red pepper and celery, 3 tablespoons each firmly packed light brown sugar and cider vinegar. Let stand at room temperature 1/2 hour before serving.

NP Tablespoon: 5 C, 0 mg CH, 1 mg S*

⊲⊺⊳ **Quick Corn Relish** *(About 3 cups):* Mix 2 cups drained cooked or canned whole kernel corn with 1/3 cup each minced yellow onion and sweet green or red pepper, 1/4 cup each minced celery and sweet pickle relish, 1/2 teaspoon salt, and 2 tablespoons each sugar and cider vinegar. Let stand at room temperature 1/2 hour before serving.

NP Tablespoon: 10 C, 0 mg CH, 55 mg S*

⊲⊺⊳ **Quick Pickled Beets** *(1 pint):* Sprinkle 1 (1-pound) can sliced beets with 1/4 teaspoon minced garlic. Add 1/3 cup hot cider vinegar mixed with 2 tablespoons sugar and 1/8 teaspoon cloves.

NP Tablespoon: 10 C, 0 mg CH, 35 mg S*

HOT MUSTARD FRUITS

6 servings   ⊠

Delicious with baked ham or boiled tongue.

2 tablespoons butter or margarine
1/3 cup firmly packed light brown sugar
3 tablespoons prepared spicy brown mustard
1 cup sliced peaches
1 cup apricot halves
1 cup drained canned pineapple slices, cut in half

Preheat oven to 325° F. Melt butter in a small saucepan over low heat, add sugar and mustard, and heat and stir about 5 minutes until sugar dissolves. Place fruits in an ungreased shallow 1-quart casserole and pour in mustard mixture. Bake, uncovered, 1/2 hour, stirring and basting fruits once or twice. Serve as a vegetable substitute.

NPS: 125 C, 10 mg CH, 120 mg S*

VARIATION

Hot Curried Fruits: Prepare as directed but add 2–3 teaspoons curry powder to melted butter along with sugar and mustard.

NPS: 125 C, 10 mg CH, 120 mg S*

FRESH HORSERADISH

1 pint ⚖

Stored in the refrigerator, this will keep almost indefinitely.

½ pound horseradish root, scrubbed and peeled
½ cup white vinegar
2 teaspoons salt

Remove any discolored parts from root with a vegetable peeler, then cut into 1″ cubes. *(Note:* If you are doing more than this amount at one time, drop horseradish into cold water to prevent browning.) Chop very fine by buzzing, a little at a time, about 30 seconds in an electric blender at high speed or by churning, all at once, in 4–5 ten-second intervals in a food processor fitted with the metal chopping blade; or put twice through the fine blade of a meat grinder. Mix with vinegar and salt. Pack into sterilized jars, cover tightly, and let ripen in refrigerator 1 week before using.

NP Tablespoon: 5 C, 0 mg CH, 140 mg S*

JELLIES

Few cooking achievements seem more magical than the transformation of plump, freshly picked fruits into sparkling, quivery jellies. Yet there is nothing mysterious about the process. Or difficult. Three essentials are needed to make jelly: *pectin* (the jelling agent found naturally in certain fruits), *acid* (also found naturally in fruits, which strengthens the pectin), and *sugar* (which stretches and tenderizes the pectin; either beet or cane sugar may be used). With a delicate balance of the three comes perfect jelly: one that quivers but does not run, is firm enough to stand alone when unmolded yet tender enough to cut easily with a spoon.

HOW TO MAKE JELLY

Suitable Fruits for Natural Jellies (those requiring no commercial liquid or powdered pectins): Tart apples, crab apples, Concord grapes, currants, quinces, blackberries, cranberries, gooseberries, and raspberries. For best results, fruits should be firm-ripe, when pectin content is at its peak. Neither green nor overripe fruits have sufficient pectin for making jelly.

Preparing the Fruit:

Apples, Crab Apples, Quinces: Wash, cutting away any blemishes; remove stems and blossom ends, then slice thin, quarter, or coarsely chop. *Do not peel, core, or seed* (these all contain pectin).

Grapes, Currants, and Berries: Stem, wash, and sort, discarding any soft or blemished fruits, then crush with a potato masher (leave skins and seeds in).

Extracting the Juice: Place prepared fruit in a large kettle, add amount of water called for in the following chart, and boil, uncovered, stirring occasionally, the recommended amount of time. Pour into a damp jelly bag suspended over a large bowl (most jelly bags come equipped with their own stands) or into a cheesecloth-lined colander set in a large bowl. Let juices drip through undisturbed; squeezing the bag to force out juices will cloud the jelly. You can, however, massage the bag *very gently* once or twice. Extracting juice is a painstaking process, so don't be alarmed if it takes an hour or more. *(Note:* If extracted juice seems cloudy, strain through several thicknesses of cheesecloth.)

Testing for Pectin: Knowing how much pectin fruit juice contains is vital to making good jelly because the pectin content determines the amount of sugar needed. There are two tests:

With a Jelmeter (the most reliable test): These, available in specialty food shops, come with full instructions; follow them. Jelmeters are calibrated glass tubes through which the extracted juice is drained, the speed of drainage indicating the pectin content and thus the quantity of sugar needed.

With Alcohol: In a small glass mix 1 teaspoon grain *(ethyl)* alcohol (available at drugstores) with 1 teaspoon room-temperature extracted juice; let stand 1 minute, then pour into a second glass. If a firm precipitate forms, juice is high in pectin and should be mixed, measure for measure, with sugar. If precipitate is curdy, use three fourths as much sugar as fruit juice and, if soft, half as much sugar as juice.

The sugar-to-juice ratios given in the accompanying table are averages and should be used as a guide only when it is not possible to make one of the more accurate pectin tests.

Cooking the Jelly: Place juice and required amount of sugar in a very large, heavy kettle (at least four times the volume of fruit put into it—jellies bubble higher and higher as

JUICE EXTRACTION TABLE

Kind of Fruit	Quantity of Prepared Fruit	Amount of Water Needed per Quart of Fruit	Recommended Boiling Time
Apples and crab apples	1 quart	1 cup	20 minutes
Quinces	1 quart	2 cups	25 minutes
Raspberries	1 quart	None	10 minutes
Blackberries, gooseberries, and cur- rants	1 quart	1/4 cup	10 minutes
Concord grapes	1 quart	1/4 cup	15 minutes
Cranberries	1 quart	1 cup	10 minutes

Note: The extracted juice (jelly stock) can be bottled and the jelly made at a later date in small quantities as needed (makes for clearer jelly). Simply heat juice to 190° F., ladle into hot sterilized jars, filling to within 1/4″ of tops, seal, and process 10 minutes in a hot water bath.* Cool, check seals, and store in a cool, dark, dry place until ready to make jelly.

they thicken and, unless kettle is big enough, will boil over). Set over low heat, insert a candy thermometer, and heat and stir, using a long-handled wooden spoon, until sugar is dissolved. Raise burner heat and boil rapidly, uncovered and without stirring, until thermometer registers 8° F. higher than the boiling point of water in your area. At sea level, the jelling temperature is about 220° F. Begin testing for sheeting, however, shortly after mixture boils (when thermometer reads about 215° F.).

Testing for Sheeting: This is the standard jelly test, fortunately a quick and reliable one. Take up a small amount of the hot mixture on a cold metal spoon, cool slightly, then tilt. When drops cling together, forming a jelly-like sheet, jelly is done.

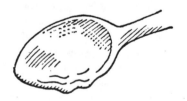

Syrupy
(not done)

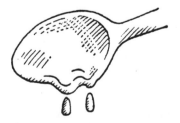

Thick Drops
(not done)

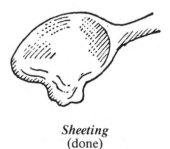

Sheeting
(done)

Preparing Jelly Jars and Closures or Jelly Glasses and Lids: These can be washed and sterilized while jelly cooks (follow directions given at beginning of this chapter). Invert sterilized glasses on a baking sheet and keep hot in a 250° F. oven until needed. Or, if you prefer, keep submerged in boiling water.

Melting Paraffin: Because hot paraffin is flammable, the melting should never be done over direct heat but in the top of a double boiler. Or, better still, in a small deep coffeepot (one used exclusively for melting paraffin) set in a saucepan of boiling water (with the coffeepot, pouring's a snap). Paraffin melted slowly and kept just at the point of liquefaction will do a far better job of sealing jellies than smoking-hot paraffin which, on hardening, will shrink from the sides of the glass, split, or crack.

Filling Jelly Glasses: Place glasses on a level counter near kettle of jelly, turn right-side-up, one by one, as you're ready to fill them. Have jelly boiling hot, then ladle into glass, holding ladle as close to glass as possible to prevent air bubbles from forming in jelly.

• *To Seal with Melted Paraffin:* Fill glasses to within 1/4″ of tops and seal with 1/8″ melted paraffin, making sure it touches

BASIC PROPORTIONS FOR JELLIES

Kind of Fruit Juice	Average Amount of Sugar Needed per Cup Extracted Juice
Apple, crab apple, cranberry, and currant	1 cup
Blackberry, gooseberry, raspberry, Concord grape, and quince	3/4 cup

glasses all round. Prick any bubbles in paraffin before it hardens so all air is sealed out. (*Note:* A single thin layer of paraffin works better than a thick one because it remains malleable, fitting itself to the contours of the cooling jelly. Thick paraffin layers are apt to become brittle on hardening and pull from sides of glasses.) Cool jelly, cap glasses, label, and store in a cool, dark, dry place.
• *To Seal in Dome-Lidded Jelly Jars:* This is the easy modern way. Simply ladle boiling hot jelly into half-pint (8-ounce) jelly or preserving jars, filling to within 1/8″ of tops. Wipe jar rims with a clean damp cloth, center dome lid on rim, then add screw band, and screw down tight. Invert jars for about 10 seconds so boiling hot jelly will destroy any microorganisms in the head space, then stand right-side-up and cool. Check seals, label, and store.

HOW TO RESCUE RUNNY JELLY

Sometimes jelly made with the greatest care refuses to jell, hardly a disaster because there are several ways to salvage it:

Without Adding Commercial Pectin: Empty jelly into a saucepan, bring to a boil, and continue cooking until mixture will sheet (see Testing for Sheeting). Ladle into clean sterilized glasses and reseal with paraffin.

With Commercial Powdered Pectin: Measure jelly and for each 1 quart measure 1/4 cup sugar, 1/4 cup water, and 4 teaspoons powdered pectin. Mix pectin and water in a large saucepan, bring to a boil, stirring constantly to prevent scorching, then mix in jelly and sugar. Boil hard for exactly 1/2 minute. Remove from heat, ladle into clean sterilized glasses, and reseal with paraffin.

With Commercial Liquid Pectin: Measure jelly and for each 1 quart measure 3/4 cup sugar, 2 tablespoons strained lemon juice, and 2 tablespoons liquid pectin. Being jelly to a full boil over high heat, quickly mix in sugar, lemon juice, and pectin, and heat, stirring constantly, until mixture comes to a full rolling boil. Boil hard 1 minute, remove from heat, ladle jelly into clean sterilized glasses, and reseal with paraffin.

JELLIES MADE WITH COMMERCIAL PECTINS

By making it possible to jell any liquid (fruit juice, vegetable juice, herb infusion), commercial pectins have revolutionized jelly making. There are two basic types: *liquid pectin,* a viscous material extracted from apples that is available in 3-ounce foil pouches, and *powdered pectin,* extracted from citrus fruits and sold in 1 3/4-ounce boxes. Latest entry: "light" pectin powder, which requires about one third less sugar to jell—a blessing to calorie counters and those who don't like their herb jellies cloyingly sweet (this new pectin product, by the way, contains no artificial sweeteners). All commercial pectins must be used with utmost care. The amounts required vary dramatically from juice to juice, depending on sweetness, tartness, and pectin content. No master recipe, alas, can be drawn up for the commercial pectins, so follow the manufacturer's recipes explicitly. *Caution: Never substitute one type of commercial pectin product for another; each works altogether differently.*

TIPS FOR MAKING BETTER JELLIES

Because so many of these tips are the same as for jams and preserves, they are included at the end of that section.

WHY THINGS SOMETIMES GO WRONG WITH JELLIES

Soft, Runny Jelly: Too little pectin or sugar or both; also undercooking.

Stiff Jelly: Too much pectin or acid or both.

Dull, Cloudy Jelly: Fruit juice not carefully extracted.

Grainy or Crystalline Jelly: Too much sugar, too little cooking.

Gummy Jelly: Overcooking.

Weepy Jelly: Fruit too acid or paraffin layer too thick.

Darkened or Off-Color Jelly: Stored at too high a temperature.

Faded Jelly: Stored in too bright a room.

JAMS, MARMALADES, FRUIT BUTTERS, PRESERVES, AND CONSERVES

These preserved fruits and fruit spreads are easy to make and foolproof enough to invite improvisation. What distinguishes one from another? Here's a fast run-down:

Jams: Crushed berries or cut-up fruits cooked with a little water and a lot of sugar until thick, slightly jelled, and of good spreading consistency.

Marmalades: Clear, tender, jelly-like spreads usually made of citrus fruits and containing shreds of rind and bits of cooked fruit.

Fruit Butters: Melba-smooth, honey-sweet spreads made by cooking strained fruit pulp with sugar and spices long and slow in an open kettle.

Preserves: Whole or cut-up fruits cooked in a sugar syrup until clear; syrup may be very thick or fairly thin.

Conserves: Jam-like spreads made of a mixture of fruits and nuts.

HOW TO MAKE JAM

Suitable Fruits: Apricots, blackberries, blueberries, carambolas, cherries, figs, gooseberries, grapes, peaches, pears, plums, raspberries, rhubarb, and strawberries. Also combinations of these.

Preparing the Fruit:

Berries and Other Soft Fruits: Wash and sort fruit, removing caps, stems, and any bruised or blemished spots, then crush.

Firm Fruits: Peel, core, and pit, then quarter, dice, or coarsely chop. (*Note:* Grapes and plums will have better texture if cooked until tender with a little water—about 1/4

cup for each quart prepared fruit—before being mixed with sugar.)

Cooking the Jam: Measure prepared fruit and for each quart add 3 cups sugar. Place in a very large, heavy kettle (at least four times volume of fruit put into it) and heat and stir over low heat until sugar dissolves. Insert a candy thermometer, then boil rapidly, uncovered, stirring often, until very thick, about 218°–222° F. on thermometer. Test for sheeting*; when mixture sheets, jam is done.

Preparing Jelly Jars or Glasses, Melting Paraffin: Follow directions given for jelly.

Filling Jars or Glasses: Remove jam from heat and let stand 1–2 minutes to settle foam; skim froth from surface, then ladle into jelly jars or glasses as directed for jelly. Cool, label, and store in a cool, dark, dry place.

HOW TO MAKE MARMALADE

(see separate recipes that follow)

HOW TO MAKE FRUIT BUTTERS

Suitable Fruits: Apples and crab apples, apricots, peaches, pears and plums, grapes and quinces.

Preparing the Fruit: Prepare as directed for jam.

Making the Fruit Pulp: Measure prepared fruit and for each 1 quart add 1/2 cup water. Cook in a large kettle, stirring now and then, until mushy; press through a sieve or purée by churning 10–15 seconds in a food processor fitted with the metal chopping blade, or by putting through a food mill.

Cooking the Fruit Butter: Measure fruit pulp and for each quart add 3 cups sugar; if you like, tie a few whole cloves, allspice, and a broken cinnamon stick in cheesecloth. Heat and stir over low heat in a large kettle until sugar dissolves, then slowly boil, uncovered, until quite thick, 1–1½ hours, stirring often to prevent scorching, especially toward the end.

Preparing Jars or Glasses, Melting Paraffin: Prepare as directed for jelly.

Filling Jars or Glasses: Remove fruit butter from heat, let stand 2 minutes, and skim off froth. Fill glasses or jars as directed for jelly. (*Note:* Many fruit butter recipes call for less sugar than this basic method; if the proportion of sugar to fruit pulp is less than 3 to 4 —3 cups sugar to 4 cups pulp—there will be less chance of spoilage if the fruit butter is poured into hot sterilized preserving jars to within 1/4″ of tops.) Seal and process in a hot water bath* about 10 minutes. Check seals after processing, then label jars and store in a cool, dark, dry place.

HOW TO MAKE PRESERVES

Suitable Fruits: Cherries, figs, peaches, pears, pineapple, raspberries, and strawberries.

Preparing the Fruit:

Cherries and Berries: Wash, stem, and sort, discarding any that are bruised or blemished. Leave sweet cherries whole but halve and pit the sour.

Figs: Wash and stem, then peel carefully, trying not to cut too close to the seeds. Leave whole.

Peaches and Pears: Peel, pit or core, and slice. *(Note:* Pears are also good cut into small chips or thin pieces.)

Pineapple: Peel, core, and cube or slice thin.

Cooking the Preserves:

Soft Fruits (Berries and Peaches): Measure prepared fruit and for each 1 quart add 3 cups sugar; mix and let stand at room temperature 10 minutes to draw some of the juices from the fruit. Set over low heat and cook and stir until sugar dissolves; cover, remove from heat, and let stand overnight so fruits will plump up. Next day, bring to a boil, add a few whole cloves and a broken cinnamon stick tied in cheesecloth, if you like, and cook slowly, stirring occasionally, until fruit is clear and syrup thick. Remove spices.

Firm Fruits: Measure prepared fruit and for each 1 quart measure 1/2 cup water and 3 cups sugar. Mix water and sugar, bring to a boil in a large kettle, stirring until sugar dissolves. Add fruit and boil, uncovered, stirring occasionally, until fruit is clear and syrup thick. If you like, tie a few whole spices in cheesecloth—cloves, allspice, a cinnamon stick—and cook along with fruits; remove when preserves are done—the fruit clear and syrup thick.

Preparing Jars or Glasses, Melting Paraffin: Prepare as directed for jelly.

Filling Jars or Glasses: Rich jam-like preserves made of small berries or fairly finely cut fruit can be ladled into jelly glasses and sealed under paraffin. But fruits preserved whole in syrup should be packed hot in hot sterilized jars. In either case, before filling jars, let preserves stand off heat 2 minutes to settle foam; skim off froth, then pack in glasses or jars as directed for jelly. *(Note:* Preserves packed in jars should be processed 10 minutes in a hot water bath.*) Cool preserves, label, then store in a cool, dark, dry place.

HOW TO MAKE CONSERVES

These are really simple variations on jams—mixtures of two or more fruits (use any suitable for jam) cooked with minced nuts and/or raisins. Prepare conserves like jam, teaming any combination of fruits you fancy, and using 3 cups sugar and 1/2 cup seedless raisins and/or chopped pecans, walnuts, or blanched almonds to each 1 quart prepared raw fruit. For better texture and flavor, add nuts during last 5 minutes of cooking.

TIPS FOR MAKING BETTER JELLIES, JAMS, PRESERVES, AND CONSERVES

In General:
• Read recipe through carefully before beginning and follow directions.
• Pick a clear, dry day for making jellies, jams, or preserves.
• Assemble equipment and ingredients before starting. Make sure jars or glasses are spotless, free of cracks and nicks.
• Make jellies, jams, and preserves in small quantities; do not double recipes.
• Measure or weigh ingredients carefully.
• Use extra-large, flat-bottomed kettles, heavy enough to reduce risk of scorching and made of an inert material, like enameled metal, hard-coat anodized aluminum, or stainless steel, that will not alter color or flavor of fruit.
• Use a candy thermometer to help determine doneness and check it for accuracy before using (for directions, see Chapter 20, Candies and Nuts).
• For soft jams and preserves, slightly undercook; for stiff ones, slightly overcook.
• If you live in a hot climate or have no cool space for storing preserves, pack in preserving jars and process 10–15 minutes in a hot

water bath* instead of ladling into jelly glasses and sealing with paraffin.

• When sealing with paraffin, make layer no more than 1/8″ thick, see that it touches glass all around and has no air bubbles.

• Wipe cooled, sealed glasses and jars with a clean damp cloth before storing.

• When cooling jars, allow plenty of space between them so air can circulate. Also, cool away from drafts.

• Test seals about 12 hours after cooling. If a jar has failed to seal, empty contents into a saucepan, bring to a boil, ladle into a clean, hot, sterile jar, reseal, and cool. Or, store in refrigerator and serve within 2 weeks.

• Store jams, jellies, and preserves in a dark, cool, dry place and let mellow several weeks before serving. Also, try to serve within a year, sooner if possible.

Jellies:

• Use firm-ripe fruit instead of fully ripe or, if you wish, one fourth slightly underripe fruit and three fourths ripe (but not overripe).

• Do not rush juice extraction but let it drip through jelly bag at its own snail's pace.

• If extracted juice lacks tartness (essential to making jelly jell), add 1 tablespoon strained lemon juice to each cup fruit juice.

• Do not overcook fruit when preparing for juice extraction—destroys pectin.

Jams, Marmalades, Fruit Butters, Preserves, and Conserves:

• To save money, use less-than-perfect fruits, *but* prepare carefully, trimming away all blemishes and moldy spots that might cause spoilage.

• When making preserves, have fruits of as uniform size and shape as possible.

• To keep fruit from floating to the top of jams and preserves, use fully ripe fruits and plump overnight in the sugar syrup.

• Watch all thick fruit mixtures closely during cooking and stir as needed to prevent scorching.

• Remove any whole spices immediately after cooling to prevent fruit from darkening.

• To reduce risks of spoilage (and make jams and preserves prettier) skim off as much froth or foam as possible before ladling into jars.

OLD-FASHIONED APPLE JELLY

5 half pints   ¢

Apples that make particularly good jelly are Rhode Island Greenings. Do not double this recipe.

5 pounds Rhode Island Greenings, washed, stemmed, and sliced thin but not peeled or cored
5 cups water
1/2 cup + 2 tablespoons lemon juice
3 3/4 cups sugar (about)

Place apples (include seeds and cores), water, and lemon juice in a very large enamel or stainless-steel kettle, cover, and boil 15–20 minutes until apples are mushy. Meanwhile, suspend 2 damp jelly bags over large, heatproof bowls or line 2 large colanders with 4 thicknesses of cheesecloth, letting ends hang over rims, and set colanders in bowls. Pour half of the apples and their juice into each bag or colander and let juice drip through. (*Note:* Cheesecloth can be tied into bags and suspended over bowls.) For sparkling, clear jelly, don't force pulp through bags. You may, however, massage bags gently, encouraging juice to trickle through. Have patience—this takes a long time. Meanwhile, sterilize 5 (8-ounce) jelly jars and their closures, and stand upside down on a baking sheet in a 250° F. oven until needed. When juice has been extracted (you should have about 5 cups; if measure is slightly short, add a little water to a jelly bag and let drip through), place the 5 cups juice in a clean, large enamel or stainless-steel kettle and stir in 3/4 cup sugar for each 1 cup juice; insert a candy thermometer. Boil mixture, uncovered, without stirring, 20–25 minutes until thermometer registers 218°–220° F.; begin testing for sheeting* after mixture has boiled 10 minutes. When jelly is done, remove from heat and skim off froth. Fill jars to within 1/8″ of tops and seal. Cool, label, and store in a cool, dark, dry place.

NP Tablespoon: 50 C, 0 mg CH, 1 mg S*

VARIATIONS

¢ **Old-Fashioned Rose Geranium Jelly:** Place a small rose geranium leaf in the bottom of each jelly jar, pour in apple jelly, press a second leaf into jelly, then seal.

NP Tablespoon: 50 C, 0 mg CH, 1 mg S*

¢ **Crab Apple Jelly:** Prepare as directed, substituting 5 pounds crab apples for Greenings (one quarter should be slightly underripe, the rest ripe) and omitting lemon juice. Test extracted juice for pectin* (crab apples contain considerable pectin) and add the quantity of sugar indicated (usually 1 cup sugar for each 1 cup extracted crab apple juice is about right). Proceed as directed.

NP Tablespoon: 55 C, 0 mg CH, 1 mg S*

¢ **Spiced Apple or Crab Apple Jelly:** Prepare as directed but, when cooking apples and water for juice, add 6–8 whole cloves, 1 broken cinnamon stick, and 2–3 whole allspice, tied in cheesecloth. Remove spice bag before pouring apples into jelly bags.

NP Tablespoon: 55 C, 0 mg CH, 1 mg S*

¢ **Minted Apple or Crab Apple Jelly:** Prepare as directed but when cooking apples and water for juice add 1 cup bruised mint leaves tied in cheesecloth; remove mint bag before pouring apples into jelly bags.

NP Tablespoon: 50 C, 0 mg CH, 1 mg S*

Quince Jelly: Prepare as directed, substituting 5 pounds coarsely chopped, unpeeled firm-ripe quinces for Greenings and omitting lemon juice; cook quinces and water (2 cups water to each quart prepared fruit) 25–30 minutes until mushy. Extract juice, test for pectin,* and add quantity of sugar indicated (usually 3/4 cup sugar for each 1 cup extracted juice). Proceed as directed.

NP Tablespoon: 45 C, 0 mg CH, 1 mg S*

OLD-FASHIONED CONCORD GRAPE JELLY

4 half pints

3 pounds Concord grapes, washed and stemmed but not peeled
3/4 cup cold water
2 1/4 cups sugar (about)

Place grapes and water in a large enamel or stainless-steel kettle and mash well with a potato masher. Cover and bring to a boil over high heat; reduce heat slightly and boil gently 15 minutes. Meanwhile, suspend 2 damp jelly bags over large heatproof bowls or line 2 large colanders with 4 thicknesses of cheesecloth, letting ends hang over rims; stand colanders in large bowls. Pour half of grape mixture into each bag or colander and let juice drip through undisturbed. *(Note: Cheesecloth can be tied into bags and suspended over bowls.)* While juice is being extracted, sterilize 4 (8-ounce) jelly jars and their closures, and stand upside down on a baking sheet in a 250° F. oven until needed. When most of the juice has dripped through, measure carefully—you should have about 3 cups; if measure is slightly short, add a little water to a jelly bag and let drip through. Place the 3 cups juice in a clean large enamel or stainless-steel kettle and add 3/4 cup sugar for each 1 cup juice; insert a candy thermometer. Bring mixture to a boil over high heat, reduce heat slightly, and boil, uncovered, without stirring, 10–15 minutes until thermometer reaches 218°–220° F. Begin testing for sheeting,* however, after 5 minutes of cooking. When jelly is done, remove from heat and skim off froth. Fill jars to within 1/8" of tops and seal. Cool, label, and store in a cool, dark, dry place.

NP Tablespoon: 35 C, 0 mg CH, 1 mg S*

JALAPEÑO JELLY

9 half pints

Plenty hot and a superb accompaniment to meats and poultry. Try it, too, on a toasted English muffin generously spread with cream cheese.

3–4 Jalapeño or other small, moderately hot chili peppers, washed and stemmed, but not cored or seeded
5–6 large sweet green peppers (about 2 pounds), washed and stemmed, but not cored or seeded
1 medium-size yellow onion, peeled
1 cup water
2 cups cider vinegar
1/4 cup sieved lemon juice
2 drops green food coloring (optional)
8 cups sugar
1/2 teaspoon unsalted butter
3 (3-ounce) pouches liquid fruit pectin

Chop peppers and onion fine by buzzing 15–20 seconds in a food processor fitted with the metal chopping blade or by putting through the medium blade of a meat grinder. Place vegetables in a large saucepan, add water, cover, and simmer 15 minutes until very soft. Cool slightly, then spoon into a damp jelly bag suspended over a heatproof bowl or into a large sieve lined with 6 thicknesses of cheesecloth and set over a heatproof bowl. Let liquid drip through undisturbed. Meanwhile, sterilize 9 (8-ounce) jelly jars and their closures; stand upside down on a baking sheet in a 250° F. oven until needed. When dripping has almost ceased, gently press bag or vegetables in cheesecloth. Measure liquid. You should have 2 1/4 cups; if slightly short, add a little water to pulp, and let it drip through. Pour the 2 1/4 cups liquid into a large enameled or stainless-steel kettle, mix in vinegar, lemon juice, food coloring, if you like, sugar, and butter. Open pouches of pectin and stand in a large measuring cup. Set kettle, uncovered, over high heat, and bring mixture to a boil, stirring constantly. Mix in pectin, then, stirring constantly, bring all to a *full rolling boil that roams up in the kettle and cannot be stirred down; boil hard 1 minute exactly,* stirring constantly. Remove from heat and quickly skim off foam with a large metal spoon. Ladle at once into jars, filling to within 1/8" of tops. Wipe rims and seal jars. Cool, check seals, then label, and store in a cool, dark, dry place.

NP Tablespoon: 45 C, 0 mg CH, 1 mg S*

VARIATION

Hot Red Pepper Jelly: Substitute sweet red peppers for the green peppers, lime juice for the lemon juice; omit food coloring, add 1 tablespoon finely grated lemon rind along with the sugar, then proceed as directed.

NP Tablespoon: 45 C, 0 mg CH, 1 mg S*

FRESH BASIL JELLY

4 half pints

This recipe uses the new "light" powdered fruit pectin (for jams and jellies with less sugar). Do not substitute regular powdered pectin or liquid pectin; they will not work in this recipe.

2 cups firmly packed young basil leaves, washed and chopped fine
1 quart water
2²/₃ cups sugar
1 (1³/₄-ounce) package powdered "light" fruit pectin (for jams and jellies with less sugar)
2 drops green food coloring (optional)

Sterilize 4 (8-ounce) jelly jars and their closures; stand upside down on a baking sheet in a 250° F. oven until needed. Heat basil and water to boiling in a covered saucepan, remove from heat, stir well, and cool, still covered, to room temperature. Line a sieve with 6 thicknesses cheesecloth, and set over a bowl; pour in basil mixture. When dripping has ceased, discard leaves and measure liquid; you should have about 3²/₃ cups; if slightly short, add a little water to round out the measure. Pour basil infusion into a large enameled or stainless-steel kettle. Combine 1/4 cup of the sugar with the pectin, slowly stir into basil infusion, then add food coloring, if you wish. Set kettle, uncovered, over high heat and bring to a boil, stirring constantly. Mix in remaining sugar, then, stirring constantly, bring mixture to a *full rolling boil that foams up in the kettle and cannot be stirred down; boil hard 1 minute exactly,* stirring all the while. Remove from heat and quickly skim off foam with a large metal spoon. Ladle at once into jars, filling to within 1/8" of tops. Wipe rims and seal

jars. Cool, check seals, then label, and store in a cool, dark, dry place.

NP Tablespoon: 35 C, 0 mg CH, 1 mg S*

VARIATION

Fresh Mint Jelly: Substitute 3 cups firmly packed fresh mint leaves, washed and chopped fine, for the basil, then proceed as directed.

NP Tablespoon: 35 C, 0 mg CH, 1 mg S*

WINE JELLY

2¹/₂ cups ⊠

Serve as a condiment with poultry, game, or game birds.

1¹/₂ cups medium-dry port, red or white wine, or 1 cup wine and 1/2 cup water
1 cup currant or grape jelly
3 whole cloves
1/2 stick cinnamon
1 tablespoon lemon juice
1 envelope unflavored gelatin softened in 1/4 cup cold water

Simmer wine, jelly, spices, and lemon juice, uncovered, 10 minutes; add gelatin and heat and stir until dissolved. Strain through a cheesecloth-lined sieve, cool, then chill until firm. Break up slightly with a fork and serve cool—not straight out of the refrigerator.

NP Tablespoon: 25 C, 0 mg CH, 1 mg S*

UNCOOKED BERRY JAM

5 half pints ⊠

This recipe can be made with a variety of berries.

1 quart berries, stemmed, washed, and drained well
2 pounds sugar
2 tablespoons lemon juice
1 (3-ounce) pouch liquid fruit pectin

Sterilize 5 (8-ounce) jelly jars and their closures, or, if you plan to store jam in freezer, freezer jars. Mash berries with a potato masher, then measure. You will need 1 pint mashed fruit. Strain out some of the seeds, if you like, but add extra mashed berries as needed to fill out the 1-pint measure. Mix berries and sugar well; combine lemon juice and pectin and add to berries; stir 3 minutes. *(Note:* A little undissolved sugar may remain.) Fill jars to within 1/4" of tops, cover with lids or rounds of foil, and let jam "set up" at room temperature; this may take 24 hours. Refrigerate and use within 3 weeks or freeze and use within 1 year.

NP Tablespoon: 45 C, 0 mg CH, 1 mg S*

ORANGE MARMALADE

4 half pints

Make only small amounts of marmalade at a time so it doesn't scorch.

2 large thick-skinned oranges (navel or Valencia are best)
1 small lemon
2 cups water
4 cups sugar (about)

Peel oranges and lemon, trim away inner white part so rind is about 3/8″ thick; cut in fine slivers about 1/2″ long. Discard pith and seeds in fruit, then chop fruit fine, saving juice. Mix rind, fruit, and juice in a very large, heavy enamel or stainless-steel kettle, add water, and simmer, uncovered, 10 minutes. Cover and let stand in a cool place overnight. Next day, wash and sterilize 4 (8-ounce) jelly jars and closures, stand upside down on a baking sheet in a 250° F. oven until needed. Measure fruit mixture and for each cup add 1 cup sugar. Return to pan, insert candy thermometer, slowly heat, uncovered, to boiling, stirring until sugar dissolves; boil slowly, uncovered, stirring now and then, 30–40 minutes until thermometer reaches 218°–220° F.; begin testing for sheeting.* When marmalade is done, remove from heat, stir 1 minute, skim off froth, and ladle into jars, filling to within 1/8″ of tops. Wipe rims and seal. Cool, check seals, label, and store in a cool, dark, dry place.

NP Tablespoon: 50 C, 0 mg CH, 1 mg S*

VARIATIONS

Bitter Orange Marmalade: Prepare as directed, using the slivered rind and chopped fruit of 4–5 Seville oranges; omit lemon. Tie seeds in cheesecloth and simmer along with rind, chopped fruit and juice, and water called for for 30–40 minutes until rind is almost tender; remove seeds and let stand overnight. Measure mixture, add enough water to total 1 quart, then proceed as directed, using 1–1 1/2 cups sugar per cup of mixture, depending on how sweet a marmalade is wanted.

NP Tablespoon: 50 C, 0 mg CH, 1 mg S*

Grapefruit Marmalade: Prepare as directed, using the rind of 2 large grapefruits instead of oranges; after trimming and slivering rind, measure 1 1/2 cups to use in the marmalade; combine with lemon rind. Bring rinds and 1 quart water to a boil in a small saucepan, then drain; repeat twice. Mix rind and chopped, seeded grapefruit sections, add the 2 cups water called for, and proceed as directed.

NP Tablespoon: 55 C, 0 mg CH, 1 mg S*

Lemon Marmalade: Prepare as directed for Orange Marmalade (above) but use the rind and chopped, seeded fruit of 4 large lemons; also use 1 1/2 cups sugar for each 1 cup fruit and rind mixture.

NP Tablespoon: 75 C, 0 mg CH, 1 mg S*

Ginger-Lime Marmalade: Prepare as directed, using the slivered rind and chopped fruit of 4–5 limes (you'll need 3 cups fruit and rind mixture) and the slivered rind and chopped fruit of 1 lemon. Use 1 1/2 cups sugar for each cup fruit mixture and add 1/3 cup slivered crystallized ginger. Cook and bottle as directed.

NP Tablespoon: 80 C, 0 mg CH, 1 mg S*

Kumquat Marmalade: Prepare as directed, using 1 quart slivered kumquat rind and chopped fruit (you'll need about 1 3/4 pounds ripe kumquats). *(Note:* The easiest way to prepare these small fruits is to halve lengthwise, scrape out seeds and core, then to sliver fruit and rind together.) Use 1 1/2 cups water and 1/2 cup lemon juice when cooking, otherwise proceed as for Orange Marmalade.

NP Tablespoon: 55 C, 0 mg CH, 1 mg S*

Calamondin Marmalade *(5 half pints):* These supertart, tiny citrus fruits, available in Florida and California, make excellent marmalade. Prepare like Kumquat Marmalade (above), substituting calamondins for kumquats, using 2 cups water instead of water *and* lemon juice, and increasing amount of sugar for each cup fruit mixture to 2–2 1/2 cups. Nutritional count not available.

GINGERED PEAR AND PINEAPPLE PRESERVES

15 half pints

Grated rind of 2 lemons
Juice of 2 lemons
10 pounds underripe pears
1 medium-size firm pineapple
1 pound crystallized ginger, coarsely chopped
5 pounds sugar

Place lemon rind and juice in a very large enamel or stainless-steel kettle. Peel, quarter, and core pears, one at a time; divide each quarter lengthwise into 3 wedges, then slice thin, letting pear fall into lemon juice in kettle and tossing occasionally to mix. Peel pineapple, quarter lengthwise, and remove hard core; cut quarters into long, slim wedges, then slice thin; add to kettle along with ginger and sugar. Set, uncovered, over moderately high heat and bring to a boil, stirring occasionally. Adjust heat so mixture boils *very gently* and boil, uncovered, stirring occasionally, 1–1¼ hours until the consistency of marmalade. Meanwhile, wash and sterilize 15 (8-ounce) jelly jars and their closures; stand upside down on a baking sheet in a 250° F. oven until needed. Ladle preserves into jars, filling to within ⅛″ of the tops; wipe rims and seal. Cool, check seals, label, and store in a cool, dark, dry place. Let stand 2–3 weeks before using.

*NP Tablespoon: 55 C, 0 mg CH, 1 mg S**

BLUE RIDGE APPLE BUTTER

4 half pints

4 pounds tart cooking apples, washed, cored, and sliced but not peeled
3 cups apple cider or water
2 cups sugar (about)
1 teaspoon cinnamon
¼ teaspoon allspice
¼ teaspoon cloves
¼ teaspoon salt

Boil apples and cider, uncovered, in a large enamel or stainless-steel kettle, stirring frequently, about 20 minutes until mushy; put through a fine sieve, pressing out as much liquid as possible. Measure apple pulp and for each 1 cup add ½–¾ cup sugar, depending on how sweet you like things. Put pulp, sugar, spices, and salt in a clean enamel or stainless-steel kettle and cook, uncovered, very slowly about 1½ hours, stirring often, until very thick (spoon a little mixture on a cold saucer, if it cools into a smooth firm mass, butter is done). Meanwhile, wash and sterilize 4 (8-ounce) jelly jars and their closures, and stand upside down on a baking sheet in a 250° F. oven until needed. Spoon apple butter into jars, filling to within ¼″ of tops, wipe rims, seal, and process in a hot water bath* 10 minutes. Cool, check seals, label, and store in a cool, dark, dry place several weeks before serving.

*NP Tablespoon: 45 C, 0 mg CH, 10 mg S**

LEMON CHEESE (LEMON CURD)

1 quart ⊠

Use as a filling for cakes, pies, sweet rolls, or as a spread for hot breads.

1 cup butter
2 cups sugar
3 tablespoons finely grated lemon rind
⅔ cup lemon juice
⅛ teaspoon salt
4 eggs

Melt butter in the top of a double boiler over simmering water. Add sugar, lemon rind, juice, and salt and stir until sugar dissolves, 2–3 minutes. Beat eggs until frothy, mix in about 1 cup lemon mixture, return to double boiler, and cook and stir 7–9 minutes until thick. Ladle into small jars, cover, and cool to room temperature. Store in refrigerator.

*NP Tablespoon: 55 C, 25 mg CH, 40 mg S**

Index

curry, 107–8
dilled deviled ham, 107
guacamole, 108
guacamole with tomato, 108
hummus, 108
sherried green cheese, 107
tapenade, 107
taramasalata, 109
empanaditas, 103–4
falafel, 551
figs and ham, 99
fruit cocktails, 110
ham fritters, Spanish, 104
health mix, 101
herring in sour cream, 375
lamb-stuffed bulgur balls, crispy, 227
mangoes and ham, 99
meat balls
    blue cheese, 105–6
    chili, 105
    chutney-nut, 105
    hot spicy, 105
    Roman, 105
melon and ham, 99
microwaving, 90
mushrooms
    dry-roasted herbed, 100
    marinated, 99
    prosciutto-stuffed, 98
mussels, cold marinated, 100
nachos, cheese
    with beans and bacon, 104
    with green chilies, 104
    potato-skin, with chilies, 104
nuts as, 97
olives
    dill and garlic, 100
    pâté, 93
    spiced, 100
Osaka skillet broccoli, 556
oysters
    cold marinated, 100
    Florentine, 410
    Remick, 410
    Rockefeller, 409–10
pasties, 178
pâté, 91–93
    about, 91
    amount needed, 91
    black olive, 93
    chicken liver, easy, 92
    country-style liver, 91–92
    egg, nut, and mushroom, 92
    fish, layered, 93
    to glaze with aspic, 91
    kinds of, 91
    pretty party, 92
    to serve, 91
    spinach, carrot, and white kidney bean, 92–93
quiche Lorraine, 450–51
    tarts, 101–2
rumakis, 106
scallops

cold marinated, 100
    rumaki, 420
Scotch woodcock, 435–36
seafood cocktails, 111
shellfish, low-calorie marinated cold, 100
shrimp
    canapés, 98
    cocktail, 111
    cold marinated, 99–100
    gingery Chinese, 421
    butterfly, 421
    mousse, 368
    pickled, à la Lorna, 422–23
    rumakis, 419–20
    sushi with cucumber and scallion, 95
    toast, 101
spreads
    about, 106
    baba ganouj, 110
    beer cheese, 108–9
    for canapés, 97
    caponata, 109–10
    egg-dill, 109
    hummus, 108
    liptauer cheese, 109
    mushroom caviar, 110
    salt cod with garlic, oil, and cream 372–73
    tapenade, 107
stuffed vegetables, 97
sushi
    salmon nori-roll, 94–95
    shrimp, cucumber, and scallion, 95
teriyaki, 160
trail mix, 101
Apple(s)
See also Applesauce
about, 712–13
baked, 725
    brown sugar glazed, 725
    stuffed, 725
brown Betty, 728
    berry-, 728
bulgur with almonds and, 466
butter, Blue Ridge, 892
cake, upside-down, 809
candied, 864
caramel, 864
-celery stuffing, baked spareribs with, 251
charlotte, Swiss, 728
chicken or turkey sandwiches with, 402
chutney, 879-80
cider. *See* Cider
clafouti, 750
cottage pudding, 750
crisp, 729
fried rings, 725
    curried, 725
fritters, 712
Indian pudding, 738
jelly

juice extraction table, 884
    minted, 889
    old-fashioned, 888
    preparing the fruit, 883
    rose geranium, 888
    spiced, 889
-lime cooler, minted, 70
-oatmeal bars, 852
omelets with brandy, 748
pancakes, 669
peeling, coring, and seeding, 710
pickled, 878
pie
    country-style, 774
    fried, 776
    kinds of apples for, 775
    spice blend for, 49
    streusel, 778
poached (stewed), 721
    dried, 722–23
pork and
    chops with raisins and, 246
    loin roast stuffed with prunes and, 238
    pot roast with apple gravy, 241
    roast shoulder stuffed with pecans and, 240
    spareribs baked with apple-celery stuffing, 251
punch, autumn, 73
-raisin stuffing, 516
red cabbage and, Flemish, 561
rutabaga and, scalloped, 611
saffron, golden, 724–25
sausage and
    baked, 288
    with onions, braised, 288–89
    soup, 138
    Russian, 138
spiced filling for coffee cakes and sweet breads, 696
strudel, 787–88
stuffing
    pecan and, 519
    with prune and cranberry, 520
    -raisin, 516
tarte tatin, 774
turnovers, 774–75
upside-down cake, 809
Waldorf salad, 641–42
yams with
    and Canadian bacon, baked, 271
    casserole with raisins, 609
Applejack, 58
Applesauce
cake, 807–8
cookies, 832–33
duck or goose with sauerkraut and, roast, 312

and chicken liver hors
d'oeuvre, 106
country-cured, 269
cream cheese and
horseradish dip with,
107
crumbles or bits of, 269
curls, to make, 23
dressing, hot: wilted spinach
salad with, 629
drippings, saving and using,
270
eggs with
creamed, with onion, 443
pie, 442
ends and pieces of, 269
fat content of, 269
flank steak pinwheels
wrapped in, 167–68
hamburgers with, 172
Irish, 269
lima beans with
carrots and, 546
sour cream and, 546
muffins, 658
to panbroil, 270
pancetta, 269
to panfry (sauté), 270
preparation for cooking, 270
rutabaga with sour cream
and, 611
sandwiches
cream cheese and, 704
with lettuce and tomato,
703
peanut butter and, 704
slab, 269
sliced, 269
-sour cream sauce, 502
spaghetti carbonara with,
478
spinach with, 613
square (jowl), 269
thick sliced, 269
thin sliced, 269
wild rice with mushrooms
and, 465
Bagna cauda, 96
Baguette, defined, 12
Bahamian conch chowder,
391–92
Bain marie, defined, 12
Bake, defined, 12
Baked Alaska, 748
Baking pans
for bread, 655–56
to line with crumbs or sugar,
23
to line with ladyfingers, 23
measuring, 20
Baking sheets, for cookies, 826
Baking soda, 35
Baklava, 792
Balinese beef on skewers, 166–
67
Balkan-style veal and chestnut
stew, 207
Ball, defined, 12

Ballotines, 305
Balmoral heart patties, 274
Banana(s)
about, 713
baked, 725
cream pie, 780
flambé, 725–26
fritters, 712
ice cream, 745
milk shake, 68
sautéed halved, 725
tea bread, 667
B & B, 58, 78–79
Bannocks, 661
Barbados sugar, 35
Barbecue(d)
beans, 550
beef
gravy for, 509
hamburgers, 172
pot roast, 180
sauce for, 508–9
spit-, 152
defined, 12
fish, 354
game birds, 344
gravy for beef, 509
lamb
burgers, smothered, 223
chops, baked, 221
oven-, 212
riblets, 231–32
pork
chops, 248
pot roast, 241
spit-, 235
tenderloin, oven-, 239
poultry
broiled or charcoal-
broiled, 315–16
spit-, 314
sauce
all-purpose, 508
for beef, 508–9
Chinese, 509
chuck wagon, 248
South American hot, 509
spice blends for, 49
Barbecuing
See also specific recipes
on gas or electric barbecues,
144
pit, 144
Barding, 12
meat, 142
poultry, 306
Bar-le-Duc, defined, 12
Barley
about, 456
and mushroom casserole,
467
soup
with lamb and pepper, 132
Scotch broth, 128
Scotch broth, thrifty, 218–
19
Barney's triple decker
sandwich, 705

Barracuda, 360
Basil
about, 44
jelly, 890
pesto
processor, 477
spaghetti with, 477
sauce of fresh cold tomato
and, hot pasta with, 477
Basque-style
Bayonne ham, 256
cabbage soup, 135
chicken, 322
eggplant, peppers, and
tomatoes, 578
garbure, 134
piperade, 440
Bass, about, 364
Baste, defined, 12
Bâtarde sauce, 498–99
Batter
definition of, 12
for fried foods, 671–72
tempura, 672
vegetable fritter, 672
Batterie de cuisine, defined, 12
Bauernwurst, 293
Bavarian cream
Charlotte Russe, 742
chocolate, 742
fruit, 742
mocha, 742
rum, 741–42
vanilla, 741
Bay leaves, about, 44
Bayonne ham, 256
Bean(s), 542–52
*See also names of specific
beans*
appetizers, 99
and bacon sandwiches, 703
baked
Boston-style, 548
casserole of sliced pork
and, 242
ham and, 265
pork chops and, 247
sandwiches with, 703, 705
cheese nachos with bacon
and, 104
dried
about, 529, 543–44
appetizers, 99
boiled, 547
cold, 547
creamed purée of, 547–48
purée of, au gratin, 548
savory, 547
equivalent measurements of,
28
fresh, about, 529, 542–43
ragoût of mutton and, 230
salad
beet and, 635
creamy, 635
dried, 634–35
Parmesan, 635
three, 634

with sour cream and
caraway seeds, 553
and bean salad, 635
boiled, 552
borscht
quick, 128–29
Russian, 128
to brighten, 24
in burgundy, 554
cold, 553
Harvard, 553
and herring à la russe, 375
with horseradish, 553
hot spicy shredded, 553
orange-glazed, 553
to parboil, 553
pickled
with eggs, 445
quick, 882
to prepare for cooking, 552
in red flannel hash, 190
with sour cream and dill,
553
Beet greens, about, 552
Beignets, 712
defined, 12
Belgian endives
about, 532, 581
au gratin, 581
with ham, 581
boiled, 581
braised, 581–82
cold, 581
low-calorie, 581
to parboil, 581
soup, cream of, 122
Swiss-style, 581
veal chops or steaks
flambéed with, 198
Belgian-style
See also Flemish-style
Waterzooie, 129
Benedictine, 58
Benne wafers, 832
Bercy butter, 504
Bercy sauce, 490
Berliner blutwurst, 294
to heat, 290
Berliner bockwurst, 294
Berliner kränze (wreaths), 845
Berry(-ies)
See also names of specific
berries
about, 713
-apple brown Betty, 728
cobbler, 727–28
ice cream, 745
jam, uncooked, 890–91
jelly, 883–85
milk shake, 68
pancakes, 669
pie
basic, 776–77
chiffon, 782
Dutch, 777
frozen, 777
poached (stewed), 721
relish, 881

soup
basic, 137
quick, 137
spiced, 138
sweet-sour, 138
Swedish cream with, 742
Beurre, defined, 12
Beurre blanc, 503
aux fines herbes, 503
Beurre manié, 488
defined, 484
Beurre noir, 504
defined, 484
Beurres composés, defined, 484
Beverages, alcoholic, 51–62
See also names of specific
beverages and types of
beverage
ale, 51
beer, 51
bitters, 59–60
brandies and liqueurs, 57–59
calorie counts for, 79
liquors, 56–57
amounts needed for
parties, 61
bottles of, 62
buying, for parties, 60
microwaving, 62
mixed
chart, 78–89
terms and techniques of,
60–61
tips for making, 78
punches, 75–77
whiskeys, 56–57
wine(s), 51–56
bottle shapes and sizes, 55
buying, for parties, 60
cooking, 54
dessert, 53–54
red, dry, 51, 56
rosé, 51, 56
serving, 55–56
sparkling, 53–54
table, 51–53
terms and techniques, 54–
55
white, dry, 51, 56
Beverages, nonalcoholic
appetizer, 71–72
coffee
See also Coffee about, 63
to make, 63–65
variations on, 65–66
coolers, 70
decorative ices and ice rings
for punch bowls, 72
equivalent measurements of,
29–30
fruit, 69–71
ice cream sodas, 68–69
lemonade, 70
microwaving, 62
milk, 67–69
mineral waters, 60
punches, 73–75
seltzers, 60

shrubs, 71
sodas, 60
tea, 66–67
tea-like, 66
tomato cocktails, 71
Bien fatigué, defined, 12
Bierwurst (Beerwurst), 294
Bigarde (orange) sauce, 494
Billi-bi, 126
Bind, defined, 13
Biscuit(s)
baking powder, 660
buttermilk, 660
cheese, 661
-corn meal, 661
chicken or turkey stew with,
331
drop, 660
extra-quick, 660
extra-rich, 660
ginger, 832
herb, 661
make-ahead, 661
microwave-baking, 657
mixing method for, 655
party, 661
reheating, 656–58
savory pinwheel, 660
stir-and-roll, 660
sweet pinwheel, 660
test for doneness, 656
topping for casseroles, 660
quick, 660
toppings for, 661
tortoni, 747
Bisque
definition of, 13, 112
shellfish, 126
Bitters, 59–60
Black bean(s)
about, 543
beef stew with piñon nuts
and, 183–84
Brazilian, 552
dip, 108
Italian-style sausage and,
289
and peppers, Florida, 552
soup
easy, 132
old-fashioned, 132
and sour cream, 547
Blackberry(-ies)
See also Berry(-ies)
about, 713
-apple brown Betty, 728
jelly, juice extraction table,
884
shrub, 71
Black bottom pie, 779
Black-eyed pea(s)
about, 543
boiled fresh, 546–47
Carolina-style, 547
hog jowl and, 271
hopping John, 547
and rice salad, 635
salad of lamb and, 219

Southern-style, 550
Black Russian, 78–79
Black velvet, 78–79
Blanch, defined, 13, 872
Blancmange, 735–36
Blanquette de veau, 206
Blaze, defined, 13
Blend, defined, 13, 796
Blini, 669–70
Blintzes
    cheese, 452
    fruit, 452
Blood (game), as thickener for
        sauces, 485
Blood sausages, 293
    heating and serving, 289–90
Bloody Mary, 78–79
Blueberry(-ies)
    See also Berry(-ies)
    about, 713
    -apple brown Betty, 728
    muffins, 659
    waffles, 670
Blue cheese
    See also Roquefort cheese
    burgers, 171
    meat balls, 105–6
    -sour cream sauce, 502
    steak, 164
    veal balls, 206
Bluefish
    about, 360
    smothered with herbs and
        cream, baked, 375
Blue Ridge apple butter, 892
Bobotie, 225
Bocconcini, 203
Bockwurst, 292
Boeuf, defined, 13
Boeuf à la Bourguignonne, 184
Boil, defined, 13
Boiled dinner
    New England-style, 189
    Polish-Style, 182
Bok choy. *See* Chinese cabbage
Bollito misto, 182
Bologna, 294
Bolognese-style tomato sauce,
        506
Bombay duck, 13
Bombay-style lamb shanks, 232
Bombe, 742
    to freeze, 743
Bone, to, defined, 13
Bones, ham, 266
Boning
    meat, 142
    poultry, 307–9
Boonekamp, 60
Borage, 48
Bordeaux wine, 51–52
Bordelaise sauce, 495
    filet steaks, tournedos, or
        filets mignons with, 158
Bordelaise-style roast lamb,
        211–12
Boreks
    beef, 102–3

cheese, 103
    spinach and mozzarella, 103
Borscht
    beef and bacon, 186
    economy, 186
    quick, 128–29
    Russian, 128
    stew, 186
    Ukrainian, country-style, 186
Boston cream pie, 802
Boston-style
    baked beans, 548
    brown bread, 668
    stuffed clams, 390–91
"Bottled in bond," meaning of,
        60
Bouchées, 770–71
Boudins blancs, 293
Bouillabaisse, 381
Bouillon
    See also Broth; Stock
    court
        for aspics, 348
        rich wine, 348
        simple, 347–48
        white wine, 348
    definition of, 112
    tomato, 71
    -vegetable, 120
Bouquet garni, about, 48–49
Bourbon, 57
    Kentucky colonels, 865
Bourguignonne (Burgundy)-
        style
    beef fondue, 159
    escargots, 425
    gougère (cheese pastry ring),
        102
    sauce, 495.
    veal, braised, 199
Boysenberry(-ies)
    See also Berry(-ies)
    about, 713
Braciolini, 169
Brains
    about, 272
    amount needed, 272
    in black butter sauce, 273
    to blanch, 272
    braised, 283
    breaded, 273
    broiled, 273, 282
    coquilles of, Mornay, 273
    creamed, 283
    to prepare for cooking, 272
    sautéed, 272
    vinaigrette, 273
Braising
    defined, 13
    meat, 145
    poultry, 318
Bran
    about, 456
    bread, 681
    flour, 34
    muffins, 659
Brandade de morue, 372–73
Brandy(-ied)

about, 58
Alexander, 78–79
    pie, 783
apple omelet with, 748
dessert sauce, 753
    hard sauce, 755
fruit compote, 723
mincemeat in cheese pastry,
        778
peaches, 878
pears, 878
Bratwurst, 292
    sauerkraut with meat and,
        241–42
Brazilian-style black beans, 552
Bread(s)
    See also Rolls; Toast
    baking tips, 655–58
    convection-oven cooking of,
        8
    cooling, 656
    corn. *See* Corn bread
    croustades, 673
    croutons, 673–74
    crumbs
        to make, 9, 24, 673
        to measure, 19
        as soup thickeners, 113
    cubes, 673
    dumplings, 671
    equivalent measurements of,
        29
    flours for, 34, 674
    garlic, 672
        cheese-, 672
        herbed, 672
    pudding
        butter, 733
        queen of puddings, 733
    quick, 658–70
        See also Biscuit(s); Corn
            bread; Muffins
        apricot-pecan, 666
        banana tea, 667
        bannocks, 661
        Boston brown bread, 668
        carrot and raisin, 667
        cinnamon coffee cake,
            667–68
        cranberry nut, 666–67
        date-nut, 666
        doughnuts, spicy, 668
        Irish soda bread, 661–62
        microwave-baking, 657
        mixing methods, 655, 656
        orange nut, 666
        pancakes, 668–70
        pizza, 689
        popovers, 662
        prune and walnut, 666
        puri, 663
        raisin or currant and nut,
            666
        scones, Hilda's Yorkshire,
            662
        test for doneness, 656
        Yorkshire pudding, 662
        zucchini-walnut, 667

Brussels sprouts
about, 530, 557
au gratin, 557
boiled, 557
with chestnuts, 557–58
dilled, in sour cream, 557
low-calorie, 557
in onion sauce, 558
parmigiana, 557
to prepare for cooking, 557
soup, cream of, 122
Bûche de Noël, 805–6
Buckwheat
about, 456
kasha
basic, 466
chick-peas and, 550–51
croquettes, 464
mushroom-, 466
Old World, 466
tofu and, 454-55
varnishkas, 466
with walnuts, baked, 466–67
pancakes, 669
pasta with sesame and snow
peas, 479
Budapest-style braised veal,
198–99
Buffalo, about, 297, 299
Buffalo fish, 364
Bulgur (cracked wheat)
with apples and almonds,
466
balls, crispy lamb-stuffed,
227
bread, fast-rising, 683
croquettes, 464
with mushrooms, 466
with onions, braised, 466
-pecan stuffing, 518
pilaf, 461
tabbouleh, 637
Bullseye, 72
Bullshot, 78–79
Buns
caramel sticky, 693
Chelsea, 693
hot cross, 692
Buñuelitos, 104
Burbot, 364
Burgers
See also Hamburgers
conch, 392
heart, Balmoral, 274
lamb, 223
to braise, 223
to broil, 223
to charcoal-broil, 223
in foil, 223
to panbroil, 223
to panfry (sauté), 223
with sausage, 223
smothered barbecue, 223
venison, 299
Burgundy-style. *See*
Bourguignonne
(Burgundy)-style

Burgundy wine
about, 52
beets in, 554
hamburgers with, 172
pot roast, 179
sparkling, 53
Burnet, 48
Burnt almond ice cream, 746
Burnt sugar cake, 806
Butter(s), 33
anchovy, 503–4
balls, to make, 23
Bercy, 504
"black," 504
sauce, brains in, 273
browned, 504
cakes. *See* Butter cakes
caper, 504
chili, 504
chive, 504
clarified, 484
curls, to make, 23
curry, 504
dill, 504
equivalent measurements of,
28
flavored, 503–5
microwaving, 487
-flavor granules, 33
fondant, 858
garlic, 504
green, 504
herb, 504
horseradish, 504
to keep from burning, 24
lemon, 504
lobster, 504
maître d'hôtel, 504
marchands de vin, 505
mushroom, 505
mustard, 505
noisette, 505
orange, 505
paprika, 505
parsley, 504
lemon-, 504
pimiento, 505
for poultry, 321
sauces, 503–5
drawn, 503
white, 503
seasoned, 505
shallot, 505
shrimp, 505
storage time for, in
refrigerator, 41
tarragon, 505
tomato, 505
watercress, 505
Butterballs, 843
Butter cakes
about, 799
chocolate, 801
mocha, 801
poppy seed, 801
three-egg, 801
two-egg, 800–1
Butter clams, 387

Buttercup squash
See also Squash, winter
about, 615
boiled, 617
Butterfish, 360
Butterflying
defined, 13
meat, 142
Buttermilk
about, 31
biscuits, 660
marinade, 509
mayonnaise, 510
pancakes, 669
rolls, 689
crusty, 689
salad dressing, 649–50
veal balls in gravy, 205
waffles, 670
Butternut squash
See also Squash, winter
about, 615
baked, 617
boiled, 617
to charcoal bake, 618
fruit-glazed, 618
parmigiana, 618–19
Butter pecan ice cream, 746
Butterscotch
cookies
brownies, 849
icebox, 847
sugar, 838
cream cake filling, 824
cream pie, 779
custard, 730
-maple chiffon cake, 813
pudding, tapioca, 736
sauce, 752
-spice cupcakes, 815
syrup, 752–53
Byrrh, 52

Cabbage
See also Chinese Cabbage;
Coleslaw; Sauerkraut
about, 530, 558
Austrian, 559
and chestnuts, 560
Colcannon, 559
corned beef and, 190
creamy, 559
Creole-style, 559
game birds braised with, 344
knabrus, Pennsylvania
Dutch, 559
low-calorie, 559
'n' kale, 584
to parboil, 558
to prepare for cooking, 558
red
and apples, Flemish, 560
to brighten, 24
and chestnuts, 560
and pork ragout, 253
steamed, 558
sweet-and-sour, 560
scalloped, 560

serving tip, 558
to shred, 9, 22
soup, 135
   Basque, 135
   cream of, 122
   German, 135
spicy East Indian baked, 560
steamed, 558
stuffed Polish rolls with
   lemon sauce, 175
Cachaça, 57
Cacik, 631
Caesar salad, 628
Café au lait, 65
Café brûlot, 65
Cake(s)
   See also Torte
   angel food, 812–13
      about, 795
   applesauce, 807–8
   baking techniques, 798–99
   Boston cream pie, 802
   bûche de Noël, 805–6
   burnt sugar, 806
   butter
      about, 799
      chocolate, 801
      mocha, 801
      poppy seed, 801
      three-egg, 801
      two-egg, 800–1
   cheese, 784
      cherry topping for, 784
      strawberry topping for,
         784
   chiffon
      about, 795
      basic, 813
      butterscotch-maple, 813
      chocolate, 813
      lemon, 813
      mocha, 813
      orange, 813
      spiced, 813
   chocolate
      butter, 801
      chiffon, 813
      Christmas log, 805–6
      crazy, 804
      devil's food, 804–5
      jelly roll, 812
      marble, 802
      -nut, 807
      Sachertorte, 805
      sponge, 810
      sponge, economy, 810
   Christmas log, 805–6
   coconut
      cream, 802
      sponge, cream, 810
   coffee. *See* Coffee cake
   convection-oven cooking of,
      8
   cooling and removing from
      pans, 799
   decorating tips for, 816–18
   devil's food, 804–5
      loaf, 805

failures, 800
filling
   about, 816
   butterscotch cream, 824
   chocolate cream, 823
   coconut cream, 824
   coffee cream, 824
   double cream, 823
   fruit cream (with milk),
      824
   fruit cream (with whipped
      cream), 824
   lemon, 824
   lemon cheese (curd), 892
   lime, 824
   Neapolitan fruit cream,
      820
   orange, 824
   pastry cream, 824
   pineapple, 824
   pineapple-coconut, 825
   poppy seed cream, 823
   rich fruit, 824
   strawberry, 824–25
   vanilla cream, 823
flour for, 34
frostings, 815–22
   application of, 816
   butter cream, 818–19
   to color, 817–18
   cream cheese, 819
   decorative, 817, 819
   fudge, 821–22
   leftover, 816
   mountain, 821
   ornamental, 822
   preparing cakes for, 815
   seafoam, 821
   7-minute, 820–21
   tips on, 815–18
   whipped cream, 819–20
fruit
   Christmas, dark, 814
   light, 813–14
génoise, 811
ginger, grandmother's soft,
   808
gingerbread, 808
   upside-down, 809
glaze
   apricot, 823
   chocolate, 823
   snow, 823
icing
   broiled, 822
   easy white, 823
   glacé, 822
   royal, 822
ingredients for, 795–96
jelly roll, 812
kinds of, 794–95
Lady Baltimore, 802
lemon. *See* Lemon, cake
marble, 802
mixing methods, 655, 794–
   95, 797
nut, 806–7
   -candied fruit, 807

chocolate-, 807
   layer, 807
   orange-, 807
   -seed, 807
   sponge, 810
orange. *See* Orange(s), cake
petits fours, 811–12
   simple, 812
pound, 803–4
rainbow, 802
Sachertorte, 805
spice(d), 806
   chiffon, 813
   layer, 808
   lemon-, 808
   raisin-, 808
sponge, 809–10
   See also génoise *above*
   about, 794, 799
   loaf, easy, 810
storing and keeping, 39, 799
terms and techniques, 796
tests for doneness, 798
Thelma's 1, 2, 3, 4 cake, 804
tips on making, 797, 800
tipsy, 820
upside-down
   apple, 809
   apricot or peach, 809
   gingerbread, 809
   pineapple, 809
wedding
   cutting procedure for, 800
   Mexican (cookies), 843–44
   white, 802–3
white or silver, 802
Cake pans, 797–99
Calabrese salami, 296
Calamari, definition of, 13
Calamondin marmalade, 891
Calcium hydroxide (slaked
   lime), 873–74
Calf's brains. *See* Brains
Calf's liver
   about, 278
   alla Veneziana, 279
   and bacon, 278
   broiled, 278
   dumplings, 139
   in English mixed grill, 221–
      22
   lightly curried, on crisp
      capellini pancakes, 279–
      80
   in mustard sauce, 278
   and onions, 278
   pâté
      country-style, 91–92
      pretty party, 92
   with prosciutto and parsley,
      279
   and rice casserole, Finnish,
      280
   sautéed, 278
California-style
   cold cracked crab, 395
   crab cioppino, 396–97
   fruit pickles, 878

roast Rock Cornish hens or
squabs, 312
sour cream dressing, 650
splits (frankfurters), 292
California wines, 52, 53
Calvados, 58
game birds with cream,
truffles, and, 343
Calzone, 451
with chèvre, 452
with ham, 452
Campagnole salami, 296
Campari, 60
soda, 78–79
Campfire broiling of meat, 144
Canadian bacon, 269
to bake, 270
baked yams, apples, and, 271
ginger-glazed, baked, 271
lime-glazed, baked, 271
orange-glazed, baked, 271
to spit-roast, 270
Canadian whisky, 57
Canapés
about, 97
amount needed, 97
garnishes for, 98
spreads for, 97
suggestions for, 98
Candied fruit
citrus peel, 864
in divinity, 860
in fruit cake, 813–14
meringue kisses with, 834
nut cake with, 807
Candy, 855–66
apple
candied, 864
caramel, 864
apricot-almond balls, 864
brittle, 862–63
butter fondant, 859
caramels, 862
Christmas divinity, 860
citrus peel, candied, 864
coconut
Chinese, 868
fudge, 861
penuche, 861
snowballs, 860
coffee fondant, 859
confetti divinity, 860
cooked, 859–64
decorating, 858
definition of, 13
divinity, 860
flavorings for, 858
fondant, 859–60
citrus-rum, 865
uncooked, 865
fruit
confetti divinity, 860
divinity, 860
fondant-stuffed, 859
frosted, 859
glazed, 868
-nut bars, spicy uncooked,
866

sugarplums, 860
fudge
blond, 861
chocolate, 860
chocolate chip, 861
coconut, 861
uncooked, 865
Kentucky colonels, 865
in microwave ovens, 856
mints
Mrs. B's pulled, 863–64
thin, 860
molasses taffy, 863
nut
bonbons, 859
caramels, 862
frosted, 859
orange-sugared, 868
penuche, 861
sugared, 868
sugared and spiced, 868
opera creams, 859
penuche, 861
peppermint taffy, 863
pinwheels, 860
pistachio divinity, 860
popcorn balls, 869
pralines, 861
seafoam, 860
snowballs, 860
spicy uncooked fruit-nut
bars, 866
sugarplums, 860
techniques for making, 856–
58
temperatures and test chart,
856
tips for making, 855–56
toffee, old English, 862
uncooked, 865–66
vanilla taffy, 863
wrapping and keeping, 859
Cannellini
about, 543
-kielbasa casserole, 291–92
in pasta e fagioli, 133–34
Cannelloni
Garibaldi, 482–83
with meat filling, 482
meatless, 483
squares, 482
Cantaloupe, about, 717
Cantonese-style
chicken, shrimp, and
vegetables, 420
lobster, 404
shrimp with vegetables, 420
Capellini: crisp pancakes of,
lightly curried calf's
liver on, 279–80
Cape Malay curried minced
lamb, 225
Caper(s)
about, 44
butter, 504
chicken and egg salad with,
638

lamb shanks braised with
sour cream and, 232
pasta shell salad with tuna,
dill, and, 636
and salmon sandwiches, 707
sauce, 489
horseradish and, 489
lemon-, German meat ball
in, 176
lemon-, quick, 500
onion and, York-style
lamb riblets smothered
in, 231
sour cream-, 502
sole or flounder paupiettes
stuffed with anchovies
and, 372
and tuna soufflé, 383–84
Capon, 301
Caponata, 109–10
Cappuccino, 66
Carambolas, about, 714
Caramel(s), 862
apples, 864
chocolate, 862
crème, 730
custard sauce, 731
defined, 13, 484
frosting
fudge, 823
7-minute, 820
-glazed ham loaf, 263
nut, 862
pudding, 735
sticky buns, 693
syrup, 753
Caramelized sugar
about, 13
to color stocks and broths,
113
to make, 113
in a microwave oven, 709–
10
Caraway seed(s)
about, 44
beets with sour cream and,
baked, 553
cake, nut-, 807
coleslaw with creamy oil and
vinegar dressing, 629–30
dumplings, 671
game birds with sauerkraut,
raisins, and, 344
and onion tart, Swabian, 451
paprika spareribs with
sauerkraut and, 251
piecrust, 767
rice, 460
Cardamom
about, 44
to crush seeds of, 24
Cardinal sauce, sole or
flounder with, 370–71
Cardoons
about, 531, 562
to cook, 562
Carob, about, 36
Carolina-style

punch, 75
sauce, chicken breasts in, 329
Chanterelles, 587
Chantilly mayonnaise, 652
Chantilly sauce, 498
Chapati, 13
Chapon, 627
definition of, 13
Charcoal, spit-roasting over
See also under specific meats and poultry
meat, 143–44
poultry, 313
chart, 316
thermometer for, 148
Charcoal broiling (grilling)
meat, 144, 147
Charcoal seasoning, 49
Charcutière sauce, 495
Chard
about, 531, 569
boiled, 569–70
cold, 570
low-calorie, 570
puréed, 570
Charleston-style
benne wafers, 832
shrimp pie, 422
Charlotte Russe, 742
Char shu ding, 243
Chartreuse, 58
Chasseur-style (hunter's style)
filet steaks, filet mignons, or tournedos, 158
sauce, 495
veal steaks or chops, 199
Chateaubriand, 156
Chateaubriand sauce, 495
Château potatoes, 603
Chaud-froid (sauce), 492
chicken breasts with, 328
pheasant breasts, 346
Chayotes
about, 570
to cook and serve, 570
Checkerboards, chocolate, 846
Cheddar cheese
-corn fritters, 575
dip, sherried green, 107
and ham soufflé, 264
and macaroni loaf, 476
-noodle ring, 474
-pimiento sandwiches, 706
rings, golden, 839
sauce
chipped beef in, 191
onions in, 592
soup, 127
spread, beer, 108–9
Welsh rabbit, 449
Cheese(s)
See also names of specific cheeses
about, 445
appetizers, 96
boreks, 103
crackers, 101

gougère (pastry ring), 102
mozzarrella cubes, fried, 102
nachos, 104
and asparagus casserole, 541
beans with, fried, 549
biscuits, 661
-corn meal, 661
blintzes, 452
"blue," 447
bread, 688
crumbs, 673
garlic-, 672
herb-, 688
onion-, 688
pimiento-, 688
cake, 784
cherry topping for, 784
strawberry topping for, 784
calzone, 451
with chèvre, 452
cannelloni, 483
chicken with
breasts stuffed with ham and, 328
fried, 316
sandwich, fried, 451
chiles rellenos with, 175
coeur à la crème, 749
convection-oven cooking of, 8, 435
crackers, 101
croque-madame, 451
croque-monsieur, 451
croquettes, 444
dip, sherried green, 107
dumplings, 671
eggplant with, 580
eggs with, deviled, 443
endives with, 581
equivalent measurements of, 28
firm, 447
fondue, 449
cheddar-beer, 450
food, process, 445
gnocchi, 467
with sage-cream sauce, 467
gougère, 102
to grate, 9, 22
ham and
calzone, 452
chicken breasts stuffed with, 329
fried sandwich, 451
grilled sandwich, 707
heroes, 265
with olives, creamed, 261–62
salad, 639
sandwiches, 702
soufflé, 264
hard (grating), 448
and hominy casserole, 469
kohlrabi with, 584
lasagne, 481–82

leeks with, 585
macaroni and
deluxe, 475–76
loaf, with cheddar, 476
loaf, with pimiento, Italian, 476
salad, 635
manicotti, 483
to microwave dishes with, 435
nachos
with beans and bacon, 104
with green chilies, 104
potato-skin, with chilies, 104
-noodle ring, 474
omelets, 437
pasteurized, 445
pastry, 766–67
brandied mincemeat in, 778
pastry ring, Burgundian, 102
pie with corn and tomatoes, 621
potatoes with, scalloped, 605
process, 445
puff, Swiss, 450
quiche
Lorraine, 450–51
to microwave, 434–35
Roquefort, 451
ravioli stuffed with, 480
reheating in a microwave oven, 435
rice and, 460
croquettes, 464
Spanish, baked, 462–63
sandwiches
chicken or turkey and, 451, 703, 707
cream cheese and bacon, 704
cream cheese and jelly, 704
cream cheese and watercress, 706
croque-madame, 451
croque-monsieur, 451
grilled, 704, 707–8
ham and, 265, 451, 703, 708
Monte Carlo, 708
Monte Cristo, 707–8
mozzarella in a carriage, 708
Parmesan and egg, 707
pimiento and, 706
plain, 704
spreads with grated cheese, 704
sauce
chipped beef in, 191
eggs in, 443
haddock baked in, 373
Italian, 491
Mornay, 489
mushroom and, 488
stuffed eggs in, 441–42

to steam by microwave, 357
stone, 395
stuffed Dungeness, 398
pilaf-, 398
stuffing for fish, 522
veal cutlets with, 204
Crab apple(s)
about, 715
jelly, 888
juice extraction table, 884
minted, 889
preparing the fruit, 883
pickled, 878
Crab boil (shrimp spice), 49
Cracked wheat. *See* Bulgur
(cracked wheat)
Crackers
cheese, 101
equivalent measurements of,
29
food processor technique for
crumbling, 9
Cranberria, 58
Cranberry(-ies)
about, 714
jelly: juice extraction table,
884
ketchup, 879
nut bread, 666–67
pork pot roast, 241
relish
corn-, 881
in fruit-nut conserve, 882
-orange, 881–82
-orange, preserved, 882
-pear, 882
-walnut, 882
salad
frozen ribbon, 646–47
spicy, molded, 645
sauce
orange-, 513
spicy whole, 513
whole, 513
shrub, 71
sparkle, 70
stuffing
with apples and prunes,
from packaged mix, 520
corn bread and, 518
wild rice and, 517
Cranberry beans
about, 542–43
boiled fresh, 546
in succotash, 574
Swedish, 550
Cranberry tomatoes, about,
619
Crappies, 365
Crayfish
about, 399–400
Finnish-style, 399
Cream
about, 32–33
crème fraîche, 32
defined, 484–85
Devonshire (clotted), 32
Dijon, turkey cutlets in, 335

equivalent measurements of,
28
heavy (whipping), 32
light (coffee), 32
pastry, 824
powdered (instant), 32
pressurized whipped, 33
sauce
curried, calf's liver on
crisp capellini pancakes
with, 280
haddock baked in, 373
horseradish, 500
lemon, mustardy Rock
Cornish hens or squabs
in, 312
sage-, gnocchi with, 467
-wine, cauliflower in, 566
-wine, scallops and
mushrooms in, 413
-wine, suprêmes of
chicken in, 329
-wine, veal birds in, 204
sour. *See* Sour cream
substitutes for, 33
whipped, sweetened, 755
chocolate, 755
decorative, 755
party, 755
plain, 755
spiked, 755
Cream, to, defined, 13, 796
Cream cheese
dip with bacon and
horseradish, 107
frosting, 819
sandwiches
with bacon, 704
with jelly, 704
watercress and, 706
spread, Liptauer, 109
with tomato and olive aspic,
643
Cream of tartar, 35
Cream puffs, 790
Crème, definition of, 13
Crème Anglaise. *See*
Custard(s), stirred
Crème brûlée, 731
Crème caramel, 730
Crème de menthe frappé, 80–
81
Crème fraîche, 32
Crème liqueurs, 58
Creole-style
See also Louisiana-style;
New Orleans-style
cabbage, 559
jambalaya, 463
pork chops and steaks, 247
sausage patties, 288
shrimp, 418–19
gumbo, 418
jambalaya, 418
tomato sauce, 506
turkey
drumsticks, 336–37
parts, 337

Crepes
asparagus, au gratin, 557
broccoli, au gratin, 556
chicken
au gratin, 331
ham and, 331
mushroom and, 330–31
dessert, 671
ham and chicken, 331
for savory fillings, 670–71
Suzette, 748–49
turkey, with mushrooms,
330–31
Crimp, definition of, 13, 758
Croaker, 360
Croissants, 690–91
Croque-madame, 451
Croquembouche, 791
Croque-monsieur, 451
Croquettes
beef
budget, 154
dressed-up, 154
bulgur, 464
cheese, 444
chicken, 332–33
curried, 333
with ham, tongue, or
shellfish, 333
chick-pea, 551
egg, 444
fish, 359
ham, crusty-crumb, 264–65
kasha, 464
potato, 603
rice, 464
cheese-, 464
main dish, 464
savory, 464
shellfish, 386
turkey, 332–33
curried, 333
Croustades, 673
Croûte, definition of, 13, 758
Croutons, 673–74
Crudités, 95–96
Crullers, 698–99
Crumb(s)
equivalent measurements of,
29
to line pans with, 23
to make, 9, 24, 673
measuring, 19
pastries, 757
piecrust, 770–71
as soup thickeners, 113
Crumbling
definition of, 13
with food processor, 9
Crumpets, 670
Crus Classés, meaning of, 54
Crush, definition of, 13
Cuarenta y Tres, 58
Cuba Libre, 80–81
Cubing, 13, 20
Cucumber(s)
about, 532, 576
aspic, 644

ring, 694
sandwiches, 706
twists, 694
Danziger Goldwasser, 58
Dash, definition of, 60
Dasheens
  about, 532, 577
  to cook, 577
Dashi, 14
Date(s)
  cookies
    Chinese chews, 850–51
    -oatmeal bars, 852
    porcupines, 853
    squares, German, 852
  muffins, 658
  -nut
    bread, 666
    fingers, Mrs. Bouldin's, 854
  pudding
    steamed, 739
    walnut and, 751
  rice, 460
Decanting, 55
Decorating
  bags, 817
  cakes, 816–18
  cookies, 828–29
  tips (or tubes), 817
Deep-fat-fry, definition of, 14
Defrosting
  breads, 657–58
  fish, 351–52
  fruit, 710
  meat, 145–46
  poultry, 305–6
Deglaze, defined, 14, 486
Degrease, defined, 485
Demi-glace, 495
  definition of, 14
Demitasse, 65
Dessert(s)
  See also Cake(s); Custard(s); Fruit(s); Pastry(-ies); Pie; Pudding; Soufflé(s), dessert; Tart(s); *other specific types of dessert, and specific recipe titles*
  choosing, 709
  convection oven cooking, 710
  crepes, 671
  frozen, 742–48
    See also Granité; Ice (dessert); Ice cream; Sherbet
    about, 742
    to freeze, 743–44
    kinds of, 742–43
  fruit, 710–29
  garnishes for, 709
  gelatin, 739–42
  microwaving, 709–10
  omelets, 439, 748
    fillings, 438
  rice pancakes, 465
  sauces. *See* Dessert sauces

soup
  apple, 138
  apple, Russian, 138
  cherry, Hungarian, 138
Dessert sauces
  See also Cream, whipped; Syrup
  apricot, Algarve, 754
  brandy, 753
  butterscotch, 752
  chocolate, 752
    basic, 752
    creamy, 752
    -nut, 752
    -peppermint, 752
  currant, 754
  eggnog, 751
    orange or lemon, 752
  hard, 755
    brandy or rum, 755
    lemon or orange, 755
  honey, 754–55
    -nut, 755
  jam or jelly, 754
  lemon, 753
    -raisin, 753–54
  lime, 753
  low-calorie, 756
  marmalade, 754
  Melba, 754
  microwaving, 751
  Nesselrode, 752
  orange, 753
  rum, 753
  strawberry, 754
  vanilla, 751
    bean, 751
    French, 751
    mousseline, 751
  zabaglione, 732
Dessert wines, 53–54
Devil, to, defined, 14
Devil's food
  cake, 804–5
  loaf, 805
Devils on horseback, 410
Devonshire (clotted) cream, 32
Dewberries
  See also Berry(-ies)
  about, 713
Dhal, 586
  and lamb curry, 229
Diable sauce, 494
Dicing, 14, 20, 21
Dijon cream, turkey cutlets in, 335
Dijon dressing: warm salad of Rock Cornish hens, endives, and watercress with, 638–39
Dijonnaise-style
  sauce, 501
  veal, braised, 199
  vegetables, 529
Dill(ed)
  about, 45
  asparagus with, 541
  beans with bacon and, 544

beets with sour cream and, 553
bread, 681
Brussels sprouts in sour cream, 557
butter, 505
carrots, 876
deviled ham dip, 107
egg
  salad, 639
  spread, 109
and garlic olives, 100
green beans, 876
lima beans with, 546
mayonnaise, 500
pasta shell salad with tuna, capers, and, 636
pickles, 874–75
  kosher, 875
  sweet, 875
roast lamb with topping of crumbs and, 212
salmon loaf with lemon and, 383
salsify with sour cream and, 612
sauce
  new potatoes in, 608
  shrimp in, 417
  sour cream-, 502
  yogurt-, 502
veal birds stuffed with ham and, 204
zucchini, 875
Dilute, definition of, 14
Dim sum, definition of, 14
Diplomate sauce, 491
Dip(s)
  about, 106
  black bean, 108
  clam
    and cream cheese, 107
    deviled, 107
  cream cheese, bacon and horseradish, 107
  for crudités, 96
  curry, 107–8
  dilled deviled ham, 107
  guacamole, 108
    with tomato, 108
  hummus (chick-pea), 108
  as sauces, 106
  sherried green cheese, 107
  tapenade, 107
  taramasalata, 109
Disjoint, definition of, 14
Dissolve, definition of, 14
Divinity, 860
Dock, about, 625
Dolma, 226
Dot, to, defined, 14, 759
Dough, definition of, 14
Doughnuts
  baking powder, spicy, 669
  yeast-raised, 699
    jelly, 699
Dragées, definition of, 14
Drain, definition of, 14

Drambuie, 58
Draw, defined, 14
Dredge, to, defined, 14, 796
Dress, defined, 14
Drippings, defined, 14
Drizzle, defined, 14
Drop, defined, 14
Drum, 360
Dubonnet, 52
Duchess potatoes, 606
Duck(ling)
 à la bigarade, 338
 à l'orange, 338
 with Bing cherry sauce, 338
 broiled, 313, 315
  chart, 316
 Chinese-style, 338
 eggs, 430
 to halve or quarter, 304
 kinds of, 302
 morello, 338
 with orange sauce, 338
 roast, 312
  chart, 313
  halves or quarters, 312
  orange-tea-glazed, 312
  with sauerkraut and
   applesauce, 312
 spit-roasting, 312, 315
 wild
  See also Game birds
  rare roast, 345
Dumplings
 basic, 671
 beef stew with, 183
 bread, 671
 caraway, 671
 cheese, 671
 chicken or turkey stew with,
  331
 farina, 139
 green peas and, 597
 ham shank stew with, 262–
  63
 Irish stew with, 230
 liver, 139
 matzo balls, 139
  Mary's, 139–40
  precooked, 140
 nockerln, 475
 parsley, boiled brisket of
  beef with, 182
 parsley or chive, 671
 potato, 139
 saffron, 671
 sage, thyme, and onion, 671
Dust, to, defined, 14
Dutch-style berry pie, 777
Duxelles
 definition of, 14
 sauce, 495

Earthenware, 2, 6
Eau de vie, 58, 59
Éclairs, chocolate, 790
Eel, about, 360
Egg(s)
 adding to hot mixtures, 432

à la king, 331
and asparagus divan, 542
in aspic, 444
 hard-cooked, 444
 stuffed or deviled, 444
 tarragon, 444
and bacon pie, 442
to bake or shirr, 433–34
to beat
 whites, 431
 whole, 430
 yolks, 431
with beets, pickled, 446
Benedict, 436
blood specks in, 429–30
to boil, 432, 434
to break, 430
and broccoli
 au gratin, 442
 casserole with sour cream
  and, 556
 parmigiana, 555
buying, 429–30
for cakes, 794
chicken and, creamed, 330
Chinese fried rice and, 463
cholesterol-free, frozen, 430
chopping in food processor,
 10
color of, 429
convection-oven cooking of,
 8, 435
to cook in shell, 432
creamed
 with bacon and onion, 443
 basic, 443
 in cheese sauce, 443
 curried, 443
 scalloped, 443
croquettes, 444
curdled mixtures with, to
 rescue, 432
curdling, to prevent, 431
custards. *See* Custard(s)
deviled, 443
 anchovy, 443
 in aspic, 444
 with cheese, 443
 curried, 443
 garnishes, 443
-dill spread, 109
dried solids, 430
drop soup, 119
duck, 430
equivalent measurements of,
 29
fertile, 430
Florentine, 436
folding in beaten whites, 431
food processor technique for
 chopping, 10
foo yung, 436
to French-fry, 433
freshness of, 429
frittata
 artichoke, 440
 ham and tomato, 440
 onion, 439

to fry, 432–34
garnishes for, 435
ham and
 creamed, 261
 frittata with tomato and,
  440
 omelet with mushroom,
  tomato, and, 439
 pie, 265
 salad with olives, 266
 sandwiches, 703
 shortcake, 262
hard-cooked, 432
hominy and bacon scramble
 with, 469
huevos rancheros, 436
leftover yolks and whites,
 432
to microwave, 434–35
-noodle ring, 474
omelets. *See* Omelet(s)
100- or 1,000-year-old
 Chinese, 430
pasta, 472
pâté with nuts and
 mushrooms, 92
pickled, 445
piperade, 440
to poach, 432, 434
and potato "pie," ranch-
 style, 442
quail, 430
quality of, 429
quiche. *See* Quiche
"red beet," Pennsylvania
 Dutch, 445
reheating in a microwave
 oven, 435
to remove a speck of yolk
 from white, 430
to remove shell fragments,
 430
salad, 639
 anchovy-, 639
 chicken, caper, and, 638
 curried, 639
 dilled, 639
 herbed, 639
 pickle-, 639
 sandwiches, 704
 shellfish, avocado, and,
  640
sandwiches
 fried, 704
 ham and, 703
 Parmesan and, 707
 salad, 704
 scrambled, or omelet, 704
sauce(s)
 thickened with eggs, 485,
  497–98
 velouté, 490
Schnitzel à la Holstein, 201
Scotch, 291
to scramble, 433, 434
to separate, 430
serving, 435
size of, 429

onion fry in sour cream, 594
Finocchio. *See* Fennel
Fish, 349–85
  See also names of specific fish
  amount needed, 349
  to bake, 352–54
    by microwave, 357–58
  barbecued, 354
  bouillabaisse, 381
  to braise, 353
  to broil, 354
  buying fresh, 349
  cakes, 359
  canned, 352
  categories of, 349
  ceviche, 382–83
  to charcoal-broil, 354
  and chips, 366
  chowder, New England, 130
  to clean, 350–51
  convection-oven cooking of, 8, 358
  cooking methods for, 352–59
  court bouillon for
    rich, 348
    simple, 347–48
    white wine, 348
  croquettes, 359
  to deep-fat-fry, 355
  federally graded, 349
  fettuccine and, 478–79
  to fillet, 350–51
  fillets
    See also specific recipes
    à la meunière, 355
    amandine, 355
    to bake, 353–54
    microwaving, 356, 357
    to poach, 355–56
  fried
    batter-, 355
    breaded, 355
    shallow-, 355
  frozen, 351–52
  leftover, 348–49
  loaf, 366
    herbed, 367
  microwaving, 356–58
  mousse
    cold, 368
    in a fish mold, 368
    velvety, 367–68
  to oven broil, 354
  to oven fry, 355
  to panfry (sauté), 355
  Peruvian raw pickled, 382–83
  pie
    with green peppers, crisp-crusted, 367
    potato-, 367
  to poach, 355–57
  Provençal, 382
  quenelles, 368–69
    à la Florentine, 369
    gratinéed, 369
    processor, 368–69
  reheating by microwave, 358
  roe. *See* Roe
  safety precautions when buying, 349
  sandwiches, 704
  scaling, 350
  scalloped
    with cheese, 366
    easy, 366
    with herbs, 366
    with lemon, 366
  to serve whole and large chunks of, 359
  soufflé
    basic, 367
    curried, 367
    lemon, 367
    microwaving, 358
  steaks
    à la meunière, 355
    amandine, 355
    to bake, 353–54
    Dugléré, 380
    microwaving, 356, 357
    to poach, 355–56
    with sour cream sauce, curried, 380
  steaks Dugléré, 380
  to steam, 356–57
  stock, 118
  storage time for
    frozen, 39
    refrigerated, 40
  stuffing
    almond, easy, 522
    bread, basic, 521
    clam, 522
    crab or shrimp, 522
    lemon bread, 521
    mushroom, 522
    vegetable, 521
  terrine, layered, 93
  test of doneness, 352
  to thaw, 351–52
  and vegetables, Japanese-style, 383
Fisherman's baked shells, 476
Fish house punch, 76
Five fragrance (five spice) powder, 49
Flageolets
  about, 543
  stew, 548
Flake, definition of, 14
Flame (flambé), definition of, 13
Flaming
  filet steaks or tournedos, 158
  steaks, 163
Flan (custard), 731
  pineapple, 732
  rum, 732
Flan (pastry)
  baking a, 760–61
  defined, 758
  fruit, Viennese, 786
  torte pastry for, 769
Flan rings, 758
  fitting pastries into, 760
Flemish-style
  beef-beer stew, 184–85
  carrots, 564
  red cabbage and apples, 561
Float for punch bowls, 72
Floating island, 732
Florentines, 835
Florentine-style
  artichoke bottoms, 538
  crab, 397
  eggs, 436
  noodles, 475
  oysters, 410
  quenelles, 369
  sole or flounder, 369
Florida-style black beans and peppers, 552
Flounder
  about, 360, 369
  à la bonne femme, 369
  à la Florentine, 369
  à l'Américaine, 370
  à la Niçoise, 369
  à la Normande, 369
  amandine, 369
  aux fines herbes, 369
  baked
    almond-crumb-topped, 371
    crumb-topped, 371
    sesame, 371
  cardinal, 370–71
  with crab sauce, 371
  en papillote, low-calorie, 371
  Marguery, 369
  Mornay, 369
  paupiettes of
    anchovy-and-caper-stuffed, 372
    mushroom-stuffed, 372
    with rosy sauce, 371–72
    shrimp-stuffed, 372
  Véronique, 369
Flour
  about, 34–35
  all-purpose, 34, 674, 795
  bread, 34, 674
  for bread, 674
  cake, 34, 795
  for cakes, 795
  equivalent measurements of, 29
  instant-type, 34
  pastry, 34, 757–58
  presifted, 34
  seasoned, defined, 17
  self-rising, 34
  substitutions for, 27
  as thickener
    for sauces, 485, 486
    for soups, 113
  to, defined, 14
  whole wheat, 34
Flower nails, 817
Fluff, definition of, 14
Fluke, 360
Flute, definition of, 14
Fold, definition of, 14

about, 714
jelly
juice extraction table, 884
Göteborg cervelat, 296
Gothaer cervelat, 296
Göttinger cervelat, 296
Gougère, 102
Goulash
Hungarian, 185
savory, 186
Transylvanian, 185–86
Yugoslav, 186
Graham cracker crust, 771
Grand Central oyster stew,
408–9
Grand Marnier, 58
soufflé, hot, 735
Granité
about, 742
coffee or tea, 744
fruit, 744
melon, 744
orange, 744
Graniteware, 2
Granola bars, honey nut, 851
Grape(s)
about, 715–16
to "frost," 24
jelly
Concord, 889
juice extraction table, 884
preparing the fruit, 883
lemonade, easy, 70
peeling, 710
pie, 776
punch, hot spicy, 73
red, in Waldorf salad, 642
Grapefruit
about, 715
and avocado salad, 641
baked, 722
broiled, 726
honey-, 726
candied peel of, 864
-ginger cooler, 70
marmalade, 891
sauce, 754
Grape leaves
game birds baked in, 343
stuffed with lamb, 226
Grappa, 58
Grasshopper, 80–81
Grasshopper pie, 782–83
Grate, definition of, 15
Grated foods, measuring, 19
Grating techniques
food processor, 9
hand, 22
Gravy
apple, pork pot roast with,
241
au jus, 493
barbecue, for beef, 509
browner, liquid, 37
buttermilk veal balls in, 205
country, panfried pork chops
with, 249
giblet, 493

herb, 493
jus lié, 493
microwaving, 487
mushroom, 493
braised whole pork
tenderloin with, 239–40
onion, 493
pan, 492–93
parsley, chicken livers with,
329–30
plantation, fried rabbit with,
299
red currant, braised stuffed
breast of veal with, 196
red-eye, country-fried ham
with, 268–69
reheating in a microwave,
487
sour cream, 493
beef birds with, 169
horseradish, pot roast
with, 180
onion-, ham steak in, 267
pork balls in, 252
tips for making, 486–87
tomato-mushroom, braised
beef liver with, 280
vegetable
braised stuffed breast of
veal with, 196
braised veal roast with,
194
wine, 493
herbed veal pot roast with,
195
Grease, definition of, 15
Grease and flour, definition of,
15
Greek-style
avgolemono soup, 127
baklava, 792
chick-peas and tomatoes,
551
karydata, 851
kourabiedes, 844
lamb
arni psito, 212
Athenian braised shoulder,
easy, 215–16
avgolemono sauce, braised
roast with, 216
dolma (stuffed grape
leaves), 226
moussaka, 223–24
pastítsio, 224–25
roast, 212
spit-roasted breast, 216
taverna-style roast leg, 212
squid stuffed with savory
rice, 427
taramasalata, 109
vegetables à la grecque, 528–
29
wheat and walnut bars, 851
Green bean(s)
about, 542, 543
amandine, 544
au gratin, 544–45

with bacon and dill, 544
boiled, 544
cold, 544
dilled, 875
Italian, about, 542, 543
low-calorie, 544
Lyonnaise-style, 545
with mushrooms, 544
in mustard sauce, 544
with oil and vinegar, 544
to parboil, 544
Provençal-style, 545
salad, 634
three-bean, 634
succotash, 574
with hominy, 574
sweet-sour, 544
with water chestnuts,
Oriental-style, 545
Green butter, 505
Green dressing, chilled scallops
with radicchio in, 414
Green goddess dressing, 654
Green mayonnaise, 654
Green pea(s)
about, 534, 596
à la Française, 597
boiled, 596
cold, 596
in cream, 597
and dumplings, 597
with mint and orange, 597
minted, 596
to parboil, 596
puréed, 597
and rice, 462
with rosemary, 596–97
soufflé, 527
soup
cream of, 122
potage Saint-Germain, 124
vegetables to team with, 597
Green peppers, sweet (bell)
about, 534, 599
black beans and, Florida,
552
Chinese beef and, 168–69
and corn
pancakes, 669
stuffing, from packaged
mix, 520
and fish pie, 367
ham with
casserole of potatoes and,
262
pineapple and, 261
marinated roasted, 600–1
in Swiss cheese sauce,
600–1
with mushrooms and onions,
589
and onions, Italian, 600
piperade, 440
pork chops with rice and,
baked, 249
relish, 880
hot, 880

tempura
    batter, 672
    sauce, 511
teriyaki sauce, 509
vegetable salad with toasted
        sesame seed dressing,
        629
Jell (gel), definition of, 15
Jellied
    consommé, 117
        about, 112
        madrilène, 118
    salad. *See* Gelatin, salads
Jelly(-ies), 883–85
    apple
        minted, 889
        old-fashioned, 888
        rose geranium, 888
        spiced, 889
    basil, 890
    with commercial pectins, 885
    crab apple, 888
        minted, 889
    and cream cheese
        sandwiches, 704
    cutouts, 838
    doughnuts, 698
    glaze for ham, 258
    hot red pepper, 890
    how to make, 883–85
    jalapeño, 889–90
    mint, 890
    omelet fillings, 438
    sauce, 754
    and peanut butter
        sandwiches, 704
    port wine, 740
    problems with, 885–86
    runny, how to rescue, 885
    roll, 812
        chocolate, 812
        lemon, 812
        orange, 812
        strawberry, 812
    tips for making better, 885,
        887–88
    wine, 890
Jelly glasses and lids, 871
    filling and sealing, 884–87
    preparing, 884
Jelly jars and closures
    filling and sealing, 884–87
    preparing, 884
Jelly-roll style, definition of, 15
Jelmeter, 883
Jerky, 189
Jerusalem artichoke(s)
    about, 529, 539
    baked, 539–40
    boiled, 539
    creamed, 540
    hashed brown, 540
    low-calorie, 539
    pickle relish, 881
    to prepare for cooking, 539
    purée, 539
    soup, cream of, 122
Jewish-style

See also Kosher
    dill pickles, 875
    kasha varnishkas, 467
    matzo balls, 140
        Mary's, 140
        precooked, 140
Jicama
    about, 533, 583
    to cook, 583
Jigger (or shot), 60
Jonnycakes, Rhode Island,
        663–64
Jowl, hog, 269
    and black-eyed peas, 271
Jubilee punch, 74
Julienne
    definition of, 15
    technique for, 21
Jumbles, 838
Juniper berries
    about, 45
    sauerkraut braised with, 562
    and scallion sauce, pigs' feet
        (trotters) in, 254–55
Junket, definition of, 15
Jus lié, 493

Kabinet, meaning of, 54
Kahlúa, 58
Kale
    about, 533, 584
    boiled, 584
    'n' cabbage, 584
    in caldo verde, 136
    low-calorie, 584
    soup, cream of, 122
Karydata, 851
Kasha
    basic, 466
    chick-peas and, 551
    croquettes, 464
    mushroom-, 466
    Old World, 466
    tofu and, 454–55
    varnishkas, 466
    with walnuts, baked, 467
Kebabs
    See also Shish kebabs
    beef, 217
    fruit, 722
Kedgeree, 374
Keel (keel bone), 308
Kentucky colonels, 865
Ketchup
    cranberry, 879
    easy, 879
    tomato, 879
Khichiri, 464
Kibbeh, 225
Kidney(s), 275–78
    about, 275
    amount needed, 275
    beef
        braised, 276–77
        braised, lower-calorie, 277
        and steak pie, 186–87
        stew, Clara's, 277–78
    lamb

breaded broiled, 276
broiled, 276
deviled, 277
en brochette, 276
in English mixed grill,
        221–22
low-calorie, 276
marinated broiled, 276
and rice stuffing, 517
sautéed, 275–76
sautéed in onion and wine
        sauce, 276
sautéed with mushrooms,
        276
pork
    braised, 276–77
    braised, lower-calorie, 277
to prepare for cooking, 275
veal
    breaded broiled, 276
    broiled, 276
    low-calorie, 276
    low-calorie braised, 277
    marinated broiled, 276
    and mushrooms, braised,
        277
    sautéed, 275–76
    sautéed in onion and wine
        sauce, 276
    sautéed with mushrooms,
        276
    stew, Clara's kidney, 277–
        78
    with vegetables, braised,
        277
Kielbasa
    about, 295
    -cannellini casserole, 291–92
Kimchi, 15
Kingfish, 361
Kippered herring, 375–76
Kir, 82–83
Kirsch, 58
Kitchen utensils. *See*
        Cookware
Kiwi fruits, about, 716
Knackwurst
    about, 295
    sauerkraut with meat and,
        241–42
Knead, definition of, 15
Knives, 3–4
    techniques for using, 20
Knob celery. *See* Celeriac
Kohlrabi
    about, 533, 584
    au gratin, 585
    boiled, 584
    creamed, 585
    low-calorie, 584
    mashed, 584
Königsberger klops, 176
Kosher
    definition of, 15
    dill pickles, 875
    salami, 296
    salt, 37
Kourabiedes, 844

Kugelhupf, 693
Kümmel, 58
Kumquat(s)
about, 716
marmalade, 891

Lady Baltimore cake, 802
Ladyfingers, 835
to line pans with, 23
Lager, 51
Lait, defined, 15
Lamb
artichokes stuffed with, 218
balls baked in tomato sauce,
Turkish, 226–27
brains. *See* Brains
bulgur balls stuffed with,
crispy, 227
burgers, 223
to braise, 223
to broil, 223
to charcoal-broil, 223
in foil, 223
microwaving, 146
to panbroil, 223
to panfry (sauté), 223
with sausage, 223
smothered barbecue, 223
casserole
eggplant and, 217–18
zucchini and, 219
chops and steaks, 219–22
à la Mexicaine, 221
amount needed, 219
to bake, 220–21
baked barbecued chops,
221
to braise, 220
to broil, 220, 221
to charcoal broil, 220, 221
financière, 221
cuts for, 219
English mixed grill, 221–
22
for extra flavor, 221
general preparation for
cooking, 219
Italian-style, 220
to panbroil, 220, 221
panfried, with minute
sauce, 220
to panfry (sauté), 220
planked lamb chops, 220
to test for doneness, 221
with vegetables, 220
with wine and herbs, 220
curry(-ied), 229
bobotie, 225
and carrot loaf, 226
with dhal, 229
roast leftovers, 218
cuts and types of, 209–10
lesser, 227
dolma, 226
fell of, 210
grape leaves stuffed with,
226
ground, 222–27

hash, 219
hearts. *See* Heart(s)
kidneys
breaded broiled, 276
broiled, 276
deviled, 277
enbrochette, 276
in English mixed grill,
221–22
low-calorie, 276
marinated broiled, 276
and rice stuffing, 517
sautéed, 275–76
sautéed in onion and wine
sauce, 276
sautéed with mushrooms,
276
leftover
roast, 217–19
shepherd's pie with, 177
liver
about, 278
broiled, 278
dumplings, 139
loaf
carrot and, curried, 226
herbed, 226
moussaka, 223–24
musk glands of, 210
neck slices braised with
limas and carrots, 230–
31
pastítsio, 224–25
pie, Lebanese, 225
pilaf, leftover, 218
recognizing quality in, 210
riblets or spareribs
barbecued, 231
charcoal-barbecued, 231–
32
York-style, smothered in
onions and caper sauce,
231
roast, 210–19
à la Bordelaise, 211–12
à la Boulangère, 212
à la Bretonne, 212
à la Provençale, 212
amount needed, 211
apricot-glazed stuffed
breast, 216–17
arni psito, 212
Athenian braised shoulder,
easy, 215–16
with avgolemono sauce,
braised, 215
baby lamb, 211
bonne femme, 212
to carve leg, 213–14
charcoal-broiled, 217
charcoal spit-roasted
breast, 216
cooking methods, 210–13
crown, 214
crown, filled with
vegetables, 214
cuts for, 210

with dill-crumb topping,
212
to give extra flavor, 211
glazes for, 211
Greek-style, 212
Greek-style spit-roasted
breast, 216
herb-stuffed rolled leg, 215
leftovers, how to use up,
216–19
Neapolitan, 212
oven-barbecued, 212
preparation for cooking,
211
Sicilian-style braised leg,
215
to spit-roast, 213
stuffed cushion shoulder,
215
stuffed leg with rice, piñon
nuts, and currants, 214–
15
taverna-style, 212
temperature when cooked,
210
with tomato sauce,
braised, 216
Turkish shish kebabs,
216–17
with vegetables, braised,
216
salad of black-eyed peas and,
219
shanks, braised, 232
Bombay, 232
with gremolata, 232
piñon- and rice-stuffed,
232
with sour cream and
capers, 232
with vegetables, 232
shepherd's pie, 219
shish kebabs
charcoal-broiled, 217
Turkish, 217
sliced
cold, 219
hot, 219
soup with pepper and
barley, 132
stew
See also curry(-ied) *above*
cassoulet, 228
couscous, 229–30
economy, 227
French-style, 228–29
Irish, 230
Irish, with dumplings, 230
Lancashire hot pot, 231
navarin of, printanier, 228
North African, 229–30
with potatoes, economy,
227
Lancashire hot pot, 231
Landjäger cervelat, 296
Lard, 33
about, 147
definition of, 15

storage time for, in
  refrigerator, 42
Larding, 142–43
Lasagne, 481–82
Lava rocks, gas and electric
  barbecuing with, 144
Lavender, 48
Leaven(ings)
  about, 35
  for cakes, 795–96
  definition of, 15
  substitutions for, 27
Lebanese-style lamb pie, 225
Leberkäse, 293
  to heat, 290
Lebkuchen, 841–42
Leek(s)
  about, 533, 585
  au gratin, 585
  boiled, 585
  cold, 585
  low-calorie, 585
  pie, 585
  soup, cream of, 122
  in soups
    cockaleekie, 129
    vichyssoise, 125
Lees, 55
Leftovers
  beef (roast)
    chow mein or chop suey,
      155
    croquettes, 154
    curry, 155
    hash, 155
    macaroni, beef, and
      tomato casserole, 154
    miroton, 152, 154
    potato and beef cakes, 154
    quick beef paprika, 154–
      55
    shepherd's pie with, 177
    and vegetable pie, 155
    vegetables stuffed with,
      155
    very small amounts, what
      to do with, 155–56
  in eggs foo yung, 436
  egg yolks and whites, 432
  fish, 348–49
  ham
    and baked beans, 265
    bok choy with, 265
    and cheese heroes, 265
    and chicken salad, 266
    Chinese cabbage with, 265
    Chinese rice and, 265
    creamed potatoes and, 265
    croquettes, crusty-crumb,
      264–65
    and egg pie, 265
    and egg salad, with olives,
      266
    mousse, 266
    and potato pie, 265
    potted, 265
    timbales, 264
    and tongue salad, 266

very small amounts, 266
  Waldorf salad, 266
lamb
  roast, 217–19
  shepherd's pie with, 177
pork (roast), 242
  casserole of baked beans
    and, 242
  Chinese fried rice, 243
  chop suey, 243
  cubed, and olives in sour
    cream, 243
  hot sandwiches, 244
  lo mein, 242
  sliced cold, 243
  sliced hot, 243–44
  subgum (10-ingredient)
    pork chow mein, 242
  very small amounts, 244
  poultry, 340–41
  rice, 459
  stuffing, 515
  wines, 56
Legumes, definition of, 15
Lemon
  about, 716
  blancmange, 736
  bread stuffing for fish, 521
  broth, veal balls in, 197
  butter, 505
    parsley-, 505
  cake
    chiffon, 813
    jelly roll, 812
    -spice, 808
    sponge, 810
  cake filling, 824
  candied peel of, 864
  cheese (curd), 892
  chicken with
    broiled, 316
    soup, Greek, 127
  cookies
    sponge squares, 850
    sugar, 838
    wafers, 830
  cupcakes, 815
  custard sauce, 731
  dessert sauce, 753
    eggnog, 752
    hard sauce, 755
    marmalade, 754
    -raisin, 753–54
  equivalent measurements of,
    28
  fish with
    scalloped, 366
    soufflé, 367
  fluff, 740–41
  food processor techniques
    for grating rind of, 11
  frosting
    butter cream, 819
    cream cheese, 819
    mountain, 821
    7-minute, 820
  glaze(d)
    carrots, 563

sugar, for cakes, 823
  granité, 744
  to grate rind with food
    processor, 11
  halibut steaks, stuffed, 380
  ice, 744
  jelly roll, 812
  -lime salad dressing, 650
  loaf, sweet, 801
  marmalade, 891
    sauce, 754
  pie
    angel, 784
    chess, 783
    chiffon, 782
    meringue, 778–79
  pork chops or steaks with
    orange and, 246
  pudding, steamed, 738
  rice pudding, 737
  salmon loaf with dill and,
    383
  sauce, 492
    avgolemono, 498
    caper, German meat balls
      in, 176
    caper-, quick, 500
    cream, mustardy Rock
      Cornish hens or squabs
      in, 312
    custard, 731
    dessert sauce. See dessert
      sauce above
    Polish stuffed cabbage
      rolls with, 175
  sherbet, 745
  soufflé, 741
  sugar glaze, 823
  Thai turkey with shiitake
    mushrooms and bean
    sprouts, 335
  turkey broiled with, 316
  veal loaf, 205
Lemonade
  grape, easy, 70
  mix, easy, 70
  pink, easy, 70
  punch, nonalcoholic, 74
Lemon balm, 48
Lemon grass, 48
Lemon verbena, 45
Lentil(s)
  about, 533, 586
  boiled, 586
  dhal, 586
  and ham, 586
  red, and rice, 586–87
  rice and, East Indian, 464
  savory, 586
  soup with ham, 133
Let down, definition of, 15
Lettuce
  cups, to make, 625
  sandwiches, 704
    with bacon and tomato,
      702
    and tomato, 704
  types of, 624

broiled, 279
mushrooms, 588
okra, 590
onions, 592
rutabaga, 611
salad dressing
fruit, 651
mustard dressing, 653
tangy, 653
Thousand Island, 653
yogurt, 650
shellfish, cold marinated, 100
sherbets, 745
shrimp, broiled, 416–17
spinach, 613
squash, summer, 615
turnips, 622
yogurt-based sauces, 502
yogurt dressing, 650
winter health salad, 628
Lyonnaise-style
artichoke bottoms, 538
beans, fresh, 545
noodles, 475
omelet, 439
potatoes, 604
sauce, 495
steak, 164
tripe, 285–86
veal, braised, 199
Lyon salami, 296

Macaroni
casserole
beef, tomato, and, 154
lamb and, 224–25
and cheese
deluxe, 475–76
loaf with Cheddar, 476
loaf with pimiento, Italian, 476
salad, 635
to cook, 471
salad
basic, 635
cheese-, 635
"deli," 635
with meat, chicken, or shellfish, 635
seashell, fisherman's baked, 476
Macaroons, 833–34
chocolate, 833
coconut, 834
Mace, about, 45
Macédoine
of fruit, 711–12
of vegetables
cold, 563
hot, 563
Macerate, definition of, 15
Mackerel (Atlantic), 361
canned, 352
Madeira
about, 53
beef tenderloin, 157
sauce, 496
mushrooms in, 589

Madeleines, 835–36
Madrilène consommé, 118
definition of, 112
jellied, 118
Magyar chicken paprika, 322
Maître d'hôtel butter, 504
Maltaise (Maltese) sauce, 498
Malted milk, 68
shakes, 68
Mango(es)
about, 717
chutney, 880
and ham, 99
Manhattan, 82–83
Manhattan clam chowder, 130–31
Manicotti
chicken-and-mushroom stuffed, 483
meatless, 483
squares, 482
Maple
-butterscotch chiffon cake, 813
frosting
butter cream, 819
mountain, 821
milk, 68
penuche, 861
sugar, 35
sweet potatoes flavored with, 608
syrup, 36
Maraschino, 59
Marble mountain frosting, 821
Marc, 55, 58
Marchands de vin butter, 505
Marchands de vin sauce, 496
Margarine, 33
storage time for frozen, 39
Margarita, 82–83
Marguerites, 840
Marigold, 48
Marinade
See also specific recipes
à la grecque, 648
beer, 510
buttermilk, 510
defined, 485
for poultry, 320, 509
for tenderizing meat, 142
Marinara sauce, 506–7
anchovy-, 507
mushroom-, 507
Marinate, definition of, 15
Marinière sauce, 490
Marjoram, about, 45
Marketing tips, 37–38
Marmalade
calamondin, 891
defined, 886
ginger-lime, 891
glaze for ham, 258
grapefruit, 891
kumquat, 891
lemon, 891
orange, 891

bitter, 891
sauce, 754
steamed pudding topped with, 739
Marmite, definition of, 16
Marron, definition of, 16
Marrons. *See* Chestnut(s)
Marrow, definition of, 16
Marsala (wine)
veal scaloppine alla, 202
zabaglione, 732
Marseilles-style squid, 427
Martini, 82–83
Maryland-style crab cakes, 398–99
Mary's matzo balls, 140
Masa harina, 34, 457
Mash, definition of, 16
Mask, definition of, 16
Mate, 66
Matzo
balls, 140
Mary's, 140
precooked, 140
definition of, 16
Maude's cookies, 831
Mayonnaise
anchovy, 499
Andalouse, 499
avocado, 499
blender or processor, 651
buttermilk, 499
caviar, 499
Chantilly, 652
chicken, 327
chutney, 499
curry, 652
dill, 499
French, 499
fruit, 652
gelatin, salmon in, 378
green, 654
herb, 499–500
homemade, 651
mustard, 652
Niçoise, 651–52
pimiento and olive, 500
rémoulade dressing with, 651
rules for making, 651
Russian, 652
sauces
about, 499
aioli, 499
lemon-caper, quick, 500
mustard, 500
shellfish cocktail, 500
thin, 652
-tuna sauce
cold roast veal in, 196–97
turkey in, 336
watercress, 500
May wine, 55
Mealy, definition of, 16
Measurements
equivalent, 26–30
metric and U.S. systems of, 25–27

Nap, definition of, 16
Napa Valley roast Rock
      Cornish hens or squabs,
      312
Napoleons, 789
Nasturtium
  about, 46, 625
  salad, 628
Naturschnitzel, 202
Navarin of lamb printanier,
      228–29
Neapolitan-style
  calzone, 451
  fruit cream filling, 820
  roast lamb, 212
  roast stuffed veal, 194
Neat, 61
Nectarine(s)
  about, 717
  flambé, 726
  fritters, 712
  Melba, 727
  peeling and pitting, 710
  pie, 776
  stewed dried, 723
Negroni, 84–85
Nesselrode sauce, 752
Nettle leaves, wilted, 577
New England-style
  See also Boston-style
  boiled dinner, 189–90
  clam chowder, 130
  clam pie, 390–91
  fish chowder, 130
  Indian pudding, 737–38
  pot roast, 180
New Orleans-style
  See also Creole-style;
      Louisiana-style
  oysters Rockefeller, 409–10
Niçoise-style
  onion tart (pissaladière), 594
  quiche, 451
  salade, 384
  sauce, 651–52
  sole or flounder, 369
  tuna, 384
Nitrosamines, 269
No-cholesterol pastry, 767–68
Nockerln, 475
Noisette(s)
  butter, 505
  definition of, 16
  noodles, 474
Nonpareilles, definition of, 16
Nonstick finishes, 2
Noodle(s)
  Alfredo, creamed, 478
  amandine, 474
  -chicken or -turkey
      casserole, 333
  chicken soup with, 119
  to cook, 472
  dough for, 473
  Florentine, 475
  fried, 474
  garlic, 474
  herbed, 474

Hungarian, 475
lo mein, pork, 242
Lyonnaise, 475
noisette, 474
Polonaise, 475
poppy seed, 474
ring, 474
  cheese-, 474
  egg-, 474
sauced, 475
savory, 474
Smetana, 475
spätzle, 475
Nori-maki, 94–95
Normandy-style
  game birds, braised, 344
  Rock Cornish hens, 337
  sauce, 490–91
  sole or flounder, 369
  tripes à la mode de Caen,
      286
North African-style
  See also Moroccan-style
  couscous, 468
  lamb stew, 229–30
Norwegian-style split pea soup
      with ham, golden, 132–
      33
Nouvelle cuisine, defined, 16
Nut(s)
  See also specific types
  about, 866
  as appetizers, 97
  bread
    cranberry, 666–67
    date-, 666
    orange, 666
    raisin or currant and, 666
  buying, 865
  cake, 806–7
    -candied fruit, 807
    chocolate-, 807
    layer, 807
    orange-, 807
    -seed, 807
    sponge, 810
  candies
    bonbons, 859
    caramels, 862
    frosted, 859
    orange-sugared, 868
    penuche, 861
    sugared, 868
    sugared and spiced, 868
  -chocolate sauce, 752
  -chutney meat balls, 105
  cookies
    -date fingers, Mrs.
      Bouldin's, 854
    -honey granola bars, 851–
      52
    kisses, 834
    meringue bars, 851
    quick, 829
    refrigerator, 846
    rings, 845
  curried chicken or turkey
      sandwiches with, 703

filling for coffee cakes and
      sweet breads, 696
food processor techniques
      for, 10
frosting
  butter cream, 819
  7-minute, 820
  whipped cream, 820
-fruit conserve, 882
and fruit whip, 734
glazed, 868
health mix, 101
muffins, 658–59
  bran-, 659
noodles with, 474
omelet fillings, 438
pancakes, 669
pastry, 767
pâté with eggs and
      mushrooms, 92
piecrust
  crumb-, 771
  toasted, 772
  preparing, 866–67
  -raisin cupcakes, 815
  rice with, 460
  sauce
    See also syrup *below*
    chocolate-, 752
    honey-, 755
  soufflé, hot, 734–35
  storage time for, in
      refrigerator, 42
  syrup
    basic, 753
    orange-, 753
    pistachio, 753
  trail mix, 101
  waffles, 670
  yogurt, 453
Nutmeg, about, 46

Oatmeal
  bannocks, 661
  bread, easy, 687
  cookies
    -apple, 852
    bars, 830
    -date bar, 852
    dropped chippies, 833
    -fig bar, 852
    icebox, 847–48
    -prune bar, 852
  herring in, 374
Oats, about, 457
O'Brien potatoes, 604
Ocean perch, 362
Octopus
  about, 426
  Mediterranean-style, 427–28
  to prepare for cooking, 426–
      27
Oeuf, definition of, 16
Oeufs à la neige, 732
Oie, definition of, 16
Oil(s)
  about, 33–34
  measuring, 19

anchovy-and-caper-stuffed,
372
mushroom-stuffed, 372
with rosy sauce, 371–72
shrimp-stuffed, 372
Véronique, 369–70
Solerization, 55
Soppressata, 296
Sorbet, 743
Sorghum, 36
Sorrel
about, 535, 612, 625
to cook, 612
soup, cream of, potage
germiny, 125–26
Soubise, 558
Soubise sauce, 489
Soufflé(s)
about, 440
cheese
basic, 440–41
deviled, 441
herbed, 441
onion and, 441
wine and, 441
chicken or turkey
basic, 334
curried, 334
with ham or tongue, 335
dessert
about, 734
basic hot, 734, 741
chocolate, cold, 741
chocolate, hot, 734
coffee, cold, 741
coffee, hot, 734
fruit, cold, 741
fruit, hot, 735
lemon, cold, 741
nut, hot, 734–35
orange, cold, 741
orange, hot, 734
for a top hat, 741
vanilla, cold, 741
vanilla, hot, 734
fish
basic, 367
curried, 367
lemon, 367
to grease or not to grease
dish for, 440
ham
and cheese, 264
top hat, 263–64
to make a top hat, 440
to microwave, 434
omelet, 439
potatoes, 605
salmon, 384
shellfish
basic, 386
herbed, 386
spinach, 527
zucchini and, breast of
veal stuffed with, 195–
96
tuna and caper, 383–84
vegetable

to bake, 525
basic, 527–28
chart, 526–27
Soup, 112–40
See also Broth; Chowder;
Consommé; Gumbo;
Potage; Stock
about, 112
almond, cream of, 121
artichoke, 135
cold, 135
au pistou, 134
avgolemono, 127
avocado, curried, 121
billi-bi, 126
black bean
easy, 132
old-fashioned, 132
borscht
quick, 128–29
Russian, 128
cabbage, 135
Basque, 135
German, 135
caldo verde, 136
Cheddar cheese, 127
chestnut, 123–24
chicken
Belgian (waterzooie), 129
cream of, 127
cream of, home-style, 127
lemon-, Greek, 127
mulligatawny, 130
noodle, 119
with rice, 119
velouté, 127
chick-pea and sausage,
hearty, 131–32
cockaleekie, 129
cucumber velouté, 124
to degrease, 113
to dilute, 113
dried bean
creamy, 131
pasta e fagioli, 133–34
rosy, 131
savory, 131
dumplings for
farina, 139
liver, 139
matzo balls, 139
matzo balls, Mary's, 139–
40
potato, 139
egg drop, 119
fruit
apple, 138
apple, Russian, 138
basic, 137
berry, quick, 137
cherry, Hungarian, 138
plum, 138
spiced, 138
sweet-sour, 138
garbure, 134
garnishes for, 115
royale custard, 138

royale custard, Indian,
139
Viennese soup "peas," 138
green pea
cream of, 122
potage Saint-Germain, 124
lamb
with pepper and barley,
132
Scotch broth, thrifty, 218–
19
lentil and ham, 133
microwaving, 114
minestrone Milanese, 133
mulligatawny, 130
mushroom, cream of
deluxe, 124
low-calorie, 124
onion, French, 120–21
au gratin, 121
oxtail, 127–28
clear, 128
pasta and bean (pasta e
fagioli), 133–34
peanut, creamy, 124–25
potato
au gratin, 136
basic, 136
cream of, 136
mashed, 136
pressure-cooking, 114
pumpkin, 125
to reduce, 113
sauerkraut, Russian, 135
Scotch broth, thrifty, 218–19
serving, 114–15
sorrel, cream of, potage
germiny, 125–26
spinach, cream of, 123
potage crème d'épinards,
126
spinach and rice, Italian-
style, 136–37
techniques for making, 112–
14
to thicken, 113
tomato
cream of, quick, 126
fresh, 137
gazpacho, Andalusian, 137
turkey
cream of, 127
cream of, home-style, 127
velouté, 127
vegetable
cream of, de luxe, 121
cream of, proportions and
master recipe for
various vegetables, 122–
23
gazpacho, Andalusian, 137
vichyssoise, 125
won ton, 119–20
Soup bowls, 114, 115
Soup spoons, 114, 115
Sour (drink), 88–89
Sour cream
about, 32

pigs' feet (basic method), 254
pigs' feet in scallion and juniper sauce, 254–55
red cabbage and pork ragout, 253
spicy turnip and, 253–54
potato topping for, 605–6
poultry, 318
rabbit, peppery, 300
to, defined, 18
tomatoes
  dressed-up, 621
  savory, 620
  with vegetables, 621
  with zucchini and eggplant à la Provençale, 578–79
turkey
  with biscuits, 331
  with dumplings, 331
  mother's, 331
veal
  blanquette de veau, 206
  with chestnuts, Balkan, 207
  French white, 206
vegetable
  Provençal-style, 578–79
  Spanish, 579
  and tomatoes, 621
  white bean, 548
Sticky buns, caramel, 693
Stiff but not dry, defined, 18
Stinger, 88–89
Stir, definition of, 18
Stir-fry, definition of, 18
Stirring beverages, 61
Stock
See also Broth
all-purpose, 116
beef, 117
  brown, 117
chicken, 116
  giblet, 116
to color, 113
definition of, 18, 112
fish, 118
giblet, 319
  chicken, 116
  from other poultry and game birds, 116
  quantity, 116–17
  turkey, 116
poultry, 319
veal (white), 117
vegetable, 118
Stockinette, 759
Stollen, 695
Stone crabs, 395
Stoneware, 2
Storage of food
breads, 657
cakes, 799
candies, 859
chocolate, 857
cookies, 828
in cupboard or pantry, 42

in freezer, 38–39
herbs, 43, 50
pies, 761
in refrigerator, 38, 40–42
spices, 43
tips for, 24
Strain, definition of, 18
Strasbourg, sausages, 295
Strawberry(-ies)
See also Berry(-ies)
about, 714
cake filling, 824–25
coeur à la crème, 750
ice cream soda, 69
jelly roll, 812
milk shake, 68
-rhubarb pie, 777
Romanoff, 724
sauce, 754
shortcake, 729
tart, Swiss, 786
topping for cheese cake, 784
Straw mushrooms, 587
Strega, 59
Streusel pie
apple, pear, or plum, 778
peach, 777–78
pecan-peach, 778
String beans. *See* Green bean(s)
Striped bass, 363
Strudel
apple, 787–88
cheese, 788
cherry, 788
jam, 788
pastry, about, 757
poppy seed, 788
Stud, definition of, 18
Stuff, to
defined, 18
poultry, 309, 311
Stuffing(s)
amount needed, 514–15
apple-celery, baked spareribs with, 251
bread
  Amish potato and, 516
  apple-raisin, 516
  apricot and, 516
  balls, 515
  basic, 515
  chestnut, 516
  with chestnuts and mushrooms, 518–19
  corn bread and, 516
  for fish, basic, 521
  for fish, lemon, 521
  herbed, from packaged mix, 519
  oyster, 516
  pecan, 516
  sage and mushroom, 516
  sage and onion, 518
  savory sausage, 516
  water chestnut, 516
corn bread
  cranberry and, 518

oyster and, 518
sausage and, 518
with wild rice and chestnuts, 517–18
for fish
  almond, easy, 522
  bread, basic, 521
  clam, 522
  crab or shrimp, 522
  lemon bread, 521
  mushroom, 522
  vegetable, 521
garlic-crumb, pork chops with, 248
leftover, 515
microwaving, 515
orange-sweet potato, 519
packaged mixes, spiced up, 519
  apple and pecan, 519
  chicken liver and mushroom, 520
  corn and pepper, 520
  giblet, 520
  herbed, 519
  herbed fruit, 520
  oyster and almond, 520
  pork chops or steaks with, braised, 246
  prune, apple, and cranberry, 520
  sausage and mushroom, 520
pecan, for ham, 260
rice
  basic, 516–17
  chicken liver and, 517
  kidney and, 517
  mushroom and, 517
  sherried, with raisins and almonds, 517
sauerkraut, 519
tips on, 514–15
wild rice
  basic, 517
  with corn bread and chestnuts, 517–18
  cranberry and, 517
  mushroom and, 517
Sturgeon, 363
Subgum (10-ingredient) pork chow mein, 242
Submarines, 705–6
Substitutions, emergency, 27
Succotash
green bean, 574
old-fashioned, 574
Suckers, 365
Suet, 33
Sugar
about, 35
brown. *See* Brown sugar
for cakes, 794
caramelized
  about, 13
  to color stocks and broths, 113
  to make, 113